FROMMERS

BUDGET TRAVEL GUIDE

EUROPE '93
ON $45 A DAY

PRENTICE HALL TRAVEL

NEW YORK • LONDON • TORONTO • SYDNEY • TOKYO • SINGAPORE

Authors

F. Lisa Beebe: Barcelona, Lisbon, Madrid
Alice Garrard: Introduction, Copenhagen, Oslo, Stockholm
Dan Levine: Athens, Florence, London, Naples, Rome, Venice
Nikolaus Lorey: Geneva, Paris, Nice, Zurich
Beth Reiber: Berlin, Budapest, Innsbruck, Munich, Salzburg, Vienna
Karl Samson: Amsterdam, Brussels, Dublin, Edinburgh

FROMMER BOOKS

Published by Prentice Hall General Reference
A division of Simon & Schuster Inc.
15 Columbus Circle
New York, NY 10023

ISBN 0-13-333576-3
ISSN 0730-1510

Design by Robert Bull Design
Maps by Geografix Inc.

FROMMER'S EUROPE ON $45 A DAY '93
Editor-in-Chief: Marilyn Wood
Senior Editors: Judith de Rubini, Alice Fellows
Editors: Thomas F. Hirsch, Paige Hughes, Sara Hinsey Raveret, Lisa Renaud, Theodore Stavrou
Assistant Editors: Margaret Bowen, Peter Katucki, Ian Wilker
Managing Editor: Leanne Coupe

Special Sales   Bulk purchases of Frommer's Travel Guides are available at special discounts. The publishers are happy to custom-make publications for corporate clients who wish to use them as premiums or sales promotions. We can excerpt the contents, provide covers with corporate imprints, or create books to meet specific needs. For more information write to Special Sales, Prentice Hall Travel, Paramount Communications Building, 15 Columbus Circle, New York, NY 10023

Manufactured in the United States of America

CONTENTS

LIST OF MAPS

INVITATION TO THE READERS

In researching this book, our authors have come across many wonderful establishments, the best of which we have included here. We are sure that many of you will also come across appealing hotels, inns, restaurants, guesthouses, shops, and attractions. Please don't keep them to yourself. Share your experiences, especially if you want to comment on places that have been included in this edition that have changed for the worse. You can address your letters to:

Author (see lists of authors on inside back cover and copyright page)
Frommer's Europe '93 on $45 a Day
Prentice Hall Travel
15 Columbus Circle
New York, NY 10023

A DISCLAIMER

Readers are advised that prices fluctuate in the course of time and travel information changes under the impact of the varied and volatile factors that affect the travel industry. Neither the authors nor the publisher can be held responsible for the experiences of readers while traveling. Readers are invited to write to the publisher with ideas, comments, and suggestions for future editions.

SAFETY ADVISORY

Whenever you're traveling in an unfamiliar city or country, stay alert. Be aware of your immediate surroundings. Wear a moneybelt and keep a close eye on your possessions. Be particularly careful with cameras, purses, and wallets, all favorite targets of thieves and pickpockets.

CHAPTER 1

BEFORE YOU LEAVE HOME

Americans have long harbored a love affair with Europe, so much so that 7.5 million of them cross the Atlantic every year to explore it, trace their roots, and soak up the incomparable culture and architecture. What's different this year is that besides discovering the Old World, you're going to encounter a new entity: the New Europe.

With the Common Market quickly metamorphosing into a Single Market, change is afoot, and travelers aren't exempt from it. They no longer have to show passports at border crossings, except in Great Britain, Ireland, Denmark, and Greece; and they'll hear English used more frequently as the unifying language.

Duty-free shopping still exists, but only until July 1999. The value-added tax, which varies from country to country and which tourists may still get refunded, will become more uniform throughout Europe, at about 15%.

To make matters even simpler for travelers, there may even be a common European currency by the year 1999. Think of the time you'll save by skipping currency-exchange windows!

Like it or not, the familiar Old World is becoming more like a "United States of Europe" every day, with 340 million inhabitants living in 12 different countries (the European Community)—Portugal, Spain, France, Italy, Greece, Luxembourg, Belgium, the Netherlands, Germany, Denmark, Great Britain, and Ireland. Sweden and Austria may be next to join to the "union."

Times—and prices—have changed since *Europe on $5 a Day* was first published in 1957, just as they had changed in 1957 from the days when Arthur Frommer first explored the continent as a young soldier on leave in the 1940s. This edition, *Europe on $45 a Day,* has been completely revised for 1993. Yet it retains the dependable Frommer emphasis: good value for your money. Traveling frugally provides rewarding opportunities to mingle with Europeans on their own turf—in their plazas, pubs, and even in their homes.

Europe on $45 a day means spending $45 on accommodations and meals only. Expect to use about half the sum on accommodations. Obviously, if two of you are traveling it's easier to achieve—$45 for accommodations and $45 for meals. Trim travel costs by taking advantage of the many low airfares to Europe, traveling off-season in January through May and October through December, planning a relatively short stay (a week to 10 days, say, instead of two weeks or more), and visiting only one country, two at most, per trip.

The first three chapters of this book alert you to travel resources, savings in airfares and rail passes, discounts, and a multitude of possibilities for squeezing the most out of your European holiday. Individual city chapters give specifics, such as when to go, where to stay, what to do, and how to save money in your favorite European cities.

Prices quoted in this book are obviously subject to change depending on inflation and currency fluctuations. For up-to-date exchange rates, check the business pages of your newspaper, contact a national tourist office, or call an office of Thomas Cook Currency Services (tel. 212/757-6915).

Bon voyage, feliz viaje, buon viaggio, and happy landing in the new Old World.

1. SOURCES OF INFORMATION IN THE UNITED STATES

TOURIST OFFICES Start with the European tourist offices in the United States (see the Appendix). If you live in New York City, you're lucky, because most of the tourist offices are located there. Some countries also have offices in Chicago, Los Angeles, Beverly Hills, San Francisco, Washington, D.C., or Dallas. If you're in a rush for information, call and ask them to send it right away. Otherwise, you may wait a couple of weeks for it to arrive. Tourist offices are excellent sources of information about weather, currency, destinations, special events, airlines, rail travel, and inexpensive lodgings.

If you're not sure which country or countries you want to visit, you can get a good overview, thumbnail sketches of each country, and transportation information from the free, 52-page *Planning Your Trip to Europe,* with color photos and maps, compiled annually by the 24-nation European Travel Commission. Order by writing to the European Planner, P.O. Box 9012, East Setauket, NY 11733.

LIBRARIES Another source of information is your public library, where you can find books and magazine articles on your destination, as well as literary works by well-known European authors, from Colette to Kazantzakis. For articles, check the *Guide to Periodical Literature* for the past few years, and look under the name of the countries or cities you plan to visit. You'll find the names of articles, where and when they were published, and the pages on which they appear in the magazine.

TRAVEL VIDEOS A relatively new but growing source, not only of information but of visual inspiration, is the travel video. It shows a country as it is today—how it and its people look—and can be invaluable in helping travelers choose which regions of a country to visit. One of the best introductions to European travel is Rick Steves's 80-minute *Europe Through the Back Door,* which was filmed on location. It costs $24.95 plus $3 shipping, and can be ordered from Small World Productions, P.O. Box 28369, Seattle, WA 98118-1369 (tel. toll free 800/866-RICK). The young, congenial, and well-traveled Steves shares tips on everything from crossing the language barrier to using foreign telephones to museum-going as he guides you on a scenic tour through the cities, towns, and landscapes of Europe. A set of five tapes, based on Steves's 13½-hour PBS series "Travels in Europe," is now available. Each tape highlights a different part of Europe (Amsterdam, Paris, and London; southwest Germany; Switzerland; and two on Italy). Each also contains travel tips, art and cultural history, and out-of-the-way attractions.

Also check local video-rental stores for travel videos. If nothing is available, request a copy of the *Complete Guide to Special Interest Video* ($14.95) from Video Learning Library, 15838 N. 62nd St., Scottsdale, AZ 85254 (tel. 602/596-9970, or toll free 800/526-7002). There is a variety of travel listings, dozens on Europe alone, as well as such related topics as adventure, birdwatching, fine arts and architecture, language, and railroading. The travel videos run 30–90 minutes, are produced by many different manufacturers, and may be rented or purchased directly from Video Learning Library.

TRAVEL AGENTS The services of an agent are free (he or she gets paid through commissions from travel suppliers such as airlines, hotels, cruise lines, and car-rental companies). A reliable agent knows about special fares, early-booking discounts, and other special offers in the constantly changing travel business. He or she can tailor travel plans to the client's individual objectives, interests, and budget, and arrange all manner of international transport, including air, sea, rail, car rental, and motorcoach; help secure travel insurance; and provide information on passport, visa, and exit-tax requirements.

In the case of last-minute or complex bookings, an agent may charge for long-distance calls, Telex, fax, or other services made on the client's behalf. Ask, if you think there might be a charge. Also check to see if there are cancellation fees on bookings made through the agency.

Seek out a travel agent much as you would an accountant or financial planner. Ask your friends and co-workers for recommendations. Meet the agent in person and consider the workspace itself, the attitude of the staff, and the agent's willingness to take time to listen to your needs and concerns.

Also look for someone affiliated with at least one of two trade organizations, the **American Society of Travel Agents (ASTA)** or the newer **Association of Retail Travel Agents (ARTA)**. ASTA has been around since 1929; its Consumer Affairs Department (tel. 703/739-2782) handles complaints from consumers about unsatisfactory service by travel agents.

If the letters "CTC" follow your agent's name, so much the better. It means that he or she is a Certified Travel Counselor, with 18 months of postprofessional training through the **Institute of Certified Travel Agents (ICTA)**.

If you are booking a tour, ask the agent if the tour operator is a member of the **United States Tour Operators Association (USTOA)**, which has 40 members and a $5-million pool to reimburse consumers if a member company goes bankrupt, leaving travelers high and dry. Also check with your local Better Business Bureau to see that the tour operator has a clean record.

Two helpful, free booklets that discuss working with travel agents and other consumer travel tips are "How to Buy Travel," available from American Express, and "Avoiding Travel Problems," from the ASTA World Headquarters, 1101 King St., Alexandria, VA 22314 (tel. 703/739-2782; fax 703/684-8319).

GUIDEBOOKS Your investment in a guidebook to Europe will repay itself many times over in both the time and the money it will save you. If the book is bulky, you may want to cut or tear out certain sections to carry with you on the trip or make photocopies of pertinent pages and leave the book at home. Some travelers take the book, but tear out pages as they go, to lighten their load. Also, get a pocket-size language guide so that you will at least be able to ask directions, understand what you're ordering on a menu, and find the nearest bathroom. (Berlitz has an outstanding series, along with its handy *European Menu Reader*.)

CATALOG-ORDER TRAVEL BOOKSTORES Most bookstores carry guidebooks and travel phrase books, but if yours doesn't or if you prefer a wider selection, as well as maps and travel products, take heart. There are some excellent travel bookstores around the country that have catalogs and mail- (or phone-) order service. They include: **Book Passage,** 51 Tamal Vista Blvd., Corte Madera, CA 94925 (tel. 415/927-0960, or toll free 800/321-9785); **Forsyth Travel Library,** 9154 W. 57th St. (P.O. Box 2975), Shawnee Mission, KS 66201-1375 (tel. 913/384-3440, or toll free 800/367-7984; **The Literate Traveler,** 8306 Wilshire Blvd., Suite 591, Beverly Hills, CA 90211 (tel. 213/398-8781); **Phileas Fogg's Books, Maps, and More for the Traveler,** 87 Stanford Shopping Center, Palo Alto, CA 94304 (tel. toll free 800/533-FOGG; request the Europe catalog); **Sandmeyer's Bookstore,** 714 S. Dearborn St., Chicago, IL 60605 (tel. 312/922-2104); **Travel Books & Language**

Center, 4931 Cordell Ave., Bethesda, MD 20814 (tel. 301/951-8533, or toll free 800/220-BOOK); and the **Traveller's Bookstore,** 22 W. 52nd St., New York, NY 10019 (tel. 212/664-0995; send $2 for catalog, free with purchase). All accept major credit cards.

Europe Through the Back Door, P.O. Box C-2009, Edmonds, WA 98020 (tel. 206/771-8303; fax 206/771-0833), sells offbeat, upbeat books by Rick Steves. It does not accept credit cards.

In Canada, contact **Ulysses Bookshop,** 4176 St. Denis, Montréal, PQ H2W 2M5 Canada (tel. 514/843-9447; fax 514/843-9448); their catalog is in English and French.

INTERNATIONAL TRAVEL NEWS This nonglossy, 100-page monthly travel magazine, also known as *ITN,* has black-and-white photos and a wealth of information for travelers provided by other travelers. Besides candid letters and articles, there are ads for everything from barge cruises in France to day hikes in the Swiss Alps to apartment rentals in London to foreign-language immersion courses. The classifieds are fun, too—essentially one big information swap. To subscribe, send $16 ($17.25 in California, $26 outside the U.S.) to International Travel News, 520 Calvados Ave., Sacramento, CA 95815 (tel. 916/457-3643, or toll free 800/366-9191 from 8am to 5pm Pacific time).

CULTURGRAMS A useful, if little-known, source of information is Culturgrams. Each Culturgram contains four pages of details on a country's customs, manners, and lifestyle, along with socioeconomic statistics, maps, and addresses of embassies and national tourist offices. Culturgrams cost $1 each for a quantity of 1–5, 50¢ each for 6–49, or $40 for a set of 102 countries (price includes UPS delivery). To request an order sheet, send a stamped, self-addressed, business-size envelope to Brigham Young University, David M. Kennedy Center for International Studies, Publication Services, 280 HRCB, Provo, UT 84602 (tel. 801/378-6528); call in an order with a credit card.

TRAVEL ADVISORIES If you are concerned that travel to a certain country may be dangerous, call the **U.S. Department of State's Citizens Emergency Center** at 202/647-5225. The center can also assist if you have a relative in an emergency situation overseas.

2. PASSPORT & OTHER DOCUMENTS

SECURING & RENEWING YOUR PASSPORT Passport applications are available from authorized post offices, clerks of court, or passport agencies. It is also possible to request an application—Form DSP-11 for a new passport or DSP-82 for a renewal—by mail, from Passport Services, Office of Correspondence, Department of State, 1425 K St. NW, Washington, DC 20522-1075. The back of the application gives the addresses of 13 agencies that can process the applications; they include Boston, Chicago, Honolulu, Houston, Los Angeles, Miami, New Orleans, New York City, Philadelphia, San Francisco, Seattle, Stamford, Conn., and Washington, D.C. Be forewarned that lines are long in these agencies, and you can get a passport more quickly and easily from a post office or courthouse. (Processing may take four to five weeks in either case.)

The passport application must be accompanied by proof of U.S. citizenship: an old passport, a certified copy of your birth certificate complete with registrar's seal, a report of birth abroad, or naturalized citizenship documents. In addition, a driver's license, employee identification card, military ID, or student ID card with photo is acceptable; otherwise, have a friend of two years' duration (who has ID) accompany you and vouch that you are who you say you are.

The application must be accompanied by two identical recent two- by two-inch photos, either color or black-and-white. Look in the *Yellow Pages* of your telephone book for places that take passport photos and expect them to be expensive (up to $9 for two).

First-time applicants over age 18 pay $65 ($55 plus a $10 first-time processing fee); under 18 the fee is $40 ($30 plus a $10 first-time fee) for a passport that's good for 10 years. Anyone 16 years or older who has an expired passport issued no more than 12 years ago may reapply by mail, submitting the old document with new photos and pink renewal form DSP-82. You must send a check or money order for $55; there is no additional processing fee. Both old and new passports will be mailed to you in three to four weeks' time.

A passport for children and adolescents under 18 is good for five years and costs $35 ($25 plus a $10 processing fee). Parents or guardians may apply for children under 13, presenting two photos for each child. Children 14 years and older must apply in person.

If your passport is lost or stolen, you must submit form DSP-64 in person to reapply. There is a $10 processing fee.

The booklet "Your Trip Abroad" (publication no. 044-000-02267-2) provides general information about passports and is available for $1 per copy from the U.S. Government Printing Office, Washington, DC 20402-9325 (tel. 202/783-3238).

For recorded passport information, or to report a lost or stolen passport, call 202/647-0518.

VISAS   Most western European countries do not require a visa, while most eastern European countries do.

The U.S. Department of State's Bureau of Consular Affairs publishes a 16-page booklet called **"Foreign Entry Requirements."** The information in it includes each country's entry requirements, from passport to onward or return ticket, to proof of sufficient funds, and it usually gives the telephone number of the country's embassy in Washington, D.C. It is noted if a visa is not required for a certain duration (30–90 days, say). Fees are given in U.S. dollars. Visa information is subject to change, so double-check requirements with tourist offices and a travel agent well in advance of departure dates. You may request "Foreign Entry Requirements" by sending your name, address, and 50¢ to the Consumer Information Center, P.O. Box 454Y, Pueblo, CO 81009. The Bureau of Consular Affairs also operates a telephone line for up-to-date visa information (tel. 202/663-1225).

If you need a visa on the spur of the moment and you don't live near an embassy, there are private services that, for about $25 (it varies from one to another), will take your passport and other required information and photo and get the visa for you, sometimes in a day's time. (You also pay the consular fee for the visa.) Such services include **Visa Services,** 1519 Connecticut Ave. NW, Suite 300, Washington, DC 20036 (tel. 202/387-0300, or toll free 800/222-VISA); **Mr. Visas,** 211 E. 43rd St., New York, NY 10017 (tel. 212/682-3895); **Trans World Visa Service,** 790 27th Ave., San Francisco, CA 94121 (tel. 415/752-6957); and **Visa Service,** 581 Boylston St., Boston, MA 02116 (tel. 617/266-7646), which asks a $45 fee.

INTERNATIONAL DRIVING PERMIT   If you plan to do any driving in Europe, you may need an International Driving Permit (IDP). Check with the embassy or consulate of the countries you plan to visit to see which driving requirements they enforce, as well as with your car-rental agency for its regulations. The International Driving Permit may be obtained from any branch of the **American Automobile Association (AAA).** You do not have to be a member of AAA. To be eligible, you must be at least 18 years old, submit two two- by two-inch photos (you can get them taken at many AAA offices), your valid U.S. driver's license, and a $10 fee. If there is no AAA office near you, call or write for an IDP application; then send it, along with a photocopy of the front and back of your driver's license, the two photos signed on the back, and the $10 fee to AAA, 1000 AAA Dr., Heathrow, FL 32746-5063 (tel.

407/444-7883, or toll free 800/AAA-HELP). The permit will be mailed back to you, and it is good for one year. It does not replace your own driver's license, however, so bring both of them with you.

3. CURRENCY/CREDIT

When you go abroad, take a mix of traveler's checks, credit cards, and cash. Take 80% of your money in traveler's checks and the rest in cash—just make sure you set aside enough cash to pay the country's exit tax (U.S. dollars are accepted), and to get home at the end of the trip. That leaves credit cards for splurges, emergencies, or as collateral when booking a hotel room or renting a car, even if you plan to pay with traveler's checks.

To figure out how much money you will need to take with you, first add up anything that has been paid for in advance, such as airline and Eurailpass tickets, and subtract that from the total amount you have budgeted to spend on vacation. Then estimate the daily cost of lodging, food, entertainment, and local transportation. (Use the prices in this book as a guide.) Multiply that estimate by the number of days you'll be abroad, then add in what you expect to spend for gifts and souvenirs. Err on the generous side; you can use the leftover traveler's checks when you return home.

If you have an ATM bank card, you may be able to use it abroad. Check with your local bank for a directory of international services. Just don't get overdrawn!

Most of the time the exchange rate is better overseas than at home, so convert only a small amount of money before departing, perhaps $50, including some small bills to use for tipping and transportation when you first arrive. That way you can avoid potentially long lines at the currency-exchange booth at the airport, grab a bus into town, and change more money at a downtown bank, where the exchange rate is likely to be better than at the airport or your hotel. (Always ask the fee for changing money before doing so; it may be so high that the rate no longer is equitable and you'll want to look elsewhere.)

If you carry cash and traveler's checks in a wallet, wrap a rubber band around the wallet so it won't slip out of your pocket easily. A front pants pocket is safer than a back one. If you carry a wallet in a purse, choose a purse with a zippered closing, and keep it zippered at all times, even if you're only removing a pen briefly to sign a traveler's check. Thieves are lightning fast and quite knowledgeable about tourists' habits. Don't get distracted during your travels and become an easy mark.

Should you become separated from your money—because of theft or simply through your own devices—a kind friend or relative at home can send you more via an American Express **MoneyGram** (tel. toll free 800/666-3947 in the U.S., 800/933-3278 in Canada). The transaction is quick; once the money is sent, you go in to a European American Express office with identification and a code word (the name of the family dog, perhaps) and pick it up, usually in the form of traveler's checks. The sender pays the service fee (figure about $40 to send $500).

TRAVELER'S CHECKS The safest way to travel with money is in the form of traveler's checks. Extra impetus for using them is that you usually get a little more foreign currency for your traveler's checks than you would for the equivalent amount of cash. (It has to do with the vagaries of the banking business.) If you lose the checks or they are stolen, the loss is only temporary. Paying with traveler's checks can be a handy budgeting tool during a trip because you can pace your spending as you see your check stock dwindling; with credit-card purchases, it's much easier to overspend.

Most traveler's checks have a standard charge. **Thomas Cook** often offers its checks for free through its travel agents, and **American Express** traveler's checks are offered free to members of the American Automobile Association (AAA) and many credit unions. This 1%–2% fee is set by the bank; some will waive the fee for

A PRECAUTION

Before you leave home, make two backup copies of each document you are carrying—your passport (copy the inside page with your photo), airline ticket, driver's license, international driving permit, youth-hostel card, prescriptions, and traveler's check numbers. Leave one set of copies at home and put the other in your luggage separate from the originals. Should the documents be lost or stolen, you'll have invaluable backup information to replace them or, in some cases, to get out of Europe and back home.

their account holders. You also may be able to buy traveler's checks with your credit card.

Find out if it's possible, or even feasible, to buy some traveler's checks in foreign currency, such as francs, Deutschmarks, or pounds sterling, to avoid the 5% fee that foreign banks may charge to change your checks into local currency. American Express traveler's checks may be obtained in British pounds, German Marks, and Swiss or French francs without paying the currency-conversion fee; you pay only a 1% commission. Thomas Cook MasterCard traveler's checks are available in German Marks, Dutch guilders, French and Swiss francs, Spanish pesetas, and British pounds. VISA checks are available in British pounds, French francs, Dutch guilders, German Marks, and Spanish pesetas.

Remember, you'll be buying foreign currency checks at the current exchange rate, which means you won't have to worry about fluctuations of the dollar. The down side is that you cannot take advantage of improving exchange rates as you travel. (Americans have not had to worry about this in recent years).

Another way to avoid an extra banking fee abroad is to cash traveler's checks at their corresponding bank. Cash VISA checks at Barclays Bank and Thomas Cook checks at Midland Bank and Thomas Cook offices (the latter two mainly in Britain), which also cash MasterCard checks at no charge. American Express Travel Service offices will change American Express checks into currency, or into traveler's checks in a foreign currency, for no fee. They also serve as refund centers and provide some emergency assistance.

Get traveler's checks in both large and small denominations. Toward the end of your stay, change the small checks so you won't be left with too much local currency. Changing dollars into foreign currency and then back into dollars means that you pay an exchange premium twice.

During the trip, divide traveler's checks up to avoid losing everything in case you are robbed; put some in your luggage and others in your wallet, and keep a list of the check numbers in an altogether separate place. Keep a record of the date of purchase of your checks, along with a hot-line number for the credit-card company to call in case they are lost. Leave a copy of this information and a list of check numbers at home with a friend, in case yours disappears. Check off the numbers as you cash the checks, so you don't accidentally claim theft for checks you actually cashed. You may be asked to show your passport in order to cash traveler's checks abroad.

For more information, contact American Express (tel. toll free 800/221-7282; request the "Ask the President" division of customer service), Barclays Bank (for Barclays' VISA traveler's checks; tel toll free 800/847-2245), and Thomas Cook MasterCard (tel. toll free 800/223-7373). For VISA and MasterCard, check with your bank.

CREDIT AND CHARGE CARDS Credit cards may prove to be a godsend abroad. You can use them for special purchases or unexpected expenses to avoid dipping into your cash fund. And if you run out of money altogether, the credit card can provide a cash advance (for which you will be charged a service fee).

Don't leave home without checking your card's expiration date, either. Travelers have had their credit cards become extinct mid-trip.

To avoid paying interest on credit-card charges that come due when you are abroad, send a check to the credit-card company before you leave home to cover what you expect your expenses to be.

Credit cards are increasingly connected to bank cash machines throughout the world, giving you easier access to funds. VISA Gold Card members may withdraw foreign currency from any ATM location in the PLUS system. Call VISA (tel. toll free 800/551-7648) for information on locations, emergency replacement, and insurance. American Express cardholders may also withdraw foreign currency from select ATMs against a line of credit (Optima card only) or their checking accounts. Call American Express for details (tel. toll free 800/CASH-NOW for locations, 800/528-4800 for other questions). MasterCard privileges vary; check with the bank that issued your card.

Reminder   The actual price tag on anything you buy with a credit card is subject to the fluctuations of the dollar. The purchase is not converted into dollars from foreign currency until it is actually received at U.S. headquarters, whether you bought it two weeks or two months earlier. Like it or not, you're dealing with a time lag. If the dollar is growing stronger abroad, buying on credit works in your favor; if it is weakening, it works against you.

4. LUGGAGE & PACKING POINTERS

LUGGAGE

If you're thinking of buying a new travel bag, keep in mind durability, packability, and practicality. If you choose wisely, the bag will last you for years and, like its owner, take on character with age.

Soft-sided luggage is popular because it can expand to hold a lot of belongings, including things collected along the way. Garment bags do well for trips of a week or two (except for train travel, when they become unwieldy); you can wedge all sorts of incidentals in the often-unused space in the corners.

Select a bag that's waterproof and lightweight but strong, with sturdy zippers or locks. Half a dozen pockets or compartments are always a plus.

Hard-sided suitcases weigh 8–10 pounds and are heavier than most of us care to handle when fully packed. If you need a second bag, choose a shoulder bag or a small backpack instead of a large bag, one that will fit under the airplane seat or in the overhead bin. The best pack converts for hand carrying.

Don't be fooled by bags that come with incredibly low price tags. They may not survive one flight. You may be able to find well-made, reasonably priced bags on sale.

WHAT TO TAKE

You can get by with three changes of clothes in complementary colors to allow for creative mixing and matching. Choose comfortable clothes that wash well and need no ironing. Pick items you like because you'll be seeing a lot of them.

If you need new clothes or shoes for the trip, buy them well enough in advance of your departure to break them in beforehand. New shoes can not only cause blisters, but they also exercise different muscles in the legs, causing soreness and inhibiting your ability to explore a new place.

Put your name and address on anything you might accidentally leave on the plane or in a restaurant or hotel room; this includes your camera, glasses case, or binoculars case. Also tuck vital tracking information in the pocket of your jacket or raincoat.

Don't expect to be able to buy any essential item abroad; as sure as you need it, you won't find it anywhere or, if you do, it'll cost twice what you'd pay at home.

Women may find skirts more comfortable, and cooler, than pants. If you need a coat or jacket, plan to wear rather than pack it. If the mercury drops, stay warm by adding layers—a T-shirt under a shirt under a sweater or jacket.

Silk long underwear is lightweight, easily packable, and warm. Bring along a hat or cap, since up to 30% of the body's temperature is lost through the head. In hot climates you'll need a hat for shade and some sunscreen.

The bare-bones packing rule on garments is two (pairs of underwear, socks, shirts): Wash one and wear one. The same goes for shoes: one pair for walking, the other more formal.

Take one extra piece of clothing for unexpected weather—a heat spell in winter or a cold front in a balmy climate. For a spot-check of the current weather and a three-day forecast for any European city, or for ski conditions at 14 European resorts, call 900-WEATHER, using a Touch-Tone telephone only. Punch in the first four letters of the city or resort name (LOND for London, for instance). The service, operated by the Weather Channel, costs 95¢ per minute; calls average three minutes.

Men can dress up a shirt with a tie or vest; women can add jewelry or scarves. Bring along a lightweight fabric bag to carry home purchases made abroad.

If you can manage to pack everything in a couple of carry-on bags, you can bypass time-consuming luggage check-in counters and baggage-claim areas at airports. You'll also have no worries about luggage arriving at your destination a few days after you do and you won't have to linger at the baggage-claim area when all you really want to do is get into town, find a room, and relax. Furthermore, if you need a personal item mid-flight, it's right at your feet or just overhead where you stowed it. Airlines have different requirements for acceptable carry-on luggage; figure about 22 by 14 by 9 inches. Some airlines allow only one carry-on bag per person, especially if a flight is fully booked. Bags are also subject to weight restrictions, usually 70 pounds.

CHECKLIST To avoid overlooking anything, modify this list to suit you; then check off items as you pack them.

Accessories (a few strategic ones)
Address book
Air/rail tickets
Air/seasickness pills
Alarm clock
Antidiarrhea medicine
Aspirin
Camera, batteries, film
Cash ($50 worth of foreign currency, enough dollars to get you to and from the airport)
Credit cards
Documents: trip itinerary, vouchers, receipts, reservation slips, Eurailpass and validation slip, traveler's check numbers, prescriptions
Eyeglasses (or contacts), with a spare set or prescription
Flashlight
Guidebook
Hat or cap
Insurance or assistance policy
International driver's license
Jacket
Jewelry (nothing too valuable)
Magnifying glass
Maps
Pajamas/nightgown/T-shirt (optional)

Pants (two or three pairs)
Passport and visas (make photocopies)
Phrase book
Plastic bags to hold damp clothes or washcloth
Prescription medicine
Raincoat or windbreaker
Sewing kit
Shawl (versatile as an accessory, wrap, bathing suit cover, and bathrobe)
Shirts, blouses, tops (two to four)
Shoes (two pairs)
Sleeping sheet, for staying in hostels
Socks/tights (two to four pairs)
Sunscreen
Sunglasses
Sweater
Swimsuit
Swiss army knife (essential for impromptu picnics)
Tie
Toiletries
Transformer and adapter plugs
Traveler's checks
Underwear (two to four sets)
Vitamins
Washcloth (European lodgings often don't supply them)
Umbrella (collapsible)

HOW TO PACK   Pack items of clothing first. Rolling articles keeps wrinkles at bay. Next, add shoes and toiletries around the sides of your bag. Put shoes in a plastic bag to keep clothes clean; do the same for toiletries, or put tape around the caps, to contain spills. Pack the tape for later use.

Stuff shoes with underwear or socks so they keep their shape. Pack an extra plastic bag for the inevitable time you have to travel with a damp swimsuit or clothing.

Always put documents, medication, traveler's checks, keys, and other valuables in your carry-on luggage. Be sure your reading material or journal is easily accessible.

To make it easier to recognize your luggage at the baggage claim (especially if it's black), tie a colorful piece of yarn on the handle.

To avoid prolonged inconvenience in case a bag is lost, include your itinerary in each piece of luggage, along with the name of your tour operator if you have one. If you are traveling with another person, pack some of each other's belongings in each bag so both will have a change of clothing if a bag is lost.

Pack and repack articles the same way each time during the trip. They'll be easier to find and will take up a predictable amount of space.

Reminder   Take half as many clothes as you think you'll need and twice as much money.

5. INSURANCE & ASSISTANCE

Don't buy insurance unless you're positive you aren't already covered. Check existing policies, as well as with credit-card companies whose cards you hold. Some of them offer automatic travel accident insurance up to $100,000 for you and your family when you purchase air, rail, or sea passage through them. You may belong to a social or professional organization through which you are covered on trips abroad.

Be aware that there are different types and degrees of coverage. What suits you? How much insurance can you afford? How much risk can you afford? How much peace of mind do you need? What about the event of an act of terrorism? What if a preexisting medical condition kicks up? While it is important to get the coverage you need, there's no reason to overinsure.

Travel *assistance* provides on-site help in the midst of a travel emergency, including emergency transport, contact with an English-speaking surgeon, arrangement for hospital admittance, or an emergency loan for medical expenses. Travel *insurance,* on the other hand, covers some or much of the cost of the emergency, but only after the fact.

Today the two types of coverage are increasingly similar, each offering options of the other—great for the consumer. Both assistance and insurance are available through travel agents, as well as insurance companies. Before you sign on the dotted line, check the fine print for what is not covered; it's just as important as what is.

Prices given below are for one or two weeks' coverage for an individual (family rates are often available).

INSURANCE/ASSISTANCE   Access America, 6600 W. Broad St., Richmond, VA 23230 (tel. toll free 800/284-8300). Coverage for individuals includes three different policies: medical, $49 for $10,000 worth of coverage for 9–15 days; medical plus trip cancellation, $89 for 9–15 days (includes $1,000 for trip interruption and $500 for flight delay of three or more hours); and a comprehensive plan for $111 for 9–15 days that incorporates the above with $1,000 baggage coverage, $100 for bag delay, and $50,000 death and dismemberment policy. Policy holders have access to a 24-hour hotline, which they may call collect from Europe. Optional additional baggage or trip cancellation, terrorism coverage, family plans, and extended-stay plans are available.

HealthCare Abroad (MEDEX), 107 W. Federal St. (P.O. Box 480), Middleburg, VA 22117 (tel. 703/687-3166, or toll free 800/237-6615). Policy holders who travel for 10–90 days pay $3 a day for $100,000 accident and sickness coverage, medical evacuation, and $25,000 accidental death or dismemberment insurance. Optional trip cancellation costs 5¢ per dollar, with a minimum $25 (for $500) coverage. Baggage coverage is $1 a day for $1,000 worth of coverage. All coverage may also be purchased separately. Ask about family and extended-stay plans.

International SOS Assistance, Eight Neshaminy Interplex, Trevose, PA 19053-6956 (tel. 215/244-1500, or toll free 800/523-8930). Strictly an assistance company, it offers a 24-hour hotline, emergency evacuation, hospital admission, return of unattended minors, and return of remains; $35 for 1–14 days. Ask about couple, family plan, and frequent-traveler rates.

Tele-Trip (Mutual of Omaha), 3201 Farnam St., Omaha, NE 68131 (tel. 402/345-2400, or toll free 800/228-9792). A sample comprehensive package including trip and flight cancellation; baggage loss or delay; accidental medical, death, and dismemberment; medical evacuation; and traveler's assistance costs $113 for a three-week trip.

Travel Assistance International (Europ Assistance), 1133 15th St. NW, Suite 400, Washington, DC 20005 (tel. 202/331-1609, or toll free 800/821-2828). It provides unlimited medical evacuation coverage up to $15,000 in medical insurance, medical referrals, legal assistance, and an emergency message center, and sends out detailed travel information before the trip. Coverage for 9–15 days costs $50. Ask about family yearly and extended-stay plans and terrorism coverage.

Travel Guard International, 1145 Clark St., Stevens Point, WI 54481 (tel. toll free 800/826-1300). A comprehensive insurance package including medical coverage, emergency assistance, accidental death, trip cancellation and interruption, and baggage loss or delay is based on 8% of the total trip cost; some limitations apply. Separate extensive medical, trip-cancellation, and baggage coverage is also available.

Travel Insurance PAK, Travelers Insurance Division, One Tower Square, 10NB, Hartford, CT 06183-5040 (toll free 800/243-3174). Travel accident and illness coverage starts at $10 for 6–10 days; $500 worth of coverage for lost, damaged, or delayed baggage costs $20 for 6–10 days; and trip cancellation costs $5.50 for $100 worth of coverage (written approval is necessary for cancellation coverage above $5,000).

A MEDICAL DIRECTORY If you decide against coverage of any kind, consider **IAMAT (the International Association for Medical Assistance to Travelers),** 417 Center St., Lewiston, NY 14092-3633 (tel. 716/754-4883), which publishes an annual directory of English-speaking doctors in more than 130 countries worldwide who offer services to members of the organization for a standard fee; in 1991 it was $45 for an office visit, $55 for a house call, and $65 for an appointment during holidays or on Sunday. There is no fee to become an IAMAT member, though the organization does accept donations. It will send a packet that includes the directory and information on climate, food, water, and immunization.

THEFT COVERAGE If you are concerned about theft, check your homeowner's, condo, co-op, or renter's insurance policy to see if it includes an off-premises–theft clause. **Allstate** has outstanding, inexpensive off-premises coverage that repays the recipient within a week of report of theft accompanied by an official police report, even if it is in a foreign language. For more information, contact any Allstate agent.

COMPUTER COVERAGE If you plan to travel with a computer, be aware that it probably is not covered by either your homeowner's, renter's, or travel insurance. (Access America does insure computers and other electronic equipment as baggage for up to $1,000.) It's possible to get coverage specifically for the computer through **Safeware,** 2929 N. High St. (P.O. Box 02211), Columbus, OH 43202 (tel. 614/262-0559, or toll free 800/848-3469).

The company offers a $90 ninety-day policy and a $200 annual policy for up to $4,000 worth of equipment, software, and disks which comes with a $250 deductible. Among the hazards covered are theft (the biggest problem where laptop computers are concerned), fire, vandalism, natural disasters, accidental damages, and damages resulting from airport x-rays. The policy goes into effect with a phone call.

6. CAMERA & FILM

From experience on past trips, determine how many rolls you're likely to shoot in a day or a week, then throw in three more for good measure. If this is your first trip with camera equipment, err on the side of abundance and allow yourself at least one roll a day. Film can be twice as expensive in foreign countries as it is in your hometown camera store or drugstore. It generally comes with processing included, though.

To protect film when going through airport x-rays, put it in a lead-laminated pouch, available in several sizes in camera stores. To be extra careful, ask the attendant to hand-handle the film. Put it in a plastic bag, either unopened in its box or completely free of packing, plastic container and all.

If you have film in your camera, pass it around the x-ray machine as well. Officials claim that the machine will not damage low-speed films—ASA 64 or 100, say—but professional photographers claim differently, and multiple doses of low-voltage x-rays do fog film.

Film is less expensive if bought in the U.S. with processing included, and with handy mailers you may even send it home as you shoot it. Kodak sold its U.S. processing plants in 1988, and mailers are now available for Kodalux, not Kodak, processing. Kodalux will, however, accept Kodak mailers.

Addresses of the processing plants around the country are given on the back of each mailer. If slides or prints are not returned to you, call Kodalux headquarters (tel. 201/797-0600; ask for customer service). Be sure to keep your mailing stub and address the mailer in indelible ink so your return address will not be obscured if the mailer gets wet.

Carry a plastic bag to protect your camera if you'll be shooting in dust or rain.

To identify what is on each roll of film, carry handy stick-on dots on which to jot down the subject matter on the roll.

7. HEALTH TIPS

When packing, don't overlook a prescription for any medicine you take on a regular basis. Ask your doctor to give you a generic prescription because European trade names of prescription drugs are different from those in the United States. Some drugs that are available over-the-counter in the United States may require a doctor's prescription in some European countries—such as antihistamines in Sweden—so pack anything you could possibly need to avoid time-consuming hassles and extra expense during the trip.

If you have ongoing or recurring physical maladies, carry a printed medical history with your Social Security number, insurance company, address, current medications with generic names and dosages, and a list of drug allergies. This will be invaluable to a foreign doctor.

The 178-page book *Health Information for the International Traveler* is available from the Superintendent of Documents, U.S. Government Printing Office, Washington, DC 10401 (tel. 202/783-3238 to order with VISA or MasterCard, or for more information); specify stock no. 017-023-00189-2.

VEGETARIAN TRAVELERS   Finding restaurants that cater to a vegetarian diet may be difficult in Europe. But markets selling fresh fruits and vegetables are more plentiful than in the U.S.

The *International Vegetarian Travel Guide* ($9.95), updated in 1991, contains 292 pages of information on restaurants and lodgings that cater to vegetarians. *Europe on 10 Salads a Day* ($9.95), published in 1991, profiles vegetarian restaurants in every major city and off the beaten track. Order either book or ask about new and additional titles from Vegetarian Times Bookshelf, P.O. Box 446, Mount Morris, IL 61054 (tel. toll free 800/435-9610); $3 postage and handling. VISA and MasterCard are accepted.

The **Vegetarian Resource Group,** P.O. Box 1463, Baltimore, MD 21203 (tel. 410/366-8343), can provide information about resources in individual European countries.

The **Vegetarian Society of the United Kingdom** is at Parkdale, Dunham Road, Altrincham, Cheshire, WA14 4QG England (tel. 061/928-073).

For more information on vegetarian-related travel, contact the *Vegetarian Times,* P.O. Box 570, Oak Park, IL 60302 (tel. 708/848-8100).

Reminder   Expect to find many more smokers in Europe than in the United States. Few restaurants provide no-smoking sections, and if you ask people in restaurants, cafés, pubs, or elevators or on airplanes to refrain from smoking, they are likely to be offended and tell you so.

8. TIPS FOR SPECIAL TRAVELERS

FOR THE DISABLED   One of the toughest parts of travel to an unfamiliar place is not knowing exactly what you're going to find. For travelers with physical disabilities, this can be especially daunting. The more they can learn about the accessibility of a place before they arrive, the better equipped they'll be to maneuver and enjoy themselves once they're there. Here are some sources of information:

Mobility International USA, P.O. Box 3551, Eugene, OR 97403 (tel. 503/343-1284, voice and TDD), can provide information for the disabled not only on travel abroad but on work camps and educational exchanges in its new and expanded edition of *A World of Options for the '90s: A Guide to International Educational Exchange, Community Service, and Travel for Persons with Disabilities,* which costs $16. It also offers *A Manual for Integrating Persons with Disabilities into International Educational Exchange Programs,* for $18, including postage and handling. The organization offers a video called *Looking Back, Looking Forward,* about a group of disabled and nondisabled travelers who visited England and Costa Rica; it costs $40 for members, $49 for nonmembers, including shipping, and is available with captions. Mobility International also sponsors its own four-week exchange programs. Membership in the organization includes a newsletter and a telephone information service, and costs $20 a year; subscription to the newsletter only is $10.

Directions Unlimited, 720 N. Bedford Rd., Bedford Hills, NY 10507 (tel. toll free 800/533-5343), and **Wings on Wheels (Evergreen Travel Service),** 4114 198th St. SW, Suite 13, Lynnwood, WA 98036 (tel. 206/776-1184, or toll free 800/435-2288), book tours to Europe for disabled travelers. Joan French, who is deaf, organizes tours for the deaf through her company, **Interpret Tours,** 1730 Citronia St., North Ridge, CA 91325 (tel. TTY 818/885-6921; if you don't have TTY, call the California Relay Service, toll free 800/342-5833, and give them her number and your message).

The **Travel Information Service** of Moss Rehabilitation Hospital, 1200 W. Tabor Rd., Philadelphia, PA 19141-3099 (tel. 215/456-9600), a center for treatment of the physically disabled, serves as a clearinghouse of information, much of it from firsthand reports, on accessible hotels, restaurants, and attractions abroad. There is a nominal fee for mailing materials.

Three out-of-print guides that are useful for general—but not current—information may be available in public libraries: ***Access to the World: A Travel Guide for the Handicapped*** by Louise Weiss (Henry Holt, 1986), ***A Travel Guide for the Disabled: Western Europe*** by Mary Meister Walzer (Van Nostrand Reinhold, 1982), and ***Frommer's Guide for the Disabled Traveler*** by Frances Barish (Prentice Hall, 1984), covering Europe, the U.S., and Canada.

FOR OLDER TRAVELERS   The following travel tips, many of them gleaned from Arthur Frommer himself, a mature traveler with a lot of miles under his seat belt, are particularly geared to the "traveler emeritus":

- Prepare for your trip by reading history and art-appreciation books. Approach a place with mature deliberation rather than youthful impetuousness.
- Pack less and enjoy more. (See Section 4, "Luggage and Packing Pointers," above.)
- Always carry proof of age—your passport, driver's license, Medicare card, or membership card for an organization for seniors—to take advantage of senior discounts.
- If you plan to travel by train but only in one European country, find out if that country offers senior passes. You could save up to 50%.
- When making your airline reservation, ask for the senior discount of 10% offered by airlines on most fares, and find out if there is a special promotional fare that is even lower.
- Combat jet lag by going to sleep for a few hours immediately upon arrival. Otherwise, you may become overly tired and unable to sleep later.
- Buy travel insurance before departing on a trip. You can insure yourself, your luggage, even the price of your trip in the event of cancellation—yours or the tour operator's. (See Section 5, "Insurance and Assistance," above.)
- Seek out the undiscovered rather than the heavily touristed. Nothing is duller than contrived nightspots, souvenir shops, and endless tours. Mature travelers especially crave good companionship more than crowds, and that is often found in out-of-the-way places not yet on the tourist circuit.

Youth hostels around the world cater to the young and the young at heart and almost all place no maximum-age limitation on membership. The facilities are clean, though generally lacking the private bath that older travelers tend to prefer. Beds are often cots or bunk beds in privacy-lacking dorms, segregated by sex. Hostel management will provide private rooms for couples or families. These may often be reserved in advance. For membership information, see "How to Save Money on Accommodations" in Chapter 2.

Retired travelers have the advantage of being able to stay longer abroad, even on a budget. If they travel off-season, they can take advantage of extended-stay bargains offered by tour operators such as **Sun Holidays,** 26 Sixth St., Stamford, CT 06905 (tel. 203/323-1166, or toll free 800/243-2057). In winter 1992 it offered 28 days in an apartment on Spain's Costa del Sol for $999 per person, including airfare from New York, Boston (for $40 more), or Miami (for $147 more)—less than $36 a day.

Sometimes the pain of traveling alone after the loss of a spouse is softened by linking up with a group or finding a travel companion through a travel club. Two companies that specialize in travel and tours for older adults include **Grand Circle Travel, Inc.,** 347 Congress St., Boston, MA 02210 (tel. 617/350-7500, or toll free 800/221-2610), and **Saga International Holidays Ltd.,** 120 Boylston St., Boston, MA 02116 (tel. toll free 800/343-0273). Call for a brochure and detailed itineraries. The latter offers some programs in conjunction with Elderhostel (see below), and offers Smithsonian Odyssey Tours (educational guided tours) in conjunction with the Smithsonian Institution.

Two educational organizations for older adults, **Elderhostel** and **Interhostel,** uniquely combine travel with education, with companionship as a natural by-product.

For more information about them and their overseas programs, see "Low-Cost Travel with a Difference" in Chapter 2.

The AARP Experience from American Express, P.O. Box 37580, Louisville, KY 50233-9895 (tel. toll free 800/927-0111 for land and air programs, 800/745-4567 for cruises, and 800/659-5678 TDD or TTY), organizes group escorted tours and hosted cruises for members, as well as independent stays (renting an apartment). People 50 and over may join the AARP (see below), a private, nonprofit organization. Tours may be booked through the AARP or any American Express travel office; you do not have to be a cardholder.

Partners-in-Travel, P.O. Box 491145, Los Angeles, CA 90049 (tel. 310/476-4869), publishes a bimonthly newsletter filled with nearly 200 travel personals in its classified section. The service is not limited to older travelers, though people over 55 number 50% of the subscribers. The cost is $40 for a one-year subscription.

For more choices still, consider the **Travel Companion Exchange,** P.O. Box 833-F, Amityville, NY 11701 (tel. 516/454-0880; fax 516/454-0170). Members, who range in age from 18 to 80, receive several hundred listings and may request extended profiles of those that particularly interest them. Membership is $6 or $11 per month for a minimum six-month period and includes listings and a bimonthly newsletter (those seeking a travel partner of the opposite sex pay the higher rate because the match-up is more time-consuming for the staff). Without becoming a member of the exchange, you may subscribe to its newsletter (without listings) at $24 for six months, or $36 for one year; both the subscription and membership include six free back issues right away plus future issues. The newsletter includes 12 pages of travel tips; information on airfare, hotel, and cruise discounts; and money-saving ideas for single travelers. Travel Companion Exchange, in existence since 1981, has 2,000 active members.

Good sources of a wide range of information for older travelers include the **American Association of Retired Persons (AARP),** 3200 E. Carson St., Lakewood, CA 90712 (tel. toll free 800/424-3410), which has a $5 membership fee and a Purchase Privilege Program with discounts on lodging and car rentals; **Mature Outlook,** 6001 N. Clark St., Chicago, IL 60660-9977 (tel. toll free 800/336-6330), for a bi-monthly magazine ($9.95 a year), newsletter, and discounts; and the **National Council of Senior Citizens,** 1331 F St. NW, Washington, DC 20004 (tel. 202/347-8800).

Reminder Retirement in Europe can be a reality. If you've ever toyed with the idea, get a copy of **The World's Top Retirement Havens,** which discusses the specifics of living in 20 different countries, more than half of them in Europe. The 460-page paperback, published in 1991, costs $15.95 from International Living, 824 E. Baltimore St., Baltimore, MD 21202 (tel. toll free 800/223-1982; fax 301/837-3879). A one-year subscription to the **International Living** monthly newsletter, with regular columns on real estate, investing, employment, and budget travel (much of it related to Europe), costs $29, and includes the free report "The Five Best Retirement Destinations for the 1990s."

FOR SINGLE TRAVELERS Traveling alone can be pure heaven for some; for others, anathema. One drawback is that solo travelers often spend more money since they have no one with whom to share expenses for food, transportation, and lodging. Hotel rooms usually are booked at a double-occupancy rate, but guesthouses and small hotels often keep prices low for single occupants, and may even have a few single rooms on the premises. Ask if there is a single supplement before agreeing to stay anywhere; it could be as high as 50%.

Even those who thrive on the freedom and solitude that traveling alone affords sometimes welcome an in-depth exchange with other people (it doesn't always happen when you're on your own). An excellent way to connect with individuals or families in foreign countries is through home stays or arranged visits of just a few hours' duration. These may be set up through organizations such as **Servas** or **Friends Overseas** (see "Low-Cost Travel with a Difference" in Chapter 2 for more information).

Singleworld, 401 Theodore Fremd Ave., Rye, NY 10580 (tel. 914/967-3334, or toll free 800/223-6490), is a travel agency and tour operator that caters, as its name implies, to single travelers, who pay a $25 yearly fee from the date of their first departure. Trips are organized in three ways: for ages 20–33, 29–49, and for all ages. You may book with Singleworld directly, or through your travel agent.

For particularly fun-loving gatherings of singles, not to mention a relaxed way to meet Europeans, consider **Club Med,** 40 W. 57th St., New York, NY 10019 (tel. toll free 800/CLUB-MED), or **Contiki Holidays,** 1432 E. Katella Ave., Anaheim, CA 92805 (tel. toll free 800/626-0611, 800/624-0611 in California). Club Med, 60% of whose guests are single, now has single rooms available at a number of its properties.

If you decide to seek out another single traveler similar to you in age and interests to share experiences and expenses, contact **Travel Companion Exchange,** whose membership includes people of all ages (for details, see "For Older Travelers," above). You may also find someone by putting up notices in youth hostels once you get to Europe.

The **Campus Travel Group** (incorporating London Student Travel), 52 Grosvenor Gardens, London SW1 W0AU (tel. 071/730-3402; fax 071/730-5739), specializes in travel for students and young independent travelers both within Great Britain and throughout Europe by plane, boat, bus, or train. The main office (mentioned above) is at the Victoria tube station; other London locations include Covent Garden tube (tel. 071/836-3343), High Street Kensington tube (tel. 071/938-2188), and Euston station (tel. 071/383-5337).

Some tour organizers cater primarily to single travelers over age 50 or 60; to find out about them, see "For Older Travelers," above.

FOR FAMILIES   Children add joys and a different level of experience to travel. They speak a universal language and will be able to communicate with other children, as well as adults, wherever you find yourself, and they will draw sometimes reticent local people like a magnet, which would probably not happen were you alone.

Taking kids along means additional, more thorough planning. Check with the child's doctor before leaving, and don't forget to pack first-aid supplies, such as a thermometer, Band-Aids, cough drops, and children's aspirin.

Help children prepare by visiting the library to read encyclopedia accounts of the country, its culture, customs, climate, and people. Make photocopies of a map of the country or of Europe and have the kids color it in; draw special attention to the places you will be visiting. Buy a tape of traditional music or stories and rent travel videos.

Make a big deal about getting your child's passport; even infants are required to have one, and a child old enough to sign his or her own name should do so on the document.

When traveling with young children, bring along a favorite (packable) toy and book for familiarity and comfort in new places. Bring plenty of disposable diapers, despite the bulkiness. You'll also be able to buy more most places you visit.

Give a child who is big enough his or her own kid-size backpack to carry some of the load. Encourage kids to send postcards to friends and family back home, to keep a journal, or to take photos with an Instamatic camera.

Get to the airport early for check-in and boarding (folks with kids get to go first). If you're traveling with a stroller, figure out ahead of time if it will fit in the overhead compartment (check when you make your reservation). Reserve bulkhead seats if possible for the extra space they afford.

You may order special children's meals (hot dogs, spaghetti, peanut butter and jelly sandwiches), but you have to request them ahead of time. Airlines don't keep baby food on board, but flight attendants will heat up any you've brought with you.

Don't bring a noisy game that will annoy passengers around you or one with myriad pieces that you'll have to look for at the end of the flight.

Throughout the flight (and the trip), keep snacks on hand: raisins, crackers, fruit, water, or juice. Limit your activities so as not to tire out the child or yourself by planning enough "down time" and ample bathroom breaks.

Try to stay in hotels that are child-friendly, with space for kids to play, such as a garden or courtyard. Check in during the afternoon so that the child can get accustomed to the new home-away-from-home.

If your child is overly dependent at the beginning of the trip, be supportive. Hold off on any long excursions until he or she feels more outgoing. When you're ready to venture out, do so early in the day, when lines tend to be shorter. If it's hot, be sure the child has a hat with a brim. If you have to wait in line, play "I Spy" or counting games to pass the time. Relax together in the unbeatable European gardens and parks.

Teach children to identify park, museum, or department store employees by their uniforms or name tags, so they will know whom to ask for help if they get lost. You can pin a small whistle to a small child's clothing with instructions to blow it in case you get separated.

Buy souvenirs at the end of the day to lessen the chance that they will break or get lost before you return to the hotel.

When you return home, put together a scrapbook with the child, including postcards, other souvenirs, and photos.

Additional resources include **Travel with Your Children (TWYCH),** 45 W. 18th St., New York, NY 10011 (tel. 212/206-0688), which publishes the newsletter *Family Travel Times* for $35 for 10 issues (subscribers with questions about travel to specific countries have access to a call-in service on Wednesday from 10am to 1pm, eastern standard time), and *Travel with Children* by Maureen Wheeler (Lonely Planet), actually about travel in Asia but the advice is universally good.

An increasingly popular vacation destination for families is **Club Med,** 40 W. 57th St., New York, NY 10019 (tel. toll free 800/CLUB-MED), which first opened in 1950 as a tent village in Majorca, Spain. There are now 45 properties in western Europe in Spain, Portugal, France, Switzerland, Austria, Italy, and Greece, as well as in Yugoslavia, Bulgaria, Turkey, and Morocco. Many of these have Mini Clubs for children ages 2–11 years, and Baby Clubs for children ages 4 through 23 months, with supervised activities especially for children. Club Med Opio, which opened on the French Riviera in 1989, has a Mini Club.

Reminder Teach kids a few key words in a foreign language, such as *bonjour, au revoir,* and *merci,* but don't get upset when they pick up more of the language than you do once you arrive.

FOR STUDENTS The **International Student Identity Card (ISIC),** available for $15 ($14 if you pay in person) from the Council on International Educational Exchange (CIEE), 205 E. 42nd St., Dept. ID/F, New York, NY 10017 (tel. 212/661-1414), enables students ages 12 and up to take advantage of discounts on transportation, lodging, and admission to attractions. (Some airfare discounts are subject to age restrictions.) Call toll free 800/GET-ANID for one of the 400 U.S. campus CIEE offices.

To be eligible for the card, you must be enrolled full time or part time in a degree program. The application must include proof of student status via a letter on school stationery carrying the school seal (a transcript or bursar's receipt is also acceptable), a $14 registration fee, and one passport-size photo. The validity of the card runs from September of one year through December of the next. The card comes with a guide listing student offices worldwide. These offices are great contact points in any city, and they can tell you how to get the most mileage out of the card in their country.

For people under the age of 26 who are not students, CIEE issues the **International Youth Identity Card (IYIC).** Applicants must send proof of age (a copy of your birth certificate, the personal data page of your passport, or driver's license), a $14 fee, a valid passport number, and one passport-size photo. The card, valid from September of one year through December of the next, comes with the handy booklet "International Youth Card Discounts for Cardholders."

Both the ISIC and IYIC cards carry basic accident and sickness insurance coverage, and cardholders have access to a worldwide hotline for help in medical, legal, and financial emergencies.

CIEE has offices in Great Britain, France, Germany, Italy, and Spain. Its European headquarters is located at 49, rue Pierre Charron, 75008 Paris (tel. 43-59-23-69).

9. RECEIVING MAIL & MESSAGES ABROAD

No matter how much you love to travel, there's nothing better than having news from home while you're away. If you plan an extended stay in Europe, arrange for friends and family to write you there.

General Delivery services (called **Poste Restante**) at main post offices will generally hold mail for travelers for a limited time, usually alphabetizing it by first letter of the last name. Ask correspondents to write on the envelope a request to hold until a certain date, one a few days *after* you plan to leave, just to make sure.

Some banks or credit-card companies handle mail for their card- or traveler's-check holders, but American embassies and consulates do not. **American Express** will hold mail for 30 days for its cardholders or people using its traveler's checks or other travel services. There is also a nominal fee for all travelers who have their mail forwarded. Renters of **Avis** cars have access to the company's free Europe Message Center, through which they may receive and leave messages while abroad.

In an emergency, American Express will send a single mailgram or international cable for a traveler. For more information about these and other services, cardholders should request the free **"American Express Traveler's Companion"** from any American Express Travel Service office or by writing American Express, P.O. Box 678, Canal Street Station, New York, NY 10013.

If you have a friend abroad (or an amenable friend of a friend), leave his or her address and telephone number, along with the dates you expect to visit. You can also leave the name and address of a hotel where you have a reservation; just alert the hotelier to hold your correspondence.

In the case of a medical emergency, your travel-insurance company may serve as a message center for you.

Before you leave home, select one to three places (depending on your length of stay and your movement abroad) where you would like to receive mail and prepare a list of places and approximate dates when you will be there to give to your friends.

10. ELECTRICITY

Electricity in the U.S. is 110–120 volts, while in Europe it generally is 220–240 volts. This means that your electric razor, hairdryer, or portable computer will burn out if you plug it into a European outlet—*if* the plug will fit in the outlet.

What you need in order to mix those electrical apples and oranges is an adapter plug *and* an electrical transformer. The adapter makes it possible to plug your appliance into the wall, while the transformer (sometimes incorrectly called a converter) changes the number of volts flowing to that appliance from 220 to 110. If you use an adapter without a transformer, you may smell a faint odor that tells you your appliance is burning out.

Buy adapters and transformers before you leave home, because they may not be readily available in Europe. In the U.S., hardware stores or electronics shops carry them, as well as travel specialty stores.

If you plan to travel with a portable computer, read the instruction manual carefully or call the manufacturer to see if you will also need to buy a special transformer. This device makes it possible for an apparatus geared to the U.S. 60-cycle current to operate on the 50-cycle current in Europe; without it, you could overheat the computer and damage it permanently.

Specify to the salesperson the countries you plan to visit. In continental Europe, wall outlets usually require two thin round pins. In Great Britain, outlets require a large plug with three flat prongs, one of them thicker than the other two and perpendicular to them.

Even a dual-voltage (110/220) appliance may need a special adapter. To find out, contact the **Franzus Company,** Dept. B50, Murtha Industrial Park (P.O. Box 142), Beacon Falls, CT 06403 (tel. 203/723-6664). Send a self-addressed, stamped envelope for the company's free pamphlet "Foreign Electricity Is No Deep Dark Secret."

A simple way to meet all your electrical needs, no matter which country you visit, is to invest in the **Franzus Travel-Lite Worldwide Converter/Adapter Set,** complete with a compact case and four international adapter plugs. The best part is the weight, a mere 8.5 ounces. It's available for $27.95 from the **Traveller's Bookstore,** 22 W. 52nd St., New York, NY 10019 (tel. 212/664-0995).

Reminder Some foreign hotels have 110-volt outlets marked "For Shavers Only" for 15- to 20-watt devices. Don't use them for anything requiring higher wattage or you may find yourself in the dark.

11. TIME ZONES

Based on eastern standard time, Great Britain, Ireland, and Portugal are five hours ahead of New York; Greece is seven hours ahead of New York. The rest of the countries featured in this book are six hours ahead of New York. For instance, when it's noon in New York, it's 5pm in London and Lisbon, 6pm in Paris, Copenhagen, and Amsterdam, and 7pm in Athens. The European countries observe daylight saving time, but Great Britain and Ireland start it a little later than continental Europe. The time change does not usually occur on the same day, and not necessarily the same month, as in the U.S.

HOW TO ENJOY EUROPE ON A BUDGET

On or off the Continent, it's reassuring to have a friend waiting at your destination. It's more fun (not to mention less frustrating and less expensive) when someone is there to draw the maps, show you the ropes, divulge the bargains, and share the magic. Consider this guidebook such a friend, pointing out ways to get the most out of your visit to Europe for less.

In this chapter you will find suggestions on how to save money on everything from accommodations to international telephone calls as well as ideas for alternative low-cost travel.

1. HOW TO SAVE MONEY ON . . .

ACCOMMODATIONS

Most tourist offices and travel agents provide listings of bed-and-breakfast accommodations, inns, farmhouses, and small hotels, where a couple might spend $20 each for a double room and another $10 each for dinner.

Keep prices down by traveling off-season and off the beaten track. And politely negotiate the price of the room, especially if you sense there are plenty of empty ones from which to choose—you might find yourself paying 25% less than you expected. Negotiate a trade-off, a lower price for a smaller room or one without a television, or one at the end of a long hallway. Ask for a better rate if you stay several nights. Perhaps they have a smaller room at a lower price or a weekend special or an off-season discount. If you're a student or an older traveler, ask for a discount. If you can't get a lower rate on a room, ask to have dinner thrown in. Be pleasant, not pushy; if the proprietor is not easily persuaded, try elsewhere or hope for better luck next time.

Motel and hotel chains are springing up around Europe, such as Camponile and the bare-bones Formule in France, and though they may lack the charm of an old inn, they are clean and reasonably priced. Others include Sleep Inn, Le Relais Bleu, Hotel Ibis, RestHotel Primevere, Hotel Arcade, Fimotel, and even Videotel. Also consider associations of small, family-run and -oriented places, such as Logis de France, and the somewhat more expensive Relais du Silence and Romantik Hotels, some of which include breakfast with the room price. Ask at the tourist office for the central reservations number of such chains and associations.

As alluring as the great cities of the world are, try to budget your time in them and get out into the countryside which, besides being beautiful, is less expensive, just like at home. For instance, in Italy, instead of going to Rome and Venice, head to Siena, Todi, and Pavia—lovely, photogenic, and historic places in miniature. Instead of visiting the Loire Valley this year, discover the Dordogne in southern France. And consider a country that is less expensive overall, not just in lodging. A room is bound to cost less in a place where you can sip a cup of coffee for 50¢ instead of $3.25 a cup, or take a two-mile taxi ride for $1.85 instead of $4.55 (check the "What Things Cost" chart in each city chapter to get a clear idea of just that).

Creative travel alternatives to hotel stays where lodging costs nothing or next to nothing include home stays, work camps, home exchanges, and educational vacations (see "Low-Cost Travel with a Difference," below).

YOUTH HOSTELS   One of the least expensive ways to keep a roof over your head and meet other travelers in an informal, relaxed atmosphere is to stay in youth hostels, which are plentiful in Europe and welcome "youth" of all ages for $8–$15 a night. Membership in **American Youth Hostels, Inc. (AYH)**, an affiliate of the International Youth Hostel Federation, costs $25 a year for people ages 18–54, $15 for those 55 and older, and $10 for those 17 and younger. Family memberships cover parents and children under 15 and cost $35. Kids as young as 5 or 6 are generally welcome at youth hostels.

The *International Youth Hostel Handbook,* Vol. I: *Europe and the Mediterranean,* costs $10.95, plus $2 for postage and handling, and is distributed by American Youth Hostels, Inc., P.O. Box 37613, Washington, DC 20013-7613 (tel. 202/783-6161).

REMINDER   Figure on spending about half your daily budget allotment on lodging. You can save a night here and there by taking an overnight train.

MEALS

If you are staying in a hotel or inn, the price of lodging may include dinner, or at least breakfast. Bone up on the different kinds of meal plans available and decide which best suits your style of travel:

   EP—European Plan, a room without meals
   CP—Continental Plan, a simple breakfast of coffee and rolls
   AP—American Plan, with three meals daily included
   MAP—Modified American Plan, which includes breakfast and dinner

The hotel may serve dinner separately, say, for $15 for a five-course meal, including tax and tip. That's more than reasonable by American standards, but you may choose to eat less at a café in town for half the price. Likewise, if a hotel breakfast costs $4 or $5, pass it up for a roll and coffee for $1 down the street.

Learn to read wine lists from the bottom up; the price of a carafe of a regional product might be one-tenth what you'd pay for export variety. In some restaurants and with fixed-price dinners, wine is included with the meal. Besides being cheaper, a local bistro, taverna, or pub is just that—more local. You'll rub elbows with the people who live there. Ask local people you meet for recommendations of places *they* like, not places they think you would like.

If you love fine food, but not necessarily by candlelight, consider having your big meal of the day at lunch. Outstanding restaurants may serve the same or similar meals for lunch and dinner, but the fixed-price lunch of four or five courses is likely to be half as expensive. Lunch reservations are easier to come by, as well. In Great Britain and Ireland, indulge in afternoon tea; it's not expensive and will cut your appetite for a huge meal later in the evening. Wherever you eat, be sure to check the menu to see if a service charge of 15% has been added; don't tip twice by accident.

On the other hand, if your day is filled with sightseeing, lunch can be as quick and simple as a chunk of cheese and a loaf of bread eaten on a park bench.

REMINDER   Never skip a meal just to save money. You might end up sick or run down, and that's the one thing you can't afford during your trip. It's bad enough to feel ill at home; in a foreign country, especially if you don't speak the language and need some over-the-counter remedy, nothing could be worse.

SIGHTSEEING

It has been said that the best things in life are free. Some of the best things in sightseeing are, too. You can't get much better than a stroll through the Luxembourg Gardens in Paris or an afternoon in the Tate Gallery in London. They're free. Get a booklet of walking tours, often at no charge from the local tourist office. Visit the tourist office for as much information as you're likely to need to sightsee on your own. Find out if admission to museums is free on a particular day and go then. Keep in mind that many European museums are closed on Monday, so check the schedule before you go.

SHOPPING

DUTY-FREE SHOPS Duty-free shopping is available in airports, on ferries and cruise ships, in downtown stores, and at international border crossings. Most of us take advantage of the savings it offers by dashing into airport duty-free shops to get rid of any foreign currency left over at the end of a trip abroad. These stores have traditionally gotten the last few guilders, francs, or schillings in the last few minutes. The only way actually to save money through duty-free shopping, however, is to know the going prices on the same merchandise at home to be able to compare. Once you're in an airport duty-free shop, you're on your way out of the country so you can't run back to town to buy for less. If you're only saving a couple of bucks, it's hardly worth it to lug the stuff home.

The limit on duty-free items Americans can bring back into the U.S. is $400, including one liter of alcohol. Beyond the allotted exemption, the next $1,000 worth of goods is taxed at a flat rate of 10%. For more information on regulations, write to the Department of the Treasury, U.S. Customs Service, Washington, DC 20299; request publication no. 512 for the handy "Know Before You Go" pamphlet or no. 514 for details on mail imports.

To take best advantage of duty-free stores, know the comparable at-home price of the item, don't judge the savings available in any given shop on just one item, and plan duty-free purchases rather than relegating them to spur-of-the-moment spending.

VALUE-ADDED TAX [VAT] First the bad news: European countries tack a Value-Added Tax, usually referred to as the VAT, to goods and services. Rates vary from country to country, beginning at about 6% for hotels and car rentals and skyrocketing up to 35% for luxury items (fortunately, budget travelers are rarely in the market for diamond-studded watches or fur coats). Most of the time, figure on paying at least 15% in tax when you buy consumer goods, an add-on that can put a serious dent in your pocketbook rather quickly.

The good news: You can get back most of the tax on purchases (not services) over a certain designated amount when you leave the country. But be aware that the process can be tricky, time-consuming, and fraught with paperwork.

Regulations vary from country to country, so check "Savvy Shopping" in the individual city chapters, and inquire at tourist offices when you arrive, for specific information. If you want to take advantage of the refund, shop in participating stores (look for a sign posted out front or in the window), ask the storekeeper for the necessary forms, save receipts, and keep the purchases for which you want the refund in their original packages.

Always ask what percentage of the tax will be refunded, if there are additional service charges, if the refund will be given to you at the airport (or train station) or mailed to you at a later date, and if the refund will be in dollars or foreign currency. If you make the purchase on your credit card, the refund may show up as a credit on the card.

When leaving the country, allow an extra hour before your departure to process the VAT-refund forms. If the money is to be mailed to you, expect a wait of several weeks to several months. Unless you've made substantial purchases, this may be one foreign experience you'd just as soon pass up.

MARKETS, AUCTIONS & SALES   Just like home, Europe has bargains if you know where to look for them, and, like home, they are often found in markets, at auctions, and at department-store sales advertised in local newspapers.

Bargaining may be more prevalent in parts of the world other than Europe, but it is still done in Spain, Portugal, and Greece, and in most other countries you will run across the occasional opportunity to haggle.

These tips will help ease the process along:

- Never appear too interested or too anxious.
- Set your goal at 50% of the vendor's asking price, and first offer only a third of the first quoted price. Slowly work your way up from there. Remember, the price never jumps up—it inches up.
- Tantalize with cash. Have the exact amount you want to pay in your hand.
- Know what you're buying, especially when it comes to antiques and gems.
- Don't take bargaining, the vendor, or yourself too seriously. There is no right or wrong approach and ideally it should be fun for everyone involved.

EVENING ENTERTAINMENT

If you're interested in the theater or ballet or opera, ask at the tourist office if discount or last-minute-sale tickets are available and where to get them, at the theater itself or a special booth. Some theaters sell standing room or discount seats on the day of the performance, and students and older travelers may qualify for special admission.

Nightclubs tend to be expensive, but you might be able to avoid a cover charge by standing at the bar rather than taking a table. If you decide to splurge, keep a lid on your alcohol intake; that's where the costs mount up astronomically. If you have arrived during a public holiday or a festival, there may be abundant free entertainment, much of it in the streets.

For leads on stretching your entertainment dollar, check "Budget Bests" and "Evening Entertainment" in each city chapter.

TIPPING

Try to get an idea about tipping before you get to your destination because you may find yourself in a "to tip or not to tip" situation as soon as you arrive. Ask the tourist board, a travel agent, or friends who have traveled in that country. Once there, ask the local tourist board, a tour guide, or local people you meet. If you don't know how much to tip, ask—and don't feel embarrassed about it.

Tour guides should be tipped, along with any guides at a church or historic site. Sometimes ushers at theaters, movies, and sporting events are tipped; take your cue from the people around you. Washroom and cloakroom attendants always receive something. Porters in airports and rail stations usually receive about $1 a bag. Taxi drivers receive no tip in some European countries and 5%–15% in others.

If no service charge has been added to your hotel bill, you might want to leave $1 a day. The owners of bed-and-breakfast establishments generally are not tipped. In a restaurant, a service charge may well be added to the bill. Always check. In France, it's *servis compris;* in Germany, *Bedienung.* If the service has been outstanding, leave a few extra coins.

On the other hand, tipping is optional, something done in appreciation for good service; when that is not the case, don't tip. When in doubt about how much to tip, err on the side of generosity and leave 15%. And remember, it's 15% of the total *before* tax; never tip on tax.

(For specific information on tipping, see the "Fast Facts" section of the individual city chapters.)

TRANSCONTINENTAL CALLS

Never pay for a transcontinental call in Europe, if you can help it. There are several less expensive alternatives. AT&T provides USA Direct, which links you directly to an

American operator. The calls are either billed to your AT&T Calling Card or made collect at U.S. rates, which are substantially lower than rates for calling direct from Europe. You must use either an access number (different for each participating country) or call from a specially designated telephone. For details, call toll free 800/874-4000 in the U.S.; in Europe, call 1-412/553-7458 collect.

Similarly, MCI offers a Call USA plan, connecting you with an English-speaking operator who then places the call for you. There is a $2 surcharge ($5 if you call collect), plus the cost of the call itself. For more information, call toll free 800/444-3333.

If USA Direct or Call USA are not available, charge the call to your international calling card, if you have one, or call collect. Calling-card calls are billed at operator-assisted station-to-station rates, while collect calls are billed at person-to-person rates. Call the billing office of your telephone company (the number should be on your latest bill) to ask about the most economical way to call from your destinations and to request a free calling card and international number. You may be able to get an international number immediately over the telephone.

One reader who recently spent several months in Scandinavia reports that credit-card calls are the least expensive way of calling home. If you have a card and access to a telephone designated for this type of call, give it a try.

Avoid paying for transatlantic calls in Europe. Charges are higher and hotels add their own surcharge, sometimes as hefty as 150%, which you may be unaware of until you are presented with the bill. Some major European hotels and chains participate with AT&T in the Teleplan program, which offers USA Direct with no surcharge, and ensures that other surcharges on other international calls are limited, uniform, and published.

If you need to place the call, talk briefly and have your party call you right back. In most countries you are charged only for the actual length of the call, so even with a 100% surcharge your initial call will not be exorbitant.

Finally, if you must pay for the call, make it from the local post office, or from a special telephone center, to avoid a surcharge. Check at the telephone desk and you will be assigned a booth in which to place your call. Afterward, you'll be told the amount you owe.

2. HOW TO SAVE MONEY GETTING AROUND

BY PLANE

For the most part, air transport within Europe remains in the realm of the business traveler and not the budget traveler. The cost is usually so prohibitively high that budget travelers consider it only as a splurge or when they're in a pinch for time. Some airlines offer **special promotions** as well as 7- and 14-day advance-purchase fares. For instance, British Airways offers its transatlantic passengers a U.K. travel pass for 3–12 flights between British cities at $66 or $85 apiece, depending on the route. Air Inter's Le France Pass offers unlimited flying for any 7 days during a 30-day period to any destination in France and Corsica for $250, but the pass must be purchased in the U.S. from a travel agent or from Jet Vacations. SAS offers a Visit Scandinavia Pass, where each trip segment (Oslo to Stockholm, say) for up to six segments costs $80; the pass is good in Denmark, Norway, and Sweden, and must be purchased in the U.S.

Unlike domestic air travel in the U.S., lower-priced airfares are available throughout Europe on **charter flights** rather than regularly scheduled ones. Look in local newspapers to find out about them and take advantage of them. For instance, the charter arm of Air France is Jet Vacations (tel. 212/830-0999, or toll free 800/JET-0999).

The sky over Europe is changing, and this year there will be an official lessening of airline regulations throughout the 12 countries of the European Community (EC). The changes will not be so drastic as those that occurred after airline deregulation in the U.S., but they should result in lower airfares, perhaps a few fare wars, and special deals and discounts for the air traveler. As this occurs, charter travel may diminish and regularly scheduled carriers may take over a larger chunk of the leisure travel market.

BY TRAIN

European trains are less expensive than those in the United States and far more genteel, imparting the essence of everyday life and rhythms in an extensive 100,000-mile rail system. With modern, high-speed trains, in many countries, including France, Germany, Italy, Sweden, and Switzerland, on journeys of less than five hours, the train is faster than a plane.

The cost of a train ride from London to Edinburgh on BritRail is $151 in first class or $99 in second class; to Brussels, it's $88 or $71. On Rail Europe, Inc., the price to travel from Paris to Amsterdam is $83 in first class, $55 in second class; and to Madrid, $167 in first class and $112 in second class. On German Rail, Inc., expect to spend $82 in first class and $53 in second class to travel between Berlin and Vienna, or $104 in first class and $69 in second class between Frankfurt and Zurich.

The difference in quality between first- and second-class seats on an international express train is small, a matter of one or two inches of extra padding at most. On the slower-moving trains, however, your pocketbook still saves but your sacroiliac may suffer. For additional ticket prices and detailed train schedules, see Appendix H.

TRAIN PASSES Almost all the countries represented in this book offer individual rail passes or discounts; regional passes, such as BritFrance Railpass, Benelux Tourrail Pass, ScanRail, and European East Pass (for Austria, Hungary, Czechoslovakia, and Poland), are also available. The most extensive (and most popular) passes remain Eurail and BritRail, and information about them is provided below. Some passes include senior discounts, some must be purchased only in the U.S., and most may be booked through travel agents.

If you plan to visit only one country or region of Europe, keep in mind that a country or regional pass will cost less than a Eurailpass. Keep the validation slip you receive as proof of purchase for replacement of your pass in case it is stolen.

Prices for 1993 are as follows:

Eurailpass: 15 days, $460; 21 days, $598; one month, $728; two months, $998; three months, $1,260. Accepted in Austria, Belgium, Denmark, Finland, France, Germany, Greece, Hungary, Ireland, Italy, Luxembourg, the Netherlands, Norway, Portugal, Spain, Sweden, and Switzerland. First class only, with access to many ferries, steamers, and buses free or at a discount.

Eurail Saverpass: 15 days, $390 per person; for two or more people traveling together October through March, or for three people traveling together April through September. Same privileges as the Eurailpass. First class only.

Eurail Flexipass: Any 5 days within 15 days, $298; any 9 days within 21 days, $496; any 14 days within one month, $676. Same privileges as Eurailpass. First class only.

Eurail Youthpass: One month, $508; two months, $698. For travelers under 26 years old. Same benefits as Eurailpass. Second class only.

The latest available prices below were for 1992, with rate increases expected for 1993.

EurailDrive Pass: Any 7 days (4 rail, 3 car) for use within 21 days, $269. Additional rail days are available for $40 per person per day; additional car days for $50 per car per day. A single traveler pays $439 for the 7 days.

Note: Children under 12 travel for half fare, and under 4 for free, on Eurailpass, Eurail Saverpass, and Eurail Flexipass.

BritRail First and Standard Pass: First Pass (first class) is 8 days, $319; 15 days, $479; 22 days, $599; one month, $689. Standard Pass (second class) is $209, $319, $399, and $465, respectively. Children under 16 ride for half fare. Purchase in the U.S.

BritRail Flexipass: Any 4 days within 8 days, $269 first class, $179 economy; any 8 days within 15 days, $379 first class, $255 economy; any 15 days within one month, $549 first class, $369 economy. Also ask about BritRail/Drive, Senior Citizen Pass, Youth Pass. All must be purchased in the U.S.

For more information, see *Baedeker's Rail Guide to Europe* (Prentice Hall) or the *Thomas Cook European Timetable,* and contact individual tourist offices or Eurailpass, P.O. Box 325, Old Greenwich, CT 06870-0325. You can get Eurailpass information and a copy of the handy *Eurail Traveler's Guide* by contacting **Rail Europe, Inc.,** 230 Westchester Ave., White Plains, NY 10604 (tel. 914/682-5172, or toll free 800/345-1990 outside New York, New Jersey, and Connecticut); **BritRail Travel International,** 1500 Broadway, 10th Floor, New York, NY 10036 (tel. 212/575-2667, or toll free 800/667-8585 outside New York State); or **German Rail, Inc.,** 747 Third Ave., 33rd Floor, New York, NY 10017 (tel. 212/308-3100). Be prepared for busy signals.

If the idea of combining train and car travel on a vacation is appealing, ask Rail Europe about its **Rail 'N' Drive** programs, in conjunction with Avis and Hertz rental-car companies.

TRAIN TIPS To make your travels by train as pleasant as possible, remember a few general rules. First, hold on to your train ticket after it has been marked or punched by the conductor. Some European railroad stations require that you present your ticket when you leave the station platform at your destination.

On an overnight trip, inquire into the availability of second-class couchettes, compartments equipped with six lightly padded ledges along the wall, on which you can stretch out full-length to sleep. Plush they're not, but they are dirt cheap and a godsend to those who can't sleep sitting up. While you sleep—or even nap—be sure your valuables are in a safe place; you might temporarily attach a small bell to each bag to warn you if someone attempts to take it. If you've left bags on a rack in the front or back of the car, consider securing them to it with a small chain and lock to deter thieves, who look at trains as happy hunting grounds. To vary the routine of a long second-class trip, retire to the dining car and order a drink or a snack; there you'll be able to sit in a cushioned chair as long as you like. Take all valuables with you.

Take a bottle of mineral water or soda with you. Few European trains have drinking fountains and the dining car may be closed. As you'll soon discover, the experienced European traveler comes loaded with hampers of food and drink and munches away through the trip.

If you leave bags in a locker in a train station, don't let anyone help you store them in it. A favorite trick among thieves is feigned helpfulness, while they pass you the key to an empty locker and pocket the key to yours.

REMINDER Some type of rail pass almost always costs less than the regular fare from one point to another in Europe. Many passes must be purchased in the U.S.

BY CAR

Budget travel and rental cars do not usually go hand in hand, but if you're traveling in a group of four you're actually better off renting a car. Besides being the cheaper form of transportation, it gives you added mobility to find a budget hotel or a comfortable spot to camp. And you can carry more bags more easily.

In Europe not only are rental cars pricey, but **gasoline** costs as much as three times more than Americans are accustomed to paying. The price may *look* similar, since gas is sold by the liter there. Just remember that 1 U.S. gallon equals 3¾ liters; in Britain, the Imperial gallon is the equivalent of 1.2 U.S. gallons. Resign yourself to allocating a chunk of your travel budget to gasoline if you drive. On the brighter side, European cars use gas more sparingly than American models.

You can get a better deal on a rental car by reserving it ahead, even a couple of days. Expect to be given a standard-shift vehicle unless you specifically ask for an automatic. Find out all the charges you are likely to incur from the car-rental company; besides the daily or weekly rental charge, consider a mileage charge, insurance, the cost of the fuel, and possible tax on the total rental bill (15% and 22% in Great Britain and France, respectively). In addition, you'll be paying for parking and tolls along the way. If you already have collision coverage on your own automobile insurance, you're most likely covered when you are behind the wheel of a rental car. So check with your insurance agent before renting a car. If you decide on European insurance, be sure it doesn't come with a $1,000 deductible.

A **collision-damage waiver** costs a hefty $12–$24 a day (up to $36 for some larger models), and can jack the price of a rental car up incredibly. The cost of the insurance, the scope of coverage, and the deductible will depend on the country, the rental company's regulations, and the size of the car. In some countries, collision insurance is required by law. The good news is that some credit- and charge-card companies (American Express is one) automatically insure their cardholders against collision damage at no additional charge when they rent a car using the card as payment. (*Note:* You will lose this coverage if you take the car-rental company's insurance.)

Travel Guard International, 1145 Clark St., Stevens Point, WI 54481 (tel. toll free 800/826-1300), offers eight days of coverage for $19 for repairs up to $25,000; after eight days, additional coverage costs $3 per day. Rental-car companies may try to sell you personal-injury insurance, but if you already have traveler's insurance or if your own automobile policy provides it (see "Insurance and Assistance," in Chapter 1), you won't need more.

You may get slightly lower prices from a European rental company, but you may have to return the car to the place where it was originally picked up, which could throw a kink in some travel plans. A larger company, either American or European, will probably offer drop-off service, which might suit your travel plans best. Try to negotiate the best possible deal with the company. There may be a discount available for keeping the car longer, for unlimited mileage (or at least some miles thrown in for free), or for a bigger car for a lower price. Usually you can get some sort of discount for a company or association affiliation. Check before you leave home and take a member identification card with you.

To begin the shopping-around process, contact some of the American car-rental companies with international branches: **Avis** (tel. toll free 800/331-1084); **Budget** (tel. toll free 800/472-3325); **Dollar Rent a Car,** or **Eurodollar** in Europe (tel. toll free 800/800-6000); **Hertz** (tel. toll free 800/654-3001); or **National,** called **Europcar** in Europe (tel. toll free 800/227-3876). You may be able to pick up a car in one country and leave it in another, and if you keep the car a couple of weeks, there may not be a drop-off charge. Budget, in its Discover Europe program, provides useful motoring itineraries for Belgium, France, Germany, the Netherlands, and Luxembourg.

Some U.S.-based companies specialize in European car rentals (and in some cases, less expensive car leasing, which you should inquire about if you are traveling for three or more weeks): **Auto-Europe** (tel. toll free 800/223-5555), **Europe by Car** (tel. 212/581-3040, or toll free 800/223-1516 outside New York State, 800/252-9401 in California), **Foremost Euro-Car, Inc.** (tel. toll free 800/272-3299), and **Kemwel** (tel. toll free 800/678-0678).

If you have friends abroad, ask them to check rental-car costs there for you; if you can get a better deal by reserving from home, do it. If you can avoid giving your credit-card number, more's the better. You may arrive, only to find that other companies offer much better rates. Try not to rent at the airport, where overheads are higher and business travelers on expense accounts do business. Often a car-rental place near the airport will send a shuttle bus to pick you up. You may want to take local transportation into town and tour on foot for a few days before renting a car.

Once behind the wheel in Europe, be prepared for fast, aggressive driving on the part of locals. Join right in and you'll do fine. Driving on the right is standard, except in Great Britain and Ireland, where you'll get the hang of the reverse situation cautiously but quickly. The freeways are fun and actually help your car get better mileage, although you do pay a toll to use them. However, backroads in Europe can be very sluggish, and you might prefer to get to your destination the quickest way possible and let others sit in the traffic. In Europe roads are marked in kilometers (km), one of which equals .62 mile (100km is 62 miles). Self-service gas stations are readily available, and prices tend to be lower off the freeway. American Automobile Association (AAA) members can get reciprocal member privileges from European auto clubs; ask your local chapter for details.

An **international driving permit** is required by some European countries, including Italy, Spain, Austria, and Germany. It may also be required by the car-rental agency, and is recommended by AAA if you plan to drive in any non-English-speaking country. It is readily available through any branch of AAA for $10; although you may never be asked to show it by either a rental-car clerk or a police officer, it doesn't hurt to have one, just in case. Remember, it doesn't take the place of your U.S. license; it simply accompanies it and serves as a translation of it.

Equally important is a good road map. The European ones are well marked and easy to read. Gas stations and local bookstores in Europe sell them. In the United States, contact **Hagstrom Map & Travel Center,** 57 W. 43rd St., New York, NY 10036 (tel. 212/398-1222); city maps are $7.95 up, and country and regional maps, $9.95 up. The AAA can provide a European planning map for its members. **Michelin Travel Publications,** with headquarters in the U.S. at P.O. Box 3305, Spartanburg, SC 29304-3305 (tel. 803/599-0850, or toll free 800/423-0485 outside South Carolina), also publishes maps and guidebooks. Maps may be ordered by mail or by phone with a credit card, and also through travel bookstores (see "Sources of Information in the United States," in Chapter 1).

The **AA Driving Tours** (Prentice Hall, $17.95), devised by the Automobile Association of England and available for France and Italy, provide up to 30 mapped tours that start and end in a major city; each tour lasts from three to five days and covers 250–500 miles.

REMINDER Never leave bags in the trunk of a car—no matter where, no matter how short the stopover.

BY BUS

Bus transportation is readily available throughout Europe; it sometimes is less expensive than the train (worth checking into if you don't have a rail pass), and it covers a more extensive area than the train. European buses, like the trains, outshine their American counterparts.

Europabus, c/o German Rail, 747 Third Ave., 33rd Floor, New York, NY 10017 (tel. 212/308-7213, or toll free 800/223-6063 outside New York State), can provide information on regular coach service or 20 different bus tours in eight European countries from 2 to 14 days long. The buses are all no-smoking, and 30% of the passengers come from North America.

Cosmos, a British operator, specializes in economical bus tours of Europe that may be booked through travel agents in the U.S. It will match single travelers who want to share a room to avoid paying a supplement. Express bus transportation is offered throughout Europe for people 18–35 by **London Student Travel,** 52 Grosvenor Gardens, London SW1W0AG (tel. 071/730-3402; fax 071/730-5739).

In 1993, **British Airways** begins offering coach-tours to its customers throughout Europe, in conjunction with British tour operator Travelers International (tel. toll free 800/COACHBA).

BY RV/CAMPING

TRAVELING BY RV Recreational touring—called caravanning in Europe—is as popular there as it is in the U.S. Campgrounds are open spring through fall, and local tourist offices can direct you to local sites. Before you leave home, ask for a map of sites from individual tourist bureaus in this country.

RV rentals may be made from the U.S. Get details from **Foremost Euro-Car,** 5430 Van Nuys Blvd., Suite 306, Van Nuys, CA 91401 (tel. toll free 800/272-3299).

The **Recreation Vehicle Industry Association,** 1896 Preston White Dr., (P.O. Box 2999), Reston, VA 22090-0999, in conjunction with the **American Association of Retired Persons (AARP),** makes available a free guide to RV driver safety; request "Safety & RV: A Moving Experience," Stock Number D-13149, from AARP Fulfillment, 1909 K St. NW, Washington, DC 20049.

Book an RV as far in advance as possible to ensure getting the kind you want, and ask the following questions:

- What sizes and configurations are available?
- Which gets the best gas mileage?
- Will the vehicle I choose be acceptable at campgrounds in all the countries I plan to visit?
- Is mileage included in the rental price?
- When is the rental fee to be paid, at pickup or drop-off?
- Is the RV equipped with linens, towels, pots and pans, and other kitchen supplies?
- Will there be an orientation session on use of the RV for first-time users?
- Is there an emergency telephone number in case of difficulties?
- Will an operator's manual be provided?
- Is there a cancellation policy?
- What is the minimum age for a driver?

When driving the RV, make an allowance for the vehicle's size when turning; the front and rear wheels are much farther apart than those of a car. Allow more time to brake, change lanes, and enter a busy highway, since the RV will take more time to slow down and accelerate.

CAMPING Tent-camping gear can be rented in Europe (tourist offices can tell you how to go about it), though it's easier to bring your own. Campgrounds are plentiful, more than 100,000 at last count. Campfires are not allowed and facilities are more functional than picturesque. If you have a cookstove, bring fuel as well. You can expect coin-operated showers, a grocery store, and often a little restaurant conducive to socializing with other campers. The charge per night is about $15—figure $5 per tent and $5 per person. Campgrounds are designated "Campings" on roadside signs and are well marked on maps.

More detailed information is available in Dennis and Tina Jaffe's *Camping in Southern Europe* and *Camping in Northern Europe* (Williamson Travel Guides, $13.95, available through the Traveller's Bookstore in New York) and from the **National Campers and Hikers Association,** 4804 Transit Rd., Building 2, Depew, NY 14043-4704 (tel. 716/668-6242). The organization offers its members an International Camping Carnet for $10; membership in the organization is $20 for individuals or families; the carnet is good for some discounts, and is useful when campground personnel ask you to leave some form of ID and you don't want to relinquish your passport. The organization can also provide a list of sources in Europe for renting or buying camping equipment and renting a car or camper.

BY BICYCLE

Reconnoitering Europe (or parts of it) by bike can be one of the most exhilarating experiences on earth, but it takes stamina and planning. At least a month before you leave home, do some test runs of 10–50 miles, increasing the distance as you increase your strength. Take a bike-maintenance refresher course. Link up with a local biking group or join outings planned by American Youth Hostels. Plan your trip when the weather is mild but not too hot.

Bring raingear, sunscreen, a helmet, biker's gloves, and a repair kit. Be sure the helmet has reflector bands; you can find them to fit across your chest as well. The bike should have reflectors and a bell for extra safety (for you and for pedestrians). A good bike lock is all-important. Ask at the hostel or inn if there is a room where you may lock your bike.

When plotting your route, try to get a good idea of the grade of the roads; try to find out about headwinds, which can slow you down, and about the availability of lodging along the way. Also see *Biking Through Europe* by Dennis and Tina Jaffe (Williamson Travel Guides, 1987, $13.95), which contains biking tours in Austria, Belgium, Denmark, France, Great Britain, West Germany, the Netherlands, and Switzerland.

Bicycle tours are available but usually out of range for budget travelers. For example, Butterfield & Robinson's nine-day Loire Valley tour in 1992 cost $3,095, land only, including breakfasts and dinners. Order the catalogs anyway and look at the itineraries to get ideas for your own trip. The photos are an inspiration in themselves, and if not this year, perhaps another year you'll be able to sign up with a tour. The best source of information on who's offering what in the way of bike tours is the magazine *Bicycle USA*'s annual **Tourfinder** March/April issue. A copy costs $5 from the League of American Wheelmen, 190 W. Ostend St., Suite 120, Baltimore, MD 21230 (tel. 301/944-3399).

Contact **Butterfield & Robinson,** 70 Bond St., Suite 300, Toronto, ON M5B 1X3, Canada (tel. toll free 800/387-1147); **Country Cycling & Hiking Tours,** 140 W. 83rd St., New York, NY 10024 (tel. 212/874-5151); **Baumeler Tours/New England Bicycle Tours,** P.O. Box D, Randolph, VT 05060 (tel. 802/728-3261); **Travent International,** P.O. Box 145, Waterbury Center, VT 05677-0305 (tel. toll free 800/325-3009, or 802/244-5420 in Vermont or Canada); and **Gerhard's Bicycle Odysseys,** P.O. Box 757, Portland, OR 97207 (tel. 503/223-2402). The **Bicycle Adventure Club,** 3904 Groton St., San Diego, CA 92110 (tel. 619/226-2175), specializes in tours for the budget-minded. **International Bicycle Tours,** 7 Champlin Sq. (P.O. Box 754), Essex, CT 06426 (tel. 203/767-7005), concentrates on tours through Holland, France, England, and Austria; some tours are specifically geared to people over 50.

REMINDER   If you plan to take your bicycle to Europe, find out the airline's regulations when booking reservations. You may be asked to disassemble part of the bike or box it up; some airlines provide boxes, while others do not.

3. INDEPENDENT VS. GROUP TRAVEL

The two major lures of packaged tours are lower cost and no planning. Tour operators buy airline seats, hotel rooms, tables in restaurants, and surface transportation in bulk and pass the savings on to the consumer. The independent traveler can essentially create the same itinerary but must rely on more modest hotels and restaurants to keep costs down.

For the latest in what's available in tours today, check the ads in the travel section of your newspaper. Tours are most often put together by airlines or charter companies, hotels, or tour operators and sold through travel agents. Before signing up for one, read the fine print carefully and investigate the following:

How reputable is the tour operator? Ask for references of people who have participated in tours run by this outfit. Call travel agents and the local Better Business Bureau. The consumer department of the U.S. Tour Operators Association (USTOA), 211 E. 51st St., Suite 12-B, New York, NY 10022 (tel. 212/944-5727), will provide information on its members. Be leery of any outfit that does not give you details of the itinerary before demanding payment. (You may also complain about a particular tour operator to the USTOA, but by mail only.)

What is the size of the tour? Decide whether you can handle an experience shared with 40 other people, or if your limit is 20. A smaller tour is a better-quality tour.

Will the same guide stay with you throughout the tour? This works better than being passed from guide to guide, city to city.

What kind of hotels will be used and where are they located? Get the names of the hotels and then look them up in guidebooks. If you sense that the hotels provide only minimal essentials, so might the entire tour. If the hotel is not conveniently located, it will be less expensive, but you may feel isolated or unsafe, and you'll spend extra money and time getting to and from attractions and nightspots.

If meals are included, how elaborate are they? Is breakfast continental or buffet? Is the menu for the group limited to a few items?

How extensive is the sightseeing? You may have the chance to get on and off the bus many times to explore a number of attractions, or you may see them only through the bus window. If you like to explore, pick an attraction you are interested in and ask the operator precisely how much time you can expect to spend there. Find out if all admissions are included in the price of the tour.

Does the itinerary suit you? The destinations should not only be of interest, but there should also be enough time scheduled to savor each one.

Are the optional activities offered at an additional price? This usually is the case, so make sure the activities that particularly interest you are included in the tour price.

What is the refund policy should you cancel?

How is the package price paid? If a charter flight is involved, make sure that you can pay into an escrow account (ask for the name of the bank) to ensure proper use of the funds, or their return in case the operator cancels the trip.

Consider mixing independent travel with a tour once you get to Europe by linking up with a European operator that specializes in low-cost bus tours or minitours. A number are based in London, among them **Globus Gateway Cosmos/Cosmos Tourama,** 177-179 Hammersmith Rd. (tel. 071/741-0507 in London, or toll free 800/556-5454 in the U.S.); **Trafalgar Tours,** 9 Bressenden Place (tel. 071/828-4388 in London, or 212/689-8977 in New York, or toll free 800/854-0103 in the U.S.); and **Trophy Tours/Frames Rickards,** 11 Herbrand St. (tel. 071/837-3111 in London, or toll free 800/527-2473 in the U.S.), which has a popular Mix 'n' Match tour program.

4. LOW-COST TRAVEL WITH A DIFFERENCE

EDUCATIONAL TRAVEL Educational travel provides one of the most invigorating ways to learn, allowing for a nice mix of schooling and vagabonding. Request the free booklet "Basic Facts on Study Abroad" from the **Institute of International Education (IIE),** 809 United Nations Plaza, New York, NY 10017 (tel. 212/883-8200). It can also provide a list of related books, including its title *Vacation Study Abroad* ($31.95). The **Council on International Educational Exchange (CIEE),** 205 E. 42nd St., New York, NY 10017 (tel. 212/661-1414), offers the free booklet "Student Travel Catalog," as well as the 500-page *Work, Study, Travel Abroad: The Whole World Handbook,* edited by Del Franz and Lázaro Hernández and updated in even-numbered years (St. Martin's Press, $12.95). The book lists about 1,000 study opportunities abroad.

Many people, especially older travelers, register for language courses at the Alliance Française or Eurocentre in Paris; the Goethe Institutes in Berlin, Munich, or Düsseldorf; the Istituto Dante Alighieri in Florence; and the Colegio de Estudios Hispanicos in Salamanca (contact the appropriate tourist office for information; see the Appendix). Some travelers choose to stay one or more weeks at the English-language "folk high school" (adult residential college) in Denmark. No exams (entrance or otherwise), no tests, no certificates—just learning for the sake of learning. Contact **Den Internationale Højskole (International People's College),** Montebello Alle 1, DK-3000 Helsingør, Denmark (tel. 45/49-21-33-61; fax 45/49-21-21-28). Still others enroll in summer courses at Oxford or Cambridge University in

England, or Trinity College in Ireland; also request the brochure **"Tours and Special Interest Holidays"** from the British Tourist Authority, 40 W. 57th St., Suite 320, New York, NY 10019 (tel. 212/581-4700).

Those age 60 and older, and their spouses of any age (or their "significant others" age 50 or older), can take advantage of the Elderhostel program abroad and at home. **Elderhostel,** 75 Federal St., Boston, MA 02110-1941 (tel. 617/426-7788), sends almost 16,000 people to school abroad every year. Courses last two to four educational weeks, starting at $2,000, including airfare, meals, lodging, daily classroom instruction, and admission fees. Elderhostel also offers, in conjunction with the Experiment in International Living (see below), educational programs with a home-stay component. Write for a free catalog. **Interhostel,** University of New Hampshire, 6 Garrison Ave., Durham, NH 03824 (tel. 603/862-1147, or toll free 800/733-9753), offers two-week educational programs for persons 50 and older. Prices are $1,375–$1,975 and include tuition, room and board, and ground transportation.

The **Folkways Institute,** 14600 SE Aldridge Rd., Portland, OR 97236 (tel. 503/658-6600, or toll free 800/225-4666), has a senior studies program for people over 55; the classes tend to be smaller than those of Elderhostel and Interhostel (8–20, compared to 20–40), and the focus is on active participation and in-the-field exploration. The organization also offers courses in natural history and life and culture abroad to participants of all ages. There are a total of about 12 European courses, lasting from one to three weeks. The cost ranges from $1,300 to $2,700, including lodging, land transportation, lecture and museum fees, and some meals, but not airfare.

The **Foundation for Field Research,** P.O. Box 2010, Alpine, CA 91903 (tel. 619/445-9264), gives participants—teenagers to octogenarians—on-site training to assist archeologists, marine biologists, anthropologists, and ornithologists. Trips to Europe last two or four weeks and start at $1,350, 75% of which goes to the research.

Earthwatch, 680 Mt. Auburn St. (P.O. Box 403N), Watertown, MA 02272 (tel. 617/926-8200), sponsors expeditions for full time work on actual digs (participants can receive tax deductions for their contributions to scientific research). It also offers hundreds of projects in all aspects of biological and ecological research, where participants assist in everything from mapping volcanoes to tracking endangered species. The expeditions to Europe average two weeks and start at about $1,300, which includes food, lodging, local transportation, and equipment, but not airfare.

Smithsonian Study Tours and Seminars, from the Smithsonian Institute, 1100 Jefferson Dr. SW, Room 3045, Washington, DC 20560 (tel. 202/357-4700), offers more than 75 European study tours. Offerings, which vary from year to year, emphasize cultural and historical study and are led by professors. You must be a member of the Smithsonian ($20 a year) to participate; members receive *Smithsonian* magazine and may request the thrice-yearly *Smithsonian Traveler* newsletter detailing the trips. Although all ages may participate, the study is geared to adults and about 70% of participants are over 50.

HOME STAYS OR VISITS The **International Visitors Information Service,** 1623 Belmont St. NW, Washington, DC 20009 (tel. 202/939-5566), provides a way for travelers to meet locals for dinner or tea, at a café, or in their homes. Far in advance of departure, send $6.50 for the *Meet the People* directory, which lists organizations in 35 countries that will put you in touch with these hosts.

Servas (from the Esperanto word meaning "to serve"), represented in the U.S. by the U.S. Servas Inc., 11 John St., Suite 407, New York, NY 10038-4009 (tel. 212/267-0252), seeks to promote friendship and goodwill through two-night home stays. The organization has 15,000 hosts in 112 countries worldwide. Membership requires an interview to make sure of the traveler's seriousness of intent. Servas travelers include singles, couples, and families; they pay $45 per person per year for membership (children under 18 pay nothing, but must be accompanied by an adult) and a refundable $25 deposit for up to five host lists, $25 for each additional five. The directories provide information on hosts, including where they live, phone number, occupation, year of birth, languages spoken, and interests. The traveler writes the host and sets up the visit. Travelers may stay with several hosts in the same city or region, and they do not have to reciprocate and become hosts themselves, though many do.

Since 1971, **Friends Overseas,** 68-04 Dartmouth St., Forest Hills, NY 11375, has put American travelers to Denmark, Norway, Sweden, and Finland in touch with Scandinavians who share the same interests and/or background. For a $25 membership, you will receive the names and addresses of a number of selected Scandinavian members and must write to them before your departure; otherwise, they may not have enough advance notice to plan a meeting with you. Some 4,000 Scandinavians— singles, couples, and families—belong to the organization. For more information, send a self-addressed, stamped business-size envelope to Friends Overseas at the above address. Those writing from overseas should include the equivalent of $1.50 (U.S.) in return postage.

Amateur radio buffs can meet their European counterparts by joining the **International Travel Host Exchange,** sponsored by the American Radio Relay League. Members of the exchange list their name, telephone number, address, and languages spoken, and state whether they can accommodate overnight visitors or merely show them the local sights (expect plenty of shop talk, too). For more information or an application, contact the American Radio Relay League, 225 Main St., Newington, CT 06111 (tel. 203/666-1541).

If you prefer group interaction to one-on-one experiences, **Friendship Force,** 575 South Tower, 1 CNN Center, Atlanta, GA 30303 (tel. 404/522-9490), can help. Throughout the year the organization, with which former President Jimmy Carter has been associated, assembles groups of 21–42 people and flies them to one- or two-week stays with families in western or eastern Europe, followed by an optional one-week organized tour of the country. The emphasis is on personal exchange; no money changes hands between guests and hosts, and the major expense for the traveler is the airfare, usually advance purchase.

Experiment in International Living/Summer Abroad, Kipling Road, Brattleboro, VT 05302 (tel. 802/257-7751, or toll free 800/345-2929 outside Vermont), places students aged 15–20 in the homes of foreign families for four to six weeks, where they participate in family life (usually there are children their age in the family), as well as get together with other program participants and their group leader at least once a week. The organization can also arrange home stays for adults. Other programs include college semester abroad, language courses, community service, and ecological study trips, including one in conjunction with Elderhostel (see above).

WORK CAMPS There's no better or more enjoyable way for someone 16 or 18 and older to participate in international cooperation and goodwill than at a work camp. Volunteers from around the world arrange and pay for their own transportation and work in exchange for room and board and the chance to perform a socially significant task. Groups generally number 5–30; volunteers generally spend two to three weeks at a camp, work a five-day, 30-hour week, and receive basic lodgings and communal meals. They may do manual or physical labor or perform a service, such as restoring hiking trails in a national park or working with underprivileged kids or the elderly. Most work camps take place May through September.

For detailed information, contact **Volunteers for Peace International Workcamps (VFP),** 43 Tiffany Rd., Belmont, VT 05730 (tel. 802/259-2759). VFP generally requires a minimum age of 18 for participants, although it will accept 16- and 17-year-olds for camps in France, Germany, and Spain. Its directory, published in April, costs $10, which includes a newsletter subscription. This cost is deducted from any later registration fee—$125 per work camp.

Also contact **SCI International Voluntary Service (SCI/IVS),** c/o Innisfree Village, Route 2, Box 506, Crozet, VA 22932 (tel. 804/823-1826 on Monday, Wednesday, and Thursday, 9am to noon), which requires volunteers abroad to be 18 years old. Its directory, which includes workcamps in western and eastern Europe, is also published in April; it costs $3. Applicants pay $75 per project.

The **Council on International Educational Exchange (CIEE),** 205 E. 42nd

St., New York, NY 10017 (tel. 212/661-1414), offers a work-camp program. The minimum age to participate is 18 (16 in Germany). Its booklet on international work camps is free but the actual application requires a $135 fee.

HOME EXCHANGES The **Vacation Exchange Club,** P.O. Box 820, Haleiwa, HI 96712 (tel. toll free 800/638-3841), can help you set up a home swap—your house or apartment for a residence in a European country for a mutually determined amount of time. The cost of a listing in the directory, which is published four times a year (January, March, June, and September), is $50. You may also receive a 10,000-entry directory for the same price.

SPECIAL-INTEREST TRAVEL For the best prices where special-interest travel is concerned, start with trips organized by local colleges and universities, led by knowledgeable professors, and focusing on everything from architecture to wine tasting.

Photography tours and adventure-travel expeditions can be expensive; they also usually focus on places considered more remote than European destinations, such as Nepal, Rwanda, or the Galápagos Islands. The cheapest of the adventure companies is the **Adventure Center,** 1311 63rd St., Suite 200, Emeryville, CA 94608 (tel. 510/654-1879, or toll free 800/227-8747). It is slower paced and more basic in its arrangements than bigger and better-known companies, but the traveler saves on the price; request its Explorer brochure, which focuses on trips to Europe. No trip attempts to cover all of Europe in one fell swoop; instead, you might go hiking in the Swiss Alps, cycling in the Loire Valley, or meandering via local ferries through the Greek isles. Land-only prices start at $650 for the two- to five-week trips.

Other adventure-travel operators that feature European trips include **Overseas Adventure Travel,** 349 Broadway, Cambridge, MA 02139 (tel. 617/876-0533, or toll free 800/221-0814); **Society Expeditions,** 3131 Elliott Ave., Suite 250, Seattle, WA 98121 (tel. 206/285-9400, or toll free 800/548-8669); **Mountain Travel Sobek,** 6420 Fairmount Ave., El Cerrito, CA 94530 (tel. 510/527-8100, or toll free 800/227-2384); **Off the Deep End,** P.O. Box 7511, Jackson, WY 83001 (tel. 307/733-8707, or toll free 800/223-6833); and **Above the Clouds,** P.O. Box 398, Worcester, MA 01602 (tel. 508/799-4499, or toll free 800/233-4499).

If you're interested in a particular tour, ask these questions about it:

- Are prices quoted in U.S. dollars?
- What does the fee cover?
- Can you make connecting air arrangements?
- Is insurance available?
- Is the group composed of amateurs as well as professionals?
- Does the leader give formal instruction or only informal interaction?
- If it is a photography tour, will film be processed en route so that images may be criticized?
- What is the ratio of leaders to participants?
- Are supplies and equipment provided?
- Are references available from people who have taken this trip with this leader?

Women 18 and older interested in traveling with other women may contact **Womentrek,** P.O. Box 20643, Seattle, WA 98102 (tel. 206/325-4772, or toll free 800/477-TREK), or, for women over 30, **Rainbow Adventures,** 1308 Sherman Ave., Evanston, IL 60201 (tel. 708/864-4570). The latter, which offers hiking tours in Europe, was founded in 1982 by a former Peace Corps volunteer and biologist. Both groups attract a mix of women in age, background, and interests.

Those looking for gay travel offerings should contact **Adventure Bound Expeditions** (outdoor trips for men), 711 Walnut St., Carriage House, Boulder, CO 80302 (tel. 303/449-0990—collect, if you like), or the **Islanders Club** (cruises for both men and women), 530 W. 23rd St., Suite 225, New York, NY 10011-1101 (tel. 212/633-8898). For upscale tour programs for men, contact **Hanns Ebensten Travel,** 513 Fleming St., Key West, FL 33040 (tel. 305/294-8174).

Published in 1991, ***Are You Two Together—A Gay and Lesbian Travel Guide to Europe,*** by Lindsy Van Gelder and Pamela Robin Brandt (Random House, $18), describes with warmth and humor the couple's adventures on the road, relates stories of famous European gay men and lesbians, and recommends hotels, restaurants, bookstores, gay centers, and other resources.

Also consult other gay guidebooks, such as *International Places for Men* or *International Places for Women,* or the special travel editions of *Outing* or *The Advocate.*

CHAPTER 3

GETTING THERE

1. BY AIR
2. BY SEA
3. TRAVEL CLUBS
4. TRAVEL
   NEWSLETTERS

This chapter explores various options for getting to Europe by air and sea, treating not only the obvious choices, but also some that you may not have thought of that can save you money.

1. BY AIR

BUCKET SHOPS With the deregulation of air travel from the United States, major scheduled airlines are increasingly making a portion—up to 40%—of their transatlantic seats available to consolidators. They in turn distribute the tickets to the public through retail discount travel agencies known as "bucket shops," at reductions of about 20%–30%.

The resulting, sharply reduced fares are now the least expensive means of traveling to Europe, lower in most instances than charter-flight fares. For example, in winter 1992 from New York, you could buy bucket-shop tickets to London on well-known international airlines for as little as $369 round-trip; figure about $549 in summer. Flying to other, more distant European cities is slightly more expensive. The tickets are restrictive, valid only for a particular date or flight, nontransferable, and nonrefundable except directly from the bucket shop.

Ads for bucket shops are small, usually a single column in width and a few lines deep, most notably in the Sunday travel section of major newspapers. They contain a list of cities and, opposite it, a list of corresponding prices. Short and to the point.

While prices for flights available through bucket shops are low, at times they may be eclipsed by special offers by the airlines. Watch for specials advertised.

Leading bucket shops selling air transportation to Europe include **Access International, Inc.,** 101 W. 31st St., Suite 1104, New York, NY 10001 (tel. 212/465-0707, or toll free 800/825-3633); **Sunline Express, Inc.,** 607 Market St., San Francisco, CA 94105 (tel. 415/541-7800, or toll free 800/SUNLINE); **Euro-Asia, Inc.,** 4203 E. Indian School Rd., Suite 210, Phoenix, AZ 85018 (tel. 602/955-2742, or toll free 800/525-3876), which also offers discount fares through travel agents.

CHARTERS The second-cheapest way to cross the Atlantic is on a charter flight. Competition from the bucket shops, not to mention fiercely competitive commercial airlines, has pared their number somewhat, but there are still plenty from which to choose. **Homeric Tours, Inc.** (tel. 212/753-1100, or toll free 800/223-5570), specializes in charters and tours to Athens and Thessalonica for $549–$699 round-trip, depending on date. **Sceptre Charters, Inc.** (tel. 718/738-9400, or toll free 800/221-0924 outside New York State), from May through mid-October operates charters to Shannon, Ireland, from only $433 round-trip, and direct to Dublin (the only operator to offer direct flights) and to Belfast from only $469 round-trip. **Balair** (tel. 212/581-3411, or toll free 800/3-BALAIR in California, Maine, and Florida) flies charters from New York, Miami, San Francisco (summer only), and Bangor, Maine (summer only) to Geneva, Zurich, and Basel, for $536–$676 round-trip (from New York). **Martinair** (tel. 516/627-8711, or toll free 800/366-4655), operates weekly charters from eight major U.S. cities and Toronto to Amsterdam at round-trip prices ranging from $619 from Tampa and $818 from Seattle and Oakland.

From New York, Boston, Washington, D.C., Chicago, Miami, Houston, San

Francisco, and Los Angeles, **Jet Vacations, Inc.** (tel. 212/830-0999, or toll free 800/JET-0999), the well-known subsidiary of Air France, operates charters to Paris, and occasionally to Nice, for one-way East Coast prices of $229–$315, depending on city, from Houston for $290–$345, and from Los Angeles for $299–$365.

A major New York operator, **Travac,** at 989 Sixth Ave., New York, NY 10018 (tel. 212/563-3303, or toll free 800/TRAV-800), operated charters from New York to London, Paris, Amsterdam, Rome, and Geneva, at round-trip rates starting at $360 in spring 1992. Travac also serves as a bucket shop and, through add-ons (cheaper connecting flights to gateway cities), offers discounts from most major U.S. cities to most major European cities.

One of America's oldest charter companies, **Council Charter,** 205 E. 42nd St., New York, NY 10017 (tel. 212/661-0311, or toll free 800/800-8222), offers a combination of charters and scheduled flights to most major European cities from a variety of gateways in the U.S. Among the cities served from New York are London, Paris, Amsterdam, Brussels, Nice, Rome, and Madrid. The company offers one-way and round-trip fares and allows passengers to fly into one city and out of another. It also offers a $30 cancellation waiver that allows passengers to cancel for any reason up to three hours prior to departure from the U.S. and receive a full refund.

For dates, departure cities, and prices for charter transportation between North America and Europe, check the Sunday travel section of a large city newspaper. *Jax Fax,* the monthly magazine of the air-chartering industry, is a comprehensive source of information. Browse through your travel agent's latest copy.

Before deciding to take a charter flight, check the restrictions. You may be asked to purchase a tour package, pay far in advance of the flight, be amenable if the day of departure or the destination is changed, pay a service charge, fly on an airline with which you are not familiar (this usually is not the case), and pay harsh penalties if you cancel but be understanding if the charter does not fill up and is cancelled up to 10 days before departure (seriously consider cancellation insurance; see "Insurance and Assistance," in Chapter 1). Summer charters fill up more quickly than others and are almost sure to fly.

Also, be sure you have received full information on the prices; some charter companies have high-season supplements; some pass airport taxes directly on to the traveler. Make sure that the flight you want is available on the days you need. If the base rate furnished is from an eastern gateway city, the company may run connecting flights either as charters or in conjunction with regularly scheduled airlines from other U.S. cities. These flights will be cheaper than independently booked flights, but you will pay an "add-on" fee.

REBATORS In another category are the rebators, companies that pass all or part of their commissions on to the consumer; some charge a fee for their services. If you know where you want to go, call and find out the rebator's asking price; unlike travel agents, rebators don't help you make plans, but they help you carry them out for a discounted price. For instance, **Travel Avenue,** 641 W. Lake St., Suite 201, Chicago, IL 60606-1012 (tel. 312/876-1116, or toll free 800/333-3335), is a rebator that gives its commissions to its customers and charges them a fixed service fee. The company deals primarily in airfares, offering a 5%–16% rebate, with a $10 fee for domestic and $25 for international flights. It has a tour and cruise department that offers an 8% rebate and charges a $25 fee for tickets under $1,000 and $50 for tickets over $1,000.

Another rebator is **The Smart Traveller,** 3111 SW 27th Ave., Miami, FL 33133 (tel. 305/448-3338, or toll free 800/226-3338).

Travel Management International, 18 Prescott St., Suite 4, Cambridge, MA 02138 (617/661-8187, or toll free 800/245-3672) offers discount tickets on major airlines.

GOING AS A COURIER Travelers who wear two caps, that of airline passenger and that of courier, stand to save a lot of money crossing the Atlantic. The courier company handles the check-in and pickup of packages at each airport, and all you have to do is give up your checked-baggage allowance and make do with carry-on. Expect to meet a courier service representative at the airport before departure to get the manifest of the checked items; upon arrival, you deliver the baggage-claim tag to a waiting courier agent. The system benefits not only travelers, but also companies transporting time-sensitive materials, such as film or documents for banks and insurance firms.

One drawback besides restricted baggage is that you have to travel alone, since only one person can take advantage of any given flight. If there are two of you, try to arrange your departures on two consecutive days; the first to arrive can secure the hotel room and learn the lay of the land.

Companies that offer frequent courier service to Europe include **Now Voyager Freelance Couriers,** 74 Varick St., Suite 307, New York, NY 10013 (tel. 212/431-1616), which flies about 18 couriers to Europe a day; or **Halbart Express,** 147-05 176th St., Jamaica, NY 11434 (tel. 718/656-8189 between 10am and 3pm), which books reservations well in advance of departure.

Most flights depart from New York, so you may have to tack on the additional cost to get to the gateway city. Prices change all the time, from low to very low. If a company needs emergency courier service and you can fly immediately, you could travel for next to nothing—say, $50 round-trip.

Sample fares for spring 1992 from Now Voyager were about $299 round-trip from New York to London, Stockholm, or Oslo; about $350 round-trip from New York to Milan, Paris, or Rome; and about $199 round-trip from New York to Copenhagen, Frankfurt, or Madrid. Now Voyager books flights up to two months in advance, but call the 24-hour-a-day number for last-minute immediate departure specials.

Foreign destinations are booked round-trip for specific dates. On occasion, the return flights have no courier delivery on the day of departure, so checked-baggage space is available; call to find out, and if so, buy a suitcase and fill it up.

For current information about courier travel and courier services, subscribe to *Travel Unlimited,* P.O. Box 1058, Allston, MA 02134, an eight-page, monthly typewritten newsletter, which has been published since 1986. The cost is $25 per year ($35 outside the U.S.) or $5 for a single issue.

"CHEAP" AIRLINES An almost equally frugal way to cross the Atlantic is to fly aboard an airline that is a relative newcomer to transatlantic routes and may not be identified by consumers with particular European destinations. To attract a little attention, these carriers drop their fares below those of the established competition. Actually, the only thing "cheap" about them is their price structure, not their service, standards, or safety. In summer 1992 **Virgin Atlantic Airways** (tel. toll free 800/862-8621) offered round-trip flights to London from New York and Boston for $569, from Miami for $679, from Orlando for $699, and from Los Angeles (midweek only) for $769. Ask about Late-Saver fares if you have to fly at the last minute and can't take advantage of the airline's lowest fares.

Continental Airlines (tel. toll free 800/231-0856) offered summer 1992 round-trip midweek flights from New York (Newark) to London starting at $558. Other Continental gateways include Houston and Denver; other European destinations include Paris, Frankfurt, Madrid, and Munich.

Tower Air (tel. 718/917-8500 in New York, or toll free 800/324-TOWER) offered summer 1992 round-trip fares from New York to Paris, Copenhagen, and Stockholm from $648 ($100 less off-season) with no restrictions.

Icelandair (tel. toll free 800/223-5500) offered 1992 winter fares of $298; 1992 Euro-Bargain midweek summer fares to Luxembourg from New York for $778, from Baltimore-Washington for $798, and from Orlando (via Baltimore) for $848. Much more of a saving for travelers with a flexible summer schedule, its Three Days Before fares, which must be booked no *earlier* than three days before the departure date, were $299 from New York and Baltimore-Washington, and $342 from Orlando. These latter fares require no minimum stay abroad, and the maximum stay is one year.

Icelandair provides complimentary bus service to selected cities in Germany; train fare to Paris is $62 round-trip, and passengers on the airline also benefit from an $84 round-trip fare ($42 one way) any place in Switzerland served by the Swiss Federal Railway.

Sometimes cut-rate fares pop up unexpectedly when a carrier inaugurates service from a new U.S. gateway, such as USAir did in January 1992 from Philadelphia to Paris; for almost two months the carrier offered a $318 round-trip midweek fare, with low-priced connecting fares to Philadelphia from other parts of the U.S. Always keep an eye out for these short-term deals.

ADVANCE-PURCHASE FARES   If you can't find an acceptable charter or bucket fare, and if no "cheap" airline flies from a gateway near you, look into advance-purchase fares, which are offered by every airline and are also known as excursion fares. Restrictions always apply. You have to purchase the ticket at least 14 to 30 days before departure and stay in Europe for a certain number of days, usually no fewer than 7 and no more than 21. The ticket may be called "nonrefundable," but some airlines will let you change the return date for $75 or so; it pays to ask when you book the ticket.

Advance-purchase fares are often higher than those mentioned in previous categories, so it behooves you to search out other possibilities first, including connecting airfare to cities served by charters, bucket shops, "cheap" airlines, or courier services. If you are a student or an older traveler, ask if you qualify for a discount. Airfares are as changeable as the weather, so it pays to call around—to both American and European carriers.

EUROPEAN CARRIERS   In shopping around for the best fares, don't overlook the European carriers themselves. Most European countries have their own national carrier, which is either partially or totally state-owned (British Airways is an exception). The European carriers fly to more destinations within Europe and have more scheduled flights within their own countries. And many of them have long been praised for outstanding service.

Do a little investigating and you may find that the European carriers offer prices comparable to U.S. airlines, and they do sometimes advertise special bargains. For example, in 1992 Alitalia offered anyone buying a round-trip (not advance-purchase) ticket to Italy the opportunity to buy a companion round-trip ticket for only $100, along with up to two flights within Italy for only $50 each. Other European carriers also offer special promotional fares within their country or region (see "How to Save Money Getting Around," in Chapter 2).

Following is a list of European countries, their national carrier, and a toll-free telephone number for it. Check what they have to offer, especially if you plan to do some flying within Europe. Some have partnership arrangements with American carriers, such as SAS with Continental. This works particularly well for the traveler departing from outside the New York area. (For example, when you board a Continental flight in Denver, you are given a boarding pass for SAS at Newark airport, and your baggage is checked through to Copenhagen.) Similarly, joint fares are offered through a number of European carriers and TWA. It pays to inquire about them.

EUROPEAN AIRLINES

Country	Airline	Toll-free Number
Austria	Austrian Airlines	800/843-0002
Belgium	Sabena	800/955-2000
England	British Airways	800/AIRWAYS
Scotland	British Airways	800/AIRWAYS
Denmark	SAS World Airlines	800/221-2350
Norway	SAS World Airlines	800/221-2350
Sweden	SAS World Airlines	800/221-2350
France	Air France	800/AF-PARIS
Germany	Lufthansa	800/645-3880
Greece	Olympic Airways	800/223-1226 (outside New York State)

Hungary	Malev Hungarian	800/262-5380 (western U.S.)
	Airlines	800/877-5429 (Midwest and South)
		800/223-6884 (eastern seaboard)
Ireland	Aer Lingus	800/223-6537
Italy	Alitalia	800/223-5730
The Netherlands	KLM Royal Dutch	
	Airlines	800/777-5553
Portugal	TAP Air Portugal	800/221-7370
Spain	Iberia	800/772-4642
Switzerland	Swissair	800/221-4750

FLY-DRIVE   A good option for the independent-spirited, budget-minded person is a fly-drive tour. A tour operator will get you to and from Europe and have a car waiting for you at a price much lower than you could get by booking airfare and a car rental on your own. You pay for the rest: food, lodging, entertainment.

CIE Tours (tel. toll free 800/CIE-TOUR, 800/447-0279 in New Jersey) goes a step further with its seven-day "self-drive vacation." For $729 per person, the company provides round-trip airfare from New York or Boston to Shannon or Dublin on Aer Lingus, a rental economy car with unlimited mileage, accommodations for six nights at a choice of over 1,000 farmhouses and town and country homes throughout Ireland, a full Irish breakfast daily, a cassette tape of driving hints and touring tips, a hardcover atlas/guidebook, a list of suggested activities (such as playing bridge with a local bridge club), and all service charges, collision-damage waiver, and taxes. (Land-only prices start at $299 per person for six nights. Vouchers allow optional upgrade in hotel accommodations for a small fee, and single rooms are available for a $10 supplement per night.)

Aer Lingus (tel. toll free 800/223-6537) offers fly-drive packages including hotel vouchers and the option to stay in farmhouses, dinner included. There is a single-room supplement.

The **British Airways** (tel. toll free 800/AIRWAYS) "London Plus" plan allows travelers to build their own vacations using discounted hotel and rental-car rates (using Avis and Europcar), as well as discounted tickets to over 30 London theater productions.

REMINDER   To lodge a complaint about a commercial airline, be it a national or international carrier, go first to the airline's consumer-relations representative. To get the name and telephone number of that person, or to complain further if you are dissatisfied with the response, contact the **Department of Transportation's Office of Intergovernmental and Consumer Affairs,** 400 Seventh St. SW, Room 10405, Washington, DC 20590 (tel. 202/366-2220).

2. BY SEA

CRUISE LINES   "One if by land, two if by sea" holds true for budget travelers to Europe. The best value for the dollar is air-borne. Still, if your big dream— undeniably, a romantic one—is to make a transatlantic crossing once in your lifetime, pursue it. Start your research by studying your travel agent's or librarian's copy of the bimonthly *Official Steamship Guide,* which has a transatlantic section that lists ships and passenger freighters, date of departure, port of embarkation, ports of call, port of debarkation, length of cruise, lowest available price, and telephone number. The guide also includes information on barge, canal, and river cruises and ferry services. For more information or a one-year subscription for $85, contact the Official Steamship Guide, 111 Cherry St., Suite 205, New Canaan, CT 06840 (tel. 203/966-9784).

Only one ship plies the Atlantic with regularity anymore—the *Queen Elizabeth 2,* from April to December—and it's not cheap. Prices start at $1,795, including return airfare, for the five-day trip. For more information, contact **Cunard**, 555 Fifth Ave., New York, NY 10017 (tel. toll free 800/5-CUNARD or 800/221-4770). However, other cruise lines reposition their ships from one port of call to another to keep them in warm waters year round, and in the process make one transatlantic crossing each way each year. The eastbound crossing to the Mediterranean occurs in April; the westbound to Florida or the Caribbean, in November. These ships generally make the crossing in twice the amount of time the *QE2* does, so the price is higher, but the cost is much less on a per diem basis.

Cunard's *Vistafjord* makes both crossings, and its *Sea Goddess* makes the spring crossing.

Other cruise lines with Europe-bound ships include **Princess** (for information, see a travel agent); **Royal Cruise Line** (tel. toll free 800/227-4534); top-of-the-line **Royal Viking,** 95 Merrick Way, Coral Gables, FL 33134 (tel. 305/447-9660 or toll free 800/422-8000 outside Florida); and **Sun Line** (tel. 212/397-6400, or toll free 800/872-6400 outside New York State). Check rates with each and ask if the prices include a return flight.

FREIGHTERS Cruise liners cross the Atlantic in about 5 days, while it takes a freighter 8–10 days. Freighters carry no more than 12 passengers (otherwise they'd be required to have a doctor on board), charge less than cruise lines (though more than airlines), and provide unbeatable service. Plus you'll have the run of the ship and form a fast camaraderie with the other passengers and the crew. On the other hand, you may find yourself at the mercy of erratic sailing schedules (some passengers have waited a week in port for their freighter to leave). Nonetheless, freighter travel is on the rise.

By freighter tradition, passengers pay for a fixed number of days; if the trip comes in early, they might receive a refund; if it takes longer, and it often does, they may get the extra days for free. Tipping is expected, as it is on cruise ships. On a freighter, you pay about half the daily cost of a passenger liner, or about $100 a day. Some budget-style ships and originating foreign freighters charge less. **Polish Ocean Lines,** c/o Gdynia America Line, 39 Broadway, 14th Floor, New York, NY 10006 (tel. 212/952-1280), offers year-round transatlantic sailings of 8–10 nights from Newark, N.J., to Le Havre, Rotterdam, and Bremerhaven for $1,010 one way.

The **Mediterranean Shipping Company,** c/o Sea the Difference, 96 Morton St., New York, NY 10014 (tel. 212/691-3760, or toll free 800/666-9333), offers one-way trips year round from Boston, calling at New York, Baltimore, Newport News, Va., Antwerp, Bremen, Hamburg, Felixstowe, and Le Havre, starting at $1,600 from Boston or New York ($1,400 from Baltimore and Newport News). The round-trip fare is $3,200 for 28 nights.

Yugoslav Great Lakes Line, c/o Freighter World Cruises, 180 S. Lake Ave., Suite 335, Pasadena, CA 91101 (tel. 818/449-3106), has a 30- to 40-day round-trip that sails from Montréal, calling at Livorno, Genoa, Naples, Trieste, and Koper and Bar Yugo, Yugoslavia. The trip costs $2,880–$3,400, or about $85 a day; limited one-way fares are available. **Mineral Shipping** (c/o Freighter World Cruises, address above) offers more basic accommodations and amenities on monthly sailings from East Coast ports to several Dutch ports from $1,050 one way to $2,950 for a round-trip voyage of 28 days. Sailings on **Container Ships Reederi** (also c/o Freighter World Cruises) from Vancouver and Long Beach, California, through the Panama Canal to ports in England, Holland, or France start at $2,085 one way and $5,975 round-trip. The prices don't seem bad at all when you consider that top-of-the-line Royal Viking's *Royal Viking Sun* made a 17-day crossing in April 1992 from Fort Lauderdale to Rome with prices starting at $6,650.

Even "cheap" freighters like those above charge considerably more than airlines, but they do provide a memorable experience. Waiting lists for freighter travel range from two weeks to four months to a year, but last-minute berths are fairly easy to come by. People who are retired or on sabbatical are prime candidates for this type of vagabonding. Most lines have a maximum age of 75-plus.

SEASICKNESS Seasickness, really motion sickness, most affects first-time travelers and children aged 10–12, and usually only when seas get rough. To avoid it, ask for an inside cabin near the water line and steer clear of large quantities of food and drink during the voyage. If you feel unsteady, lie down and keep your head still. Check with your doctor about taking anti-seasickness drugs.

Most people who feel queasy on a ship or freighter get their sea legs after a couple of days. Some even experience "land sickness" once they reach their destination.

3. TRAVEL CLUBS

Members of travel clubs are doubly fortunate: their lifestyle permits them to pick up and travel at the last (or next-to-last) minute, and through their club, they can choose from bookings all over the world. The offerings are usually within a few weeks of departure, when remaining seats, rooms, or berths need to be filled, and the discounts are impressive—from 20% to 40%.

Bookings are done entirely by telephone, so you might find yourself on hold for five minutes, waiting your turn. The closer it gets to departure time, the better the discount.

Most travel clubs charge $45–$50 a year for membership. When deciding which one to join, consider the following:

- What kinds of travel are available?
- How are members notified of offerings?
- Is there a newsletter?
- Is there a toll-free hotline?
- How often is it updated?
- How difficult is it to get through on the hotline?
- Is there a service charge for overnight delivery of a ticket?
- Can a ticket be left at the airport for immediate pickup and use? Is there a charge?
- May a companion who is not a member of the club travel at the same rate? How about more than one other person?
- How soon and how far into the future can a member book a trip?
- What is the method of payment?
- What are the primary gateways?
- Are car-rental discounts offered?
- Is it possible to register for a particular destination or cruise and be notified when it is available? Is there an extra charge?
- What is the cancellation policy?

Travel clubs nationwide include the following:

Discount Travel International, 114 Forrest Ave., Narberth, PA 19072 (tel. 215/668-2182, or toll free 800/334-9294). Annual membership: $45. Members receive a 5% bonus on regular flights and a 7% bonus on charter flights booked through the club.

Last Minute Travel, 1249 Boylston St., 3rd Floor, Boston, MA 02215-3410 (tel. 617/267-9800, or toll free 800/LAST-MIN). There is no membership fee.

Last Minute Travel Connection, 601 Skokie Blvd., Suite 224, Northbrook, IL 60062-2818 (tel. 708/498-9216; fax 708/498-5856), has three services: a 900-number hotline for travel bargains on airfares, cruises, hotels, package tours, and condominiums; a registration service for specific destinations ($15 for five notifications); and a $40 annual subscription for a listing of monthly bargains ($200 if you want weekly listings). The hotline (tel. 900/446-8292) costs $1 per minute; calls average three to five minutes (call 708/498-3883 for a demonstration).

Moment's Notice, 425 Madison Ave., Suite 702, New York, NY 10017 (tel. 212/486-0503). Members have access to a hotline, but it's not toll free. The annual fee is $45.

Sears Discount Travel Club, 3033 S. Parker Rd., Suite 1000, Aurora, CO 80014 (tel. toll free 800/433-9383). Members receive a quarterly catalog, maps for trip routing, a 5% cash bonus on all purchases, and discounts on some hotels. Membership is $49.

Travelers Advantage, 3033 S. Parker Rd., Suite 1000, Aurora, CO 80014 (tel. toll free 800/548-1116). Membership is $49 a year, and besides the going discounts, members receive a 5% cash bonus on air, hotel, and car rentals booked through the club's reservations system.

Vacations to Go, 2411 Fountain View, Houston, TX 77057 (tel. 713/974-2121, or toll free 800/338-4962 outside Texas). Annual membership is $19.95, or $50 for three years, and includes four issues of *Vacation* magazine and their cruise catalog, plus discounts on car or RV rentals and airline tickets. They specialize in cruises.

Worldwide Discount Travel Club, 1674 Meridian Ave., Miami Beach, FL 33139 (tel. 305/534-2082). A toll-free number is available to members, who receive a travelogue with 200 listings every three weeks. Individual membership is $40 per year; families pay $50.

Encore Marketing International, 4501 Forbes Blvd., Lanham, MD 20706 (tel. 301/459-8020, or toll free 800/638-8976), operates four specialty discounting organizations: Short Notice provides last-minute discounts on tour packages and organized trips (annual membership, $36); Encore offers additional free nights or up to 50% discounts at about 700 European hotels and discounts on car rentals and airfares (annual membership, $48); and Villas of the World provides 20%- to 25%-per night discounts on villas, condos, and resorts ($60 for one year); while Villas with Meals offers a 15% discount on restaurants in villas.

REMINDER Airfares and other travel costs are at their peak when the tourist season is. In Europe, that's June through September. Fortunately, that's when travel clubs have the most discounts available for Europe. Those who can leave on short notice pay a fraction of the normal fares.

4. TRAVEL NEWSLETTERS

Worth the subscription investment, travel newsletters whet your appetite for travel and keep you informed about the latest offers and savings available.

Consumer Reports Travel Letter, Subscription Department, P.O. Box 53629, Boulder, CO 80322 (tel. 303/447-9330, or toll free 800/234-1970). Particularly useful for airfare discounts, it is published monthly, with a yearly subscription price of $37; for two years, $57.

Travel Companions, P.O. Box 833-F, Amityville, NY 11701 (tel. 516/454-0880; fax 516/454-0170). Published by Travel Companion Exchange (members receive listings of potential travel buddies; subscribers don't), it comes out every two months and offers money-saving tips and information on discounts, as well as savings for single travelers. A sample copy costs $4; a six-month subscription, $24; a one-year subscription, $36. Every new subscriber or member receives six back issues, each one containing many European travel tips.

Travel Smart, 40 Beechdale Rd., Dobbs Ferry, NY 10522 (tel. 914/693-8300, or toll free 800/327-3633). One of the oldest travel newsletters, it is published monthly, with an introductory subscription rate of $37; the renewal rate is $44. Write for a free copy.

AMSTERDAM

"I n Rotterdam they work, in The Hague they rule, but in Amsterdam they live." This old saying was shared with me by a Dutch doctor I met on a train in the Netherlands, and you'll find that it's very true. Amsterdammers have a zest for life that is evident in their bustling nightlife, their numerous museums, and their thousands of restaurants serving foods from all over the world. In summer the sidewalks and squares of Amsterdam are filled with tables and chairs as café-sitters enjoy the warm air while sipping a Heineken or a coffee. In winter they strap on their skates and race down the frozen canals (if it gets cold enough). And at any time of year these health-conscious people take to the streets on their bicycles. It's impossible to visit Amsterdam without falling under its spell and joining Amsterdammers as they enjoy their lively city.

Amsterdam is also a city that takes pride in its history. Not only are there dozens of museums, but the entire center city itself is one large historic district of restored buildings, most of which date from Amsterdam's golden age in the 17th century. At that time Amsterdam was the most prosperous port in the world, and the wealthy merchants built a beautiful city of elegant canal mansions that are preserved for all to enjoy. The preservation process continues today as young and energetic Amsterdammers restore the Jordaan neighborhood.

Lively Amsterdam, with its countless shops and brown cafés, excellent museums, and restaurants serving food from all over the world, is an exciting, cosmopolitan city where you'll find plenty to see and do while staying within your budget.

1. FROM A BUDGET TRAVELER'S POINT OF VIEW

AMSTERDAM BUDGET BESTS

Amsterdam's best deal by far is simply to stroll along the shady canals with their beautiful 17th-century canal houses. Few cities in the world have so many buildings of this vintage still standing. While you stroll the streets, you will likely see many street performers, from marionettes to five-piece rock 'n' roll bands. The entertainment costs only as much as you wish to toss into the hat.

WHAT THINGS COST IN AMSTERDAM — U.S. $

	U.S. $
Taxi from the airport to the city center	30.30
Metro from Centraal Station to Waterlooplein	1.20
Local telephone call	.15
Double room at the Amsterdam Sonesta (deluxe)	293.95
Double room at the Hotel Seven Bridges (moderate)	96.95
Double room at the Prinsenhof Hotel (budget)	60.60
Lunch for one at Sama Sebo (moderate)	16.50
Lunch for one at Broodje van Kootje (budget)	5.50
Dinner for one, without wine, at Dikker & Thijs (deluxe)	40.00
Dinner for one, without wine at Haesje Claes (moderate)	16.00
Dinner for one, without wine, at the Egg Cream (budget)	9.00
Glass of beer	1.50
Coca-Cola	1.35
Cup of coffee	1.35
Roll of ASA 100 color film, 36 exposures	9.10
Admission to the Rijksmuseum	3.95
Movie ticket	7.90
Theater ticket to the Concertgebouw	12.10–30.30

SPECIAL DISCOUNT OPPORTUNITIES

FOR STUDENTS   If you are under 26, and not necessarily a student, you can purchase a **Cultureel Jongeren Passport (CJP)** or Cultural Youth Passport, which entitles you to free admission to many of the city's museums, as well as to discounts on theater performances, concerts, and other events. The cost is only Dfl 15 ($9.10) and the passport is good for one year. You can get your CJP at the Amsterdam Uit Buro (AUB) on the Leidseplein. Be sure to bring your passport and a passport-size photo of yourself.

If you're under 26, you can also get a **Museum Card,** good for one year, for only Dfl 15 ($9.10). The Museum Card allows you free admission to most of the major museums in Amsterdam.

FOR SENIOR CITIZENS   Almost all museums in Amsterdam have reduced admission for senior citizens, and there is also a senior citizens' **Museum Card** available for Dfl 25 ($15.15).

FOR EVERYONE   The **National Museum Card** gives free admission to more than 350 museums all over Holland for one year. The normal adult rate for the card is Dfl 45 ($27.30). If you plan to visit more than five or six museums in Amsterdam, you'll save money by purchasing this card. Museum Cards are available from museum ticket windows and at the VVV Tourist Information Center in front of Centraal Station.

For getting around town on the public transit system, which includes trams, buses, and a subway system, buy either the **dagkaart (day card)** for Dfl 9.50 ($5.75), or a 15-strip **strippenkaart** for Dfl 9.85 ($5.95). The dagkaart is good for one day's unlimited travel in the city, and the strippenkaart is good for as many as seven trips, with no time limit. A dagkaart is available from bus and tram drivers and in Metro

WHAT'S SPECIAL ABOUT AMSTERDAM

Canals
- [ ] Attractive old homes lining the city's five main canals.
- [ ] Canal tours, canal buses, canal taxis, and canal bikes.

Museums
- [ ] The Rijksmuseum Vincent van Gogh, the Amsterdam Historisch Museum, and the Tropenmuseum.

The Netherlands
- [ ] Windmills, tulips, and people in wooden shoes within an hour or so of Amsterdam.

***Patats Frites* [French Fries]**
- [ ] Better than the much-acclaimed Brussels fries (if you're visiting both cities, you can make your own taste comparison).

Nightclubs
- [ ] Melkweg, Paradiso, and Kosmos, still going strong after all these years.
- [ ] Lectures, classes, food, galleries, film presentations, and live concerts in addition to music.

Concertgebouw
- [ ] The center of Amsterdam's music scene, with some of the best acoustics of any concert hall in the world; performances almost every night.

Bicycles
- [ ] The best way to get around Amsterdam.
- [ ] Reasonable rates at bike-rental shops.

stations. The strippenkaart is available in tobacco shops, at the ticket office in front of Amsterdam's Centraal Station, and at post offices.

The **Holland Leisure Card** costs $15 in the U.S., and provides discounts on everything from car rental to rail passes. Included in the Leisure Card are 25% discounts on sightseeing excursions by bus and boat, free admission to the Aalsmeer flower auction, and a 40% discount on a one-day Dutch Rail Day Pass. The Holland Leisure Card can be ordered from the Netherlands Board of Tourism, 355 Lexington Ave., 21st Floor, New York, NY 10017 (tel. 212/370-7367).

WORTH THE EXTRA BUCKS

Amsterdam is a city of canals—in fact there are more here than in Venice. It would be a shame to visit this watery city without staying in a hotel overlooking one of the canals, especially since these **canal-house hotels** are generally in 300-year-old buildings. So if you really want to experience Amsterdam, splurge a bit, even if it's only for one night, and stay at one of the canal-house hotels recommended below.

The other splurge you won't want to miss in Amsterdam is an **Indonesian rijstaffel dinner.** This dining extravaganza includes 15–20 different courses and will cost you between Dfl 40 and Dfl 50 ($24.25 and $30.30).

2. PRETRIP PREPARATIONS

DOCUMENTS   Citizens of the United States, Canada, Australia, and New Zealand need only a valid passport for a visit to the Netherlands for stays of less than three months.

WHAT TO PACK   Amsterdam is a very relaxed city where almost anything goes, especially when it comes to clothing. The only absolute must for a trip to Amsterdam is an umbrella or raincoat. In the winter, be sure to bring a warm coat since temperatures stay around freezing and can get considerably colder.

WHEN TO GO   You'll see from the climate chart that Amsterdam gets plenty of rain all year. Although July and August receive the most rainfall, they also receive plenty of sunshine, making summer the best time of year for sidewalk café-sitting. In addition, many excursions from Amsterdam operate only during the summer; this is when the Alkmaar Cheese Market and the Zuiderzee Museum in Enkhuizen are both open.

Amsterdam's Average Daytime Temperature & Days of Rain

	Jan	Feb	Mar	Apr	May	June	July	Aug	Sept	Oct	Nov	Dec
Temp. (°F)	36	36	41	46	54	59	62	62	58	51	44	38
Days of Rain	21	17	19	20	19	17	20	20	19	20	22	23

Special Events   The most popular time of year to visit the Netherlands is the **bulb-flowering season.** From the end of March to mid-May the bulb fields—tulips, hyacinths, daffodils, and crocuses—are in full bloom. There are plenty of excursions available from Amsterdam to view the colorful fields, and at the end of April each year there is a **Flower Parade** from Haarlem to Noorwijk.

April 30 is **Queen's Day,** when Amsterdam takes to the streets for a day of merry-making with performances, exhibits, parades, and markets.

Throughout June, Amsterdam celebrates the **Holland Festival** with cultural and musical events all over the city.

BACKGROUND READING   Anyone interested in the Holocaust and World War II will want to read *Anne Frank: The Diary of a Young Girl* (Washington Square Press). Written by a 14-year-old Jewish girl while her family was in hiding from the Germans during World War II, the diary provides a feel for life in occupied Amsterdam. Once you arrive here, you can visit the house where Anne and her family lived until they were discovered. Another fascinating war diary is *An Interrupted Life* (Pocket Books) by Etty Hillesum, a young Jewish woman who lived in Amsterdam until she was taken to Auschwitz where she died.

For those interested in history, Simon Schama's *The Embarrassment of Riches* (Knopf) is an extremely accessible examination of golden age Amsterdam.

Novels set in and around Amsterdam include Janwillem van de Wetering's *Corpse on the Dike* and *Hard Rain* (Ballantine), both enjoyable, offbeat detective stories.

---

3. ORIENTATION & GETTING AROUND

ARRIVING IN AMSTERDAM

FROM THE AIRPORT   If you fly into Amsterdam, you'll arrive at the efficient **Schiphol Airport.** The runways here are 16 feet below sea level, on the floor of what was once a large lake. For many years Schiphol Airport has been voted the best airport in Europe, in part because of its massive duty-free shopping center.

Making Schiphol even more convenient is the **train** that connects the airport with Amsterdam's Centraal Station. Leaving directly from the air terminal, this train costs Dfl 5 ($3.05) one way in second class. It's also possible to catch trains to other European cities directly from the airport.

FROM THE TRAIN STATION   Whether you fly into Amsterdam or take a train from another city in Europe, you'll find yourself at Amsterdam's massive **Centraal**

Station, which was built a little over 100 years ago on an artificial island. Inside the terminal you'll find a currency-exchange counter and a railway information center. Directly in front of the station is the VVV Tourist Information Center, a Metro station, and a ticket office where you can purchase a strippenkaart or dagkaart for use on the trams and buses. These cards are less expensive here than when bought from tram and bus drivers. Many tram and bus stops are also located in front of Central Station.

INFORMATION

The **VVV Amsterdam Tourist Information Center** (tel. 626-64-44) is directly in front of Central Station in a small white building that also contains a coffee shop and boat dock. Hours vary with the season, but throughout the year they are open daily—in summer from 9am to 11pm; in other months they close earlier. Here you can get maps and information about the city, as well as book hotels and tours. They also have a window for buying theater and concert tickets. There is another information center at 106 Leidsestraat.

Be sure to pick up a copy of **What's On in Amsterdam** for Dfl 2.50 ($1.50). This small magazine is full of information about the week's art exhibitions, concerts, and theater performances, and lists popular bars, discos, and restaurants.

Another great source of information for the young and the budget-conscious is the **Use It** youth information guide, available at the Tourist Information Center and at the Sleep-In, 51 s'Gravesandestraat. Aimed specifically at students and young travelers, this booklet is crammed with great information for everyone.

For additional information on cultural events in Amsterdam or to make reservations, stop by the **Amsterdam Uit Buro (AUB),** on the Leidseplein, open Monday through Saturday from 10am to 6pm.

CITY LAYOUT

When you step out of the Central Station main entrance you are facing the center of Amsterdam. Using this point as a reference, the city is laid out along five concentric semicircles of canals called **Singel, Herengracht, Keizersgracht, Prinsengracht,** and the outermost, **Singelgracht** (*gracht* means "canal"). It was along these canals that the wealthy merchants of the 17th century built their elegant homes, which are still standing today. The largest and most stately of the canal houses are along the Herengracht. Within these canals are many smaller canals radiating out from the center. The area within Singelgracht is known as the old city.

Leading away from Centraal Station is **Damrak,** a very busy tourist street that leads to **Dam Square,** location of the former dam on the Amstel River that gave Amsterdam its name. To the left of the Damrak is Amsterdam's famous **red-light district,** where government-licensed prostitutes sit in their windows with red lights glowing. One block to the right of the Damrak is **Nieuwendijk** (which becomes **Kalverstraat** when it crosses Dam Square), a pedestrians-only shopping street. If you follow Kalverstraat to the end, you'll find yourself at **Muntplein** beside the old Mint Tower. Cross the Singel and continue in the same direction and you'll reach **Rembrandtplein** (*plein* means "square"), one of Amsterdam's main evening-entertainment areas.

The other main nightlife area is **Leidseplein,** which is on the last of Amsterdam's concentric canals, the Singelgracht (not to be confused with the Singel, which is the first of the concentric canals). Leidseplein is at the end of **Leidsestraat,** another pedestrian shopping street that leads from the Singel to Singelgracht. Leidsestraat is reached from Kalverstraat by **Heiligeweg,** another short pedestrian shopping street.

Museumplein, where you'll find Amsterdam's three most famous museums—the Rijksmuseum, the van Gogh Museum, and the Stedelijkmuseum—is a five-minute walk along Singelgracht from Leidseplein.

One other area worth mentioning is the **Jordaan,** a quickly developing old neighborhood now filled with inexpensive restaurants, unusual shops, and small galleries. You'll find the Jordaan between Prinsengracht and Singelgracht in the area bounded by **Rozengracht** and **Brouwersgracht.** To reach this area, turn right off Damrak at any point between Centraal Station and Dam Square. When you cross Prinsengracht, you are in the Jordaan.

GETTING AROUND

Amsterdam offers many options for getting around the city. Trams and buses are generally the most convenient and bicycles are the most fun.

BY SUBWAY   Amsterdam's subway system, which is called the **Metro,** unfortunately doesn't serve most areas that tourists want to visit. You can, however, use it to reach Waterlooplein or the Amstel Station from Centraal Station. Both of these stops are within Zone 1 and require two boxes on a strippenkaart (see below).

BY BUS & TRAM   There are 16 tram lines and 30 bus lines serving Amsterdam. The buses and trams are the most convenient means of getting around the city, although they can be slow during rush hours. Tram nos. 1, 2, 4, 5, 9, 13, 16, 17, 24, and 25 and bus nos. 18, 21, 32, 33, 34, 35, 39, and 67 all originate at Centraal Station.

Now comes the confusing part. How do you pay for your ride? A single ticket is Dfl 2 ($1.20), but the best idea is to buy a **strippenkaart** for Dfl 9.85 ($5.95) at a tobacco shop, newsstand, post office, or at the Centraal Station public transportation ticket office, opposite the main entrance to the station. Before boarding a bus or tram, consult the map that's posted at every stop to determine how many zones you will be traversing. Fold your strippenkaart so that one more box than the number of zones you are traveling through is facing up and stick this end into the yellow box near the door as you enter. The machine will stamp your card. If you are traveling through one, two, or three zones, your card is good for one hour and as many transfers as you need. On buses, have the driver stamp your card. If you don't have a strippenkaart, you can buy 2-, 3-, and 10-strip cards from the driver, but this is a more expensive option than buying the strippenkaart ahead of time.

Want a less complicated solution? For Dfl 9.50 ($5.75), a **dagkaart** is available from bus and tram drivers, good for 24 hours and as many rides across as many zones as you like. Be sure to get it stamped the first time you use it. There are also tickets good for two to nine days, ranging in price from Dfl 12.60 to Dfl 33 ($2.65 to $20).

Should you be considering not paying the fare, keep in mind that inspectors, sometimes undercover inspectors, may demand to see your ticket at any time. If you haven't paid the proper fare, you will be fined Dfl 100 ($60.60). They will not accept the fact that you are a tourist as an excuse for not paying.

ON FOOT   When you look at a map of Amsterdam, it's easy to think that the city is too large to see on foot. This simply isn't true. In fact it's possible to see almost every important sight in the city on a four-hour walking tour. One important thing to remember when walking around town is that cars and bicycles have the right of way when turning. Don't step in front of one thinking that it's going to stop for you.

BY BICYCLE   Of the 700,000 people in Amsterdam, 550,000 own bicycles. You'll see children barely old enough to walk, their great-grandparents, even businesswomen in high heels pedaling around the city in any weather. A bicycle is one of the best ways of getting around in this flat city where too many cars clog the narrow streets. There are two things to remember, though: Watch out for unpredictable drivers, and always lock your bike—theft is a common problem.

Bikes can be rented all over Amsterdam, but the following shops offer good rates: **Take a Bike,** in the basement of Centraal Station, to the right of the main entrance as you are facing the station (tel. 624-83-91), charges only Dfl 7 ($4.25) per day plus a Dfl-200 ($121.10) deposit. **MacBike,** 116 Nieuwe Uilenburgerstraat (tel. 620-09-85), charges Dfl 9 ($5.45) per day plus an ID card and a Dfl-50 ($30.30) deposit.

Even more fun than cycling around the city is touring the countryside. Ask at the VVV tourist office in front of Centraal Station for brochures outlining cycling routes, then head off on your own. If you prefer to be guided, however, contact **Ena's Bike Tours** (tel. 015/14-37-97). The tours travel down scenic country lanes and into old

Dutch villages. Ena's tours are offered from June 1 to October 1, and start from the Amstel Station at 10am. Tours are Dfl 37.50 ($22.75), excluding the price of lunch. A similar tour is offered by **Yellow Bike Guided Tours,** 66 Nieuwezijds Voorgurgwal (tel. 620-69-40) for Dfl 39 ($23.65). This company also offers bicycle tours of Amsterdam for Dfl 25 ($15.15).

Amsterdam has one other pedal-powered means of transportation—**canal bikes.** These are small pedal boats for two to four people that are available on Leidseplein, near the Rijksmuseum, on Prinsengracht near the Anne Frank House, and on Keizersgracht near Leidsestraat. Canal bikes are available from 9am to 7pm in spring and autumn and until 11pm in summer. Rates are Dfl 18.50 ($11.20) per hour for a two-person boat and Dfl 27.50 ($16.65) per hour for a four-person boat. There is also a Dfl-50 ($30.30) refundable deposit.

BY CAR   A car is a good way to see the nearby countryside, and in Holland everything is nearby. On a day trip from Amsterdam it's possible to visit almost any area of the country. All the major car-rental agencies have offices in Amsterdam, and there are a number of smaller companies that offer rates as low as Dfl 45–60 ($27.30–$36.35) per day for very economical subcompact cars. These rates do not, however, include the mileage cost or the 18.5% tax. Try **Diks,** 278-280 van Ostadestraat (tel. 662-33-66), or **AutoRent,** 232 van Ostadestraat (tel. 671-07-33 or 679-98-09).

BY BOAT   There is one last means of getting around in Amsterdam, and that is by boat. The best option for tourists is the **Museumboat** (tel. 622-21-81), which stops near virtually all of Amsterdam's museums and attractions. The boats leave from behind the Tourist Information Center in front of Centraal Station every 30 minutes between 10am and 5pm. Tickets are available at the Lovers Canal Cruises counter near the dock. A day ticket costs Dfl 15 ($9.10) for adults and Dfl 13 ($7.90) for children 13 and under. This ticket also allows you half-price admission at most of the museums. There is also a combi-ticket for Dfl 25 ($15.15), which includes free admission to three museums. However, this is only a bargain if you choose to visit three of the most expensive museums, such as the Rijksmuseum, the Rijksmuseum Vincent van Gogh, or Anne Frank Huis. There are English-speaking guides on the boats.

There are also **water taxis,** but these are quite expensive. If you feel like a splurge, call 675-09-09.

The **Canal Bus** (tel. 623-98-86), a boat operating on a fixed route, stops at the Rijksmuseum, Leidseplein, Leidsestraat/Keizersgracht, Westerkerk/Anne Frank Huis, Centraal Station, and City Hall/Rembrandthuis. A ticket costs Dfl 12.50 ($4.20) and is good all day.

FAST FACTS   AMSTERDAM

Babysitters   A student babysitting service, Kriterion, 24 Tweede Rozendwaarstraat (tel. 624-58-48), takes calls daily from 5:30 to 7pm.

Banks   Three convenient banks are: Amro Bank, 82 Rokin (tel. 624-25-90), open Monday through Friday from 9am to 4pm; ABN Bank, 16 Rokin (tel. 624-15-52), open Monday through Friday from 9am to 5pm; and Rabobank, 16 Dam (tel. 626-87-31), open Monday through Friday from 9am to 4pm, and on Thursday also from 5:30 to 7:30pm.

Business Hours   **Banks** are open Monday through Friday from 9am to 4 or 5pm, and occasionally later on late-night shopping evenings. **Shops** are generally open Monday through Friday from 8:30 or 9am to 5:30 or 6pm and on Saturday from 8:30 or 9am to 4 or 5pm. Almost all shops are closed on Sunday, and many don't open until 11:30am on Monday and stay open until 9pm on Thursday or Friday.

Consulates   The Hague is the seat of government of the Netherlands and that's where all embassies are located. But there are a few consulates in Amsterdam, including the **United States,** 19 Museumplein (tel. 664-56-61), open Monday through Friday from 8:30am to noon and 1:30 to 3:30pm; and **Great Britain,** 44 Koningslaan (tel. 676-43-43), open Monday through Friday from 9am to noon and 2 to 4pm.

Currency　　The Netherlands **guilder** (abbreviated **f.** or **Dfl** for florin or Dutch florin, which was the old name of the currency) is the basic monetary unit. The guilder is divided into 100 cents and there are coins of 5, 10, and 25 cents, as well as 1, 2.50, and 5 guilders. Paper-note denominations include 5, 10, 25, 50, 100, 250, and 1,000 guilders.

When changing money, be absolutely sure to ask the exchange rate and the service charge. Rarely will a currency-exchange office give you the official rate, so shop around. Banks are usually best, followed by windows in train stations and tourist information centers. American Express and Thomas Cook also offer good rates, and can be found at several locations in Amsterdam.

Emergencies　　For 24-hour doctor and dentist referrals, call 664-21-11 or 679-18-21. For police emergencies, call 622-22-22. For an ambulance or in case of a fire, call 06-11. Before and after regular pharmacy hours (Monday through Friday from 9am to 5:30pm), call 694-87-09 for information on where you can get a prescription filled.

Eyeglasses　　If you need to have your glasses repaired or replaced, contact Gebr. Prins Brillen B.V., 224 Koninginneweg (tel. 662-26-51) or FA J.M. Schmidt, 72 Rokin (tel. 623-19-81).

Holidays　　Public holidays in Amsterdam include New Year's Day, Good Friday, Easter Monday, Queen's Day (Apr 30), Ascension Day, Whit Sunday and Monday, Christmas Day, and Boxing Day (Dec 26).

Hospitals　　The following hospitals have a first-aid department: Academisch Medisch Centrum, 9 Meibergdreef (tel. 566-91-11), and Onze Lieve Vrouwe Gasthuis, 179 1e Oosterparkstraat (tel. 599-91-11).

Information　　The **VVV Amsterdam Tourist Information Center** is directly in front of Centraal Station in a small white building that also contains a coffee shop and boat dock. See "Orientation and Getting Around," above, for details.

Laundry/Dry Cleaning　　When it's time to clean up those travel-weary clothes, head to a *wasserette*. Most are open Monday through Friday from 8am to 8pm and on Saturday until 3pm. Convenient locations include the following: 9 Ferdinand Bolstraat, near the Heineken brewery, where 13 pounds costs Dfl 7 ($4.25); 59 Rozengracht, on the edge of the Jordaan area, where you can do 9 pounds for Dfl 8 ($4.85); and 104 Haarlemerdijk, at the north edge of the Jordaan, charging Dfl 11 ($6.65) for 11 pounds if you drop off your laundry.

Get your dry cleaning done at the Clean Center, 59-61 Elandsgracht (tel. 625-07-31), or at 9 Ferdinand Bolstraat (tel. 662-71-67), near the Heineken brewery. Klardinette, 23 Rozengracht (tel. 627-82-71), is another convenient choice.

Lost and Found　　There is a general lost-and-found office at 11 Waterlooplein (tel. 559-80-05), open Monday through Friday from 11am to 3:30pm. For items lost on a tram, bus, or the Metro, go to the GVB head office at 108-114 Prins Hendrikkade (tel. 627-27-27). It's open Monday through Friday from 8:30am to 4:30pm. For items lost on trains, check at 1 Stationsplein (tel. 557-85-44) between 7am and 10pm.

Mail　　The PTT—Main Post Office is located at 250 Singel at the corner of Radhuisstraat. It's open Monday through Friday from 8:30am to 6pm (on Thursday to 8:30pm) and on Saturday from 9am to noon. Branch offices are open Monday through Friday from 9am to 5pm. A letter to the U.S. will cost Dfl 1.40 (85¢) and a postcard to the U.S., Dfl .80 (50¢).

Newspapers　　You'll find plenty of English-language newspapers, magazines, and books at W. H. Smith, 152 Kalverstraat (tel. 638-38-21), open on Monday from 1 to 6pm, Tuesday through Friday from 9am to 6pm (on Thursday to 9pm), and on Saturday from 10am to 5pm.

Photographic Needs　　You will find one-hour photo processing all along

THE GUILDER & THE DOLLAR

At this writing $1 = approximately 1.65 guilders (or 1 guilder = 60½¢), and this was the rate of exchange used to calculate the dollar values given in this chapter (rounded to the nearest nickel). This rate fluctuates from time to time and may not be the same when you travel to Holland. Therefore the following table should be used only as a guide:

Dfl	U.S.	Dfl	U.S.
.25	.15	30	18.18
.50	.30	35	21.21
.75	.45	40	24.24
1	.61	45	27.27
2	1.21	50	30.30
3	1.82	55	33.33
4	2.42	60	36.36
5	3.03	65	39.39
6	3.64	70	42.42
7	4.24	75	45.45
8	4.85	80	48.48
9	5.45	85	51.52
10	6.06	90	54.55
15	9.09	95	57.58
20	12.12	100	60.61
25	15.15	125	75.76

Damrak, Leidsestraat, Nieuwendijk, and Kalverstraat. Swank Shot Studios, 4 Spui (tel. 623-69-26) and 22 Rokin (tel. 624-40-00), are convenient camera stores.

Police   For police emergencies, dial 622-22-22.

Radio/TV   There are 16 cable TV stations in Amsterdam, including three British and one American station. There are only a few local radio stations, but the programming is fairly diverse.

Religious Services   Churches with services in English include St. John and St. Ursula, 30 Begijnhof (tel. 622-19-18); the English Reformed Presbyterian/Church of Scotland, 48 Begijnhof (tel. 624-96-65); and the Anglican Church, 42 Groenburgwal (tel. 624-88-77).

Shoe Repair   Get shoes repaired at Schoenreparatie 2000, 72 Kerkstraat (tel. 623-51-37), open Monday through Friday during regular business hours. Other shoe-repair shops can be found at 4 Kalverstraat and 5 Spui.

Tax   Look for the HOLLAND TAX-FREE SHOPPING sign in shop windows around Amsterdam. These shops will provide you with the form you need for recovering the VAT (Value-Added Tax) when you leave the country. Refunds are available only when you spend more than Dfl 300 ($181.80) in a store. For more information, see "Savvy Shopping," below.

Taxis   You can get a taxi in front of any major hotel, or at Leidseplein, Rembrandtplein, or Centraal Station. To phone for a cab, call 677-77-77. Rates start at Dfl 4.60 ($2.80) and increase by Dfl .23 (15¢) per 100 meters.

Telephone   A **local phone call** costs Dfl .25 (15¢) for three minutes. Telephone instructions are in English, and machines accept 25-cent and Dfl-1 coins. For **international phone calls,** there is the PTT Telehouse at 48-50 Raadhuisstraat, open daily 24 hours. There is another phone center at 101 Leidsestraat. A three-minute call to the U.S. costs Dfl 13.50 ($8.20). You can reach an AT&T operator by dialing 06 (wait for the tone), then 022-9111.

Tipping In almost all restaurants, a service charge is included in the price of the meals, so it's not necessary to leave any tip. However, if service is exceptionally good, you may want to leave a small tip, depending on the price of the meal. Taxi fares include a service charge, but drivers expect a small tip as well.

4. BUDGET ACCOMMODATIONS

Be prepared to climb steep stairways if you want to save money in Amsterdam. Narrow and steep as ladders, Amsterdam's stairways were designed to conserve space in the narrow houses along the canals. Today they are an anomaly that will make your stay in Amsterdam even more memorable. There was a time when the canal-house hotels of Amsterdam were quite cheap, but those days are now gone. Most canal-house hotels have raised their rates beyond the budget range, but you will still find a few listed here. Even if you don't stay in a canal house, you will most likely stay in a building built 250–350 years ago during Amsterdam's golden age. If you have difficulty climbing stairs, ask for a room on a lower floor.

In most cases a large Dutch breakfast is included in the rate for a night. These hearty repasts usually include ham, cheese, a boiled egg, several types of bread, butter, milk, and sometimes chocolate sprinkles, which are very popular.

DOUBLES FOR LESS THAN DFL 100 [$60.60]

NEAR DAM SQUARE

HOTEL DE WESTERTOREN, 35b Raadhuisstraat, Amsterdam 1016 DC. Tel. 020/624-46-39. 8 rms (4 with shower). **Tram:** 13, 14, or 17 to Westermarkt.
$ Rates (including breakfast): Dfl 50 ($30.30) single without shower; Dfl 80 ($48.50) double or twin without shower, Dfl 90 ($54.55) double or twin with shower but shared toilet. You will get a discount if you mention this book. EURO, MC, V.
Perhaps the best of the hotels on this block is the Westertoren, which was recently renovated. The two rooms in the front with balconies are attractive but tend to be a bit noisy. The quieter rooms in the back are large and bright. A full Dutch breakfast is served in the rooms, and proprietors Tony and Chris van der Veen, who both speak English, will share a wealth of information about the city.

HOTEL PAX, 37 Raadhuisstraat, Amsterdam 1016 DC. Tel. 020/624-97-35. 8 rms (none with bath). **Tram:** 13, 14, or 17 to Westermarkt.
$ Rates: Dfl 45 ($27.30) single; Dfl 80 ($48.50) double. AE, MC, V.
Most of the rooms here are quite large and all are simply furnished and clean. Two of the eight rooms have small balconies overlooking the street. Room 19, with four beds and plenty of space on the top floor, is particularly well suited to students or young people traveling together. Mr. Veldhuizen has been in business for nearly 30 years.

NEAR THE RIJKSMUSEUM

HOTEL ASTERISK, 14-16 Den Texstraat, Amsterdam 1017 ZA. Tel. 020/624-17-68. 25 rms (19 with bath). TEL **Tram:** 16, 24, or 25 or Weteringcircuit.
$ Rates (including full breakfast): Dfl 60–75 ($36.35–$45.45) single without bath;

Dfl 75–90 ($45.45–$54.55) single with bath; Dfl 75–95 ($45.45–$57.60) double without bath, Dfl 100–155 ($60.60–$93.95) double with bath; Dfl 125–185 ($75.75–$112.10) triple with bath. EURO, V.

This is the nicer of the Texstraat options. There are new carpets and furniture in all 25 rooms, and a buffet Dutch breakfast, with at least five types of bread as well as meats and cheeses, is served every morning. The breakfast room is bright, and over the years visitors from all over the world have tacked pieces of their own money on the wall. There are a few rooms on the ground floor, an elevator, and babysitters available, making this a good choice for older travelers and families alike.

HOTEL CASA-CARA, 24 Emmastraat, Amsterdam 1075 HV. Tel. 020/ 662-31-35. 9 rms (6 with bath). **Tram:** 2 or 16 to Emmastraat.

$ Rates (including full breakfast): Dfl 55 ($33.35) single without bath; Dfl 75 ($45.45) double without bath, Dfl 105 ($63.65) double with bath; Dfl 160 ($96.95) quad with bath. No credit cards.

Another inexpensive choice in this area is the Hotel Casa-Cara, which offers spacious, clean rooms with large windows, high ceilings, and a full breakfast, all in a very quiet residential neighborhood.

VAN OSTADE BICYCLE HOTEL, 123 Van Ostadestraat, Amsterdam 1072SV. Tel. 020/679-34-52. 15 rms (3 with shower but no toilet). **Tram:** 24 or 25 to the Ceintuurbaan stop.

$ Rates (including breakfast): Dfl 60 ($36.35) single without shower; Dfl 90 ($54.55) double without shower, Dfl 100 ($60.60) double with shower. No credit cards.

The young owners of this budget hotel have hit upon an interesting idea. They cater to visitors who wish to explore Amsterdam on bicycles. Their guests can rent bicycles for only Dfl 6 ($3.65) per day and a deposit is not required. They also are helpful in planning bicycling routes. The guest rooms have all been recently renovated and feature new carpets and comfortable modern furnishings. Some rooms have small balconies and there are large rooms for families. Though the Van Ostade is only a few blocks from the Albert Cuypstraat market, it's unfortunately not in a particularly attractive neighborhood.

NEAR LEIDSEPLEIN

HOTEL IMPALA, 77 Leidsekade, Amsterdam 1017 PM. Tel. 020/623- 47-06 or 622-40-22. 16 rms (7 with bath). **Tram:** 1, 2, or 5 to Leidseplein.

$ Rates (including full breakfast): Dfl 50–80 ($30.30–$48.50) single; Dfl 75–130 ($45.45–$78.80) double; Dfl 110–145 ($66.65–$87.90) triple; Dfl 150–190 ($90.90–$115.15) quad. EURO, V.

Just around the corner from Leidseplein, the Impala overlooks the junction of two canals. The singles and doubles here are small, but the triples and quads are quite large, and one is particularly popular with its bay window overlooking the canals. The furnishings in the rooms are eclectic and a bit aged, and the rooms are not always clean. However, younger travelers will find it to be a good value. The full Dutch breakfast is served in a large breakfast room with a hardwood floor, huge aquarium, and an unusual modern tapestry on the wall.

HOTEL DE LEYDSCHE HOF, 14 Leidsegracht, Amsterdam 1016 CK. Tel. 020/623-21-48. 10 rms (4 with shower but no toilet). **Tram:** 1, 2, or 5 to Keizersgracht.

$ Rates: Dfl 90 ($54.55) double without shower, Dfl 100 ($60.60) double with shower; Dfl 150 ($90.90) triple with shower; Dfl 180 ($109.10) quad with shower. No credit cards.

Built in 1665 and overlooking the Leidsegracht, this old home has long been an excellent budget hotel. Rooms vary in size, and the large rooms have high ceilings and

FROMMER'S SMART TRAVELER: HOTELS

VALUE-CONSCIOUS TRAVELERS SHOULD
TAKE ADVANTAGE OF THE FOLLOWING:

1. Hotels listed in this book or recommended by the Amsterdam VVV tourist information center in front of the train station. Politely decline the offers of young men and women in the train stations who will want to take you to a hotel.
2. Hotels near the Jordaan and the Leidseplein.

big windows. Many of the rooms have wood paneling that makes them look a bit like saunas, but original plasterwork and old (unused) fireplaces in some rooms hint at the building's past. If you need a firm mattress, you might want to look somewhere else. The most interesting feature of the hotel is its intricately carved stairway railing. Note that breakfast is not included here.

NEAR THE JORDAAN

HOTEL SCHRODER, 48B Harlemmerdijk, Amsterdam 1013 JE. Tel. 020/626-62-72. Fax 020/620-76-83. 9 rms (none with bath). **Bus:** 22 from Centraal Station to the third stop.
$ Rates: Dfl 50 ($30.30) single; Dfl 80 ($48.50) double; Showers Dfl 2 ($1.20) for 8 min. No credit cards.
On a street lined with all sorts of shops, on the edge of the Jordaan, is the inexpensive Hotel Schroder. This is a very basic hotel, but tile floors throughout and small tables and chairs in all nine rooms make it quite comfortable. The rooms are small, but considering the rates this is an exceptional deal. A full Dutch breakfast is served in the guest rooms.

DOUBLES FOR LESS THAN DFL 120 [$72.70]

NEAR WATERLOOPLEIN

HOTEL ADOLESCE, 26 Nieuwe Keizersgracht, Amsterdam 1018 DS. Tel. 020/626-39-59. Fax 020/627-42-49. 23 rms (11 with bath). **Metro:** Waterlooplein.
$ Rates (including full breakfast): Dfl 100 ($60.60) double without bath, Dfl 140 ($84.85) double with bath; Dfl 140 ($84.85) triple without bath; Dfl 160 ($96.95) quad without bath. No credit cards. **Closed:** Nov–Mar.
A good choice is this hotel, which began as a student hotel but is now more family oriented. The 23 rooms are outfitted with attractive new furnishings. A large breakfast room with skylights, a small bar, a patio garden, and a TV lounge make this an outstanding value. This six-story building has steep stairs and no elevator, but there are some rooms on the ground floor, including two on the patio.

HOTEL BARBACAN, 89 Plantage Muidergracht, Amsterdam 1018 TN. Tel. 020/623-62-41. Fax 020/627-20-41. 20 rms (13 with bath). TEL **Tram:** 9 to Artis Zoo.
$ Rates (including full breakfast): Dfl 65 ($39.40) single without bath; Dfl 100 ($60.60) double without bath, Dfl 145 ($87.90) double with bath. AE, EURO, MC, V.

The guest rooms here are clean, modern, and quiet, with new carpets and contemporary furnishings. The breakfast room has been completely redecorated and there is even a small gift shop.

HOTEL PRINSENHOF, 810 Prinsengracht, Amsterdam 1017 JL. Tel. 020/623-17-72 or 627-65-67. Fax 020/638-33-68. 10 rms (2 with bath). **Tram:** 4 to Prinsengracht.

$ Rates (including full breakfast): Dfl 75 ($45.45) single without bath; Dfl 100–105 ($60.60–$63.65) double without bath. Dfl 150–155 ($90.90–$93.95) double with bath; Dfl 160 ($96.95) triple without bath, Dfl 185 ($112.10) triple with bath; Dfl 220 ($133.35) quad with bath. No credit cards.

One of the best deals in Amsterdam, the Prinsenhof is located not far from the Amstel River in a renovated canal house. Most of the rooms are quite large, with beamed ceilings, and the front rooms look out onto the Prinsengracht, where colorful small boats are docked. The rates here include a large breakfast in a very attractive blue-and-white dining room. The friendly proprietors, Mr. vand der Jagt and Mr. Schulz, take pride in the quality of their hotel and will make you feel comfortably at home. A pulley will haul your bags to the upper floors.

NEAR REMBRANDTPLEIN

HOTEL KEIZERSHOF, 618 Keizersgracht, Amsterdam 1017 ER. Tel. 020/622-28-55. 4 rms (2 with shower only). **Tram:** 1, 2, or 5 to Keizersgracht.

$ Rates (including full breakfast): Dfl 60 ($36.35) single without shower; Dfl 115 ($69.70) double without shower. Dfl 130 ($78.80) double with shower. No credit cards.

This hotel, in a large old canal house, is run by the genial Mrs. de Vries. The four rooms are named after movie stars, and there are several other special touches that make a stay here very memorable. The hotel is entered through a street-level door, and to reach the upper floors you must climb a wooden spiral staircase built from a ship's mast. The ceilings of most rooms have exposed beams. A full Dutch breakfast is served in the ground-floor breakfast room.

IN THE JORDAAN

In the area called the Jordaan, only a few blocks west of the city center, are several fine hotels with economical rates. On a very picturesque small canal, Bloemgracht, are two hotels run by the same friendly Dutch manager.

HOTEL ACACIA, 251 Lindengracht, Amsterdam 1015 KH. Tel. 020/622-14-60. Fax 020/638-07-48. 14 rms (all with bath). **Bus:** 18 to Nieuwe Willems Straat.

$ Rates (including full breakfast): Dfl 80–90 ($48.50–$54.55) single; Dfl 100–110 ($60.60–$66.65) double; Dfl 140 ($84.85) triple; Dfl 180 ($109.10) quad. EURO, MC, V (add 5% to rates).

This unusual triangular corner building faces a small, picturesque canal. The young Dutch owners, Hans and Marlene van Vliet, are proud of their hotel, and it shows. All 14 rooms are furnished with modern beds, small tables, and chairs, as well as attractive new carpets. The large front-corner rooms sleep as many as six and have windows on three sides. On the ground floor is a cozy Old Dutch–style breakfast room where a full breakfast is served at long wooden tables.

HOTEL VAN ONNA, 102 Bloemgracht, and HOTEL VAN HULSSEN, 108 Bloemgracht, Amsterdam 1015 TN. Tel. 020/626-58-01 for both. 18 rms. **Tram:** 13, 14, or 17 to Westermarkt.

$ Rates (including full breakfast): Dfl 50 ($30.30) per person—single, double, or triple. No credit cards.

These two hotels share a breakfast room and have a total of 18 guest rooms available. Mr. Loek van Onna, the proprietor, has lived at no. 102 since he was a small boy. The van Hulssen was designed 350 years ago by the same architect who designed the nearby Westerkerk. The rooms here have new furniture, carpeting, and wallpaper. The large windows of the front rooms offer a wonderful view of the canal. The van Onna was built as a millstone factory about 300 years ago. Rooms here are not as attractive as the rooms two doors away, but the attic rooms with their exposed beams will give you a feel for life in a canal house.

NEAR THE RIJKSMUSEUM

EUPHEMIA BUDGET HOTEL, 1-9 Fokke Simonszstraat, Amsterdam 1017 TD. Tel. 020/622-90-45. 26 rms (none with bath). **Tram:** 16, 24, or 25 to Prinsengracht.

$ Rates: Dfl 90 ($54.55) double; Dfl 95–110 ($57.60–$66.65) quad. Breakfast Dfl 5 ($3.05) extra. AE, DC, EURO, MC, V.

Five minutes' walk from the Rijksmuseum, the Euphemia is popular with students and young travelers. A bit frayed around the edges, this is still a clean and inexpensive place to stay. In addition to the color TV in most rooms, there is also a TV and VCR in the breakfast room. You can even rent videos from the hotel, and inexpensive snacks are sold during the afternoon and evening.

HOTEL KAP, 5B Den Texstraat, Amsterdam 1017 XW. Tel. 020/624-59-08. 17 rms (4 with bath, 1 with shower only). **Tram:** 16, 24, or 25 to Weteringcircuit.

$ Rates (including full breakfast): Dfl 60 ($36.35) single without shower or bath; Dfl 90 ($54.55) double without shower or bath; Dfl 135 ($81.80) triple without shower or bath; Dfl 170 ($103.05) quad without shower or bath. Rooms with shower or bath are more expensive. AE, DC, EURO, V.

Across the street from the Hotel Asterisk, this hotel has several large family rooms as well as smaller rooms. Simply furnished and decorated, the rooms are clean and comfortable. Dark wooden tables and chairs fill the breakfast room where a full Dutch breakfast is served.

KOOYK HOTEL, 82 Leidsekade, Amsterdam 1017 PM. Tel. 020/623-02-95 or 622-67-36. 19 rms (none with bath). **Tram:** 1, 2, or 5 to Leidseplein.

$ Rates (including full breakfast): Dfl 70 ($42.40) single; Dfl 100–105 ($60.60–$63.65) double; Dfl 130–135 ($78.80–$81.80) triple; Dfl 155–175 ($93.95–$106.05) quad. MC, V (add 4% to rates).

Another good value is the Kooyk Hotel. Most of the rooms here have TVs, and all have been refurnished and redecorated. Reproductions of Dutch paintings, old photographs of Amsterdam, and photos of American movie stars hang on the walls. There is a huge four-bed room in front that overlooks the Singelgracht. A full Dutch breakfast is served in the ground-floor breakfast room.

HOTEL LINDA, 131 Stadhouderskade, Amsterdam 1074 AW. Tel. 020/662-56-68. 17 rms (2 with bath, 5 with shower only). **Tram:** 4, 16, 24, or 25 to Stadhouderskade.

$ Rates (including full breakfast): Dfl 105 ($63.65) double without bath or shower, Dfl 130 ($78.80) double with shower, Dfl 155 ($93.95) double with bath. No credit cards. **Closed:** Nov–Jan.

A bit farther down the street away from the Rijksmuseum, the Hotel Linda is an elegant but moderately priced hostelry overlooking the canal. The front door's huge, old-fashioned key for a handle makes it impossible to miss. Inside there are Persian carpets on the floors, a marble entrance, and stained-glass doors. The rooms are well furnished, and a delicious Dutch breakfast is served each morning.

HOTEL MUSEUMZICHT, 22 Jan Luykenstraat, Amsterdam 1071 CN. Tel. 020/671-29-54. 14 rms (3 with bath). **Tram:** 1, 2, or 5 to Leidseplein.

$ Rates (including full breakfast): Dfl 60 ($36.35) single without bath; Dfl 95 ($57.60) double or twin without bath; Dfl 120 ($72.70) double with bath; Dfl 125 ($75.75) triple without bath; Dfl 150 ($90.90) triple with bath. AE, EURO, MC, V.

This hotel is ideal for museum-goers since it's right across from the back of

Amsterdam's famous Rijksmuseum. The breakfast room commands an excellent view of the museum with its numerous stained-glass windows. Robin de Jong, the proprietor, has furnished the 14 rooms with an interesting collection of items, from 1930s English wicker to 1950s modern. The furnishings and the proximity to the museum make this one of the better budget choices in the area.

HOTEL WYNNOBEL, 9 Vossiusstraat, Amsterdam 1071 AB. Tel. 020/ 662-22-98. 12 rms (none with bath). **Tram:** 1, 2, or 5 to Leidseplein; then walk south along Singelgracht for three blocks.

$ Rates (including full breakfast): Dfl 70–75 ($42.40–$45.45) single; Dfl 95–100 ($57.60–$60.60) twin; Dfl 130 ($78.80) triple; Dfl 160 ($96.95) quad. No credit cards.

The Wynnobel is just around the corner from the chic boutiques of P. C. Hoofstraat and only a few minutes' walk from the Rijksmuseum. It overlooks part of Vondelpark and is run by friendly Pierre Wynnobel and his wife. The large rooms are all furnished with old or antique furniture, and a large Dutch breakfast is served in your room. A beautiful central stairway winds around to the hotel's four floors, and the first floor is only a short climb. Mr. Wynnobel sees to it that the hotel is kept clean, and a stay here is always pleasant.

SUPER-BUDGET CHOICES
STUDENT HOTELS & YOUTH HOSTELS

If you plan to stay in a hostel or student hotel in the summer, it's imperative that you look for a room early in the day—by late afternoon, hostels are usually full. Try to avoid arriving in Amsterdam after dark since this will make finding a place to stay very difficult. Amsterdam has two IYHF (International Youth Hostel Federation) youth hostels. Nonmembers pay Dfl 5 ($3.05) extra per night for the first six nights.

EBEN HAEZER, 179 Bloemstraat, Amsterdam 1016 LA. Tel. 020/624- 47-17. 114 beds. **Tram:** 13 or 17 to Marnixstraat.

$ Rates (including full breakfast): Dfl 13.50 ($8.20) dorm bed, plus a refundable deposit of Dfl 10 ($6.05). No credit cards.

This is the nicer of the two Christian Youth Hostels, and is located on the edge of the Jordaan area, a 10-minute walk from Dam Square. The beds are bright-red bunk beds in large dormitories with huge windows. There is a midnight curfew Sunday through Thursday night (1am on Friday and Saturday), and the dorms are closed for cleaning every day between 10am and 2pm. New showers, central heating, a small lounge, a large, quiet dining hall serving three meals a day, and a peaceful patio all add up to a great deal if you don't mind sleeping in a dorm.

HANS BRINKER HOTEL, 136 Kerkstraat, Amsterdam 1017 GR. Tel. 020/622-06-87. Fax 020/638-20-60. 115 rms (28 with bath). **Tram:** 1, 2, or 5 Leidseplein.

$ Rates (including continental breakfast): Dfl 115 ($69.70) double without bath, Dfl 145 ($87.90) double with bath; Dfl 38 ($23.05) for a dorm bed. AE, EURO, V.

This hotel is very conveniently located only a few blocks from Leidseplein. There are 255 beds available here, most in four-bed rooms that share a shower with one other room. The showers are between the rooms and have doors from each room, so be sure to lock up when you take a shower.

INTERNATIONAL BUDGET HOTEL, 76 Leidsegracht, Amsterdam 1016 CR. Tel. 020/624-27-84. 67 beds. **Tram:** 1, 2, or 5 to Leidseplein.

$ Rates: Dfl 55 ($33.35) single; Dfl 70–95 ($42.40–$57.60) double; Dfl 105 ($63.65) triple; Dfl 30 ($18.20) for a dorm bed. Breakfast Dfl 2–5 ($1.20–$3.05) extra. No credit cards.

Rooms here are very basic and most are shared four-bed rooms, but there are a few single and double rooms that come with their own TVs. There is also a lounge with several large sofas, a TV, VCR, and videotapes for rent, and a breakfast room where a large breakfast is served. This hotel is popular with students and is housed in a restored former canal warehouse with large shutters and windows facing Leidsegracht.

THE SHELTER, 21 Barndesteeg, Amsterdam 1012 BV. Tel. 020/625-32-30. 166 beds. **Metro:** Nieuwmarkt.
$ Rates (including full breakfast): Dfl 13.50 ($8.20) dorm bed, plus a refundable deposit of Dfl 10 ($6.05). No credit cards.
The other Christian Youth Hostel is in the heart of the red-light district, only a block from the Nieuwmarkt. The management here is very friendly, and they accept people between 18 and 35. Large dormitories filled with bunk beds can accommodate up to 166 visitors. No alcohol is allowed on the premises, and there is a midnight curfew Sunday through Thursday night (1am on Friday and Saturday). There is a garden with a large fish pond, a recreation room, and a restaurant where lunch and dinner are served. The Shelter's location may make some people uncomfortable; unaccompanied women, especially, may be bothered at night.

STADSDOELEN, 97 Klovienersburgwal, Amsterdam 1011 KB. Tel. 020/624-68-32. 190 beds.
$ Rates (including full breakfast): Dfl 20 ($12.10) for a dorm bed for IYHF members. No credit cards. **Closed:** Jan–Feb.
Amsterdam's other official youth hostel is located on the edge of the red-light district, and for that reason unaccompanied women may be uncomfortable staying here. Situated on a canal, the hostel offers standard dorm accommodations, and has large lockers and a self-catering kitchen.

VONDELPARK, 5 Zandpad, Amsterdam 1054 GA. Tel. 020/683-17-44. Fax 020/616-65-91. 320 beds. **Tram:** 1, 2, or 5 to Leidseplein.
$ Rates (including full breakfast): Dfl 20 ($12.10) for a dorm bed for IYHF members. No credit cards.
This is by far the nicer of the two hostels, with its own entrance gate from the large Vondelpark. Housed in an imposing old school building, the hostel has 320 beds primarily in 8-, 12-, and 14-bed dorms outfitted with metal bunk beds. The new furnishings and carpets and the cleanliness make this an exceptional deal. There are even a few double and quad rooms available for the same price, which includes a full Dutch breakfast. Other amenities include sturdy lockers for only 25¢ per day, a self-service kitchen, a bar at night with a small dance floor, a no-smoking reading room, and a covered bicycle shed.

IN SUMMER ONLY

THE SLEEP-IN, 51 s'Gravesandestraat, Amsterdam 1092 AA. Tel. 020/694-74-44. Fax 020/663-26-49. 522 beds. **Tram:** 6 or 10 to Weesperplein.
$ Rates: Dfl 20 ($12.10) dorm bed. No credit cards. **Open:** Easter, Whit Sunday, late June to early Sept, Christmas.
This large and very basic hostel is operated by the city every summer to handle the overflow of young travelers who find their way to Amsterdam. The low rate here does not include breakfast, but it does include free showers. A bar, restaurant, video lounge, free luggage check, and live music in the evenings all combine to make this a fun place for young people to stay. It's open all night, but closed from noon to 4pm.

ROOMS IN PRIVATE HOMES

Some of Amsterdam's best deals are to be found in private homes not far from the center of the city. If you're missing the personal touch and want to feel like a visiting friend rather than a guest, head out to one of these homes 10–15 minutes from the city center.

ARK OASE, opposite 216 Da Costakade, Amsterdam 1053 XK. Tel. 020/616-76-14. 2 rms. **Tram:** 17 to Bilderkijkstraat.

$ Rates (including full breakfast): Dfl 40 ($24.25) per person. No credit cards.

One of the few houseboats in Amsterdam that still accepts paying guests, Ark Oase looks a bit like a floating mobile home, but it's an Amsterdam experience worth trying. The rooms are homey, and the owner, Mr. H. J. Steens, is very friendly.

JEKATERINA SCHMICHOVA, 87 Marco Polostraat, Amsterdam 1057 WG. Tel. 020/616-76-91. 3 rms. **Tram:** 13 to Marco Polostraat; then walk south for three minutes.

$ Rates (including full breakfast): Dfl 27 ($16.35) per person. Mrs. Schmichova will do nine pounds of laundry for Dfl 5 ($3.05). No credit cards.

Mrs. Schmichova, who is from Russia and speaks excellent English, can usually find room for you in one of her spotlessly clean rooms. A large breakfast includes meat, cheese, tomato, honey, egg, orange juice, and coffee, tea, or hot chocolate. Mrs. Schmichova is a gracious hostess who makes her guests feel right at home.

MRS. J. SLOOF, 353 Willem de Zwijgerlaan, Apt. 2, Amsterdam 1055 RB. Tel. 020/684-11-66. 1 rm. **Bus:** 21 to Charlotte Bourbonstraat.

$ Rates (including full breakfast): Dfl 40 ($24.25) per person. Minimum stay two nights. Showers Dfl 1 (60¢) each. No credit cards.

Situated in a large modern apartment building, Mrs. Sloof's apartment is very close to one of the last windmills in Amsterdam. The one room has modern furnishings and is clean and comfortable.

MRS. S. BORG, 247 Admiralengracht, Amsterdam 1056 DX. Tel. 020/ 618-93-82. 4 rms. **Tram:** 13 to Marco Polostraat.

$ Rates (including full breakfast): Dfl 30 ($18.20) per person. No credit cards.

This is another good choice for those who prefer to stay in someone's home. Two of the rooms are in the basement, but they are nonetheless attractively furnished and carpeted. Guests can even iron their clothes here. Breakfasts are American style.

WORTH THE EXTRA BUCKS

HOTEL AGORA, 462 Singel, Amsterdam 1017 AW. Tel. 020/627-22-00. Fax 020/627-22-02. 15 rms (12 with bath). TV TEL **Tram:** 1, 2, or 5 to Spui.

$ Rates (including full breakfast): Dfl 110–118 ($66.65–$71.50) double without bath, Dfl 173–210 ($104.85–$127.30) double with bath; Dfl 210–245 ($127.30–$148.50) triple with bath; Dfl 278 ($168.50) quad with bath. AE, DC, EURO, MC, V.

Two houses built in 1735 have been fully restored to create this fine hotel, which is only steps away from the floating flower market. There are 3 rooms that fall within our budget and 12 more (all with private bath) that are worth the extra money. All rooms are carpeted and attractively furnished with new beds and a few antiques. The large family room has three windows overlooking the Singel canal. The hotel is efficiently run and well maintained by Giorgio Campeggi from Italy and Pierre Giauque from Switzerland. The Dutch breakfast is served on marble-top tables in the ground-floor breakfast room.

HOTEL AMSTERDAM WIECHMANN, 328 Prinsengracht, Amsterdam 1016 HX. Tel. 020/626-33-21. Fax 020/627-22-02. 36 rms (all with bath). TV TEL **Tram:** 1, 2, or 5 to Prinsengracht.

$ Rates (including full breakfast): Dfl 140–200 ($84.85–$121.20) double; Dfl 250 ($151.50) triple or quad. AE, EURO, V.

This hotel is constructed from three canal houses, and offers 36 attractively furnished and recently redecorated rooms, all with private bath. The hotel is owned and operated by American Ted Boddy and his English-speaking Dutch wife. They are extremely knowledgeable about Amsterdam and the rest of Holland. The breakfast here is a buffet that includes cereal, juice, meat, eggs, cheese, breads, honey cakes, and, of course, plenty of Dutch butter.

HOTEL SEVEN BRIDGES, 31 Reguliersgracht, Amsterdam 1017 LK. Tel. 020/623-13-29. 11 rms (6 with bath). **Tram:** 16, 24, or 25 to Keizersgracht. **$ Rates** (including full breakfast): Dfl 90 ($54.55) single without bath, Dfl 130 ($78.80) single with bath; Dfl 110 ($66.65) double without bath, Dfl 160 ($96.95) double with bath. No credit cards.

This may be the best hotel value in all of Amsterdam. If you're going to splurge for a room with an attached bath, this is the place to do it. Each of the huge rooms is unique, with antique furnishings, plush carpets, and reproductions of modern art on the walls. One room even has a bathroom with a skylight and wooden walls similar to those in a sauna. The front rooms overlook a small canal and the rear rooms overlook a garden. Your large Dutch breakfast will be served to you in your room at the time you request. Proprietors Pierre Keulers and Gunter Glaner are extremely helpful. An added bonus is that the hotel is only two blocks from the busy Rembrandtplein.

5. BUDGET DINING

Amsterdammers love to eat. Not only are there plenty of traditional Dutch restaurants, but there are also dozens of ethnic restaurants serving everything from Argentine to Tunisian food. Two very good areas for discovering new restaurants are around Leidseplein and in the Jordaan.

Indonesian food is extremely popular in Amsterdam. Even if you're on a tight budget, try to have at least one *rijstaffel* dinner, a traditional "rice table" banquet of as many as 20 different succulent and spicy foods served in tiny bowls. Pick and choose from among the bowls and add your choice to the pile of rice on your plate. It's almost impossible to eat all the food that's set on your table, but give it a shot—it's delicious. For an abbreviated version of rijstaffel served on one plate, try *nasi rames*. At lunch, the standard Indonesian fare is *nasi goreng* (fried rice with meat and vegetables) or *bami goreng* (fried noodles prepared in the same way).

Amsterdam's favorite lunch is a *broodje*, a small sandwich made with a soft roll or French bread and filled with meat or fish. You'll find these tasty and inexpensive sandwiches in restaurants and at street stands throughout Amsterdam. An especially popular street food is *broodje haring*, raw herring and onions in a soft bun. The traditional method for eating herring is to tip your head back and lower the fish head-first into your mouth.

Another traditional Dutch lunch to try is *uitsmijters* (pronounced out-*smay*-ters), which consists of two pieces of toast topped with ham or cheese and two fried eggs, and often served with a small salad.

If you want to experience Amsterdam conviviality at its finest, head to one of the city's hundreds of brown cafés. A brown café is a local bar that gets its name from the predominantly brown coloring of the interior. Why are the interiors of these cafés brown? Hundreds of years of thick tobacco smoke have stained the walls and furniture, and continue to do so today.

LOCAL BUDGET BETS

BROODJE RESTAURANTS

BROODJE VAN KOOTJE, 20 Leidseplein. Tel. 623-20-36.

Cuisine: DUTCH (BROODJES).
$ Prices: Dfl 4–9 ($2.40–$5.45). No credit cards.
Open: Sun–Thurs 9:30am–1am, Fri–Sat 9:30am–3am.

This is basically a fast-food restaurant Dutch style. Brightly lit and with only a few tables, Broodje van Kootje is very popular with Amsterdammers on the go. If you can't stomach the idea of eating a raw herring from a street vendor, maybe it will seem more palatable here. Another specialty is the creamy croquette broodje.

There's another, equally popular location at 28 Spui (tel. 626-96-20).

CALYPSO SANDWICH SHOP, 15 Zoutsteeg. Tel. 626-33-88.

Cuisine: DUTCH (BROODJES).
$ Prices: Dfl 4–11 ($2.40–$6.65). No credit cards.
Open: Daily 8am–7pm.

If you're looking for an inexpensive place for a quick broodje or two while strolling along the Nieuwendijk, duck into one of the many little alleys that lead toward Damrak. There are at least two or three sandwich shops on most alleys. This is one of the nicest little sandwich shops, with plenty of seating inside and a few tables out front. They serve a wide selection of broodjes, uitsmijters, and croquettes.

NOORDZEE, 122 Kalverstraat. Tel. 623-73-37.

Cuisine: DUTCH (SEAFOOD BROODJES).
$ Prices: Dfl 5–8 ($3.05–$4.85). No credit cards.
Open: Mon–Wed and Fri–Sat noon–7pm, Thurs noon–10pm.

If you're walking down the crowded Kalverstraat and your eyes are suddenly drawn to the most colorful sandwiches you've ever seen, you have undoubtedly stumbled upon the Noordzee. Herring and mackerel—served raw, smoked, or cooked—shrimp, tuna, and crab are delicious.

BROWN CAFES

CAFE DE PILSERIJ, 10 Gravenstraat. Tel. 625-00-14.

Cuisine: DUTCH.
$ Prices: Dfl 10–22 ($6.05–$13.35). No credit cards.
Open: Mon–Fri noon–midnight, Sat noon–8pm.

This high-ceilinged café and bar may look as though it has been here forever, but not too long ago it was a stationery store. Inside you'll find tables in front and back, with hanging plants adding a bit of color to the dark interior. Old jazz recordings are a favorite with the bartender. Located behind the Nieuwekirk and only steps from the Nieuwendijk pedestrian shopping street, this café is an excellent place to try a traditional Dutch lunch of uitsmijters.

INDONESIAN RESTAURANTS

BOJO, 5 Lange Leidsedwarsstraat, Tel. 622-74-34.

Cuisine: INDONESIAN.
$ Prices: Main courses Dfl 12–18 ($7.25–$10.90). No credit cards.
Open: Sun–Thurs 5pm–2am, Fri–Sat 5pm–5:30am.

Not only is this excellent Indonesian restaurant inexpensive and conveniently located near the Leidseplein, but it's also open all night on the weekend. So if hunger strikes you after a late night out on the town, drop in for a flavorful longtong rames special (served with chewy rice cakes). If it looks too crowded when you stop by, be sure to check the adjoining dining room, which has its own separate entrance.

PADI, 50 Haarlemmerdijk. Tel. 625-12-80.

Cuisine: INDONESIAN.
$ Prices: Dfl 15–35 ($11.10–$21.20) rijstaffel Dfl 32 ($19.40); nasi rames Dfl 16 ($9.70). No credit cards.
Open: Dinner only, daily 5–10pm.

This small Indonesian restaurant in the vicinity of the Jordaan is especially convenient if you are staying at the Hotel Schroder. The 11-dish rijstaffel is a good deal, as is the nasi rames, the less spectacular version of rijstaffel.

SAMA SEBO, 27 P. C. Hoofstraat, Tel. 662-81-46.
   Cuisine: INDONESIAN.
$ Prices: Dfl 25–45 ($15.15–$27.30); rijstaffel Dfl 45 ($27.30). AE, DC, EURO, MC, V.
   Open: Lunch Mon–Sat noon–3pm; dinner Mon–Fri 5–10pm, Sat 5–11pm.

 Sama Sebo serves the best bami goreng and nasi goreng in Amsterdam (but only at lunch). A meal here is a very worthwhile splurge. When you order either of the two lunch specials, you get a heaping mound of food that's really a nasi rames (one-plate rijstaffel). There are two sections to the restaurant—the main dining room with its Indonesian motif and the bar area for more casual dining.

SPECIAAL, 142 Leliestraat. Tel. 624-97-06.
   Cuisine: INDONESIAN.
$ Prices: Dfl 20–40 ($12.10–$24.25); rijstaffel Dfl 39.50–47 ($23.95–$28.50). AE, EURO, MC, V.
   Open: Dinner only, daily 5:30–11pm.
For an Indonesian meal in the Jordaan, try this tiny restaurant. The walls are woven bamboo and hung with framed batiks and photos of Indonesia. There are also batik tablecloths. Besides the standard Indonesian dishes, they have some unusual offerings for those who are already very familiar with Indonesian food.

MEALS FOR LESS THAN DFL 16 [$9.70]

EGG CREAM, 19 St. Jacobsstraat. Tel. 623-05-75.
   Cuisine: VEGETARIAN.
$ Prices: Dfl 10–20 ($6.05–$12.10); daily special Dfl 11 ($6.65) at lunch, Dfl 16 ($9.70) at dinner. No credit cards.
   Open: Wed–Mon 11am–8pm.
This tiny restaurant down a nondescript alleyway off the Nieuwendijk is a holdover from Amsterdam's hippie heyday and it still attracts a young crowd. Lots of varnished wood and a notice board advertising everything from meditation classes to apartments for rent give it the feel of a university hangout. Simple surroundings and basic vegetarian meals at extremely low prices are the main attractions of this place.

KEUKEN VAN 1870, 4 Spuistraat. Tel. 624-89-65.
   Cuisine: DUTCH.
$ Prices: Dfl 10–20 ($6.05–$12.10). AE, DC, EURO, MC, V.
   Open: Mon–Fri 11:30am–8pm, Sat–Sun 4–9pm.
In business for more than 120 years, this restaurant is one of the cheapest you'll find in Amsterdam. At one time the restaurant was primarily for feeding the poor, but today

---

Ⓕ FROMMER'S SMART TRAVELER: RESTAURANTS

VALUE-CONSCIOUS TRAVELERS SHOULD
TAKE ADVANTAGE OF THE FOLLOWING:

1. A quick lunch from an automat.
2. Broodjes and uitsmijters.
3. Dutch cheese—it's wonderful and makes ideal picnic food.
4. A cone of hot fries, a filling and inexpensive snack.
5. Tourist menus, which are usually three-course fixed-price meals that will allow you to eat in a restaurant that would otherwise be out of your range.

it is frequented by working people, students, and shoppers from the Nieuwendijk two blocks away, all of whom line up for the inexpensive self-service meals. A large and spartan dining area has seating for more than 100 people.

MOEDER'S POT, 119 Vinkenstraat. Tel. 623-76-43.
  Cuisine: DUTCH.
$ **Prices:** Dfl 10–30 ($6.05–$18.20). No credit cards.
  Open: Dinner only, Mon–Fri 5–10pm, Sat 5–9:30pm.
The restaurant is tiny but the meals are huge. Moeder's Pot has been around for years and is a very popular neighborhood hangout. The daily specials are a particularly good deal. This is close to Haarlemer Square and especially convenient if you're staying at the Hotel Schroder or Hotel Acacia.

PANCAKES

PANCAKE BAKERY, 191 Prinsengracht. Tel. 625-13-33.
  Cuisine: PANCAKES.
$ **Prices:** Dfl 8–20 ($4.85–$12.10). No credit cards.
  Open: Daily noon–9:30pm.
⭐ In the basement of a 17th-century canal warehouse is a long, narrow restaurant that serves some of the most delicious and unusual pancakes you'll ever taste.
There are several dozen varieties on the menu, almost any one of which is a complete meal. Choices include such concoctions as salami and cheese, cheese and ginger, chestnuts with whipped cream, and advokaat (a Dutch egg nog–like cocktail). In summer there are a few tables in front of the restaurant overlooking the canal.

CAFETERIAS

THE ATRIUM, 237 Grimburgwal. Tel. 525-39-99.
  Cuisine: DUTCH.
$ **Prices:** Dfl 6–8 ($3.65–$4.85). No credit cards.
  Open: Mon–Fri 9am–7pm.
This spectacular facility is the university cafeteria for Amsterdam. On the grounds of Amsterdam's old university, a courtyard between four restored buildings has been covered over. High above your head is a glass roof that lets in plenty of light all year. To reach the food lines, walk up the stairs just inside the door and across the pedestrian bridge.

HEMA DEPARTMENT STORE, 174 Nieuwendijk. Tel. 623-41-76.
  Cuisine: DUTCH.
$ **Prices:** Dfl 7–14 ($4.25–$8.50). No credit cards.
  Open: Mon 11am–6pm, Tues–Wed and Fri 9:30am–6pm, Thurs 9:30am–9pm, Sat 9am–5pm.
This second-floor cafeteria is just what one would expect from a discount department store. Still, the prices are low and the food is quite acceptable, especially such Dutch specialties as pea soup with bread and bacon. The steak dinner with mushrooms, potatoes, and green beans is a real bargain.

THE STATION, Platform 1, Centraal Station. Tel. 627-33-06.
  Cuisine: DUTCH.
$ **Prices:** Dfl 6–20 ($3.65–$12.10). No credit cards.
  Open: Mon–Sat 7am–10pm, Sun 8am–10pm.
⭐ Large, clean, and quiet, this cafeteria offers a wide choice of hot meals, sandwiches, salads, and pastries. The selection of meals is unusually varied, with half a dozen different types of salads as well as specials that change daily and monthly. You can even have wine with your meal here. The carpeting keeps the large eating hall quiet—you'd hardly know you were in a train station.

MEALS FOR LESS THAN DFL 26 [$15.75]
BOLHOED RESTAURANT, 60 Prinsengracht. Tel. 626-18-03.

Cuisine: VEGETARIAN.
$ Prices: Dfl 24–30 ($14.55–$18.20); lunch about half price. No credit cards.
Open: Lunch daily noon–3pm; dinner daily 5–9pm.

You may be hesitant to enter this restaurant when you see how badly it's leaning (a common problem in a city built on wooden pilings), but the owner assured me that the building had been that way for hundreds of years. High ceilings, large windows, and blond hardwood floors give this restaurant a bright and airy feeling. There is often live piano music in the evenings.

CASA DI DAVID, 426 Singel. Tel. 624-50-93.
Cuisine: ITALIAN.
$ Prices: Dfl 16–40 ($9.70–$24.25). AE, DC, EURO, MC, V.
Open: Dinner only, daily 5–11:30pm.

Directly across the canal from the Spui is one of the best Italian restaurants in Amsterdam. Be sure to try the individual-size pizzas. The vegetarian pizza with artichokes, mushrooms, zucchini, eggplant, and olives is outstanding. Wine casks, checked tablecloths, and subdued lighting add to the ambience of this canalside restaurant.

DE BLAUWE HOLLANDER, 28 Leidsekruisstraat. Tel. 623-30-14.
Cuisine: DUTCH.
$ Prices: Dfl 17–32 ($10.30–$19.40); tourist meals Dfl 14.50 ($8.80). No credit cards.
Open: Dinner only, daily 5–10pm.

The atmosphere here is casual and relaxed, and it's popular with the younger set who are on their way out for a night of bar-hopping around the nearby Leidseplein. Along the front window is a long table piled with magazines in several languages to read over tea, coffee, or a beer, or while you wait for your meal. Best of all, they offer special tourist meals which might include pea soup, ribs, bacon, black bread and butter, or meatballs, potatoes, and a salad or vegetable.

DE BOEMERANG, 171 Weteringschans. Tel. 623-42-51.
Cuisine: MUSSELS.
$ Prices: Dfl 25–40 ($15.15–$24.25). AE, EURO, V.
Open: Mon–Fri noon–9pm, Sat–Sun 4–9pm.

 If you like mussels, this legendary restaurant is the place to go in Amsterdam. The decor is old and eclectic and the selection on the jukebox is 20 years old, but you don't come here for the atmosphere. You come for the most succulent mussels you've ever tasted, served in huge pots in a quantity that's almost impossible to finish. Choose from among a number of different dipping sauces, all of which are a delicious complement to the fresh mussels.

EETCAFE DE PLATVINK, 59 Lindengracht. Tel. 623-78-38.
Cuisine: DUTCH.
$ Prices: Full three-course dinner Dfl 15 ($9.10); main courses Dfl 20–24 ($12.10–$14.55). No credit cards.
Open: Dinner only, Thurs–Tues 4pm–midnight.

If you crave a good old-fashioned Dutch meat-and-potatoes meal, you'll definitely find satiation at De Platvink (a peculiar name that translates as "Flat Finch"). This is a tiny place in the heart of the Jordaan, and if you stick with the Dfl-15 daily special, you can't help but go away happy and full. Single diners can sit at the eating bar.

HAESJE CLAES, 320 Nieuwe Zijds Voorburgwal. Tel. 624-99-98.
Cuisine: DUTCH.
$ Prices: Dfl 20–35 ($12.10–$21.20). AE, DC, EURO, MC, V.
Open: Mon–Sat noon–midnight, Sun 5pm–midnight.

Dark-wood paneling, low, beamed ceilings, and stained-glass windows create just the right atmosphere for your meal of traditional Dutch food. The meals are hearty and the portions large enough to satisfy even the hungriest person.

The restaurant is popular with everyone from executives in suits to shoppers from the nearby Kalverstraat, who fill the small tables in the two dining rooms. They come for the delicious food and reasonable prices.

SUPER-BUDGET MEALS

For the cheapest food in Amsterdam, stop by one of the city's many snack bars, known as **automatiek,** which are reminiscent of the Automats that long ago disappeared from the American scene. Walls of little glass boxes display croquettes, broodjes, and other snacks. Just drop your coins in the slot and take your pick. Croquettes are Dfl 1.50 (90¢) and broodjes, Dfl 2.50 ($1.50). These snack bars also sell delicious fries. For Dfl 2.50 ($1.50) you get a large container or cone of fries with your choice of ketchup or the Dutch mayonnaiselike sauce that's traditionally served on fries here.

Febo, the best known of the automatieks, can be found at 142 Kalverstraat, 94 Leidsestraat, 220 Nieuwendijk, and 38 Reguliersbreestraat.

PICNIC SUPPLIES & WHERE TO EAT THEM

You can pick up almost anything you might want for a picnic, from cold cuts to a bottle of wine, at the **Mignon supermarket,** 74 Leidsestraat. Then head over to the **Vondelpark,** only a 15-minute walk away. If it's summer you might even catch a free concert at the outdoor theater.

WORTH THE EXTRA BUCKS

D'THEEBOOM, 210 Singel. Tel. 623-84-20.
   Cuisine: FRENCH.
   $ Prices: Fixed-price dinner Dfl 44 ($26.65). AE, DC, EURO, MC, V.
   Open: Lunch Mon–Fri noon–2:30pm; dinner daily 6–10:30pm.

★ When you're tired of pork chops and potatoes and want a worthwhile splurge, you can't do better than this modern French restaurant. The cuisine is nouvelle and the decor is moderne. The three-course dinner includes soup or salad, main course, an assortment of vegetables, and dessert. Everything is superbly prepared and artfully presented.

---

6. ATTRACTIONS

SUGGESTED ITINERARIES

IF YOU HAVE ONE DAY The very first thing you should do in Amsterdam is take a boat tour of the canals. After your tour, head to the Rijksmuseum and see several Rembrandts and the museum's large collection of paintings by such 17th-century Dutch masters as Vermeer, Jan Steen, and Frans Hals. After lunch, visit the Rijksmuseum Vincent van Gogh. Finish your day with a visit to the Rembrandthuis Museum. Not only will you get a look at virtually all the prints that Rembrandt made but you'll also get to see the inside of the restored 17th-century house where he once lived.

IF YOU HAVE TWO DAYS For your first day, follow the itinerary above. On your second day, visit the famous Anne Frank House Museum, where the Jewish Frank family hid from the Nazis during World War II. After visiting the museum, stroll around the Jordaan area, an old section of Amsterdam that has only been restored in the past few years. Have lunch at one of the many restaurants in the Jordaan, then head for the Amsterdam Historical Museum on Kalverstraat. This excellent museum

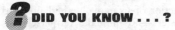
DID YOU KNOW . . . ?

- About half the area of the Netherlands is below sea level; only the dikes stop the country from being swallowed by the sea.
- There are 600,000 flower bulbs in public parks and gardens in Amsterdam.
- The word "yacht" comes from the old Dutch *jaght*; the first yacht race ever—between the English and the Dutch—took place in 1662 on the Thames.
- Amsterdam boasts 2,400 houseboats.
- KLM, Royal Dutch Airlines, is the world's oldest airline—service was initiated between Amsterdam and London in 1920.
- There are 206 van Gogh paintings in Amsterdam.
- The Pilgrims, though they were English, lived in Holland for 11 years before sailing for America.
- There are more than 12 million bicycles in the Netherlands.
- Two-thirds of the cut flowers sold in the world come from the Netherlands.
- Though Amsterdam is the official capital of the Netherlands, the seat of government is The Hague.

covers several hundred years of local Amsterdam history. When you leave, be sure to take a stroll around the Begijnhof, a peaceful courtyard surrounded by old houses. Since you're on Kalverstraat, Amsterdam's busiest pedestrian shopping street, you might want to get in a bit of shopping.

IF YOU HAVE THREE DAYS   After your canal tour, spend the rest of your first day on the Museumplein. Visit the Rijksmuseum, the van Gogh Museum, and the Stedelijk, Amsterdam's impressive museum of contemporary art.

On Day 2, visit the Rembrandthuis and the Jewish Historical Museum, which is only a few blocks away. While you're in this area, you can stroll around the Waterlooplein flea market. If you are interested, this would be a good time, and much safer than at night, to stroll through Amsterdam's famous red-light district, where the women sit in their windows. Take precautions if you visit the red-light district—night or day. In the afternoon, visit the Amsterdam Historical Museum and the Begijnhof.

On your third day, visit the nearby museum village of Zaanse Schans in the morning. Working windmills and Dutch artisans are two of the attractions in this beautiful little village only 20 minutes from the city. In the afternoon visit the Anne Frank House Museum and tour the Jordaan.

IF YOU HAVE FIVE DAYS   On your fourth day, get up early and take the bus to the flower auction in Aalsmeer, the largest flower auction in the world. Back in town, visit the Tropenmuseum, Amsterdam's museum of the tropics. To continue your exotic journey, visit the Albert Cuypstraat open-air market next. This market is lined with vendors selling all manner of goods, from fresh fish to Japanese electronics. You might even be able to catch a tour of the Heineken Brewery if you time things well.

On Day 5, try an all-day excursion to Enkheuisen's Zuiderzee Museum, a restored village featuring more than 100 houses and other buildings from around the former Zuiderzee. An alternative to this is a trip to Rotterdam and The Hague, with a visit to the miniature village of Madurodam.

TOP ATTRACTIONS

The Netherlands calls itself "Museum Land," and Amsterdam, with 42 museums, is its de facto capital. These museums range from the grandiose Rijksmuseum to the fascinating little Amstelkring, also known as Our Lord in the Attic. Even if you plan to visit only the first six museums listed below, you should purchase a **Museumkaart (museum card),** which entitles you to free admission to more than 350 museums all over the Netherlands, including the first six below and many others in Amsterdam. The pass costs Dfl 40 ($24.25) for adults, Dfl 15 ($9.10) for those under 18, and Dfl 25 ($15.15) for those over 65.

THE RIJKSMUSEUM, 42 Stadhouderskade. Tel. 673-21-21.

⭐ This is the largest and most important collection of art in the Netherlands, and the focus, of course, is on the Dutch masters—Rembrandt, Vermeer, Frans Hals, Jan Steen, and others. In addition, there are large collections of sculpture and applied arts, Asian art, prints and drawings, and Dutch antiquities. Built between 1877 and 1883, the museum is a cathedral to the arts.

Although the museum has literally hundreds of rooms full of art, first-time visitors invariably head for *The Night Watch,* Rembrandt's most famous masterpiece. Painted in 1642 and, since 1947, correctly titled *The Shooting Company of Captain Frans Banning Cocq and Lieutenant Willem van Ruytenbuch,* this large canvas was commissioned as a group portrait to hang in a guild hall. In the two small rooms directly preceding *The Night Watch* room are several of Rembrandt's most beautiful paintings, including *The Jewish Bride, Anatomy Lesson of Dr. Tulp,* and *Self-Portrait as the Apostle Paul.* Rembrandt was a master of light and shadow and these paintings from late in his life show some of his finest work.

Leading up to *The Night Watch* is the Gallery of Honor, in which you can see paintings by such great non-Dutch artists as Goya, Fra Angelico, Tiepolo, Rubens, and van Dyck. In the rooms to the left of *The Night Watch* are more works by Rembrandt and the other Dutch masters of the 17th century.

Admission: Dfl 6.50 ($3.95) adults, Dfl 3.50 ($2.10) senior citizens and children. **Open:** Tues–Sat 10am–5pm, Sun 1–5pm. **Closed:** Jan 1. **Tram:** 2, 5, or 16 to Museumplein.

RIJKSMUSEUM VINCENT VAN GOGH, 7 Paulus Potterstraat. Tel. 676-48-81.

⭐ This modern museum houses the world's largest collection of works—200 paintings and 500 drawings—of the most important Dutch artist of the 19th century. The museum gives both a chronological and thematic presentation of van Gogh's Dutch and French periods. Also displayed is his private collection of Japanese prints, magazine illustrations, and books. The museum displays works by contemporaries who both influenced him and in turn were influenced by him. The periods before he was born and after his death are also represented. As you view the paintings on display, you will see van Gogh's early, gloomy style slowly change to one of vibrant colors, and see his brush strokes getting bolder as he develops his own unique style.

Admission: Dfl 10 ($6.05) adults, Dfl 5 ($3.05) senior citizens and children. **Open:** Tues–Sat 10am–5pm, Sun 1–5pm (ticket office closes at 4pm). **Closed:** Jan 1. **Tram:** 2, 5, or 16 to Museumplein.

STEDELIJK MUSEUM, 13 Paulus Potterstraat. Tel. 6573-29-11.

Focusing on modern art from 1850 to the present, the Stedelijk is Amsterdam's most innovative major museum. Virtually all the museum's extensive permanent collection—including works by Chagall, Picasso, Monet, Manet, Cézanne, Mondrian, Matisse, Dubuffet, De Kooning, Appel, and Rauschenberg, among many others—is on display every summer. In the winter, many works are put into storage to make way for temporary exhibits and installations by artists from the current art scene. The most recent trends in European and American art are well represented, so be prepared for exhibitions of the most daring of today's artists. In addition to the paintings, sculptures, drawings, and engravings, there are exhibits of applied arts, videos, industrial design, and photography.

Admission: Dfl 7 ($4.25) adults, Dfl 3.50 ($2.10) senior citizens and children. **Open:** Daily 11am–5pm. **Closed:** Jan 1. **Tram:** 2, 5, or 16 to Museumplein.

REMBRANDTHUIS MUSEUM, 4-6 Jodenbreestraat. Tel. 624-94-86.

When Rembrandt van Rijn moved into this three-story house in 1639, he was already a well-established and wealthy artist. However, the cost of buying and furnishing the house eventually led to his financial downfall in 1656. When Rembrandt was declared insolvent that year, an inventory of the contents of the house was drawn up, which listed more than 300 paintings by Rembrandt himself and some by his teacher, Pieter Lastman, and his friends, Peter Paul Rubens and Jan Lievens. The following year Rembrandt was forced to sell the house and most of his possessions to meet his debts. He remained in the house until 1660, and then moved to much less grandiose accommodations on Rozengracht, in the Jordaan.

The museum houses a nearly complete collection of Rembrandt's etchings. Of the 280 prints he made, 250 are on display here, along with paintings by his teachers and pupils. Rembrandt's prints show amazing detail, and you can see his use of shadows and light for dramatic effect. Wizened patriarchs, emaciated beggars, children at play, and Rembrandt himself in numerous self-portraits are the subjects that you will long remember after a visit to the Rembrandthuis.

Admission: Dfl 4 ($2.40) adults, Dfl 2.50 ($1.50) senior citizens and children. **Open:** Mon–Sat 10am–5pm, Sun and hols 1–5pm. **Closed:** Jan 1. **Metro:** Waterlooplein. **Tram:** 9 to Waterlooplein.

AMSTERDAM HISTORISCH MUSEUM, 92 Kalverstraat. Tel. 523-18-22.

Of all Amsterdam's many museums, none is so well designed as this former orphanage that now houses exhibits covering nearly 700 years of the city's history. Items in the collection range from a pair of old leather shoes found in the mud of a building foundation to huge canvases depicting 17th-century Civic Guards. The museum halls are laid out so that visitors can go chronologically through the history of Amsterdam, with the main focus on the golden age of the 17th century. During this century Amsterdam was the richest city in the world, and some of the most interesting exhibits are of the trades that made Amsterdam so rich. In short, everything you might want to know about the history of this fascinating city is housed in these buildings.

Admission: Dfl 5 ($3.05) adults, Dfl 2.50 ($1.50) senior citizens and children. **Open:** Daily 11am–5pm. **Closed:** Jan 1. **Tram:** 1, 2, or 5 to Spui.

JOODS HISTORISCH MUSEUM, 2-4 Jonas Daniel Meijerplein. Tel. 626-99-45.

The Jewish Historical Museum in Amsterdam is housed in four Orthodox synagogues. The neighborhood surrounding the museum was the Jewish quarter of Amsterdam for 300 years until the Nazi occupation during World War II emptied the city of its Jewish population. The oldest of the museum's four synagogues, built in 1670, is the oldest public synagogue in western Europe. The newest of the four was built in 1752. Inside the restored synagogues are exhibits covering the history of Jews in the Netherlands, including their persecution throughout Europe under Hitler. Jewish religious artifacts are a major focus of the museum.

Admission: Dfl 7 ($4.25) adults, Dfl 3.50 ($2.10) senior citizens and children. **Open:** Daily 11am–5pm. **Closed:** Yom Kippur. **Metro:** Waterlooplein. **Tram:** 9 to Waterlooplein.

MUSEUM AMSTELKRING, 40 Oudezijds Voorburgwal. Tel. 624-66-04.

⭐ Although Amsterdam has been known as a tolerant city for many centuries, just after the Protestant Reformation Roman Catholics fell into disfavor. Forced to worship in secret, they devised ingenious ways of gathering for Sunday services. In an otherwise ordinary-looking 17th-century canal house in the middle of Amsterdam's red-light district is the most amazing of these clandestine churches, known to the general public as "Our Lord in the Attic." The three houses that comprise this museum were built in the 1660s by a wealthy Catholic merchant specifically to house a church. Today the buildings are furnished much as they would have been in the mid-18th century. Nothing prepares you for the mini-cathedral you come upon so unexpectedly when you climb the last flight of stairs into the attic. A large baroque altar, religious statuary, pews to seat 200, even an 18th-century organ and an upper gallery complete this miniature church in an attic.

Admission: Dfl 4.50 ($2.75) adults, Dfl 3 ($1.80) senior citizens, students, and children. **Open:** Mon–Sat 10am–5pm, Sun 1–5pm. **Closed:** Jan 1. **Directions:** From Centraal Station, walk down Damrak, turn left on Oudebrugsteeg, and then right onto the far side of the Oudezijds Voorburgwal.

THE
NETHERLANDS

 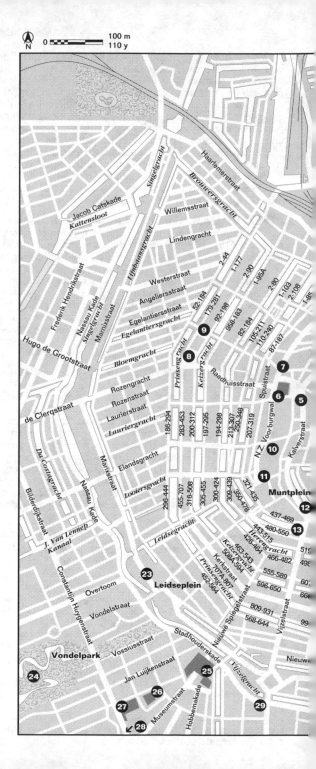

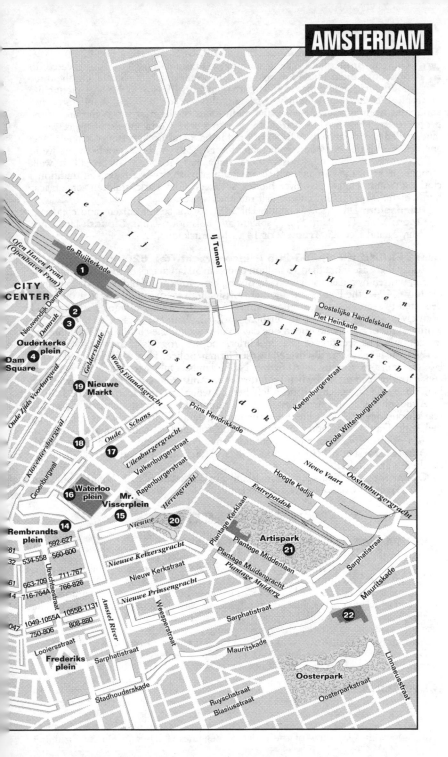

AMSTERDAM

TROPENMUSEUM, 2 Linnaeusstraat. Tel. 568-82-95 or 568-82-00.

⭐ One of Amsterdam's finest and most unusual museums is dedicated to presenting the tropics to people living in a very different climate. On the three floors surrounding the main hall are numerous life-size tableaux depicting life in tropical countries. Although there are displays of beautiful handcrafts and antiquities from all these regions, the main focus of the museum is the life of the people today. There are hovels from the ghettoes of Calcutta and Bombay, as well as mud-walled houses from the villages of rural India. Bamboo huts from Southeast Asia and crowded little shops no bigger than closets show you how people today live in such countries as Thailand, Pakistan, Guatemala, and Morocco. You are able to walk through many of the exhibits, which are peopled with life-size figures in traditional clothing. Sound effects play over hidden speakers: dogs bark, children scream, car horns blare, frogs croak, vendors call out their wares.

Admission: Dfl 6 ($3.65) adults, Dfl 3 ($1.80) for senior citizens and children.

Open: Mon–Fri 10am–5pm, Sat–Sun and hols noon–5pm. **Closed:** Jan 1, Apr 30, May 5, and Dec 25. **Tram:** 9 or 14 to Mauritskade.

ANNE FRANK HUIS, 263-265 Prinsengracht. Tel. 626-45-33.

Today there are more than 13 million copies in 50 languages of *The Diary of Anne Frank,* written by a teenage Jewish girl during her two years of hiding in this building. On July 6, 1942, the Franks and another Jewish family went into hiding to avoid being deported to German concentration camps. Anne, the youngest Frank daughter, had been given a diary for her 13th birthday in 1942. With the eyes of a child and the writing skills of a girl who hoped one day to be a writer, she chronicled life in hiding, the continued persecution of Jews by Hitler, and the progress of the war. On August 4, 1944, the Franks were discovered by the German police. They were deported on the last transport to Auschwitz from the Netherlands. Only Mr. Frank survived the concentration camps, and when he returned to Amsterdam a former employee gave him Anne's diary, which had been left behind when the police arrested the family.

Although the rooms here contain no furniture, the exhibits, including a year-by-year chronology of Anne's life, fill in the missing details. The museum is operated by the Anne Frank Foundation, an organization founded to eliminate anti-Semitism, fascism, and neo-Naziism, and to continue Anne Frank's struggle for a better world.

Admission: Dfl 6 ($3.65) adults, Dfl 3 ($1.80) students ages 10–17, free for children 9 and under.

Open: Mon–Sat 9am–5pm, Sun 10am–5pm. **Closed:** Jan 1, Yom Kippur, and Dec 25. **Tram:** 13 or 17 to Westermarkt.

MORE ATTRACTIONS

ROYAL PALACE, Dam Sq. Tel. 624-86-98.

Built in the 17th century on top of 13,659 wooden pilings to prevent it from sinking into the soft Amsterdam soil, the Royal Palace was originally the Town Hall. At the time it was built, it was referred to as the Eighth Wonder of the World because of its immense size (it was the largest town hall ever built) and the fact that it used so many pilings to support it. In 1808 the building was converted into a palace. The dazzling interior is filled with sculptures, frescoes, and furniture. In the summer, and occasionally in other months, there are conducted tours.

Admission: Dfl 5 ($3.05) adults, Dfl 3 ($1.80) senior citizens and children.

Open: Early June to late Aug, daily 12:30–4pm; Sept–May, only by guided tour given Wed at 2pm. **Directions:** Walk down Damrak from Centraal Station.

THE BEGIJNHOF, Spui.

Only steps away from Amsterdam's busiest pedestrian shopping street is the most tranquil spot in the city. Hidden behind a nondescript facade is a courtyard ringed with old restored almshouses. Since the 14th century the Begijnhof has been home to poor widows and lay nuns of the order of Beguines (Begijns in Dutch; Begijnhof

means Beguine Court). The oldest and one of the last remaining wooden houses in Amsterdam is here at no. 34, built in 1475. In the center of the courtyard are a clandestine Roman Catholic church and an English Presbyterian church.
Admission: Free.
Open: Daily. **Tram:** 1, 2, or 5 to Spui.

MUSEUM WILLET-HOLTHUYSEN, 605 Herengracht. Tel. 523-18-22.

For a glimpse of what life was like for Amsterdam's wealthy merchants during the 18th and 19th centuries, pay a visit to this elegant canal-house museum. Each of the rooms is furnished much as it would have been 200 years ago. In addition there is an extensive collection of ceramics, china, glass, and silver. Of particular interest are the large old kitchen and the formal garden in back.
Admission: Dfl 2.50 ($1.50) adults, Dfl 1.50 (90¢) senior citizens and children.
Open: Daily 11am–5pm. **Tram:** 4 to Herengracht.

NETHERLANDS THEATER INSTITUTE, 166 Herengracht. Tel. 623-51-04.

Splendid marble corridors, wall and ceiling frescoes, and ornate plasterwork make this patrician canal house one of the most beautiful in the city. Richly ornamented roof gables of different styles were a sign of wealth during Amsterdam's golden age, and crowning this building is the oldest extant example of an ornate neck gable. Although it's worth visiting this museum simply to see how the wealthy once lived, there are also many interesting exhibits pertaining to theater in the Netherlands over the centuries. Be sure to press the buttons of the miniature stage sets. You'll see how waves once rolled across the stage and other equally dramatic effects.
Admission: Dfl 5 ($3.05) adults, Dfl 3 ($1.80) senior citizens and children.
Open: Tues–Sun 11am–5pm. **Tram:** 13, 14, or 17 to Dam Square.

OUDE KERK, 23 Oudekerksplein. Tel. 624-91-83.

This Gothic church is the oldest in the city, dating from the 13th century. The many stained-glass windows are particularly beautiful. Inside the church are monumental tombs, including that of Rembrandt's wife, Saskia van Uylenburg. The organ, built in 1724, is played regularly in the summer. Many connoisseurs believe that it has the best tone of any organ in the world. During the summer you can climb the 230-foot-high tower for an excellent view of Old Amsterdam.
Admission: Dfl 2.50 ($1.50).
Open: Easter–Oct, Mon–Sat 11am–5pm; Oct–Easter, daily 1–3pm. **Directions:** Walk three blocks from Damrak to the middle of the red-light district.

NIEUWE KERK, Dam Square. Tel. 626-81-68.

This church across the street from the Royal Palace is new in name only. Construction on this late Gothic structure was begun about 1400, but much of the interior, including the organ, dates from the 17th century. Since 1815 all Dutch kings and queens have been crowned here. Today the church is used primarily as a cultural center where special art exhibits are held. There are also regular performances on the church's huge organ in the summer.
Admission: Varies.
Open: Mon–Sat 11am–4pm, Sun noon–5pm. **Closed:** Jan–Feb. **Directions:** Walk down Damrak from Centraal Station.

WESTERKERK, 279 Prinsengracht. Tel. 624-77-66.

Built between 1620 and 1630, this church is a masterpiece of Dutch Renaissance style. At the top of the 275-foot-high tower is a giant replica of the imperial crown of Maximilian of Austria. Somewhere in this church (no one knows exactly where) is the grave of Rembrandt. During the summer there are regular organ concerts played on a 300-year-old instrument. Also in summer, you can climb the tower.
Admission: Church, free; tower, Dfl 1 (60¢).

Open: May 15–Sept 15, Mon–Sat 10am–4pm. **Closed:** Rest of year. **Tram:** 13 or 17 to Westermarkt.

PARKS & GARDENS

When the sun shines in Amsterdam, people head for the parks. The most popular and conveniently located of Amsterdam's 20 parks is the **Vondelpark,** which is only a short walk from Leidseplein and covers 122 acres. Lakes, ponds, and streams are surrounded by meadows, trees, and colorful flowers. This park, open daily from 8am to sunset, is extremely popular with young people from all over the world in the summer months.

Farther from the city center are many more large parks, such as the huge **Amsterdamse Bos,** covering more than 2,000 acres and providing hiking, biking, and horseback riding trails, as well as picnic areas and campgrounds. Closer to the city center are the **Rembrandtpark, Artis Zoo,** and **Oosterpark.**

SPECIAL-INTEREST SIGHTSEEING

FOR THE JEWISH HISTORY ENTHUSIAST Anyone interested in Jewish history will find Amsterdam a fascinating city. The centerpiece of Jewish history in Amsterdam is the **Jewish Historical Museum,** at 2-4 Jonas Daniel Meijerplein (tel. 626-99-45), directly across the street from the Portuguese Synagogue. The plight of Jews in Amsterdam during World War II is brought poignantly home at **Anne Frank Huis,** 263-265 Prinsengracht (tel. 626-45-33). See above for details on both museums.

FOR THE ARCHITECTURE LOVER Amsterdam is an architecture lover's dream. The fascinating narrow **canal houses** and warehouses built primarily during the 17th century are not only beautiful to look at (and best viewed from a boat cruising the canals), but also delightful to stay in. All the canal-house hotels listed above feature steep narrow stairways and other original period touches. You'll have to crane your neck a bit to appreciate the beauty of these old houses fully since their most striking features are their gables. The largest canal houses are on Herengracht, but, in my opinion, the smaller houses on other canals (especially in the Jordaan area) are much more interesting architecturally.

To see the inside of some restored canal houses, visit the **Theater Museum,** 166 Herengracht; the **Willet-Holthuysen Museum,** 605 Herengracht (see above for details on hours and admission fees); or the **Museum van Loon,** 672 Keizersgracht. An interesting contrast to these grand mansions is the narrowest house in Amsterdam (only a yard wide) at 7 Singel, behind the Sonesta Hotel.

Another architecturally interesting spot off the canals is the **Begijnhof,** just off the busy Kalverstraat shopping area. In this peaceful courtyard lay nuns and elderly women have lived since the 14th century. Number 34 is Amsterdam's oldest home, built in 1475 (see above for details). Also fascinating for architecture fans are the **Rijksmuseum** and **Centraal Station,** which were designed by the same architect in the late 19th century.

ORGANIZED TOURS

WALKING TOURS Although it's possible to see most of the important sights of Amsterdam in a single long walking tour, it's best to break the city up into different smaller tours. Luckily, the VVV tourist office has done the work for you. For only Dfl 2.75 ($2.40) you can buy a brochure outlining one of seven different walking tours. These include "Voyage of Discovery Through Amsterdam," "A Walk Through Jewish Amsterdam," "A Walk Through the Jordaan," and "A Walk Through Maritime Amsterdam." If you have your own portable tape player, you might want to consider buying one of the VVV's taped tours of the city. There are two different 2½-hour tours available for Dfl 30 ($18.20) per tape.

BUS TOURS For a much faster tour that covers much of the same ground as the walking tours, try one of the three-hour guided bus tours offered by **NZH Travel,** Damrak between Centraal Station and the Scandic Crown Hotel (tel. 625-07-72), or **The Best of Holland Excursions,** 34 Damrak (tel. 623-15-39). In addition to pointing out the major sights of Amsterdam, tours include a visit to a diamond cutter. Tours cost Dfl 25 ($15.15).

BOAT TOURS   Gazing up from a boat on a canal is absolutely the best way to view the old houses and warehouses of Amsterdam. If you have to choose between a walking tour, a bus tour, and a boat tour, definitely take the boat. This is a city built on the shipping trade, so it's only fitting that you should see it from the water, just as the merchants of the 17th century's golden age saw their city. Not only will you get a sense of Amsterdam as a city of canals, but you will also see the city's international harbor.

There are canal-boat docks all over the city, all of which have signs stating the time of the next tour. Tours last 1 to 1½ hours and cost Dfl 9–12 ($5.45–$7.30). The greatest concentration of canal-boat tour operators is along Damrak a block from Centraal Station. Since the tours are all basically the same, simply pick the one that's most convenient for you.

A BREWERY TOUR   The **Heineken Brewery Museum,** 78 Stadhouderskade, is a short walk along Singelgracht from the Rijksmuseum. Tours are held Monday through Friday at 10am and 2pm and the only charge is a Dfl-2 ($1.20) donation that is given to several different charities. Heineken opened its first Amsterdam brewery in 1864, and over the years it expanded as its beer gained popularity. The guides thoroughly explain the brewing process as they take you through the old brewing facilities. After the short tour, visitors see a film about the company while sipping cold beers in a large drinking hall overlooking the city.

DIAMOND FACTORY TOURS   For more than 400 years Amsterdam has been associated with diamonds, and while you are here be sure to take a tour of a diamond-cutting and -polishing facility. Tours are offered daily at many of the city's largest diamond companies. The tours show you how the rough stones are cut and then polished, a process that reduces 50% of every stone to diamond dust. There is no pressure to buy stones or jewelry when you are taken to the company's showroom as part of the tour. Here your guide will show you the different cuts and how to determine the quality of a diamond. Diamond cutting is a very specialized skill and to this day it is still done by hand.

Diamond factories offering free individual and group tours include: the **Amsterdam Diamond Center,** 1 Rokin (tel. 624-57-87), just off Dam Square, down Damrak from Centraal Station, open daily from 10am to 5:30pm (on Thursday to 8:30pm); **Coster Diamonds,** 2-4 Paulus Potterstraat (tel. 676-22-22), reachable by tram no. 1, 2, or 16 to Museumplein, open daily from 9am to 5pm; and **Van Moppes Diamonds,** 2-6 Albert Cuypstraat (tel. 676-12-42), near the Albert Cuypstraat stop on tram no. 16, 24, or 25, and open daily from 9am to 5pm.

SPECIAL & FREE EVENTS

In keeping with Amsterdammers' enthusiasm about life, every day is filled with special events. Some of Amsterdam's best freebies are its **street performers.** You'll find them primarily in front of Centraal Station during the day and on Leidseplein and Rembrandtplein in the evening.

April 30 is **Queen's Day** and the city crowds the streets to enjoy performances, parades, markets, and general merrymaking.

The single most important annual event in the Netherlands is the **flowering of the bulb fields** each spring from March to mid-May. Two-thirds of all the cut flowers sold in the world come from the Netherlands. The best flower-viewing areas are between Haarlem and Leiden and between Haarlem and Den Helder. The highlight of the bulb season is the annual **flower parade** from Haarlem to Noorwijk in late April. There's another flower parade from Aalsmeer (home of the world's largest flower auction) to Amsterdam on the first Saturday in September.

In June, July, and August there are **open-air concerts** in Vondelpark. Check at the Tourist Information Center for times and dates. In June the city hosts the **Holland Festival,** an extravaganza of music, dance, and other cultural offerings that take place all over the city and feature a different theme each year. In September, the **Jordaan Festival** showcases this old neighborhood where small inexpensive restaurants, secondhand shops, and unusual boutiques and galleries are found.

7. SAVVY SHOPPING

As you stroll the streets of Amsterdam, you could easily get the impression that the city is simply one giant outdoor shopping mall. Everywhere you look there are shops ranging in price and variety from the used-clothing and book stores of the Jordaan to the designer boutiques of P. C. Hoofstraat. Unfortunately, because of the weak dollar, most of these stores offer little in the way of bargains. However, there are many typically Dutch souvenirs and gift items that might appeal to you and can be real bargains if you shop around.

The main shopping areas of the city include **Nieuwendijk** and **Kalverstraat.** On these two streets you'll find many souvenir shops as well as stores selling inexpensive clothing. The upscale shopping area of Amsterdam is **P. C. Hoofstraat,** near Museumplein. This street is lined with designer boutiques and expensive restaurants. For secondhand goods, wander the streets of the **Jordaan,** and for pricey antiques, it's **Nieuwe Spiegelstraat,** which leads to the Rijksmuseum. **The Bijenkorf** and **C&A,** two of Amsterdam's largest department stores, face each other on Damrak near Dam Square.

Most shops that deal with tourists will be happy to **ship your purchases home** for an additional charge. If you want to ship something yourself, go to the Main Post Office where there is a special counter selling boxes and packing materials. They will also provide you with the necessary Customs forms to fill out.

Watch for the TAX FREE FOR TOURISTS signs in shop windows. These stores will provide you with a form for claiming a **refund of the VAT** (Value-Added Tax). This refund amounts to 15.6% of the total cost of purchases in Amsterdam and throughout the Netherlands. However, before you can get a refund, you will have to make a purchase of at least Dfl 300 ($181.80) in any participating store. When you are leaving the country by air, you must present the form and the goods to Customs. After Customs has stamped your form, you put the form in an envelope and mail it directly from Customs. Your refund will be mailed to you within 10 days. If you leave the country by rail or train, you can claim an immediate cash refund at any GWK office. These offices are located at all major border crossings into Germany and Belgium.

MARKETS Amsterdam's two most famous markets are the **Waterlooplein flea market** and the **open-air market on Albert Cuypstraat.** Both these markets generally sell the same sorts of goods, but you can still find a few antiques and near-antique objects for sale on Waterlooplein. The flea market surrounds the modern Muziektheater building. Most of what's offered here these days is used and cheap clothing. On Albert Cuypstraat you'll find more cheap clothing than you could ever want to look at, but also fresh fish, Asian vegetables, fresh-cut flowers, electronics, cosmetics, and all the assorted people who buy and sell such an array of products. Both the flea market and the Albert Cuypstraat market are open Monday through Saturday from 9am to 5pm.

Other markets in Amsterdam include the Sunday **Antiques Market,** by the Weigh House on the Nieuwmarkt, which is open May to October from 10am to 4pm. The **Floating Flower Market** is along the Singel between Muntplein and Leidsestraat, open Monday through Friday from 9am to 6pm (on Thursday until 9pm) and on Saturday until 5pm. The **Bird Market,** on the Noordermarkt in the Jordaan, takes place every Saturday morning. There is also a **flea market** here on Monday morning and a **farmer's market** on Saturday from 10am to 3pm. There is a **Book**

Market on Oudemanhuispoort between Oudezijds Voorburgwal and Kloveniersburgwal on the edge of the red-light district, held Monday through Saturday from 10am to 4pm. On Sunday from 10am to 5pm there is an **art market** on the Spui.

8. EVENING ENTERTAINMENT

For listings of the week's performances in Amsterdam's many theaters and concert halls, consult **What's On in Amsterdam,** a magazine available for Dfl 2.50 ($1.50) at the VVV Tourist Information Center in front of Centraal Station or at the AUB reservation office on Leidseplein. At these two locations you can also make reservations and buy tickets for shows at many venues in Amsterdam.

THE PERFORMING ARTS

THEATER

CARRÉ, 115-125 Amstel. Tel. 622-52-25.
The Carré, a huge old domed theater on the Amstel River near the Skinny Bridge, occasionally presents touring plays from Broadway or London's West End. Performances.
Prices: Tickets, Dfl 25–87 ($15.15–$52.75).
Open: Box office, daily 10am–7pm. **Metro:** Weesperplein.

CLASSICAL MUSIC

CONCERTGEBOUW, 2-6 Concertgebouwplein. Tel. 671-83-45.
This world-famous concert hall, with its ornate Greek Revival facade, is said to have some of best acoustics of any hall in the world. Performances, including those by the renowned Concertgebouw Orchestra, are held almost every night in the building's two halls. There are free lunchtime concerts on Wednesday at 12:30pm.
Prices: Tickets, Dfl 17.50–60 ($10.60–$36.35).
Open: Box office, daily 10am–7pm. **Tram:** 2.

BEURS VAN BERLAGE, 213 Damrak. Tel. 627-04-66.
This impressive building on the Damrak was once the Amsterdam stock exchange, but a few years ago it was converted into two concert halls that host frequent symphony performances.
Prices: Dfl 18–40 ($10.65–$24.25).
Open: Box office, Tues–Fri 12:30–6pm, Sat 12:30–5pm. **Tram:** 4.

OPERA & DANCE

MUZIEKTHEATER, 3 Amstel. Tel. 625-54-55.
This ultramodern 1,600-seat hall caused quite a stir when it was built. Amsterdammers thought the architecture clashed with the neighborhood. Both the Dutch National Opera and Dutch National Ballet perform here.
Prices: Tickets, Dfl 20–80 ($12.10–$48.50).
Open: Box office, daily 10am–8pm. **Tram:** 9 or 14.

STADSSCHOUWBURG, 26 Leidseplein. Tel. 624-23-11.
Amsterdam's former opera and ballet theater is a neoclassical building with Dutch Renaissance features built in 1894. Performances include plays in Dutch and English, and music and dance performances by international companies.
Prices: Dfl 11–50 ($6.65–$30.30).
Open: Box office, daily 10am–6pm. **Tram:** 1, 2, or 5.

ROCK & JAZZ

For many years the main venues for rock music in Amsterdam have been the **Melkweg,** 234a Lijnbaangracht (tel. 624-17-77), and the **Paradiso,** 6-8 Weteringschans (tel. 626-45-21), both of which are only a short walk from Leidseplein. These massive clubs have live music several nights a week. Check the calendars in front of each club for listings of upcoming performances. Admission to each club ranges from Dfl 12 to Dfl 25 ($7.25 to $15.15). (See "Networks and Resources," below, for additional information.)

For jazz, the **Bamboo Bar,** 64 Lange Leidsedwarstraat (tel. 624-39-93), and the **Café Alto,** 115 Korte Leidsedwarstraat (tel. 626-32-49), both near Leidseplein, are the most popular spots in town. Both have live music several nights a week, with no cover charge or only a few guilders. Drinks start at Dfl 2.50 ($1.50).

MOVIES

Amsterdam always has a good selection of the best films from all over the world, and foreign films are shown in their original language with Dutch subtitles. In front of every theater is a list of all the films playing that week in Amsterdam. The greatest concentration of theaters is on Leidseplein. You can save money by going to a matinee or a Wednesday-night show. At these times tickets are only Dfl 10 ($6.05). Also, keep in mind that there are 15–30 minutes of commercials and previews before the film starts. The posted times are when the commercials, not the film, begin.

If you see only one movie while you're in Amsterdam, try to see it at the **Tuschinski Theater,** 26-28 Reguliersbreestraat (tel. 626-26-33), just off Rembrandtplein, a beautiful art deco movie palace built in 1921.

BARS & BROWN CAFES

To experience Amsterdam conviviality at its finest, head to one of the city's hundreds of brown cafés. Here you'll encounter a warm and friendly atmosphere where you can sit and sip a glass of beer or a mixed drink, and even get a cheap meal.

There are countless bars in Amsterdam, most around Leidseplein and Rembrandtplein. Bars in Amsterdam don't start to get busy until at least 10pm, although they usually open at noon and stay open all day. In both the cafés and the bars the most popular drink is draft Heineken served in small glasses with two fingers of head on top for around Dfl 2.50 ($1.50). Also popular is *genever* (Dutch gin) available in *jonge* (young) and *oude* (old) varieties—oude is quite a bit stronger in taste and alcoholic content. Genever shots start at Dfl 2.50 ($1.50) as well.

Most cafés and bars are open on Friday and Saturday from noon to 2am and Sunday through Thursday from noon to 1am. On Sunday nights from about 6pm on, there is live traditional Dutch music in several bars on the Rembrandtplein.

DE TWEE ZWAANTJES, 114 Prinsengracht. Tel. 625-27-29.

In the Jordaan, this small brown café is very popular with neighborhood locals and tourists alike for its weekend sing-alongs. Late in the evening the musical instruments begin to show up, and once everyone has had enough Heineken and genever, the old music begins. You're welcome to join in and learn a few traditional Amsterdam favorites while the accordion wheezes away.

HOPPE, 18-20 Spui. Tel. 624-07-56.

Although you will see signs for Hoppe genever in front of most cafés, there is only one Café Hoppe. This is one of Amsterdam's oldest, most traditional, and most popular brown cafés. The dark walls, low ceilings, and old wooden furniture are literally unchanged since the café opened in 1670. If you want to feel as though you stepped into a painting by Breughel, this is the place for you.

DE DRIE FLESCHJES, 16 Gravenstraat. Tel. 624-84-43.

This establishment is located between the Nieuwe Kerk and the Nieuwendijk. Originally a tasting house where people could try different liqueurs distilled and aged on the premises, De Drie Fleschjes has been in business for more than 300 years. One wall of this bar is lined with old wooden aging barrels. De Drie Fleschjes is popular with businesspeople and journalists, who stop by to sample the wide variety of oude and jonge genevers. De Drie Fleschjes closes at 10pm and is closed all day Sunday.

CAFE PAPENEILAND, 2 Prinsengracht. Tel. 624-19-89.

Located on the corner of the Prinsengracht and the Brouwersgracht, Papeneiland is the oldest café in Amsterdam. Since 1600 or thereabouts, folks have been dropping by for shots of genever and glasses of beer. The walls near the huge front windows are covered with blue-and-white tiles and there is an old woodstove. If you have a feeling of déjà vu while you're here, it's probably because you saw the same view in a painting in the Amsterdam Historisch Museum.

DE KROON ROYAL CAFE, 17-I Rembrandtplein. Tel. 625-20-11.

The concept of the "Grand Café" has recently taken Amsterdam by storm. New Amsterdammers, tired of cramped and crowded brown cafés, have been flocking to these new large cafés. De Kroon is one of the best. On the second floor of a building overlooking the Rembrandtplein, it features such unusual decor as old display cabinets full of stuffed animals and human anatomy models. Whether you're in jeans or theater attire, you'll feel comfortable here.

DISCOS

You'll find dozens of large and small discos clustered around the Leidseplein and Rembrandtplein areas. These rise and fall in popularity, so ask someone in a café what the current favorite is and check it out.

ROXY, 465-467 Singel. Tel. 620-03-54.

When last I visited Amsterdam, this was *the* place to go dancing. The Roxy is a huge multilevel disco created from an old movie theater. Inside there's room for more than 1,000 people, and the place stays packed on weekends.

Prices: A small glass of Heineken Dfl 2.50 ($1.50); mixed drinks Dfl 8 ($4.85) and up. **Admission:** Dfl 5 ($3.05) Sun–Wed, Dfl 10 ($6.05) Thurs–Sat.

Open: Wed–Sun 11pm–4am.

ESCAPE, Rembrandtplein. Tel. 622-35-42.

This disco is equally large and equally popular. Here you have a choice of several dance floors, all with plenty of flashing lights and a great sound system. Thursday is students' night—if you have an ID, you can get in for free.

Prices: A small glass of Heineken Dfl 2.50 ($1.50); mixed drinks Dfl 8 ($4.85) and up. **Admission:** Dfl 10 ($6.05); free for students on Thurs.

Open: Thurs 10pm–4am, Fri–Sat 10pm–5am.

9. NETWORKS & RESOURCES

STUDENTS

Student activities in Amsterdam do not revolve around a university. This is because the city's main university has relocated many miles outside the center of Amsterdam and is no longer convenient to the bars, cafés, discos, theaters, and other places that young people in Amsterdam frequent. However, classes are still held in various buildings around the city, and because of this you will find students gathering at two student restaurants within the city. The **Atrium,** at 237 Grimburgwal on the campus of the old university, only a block off the Rokin at the foot of the Oudezijds Voorburgwal canal, is open daily from noon to 7pm. The other student cafeteria is a short walk from Waterlooplein at 15 Roetterstraat, open only Monday through Friday from 5 to 7:30pm.

For information about cultural events in Amsterdam, visit the **AUB,** on Leidseplein at Marnixstraat. If you are under 26 you can pick up a CJP (Cultural

Youth Pass) here for Dfl 15 ($9.10). The CJP is good for free admission to most of the city's museums and for discounts on most cultural events. The AUB is open Monday through Saturday from 10am to 6pm. If you are young and in trouble or just want someone to talk to, contact the **JAC (Youth Advice Center)**, at 30 Amstel (tel. 624-29-49), located along the river near Rembrandtplein.

In the late '60s and '70s three names summed up the student scene in the Amsterdam cultural universe—Kosmos, Melkweg (Milky Way), and Paradiso. If these three huge clubs are dear to your heart, you'll be happy to know they're still going strong. They have, however, changed with the times and now attract a much different crowd. If you're new to Amsterdam, you may want to join the thousands of people who flock to these three clubs nightly to find out what it's all about.

KOSMOS, 142 Prins Hendrikkade. Tel. 626-74-77.
This building overlooking Amsterdam harbor is now the city's premier New Age Center, although there is still dancing on Saturday night. Courses in meditation, yoga, holistic health, and other esoteric studies are held regularly. There is also a bookstore in the basement with many English-language books for sale, and a restaurant serving inexpensive vegetarian meals. Admission depends on whether you are taking a course, attending a lecture, or just want to go dancing.
Admission: Dfl 10–15 ($6.05–$9.10).
Open: Daily 10:30am–11pm.

MELKWEG, 234a Lijnbaangracht. Tel. 624-17-77.
This is the most popular of the three clubs these days, with activities starting at 11am and continuing until the early hours of the morning. You can see films, dance to recorded music, hang out in the café, view the changing art exhibits, hear a live band, or attend a workshop. There is a bookshop, a restaurant, and a café here also. Melkweg is just off Leidseplein behind the Stadsschouwburg.
Admission: Dfl 7.50–25 ($4.55–$15.15) plus Dfl 3 ($2.10) monthly membership.
Open: Wed–Sun 11am–3am.

PARADISO, 6-8 Weteringschans. Tel. 626-45-21.
This club has also changed its image considerably since it first opened. It is now more a venue for political forums and lectures, in addition to frequent rock, pop, and jazz concerts.
Admission: Dfl 12–20 ($7.30–$12.10), plus Dfl 3 ($2.10) monthly membership.
Open: Wed–Sat 8pm–1am.

GAY MEN & LESBIANS

Amsterdam bills itself as the gay capital of Europe, and there are dozens of gay bars and discos all over the city, with a concentration near the Rembrandtplein. To find out more about the gay and lesbian scenes in Amsterdam, stop by **COC**, 14 Rozenstraat (tel. 626-30-87), two blocks from the Westerkerk. This center offers gay men and lesbians plenty of information, plus a coffee shop, pub, and disco.

You can also call the **Gay and Lesbian Switchboard** (tel. 623-65-65), which is open 24 hours a day to provide information and advice.

The *Use It* guide available at the VVV Tourist information Center in front of Centraal Station also has listings of popular gay and lesbian bars, discos, baths, and bookstores.

WOMEN

There are several women's centers around the city, including **Vrouwenhuis**, 95 Nieuwe Herengracht (tel. 625-20-66), near Waterlooplein, open Monday, Tuesday, and Thursday from 2 to 5pm. There is also a women-only restaurant here on Thursday night.

At the **Vrouwencentrum de Pijp**, 52 Karel du Jardinstraat (tel. 679-57-22), a women's library is open Tuesday through Saturday from 2 to 5pm (on Thursday to 8pm).

Saarein, 119 Elandstraat (tel. 623-49-01), near Leidseplein, is a women-only bar, open on Monday from 8pm to 1am, Tuesday through Thursday from 3pm to 1am, on Friday and Saturday from 3pm to 2am, and on Sunday from 3pm to 1am.

Xantippe, 290 Prinsengracht (tel. 623-58-54), is a women's bookstore selling more than 8,000 titles in five different languages, including English.

10. EASY EXCURSIONS

If Amsterdam is the only stop you plan to make in the Netherlands, try to make at least one excursion into the countryside. You'll be amazed at how easily you can leave the crowded city behind. Dikes, windmills, and people who actually wear wooden shoes await you just beyond the city limits in some of Holland's quaintest villages.

ZAANSE SCHANS   If you have time for only one excursion out of the city, make this the one. Zaanse Schans is a beautiful little village on the banks of the River Zaan 15 miles north of Amsterdam. Along the riverbank are six windmills, two of which are still operating and can be visited. Surrounding the village are pastures where cows graze, and the nearby cocoa factory fills the air with the smell of chocolate.

Zaanse Schans is open daily from April to November 1, only on weekends during the rest of the year. The best way to get here is by train from Amsterdam's Centraal Station. There are departures every 30 minutes, and the trip takes 15 minutes. Take a train bound for Alkmaar that makes local stops, and get off at the Koog-Zaandijk station. From the station, follow the signs. It's about an 8-minute walk. The round-trip fare is only Dfl 6.50 ($3.95). A railway excursion ticket, available for Dfl 17.60 ($10.65), includes round-trip rail fare, a 45-minute cruise on the River Zaan, coffee and a pancake in the De Krai pancake restaurant, and admission to the Zaandam Clockwork Museum.

ENKHUIZEN   If you have more time, you should visit the **Zuiderzee Museum** in Enkhuizen. The famous Zuiderzee was once a very tempestuous sea, until ingenious Dutch engineers closed it off from the open sea in 1932, forming the freshwater IJsselmeer. This museum preserves the history of the Zuiderzee in 134 typical houses, shops, and workshops from the many fishing villages that once dotted this coastline. Several former warehouses house an indoor museum displaying model ships, costumes, pottery, paintings, and furniture from the Zuiderzee fishing villages.

The Zuiderzee Museum is open daily from 10am to 5pm between April and October. Admission, including the cost of the boat to the museum, is Dfl 11 ($6.65) for adults, Dfl 8 ($4.85) for seniors and children 6–18, and free for children under 6. Trains leave Amsterdam's Centraal Station every hour for Enkhuizen, and the trip takes about an hour. The round-trip fare is Dfl 23.50 ($14.25). There is also a Dfl-26.50 ($16.05) railway excursion ticket that includes the train fare, museum ferry, and museum admission.

AALSMEER FLOWER AUCTION   The Netherlands is the world's largest exporter of cut flowers, and nearly 50% of the flowers that leave the country are sold at this massive auction house. Nothing could adequately prepare you for the sight of these acres of cut flowers stacked three tiers high on constantly moving carts. In six auction halls, hundreds of buyers from all over the world compete for the best flowers at the lowest prices. The Flower Auction is open Monday through Friday from 7:30 to 11am. Admission is Dfl 4 ($2.40).

To reach the Flower Auction in Aalsmeer, take bus no. 171 from in front of the Victoria Hotel across the square from Centraal Station. Get off at the Hortensieplein stop in Aalsmeer, transfer to bus no. 140, and ask the driver to let you off at the *bloemveiling* (flower auction). The entire trip will take five strips on your strippenkart.

ALKMAAR   One of the most popular summer excursions is to the **open-air cheese market** in Alkmaar. Held every Friday morning between April 21 and

September 15 from 10am to noon, the cheese market attracts thousands of picture-taking visitors to this historic old town. Huge piles of yellow cheese cover the paving stones of Alkmaar's main square while men in white suits and red, yellow, or blue hats rush about carrying wooden platforms stacked with still more rounds of cheese. When the auction is over, be sure to take time to explore the town.

Trains leave regularly from Amsterdam's Centraal Station for the 45-minute trip to Alkmaar. A round-trip ticket is Dfl 15.50 ($9.40).

GUIDED TOURS AROUND HOLLAND   There are more than 20 organized tours available from Amsterdam, ranging in length from a few hours to a few days. The largest tour operator is **Holland International,** 7 Damrak and 10 Dam Square (tel. 625-30-35 or 622-25-50). Stop by their offices and pick up their brochure.

Some of their more popular tours are to **Marken and Volendam,** two Zuiderzee fishing villages. In summer this trip can be done by boat and bus. Another interesting tour is the all-day trip **around the former Zuiderzee.** This tour allows you to see the amazing Afsluitdijk, the Enclosure Dike that turned the Zuiderzee from a stormy sea into a placid lake.

ATHENS

Visitors to Athens are immediately confronted with colorless concrete buildings, congested streets, and sometimes stifling smog—not the romantic wonderland you dreamed about when planning your trip to the city of the gods. But suddenly you catch a glimpse of the Acropolis, your heart skips a beat, and in a magic moment you're right where you had imagined. Climbing toward the Parthenon, you can't help but imagine yourself walking in the footsteps of Socrates and Aristophanes. And even if you've never been interested in the history of Western civilization, you'll find yourself asking questions, reading brochures, and even buying books about early times.

While Athens may not be beautiful physically, it does have its attractions. It's packed with some of the most boisterous, friendly, and fun people in the world, and few cities can boast livelier restaurants, a more bustling café culture, or more energetic nightclubs. Athens's good food and relatively inexpensive accommodations will also be welcomed by budget travelers. Seldom does Europe offer such abundance without putting a strain on your pocketbook.

1. FROM A BUDGET TRAVELER'S POINT OF VIEW

ATHENS BUDGET BESTS

From hotels to restaurants, transportation facilities, and sights, the entire city of Athens is a great value. The meticulous budgeteer could live for far less than $45 a day here, and those who spend their full allotment should live quite comfortably.

SPECIAL DISCOUNT OPPORTUNITIES

FOR STUDENTS & YOUNG PEOPLE If you hold an International Student Identification Card (ISIC) you can realize a substantial **discount on museum fees**—usually 50%.

If you are under 26, student or not, you can purchase rail, coach, airline, and ship tickets for up to 40% below the official prices by visiting the **Transalpino Travel Office,** 28 Nikis St. (tel. 322-0503), two blocks from Syntagma Square. It's open June 15 through October, Monday through Friday from 8am to 7pm and on Saturday from 8:30am to 1pm; the rest of the year, Monday through Friday from 9am to 5pm and on Saturday from 8:30am to 1pm.

FOR SENIORS Most **museums** grant 30%-50% ticket discounts to senior citizens—women over 60 and men over 65.

WHAT THINGS COST IN ATHENS   U.S. $

Taxi from the airport to Syntagma Square	6.85
Taxi from Larissis train station to hotel	2.65
Public transportation (bus or metro)	.40
Local telephone call	.05
Double room at the Hotel Hilton (deluxe)	197.35
Double room at the Hotel Dorian Inn (moderate)	91.60
Double room at Tempi (budget)	23.15
Continental breakfast	2.65
Meal for one, without beverage, at the Hotel Hilton (deluxe)	25.00
Meal for one, without beverage, at Nea Olympia (moderate)	8.70
Meal for one, without beverage, at Bairaktaris (budget)	5.80
Half a liter of beer	1.60
Half a liter of retsina (wine)	.95
Coca-Cola in a restaurant	.85
Cup of coffee in a restaurant with table service	.75
Roll of ASA 100 color film, 36 exposures	5.50
Admission to the Acropolis	7.90
Movie ticket	5.25

2. PRETRIP PREPARATIONS

DOCUMENTS   U.S. and Canadian citizens simply need a valid passport for stays up to three months.

WHAT TO PACK   Between April and October, pack warm-weather clothes plus a light jacket for cool nights. From late October to early April, heavier clothing is recommended. Sunglasses and a hat are musts in summer.

WHEN TO GO   March through May is pleasant and mild, while June to October can be dry and hot. Even during summer there is relief in the afternoons and evenings when a cool breeze blows in from the nearby sea. December through February are not terribly cold, but it rains a lot and it can be very windy.

Athens's Average Daytime Temperature & Days of Rain

	Jan	Feb	Mar	Apr	May	June	July	Aug	Sept	Oct	Nov	Dec
Temp. (°F)	52	54	58	65	74	86	92	92	82	72	63	56
Days of Rain	14	12	11	9	8	5	2	3	4	9	12	14

Special Events   Every evening (except when there's a full moon) from April through October (usually at 9pm) a spectacular **sound-and-light show** is performed near the Pnyx, a small hill on the south side of the Acropolis. The 45-minute show, which costs 800 Dr ($4.20), is a commentary on Athens's history. For confirmation of the schedule, call 322-1459 or 322-3111 ext. 240, or drop by the tourist information office in Syntagma Square.

✓ WHAT'S SPECIAL ABOUT ATHENS

Ancient Monuments
- ☐ The Acropolis. Need I say more?
- ☐ The Ancient Agora, Socrates' old stomping ground and the marketplace of ancient Athens.
- ☐ Delphi, three hours from Athens, the Greeks' center of the universe.

Museums
- ☐ National Archeological Museum, a huge collection of the best ancient Greek relics anywhere.

Natural Landmarks
- ☐ Lycabettus Hill, for the great views from its summit.

Neighborhoods
- ☐ Plaka, a quaint area of pedestrian streets, small stores, restaurants, and cafés.

Shopping
- ☐ The Flea Market, filled with small stores and tourist trinkets.

From mid-July to mid-September, the annual **Athens Festival** takes place in the Odeon of Herodes Atticus, built in A.D. 161. World-renowned orchestras, ballet companies, singers, and dancers perform in this unique setting. Seats cost 1,000–5,000 Dr ($5.25–$26.30).

The Odeon of Herodes Atticus is in the shadow of the Acropolis off Dionisiou Areopagitou Street. For information and tickets, inquire at 4 Stadiou St. (tel. 01/322-1459). You can also buy tickets at the theater starting at 8pm on evenings of performances (which begin at 9pm).

BACKGROUND READING   *The Iliad* and *The Odyssey* (Penguin) are obvious Greek travel companions. Plato and Aristotle are also good reads, though not light beach material.

Modern works on Greece include Henry Miller's *The Colossus of Maroussi* (New Directions) and Mary Renault's many historical novels, including *The King Must Die* and *The Mask of Apollo* (Random House). For a more detailed guide to the city, see *Frommer's Athens* (Prentice Hall).

3. ORIENTATION & GETTING AROUND

ARRIVING IN ATHENS

FROM THE AIRPORT   Nearly 85% of all visitors arrive in Athens by plane at one of two airports. All domestic and international flights of the national airline, Olympic, arrive at **Hellinikon (or West) Airport** (tel. 01/981-1201), seven miles southeast of the city. Several banks in the arrivals area are open daily from 7am to 11pm. A Greek Tourist Office (tel. 979-9264) offers city maps and other information on an erratic schedule. A blue express bus connects the airport with downtown Athens every 20–30 minutes from 6am to midnight for only 190 Dr ($1), and hourly after midnight for 270 Dr ($1.40). The bus stops at Amalias Avenue near Syntagma Square and at Stadiou Street near Omonia Square; during the summer the bus also adds stops at the train and bus stations. Hard-core budgeteers may wish to take local bus no. 122 or 133 into town for only 75 Dr (40¢).

If you're flying any carrier other than Olympic, you'll arrive and depart from **East Airport** (tel. 01/969-9111), located about eight miles from the city center. As at the other airport, you'll find at least one bank here open from 7am to 11pm daily. You can get information from the Greek Tourist Office (tel. 01/979-9500 or 970-2395) to the left after exiting Customs. The express bus to downtown runs on the same schedule with the same stops as at the West Airport, for the same price. Local bus no. 121 also makes the journey.

Taxis from the airport to town should cost no more than 1,200 Dr ($6.30)—but read the warnings in "Getting Around" "By Taxi," below, before entering.

To get between the two airports, take yellow bus no. 19 for 190 Dr ($1). This bus also goes to the port at Piraeus, so make sure you ask if it's going in the right direction.

FROM THE TRAIN STATION There are two train stations, located a few blocks from each other about a mile northwest of Omonia Square. The main station, **Larissis,** services northern Greece (Larissa, Saloniki, and Volos) and provides connections to Vienna, Zurich, and Paris. Here you'll find a currency-exchange office open daily from 8am to 9:15pm with high commission rates, and a luggage-storage office charging 200 Dr ($1.05) per bag per day, open from 6:30am to 9:30pm. The **Peloponnese** station, just to the south, services trains to and from the Peloponnese (Corinth, Patras, and Olympia).

Yellow trolleybus no. 1 connects the stations with Syntagma Square; a taxi into town should cost about 500 Dr ($2.65).

FROM THE HARBOR Athens's main seaport, **Piraeus,** seven miles southwest of town, is a 15-minute subway ride from Omonia and Monastiraki Squares. Ships from European and overseas harbors arrive and depart here. The subway runs from about 5am to midnight, and costs 75 Dr (40¢).

INFORMATION

The **Tourist Information Office,** 2 Karageorgi St. (tel. 322-2545), at the northwest corner of Syntagma Square, is inside the National Bank of Greece. Look for the modern 10-story building next to the Lufthansa office. Information about Athens, free city maps, hotel lists, and other general information booklets are available in English. The office is usually open in summer, Monday through Thursday from 8am to 2pm and 3:30 to 8pm, on Friday from 8am to 1:30pm and 3 to 8pm, on Saturday from 9am to 3pm, and on Sunday from 9am to 2pm; from November to the end of Easter, hours are 8am to 2pm and 3:30 to 6:30pm Monday through Thursday, 8am to 1:30pm and 3:30 to 6:30pm on Friday, 9am to 2pm on Saturday, and 9am to 1pm on Sunday.

The Hellenic Chamber of Hotels staffs an adjacent window and books hotel rooms in all price categories (see "Budget Accommodations," below, for details).

CITY LAYOUT

Athens has two hearts: **Syntagma (Constitution) Square** and **Omonia Square.** Approximately a mile apart, these two squares are connected by two parallel avenues, **Stadiou Street** and **Panepistimiou Street.** From Syntagma Square, **Mitropoleos Street** leads, slightly downhill, to **Monastiraki Square,** near the flea market and the Plaka district. From Monastiraki Square, mile-long **Athinas Street** leads to Omonia Square. In the triangle formed by these three squares—Syntagma, Omonia, and Monastiraki—lies Athens's inner city, its shopping area, the central market, the main department stores, the post offices, banks, and many of the hotels, pensions, tavernas, and restaurants listed in this chapter.

Two helpful orientation landmarks are the **Acropolis** and **Lycabettus Hill** (the latter with the small white church and the Greek flag on top). Both are visible from most parts of the city.

Finding your way around most of Athens is relatively easy, despite signs that look "Greek" to you. An exception is Plaka, with its small winding streets at the foot of the Acropolis, a labyrinth that will challenge even the best navigators. Most maps do not include all of Plaka's streets, so if you're concerned about getting lost, invest in the pricey German-published *Falk-plan* (available in some bookstores), which costs a whopping 2,000 Dr ($10.55).

GETTING AROUND

BY BUS, TROLLEYBUS, OR SUBWAY The public transportation system is composed of buses, trolleybuses, and a subway line, all charging 75 Dr (40¢) per one-way ticket. Generally, the **orange trolleybuses** (which are directly connected to electric lines above) service areas in the center that you'll be visiting, and the **blue buses** go to more remote areas. For either, you must buy tickets in advance from news kiosks or special bus-ticket kiosks, but in a pinch a local might agree to sell you a ticket. The same ticket works on all transportation lines. When you board, cancel the ticket in an automatic machine. Buses run all the time but with limited night service. You probably won't use the bus too often as many sights of interest can be reached on foot.

The **subway** is useful primarily as a link with Piraeus, the seaport of Athens. The line originates in suburban Kiffisia and passes through Athens, stopping at Victoria, Omonia, and Monastiraki before going on to Piraeus. The subway runs about every 10 minutes from 5am to midnight.

BY TAXI Taxis are very inexpensive in Athens. However, many travelers have complained of special "tourist prices," facilitated by an illegally fast meter or unheard-of "supplements" to the fare; upon your arrival, some drivers may also try to steer you away from your hotel to their "favorite," where they receive a kickback.

As of this writing, the minimum fare is 300 Dr ($1.60), the typical fare for a short hop in central Athens. Various additional charges include a luggage fee of 40 Dr (20¢) per 22-lb. bag, and an extra 100–200 Dr (50¢–$1.05) for stops at transportation centers such as the airport or train station. Of course these rates could change by the time you arrive, so the best thing to do is to ask locals what the fare should be before you enter a taxi. If you have a problem or dispute, insist on a receipt, write down the driver's license-plate number, and then ask the tourist office for advice.

You may see locals shouting at the windows or running alongside taxis trying to get in a word with the driver. What's going on? Taxis can pick up several passengers at the same time, and these people are trying to see if the taxi is going their way. If you are picked up halfway through another passenger's ride, note the amount on the meter as you board and subtract it from the final fare.

ON FOOT Like so many other European cities, Athens is creating pedestrian zones, mostly in major shopping areas, making window-shopping and strolling a real pleasure.

Most sightseeing in Athens can be done on foot. Watch out for heavy street traffic (cars, trolleybuses, trucks, and buses), especially during rush hours. When crossing a street, keep in mind that in Athens a red traffic light does not necessarily mean that cars will stop. Also remember that the confusing streets of Plaka may require a bit more patience than usual to find your way around.

BY CAR & MOPED Not far from Syntagma Square, **Avis,** at 48 Amalias St. (tel. 322-4951), charges from $325 per week with unlimited mileage, not including about $7 for daily insurance, plus 16% tax. **Pappas,** two doors down at 44 Amalias St. (tel. 323-4772 or 322-0087), is cheaper, charging about $312.50, not including insurance and tax. Both rent for less money in the off-season. Avis is open from 7:30am to 8:30pm daily, and Pappas, from 8am to 9pm daily.

Mopeds can be rented from **Meintanis,** 4 Dionisiou Aeropagitou in Plaka, at the foot of the Acropolis near the intersection with Amalias Street (tel. 323-2346), for about $16 per day, or $100 per week, depending on the time of year. They require a deposit of 8,000 Dr ($42.10) or a credit card. They're open Monday through Saturday from 9am to 8pm and on Sunday from 11am to 3pm.

Street parking is a problem in Athens. Ask at your hotel for the nearest parking place, which will cost up to 1,000 Dr ($5.25) per day.

 FAST ATHENS

Banks Banks are generally open Monday through Thursday from 8am to 2pm and on Friday from 8am to 1:30pm. All banks have currency-exchange counters. The American Express office, 2 Ernou St. (tel. 324-4975), offers currency-exchange and other services Monday through Friday from 8:30am to 4pm and on Saturday from 8:30am to 1:30pm. Avoid changing money on Sunday and holidays; the exchange rates offered by illegal street agents are outrageous.

Business Hours In winter, **shops** are generally open on Monday and Wednesday from 9am to 5pm; on Tuesday, Thursday, and Friday from 10am to 7pm; and on Saturday from 8:30am to 3:30pm. In summer, shops are generally open on Monday, Wednesday, and Saturday from 8am to 3pm; and on Tuesday, Thursday, and Friday from 8am to 1:30pm and 5:30 to 10pm. Note that many shops geared to tourists keep especially long hours, and some shops close for "siesta" from about 2 to 5pm. Most **food stores and the central market** are open on Monday and Wednesday from 9am to 4:30pm, on Tuesday from 9am to 6pm, on Thursday from 9:30am to 6:30pm, on Friday from 9:30am to 7pm, and on Saturday from 8:30am to 4:30pm. Many small shops, such as groceries and bakeries, are open on Sunday, too.

Currency The **drachma (Dr)** is the Greek national currency. Coins are issued in 1, 2, 5, 10, 20, and 50 Dr; bills are denominated in 50, 100, 500, 1,000, and 5,000 Dr.

Embassies As a capital city, Athens is home to the embassies of many foreign countries, including: the **U.S. Embassy,** 91 Vas. Sofias Ave. (tel. 721-2951, 721-2959, or 721-8400); the **Canadian Embassy,** 4 Ioannou Genadiou St. (tel. 723-9511 or 723-9519); the **Embassy of the U.K.,** 1 Ploutarchou St. (tel. 723-6211 or 723-6219); the **Australian Embassy,** 37 D. Soutsou Ave. (tel. 644-7303); and the **New Zealand Embassy,** 15 Tsoha St. (tel. 641-0311).

Emergencies In an emergency, dial 100 for the police, 199 to report a fire, and 166 for an ambulance and hospital. If you need an English-speaking doctor, call your embassy for advice.

A centrally located pharmacy is at 2 Ermou St. (tel. 322-3339), next to the American Express office, half a block from Syntagma Square. It's open on Monday and Wednesday from 8am to 2:30pm, and on Tuesday, Thursday, and Friday from 8am to 2:30pm and 5 to 8pm. At other times, consult the list of pharmacies open on Saturday and Sunday posted on the door, or dial 107 for the address of an open pharmacy.

Holidays Public holidays in Athens include New Year's Day (Jan 1), Epiphany (Jan 6), Ash Wednesday, Independence Day (Mar 25), Good Friday, Greek Orthodox Easter Sunday and Monday (usually one week after Catholics and Protestants celebrate Easter), Labor Day (May 1), Assumption Day (Aug 15), National Day (Oct 28), and Christmas (Dec 25–26).

Information The main Tourist Information Office is at 2 Karageorgi St., in Syntagma Square. See "Orientation and Getting Around," above, for details.

Laundry The laundry at 10 Angelou Geronda St., off Kidathineon Street, in Plaka (tel. 324-7896), is open daily from 8:30am to 8pm. They charge 800 Dr ($4.20) for wash, dry, and soap. Another self-service laundry is Maytag Launderette, at 46 Didotou St., near Omonia Square, three blocks off Akadimias Street (tel.

THE DRACHMA & THE DOLLAR

At this writing $1 = approximately 190 Dr (or 1 Dr = 0.5¢), and this was the rate of exchange used to calculate the dollar values given in this chapter (rounded to the nearest nickel). This rate fluctuates from time to time and may not be the same when you travel to Greece. Therefore the following table should be used only as a guide:

Dr	U.S.	Dr	U.S.
5	.02	1,500	7.89
10	.05	2,000	10.53
15	.07	2,500	13.16
20	.10	3,000	15.79
25	.13	3,500	18.42
50	.26	4,000	21.05
75	.39	4,500	23.68
100	.53	5,000	26.32
150	.79	6,000	31.58
200	1.05	7,000	36.84
250	1.32	8,000	42.11
300	1.58	9,000	47.37
400	2.11	10,000	52.63
500	2.63	12,500	65.79
750	3.95	15,000	78.95
1,000	5.26	17,500	92.11

361-0661), which charges 1,000 Dr ($5.25) for you to wash and dry 5 kilos (11 lb.) or 1,500 Dr ($7.90), if they do the work. It's open Monday through Saturday from 8am to 9pm.

Lost and Found   If you lose something on the street or on public transportation, contact the Police Lost and Found Office, 173 Leoforos Alexandras St. (tel. 770-5771 or 644-5940), open Monday through Saturday from 9am to 3pm. If you lost it on a bus or train, call 642-1616. Lost passports and other documents are returned by the police directly to the appropriate embassy, so check there, too.

Mail   The main post office, on Syntagma Square (tel. 324-1014), is open Monday through Friday from 7:30am to 8pm and on Saturday and Sunday from 9am to 2pm. There's also a little mobile post office on Monastiraki Square, open Monday through Saturday from 8am to 6pm and on Sunday from 8am to 5pm. Letters cost 80 Dr (40¢) to other parts of Europe and 100 Dr (55¢) to America and the South Pacific. Postcard postage is 80 Dr (40¢) to Europe, 100 Dr (55¢) to all other areas.

Friends and family can write to you in Athens care of American Express, 2 Hermou St., Athens 10225 (tel. 01/324-4976; fax 01/322-7893). If you have an American Express card or traveler's checks, the service is free; otherwise, each collection costs a steep 400 Dr ($2.10). It's open Monday through Friday from 8:30am to 4pm and on Saturday from 8:30am to 1:30pm.

The parcel post office (for packages over 1 kilo, 2.2 lb), 4 Stadiou St., inside the arcade (tel. 322-8940), is open Monday through Friday from 7:30am to 8pm. Note that they sell four sizes of boxes here as well.

Newspapers/Magazines   There is no shortage of English-language news. Most central-Athens newsstands carry the local daily *Athens News*, along with the *International Herald Tribune* and *USA Today*. Local weeklies include the *Greek News* and *Greece's Weekly*, both good for in-depth local news and entertainment listings.

Police   In an emergency, dial 100.

Radio/TV   There are six Greek TV stations in Athens. In addition, a staggering array of foreign-language channels includes transmissions from Italy, France, Germany, and even Russia. CNN broadcasts in English around the clock on Channel 14, and American movies on Greek television are usually with the original soundtrack and Greek subtitles.

Tax   Value-Added Tax (VAT) is included in the ticket price of all goods and services in Athens, ranging from 13% to 36% on certain luxury items.

Telephone   At just 10 Dr (5¢) **local telephone calls** in Athens are the cheapest in western Europe. Most newspaper stands are equipped with telephones, perhaps your best bet since public pay phones are often out of order.

You can place **international telephone calls** at the Overseas Telephone Exchange (O.T.E.), 15 Stadiou St. (tel. 322-1002), three blocks from Syntagma Square. The office is open Monday through Friday from 7am to midnight, and on Saturday, Sunday, and holidays from 8am to midnight. North Americans can phone home directly by contacting an MCI (tel. toll free 00-800-1211) or AT&T (tel. toll free 00-800-1311) operator. Both companies allow collect calls or will bill your telephone credit card.

Tipping   Restaurants already include a service charge in the bill, but many locals round up tabs larger than 1,000 Dr ($5.25) to the nearest 100 Dr (55¢). You might also want to round off a taxi fare by adding some extra drachmas.

4. BUDGET ACCOMMODATIONS

Good news greets you upon your arrival at one of Athens's budget hotels: some of the lowest prices of any capital in Europe. Indeed, prices are so low that Athens compares favorably to other low-cost Balkan capitals, such as Belgrade, Bucharest, and Sofia! Don't expect too much comfort for these incredible rates. Most rooms are rather plain, usually free of decoration, and with furniture and decor from the 1950s or 1960s. English is spoken by some, but not all, receptionists who work in these hotels.

As many of these hotels are similar in physical layout, location in Athens becomes an important consideration. As my first choice I prefer Plaka, with twisting lanes and small houses at the foot of the Acropolis. Second, I suggest hotels in two areas adjacent to Plaka: between Monastiraki Square and Omonia Square, or around Syntagma Square. Finally, because of its distance from ancient Athens (but still only 15–20 minutes on foot), I leave as a third choice the area near Omonia Square. This last neighborhood is close to many stores and the heart of modern Athens, so it, too, has its own virtues. You'll occasionally find a good budget pick outside these areas, and several are listed below.

If you arrive without a reservation, either contact one of the hotels listed below or visit the service window of the **Hellenic Chamber of Hotels,** adjacent to the Tourist Information Office inside the National Bank of Greece on Syntagma Square at 2 Karageorgi St. (tel. 01/323-7193). This for-profit agency can reserve you a room on the spot, based on price and other specifics, for which you pay a deposit of a third or half the cost of your stay; no additional charges are levied (they take a commission from the hotel). Note that they deal with many of the budget hotels in this chapter, but not the very smallest ones. They can also make reservations for hotels elsewhere in Greece. The office is open Monday through Saturday from 10am to 4pm in low season, from 8:30am to 8pm in high season; closed Sunday. To write ahead for a reservation, the mailing address is 24 Stadiou St., Athens 10564 (fax 01/322-5449).

FROMMER'S SMART TRAVELER: HOTELS
VALUE-CONSCIOUS TRAVELERS SHOULD
TAKE ADVANTAGE OF THE FOLLOWING:

1. Hotels near Plaka, the most charming area of town.
2. The service window of the Hellenic Chamber of Hotels, which will reserve rooms without charging the usual commission fee.
3. Negotiable hotel rates—always ask whether they have something cheaper.

One final piece of advice: Since many of our budget hotels are on small side streets that can be difficult to find at first, or are located 5–15 minutes by foot from the main public transportation hubs of Omonia or Syntagma Square, you might consider taking a taxi to your hotel if you have a lot of luggage when you first arrive. A short hop within the center from Syntagma or Omonia Square often costs as little as 500 Dr ($2.65).

DOUBLES FOR LESS THAN 6,700 DR [$35.25]

IN PLAKA

DIOSKOUROS HOTEL, 6 Pittakou St., Athens 10558. Tel. 01/324-8165
or 324-6582. 14 rms (none with bath). **Directions:** See below.
$ Rates: June–Oct 15, 4,800 Dr ($25.25) single; 5,400 Dr ($28.40) double; 6,000 Dr ($31.60) triple. Oct 16–May, prices drop about 30%. No credit cards.
At the Dioskouros you'll find a very quiet ambience, as most rooms face an interior courtyard or garden. The rooms are bare and a bit dirty, however, with wooden floors and high ceilings. Eurailers, and other travelers in small groups, especially will find it suitable here.
To get there, from Syntagma Square, walk south on the large Boulevard Leof. Amalias past seven streets to your right (many of them rather small lanes), and on the eighth, turn down Thalou and take the first right to find Pitakou (which, incidentally, is not indicated on any map I've seen).

GUEST HOUSE KOUROS, 11 Kodrou St., Athens 10558. Tel. 01/322-7431. 10 rms (none with bath).
$ Rates: 4,200 Dr ($22.10) single; 6,000 Dr ($31.60) double. No credit cards.
On a narrow, pretty pedestrian street in the heart of Plaka, this 200-year-old house has 10 basic rooms and three balconies, the uppermost of which has a nice view over the quiet neighborhood. Some rooms have molded ceilings high above—a nice touch in such a modest hotel. The front rooms are best, as they let in gulps of light.

BETWEEN MONASTIRAKI & OMONIA SQUARES

HOTEL HERMION, 66c Ermou St., Athens 10551. Tel. 01/321-2753. 29 rms (none with bath). **Directions:** Walk 10 minutes down Ermou from Syntagma Square.
$ Rates: May–Oct, 3,950 Dr ($20.80) single; 5,650 Dr ($29.75) double; 7,000 Dr ($36.85) triple. Nov–Apr, 2,750 Dr ($14.50) single; 4,200 Dr ($22.10) double; 5,600 Dr ($29.50) triple. No credit cards.
The rooms in this old building located near Monastiraki Square take you through a

budget-hotel time warp as they have changed little over recent decades. Some rooms have so many tiny cracks in the paint that, combined with the dim lighting, there appears to be a pattern on the walls! The hotel does have a few virtues though: Those who walk up to the fourth floor may be rewarded with a view of the Acropolis, and owner Yeorgo Mouroulis speaks perfect English, complete with an American twang.

HOTEL TEMPI, 29 Eolou St., Athens 10551. Tel. 01/321-3175. Fax 01/321-4705. 24 rms (8 with shower). **Subway:** Monastiraki.

$ Rates: May–Sept, 2,800 Dr ($14.75) single without shower; 4,400 Dr ($23.15) double without shower, 5,000 Dr ($26.30) double with shower. Oct–Apr, 2,650 Dr ($13.95) single without shower; 3,100 Dr ($16.30) double without shower, 4,050 Dr ($21.30) double with shower. AE, MC, V.

In Plaka, next to Monastiraki Square, this three-story house (no elevator) has simply furnished rooms. Managed by Yannis and Katerina, a friendly, helpful, and English-speaking husband-and-wife team, the Hotel Tempi has a rooftop lounge with a view of the Acropolis, laundry facilities, free luggage storage, and a book exchange that includes a number of travel guides. Ten rooms have balconies overlooking a church and the street in front, recently converted into a pedestrian lane.

NEAR OMONIA SQUARE

ATHENS HOUSE HOTEL, 4 Aristotelous St., Athens 10432. Tel. 01/524-0539. 14 rms (none with bath). **Directions:** See below.

$ Rates: May–Sept, 3,000 Dr ($15.80) single; 6,600 Dr ($34.75) double; 7,800 Dr ($41.05) triple. Breakfast 800 Dr ($4.20) extra. No credit cards.

This pension is located on the fifth floor of an old apartment building. There's elevator access to the rooms, which are basic, but clean, with one or two prints on the aging painted walls. The central attraction here is the very low rates. The owner, Basel, also speaks English.

To get here, from Omonia Square, walk north up Septemvriou Street, take the third left down Chalkokondyl, and then take the first right onto Aristotelous Street. The hotel will be immediately on your right.

ELSEWHERE AROUND TOWN

PENSION MARBLE HOUSE, 35 Zinni St., Athens 11741. Tel. 01/923-4058. 15 rms (9 with shower). **Bus:** 1 or 5 from Syntagma Square.

$ Rates: Summer, 3,500 Dr ($18.40) single without shower, 4,300 Dr ($22.65) single with shower; 5,300 Dr ($27.90) double without shower, 6,200 Dr ($32.65) double with shower. 15%–20% discount during the winter. Breakfast 500 Dr ($2.65) extra. No credit cards.

As the name suggests, at this hotel you'll find marble on the floors, reception counter, and stairs. The rooms are quite clean, with wood-frame beds, stone floors, baby-blue walls, and balconies overlooking the quiet though unexceptional neighborhood. There is a small English-language book exchange. You'll find the hotel at the back left-hand corner of a very quiet dead-end lane that begins at no. 35 Zinni, not far from the Olympic Airways terminal on Syngrou Avenue. Pension Marble has no elevator.

DOUBLES FOR LESS THAN 9,000 DR
[$47.35]

IN PLAKA

ADAMS HOTEL, Herefontos and Thalou Sts., Athens 10558. Tel. 01/322-5381 or 324-6582. 15 rms (all with bath). **Directions:** See below.

$ Rates: 6,000 Dr ($31.60) single with bath outside room, 6,600 Dr ($34.75) single with bath inside room; 7,200 Dr ($37.90) double with bath outside room, 7,800 Dr ($41.05) double with bath inside room. Breakfast 600 Dr ($3.15) additional. No credit cards.

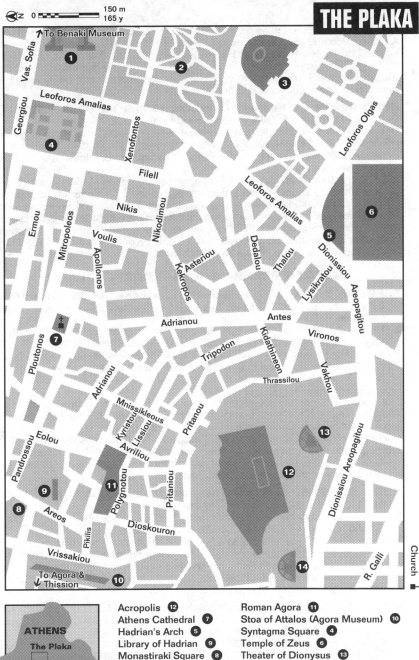

THE PLAKA

0 — 150 m
0 — 165 y

↑To Benaki Museum

Vas. Sofia
Georgiou
Leoforos Amalias
Xenofontos
Filell
Ermou
Mitropoleos
Nikis
Voulis
Apollonos
Nikodimou
Asteriou
Kekropos
Leoforos Amalias
Leoforos Olgas
Dedalou
Thalou
Lysikratou
Dionissiou Areopagitou
Adrianou
Antes
Vironos
Ploutonos
Adrianou
Tripodon
Kidathineon
Thrassilou
Vakhou
Mnissikleous
Kyristou
Lissiou
Avriliou
Pritanou
Pritaniou
Eolou
Pandrossou
Polygnotou
Pikilis
Areos
Dioskouron
Dionissiou Areopagitou
Vrissakiou

↓To Agora &
Thission

R. Galli
Church
+

ATHENS
The Plaka

Acropolis	12	Roman Agora	11
Athens Cathedral	7	Stoa of Attalos (Agora Museum)	10
Hadrian's Arch	5	Syntagma Square	4
Library of Hadrian	9	Temple of Zeus	6
Monastiraki Square	8	Theater of Dionysus	13
National Garden	2	Theater of Herodes Atticus	14
Parliament Building	1	Zapion	3

Good views of the Acropolis and the city can be had from almost every room here. All have balconies, and some, most notably Room 303, have large terraces. There is a big bar in the lobby lounge, and English is spoken fluently. There is a 2am curfew.

To get here, from Syntagma Square, walk south on the large Boulevard Leof. Amalias past seven streets to your right (many of them rather small lanes), and on the eighth, turn down Thalou and continue straight to the hotel.

HOTEL ADONIS, 3 Kodrou St., Athens 10558. Tel. 01/324-9737. Fax 01/323-1602. 26 rms (all with shower and toilet). TEL

$ Rates: 6,000 Dr ($31.60) single without shower, 6,600 Dr ($34.75) single with shower; 7,200 Dr ($37.90) double without shower, 7,800 Dr ($41.05) double with shower. 10% discount for stays longer than two nights. Breakfast 500 Dr ($2.65) extra. No credit cards.

Just a few short blocks off Syntagma Square, Hotel Adonis features well-maintained rooms, small balconies, and clean bathrooms in an appealing location. Although you might not have chosen the tan-and-brown wallpaper for your own home, you'll certainly appreciate the view from the lovely breakfast roof garden that overlooks both the Acropolis and Lycabettus Hill. The receptionist speaks English, another plus, making this a highly recommended mid-budget-range choice. You'll see a group of flags flying out front.

BETWEEN OMONIA & MONASTIRAKI SQUARES

CAROLINA HOTEL, 55 Kolokotroni St., Athens 10560. Tel. 01/322-0837, 322-0838, or 322-8148. 31 rms (16 with shower, 4 with private shower across the hall). TEL

$ Rates: July–Oct, 5,000 Dr ($26.30) single without shower, 5,850 Dr ($30.80) single with shower; 6,750 Dr ($35.50) double without shower, 7,800 Dr ($41.05) double with shower. Apr–June, 4,000 Dr ($21.05) single without shower, 5,000 Dr ($26.30) single with shower; 5,800 Dr ($30.50) double without shower, 6,750 Dr ($35.50) double with shower. Nov–Mar, further discounts available. No credit cards.

The Carolina is not the most comfortable hotel in this area, but it's clean and adequate, and it has a lounge with a snack bar. Rooms all have balconies. The furniture dates back several decades and the lighting is dim. The three floors are reached by elevator. Co-owner George Papagiannoulas (who runs the place with his brother) worked in Australia for 10 years and speaks English well. Another virtue of the hotel is a luggage checkroom where you can leave your things if you go away for a few days. Kolokotroni Street runs between Stadiou and Eolou.

HOTEL ALKISTIS, 18 Platia Theatrou, Athens 10552. Tel. 01/321-9811. 128 rms (all with shower and toilet). TEL

$ Rates (including continental breakfast): 5,000 Dr ($26.30) single; 7,500 Dr ($39.50) double. AE, DC, MC, V. **Closed:** Nov–Jan.

This is one of the largest hotels in town, with 10 floors of comfortably furnished rooms reached by two elevators. All rooms have small aging bathrooms and most have medium-size terraces. There's also a fan attached to the wall to fight the summertime heat. The small street is about halfway between Omonia and Syntagma Squares, between Menandrou and Sokratous Streets.

HOTEL ATTALOS, 29 Athinas St., Athens 10554. Tel. 01/321-2801. 80 rms (all with shower or bath and toilet). TEL **Directions:** From Syntagma Square, walk down Ermou and turn right after the second traffic light.

$ Rates: Apr–Oct, 6,000 Dr ($31.55) single; 8,400 Dr ($44.20) double; 10,100 Dr ($53.15) triple. Nov–Mar, 5,000 Dr ($26.30) single; 6,400 Dr ($33.70) double; 6,450 Dr ($33.95) triple. Breakfast 800 Dr ($4.20) extra. V.

 The Attalos is a modern six-story building with nicely furnished rooms (elevator accessible) with a print and mirror in each room adding a bit more pizzazz than usual for a budget hotel in Athens. Twelve rooms in the back have

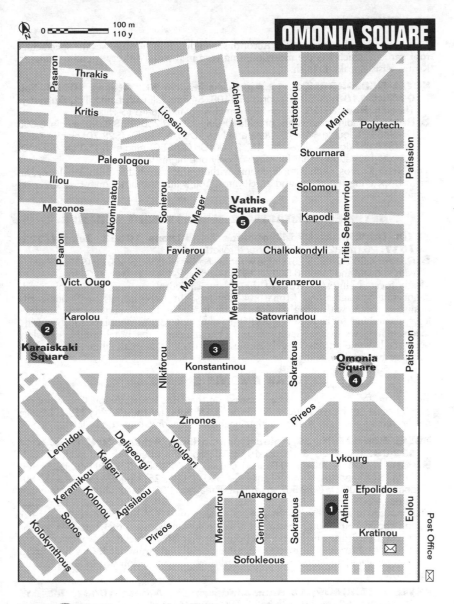

OMONIA SQUARE

0 ⸺ 100 m
⸺ 110 y

Pasaron
Thrakis
Kritis
Liossion
Acharnon
Aristotelous
Marni
Polytech.
Patission
Paleologou
Stournara
Iliou
Sonierou
Akominatou
Mager
Solomou
Mezonos
Vathis Square ⑤
Kapodi
Tritis Septemvriou
Psaron
Favierou
Chalkokondyli
Vict. Ougo
Marni
Menandrou
Veranzerou
Karolou
Satovriandou
② Karaiskaki Square
③
Nikiforou
Konstantinou
Sokratous
Omonia Square ④
Patission
Zinonos
Pireos
Leonidou
Deligeorgi
Voulgari
Lykourg
Kalgeri
Keramikou
Kolonou
Agisilaou
Menandrou
Anaxagora
Gerniou
Sokratous
Athinas
Efpolidos
Eolou
Sonos
①
Post Office
Kolokynthous
Pireos
Kratinou
Sofokleous

ATHENS

Omonia Square

① City Hall
② Karaiskaki Square
③ National Theater
④ Omonia Square
⑤ Vathis Square

large balconies with views of the Acropolis, and the same view blesses the spectacular roof garden, which has the most stunning vista in town. The very friendly manager, Kostas Zisis, speaks English.

HOTEL NEON-KRONOS, 12 Agion Asomaton St., Athens 10553. Tel. 01/325-1106, 325-1107, or 325-1108. 54 rms (all with bath). TEL **Subway:** Thission. **Bus:** 25, 26, 27, or 28 from Syntagma Square to Thission.

$ **Rates** (including continental breakfast): July–Oct, 6,250 Dr ($32.90) single; 8,600 Dr ($45.25) double. Mar 16–June and Nov–Dec, 5,450 Dr ($28.70) single; 7,000 Dr ($36.85) double. Jan–Mar 15, 3,900 Dr ($20.50) single; 5,150 Dr ($27.10) double. 10% supplement for stays of only one night. V.

The Neon-Kronos offers simple rooms without decoration but with a balcony, an English-speaking reception, and an elevator. You'll find the hotel on a side street off Ermou Street.

BETWEEN SYNTAGMA & MONASTIRAKI SQUARES

HOTEL IMPERIAL, 46 Mitropoleos St., Athens 10563. Tel. 01/322-7617. 25 rms (22 with shower and toilet).

$ **Rates:** 4,800 Dr ($25.25) single without shower or toilet, 5,400 Dr ($28.40) single with shower and toilet; 6,500 Dr ($34.20) double with shower. MC, V.

Ideally located almost in front of the Athens cathedral, on one of the main roads connecting Syntagma and Monastiraki Squares, the Imperial has small but cozily furnished rooms with aging patterned wallpaper. The hotel's services and facilities leave something to be desired, and if it were not for its premiere location, and spectacular views of the Acropolis and church below, the hotel would be wildly overpriced. Some rooms have balconies, and there is a small library of English-language books downstairs.

NEAR OMONIA SQUARE

Two of the following choices are located on the same street, Agiou Constantinou, which begins on the west side of Omonia Square (look for the 10-story Hotel Mirage on the square and take the street that begins a few storefronts to the left).

HOTEL ACHILLION, 32 Agiou Constantinou, Athens 10437. Tel. 01/523-0971, 522-5618, or 522-1918. 56 rms (all with shower and toilet). TEL

$ **Rates:** Mar 15–Oct, 6,000 Dr ($31.60) single; 7,200 Dr ($37.90) double; 14,400 Dr ($75.75) apartment. Nov–Mar 14, 4,800 Dr ($25.25) single; 5,800 Dr ($30.50) double; 11,500 Dr ($60.50) apartment. Breakfast 600 Dr ($3.15) extra. No credit cards.

This modern seven-story building has a restaurant, a TV lounge, and a small bar behind the marble-floored reception area. Interestingly, the hotel caters to groups from eastern Europe and Russia, and the entrance area is decorated with city flags from these countries. The apartments are especially recommended; they hold up to four people each, and most have large bathtubs. The reception can be disorganized and slow.

HOTEL EPIDAUROS, 14 Koumoundouru St., Athens 10437. Tel. 01/523-0421. 50 rms (36 with bath). TEL **Directions:** From Omonia Square, walk down Agiou Constantinou for four blocks and then turn left onto Koumoundouru Street.

$ **Rates:** 6,800 Dr ($35.80) single without bath, 8,150 Dr ($42.90) single with bath; 8,800 Dr ($46.30) double without bath, 10,150 Dr ($53.40) double with bath. Breakfast 500 Dr ($2.65) extra. No credit cards.

Here all rooms come with light-brown wallpaper, two prints on the wall, and a small desk, and most have a tiny bathroom and small balcony. The seven-story building has two elevators and a small bar at the back of the lobby. The desk clerk speaks English. Note that rates here are extremely negotiable during the off-season.

HOTEL PYTHAGORION, 28 Agiou Constantinou St., Athens 10437. Tel.

01/524-2811, or 524-2814. Fax 01/524-5581. 56 rms (all with shower and toilet). A/C

$ **Rates:** Apr–June 15, 6,650 Dr ($35.00) single; 8,500 Dr ($44.75) double. June 16–Sept, 7,100 Dr ($37.35) single; 9,650 Dr ($50.80) double. Oct–Mar, 3,600 Dr ($18.95) single; 6,000 Dr ($31.55) double. Triples cost about 1,500 Dr ($7.90) more than doubles, year round. DC.

This hotel three blocks from Omonia Square specializes in accommodating large groups of (mostly) European travelers. The rooms in this modern seven-story building are all spacious and simply furnished, and feature soundproof windows. Some rooms feature large terraces, and the hotel staff speaks English.

ELSEWHERE AROUND TOWN

CLARE'S HOUSE, 24 Sorvolou St., Athens 11636. Tel. 01/922-2288 or 922-0678. 20 rms (7 with shower and toilet). TEL **Directions:** See below.

$ **Rates** (including continental breakfast): 5,950 Dr ($31.30) single without shower or toilet; 7,800 Dr ($41.05) double without shower or toilet, 9,900 Dr ($52.10) double with shower and toilet. No credit cards.

This very modern four-story house, built in 1988, is near the Athens Stadium, a 15- to 20-minute walk from Syntagma Square. Clare's captures a homey feel of a modern university dorm. When I last visited, a group of American students living here for the semester were watching television and eating lunch they had prepared in the public kitchen. The helpful, English-speaking owner will do your laundry for 600 Dr ($3.80) a load.

The drawback to this pleasant choice is its hard-to-find location, in the "Mets" area of town. Take bus no. 2, 4, or 11 from Syntagma Square to Olgas Street in front of the stadium, and at the end of Olgas turn right onto Arditou. Sorvolou is nearby after a staircase leading up from Arditou, but it's best to ask for exact directions. There's no sign in front, just a big glass door.

TONY'S PENSION, 26 Zacharitsa St., Athens 11741. Tel. 01/923-6370, 923-0561, or 923-5761. 14 rms (all with shower and toilet, 11 with kitchenette). **Trolleybus:** 1 to Zinni Street.

$ **Rates:** 6,000 Dr ($31.60) single; 8,400 Dr ($44.20) double, 10,800 Dr ($56.85) double with kitchenette; 13,500 Dr ($71.05) triple; 17,550 Dr ($92.35) quad. Breakfast 800 Dr ($4.20) extra. AE, DC, EURO, MC.

A modern three-story house with a roof garden and simple, clean rooms, Tony's Pension gets marks for its friendly English-speaking staff. They offer a large selection of English-language paperbacks and guides, and a small bar in the entrance area. One floor has a public kitchen and refrigerator open to all. Rooms with kitchenette, which sleep two to four, are a particularly good buy, and include a fully equipped kitchen and bathroom. The pension is at the foot of the Philopappos Hill, not far from the Acropolis and a five-minute walk from the Olympic Airways terminal.

SUPER-BUDGET CHOICES

HOSTELS

ATHENS YOUTH HOSTEL, 57 Kypselis St., Athens 11361. Tel. 01/822-5860. 180 beds. **Bus:** 2, 4, or 9 from Syntagma Square to one stop after "Museum"; then turn right.

$ **Rates:** 950 Dr ($5) per person with the IYHF membership card, 1,400 Dr ($7.35) per person without one. You can buy a IYHF card here for 1,800 Dr ($9.50). No credit cards.

This spacious three-story house, located four blocks behind the National Archeological Museum, is the only official youth hostel in Athens. Each dorm room has 6–12 bunk beds, and the first and second floors are segregated by sex. Facilities include a laundry room, free showers, and a cafeteria in the basement seating 70. The hostel is closed between 10:30am and 1:30pm, and there is a midnight curfew.

HOTEL IDEAL, 39 Eolou St., Athens. Tel. 01/321-3195 or 322-0542. 32 rms (none with bath).

$ Rates: 2,750 Dr ($14.50) single; 5,700 Dr ($30.00) double; 7,450 Dr ($39.20) triple; 8,600 Dr ($45.25) quad. No credit cards.

There are no frills at this hostellike hotel in a three-story house 10 minutes' walk from Syntagma Square. There are sinks in 31 of the rooms, but cold water only; use of the hot showers on each floor is free. The building, which was constructed in 1836, has marble stairs (no elevator). The rooms are stuffy with ugly yellow the latest color on the much-painted walls. A few have balconies, and there is no curfew here. Breakfast is not available in the hotel, but there are three coffee shops just around the corner that serve a continental breakfast for 500 Dr ($2.65).

PENSION ARGO, 25 Victor Hugo (Victoros Ougo) St., Athens 10437. Tel. 01/522-5939. 18 rms (4 with shower and toilet). **Directions:** See below.

$ Rates: May 15–Oct 15, 3,400 Dr ($17.90) single; 4,300 Dr ($22.65) double without shower; 5,050 Dr ($26.60) double with shower; 5,400 Dr ($28.40) triple; 1,500 Dr ($7.90) per person quad. Oct 16–May 14, 2,500 Dr ($13.15) single, 3,100 Dr ($16.30) double, 4,200 Dr ($22.10) triple; 1,250 Dr ($6.60) per person quad. Rooms with shower and toilet 230 Dr ($1.45) extra; breakfast, 500 Dr ($2.65). No credit cards.

Located in a rather shabby building between Larissis Station and Omonia Square, Pension Argo is acceptable as a spartan money-saver. Facilities include free showers and a self-serve laundry in the basement—800 Dr ($4.20) for 5 kilos (11 lb.). There is no elevator to the three floors. Kostas, the co-owner, speaks English well.

If you take the bus from the airport, get off at Karaiskaki Square and the pension will be only two blocks away.

STUDENT AND TRAVELERS INN, 16 Kidathineon St., Athens 10558. Tel. 01/324-4808. 35 rms. **Directions:** From Syntagma Square, walk south down Filellinon Street for three blocks and turn right on Kidathineon.

$ Rates: 2,550 Dr ($13.40) single; 4,300 Dr ($22.65) double; 2,000 Dr ($10.50) per person triple. Breakfast 500 Dr ($2.65) extra. No credit cards.

⭐ My top super-budget choice in Athens is the Student and Travelers Inn, mostly because of its enviable location in the heart of Plaka, a 10-minute walk from Syntagma Square. In addition, it offers an appealing garden in back covered by a trellis for morning breakfast and afternoon relaxation. Almost all the basic but clean rooms have balconies, and the place even has an elevator. To top off this budget find, lively owner Spiros Mavromates speaks perfect English—the result of 25 years' living in New York City.

WORTH THE EXTRA BUCKS

HOTEL ARETHUSA, 6 Metropoleos St., Athens 10563. Tel. 01/322-9431 or 322-9438. Fax 01/322-9439. 87 rms (all with bath). A/C TEL

$ Rates: Mar 15–Oct (including continental breakfast), 10,200 Dr ($53.70) single; 14,400 Dr ($75.80) double. Nov–Mar 14, 7,150 Dr ($37.65) single; 10,400 Dr ($54.75) double; breakfast 700 Dr ($3.70) extra. AE, DC, EURO, MC, V.

⭐ Located just off Syntagma Square at the corner of Nikis Street is this fairly modern hotel with eight floors (elevator access). All the rooms here have air conditioning and radio, and although the room decor is a throwback to the 1950s, you'll find the hotel a comfortable and well-located place. Breakfast is served in a roof garden which affords spectacular views of the Acropolis. A few rooms on the top floor also have good views.

HOTEL DORIAN INN, 17 Pireos St., Athens 10552. Tel. 01/523-9782 or 523-9784. 146 rms (all with bath and toilet). TEL

$ Rates (including complete breakfast): Apr–Oct, 11,500 Dr ($60.50) single; 17,400 Dr ($91.60) double; 20,900 Dr ($109.90) triple. Nov–Mar, 7,200 Dr ($37.90) single; 10,800 Dr ($56.85) double; 13,000 Dr ($68.40) triple. AE, DC, EURO, MC, V.

This 12-story hotel (elevator access) has spacious, well-furnished rooms, all of which have a pleasant sitting area with a writing desk. Ceiling-to-floor windows let in lots of light, but the rooms themselves are slightly worn (some with balcony). The Dorian Inn is unique among my listings in that it has a swimming pool, free to guests. There are two bars, and a restaurant serving three meals daily. You'll find the hotel just three blocks from Omonia Square, behind a large glass facade.

5. BUDGET DINING

Happily, Athens is a city of many inexpensive restaurants. You'll find the most charming of these in the heart of Plaka, many featuring traditional Greek ambience inside and outdoor seating. Unfortunately, these restaurants tend to attract many tourists and several close for the winter. The budget restaurants near Syntagma and Omonia Squares listed here often cook up just as good food, but in simpler settings that often recall the 1950s or early 1960s in decor.

Most places I've listed have menus printed in Greek and English. When in doubt, ask for *moussaka,* a staple served in all tavernas (smaller and unpretentious restaurants) and 95% of the self-service and table-service cafeterias and restaurants. Moussaka consists of baked ground meat covered with vegetables and spices, and sometimes topped with a layer of dough or mashed potatoes. Its quality varies from place to place, but when it's good, it makes a wonderfully tasty meal. And it's filling: You'll be more than stuffed if for dinner you have a plate of moussaka, a tomato salad, bread, and wine. Eaten in a normal taverna or restaurant, that combination should rarely cost more than 1,400 Dr ($7.35). Another staple is *dolmothakia* (rice and meat in grape, or sometimes cabbage, leaves). For a lighter snack, ask for *souvlaki* (roast and spitted chunks of lamb spiced with oregano). A popular Greek table wine is *retsina,* a white wine flavored with pine resin—if you don't like its taste, ask for *aresinato* (wine without resin). The Greek before-meal drink is *ouzo,* about 200–300 Dr ($1.05–$1.60) a shot, taken either straight or with water, which turns it cloudy white.

Coffee shops are found in abundance in Athens. By far the largest concentration of them is on Syntagma Square, with seating for over 1,000. On summer evenings all the seats are occupied by Athenians and tourists alike. In addition to coffee, you can usually get soft drinks, sandwiches, ice cream, and beer. Expect to pay about 650 Dr ($3.40) for a coffee with milk; if you stand up you'll pay considerably less.

MEALS FOR LESS THAN 1,250 DR ($6.60)

IN PLAKA

PLATANOS RESTAURANT, 4 Diogenes St. Tel. 322-0666.
   Cuisine: GREEK.

FROMMER'S SMART TRAVELER: RESTAURANTS

VALUE-CONSCIOUS TRAVELERS SHOULD
TAKE ADVANTAGE OF THE FOLLOWING:

1. Restaurants in the heart of Plaka and near Syntagma and Omonia Squares.
2. Coffee shops on Syntagma Square.
3. Moussaka, a filling, tasty meal.

$ Prices: 550–1,350 Dr ($2.90–$7.10). No credit cards.
Open: Lunch Mon–Sat noon–4:30pm; dinner Mon–Sat 8pm–midnight.

⭐ Its location on a lovely, quiet pedestrian square makes this one of my favorite romantic spots in Plaka. Established in 1932, the restaurant recently saw an interior facelift, creating a pleasant ambience of paintings, photos, and certificates on the walls beneath the modern wooden ceiling. If it's a nice day, sit at a table on the square in front. Platanos is famous for its Greek specialties and its large list of white, red, and rosé wines.

RESTAURANT EDEN, 3 Flessa St. Tel. 324-8858.
Cuisine: VEGETARIAN.
$ Prices: 750–1,100 Dr ($3.95–$5.80). No credit cards.
Open: Wed–Mon noon–midnight.

⭐ One of the few solely vegetarian restaurants in Greece, this place serves up good low-cost food in appealing surroundings. The attractive decor of the two-level restaurant includes 1920s-style prints and mirrors, hanging wrought-iron lamps, and views over nearby rooftops. Greeks and tourists alike gather here to sample a large variety of delicious dishes, including minestrone soup, soy moussaka, mushroom pie, salads, juices, and desserts. Owner Theodore Kamperidis lived on Cape Cod for eight years and speaks good English, as does much of the staff.

TAVERNA BAIRAKTARIS, 2 Platia Monastiraki. Tel. 321-3036.
Cuisine: GREEK.
$ Prices: 400–1,350 Dr ($2.10–$7.10). No credit cards.
Open: Daily 7am–2am.
One of the most popular and best-value tavernas in Plaka, facing the Monastiraki Square subway station, Taverna Bairaktaris is a boisterous place where the owner often stands at the door clapping his hands to attract new customers. The open kitchen enables diners to walk up to the glass counter of Greek specialties and tell the cook what they want; just to the left of the entrance you'll see another chef grilling meats. They also have tables under a tent on busy Monastiraki Square out front. Greek music plays on the radio, adding to the typical Hellenic atmosphere here. Retsina, stored in five large wooden barrels in the inside dining room, is produced in the owner's vineyard. Several waiters speak English.

NEAR SYNTAGMA SQUARE

DIROS RESTAURANT, 10 Xenophonos St. Tel. 323-2392.
Cuisine: GREEK.
$ Prices: 900–3,400 Dr ($4.75–$17.90). AE, DC, V.
Open: Daily noon–midnight.
Many demanding Greek regulars frequent this air-conditioned restaurant two blocks from Syntagma Square, so you can count on getting good, simple, home-cooked food here. Items on the menu include avgolemono (rice, egg, and lemon soup), bean soup, a large selection of spaghetti dishes, and roast chicken with french fries. There is seating for 50 both inside and out, and the waiter and manager speak some English. The plain decor suggests an upscale cafeteria with its imitation wood paneling and bright light.

WENDY'S, 4 Stadiou St., at Syntagma Sq. Tel. 323-9322.
Cuisine: AMERICAN FAST FOOD
$ Prices: Salad bar 700–1,100 Dr ($3.70–$5.80); burgers 400–950 Dr ($2.10–$5).
Open: Sun–Thurs 6am–3am, Fri–Sat 7am–4am. No credit cards.
Bright, clean, loud, and neon-lit, this American fast-food restaurant looks very much like other Wendy's franchises around the world—except this one's packed, almost around the clock. Opened in 1991, Wendy's gets mention here for its well-maintained salad bar, perhaps the only one in all of Greece, a welcome respite from the heavy, meaty fare served most everywhere else. Baked potatoes and burgers are also sold.

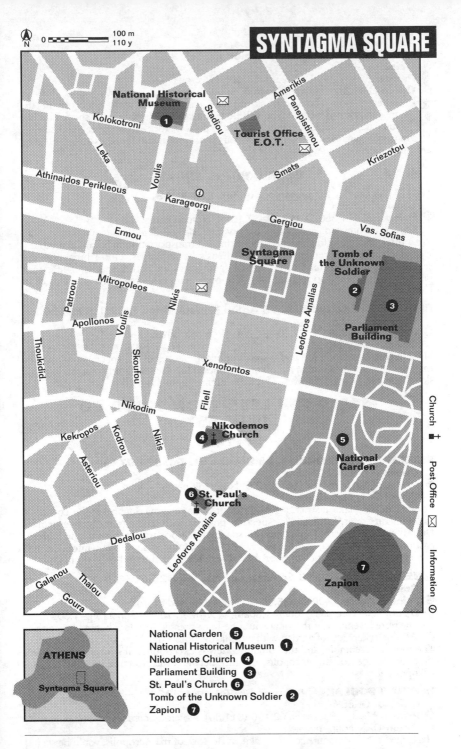

SYNTAGMA SQUARE

0 ——— 100 m
N   110 y

National Historical Museum
Amerikis
Panepistimou
Kolokotroni
Stadiou
Tourist Office E.O.T.
Leka
Kriezotou
Athinaidos Perikleous
Voulis
Smats
Karageorgi
Gergiou
Vas. Sofias
Ermou
Syntagma Square
Tomb of the Unknown Soldier
Mitropoleos
Patroou
Nikis
Leoforos Amalias
Parliament Building
Apollonos
Voulis
Skoufou
Xenofontos
Thoukidid.
Nikodim
Filell
Kekropos
Kodrou
Nikodemos Church
Nikis
National Garden
Asteriou
St. Paul's Church
Dedalou
Leoforos Amalias
Galanou
Thalou
Zapion
Goura

Church   ■ †
Post Office   ⊠
Information   ⓘ

ATHENS
Syntagma Square

National Garden ❺
National Historical Museum ❶
Nikodemos Church ❹
Parliament Building ❸
St. Paul's Church ❻
Tomb of the Unknown Soldier ❷
Zapion ❼

WILLIAM OF ORANGE, 4 Apolonos St. Tel. 323-8743.
  Cuisine: GREEK.
$ **Prices:** 550–1,350 Dr ($2.90–$7.10). No credit cards.
  Open: Daily 8am–11pm. **Closed:** Sun in winter.
  Whether you choose to sit on the carpeted sidewalk patio or in the air-conditioned interior, you will be treated to traditional Greek specialties like souvlaki and various spinach dishes in a New York–style coffee-shop setting. Hamburgers, spaghetti, and other more tourist-accessible foods are also available, and are often prepared by William himself.

NEAR OMONIA SQUARE

FONTANA CAFE, 20 Omonia Sq. Tel. 522-4349.
  Cuisine: GREEK.
$ **Prices:** 550–1,350 Dr ($2.90–$7.10). No credit cards.
  Open: Summer, daily 5:30am–3am; winter, daily 6:30am–midnight.
With three floors overlooking the city's principal transportation hub, Fontana offers a welcome touch of serenity in one of Athens's busiest areas. Good breakfasts are served here, as are a number of toasted sandwiches and other snacks. The café is popular with locals who relax all day here over a cup of coffee and a sweet piece of baklava.

RESTAURANT GIANAKIS, 15 Agiou Konstantinou St. Tel. 522-3895.
  Cuisine: GREEK.
$ **Prices:** 550–800 Dr ($2.90–$4.20). No credit cards.
  Open: Daily 7am–11pm.
Here in true fast-food style you'll see illuminated photos of the specialties above the cashier, highlighting some of the 30 main dishes. The place is slightly less modern and sleek than the Fontana (above). The large dining room seats 200.

MEALS FOR LESS THAN 2,000 DR ($10.55)

IN PLAKA

PICCOLINO RESTAURANT, 26 Sotiros St. Tel. 324-9745.
  Cuisine: ITALIAN/GREEK.
$ **Prices:** 950–1,750 Dr ($5–$9.20). No credit cards.
  Open: Daily 6pm–3am.
Located in the Plaka district, a few blocks from Syntagma Square, at the corner of Kidathineon Street, Piccolino is especially popular with students and young people. Dishes include generous portions of spaghetti carbonara, macaroni and cheese, pastitsio (fried noodles), octopus with french fries, mussels stewed in white wine, fish and chips, and 10 varieties of pizza baked in a traditional wood-fired oven.

TAVERNA ATTALOS, 16 Erechttheos St. Tel. 325-0353.
  Cuisine: GREEK.
$ **Prices:** 1,100–3,400 Dr ($5.80–$17.90). No credit cards.
  Open: Apr–Oct, daily 10am–1:30am; Nov–Mar, Thurs–Sun 11am–1:30am.
For the pure loveliness of the view you'll be hard-pressed to find a better choice than the Attalos, where a roof garden with a trellis overlooks the Acropolis in the distance. The food is acceptable, and the romantic view is exceptional. It's located on a small street at the foot of the Acropolis, roughly between the Athens cathedral and the Acropolis.

TAVERNA POULAKIS, 6 Panos St. Tel. 321-3222.
  Cuisine: GREEK.
$ **Prices:** Meals for less than 2,150 ($11.30). No credit cards.
  Open: Daily noon–midnight.
Here, next to the Roman Agora in Plaka, at the foot of the Acropolis, you'll be served

home-cooked Greek food, which you can select at the counter. The menu includes dolmades (cabbage leaves stuffed with ground meat), pastitsio (macaroni stew), and farmer's salad with feta cheese. This typical taverna has seating for 20 inside and 100 outside.

TRATTORIA RESTAURANT, 4 Farmaki St. Tel. 324-5474.
   Cuisine: ITALIAN.
$ Prices: 700–2,100 Dr ($3.70–$11.05). AE, V.
   Open: Daily 10am–midnight.
      For a change of pace from Greek food, you may enjoy the selection of spaghetti, soups, and eight varieties of pizza at this restaurant in the heart of Plaka. Paintings of Venice and other Italian scenes adorn the interior walls, and outside tables spill onto an attractive, though much-touristed, pedestrian square. You'll find the square just off Kidathineon Street in Plaka.

NEAR SYNTAGMA SQUARE

DELFI RESTAURANT, 13 Nikis St. Tel. 323-4869.
   Cuisine: GREEK.
$ Prices: 700–2,700 Dr ($3.70–$14.20). AE, DC, MC, V.
   Open: Mon–Sat 11am–11 or 11:30pm.
Waiters in green jackets and black ties (some of whom speak English) serve tasty dishes in this restaurant popular with businesspeople. The L-shaped eatery is styled with attractive wood paneling on some walls and stretches of imitation red brick on others. Taped music plays in the background.

GOLDEN FLOWER, 30 Nikis St. Tel. 323-0113.
   Cuisine: CHINESE.
$ Prices: 1,350–2,700 Dr ($7.10–$14.20); complete meal for two 5,400 Dr ($28.40). DC.
   Open: Lunch Mon–Fri noon–3:30pm; dinner daily 7pm–midnight.
At the Golden Flower, one of the few Cantonese restaurants in central Athens, the Chinese cooks and staff serve up some tasty dishes to eat in or take out. The decor includes all the Chinese-restaurant classics: hanging red lamps, dragons on the ceilings, a red archway separating two sides of the restaurant, and many other small decorations. Chinese pop music plays in the background.

RESTAURANT CORFU, 6 Kriezotou St. Tel. 361-3011.
   Cuisine: GREEK/FISH. **Reservations:** Recommended.
$ Prices: 1,350–2,100 Dr ($7.10–$11.05). AE, DC, V.
   Open: Mon–Fri noon–midnight, Sat noon–5pm.
Everyone from top government officials from the nearby Parliament to local workers favors this restaurant near Syntagma Square. Some clients have been coming here for 25 years, and to cater to their conservative regulars, the management has left the decor much as it was when the place opened in 1964. Waiters in white jackets and black ties provide an elegant touch, and several different areas provide romantic corners for those who prefer a bit of quiet.

RESTAURANT KENTRIKON, 3 Kolokotroni St. Tel. 323-2482.
   Cuisine: GREEK.
$ Prices: 950–2,700 Dr ($5–$14.20). No credit cards.
   Open: Sun–Fri noon–6pm.
The decor here will march you back to the early 1960s with its large open dining room with wood panels covered by prints of ancient Athens on the walls and glass balls hanging above for lights. Since the restaurant is open for lunch only, it caters mostly to local workers and businesspeople.

NEAR OMONIA SQUARE

RESTAURANT NEA-OLYMPIA, 3 Emanuel Benaki St. Tel. 321-7972.
   Cuisine: INTERNATIONAL.

$ Prices: 950–2,300 Dr ($5–$12.10). No credit cards.
Open: Mon–Fri 11am–midnight, Sat 11am–4pm.

Off Stadiou Street, two blocks off Omonia Square, is one of the largest restaurants in town, with a slightly more attractive decor than some of the other budget picks in the area. Glass windows overlook the street, and Greek prints adorn the shiny, blond-wood walls. Daily specials are posted at each table in Greek, so make sure to ask the waiter for a translation; the regular menu is in English.

IN KOLONAKI

GRAND CAFE, 19 Sina St., Kolonaki. Tel. 645-0776.
   Cuisine: INTERNATIONAL. **Directions:** See below.
$ Prices: 500–1,200 Dr ($2.65–$6.30). No credit cards.
   Open: Mon–Sat 10am–2am, Sun 6pm–2am.

One of Kolonaki's most stylish cafés is also one of the newest. Occupying the second and third floors of a pretty white corner building, the contemporary café features high ceilings, well-stocked bars, and good-looking, uncomfortable furniture that epitomizes form over function. Drinks, hot and cold, are the menu's main feature, but competently prepared sandwiches and omelets are also served.

The Grand Café is located in Athens's Kolonaki area. Exit Syntagma Square on Stadiou Street and, after one block, turn right onto Voukourestiou Street. Continue uphill for six blocks and turn left onto Skoufa Street. The café is about five blocks ahead on your right, on the corner of Sina Street.

TAVERNA DIMOKRITOS, 23 Dimokritou St., Kolonaki. Tel. 361-3588 or 361-9293.
   Cuisine: GREEK. **Directions:** See below.
$ Prices: Appetizers 500–850 Dr ($2.65–$4.50); main courses 950–1,550 Dr ($5–$8.15). No credit cards.
   Open: Lunch Mon–Sat 1–5pm; dinner Mon–Sat 8pm–1am.

Overlooking a small park, facing Skoufa Street, this two-room traditional Greek taverna serves some of the finest food to a dedicated clientele. The large menu, which is in both Greek and English, features grilled veal, rabbit, fish, and lamb, but many knowledgeable locals swear by the swordfish souvlaki. A variety of Greek salads, in a case by the entrance, welcome you into a spotless, and pretty interior.

Taverna Dimokritos is located in Athens's Kolonaki area. Exit Syntagma Square on Stadiou Street and, after one block, turn right onto Voukourestiou Street. Continue uphill for six blocks and turn left onto Skoufa Street. After one block, turn right onto Dimokritou Street. The restaurant is on your left, up a short flight of stairs, and is marked only by the word TAVERNA on its doors.

ELSEWHERE AROUND TOWN

RESTAURANT COSTOYANIS, 37 Zaimi St. Tel. 822-0624.
   Cuisine: GREEK. **Trolleybus:** 3 or 5 to the National Archeological Museum.
$ Prices: 800–2,300 Dr ($4.20–$12.10). No credit cards.
   Open: Mon–Sat 8am–2am.

As you enter the Costoyanis you'll see an impressive display of fish and other foods, and you can choose the items you'd like to sample. You can also order from the menu while seated in the attractive dining room with wooden beams on the ceiling and a long array of windows covered by curtains to one side. This well-known gourmet restaurant is located a few blocks behind the National Archeological Museum.

PICNIC SUPPLIES & WHERE TO EAT THEM

The best place to buy picnic supplies is the **Central Market** on Athinas Street, between Monastiraki and Omonia Squares. The market, which is one of the best in

Europe, is open on Monday and Wednesday from 9am to 4:30pm, on Tuesday from 9am to 6pm, on Thursday from 9:30am to 6:30pm, on Friday from 9:30am to 7pm, and on Saturday from 8:30am to 4:30pm. Another option is the food store in the basement of the **Minion Department Store,** at 28 Oktovriou St. near Omonia Square, open on Monday and Wednesday from 9am to 5pm; on Tuesday, Thursday, and Friday from 10am to 7pm; and on Saturday from 8:30am to 3:30pm. On Sunday many grocery stores, fruit stores, and bakeries around Plaka are open.

The best place for a picnic is Athens's **National Garden,** near Syntagma Square. It is the largest public park in the city, with trees, lawns, ponds, and even a few peacocks.

6. ATTRACTIONS

SUGGESTED ITINERARIES

IF YOU HAVE ONE DAY   Head right up the mighty Acropolis to visit the Parthenon. Afterward, explore Plaka, down below, Athens's most charming neighborhood. Visit the ancient agora nearby, and consider lunch or dinner in one of Plaka's romantic restaurants.

IF YOU HAVE TWO DAYS   It's worth spending three or four hours of your second day at the National Archeological Museum. If you're not too tired, take the funicular to the top of the 1,000-foot Lycabettus Hill for a marvelous view of Athens, Piraeus, and beyond. Also consider another museum or two, listed below. If you're a photography buff, you might also return during the late afternoon to the Acropolis for the best lighting of the Parthenon facade.

IF YOU HAVE THREE DAYS OR MORE   Visit more of the museums listed below, or consider a day trip to one of the great sights of antiquity, such as Delphi, Corinth, Mycenae, or Epidaurus (see "Easy Excursions," below, for details). Or take a day-long excursion by boat to the three islands of Aegina, Poros, and Hydra in the nearby Saronic Gulf.

TOP ATTRACTIONS

THE ACROPOLIS, above Plaka. Tel. 321-0219.

⭐   Originally the residence and fortress of the king from as far back as the 13th century B.C., the Acropolis ("high point of the city") gradually grew into a religious sanctuary. A visit to the remaining 5th-century B.C. temples built during Athens's golden age is breathtaking—both in the discovery of such well-preserved antiquity and in the rigorous climb up the mighty hill at Athens's center.

The Parthenon: Crowning the Acropolis is the beautifully proportioned Doric Parthenon, built of Pentellic marble under Pericles, the Athenian leader, between 447 and 432 B.C. The highest achievement of classical form with its massive, powerful columns, the Parthenon has served as a model and prototype for Western architecture—civic, religious, and private—for almost 2,500 years. After the decline of ancient Athens, the Parthenon, originally dedicated to the goddess Athena, underwent many transformations. In A.D. 450 Christians consecrated it as a church, and by 1458 the Turks had converted it into a mosque (a circular staircase of a minaret remains to this day inside the Parthenon, unseen from outside).

Years of use and battle took their toll on the Parthenon. In 1687 the Venetians attacked the Acropolis to destroy Turkish gunpowder storerooms (which subse-

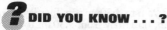
DID YOU KNOW . . . ?

- Athens is the southernmost capital in Europe.
- The ancient Olympiad originated around the 13th century B.C.
- Athens hosted the first modern Olympic Games, in 1896.
- When the Turks captured Athens in 1456, the Parthenon was turned into a mosque.
- The white marble, horseshoe-shaped stadium built in A.D. 143 is still used for athletic events.

quently exploded), and in the 1820s Greeks and Turks warred here. These battles scattered temple fragments over a wide area around the Acropolis—disasters from which restorers are still, quite literally, picking up the pieces.

Theft by zealous archeologists also took its toll on the Acropolis, most notably in the removal of the Parthenon's spectacular pediment sculptures, popularly known as the **Elgin Marbles.** Yet this heist was no middle-of-the-night caper. In the beginning of the 19th century, the British Earl of Elgin gained permission from the Ottoman Turks (who ruled over Greece at the time) to remove large pieces of the Acropolis. Lord Elgin and his men hacked off tons of marble, including the Parthenon pediment, which he sold at a profit to the British government (they remain in the British Museum today). Nearly two centuries later, the Greek government continues to press the British for the return of these antiquities.

Other Temples on the Acropolis: Several other temples adorn the top of the Acropolis. The **Propylaea** is the graceful gateway to the Acropolis, and overlooking the approach is the **Temple of Athena Nike** (Victory). Also on the Acropolis is the **Erechtheum,** an Ionic temple built to house cults to both Athena and Poseidon.

Acropolis Museum: Don't miss the Acropolis Museum, on the back right-hand corner of the Acropolis. Here you'll find a small but important collection of ancient sculpture, pediments of Greek temples, pottery, and other artifacts from several different eras. One highlight is four of the six original Caryatids from the Erechtheum (one is in the British Museum in London, and one is currently under restoration).

Admission: 1,500 Dr ($7.90) adults, 800 Dr ($4.20) students and youths 12–16, free for children under 12.

Open: Apr–Oct, Mon 11:30am–7pm, Tues–Fri 8am–7pm, Sat–Sun 8:30am–2:30pm; Nov–Mar, Mon 11:30am–4:30pm, Tues–Fri 8am–4:30pm, Sat–Sun 8:30am–2:30pm. **Subway:** Thission. **Bus:** 5 or 9 from Syntagma Square to Makrigiani; then a 15-minute walk uphill.

NATIONAL ARCHEOLOGICAL MUSEUM, 1 Tositsa St. Tel. 821-7717.

⭐ This museum houses a magnificent collection of Greek artifacts from the ancient world. Among the most fabulous treasures are the gold masks, cups, dishes, and jewelry unearthed in Mycenae by Schliemann in the 19th century. Also displayed are sculptures found on the Greek islands, including a Zeus, an Apollo, a Hygeia, a jockey, and many hand-painted vases. Recent additions to the collection include remarkably well preserved 3,500-year-old frescoes found on Santorini.

Admission: 1,500 Dr ($7.90) adults, 800 Dr ($4.20) students and youths 12–16, free for children under 12.

Open: Summer, Mon 12:30–7pm, Tues–Fri 8am–7pm, Sat–Sun 8:30am–3pm; winter, Mon 11am–5pm, Tues–Fri 8am–5pm, Sat–Sun 8:30am–3pm. **Bus:** 2, 4, 5, or 9 from Syntagma Square.

ANCIENT AGORA, between the Acropolis and Monastiraki Sq. in Plaka. Tel. 321-0185.

⭐ A visit to Athens's ancient agora (marketplace and city center) comprises the Temple of Hephaestus, overlooking the agora from the west, and the Stoa of Attalos, on the east side. The Temple of Hephaestus, built in the first half of the 5th century B.C., is one of the best-preserved ancient buildings in Greece. The Stoa of Attalos, a long, open colonnade designed to offer shelter from all kinds of weather while providing a place for informal discussion, was rebuilt to serve as a museum. The Stoa of Attalos is the setting for many of Plato's *Dialogues.*

Admission: 800 Dr ($4.20) adults, 400 Dr ($2.10) students and youths 12–16, free for children under 12.
Open: Tues–Sun 8:30am–3pm. **Subway:** Thission.

MORE ATTRACTIONS

BYZANTINE MUSEUM, 22 Vassilissis Sophias Ave. Tel. 721-1027.
Housed in a former ducal residence, this museum is devoted entirely to the art and history of Byzantium. Exhibited on three floors and in a courtyard are decorative sculptures, altars, mosaics, bishops' garments, bibles, and a small-scale reconstruction of an early Christian basilica.
Admission: 1,000 Dr ($5.25) adults, 500 Dr ($2.65) students and youths 12–16, free for children under 12.
Open: Summer, Tues–Fri 8am–7pm, Sat–Sun 8:30am–3pm; winter, Tues–Sun 8:30am–3pm. **Trolleybus:** 3; or a 10-minute walk from Syntagma Square.

BENAKI MUSEUM, 1 Koumbari St. Tel. 361-1617.
This museum houses a collection of folk art, costumes, jewelry, pottery, and relics from the Greek War of Independence in 1821, including Lord Byron's writing desk and pen.
Admission: 400 Dr ($2.10) adults, 200 Dr ($1.05) students and youths 12–16, free for children under 12.
Open: Wed–Mon 8:30am–2pm. **Trolleybus:** 3; or a five-minute walk from Syntagma Square.

NATIONAL HISTORICAL MUSEUM, 13 Stadiou St. Tel. 323-7617.
Located in the former Parliament buildings, halfway between Omonia Square and Syntagma Square, this museum represents Greek history with objects from the Byzantine era, the Turkish occupation, the Balkan War, and the War of Independence.
Admission: 200 Dr ($1.05) adults, 100 Dr (50¢) students and youths 12–16, free for children under 12; free for everyone Tues.
Open: Tues–Fri 9am–1:30pm, Sat–Sun 9am–12:30pm. **Bus:** 1, 2, or 4 to the first stop going toward Omonia Square; or a five-minute walk from Syntagma Square.

GREEK FOLK ART MUSEUM, 17 Kidathineon St. Tel. 322-9031.
In Plaka, just four blocks from Syntagma Square, this museum is housed in a former Turkish mosque. Greek costumes, jewelry, paintings, and stamps are on display.
Admission: 400 Dr ($2.10) adults, 200 Dr ($1.05) youths 12–16, free for students and children under 12.
Open: Tues–Sat 10am–2pm. **Directions:** Walk up Filellinon Street, five minutes from Syntagma Square.

ATHENS CATHEDRAL, Mitropoleos St., between Syntagma and Monastiraki Sqs.
A beautiful Byzantine-style cathedral, Athens's Greek Orthodox headquarters features a modern stone facade and is decorated with silver votive offerings. The smaller cathedral in its shadow, built in the 13th century, is a gem from the Byzantine era. Its white marble and red-brick facade and cupolas are an eye-catching sight amid the modern apartment buildings.
Admission: Free.
Open: Daily 6am–1pm and 4–7pm. **Directions:** Walk five minutes downhill from Syntagma Square.

LYCABETTUS HILL, Plutarchou St. Tel. 722-7065.
This hill, with the highest elevation in Athens, provides superb views of the city, Piraeus, and beyond. A funicular (called a *teleferik*), runs every 10 minutes, and transports you from the foot of the hill to the white St. George's Church, with its huge Greek flag, at the top, a landmark clearly visible from almost everywhere in Athens.

GREECE

Athens

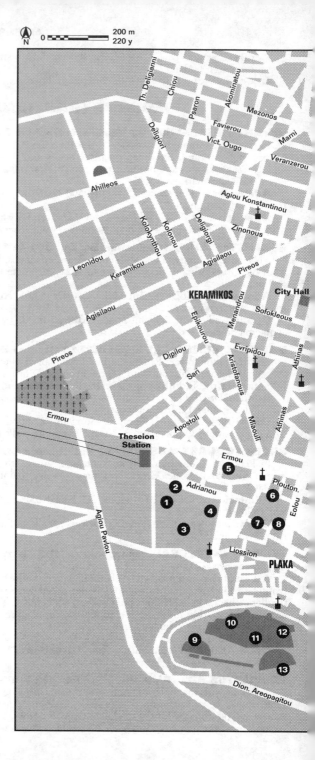

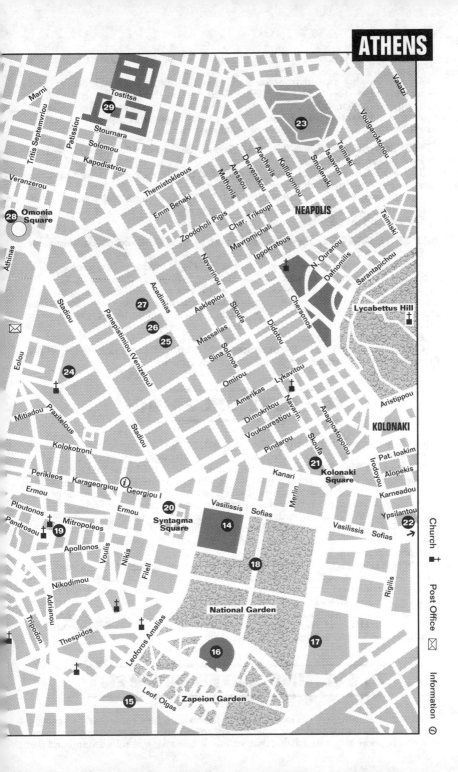

ATHENS

Church **⊫**

Post Office ⊠

Information ⊘

Admission: Lycabettus Hill, free; funicular, 300 Dr ($1.55) round-trip (walking is free).

Open: Viewing area in front of St. George's, daily 24 hours. Funicular, June 7–Sept 15, Mon–Tues 9:30am–12:45am, Wed 8:45am–12:45am, Thurs 10:30am–12:45am, Fri 9:30am–12:45am, Sat–Sun 8:45am–12:45am; Sept 16–June 6, stops running at 12:15am nightly. **Bus:** 3, 7, or 13 from Syntagma Square to Leoforos Vassilissis Sofias Street at the corner of Plutarchou Street.

CEMETERY OF KERAMIKOS, 148 Ermou St., near Monastiraki Sq. in Plaka. Tel. 346-3552.

The oldest gravestones in Greece are located in this ancient burial ground. An interesting and unusual sight.

Admission: 400 Dr ($2.10) adults, 200 Dr ($1.05) students and youths 12–16, free for children under 12.

Open: Tues–Sun 8:30am–3pm.

NATIONAL GARDEN, Amalias St., next to the Parliament Building off Syntagma Sq.

When Greece was a monarchy, this was the king's private palace garden. Now public, the area combines a park, garden, and zoo, with shady trees, benches, a café, small lakes and ponds with ducks, swans, and a few peacocks. A favorite meeting place for young and old Athenians on hot summer days, it's a good spot for picnics and for jogging. The huge palacelike building in the middle of the garden is an exhibition and reception hall.

Admission: Free.

Open: Daily 7am–10pm. **Directions:** Walk from Syntagma Square to the yellow Parliament House, then turn right onto Leoforos Amalias Street.

7. SAVVY SHOPPING

Athens is not especially known for shopping but, like any big city, it has a variety of mainstream and offbeat shops. The most unique items, at the best prices, are sold in and around the **Flea Market,** a daily spectacle starting at Monastiraki Square. It's best on Sunday, when it's packed with locals. Other days are good too, offering the usual tourist-oriented trinkets, statues, jewelry, sandals, and various handmade goods. Poke around some of the nearby side streets for antiques and other finds.

Inexpensive to mid-priced fashions can be found on the many streets within the Omonia Square/Syntagma Square/Monastiraki Square triangle. For top-of-the-line goods, wander around the smaller streets near Kolonaki Square, located between Syntagma Square and Lycabettus Hill.

Athens has an excellent English-language bookstore, selling both new and used fiction and nonfiction. **Compendium,** 28 Nikis St. (tel. 322-1248), is close to Syntagma Square. In winter it's usually open on Monday and Wednesday from 9am to 5pm, on Tuesday, Thursday, and Friday from 10am to 7pm, and on Saturday from 9am to 3:30pm; in summer, on Monday and Wednesday from 9am to 3pm, on Tuesday, Thursday, and Friday from 9am to 1:30pm and 5:30 to 8:30pm, and on Saturday from 9am to 3:30pm.

8. EVENING ENTERTAINMENT

When it comes to nightlife, Greeks may be the world's best partiers. An evening's activities usually start with dinner around 9pm, an extremely leisurely event that often seems to be more about socializing than eating. When midnight rolls around and the last glass of ouzo is emptied, revelers seek out a *bouzoukieria* for some traditional entertainment, or else head to a dance club, bar, or café. Travelers in their 20s will find their Greek compatriots hanging around the cafés in Kolonaki Square, where it's sometimes hard to find an empty seat among hundreds of chairs. Cafés on Syntagma and Monestiraki Squares also front busy street scenes, and are good places to idle an evening away. Check the daily **Athens News,** sold at most major newsstands, for current cultural and entertainment events, including films, lectures, theater, music, and dance.

THE PERFORMING ARTS

ATHENS OPERA HOUSE, 59 Acadimias St. Tel. 360-0180.

The capital's primary stage for traditional and contemporary opera and theater sponsors productions from the middle of November to the end of April. An English-speaking public relations officer can tell you what's on.

Prices: Tickets, 650–1,900 Dr ($3.40–$10).

Open: Box office, Mon–Sat 9am–1pm and 5–7pm, Sun 10am–1pm and 5–7pm.

BOUZOUKIERIA

TAVERNA MOSTROU, 22 Mnisikleos St. Tel. 322-5337.

One of the largest, oldest, and best-known clubs for traditional Greek music and dancing. Shows here begin about 11pm and last into the wee hours. The entrance cost includes a fixed-menu supper. A la carte dining is available, but expensive.

Admission: 3,500 Dr ($18.40).

REBETIKI ISOTORIA, 181 Ippocratous St. Tel. 642-4937.

Housed in a neoclassical building, this down-scale, smoke-filled room offers old-style live music, played to a mixed crowd of older regulars and younger students and intellectuals. The music usually starts at 11pm, but arrive earlier to get a seat.

Admission: 1,400–2,800 Dr ($7.35–$14.75).

DANCE CLUBS

ALARM, 9 Spiliotopoulou St. Tel. 771-1315.

A converted cinema is now the setting for live local music played to a young, fashion-unconscious crowd. Beer costs 900 Dr ($4.75) and bands usually start around midnight.

Admission: Around 1,700 Dr ($8.95).

ACTUEL CLUB, 44 Kleomenous St., Kolonaki. Tel. 724-9861.

This trilevel club features a sedate piano bar/restaurant up top, a trendy café/bar in the middle, and a pint-sized disco underneath. Good Greek rock plays to Athens's best-looking crowd. Music usually starts around 10:30pm, and drinks cost a steep 1,200 Dr ($6.30).

Admission: Small cover charge on weekends.

AUTOKINISIS, 7 Kifisias Ave, Plothei. Tel. 681-2360.

Athens's trendy 20-something crowd packs shoulder-to-shoulder into this New York–style dance club. There is no dance floor per se; rather, the entire club hops to the beat. The place really goes wild around 2am when new American sounds give way to traditional Greek music. The club is open from 11pm to 3am Tuesday through Saturday, and drinks cost 1,500 Dr ($7.90).

Admission: Cover charge 2,400 Dr ($12.65) on the weekends.

FILM

Movies are popular in Athens, and shows during the evening are often sold out. Most of the movie houses are near Omonia Square, on Stadiou or Patisson Street. Films are usually screened in their original language and tickets cost 1,000 Dr ($5.25).

9. EASY EXCURSIONS

Located as it is right in the center of the country, Athens makes a perfect launching pad for explorations throughout Greece. Ferries leave from Athens's port, Piraeus, for a myriad idyllic islands, and Olympic Airways' domestic flights to the islands and other destinations in Greece are refreshingly moderate in price. For a list of ferry or long-distance bus routes and times, drop by the information window of the National Tourist Organization of Greece, in Syntagma Square. For flight schedules, try any Olympic Airways office.

DELPHI

Everyone's favorite excursion is to Delphi, just three hours from Athens by bus. The bus to Delphi leaves from the station at 260 Lission St. (take bus no. 24 from Amalias Street in front of the National Gardens to the bus station).

Famous in antiquity for its oracle, which made divine prophesies, Delphi has attracted pilgrims for several millennia and was consulted by many of the greatest figures in ancient history. Inscriptions on the temple pediments advised visitors "Know thyself" and "Nothing in excess." Today Delphi is one of Greece's most exciting ancient sites.

The main archeological site is a 10- to 15-minute walk from the bus stop, from where two roads slope upward at a fork in the highway. Walk up the road on the right, straight through town and beyond. After you exit the small town you'll pass the museum on your left and soon afterward you'll arrive at the ruins. The lovely Temple of Athena Pronaia is about another 10 minutes farther down the road.

You'll pass the **tourist office,** in the center of town at Pavlou and 44 Frederikis St. (tel. 0265/82-900), where you can pick up a pamphlet on Delphi with a map of the ruins, as well as bus and other information. The tourist office is open April to September, daily from 8am to 9pm; and October to March, Monday through Saturday from 8am to 8pm and on Sunday from 10am to 3pm.

ATTRACTIONS

THE ARCHEOLOGICAL SITE. Tel. 0265/82-313.
After passing along the Sacred Way, with important civic religious buildings, you'll arrive at the Temple of Apollo, site of the ancient oracle of Delphi. Six columns remain, only one its original height. The setting is stunning, with a valley in front and tall rocky mountains rising immediately behind, with more in the distance. Behind the Temple of Apollo is the well-preserved theater, with complete tiers of seating. A short hike up the hill from the main site brings you to an impressive, long oval stadium with seating still intact.

Admission: 1,000 Dr ($5.25).
Open: Summer, Mon–Sat 8am–7pm, Sun 8:30am–3pm; rest of the year, Mon 7:30am–5pm, Tues–Fri 7:30am–5:30pm, Sat–Sun 8:30am–3pm.

DELPHI MUSEUM. Tel. 0265/82-313.
After your visit to the archeological site, you can examine some of the fine architectural detail of the Sanctuary of Delphi from the 6th century B.C., including various friezes, sculptures, votive offerings, and more.

Admission: 1,000 Dr ($5.25).
Open: Summer, Mon noon–7pm, Tues–Sat 8am–7pm, Sun 8:30am–3pm; rest of the year, Mon 11am–5pm, Tues–Fri 7:30am–5:30pm, Sat–Sun 8:30am–3pm.

OTHER DAY TRIPS

Delphi is just the beginning of the rich antiquity that can be explored around Athens. Other famous sites include **Corinth,** with its mostly 1st century A.D. ruins of a powerful Greek city; **Mycenae,** the city of Agamemnon, with ruins of the royal citadel and "beehive" tombs dating from 1200 B.C.; and **Epidaurus,** home to the best-preserved ancient theater in Greece, with seating for 14,000.

Buses serve all these destinations; ask the tourist office for the latest schedule (note that buses leave from two different stations in Athens). You can also join a tour offered by the **Viking Travel Office,** 3 Filellinon St. (tel. 322-9383). There are tours to Delphi, and one to three islands for about 9,000 Dr ($47.35) in high season without lunch, 9,500 Dr ($50) with lunch. Note that these are special prices for Frommer's readers, and in fact Viking offers discounts on all tours for those bearing this guide: 10% off the cost of half- and full-day city sightseeing tours and cruises (such as the Athens City Tour, Cape Sounion, and a three-island cruise); 10% off the cost of a four-day coach tour to Delphi, Epidaurus, Mycenae, Corinth, and Eleusis, with an English-speaking guide and half-board accommodations; and about 40% off the cost of a seven-day discovery cruise to Mykonos, Santorini, and the Cyclades, including accommodations, breakfast and light lunch, harbor fees, and an English-speaking guide (available only a week before departure). Viking Travel Office is open in summer, daily from 8am to 6pm; October to March, Monday through Friday from 8am to 4pm.

BARCELONA

With the Olympic Games well over, Barcelona can now savor the multitude of enhancements and improvements it made in preparation for that international event. Several times in the course of its 2,000-year-plus history Barcelona has similarly seized the moment and squeezed the most out of it. In 1888 and 1929 it hosted World Exhibitions that, like last year's Olympic Games, altered the face of the city forever.

In A.D. 874 Barcelona was nicknamed "La Ciudad Condal" for the counts who negotiated its independence. In the 13th and 14th centuries it was the capital of the Kingdom of Catalonia and Aragón, whose colonial influence extended to Sicily and Greece. In 1259 it promulgated the first code of European maritime law, upon which other Mediterranean states modeled their own.

Long Spain's most progressive and "European" city, Barcelona, the Mediterranean's third-largest port, was also the country's first industrial enclave in the late 19th century.

From the Gothic cathedral to Gaudí's Sagrada Familia to Ricardo Bofill's new National Theater, Barcelona demonstrates an enviable flair for eye-catching architecture. From Picasso to Miró to Tàpies, it has fostered a great deal of artistic genius.

Now eager to be a key player within Spain, the European Community, and the world beyond, Barcelona has everything going for it—good looks, good business sense, an appreciation for culture in all its forms, and an unerring eye for style.

1. FROM A BUDGET TRAVELER'S POINT OF VIEW

BARCELONA BUDGET BESTS

At lunch, the three-course *menu del día* is usually a bargain. Make this your main meal and stick to snacks, sandwiches, pizzas, or *tapas* (assorted hors d'oeuvres) in the evening.

January, February, and July are sale months. Toward the end of these months prices are truly rock-bottom.

SPECIAL DISCOUNT OPPORTUNITIES

FOR STUDENTS Students with appropriate ID enjoy reduced or free admission at most of the city's museums and monuments.

The **"Youth Card"** issued by the Generalitat of Catalonia makes it easy and cheap for young people to get the most out of their stay. The "Youth Card" guide lists almost 8,000 establishments offering special discounts. For information, contact Direcció General de Joventut, Generalitat de Catalunya, Viladomat, 319, 08029 Barcelona (tel. 3/322-90-61), open Monday through Friday from 9am to 2pm and 3 to 7pm.

WHAT THINGS COST IN BARCELONA	U.S. $
Taxi from the airport to Les Rambles	18.75
Metro fare	1.05
Local telephone call	.20
Double room at the Hotel Havana Palace (deluxe)	385.00
Double room at the Hotel Colón (moderate)	245.00
Double room at the Hostal-Residencia Windsor (budget)	63.00
Continental breakfast	4.95
Lunch for one, without wine, at La Poma (moderate)	14.30
Lunch for one, without wine, at Self Naturista (budget)	6.90
Dinner for one, without wine, at El Dorado Petit (deluxe)	75.00
Dinner for one, without wine, at Tramonti 1980 (moderate)	36.45
Dinner for one, without wine, at Pitarra Restaurant (budget)	20.00
Pint of beer (caña)	1.15–1.40
Coca-Cola in a restaurant	1.40
Cup of coffee	.95
Roll of ASA 100 color film, 36 exposures	5.65
Admission to Museu de Picasso	5.70
Movie ticket	3.65–6.50
Theater ticket	8.60 and up

The following establishments also offer special services and discounts to young travelers: the **Youth Travel Office** (Oficina de Turisme Juvenil—TIVE), Gravina, 1, 08001 Barcelona (tel. 3/302-06-82), open Monday through Friday from 9am to 1pm and 4 to 5:30pm; and **Information Service and Youth Activities** (SIPAJ), Rble. Catalunya, 5-Pral., 08007 Barcelona (tel. 3/301-40-46), open Monday through Friday from 5 to 9pm.

FOR EVERYONE TAP Air Portugal (tel. toll free 800/221-7370) has increased its service to Spain, so look for special fares to Barcelona via Lisbon. Also ask about Iberia's (tel. toll free 800/772-4642) "Barcelona Amigo" offer.

WORTH THE EXTRA BUCKS

Performances at the Gran Teatre del Liceu and the Palau de la Música Catalán are definitely worth spending a bit more for. Sampling Catalonia's fine *cavas* (champagnes) in one of the city's sophisticated *champañerías* also makes a good splurge.

2. PRETRIP PREPARATIONS

DOCUMENTS Citizens of the U.S. and Canada need only a valid passport for stays of up to three months.

WHAT TO PACK In summer take light clothing. In spring and fall take clothes that can be layered in the event of the occasional cooling rain. In winter a light coat or lined raincoat teamed with a sweater should be sufficiently warm. For the Old Town's cobblestone streets take sensible walking shoes.

WHEN TO GO   Temperatures are mild most of the year but the humidity is high, so the heat of July and August can be oppressive. Rain is most likely to fall in spring and autumn, but these are still the best times to go.

Barcelona's Average Daytime Temperature

	Jan	Feb	Mar	Apr	May	June	July	Aug	Sept	Oct	Nov	Dec
Temp. (°F)	49	51	54	59	64	72	76	76	72	64	57	51

Special Events   Locals gather regularly to **dance the *sardanas,*** a sedate, regional folk dance. Watch them in front of the cathedral on Saturday at 6:30pm and on Sunday at noon; at Plaça Sant Jaume on Sunday and holidays at 7pm in summer and 6:30pm in winter; and at Plaça Sant Felip Neri the first Saturday of the month at 6pm.

The night of June 23 Barcelona celebrates the **Verbena de Sant Joan** with bonfires in the streets and plazas. It is customary to eat the coca, a special sweet made from fruit and pine nuts, and attend the festivities on Montjuïc that culminate in an impressive fireworks display.

Every year during the second half of June there is a **Festival de Flamenco** (tel. 317-57-57 for information).

During the week of September 24 are the celebrations of the **fiestas de la Mercé,** Barcelona's most important and popular festival. Concerts and theatrical performances animate the Plaças Sant Jaume, de la Seu, del Rei, Sot del Migdia, Escorxador, and Reial, and giants, devils, dragons, and other fantastic creatures parade through the Old Town. At the end of it all is a music pageant and fireworks.

During the month of November, the **Festival Internacional de Jazz de Barcelona** takes place in the Palau de la Música Catalana.

BACKGROUND READING   For insight into Catalonia's role in the Spanish Civil War, read George Orwell's *Homage to Catalonia* (Harcourt Brace Jovanovich). For general insight into Spain, pick up Nikos Kazantzakis's *Spain.* See also "Background Reading" in "Pretrip Preparations" in the Madrid chapter.

3. ORIENTATION & GETTING AROUND

ARRIVING IN BARCELONA

FROM THE AIRPORT   **El Prat Airport** is about 7½ miles from center city. A train runs between the airport and the Estació Sants every 30 minutes between 6am and 11pm. The trip takes about 15 minutes and costs 240 ptas. ($2.50). A convenient, comfortable bus runs between the airport and Plaça Catalunya every 15 minutes Monday through Friday between 5:30am and 11pm, and on Saturday, Sunday, and holidays every 30 minutes from 6am to 10:45pm. The trip takes about 15 minutes and costs 440 ptas. ($4.60). A taxi into town costs about 1,800 ptas. ($18.75).

FROM THE TRAIN STATION   Most national and international trains arrive at **Estació Sants,** Estació de França, or the passeig de Gràcia stations, all centrally located and linked to the municipal metro network.

INFORMATION

The following **tourist offices** offer basic maps, materials, and timely information on exhibitions and other cultural events: Estació Sants, open daily from 8am to 8pm;

WHAT'S SPECIAL ABOUT BARCELONA

Architectural Highlights
- [ ] Gaudí's Sagrada Familia, an immense, modernist cathedral crawling its way to completion.
- [ ] Palau de la Música Catalana, an outstanding example of modernism and one of the world's finest concert halls.

Attractions
- [ ] La Rambla, one of the world's most entertaining boulevards.
- [ ] The Gothic cathedral, noted for its cloisters, *Cristo de Lepanto*, and tomb of Santa Eulàlia, one of the city's patron saints.

Museums
- [ ] Museu Picasso, home to an enlightening collection of the master's works.
- [ ] Fundació Joan Miró, with more than 10,000 works by this Catalan artist.

Vistas
- [ ] From the top of Montjuïc.

- [ ] From the top of Mount Tibidabo.
- [ ] From the Transbordador del Puerto.
- [ ] From Parc Güell.

Parks
- [ ] Parc de la Ciutadella, home to the zoo, the Museu d'Art Modern, and many attractive sculptures and fountains.

Neighborhoods
- [ ] Barri Gòtic, a maze of medieval streets sprouting growing numbers of shops.

Transportation
- [ ] *Tramvía blau*, running amid the stately modernist mansions of Avinguda Tibidabo.

Excursions
- [ ] Montserrat Monastery, a popular pilgrimage destination and home of the Black Virgin, one of Catalonia's patron saints.

Ajuntament de Barcelona, Plaça Sant Jaume, open June 24 to September 30, Monday through Friday from 9am to 8pm and on Saturday from 8:30am to 2:30pm; Estació de França, avinguda Marqués de l'Argentera, open daily from 8am to 8pm; the Centre de Informació, Palau de la Virreina, La Rambla, 99, open June 24 to September 30, Monday through Friday from 9:30am to 9pm and on Saturday from 10am to 2pm; and the airport information office, open Monday through Saturday from 9:30am to 8pm and on Sunday and holidays from 9:30am to 3pm.

For information on Barcelona, Catalunya, and the rest of Spain, the **Oficina de Informació Turística,** Gran Via C.C., 658 (tel. 301-74-43), open Monday through Friday from 9am to 7pm and on Saturday from 9am to 2pm.

If you want to phone for information, this last office is your best bet. Or call **Tourist Information** (tel. 490-91-71). For information on cultural activities and museums, call 301-12-21.

During the summer, uniformed **"roving hosts"** in the principal tourism areas offer assistance in various languages.

For **24-hour information** on what's happening in Barcelona, dial 010.

CITY LAYOUT

Barcelona took municipal shape under the Romans and later expanded from a medieval core at the water's edge. Between the harbor and the ordered grid of the 19th-century Eixample lies the **Ciutat Vella (Old Town).** Bordered by the Parc de la Ciutadella to the northeast and the fortress-topped hill of Montjuïc to the southwest, its focal point is the medieval **Barri Gòtic.**

To the east is the **Barri de la Ribera,** focal point of Barcelona's 13th- and

14th-century colonial and commercial expansion. Below the Parc de la Ciutadella and east of the harbor is **Barceloneta,** home to the city's seafarers and a proliferation of seafood restaurants—most of them mediocre—at the edge of the Vila Olímpica.

At the Barri Gòtic's western edge is **La Rambla,** which bisects the Old Town. On the other side, down by the port, is the notorious **Barri Xinés** (Barrio Chino in Spanish), a sometimes-dangerous neighborhood, best avoided at night.

To the north of Plaça Catalunya is the **Eixample,** a grid of wide streets that is the product of Barcelona's 19th-century industrial prosperity. North of the Eixample are **Gràcia,** an area of small squares and lively bars and restaurants that was once a separate village, and **Tibidabo,** Barcelona's tallest mountain.

GETTING AROUND

You can easily get around by metro, bus, funicular, cable car, taxi, train, or on foot. Given the city's frequent traffic congestion, the metro and walking are quickest. Note that public transport fares are slightly higher on weekends and holidays. Call 412-00-00 Monday through Friday from 7:30am to 8:30pm and on Saturday from 8am to 2pm for general information on public transportation throughout the city.

A guide indicating all bus, train, and metro lines is available for 85 ptas. (90¢) at newsstands, bookstores, and the Ronda Sant Pau, Plaça Universitat, and Sants-Estació metro stops.

BY SUBWAY The metro and integrated commuter train lines (called FF.CC. de la Generalitat) operate Monday through Thursday from 5am to 11pm; on Friday, Saturday, and holiday eves from 5am to 1am; on weekday holidays from 6am to 11pm; and on Sunday from 6am to midnight. The one-way fare is 95 ptas. ($1), but two **10-trip cards (Tarjetas T-1 and T-2)** will save you money. Tarjeta T-1, which costs 560 ptas ($5.85), entitles you to travel by bus, metro, tramvía blau, Montjuïc funicular, and the FF.CC. de la Generalitat within the city limits; Tarjeta T-2, which costs 500 ptas. ($5.20), permits travel on all the same transport except the bus. **Special one-, three-, and five-day passes (*abono temporales*),** costing 385, 1,075, and 1,500 ptas. ($4, $11.20, and $15.60) respectively, permit unlimited travel on the metro and buses. These are sold at the following TMB (Transports Metropolita de Barcelona) offices: Ronda Sant Pau, 43; Plaça Universitat (vestibule of the metro station); and Sants-Estació (vestibule of metro Line 5). A metro map is available free at most metro stations.

BY BUS Barcelona's color-coded buses run daily from 6:30am to 10pm, with night service on the main thoroughfares until 4am (or in some cases all night). Red buses originate or pass through the heart of the city; yellow buses cut across the city beyond the central districts; green buses serve the periphery; and yellow buses run at night through the city center. The fare is 100 ptas. ($1.05).

BY TELEFÉRICO, TRAMVÍA BLAU & FUNICULAR The **Transbordador del Puerto** runs between Barceloneta and Montjuïc with an intermediate stop on the Moll de Barcelona near the Columbus Monument. It's in operation October to March, Monday through Friday from noon to 5:45pm, on Saturday from 11:45am to 7pm, and on Sunday and holidays from 11:15am to 7pm; April to June 22, Monday through Friday from noon to 7pm and on Saturday, Sunday, and holidays from 11:30am to 8pm; June 23 to September 17, Monday through Friday from noon to 7:30pm and on Saturday, Sunday, and holidays from noon to 8:30pm; September 18–30, Monday through Friday from noon to 6:45pm, on Saturday from noon to 7:45pm, and on Sunday and holidays from noon to 7:15pm. It runs about every 15 minutes and the one-way fare ranges from 630 ptas ($6.55) to 740 ptas ($7.70), depending on the distance traveled.

The **Montjuïc funicular** runs between the Paral.lel metro stop (Line 3) and the amusement park at the top of Montjuïc on weekends from September 30 to June and daily in summer, during the Christmas holidays, and during Holy Week from 11am to 9:30pm. The weekday fare is 135 ptas. ($1.40). The **Teleférico de Montjuïc** (cable

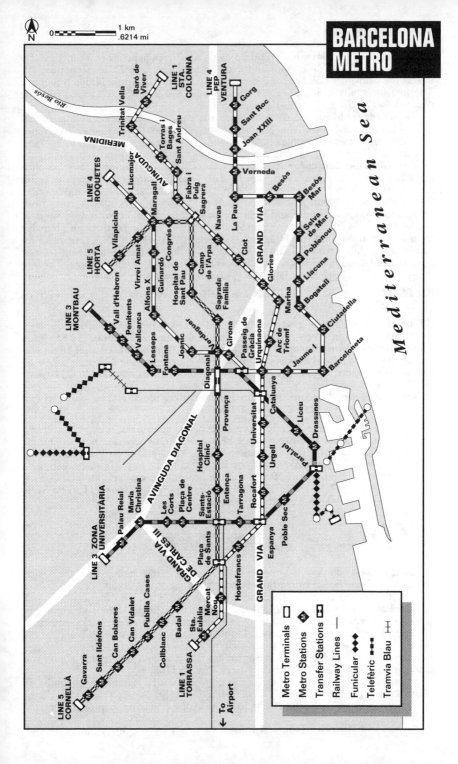

car) linking the funicular with Montjuïc castle runs from September 30 to June 21, weekends from 11am to 2:45pm and 4 to 7:30pm; and June 22 to September 29, during the Christmas holidays, and during Holy Week, daily from 11:30am to 9pm. The fare for adults is 300 ptas. ($3.10) one way, 540 ptas. ($5.60) round-trip; for children 4–12, 350 ptas. ($3.65) round-trip.

The **tramvía blau,** which runs from passeig de Sant Gervasi/avinguda del Tibidabo to the bottom of the Tibidabo funicular, operates weekends all year and daily during summer, Christmas holidays, and Holy Week from 7:05am to 9:55pm. The fare is 150 ptas. ($1.55) one way, 240 ptas. ($2.50) round-trip.

The **Tibidabo funicular** runs to the top of Tibidabo mountain at least once every half hour: September 25 to May 31, daily from 7:15am to 9:45pm; June 1–26, Monday through Friday from 7:15 to 9:45pm, and on Saturday, Sunday, and holidays from 7:15am to 11:30pm; June 28 to September 15, Monday through Thursday from 7:15am to 2:30am, on Friday and Saturday from 7:15am to 3:30am, and on Sundays and holidays from 7:15am to 11:30pm; September 16–24, Monday through Thursday from 7:15am to 9:45pm, on Friday and Saturday from 7:15am to 3:30am, and on Sunday and holidays from 7:15am to 11:30pm. On June 23 (Verbena de Sant Joan) it operates until 4:30am; on September 23 (Puente de la Mercè), until 11:30pm. The fare is 240 ptas. ($2.50) one way, 390 ptas. ($4.05) round-trip.

ON FOOT   Barcelona's Ciutat Vella can easily be covered on foot, as can much of the Eixample.

BY TAXI   Most Barcelona taxis are black and yellow. When available, they display a LIBRE sign and/or lit green roof light. The initial charge is 275 ptas. ($2.85); each additional kilometer is 80 ptas. (85¢). This jumps to 100 ptas. ($1.05) after 10pm and on Saturday, Sunday, and holidays. Supplemental charges include 325 ptas. ($3.40) to and from the airport, 75 ptas. (80¢) when departing from a train station, and 110 ptas. ($1.15) for each large bag.

Taxi stands are abundant, you can hail a cab on the street, or you can call 386-50-00, 330-08-04, 321-88-33, or 300-38-11.

BY CAR   Having a car in Barcelona is a burden, and renting one is expensive. If you must have one, book a fly/drive package before you go. Otherwise, shop around for the best deal among the following agencies with in-town and airport offices: **Atesa,** carrer de Balmes, 141 (tel. 237-81-40, or 302-28-32 at the airport); **Avis,** carrer de Arugó, 235 (tel. 215-84-30, or 379-40-26 at the airport); **Europcar,** carrer de Consell de Cent, 363 (tel. 317-58-76, or 379-90-51 at the airport); and **Hertz,** Estació Sants (tel. 490-86-62, or 241-13-81 at the airport).

 FAST *BARCELONA*

Addresses   In Spain, street numbers follow street names and the ° sign indicates the floor. *Dcha.* or *izqda.* following the floor means "right" or "left." *Baja* refers to the ground floor, and the Spaniard's first floor (1°) is the American's second.

Banks   Money can be changed at any bank advertising CAMBIO; a commission is always charged, which makes cashing small amounts of traveler's checks expensive. When banks are closed (see "Business Hours," below), you can change money at the Estació Sants: in winter, daily from 8am to 8pm; in summer, Monday through Saturday from 8am to 10pm and on Sunday from 8am to 2pm and 4pm to 10pm. You can change money at the airport daily from 7am to 11pm.

If you're really stuck, there are Chequepoint offices at La Rambla, 5, 64, and 130, where you can change money daily from 9am to midnight; although they don't charge a commission, their exchange rate is lower than the prevailing rate offered by the banks.

Business Hours   Hours at **banks** vary, but are usually Monday through

Friday from 8:30am to 2pm and on Saturday from 8:30am to 1pm (except in summer). Typical **office** hours are Monday through Friday 9am to 1:30pm and 4 to 7pm, but some offices have special summer hours from 8am to 3pm. **Shop** hours vary widely, but the norm is from 10am to 1:30pm and 5 to 8pm.

Consulates The **U.S. Consulate,** via Laietana, 33 (tel. 319-95-50), is open Monday through Friday from 9am to 12:30pm and 3 to 5pm. The **Canadian Consulate,** at via Augusta, 125 (tel. 209-06-34), is open Monday through Friday from 9am to 1pm. The **Consulate of the U.K.,** at avinguda Diagonal, 477 (tel. 322-21-51), is open Monday through Friday from 9:30am to 1:30pm and 4 to 5pm.

Currency The unit of currency is the Spanish **peseta (pta.),** with coins of 1, 5, 25, 50, 100, 200, and 500 ptas. Be aware that the 500-peseta coin is easily confused with the 100-peseta coin. Notes are issued in 500 (rare nowadays), 1,000, 2,000, 5,000, and 10,000 denominations. Watch out for the new 1- and 5-peseta coins: The former is tin-colored and tiny, the latter pale bronze and much smaller than the familiar 5 pesetas.

Doctors Call 212-85-85 for a doctor or 417-19-94 for a nurse. If you require hospital attention, go to Hospital Clínic i Provincial, Casanova, 143 (tel. 323-14-14), or Hospital Creu Roja de Barcelona, Dos de Maig, 301 (tel. 433-15-51).

Emergencies In a medical emergency, call 061. For the **police,** call 091 or 092. In the event of **fire,** call 080.

Holidays For local holidays see "Special Events" in "Pretrip Preparations," above. Others include: January 1, January 6, Good Friday, Easter Monday, May 1, May 15, Corpus Christi (May or June), June 24, August 15, September 11, October 12, November 1, December 6, December 8, and December 25–26.

Hospitals See "Doctors," above.

Information See "Orientation and Getting Around," above.

Language Catalan, the indigenous language of Barcelona and Catalonia, is the second official language of the region, and most signs appear either solely in Catalan or in both Catalan and Spanish.

THE PESETA & THE DOLLAR

At this writing $1 = approximately 96 ptas. (or 1 pta. = 1¢), and this was the rate of exchange used to calculate the dollar values given in this chapter (rounded to the nearest nickel). This rate fluctuates from time to time and may not be the same when you travel to Spain. Therefore the following table should be used only as a guide:

Ptas.	U.S.	Ptas.	U.S.
5	.05	1,000	10.42
10	.10	1,500	15.63
15	.16	2,000	20.83
20	.21	2,500	26.04
25	.26	3,000	31.25
30	.31	3,500	36.46
40	.42	4,000	41.67
50	.52	4,500	46.88
75	.78	5,000	52.08
100	1.04	5,500	57.29
150	1.56	6,000	62.50
200	2.08	6,500	67.71
250	2.60	7,000	72.92
500	5.21	7,500	78.13

Laundry/Dry Cleaning Lavandería/Tintorer ía Molas, carrer de les Moles, 8 (tel. 301-20-92), near the Plaça de Catalunya, offers both laundry and dry-cleaning services Monday through Friday from 9am to 2pm and 4:30 to 8pm, and on Saturday from 9am to 2pm. Up to 7 kilos (15½ lb.) of laundry, washed and dried, costs 1,100 ptas. ($11.45). Autoservicio Lavandería Roca, Raurich, 20 (tel. 231-82-94), in the Barri Gòtic, offers self-service facilities Monday through Saturday from 8am to 7pm (closed Saturday in July and August).

Lost and Found If you've lost something, dial 317-38-79. If you've lost something on public transportation, contact the metro office in Plaça Catalunya across from Carrer Bergara (tel. 318-52-93).

Mail Post offices are generally open Monday through Friday from 9am to 2pm. The central post office in Plaça Antoni López (tel. 318-38-31) is open Monday through Friday from 9am to 10pm and on Saturday from 9am to 2pm. Letters and postcards to the U.S. cost 100 ptas. ($1.05).

Newspapers Barcelona's leading dailies are *La Vanguardia* and *El Periódico.* The national *El País,* Spain's leading daily, prints a Barcelona edition. Foreign-language newspapers are readily available at newsstands along La Rambla and throughout the Eixample.

Photographic Needs Panorama, La Rambla, 125 (tel. 317-89-24), is open Monday through Saturday from 9:30am to 8pm to satisfy most of your photographic needs, including processing. Two Panorama branches offer the same services and hours: passeig de Gràcia, 4 (tel. 318-37-00) and Calvet, 15 (tel. 202-03-30).

Police Call 091 or 092. The police station at La Rambla, 43 (tel. 301-90-60), offers 24-hour service. You will also see small, roving trailers marked OFICINA DE DENUNCIAS where you can seek assistance or report a crime.

Radio/TV Private television stations have just come to Spain and the offering in Catalan, Spanish, and other languages is growing by the day.

Religious Services Most of Barcelona's churches are Roman Catholic. Masses are generally held between 7am and 2pm and between 7 and 9pm on Sunday and holidays, and between 7 and 9pm on Saturday. Mass in English is held at 10:30am on the first and third Sunday of the month at Paroisse Française, Anglí, 15 (tel. 204-49-62), and Anglican Mass in English is celebrated every Sunday at 11am and every Wednesday at 11:30am at Saint George Church, Sant Joan de la Salle, 41 (tel. 417-88-67).

Shoe Repair For a quick fix, go to Rápido López, plazueleta de Montcada, 5, open Monday through Friday from 9am to 1pm and 4:30 to 8pm, and on Saturday from 9am to 1pm.

Tax For information on the value-added tax (VAT), known as IVA in Spain, see "Savvy Shopping," below. It runs from 6% on restaurant bills to 33% on luxury items.

Taxis See "Orientation and Getting Around," above.

Telephone Barcelona's **area code** is 93 when calling from elsewhere in Spain, 3 when calling from abroad.

If you call long distance from your hotel or hostal, expect a hefty surcharge. Most **public phone** *"cabinas"* have clear instructions in English. Place at least 15 pesetas' worth of coins in the rack at the top for a local call, and they will roll in as required.

To make an **international call,** dial 07, wait for the tone, and dial the area code(s) and number. Note, however that an international call from a phone booth requires stacks and stacks of heavy 100-peseta coins. As an alternative, international calls can be made at carrer Fontanella, 4, Monday through Saturday from 8:30am to 9pm. You can pay with a credit card, and there is one USA Direct phone which immediately connects you with an AT&T operator. (The lines here are often long.)

Tipping Tipping is by no means obligatory and large tips are not expected. A bellhop should get 50 ptas. (50¢) per bag. Taxi drivers don't get surly if you don't tip them, but 5%–10% is customary. Virtually all restaurants include a service charge in the bill, so a 5% tip usually suffices. At bars and cafeterias, tip 10–100 ptas. (10¢–$1.05), depending on the amount of the bill. The percentage left as a tip decreases as the amount of the bill increases.

Useful Telephone Numbers Airport information (tel. 301-39-93), RENFE (Spanish railways) information (tel. 490-02-02).

4. BUDGET ACCOMMODATIONS

Budget accommodations were never abundant in Barcelona and, in the wake of the Olympic Games, are even less so now as many hostelries upgraded their facilities to capitalize on the wave of 1992 visitors. Most of the low-priced digs are in the Old Town, with a few scattered throughout the Eixample. Rooms without a shower or bath will usually have at least a washbasin.

Note: Unless otherwise indicated, rates below do *not* include breakfast and 6% VAT.

DOUBLES FOR LESS THAN 4,700 PTAS. [$48.95]

HOSTAL DON QUIJOTE, La Rambla, 70, 08002 Barcelona. Tel. 3/302-55-99. 34 rms (17 with tub or shower). **Metro:** Liceu.
$ Rates (including VAT): 2,200 ptas. ($22.90) single; 4,400 ptas. ($45.85) double; 4,950 ptas. ($51.55) triple. No credit cards.
The entrance here, across from the Liceu Theater, is one flight up, and the rooms (threadbare in places) occupy two floors (no elevator). The colorful tile floors and commendable cleanliness rescue these quarters from potential shabbiness. An occasional fanciful furnishing (like a marble-top dresser or similar family heirloom) also helps. No breakfast is served. None of the rooms have toilets.

HOSTAL LAYETANA, Plaça Ramón Berenguer el Gran, 2, 08002 Barcelona. Tel. 3/319-20-12. 20 rms (none with bath). **Metro:** Jaume I.
$ Rates (including VAT): 1,980–2,200 ptas. ($20.60–$22.90) single. 3,300–3,740 ptas. ($34.40–$38.95) double. No credit cards.

ⓕ FROMMER'S SMART TRAVELER: HOTELS

VALUE-CONSCIOUS TRAVELERS SHOULD
TAKE ADVANTAGE OF THE FOLLOWING:

1. Reductions at some hotels if you pay cash instead of with a credit card.
2. Long-term discounts if you're planning to stay more than a week.
3. Bargaining—especially off-season.

QUESTIONS TO ASK IF YOU'RE ON A BUDGET

1. Is there a surcharge for local or long-distance telephone calls? Usually there is, and it can be as high as 40%. Make your calls at the nearest telephone office instead.
2. Is service included or will it be added to your final bill. Likewise, are all taxes included, or will you be billed extra?

Several elevatorless flights up, this hostal has somewhat more spacious rooms than other hotels of its low-priced ilk. It would not be my first choice, but it's among the most economical around, and recent renovations have made it more palatable. All rooms have sinks.

HOSTAL MARITIMA, La Rambla, 4, 08001 Barcelona. Tel. 3/302-31-52. 16 rms (3 with shower). **Metro:** Drassanes.

$ Rates: 1,730 ptas. ($18) single; 2,885 ptas. ($30.05) double; 3,800 ptas. ($39.60) triple; 4,620 ptas. ($48.10) quad. No credit cards.

Exuberant Italian proprietor Vittorio Rosellini runs a clean, disciplined establishment in the lower Rambla near the wax museum. The high-ceilinged rooms with sinks are bare-bones basic but still somehow friendly. This is a favorite with young travelers. There are laundry facilities on the premises, and you can have a load done for 600 ptas. ($6.25). The hostal is two flights up; there's no elevator.

HOSTAL PARISIEN, La Rambla, 114, Pral., 08002 Barcelona. Tel. 3/301-62-83. 15 rms (some with tub or shower only). **Metro:** Liceu.

$ Rates (including VAT): 1,650 ptas. ($17.20) single without tub or shower; 3,300 ptas. ($34.35) double without tub or shower; 3,850 ptas. ($40.10) double or triple with tub or shower. No credit cards.

The entrance to these slightly dingy digs is a few flights up, but the price is right for central accommodation. All rooms have sinks, but none has a toilet. The makeshift furnishings don't seem to faze the hostal's predominantly young clientele, and in general, the camaraderie makes up for some shortcomings in comfort. A washer and dryer are at the disposal of guests, with each load costing 550 ptas. ($5.70).

HOSTAL R. RAMOS, carrer Hospital, 36, 08001 Barcelona. Tel. 3/302-04-30. 15 rms (all with bath). TEL **Metro:** Liceu.

$ Rates (including VAT): 2,750 ptas. ($28.65) single; 4,620 ptas. ($48.10) double; 6,050 ptas. ($63) triple. MC, V.

At a quiet remove from the nearby Rambla, this small hostal offers small rooms (13 doubles, two triples) with truncated tubs in the bath. If you don't mind being a bit cramped, you may be quite comfortable here. No breakfast is served.

PENSION AROSA, Portal de L'Angel, 14, 1°, 08002 Barcelona. Tel. 3/317-36-87. 7 rms (with varying bath facilities, including some doubles with complete bath). **Metro:** Catalunya.

$ Rates: (including VAT): 1,650 ptas. ($17.20) single; 3,300 ptas. ($34.35) double. Additional person 1,000 ptas. ($10.40) extra. No credit cards.

All is clean, comfortable, and quiet at this intimate pension between the Barri Gòtic and the Eixample. The entrance is several flights up (no elevator). All rooms have settees in addition to various combinations of single and double beds. No. 7 is the largest room. Front rooms have balconies.

DOUBLES FOR LESS THAN 6,000 PTAS. ($62.50)

HOSTAL REY DON JAIME I, carrer Jaume I, 11, 08002 Barcelona. Tel. 3/315-41-61. 30 rms (with bath or with shower and toilet). TEL **Metro:** Jaume I.

$ Rates: 3,630 ptas. ($37.80) single with shower and toilet, 4,180 ptas. ($43.55) single with bath; 5,170 ptas. ($53.85) double with shower and toilet, 5,830 ptas. ($60.70) double with bath. Additional person 1,000 ptas. ($10.40) extra. No credit cards.

A solid choice in an excellent location where the recently renovated rooms (all with bright, cheery baths) occupy three floors; there is no elevator. All rooms have a small balcony. Rooms in the back are quieter.

HOSTAL-RESIDENCIA ALHAMBRA, carrer Junqueres, 13, 08003 Bar-

celona. **Tel. 3/317-19-24.** Fax 3/241-22-04. 31 rms (21 with bath, 6 with shower only). TEL **Metro:** Urquinaona.
$ Rates (including VAT): 2,100 ptas. ($21.90) single without bath, 3,730 ptas. ($38.85) single with shower only, 4,475 ptas. ($46.60) single with bath; 4,850 Ptas. ($50.50) double with shower only, 5,595 ptas. ($58.30) double with bath; 4,230 ptas. ($75.30) triple with bath. EURO, V.
This is a basic, clean choice in a nice neighborhood near the Palau de la Música Catalana. The rooms occupy four floors; there is no elevator. One of the best rooms is no. 106; it has a double bed, a single bed, and a terrace facing the back. Some rooms are newly renovated.

HOTEL COSMOS, carrer dels Escudellers, 19, 08002 Barcelona. Tel. 3/317-18-16. Fax 3/412-50-39. 67 rms (all with shower or bath). TEL **Metro:** Drassanes.
$ Rates: 2,970 ptas. ($30.95) single; 4,785 ptas. ($49.85) double; 6,460 ptas. ($67.30) triple. AE, DC, MC, V.
Located near the lower, seedier end of La Rambla, the Cosmos offers no-frills budget digs amid undecorated halls. The white walls of the rooms themselves do much to brighten the clean but rather cramped quarters.

HOTEL INGLÉS, carrer de Boquería, 17-19, 08002 Barcelona. Tel. 3/317-37-70. Fax 3/302-78-70. 29 rms (20 with bath, 9 with sink only). TEL **Metro:** Liceu
$ Rates (including VAT): 2,935 ptas. ($30.55) single with sink only; 4,950 ptas. ($51.55) double with bath; 6,600 ptas ($68.75) triple. AE, DC, MC, V.
Spread across four floors serviced by an elevator, the Inglés's eclectically furnished rooms have tiled floors. Tucked in a narrow side street off La Rambla, the hotel's rooms, especially the interior rooms with a terrace, are quiet.

HOTEL RESIDENCIA NEUTRAL, Rambla de Catalunya, 42, 08007 Barcelona. Tel. 3/487-63-90. 28 rms (most with bath but no toilet). TEL **Metro:** Passeig de Gràcia.
$ Rates: 2,400 ptas. ($25) single with shower only; 3,850 ptas. ($40.10) double with shower only, 5,050 ptas. ($52.60) double with bath; 5,200 ptas. ($54.15) triple with shower only, 6,830 ptas. ($71.15) triple with bath. No credit cards.
A budget choice in a luxury area, the Neutral's entrance is one flight up. Colorful antique floor tiling helps brighten the high-ceilinged rooms furnished with assorted odds and ends. The rooms are small, but the breakfast room with its impressive coffered ceiling and the adjacent TV room are spacious.

PENSION MONT-THABOR, La Rambla, 86, 1a, 08002 Barcelona. Tel. 3/317-66-66. 8 rms (3 with bath, 5 with sink and tub). **Metro:** Liceu.
$ Rates: 1,650 ptas. ($17.20) single; 3,850–4,400 ptas. ($40.10–$45.85) double with sink and tub, 4,730 ptas. ($49.25) double with bath. No credit cards.
Though there are no frills here, all is clean and cozy. This is a solid, pleasant, cheap lodging. There's no elevator.

DOUBLES FOR LESS THAN 9,900 PTAS. [$103.10]

HOSTAL-RESIDENCIA CIUDAD CONDAL, carrer Mallorca, 255, 08008 Barcelona. Tel. 3/215-10-40. 11 rms (singles with shower and toilet; doubles with bath). TEL **Metro:** Passeig de Gràcia.
$ Rates (including VAT): 4,565 ptas. ($47.55) single with shower and toilet; 6,105 ptas. ($63.60) double with bath; 7,920 ptas. ($82.50) triple. No credit cards.
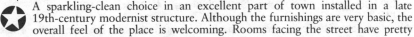 A sparkling-clean choice in an excellent part of town installed in a late 19th-century modernist structure. Although the furnishings are very basic, the overall feel of the place is welcoming. Rooms facing the street have pretty

balconies. Interior rooms face a lovely garden. This hostal is two elevatorless flights up, though.

HOSTAL-RESIDENCIA OLIVA, passeig de Gràcia, 32, 4, 08007 Barcelona. Tel. 3/488-01-62. 16 rms (some with half bath, some with complete bath). **Metro:** Passeig de Gràcia.

$ Rates: (including VAT): 2,200–3,300 ptas. ($22.90–$34.35) single without bath; 4,400–6,600 ptas. ($45.85–$68.75) double without bath; 5,720–7,920 ptas. ($59.60–$82.50) double with shower or bath. Additional person 2,200 ptas. ($22.90) in triple or quad. Shower or bath (if room doesn't have one) 350 ptas. ($3.65) extra. No credit cards.

⭐ Located in a beautiful vintage Eixample building with a correspondingly beautiful vintage elevator, the Oliva offers comely, high-ceilinged rooms with tile floors, lace curtains, and sinks.

HOSTAL-RESIDENCIA WINDSOR, Rambla de Catalunya, 84, 08008 Barcelona. Tel. 3/215-11-98. 15 rms (some with shower and toilet). **Metro:** Passeig de Gràcia or Provença.

$ Rates: 2,750 ptas. ($28.65) single without shower or toilet, 3,520 ptas. ($36.65) single with shower and toilet; 4,950 ptas. ($51.55) double without shower or toilet, 6,050 ptas. ($63) double with shower and toilet. Additional person 1,500 ptas. ($15.60) extra. No credit cards.

⭐ The singles here are small, but quiet and comfortable. The lobby, halls, and TV room are elegantly outfitted. Rooms without a bath share a bath with one other room. All are carpeted. The location is upscale.

HOTEL CATALUÑA, carrer de Santa Anna, 24, 08002 Barcelona. Tel. 3/301-91-50. Fax 3/302-78-70. 40 rms (all with bath). TEL **Metro:** Plaça Catalunya.

$ Rates (including breakfast and VAT): 4,600 ptas. ($47.90) single; 7,940 ptas. $82.70 double. AE, DC, MC, V.

About a block east of the upper Rambla, this spotless budget choice has colorful rugs to brighten the halls.The 40 rooms (including 16 singles) are simply furnished, but all is well maintained.

HOTEL CORTÉS, carrer de Santa Anna, 25, 08002 Barcelona. Tel. 3/317-91-12. Fax 3/302-78-70. 46 rms (all with bath). TEL **Metro:** Plaça Catalunya.

$ Rates: (including breakfast and VAT): 5,305 ptas. ($55.25) single; 8,875 ptas. ($92.45) double; 12,115 ptas. ($126.20) triple. AE, DC, MC, V.

Just off La Rambla, the Cortés is popular with American students on youth tours. All rooms are clean, have modern tile baths, and are being renovated.

HOTEL CONTINENTAL, La Rambla, 138, 2a, 08002 Barcelona. Tel. 3/301-25-70. Fax 3/302-73-60. 32 rms (all with bath). TV TEL **Metro:** Liceu or Plaça Catalunya.

$ Rates (including breakfast): 7,205–10,175 ptas. ($75.05–$106) single; 8,965–10,505 ptas. ($93.40–$109.40) double; 10,395–12,045 ptas. ($108.30–$125.45) triple; 11,715–13,585 ptas. ($122.05–$141.50) quad. AE, MC, V.

⭐ The rooms, all with new baths, cover two floors and have ceiling fans and old-fashioned charm. Among the furnishings that look as if they've been passed down from grandma are brass beds. A cozy salon off the reception area overlooks the Rambla and doubles as a breakfast room, where an ample buffet breakfast is offered. Don't be put off by the hotel's rather worn-looking entrance.

HOTEL RESIDENCIA INTERNACIONAL, La Rambla, 78-80, 08002 Barcelona. Tel. 3/302-25-66. Fax 3/317-61-90. 60 rooms (all with bath).

$ Rates (including breakfast and VAT): 6,920 ptas. ($72.10) single; 9,020 ptas ($93.95) double; 12,306 ptas. ($128.20) triple; 14,400 ptas. ($150) quad. AE, DC, MC, V.

Although somewhat pricey for the parameters of this guide, the Internacional has harbored many Frommer readers over the years, and, with the discount offered them, comes close to this book's budget criteria. The hotel's newly refurbished rooms are bright and cheery (if a bit functional) and feature ample baths. The large, friendly breakfast room overlooks La Rambla where, in the summer, the hotel also runs an al fresco café.

HOTEL SAN AGUSTIN, Plaça Sant Augustí, 3, 08001 Barcelona. Tel. 3/318-16-58. Fax 3/317-29-28. 77 rms (all with bath). A/C TV TEL **Metro:** Liceu.
$ Rates (including breakfast): 5,445–5,665 ptas. ($56.70–$59) single; 8,170–8,580 ptas. ($85.10–$89.35) double; 9,775–10,150 ptas. ($101.80–$105.70) triple; 12,125–15,180 ptas. ($126.30–$158.10) quad; 17,215–17,765 ptas. ($179.30–$185.05) quint. AE, EURO, MC, V.

⭐ Close to La Rambla, but at a quiet remove, this was once a convent but has been a hotel for more than 100 years. It sports a new, inviting entrance and friendly renovated rooms with gleaming white walls and rustic ceiling beams. Highly unusual for a two-star hotel is the large, commendable restaurant offering daily fixed-price lunch and dinner menus with a choice of appetizers, main courses, and desserts. Prices climb in August and during trade fairs, but bearers of this guidebook get a 10% discount if they show it when checking in.

SUPER-BUDGET CHOICES

A YOUTH HOSTEL

ALBERG MARE DE DÉU DE MONTSERRAT, passeig Mare de Déu del Coll, 41-51, 08023 Barcelona. Tel. 3/213-86-33. 160 beds. **Metro:** Vallcarca. **Bus:** 25 or 28.
$ Rates (including breakfast): 935 ptas. ($9.75) per person under 26 with a youth hostel card, 1,400 ptas. ($14.60) per person over 26 with a youth hostel card. Surcharge of 300 ptas. ($3.15) per night for six nights for those without a card (the surcharge applies toward the purchase of a youth hostel card). No credit cards.
This hostel occupies a former modernist mansion in a northern area of the city. The lobby area is colorfully Moorish. There are great views here and there. The hostel closes at midnight, but opens its doors for night owls at 1am and 2am.

CAMPING

Campgrounds are rated luxury, first, second, and third class. All have the following facilities and basic services: drinking water, wash basins, showers, toilets, sinks, wash-houses, electricity, daily rubbish collection, fences, around-the-clock surveillance, medical assistance, a small pharmacy, safekeeping for valuables, and fire extinguishers. Most campgrounds offer special rates outside the peak season—June, July, and August—and discounts for children under age 10.

BARCINO, Cra. Nacional II, km. 616.6, 08950 Esplugues de Llobregat. Tel. 3/372-85-01. 72 stands for camping.
$ Rates: 325–500 ptas ($3.40–$5.20) per adult, 225–400 ptas ($2.35–$4.15) per child under 10; 500 ptas. ($5.20) per tent and car. No credit cards.
Much smaller than the one above, this campground is just at the edge of the city limits and offers a supermarket, bar, and adult and children's pools. It also accepts reservations.

ESTRELLA DE MAR, Autovia Castelldefels, km 16.7, 08860 Castelldefels. Tel. 3/665-32-57. 525 stands for camping.
$ Rates: 425 ptas. ($4.40) per adult, 300 ptas. ($3.10) per child under 10; 425 ptas. ($4.40) per tent and car. No credit cards.

Located by the beach, it offers a supermarket, restaurant, bar, swimming pool, child's pool, and tennis. Reservations are accepted.

LONG-TERM STAYS

Students can stay in any of the following dormitory facilities open all year: **Residencia Universitaria "Athenea"** (women only), Baró de la Barre, 5-7, 08023 Barcelona (tel. 3/210-72-53); **Colegio Mayor "Bonaige"** (women only), Jiménez i Iglesias, 3,08034 Barcelona (tel. 3/204-91-08); **Residencia "Bonanova"** (men only), Sant Joan La Salle, 37, 08022 Barcelona (tel. 3/417-52-21); **Colegio Mayor C.D. "Influencia Católica"** (mixed), Santaló, 27, 08021 Barcelona (tel. 3/209-04-00); **Colegio Mayor Ramón Llull** (mixed), Comte d'Urgell, 187, 08036 Barcelona (tel. 3/430-84-00); and **Colegio Mayor Sant Raímon de Penyafort** (mixed), avinguda Diagonal, 643, 08028 Barcelona (tel. 330-87-11.

WORTH THE EXTRA BUCKS

HOTEL R. REGENCIA COLÓN, Sagristans, 13-17, 08002 Barcelona. Tel. 3/318-98-58. Fax 3/317-28-22. 55 rms. A/C MINIBAR TV TEL **Metro:** Urquinaona or Jaume I.

$ **Rates** (including breakfast): 9,295 ptas. ($96.80) single with shower and toilet; 10,615 ptas. ($110.55) single with bath; 16,060 ptas ($167.30) double with bath; 21,835 ptas. ($227.45) triple with bath. AE, DC, MC, V.

The Regencia Colón's proximity to the cathedral and its bright, cheerful, sound-insulated rooms recommend it as a splurge.

Reservations: Contact Marketing Ahead, 433 Fifth Ave., New York, NY 10016 (tel. 212/686-9213).

5. BUDGET DINING

Eating well in Barcelona is easy. Eating inexpensively is a bit more challenging. The city's restaurants offer a wealth of dishes that are primarily Mediterranean in their basic ingredients—olive oil, almonds, garlic, aromatic herbs, and tomatoes. Sausages like the *butifarra,* succulent roasts, robust game, delicate seafood, savory rice dishes and stews, and myriad renditions of mushrooms are the mainstays of Catalan cuisine. You'll find the highest concentration of low-priced eateries in Ciutat Vella.

Note: More and more restaurants are charging a "cover." They say it's for bread and such, but it's really a most regrettable way to boost the bill.

MEALS FOR LESS THAN 1,600 PTAS. [$16.65]

BAR PINOCHO, La Boquería Market. Tel. 317-17-31.
Cuisine: SPANISH. **Metro:** Liceu.
$ **Prices:** Under 1,100 ptas. ($11.45). No credit cards.
Open: Mon–Sat 6am–6pm. **Closed:** Hols and the first two weeks in Aug.

A Barcelona institution. As you enter the market, take a right. There's no sign—just a picture of Pinocchio. There's also no menu. The owner, Juanito, will gladly let you sample what's cooking on the stove. As there are only eight stools, you'll probably have to eat and run. A good place for breakfast, too.

BAR RESTAURANTE EL NIAGARA, carrer de les Moles, 21. Tel. 318-85-81.
Cuisine: SPANISH/SNACKS. **Metro:** Plaça de Catalunya.

$ Prices: Appetizers 350–600 ptas. ($3.65–$6.25); pizzas 600–750 ptas. ($6.25–$7.80); combination platters 525–875 ptas. ($5.45–$9.10); *menus del día* 950 and 1,050 ptas. ($9.90 and $10.95). No credit cards.
Open: Mon–Sat 8:30am–10pm.
You can enjoy everything from sandwiches, salads, and pizza to a three-course *menu del día* at this very pleasant restaurant where a medieval facade gives way to a contemporary interior decor.

CAN TRIPES, Carrer Sagues, 16. Tel. 200-85-40.
Cuisine: SPANISH/CATALAN. **Metro:** Diagonal or Hospital Clinic.
$ Prices: Appetizers 200–500 ptas. ($2.10–$5.20); main courses 500–1,200 ptas. ($5.20–$12.50). No credit cards.
Open: Lunch daily 1–4pm; snacks daily 4–9pm; dinner daily 9–11pm.
This super-budget bet is the place to go for home-cooking Catalan style. Quaintly decorated with tiles and plaid tablecloths, it's rustic and friendly. The savory escudella is a cross between soup and stew with garbanzos, beans, and potatoes.

THE CHICAGO PIZZA PIE FACTORY, carrer Provença, 300. Tel. 215-94-15.
Cuisine: AMERICAN. **Metro:** Passeig de Gràcia.
$ Prices: Pizzas 775–1,225 ptas. ($8.05–$12.75) individual up to 2,600 ptas. ($27.10) large (for three or four people); main dishes under 1,100 ptas. ($11.45). No credit cards.
Open: Sun–Thurs 12:30pm–1am, Fri–Sat 12:30pm–1:30am.
This sister establishment to Henry J. Bean's Bar and Grill offers pizzas, salads, and such American classics as chili con carne and fried chicken.

FOSTER'S HOLLYWOOD, avinguda Diagonal, 495. Tel. 322-10-15.
Cuisine: AMERICAN. **Metro:** Hospital Clínic.
$ Prices: Main courses under 1,175 ptas. ($12.25). No credit cards.
Open: Daily 1pm–1:15am.
A taste of home. Hamburgers come in quarter- and half-pound versions served with cole slaw, onion rings, and french fries. Also offers spareribs, filet mignon, shish kebab, and a children's menu.

HENRY J. BEAN'S BAR AND GRILL, carrer La Granada del Penedés, 14-16. Tel. 218-29-98.
Cuisine: AMERICAN. **Metro:** Diagonal or FF.CC., Gràcia Station.
$ Prices: Main courses 500–1,300 ptas. ($5.20–$13.55). No credit cards.
Open: Mon–Thurs 12:30pm–1am, Fri–Sat and hols 12:30pm–1:30am.
The atmosphere is English pub, the food American fast. At the bar they serve Budweiser and American tapas (nachos and potato skins), and during the 7–9pm happy hour drinks and tapas are half price. From the salad bar to the burgers, chili, and mud pies, you'll feel right at home.

LA FINESTRA, carrer de les Moles, 25. Tel. 317-58-66.

Ⓕ FROMMER'S SMART TRAVELER: RESTAURANTS

VALUE-CONSCIOUS TRAVELERS SHOULD TAKE ADVANTAGE OF THE FOLLOWING:

1. The three-course *menu del día* offered at lunch.
2. Eating or drinking standing up. Many establishments have two prices: *mesa* (table) and *barra* (bar).

Cuisine: CATALAN. **Metro:** Plaça de Catalunya.
$ **Prices:** Daily specials 440–1,650 ptas. ($4.60–$17.20); *menu del día* 960 ptas. ($10). No credit cards.
Open: Mon–Fri 8am–5pm.
This quaint, charming eatery adorned with tiles and flowers offers primarily fixed-price menus and daily specials at very reasonable prices in a very central location. A good breakfast choice, too.

MANA MANA, passeig de Gràcia, 7. Tel. 215-63-87.
Cuisine: PIZZA/PASTA. **Metro:** Passeig de Gràcia.
$ **Prices:** Sandwiches from 295 ptas. ($3.05); pizzas 740–875 ptas. ($7.70–$9.10); pastas 835–1,090 ptas. ($8.70–$11.35); main courses 870–2,145 ptas. ($9.05–$22.35); *menu del día* 1,235 ptas. ($12.85). EURO, MC, V.
Open: Lunch daily 1–4pm; dinner daily 9pm–midnight.
Mana Mana specializes in sandwiches, pizzas, pastas, ice cream, sorbet, and a delicious assortment of coffee concoctions.

RESTAURANTE EGIPTE, carrer Jerusalem, 3. Tel. 317-30-33.
Cuisine: CATALAN/SPANISH. **Metro:** Liceu.
$ **Prices:** Main courses 495–1,800 ptas. ($5.15–$18.75); *menu del día* 785 ptas. ($8.15). No credit cards.
Open: Lunch Mon–Sat 1–4pm; dinner Mon–Sat 8:30pm–12:30am. **Closed:** Hols and Mon in July and Aug.
One of three restaurants by the same name (the others are at La Rambla, 79 and carrer Jerusalem, 12) that all offer similar fast, economical fare. The gazpacho and chicken with mustard-herb sauce are very good.

SELF NATURISTA, carrer de Santa Anna, 11-15. Tel. 318-23-88.
Cuisine: VEGETARIAN. **Metro:** Plaça Catalunya.
$ **Prices:** Appetizers 140–500 ptas. ($1.45–$5.20); main courses 210–500 ptas. ($2.20–$5.20); *menu del día* 650 ptas. ($6.75). No credit cards.
Open: Mon–Sat 11:30am–10pm. **Closed:** Hols.
Off the upper Rambla, this self-service vegetarian restaurant is extremely cheap and extremely good. The ample selection of salads, main courses, and desserts varies daily, and there is a healthy choice of fresh fruit juices. Seating is McDonald's style.

MEALS FOR LESS THAN 2,000 PTAS.
[$20.85]

EL TURIA, carrer Petxina, 7. Tel. 317-95-09.
Cuisine: SPANISH. **Metro:** Liceu.
$ **Prices:** Main courses 450–2,500 ptas. ($4.70–$26.05); *menu del día* 825 ptas. ($8.60). No credit cards.
Open: Oct–May, lunch Mon–Sat 1–4pm; dinner Mon–Sat 8–11pm. June–Aug 15 and Sept 16–30, lunch Mon–Sat 1–4pm; dinner Mon–Sat 8:30–11:30pm. **Closed:** Aug 16–Sept 15 and for dinner on hols.
Especially lively at lunch, this restaurant is frequented by actors, writers, and other "arty" professionals who live and work nearby. The fare is simple and uneven. Grilled meats are featured.

ES RECO DE LA POMA, in the Royal Hotel, La Rambla, 117. Tel. 301-94-00.
Cuisine: PIZZERIA/GRILL. **Metro:** Plaça Catalunya.
$ **Prices:** Main courses 600–2,000 ptas. ($6.25–$20.85); *menu del día* 1,375 ptas. ($14.30); continental breakfast with orange juice 500 ptas. ($5.20). MC, V.
Open: Downstairs, daily 9am–1am. Upstairs, lunch daily 1–4pm; dinner daily 8–11pm.

Installed in the Royal Hotel, this eatery features salads, pizza, and pasta downstairs and additional Catalan and Spanish dishes upstairs.

GOVINDA, Plaça Vila de Madrid, 4-5. Tel. 318-77-29.
   Cuisine: INDIAN/VEGETARIAN. **Metro:** Plaça Catalunya.
$ Prices: Pizzas 740–1,000 ptas. ($7.70–$10.40); Indian dishes 935–990 ptas. ($9.75–$10.30). AE, DC, MC, V.
   Open: Breakfast Mon–Sat 9:30am–noon; lunch Mon–Sat 12:30–4pm; dinner Mon–Sat 8:30pm–midnight. **Closed:** Most of Aug.

Though largely Indian and completely vegetarian, the menu has some surprises, like pizzas and a Spanish *menu del día.* The house specialty is the thali, a tray of various Indian dishes that constitute a meal. The "natural" breakfast features sandwiches and cereals.

LA LLESCA, avinguda Gaudí, 12. Tel. 255-31-30.
   Cuisine: CATALAN/SPANISH. **Metro:** Sagrada Familia.
$ Prices: Main courses 560–1,750 ptas. ($5.85–$18.20); *menu del día* 765 ptas. ($7.95). No credit cards.
   Open: Fri–Wed 9am–5pm (lunch served 1–4pm); dinner Mon–Wed and Fri–Sat 8–11pm. **Closed:** Aug and the first two weeks of Sept.

A typical tapas bar and restaurant that is proud of its escalivada (a pepper-eggplant-onion concoction), terrasco al horno (roasted lamb's back), homemade canelones, and pollo al champán (chicken in champagne sauce).

LA PIZZA NOSTRA, carrer Montcada (between Museu Picasso and passeig del Born). Tel. 319-90-58.
   Cuisine: PIZZA/PASTA. **Metro:** Jaume I.
$ Prices: Salads 545–1,025 ptas. ($5.65–$10.65); pizzas 875–1,430 ptas. ($9.10–$14.90); pastas 950–1,290 ptas. ($9.90–$13.45). MC, V.

Within the romantic confines of a medieval mansion you can enjoy some of the best pizza in town served up with all manner of exotic toppings. If you can't make up your mind, you can have half the individual-sized pizza one way and the other half another. The desserts are also some of the best in town.

MOKA RESTAURANT CAFETERIA, La Rambla, 126. Tel. 302-68-86.
   Cuisine: CONTINENTAL. **Metro:** Plaça Catalunya.
$ Prices: Salads and pizzas 625–1,075 ptas. ($6.50–$11.20); main courses 990–2,970 ptas. ($10.30–$30.95); *menu del día* 1,375–1,760 ptas. ($14.30–$18.35); *menu turística* 880 ptas. ($9.15). No credit cards.
   Open: Sun–Fri 8am–1:30am, Sat 8am–2pm (Dec 25 7pm–1:30am).
This clean, airy, well-lit place features salads, pizzas, pastas, and *platos combinados* (Spain's version of a diner dinner). Main courses cover the full range of fish and meats.

PITARRA RESTAURANT, carrer D'Avinyó, 56. Tel. 301-16-47.
   Cuisine: CATALAN. **Metro:** Liceu, Drassanes, or Jaume I.
$ Prices: Appetizers 550–990 ptas. ($5.70–$10.30); main courses 700–2,500 ptas. ($7.30–$26.05). AE, DC, MC, V.
   Open: Lunch Mon–Sat 1–4pm; dinner Mon–Sat 8:30–11pm. **Closed:** Aug.

Occupies the former home and watch shop of the prolific and prized Catalan playwright and poet, Federic Soler Hubert (pseudonym "Pitarra"). The atmosphere is friendly, the service attentive, and the food very good. The menu is seasonal—look for game in the winter.

THE CHAINS

Burger King has two outposts: La Rambla, 135, near Plaça Catalunya (tel. 302-54-29), and passeig de Gràcia, 4, on the opposite side of Plaça Catalunya (tel.

317-18-57), both open Monday through Thursday from 11am to midnight, on Friday and Saturday from 11am to 1:30am, and on Sunday from noon to midnight.

Kentucky Fried Chicken, at La Rambla, 60, offers three pieces of chicken for 560 ptas. ($5.85) and combination platters for 525–765 ptas. ($5.45–$7.95). It's open Sunday through Thursday from 11am to midnight and on Friday and Saturday from 11am to 1am.

McDonald's has three Barcelona outposts: carrer de Pelai, 62, near Plaça Catalunya (tel. 318-29-90); La Rambla, 62; and Portal De L'Angel, 36. All are open daily from 11am to 11pm, offering hamburgers for 165–355 ptas. ($1.70–$3.70).

Pizza Hut has numerous outposts. The most central are: Diagonal, 646 (tel. 280-19-14); Urgel, 239 (tel. 410-62-20); passeig de Gràcia, 125-127 (tel. 238-30-05); Rambla de Catalunya, 91-93 (tel. 487-31-08); and avinguda Paralelo, 87 (tel. 241-73-04).

PICNIC SUPPLIES & WHERE TO EAT THEM

Stock up at the incomparable La Boquería market on La Rambla and head for the Parc de la Ciutadella or the park at the Montjuïc end of the Transbordador del Puerto.

WORTH THE EXTRA BUCKS

CASA LEOPOLDO, carrer San Rafael, 24. Tel. 241-30-14.
  Cuisine: CATALAN/SEAFOOD. **Metro:** Liceu.
$ Prices: Main courses 840–8,225 ptas. ($8.75–$85.65); *menu del día* 1,100 ptas. ($11.45). AE, V.
  Open: Tues–Sat 1:30–11:30pm, Sun 1:30–5pm. **Closed:** Holy Week and Aug.
Beautiful tiles adorn this otherwise plain restaurant where the food is on a par with that of some of the tonier restaurants around town. Its claim to fame is the *parrilladas* (platters) of seafood and fish.

6. ATTRACTIONS

SUGGESTED ITINERARIES

If you don't have time to visit a single museum or monument, take a stroll along La Rambla. The spectacle is real street theater. If you have more time, the city's monuments, museums, trendy bars, and crowded cultural calendar will keep you busy.

IF YOU HAVE ONE DAY   In the morning, stroll along La Rambla where Spain's *paseo* tradition runs from the seedy to the sublime, and take in the Columbus Monument, La Boquería, and a tour of the Gran Teatre del Liceu. In the afternoon, head for the Museu Picasso and the cathedral.

IF YOU HAVE TWO DAYS   Spend the first day as suggested above. On the morning of the second day, visit the Sagrada Familia and stroll along passeig de Gràcia to see some of the masterpieces of modernist architecture. In the afternoon, head for Montjuïc and visit the Museu d'Art de Catalunya, the Fundació Miró, and the Poble Espanyol.

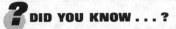

DID YOU KNOW . . . ?

- After his first voyage to the New World, Columbus returned to Barcelona.
- Raising the roof of the Palau Sant Jordi took 12 cranes and 10 days.
- The world's first submarine was immersed in the port of Barcelona on September 23, 1859.
- Barcelona also bid for the 1924, 1936, and 1972 Olympic Games.

IF YOU HAVE THREE DAYS Spend the first two days as indicated above. The third morning, head north to the Museu-Monestir de Pedralbes and Museu de Cerámica, and spend the afternoon wandering leisurely around the Barri Gòtic and visiting the Saló del Tinell, Capilla de Santa Agueda, Museu Frederic Marès, and Museu de l'Historia de la Ciutat.

IF YOU HAVE FIVE DAYS Spend the first three days as indicated above. On the fourth day, explore the Ribera barrio, visiting its Santa María del Mar Church and Museu Textil i d'Indumentària. Then stroll through the Parc de la Ciutadella and visit the zoo. Have lunch in Barceloneta and, weather permitting, take to the beach or stroll along the waterfront's Moll de la Fusta and make a trip in Las Golondrinas to the breakwater and back.

On the fifth day, tour the modernist works of the Eixample (see "A Stroll Through the Barri Gòtic," below) and visit Parc Güell in the morning. For lunch, go to the top of Tibidabo Mountain and spend the afternoon enjoying the views and, if you have children, the amusement park. One night be sure to see the Fuentes de Montjuïc, one of the city's most unique spectacles. They're illuminated October to May on Saturday and Sunday from 8 to 11pm (9 to 10pm with music) and June to September on Thursday, Saturday, and Sunday from 9pm to midnight (10 to 11pm with music). Note: The music really enhances the experience.

TOP ATTRACTIONS

All municipal museums are free for those under 18, students with international ID cards, and International Council of Museums (ICOM) members. Municipal museums are closed January 1, April 17 and 20, May 1, June 8 and 24, and December 25–26.

MUSEU PICASSO, carrer de Montcada, 15-19. Tel. 319-63-10.

Barcelona's most popular attraction, this museum reveals much about this artist whose long, prolific career extends well beyond cubism. Ensconced in three Gothic mansions, the museum's collection contains paintings, drawings, engravings, and ceramic creations.

Admission: 550 ptas. ($5.70) adults, free for children under 18.
Open: Tues–Sat 10am–8pm, Sun and hols 10am–3pm.

CATEDRAL, Plaça de la Seu. Tel. 315-35-55.

Begun at the end of the 13th century and completed around the middle of the 15th (except for the main facade, which dates from the early 20th century), this Gothic cathedral largely reflects the splendor of medieval Barcelona. Its main points of interest are the central choir; the crypt of Santa Eulàlia, whose white alabaster sepulcher is of 14th-century Italian craftsmanship; the *Cristo de Lepanto,* whose twisted torso allegedly dodged a bullet during the battle of the same name; and the unusual cloisters studded with palm trees, magnolias, medlars, a fountain erupting from a moss-covered rock, and a gaggle of geese. Try not to miss the cathedral when it's illuminated on a Thursday, Saturday, or Sunday evening.

Admission: Cathedral, free; Museu de la Catedral, 25 ptas. (25¢).
Open: Cathedral, daily 7:45am–1:30pm and 4–7pm; museum, daily 11:45am–1pm. **Metro:** Jaume I. **Bus:** 16, 17, 19, 22, or 45.

LA SAGRADA FAMILIA, carrer de Mallorca, 401. Tel. 455-02-47.

BARCELONA

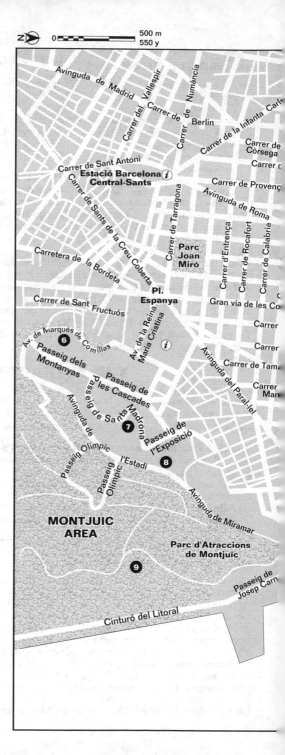

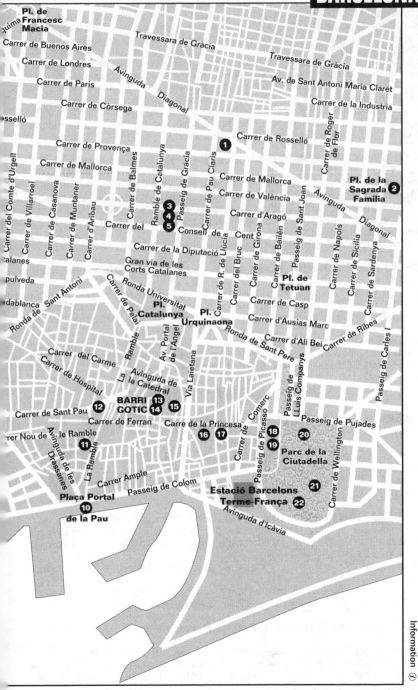

Pl. de **Francesc Macia**

quima

Carrer de Buenos Aires

Carrer de Londres

Carrer de Paris

Carrer de Còrsega

sselló

Travessara de Gràcia

Travessara de Gràcia

Av. de Sant Antoni Maria Claret

Carrer de la Industria

Avinguda

Diagonal

Carrer de Provença

Carrer de Mallorca

Carrer de Rosselló

1

Carrer de Mallorca

Carrer de València

Carrer d'Aragó

Consell de

Cent

Carrer de la Diputació

Gran via de les Corts Catalanes

Ronda Universitat

Pl. de la Sagrada Familia 2

Avinguda

Diagonal

Carrer de Napols

Carrer de Sicilia

Carrer de Sardenya

Carrer de Roger de Flor

Carrer de Bailèn

Passeig de Sant Joan

Carrer de Girona

Carrer del Bruc

Carrer de R. de Llúcia

Carrer de Balmes

Ramble de Catalunya

Passeig de Gracia

Carrer de Pau Claris

Carrer del

3
4
5

Carrer del Comte d'Urgell

Carrer de Villarroel

Carrer de Casanova

Carrer de Muntaner

Carrer d'Aribau

calanes

pulveda

dablanca

Ronda de Sant Antoni

Carrer de Pelai

Pl. Catalunya

Pl. Urquinaona

Pl. de Tetuan

Carrer de Casp

Carrer d'Ausias Marc

Ronda de Sant Pere

Carrer d'Ali Bei

Carrer de Ribes

Passeig de Carles I

Carrer del Carme

Carrer de Hospital

Carrer de Sant Pau

rer Nou de le Ramble

11

La Ramble

Av. Portal de l'Angel

Avinguda de la Catedral

Via Laietana

BARRI GOTIC

12

13
14
15

Carrer de Ferran

Carre de la Princesa

16 **17**

Carrer de Comerç

Carrer de Picasso

Passeig de Lluis Companys

Passeig de Pujades

18
19

20

Parc de la Ciutadella

21

Carrer de Wellington

Avinguda de les Drassanes

Carrer Ample

Passeig de Colom

Plaça Portal de la Pau

10

Estació Barcelons Terme-França 22

Avinguda d'Icàvia

★ An ambitious work in perpetual progress, this modernist rendition of a cathedral will, if finished, be Europe's largest. Work began in 1882; two years later Gaudí took over and projected a temple of immense proportions (the dome is slated to be 525 feet high) and profound religious symbolism. But to date it remains a shell of a cathedral and controversy swirls around its completion. Since Gaudí died in 1926 leaving no detailed plans, construction has continued by fits and starts. Within one of the towers an elevator ascends to a magnificent view. The **Museu del Templo** in the crypt chronicles the cathedral's structural evolution.

Admission: Church 440 ptas. ($4.60); elevator 125 ptas. ($1.30).

Open: Sept–Mar, 9am–6pm; Apr–June, 9am–7pm; July–Aug, 8am–9pm. **Metro:** Sagrada Familia. **Bus:** 19, 34, 43, 50, 51, or 54.

MUSEU D'ART DE CATALUNYA, Palau Nacional, Parc de Montjuïc. Tel. 423-18-24.

Within this building built for the 1929 World's Fair and newly redesigned inside by Gae Aulenti is a collection of Catalan art from the Romanesque, Gothic, and 16th- to 18th-century periods, along with a smattering of works by such high-caliber non-Catalan artists as El Greco, Velázquez, Zurbarán, and Tintoretto.

Admission: 550 ptas. ($5.70).

Open: Undergoing renovation at this writing; check new hours. **Metro:** Espanya.

FUNDACIÓ JOAN MIRÓ, Plaça Neptú, Parc de Montjuïc. Tel. 329-19-08.

A tribute to the Catalan abstractionist Joan Miró, this museum follows his work from 1914 to 1978 and includes many sculptures, paintings, and multimedia tapestries. Temporary exhibitions of other contemporary artists are also held here on a regular basis.

Admission: 450 ptas. ($4.70) adults, 200 ptas. ($2.10) students.

Open: Tues–Wed and Fri–Sat 11am–7pm, Thurs 11am–9:30pm, Sun and hols (Mon hols too) 10:30am–2:30pm. **Bus:** 61 from Plaça Espanya.

MORE ATTRACTIONS

GRAN TEATRE DEL LICEU, La Rambla. 61-65. Tel. 318-91-22.

★ Barcelona's majestic opera house dates from the 19th century. A study in Victorian opulence, it features blue silk walls in the entrance hall, a sweeping staircase leading to a salon of mirrors, and one of Europe's largest stages.

Admission: 225 ptas. ($2.35).

Open: Guided half-hour tours in English Mon–Fri at 11:30am and 12:15pm. **Metro:** Liceu.

COLUMBUS MONUMENT, Plaça Portal de la Pau. Tel. 302-52-24.

This municipal landmark commemorates Columbus's triumphant return after his first expedition to the New World. After sailing into Barcelona, he delivered news of his discoveries to Queen Isabella.

Admission: 225 ptas. ($2.35) adults, 80 ptas. (85¢) children 4–12 and senior citizens over 60, free for children under 4.

Open: June 24–Sept 24, daily 9am–9pm; Sept 25–June 23, Tues–Sat 10am–2pm and 3:30–6:30pm, Sun and hols 10am–7pm. **Metro:** Drassanes.

MUSEU MARÍTIM, Drassanes Reials, Portal de la Pau, 1. Tel. 301-64-25.

Installed in the Drassanes (medieval shipyards of the 13th century), this museum's collection of seafaring paraphernalia is distinguished by a reconstruction of *La Galería Real* of Don Juan of Austria, which took part in the Battle of Lepanto, and a map owned by Amerigo Vespucci.

Admission: 165 ptas. ($1.70).

Open: Tues–Sat 10am–2pm and 4–7pm, Sun and hols 10am–2pm. **Metro:** Drassanes.

MUSEU-MONESTIR DE PEDRALBES, Baixada del Monestir, 9. Tel. 203-92-82.

This 14th-century monastery was founded by Queen Elisenda de Montcada, whose sepulcher is found in the church. The cloisters contain a museum featuring 14th-century murals in Saint Michael's Chapel, re-creations of an apothecary and several monks' cells, an impressive kitchen, and a 16th-century sick room.

Admission: 275 ptas. ($2.85), free for children under 13.

Open: Tues–Sun 9:30am–2pm. **Closed:** Good Friday, May 1, June 24, and Dec 25–26. **Bus:** 22 or 64. **FF.CC.:** Line Sarrià–Reina Elisenda, Reina Elisenda stop.

MUSEU DE CERAMICÀ, avinguda Diagonal, 686. Tel. 280-16-21.

Located in a vintage 1920s palace, this museum's collection traces the history of Spanish ceramics from to 13th century to the present. It is considered the most important of its kind in Europe.

Admission: 275 ptas. ($2.85); free for those under 18.

Open: Mon 9am–8pm, Tues–Thurs and Sun 9am–2am, Fri–Sat 9am–6pm. **Bus:** 61 from Plaça Espanya or the free double-decker Poble Espanyol shuttle bus.

POBLE ESPANYOL, avinguda Marqués de Comillas, Montjuïc. Tel. 325-78-66.

⭐ This architectural microcosm of Spain was conceived for the 1929 World's Fair, but nowadays it is much more than an open-air museum. In fact, it's almost a village in its own right, with working artisans, lots of crafts shops, and various nightclubs and bars that are much in vogue.

Admission: 550 ptas. ($5.70) adults, 275 ptas. ($2.85) children 7–14, free for children under 7.

Open: Mon 9am–8pm, Tues–Thurs and Sun 9am–2am, Fri–Sat 9am–6am. **Bus:** 61 from Plaça Espanya or the free double-decker Poble Espanyol shuttle bus.

MUSEU TEXTIL I D'INDUMENTÀRIA, carrer de Montcada, 12-14. Tel. 310-45-16.

Occupying two 13th-century Gothic palaces near the Museu Picasso, this museum contains a fascinating collection of textiles ranging from ancient times to the 20th century. Particularly impressive are the clothing and accessories from the 18th to the 20th century and the lace collection dating back to the 16th century.

Admission: 275 ptas. ($2.85).

Open: Tues–Sun 10am–2pm and 4:30–7pm. **Metro:** Jaume. Bus: 16, 17, or 45.

MUSEU D'ART MODERN, Parc de la Ciutadella. Tel. 319-57-28.

This museum contains primarily the work of 20th-century Catalan painters, along with some fine examples of modernist furniture.

Admission: 550 ptas. ($5.70).

Open: Mon 3–7:30pm, Tues–Sat 9am–7:30pm, Sun and hols 9am–3pm. **Metro:** Arc de Triomf.

LAS GOLONDRINAS, Moll de la Fusta. Tel. 412-59-44.

Both children and adults enjoy the 30-minute round-trip boat ride from the Moll de la Fusta to the breakwater.

Admission: 225 ptas. ($2.35).

Open: Winter departures daily every half hour Mon–Fri 11am–5pm, Sat–Sun 11am–6pm; summer departures daily every half hour 11am–9pm. **Metro:** Drassanes.

PARKS & GARDENS

Parc de la Ciutadella occupies the former site of the city's citadel, some remnants of which remain. Here, too, you'll find the Museu d'Art Modern, the Museu de

Zoología, the Museu de Geología, the Parliament, the zoo, and a fantastic fountain, in part the work of Gaudí.

Parc Güell, in Barcelona's Gràcia section, was to be a suburb of 60 homes with the full complement of roads, markets, and schools. Financed by Eusebi Güell and designed by Gaudí, the project was aborted after only two houses and a smattering of public areas were built. One of the two houses is now the Casa-Museu Gaudí. Don't miss the park's entrance stairway, the Hall of a Hundred Columns, and the view from the plaza above.

SPECIAL-INTEREST SIGHTSEEING

Architecture enthusiasts will want to make a tour of modernist Barcelona. Brochures on the most important examples of this turn-of-the-century style and suggested itineraries are available from the tourist information offices (see "Orientation and Getting Around," above).

A STROLL THROUGH THE BARRI GÒTIC

This two-hour walk takes in the quarter's most important structures. Begin at the **Plaça Nova** where you'll see remnants of the Roman wall. As you pass onto carrer del Bisbe you are crossing the threshold that was the city's oldest entrance gate. The first building on the right is the **Palau Episcopal (Bishop's Palace),** whose 18th-century portal opens onto an attractive courtyard with Romanesque construction below and Gothic above. At the top of the stairway is a patio with a 13th-century mural and a splendid coffered ceiling. The courtyard is open to the public daily from 10am to 1:30pm.

Now take carrer Santa Llúcia to the **Capilla de Santa Llúcia** (open daily from 8am to 1:30pm and 4 to 7:30pm), a vestige of the 11th-century Romanesque cathedral preceding the current one. Exiting the chapel at the far side, you'll find yourself in the cathedral cloisters (see "Top Attractions," above). Enter the **cathedral** through the door by the fountain and exit through the main entrance.

Turn right up carrer dels Comtes (look up to see some classic Gothic gargoyles) and right again down carrer de la Pietat behind the cathedral. Leading off to the left is carrer Paradís where, at no. 10 in the **Centre Excursionista de Catalunya,** you can see several Roman columns in the courtyard, remnants of the city's largest Roman temple, honoring Augustus. Return to carrer de la Pietat and continue to the left behind the cathedral.

Continue along carrer del Bisbe to Plaça de Sant Jaume where you'll find the **Palau de la Generalitat,** seat of the regional Catalan government, whose main 16th-century Renaissance facade faces the plaza and the **Casa de la Ciutat (City Hall),** whose 19th-century neoclassical facade supersedes a Gothic one. To the left off carrer de la Ciutat runs the narrow carrer d'Hercules, leading into **Plaça Sant Just.** Notice the 18th-century mansions with the sgraffito decoration and the Sants Just i Pastor Church.

Now turn left onto carrer Daguería and cross carrer Jaume I and carrer de la Llibretería and continue along carrer Frenería. Turn right onto the Baixada de Santa Clara and you'll soon find yourself in the Plaça del Rei, where you'll find the **Palau Reial Major,** former residence of the condes (counts) de Barcelona and the kings of Aragón, the **Saló del Tinell** where Queen Isabella and King Ferdinand allegedly received Columbus upon his return from the New World, and the **Capilla de Santa Agueda,** built atop the Roman wall and featuring a beautiful 15th-century retablo.

Turn right on carrer del Veguer to the **Museu de l'Historia de la Ciutat** (tel. 315-11-11), open on Monday from 3:30 to 8pm, Tuesday through Saturday from 9am to 8pm, and on Sunday and holidays from 9am to 1:30pm. Admission is 300 pesetas ($3.10). Housed in a 15th-century mansion moved here stone by stone from carrer Mercaders, this museum features below-ground excavations of Roman and Visigothic remains and a veritable maze of municipal memorabilia on its upper floors.

Returning to the Baixada de Santa Clara, turn right on carrer dels Comtes. Alongside the cathedral in the Plaça de Sant Iu is the **Museu Frederic Marès** (tel. 310-58-00), open Tuesday through Saturday from 9am to 2pm and 4 to 7pm, and on Sunday and holidays from 9am to 2pm; admission is 300 ptas. ($3.10). It houses the impressive collection of antiquities and curios of Marès, a Catalan sculptor in his 90s. At the far end of the exterior courtyard is a section of Roman wall.

TOURS

AERIAL TOURS The Montjuïc cable car, the Transbordador del Puerto, and the Tibidabo funicular are fine ways to survey the city, sea, and surrounding mountains from on high.

BUS TOURS From June to September, look for the bargain **bus no. 100.** A single ticket permits unlimited travel on this special tourist bus, the tramvía blau (blue tram), the Montjuïc funicular and cable car, and the Tibidabo funicular. Originating at Plaça del Palau, bus no. 100 makes a sweep of the entire city, passing through the Barri Gòtic, along La Rambla and passeig de Gràcia, by the Sagrada Familia, along avinguda del Tibidabo and avinguda Diagonal, by the Estació Sants, through the Parc de Montjuïc, and along the passeig de Colom. It makes 16 stops along its two-hour route, and you can get on and off as you please. It runs daily every half hour from 9am to 7:30pm. An all-day ticket costs 900 ptas. ($9.35); a half-day ticket, valid after 2pm, costs 675 ptas. ($7.05). Tickets are available on the bus, at the Poble Espanyol's information office, or between 8am and 7pm at the following TMB offices: Ronda Sant Pau, 43; Plaça Universitat (vestibule of the metro station); and Sants-Estació (vestibule of metro station Line 5).

7. SAVVY SHOPPING

Barcelona's value-added tax, known as IVA in Spain, runs 6%–33%. VAT recovery is possible for residents of non-EC countries on single purchases of more than 78,800 ptas. ($820.85). There are two ways to recover the tax. If you are leaving from Barcelona's El Prat Airport, you can present the store's signed and stamped official bill—along with your passport and the article(s) purchased—for endorsement at Spanish Customs before check-in. The Customs official will return the duly signed blue copy of the bill to you. You then present it to the Banco Exterior de España offices inside the airport terminal and they will refund the tax to you in the currency of your choice. The other possibility is to mail the blue copy of the bill endorsed by the Customs official to the store and wait for a check to be sent to your home within (one hopes) 60 days.

The **main shopping streets** in the Old Town are La Rambla, avinguda Portal de l'Àngel, carrer Portaferrissa, carrer del Pi, carrer de la Palla, and carrer Pelai. In the Eixample they are passeig de Gràcia and Rambla de Catalunya. In the northern reaches of town, avinguda de la Diagonal, via Augusta, travessera de Gràcia, carrer de Balmes, and carrer Muntaner.

The big department stores are **El Cortes Inglés,** Plaça Catalunya, 14 (tel. 302-12-12), and avinguda de la Diagonal, 617-619 (tel. 419-52-06), and **Galerías Preciados,** avinguda Portal de l'Àngel, 19-21 (tel. 317-00-00), and avinguda de la Diagonal, 471-473 (tel. 322-30-11). Both are open Monday through Friday from 10am to 8pm and on Saturday from 10am to 9pm.

Barcelona's fortes are fashion and design. **Vinçon,** passeig de Gràcia, 96 (tel. 215-60-50), carries the latest gadgets and home furnishings.

MARKETS La Boquería, officially the Mercat de Sant Josep, is one of the world's cleanest, most extensive, and most fascinating produce markets. Antiques lovers will enjoy the open-air **Mercat Gòtic de Antigüedades** by the cathedral, held every Thursday from 9am to 8pm except during August.

8. EVENING ENTERTAINMENT

Barcelona's nightlife runs from the campy burlesque of El Molino to the opulence of one of Europe's most magnificent opera houses. For the latest information on concerts and other musical events, call the **Amics de la Música de Barcelona** (tel. 302-68-70 Monday through Friday from 10am to 1pm and 3 to 8pm). For information on performances by the **Ballet Contemporáneo de Barcelona,** call 322-10-37. For a comprehensive listing of evening activities, pick up a copy of the weekly *Guía del Ocio* or the entertainment guide offered with the Thursday edition of *El País.* For a guide to the gay scene, pick up a map of gay Barcelona at Sextienda, carrer Raurich 11.

THE PERFORMING ARTS

PALAU DE LA MÚSICA, Amadeu Vives, 1. Tel. 301-11-04, or 268-10-00 for reservations.

This magnificent modernist concert hall is among the world's finest. The work of Catalan architect Lluís Domènech i Montaner, its distinctive facade is a tour de force of brick, mosaic, and glass. But it is the drama and elegance within that truly set it apart from its peers. The interplay of ceramic mosaics, stained glass, and a central skylight build to the stunning crescendo of carvings that frame the stage. Throughout the year a variety of concerts and recitals are held here. Tickets are also available at all Caixa de Catalunya offices (for Caixa reservations, call 310-12-12).

Prices: Tickets, 500–5,000 ptas. ($5.20–$52.10).
Metro: Urquinaona.

GRAN TEATRE DEL LICEU, La Rambla, 61-65. Tel. 318-91-22.

November to March is opera season. Look for ballet in the spring and in September and October. Concerts and recitals are held all year.

Prices: Tickets, 400–10,000 ptas. ($4.15–$104.15).
Metro: Liceu.

MUSIC CLUBS

The **Poble Espanyol** offers "one-stop shopping" for everything from jazz to flamenco to discos to designer bars; the latest rage here is the Torres de Avila bar at the entrance. Also commendable are:

EL TABLAO DE CARMEN, Poble Espanyol, Arcos, 9. Tel. 325-68-95.

This is the best place in Barcelona to see flamenco, the flamboyant, traditional dance of southern Spains Andalucía region.

Admission: 6,500 ptas. ($67.70) dinner and first show, 3,900 ptas. ($40.60) first show and one drink.

Open: Dinner begins at 9pm; the first show is at 10:30pm; the second at 1am.

HARLEM JAZZ CLUB, Comtessa Sobradiel, 8. Tel. 310-07-55.

A hole-in-the-wall filled with aficionados who come for the fine jazz.

Admission: Free.

Open: Tues–Thurs 8pm–3am, Fri–Sat 8pm–4am, Sun 8pm–2am; live performances Tues–Thurs at 10 and 11:30pm, Sun at 9:30 and 11pm. **Metro:** Jaume I.

MOVIES

Most first-run movies are dubbed into Spanish. The following cinemas often show English-language movies: **Arkadin,** travessa de Gràcia, 103 (tel. 218-62-42); **Casa-**

blanca I & II, passeig de Gràcia, 115 (tel. 218-43-45); **Malda,** Pi, 5 (tel. 317-85-29); and **Verdi,** Verdi, 32 (tel. 237-05-16).

THE BAR SCENE

In summer, the lower end of Rambla de Catalunya blossoms with outdoor café-bars that are the highlight of every night. The bars of carrer Santaló are popular with the younger crowd. Among "designer" bars, check out:

TICKTACKTOE, Roger de Llúria, 40. Tel. 318-99-47.

A multidimensional, ultramodern nightspot that is part bar, part restaurant, and part billiard hall.

Open: Mon–Thurs 7pm–2:30am, Fri–Sat 7pm–3am. **Metro:** Urquinaona.

UNIVERSAL, Marià Cubí, 182-184. Tel. 201-46-58.

Universal's postmodern punk decor is so minimalist it seems threatened with extinction. Frankly, it recalls a converted warehouse. The crowd is young, the music loud, the trendiness tenacious.

Open: Daily 11pm–3am. **FF.CC. Generalitat:** Gràcia.

VELVET, Balmes, 161. Tel. 217-67-14.

Installed in a modernist structure, Velvet has a dance floor and two bars lined with buttocks-shaped bar stools. Don't miss the bathrooms.

Open: Mon–Thurs 7:30pm–4:30am, Fri–Sat 7:30pm–5am, Sun 7pm–4:30am. **Metro:** Diagonal.

CHAMPAÑERIAS

These establishments specialize in *cavas* (sparkling wines) from Catalonia and some foreign champagnes.

LA CAVA DEL PALAU, Verdaguer i Callis, 10. Tel. 310-09-38.

It stocks over 40 different regional cavas, 40 French champagnes, and some 350 appellation wines from Spain, France, and Chile. Champagne connoisseurs will want to try the *brut natures,* the driest and most natural of all cavas. To accompany the libations you'll find a selection of cheese, pâtés, and caviar for 1,000–2,000 ptas. ($10.40–$20.85) per *ración* (larger than a tapa portion). A glass of cava averages about 575 ptas. ($6).

Open: Mon–Thurs 7pm–2:30am, Fri–Sat 7pm–3:30am, with live piano music starting at 11:30pm. **Closed:** Holy Week and Aug. **Metro:** Urquinaona.

LA XAMPANYERÍA, Provença, 236, at the corner of Enric Granados. Tel. 253-74-55.

The "blue lagoon" of champagne bars, this place is lively, especially after midnight on weekends. In addition to over 40 types of cava, it serves pâtés, cured ham, and chocolates averaging about 1,000 ptas. ($10.40) per *ración*. A glass of cava averages 475 ptas. ($4.95).

Open: Mon–Sat 7pm–3am. **Closed:** Hols and Aug. **FF.CC. Generalitat:** Provença.

DANCE CLUBS

In addition to discos galore, Barcelona has some classic dance halls. Don't miss:

LA PALOMA, Tigre, 27. Tel. 301-68-97.

A Barcelona institution since 1903, this campy dance hall has a certain passé elegance. The music is always live, and local tradition calls for Barcelona wedding parties to stop here at some time. Birthday parties, bachelor parties, and retirement parties are regularly announced between dance numbers.

Admission: 450–650 ptas. ($4.70–$6.75).

Open: Thurs–Sun and hols 6–9:30pm and 11:30pm–3:30am. **Metro:** Universitat.

9. EASY EXCURSIONS

MONTSERRAT MONASTERY The Montserrat Monastery complex, 35 miles northwest of Barcelona, is vast, containing a basilica with the venerated Black Virgin, a museum, numerous hotels for pilgrims, restaurants, and a wealth of souvenir shops and food stalls. The monastery is situated at 725 meters (2,398 ft.) up Montserrat ("serrated mountain"). One of its noted institutions is the Boys Choir, established in the 13th century. If you time your visit right, you can hear them sing at 1pm or 7:10pm. Numerous funiculars and paths lead to some 13 hermitages and numerous shrines scattered across the mountain.

The best way to get here is via bus tour. **Julià,** Ronda Universitat, 5 (tel. 316-64-54), and **Pullmantur,** Gran Via C.C., 635 (tel. 317-12-97), offer half-day bus tours leaving daily all year long. The cost is 4,050 ptas. ($42.20).

SITGES A popular beach destination just 25 miles south of Barcelona, Sitges really swings in the summer. By mid-October it hibernates, but its scenic charms and museums are still motive enough for a visit. The **Museu Cau Ferrat,** Fonollars (tel. 894-03-64), is the legacy of the well-known Catalan painter Santiago Rusiñol, who lived and worked in this 19th-century house fashioned of two 16th-century fishermen's homes. His collection includes not only his own works, but several pieces by Picasso and El Greco, wrought iron, tiles, and archeological artifacts. Next door is the **Museu Maricel de Mar** (tel. 894-03-64), the legacy of Dr. Pérez Rosales, whose impressive collection of furniture, porcelain, lamps, and tapestries draws largely from the medieval, Renaissance, and baroque periods. There are also Romanesque frescoes and an entire 14th-century chapel. Both museums are open Tuesday through Saturday from 9:30am to 2pm and 4 to 6pm, and on Sunday from 9:30am to 2pm. Admission to each is 150 ptas. ($1.55).

Trains run daily to Sitges from the Estació Sants; round-trip fare is 475 ptas. ($4.95).

CAVA COUNTRY The wineries in Sant Sadurní d'Anoia, just 25 miles from Barcelona, produce Catalonia's fine *cavas*. **Freixenet** (tel. 891-07-00) and **Codorniu** (tel. 891-01-25) offer the best tours and tastings. Call for hours.

Trains run daily to Sant Sadurní d'Anoia (the station is right next to Freixenet) from the Estació Sants. Round-trip fare is 475 ptas. ($4.95). To visit Codorniu you really need a car, as taxis from the Sant Sadurní d'Anoia train station are unreliable.

BERLIN

The history of Berlin this century—particularly given the events within the past four years—is certainly one of the most compelling and riveting stories of our time. Just a few years ago, who would ever have imagined that the Wall would come tumbling down, that communism would meet with defeat throughout eastern Europe, and that the two Germanys would reunite in our lifetime, with Berlin as the new capital?

Berlin started out as a divided city back in the 13th century, when two settlements were founded on opposite banks of the Spree River. These settlements grew and eventually merged. Berlin served as capital of Prussia under the Hohenzollern kings and then as capital of the German nation. After the turn of this century, Berlin began to challenge Munich as the cultural capital as well, attracting such artists as Max Liebermann, Lovis Corinth, and Max Slevogt. Max Reinhardt came to Berlin to take over as director of the Deutsches Theater, Richard Strauss became conductor at the Royal Opera, and Albert Einstein became director of physics at what later became the Max Planck Institute.

After the Germans were defeated in World War II, Germany and its former capital were carved into four sectors: Soviet, American, French, and British. Berlin, buried in the Soviet sector, was divided into East and West, with East Berlin serving as the capital of East Germany. In 1961, after a series of disputes and standoffs, a wall 29 miles long and 13 feet high was erected around West Berlin, in part to stop a mass exodus of East Germans to the West. Three million had already fled, most of them young, draining East Germany of many of its brightest and most educated. How ironic that in 1989 it was another exodus from the East to the West that triggered the Wall's sudden demise.

Today Berlin is changing so rapidly that it's difficult—if not impossible—to keep up. Berlin is packed with visitors, from the East, the West, and overseas. It is now the lively city it once was. It has some of the best museums in the world, a thriving nightlife, and a rich cultural legacy. And things are only going to get better.

1. FROM A BUDGET TRAVELER'S POINT OF VIEW

BERLIN BUDGET BESTS

One of the most wonderful things about sightseeing in West Berlin is that many of its **museums** are absolutely free. These include the cluster of famous museums in

Dahlem, the Nationalgalerie's permanent collection, and the Egyptian Museum with its priceless bust of Queen Nefertiti. Admission to East Berlin's state museums is only 60¢–$1.25.

Another bargain in Berlin is its **theaters, operas, and concerts.** Opera tickets start at around $7.50, while tickets to the Schiller-Theater begin at $5.60. Because most theaters are small, the cheaper tickets are perfectly acceptable.

WHAT THINGS COST IN BERLIN	U.S. $
Taxi from Tegel Airport to Bahnhof Zoo train station	19.00
Underground from Kurfürstendamm to Dahlem	1.85
Local telephone call	.20
Double room at the Bristol Hotel Kempinski (deluxe)	312.50
Double room at the Hotel-Pension Fasanenhaus (moderate)	87.50
Double room at the Pension München (budget)	46.85
Lunch for one at Café Hardenberg (moderate)	8.50
Lunch for one at Rogacki (budget)	4.50
Dinner for one, without wine, at Fioretto (deluxe)	53.00
Dinner for one, without wine, at Hardtke (moderate)	17.00
Dinner for one, without wine, at the Athener Grill (budget)	5.00
Half liter of beer	2.80
Glass of wine	3.10
Coca-Cola in a restaurant	1.70
Cup of coffee	2.05
Roll of 200 ASA color film, 36 exposures	5.60
Admission to Dahlem Picture Gallery	free
Movie ticket	5.60
Ticket to the Berlin Philharmonic Orchestra	7.50

As for dining, your ticket to cheaper meals is the **Imbiss,** which is a food stand or tiny locale serving food for take-out or to customers who eat standing up at chest-high counters. Sausages, Berliner Boulettes, hamburgers, french fries, pizza by the slice, Turkish pizza, and other finger foods are common fare, as well as beer and soft drinks. You can easily dine for less than 5 DM ($3.10). You'll find Imbisse along side streets of the Ku'damm, as well as Alexanderplatz, Savignyplatz, and many other thoroughfares throughout Berlin.

SPECIAL DISCOUNT OPPORTUNITIES

FOR STUDENTS   For museums that do charge an admission (the Berlin Museum, Museum at the Wall, and Charlottenburg), students can obtain cheaper admission with presentation of an International Student Identity Card. In addition, some theaters (such as the Schiller-Theater) offer unused tickets to students at 50% off the normal ticket price.

If you've arrived in Berlin without an International Student Identity Card and can show proof of current student status, you can obtain the card at **ARTU,** Hardenbergstrasse 9 (tel. 31 04 66), a travel agency located in the university district not far from the train station. It also offers discount plane fares around the world, as well as cheap train tickets to people under 26 years old. It's open Monday through Friday from 10am to 6pm (on Wednesday from 11am to 6pm) and on Saturday from 10am to 1pm.

WHAT'S SPECIAL ABOUT BERLIN

Museums
- [ ] The famous Pergamon Museum in East Berlin, with the Pergamon Altar, the Market Gate, and other architectural wonders of the ancient world.
- [ ] The Gemäldegalerie in Dahlem, with 20-some paintings by Rembrandt.
- [ ] The Egyptian Museum, with the bust of Nefertiti.
- [ ] And dozens of other first-rate museums.

Nightlife
- [ ] Famous opera houses and concert halls, including the Deutsche Oper Berlin and the Philharmonie.
- [ ] Cabarets, a Berlin tradition.

- [ ] A number of live-music houses, featuring jazz and rock.
- [ ] Bars and pubs, open all night.
- [ ] Discos for all ages.

Shopping
- [ ] KaDeWe, the largest department store on the European continent.
- [ ] The Ku'damm, one of Europe's most fashionable streets, and Wilmersdorfer Strasse, a pedestrian lane lined with boutiques and department stores.
- [ ] The Europa-Center, a large mall with 70 shops, restaurants, and bars.
- [ ] Outdoor and indoor markets, a treasure trove for antiques, junk, and crafts.

2. PRETRIP PREPARATIONS

DOCUMENTS The only document needed for citizens of the United States, Canada, Australia, and New Zealand is a valid passport, which allows stays up to three months. Visitors from the United Kingdom need only an identity card.

Students should be sure to bring an International Student Identity Card as well.

WHAT TO PACK Berlin has a continental climate, which means it's pleasantly warm in the summer and cold in the winter. Dress is fairly casual, but if you're going to the theater you'll want to pack one dressy outfit. At all times of year it's wise to bring an umbrella.

WHEN TO GO At about the same latitude as Vancouver, Berlin is a tourist destination throughout the year. Its temperature and amount of rainfall, however, can vary widely from year to year. The following averages may help you plan your trip.

Berlin's Average Daytime Temperature & Rainfall

	Jan	Feb	Mar	Apr	May	June	July	Aug	Sept	Oct	Nov	Dec
Temp. (°F)	30	32	40	48	53	60	64	62	56	49	40	34
Rainfall "	2.2	1.6	1.2	1.6	2.3	2.9	3.2	2.7	2.2	1.6	2.4	1.9

Special Events Festivals in Berlin revolve around its cultural calendar, beginning with the **International Film Festival** held at the end of February. The biggest event is the **Berlin Festival,** which recognizes excellence in all fields of art and is held from the end of August to October. The **Berlin Jazzfest,** which takes place in November, attracts musicians from both Europe and the United States. If you come to Berlin during any of these festivals, you should reserve a room in advance to avoid disappointment or wasting time searching for a hotel. If you come to Berlin any time between December 1 and Christmas Eve, you'll be treated to the colorful **Christmas market,** with more than 150 booths set up around the Kaiser Wilhelm Memorial Church selling ornaments and candies.

BACKGROUND READING   In the 1920s Berlin was the third-largest city in the world. Otto Friedrich's *Before the Deluge: A Portrait of Berlin in the 1920s* (Fromm International, 1986, $12.95) describes this interesting and intriguing chapter in Berlin's history, a time when such well-known people as Marlene Dietrich, Albert Einstein, Greta Garbo, Bertolt Brecht, Walter Gropius, Kandinsky, and Klee all made their homes here. For accounts of Berlin's more recent history, read *The Berlin Wall: Kennedy, Khrushchev, and a Showdown in the Heart of Europe* (Touchstone, 1986, $8.95) by Norman Gelb, and *Living with the Wall: West Berlin 1961–1985* (Duke Publishing Co., 1985, $32.50) by Richard and Anna Merritt.

If you like the movie *Cabaret,* you may wish to read Christopher Isherwood's *Goodbye to Berlin* (New Directions, $7.95), a fictionalized account of the last days of the Weimar Republic upon which the movie was based.

3. ORIENTATION & GETTING AROUND

ARRIVAL IN BERLIN

FROM THE AIRPORT   If you're flying to Berlin on Lufthansa or any of the other airlines that serve Berlin from Frankfurt, western Europe, or the United States, most likely you'll arrive at **Tegel Airport** (tel. 030/410 11). It's located only five miles from the city center, and the best and easiest way to get into town is on city bus no. 109, which departs about every 10–15 minutes from right outside the arrivals hall. Fare is 3 DM ($1.85) one way, and the bus travels to Stuttgarter Platz and along Kurfürstendamm, where most of Berlin's hotels are concentrated, all the way to Bahnhof Zoologischer Garten (Berlin's main train station, usually called simply "Bahnhof Zoo"). The trip by taxi from Tegel Airport to Bahnhof Zoo will cost about $17.

Schönefeld Airport (tel. 030/67 87-0), which once served as East Berlin's major airport, is still the destination for most flights from eastern Europe, Asia, and Latin America. The easiest way to get from Schönefeld Airport to Bahnhof Zoo and the center of Berlin is via the S-Bahn from Schönefeld Station (a five-minute walk from the airport) to Alexanderplatz, transferring there to other lines to reach your destination. The fare is 3 DM ($1.85).

And finally, because of Berlin's sudden rise in status to capital of Germany, **Templehof Airport** (tel. 030/69 09-1) has been resurrected for commercial use, serving flights from Amsterdam, Basel, Brussels, and several cities in Germany. Transportation from the airport is either bus no. 119, which travels the length of the Ku'damm, or via U-Bahn from Platz der Luftbrücke station. In either case, the fare is 3 DM ($1.85).

FROM THE TRAIN STATION   If you're arriving by train from western Europe, you'll probably end up at the **Bahnhof Zoologischer Garten,** Berlin's main train station, popularly called **Bahnhof Zoo.** Travel time from Hamburg is less than five hours, and from Frankfurt, less than eight.

Bahnhof Zoo is located in the center of town, not far from Kurfürstendamm with its hotels and nightlife. Both a subway and bus system connect the train station to the rest of the city. Both a post office and a money-exchange office are located in the train station. For information on train schedules, call 194 19.

If you're arriving in Berlin from eastern Europe, you may arrive at **Berlin**

Hauptbahnhof or **Berlin-Lichtenberg,** where you'll find S-Bahn connections to take you on to your final destination. S-Bahn 3 will take you to Bahnhof Zoo.

INFORMATION

Berlin's **main Tourist Information Office** is located in the Europa-Center, with its entrance on Budapester Strasse (tel. 262 60 31), just a few minutes' walk from Bahnhof Zoo. In addition to stocking maps and brochures about the city, the tourist office will also book a room for you for a 5 DM ($3.10) fee. It's open Monday through Saturday from 8am to 10:30pm and on Sunday from 9am to 9pm. Other tourist offices are located at Tegel Airport (tel. 410 131 45) and Bahnhof Zoo train station (tel. 313 90 63), both open daily from 8am to 11pm and also able to book you a room.

In the eastern part of Berlin, you'll find a convenient **Information Center** at the TV tower on Alexanderplatz (tel. 212 45 12 or 212 46 75). It's open daily from 8am to 8pm and can best answer questions regarding museums and restaurants that are in what used to be East Berlin.

Unfortunately, there's nothing available in English that gives the latest information on cultural events in Berlin. Your best bet for information on current plays, operas, concerts, and other happenings is probably **Berlin Programm,** available at the tourist office and at magazine kiosks for 2.80 DM ($1.75). Issued monthly, it also lists museums and their opening hours. Other German publications include city magazines *tip* and *zitty,* which come out on alternating weeks with information on fringe theater, film, rock, folk, and all that's happening on the alternative scene. *Zitty* costs 3.30 DM ($2.05); *tip* costs 3.40 DM ($2.10).

CITY LAYOUT

One of the most famous streets in Berlin is **Kurfürstendamm,** affectionately called the **Ku'damm.** About 2.5 miles long, it starts at the Kaiser-Wilhelm Gedächtniskirche (Memorial Church), a ruined church that has been left standing as a permanent reminder of the horrors of war. Near the Memorial Church is Bahnhof Zoo (West Berlin's main train station), a large park called the Tiergarten, and the Europa-Center, a 22-story building with shops, an observation platform, and the Berlin Tourist Information Office. Along the Ku'damm are many of the city's smartest boutiques, as well as most of its hotels. Note that the numbering system of buildings runs on one side of the street all the way to the end, then jumps to the other side of the street all the way back. For example, across the street from 11 Ku'damm is 230 Ku'damm. It's a bit complicated at first, but numbers for each block are posted on street signs.

The Ku'damm has Berlin's most exclusive shops, but **Wilmersdorfer Strasse** is where most of the natives shop. A pedestrian street located near a U-Bahn station of the same name, Wilmersdorfer Strasse boasts several department stores, numerous shops, and restaurants.

Not far away is **Charlottenburg Palace** and a cluster of fine museums, including the Egyptian Museum (with the famous bust of Nefertiti) and the Bröhan Museum (with its art nouveau collection). The area around the Ku'damm Wilmersdorfer Strasse, and Charlottenburg Palace is part of Charlottenburg, West Berlin's most important precinct.

Berlin's other well-known street—and historically much more significant—is **Unter den Linden.** This was the heart of Old Berlin before World War II, its most fashionable and liveliest street, and thereafter was part of East Berlin. The Brandenburg Gate is its most readily recognized landmark, and buildings along the tree-lined street have been painstakingly restored. Unter den Linden leads past **Museum Island,** which boasts the outstanding Pergamon Museum and a number of other great museums, to the modern, spacious square called **Alexanderplatz,** with its tall television tower and Information Center. Nearby is the **Nikolai Quarter,** a reconstructed neighborhood of shops, bars, and restaurants built to resemble Old Berlin.

Berlin's other important museum districts, **Tiergarten** and **Dahlem,** are within easy reach of the city center by subway or bus. Spread along the southwestern edge of the city and accessible by S-Bahn are Berlin's most famous woods, the **Grünewald,** and waterways, the Havel and Wannsee. In the East, the **Spreewald** is a huge refuge of waterways and woods.

By the way, if you're wondering where Berlin's Wall stood before Germany reunited in 1990, it divided the city into eastern and western sectors at the Brandenburg Gate and stretched north and south from there. Keep in mind that the names of streets are changing in the eastern part.

GETTING AROUND

Berlin has an excellent public transport network, including buses, the U-Bahn (underground) and the S-Bahn (inner-city railway). All are run by Berlin's Public Transport Company, the BVG (tel. 216 50 88), and you can use one ticket for transfer to all other lines to your reach your destination. A **single ticket** costs 3 DM ($1.85) and is good up to two hours, allowing transfers, round-trips, or even an interruption of your trip (you could, for example, go to Dahlem for an hour or so and then return to the center with the same ticket). If you're traveling only a short distance (six stops by bus or three stops by subway), you can purchase a **Kurzstreckenkarte** for 2 DM ($1.25).

However, if you plan on traveling frequently by bus or subway you're better off buying a **Sammelkarte,** a card with four tickets for 10.40 DM ($6.50). A Sammelkarte with four short-distance tickets costs 6.40 DM ($4). In addition, there's also a special Ku'damm ticket costing only 1 DM (60¢), valid for travel on all buses that traverse the Ku'damm between Wittenbergplatz and Rathenauplatz.

You can also buy a **24-hour ticket** for 12 DM ($7.50), good for Greater Berlin, including trips to Potsdam.

Single tickets and Sammelkarte are available from automatic machines at U-Bahn and S-Bahn stations, ticket windows, and even at some automatic machines at bus stops (most common at bus stops along the Ku'damm). You can also purchase tickets at the BVG kiosk located in front of Bahnhof Zoo, as well as other tickets. Stop here, also, for information on transportation in Berlin, including night buses. It's open daily from 8am to 8pm.

BY S-BAHN & U-BAHN The U-Bahn has eight lines with a total of 116 stations. Lines run from about 4 or 5am until midnight or 1am. The S-Bahn stretches throughout Greater Berlin, and is useful for trips to Wannsee or from Bahnhof Zoo directly to Friedrichstrasse, and onward throughout eastern Berlin. Be sure to validate your ticket yourself by punching it in one of the small machines at the entrance to the platforms.

BY BUS Many of Berlin's buses are double-deckers, affording great views of the city. You can purchase a ticket from the bus driver, or use your Sammelkarte (described above). If you're transferring, simply show the bus driver your ticket. Apart from the normal day services, there are also special night buses (*Nachtbusse*) that run the entire night. You can pick up the schedule at the BVG office in front of Bahnhof Zoo station. In summer there are special excursion buses marked with a triangle that make fast and convenient runs from Theodor-Heuss-Platz to recreation areas at Grünewald, from Wannsee station to Pfaueninsel, and from Nikolassee station to Wannsee Beach. Bus no. 100, a double-decker, travels 24 hours a day between Bahnhof Zoo and Alexanderplatz. It's an interesting ride and is a good way to travel between the eastern and western parts of the city.

BY BICYCLE **Fahrradbüro Berlin,** Hauptstrasse 146, in Schöneberg near the Kleistpark U-Bahn station (tel. 784 55 62), rents bicycles by the day. The rate is 12 DM ($7.50), plus a deposit. Open Monday through Wednesday and Friday from 10am to 6pm, on Thursday from noon to 7:30pm, and on Saturday from 10am to 4pm.

BY TAXI   You shouldn't have to take a taxi, but if you do, there are four taxi companies with the following telephone numbers: 6902, 26 10 26, 69 10 01, or 21 02 02. The meter starts at 3.60 DM ($2.25), plus 1.69 DM ($1.05) per kilometer. Luggage costs 1 DM (60¢) extra.

FAST **BERLIN**

Babysitters   For a babysitter in Berlin, call the **Baby-Sitters Service**, Claudiusstrasse 6 (tel. 393 59 81).

Banks   Banks are open Monday through Friday from 9am to 1 or 3pm, with slightly longer hours one or two days a week, depending on the bank. The **American Express** office is located across the plaza from the Gedächtniskirche in the center of town at Kurfürstendamm 11 (tel. 882 75 75), up on the first floor (entrance is not directly on the Ku'damm, but around the corner on the plaza). It's open Monday through Friday from 9am to 5:30pm and on Saturday from 9am to noon. You can have your mail sent here free if you have American Express traveler's checks or its credit card. Otherwise the service costs 2 DM ($1.25) per inquiry.

If you need to exchange money outside these hours, your best bet is the **Deutsche Verkehrs-Kredit-Bank** (tel. 881 71 17), the exchange office at Bahnhof Zoo. It's open Monday through Saturday from 8am to 9pm and on Sunday and holidays from 10am to 6pm.

Business Hours   Downtown businesses and shops are open Monday through Friday from 9 or 10am to 6 or 6:30pm and on Saturday from 9am to 2pm. On the first Saturday of the month (called *langer Samstag*), shops remain open until 6pm. In addition, some shops remain open longer on Thursday, until 8:30pm.

Consulates   The **U.S. Consulate** is in Dahlem at Clayallee 170 (tel. 832 40 87). It's open for Americans who have lost their passports Monday through Friday from 8:30 to 11:30am, while its visa section is open Monday through Friday from 8:30 to 10:30am. The **Canadian Consulate** is on the 12th floor of the Europa-Center (tel. 261 11 61), open Monday through Friday from 8:15am to 12:30pm and 1:30 to 5pm. The **U.K. Consulate** is at Uhlandstrasse 7-8 (tel. 309 52 93 or 309 52 92), open Monday through Friday from 9am to noon and 2 to 4pm (visa section, only in the morning).

Currency   The German **Deutsch Mark (DM)** is divided into 100 **Pfennig.** Coins come in 1, 2, 5, 10, and 50 Pfennig, and 1, 2, and 5 DM. Notes are issued in 5, 10, 20, 50, 100, 200, 500, and 1,000 DM. Note that new banknotes were issued in late 1990 that are valid along with the older ones.

Dentists and Doctors   The Berlin Tourist Information Office in the Europa-Center has a list of English-speaking doctors and dentists in Berlin. If you need a doctor in the middle of the night or in an emergency, call 31 00 31.

Emergencies   In Berlin, important numbers include 110 for police, 112 for the fire department or an ambulance, and 31 00 31 for an emergency doctor. To find out which pharmacies are open nights, call 1141.

Holidays   New Year's (Jan 1), Good Friday, Easter Sunday and Monday, Ascension Day, Whit Sunday and Monday, Labor Day (May 1), German Reunification Day (Oct 3), Day of Prayer and Repentance (third Wednesday in Nov), and Christmas (Dec 25–26).

Information   For information regarding Berlin's tourist offices and useful publications on what's going on in the city, see the "Information" section of "Orientation and Getting Around," above.

Laundry/Dry Cleaning   Ask the staff of your pension or hotel where the most conveniently located self-service laundry is. Otherwise, **Wasch Center** is near the center of town at Leibnizstrasse 72 (on the corner of Kantstrasse) and at Uhlandstrasse 53 (between Pariser Strasse and Düsseldorfer Strasse). Hours for both

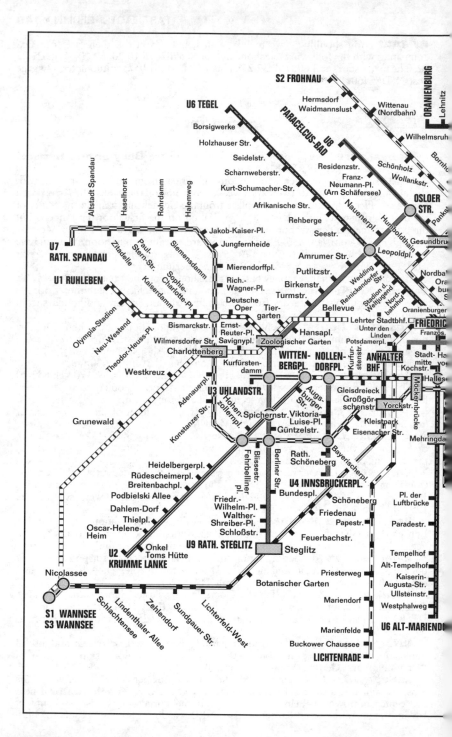

THE U-BAHN AND THE S-BAHN

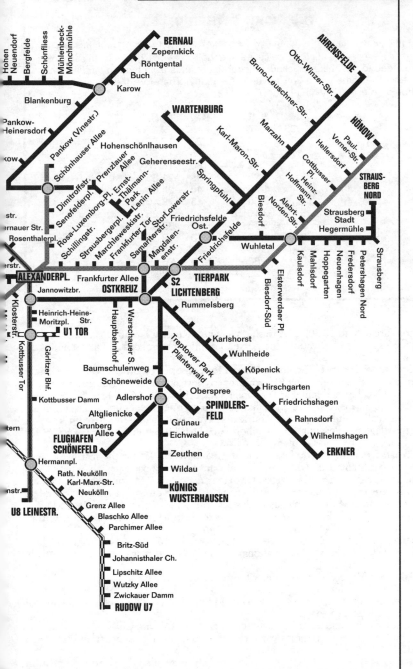

THE MARK & THE DOLLAR

At this writing $1 = approximately 1.60 DM (or 1 DM = 62¢), and this was the rate of exchange used to calculate the dollar values given in this chapter (rounded to the nearest nickel). This rate fluctuates from time to time and may not be the same when you travel to Germany. Therefore the following table should be used only as a guide:

DM	U.S.	DM	U.S.
.25	.16	15	9.35
.50	.31	20	12.50
.75	.47	25	15.60
1	.62	30	18.75
2	1.25	35	21.85
3	1.85	40	25.00
4	2.50	45	28.10
5	3.10	50	31.25
6	3.75	60	37.50
7	4.35	70	43.75
8	5.00	80	50.00
9	5.60	90	56.25
10	6.25	100	62.50

locations are 6am to 10:30pm. A wash cycle with detergent is 5.50 DM ($3.45), 1 DM (60¢) for a spin, and 1 DM (60¢) for a dryer. For information, call 213 88 00 or 854 26 57.

Lost and Found   Berlin's **general lost-property office** is at Tempelhofer Damm 3 (tel. 699 364 44 or 69 91). For property lost on public transportation services, check the BVG lost-and-found at Potsdamer Strasse 184 (tel. 216 14 13).

Mail   The **post office** in Bahnhof Zoo is open 24 hours a day for mail, telephone calls, and telegrams. You can have your mail sent here in care of Hauptpostlagernd, Postamt 120 Bahnhof Zoo, D-1000 Berlin 12 (tel. 313 97 99 for inquiries). Mailboxes in Germany are yellow.

Airmail letters to North America cost 1.65 DM ($1.05) for the first five grams, while postcards cost 1.05 DM (65¢). If you want to mail a package, you'll have to go to one of the city's larger post offices at Goethestrasse 2-3 or Marburger Strasse 12-13, which is near the Europa-Center. At these post offices you can buy boxes, complete with string and tape. Boxes come in five sizes and range in price from 1.10 DM (70¢) to 3.60 DM ($2.25). Both these post offices are open Monday through Friday from 8am to 6pm and on Saturday from 8am to 1pm.

Newspapers   **Europa Presse Center** (tel. 216 30 03), on the ground floor of the Europa-Center, sells international newspapers and magazines. It's open daily from 9am to 11pm.

Police   The emergency number for police in both East and West Berlin is 110.

Radio/TV   Tune in to 90.2 FM (87.6 for cable) for the BBC, 87.9 AM (94 on cable) for the American Forces Network, and 98.8 FM (102.85 cable) for the British Forces Broadcasting Services.

Many medium- and upper-range hotels offer cable TV with CNN news broadcasts from the United States, a sports channel in English, Super Channel from the United Kingdom, and MTV, a music channel.

Shoe Repair   For quick service on shoe repairs, head for **Wertheim** department store, Kurfürstendamm 231, or either **Karstadt** or **Hertie** department store on Wilmersdorfer Strasse, where you'll find a Mister Minit specializing in repairs.

Tax   Germany's 14% government tax is included in the price at restaurants and most hotels, including all the locales listed in this chapter. You can recover part of the 14% Value-Added Tax added to most goods—check "Savvy Shopping," below, for more information.

Taxis   See "Orientation and Getting Around," above.

Telephone   Local telephone calls cost 30 Pfennig (20¢) for the first three minutes. If you want to make an **international call,** look for phone booths with the green "International" sign or go to the post office. The main post office at Bahnhof Zoo is open 24 hours. It costs 12.60 DM ($7.85) to make a three-minute long-distance phone call to the United States.

If you're going to make a lot of phone calls or wish to make an international call from a phone booth, you might wish to purchase a **telephone card.** Available for sale at post offices, they come in values of 12 DM ($7.50) and 50 DM ($31.25). Simply insert them into the telephone slot. Telephone cards are becoming so popular in Germany that many public telephones no longer accept coins. The 12-DM card gives you approximately 40 minutes of local telephone calls; the 50-DM card is useful for long-distance calls.

At press time, the country code for former West Germany was 49 and for former East Germany was 37. Note, however, that all of Germany will probably have the same country code by 1993, and that it will probably be 49. If in doubt, call your operator.

The area code for all of Berlin is 30 if you're calling from the United States or from countries outside Germany, 030 if you're calling from within Germany.

Note, too, that in 1992 it was necessary to first dial 9 when calling from West to East Berlin; from eastern Berlin, it was necessary to first dial 849 for west Berlin. That is expected to have changed by 1993, when all you'll have to do is dial the actual telephone number for all numbers within Greater Berlin. If in doubt, ask at your hotel or the tourist office for the latest information. For information on telephone numbers in Berlin (those in the east are slowly being changed), call 11 88.

Incidentally, if you come across a number with a dash, the number following the dash is simply the extension number, which you can reach directly simply by dialing the entire number.

Note: The area codes given in this chapter are for calling from the United States.

Tipping   Since service is already included in hotel and restaurant bills, you are not obliged to tip. However, it is customary to round up restaurant bills to the nearest mark; if a meal costs more than 20 DM ($12.50), most add a 10% tip. For taxi drivers, round up to the nearest mark. Porters receive 2 DM ($1.25).

4. BUDGET ACCOMMODATIONS

Most of Berlin's pensions and hotels are clustered along and around the city's main street, Kurfürstendamm, called Ku'damm for short. Even those establishments farther away are not very far, usually within a 5- or 10-minute ride by subway to Bahnhof Zoo (Bahnhof Zoologischer Garten, West Berlin's main station).

You can save lots of money by taking a room without a private bath, and unlike cheaper accommodations in Munich, you rarely have to pay extra for a shower in Berlin. A pension is usually a smaller establishment with fewer rooms and lower prices than a hotel, though sometimes there is only a fine line between the two. Continental breakfast is often optional in the low-priced establishments—therefore, if there are two or more of you who like breakfast, you might be as well off taking a more expensive room that offers breakfast in the price. In any case, all prices include tax and service charge.

However, keep in mind that although every effort was made to be accurate, prices for rooms may go up during the lifetime of this book. Since the fall of the Wall room rates have shot upward, a reflection of the fact that Berlin has become such a popular destination that the demand for rooms has sometimes exceeded the supply. In addition, real estate in Berlin has skyrocketed, making it difficult for small pension owners to make ends meet. Be sure, therefore, to ask about the exact rate when making your reservation. At the most, prices should be no more than 10–15 DM ($6.25–$9.35) higher than those given below.

Note that in Germany, floors are counted beginning with the ground floor (which would be the American first floor) and go up to the first floor (the American second) and beyond. And remember, if the recommendations below are full, the tourist office will find you a room for a 5-DM ($3.10) fee.

Area codes given are for use from the United States. See "Fast Facts," above, for codes for calling from within Germany.

DOUBLES FOR LESS THAN 86 DM ($54)

NEAR SAVIGNYPLATZ & THE KU'DAMM

About a 10-minute walk from Bahnhof Zoo and 5 minutes from the Ku'damm, Savignyplatz is an interesting small square with some good restaurants and bars. Near the square is the S-Bahn Savignyplatz station, with direct service to Bahnhof Zoo (one stop) and to Friedrichstrasse Station and Alexanderplatz in eastern Berlin. If you're coming from Tegel Airport, take city bus no. 109 to Kurfürstendamm or Bahnhof Zoo.

HOTEL PENSION BIALAS, Carmerstrasse 16, 1 Berlin 12, Tel. 30/312 50 25 or 312 50 26. Telex 186506. 40 rms (2 with toilet only, 10 with shower and toilet). **S-Bahn:** Savignyplatz. **Bus:** 109 from Tegel Airport to Bahnhof Zoo; then a seven-minute walk.
$ Rates: (including continental breakfast): 60 DM ($37.50) single without shower or toilet, 80 DM ($50) single with shower and toilet; 70–100 DM ($43.75–$62.50) double without shower or toilet, 130 DM ($81.25) double with shower and toilet). No credit cards.

Located on a quiet street off Savignyplatz, this establishment is a cross between a hotel and a pension. An older building with large, simple rooms spread over several floors, its cheapest rooms are on the fifth floor (no elevator).

PENSION CENTRUM, Kantstrasse 31, 1 Berlin 12. Tel. 30/31 61 53. 7 rms (1 with shower). **S-Bahn:** Savignyplatz. **Bus:** 109 from Tegel Airport or Bahnhof Zoo to Bleibtreustrasse (or a 10-minute walk from Bahnhof Zoo).
$ Rates: 40–45 DM ($25–$28.10) single without shower; 70–85 DM ($43.75–$53.10) double without shower, 100 DM ($62.50) double with shower. Breakfast 7.50 DM ($4.70) extra. No credit cards.

Built in 1880, this house has stucco ceilings and double-paned windows. Formerly run by the Schmückers, who recently retired after 18 years, it's now managed by their English-speaking daughter and her Dutch husband, who hope to add showers to more of the rooms. It's an old-fashioned place with plenty of charm—but call first for a reservation. Because of an incredible increase in rent, the owners may have to close the pension in 1993.

PENSION CORTINA, Kantstrasse 140, 1 Berlin 12. Tel. 30/313 90 59.

21 rms (5 with shower). **S-Bahn:** Savignyplatz. **Bus:** 109 from Tegel Airport or Bahnhof Zoo to Schlüterstrasse.

$ Rates (including continental breakfast): 55–60 DM ($34.35–$37.50) single without shower; 85–95 DM ($53.10–$60) double without shower, 100–110 DM ($62.50–$68.75) with shower; 120 DM ($75) triple without shower, 150 DM ($93.75) triple with shower. No credit cards.

This building is 100 years old, but the breakfast room has been remodeled in bright colors and some showers were recently installed. Run the last 25 years by a Berlin native and her Italian husband, it offers mostly large rooms, each one different. There are several larger rooms that can sleep four or more people, including one facing the front that even has a balcony planted with flowers. The reception is up on the first floor. The location of this place is great.

NEAR EUROPA-CENTER

PENSION FISCHER, Nürnberger Strasse 24a, 1 Berlin 30. Tel. 30/218 68 08. Fax 30/213 42 25. 10 rms (8 with shower). **U-Bahn:** Augsberger Strasse; then a one-minute walk. **Bus:** 109 from Tegel Airport to Kurfürsten/Nürnberger Ecke (or a seven-minute walk from Bahnhof Zoo).

$ Rates: 40 DM ($25) single without shower; 50 DM ($31.25) single with shower; 70 DM ($43.75) double without shower, 70–90 DM ($43.75–$56.25) double with shower; 105 DM ($65.60) triple with shower; 120 DM ($75) quad with shower. Breakfast 6–8 DM ($3.75–$5) extra. No credit cards.

Rooms here are roomy and clean with large windows, each with an old-fashioned tiled heater, the kind that used to heat all German homes. There's an automatic machine for coffee or hot chocolate, and the breakfast room is pleasant with plants and flowers and a TV. Reception is on the second floor.

PENSION ZIMMER DES WESTENS, Tauentzienstrasse 5, 1 Berlin 30. Tel. 30/214 11 30. 8 rms (2 with shower). **U-Bahn:** Wittenbergplatz; then a one-minute walk.

$ Rates (including continental breakfast): 60–70 DM ($37.50–$43.75) single with shower; 85–90 DM ($53.10–$56.25) double without or with shower. Extra bed 36 DM ($22.50). No credit cards.

This reasonably priced pension is tucked away in an inner courtyard on busy Tauentzienstrasse, up three flights of rickety stairs. The pension itself is clean and pleasant, and since rooms with shower are slightly smaller, they're the same price as those without. All in all, a good value and a great location, between the Europa-

---

ⓕ FROMMER'S SMART TRAVELER: HOTELS

VALUE-CONSCIOUS TRAVELERS SHOULD
TAKE ADVANTAGE OF THE FOLLOWING:

1. Rooms without private bathroom, which are much cheaper.
2. Inexpensive lodging in the heart of town.
3. Winter discounts.

QUESTIONS TO ASK IF YOU'RE ON A BUDGET

1. Is breakfast included in the price? Is it buffet style, allowing you to eat as much as you wish?
2. How much is the surcharge on local and long-distance telephone calls?

Center and KaDeWe department store, about a seven-minute walk from Bahnhof Zoo.

SOUTH OF CITY CENTER

PENSION MÜNCHEN, Güntzelstrasse 62, 1 Berlin 31. Tel. 30/854 22 26. 8 rms (3 with shower and toilet). **U-Bahn:** Güntzelstrasse.

$ Rates: 50 DM ($31.25) single without shower or toilet; 75–85 DM ($46.85–$53.10) double without shower or toilet, 115–130 DM ($71.85–$81.25) double with shower and toilet. Breakfast 8 DM ($5) extra. No credit cards.

⭐   This pension is about a half-hour walk from the Ku-Damm, or just two stops on the U-Bahn. You can tell immediately upon entering that it's run by an artist: There's artwork on the walls and flowers in vases, and everything is tastefully done. Frau Renate Prasse, the charming proprietor, is indeed a sculptor and her rooms are bright, white, and spotless. The pension is located on the third floor, reached by elevator. Highly recommended.

IN KREUZBERG

HOTEL TRANSIT, Hagelberger Strasse 53-54, 1 Berlin 61. Tel. 30/785 50 51. 39 rms (all with shower). **U-Bahn:** U-1 from Bahnhof Zoo to Möckernbrücke, then U-7 from Möckernbrücke to Mehringdamm. **Bus:** 119 from the Ku'damm to Mehringdamm, or 109 from Tegel Airport to Adenauerplatz and then 119 from Adenauerplatz to Mehringdamm.

$ Rates (including buffet breakfast): 55–65 DM ($34.35–$40.60) single; 85–95 DM ($53.10–$59.35) double; 115–130 DM ($71.85–$81.25) triple; 30 DM ($18.75) per person in six-bed rooms. AE, MC, V.

Just two blocks away from Pension Kreuzberg, and also under youthful ownership, the Hotel Transit opened in 1987 in a converted former tobacco factory. It's located in the inner courtyard of an old brick building, up on the third floor reached via elevator. The single and double rooms are a bit expensive, but there are economical dormitory-style rooms that sleep six. All rooms are painted white, a bit stark and factorylike in style, but all have huge windows, high ceilings, and new fixtures. The airy breakfast room features a buffet offering as much coffee or tea as you want, and there's also a bar. This hotel is great for the price, and attracts young people from around the world.

PENSION KREUZBERG, Grossbeerenstrasse 64, 1 Berlin 61. Tel. 30/251 13 62. 13 rms (none with bath). **Bus:** 119 from the Ku'damm to Grossbeerenstrasse, or 109 from Tegel Airport to Adenauerplatz and then 119 from Adenauerplatz to Grossbeerenstrasse.

$ Rates: 50 DM ($31.25) single; 71 DM ($44.35) double; 90 DM ($56.25) triple; 120 DM ($75) quad. Breakfast 7 DM ($4.35) extra. No credit cards.

Housed in an older building with character, this 50-year-old pension has recently been acquired by Armin and Dieter, two energetic young men who are renovating the place themselves. Rooms are perfectly acceptable, especially for the younger backpacking generation. This is one of Berlin's best values.

IN EASTERN BERLIN

HOTEL NEUES TOR, Invalidenstrasse 102, 1040 Berlin. Tel. 30/282 38 59. 6 rms (2 with shower and toilet, 1 with shower only). TV **U-Bahn:** Zinnowitzerstrasse; then a one-minute walk. **S-Bahn:** Friedrichstrasse or Lehrter Stadtbahnhof; each about a 10-minute walk away.

$ Rates: 75 DM ($46.85) double without shower or toilet, 100 DM ($62.50) double with shower only, 125 DM ($78.10) double with shower and toilet. Breakfast 7 DM ($4.35) extra. No credit cards.

This pension, once located practically next to the Wall, is a good place to stay if you want to live in what was once East Berlin. Although a bit dated, the rooms are clean and comfortable, each equipped with a television and radio. Two rooms even boast new tiled bathrooms. The couple running the pension is friendly and accommodating, and will serve breakfast in your room.

DOUBLES FOR LESS THAN 120 DM ($75)

ON OR NEAR THE KU'DAMM AND SAVIGNYPLATZ

ARCO, Kurfürstendamm 30, 1 Berlin 15. Tel. 30/882 63 88. Fax 30/881 99 02. 20 rms (10 with shower only, 6 with shower and toilet). TEL **U-Bahn:** Uhlandstrasse; then a one-minute walk. **Bus:** 109 from Tegel Airport to Uhlandstrasse; then a one-minute walk.

$ **Rates** (including continental breakfast): 70 DM ($43.75) single without shower or toilet, 115 DM ($71.85) single with shower only, 140 DM ($87.50) single with shower and toilet; 110 DM ($68.75) double without shower or toilet, 138 DM ($86.60) double with shower only, 170 DM ($106.55) double with shower and toilet. Extra bed 35 DM ($21.85). AE, DC, MC, V.

⭐ This delightful third-floor pension (there is no elevator) has a great location right on the Ku'damm. Both the reception room with its muraled ceiling and the breakfast room serve as an art gallery, and breakfast is served unusually long for Berlin, from 6 to 11am. Rooms are spacious and tastefully decorated. Four of the seven rooms overlooking the Ku'damm have balconies, but those facing the back courtyard are much quieter.

HOTEL ALPENLAND, Carmerstrasse 8, 1 Berlin 12. Tel. 30/312 39 70 or 312 48 98. Fax 30/313 84 44. 43 rms (6 with shower only, 6 with shower and toilet). **S-Bahn:** Savignyplatz; then a three-minute walk. **Bus:** 109 to Uhlandstrasse; then a five-minute walk (or a 10-minute walk from Bahnhof Zoo).

$ **Rates** (including continental breakfast): 80 DM ($50) single without shower or toilet, 90 DM ($56.25) single with shower only; 115 DM ($71.85) double without shower or toilet. 125 DM ($78.10) double with shower only, 175 DM ($109) double with shower and toilet. Extra bed 55–65 DM ($34.35–$40.60). No credit cards.

True to its name, the lobby and breakfast room of this hotel are decorated in Tyrolean fashion, with lots of wood, some antiques, and dried-flower arrangements. Rooms are spread over four floors (there's no elevator) and are simple and comfortable. Rooms that face toward the back are quieter but the view is duller; some rooms have telephones. The building is old and a bit run-down, but the hotel itself is clean. It caters largely to group travelers.

HOTEL BOGOTA, Schlüterstrasse 45, 1 Berlin 15. Tel. 30/881 50 01. Fax 30/883 58 87. Telex 0184946. 130 rms (12 with shower only, 65 with shower and toilet). TEL **Bus:** 109 from Tegel Airport or Bahnhof Zoo to Bleibtreustrasse.

$ **Rates** (including continental breakfast): 65 DM ($40.60) single without shower or toilet, 105 DM ($65.60) single with shower only, 120 DM ($75) single with shower and toilet; 107 DM ($66.85) double without shower or toilet, 155 DM ($96.85) double with shower only, 185 DM ($115.60) double with shower and toilet; 135 DM ($84.35) triple without shower or toilet, 170 DM ($106.25) triple with shower only, 220 DM ($137.50) triple with shower and toilet. AE, DC, MC, V.

⭐ Located just off the Ku'damm, this older hotel is well maintained and has a friendly staff. The building itself is a century old, with a stairway that wraps itself around an old-fashioned elevator and lobbies on each floor that are reminiscent of another era. Each room is different, and there's a cozy TV room where you can spend a quiet evening.

HOTEL CRYSTAL, Kantstrasse 144, 1 Berlin 12. Tel. 30/312 90 47 or 312 90 48. Fax 30/312 64 65. Telex 184022. 32 rms (18 with shower only, 10 with tub or shower and toilet). TEL **Bus:** 109 from Tegel Airport to Bleibtreustrasse, or 149 from Bahnhof Zoo to Savignyplatz (three stops).

$ Rates (including continental breakfast): 65 DM ($40.60) single without shower or toilet, 80 DM ($50) single with shower only, 90–130 DM ($56.25–$81.25) single with tub or shower and toilet; 90 DM ($56.25) double without shower or toilet, 110–120 DM ($68.95–$75) with shower only. 130–150 DM ($81.25–$93.75) double with tub or shower and toilet; 190 DM ($118.75) triple with tub or shower and toilet. Crib available. AE, MC, V.

Although this is an older pension in a building dating from the early 1900s, its present owners took over in 1988. John and Dorothee Schwarzrock (John is an American) are real characters, friendly and outgoing, and happy to see American guests. Rooms are simple with just the basics, and they're kept spotlessly clean. There's a small bar for hotel guests just off the lobby.

HOTEL MEDENWALDT, Kurfürstendamm 225, 1 Berlin 15. Tel. 30/881 70 34 or 881 70 35. Fax 30/881 42 59. 29 rms (18 with shower only, 4 with shower and toilet). TEL **U-Bahn:** Kurfürstendamm. **Bus:** 109 from Tegel Airport to Ecke Joachimstaler Strasse (or a five-minute walk from Bahnhof Zoo).

$ Rates (including buffet breakfast): 85 DM ($53.10) single without shower or toilet, 110 DM ($68.75) single with shower only; 120 DM ($75) double without shower or toilet, 150 DM ($93.75) double with shower only, 200 DM ($125) double with shower and toilet. Extra bed 35 DM ($21.85). AE, MC, V.

This older hotel has a great location right on the Ku'damm, not far from the Kaiser Wilhelm Memorial Church. A few rooms face toward the Ku'damm, and have double windows to help cut down on noise, but if you prefer a quieter location, choose one of the rooms that face toward the back of the building. Rooms have those tall ceilings from another era, some with antique furnishings and stucco decoration and some with TVs. There's an elevator.

HOTEL-PENSION BREGENZ, Bregenzer Strasse 5, 1 Berlin 15. Tel. 30/881 43 07. Fax 30/882 40 09. 22 rms (5 with shower only, 10 with shower and toilet). MINIBAR TV TEL **U-Bahn:** Adenauerplatz; then a five-minute walk. **Bus:** 109 from Tegel Airport or Bahnhof Zoo to Leibnitzstrasse.

$ Rates (including continental breakfast): 65 DM ($40.60) single without shower or toilet, 95 DM ($59.35) single with shower and toilet; 99 DM ($61.85) double without shower or toilet, 130 DM ($81.25) double with shower only, 160 DM ($100) double with shower and toilet. Extra person 35 DM ($21.85). Crib available. MC.

Located on a quiet residential street south of Olivaer Platz and the Ku'damm, this small, friendly hotel is located on the fourth floor (there's an elevator). Rooms are clean and roomy, and the staff will make bookings for the theater and sightseeing tours.

HOTEL-PENSION DITTBERNER, Wielandstrasse 26, 1 Berlin 15. Tel. 30/881 64 85. 22 rms (13 with shower only, 7 with tub or shower and toilet). TEL **U-Bahn:** Adenauerplatz; then a six-minute walk. **Bus:** 109 from Tegel Airport or Bahnhof Zoo to Leibnitzstrasse.

$ Rates (including continental breakfast): 90 DM ($56.25) single with shower only, 120–130 DM ($75–$81.25) single with tub or shower and toilet; 110 DM ($68.75) double without shower or toilet, 130–140 DM ($81.25–$87.50) double with shower only, 140–200 DM ($87.50–$125) double with tub or shower and toilet. No credit cards.

This small pension is like a gallery—a Japanese screen and artwork in the small lobby, woodblock prints and posters in the corridors. Little wonder! The owner's husband runs the gallery downstairs. The breakfast room is grandly decorated with thick upholstered chairs, white tablecloths, and fresh flowers on each table. Guests return time and time again to this 30-year-old pension. The reception is on the third floor; guests received a special key for the elevator.

HOTEL-PENSION FUNK, Fasanenstrasse 69, 1 Berlin 15. Tel. 30/882

71 93. Fax 30/882 71 93. 15 rms (11 with shower only, 1 with shower and toilet).
TEL **Bus:** 109 from Tegel Airport or Bahnhof Zoo to Uhlandstrasse (or an
eight-minute walk from Bahnhof Zoo).

$ Rates (including continental breakfast): 65 DM ($40.60) single without shower or
toilet, 75 DM ($46.85) single with shower only; 100 DM ($62.50) double without
shower or toilet, 115–120 DM ($71.85–$75) double with shower only; 130 DM
($81.25) double with shower and toilet. No credit cards.

This clean and orderly pension features a sweeping white-marbled staircase in the
entranceway, tall ceilings, and flowered wallpaper. Rooms are large, with French
provincial furnishings.

**HOTEL-PENSION JUWEL, Meinekestrasse 26, 1 Berlin 15. Tel. 30/882
71 41.** 22 rms (15 with shower only, 3 with shower and toilet). TEL **Bus:** 109
from Tegel Airport or Bahnhof Zoo to Uhlandstrasse (or less than a 10-minute walk
from Bahnhof Zoo).

$ Rates (including continental breakfast): 75 DM ($46.85) single without shower or
toilet, 85 DM ($53.10) single with shower only, 130 DM ($81.25) single with
shower and toilet; 110 DM ($68.75) double without shower or toilet, 140 DM
($87.50) double with shower only. 170 DM ($106.25) double with shower and
toilet. Crib available. No credit cards.

Rooms here are simple, with high ceilings and pictures of local Berlin artists adorning
the walls. Since all but two rooms face a back street, the location is very quiet. The
breakfast room is decorated with owner Roswitha Schreiterer's patchwork quilts, and
breakfast is served by waitresses dressed in black wearing white aprons.

**HOTEL-PENSION MODENA, Wielandstrasse 26, 1 Berlin 15. Tel. 30/88
57 01-0.** Fax 30/881 52 94. 21 rms (9 with shower only, 5 with shower and toilet).
U-Bahn: Adenauerplatz. **Bus:** 109 from Tegel Airport or Bahnhof Zoo to
Leibnitzstrasse.

$ Rates (including continental breakfast): 60–70 DM ($37.50–$43.75) single
without shower or toilet, 80 DM ($50) single with shower only, 90–100 DM
($56.25–$62.50) single with shower and toilet; 100–110 DM ($62.50–$68.75)
double without shower or toilet, 120 DM ($75) double with shower only, 140–160
DM ($87.50–$100) double with shower and toilet; 150 DM ($93.75) triple with
shower only, 190 DM ($118.75) triple with shower and toilet. No credit cards.

The Hotel-Pension Modena, on the second floor, is a good place to stay in terms of
location and price. Managed by Frau Kreutz, this small pension offers spotlessly clean
rooms. It's located on the western edge of the Ku'damm, near Olivaer Platz.

NEAR EUROPA-CENTER

**PENSION NÜRNBERGER ECK, Nürnberger Strasse 24a, 1 Berlin 30.
Tel. 30/218 53 71.** 8 rms (none with bath). **U-Bahn:** Augsberger Strasse; then
a one-minute walk. **Bus:** 109 from Tegel Airport to Kurfürsten/Nürnberger Eck (or
a seven-minute walk from Bahnhof Zoo).

$ Rates: 55–60 DM ($34.35–$37.50) single; 100–110 DM ($62.50–$68.75)
double; 130–150 DM ($81.25–$93.75) triple. Breakfast 8 DM ($5) extra. No
credit cards.

Fresh flowers decorate the hallway of this second-floor pension (there is no elevator),
and rooms are very nice with comfortable old-style furniture. Note the huge doors
and stucco ceilings, typical of Old Berlin.

NEAR BAHNHOF CHARLOTTENBURG

**HOTEL CHARLOTTENBURGER HOF, Stuttgarter Platz 14, 1 Berlin 12.
Tel. 30/324 48 19.** Fax 30/323 37 23. 45 rms (38 with shower and toilet). TV
S-Bahn: Charlottenburg. **Bus:** 109 from Tegel Airport or Bahnhof Zoo to
Charlottenburg.

$ **Rates:** 70 DM ($43.75) single without shower or toilet, 90–110 DM ($56.25–$68.75) single with shower and toilet; 90–110 DM ($56.25–$68.75) double without shower or toilet, 110–150 DM ($68.75–$93.75) double with shower and toilet; 40 DM ($25) per person triple or quad without shower and toilet, 45 DM ($28.10) per person triple or quad with shower and toilet. Discounts available during the winter and for longer stays. No credit cards.

This is one of Berlin's most modern budget hotels. Its staff is young and friendly, and rooms are white and bright with modern furniture and colorful pictures adorning the walls. Rooms with bath have telephones, and all rooms have televisions with cable offering English programs, but there's also a TV lounge. Breakfast is not included in the price, but you may want to go to the adjoining Café Voltaire with its large windows, plants, and artwork, where breakfast costs 5 DM ($3.10). The café is open 24 hours a day. The triples and quads are of particularly good value.

SOUTH OF CITY CENTER

HOTEL PENSION POSTILLON, Gasteiner Strasse 8, 1 Berlin 31. Tel. 30/87 52 32. Fax 30/87 38 59. Telex 182946. 24 rms (5 with shower only, 4 with shower and toilet). TEL **U-Bahn:** U-9 from Bahnhof Zoo to Berliner Strasse and then U-7 from Berliner Strasse to Blissestrasse. **Bus:** 109 from Tegel Airport to Jakob-Kaiser-Platz (first stop) and then U-Bahn U-7 from Jakob-Kaiser-Platz to Blissestrasse.

$ **Rates** (including buffet breakfast): 70 DM ($43.75) single without shower or toilet, 80 DM ($50) single with shower only, 90 DM ($56.25) single with shower and toilet; 110 DM ($68.75) double without shower or toilet, 125 DM ($78.10) double with shower only, 150 DM ($93.75) double with shower and toilet. Extra bed 40–45 DM ($25–$28.10). No credit cards.

Although it's a bit far from the city center (about a 20-minute walk from the Ku'damm), Postillon is easily reached by U-Bahn. The building here is a bit old (the exterior was undergoing renovation during my last visit) and rooms are simple, but those that face the front have balconies. Breakfast is served buffet style. The pension is owned by English-speaking Herr Bernd Lucht.

HOTEL-PENSION STEPHAN, Güntzelstrasse 54, 1 Berlin 31. Tel. 30/87 41 21. 8 rms (3 with shower only). **U-Bahn:** Güntzelstrasse.

$ **Rates** (including continental breakfast): 50 DM ($31.25) single; 95 DM ($59.35) double; 140 DM ($87.50) triple. No credit cards.

Located about a 20-minute walk from the Ku'damm or just three stops from Bahnhof Zoo by U-Bahn, this small pension has super-high ceilings. The singles are fairly small here. A couple of the other rooms are furnished with antiques. Breakfast is served in a cozy room with lots of plants and flowers and a color TV.

NEAR POTSDAMER PLATZ

JUGENDHOTEL INTERNATIONAL, Bernburgerstrasse 27-28, 1 Berlin 61. Tel. 30/262 30 81 or 262 30 82. Fax 30/262 61 57. Telex 186575. 70 rms (12 with shower and toilet). **Bus:** 109 from Tegel Airport to Bahnhof Zoo and then 29 from Bahnhof Zoo to Anhalter Bahnhof.

$ **Rates** (including continental breakfast): 55 DM ($34.35) single without shower or toilet, 105 DM ($65.60) single with shower and toilet; 100 DM ($62.50) double without shower or toilet, 150 DM ($93.75) double with shower and toilet; 130 DM ($81.25) triple without shower or toilet, 215 DM ($134.35) triple with shower and toilet. No credit cards.

Rooms here are nicely furnished with natural-wood furniture, and those with private bathrooms even have a telephone, color TV, and a table with chairs. All rooms—

singles, doubles, and triples—have sinks. Located near Potsdamer Platz, it welcomes youth groups, individuals, and families.

SUPER-BUDGET CHOICES

YOUTH HOTELS

Although catering largely to youth groups, most of these youth hotels will also take individual travelers of any age; most have single and double rooms in addition to multibed dormitory rooms.

JUGENDGÄSTEHAUS AM ZOO, Hardenbergstrasse 9a, 1 Berlin 12. Tel. 30/312 94 10. 58 beds. **Bus:** 109 from Tegel Airport to Bahnhof Zoo; then a 10-minute walk.

$ Rates: 50 DM ($31.25) single; 93 DM ($58.10) double; 35 DM ($21.85) per person for rooms sleeping three to eight people. No credit cards.

This no-frills establishment is easy to overlook—there's no big sign on the outside and the building itself looks a bit run-down and neglected. But its prices can't be beat. And neither can its location—a 10-minute walk from Bahnhof Zoo. The reception is up on the fourth floor (the elevator doesn't always work) and there's a bar open from 9:30pm to 6am. Although this hostel is intended for people younger than 27, any age is welcome if there's room.

JUGENDGÄSTEHAUS CENTRAL, Nikolsburger Strasse 2-4, 1 Berlin 31. Tel. 30/87 01 88. 456 beds. **U-Bahn:** Güntzelstrasse, Spichernstrasse, or Hohenzollernplatz; then a five-minute walk.

$ Rates: 35 DM ($21.85) per person in multibed dorms (including three meals), 31 DM ($19.35) per person (including breakfast). Sheets 7 DM ($4.35) extra for stays of one or two nights, free for stays of three nights or longer. No credit cards.

This dormitory-style accommodation caters to school groups with multibed rooms, but will accept single travelers if there's room. Note, however, that it's open only to those under 25 or bona-fide students, and there's a 1am curfew. Rooms sleep 8–12 people, and you'll need your own towel here. If you take your meals here, it's really cheap—and lunch boxes will be prepared for those who are gone all day. It's located just two subway stops or a 20-minute walk south of the Ku'damm.

JUGENDGÄSTEHAUS FEURIGSTRASSE, Feurigstrasse 63, 1 Berlin 62. Tel. 30/781 52 11. 200 beds. **U-Bahn:** Kleistpark; then about a five-minute walk. **Bus:** 146 from Bahnhof Zoo to Dominicusstrasse.

$ Rates (including buffet breakfast): 30–40 DM ($18.75–$25) per person in multibed rooms. Sheets 5 DM ($3.10) extra. No credit cards.

Located in Schöneberg, this youth hotel caters primarily to school groups but will also take individuals if there's room, giving preference to younger people. There's no curfew here, and rooms sleep 4–12 people.

STUDENTEN-HOTEL BERLIN, Meininger Strasse 10, 1 Berlin 62. Tel. 30/784 67 20 or 784 67 30. Telex 0181287. 50 rms (none with bath). **Bus:** 109 from Tegel Airport to Bahnhof Zoo and then 149 from Bahnhof Zoo to JFK Platz.

$ Rates (including breakfast and sheets): 35 DM ($21.85) per person in multibed dorms; 39 DM ($24.35) per person double. No credit cards.

Although it's called a student hotel, you don't have to be a student to stay here and any age is welcome. It has 20 double rooms; the remaining rooms have four or five beds each. A game room is outfitted with a pool table, soccer game, and pinball machine. The hotel is located near John F. Kennedy Platz and Rathaus Schöneberg.

YOUTH HOSTELS

You have to have a youth hostel card to stay at Berlin's youth hostels, which you can purchase for 30 DM ($20) at the youth hostels themselves, and there's no age limit (though "seniors" pay more). Keep in mind that curfew at these youth hostels is midnight.

JUGENDGÄSTEHAUS AM WANNSEE, Badeweg 1, 1 Berlin 38. Tel. 30/803 20 34. Telex 186606. 264 beds. **S-Bahn:** Nikolassee; then a seven-minute walk.

$ Rates (including breakfast and sheets): 25 DM ($15.60) per person for "juniors" (up to and including 26 years of age), 30.50 DM ($19.05) per person for "seniors" (age 27 and older). Lunch or dinner 7.50 DM ($4.70) extra. No credit cards.

Berlin's newest youth hostel, this handsome brick building with red trim is located close to Wannsee, a lake popular for swimming and boating in the summer. Rooms have four beds each and showers are plentiful.

JUGENDGÄSTEHAUS BERLIN, Kluckstrasse 3, 1 Berlin 30. Tel. 30/261 10 97. 364 beds. **U-Bahn:** Kurfürstenstrasse; then a 12-minute walk. **Bus:** 109 from Tegel Airport to Bahnhof Zoo and then 129 from Bahnhof Zoo to Kluckstrasse.

$ Rates (including breakfast and sheets): 25 DM ($15.60) per person for "juniors" (up to and including 26 years of age), 30.50 DM ($19.05) per person for "seniors" (27 years and older). Lunch or dinner 7.50 DM ($4.70) extra. No credit cards.

This is the most conveniently located youth hostel in the city. A modern, white-and-black building not far from the Kurfürstenstrasse station, it's so popular that you should write one month in advance to reserve a bed between February and November. All rooms are dormitory style with four to six beds per room, and everyone gets a locker with a key.

JUGENDHERBERGE ERNST REUTER, Hermsdorfer Damm 48-50, 1 Berlin 28. Tel. 030/404 16 10. 110 beds. **Directions:** From Bahnhof Zoo, U-Bahn U-9 to Leopoldplatz, then U-6 from Leopoldplatz to Tegel (last stop), and then bus no. 125 to Jugendherberge; from Tegel Airport, bus no. 128 to Kurt Schumacher Platz, then U-Bahn U-6 to Tegel (last stop), and then bus no. 125 to Jugendherberge.

$ Rates (including breakfast and sheets): 20 DM ($12.50) per person for juniors (up to and including 26 years of age), 24.50 DM ($15.30) per person for "seniors" (age 27 and older). Dinner or a lunch box 7.50 DM ($4.70) extra. No credit cards.

Surrounded by woods on the far outskirts of Berlin, this youth hostel is about 35 minutes from the city center—if you make good connections. All rooms have eight beds; facilities include table tennis and a TV.

YOUTH CAMP

INTERNATIONALES JUGENDCAMP, Ziekowstrasse 161, 1 Berlin 27. Tel. 30/433 86 40. Directions: U-Bahn 6 to Tegel (last stop); then bus no. 125 to the Titusweg stop (three stops).

$ Rates (including sheets): 8 DM ($5) per person. **Open:** Mid-June to the end of Aug.

This youth camp consists of a large tent, with mattresses and sheets provided. Showers are free. Guests must be between the ages of 14 and 26 and must leave the premises during the day, from 9am to 5pm. No written reservations are accepted, so call when you get to Berlin.

WORTH THE EXTRA BUCKS

HOTEL LES NATIONS, Zinzendorfstrasse 6, 1 Berlin 21. Tel. 30/392 20 26. Fax 30/392 50 10. Telex 186861. 42 rms (5 with shower only, 14 with shower and toilet). TEL **U-Bahn:** Turmstrasse; then a five-minute walk. **Bus:** 245 from Bahnhof Zoo to Alt Moabit.

$ Rates (including continental breakfast): 70 DM ($43.75) single without shower or toilet, 95 DM ($59.35) single with shower only, 115 DM ($71.85) single with shower and toilet; 120 DM ($75) double without shower or toilet, 140 DM ($87.50) double with shower only, 175 DM ($109.35) double with shower and toilet. Extra bed 20 DM ($12.50); crib free. AE, DC, MC, V. **Parking:** Free.

This small, modern, comfortable hotel offers clean, pleasant rooms. They are carpeted, some have TVs, and those with private shower and toilet facing the front street even have small balconies. There is also a bar. Proprietor Frau Hilde Meier speaks English, as does her front-desk staff. It's located north of the Tiergarten park, just two stops from Bahnhof Zoo on the U-Bahn.

HOTEL-PENSION FASANENHAUS, Fasanenstrasse 73, 1 Berlin 15. Tel. 30/881 67 13. Fax 30/882 39 47. 25 rms (15 with shower only, 10 with shower and toilet). **Bus:** 109 from Tegel Airport or Bahnhof Zoo to Uhlandstrasse (or a seven-minute walk from Bahnhof Zoo).
$ Rates (including continental breakfast): 125 DM ($78.10) single with shower and toilet; 145 DM ($90.60) double with shower only, 190 DM ($118.75) double with shower and toilet. Extra bed 40 DM ($24.80). Crib available. No credit cards.

Located near the Käthe-Kollwitz Museum (one of my favorite German artists), this delightful pension has a great location not far from the very expensive Hotel Kempinski. The building itself has an incredibly ornate entry stairway, and the rooms are large. The breakfast room is pleasant with wooden ceiling beams, and the homey living room has large French doors that open onto a balcony with potted plants.

PENSION KNESEBECK, Knesebeckstrasse 86, 1 Berlin 12. Tel. 30/31 72 55. 15 rms (none with bath). **S-Bahn:** Savignyplatz; then a three-minute walk. **Bus:** 109 from Tegel Airport or Bahnhof Zoo to Uhlandstrasse (or a seven-minute walk from Bahnhof Zoo).
$ Rates (including continental breakfast): 85 DM ($53.10) single; 130 DM ($81.25) double; 55 DM ($34.35) per person in a family room. AE.

English-speaking, friendly Jutta Jorende took over this older pension a couple of years ago, making it more livable and pleasant. She put plants and modern lighting in the breakfast room, and 10 of her rooms face an inner courtyard, making them very quiet. There's also a large family room with four beds, two rooms have telephones, and televisions are available upon request. You can't go wrong here.

---

5. BUDGET DINING

There are an estimated 6,000 restaurants in Berlin, and a great many of these are ethnic restaurants serving international cuisine—not surprising, considering the large foreign population in Berlin. Even young Germans are more likely to go out for Greek or Italian food than they are for their own heavier cuisine. What's more, ethnic restaurants are often cheaper than their German counterparts.

You'll find many restaurants clustered along the Ku'damm area, as well as on the pedestrian street of Wilmersdorfer Strasse and around Savignyplatz. The cheapest of these is the *Imbiss,* a stand-up eatery where everything from sausages to fish sandwiches might be offered.

In addition to the restaurants below, several nightspots in the "Evening Entertainment" section (below) offer food as well. In fact, a few of the bars specialize in breakfast for those who stay out all night.

FAVORITE MEALS

Most main dishes served in a German restaurant come with side dishes such as potatoes and/or sauerkraut. One of Berlin's best-known specialties is *Eisbein* (pig's knuckle), usually served with sauerkraut and potatoes or puréed peas. *Kasseler Rippenspeer* is smoked pork chops, created by a butcher in Berlin named Kassel. *Bockwurst*, also created in Berlin, is a super-long sausage, and *Boulette* is a type of meatball. Other foods you might encounter on a menu include *Sauerbraten* (marinated beef in sauce), *Leberkäs* (a Bavarian specialty, a type of meatloaf), and *Schnitzel* (breaded veal cutlet). In any case, most main dishes in a German restaurant include one or two side dishes, and make a meal. And by all means, try a *Berliner Weisse*—a draft beer with a shot of raspberry.

AFTERNOON COFFEE   Just as the British have their afternoon tea, the Germans love their afternoon coffee, which of course requires a slice of cake or pie to accompany it.

If you're a caffeine addict, the cheapest place for a cup of coffee is at **Tschibo,** a chain coffee shop that sells both the beans and the brew, and often small cakes as well. Coffee or espresso is just 1.95 DM ($1.20), which you can drink at one of the stand-up counters. You can find Tschibo shops at Ku'damm 11 (near the American Express and Memorial Church) and Wilmersdorfer Strasse 117.

Another place for afternoon coffee is at one of the department-store restaurants, which are described below. But if you want to splurge, then go to **Café Kranzler,** Kurfürstendamm 18-19 (tel. 882 69 11), one of the few cafés to have survived the ravages of World War II. It's the favored people-watching spot on the Ku'damm, and in the summer you can sit outside. Coffee starts at 3 DM ($1.85), with cakes costing more. It's open daily from 8am to midnight.

In eastern Berlin, the place to go is the newly renovated **Opernpalais,** Unter den Linden 5 (tel. 200 22 69). One of Berlin's most celebrated cafés, it's part of a palace that was built in 1733, destroyed during World War II, and then rebuilt. On the ground floor is an opulent coffee shop, where a breakfast buffet is offered until noon. Coffee here is 3 DM ($1.85), but the main attraction is the more than 40 different tortes prepared daily. In summer there's an outdoor imbiss selling coffee, drinks, and snacks and outdoor seating.

LOCAL BUDGET BETS

DEPARTMENT STORES

HERTIE, Wilmersdorfer Strasse 118-119. Tel. 311 050.
   Cuisine: GERMAN. **U-Bahn:** Wilmersdorfer Strasse.
$ Prices: 8–13 DM ($5–$8.10). No credit cards.
   Open: Mon–Wed and Fri 9am–6pm, Thurs 9am–8pm, Sat 9am–1:30pm (to 5:30pm the first Sat of the month).
Hertie's Le Buffet, a restaurant with waitress service, is on the first floor. Every day it offers a different meal for 9 DM ($5.60), as well as about 10 other changing dishes such as fish, sausages, spaghetti, kidney ragoût, or Schnitzel. There's a salad bar.

QUELLE, Wilmersdorfer Strasse 54. Tel. 320 05 11.
   Cuisine: GERMAN. **U-Bahn:** Wilmersdorfer Strasse.
$ Prices: 9–15 DM ($5.60–$9.35). No credit cards.
   Open: Mon–Wed and Fri 9am–6pm, Thurs 9am–7:30pm, Sat 9am–1:30pm (to 5:30pm the first Sat of the month).
Across the street from Hertie is Quelle's Die Buffeteria on the second floor, a cafeteria offering fish, chicken, steaks, daily specials, and a help-yourself salad bar. This is the most cheerful, if a bit kitschy, of the department store restaurants, with its white interior, fake plants, and summertime feel to it.

KADEWE, Wittenbergplatz. Tel. 212 10.
   Cuisine: INTERNATIONAL. **U-Bahn:** U-1, U-2, or U-3 to Wittenbergplatz.

 **FROMMER'S SMART TRAVELER:
RESTAURANTS**

VALUE-CONSCIOUS TRAVELERS SHOULD
TAKE ADVANTAGE OF THE FOLLOWING:

1. Stand-up food stalls (*Imbiss*), many in the area of the Ku'damm.
2. The special menu of the day (*Tageskarte*), which may not be on the menu.
3. Food counters and restaurants in department stores, an especially good value in Berlin.
4. Coffee-shop chains such as Tschibo, with coffee costing 1.95 DM ($1.20) a cup.

QUESTIONS TO ASK IF YOU'RE ON A BUDGET

1. Is there an extra charge for each piece of bread?
2. Does the entrée come with side dishes?

$ Prices: 4–20 DM ($2.50–$11.85). No credit cards.
Open: Mon–Wed and Fri 9am–6:30pm, Thurs 9am–8:30pm, Sat 9am–2pm (to 6pm the first Sat of the month).

KaDeWe is short for Kaufhaus des Westens, and on the top floor of this large department store is the largest food department in continental Europe. It's so amazing that it may be worth coming to Berlin just to see it—sausages galore (the Germans must make more types of sausages than anyone else in the world), cheeses, teas, breads, jams, sweets, vegetables, coffees, spices, wines, salads, meats (including more cuts of pork than I can count), tanks full of live fish, and much more. And in the middle of all these sections are sit-down counters serving a wide variety of food and drink, specializing in such things as salads, pasta, ice cream, potato dishes, coffee, seafood, grilled chicken, and wines. There are many more counters, but I couldn't keep track of them all! At any rate, this place is overwhelming—and you'll find the profusion of food either wonderful or decadent.

KARSTADT, Wilmersdorfer Strasse 109-111. Tel. 31 891.
Cuisine: GERMAN. **U-Bahn:** Wilmersdorfer Strasse.
$ Prices: 7–19 DM ($4.35–$11.85). No credit cards.
Open: Mon–Wed and Fri 9am–6pm, Thurs 9am–8pm, Sat 9am–1:30pm (to 5:30pm the first Sat of the month).

Located on Berlin's best-known pedestrian shopping lane, this department store's restaurant-café with waiter service is on the fourth floor and offers daily specials that may include such dishes as Schnitzel, rumpsteak, chicken fricassee, fish, or spaghetti starting at about 10–12 DM ($6.25–$7.50). It also serves salads and cakes, and breakfast until 11:30am.

WERTHEIM, Kurfürstendamm 231. Tel. 88 20 61.
Cuisine: GERMAN/SNACKS. **U-Bahn:** Kurfürstendamm.
$ Prices: 6–25 DM ($3.75–$15.60). No credit cards.
Open: Mon–Wed and Fri 9am–6pm, Thurs 9am–8pm, Sat 9am–2pm (to 6pm the first Sat of the month).

This store's food department is in the basement, with counters serving various types of snacks and meals. Salads, stews, pasta, potato pancakes, sandwiches, grilled chicken, wine, beer, and German specialties are just some of the items you can eat here. There are tables where you can sit after you've made your purchase. The Club Culinar counter offers soup and choices of several main dishes, including vegetarian.

GERMAN MEALS FOR LESS THAN 10 DM ($6.25)

ON WILMERSDORFER STRASSE

These simple restaurants are convenient if you're shopping on Berlin's most popular shopping street, Wilmersdorfer Strasse. In addition, be sure to read over "Local Budget Bets," above, for department stores here with food service.

JOSEPH LANGER, Wilmersdorfer Strasse 118. Tel. 31 67 80.
Cuisine: GERMAN. **U-Bahn:** Wilmersdorfer Strasse.
$ Prices: 1.60–8 DM ($1–$5). No credit cards.
Open: Mon–Fri 9am–6:30pm, Sat 8:30am–2pm (to 6pm the first Sat of the month).
This small butcher shop sells inexpensive and simple meals, which you can eat standing up at one of its stand-up tables or take out. Cheapest are the Wurst selling for 1.60 DM ($1) a pair. Entrées include Leberkäs, Gulasch soup, Schnitzel, Boulette, and Eisbein.

NORDSEE, Wilmersdorfer Strasse 58. Tel. 323 10 44.
Cuisine: FISH. **U-Bahn:** Wilmersdorfer Strasse.
$ Prices: 6.50–11 DM ($4.05–$6.85). No credit cards.
Open: Mon–Wed and Fri 9am–7pm, Thurs 9am–8:30pm Sat 9am–3pm (to 6:30pm the first Sat of the month).
Nordsee is part of a national chain of fast-food fish restaurants, where ordering is made easy with an illustrated menu behind the cashier. Simply go through the cafeteria line and order one of the dozen choices, such as fried haddock, fish soup, or fish sticks. There's also take-out service, with all kinds of fish sandwiches starting at about 2.50 DM ($1.55).

ROGACKI, Wilmersdorfer Strasse 145-146. Tel. 341 40 91.
Cuisine: GERMAN. **U-Bahn:** Bismarckstrasse.
$ Prices: 4–15 DM ($2.50–$9.35). No credit cards.
Open: Mon–Fri 9am–6pm, Sat 8am–2pm.
This immensely popular stand-up cafeteria is actually a shop selling all kinds of meats, Wurst, fish, stews, salads, cheese, bread, and more, with a buffet in the left-hand corner. There's great variety, and prices are about the best in Berlin. It has been around for 60 years and is located about a seven-minute walk north of the Wilmersdorfer Strasse pedestrian section between Bismarckstrasse and Zillestrasse (look for the blue fish on its facade).

NEAR THE UNIVERSITY

IHRE FRISCH-BACKSTÜBE, Knesebeckstrasse 12. Tel. 31 06 00.
Cuisine: GERMAN.
$ Prices: 2.50–7 DM ($1.55–$4.35). No credit cards.
Open: Mon–Sat 6:30am–6:30pm, Sun noon–6pm.
Located on the corner of Knesebeckstrasse and Goethestrasse north of Savignyplatz, this cheerful self-service restaurant offers a wide variety of breads, cakes, pizza by the slice, sandwiches, and a changing menu of warm dishes, which may range from smoked pork chops to Leberkäs. There are tables where you can sit and eat or you can take it with you. It's a 10-minute walk north of the Ku'damm.

MENSA, Technische Universität, Hardenbergstrasse 34. Tel. 3140.
Cuisine: GERMAN.
$ Prices: 2.70–4.50 DM ($1.70–$2.80). No credit cards.
Open: Lunch only, Mon–Fri 11:15am–2:30pm.

This student cafeteria serves fixed-price meals to anyone in its more upscale restaurant on the top floor. Simply walk through the ground floor and then follow the signs for RESTAURANT up the stairs. Pick up a tray and choose from one of the daily changing menus, complete meals that range from Gulasch or curry rice to liver or vegetarian ragoût. While not an aesthetic place for a meal (it looks like the student establishment that it is), this is one of the cheapest restaurants in Berlin. It's just a 10-minute walk from Bahnhof Zoo.

NEAR WITTENBERGPLATZ

In addition to this simple restaurant, KaDeWe (listed above under "Local Budget Bets") has many sit-down counters on the sixth floor.

ZUM AMBROSIUS, Einemstrasse 14. Tel. 261 29 93.
    Cuisine: GERMAN. **U-Bahn:** Nollendorfplatz, then a five-minute walk; or Wittenbergplatz, then an eight-minute walk.
    $ Prices: 7–15 DM ($4.35–$9.35). No credit cards.
    Open: Daily 11:30am–11:30pm (last order).
This simple and unpretentious restaurant/bar, located on the corner of Kurfürstenstrasse and Einemstrasse, has been here about 50 years and has changed little. This is a working-person's establishment, evident in its hearty platters of Eisbein, Schnitzel, smoked pork chops, Leberkäs, Knödel (dumplings), spaghetti, Bauernfrühstuck (a kind of omelet with potatoes and sausage), and changing daily specials. In summer there are seats outside.

IN EASTERN BERLIN

CASINO, in the Staatsbibliothek, Unter den Linden 8. Tel. 2037 83 10.
    Cuisine: GERMAN. **Bus:** 100 or 157 to the Staatsoper stop.
    $ Prices: Soup or salad 2.50–5.50 DM ($1.55–$3.45); main courses 6–10 DM ($3.75–$6.25). No credit cards.
    Open: Mon–Fri 9am–6pm, Sat 10am–4:30pm.
This inexpensive cafeteria, located in a public library right on Unter den Linden, offers a limited number of soups, a salad, and daily specials, written on a blackboard. Offerings may include Schnitzel, rumpsteak, or fish. Coffee is a cheap 1.30 DM (80¢) a cup. It's a small place, so you may want to avoid the lunch-hour rush. Convenient for sightseeing jaunts along Unter den Linden and to Museum Island.

NORDSEE, Spandauer Strasse 4. Tel. 212 68 81.
    Cuisine: FISH. **S-Bahn and U-Bahn:** Alexanderplatz. **Bus:** 100.
    $ Prices: 7–12 DM ($4.35–$7.50). No credit cards.
    Open: Mon–Sat 10am–9:30pm, Sun 11am–7pm.
One of the first chain restaurants to open in what was formerly East Berlin, this Nordsee is bigger than most, offering plenty of tables and doing a brisk business. Like others in this chain, it has an illustrated menu behind the self-service counter, showing pictures of fried haddock, fish soup, fish sticks, and half a dozen other choices. There's also salad and fish sandwiches.

SUPPENTERRINE, Alexanderplatz 2. Tel. 212 40 32.
    Cuisine: GERMAN STEWS. **S-Bahn and U-Bahn:** Alexanderplatz.
    $ Prices: 3.80–5 DM ($2.35–$3.10). No credit cards.
    Open: Mon–Fri 11am–6pm, Sat noon–5pm.
This is a simple establishment, right on Alexanderplatz, across from the Hotel Stadt Berlin. It offers seating along a counter, where customers eat Eintöpfe, or one-pot stews. The limited number of stews change, but may include Linseneintopf (lentil stew), Hungarian Gulasch, Sauerkraut soup, potato soup, or Serbian bean soup. This place is often crowded, so you may have to wait for a seat to be vacated.

ETHNIC MEALS FOR LESS THAN 12 DM
[$7.50]
ON OR NEAR THE KU'DAMM & SAVIGNYPLATZ

ASHOKA, Grolmanstrasse 51. Tel. 313 20 66.
Cuisine: INDIAN. **S-Bahn:** Savignyplatz.
$ **Prices:** 4.50–11 DM ($2.80–$6.85). No credit cards.
Open: Daily noon–2am.
This is a tiny hole-in-the-wall Indian restaurant where the open kitchen takes up half the place. It's popular with the students of the area, and there are more than a dozen offerings of vegetarian dishes alone. Good for a hot-and-spicy fix.

ASIA-QUICK, Lietzenburgerstrasse 96. Tel. 882 15 33.
Cuisine: CHINESE.
$ **Prices:** 9–15 DM ($5.60–$9.35). No credit cards.
Open: Mon–Fri noon–midnight.
This simple place is, as its name implies, quick to serve soups and dishes of fish, pork, beef, chicken, rice, and noodles. Most meat dishes come in three styles: chop suey (with soy sauce), sweet-and-sour, and Szechuan (spicy). There are also vegetarian selections. There's a TV in the corner (just like most restaurants in Asia), and you can either eat here or take it out. It's a three-minute walk south of the Ku'damm, near Bleibtreustrasse.

ATHENER GRILL, Kurfürstendamm 156. Tel. 892 10 39.
Cuisine: GREEK/ITALIAN. **U-Bahn:** Adenauerplatz; then a one-minute walk.
$ **Prices:** 4–15 ($2.50–$9.35). AE, DC, MC.
Open: Daily 11am–5am.
If you can't decide whether you want Greek or Italian food, or if you want both, or if you want a meal at 3am, head for the Athener Grill. It's located toward the western end of the Ku'damm on the corner of Albrecht-Achilles-Strasse (look for a modern brick building). Its menu is on the wall—decide what you want, pay the cashier, and then hand your ticket to the cook at the respective counter. Counters are divided into various specialties, with Greek food at one counter, pizzas at another, etc. It has a cheerful interior, and Greek wines start at 2.50 DM ($1.55).

AVANTI, Rankestrasse 2. Tel. 883 52 40.
Cuisine: ITALIAN. **U-Bahn:** Kurfürstendamm.
$ **Prices:** 5.50–16 DM ($3.45–$10). No credit cards.
Open: Daily 11am–2am.
With the possible exception of Turkish Imbisse, I wouldn't be surprised to hear that there are more self-service Italian cafeterias than any other ethnic restaurant in Berlin; they're seemingly on every corner. This one has a great location just off the Ku'damm near the Gedächtniskirche and Wertheim department store. It's clean and modern, with contemporary artwork on the walls and an ice-cream/cocktail bar. Pizzas and pastas are all priced under 10 DM ($6.25), and there's a salad bar where you can help yourself at 5 DM ($3.10) for a small plate. There are also daily specials.

ITALIA SNACK, Kurfürstendamm 63. Tel. 881 18 42.
Cuisine: ITALIAN. **U-Bahn:** Adenauerplatz; then a three-minute walk.
$ **Prices:** 9–18 DM ($5.60–$11.25). No credit cards.
Open: Sun–Thurs 11am–2am, Fri–Sat 11am–3am.
This is yet another self-service Italian restaurant, though it's a bit more expensive, perhaps because of its prime location on the Ku'damm and also its more varied meat dishes. In any case, all the pizzas and pastas are under 12 DM ($7.50), and a slice of pizza is 2 DM ($1.25). Many of the dishes are visible behind the glass counter, which makes choosing and ordering easy.

JIMMY'S DINER, Pariser Strasse 41. Tel. 882 31 41.
Cuisine: AMERICAN/MEXICAN.

$ Prices: 8–20 DM ($5–$12.50). No credit cards.
Open: Sun–Thurs 4pm–4am, Fri–Sat 4pm–6am.
Come here for a bit of 1950s Americana. It looks like a diner, with its blood-red furniture and chrome, drive-in speakers hanging above the window, and old advertisements on the wall. Its menu is eclectic, from corn on the cob and Aunt Mary's chicken salad to huge "Quarter pow7ders," sandwiches, spareribs, spaghetti, tacos, enchiladas, and chili con carne, most under 10 DM ($6.25). This place, a five-minute walk from the Ku'damm, on the corner of Sächsische Strasse and Pariser Strasse, is popular with Berlin's young student crowd.

KARAVAN, Kurfürstendamm 11. Tel. 881 50 05.
   Cuisine: TURKISH. **U-Bahn:** Kurfurstendamm or Bahnhof Zoo.
$ Prices: 4–9 DM ($2.50–$5.60). No credit cards.
   Open: Daily 8am–1am.
This is a tiny Turkish take-out establishment where you can sample this ethnic food at very low prices. I especially recommend the Turkish pizza, which has a thick, soft crust with a thin spread of meat and spices. There's also a changing daily special available for 9 DM ($5.60). Since all the food is visible behind the glass counter, just choose and point.
   Karavan is located next to the American Express office, across from the Gedächtniskirche. There's another branch called **Meister Snack** at the corner of Joachimstaler Strasse and Kantstrasse, under the eaves of the Bilka Department Store.

PICCOLA TAORMINA TAVOLA CALDA, Uhlandstrasse 29. Tel. 881 47 10.
   Cuisine: ITALIAN. **U-Bahn:** Uhlandstrasse.
$ Prices: 5–14 DM ($3.10–$8.75). No credit cards.
   Open: Daily 10am–2am.
This is one of the cheapest places in town for Italian pizza, pasta, and risotto. The menu is written on the wall: After deciding what you want, just order from the counter opposite. These guys—all Italian—are fast and will have your order ready in no time. You can take out your meal—one slice of pizza is only 2 DM ($1.25)—or sit down at one of the wooden tables. As for the food, the crowd at this casual eatery a three-minute walk south of the Ku'damm speaks for itself. Beer and wine available.

SAN MARINO, Savignyplatz 12. Tel. 313 60 86.
   Cuisine: ITALIAN. **S-Bahn:** Savignyplatz.
$ Prices: 7.50–35 DM ($4.70–$21.85). AE, MC, V.
   Open: Daily 11am–1am.
All the pizza and pasta dishes are priced under 15 DM ($9.35), but if you feel like splurging you can also order the much higher priced steaks and seafood. The restaurant is pleasant and artsy, and in summer you can sit outside with a view of Savignyplatz.

NEAR WILMERSDORFER STRASSE & BAHNHOF CHARLOTTENBURG

TY BREIZH, Kantstrasse 75. Tel. 323 99 32.
   Cuisine: FRENCH. **U-Bahn:** Wilmersdorfer Strasse. **S-Bahn:** Charlottenburg.
$ Prices: 7–25 DM ($4.35–$15.60). No credit cards.
   Open: Mon–Fri 5pm–1am, Sat 6pm–midnight.
This simple French restaurant is owned by Patrick Matteï, who speaks English, Italian, French, German, and Finnish and still finds time to work as chef of his restaurant. His specialty is an appetizer of mushrooms with shrimp and cheese. Other dishes on the menu include eggplant with paprika, onions, and tomato; quiche; beef cooked in a burgundy-wine sauce with onions; and crêpes and omelets.

NEAR WITTENBERGPLATZ

EINHORN, Wittenbergplatz 5-6. Tel. 218 63 47.

Cuisine: VEGETARIAN. **U-Bahn:** Wittenbergplatz; then a one-minute walk.
$ Prices: 6.50–9 DM ($4.05–$5.60). No credit cards.
Open: Mon–Fri 10am–6pm, Sat 10am–2pm.

This natural-foods shop, on the opposite end of the square from KaDeWe, sells daily specials of ready-made vegetarian dishes which may include curry risotto with vegetables, spinach canneloni, vegetarian lasagne, stews, salads, and fruit juices. You can eat at its stand-up counter or take it outside and sit on one of the benches lining the square.

LEKKERBEK, Ansbacherstrasse 11. Tel. 211 90 34.
Cuisine: SANDWICHES/INTERNATIONAL. **U-Bahn:** Wittenbergplatz; then about a three-minute walk.
$ Prices: 3.50–10 DM ($2.20–$6.25). No credit cards.
Open: Mon–Fri 7:30am–8pm, Sat 9am–8pm.

Located on a side street just off Wittenbergplatz, this inexpensive cafeteria specializes in sandwiches, with a dozen or so fillings prepared fresh each day such as egg, salami, ham, or tuna fish. There are also salads and daily specials that may include lasagne, moussaka, or rice pilaf with chicken. There's also pizza, and wonder of wonders, a no-smoking section.

GERMAN MEALS FOR LESS THAN 20 DM ($12.50)

NEAR THE KU'DAMM

HARDTKE, Meinekestrasse 27 a/b. Tel. 881 98 27.
Cuisine: GERMAN. **U-Bahn:** Uhlandstrasse; then less than a two-minute walk.
$ Prices: 11.50–30 DM ($7.20–$18.75). No credit cards.
Open: Daily 10am–1am.

Located just off the Ku'damm, this typical German eatery has been here more than 35 years and is very popular with German visitors to Berlin. It has its own butcher shop, assuring the freshest cuts; its sausages are excellent. Although you could spend up to 30 DM ($18.75) here for dinner of Eisbein, Schnitzel, and Schweinebraten on a splurge, you can also dine on sausages for under 12 DM ($7.50) (available only until 6pm). Either way, you're in for a treat.

WIRTSHAUS ZUM LÖWEN, Hardenbergstrasse 29. Tel. 262 10 20.
Cuisine: GERMAN. **U-Bahn:** Kurfürstendamm or Bahnhof Zoo.
$ Prices: 10–20 DM ($6.25–$12.50). DC, MC, V.
Open: Sun–Thurs 9am–midnight, Fri–Sat 9am–2am.

If your fantasies of Germany include mugs of foaming German beer and a traditional Bavarian band, this is the beer hall for you. Its interior is constructed to resemble a tree-filled Bavarian plaza, and there's outdoor seating in summer. Hearty platters of Schweinshaxe, Eisbein, Grillhendl (grilled chicken), Leberknödel, Wurst, Tafelspitz, Schnitzel, Cordon Bleu dishes, and other dishes are available, all with side dishes. It's conveniently located across from the Gedächtniskirche.

NEAR THE UNIVERSITY

CAFE HARDENBERG, Hardenbergstrasse 10. Tel. 312 33 30.
Cuisine: VARIED.
$ Prices: 8–14 DM ($5–$8.75). No credit cards.
Open: Daily 9am–midnight.

Located in the university district less than a 10-minute walk from Bahnhof Zoo, this popular café is always packed with students and people who work nearby. The portions of the daily specials are hearty, and it's decorated with museum posters, plants, and ceiling fans. Classical music can be heard until 4pm, after which it's

20th-century music. In the evening the atmosphere is more like that of a bar—beer and cocktails are served in addition to dinner. In the summer you can sit outside.

NEAR CHARLOTTENBURG S-BAHNHOF

TEGERNSEER TÖNNCHEN, Mommsenstrasse 34. Tel. 323 38 27.
   Cuisine: GERMAN. **S-Bahn:** Charlottenburg. **U-Bahn:** Wilmersdorfer Strasse.
$ **Prices:** 10–20 DM ($6.25–$12.50). No credit cards.
   Open: Daily 11:30am–midnight.
This German restaurant dishes out huge portions of local and Bavarian favorites such as Eisbein or Leberkäs, with a traditional decor to match. A good place to come if you're hungry, it's located just off Wilmersdorfer Strasse.

NEAR CHARLOTTENBURG PALACE

LUISEN-BRÄU, Luisenplatz 1. Tel. 341 93 88.
   Cuisine: GERMAN. **Bus:** 109, 121, 145, or 204.
$ **Prices:** 8–20 DM ($5–$12.50). No credit cards.
   Open: Daily 11am–midnight.
★ Located southeast of Charlottenburg Palace on the corner of Spandauer Damm, Luisen-Bräu brews its own beer on the premises (you can see the stainless-steel tanks) and sells German dishes to go along with it. The food, offered buffet style, changes daily but may include such choices as Spiessbraten (skewered meat and vegetables), Kasseler Rippenspeer (pork chops), Schweinebraten (pot-roasted pork), Boulette (a meatball), salads, and stews. Dining is at long wooden tables (which induces conversation with neighbors) or, in summer, outside. This place is convenient if you're visiting the palace or the many museums in the area.

IN DAHLEM

LUISE, Königin-Luise Strasse 40. Tel. 832 84 87.
   Cuisine: GERMAN/INTERNATIONAL. **U-Bahn:** Dahlem-Dorf; then about a one-minute walk.
$ **Prices:** 9–20 DM ($5.60–$12.50). No credit cards.
   Open: Mon–Sat 10am–11pm, Sun and hols 10am–3:30pm and 5–11pm.
This is a good choice in restaurants if you're visiting the many museums in Dahlem. It's a popular watering hole for people who live in the area (as crowded as it can get on a weekday afternoon, I wonder whether any of them work), but also serves snacks and main courses, including spaghetti, chili con carne, grilled chicken, Schnitzel, roast beef, fish, and daily specials. The indoors tends to be smoky since every other German smokes, but in fine weather Luise boasts a very large outdoor beer garden.

IN EASTERN BERLIN

RAABE-DIELE ERMELER HAUS, Märkisches Ufer 10. Tel. 279 36 17.
   Cuisine: GERMAN/INTERNATIONAL. **Reservations:** Recommended. **U-Bahn:** Märkisches Museum.
$ **Prices:** 10–22 DM ($6.25–$13.75). No credit cards.
   Open: Daily noon–midnight.
Go to the basement of this ornate, rococo-style house facing a small river to get hearty platters of typical German fare served in rustic surroundings. The menu includes Berliner Eisbein, lentil soup with sausage, cabbage rolls with potatoes, fish, and other local favorites. If you desire finer surroundings, the first-floor Weinrestaurant serves wild game and more elaborate meals, but with correspondingly higher prices, with main courses starting at 30 DM ($18.75).

WIENERWALD, Rathausstrasse 5. Tel. 212 32 91.
   Cuisine: GERMAN. **S-Bahn and U-Bahn:** Alexanderplatz.

$ Prices: Soups and salads 3.50–14 DM ($2.20–$8.75); main courses 9–18 DM ($5.60–$11.25). No credit cards.
Open: Daily 10am–midnight.
Wienerwald is a successful chain of restaurants specializing in grilled chicken, so it's not surprising that they've opened a branch here just off Alexanderplatz. Its menu includes a variety of chicken dishes, fish, soups, and a salad bar.

ZUR LETZTEN INSTANZ, Waisenstrasse 14-16. Tel. 242 55 28.
  Cuisine: GERMAN. **U-Bahn:** Klosterstrasse; then about a two-minute walk.
  $ Prices: 6–20 DM ($3.75–$12.50). No credit cards.
  Open: Mon 4pm–midnight, Tues–Sun 11am–midnight.

⭐ Open since 1621, this tiny restaurant claims to be Berlin's oldest *Gaststätte*. Its rooms are rustic, with plank floors, wainscoting, and a few antiques here and there. Its menu offers Berlin specialties, including Boulette, Kohlroulade (stuffed cabbage rolls), Paprikaschote (stuffed green peppers), and Berliner Eisbein. In summer, there are a few tables outside. It's located about a five-minute walk from Alexanderplatz, behind the Rathaus.

ETHNIC MEALS FOR LESS THAN 20 DM ($12.50)

ON OR NEAR THE KU'DAMM

CHUNG, Kurfürstendamm 190. Tel. 882 15 55.
  Cuisine: CHINESE. **U-Bahn:** Uhlandstrasse or Adenauerplatz.
  $ Prices: Main courses 15–30 DM ($9.35–$18.75); fixed-price lunch 10.50–14 DM ($6.55–$8.75). AE, MC, V.
  Open: Daily 11:30am–midnight.
This ornately decorated Chinese restaurant with hanging lanterns and a red-and-black ceiling occupies a prime spot on the Ku'damm. In fact, it extends over half the sidewalk, offering a good view of the famous boulevard. A special lunch menu is offered Monday through Friday from 11:30am to 3pm, which includes an appetizer and a choice of almost two dozen main courses. There's an English menu, so ordering is no problem. Chung is near Schlüterstrasse.

RESTAURANT MARCHE, Kurfürstendamm 14-15. Tel. 882 75 79.
  Cuisine: INTERNATIONAL. **U-Bahn:** Kurfürstendamm; then a one-minute walk.
  $ Prices: Main dishes 8–15 DM ($5–$9.35). V.
  Open: Daily 8am–midnight.
This is one of my favorite places for a bite to eat on the Ku'damm. A cafeteria, it imitates the neighborhood market, with various stands of fresh meals—most prepared in front of the customers. There's a salad bar, a vegetable stand, and counters offering a selection of meat dishes, soups, pasta, salads, daily specials, cakes, ice cream, desserts, and more. Simply grab a tray and walk around to the various counters. It's a good place to load up on veggies; there are also freshly squeezed fruit and vegetable juices.

TAVERNA PLAKA, Joachimstaler Strasse 14. Tel. 883 15 57.
  Cuisine: GREEK. **U-Bahn:** Kurfürstendamm.
  $ Prices: Appetizers and salads 5–13 DM ($3.10–$8.10); main courses 15–28 DM ($9.35–$17.50). No credit cards.
  Open: Mon–Fri 4pm–1am, Sat–Sun and hols noon–2am.
Although most dishes are 16 DM ($10) or more, I recommend ordering the plentiful mesedes Plaka for 10 DM ($6.25). It's an appetizer plate, with dolmades (stuffed grape leaves), eggplant salad, feta cheese, and a sampling of other Greek delicacies—the waiter didn't blink twice when that's all I ordered. An alternative is to order the huge Greek salad (called *choriatiki*). There's also moussaka, fish, souvlaki, and gyros. In any case, this first-floor restaurant is decorated in Mykonos white-and-blue, with flowers and candles on each table. The service is friendly, and the recorded music is, of course, cheerfully Greek. Greek wines available.

STREET FOOD

There are a number of food stalls (*Imbiss*) up and down the Ku'damm and on Alexanderplatz selling Wurst, french fries, Turkish specialties, and beer. Prices are under 4 DM ($2.50). In addition, a number of restaurants described above—including Nordsee, Joseph Langer, Rogacki, Piccola Taormina Tavola Calda, Italia Snack, Asia-Quick, and Karavan—all sell take-out food at low prices.

PICNIC SUPPLIES & WHERE TO EAT THEM

All the department stores above have large food departments (especially KaDeWe) and counters serving prepared meats, salads, and take-out food. You can also buy take-out food at the stand-up establishments listed above.

As for places to eat your purchases, the most convenient green space is the **Tiergarten,** a park located just northwest of Bahnhof Zoo.

WORTH THE EXTRA BUCKS

ZITADELLE, Am Juliusturm, Spandau. Tel. 334 21 06.
   Cuisine: GERMAN. **Reservations:** Recommended. **U-Bahn:** Zitadelle.
$ **Prices:** Main courses 20–40 DM ($12.50–$32.80); fixed-price banquet 65–85 DM ($40.60–$53.10). AE, DC, MC, V.
   Open: Daily 11:30am–11pm.
   Imagine sitting in the bowels of a 700-year-old medieval fortress with stone walls and an open fireplace and eating fish or skewered grilled meat, much like people did centuries ago. The Zitadelle is just that, a medieval fortress that offers an à la carte menu during the week and a medieval banquet on Friday, Saturday, and Sunday evening with ballad-singing and special entertainment. The weekends, therefore, are the most fun and it's best to make a reservation. Although Spandau is on the outskirts of Berlin and was its own city until incorporated in 1920, it is easily reached by subway.

---

6. ATTRACTIONS

SUGGESTED ITINERARIES

Berlin is compact, with an efficient public transportation system, so you can see quite a lot of the city in a few days. To help you get the most out of your visit, here are some suggested itineraries to guide you to the most important attractions.

IF YOU HAVE ONE DAY   Your first destination should be Dahlem, where you'll find the Gemäldegalerie (Picture Gallery) with its masterpieces from the 13th to the 18th century. From Dahlem, head for Charlottenburg, stopping off first for a quick look at the famous bust of Queen Nefertiti in the Egyptian Museum. Across the street from the Egyptian Museum is Charlottenburg Palace, where you should visit the Knobelsdorff Flügel and the Schinkel Pavilion for a look at how Prussian royalty lived.

Before the day ends, go to the Brandenburger Tor (Gate), built in the 1780s as the finishing touch to the avenue Unter den Linden, one of Berlin's most famous boulevards. Finish off the day with an evening stroll along the Ku'damm.

IF YOU HAVE TWO DAYS   Devote your entire first morning to Dahlem, adding the Ethnological Museum, the Museum of Prints and Drawings, or one of the museums for Asian art to your itinerary. In the afternoon head for Charlottenburg, where in addition to the palace and the Egyptian Museum there's also the Museum of

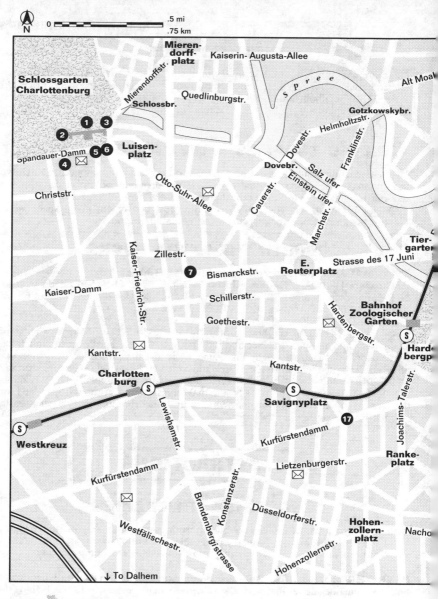

0 |▬▬▬▬▬| .5 mi
0 |▬▬▬▬▬| .75 km
N

Schlossgarten Charlottenburg

Mieren-dorff-platz

Kaiserin- Augusta-Allee

Spree

Alt Moal

Mierendorffstr.

Schlossbr.

Quedlinburgstr.

Gotzkowskybr.

Helmholtzstr.

Dovestr.

Franklinstr.

Luisen-platz

Spandauer-Damm

Dovebr.

Salz ufer

Otto-Suhr-Allee

Cauerstr.

Einstein ufer

Marchstr.

Christstr.

Tier-garten

Kaiser-Friedrich-Str.

Zillestr.

Strasse des 17 Juni

E. Reuterplatz

Bismarckstr.

Schillerstr.

Bahnhof Zoologischer Garten

Kaiser-Damm

Goethestr.

Hardenbergstr.

Hard bergp

Kantstr.

Charlotten-burg

Kantstr.

Lewishamstr.

Savignyplatz

Joachims-Talerstr.

Westkreuz

Kurfürstendamm

Ranke-platz

Kurfürstendamm

Lietzenburgerstr.

Konstanzerstr.

Brandenburgstrasse

Düsseldorferstr.

Hohen-zollern-platz

Nacho

Westfälischestr.

Hohenzollernstr.

↓ To Dalhem

Berlin ★
GERMANY

Ägyptisches Museum
(Egyptian Museum) ⑥
Akademie der Künste ⑧
Antikenmuseum ⑤
Brandenburg Tor ⑬
Bröhan Museum ④
Charlottenburg Palace ❶
Deutsche Oper Berlin ❼

Englischer Garten ⑨
Europa Center ⑯
Kaiser Wilhelm
  Gedachtniskirche ⑮
Kunstgewerbemuseum ❸
Kurfürstendamm
  (Ku-Damm) ⑰

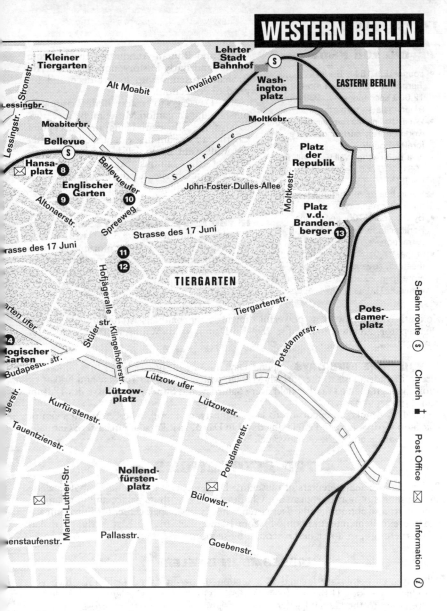

WESTERN BERLIN

Kleiner Tiergarten

Alt Moabit

Invaliden

Lehrter Stadt Bahnhof (S)

Washington platz

EASTERN BERLIN

Lessingstr.

Stromstr.

Lessingbr.

Moabiterbr.

Bellevue (S)

Hansa-platz ⊠ 8

Englischer Garten

9

10

Moltkebr.

Spree

Platz der Republik

Altonaerstr.

Spreeweg

Bellevueufer

John-Foster-Dulles-Allee

Moltkestr.

Platz v.d. Branden-berger 13

Strasse des 17 Juni

rasse des 17 Juni

11

12

Hofjägeralle

TIERGARTEN

Tiergartenstr.

Pots-damer-platz

arten ufer

4

logischer Garten

Budapest... str.

Stüler str.

Klingelhöferstr.

Lützow-platz

Lützow ufer

Potsdamerstr.

...yerstr.

Kurfürstenstr.

Lützowstr.

Tauentzienstr.

Martin-Luther-Str.

Nollend-fürsten-platz

⊠

Bülowstr.

Potsdamerstr.

...enstaufenstr.

Pallasstr.

Goebenstr.

S-Bahn route (S)

Church ■†

Post Office ⊠

Information ①

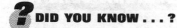

Greek and Roman Antiquities, the Museum of Pre- and Early History, and the wonderful Bröhan Museum with its art deco and Jugendstil collection.

On Day 2 go to eastern Berlin, visiting its outstanding Pergamon Museum. Be sure, too, to visit the Museum Haus am Checkpoint Charlie, a museum first established soon after the Wall went up in 1961 and located near one of the famous border checkpoints, Checkpoint Charlie. It's the best place to gain an understanding of what Berlin was like during those decades of the Wall.

IF YOU HAVE THREE DAYS   Spend Days 1 and 2 as outlined above. On Day 3, include the Nationalgalerie in your morning activities for a look at German and European artists of the 19th and 20th centuries. Spend the rest of the day according to your own special interests: the Berliner Museum for more about the history of this unusual city; the Käthe-Kollwitz Museum with its powerful drawings; the Bauhaus-Archiv and the Hansa Quarter for architectural buffs; the Ku-Damm and Wilmersdorfer Strasse for shopping.

IF YOU HAVE FIVE DAYS   Spend Days 1–3 as outlined above. In addition, be sure to include a visit to the Turkish Market, which is held on Tuesday and Friday, or stroll through the flea market held every Saturday and Sunday on Strasse des 17. Juni near Tiergarten park.

On Day 4, take an excursion to lake Wannsee or Havel, where you can swim or take a boat trip and spend a relaxing day. On Day 5, visit Potsdam in eastern Germany with its palace and park of Sanssouci.

TOP ATTRACTIONS

Berlin has four major centers of museums: Dahlem, with its famous Gemäldegalerie and museums of non-European art; Charlottenburg, with its palace and museums of ancient art and antiquities; the Tiergarten, a newly developed center for European art; and the excellent museums on Museum Island, formerly of East Berlin. It makes sense, therefore, to cover Berlin section by section.

MUSEUMS IN DAHLEM

All museums below are located in a section of Berlin called Dahlem, which you can reach by taking U-Bahn 2 from Wittenbergplatz to the Dahlem-Dorf station. If you're going to the Gemäldegalerie, take a right out of the station, cross Brümmerstrasse, and walk down Jltisstrasse to the end. Take a right on Lannstrasse, a left on Fabeckstrasse, and another right onto Arnimallee. Under the same sprawling roof with the Gemäldegalerie are the museums for sculpture, ethnology, and for East Asian, Islamic, and Indian arts. Although they can be reached by walking through the Gemäldegalerie, most of these also have their own entrance on Lansstrasse.

Note that several of the Dahlem museums will be moved to new quarters near the Tiergarten in the 1990s. The Kupferstichkabinett (Museum of Prints and Drawings) has already closed down in Dahlem and will reopen its doors in the Tiergarten in mid-1993 (inquire at the tourist office for details). Next will be the Gemäldegalerie in 1995, followed by the Skulpturengalerie at the end of the century. Thus Tiergarten will be the center for European art, while Dahlem will house collections of non-European art. Charlottenburg will continue serving as the place to go for ancient and early art.

GEMÄLDEGALERIE (Picture Gallery), Arnimallee 23-27. Tel. 830 11.

✪ West Berlin's top museum, this famous collection offers a comprehensive survey of European painting from the 13th to the 18th century. Although 400 major works were destroyed in World War II and the remaining collection was divided between East and West Berlin in the aftermath of the war, the gallery still owns more than 1,500 paintings, half of which are on display (more will be shown when it moves into its new home).

Included in the German, Netherland, Italian, French, English, Flemish, Dutch, and Spanish works are paintings by Dürer, Cranach, Holbein, Gainsborough, Brueghel, Botticelli, Raphael, Rubens, Vermeer, Murillo, and Velázquez, to name only a few. The top attraction of the Dutch section are the 20-some paintings by Rembrandt, one of the world's largest collections by this master. Look for his self-portrait, and my favorite, his portrayal of Hendrickje Stoffels, a woman who lived commonlaw with the painter—the intimacy of their relationship is captured in her face as she gazes at Rembrandt. The famous *Man with the Golden Helmet* is no longer attributed to Rembrandt.

Another one of my favorites is Lucas Cranach's *Fountain of Youth* (Der Jungbrunnen), which shows old women being led to the fountain, swimming through it, and then emerging youthful and beautiful. Note that apparently only women need the bath—men regain their youth through relations with younger women! Other highlights of the collection include Botticelli's *Venus,* Dürer's portrait of a Nürnberg patrician, and Hans Holbein's portrait of merchant Georg Gisze. Of course, these are only a fraction of what the museum offers.

Admission: 4DM ($2.50) adults, 2DM ($1.25) students and children.
Open: Tues–Fri 9am–5pm, Sat–Sun 10am–5pm. **U-Bahn:** Dahlem-Dorf.

SKULPTURENGALERIE (Sculpture Gallery), Arnimallee 23-27. Tel. 830 11.

This museum contains European sculptures from the early Christian and Byzantine periods to the end of the 18th century and rates as one of the foremost sculpture collections in Germany. Particularly well represented are works from the Italian Renaissance and German Gothic era (including carvings by Riemenschneider), but there are also ivories and bronzes.

Admission: 4 DM ($2.50) adults, 2 DM ($1.25) students and children.
Open: Tues–Fri 9am–5pm, Sat–Sun 10am–5pm. **U-Bahn:** Dahlem-Dorf.

MUSEUM FÜR VÖLKERKUNDE (Ethnological Museum), Lansstrasse 8. Tel. 830 11.

One of the world's largest ethnological museums, it possesses half a million items from around the world, including those from ancient America, Africa, the South Seas, and Asia. Particularly fascinating are the life-size boats from around the world, and dwellings and facades from various corners of the earth.

Admission: 4 DM ($2.50) adults, 2 DM ($1.25) students and children.
Open: Tues–Fri 9am–5pm, Sat–Sun 10am–5pm. **U-Bahn:** Dahlem-Dorf.

MUSEUM FÜR ISLAMISCHE KUNST (Museum of Islamic Art), Lansstrasse 8. Tel. 830 13 92 or 830 11.

Carpets, sculpture, examples of Arabic script, pottery, glass, jewelry, miniatures, and other applied art from the 8th to the 18th century are on display, with works of art from all Muslim countries represented.

Admission: 4 DM ($2.50) adults, 2 DM ($1.25) students and children.
Open: Tues–Fri 9am–5pm, Sat–Sun 10am–5pm. **U-Bahn:** Dahlem-Dorf.

MUSEUM FÜR INDISCHE KUNST (Museum of Indian Art), Lansstrasse 8. Tel. 830 13 61 or 830 11.

The most significant collection of Indian art in Germany, this museum covers a period of almost 4,000 years with its displays of terra-cotta and stone sculptures, miniatures, bronzes, and frescos from Turfan. Included are items from throughout India and Nepal, Tibet, Burma, Thailand, Indonesia, and other centers of Buddhism.
Admission: 4 DM ($2.50) adults, 2 DM ($1.25) students and children.
Open: Tues–Fri 9am–5pm, Sat–Sun 10am–5pm. **U-Bahn:** Dahlem-Dorf.

MUSEUM FÜR OSTASIATISCHE KUNST (Museum of Far Eastern Art), Lansstrasse 8. Tel. 830 13 61 or 830 11.

Works from China, Korea, and Japan from 3000 B.C. to the present are on display, including woodcuts, paintings, bronzes, ceramics, lacquerware, and sculptures.
Admission: 4 DM ($2.50) adults, 2 DM ($1.25) students and children.
Open: Tues–Fri 9am–5pm, Sat–Sun 10am–5pm. **U-Bahn:** Dahlem-Dorf.

MUSEUM FÜR DEUTSCHE VOLKSKUNDE (Museum of German Ethnology), Im Winkel 6-8. Tel. 839 01 287 or 83 20 31.

Whereas Charlottenburg Palace contains objects and furniture that belonged to the ruling class, this museum is devoted to past generations of middle- and lower-class Germans, including farmers, artisans, and homemakers. It contains items used in work, religious celebrations, and in leisure time, including peasant furniture, clothing, pottery, household items, and utensils used in making butter and turning flax into linen. On display are items collected from throughout Germany and Austria. It's a fascinating exhibit. Unfortunately, explanations are in German only, but there's an English pamphlet.
Admission: 4 DM ($2.50) adults, 2 DM ($1.25) students and children.
Open: Tues–Fri 9am–5pm, Sat–Sun 10am–5pm. **U-Bahn:** Dahlem-Dorf; then a five-minute walk (follow the signs).

SIGHTS IN CHARLOTTENBURG

To get to the attractions below, take city bus no. 109, 121, 145, or 204. An alternative is to take U-Bahn 1 to Sophie-Charlotte-Platz and then walk 10 minutes up Schloss Strasse to Spandauer Damm. Most of the museums below are on the corner of Schloss Strasse and Spandauer Damm.

CHARLOTTENBURG PALACE, Spandauer Damm. Tel. 32 09 11.

Berlin's most beautiful baroque building, Charlottenburg Palace was built in 1695 for Sophia Charlotte, wife of the future King of Prussia, Frederick I. Later it was expanded and served as the summer residence of the Prussian kings. Skip the Historical Apartments, which were the private living quarters of Sophia Charlotte and her husband, unless you have a lot of time—they can be seen only on a guided tour conducted in German and there isn't much there. Instead, walk toward the right of the main building to the **Knobelsdorff Flügel** (the New Wing), where you can wander through more royal living quarters, the state dining hall, and the elaborate ballroom, as well as through the Gallerie der Romantik (free admission) with its paintings from the 19th century.

Next head for the **Schinkel Pavilion,** located on the far east end of the palace (to the left as you exit the New Wing). This small and delightful summer house, built in the style of an Italian villa, has small, cozy rooms, each one different. After strolling through the park (laid out in the French style in 1697 and restored to its baroque form after World War II), visit the **Belvedere,** a former teahouse that now contains Berlin porcelain of the 18th and 19th centuries. On the west side of the park is the Mausoleum with the tombs of King Frederick William III and Queen Louise.

Admission: Combination ticket covering all the above, 7 DM ($4.35) adults, 3 DM ($1.85) children and students; for either the Schinkel Pavillon or the Knobelsdorff

DAHLEM MUSEUMS

TOP FLOOR
(not shown)

UPPER FLOOR

3 Museum für Völkerkunde
(South Seas)
4 Skulpturengalerie
5 Gemäldegalerie
7 Museum für Völkerkunde
(Africa)
9 Museum für Islamische Kunst
10 Museum für Ostasiatische
Kunst
11 Museum für Völkerkunde
(Southeast Asia)
12 Special exhibitions

GROUND FLOOR

1 Museum für Indische Kunst
2 Museum für Völkerkunde
(America)
3 Museum für Völkerkunde
(South Seas)
4 Skulpturengalerie
5 Gemäldegalerie

LOWER FLOOR

A Lecture Room
B Young People's Museum
C Cafeteria
D Museum for the Blind

UPPER FLOOR

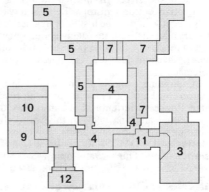

GROUND FLOOR

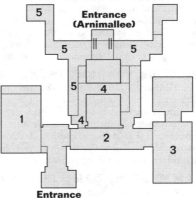

LOWER FLOOR

Flügel, 2.50 DM ($1.55) each for adults, 1.50 DM (95¢) each for students and children.
   Open: Tues–Sun 10am–5pm. **Closed:** Mausoleum closed Nov–Mar. **U-Bahn:** Sophie-Charlotte-Platz; then a 10-minute walk. **Bus:** 109, 121, 145, or 204.

EGYPTIAN MUSEUM, Schloss Strasse 70. Tel. 320 91 261 or 32 09 11.
   ⭐ Across the street from Charlottenburg Palace is this collection illustrating Egyptian cultural history. Berlin's most famous art object is here—Queen Nefertiti—up on the first floor in a dark room all by herself. Created more than 3,300 years ago, the bust amazingly enough never left the sculptor's studio but rather served as a model for all other portraits of the queen, and was left on a shelf when the ancient city became deserted. The bust was discovered early this century by German archeologists.
   In an adjoining room of the museum you can see smaller likenesses of Pharaoh Akhenaton (husband of Nefertiti) and the royal family, including Nefertiti's eldest daughter, Princess Meritaton. Look also for Queen Tiy, Akhenaton's mother. There are many other amazing items in this wonderful museum, including the Kalabasha Gate, bronzes, vases, burial objects, and tools used in everyday life.
   Admission: 4 DM ($2.50) adults, 2 DM ($1.25) students and children.
   Open: Mon–Thurs 9am–5pm, Sat–Sun 10am–5pm. **U-Bahn:** Sophie-Charlotte-Platz; then a 10-minute walk. **Bus:** 109, 121, 145, or 204.

ANTIKENMUSEUM (Museum of Greek and Roman Antiquities), Schloss Strasse 1. Tel. 320 91 215 or 32 09 11.
   Located directly across from the Egyptian Museum, this museum contains pottery, ivory carvings, glassware, jewelry, wood and stone sarcophagi, and small statuettes in marble. Particularly outstanding are the Attic red-figure vases of the 5th century B.C. and the treasury (in the basement) with its silver and exquisite gold jewelry from about 2000 B.C. to late antiquity.
   Admission: 4 DM ($2.50) adults, 2 DM ($1.25) students and children.
   Open: Mon–Thurs 9am–5pm, Sat–Sun 10am–5pm. **U-Bahn:** Sophie-Charlotte-Platz; then a 10-minute walk. **Bus:** 109, 121, 145, or 204.

MUSEUM FÜR VOR- UND FRÜHGESCHICHTE (Museum of Pre- and Early History), Spandauer Damm. Tel. 32 09 11 or 320 91 233.
   Located to the left of Charlottenburg if you stand facing the palace, this museum houses archeological finds from the Stone Age, Bronze Age, and late Iron Age, with objects illustrating life during the prehistoric age in Europe and the Near East.
   Admission: 4 DM ($2.50) adults, 2 DM ($1.25) students and children.
   Open: Mon–Thurs 9am–5pm, Sat–Sun 10am–5pm. **U-Bahn:** Sophie-Charlotte-Platz; then a 10-minute walk. **Bus:** 109, 121, 145, or 204.

BRÖHAN MUSEUM, Schloss Strasse 1a. Tel. 321 40 29.
   ⭐ Next to the Antikenmuseum is the only private museum of the bunch. It specializes in objects of the art nouveau (*Jugendstil* in German) and art deco periods, with exquisite vases, glass, furniture, silver, paintings, and other works of art from the turn of the century through the 1930s. It's a joy to walk through the rooms, which serve as a welcome change from the antiquities of the surrounding museums. Don't miss it.
   Admission: 5 DM ($3.10) adults, 2.50 DM ($1.55) students.
   Open: Tues–Sun 10am–6pm (Thurs to 8pm). **U-Bahn:** Sophie-Charlotte-Platz; then a 10-minute walk. **Bus:** 109, 121, 145, or 204.

SIGHTS IN EASTERN BERLIN

To see the sights below, I suggest that you start your tour with a stroll down Unter den Linden (the closest S-Bahn station is Unter den Linden, or take bus no. 100), where you'll see the Brandenburg Gate and pass the Neue Wache, dedicated to those who gave their lives to fight fascism. Farther down is Museum Island with the excellent Pergamon Museum. Alexanderplatz, the concrete modern heart of eastern Berlin, is just a five-minute walk farther west on Karl-Liebknecht-Strasse and is where you'll find the tourist office at the base of the TV tower. Nearby is also the Nikolai Quarter, a reconstructed neighborhood of Old Berlin (see "Evening Entertainment," below).

Note that because of the changes taking place in Berlin, the prices of museums may change (as in most Berlin museums, they may be free in the future). However, at the latest check, all state museums in eastern Berlin charge 1 or 2 DM (60¢ or $1.25) for adults and 50 Pfennig (30¢) or 1.50 DM (95¢) for children.

PERGAMON MUSEUM, Bodestrasse 1-3, on Museum Island. Tel. 203 55-0.

✪ Entrance to Berlin's most famous museum is via the bridge on Kupfergraben, behind and to the left of Das Alte Museum. It's named after its most prized possession, the Pergamon Altar, a magnificent masterpiece of Hellenistic art of the 2nd century B.C. and certainly one of the wonders of the ancient world. Essentially a museum of architecture, the Pergamon also contains the Market Gate of Milet, as well as the dazzling Babylonian Processional Way leading to the Gate of Ishtar. There's also an Islamic section and an East Asian collection.

Admission: 2 DM ($1.25) adults, 1.50 DM (95¢) children.

Open: Daily 10am–6pm (on Mon and Tues only for those sections of the museum containing the Pergamon Altar, Market Gate, and Gate of Ishtar). **S-Bahn:** Marx-Engels-Platz or Friedrichstrasse; then a 10-minute walk. **Bus:** 100 to the Deutsche Staatsoper stop.

BODE MUSEUM, Bodestrasse 1-3, on Museum Island. Tel. 203 55-0.

This is several museums in one, housing the Egyptian Museum, the Papyrus Collection, the Early Christian and Byzantine Collection, the Museum for Primeval and Early History, and the Picture Gallery with art from the 14th to the 18th century.

Admission: 1 DM (60¢) adults, 50 Pfennig (30¢) children.

Open: Wed–Sun 10am–6pm. **S-Bahn:** Marx-Engels-Platz or Friedrichstrasse; then a 10-minute walk. **Bus:** 100 to the Deutsche Staatsoper stop.

ALTE NATIONAL GALLERY, Bodestrasse, on Museum Island. Tel. 203 55-0.

Looking much like a Corinthian temple, the National Gallery is devoted to painting and sculpture of the 19th and 20th centuries, by artists of Germany, France, and other European countries.

Admission: 1 DM (60¢) adults, 50 Pfennig (30¢) children.

Open: Wed–Sun 10am–6pm. **S-Bahn:** Marx-Engels-Platz or Friedrichstrasse; then a 10-minute walk. **Bus:** 100 to the Deutsche Staatsoper stop.

DAS ALTE MUSEUM, Museum Insel. Tel. 203 55-0.

This is the first museum you see on Museum Island if you approach from Unter den Linden. It offers changing exhibitions, devoted mainly to art and objects of ancient times.

Admission: 1 DM (60¢) adults, 50 Pfennig (30¢) children.

Open: Wed–Sun 10am–6pm. **S-Bahn:** Marx-Engels-Platz or Friedrichstrasse; then a 10-minute walk. **Bus:** 100 to the Deutsche Staatsoper stop.

BRANDENBURG GATE, Unter den Linden.

During the decades of the Wall, the Brandenburger Tor stood in a no-man's land, marking the boundary of East and West Berlin and becoming the symbol of a divided Germany. After the November 1989 revolution and the fall of the Wall, it was here that many Berliners gathered to rejoice and to dance together on top of the Wall. The Gate was built in 1788–91 by Carl Gotthard Langhans as the western entrance onto Unter den Linden.

S-Bahn: Unter den Linden. **Bus:** 100 to the Unter den Linden/Brandenburger Tor stop.

REICHSTAG [Parliament], Platz der Republik. Tel. 39 77-0.

Although technically in western Berlin, the Reichstag is most easily combined with

a trip to eastern Berlin. Completed in 1894 in Neo-Renaissance style to serve the needs of Bismarck's united Germany, today it once again serves occasionally for sittings of parliament. Since 1971 it has also housed an exhibit called "Fragen an die deutsche Geschichte" (Questions Concerning German History), with displays relating to German history from 1800 to the Cold War (entrance to the exhibit is on the north side of the Reichstag). Displays are only in German, but you can rent a cassette for 2 DM ($1.25) that provides a 45-minute commentary on the exhibit, making it well worth it.
Admission: Free.
Open: Tues–Sun 10am–5pm (enter by 4pm). **Closed:** During sessions of parliament. **S-Bahn:** Unter den Linden. **Bus:** 100 to the Reichstag stop.

MORE ATTRACTIONS

NEAR TIERGARTEN

NEUE NATIONALGALERIE (New National Gallery), Potsdamer Strasse 50. Tel. 2666.
This was one of the first museums to open in the new museum area near the Tiergarten. A starkly modern building designed by Mies van der Rohe and set into a vast square surrounded by a sculpture garden, the Nationalgalerie houses art of the 19th and 20th centuries. The ground floor is devoted to changing exhibitions, while the permanent collection in the basement shows the works of Adolph Menzel (the largest of any museum collection), Lovis Corinth, Max Liebermann, Max Slevogt, Monet, Manet, Pissarro, Renoir, Kirchner, Max Beckmann, Munch, and Klee.
Admission: 4 DM ($2.50) adults, 2 DM ($1.25) students and children; temporary special exhibits, varies.
Open: Tues–Fri 9am–5pm, Sat–Sun 10am–5pm. **U-Bahn:** Kurfürstenstrasse; then bus no. 148 or 248. **Bus:** 129 from the Ku'damm.

KUNSTGEWERBE MUSEUM, (Museum of Applied Arts), Tiergarten-strasse 6. Tel. 266 29 11.
Located just a five-minute walk from the Nationalgalerie above, this museum is housed in a modern red-brick building. It's devoted to European applied arts from the early Middle Ages to the present day and includes glassware, porcelain, beer steins, tableware, and measuring instruments. The collection of medieval goldsmiths' works is particularly outstanding, as are the displays of Venetian glass, early Meissen porcelain, and art deco (*Jugendstil*) vases and objects. The bottom floor features changing exhibits of contemporary crafts and product design, from typewriters to tea pots or furniture.
Admission: 4 DM ($2.50) adults, 2 DM ($1.25) students and children.
Open: Tues–Fri 9am–5pm, Sat–Sun 10am–5pm. **U-Bahn:** Kurfürstenstrasse; then bus no. 148 or 248. **Bus:** 129 from the Ku'damm.

IN OR NEAR KREUZBERG

BERLIN MUSEUM, Lindenstrasse 14. Tel. 258 62 839.
Housed in an impressive yellow-and-white building dating from 1735, the Berlin Museum depicts local history with displays of furniture, toys, porcelain, paintings, Jewish ceremonial art, and other artifacts relating to life here since the 17th century. Berlin's Biedermeier days, life under the Nazis, and the Cold War are all documented. For refreshment, drop by the museum's Alt-Berliner Weissbier Stube, an original Old Berlin–style bar where a special wheat beer is served.
Admission: 4 DM ($2.50) adults, 2 DM ($1.25) students.
Open: Tues–Sun 10am–8pm. **U-Bahn:** U-1 to Hallesches Tor; then bus no. 141 or a 10-minute walk. **Bus:** 129 from the Ku'damm to Charlottenstrasse; then a 10-minute walk.

MUSEUM HAUS AM CHECKPOINT CHARLIE, Friedrichstrasse 44. Tel. 251 10 31.

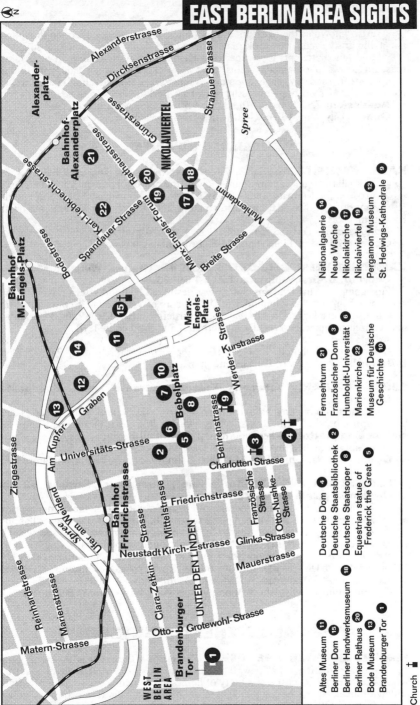

EAST BERLIN AREA SIGHTS

Nationalgalerie **14**
Neue Wache **7**
Nikolaikirche **17**
Nikolaiviertel **19**
Pergamon Museum **12**
St. Hedwigs-Kathedrale **9**

Fernsehturm **21**
Französischer Dom **2**
Humboldt-Universität **6**
Marienkirche **22**
Museum für Deutsche
Geschichte **10**

Deutsche Dom **4**
Deutsche Staatsbibliothek **3**
Deutsche Staatsoper **8**
Equestrian statue of
Frederick the Great **5**

Altes Museum **11**
Berliner Dom **15**
Berliner Handwerksmuseum **18**
Berliner Rathaus **20**
Bode Museum **13**
Brandenburger Tor **1**

Church ✝ ■

✪ Also known as the Museum at the Wall, this important collection documents the grisly events that took place around the Berlin Wall, including successful and failed attempts to escape from East Berlin. With displays in English, the museum shows photographs, items used in escapes (such as cars with hidden compartments), and newspaper clippings. A must-see, it's located beside what was the most frequently used border crossing into East Berlin, Checkpoint Charlie.
Admission: 7.50 DM ($4.70) adults, 4.50 DM ($2.80) students.
Open: Daily 9am–10pm. **U-Bahn:** Kochstrasse.

NEAR THE KU'DAMM

KÄTHE-KOLLWITZ MUSEUM, Fasanenstrasse 24. Tel. 882 52 10.
✪ A small but significant museum showing the powerful drawings and sketches by artist Käthe Kollwitz (1867–1945), a Berliner who managed to capture human emotions both tender and disturbing in her subjects. It's located just off the Ku'damm.
Admission: 6 DM ($3.75) adults, 3 DM ($1.85) students.
Open: Wed–Mon 11am–6pm. **U-Bahn:** Uhlandstrasse.

KAISER-WILHELM GEDÄCHTNISKIRCHE (Kaiser Wilhelm Memorial Church), Breitscheidplatz. Tel. 24 50 23.
First completed in 1895, this church was destroyed by bombs during World War II and was left in ruins as a reminder of the horrors of war. Today it contains a small museum with displays related to war and destructions. Beside the ruined church is a new church designed by Prof. Egon Eiermann and finished in 1961.
Admission: Free.
Open: Ruined church, Tues–Sat 10am–6pm; new church, daily 9am–7:30pm.
U-Bahn: Bahnhof Zoo or Kurfürstendamm.

EUROPA-CENTER, between Tauentzienstrasse and Budapester Strasse.
This mammoth building houses numerous shops, restaurants, pubs, cabarets, and, most important, the Berlin tourist office. On the 20th floor of Europa-Center is a **sightseeing platform** where you have a view of all Berlin.
Admission: Sightseeing platform, 3 DM ($1.85).
Open: Daily 9am–midnight. **U-Bahn:** Bahnhof Zoo or Kurfürstendamm.

ZOOLOGISCHER GARTEN (Berlin Zoo), Budapester Strasse 32 and Hardenbergplatz 8. Tel. 25 40 10.
✪ The Berlin Zoo is considered one of Europe's best, and is one of my favorites. Founded in 1844 and located just a short walk from the Ku'damm or Bahnhof Zoo, it's home to more than 11,000 animals of almost 2,000 species. The Aquarium contains more than 6,000 fish, reptiles, and amphibians.
Admission: A combination ticket for both the zoo and aquarium, 12.50 DM ($7.80) adults, 11 DM ($6.85) students, 6 DM ($3.75) children; zoo only, 8 DM ($5) adults, 7 DM ($4.35) students, 4 DM ($2.50) children.
Open: Summer, daily 9am–6:30pm; winter, daily 9am–5pm. **U-Bahn:** Bahnhof Zoo.

SPECIAL-INTEREST SIGHTSEEING

FOR THE ARCHITECTURE LOVER The **Hansa Quarter** is the result of an international gathering in 1957 by 50 leading architects from more than 20 countries, who were asked to design a community of homes, apartments, and shops for Berliners still without adequate housing as the result of World War II. Corbusier's design, however, was too large and was therefore built in the western end of the city near the Olympic Stadium; it's West Berlin's largest housing project, with 530 apartments. The

Hansa Quarter is located just north of the Tiergarten park, and the nearest U-Bahn station is Hansaplatz.

Another good choice is the **Bauhaus-Archiv,** Klengelhöfer Strasse 13-14 (tel. 261 16 18 or 254 00 233). The Bauhaus school of design, founded by Walter Gropius in Weimar in 1919 and disbanded in Berlin in 1933, revolutionized the teaching of architecture and industrial design. Here, works of art by Bauhaus masters and students are on display, including tubular steel chairs, tea pots, and lamps. There are also special exhibitions. Admission is 3.50 DM ($2.20) for adults and 1.50 DM (95¢) for students; free for all on Monday. It's open Wednesday through Monday from 10am to 5pm. Get there by bus no. 106, 129, 219, or 341 to Lützowplatz.

FOR THE VISITING AMERICAN   John F. Kennedy gave his famous "Ich bin ein Berliner" speech in front of **Schöneberg Rathaus** (tel. 7831) on June 26, 1963, just months before he was assassinated. The square in front of the Rathaus is now called John F. Kennedy Platz, and inside the Rathaus tower is a replica of the Liberty Bell, given to Berlin by the American people in 1950 and called the Freedom Bell. There isn't much to see here, but if you're a history buff and you don't mind heights, you can climb the steps to the top of the bell tower on Wednesday and Sunday between 10am and 3:30pm (follow the signs ZUM TURM) where you have a good view of the city. It's free. Take the U-Bahn to Rathaus Schöneberg.

ORGANIZED TOURS

BY BUS   Sightseeing tours of Berlin and Potsdam are offered by a number of tour companies, with buses departing from the Ku'damm area. Oldest and largest of these is **Severin + Kuhn,** Kurfürstendamm 216 (tel. 883 10 15), which is open daily from 9am to 7pm. A 2½-hour tour of Berlin, for example, costs 30 DM ($18.75), while a 4-hour tour with a stop at the Pergamon Museum is 42 DM ($26.25).

If you're in Berlin for several days, consider taking the trip to historic **Potsdam,** favored residency of Prussian royalty, where you'll visit Frederick the Great's rococo palace, Sanssouci. Days and times vary according to the year—it's 49 DM ($30.60) for a four-hour tour. Contact Severin + Kuhn for more information.

BY BOAT   If you're in Berlin from April to the end of October, you can climb aboard one of the many boats plying the River Spree and Havel and Wannsee lakes. One of the most popular trips is from Wannsee (near the U-Bahn station) to Glienicker Brücke and back, operated by **Stern und Kreisschiffahrt** (tel. 810 00 40 or 803 87 50).

Also available are two-, three-, and four-hour boat trips along the Spree River, offered throughout the year with departure directly in front of the Kongresshalle near the Tiergarten and operated by **Horst Duggen** (tel. 394 49 54). The three-hour tour, which costs 10 DM ($6.25) for adults, half price for children, travels on the Spree past the Reichstag building all the way to Museum Island and back.

7. SAVVY SHOPPING

If it exists, you can buy it in Berlin. At least, that's what they say. A look inside the KaDeWe, the largest department store on the continent, made a believer out of me. The food department alone offers 1,000 different kinds of sausages. Start your shopping spree in the **KaDeWe,** on Wittenbergplatz—with a merchandise inventory of 250,000 items, it may be as far as you get.

But that would mean you'd miss the **Ku'damm** just around the corner, the showcase of western Berlin's fashionable and elegant boutiques and art galleries. They may be beyond our budget, but window-shopping and people-watching are free. Another shopping street is the pedestrians-only **Wilmersdorfer Strasse,** where you'll find the Karstadt, Hertie, and Quelle department stores in addition to many smaller shops and restaurants.

Typical souvenirs of Berlin are stuffed toy bears (the city mascot), porcelain freedom bells (fashioned after the Freedom Bell hanging in Schöneberg Rathaus), and the Brandenburg Gate pictured on ashtrays and bowls. If kitsch doesn't appeal to you, other items Germany is known for are kitchen gadgets and cutlery, linens, those luxuriously fluffy Federbetten (feather beds), binoculars and telescopes, cameras, and toys (model trains, tin soldiers, building blocks). If you like porcelain, brands to look for include Rosenthal, antique Meissen, and Staatliche Porzellan Manufaktur—assuming, of course, you have a Swiss bank account.

If you purchase more than 60 DM ($40) worth of goods from any one store and you're taking your purchases out of the country, you're entitled to partial recovery of the Value-Added Tax (VAT), which is 14% in Germany. Most stores will issue a Tax Cheque at the time of the purchase. Fill in the reverse side, and upon leaving Germany present the Tax Cheque, receipt from the store, and the purchased articles to Customs. Airports in Berlin, Frankfurt, and other large cities will refund your money immediately. If you're leaving Germany by train, ask the Customs official who comes into your train compartment to stamp your check.

MARKETS

Berlin's best buys are found at the many antiques and flea markets. Some are indoor and are held almost daily. Others are just open one or two days a week.

STRASSE DES 17. JUNI, just east of the Tiergarten S-Bahn station. Tel. 322 81 99.

 Silverware, books, china, glass, original artwork, jewelry, clothing, and junk are offered for sale at this weekend market, Berlin's best known. Don't miss it. I love this market!
Open: Sat–Sun 10am–5pm. **S-Bahn:** Tiergarten.

TURKISH MARKET, on the banks of Maybachufer in Kreuzberg.

Kreuzberg is Berlin's "Little Istanbul," home of much of the city's Turkish population. The Turkish Market is probably Berlin's most fascinating, with both German and Turkish vendors selling vegetables, noodles, spices, clothing, and Turkish fast food. Try a Turkish pizza, a donner kebap, or felafel from one of the food vendors.
Open: Tues and Fri noon–6:30pm. **Directions:** U-Bahn to Kottbusser Tor; then walk south on Kottbusser Strasse until you cross the bridge, where you'll see the stalls spread along the bank of the river.

WINTERFELDPLATZ, in Schöneberg.

Berlin's largest weekly market of fruits, vegetables, meat, flowers, clothing, and accessories is located a five-minute walk south of the Nollendorfplatz U-Bahn station.
Open: Wed and Sat dawn–1pm. **U-Bahn:** Nollendorfplatz.

WEIHNACHTSMARKT, Breitscheidplatz and from Nürnberger Strasse to Joachimstaler Strasse.

Every December from the beginning of the month to Christmas Eve there's a Christmas market in the inner city that radiates out from the Gedächtniskirche onto side streets. Christmas decorations, candles and cookies, sausages, and other goodies are sold from colorful booths. (Other Christmas markets are held in Spandau and Alexanderplatz.)
Open: Dec 1–24, daily 11am–9pm. **U-Bahn:** Kurfürstendamm, Bahnhof Zoo, or Wittenbergplatz.

ANTIK & FLOHMARKT, at the Friedrichstrasse S-Bahn station. Tel. 215 02 130 or 215 02 129.

Due to open by 1993, this new flea market features approximately 100 vendors who once occupied the train platform at Nollendorfplatz. Antiques, curios, and junk are sold, including jewelry, porcelain, furniture, glass, lighters, and odds and ends. If you get thirsty, drop by Nolle, a pub that also sells food.

Open: Hours not yet established at press time, but probably from 11am to about 6pm, closed one day a week (most likely Mon or Tues). Inquire at the Berlin tourist office for exact details. **S-Bahn:** Friedrichstrasse.

8. EVENING ENTERTAINMENT

Berlin never sleeps. There are no closing hours for nightclubs, discos, and bars, so you can stay out all night if you want to. In fact, a native Berliner once told me, "The reason everyone comes to Berlin is its nightlife"—and he was serious. When I pointed out that people might come also because of Berlin's excellent museums, it appeared to be a possibility he had never considered.

Nightlife in Berlin means everything from far-out bars or cozy wine cellars to world-renowned opera and theater. To find out what's going on in the traditional performing arts, pick up a copy of *Berlin Programm*. Rock concerts, experimental theater, and avant-garde happenings are covered in city magazines *tip* and *zitty*.

THE PERFORMING ARTS

If you don't mind paying a commission, convenient **ticket box offices** can be found at Centrum, Meinekestrasse 25 (tel. 882-7611); in the Europa-Center, Tauentzienstrasse 9 (tel. 261 70 51); KaDeWe Department Store, Wittenbergplatz (tel. 24 80 36); and Wertheim Department Store, Kurfürstendamm 231 (tel. 882 25 00).

Tickets for theater and opera, sometimes with student discounts, are also available during box-office hours and about an hour before the performance starts. At the Schiller-Theater, on the night of the performance students can get 50% reduction on tickets regularly costing 18 DM ($11.25) or more.

OPERA

DEUTSCHE OPER BERLIN, Bismarckstrasse 35. Tel. 34381 for information, 341 02 49 for tickets.

There are performances of opera virtually every evening, except when there's ballet.

Prices: Tickets, 10–125 DM ($6.25–$78.10), 50% reduction for students.

Open: Box office, Mon–Sat 11am–8pm, Sun 10am–2pm; performances usually at 7:30 or 8pm. **U-Bahn:** Deutsche Oper.

DEUTSCHE STAATSOPER, Unter den Linden 7. Tel. 200 47 62.

The German State Opera, located on the famous Unter den Linden boulevard, has long been one of Berlin's famous opera houses, featuring opera, ballet, and concerts.

Prices: Tickets, 5–45 DM ($3.10–$28.10).

Open: Box office, Mon–Sat noon–6pm, Sun 2–6pm; performances usually at 7 or 7pm. **Bus:** 100 to the Deutsche Staatsoper stop.

KOMISCHE OPER, Behrenstrasse 55-57. Tel. 229 26 03 for information, 229 25 55 for tickets.

This innovative opera company in eastern Berlin serves as an alternative to the grander, more mainstream productions of Berlin's two other opera houses, presenting a varied program of light opera, operetta, and ballet.

Prices: 5–60 DM ($3.10–$37.50).

Open: Box office, Tues–Sat noon–6pm; performances at 7 or 7:30pm. **U-Bahn:** Französische Strasse. **S-Bahn:** Unter den Linden. **Bus:** 100.

THEATER

SCHILLER-THEATER, Bismarckstrasse 110. Tel. 319 52 36.

One of Berlin's best-known theaters, with performances of classical and modern drama, both German and foreign.

Prices: Tickets, 9–55 DM ($5.60–$34.35), 50% reduction for students.
Open: Box office, daily 10am–7pm; performances at 8pm. **U-Bahn:** Ernst-Reuter-Platz.

THEATER DES WESTENS, Kantstrasse 12. Tel. 319 03 193.
Popular productions, musicals, and operettas.
Prices: Tickets, 15–70 DM ($9.35–$43.75).
Open: Box office, Tues–Sat noon–6pm, Sun 3–6pm; performances at 8pm.
U-Bahn: Bahnhof Zoo.

CLASSICAL MUSIC CONCERTS

Performances of the Berlin Philharmonic Orchestra and the Radio Symphony Orchestra Berlin take place at the **Philharmonie,** Matthaikirchstrasse 1 (tel. 26 92 51 or 261 43 83). Tickets begin at 12 DM ($7.50). The box office is open Monday through Friday from 3:30 to 6pm, and on Saturday, Sunday, and holidays from 11am to 2pm. Performances are usually at 8pm, with a matinee on Sunday. You can get to the hall on bus no. 129, 148, or 248.

CABARET

DIE STACHELSCHWEINE, basement of Europa-Center. Tel. 261 47 95.
Its name means "Porcupine," and it has been around for 40 years. You have to speak German if you want to understand its political commentaries.
Prices: Tickets, 22–38 DM ($13.75–$23.75).
Open: Shows Mon–Sat at around 7:30pm. **U-Bahn:** Bahnhof Zoo or Kurfürstendamm.

DOLLYWOOD, Kurfürstenstrasse 116. Tel. 24 89 50.
Located beside the Hotel Sylter Hof on Kurfürstenstrasse (not to be confused with the Ku'damm) is this cabaret that specializes in transvestite variety shows. The performers come from around the world, and many of the performances are in English.
Prices: Drink minimum, Tues–Thurs and Sun 20 DM ($12.50), Fri–Sat 30 DM ($18.75).A beer costs 10 DM ($6.25). **Admission:** 15 DM ($9.35).
Open: Shows, Sun and Tues–Thurs at 9:30pm, 11pm, and 1am; Fri–Sat at 9:30pm, 11pm, 12:30am, and 2am. **U-Bahn:** Wittenbergplatz; then a five-minute walk.

LIVE-MUSIC HOUSES

GO-IN, Bleibtreustrasse 17. Tel. 881 72 18.
One of the old standbys, it opened in 1968 and has offered live folk concerts ever since. Jazz, blues, bluegrass, Spanish flamenco, Greek, German, international folk songs—it's all considered folk, and entrance is usually free on Wednesday. Bleibtreustrasse is just off the Ku'damm.
Prices: Beer from 4.20 DM ($2.60). **Admission:** Usually free Wed, 5–12 DM ($3.10–$7.50) Thurs–Tues.
Open: Daily 8pm–3am; music begins at 9pm.

QUASIMODO, Kantstrasse 12a. Tel. 312 80 86.
Dwarfed by the large Theater des Westens next to it, Quasimodo features contemporary jazz and rock groups. Check *tip* or *zitty* for concert information.
Admission: 10–25 DM ($6.25–$15.60), depending on the band.
Open: Daily from 9pm; concerts usually around 10pm. **U-Bahn:** Bahnhof Zoo.

EIERSCHALE, Rankestrasse 1. Tel. 882 53 05.
Located just off the Ku'damm across the street from the Gedächtniskirche, this

popular music house offers contemporary jazz, Dixieland jazz, blues, and popular music. It's also a good place to come for breakfast, especially on Sunday when there's live music all day long.

Admission: 4 DM ($2.50) when there's live music, which goes toward the first drink.

Open: Sun–Thurs 8am–2am, Fri–Sat 8am–4am; live music from 9:30pm. **U-Bahn:** Bahnhof Zoo or Kurfürstendamm.

MOVIES

Although there are plenty of cinemas showing the latest movies from Hollywood and German producers, Berlin's main cinematic attraction lies in its "Off-Ku'damm" cinemas, those that specialize in the classics of film history as well as new German and international productions of independent filmmakers. Check *tip* and *zitty* for listings of current films. (*OF*) means that the film is in the original language, and (*OmU*) means it's in the original language with German subtitles. Two well-known cinemas:

ARSENAL, Welserstrasse 25. Tel. 24 68 48.
The original Off-Ku'damm cinema, with extensive retrospectives, film series, and avant-garde films.
Admission: 9 DM ($5.60).
U-Bahn: Wittenbergplatz.

ODEON, Hauptstrasse 116. Tel. 781 56 57.
This theater specializes in recent English-language releases.
Admission: 10 DM ($6.25).
U-Bahn: Innsbrucker Platz.

PUBS & BARS
AROUND THE KU'DAMM & SAVIGNYPLATZ

CAFE BLEIBTREU, Bleibtreustrasse 45. Tel. 881 47 56.
This café/bar has a warm, pleasant feel to it, with plants, ceiling fans, and large front windows. One of the first so-called café/bars to open, in 1972, it's popular with the 30-ish crowd and also serves breakfast until 2pm.
Prices: Wine from 4.90 DM ($3.05); a half liter of beer 4.50 DM ($2.80).
Open: Sun–Thurs 9:30am–1am, Fri–Sat 9:30am–2:30am. **S-Bahn:** Savignyplatz.

MUSEUMSKNEIPE, in the Ku'damm Karree, Lietzenburgerstrasse 86. Tel. 881 41 71.
This bar is located in the back of a shopping mall. Appropriately enough, its ceiling and walls are lined with antiques and junk, a museum of relics often found in attics. There's live music on Sunday afternoon and every night at 9pm, and the action keeps going until the manager decides he's had enough, usually in the wee hours of the morning.
Prices: Beer 5.50 DM ($3.40). **Admission:** Free Sun–Thurs, 5 DM ($3.10) Fri–Sat.
Open: Mon–Fri from 7pm, Sat–Sun from 3pm. **U-Bahn:** Uhlandstrasse.

NEW YORK, Olivaer Platz 15. Tel. 883 62 58.
This is one of the "in" bars, casual yet trendy, a place for people in their 20s and 30s to hang out. This is the place to go if you want a drink in the middle of the day, with large windows letting in plenty of sunshine. There's a pool table, pinball machines, and video games. It's located just off the Ku'damm.
Prices: Half liter of beer from 4 DM ($2.50); wine from 6 DM ($3.75).
Open: Daily 10am–4am. **U-Bahn:** Adenauerplatz.

KU'DORF, Joachimstaler Strasse 15. Tel. 883 66 66.
Some 18 different bars are located in this basement "village," which consists of several "lanes" with one tiny bar after the other, each decorated in a different theme.

At one end is a disco, and at the other is the Klostergarten, a beer garden with live music that's popular with the middle-aged generation. Most of the people who come here are tourists, perhaps because the place is so convenient.
Prices: Half liter of beer 6.70 DM ($4.20). **Admission:** 4 DM ($2.50).
Open: Tues–Thurs 8pm–2am, Fri–Sat 8pm–4am. **U-Bahn:** Kurfürstendamm.

WIRTSHAUS ZUM LÖWEN, Hardenbergstrasse 29. Tel. 262 10 20.

This beer hall is reminiscent of those in Munich and even serves Bavarian beer—Löwenbräu. There's outdoor seating in summer, but even the interior is ingeniously constructed to resemble a beer garden. There's traditional Bavarian music beginning at 7pm, and though there's no cover charge, prices for beer are higher in the evenings. Hearty platters of German food are served. It's located across the street from the Gedächtniskirche.
Prices: Half liter of beer 5.50 DM ($3.45) in the day, 6.50 DM ($4.05) at night; food platters 10–20 DM ($6.25–$12.50). **Admission:** Free.
Open: Sun–Thurs 10am–midnight, Fri–Sat 10am–2am. **U-Bahn:** Bahnhof Zoo or Kurfürstendamm.

EXTRA DRY, Mommsenstrasse 34. Tel. 324 60 38.

Extra Dry serves no alcohol and *is for women only*. Opened in 1987, it has a bright and cheerful interior and serves milkshakes, fruit cocktails, and light snacks. As part of a program to help women who have been drug-dependent and need a clean environment in which to socialize, it's a good place for any women traveling alone or tired of the usual bar scene.
Prices: Drinks 3–4 DM ($1.85–$2.50).
Open: Tues–Sun noon–11pm. **S-Bahn:** Charlottenburg. **U-Bahn:** Wilmersdorfer Strasse.

ZWIEBELFISCH, Savignyplatz 7-8. Tel. 31 73 63.

This is one of Berlin's oldest new bars, which means it's been around for about 20 years and still enjoys great popularity. Because it stays open later than other bars in the area, it's where everyone ends up and can be quite packed at 4am.
Prices: Half liter of beer 4.10 DM ($2.55); wine 5 DM ($3.10).
Open: Daily noon–6am. **S-Bahn:** Savignyplatz.

DICKE WIRTIN, Carmerstrasse 9. Tel. 312 49 52.

Named after the rather large barmaid who used to run the place, this old-style German pub is still popular and is known for its stews.
Prices: Bowl of stew 4 DM ($2.50); half liter of beer 3.90 DM ($2.45).
Open: Daily noon–4am. **S-Bahn:** Savignyplatz.

SCHWARZES CAFE, Kantstrasse 148. Tel. 313 80 38.

The Black Café is true to its name, with a black interior and unconventional hours. Its specialty is its breakfasts, available anytime and ranging from a continental to the works. It also has a large selection of coffees (including concoctions with alcohol).
Prices: Continental breakfast 6 DM ($3.75); full breakfast 14.50 DM ($9.05); cup of coffee from 2.70 DM ($1.70).
Open: Daily around the clock, except Tues 3am–9pm. **S-Bahn:** Savignyplatz.

WINTERFELDPLATZ

SLUMBERLAND, Winterfeldplatz. Tel. 216 53 49.

The gimmick here is a floor with real sand, along with fake banana trees and palms. The music is African, Caribbean, reggae, and calypso, and it's most crowded in the very late (or early, depending on how you look at it) hours.
Prices: Half liter of beer 5 DM ($3.10); wine from 4.50 DM ($2.80); Coke 3 DM ($1.85).
Open: Sun–Fri 9pm–4am, Sat 11am–5pm and 9pm–4am. **U-Bahn:** Nollendorfplatz.

CAFE SIDNEY, Winterfeldstrasse 40. Tel. 216 52 53.

Also on Winterfeldplatz is this café/bar, modern and breezy with palm trees, two pool tables, and split-level seating. It's open all day and serves breakfast until 5pm.
Prices: Half liter of beer 6 DM ($3.75); wine from 4 DM ($2.50).
Open: Daily 9am–4am. **U-Bahn:** Nollendorfplatz.

IN KREUZBERG

LEYDICKE, Mansteinstrasse 4. Tel. 216 29 73.

⭐ Opened in 1877, this bar claims to be Berlin's oldest bar. It certainly looks like a likely contender, with its dark wainscoting, decorated ceiling, and long bar. Note the bottles of wine behind the counter—Leydicke even sells its own wine and liqueur, produced in Berlin using grapes and fruit imported from western Berlin. The bottles you see are for sale, certainly a unique souvenir of Berlin.
Prices: Glass of wine 3–5 DM ($1.85–$3.10).
Open: Mon and Fri noon–2pm and 4pm–midnight, Tues and Thurs 4pm–midnight; Wed and Sat–Sun 11am–1am. **U-Bahn:** Yorckstrasse; then a five-minute walk. **Bus:** 119 from the Ku'damm to the Mansteinstrasse stop.

IN THE NIKOLAI QUARTER

These three bars are in a reconstructed neighborhood called the Nikolai Quarter. Conveniently located just off Alexanderplatz near the Rathaus in eastern Berlin, the Nikolai Quarter features several bars, restaurants, and shops and is essentially tourist-oriented. However, it's a good place to imbibe a beer or two.

ZUM NUSSBAUM, Propstrasse. Tel. 2431 33 28.
This is my favorite bar in the Nikolai Quarter and was modeled after a bar dating from 1571 that was destroyed during World War II. It is pleasant and cozy, with wood-paneled walls and tiny rooms. There are a few tables outside, where you have a view of the Nikolai Church.
Prices: Third of a liter of beer from 3.30 DM ($2.05).
Open: Daily noon–2am. **Closed:** Second Tues of the month. **U-Bahn:** Alexanderplatz or Klosterstrasse.

ZUM PADDENWIRT, Eiergasse. Tel. 2431 32 31.
Another lively place to drink, simply decorated as taverns were in former times. It also serves German food. It's located behind the Nikolai Church.
Prices: Third of a liter of beer from 4.20 DM ($2.60).
Open: Daily 11am–midnight. **U-Bahn:** Alexanderplatz or Klosterstrasse.

ZUR RIPPE, Mühlendamm and Poststrasse. Tel. 2431 32 35.
Named after a medieval inn first mentioned in documents in 1672, this bar also offers daily specials of German cuisine. Most people, however, come here mainly to drink.
Prices: Third of a liter of beer from 3.90 DM ($4.05).
Open: Daily 11am–midnight. **U-Bahn:** Alexanderplatz or Klosterstrasse.

DISCOS & DANCE CLUBS

METROPOLE, Nollendorfplatz 5. Tel. 216 41 22.
It's hard to miss this place—a colossal, striking building converted from a former theater. Very popular, on weekends it features a giant-size disco with all kinds of technical gags, including a laser show. There are also live concerts through the week (check *tip* or *zitty*).
Prices: Drinks from 5 DM ($3.10). **Admission:** 10 DM ($6.25).
Open: Fri–Sat 10pm–6am. **U-Bahn:** Nollendorfplatz.

BIG EDEN, Kurfürstendamm 202. Tel. 882 61 20.
Opened in 1968, this place has a large dance floor and a strict front-door policy that won't admit anyone who even looks like they're drunk. It attracts young people of every nationality.

Prices: Beer from 7 DM ($4.35). **Admission:** 4 DM ($2.50) Sun–Thurs, 9 DM ($5.60) Fri–Sat, which includes a ticket good for 4 DM ($2.50) toward the first drink. Unaccompanied women admitted free.

Open: Sun–Thurs 8pm–4am, Fri–Sat 8pm–7am. **U-Bahn:** Uhlandstrasse.

CAFE KEESE, Bismarckstrasse 108. Tel. 312 91 11.

Located about a 15-minute walk from the Ku'damm (close to the Ernst Reuter U-Bahn station), this large dance hall is popular with the middle-aged and here it's always the women who ask the men to dance (except for the hourly "Men's Choice," when the green light goes on). This Café Keese opened in 1966, a sister to one that has been in operation in Hamburg since 1948, and both claim that in the past 40 years more than 95,000 couples have met on their dance floors and married. Who knows, maybe this will be your night. No jeans or tennis shoes are allowed; most men are in coat and tie, and women are dressed up. If you're over 30, you'll probably get a kick out of this place. Live band most evenings.

Prices: Drink minimum 7 DM ($4.35) Sun–Thurs, 10 DM ($6.25) Fri–Sat and hols. **Admission:** Free Sun–Thurs, 14 DM ($8.75) Fri–Sat.

Open: Mon–Thurs 8pm–3am, Fri–Sat 8pm–4am, Sun 4pm–1am. **U-Bahn:** Ernst-Reuter-Platz.

9. EASY EXCURSIONS

POTSDAM Located only 15 miles southwest of Berlin, Potsdam was once Germany's most important town, serving as both a garrison and as the residence of Prussia's kings and royal families throughout the 18th and 19th centuries. Its most famous resident was Frederick the Great, who succeeded in uniting Germany under his rule, and who built himself a delightful rococo palace in Potsdam called Sanssouci ("without worry"). Frederick the Great retreated to Sanssouci whenever he felt that the rigors of war and government were too much for him and he needed a place for quiet meditation.

Today **Sanssouci** (tel. 03733/23 931 or 22 051) is Potsdam's most famous attraction and is open only for guided tours throughout the year. These tours, *in German only*, last 40 minutes, depart every 20 minutes, and cost 6 DM ($3.75). The palace is open daily: April through September from 9am to 5pm; October, February, and March from 9am to 4pm; and November through January from 9am to 3pm. Note that it's closed the first Monday of every month.

Other places of interest in Potsdam include **Sanssouci Park;** the **Neues Palais,** which was built after the Seven Years' War as a show of Prussian strength; and **Cecilienhof,** headquarters of the Potsdam Conference in 1945 where Truman, Stalin, and Churchill met to discuss the disarmament and future of a divided Germany.

To reach Potsdam, take the S-Bahn to Wannsee station, changing there to bus no. 113 which travels to Potsdam in less than a half hour. Sanssouci is about a 20-minute walk from the Potsdam bus depot.

CHAPTER 8

BRUSSELS

Would you visit the United States without seeing Washington, D.C.? England without seeing London? France without seeing Paris? Italy without seeing Rome? No? Then would you visit Europe without seeing its capital?

If you haven't already heard, Brussels is the capital of the European Community (EC), which in 1992 created a new Europe when it eliminated border and trade restrictions between its member countries. With its newfound importance, Brussels has become very cosmopolitan. No longer is it the staid old city that travelers brushed off as devoid of nightlife or excitement. From the narrow cobblestone streets of the "low town" to the wide boulevards of the "upper town," you can sense excitement in the air as Brussels takes its place among the most important cities of Europe.

With buildings dating back to the early 15th century, the Grand' Place, which Victor Hugo called "the most beautiful square in the world," is the heart of Brussels. Even more tempting are the cafés of Brussels. At the turn of the century Brussels was at the forefront of art nouveau design. Many of the city's most popular cafés date from this period.

Sitting at a small table in one of these cafés, you may be confused by the language you overhear. Is it French or Dutch? In Brussels they speak both, occasionally combining the two. The population is made up of French-speaking Walloons (80%) and Dutch-speaking Flemish (20%). You'll find every sign in Brussels in both languages, which can be a bit confusing at first. However, it's partly because Brussels is at the heart of Europe, a mixing pot of Germanic peoples from the north and Latin peoples from the south, that it was chosen to be the capital of Europe. This mixing of cultures gives Brussels much of its vibrancy, and as the capital of a continent, it can only become more exciting and cosmopolitan in the upcoming years.

1. FROM A BUDGET TRAVELER'S POINT OF VIEW

BRUSSELS'S BUDGET BESTS To begin with, Brussels's great masterpiece, the **Grand' Place,** doesn't cost anything, and you can enjoy a wide variety of events there—from the summer "sound and light" shows to the Sunday bird market—without ever reaching for your wallet.

Brussels's many **markets** are a source of free amusement, as are its state museums, such as the Musée Royaux des Beaux-Arts and the Musée Instrumental.

Belgium's **cafés** are a bargain, for they allow you to spend hours lingering over just one drink. And Belgium's excellent beers are moderately priced and widely available. Further, the superb Belgian frites (which we mistakenly call "french fries") sold on the street cost only about 50F–65F ($1.70–$2.25).

The **Cinema Museum** screens movie classics for 80F ($2.75) a showing.

WHAT THINGS COST IN BRUSSELS	U.S. $
Taxi from the airport to the city center	34.50
Underground from train station to outlying neighborhood	1.40
Local telephone call	.35
Double room at the Hotel Amigo (deluxe)	227.60
Double room at the Hôtel La Madeleine (moderate)	89.50
Double room at the Hotel Pacific (budget)	48.30
Lunch for one at Falstaff (moderate)	12.05
Lunch for one at King Sandwich (budget)	4.00
Dinner for one, without wine, at Villa Lorraine (deluxe)	105.00
Dinner for one, without wine, at Aux Arcades (moderate)	27.60
Dinner for one, without wine, at Restaurant Istanbul (budget)	10.35
Glass of beer	2.25
Coca-Cola in a café	2.05
Cup of coffee in a café	2.05
Roll of ASA 100 color film, 36 exposures	8.30
Admission to the Museum of Lace	2.75
Movie ticket	7.60
Opera ticket	8.60–96.55

SPECIAL DISCOUNT OPPORTUNITIES **Students** enjoy half-price tickets to many cultural events, as well as discounts on train and plane fares and certain tours.

Select cultural arenas, cinemas, and some museums offer **senior discounts.**

Every Friday through Sunday night throughout the year, and daily in July and August, many first-class hotels rent their rooms at half price in order to fill vacancies when business travelers are away. **Anyone** can book these discounts through the Brussels Tourist Office.

WORTH THE EXTRA BUCKS You can enjoy a memorable 20-minute horse-and-carriage tour of the historic center for 450F ($15.50).

2. PRETRIP PREPARATIONS

DOCUMENTS Americans, British subjects, Canadians, Australians, and New Zealanders just need a valid passport to enter Belgium.

WHAT'S SPECIAL ABOUT BRUSSELS

Cafés
- ☐ Sip delicious Belgian beers or an elegantly served cup of hot chocolate.
- ☐ Art nouveau and art deco surroundings.

Grand' Place
- ☐ The heart of Brussels and one of the most beautiful squares in Europe.
- ☐ The daily flower market and the Sunday bird market.
- ☐ Cafés and restaurants, where you can sip beer by a fire.

Art Nouveau
- ☐ The Horta Museum and the Belgian Comic Strip Museum building, among others.
- ☐ Tours given by ARAU Tourville.

Comic Books
- ☐ The Belgian Comic Strip Museum, a comic-book museum.

- ☐ The irresistible hard-cover adventures of Tintin, Asterix, and other comic-book heroes.
- ☐ Comic-book stores all over the city.

Patats Frites [French Fries]
- ☐ Traditionally served in paper cones and smothered with mayonnaise.

Musée d'Art Moderne
- ☐ The extensive collection of surrealist paintings by René Magritte.

Bruparck
- ☐ Nearly 30 movie theaters, a water amusement park, a restaurant and café complex, a miniature Europe, a planetarium, and the fantastic Atomium.

Beer
- ☐ Many flavored with fruit, tasting a bit like sweet sparkling wine. Order as many different types as you can.

WHAT TO PACK A raincoat, umbrella, swimsuit (in summer), good walking shoes (not high heels, which are uncomfortable on the city's cobblestone streets), and a sweater for summer evenings are necessary additions to your typical travel wardrobe.

WHEN TO GO May to September is the best time of the year to visit as the weather grows warm and the city more lively. However, as it never becomes overly cold in winter, you might consider an off-season visit as well.

Brussels's Average Daytime Temperature & Days of Rain

	Jan	Feb	Mar	Apr	May	June	July	Aug	Sept	Oct	Nov	Dec
Temp. (°F)	35	38	43	49	56	61	63	63	60	52	43	37
Days of Rain	19	16	18	17	15	15	17	16	15	17	18	20

Special Events July and August are especially active months in Brussels. On the first Thursday in July you can watch the **Ommegang** in the Grand' Place, a parade of noble families dressed in historic costumes around the square; July 21, **National Day,** is marked by various celebrations, including fireworks; July 21 to August 20 brings the bustling **Brussels Fair** near Gare du Midi; on August 9 the Bruxellois celebrate the raising of the **"Meiboom,"** a tradition marked by planting a tree at the intersection of rue des Sables and rue du Marais, as bands and various other activities celebrate the event.

For the most up-to-date information on this year's special events, contact the Belgian National Tourist Office, 745 Fifth Ave., New York, NY 10151 (tel. 212/758-8130).

BACKGROUND READING   Mystery lovers will enjoy the novels of Georges Simenon, whose Inspector Jules Maigret has often walked the streets of Brussels in his quest to solve crime.

For many Belgians, comic-book figure Tintin by Hergé is a "national hero" whose exploits show off Belgian characteristics of calculated savvy rather than rash action or brute force to solve problems.

History lovers may consider reading about 16th-century Belgium when Brussels was at its heyday, or brush up on accounts of the Battle of Waterloo.

3. ORIENTATION & GETTING AROUND

ARRIVING IN BRUSSELS

FROM THE AIRPORT   Brussels's **National Airport** at Zaventem is just under 8 miles from the city center. A convenient 20-minute shuttle-train service connects first with Gare du Nord and then Gare Centrale every 30 minutes from 5:24am to 11:46pm. Second-class tickets cost 75F ($2.60), 55F ($1.90) for children; buy your tickets at the tourist office in the airport or at the ticket window near the entrance to the train.

Several windows at the airport offer money exchange, and a **National Tourist and Information Office** (tel. 02/722-3000), open Monday through Friday from 8am to 9pm and on Saturday and Sunday from 8am to 8pm, provides information, maps, and brochures, as well as hotel reservations.

FROM THE TRAIN STATION   Brussels has three major train stations (as well as several smaller ones), but you should try to arrive at Gare Centrale (Central Station), as it's the most centrally located and in the best neighborhood. Trains leave from Gare Centrale back to the airport three times an hour starting at 5:39am and continuing until 11:14pm.

Gare Centrale [Central Station]   If you're staying in the area near the Grand' Place, your hotel may be within walking distance of Central Station. To reach the Grand' Place from the station, head toward the tower (the top of the Town Hall, probably still covered in scaffolding) a few blocks away.

If you're going elsewhere in town, you can connect to the metro. When you arrive at Gare Centrale, climb the stairs to the main hall and look for signs to the metro.

Gare du Nord [North Station]   To catch the metro, go to the area adjacent to the central ticket hallway. If you prefer to walk into town (a 20-minute stroll), follow the sign reading CENTRE, which leads you through a block-long elevated pedestrian walkway, and then points you toward town.

Gare du Midi [South Station]   Because one of Brussels's worst neighbor-hoods surrounds the South Station, it's usually best to arrive at other stations in town. Yet you may find it useful to get off here to catch a direct metro to the east side of town (also called "upper Brussels"), site of several budget hotels. You catch the metro from the exit of the station; ask to make sure you're heading the right way.

INFORMATION

TIB, the Tourist Information Office of Brussels, Hôtel de Ville de Bruxelles (the Town Hall), Grand' Place (tel. 02/513-8940), in addition to answering questions of all sorts about Brussels, also gives out the entertainment guide *What's On,* and sells a small *Brussels Guide and Map.* They can reserve you a room (see "Budget Accommodations," below) or reserve concert and theater tickets for a 25F (85¢) service fee. In addition, you can buy tram, metro, and bus tickets. The office is on the ground floor of the Town Hall right in the Grand' Place. It is open March to September, daily from 9am to 6pm; in October and November, Sunday hours are 10am to 2pm; and December through February, it's closed on Sunday.

The **Tourist Information Office,** 63 rue Marché-aux-Herbes, 1000 Bruxelles (tel. 02/504-0390), also reserves hotel rooms in Brussels as well as the rest of Belgium without a service charge, although they do require a deposit. As opposed to the office above, this one specializes in all of Belgium, so it's the place to come before planning side trips. They give out a wide variety of Belgian brochures. This office is just one block from the Grand' Place. It's open June to September, Monday through Friday from 9am to 8pm and on Saturday and Sunday from 9am to 7pm; March to May and October, daily from 9am to 6pm; and November to February, Monday through Saturday from 9am to 6pm and on Sunday from 1 to 5pm.

CITY LAYOUT

Brussels is not laid out in an organized grid, so a brief assessment of its major streets and landmarks may come in handy.

The small cobblestone streets in the center of the city are clustered around the magnificent **Grand' Place.** Two of the most traveled lanes nearby are the restaurant-lined **rue des Bouchers** and **petite rue des Bouchers.** Just a block from the Grand' Place you'll see the classical colonnaded **Bourse,** Belgium's most important stock exchange; there's also a major metro stop on this square, which takes its name from the stock exchange. A few blocks north you'll reach another important landmark, the **National Opera** on **place de la Monnaie** (named after the mint that once stood on the square). Brussels's busiest shopping street, **rue Neuve,** starts from this square and runs north for several blocks.

Brussels's uptown, although located to the southeast of the center, is literally atop a hill. Here you'll find Brussels's second great square, **place du Grand-Sablon,** as well as the Royal Museums of Fine Arts and the Royal Palace. A few blocks to the south you'll see an easy point of reference in the huge white Palace of Justice lined with dozens of classical columns. It's just a few blocks from the start of **avenue Louise,** site of Brussels's ritziest stores.

To make navigating challenging, maps list street names in both French and Dutch. For consistency and ease, I have used the French names in this chapter, and in mailing addresses I have used the French name of the town itself—Bruxelles.

GETTING AROUND

BY METRO Brussels's pleasant metro system consists of three major lines in the center, spruced up with art and music in many stations. There are stops at the three major train stations; other important stations include Bourse, the stock exchange; De Brouckere, near the Opera House and the start of the rue Neuve pedestrian street; Rogier, at the other end of rue Neuve; and place Louise, near the Palace of Justice and avenue Louise.

Rides cost 40F ($1.40) and allow transfers onto all modes of transportation for 1 hour. You can also buy a five-ticket card for 175F ($6.05), a 10-journey card for 250F ($8.60), or an unlimited day pass for 160F ($5.50). The metro runs daily from 6am to midnight. Signs showing a white "M" surrounded by blue indicate the stations. Keep an eye on your wallet or bag.

BY BUS & TRAM A web of buses and trams service areas where the metro does not go. If the stop says "sur demande," you must flag down the bus. Fares are the same as on the metro, and make sure to watch your wallet or bag.

ON FOOT   You'll find no better way to explore the historic core of the town than on foot, especially around the Grand' Place. You'll also enjoy strolling uptown around the place du Grand-Sablon.

BY BICYCLE   Because of the many hills in Brussels and its aggressive car drivers, few locals get around by bicycle.

BY TAXI   The fare starts at 90F ($3.10) and then increases rapidly by 35F ($1.20) per kilometer inside the city or 70F ($2.40) outside the city limits. A typical fare from one point to another in the center costs 175F–225F ($6.05–$7.75).

BY CAR   Brussels's proximity to the rest of the country, as well as to France, Germany, and Holland, make a car an attractive transportation option for continuing on from Brussels. All the top American firms rent in Belgium—including Hertz, Avis, and Budget. Note that car rentals are taxed 25% in Belgium. The smallest car at **ABC Rent a Car,** rue d'Anderlecht, 133 (tel. 513-1954), rents for 1,675F ($57.75) a day, with unlimited mileage and VAT included.

FAST BRUSSELS

Babysitters   If you need a babysitter while in Brussels, contact **ULB babysitting service** (tel. 642-2171).

Banks   There are several banks in the area around the Grand' Place and the Bourse, including **Crédit Générale Bank,** Grand' Place, 5 (tel. 516-1211), open Monday through Friday from 8:45am to 4:30pm; and **Kredietbank,** Grand' Place, 19 (tel. 517-4111), open Monday through Thursday from 9am to 4:30pm and on Friday from 9am to 5:15pm.

Business Hours   **Stores** are open Monday through Saturday from 10am to 6 or 7pm; some larger stores stay open on Friday to 8 or 9pm. **Post offices** are open Monday through Friday from 9am to 5pm. **Banks** are open Monday through Friday from 9:15am to 3:30pm; some branches have Saturday-morning hours.

Consulates   If you should need to contact your home government, you'll find the **U.S. Consulate** at boulevard du Régent, 25 (tel. 02/513-3830); the **Canadian Consulate** at avenue Tervueren, 2 (tel. 02/735-6040); the **Consulate of the U.K.** at Britannia House, rue Joseph-II, 28 (tel. 02/217-9000); the **Australian Consulate** at rue Guimard, 6 (tel. 02/231-0500); the **New Zealand Consulate** at boulevard du Régent, 47 (tel. 02/512-1040); and the **Irish Consulate** at Kanselarij Luxemburgstrasse 19 (tel. 513-6633).

Currency   The Belgian currency is the **Belgian franc (F),** made up of 100 **centimes.** Coins come in 50 centimes and 1, 5, 10, and 20 francs; bills are denominated in 50, 100, 500, 1,000, and 5,000 francs.

Banks charge a 150F ($5.15) commission on traveler's checks, and nothing on cash. Currency-exchange offices charge a lower commission (or none at all), but give a lower rate per dollar. If you're changing a small amount of money you may save at an exchange office, but for several hundred dollars or more you'll do best at a bank. Remember to shop around, as exchange rates and commissions differ widely.

Emergencies   If you need a **doctor,** dial 479-1818 or 648-8000. If you need a **dentist,** dial 426-1026 or 428-5888 (evening and weekends only). For the **police,** dial 101. For an **ambulance** or in case of a **fire,** dial 100.

Eyeglasses   There are several opticians in and near the City 2 shopping mall.

Holidays   In Brussels the following are official holidays: New Year's Day, Easter Monday, Labor Day (May 1), Ascension (sixth Tuesday after Easter), Whit Monday (seventh Monday after Easter), National Day (July 21), Assumption (Aug 15), All Saints' Day (Nov 1), Armistice Day (Nov 11), and Christmas Day.

Hospitals   If you need a hospital, contact **Cliniques Universitaires St-**

THE BELGIAN FRANC & THE DOLLAR

At this writing $1 = approximately 29 francs (or 1 franc = 3.5¢), and this was the rate of exchange used to calculate the dollar values given in this chapter (rounded to the nearest nickel). This rate fluctuates from time to time and may not be the same when you travel to Belgium. Therefore the following table should be used only as a guide:

Francs	U.S.	Francs	U.S.
1	.03	150	5.17
5	.17	200	6.90
10	.35	250	8.62
15	.52	500	17.24
20	.69	750	25.86
25	.86	1,000	34.48
30	1.03	1,250	43.10
35	1.21	1,500	51.72
40	1.38	1,750	60.34
45	1.55	2,000	68.97
50	1.72	2,250	77.59
75	2.59	2,500	86.21
100	3.45	2,750	94.83

Luc, avenue Hippocrate, 10 (tel. 764-1111), or **Clinique St-Michel,** rue L. de Lantsheere, 19 (tel. 739-0711).

Information See "Information" under "Orientation and Getting Around," above, for details.

Laundry/Dry Cleaning Self-service laundries can be found throughout Brussels. **Ipsomat,** rue de Flandre, 51, a block from place Ste-Catherine (and just two blocks from the Bourse), charges 110F ($3.80) for 5 kilos (11 lb.); it's open daily from 7am to 10pm. Ipsomat also has a branch at chausée de Wavre, 123, on the other side of town, open daily from 7am to 10pm. **Lav-o-Net,** rue Antoine-Dansaert, 157, charges 115F ($3.95) to wash 6 kilos (13¼ lb.); it's open daily from 7am to 10pm.

The chain of stores called **5 à Sec** offer some of the city's best-priced dry cleaning in 1-day service. There's one on rue du Marché-aux-Herbes, off the Grand' Place, open from 7:30am to 6pm Monday through Friday only. You'll find another branch at chaussée de Charleroi, 37, in the place Louise area, open from 7:30am to 6pm Monday through Friday.

Lost and Found If you lost something on a plane, call Brussels National Airport (tel. 723-6011); in the airport, call 722-3940; on the metro or a tram, call 515-2394; on a train, call 219-2880 (or after a week, 218-6050); on the highway, call 517-9611.

Mail Two conveniently located post offices are at Gare Centrale (open Monday through Friday from 9am to 6pm) and at the Bourse (open Monday through Friday from 9am to 5:30pm). Postage for a postcard to the United States is 28F (95¢) and for a letter it's 47F ($1.60).

You can receive mail at **American Express,** place Louise, 2, 1050 Bruxelles (tel. 02/512-1740). If you're not an American Express client, they'll charge a 50F ($1.70) fee. You'll also find an American Express cash machine outside their office. The American Express office is open Monday through Friday from 9am to 5pm and on Saturday from 9:30am to noon.

Newspapers You'll find plenty of English-language newspapers, magazines, and books at **W. H. Smith,** boulevard Adolphe-Max, 75 (tel. 219-2708), open

Monday through Saturday from 9am to 6pm (on Tuesday from 10am and on Friday to 7pm).

Photographic Needs   Try **Technaphot,** boulevard Anspach, 23 (tel. 217-6800), open Monday through Saturday from 10am to 6:30pm. There are also 1-hour photo-processing centers along rue Neuve and in City 2.

Police   In an emergency, dial 101 to reach the police.

Radio/TV   There are several local radio and TV stations, including the BBC.

Religious Services   Call **Bruxelles Accueil,** rue de Tabora, 6 (tel. 511-2715), for timetables of religious services at churches all over Brussels.

Shoe Repair   You can get your shoes repaired in the basement of City 2 shopping center.

Tax   You can get a tax refund for purchases once you leave Belgium by asking the shopkeeper to give you a tax-free form. At the border or airport, show the Customs officials your purchase and they will stamp the form. Then you can mail this form back to the Belgian Tax Bureau (the address is on the form) or, if you are leaving via the airport, bring it directly to the "Advantage Bureau," which charges a small commission but gives you an on-the-spot refund. The Belgian VAT ranges from 6% to 33%.

Taxis   See "Orientation and Getting Around," above.

Telephone   A **local phone call** costs 10F (35¢) for 3 minutes.

To make **international calls,** walk one block north of Gare Centrale to boulevard de l'Impératrice, 17 (tel. 02/513-4490) to the large PTT telegraph, telephone, and Telex office, open from 8am to 10pm daily. It costs 179F ($6.15) for a 3-minute call to the U.S., or 150F ($5.15) with a **PTT telecard,** which is available at PTT offices. You can also make international calls from the PTT office at the airport. In addition, you can dial an American operator using **AT&T's "USA Direct" service,** which allows collect and credit-card calls at the local number 11-0010.

Tipping   The prices on **restaurant** menus already include a service charge of 16%, along with a value-added tax (called TVA in Belgium) of 19% (you'll see a little note on the menu reading "T.V.A. et service compris"), so it's not necessary to tip. It is acceptable to round up if you want to. Service is included in your hotel bill as well.

4. BUDGET ACCOMMODATIONS

You shouldn't have too much trouble finding a place within your budget, thanks to the city's many family hotels in old town houses. Although some of these feature charming vintage furniture, most offer modest comfort in a friendly atmosphere, usually with an English-speaking staff. It's best to arrive during the day, since some receptions close once the owner has gone to bed.

You'll find a few budget offerings in the Grand' Place area, the most charming part of Brussels, and more in the area around avenue Louise.

Some of the best youth hostels in Europe are in Brussels, offering another viable option.

If you arrive in Brussels without a reservation, you might want to stop by the **TIB (Office de Tourisme et d'Information),** Hôtel de Ville de Bruxelles, Grand' Place, 1000 Bruxelles (tel. 02/513-8940), where you can make a hotel-room reservation. The TIB will ask you how much you want to spend; after they've made the booking, they'll ask for a 5% deposit. The TIB is open March to September, daily from 9am to 6pm; October to February, Monday through Saturday from 9am to 6pm (in October and November, also on Sunday from 10am to 2pm).

You can also write ahead to **Belgium Tourist Reservations,** B.P. 41, 1000 Bruxelles 23 (tel. 02/230-5029).

DOUBLES FOR LESS THAN 1,450F [$50]

NEAR THE GRAND' PLACE

HOTEL PACIFIC, rue Antoine-Dansaert, 57, 1000 Bruxelles. Tel. 02/ 511-8459. 18 rms (some with shower, none with toilet). **Metro:** Bourse.
$ Rates (including breakfast): 850F ($29.30) single without shower; 1,400F ($48.30) double without shower, 1,800F ($62.05) double with shower. Showers cost 100F ($3.45) extra for those in rooms without shower. Lower rates without breakfast. No credit cards.

An excellent value in an unbeatable location, just a 5-minute walk from the Grand' Place and two blocks from the Bourse, the Pacific has a friendly, soft-spoken owner, Paul Pauwels. Unfortunately, he usually enforces a midnight curfew. Most rooms are large, with plumbing fixtures dating from 80 years ago. The rooms in the front part of the building also have small balconies.

SOUTH OF GARE DU NORD

HOTEL-RESIDENCE ALBERT, rue Royale-Ste-Marie, 27-29, 1030 Brux-elles. Tel. 02/217-9391. Fax 02/219-2017. 22 rms (10 with shower and toilet, 12 with shower only), 16 apartments. TEL **Directions:** From Gare du Nord, walk 5 min. up a hill on rue Dupont.
$ Rates (including breakfast): 970F ($33.45) single with shower only, 1,000F ($34.50) single with shower and toilet; 1,240F ($42.75) double with shower only, 1,480F ($51.05) double with shower and toilet; 1,600F–1,700F ($55.15–$58.60) apartment. No credit cards.
The rooms are free of decoration and have tiny writing desks; other furnishings are new. The private bathrooms are separated only by a curtain, and rooms with shower have only a free-standing unit in the room. The 16 apartments are suitable for one or two guests. For maximum quiet, ask for the rooms in the back away from the busy street. There is a bar on the premises.

HOTEL SABINA, rue du Nord, 78, 1000 Bruxelles. Tel. 02/218-2637. Fax 02/219-3239. 24 rms (22 with shower and toilet, 2 with shower only). TEL **Metro:** Madou.
$ Rates (including breakfast): 1,350F–1,500F ($46.55–$51.70) single; 1,350F–1,750F ($46.55–$60.35) double. MC, V.
The owners of this excellent uptown choice speak English, and the accommodations are modern and very clean. Most rooms have a closet-sized shower and toilet. The small breakfast room has a large wood fireplace, a wood-beam ceiling, and a TV to the side. You'll find the street off place des Barricades.

IN THE AVENUE LOUISE AREA

HOTEL BERCKMANS, rue Berckmans, 12, 1060 Bruxelles. Tel. 02/537-8948. 23 rms (6 with shower and toilet, 15 with shower only). TEL **Metro:** Place Louise. **Bus:** 60.
$ Rates (including breakfast): 700F ($24.15) single without shower or toilet, 1,000F ($34.50) single with shower only, 1,400F ($48.30) single with shower and toilet; 1,100F ($37.95) double without shower or toilet, 1,400F ($48.30) double with shower only, 1,650F ($56.90) double with shower and toilet. ACCESS, AE, DC, EURO, MC, V.
Despite the upscale tone of the avenue Louise district, it's still possible to get an

inexpensive room in the area. The Hotel Berckmans is comfortable. Rooms vary in size, and those with private shower and toilet have the facilities behind a curtain rather than in a separate room. A few of the rooms have TVs.

DOUBLES FOR LESS THAN 1,800F [$62.05]

NEAR THE GRAND' PLACE

PENSION DES EPERONNIERS, rue des Eperonniers, 1, 1000 Bruxelles. Tel. 02/513-5366. 26 rms (9 with full bath, 10 with toilet only, 3 with shower only).

$ **Rates** (including breakfast): 1,000F ($34.50) single without bath, 1,100F ($37.95) single with shower or toilet only, 1,250F ($43.10) single with bath; 1,400F ($48.30) double without bath, 1,500F ($51.70) double with shower or toilet only, 1,650F ($56.90) double with bath. MC, V.

Just one block from the Grand' Place, this pension, opened in 1987, offers just about the lowest prices in the area. The rooms are large and clean, some with a few older pieces of furniture. The reception is quite friendly, if in limited English.

SOUTH OF GARE DU NORD

HOTEL INTERNATIONAL, rue Royale, 344, 1030 Bruxelles. Tel. 02/217-3344 or 217-1484. 25 rms (all with sink and bath but no toilet). **Metro:** Botanique.

$ **Rates** (including breakfast): 1,150F ($39.65) single; 1,400F–1,500F ($48.25–$51.70) double; 1,850F ($63.80) triple. ACCESS, DC, EURO, MC.

This is an older pension-style hotel with sink, bath, and bidet curtained off to the side of the rooms. It's located on a busy traffic avenue across from St. Marie's Church and near the Hôtel Albert, a 10-minute walk from the Gare du Nord.

HOTEL LA GASCOGNE, bd. Adolphe-Max, 137, 1000 Bruxelles. Tel. 02/217-6962 or 217-4363. 13 rms (none with bath). **Metro:** Rogier.

$ **Rates** (including breakfast): 1,100F ($37.95) single; 1,600F ($55.15) double. AE, DC, EURO, V.

Located on a bustling street parallel to rue Neuve, La Gascogne features spacious rooms with furniture from the 1940s and 1950s, floral wallpaper, and large windows with small balconies overlooking the street. You enter the hotel through the restaurant on the first level. Unfortunately, this block is also the site of several porno theaters.

RELAIS LA TASSE D'ARGENT, rue du Congrès, 48, and HOTEL MADOU, rue du Congrès, 45, 1000 Bruxelles. Tel. 02/218-8375 or 217-3274. 16 rms (all with bath). **Metro:** Madou.

$ **Rates:** 1,300F ($44.80) single; 1,550F–1,650F ($53.45–$56.90) double; 1,950F ($67.25) triple. Breakfast costs 125F ($4.30) extra. No credit cards.

⭐ Built in two old family houses, these small hotels really make you feel as though you're a guest in a friend's home. The rooms feature half-size bathtubs and large windows overlooking the street. The lovely breakfast room at no. 48 has a grandfather clock and chintz seating, helping to make this an excellent choice. All the rooms in both hotels are newly decorated.

NORTH OF GARE DU MIDI

HOTEL A LA GRANDE CLOCHE, place Rouppe, 10-12, 1000 Bruxelles. Tel. 02/512-9131 or 512-6140. Fax 02/512-6591. 47 rms (4 with bath, 26 with shower only). TEL **Metro:** Anneessens.

$ Rates (including breakfast): 1,500F ($51.70) single with shower only; 1,525F ($52.60) double without bath, 2,100F ($72.40) double with shower only, 2,600F ($89.65) double with bath. AE, EURO, MC, V.

This hotel, located on a small traffic circle 10 minutes on foot from Gare du Midi and another 10 minutes from the Grand' Place, offers clean, modern rooms, most with small shower and sink areas. The double with bath also has a TV. The elevator-equipped building even has hairdryers in the hallways and some rooms. This is a very good choice.

HOTEL GEORGE-V, rue t'Kint, 23, 1000 Bruxelles. Tel. 02/513-5093 or 513-4974. 17 rms (14 with bath, 3 with toilet only). **Metro:** Bourse.
$ Rates (including breakfast): 1,750F ($60.35) single or double with toilet, 1,980F– 2,200F ($68.30–$75.85) single or double with bath. EURO, V. **Parking:** 140F ($4.85) per 24 hours.
A four-story white structure on a residential street, this elevator building is just a 5- to 10-minute walk from the Bourse metro stop. The hotel was completely remodeled in 1991 and is now very elegant for a budget hotel. Dark wood, polished brass, and marble are just some of the fine touches. Public areas include a TV lounge and bar.

HOTEL VAN BELLE, chaussée de Mons, 39, 1070 Bruxelles. Tel. 02/521-3516. 140 rms (112 with bath). TV
$ Rates: 1,200F ($41.40) single without bath, 2,100F–2,400F ($72.40–$82.75) single with bath; 1,650F ($56.90) double without bath, 2,325F–3,050F ($80.15–$105.15) double with bath. There's a 5% discount on these rates to Frommer's readers paying cash. AE, DC, EURO, V. **Parking:** 150F ($5.15) in an underground lot.

A larger and more formal hotel than most choices in this chapter, the Van Belle offers hotel services such as photocopying and fax machines that smaller budget hotels do not provide. The smaller, cheaper rooms without bathrooms in the old wing have a sink and aging carpets, but bright lighting. The larger rooms in the modern wing have two chairs and a small writing table. It's about a 10-minute walk north of Gare du Midi.

DOUBLES FOR LESS THAN 2,000F [$68.95]

NEAR THE GRAND' PLACE

HOTEL MIRABEAU, place Fontainas, 18-20, 1000 Bruxelles. Tel. 02/511-1972. 30 rms (24 with bath, 6 with shower only). TV TEL **Metro:** Anneessens.
$ Rates: 1,350F–1,520F ($46.55–$52.40) single; 2,050F ($70.70) double. AE, DC, EURO, MC, V.
A good value for those who want a private bathroom, this hotel is set off the busy boulevard Le-Monnier by a small square. Some rooms have a large series of windows and all have a small writing desk, new carpets, and tiny modern bathrooms.

RESIDENCE LA VIEILLE LANTERNE, rue des Grands-Carmes, 29, 1000 Bruxelles. Tel. 02/512-7494. 6 rms (all with bath).
$ Rates: 1,400F ($48.30) single; 1,900F ($65.50) double. Breakfast 100F ($3.45) extra. AE, DC, EURO, MC, V.

A tiny inn with two rooms per floor, this find is diagonally across from the *Manneken Pis*. It can be hard to spot at first—you enter the hotel through the side door of a trinket shop selling hundreds of *Mannekin Pis* replicas. You'll feel right at home in the rooms with their old-style windows and fully equipped bathrooms. It's a good idea to write ahead to reserve a room; and if you'll be arriving after 2pm, a deposit is required.

IN THE AVENUE LOUISE AREA

HOTEL WINDSOR, place Rouppe, 13, 1000 Bruxelles. Tel. 02/511-2014 or 511-1494. 24 rms (9 with shower). **Metro:** Anneessens.
$ Rates (including breakfast): 1,220F ($42.05) single without shower, 1,465F ($50.50) single with shower; 1,580F ($54.50) double without shower, 1,925F ($66.40) double with shower. EURO, MC, V.

You pass through a quiet little bistro restaurant to get to the guest rooms at this recently renovated hotel. New furnishings, carpets, and wallpaper give the hotel a very contemporary feel, and though there are no rooms with full bath (toilets are down the hall), those rooms that do not have a shower do have a bidet. Most rooms also have a phone and a clock radio.

RESIDENCE LES BLUETS, rue Berckmans, 124, 1060 Bruxelles. Tel. 02/539-3258. 9 rms (8 with bath, 1 with shower only). **Metro:** Hôtel des Monnaies.
$ Rates (including breakfast): 1,000F ($34.50) single with shower only, 1,650F ($56.90) single with bath; 1,950F ($67.25) double with bath and TV. No credit cards.

⭐ A three-story building on a residential street, Les Bluets is attractive, with antique furniture and moldings in its rooms, all of which have new carpets and were repainted in 1991. Some rooms have TVs and others have 14-foot ceilings that give the rooms a very spacious feel.

PRIVATE ROOMS

Private rooms in Belgium do not represent the substantial savings over hotels that they do in certain other countries such as Denmark and Sweden, but they provide a colorful alternative to the formal atmosphere of a hotel.

La Rose au Vent (The Windrose), avenue des Démineurs, 1A, 1090 Bruxelles-Jette (tel. 02/425-4071; fax 02/425-4071), rents 50 rooms in Brussels itself and across the country. To reserve a room it's best to write them at least 2 weeks in advance. You must make a minimum 2-night reservation, and send a 25% deposit and a 350F ($12.05) reservation fee. Alternatively, you can call when you arrive in town, and then call back a few hours later to see if they have found a room for you. Room rates—including breakfast—run 1,000F–2,000F ($34.50–$68.95) for a single and 1,600F–3,400F ($55.15–$117.25) for a double, without or with a bath. The agency accepts no credit cards.

SUPER-BUDGET CHOICES

HOSTELS

Brussels offers students and the young-at-heart a powerful lineup of excellent hostels in central locations, most with everything from single rooms to large "sleep-in" rooms.

AUBERGE DE JEUNESSE JAN BRUEGHEL, rue du Saint-Esprit, 2, 1000 Bruxelles. Tel. 02/511-0436. 135 beds (no rms with bath).
$ Rates (including breakfast): 600F ($20.70) single; 495F ($17.05) per person double; 415F ($14.30) per person quad; 370F ($12.75) per person in a 12-bed room. Those without an IYHF card pay 80F ($2.75) extra. Sheets 120F ($4.15) extra; towels, 30F ($1.05); dinner, 230F ($7.95). No credit cards.

This hostel is located in an attractive brick building at the side of the Eglise Notre-Dame-de-la-Chapelle, where Jan's father, the great Pieter Brueghel, is buried. Rooms have cinder-block walls, bunk beds, a sink, and large windows. Each floor has a TV lounge, and there's a cafeteria on the premises. Just one word of caution: Don't

FROMMER'S SMART TRAVELER: HOTELS
VALUE-CONSCIOUS TRAVELERS SHOULD
TAKE ADVANTAGE OF THE FOLLOWING:

1. Hotels in the residential neighborhood along Avenue Louise.
2. Youth hostels, which are excellent bargains and offer quite a few single and double rooms for those who want to save money but don't want to sleep in a dorm.
3. Hotels within a block or two of the Grand' Place—if you're willing to spend a little more money.

change money at the reception, which is open from 7:30 to 10am and 2pm to midnight—they offer terrible rates. The hostel is only a 10-minute walk from Gare Centrale.

CHAB (CENTRE D'HEBERGEMENT DE L'AGGLOMERATION BRU-XELLOISE), rue Traversière, 8, 1030 Bruxelles. Tel. 02/217-0158. 280 beds (no rms with bath). **Bus:** 65 or 66 from Gare Centrale.
$ Rates (including breakfast): 580F ($20) single; 480F ($16.55) per person double; 400F ($13.80) per person triple or quad; 280F–340F ($9.65–$11.75) per person in larger rooms. Sheets cost 80F ($2.75) extra. V.
Located in two different buildings across the street from each other, CHAB offers very pleasant, clean rooms with large windows that open like doors onto the street. Both buildings have little gardens in back, and one has a modest kitchen and a snack bar serving meals for 160F–200F ($5.50–$6.90) daily from noon to 2:30pm and 6:30 to 10pm. The friendly reception gives advice on Brussels's hot spots. Only guests under 35 years of age are accepted, and a 2am curfew is enforced. CHAB is 10 minutes on foot from Gare du Nord.

CENTRE INTERNATIONAL D'ACCUEIL POUR JEUNES JACQUES BREL, rue da la Sablonnière, 30, 1000 Bruxelles. Tel. 02/218-0187. Fax 02/217-2005. 139 beds. **Bus:** 65 or 66 from Gare Centrale to Chèques Postaux.
$ Rates (including breakfast): 600F ($20.70) single; 495F ($17.05) per person double; 415F ($14.30) per person quad; 370F ($12.75) per person in a dorm. Those without an IYHF card pay a one-time supplement of 20F (70¢). Sheets 120F ($4.15) extra. MC, V.
Opened in 1987, this youth hostel was formerly a hospital—it still has special facilities for the disabled. Public facilities include a bar, washing machines, a TV room, and two small sun decks. The rooms (with 1–14 beds) have large windows, allowing in lots of light, and showers. A 1am curfew is enforced, but the reception is open throughout the day. This hostel is located in the elegant "upper Brussels" area of the city, a 10- to 15-minute walk from Gare Centrale.

MAISON INTERNATIONALE, chaussée de Wavre, 205, 1040 Bruxelles. Tel. 02/648-9787. 82 beds (no rms with bath). **Metro:** Namur. **Bus:** 38 from Gare Centrale.
$ Rates (including breakfast): 360F ($12.40) single; 310F ($10.70) per person double. Sheets 80F ($2.75) extra. You can camp in the backyard for 230F ($7.95) per person. No credit cards.
Although not as new and spiffy as some of Brussels's other youth hostels, the former monastery Maison Internationale offers the lowest year-round prices in town. What's more, travelers of all ages are welcomed and the IYHF card is not required. They do have a 12:30am curfew and a 9:30am–4pm lockout. All rooms have sinks, but only the singles have hot as well as cold water.

SLEEP WELL, rue de la Blanchisserie, 27, 1000 Bruxelles. Tel. 02/218-

5050. Fax 02/218-1313. Telex 62108. 130 beds (no rms with bath). **Metro:** Rogier.

$ Rates (including breakfast): 460F ($15.85) single; 410F ($14.15) per person double; 350F ($12.05) per person in a 4- to 6-bed room; 300F ($10.35) per person in a 10- to 18-bed room. Sheets 80F ($2.75) extra. There's a 10% discount for holders of an FIYTO card or ISIC. No credit cards.

⊛ Located just behind the huge City 2 shopping mall and one block from the bustling rue Neuve, Sleep Well enjoys probably the best location of all of Brussels's well-placed hostels. Guests of all ages are welcomed, but a 1am curfew and a 10am–4pm close-out are maintained. Downstairs, the evening café serves 15 types of beer for 35F–65F ($1.20–$2.25). They also sponsor 2-hour city tours in the summer for only 60F ($2.05) per person! There were plans to move the hostel around the corner in late 1992, so call for the new address.

UNIVERSITY ACCOMMODATIONS

STUDENT HOMES OF THE FREE UNIVERSITY OF BRUSSELS, bd. du Triomphe, 1, Housing Department, Entrance 7, 1050 Bruxelles. Tel. 02/641-2831. All rms are singles with bath. **Metro:** Pétillon.

$ Rates: 500F ($17.25) per person per day for up to 7 days, 450F ($15.50) per additional day. Breakfast 110F ($3.80) extra; lunch, 220F ($7.60). No credit cards. **Open:** July 15–Sept 15.

A great summer value, the Student Homes offer the privacy and comfort of a fully equipped hotel room, yet charge youth-hostel prices. The rooms have access to a kitchen. Unfortunately, the location is a bit remote at the Oefenplein campus. When you get to the campus, follow the signs for *studentenhomes* to reach the reception.

WORTH THE EXTRA BUCKS

HOTEL LA MADELEINE, rue de la Montagne, 22, 1000 Bruxelles. Tel. 02/513-2973. 52 rms (37 with bath, 10 with shower only). TEL

$ Rates (including breakfast): 1,225F ($42.25) single without bath, 1,895F ($65.35) single with shower only, 2,295F ($79.15) single with bath; from 2,595F ($89.50) double with bath. ACCESS, AE, EURO, MC, V.

In a superb location, La Madeleine is just one block from the Grand' Place and a few minutes on foot from Gare Centrale. The facilities are generally modest but clean; there's a cheery breakfast room with white wooden ceilings and a red bar area.

HOTEL MARIE-JOSE, rue de Commerce, 73, 1040 Bruxelles. Tel. 02/512-0843. Fax 02/512-4604. 23 rms (all with bath). TV **Metro:** Arts-Loi or Luxemburg.

$ Rates (including breakfast): 1,300F–2,700F ($44.85–$93.10) single; 1,800–3,200F ($62.05–$110.35) double. AE, DC, EURO, MC, V.

A three-story structure on a quiet side street that's a 10- or 15-minute walk from Gare Centrale (through the Parc de Bruxelles in the center), this hotel welcomes visitors with a cozy lobby graced with flowers, a fish tank, and a grandfather clock, as well as an upscale restaurant. The room TVs have remote-control units.

5. BUDGET DINING

Although it's not among the least expensive cities of Europe, Brussels has a substantial number of restaurants where you can dine well at a reasonable cost.

Belgians cook up ingenious specialties, everything from poultry sautéed in beer to tasty mussels prepared in dozens of sauces. One favorite is mussels steamed in a vegetable broth, served in a sturdy iron pot. When ordering mussels (a kilo, 2.2 lb., is a typical portion), note that the best time is from September through the winter; mussels served in the summer are often imported and not as good.

The Belgians also deserve credit for perfecting a mighty culinary quintet of cheese, waffles, fried potatoes, chocolate, and beer, and no visit to Brussels is complete without a generous sampling of each.

In American lingo the French may have their name attached to fried potatoes, but it's the Belgians who mastered the art. Brussels is dotted with dozens of fast-food stands serving Belgian frites wrapped in paper cones. Belgians usually eat their fries with mayonnaise rather than ketchup; although this method may cause apprehension at first, once having tried it you may well be converted forever. Prices run 50F–70F ($1.70–$2.40), depending on the portion and where you buy them; the topping (which you must specifically ask for) costs 10F–15F (35¢–50¢).

Belgium is also famous for its 400 different brands of beer, produced by hundreds of small breweries throughout the country. Many of these brews are considerably stronger than those we know in America—the alcohol content can be as high as 12%. Belgian Trappist monks produce 30–40 brands of the country's most expensive and strongest beers (thanks to heavy fermentation).

Since you'll see dozens of beer offerings on the menu of many restaurants, it's a good idea to ask the waiter for suggestions—but remember also to check the price, for certain brands are quite expensive.

MEALS FOR LESS THAN 250F ($8.60)

DEN TEEPOT, rue des Chartreux, 29. Tel. 511-9402.
   Cuisine: VEGETARIAN. **Metro:** Bourse.
   $ Prices: Plat du jour 200F ($6.90) large, 150F ($5.15) small. No credit cards.
   Open: Lunch only, Mon–Sat noon–2pm.
If meat and potatoes are not your favorite fare and greasy french fries leave you cold, Den Teepot may be just the place you're seeking. Rice and beans and veggies, organically grown and macrobiotically prepared, are the staples here, but surprisingly, you can also get a beer with your meal. Though they're a bit pricey, you should try one of the fresh juices. The carrot juice is usually extremely spicy.

RESTAURANT ISTANBUL, chaussée de Haecht, 16. Tel. 218-7286.
   Cuisine: TURKISH. **Reservations:** Recommended on Fri and Sat night.
   $ Prices: 225F–410F ($7.75–$14.15); plat du jour 295F ($10.15). No credit cards.
   Open: Lunch daily 11:30am–3pm; dinner daily 6pm–1am.
A long restaurant with small Turkish carpets and ornaments on the wall, Istanbul serves tasty grilled fare. Turkish music plays on the radio for most meals, and on Friday and Saturday night there's live Turkish music and belly dancing starting at 8pm—at no extra charge. Located around the corner from the CHAB youth hostel, south of Gare du Nord, Istanbul is one of several low-cost Turkish and Middle Eastern restaurants in the area.

QUICK BITES

There are numerous fast-food Greek places near the Grand' Place that make gyros, falafels, and other low-cost items for about 120F ($4.15) each.

The many inexpensive cafeterias and fast-food restaurants in **City 2,** a huge American-style shopping mall on rue Neuve, makes it one of Brussels's great budget centers. The mall, as well as most of its restaurants, is open daily from 10am to 7pm (on Friday to 8pm). Here's a sampling:

   City Grill, on the basement level, is a self-service cafeteria. Main courses cost around 230F–400F ($7.95–$13.80), the salads are 110F–330F ($3.80–$11.40), and the menu of the day, which might be a soup, veal dish, and apple cake, costs 230F–300F ($7.95–$10.35).

Inno Department Store Cafeteria, on rue Neuve, and linked by a pedestrian bridge to City 2, is a self-service cafeteria with many offerings, including pork burgers and anchovies, rumpsteak garni, and other cafeteria specials. Prices are moderate— 210F–375F ($7.25–$12.95)—which often attracts a long line of people. It's open Monday through Saturday from 9:30am to 6:30pm (on Friday to 7:30pm).

King Sandwich, also in the basement, specializes in—you guessed it— sandwiches, for 50F–100F ($1.70–$3.45).

You'll also find several other restaurants on other floors of City 2, including **Mister Grill and Buffets,** which specializes in pork goulash and fries, and half a chicken with garnishes, in the 200F–400F ($6.90–$13.80) range.

At **Pizzeria Donnini,** on the basement level, which specializes in pizza and pasta, you order from a pictorial menu that shows the exact size of the portions, which are huge. Prices run 60F–220F ($2.05–$7.60).

MEALS FOR LESS THAN 350F ($12.05)

NEAR THE GRAND' PLACE

AU BAMBOU FLEUR, rue Jules-van-Praet, 13. Tel. 502-2951.
   Cuisine: VIETNAMESE. **Metro:** Bourse.
$ **Prices:** 350F–500F ($12.05–$17.25); lunch special 225F ($7.75). No credit cards.
   Open: Daily noon–2am.
In recent years there has been quite a proliferation of Vietnamese restaurants in Brussels. They're almost always the cheapest restaurants around, and their lunch specials are always a good deal. Au Bambou Fleur is just three blocks from the Grand' Place, and thus is very convenient. To help you make a decision, the menu, which is posted in the front window, has photos of all the dishes.

BETWEEN AVENUE LOUISE & CHAUSSEE DE WAVRE

LA CUCCAGNA, chaussée de Wavre, 39. Tel. 513-3110.
   Cuisine: ITALIAN. **Reservations:** Recommended at lunch.
$ **Prices:** Pizza and pasta courses 150F–230F ($5.15–$7.95); meat and fish courses 320F–430F ($11.05–$14.85). AE, DC, EURO, MC, V.
   Open: Lunch Mon–Sat noon–2:30pm; dinner Mon–Sat 6–11pm.
Staffed and run by Italians, La Cuccagna features a modern decor of pastel colors and

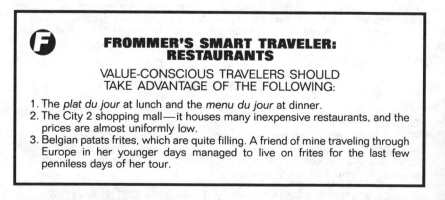

(F) **FROMMER'S SMART TRAVELER:**
RESTAURANTS

VALUE-CONSCIOUS TRAVELERS SHOULD
TAKE ADVANTAGE OF THE FOLLOWING:

1. The *plat du jour* at lunch and the *menu du jour* at dinner.
2. The City 2 shopping mall—it houses many inexpensive restaurants, and the prices are almost uniformly low.
3. Belgian patats frites, which are quite filling. A friend of mine traveling through Europe in her younger days managed to live on frites for the last few penniless days of her tour.

a few faux columns. I enjoyed a huge bowl of rigatoni, which easily made a meal in itself, for 225F ($7.75). Italian music plays in the background, and occasionally a Sicilian guitarist performs in the evening.

ROTISSERIE COUCOU, av. de la Toison d'Or, 6. Tel. 511-5222.
   Cuisine: BELGIAN. **Metro:** Namur.
$ **Prices:** Main courses 175–250F ($6.05–$8.60); complete meal specials 360F–485F ($12.40–$16.70). AE, DC, EURO, MC, V.
   Open: Daily 11am–10pm.
This is a cross between a cafeteria and a restaurant. There are paper place mats and a well-worn floor, but the wooden rafters are attractive. Coucou grills a good-quality, reasonably priced chicken behind the counter as you enter.

MEALS FOR LESS THAN 500F ($17.25)

WEST OF LA BOURSE

IN'T SPINNEKOPKE, place du Jardin-aux-Fleurs, 1. Tel. 511-8695.
   Cuisine: BELGIAN. **Metro:** Bourse.
$ **Prices:** 300F–575F ($10.35–$19.85). AE, DC, EURO, MC, V.
   Open: Lunch Mon–Fri noon–3pm; dinner Mon–Sat 6–11pm. Bar Mon–Fri 11am–11pm, Sat 6–11pm. **Closed:** Aug.

✪ My favorite typical local place in town, this restaurant serves excellent food in a building that dates from 1762. Wood beams, wood paneling, pink floral wallpaper, pink tablecloths, candles, and roses serve as decorations, capturing a European charm that makes for a special evening out. The restaurant serves a large variety of beers, and even cooks with some beer sauces. Prices are a bit high, but worth it. The restaurant is about a 5-minute walk from the Bourse metro stop.

NEAR THE GRAND' PLACE

**AUBERGE DES CHAPELIERS, rue des Chapeliers, 1-3, off the Grand'
   Place. Tel. 513-7338.**
   Cuisine: BELGIAN. **Reservations:** Recommended.
$ **Prices:** 250F–610F ($8.60–$21). ACCESS, AE, DC, EURO, MC, V.
   Open: Lunch daily noon–2:30pm; dinner Sun–Thurs 6–11pm, Fri–Sat 6pm–midnight.
Located in a 17th-century building where Brussels's best artisans once designed hats, the Auberge des Chapeliers (Inn of the Hat Makers) preserves a charming feel. Behind a beautiful brick facade, the first two floors of the restaurant are graced with wooden beams and paneling and are connected by a very narrow wooden staircase. The third floor has windows overlooking the nearby streets. Excellent fries accompany the typical Belgian cuisine. Don't miss this conveniently located and reasonably priced choice.

CAP DE NUIT, place de la Vieille Halle-aux-Blés, 28. Tel. 512-9342.
   Cuisine: ITALIAN/BELGIAN.
$ **Prices:** 270F–590F ($9.30–$20.35). AE, DC, EURO, MC, V.
   Open: Daily 6pm–7am.
Cap de Nuit assures that you'll never go hungry late at night, as it serves up pasta and other dishes all the way to 7am, the latest of any restaurant in town! The modern decor, late hours, and the 28 varieties of beer attract a crowd between the ages of 20 and 40.

RESTAURANT FALSTAFF, rue Henri-Maus, 25-27. Tel. 511-8788 or
   511-8789.
   Cuisine: BELGIAN. **Reservations:** Recommended.

$ Prices: Main courses 245F–625F ($8.45–$21.55); complete lunch special 350F ($12.05); sandwiches 60F–120F ($2.05–$4.15). AE, DC, EURO, MC, V.
Open: Daily 7am–5am (lunch special served noon–3pm).

 An art nouveau masterpiece with carved wooden ceilings, painted glass, and mirrors, Falstaff attracts a boisterous crowd. The best value of the day is the *plat du jour,* or if you come for dinner, the complete *menu du jour.* The restaurant has two halves, each with a different menu: an art nouveau part from 1903 and a newer section from 1965. Service can be slow and impersonal, but the place still captures that Belgian joie de vivre.

SHAMROCK, rue Jules-van-Praet, 27-29. Tel. 511-4989.
Cuisine: INDIAN. **Metro:** Bourse.
$ Prices: 300F–600F ($10.35–$20.70). No credit cards.
Open: Lunch daily noon–3pm; dinner daily 7pm–midnight.
Neither the name nor the publike decor even hints that this might be an Indian restaurant, but don't worry—once you see the menu, you'll know you're at the right place. As soon as you sit down, you'll be brought a papadam (crisp lentil chip) with three different sauces to spread on it. It's best if you have several people in your group when you eat here so that you can try as many succulent and spicy dishes as possible.

T'KELDERKE, Grand' Place, 15. Tel. 513-7344.
Cuisine: BELGIAN. **Reservations:** Recommended, if possible.
$ Prices: Main courses 225F–475F ($7.75–$16.40); weekday lunch special 250F ($8.60); mussels 595F–725F ($20.50–$25). AE, EURO, MC, V.
Open: Daily noon–2am (weekday lunch special offered noon–2pm or until they run out).
T'Kelderke (The Little Cellar) is, as its name implies, a brick-vaulted cellar just a few steps down from the square (on the "upper" side of the square). The food is good and the place features a mix of locals and tourists.

TAI-HON, rue des Eperroniers, 45. Tel. 514-5058.
Cuisine: CHINESE.
$ Prices: 250F–450F ($8.60–$15.50); daily special 150F ($5.15). AE, DC, EURO, MC, V.
Open: Tues, Sun 7–11:30pm, Mon, Wed, Sat noon–11:30pm.
This small and unusual Chinese restaurant offers original dishes in the Taiwan, or simple Chinese, style. Photos of the artistically arranged dishes are pasted in the front window, and the Zenlike interior provides an oasis of calm. The *plat du jour* is a good deal, or you can choose from such dishes as steamed salmon and shrimp scampi with pepper. Take-out service is also available.

RUE DES BOUCHERS & PETITE RUE DES BOUCHERS

These two streets boast dozens of inviting restaurants, many with frosted windows and ornate displays of fresh fish outside. Unfortunately, most of these tourist-oriented restaurants are substantially overpriced, often serving food of uneven quality. On the whole, I suggest a stroll through the area to work up your appetite, and then a walk to another area of town to find a more reasonably priced restaurant. If you do want to enjoy one mini-splurge here, however, try. . . .

CHEZ LEON, rue des Bouchers, 18-22. Tel. 511-1415 or 513-0848.
Cuisine: BELGIAN.
$ Prices: Mussel dinner 310F–610F ($10.70–$21.05); plat du jour 310F ($10.70). AE, DC, EURO, MC, V.
Open: Daily noon–midnight.
In 1990 Chez Leon served more than 800,000 pounds of mussels, making it Brussels's true king of mussels! Many tourists frequent this bubbling bistro, where the waiters run to and fro at a frantic pace. The dining rooms feature

tables with paper tablecloths and wooden stall seating. The kitchen is to the side as you enter the restaurant.

FOR DESSERT

Many connoisseurs consider Belgium the world's greatest chocolate confectioner. For Belgians, the real art comes in not merely producing a quality bar of chocolate but in filling that chocolate with goodies inside, creating the perfect praline.

The chain of stores called **Leonidas** sells excellent Belgian pralines for the lowest prices in town, 360F ($12.40) per kilo (2.2 lb.). They have 10 branches in town, including boulevard Anspach, 46, off the Bourse (tel. 218-0363); boulevard Adolphe-Max, 49-51, parallel to rue Neuve (tel. 217-9555); and chaussée d'Ixelles, 5, off Porte Namur (tel. 511-1151).

Also, look for signs throughout the city that read **Vigaufra,** where they sell fresh waffles for about 35F ($1.20).

PICNIC SUPPLIES

You'll find a huge supermarket with a large cold-cut-and-cheese counter perfect for assembling a picnic lunch in **GB,** in the basement of City 2 on rue Neuve. It's open from 10am to 7pm daily (on Friday to 8pm). There's another **GB** at the corner of rue de Marché-aux-Pullets and rue des Halles, one block from the Bourse.

You'll also find ample gourmet food stores in the streets around the Grand' Place.

6. ATTRACTIONS

SUGGESTED ITINERARIES

IF YOU HAVE ONE DAY   You'll want to spend your first hours in Brussels at the magnificent Grand' Place, whose elaborate buildings and ornate details are a fairy tale come true. In particular, visit the Gothic Hôtel de Ville de Bruxelles and the Musée de la Ville de Bruxelles (Museum of the City of Brussels).

From the Grand' Place, pay a visit to the defiant *Manneken Pis,* and then after lunch, head uptown to the impressive Musées Royaux des Beaux-Arts to see their collection of old masters and modern artists. After a few hours in the museum, walk over to the attractive place du Grand-Sablon and its diminutive neighbor, place du Petit-Sablon.

IF YOU HAVE TWO DAYS   Spread the above activities at a more relaxed pace over 2 days, and stop in at the Notre-Dame du Sablon church while on place du Grand-Sablon. Also visit the Cathédrale St-Michel et Ste-Gudule near Gare Centrale. Then explore rue Neuve, Brussels's main pedestrian street, and wander about the nearby streets. If you still have extra time, consider a visit to the Musée Instrumental.

IF YOU HAVE THREE DAYS   Spend your first 2 days as outlined above, and then on the third day head out to the museum complex at Parc du Cinquantenaire where you can admire the varied collection of the Musées Royaux d'Art et d'Histoire, the superb Musée Royal de l'Armée et d'Histoire Militaire, and the fun Autoworld. Also consider the Musée du Costume et de la Dentelle (Costume and Lace Museum), near the Grand' Place, and a stroll on the elegant avenue Louise.

IF YOU HAVE FIVE DAYS   Visit the massive Atomium from the 1957 Brussels World's Fair and stop in at the Bruparck amusement center directly opposite the Atomium. Consider a picnic in one of Brussels's parks.

BELGIUM

★ Brussels

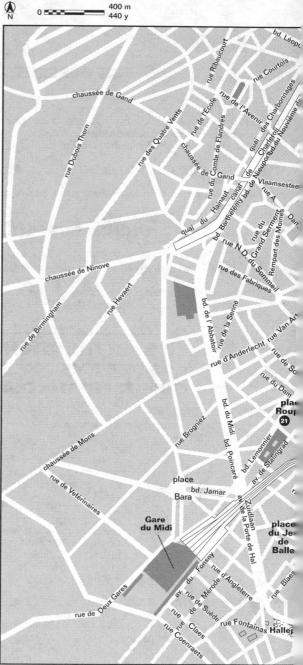

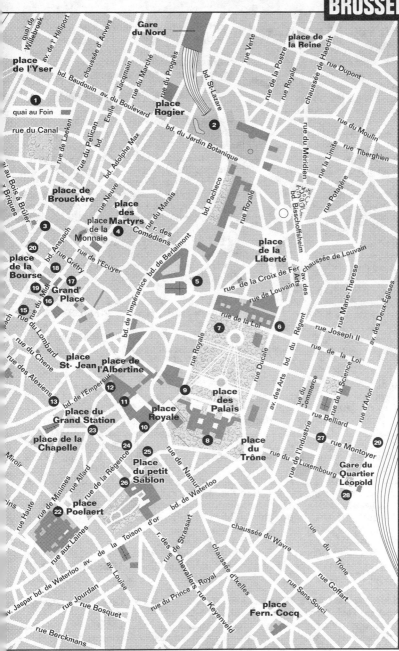

BRUSSELS

quai de Willebroek · av. de l' Héliport · Gare du Nord · chaussée d'Anvers · place de la Reine · chaussée de Haecht · rue Dupont

place de l'Yser · bd. Baudouin · av. du Boulevard · Jacqmain · rue du Marché · rue du Progrès · rue Verte · rue de la Poste · rue Royale · rue du Moulin

1 quai au Foin · rue de Laeken · bd. Emile Jacqmain · **place Rogier** · bd. St-Lazare · bd. du Jardin Botanique · rue de la Limite · rue Tiberghien

rue du Canal · rue du Pélican · **2** · bd. Pacheco · rue du Méridien · bd. Bischoffsheim · bd. Bisschoffsheim · rue Potagère

ai au Bois à Brûler · y Briques · **place de Brouckère** · rue Neuve · bd. Adolphe Max · rue du Marais · bd. Pacheco · rue Royale · **place de la Liberté** · chaussée de Louvain

3 · bd. Anspach · **place des Martyrs** · **place de la Monnaie** · r. des Comédiens · bd. de Berlaimont · av. des

20 · rue Grétry · rue de l'Ecuyer · rue de la Croix de Fer · Arts · av. Marie-Thérèse · rue Marie-Thérèse · des Deux-Églises

place de la Bourse · **18** · **17** · **5** · rue de Louvain · rue Joseph II

19 · **16** · **Grand' Place** · bd. de l'Impératrice · rue de la Loi · **6** · rue Joseph II

15 · rue du Midi · rue du Lombard · rue du Chene · rue de la Loi · **7** · rue Royale · av. du Régent · rue de la Loi · rue d'Arlon

rue des Alexiens · **place St- Jean** · **place de l'Albertine** · **12** · bd. de l'Empereur · **9** · **place des Palais** · av. des Arts · bd. du Commerce · rue de la Science · rue Belliard

13 · **11** · **place du Grand Station** · **place Royale** · **10** · rue du Luxembourg · rue de l'Industrie · **27** · rue Montoyer · **29**

23 · **place de la Chapelle** · **24** · **25** · **8** · **place du Trône** · **Gare du Quartier Léopold**

Miroir · rue Allard · rue de la Régence · **Place du petit Sablon** · rue de Namur · bd. de Waterloo · **28**

rue Haute · rue de Minimes · **26** · **place Poelaert** · **22** · rue aux Laines · av. de la Toison d'or · r. des de Strassart · chaussée du Wavre

av. Jaspar bd. de Waterloo · rue Jourdan · rue Bosquet · av. Louise · rue du Prince Royal · rue Keyenveld · chaussée d'Ixelles · rue du Trône · rue Goffart · rue Sans-Souci

rue Berckmans · **place Fern. Cocq**

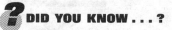

DID YOU KNOW . . . ?

- About the size of Maryland, Belgium is the second-smallest country in the European Community.
- Belgium has the last Roman Catholic monarchy in northern Europe.
- The "French" fry is actually a Belgian specialty and reaches its zenith in Brussels.
- The word *spa* comes from the Belgian city of Spa, which is known for its mineral waters and springs.
- Europe's oldest covered shopping arcade is in Brussels.
- Adolphe Sax, a Belgian, invented the saxophone.
- Brussels was the birthplace of the art nouveau style of architecture and design.
- Flemish- and French-speaking Brussels is one of the few officially bilingual capitals in the world.
- In 1990 King Baudoin abdicated for 1 day to avoid signing a pro-abortion law that he morally opposed.

Virtually all of Belgium can be visited on a day trip from Brussels, and I suggest spending at least one of your extra days in Brussels seeing another part of the country, such as the medieval wonders of Ghent and Brugge.

TOP ATTRACTIONS

The **Grand' Place** has been the center of the city's commercial life as well as public celebrations since the 12th century. Most of it was destroyed in 1695 by express order of France's Louis XIV; it was rebuilt over the next few years. Prominent merchants and artisans, as well as important guilds, owned these buildings, and each competed to outdo the others with highly ornate facades of gold leaf and statuary, often with emblems of their guilds. Thanks to the town's close monitoring of these reconstructions and later alterations, each building on the square preserves its original baroque splendor.

HOTEL DE VILLE DE BRUXELLES [Town Hall], Grand' Place. Tel. 512-7554.

One of the few buildings to survive the 1695 bombardment, the brilliant Town Hall dates from 1402. Its facade shows off Gothic intricacy at its best, complete with dozens of statues and arched windows. A 215-foot tower (temporarily covered with scaffolding) sprouts from the middle, yet it's not placed directly in the center (you'll see 10 windows to the left and 7½ windows to the right of the tower). Legend has it that when the architect realized his error, he jumped from the summit of the tower.

You may visit the interior on 30- to 40-minute tours, which start in a room full of paintings of the past foreign rulers of Brussels, who have included the Spanish, Austrians, French (under Napoleon), the Dutch, and finally the Belgians. In the Council Hall you'll see baroque decoration, and in several chambers such as the Maximilian Room you'll marvel at 17th-century tapestries so detailed that they even provide perspective. In the room before the mayor's office you'll see a 19th-century painting of Brussels with a river in the town center—a stream later covered up in an attempt to curb malaria. The entire building is still used as the seat of the civic government, and its wedding room remains a popular place to tie the knot.

Admission: 75F ($2.60) adults, 50F ($1.70) children.

Open: Tues–Fri 9:30am–12:15pm and 1:45–4pm, Sun 10am–noon and 4–6pm. Call or drop by for the exact hours of the English-language tours. **Closed:** Jan 1, May 1, Nov 1 and 11, Dec 25.

MUSEE DE LA VILLE DE BRUXELLES (Museum of the City of Brussels), Maison du Roi, Grand' Place. Tel. 511-2742.

This 19th-century structure has served as both a covered bread market and as a prison in its previous incarnations. Today it displays a mixed collection associated with the art and history of Brussels. On the ground floor you can admire detailed tapestries from the 16th and 17th centuries, as well as porcelain, silver, and stone statuary. After climbing a beautiful wooden staircase to the second floor, you can trace the history of Brussels in old maps, prints, photos, and models. And on the third floor, the museum shows off dozens of costumes that have been given to the *Manneken Pis* since 1698, including a hotel receptionist uniform, 18th-century ball costumes, and a Japanese kimono complete with headband.

Admission: 80F ($2.75) adults, 50F ($1.70) children.

Open: Apr–Sept, Mon–Fri 10am–12:30pm and 1:30–5pm, Sat–Sun 10am–1pm; Oct–Mar, Mon–Fri 10am–12:30pm and 1:30–4pm, Sat–Sun 10am–1pm. **Closed:** Jan 1, May 1, Nov 1 and 11, Dec 25.

THE MANNEKEN PIS, rue de l'Etuve, at the corner of rue du Chêne.

⭐ A small bronze statue of a urinating child, the *Manneken Pis* has come to symbolize the city of Brussels. No one knows when this child first came into being, but it's clear that he dates from quite a few centuries ago—the 8th century, according to one legend. Thieves have made off with the tyke several times in history. One criminal who stole and shattered the statue in 1817 was sentenced to a life of hard labor! (The pieces were used to recast another version.)

The *Manneken Pis* owns a vast wardrobe, which he wears on special occasions (during the Christmas season he dons a Santa suit, complete with white beard). You can see part of his vast collection in the Musée de la Ville de Bruxelles in the Maison du Roi (see above). You'll find the statue at the intersection of rue de l'Etuve and rue du Chêne, four blocks from the Grand' Place. If you want to read about the many legends of the *Manneken Pis,* you'll find an illustrated book for sale in the Musée de la Ville de Bruxelles.

Incidentally, the *Manneken Pis* now has a female counterpart called the **Jeanneke Pis,** located on the dead-end impasse de la Fidélité off rue des Bouchers. It was the 1987 brainstorm of a local restaurateur who wanted to attract business; its lack of grace is an embarrassment to many Bruxellois.

MUSEES ROYAUX DES BEAUX-ARTS, rue de la Régence, 3. Tel. 513-9630.

⭐ In a vast museum of several buildings, this complex combines the Musée d'Art Ancien (Classical Art) and the Musée d'Art Moderne (Modern Art) under one roof, showing off works from the 14th to the 20th century. The collection starts with Hans Memling's portraits from the late 15th century, which are marked by sharp, lifelike details, as well as works by Hieronymus Bosch and Lucas Cranach's *Adam and Eve.*

You'll admire the subsequent rooms featuring Pieter Brueghel, including his *Adoration of the Magi.* Don't miss the very unusual *Fall of the Rebel Angels,* with its grotesque faces and beasts. But don't fear—many of Brueghel's paintings are of a less fiery nature, such as the scenes depicting Flemish village life.

Later artists represented in the collection include Rubens, van Dyck, Frans Hals, and Rembrandt.

The museum's modern collection is housed in a circular building connected to the main entrance. The overwhelming collection includes works by Matisse, Dalí, Yves Tanguy, Max Ernst, Marc Chagall, and René Magritte. You may want to purchase a museum plan for 10F (35¢) to help you navigate your way through.

Admission: Free.

Open: Musée d'Art Ancien, Tues–Sun 10am–noon and 1–5pm; Musée d'Art Moderne, Tues–Sun 10am–1pm and 2–5pm. **Closed:** Jan 1, May 1, Nov 1 and 11, Dec 25. **Tram:** 92, 93, or 94. **Bus:** 20, 34, 38, 71, 95, or 96.

MORE ATTRACTIONS
MUSEUMS

MUSEE INSTRUMENTAL [Instrument Museum of the Royal Music Conservatory], place du Petit-Sablon, 17. Tel. 512-0848.

Only 5% of the museum's immense collection is shown at one time, so the collection rotates periodically. In the permanent exhibit you'll see a piano that fits into a book, a viola with a map of Paris inlaid on the back, one of the first lutes in the world (from the 16th century), and two of the earliest models of a keyboard. In the wind instruments section you'll learn that it was a Belgian, Adolphe Sax, who invented the saxophone. On weekends small demonstrations are given and the instruments are explained.

Admission: Free.

Open: Tues–Sat 2:30–4:30pm, Sun 10:30am–12:30pm. **Tram:** 92, 93, or 94. **Bus:** 20, 34, 71, 95, or 96.

MUSEE ROYAL DE L'ARMEE ET D'HISTOIRE MILITAIRE, Parc du Cinquantenaire, 3. Tel. 733-4493.

One of Brussels's often-forgotten museums, its huge military collection is one of the finest in Europe. It includes an extensive display of armor, uniforms, and weapons from various Belgian campaigns (such as the Congo), a massive clutter of World War I artillery pieces, an aircraft hangar full of 130 impressive airplanes, and a World War II collection of Nazi flags that brings the Nuremberg rallies to mind. Anyone interested in military history shouldn't miss the superb, though sometimes cluttered, collection.

Admission: Free.

Open: Tues–Sun 9am–noon and 1–4:45pm (to 4pm in winter). **Closed:** Jan 1, May 1, Nov 1 and 11, Dec 25. **Metro:** Merode; it's opposite Autoworld.

MUSEES ROYAUX D'ART ET D'HISTOIRE, Parc du Cinquantenaire, 10. Tel. 741-7211.

A vast, poorly organized museum that opens half its collection one day and the other half on the next, this museum shows off antiques, decorative arts (such as tapestries, porcelain, silver, and sculptures), and archeology. Highlights include an Assyrian relief from the 9th century B.C., a Greek vase from the 6th century B.C., the A.D. 1145 reliquary of Pope Alexander, some exceptional tapestries, and colossal statues from Easter Island dating from centuries before Christ. This museum is the largest in Belgium.

Admission: Free.

Open: Tues–Fri 9:30am–5pm, Sat–Sun 10am–5pm. **Metro:** Merode; it's around the corner from the Military Museum and Autoworld.

AUTOWORLD, Parc du Cinquantenaire, 11. Tel. 736-4165.

I'm not a car fanatic, but I found this display of an aircraft hangar full of 500 historic cars fascinating. The collection starts with early motorized tricycles of 1899, and moves on to a 1911 Model T Ford, a 1924 Renault, a 1938 Cadillac that was the official White House car for FDR and Truman, a 1956 Cadillac used by Eisenhower, as well as by Kennedy during his June 1963 visit to Berlin, and more.

Admission: 150F ($5.15) adults, 100F ($3.45) students.

Open: Apr–Oct, daily 10am–6pm; Nov–Mar, daily 10am–5pm. **Metro:** Merode; it's across from the Military Museum.

MUSEE COSTUME ET DE LA DENTELLE (Costume and Lace Museum), rue de la Violette, 6 (near the Grand' Place). Tel. 512-7709.

Honoring the once-major industry (some 10,000 Bruxellois made lace in the 18th century) that now operates in a reduced but still-prominent fashion, this museum shows off particularly fine lace and costumes from 1599 to the present, with frequent changing exhibitions.

Admission: 80F ($2.75) adults, 50F ($1.70) children.

Open: Apr–Sept, Mon–Fri 10am–12:30pm and 1:30–5pm, Sat–Sun 2–4:30pm; Oct–Mar, Mon–Fri 10am–12:30pm and 1:30–4pm, Sat–Sun 2–4:30pm. **Closed:** Jan 1, May 1, Nov 1 and 11, Dec 25.

LA MAISON DES BRASSEURS (Brewery Museum), Grand' Place, 10. Tel. 511-4987.

This museum dedicated to beer depicts a tiny brewery from the 18th century in a

single room. You are given a beer at the end of what will be a brief visit. It's located on the same side of the Grand' Place as the Town Hall.
Admission: 50F ($1.70).
Open: Apr–Oct, Mon–Fri 10am–noon and 2–5pm, Sat 10am–noon; Nov–Mar, Mon–Fri 10am–noon and 2–5pm.

CHURCHES

CATHEDRALE ST-MICHEL ET STE-GUDULE, set back off bd. de l'Impératrice near Gare Centrale. Tel. 217-8345.
Dating from 1226, St-Michel is a Gothic masterpiece, highlighted by very detailed, 16th-century stained-glass windows that are some of the finest examples in the world. The 15th-century facade of the two matching towers appears strangely unfinished as they end in square tops rather than long points—yet this is exactly how it was designed. In 1983 extensive cleaning and restorations were started; the process uncovered archeological remains of a Roman church below the cathedral floors. Until the restoration is completed (possibly in 1993), half of the interior remains closed. You enter from the door on the right-hand side of the church.
Admission: Free.
Open: Mon–Fri 7am–6pm, Sat 7am–4pm, Sun 2–6pm for tourist visits. On Sun at 10am they celebrate the Eucharist with a choir, and Aug–Oct they perform chamber music or organ concerts occasional weekdays at 8pm.

NOTRE-DAME DU SABLON, rue de la Régence, 3B, off place du Grand-Sablon. Tel. 511-5741.
A late Gothic 15th-century structure, the church is noted for its rich collection of mosaic windows, which brightly contrast with the gray-white Gothic arches and walls of the interior.
Admission: Free.
Open: Mon–Fri 7am–6:30pm, Sat–Sun 9am–7pm.

PALAIS ROYAL

MUSEE DE L'HOTEL DE BELLEVUE, place des Palais, 7. Tel. 511-4425.
Built in 1820 to replace a previous structure that had burned down, this palace serves as a regal reception and ceremonial area rather than as the king's actual home. Today you can visit part of the palace and see 18th- and 19th-century objects belonging to the royal family.
Admission: Free.
Open: Sat–Thurs 10am–4:45pm. **Tram:** 92, 93, or 94. **Bus:** 20, 34, 38, 71, 95, or 96.

BRUPARCK & THE ATOMIUM

To the northwest of the center you can enjoy some frivolity at the Bruparck amusement center and a visit to the symbol of the Atomic Age, the Atomium.

BRUPARCK, bd. du Centenaire, 20. Tel. 477-0377.
A Belgian Disneyworld of sorts that opened in 1988, Bruparck hosts the largest cinema complex in the world (called Kinepolis; see "movies," in "Evening Entertainment," below), a water-sports pavilion, a planetarium, and a "Mini-Europe" village that reassembles some of Europe's great sights on a scale of one-25th of the original. The Bruparck village also contains several restaurants (including one within an original 1930s *Orient Express* car), cafés, stores, and a disco.
Admission: Mini-Europe, 340F ($11.70) adults, 290F ($10) children.
Open: July–Aug, Sun–Thurs 9am–8pm, Fri–Sat 9am–9pm; Sept–June, daily 9am–6pm. **Metro:** 1A to Heysel, the last stop.

THE ATOMIUM, Heysel, Laeken. Tel. 477-0977.

✪ Built in 1958 for the Brussels World's Fair, the 335-foot-high Atomium portrays an iron molecule magnified 165 billion times, and seems like a giant plaything of the gods that tumbled down to earth. You can explore the interior as elevators and escalators connect the individual atoms, the top of which sports a restaurant with a great panorama over Brussels. In a $3.5-million project, the interior exhibition areas were recently rebuilt, replacing the stale science exhibits from 1958 (they had become a local embarrassment). Today the interior has exhibits on current medical and research issues.

Admission: 150F ($5.15) adults, 120F ($4.15) children.

Open: Apr–Sept, daily 9:30am–10pm; Oct–Mar, daily 9:30am–6pm. **Metro:** 1A to Heysel, the last stop.

PARKS & GARDENS

The most attractive park in town is the **Parc de Bruxelles,** which extends in front of the Palais Royale. Once the property of the dukes of Brabant, this well-designed park with geometrically divided paths running through it became public in 1776. The many park benches make a fine place to stop for a small picnic. It's also historic; Belgium's first battle for independence (in 1830) was fought here.

A nice park in the center is the **Jardin d'Egmont.** It's often overlooked because it's hidden behind buildings—there are only two small entrance paths. You'll find this sculptured garden between the Palace of Justice and the Royal Palace; enter from rue du Grand-Cerf, or a small footpath off boulevard du Waterloo.

Outside the Musée Instrumental you'll see **place du Petit-Sablon,** with a small sculptured garden at the center surrounded by a wrought-metal gate. Forty-eight statues of ancient guilds surround the quaint garden.

SPECIAL-INTEREST SIGHTSEEING

FOR THE HISTORY BUFF One of Brussels's great sights for the history buff is the **Waterloo Battlefield** and its nearby museums, which are detailed under "Easy Excursions," below.

FOR THE ARCHITECTURE LOVER The **Horta Museum,** rue Américaine, 25 (tel. 537-1692), shows off the art nouveau designs, often in iron and glass, of Victor Horta and contains information pertaining to his life and work. Admission is 100F ($3.45), and it's open Tuesday through Saturday from 2 to 5:30pm. To get there, take tram no. 37, 81, 93, or 94; or bus no. 54.

Brussels boasts a rich array of other art nouveau and art deco structures. For a list of some of these buildings, refer to the *Brussels Guide and Map,* available from the tourist office.

FOR THE COMIC BOOK LOVER At the **Belgian Comic Strip Museum,** Waucquez Warehouse, rue des Sables, 20 (tel. 219-1980), lovers of Tintin and other Belgian comic-book heroes can see their favorite stars at this unique museum that opened in late 1988. The building was designed by art nouveau architect Victor Horta. Admission is 120F ($4.15) for adults and 60F ($2.05) for children. It's open daily 10am to 6pm. Take the metro to Rogier or Botanique.

ORGANIZED TOURS

BUS TOURS **Brussels City-Tours,** rue de la Colline, 8, off the Grand' Place (tel. 02/513-7744), sponsor a 2½-hour tour of Brussels for 650F ($22.40) and offer several options for day trips across Belgium.

For do-it-yourself walking tours of Brussels, refer to the tourist office's *Brussels Guide and Map.*

ALTERNATIVE TOURS **ARAU Tourville,** rue H-Maus, 37 (bte 7), 1000 Bruxelles (tel. 02/513-4761), organizes a social tour that attempts to help you "discover not only Brussels's countless treasures, but also problems the city faces."

They also run specialized art tours, such as "Brussels of the 1930s." Tours cost 500F ($17.25).

SPECIAL & FREE EVENTS

ON THE GRAND' PLACE   It is only natural that Brussels's magnificent Grand' Place should host some of the city's most memorable free events. If you visit during the summer, you can watch a free evening **"Sound and Light" show.** Classical music plays as the square's buildings are dramatically highlighted. Or you can stop by at noon when the tower of the Maison du Roi plays golden carillon chimes reminiscent of an earlier European era.

However, the most spectacular event on the Grand' Place is the annual **Ommegang** pageant on the first Thursday in July. During the pageant, noble families dress in historic costumes and parade around the square.

The square still functions as an important **marketplace.** Tuesday through Sunday from 8am to 6pm the Grand' Place hosts a flower market, and on Sunday (as detailed below under "Savvy Shopping"), a bird market. During Christmas a large tree is erected at the center and a crèche nativity scene is placed at the lower end of the square.

7. SAVVY SHOPPING

BRUSSELS'S BEST BUYS   Brussels has several **outdoor markets,** where half the fun is finding an alluring item and the other half is bargaining down the price. Of course, you'll also enjoy a stroll along the modern shopping promenades, the busiest of which is the pedestrian **rue Neuve,** which starts at place de la Monnaie, the site of the Opera House, and runs north to place Rogier. Here you'll find numerous boutiques as well as department stores, including **City 2,** a huge shopping mall full of stores and inexpensive restaurants (see "Budget Dining," above, for details on the latter).

Other interesting shopping malls include the **Anspach Center,** off place de la Monnaie, diagonally across from the Opera House; the **Centre Monnaie,** across the street; and the **Galeries Saint-Hubert,** the first covered shopping arcade in Europe (from 1845), off rue du Marché-aux-Herbes.

For luxury shopping, try the stores on **avenue Louise** and the nearby streets, where you'll find such names as Cartier, Burberry's, Louis Vuitton, Benetton, and Valentino. You may not find any bargains, but there's lots to look at.

You'll find an interesting street for window-shopping near the Grand' Place, **rue des Eperonniers,** which hosts many small shops including antiques, toy, old book, and clothing stores.

Lace is the overwhelming favorite among visitors to Brussels, followed by **crystal, pewter, jewelry,** and **antiques. Chocolate, beer,** and other foods are a more economical favorite of foreign shoppers.

Belgians view **comic books** quite seriously. Hard covers bind comic books—you are meant to treasure and preserve them. Thin, colorful volumes often cost about $10, although you can also find used ones for less. You can also buy comics at several stores between nos. 132 and 206 chaussée de Wavre, between rue du Trône and rue Goffart.

OUTDOOR MARKETS   Flea Market   My favorite outdoor market is the flea market on place du Jeu-de-Balle, a large cobblestone square a few blocks from Gare du Midi. Like all flea markets, you'll have to sift through lots of junk but you can make real finds in the old postcards, comic books, clothes, furniture, African masks, brass fixtures, and other items. The market is set up daily from 7am to 2pm.

Antiques Market   For better-quality goods at decidedly higher prices, check out the antiques market on place du Grand-Sablon, open Saturday and Sunday. You'll also find quite a few antiques stores, open throughout the week, on streets in the nearby area (try, for example, rue de Rollebeek). Prices are high, but it's a fun place to look around. On Saturday the market is open from 9am to 6pm; on Sunday, from 9am to 2pm.

Bird Market   As you near the Grand' Place on Sunday morning, the loud chirping and whistling of birds makes it sound as though you're entering a tropical jungle. Yet it's only the bird market, where you can admire thousands of birds—from parakeets to ducks. It's an unusual market in the very center of town, and is certainly amusing. Open on Sunday from 7am to 2pm.

Sunday Casbah   Every Sunday hundreds of merchants assemble their wares along the railroad tracks leading to the Gare du Midi, and because many of the merchants are Arabs and southern Europeans, the scene resembles a Middle Eastern casbah. You'll find many excellent food bargains, making it a perfect place to gather provisions for a few days. You can also find household items and many odds and ends at low cost. Hold onto your wallet (busy markets the world over attract pickpockets) and bargain.

The market starts where boulevard du Midi crosses the rail tracks at place de la Constitution, and continues on both sides of the tracks for several blocks. Lemonnier is the nearest metro stop. It's open on Sunday from 6am to 1pm. For a list of other markets, see the *Brussels Guide and Map,* sold at the Brussels Tourist Office.

8. EVENING ENTERTAINMENT

Although Brussels is too conservative and traditional to go really wild at night, it offers a full array of things to do in the evening hours. The best list of upcoming events is the weekly English-language **What's On** magazine, available free from the tourist office. It lists dance, opera, live music, film, and television events for the week, both for Brussels and for the rest of Belgium. You'll also find monthly listings in the tourist office's **Key to Brussels** brochure.

The French-language magazine **Kiosque** lists upcoming events with more detailed descriptions and photos than the English-language publications. You can buy it at newsstands for 50F ($1.70).

Keep in mind that the tourist office in the Town Hall on the Grand' Place sells concert and theater tickets.

THE PERFORMING ARTS
OPERA, BALLET & CONCERTS

The **Opera National,** in place de la Monnaie (tel. 218-1211 or 218-1202), offers performances of opera and ballet, and concerts of the National Orchestra. Tickets cost 150F–2,800F ($5.15–$96.55); a half hour before the show (usually at 7:30pm), people under age 25 may purchase tickets for 200F ($6.90). The box office, open Monday through Saturday from 11am to 6pm, accepts several major credit cards. They'll also give you a free copy of their program of upcoming events, called "De Munt–La Monnaie."

JAZZ

BIERODROME, place Fernand-Cocq, 21. Tel. 512-0456.

An active beer pub and favorite of jazz connoisseurs, the Bierodrome features live jazz 4 nights a week. When there are no live acts, the club's owner plays tunes from his collection of 10,000 jazz records.

Admission: 200F ($6.90), including a glass of wine; free Sun. Drink prices go up during concerts.

Open: Tues–Sun noon–3am. Music starts at 10pm Fri–Sun.

TRAVERS, rue Traversière, 11. Tel. 218-4086.

On the other end of the spectrum, Travers is a quintessential small and smoky jazz club with fewer than a dozen tables lit by candles placed in champagne bottles. Modern art adorns the walls. Between two and five concerts are performed a week; call for the exact schedule. There are also occasional rock and reggae shows.

Admission: 300F–600F ($10.35–$20.70), except Mon when they perform a jam session for free (although drinks are slightly more expensive Mon).

Open: Mon–Sat 9pm–2am or later. Concerts start at 10pm.

L'ESTAMINET DU KELDERKE, Grand' Place, 14. Tel. 512-3694.

At the upper end of the Grand' Place in a basement that looks as if it could have been a wine cellar at one time, there are nightly jazz concerts covering the jazz spectrum from Dixieland to boogie to mainstream to modern. This place isn't very big, so you might want to arrive early. Drinks cost 100F–180F ($3.45–$6.20).

Admission: Free.

Open: Mon–Sat 6pm–1am, Sun 6pm–midnight.

MOVIES

Most foreign films are subtitled in French and Flemish and cost 220F–250F ($7.60–$8.60), except on Monday when prices fall to 150F–170F ($5.15–$6.05). Some cinemas offer students under age 26 and senior citizens discount tickets of 150F ($5.15).

For a completely different cinema experience, consider a viewing of the sensational IMAX (maximum image) film technology in the **Kinepolis,** boulevard du Centenaire, 1, in Bruparck (tcl. 479-7669). Films are shown every hour on the hour from 11am to 5pm and 8 to 10pm in either French or Dutch. English versions are occasionally shown; call ahead for details. Admission is 240F ($8.30) for adults, 200F ($6.90) for students and children. To get there, take metro 1A to Heysel, the last stop.

Bruparck also sports 23 regular cinemas in Kinepolis, making it the largest movie palace in the entire world! (See "More Attractions," above, for descriptions of the other amusements in Bruparck.)

The **City 2** shopping mall, on rue Neuve, houses eight cinemas.

Musée du Cinema, in the Palais des Beaux-Arts, rue Baron-Horta, 9 (tel. 507-8370), plays classic films in their original languages every evening, and silent films in a different screening room. Only 50F ($1.70) is charged in advance or 80F ($2.75) on the evening of the show. Children under 16 are not admitted.

CAFES & BARS
IN & NEAR THE GRAND' PLACE

It's always satisfying to grab a chair at a sidewalk café in the Grand' Place and drink in the beauty of the floodlit, golden buildings that ring the square. After you've ordered one drink, you can remain for as long as you wish.

LE ROY D'ESPAGNE, Grand' Place, 1. Tel. 513-0807.

⭐ The oldest café here in a building dating from 1690 (once home to Brussels's bakers), Le Roy d'Espagne accommodates guests in several areas. In addition to the outdoor café tables, you can drink in a room that preserves a Flemish interior style of the 17th century—a masterpiece of wooden architecture with a wooden walkway and beams above and a fireplace covered by a black metal hood. Another room, the beer cellar, attracts many youth. So if inclement weather forces you inside, your visit won't be a total wash!

Prices: Beer 60F–140F ($2.05–$4.80).

Open: Daily 10am–1am.

A LA MORT SUBITE, rue Montagne-aux-Herbes-Potagères, 7. Tel. 513-1318.

★ A café from 1911 with columns, neoclassical ornaments and mirrors, and old small wooden tables in a style that recalls the prewar epoch, A la Mort Subite is a good place to enjoy an afternoon coffee or an evening beer.
Prices: Coffee 60F ($2.05); beer 55F–110F ($1.90–$3.80).
Open: Daily 10am–1am.

A L'IMAIGE NOSTRE-DAME, 8 rue du Marché-aux-Herbes, 6. Tel. 219-4249.

In this house dating from 1642, just a block from the Grand' Place, people of all ages enjoy reasonably priced beers amid wooden beams on the ceiling, old wooden tables, painted windows, and an antique ceramic fireplace.
Prices: Beer 70F–125F ($2.40–$4.30).
Open: Daily noon–midnight.

LE CERCUEIL (The Coffin), rue des Harengs, 10-12. Tel. 513-3361.

For those with a mischievous sense of humor for the macabre, this bar just off the Grand' Place provides an atmosphere like no other. The tables are glass panes placed over coffins, and when you order certain drinks you'll be served in a ceramic skull. Purple fluorescent lighting keeps the rooms very dim, and ecclesiastical music, especially organ music, plays in the background, helping to create an eerie atmosphere of a horror movie. Prices are a little high.
Prices: Half a liter of beer 80F–180F ($2.75–$6.20).
Open: Daily 11am–3am.

ELSEWHERE

LA FLEUR EN PAPIER DORE, rue des Alexiens, 53. Tel. 511-1659.

A café located in a 17th-century building, this typical beer bar tries to create a "temple of surrealism" with old prints, plates, horns, porcelain, and other objects covering every inch of the walls. The three small rooms house fewer than a dozen tables. On Friday and Saturday from 9 or 10pm an accordion player pumps out some tunes. You'll find this typically charming place off place de la Chapelle.
Prices: Beer 55F–95F ($1.90–$3.30); glass of wine 55F–85F ($1.90–$2.95).
Open: Daily 10:30am–2am.

DE ULTIEME HALLUCINATIE, rue Royale, 316. Tel. 217-0614.

In what was a turn-of-the-century private house is now a restaurant resplendent in art nouveau as well as an old garden café. Rocky walls and plants decorate one side and a long marble bar occupies the other. There's also a more futuristic bar area downstairs with fluorescent lighting and abstract, outer space–style art, a small outdoor café area, and a charming section behind the garden. They have a wide selection of beers, as well as wine, coffee, and a few snacks.
Prices: Beer from 50F ($1.70); glass of wine 75F ($2.60); coffee 60F ($2.05).
Open: Café, Mon–Fri 11am–3am, Sat–Sun 4pm–3am.

CLUBS & DISCOS

LE GARAGE, rue Duquesnoy, 16. Tel. 512-6622.

The first large disco opened in Brussels (in 1983), Le Garage accommodates a car to the side of the dance floor and a video screen. The disco attracts for the most part people aged 18–30.
Admission: 100F ($3.45) Sun–Thurs, 300F ($10.35) Fri–Sat, which includes one mixed drink.
Open: Daily 11pm–6am, although it doesn't pick up until 12:30 or 1am.

DNA, rue Plattesteen, 182. Tel. 512-1451.

A youth and student favorite, DNA is reputed to have the largest collection of rock 'n' roll records in Brussels, which they play at high volume. "It's the only decent music in town," one leather-clad youth told me.
Prices: Most beers 50F–75F ($1.70–$2.60). **Admission:** Free.
Open: Sun–Thurs 6pm–3am, Fri–Sat 4pm–6am.

9. NETWORKS & RESOURCES

STUDENTS   As mentioned previously in "Budget Accommodations," students visiting Brussels enjoy an excellent setup of youth hostels, which provide not only a cheap bed but also a great place to meet other students.

  Acotra, rue de la Madeleine, 51, B-1000 Bruxelles (tel. 02/512-8607 or 512-5560), sells discount student train, plane, boat, and bus tickets, and also books places in youth hostels and private rooms. They also sell the ISIC (International Student Identity Card) and FIYTO (Federation of International Youth Travel Organizations) card here. You'll find this office across a small park from Gare Centrale, toward the Grand' Place. It's open Monday through Friday from 10am to 6pm (on Thursday to 7pm) and on Saturday from 10am to 1pm; closed Sunday.

GAY MEN   **Rue des Riches-Claires** and **rue du Marché-au-Charbon** (not far from the Bourse) hosts a few gay establishments, including a community center (**Homocentrum**) at 81 rue du Marché-au-Charbon (tel. 512-4809) and a leather clothing store.

  Macho 2, rue du Marché-au-Charbon, 108, a block from rue des Riches-Claires (tel. 513-5667), houses a gay men's sauna, swimming pool, steam room, and café. It's open Monday through Thursday from noon to 2am, on Friday and Saturday from noon to 6am, and on Sunday from 2pm to midnight. Admission is 400F ($13.80), 350F ($12.05) for students.

  Ask any of the above places for the French-language magazine *Regard,* which lists other gay events in town.

10. EASY EXCURSIONS

WATERLOO   On June 18, 1815, the Grand Alliance of British, Dutch, and Prussian forces, along with a smattering of soldiers from the German principalities, defeated mighty Napoleon Bonaparte and his 74,000 French troops, leaving 40,000 dead. Napoleon himself survived, but his attempt to rebuild his empire was crushed; he was sent to the island of Sainte-Hélène, where he died 6 years later at the age of 52.

  Bus "W" leaves on the half hour and the hour from a small bus terminal on avenue de Stalingrad in Brussels, one block to the south of place Rouppe. The 11-mile ride takes 50 minutes and costs 80F ($2.75). You can fill up with the details of the battle at the **Wellington Museum,** chaussée de Bruxelles, 147 (tel. 02/354-7806); study a 360° mural at the **Battlefield Panorama,** rue des Vertes Bornes, 90 (tel. 02/384-3139); and then survey the actual battlefield from atop the **Lion's Mound,** route du Lion, 252-254 (tel. 385-1912), a pyramidlike hill opposite the Battlefield Panorama.

OTHER EXCURSIONS   Most of Belgium is just a short distance outside Brussels, making the choices for side trips so many that I can only highlight the possibilities. Consider **Ghent,** often called the "Venice of the North" for its canals and charm; **Bruges,** another medieval monument with a beautiful market square and Michelangelo statue; modern **Antwerp,** the hometown of the 17th-century art master Peter Paul Rubens (you can still visit his impressive house), a diamond capital, and a massive port; and **Leuven,** a quaint university town with 22,000 students and architecture dating from hundreds of years ago.

  Belgium's excellent rail network quickly links you up with all of these towns: Leuven is just 20 minutes away; Antwerp, 30 minutes; Ghent, 40 minutes; and Bruges, 55 minutes.

  The national rail company, SNCB, provides several excursion-ticket possibilities to facilitate low-cost trips from Brussels, including: "A Weekend at the Sea or

Ardennes," which allows half-price travel to those destinations on the weekend; or "Un beau jour à . . ."—day-long excursions to various cities across Belgium. You can also buy a railpass that allows 5 days of travel over a 17-day span. Ask for details at either the tourist office or at any train station.

You can even leave Belgium entirely and be back in Brussels for a late supper that same day—albeit a very ambitious outing. On a rapid train, Paris is only 2½ hours away, and Amsterdam and Luxembourg are just under 3 hours.

BUDAPEST

A stately, elegant, traditional city, which spreads impressively along both sides of the huge Danube River (called Duna in Hungary), Budapest is a grand capital in the tradition (and appearance) of Vienna. It's also a logical next stop from Vienna, so close by train or Danube river steamer that it makes little sense not to visit if you're in Vienna. Slightly larger than Austria, but smaller than Kentucky, Hungary has 10 million inhabitants, of whom 2.2 million live in Budapest. Budapest was, early on, a Roman colony. Thereafter it was ruled successively by Mongols, Turks, and the Habsburgs, and from 1945 to 1990 was a reluctant member of the Eastern bloc. Hungarians, however, always enjoyed greater freedom than many of their Eastern neighbors and helped lead the way in one of the most amazing stories of our time—the decline of communism and the opening of eastern Europe to democratic reform. Since its first free elections in more than four decades were held in March 1990, the country has been in the midst of even greater changes. If it has been 10 years since you've been to Hungary—or even just 2—you're in for some big surprises. It's an exciting time to visit Budapest and witness history in the making.

1. FROM A BUDGET TRAVELER'S POINT OF VIEW

DISCOUNT OPPORTUNITIES AND BUDGET BESTS   Very few discount opportunities are available in Budapest. This shouldn't worry you because, as you will see, prices are already very low, making Budapest itself a budget best. Even though Hungary is beset with galloping inflation and rising prices for everything from milk to gasoline, the country is still very affordable. In fact, don't be surprised if your money goes farther here than in any of the other destinations described in this book.

2. PRETRIP PREPARATIONS

DOCUMENTS   As of 1990 American, Canadian, and British travelers need only a valid passport to enter Hungary. However, at press time, Australian and New Zealand citizens were still required to obtain a visa. Entry procedures may become easier in the future; you'd be wise to check on visa requirements before your trip.

WHAT THINGS COST IN BUDAPEST	U.S. $
Taxi from Ferihegy Airport to Budapest city center	19.00
Public transportation within the city	.25
Local telephone call	.06
Double room at the Duna Inter-Continental (deluxe)	260.00
Double room at the Hotel Nemzeti (moderate)	125.00
Double room in the home of Dr. Walter Fleps, with breakfast (budget)	25.00
Lunch for one, without wine, at Múzeum Kávéház Etterem (moderate)	10.00
Lunch for one, without wine, at Central Restaurant (budget)	2.00
Dinner for one, without wine, at Café New York (deluxe)	30.00
Dinner for one, without wine, at Matyas Pince (moderate)	14.00
Dinner for one, without wine, at Metropol Etterem (budget)	3.60
Glass of wine	1.00
Half liter of beer	1.50
Coca-Cola in a street café or self-service restaurant	.45
Cup of coffee with milk	.65
Roll of ASA 100 color film, 36 exposures	5.25
Admission to the National Museum	.40
Movie ticket (depending on the seat)	1.10–2.70
Theater ticket (Hungarian State Opera)	2.00

Visas can be obtained from any Hungarian embassy, consulate, or from IBUSZ, the official Hungarian Travel Office. If you're arriving by plane, you can also obtain a visa at Budapest's Ferihegy Airport; likewise, if you're traveling by car or boat, you can apply for a visa at the border. If you're traveling by train or bus, however, you must obtain your visa prior to your trip.

Within Europe, one of the easiest places to obtain a visa is in Hungary's neighboring country, Austria. There's an IBUSZ right in the heart of Vienna at Kärntner Strasse 26 (tel. 0222/51-5550), open in the winter months Monday through Friday from 9am to 5pm, and in the summer, Monday through Friday from 8:30am to 5:30pm and on Saturday from 9am to noon. It takes approximately two days to obtain a visa here, which costs 250 Austrian Schillings (about $23) and requires two photographs; you can obtain a visa in one day for an additional 110 Schillings ($10).

WHAT TO PACK An ideal wardrobe includes a light jacket, a sweater for evenings, and an umbrella or raincoat. For fall, winter, and early spring, take a moderately heavy coat, gloves, hat, and boots with you (winter, especially, can be bitterly cold). If you plan on staying in a private home, be sure to pack your own bath towel.

WHEN TO GO The best time for visiting Budapest and Hungary is early May to mid-October, when weather conditions are generally good. Prolonged rainfall is rare, but there are frequent thunderstorms during the summer.

Budapest's Average Daytime Temperature

	Jan	Feb	Mar	Apr	May	June	July	Aug	Sept	Oct	Nov	Dec
Temp (°F)	30	35	42	55	64	68	74	71	65	54	46	35

Special Events   With the exception of the Grand Prix car race and the European soccer matches once or twice a year, Budapest has only a few special events. The **Spring Festival** in March is Budapest's most famous festival, offering outstanding performances in the theater, opera, ballet, folk dancing, art exhibits, and concerts. Past Spring Festivals have featured international greats from piano virtuoso Zoltán Kocsis to Keith Jarrett and Joe Cocker. What's more, prices for tickets are so low that you can attend virtually every event for what it would cost to attend one musical extravaganza in Salzburg.

3. ORIENTATION & GETTING AROUND

ARRIVING IN BUDAPEST

FROM THE AIRPORT   **Ferihegy Airport,** 10 miles southeast of the city, is linked with the Pest air terminal at Erzsébet tér (formerly Engels tér) by a public bus that costs 100Ft ($1.35). Buses depart every half hour or hour and the trip takes about 35 minutes. Tickets can be bought from the driver. The same trip by taxi will set you back about 1,400 Ft ($19).

FROM THE TRAIN STATION   There are three train stations: the **Keleti (East) Station,** in Pest, for trains to and from Vienna, Paris, Frankfurt, or Rome; the **Nuygati (West) Station,** in Pest, for trains to and from Prague or East Berlin; and the **Déli (South) Station,** in Buda, for connections with Lake Balaton. Each railroad station is also the location of a subway station.

ARRIVING BY BOAT   Although this boat trip is not covered by Eurailpass, you might want to splurge and travel to Budapest from Vienna by boat along the Danube. The trip by hydrofoil, which departs daily from April 1 to October 1, takes 4½ hours and costs 690 Austrian Schillings ($62.70) one way. There are also Hovercrafts which cost slightly more. You can make bookings at the IBUSZ office in Vienna, Kärntner Strasse 26 (tel. 0222/51-5550).

In any case, you'll arrive in Budapest on the Pest side, just south of the Erzsébet híd (Elizabeth Bridge). From there you can walk 10 minutes or take a taxi to the main IBUSZ office at Petőfi tér (square), described below.

INFORMATION

For all kinds of information related to your stay in Budapest, including sightseeing, brochures, maps, museums, cultural programs, weather, and emergencies, visit or phone **Tourinform,** Süto utca 2 (tel. 117-9800), near Deák Ferenc tér in Pest, open daily from 8am to 8pm.

For detailed information on hotels, sightseeing tours, and currency rates and exchange, call or go to the **IBUSZ Hotel Service Office,** Petőfi tér 3 (tel. 118-5707 or 118-4842), near the Duna Inter-Continental Hotel in Pest, open daily 24 hours.

For information on Budapest's events, including concerts, the opera, and special exhibitions, pick up a free copy of ***Programme in Hungary*** at Tourinform, published monthly. For even more detailed information, purchase ***Budapest Week,*** an English weekly sold at Tourinform and at selected newsstands for 48 Ft (65¢). It

✓

WHAT'S SPECIAL ABOUT BUDAPEST

Its Prices
☐ A subway ticket for 25¢.
☐ Accommodations in private homes for less than $10 per person a night.
☐ Eating like a king for less than $5.
☐ Admission fees to museums of less than 50¢.

Dining
☐ Café New York, one of the most splendid dining halls in Europe, with prices that can't be beat.

Thermal Baths
☐ 200 in Budapest; you can get a 30-minute massage in Budapest for less than $5.

Museums
☐ The Hungarian National Gallery, with the world's most complete collection of Hungarian art.
☐ The Museum of Fine Arts, with works of European masters.

---

appears on Thursday afternoons and contains all the latest information on everything from films and opera to ballet, folk dancing, pop, rock, and classical music. It also lists all venues, complete with addresses.

CITY LAYOUT

Budapest is bisected by the **Duna (Danube) River** into a right bank and a left bank. Of the city's three main districts, two—**Buda** and **Óbuda**—are found on the left bank, while **Pest** is on the right bank. In terms of major attractions, most of the main shopping streets, the House of Parliament, the National Museum, Museum of Applied Arts, and Museum of Fine Arts, are located in Pest, on the right bank. Buda, on the left bank, is the location of Castle Hill, Fishermen's Bastion, Matthias Church, and the National Gallery.

In other words, Pest is the center for shopping, dining, banking, and nightlife, and it's where most of the major hotels are located. Buda, on the other hand, is the historical and cultural part of the city, and Castle Hill has been beautifully renovated with a number of fine buildings. You will probably want to divide your time equally between the two.

Budapest is divided into districts, reflected in postal addresses. District V is the business center of Pest encompassing the area around Roosevelt tér and Váci út, while District I is Buda's Castle Hill area.

The main streets in Pest are **Rákóczi út** (and its extension, Kossuth L. u.), stretching a mile from Keleti Station to Erzsébet híd; **Teréz körút** (and its extension, Erzsébet Körút), running from Blaha L. tér to Nyugati Station, with the Oktogon subway station halfway along; and the two-mile-long and more than 100-yard-wide **Andrássy út**, lined with theaters, high schools, embassies, and palacelike buildings, which begins near **Deák Ferenc tér** and leads to the monumental **Hősök tere** (Heroes' Square), site of mass rallies on official holidays. The main shopping street, now also a pedestrian zone, and as elegant as the Merceria in Venice or the Faubourg-St-Honoré in Paris, is **Váci ut,** running parallel to the Danube from near Erzsébet híd to Vörösmarty tér.

Incidentally, several dozen street and plaza names were changed after Hungary became a democracy. With Lenin and Engels out of favor, Lenin körút became Teréz körút and Erzsébet körút, and Engles tér became Erzsébet tér. Likewise, Népköztársaság became Andrássy út, Tanács körút became Károly körút, and November 7 tér became Oktogon. The old names still appear on most maps, and some street signs have yet to be changed.

The Hungarian word for street is **utca** (abbreviated "u.") or **út.** A larger boulevard is **körút,** abbreviated krt., while a square is **tér.** The word for bridge is **híd.**

Of the six **bridges** spanning the Danube, only four are of importance for travelers. They are (from south to north): Szabadság híd, linking Dimitrov tér in Pest with Gellért tér in Buda; Erzsébet híd, connecting Március tér in Pest with the Gellért Hill area in Buda; Széchenyi lánchíd, reaching from Roosevelt tér in Pest to Clark Adam tér in Buda; and Margit híd, which spans the river from Jaszai Mari tér, near the Parliament Building in Pest, via Margit-sziget (Margaret Island), to the Buda side of the river.

GETTING AROUND

BY BUS, STREETCAR & SUBWAY   Although prices could go up by 1993, public transportation within the city is incredibly cheap. At press time, buses, trams, and subways cost only 18 Ft (25¢). Tickets for all three are sold at newsstands, tobacco shops, and major subway stations, but never aboard the conveyance. They must be punched or validated in small machines at the subway turnstiles and aboard the trams and buses.

Tickets are good for only one journey and do not allow a transfer, so you're best off buying several tickets and keeping them on hand. If you'll be traveling a lot, purchase a day ticket for 150 Ft ($2), which allows you to use all buses, streetcars, and subways throughout the capital. You'll probably end up using the subways the most—there are three lines, all number- and color-coded, and all converging at Deák Ferenc tér. It's virtually impossible to get lost. The free map issued by Tourinform shows locations of some of the major subway stations. However, if you're going to be in Budapest for any length of time, you may wish to purchase a more detailed map of the city, also available at Tourinform.

BY TAXI   Taxis are also incredibly inexpensive. The fare from Keleti train station to any of the hotels or private homes listed in the accommodations section should not exceed 300 Ft ($4.05). If you hail a taxi in the street or go to a taxi stand, the fare starts at just 20 Ft (25¢). If you telephone for a taxi, the meter starts at 30 Ft (40¢). You can call a taxi by dialing 122-2222, 166-6666, 122-8855, 129-4000, or 155-5000. If you want to order a taxi in advance, such as a trip to the airport the next day, call 118-8888.

BY CAR   **Avis,** located at Martinelli tér 8 (tel. 118-4158), in Pest near the Duna Inter-Continental Hotel, rents a compact Toyota Corolla for a daily price of $30, plus 30¢ per kilometer. The office is open Monday through Saturday from 8am to 8pm and on Sunday from 8am to 2pm.

Other car-rental agencies with similar prices include **Hertz,** Kertesz u. 24 (tel. 111-6116), and **Europcar,** Vaskapu u. 16 (tel. 133-4783).

FAST BUDAPEST

Babysitters   There is no babysitting service in Budapest. However, some of the five-star hotels provide babysitting services for their customers.

Banks   The National Bank of Hungary has a main office at Szabadság tér 8-9 (tel. 153-2600 or 112-3223), in Pest. However, because banks have such short business hours you'll probably find it more convenient to change your money at one of the many travel agencies such as the IBUSZ Hotel Service, Petofí tér 3 (tel. 118-5705 or 118-4842), open 24 hours daily. You can also exchange money at any hotel, at slightly less favorable rates than those offered by banks and travel agencies.

There are even automatic money changers in Budapest now. The most convenient is at the K & H Bank, located at Károly krt. 20 in the heart of Pest (across from the Viking Söröző Tuborg restaurant) and open 24 hours. It exchanges U.S. and Canadian dollars, British pounds, and many other currencies, including Japanese yen, into forints at a competitive exchange rate. U.S. $5, $10, and $50 bills are accepted.

There's a 24-hour automatic cash machine for American Express credit-card holders at American Express, conveniently located in the heart of Pest's business district at Deák Ferenc út 10 (tel. 117-3539), just off Vörösmarty Square. Its office is open Monday through Friday from 9am to 5pm and on Saturday from 9am to noon.

Note: As you walk around Budapest, you may be approached by people on the street asking whether you wish to exchange dollars for forint at a much more favorable rate than that offered by banks. *Don't be tempted!* Not only do tourists report being short-changed and cheated in the bargain, but it's against the law.

Business Hours   **Shops** selling food are open Monday through Friday from 7am to 7pm and on Saturday from 7am to 2pm. Other stores and department stores are open Monday through Friday from 10am to 6pm and on Saturday from 9am to 1pm. Many stay open on Thursday until 8pm. **Banks** are open Monday through Friday from 9am to 12:30 or 1pm.

Currency   Hungary's official currency is the **forint (Ft)**, and 1 forint equals 100 **fillérs** (but you'll rarely see a fillér, as they no longer have any practical value). Coins come in 10, 20, and 50 fillérs and 1, 2, 5, 10, and 20 Ft. Banknote denominations are issued for 10, 20, 50, 100, 500, 1,000, and 5,000 Ft.

Customs Regulations   There are no special Customs restrictions when entering Hungary. You can import reasonable amounts of tobacco, alcohol, and gifts, and unlimited amounts of non-Hungarian currency. When leaving Hungary, you cannot carry more than 500 Ft ($6.75) with you, and no more than 3,000 Ft ($40.55) worth of gifts or goods purchased in Hungary. My guess is that as border restrictions relax, Customs regulations will also become more lenient. If in doubt, ask IBUSZ or Tourinform for information on the latest developments.

Dentist   If you need to see a dentist, your best bet is the Stomatological Institute, Mária u. 52 (tel. 133-0189). Otherwise, for a list of English-speaking dentists, call your embassy.

Doctor   Contact your embassy for a list of English-speaking doctors.

Embassies   As a capital city, Budapest is home to the embassies of many foreign countries, including: the United States, Szabadság tér 12 (tel. 112-6450); Canada, Budakeszi u. 32 (tel. 176-7711); Great Britain, Harmincad u. 6 (tel. 118-2888); and Australia, Délibáb u. 30 (tel. 153-4233).

Emergencies   If you need police assistance, phone 07. For the fire department, call 05; for a hospital or an ambulance, 04. The pharmacy at Rákósczi út 86 (tel. 122-9613), near the plush Hungaria Hotel and Keleti Station, is one of the easiest to find. It's open Monday through Friday from 8am to 8pm and on Saturday from 8am to 2pm. A list of pharmacies open on Sunday is posted on the door.

Holidays   The following holidays are celebrated in Budapest: New Year's Day (Jan 1), Revolution Day (Mar 15), Easter Monday, Labor Day (May 1), Constitution Day (Aug 20), Hungarian Revolution of New Republic Day (Oct 23), and Christmas (Dec 25–26).

Hospitals   Foreigners in need of first aid are handled at any hospital free of charge, though fees are levied for more involved treatment and medical examination. If you need to go to a hospital, the best policy is to call an ambulance, which will deliver you to the nearest hospital.

Information   For all kinds of information related to your stay in Budapest, see "Orientation and Getting Around," above, where you will find addresses for both IBUSZ and Tourinform.

Laundry/Dry Cleaning   There are many dry cleaners in Budapest, but few self-service laundries (*patyolat* in Hungarian). One of the few, and the most centrally located, is the Irisz Szalon at Rákóczi út 8 (tel. 122-1840), near the Astoria subway station. It has 10 self-service machines, is open Monday through Friday from 7am to 7pm, and charges 150 Ft ($2) for 5 kilos (11 lbs.) washed and dried, including detergent. It even has a sheet of instructions in English—ask one of the attendants to get it for you.

If you are staying at a private home or guesthouse, your landlord will probably do your laundry for a more reasonable price.

Lost and Found If you lose something on public transportation (subway, tram, bus), go to BKV, Akácfa u. 18 (tel. 122-6613), near the Oktogon subway stop. If you lose something in a taxi, go to Engels tér 5 (tel. 117-4961). Contact the information window of the train station for items lost on a train. At Keleti Station, phone 122-5615; at Nyugati Station, phone 149-0115; and at Déli Station, go to the office near Track 12 (no phone). Hours are Monday through Friday from 8am to 6pm and on Saturday from 8am to 2pm.

For objects lost on the street, in shops, or in museums, contact Tourinform, Sütő utca 2, near Deák Ferenc tér (tel. 117-9800). They are staffed with English-speaking personnel.

Mail Most post offices in Hungary are open Monday through Friday from 8am to 6pm and on Saturday from 8am to 2pm. The **Central Post Office** is conveniently located in the business district of Pest at Petőfi Sandor u. 13 (tel. 117-5500). It's open Monday through Friday from 8am to 8pm and on Saturday from 8am to 1pm. The post offices beside Nyugati Station on Teréz körút and at Keleti Station at Baross tér 11 are open 24 hours. An airmail letter to the United States costs 32 Ft (45¢) for the first five grams; a postcard costs 22 Ft (30¢). Mailboxes are red in Hungary.

The **postal code** for Budapest varies according to the district, with 1052 referring to the heart of Pest around the Duna Inter-Continental Hotel, District V. If you're not sure of the postal code, your best bet is to address a letter to Budapest with H-1000.

Newspapers *Budapest Week,* an English-language weekly that appears on newsstands and at Tourinform on Thursday afternoon for 48 Ft (65¢), contains information on what's going on in the Hungarian capital, including the performing arts, movies, and concerts.

Another local newspaper is the *Daily News,* which, despite its name, became a weekly in 1992 to cut costs. Begun as a government news agency newspaper more than 25 years ago, it has been seeking backers with hopes of becoming a daily newspaper once again and increasing its size (note that its name may change in the process, probably to the *Hungarian Times*).

Selected newsstands and hotels carry issues of *Budapest Week,* the *Daily News,* and such well-known English-language newspapers as the *International Herald Tribune.* Libri International Bookshop, located in the heart of Pest at Váci u. 32 (tel. 118-2718), carries English-language newspapers, as well as guide books and fiction in English. It's open Monday through Friday from 10am to 6pm (to 8pm on Thursday) and on Saturday from 9am to 2pm.

Photographic Needs Fotex is a chain of film-processing stores that also deals in Kodak film and processing. A conveniently located Fotex at Váci u. 9 (tel. 137-5641), Budapest's main shopping street, is open Monday through Saturday and on Sunday from 9am to 2pm. Another Fotex in Pest is at Petőfi Sandor u. 11 (tel. 117-8849), near the main post office, open Monday through Friday from 8am to 8pm and on Saturday from 10am to 2pm.

Police The emergency number for the police is 07.

Radio/TV An English broadcast of the news is aired daily in summer at noon on Petőfi Station, 66.62 MHz.

Shoe Repair Most shoe-repair shops in Budapest are small, servicing the local neighborhood. Ask at your hotel for the nearest repair shop. Otherwise, there's a Mister Minit (an international chain of shoe-repair shops) in the Centrum-Corvin department store at Blaha L. tér.

Tax Hotels, private accommodations, and restaurants include a 15% tax in their rates while restaurants add a 25% tax to their bills. As for goods, there's a Value-Added Tax of 10%–30% included in the price, with the highest taxes applied to luxury goods. Foreigners are not entitled to a refund of the VAT, unlike in most other countries.

Taxis Refer to "Orientation and Getting Around," above, for information on calling a taxi and prices.

Telephone Public telephones and booths are found on streets, in subway

THE FORINT & THE DOLLAR

At this writing $1 = approximately 74 Ft (or 1 Ft = 1.3¢), and this was the rate of exchange used to calculate the dollar values given in this chapter (rounded to the nearest nickel). This rate fluctuates from time to time and may not be the same when you travel to Hungary. Therefore the following table should be used only as a guide:

Ft	U.S.	Ft	U.S.
1	.01	500	6.45
5	.06	750	10.13
10	.13	1,000	13.51
15	.20	1,250	16.89
20	.27	1,500	20.27
25	.34	1,750	23.65
30	.40	2,000	27.03
35	.47	2,250	30.40
40	.54	2,500	33.78
45	.61	2,750	37.16
50	.67	3,000	40.55
75	1.01	3,500	47.30
100	1.35	4,000	54.05
150	2.03	4,500	60.80
200	2.70	5,000	67.55
250	3.37	5,500	74.32

stations, and in Budapest's hotels. For a **local call,** insert a 5-Ft (6¢) coin. Note that a few years back, all telephone numbers for Budapest were changed from six-digit to seven-digit numbers by adding a 1 in front of each number. Thus, if you come across an old number with only six digits, be sure to dial a 1 first.

The **international country code** for Hungary is 36, while the **city code** for Budapest is 1.

For **international telephone calls,** head for the International Telephone Office, located near the main post office at Petőfi Sandor u. 17 in Pest (tel. 118-7533 or 117-1606), on the second floor. The staff is helpful and will tell you how to make an international call. It's open Monday through Friday from 8am to 8pm and on Saturday and Sunday from 9am to 3pm. Otherwise, if you need an English-speaking operator to assist you, dial 118-6977 or 117-2200. A three-minute telephone call to North America costs 450 Ft ($6.10).

Tipping Although service is included in restaurant bills, everyone expects to be tipped. As a general rule, add 10% to your taxi fare or restaurant bill, or at least add what Budapesters call a "tenner"—a 10-Ft (15¢) coin.

4. BUDGET ACCOMMODATIONS

One of the changes that we can hope will come to Budapest in the near future is more and better accommodations. While there are the usual first-class hotels that are beyond the budget traveler's pocket, Budapest does not have nearly enough medium-and lower-priced hotels to accommodate the growing number of tourists who are flocking to Europe's "undiscovered" capital. Summers are especially overcrowded and overbooked.

Budapest, therefore, relies more heavily on private accommodations to house its tourists than any other major city in Europe. Everyone in town, it seems, rents out rooms to visitors. Officially, these private entrepreneurs must have a special permit from the government. Unofficially, there are many individuals without permits who meet incoming trains to try and rent rooms, and the officials for the most part seem simply to look the other way. On my last several trips to Budapest I was approached by individuals at least six times before I even made it from the train platform to the IBUSZ office at the train station. In the summer, when accommodations are tight and there are long lines of tourists at travel agencies trying to book a room, you are best off trying your luck with an individual. Be sure to ask how far away the room is (you don't want to waste time traveling to the center of town via a long bus ride), and whether there's a shower you can use. How much you end up paying depends largely on the time of the year—but it will probably be anywhere from $10 to $15 (usually in Western currency) a night for two people.

IBUSZ can book hotel rooms or private accommodations, but travelers should be aware that in the summer months the cheaper accommodations fill up fast. A staff member of IBUSZ suggested trying to arrive early in the morning, since by afternoon all rooms may be filled. (You might have to take a more expensive accommodation the first night and then return to IBUSZ early the next morning.) There's an IBUSZ at Keleti Station, open Monday through Friday from 8am to 7pm and on Saturday and Sunday from 8am to 5pm. A larger **IBUSZ Hotel Service Office** is located at Petőfi tér 3 (tel. 118-5707 or 118-4865), open 24 hours daily. Different IBUSZ offices handle different private-room accommodations; the one at Petőfi tér has one of the largest lists of private rooms in the city, is usually less crowded, and accepts all major credit cards for payment of accommodations, whether for a private home or a hotel. There is no fee for the booking service, but you must pay for your room at IBUSZ; they will then issue your accommodations voucher. Private rooms booked through IBUSZ, costing 1,200–1,500 Ft ($16–$20) for a double, and are available for check-in only after 5pm and for a minimum of two nights.

DOUBLES (IN PRIVATE HOMES) FOR LESS THAN 2,450 FT ($32)

Although you may stand a better chance of finding an empty room in a private home if you book through IBUSZ, you might wish to try one of the following four recommendations if you want to reserve a room in advance or if you prefer knowing what a place is like before you get there (rooms booked through IBUSZ range from minuscule to spacious). All five private homes here prefer payment in U.S. dollars, and rates are much higher than those charged by IBUSZ.

IN PEST

MR. AND MRS. KÁROLY SZELES, Becsi u. 1, 1052 Budapest. Tel. 1/137-4353 or 3636/16559. 1 rm in winter; 1 apt. in summer. TV **Subway:** Deák Ferenc tér.

$ Rates (including shower): Winter, $35 double; summer, $120–$150 apt. No credit cards.

✪ You can't get much more centrally located than this, in between Vörösmarty and Deák Ferenc Squares in the heart of Pest. The Szeleses are friendly, retired English-speaking economists who rent a large double room with color TV and plants during the winter and the entire apartment during the summer (they are away in Eger). Their apartment is on the third floor (there's an elevator). By the way, if the Szeleses' home is booked, they can also recommend other private rooms in the homes of Mr. Szeles's two brothers in Budapest.

SÁNDOR AND MARGARITTE TOTH, Baross u. 98, 1082 Budapest. Tel. 1/133-3873. 2 rms. TV **Streetcar:** 23, 24, or 36 from Keleti Station to the third stop.
$ Rates (including continental breakfast and shower): $20–$24 double.
Centrally located, south of Keleti Station, the Toths are an older couple who rent very small, basic, and adequately furnished rooms, one with color TV and radio. Both hosts are friendly, and their son, Zoltan, speaks English. Take the elevator to the third floor, then look for no. 5 via an open-air corridor facing the inner courtyard.

TOWNHOUSER'S LODGE, Attila u. 123, 1162 Budapest. Tel. 1/169-7387. 5 rms. **Directions:** Subway to Örs Vezéer Tér, then bus no. 31 to György utca (fifth stop).
$ Rates (including breakfast, shower, and laundry): $10 single; $20 double; $30 triple. No credit cards.
Although located on the eastern outskirts of Pest, this reasonably priced, family-run pension is easy to get to and has a number of features that highly recommend it. It's actually a house, home of Béla Tanhauser, his wife, Rose, two daughters, and Dino the dog. The house, located in a quiet residential area, has a nice garden where guests can relax in summer and eat breakfast, and there's even a refrigerator and cooking facilities for guest use and free use of a washing machine. Béla offers customized sightseeing tours of Budapest and the surrounding area in his van, including trips to Szentendre and a day's sail on Lake Balaton (city tours cost $10 a person; the trip to Lake Balaton, $25). Rooms, which come in various sizes and include radios (TVs available), are up on the first and second floors—the only disadvantage is the rather steep stairs.

IN BUDA

DR. WALTER FLEPS, Bogár u. 20b, 1022 Budapest. Tel. 1/115-3887. 2 rms. **Directions:** Subway to Batthyany tér, then bus no. 11 to the eighth stop; or bus no. 91 from Nyugati Station.
$ Rates: $25 double. Breakfast $3 extra. No credit cards.
My best private home selection in Budapest is this ultramodern, spotlessly clean, partially glassed-in house with large balconies overlooking the entire city, in a rather elegant residential district (where, incidentally, Rubik, of Cube fame, lives). Dr. Fleps, a retired lawyer, speaks excellent English and is extremely helpful with information and tips. The rooms, bright and sunny, are furnished with

---

ⓕ FROMMER'S SMART TRAVELER: HOTELS

VALUE-CONSCIOUS TRAVELERS SHOULD
TAKE ADVANTAGE OF THE FOLLOWING:

1. Discounts in the winter months (even major hotel operators grant significant price reductions in the off-season).
2. Rooms in private homes, the cheapest way to go.

QUESTIONS TO ASK IF YOU'RE ON A BUDGET

1. Are there hotel rooms without shower? (Staff may assume that you want one of the more expensive rooms.)
2. Where is the hotel or private room located? (If you're willing to spend more time traveling to the city center, you may spend less money for your room.)
3. Is breakfast included?

antiques. It's located about two miles northwest of the city center. There is ample parking on the street.

MRS. MAGDA PALFFY, Ménesi u. 98, 1118 Budapest. Tel. 1/165-8870.
  3 rms. **Directions:** Bus no. 7 from Keleti Station to Móricz tér, then streetcar no. 61.
  $ Rates (including breakfast and shower): $30 double. No credit cards.

Mrs. Palffy is a friendly, gregarious sculptor and painter who speaks fluent German and understands English, and who welcomes travelers into her home. She offers one private room with a shower and toilet, and if it's taken she'll put up guests in her living room and bedroom and move into her studio in the same building. Her home is located in a residential area behind Gellért Hill.

DOUBLES FOR LESS THAN 4,440 FT ($60)

IN PEST

HOTEL METROPOL, Rákóczi út 58, 1074 Budapest. Tel. 1/142-1175.
  Fax 1/142-6940. Telex 22-6209. 102 rms (10 with tub or shower and toilet, 24 with shower only). TEL **Subway:** Blaha L Lujza tér (or about a 15-minute walk from Keleti Station).
  $ Rates (including breakfast and shower): 2,530 Ft ($34) single without tub/shower or toilet, 3,080 Ft ($42) single with tub or shower and toilet; 3,400 Ft ($46) double without tub/shower or toilet, 4,070 Ft ($55) double with shower only, 4,300 Ft ($58) double with tub or shower and toilet; 5,370 Ft ($73) triple with shower only. AE, DC, MC, V.

Conveniently located a few blocks from Keleti Station, the Hotel Metropol has rooms on four floors (elevator access). The receptionists and waiters speak English. All rooms are spacious and comfortable, though simple. Those facing away from Rákóczi út are quieter. Facilities include three restaurants and a bar.

PARK HOTEL, Baross tér 10, 1087 Budapest. Tel. 1/113-1420 or 113-5619. Fax 1/113-5619. Telex 22-6274. 172 rms (16 with shower and toilet, 45 with shower only). TEL **Subway:** Keleti pu (station).
  $ Rates (including breakfast and shower): 2,700 Ft ($37) single without shower or toilet, 3,300 Ft ($45) single with shower only; 3,700 Ft ($50) double without shower or toilet, 4,400 Ft ($59) double with shower only, 4,700 Ft ($63) double with shower and toilet. AE, DC, MC, V.

The main advantages to staying in this older hotel are that it's located right across the street from Keleti Station and that the front-desk staff speaks English. The hotel dates from 1914 and looks it, with worn carpets and wallpaper that has seen better days. But the rooms are adequate and come with telephone and radio, and those with bathrooms also have TVs. Request a room that faces away from the street and traffic noise. Facilities include a restaurant and two bars.

IN BUDA

GABOR GUBACSI'S PRIVATE GUESTHOUSE, Fullank u. 7, 1026 Budapest. Tel. 1/176-4718. 3 rms (all with shower and toilet). **Bus:** 11 from Batthyany tér or 91 from Nyugati Station.
  $ Rates: $48 double. Breakfast $3 extra. No credit cards.

⭐ This villalike house with three floors, built in 1986, is located two miles northwest of the city center. Rooms are all on the mezzanine floor, only a few steps up from street level. This is the most modern of my hotel selections (it's a guesthouse with the comfort of a hotel), and all the rooms are adequately furnished, with kitchenette, TV lounge, and balconies for sunbathing. The owners speak English. This is a good choice for families of up to six people, or for longer-staying guests. The only disadvantage is that it's a bit far out, in a residential area of Budapest.

HOTEL IFJÚSÁG, Zivatar u. 13, 1024 Budapest. Tel. 1/135-3331. 100

rms (all with shower and toilet). **Bus:** 11 from the Batthyany tér subway station or 91 from Nyugati Station.

$ Rates (including breakfast): 4,070 Ft ($55) single; 4,440 Ft ($60) double; 9,170 Ft ($124) triple. No credit cards.

Although more expensive than the other hotels in this category, this simple hostelry has a convenient location on a hill overlooking the city and rooms facing the Duna River even have balconies. Although the exterior of the hotel resembles a college dormitory, the rooms are being renovated one floor at a time, complete with telephone, clock radio, and new, comfortable furnishings. Facilities include a restaurant and espresso bar.

PENSION KORONA, Sasadi út 127, 1112 Budapest. Tel. 1/186-2460 or 181-2788. 14 rms (all with shower and toilet). MINIBAR TV **Bus:** 7 from Keleti Station to Móricz tér, then bus no. 53.

$ Rates (including breakfast): $40 single; $50–$60 double. No credit cards.

⭐ The charming couple running this pleasant spotlessly clean, hotellike pension with a garden speaks English. There is a free shoe-shine machine and a laundry (175 Ft/$2.35 per load, washed and dried), and barbecues are held on the lawn. All rooms have a TV with satellite reception and a private terrace or balcony. A restaurant serves excellent Hungarian meals for 500 Ft ($6.75), wine included. The Korona is located in the southwestern part of town. There is ample parking at the hotel.

PENSION VADVIRÁG, Nagybanyai út 18, 1025 Budapest. Tel. 1/176-4292. 8 rms (all with shower and toilet). **Directions:** Subway to Moszkva tér and then bus no. 5 to Pasaréti tér, from which it's a 10-minute walk.

$ Rates (including continental breakfast): 2,880 Ft ($39) single; 4,070 Ft ($55) double; 4,800 Ft ($65) apt. Use of the sauna in the basement 300 Ft ($4.05) extra. No credit cards.

⭐ This very nice and modern two-story house in the northwestern part of Buda, built in 1988, is managed by an English-speaking husband-and-wife team. All the rooms have modern furniture, wall-to-wall carpeting, and plenty of wardrobe space, and three rooms even have their own private balcony, including a larger, apartment-size room which also has a TV. There's a pleasant garden surrounding the pension where you can sunbathe in summer, and breakfast is served on a terrace overlooking the town. The Vadvirág ("Wildflower") is ideal for families or small groups.

SUPER-BUDGET CHOICES

CITADELLA SZÁLLÓ, Citadella sétány, 1118 Budapest. Tel. 1/166-5794. 15 quad rms (all with shower) 60 dormitory beds. **Bus:** 7 from Keleti Station to Móricz tér, then 27 up the hill to the fortress.

$ Rates: 2,140 Ft ($29) quad; 277 Ft ($3.75) per person in dormitory. No credit cards.

High above the city on Gellért Hill in Buda, this youth hostel is actually located in a 150-year-old fortress built by the Habsburgs. Youth-hostel cards are not required and there's no age limit. Dormitory rooms are large and packed with beds, with up to 18 people to a room, and there are also four-bed rooms with showers. You can't beat the price and it's open all year. Write or call in advance for a reservation.

DIÁKSPORT HOTEL, Dózsa György u. 152, 1134 Budapest. Tel. 1/120-8425 or 140-8585. 17 rms (6 with shower), 60 dormitory beds. **Subway:** Dózsa György út. **Streetcar:** 79.

$ Rates: 330 Ft ($4.45) single without shower, 380 Ft ($5) single with shower; 550 Ft ($7.45) double without shower, 800 Ft ($10.80) double with shower; 250 Ft ($3.35) per person in dormitory. No credit cards.

This inexpensive hostelry caters primarily to young people who are used to youth-hostel accommodations, with sparsely furnished, cell-like rooms that hardly provide enough space to unpack. All rooms, however, have windows, and some of the single and double rooms even have a private shower. Most of the rooms, however, are dormitory style. No youth-hostel cards are required, and it's located north of the city center; entrance to the hotel is on a side street, Angyalföldi út.

CAMPING

CAMPING HARS-HEGY, Hars-Hegy u. 5, 1021 Budapest. Tel. 1/115-1482 or 176-1921. Sites for 100 RVs and 500 tents, 35 chalets. **Directions:** Subway from Keleti Station to Moszkva tér, then bus no. 22.

$ Rates: Tent sites for two people 460–920 Ft ($6.20–$12.45); from 2,800 Ft ($38) chalets. **Closed:** Mid-Oct to mid-Apr.

In the Buda hills, two miles northwest of the city, is this huge parklike area with sites for RVs and tents. Also available are 35 modern wooden chalets, equipped with showers, toilets, kitchenettes, and refrigerators. Campground facilities include hot public showers, cooking facilities, a snack bar, restaurant, refrigerators for rent, tennis court, a playground, and laundry facilities. Note, however, that the campground is open only from mid-April to mid-October.

MIKRO CAMPING, Rozgonyi P. u. 19, 1031 Budapest. Tel. 1/160-9440. 10 tent sites, 4 rms. **Directions:** Subway to Batthyany tér, then HEV local train 20 minutes to the Romai Furdo stop; then a five-minute walk.

$ Rates: Tent sites for two people $6; double rooms $10. Showers 15 Ft (25¢) extra. **Closed:** Oct–May 15.

Located about 20 minutes north of Buda on the HEV local train, this small, family-owned establishment is ideally suited for backpackers and cyclists. Only a few minutes' walk from the Danube, it offers both tent sites and four private rooms, and there are several outdoor swimming complexes nearby. Write beforehand for reservations. Groups welcome.

WORTH THE EXTRA BUCKS

Because the exchange rate fluctuates in Hungary, these hotels quote dollars for their room rates.

HOTEL NEMZETI, József körút 4, 1088 Budapest. Tel. 1/133-9160 or 133-9169. Fax 1/114-0019. Telex 22-7710. 76 rms (all with tub or shower and toilet). MINIBAR TV TEL **Subway:** Blaha Lujza tér.

$ Rates (including breakfast): $90 single; $125 double. Extra person $25. Winter discounts available. AE, DC, MC, V.

This is my pick for a romantic splurge, especially if you like elegant, older hotels. Built at the turn of the century in ornate, art nouveau style, it boasts a lobby full of old-world charm, with marbled pillars soaring to arched ceilings etched in gilded stucco and hung with chandeliers. An impressive grand staircase leads to rooms upstairs (there are elevators, too), where you'll find spacious rooms with all the modern conveniences. Most rooms face a quiet inner courtyard. The front desk speaks English and can book sightseeing tours, make restaurant reservations, and help obtain theater and opera tickets. Its restaurant is alone worth the visit to this hotel. Highly recommended, this hotel is located in the heart of Pest off busy Rákóczi út.

HOTEL STADION, Ifjúság u. 1, 1148 Budapest. Tel. 1/251-2222 or 252-9333. Fax 1/251-2062. Telex 22-5685. 372 rms (all with shower and toilet). MINIBAR TV TEL **Subway:** Népstadion.

$ Rates (including breakfast): $80 single; $111 double. Winter discounts available. AE, CB, DC, MC, V.

You'll spot this modern seven-story hotel complex immediately because of its size and twin towers. It is very centrally located in Pest, next to the Népstadion subway stop. Facilities include an indoor swimming pool, solarium, sauna, bowling alley, restaurant, bar, three elevators, and an English-speaking staff. The hotel doesn't have much character, but it's clean and functional.

5. BUDGET DINING

Restaurant critics worldwide agree that Hungarian cuisine is among the tastiest in Europe. Equally important is the fact that the price for that cuisine is extremely low. For 400 Ft ($5.40) per meal you can eat well, and for 1,500 Ft ($20), magnificently.

The basic ingredient in Hungarian food is red pepper, called paprika—you'll find it in soups, main dishes, and even some desserts. Among the most popular specialties, listed on every menu, are *paprika gulyas,* a soup made of beef, onions, paprika, potatoes, and spices; *fogas,* whitefish soup and paprika; *lecso,* a cooked vegetable stew (with paprika); *paprika chicken; cabbage leaves* stuffed with bacon, pork, rice, and herbs; *rétes* (apple strudel); and omelets filled with cottage cheese, ground nuts, and topped with a hot-chocolate sauce.

A restaurant is called an *etterem* in Hungarian; if you're looking for a cup of coffee, look for a sign saying KAVE outside the eatery door. Most restaurants in Budapest are open from about noon to 7 or 10pm.

Excellent wines are the *tokay* (white) and *bikaver* (red, literally meaning "bull's blood"). Hungary's most famous apéritif is an apricot brandy, called *barack.*

MEALS FOR LESS THAN 400 FT [$5.50]

IN PEST

CENTRAL RESTAURANT, Károly krt. 7. Tel. 122-6273.
   Cuisine: HUNGARIAN/FAST FOOD. **Subway:** Astoria.
$ **Prices:** Main courses 40–100 Ft (55¢–$1.35); fixed-price meals 140–400 Ft ($1.90–$5.40). No credit cards.
   Open: Daily 8:30am–7pm.
Budapest's largest self-service restaurant has seating for 80 inside and another 80 on the sidewalk. Food selections, which are lined up on a 30-foot serving counter, include soups, spaghetti pomodoro, beef stew, pork sausage with cabbage, fried chicken, salads, desserts, and beverages. The staff does not speak English—just point to the dish you want. The restaurant is furnished simply, but the food is of good quality and hearty quantity.

CITY GRILL, Váci u. 20. Tel. 138-4999.
   Cuisine: FAST FOOD. **Subway:** Vörösmarty tér.
$ **Prices:** 50–100 Ft (65¢–$1.35). No credit cards.
   Open: Mon–Fri 7am–10pm, Sat 8am–11pm, Sun 9am–9pm.
This fast-food cafeteria, located next to the Taverna Hotel, is a local alternative to McDonald's and Burger King, both of which have gained strong footholds in capitalist Hungary. It serves the usual hamburgers, chicken nuggets, sausage, and gravy, as well as such local choices as Hungarian-style hamburgers and fried pancakes stuffed with cheese. Simple, fast, cheap, and convenient.

EMKE BISZTRO, in the Hotel Emke, Akácfa u. 1. Tel. 122-9230.
   Cuisine: FAST FOOD. **Subway:** Blaha Lujza tér.
$ **Prices:** 30–130 Ft (40¢–$1.75). No credit cards.
   Open: Daily 7am–9pm.
Located on the corner of Rákóczi út just off busy Blaha Lujza tér, this simple cafeteria won't win any aesthetic awards but it's modern and clean, and its prices can't be beat. Popular with the locals, many of whom come just for the 48-Ft (65¢) beer, it offers sandwiches, salads, grilled chicken, pizza, and desserts. A Coke is just 29 Ft (40¢).

MAGALLO RESTAURANT, Károly krt. 23. Tel. 122-3015.
   Cuisine: HUNGARIAN. **Subway:** Astoria or Deák Ferenc tér.

$ Prices: 80–340 Ft ($1.10–$4.60). No credit cards.
Open: Mon–Sat 11am–11pm.
Located a few blocks from Central Restaurant, Magallo is a popular eatery, frequented by locals working in this busy area of Pest. Typical of many inexpensive restaurants in Budapest, they don't bother with changing the tablecloths after each customer, so if you like pristine dining rooms go someplace else. But people don't come for the ambience—rather for the cheap prices. An English menu lists Hungarian kettle goulash, sholet beans with Hungarian beef stew, Hungarian mutton or pork stew, fried chicken, wienerschnitzel, Hungarian paprika veal with gnocchi, stuffed pork cutlets, and frogs' legs, but whether all the dishes are always available is another story. You might find yourself eating one of the daily specials.

HOTEL METROPOL ETTEREM, Rákóczi út 58. Tel. 142-1175.
Cuisine: HUNGARIAN. **Subway:** Blaha Lujza tér.
$ Prices: 150–500 Ft ($2–$6.75). No credit cards.
Open: Daily noon–9pm.
The English menu of this bistro, where the waiters speak some English, changes but may include mutton stew, egg with risotto, fried fish with french fries, knuckle of pork, Cordon Bleu, Hungarian stew of tripe with boiled potatoes, turkey breast, and rumpsteak with fried onions and potatoes. This simple restaurant is a part of the Hotel Metropol next door, but has its own street entrance. Look for the sign GYORS ETTEREM.

RESTAURANT NAPOLETANA, Petofí tér 3. Tel. 118-5714.
Cuisine: ITALIAN. **Subway:** Vörösmarty tér.
$ Prices: Pasta from 250 Ft ($3.35); pizza from 240 Ft ($3.25); main courses 370–700 Ft ($5–$9.45). AE, DC, MC, V.
Open: Daily 11am–11pm.
Located right next to IBUSZ, this Italian restaurant serves various pizzas, pastas, beef dishes, and fish. Although the orange decor is blinding and the pizzas could be better, this place is good for a fix if you're tired of Hungarian paprika.

IN BUDA

VÖRÖS SÜN DRINKBÁR, Táncsics M. u. 2. Tel. 156-9993.
Cuisine: SOUPS/SALADS/SNACKS. **Bus:** Special "Varbusz MM" minibus from Moszkva tér.
$ Prices: Soup and salads 150–200 Ft ($2–$2.70); main courses 350–450 Ft ($4.70–$6.10).
Open: Tues–Fri 5pm–1am, Sat 3pm–1am, Sun noon–1am.
Located on Castle Hill, where most restaurants cater to tourists with money, this is a

---

 FROMMER'S SMART TRAVELER: RESTAURANTS

VALUE-CONSCIOUS TRAVELERS SHOULD
TAKE ADVANTAGE OF THE FOLLOWING:

1. Budapest's low prices—this is the place to splurge since meals here cost a third of what they'd be in Austria or Germany.
2. Cafeterias for simple dining.
3. Local wines and Hungarian beer instead of imports.

good place for lunch or a snack if you're visiting nearby Matthias Church and Fishermen's Bastion. Just a stone's throw from the Hilton Hotel (look for its red sign), this tiny bar offers soups, salads, and a few main dishes, which may include goulasch, bean soup, turkey-breast salad, beef steak, roast pork, and shrimp cocktail. It also offers the usual apéritifs, spirits, beer, and Hungarian wines. The building is 400 years old, but the interior has been tastelessly modernized. What a pity.

MEALS FOR LESS THAN 1,000 FT [$13.50]

IN BUDA

ARANYHORDÓ, Tárnok u. 16. Tel. 156-1367.

Cuisine: HUNGARIAN. **Bus:** Special "Varbusz MM" minibus from Moszkva tér.
$ **Prices:** Main courses 450–1,200 Ft ($6.10–$16.20). AE, MC, V.
Open: Restaurant, daily 10am–midnight (to 10pm in winter); wine cellar, daily 7pm–midnight (to 10pm in winter).

Located on Castle Hill not far from the Fishermen's Bastion, this is a convenient restaurant if you're visiting the many nearby attractions. It's actually three establishments in one building, all with the same menu—a ground-floor brasserie, an upstairs formal restaurant, and a wine cellar open only in the evening. I prefer the wine cellar, which resembles the interior of a cave as it winds from room to tiny room. There's gypsy and accordion music every evening, and the English menu includes paprika chicken, fish, Hungarian beef stew, pork cutlet, goose liver Hungarian style, grilled dishes, and turkey breast.

PARK ETTEREM RESTAURANT, Kosztolanyi Dezsö tér 2. Tel. 166-9470.

Cuisine: HUNGARIAN. **Bus:** 7 from Rákóczi út in Pest.
$ **Prices:** Main courses 250–600 Ft ($3.35–$8.10). AE, DC, MC, V.
Open: Daily noon–11pm.

Park Restaurant is in Buda, on a pond-size lake surrounded by weeping willows and reed grass, in a park with flowerbeds. It's one of the most popular outdoor restaurants and cafeterias, with 80 seats inside and 150 outside on a sun terrace overlooking the pond and a fountain (terrace open May to September only). A la carte selections include wienerschnitzel with french fries, gulash in sweet- or sour-cream sauce, spaghetti, rumpsteak, and chicken. Note, however, that at press time the restaurant was making the transition from national to private ownership—telephone before making the trip.

IN PEST

APOSTOLOK, Kigyo u. 4. Tel. 118-3704.

Cuisine: HUNGARIAN.
$ **Prices:** Main courses 230–1,000 ($3.10–$13.50). AE, DC, MC, V.
Open: Daily 10am–midnight.

Located in the heart of Pest just off the Váci útca shopping street, near Felszabadulas tér, this is a beautifully decorated restaurant in the style of the Old World—stained-glass windows, carved wooden booths and dark-stained wainscoting, an intricately tiled floor, and wrought-iron chandeliers. Its English menu includes all the Hungarian specialties, including Hartobágy pancakes, fried carp filet, paprika chicken with gnocchi, roast duck, sholet beans with smoked pork chop, fried chicken, and Hungarian beef stew with potatoes. If you watch what you eat, you can dine here for less than 500 Ft ($6.75).

KISPIPA VENDÉGLÖ, Akácfa u. 38. Tel. 142-2587.

Cuisine: HUNGARIAN. **Reservations:** Recommended at dinner. **Subway:** Blaha Lujza tér.
$ **Prices:** Main courses 230–645 Ft ($3.10–$8.70); fixed-price meals 300–400 Ft ($4.05–$5.40). No credit cards.
Open: Mon–Sat noon–midnight.

★ Located in a modest neighborhood and simply furnished by Western standards, this establishment is a favorite among Hungarians, and a good place to celebrate a special occasion. A pleasant restaurant with a 1920s ambience, it features live piano music and is decorated with Hungarian advertisements from the first few decades of the century. An English menu lists frogs' legs, pheasant, venison, grilled trout, duck, veal cutlets, mutton, roast pork, and other exotic dishes. You're best off making a reservation for dinner.

MÚZEUM KÁVÉHÁZ ETTEREM, Múzeum körút 12. Tel. 138-4221 or 118-5202.

Cuisine: HUNGARIAN. **Subway:** Astoria or Kalvin tér.

$ Prices: 380–1,000 Ft ($5.15–$13.50). AE.

Open: Mon–Sat noon–1am.

Located right beside the Hungarian National Museum, this cheerful restaurant with an English menu is gaily decorated with colored tiles, etched crossbeams, wainscoting, and a wooden floor. In addition to daily specials, it also offers stuffed green peppers with homemade sausage, pickled salmon, sirloin of beef, rabbit gulasch with gnocchi, chicken, roast duck, fish, and gulasch with potatoes. If you want, you can also order simply a cup of coffee or a beer.

NEMZETI HOTEL RESTAURANT, József körút 4. Tel. 133-9160.

Cuisine: HUNGARIAN. **Subway:** Blaha Lujza tér.

$ Prices: 400–1,000 Ft ($5.40–$13.50). AE, DC, MC, V.

Open: Daily 7am–11pm.

★ Come here if you want a special, romantic evening but find Café New York too expensive (see "Worth the Extra Bucks," below). Located in the Nemzeti Hotel but with its own sidewalk entrance, this is a refined dining establishment, with tall ceilings, subdued lighting, live music in the evenings, and booths. You might wish to start with Hortobágy pancakes or chicken liver risotto, followed by Jokai bean soup, and topped with main dishes ranging from fish, paprika chicken, and Hungarian stew to crispy roast duckling, stuffed cabbage, and pork tenderloin. The food is excellently prepared and nicely presented. One of my favorites.

PILSNER URQUELL SORFORRAS, Váci út 15. Tel. 118-3814.

Cuisine: HUNGARIAN. **Subway:** Vörösmarty tér.

$ Prices: Appetizers and soups 80–130 ($1.10–$1.75); main dishes 230–700 ($3.10–$9.45). No credit cards.

Open: Daily 10am–11pm.

This new restaurant on Pest's main shopping boulevard offers comfortable dining at reasonable prices. Its dining area is clean and bright, decorated in black and lavender with the ubiquitous fake plants. The limited menu offers the standard Hungarian fare, as well as soups, appetizers, and a salad bar—a small plate costs 120 Ft ($1.60). The establishment's main attraction, however, is its Pilsner Urquell beer on draft; a half-liter mug costs 100 Ft ($1.35).

RESTAURANT MATYAS PINCE, Március 15 tér 7. Tel. 118-1693.

Cuisine: HUNGARIAN/INTERNATIONAL. **Reservations:** Recommended.

Subway: Felszabadulas tér.

$ Prices: Main courses 390–900 Ft ($5.25–$12.15). AE, DC, MC, V.

Open: Lunch daily noon–3pm; dinner daily 7pm–midnight.

In Pest, near the Erzsébet híd (bridge), is this first-class restaurant, with a beautiful interior, 100 seats, English-speaking waiters, and Gypsy music most nights. Phone for a reservation, since this place is often booked by tour groups. The English menu primarily includes Hungarian specialties, from Hungarian paprika chicken or sholet beans with roast duck to smoked pork. Top off your meal with sponge cake with vanilla sauce. There are several dining halls here, including an ornate beer cellar with the same menu as the restaurant but open throughout the day from noon to midnight.

TUBORG VIKING SÖRÖZÖ-SÖBÁR, Károly krt. 5. Tel. 142-6192.

Cuisine: INTERNATIONAL. **Subway:** Astoria.

$ Prices: Main courses 280–550 Ft ($3.80–$7.45). AE, DC, MC, V.
Open: Daily noon–2am.

This is another one of Budapest's newer, modern establishments, with a bar and café on the ground floor and a restaurant in the basement. The restaurant is pleasant, and there's even live piano music several evenings a week. The English menu lists Hungarian, German, and Dutch dishes ranging from turkey breast and Wienerschnitzel to tenderloin steak, Hungarian rumpsteak, or pork cutlets Budapest style. Greek salad is offered for those who miss their veggies. A half liter of draft beer is 105 Ft ($1.40).

VEGETARIUM ETTEREM, Cukor utca 3. Tel. 138-3710.
Cuisine: VEGETARIAN. **Subway:** Felszabadulas tér; then walk a few minutes south.
$ Prices: Appetizers and salads 100–170 Ft ($1.35–$2.30); main courses 210–400 Ft ($2.85–$5.40). AE, MC.
Open: Daily noon–10pm.

This pleasant restaurant is a great alternative to the heavier Hungarian cuisine—and about your only alternative if you're a vegetarian. Wonder of wonders, no smoking is allowed here (a rarity in Europe), and it's decorated with original artwork, huge wooden booths for added privacy, and paper lanterns, all of which give it an earthy, healthy atmosphere. The menu includes starters such as green paprika stuffed with cottage cheese, stuffed mushrooms, and fried tofu, while main dishes range from French bean ragoût and soybean burgers to tempura and macrobiotic platters, including a seaweed platter. There are also healthy beverages, including apple cidar and other fruit drinks.

COFFEEHOUSES

CAFE GERBEAUD, Vörösmarty tér 7. Tel. 118-1708.
Cuisine: COFFEEHOUSE/SNACKS.
$ Prices: Coffee with milk 75 Ft ($1); pastry 50–90 Ft (65¢–$1.20).
Open: Daily 9am–11pm.

Located on a fashionable square in downtown Pest, Café Gerbeaud was founded in 1858 by a French entrepreneur, and its white marble tables, mirrored rooms, and stucco ceilings strongly resemble other famous coffeehouses in western Europe also established in the mid-19th century. Coffee and pastry here are first class; try a generous helping of apple strudel (or one of 25 other tempting choices). This is a favorite hangout of reporters, critics, and other literary-minded people.

CAFE RUSZWURM, Szentháromság u. 7. Tel. 175-5284.
Cuisine: COFFEEHOUSE/SNACKS. **Bus:** "Warbuz MM" minibus from Moszkva tér.
$ Prices: Coffee with milk 50 Ft (65¢); pastry 25–70 Ft (35¢–95¢).
Open: Thurs–Tues 10am–7pm.

Café Ruszwurm is located on Castle Hill, near Matthias Church in Buda, in a 17th-century house with Biedermeier furnishings. It's a small place with only two rooms, and its homemade pastries are the best in town. Fruit cake topped with whipped cream, poppyseed strudel, cinnamon pies, and walnut tarts are among the most popular items here. If you don't find a vacant seat, go to the take-out counter and carry some of the tempting pastries to the nearby stone seats of the Fishermen's Bastion. Munch them there while enjoying the panoramic view over Pest and the Danube.

WORTH THE EXTRA BUCKS

CAFE NEW YORK, Erzsébet krt. 9. Tel. 122-3849.
Cuisine: HUNGARIAN. **Subway:** Blaha Lujza tér.
$ Prices: Main courses 450–2,000 Ft ($6.10–$27). AE, CB, DC, MC, V.

Open: Restaurant, lunch daily noon–3pm; dinner daily 6:30–11pm. Café, daily 9am–10pm.

✪ Don't miss this place! Located in Pest, near Blaha Lujza tér, this is one of the most famous restaurants in Europe. It first opened in 1894, and now has a lovely baroque interior, marble pillars, huge mirrors in gilded frames, and thick carpets. Try to book a seat in the lavishly decorated lower part, called "Deep Water," reached via a wide staircase and illuminated by crystal chandeliers. The waiters are attentive, and there's Hungarian music in the evenings. You might wish to try a cup of turtle soup flavored with cognac as a starter, followed by chateaubriand with béarnaise sauce, served with sautéed broccoli, pancakes à la Hortobágy (filled with minced meat and served with a creamy pepper sauce), a small bottle of Tokay wine, mineral water, and coffee. Those who have dined here include Charlie Chaplin, Jackie Coogan, Marcello Mastroianni, Anthony Perkins, and Luciano Pavarotti. Granted, the restaurant now caters primarily to tourists and dishes are a bit pricey, but even if you don't dine here, you should at least come for a cup of coffee in the ground-floor coffee shop, where you'll have a bird's-eye view of the dining hall below. Open daily from 9am to 10pm, the coffee shop offers a large coffee with milk for 75 Ft ($1), as well as a limited menu of sandwiches, soups, and such dishes as veal goulash with gnocchi or pork with mushrooms, with prices ranging from 140 Ft to 500 Ft ($1.90 to $6.75).

CITADELLA RESTAURANT, on top of Gellért Hill. Tel. 166-7736.
   Cuisine: HUNGARIAN/INTERNATIONAL. **Bus:** 27 to Citadella.
$ Prices: Main courses 500–1,200 Ft ($6.75–$16.20). AE, DC, MC, V.
   Open: Daily noon–midnight.
This restaurant has a most unusual setting—it's deep in the bowels of a 150-year-old fortress that sits atop a hill in Buda. Medieval in appearance, with vaulted brick ceilings and candles on the tables, it offers an English menu with soups such as gulasch or French onion, appetizers like Russian caviar or shrimp cocktail, and dishes that include paprika chicken, veal knuckle, beef roulade, beef steak Budapest style, shashlik (Hungarian pork shish kebab), and haunch of venison. For dessert, try mixed strudel or sponge cake. Next to the restaurant is a nightclub with a dance floor, open from 10pm to 4am, as well as a casino open from 6pm to 4am. Most of the waiters here speak English. Bus no. 27 stops in front of the restaurant, but you may prefer to take a taxi.

LUGAS RESTAURANT, Szilágyi Erzsébet fasor 77. Tel. 154-4765.
   Cuisine: HUNGARIAN/ITALIAN. **Directions:** Subway to Moszkva or Déli Station, then streetcar no. 18 to the last stop (or bus no. 22 from Moszkva).
$ Rates: Appetizers 270–600 Ft ($3.65–$8.10); main courses 500–1,300 Ft ($6.75–$17.55). AE.
   Open: Daily noon–midnight.
This is a delightful place for a meal on a warm, sunny day—it has an outdoor terrace. Inside is much more upscale and formal, with tables decked with pink tableclothes and black tableware and attentive waiters and waitresses. The lunch clientele is likely to be businessmen in suits. In the evenings there's live piano music. The English menu lists goulash soup, Hungarian pancakes, spaghetti, lasagne, grilled pike perch, smoked trout, salmon steak, sole, chicken stew with gnocchi, turkey breast with brocolli, pork medallions Hungarian style, stuffed cabbage, and Hungarian veal stew with gnocchi.

---

6. ATTRACTIONS

SUGGESTED ITINERARIES

IF YOU HAVE ONE DAY If you have only one day to devote to Budapest, spend the morning in Buda on Castle Hill, a picturesque, old part of town that has been lovingly restored. Here you'll find Matthias Church, the Fishermen's Bastion next

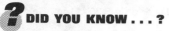

DID YOU KNOW . . . ?

- Buda, Pest, and Óbuda, on both sides of the Danube, did not become one city until 1873.
- Hungarian is not related to most European languages: it resembles languages spoken in western Siberia.
- Budapest's Nyugati Station was built by the Eiffel Company.
- The Parliament Building, erected in 1904, was at the time the largest one in the world.
- As a result of World War I, Hungary lost 68% of its land and 58% of its population.
- Only about one-quarter of Budapest's buildings remained intact after German and Russian fighting during World War II.
- During the 1956 anti-Communist uprising, 190,000 Hungarians fled the country.
- There are 128 listed thermal springs in Budapest.
- Budapest's subway, completed in 1896, was the first in continental Europe. Only London's subway (1890) is older.

door, as well as the Hungarian National Gallery with its art treasures and the Budapest History Museum tracing the history of the city since Roman times. In the late afternoon, head toward the Pest end of town and stroll down the fashionable Váci pedestrian lane, topping it off with a cup of coffee at Café Gerbeaud. Splurge for dinner at the Café New York.

IF YOU HAVE TWO DAYS   Spend the first day as described above. On the second day, spend the day in Pest, taking in the city's other major attractions like the National Museum, the Museum of Fine Arts, and St. Stephen's Basilica. End the day with a soak in one of Budapest's famous thermal baths.

IF YOU HAVE THREE DAYS   Spend Days one and two as outlined above. On your third day, go to the ancient Roman settlement of Aquincum, in Óbuda, where you can see the ruins of a large amphitheater and visit a museum of Roman archeological finds. In the afternoon, head for Margaret Island, Budapest's most popular recreation area, located right in the middle of the Danube, where you can relax, go swimming, and have a picnic. If it's wintertime (the Aquincum is open only from May through October), spend the day following your own pursuits or exploring the shops along the Váci.

IF YOU HAVE FIVE DAYS   Explore the environs of Budapest. Take the Danube Bend Excursion by boat or by bus, or skip the tour and head straight for Szentendre, a village with a ceramics museum, an outdoor museum, and lots of shops and boutiques. Another populr destination is Lake Balaton, central Europe's largest freshwater lake and a wine-growing region. See "Easy Excursions," below, for details.

TOP ATTRACTIONS

ON BUDA'S CASTLE HILL

From Moszkva tér, a special minibus called "Varbusz MM," with a picture of a castle on it, makes runs to and along the ridge of Castle Hill. You can also reach Castle Hill from the Pest side by taking bus no. 16 from Erzésbet tér to the Disz tér stop on Castle Hill.

MÁTYÁS TEMPLON (Matthias Church). Tel. 155-5657.

Built in the Gothic style in the 13th century with a gold-tiled roof, the Matthias Church has witnessed many royal marriages (starting with King Matthias in 1475) and coronations (Maria Theresia in 1740, Franz Josef in 1876, and Karl in 1916, to name but a few). During the Turkish occupation (1542–1686) it was converted into a mosque. Today, Catholic mass is held here regularly, and organ concerts of music by Liszt and Kodaly are presented on Friday in the summer. The baroque column in

front of the church was erected to commemorate the end of a plague in the 18th century.
Admission: Free.
Open: Daily 9am–7pm. **Bus:** Special "Varbusz MM" minibus from Moszkva tér, or 16 from Erzsébet tér in Pest and Moszkva tér to Disz tér.

HALÁSZ BÁSTYA (Fishermen's Bastion), next to the Matthias Church.
Completed in 1901 in Neo-Romanesque style on the site of an old fish market, Fishermen's Bastion is the city's landmark. Its arcades, walls, and turrets overlook Pest and the Danube from a unique vantage point, perfect for taking photos of the most attractive areas of Budapest.
Admission: Free.
Open: Daily, 24 hours. **Bus:** Special "Varbusz MM" minibus from Moszkva tér, or 16 from Erzsébet tér in Pest and Moszkva tér to Disz tér.

MAGYAR NEMZETI GALERIA (Hungarian National Gallery), in Wings B, C, and D of Buda Castle Palace. Tel. 175-7533.

⭐ Devoted solely to Hungarian artists, the National Gallery exhibits Hungary's most treasured artworks. Beginning with early Gothic winged altars of the 11th century, the entire history of Hungarian painting and sculpture is represented, including stone carvings, frescoes, and room upon room of paintings from the late Renaissance to the 20th century. This place is large, with portraits of famous Hungarians and works by István Ferenczy, Mihály Munkácsy, László Paál, Pál Szinyei Merse, and many more. You'll want to spend several hours here.
Admission: 20 Ft (25¢).
Open: Summer, Tues–Sun 10am–6pm; winter, Tues–Sun 10am–4pm. **Bus:** Special "Varbusz MM" minibus from Moszkva tér, or 16 from Erzsébet tér in Pest and Moszkva tér to Disz tér.

LEGÚJABBKORI TÖRTENETI MÚZEUM (Contemporary Historical Museum of Hungary), in Wing A of Buda Castle Palace. Tel. 175-7533.
This newly opened museum on Castle Hill is Budapest's only museum devoted exclusively to modern and contemporary art and photography, with changing exhibits. There are also changing exhibits relating to Hungary's history.
Admission: Fees vary according to what's being shown, but average about 60 Ft (80¢).
Open: Summer, Tues–Sun 10am–6pm; winter, Tues–Sun 10am–4pm. **Bus:** Special "Varbusz MM" minibus from Moszkva tér, or 16 from Erzsébet tér in Pest and Moszkva tér to Disz tér.

TÖRTÉNETI MÚZEUM (History Museum), in Wing E of Buda Castle Palace. Tel. 175-7533.
Located next to the National Gallery, this museum traces 2,000 years of Budapest's history, beginning with excavational finds of the Roman settlement Aquincum, including a Roman helmet, bowls, vases, and a wall mosaic. Be sure to go down into the basement, since the museum is located in the old castle and it's here that you'll find the Albrecht Cellar, constructed in the first half of the 18th century. Its architecture is as interesting as the museum itself, which also contains weapons, sculptures, and ceramics.
Admission: 30 Ft (40¢).
Open: Summer, Tues–Sun 10am–6pm; winter, Tues–Sun 10am–4pm. **Bus:** Special "Varbusz MM" minibus from Moszkva tér, or 16 from Erzsébet tér in Pest and Moszkva tér to Disz tér.

IN PEST

MAGYAR NEMZETI MÚZEUM (Hungarian National Museum), Múzeum krt. 14. Tel. 138-2122.

HUNGARY

Budapest

Budapest History
Museum **22**
Citadella **26A**
Déli Train Station **3**
Engels Tér Bus Station **4**
Express **7**
Ferenc Liszt Memorial
Museum **15**
Franz Liszt Academy
of Music **29A**
Gellért Baths **29B**
Great Synagogue **23**
Hév Suburban Rail
Station **2**
Hungarian National
Museum **26**
Hungarian State Opera
House **30**
IBUSZ **9**
Inner City Parish Church **24**
Jubileumi Park **25**
Keleti (Eastern) Train
Station **5**
Margaret Island **10**
Matthias Church **19**
Military Museum **18**
Museum of Applied Arts **27**
Museum of
Contemporary History **20**
Museum of Fine Arts **14**
Museum of
Hungarian Art **21**
Musical Instruments
Museum **17**
Nyugati Train Station **1**
Parliament **19**
Pest Vigadó Concert Hall **32**
Petőfi Youth Center **31**
St. Stephen's Basilica **18**
Széchenyi Baths **11**
Tourinform **8**
Transport Museum **12**
Városliget Park **13**
Vigadó tér Boat Station **6**

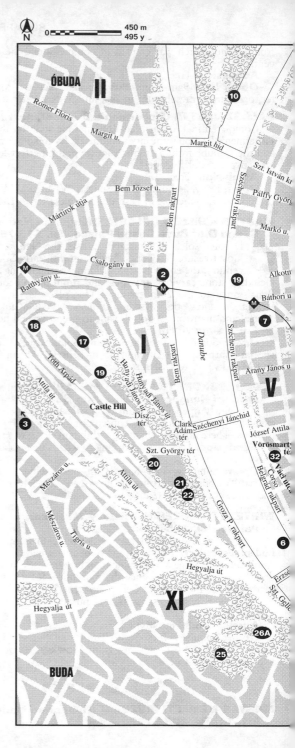

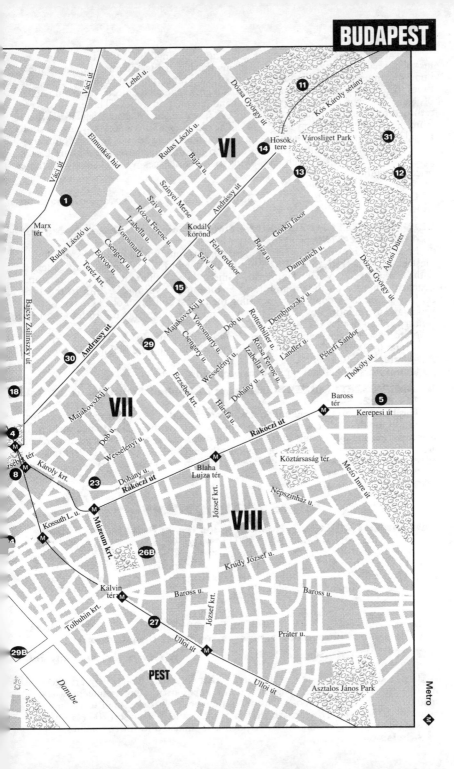

BUDAPEST

VI

VII

VIII

PEST

Váci út

Lehel u.

Dózsa György út

Kos Károly sétány

Elmunkás híd

Rudas László u.

Bajza u.

Hősök tere

Városliget Park

Szinyei Merse

Szív u.

Rózsa Ferenc u.

Izabella u.

Vörösmarty u.

Csengery u.

Eötvös u.

Teréz krt.

Andrássy út

Kodály körönd

Felső erdősor

Szív u.

Gorkíj fasor

Bajza u.

Damjanich u.

Ajtósi Dürer

Dózsa György út

Marx tér

Rudas László u.

Bajcsy Zsilinszky út

Andrássy út

Majakovszkij u.

Vörösmarty u.

Csengery u.

Erzsébet krt.

Wesselényi u.

Dob u.

Rottenbiller u.

Rózsa Ferenc u.

Izabella u.

Dembinszky u.

Landler u.

Péterffy Sándor

Thököly út

Majakovszkij u.

Dob u.

Wesselényi u.

Dohány u.
Rákóczi út

Harsfa u.

Dohány u.

Baross tér

Kerepesi út

Mező Imre út

Rákóczi út

Köztársaság tér

Blaha Lujza tér

Népszínház u.

Károly krt.

Kossuth L. u.

Múzeum krt.

József krt.

Krúdy József u.

Baross u.

Tolbuhin krt.

Kálvin tér

Baross u.

Ferenc krt.

Üllői út

Práter u.

Üllői út

Asztalos János Park

Damube

Marx tér

Erzsébet tér

Metro

I wish this museum had more explanations in English, but at least there's an inexpensive booklet available that explains the highlights. This is Hungary's most important museum, detailing the history of the Hungarian people from prehistoric times to 1849. It contains the nation's most highly venerated objects, the royal regalia of King Stephen: crown, scepter, orb, and coronation robes. These items were returned to Hungary from Fort Knox in 1987, where patriots had safeguarded them from the invading Red Army since 1945. The oldest exhibit is a 50,000-year-old skull found in Hungary. Other objects include a Roman mosaic floor, a Turkish commander's colorful tent, clothing, furniture, a piano used by Beethoven, and Franz Liszt's golden baton. You'll see, each day, Hungarians of all ages walking slowly by these priceless symbols.

Admission: 30 Ft (40¢).

Open: Tues–Sun 10am–6pm. **Subway:** Kálvin tér; then a short walk up Múzeum krt.

SZEPMUVESZETI MÚZEUM (Museum of Fine Arts), Dózsa György út 41. Tel. 142-9759 or 117-5222.

Located on Hösök tere (Heroes' Square), this museum shows works of the old masters, from the 14th to the 19th century. It's one of Europe's greatest art galleries, with works by da Vinci, Tintoretto, Ghirlandaio, Bellini, Raphael, Dürer, and Cranach exhibited on the ground floor. Spanish masters from the 14th to the 17th century are on the second floor, including the largest collection of El Grecos outside Spain, and five paintings by Goya. Drawings and engravings from the 16th to the 19th century are on display on the top floor.

Note that this museum has been closed for renovation, with an expected reopening by 1993. Ask Tourinform whether it's open before making the trip.

Admission: 30 Ft (40¢).

Open: Tues–Sun 10am–5pm. **Subway:** Hösök tere.

IPARMÜVÉSZETI MÚZEUM (Museum of Applied Art), Üllöi út 33. Tel. 117-5222.

This beautiful art nouveau building was constructed before the turn of the century especially for this collection, and is bright and airy with a glass-domed atrium. It features changing exhibitions of furniture, glassware, tapestries, and other decorative arts, so there's always something new. Both the building and its collections are testimony of the important role Budapest played in European history.

Admission: 20 Ft (25¢).

Open: Tues–Sun 10am–6pm.

MORE ATTRACTIONS

PARLIAMENT BUILDING, Kossuth Lajos tér, in Pest. Tel. 112-0600.

Constructed in Neo-Gothic style 100 years ago when Budapest was part of the Austro-Hungarian Empire, the Parliament Building is 820 feet long, 387 feet wide, and 315 feet high, with 27 gates and 88 statues of Hungarian kings and noblemen on the outside walls. Visitors are allowed inside only in groups (and when the Parliament is not in session), on tours offered by Budapest Tourist, Roosevelt tér 5 (tel. 117-3555), or by IBUSZ.

Admission: Budapest Tours, 650 Ft ($8.80).

Open: Tours given Apr–Sept, Wed and Fri at 10:45am and 1:45pm. **Directions:** Tours depart from Roosevelt tér 5, near the Vörösmarty subway station.

SZT. ISTVÁN (St. Stephen's Basilica), Szent István tér, in Pest. Tel. 111-0839.

This is the largest church in the city, with two spires, built 150 years ago and named after Hungary's first king. It is a combination of many architectural styles, mainly neoclassical and Neo-Renaissance. Be sure to visit the small room near the altar end of the church; there's a small display there, and if you insert 20 Ft (30¢) into a glass showcase, a hand bone of St. Stephen is illuminated for three minutes.

Admission: Free.

Open: Summer, Mon–Sat 9am–5pm, Sun 1–4pm; winter, Mon–Sat 10am–4pm, Sun 1–4pm. **Subway:** Deák Ferenc tér.

GELLÉRT HILL, in Buda.

On top of the 770-foot hill is the Liberation Monument, which honors Soviet soldiers who were killed while liberating Budapest from Nazi occupation in 1944. Next to the monument is the Citadel, a fortress and former prison built 140 years ago by the Habsburgs and now a restaurant and youth hostel. All tour buses stop here to allow tourists to take photographs. Gellért Hill is the place to go for the best panoramic views of Pest and the Danube.

Admission: Free.

Open: Daily, 24 hours. **Bus:** 27 from Móricz tér to the last stop.

AQUINCUM, Kórvin utca, in Óbuda. Tel. 168-8241.

Near the Arpad Bridge are the ruins of this Roman city, which 2,000 years ago had 50,000 inhabitants. Excavation work has been ongoing at this open-air museum since 1870, and discoveries include an amphitheater with a seating capacity of 15,000 and a thermal bath (Budapest has 120 active thermal springs). Most of the Roman finds are in the National Museum in Pest, but some smaller artifacts—weapons, tools, pottery, jewelry, and the like—are exhibited in the nearby Roman Camp Museum, at Szentendrei u. 139 (tel. 180-4650). The day-long Danube Bend bus tour takes you along the Roman excavation area.

Admission: 30 Ft (40¢).

Open: May–Oct, Tues–Sun 10am–6pm. **Train:** HEV local train from Battyány tér to the Aquincum station.

MARGIT-SZIGET (Margaret Island), in the Danube River.

Located between Buda and Pest in the middle of the Danube, this 1½-mile-long island is Budapest's most popular park and largest resort area, with gardens, a swimming pool, hot springs, tennis courts, meadows, a small zoo, and open-air restaurants. It's ideal for a picnic or relaxing, right in the heart of the city.

Admission: Free.

Open: Daily, 24 hours. **Directions:** Walk across Margit híd (bridge) or take bus no. 26 or streetcar no. 6.

VAROSLIGET (City Park), behind Hösök tere, in Pest.

This is Budapest's second-largest park, with a boating lake, swimming pool, hot spring spa, a **zoo** with over 3,000 animals, a botanical garden, and a castle reminiscent of Walt Disney World (it houses an agricultural museum, wine cellar included). Adjacent to it is a big **amusement park,** open daily from 10am to 7:30pm (in summer to 9pm), with roller coasters, fun houses, shooting ranges, puppet shows, and dance floors.

Admission: Park, free; zoo, 50 Ft (65¢) adult, 25 Ft (35¢) children.

Open: Park, daily 24 hours; zoo, daily 9am–5:30pm. **Closed:** Wed in winter. **Subway:** Hösök tere.

ORGANIZED TOURS

May through October there are many interesting tours in and around Budapest, including a two-hour walking tour of the Parliament Building (when not in session), Matthias Church, the National Gallery, and Castle Hill.

Other tours include the following, all of which are conducted by an English-speaking guide. Book through IBUSZ.

City Tour, by bus, which takes you to the most important sights, such as Heroes' Square, Matthias Church, Fishermen's Bastion, Castle Hill, and the Citadel. The tour departs daily at 10am, lasts three hours, and costs $17.

Goulash Party Tour, an evening of folklore at a typical Hungarian restaurant, featuring Gypsy music, costumes, dances, and jokes, with an English-speaking master of ceremonies. You'll enjoy goulash soup, cold cuts, various sorts of bread, strudel for dessert, and all the wine you can drink. The party begins nightly May through October at 8pm, lasts three hours, and costs $45.

Budapest by Night Tour, which begins with dinner with live music and continues to a nightclub with floor shows. The fun starts nightly at 7:30pm May through October and on Wednesday and Saturday the rest of the year. The price is $65.

SPORTS & RECREATION

THERMAL BATHS This is my kind of sport! No respectable European would dream of coming to Budapest and not take advantage of the city's famous thermal baths—and you should follow suit. Altogether there are approximately 200 medicinal baths in Budapest, where everyone from janitors to politicians can soak away their cares. There are dozens of public baths, but one of the most famous, and certainly most ornate, is the bath at the **Hotel Gellért,** Szent Gellért tér 1 (tel. 166-6166), located in Buda at the base of Gellért Hill beside the Danube. Built in elaborate art nouveau after the turn of the century, the thermal indoor bath has a glass roof that can be removed in fine weather. There's also a large outdoor swimming pool with artificial waves. Admission to the thermal baths is 120 Ft ($1.60); if you want a massage, it's 100 Ft ($1.35) extra for 10 minutes and 300 Ft ($4.05) for 30 minutes. Both bathing suits and towels are available for rent. The baths are open Monday through Friday from 6am to 8pm (you must enter by 7pm) and on Saturday and Sunday from 6:30am to 1pm (you must enter by noon). Massages are given Monday through Friday only.

Another famous bath is the **Király Fürdö,** Fó utca 84 (tel. 115-3000), which features a splendid cupola above an octagonal bath and thermal tubs, salt baths, and massage. It's open for men only on Monday, Wednesday, and Friday, while women get their chance to soak on Tuesday, Thursday, and Saturday. Hours are 6:30am to 6pm (closed Sunday).

For a list of more thermal baths, consult the *Programme in Hungary,* distributed free at Tourinform.

7. SAVVY SHOPPING

There are many shopping streets in Budapest, but for a visiting tourist the heart of the **shopping district** is in Pest, in a quadrangle formed by the Danube, József Attila utca, Károly körút, and Kossuth Lajos utca, all near the Deák Ferenc tér subway stop. Váci utca in particular, now a pedestrian zone, is a good hunting ground for souvenir shoppers.

What are Budapest's best bargains? Hand-embroidered handkerchiefs and table-cloths, dolls in Puszta costumes, sheepskin jackets, Tokay wine bottles, packages of paprika, porcelain, pottery,and jewelry.

Try **Népmüveszet Folk Art Centrum,** Váci utca 14 (tel. 118-5840), for a wide selection of Hungarian embroidery, wood carvings, clothing, pottery, and other native products. It's open Monday through Friday from 9:30am to 6pm, on Saturday from 9:30am to 5pm, and on Sunday from 9:30am to 2pm. Castle Hill also has souvenir and antique shops.

MARKETS Budapest's largest and best-known flea market, **Hasznaltcikk Piac,** is held on the southern outskirts of Budapest at Nagykörosi utca 156. Here you'll find stalls selling silver, china, old books, jeans, leather jackets, antiques, and junk, and since the dealers know their wares and their value, you probably won't find any undiscovered treasures. However, it's fun just to browse. It's open Monday through Friday from 8am to 4pm and on Saturday from 8am to 2pm. To reach it, take bus no. 54 from Boráros tér to the Hasznaltcikk Piac stop, about a 25-minute ride. The market is at the end of Nagykörosi utca, on the left side of the street. Keep your eyes peeled, because it's easy to miss.

8. EVENING ENTERTAINMENT

Because of Hungary's low prices, you should take advantage of Budapest's wonderful concert and stage offerings. There is something going on musically in Budapest virtually every evening of the year, with tickets for many performances ranging as low as 120–300 Ft ($1.60–$4.05). Particularly outstanding are performances of the Hungarian National Symphony Orchestra, the Budapest Symphony Orchestra, and the Hungarian State Opera. For information regarding concerts, recitals of guest performers, opera, ballet, and dance, pick up a free copy of the monthly booklet *Programme in Hungary* at Tourinform. Other sources of information for what's going on in the capital are *Budapest Week* and *Daily News,* both published weekly and containing entertainment sections listing concerts, movies, and other events.

Upon arrival in Budapest, one of your first stops should be the **Philharmonia Booking Office** (Nemzeti Filharmonia) at Vörösmarty tér 1 (tel. 117-6222), where you can purchase tickets for concerts. Tickets for opera and ballet can be purchased either at the door or at the **Central Theater Booking Office,** Andrássy út 18.

THE PERFORMING ARTS

THEATERS & CONCERT HALLS

HUNGARIAN STATE OPERA, Andrássy út 22, in Pest. Tel. 153-0170.
This major theater hosts opera, concerts, and ballet.
Prices: Tickets, 150–800 Ft ($2–$10.80).
Subway: Arany János.

PESTI VIGADÓ (Pester Redoute), Vigadó tér 2, in Pest. Tel. 117-6222.
This hall, near the Duna Inter-Continental Hotel, specializes in folklore shows and classical music.
Prices: Tickets, 200–800 Ft ($2.70–$10.80).
Subway: Vörösmarty tér.

ACADEMY OF MUSIC, Liszt tér 8, in Pest. Tel. 142-0179.
The Academy presents concerts regularly, including chamber music and string quartets.
Prices: Tickets, 200–500 Ft ($2.70–$6.75).
Subway: Oktogon.

MADACH THEATER, Erzsébet krt. 31-33, in Pest. Tel. 132-1147.
This theater performs musicals such as *Les Misérables* and *Cats*.
Prices: Tickets, 550–900 Ft ($7.45–$12.15).
Subway: Blaha Lujza tér.

NIGHTCLUBS & MUSIC SHOWS

MAXIM VARIETE, Akácfa u. 3. Tel. 122-7858.
This Pest cabaret/nightclub features two shows. The first program begins at 9:30pm and features a circuslike atmosphere with acrobatics and a magic show; the second show, which begins at midnight, is a bit more risqué, with a revue of dancing girls. In addition to paying admission, customers are expected to order a drink.
Prices: Beer 400 Ft ($5.40); cocktails 1,000 Ft ($13.50). **Admission:** 1,000 Ft ($13.50).
Open: Mon–Sat 8pm–3am. **Subway:** Blaha Lujza tér.

MOVIES

Cinemas charge 100–190 Ft ($1.35–$2.55), depending on where you sit, for an evening show, half that for a matinee. Movies are shown in their original version, with

Hungarian subtitles. Most of the cinemas are found in Pest. Check the *Daily News* or *Budapest Week* for a listing of movies being shown throughout the city in English.

GAMBLING

The **Budapest Casino,** in the Hilton Hotel, Castle Hill in Buda (tel. 175-1000), boasts the usual games of roulette, baccarat, blackjack, and one-arm bandits. The minimum stake is $1.50. The doorman at the door will check your passport before letting you in. Admission is $6.50, which goes toward chips for games. It's open daily from 5pm to 4am. Jacket and tie are required for men.

In Pest, there's **Gresham Palast,** Roosevelt tér 5 (tel. 117-2502), located near the Atrium Hyatt Hotel. Open daily from 2pm to 4am, it also charges $6.50 admission, which goes toward chips. No jeans or sports shoes are allowed, and after 8pm men must wear jackets. Be sure to bring your passport.

LIVE MUSIC

MINIATÜR ESPRESSO, Buday László u. 10. Tel. 135-1134.

With a history stretching back 40 years, this cozy, tiny piano bar is an institution and is a favorite for travelers who come to Budapest again and again. They come for a bit of nostalgia, confident that little has changed here over the decades, from the lace tablecloths, red wallpaper, and overstuffed red chairs to the soft lighting and soothing piano music. For the past 40 years it has been run by the motherly Manyi Néni, who has recently passed on the duties to her daughter, Mária. Most likely you'll find both of them there. A very civilized place, it's located in Buda, on a hill west of Margit Híd.

Prices: Cocktails 280 Ft ($3.80). **Admission:** Free.

Open: Mon–Sat 7pm–3am. **Streetcar:** 4 or 6 to the Mechwart liget stop.

ROCK CAFE, Dohány u. 20.

Catering to a much younger crowd is this basement establishment simply decorated in yellow and black and featuring a pool table, pinball machine, and music videos. Its stage is small, the venue for live Hungarian rock and blues bands.

Prices: Beer from 80 Ft ($1.10). **Admission:** 160 Ft ($2.15) for evening performances.

Open: Daily noon–4am (music daily 10:30pm–12:30am). **Subway:** Astoria.

9. EASY EXCURSIONS

The easiest way to see the countryside around Budapest is to join one of the several tours offered by IBUSZ. The **Danube Bend Tour by Boat,** for example, is a nine-hour trip along the Danube, with a stop at Szentendre with its Kovács Margit Ceramics Museum and shops. It's offered May through October on Wednesday, Friday, and Saturday at 8:30am. If you prefer to travel by bus, there's the **Danube Bend Tour by Coach,** which takes in Szentendre, Esztergom with its famous cathedral, and Visegrad with its royal castle ruins. This tour departs May through October on Tuesday, Thursday, and Saturday at 9am; during the winter months it departs on Saturday only, at 9am. Price for both tours is $55.

For further information, contact any IBUSZ office. They will also be able to tell you about full-day tours to Hungary's largest lake, **Balaton,** and to a famous stud farm in **Tok,** complete with an equestrian show. They also have information on hydrofoil trips on the Danube to Vienna and by cruise ship to Passau, Germany, via Czechoslovakia and Austria.

SZENTENDRE Located on the Danube River just north of Budapest, "Saint Andrew" is known for its artists' colony, art shops, and small-town ambience. Its gaily painted houses hold a number of shops, cafés, and galleries. Foremost among its attractions is the **Szabadteri Néprajzi Múzeum (Open-Air Village Museum),**

Szabadságforrás út, with its collection of peasant houses and cottages from all over Hungary. It's open from April to October, Tuesday through Sunday from 9am to 5pm.

Be sure, too, to visit the **Kovács Margit Ceramic Museum,** Vastagh György utca 1, with the works of Hungary's most famous ceramicist, including her realistic portraits, biblical figures, grotesque figurines, and jugs and plates with fairy-tale decorations.

To reach Szentendre, take the HEV local train from Battyány tér, a trip of about 45 minutes.

LAKE BALATON   After Budapest, Lake Balaton receives more visitors than any other place in Hungary. The largest freshwater lake in Central Europe, it is 43 miles long but only 3 miles wide. Its mostly shallow waters warm quickly in the sun, making it popular for swimming, sunbathing, and other summertime pursuits. Its shores are surrounded by hotels and restaurants, while the hills beyond are famous for their vineyards. The main tourist season is from mid-May to about mid-September. Both buses and trains connect the north end of Lake Balaton to Budapest in about 1½–2 hours. Contact Tourinform for tourist information and IBUSZ if you wish to book accommodations.

COPENHAGEN

For a moment, let's have some fun and create the perfect city. First, we'll lay down a vast network of pedestrian streets, lined with great stores and cafés. Bicycle lanes will span the city, encouraging a quiet, nonpolluting means of transport, and we'll generously spread royal palaces and rich museums throughout. Of course, we'll build our city along a pretty, yet functional harbor. Just for fun, let's put an amusement park right in the city center, making carnival rides and concerts accessible to all. Finally, we'll govern our city with a socially minded philosophy that virtually eliminates poverty, crime, and begging.

As you have probably guessed, this is no fantasy—this is Copenhagen. And without a doubt, this very real city's richest gift is its quality of life.

Copenhageners are a reflection of a kind and gentle lifestyle. They smile easily, laugh a lot, and will often go out of their way to help a stranger. Copenhageners are known for their terrific sense of humor—they like to poke fun at themselves and others, especially American travelers. The city itself is the "jazz capital" of Europe, boasting more than its fair share of exceptional talent. And as every stroller along Strøget will discover, the city attracts some of the best street performers in the world.

Even for the value-minded tourist, Copenhagen is a city to love and savor. Getting around is relatively easy—you can walk to almost everything. Hotels and restaurants cater to a variety of pocketbooks and maintain some of the highest standards in Europe. And the bars and clubs serve some of Europe's best brews at a fraction of the price of other Scandinavian cities. This chapter will prove that "wonderful, wonderful" Copenhagen can be enjoyed on a budget.

1. FROM A BUDGET TRAVELER'S POINT OF VIEW

COPENHAGEN BUDGET BESTS

Tivoli, the city's biggest tourist draw, provides one of Copenhagen's cheapest thrills. You can get in for 33 Kr ($5.45), half that for kids, and spend the entire day. See "Attractions," below.

The two city brewery tours are informative, intoxicating, fun, and free. See "Special-Interest Sightseeing," in "Attractions," below.

You can see an opera, ballet, or play at the Royal Theater for as little as 40 Kr ($6.30). See "Evening Entertainment," below.

WHAT THINGS COST IN COPENHAGEN

U.S. $

Taxi from Central Station to Kongens Nytorv	7.10
Underground from Central Station to outlying neighborhood	1.25
Local telephone call	.08
Double room at the SAS Royal Hotel (deluxe)	340.00
Double room at Saga (moderate)	99.35
Double room at 9 Små Hjem (summer only) (budget)	66.25
Lunch for one at Københavnercaféen (moderate)	8.15
Lunch for one at Sabines Cafeteria (budget)	5.50
Dinner for one, without wine, at Els (deluxe)	30.30
Dinner for one, without wine, at Pasta Basta (moderate)	10.90
Dinner for one, without wine, at Shezan (budget)	9.45
Pint of beer	2.70
Glass of wine	3.15
Cup of coffee in a café	1.90
Coca-cola in a restaurant	2.35
Roll of ASA 100 color film, 36 exposures	12.80
Admission to Tivoli	4.75
Admission to the Ny Carlsberg Glyptotek Museum	2.35
Movie ticket	9.45
Theater ticket (at Royal Theater)	6.30

SPECIAL DISCOUNT OPPORTUNITIES

FOR STUDENTS   By flashing an International Student Identification Card, young people can get discounts at most of the city's museums, at some concert halls, and on planes, trains, and ferries from Denmark. Check listings throughout this chapter for special student rates.

FOR SENIORS   People over age 67 are entitled to half-price tickets at the Royal Theater, reduced admission to some museums, and discounts on ferry trips to Sweden. See individual listings below for details.

FOR EVERYONE   The **Copenhagen Card** entitles tourists to free museum entry, free public transportation, and good discounts on a variety of activities throughout the capital. The card is for one, two, or three days and costs 120 Kr ($18.90), 200 Kr ($31.55), and 250 Kr ($39.45) respectively. Children 5–11 years old pay half price. Cards can be bought at the Room Service office in Central Station, the Danish Tourist Board (see "Information," in "Orientation and Getting Around," below), and at many hotels and S-tog stations.

WORTH THE EXTRA BUCKS

A trip to the Louisiana Museum in Humlebæk in North Zealand is definitely worthwhile. For details about this stunning repository of modern art and sculpture, see "Easy Excursions," at the end of this chapter.

2. PRETRIP PREPARATIONS

DOCUMENTS   Citizens of the United States, Canada, New Zealand, and Australia need only a passport to enter Denmark.

WHAT TO PACK Since summers are cooler here than in most of Europe, always pack a sweater and bring a coat appropriate to the season; a lined raincoat is always practical. At the height of winter, temperatures usually hover around the freezing mark. Pack warm clothes, and bring boots suitable for walking in snow.

WHEN TO GO Copenhagen is at its best from the end of April to the beginning of September. Days are long, Tivoli is open, and sidewalk cafés buzz late into the night. Of course, other seasons have their charm as well, including less precipitation, fewer tourists, and, in general, lower prices. Christmas in Copenhagen is especially endearing.

Copenhagen's Average Daytime Temperature & Rainfall

	Jan	Feb	Mar	Apr	May	June	July	Aug	Sept	Oct	Nov	Dec
Temp (°F)	32	31	36	44	53	60	64	63	57	49	42	37
Rainfall "	1.9	1.5	1.2	1.5	1.7	1.8	2.8	2.6	2.4	2.3	1.9	1.9

Special Events Most of the city's special events are staged during the summer, when the tourist season is in full swing. Festivities begin at the end of May with the **Copenhagen Carnival,** a raucous Mardi Gras party replete with costumes and sambas. **Free park concerts** start in June, including a weekly Saturday rock music festival at Femøren and Sunday concerts in Fælledparken. Free concerts are sometimes held in Nikolaj Church. The **Copenhagen Jazz Festival,** during the first part of July, and the **Copenhagen Summer Festival,** which emphasizes classical music from late July to mid-August, highlight the summer's festivities. See "Special and Free Events" in "Attractions," below, for other happenings, and visit the Danish Tourist Board and Use-It (addresses under "Information" in "Orientation and Getting Around," below) for free event schedules.

BACKGROUND READING Hans Christian Andersen (1805–75) is Denmark's most famous author. His endearing fairy tales include *The Emperor's New Clothes, The Little Mermaid,* and *The Ugly Duckling,* available individually or in Andersen anthologies.

Søren Kierkegaard (1813–55) was a seminal existentialist, deeply influencing later thinkers and future generations. Baroness Karen Blixen, better known by her pseudonym, Isak Dinesen, was another notable Danish author perhaps best known for *Out of Africa.*

Look for *H. C. Andersen's Copenhagen—A Fairy Tale Walk* by Bente Kjølbye (Høst & Son), available in English and German in local bookstores.

3. ORIENTATION & GETTING AROUND

ARRIVING IN COPENHAGEN

FROM THE AIRPORT Is it a top-of-the-line department store or is it an airport? It's both! It's **Copenhagen Airport** (tel. 33-50-93-33), six miles from the city center and the fanciest place to land in Europe.

The bank in the Arrivals Hall offers reasonable rates; it's open daily from 6:30am to 10pm. Public telephones accept a number of foreign coins—including American quarters. There is also a bar-café; a small market; lockers; rental-car counters, including Avis, Budget, Europcar, Hertz, and Pitzner (a Danish company that claims to have the lowest airport prices); and courtesy baggage carts.

In the adjacent Departure Hall, the Left Luggage Office (tel. 31-50-88-89), open

WHAT'S SPECIAL ABOUT COPENHAGEN

Strøget
☐ World-class shopping and some of Europe's best street performers.

Palaces
☐ Rosenborg Palace, home of the Crown Jewels and a beautiful park.
☐ Christiansborg Palace, with its 800 years of history and impressive state rooms.
☐ Frederiksborg Palace, the "Versailles of northern Europe," 45 minutes from Copenhagen.

Museums
☐ The Ny Carlsberg Glyptotek, with its ancient and modern art, and serene courtyard.

☐ The Louisiana Museum of Modern Art, one hour by train from Copenhagen's Central Station and really worth the trip.

Tivoli
☐ The geographical and spiritual heart of Danish culture, it comes alive nightly in summer with music, dance, food, and merriment.

---

daily from 6:30am to 10:30pm, charges 20 Kr ($3.15) per bag per day, 30 Kr ($4.75) for bikes and skis. Opposite it, a post office (enter through the red door) is open Monday through Friday from 9am to 5:30pm and on Saturday from 9am to noon.

The **SAS Airport Bus** (tel. 32-52-00-66) departs every 15 minutes and runs between the main terminal and Copenhagen's Central Station; the trip takes about 25 minutes and costs 26 Kr ($4.10); children under 12 ride free. There are usually several SAS buses parked out front, so be sure you're on the one going downtown; it's marked HOVEDBANE GARDEN/CITY.

City bus no. 32 also makes the run between the airport and the city center (Town Hall Square); buses depart every 10–20 minutes and the 45-minute journey costs just 13.50 Kr ($2.10). From here, you can connect with other buses and the S-tog trains.

A **taxi** into town will run you about 120 Kr ($18.90), which is reasonable if you are three or four adults.

FROM THE TRAIN STATION **Central Station** is relatively easy to negotiate. Lockers and shops are located in the center of the station, while more shops, banks, ticket windows, and platform entrances are located around the perimeter. The information window is open daily from 7am to 9pm; the hotel reservations window, daily from 9am to midnight May through August and 9am to 10pm September to April.

The **luggage-storage office** is open daily from 6:30am to midnight. The rates are 15 Kr ($2.35) per bag or 20 Kr ($3.15) per backpack per day. Alternatively, lockers are available for 10 Kr ($1.60) per day.

Den Danske Bank exchange office, on the station's platform side, is open daily from 7am to 9pm (to 10pm in summer). Commission rates are competitive with other area banks Monday through Wednesday, and Friday from 9:30am to 4pm and on Thursday from 9:30am to 6pm; rates rise from 20 Kr ($3.15) for cash and 35 Kr ($5.50) for traveler's checks to 25 Kr ($3.95) and 40 Kr ($6.30), respectively outside these "normal" banking hours.

From mid-June to mid-September, travelers can relax and shower free at the **Interrail Center,** a popular meeting point for backpackers. It's open daily from 6:30am to midnight.

Other station facilities include: a supermarket, open daily from 8am to midnight; a post office, open Monday through Friday from 8am to 10pm, on Saturday from 9am to 4pm, and on Sunday and holidays from 10am to 5pm; and an international telephone bureau called **TeleCom,** open Monday through Friday from 8am to 10pm and on Saturday, Sunday, and holidays from 9am to 7pm.

At the train station, you can also get a passport photo taken, rent bicycles, get a shoe shine, buy flowers, buy a novel, enjoy a meal (from a commendable pizza at City Pizza to a delectable Danish buffet at the Bistro), and rent a luggage cart for a refundable 10 Kr ($1.60).

The city's **subway (S-tog)** lines converge at Central Station. Go to Platforms 9 through 12 to catch one of these trains.

INFORMATION

In spring 1992, the **Danish Tourist Board** moved its information office from Tivoli's Hans Christian Andersen Castle to a new location near Tivoli's main entrance, Bernstorffsgade 1 (tel. 33-11-13-25; fax 33-93-49-69). Their most useful publication is the free guide **Copenhagen This Week,** which is also available in hotels and tourist spots around town. The staff is patient and helpful and will provide information on everything from hostels and hotels to activities and nightlife to day trips and longer excursions. The office is open May through September, daily from 9am to midnight; October and April, Monday through Saturday from 9am to 5pm; and November through March, Monday through Friday from 9am to 5pm and on Saturday from 9am to noon.

Use-It, on the second floor of Huset (The House), Rådhusstræde 13 (tel. 33-15-65-18), is Copenhagen's "alternative" information office. Although the office may appear youth oriented, the information is geared toward budget travelers of all ages and is often superior to that of the tourist board. A number of useful and free publications are distributed here, including **Playtime,** a newspaper with advice on low-cost restaurants, hotels, and sightseeing activities; and a city map. The energetic young staff can counsel travelers on getting a job, renting an apartment, and almost anything else. Other useful services include a ride board for travelers needing rides or companions to other points in Europe and a terrific room-finding service (see "Budget Accommodations," below). Unfortunately, lines here can be very long, especially in summer, so unless you want to chat, head straight for the publications and move on. There is a big table where you may relax and read the materials; there's also a basket with condoms in it. Another handy service is a free locker for a day, with a 50-Kr ($7.90) refundable deposit; you can leave belongings for a longer period for 10 Kr ($1.60) per day. Use-It is open June 15 to September 14, daily from 9am to 7pm; the rest of the year, Monday through Friday only from 10am to 4pm.

CITY LAYOUT

Copenhagen revolves around **Strøget,** a mile-long pedestrian thoroughfare right in the heart of town. Strøget is actually a string of several streets: Østergade, Amagertorv, Vimmelskaftet, Nygade, and Frederiksberggade. And although this strip seems like a centuries-old essential part of city life, it was only declared free of automobiles in 1962.

Strøget's eastern end runs into **Kongens Nytorv** (the King's Square), site of the Royal Theater and the Magasin du Nord department store, and the beginning of **Nyhavn**—once Copenhagen's wild sailors' quarter, now a redeveloped pedestrian area.

Købmagergade, another pedestrian avenue, branches north from Strøget's middle, and itself spawns several smaller pedestrian streets.

A new pedestrian street called **Strædet** (it means "the Street," and the word is a combination of Læderstræde and Kompagnistræde) runs parallel to Strøget and is best known for its antiques shops and antiquarian bookshops.

The island of **Slotsholmen** lies just a few blocks south of Strøget, and contains Christianborg Palace, the National Library, and a number of museums.

Strøget's western terminus opens onto **Rådhuspladsen,** the Town Hall Square. The very wide **Vesterbrogade** continues west past **Tivoli Park,** Central Station (Hovedbanegården), and into Frederiksberg. Many of the suggested hotels are clustered just southwest of Central Station.

GETTING AROUND

BY SUBWAY [S-TOG] AND BUS   Copenhagen is served by an extensive bus and subway network. Regular service begins daily at 5am (at 6am on Sunday) and continues until 12:30am. At other times there is a limited night-bus service departing from Town Hall Square.

Fares are based on a zone system; rates rise the farther you go. Most destinations in central Copenhagen will cost the minimum 9 Kr ($1.40). Buses and subway trains use the same tickets and you can transfer as much as you like for up to one hour.

The subway—called the S-tog—works on the honor system. Either pay your fare in the station you're departing from, or stamp your own strip ticket in the yellow box on the platform. In Central Station, the S-tog departs from Platforms 9 through 12.

Similarly, when you board a bus, either pay the driver or stamp your ticket in the machine. It's easy to get away without paying, but beware: Fines for fare dodging are stiff! Bus drivers are exceptionally nice and helpful. Most speak some English, and even if they don't, they have an uncanny ability to know where it is you want to go.

If you plan on traveling by train or bus a lot, buy a 10-ticket strip for 70 Kr ($11.05). Tickets can be bought on buses and at all rail stations. Children under 12 always ride for half price; those under 7 ride free on buses; under 5, free on local trains.

Dial 36-45-45-45 for bus information and 33-14-17-01 for S-tog information.

ON FOOT   The compact city center and many pedestrian thoroughfares make walking a breeze. You may be interested in picking up a copy of "Copenhagen on Foot," a well-written booklet of walking tours distributed free by Use-It (see "Information," above).

BY BICYCLE   Wide bike lanes, long green traffic lights, and beautiful surroundings encourage bike riding for both transportation and recreation. About half of all Danes ride regularly, and even high government officials can sometimes be seen pedaling to work. A guide to biking in and around Copenhagen is distributed free by Use-It (see "Information," above). Look for the new free-use bike stands on many corners. Or rent a three-speed at Central Station from **Københavns Cyklebors,** Reventlowsgade 11 (tel. 33-14-07-17), for 50 Kr ($7.90) for one day, less if you keep the bike longer or opt for one speed; open daily.

BY TAXI   The basic taxi fare for up to four people is 12 Kr ($1.90) at the flag drop (make sure your cab has a meter), then 7.20 Kr ($1.15) per kilometer (.62 mile) between 6am and 6pm, or 9.60 Kr ($1.50) between 6pm and 6am and on Saturday and Sunday. Payment by credit card is acceptable. A cab available for hire displays the word FRI. To order a taxi in advance, dial 31-10-10-10, 31-35-35-35, or 31-22-55-55.

BY CAR   Unless you're planning an extended trip outside Copenhagen, you will find that keeping a car in the city is more trouble than it's worth. Most major U.S. car-rental firms, including Hertz and Avis, have offices in Copenhagen. Compare big-company prices with those charged by local car companies, listed in the "Transport" section of the tourist board publication *Copenhagen This Week.*

In Denmark, drivers must use their lights at all times, even in daytime, and all occupants of the car, including those in the backseat, must buckle their seatbelts.

COPENHAGEN

American Express   The American Express Card & Travel Service office is conveniently located in the middle of Strøget, at Amagertorv 18 (tel. 33-11-50-05), open Monday through Friday from 9am to 5pm and on Saturday from 9am to noon. To report a lost card, call 80-01-00-21.

Babysitters   Minerva (Students) (tel. 31-22-96-96) is a multilingual babysitter clearinghouse charging 25 Kr ($4.40) per hour, plus a 25-Kr ($4.40) booking fee. Reserve Monday through Thursday from 6 to 9am and 3 to 6pm, on Friday from 3 to 7pm only. On Saturday the office is open from 3 to 5pm only. The student sitters are all ages.

Banks   Banks are usually open Monday through Friday from 10am to 4pm (on Thursday until 6pm). Outside these hours, the best place to change money is either the American Express office, Amagertorv 18, at Hemmingsens Gade (tel. 33-11-50-05), open Monday through Friday from 9am to 5pm, and on Saturday from 9am to noon; or the exchange office in Central Station, open daily from 7am to 9pm (until 10pm from April through September).

Bookstores   Copenhagen has a wealth of bookstores, called *boghandel,* that carry a good selection of travel books and fiction and nonfiction books in English. Tops among them are Boghallen, in the Politiken building, Rådhuspladsen 37, a block from Strøget (tel. 33-11-85-11), and Arnold Busck, Kobmagergade 49 (33-12-24-53). Prices for paperbacks range from 49 Kr to 99 Kr ($7.70 to $15.60).

Business Hours   **Shops** are usually open Monday through Thursday from 9am to 5:30pm (department stores, until 6pm), on Friday from 9am until 7 or 8pm, and on Saturday from 9am until 1 or 2pm. **Offices** are open Monday through Friday from 9 or 10am until 4 or 5pm, and sometimes on Saturday until noon or 1pm (the first Saturday of the month, until 5pm).

Currency   The Danish currency is the **krone** (crown), or **kroner (Kr)** in its plural form, made up of 100 **øre.** Banknotes are issued in 20, 50, 100, 500, and 1,000 kroner. Coins come in 25 and 50 øre, and 1, 5, 10, and 20 kroner.

Dentists   Emergency dental care is provided by Tandlægevagten, Oslo Plads 14 (tel. 31-38-02-51). The office, located near Østerport Station, is open Monday through Friday from 8 to 9:30pm, and on Saturday, Sunday, and holidays from 10am to noon.

Doctors   To reach a doctor outside normal hours, dial 33-93-63-00 Monday through Friday from 8am to 4pm; other times, call 33-12-00-41.

Embassies   Denmark's capital is home to the embassies of many nations, including: the **U.S. Embassy,** Dag Hammerskjölds Allé 24 (tel. 31-42-31-44); the **Canadian Embassy,** Kristen Bernikowsgade 1 (tel. 33-12-22-99); the **British Embassy,** Kastelsvej 40 (tel. 31-26-46-00); and the **Australian Embassy,** Kristaniagade 21 (tel. 31-26-22-44). The nearest embassy of New Zealand is in The Hague, Netherlands.

Emergencies   Dial 000 for police, fire, or ambulance service. No coins are needed when dialing from a public phone. Steno Apotek, Vesterbrogade 6C (tel. 33-14-82-66), is a 24-hour pharmacy located just across from Central Station.

Eyeglasses   Several optical shops are located in and around Strøget. Synoptik, Købmagergade 22 (tel. 33-15-05-38), has a particularly large selection of modern frames. It's open Monday through Thursday from 9:30am to 6pm, on Friday from 9:30am to 7pm, and on Saturday from 9:30am to 2pm.

Holidays   New Year's Day, Maundy Thursday, Good Friday, Easter Sunday and Monday, Common Prayer Day (late Apr), Ascension Day, Whit Sunday and Monday (mid-May), Constitution Day (June 5), and Christmas Eve and Christmas Day.

Hospitals   Even foreigners staying temporarily in Denmark are entitled to free hospital care in the event of a sudden illness. Rigshospitalet, Blegdamsvej 9 (tel. 35-45-35-45), is the most centrally located hospital.

Information   See "Orientation and Getting Around," above, for tourist and

THE KRONE & THE DOLLAR

At this writing $1 = approximately 6.34 kroner (or 1 krone = 16¢), and this was the rate of exchange used to calculate the dollar values given in this chapter (rounded to the nearest nickel). This rate fluctuates from time to time and may not be the same when you travel to Denmark. Therefore the following table should be used only as a guide:

Kr	U.S.	Kr	U.S.
1	.16	100	15.77
2	.32	125	19.72
3	.47	150	23.66
4	.63	175	27.60
5	.79	200	31.55
6	.95	225	35.49
7	1.10	250	39.43
8	1.26	275	43.38
9	1.42	300	47.32
10	1.58	325	51.26
15	2.37	350	55.21
20	3.15	375	59.15
25	3.94	400	63.09
50	7.89	500	78.86

transportation information. Other important addresses and telephone numbers can be found under the appropriate headings below.

Laundry/Dry Cleaning   Copenhagen has laundries in all different areas of town; look for the word *vask* (wash) such as *møntvask* or *vaskeri*. A convenient one, Tre-stjernet Montvask, is only two blocks from Central Station, in the basement of the Saga Hotel (separate entrance), at Colbjørnsensgade 20; it costs about 30 Kr ($4.75) for soap, washing, and drying.

For dry cleaning, go to Buen, Vester Farimagsgade 3 (tel. 33-12-45-45), just one block from Central Station. It's open Monday through Friday from 8am to 6pm and on Saturday from 10am to 2pm, but it's not cheap at about 95 Kr ($15) for a jacket or sweater and a pair of pants.

Lost and Found   If you lost it on a train or bus, try the Lost Property Office at Lyshojgardsvej 80, Valby (tel. 36-44-20-10 for trains, 36-45-45-45 for buses). It's open Monday through Friday from 10am to 5pm. If you lost it somewhere else, try the Copenhagen police at Carl Jocobsensvej 20, Valby (tel. 31-16-14-06), open Monday through Friday from 9am to 3pm (on Thursday to 5pm).

Mail   Post offices are usually open Monday through Friday from 9 or 10am until 5 or 5:30pm. Some are also open on Saturday from 9am to noon. Letters weighing under 20 grams cost 4.75 Kr (75¢) to North America and Australia; postcards require 3.75 Kr (60¢).

You can receive mail marked "Poste Restante" most conveniently (in terms of location and hours) at the post office in Central Station, Monday through Friday from 8am to 10pm, on Saturday from 9am to 4pm, and on Sunday and holidays from 10am to 5pm. Holders of American Express cards or traveler's checks can pick up personal mail at that company's main office (see "American Express," above), which will hold it for 30 days and forward it to you elsewhere for 35 Kr ($5.50). American Express does not accept parcels.

Newspapers   There are no English-language newspapers printed in Denmark. However, the *International Herald Tribune, USA Today, The European,* and other papers are widely available. Newsstands on Nytorv (Strøget), opposite Town Hall, and in major hotels have good selections.

You can read newspapers and magazines free at Hoved Biblioteket, Kultorvet 2 (tel. 33-93-60-60), the main public library. It's open Monday through Friday from 10am to 7pm, and on Saturday from 10am to 2pm.

Photographic Needs On a major pedestrian street, Kontant Foto, Købmagergade 44 (tel. 33-12-00-29), is the largest camera supply and photo store in Copenhagen. It's open Monday through Friday from 10am to 5:30pm and on Saturday from 10am to 2pm. Foto Quick, in Rådhusarkaden, at H. C. Andersens Boulevard and Vesterbrogade, offers one-hour processing but exacts a hefty price: 118 Kr ($18.60) for 24 exposures, 165 Kr ($26) for 36 exposures; it's open Monday through Friday from 9am to 5:30pm and on Saturday from 10am to 2pm.

Police In an emergency, dial 000 from any phone—no coins are needed. For other police matters, call Police Headquarters, Polititorvet (tel. 33-14-14-48).

Radio English-language newscasts are broadcast Monday through Friday at 8:10am on 90.8 FM.

Religious Services The Cathedral of Copenhagen (Danish Protestant), Nørregade, is Denmark's most important church; services are held on Sunday at 10am and 5pm and Friday at 11am; open daily from 8:30am to 5pm. The Christian Church Copenhagen, Baggensgade 7 (tel. 31-75-07-01), is an interdenominational Protestant church with services in English. Roman Catholic services are held in Danish at St. Ansgar Church, Bredgade 64 (tel. 33-13-37-62), on Saturday at 5pm and on Sunday at 10am; Catholic services in English are held at the Sacraments Church, Norrebrogade 27 (tel. 31-35-68-25), on Sunday at 6pm, and at St. Anne's Church, Hans Bogbinders Alle 2 (tel. 31-58-21-02), on Saturday and Sunday at 5pm; take bus no. 2 or 13. The largest Jewish synagogue is at Krystalgade 12 (tel. 33-12-88-68). The Muslim Cultural Institute, Vesterbrogade 107 (tel. 31-24-67-86), holds services and acts as a resource center for Copenhagen's Islamic community. The city's "gay church," Metropolitan Community Church, Knabrostræde 3 (tel. 31-83-32-86), has services in Danish on Sunday at 5pm; the minister, Mia Andersen, speaks English.

Shoe Repair There is a shoe-repair shop (tel. 31-91-02-20) in Cityarkaden, near the end of Strøget, at Ostergade 32, as well as a Mister Minit (tel. 33-11-21-08) in the center of Central Station, which is open from 8am to 8pm Monday through Friday, 9am to 6pm on Saturday, and 10am to 6pm on Sunday.

Sundries The grocery store in Cityarkaden, Ostergade 32, can supply miscellaneous items such as towels, socks, underwear, wine, candles, and snacks. Dælls Varehus department store, Nørregade 12 (tel. 31-12-78-25), has anything else you might need. The best of the generic souvenir shops is Kobenhavn Souvenir, Frederiksberggade 28 (Strøget).

Tax Denmark's 22% Value-Added Tax is called MOMS (pronounced "mumps"), and is usually included in the prices listed in hotel tariffs and restaurant menus. Many stores offer tourists the opportunity to reclaim sales tax on purchases over 600 Kr ($94.65). See "Savvy Shopping," below, for details.

Taxis See "Orientation and Getting Around," above.

Telephone The most important thing to note is that in Denmark *you must always dial the area code (31, 32, 33, etc.) before the number,* even when calling from next door.

To make **local telephone calls** costs a minimum of 50 øre (8¢) for about 2½ minutes. Deposit either two 25-øre coins, or splurge on a whole krone; a tone will sound when you have to add more coins. On older phones, deposit coins before dialing; although unused coins are not returned even if you reach a busy signal, they are credited toward another call. On newer phones—recognizable by their yellow front plate—wait for the answering party to pick up before inserting money. Local directory assistance is 0033. It costs five times as much to make a local call from a hotel room as it does from a pay phone, which you will usually find in the hotel lobby. The bad news about pay phones is that you don't always get your coin back when there's no answer.

As for **international calls,** it costs about 12 Kr ($1.90) per minute to call the United States and Canada and about 5 Kr (80¢) to call Europe. The easiest way to call North America is via AT&T's "USA Direct" service. If you have an AT&T Calling

Card, or call collect, you can reach an American operator from any phone by dialing 08001-0010. Deposit 50 øre before dialing. Alternatively, you can make long-distance calls from the Central Station's TeleCom Center (tel. 33-14-20-00), located inside the station; it's open Monday through Friday from 8am to 10pm and on Saturday, Sunday, and holidays from 9am to 9pm. A second TeleCom Center, a couple of blocks from Strøget at Købmagergade 37, is open Monday through Friday from 8am to 10pm; it has telephone directories from many countries in Europe, which can be helpful if you plan to do more traveling abroad.

Time   There is a six-hour time difference between Denmark and the east coast of the United States (eastern standard time). Daylight saving time is in effect in Denmark from the end of March until the end of September.

Tipping   It's usually not necessary. A 15% service charge is automatically added to most restaurant bills. If service has been extraordinary, you might want to round up the bill.

Useful Telephone Numbers   AIDS Information (tel. 33-91-11-19); **Alcoholics Anonymous** (tel. 31-81-81-92); **Lost Credit Cards,** American Express (tel. 80-01-00-21), and Access, Eurocard, MasterCard, and VISA (tel. 44-89-25-00).

4. BUDGET ACCOMMODATIONS

By now, Copenhagen is used to its annual invasion of tourists. It's nice to know that there are enough budget accommodations to house everyone. As with most other European cities, Copenhagen offers several accommodation alternatives, the most economical of which is probably renting a room in a private home.

Room Service (Værelseanvisning), beside Tivoli's main entrance, at Bernstorffsgade 1 (tel. 33-12-28-80; fax 33-12-97-23), specializes in booking private rooms, as well as same-day discounted hotel rooms. The office rents up to 160 private rooms, most of which are 10–15 minutes by bus or S-tog from the city center, with rates rarely topping 150 Kr ($23.65) per person, not including breakfast. Room Service also works with some of the best hotels in the city, selling same-day space that would otherwise remain empty. There is a 13-Kr ($2.05) per-person booking fee and a small deposit required at time of booking. Hotels (not private homes) may be booked in advance by writing to **Hotelbooking København,** Hovedbanegården, DK-1570 København V. It's open May through August, daily from 9am to midnight; in September, daily from 9am to 10pm; in April and October, Monday through Saturday from 9am to 5pm; and November through March, Monday through Friday from 9am to 5pm and on Saturday from 9am to noon.

DOUBLES FOR LESS THAN 300 KR ($47.30) IN PRIVATE HOMES

Use-It, in Huset, Rådhusstræde 13 (tel. 33-15-65-18), the alternative youth information office, rents about 70 private rooms for the lowest rates in town. Best of all, there's no commission charge. Moreover, private rooms listed here have proved to be every bit as suitable as the Central Station's more costly private accommodations. Rooms cost about 125 Kr ($19.70) for a single, 200 Kr ($36.55) for a double. The Use-It office also has information about apartment shares, a good possibility if you plan to stay in Copenhagen for a month or longer. You could stay about 10 minutes from downtown for about 1,800 Kr ($283.90) a month; that works out to less than $10 a day. From

June 15 to September 14 the office is open daily from 9am to 7pm; the rest of the year, Monday through Friday only from 10am to 4pm.

Last but not least, you can contract a private room directly. Some of the best are listed below. Remember that each of these homes has only a handful of rooms available, so always call ahead to avoid disappointment.

IN THE CENTER

Staying in a room in a private home has several advantages: low cost; a more intimate environment than a hotel, but with privacy; and the opportunity to get to know a Danish host. All the hosts listed below are English-speaking and well traveled. There is also a strong network among hosts, and if one is booked, she will be able to direct you to another. Out of courtesy to hosts, always let them know when you plan to arrive so that you don't tie up their whole day or evening. (And be understanding if they cannot spend as much time socializing with you as you'd like.) You'll be more than impressed with the lodging they provide and their sophistication as hosts.

MS. GITTE KONGSTAD, Skt. Annægade 1b (4th Floor), Christianshavn, 1416 København K. Tel. 31-57-24-66. Fax 31-57-24-86. 3 rms. TV **Bus:** 2 or 8 from City Hall; get off one stop after Knippels Bridge.

$ Rates: 210 Kr ($33.10) single; 275 Kr ($43.40) double. Additional person 100 Kr ($15.80) extra. Breakfast with eggs 40 Kr ($6.30) extra, 25 Kr ($3.95) for kids.

Beam ceilings, hardwood floors, and an abundance of bookshelves, flowers, and floral curtains and wallpaper make this place look like a spread from *Country Living*, yet it's a home above all else, and you'll feel welcome from the moment you arrive. The building itself, originally erected as an East India Trading Company warehouse in 1782, has been converted into condominium flats. Although the apartment is a fourth-floor walk-up, the rooms, beautifully furnished in lush floral fabrics, have a private entrance, cable TV, makeup mirror, and coffee- and cocoa-making facilities. Guests particularly like chatting over breakfast. Charming, helpful, and quite knowledgeable about the city, Gitte welcomes children (her family room has a sleeping nook for kids), and provides free coffee and tea for her guests. The apartment is just 10 minutes from Copenhagen's busy shopping streets.

MS. MARGRETHE KAAE CHRISTENSEN, Amaliegade 26 (3rd Floor), 1256 København K. Tel. 33-13-68-61. 2 rms. **Bus:** 1 or 6 from Central Station to Amalienborg Palace.

$ Rates: 225 Kr ($35.50) single; 300 Kr ($47.30) double. A breakfast of bread, bacon, and eggs 40 Kr ($6.30) extra.

This is about as close as most of us will get to living at the royal Amalienborg Palace—just 50 yards away and directly across from the Italian Embassy. You'll be greeted by the exceedingly friendly and lively Ms. Christensen, whose elegant accommodations include a bath with tub and shower and use of the kitchen. One room has a sink and double bed; the other, two single beds and a private entrance. Both have coffee-, tea-, and soup-making facilities.

MS. TESSIE MEILING, Sølvgade 34b, 1307 København. Tel. 33-15-35-76 at home, 33-15-28-42 at work. 1 rm. **Bus:** 10 from Central Station to Kronprinsessegade, near the State Museum of Art.

$ Rates: Daily, 110 Kr ($17.35) single; 165 Kr ($26) double. Weekly, 550 Kr ($86.75) single; 770 Kr ($121.45) double.

Kindergarten teacher Tessie Meiling offers one of the city's best values for a stay of a week or more. The garret apartment, a three-story walk-up in a house built in 1845, has a country kitchen with board floors. Wooden cabinets, chests, and tables—and Tessie's artistic hand—are everywhere. Unfortunately there is only one comfortable room for rent here, furnished with two single beds, color TV, cassette player, and good reading lamp. The rates do not include breakfast, but you are more than welcome to use the kitchen. The shower is in the kitchen, but you have privacy when you use it. The building is near the State Museum of Art and

FROMMER'S SMART TRAVELER: HOTELS

VALUE-CONSCIOUS TRAVELERS SHOULD
TAKE ADVANTAGE OF THE FOLLOWING:

1. Private homes, recommended if you're on a tight budget.
2. Hotels that are immediately southwest of Central Station, along Colbjørnsensgade and Helgolandsgade (off Istedgade). Although many are above our price range, some offer excellent values. The area has several pornographic bookstores and video shops, but it is safe.
3. Hotel rooms without a private bath; you usually get a sink. Be sure the bath is nearby and well maintained.

Botanical Garden, and across the street from Rosenborg Palace and Garden; the entrance is at the back of a courtyard.

MS. TURID ARONSON, Brolæggerstræde 13, 1211 København K. Tel. 33-14-31-46. 3 rms. **Bus:** 6 from Central Station to the canal.

$ Rates: 160 Kr ($25.25) single; 270 Kr ($42.60) double; 360 Kr ($56.80) triple. Breakfast 30 Kr ($4.75) extra.

You will find more upscale lodging in the other private homes listed here, but none more convenient, only one block from Strøget. Two of the three rooms are adjacent to the bathroom, which is tiled with a shower. The rooms are comfortable, spacious, and stocked with brochures of local attractions; and guests enjoy sitting around the kitchen table. Brolæggerstræde is a short street, only two blocks long, and around the corner from Huset.

IN FREDERIKSBERG

Bus no. 1, which stops at most of the homes listed below, is particularly convenient because it also stops at many of Copenhagen's most popular tourist attractions.

GURLI AND VIGGO HANNIBAL, Folkets Allé 17, 2000 Frederiksberg. Tel. 31-86-13-10. 2 rms. **S-tog:** Line C to Peter Bangsvej (toward Ballerup C—not Cx). **Bus:** 1 from Town Hall or Central Station.

$ Rates: 250 Kr ($39.45) per room. Extra bed 80 Kr ($12.60). Single travelers may get a discount during the off-season. Breakfast 35 Kr ($6.15) per person extra.

This helpful couple offers a memorable stay in their modern home. Rooms have blond-wood furniture and lots of closet space. Room 12 features a private bath and a small anteroom with a hotplate for boiling water, but slightly smaller Room 11 is equally inviting, with a cute full bath downstairs. The bath has a tub and shower, and the pipe-and-cork stairway and framed puzzles in the rooms are particularly unusual. Guests are welcome to borrow from the home's small English-language library. If you call ahead, they may pick you up at the S-tog stop. The Hannibals are smokers, so smokers will feel particularly at home here.

MS. BETTY WULFF, Jyllandsvej 24, 2000 Frederiksberg. Tel. 31-86-29-84. 3 rms. TV **Bus:** 1 from Central Station toward Frederiksberg to P. G. Ramms Allé.

$ Rates: 240 Kr ($37.85) double.

★ The wood ceilings and walls make the rooms particularly cozy. Beds are fitted with Swedish health mattresses, and two of the rooms are linked together, making them ideal for families. Betty, a scientist with the World Health Organization who has worked at the Scripps Institute in La Jolla, California, serves free coffee and tea in the morning; you can buy pastries down the street. You're welcome to store cold food. If the house is full, ask about a room in her house (built in 1912, now renovated) off Vesterbrogade, near Frederiksberg Park at Jacobys Allé 23 (tel. 31-86-29-84 or 31-31-32-10); the six double rooms have TV (some have a private balcony), and guests may make breakfast in the kitchen and use the garden; prices range from 200 Kr to 300 Kr ($31.55 to $47.30) double.

MS. ELSE SKOVBORG, Jyllandsvej 29, 2000 Frederiksberg. Tel. 31-46-25-72. 1 rm. **Bus:** 1 from Central Station toward Frederiksberg to P. C. Ramms Allé; then walk three blocks.

$ Rates: 300 Kr ($47.30) single or double.

Talkative and friendly, Ms. Skovborg rents a room with a double bed, Danish cabinets, and a collection of English books. Guests are free to sit in the large back garden filled with apple trees. Ms. Skovborg, an artist, and her husband designed the house. There is a tiny bath with shower only for guests.

MS. HANNE LOYE, Ceresvej 1, 1863 Frederiksberg C. Tel. 31-24-30-27. 3 rms. **Bus:** 1 from Central Station; get off seven stops later in front of the Frederiksberg City Hall.

$ Rates: 310 Kr ($48.90) double. Extra bed 155 Kr ($24.45).

Antique furniture punctuates the pretty rooms on the second floor of this 60-year-old home. Ms. Loye, an actress, does not offer breakfast, but you'll find many stores nearby, including restaurants, bakeries, and a supermarket. Rooms are supplied with plates, cups, silverware, and glasses. You can luxuriate in the large tub and read one of the books in English that are scattered about. Two self-service laundries are within walking distance, and the house is only three blocks from the bus stop. Call ahead.

NILS AND ANNETTE HAUGBØLLE, Hoffmeyersvej 33, 2000 Frederiksberg. Tel. 31-74-87-87. 4 rms. **S-tog:** Line C to Peter Bangsvej, five stops from Central Station.

$ Rates: 100–150 Kr ($15.80–$23.65) single; 240 Kr ($37.85) double. **Open:** June to mid-Sept.

Rooms in this charming, modern two-story home are attractive, and one even has a TV and a balcony. The owners, a doctor and nutritionist, live downstairs with their three children, away from the second-floor rented rooms. Check out their handy homemade reference file for tourists, complete with maps and brochures. The wood-and-tile bath has a tub and shower. Complimentary tea or coffee is available, and two bakeries and a self-service laundry are nearby. The Haugbølles rent rooms June through mid-September only, and prefer advance reservations.

NORTH OF THE CENTER [NEAR THE BEACH]

MS. DAPHNE PALADINI, Dyrehavevej 20, 2930 Klampenborg. Tel. 31-64-07-44. 5 rms (none with bath). **S-Tog:** Klampenborg.

$ Rates: 160 Kr ($25.25) per person. Breakfast 45 Kr ($7.10) extra. **Open:** Apr–Dec.

Congenial Ms. Paladini, who is fluent in seven languages (she taught the queen Spanish), rents out three large rooms and two singles. The two double rooms downstairs have a separate entrance and southern exposure. One of the two full baths features a tub and is the size of a studio apartment. Guests have access to a kitchen and barbecue, and the beach is a 5-minute walk away. The train ride to Klampenborg takes 20 minutes; to get to the house, another 3. Cross the street that fronts the station, then follow Dyrehavevej (to your left) and look for the white gate and white house set back from the street. Rooms are available April through December only.

PETER AND LILLIAN PRETZSCH, Christiansvej 36, DK 2920 Charlottenlund. Tel. 31-63-51-48. 4 rms. **S-tog:** Charlottenlund, about a 10-minute walk from the house.

$ Rates: 155 Kr ($24.45) single; 270 Kr ($42.60) double. Extra bed 90 Kr ($14.20). Full breakfast 40 Kr ($6.30) extra; a modified breakfast costs less.

Two double and two single rooms occupy the entire second floor of this pretty, quiet home, which is located near two parks. The bath has a separate tub and shower, and there are two toilets. Guests enjoy the comfortable living room, pretty breakfast room, and large garden out back. The beach is a 25-minute walk away. Besides being a gracious host, Peter Pretzsch is a champion javelin thrower, undefeated in Denmark for 17 years. If booking far in advance, send a deposit check in kroner for one night's lodging. The train ride out takes 15 minutes.

HOTEL DOUBLES FOR LESS THAN 312 KR [$49.20]

HOTEL KFUM SOLDATERHJEM, Gothersgade 115, København K. Tel. 33-15-40-44. Fax 33-15-44-74. 10 rms (none with bath). **S-tog:** Nørreport.
$ Rates: 185 Kr ($29.20) single; 305 Kr ($48.10) double. No credit cards.

⭐ Although it was originally intended for soldiers, KFUM Soldaterhjem has been taken over by businesspeople and budget travelers searching for the best value in town. Rooms (eight singles and two doubles) here are devoid of decoration, but are spic-and-span clean. The reception, on the second floor, doubles as a do-it-yourself piano and TV lounge and snack bar (serving short-order meals for less than $5). Rooms are on the fifth floor, a hearty climb. Rosenborg Palace is across the street from the hotel, and the clean-cut young men of the Royal Guard hang out in the lounge. Reception hours are 8:30am to 11pm Monday through Friday and 3 to 11pm on Saturday, Sunday, and holidays; enter the door marked KFUM SOLDATERHJEM. The hotel and café are run by the friendly, competent husband-and-wife team, Preben Nielsen and Grethe Thomasen. This is the only YMCA hotel in Denmark; families are welcome.

HOTEL 9 SMÅ HJEM, Classensgade 40, DK-2100 København Ø. Tel. 31-26-16-47. Fax 35-43-17-84. 60 rms (30 with bath). TV **Bus:** 40 from Central Station to Classensgade; then walk one block.
$ Rates (including VAT): Without breakfast or private bath daily, 200 Kr ($31.55) single, 312 Kr ($49.20) double; weekly, 1,106 Kr ($174.45) single, 1,876 Kr ($295.90) double. Including breakfast and private bath daily, 298 Kr ($47) single, 420 Kr ($66.25) double; weekly, 1,624 Kr ($256.15) single, 2,198 Kr ($346.70) double. Apartments with kitchen included also available. ACCESS, DC, EURO, MC, V.

⭐ Clean, attractive, spacious rooms make this hotel (named "9 Small Homes") the best value in town, especially since most rates include breakfast, summer rates are low, and there's a kitchen on each floor for guests' use. Bathrooms have showers, not tubs. Contemporary furniture, stately wall maps and prints, modern conveniences like TVs and direct-dial phones, friendly management, and a good neighborhood bakery across the street make this an unbelievable find. What's the catch? The reception hours are limited to weekdays from 8am to 5:30pm, and chamber service is available at an additional cost. There is no sign marking the building (look for the big "40" above the entry); the reception is on the second floor. Reserve three months ahead in summer.

HOTEL DOUBLES FOR LESS THAN 435 KR [$76.30]

HOTEL SANKT JØRGEN, Julius Thomsensgade 22, DK-1632 København V. Tel. 35-37-15-11. 20 rms (none with bath). **Bus:** 2 from Town Hall Square, or 13 from Central Station (just two stops away).
$ Rates (including breakfast): 350 Kr ($52.20) single; 450 Kr ($71) double. Extra bed 125 Kr ($19.70).

This simple but pleasant pension-style hotel represents another top value. The public hallways have old-fashioned lamps, mirrors, and chairs, while the large, comfortable rooms feature big windows and sinks. The shared baths are squeaky clean. Friendly owner/manager Brigitte Poulenard serves breakfast herself. Take the elevator to the third-floor reception. The hotel is a 10-minute walk from Town Hall.

SØFOLKENES MINDEHOTEL, Peder Skrams Gade 19, 1054 København

K. Tel. 33-13-48-82. 70 rms (none with bath). **Bus:** 27, 28, or 40 from Central Station to Havnegade.

$ Rates (including breakfast): 225 Kr ($35.50) single; 390 Kr ($61.50) double; 550 Kr ($86.75) triple; 660 Kr ($104.10) quad. AE, EURO, MC, V.

This hotel for Danish sailors and international travelers boasts one of the best locations in the city, just two blocks from Nyhavn and the Royal Theater and close to Strøget. Rooms are modest but comfortable, with good reading light; each has a sink, and by 1993 all should have a fresh coat of paint, and some may even have private bath. There is a TV room and a breakfast room. The 42 single rooms (at reasonable rates) make this a particularly good choice for solo travelers; there are also 17 doubles and 11 family rooms.

HOTEL DOUBLES FOR LESS THAN 475 KR [$74.90]

NEAR CENTRAL STATION

The hotels near Central Station are reasonably priced by Copenhagen standards; offer clean, comfortable lodging with breakfast; and are well situated within walking distance of the city's major attractions, including Tivoli, Strøget, and palaces and museums, as well as the Tourist Office and the Scala Center. The area attracts transients, but don't let that put you off. (*Note:* For less than 500 Kr, don't expect a private bath.)

SAGA HOTEL, Colbjørnsensgade 20, DK-1625 København V. Tel. 31-24-49-44. Fax 31-24-60-33. 77 rms (13 with bath). TEL **Directions:** One block from Central Station.

$ Rates (including breakfast): 275–380 Kr ($43.40–$59.95) single without bath, 420–580 Kr ($66.25–$91.50) single with bath; 400–510 Kr ($63.10–$80.45) double without bath, 630–800 Kr ($99.35–$126.20) double with bath; 200 Kr ($31.55) per person triple or quad. ACCESS, AE, DC, EURO, MC, V.

This perennial standby has long welcomed Frommer's readers with comfortable rooms (6 singles, 53 doubles, 9 triples, 9 quads), a good breakfast, and a 5% discount. Rooms with full bath also have cable TV. The owners/managers, Susanne and Søren Kaas (sister and brother) and Boye Birk, are young and extremely knowledgeable about Copenhagen and ways to save money here, and they are accommodating as can be. The hotel, decorated in soft colors throughout, has a pleasant breakfast/dining room, where it serves a filling Danish supper Monday through Wednesday for 45 Kr ($7.10); it also has a café and bar, and sells souvenirs as well as amber and silver jewelry from Poland. The Saga attracts a congenial clientele of all ages and nationalities.

IN VESTERBRO

HOTEL CAPRIOLE, Frederiksberg Allé 7, 1621 København V. Tel. 31-21-64-64. Fax 33-25-64-60. 25 rms (all with bath). TV TEL. **Bus:** 27 or 28 from Central Station (just two or three stops); walk if your luggage is light.

$ Rates (including breakfast): 365 Kr ($57.60) single; 475 Kr ($74.90) double.

This pretty four-story building adorned with faux classical columns is a 15-minute walk from Central Station; if you're tired or loaded down, the bus stops half a block away. All the rooms were renovated in 1992, so that each now has a full bath with shower, but the place retains its old-fashioned charm.

IN FREDERIKSBURG

CAB-INN, Danasvej 32-34, 1910 Frederiksberg C. Tel. 31-21-04-00. Fax

31-21-74-09. 86 rms (all with bath). A/C TEL TV **S-tog:** Vesterport; the hotel is a five-minute walk away. **Bus:** 29; it stops 10 yards away.

$ Rates: 375 Kr ($59.15) single; 450 Kr ($71) double; 600 Kr ($94.65) family room for up to four people. Breakfast 30 Kr ($4.75) extra. ACCESS, DC, EURO, MC, V. **Parking:** 30 Kr ($4.75).

Small and tidy, its tiny high-tech rooms, accessible by magnetic cards, are reminiscent of cabins on trains or ships, with everything built in. The toilet-and-shower combo is extremely compact. If claustrophobia isn't a problem, you can save money by staying here, where the motto is "Sleep cheap in luxury." The hotel has a lobby café open 24 hours for guests and a service counter selling newspapers, toiletries, and snacks, and renting videos. Complimentary coffee- and tea-making facilities are in the rooms. Rooms for disabled travelers are available, and a dance/aerobics studio and solarium are on the premises. Town Hall Square is a 15-minute walk away.

HOTEL DOUBLES FOR LESS THAN 575 KR [$88.45]

BY NØRREPORT

IBSENS HOTEL, Vendersgade 25, DK-1363 København K. Tel. 33-13-19-13. Fax 33-13-19-16. 49 rms (6 with bath). TV TEL **S-tog:** Nørreport.

$ Rates (including breakfast): 420 Kr ($66.25) single without bath; 525 Kr ($82.80) double without bath, 630 Kr ($99.35) double with shower only, 840–990 Kr ($132.50–$156.15) double with shower and toilet. ACCESS, AE, DC, EURO, MC, V.

Managed by three women—Sine Manniche, Anni Kjær, and Helle Pedersen—Ibsens is a good choice because of its location. Huge antique wooden dressers and decorative cabinets are liberally dispersed throughout. Breakfast—an all-you-can-eat affair—is served in an eclectically decorated dining room. Honeymooners like Room 217. The reception area is on the second floor, and there is no elevator. Ørsteds Park and the Botanical Garden are nearby, and downtown is a 10-minute walk away.

NEAR CENTRAL STATION

NEBO MISSIONSHOTELLET, Istedgade 6, 1650 København V. Tel. 31-21-12-17. Fax 31-23-47-74. 97 rms (about half with bath). TEL

$ Rates (including breakfast): May to mid-Sept, 360 Kr ($56.80) single without bath, 530 Kr ($83.60) single with bath; 560 Kr ($88.30) double without bath, 820 Kr ($129.35) double with bath. Mid-Sept to Apr, prices fall 20%–30%. ACCESS, AE, DC, EURO, MC, V.

The Nebo offers comfortable budget rooms (43 singles and 54 doubles) with clock radios, sinks, and phones. This is tops of the three hotels in the area owned by the Danish Church, and is capably run by a friendly staff. A few rooms are without TVs, but guests are free to use the one in the pretty lobby lounge. If you get a courtyard room, you can enjoy the relaxing sounds of the gurgling fountain outside. Baths, by the way, have shower only. Breakfast is a traditional all-you-can-eat buffet served in a pretty room adjacent to a garden, where you can eat outside in summer. The Nebo is half a block from Central Station.

SUPER-BUDGET CHOICES

HOSTELS

Copenhagen has three International Youth Hostel Federation (IYHF) hostels, open to visitors of all ages. Unfortunately, they are not particularly well located, but good transportation links and good rates counter this setback. Rates differ slightly from one hostel to the next, and preferential prices are given to IYHF cardholders. Sleeping bags are not permitted on the hostels' beds; you must supply your own sheet or rent one from the reception for about 30 Kr ($4.75). IYHF cards can be purchased at any hostel for about 115 Kr ($18.15). In summer, reserve a bed in advance, or you may have to go as far as Roskilde (a half-hour train ride away) to find a hostel that can accommodate you. Throughout Denmark, a three-day-maximum hostel stay is usually imposed in summer.

BELLAHØJ HOSTEL, Herbergvejen 8, 2700 København. Tel. 31-28-97-15. 295 beds. **Bus:** 2 from City Hall Square; from the bus stop, walk to the corner, turn right, and follow Fuglesangs Allé to the hostel.
$ **Rates:** 55 Kr ($8.70) per person with the IYHF card, 75 Kr ($11.80) without the IYHF card. Breakfast 35 Kr ($5.50) extra; dinner, 55 Kr ($8.70). **Closed:** Nov 20–Dec 20.

Located in a residential area northwest of the city center and across from a park, the Bellahøj has a large, pleasant lobby lounge, laundry facilities, a TV room, table-tennis room, vending machine, four showers for men and women on each floor, and lockers. There's no kitchen. The hostel is open 24 hours but rooms are off-limits from 10am to noon. The 30 rooms (a little on the dingy side) contain 4–14 beds each. Families pay 5 Kr (80¢) per person extra to have their own room. Allow 20–30 minutes' arrival time by bus from downtown Copenhagen.

COPENHAGEN HOSTEL, Vejlands Allé 200, 2300 København S. Tel. 32-52-29-08. Fax 32-52-27-08. 528 beds. **Bus:** 46 from Central Station from 6am to 6pm only; other times, 16 to Mozarts Plads and change to no. 37.
$ **Rates:** 60 Kr ($9.45) per person with the IYHF card, 83 Kr ($13.10) without the IYHF card. Breakfast 36 Kr ($5.70) extra; dinner, 40 or 57 Kr ($6.30 or $9). **Closed:** Dec 20–Jan 2.

Copenhagen's newest hostel, 12 years old, has no curfew, but its location, in the middle of a park 2½ miles south of the city center, can make getting home after midnight tedious. In addition to 60 double and 80 five-bed rooms, there are laundry and cooking facilities, a TV room, kiosk, and table-tennis tables. Check-in is from 1pm to late evening; try to book in advance.

LYNGBY HOSTEL, Radvad 1, 2800 Lyngby. Tel. 42-80-30-74. 94 rms.
S-tog: Lyngby; then change to bus no. 182 or 183 toward Hjortekær.
$ **Rates:** 54 Kr ($8.50) per person with the IYHF card, 74 Kr ($12.30) without the IYHF card. Families 5 Kr (80¢) per person extra. Breakfast 40 Kr ($6.30) extra; dinner, 62 Kr ($9.80). **Closed:** Dec 23–Jan 2.

The smallest of Copenhagen's hostels has fewer than 100 beds in four dorms and 14 family rooms. Advance reservations are necessary from September through mid-May. Check-in is between 9:30am and noon, and 4 to 9pm.

OTHER YOUTH CHOICES

Copenhagen has three "unofficial" youth hostels that are good picks for young Eurailers and hearty others. One, also a hotel, is open year round.

COPENHAGEN SLEEP-IN, Per Henrik Lings Allé 6, 2100 København Ø. Tel. 31-26-50-59. 776 beds. **S-tog:** Nørdhavn. **Bus:** 1, 6, or 14 to Idrætsparken.
$ **Rates** (including breakfast): 80 Kr ($13.20) per person. **Open:** Late June to Aug.

Established by the government to alleviate tight tourist housing, the Copenhagen Sleep-in offers one of the cheapest places to sleep in the city. The four-bed rooms are only open in summer, and close during the day from noon to 4pm. The location, in Fælled Park, is not as inconvenient as the IYHF hostels, and the price includes breakfast, hot showers, and a guarded luggage-storage room. There are no kitchen facilities, and sleeping bags are required. No curfew.

JØRGENSEN HOTEL, Rømersgade 11, 1362 København K. Tel. 33-13-81-86. Fax 33-15-51-05. 22 rms (15 with bath). **S-tog:** Nørreport.

$ Rates (including breakfast): Dorm rooms, 90 Kr ($15.45) per person (cash only). Family rooms, 125 Kr ($19.70) per person; sheets 30 Kr ($4.75) extra. Hotel rooms, 350 Kr ($55.20) single without bath; 450 Kr ($71) single with bath; 450 Kr ($71) double without bath, 550 Kr ($86.75) double with bath. MC, V.

A block from pretty Ørsteds Park, this hotel is particularly popular with youth-hostel devotees in summer and school groups off-season. The dorm rooms have four to nine beds, lockers, and usually a refrigerator. The hotel rooms are basic, with a sink and refrigerator but little decoration, and if you choose to stay in one, those without private bath offer best value for the money. The shared baths, however, could use a little more attention. The hotel's café serves dinner and often features piano music. A self-service laundry is down the street, and Strøget just 10 blocks away via Købmagergade. The hotel entrance is on the corner.

VESTERBRO UNGDOMSGARD (City Hostel), Absalonsgade 8, 1658 København V. Tel. 31-31-20-70. 200 beds. **Directions:** From Central Station, walk nine blocks along Istedgade to Absalonsgade or take bus no. 6.

$ Rates (including use of lockers and showers): 85 Kr ($13.40) per person. Breakfast 15 Kr ($2.35) extra. **Open:** Early May to Aug.

Of Copenhagen's super-budget choices, this private hostel boasts the best location, within walking distance of Central Station. But this also makes it the most expensive of the lot. There are 5–10 beds in most rooms, plus a 60-bed dorm.

CAMPING

As always, camping is the cheapest accommodations option, though in Copenhagen it's only practical during the summer. Sites charge an average of 40 Kr ($6.30) per night. You'll also need a camping pass, which is issued by any camp manager, is good for a year, and costs about 30 Kr ($4.75) per person or 50 Kr ($7.90) per family. A full list of legal spots is available from the tourist board, and **Bellahøj Camping,** Hvidkildevej, 2400 København NV (tel. 31-10-11-50), about three miles from the city center, is the closest and cheapest campground. It's open June through August, daily from 7am to 10pm. Take bus no. 2 or 8 from Town Hall Square to the "Camping" stop. (And it's nice to know that the Bellahøj hostel is nearby, in case of serious rain or a sudden cold snap.)

FARM & COUNTRY HOLIDAYS

You can set up a farm or country holiday in Denmark, in which you either stay with a family and share breakfast only or breakfast and supper with them, or rent a separate cottage on their property and do your own cooking. Rates are quite reasonable, starting at 150 Kr ($26.30) per person for a room with breakfast included; a house for four to six people for a week starts at 1,600 Kr ($280.70) in summer. For more information, contact the Danish Tourist Board.

LONG-TERM STAYS

If you plan on staying in Copenhagen for some time, visit the **Use-It** office in Huset (see "Information" in "Orientation and Getting Around," above). They can help you with low-cost accommodations in either a student hall or a private apartment.

WORTH THE EXTRA BUCKS

EXCELSIOR, Colbjørnsensgade 4, 1652 København. Tel. 31-24-50-85. Fax 31-24-50-87. 100 rms (89 with bath). MINIBAR TV TEL

$ Rates (including breakfast): 375 Kr ($59.15) single without bath, 650–770 Kr ($102.50–$121.45) single with bath; 575 Kr ($90.70) double without bath, 770–865 Kr ($121.45–$136.45) double with bath. ACCESS, AE, DC, EURO, MC, V.

Two blocks from Central Station, this place wins as the most fun for kids, with bright colors throughout, a patio garden with swing and deck chairs, and a play area complete with Lego blocks in the lobby. Kids also love the theme rooms, with decor corresponding to the name on the door; favorites include Parrot, Rainbow, and Pyramid. Each room has a safe in it; some baths have tubs. The newer section, which opened in 1991, has 30 modern double rooms and 10 singles, all with twin beds and showers and a big patio. The hotel also offers laundry service.

JOSTY, Pile Allé 14, 2000 Frederiksberg. Tel. 31-86-90-90. 5 rms (all with bath), 2 suites. **Bus:** 6, 28, or 41.

$ Rates (including breakfast): 450 Kr ($71) single; 600 Kr ($94.65) double or suite. ACCESS, DC, EURO, MC, V.

A country inn (1813) set in Frederiksberg Garden, a 10-minute bus ride from downtown Copenhagen, it has five double rooms and two large suites, all furnished in old-fashioned decor and overlooking the garden. It's perfect for early-to-bedders who relish peace and quiet; the doors close at midnight. The restaurant on the premises serves Danish food for lunch and dinner.

SELANDIA HOTEL, Helgolandsgade 12, 1653 København V. Tel. and fax 31-31-46-10. 90 rms (56 with bath). TEL TV

$ Rates (including breakfast): 390 Kr ($61.50) single without bath, 550–650 Kr ($86.75–$102.50) single with bath; 540 Kr ($85.20) double without bath, 850 Kr ($134.05) double with bath. Extra bed 200 Kr ($31.55). Children 4–12 pay half price.

This inviting small hotel two blocks from Central Station has cheerful yellow hallways with colorful prints and a pleasant breakfast room. Rooms are comfortable and all have a pants press. The larger Absalon Hotel, across the street, is under the same ownership but caters more to business travelers and groups.

5. BUDGET DINING

Denmark is more famous for its drink than its food, and indeed, the native eateries are easily outnumbered by bars and restaurants with continental cuisine. It follows that many of Copenhagen's best restaurants are of foreign origin. But rather than lament the lack of Danish choices, celebrate the city's terrific culinary diversity and find solace in the fact that many ethnic food places are less expensive than their Danish counterparts.

But by all means sample the Danish fare whenever possible. A typical Danish buffet begins with fish, then meat, cheese, fruit, and dessert, and a new plate is provided for each course. A popular, filling dish called *biksemad* consists of meat, potatoes, and onions. *Grov birkes* are a tasty, nonsweet breakfast roll, and the pastries are rich and wonderful, no matter which you select ("Napoleon's Hat," for one, is delicious).

No matter what you eat, however, you may wish to follow the Danish custom of drinking a cool pilsner beer and a shot of akvavit—a 90-proof potato-based schnapps. You'll have to resign yourself to expecting no free coffee refills; that's the custom here.

Remember that tax and tip are included in the price. You don't have to add anything extra.

LOCAL BUDGET BEST

Smørrebrod, translated literally as "bread and butter," is Denmark's most famous culinary delicacy. These open-face sandwiches come in dozens of varieties, topped

---

Ⓕ **FROMMER'S SMART TRAVELER: RESTAURANTS**

VALUE-CONSCIOUS TRAVELERS SHOULD TAKE ADVANTAGE OF THE FOLLOWING:

1. Small, inconspicuous places off the beaten path.
2. Restaurants clustered around Vesterbrogade, northwest of Central Station.
3. Restaurants around Grabrodretorv, two blocks north of the middle of Strøget.
4. Smörgåsbords and other all-you-can-eat restaurants. Although they're not particularly cheap, they offer terrific values.

---

with everything from a single slice of cheese to mounds of sweet shrimp, and can be found almost everywhere. Even though it takes two or three servings to make a meal, you'll find that smørrebrod play an important part in the budget traveler's diet. Remember that smørrebrod are eaten with a knife and fork, and most of the shops that sell them are only open during the day. Below is a favorite:

TH SØRENSEN, Vesterbrogade 15. Tel. 31-31-17-02.
Cuisine: DANISH. **Bus:** 16.
$ Prices: 20–45 Kr ($3.15–$7.10). No credit cards.
Open: Mon–Fri 8am–8pm, Sat 10am–6pm.
Located on the main street, just west of Central Station, this shop's copious mouth-watering window display will stop you in your tracks. No need to worry about reading the menu—just point, pay, and enjoy! You may also get salad and American-style heros. It's at Helgolandsgade; there's also a branch in the Scala Center (see below) that's open until midnight (tel. 35-15-76-84).

MEALS FOR LESS THAN 45 KR [$7.10]

CAFES & SHORT-ORDER SPOTS

Most cafés offer sandwiches, smørrebrod, and a few hot dishes—enough for a good lunch or light meal.

BANANREPUBLIKKEN, Norrebrogade 13. Tel. 31-39-79-21.
Cuisine: INTERNATIONAL.
$ Prices: Lunch 22–42 Kr ($3.50–$6.60); dinner 60–118 Kr ($9.45–$18.60). No credit cards.
Open: Sun–Wed 11am–2am, Thurs–Sat 11am–4am (lunch 11:30am–4pm; dinner 6–10pm).
Not to be confused with the trendy safari-clothing store, this is a rustic café with a blackboard menu featuring salads, sandwiches, guacamole, and homemade cakes. African, Far Eastern, and Latin American dishes are served at dinner. Live bands perform Latin music and reggae here several nights a week; there's a 40-Kr ($7) cover on Thursday and Saturday; free admission on Tuesday, but the price of beer goes up 4 Kr (70¢).

DEN GRONNE KÆLDER (The Green Cellar), Klareboderne 10. Tel. 33-15-21-81.
Cuisine: VEGETARIAN.
$ Prices: 28–35 Kr ($4.90–$6.15). No credit cards.
Open: Mon–Fri 11am–6:30pm, Sat 11am–2pm.
Small and to the point, with six tables and take-out service, Den Gronne Kælder

serves such main courses as quiche, pizza, and lasagne, with salad. There are half a dozen main-course salads from which to choose, along with soup and fruit or vegetable juices.

KLAPTRÆET, Kultorvet 11. Tel. 33-13-31-48.

Cuisine: LIGHT FARE.
$ Prices: 25–52 Kr ($3.95–$8.20). No credit cards.
Open: Mon–Wed 9am–2am, Thurs 9am–3am, Fri–Sat 10am–3am, Sun 11:30am–midnight.

Downstairs from an alternative movie house, this bohemian café serves cheap breakfasts, lunches, and light meals to students, travelers, and assorted others. Chili con carne, salads, soups, and sandwiches are among the offerings. Old movie posters and newspapers double as wallpaper. Order and pay at the bar; they'll bring your food. Kultorvet is a traffic-free pedestrian square, two blocks southeast of Nørreport Station.

LARSBJØRNSSTRÆDES SALATBAR, Larsbjørnsstræde 7. Tel. 33-32-11-32.

Cuisine: LIGHT FARE/SNACKS.
$ Prices: 26–36 Kr ($4.10–$5.70). No credit cards.
Open: Mon–Fri 10:30am–5:30pm, Sat 11am–2:30pm.

Cheese, humus, roast beef, turkey, chicken, ham, salmon, and tuna are the popular smørrebrod fillings at this cozy café with only half a dozen tables. All are served on French bread. There's also fresh-squeezed orange, apple, and carrot juice, carrot cake (in winter), and all kinds of salads. The eatery is two short blocks north of Frederiksberggade, near the Town Hall side of Strøget.

SABINES CAFETERIA, Teglegardsstræde 4. Tel. 33-12-82-71.

Cuisine: LIGHT FARE/SNACKS.
$ Prices: 20–35 Kr ($3.15–$5.50). No credit cards.
Open: Mon–Fri 7:30am–2am, Sat 9am–2am, Sun noon–2am.

 This small, undecorated place is not a cafeteria at all (though it used to be, when Sabine ran it), but a licensed local café with a mixed crowd that has included Mick Jagger. The morning buffet breakfast special includes toast, honey, cheese, hard- or soft-boiled egg, yogurt, coffee, and juice or milk, and sells for just 35 Kr ($5.50). Daily specials include smoked salmon, paprika chicken, and smoked ham. Copenhageners like to drop in here after a movie; that's a good time for coffee and brandy, which runs 25 Kr ($3.95). Teglegardsstræde runs perpendicular to Nørre Voldgade, just south of Ørsteds Park.

FAST FOOD

KFUM SOLDATERHJEM CAFE, Gothersgade 115 (2nd Floor). Tel. 33-15-40-44.

Cuisine: FAST FOOD/DANISH.
$ Prices: 16–42 Kr ($2.50–$6.60). No credit cards.
Open: Daily 10am–9:30pm for hot food; snacks until 11pm.

A real find for low prices and pleasant, if a bit noisy, surroundings. You can order burgers, chicken, fish, salads, and even Danish hot meals. The dining room is pleasant and casual, the portions are ample, and the crowd is mostly well-scrubbed young men of the Royal Guard.

PIZZA HUSET, Gothersgade 21. Tel. 33-15-35-10.

Cuisine: ITALIAN.
$ Prices: 20–45 Kr ($3.15–$7.10). No credit cards.
Open: Daily 11am–6am.

Because of its late hours this take-out spot is a favorite with weekend night owls. Try the pizza sandwich, an oven-baked combination of ham, salad, and cheese.

SCALA CENTER, Axeltorv 2. Tel. 33-15-12-15.
Cuisine: INTERNATIONAL.
$ Prices: 26–52 Kr ($4–$8).
Open: Daily 7am–1 or 2am (later on weekends).

 Located across from the main entrance to Tivoli, with an entrance on Vesterbrogade, this sparkling center of activity houses a good variety of fast-food stands adjacent to more expensive cafés and international restaurants. Pizza, pasta, smørrebrod, chicken, quiche, hamburgers, and other favorites are all available at moderate prices. Communal tables mean that you can satisfy everyone and still eat together. Scala's ground level features bargain eateries, tops among them Streckess, Shawarma Scala, and a popular gelati counter, Bravissimo. Its third floor is home to more expensive sit-down places. The sculpture in front of Scala, by Mogens Møller, symbolizes the sun and the nine planets of the solar system, placed at their equivalent (in small scale) actual distance from the sun.

SHAWARMA GRILL HOUSE, Frederiksberggade 36. Tel. 33-12-63-23.
Cuisine: MIDDLE EASTERN.
$ Prices: 22–65 Kr ($3.50–$10.25). No credit cards.
Open: Daily 11am–11pm.
You will see a lot of fast-food Middle Eastern places around the city, with almost identical menus and prices. This one has more counter seating than most and is located just off Town Hall Square at the beginning of Strøget.

MEALS FOR LESS THAN 70 KR [$10.75]

ALEXANDER'S ORIGINAL PIZZA HOUSE, Lille Kannikestræde 5. Tel. 33-12-55-36.
Cuisine: PIZZA.
$ Prices: Pizza and salad buffet 58 Kr ($9.15). AE, DC, EURO, MC, V.
Open: Daily noon–midnight.

Only pizza and salad are on the menu here, and Alexander's best deal is the self-service all-you-can-eat buffet. Since most of the pizzas on the menu are offered at the buffet (along with a copious salad bar), only the pickiest eaters should order à la carte. The restaurant's dark, wood interior, complete with an upright piano, old beer barrels, and wagon wheel, is reminiscent of a saloon from America's Old West. Evenings from 6 to 8:30pm get busy, as an eternal line surrounds the serving area. Alexander's has three other locations around the city, each with its own memorable interior and ambience.

AMERICAN PIZZA, Vingårdsstræde 21, at Nikolaj Plads. Tel. 33-12-55-97.
Cuisine: AMERICAN.
$ Prices: All-you-can-eat 51 Kr ($8.05). ACCESS, AE, EURO, MC, V.
Open: Daily noon–11pm.

"This place encourages pig-outs," the vivacious hostess told me on my first visit here. That it does, with a large, fresh salad bar and assorted pizzas that include ham, pepperoni, and ground beef. You can request vegetarian or deep-dish varieties. The decor includes red tablecloths and curtains and a large poster of the Brooklyn Bridge; music by Johnny Mathis or Crystal Gale is likely to be playing in the background.

CAFE WILDER, Wildersgade 56 and Sankt Anne Gade, on Christianshavn. Tel. 31-54-71-83.
Cuisine: LIGHT FARE.
$ Prices: 22–85 Kr ($3.50–$13.40). No credit cards.
Open: Mon–Fri 9am–2am, Sat–Sun noon–2am.
This corner café offers everything from soup and sandwiches to cheese plates to cold

salads including chicken pesto. Hot dishes are served from 6:30 to 9:30pm only. It attracts all ages, many of whom arrive by bike, as well as young parents with a baby carriage in tow. The daily fare is displayed in the counter.

KASHMIR INDIAN RESTAURANT, Nørrebrogade 35. Tel. 35-37-54-71.

Cuisine: INDIAN. **Reservations:** Recommended at dinner. **Bus:** 7 from Town Hall, or 16 from Town Hall or Central Station, to Nørrebrogade in the Nørrebro area of town.

$ Prices: 45–98 Kr ($6.90–$15.10). AE, DC, EURO, MC, V.

Open: Lunch daily 11am–3pm; dinner daily 3–11:30pm.

Outstanding food is served in an authentic Indian environment, sitar music and all. And although owner Mohan Bains boasts that he has served the Queen of Denmark, it's the locals who keep him in business—they come in droves. The lunch special changes daily, but always includes a main course, rice, bread, and salad.

KØBENHAVNERCAFÉEN (Copenhagen Café), Badstuestræde 10. Tel. 33-32-80-81.

Cuisine: DANISH.

$ Prices: Daily special 59 Kr ($10.35) with five items, 89 Kr ($15.60) with seven items; main courses 37–68 Kr ($5.85–$10.70). AE, DC, EURO, MC, V.

Open: Daily 10am–midnight (kitchen open 11:30am–10pm).

This café is only half a block from Strøget, yet seemingly miles from the hustle and modernity outside. The menu comes with an English translation, and you won't leave hungry. The daily special features herring, fried filet of fish, roast pork, and bread; the deluxe version adds roast beef, Danish meatballs, chicken, salad, and cheese. The small café fills up with customers and easy conversation, and it can get smokey. There's free piano music on Sunday in winter; otherwise, guests are free to play whenever the mood strikes.

QUATTRO FONTANE, Guldbergsgade 3. Tel. 31-39-49-41.

Cuisine: ITALIAN. **Bus:** 5 or 16 along Nørrebrogade to Elmergade and walk one block north.

$ Prices: 36–72 Kr ($6.30–$12.65). No credit cards.

Open: Daily 4–midnight.

Despite its decor including hanging wax grapes, chianti bottles, and boot-shaped map, this place is really popular. Mid-priced meat and fish dishes are available, or stick to their well-priced pasta and pizza, both made fresh on the premises. Ask about the daily special. The restaurant is well worth the bus ride from the city center. Reservations are not accepted.

NOSTRADAMUS, Nyhavn 31. Tel. 33-14-52-44.

Cuisine: ITALIAN.

$ Prices: Pizza 53–67 Kr ($8.35–$10.55); meat dishes 67–167 Kr ($10.55–$26.35). AE, EURO, MC, V.

Open: Daily 11am–midnight.

This is a restaurant, steakhouse, and pizzeria rolled into one, and you'll do fine price-wise if you stick to the pasta and pizza dishes. Relaxed and cozy, it features exposed beams and brick walls, two dining levels, a fireplace and a nice view of the canal, and a striking glass facade.

RESTAURANT SHEZAN, Victoriagade 22, at the corner of Istedgade. Tel. 31-24-78-88.

Cuisine: PAKISTANI.

$ Prices: 35–70 Kr ($5.50–$11.05). EURO, MC, V.

Open: Daily 11am–11pm.

One of the cheapest, most popular sit-down restaurants in town, Shezan serves good food that doesn't spare the spices. Specialties include spicy lamb, chicken, beef, and curry dishes. Arched windows and room dividers add to the pleasant interior. If you're walking from the train station, come via Vesterbrogade to avoid the sex-shop strip along Istedgade. The restaurant, which draws primarily a young crowd, is at the corner of Victoriagade and Istedgade, where it has been since 1978; look for the blue-and-white facade.

RESTAURANT SPORVEJEN, Gråbrødre Torv 17. Tel. 33-13-31-01.
   Cuisine: AMERICAN.
$ **Prices:** 31–71 Kr ($4.90–$11.20). No credit cards.
   Open: Daily 11am–midnight.
Located in an authentic old tram car inside a building, complete with poles and straps, and Sporvejen's "tin-can" interior is reminiscent of an American diner. The chef, cooking on a small grill near the front door, dishes your dinner right onto the plate in front of you. Specialties include hamburgers and omelets. It's licensed.

MEALS FOR LESS THAN 90 KR [$13.85]

AXELBORG BODEGA, Axeltorv 1. Tel. 33-11-00-96.
   Cuisine: DANISH.
$ **Prices:** 35–110 Kr ($5.50–$17.35). AE, DC, EURO, MC, V.
   Open: Sun–Thurs 10am–1am, Fri–Sat 10am–2am (the kitchen closes at 9:30pm); lunch special served 11am–5pm.
Considering that the Circus is just across the street, it seems appropriate that this place is loud and boisterous. The tavern's clientele cheer and joke with one another while downing beers the whole time. The Danes use the word *bodega* to refer to a local bar. The menu at this one features ham and eggs and omelets for lunch, and roast beef, fried fish, pork chops, and veal for dinner, which cost about $10 when you order with care.

BISTRO, in Central Station. Tel. 33-14-12-32.
   Cuisine: DANISH.
$ **Prices:** Buffets 56 Kr ($8.85) salad, 70 Kr ($11.05) fish and cheese; daily specials (served all day) 49–60 Kr ($7.70–$9.45); main courses 84–123 Kr ($13.25–$19.40), with complimentary salad buffet (half price for kids under 12 who get the same dish as their parents); cold Danish buffet 125 Kr ($19.70). ACCESS, AE, DC, EURO, MC, V.
   Open: Daily 11:30am–9:30pm.
If you think an outstanding restaurant in a train station is an oxymoron, you're in for a pleasant surprise. At the elegant, airy Bistro, with its columns, arched ceiling, and lights resembling hanging artichokes, choose from several buffets (the restaurant is best known for its cold buffet, priced above budget but worth the splurge). You may also order à la carte. Menu offerings include roast beef or pork, turkey, duck, halibut steamed in white wine, and grilled salmon. On Sunday a special three-course family dinner costs 89 Kr ($14.05) per person.

CAFE LUNA, Skt. Annægade 5, Christianhavn. Tel. 31-54-20-00.
   Cuisine: CONTINENTAL.
$ **Prices:** Appetizers 35–50 Kr ($5.50–$7.90); main courses 50–105 Kr ($7.90–$16.55); three-item smørrebrod 25 Kr ($3.90). EURO, MC, V.
   Open: Lunch daily 10am–3pm; dinner daily 5–10pm.

Cafe Luna excels in tasty food, ample portions, and something travelers rarely get enough of—vegetables. Start with an appetizer of escargots, French onion soup, or octopus, and move on to a main course of chopped steak, turkey, or fish. The sliced turkey breast in wine sauce that I was served at dinner came with whole-grain bread, broccoli, cauliflower, green beans, cherry tomatoes, red-leaf lettuce, and a side dish of potatoes. Lunch offerings include sandwiches, omelets, and salads. The congenial café, a short bus ride or 20-minute walk from Town Hall Square, has half a dozen tables and a funky frieze that adds spice to the decor.

CAFE PETERSBORG, Bredgade 76. Tel. 33-12-50-16.
Cuisine: DANISH.
$ Prices: Open-face sandwiches 18–55 Kr ($4.40–$8.70); hot meals at lunch and dinner 52–120 Kr ($8.20–$18.90); daily specials 65–80 Kr ($10.25–$12.50). AE, DC, MC, V.
Open: Lunch Mon–Fri noon–3pm; dinner Mon–Fri 5–7:45pm.

A congenial place off the beaten track, it has good home-cooking, a lively local crowd, and inviting decor—dark paneling and furniture, exposed beams, three dining areas, and tables trimmed with candles and flowers. Come before or after a visit to the *Little Mermaid*, which is nearby. It's licensed.

EL GRECO, Skindergade 20. Tel. 33-32-93-44.
Cuisine: GREEK. **Reservations:** Recommended Thurs–Sat nights.
$ Prices: All-you-can-eat buffet 59 Kr ($9.30) 11:30am–3pm, 98 Kr ($15.45) from 4pm. EURO, V.
Open: Daily 11am–midnight (last orders at 11pm).

Amid white stucco walls, wood-beamed ceilings, and Mediterranean farmhouse decor, you can enjoy a large "Greek smörgåsbord" with more than 20 hot dishes. Help yourself to meats, fish, chicken, rice, potatoes, and other specially prepared Greek foods, and eat as much as you like. This popular restaurant is well situated; choose a seat upstairs.

GREENS, Grønnegade 12-14. Tel. 33-15-16-90.
Cuisine: VEGETARIAN.
$ Prices: 42–129 Kr ($6.45–$19.85), all-you-can-eat lunch salad buffet 75 Kr ($11.55). AE, EURO, MC, V.
Open: Lunch Mon–Sat 11:30am–5pm; dinner Mon–Sat 5:30–9pm.

This vegetarian restaurant serves up attractive, healthful food in an equally pretty, smoke-free environment. Several different rooms are all united by comfortable furnishings, wood floors, and pretty potted plants. The all-you-can-eat self-service lunch is more filling, and significantly less expensive, than the more formal dinner. And orders to go are even cheaper than eating in.

PASTA BASTA, Valkendorfsgade 22. Tel. 33-11-21-31.
Cuisine: ITALIAN.
$ Prices: 60–200 Kr ($9.45–$31.55); Pasta Basta table 69 Kr ($10.90). ACCESS, DC, EURO, MC, V.
Open: Sun–Wed 11:30am–3am, Thurs–Sat 11:30am–3am.

Except for its name, Pasta Basta has everything going for it: a tastefully decorated, modern interior, large windows overlooking a romantic cobblestone street, and an all-you-can-eat buffet with top-notch food. For reasons unexplained, some diners order a hot pasta dish in addition to the Pasta Basta table. Help yourself to the house wine that's automatically placed on each table. Measuring stripes down the side mean that you only pay for as much as you drink. The restaurant is located near Strøget, behind Holy Ghost Church.

MEALS FOR LESS THAN 110 KR [$19.30]

BARCELONA, Fælledvej 21. Tel. 31-35-76-11.
Cuisine: CONTINENTAL.
$ Prices: Tapas (appetizers) 45 Kr ($7.10); main courses 75–90 Kr ($11.80–$14.20); three-course meal 95 Kr ($15) at lunch, 145 Kr ($22.90) at dinner.
Open: Dinner only, daily 5–11pm.

More affordable for budget travelers at lunchtime, when it's a lively tapas bar, Barcelona, with its board floors and mixed crowd, is a colorful café in the increasingly popular Nørrebro part of town. The dinner menu changes monthly. The restaurant's downtown counterpart is more upscale, catering primarily to a business clientele but with the same outstanding cuisine.

LA ROSE DE TUNIS, Vesterbrogade 120. Tel. 31-24-06-51.
   Cuisine: TUNISIAN/FRENCH. **Reservations:** Recommended on Sat–Sun.
   Bus: 6 from Central Station to the fourth stop.
$ **Prices:** 80–145 Kr ($12.60–$22.90). AE, DC, EURO, MC, V.
   Open: Dinner only, daily 5–10pm.
Uneven whitewashed walls, tile mosaics, hand-woven rugs, and traditional music mimic an upper-class Tunisian home. Owner Kwame Adams directs an excellent kitchen, and although dishes are not cheap, the food is terrific. Try the brik (thin, crisp pancakes stuffed with tuna, chicken, or meat), or the couscous (pastina made of grain flour topped with meats and/or vegetables). This restaurant, with flowers, candles, and white linen napkins and tablecloths, provides an elegant night out.

NYHAVNS FÆRGEKRO, Nyhavn 5. Tel. 33-15-15-88.
   Cuisine: DANISH.
$ **Prices:** Buffet (with 10 choices of herring) 65 Kr ($10.25); main courses 125–135 Kr ($19.70–$21.30); sandwiches 19-53 Kr ($3–$8.35). ACCESS, DC, EURO, V.
   Open: Lunch daily 11:30–4pm; dinner daily 5–11:30pm.
This place is unique for two reasons: First, it serves French champagne by the glass and, second, a decadent, delectable desserts-only buffet featuring such temptations as white-chocolate mousse, profiterole, and a tart of the day. The champagne costs 32 Kr ($5.05) a glass; unlimited visits to the dessert table with its 10 selections, 67 Kr ($10.55). Less indulgent fare for the strong-willed includes 15 different open-face sandwiches and traditional Danish meals. The restaurant itself is striking, with a black-and-white marble floor, spiral stairway from an old streetcar, and lights that serve as "call buttons" for the servers. Friendly service, too.

FOR DESSERT

Just look at all the delicious bakeries around Copenhagen and you'll understand why Denmark's pastries are world famous. Don't ask for a danish, though—just point to the dessert that catches your fancy.

AMAGERTORV TEA ROOM, in the Royal Copenhagen Building, Oster-gade 15 (3rd Floor). Tel. 31-12-44-77.
   Cuisine: DESSERT.
$ **Prices:** 12–30 Kr ($1.90–$4.75).
   Open: Daily 11am–5pm (music 1:30–4:30pm).
This long, elegant room with Venetian chandeliers, large mirrors, and windows punctuated by palms, gazes out at the rooftops of old Copenhagen. To sit in it is to drift back in time a few centuries. The pastries—pies, cakes, eclairs, and almond confections—are beautifully displayed in the center of the room, and served on Royal Copenhagen porcelain, of course. The tea room, which is licensed, provides the perfect setting for sipping wine, sherry, or brandy while listening to strains of "Fly Me to the Moon" or "Bewitched, Bothered, and Bewildered" on the piano. They even serve martinis.

CONDITORI LA GLACE, Skoubogade 3-5. Tel. 33-14-46-46.
   Cuisine: DESSERT.
$ **Prices:** Cakes 8–24 Kr ($1.25–$3.80); coffee or hot chocolate 22 Kr ($3.50). No credit cards.
   Open: Mon–Thurs 8am–5:30pm (last serving at 5pm); Fri 8am–6pm (last serving at 5:30pm), Sat 8:30am–4pm.
Founded in 1870, this dignified café maintains the elegance of a bygone era. Order at the counter and take a seat. When your food is ready, it's brought to your table. Real

dessert lovers should try "Sports Cake," the house specialty, whipped cream–topped caramel cream puffs that have been made every day since November 18, 1891. The café has smoking and no-smoking rooms. Skoubogade is a small street off Strøget.

CONDITORI H. C. ANDERSEN, in Rådhusarkaden, H. C. Andersens Blvd. and Vesterbrogade. Tel. 33-32-80-98.
 Cuisine: DESSERT.
$ **Prices:** 12–18 Kr ($2.10–$3.15).
 Open: Mon–Sat 8am–6pm, Sun 1–5pm.

Everything from the pastries to the ice-cream sundaes to the loaves of homemade bread (10 kinds) looks enticing in this modern, bright spot. There's a large painting of the author. Seating is inside and in the mall—a great spot for people-watching and sipping delicious hot chocolate. Light fare is also served.

PICNIC SUPPLIES

Aldi and Netto are the two most reasonably priced supermarket chains. Other markets such as Irma and Brugsen may have a more extensive selection. A fairly convenient **Netto** supermarket is located at Kampmannsgade 1, near Sankt Jørgens Lake; it's open Monday through Friday from 9am to 7pm and on Saturday from 8am to 2pm. Closer, but more expensive, **Brugsen** is one block from Tivoli on Hammerichsgade.

For gourmet picnic supplies, check out **Meals,** an indoor/outdoor market in a passageway off Strøget, at Østergade 26 (tel. 33-32-62-21). Here you'll find all manner of take-out, from whole meals to pastas, salads, and herrings. There's also a soup-and-sandwich bar and organic veggies. Some items are pricey; others, such as a small quiche for 10 Kr ($1.60) and a large one for 35 Kr ($5.50), reasonable. The smell of fresh dill permeates the shop.

WORTH THE EXTRA BUCKS

ELS, Store Strandstræde 3. Tel. 33-14-13-41.
 Cuisine: DANISH. **Reservations:** Recommended.
$ **Prices:** Quick lunch 101 Kr ($15.95); main course at lunch 132 Kr ($20.80); fixed-price lunch 157 Kr ($24.75) for two courses, 181 Kr ($28.55) for three courses; fixed-price dinner, 192 Kr ($30.30) for two courses, 220 Kr ($34.70) for three courses. AE, DC, EURO, MC, V.
 Open: Lunch daily 11:30am–3pm; dinner daily 5:30pm–1am.

Visually and culinarily memorable, Els is also outstanding for its location (near Kongens Nytorv), atmosphere, and romance. The original decor dates from 1853, with six murals of women depicting the four seasons and the twin muses of dance and music. The fixed-price menu changes daily (the lunchtime smörgåsbord monthly), ensuring the freshest foods available. At dinner, expect such dishes as duck-liver pâté, caviar, crab bisque, pheasant, and filet of sole. The last dinner orders are taken at 10pm.

ORTMANNS HUS, Gothersgade 41. Tel. 33-13-61-14.
 Cuisine: FRENCH/DANISH.
$ **Prices:** Smørrebrod 28–48 Kr ($4.40–$7.60); five-item Danish lunch sampler 100 Kr ($15.80); appetizers 55–70 Kr ($8.70–$11.05); main courses 135–178 Kr ($21.30–$28.10); special three-course meal 235 Kr ($37.05). ACCESS, AE, DC, EURO, MC, V.
 Open: Mon–Fri 11:30am–11:30pm, Sat 11:30am–2:30pm.

Ortmanns Hus is small and impeccably memorable for the food above all, prepared by French chef Thierry Ravasco, and followed closely by the ambience of the 1773 timbered house, the size (only eight tables seating 25 people), the soft lighting, and the unusually friendly service. These folks do everything by hand: They bake their own bread, make their own desserts (including ice cream), roll their own cold cuts (lacing them with cardamon), and even hand-paint the menus. Ortmanns Hus is particularly known for its sweetbreads and good sauces, and for food that is, they stress, "rich and good, not something people would have at home." To accompany it, there are some fine French wines, starting at 160 Kr ($25.25).

6. ATTRACTIONS

SUGGESTED ITINERARIES

In addition to the shopping streets of Strøget and the wonderful walks of Tivoli, Copenhagen's main sights are three royal palaces, two breweries, one *Little Mermaid,* and several marvelous museums.

IF YOU HAVE ONE DAY   Start your morning along Strøget, the world's longest pedestrian street, then explore Kongens Nytorv (King's New Square) and Nyhavn, the old sailors' quarters and one of the most charming parts of the city. After lunch (and this is a terrific area for it), take an imperial tour of Christiansborg Palace, visiting the queen's reception rooms and the ancient palace foundations. The evening is for Tivoli, where you can enjoy everything from old-time carnival fun to concerts featuring the world's top performers.

IF YOU HAVE TWO DAYS   Start your second day at the mighty Gefion Fountain and the demure *Little Mermaid* (if you're early enough, you might miss the tour buses). Then make your way to the queen's residence, Amalienborg Palace, by noon to see the Changing of the Guard. Continue your palace perusal with fairytalelike Rosenborg Palace to see the Crown Jewels and opulent royal interiors. Back in the city center, climb the Round Tower for the best view of Copenhagen, and if you still have time, visit the Ny Carlsberg Glyptotek to see ancient sculptures and French and Danish art of the 19th and early 20th centuries.

IF YOU HAVE THREE DAYS   Make time to visit Denmark's Fight for Freedom Museum on your way to or from the *Little Mermaid.* Then consider a trip to one of the city's breweries, Carlsberg or Tuborg, or to the beautiful Botanical Gardens and the nearby State Museum of Fine Art and the Hirschsprung Collection. If your curiosity is piqued, visit Christiania, Copenhagen's experimental community on Christianshavn.

IF YOU HAVE FIVE DAYS   With your additional time, visit Copenhagen's Town Hall and the National Museum as well. If you can, take a trip to the Louisiana Museum of Modern Art, the Karen Blixen Museum, or Helsingør (site of Shakespeare's *Hamlet*) in North Zealand.

TOP ATTRACTIONS

TIVOLI, Vesterbrogade 3. Tel. 33-15-10-01.

When Tivoli opened in 1843, the park was well outside the city center. Today, of course, it is Copenhagen's centerpiece, attracting over 4.5 million visitors annually. And although the grounds are full of white-knuckle rides, few would relegate Tivoli to the category of "amusement park." Tivoli is an integral part of Copenhagen, and is the city's main showcase for Danish culture, music, and entertainment. Every day brings with it a full program of open-air concerts, cabaret theater, dancing, pantomime, and other special events. Most are free or fairly priced.

The majority of the performances are staged at night, when the park takes on truly

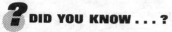

DID YOU KNOW . . . ?

- Denmark is the smallest country in Scandinavia, but Copenhagen (pop. 500,000) is the second-largest city.
- Denmark has the highest standard of living of any EC country.
- Three-quarters of Denmark's land area is devoted to agriculture.
- Denmark has no mountains or rivers, and on average it is only 98 feet above sea level.
- In 1972, Queen Margrethe became the first female monarch in Denmark's history.
- Thanks to an enormous national effort, only 53 Danish Jews died in World War II.
- The Danes love candles, and burn them even at breakfast.
- The average Danish family has 1.2 kids and five bicycles.
- 90% of Danes own their own homes.
- The legal requirement for marriage in Copenhagen is one week's residency.
- Denmark is the world's largest exporter of insulin and windmills.
- Homosexual marriages have been legal in Denmark since 1989.

magical proportions. Thousands of lights shimmer through the trees, and every Wednesday, Friday, and Saturday night fireworks light the sky with a cavalcade of color. Don't overlook an afternoon visit, however, especially from May to the first half of June when 100,000 brightly colored tulips organically paint the park.

Finally, when you're ready for thrills, hop on the old wooden roller coaster. Built in 1914, its incessant creaking gives riders a reason to scream.

Groften and Slukefter are popular spots for a drink. The former, parts of which are open year round, serves Danish food, and the latter, beside the main entrance to Tivoli, features jazz and blues year round. The Tivoli Museum will open at H. C. Andersens Blvd. 22 in May 1993.

The **Tivolis Billetcenter (Tivoli Ticket Center)**, Vesterbrogade 3 (tel. 33-15-10-12), sells tickets to concerts and special events in the park. This office also distributes a free daily schedule, and is located next to the park's main entrance.

Admission: Before 1pm, 23 Kr ($3.80) adults, 12 Kr ($2) children; after 1pm, 33 Kr ($5.45) adults, 17 Kr ($2.80) children. Rides 10–15 Kr ($1.65–$2.50) each; unlimited-ride ticket available.

Open: Park, daily 10am–midnight; Ticket Center, Mon–Sat noon–6pm (also on Sun when events are scheduled). **Closed:** Mid-Sept to late Apr. **Directions:** Walk from the city center.

ROSENBORG PALACE, Øster Voldgade 4a. Tel. 33-15-32-86.

The summer residence of King Christian IV (1577–1648) was built during his reign and served as the official royal residence throughout the 17th century. Today visitors may wander through the opulently furnished State Apartments and a dungeon containing the kingdom's most valued jewels and possessions, including jewel-encrusted swords, dazzling crowns, opulent necklaces, and other priceless possessions of the royal family. Be sure to see the display featuring the clothing Christian IV wore on the day he lost an eye (an event well known by Danish schoolchildren) and the earrings he had made for his mistress from the bullet fragments. There are no electric lights in the palace, so try to come on a sunny day, and allow time to ramble in the sculpted gardens.

Admission: 35 Kr ($5.50) adults, 20 Kr ($3.15) students, 7 Kr ($1.10) children under 15. Prices are about 30% lower in winter.

Open: June–Aug, daily 10am–4pm; May and Sept to late Oct, daily 11am–3pm; the rest of the year, Tues, Fri, and Sun 11am–2pm (the imperial jewels open to view Tues–Sun 11am–3pm). **S-tog:** Nørreport. **Bus:** 5, 7, 10, 14, 16, 17, 43, or 84.

AMALIENBORG PALACE, Slotsplads.

The official residence of Denmark's Queen Margrethe II and her husband, Prince Henrik, is an outstanding example of rococo architecture. Amalienborg is actually a complex of four mansions dating from 1760 that ring a large cobblestone square. An equestrian statue of Frederik V stands at the center of the square, while the Queen's

Guards—bearskin hats and all—stand watch around the perimeter. The noontime Changing of the Guard at Amalienborg is as spirited as any, full of pomp and pageantry, but it is performed only when the queen is in residence (mainly during the colder months). The palace interiors are not open to the public.

Amaliehavens Kiosk, a block from the palace, at Toldbodgade 34 (tel. 33-11-34-40), where the tour buses stop, sells cards, souvenirs, stamps, sandwiches, and ice cream, and has a telephone and rest room; friendly owner Poul Jensen is a wealth of information.

Bus: 1, 6, 9, or 10; or walk from Strøget.

RUNDETÅRN (The Round Tower), Købmagergade. Tel. 33-93-66-60.

There are taller buildings in the city, boasting more spectacular views, but none has more charm and history than this ancient observatory. Built by King Christian IV in 1642, the Round Tower has long been loved by locals as an integral part of the cityscape. The observation platform up top can only be reached by climbing the tower's 687-foot internal spiral ramp. En route, you'll pass a large gallery with changing exhibits; it's free and worth a look. At the observation platform, maps point out prominent rooftops around the old city, Rosenborg Palace in the foreground, and Frederiksberg Castle on the horizon.

Admission: 12 Kr ($1.90) adults, 5 Kr (80¢) children.

Open: Apr–May and Sept–Oct, Mon–Sat 10am–5pm, Sun noon–4pm; June–Aug, Mon–Sat 10am–8pm, Sun noon–8pm; Nov–Mar, Mon–Sat 10am–4pm, Sun noon–4pm. **Directions:** Walk from the city center.

DEN LILLE HAVFRUE (Little Mermaid), Langelinie on the harbor.

Like famous monuments the world over, this simple green statue on a rock off the shore will seem smaller than you had imagined it, but it will make you smile all the same. Locals poke fun at the statue's popularity, and at times have even vandalized it. Still, this frail bronze figure, created in 1913 by Erik Erikson and inspired by the Hans Christian Andersen fairy tale, remains the most famous monument in Copenhagen. Industrial tanks on the opposite shore create an unsightly background, but adjacent **Kastellet Park,** laid out on the remains of Copenhagen's old ramparts, is a beautiful area for strolling and picnicking. Don't miss Gefion Fountain or the bust of Winston Churchill, adjacent to St. Alban's Church.

Bus: 1, 6, or 9; during the summer a shuttle bus operates between Town Hall Square and the statue. **S-tog:** Østerport; then walk through the park.

CHRISTIANSBORG PALACE, Christiansborg Slotsplads, on Slotsholmen. Tel. 33-92-64-92.

⭐ Rebuilt early in this century on top of ancient foundations, Christiansborg Palace was home to the royal family until 1794. The ring of water surrounding the tiny island of Slotsholmen resembles a protective moat. Most of the palace's rooms are now used as offices by parliamentary and supreme court officials, though a few of the glamorous royal reception rooms still serve their original purpose. For tourists, admission to the reception rooms is by guided tour only, and features the Throne Room, where the queen receives foreign ambassadors; the Velvet Room, named for its hanging tapestries; and the Banquet Hall, still used by the royal family and their guests of honor. These, and other rooms, are resplendent with Murano chandeliers, Flemish tapestries, and other impressive details. The palace entrance is beyond the large courtyard, on the left side of the building.

You can also visit the well-preserved palace ruins (the original foundations of Bishop Absalon's 1167 castle) for an additional charge.

Admission: 27 Kr ($4.25) adults, 10 Kr ($1.60) children.

Open: Tours in English given Oct–Apr, Tues, Thurs, and Sun at 11am and 1pm; May–Sept, Tues–Sun at 11am and 1 and 3pm. **Closed:** Jan. **Bus:** 1, 2, 6, 8, 9, 10, 28, 29, 31, 37, 41, or 43; or walk from the city center.

NY CARLSBERG GLYPTOTEK, Dantes Plads 7, across from the back entrance to Tivoli. Tel. 33-91-10-65.

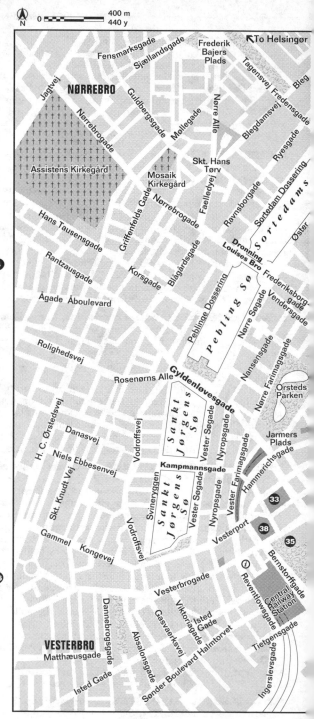

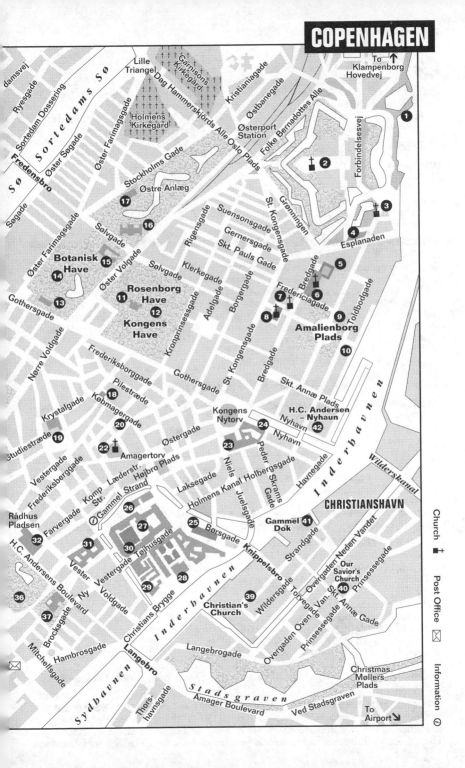

COPENHAGEN

Church † Post Office ⊠ Information ⓘ

★ Specializing in ancient art and French and Danish art of the 19th and early 20th centuries, the Glyptotek has impressive collections of Greek statues, Roman portrait busts, and Egyptian and Etruscan art. Founded by brewer/arts patron Carl Jacobsen in 1882, the collection of antiquities has continued to grow and includes Near Eastern, Palmyrene, and Cypriot art, along with extensive works from more recent times. The French sculpture collection features 35 works by Rodin and the complete ouevre of Degas. The second-floor modernists are mainly French and include Gauguin, Corot, Courbet, Manet, Monet, Cézanne, and Renoir; don't miss Gallery 28. The museum is built around a glass-domed conservatory that compels some folks to visit the Glyptotek with little intention of looking at art.

Admission: 15 Kr ($2.35); free Wed and Sun, and at all times for children.

Open: May–Aug, Tues–Sun 10am–4pm; Sept–Apr, Tues–Sat noon–3pm, Sun 10am–4pm. **Closed:** Good Friday, Easter Sunday, Whitsunday, June 5, and Christmas Day. **S-tog:** Hovedbanegård. **Bus:** 1, 2, 5, 10, 14, 16, 28, 29, 30, 32, 33, 34, or 41.

STATENS MUSEUM FOR KUNST (State Museum of Fine Arts), Sølvgade 48-50. Tel. 33-91-21-26.

★ The country's largest art museum occupies a monumental building in the Østre Anlæg park. The Danish art is separated from all the rest, and although there is heavy emphasis on works from the late 18th century, most are overshadowed by outstanding 19th-century landscapes. The foreign-art section is heavy on Dutch and Flemish paintings, though other European modernists (especially French), such as Matisse and Braque, are also well represented. Look for special changing exhibitions.

Admission: 20 Kr ($3.15) adults, free for children under 16.

Open: Museum, Tues–Sun 10am–4:30pm; sculpture garden, daily 10am–4:30pm. **Bus:** 10, 24, 43, or 184.

MORE ATTRACTIONS

FRIHEDSMUSEET (Denmark's Fight for Freedom Museum 1940–1945), Churchillparken. Tel. 33-13-77-14.

This small but fascinating collection chronicles the nation's underground fight against the Germans who, despite Denmark's pledge of neutrality, occupied the country in 1940. Computerized information, an audiovisual show, and displays on sabotage efforts and prison life, along with a plethora of pictures, are featured. The museum also celebrates the nation's unique efforts to save the country's Jewish citizens. A 40-page guide is available for 15 Kr ($2.35).

Admission: Free.

Open: May to mid-Sept, Tues–Sat 10am–4pm, Sun 10am–5pm; mid-Sept to Apr, Tues–Sat 11am–3pm, Sun 11am–4pm. **S-tog:** Østerport. **Bus:** 1, 6, or 9.

NATIONAL MUSEUM, Ny Vestergade 10, Tel. 33-13-44-11.

Cataloguing life in Denmark since the Stone Age, this vast museum, located across from Christiansborg Palace, includes prehistoric finds, ancient burial chambers, traditional farmers' tools, and centuries-old porcelain, furniture, and housewares. Interesting, too, are the displays on the colonization of Greenland, as well as the Victorian House, with its original interior dating from 1890 (tours of it are available). The museum keeps limited hours, and even though it's often jammed with schoolchildren during the week, it's still worth a visit. There are guided tours in English in July and August.

Admission: Museum, 20 Kr ($3.15) adults, 15 Kr ($2.35) students, free for children; Victorian House, an additional 15 Kr ($2.35) adults.

Open: Tues–Sun 10am–5pm. The Victorian House has restricted hours. **Bus:** 1, 2, 5, 6, or 10.

KØBENHAVNS RÅDHUS (Town Hall), Rådhuspladsen. Tel. 33-15-38-00.

Copenhagen's imposing red-brick Town Hall (1905) is one of the best-known structures in the city because of its clock tower and location in the heart of town. There's no need to look inside, unless you are a clock fan. The Town Hall is most famous for **Jens Olsen's World Clock,** a gigantic silver-and-gold timepiece located on the ground floor. It began ticking in 1955, and is accurate to within half a second every 300 years! The pillar just east of Town Hall is topped by two men playing lurs, instruments found only in Scandinavia.

Admission: Town Hall, free; clock, 8 Kr ($1.25) adults, 4 Kr (65¢) children.

Open: Guided tours, Mon–Fri at 3pm, Sat at 10am; Jens Olsen's World Clock, Mon–Fri 10am–4pm, Sat 10am–1pm.

H. C. ANDERSEN–NYHAVN, Nyhavn 69. Tel. 33-33-01-60.

✪ This cultural center devoted to Copenhagen's premier storyteller appeals more to adults than to children, though the bed from *The Princess and the Pea* is on display, and there are videos and special activities for small fry. There are excellent exhibits about the author's life and works, including many photographs (fortunately for archivists, Andersen adored having his picture taken). Texts are in Danish and English. In the afternoon there are musical presentations of his songs (in Danish). Andersen, who wrote 167 fairy tales, translated into more than 100 languages, never actually lived in this building, which has been impeccably renovated, but he lived next door, at no. 67, and in two other buildings on Nyhavn, nos. 18 and 20. The center has a small shop and an inviting attic café.

Admission: 35 Kr ($5.50) adults, 20 Kr ($3.15) students and children 8–14.

Open: Spring, summer, and autumn, Wed–Sun 10am–5pm; winter, Wed–Sun noon–5pm.

GRUNDTVIGS KIRKE (Grundtvig's Church), Pa Bjerget. Tel. 31-81-54-42.

This impressive blond-brick structure, a cross between a simple Danish church (no stained glass, no grand altar) and a Gothic cathedral, was completed in 1940 in honor of N. F. S. Grundtvig, the Lutheran parson and poet who wrote 36% of the Danish hymnbook and founded the folk high school movement. The model ship hanging inside was a gift from Queen Alexandrine (Queen Margrethe's grandmother). The church measures 22 meters (70 ft.) high on the inside, with a tower soaring 35 meters (111 ft.). Each of its massive columns is made of 10,000–12,000 bricks. Concerts are held here in summer.

Admission: Free.

Open: Mid-May to mid-Sept, Mon–Sat 9am–4:45pm, Sun noon–4pm; mid-Sept to mid-May, Mon–Sat 9am–4pm, Sun noon–1pm. **Closed:** When there is an official church function. **Bus:** 19 from Town Hall, or 10, 16, or 43.

CHRISTIANIA, Christianshavn.

Organized squatters took over dozens of disused army buildings on the island of Christianshavn in 1971, creating the "Free State of Christiania." The public, both critical of the city's housing situation and curious about this new solution, generally supported the group, pressuring the government against taking any action. Today, Christianians, some 900 of them, support their own government, paying taxes and rent to Christiania instead of to the Danish government, and the area, with its piles of garbage, dirt, graffiti, unpaved streets, and sometimes open drug use, looks more like an undeveloped nation than modern Denmark. But these unsightly things are offset by interesting murals and wonderfully painted houses, and nightspots. Tourists are welcome, but they are asked not to take photographs, especially along the main drag, known as "Pusher Street." A restaurant and a jazz club, **Spiseloppen** and **Loppen,** respectively, are located in the building to your right just inside the main entrance to Christiania; rest rooms and a small gallery are in the same building.

Bus: 8 from Town Hall Square; get off at the second stop after the bridge.

PARKS & GARDENS

In addition to the gardens of **Tivoli,** Copenhagen boasts several other greens that are perfect for picnicking. On the grounds of Rosenborg Palace the sculptured gardens of **Kongens Have (King's Garden)** attract ducks, swans, gulls, and people. This is the city's oldest park, and is as popular as ever with hand-holders and strollers alike.

The charming, wooded **Botanisk Have (Botanical Garden),** behind the State Museum of Fine Arts, is particularly nice on hot summer days. The gates are open daily from 8:30am to 6pm, April to October; until 4pm the rest of the year.

Like most parks in the city, the **Park of the Citadel (Kastellet),** behind the *Little Mermaid,* is laid out on Copenhagen's old ramparts. Adjacent **Churchill Park,** to the south, is noted for St. Alban's English Church and the impressive Gefion Fountain, depicting the legend of the founding of Denmark. And don't overlook the small but winsomely bulldoggish bust of Sir Winston himself in the park.

A ribbon of three artificial lakes cuts through Copenhagen (all rectangular and uninspiring); the most appealing, **Lake Peblinge,** is the scene of enthusiastic boating, strolling, sitting, and duck-feeding in summer. Nearby, **Ørsteds Park,** with its small lake, pleasant paths, and statues, invites meandering. Cemetery lovers won't be disappointed by the parklike **Assistens Kirkegard,** at Nørrebrogade and Kapelvej, the final resting place of Hans Christian Andersen, Søren Kierkegaard, physicists H. C. Ørsted and Niels Bohr, and tenor sax player Ben Webster. Nearby, **Fælledparken** is the scene of exuberant outdoor concerts in the summertime.

Frederiksberg Park, adjacent to the zoo, is one of the city's prettiest green spots. Get there quickly and easily from Central Station via bus no. 28 or 41.

North of the city center on Tuborgvej is **Mindelunden i Ryvangen** (the Memorial Park), dedicated to Danish civilians who lost their lives during the German occupation of Denmark from April 9, 1940, to May 5, 1945. Among the 158 graves here are those of 31 Danish Jews who died in concentration camps. The location of the park is a former Nazi execution site. To visit, take the S-tog to Ryparken.

KIDS' COPENHAGEN

LOUIS TUSSAUD'S WAX MUSEUM, H. C. Andersens Blvd. 22. Tel. 33-14-29-22.

Kids love the fairytale exhibits here, and sound effects add to the wonder of scenes from the Brothers Grimm, "Sleeping Beauty," "Jack and the Beanstalk," and "The Snow Queen." For the very brave, there's a spooky Chamber of Horrors.

Admission: 42 Kr ($6.60) adults, 20 Kr ($3.15) children.

Open: Mid-Sept to late Apr, daily 10am–4:30pm; late Apr to mid-Sept, daily 10am–11pm. **S-tog:** Hovedbanegård.

TYCHO BRAHE PLANETARIUM, Gammel Kongevej 10. Tel. 33-12-12-24.

Another lure for young folks is western Europe's largest planetarium, with showings of Omnimax movies. Nearly all the shows have an audio cassette translation in English.

Admission: Planetarium, 10 Kr ($1.60) adults or children; for Omnimax, add another 45–85 Kr ($7.10–$13.40), depending on the show.

Open: Sun–Mon 10:30am–9pm, Tues–Thurs 9:30am–9pm, Fri–Sat 10:30am–10pm. **S-tog:** Vesterport. **Bus:** 1 or 14.

EKSPERIMENTARIUM, in the Tuborg Brewery, Strandvejen 54, Hellerup. Tel. 39-27-33-33.

Opened in 1991 and housed in an old bottling hall of the Tuborg Brewery, the Eksperimentarium fuels kids' interest in the natural sciences and modern technology with hands-on exhibits (many explanations in English), microscope-equipped labs, demonstrations (the dissection of a cow's eye, for instance), computer workshops, and a video room. There's also a shop and a cafeteria.

Admission: 50 Kr ($7.90) adults, 35 Kr ($5.50) children under 15; special family ticket 70 Kr ($11.05) for one adult and one child Tues–Fri before 1pm.

Open: Mon, Wed, and Fri 9am–6pm; Tues and Thurs 9am–9pm; Sat–Sun 11am–6pm. **S-tog:** Hellerup.

LEGETØJSMUSEET (Toy Museum), Valkendorfsgade 13. Tel. 33-14-10-09.

The Toy Museum houses almost 5,000 toys from Denmark, Germany, England,

and the U.S. in a converted 200-year-old warehouse. The first floor is a re-created Danish village with 14 houses, each displaying toys with a different theme. Dolls and dollhouses fill the top floor. The oldest toy dates from 1540, and the 1740 Noah's Ark still has all its animals. One exhibit, called "Doll Doctor," is a 1920s doll shop stocked with spare doll parts.

Admission: 20 Kr ($3.15) adults, 10 Kr ($1.60) children.
Open: Mon–Thurs 9am–4pm, Sat–Sun 10am–4pm. **S-tog:** Nørreport. **Bus:** 2, 5, 14, 16, or 43.

COPENHAGEN ZOO, Roskildevej 32. Tel. 36-30-20-01.
Founded in 1859 and modernized in recent years, the Copenhagen Zoo is home to 2,000 animals, from Nordic species to Asiatic black bears to South American llamas. There is a special activity area for children.

Admission: 45 Kr ($7.10) adults, 22 Kr ($3.50) children.
Open: Summer, daily 9am–6pm; winter, daily 9am–4pm. **S-tog:** Valby. **Bus:** 27, 28, 39, or 175.

DANMARKS AKVARIUM (Denmark Aquarium), Charlottenlund Fort Park, Strandvejen, Charlottenlund. Tel. 31-62-32-83.
Opened in 1959, the Denmark Aquarium features fish that inhabit waters around the world, along with some turtles and terrapins. For those with a fascination with bloodthirsty fish, there's a tank of South American piranyas. The train ride to Charlottenlund takes 15 minutes.

Admission: 30 Kr ($4.75) adults, 15 Kr ($2.35) children.
Open: Mar–Oct, daily 10am–6pm; Nov–Feb, Mon–Fri 10am–4pm, Sat–Sun 10am–5pm. **S-tog:** Charlottenlund. **Bus:** 6 to Charlottenlund Fort.

PROFESSOR OLSEN'S SPILLERLAND, in Scala Center, Axeltorv 2 (3rd Floor). Tel. 33-15-12-15.
A family-entertainment arcade with everything from pinball machines to carnival games. There's even a miniature carousel with four horses. Kids love it—and they get in for free.

Admission: 30 Kr ($4.75) adults, which buys six tokens for the pinball machines; free for children under 12.
Open: Noon–midnight.

SPECIAL-INTEREST SIGHTSEEING
FOR HISTORY BUFFS

TØJHUSMUSEET (Royal Arsenal Museum), Tøjhusgade 3. Tel. 31-11-60-37.
Those who believe the history of humanity is the history of war will find much of interest here. Housed in the king's arsenal, completed in 1604 with the longest arched hall in Europe, this museum displays a vast collection of weapons spanning several centuries. The first floor, a veritable forest of steel, features tank and artillery displays as well as a long series of cannons. Several airplanes, including two 1927 craft and a 1911 propeller plane, hang from the ceiling. The thousands of personal weapons on the second floor include armor pieces, guns, and swords. Older kids like this museum, too.

Admission: 20 Kr ($3.15) adults, 10 Kr ($1.60) students and seniors, 5 Kr (80¢) children 6–17.
Open: Mid-June to mid-Sept, Tues–Sun 10am–4pm; mid-Sept to mid-June, Tues–Fri 1–3pm, Sat–Sun noon–4pm. **Bus:** 1, 2, 5, 6, 10, 31, 37, or 43.

ARBEJDERMUSEET (The Workers' Museum), Rømersgade 22. Tel. 31-93-33-88.
This museum provides a look at the cultural and social history of Copenhagen's middle class in three permanent exhibits: "For Life and Bread," about the effect of industrialization in 1870; "Meager Times," about unemployment in the 1930s; and "The 1950s," depicting the prosperous times following World War II. Café &

Øl-Halle 1892, the on-premises eatery, looks like the cafés did 100 years ago and serves food and drink from that era as well. Guided tours, available in July only, include a traditional meal.

Admission: 25 Kr ($3.95) adults, 15 Kr ($2.35) children.
Open: Tues and Thurs–Fri 10am–3pm, Wed 10am–8pm, Sat–Sun 11am–4pm.
S-tog: Nørreport.

FOR ART & ARCHITECTURE BUFFS

THORVALDSEN MUSEUM, Slotsholmen. Tel. 33-32-15-32.

★ The personal museum of Bertel Thorvaldsen (1770–1844), Denmark's most celebrated sculptor, features the artist's graceful creations as well as other works from his private collection. Notable are Thorvaldsen's plaster casts of large monuments from around the world. Among the most striking are his portrayals of Hercules, Venus, Jason, Mars, Vulcan, Mercury, and Christ and the Apostles. Don't miss the monumental equestrian statues or the exhibits in the basement: his personal effects, including two silver spoons (the only cutlery he owned), two flintlock pistols, a silver lorgnette, and a gold snuffbox with his monogram in diamonds (a gift from the city of Turin); his work techniques; and his achievements as a young artist. Audio guides in English are available for a small charge. The museum, which has arched ceilings and striking interiors, is adjacent to Christiansborg Palace. Splendid works in marble by Thorvaldsen may be seen in Copenhagen Cathedral (Church of Our Lady).

Admission: Free.
Open: Tues–Sun 10am–5pm. **Bus:** 1, 2, 6, 8, 10, 28, 29, or 41; or walk from the town center.

KØBENHAVNS BYMUSEUM (Copenhagen City Museum), Vesterbrogade 59. Tel. 31-21-07-72.

Many pictures, prints, maps, and models of Copenhagen illustrate the development of the city from antiquity to the present day. A separate, permanent display features objects associated with the life of philosopher and author Søren Kierkegaard. Outside the building in summer is a large-scale model of the city that deserves a look.

Admission: Free.
Open: May–Sept, Tues–Sun 10am–4pm; Oct–Apr, Tues–Sun 1–4pm. **Bus:** 6, 16, 27, or 28.

DEN HIRSCHSPRUNGSKE SAMLING (The Hirschsprung Collection), Stockholmsgade 20. Tel. 31-42-03-36.

★ Tobacco manufacturer Heinrich Hirschsprung bequeathed his vast collection of 19th-century Danish art, notably paintings of people and landscapes, to Denmark in 1911. The striking building constructed specifically to house the collection has 16 exhibition areas, a particularly large one devoted to the works of P. S. Krøyer. Works by Anna and Michael Ancher, Viggo Johansen, and Vilhem Hammershoi are prominently displayed. Furniture designed by the artists—chests, chairs, tables—is exhibited along with the art.

Admission: 20 Kr ($3.15) adults, 10 Kr ($1.60) students, free for children 15 and younger.
Open: Wed–Sat 1–4pm, Sun 11am–4pm. **S-tog:** Østerport or Nørreport. **Bus:** 10, 14, 40, 42, 43, or 184.

DAVIDS SAMLING (The David Collection), Kronprinsessegade 30. Tel. 33-13-62-13.

This former home of lawyer, businessman, and art collector C. L. David, who died in 1960, across the street from the King's Garden and purportedly houses the largest collection of Islamic art in Northern Europe. Beautiful calligraphy, pottery, tiles, and tapestries are on the fourth floor; the first three floors are devoted to Danish, French, and English art and decorative arts, respectively.

Admission: Free.
Open: Tues–Sun 1–4pm. **Bus:** 7, 10, or 43.

GAMMELDOK(DanishArchitectureCenter),Strandgade27B,Christians-havn. Tel. 31-57-19-30.

The focus here is modern—be it design, architecture, interiors, textiles, or furniture—as the changing exhibits attest. The term *gammel dok* means "old dock," and the center is on one, in half of a converted warehouse (1882); the other half is studio space for artists. A bookstore/shop (selling high-tech items) and café fill the ground level. The exhibition space and fine views of Copenhagen are on the second floor. The center usually mounts a large, summer-long exhibition.

Admission: 20 Kr ($3.15) adults, 10 Kr ($1.60) seniors, free for students and children under 16.

Open: Tues and Thurs–Sun 10am–5pm, Wed 10am–10pm. **Bus:** 2, 8, 9, 31, or 37.

CHARLOTTENBORG PALACE AND EXHIBITION HALL, Nyhavn 2. Tel. 33-13-40-22.

Right on Kongens Nytorv, between Nyhavn and the Royal Theater, this former residence of the royal family, completed in 1683, is now home to the Royal Academy of Fine Arts. In the artist-run Exhibition Hall, changing exhibits devoted to art, architecture, decorative arts, and design fill spacious galleries with 10- to 24-foot ceilings. The avant garde is alive and well here. There's a pleasant café on the ground floor.

Admission: 20 Kr ($3.15) adults, 10 Kr ($1.60) seniors and students, free for children.

Open: Daily 10am–5pm. **Bus:** 1, 6, 7, 9, 10, or 31.

ORGANIZED TOURS

WALKING TOURS

Copenhagen on Foot, Kongelundsvej 91 (tel. 31-51-25-90), under the direction of Mr. H. S. Jacobsen, offers a diverse selection of English-language walking tours daily in summer and on weekends in spring and autumn. Each walk lasts about two hours. Prices are usually 30 Kr ($4.75) for adults, 20 Kr ($3.15) for students to 23 years old, free for children. Walks are listed in the tourist board publication *Copenhagen This Week*. No advance booking.

"Copenhagen on Foot," an excellent brochure distributed free by Use-It (see "Information" in "Orientation and Getting Around," above, for address), will guide you through the streets of the city at your own pace.

BUS TOURS

Use-It's free **"Copenhagen by Bus"** brochure takes you through a do-it-yourself tour of all the major sights using city bus no. 6. Those looking for more structure can choose from over a dozen guided bus tours. **Vikingbus** (tel. 31-57-26-00) offers a 2½-hour "Grand Tour of Copenhagen" at 150 Kr ($23.65) for adults, half price for children under 12. Tours depart from Town Hall Square April through October, daily at 11am and 1:30pm (also at 3pm from mid-September to mid-October); the rest of the year, daily at 11am (on Saturday also at 1:30pm).

The company offers a shorter, less expensive 1½-hour city tour for 110 Kr ($17.35), departing Town Hall Square daily at 10am, noon, and 4pm in summer, at 10am and 4pm daily the rest of the year.

CANAL TOURS

Though no longer as active as it was years ago, the city's waterfront has remained as impressive and interesting as ever. Complemented by a vast network of canals running through the old part of the city, boat tours offer both a relaxing cruise and a good education on the history of the city. Guided tours run from May to the middle of September only, and a quite reasonable one is offered by **Netto-Badene** (tel. 31-54-41-02), departing daily from Holmens Church, opposite the Stock Exchange). The tour lasts 50 minutes and costs only 20 Kr ($3.15) for adults and 10 Kr ($1.60) for children.

Other guided boat tours, also of 50 minutes' duration, leave from Gammel Strand and Kongens Nytorv, but they cost twice as much (tel. 33-13-31-05). There is also a half-hour unguided tour to the *Little Mermaid* for 15 Kr ($2.35); another, called "Under 12 Bridges," also unguided, explores the city's canals for 20 Kr ($3.15); kids pay half price for either. Check with the tourist board for current times and itineraries for all tours.

BREWERY TOURS

CARLSBERG BREWERY, Valby Langgade 1. Tel. 31-21-12-21, ext. 1313.

This guided tour shows how barley, hops, yeast, and water are combined to make the famous Carlsberg beer. The main brewing hall dates from the turn of the century and is dominated by huge copper kettles and a pungent aroma. The hour-long tour, which involves maneuvering lots of stairs, concludes with a visit to the beer museum, and free samples of the brewery's products. Additional highlights are the unique Elephant Gate and the original Little(r) Mermaid.

A visit here may easily be combined with a walk to nearby public parks (Sondermarken and Frederiksberg) and the zoo, if you start early enough in the day.

Admission: Free.

Open: Tours given Mon–Fri at 11am and 2pm (call to confirm these hours). **Bus:** 6 from Town Hall Square.

TUBORG BREWERY, Strandvejen 54, Hellerup. Tel. 31-29-33-11, ext. 2212.

✪ Carlsberg and Tuborg merged in 1970, but the two companies still maintain separate breweries and labels. Of the two tours, Tuborg's, which includes two brief slide presentations, seems more authentic and folksy (though its buildings are more modern) as it winds its way through narrow passageways and refrigerators. The "Largest Beer Bottle in the World," holding the equivalent of about a million regular-size bottles of beer, is also on the premises. Like all good brewery tours, this one, which lasts 1¾ hours, concludes with a sampling.

You may combine the Tuborg tour with a visit to the **Eksperimentarium.** Housed in the brewery's old bottling hall, it's a hands-on science and technology laboratory with "please touch" exhibits and special activities for children (see "Kids' Copenhagen," above).

Tuborg is a short S-tog ride to Ryparken, where you'll find the **Memorial Park,** dedicated to Danish civilians who lost their lives during the German occupation of Denmark from April 9, 1940, to May 5, 1945. Among the 158 graves are those of 31 people who died in concentration camps.

Admission: Free (the Experimentarium has a separate admission.)

Open: Tours given Mon–Fri at 10am, 12:30pm, and 2:30pm. **Bus:** 6 toward Hellerup; it stops half a block away (allow a half hour to arrive).

SPECIAL & FREE EVENTS

Grabrødre Torv, a square in the very center of Copenhagen, comes alive each summer day with street entertainers, outdoor cafés, and occasional live music concerts. Renovated in traditional Danish style, Grabrødre Torv is a beautiful meeting place for people of all ages.

Nyhavn (the New Harbor), off Kongens Nytorv, is a dead-end canal lined by historic buildings and another summer favorite. Once the raucous sailors' quarter, Nyhavn has become an upscale strolling area lined with fairly expensive cafés and restaurants. During the summer the cafés lining Nyhavn's pedestrian street appear to specialize in ice cream and beer. Majestic, tall, fully rigged ships are moored all along the canal, and you can also see where Hans Christian Andersen lived during different periods of his life—at nos. 18, 20, and 67 Nyhavn.

Peek into the courtyards at nos. 18 and 20. In late 1991 the **Hans Christian Andersen–Nyhavn** center opened at Nyhavn 69, next door to one of the houses where Andersen once lived.

Nyhavn's wild maritime past is still evidenced by a couple of old-time bars and tattoo parlors, such as the one at Nyhavn 17, which has been decorating bodies since 1878 with everything "from wild to mild."

See the tourist board's publication *Copenhagen This Week,* and "Special Events," above, for more information on unique and interesting city activities.

7. SAVVY SHOPPING

Copenhagen's stores and selections are as wide and varied as any. Everything has its price, however, and here it's usually higher than it is Stateside. Heavy import duties make foreign goods very expensive, which actually is all right, because the most unusual objects here are those of Danish design. Be sure to check out the native silver, porcelain, glassware, and antiques.

SHOPPING STREETS Strøget All shopping tours should begin on Strøget, the city's mile-long pedestrian thoroughfare and the address of many exclusive stores, such as **Royal Copenhagen, Bing & Grondahl, Georg Jensen, Holmegaard,** and the upscale department store **Illum's** (peek inside at the marble atrium with its chandeliers and fountain) and the home-furnishings specialty store, **Illum's Bolighus.** Just off Strøget and a block from the American Express office is **Pamfilius,** at Valkendorfsgade 19, a good source for reasonably priced gifts. Fashionable **Magasin du Nord,** at Kongens Nytorv opposite the Royal Theater, is the largest department store in Scandinavia; it also owns Illum's.

Other Shopping Streets Perpendicular to Strøget, branching north to the Nørreport S-tog, is **Købmagergade,** also free of cars. Several other city shopping streets are reserved exclusively for walkers. They are marked in red on most tourist maps.

Besides the upscale shops, Copenhagen has a good number of secondhand stores and small "vintage" boutiques, especially in and around **Larsbjørnsstræde.** Two favorites are the small shop in Kvindehuset (Women's House), Gothersgade 37, only open Monday through Wednesday from noon to 6pm, and the well-stocked UFF at Kultorvet 13 (come here for replacement jeans or Nordic sweaters) or Vesterbrogade 37 at Viktoriagade. Other fertile hunting grounds are the shops along **Vesterbrogade.**

More Shopping Areas And by no means overlook the **museum shops** (the one at the National Museum is particularly good for jewelry modeled on Viking amulets) and the outstanding selection of duty-free shops, about 30 in all, at **Copenhagen Airport.** Bicycle connoisseurs might consider the triangulated, cantilever-frame Copenhagen Pedersen, which sells for about 2,500 Kr ($394.30) at the **Cycle Smithy** in counterculture **Christiania.**

Store Hours In general, stores are open Monday through Thursday from 9:30am to 5:30pm, on Friday until 7pm, and the first Saturday of each month from 9:30am to 5pm, every Saturday in August. Note that on Monday several shops don't open until 10am and, strangely, many bakeries don't open at all.

Taxes Many stores offer non-Scandinavian tourists the opportunity to recover the Value-Added Tax (VAT) on purchases over 600 Kr ($94.65). Here's how to get the refund: After paying, ask the retailer for a Tax Free Check, and leave your purchase sealed until you leave the country. When departing from Denmark by train, show both the check and the purchase to an official on board. He or she will validate the check, which must then be returned to the store. If you're flying from Copenhagen, you'll get a cash refund (minus a small commission charge) at the airport's Tax Free Shopping office. Remember not to check luggage containing the purchase until you have received your refund! Questions about tax refunds can be answered by Europe Tax-free Shopping (tel. 33-52-55-66).

DENMARK'S LARGEST MALL   In addition to housing a myriad cafés and restaurants (see "Budget Dining," above), the modern **Scala Center,** Axeltorv 2 (tel. 33-15-12-15), supports a variety of shops and a multiplex cinema. Several stories surround a large atrium where live music is sometimes performed, and plenty of well-placed café tables encourage shoppers to linger. The stores are open on Monday from 10am to 7pm, Tuesday through Thursday from 10am to 6pm, on Friday from 10am to 8pm, and on Saturday from 10am to 2pm. Scala Center itself is open daily from 10am to midnight.

AN OUTDOOR MARKET   The **Copenhagen Fleamarket,** on Israels Plads, is open every Saturday from May to October. The market specializes in antiques and bric-a-brac; for the best selection, visit between 8am and 2pm. Other days it's a fruit and vegetable market. S-tog: Nørreport.

8. EVENING ENTERTAINMENT

In Copenhagen, a good night means a late night. On warm weekends hundreds of rowdy revelers crowd Strøget until sunrise, and merrymaking is not just for the younger crowd: jazz clubs, traditional beer houses, and wine cellars are routinely packed with people of all ages. The city has a more serious cultural side as well, exemplified by excellent theaters, operas, ballets, and a circus that shouldn't be missed.

Half-price tickets for some concerts and theater productions are available the same day of the performance from the ticket kiosk opposite the Nørreport rail station, at Nørrevoldgade and Fiolstræde. It's open Monday through Friday from noon to 7pm and on Saturday from noon to 3pm.

On summer evenings there are outdoor concerts in Fælled Park near the entrance near Frederik V's Vej; inquire about dates and times at the tourist office.

THE PERFORMING ARTS

THEATER, OPERA & BALLET

DET KONGELIGE TEATER (Royal Theater), at the south end of Kongens Nytorv. Tel. 33-14-10-02 after 1pm.

Copenhagen's cultural scene is dominated by a single theater, the Royal Theater, home of the famed Royal Danish Ballet, one of the few places in the world regularly staging theater, opera, and ballet under the same roof. Founded in 1748, the theater alternates productions between its two stages. Regular premières and popular revivals keep the stage lit almost every night of the season. To get tickets at the box office, pick up a number at the entrance—low numbers are to pick up a reserved seat; high numbers, to buy a ticket.

Prices: Tickets, 40–230 Kr ($6.30–$36.30); half price up to one week prior to the performance for those under 26 and over 67 years old.

Open: Box office, Sept–May, Mon–Sat 1–8pm. **Closed:** June–Aug.

MERMAID THEATER, Sankt Peders Stræde 27. Tel. 33-11-43-03 from noon to 4pm.

The Mermaid is known for English-language stage plays, including productions of

Dorothy Parker's *A Telephone Call,* August Strindberg's *The Stronger,* James Joyce's *Molly,* Harold Pinter's *Landscape,* and Mark Twain's *Made of Dirt.* Check with the tourist board or newspaper for current offerings.

Prices: Tickets, 65–90 Kr ($10.25–$14.20) for benches, 110–120 Kr ($17.35–$18.90) for chairs.

Open: Usually Mon–Sat at 8:30pm in summer, 8pm in winter. Check with the theater or ask the tourist board for current schedules and show times.

JAZZ, BLUES & ROCK

Copenhagen's love affair with jazz and blues is the most passionate in Europe. Danes have whole-heartedly embraced jazz as their own, and even though this capital's clubs are not as plentiful as those in New Orleans or Chicago, they challenge the American variety in both quality and enthusiasm.

DE TRE MUSKETERER, Nicolaj Plads 25. Tel. 33-12-50-67.

This is a top jazz club featuring traditional swing styles. Bopping along for more than 20 years, the Three Musketeers attracts an upbeat, middle-aged crowd with its easy atmosphere and good dance floor. It's opposite St. Nicholas Church.

Admission: 35–80 Kr ($5.50–$12.60).

Open: Tues–Thurs 8pm–2am, Fri–Sat 8pm–3am, Sun 3–6pm.

CA'FEEN FUNKE, Sankt Hans Torv. Tel. 31-35-17-41.

This small local favorite is rarely visited by tourists. Live bands usually perform blues, jazz, soul, or funk on Thursday and Saturday. Best of all, there's never a cover charge. Look for the blue facade, and arrive early if you want to sit.

Admission: Free.

Open: Daily 11am–2am; music usually starts at 9pm. **Bus:** 5, 10, or 16 from Nørreport to Blegdamsvej.

DIN'S, Lille Kannikestræde 3. Tel. 33-93-87-87.

Din's is a restaurant and bar with a very active stage. Although rock bands sometimes perform here, the intimate back room is best suited to the jazz and blues performances held weeknights (except Tuesday, which is devoted to stand-up comedy). On weekends, rock 'n' roll takes center stage. The music starts at 11pm.

Admission: 30 Kr ($4.75), which includes a beer.

Open: Mon and Wed 4pm–1am, Tues 4pm–2am, Thurs 4pm–3am, Fri 4pm–4am, Sat 2pm–4am.

HAND I HANKE, Griffenfeldtsgade 20. Tel. 35-37-20-70.

Blues and rock make up the main agenda at this local bar with board floors, wooden tables and benches, and plants in the windows. All ages feel at home here. The music takes place downstairs, hanging out and playing backgammon upstairs. There's a bar menu, and a backgammon tournament takes place every Sunday for a small admission fee. ·

Admission: Free or 35–65 Kr ($5.80–$10.70), depending on the band; prices include a beer or glass of wine.

Open: Daily 2pm–1am; music from 9pm Tues–Sat. **Bus:** 5, 7, or 16 to Nørreport.

INDUSTRIEN, Bolten's Gård, Gothersgade 8, Kongens Nytorv. Tel. 33-91-91-55.

Part of the trendy Bolten's Court, tucked off Kongens Nytorv in a courtyard surrounded by 18th-century houses, Industrien is a popular late-night spot for jazz, rhythm and blues, funk, and rock. In the city's former House of Industry, the renovated space has a unique diamond-shaped stage that opens to Bolten's main courtyard, perfect for outdoor concerts in mild weather. Besides Industrien, Bolten's Court is home to cafés, eateries (from fast food to fancy), galleries, and a theater—enough variety to induce anyone who enters to stay and explore. Industrien has public restrooms, on the main floor to the left.

Admission: Varies with entertainment.
Open: Daily 9:30pm–5am.

COPENHAGEN JAZZ HOUSE, Niels Hemmingsensgade 10. Tel. 33-15-26-00.

A new addition to the Copenhagen music scene opened in 1991. Expect to hear Danish jazz here 75% of the time, foreign jazz the rest of the time. Once the bands pack up and go home, the disco fires up and goes strong until the wee hours. There's a café at street level. The concert hall in the basement seats 300.

Admission: 50–200 Kr ($8–$32)
Open: Tues–Thurs 8:30pm–midnight, Fri–Sat 9:30pm–1am; the jazz disco is open until 5am.

FREE ENTERTAINMENT

Open since 1989, the modern, multilevel **Scala Center,** Axeltorv 2 (tel. 33-15-12-15), has become a magnet for shopping, dining, entertainment, and people-watching. Numerous balconies provide a spot to stand or sit and enjoy the wide range of talented musicians who perform everything from jazz to classical guitar to pop several evenings a week on the second-level balcony. Or hop in one of the glass-enclosed elevators and observe the colorful scene as you glide up and down the airy atrium. Admission is free and the center is open from 7am to midnight.

MOVIES

Copenhagen is a movie city, and most films are in English with Danish subtitles. The going price of a ticket is about 60 Kr ($9.45), but in some places, such as **Palads,** Axeltorv 9 (tel. 33-13-14-00), the building near the Scala Center that looks like a psychedelic wedding cake and features 19 small cinemas, you pay only 30–40 Kr ($4.75–$6.30) for features that begin before 6pm and on Monday night. Equally good discounts, but more comfortable seating, are available at the five movie theaters at the **Scala Center,** Axeltorv 2 (tel. 33-13-81-00). Independent cinemas include the arty **Grand Teatret,** Mikkel Bryggersgade 8 (tel. 33-15-16-11), a block from Strøget near Town Hall Square; **Delta Bio,** Kompagnistræde 19 (tel. 33-93-06-41); and **Klaptræet,** Kultorvet 11 (tel. 33-13-00-09).

THE BAR SCENE

"IN" SPOTS

KRASNAPOLSKY, Vestergade 10. Tel. 33-32-88-00.

This popular restaurant and bar, with minimal decor and a pool table in back, can be laid-back and low-key or loud and boisterous. Drinks from the long, well-stocked bar are surprisingly well priced. For many, Krasnapolsky, with its popular jukebox, is just a way to warm up before visiting U-Matic disco, next door.

Prices: Beer 20 Kr ($3.15); wine 22 Kr ($3.50).
Open: Mon–Sat 10am–2am, Sun 8pm–2am.

CAFE DAN TURRELL, Store Regnegade 3-5. Tel. 33-14-10-47.

Opened in 1977 and named after the contemporary Danish author of westerns and murder mysteries, it attracts mostly art and architecture students and other young intellectuals, who converse over cheeseburgers, pastrami sandwiches, and chili. Turrell's dust jackets decorate the wall behind the bar, where it's easy to imagine James Dean propped.

Prices: Light fare 42–48 Kr ($6.60–$7.60).
Open: Daily 11am–1:45am (kitchen closes at 10pm).

PEDER OXE VINKÆLDER, Grabrødretorv 11. Tel. 33-11-11-93.

Both unabashedly upbeat and terminally crowded, the Vinkælder's basement bar is one of the best in the city. The bulk of the crowd is too young to afford dinner at the popular and pricey restaurant above. Weekend nights require a strong voice to be heard over the music and the crowd.

Prices: Beer 20 Kr ($3.15); mixed drinks 39 Kr ($6.15).
Open: Daily noon–1am.

CAFE VICTOR, Ny Østergade 8. Tel. 33-13-36-13.

Trendiest of these listings, the Café Victor serves crêpes, quiches, and omelets to Copenhagen's young professionals, schmoozing elbow to elbow. Ceiling-to-floor windows look onto the street, and singles and sightseers often drink or enjoy a small meal at the 1950s-style bar.

Prices: Beer and wine 20 Kr ($3.15).
Open: Mon–Sat 9am–2am.

HUSET (The House), Rådhusstræde 13. Tel. 33-32-00-66 or 33-15-20-02.

A Copenhagen phenomenon, this active student information, entertainment, and cultural center attracts students and alternative folks of all ages to its clubs, restaurant, café, theater, cinema, and video gallery with 80 selections. **Musikcafeen** features top jazz and rock bands nightly; **Bar Bue** goes in for live punk, rap, and new wave music during the week, disco on weekends; **Kafe Par Zalu** (a spoof on Port Salud), a lively weekend meeting spot for people in their early 20s, often has a live band (usually jazz) on Sunday afternoon. By contrast, **Café Rosa** is a small, quiet bar open Tuesday through Saturday. A new café, **Salon K,** featuring cabaret and stand-up comedy, has opened in the complex.

Admission: Free–60 Kr ($9.45), depending on the entertainment.
Open: Daily 10am–2am; call or drop by for specific hours of individual entities.

OLD-TIME BARS

VINSTUEN 90'EREN, Gammel Kongevej 90. Tel. 31-31-84-90.

This place is for beer lovers. If you think you've tried them all, belly up to this bar and order Fadøl, a creamy, frothy beer that's like no other. A half liter of draft takes so long to pour (about 15 minutes) that patrons are advised to order a bottle of Carlsberg while waiting for the heavy foam to subside. The 77-year-old bar attracts everyone from dispirited drunkards to artists and actors (often one and the same).

Prices: Half liter of Fadøl 33 Kr ($5.20).
Open: Mon–Wed 10am–1:30am, Thurs–Sat 10am–2am, Sun and hols noon–1:30am.

HVIIDS VINSTUE, Kongens Nytorv 19. Tel. 33-15-10-64.

This is Copenhagen's most historic wine cellar, faithfully serving citizens since 1723. It's no miracle that Hviids is still open as it's a great place to drink. The large crowd of locals and visitors always includes a good share of the audience from the Royal Theater across the street. One cozy seating area leads to another.

Prices: Beer and wine 19 Kr ($3).
Open: Sun–Thurs 10am–1am, Fri–Sat 10am–1:45am. **Closed:** Sun May–Aug.

NYHAVN 17, Nyhavn 17. Tel. 33-12-54-19.

Although sailors have been replaced by landlubbers, the spirit of the city's past as an important port still lingers here. Entertainment is provided by an organist and singer. Paintings of sailors and exotic women overlook the dance floor, which gets crowded on Friday and Saturday nights.

Prices: Beer 21 Kr ($3.30); whisky 23 Kr ($3.60).
Open: Tues–Sun 2pm–1am; music from 8pm.

GAMBLING

CASINO COPENHAGEN, in the SAS Scandinavia Hotel, Amager Blvd. 70. Tel. 33-11-23-24.

Denmark's first fully licensed casino opened in 1990, with blackjack, roulette, and baccarat. It's run by Casinos Austria International, the world's largest casino operator.

Admission: 40 Kr ($6.30).

Open: Daily 2pm–4am.

DANCE CLUBS

As in other major cities, dance clubs come and go as fast as hiccups, and once gone, are just as quickly forgotten. If you're really into this scene, ask around and check the local glossy giveaways (available in most clubs and record stores). Below is a tried-and-true option:

U-MATIC, Vestergade 10. Tel. 33-32-88-00.

This good late-night dance club is owned by the adjacent Krasnapolsky (see above). A long bar runs along one wall, leaving just enough room for the tables and dance floor. Most important, the sound is good, and there are several video screens. It has two DJs and two dance floors, attracts an arty crowd, and offers gay evenings on Thursday.

Admission: 40 Kr ($6.30) Thurs, 50 Kr ($7.90) Fri–Sat, free Wed.
Open: Wed–Sat 11pm–4:30am.

GAY NIGHTLIFE

Copenhagen has numerous gay bars and clubs. Those listed below are tried and true. For the newest additions to the gay nightlife scene, drop by the **Bogcafe**, at Knabrostræde 3 (see "Networks and Resources"), in the same complex as Cafe Pan and Disco, listed below, and ask for a copy of the free "Copenhagen Gay Guide."

CAFE PAN AND DISCO, Knabrostræde 3. Tel. 33-32-49-08.

The café has a relaxed atmosphere and comfortable surroundings, and serves snacks and sandwiches all day, while in the disco there's dancing till the wee hours. Thursday night is for women only. It's conveniently located half a block from Strøget.

Admission: 30 Kr ($4.75).
Open: Café, Sun–Tues 1pm–3am, Wed–Thurs 1pm–2am, Fri–Sat 1pm–5am; disco, daily 10pm–5am.

PINK CLUB, Farvergade 10. Tel. 33-11-26-07.

This large, popular bar attracts gay men primarily.
Admission: Free.
Open: Daily 4pm–4am.

CAFE BABOOSHKA, Turensensgade 6. Tel. 33-15-05-36.

One of the only clubs in town primarily for lesbians, it serves hot and cold food and is fully licensed. Changing monthly exhibits feature paintings, graphics, and photographs by women, and from time to time there's live music in the evening.
Admission: Free.
Open: Mon–Sat 4pm–1am; Sun 2–11pm.

9. NETWORKS & RESOURCES

STUDENTS   Huset, Rådhusstræde 13 (tel. 33-32-00-66), is a unique city-subsidized building completely dedicated to students and young people. The building houses an information office, cafés, restaurants, and evening music spots, several of which are listed above under their appropriate headings. The Use-It office (see "Information" in "Orientation and Getting Around," above) also makes its home here, and shouldn't be missed.

The **International Student Center,** Frederiksborggade 52 (tel. 33-15-32-16), organizes monthly activities for students, including concerts, films, and excursions to nearby and farther flung locales, from Christiania to Roskilde.

Danish-language courses are readily available from several sources in

Copenhagen, among them **K.I.S.S. (Danish Language School)**, Nørregade 20 (tel. 33-11-44-77), where courses last 2½ weeks and cost 235 Kr ($37.05), including materials. Ask for the "Danish Courses for Foreigners" pamphlet at the Use-It office.

Den Internationale Hojskole (an international folk high school), Montebello Allé 1, DK-3000 Helsingør (tel. 32-21-33-61), has a multilingual staff and offers courses in English and other languages.

Transalpino Rejiser, Skoubogade 6 (tel. 33-14-46-33), specializes in discount train and plane tickets for travelers under 26. **Kilroy Travels Denmark,** Skindergade 28 (tel. 33-11-00-44), also offers bus, train, plane, and boat discounts to students and people under 26. There is a travel library/bookstore next door called **Kupeen,** where you can research your upcoming journeys, check a ride board for travel companions, and buy English-language travel books (if you have an international student card, you get a 10% discount). Both Kilroy Travels Denmark and Transalpino Rejiser are open Monday through Friday from 10am to 5pm.

The main building of **Copenhagen University,** dating from 1479, is right in the heart of the city, next to Copenhagen Cathedral. Unfortunately, like many urban schools, the campus lacks the bustle and energy of student life; students prefer to hang out in nearby cafés.

GAY MEN & LESBIANS The best source of information about gay and lesbian activities in Copenhagen is the **Pan Center,** which houses Denmark's **National Organization for Gay Men and Lesbians.** Of most immediate help to out-of-towners is the Pan Center's bookstore, called the **Pan Bogcafe,** Knabrostræde 3 (tel. 33-13-19-48), open Monday through Friday from 5 to 7pm. The staff is knowledgeable about gay goings-on and meeting places in the city and will give you the free "Copenhagen Gay Guide" and the free monthly gay newspaper *Pan-Bladet.* Besides books, many in English, the shop also sells magazines, postcards, posters, and T-shirts, and there's usually coffee available for a small charge.

Just across the portal from the Bogcafe, the Pan Center **library** (tel. 33-11-19-61) has books and periodicals from all over the world; it's open Monday through Friday from 5 to 7pm (until 8pm on Wednesday) and on Saturday from 1 to 3pm.

There is also a **general information number** that may be called Monday through Friday nights from 8pm to midnight only: 33-13-01-12. The **AIDS information** number is 33-91-11-19.

The city's "gay church" is the **Metropolitan Community Church,** Knabrostræde 3 (tel. 31-83-32-86). Services, on Sunday at 5pm, are in Danish, but the minister, Mia Andersen, speaks excellent English.

Since May 1989, gay unions (called "registered partnerships," but essentially marriages) and divorces have been legal in Denmark. Gay and lesbian couples have most of the rights of heterosexual married couples, except that they cannot adopt or gain custody of children or have a church wedding.

WOMEN Kvindehuset (Women's House), Gothersgade 37 (tel. 33-14-28-04), is a center for women's exchange, informal discussions, and scheduled seminars and classes. There's a small but selective thrift shop on the premises and a table and chairs where you may sit and share coffee and conversation with other women. The Women's House is open Monday through Wednesday from noon to 6pm; and its café is open on Monday and Thursday from 6 to 10pm; call to double-check hours.

10. EASY EXCURSIONS

For a leisurely trip through the Danish countryside, your best bet may be the **Danish State Railways (DSB) "Special Excursion" ticket.** Not every destination is covered, but trips to the Louisiana Museum of Modern Art, Legoland, Odense, and other highly touristed destinations certainly are. Call DSB (tel. 33-14-17-01) for further information.

HUMLEBÆK Located in North Zealand about an hour from Copenhagen's Central Station is the stunning **Louisiana Museum of Modern Art,** Gammel Strandvej 13 (tel. 42-19-07-19), which claims to be the most-visited museum in Denmark. The wonderful permanent collection includes works by Warhol, Lichtenstein, Calder, and Giacometti, though the world-class special exhibitions are the main draw, and have included a Chagall retrospective and a Warhol exhibition. The museum itself, on a spectacular piece of land overlooking the sea, is beautiful. During warmer months, you can picnic on the sprawling grounds.

The museum is open Thursday through Tuesday from 10am to 5pm and on Wednesday from 10am to 10pm. Admission is 42 Kr ($6.30) for adults, free for children. A special round-trip train fare is 74 Kr ($11.70).

Take the train from Central Station Platform 1 or 2, then bus no. 388 from Humlebæk Station (or a scenic one-mile walk).

HELSINGØR [ELSINORE] "Four-hundred years of legal piracy," from the 15th through the 19th century, made Helsingør rich from tolls assessed on passing ships. Today, a walk around this carefully restored old town is proof enough that this was at one time Denmark's most important parcel. A wonderful architectural legacy and other indelible marks have been made on this seaside village by traders from around the world. But Helsingør is most famous for its regal 16th-century **Kronborg Castle** (tel. 49-21-30-78), supposedly the setting for Shakespeare's *Hamlet*. Whether or not this is true, it is inarguable that the castle is nothing less than majestic. The castle tour features the royal apartments (with paintings and tapestries from the 16th and 17th centuries), the ballroom, the chapel, and other ancient areas. Located on the Danish coast 28 miles north of Copenhagen, Helsingør may be reached by train from Central Station in about an hour.

The castle is open May through September, daily from 10:30am to 5pm; in April and October, daily from 11am to 4pm; and the rest of the year, Tuesday through Sunday from 11am to 3pm. Admission is 20 Kr ($3.15) for adults, 10 Kr ($1.60) for children. Joint admission to the castle and the **Danish Maritime Museum** is 34 Kr ($5.35) for adults, half price for children. A visit in August might even coincide with a production of *Hamlet*.

RUNGSTEDLUND A visit to the **Karen Blixen Museum** in Rungstedlund may easily be combined with a trip to Kronborg Castle or the Louisiana Museum of Modern Art. The Karen Blixen Museum, at Rungsted Strandvej 111 (tel. 42-57-10-57), is the memorabilia-filled home of the late author (alias Isak Dinesen, 1885–1962) of *Seven Gothic Tales* and the autobiographical *Out of Africa*, opened to the public in 1991. Except for the years she spent in Kenya, Blixen lived here all her life. You may visit the house and grounds, including her grave, May through September, daily from 10am to 5pm; October to April, daily from 1 to 5pm. Admission is 30 Kr ($4.75) for adults, free for children under 12; the Copenhagen Card is accepted.

Take the train to Rungsted Kyst, or change at Klampenborg for bus no. 388; the bus stop is about a block from the museum, which is well marked (walk in the direction the bus is traveling).

HILLERØD A not-so-scenic 45-minute ride from Copenhagen is **Frederiksborg Palace** (tel. 42-26-04-39), which has been called the "Versailles of Northern Europe." It was built in Dutch Renaissance style as a royal residence from 1600 to 1620 for Christian IV, who was king of Denmark and Norway for 60 years. Of particular interest are the immense Neptune Fountain, the elaborate, restored three-dimensional ceiling in the Knights Hall, and the chapel, looking just as it did when Christian IV used it.

The palace is open in April and October, daily from 10am to 4pm; May through September, daily from 10am to 5pm; and November through March, daily from 11am to 3pm. Admission is 30 Kr ($4.75) for adults, 10 Kr ($1.60) for students, and 5 Kr (80¢) for children 6–14. Tour cassettes are available in English and other languages for 25 Kr ($3.95).

ROSKILDE For centuries Danish kings and queens have been laid to rest at the red-brick **cathedral** in Roskilde, most recently King Frederik IX in 1985. Today people visit Roskilde, which lies due west of Copenhagen and a mere half-hour train ride away, primarily to see the cathedral and royal tombs and the **Viking Ship Museum,** on Strandengen. The museum, open daily, houses five ships raised from the Roskilde Harbor in 1962. Purposefully sunk as barricades around A.D. 1000, they include two warships, two merchant ships, and a small vessel that was either a ferry or fishing boat. Films in English, German, French, Italian, and Spanish about the excavation of the ships are shown.

The **main square** of Roskilde becomes a fruit, flower, vegetable, and flea market on Wednesday and Saturday mornings. Its **palace,** which now houses a collection of paintings and furniture from local merchant families, was built in 1733, its town hall in 1884.

In summer, excursion boats ply the Roskilde Fjord, and concerts are held throughout the venerable old city, as well as in Roskilde Park on Tuesday night. The enormously popular, four-day **Roskilde Festival** (tel. 42-37-05-48) is held at the end of June every year. While the emphasis is on rock music, there is also folk, blues, and jazz, along with film presentations and theatrical performances. The festival is one of the oldest and largest in northern Europe, attracting top performers.

The **tourist office** (tel. 42-35-27-00) is near the cathedral. Trains run frequently between Copenhagen and Roskilde; if you want to explore this area further, take the bus from Roskilde 7km (4.3 miles) west to the charming village of **Gammel Lejre.**

DRAGØR   For a quick change of scene, hop on the no. 30 or 33 bus at Town Hall Square (no charge with the Copenhagen Card), and in 40 minutes you'll be strolling the cobblestone walkways of the quaint seaside town of Dragør (rhymes with "sour"), with its small houses with red-tile or thatched roofs.

It's possible to see everything in an hour or two, or linger for lunch or supper in the flower-filled courtyard of the **Hotel Dragør Kro** (1721) or at the **Strand Hotel,** overlooking the harbor. Either of these inns can also provide lodging for the night.

The small **Dragør Museum,** at the harbor, is open May through September, Tuesday through Friday from 2 to 5pm and on Saturday and Sunday from noon to 6pm. There's a small, good camera store, **Dragør Foto,** on the main drag, Kongevejen 17 (tel. 31-53-78-00).

The pleasant bus ride to Dragør takes you through tidy Danish communities and then farmland. Bus drivers accept the Copenhagen Card.

MALMÖ, SWEDEN   Sweden's third-largest city—undeniably modern but with a 13th-century core—lies directly across the channel from Copenhagen. Visitors particularly enjoy the architecture in the old part of town, as well as the Malmö Museum at Malmöhus, a 15th-century castle. The city has several parks and a 4.2-mile (7km) stretch of sandy beach.

It's actually possible to visit Malmö in less than an hour or two by boat or hydrofoil. Both services depart from Havnegade, at the corner of Nyhavn in Copenhagen. For a more in-depth look at the two countries, ask DSB about **''Around the Sound,''** an inexpensive two-day excursion ticket to Sweden and back via boat and train. Remember to bring your passport! You'll also have to change money in Sweden.

The **ferryboat** takes 90 minutes and costs 55 Kr ($9.65) one way. The **high-speed craft (flyvebadene),** at Havngade 40 (tel. 33-14-77-70), takes only 45 minutes but costs 85 Kr ($13.40) each way (children under 16 pay half price). Senior citizens are entitled to a special one-day round-trip fare of 45 Kr ($7.10), but they must travel between 6am and 3pm. Reserve in advance.

DUBLIN

In Dublin there are no spectacular monuments, no grandiose museums, no hilltop castles, and no temples. Yet Dublin has a subtle charm that grows on you as you walk its streets and meet its citizens. Although it's a fast-paced capital and the largest city in Ireland, with more than a million people (nearly one-quarter of Ireland's population), Dublin remains compact and accessible to the visitor. Unlike most cities of this size, Dublin has not sprouted forests of skyscrapers. It is characterized primarily by low-rise, 18th-century buildings and, consequently, has a distinctly old European feel. In large part the ambience of Dublin is due to its inhabitants, 25% of whom are under the age of 26. They preserve their national heritage in their theater, their literature, their music, and even in the beer they drink.

Founded just over 1,000 years ago, Dublin has long been an important city. The name Dublin comes from the Irish *Dubh Linn* (Dark Pool), named for the black waters of the Liffey River where the first inhabitants built a trading port. Although the Vikings were the first to settle here, Dublin was also home to the Anglo-Normans who, in the 12th century, built Christ Church and St. Patrick's Cathedral.

The Irish are a proud people who for centuries struggled against British rule before finally winning their independence in 1949. Much of the conflict, especially during the early years of this century, took place in Dublin. The Irish Nationalist movement, Sinn Féin, was born here, and in 1916 Dublin was the location of the famous Easter uprising, which stimulated Irish nationalism greatly.

The British left a legacy in the architecture of Dublin. The simple but elegant Georgian town houses surrounding St. Stephen's Green and Merrion Square, Leinster House (the seat of Irish government), and Dublin Castle's State Apartments are just a few of Dublin's important buildings that were constructed by the British.

---

1. FROM A BUDGET TRAVELER'S POINT OF VIEW

DUBLIN BUDGET BESTS   The best values in Dublin by far are the city's many bed-and-breakfasts. These are generally small establishments with six or fewer rooms, but what they lack in size they more than make up for in homeyness. To stay in a Dublin bed-and-breakfast is to meet the Irish in their own homes, and there is no better way to get to know Ireland than to sit around the breakfast table chatting with your hosts over a huge meal of porridge, soda bread, thick bacon, and delicious sausages, eggs, juice, and coffee.

WHAT THINGS COST IN DUBLIN	U.S. $
Taxi from the airport to the city center	16.00
Local telephone call	.36
Double room at the Shelbourne Hotel (deluxe)	270.00
Double room at Georgian House (moderate)	130.00
Double room at Mrs. Fitzgibbon's (budget)	52.20
Continental breakfast at Kylemore Café	1.50
Lunch for one at Rudyard's (moderate)	14.40
Lunch for one at Bewley's (budget)	7.20
Dinner for one, without wine, at Coq Hardi (deluxe)	57.60
Dinner for one, without wine, at Flanagan's (moderate)	21.60
Dinner for one, without wine, at Old Stand (budget)	14.40
Pint of beer	3.00
Coca-Cola (in a restaurant)	1.00
Cup of coffee	1.00
Roll of 100 ASA color film, 36 exposures	8.60
Admission to Dublin Castle	1.80
Movie ticket	7.20
Theater ticket	14.40–23.40

SPECIAL DISCOUNT OPPORTUNITIES Dublin's best special discounts are for traveling on the city's extensive network of buses and commuter trains. There are several different passes available, but the best deal is for students. For IR£8.50 ($15.30), students can get a weekly bus ticket allowing unlimited travel on all buses except the airport coach. You must have a U.S.I.T. card with a C.I.E. Travel Save stamp in order to get one of these passes. There is also a 1-day family pass for IR£5.50 ($9.90) that allows two adults and up to four children unlimited use of the bus and suburban rail system during off-peak hours.

WORTH THE EXTRA BUCKS Escorted bus tours, especially those visiting the Wicklow Mountains, are well worth the cost since they will give you an indication of why Ireland is called the Emerald Isle. If you are traveling with a group and you don't want to take the bus tour, renting a car for a day can be quite affordable. It takes very little time to get out of the city and into the green countryside. Tours cost between IR£6 and IR£22 ($10.80 and $39.60).

2. PRETRIP PREPARATIONS

DOCUMENTS Citizens of the United States, Great Britain, Canada, Australia, and New Zealand need only a valid passport to visit Ireland.

WHAT TO PACK The only essential item to pack for a trip to Dublin is an umbrella or raincoat. A sweater also comes in handy year round, although you might prefer to buy your Irish wool Aran sweater while you're here.

Dubliners, although often quite stylish, tend to dress more informally than the residents of many other European cities. Very casual, comfortable clothes will do in most situations here. Bring something dressy if you plan to attend the theater.

✓ WHAT'S SPECIAL ABOUT DUBLIN

The Book of Kells
☐ A 1,000-year-old copy of the New Testament, one of Ireland's most important treasures.

Irish Music
☐ Traditional Irish music any night of the week in pubs all over Dublin, most of the time absolutely free.

James Joyce
☐ A map marking locations from *Ulysses* available from the tourist office.

☐ A James Joyce museum in the nearby town of Sandy Cove.

Wool Sweaters
☐ A large selection at the Dublin Woolen Mills shop by the Ha'penny Bridge.

Live Theater
☐ Productions from a wealth of Irish playwrights past and present are performed.

WHEN TO GO   It can be cool and rainy any time of year in Dublin, so be sure to bring clothes for "damp" days, as Dubliners call their cool wet days.

Dublin's Average Daytime Temperature & Days of Rain

	Jan	Feb	Mar	Apr	May	June	July	Aug	Sept	Oct	Nov	Dec
Temp. (°F)	45	45	49	53	58	63	65	65	62	57	50	47
Days of Rain	17	14	15	14	15	14	14	16	15	16	16	18

Special Events   The most important event in Dublin, and all of Ireland, is **St. Patrick's Day,** March 17. Wherever you are, there will be plenty of celebrating on this date. Dubliners celebrate their literary heritage each June with the **Dublin Literary Festival.** The focal point of the festival is Bloomsday, June 16, which memorializes James Joyce's character Leopold Bloom. In late September and early October is the **Dublin Theatre Festival.**

BACKGROUND READING   Over the years Dublin has been home to an impressive number of playwrights, poets, and novelists. Most notable of them all is James Joyce, who wrote about his turn-of-the-century Dublin in the weighty novel *Ulysses* and the more accessible *Dubliners,* a collection of short stories. Other famous literary figures include W. B. Yeats, Samuel Beckett, Oscar Wilde, J. M. Synge, George Bernard Shaw, and Sean O'Casey. Yeats, Beckett, and Shaw all received Nobel Prizes in literature. Jonathan Swift, author of *Gulliver's Travels,* was dean of St. Patrick's Cathedral from 1713 to 1745. For general background on Ireland, try Leon Uris's *Trinity.*

3. ORIENTATION & GETTING AROUND

ARRIVING IN DUBLIN

From **Dublin Airport,** 7 miles north of the city, buses run a regular schedule to the **Busáras Central Bus Station.** You can take either the express bus for IR£2.30 ($4.15), which will get you into town in under 30 minutes, or bus no. 41A, which can take as long as an hour but costs only IR£1.10 ($2). A taxi into town will cost IR£10 ($18).

INFORMATION

The **Irish Tourist Board (Bord Fáilte)** has its main information center at 14 Upper O'Connell St. (tel. 747-733), where you can find all sorts of information about Dublin and the rest of Ireland. Facilities include a currency-exchange counter, a car-rental counter, and a hotel-reservations desk. Books and maps for sale here can help you learn more about the city. Bord Fáilte also maintains offices at Dublin Airport (tel. 376-387) and at the ferry dock in Dun Laoghaire (tel. 280-6984). The hours for each of the tourist information centers vary depending on the month, but they are generally open Monday through Saturday from 9am to 6pm.

You can also pick up a copy of **Tourism News,** a free tourist information newspaper, and the **Dublin Event Guide,** a free biweekly entertainment guide, at any of the tourist centers.

CITY LAYOUT

The **River Liffey** flows through the city, dividing it north-south. On the **north bank** is the new city, which has as its focal point **O'Connell Street,** a busy street lined with shops and restaurants. The Busáras Central Bus Station is also on the north side. Connecting the north and south banks of the river are 11 bridges, the largest of which is the O'Connell Street Bridge and the smallest of which is the nearby pedestrians-only Ha'Penny Bridge. On the **south bank** in the old city are most of Dublin's important sites such as Trinity College, Dublin Castle, Christ Church Cathedral, St. Patrick's Cathedral, the National Gallery, and the National Museum.

GETTING AROUND

Dublin is a very crowded city and getting around by bus or car can be very time-consuming. If you are going a short distance it's almost always better to walk, especially given the fact that most of the tourist attractions are clustered within the old city. For longer distances, there are a number of transportation options.

BY DART   The Dublin Area Rapid Transit, or DART, commuter train is the best way to get in and out of Dublin if you are staying in Dun Laoghaire or want to take a trip out to Howth Head or Bray Head for a bit of walking around outside the city. Unfortunately, it's not very useful for travel within the city itself. There are only three stops convenient to tourist sites—Pearse Station, beside Trinity College; Tara Station, on the south bank of the Liffey one block from O'Connell Bridge; and Connolly Station. DART costs about the same as the bus (see below). The fare to Dun Laoghaire is IR£1 ($1.80).

BY BUS   Because of the traffic congestion in the center of Dublin, public buses can be agonizingly slow, but they are still the best way to travel around the city. Almost all the tourist sites can be easily reached by bus. The fare varies according to your destination, with an average fare of 80p ($1.45). The trip to Dun Laoghaire will cost IR£1.10 ($2). Exact change is suggested but not necessary.

There are several different **discount bus passes** that allow unlimited travel for 1, 4, or 7 days. These passes range in price from IR£2.80 ($5.05) for a 1-day bus pass to IR£10 ($18) for a 4-day bus and DART pass. You can pick up passes at the main bus office on Upper O'Connell Street across from the Irish Tourist board information center. Combination bus and DART passes are available at all DART stations. To use your bus pass, simply insert it into the small box just inside the door of the bus. The box will stamp your ticket and return it to you.

ON FOOT   Dublin, though a compact city that can easily be explored on foot, is not an easy city to find your way around. A street in Dublin may change names three times within three blocks, and the street signs, when they're there at all, are posted on the second-floor wall of a corner building. Adding to the confusion is the lack of numbers on buildings in many places and the fact that many streets in Dublin are numbered up one side of the street and down the other, rather than alternating sides. There are exceptions, but they are primarily in the suburbs.

BY BICYCLE   Riding a bicycle in Dublin is not recommended. Traffic is very heavy, streets are narrow, and pedestrians crowd every corner in the city center. If you are determined to take to the streets on wheels, however, you can rent a bicycle for IR£5 ($9) per day or IR£22 ($39.60) per week at the **Bike Store,** 58 Lower Gardiner St. (tel. 725-399), just around the corner from the Dublin Tourist Hostel. The Bike Store is open Monday through Saturday from 9:30am to 6pm.

CAR RENTAL   Renting a car in Dublin is not advisable because of traffic congestion and parking problems, but when exploring the countryside you may wish to go by car. **Argus Automobiles,** at the Tourist Office at 14 Upper O'Connell St. (tel. 744-468), is convenient and has good rates. Their most economical car is IR£31 ($55.80) per day in high season. If you do rent a car in Dublin, be sure you can park it off the street. Car theft and break-ins are all too frequent.

   If you are staying in Dun Laoghaire, try **South County Rentals,** Rochestown Avenue (tel. 280-6005). Their least expensive car rents for IR£26 ($46.80) per day (though mileage is extra unless you rent for 4 days or more).

FAST DUBLIN

Banks   The **Bank of Ireland,** 28 Lower O'Connell St. (tel. 728-344), and **Allied Irish Bank,** 63 Upper O'Connell St. (tel. 731-500), are open Monday through Friday from 10am to 12:30pm and 1:30 to 3pm (on Thursday until 5pm).

Business Hours   Regular **office hours** in Dublin are Monday through Friday from 9am to 5pm. **Shops** generally stay open Monday through Saturday from 9am to 6pm and many offer late shopping until 8 or 9pm 1 or 2 nights a week.

Currency   The basic unit of currency in Ireland is the **punt,** or **Irish pound (IR£),** which is divided into 100 **pence (p).** There are 1p, 2p, 5p, 10p, 20p, 50p, and IR£1 coins and notes of 5, 10, 20, 50, and 100 pounds. We use the symbol IR£ to distinguish the Irish pound from the English pound. Currency can be exchanged at banks, and at the Irish Tourist Board at 14 Upper O'Connell St. (see "Information," above, for details).

Embassies   The **U.S. Embassy** is at 43 Elgin Rd. (tel. 688-777); the **Australian Embassy** is at Fitzwilton House, Wilton Terrace (tel. 761-517); the **Canadian Embassy** is at 65 St. Stephen's Green (tel. 781-988); and the **British Embassy** is at 31 Merrion Rd. (tel. 269-5211).

Emergencies   Dial **999** for **fire, police,** and **ambulance.** For the name and phone number of a physician on duty, ask at your hotel. **O'Connell's Pharmacy,** 55 Lower O'Connell St. (tel. 730-427), is open Monday through Saturday from 8:30am to 10pm and on Sunday from 10am to 10pm.

Eyeglasses   See **Boylan Flanagan Ltd.** at 19a Talbot St. (tel. 786-056) if you need your glasses repaired or replaced. They are open Monday through Friday from 9am to 5:30pm and on Saturday from 9am to 1pm.

Holidays   Public holidays in Dublin are January 1; March 17 (St. Patrick's Day); Good Friday; Easter Monday; the First Mondays in June, August, and October; and December 25–27.

Hospitals   The **Mater Misericordiae Hospital,** 7 Eccles St. (tel. 301-122), is a general hospital with an outpatient clinic.

Information   The main information center for the **Irish Tourist Board (Bord Fáilte)** is at 14 Upper O'Connell St. (tel. 747-733). Bord Fáilte also maintains offices at the airport (tel. 376-387), and at the ferry dock in Dun Laoghaire (tel. 280-6984). See "Information," above, for details.

THE PUNT [IRISH POUND] & THE DOLLAR

At this writing $1 = approximately 55½p (or IR£1 = $1.80), and this was the rate of exchange used to calculate the dollar values given in this chapter (rounded to the nearest nickel). This rate fluctuates from time to time and may not be the same when you travel to Ireland. Therefore the following table should be used only as a guide:

IR£	U.S. $	IR£	U.S. $
.25	.45	6	10.80
.50	.90	7	12.60
.75	1.35	8	14.40
1	1.80	9	16.20
2	3.60	10	18.00
3	5.40	15	27.00
4	7.20	20	36.00
5	9.00	25	45.00

Laundry/Dry Cleaning   The **laundrette** at 10 Lower Dorsett St. is open Monday through Wednesday from 9am to 7pm, on Thursday and Friday from 9am to 8pm, and on Saturday from 9am to 6:30pm. Take dry cleaning to **Marlowe Cleaners,** 58 O'Connell St. (tel. 731-050), open Monday through Saturday from 8am to 6pm. They also do shoe repairs.

In Dun Laoghaire, the **Star Laundry** is at 47 Upper Georges St. It's open daily from 8:30am to 6pm.

Lost and Found   The **Dublin Bus Lost Property Office** is on Marlborough Street between Marlborough Place and Sackville Place, open Monday through Friday from 8:45am to 12:45pm and 1:30 to 5pm. You can also inquire about lost property at the **Irish Tourist Board,** at 14 Upper O'Connell St.

Mail   The **General Post Office** is located on O'Connell Street at the corner of Henry Street. It's open Monday through Saturday from 8am to 8pm and on Sunday from 10:30am to 6:30pm. An airmail letter to the United States will cost 52p (95¢) and a postcard to the U.S. will cost 38p (70¢). There is also a foreign-currency exchange here that keeps the same hours as the post office.

Newspapers   The *Irish Independent* and the *Irish Times* are the most informative newspapers.

Photographic Needs   The **Camera Shop,** 70 Lower Gardiner St. (tel. 747-248), is open Monday through Saturday from 9am to 6pm.

Police   Dial 999.

Radio/TV   Two national, three local, and BBC radio stations are broadcast. TV choices include the BBC, Irish programming, and satellite programming.

Religious Services   **St. Patrick's Cathedral,** St. Patrick's Street (tel. 754-817), has Anglican services daily at 8:30am and on Sunday also at 11:15am. **St. Mary's Pro-Cathedral,** Marlborough Street (tel. 745-441), has Catholic services with a choir on Sunday at 11am. There is an orthodox synagogue, **Dublin Hebrew Congregation,** at 37 Adelaide Rd. (tel. 761-734).

Shoe Repair   **Rapid Shoe Repair,** 5 Sackville Place, will repair shoes Monday through Saturday from 9am to 6pm.

Tax   Ireland's VAT (Value-Added Tax) ranges from 12.5% to 21%, depending on the goods purchased. Many stores will refund this amount to foreign visitors. For details, see "Savvy Shopping," below.

Taxis   Taxis are IR£1.80 ($3.25) to start and 75p ($1.35) per mile after that. Bags are 40p (70¢) extra and there is a 40p (70¢) extra charge for trips at night and on

Sunday. There are taxi stands along O'Connell Street and in front of major hotels. Cab companies you can call include **Co-op Taxis** (tel. 766-666), and **VIP Taxi Co.** (tel. 783-333).

Telephone   Dublin is in the process of adding a seventh digit to its six-digit phone numbers. If your call does not go through, contact an operator.

There is a **local and international phone center** at the General Post Office on O'Connell Street. A local phone call costs 20p (36¢). Pay phones accept either a variety of coins or a phone card (available at post offices). A call to the U.S. will cost about IR£4.05 ($7.30) for 3 minutes.

Tipping   In restaurants that do not add a service charge, 10% is the acceptable amount to tip if the service has been good. Taxi drivers do not expect a tip, but if you wish to give one, again, 10% is appropriate.

4. BUDGET ACCOMMODATIONS

All over Ireland you will discover delightful bed-and-breakfasts, and Dublin is no exception. The Irish, born with the gift of the gab, are an outgoing lot, and perhaps the best way to get to know a few is to stay in a bed-and-breakfast. For the most part, these are family homes whose owners strive to make you feel at home.

Gardiner Street, which begins only a few short blocks from Dublin's main bus terminal, is the city's center for budget accommodations. This area has experienced a pronounced decay over the past few years and is a bit run-down, but most guesthouses on this street still maintain their high standards. These 150- to 200-year-old homes, with their high ceilings and ornate plasterwork, offer a glimpse into Dublin's Georgian years. For those who like to be close to the action and are accustomed to the vagaries of inner-city life, this is the place to look for accommodations.

On the other hand, if you prefer to stay in a smaller family home on a quiet, residential street, enjoy electric blankets and down comforters, and don't mind a 15-minute commute, then by all means head for Dublin's suburbs. Two towns in particular offer excellent accommodation and value—**Clontarf** to the north and **Dun Laoghaire** (pronounced Dun Leary) to the southeast. Clontarf is connected to the city by bus no. 30 and Dun Laoghaire is connected by the speedy DART commuter train and bus nos. 7, 7A, and 8.

Remember that Dublin is in the process of changing its phone numbers. If your call does not go through, call the operator and ask for the new number.

DOUBLES FOR LESS THAN IR£31 [$55.80]

IN THE CITY CENTER

CASSIDY'S GUESTHOUSE, 4 Ardmore Ave., Dublin 7. Tel. 01/388-846.
    4 rms (none with bath). **Bus:** 10.
    $ Rates (including full Irish breakfast): IR£9.50 ($17.10) per person—single, double, triple, or quad. No credit cards.
With the cost of rooms steadily climbing and the dollar very weak, this pleasant guesthouse on a quiet residential street is a real find. Run by Aine Cassidy (with help from her husband and three young children), the guesthouse is a good choice for young travelers who are tired of hostels.

HARVEY'S GUESTHOUSE, 11 Upper Gardiner St., Dublin 1. Tel. 01/748-384. 5 rms (none with bath).

$ Rates (including full Irish breakfast): IR£15–IR£17 ($27–$30.60) single; IR£12.50–IR£14.50 ($22.50–$26.10) per person—double, triple, quad, or quint. No credit cards. **Parking:** Free.

A 10-minute walk from the bus terminal, Harvey's has been in operation for more than 20 years, and its small size assures personal attention from owners Mr. and Mrs. Eilish Flood. This is a good guesthouse for families or groups since two of the large rooms can sleep up to five people each. Floral sheets and warm duvets are nice touches.

SINCLAIR HOUSE, 3 Hardwicke St., Dublin 1. Tel. 01/788-412. 6 rms (none with bath).
$ Rates (including full Irish breakfast): IR£13.50–IR£18 ($24.30–$32.40) single; IR£27 ($48.60) double. No credit cards.
Less than a 15-minute walk up O'Connell Street from the bridge is this pleasant guesthouse run by Mrs. Maria McMahon. The Sinclair is an old Georgian town house built in the 18th century. A full Irish breakfast is served in a large dining room and there is a comfortable TV lounge where guests can relax, watch TV, or visit with other guests and the hosts. Rooms have clock radios and attractive bedspreads.

ALONG CLONTARF ROAD

Clontarf Road runs along the north side of Dublin Bay and is about 20 minutes by bus from O'Connell Street. A park with beautiful green lawns located between the bay and the roadway is delightful for evening strolls in the summer. Unfortunately, the view across the bay for much of the road's length is of the industrial port of Dublin. Take bus no. 30 from Abbey Street to reach any guesthouse on Clontarf Road.

BAYVIEW, 265 Clontarf Rd., Dublin 3. Tel. 01/339-870. 3 rms (2 twins with bath). **Bus:** 30.
$ Rates (including full Irish breakfast): IR£18 ($32.40) single without bath, IR£20 ($36) single with bath; IR£28 ($50.40) double without bath, IR£32 ($57.60) double with bath. No credit cards.
In another of the small guesthouses along Clontarf Road, you will be greeted by genial Mrs. Carmel Drain. Rooms 2 and 3 both have large bay windows that look out across the bay. Coffee (all day) and Irish breakfast are both available at 6am for early risers.

SEA BREEZE, 312 Clontarf Rd., Dublin 3. Tel. 01/332-787. 4 rms (3 with shower only). **Bus:** 30
$ Rates (including full Irish breakfast): IR£21 ($37.80) single; IR£30 ($54) double. No credit cards.
Sea Breeze is operated by Mrs. Myra O'Flaherty, who goes out of her way to take care of her guests. Of the Clontarf Road guesthouses listed, this 100-year-old house has the best view; try to get Room 4 with the bay window. The sitting room and dining room are both quite spacious. For IR£7 ($12.60), Mrs. O'Flaherty will prepare a four-course meal, though there are also several nearby restaurants.

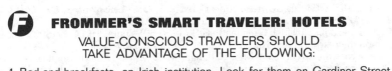

FROMMER'S SMART TRAVELER: HOTELS

VALUE-CONSCIOUS TRAVELERS SHOULD
TAKE ADVANTAGE OF THE FOLLOWING:

1. Bed-and-breakfasts, an Irish institution. Look for them on Gardiner Street near the bus station, along Clontarf Road northeast of downtown, and not far outside the city in the town of Dun Laoghaire.
2. Accommodations outside of downtown Dublin, if you prefer not to climb steep flights of stairs.

SOUTH OF CITY CENTER

MRS. MAI BIRD'S GUESTHOUSE, 25A Oakley Rd., Ranelagh, Dublin 6.
Tel. 01/972-286. 5 rms (none with bath). **Bus:** 13 from O'Connell Street.
$ Rates (including full Irish breakfast): IR£21 ($37.80) single; IR£14 ($25.20) per person—double, triple, or quad. No credit cards.

Dublin's southern district of Ranelagh, about 15 minutes south of city center, with narrow stone-walled lanes, is a neighborhood with the feel of a country village. In Mrs. Bird's small red-brick cottage the lace-trimmed breakfast room, tile-and-iron fireplaces, and attractively decorated rooms make a stay here quite enjoyable.

IN DUN LAOGHAIRE

This Victorian seaside resort, only 15 minutes by DART train from Dublin city center, is also the port for ferries to Liverpool and Holyhead in Great Britain. The greatest concentration of guesthouses here is on Rosmeen Gardens, a 3-minute walk from the Sandycove DART station.

MRS. ANNE D'ALTON, Annesgrove, 28 Rosmeen Gardens, Dun Laoghaire, Co. Dublin. Tel. 01/280-9801. 4 rms (none with bath). **DART:** Sandycove.
$ Rates (including full Irish breakfast): IR£17 ($30.60) single; IR£14.50 ($23.20) per person in shared rooms. No credit cards.

You'll feel right at home in Mrs. D'alton's cheerful home. All the rooms are very comfortable, and there are warm duvets on all the beds. There's a cozy TV lounge, and out back, a pleasant garden. A filling Irish breakfast will keep you going through hours of sightseeing.

MRS. GRETA MCGLOUGHLIN, 27 Rosmeen Gardens, Dun Laoghaire, Co. Dublin. Tel. 01/804-333. Fax 01/280-9331. 3 rms (1 with bath). TV **DART:** Sandycove.
$ Rates (including full Irish breakfast): IR£20 ($36) single; IR£14.50 ($26.10) per person in shared room without bath, IR£18 ($32.40) per person in shared room with bath. No credit cards. **Closed:** Dec–Jan.

Operated by a former Aer Lingus airline hostess, this B&B features a bright and cheery breakfast room overlooking the garden. Guest rooms are comfortably and attractively furnished.

MRS. HELEN CALLANAN, 1 Rosmeen Gardens, Dun Laoghaire, Co. Dublin. Tel. 01/280-6083. 6 rms (1 with bath). **DART:** Sandycove.
$ Rates (including full Irish breakfast): IR£18 ($32.40) single; IR£14.50 ($23.20) per person in shared rooms. No credit cards.

Mrs. Helen Callanan started out at 5 Rosmeen Gardens and continues to take in guests at her new address. This spacious red-brick house, built in 1900, affords views of the bay from its colorfully decorated rooms, one of which even has a large comfortable couch. A full Irish breakfast is served from 7am on.

MRS. MARIE DUNN, 30 Rosmeen Gardens, Dun Laoghaire, Co. Dublin. Tel. 01/280-3360. 4 rms (none with bath). **DART:** Sandycove.
$ Rates (including full Irish breakfast): IR£17 ($30.60) single; IR£14.50 ($23.20) per person in shared rooms. No credit cards. **Closed:** Nov–Mar.

Directly across the street from Mrs. Callanan, Mrs. Marie Dunn is open only from April to October. Rooms here are clean and comfortable. A full Irish breakfast is served in the cozy dining room.

RATHOE HOUSE, 12 Rosmeen Gardens, Dun Laoghaire, Co. Dublin. Tel. 01/280-8070. 4 rms (none with bath). **DART:** Sandycove.
$ Rates (including full Irish breakfast): IR£18 ($32.40) single; IR£14.50 ($23.20) per person in shared rooms. No credit cards.

★ You will be made to feel like a long-lost relative the moment you walk through the door of Mrs. Fitzgibbon's Rathoe House. All beds come with electric blankets and down comforters. Mrs. Fitzgibbon is happy to take the time to help you get your bearings in Dublin and serves large Irish breakfasts.

ROSMEEN HOUSE, 13 Rosmeen Gardens, Dun Laoghaire, Co. Dublin. Tel. 01/280-7613. 5 rms (1 double with bath). **DART:** Sandycove.
$ Rates (including full Irish breakfast): IR£17 ($30.60) single; IR£14.50 ($23.20) per person in shared rooms. No credit cards. **Closed:** Dec 15–Feb 1.
Rosmeen House is right next door to the Rathoe House. This house was built in the 1920s, and guests have use of a drawing room and sun room as well as the dining room. Mrs. Murphy keeps her home immaculately clean. The orthopedic beds all have electric blankets.

DOUBLES FOR LESS THAN IR£33 ($59.40)

STELLA MARIS, 13 Upper Gardiner St., Dublin 1. Tel. 01/740-835. 8 rms (2 with bath). **Parking:** Free, in the back.
$ Rates (including full Irish breakfast): IR£16–IR£17 ($28.80–$30.60) single; IR£14–IR£16 ($25.20–$28.80) per person, double or triple. No credit cards.

★ In one of the old Georgian town houses along Upper Gardiner Street is the friendly Stella Maris, efficiently run by Mrs. Breda Smith. Mrs. Smith was in the hotel business long before she opened her own bed-and-breakfast, and she brings her years of experience into use here. Most of the rooms are large and comfortable, with high ceilings and large windows.

WAVERLY HOUSE, 4 Hardwicke St., Dublin 1. Tel. 01/746-132. 6 rms (4 with shower).
$ Rates (including full Irish breakfast): IR£14–IR£16 ($25.20–$28.80) single without shower; IR£12–IR£15 ($21.60–$27) per person double without shower. IR£12–IR£17 ($21.60–$30.60) per person, double or triple, with attached shower. No credit cards.
Hardwicke Street is a few blocks from Gardiner Street and in a more attractive area. At the end of this quiet street is a large old church with a picturesque steeple. The Waverly is in a modernized Georgian town house with a long history of accepting paying guests. In 1903 James Joyce stayed here when the building was used as a boardinghouse.

SUPER-BUDGET CHOICES

HOSTELS

DUBLIN INTERNATIONAL YOUTH HOSTEL, 61 Mountjoy St., Dublin 7. Tel. 01/301-766. 500 beds. **Bus:** 10 from O'Connell Street.
$ Rates (including continental breakfast): IR£7.50–IR£9.50 ($13.50–$17.10) for IYHF members; rates vary with the season, and smaller rooms are more expensive. EURO, MC, V.
This is Dublin's newest hostel, housed in a converted convent. Most of the accommodations are in large dormitories, but there are also a few doubles, triples, and quads. The dining room here is a beautiful converted chapel, and the pay phone is in an old confessional booth. Other amenities include discount train fares to other parts of Ireland (a real deal, and not available anywhere else) and a courtesy bus to the ferry ports in summer.

If you are not a member of the IYHF, instead of paying the single IR£7.50 ($13.50) membership fee at one time, you can now buy a guest stamp for IR£1.25 ($2.25) per night. When you have purchased six guest stamps, you are considered a member.

ISAAC'S DUBLIN TOURIST HOSTEL, 2-5 Frenchman's Lane, Dublin 1. Tel. 01/749-321 or 363-877. 250 beds.
$ Rates: IR£6 ($10.80) per person in dorms (sheets for an additional charge); IR£17

($30.60) single; IR£26 ($46.80) double (Single and double rates include full breakfast.) Continental breakfast costs IR£1.30 ($2.35) extra; a full Irish breakfast, IR£2 ($3.60). No credit cards.

⭐ Dublin's best value is this restored wine-storage warehouse that was built in the 1700s. The hostel is only 50 yards from the main bus terminal, requires no youth-hostel card, and accepts people of all ages. The ground-floor restaurant and lounge is reminiscent of a German rathskeller with stone walls and huge exposed beams overhead. The self-service restaurant is open to the public. A spacious self-catering kitchen and television lounge are available to guests. There are some singles and doubles, but mostly six-bed dorms.

KINLAY HOUSE, 2-12 Lord Edward St., Dublin 2. Tel. 01/679-6644. Fax 01/778-908. 150 beds. **Bus:** 50 or 54.

$ Rates (including an all-you-can-eat continental breakfast): IR£8 ($14.40) per person in dorms; IR£10 ($18) per person in quads. No credit cards.

⭐ Located across the street from Christ Church Cathedral is this 100-year-old building that was originally a charitable boys' home. It accepts guests of both sexes and all ages, and no hostel card is necessary. All rooms are carpeted, clean, and attractively furnished. Most of the accommodations are in four- and six-bed rooms. There is a large, bright dining hall and a self-catering kitchen. There is also a television lounge, a study lounge, and a recreation room. Unfortunately, it's situated on a busy street and the noise may bother light sleepers. The hostel is on the edge of the Temple Bar area, Dublin's "left bank," where you'll find plenty of interesting restaurants and shops.

YOUNG TRAVELLER, Western Way, on St. Mary's Place, Dublin 7. Tel. 01/305-000. 58 beds. **Bus:** 10 from O'Connell Street.

$ Rates (including continental breakfast): IR£9 ($16.20) per person in dorms. V.

This hostel is a bit away from the center but easily reached in about 10 minutes by bus. It's on Western Way, a tiny street located just north of Dorset Street with an old church on a square only steps from its door. There are 58 beds here in 14 quads and one twin, and each room has its own shower. The rooms are quite attractive, with carpeting and matching curtains and duvets. The hostel is open daily 24 hours all year and requires no youth-hostel card. All ages are accepted.

WORTH THE EXTRA BUCKS

MRS. ELSIE O'DONOGHUE, 41 Northumberland Rd., Ballsbridge, Dublin 4. Tel. 01/681-105. 8 rms (none with bath). **Bus:** 5, 6, 7, or 8.

$ Rates (including full Irish breakfast): IR£23 ($41.40) single; IR£38 ($68.40) double, IR£51 ($91.80) triple, IR£68 ($122.40) quad. No credit cards.

⭐ In the posh Ballsbridge district of Dublin not far from the deluxe Jurys Hotel and the American Embassy, 15 minutes south of center city, is one of the best splurge bed-and-breakfasts in the city. Elsie O'Donoghue's large Victorian home was built in 1877 and it features the finest plasterwork ceilings of any guesthouse listed here. Breakfast is served in a huge room with a massive mirror over the fireplace. Mrs. O'Donoghue is extremely helpful to her guests and will make sure that you enjoy your stay in Dublin.

5. BUDGET DINING

From pub grub to haute cuisine, Dublin has it all, but the name of the game for cheap eating here is self-service. Many very good and inexpensive restaurants, ranging in size from the massive Bewley's Café on Grafton Street to the tiny Cunningham's Coffee Shop across from the National Museum, offer self-service meals. Also keep in mind that since breakfast is included in the cost of your room, you can save money for more expensive destinations or splurge a bit on food while you're here in Dublin.

LOCAL BUDGET BETS

FISH & CHIPS

BESHOFF'S, 14 Westmoreland St. and 7 Upper O'Connell St. Tel. 778-026.
   Cuisine: FISH AND CHIPS.
$ **Prices:** IR£3–IR£5.50 ($5.40–$9.90). No credit cards.
   Open: Daily 11:30am–1am.

Beshoff's is one of Dublin's oldest and most popular fish-and-chips restaurants, and it now offers two locations on either side of the O'Connell Street Bridge. The first Beshoff's was founded in 1913 by Russian immigrant Ivan Beshoff. Today the two always-crowded restaurants offer as many as 20 varieties of fish and chips in an Edwardian oyster-bar atmosphere of black-and-white tiles and marble-top tables. On any given day the catch might include plaice, mackerel, smoked mackerel, shrimp, and monkfish.

MEALS FOR LESS THAN IR£5 [$9]

ON THE NORTH BANK

KYLEMORE CAFE, 1-2 Upper O'Connell St. Tel. 722-138.
   Cuisine: IRISH.
$ **Prices:** IR£2.50–IR£5 ($4.50–$9). No credit cards.
   Open: Mon–Sat 8am–9pm, Sun noon–8pm.

This large restaurant on busy O'Connell Street bills itself as a new concept in self-service dining, and it is indeed a cafeteria with style. Floor-to-ceiling windows flood the large and always-crowded dining room with light. There are plenty of marble-top tables to seat the throngs of diners who fill the restaurant all day long, so don't be discouraged if it looks full.

ON THE SOUTH BANK

THE ATRIUM, Trinity College. Tel. 773-787.
   Cuisine: IRISH.
$ **Prices:** IR£2–IR£2.50 ($3.20–$4). No credit cards.
   Open: Mon–Thurs noon–7:15pm, noon–6:30pm.
Another exceptional bargain is this huge student cafeteria on the Trinity College campus. It's to the left of the campanile just inside the main gate to the college, and inside you'll find large portraits of former deans hung high on the walls of the bright room. The prices are incredibly reasonable, and if you're a student, the prices are even better. If you aren't hungry enough for a big lunch, visit the snack bar in the basement where you can pick up a small sandwich for less than IR£1 ($1.80).

BEWLEY'S CAFE, 78 Grafton St. Tel. 776-761.
   Cuisine: IRISH.
$ **Prices:** IR£2–IR£4.50 ($3.60–$8.10). No credit cards.
   Open: Mon–Fri 7:30am–9pm (Thurs until 10pm), Sat 8am–8pm, Sun 10am–7pm.

Bewley's is a Dublin institution and as such is always jammed with people despite its 350 seats and three dining areas. It specializes in coffees, teas, and pastries, but you can also get sandwiches, salads, and hot lunches at their self-service restaurants. There are tables and large booths, and no one will mind if you linger over coffee and the newspaper or a book for several hours.

Other Bewley's locations include 11-12 Westmoreland St. and 12 Georges St.

CUNNINGHAM'S COFFEE SHOP, 35A Kildare St. Tel. 762-952.

Cuisine: IRISH.
$ Prices: IR£1.75–IR£4.50 ($3.15–$8.10). No credit cards.
Open: Mon–Fri 8:45am–5:30pm.

This tiny restaurant is hardly bigger than a closet, but it's very convenient to the National Museum, which is directly across the street. Duck in if you're in a hurry.

THE WELL FED CAFE, 6 Crow St. Tel. 771-974.

Cuisine: VEGETARIAN.
$ Prices: IR£2.50–IR£5.50 ($4.50–$9.90). No credit cards.
Open: Tues–Fri 10am–8:30pm, Sat 10am–4:30pm.

More than just a restaurant, the Well Fed Café is a gathering place for those who espouse a natural way of life. The restaurant specializes in home-cooked vegetarian meals and offers three-course meals. If you're looking for long-term accommodations or are interested in a yoga class or a lecture on Marxism in Ireland, check the extensive bulletin boards here.

MEALS FOR LESS THAN IR£10 ($18)

ON THE SOUTH BANK

BAD ASS CAFE, 9-11 Crown Alley. Tel. 712-596.

Cuisine: IRISH.
$ Prices: IR£3.50–IR£9 ($6.30–$16.20). ACCESS, AE, EURO, MC, V.
Open: Daily 9am–midnight.

 This restaurant is popular with students and families alike. The split-level dining room is spacious and painted red, white, and blue. Along one wall is a large notice board covered with flyers for interesting events in and around Dublin. Reading the menu is half the fun of eating here, and there's live music Tuesday and Thursday nights. Remember that service is *not* included here.

GALLAGHER'S BOXTY HOUSE, 20-21 Temple Bar. Tel. 772-762.

Cuisine: IRISH.
$ Prices: IR£5.50–IR£10 ($9.90–$18). EURO, MC, V.
Open: Mon–Fri 7:30am–11pm, Sat–Sun 12:30–11pm.

Boxty is a traditional Irish dish made from—you guessed it—potatoes. In this case the potatoes are made into a pancake and rolled around a filling to form an Irish filled crêpe. Get your boxty filled with beef and horseradish, bacon and cabbage, Indian chickpeas, or any of many other fillings. The stone walls and stained glass give the restaurant the feel of an old inn or tavern.

NATIONAL GALLERY FITZERS, Merrion Sq. W. Tel. 686-481.

Cuisine: INTERNATIONAL.
$ Prices: IR£4.75–IR£6 ($8.55–$10.80). ACCESS, AE, DC, EURO, MC, V.

ⓕ ### FROMMER'S SMART TRAVELER: RESTAURANTS

VALUE-CONSCIOUS TRAVELERS SHOULD
TAKE ADVANTAGE OF THE FOLLOWING:

1. Self-service dining.
2. Tourist menus, which provide limited choices but substantial savings.
3. Pub grub, which can often be surprisingly sophisticated, and costs less than restaurant fare.

Open: Coffee daily 10am–noon; lunch daily noon–4:30pm; tea Mon–Wed and Fri–Sat 3–5:30pm Thurs 3–8:30pm, Sun 2–4:30pm.

Strategically located between two galleries full of paintings at the National Gallery on Merrion Square, Fitzers rapidly became one of Dublin's "in" lunch spots after it opened. In between Goyas and El Grecos you can try coq au vin or hake Mallorca. Beef cannelloni or vegetarian lasagne might be the perfect accompaniment to a Gainsborough. There is live piano music on Thursday evening and Saturday afternoon, and lots of plants and latticework give Fitzers a garden-party feeling.

THE OLD STAND, 37 Exchequer St. Tel. 777-220.
Cuisine: PUB GRUB.
$ Prices: IR£4–IR£9 ($7.20–$16.20). ACCESS, EURO, MC.
Open: Lunch Mon–Fri 12:30–2:30pm; dinner Mon–Fri 5–9:30pm, Sat 12:30–8:30pm. No food served Sun.

★ This pub is extremely popular not so much for its atmosphere or its drinks, but for the meals it serves. The selections might include the soup of the day, smoked salmon or trout salad, and an apple tart with cream. Close to Grafton Street, this is some of the best pub food in Dublin.

RUDYARD'S, 15-16 Crown Alley. Tel. 710-846.
Cuisine: IRISH.
$ Prices: IR£9–IR£15 ($16.20–$27). ACCESS, AE, DC, EURO, MC, V.
Open: Lunch Mon–Fri 12:30–2:30pm; dinner Mon–Thurs 5–10:30pm, Fri–Sat 5–11pm.

This elegant bistro looks tiny when you glance through the front window, but there are actually three floors of tables, including a wine bar. The candles on the tables, the marble floor, and the specials listed on the menu out front should be enough to draw you inside. Stop by for dinner and enjoy live jazz in the wine bar or save money by having lunch instead.

TRATTORIA PASTA PASTA, 42 Exchequer St. Tel. 679-2565.
Cuisine: ITALIAN.
$ Prices: IR£4–IR£10 ($7.20–$18). ACCESS, AE, DC, EURO, MC, V.
Open: Mon–Sat noon–12:30am.

Just a few doors away from the Old Stand, this restaurant features an excellent variety of Italian foods, from light lunches to filling pasta dinners. Bright and airy, the two-level restaurant is decorated with colorful murals. At lunch and dinner the restaurant is filled with Dubliners who have forsaken the potato for pasta.

PICNIC SUPPLIES

In the basement of the **Dunnes Market** on North Earl Street, two doors from O'Connell Street, you'll find almost everything you need for a picnic. Wait to buy your bread across the street at the **Kylemore Bakery,** where they have delicious breads and pastries. When you have everything you need, take bus no. 10 to Phoenix Park.

6. ATTRACTIONS

In A.D. 988 Dublin was founded by traders who settled on the banks of the Liffey River. Since then the city has had a turbulent history as the people constantly struggled for home rule first against the Vikings, then the Normans, and most recently the British. This history is captured in many of the city's important landmarks.

SUGGESTED ITINERARIES

IF YOU HAVE ONE DAY Start your day at Trinity College Library where the *Book of Kells* is on display. Then walk over to the National Museum to see exhibits of Irish antiquities. If you have time, visit the nearby National Gallery briefly, with its fine

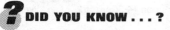 **DID YOU KNOW . . . ?**

- No point in Ireland is more than 70 miles away from the ocean.
- There are no snakes in Ireland; according to tradition, St. Patrick banished them from the island.
- Swift, Yeats, and Joyce were all born in Dublin.
- All official documents are published in both Irish and English.
- More than four times as many Irish citizens live outside Ireland as live within the country.
- Dublin was founded by Vikings.

collection of old masters and important Irish artists. After lunch, tour Dublin Castle and then visit St. Patrick's Cathedral and Christ Church Cathedral.

IF YOU HAVE TWO DAYS If you have 2 days, start your first day at the Trinity College Library, then walk over to the National Museum and National Gallery. After lunch, stroll around Merrion Square and St. Stephen's Green. Around these two public parks are a number of dignified Georgian town houses. Walk down Grafton Street, perhaps visiting the St. Stephen's Green Centre or the Powerscourt Town House Centre. Both of these are elegant shopping centers created from old buildings. Afterward tour Dublin Castle.

Start Day 2 with visits to Christ Church Cathedral and St. Patrick's Cathedral. Have lunch at the Brazen Head, Dublin's oldest pub, then visit the Guinness Hop Store Gallery to see how stout, Dublin's favorite drink, is brewed. Finish the day at the National Museum of Modern Art.

IF YOU HAVE THREE DAYS Spend Days 1 and 2 as described above. On your third day, take a day trip to the Boyne Valley and the north coast to visit burial mounds at Newgrange, the site of the Battle of the Boyne, King William's Glen, and other sites. This trip is also worthwhile for the glimpse of the Irish countryside it affords.

IF YOU HAVE FIVE DAYS Schedule another day trip to see the fabulous Irish countryside. Glendalough and the Wicklow Mountains make an excellent excursion. You can visit historic Glendalough, a former monastic city, and see Dublin's own mountains.

On the morning of your fifth day, take a trip out to Sandycove to see the James Joyce Museum and the Victorian harbor town of Dun Laoghaire. In the afternoon return to Dublin and visit the Municipal Gallery of Modern Art and the crypts of St. Michan's Church.

TOP ATTRACTIONS

NATIONAL MUSEUM, Kildare St. Tel. 618-811.

This museum is only half a block south of the Trinity College campus and among other exhibits has displays of early Viking life in Dublin. Be sure to watch the video of the excavation of the original site of Dublin that was discovered during construction of an office building. Housed in the same building is the Treasury, which holds the famous gold Tara Brooch and other Irish antiquities of particular value and beauty.

Admission: Museum, free; treasury, IR£1 ($1.80) adults, 30p (55¢) children, free for senior citizens and free for all on Tues.

Open: Tues–Sat 10am–5pm, Sun 2–5pm.

NATIONAL GALLERY, Merrion Sq. W. Tel. 615-133.

This gallery houses a collection of old masters, Irish artists, and the National Portrait Gallery. Among the many works displayed here are pieces by Rembrandt, Brueghel, Rubens, El Greco, Gainsborough, and Monet. Near the museum entrance is a statue of George Bernard Shaw, who left one-third of his estate to the museum when he died, saying that he owed his education to the gallery. There is an excellent and moderately priced self-service restaurant here in the gallery (see "Budget Dining," above, for details).

Admission: Free.

Open: Mon–Sat 10am–6pm (on Thurs until 9pm), Sun 2–5pm.

TRINITY COLLEGE LIBRARY, Trinity College Campus. Tel. 772-941.

Trinity College Library, built between 1712 and 1732, is to the right and behind the campanile just inside the front gate of Trinity College. Housed in the library's Long Room is the *Book of Kells,* an illustrated and illuminated copy of the gospels created by Irish monks in the early 9th century at the monastery of Kells. This exquisitely ornamented book is the rarest and most important book in Ireland. On the main floor is a bookstore that sells books by Irish authors, books about Ireland, and other gifts.

Stroll around the campus of Trinity College, founded 400 years ago, and glance into some of the old buildings to see some of the finest architecture in the city. The massive dining hall to the left of the campanile is open to the public (see "Budget Dining," above).

Admission: IR£1.75 ($3.15) adults, IR£1.50 ($2.70) students and senior citizens, free for children.

Open: Mon–Fri 9:30am–4:30pm, Sat 9:30am–12:30pm.

DUBLIN CASTLE, Dame St. Tel. 777-129.

Dublin Castle is located about midway between O'Connell Bridge and St. Patrick's Cathedral. The round tower beside the castle's chapel was built by the Normans in the early 13th century and is the oldest part of the castle. Most of the present building, however, was erected in the 18th century by the British as the residence of the viceroys. The castle now houses the State Apartments, and it is used for inaugurations of Irish presidents. The apartments are open to the public, with guided tours held throughout the day. Some fine Georgian plasterwork ceilings can be seen here. Around the outside wall of the attached chapel are more than 90 carved stone busts of British monarchs and other important historical figures.

Admission: IR£1 ($1.80) adults, 50p (90¢) children.

Open: Mon–Fri 10am–12:15pm and 2–5pm, Sat–Sun 2–5pm.

CHRIST CHURCH CATHEDRAL, Christ Church Place. Tel. 778-099.

One block west of Dublin Castle, on a ridge above the site of the original Norse town of Dublin, stands Christ Church Cathedral. Founded in 1038, the present building dates from 1172 and it was substantially renovated between 1871 and 1878. Inside you will find a monument to Strongbow, the ruler who had the cathedral built, and in the crypt you will see the stocks that once stood nearby. You may notice that the north interior wall has a very pronounced outward lean. Don't worry—it has been like this for hundreds of years and the building is in no danger of falling.

Admission: 50p (90¢) adults, 25p (45¢) students.

Open: Daily 10am–5pm; tours available by request. **Bus:** 21A, 50, 54, 54A, 78, or 78A.

ST. PATRICK'S CATHEDRAL, St. Patrick St. Tel. 754-817.

This cathedral was built less than 25 years after Christ Church Cathedral in an attempt to outdo that building. Jonathan Swift, author of *Gulliver's Travels,* was dean here from 1713 to 1745 and his tomb is to be found within the walls of this impressive Norman cathedral.

Admission: 80p ($1.45) adults, 30p (50¢) students.

Open: Mon–Fri 9am–6pm, Sat 9am–5pm (to 4pm in winter), Sun 10–11am (Easter–Oct, also 12:45–3:15pm; in winter, 10:30–11am only). **Bus:** 50, 50A, 54A, or 56A.

GUINNESS HOP STORE GALLERY, Crane St. Tel. 536-700, ext. 5238.

Three blocks west of Christ Church Cathedral, the Guinness Brewery is one of Dublin's most important institutions. The brewery itself is not open for tours, only the brewery museum where you can learn all about the famous "black porter" or stout

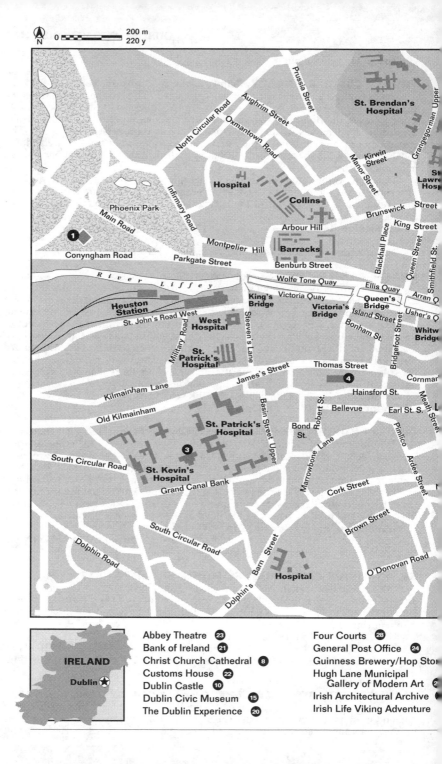

N 0 | 200 m
          220 y

St. Brendan's Hospital

Prussia Street

Aughrim Street

Oxmantown Road

North Circular Road

Infirmary Road

Kirwin Street

Manor Street

St. Lawre Hosp

Grangegorman Upper

Brunswick Street

King Street

Hospital

Collins

Arbour Hill

Barracks

Benburb Street

Blackhall Place

Queen Street

Smithfield St.

Phoenix Park

Main Road

Montpelier Hill

Conyngham Road

Parkgate Street

1

River Liffey

Wolfe Tone Quay

Ellis Quay

Arran Q

Victoria Quay

King's Bridge

Queen's Bridge

Usher's Q

Heuston Station

St. John's Road West

St. John's Road West

Island Street

Victoria's Bridge

Bonham St.

Whitw Bridge

West Hospital

Steeven's Lane

Military Road

Bridgefoot Street

St. Patrick's Hospital

Thomas Street

4

Cornmar

Hainsford St.

James's Street

Bellevue

Earl St. S.

Meath Street

Kilmainham Lane

Robert St.

Bond St.

Old Kilmainham

Basin Street Upper

St. Patrick's Hospital

Pimlico

Marrowbone Lane

Ardee Street

South Circular Road

3

St. Kevin's Hospital

Grand Canal Bank

Cork Street

Brown Street

South Circular Road

O'Donovan Road

Dolphin Road

Barn Street

Dolphin's

Hospital

IRELAND

Dublin ★

Abbey Theatre ㉓
Bank of Ireland ㉑
Christ Church Cathedral ⑧
Customs House ㉒
Dublin Castle ⑩
Dublin Civic Museum ⑮
The Dublin Experience ⑳

Four Courts ㉘
General Post Office ㉔
Guinness Brewery/Hop Stor
Hugh Lane Municipal
  Gallery of Modern Art ㉕
Irish Architectural Archive
Irish Life Viking Adventure

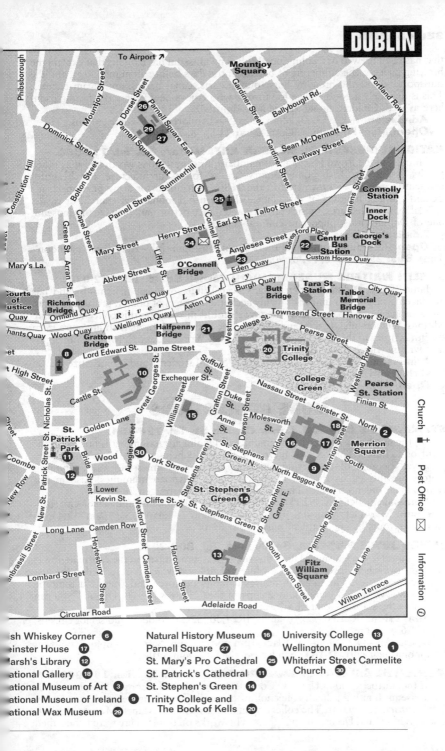

DUBLIN

To Airport ↗

Mountjoy Square

Phibsborough

Dominick Street

Constitution Hill

Mountjoy Street

Dorset Street

Parnell Square East

Parnell Square West

Bolton Street

Capel Street

Green St.

Arran St. E.

Mary's La.

Courts of Justice

Quay

hants Quay

Wood Quay

High Street

Castle St.

Coombe

New Row

New St.

St. Nicholas St.

St. Patrick Street

Bride Street

Golden Lane

St. Patrick's Park

Wood

Lower Kevin St.

Long Lane

Camden Row

nbrassil Street

Heytesbury Street

Lombard Street

Circular Road

Gardiner Street

Ballybough Rd.

Portland Row

Sean McDermott St.

Railway Street

Amiens Street

Connolly Station

Inner Dock

George's Dock

Summerhill

Parnell Street

O'Connell Street

Earl St. N. Talbot Street

Henry Street

Mary Street

Anglesea Street

Beresford Place

Central Bus Station

Custom House Quay

Abbey Street

Liffey St.

Eden Quay

City Quay

Richmond Bridge

Ormand Quay

Ormand Quay

Wellington Quay

River Liffey

Burgh Quay

Butt Bridge

Tara St. Station

Talbot Memorial Bridge

Gratton Bridge

Halfpenny Bridge

Aston Quay

Westmoreland

College St.

Townsend Street

Hanover Street

Lord Edward St.

Dame Street

Exchequer St.

Suffolk St.

Great Georges St.

William Street

Grafton St.

Duke St.

Anne St.

Dawson Street

Nassau Street

Pearse Street

Trinity College

College Green

Pearse St. Station

Westland Row

Finian St.

Finian St.

Molesworth St.

Leinster St.

Kildare St.

Merrion Street

Merrion Square

Aungier Street

York Street

St. Stephens Green W.

St. Stephens Green N.

North Baggot Street

North

St. Patrick's

Cliffe St.

St. Stephens Green S.

St. Stephen's Green

St. Stephens Green E.

Pembroke Street

Merrion Square South

Wexford Street

Camden Street

Harcourt Street

Hatch Street

Adelaide Road

Fitz William Square

South Leeson Street

Lad Lane

Wilton Terrace

Church ☩

Post Office ⊠

Information ⊙

ish Whiskey Corner ⑥

einster House ⑰

arsh's Library ⑫

ational Gallery ⑱

ational Museum of Art ③

ational Museum of Ireland ⑨

ational Wax Museum ㉙

Natural History Museum ⑯

Parnell Square ㉗

St. Mary's Pro Cathedral ㉕

St. Patrick's Cathedral ⑪

St. Stephen's Green ⑭

Trinity College and
   The Book of Kells ⑳

University College ⑬

Wellington Monument ①

Whitefriar Street Carmelite
   Church �30

that has been brewed in Dublin since 1769. The museum has exhibits that explain the brewing process, the coopering of barrels in the days before aluminum kegs, and the transportation of the brew by horse-drawn carts, canal barges, and steam engines. This is definitely a good choice for anyone who enjoys beer. There is a tasting room here as well. Children under 12 are not admitted.

Admission: IR£2 ($3.60) adults, 50p (90¢) children and senior citizens.
Open: Mon–Fri 10am–4:30pm. **Bus:** 21A, 78, 78A, or 78B.

NATIONAL MUSEUM OF MODERN ART, Military Rd. Tel. 718-666.

Housed in the Royal Hospital Kilmainham, this museum is worth a visit as much for its displays of Irish contemporary art as for its architecture and beautiful manicured grounds. Constructed in the 1680s as a home for army pensioners, it's Ireland's largest building of this vintage that is not a monastery, church, or castle. Special exhibits, lectures, music concerts, and dance performances make this museum one of Dublin's most important cultural centers.

Admission: Free.
Open: Tues–Sun 11am–6pm; tours Sun noon–3pm (July–Aug, Tues–Sun noon–3pm). **Bus:** 21A, 23, 78, 79, or 90.

DUBLIN WRITERS MUSEUM, 18/19 Parnell Sq. N. Tel. 722-077.

James Joyce, William Butler Yeats, Oscar Wilde, Brendan Behan—Ireland has produced a surprising number of highly acclaimed writers of poetry, prose, and plays. No aspiring writer or student of literature should miss seeing this collection of rare editions, memorabilia, letters, and photos. The collection covers Irish literature from the 9th century to the present. The adjacent Irish Writer's Centre provides contemporary writers with a place to meet and work.

Admission: IR£2 ($3.60) adults, IR£1 ($1.80) students and senior citizens, 50p (90¢) children 12 and under.
Open: Mon–Sat 10am–5pm, Sun 2–6pm.

MORE ATTRACTIONS

ST. MICHAN'S CHURCH, Lower Church St. Tel. 724-154.

On the north side of the river is an unusual Dublin attraction that is housed in the crypt of a church. The corpses interred in the vaults here at St. Michan's have been preserved because of the drying action of the porous limestone walls. Ghoulish visitors are thrilled by these Irish equivalents of Egyptian mummies. Also in this church is an organ on which Handel performed his Dettingen *Te Deum*.

Admission: IR£1.20 ($2.15) adults, IR£1 ($1.80) students and senior citizens.
Open: Mar–Oct, Mon–Fri 10am–12:45pm and 2–4:45pm, Sat 10am–12:45pm; Nov–Feb, tours by appointment only. **Bus:** 34 or 34A.

JAMES JOYCE MUSEUM, Sandycove. Tel. 809-265.

No James Joyce fan should miss this small museum housed in the Martello Tower in Sandycove where Joyce lived for a while in 1904 and which is described in the first chapter of *Ulysses*. The museum houses exhibits on Joyce and Dublin at the time *Ulysses* was written. If you pick up a copy of the "*Ulysses* Map of Dublin," you can make this the starting point of a Joyce tour of the city.

Admission: IR£1.60 ($2.90) adults, IR£1.30 ($2.35) students and senior citizens, 90p ($1.60) children.
Open: Apr–Oct, Mon–Sat 10am–1pm and 2–5pm, Sun 2:30–6pm; Nov–Mar by appointment only. **DART:** Sandycove, then a 5-min. walk.

MUNICIPAL GALLERY OF MODERN ART, Parnell Sq. Tel. 741-903.

At the northern end of Upper O'Connell Street in an old Georgian mansion stands this museum housing a small collection of primarily French impressionists and early 20th-century Irish artists. The collection includes works by Manet, Monet, Morisot, Corot, Renoir, and Degas, among others. The works on display here were bequeathed to the city of Dublin by Sir Hugh Lane, who drowned in the sinking of the *Lusitania* at the beginning of World War I.

Admission: Free.

Open: Tues–Fri 9:30am–6pm, Sat 9:30am–5pm, Sun 11am–5pm.

PARKS & GARDENS

Phoenix Park, in western Dublin, is one of the largest urban parks in the world. In such a gray city as Dublin, this vast expanse of green, which can be reached by bus no. 10 from O'Connell Street, is a welcome change. Here you will find the zoo, as well as the residences of the president of Ireland and the U.S. ambassador. Rolling green hills, ponds where ducks and swans beg for handouts, and a herd of free-roaming deer all make this an excellent place for a picnic.

The **National Botanical Gardens** (tel. 374-388) are in the northern suburb of Glasnevin and can be reached by bus no. 19 from O'Connell Street. Founded in 1795, the gardens contain more than 20,000 different species of plants and a beautiful large greenhouse more than 400 feet long. The Botanical Gardens are open daily except December 25. There is no admission charge.

SPECIAL-INTEREST SIGHTSEEING

A JAMES JOYCE TOUR   Fans of James Joyce won't want to miss the opportunity to tour Joyce's Dublin. This is especially easy with the **"*Ulysses* Map of Dublin."** The map lists 22 sights mentioned in the character Leopold Bloom's travels around Dublin on June 16, 1904. The starting point on the map is the **James Joyce Museum,** in the Martello Tower in Sandycove, open Monday through Saturday from 10am to 1pm and 2 to 5pm, and on Sunday from 2:30 to 6pm May to September (other months, by appointment only). Joyce's letters, documents, personal possessions, and photographs, as well as many items associated with *Ulysses,* are on display. The map is available at the Irish Tourist Board, 14 Upper O'Connell St., for 50p (90¢).

ORGANIZED TOURS

WALKING TOURS   Dublin is a fairly compact city. With a good pair of shoes you can see most of the city's important sights in a long day's walk. First stop by the Irish Tourist Board for a good map and a copy of *The Dublin Guide,* a booklet listing several walking tours of the city. For a good overview of the city, try combining Tours 1 and 2, which will show you the old town, the Georgian squares, and the cathedrals.

BUS TOURS   For the standard fast-paced, see-it-all-in-under-3-hours bus tour of Dublin, climb aboard the **Dublin Bus** open-deck sightseeing coach. Tours leave from the Dublin Bus office at 59 Upper O'Connell St. (tel. 720-000, ext. 3028) from April to December daily at 10:15am and 2:15pm. You can purchase your ticket at the office or on the bus for IR£7 ($12.60) for adults, IR£3.50 ($6.30) for children. This tour takes in most of the important sights in Dublin but doesn't stop at any of them.

SPECIAL & FREE EVENTS

Of all the holidays celebrated in Dublin, **St. Patrick's Day** is the one celebrated with the most enthusiasm. The parade itself is held on March 17, but there are festivities for several days before and after.

Another favorite of Dubliners is the **Liberties Festival,** celebrating life in the Liberties, Dublin's oldest neighborhood. Held each year in mid-June, the festivities include outdoor concerts, exhibitions, guided walks, pageants, and other events.

For fans of James Joyce, June 16 is the day to be in Dublin. On this date the city celebrates **Bloomsday,** in memory of Leopold Bloom, Joyce's protagonist who, in the novel *Ulysses,* travels around Dublin on June 16, 1904. Bloomsday is part of the larger **Dublin Literary Festival,** held in mid-June.

In late September and early October, the **Dublin Theatre Festival** is the focus of all Ireland. Featured are new Irish plays, classic revivals, and performances by overseas touring companies.

For free events, nothing in Dublin can beat the free **traditional Irish music** that can be heard every night of the week in pubs all over the city. See the "Evening Entertainment" section for details.

7. SAVVY SHOPPING

Grafton Street, a pedestrians-only zone near Trinity College, is Dublin's chic shopping district. Trendy boutiques, expensive restaurants, and specialty shops continue to proliferate here. **Powerscourt Townhouse Centre** and **St. Stephen's Green Centre** are this area's newest focal points and prime examples of Dublin's ongoing renovation and gentrification.

Visit some of the shops that advertise in *Tourism News,* a free newspaper available at the tourist office. There are unusual shops selling imported goods, secondhand clothes, and hard-to-find records in the **Temple Bar area** of the south bank.

RECOVERING VAT & SHIPPING IT HOME   Obtaining a VAT (Value-Added Tax) refund is quite easy in Ireland. Whenever you make a large purchase in a shop, ask for a **Cashback voucher.** Be aware that you may have to spend a minimum of IR£100 ($180) before the store will give you a voucher. Refunds may be claimed at the airport Cashback windows before you leave the country, or by mail after your return home. If you are leaving by ferry, you must mail the Cashback voucher for a refund. Also, remember that you may have to show your purchases to Customs before leaving the country in order to get the refund. Look for the CASHBACK TAX FREE SHOPPING sign in shop windows and read the instructions carefully.

If you don't want to carry your purchases with you while you're traveling, take advantage of the mailing service offered by most shops for an additional charge.

MARKETS   The largest and most popular **flea market** in the Dublin area is held every Saturday and Sunday from 10am to 5:30pm in Blackrock at 19a Main St. More than 100 vendors sell a wide variety of old and new goods at great prices. Take the DART train to the Blackrock station.

There is a very lively and colorful **produce market** on Moore Street beside the ILAC Centre. Moore Street is famous as the market from which Molly Malone wheeled her wheelbarrow down streets broad and narrow. You'll still find the produce vendors shouting out the prices of their offerings. The scene is in sharp contrast to the adjacent modern shopping mall.

8. EVENING ENTERTAINMENT

From singing pubs to opera to buskers to Broadway-style theater, Dublin has a wealth of after-dark activities to satisfy tastes of all ages. To find out what's going on, pick up a copy of the biweekly *Dublin Events Guide* magazine, available free at the Tourist Information Office. Here you'll find listings for music performances, stage productions, movie theaters, museum and gallery exhibits, and even television listings.

THE PERFORMING ARTS

THEATER, OPERA & CLASSICAL MUSIC

ABBEY THEATRE, Lower Abbey St. Tel. 787-222.
Dublin has been known as a theater center ever since the Abbey Theatre opened in

1904 with W. B. Yeats as its first director. The current theater was built in 1966, 15 years after the original theater burned down. There are two stages here where you can see the best and latest in contemporary Irish theater.

Prices: Tickets, IR£8–IR£13 ($14.40–$23.40), IR£5 ($9) for student standby.
Open: Box office, Mon–Sat 10:30am–7pm.

GAIETY THEATRE, S. King St. Tel. 771-717.

This is Dublin's other main venue for contemporary Irish theater and is located not far from St. Stephen's Green.

Prices: Tickets, IR£8–IR£13 ($14.40–$23.40).
Open: Box office, Mon–Sat 11am–7pm.

GATE THEATRE, Cavendish Row. Tel. 744-045.

Dublin's opera house is housed in a 200-year-old building that was built as part of the adjacent Assembly Rooms, which themselves were built to help fund the Rotunda Hospital, the first maternity hospital in Europe.

Prices: Tickets, IR£8–IR£12 ($14.40–$21.60).
Open: Box office, Mon–Sat 10am–7pm.

NATIONAL CONCERT HALL, Earlsfort Terrace. Tel. 711-533.

Dublin's main venue for classical music was originally part of University College, Dublin. The hall stays busy with performances several nights a week for much of the year.

Prices: Tickets, IR£3–IR£15 ($5.40–$27).
Open: Box office, Mon–Sat 11am–7pm.

FOLK, ROCK & JAZZ

There are dozens of clubs and pubs all over town that feature rock, folk, jazz, and traditional Irish music. Any night of the week you can hear almost any type of music.

At the **Baggot Inn,** Baggot Street (tel. 761-430), most nights of the week there is live music (primarily rock) on both floors of this popular club. The Baggot Inn is just a short walk from St. Stephen's Green. Admission is IR£2–IR£4 ($3.60–$7.20), and it's open Monday through Saturday from 11am to 1am and on Sunday from noon to 11pm.

MOVIES

Movies in Dublin cost IR£4 ($7.20) for adults after 5pm and IR£2.50 ($4.50) before 5pm. There are two multiplex theaters on O'Connell Street and another one two blocks away on Mid Abbey Street.

PUBS

You can hardly walk a block without encountering a pub in Dublin. Not only are they watering holes for sipping the dark Guinness stout, but they also offer snacks and meals. Best of all, many of them host live music at night. In any of these pubs music starts around 9pm and continues until 11pm. There's sometimes a small cover charge of IR£1–IR£3 ($1.80–$5.40). A pint of Guinness will cost around IR£1.75 ($3.15).

Brazen Head, 20 Lower Bridge St. (tel. 679-5186). A couple of long blocks past Christ Church Cathedral and down by the Liffey, you'll find Dublin's oldest pub. There are several rooms here, each with a slightly different atmosphere. You can have a quiet pint or a meal in one room and join in the music in another.

O'Donoghue's, 15 Merrion Row (tel. 614-303). For fans of traditional Irish music, this pub is a must. The Dubliners, one of Ireland's favorite traditional bands, had their start here, and impromptu music sessions continue here almost every night. Sometimes there are bands playing in both the front and back rooms.

Slattery's, 129 Capel St. (tel. 727-971). Although Capel Street is looking a bit down at the heels these days, Slattery's continues to be popular for live music of all types, which may be heard in either the upstairs or downstairs lounge. Traditional Irish music is still the most popular sound here.

Davy Byrne's, 21 Duke St. (tel. 775-217). This pub figured prominently in James Joyce's *Ulysses* and has been famous ever since. Unfortunately it recently underwent a total interior renovation and now lacks the atmosphere one would hope to find in a Dublin pub. Pastel walls, potted plants, and Dublin's upscale singles give this pub a very American ambience.

DISCOS

Discos in Dublin are generally open Thursday through Sunday from 11pm to 3am. Admission is usually IR£6 ($10.80), with drinks costing IR£1.75–IR£2.50 ($3.15–$4.50). Since discos tend to come and go with regularity, it's best to ask what the "in" place is when you visit. **Leeson Street,** which begins at the southeast corner of St. Stephen's Green, has a concentration of nightspots, several of which are always popular, making this a good place to start searching for an appealing disco.

9. NETWORKS & RESOURCES

STUDENTS **Trinity College** is the focus of student life in Dublin. Located on the south side of the Liffey, at the top of Dame Street, the large campus with its many 18th-century buildings is in the heart of Dublin's old city. There is an information office just inside the main gate where you can find out more about what is going on at the college.

For general information about the city, young people should check at the **Community & Youth Information Centre,** on Sackville Place at Marlborough Street (tel. 786-844), two blocks from O'Connell Street. The hours here are Monday through Wednesday from 9:30am to 6pm and Thursday through Saturday from 9:30am to 5pm.

GAY MEN & LESBIANS For information on the gay and lesbian scene in Dublin, stop by the **Well Fed Café,** 6 Crow St., and glance at the bulletin boards. The **Gay Switchboard** (tel. 721-055) is open Monday through Friday from 6 to 10pm.

10. EASY EXCURSIONS

To understand why Ireland is called the Emerald Isle, you must venture beyond the gray walls of urban Dublin into the verdant countryside. There are several day-long excursions that can be made easily from Dublin.

The budget-conscious can hop on the DART train and ride it to the end of the line in either direction. To the north is the peninsula of **Howth,** the northern arm of Dublin Bay. From the Howth station, catch the DART feeder bus to the summit of Howth Head and from there you can walk along quiet paths through green fields back to the village of Howth. At the southern end of the DART line is the village of **Bray.** From here there is a 3-mile walk around Bray Head to the village of Greystones.

Bus Eireann, Busáras Central Bus Station (tel. 302-222), offers about 20 different half-day and full-day excursions from Dublin. Some of the more worthwhile tours are those to the beautiful Powerscourt Gardens in the Wicklow Mountains, the Glendalough and Wicklow Gap tour, and the most interesting one, the Boyne Valley and North Coast tour. Besides driving through gorgeous green countryside, you will visit the massive gravesites of Newgrange dating from 2500 B.C. You will also visit the site of the Battle of the Boyne, and other sites of historical significance. The tours are offered on different days of the week and cost IR£6–IR£22 ($10.80–$39.60).

EDINBURGH

Edinburgh is a city with a long and stormy past. You'll be reminded of that past every time you gaze up at Edinburgh Castle, one of the most arresting sights in Europe. You'll recall the city's history when you follow in the footsteps of Mary Queen of Scots through the Palace of Holyroodhouse. In the Old Town the narrow, winding alleys called closes will lead you from the 20th-century traffic back to the city's medieval days. In striking contrast to the Old Town's jumble of twisted streets are the wide boulevards and stately town houses of the Georgian New Town. Together the Old and New Towns, joined by the sloping lawns and ancient trees of Princes Street Gardens, make Edinburgh one of Europe's most historically fascinating cities.

Even though Edinburgh takes care to preserve its history, it does not ignore the finer things of life. The Edinburgh International Festival, held every August, is one of the most popular cultural festivals in the world. And in the other 11 months of the year Edinburgh's many theaters, concert halls, live-music clubs, galleries, and museums are busy catering to the cultural appetite of the Scots. Every block seems to have its own pub, where you can sometimes hear a bit of traditional highland music while you sip your pint of ale. Elegant and expensive shops line Princes Street in the New Town, while in the Old Town, antiques shops, boutiques, and unusual import stores prevail.

Historic and lively, Edinburgh has much to offer the visitor, and if the sun should be shining when you visit, consider yourself very lucky: You will have seen one of Europe's most stunning sights.

1. FROM A BUDGET TRAVELER'S POINT OF VIEW

EDINBURGH BUDGET BESTS The best values in Edinburgh are the city's many free museums and galleries. These include the two Royal Museums, the National Gallery, and the Museum of Childhood. Other budget bests include free live music in pubs and clubs, and lunch in almost any pub.

SPECIAL DISCOUNT OPPORTUNITIES If you plan to use the public buses in Edinburgh, be sure to buy a silver **Freedom Ticket,** which costs only £1.80 ($3.40) and is good for a day. If you plan to be around for a week, you can get a **City Ridacard** at £8 ($15.20) for adults or £4.60 ($8.75) for juniors. There is also a

Touristcard, good for up to 13 days, which includes unlimited travel and discount vouchers for bus tours, restaurants, shops, museums, and theaters. Touristcards cost £4.50 ($8.55) for adults and £3.50 ($6.65) for children for 2 days, up to £17 ($32.30) for adults and £12.50 ($23.75) for children for 13 days.

WHAT THINGS COST IN EDINBURGH	U.S. $
Taxi from the airport to the city center	22.80
Local telephone call	.20
Double room at the Edinburgh Sheraton (deluxe)	260.00
Double room at the Ailsa Craig (moderate)	95.00
Double room at Castle Guest House (budget)	57.00
Continental breakfast in a hotel	5.00
Lunch for one at the Royal Mile (moderate)	9.50
Lunch for one at the Baked Potato (budget)	4.75
Dinner for one, without wine at Pompadour (deluxe)	78.00
Dinner for one, without wine at Pierre Victoire (moderate)	23.00
Dinner for one, without wine at Henderson's (budget)	9.00
Pint of beer	2.95
Coca-Cola	1.15
Cup of coffee	1.15
Roll of ASA 100 color film, 36 exposures	7.00
Admission to Edinburgh Castle	5.30
Movie ticket	6.25
Theater ticket at King's Theatre	7.60–30.40

WORTH THE EXTRA BUCKS   If you're in the mood for a hotel splurge, Edinburgh offers a couple of fine choices on Royal Terrace. Try the Terrace or the Halcyon for excellent value.

2. PRETRIP PREPARATIONS

DOCUMENTS   Citizens of the United States, Canada, Australia, and New Zealand need only a valid passport for travel to Edinburgh.

WHAT TO PACK   You'll see from the climate chart below that Edinburgh is cool and wet all year, so be sure to bring an umbrella. In summer you should have a sweater or light jacket with you for the cool evenings, and in winter you'll definitely need a heavy coat. Strong winds make winter in Edinburgh seem even colder.

Edinburgh is not as fashion-conscious as London. You'll fit right in with the Scots here in casual clothes. Good walking shoes are a must since you will want to walk the length of the Royal Mile at least, and may even climb Salisbury Crags.

WHEN TO GO   Although it rains all year here and can be gray and overcast for long stretches at a time, summer can also be gloriously sunny and warm. There are even times in the winter when the sun shines for several days in a row.

If you're a culture vulture, you won't want to miss the **Edinburgh International Festival** in August. If you're interested in attending the festival, be sure to make hotel and airline reservations months in advance. The city is absolutely packed to overflowing during the 3 weeks of the festival.

WHAT'S SPECIAL ABOUT EDINBURGH

Edinburgh Castle
- ☐ A fabulous sight, set atop a rocky crag in the middle of the city.
- ☐ An active military base with historically interesting buildings open to the public.

Palace of Holyroodhouse
- ☐ Home of Mary Queen of Scots and still used by Queen Elizabeth II when she visits Edinburgh.

Woolens
- ☐ Numerous Mill Shop stores providing the city's best shopping deals—discount woolens direct from the mills.

Edinburgh Festival
- ☐ Cultural extravaganza every summer attracting culture vultures from the world over.

Views from Princes Street Gardens
- ☐ A stunning sight when the pale northern sunshine sets the stone bulding of Edinburgh's old city aglow.

Ghostly Ghoulish Tours
- ☐ Nighttime walking tours of some of the more infamous locations in Edinburgh's Old City, where witch burning was once the favorite spectator sport!

The Royal Mile
- ☐ A fascinating collection of medieval buildings, narrow alleys known as closes, museums, shops, and pubs along the mile-long street that connects the Palace of Holyroodhouse and Edinburgh Castle.

Royal Botanic Garden
- ☐ Everything from the giant water lillies of Amazonia to desert succulents.

Edinburgh's Average Daytime Temperature & Days of Rain

	Jan	Feb	Mar	Apr	May	June	July	Aug	Sept	Oct	Nov	Dec
Temp. (°F)	38	38	41	45	50	56	58	58	55	50	42	40
Days of Rain	12	11	11	12	12	10	10	13	11	12	13	13

Special Events   The main focal point of the Edinburgh cultural calendar is the annual **Edinburgh International Festival,** which goes on for 3 weeks in late August and early September. See "Special and Free Events," below, for more information.

BACKGROUND READING   Sir Walter Scott is Edinburgh's most beloved literary figure and his Waverly novels are its most popular works. Almost as popular is Robert Louis Stevenson, whose collection of poems *A Child's Garden of Verses* (Macmillan, 1981), evokes his childhood in the city. Stevenson's novel *The Strange Case of Dr. Jekyll and Mr. Hyde* (Oxford University Press, 1979) is based on a famous local criminal, Deacon Brodie. Robert Burns, idolized by the Scots, brings 18th-century Edinburgh and Scotland to life in such poems as his famous "Scots Wha Ha'e." Sir Arthur Conan Doyle based his character Sherlock Holmes on an Edinburgh surgeon, Dr. Joseph Bell.

3. ORIENTATION & GETTING AROUND

ARRIVING IN EDINBURGH

FROM THE AIRPORT **Edinburgh Airport** is located 10 miles northwest of the city. You may wish to stop by the Edinburgh Tourist Information Desk here before heading into the city.

White double-decker **Airlink** buses regularly make the 25-minute trip into the city. The one-way fare is £3 ($5.70). Waverly Bridge is the last stop and is centrally located between the Old Town and the New Town.

There are also airport **taxis** that will take you into the city center for about £12 ($22.80). If you can get one of the standard black taxis to give you a ride, you'll save a couple of dollars, but these taxis are not supposed to pick up fares at the airport.

FROM THE TRAIN STATION There are two main train stations in Edinburgh, **Waverly Station** and **Haymarket Station.** Waverly Station is the more conveniently located of the two. If you follow the exit signs up the automobile ramp, you'll find yourself on Waverly Bridge. Princes Street and the New Town are to your right, and the Old Town is to your left.

INFORMATION

The main **Edinburgh Tourist Information Centre** (tel. 031/557-1700) is at the corner of Princes Street and Waverly Bridge on the top of the modern underground Waverly Market shopping center. The tourist center hours are Monday through Saturday from 9am to 6pm.

For information on events while you're in town, pick up a free copy of **What's On in Edinburgh** at the Tourist Information Centre. It lists events, exhibitions, theater, and music in the city. For more detailed listings, try the magazine **The List,** which is available at the Tourist Information Centre for £1 ($1.90).

Students who want to find out more about the university scene in Edinburgh, head over to the **Edinburgh University Student Centre,** on Bristo Square. There is a large notice board listing events of interest to students. If you are looking for an apartment for a few months or longer, you'll find ads for roommates here.

CITY LAYOUT

Edinburgh is a very easy city to find your way around. The city is divided into an **Old Town** and a New Town, which are separated from each other by Princes Street Gardens. Dominating the Edinburgh skyline is **Edinburgh Castle,** standing high on a hill at the western end of the Old Town. At the opposite end of the Old Town and connected to the castle by the **Royal Mile,** a single street that bears four different names along its length, is the **Palace of Holyroodhouse,** the Scottish residence of Queen Elizabeth II and many kings and queens past.

Princes Street is the main thoroughfare of the **New Town** and is bordered on the north side by department stores and some of Edinburgh's most elegant clothing stores. Running the length of Princes Street on the south side is **Princes Street Gardens,** a beautiful park that fills the valley between the two sections of the city.

GETTING AROUND

BY BUS Burgundy-and-white Lothian Region Transport double-deckers run frequently to all parts of the city and outlying suburbs. Fares vary according to the number of stops you travel, and range from 35p (65¢) to £1.75 ($3.35). You are expected to have the correct fare when boarding. Deposit your coins in the slot beside the driver and take your ticket. Be sure to hang on to this ticket in case an inspector asks to see it.

You probably won't know how many stops you will be traveling, and consequently won't know how much to pay. With plenty of change in hand, ask the driver how much the fare is to your destination, or purchase a **Freedom Ticket** at the Tourist Information Centre for £1.80 ($3.40) and don't worry about the fare. The Freedom Ticket is good for one day and allows you to use the LRT buses as frequently as you like. Freedom Cards are also available at the Ticket Centre, at Waverly Bridge.

Monday through Thursday and on Sunday, the buses stop running a little after 11pm, but on Friday and Saturday some buses run all night. Night fare is £1.20 ($2.30).

ON FOOT   Edinburgh, especially the narrow lanes and closes of Old Town, is best explored on foot. Almost everything you will want to see is either along or just a few blocks from the Royal Mile, along Princes Street, or on the nearby streets of the New Town.

BY BICYCLE   Because Edinburgh is built on a series of hills and ridges, bicycling around the city is not recommended. However, exploring the surrounding countryside by bike is very pleasant. **Central Cycle Hire,** 13 Lochrin Place (tel. 228-6333), rents bicycles for £6–£20 ($11.40–$38) depending on the type of bicycle. They will also help you pick out a route for a day's cycling. Hours May to August are Monday through Saturday from 10am to 5:30pm and on Sunday from 10am to noon and 5 to 7pm; September to April, closed Sunday and Tuesday. You can reach the shop by bus no. 9, 10, 11, 16, 18, 23, 27, 30, or 45 from Princes Street. Get off by the Cameo Cinema.

CAR RENTAL   For excursions farther afield, you might want to rent a car. **Melville's Self Drive,** 9 Clifton Terrace (tel. 337-5333), and **Total Self Drive,** 45 Lochrin Place (tel. 229-4548), offer their smallest cars at rates of under £20 ($38) per day with 150 miles free.

 EDINBURGH

Babysitters   If you need a babysitter in Edinburgh, contact **Guardians Babysitting,** 28 Strathalmond Park (tel. 339-2288).

Banks   There are several banks along Princes Street that will change money. They offer the best exchange rate in town and charge a small commission. The **Royal Bank of Scotland,** 142-144 Princes St. (tel. 226-2555), is open Monday through Friday from 9:15am to 4:45pm (on Thursday to 5:30pm); the **Bank of Scotland,** 141 Princes St. (tel. 225-6204), is open the same hours.

Business Hours   **Shops** are generally open Monday through Saturday from 10am to 5:30 or 6pm (on Thursday to 7:30pm). **Offices** are open Monday through Friday from 9am to 5pm. Some smaller shops may close for lunch.

Consulates   The **U.S. Consulate** is at 3 Regent Terrace (tel. 556-8315), which is an extension of Princes Street beyond Nelson's Monument. The **Australian Consulate** is in Hobart House, 80 Hanover St. (tel. 226-6271).

Currency   The basic unit of currency in Scotland is the **pound sterling (£),** which is divided into 100 **pence (p).** There are 1p, 2p, 10p, 20p, 50p, and £1 coins; banknotes are issued in £1, £5, £10, £20, and £50.

There are **currency-exchange counters** at the Tourist Information Centre in Waverly Market, at the Central Post Office at the north end of North Bridge, and at many banks in the Princes Street and Royal Mile areas. Although they all offer about the same rate, the banks tend to charge a smaller fee.

Dentists   See "Emergencies," below.
Doctors   See "Emergencies," below.

Emergencies   If you need a **doctor** or **dentist** check the *Yellow Pages* or ask at your hotel. For **police** assistance or an **ambulance,** dial 999.

There are no 24-hour pharmacies in Edinburgh. **Boots,** 48 Shandwick Place (tel. 225-6757), is a pharmacy that is open Monday through Friday until 9pm.

Eyeglasses   Boots Opticians, 101-103 Princes St. (tel. 225-6397), open Monday through Saturday from 9am to 5:30pm (on Thursday to 7:30pm) can repair or replace your eyeglasses.

Holidays   New Year's Day, January 2, May Day, May 8 (Victoria Day), Christmas and December 26 (Boxing Day), and the spring and autumn bank holidays, which fall in mid-April and mid-September respectively.

Hospital   The **Royal Infirmary,** 1 Lauriston Place (tel. 229-2477), is one of the most convenient hospitals.

Information   The **Edinburgh Tourist Information Centre** is located on the top (Princes Street level) of the modern Waverly Market shopping mall. See the information section of "Orientation and Getting Around," above, for details.

Laundry/Dry Cleaning   In the Dalkeith Road area, there is a laundry, simply named **Laundrette,** at 210 Dalkeith Rd. Hours are Monday through Friday from 8:30am to 5pm, on Saturday from 9am to 2:30pm, and on Sunday from 10am to 2:30pm. In the Princes Street area there is the **Laundromat,** at 54 Leith Walk, which is an extension of Leith Street one block past Royal Terrace. They're open Monday through Saturday from 8am to 7pm (on Wednesday to 6pm), and on Sunday from 9:30am to 5pm.

For dry cleaning, try **Pullars & Sons,** 23 Frederick St. (tel. 225-8095), open Monday through Friday from 8:30am to 5:30pm and on Saturday from 8:30am to 5pm.

Lost and Found   The first place to check if you have lost something in Edinburgh is the **Lothian and Borders Police Headquarters,** on Fettes Avenue (tel. 311-3131). Another place to try is the **Edinburgh Tourist Information Centre,** at Waverly Market.

Mail   The **Central Post Office** is at 2-4 Waterloo Place, at the north end of North Bridge. It's open Monday through Thursday from 9am to 5:30pm, on Friday from 9:30am to 5:30pm, and on Saturday from 9am to 12:30pm. A letter to the U.S. costs 39p (75¢); a postcard, 33p (65¢).

Newspapers   Edinburgh's most informative newspapers are *The Scotsman* and *The Independent.*

Photographic Needs   Edinburgh Cameras, 55 Lothian Rd. (tel. 229-4416), open Monday through Saturday from 9am to 5:30pm (on Thursday to 7pm) and on Sunday from noon to 5pm, will meet all your photo needs.

Police   To reach the police, in an emergency dial 999; otherwise dial 311-3131.

Radio/TV   Edinburgh has several radio and television stations offering a wide range of programming.

Religious Services   For information on churches and synagogues in Edinburgh, contact the **Tourist Information Centre** at Waverly Market (tel. 557-1700). An extensive listing of times and locations of services is maintained there.

Shoe Repair   Only a few blocks from the east end of Princes Street, **Mister Minit,** 22 Frederick St. (tel. 226-6741), is a convenient place to get your shoes repaired. It's open Monday through Friday from 8am to 5:30pm and on Saturday from 8am to 5pm.

Tax   Getting your VAT refund can be complicated, but most shops selling to tourists are quite willing to make it as easy as possible. Be sure to ask the cashier for the proper forms to fill out. Look for the TAX-FREE SHOPPING sign in store windows. For details, see "Savvy Shopping," below.

Taxis   There are taxi stands along Princes Street and at Waverly Station. Fares start at 90p ($1.70) and increase by 10p (20¢) every 300 yards. You can also phone 229-2468 for a cab.

Telephone   Public telephones cost 10p (20¢) for the first 3 minutes and accept coins of various denominations. You can also purchase a phone card, for use in special

THE POUND & THE DOLLAR

At this writing $1 = approximately 53p (or £1 = $1.90), and this was the rate of exchange used to calculate the dollar values given in this chapter (rounded to the nearest nickel). This rate fluctuates from time to time and may not be the same when you travel to the U.K. Therefore the following table should be used only as a guide:

£	U.S. $	£	U.S. $
.01	.02	6	11.40
.05	.10	7	13.30
.10	.19	8	15.20
.25	.48	9	17.10
.50	.95	10	19.00
.75	1.43	15	28.50
1	1.90	20	38.00
2	3.80	25	47.50
3	5.70	30	57.00
4	7.60	40	76.00
5	9.50	50	95.00

phones, at post offices and newsstands. A 3-minute phone call to the United States will cost about £3.90 ($7.40). Alternatively, you can reach an AT&T operator, and receive U.S. rates for collect or credit-card calls, by dialing 0800-89-0011.

Tipping   In most restaurants, tax and service charge are included in the price of the meal, so it's unnecessary to leave any further tip. If a service charge has not been included in the bill, the standard tip here is 10%. Taxi drivers expect a 20% tip.

4. BUDGET ACCOMMODATIONS

There are few centrally located budget guesthouses in Edinburgh, and most of these have a drawback for many older travelers—stairs. Three guesthouses listed here are only a short walk from Waverly Station, but they are all on the upper floors of old town houses. Also close to Princes Street are a number of small bed-and-breakfast hotels that are splurges—worthwhile but outside our normal budget guidelines. The best deals in Edinburgh are to be had 5 to 15 minutes by bus from the center, where you'll find spacious rooms and lower rates.

The cheapest accommodations in Edinburgh, aside from hostels, are home stays. People with an extra bedroom or two in their home will take in paying guests for about £12 ($22.80) per person per night. Home stays are generally available only in the summer, but occasionally in other months as well. The **Edinburgh Tourist Information Centre** in Waverly Market (tel. 031/557-1700) has a list of hundreds of home stays, and they will also make reservations for you; stop by or phone.

DOUBLES FOR LESS THAN £33 [$62.70]

IN THE CITY CENTER

CAFE ROYAL GUEST HOUSE, 5 W. Register St., Edinburgh EH2 2AA. Tel. 031/556-6894. 20 rms (none with bath).

$ Rates (including continental breakfast: £15–£20 ($28.50–$38) single; £30–£40 ($57–$76) double. No credit cards.

You'll have to be young and athletic to stay at this very centrally located guesthouse. To reach the registration desk, you must first ascend four flights of stairs. This climb and the guesthouse's proximity to two of Edinburgh's most popular pubs make it a good choice for younger travelers. There are also plenty of flyers on the walls of the stairwell, so that guests can stay in touch with local happenings. Rooms are spartanly furnished with modern furniture in a bold red-and-white theme.

CASTLE GUEST HOUSE, 38 Castle St., Edinburgh EH2 3BN. Tel. 031/ 225-1975. 7 rms (none with bath) TV

$ Rates (including full breakfast): £17 ($32.30) single; £30 ($57) double. No credit cards.

Mr. and Mrs. J. C. Ovens have been accepting guests into their 200-year-old home for more than 30 years. The seven rooms are all quite cozy and have tea-making facilities and central heating, as well as TV. You can choose from among six different breakfasts here. Castle Guest House is less than two blocks from Princes Street and about 10 minutes from Waverly Station. The street affords an excellent view of the castle.

ALONG DALKEITH ROAD

CRION GUEST HOUSE, 33 Minto St., Edinburgh EH9 2BT. Tel. 031/667-2708. 6 rms (none with bath). TV **Bus:** 3, 7, 8, 18, 31, or 37.

$ Rates (including full breakfast): £16–£18 ($30.40–$34.20) single; £26–£30 ($49.40–$57) double. No credit cards.

Minto Street is one of Edinburgh's budget guesthouse districts and the Crion is one of the best on the street. The proprietess, Mrs. Cheape, is friendly and has done much to make her small guesthouse as homey as possible. Floral-print draperies with matching valences and bedspreads give the guest rooms a country flavor, while in the breakfast room you'll find classic Edinburgh plasterwork wainscoting and an elegant fireplace. The availability of a first-floor room makes this a good choice for travelers who have problems with stairs.

GIFFORD GUEST HOUSE, 103 Dalkeith Rd., Edinburgh EH16 5AJ. Tel. 031/667-4688. 6 rms (3 with shower). TV **Bus:** 14, 21, or 33 to Royal Commonwealth Pool. **Parking:** Free.

$ Rates (including full breakfast): £14–£21 ($26.60–$39.90) single without shower; £26–£32 ($49.40–$60.80) double without shower; £30–£36 ($57–$68.40) double with shower; £48–£60 ($91.20–$114) quad without shower, £52–£64 ($98.80–$121.60) quad with shower. No credit cards.

This spacious old home has a beautiful stairwell topped by a huge skylight. Mrs. Margaret Dow, the friendly manager, has three rooms with their own showers. All the rooms are quite large, with high ceilings, central heating, and tea-making facilities. Most rooms have been redecorated recently and have attractive matching duvets on the beds. The rooms in back offer a view of Arthur's Seat and Salisbury Crags.

ROSEHALL HOTEL, 101 Dalkeith Rd., Edinburgh EH16 5AJ. Tel. 031/ 667-9372. 10 rms (4 with shower only, 2 with shower and toilet). **Bus:** 14, 21, or 33 to Royal Commonwealth Pool.

$ Rates (including full breakfast): £16–£17 ($30.40–$32.30) single without shower or toilet; £30–£32 ($57–$60.80) double or twin with shower only; £15–£16 ($28.50–$30.40) per person triple, quad, or quint without shower or toilet, £17–£19 ($32.30–$36.10) per person triple, quad or quint with shower and toilet. EURO, MC, V.

Next door to the Gifford, proprietors Mr. and Mrs. Officer offer 10 large rooms. Each is recently decorated and the rooms that front on the street have double-glazing on the windows to keep down the noise. There are two singles, two doubles and two twins, a triple, two quads, and a five-bed room.

NORTH OF CITY CENTER

DENE GUEST HOUSE, 7 Eyre Place, Edinburgh EH3 5ES. Tel. 031/556-2700. 7 rms (2 with shower and toilet). TV **Bus:** 23 or 27 from Hanover Street.
$ **Rates** (including continental breakfast): £19 ($36.10) single without shower or toilet; £32 ($60.80) double without shower or toilet, £40 ($76) double with shower and toilet. No credit cards.

Five minutes north of Waverly Station by bus is the Dene Guest House, operated since 1960 by the friendly Donaghue family. There are seven simply decorated and cozy rooms, and the two four-bed family rooms now have attached baths. The guesthouse has been completely redecorated. Eyre Place is only three stoplights down the hill and just beyond the modern buildings on the right.

DOUBLES FOR LESS THAN £39 ($74.10)

IN THE CITY CENTER

ELDER YORK GUEST HOUSE, 38 Elder St., Edinburgh EH1 3DX. Tel. 031/556-1926. 14 rms (3 with shower only, 3 with shower and toilet). TV
$ **Rates** (including full breakfast): £19 ($36.10) single without shower or toilet; £38 ($72.20) double without shower or toilet, £46 ($87.40) double with shower and toilet. No credit cards.

A little bit closer to Waverly Station than the first two city-center guesthouses listed above, and again on the upper floors of an old town house, this guesthouse, run by Mr. McCue, offers 14 small but adequately furnished rooms with TVs and tea-making facilities. Several of the rooms come with their own showers, and all are quite clean. Comfortable chairs are good for relaxing in after a day of walking around the city.

IN THE DALKEITH ROAD AREA

AVON HOTEL, 1-2 Spence St., Edinburgh EH16 5AG. Tel. 031/667-8681. 12 rms (2 with shower and toilet). TV **Bus:** 14, 21, or 33 to Royal Commonwealth Pool.
$ **Rates** (including full breakfast): £20 ($38) single without shower or toilet; £38 ($72.20) double without shower or toilet; £45 ($85.50) triple without shower or toilet. Rooms with shower and toilet cost a few dollars extra. AE.

⭐ Directly across the street from the other two Dalkeith Road hotels listed in this chapter is the Avon. Opened by Mr. and Mrs. Adam in 1987, the Avon is a very attractive little hotel and is highly recommended. The Adams put a lot of work into renovating their hotel and it shows. The 12 rooms are spotlessly clean, and each has tea-making facilities. There are two singles, six doubles, and four triples (one with shower and toilet).

NORTH OF CITY CENTER

ARDENLEE GUEST HOUSE, 9 Eyre Place, Edinburgh EH3 5ES. Tel. 031/556-2838. 8 rms (2 with shower and toilet). TV **Bus:** 23 or 27 from Hanover Street.
$ **Rates** (including full breakfast): £17 ($32.30) per person single, double, or triple without shower or toilet, £19 ($36.10) per person single, double, or triple with shower and toilet. No credit cards.

Next door to the Dene is this equally comfortable three-floor guesthouse run by David and Judy Dinse. Here you will find eight large and attractively decorated rooms. Potted plants are a nice touch. All the rooms have tea-making facilities. You have your choice of how you would like your eggs fixed each morning.

SOUTHWEST OF CITY CENTER

KARIBA GUEST HOUSE, 10 Granville Terrace, Edinburgh EH10 4PQ.

FROMMER'S SMART TRAVELER: HOTELS

VALUE-CONSCIOUS TRAVELERS SHOULD
TAKE ADVANTAGE OF THE FOLLOWING:

1. Home stays, which are usually available only in summer. Check the tourist office for availability.
2. Accommodations about a 10- to 15-minute bus ride out of the city center.
3. Guesthouses along Dalkeith Road, near the university residence halls.

Tel. 031/229-3773. 9 rms (3 with shower and toilet, 6 with shower only). TV
Bus: 9, 10, or 27.
$ **Rates** (including full breakfast): £32–£34 ($60.80–$64.60) double with shower only, £36–£38 ($68.40–$72.20) double with shower and toilet; £48–£51 ($91.20–$96.90) triple with shower only, £54–£57 ($102.60–$108.30) triple with shower and toilet. ACCESS, EURO, MC.

This small Victorian guesthouse has a very warm, homey atmosphere thanks to its owners, Jack and Molly Sinclair, who are friendly and full of helpful information for visitors to Edinburgh. They offer nine rooms with TVs and tea-making facilities. Mr. Sinclair has put a lot of time and energy into restoring this Victorian home to its former glory, and the plasterwork cornices and ceilings are particularly attractive. Breakfast is served in the large dining room.

RAVENSDOWN BED AND BREAKFAST, 248 Ferry Rd., Edinburgh EH5 3AN. Tel. 031/552-5438. 7 rms. **Bus:** 23 from Hanover Street.
$ **Rates** (including full breakfast): £21 ($39.90) single; £36 ($68.40) double; £48 ($91.20) triple; £60 ($114) quad. No credit cards.
The friendly and helpful proprietors, Mr. and Mrs. Leonardo Welch, operate a very pleasant guesthouse offering large, comfortable, and clean rooms. All rooms come with tea-making facilities and comfortable chairs for relaxing. Try to get one of the south-facing rooms—the view of the Edinburgh skyline is magnificent.

SUPER-BUDGET CHOICES

HOSTELS

Edinburgh's two Y.H.A. hostels are both located 15 minutes from the city center in very elegant and quiet surroundings.

BRUNTSFIELD YOUTH HOSTEL, 7 Bruntsfield Crescent, Edinburgh EH10 4EZ. Tel 031/447-2994. 172 beds. **Bus:** 11 or 16 from Princes Street to Forbes Road, or 15 to Bruntsfield Hospital.
$ **Rates:** £7.10 ($13.50) per night for Y.H.A. members; £8.60 ($16.35) for nonmembers for the first 6 nights, after which they receive a membership card. No credit cards. **Closed:** Jan.
This hostel offers accommodations in dorms on four floors with rooms holding 8 to 26 beds each. There is a self-catering kitchen, large lounge, and TV room, all of which are very clean.

EGLINTON YOUTH HOSTEL, 18 Eglinton Crescent, Edinburgh EH12 5DD. Tel. 031/337-1120. 180 beds. **Bus:** 3, 4, 12, 13, 22, 26, 28, 31, 33, or 44 to Palmerston Place.
$ **Rates:** £8 ($15.20) per night for Y.H.A. members; £9.50 ($18.05) for nonmembers for the first 6 nights, after which they receive a membership card. No credit cards. **Closed:** Dec.
This is the larger of the two official hostels in town. It's located about 400 yards from

the Haymarket train station and the same distance from the Gallery of Modern Art. There are 180 beds on three floors, with accommodations in dorms of 6 to 12 beds each. There is a self-catering kitchen, TV lounge, self-service laundry, small grocery, and central heating. Eglinton Crescent is the second left off Palmerston Place.

HIGH STREET HOSTEL, 8 Blackfriars St., Edinburgh EH1 1NE. Tel. 031/557-3984. 160 beds. **Directions:** See below.
$ Rates: £8 ($15.20) per person per night. Breakfast £2–£2.25 ($3.80–$4.30) extra. No credit cards.

Edinburgh's third hostel is independently operated, and although not so clean or spacious as the two above, it is very conveniently located just off the Royal Mile. No hostel card is necessary to stay here. Beds are in dorms that sleep 6 to 38 people. The nightly rate doesn't include breakfast but it does include showers, luggage-storage facilities, and a self-catering kitchen. Two lounges provide plenty of room for meeting other travelers, and blackboards and bulletin boards have postings of what's going on in Edinburgh that week.

From Waverly Station, cross North Bridge and turn left on High Street (the second intersection). Blackfriars Street is the second street on the right.

POLLOCK HALLS, 18 Holyrood Park Rd., Edinburgh EH16 5AY. Tel. 031/667-1971. 1,000 rms. **Bus:** 14, 21, or 33 to Royal Commonwealth Pool.
$ Rates (including full breakfast): £21 ($39.90) per person per night. **Open:** June–Sept.

For most of the year these are the dormitories for Edinburgh University, but during the summer months, from June to the end of September, the 1,000 single rooms are available to the public. This rate includes breakfast and showers. There are plenty of facilities including a self-service laundry, TV rooms, lounges, and bars. Many of the rooms have excellent views of the nearby Salisbury Crags and Arthur's Seat. The entrance gate is just beyond the Royal Commonwealth Pool complex. Once through the gates, follow the signs to St. Leonard's Hall.

WORTH THE EXTRA BUCKS

On Royal Terrace, only 5 minutes from Waverly Station, are a number of small hotels that are very elegant and just a bit more expensive than others in this area. If you can afford it, these are definitely worth the additional cost. The two listed here offer the best value on the block.

TERRACE HOTEL, 37 Royal Terrace, Edinburgh EH7 5AH. Tel. 031/556-3423. 14 rms (11 with bath). TV
$ Rates (including full breakfast): £20–£22 ($38–$41.80) single without bath, £25–£29 ($47.50–$55.10) single with bath, £42–£45 ($79.80–$85.50) double without bath, £50–£56 ($95–$106.40) double with bath. ACCESS, V.

This small Georgian-style hotel has the most for the money in this neighborhood. Owner Annie Mann is constantly improving the hotel and she always keeps it immaculately clean. There is a spacious lounge and breakfast room featuring beautiful fireplaces. A full breakfast is served every morning. The rooms range from roomy to spacious, and include TVs and tea-making facilities.

THE HALCYON, 8 Royal Terrace, Edinburgh EH7 5AB. Tel. 031/556-1032 or 556-1033. 16 rms (5 with shower only).
$ Rates (including full breakfast): £24–£27 ($45.60–$51.30) per person in rooms without shower, £27 ($51.30) per person in rooms with shower. Children are charged according to their age—£1 ($1.90) per year—and lower rates are available in triples. No credit cards.

Your next best bet on this street is run by the very engaging Peggy Reed. There are thick carpets and matching duvets in all the rooms. The third-floor rooms in front have fine views across the Firth of Forth that are well worth the walk up. An attractive garden leads to a private park where tennis courts are available to guests.

5. BUDGET DINING

Edinburgh is basically a meat-and-potatoes town. Most restaurants and pubs serve the same foods that you'd find in London. The local specialty is *haggis,* a concoction of the heart, liver, and lungs of a sheep, minced and cooked in the sheep's stomach with oatmeal, onions, and seasonings. The Scots love it, and I've eaten it and survived.

LOCAL BUDGET BETS & FAVORITE MEALS
TRADITIONAL SCOTTISH FOOD

THE SCOTS PANTRY, Waverly Market food court. Tel. 557-5130.
  Cuisine: SCOTTISH.
$ Prices: £2–£3.75 ($3.80–$7.15). No credit cards.
  Open: Mon–Sat 9am–6pm (on Thurs to 7pm), Sun 9am–5pm.

⭐ If you have a hankering for some traditional Scottish food, but you don't want to eat in a pub, try this fast-food counter on the bottom floor of the shopping mall beside the train station. If you aren't in the mood for haggis, neeps (turnips) and tatties (potatoes), or mince and stovies, there are plenty of other foods available here at equally low prices. Once you have your food, find an empty seat and enjoy this truly Scottish taste treat. There might even be live music at lunch.

PUB GRUB

Pubs along the Royal Mile and Rose Street, which runs parallel to Princes Street, offer plenty of local atmosphere and good prices.

THE CAFE ROYAL BISTRO, 17 W. Register St. Tel. 557-4792.
  Cuisine: PUB GRUB.
$ Prices: £2–£4 ($3.80–$7.20). No credit cards.
  Open: Mon–Sat 11:30am–6pm.
Located behind the Wimpy fast-food restaurant across from Waverly Market, this café is above the very elegant and slightly more expensive Guildford Arms pub. Very popular with young working people and students, its rooms have an old lived-in feel to them, and the high ceilings give the pub an open, airy feel.

THE ROYAL MILE, 127 High St. Tel. 556-8274.
  Cuisine: SCOTTISH.
$ Prices: £5–£6 ($9.50–$11.40); daily special £3.50 ($6.65). No credit cards.
  Open: Mon–Wed 11am–11pm, Thurs–Sat 11am–midnight, Sun 12:30–2:30pm and 6:30–11pm.
In this traditional Old Town pub you'll find very good traditional Scottish fare, and the location, midway between the castle and the palace, makes it an ideal lunch spot. The daily special includes soup, main course, vegetables, and dessert. This surprisingly elegant pub is popular with government employees from nearby offices.

MEALS FOR LESS THAN £5 [$9.50]

THE BAKED POTATO SHOP, 56 Cockburn St. Tel. 225-7572.
  Cuisine: STUFFED POTATOES.
$ Prices: £2–£2.50 ($3.80–$4.75). No credit cards.
  Open: Daily 9am–9pm.
If you're in a need of some cheap eats while wandering the Royal Mile, you can hardly do better than this hole in the wall. Little bigger than a closet, and with seating for only four people, the Baked Potato Shop is primarily a take-out place. The potatoes are huge and stuffed with vegetarian fillings such as curry, cauliflower and cheese, or chili. However, try the vegetarian haggis—it tastes just like the real thing.

THE TEA ROOM, in the Royal Museum of Scotland, Chambers St. Tel. 225-7534.
Cuisine: SANDWICHES.
$ Prices: £1–£2.50 ($1.90–$4.75). No credit cards.
Open: Mon–Sat 10am–4:30pm. Sun 2–4:30pm.
At the back of the museum on the ground floor, this bright split-level restaurant provides a convenient and inexpensive spot to grab a quick lunch. Since there is no entrance charge for the museum, you could eat here any time you're in the area.

CAFETERIAS

All the major department stores along Princes Street have cafeterias serving economical meals. In addition, many of the smaller stores also have small cafés with equally good prices.

BHS, 64 Princes St. Tel. 226-2621.
Cuisine: ENGLISH.
$ Prices: £2–£4 ($3.80–$7.60). ACCESS, EURO, MC, V.
Open: Mon–Wed 9am–5:30pm, Thurs 9am–9pm, Fri–Sat 9am–6pm, Sun 12:30–5pm.
Up an escalator at the back of this store you'll find a large modern restaurant with the lowest prices of the department-store cafeterias.

BURTON'S, 30 Princes St. Tel. 557-4578.
Cuisine: ENGLISH.
$ Prices: £2–£5 ($3.80–$9.50). ACCESS, V.
Open: Mon–Sat 9am–5:30pm (on Thurs to 7:30pm).
On the fifth floor of this store, reached by an elevator, is the best of the department-store cafeterias. There is a fabulous view of Princes Street Gardens, the castle, and the Old Town. On top of that, the food is good and the servings are generous. As with most cafeterias, desserts are plentiful and cheap.

JENNER'S, 47 Princes St. Tel. 225-2442.
Cuisine: ENGLISH.
$ Prices: £2–£6.50 ($3.80–$12.35). ACCESS, AE, DC, V.
Open: Mon–Sat 9am–5:30pm (on Thurs to 7pm).
This department store doesn't have just one cafeteria—it has five restaurants and coffee shops scattered throughout its large complex. There are menus posted at the Princes Street doors so you can decide which of the restaurants best fits your immediate craving or budget. The Rose Street Restaurant on the first floor offers a selection of different hot dishes daily. Comfortable but noisy.

TEVIOT BAR, Bristo Sq. Tel. 650-4673.
Cuisine: ENGLISH.
$ Prices: £1–£3 ($1.90–$5.70).

 FROMMER'S SMART TRAVELER: RESTAURANTS

VALUE-CONSCIOUS TRAVELERS SHOULD
TAKE ADVANTAGE OF THE FOLLOWING:

1. Early meals. Many of the restaurants listed here close at 5:30 or 6pm.
2. Department stores along pricey Princes Street, surprisingly inexpensive places to eat.
3. Pub grub or fast food on Sunday, as finding a place to eat on Sunday can be a real problem in Edinburgh.

Open: Mon–Fri 8:30am–7:30pm.

The prices at this student cafeteria are incredibly low and the modern dining hall on the second floor of the student center has plenty of room.

To reach the university refectory from Waverly Station, cross North Bridge and follow South Bridge to South College Street, where you make a right turn. Bristo Square is only a block ahead and the cafeteria is in the old student union building.

MEALS FOR LESS THAN £7 [$13.30]

VEGETARIAN & NATURAL FOODS

HENDERSON'S SALAD TABLE AND WINE BAR, 94 Hanover St. Tel. 225-2131.

    Cuisine: VEGETARIAN.

$ Prices: £2.50–£5 ($4.75–$9.50).

    Open: Mon–St 8am–10:45pm.

    This is another excellent change from the meat-and-potatoes diet. A delicious assortment of salads (served by the scoop) and hot meals are available all day in this large basement restaurant. Batik and stained-glass room partitions, live jazz, and colorful wall hangings create a very relaxing atmosphere. Tempting cakes and pies and a large variety of herbal teas are ideal for afternoon tea or dessert.

SUNFLOWER COUNTRY KITCHEN, 4-8 S. Charlotte St. Tel. 220-1700.

    Cuisine: NATURAL FOODS.

$ Prices: £2.75–£5 ($5.25–$9.50). No credit cards.

    Open: Mon–Sat 8am–6pm.

    On Charlotte Street, around the corner from Princes Street (at the end nearest the castle), is this spacious self-serve natural-foods restaurant. Here you will find excellent and healthy meals at reasonable prices. If you're on a diet, you'll appreciate the calorie counts on the menu. Don't be discouraged if it looks too busy—they have two serving areas and the lines move quickly even at lunch when they're packed with shoppers and businesspeople from the area.

PICNIC SUPPLIES & WHERE TO EAT THEM

MARKS & SPENCER, 53 Princes St. Tel. 225-2301.

    Cuisine: SANDWICHES/SALADS.

$ Prices: £1–£1.75 ($1.90–$3.35). No credit cards.

    Open: Mon–Tues 9:30am–5:30pm, Wed 9am–5:30pm, Thurs 9am–8pm, Fri 8:45am–8pm, Sat 8:30am–6pm.

In the basement of this department store is a supermarket with cooler after cooler of freshly made sandwiches, salads, pasta salads, cakes, cookies, fruits, vegetables, and anything else you might want for a picnic. Best of all, the prices are extremely low and Princes Street Gardens is right across the street. If you're feeling like a walk before eating, head up to the top of Salisbury Crags or Aurthur's Seat.

6. ATTRACTIONS

SUGGESTED ITINERARIES

IF YOU HAVE ONE DAY   Don't worry. Even if you have only 1 day in town, you can still see the two most important sights and maybe even a few less important ones. Start the day at Edinburgh Castle, approaching through the Princes Street

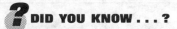

DID YOU KNOW . . . ?

- Greyfriar's Bobby, a Skye terrier, kept a 14-year vigil at his master's grave.
- Princes Street Gardens was once a lake.
- More than 17,000 supposed witches were executed in Scotland between the years 1479 and 1722.
- *The Strange Case of Dr. Jekyll and Mr. Hyde* is based on a historical Edinburgh resident.
- Edinburgh's zoo boasts the world's largest colony of penguins in captivity.
- Golf has existed since the 15th century. The Royal and Ancient Golf Club in St. Andrews, north of Edinburgh, was founded in 1754.

Gardens, which have a gate opening onto the castle parking lot. This will give you the best feel for the loftiness of Castle Hill. After spending a couple of hours at the castle, head down the Royal Mile, stopping at the Royal Mile pub for lunch. After lunch, tour the Palace of Holyroodhouse, once the home of Mary Queen of Scots.

IF YOU HAVE TWO DAYS With 2 days you can split the Royal Mile into two royal half miles, covering one on the first day and one on the second. This gives you more time to explore the medieval closes and stop at the many small museums along the way. I recommend Lady Stair's House, Huntly House, the John Knox House, St. Giles's Cathedral, and if you have time, a visit to the Brass Rubbing Centre to make your own rubbing. On one of your 2 days you should also try to visit the National Gallery of Scotland and climb the Scott Monument, both of which are in the New Town along Princes Street Gardens.

IF YOU HAVE THREE DAYS Spend 2 days in the Old Town visiting the sights already mentioned. On your third day take a trip outside the city to see the Scottish highlands and a loch or two, preferably Loch Ness, for a chance to glimpse Nessie, the elusive creature rumored to live in the depths of those waters.

IF YOU HAVE FIVE DAYS Follow the suggestions above, but add to these a day in the New Town visiting the Georgian House, the Royal Museum of Scotland and National Portrait Gallery, and the Royal Botanic Gardens. If one of your five days happens to be sunny, change your plans and take a picnic lunch up on Salisbury Crags. You can't beat the view from up there! The rest of the day, you might visit the Scottish Gallery of Modern Art or visit a few more sights along the Royal Mile.

TOP ATTRACTIONS

EDINBURGH CASTLE, Castle Hill. Tel. 225-9846.
Perched on a hill overlooking Edinburgh, the castle constantly draws the eye to it. Whether it's catching the first rays of the sun, enshrouded in fog, or brightly illuminated at night, Edinburgh Castle is the most striking sight in the city. St. Margaret's Chapel is the oldest building inside the castle walls, dating from the early 12th century. Housed within the Royal Palace here are the Scottish crown, scepter, and sword.

Admission: £2.80 ($5.30) adults, £1.40 ($2.65) children and senior citizens.
Open: Mon–Sat 9:30am–5:05pm, Sun 11am–5:05pm. **Bus:** 1 or 6.

PALACE OF HOLYROODHOUSE, Canongate. Tel. 556-1096.
Built more than 300 years ago for the kings and queens of Scotland, this palace is still the official residence of the queen when she visits Edinburgh each summer. This was the home of Mary Queen of Scots, Bonnie Prince Charlie, and Queen Victoria. Uniformed guides will delight in describing to you the grisly death of Queen Mary's personal secretary, David Rizzio, who was murdered by associates of her jealous husband in 1566. Elsewhere in the palace are massive tapestries, ornate plasterwork

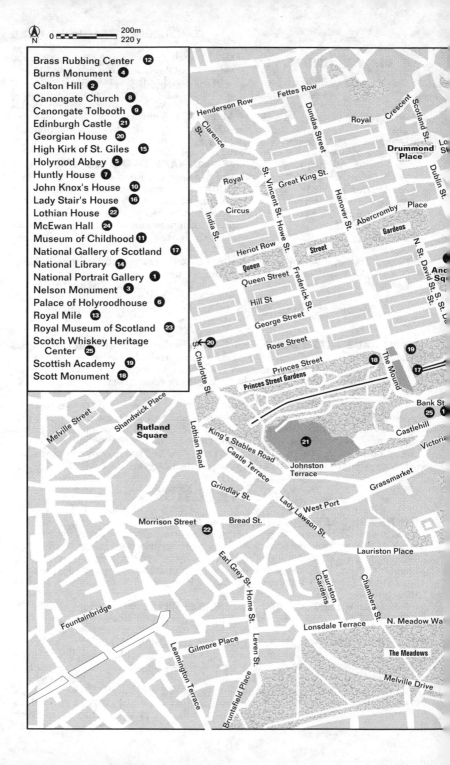

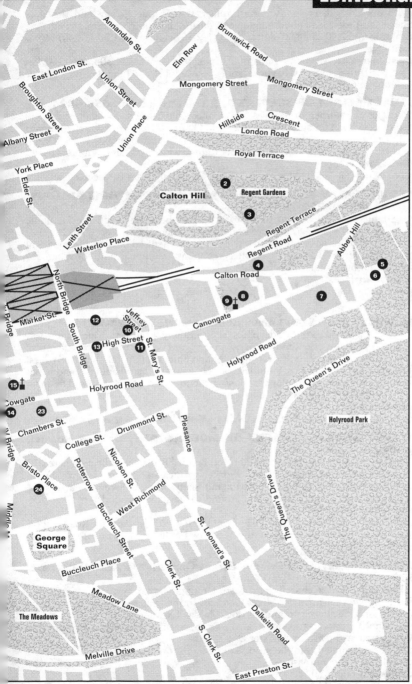

EDINBURGH

ceilings, a portrait gallery of the Stuart rulers, the Throne Room, and the State Apartments, still used for entertaining guests during the queen's summer residency.
Admission: £2.40 ($4.55) adults, £1.20 ($2.30) children, £1.80 ($3.40) senior citizens.
Open: Mar–Oct, Mon–Sat 9:30am–5:15pm, Sun 10:30am–4:30pm; Nov–Mar, Mon–Sat 9:30am–3:45pm. **Closed:** Jan 1–3, May 13–28, June 17–July 7, Dec 25–26. **Bus:** 1, 6, or 60.

NATIONAL GALLERY OF SCOTLAND, 2 The Mound. Tel. 556-8921.

Located at the corner of Princes Street and The Mound, the gallery has an outstanding collection for such a small museum. On display are works by Rembrandt, Raphael, Titian, El Greco, Rubens, van Dyck, Goya, Gainsborough, Monet, Degas, Gauguin, van Gogh, and the Scottish artists Ramsay, Raeburn, and Wilkie.
Admission: Free.
Open: Mon–Sat 10am–5pm, Sun 2–5pm. **Bus:** Any Princes Street bus.

ROYAL MUSEUM OF SCOTLAND AND NATIONAL PORTRAIT GALLERY, 1 Queen St. Tel. 225-7534.

The exhibits here all pertain to Scottish history, beginning with the Neolithic period nearly 6,000 years ago and continuing up to the present. Viking, Celtic, and Roman artifacts tell a fascinating story that is an excellent adjunct to the medieval history of Edinburgh. The portrait gallery contains traditional and some not-so-traditional paintings of famous Scots.
Admission: Free.
Open: Mon–Sat 10am–5pm, Sun 2–5pm. **Bus:** 2/12, 4, 10A, 11, 15, 16, 42/46, or 43/44.

ROYAL MUSEUM OF SCOTLAND, Chambers St. Tel. 225-7534.

A Venetian Renaissance facade hides an unusually bright and airy Victorian interior at this museum of natural history, industry, and decorative arts on Chambers Street two blocks south of the Royal Mile. Stuffed animals, minerals, steam engines, Egyptian artifacts, and working models of the engines that made the Industrial Revolution possible are on display throughout the museum's three floors. The main hall of the museum is itself reason enough to visit.
Admission: Free.
Open: Mon–Sat 10am–5pm, Sun 2–5pm. **Bus:** Lawnmarket or Tron bus.

SCOTTISH NATIONAL GALLERY OF MODERN ART, Belford Rd. Tel. 556-8921.

Housed in an 1820s neoclassical building on Belford Road, the collection here is as fine as that in the National Gallery. Works by Picasso, Matisse, Miró, David Hockney, Henry Moore, Roy Lichtenstein, and many other 20th-century artists are on display both inside the museum and around the spacious grounds.
Admission: Free.
Open: Mon–Sat 10am–5pm, Sun 2–5pm. **Bus:** 41 to Queensferry Road (get off at Belford Road, just before crossing the Water of Leith; the museum is a 5-minute walk up Belford Road).

SCOTT MONUMENT, East Princes Street Gardens. Tel. 225-2424, ext. 6596.

Looking more like a church spire than a monument to a writer, this Gothic structure dominates East Princes Street Gardens. In the center of the spire is a large seated statue of Sir Walter Scott and his dog, Maida. The monument rises to a height of more than 200 feet. Visitors are treated to a spectacular view of the city from an observation area at the top of 287 steps.
Note: The monument is in the process of being restored, and may still be covered with scaffolding when you visit.
Admission: 60p ($1.15).
Open: Apr–Sept, Mon–Sat 9am–6pm; Oct–Mar, Mon–Sat 9am–3pm. **Bus:** 2/12, 3, 3A, 4, 4A, 10, 11, 15, 15A, 16, 43, 44, 80, or 80A.

NELSON MONUMENT AND THE NATIONAL MONUMENT [EDINBURGH'S DISGRACE], Calton Hill. Tel. 556-2716.

Erected in memory of Admiral Lord Horatio Nelson, victor at the Battle of Trafalgar, this 106-foot-tall tower atop Calton Hill was built to resemble a telescope, and it offers superb views over the city. The "Greek" ruins beside the monument are all that was built of a monument to commemorate Scottish soldiers and sailors who died in the Napoleonic Wars. Lack of funds prevented its completion and now it is one of the most eye-catching structures in all of Edinburgh, going by the name of Edinburgh's Disgrace.

Admission: Nelson Monument, 60p ($1.15); National Monument, free.

Open: Oct–Mar, Mon–Sat 10am–3pm; Apr–Sept, Mon 1–6pm, Tues–Sat 10am–6pm. **Bus:** 26, 85, or 86.

GEORGIAN HOUSE, 7 Charlotte Sq. Tel. 225-2160.

Edinburgh's New Town is a model of 18th-century urban planning. In contrast to the Old City, symmetry reigns in the grand boulevards, parks, squares, and elegant rowhouses on this side of Princes Street Gardens. Furnished in original Georgian style, this house shows what life was like in the New Town 200 years ago when it was indeed new. Furnishings include Chippendale, Hepplewhite, and Sheraton styles, as well as porcelain by Derby and Wedgwood.

Admission: £2.40 ($4.55) adults, £1.20 ($2.30) children and students.

Open: Apr–Oct, Mon–Sat 10am–5pm, Sun 2–5pm. **Closed:** Nov–Apr. **Directions:** Walk two blocks over from the west end of Princes Street. **Bus:** 13, 18, 40, or 41A.

MORE ATTRACTIONS

Between Edinburgh Castle and the Palace of Holyroodhouse, along the **Royal Mile,** you'll find dozens of interesting shops, old pubs, fascinating little museums, and Edinburgh's oldest cathedral. You'll find many of the sights listed here down the narrow closes (alleyways) that lead off the Royal Mile. Regardless of whether they have a specific attraction to visit, all the closes are worth exploring simply for their medieval atmosphere.

ST. GILES'S CATHEDRAL, High St. Tel. 225-4363.

Located on High Street, this cathedral is the spiritual heart of the Church of Scotland. A church has existed on this site since the 9th century, but this building dates only from 1385. Since then many alterations have changed the building immensely. Scottish religious reformer John Knox, who established the Protestant religion in Scotland, became the minister here in 1560. The unusual main spire is in the form of a thistle, one of the symbols of Scotland.

Admission: Cathedral, free; the small Thistle Chapel inside, 30p (60¢).

Open: Mon–Sat 9am–5pm, Sun 7:30am–9pm. **Bus:** 1, 6, 34, or 35.

JOHN KNOX'S HOUSE, 43 High St. Tel. 556-9579.

Tradition has it that John Knox, leader of the Protestant Reformation in Scotland, lived here between 1561 and 1572. Built in 1490 and a museum since 1853, this may be the oldest house in Edinburgh. The wooden gallery surrounding the upper floors is the last of its kind in the city. Inside are paintings and lithographs of Knox, along with his letters, sermons, and early tracts.

Admission: £1.20 ($2.30) adults, 50p (95¢) children.

Open: Mon–Sat 10am–4:30pm. **Bus:** 1, 3, 5, 6, 7, 8, 14, 21, 31, 33, 34, 35, 80, 81, 82, 87, 88, or 132.

HUNTLY HOUSE, Canongate. Tel. 225-2424, ext. 6689.

To learn more about the history of Scotland, and Edinburgh in particular, head for this small museum on Canongate (the lower section of the Royal Mile). In this restored 16th-century town house are exhibits and rooms set up to show how citizens of Edinburgh lived in different centuries of the house's history.

Admission: Free.

Open: June–Sept, Mon–Sat 10am–6pm; Oct–May, Mon–Sat 10am–5pm. **Bus:** 1 or 6.

LADY STAIR'S HOUSE, Lawnmarket. Tel. 225-2424, ext. 6593.

Located in Lady Stair's Close off the Lawnmarket, less than 100 yards from George IV Bridge, this museum is a must for fans of Scottish literature. Robert Burns, Sir Walter Scott, and Robert Louis Stevenson are commemorated with collections of their works, their personal effects, and portraits.

Admission: Free.

Open: June–Sept, Mon–Sat 10am–6pm; Oct–May, Mon–Sat 10am–5pm. **Bus:** 1, 6, 23, 27, 30, 34, 35, 40, 41, 42, 46, or 89.

OUTLOOK TOWER AND CAMERA OBSCURA, Castle Hill. Tel. 226-3709.

The camera obscura, a device that produces an upside-down image on the wall of a black room, was installed in 1850 and has been a popular attraction ever since. It's like walking inside a huge camera. Also here are exhibits on pinhole photography and holography.

Admission: £2.50 ($4.75) adults, £1.25 ($2.40) children.

Open: Daily 10am–6pm. **Bus:** 1, 6, 23, 27, 30, 34, 35, 40, 41, 42, 46, or 89.

BRASS RUBBING CENTRE, Chalmer's Close, High St. Tel. 556-4364.

The center provides instruction and replicas of medieval church brasses and Neolithic Scottish stone carvings in all sizes for you to make your own rubbings. There are also ready-made rubbings for sale. The center is housed in an old church and has a number of rubbings and old brasses on display.

Admission: Free; rubbings vary in price.

Open: June–Sept, Mon–Sat 10am–6pm; Oct–May, Mon–Sat 10am–5pm. **Bus:** 1, 6, or 60.

PARKS & GARDENS

Edinburgh is filled with parks and gardens. The largest is **Holyrood Park,** which begins behind the Palace of Holyroodhouse. With rocky crags, a loch, sweeping meadows, and the ruins of an old chapel, it's a wee bit of the Scottish countryside in Edinburgh. **Arthur's Seat,** at 823 feet, and the **Salisbury Crags** offer unbeatable views over Edinburgh to the Firth of Forth. This is a great place for a picnic.

PRINCES STREET GARDENS.

These tranquil gardens separate the Old Town from the New Town. Old trees and brilliant green lawns fill the valley between the two sections of the city. There are dozens of wooden benches given in memory of loved ones by the people of Edinburgh along the paved footpaths of the gardens, making this an excellent place to sit and relax and enjoy the views of the city.

Admission: Free.

Open: Daily dawn–dusk.

ROYAL BOTANIC GARDENS, Inverleith Row. Tel. 552-7171.

Edinburgh's 70-acre botanical garden is known for its large collection of rhododendrons, which flower profusely every spring. With a large arboretum, research facilities, and wild areas providing a sharp contrast to the neatly manicured gardens, this is one of the finest botanical gardens in Europe. It's also the second-oldest botanical garden in Britain, established as a physic garden in 1670 by two physicians who used the plants for treating illnesses.

Admission: Free.

Open: Mon–Sat 9am–sunset (1 hour before sunset in summer), Sun 11am–sunset (1 hour before sunset in summer). **Bus:** 8, 19, 23, 27, or 29.

EDINBURGH ZOO, 134 Corstorphine Rd. Tel. 334-9171.

The Edinburgh Zoo covers 80 acres of parkland and houses more than 2,000 animals. The main attraction of the zoo is the **penguin parade,** which takes place daily at 2:30pm from April to September. With more than 100 penguins, this is the world's largest self-supporting captive penguin colony, and they're an unforgettable sight when they go for their afternoon stroll.

Admission: £4.20 ($8) adults, £2.10 ($4) children.

Open: Mon–Sat 9am–6pm, Sun 9:30am–6pm (to dusk in winter). **Bus:** 12, 26, 31, 85, or 86.

SPECIAL-INTEREST SIGHTSEEING

Literary fans should not miss Lady Stair's House, a small museum devoted to **Scottish writers** Robert Burns, Sir Walter Scott, and Robert Louis Stevenson. In addition, if you have the stamina, make a pilgrimage to the top of the Scott Memorial in Princes Street Gardens. And on the corner of Lawnmarket and Bank Street is Deacon Brodie's Tavern, named for the criminal who inspired Robert Louis Stevenson to write *The Strange Case of Dr. Jekyll and Mr. Hyde.*

ORGANIZED TOURS

WALKING TOURS   Three interesting walking tours of Edinburgh are offered by **Robin's Walking Tours** (tel. 661-0125), all of which last about 2 hours, cost £3 ($5.70) per person, and start from the fountain in front of the Waverly Market Tourist Information Centre. The "Royal Mile Tour" introduces you to the Edinburgh of Queen Mary. The "18th Century Edinburgh" covers the fine exterior and interior architecture of the mid-18th century and follows the footsteps of Robert Louis Stevenson. "Dr. Jekyll's Horror Walk" covers famous murders and other macabre and bizarre events throughout Edinburgh's history.

Similar tours are offered by **The Cadies** (tel. 225-6745). Their tours of haunted Edinburgh last 1¼ hours, cost £4 ($7.60) and leave from in front of the Witchery Restaurant just outside the gate to Edinburgh Castle. Reservations are required.

BUS TOURS   For a quick, 2-hour overview of the main sights of Edinburgh, you can take a **Lothian Region Transport** bus tour that will show you the Royal Mile, some other streets in the Old Town, a bit of the Georgian New Town, and either Edinburgh Castle or the Palace of Holyroodhouse. Adults pay £7 ($13.30), which includes admission to the castle or the palace. Tours start from Waverly Bridge, and tickets are available from the Ticket Centre on Waverly Bridge.

A less expensive option is to choose the "Edinburgh Classic Tour," which is a day pass for an open-topped double-decker bus that makes a regular circuit past all the major tourist attractions in both Old Town and New Town. You can get on and off the bus to visit an attraction and then catch a later bus. Tickets cost £3.50 ($6.65) for adults and £1.50 ($2.85) for children.

SPECIAL & FREE EVENTS

For 3 weeks every August, Edinburgh goes on a cultural binge. I am referring, of course, to the world-renowned **Edinburgh International Festival,** which is not just one festival but five different festivals all rolled up into one. There is the official festival, the Festival Fringe, the Film Festival, the Edinburgh Book Festival, and the International Jazz Festival. During the 3 weeks of the festival, hundreds of theater, dance, opera, and mime companies give thousands of performances. The finest in classical and jazz music fills dozens of halls and special art exhibits and a book festival give the visual and literary arts their due. One of the most popular performances is the Edinburgh Military Tattoo, a military musical extravaganza held on the esplanade in front of the castle just before dusk. The Fringe, featuring premieres of new plays, is rapidly becoming the most popular part of the festival.

For information on the Edinburgh International Festival, contact the Festival Society, 21 Market Street, Edinburgh, Scotland (tel. 031/226-4001). For more information on the **Edinburgh Tattoo,** contact the Tattoo Office, 22 Market St.,

Edinburgh EH1 1QB (tel. 031/225-1188); for the **Edinburgh Festival Fringe,** contact the Edinburgh Festival Fringe, 180 High St., Edinburgh EH1 1QS (tel. 031/226-5257).

7. SAVVY SHOPPING

Princes Street in the New Town is Edinburgh's main shopping area, with several large department stores and dozens of shops selling designer clothes and other equally expensive items.

Victoria Street and **Grassmarket** in the Old Town both have some unusual shops.

VAT REFUNDS In shops all over Edinburgh you will see signs saying TAX-FREE SHOPPING. These signs refer to the process by which you as a visitor can recover the Value-Added Tax that amounts to about 17.5% of everything you buy. Usually shops will require a minimum purchase of £30–£50 ($57–$95) before they will fill out the tax-refund forms for you. Once the forms are filled out, present them to Customs before leaving the country, along with the purchases themselves. After the forms have been stamped by Customs, mail them back to the store with the envelope provided by the store. Within a few weeks your refund will be mailed to your home address in the form you have requested (such as a check in U.S. dollars).

8. EVENING ENTERTAINMENT

For a city of its size, Edinburgh (pop. 450,000) has an overwhelming array of evening entertainment. Whether your interest is theater, dance, or folk, classical, or rock music, Edinburgh will entertain you for next to nothing. On any given night you might see a play for £4 ($7.60), stop by a pub for a bit of free traditional music, and then head to a disco (get there before 11pm to get in for £2/$3.80) for some late-night dancing—a jam-packed night out for only £6 ($11.40), not including drinks.

Pick up a free copy of **What's On in Edinburgh** at the Tourist Information Centre at Waverly Market. This pocket-size booklet comes out every month and lists exhibitions, theater, music, films, sports events, and other information helpful to tourists. Another good source of information is the biweekly magazine **The List,** also available at the Tourist Information Centre, for £1 ($1.90). Here you'll find the same sort of information in more detail, plus reviews.

THE PERFORMING ARTS

THEATER

Edinburgh is a theater-goer's dream come true—fine performances and low prices. This is not surprising considering Edinburgh's love of theater, the culmination of which is the annual summer **Edinburgh International Festival.** Tickets start as low as £4 ($7.60) at many theaters, and even the most expensive theaters have tickets for under £6 ($11.40) to most performances. Shows start at 7:30pm Monday through Saturday (no performances on Sunday). It's sometimes possible to catch a free preview. Check *The List* (see above) to find the best deals while you're in town.

KING'S THEATRE, 2 Leven St. Tel. 229-1201.

This Victorian theater has about 1,600 seats and features a wide variety of performances by different repertory companies. Ballet, opera, light opera, pantomime, and drama all show up here.

Prices: Tickets, £4–£16 ($7.60–$30.40).

Open: Box office, Mon–Sat 10am–7:30pm on performance days, 10am–6pm on nonperformance days.

ROYAL LYCEUM THEATRE, Grindlay St. at Lothian Rd. Tel. 229-9697.

Edinburgh's main playhouse seats 1,200 and features plays and operas by the resident company.

Prices: Tickets, £4–£12 ($7.60–$22.80).

Open: Box office, Mon–Sat 10am–8pm.

TRAVERSE THEATRE, Cambridge St., off Lothian Rd. Tel. 226-2633.

You can catch new and experimental theater productions by English and Scottish playwrights at this small theater.

Prices: Tickets, £4–£6 ($7.60–$11.40).

Open: Box office, Tues–Sat 10am–8pm, Sun 6–8pm.

THE NETHERBOW ARTS CENTRE, 43 High St. Tel. 556-9579.

This is another location for new Scottish theater, and even has lunchtime performances.

Prices: Tickets, £2.50–£5 ($4.75–$9.50).

Open: Box office, Mon–Sat 10am–6pm.

CLASSICAL MUSIC

There are two major halls for performances of classical music: **Usher Hall,** on Lothian Road (tel. 228-1155), where the Scottish National Orchestra plays; and the **Queen's Hall,** Clerk Street (tel. 668-2019), which is the home of the Edinburgh Symphony Orchestra and showcases other groups as well. Both have performances at 7:30pm (check *What's On in Edinburgh* or *The List* for schedules and programs), and tickets at both start at £4–£5 ($7.60–$9.50).

FOLK, ROCK & JAZZ

Fans of folk, rock, and jazz can have a field day in Edinburgh, where most clubs offer free live music every night. At most you might have to pay £1 ($1.90) on a Friday or Saturday night for the top local bands. Music usually starts around 11pm.

Also keep your eyes out for the *Gig Guide,* a free monthly schedule of performances of rock, pop, folk, and jazz music in nightclubs, pubs, and bars.

PRESERVATION HALL, 9a Victoria St. Tel. 226-3816.

In an old church (you can't miss it) that has been converted into a commercial building is one of Edinburgh's most popular spots for live rock music and blues.

Admission: £1 ($1.90) most nights.

Open: Daily 9pm–2am.

FIDDLERS ARMS, 11-13 Grassmarket. Tel. 229-2665.

For fine traditional music, try this pub a block west of the end of Victoria Street. On Monday nights local musicians get together to play old favorites in a corner of the pub's front room.

Admission: Free.

Open: Mon–Wed 11am–11pm, Thurs–Sat 11am–midnight, Sun 12:30–11pm.

MALT SHOVEL, 13 Cockburn St. Tel. 225-6843.

This small, dark pub is an Edinburgh legend that has spawned at least two companion pubs in the area. Besides the free live jazz and traditional music, there is one of the best selections of single-malt whiskeys in town.

Admission: Free.

Open: Mon–Sat noon–12:30am.

MOVIES

The most easily accessible for visitors are the **Cannon** on Lothian Road, which starts at the western end of Princes Street; the **Cameo** on Home Street (an extension of

Lothian Road); and the **Odeon** on Clerk Street, which is close to Dalkeith Road. The **Edinburgh Filmhouse** on Lothian Road shows foreign films.

Tickets range from £2.10 ($4) to £4 ($7.60). Early shows are usually less expensive.

EDINBURGH'S PUBS

There is a pub on nearly every block in Edinburgh, and many of them have live music at least 1 night a week. In all of them, either a pint of ale or a shot of scotch whiskey will cost £1.20–£1.60 ($2.30–$3.05). Most pubs also serve lunch from noon to 2:30pm. Rose Street is famous for its pubs, or try these:

THE GREEN TREE, 184 Cowgate. Tel. 225-1294.

This atmospheric pub with low ceilings and dark brick walls is directly under South Bridge, literally in the foundation of the bridge. There is often live traditional music here in the evenings. Popular with students from the nearby university.

Open: Mon–Sat 11am–11pm.

THE GUILDFORD ARMS, 1 W. Register St. Tel. 556-4312.

This ornate Victorian pub, located behind the Wimpy restaurant by North Bridge, is popular with an older and more upscale clientele. You can't miss the beautiful etched-glass windows. Once inside you'll be astounded by the sumptuous decor.

Open: Mon–Thurs 11am–11pm, Fri–Sat 11am–midnight, Sun 12:30–2:30pm and 6:30–11pm.

CAFE ROYAL, 17 W. Register St. Tel. 556-1884.

On the same tiny block as the Guildford Arms, the ever-popular Café Royal, known for its circle bar, appeals to a more casual clientele. Stained-glass windows and unusual painted tiles of famous inventors make the Café Royal a particularly interesting spot to down a pint. There is also live folk music here on Wednesday at 8pm, when there is an admission charge of £3.50 ($6.65).

Open: Mon–Sat 10am–11pm, Sun 11am–11pm.

DISCOS

Discos in Edinburgh generally open their doors around 10pm and stay open until 3 or 4am. Drinks average £1.50 ($2.85) for beer or hard liquor, and many offer special drink prices on certain nights or early in the evening.

CENTURY 2000, 31 Lothian Rd. Tel. 229-7670.

This is the largest disco in Edinburgh, and one of the most popular.

Admission: £5 ($9.50), £3 ($5.70) before midnight.

Open: Fri–Sat 10pm–4am.

BUSTER BROWN'S, 25-27 Market St. Tel. 226-4224.

Buster Brown's is popular with the under-25 group and features mainstream top-40 dance music.

Admission: £3 ($5.70) Fri and Sun, £2 ($3.80) before 11:30pm; £4 ($7.60) Sat, £2 ($3.80) before 11:30pm.

Open: Fri–Sun 10:30pm–3:30am.

9. EASY EXCURSIONS

Lothian Region Transport, 14 Queen St. (tel. 554-4494), offers more than 20 different excursions from Edinburgh. Among the best of these is the tour to **Loch Ness and the Grampian Mountains.** This tour is available only from early April through early November. The trip costs £20 ($38) for adults and £16 ($30.40) for children. Along the way toward the home of the fabled Loch Ness monster, the coach travels through beautiful mountains, forests, fields, and farmland.

For a less expensive all-day excursion, try the trip to beautiful **Loch Lomond.** In summer the tour is combined with a visit to either the Argyllshire or Trossachs mountains. In winter the tour travels through the Argyllshire mountains. The cost is £12.50 ($23.75) for adults and £8 ($15.20) for children.

You can also book your tour at the Ticket Centre on Waverly Bridge (tel. 220-4111).

CHAPTER 13

FLORENCE

Five hundred years ago, Florence was the center of European culture. It was here in the 14th, 15th, and 16th centuries that many of the most important developments in modern art and architecture took place. Indeed, today we refer to their time as the Renaissance, or "rebirth."

Florence is no longer the axis around which the artistic world revolves, but the taste, elegance, and aesthetic sensibilities that marked the Renaissance are still alive and well. Today elegant young Florentines saunter through the narrow cobblestone streets, through its spacious piazzas, and past its great *palazzi* with the same confidence and pride as their forebears.

Europe's cultural revolution was financed in large part by the Medicis, Florence's ruling family throughout much of the Renaissance. They came to power as bankers, and used their wealth to foster the arts. The city is swimming in their heritage, with fully half a dozen different museums housing major paintings and sculptures of the period.

But it's not only the sights and the history that make Florence a special place for budget travelers. It's also the nuts and bolts of where you stay and what you eat that will make this city special around the clock. Many of the budget hotels listed here are housed in the same 15th- and 16th-century *palazzi* where the Medicis and the Michelangelos lived. Modern visitors often find themselves sleeping beneath ceilings decorated with colorful frescoes, or in beds old enough to have been slept in by Botticelli. The cuisine in this city, situated in the heart of the nation's most fertile agricultural land, is arguably the finest in Italy.

Just as Florence inaugurated a rebirth of creative thought in Europe five centuries ago, it will raise your spirits and lift your thoughts in 1993.

1. FROM A BUDGET TRAVELER'S POINT OF VIEW

FLORENCE BUDGET BESTS   You're likely to find bargains on almost everything in this shopper's paradise. Florence's enormous open-air market stretches for half a dozen blocks, with hundreds of stalls hawking everything from $8 souvenir T-shirts to $400 designer leather coats, often at about half what you'd pay for comparable quality back home. Hand-knit all-wool sweaters, at about $30, and fashionable leather jackets, beginning at around $200, are the best buys, but budget shoppers will be able to find just about anything here, at very reasonable prices.

You can always save money on food and drink by consuming them standing up at one of the city's ubiquitous bars. A 2,500-lira ($2.15) *panino* (sandwich) and a 1,500-lira ($1.30) cappuccino make a quick and satisfying lunch. Prices double—at least—if you sit down.

Finally, Florence is especially well suited to the one tourist activity that never costs a cent—walking. With its 15th-century *palazzi* lining cobblestone streets that are even older, Florence is one of the most delightful cities in Europe to explore on foot.

WHAT THINGS COST IN FLORENCE	U.S. $
Taxi (from the train station to piazza della Signoria)	8.70
Public bus (from any point within the city to any other point)	.85
Local telephone call	.18
Double room at the Excelsior (deluxe)	390.00
Double room at the Hotel Morandi Alla Crocetta (moderate)	118.70
Double room at the Locanda Mia Cara (budget)	40.20
Continental breakfast (cappuccino and croissant)	
(at any café or bar)	2.15
(at most hotels)	5.20
Lunch for one at Trattoria del Pennello (moderate)	18.25
Lunch for one at any café (budget)	4.35
Dinner for one, without wine, at Enoteca Pinchiorri (deluxe)	105.00
Dinner for one, without wine, at Ristorante Acqua Al Due (moderate)	25.75
Dinner for one, without wine, at Trattoria da Giorgio (budget)	10.45
Pint of beer (at Fiddler's Elbow)	5.20
Glass of wine (at Chiodo Fisso)	3.50
Coca-Cola to take out (at any café in town)	1.75
Cup of coffee (cappuccino) (at any café in town)	1.30
Roll of ASA 100 color film, 36 exposures	7.85
Admission to the Uffizi Galleries	8.70
Movie ticket (at the Astro Cinema)	6.50
Theater ticket (at the Teatro Communale)	8.70

WORTH THE EXTRA BUCKS   To gourmets and gourmands alike, Florence is the culinary capital of Italy. In "Budget Dining," below, you'll find half a dozen restaurants that are particularly worth a splurge.

Florence also has an outstanding selection of charming, one-of-a-kind hotels. If you can afford to spend a little bit more on accommodations, you'll inevitably be treated to an extraordinary and memorable stay.

Finally, don't miss the *gelato* (ice cream). At about 3,000 lire ($2.60) per serving, this light, delicious local delicacy is worth every lira.

2. PRETRIP PREPARATIONS

DOCUMENTS/WHAT TO PACK   For suggestions on documents and wardrobe, see the Rome chapter.

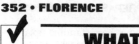

WHAT'S SPECIAL ABOUT FLORENCE

The City Itself

☐ The most significant and most captivating architecture in Italy.

☐ The surrounding Tuscan countryside, home to some of the most delightful scenery in Italy.

☐ Watching the sun set over the red-tile roofs of the city.

☐ Taking a *passeggiata* (stroll) along via Calzaiuoli on a warm summer night.

Sights

☐ Michelangelo's *David* at the Accademia Gallery, which, despite the crowds, is worth the wait.

☐ The Botticelli Galleries at the Uffizi, some of the brightest and most refreshing museum rooms in Europe.

☐ The rich color and architecture of the Duomo and the adjacent Baptistery and Campanile.

Film Locations

☐ The piazza della Signoria, where one of the key opening scenes in *A Room with a View* takes place.

Shopping

☐ The incomparable prices and variety at the enormous, sprawling San Lorenzo Market.

☐ The extraordinary quality of the leather goods available throughout the city.

☐ The trendy boutiques that line via Calzaiuoli and the surrounding streets.

Events/Festivals

☐ The raucous twice-annual Palio horse race in nearby Siena.

Cuisine

☐ Enjoying a languorous, multicourse meal at any one of the city's terrific restaurants.

☐ Rich, delicate, cream-based pasta sauces.

☐ Incomparable *gelato*.

WHEN TO GO Florence remains popular and comfortable from April through October, and, thankfully, July and August are not nearly so sweltering as in Rome. As the inhabitants of many other Italian cities do, Florentines desert Florence in August, when many restaurants may be closed for three or more weeks of vacation.

Florence's Average Daytime Temperature & Rainfall

	Jan	Feb	Mar	Apr	May	June	July	Aug	Sept	Oct	Nov	Dec
Temp. (°F)	45	47	50	60	67	75	77	70	64	63	55	46
Rainfall "	3	3.3	3.7	2.7	2.2	1.4	1.4	2.7	3.2	4.9	3.8	2.9

Special Events The highlight of June 24, the feast day of Florence's patron saint, John the Baptist, is the **Calcio Storico,** a rough-and-tumble medieval cross between rugby and soccer played with a wooden ball and few (if any) rules. Teams representing the four original parishes of Florence, clad in 16th-century costume, square off against one another in piazza Santa Croce, competing vigorously for that year's bragging rights. Later on, fireworks light up the night sky.

Nearby Siena has its own medieval grudge match, the **Palio,** on July 2 and August 16. Horses representing 10 of the city's historic districts (*contrade*) race once around the sloping, oval main square. The race itself is very brief, but the preparations, parades, and post-Palio celebrations seem to go on forever. Indeed, travelers who have journeyed to Siena in the weeks before a Palio have been known to happen upon impromptu street demonstrations by a hopeful *contrada's* neighborhood marching band.

BACKGROUND READING & VIEWING   Put yourself in the mood to savor this wonderful city by viewing the wonderfully romantic *A Room with a View,* from E. M. Forster's novel of the same name (Bantam). The film evokes the extraordinary charm of one of Europe's most seductive cities.

Mary McCarthy's *The Stones of Florence* (Harcourt Brace Jovanovich) is very readable, and an excellent source of background on the history and culture of the city.

Irving Stone's biography of Michelangelo, *The Agony and the Ecstasy* (New American Library), adds a fourth dimension to his masterpieces, which you'll be viewing at seemingly every turn in this rich city. *The House of Medici: Its Rise and Fall* (Morrow) by Christopher Hibbert is the best book on Florence's ruling class.

Luigi Barzini's classic *The Italians* (Macmillan) offers a frank, refreshing, and opinionated discussion of the history and culture of his homeland, past and present.

Finally, turn to *Frommer's Italy* for more on this special city.

3. ORIENTATION & GETTING AROUND

ARRIVING IN FLORENCE

Most Florence-bound trains roll into the **Stazione Santa Maria Novella,** which you'll often see abbreviated "S.M.N." The station is on the western edge of the city's compact historical center, a leisurely 10-minute walk from the Duomo and just 15 minutes from piazza della Signoria and the Uffizi Galleries.

With your back toward the tracks, you'll find an Ufficio Turismo information and accommodations service office (tel. 28-2893) toward the station's left exit. They're open April through October, daily from 8:15am to 9:30pm; November through March, the office closes at 9pm. The train information office is located near the right exit. Walk straight, through the large glass doors, into the outer hall for tickets and a bank that changes money Monday through Saturday from 8:20am to 7:20pm. There is an Albergo Diurno, or day hotel, where you can wash up or take a shower after a long train ride adjacent to Track 16. There is also a luggage depot at the head of Track 16, where you can drop your bags while you search for a hotel. They charge 1,500 lire ($1.30) per piece, and are open 24 hours.

Some trains stop at **Stazione Campo di Marte,** on the east side of the city. There is 24-hour bus service between the two stations.

INFORMATION

The main train station's **Ufficio Turismo (I.T.A.)** information and accommodations service office, listed above, distributes fairly good, free city maps, answers simple questions, and makes hotel reservations for a 2,000- to 3,000-lira ($1.75–$3.50) fee (depending on the quality of the hotel). Especially during crowded summer months, however, travelers arriving by train may wish to bypass this office and walk a few steps farther to a second I.T.A. office just outside the station. With your back to the tracks, take the left exit, cross onto the concrete median, turn right, and the office will be about 100 feet ahead. This alternative information center distributes a wider variety of government tourist publications, including *Firenze Oggi* (*Florence Today*), a helpful 2,000-lira ($1.75) bimonthly. They're usually open April through October, daily from 8:15am to 7:17pm; November through March, from 8:15am to 1:45pm.

The city's largest tourist office is the **Main I.T.A. Office,** Cavor, 1r (tel. 276-0301), located about three blocks north of the Duomo. They are less harried then the busy station offices, offer lots of literature, and boast an unusually helpful staff. The office is usually open Monday through Saturday from 8am to 7:30pm.

The bilingual **Concierge Information** magazine, available free from the concierge desks of top hotels, contains a monthly calendar of events, as well as information on museums, sights, and attractions. **Firenze Spettacolo,** a 2,500-lira ($2.15) Italian-language monthly sold at most city newsstands, lists the latest in nightlife, arts, and entertainment.

CITY LAYOUT

Florence is a compact city that is best negotiated on foot. No two sights are more than a 20- or 25-minute walk apart, and all the hotels and restaurants listed in this chapter are located in the downtown area.

The city's relatively small, beautiful, and touristy **Centro Storico,** or Historic Center, is loosely bounded by the S.M.N. Train Station to the northwest, piazza della S.S. Annunziata to the northeast, and the Arno River to the south. The area leading up to the Pitti Palace, located just across the river, a few blocks past the Ponte Vecchio, is also popular tourist territory.

Piazza del Duomo, which is dominated by Florence's largest and most famous church and ancillary Baptistery, is situated at the center of the tourist's city. During your stay, you will inevitably walk along many of the streets that radiate out from this imposing square.

Borgo San Lorenzo, which runs north from the Baptistery, is best known for its excellent outdoor market, which sells everything from marbleized paper-wrapped pencils to leather jackets.

Via Calzaiuoli, Florence's most popular pedestrian thoroughfare and shopping street, runs south from the Duomo, connecting the church with the romantic, statue-filled **piazza della Signoria.** At its midsection, via Calzaiuoli is bisected by the short via Speziali, which opens into **piazza della Repubblica,** a busy shop and café-ringed square surrounded by expensive shopping streets.

Back on piazza della Signoria, follow the crowds onto via Vaccereccia, turn left, and walk south two blocks to the **Ponte Vecchio** (Old Bridge), the Arno River's most famous span. Topped with a cluster of tiny jewelry shops, the bridge crosses over to the **Oltrarno** area, best known for the Pitti Palace, located just a few blocks past the bridge.

Confused? Climb up through Boboli Gardens, located behind the Pitti Palace, and you'll be rewarded with a beautiful bird's eye view of Florence that will help you navigate your way around the city.

STREET NUMBERING   There are two systems of street numbering: blue or black (*blue* or *nero*) and red (*rosso*). Blue or black numbers are used for residential and office buildings, including hotels, while red numbers are used to identify all commercial enterprises, including restaurants. In this chapter, red-numbered addresses are indicated by a lowercase "r" following the number.

GETTING AROUND

BY BUS   You'll rarely need to take advantage of Florence's efficient **A.T.A.F. bus system,** since the city is so wonderfully compact. Bus tickets cost 1,000 lire (85¢) and must be purchased before you board. An eight-pack of tickets will run you 7,500 lire ($6.50), while a 24-hour pass costs 5,000 lire ($4.35). Tickets are sold at the A.T.A.F. booth at the head of Track 14 in the train station, and at tobacco shops (*tabacchti*) and most newsstands. Once on board, validate your ticket in the box near the rear door.

Bus nos. 13, 14, and 19 run from the train station (most stop outside the exit by Track 16) to piazza del Duomo and from there, down via del Proconsolo and past the Bargello to the back side of piazza della Signoria. Bus nos. 15, 35, and 36 continue across the Arno and on to the Pitti Palace, in the Oltrarno.

BY TAXI   Cabs can be hailed in the street, or called to your restaurant or hotel by dialing 4798 or 4390. Taxis charge 1,250 lire ($1.10) per kilometer, but there is a minimum fare of 6,000 lire ($5.20), and most hops around the city average about 10,000 lire ($8.70), including a 10% tip.

ON FOOT Florence is a very compact city. A leisurely walk will take you from one end of the tourist area to the other—from the train station to piazza Santa Croce—in about 25 minutes. The free map given out by the tourist office lacks a street index, but may be all you need. The best full map of the city is the yellow-jacketed map by Studio F.M.B. Bologna, available at most newsstands for 7,000 lire ($6.10).

CAR RENTAL Auto-rental agencies in Florence are centered around the Europa Garage on borgo Ognissanti. **Avis** is no. 128r (tel. 21-3629) and **Budget** is nearby at no. 134r (tel. 28-7161); **Eurodollar** has offices across the street at no. 133r (tel. 21-8665 or 28-4543). Rates start at a steep 112,500 lire ($97.80) per day with unlimited mileage, plus 13,500 lire ($11.75) per day for insurance. Avis and Budget are open Monday through Saturday from 8am to 8pm and on Sunday from 8am to 1pm and 5 to 8pm. Eurodollar is open Monday through Saturday from 8am to 1pm and 2 to 8pm, and on Sunday from 8am to 1pm only.

Rates are sometimes lower if you make reservations from home at least 48 hours in advance. Plan ahead, or consider phoning a friend or relative back home to have the reservations made for you.

Florence's historic center, where most hotels are located, is strictly off-limits to all vehicular traffic, except that of local residents. **Parking** near the center will cost about 23,000 lire ($20) per day. The most convenient garage to the Historic Center is the Europa, at borgo Ognissanti, 96, next to Avis; it's open daily 6am to 2am. The International Garage, at via Palazzuolo, 29, just west of via Porcellana, is only a few blocks away.

FAST FACTS: FLORENCE

Banks Standard bank hours are Monday through Friday from 8:20am to 1:20pm and 2:45 to 3:45pm; only a few banks are open on Saturday. The **Banca Nazionale delle Communicazioni,** in the outer hall of the train station, is open Monday through Saturday from 8:20am to 7:20pm. The **state railway** will change money at any hour at Window 19. American Express, at via Guicciardini, 49r (tel. 27-8751), exchanges its traveler's checks fee-free, and is open Monday through Friday from 9am to 5:30pm and on Saturday from 9am to 12:30pm.

Business Hours In summer, most **businesses and shops** are open Monday through Friday from 9am to 1pm and 4 to 8pm; on Saturday, shops are open in the morning only. From mid-September through mid-June, most shops are open Tuesday through Saturday from 9am to 1pm and 3:30 to 7:30pm; on Monday during the winter, shops don't open until the afternoon. The exception to this winter rule are *alimentari* (small grocery stores), which are open on Monday morning in low season but closed Wednesday afternoon. In Florence, as throughout Italy, just about everything is closed on Sunday. **Restaurants** are required to close at least one day per week, though the particular day varies from one trattoria to another.

Consulates The **U.S. Consulate** is located at lungarno Amerigo Vespucci, 38 (tel. 29-8276), near its intersection with via Palestro; it's open Monday through Friday from 9am to noon and 2 to 4pm. Britons will find the **British Consulate** at lungarno Corsini, 2 (tel. 28-4133), near piazza Santa Trinità; it's open Monday through Friday from 9:30am to 12:30pm and 2:30 to 4:30pm.

Citizens of **Australia, New Zealand,** and **Canada** should consult their missions in Rome.

Currency The Italian unit of currency is the **lira,** almost always used in the plural form, **lire.** The lowest unit of currency these days is the silver 50-lira coin. There is also a silver 100-lira piece, a gold 200-lira coin, and a combination silver-and-gold 500-lira coin. Notes come in the following denominations: 1,000, 2,000, 5,000, 10,000, 50,000, and 100,000 lire.

Dentists/Doctors   For a list of English-speaking dentists or doctors, ask at the U.S. or British Consulate, or at the American Express office.

Emergencies   In Florence, as throughout Italy, dial 113 for the police. Some Italians recommend the military-trained *Carabinieri* (tel. 112), whom they consider a better police force. To report a fire, dial 115. For an ambulance, dial 21-2222.

For a pharmacy, the Farmacia Communale, at the head of Track 16 in the train station, is open 24 hours daily.

Holidays   See the Rome chapter for details.

Information   For the location of the tourist information offices, see "Information" in "Orientation and Getting Around," above.

Laundry/Dry Cleaning   The **Lavanderia Superlava Splendis,** via del Sole, 29r (tel. 21-8836), off piazza Santa Maria Novella, is the most convenient self-service laundry to hotels in the train station area. It's open Monday through Friday from 8am to 7:30pm, offers one-day service, and charges about 15,000 lire ($13.05) to wash and dry up to 4 kilos (about 9 lb.). Also near the station, with same-day service and slightly lower prices, is the nameless **lavanderia** at borgo Ognissanti, 110r (tel. 29-4143), on the block between via Finiguerra and via Santa Lucia, near the Ponte Amerigo Vespucci. This laundry, which charges 15,000 lire ($13.05) for up to 5 kilos (11 lbs.), is open Monday through Friday from 8am to 1pm and 3:30 to 7:30pm. This place also does dry cleaning. You'll find yet another laundry, the **Lavanderia Elen-Sec,** at via dei Neri, 46r (tel. 28-3747), on the other side of piazza della Signoria, near Santa Croce. They charge 4,000 lire ($3.50) per kilo, with a 3-kilo minimum. It's open Monday through Friday from 8:30am to 1pm and 4 to 7:30pm (in winter, from 3:30 to 7:30pm); they're closed for three weeks in August.

Lost and Found   **Oggetti Smarriti** is located at via Circondaria, 19 (tel. 36-7943), in the area behind the train station.

Mail   Florence's **main post office** is located on via Pellicceria, off the southwest corner of piazza della Repubblica. Purchase stamps (*francobolli*) at Windows 21–22. Letters sent "Fermo Posta" (Italian for General Delivery) can be picked up at Windows 23–24. The post office is open Monday through Friday from 8:15am to 7pm and on Saturday from 8:15am to noon.

All packages heavier than 1 kilo (2.2 lb.) must be properly wrapped and brought around to the **parcel office** at the back of the building (enter at via dei Sassetti, 4, which is also known as piazza Davanzati). If you're uncertain about Italy's complex parcel-post standards, take your shipment to **Filippo's Pacco Parcel,** via dei Canacci, 4r (tel. 21-1912), off via della Scala near the station, where they'll wrap your shipment for 5,000–10,000 lire ($4.35–$8.70). May through September, Filippo is open Monday through Saturday from 9am to 6:30pm; October through April, Monday through Friday from 9:30am to 1pm and 3 to 6pm.

Remember that you can buy stamps at any *tabacchi* with no additional service charge; ask at your hotel about the current postal rates.

Police   Throughout Italy, dial 113 for the police. Some Italians recommend the *Carabinieri* (tel. 112), whom they consider a better-trained police force.

Shoe Repair   For resoling or sewing, try Riparazioni Scarpe II Ciabattino, at via del Moro, 88r, located near piazza Santa Maria Novella, not far from the train station. They're open Monday through Friday from 8:30am to noon and 2:30 to 7:30pm, and on Saturday from 8:30am to noon.

Student Networks and Resources   Florence's university is located between the Mercato Centrale and piazza San Marco, the latter being the center of student activity in Florence. The *mensa*, or cafeteria, where students congregate at mealtimes is at via San Gallo, 25a. There is a sizable community of American students in Florence for study-abroad programs.

The Centro Turistico Studentesco (C.T.S.), at via dei Ginori, 11r (tel. 28-9570), across the street from the Medici-Riccardi Palace near the San Lorenzo market, is the best budget travel agent in Florence, selling reduced-price train, air, and ferry tickets. They specialize in youth and student fares, but are helpful to thrifty travelers of all ages. Note that they don't make train reservations, and don't accept

THE LIRA & THE DOLLAR

At this writing $1 = approximately 1.150 lire (or 100 lire = 0.9¢), and this was the rate of exchange used to calculate the dollar values given in this chapter (rounded to the nearest nickel). This rate fluctuates from time to time and may not be the same when you travel to Italy. Therefore the following table should be used only as a guide:

Lire	U.S. $	Lire	U.S. $
50	.04	10,000	8.70
100	.09	15,000	13.04
200	.17	20,000	17.39
300	.26	25,000	21.74
400	.35	30,000	26.09
500	.43	35,000	30.43
750	.65	40,000	34.78
1,000	.87	45,000	39.13
1,500	1.30	50,000	43.48
2,000	1.74	55,000	47.82
2,500	2.17	60,000	52.17
3,000	2.61	65,000	56.52
4,000	3.48	70,000	60.87
5,000	4.35	75,000	65.21

credit cards. They're open Monday through Friday from 9:30am to 1pm and 4 to 7pm, and on Saturday from 9:30am to noon.

Tax   See the Rome chapter for more information.

Telephone   There are two types of public pay phones in regular service. The first accepts coins or special slugs, called *gettone,* which you will sometimes receive in change. The second operates with a phonecard, available at *tabacchi* and bars in 5,000-lira ($4.35) and 10,000-lira ($8.70) denominations. Break off the perforated corner of the card before using it. Local phone calls cost 200 lire (18¢). To make a call, lift the receiver, insert a coin or card, and dial.

Long-distance and international phone calls can be placed at the ASST office inside the main post office (see "Mail," above). Several countries also have direct operator service, allowing callers to use telephone calling cards or call collect (reverse charges) from almost any phone. Consult "Fast Facts" in the Rome chapter for complete information.

The telephone area code for Florence is 055.

Tipping   See the Rome chapter for more information.

4. BUDGET ACCOMMODATIONS

There's a large concentration of budget hotels in the area immediately to the left as you exit the train station. You'll find most of the hotels in this convenient, if charmless, area on the noisy **via Nazionale,** and the first two side streets off via

Nazionale, **via Fiume** and **via Faenza.** The area between the Duomo and piazza della Signoria, particularly along and near **via Calzaiuoli,** is also a good place to look, and is a quieter, more pleasant place to spend your evenings.

During the peak summer months it's important to arrive early as many hotels fill up for the next night even before all their guests from the previous evening have checked out. If you have trouble or are intimidated by the language barrier, try the **room-finding office** in the train station, near Track 16 (see "Information" in "Orientation and Getting Around," above).

A continental breakfast in an Italian hotel is one of the great disappointments of Florence. The usual rate for a roll, butter, jam, and coffee is 6,000 lire ($5.20). You can get the same breakfast for about half that price at any café. Unfortunately, many of the hotels listed in this chapter, especially in the medium- and high-priced categories, do not make breakfast optional. In the descriptions below, if prices are listed "including continental breakfast," you can assume that breakfast is more or less obligatory. If it's optional, almost without exception it's not worth the price.

DOUBLES FOR LESS THAN 59,000 LIRE [$51.30]

NEAR THE DUOMO

LOCANDA ORCHIDEA, borgo degli Albizi, 11 (1st Floor), 50122 Firenze. Tel. 055/248-0346. 10 rms (1 with shower). **Bus:** 14 or 23 from the train station; get off at the first stop on via del Proconsolo.

$ **Rates:** 31,500 lire ($27.40) single without shower, 33,600 lire ($29.20) single with shower; 47,300 lire ($41.15) double without shower, 50,400 lire ($43.80) double with shower; 65,100 lire ($56.60) triple without shower, 69,300 lire ($60.25) triple with shower. No credit cards.

Maria Rosa Cook, the friendly, professional proprietor who operates this cozy and exceptionally clean pensione, will happily tell you the history of this 12th-century palazzo where Dante's wife was born. Four of her 10 rooms overlook a lovely garden, which all guests are welcome to use. These are the best beds in the house, with especially large windows that let in buckets of sunlight. Ms. Cook, who speaks English and French, is quite fond of Yankee guests (Red Sox fans are another matter though). No curfew.

SOGGIORNO BRUNORI, via del Proconsolo, 5 (2nd Floor), 50122 Firenze. Tel. 055/28-9648. 9 rms (1 with bath). **Bus:** 13, 14, or 19.

$ **Rates:** 53,000 lire ($47.70) double without bath, 60,000 lire ($54) double with bath; 72,000 lire ($64.80) triple without bath, 85,500 lire ($76.50) triple with bath; 92,000 lire ($82.80) quad without bath, 108,000 lire ($97.20) quad with bath. Slight reduction for guests who don't take showers. Breakfast 8,000 lire ($7.20) extra. No credit cards. **Closed:** Jan–Feb.

The rooms are a bit tired and show the wear and tear of countless backpackers, but the prices are among the lowest around. The two young owners, Leonardo and Giovanni, are exceptionally friendly, full of helpful hints, and speak excellent English. They'll sell you stamps, help you decipher the train schedules they keep on hand, and offer you a free city map at check-in. Their unusually spacious rooms make this a fine selection for backpacking groups. You may want to ask for one of the three rooms away from the noisy street. There's a 12:30am curfew.

ON VIA FAENZA

There are more hotels on via Faenza than on any other block in Florence, as some buildings house as many as six pensiones. Three at no. 56 via Faenza fit into the lowest

FROMMER'S SMART TRAVELER: HOTELS

VALUE-CONSCIOUS TRAVELERS SHOULD
TAKE ADVANTAGE OF THE FOLLOWING:

1. Budget hotels in the area immediately to the left as you exit the train station.
2. The room-finding office in the train station, near Track 16.
3. Breakfast at one of Florence's cafés, rather than at your hotel (unless it's obligatory).

budget category, while the Albergo Anna and the Albergo Marini, in the same building, are fine choices for those with a bit more money to spend. In the area immediately to the left as you exit the train station, via Faenza is the second left off via Nazionale.

ALBERGO AZZI, via Faenza, 56 (1st Floor), 50123 Firenze. Tel. 055/21-3806. Fax 055/21-3806. 11 rms (none with bath).
$ Rates (including breakfast): 58,800 lire ($61.15) double; 83,000 lire ($72.15) triple; 29,400 lire ($25.55) per person in dormitory rooms. No credit cards.
Reno Mazzapicchio and his partner, Monica Rocchini, operate their cozy, if not always impeccable, dormitory-style pensione. While double rooms are available, most guests pay a flat 29,400 lire ($25.55) per person, in rooms shared with three to five other budget travelers. That's the cheapest bed outside a youth hostel.

ALBERGO MARCELLA, via Faenza, 58 (3rd Floor), 50123 Firenze. Tel. 055/21-3232. 7 rms (1 with bath).
$ Rates: 31,500 lire ($27.40) single without bath; 47,300 lire ($41.15) double without bath, 52,500 lire ($45.65) double with bath; 63,000 lire ($54.80) triple without bath, 69,300 lire ($60.25) triple with bath. No credit cards.
Signor Noto Calogero and his family are always warm and welcoming, and offer adequate rooms at very low prices. This is a classic ultra-budget-traveler's pensione, in better condition than most others in its class. The management speaks perfect English.

ALBERGO MERLINI, via Faenza, 56 (3rd Floor), 50123 Firenze. Tel. 055/21-2848 or 28-3939. 12 rms (2 with bath).
$ Rates: 36,800 lire ($32) single without bath; 57,500 lire ($50) double without bath, 69,300 lire ($60.25) double with bath; 71,400 lire ($62.10) triple without bath, 81,900 lire ($71.20) triple with bath. Breakfast 10,000 lire ($8.70) extra. No credit cards.
Signora Mary's furnishings would be the envy of any antique collector. Breakfast, which is optional, is served on a terrace decorated with frescoes by American art students. All in all, though not the best value on the street, this is probably the best value in the building. Perhaps that's why I get so many letters from readers praising this place.

ALBERGO MIA CARA, via Faenza, 58 (2nd Floor), 50123 Firenze. Tel. 055/21-6053. Fax 230-2601. 50 rms (20 with bath).
$ Rates: 33,100 lire ($28.75) single without bath, 39,900 lire ($34.70) single with bath; 46,200 lire ($40.20) double without bath, 57,800 lire ($50.25) double with bath. Breakfast 7,000 lire ($6.10) extra. No credit cards.
In Florence you can easily pay quite a bit more and get a lot less than you do here at Pietro Noto's unusually large and modern hotel. He has laid new stonework tiles in every room, installed the latest in modern plumbing equipment, and has even stripped

and stained all the window frames. This all might not be so special if his prices weren't among the lowest in town.

If everything goes according to schedule, a large hostel with dormitory rooms will open this summer. Brand-new rooms and a winning location make this a good place to stay.

ALBERGO MONICA, via Faenza, 66B (1st Floor), 50123 Firenze. Tel. 055/28-3804. 16 rms (all with shower or shower and toilet). TEL
$ Rates: 42,000 lire ($36.50) single without shower or toilet, 44,100 lire ($38.35) single with shower only, 47,300 lire ($41.15) single with shower and toilet; 57,800 lire ($50.25) double without shower or toilet, 68,300 lire ($59.40) double with shower only, 73,500 lire ($63.90) double with shower and toilet; 89,300 lire ($77.65) triple with shower only, 105,000 lire ($91.30) triple with shower and toilet. Air conditioning 5,000 lire ($4.35) extra; breakfast 10,000 lire ($8.70). Bearers of this book receive a 5% discount Apr–Oct and a 10% discount Nov–Mar. AE, MC, V.

Gracious owner Giovanna Rocchini and her charming English-speaking niece, Monica, run a truly exceptional hotel, complete with spacious rooms that are kept quite clean and very competitively priced. Public areas include a café and a nice outdoor terrace. The quietest rooms are in the back, but this albergo is a good value no matter which room you occupy.

NEAR THE TRAIN STATION

PENSIONE MARY, piazza Independenzia, 5 (2nd Floor), 50129 Firenze. Tel. 055/49-6310. 12 rms (8 with bath). **Directions:** See below.
$ Rates: 33,600 lire ($29.20) single without bath, 43,100 lire ($37.50) single with bath; 50,400 lire ($43.80) double without bath, 63,000 lire ($54.80) double with bath; 68,300 lire ($59.40) triple without bath, 85,100 lire ($74) triple with bath. Breakfast 9,000 lire ($7.85) extra. No credit cards.

Located on the top floor of an elevatorless three-story building on one of Florence's largest squares, this well-lit pensione is popular with students and young-minded others. Wood-paneled halls open into good-sized, clean rooms.

From the train station's front exit, turn left onto via Nazionale. The hotel is five blocks ahead, on the east side of piazza Indepenzia.

PENSIONE SOLE, via del Sole, 8 (3rd Floor), 50123 Firenze. Tel. 055/239-6094. 8 rms (2 with bath). **Directions:** From the train station, walk to piazza Santa Maria Novella; via del Sole begins at the far left corner of the piazza.
$ Rates: 34,500 lire ($30) single without bath; 51,800 lire ($45.05) double without bath, 54,100 lire ($47.05) double with bath; 69,000 lire ($60) triple without bath, 75,900 lire ($66) triple with bath. Showers (for those in bathless rooms) 3,000 lire ($2.60) extra. No credit cards.

Situated on a relatively quiet street just minutes from the train station, this is one of the better budget recommendations in the area, with simply furnished but very clean rooms. Its charming and exceptionally friendly owners, Anna and Michele Giuralarocca, don't speak much English, but their teenage daughters are usually standing by to help translate. Note that there's no elevator to this third-floor pensione, and a 1am curfew.

DOUBLES FOR LESS THAN 88,000 LIRE [$76.50]

NEAR THE TRAIN STATION

ALBERGO CENTRALE, via dei Conti, 3 (2nd Floor), 50123 Firenze. Tel. 055/21-5216 or 21-5761. 18 rms (9 with bath). TEL **Directions:** Walk along via de' Panzani, which quickly becomes via de' Cerretani; via dei Conti is the second left.

$ Rates: 55,200 lire ($48) single without bath, 66,700 lire ($58) single with bath; 87,400 lire ($76) double without bath, 104,700 lire ($91.05) double with bath; 126,500 lire ($110) triple without bath, 146,100 lire ($127.05) triple with bath. Bearers of this book receive a 5% discount. AE, MC, V.

Normandy-born manager Mariethérèse Blot is wonderfully obliging and speaks excellent English. She has added a charming French touch to her 18 exceptionally large rooms in this former patrician residence known as the Palazzo Malaspina. All rooms come complete with attractive floral wallpaper, and some feature views of the nearby San Lorenzo Church. The Centrale is particularly well suited for traveling families, and curfew is 1:30am.

HOTEL AUSONIA, via Nazionale, 24 (3rd Floor), 50123 Firenze. Tel. 055/49-6547 or 49-6324. 20 rms (12 with bath). **Directions:** See below.

$ Rates (including continental breakfast): 43,100 lire ($37.50) single without bath, 52,500 lire ($45.65) single with bath; 67,200 lire ($58.50) double without bath, 79,800 lire ($69.40) double with bath; 92,400 lire ($80.35) triple without bath, 110,300 lire ($95.90) triple with bath. Bearers of this book receive a 5% discount mid-Mar to Nov 14 and a 10% discount Nov 15 to mid-Mar. AE, MC, V.

Run by the friendly, English-speaking Delli family, this hotel occupies two floors on one of the city's busiest streets. Though equally nice, the rooms downstairs are not as modern as those above. Even though front rooms are equipped with double-paned glass, you might want to request accommodations in back, where it's extra-quiet.

From piazza della Stazione, in front of the train station, turn left on via Nazionale. The pensione is four blocks ahead on your right.

HOTEL NUOVA ITALIA, via Faenza, 26, 50123 Firenze. Tel. 055/26-8430 or 28-7508. 21 rms (all with bath). TEL **Directions:** Turn right onto via Faenza from via Nazionale and the hotel will be on your left after a few steps.

$ Rates: 53,900 lire ($46.85) single; 79,200 lire ($68.85) double; 106,700 lire ($92.80) triple; 134,800 lire ($117.20) quad. Breakfast 12,000 lire ($10.45) extra. AE, DC, MC, V.

This is one of the standouts near the train station, with its modern furniture, wall-to-wall carpeting, and tasteful art reproductions and posters in every room. Signora Elida Viti watches over all, assisted by her son, Luciano, his Canadian-born wife, Eileen, and her granddaughter, Daniela. Eileen met Luciano more than 30 years ago when she stayed at the Nuova Italia, on the recommendation of *Europe on $5 a Day.* That may be one reason why Signora Viti has such a fondness for readers of this book, who can expect to be treated like visiting royalty. "We are always there to help you," the signora insists. This is an ideal selection for families. The hotel is open all night.

ON VIA FIUME

There are fewer hotels on this street than on the adjacent via Faenza, but two budget-priced places stand out. Via Fiume is the first left off via Nazionale as you walk away from the train station.

ALBERGO ADUA, via Fiume, 20 (2nd Floor), 50123 Firenze. Tel. 055/28-7506. 7 rms (4 with bath).

$ Rates: 54,100 lire ($47.05) single without bath; 72,500 lire ($63.05) double without bath, 92,000 lire ($80) double with bath; 96,600 lire ($84) triple without bath, 120,800 lire ($105.05) triple with bath. No credit cards.

This place is plain and a little overpriced for a one-star lodging, but its high carved ceilings, enormous rooms, bathrooms, and windows, and its remarkably quiet location near the train station, make it noteworthy. Owners Anna Pianigiani and feel of a budget American chain hotel. Recently renovated rooms, outfitted with Otello Bartarelli are unusually gracious, and the view of the surrounding rooftops from their rooms is pleasant.

ALBERGO FIORITA, via Fiume, 20 (3rd Floor), 50123 Firenze. Tel. 055/28-3693. 11 rms (1 with bath).
$ **Rates** (including continental breakfast): 44,900 lire ($39.05) single without bath; 75,900 lire ($66) double without bath, 90,900 lire ($79.05) double with bath; 96,600 lire ($84) triple without bath; 138,000 lire ($120) quad without bath. No credit cards.

The friendly Masselli family speaks excellent English, and offers visitors large rooms with particularly pretty ceilings and favorable rates. The hotel locks up at midnight.

AT VIA FAENZA, 56

In the area immediately to the left as you exit the train station, via Faenza is the second left off via Nazionale.

ALBERGO ANNA, via Faenza, 56 (2nd Floor), 50123 Firenze. Tel. 055/239-8322. 7 rms (2 with bath, 5 with shower).
$ **Rates** (including full breakfast): 49,400 lire ($42.95) single; 77,700 lire ($67.55) double; 109,200 lire ($94.95) triple; 139,700 lire ($121.50) quad. No credit cards.

Owner Silvestri Petri offers the warmest sort of welcome—he has been known to hand guests a piece of cold watermelon as they return from a hot day of sightseeing. And the spotless marble floors, the fresh-cut flowers in the reception area, and the abundant breakfast each morning speak a universal language. Ask for Room 1, which features a frescoed ceiling. One of the best values on this street.

PENSIONE ARMONIA, via Faenza, 56 (1st Floor), 50123 Firenze. Tel. 055/21-1146. 7 rms (none with bath).
$ **Rates** (including continental breakfast): 75,600 lire ($65.75) double; 94,500 lire ($82.15) triple; 126,000 lire ($109.55) quad. No credit cards.

Owned by a young, English-speaking brother-and-sister team, this small, spotless pensione is more expensive than some others in the building, but a step above. Their whitewashed rooms and sparkling tile floors will brighten your day no matter how high the temperature or how thick the crowds.

NEAR THE DUOMO

ALBERGO COSTANTINI, via Calzaiuoli, 13 (2nd Floor), 50122 Firenze. Tel. 055/21-5128. 14 rms (7 with bath, 2 with shower). TEL
$ **Rates:** 42,000 lire ($36.50) single without bath, 52,500 lire ($45.65) single with shower or full bath; 57,800 lire ($50.25) double without bath, 78,800 lire ($68.50) double with shower or full bath; 106,100 lire ($92.25) triple with full bath; 98,200 ($85.40) quad without bath. 5% discount Nov–Feb. No credit cards.

The sturdy cot-style beds don't earn raves here, but the perfect location, steps from the Duomo and piazza della Signoria, can't be beat. Recent fixings include new tiling, and excellent English is spoken by Nadia, the friendly manager. This is a good selection for older travelers, which the management in fact prefers. Renaissance fans might request one of the hotel's three rooms with frescoed ceilings. The hotel is open all night.

HOTEL FIRENZE, via del Corso/piazza Donati, 4, 50122 Firenze. Tel. 055/26-8301 or 21-4203. Fax. 055/21-2370. 70 rms (20 with bath). TEL
$ **Rates** (including continental breakfast): 43,100 ($37.50) single without bath, 52,500 lire ($45.65) single with bath; 67,200 lire ($58.50) double without bath, 78,800 lire ($68.50) double with bath; 94,500 lire ($82.20) triple without bath, 110,300 ($95.90) triple with bath. No credit cards.

Perfectly located two blocks south of the Duomo, this sparkling, simple lodge has the blatantly inexpensive furnishings contrast with the building's stylish, centuries-old facade. Rooms with private bath come with televisions, and are, in general, nicer than the bathless rooms.

PENSIONE MARIA LUISA DE' MEDICI, via del Corso, 1, 50122 Firenze. Tel. 055/28-0048. 10 rms (2 with bath). TEL

$ Rates (including full breakfast): 81,900 lire ($71.20) double without bath, 93,500 lire ($81.30) double with bath; 115,500 lire ($100.45) triple without bath, 130,200 lire ($113.20) triple with bath; 147,100 lire ($127.90) quad without bath, 161,800 lire ($140.70) quad with bath. No credit cards.

⭐ This charming pensione, named after the very last Medici princess, is perhaps the most imaginative, eclectic, and unique place to sleep in all of Italy. Each of its 10 enormous rooms is named after a different member of the Medici clan, and includes a portrait of that prince or princess. The owner, Dr. Angelo Sordi—retired physician, amateur historian, and design buff—has furnished each of the rooms with avant-garde Italian furniture that contrasts with the occasional antique, oversize original Renaissance-style oil paintings, and floor-to-ceiling velvet drapes (handmade by his Welsh partner, Evelyn Morris). With 10 enormous rooms, including three triples, two quads, and two rooms that can sleep five, the Maria Luisa is an ideal choice for families on a budget. By the way, Angelo and Evelyn will send you off each morning with a full breakfast that includes cereal and juice.

The pensione is perfectly situated steps from piazza della Repubblica.

NEAR PIAZZA DELLA SIGNORIA

SOGGIORNO CESTELLI, borgo SS. Apostoli, 25, 50123 Firenze. Tel. 055/21-4213. 7 rms (2 with bath).

$ Rates (including continental breakfast): 43,100 lire ($37.50) single without bath; 68,300 lire ($59.40) double without bath, 81,900 lire ($71.20) double with bath; 110,300 lire ($95.90) triple with bath; 141,800 lire ($123.30) quad with bath. No credit cards.

⭐ Staying at Ada Cestelli's tiny seven-room pensione is like stepping back in time. She has packed more old-world elegance into her seven enormous antique-filled rooms than many four-star, 40-room hotels. You'll sleep on huge antique beds under richly embroidered spreads. And finally, her nephew Luciano, who helps her run the place, is a classical music aficionado who will share his enthusiasm and his library with guests. The exceptionally low rates and unbeatable location make it one of the best bargains in this book. There is one catch though: Signora Cestelli will rarely take reservations—not even with prepayment, not even if you phone ahead a few days before. You must simply show up, and if someone happens to be leaving that day, well, consider yourself blessed. Borgo SS. Apostoli begins where via Tornabuoni meets piazza Santa Trinita, a block from the Arno.

IN THE OLTRARNO

PENSIONE LA SCALETTA, via Guicciardini, 13 (2nd Floor), 50125 Firenze. Tel. 055/28-3028 or 28-9562. Fax 055/28-3028. 12 rooms (11 with bath). TEL **Bus:** 3 or 15 from the train station.

$ Rates (including continental breakfast): 59,900 lire ($52.10) single without bath; 72,500 lire ($63.05) single with bath; 87,200 lire ($75.80) double without bath, 110,300 lire ($95.90) double with bath; 147,000 lire ($127.80) triple with bath; 173,300 lire ($150.70) quad with bath. MC, V.

⭐ Here you'll eat breakfast each morning on the roof, overlooking Florence with a stunning view of the Pitti Palace and the Boboli Gardens fanning up the hillside. Owner Barbara Barbieri and her family keep their 12 large, high-ceilinged rooms spotless, just as they do each of their half dozen little sitting rooms that you'll find scattered throughout this cozy, quiet pensione. La Scaletta is located in the Oltrarno, next door to the American Express office and a short block from the Pitti Palace.

PENSIONE SORELLE BANDINI, piazza S. Spirito, 9, 50125 Firenze. Tel. 055/21-5308. 12 rms (3 with bath). **Bus:** 3 or 15 from the train station.

$ Rates (including continental breakfast): 56,700 lire ($49.30) single without bath; 87,200 lire ($75.80) double without bath, 99,800 lire ($86.80) double with bath; 121,800 lire ($105.90) triple without bath, 139,700 lire ($121.50) triple with bath; 157,500 lire ($136.95) quad without bath, 178,500 ($155.20) quad with bath. No credit cards.

⭐ Unassuming from the outside, this cavernous castle, with sweeping views over red rooftops below, is one of Florence's most unusual finds. Everything is oversize here, from the rooms to the furnishings, to the gigantic balcony that wraps around half the building. Enter through the giant iron gates and take the elevator to the second floor. Highly recommended.

The pensione is located across the Ponte Vecchio, two blocks northwest of the Pitti Palace.

SUPER-BUDGET CHOICES

In addition to the inexpensive multibedded accommodations of Albergo Mia Cara and Albergo Azzi (both listed above), look to the following hotels for cheap, dorm-style bedrooms.

YOUTH HOSTELS

OSTELLO SANTA MONACA, via Santa Monaca, 6, Firenze. Tel. 055/26-8338 or 239-6704. 111 beds. **Directions:** See below.

$ Rates: 16,000 lire ($13.90) per person, plus a one-time sheet-rental fee of 2,000 lire ($1.75)—unless you bring your own, of course. Breakfast not available. No credit cards.

Much more convenient if not so clean as the remote IYHF youth hostel, this privately run hostel is a lively gathering spot for travelers from all over the world, and a great place to trade budget tips and meet travel companions. Rooms are closed from 9:30am to 1pm, and the building itself is locked up from 1 to 4pm. If you arrive before 1pm, leave your passport or some other form of ID in the red safety-deposit box next to the reception desk *and* add your name to the sign-up list for that day; come back to register between 4 and 5:30pm. There's an airtight midnight curfew, and the doors aren't reopened until 6:30am.

The hostel is located in the Oltrarno, a 10-minute walk from the station: Walk around to piazza Santa Maria Novella; go along via dei Fossi, which begins at the far left corner of the piazza until that street ends on the banks of the Arno; cross the Ponte alla Carraia bridge, and walk along via de' Serragli; via Santa Monaca will be the third right.

OSTELLO VILLA CAMERATA, viale Augusto Righi, 2-4, Firenze. Tel. 055/60-1451. 400 beds. **Bus:** 17B to the end (*capolinea*) of the route; then a half-mile walk.

$ Rates (including continental breakfast): 19,000 lire ($16.50) per person, including sheets. No credit cards.

Florence's stunningly beautiful IYHF youth hostel is housed in a mammoth 15th-century villa surrounded by a large park and garden. The views in the morning from this hilltop location are fantastic. The hostel is almost a community unto itself, with movies in English every evening, a bar, and an ultra-budget restaurant serving two meals a day. The hostel accepts IYHF members only, but you can buy a card (valid for a full year) on the premises for 30,000 lire ($26.10), or become a member for the night for 5,000 lire ($4.35). In summer, arrive by 2pm when the reception opens in order to secure a bed; this popular, peaceful, and dift-cheap hostel fills quickly. Curfew is 11:30pm year round, and the 12,000-lire ($10.45) dinner is served from 6:30 to 8pm. This is one of the most comfortable, least institutional hostels I've seen in Europe, and the only one with private baths in some rooms (four to eight beds per room).

WORTH THE EXTRA BUCKS

If you blow your budget in one Italian city, make it Florence, and do it at one of these two hotels:

HOTEL MARIO'S, via Faenza, 89 (1st Floor), 50123 Firenze. Tel. 055/ 21-6801. Fax 055/21-2039. 16 rms (all with bath). TEL
$ Rates (including full breakfast): 120,000 lire ($104.35) single; 165,000 lire ($143.50) double; 220,000 lire ($191.30) triple; 250,000 lire ($217.40) quad. Significant low-season discount for bearers of this book. AE, DC, MC, V.
Traditional Florentine furnishings are everywhere at Mario's, right down to the wrought-iron headboards. Most rooms look out onto a peaceful garden, a welcome respite from the busy street outside. The beamed ceilings date from the 17th century, but the hotel has been in operation only (!) since 1872. Owner Mario Noce and family run a first-rate ship, cheap by three-star standards, complete with in-room hairdryers and air conditioning. I have received more letters of praise for Mario's than for any other hotel in Florence. Perhaps it's the fresh fruit that they always keep stocked in the rooms.

HOTEL MORANDI ALLA CROCETTA, via Laura, 50 (1st Floor), 50121 Firenze. Tel. 055/234-4747. Fax 055/248-0954. 10 rms (all with bath). TV TEL **Directions:** See below.
$ Rates: 89,300 lire ($77.65) single; 136,500 lire ($118.70) double; 184,800 lire ($160.70) triple. Breakfast 15,000 lire ($13.05) extra. AE, DC, MC, V.
✪ British expatriate Kathleen Doyle has been living in Italy and serving its visitors since 1929. She boasts that "no one who has come here yet has been disappointed," and it's certainly easy to see why. Each room has its own character, thoroughly unique and meticulously planned—a stained-glass door here, a priceless antique table there. Indeed, the only common thread is the fresh flowers placed in every room each day, carefully chosen to match the colors in that room. Mrs. Doyle's son, an officer in the Italian navy, knows exactly what is needed to furnish a particular room, and quite literally has searched the world until he has found the perfect item.
The Hotel Morandi is on a quiet street near piazza San Marco, which is reached from the train station by bus nos. 17 and 25. From piazza San Marco, walk across to piazza SS. Annunziata. Go left at the piazza onto via Gino Capponi. Via Laura will be the first right, and you'll find the hotel 200 yards along on your left.

5. BUDGET DINING

For important information on dining in Italy, see the introduction to "Budget Dining" in the Rome chapter.
Top among Florence's culinary specialties is *bistecca alla fiorentina,* an inch-thick, charcoal-broiled steak. The hills surrounding Florence produce the best beef in the country, which is sold by weight, and is usually the most expensive item on the

menu. Many Florentines sing the praises of *trippa alla fiorentina,* but calves' intestines, cut into strips and served with onions and tomatoes, are not for everyone. *Paglia e fieno,* a mixture of green (spinach-based) and white (egg-based) pasta served in a cream sauce of ham, peas, and (sometimes) mushrooms, is the region's best-known pasta dish. Hearty Tuscan peasant dishes, including *ribollita,* a rich soup of boiled-twice cabbage and bread, and *fagioli all' uccelletto,* a tasty dish of pinto beans smothered in a sauce of tomato, rosemary (or sage), and olive oil, also deserve a try. *Crostini di fegatini,* chicken liver pâté served on small pieces of toasted bread, is a favorite Florentine antipasto (appetizer). Tuscany's wines—the most famous of which bear the black rooster seal of a true chianti—are as distinctive as the region's meals. Finally, whatever you do, don't miss Florence's gelato—light, airy, unforgettable ice cream.

There's no one dish or neighborhood that equals good budget dining in Florence. Your best bet is to choose one of the eateries listed below where they'll allow you to order just one course—though whether a modest pasta dish will satisfy your appetite may be another matter. While not always the cheapest way to dine, the ubiquitous *menu turistico* (a three-course fixed-price meal) is a good way to contain costs.

Keep in mind that in the listings below, prices are for pasta and meat courses only. Don't forget to add in charges for bread and cover, service, and vegetable side dishes when calculating what you should expect to pay.

MEALS FOR LESS THAN 12,000 LIRE ($10.45)

NEAR THE TRAIN STATION

ITALY AND ITALY, piazza della Stazione, 25-37r.
   Cuisine: ITALIAN. **Directions:** Exit the train station by Track 16 and cross the street.
$ **Prices:** 2,500–6,300 lire ($2.15–$5.50). No cover charge. No credit cards.
   Open: Wed–Mon 10am–1am.
"Italian fast food" may sound sacrilegious, but that's what this cafeteria specializes in. Right down to the green modular plastic furniture and the matching staff uniforms, this place will seem like any roadside hamburger stand in North America. But actually the food isn't half bad. In addition to burgers you can choose pizzotto (their own invention, similar to a calzone, stuffed with tomato sauce, cheese, and some meat), spaghetti with three different toppings and even french fries (yes, that's right). A hamburger alone will set you back 2,400 lire ($2.10).

RISTORANTE-PIZZERIA LA LAMPARA, via Nazionale, 36r.
   Cuisine: ITALIAN.
$ **Prices:** Pizza and pasta courses 7,000–8,000 lire ($6.10–$6.95); meat courses 14,000–18,000 lire ($12.15–$15.65). AE, DC, MC, V.
   Open: Wed–Mon 12:30–11pm. **Closed:** Second half of Dec.
This eatery, located only steps from the train station, is on the expensive side as pizza goes, but it's one of the most pleasant and welcoming pizzerias around. As you walk in, you'll see bowls of fresh ingredients spread out proudly on the counter in front of the pizza chef and the traditional open-mouthed, wood-burning pizza oven. The fresh, bright main dining room is made more attractive still by the jungle of plants growing in a small courtyard on the opposite side of a room-long glass wall. And the pizza tastes great!

ON VIA PALAZZUOLO, BETWEEN THE TRAIN STATION & THE RIVER

MENSA SAN FRANCESCO, piazza Sant'Annunziata, 2.
   Cuisine: ITALIAN.

FROMMER'S SMART TRAVELER: RESTAURANTS

VALUE-CONSCIOUS TRAVELERS SHOULD
TAKE ADVANTAGE OF THE FOLLOWING:

1. One of the eateries listed below, where they'll allow you to order just one course.
2. The ubiquitous *menu turistico*.

$ Prices: Fixed-price meal (including three courses and wine) 12,000 lire ($10.45). No credit cards.
Open: Lunch only, Mon–Fri noon–2pm. **Closed:** Aug, and the last two or three weeks in Dec.

Operated by a local religious order, this mensa may be the best lunch value in Florence. For just 12,000 lire ($10.45) you'll feast on a pasta course, a main course, vegetable, bread, and wine or water. Everyone is welcome here, from priests to local laborers, and from students at the nearby university to elderly pensioners, with a handful of tourists and thrifty professionals thrown in. Note that few waiters speak English, and that the mensa is open just for lunch, weekdays only.

TRATTORIA, via Palazzuolo, 69r.
Cuisine: ITALIAN. **Directions:** Walk two short blocks from the train station, between via dell' Albero and via de' Canacci.
$ Prices: *Menu turistico* 12,000 lire ($10.45). No credit cards.
Open: Lunch Sun–Fri 11am–3pm; dinner Sun–Fri 7pm–midnight. **Closed:** Aug.
This nameless one-room trattoria features the cheapest *menu turistico* (its only offering) in Florence, which includes three courses and wine. There's no à la carte menu. Expect to wait outside this colorful hole-in-the-wall with a cadre of hungry locals unless you come early.

TRATTORIA DA GIORGIO, via Palazzuolo, 100r.
Cuisine: ITALIAN.
$ Prices: *Menu turistico* 12,000 lire ($10.45). No credit cards.
Open: Lunch Mon–Sat 10am–3:30pm; dinner Mon–Sat 6:30–10pm. **Closed:** Aug.
If you can't find a seat at the nameless trattoria listed above, try its livelier, slightly larger rival, located on the same block on the opposite side of the street. Da Giorgio boasts the same 12,000-lira ($10.45) fixed-price meal, including wine, but in a more comfortable setting. Again there's no à la carte menu.

NEAR PIAZZA DEL DUOMO

YELLOW SNACK BAR, via del Proconsolo, 39r. Tel. 21-1766.
Cuisine: ITALIAN.
$ Prices: Pizza 7,700–12,100 lire ($6.70–$10.50); pasta courses 8,800 lire ($7.65); meat courses 8,300–17,600 lire ($7.20–$15.30). No credit cards.
Open: Wed–Mon 7:30pm–2am. **Closed:** Aug.

This curious, popular new saloon is like a cross between an Italian café, a German beer hall, and an American jazz club. In fact, their card lists "piano bar, American bar, pizza, restaurant, and beer-house" as the entertainment credentials. But it's not a bar, serves meals (not snacks), and isn't even very yellow. It is an outstanding place to eat, with *pasta fresca* (fresh pasta) made continuously on the premises, and reasonably tasty pizza as well. The piano music that begins at 10:30pm most nights is a sideline to the cuisine. While there's no pressure here to order a full meal, they frown on patrons who come just to drink, and are likely to turn you away before about 11pm. Yellow is located at the intersection of via del Proconsolo and borgo degli Albizi, near the Bargello.

MEALS FOR LESS THAN 18,500 LIRE ($16.10)

NEAR THE DUOMO

RISTORANTE-PIZZERIA I GHIBELLINI, piazza San Pier Maggiore, 8-10r. Tel. 21-4424.
  Cuisine: ITALIAN.
$ **Prices:** Pizza 4,900–9,900 lire ($4.25–$8.60); pasta courses 3,900–7,700 lire ($3.40–$6.70); meat courses 7,200–12,100 lire ($6.25–$10.50). AE, DC, MC, V.
  Open: Lunch Thurs–Tues noon–4pm; dinner Thurs–Tues 7pm–midnight.

⭐ I Ghibellini serves some of the most delicate pasta sauces in Florence in the medium-priced range. Its excellent food, combined with its outdoor tables on a quiet piazza, its four bright, air-conditioned rooms inside, and its long hours, make this one of the most recommendable restaurants in Florence. You'll find it at the end of borgo degli Albizi, which stretches east from via del Proconsolo.

TRATTORIA LE MOSSACCE, via del Proconsolo, 55r. Tel. 29-4361.
  Cuisine: ITALIAN.
$ **Prices:** Pasta courses 4,900–5,500 lire ($4.25–$4.80); meat courses 8,800–9,400 lire ($7.65–$8.15); *menu turistico* 17,600 ($15.30), available only on request. No credit cards.
  Open: Lunch Mon–Sat noon–2:30pm; dinner Mon–Sat 7–9:30pm. **Closed:** Aug.
Ask Florentines about this place and they'll tell you: "Everyone goes there." In fact, most Florentines have been coming here for so long and are so loyal that they still know and refer to it by its former name, "Gastone." Don't be fooled by its narrow doorway or its bright, ordinary dining room. The food is anything but ordinary here, however. Le Mossacce is very conveniently located, one block from the Duomo.

BETWEEN PIAZZA DELLA SIGNORIA & PIAZZA SANTA CROCE

This is the one area in Florence where you'll find scads of moderately priced restaurants. The greatest concentration of *trattorie* is along via dei Neri, which connects piazza della Signoria with piazza Santa Croce, and its main cross street, via dei Leoni.

RISTORANTE MONTECATINI, via dei Leoni, 6r. Tel. 28-4863.
  Cuisine: ITALIAN.
$ **Prices:** Pasta courses 3,900–5,500 lire ($3.40–$4.80); meat courses 7,200–11,000 lire ($6.25–$9.60); *menu turistico* 19,000 lire ($16.50). AE, DC, V.
  Open: Lunch Thurs–Tues noon–3pm; dinner Thurs–Tues 7–11pm. **Closed:** Feb.
If you plan to go with a *menu turistico* in this neighborhood, this is the place to try. They offer an unusually extensive menu, including spaghetti al pesto (a spicy basil sauce from the Genoa region), lasagne, and chicken cacciatore. Wine bottles line the walls, the linen tablecloths are changed after each party, and the service is remarkable. Montecatini is located steps from the intersection of via dei Leoni and via dei Neri.

ROSTICCERIA-TRATTORIA MARIO, via dei Neri, 74r. Tel. 26-2723.
  Cuisine: ITALIAN.

$ Prices: Pasta courses 3,900–4,400 lire ($3.40–$3.80); meat courses 5,500–8,800 lire ($4.80–$7.65); *menu turistico* (with wine) 13,200 lire ($11.50), available only on request. MC, V.
Open: Tues–Sun noon–9pm. **Closed:** Jan 1–15.

This is the smallest and most intimate of the four places I've listed in this neighborhood, with a country-kitchen atmosphere. They're proud of their authentic cuisine here, and prove it by spreading their offerings out on tables in the main dining room. Walk up and indicate the chop or vegetable of your choice. A cozy place, with vaulted ceilings, Mario is also very reasonably priced, with the cheapest *menu turistico* in the neighborhood. Mario is located just steps from the Palazzo Vecchio on via dei Neri.

TRATTORIA DA BENVENUTO, via dei Neri, 47r. (also via della Mosca, 16r). Tel. 21-4833.
Cuisine: ITALIAN.
$ Prices: Pasta courses 3,900–4,400 lire ($3.40–$3.80); meat courses 6,600–7,000 ($5.75–$6.70). No credit cards.
Open: Lunch Mon–Tues and Thurs–Sat 12:15–3pm; dinner Mon–Tues and Thurs–Sat 7:15–10pm.

Of the half dozen restaurants in this immediate area, Benvenuto's offers the least expensive à la carte dining (though they do insist that you take a full meal), and is the most popular place among Italians. The atmosphere is simple and unassuming, but the food is anything but that. The restaurant is situated at the corner of via dei Neri and via della Mosca.

TRATTORIA ROBERTO, via Castellani, 4r. Tel. 21-8822.
Cuisine: SEAFOOD.
$ Prices: Pasta courses 6,600–8,800 lire ($5.75–$7.65); meat courses 8,800–15,400 lire ($7.65–$13.40); fish courses 11,000–22,000 lire ($9.60–$19.15); *menu turistico* (including fish course, wine, and dessert) 17,500 lire ($15.20). MC, V.
Open: Lunch Thurs–Tues noon–3pm; dinner Thurs–Tues 7–11pm. **Closed:** Possibly Aug.

Fittingly enough, this restaurant just half a block from the river specializes in fish. Their card says so, it's written in bold letters across their front window, and their display case, placed strategically just inside the door, speaks for itself. Florence is not exactly the seafood capital of Italy, but this is one of the best places in town to indulge your oceanic palate. The attentive, helpful service and the pleasant atmosphere make this one of the best bets in the area. Via Castellani is an extension of via dei Leoni toward the river.

NEAR THE TRAIN STATION

TRATTORIA ENZO E PIERO, via Faenza, 105r. Tel. 21-4901.
Cuisine: ITALIAN. **Directions:** Walk up via Nazionale from the station; via Faenza is the second street on your left.
$ Prices: Pasta courses 4,400–6,600 lire ($3.80–$5.75); meat courses 6,600–11,000 lire ($5.75–$9.60); *menu turistico* 16,000 lire ($13.90). AE, DC, MC, V.
Open: Lunch Mon–Sat noon–3pm; dinner Mon–Sat 7–10pm.

The atmosphere here is pleasant and the service is unusually friendly. The menu is in Italian and English, and most of the waiters speak English, and will be happy to help you make your selections. The desserts (*dolce*) are especially good here (my favorite is *tiramisu*). This is a good bet if you'd like to dine in a genuine and reasonably priced trattoria without straying far from the train station.

TRATTORIA ZA-ZA, piazza Mercato Centrale, 26r. Tel. 21-5411.
Cuisine: ITALIAN.

$ Prices: Pasta courses 5,300–9,500 lire ($4.60–$8.25); meat courses 9,000–13,000 lire ($7.80–$11.30). AE, DC, MC, V.

Open: Lunch Mon–Sat noon–2:30pm; dinner Mon–Sat 7–10pm. **Closed:** Aug. The walls of this popular locale are lined with chianti wine bottles and photographs of not-so-famous patrons. At the restaurant's long wooden tables sits an eclectic mix of tourists and local workers. Convenient to the San Lorenzo open-air market, this typical Florentine eatery serves hearty meals such as ribollita and crostini caldi misti at reasonable prices in a rustic setting. While you're waiting to be served, watch the show put on daily in the open kitchen by English-speaking chef Stefano Bondi.

PICNIC SUPPLIES & WHERE TO EAT THEM

Doing your own shopping for food in Italy can be an interesting cultural experience in itself, since there's no such thing as a supermarket. Cold cuts are sold at a *salumeria*. To pick up cheese or yogurt, you'll have to find a *latteria*. Vegetables can usually be found at an *alimentari*, the closest thing Italy has to a grocery store. For bread to put all that between, visit a *panetteria*. Wander into a *pasticceria* to find dessert. And for a bottle of wine to wash it down, search out a *vinatteria*. **Via dei Neri,** which begins at via de' Benci near piazza Santa Croce and stretches over to the Palazzo Vecchio, is lined with small specialty food shops, and is one of the best areas for purchasing food for an outing.

If you prefer to find all that you need under one roof, visit the colorful **Mercato Centrale,** Florence's huge, block-long central marketplace. The market, open Monday through Saturday from 7am to 2pm and on Saturday from 4 to 8pm, is located at via dell' Ariento, 12, in the midst of the San Lorenzo open-air market, on the block between via San Antonino and via Panicale.

The **Boboli Gardens,** located on the opposite side of the Arno (see "Parks and Gardens" in "Attractions," below), is without a doubt the pest picnic spot in town.

WORTH THE EXTRA BUCKS

FIASCEHETTERIA DA IL LATINI, via Palchetti, 6r. Tel. 21-0916.

Cuisine: ITALIAN. **Directions:** See below.

$ Prices: Pasta courses 5,500–7,700 lire ($4.80–$6.70); meat course 11,000–13,200 lire ($9.60–$11.50); seven-course fixed-price meal 40,000 lire ($34.80). No credit cards.

Open: Lunch Wed–Sun noon–3pm; dinner Tues–Sun 7:30–10:30pm. **Closed:** July 20–Aug 10.

Narcisio Latini and his sons, Giovanni and Torello, operate what must certainly be the busiest, most popular restaurant in town. Even in the dead of winter you'll see a long line of Italian tourists waiting for a cramped seat at one of the long wooden tables inside. Once you get a table—the wait can be an hour or more—settle in for a raucous, delicious adventure in eating that you won't soon forget. Papa Latini watches over the operation with an eagle eye, shouting commands, talking to four people at once, placing telephone orders to the Latini family farm 20 miles away (where the wine and most of the food is produced), and never losing control over the wonderful chaos.

There is no written menu; one of the brothers will explain the selection, in rough English, for you. It's all hearty, meaty fare, and you'll spend about 40,000 lire ($34.80) for an unforgettable seven-course feast: an antipasto of prosciutto crudo (ham) and sausage, followed by a pasta course, a main course, a vegetable, ice cream, an aperitivo (after-dinner wine), biscotti (almond cookies), coffee, and all the wine and mineral water you can drink. Expect to leave with a too-full stomach, unless you can get their attention long enough to explain that you'd prefer a more modest meal.

Il Latini is hard to find, but worth every effort. With your back to the Ponte Vecchio, turn left along the river and then right into piazza C. Goldoni (opposite

Carraia Bridge). Walk one block along via Vigna Nuova, and take the first left onto via Palchetti.

LA VIE EN ROSE, borgo Allegri, 68r. Tel. 24-5860.
Cuisine: INTERNATIONAL. **Directions:** See below.
$ Prices: 7,700 lire ($6.70) for first courses, 16,500 lire ($14.35) for second courses. AE, DC, MC, V.
Open: Wed–Mon 7:30pm–1am. **Closed:** Aug.

Teresa and Stefano's terrifically creative nouveau Italian kitchen is a terrific find in a moderate price category. Fresh pastas, like homemade tortelli, are topped with imaginative sauces. Other dishes may include chicken breast marsala, or a lightly cooked beef carpaccio, topped with rosemary, arugula, and olive oil. A short, but well-selected wine list includes several good buys. La Vie en Rose also happens to be one of the few places where you can eat a full meal after 10 or 11pm.

To find it from piazza Santa Croce, walk along the north side of the church (the left if you're facing it) and borgo Allegri will be the third street on your left; it's about a 10-minute walk. From piazza del Duomo it will take 15 or more minutes: Walk out via dell' Oriuolo, continue straight across piazza Salvemini onto via Martiri del Popolo, and turn right onto borgo Allegri at piazza dei Ciompi. If you're asking directions, inquire after the nearby Mercato della Pulce, a well-known landmark.

RISTORANTE ACQUA AL DUE, via della Vecchia, 40r (at via dell'Acqua), Tel. 28-4170.
Cuisine: ITALIAN. **Reservations:** Required.
$ Prices: Pasta courses 6,300–7,400 ($5.50–$6.45); meat courses 9,900–16,000 lire ($8.60–$13.90); *assaggios* 9,000 ($7.80) for pasta, 6,300 ($5.50) for dessert. No credit cards.
Open: Lunch Tues–Sun 12:30–3pm; dinner Tues–Sun 7:30–1am. **Closed:** Aug.

Italy, of course, is most famous for its pasta, and this is the place to discover what you like best. The specialty of the house is the *assaggio,* a sampling of five different types of pasta in various sauces. They also offer a three-part salad assaggio, as well as an assaggio di dolce (desserts) of four super-sweet offerings. There's no English menu, but most of the waiters here speak English. No matter how cold it is outside, no matter how hard it's raining, if you don't have a reservation you'll be turned away at this place, one of Florence's best-known eateries. The busy, yet comfortable restaurant is especially popular with the under-30 crowd. Guests of any age can expect to leave here very satisfied, and usually about 30,000 lire ($26.10), including wine, poorer per person. Acqua al Due is tucked away on the street that runs behind the Bargello.

RISTORANTE ORCAGNA, piazza della Signoria, 1r Tel. 239-2188.
Cuisine: ITALIAN.
$ Prices: Pasta courses 5,500–9,900 lire ($4.80–$8.60); meat courses 9,900–17,600 lire ($8.60–$15.30); *menu turistico* 28,000 lire ($24.35), including wine and fruit or coffee, AE, DC, MC, V.
Open: Lunch Mon–Sat noon–2:30pm; dinner Mon–Sat 7–10pm.
This restuarant is "worth the extra bucks" for one reason—its one-of-a-kind location right on piazza della Signoria. You can eat outdoors on a piazza in any city in Italy, but this is the only place where you can do so under the watchful gaze of so much of the Renaissance's finest sculpture, including Cellini's *Perseus Holding Medusa's Head,* and the best copy of Michelangelo's *David.* The food seems an afterthought here at what could be the most romantic dining spot in the country.

RISTORANTE OTTORINO, via dell'Oche, 20r. Tel. 21-8747 or 21-5151.
Cuisine: ITALIAN.
$ Prices: Pasta courses 8,800–9,900 lire ($7.65–$8.60); meat courses 16,500–24,200 lire ($14.35–$21). AE, DC, MC, V.

Open: Lunch Mon–Sat 12:15–2:30pm; dinner Mon–Sat 7:15–10:30pm. **Closed:** 15 days in mid-Aug.

Arguably, this is the best restaurant in Florence. You'll spend more here than at any other splurge choice listed in this chapter—easily 44,000 lire ($38.25) per person for three courses with wine—for food that is always excellent and often exquisite. Among the half dozen specialties listed at the top of the menu, my favorites are paglia e fieno all'Ottorino (green and white pasta in a cream sauce of ham and peas) and scaloppine vitella Ottorino e tartufo (thinly sliced medallions of veal in a wine-and-mushroom sauce). Ottorino has been recently remodeled to include exposed brick walls, high ceilings, bright lighting, and modern furnishings—a pleasant alternative to many of the older, more rustic restaurants listed in this chapter. Via dell'Oche is the first left off via Calzaiuoli as you walk from piazza del Duomo.

TRATTORIA DEL PENNELLO, via Dante Alighieri, 4r. Tel. 239-4848.
    Cuisine: ITALIAN. **Directions:** See below.
$ Prices: Antipasto prices vary with quantity and dish, but expect to spend 11,000 lire ($9.60) for a healthy sampling. Pasta courses 3,900–4,400 lire ($3.40–$3.80); meat courses 11,000–16,500 lire ($9.60–$14.35); *menu turistico* 21,000 lire ($18.25) and 26,000 lire ($22.60). No credit cards.
    Open: Lunch Tues–Sun 11am–3pm; dinner Tues–Sat 7pm–midnight. **Closed:** Aug.

Though his house was just across the street, Dante never dined here. That was his loss. An enormous amount of energy and effort goes into the food at del Pennello, an attractive restaurant with plain white walls, a bright interior, and unassuming plain white curtains. The specialty here is an extraordinary array of two dozen delicious antipasti (appetizers), which are displayed in the dining room each evening. The assortment changes daily, as does the entire menu for that matter. Try to get an English-speaking waiter. For a full meal, with a good sampling of antipasti, expect to spend about 38,500 lire ($33.50) per person.

From via dei Calzaiuoli, turn onto via dei Tavolini, which becomes via Dante Alighieri. If you get lost, just ask anyone for directions to the Casa di Dante, across the street.

TRATTORIA SOSTANZA, via del Porcellana, 25r. Tel. 21-2691.
    Cuisine: ITALIAN.
$ Prices: Pasta courses 6,600–7,700 lire ($5.75–$6.70); meat courses 8,800–15,400 lire ($7.65–$13.40) No credit cards.
    Open: Lunch Mon–Fri noon–2:30pm; dinner Mon–Fri 7:30–9:30pm. **Closed:** Aug. and 12 days around Christmas.

Ronald Reagan ate here, as have countless other movies stars, cowboys, and heads of state. The walls of this 120-year-old, one-room place are literally covered with photos and autographs of all the famous people who have dined here. The handwritten menu changes daily, and there's usually someone around to translate. They insist that you take a full meal, which will run 33,000–44,000 lire ($28.70–$38.25) with wine. Trust me, you won't be disappointed.

Sostanza is located on via del Porcellana between via Palazzuolo and borgo Ognissanti. Via del Porcellana begins at via della Scala, near piazza Santa Maria Novella.

FOR GELATO (ICE CREAM)

VIVOLI, via Isole dei Stinche, 74. Tel. 239-2334.
    Cuisine: ITALIAN GELATO.
$ Prices: 3,000 lire ($2.60) for a medium-sized dish. No credit cards.
    Open: Tues–Sun 9am–1am. **Closed:** Aug, and Jan to early Feb.

Vivoli is the Michelangelo of ice creams. Tucked away one block up via dell' Anguillara from piazza Santa Croce, Vivoli is world famous and rightly so. The gelato here is just plain terrific. Exactly how world renowned is that small, brightly lit shop? Well, they keep a postcard taped to their wall, which, although it bore only "Vivoli, Europa" for the address, was successfully and promptly delivered to the world capital of ice cream. Note that you must pay first here.

FESTIVAL DEL GELATO, via del Corso, 75r. Tel. 239-4386.
   Cuisine: ITALIAN GELATO.
$ Prices: 3,000 lire ($2.60) for a medium-sized dish. No credit cards.
   Open: Summer, Tues–Sun 8am–1am; winter, Tues–Sun 11am–1am.
Located just off via Calzaiuoli, Festival del Gelato is more scene than substance, with pounding pop music and blinding neon. But with about 100 flavors, a number of which match the neon, and the trendiest clientele in Florence, Festival is worth a stop on your way from piazza Signoria to the Duomo.

PERCHE NO, via dei Tavolini, 19r. Tel. 239-8969.
   Cuisine: ITALIAN GELATO.
$ Prices: 3,000 lire ($2.60) for a medium-sized dish. No credit cards.
   Open: Wed–Mon 8am–12:30am.
Also just off via Calziuoli is this fine gelateria, called "Why Not?"—which is a good question.

GELATERIA IL TRIANGOLO DELLE BERMUDE, via Nazionale, 61r. Tel. 28-7490.
   Cuisine: ITALIAN GELATO.
$ Prices: 3,000 lire ($2.60) for a medium-sized dish. No credit cards.
   Open: Summer, Tues–Sun 8am–1am; winter, Tues–Sun 8am–midnight.
   Closed: Jan.
Last but not least, the "Bermuda Triangle" is a must for any ice cream lover on a gelateria crawl.

6. ATTRACTIONS

SUGGESTED ITINERARIES

Seeing all of Florence in a short time requires organization. It's not just that there is so much to see in this great city; it's also that the museums keep short, capricious hours. With the notable exception of the Uffizi Galleries, most museums in Florence close at 2pm, with the last entrance at least 30 minutes (and sometimes 45–60 minutes) before closing. In addition, each museum is closed a particular day of the week, many on Monday. Churches and the markets are the best places to spend your afternoon touring time, since they usually remain open until 7pm.

IF YOU HAVE ONE DAY This is a dilemma if ever there was one. There is so much to see in Florence, all of it as historically significant and aesthetically captivating as the next attraction, that the best approach to one day may be to flip a coin, or to write the names of sights on slips of paper and pull them out of a hat.
    You might begin your day at the Uffizi Galleries, the most important art museum in Europe after the Louvre in Paris. You'd have to race at breakneck speed through the musuem's 45 rooms to see everything, so I suggest that you choose a particular period or painter to study and reflect upon. Then head over to the Accademia, where there are eight pieces by Michelangelo, one of which is his *David*, considered one of the greatest Renaissance sculptures. The last visitors are admitted at 1:30pm, and lines can be up to an hour long in summer, so plan to leave the Uffizi by shortly after noon, or visit here first.
    Have lunch on piazza della Signoria, in the shadow of the Palazzo Vecchio and the Uffizi, for a memorable break from sightseeing. Find time after lunch to visit the

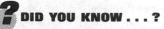 **DID YOU KNOW . . . ?**

- From 1865 to 1870, Florence was the capital of Italy.
- Florentine writers like Dante, Petrarch, and Boccaccio helped turn the Tuscan dialect into Italy's literary language.
- Giotto, da Vinci, Michelangelo, Machiavelli, Donatello, and Galileo were all residents of Florence.
- Although the construction of the cathedral of Santa Maria del Fiore was begun in 1294, the facade was not finished until 1875.
- Florence's Biblioteca Nazionale Centrale serves as the nation's official library; a copy of every book published in Italy is sent here.
- Despite its historic and artistic importance, Florence is only the eighth-largest city in Italy.
- Poet Elizabeth Barrett Browning is buried in Florence's English cemetery.

Duomo and Baptistery, which remain open until 5pm.

In the late afternoon, head over to the sprawling open-air Mercato San Lorenzo, open until 7pm, to take advantage of the bargains—on leather goods and wool sweaters in particular.

Otherwise, create your own walking tour. Cross the Ponte Vecchio into the Oltrarno, Florence's quieter, more workaday quarter, or stroll among the boutiques and *palazzi* in the area between the Duomo and the river. Finally, don't miss an opportunity to take in a hearty Tuscan meal at any one of the restaurants listed above.

IF YOU HAVE TWO DAYS You may want to spend part of your second day at the Uffizi Galleries again. There is so much to see and to savor here that many people find it most enjoyable and instructive to return to the Uffizi several times, focusing on a different period or style at each visit.

While you're back in the area of the Uffizi, stop at the Palazzo Vecchio. Or visit the many museums of the Pitti Palace, which could easily keep you occupied until 2pm when they close. Try to make time before 2pm to visit the Bargello, Florence's main sculpture museum, and the Casa Buonarroti, home to an excellent collection of early and lesser works by Michelangelo. After a picnic lunch in the Boboli Gardens behind the Pitti Palace, take in the expansive collection of the Duomo Museum, which is open into the evening.

Also consider that the one-day schedule outlined in the previous section is quite busy. You may want to stretch it over two days.

IF YOU HAVE THREE DAYS The treasures of Florence's half dozen most important churches can easily consume your third day in Florence. Fra Angelico's frescoes at San Marco, the tombs of Macchiavelli and Dante at Santa Croce, the Spanish Chapel at Santa Maria Novella, the legacy left by the Medici dynasty at their own San Lorenzo and the nearby Medici-Riccardi Palace, and the Gothic Orsanmichele will easily combine for a splendid Day 3 of sightseeing in Florence.

IF YOU HAVE FIVE DAYS Some visitors have fallen so deeply in love with Florence that on their fifth day they've been known to begin selling their possessions, and have been seen sitting at a café on piazza della Signoria searching the classified ads looking for a job and an apartment.

If you have a full five days, I suggest that you stretch the hectic three-day itinerary sketched above over four days. On the fifth day, despite Florence's unique pleasures and charms, get out of town. Pisa, Siena, San Gimignano, and nearby Fiesole are all lovely towns worth a visit, and all can easily be reached on a day trip (see "Easy Excursions," below).

TOP ATTRACTIONS

UFFIZI GALLERIES, piazzale degli Uffizi, 6. Tel. 21-8341.

The Uffizi is one of the most important art museums in the world, and should be the first stop in Florence for anyone interested in the rich artistic heritage of the Renaissance. Four centuries of artistic development are housed in this impressive building, which was originally commissioned by Duke Cosimo de' Medici to house the city's administrative offices (in fact, *uffizi* translates as "offices" in English).

The museum's superb collection begins in Room 2 with Giotto's early 14th-century *Madonna*, looked to by most scholars as the first painting to make the transition from the Byzantine period to the Renaissance style. Look for the differences between Giotto's work and his teacher Cimabue's *Madonna in Maestà* on the opposite wall.

For many, the Botticelli rooms (Rooms 10–14) are the axis around which this extraordinary museum revolves. The most stunning and significant of the breathtaking works that fill these rooms are the restored *Primavera* (The Allegory of Springtime) and *The Birth of Venus*.

Other notable works include Leonardo da Vinci's unfinished *Adorazione dei Magi* in Room 15, Rosso Fiorentino's *Putto che Suona in Tribuna* (Cherub Playing a Lute) in Room 18, Lukas Cranach's *Adame e Eva* in Room 20, Michelangelo's *Sacra Famiglia* (Holy Family) in Room 25, Raphael's *Autoritratto* (Self-portrait) in Room 26, Titian's *Flora* and *La Venere di Urbino* (Venus of Urbino) in Room 28, Tintoretto's *Leda* in Room 35, Caravaggio's *Medusa* and *Bacco* in Room 43, Rembrandt's *Autoritratto* (Self-portrait) in Room 44, and Canaletto's *Veduta del Palazzo Ducale di Venezia* (View of the Ducal Palace in Venice) in Room 45.

It makes all the difference in the world if you learn a little something about Renaissance painting before taking on the Uffizi. American expatriate Kirk von Dürer offers the best capsule course around, lecturing nightly at 8:30pm at his Penthouse Galleria (see below).

For a break from this exhaustive and exhausting collection, savor a cappuccino or Campari at the bar tucked away beyond Room 45, where you'll enjoy a view of the Palazzo Vecchio, the Duomo and Campanile, and the hills of Fiesole from the rooftop terrace.

Admission: 10,000 lire ($8.70).

Open: Tues–Sat 9am–7pm, Sun 9am–1pm. Ticket office closes 45 minutes before the museum.

GALLERIA DELL'ACCADEMIA, via Ricasoli, 60. Tel. 21-4375.

⭐ A cynic would observe that nowhere else in Europe do so many wait in line for so long to see so little. The Accademia is home to Michelangelo's *David*, considered by many to be the greatest sculptor's greatest work. *David* looms in stark perfection beneath the rotunda of the main room. The statue has recently been protected by a high glass screen, after an attack in 1991 that damaged its left foot. The museum houses seven other pieces by Michelangelo, including *The Prisoners*, in the arcade, and the second of his four versions of the *Pietà*. The line to get in to see *David* can be up to an hour long. Try getting there before the museum opens in the morning, or around midday. The Accademia is located between piazza del Duomo and piazza San Marco.

Admission: 10,000 lire ($8.70).

Open: Tues–Sat 9am–2pm, Sun 9am–1pm. Last entrance 30 minutes before closing.

A SPECIAL NOTE ON HOURS

With the exception of churches, all the sights listed below stop admitting visitors at least 30 minutes, and in some cases as much as 60 minutes, before the stated closing time. Tourists can remain inside until the posted closing time, but entrance is forbidden in the last half hour or more.

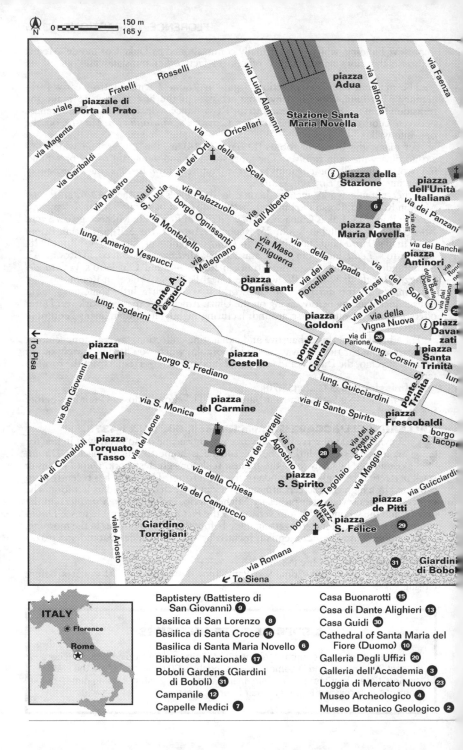

0 — 150 m / 165 y
N

Rosselli
Fratelli
viale Magenta
viale di **Porta al Prato**
via Magenta
via Garibaldi
via Palestro
via di S. Lucia
via Montebello
via dei Orti della Scala
via Oricellari
via Luigi Alamanni
via Valfonda
via Faenza

piazza Adua

Stazione Santa Maria Novella

(i) **piazza della Stazione**
piazza dell'Unità Italiana
via dei Panzani

6

via dell'Alberto
via Palazzuolo
borgo Ognissanti
lung. Amerigo Vespucci
via Melegnano
via Maso Finiguerra

piazza Santa Maria Novella

via della
via dei Avelli
via dei Banchi
piazza Antinori
via dei Porcellana
via dei Spada
via del Sole
via Tornabuoni
via della Bella Donna
via Ronc ne

piazza Ognissanti

Ponte A. Vespucci
lung. Soderini

via dei Fossi
via del Morro
via della Vigna Nuova
via di Parione
26
lung. Corsini

piazza Goldoni

(i) **piazz Dava zati**
piazza Santa Trinità

← To Pisa

piazza dei Nerli

borgo S. Frediano

piazza Cestello

ponte alla Carraia

lung. Guicciardini

ponte S. Trinità
lun

via San Giovanni
via S. Monica
via del Leone
via di Camaldoli

piazza del Carmine

via di Santo Spirito

piazza Frescobaldi
borgo S. Iacopo

27

via dei Serragli
via S. Agostino
via dei Presto di S. Martino

piazza Torquato Tasso

28
Tegolaio
via Maggio
via Guicciardi

via della Chiesa
piazza S. Spirito

via del Campuccio

Giardino Torrigiani
viale Ariosto

borgo Mazz etta
piazza de Pitti

piazza S. Felice
29

31
Giardini di Bobol

via Romana

← To Siena

Baptistery (Battistero di San Giovanni) **9**
Basilica di San Lorenzo **8**
Basilica di Santa Croce **16**
Basilica di Santa Maria Novello **6**
Biblioteca Nazionale **17**
Boboli Gardens (Giardini di Boboli) **31**
Campanile **12**
Cappelle Medici **7**

Casa Buonarotti **15**
Casa di Dante Alighieri **13**
Casa Guidi **30**
Cathedral of Santa Maria del Fiore (Duomo) **10**
Galleria Degli Uffizi **20**
Galleria dell'Accademia **3**
Loggia di Mercato Nuovo **23**
Museo Archeologico **4**
Museo Botanico Geologico **2**

FLORENCE ATTRACTIONS

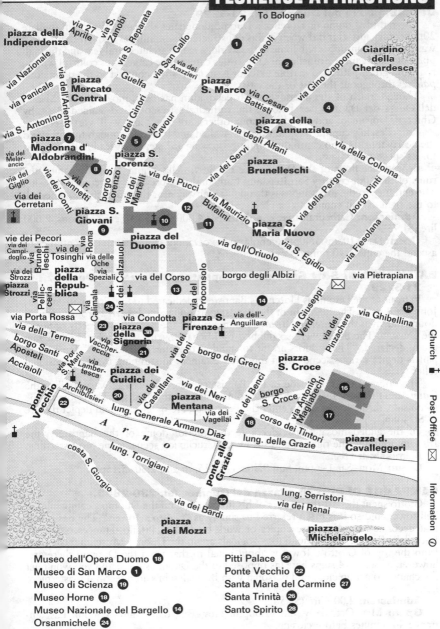

To Bologna

Museo dell'Opera Duomo 18
Museo di San Marco 1
Museo di Scienza 19
Museo Horne 18
Museo Nazionale del Bargello 14
Orsanmichele 24
Palazzo Medici-Riccardi 5
Palazzo Strozzi 25
Palazzo Vecchio 21
Piazza della Signoria 38

Pitti Palace 29
Ponte Vecchio 22
Santa Maria del Carmine 27
Santa Trinità 26
Santo Spirito 28

Church ■✝
Post Office ⊠
Information ⊙

DUOMO, piazza del Duomo. Tel. 21-3229.

The red-tiled dome of Florence's Duomo dominates the city's skyline in the late 20th century just as it did when it was constructed five centuries ago. At that time it was the largest unsupported dome in the world, a major architectural feat and the high point of the architect Brunelleschi's illustrious career. The cathedral's colorful white-, red-, and green-patterned marble exterior is an interesting contrast to the dark-stone *palazzi* throughout the rest of the city.

Though much of the interior church decoration has been moved to the Museo dell'Opera del Duomo (see below), the cathedral's frescoes and stained glass, by Ghiberti, Donatello, and Uccello, among others, are intact and well worth seeing.

Brunelleschi's cupola was built double-walled and is strong enough to withstand the hearty tourists who climb the spiraling, dizzying 463 steps that lead to the summit for its spectacular view.

Beneath the floor of the Duomo are the Scavi della Cripta di San Reparata, the ruins of the 10th-century San Reparata Cathedral that previously occupied this site. The entrance to the excavations is through a stairway near the front of the cathedral, to the right as you enter.

Admission: Cathedral, free; cupola ascent 4,000 lire ($3.50); excavations, 2,000 lire ($1.75).

Open: Daily 10am–5:40pm (cupola and excavations closed Sun). Last entrance to ascend the cupola 40 minutes before closing.

BATTISTERO DI SAN GIOVANNI (Baptistery), piazza del Duomo. Tel. 21-3229.

In front of the Duomo is Florence's Baptistery, dedicated to the city's patron saint, John the Baptist. The highlight of the Baptistery is Lorenzo Ghiberti's bronze exterior doors known as the *Gates of Paradise*, on the side of the Baptistery directly opposite the Duomo. The doors were so dubbed by Michaelangelo, who, when he first saw them, declared, "These doors are fit to stand at the gates of Paradise." Ten bronze panels depict various scenes from the Old Testament in stunning three-dimensional relief.

The doors at the north side of the Baptistery were Ghiberti's "warm-up" to the *Gates,* and the work that won him the commission for the final set. The doors on the south side, through which you enter the Baptistery, are by Pisano, and depict the life of St. John.

Of the gilded mosaics that decorate the interior dome of the Baptistery, the *Inferno,* found to the right of and below the Crucifixion scene, is the most startling.

Admission: Free.

Open: Mon–Sat 1–6pm, Sun 9:30am–12:15pm and 2:30–5:15pm.

CAMPANILE DI GIOTTO, piazza del Duomo. Tel. 230-2885.

Giotto spent the last three years of his life working on the Duomo's campanile, or bell tower, and so it is often referred to simply as "Giotto's Tower." The bas-reliefs that decorate its exterior are copies of work by Andrea Pisano, Francesco Talenti, Luca della Robbia, and Arnoldi (the originals are in the Duomo Museum). The view from the top of Giotto's Tower is about equal to that from the Duomo; there are, however, a mere 414 steps here (as opposed to the Duomo's 463), and you won't get the chance to get up close and personal with Brunelleschi's architectural masterpiece here.

Admission: 4,000 lire ($3.50).

Open: Mar–Oct, daily 9am–7:30pm; Nov–Feb, daily 9am–5:30pm. Last entrance 40 minutes before closing.

MUSEO DELL'OPERA DEL DUOMO, piazza del Duomo, 9. Tel. 230-2885.

Easily overlooked, this quiet, airy museum behind the cathedral contains all the art and furnishings that once filled the spacious Duomo. Even in the ticket office there's a bust of Brunelleschi, and over the door hang two glazed della Robbia terra-cottas. In the second inner room to your left you'll find the remains of the old facade of the cathedral (destroyed in 1587), including work by the original architect, Arnolfo di Cambio. Also here is a weather-worn but noble *St. John* by Donatello, and Nanni di Banco's intriguing *San Luca*.

The highlight of the center room upstairs is the enchanting twin marble choirs by Donatello and Luca della Robbia. In the next room to the left are the original bas-reliefs that decorated the first two stories of the exterior of the campanile. Another priceless and fascinating masterpiece, in the last room on the second floor, is the silver altarpiece with scenes from the life of St. John by Michelozzo and friends.

Among many other points of interest is Donatello's exotic wooden statue of Mary Magdalen, and Michelangelo's final *Pietà*, sculpted when he was more than 75 years old. The haunting figure of Joseph is thought to be a self-portrait of the artist—old, tired, and nearly blind. In fact, it's rumored that Michelangelo later tried to destroy the work, and it is generally accepted that Mary may be partially or wholly the work of one of his students.

Admission: 4,000 lire ($3.50) Mon–Sat, free Sun.

Open: Mar–Oct, Mon–Sat 9am–8pm, Sun 10am–1pm; Nov–Feb, Mon–Sat 9am–6pm, Sun 10am–1pm. Last entrance 60 minutes before closing.

PIAZZA DELLA SIGNORIA, PALAZZO VECCHIO, and ORCAGNA'S LOGGIA, piazza della Signoria. Tel. 276-8465.

In Italy, all roads lead to Rome, but in Florence at least, all roads lead to the spacious, elegant piazza della Signoria, the cultural and physical heart of the city since the 15th century.

The square is dominated by the rough-hewn fortress architecture of the Palazzo Vecchio, Florence's city hall for many years, and home to Duke Cosimo de' Medici for 10 years. You'll enter through the stunning main courtyard of the palazzo, with its intricately carved columns and extraordinarily colorful ceilings. The highlight of the interior is the massive, lavish Salone dei Cinquecento, formerly the city's council chambers, and still used today for government and civic functions. The richly decorated back rooms of the palazzo on beyond the Salone offer an intriguing glimpse into how the ruling class of Renaissance Florence lived. The Palazzo Vecchio also houses a modest museum of ancient musical instruments.

A small disc in the ground in front of Ammanati's enormous *Neptune* fountain marks the spot where the tyrant Savonarola was burned at the stake in 1498. Opposite the Palazzo Vecchio is Orcagna's Loggia (also known as the Loggia dei Lanzi), Florence's captivating outdoor sculpture gallery.

Admission: Piazza della Signoria, free; Palazzo Vecchio, 5,000 lire ($4.35) Mon–Fri, free Sun.

Open: Piazza della Signoria, daily 24 hours; Palazzo Vecchio, Mon–Fri 9am–7pm, Sun 8am–1pm (closed Sat).

PITTI PALACE, piazza de'Pitti. Tel. 21-3440.

Begun in 1458 for the wealthy banker Luca Pitti, and later occupied by the Medici family and the Royal House of Savoy, this enormous palace today houses a complex of museums.

The **Galleria Palatina,** on the first floor (tel. 21-0323), is the star attraction, home to one of the finest collections in Italy after the Uffizi. In addition to the outstanding Raphaels displayed here, including *Madonna of the Chair, Angelo and Maddalena Doni,* and *Tommaso Inghirami,* the museum's treasures include: a large collection of works by Andrea del Sarto; Fra Bartolomeo's beautiful *Deposition from the Cross* and *San Marco;* some superb works by Rubens, including *The Four Philosophers* and his famous *Isabella Clara Eugenia;* canvases by Tintoretto and Veronese; and some absolutely stunning portraits by Titian, including *Pope Julius II, The Man with the Gray Eyes,* and *The Music Concert.*

The **Appartamenti Monumentali (Royal Apartments)** (tel. 21-0323) are ornate, gilded, and chandeliered, with portraits of the Medicis and furnishings from the days of the House of Savoy. (The apartments may be closed for restoration in 1993). Upstairs, the **Galleria d'Arte Moderna** (tel. 28-7096) houses an interesting array of Italian impressionist and 20th-century art. Visit the **Museo degli Argenti (Silver Museum)**, on the ground floor (tel. 21-2557), for a look at the treasure of the Medici family. The **Museo delle Berline** displays the Savoy carriages.

Admission: Palatina, 8,000 lire ($6.95); Modern Art Gallery, 4,000 lire ($3.50); Argenti, 6,000 lire ($5.20).

Open: Tues–Sat 9am–2pm, Sun 9am–1pm. Last entrance 45 minutes before closing. **Directions:** Walk across the Ponte Vecchio, the only bridge in Florence that survived World War II, and continue up via Guicciardini for a quarter of a mile.

IL BARGELLO, via del Proconsolo, 4. Tel. 21-0801.

If a visit to the Accademia has whetted your appetite for more fine Renaissance sculpture, then you'll be interested in the outstanding collection on view at the national museum, called Il Bargello. This stark, medieval-style building served as the city's jail in earlier times. Today it houses a number of treasures by Michelangelo, including his first attempt at *David* and his unfinished *Martyrdom of St. Andrew,* as well as *Bacco, Brutus,* and *Madonna Teaching Jesus and San Giovanni to Read.* Among the other important sculptures here are Ammanati's *Leda and the Swan,* Giambologna's *Mercury,* and Donatello's *San Giorgio.* The Bargello is on via del Proconsolo at via Ghibellina, near the Uffizi.

Admission: 6,000 lire ($5.20).

Open: Tues–Sat 9am–2pm, Sun 9am–1pm.

MORE ATTRACTIONS

MUSEO DI SAN MARCO, piazza San Marco, 1. Tel. 21-0741.

Located directly next door to the San Marco Basilica in what was once a monastery, this small museum is a monument to the work of Fra Angelico.

Directly to your right upon entering is a room containing the largest collection of his movable painting in Florence. The chapter room nearby is home to Angelico's large and impressive *Crucifixion* fresco. At the top of the stairs leading to the monks' cells on the second floor is his stunning and beautiful masterpiece, *The Annunciation.* Each of the cells upstairs is decorated with a fresco painted either by Fra Angelico or one of his assistants under the master's direction.

At the end of the corridor is Savonarola's cell, which includes a stark portrait of the monastery's former prior by his convert, Fra Bartolomeo, as well as his sleeping chamber, notebook, rosary, and remnants of the clothes worn at his execution.

Piazza San Marco is at the end of via Ricasoli, which begins at piazza del Duomo.

Admission: 6,000 lire ($5.20)

Open: Tues–Sat 9am–2pm, Sun 9am–1pm (closed Mon). The ticket office closes 30 minutes before the museum.

BASILICA DI SANTA CROCE AND THE PAZZI CHAPEL, piazza Santa Croce. Tel. 24-4619.

The most interesting features of the interior of the Basilica di Santa Croce, which dominates Florence's largest pedestrian piazza, are the two restored chapels by Giotto to the right of the altar. Santa Croce is also the final resting place for many of the most renowned figures of the Renaissance. Michelangelo's tomb is the first on the right as you enter the church. Dante's empty tomb is right next to him, while Machiavelli rests in the fourth. Galileo and Rossini, among others, were also laid to rest here.

The entrance to the tranquil Pazzi Chapel (marked OPERA DI SANTA CROCE) is to the left as you leave the church. Commissioned by Andrea de' Pazzi, a key rival of the Medici family, the chapel is today considered significant mostly as an excellent example of early Renaissance architecture. Designed by Filippo Brunelleschi, the chapel today serves as the church's museum. It houses just a few of Cimabue's fine works, including his *Crucifixion,* which suffered serious damage in the 1966 flood.

Admission: Basilica, free; Pazzi Chapel, 3,000 lire ($2.60).

Open: Basilica, daily 8am–12:30pm and 3–6:30pm. Pazzi Chapel, Mar–Sept, Thurs–Tues 10am–12:30pm and 2:30–6:30pm; Oct–Feb, Thurs–Tues 10am–12:30pm and 3–5pm.

BASILICA DI SANTA MARIA NOVELLA, piazza Santa Maria Novella. Tel. 28-2187.

The richly decorated interior of this church, located around the corner from the train station, is covered with frescoes by Lippi, Ghiberti, Ghirlandaio, Brunelleschi, Massaccio, and Giotto, among others. The highlight of the church is the Cappellone degli Spagnoli (Spanish Chapel), covered with an important and captivating series of early Renaissance frescoes by Andrea de Bonaiuto illustrating the history of the Dominican church. The entrance to the Spanish Chapel is immediately to the right as you exit the basilica.

Admission: Basilica, free; Spanish Chapel, 4,000 lire ($3.50).

Open: Basilica, Mon–Fri 7–11:30am and 3:30–6:30pm, Sat 7–11:30am and 3:30–5pm, Sun 8:30am–noon and 3:30–5pm; Spanish Chapel, Mon–Thurs and Sat 9am–2pm, Sun 8am–1pm.

BASILICA DI SAN LORENZO AND THE CAPPELLA DEI PRINCIPI (Medici Chapels), piazza Madonna. Tel. 21-3206.

The San Lorenzo Basilica was the Medici family's cathedral, and the final resting place for most of the clan. The key feature of the main part of the church is the **Biblioteca Laurenziana,** a stunning bit of architecture by Michelangelo. The entrance to this main part of San Lorenzo, including the Biblioteca Laurenziana, is at the end of borgo San Lorenzo, near the Medici-Riccardi Palace.

San Lorenzo is best known, however, for the **Medici Chapels.** To reach them today, visitors must walk around to the back of the church to piazza Madonna degli Aldobrandini. Visit the New Sacristy first, which contains Michelangelo's tomb for Lorenzo de Medici, with the figures of *Dawn* and *Dusk;* and Giuliano de Medici, whose tomb features figures of *Night* and *Day.* The other chapels, decorated to their baroque teeth, are less interesting, as are the two rooms behind the altar containing various treasures and religious relics.

Admission: San Lorenzo and the Biblioteca Laurenziana, free; Medici Chapels, 8,500 lire ($7.40).

Open: Biblioteca Laurenziana, Mon–Sat 9am–1pm; Medici Chapels, Tues–Sat 9am–2pm, Sun 9am–1pm; the main part of San Lorenzo Basilica, hours are erratic, as restoration is under way.

MEDICI-RICCARDI PALACE, via Cavour, 1. Tel. 2-7601.

Built for Cosimo the Elder by Brunelleschi's student Michelozzo, this mid-15th-century palazzo became the prototype for subsequent noble homes. The chapel is covered with magnificent frescoes by Benozzo Gozzoli, who worked several members of the Medici family into his depictions of the Wise Men. Across the courtyard is a second-floor baroque gallery covered with Luca Giordano's frescoes illustrating the *Apotheosis of the Medici Dynasty.* The entrance to the palace is one block up via de' Martelli from the Duomo.

Admission: Free.

Open: Mon–Tues and Thurs–Sat 9am–1pm and 3–5pm, Sun 9am–noon.

CHIESA DI ORSANMICHELE, via de' Calzaiuoli.

✪ Just a few short blocks up from piazza della Signoria on via de' Calzaiuoli, between via dei Lamberti and via Orsanmichele, is the 14th-century Orsanmichele Church, the last remnant of Gothic architecture in Florence and originally built to do double duty as a granary. Inside, among the vaulted Gothic arches, stained-glass windows, and 500-year-old frescoes is the colorful, sumptuous tabernacle by Andrea Orcagna. The niches surrounding the exterior of the church are a virtual history of Florentine sculpture from the 14th through the 16th century. Note Ghiberti's *St. John* (left) and Verrocchio's *St. Thomas* (right) on the front facade.

Admission: Free.

Open: Daily 8am–noon and 3–6pm.

MUSEO DELLA CASA BUONARROTI, via Ghibellina, 70. Tel. 24-1752.
This graceful house, which Michelangelo bought and designed for his nephew, was turned into a museum by his heirs. Today it houses two of the master's most important early works. *Madonna alla Scala* (Madonna on the Steps) and *Battaglia dei Centauri* (Battle of the Centaurs) were sculpted in his teenage years, when he was still working in relief. The museum also houses a sizable collection of his drawings and scale models.
   Admission: 5,000 lire ($4.35) adults, 3,000 lire ($2.60) students.
   Open: Wed–Mon 9:30am–1:30pm. **Directions:** Via Ghibellina begins alongside the Bargello; the Casa Buonarroti is five short blocks down this street. If you're coming from piazza Santa Croce, you'll find Casa Buonarroti at the top of via delle Pinzochere, two blocks from the piazza.

PARKS & GARDENS

The lush **Giardini Boboli** (tel. 21-3440) begin behind the Pitti Palace and fan upward to the Belvedere Fortress (tel. 234-2822), which crowns the hill. Enter the gardens via the rear exit to the Pitti Palace. The gardens, particularly beautiful in the spring, are the best spot in Florence for a picnic lunch. The view from the fortress is stunning, but there's not much to see inside unless there's a special exhibition; ask at the tourist office or look for posters around town.
   The Boboli Gardens are open daily, from sunrise to sunset; fortress hours vary with exhibitions. Admission to the gardens is free; fortress admission is free as well, while exhibition admission varies.

SPECIAL-INTEREST SIGHTSEEING

Florence's 19th-century **Jewish Synagogue,** an excellent and delightful, if incongruous, example of Moorish architecture, is located at via Farini, 4 (tel. 24-5252). The synagogue's caretaker will modestly tell you that "this is the most beautiful synagogue in all of Europe," and she may be right. Call to verify the synagogue's erratic hours, which, when I last visited, were Sunday through Thursday from 11am to 1pm and 2 to 5pm, and on Friday from 11am to 3pm.
   A visit to the synagogue, situated at the intersection of via Farini and via Pilastri, is best combined with a visit to piazza Santa Croce (walk straight up via de' Pepi, and turn right when it ends at via Pilastri) or the piazza San Marco/piazza Sant'Annunziata area (walk out via della Colonna and take the third right at via Farini). Admission is free.
   Literary enthusiasts especially will enjoy a pilgrimage to the **Casa Guidi,** the home of Elizabeth Barrett and Robert Browning, currently in the process of being restored to its original state after a century of disuse. The famous couple came to the Casa Guidi in 1847 and remained until 1861, when Barrett passed away. Their home was the center of the Anglo-Florentine community, where they hosted Nathaniel Hawthorne, Margaret Fuller, and other great figures in English and American literature. Whether or not the place can be restored to its state in the middle of the last century, it's still a must for literary pilgrims, as this is where Barrett did most of her work, and where a considerable portion of Browning's material was penned.
   For the record, Guidi was the family that owned the *palazzo* in the days of the Medicis. This notable place, which is always staffed by an American or British expatriate, is open Monday through Friday from 3 to 6pm, and at the other times by appointment; verify the winter hours. Admission is free. The house is located on piazza San Felice (tel. 28-4393), in the Oltrarno. Piazza San Felice is at the intersection of via Romana, via Mazzetta, and via Maggio, opposite the Pitti Palace.
   While Florence is best known and most often visited for its legacy of art and architecture, the collection of its **Museo di Storia della Scienze (History of Science Museum),** piazza dei Giudici, 1 (tel. 29-3493), on the river behind the Uffizi, is interesting and worth a visit for those with a special interest in the roots of technology. Its halls are filled with 16th- and 17th-century clocks, microscopes, telescopes, surveying instruments, and models of the solar system—all lovely as works

of art, in addition to having historical and scientific value. The museum is open Monday through Saturday from 9:30am to 1pm; on Monday, Wednesday, and Friday it is also open from 2 to 5pm. Admission is 10,000 lire ($8.70).

ORGANIZED TOURS

Florence is such a small city, and walking through its streets is such a pleasure, that a bus tour is not the most enjoyable way to see this wonderful city.

C.I.T., at the corner of piazza della Stazione and piazza dell'Unità Italiana (tel. 21-0964), offers two separate half-day bus tours of the city, including visits to the Uffizi Galleries, the Medici Chapels, and the breathtaking piazzale Michelangelo overlooking the city. Each tour is 35,000 lire ($30.45). C.I.T. is also the place to inquire about organized tours to other areas of Tuscany. It's open Monday through Friday from 8:30am to 12:30pm and 3 to 6:30pm, and on Saturday from 8:30am to noon.

SPECIAL & FREE EVENTS

The **Maggio Musicale,** or "Musical May," is Italy's oldest musical festival. Events take place at various outdoor locations throughout Florence, including piazza della Signoria and the courtyard of the Pitti Palace. Zubin Mehta often conducts Florence's own Maggio Musicale Orchestra, and guest conductors and orchestras appear throughout the festival, which, despite its moniker, runs from late April into July. For schedules and ticket information, inquire at one of the tourist offices.

From June through August, the Roman theater in nearby Fiesole comes alive with dance, music, and theater for the **Estate Fiesolana,** or "Summer in Fiesole." A.T.A.F. bus no. 7 travels to Fiesole from the train station and piazza del Duomo. Again, check with the tourist office for details.

7. SAVVY SHOPPING

In terms of shopping, Florence is easy to categorize: It's paradise. This capitalist capital, where modern banking and commerce began, has something for every taste and price range. Whether you can afford little more than a bargain-priced wool sweater in the open-air market or are looking to carry home your own little piece of the Renaissance's artistic wealth, Florence is for you.

BEST BUYS

Haute couture in Florence is alive and well and living on **via Tornabuoni,** where some of the most recognized names in Italian and international design and fashion share space with the occasional bank, which you may have to rob to afford anything on this chic boulevard.

Via Calzaiuoli is lined with fashionable jewelry and clothing stores and is the city's main shopping street. Stores here are not quite as high fashion or as high priced as on the gilded via Tornabuoni.

Via del Corso and its extension on the opposite side of via del Proconsolo, **borgo degli Albizi,** is another major shopping street, boasting many of the more avant-garde boutiques in this fashion capital.

If you've arrived in Florence with a Medici-size fortune and hope to leave with a collection to rival the Uffizi, shop on **borgo Ognissanti** near the Arno and **lungarno Corsini** and **lungarno Acciaiuoli** along the river, where you'll find merchants offering fine paintings and sculpture, objets d'art, and antiques.

Leather is perhaps what Florence is most famous for. As you get closer and closer to the city, the din of the rumor mill rises to a dull roar, reaching a crescendo when you finally arrive, by which time many travelers have been happily convinced that they *must* buy a leather coat during their stay. All this is for good reason—for quality, price, and selection, no European city can hold a candle to Florence. Expect to spend $200–$300 for a leather jacket.

The **area around piazza Santa Croce** is the best place to shop for leather, and not much more expensive than the pushcarts at the San Lorenzo market. Of the many shops that surround this square, I hear the most praise for **Fibbi Brothers,** corso dei Tintori, 21r (tel. 24-4231), located one block from the square, toward the river. Fibbi is open daily from 9am to 7pm April through October; November through March, they're closed Sunday and Monday, and for lunch from 1 to 3pm.

Jewelry shops line both sides of the pedestrian **Ponte Vecchio,** the only bridge in Florence that escaped destruction in World War II.

MARKETS

There's nothing in Italy, and indeed perhaps nothing in Europe, to compare with Florence's bustling, sprawling, open-air **Mercato San Lorenzo.** Hundreds of pushcarts crowd together along the streets around the San Lorenzo Church and the Mercato Centrale, offering countless varieties of hand-knit wool and mohair sweaters, leather jackets, handbags, wallets, gloves, and briefcases—not to mention the standard array of souvenir T-shirts and sweatshirts, wool and silk scarves, and other souvenirs.

The market stretches for six blocks between piazza San Lorenzo behind the Medici Chapel to via Nazionale, along via Canto de' Nelli and via dell' Ariento, with stalls also set up along various side streets in between.

The days of bargaining have passed here at the open-air market. Getting a pushcart salesperson to knock 10% or 15% off the posted price should be considered a major accomplishment, and one that only happens in the off-season.

Each vendor keeps his or her own schedule, but the market generally operates more or less from 9am to 7pm daily from mid-March through October (closed on Sunday and Monday the rest of the year). Almost all vendors accept credit cards.

Much smaller, but still worth a look, is the outdoor **Mercato del Porcellino,** also known as the **Straw Market,** where about 100 pushcarts crowd together beneath an arcade near piazza della Repubblica. Vendors here offer mostly handbags, scarves, lace products, and souvenirs. The market is named for the bronze boar (*porcellino*) on the river side of the arcade, whose snout has been worn smooth by the countless Florentines who have touched it for good luck.

The Mercato del Porcellino is listed on most maps as "piazza del Mercato Nuovo." From piazza della Repubblica, walk two blocks toward the river and the Ponte Vecchio on via Calimala, which begins at the corner of the piazza with the Cinzano and Campari signs. Hours here are generally 9am to 6pm, daily from mid-March to November 3 and Tuesday through Saturday the rest of the year.

ENGLISH BOOKSTORES

LIBRERIA INTERNAZIONALE SEEBER, via Tornabuoni, 68r. Tel. 21-5697.

The biggest English bookstore in town, the Seeber is located opposite the main tourist office.

Open: Mon 2–7:30pm, Tues–Sat 9:30am–7:30pm.

BM LIBRERIA BOOK SHOP, borgo Ognissanti, 4r. Tel. 29-4575.

This shop at piazza Goldoni is the best place in town to pick up travel guidebooks.

Open: Summer, daily 8am–1pm and 3:30–7:30pm; winter, Tues–Sat 8am–1pm and 3:30–7:30pm.

AFTER DARK, via del Moro, 86r. Tel. 29-4203.

This is my favorite bookstore in Florence. Near piazza Santa Maria Novella, it stocks magazines, posters, and gifts that you may not be able to find anywhere else in Italy. The British expatriate owner also carries gay literature, and will trade for your used paperbacks.

Open: Daily 10am–7pm (usually closed for lunch 1:30–2:30pm)

8. EVENING ENTERTAINMENT

THE PERFORMING ARTS

The two principal performing arts festivals in Florence are the **Maggio Musicale** and the **Estate Fiesolana.** For more information on both, see "Special and Free Events" in "Attractions," above.

The **Teatro Comunale,** corso Italia, 16 (tel. 277-9236), is Florence's main theater, with productions in Italian. Prices of course vary with the production, but most tickets run 10,000–30,000 lire ($8.70–$26.10). The box office is open Tuesday through Saturday from 9am to 1pm, and from one hour before showtime.

Visitors should also check the theater and concert listings of *Welcome to Florence,* available free at the tourist office, for information on concerts, recitals, and other productions in churches and other venues throughout the city.

MOVIES

The **Astro Cinema,** across the street from the world-famous Gelateria Vivoli on tiny via Isole dei Stinche, screens films in English every night but Monday, for 8,000 lire ($6.95). They open a new film every three to six days, so stop by to pick up their latest program (sorry, no telephone). To find the Astro, which is closed in August, walk along via Ghibellina, which begins behind the Bargello Museum; via Isole dei Stinche will be the first street on the right.

BARS, NIGHTCLUBS & DISCOS

Nightlife is not Florence's strongest suit. This city is more a place for spending a quiet evening at an outdoor café, or enjoying a long, leisurely meal at your favorite trattoria. Nonetheless, below are listed several favorites among budget travelers.

THE RED GARTER, via de' Benci, 33r. Tel. 234-4904.

With live music and dancing nightly, and scores of young American travelers spilling draft beer all over the sawdust- and popcorn-covered floors, the Red Garter looks, smells, and feels every bit like a campus saloon in an American college town. There's no place like it anywhere else in Italy.

The Red Garter is located on via de' Benci between piazza Santa Croce and the Ponte alle Grazie bridge.

Prices: Draft beer (.41, 14 oz.) 6,000 lire ($5.20); bottled beer 7,000 lire ($6.10); glass of wine 5,000 lire ($4.35); mixed drinks 7,000 lire ($6.10). **Admission:** Free (no cover charge).

Open: Daily 8pm–1am; happy hour is 8–9:30pm.

SPACE ELECTRONIC DISCO, via Palazzuolo, 37. Tel. 29-3082.

Revelers will find a more balanced combination of tourists and Italians at this wildly decorated pleasure palace. Its motley collection of artifacts and electronics includes two enormous carnival faces plucked right from an American boardwalk, an open parachute that hangs from the ceiling, an imitation space capsule that sails back and forth across the dance floor, and of course the requisite video screens and lasers. Not to mention the fish tank loaded with piranhas that doubles as the bar.

Prices: Draft beer 6,000 lire ($5.20); mixed drinks 8,000 lire ($6.95). **Admission:** 20,000 lire ($17.40), which includes the first drink; there's a 5,000-lire ($4.35) discount for bearers of this book.

Open: Mar–Aug, daily 9:30pm–1:30am; Sept–Feb, Tues–Sun 9:30pm–1:30am.

CHIODO FISSO, via Dante Alighieri, 16r. Tel. 26-1290.

A self-proclaimed "guitar club," this cozy and intimate wine cavern is about the only place to listen to live folk music in Florence. There's no admission charge but relatively steep drink prices; chianti is the only wine they serve.

Via Dante Alighieri runs between via dei Calzaiuoli and via del Proconsolo, one block toward the river from via del Corso.

Prices: Bottle of chianti 25,000 lire ($21.75); minicarafe (basically two glasses) of chianti 6,000 lire ($5.20); glass of chianti 4,000 lire ($3.50); beer and mixed drinks 10,000 lire ($8.70). **Admission:** Free.

Open: Daily 9:30pm–3am. **Closed:** Two weeks in Aug.

FIDDLER'S ELBOW, piazza Santa Maria Novella, 7r. Tel. 21-5056.

This Irish-style pub is one of Florence's newest watering holes. Perpetually packed with international travelers and assorted locals, it's one of the few places in town where you can find an authentic pint of Guinness. It's located about three blocks from the train station.

Prices: Pint of beer 6,000 lire ($5.20). **Admission:** Free.

Open: Thurs–Tues 4:30pm–12:15am.

9. EASY EXCURSIONS

Tuscany is considered by many to be the most beautiful region of Italy. Four towns, all of which can be reached from Florence on a day trip, are particularly noteworthy.

PISA Everybody knows what to see in Pisa, an hour away by train for 10,000 lire ($8.70), round-trip. It's too bad that Pisa is so renowned for its mistakes, though. Were it not for the tilt of the infamous **Leaning Tower,** Pisa's **piazza del Duomo** would be one of the loveliest squares in the country. To reach it, take the bus marked "Duomo" from the train station in Pisa.

SIENA The "musts" to see in lovely Siena include its stunning **Duomo** and adjacent museum, as well as the **Palazzo Pubblico,** which dominates the unique oval central square, known as the **Campo.** And if you've dodged one too many errant taxis, you'll especially enjoy the fact that the historic quarter of Siena is car-free.

There is train service from Florence to Siena, but buses are more convenient, since they will drop you off much closer to the center than the remote train station. S.I.T.A. buses leave Florence for Siena about every 30 minutes from the station at via Santa Caterina da Siena, 15r (tel. 21-1487), located near the train station; exit the station by Track 5, turn left and then right at the next corner, and the bus depot will be right there. The bus journey takes about 75 minutes and costs 7,000 lire ($6.10) each way.

SAN GIMIGNANO San Gimignano is a charming, immensely fortified medieval hill town a bit farther away than Siena, and only accessible via S.I.T.A. bus. Travelers must change coaches at Poggibonsi. Buses leave Florence every 60–90 minutes, arrive an hour and 45 minutes later, and cost 7,000 lire ($6.10) one way.

FIESOLE Fiesole, in the hills just above Florence, can be reached by taking municipal bus no. 7 to the end of the line. There's not much to do here—but then, that's the whole point.

GENEVA

Cool, peaceful Geneva is the quintessential international city. Ever since it hosted its first conference in the 8th century, Geneva has been a privileged site for summit meetings and a favored headquarters of international organizations. Both the Red Cross and the League of Nations were founded here, and the city is home to the multilingual, multinational workers of the World Health Organization (WHO), the Centre Européen de Recherches Nucléaires (CERN), and countless other representations from the world of acronyms. When Reagan and Gorbachev met for the first time, they chose peace-loving Geneva as their stage.

Yet despite these ties with the entire world, few places are as conscious as Geneva of its essential quality—that of being first and foremost its own city. Surrounded almost totally by France, Geneva did not join the Swiss Confederacy until 1815, and it still displays its official name with pride: *Republic* and Canton of Geneva. Separatism is not unheard of. On the Ile Rousseau, the statue of Jean-Jacques Rousseau bears an inscription describing the philosopher simply as a citizen of Geneva—*citoyen de Genève*. Other citizens have included Voltaire, Byron, Lenin, Richard Burton, Alain Delon, Audrey Hepburn, and Romania's exiled King Michael.

Argentine writer Jorge Luís Borges lived here as a child, during World War I, and returned in his 80s, just a few months before his death; he loyally proclaimed Geneva as the one place in the world "most propitious for happiness." When you see the deep blue lake, with the snowcapped Alps in the distance and the jet d'eau arcing gracefully above the very proper skyline, you may think so, too.

1. FROM A BUDGET TRAVELER'S POINT OF VIEW

Geneva on $45 a day? A friend who works at the United Nations did not believe it could be done until I showed her how. It is indeed possible if you know where to look for the bargains.

In this chapter you'll find a number of inexpensive hotels with double rooms for 80 Swiss francs ($57.15), and this rate includes a continental breakfast. With your remaining francs, you should be able to get lunch and dinner and stay within your budget.

WHAT THINGS COST IN GENEVA

U.S. $

Taxi from airport to city center	28.55
Public transportation for an average trip within the city	1.40
Local telephone call	.28
Double room at Le Richemond (deluxe)	380.00
Double room at Hôtel de Clos Voltaire (moderate)	140.00
Double room at Hôtel de la Cloche (budget)	54.00
Lunch for one, without wine, at Café des Antiquaires (moderate)	12.15
Lunch for one, without wine, at Restaurant Manora (budget)	7.50
Dinner for one, without wine, at La Perle du Lac (deluxe)	45.00
Dinner for one, without wine, at Les Armures (moderate)	25.00
Dinner for one, without wine, at La Cave Valaisanne (budget)	14.00
Glass of wine	2.50
Coca-Cola	2.10
Cup of coffee	1.90
Roll of ASA 100 color film, 36 exposures	5.00
Admission to Red Cross Museum	5.70
Movie ticket	10.00
Theater ticket	14.00

GENEVA BUDGET BESTS The best bargains in Geneva are undoubtedly the **museums**—most of them are free. One exception is the must-see Red Cross Museum; it's one of the most expensive in the city at SFr 8 ($5.70) for adults.

If you plan to visit far-flung sections of the city by bus or tram, you'll save money by purchasing a one-, two-, or three-day **transit pass** valid on buses and trams, and good for unlimited rides within the city. For only SFr 2 ($1.40) you can have an inexpensive boat ride across the blue-green waters of Lake Geneva from one bank to the other.

In summer, head to the parks and quays along the banks of the lake for another Geneva bargain—**free music.** Classical, jazz, and pop music are all performed throughout the summer and make a wonderful accompaniment to a picnic dinner. In addition, there are free concerts from June to September on Saturday at 6pm at the Cathédrale de St-Pierre and on Sunday and Monday evening at the Eglise de St-Germain, only a block from the cathedral.

And last, don't pass up the opportunity to have Geneva's delicious **cheese fondue** at least once. This meal is not only both filling and entertaining, but it's also one of Geneva's best food bargains.

WORTH THE EXTRA BUCKS You can get a taste of life in a country home if you stay at the Hôtel de Clos Voltaire, which is surrounded by a small garden and also has private access to the quiet park of the Voltaire Museum.

2. PRETRIP PREPARATIONS

DOCUMENTS Citizens of the United States, Great Britain, Canada, Australia, and New Zealand need only a valid passport. Remember to carry your passport if you visit

WHAT'S SPECIAL ABOUT GENEVA

Lake Geneva
☐ One of Europe's most beautiful lakes.
☐ Great for boat excursions.

The Old City
☐ Narrow cobblestone streets and pretty fountains.
☐ A nice place for a stroll.

The Parks
☐ Some 37 acres alongside the lake, with views of the Alps.
☐ Great for picnicking and strolling.

The Alps
☐ Both the French and Swiss versions very close to the city.
☐ Great for day trips and skiing.

The International Institutions
☐ The U.N. and the Red Cross Museum, representative of Geneva's multinational spirit.

An International City
☐ People from all over the world, ethnic restaurants, and more.

Chamonix or the Salève, both of which are in France, or if you take a boat excursion that stops at any of the French villages on the south shore of Lake Geneva.

WHAT TO PACK   Genevans tend to dress a bit more conservatively than people in other European cities. If you are visiting in the winter, bring warm clothing. You'll see more fur coats in Geneva than in almost any other city in the world. In summer, don't forget your bathing suit: A visit to Geneva wouldn't be complete without at least a quick dip in the lake. An umbrella or raincoat is a must in Geneva at any time of year.

WHEN TO GO   Despite its proximity to the Alps, Geneva itself is at a relatively low elevation, less than 3,000 feet. Consequently, the climate is relatively mild and rainfall is fairly evenly distributed throughout the year. In the winter the rain is often mixed with snow.

Geneva's Average Daytime Temperature & Rainfall

	Jan	Feb	Mar	Apr	May	June	July	Aug	Sept	Oct	Nov	Dec
Temp. (°F)	34.7	28.8	40.5	44.4	59.7	63.0	67.7	65.1	60.0	53.2	41.0	36.1
Rainfall ″	2.6	2.4	2.8	2.6	2.8	3.3	3.0	3.9	3.8	3.4	3.6	3.2

Special Events   The annual **Fêtes de Genève** in the first week of August and **l'Escalade** in mid-December are Geneva's biggest and most popular festivals. The Fêtes de Genève feature live music all over the city, while the focus of the Escalade is a torchlit parade through the streets of the Old City, with hundreds of Genevans dressed in 17th-century costumes. Both celebrations are well worth a special visit.

BACKGROUND READING   George Mike's *Switzerland for Beginners* (André Deutsch, 1987) is an amusing collection of essays on diverse aspects of Swiss life. H. M. Waidson's *Anthology of Modern Swiss Literature* (St. Martin's Press, 1985) is a comprehensive introduction in English to the multilingual literature of Switzerland.
Writers from all over the world have written about Geneva—Rousseau, Stendhal, Victor Hugo, Hans Christian Andersen, Rilke. If you read French, you might consider getting a copy of *Genève: Un Guide Intime* (Autrement, 1986), which is part of the collection "L'Europe des Villes Rêvées"; it's a highly personal vision of the city by the French author Michel Butor, and it includes an anthology of short pieces on Geneva by the writers mentioned above.

3. ORIENTATION & GETTING AROUND

ARRIVING IN GENEVA

With only 170,000 residents, Geneva is a small city. **Geneva-Cointrin Airport,** though quite busy with all the comings and goings of employees and visitors to the city's numerous international organizations, is a compact and easily negotiated airport.

Getting into the city from the airport is a breeze. In the basement of the air terminal is a train station with trains leaving about every five minutes for the six-minute trip to the **Cornavin Train Station** (tel. 731-6450) in the city. If you happen to be heading for another city in Switzerland, you may be able to depart directly from the airport train station without having to change trains at Cornavin Station. The train from the airport into the city costs SFr 4.40 ($3.15) one way and runs from 5:30am to 12:20am. So whether you arrive by air or by train, you'll find yourself at Cornavin Station, on the right bank of Geneva.

Taking a taxi into town is highly inadvisable. They take much longer than the train and, at SFr 40 ($28.55), are much more expensive.

INFORMATION

The **main tourist office,** located in the train station (tel. 738-52-00), is open October through June, Monday through Saturday from 9am to 6pm; July through September, daily from 8am to 8pm. The extremely helpful staff will make hotel reservations in the city for SFr 5 ($3.55) and elsewhere in Switzerland for SFr 10 ($7.15). Here you can also pick up a free copy of *This Week in Geneva,* a very useful publication with information on sightseeing, the performing arts, and other special events.

From June 15 to September 15, **CAR (Centre d'Accueil et de Rencontres)** (tel. 731-46-47) provides information from a car parked on rue du Mont-Blanc in front of the train station. Hours are daily from 8:30am to 11pm.

Infor Jeunes, 13, rue Verdaine (tel. 321-22-30), near place Bourg-de-Four in the Old City, is an information center for young travelers. They can answer all sorts of questions you might have about Geneva.

CITY LAYOUT

Geneva is located at the western end of **Lake Geneva,** known in French as Lac Léman, site of the impressive *jet d'eau.* The blue-green waters of the lake meet the **Rhône River,** which divides the city into a left and a right bank. On the **rive gauche** (left bank) are the Old City, some major shopping streets, the famous flower clock, the university, and several important museums. On the **rive droite** (right bank) are the train station, the major international organizations, and many attractive parks.

GETTING AROUND

BY BUS & TRAM Geneva is not very big, so you will be able to walk almost everywhere. For longer distances, the **Transports publics genevois (TPG)** (tel. 21-08-44) offers a fine network of buses and trolleys, as well as one tram—the smoothly gliding no. 12. If you're going three stops or fewer, the fare is SFr 1.20 (85¢); for more than three stops the ticket costs SFr 2 ($1.40) and is good for one hour with no limits on transfers. Tickets are dispensed from coin-operated machines at every stop.

There is also a series of **cartes journalières,** or day passes. A one-day pass is available for SFr 8.50 ($6.05), a two-day pass for SFr 15 ($10.70), and a three-day pass for SFr 19 ($13.55). Another option are the **cartes multiparcours,** 12 three-stop tickets for SFr 12 ($8.55) or six one-hour tickets for SFr 11 ($7.85). Those staying for longer periods should consider the monthly passes. The **carte orange** costs SFr 53 ($37.85), while the **carte vermeil** (for senior and disabled citizens) costs SFr 36 ($25.70) and the **carte azur** (for those 25 years of age and under), SFr 30 ($21.40).

ON FOOT   Unless you want to see both the Old City on the left bank and the international organizations on the right bank in one day, Geneva can easily be explored on foot.

BY BICYCLE   A bicycle is an excellent way to visit the countryside around Geneva, but for sightseeing in the city, where the streets of the Old City are steep and made of cobblestones, it's not practical. For cycling in the countryside, pick up a map of the canton of Geneva from the tourist office and head out through farmland and vineyards to the many picturesque, small villages.

Multispeed bicycles can be rented at **Cornavin Station** for SFr 11 ($7.85) for a half day or SFr 16 ($11.40) for a full day. Mountain bikes and tandems are also available, for SFr 27 ($19.30).

Horizon Motos, at 22, rue de Paquis (tel. 731-23-39), also rents mountain bikes, as well as mopeds and motorcycles. The mountain bikes and mopeds are SFr 30 ($21.40) per day and SFr 140 ($100) per week. Unless you pay for the rental with a credit card, you'll have to leave a SFr-500 ($360) refundable deposit. Motorcycles start at SFr 27 ($28.55) per day. This rate does not include insurance, and you'll need a valid motorcycle license.

BY BOAT   Shuttling back and forth between the right and left banks of the city in the summer months are small boats known as **Mouettes Genevoises.** These water buses are the cheapest way to take a cruise on the lake. For as little as SFr 2 ($1.40) you can cross from one side of the lake to the other, or for SFr 10 ($7.15) you can get a round-trip ticket that allows you to get off at any of the five stops and get back on a later boat.

BY CAR   Most of the major international car-rental agencies have offices in Geneva. For budget car rentals, try **Léman,** at 6, rue Amat (tel. 732-01-43), where you can rent a Peugeot 205 for SFr 96 ($68.55) per day, with unlimited mileage and gas included. Open Monday through Saturday from 8am to 7pm and on Sunday from 9am to noon.

 GENEVA

Babysitters   The tourist office lists several agencies, including Service de Placement de l'Université, 4, rue de Candolle (tel. 329-39-70 or 705-77-02), which you must call by 8:30am for service that evening; and Baby Call, 4, rue du Vieux-Billard (tel. 781-06-66), open from 2 to 6pm.

Business Hours   Hours for most shops are Monday through Saturday from 8:30am to 6:30pm. Offices are open Monday through Friday from 8am to noon and 2 to 6pm.

Consulates   Because of Geneva's important position in global politics, many consulates, as well as missions to the United Nations, are here. These include the Australian Consulate, 56-58, rue Moillebeau (tel. 734-62-00); the British Consulate, 37-39, rue Vermont (tel. 734-38-00); the Canadian Consulate, 11, chemin du Pré-de-la-Bichette (tel. 733-90-00); the New Zealand Consulate, 28, chemin du Petit-Saconnex (tel. 734-95-30); and the U.S. Consulate, 1-3, avenue de la Paix (tel. 738-76-13).

Currency   The basic unit of currency in Switzerland is the Swiss franc (SFr), which is divided into 100 centimes. There are banknotes of SFr 10, 20, 50, 100, 500, and 1,000, and coins of SFr ½, 1, 2, and 5, and 5, 10, and 20 centimes. Banks all over Geneva have currency-exchange windows and offer good rates.

Emergencies　Dial 117 for the police, 118 for the fire department. In medical emergencies, dial 320-25-11, or go to the Hôpital Cantonal, 24, rue Micheli-du-Crest (tel. 382-33-11). If you need a dentist, go to one of the *cliniques dentaires* at 5, chemin Malombré (tel. 346-64-44) and 60, avenue Wendt (tel. 733-98-00); both are open daily from 7:30am to 8pm.

This Week in Geneva contains the addresses of pharmacies open until 9 or 11pm that week; in emergencies, dial 111 or 144.

Holidays　Public holidays in Geneva include New Year's Day (Jan 1), Good Friday, Easter Monday, and Christmas Day (Dec 25).

Hotlines　La Main Tendue (tel. 28-28-28 or 143) is a hotline for those in need.

Information　See "Orientation and Getting Around," above.

Laundry　Known in Geneva as a *Salon Lavoir,* a laundry is usually self-service. The Salon Lavoir, 4, rue de Montbrillant, on the first street behind Cornavin Station, will do your laundry for you for SFr 16 ($11.40). It's open Monday through Friday from 7:30am to 6:30pm (on Thursday to noon), and on Saturday from 8am to 2pm.

Two laundries in the Plainpalais area are open daily from early morning to late at night and charge only about SFr 12 ($8.55) for you to wash and dry your own clothes. They're located at the end of rue des Voisins at 10, rue Jean-Violette, and 200 yards from the place du Cirque at 61, rue St-Georges.

In the Eaux-Vives district there's one at 8, rue du 31 Decembre that's open daily from 6:30am to 10pm and charges SFr 10 ($8) to wash and dry.

Lost and Found　Geneva's efficient Service cantonal des objets trouvés, 7, rue des Glacis-de-Rive (tel. 787-60-00), is open Monday through Thursday from 8am to noon and 1 to 4:30pm, on Friday to 4pm. Check here for items lost in shops, restuarants, taxis, buses, and on the street. There are other Lost Property Offices in the airport and the central station.

Mail　The main post office is at 18, rue du Mont-Blanc, two blocks from Gare

---

THE SWISS FRANC & THE DOLLAR

At this writing $1 = approximately SFr 1.40 (or SFr 1 = 71¢), and this was the rate of exchange used to calculate the dollar values given in this chapter (rounded to the nearest nickel). This rate fluctuates from time to time and may not be the same when you travel to Switzerland. Therefore the following table should be used only as a guide:

SFr	U.S.$	SFr	U.S.$
1	.71	35	25.00
2	1.42	40	28.57
3	2.14	45	32.14
4	2.85	50	35.71
5	3.57	55	39.28
6	4.28	60	42.85
7	5.00	65	46.42
8	5.71	70	50.00
9	6.42	75	53.57
10	7.14	80	57.14
15	10.71	85	60.71
20	14.28	90	64.28
25	17.85	95	67.85
30	21.42	100	71.42

Cornavin. It's open Monday through Friday from 7am to 7pm and on Saturday from 7 to 11am.

Police   In an emergency, dial 117 for the police.

Religious Services   For details, contact the American Church, 3, rue de Monthoux (tel. 732-80-78); the Roman Catholic John XXIII Centre, 35, chemin Adolphe-Pasteur (tel. 733-04-83); or the Jewish Liberal Community, 12, quai du Seujet (tel. 732-04-83).

Tax   The VAT (Value-Added Tax) of 6.2%, levied on items above SFr 500 ($357.15), is refundable; simply ask the store for a VAT form and present it to the Customs official when leaving the country.

Taxis   Taxicabs are easy to find, but not cheap. If you need one, call 141.

Telephone   There is a large long-distance phone center located at Gare Cornavin, open daily from 7am to 10:30pm. You can also make long-distance calls at the main post office on rue du Mont-Blanc, two blocks from the station. Local calls start at 40 centimes (28¢); telephones accept coins in various denominations. The telephone area code for Geneva is 022.

Tipping   A service charge is usually added to restaurant bills and taxicab fares in Geneva, so it's unnecessary to leave a tip beyond the few centimes you might receive back when you break a franc. However, if a special service is performed by a waiter or cabdriver, a larger tip would be appropriate.

Useful Telephone Numbers   General information, 111; exchange rates, 160; time, 161; weather, 162; road conditions, 163.

4. BUDGET ACCOMMODATIONS

Despite its reputation as one of the more expensive cities in the world, Geneva has a few inexpensive hotels. The choices are even better in the summer when many student dormitories open up to tourists. These are often the best deals, with attached baths for less than you'd spend for a room without bath in a regular hotel.

It's a good idea to reserve in advance. If you have trouble finding a room when you arrive in the city, remember that the **tourist office** will make hotel reservations for SFr 5 ($3.55); see "Orientation and Getting Around," above.

DOUBLES FOR LESS THAN SFR 100 [$71.40]

ON THE RIGHT BANK

HOTEL DES TOURELLES, 2, bd. James-Fazy, 1201 Genève. Tel. 022/ 732-44-23. 23 rms. **Directions:** See below.

$ Rates (including continental breakfast): SFr 60 ($42.85) single without bath, SFr 75 ($53.55) single with bath; SFr 90 ($64.30) double without bath, SFr 110 ($78.55) double with bath; SFr 120 ($85.70) triple without bath, SFr 135 ($96.40) triple with bath. AE, EURO, MC, V.

Named after the turrets on the corner of the building, this is one of Geneva's best budget hotels. The turret rooms are huge, with seating alcoves and views of the river and the Old City. Some rooms have bay windows and antiques. The hotel is clean and the management friendly.

To reach the hotel, turn right when you come out of Gare Cornavin, staying to the right of the large church on boulevard James-Fazy. The Tourelles is on the left side of the street just before the bridge over the river.

HOTEL DE LA CLOCHE, 6, rue de la Cloche, 1201 Genève. Tel. 022/732-94-81. 8 rms (none with bath). **Bus:** 1 from Gare Cornavin; for walking directions, see below.

$ Rates (including continental breakfast): SFr 50 ($35.70) single; SFr 75 ($53.55) double; SFr 95 ($67.85) triple; SFr 115 ($82.15) quad. Showers SFr 2 ($1.40) if you stay one night, free for longer stays. No credit cards.

Built in the 1880s, the small Hôtel de la Cloche was once the apartment of the director of the Grand Casino. Many luxurious features remain, like the beautiful blue-and-white porcelain sink in the toilet near the entrance (some guests have offered to buy it, according to managers M. and Mme Chabbey).

From Gare Cornavin, walk down rue du Mont-Blanc, turn left onto quai du Mont-Blanc and left again at the fifth street, which is rue de la Cloche; the Hôtel de la Cloche is directly across the street from the Noga Hilton.

HOTEL RIO, 1, place Isaac-Mercier, 1201 Genève. Tel. 022/732-32-64. 32 rms (all with shower only). **Directions:** Leave the Central Station and turn right onto boulevard James-Fazy, which leads right to the hotel.

$ Rates (including continental breakfast): SFr 70 ($50) single; SFr 90 ($64.30) double; SFr 125 ($89.30) triple.

The hotel is spread over three floors of a corner house about a three-minute walk from the Central Station. The reception is one flight up, and there's an elevator. The rooms are basic, but there are friendly, English-speaking owners.

HOTEL ST-GERVAIS, 20, rue des Corps-Saints, 1201 Genève. Tel. 022/732-45-72. 30 rms. **Directions:** See below.

$ Rates (including continental breakfast): SFr 60 ($42.85) single without bath; SFr 70 ($50) double without bath, SFr 90 ($64.30) double with shower only, SFr 100 ($71.40) double with bath. AE, EURO, MC, V.

Situated on seven floors of a building with an elevator, the St-Gervais features recently remodeled rooms, most of which are small and geometrically creative: Few are square. The carpets are pretty, the furniture is modern, and everything is very clean. The English-speaking management is friendly. Gare Cornavin is only a three-minute walk away.

To reach the hotel, turn right as you exit the station, walk down rue Cornavin to rue des Corps-Saints, which veers off from it where rue Cornavin turns toward the river.

ON THE LEFT BANK

HOTEL BEAU SITE, 3, place du Cirque, 1204 Genève. Tel. 022/328-10-08. 54 beds. **Bus:** 1 from Gare Cornavin to place du Cirque.

$ Rates (including continental breakfast): SFr 55 ($39.30) single without bath, SFr 60 ($42.85) single with shower, SFr 75 ($53.55) single with bath; SFr 75 ($53.55) double without bath, SFr 80 ($57.15) double with shower, SFr 95 ($67.85) double

---

Ⓕ FROMMER'S SMART TRAVELER: HOTELS

VALUE-CONSCIOUS TRAVELERS SHOULD
TAKE ADVANTAGE OF THE FOLLOWING:

1. Student dormitories, which are available for tourists during the summer.
2. The tourist office, which will make reservations for a small fee.

with bath; SFr 90 ($64.30) triple without bath, SFr 92 ($65.70) triple with shower, SFr 115 ($82.15) triple with bath; SFr 100 ($71.40) quad without bath, SFr 108 ($77.15) quad with shower. EURO, MC, V.

This is a funky old place popular with young travelers. Large high-ceilinged rooms with parquet floors, doors painted red and gray, an antique sewing machine, and a TV lounge with a large overstuffed couch all contribute to the antique atmosphere. If manager Denise Ray is not around, someone at the desk who speaks enough English will check you in.

HOTEL DU LAC, 15, rue des Eaux-Vives, 1207 Genève. Tel. 022/735-45-80. 26 rms (none with bath). **Bus:** 6 from Gare Cornavin to place des Eaux-Vives.

$ Rates (including continental breakfast): SFr 58 ($41.40) single; SFr 78 ($55.70) double; SFr 98 ($70) triple. No credit cards.

The immaculately clean and well-maintained Hôtel du Lac is located on the sixth and seventh floors of an elevator-equipped modern apartment building. Owners M. and Mme Cagnoli-Spiess are responsible for making this such a delightful place to stay. They take great pride in keeping their hotel in top shape, doing much of the work themselves. All the rooms on the sixth floor have balconies, and many of the rooms have connecting doors so that families or two couples can share two rooms.

HOTEL LE GRENIL, 7, av. de Sainte-Clothilde, 1205 Genève. Tel. 022/28-30-55. 50 rms. **Bus:** 1 from Gare Cornavin to place du Cirque; then walk down boulevard St-Georges to avenue de Sainte-Clothilde.

$ Rates (including continental breakfast): SFr 85 ($60.70) single without bath, SFr 105 ($75) single with bath; SFr 98 ($70) double without bath, SFr 130 ($92.85) double with bath; SFr 115 ($81.15) triple without bath, SFr 145 ($103.55) triple with bath; SFr 130 ($92.85) quad without bath, SFr 160 ($114.30) quad with bath; SFr 25 ($17.85) per person in an eight-bed room. AE, DC, EURO, MC, V.

Rooms here are amazingly similar to those you might find in any modern hotel in North America; even more surprising is that le Grenil is sponsored by the YMCA and the YWCA of Geneva. Besides standard rooms—most with radio and telephone—the hotel has rooms for the disabled and two dormitories. Other amenities include a TV lounge, a dining room serving lunch and dinner (half board available), an art gallery off the large lobby, and a theater in the basement.

HOTEL LE PRINCE, 16, rue des Voisins, 1205 Genève. Tel. 022/329-85-44 or 29-85-45. 20 rms (all with bath or shower). TV TEL **Bus:** 1 from Gare Cornavin to Pont d'Arve; then walk across rue de Carouge and turn left at the next intersection.

$ Rates: SFr 75 ($53.55) single; SFr 100 ($71.40) double; SFr 125 ($89.30) triple. Continental breakfast SFr 6 ($4.30) extra. AE, MC, V.

Near the university in the Plainpalais district, the Hôtel le Prince is an excellent deal. The management is wonderfully friendly and many rooms have lots of light and minibars—some will be remodeled soon. Everything here smells good, and the restaurant next door is an added plus.

DOUBLES FOR LESS THAN SFR 110 [$78.55]

ON THE RIGHT BANK

HOTEL TOR, 3, rue Lévrier, 1201 Genève. Tel. 022/732-39-95. 23 rms (all with tub or shower and toilet). TV TEL **Directions:** From Gare Cornavin, walk down rue du Mont-Blanc and turn left onto rue Lévrier.

$ Rates (including continental breakfast): SFr 75–100 ($53.55–$71.40) single; SFr 90–130 ($64.30–$82.85) double; SFr 150 ($107.15) triple; SFr 170 ($121.40) quad. EURO, MC, V.

Located on the third floor of an elevator-equipped building, the Hôtel Tor is spacious and well furnished. All rooms have TVs and their own tubs or showers and private toilet. The management is pleasant and speaks excellent English. The Tor is located close to the station and the lake.

ON THE LEFT BANK

HOTEL CENTRAL, 2, rue de la Rôtisserie, 1204 Genève. Tel. 022/21-45-94. 29 rms (all with bath). TV **Bus:** 5 from Gare Cornavin to Bel-Air.

$ Rates (including continental breakfast): SFr 78–90 ($55.70–$64.30) single; SFr 90–120 ($64.30–$85.70) double; SFr 130–150 ($92.85–$107.15) triple; SFr 140–170 ($100–$121.40) quad. No credit cards.

Located on the edge of the Old City one block from rue du Marché—one of Geneva's two main shopping streets—the businesslike Hôtel Central is convenient for touring and shopping. The rooms, which are small, are spotlessly clean and have private baths, new carpets, and modern furnishings. The hotel is on the upper floors of an elevator-equipped building with a shopping arcade on the ground floor.

HOTEL DE L'ETOILE, 17, rue des Vieux-Grenadiers, 1205 Genève. Tel. 022/28-72-08. 30 rms (all with shower and toilet). **Bus:** 1, 4, or 44 from Gare Cornavin to Ecole-de-Médecine.

$ Rates: SFr 70 ($50) single; SFr 105 ($75) double; SFr 130 ($92.85) triple. Continental breakfast SFr 7 ($5) extra. EURO, V.

Located in the Plainpalais area, the Hôtel de l'Etoile is much nicer than the street it's on. Refurbished not long ago, the rooms are pleasant and come with shower and toilet. Owners M. and Mme Dousse both speak English.

HOTEL PAX, 68, rue du 31-Décembre, 1207 Genève. Tel. 022/735-44-40. 70 beds. TV **Bus:** 9 from Gare Cornavin to rue du 31-Décembre.

$ Rates: SFr 70 ($50) single without bath, SFr 105 ($75) single with bath; SFr 95 ($67.85) double without bath, SFr 126 ($90) double with bath; SFr 105 ($75) triple without bath, SFr 150 ($107.15) triple with bath. AE, DC, EURO, MC, V.

Not as close to the center as some of the hotels listed here, the Pax is certainly acceptable and moderately priced. Many of the rooms are quite spacious and have large windows. The color TVs in every room cost an additional SFr 7 ($5) per day.

SUPER-BUDGET CHOICES

OPEN ALL YEAR

AUBERGE DE JEUNESSE, 28, rue Rothschild, 1202 Genève. Tel. 022/732-62-60. 350 beds. **Directions:** See below.

$ Rates (including continental breakfast): SFr 66 ($47.15) double with bath for IYHF members, SFr 80 ($57.15) for nonmembers; SFr 79 ($56.40) quad with bath for IYHF members, SFr 86 ($61.40) for nonmembers; SFr 18 ($12.85) per person for IYHF members in a 6-, 8-, or 10-bed dorm, SFr 25 ($17.85) per person for nonmembers. Youth hostel membership costs SFr 30 ($21.40). No credit cards.

Geneva's official youth hostel has an excellent location less than a 15-minute walk from Gare Cornavin and two blocks from the lake. Opened in 1987, it's housed in a former hospital and a modern building designed specifically as a youth hostel. Outstanding features include a large glass-walled and glass-ceilinged lobby, TV lounge, no-smoking library and quiet room, self-catering kitchen, rooms for the disabled, and a self-service restaurant featuring *plats du jour* for only SFr 9 ($6.40). There is a midnight curfew here, and the hostel is also closed from 10am to 4pm.

From Gare Cornavin, turn left and walk six blocks up rue de Lausanne, or take bus no. 1 two stops, turning right two blocks past the bus stop.

ST. BONIFACE CENTER, 14, av. du Mail, 1205 Genève. Tel. 022/28-26-36. 140 beds. **Bus:** 1 from Gare Cornavin to place du Cirque; then walk down avenue du Mail three blocks.

$ Rates (including continental breakfast): SFr 50 ($35.70) single; SFr 75 ($53.55) double; SFr 22 ($15.70) per person in the dorms, SFr 19.50 ($13.90) if you provide your own sheets. No credit cards.

Open all year, the Pension St-Boniface is almost always full, but it's worth a try. There are 140 beds—in dormitories, singles, and doubles. Kitchen facilities are available to guests who want to do their own cooking, and a laundry service is provided for only SFr 2.50 ($1.80) per load.

SUMMER-ONLY ROOMS

CITE UNIVERSITAIRE DE GENEVE, 46, av. Miremont, 1206 Genève. Tel. 022/46-23-55. 550 rms (none with bath). **Bus:** 3 from Gare Cornavin to Cité Universitaire, the last stop.

$ **Rates:** SFr 28 ($20) single, SFr 41 ($29.30) double, for students with official ID card; SFr 34 ($24.30) single, SFr 47 ($33.55) double, for nonstudents. Studios SFr 56 ($40), single or double. There's a SFr 30 ($21.40) refundable key deposit and a three-night minimum stay. Breakfast SFr 5 ($3.55) extra; lunch or dinner, SFr 10 ($7.15). No credit cards. **Open:** July–Sept.

This is the largest and best establishment in this category, open to tourists from July to the end of September. Each room has its own sink, single bed, and desk with chair, and most have fantastic views of the Salève. Studios have small kitchens. Doubles can be arranged by adding another bed to the room. Breakfast, lunch, and dinner are available in the ground-floor cafeteria.

WORTH THE EXTRA BUCKS

HOTEL DE CLOS VOLTAIRE, 49, rue de Lyon, 1203 Genève. Tel. 022/44-70-14. 41 rms.

$ **Rates** (including continental breakfast): SFr 60 ($42.85) single without bath, SFr 85 ($60.70) single with bath; SFr 120 ($85.70) double without bath, SFr 140 ($100) double with bath. AE, DC, EURO, MC, V.

⭐ The Hôtel de Clos Voltaire is an old building on the right bank with green shutters and stucco walls. The hotel is located inside an intimate walled garden with its own gate to the park surrounding the Voltaire Museum, which was once this writer's home. This is the closest you can get to château living on a budget in Geneva. Rue de Lyon starts behind Gare Cornavin.

5. BUDGET DINING

Situated in the middle of Europe and containing a bit of the culture of France and Italy—and many other nations—Geneva offers a large variety in the way of food. However, there are many typically Swiss meals that are exceptional bargains.

Most popular is *fondue* in its three varieties: cheese fondue, into which bread is dipped; beef fondue, in which beef is cooked in a pot of hot oil; and Chinese fondue, in which meat and vegetables are cooked in a broth. One thing you won't find is chocolate fondue. Though they have wonderful chocolate and love fondue, the Swiss leave the combining of the two to chocoholic Americans. Other Swiss specialties include *raclette,* another cheese dish that features melted cheese over potatoes, and *rösti,* a sort of hash-browned potatoes with onions.

To save money it's a good idea to stick to the *plat du jour,* or, if you're very hungry, the *menu complet,* which consists of the plat du jour with a soup or appetizer and a dessert. Plats du jour are often available only at lunch, so to save money you might want to eat a large meal at noon and something light in the evening.

MEALS FOR LESS THAN SFR 12 [$8.55]
ON THE LEFT BANK

CAFE DU MOLARD, 4, place du Molard. Tel. 28-35-53.
Cuisine: ITALIAN.

$ Prices: SFr 11–37 ($7.85–$26.40). AE, DC, EURO, V.
Open: Daily 10:30am–midnight.

If you are craving good old-fashioned Italian cooking, try this very popular restaurant, which features fresh, homemade pasta dishes as well as 15 different types of pizza. This is a very popular place for young Genevans, who often start a night out on the town here. In the summer you can eat at a table out on the square.

GRAND PASSAGE, 50, rue du Rhône. Tel. 310-66-11.
Cuisine: SWISS.
$ Prices: SFr 6–16 ($4.30–$11.40). AE, DC, EURO, V.
Open: Mon–Fri 8:30am–6:30pm, Sat 8am–5pm.

This department-store cafeteria is the place to stop for an inexpensive lunch in the heart of Geneva's shopping district. Don't confuse this self-service restaurant with the slightly more expensive Restaurant Francais in the same building. Here you can get tasty plats du jour for about SFr 12 ($8.55). At the place du Molard entrance to the store there are several booths selling Middle Eastern fast food for about SFr 7.50 ($5.35).

LA ZOFAGE, 6, rue des Voisins. Tel. 29-51-13.
Cuisine: SWISS.
$ Prices: SFr 8–15 ($5.70–$10.70). No credit cards.
Open: Daily 11am–midnight.

This is one of the least expensive restaurants in the city. Down a few steps from street level, the restaurant is frequented mostly by students and is simply furnished. The plat du jour costs about SFr 12 ($8.55) and might be chicken Cordon Bleu with vegetables or potatoes, or cannelloni au gratin with a salad.

ON THE RIGHT BANK

Although the greatest concentration of budget restaurants is on the left bank, two establishments on the right bank offer excellent deals.

MIGROS, 41, rue des Pâquis. Tel. 731-79-50.
Cuisine: SWISS.
$ Prices: SFr 6.80–15 ($4.85–$10.70). No credit cards.
Open: Mon 1–6:45pm, Tues–Fri 8am–6:45pm, Sat 8am–5:45pm.

This branch of the popular Migros department store found all over Geneva is only a five-minute walk from rue du Mont-Blanc. Here the plats du jour start at SFr 6.80 ($4.85), and each day there are a number of unusual and very inexpensive specials such as paella or boeuf bourguignon with rice pilaf.

On the left bank there is a Migros at 29, rue de la Terrassière; tram no. 12 stops right in front.

RESTAURANT MANORA, 4, rue Cornavin. Tel. 731-31-46.
Cuisine: SWISS.
$ Prices: SFr 6.50–16 ($4.65–$11.40). No credit cards.
Open: Daily 9am–9pm.

FROMMER'S SMART TRAVELER: RESTAURANTS

VALUE-CONSCIOUS TRAVELERS SHOULD
TAKE ADVANTAGE OF THE FOLLOWING:

1. Fondue, raclette, and rösti, Swiss meals that are exceptional bargains.
2. The *plat du jour*, or, if you're very hungry, the *menu complet*.

⭐ Manora is a large self-service restaurant that's packed with people day and night. It's one of Geneva's best. The reason for its popularity is its prices. Plats du jour start at an incredibly low SFr 8 ($5.70) for risotto and a vegetable. A filling medium-sized plate from the outstanding salad bar costs only SFr 7.50 ($5.35), and even a large plate of entrecôte steak with fries and a vegetable costs only SFr 16 ($11.40). A large selection of cakes and desserts will tempt you.

MEALS FOR LESS THAN SFR 19 [$13.55]
ON THE LEFT BANK

AU CARNIVORE, 30, place du Bourg-de-Four. Tel. 311-87-58.
   Cuisine: SWISS.
$ **Prices:** SFr 15–40 ($10.70–$28.55). AE, EURO, MC, V.
   Open: Daily 11am–11:30pm.
The bilevel place du Bourg-de-Four is one of the most beautiful squares in the Old City, and a great dining spot popular with students, businesspeople, and tourists. As its name implies, Au Carnivore specializes in meats. Although many of the menu items are beyond our budget, there are a few low-priced items that are excellent deals. Try the tagliatelle arrabbiate for SFr 18 ($12.85) or the entrecôte with french fries for SFr 29 ($20.70).

CAFE BOURG-DE-FOUR, 13, place Bourg-de-Four. Tel. 20-01-98.
   Cuisine: SWISS.
$ **Prices:** SFr 13.50–22 ($9.65–$15.70). No credit cards.
   Open: Daily noon–10pm.
⭐ This little restaurant is an excellent place to try rösti, a Swiss version of potato pancakes. You can get this typical dish topped with two eggs for SFr 13 ($9.30) or topped with ham and two eggs for SFr 15 ($10.70). They also have large salads, a plat du jour for both lunch and dinner, and Yugoslav dishes in the evenings.

CAFE DES ANTIQUAIRES, 35, Grand' Rue. Tel. 28-50-98.
   Cuisine: SWISS.
$ **Prices:** SFr 13–20 ($9.30–$14.30). No credit cards.
   Open: Mon–Fri 7am–midnight, Sat
Close to the Hôtel de Ville (City Hall) is this small dark café popular with locals, who get their own large reserved table just inside the front door (don't sit down at the table with the black wrought-iron ashtray). The house specialty is cheese fondue for a reasonable SFr 17 ($12.15), and there are also plats du jour for about SFr 15 ($10.71). Be sure to have a glass of kirsch after your meal to help digest all that cheese—the Swiss would hardly dream of having fondue without this sweet apéritif. In fact, they often have their kirsch in the middle of the meal, calling it "coupe de milieu."

DENT DE LION, 25, rue des Eaux-Vives. Tel. 736-72-98.
   Cuisine: VEGETARIAN.
$ **Prices:** SFr 14–23 ($10–$16.40). No credit cards.
   Open: Mon–Sat noon–10pm.
This small vegetarian restaurant is always packed at lunch with local businesspeople who wedge themselves into the tiny tables. A plat du jour is SFr 15 ($10.70) and the menu complet, which features the same main dish with a soup and a dessert included, is SFr 20 ($14.30). The plat du jour might be tofu Stroganoff served on a large mound of brown rice with a salad on the side.

LA CAVE VALAISANNE, Chalet Suisse, place du Cirque. Tel. 28-12-36.
   Cuisine: SWISS.
$ **Prices:** SFr 12.50–20 ($8.90–$14.30). AE, CB, DC, EURO, MC, V.
   Open: Daily 11am–1am.
This is a very popular Swiss restaurant where the specialty is fondue. They offer numerous varieties of this cook-it-yourself meal, with the basic cheese fondue being the house favorite. Raclette is also available. Their "lunch-affaire"—oeuf mayonnaise or soup, an entrée, and ice cream—for SFr 17 ($12.15) is a very good deal.

RESTAURANT LE PRINCE, 16, rue des Voisins. Tel. 329-85-44.
   Cuisine: ITALIAN/SWISS. **Bus:** 1 from Gare Cornavin to the Pont d'Arve stop.
   $ Prices: SFr 13 ($9.30)–SFr 15.50 ($11.10); tourist menu SFr 27 ($19.30). AE, MC, V.
   Open: Mon–Sat noon–2pm and 6:30–10pm.
Attached to the budget Hôtel le Prince is this wonderful family-run establishment. Everything here is fresh. Plats du jour, served for lunch and dinner, include beef bourguignon with French fries and lamb chops with salad. A special tourist menu is offered; soup, a main course, dessert, wine, a soft drink, and coffee are included. Always crowded, mostly with students, the restaurant is highly recommended.

TAVERNE DE LA MADELEINE, 20, rue Toutes-Ames. Tel. 28-40-32.
   Cuisine: SWISS.
   $ Prices: SFr 11–20 ($7.85–$14.30). No credit cards.
   Open: Mon–Fri 11:45am–7:30pm, Sat 11:45am–2pm.
✪   The simple, cozy Taverne de la Madeleine is the oldest restaurant in Geneva. It's tucked into a small terrace below the Cathédrale de St-Pierre and across the street from the much smaller Madeleine Church. Although it doesn't serve alcohol, it's still very popular, especially at lunch. The restaurant offers several daily specials, including two vegetarian meals. Try the succulent little filets of the Lake Geneva perch, with salad and a huge pile of fries, for SFr 19.50 ($13.90). Large salads with ham, bacon, eggs, and cheese are SFr 16 ($11.40), while the vegetarian plats du jour average SFr 13–16 ($9.30–$11.40).

PICNIC SUPPLIES & WHERE TO EAT THEM

Picnics are your best budget-dining bet in Geneva, and with plenty of beautiful parks around the city, try to enjoy at least one picnic while you're here. Moreover, shopping for picnic supplies can be one of the highlights of your trip if you pick them up at the **Halle de Rive** on place du Rive on the left bank. This huge marketplace extends through the whole block and is filled with all kinds of delicacies. Stroll through the aisles before making your choices. On market days, Wednesday and Saturday, the place du Rive fills with stalls as farmers from all over the region display and sell the most beautiful produce. In the huge Halle de Rive you'll find dozens of stalls selling fresh breads, cheese, hams, and sausages by the 100 grams or even by the slice. Pick up some beautiful, delicious fresh fruit and a bottle of wine, and you're all set.

WORTH THE EXTRA BUCKS

LES ARMURES, 1, rue du Puits-Saint-Pierre. Tel. 310-34-42.
   Cuisine: SWISS.
   $ Prices: SFr 17–32 ($12.15–$22.85). AE, CB, DC, EURO, MC, V.
   Open: Lunch daily 11:45am–3pm; dinner daily 6–11:45pm.
✪   In the heart of the Old City, beside the arsenal, is a favorite of Genevans. This two-story restaurant is decorated with suits of armor, swords, shields, and lances, like a real armory. Although there is a wide assortment of pizza, costing only SFr 12–15 ($8.55–$10.70), Swiss dishes are the specialty here: fondue, raclette, and viande séchée (air-dried beef) for SFr 16 to 22 ($11.10–$15.70). Another popular Swiss specialty is choucroute garni, a dish of sauerkraut accompanied by several types of ham and sausage, for SFr 18 ($12.85).

6. ATTRACTIONS

SUGGESTED ITINERARIES

IF YOU HAVE ONE DAY   For an overview of Geneva, head first to the Old City. Strolling the narrow cobblestone lanes and climbing the stairways of this once-

fortified city on a hill provides a glimpse into the medieval history of Geneva. In the afternoon, head over to the right bank for a visit to the Palais des Nations or the Red Cross Museum, two institutions representative of Geneva's international spirit. Save time to stroll through the lakeside parks and view the jet d'eau and the flower clock, both of which are the symbols of Geneva.

IF YOU HAVE TWO DAYS In the morning visit another of Geneva's fine museums, such as the Watch and Clock Museum or the Museum of Art and History, and view the Reformation Monument below the walls of the Old City. In the afternoon try to take a lake cruise to see the beautiful surroundings of Geneva.

IF YOU HAVE THREE DAYS Take a trip to the Alps for some stunning vistas or maybe even some skiing. Mont Blanc, the continent's rooftop, is possible in a long day, or the Salève, which can be reached much more conveniently. Both are in France, so be sure to take your passport.

IF YOU HAVE FIVE DAYS Geneva's lesser-known museums—the Musée d'Instruments Anciens de Musique, the Collections Baur, the Voltaire Museum—may entice you. And then there are the parks, such as the Jardin Botanique. Also try to visit the suburb of Carouge, an unusual old enclave within the modern city. Another possibility is an all-day excursion to the Jura Mountains and the Genevan countryside, or to Lausanne or Montreux, two beautiful cities on Lake Geneva.

TOP ATTRACTIONS

THE OLD CITY

With its narrow cobblestone streets and tiny stairways, the Old City of Geneva is a great place to stroll around. Pretty fountains dot the streets, and colorful Swiss and Genevan flags wave between the old buildings. There are art galleries and inviting bistros, and bibliophiles will appreciate the bookshops selling rare books. Geneva was for many centuries a walled city, and you can see part of the walls by walking along rue de la Croix Rouge.

Wandering is the best strategy for knowing the Old City, but there are also several sites you may want to visit: Calvin's church, the 12th-century **Cathédrale de St-Pierre;** the 16th-century **Hôtel de Ville** (City Hall), where the Red Cross was founded; the **place du Bourg-de-Four,** which was probably the ancient Roman forum and today is filled with sidewalk cafés; the **Maison Tavel,** Geneva's oldest house and now a museum; and the old **City Arsenal,** with its covered patio, wall mosaics, and cannons.

MAISON TAVEL, 6, rue du Puits-Saint-Pierre. Tel. 28-29-00.
This museum is located in Geneva's oldest house. One of the most interesting exhibits is a large model of the city circa 1850. Made of copper and nickel, the model was built by one man as a hobby. There is also an unusual display of ornately carved doors from several old houses.
   Admission: Free.
   Open: Tues–Sun 10am–5pm.

OUTSIDE THE OLD CITY

MUSEE DE L'HORLOGERIE ET DE L'EMAILLERIE [Watch and Clock Museum], 15, route de Malagnou. Tel. 736-74-12.

A visit to Geneva would not be complete without a trip to this museum to see the extensive collection of clocks, watches, enamel watch cases, and musical snuff boxes. Exquisite clocks and watches that are works of art rather than mere timepieces are displayed on two floors of an old château surrounded by a quiet park. The ticking of timepieces immediately greets you upon entering, and as you wander through the rooms you'll find yourself rushing from one clock to the next as they each mark the hours, half hours, and quarter hours with sonorous chimes and dancing figures.

Admission: Free.
Open: Wed–Mon 10am–5pm.

FLOWER CLOCK, Jardin Anglais.

For years Geneva and watches have been synonymous, so it's fitting that one of the sights most associated with this city is the flower clock in the Jardin Anglais (English Garden). All year this clock ticks away with as many as 6,300 flowers filling the area within its 50-foot circumference. The Jardin Anglais is on the left bank at the foot of the pont du Mont-Blanc. From this spot you can walk through one park after another for more than a mile along the left bank of Lake Geneva.

JET D'EAU, quai des Eaux-Vives.

No other sight is more representative of Geneva than this huge fountain of water that rises 390 feet into the air. Visible from all over the city, the jet d'eau rises from the Eaux-Vives Jetty on the left bank but is best seen from the right bank with the Alps and the Old City as a backdrop. The jet d'eau pumps 132 gallons of water per second into the air, and at any given moment 7 tons of water is suspended above the waters of Lake Geneva. The water jet operates from the beginning of March until the first Sunday of October, but may be turned off when the weather is bad.

PALAIS DES NATIONS, avenue de la Paix. Tel. 736-60-11, ext. 4539.

This massive art deco building was built between 1929 and 1936 as the headquarters of the League of Nations, the predecessor of the United Nations, and today it is the U.N.'s European headquarters. Inside are huge conference halls and assembly rooms. An organized tour of the palais is available in several languages, which will give you an idea of the large role Geneva plays in international peace keeping. Although this is the center of the U.N. in Geneva, there are many more affiliated organizations all over the city. Be sure to call ahead to find out when there will be a tour in the language you prefer.

Admission: SFr 8 ($5.70) adults, SFr 6 ($4.30) students, SFr 3.50 ($2.50) children, free for children under age 6.
Open: July–Aug, daily 9am–noon and 2–6pm; Sept–June, daily 10am–noon and 2–4pm. **Bus:** 8 or F from Gare Cornavin.

MUSEE INTERNATIONAL DE LA CROIX-ROUGE ET DU CROISSANT-ROUGE [International Red Cross and Red Cresent Museum], 17, av. de la Paix. Tel. 734-52-48.

Opened in November 1988, the very modern International Red Cross and Red Crescent Museum is directly across the street from the visitors' entrance to the Palais des Nations. The museum chronicles the history of the Red Cross from its founding in Geneva in 1863 by Henri Dunant. The exhibits are minimal while numerous audiovisual presentations, including film footage of wars and natural disasters, give visitors a dramatic look at the work that the Red Cross does. This is the most expensive museum in Geneva, but definitely worth the expense. Few museums anywhere are as moving.

Admission: SFr 8 ($5.70) adults, SFr 4 ($2.85) students.
Open: Wed–Mon 10am–5pm. **Bus:** 8 or F from Gare Cornavin.

MONUMENT DE LA REFORMATION, promenade des Bastions.

⭐ Located on the promenade des Bastions below the highest remaining walls of the Old City, this massive wall more than 330 feet long commemorates one of Geneva's most important historical events—the Protestant Reformation, as preached by John Calvin. Construction of the wall was begun in 1909 on the 400th anniversary of the birth of Calvin, who, though not born in Geneva, lived here for nearly 30 years in the mid-16th century. In the center are four massive statues of Calvin and fellow Reformation leaders Farel, Beza, and Scottish reformer John Knox. On each side of these central figures are smaller statues of important Protestant figures from other nations.

Admission: Free.
Tram: 12 to place Neuve.

MORE ATTRACTIONS

INSTITUT ET MUSEE VOLTAIRE, 25, rue des Délices. Tel. 344-71-33.

From 1755 to 1760 the French philosopher Voltaire lived in Geneva and his home is now a museum. Four rooms display original documents relating to Voltaire's life, first editions of his writings, and other manuscripts, prints, and objects from the 18th century. One of the highlights of the museum is a life-size statue of Voltaire, dressed in a suit once owned by the great philosopher and sitting at his former desk.

Admission: Free.
Open: Mon–Fri 2–5pm. **Bus:** 7 to Délices or 6 to Prairie.

MUSEE HISTORIQUE DE LA REFORMATION ET MUSEE JEAN-JACQUES ROUSSEAU, University Library, promenade des Bastions. Tel. 20-82-66.

If you are interested in the philosopher Rousseau and can read French, you'll find this two-room museum quite interesting. Documents pertaining to the Reformation, portraits of important figures, and a case filled with busts of Rousseau are among the items on display here. In an adjoining room you'll also see a folio from a 2nd-century manuscript of Homer's *Iliad*. The museum is on the ground floor of the library, straight ahead as you enter. If the doors are locked during normal hours, ask at the desk to be let in.

Admission: Free.
Open: Mon–Fri 9am–noon and 2–5pm, Sat 9am–noon. **Tram:** 12 to place Neuve; the museum is inside the park on the right and directly across from the Reformation Museum.

MUSEE D'ART ET D'HISTOIRE, 2, rue Charles-Galland. Tel. 29-00-11.

This is Geneva's largest museum, housing a wide variety of art and antiquities. Exhibits range from Egyptian mummies to entire rooms from Swiss châteaux, complete with paneling, antique heating systems, furniture, and the art that was in the rooms when they were acquired by the museum. Wandering from one lavishly furnished room to the next provides an excellent glimpse of the château lifestyle. Another large hall contains all manner of arms and armor from past centuries, including one of the folding ladders used by the Savoyards to scale the walls of the city when they attacked Geneva in 1602. Upstairs in the galleries, several rooms are devoted to turn-of-the-century Swiss artist Ferdinand Hodler. His Alpine landscapes in shades of lavender and blue are especially beautiful. The museum is located three blocks from place du Bourg-de-Four in the Old City.

Admission: Free.
Open: Tues–Sun 10am–5pm.

SITE ARCHEOLOGIQUE DE ST-PIERRE, at the Cathédrale de Saint-Pierre. Tel. 29-42-80.

Right in the center of Geneva's Old City you'll find one of the largest archeological

SWITZERLAND

★ Bern

● Geneva

Cathédral Saint-Pierre ⑨
Eglise Russe ⑦
Flower Clock ④
Hôtel-de-Ville ⑩
Jardin Anglais ③
Jet d'Eau ②
Maison Tavel ⑪
Monument Brunswick ⑤
Monument de la
Réformation ⑫
Musée d'Art et
d'Histoire ⑧
Musée d'Ethnographie ⑭
Musée de l'Horlogerie ⑥
Palais des Nations ①
Université ⑬

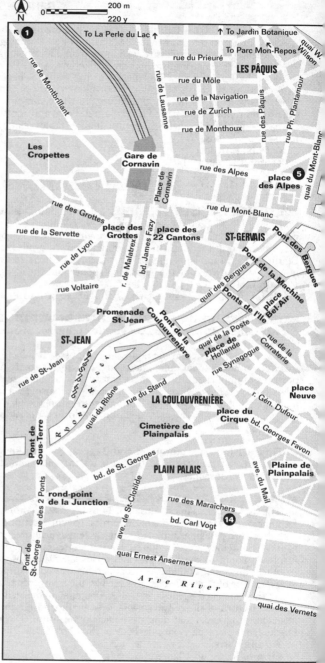

GENEVA

parc la Grange

ave. William Favre

LES EAUX-VIVES

Lake Geneva

rue des Eaux-Vives

rue de Montchoisy

quai Gustave Ador

rte. de Frontenex

Gare des
Eaux-Vives

promenade du Lac

3

place du
Jargonnant

rte. de Chêne

Pont du Mont-Blanc

4

Jardin
Anglais

place des
Eaux-Vives

ave. de Frontenex

VILLEREUSE

quai Général Guisan

rue du Rhône

rue d'Italie

rond-point
de Rive

carrefour
de Rive

rue de la Terrassière

CONTAMINES

rue de la Croix-a'or

rue de Rive

rue de Villereuse

6

rue F. Hodler

rte. Malagnou

11

Grand Rue

9

rue des Granges

10

place du
Bourg-de-Four

rue Jaques Dalcroze

8

bd. Helvétique

7

rue F. le Fort

rue le Fort

FLORISSANT

12

ST-LEGER

rte. de Florissant

promenade des Bastions

bd. des Tranchées

MALOMBRÉ

13

rue de Candolle

av. J. Crosnier

Parc
A. Bertrand

rond-point de
Plainpalais

bd. des Philosophes

ave. Peschier

place des
Philosophes

ave. Henri Dunant

rue de Carouge

Pont d'Arve

bd. du

rue Prévost-Martin

bd. de la Cluse

ave. de la Roseraie

Chemin Thury

ave. de Champel

rue Dancet

ch. des Crêts

ch. des Crêts

bd. des Acacias

quai Charles Page

Arve River

rue Barthélémy Menn

Church

■+

Post Office

⊠

2

sites in Europe. The cathedral itself dates only from 1160, but during a renovation project evidence was unearthed of a church on this site as long ago as the 5th century. Visitors can now walk through the ages beneath the cathedral and an adjacent chapel and street. Layer upon layer of history has been exposed and left as if the archeologists were still digging. Old wells and a large mosaic floor are evidence of Roman occupation of the site. Located beneath the cathedral, the archeological site has its own entrance, to the right side of the cathedral's main steps.

Admission: SFr 5 ($3.55) adults, SFr 3 ($2.15) children.
Open: Tues–Fri 10am–1pm and 2–6pm.

MUSEE D' INSTRUMENTS ANCIENS DE MUSIQUE, 23, rue Lefort. Tel. 46-95-65.

Musicians and anyone else who appreciates the artistry of instrument making will want to visit this small museum beside the Russian church. More than 350 musical instruments, primarily from the 16th to the 19th century, are on display here, most of them in working condition. Guides play many of the instruments during tours of the museum, and monthly concerts using the museum's instruments are held from October to June.

Admission: SFr 2 ($1.40) adults, free for students.
Open: Tues 3–6pm, Thurs 10am–noon and 3–6pm, Fri 8–10pm, and by appointment.

EGLISE RUSSE [Russian Church], rue des Délices.

Directly across the street from the Museum of Ancient Musical Instruments is this little, jewel-box-like church. With its gold domes and spires, the church seems oddly out of place in Geneva. It is especially beautiful at night when bright lights illuminate the gold domes.

Admission: Free.
Open: Daily.

COLLECTIONS BAUR, 8, rue Munier-Romilly. Tel. 46-17-29.

In a former private home near the Museum of Art and History you'll find this excellent collection of Asian art and ceramics. The collection displays more than 1,000 years of Chinese ceramics as well as exhibiting beautiful antique jade pieces. Watch for the large jade vase with its high-relief images. Japanese swords, lacquer boxes, and objects for tea ceremonies are also on display.

Admission: SFr 5 ($3.55) adults, SFr 2.50 ($1.80) students.
Open: Tues–Sun 2–6pm. **Bus:** 1 to Florissant.

CAROUGE

Once a separate village on the far side of the narrow Arve River, Carouge was incorporated into the city of Geneva in the early 19th century. However, despite the presence of modern buildings on all sides, Carouge still manages to maintain the feel of a small village much removed from the city. Of particular interest is the Italian **architecture** here, reminiscent of the island of Sardinia, which ruled Carouge in the 18th century. Most of the village's old buildings have been restored and now contain shops, boutiques, restaurants, and discos.

Wednesday and Saturday are **market days** in Carouge and an especially fun time to visit. Farmers sell their produce under the curiously trimmed plane trees on the place du Marché, in the center of which is a small fountain.

You may also want to visit the **Museum of Carouge,** 2, place de Sardaigne (tel. 342-33-83), which contains artifacts pertaining to the history of the village as well as temporary exhibits by local artists. It's open Tuesday through Sunday from 2 to 6pm, and admission is free.

PARKS & GARDENS

The founders of the city of Geneva are to be congratulated for their forethought in preserving the banks of Lake Geneva. Stretching along both banks of the lake are several miles of promenades connected to several parks. Many of these parks have been created from the grounds of ancient châteaux, while others surround the modern buildings of the international organizations headquartered here.

ON THE RIGHT BANK   Formerly the grounds of a château, the ☼ **Parc de l'Ariana** surrounds the Palais des Nations on the right bank. When the last owner of the château died without an heir, he donated the grounds to the city to be used as a park, on the condition that it be opened to the public forever. Today you can stroll beneath centuries-old cypress and cedar trees and enjoy the peace and quiet surrounding the United Nations' European headquarters.

Directly adjacent to this park is the **Jardin Botanique,** where thousands of trees, shrubs, and flowers from all over the world are on display.

ON THE LEFT BANK   On the left bank, you can walk along quai Gustave-Ador past the jet d'eau and on to the **Parc La Grange** and the adjacent **Parc des Eaux-Vives.** Here you will find a large rose garden and a beautiful 18th-century château that is now a popular and expensive restaurant. If it's a warm day and your stroll through the parks has you longing for a dip in the cool waters of the lake, continue another 100 yards or so beyond the Parc des Eaux-Vives to **Genève-Plage,** Geneva's favorite beach.

SPECIAL-INTEREST SIGHTSEEING

John Calvin, who settled in Geneva in 1536, changed the city forever when he split from the Roman Catholic church and devoted himself to the Reformation. For centuries afterward, Geneva was forced to defend itself against the frequent attacks of its Roman Catholic neighbors who were bent on returning Geneva to the fold. Anyone interested in the Geneva of Calvin can arrange for a special guided tour with the Geneva Tourist Office. The tour visits the Calvin Auditorium where he preached, the Reformation Wall, and other sites associated with this famous religious reformer.

People interested in philosophy and literature will want to visit two museums dedicated to Geneva's other famous residents, **Jean-Jacques Rousseau and Voltaire.** See "More Attractions," above, for more information about these two small museums.

The Argentine writer **Jorge Luís Borges** lived in Geneva as a child and returned here in his mid-80s. He died in 1986 and is buried in the Cimetière de Plainpalais, on the left bank.

WALKING TOURS

Geneva is divided into two very distinct sections—the old and the new. The Old City preserves Geneva's medieval history with its narrow streets and houses dating from the 13th century. Because buses are not allowed in the Old City, it is necessary to get out and walk.

The **Geneva Tourist Office** offers a recorded tour for a cassette player that allows you to hear the history of the Old City as you explore at your own pace. In about 2½ hours the recorded tour covers 2,000 years of Genevan history and provides information on 26 points of interest. For SFr 10 ($7.15) you will be provided with the tape and a map of the Old City. If you don't have your own tape player, you can use one of the tourist office's, but you'll have to present your passport and leave a SFr-50 ($35.70) refundable deposit. Pick up the tape at the Tourist Information Center in Cornavin Station.

An alternative to this self-guided tour is the two-hour guided tour offered by the tourist office on Monday, Wednesday, and Friday at 5pm from June to September. The cost of this tour is SFr 10 ($7.15) for adults, SFr 7 ($5) for students, and SFr 4 ($2.85) for children under 12. In addition to visiting the major sites in the Old City, this tour includes a visit to a private collection of 18th-century furniture and Chinese cloisonné, and ends with a sampling of Genevan wines. The tour starts in front of the Town Hall at 2, rue de l'Hôtel-de-Ville.

In addition to these two tours, there are specialized walking tours of the Old City focusing on different periods of history. Contact the Geneva Tourist Office Information Desk in Cornavin Station for details.

BUS TOURS

Keytours, 7, rue des Alpes (tel. 731-41-40), on the right bank, offers a two-hour bus tour pointing out the highlights of both the left and right banks of Geneva daily at 10am and 2pm from April to October. In winter (November to March) the tour runs only once a day, and in spring and fall, twice a day. The tour quickly shows you the highlights of Geneva and includes a brief walk through the Old City. You will see the shores of the lake with their numerous parks, the flower clock, the jet d'eau (if you visit between March and October), the modern buildings of Geneva's international organizations, monuments, and commercial centers. The cost of the tour is SFr 23 ($16.40) for adults and SFr 12 ($8.55) for children.

SPECIAL & FREE EVENTS

Despite its reputation as one of Europe's most expensive cities, Geneva has a wealth of **free concerts** and other events throughout the year, and especially in the summer. Along the quays that line both sides of the lake and in the parks that extend back from the quays there are regular concerts in bandshells and on the lawns. On Saturday nights there are **concerts and organ recitals** at the Cathédrale de St-Pierre in the center of the Old City, and at the much smaller Eglise de St-Germain, only a block away on the Grand' Rue, there are concerts on Sunday and Monday at 6pm in the summer. For a listing of events around town, check *This Week in Geneva* or *The Geneva List of Events* (where free events are marked by a small circle with a dot in the middle).

Geneva also has numerous festivals throughout the year, the most popular of which are the **Fêtes de Genève** during the first week of August and **l'Escalade** held each year in mid-December. The former celebration is marked by revelry and numerous free concerts all over the city. L'Escalade celebrates Geneva's defeat of invading forces in 1602. The festival features hundreds of people in period costumes marching through the streets by torchlight, children in Halloween-like costumes, special meals, and candies. Both events are rather a departure for staid Geneva, and they offer a glimpse of Genevans when they let their hair down.

7. SAVVY SHOPPING

BEST BUYS   Watches, knives, cheese, and chocolate are among your best buys in Geneva. These are the products for which Switzerland is famous, and you'll find them here in abundance. Check prices carefully, though: Unfortunately many Swiss watches are currently cheaper in the United States than they are in Switzerland. Swiss army knives are still a good deal, and as for chocolate—well, Swiss chocolate is incomparable and just isn't the same when you buy it in another country, so indulge yourself while you're here.

The **Chocolatier du Rhône,** at 3, rue de la Confédération, with its own tiny café, sells what many consider the best chocolate in the world. A pound of their delectable product costs around SFr 49 ($28.55), but you don't have to buy such a large quantity. Pick and choose a few of your favorites. Make sure you try their prize-winning mocca glacé. A small assortment will cost less than SFr 15.50 ($11.05).

Geneva's left-bank shopping area is along the exclusive **rue du Rhône** and adjacent streets. Here you'll find shop after shop of designer fashions and expensive watches. Along the winding streets of the **Old City,** you'll find antiques stores and galleries.

For Swiss army knives and watches (if the dollar strengthens), stroll along the pedestrians-only **rue du Mont-Blanc** on the right bank. Shop window after shop window is filled with an endless assortment of watches, knives, and other souvenirs and all at comparable prices.

Before you head out for a day of shopping, remember that shops in Geneva don't open until 1pm on Monday and many of the smaller shops close for lunch between noon and 2pm.

MARKETS   A rare experience is a visit to a Swiss **street market** offering the most perfect produce you'll ever see. You'll find these bustling and beautiful markets near the Cours de Rive on Wednesday and Saturday and in Carouge on place du Marché on Saturday.

Wednesday and Saturday are the days for Geneva's large and busy **flea market,** which is located on place de Plainpalais. In the summer there is a **book market** on place de la Madeleine on the edge of the Old City below the Cathédrale de St-Pierre. In the winter months you are likely to find crafts from all over the world on this square. If you're looking for **local crafts,** you'll find them for sale on rue du Rhône near place du Molard on Thursday.

8. EVENING ENTERTAINMENT

Geneva is not known for its nightlife. Very few plays are performed in English, and there is very little in the way of live popular music. There are, however, regular ballet, opera, and classical-music performances, as you would expect from such a sophisticated city. The tourist office's monthly *List of Events* has very thorough listings.

THE PERFORMING ARTS
CLASSICAL MUSIC & BALLET

VICTORIA HALL, 14, rue du Général-Dufour. Tel. 28-81-21.
This is Geneva's main venue for classical-music performances.
Prices: Tickets, SFr 15–25 ($10.70–$17.85).

GRAND-THEATRE DE GENEVE, place Neuve. Tel. 311-23-11.
This is another hall to try for classical-music performances.
Prices: Tickets, SFr 18–90 ($12.85–$64.30) for opera, SFr 14–75 ($10–$53.55) for ballet.

FOLK, ROCK & JAZZ

For free live jazz, try **Halles de l'Ile,** place de l'Ile (tel. 21-52-21), a sophisticated restaurant on an island in the middle of the Rhône River. The building was formerly a marketplace and it features a splendid location with large windows opening onto the rushing blue-green waters of the river. Drinks start at SFr 4 ($2.85) for beer or wine. Open Monday through Saturday from 8pm to midnight.

MOVIES

Read the listings carefully before you go to the movies. Movies are shown both dubbed into French and in the original language with French subtitles. If the original language of the film you are attending happens to be German and you speak neither German nor French, you'll be out of luck. American and English films are usually shown with subtitles at 6:45 and 10pm. Check the listings in *Geneva This Week.* Subtitled films carry the notation "V.o.s.-tit" ("Version originale, sous-titres"). Tickets cost SFr 14 ($10).

BARS & DISCOS

Your best option for bars and discos is the area known as **Carouge** (take tram no. 12). Here, on rue Vautier just off place du Marché you'll find a half dozen or more bars and discos that feature live or recorded rock music. Admission is generally free or only a few francs. Drink prices vary, generally SFr 4–15 ($2.85–$10.70), depending on the night's entertainment.

9. EASY EXCURSIONS

Geneva is surrounded by water and mountains, and if you are visiting for more than a day, try to make an excursion to the Alps or cruise around Lake Geneva on one of the many excursion boats that ply the blue-green waters every summer. If you are in town for three days or more, try to do both a mountain trip and a lake trip.

THE SALEVE Standing on Geneva's right bank gazing across at the Old City on the left bank, you cannot help but be awed by the massive wall of rock that rises at the city's back. This is the Salève, which rises nearly 4,500 feet and commands a spectacular view of Geneva, the lake, the Rhône River, and miles of French and Swiss countryside. To the south the panorama of the Alps with Mont-Blanc rising above the surrounding peaks, and to the north are the Jura Mountains. The peak of the Salève is reached by cable car from the base of the mountain in only three minutes. At the top is a modern observatory, restaurant, and walking and cross-country ski trails. Because the Salève is across the French border, you'll need to bring your passport with you. However, it's not necessary to change any money for this excursion; they will accept your Swiss francs at the cable-car ticket window. The round-trip fare is SFr 14.50 ($10.35) for adults and SFr 8.60 ($6.15) for children and senior citizens.

To reach the Salève, take bus no. 8 from Geneva to the last stop at the town of Veyrier, which is still on the Swiss side of the border. When you get off the bus, you'll see the border station. Walk through and then follow the signs marked TELEPHERIQUE. It's less than a 10-minute walk.

CHAMONIX & MONT-BLANC If the Salève whets your appetite for more mountains, a trip into the heart of the French Alps may be just the thing you need. The ski resort of Chamonix at 3,370 feet lies at the foot of the Mont-Blanc massif, which rises to 15,625 feet. Surrounding Chamonix are dozens of lesser peaks and glaciers. Although most popular in the winter months when skiers flock to the many slopes, this area is beautiful year round. In summer flowers fill the green meadows and tiny Alpine lakes sparkle in the sunlight. But whether you go in summer or winter, pick a sunny day for your visit, for it is under clear skies that you can most fully appreciate the views of the surrounding peaks.

Trains from Geneva to Chamonix leave not from Cornavin Station but from the Eaux-Vives Station on the left bank. Tram no. 12 stops in front of this station, but to take this tram you must first be on the left bank, since it doesn't cross the river. There is no direct train to Chamonix from Geneva; it's necessary to change trains twice. Your best trains to take for a day in the mountains leave Geneva at 6:40am, 8:26am, 2:43pm, and 5:35pm. The entire journey takes about 2½ hours; round-trip fare is SFr 46 ($32.85).

From Chamonix, there are three possible ascents out of the valley, all of which present unsurpassed views of peaks and glaciers. The longest and most expensive of these is the ascent by cable car to L'Aiguille du Midi at 12,500 feet. The trip is in two stages and costs 150 French francs ($27.75) round-trip, or you can choose to stop at the halfway point, Plan de l'Aiguille (7,500 feet), for a round-trip fare of only 60 French francs ($11.10). The last ascent out of the valley is to the resort of Montenvers overlooking the Mer de Glâce glacier, which is nearly 4½ miles long and averages 3,900 feet in width. This is done by electric rack railway. By far the best view and value is from Le Brevent, with its stunning panorama of Mont-Blanc, Chamonix nestled in the valley below, and the fingerlike glaciers that reach down from the peaks.

Expensive all-day tours to Chamonix are offered from Geneva by **Keytours,** 7, rue des Alpes (tel. 731-41-40), with the cost depending on which ascent you make out of the valley. The excursion for SFr 120 ($85.70) includes a trip either to Le Brevent or to La Mer de Glâce. For SFr 142 ($101.40) you will climb to L'Aiguille du Midi, and for SFr 169 ($120.70) you can continue past L'Aiguillle du Midi, again by cable car, to Helbronner Point on the French-Italian border. This is an additional 5.5km (3¼-mile) trip across snowfields and glaciers. Whether you go by train or escorted motorcoach, don't forget to take your passport—Chamonix is in France.

LAKE CRUISES   Lake Geneva is a 45-mile-long, crescent-shaped body of water, the entire north shore and either end of which are in Switzerland, while the south shore is in France. All along both shores are small villages, châteaux, fields, farms, and vineyards, and framing it all are the ever-present mountains, both the Alps and the Juras. There are numerous tours of the lake, ranging from a short 40-minute trip in a little *mouette* (water bus) to all-day cruises of the entire lake on sleek yachts. The 40-minute trip leaves from the dock near the flower clock on the left bank and costs SFr 7 ($5). The castle of Baron M. de Rothschild, the villa of Empress Joséphine, and Diodati Villa where Lord Byron stayed in 1816 are some of the sights pointed out on this brief cruise. A two-hour cruise costing SFr 22 ($15.70) passes more beautiful villas and châteaux and travels as far as the start of the French portion of the lake's south shore. These cruises leave from quai du Mont-Blanc on the right bank at 10:15am and 3pm from March to November. The all-day cruise costs SFr 50 ($35.70) and leaves from the quai du Mont-Blanc at 9:15am and returns at 10:50pm. This cruise is available daily between May 29 and September 25.

INNSBRUCK

Encircled by snowcapped peaks or wildflower-strewn meadows, depending on the season, this small city with only 120,000 people is one of Europe's most scenic places. For much of its history, Innsbruck, the capital of Tyrol, was a major crossroads of the Holy Roman Empire, and still today nearly everyone traveling from Munich to Rome or from Zurich to Vienna by car or train passes through it, making it a convenient stopover. What's more, Innsbruck is an Alpine village in the true sense of the word, with bracing fresh air, narrow cobblestone streets, centuries-old buildings, and mountains on all sides.

The Winter Olympics were held here in 1964 and 1976—and with good reason. It's a skier's mecca year round, because of the Stubai Glacier 10 miles south. Thus while much of the Alps may suffer heavily from lack of snow, in Innsbruck it has been business as usual. In fact, if you want to go skiing in the middle of the summer, this is the place to go. Even if you don't ski you'll be treated to a spectacular Alpine panorama, museums, a picturesque old town, and a relaxing pace of life. If you're tired of big cities, come to Innsbruck to unwind.

1. FROM A BUDGET TRAVELER'S POINT OF VIEW

INNSBRUCK BUDGET BESTS If you're willing to stand up to eat and drink, you can save money: Two wieners and a roll, for which you'll pay 40 S ($3.65) in a sit-down restaurant, costs only 25 S ($2.25) at an *Imbiss* (food stand), and half a liter of beer costs 25 S ($2.25) instead of 30 S ($2.70). And if you order from the posted daily menu (*Tagesgericht*), usually a one-plate meal such as spaghetti bolognese, instead of choosing the same dish from the menu card, you can save up to 26 S ($2.35). Relaxing over a coffee and Sachertorte in one of Innsbruck's open-air coffee shops, such as the Hofgartencafe in the middle of Innsbruck's most beautiful public garden (open in summer daily from 9am to 9pm), is a delightful and inexpensive experience not to be missed.

For bargains on entertainment, check with the Innsbruck Information Office, Burggraben 3 (tel. 5356), to see if any free cultural performances are scheduled for the day: You may discover a free concert outside in a park, or in a church, music hall, or theater. From mid-June to the beginning of September, for example, there's the free Tyrolean Folkloric Evening held outdoors in front of the Goldenes Dachl every Thursday at 8:30pm, featuring Tyrolean music and folk dances. In addition, the

Tyrolean Landesmuseum hosts a concert of old traditional musical instruments twice a month on Sunday at 10am. Contact the tourist office for more information.

WHAT THINGS COST IN INNSBRUCK	U.S. $
Taxi from the airport to the train station	11.80
Public transportation (bus, tram)	1.55
Local telephone call	.09
Double room, with continental breakfast, at Weisses Rössl (deluxe)	94.55
Double room, with continental breakfast, at Pension Steffi (moderate)	52.70
Double room, with continental breakfast, at Pension Paula (budget)	38.20
Lunch for one, without wine, at Al Dente (moderate)	10.00
Lunch for one, without wine, at Zach (budget)	5.90
Dinner for one, without wine, at Schwarzer Adler (deluxe)	20.00
Dinner for one, without wine, at Riese Haymon (moderate)	11.40
Dinner for one, without wine, at Shere Punjab (budget)	8.00
Glass of wine	1.90
Coca-Cola in a restaurant	1.80
Cup of coffee with milk (in a restaurant or coffeehouse with table service)	2.25
Roll of ASA 100 color film, 36 exposures	6.25
Admission to the Tyrolean Folkloric Museum	1.80
Movie ticket (depending on the seat)	6.35–8.20
Theater ticket	13.20

SPECIAL DISCOUNT OPPORTUNITIES   Students and children under 15 pay **reduced admission** (usually 20%–50% off) to museums, cable cars, and the zoo.

Anyone under 26 can obtain considerable savings by buying airline and train tickets at **Ökista** (Student Travel Office), Josef Hirn Strasse 5 (tel. 588997), in the university area, a 20-minute walk from the train station. The office is open Monday through Friday from 9:30am to 5:30pm.

Anyone spending at least three nights in one of Innsbruck's pensions or hotels can become a member of **Club Innsbruck** free of charge, which entitles members to discounts for lifts and cable cars, museums, and several sports facilities, as well as guided hikes and events sponsored by the club. Contact the Innsbruck Information Office for more information.

WORTH THE EXTRA BUCKS   If you're here to ski, take advantage of the **"Stubai Package"** offered by the Innsbruck Information Office for 620 S ($56.35), which includes ski rental, lift tickets, and transportation to and from Stubai Glacier.

Even if you don't ski, it's worth it to take the **cable car to the top of the Hafelekar,** Innsbruck's most impressive mountain—you can't miss seeing it when you arrive by train. A round-trip costs 257 S ($23.35) if you buy it directly at the lift. But you can save 18 S ($1.65) if you purchase your lift ticket at the Innsbruck Information Office at Burggraben or the train station, in which case it costs only 207 S ($21.70). A trip to Innsbruck without a ride up the Hafelekar is like visiting Paris without riding to the top of the Eiffel Tower. For details, see "Easy Excursions," below.

2. PRETRIP PREPARATIONS

DOCUMENTS   Citizens of the United States, Britain, Canada, Australia, and New Zealand need only a valid passport for stays of up to three months.

WHAT TO PACK   For your ideal wardrobe, see the Munich chapter. However, keep in mind that temperatures tend to be a bit brisker here. You will definitely need a heavy jacket or coat in winter; in summer be sure to bring a sweater. As for ski equipment, boots and skis are readily available for rent.

WHEN TO GO   This will depend on your favorite pastime. Obviously, winter and spring are great for skiing enthusiasts, and spring through fall are best for hikers and mountaineers.

Innsbruck's Average Daytime Temperature & Rainfall

	Jan	Feb	Mar	Apr	May	June	July	Aug	Sept	Oct	Nov	Dec
Temp. (°F)	30	35	42	48	55	65	70	70	65	48	38	32
Rainfall ″	3.4	2.5	3.2	4.1	4.5	5.4	5.8	5.3	4.2	3.5	3.3	3.7

Special Events   The new year in Innsbruck kicks off with an annual **Ski Jump Competition,** held in January (the 1964 Olympic ski jump is right on the edge of town). If you're a music fan or history buff, you'll want to take advantage of the **Festival of Early Music,** held annually in July and August, with concerts at Castle Ambras, the Hofburg, and the Tyroler Landestheater. It features everything from baroque operas to concerts with historical instruments. And from the end of November until Christmas, there's the annual **Christmas market** in Old City.

3. ORIENTATION & GETTING AROUND

ARRIVING IN INNSBRUCK

FROM THE AIRPORT OR TRAIN STATION   The city's small **airport,** two miles west of downtown, is used only for commuter flights to and from Vienna, Zurich, and Frankfurt (the closest major airport is Munich). A taxi from Innsbruck's airport to either the train station or downtown is 130 S ($11.80). Much cheaper is public bus F, which costs 17 S ($1.55) and travels to Maria-Theresien-Strasse in the center of town.

Innsbruck's **train station,** called the Hauptbahnhof (Central Station), is conveniently located in the city center. From here, you can catch a streetcar or tram, bus, or taxi to your final destination. For train information and schedules, call 1717.

INFORMATION

If you're arriving in Innsbruck by train, your first stop should be the **Innsbruck Information Office** (tel. 583766), located to the left as you exit the station. Open

WHAT'S SPECIAL ABOUT INNSBRUCK

The Alps
- [ ] Site of the 1964 and 1976 Winter Olympics.
- [ ] Beautiful Alpine scenery.
- [ ] Skiing year round.

Sports
- [ ] Skiing resorts surrounding Innsbruck, with complimentary bus transportation in winter.
- [ ] More winter sports, such as ice skating, tobogganing, cross-country skiing, bobsledding.
- [ ] Summer sports, including swimming, mountain climbing, archery, ice skating, golf, bowling, tennis, bike riding, and skiing.

Picturesque Old City
- [ ] Pedestrians-only cobblestone lanes, centuries-old buildings.
- [ ] Innsbruck's best museums and historical sites.
- [ ] Restaurants, cafés, bars, and shops, all centrally located.

Scenic Outlooks
- [ ] Stadtturm, 100-foot-high city tower, with views of the Old City.

- [ ] Hafelekar, the 7,700-foot-high mountain north of Innsbruck, with a funicular and cable car.
- [ ] Patscherkofel, the 7,400-foot-high mountain in the village of Igls, known for skiing and hiking.

Alpenzoo
- [ ] Europe's only Alpine zoo, where children and adults alike can learn about animals native to the region.

Austrian Folklore
- [ ] Tiroler Volkskunstmuseum, one of Austria's best folkloric museums, with displays relating to life in the Tyrolean Alps.
- [ ] Tyrolean Folkloric Evening, free entertainment of music and dance on Thursday evenings in the summer.
- [ ] Tiroler Alpenbühne, typical Tyrolean entertainment every evening in the summer.

daily from 8am to 10pm in summer and 9am to 10pm in winter, it offers maps of the city and information on tours, excursions, and evening entertainment. It will also reserve accommodations for you for a 30-S ($2.70) fee, and has the extra convenience of a message board, great for communicating with friends you might be meeting in Innsbruck.

Once you're in the city, there's another convenient **Innsbruck Information Office** at Burggraben 3 (tel. 5356), just off Maria-Theresien-Strasse near Old City. At this well-organized and helpful main office, you can also pick up maps, brochures, and make hotel reservations. Be sure to pick up their monthly brochure "Veranstaltungen" ("Events"). You can also purchase bus tickets here, and exchange money daily at the same rates as at banks. This office is open daily from 8am to 7pm.

If you plan on traveling or hiking outside Innsbruck in the surrounding province of Tyrol, contact **Tirol Info,** Wilhelm-Greil-Strasse 17 (tel. 53200), for brochures and maps. It's open Monday through Friday from 8:30am to 6pm and on Saturday from 9am to noon.

CITY LAYOUT

The **Inn River** divides the city into right and left banks. Most of Old Innsbruck (the name means "Inn Bridge"), including the Hofkirche, Goldenes Dachl, and the main train station, are on the right bank. Salurner Strasse and Brixener Strasse lead from the train station to the city's main street, **Maria-Theresien-Strasse.** From there **Burggraben** goes down to the river and the **Alte Innbrücke** (Old Inn Bridge). This bridge and the **Universitätsbrücke** are the two most important river crossings; the other six are on the outskirts.

You will undoubtedly spend most of your time in the neighborhood of the **Altstadt,** or Old City. It's bounded on the south by Marktgrabben and Burggraben and to the north by the Inn River. It's easily navigable on foot—indeed, much of it now is made up of pedestrians-only cobblestone streets. The heart of the city is along **Herzog-Friedrich-Strasse** and **Hofgasse,** Innsbruck's most picturesque streets.

GETTING AROUND

BY TRAM & BUS   Trams (streetcars) and buses provide public transportation. A single ticket, which permits transfers, costs 17 S ($1.55) and may be purchased from the driver. You can save money by buying a four-day ticket for 88 S ($8) or four tickets for 42 S ($3.80). The different ticket options are available from the tourist office, where you can also pick up a free transportation map, which shows all the lines and stops, and has a schedule and prices. For more information on tram and bus tickets or travel routes, contact the **Innsbrucker Verkehrsbetriebe** (tel. 5307-80 or 5356).

BY TAXI   The average taxi fare within the city limits is 65 S ($5.90). To or from the airport, expect to pay 130 S ($11.80), and not more than 100 S ($9.10) for trips to the outskirts of town. From Innsbruck's train station to the village of Igls costs about 130 S ($11.80).

ON FOOT OR BY BICYCLE   Many of the downtown streets have been closed to traffic, making for really pleasant walking.

Bikes are available for rent from April to October at the main train station. It costs only 45 S ($4.10) if you have a Eurailpass or are in possession of a train ticket for that day. Otherwise, a day's rental is 90 S ($8.20).

CAR RENTAL   It's much cheaper to rent a car in Europe if you make arrangements before you leave home. However, if you need one in Innsbruck, go to **Avis,** Salurner Strasse 15 (tel. 571754). They are open Monday through Friday from 7:30am to 7pm, on Saturday from 8am to noon and 1 to 6pm, and on Sunday from 9am to noon and 1:30 to 6pm. One-day rental of an Opel Corsa with unlimited mileage is 846 S ($76.90), including 20% Value-Added Tax.

Hertz, with prices starting at 648 S ($58.90) for a one-day rental, including unlimited mileage and tax, is located across the street from the main train station at Südtirolerplatz 1 (tel. 580901). It's open Monday through Friday from 7:30am to 6pm, on Saturday from 8am to 3pm, and on Sunday from 8am to noon (closed Sunday in winter).

Since there are often special holiday packages, weekend rates, and other deals, it pays to shop around.

FAST INNSBRUCK

Babysitters   For babysitting in Innsbruck, call the **Babysitter Zentrale** (tel. 894132).

Banks   Banks are open Monday through Friday from 7:45am to 12:30pm and 2:15 to 4pm. If you want to exchange money outside these hours, your best bet is the Innsbruck Information Office, Burggraben 3 (tel. 5356), open daily from 8am to 7pm, and at the money-exchange counter at the main train station, open daily from 7:30am to 8pm in winter and 7:30am to 9pm in summer.

The American Express office, where you can exchange money or pick up mail, is at Brixner Strasse 3 (tel. 582491). It's open Monday through Friday from 9am to 5:30pm and on Saturday from 9am to noon.

Business Hours   Banks are open Monday through Friday from 7:45am to 12:30pm and 2:15 to 4pm. Shops and most businesses are open Monday through Friday from 8:30 or 9am to noon and 2 to 6pm (some shops in the center of town remain open during the lunch hours) and on Saturday from 8:30 or 9am to noon. On the first Saturday of the month, many shops remain open until 5pm.

Consulates   There are no U.S., Australian, Canadian, or New Zealand consulates in Innsbruck. The nearest are in Munich or Vienna. The **British Consulate** is at Mathias-Schmid-Strasse 12 (tel. 588320), open Monday through Friday from 9am to noon.

Currency   The Austrian currency is the **Schilling,** written ASch, ÖS, or simply S (as I have done). A Schilling is made up of 100 **Groschen** (which are seldom used). Coins are minted as 10 and 50 Groschen, and 1, 5, 10, and 20 Schilling. Banknotes appear as 20, 50, 100, 500, 1,000, and 5,000 Schilling.

Dentists/Doctors   If you are in need of an English-speaking doctor or dentist, contact the Innsbruck Information Office. Otherwise, call the University Clinic, Anichstrasse 35 (tel. 504).

Emergencies   For urgent medical assistance, including an English-speaking doctor or dentist, call the University Clinic (tel. 504). For an ambulance, call 144; for the police, call 133; and for the fire department, 122.

There is a centrally located pharmacy, St. Anna Apotheke, at Maria-Theresien-Strasse 4 (tel. 585847), open Monday through Friday from 8am to 12:30pm and 2:30 to 6pm, and on Saturday from 8am to noon. A list of pharmacies that are open late at night or on Sunday is posted on the door of every pharmacy.

Holidays   Bank holidays in Innsbruck are New Year's Day (Jan 1), Epiphany (Jan 6), Easter Monday, Labor Day (May 1), Ascension Day, Whit Monday, Corpus Christi, Assumption Day (Aug 15), Austria Day (Oct 26), All Saints' Day (Nov 1), Immaculate Conception (Dec 8), and Christmas (Dec 25–26).

Hospitals   The General Hospital (and University Clinic) is located at Anichstrasse 35 (tel. 504). Another hospital is the Sanatorium der Barmherzigen Schwestern, Sennstrasse 1 (tel. 59380).

Information   The main tourist office, the Innsbruck Information Office, located at Burggraben 3 (tel. 5356), is described in more detail in the "Orientation and Getting Around" section, above.

Laundry   There is a conveniently located coin-operated laundry in central Innsbruck, Münzwäscherei Hell, located at Amraser Strasse 15 (tel. 41367), a few blocks behind the train station. For 130 S ($11.80) you can have 5 kilos (11 lb.) washed and dried. They're open Monday through Friday from 8am to 6pm and on Saturday from 8am to 1pm. Wäscherei Dellemann, Colin Gasse 9, at Burger Strasse (tel. 580983), provides overnight service for slightly higher rates. They're open Monday through Friday from 8am to 1pm and 2 to 6pm, and on Saturday from 9am to noon.

At many of the pensions on the outskirts, the proprietor will wash and dry your laundry or allow you to do so.

Lost and Found   If you lose something, check with the main police station (Bundespolizeidirektion), Kaiserjägerstrasse 8 (tel. 5900). If you lose something on a bus, try the bus station's lost and found at Maximilian Strasse 23 (tel. 585325); if you lose something on a train, go to the main train station on Südtirolerplatz (tel. 503 5357).

Mail   Innsbruck's main post office, open daily 24 hours, is at Maximilian Strasse 2 (tel. 5000), four blocks from the train station. "Poste Restante" mail can be picked up here. Additionally, there's another post office located beside the train station (to your left if facing the station) at Brunecker Strasse 1 (tel. 599340), open Monday through Saturday from 7am to 8pm.

The city postal code for Innsbruck is 6020.

Newspapers   English-language newspapers readily available in Innsbruck include the *International Herald Tribune* and *USA Today*. The best place to read over the day's newspaper—and it's free—is at Café Central, Gilmstrasse 5 (tel. 5920), a coffeehouse in the center of the city open daily from 8am to 11pm.

Photographic Needs   Because Innsbruck is a tourist-oriented town, there are photography and film shops everywhere. For film, try the conveniently located Kaufhaus Tyrol, a department store at Maria-Theresien-Strasse 33 (tel. 581401).

Police   The emergency number for the police is 133.

Shoe Repair   If your shoes wear out and need repair work, quick service is provided by Mister Minit, a chain of shoe-repair stores throughout Austria. The most convenient Mister Minit is located in Kaufhaus Tyrol, at Maria-Theresien-Strasse 33 (tel. 581401).

Tax   Government tax and service charge are already included in restaurant and hotel bills. If you have purchased goods for more than 1,000 S ($90.90), you're entitled to a refund of part of the Value-Added Tax, which runs 20%–32% depending on the item. See "Savvy Shopping," below, for more information.

Taxis   If you need a taxi in Innsbruck, call 5311, 45500, 41168, 61333, or 41541. For a discussion of fares, refer to "Orientation and Getting Around," above.

Telephone   Public telephones are found throughout the city, including in booths on sidewalks and in hotels and coffee shops. For local calls, insert one 1-Schilling coin for a one-minute call (insert more for longer calls—unused coins will be returned). Since hotels usually add a stiff fee to phone calls, make long-distance calls from post offices (the main post office, located at Maximilian-Strasse 2, is open 24 hours). The cost of a telephone call to the United States is 18 S ($1.65) per minute, or 54 S ($4.90) for three minutes.

If you need to make a lot of local calls (and don't want to bother with coins) or wish to make long-distance calls from a public telephone, you can purchase a **telephone card** from any post office for 50 S ($4.55) or 100 S ($9.10); the card can be inserted into slots on specially designated telephones.

Note: Telephone numbers are slowly being changed in Innsbruck. If you need information on a telephone number in the city, dial 08. And incidentally, if you come across a number with a dash—as in 5307-03—the number following the dash is the extension number. Treat it as you would any number and simply dial the whole number.

Innsbruck's **city telephone code** is 0512. If you're calling Innsbruck from outside Austria, you need dial only 512.

Tipping   A service charge is included in hotel and restaurant bills, and taxi fares. Still, it's customary to round up to the nearest 10 Schilling for both restaurant bills and taxi fares. If you feel a tip is necessary, add only 10% to any bill.

4. BUDGET ACCOMMODATIONS

Most of Innsbruck's budget accommodations are located on the outskirts of town and in neighboring villages, easily reached in less than 30 minutes by public transportation. The cheapest rooms are those rented out in private homes, with a shared bathroom down the hall. A bit higher priced are bathless rooms in smaller pensions (often called a *Gasthof* or *Gästehaus*), also located on the outskirts. Finally, if you'd rather stay in the center of Innsbruck near the Old City and feel like pampering yourself a bit, there are some good choices for a splurge.

Remember that if the recommendations below are full, the Innsbruck Information Offices at the train station and on Burggraben will reserve accommodations for you for a 30-S ($2.70) fee.

Remember, too, that telephone numbers are being changed in Innsbruck. If you can't reach any of the pensions or private homes below, call information at 08 to inquire whether the telephone number has been changed.

Finally, you may be approached at the train station by people asking whether you

THE SCHILLING & THE DOLLAR

At this writing $1 = approximately 11 S (or 1 S = 9¢), and this was the rate of exchange used to calculate the dollar values given in this chapter (rounded to the nearest nickel). This rate fluctuates from time to time and may not be the same when you travel to Austria. Therefore the following table should be used only as a guide:

S	U.S.$	S	U.S.$
1	.09	100	9.09
2	.18	150	13.63
3	.27	200	18.18
4	.36	250	22.72
5	.45	300	27.27
6	.54	350	31.82
7	.64	400	36.36
8	.73	450	40.90
9	.82	500	45.45
10	.91	600	54.54
15	1.36	700	63.63
20	1.81	800	72.72
25	2.27	900	81.81
50	4.54	1,000	90.90

need a room for the night. If you've already made reservations at one of the accommodations in this book, it's only fair to honor the reservation by showing up.

DOUBLES (IN PRIVATE HOMES) FOR LESS THAN 370 S ($33.65)

IN INNSBRUCK

HAUS SCHWARZ, Lindenbühelweg 12, 6020 Innsbruck. Tel. 0512/ 85535 or 285535. 4 rms (none with bath). **Bus:** H from the train station (leaving every hour on the hour) to Grauer Stein and then a three-minute walk; or A from the train station to Grosser Gott, followed by a seven-minute walk.
$ Rates (including continental breakfast and showers): 200 S ($20) single; 360–380 S ($32.70–$34.55) double; 540–570 S ($49.10–$51.80) triple. 20-S ($1.80) supplement for a one-night stay. No credit cards.
Ten minutes from the train station by bus, this private home is up on a hill overlooking the city, and two of its rooms even have a balcony. Better yet is the indoor heated pool hotel guests can use for 30 S ($2.70) (open only from May to October), with sliding glass doors opening onto a yard with a view of the city. The owner, who speaks English, has put together an album complete with all the things to do in Innsbruck, including recommendations for restaurants and excursions. Three of the rooms have their own sinks. Note that the owner here requests a check for your first night's reservation. She cashes it only if you don't show up—otherwise you'll get it back upon arrival and will be asked to pay for the total amount of your stay in cash.

LYDIA PRANTL, Hörmann Strasse 7, 6020 Innsbruck. Tel. 0512/ 419195. 2 rms (none with bath). **Directions:** See below.
$ Rates (including continental breakfast): 230 S ($20.90) single; 300 S ($27.25) double. Showers 20 S ($1.80) extra. No credit cards.
This fifth-floor apartment (there's an elevator) offers two rooms for travelers, a single

and a double. Frau Prantl, who speaks English, is an older, friendly woman who has been renting these rooms for more than 20 years.

To reach her flat (about a 10-minute walk), take a right out of the station, turn right at the first corner and walk under the underpass, turn right again and go over the bridge; turn right once more, and then turn left at the first street. It's the first house on the left.

OUTSIDE INNSBRUCK

FREMDENHEIM ANNE KALTENBERGER, Schulgasse 15, 6162 Mutters. Tel. 0512/575547. 6 rms (2 with shower). **Tram:** STB from the train station to Mutters.

$ Rates (with continental breakfast): 165 S ($15) single; 300 S ($27.25) double; 480 S ($43.65) triple. Showers 20 S ($1.80) extra. No credit cards.

This lovely Tyrolean-style house is modern and spotless, with scenic views of the surrounding Alps. Every room has a balcony and its own sink. Mutters, a 20-minute ride from Innsbruck, is a small village atop a plateau.

HAUS ROSSMANN, Schulgasse 13, 6162 Mutters. Tel. 0512/562625. 4 rms (none with bath). **Tram:** STB from the train station to Mutters.

$ Rates (including continental breakfast and showers): 190 S ($17.25) single; 360 S ($32.70) double; 540 S ($49.10) triple. No credit cards.

This lovely guesthouse, run by an English-speaking proprietor, is located next to the Fremdenheim Kaltenberger, listed above, and also offers spotless rooms with sinks and balconies offering spectacular views.

KÄTHE WOLF'S GUESTHOUSE, Dorfstrasse 48, 6162 Mutters. Tel. 0512/584088. 8 rms (none with bath). **Tram:** STB from the train station to Birchfeld.

$ Rates (including continental breakfast): 150 S ($13.65) single; 300 S ($27.25) double; 450 S ($40.90) triple; 600 S ($54.55) quad. First shower free; additional showers 5 S (45¢) each. No credit cards.

Käthe's guesthouse has been a favorite of readers, especially backpackers, since 1970, primarily thanks to Käthe's caring, easy-going, and friendly personality. Her large, older home is nothing fancy, but rooms come with sinks, there's a large yard for sunning, and her German shepherd responds only to English. If you phone ahead, Käthe will pick you up from Innsbruck's train station free of charge. This place is highly recommended for those in need of a bit of mothering.

DOUBLES FOR LESS THAN 500 S [$45.45]

IN INNSBRUCK

GASTHOF INNBRÜCKE, Innstrasse 1, 6020 Innsbruck. Tel. 0512/281934. 20 rms (6 with shower and toilet). **Bus:** A to Innbrücke; then walk across the bridge.

$ Rates (including continental breakfast and showers): 240 S ($21.80) single without shower or toilet; 300 S ($27.25) single with shower and toilet; 440 S ($40) double without shower or toilet, 590 S ($53.65) double with shower and toilet; 630 S ($57.25) triple without shower or toilet, 780 S ($70.90) triple with shower and toilet. AE, DC, MC, V.

With a great location right beside the Inn River and only a five-minute walk from Altstadt, this guesthouse occupies three floors of a building whose foundations date from 1425 and has been managed by the same family for four generations. Rooms with a view of the river are the same price as quieter, smaller rooms that face toward the back of the hotel. There's a restaurant and a small bar.

GASTHOF RIESE HAYMON, Haymon Gasse 4, 6020 Innsbruck. Tel. 0512/589837. 20 rms (3 with shower). **Tram:** 1 to Konzertstrasse; or a 15-minute walk south of the train station, past Südbahnstrasse and Leopoldstrasse.

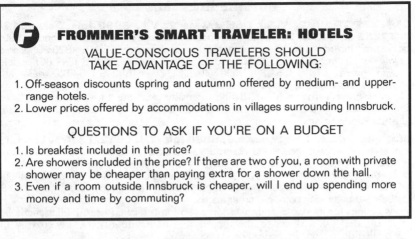

FROMMER'S SMART TRAVELER: HOTELS

VALUE-CONSCIOUS TRAVELERS SHOULD
TAKE ADVANTAGE OF THE FOLLOWING:

1. Off-season discounts (spring and autumn) offered by medium- and upper-range hotels.
2. Lower prices offered by accommodations in villages surrounding Innsbruck.

QUESTIONS TO ASK IF YOU'RE ON A BUDGET

1. Is breakfast included in the price?
2. Are showers included in the price? If there are two of you, a room with private shower may be cheaper than paying extra for a shower down the hall.
3. Even if a room outside Innsbruck is cheaper, will I end up spending more money and time by commuting?

$ Rates (including continental breakfast and showers): 280 S ($25.45) single without shower; 480 S ($43.65) double without shower, 550 S ($50) double with shower. No credit cards.

This looks like an ancient building, with knights in armor painted on its facade and a heavy stone portal, and rooms are simple and sparsely decorated. It's on the edge of town, near two beautiful baroque churches and not far from the Olympic ski jump.

PENSION BISTRO, Pradler Strasse 2, 6020 Innsbruck. Tel. 0512/ 46319. 9 rms (none with bath).

$ Rates (including continental breakfast and showers): 320 S ($29.10) single; 490 S ($44.55) double; 680 S ($61.80) triple; 700 S ($66.65) quad. AE, MC, V.

All rooms here have sinks, and some even have panoramic views of the Alps as well. The pension has a pleasant modern restaurant serving Austrian, Italian, and French food. The only disadvantage is that it's a bit far from the center of town, about a 15-minute walk northeast of the train station, past the overhead tracks and the Sill River.

PENSION HEIS, Dorfgasse 11, Hötting, 6020 Innsbruck. Tel. 0512/ 285345. 9 rms (2 with shower and toilet). **Bus:** A from the train station to Daxgasse.

$ Rates (including continental breakfast and showers): 430 S ($39.10) double without shower or toilet, 520 S ($47.25) double with shower and toilet; 600 S ($54.55) triple without shower or toilet; 800 S ($72.70) quad without shower or toilet. No credit cards.

Located on a hill with great views over the city, this Tyrolean-style pension offers roomy accommodations, most with balcony and five overlooking the city. The friendly owner speaks some English.

PENSION PAULA, Weiherburggasse 15, 6020 Innsbruck. Tel. 0512/ 892262. 14 rms (3 with shower and toilet, 3 with shower only). **Bus:** K from the train station to Schmelzergasse.

$ Rates (including continental breakfast and showers): 260 S ($23.65) single without shower or toilet; 420 S ($38.20) double without shower or toilet, 500 S ($45.45) double with shower only, 560 S ($50.90) double with shower and toilet. AE, DC, MC, V.

This country-style chalet, located on a hill, offers splendid panoramic views of Innsbruck and the surrounding mountainside. Try to get one of the rooms facing the front with a balcony. The proprietor is fluent in English. Highly recommended.

OUTSIDE INNSBRUCK

GASTHOF TRAUBE, Viller Dorfstrasse 2, Vill, 6080 Igls. Tel. 0512/ 77252 or 377252. 24 rms (8 with shower). **Bus:** from the train station to Vill.
$ Rates (including continental breakfast and showers): 230 S ($20.90) single without shower; 420 S ($38.20) double without shower, 460 S ($41.80) double with shower; 570 S ($51.80) triple without shower, 600 S ($54.55) triple with shower. No credit cards.

This storybook Tyrolean house, dating originally from the 14th century but since rebuilt, is located in a tiny village called Vill, near Igls. It's about a 20-minute ride from Innsbruck, and rooms are simple.

HAUS MARIA, Bilgeri Strasse 9, 6080 Igls. Tel. 0512/77186. 11 rms (3 with tub or shower and toilet). **Bus:** J from the train station to Igls, the last stop. **Tram:** 6 from the train station to Igls.
$ Rates (including continental breakfast and showers): 440 S ($40) double without bath, 480 S ($43.65) double with bath; 680 S ($61.80) quad without bath, 760 S ($69.10) quad with bath. No credit cards.

Igls is famous for its skiing, and this simple pension is located near the Patscherkofel cable car that takes skiers to the top of the mountain. Rooms are cozy, with down-filled duvets on the beds. The owner speaks English.

PENSION RIMML, Harterhof Weg 82, Kranebitten, 6020 Innsbruck. Tel. 0512/284726. 12 rms (10 with shower and toilet). **Bus:** LK from Bozner Platz (near the train station) to Klammstrasse, about 20 minutes.
$ Rates (including continental breakfast and showers): 225 S ($20.45) single without shower or toilet, 300 S ($27.25) single with shower and toilet; 450 S ($40.90) double without shower or toilet, 600 S ($54.55) double with shower and toilet. No credit cards.

⭐ All rooms in this rural-style guesthouse are on the ground floor and have their own sinks. There's a peaceful garden for sunning, as well as bicycles you can use for free. The couple who run this place are both fluent in English and will pick you up free from the train station if you call them.

DOUBLES FOR LESS THAN 700 S [$63.65]

IN INNSBRUCK

GÄSTEHAUS TAUTERMANN, Stamser Feld 5, Hötting, 6020 Innsbruck. Tel. 0512/281572. Fax 0512/281572-10. 28 rms (all with shower and toilet) TV TEL **Bus:** A from the train station to Höttinger Kirche.
$ Rates (including continental breakfast): 700 S ($63.65) double; 800 S ($72.70) triple; 1,000 S ($90.90) quad. AE, DC, MC, V.

Located across the Inn River just a six-minute walk from Old City, this simply furnished, clean guesthouse offers rooms spread over three floors of a modern apartment house (there's no elevator). Half the rooms have minibars and clock radios, and its televisions are hooked up to cable with some programs in English. The owners speak English.

OUTSIDE INNSBRUCK

PENSION STEFFI, Dorfplatz 2, 6161 Natters. Tel. 0512/546770 or 589402. 10 rms (all with shower and toilet). **Tram:** STB from the train station to Natters, about a 30-minute ride; or a 15-minute taxi ride.
$ Rates (including continental breakfast): 300 S ($27.25) single; 580 S ($52.70) double; 780 S ($70.90) triple; 1,000 S ($90.90) quad. No credit cards.

⭐ This delightful pension, located only three miles south of Innsbruck and beautifully decorated with dried-flower arrangements, plants, and antiques, is owned and managed by a charming young couple named Brigitte (who wears dirndls in summer) and Edwin Klien-Frech, both formerly English teachers, who speak excellent English. Rooms, all equipped with radio, are cozily furnished with natural-wood furnishings, and there's a sun terrace and garden with folding chairs. If you give advance notice, you'll be picked up at the train station, a 15-minute ride away. You'll love this place.

SUPER-BUDGET CHOICES
YOUTH HOSTELS & YOUTH HOTELS

INTERNATIONALES STUDENTENHAUS, Rechengasse 7, 6020 Innsbruck. Tel. 0512/594770. 600 beds (some rms with bath). **Bus:** C from the train station to Studentenhaus.

$ Rates (including breakfast, sheets and showers): 230 S ($20.90) single without bath, 290 S ($26.35) single with bath; 460 S ($41.80) double without bath, 580 S ($52.70) double with bath. No credit cards. **Open:** July–Sept.

University students live here during the school year, but July through September rooms are available to tourists. Rooms are spartan but adequate, and there's no curfew.

JUGENDHERBERGE INNSBRUCK (IYHF), Reichenauer Strasse 147, 6020 Innsbruck. Tel. 0512/46179 or 46180. 190 beds. **Bus:** O to Jugendherberge.

$ Rates (including breakfast, sheets, and showers): 121 S ($11) per person the first night, 91 S ($8.25) each additional night. No credit cards.

You're supposed to have a youth-hostel card to stay in one of its dormitory-style rooms, but if you don't, you can buy a "guest" membership for an extra 30 S ($2.70) per night. This ultramodern hostel is closed from 10am to 5pm, has an 11pm curfew, and is open year round.

MK–AM JESUITENKOLLEG INNSBRUCK, Sillgasse 8a, 6020 Innsbruck. Tel. 0512/571311. 100 beds.

$ Rates (including breakfast, sheets, and showers): 130 S ($11.80) per person. No credit cards. **Open:** July to mid-Sept.

Although youth-hostel members are desired at this privately owned hostel, it accepts other guests for 20 S ($1.80) additional. Rooms are outfitted with 6–14 beds. This hostel has a great location, right in the center of the city just a five-minute walk northwest of the station, off Museumstrasse (saving on bus fare), but is open only from July to mid-September.

TORSTEN-ARNÉUS-SCHWEDENHAUS, Rennweg 176, 6020 Innsbruck. Tel. 0512/585814. 80 beds. **Bus:** C from the train station to the Handelsakademie.

$ Rates (including breakfast, sheets, and showers): 150 S ($13.65) per person. No credit cards. **Open:** July–Aug.

This modern, bungalow-style house is open only in July and August, with rooms of four to eight costs each. It's located north of the city center, near the Inn River.

CAMPING

There are two camping opportunities around Innsbruck, open from about mid-March or April to the end of October. These are **Camping Reichenauerstrasse,** Reichenauerstrasse and Langer Weg (tel. 0512/46252), located in town on the Inn River; and **Camping West,** Kranebitterallee 214, in Kranebitten (tel. 0512/284180). All begin at 55 S ($5) per person per night, plus 35–50 S ($3.20–$4.55) per night for a tent or camper and 35 S ($3.20) per automobile.

WORTH THE EXTRA BUCKS

GASTHAUS WEISSES RÖSSL, Kiebachgasse 8, 6020 Innsbruck. Tel. 0512/583057. Fax 0512/5830575. 14 rms (all with tub or shower and toilet). TEL, TV

$ Rates (including breakfast): 680–750 S ($61.80–$68.20) single; 1,040–1,200 S

($94.55–$109.10) double; 1,300–1,500 S ($118.20–$136.35) triple; 1,600–1,800 S ($145.45–$163.65) quad. AE, DC, MC, V.

⭐ This is a delightful inn for a splurge, located in the center of Old City. The house, first built in 1410 and called the Weisses Rössl ("White Horse") since 1590, was recently renovated to enhance its original rustic splendor. The second floor has its original wood ceiling, and there's even a "light well"—an empty open shaft that used to provide the only light to the floors below before the advent of electricity. It boasts a fine traditional restaurant, with an outdoor terrace for summer dining. This place is a true find, just a 10-minute walk from the train station.

5. BUDGET DINING

Most budget restaurants are concentrated on the right bank of the Inn, clustered around the train station and the university, or in the Old City.

Many of the specialties are such familiar Austrian dishes as Wiener Schnitzel, Gulasch, and Backhendl (grilled and breaded chicken), but there are some local specialties to look for, too—omelets filled with cranberries or Tiroler Knödel with Gröstl, for example. The latter consists of tennis-ball-size dumplings made of white bread, flour, smoked bacon, milk, egg, and salt, served with a stew made of potatoes, beef, and onions. The beverage of choice is beer from the barrel, served either in a small glass called a *Seidel* (a third of a liter) or in a medium-sized glass or earthenware mug called a *Krügerl* (half a liter).

A LOCAL BUDGET BET

UNIVERSITY MENSA, Herzog-Sigmund-Ufer 15. Tel. 584375.
   Cuisine: AUSTRIAN.
$ **Prices:** Fixed-price meals 25–45 S ($2.25–$4.10). No credit cards.
   Open: Lunch only, Mon–Fri 11am–2pm. **Closed:** Aug 15–Sept 15.
This place serves absolutely the cheapest meals in Innsbruck and requires no student or other identification. Nonstudents simply pay a bit more (the nonstudent prices are written in parentheses on the chalk board containing the daily menu). There are usually three complete meals offered, as well as a few items à la carte. Traditional meals include Gemüsesuppe (vegetable soup) and Gulasch (beef stew in spicy sauce). The mensa is located near Universitätsbrücke (University Bridge), upstairs in the gray building facing the river, just a 10-minute walk from the train station.

MEALS FOR LESS THAN 70 S [$6.35]

NORDSEE, Maria-Theresien-Strasse 11. Tel. 572881.
   Cuisine: SEAFOOD.
$ **Prices:** 50–100 S ($4.55–$9.10). No credit cards.
   Open: Mon–Fri 9am–7pm, Sat 9am–1:30pm (to 5pm the first Sat of the month).
This pleasant self-serve restaurant offers such reasonably priced and tasty dishes as fried sole with potato salad, fish cakes with green salad, fish sandwiches, and paella. Ordering is easy, since all dishes are pictured on an illustrated sign board above the counter.

ZACH, Wilhelm-Greil-Strasse 11. Tel. 583054.
   Cuisine: AUSTRIAN.
$ **Prices:** 25–90 S ($2.25–$8.20). No credit cards.
   Open: Mon–Fri 7:30am–6:15pm, Sat 7:30am–12:15pm.
Conveniently located about halfway between the train station and Old City, this well-known butcher shop sells meats on one side of the store and offers simple dishes and complete meals from a self-service counter on the other side of the shop. An English menu lists chicken with salad or potatoes, meatloaf, roast pork, large salad,

---

FROMMER'S SMART TRAVELER: RESTAURANTS

VALUE-CONSCIOUS TRAVELERS SHOULD TAKE ADVANTAGE OF THE FOLLOWING:

1. Innsbruck's many stand-up food stands (called *Imbiss*), serving everything from Wurst to pizza and beer (try the Imbiss at the Kaufhaus Tyrol department store, Maria-Theresien-Strasse 33).
2. The special menu of the day (*Tagesgericht*), which is often a complete meal in itself.
3. Butcher shops and food departments of department stores, which usually offer cooked foods for take-out.
4. Coffee-shop chains such as Eduscho, which sell both the beans and inexpensive cups of coffee.

QUESTIONS TO ASK IF YOU'RE ON A BUDGET

1. Is there a charge for each piece of bread consumed? (Most restaurants charge for each piece of bread.)
2. Does the entrée come with vegetables or side dishes?

---

frankfurters with roll, and Wiener Schnitzel with fries. There are also daily specials costing about 60–70 S ($5.45–$6.35) for a complete meal, available from 11am to 2pm. These may range from lasagne or a beef Gulasch to spinach dumplings. Although there are a few seats for sit-down dining, most people stand at one of the chest-high tables. Avoid the busy lunch hour if you want to sit down.

MEALS FOR LESS THAN 130 S [$11.80]

AL DENTE, Meraner Strasse 7. Tel. 584947.
   Cuisine: PASTA. **Directions:** Walk a couple of minutes from the train station toward Maria-Theresien-Strasse.
$ Prices: Main courses 75–110 S ($6.80–$10). No credit cards.
   Open: Daily 11am–10:30pm.
This combination café/restaurant is small and pleasant, and is a good place for a meal or a cappuccino. As its name suggests, it specializes in pasta dishes, as well as a great variety of salads. If you're craving tagliatelle and a tunafish salad, this is the place.

GASTHAUS WEISSES RÖSSL, Kiebachgasse 8. Tel. 583057.
   Cuisine: AUSTRIAN.
$ Prices: Soups and appetizers 30–100 S ($2.75–$9.10); main dishes 75–160 S ($6.20–$14.55). AE, DC, MC, V.
   Open: Lunch Mon–Sat 11am–2pm; dinner Mon–Sat 6–10pm.
   This is a great place for a traditional meal in the heart of the city. Located up on the first floor of an old inn, this old-fashioned restaurant features a wooden ceiling and wooden benches and is decorated with antiques, pewter plates, and antlers. Its English menu includes fish, rumpsteak, Schnitzel, beef filet with onions and potatoes, Cordon Bleu, Gulasch, and grilled sausages. There's also a children's plate of Wiener Schnitzel and french fries for 65 S ($5.90). Since it's a popular place, you're best off making a reservation.

GASTHOF RIESE HAYMON, Haymon Gasse 4. Tel. 589837.
   Cuisine: AUSTRIAN. **Tram:** 1 to Konzerstrasse.
$ Prices: Main courses 60–120 S ($5.45–$10.90). No credit cards.

Open: Daily 11am–9pm.

This is one of the best budget restaurants with table service in town. And you shouldn't have a problem getting a table here: There is seating for 60 inside and for 200 outside, weather permitting. Choose between two- or four-course menus (*Stammessen*), or à la carte, with most entrées including a side dish. The latter includes Schnitzel, fish, omelets, Gulasch, and Tiroler Bauernschmaus (a Tyrolean specialty). It's a 15-minute walk south of Old City.

PHILIPPINE, Tempelstrasse 2. Tel. 589157.
  Cuisine: VEGETARIAN.
$ Prices: Lunch main courses 75–110 S ($6.80–$10); dinner 90–160 S ($8.20–$14.55). No credit cards.
  Open: Lunch Mon–Sat 11:30am–2:30pm; dinner Mon–Sat 6–10:30pm.

⭐ If you're tired of the hearty and somewhat heavy Austrian cuisine, try this vegetarian restaurant for a unique change of pace. A pleasant, airy restaurant up on the first floor, it offers a lunch menu with slightly lower prices that includes vegetarian pasta, tofu, and vegetable dishes. For dinner, try the Chinese vegetables with wild rice, a pasta dish or a Schnitzel made with wheat. There's also a salad bar. On the ground floor of the restaurant is a café, open Monday through Saturday from 10am to 11pm for snacks, drinks, and salads. It's just a minute's walk south of Maria-Theresien-Strasse, on the corner of Müllerstrasse and Tempelstrasse.

SHERE PUNJAB, Inn Strasse 19. Tel. 82755.
  Cuisine: INDIAN.
$ Prices: Main courses 65–110 ($5.90–$10). AE, DC, MC, V.
  Open: Lunch daily 11am–2pm; dinner daily 5–11pm.

This small, family-run restaurant faces the Inn River. Try the chicken tikka or the lentil soup for an appetizer, followed by one of the many lamb, beef, fish, chicken, or vegetable dishes, all served with rice. Strangely enough, there's also pizza and Wiener Schnitzel. Monday through Friday from 11am to 2pm, there's a special fixed-price lunch menu available for 65 S ($5.90) that includes a soup, main course, rice, and dessert. The restaurant is located just a four-minute walk from Old City, across the Inn River.

WIENERWALD, Museum Strasse 24 (tel. 584165) and Maria-Theresien-Strasse 12 (tel. 584165).
  Cuisine: AUSTRIAN.
$ Prices: 70–110 S ($6.35–$10). AE, DC, MC, V.
  Open: Daily 10am–midnight.

Wienerwald made a name for itself with its chicken—grilled with or without breadcrumbs—but now other traditional dishes are also available, such as Gulasch and Wiener Schnitzel as well as a salad bar. The daily-changing two-course menu is a good buy. Wienerwald is one of a chain of restaurants found throughout German-speaking Europe. Both of these are within a five-minute walk of the train station.

STREET FOOD

There are food stands (called an *Imbiss*) in every city in Austria. During the day, try the **Imbiss at Kaufhaus Tyrol,** Maria-Theresien-Strasse 33 (tel. 581401), located at the entrance of this large department store. It offers Bratwurst, pizza by the slice, Schnitzelburger, beer, and more, with most prices under 32 S ($2.90). It's open the same hours as the store: Monday through Friday from 8:30am to 6:30pm and on Saturday from 8:30am to 12:30pm (to 5pm the first Saturday of the month).

In the evenings, try the Wurst stand in the Old City, right in front of the Goldenes Dachl on Herzog-Friedrich-Strasse.

CAFES/KONDITOREIS

If all you want is a cheap cup of coffee, head for **Eduscho,** a coffee shop that sells both the brew and the beans. Located just south of the Old City at Maria-Theresien-

Strasse 1 (tel. 563943), it's open Monday through Friday from 8:30am to 6:30pm and on Saturday from 8:30am to 12:30pm (to 5pm the first Saturday of the month). A cup of coffee or espresso consumed at one of its stand-up tables is just 6 S (55¢).

CAFE CENTRAL, Gilmstrasse 5. Tel. 5920.
   Cuisine: COFFEEHOUSE
$ Prices: *Brauner* 21 S ($1.90).
   Open: Daily 8am–11pm.
At this conveniently located café, halfway between the train station and the Old City, you can read English-language newspapers while enjoying a cup of excellent coffee or tea. This is Innsbruck's oldest coffeehouse, founded in 1878, and features live piano music on Sunday evenings. You can come here for just a cup of coffee—a small *Brauner* (a small cup of strong, black coffee with whipped cream) is just 21 S ($1.90)—or eat a complete meal of spaghetti or an omelet or maybe just an Apfelstrudel.

CAFE MUNDING, Kiebachgasse and Schlossergasse. Tel. 584118.
   Cuisine: COFFEEHOUSE
$ Prices: A large coffee with mild 22 S ($2).
   Open: Daily 8am–9pm.
This is one of the nicest coffeehouses in town, with walls that serve as a gallery for local artists. The building itself, which has been renovated, is in the middle of the Old City and dates from the Middle Ages; in the summer you can sit outside. There are various coffees, including Irish coffee and Viennese blends. A specialty is homemade ice cream (more than 20 kinds) and cakes.

STADTCAFE, Rennweg 2. Tel. 586869.
   Cuisine: COFFEEHOUSE
$ Prices: Coffee with milk 23 S ($2.10); cakes and strudels 30 S ($2.70).
   Open: Summer, daily 9am–midnight; winter, Mon 10am–8pm, Tues–Sun 10am–midnight.
The Stadtcafe specializes in cakes and strudels, all priced about 30 S ($2.70) per serving. It's located across the street from the Hofburg, with outdoor seating in summer.

PICNIC SUPPLIES & WHERE TO EAT THEM

Innsbruck's largest department store, **Kaufhaus Tyrol,** is situated in the center of town at Maria-Theresien-Strasse 33 (tel. 581401) and has a well-stocked food department in its basement. In addition to its fruits, vegetables, cheeses, and sausages it also has counters selling take-out food, including salads and meat dishes. It's open Monday through Friday from 8:30am to 6:30pm and on Saturday from 8:30am to 12:30pm (to 5pm the first Saturday of the month).

   Not far away is **Hörtnagel,** Burggraben 4 (tel. 59729), near the Innsbruck Information Office. It offers the usual cheeses, Wursts, and fruits, as well as a delicatessen. Hours here are Monday through Thursday from 7:30am to 12:30pm and 3 to 6:30pm, on Friday from 7:30am to 6:30pm, and on Saturday from 7:30am to noon.

   And where to eat your goodies? The best place is along the **Inn River,** where there are public benches, and the **Hofgarten.**

WORTH THE EXTRA BUCKS

SCHWARZER ADLER, Kaiserjägerstrasse 2. Tel. 587109.
   Cuisine: AUSTRIAN.
$ Prices: Main courses 150–240 S ($13.65–$21.80). AE, DC, MC, V.
   Open: Lunch Mon–Sat 11am–2pm; dinner Mon–Sat 6–11pm.
   There are two choices for dining in this well-known hotel restaurant, both with the same menu. On the ground floor are cozy parlorlike rooms; in the basement is the K. K. Keller with its vaulted ceilings. In any case, there are antiques

throughout and the decor is traditionally Austrian. There's an English menu that changes weekly and always includes natural organic selections as well as Tyrolean and Austrian dishes. Specialties include trout, garlic-cream soup, sirloin steak, and Schnitzel. Schwarzer Adler is within a three-minute walk east of the Old City.

---

6. ATTRACTIONS

SUGGESTED ITINERARIES

IF YOU HAVE ONE DAY   If you have only one day, spend it in the Old City, where you'll find most of Innsbruck's top attractions and historic buildings, including the Goldenes Dachl, the Olympic Museum, the Tyrolean Folkloric Museum, and the Hofburg. Top the day with a meal in a traditional Austrian restaurant.

IF YOU HAVE TWO DAYS   Spend the first day as described above. On Day 2, spend it in the Alps for which Innsbruck is famous. If you ski, head straight for Stubai Glacier, where you can ski every day of the year. If you don't ski, take the funicular and then the cable car to Hafelekar, a 7,700-foot-high peak just north of the city, where you'll have a breathtaking view of the Alps. If it's a Thursday in the summer, see whether the Tyrolean Folkloric Evening is taking place in front of the Goldenes Dachl.

IF YOU HAVE THREE DAYS   Spend the first two days as outlined above. On the third day, go to the Alpenzoo, where you will see animals native to the Alps. In the afternoon, head for Ambras Castle, built in the 16th century and housing a collection of arms and armor.

TOP ATTRACTIONS

GOLDENES DACHL (Golden Roof), Herzog-Friedrich-Strasse 15.

In the heart of the Old City is this Innsbruck landmark, a gleaming, gold-roofed balcony made of 2,657 gilded tiles. Built in the late 15th century for Emperor Maximilian to celebrate his marriage to Bianca Maria Sforza, it was used as a royal box for watching civic events in the square below, including tournaments between armor-clad knights. Although visitors aren't allowed inside the balcony, the building's facade is the most-photographed building in Innsbruck. On Thursday evenings in the summer, Tyrolean Folkloric Evenings are staged in the square in front of the building.

The best thing to do at the Goldenes Dachl is go inside to see the **Olympia-Museum** (tel. 5360575), where you can watch 14-minute videos of the most interesting scenes of the Winter Olympics held in Innsbruck in 1964 and 1976. There's also an international Olympic stamp collection. Note that you can buy a combination ticket that will also allow you to visit the Stadtturm, described below.

Admission: Olympia-Museum, 22 S ($2) adults, 11 S ($1) students and children; combination ticket to Olympia-Museum and Stadtturm, 32 S ($2.90) adults, 16 S ($1.45) children.

Open: Daily 9:30am–5:30pm. **Closed:** Mon Nov–Feb.

STADTTURM (City Tower), Herzog-Friedrich-Strasse 21. Tel. 575962.

Located almost catercorner from the Goldenes Dachl, the Stadtturm was built in 1560 and measures 100 feet high. At one time it held a prison, but today its viewing platform offers panoramic views of the city and Alps.

Admission: 18 S ($1.65) adults, 9 S (80¢) children; combination ticket to Olympia-Museum and Stadtturm, 32 S ($2.90) adults, 16 S ($1.45) children.

Open: Mar–Oct, daily 10am–5pm (to 6pm July–Aug). **Closed:** Nov–Feb.

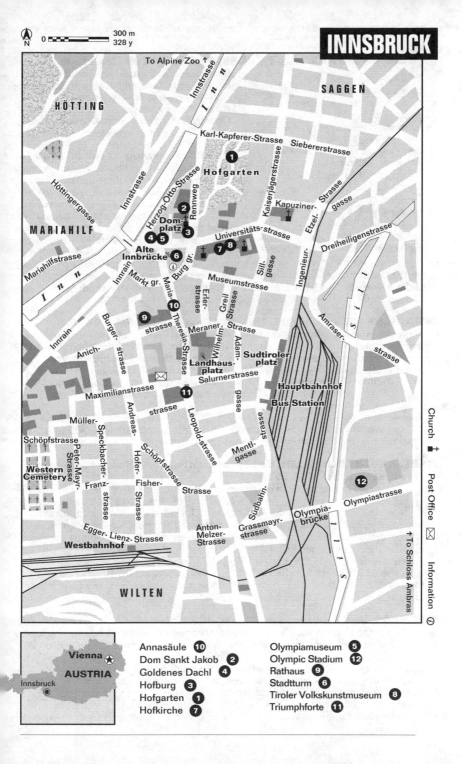

INNSBRUCK

0 ——— 300 m
N 328 y

To Alpine Zoo ↑

SAGGEN

HÖTTING

Innstrasse

Karl-Kapferer-Strasse   Sieberersstrasse

Höttingergasse

Herzog-Otto-Strasse   Rennweg   Kaiserjägerstrasse

Kapuziner-   Strasse gasse

Hofgarten   ❶

MARIAHILF

Mariahilfstrasse

Innstrasse

Inn

❷
**Dom-
platz**   ❸

❹ ❺

**Alte
Innbrücke**   ❻

Universitäts-strasse   Etel-   Dreiheiligenstrasse

❼ ❽

Ingenieur-

Innrain   Markt gr.   Burg gr.   Maria-

Museumsstrasse   Sill-
gasse

Erler-
strasse

Greil
Strasse   Amraser-

Burger-   strasse   ❿

❾   strasse

Anich-   strasse

Theresia-Strasse

Meraner   Strasse

Wilhelm   Adam-   Strasse

**Sudtiroler
platz**

**Landhaus-
platz**

✉   Salurnerstrasse

Maximilianstrasse   ⓫   **Hauptbahnhof**

Bus Station

Andreas-   strasse

Leopold-strasse

Mentl-
gasse

Müller-
Schöpfstrasse   Schöpf strasse

Peter-Mayr-
Strasse

Speckbacher-
Strasse   Hofer-
Strasse

Fisher-
Strasse

Sudbahn-
strasse

**Western
Cemetery**

Franz-
strasse

Egger- Lienz- Strasse

Westbahnhof

Anton-
Melzer-
Strasse

Grassmayr-
strasse

Olympia-
brücke

Olympiastrasse   ⓬

→ To Schloss Ambras

WILTEN

Church ☩   Post Office ✉   Information ⓘ

Vienna ★
AUSTRIA

Innsbruck

Annasäule ❿	Olympiamuseum ❺
Dom Sankt Jakob ❷	Olympic Stadium ⓬
Goldenes Dachl ❹	Rathaus ❾
Hofburg ❸	Stadtturm ❻
Hofgarten ❶	Tiroler Volkskunstmuseum ❽
Hofkirche ❼	Triumphforte ⓫

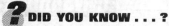 **DID YOU KNOW . . . ?**

- Innsbruck developed rapdily because of its position near the crossroads of several transalpine routes
- Innsbruck is the gateway to the Brenner Pass, the most frequently used pass over the central Alps.
- Innsbruck hosted the winter Olympics in 1964 *and* 1976
- Only the Soviet Union, East Germany, and Switzerland won more medals than Austria in the 1988 Winter Olympic Games.
- The Alps cover nearly 75% of Austrian territory.

DOM SANKT JAKOB, Domplatz.

Innsbruck's cathedral was built in the baroque style in the early 18th century. The carillon is hear daily at 4 or 4:15pm.

Admission: Free.

Open: Daily 8am–7pm. **Closed:** Until beginning of 1993 for renovation.

HOFBURG, Rennweg 1. Tel. 587186.

This royal residence, originally constructed by Emperor Maximilian in the 1500s, is to Innsbruck what Versailles is to Paris—but on a smaller scale. It was reconstructed in the rococo style by Empress Maria Theresia in the mid-18th century. Of particular note is the main hall, lavishly decorated in rococo style with elaborate stucco designs and its painted ceilings. Tapestries and paintings adorn the walls of the rooms. The Hofburg is in the heart of Old City.

Admission: 30 S ($2.70) adults, 10 S (90¢) students, 5 S (45¢) children.

Open: Daily 9am–4pm. **Closed:** Sun and hols Oct 16–May 15.

HOFKIRCHE (Court Church), Universitätsstrasse 2. Tel. 584302.

Near the Hofburg is the royal Court Church, built in the mid-16th century and containing the tombs of Emperor Maximilian I and Tyrolean freedom fighter Andreas Hofer. Surrounding the emperor's tomb are 28 larger-than-life bronze statues of his ancestors and relatives. Be sure to see the Silberne Kapelle (Silver Chapel), final resting place of Archduke Ferdinand II and his wife. Note that the Hofkirche is located through the same entryway as the Volkskunstmuseum described below; the combination ticket for both offers a reduction.

Admission: 20 S ($1.80) adults, 14 S ($1.25) students, free for children to 15 years; combination ticket for Hofkirche and Volkskunstmuseum, 30 S ($2.70).

Open: Mon–Sat 9am–5pm, Sun noon–5pm.

TIROLER VOLKSKUNSTMUSEUM (Tyrolean Folkloric Museum), Universitätsstrasse 2. Tel. 584302.

This is my favorite museum in Innsbruck. Certainly it's one of the best folkloric museums in the country, with its collection of items used by common folk from the Middle Ages to this century. Included are sleighs; a beautiful collection of painted furniture (*Bauernmöbel*); ornamental bells for sheep, goats, and cows (you should see the size of some of these); farming tools and cooking utensils; religious artifacts; and clothing.

Admission: 20 S ($1.80) adults, 14 S ($1.25) students, free for children to 15 years; combination ticket for Hofkirche and Volkskunstmuseum, 30 S ($2.70).

Open: Mon–Sat 9am–5pm, Sun 9am–noon. **Closed:** New Year's Day, Easter Sunday, May 5, Corpus Christi, Nov 1, Dec 25.

ALPENZOO, Weiherburggasse 37. Tel. 892323.

This is the place to see all those animals native to the Alps and Alpine region, including European bison, wildcats, wolves, otters, beavers, vultures, owls, eagles, buzzards, elk, Alpine ibex, rabbits, brown bears, and dozens of fish (in an aquarium). The easiest way to get to the zoo, located above the city on the slopes of the Hungerburg and boasting a great view, is via a funicular, which is free if you purchase your zoo ticket at the funicular gate. An alternative is to purchase your ticket in advance at the Innsbruck Information Office. Costing 60 S ($5.45) for adults and 30 S ($2.70) for children, this ticket allows free round-trip transportation from anywhere in Innsbruck or Igls to the Alpenzoo, including the ride on funicular and admission to the zoo. The ticket is actually a postcard, which you can then use after your visit to write to the folks back home.

Admission: Zoo and funicular, 56 S ($5.10) adults, 28 S ($2.55) students and children.

Open: Daily 9am–6pm (to 5pm in winter). **Directions:** Tram 6 or 1 or bus C to Hungerburgbahn.

SCHLOSS AMBRAS, Schloss Strasse 20. Tel. 41215 or 48446.

Two miles east of Innsbruck in a district called Amras is this fortresslike castle, built in 16th century. Inside is a large collection of arms, armor, tournament equipment, tapestries, Renaissance paintings, and manuscripts.

Admission: 30 S ($2.70) adults, 10 S (90¢) children.

Open: May–Sept, Wed–Mon 10am–5pm. **Closed:** Oct–Apr. **Tram:** 3 or 6 from the Innsbruck train station.

PARKS & GARDENS

The two largest and most famous parks are the **Hofgarten,** in the Old City, and the **Amraser Schlosspark,** two miles east of town, next to Schloss Ambras. Smaller parks are the **Rapoldipark,** behind the train station, and **Walther Park,** on the left riverbank, near Alte Innbrücke. All feature restaurants and coffee shops, and are popular hangouts during the summer months. Enjoying a beer or a soft drink, watching the locals, and admiring the Alpine panorama is not only relaxing, but is a good opportunity to make new friends.

ORGANIZED TOURS

If you have a limited amount of time, take the two-hour tour of city highlights, accompanied by an English-speaking guide. It leaves from the train station daily at noon, with additional departures at 10am and 2pm during the summer. The price is 140 S ($12.70) for adults, 70 S ($6.35) for children aged 7–14. The bus stops for 20 minutes both at the Olympic ski jump, built for the 1964 Games, and in the Old City. Tickets for the tour are available at the Innsbruck Information Office at Burggraben 3 and the train station.

SPECIAL & FREE EVENTS

If you're in Innsbruck in summer on a Thursday, be sure to head to Herzog-Friedrich-Strasse in front of the Goldenes Dachl for the **Tyrolean Folkloric Evening.** It begins at 8:30pm on Thursday from mid-June to September and includes free entertainment of Tyrolean music and folkloric dancing.

7. SAVVY SHOPPING

Innsbruck is not a bargain town for Austrian souvenirs and goods—prices are simply too high. However, it's fun to look and you might find something worth the extra bucks. The best place to look for stores is in the Old City and along Maria-Theresien-Strasse. Austrian products include sweaters, Gmünder ceramics, petit-point items, and enamel jewelry. If you purchase goods at any one store for more than 1,000 S ($90.90), you're entitled to a refund of part of the Value-Added Tax (VAT), which ranges from 20% to 32%. Ask the clerk to give you a U-34 Customs form. Upon leaving Austria, have it stamped by Customs, whether you leave by train, car, or plane.

8. EVENING ENTERTAINMENT

For theater and musical performances, pick up the free monthly **"Veranstaltungen"** ("Events"), a publication listing theater, concerts, dance, and other cultural programs at the Innsbruck Information Office at Burggraben 3. For movie programs, buy a local paper (*Tiroler Tageszeitung*) or check the cinema posters near the train station.

THE PERFORMING ARTS

TIROLER LANDESTHEATER, Rennweg 2. Tel. 520744.

Located in the heart of the city across from the Hofburg, the Tiroler Landestheater is Innsbruck's most important venue for performances of opera, operetta, and theater, including one-act plays, comedies, and such lighthearted productions as the 1990 showings of *Peter Pan*. There are two theaters, the Grosses Haus for opera and large productions, and the Kammerspiele for plays.

Prices: Tickets, opera 250 S ($22.70) (second-balcony seat); theater productions 145–210 S ($13.20–$19.10).

Open: Box office, Mon–Sat 8:30am–8:30pm; performances usually at 7:30 or 8pm, with a matinee about once a week at 3pm.

TIROLER ALPENBÜHNE, in the Sandwirt Inn at Reichenauerstrasse 151, in the Messe-Saal on Etzel Strasse, or in the Hotel-Gasthof Sailer at Adam Gasse 8. Tel. 63263 or 63497.

An evening of Tyrolean entertainment offers traditional music, yodeling, and folk dancing. Contact the Innsbruck Information Office or call one of the numbers above to find out where the evening's program will be held and how to get there.

Prices: 190 S ($17.25), which includes one free drink.

Open: June–Aug, daily 9–11pm; Sept–May, once a week.

TREIBHAUS, Angerzellgasse 8. Tel. 586874.

This is one of the best places in town for live music, from jazz or blues to folk music, with free jazz concerts every Sunday from 10am to 1pm. In addition, there are frequent cabaret and other theatrical productions. This place is hidden away on a side street in the heart of Innsbruck just a block from Burggraben. Since the stage is located in what is actually a large tent (heated in winter), it becomes a pavilion in summer, with outdoor seating. More than 30 different kinds of pizza are offered on a limited menu. Check "Veranstaltungen" for current concerts and productions.

Prices: Half liter of beer, 28 S ($2.55). **Admission:** Concerts, 80–150 S ($7.25–$13.65).

Open: Café, Mon–Sat 4pm–1am, Sun 10am–1pm; performances usually at 7:30 or 8pm. **Directions:** Walk one block east of Burggraben, off Museum Strasse.

MOVIES

All of Innsbruck's 18 city cinemas are on the right bank. The most accessible are on Maria-Theresien-Strasse and near Bozener Platz. Average price for tickets is 70–90 S ($6.35–$8.20). **Cinematograph,** at Museum Strasse 31 (tel. 578500), often shows foreign movies in the original language (including English), usually at 6, 8, and 10pm. A leaflet of its monthly program is available outside its door. Tickets here are 60 S ($5.45).

BARS & CLUBS

LA COPA, Badgasse 4. Tel. 587495.

This small bar, located behind the Goldenes Dachl on a small alleylike street, is popular with Innsbruck's younger crowd (is 30 still young?). Cozy with vaulted ceilings, this is a good place for that après-ski drink; the crowds start pouring in after

10pm. There's live music several times a week. The house specialty is a drink called the B-52, with a secret recipe.

Prices: A Seidel (a third of a liter) of beer 23 S ($2.10). **Admission:** Free.
Open: Daily 7pm–1am.

PIANO, Herzog-Friedrich-Strasse 5. Tel. 571010.

This is a trendy bar, the place to see and be seen for Innsbruck's professional yuppie crowd. It's located near the Goldenes Dachl, its entryway buried between the stores along the covered sidewalk.

Prices: A Seidel of beer 21 S ($1.90); wine from 21 S ($1.90). **Admission:** Free.
Open: Mon–Sat 10am–1am.

CLUB FILOU, Stift Gasse 12. Tel. 580256.

Club Filou has a small bar on the ground floor, but the real action is in the basement at its disco. The dance floor is small, but that doesn't hinder the crowds that pour into this place. The action here continues full swing until the wee hours of the morning. In summer there's an outdoor garden. Club Filou is also in the Old City.

Prices: A Seidel (a third of a liter) of beer at the bar 26 S ($2.35); a Seidel of beer in the disco, 45 S ($4.10). **Admission:** Disco, free Sun–Thurs, 100 S ($9.10) Fri–Sat, which goes toward 100 S worth of drinks or food.

Open: Bar, daily 6pm–4am; disco, daily 9pm–4am.

9. EASY EXCURSIONS

Hafelekar, Innsbruck's "house mountain," 7,700 feet above sea level, is three miles north of the city center. Take bus C from the train station to the Hungerburg stop, where you board the funicular and then the cable car to the peak. The round-trip price is 257 S ($23.35), less for Eurailpass holders or if you purchase your ticket at the Innsbruck Information Office. The panoramic view of Tyrol's Alps is breathtaking.

Patscherkofel mountain, 7,400 feet above sea level, is three miles southeast of Innsbruck. Take tram no. 6 or bus J from the train station to Igls to board the cable car to the top. The round-trip price is 170 S ($15.45) 15% less for Eurailpass holders. The view is impressive, but Hafelekar is better.

The **Schwazer Silberbergwerk (Schwaz Silver Mines),** located in the village of Schwaz, less than a 20-minute train ride from Innsbruck, were once the largest medieval silver mines in central Europe. In the early 1500s Schwaz boasted 10,000 miners and was the second-largest town in Austria after Vienna, its silver forming the financial basis of the Habsburg empire. Today, part of the mines' 300-mile network of tunnels have been opened to 1½-hour tours, which begin with an impressive seven-minute train ride through a narrow tunnel that took a whole generation of miners 26 years to dig. The tour continues on foot, with displays and explanations of the lives of the miners and problems they faced, from the transportation of ore and dead rock to water seepage and ventilation. Although tours are given only in German, an accompanying booklet with English translations is available.

Participants are given hard hats and waterproof jackets, and good walking shoes are recommended. Tours are given in summer, Monday through Friday from 8:30am to 4pm and on Saturday and Sunday from 8:30am to 5pm; in winter, daily from 10am to 4pm. Cost of the tour is 120 S ($10.90) for adults and 60 S ($5.45) for students and children. For more information, call the Schwazer Silberbergwerk at 05242/72372-0.

LISBON

Despite its location on the Atlantic, Lisbon (pop. 1.5 million) has a decidedly Mediterranean mien. Vibrant beneath a cerulean sky gleam the bright-orange roofs, pretty pastel houses, abundant *azulejos* (tiles), and decorative mosaic sidewalks that make Lisbon one of Europe's most winsome capitals. Straddling seven notable hills and some two dozen lesser ones, the city is replete with fabulous vistas that sneak up on you as you negotiate the benign maze of staircased streets and aged, twisting alleyways that meander through the city's historic core.

Legend has it that Ulysses founded Lisbon, but recorded history points to a Roman origin in the 3rd century B.C. In the centuries since, the former Roman city of Olisipo passed through the hands of the Vandals, Visigoths, and Moors en route to becoming the nation's capital in 1260. Echoed in the city's monuments and museums is the 16th-century imperial majesty of a nation whose empire once stretched across many seas and was more than 100 times its own size.

After a devastating 1755 earthquake, which leveled much of the city, Lisbon arose anew under the supervision of the Marquês de Pombal, whose enlightened urban planning continues to serve Lisbon well. The Baixa is an orderly grid of shopping streets; the broad, tree-lined avenida da Liberdade, flanked with outdoor cafés, invites you to linger; and throughout the city, abundant parks and gardens and lively plazas ward off municipal monotony.

The pace now is picking up in Lisbon. Shops are becoming increasingly chic, restaurants more sophisticated, and the nightlife hours longer. Perhaps the most telling, and, in my opinion, regrettable, sign of the progressive times is the debut of a McDonald's franchise.

Clearly, Lisbon is on the move. Life once percolated through its romantic streets. It's now beginning to pulse.

1. FROM A BUDGET TRAVELER'S POINT OF VIEW

LISBON BUDGET BESTS If you don't mind potent olive oil and abundant garlic, *restaurante-cervejarias* are inexpensive eateries. In some budget restaurants, younger children can eat from their parents' plates and half portions are available; where portions are large, sharing is sometimes permitted. In establishments where you can sit or stand, standing is cheaper.

Because Lisbon's touristic nucleus is so compact, most things can be seen and done on foot or for the modest price of a subway or bus ticket.

WHAT THINGS COST IN LISBON	U.S. $
Taxi from the airport to the Hotel Tivoli on avenida da Liberdade	6.40
Metro from Rotunda to Rossio	.40
Local telephone call	.08
Double room at the Hotel Tivoli (deluxe)	320.00
Double room at the Eduardo VII (moderate)	130.00
Double room at Residêncial Dinastia-I (budget)	30.55
Continental breakfast	1.60
Lunch for one, without wine, at Cervejaria da Trindade (moderate)	13.25
Lunch for one, without wine, at Tasca Marinheiro (budget)	7.70
Dinner for one, without wine, at Tavares Rico (deluxe)	68.25
Dinner for one, without wine, at Casanostra (moderate)	22.05
Dinner for one, without wine, at Cervejeria a Cubata (budget)	9.95
Glass of beer	.55
Coca-Cola in a restaurant	1.00
Cup of coffee	.65
Roll of ASA 100 color film, 24 exposures	5.35
Admission to Mosteiro dos Jerónimos	2.00–3.30
Movie ticket	2.00–3.10
Theater ticket	7.30–18.25

SPECIAL DISCOUNT OPPORTUNITIES   For Students   Tagus Turismo Juvenil, praça de Londres, 9b, between the Campo Pequeno and Areeiro metro stops (tel. 848-49-57), is Lisbon's youth and student travel agency, offering special rates on flights, car rentals, and sightseeing tours in Portugal and abroad. They're open Monday through Friday from 10am to 1pm and 2:30 to 6pm.

Some museums offer free admission to students and senior citizens, so bring along the appropriate ID.

For Everyone   Most museums are free Sunday morning, and some are free on Wednesday morning.

WORTH THE EXTRA BUCKS   An evening at a **fado club** (with dinner and entertainment) may run 2,500–5,000 Esc ($18.25–$36.50) per person, but you should experience this Portuguese song form at least once. A dinner reservation will guarantee you a seat, but you can go around 11pm just for drinks and pay a minimum, typically 1,000–1,700 Esc ($7.30–$12.40). The music usually goes on until at least 3am.

2. PRETRIP PREPARATIONS

DOCUMENTS   Citizens of the United States, Canada, the U.K., Australia, and New Zealand require only a valid passport.

✓ WHAT'S SPECIAL ABOUT LISBON

Architectural Highlights
☐ Mosteiro dos Jerónimos (Jerónimos Monastery), a fine example of the 16th-century Manueline architectural style inspired by Portugal's maritime prowess and vast colonial empire.

Monuments
☐ Padrão dos Descobrimentos (Monument of the Discoveries), an impressive tribute to Portugal's imperial past coupled with a sidewalk depiction that summarizes that past.

Museums
☐ Museu da Fundação Calouste Gulbenkian (Gulbenkian Foundation Museum), a gem of a museum custom-designed to display its eclectic collection.
☐ Fundação Ricardo Espirito Santo (Museum of Decorative Arts), where you can order a reproduction of anything that strikes your fancy.

Vistas
☐ From Saint George's Castle.
☐ From the top of the Santa Justa Elevator.
☐ From São Pedro de Alcantara park.

Engineering Highlights
☐ Ponte 25 de Abril, one of the longest single-span suspension bridges in the world.

Neighborhoods
☐ Strolling through the Alfama's maze of narrow streets for an intimate glimpse of daily Lisbon life.

After Dark
☐ Fado, Portugal's traditional song form, steeped in the full range of human emotion.

Great Towns/Villages
☐ Sintra, a mountain retreat stocked with romantic palaces and beautiful gardens.

Spectacles
☐ The bullfight, which in Portugal offers the full panoply of color and excitement without the fatal dénouement.

Transportation
☐ The colorful trams, especially no. 28, which traverses Lisbon's oldest neighborhoods.

WHAT TO PACK Make sure you bring flat, comfortable shoes for the many cobblestone streets and mosaic sidewalks.

Except in summer, pack clothing that can be layered. As summer nights are often cool, bring a shawl or light jacket. In winter, a lined raincoat (perhaps with a sweater) should suffice. In the spring, be prepared for rain.

Shorts are not considered in good taste as street attire.

WHEN TO GO July and August are the peak tourist months, and the hottest (though nights are cool). Spring and fall are ideal as the city is often at its greenest.

Lisbon's Average Daytime Temperature & Rainfall

	Jan	Feb	Mar	Apr	May	June	July	Aug	Sept	Oct	Nov	Dec
Temp. (°F)	57	59	63	67	71	77	81	82	79	72	63	58
Rainfall "	4.3	3.0	4.2	2.1	1.7	0.6	0.1	0.2	1.3	2.4	3.7	4.1

Special Events June 12 and 13 Lisbon celebrates the **Feast Day of St. Anthony** with *marchas* (strolling groups of singers and musicians). On the evening of June 12 revellers parade in costume along avenida da Liberdade. Festivities include dances, bonfires, and general merriment in the taverns until dawn, especially in the Alfama district. Festivities on **June 24** and **June 29** in the Alfama honor Lisbon's other popular saints—John, Peter, and Paul.

In July, Sintra holds its annual **music festival.** In August, Estoril does likewise. In the fall, Cascais holds an annual **jazz festival.** Check newspapers for details.

3. ORIENTATION & GETTING AROUND

ARRIVING IN LISBON

FROM THE AIRPORT   From **Portela Airport** to the heart of town is only about six miles. Expect to pay about 1,000 Esc ($7.30) for a taxi. The Linha Verde (Green Line) bus costs 260 Esc ($1.90) and runs from the airport to Santa Apolónia Station every 15 minutes from 7am to 9:20pm.

FROM THE TRAIN STATION   From Madrid or Paris you'll arrive at **Santa Apolónia Station,** Lisbon's major terminal, located by the river near the Alfama.

In addition to Santa Apolónia, which serves Lisbon's northern environs, there are three other stations—**Rossio** (with trains to Sintra), **Cais do Sodre** (with trains to the Estoril Coast), and **Sul e Sueste** (with trains to the Algarve).

INFORMATION

The main **Portuguese Tourist Office,** at Palácio Foz, praça dos Restauradores (tel. 01/346-63-07 or 01/346-36-43), is the best source of information. It's open Monday through Saturday from 9am to 8pm and on Sunday from 10am to 6pm.

For a listing of useful information, addresses, phone numbers, and events, pick up *What's On in Lisbon* at the tourist office or any major hotel. The best source of up-to-the-minute information on entertainment around town is *Diário de Noticias.*

CITY LAYOUT

The heart of the city extends some two miles from **praça do Comércio** to **praça do Marquês de Pombal** (named after the prime minister who rebuilt the town after the 1755 earthquake). Between praça do Comércio and **Rossio Square** is the **Baixa,** a grid of small shopping streets. From Rossio Square to praça do Marquês de Pombal runs **avenida da Liberdade,** Lisbon's rendition of the Champs-Elysées.

Looking at Lisbon from the waterfront, to the right is the **Alfama,** crowned by the Castelo São Jorge (St. George's Castle); to the left is the **Bairro Alto,** the old, inner-city business district that still houses most of the newspaper publishers and fado clubs and has recently become home to chic restaurants, bars, and clubs.

NEIGHBORHOODS   The **Baixa** (literally "Lower Town") stretching from the river to Rossio Square (site of the Inquisition's auto-da-fés) is a bustling enclave of shops. Such streets as rua do Ouro (Street of Gold) and rua da Prata (Street of Silver) have now diversified their consumer offerings. For your shopping convenience, rua Augusta and rua de Santa Justa are pedestrian streets lined with boutiques and shops selling leather goods, real and faux jewelry, assorted handcrafts, and more.

The shopping continues along rua do Carmo, rua Garrett, and largo do Chiado, which link the Baixa with the **Bairro Alto** (literally "Upper Town"). Many years ago its steep, claustrophobic streets harbored unsavory characters, but today the Bairro Alto has been gentrified to a tasteful trendiness.

To the north of both the Baixa and Bairro Alto extends the ample **avenida da Liberdade,** where banks, airline offices, and tour operators rub elbows with kitschy souvenir shops, first-run cinemas, and the occasional sidewalk café.

Rising steep and narrow at the foot of Saint George's Castle is the **Alfama,** the Lisbon of yestercentury. Having miraculously escaped the devastation of the 1755 earthquake, its medieval aspect remains intact, making it one of Lisbon's most colorful neighborhoods. Except for a handful of churches, museums, and a smattering of shops and restaurants catering to tourists, this is largely a working-class neighborhood festooned with colorful garlands of drying laundry.

Six kilometers (four miles) from praça do Comércio is **Belém** (which means Bethlehem), a Lisbon district that has almost taken on an urban identity of its own. The focal point of Portugal's 16th-century maritime activities, Belém appropriately offers several museums and monuments commemorating the enterprise of Portugal's colonial heyday. Once you've seen them, and Europe's longest single-span suspension bridge, the **Ponte 25 de Abril,** there is little reason to linger in Belém.

GETTING AROUND

Taxis are so inexpensive that you may choose to forgo the efficient public transport.

BY SUBWAY   The V-shaped subway system is Europe's cheapest—40 Esc (29¢) per ticket if you buy 10 at a time or 45 Esc (33¢) from the vending machine, 50 Esc (36¢) otherwise. It operates daily from 6:30am to 1am.

BY BUS & TRAM   Far more extensive are the bus and tram networks. A module of 10 tickets, good for two to four zones of travel, costs 580 Esc ($4.25) at booths located in most of the major squares (such as Rossio and Figueira) and by the Santa Justa Elevator; route maps are available there as well. You can also buy a block of 20 tickets for the same price, but each ticket is then good for one zone only. Tickets purchased on the bus cost 130 Esc (95¢); on the tram, 110 Esc (80¢). Buses and trams run daily from 6am to 1am.

SANTA JUSTA ELEVATOR & FUNICULAR CARS   Near Rossio Square, the **Santa Justa Elevador** links rua do Ouro with praça do Carmo. The fare is 30 Esc (22¢).

Lisbon's three **funicular cars** are the Gloria, from praça dos Restauradores to rua São Pedro de Alcantara; the Lavra, from the east side of avenida da Liberdade to campo Martires da Pátria; and the Bica, from calçada do Combro to rua da Boavista. The fare is also 30 Esc (22¢).

SPECIAL TOURIST TICKET   **Four-** and **seven-day tickets** valid for all city buses, trams, subways, the Santa Justa Elevator, and the funicular cars cost 1,155 Esc ($8.45) and 1,625 Esc ($11.85), and are sold at the Santa Justa Elevator daily from 8am to 8pm.

Travelers staying in Lisbon a month or more should purchase one of the **Social Passes (*Passes Sociais*),** which are valid for one month on all forms of public transportation. Adult passes cost 2,635–5,010 Esc ($19.25–$36.55); passes for children ages 4–12, 1,980–3,760 Esc ($14.45–$27.45). Social Passes can be purchased at the foot of the Santa Justa Elevator and at ferry, tram, bus, and railroad terminals.

BY TAXI   The initial cost is 135 Esc ($1), and each additional 135 meters or 34 seconds of waiting time costs 7 Esc (5¢). Luggage weighing over 30 kilos (66 lb.) commands a 50% surcharge. Fares increase 20% between 10pm and 6am.

There are taxi stands on the east side of Rossio Square near the train station, in the largo do Chiado, and near the San Roque Church. Taxis are available when the green roof lights are off.

ON FOOT   The tourist area of Lisbon is compact enough that you can comfortably cover most of it on foot. Only the sights in the area of Parque Eduardo VII and the Belém district require public transportation or a car.

CAR RENTAL   Most international car-rental companies have offices at the airport. Some in-town addresses are: **Avis,** avenida Praia da Victoria, 12C (tel. 356-76-11), open daily from 8am to 7pm in town and daily from 6am to 1am at the airport (tel. 89-99-47); **Europcar,** avenida António Augusto Aguiar, 24 (tel. 52-45-58), open Monday through Saturday from 8am to 8pm and on Sunday and holidays from 8am to 6:30pm in town, and daily from 7am to 1am at the airport (tel. 80-11-76); and **Hertz,** avenida 5 de Outubro, 10 (tel. 57-90-77), open Monday through Friday from 8am to 7pm and on Saturday and Sunday from 9am to 1pm and 2 to 7pm in town, from 6am to midnight at the airport (tel. 89-27-22).

Expect to pay a minimum base rate of about 4,200 Esc ($30.65) per day, plus extras and tax. Shop around for any special rates.

 LISBON

Addresses Lisbon addresses consist of a street name, number, and story, denoted by a numeral and the symbol °. "Rua Rosa Araújo, 2-6°" means the sixth floor at no. 2 on that street. Remember that in Europe the ground floor is not counted as the first floor—6° actually means seven stories up.

Banks Banks are open Monday through Friday from 8:30am to 2:45pm; some offer a foreign-exchange service Monday through Saturday from 6 to 11pm. The bank at the airport is always open. You can change money on Saturday and Sunday from 8:30am to 8:30pm at the bank at Santa Apolónia Station (tel. 86-84-50). The American Express Travel Representative office is at Star Travel, praça dos Restauradores, 14 (tel. 346-03-36), open Monday through Friday from 9am to 12:30pm and 2 to 6pm.

Business Hours Shops are typically open Monday through Friday from 9am to 1pm and 3 to 7pm (though some are now open through lunch) and on Saturday from 9am to 1pm. Restaurants are open from noon to 3pm and 7 to 11pm or midnight. Offices are generally open Monday through Friday from 9am to 1pm and 3 to 5:30pm or 6pm.

Currency The Portuguese currency unit is the escudo (Esc), written 1$00. Fractions of an escudo (centavos) follow the "$"; for example, 100 escudos is written "100$00." Coins are minted in 50 centavos, and 1, 5, 10, 20, 25, and 50 escudos. Notes are printed in 100, 500, 1,000, 5,000, and 10,000 escudos.

Doctors English-speaking doctors can be found at the British Hospital, rua Saraiva de Carvalho, 49 (tel. 60-20-20).

Embassies The **U.S. Embassy** is on avenida das Forças Armadas (tel. 726-66-00), open Monday through Friday from 8:30am to 12:30pm and 1:30 to 5:30pm. The **Embassy of the U.K.** is at rua São Domingos a Lapa, 37 (tel. 396-11-91), open Monday through Friday from 9am to 1pm and 2:30 to 5:30pm; the British Consulate, rua da Estrela, 4 (tel. 395-40-82), is open Monday through Friday from 10am to 12:30pm and 3 to 4:30pm. The **Canadian Embassy,** avenida da Liberdade, 144-56, 4° (tel. 347-48-92), is open Monday through Friday from 8:30am to 12:15pm and 1pm to 5pm. The **Australian Embassy,** at avenida da Liberdade, 244-4° (tel. 52-33-50), is open Monday through Thursday from 9am to 12:30pm and 1:30 to 5pm, and on Friday from 9am to 12:30pm.

Emergencies Call 115 for an ambulance, the fire department, and the police.

Look in any newspaper or dial 16 for 24-hour pharmacies. Closed pharmacies post notices indicating the nearest open one.

Holidays Holidays in Lisbon are: New Year's Day (Jan 1), Freedom Day (Apr 25), Worker's Day (May 1), Camões and Portugal Day (June 10), Assumption Day (Aug 15), Day of the Republic (Oct 5), All Saints' Day (Nov 1), Feast of the Immaculate Conception (Dec 8), and Christmas (Dec 25). Other public holidays with shifting dates are Good Friday, Shrove Tuesday, and Corpus Christi.

Hospitals See "Doctors," above.

Information See "Orientation and Getting Around," above.

THE ESCUDO & THE DOLLAR

At this writing $1 = approximately 137 Esc (or 1 Esc = 0.72¢), and this was the rate of exchange used to calculate the dollar values given in this chapter (rounded to the nearest nickel). This rate fluctuates from time to time and may not be the same when you travel to Portugal. Therefore the following table should be used only as a guide:

Esc	U.S.$	Esc	U.S.$
5	.03	1,500	10.95
10	.07	2,000	14.60
15	.10	2,500	18.25
20	.15	3,000	21.90
25	.18	3,500	25.55
50	.36	4,000	29.20
75	.55	4,500	32.85
100	.73	5,000	36.50
150	1.09	6,000	43.80
200	1.46	7,000	51.10
250	1.82	8,000	58.40
500	3.65	9,000	65.70
1,000	7.30	10,000	72.99

Laundry/Dry Cleaning   Pestox, rua Bernardim Ribeiro, 93b (tel. 55-66-03), about 500 yards east of the Rotunda, is open weekdays from 9am to 7pm and charges 800 Esc ($5.85) for 4–5 kilos (8–11 lb.) of laundry on a self-service basis, and 300 Esc ($2.20) per kilo (2.2 lb.), for a minimum of 3 kilos (6.6 lb.) of laundry washed and dried for you. *Tinturaria* is the Portuguese term for dry cleaning.

Lost and Found   Check for lost property at the municipal Governo Civil, next to the São Carlos Opera House, or at the Anjos Police Station, rua dos Anjos, 56; they are open from 9am to noon and 2 to 6pm. For items lost on public transportation, check at Seeção de Achados da P.S.P. Olivais Sul, Pr. Cidade Salazar Lote, 180 (tel. 33-54-03), Monday through Friday from 9am to noon and 2 to 6pm.

Mail   The Central Post Office (Correio), parça dos Restauradores, 58, is open daily from 8am to 10pm. The post office at the airport is open 24 hours daily. Letters and postcards to North America cost 115 Esc (85¢).

Newspapers   *Diário de Noticias* is Lisbon's leading daily. The *Anglo-Portuguese News* is a local English-language paper. You'll find foreign-language newspapers at most newsstands.

Photographic Needs   Fotosport, Terminal de Rossio, Loja (Shop) 120 (tel. 342-78-70), is open Monday through Friday from 8am to 10pm and on Saturday, Sunday, and holidays from 9am to 8pm.

Police   Call 115 for the police.

Radio/TV   Every morning at 8am Radio Comercial broadcasts up-to-the-minute information on Lisbon events in several languages, including English.

Religious Services   Since Portugal is predominantly Roman Catholic, finding a mass (in Portuguese) is easy. Other opportunities for worship include: the Baptist Evangelical Church, rua Filipe Folque, 36, with services on Wednesday at 7:30pm and on Sunday at 11am and 7:30pm; St. George's Church (Church of England), rua de São Jorge, 6, with services on Sunday at 11am; the Mosque of Lisbon, avenida José Malhoa, with services every day and a special service on Friday; and Shaare Tickva Synagogue, rua Alexandre Herculano, 59, with services on Friday from 7:30 to 8pm and on Saturday at 10:30am.

Shoe Repair   Silva e Neves Lopes, Lda., rua Rodrigo da Fonseca, 182B (near the Hotel Ritz) (tel. 68-70-55), is open Monday through Friday from 7am to 8:30pm and on Saturday from 7am to 1pm.

Tax The Value-Added Tax (I.V.A. in Portugal) is about 17%. See "Savvy Shopping," below, for refund information.

Taxis See "Orientation and Getting Around," above.

Telephone There is a central telephone office at Rossio Square 68, diagonally across from the National Theater, open daily from 8am to 11pm. Local calls cost 8¢; for long distance within the country, dial "0" before the two-digit area code and then the number.

To call internationally, dial 00 and then the country and city codes and the number. Some phones are equipped for credit-card (American Express, VISA, etc.—not phone-company cards) calls. A three-minute call to the U.S. costs 950 Esc ($6.95) Monday through Friday from 10pm to 8am, on Saturday from 1pm to 8am, and all day Sunday (discount periods); 1,150 Esc ($8.40) at all other times. If you call direct from your hotel, however, you may pay steep surcharges.

To call collect, or at more economical U.S. calling-card rates, place your call through AT&T's USA Direct by dialing 05017-1-288 or through MCI's Call USA by dialing 05017-1-234. You can also call collect, or at U.S. calling-card rates, through an international operator by dialing 098.

The dial tone for long distance calls may be unusual, but make sure there is a tone before you begin dialing and that the tone stops once you begin to dial. Dial steadily, without long pauses; the connection can take up to a minute, during which time you may hear some unfamiliar tones. Any persistent tone means that your call has failed.

In post offices and scattered "Credifone" locations, special phones take prepaid cards in 50- and 120-unit denominations (750 and 1,725 escudos—$5.45 and $12.60) sold at post offices; 120 units buys about 3 minutes to the U.S. at standard rates and over 3½ minutes during the discount periods. You can also make international calls at the Central Post Office, praça dos Restauradores, daily from 8am to 10pm.

Tipping Although restaurant prices usually include a service charge, it is considered polite to tip an additional 5%–10%. Taxi drivers get about 10% for long rides and 15%–20% on short rides; a minimum tip of 25–30 Esc (20¢–25¢) is suggested. You should give 100–200 Esc (75¢–$1.50) to porters and bellhops.

Useful Telephone Numbers TAP Air Portugal (tel. 54-40-80); airport information (tel. 80-20-60); train information (tel. 87-60-25); camping and caravanning information (tel. 315-27-15).

4. BUDGET ACCOMMODATIONS

Budget accommodations abound throughout the city, but the most convenient areas to stay are around the Parque Eduardo VII, along avenida da Liberdade, around Rossio Square, and in the Bairro Alto. Don't judge a hotel by its facade. Go in and ask to see several rooms before deciding. Ask which rooms are quietest and if any have been renovated recently. Many budget lodgings will serve breakfast in your room upon request.

Long-Term Stays Residências are geared for long-term stays and offer discounts of 10% or more.

DOUBLES FOR LESS THAN 6,000 ESC [$43.80]

NEAR ROSSIO SQUARE

RESIDÊNCIA DO SUL, praça Dom Pedro IV, 59-2° Esq., 1100 Lisboa.

Tel. 01/342-25-11. 21 rms (15 with bath, 6 with sink and bidet). **Metro:** Rossio.

$ Rates (including service and VAT): 2,420 Esc ($17.65) single with sink and bidet, 3,520 Esc ($25.70) single with bath; 2,860 Esc ($20.90) double with sink and bidet, 3,960 Esc ($28.90) double with bath; 4,400 Esc ($32.10) triple with shower, 5,110 Esc ($37.75) triple with bath. No credit cards.

In the heart of Lisbon, this very basic lodging shares its entrance with a gift shop. The rooms are adequate and clean, but somewhat dreary, with the occasional battered furnishing. The price is right, however, and you may find a room here in peak season (July and August) when vacancies are at a premium.

There are two additional Residências do Sul: avenida da Liberdade, 53-2° (tel. 01/346-56-47) (Metro: Restauradores), and avenida Almirante Reis, 34 (tel. 01/814-72-53) (Metro: Anjos).

IN BAIRRO ALTO

PENSÃO SEVILHA, praça da Alegria, 11-2°, 1200 Lisboa. Tel. 01/346-95-79. 32 rms (15 with bath). TEL **Metro:** Avenida.

$ Rates (including service and VAT): 1,735 Esc ($12.65) single without bath; 2,860 Esc ($20.85) single with bath; 2,860 Esc ($20.85) double without bath, 4,040 Esc ($29.50) double with bath; 5,195 Esc ($37.90) triple with bath; 5,775 Esc ($42.15) quad with bath. No credit cards.

Just off avenida da Liberdade, this no-frills pension in praça da Alegria (literally, "Fun Square") is ideal for seasoned budget travelers and heaven for backpackers seeking lodging in a central area. The modern baths are a comfortable notch above the dorm-style accommodations, and you'll need to go up several flights of stairs to your quarters. Most of the rather large rooms overlook the square. Prices are by no means firm, especially off-season—so bargain.

AROUND PARQUE EDUARDO VII

RESIDÊNCIA DUBLIN, rua de Santa Marta, 45, 1100 Lisboa. Tel. 01/355-54-89. 42 rms (21 with bath, 6 with shower and bidet). **Metro:** Rotunda.

$ Rates (including breakfast, service, and VAT): 3,850 Esc ($28.10) single without bath, 4,400 Esc ($32.10) single with shower and bidet, 4,950 Esc ($36.15) single with bath; 4,400 Esc ($32.10) double without bath, 4,950 Esc ($36.15) double with shower and bidet, 5,500 Esc ($40.15) double with bath; 7,700 Esc ($56.20) triple with bath; 8,690 Esc ($63.45) suite for six with bath. No credit cards.

Near the Rotunda, the Dublin's rooms are small, basic, and impersonal. Though dimly lit, they are quite clean.

RESIDENCIAL ALELÚIA, rua Luciano Cordeiro, 32, 1100 Lisboa. Tel. 01/57-37-02. 14 rms (all with bath, some with kitchenette), 1 apartment. MINIBAR TV TEL **Metro:** Rotunda.

$ Rates (including service and VAT): 3,300 Esc ($24.10) single; 4,400–6,600 Esc

---

Ⓕ FROMMER'S SMART TRAVELER: HOTELS

VALUE-CONSCIOUS TRAVELERS SHOULD
TAKE ADVANTAGE OF THE FOLLOWING:

1. *Residências*, which often offer discounts of at least 10% to guests staying more than a week.
2. Bargaining—hoteliers will not be offended—especially off-season.

($32.10–$48.15) double; 6,050–8,250 Esc ($44.15–$60.20) triple; 6,600–8,800 Esc ($48.15–$64.25) quad; 7,700 Esc ($56.20) apartment for up to six. Continental breakfast 250 Esc ($1.80) extra, 350 Esc ($2.55) with fruit. No credit cards. As you pass through the building's portal, the Alelúia's reception area is to the right. Many of its rooms feature gilded headboards and marble-top tables, but readers have been complaining of late about slipping maintenance and being put up in rooms that are undergoing renovation. The quality and charm of the rooms are uneven, so have a look at a few before you decide. The renovated rooms have pretty tilework on the walls. The maze of halls, studded with more tiles and decorative wrought iron, harbors several intimate salons with TVs and a cozy bar. Owner António Morais, who speaks excellent English, provides free transportation from the airport or train station if you call upon arrival. Readers consistently rave about his friendliness and helpfulness.

RESIDENCIAL DINASTIA-I, rua Dom João V, 7, 1200 Lisboa. Tel. 01/68-50-67. 26 rms (16 with bath, 7 with shower only). TEL **Metro:** Rotunda. **Tram:** 25 or 26. **Bus:** 20 or 22.
$ **Rates** (including breakfast, service, and VAT): 2,750 Esc ($20.05) single without bath, 3,630 Esc ($26.50) single with shower only, 4,180 Esc ($30.50) single with bath; 3,300 Esc ($24.10) double without bath, 3,850 Esc ($28.10) double with shower only, 4,400 Esc ($32.10) double with bath; 4,400 Esc ($32.10) triple with shower only, 5,060 Esc ($36.95) triple with bath. No credit cards. **Parking:** Free.
A short walk from the Rotunda, this unpromising-looking pension has rather spacious rooms that are gradually being renovated; the new ones have nice terracotta floors. For maximum quiet, ask for a room in the back. Rooms 105, 305, and 306 feature large baths.

PENSÃO PÁTRIA, avenida Duque de Avila, 42-6°, 1000 Lisboa. Tel. 01/53-06-20. 30 rms (3 with bath, 27 with bidet and sink only). TEL **Metro:** Saldanha. **Bus:** 16, 18, 26, or 42.
$ **Rates** (including breakfast, service, and VAT): 4,040 Esc ($29.50) single with bidet and sink, 4,400 Esc ($32.10) single with bath; 4,800 Esc ($35.05) double with bidet and sink, 5,500 Esc ($40.15) double with bath. No credit cards.
The Pátria's rooms are very basic and cramped, but clean. Little English is spoken here, but the management is friendly. There is also a restaurant serving lunch and dinner, as well as breakfast.

NEAR AVENIDA DA LIBERDADE

RESIDENCIAL FLORESCENTE, rua Portas São Antão, 99, 1100 Lisboa. Tel. 01/342-66-09. 115 rms (20 with bath, 40 with shower only, 55 with sink and bidet only). **Metro:** Restauradores.
$ **Rates** (including service and VAT): 3,850 Esc ($28.10) single or double with sink and bidet only, 4,400 Esc ($32.10) single or double with shower, 4,400–6,600 Esc ($32.10–$48.15) single or double with bath. EURO, MC, V.
⭐ Centrally located off praça dos Restauradores, the Florescente offers small, clean rooms on four floors (no elevator, but an attractive tiled stairway). Some rooms are more pleasant than others (some have TV or piped-in music), so see a few before deciding. No breakfast is served, but there are numerous coffee shops nearby.

DOUBLES FOR LESS THAN 8,000 ESC [$58.40]

IN BAIRRO ALTO

PENSÃO LONDRES, rua Dom Pedro V. 53, 1200 Lisboa. Tel. 01/346-22-03. 40 rms (12 with bath, 10 with shower). **Tram:** 20 or 24. **Bus:** 15 or 19.
$ **Rates** (including breakfast, service, and VAT): 3,750 Esc ($20.10) single without

bath, 3,850 Esc ($28.10) single with bath; 3,520 Esc ($25.70) double without bath, 4,400 Esc ($32.10) double with shower, 6,050 Esc ($44.15) double with bath; 7,700 Esc ($56.20) triple with bath; 9,570 Esc ($69.85) quad with bath; 12,100 Esc ($88.30) six-bed room with bath. No credit cards.

⭐ Located near the belvedere San Pedro de Alcantara, this is a choice hostelry with sculptured ceilings and fine furnishings in most of the rooms, some with telephones and all with sink. For a splendid view, ask for a room on the fourth floor; there's only one six-bed room. Owner Manuela D. Ferreira makes sure that all is super-clean. Reception is on the second floor.

RESIDENCIAL CAMÕES, trav. do Poço da Cidade, 38-1°, 1200 Lisboa. Tel. 01/346-75-10, or 01/346-40-48 for reservations. 18 rms (8 with bath, 6 with shower only), 2 suites. TEL **Metro:** Rossio. **Tram:** 24. **Bus:** 100.
$ **Rates** (including breakfast and service): 3,465 Esc ($26.45) single without bath, 6,615 Esc ($50.50) single with bath; 5,775 Esc ($44.10) double without bath, 7,665 Esc ($58.50) double with bath; 6,300 Esc ($48.10) triple without bath, 7,665 Esc ($58.50) triple with bath; 9,975 Esc ($76.15) suite for four; 11,025 Esc ($84.15) suite for six. No credit cards.

Friendly tiles greet guests at this hostelry in the heart of Lisbon. Though the rooms (divided among three floors, no elevator) are somewhat cramped, they are clean and comfortable. A cheery breakfast room gets each day off to a bright start. Discounts are readily offered for longer stays.

RESIDENCIAL SANTA CATARINA, rua Dr. Luís de Almeida e Albuquerque, 6, 1200 Lisboa. Tel. 01/346-61-06. 16 rms (all with shower and toilet). TEL **Directions:** See below.
$ **Rates** (including breakfast, service, and VAT): 4,400 Esc ($32.10) single; 6,820 Esc ($49.80) double; 8,250 Esc ($60.20) triple; 9,900 Esc ($72.25) quad. 10% discount on single rooms and a 15% discount on other rooms for bearers of this book. No credit cards.

⭐ Tucked away on a short, quiet street in the vicinity of praça Luís de Camões, this petite pension is attractively furnished and very well maintained. Manager/ owner "Mr. Charles" serves breakfast in the very pleasant haciendalike bar/lounge.

To get here, take tram no. 28 to largo do Calhariz; then walk left up rua Marechal Saldanha and turn right onto rua Dr. Luís de Almeida e Albuquerque.

AROUND PARQUE EDUARDO VII

RESIDENCE LISBONENSE, rua Pinheiro Chagas, 1, 1000 Lisboa. Tel. 01/54-46-28. 30 rms (15 with bath, 7 with shower only). TEL **Metro:** Saldanha.
$ **Rates** (including breakfast, service, and VAT): 2,860 Esc ($20.85) single without bath, 3,410 Esc ($24.90) single with shower only, 3,960 Esc ($28.90) single with bath; 4,510 Esc ($32.90) double without bath, 5,170 Esc ($37.75) double with shower only, 6,160 Esc ($44.95) double with bath. No credit cards.

⭐ Ensconced in a rather stylish old Lisbon building, the well-maintained Lisbonense occupies four floors (there's an elevator). Reception is on the third floor, and you'll likely find someone who speaks English. The smallish rooms are clean, neat, and quaintly charming because of their warm wood furnishings. Number 311 is a large, suitelike room with a large bath. The petite TV room doubles as the breakfast room.

RESIDÊNCIA NAZARETH, avenida António Augusto de Aguiar, 25-4°/ 5°, 1000 Lisboa. Tel. 01/54-20-16. Fax 01/356-08-36. 32 rms (all with bath). A/C TV TEL **Metro:** Parque. **Bus:** 31, 41, or 46.
$ **Rates** (including breakfast, service, and VAT): 5,500–7,150 Esc ($40.15–$52.20) single; 7,150–8,250 Esc ($52.20–$60.20) double; 9,900–10,450 Esc ($72.25–

$76.25) triple; 12,100–13,750 Esc ($88.30–$100.35) quad. AE, DC, EURO, MC, V.

⭐ A Middle Eastern motif of stucco walls and abundant arches in the reception and bar areas fades to just a hint of the Arabic in the ample rooms and baths. The owners, Senhor Nazir and Senhor Basir of Mozambique, and most of the reception staff are fluent in English. Laundry service is available.

DOUBLES FOR LESS THAN 10,500 ESC [$76.65]

AROUND PARQUE EDUARDO VII

RESIDÊNCIA ASTÓRIA, rua Braamcamp, 10, 1297 Lisboa. Tel. 01/52-13-17. Fax 01/53-54-91. 85 rms (all with bath). TEL **Metro:** Rotunda.
$ **Rates** (including breakfast, service, and VAT): 5,500–7,150 Esc ($40.15–$52.20) single; 8,800–9,900 Esc ($64.25–$72.25) double; 8,800–13,200 Esc ($64.25–$96.35) triple; 13,750–16,500 Esc ($100.35–$120.45) quad. No credit cards.
Just off the Rotunda, the Astória has small, squeaky-clean rooms furnished in light wood. Sculptured ceilings interject a note of old-world charm in this otherwise contemporary lodging. You can usually find someone who speaks English behind the reception desk—if not, ask for the owner, Senhor Caldeira.

RESIDÊNCIA CARAVELA, rue Ferreira Lapa, 38, 1100 Lisboa. Tel. 01/53-90-11. Fax 01/315-03-19 (for reservations). 45 rms (all with shower or bath). TV TEL **Metro:** Rotunda. **Bus:** 20 or 22.
$ **Rates** (including breakfast, service, and VAT): 6,600–7,700 Esc ($48.15–$56.20) single; 7,700–8,800 Esc ($56.20–$64.25) double; 8,800–9,900 Esc ($64.25–$72.25) triple; 9,900–11,000 Esc ($72.25–$80.30) quad. AE, D, MC, V.
Off avenida Duque de Loulé, and around the corner from the Centro Cultural Americano (where you can peruse U.S. newspapers and magazines), the Caravela's exterior makes an unprepossessing first impression, but its carpeted rooms are comfortable, albeit a bit dark and worn here and there. The triples have good-sized baths; 14 rooms have showers instead of tubs. There is a pleasant bar for evening socializing.

RESIDÊNCIA IMPERADOR, avenida 5 de Outubro, 55, 1000 Lisboa. Tel. 01/352-48-84. Fax 01/352-65-37. 43 rms (all with bath). A/C TV TEL **Metro:** Saldanha. **Bus:** 21 or 44, or 36 Linha Verde.
$ **Rates** (including breakfast, service, and VAT): 6,600–7,700 Esc ($48.15–$56.20) single; 7,700–8,800 Esc ($56.20–$64.25) double. AE, DC, EURO, MC, V.
Just a few blocks from the Pensão Pátria (see above), the Imperador's standardized rooms have luggage racks, desks, and sundry furnishings affixed to the wall in the manner of a business hotel. The baths are quite cheerful, and the staff has some knowledge of English.

PENSÃO CASAL RIBEIRO, rua Braamcamp, 10-R/C. Dto., 1200 Lisboa. Tel. 01/54-85-44. 30 rms (all with bath). TEL **Metro:** Rotunda.
$ **Rates** (including breakfast, service, and VAT): 6,600 Esc ($48.15) single; 8,250 Esc ($60.20) double; 9,350–9,900 Esc ($68.25–$72.25) triple. No credit cards.
⭐ Don't be deterred by the somewhat dilapidated exterior. This excellent hostelry offers very pleasant, compact rooms equipped with radios and baths beyond one's expectations in the budget category.

IN BAIRRO ALTO

RESIDÊNCIA ROMA, travessa da Glória, 22-A, 1°, 1200 Lisboa. Tel. 01/346-05-57. Fax 01/346-05-57. 24 rms (all with bath). TV TEL **Metro:** Restauradores.

$ **Rates** (including breakfast, service, and VAT): 7,260–8,140 Esc ($53–$59.40) single; 9,900–10,780 Esc ($72.25–$78.70) double; 12,980–14,190 Esc ($94.75–$103.55) triple. AE, EURO, MC, V.

Just off avenida da Liberdade, the Roma is a very clean, comfortable place to bed down. Rooms 201, 202, and 208 are the most spacious doubles. English is spoken with great fluency at the front desk, and the cozy bar offers 24-hour service.

SUPER-BUDGET CHOICES

A YOUTH HOSTEL

CATALAZETE YOUTH HOSTEL, Estrada Marginal, 2780 Oeiras. Tel. 01/443-06-38. 104 beds.

$ **Rates:** High season (Dec 15–Jan 8, Mar 19–Apr 2, and June–Sept), 1,375 Esc ($10) single; 4,125 Esc ($30.10) double. Low season (Oct–Dec 14, Jan 9–Mar 18, and Apr 3–May), 1,100 Esc ($8) single; 3,300 ($24.10) double.

This hostel, located in Oeiras, about half an hour from Lisbon and 15 minutes from Estoril, is open only to members of the International Youth Hostel Federation. They close at midnight; lights out between midnight and 7am. Smoking, eating, and drinking alcoholic beverages are prohibited. There are five double rooms; all other rooms have four or six beds. Guests must use a sleeping bag or two sheets when utilizing the hostel's blankets. All three meals are served.

A CAMPGROUND

PARQUE DE CAMPISMO DE MONSANTO, off the Estoril autostrada. Tel. 01/70-20-61 or 01/70-20-62.

$ **Rates:** Oct–Apr, 105 Esc (75¢) per person; 105 Esc (75¢) per tent; 85 Esc (60¢) per car. May–Sept, 315 Esc ($2.30) per person; 315 Esc ($2.30) per tent; 210 Esc ($1.55) per car. Showers 90 Esc (65¢) extra.

This campground includes all facilities for camping.

WORTH THE EXTRA BUCKS

ALBERGARIA DA SENHORA DO MONTE, calçada do Monte, 39, 1100 Lisboa. Tel. 01/86-60-82. Fax 01/87-77-83. 28 rms (all with bath), 4 suites. TEL **Tram:** 28. **Bus:** 12, 17, 26, or 35.

$ **Rates** (including VAT and breakfast): 9,900–11,550 Esc ($72.25–$84.30) single; 13,200–15,400 Esc ($96.35–$112.40) double; 16,500–19,250 Esc ($120.45–$140.50) double with terrace; 19,250 Esc ($140.50) suite (triple) with sitting room. AE, DC, EURO, MC, V.

Only five rooms lack a view in this panoramically perched establishment overlooking all of Lisbon; the top-floor bar and restaurant in particular offer beautiful sunset views. Every room has a beautifully tiled bath, 11 rooms have balconies, and 4 have terraces; some have air conditioning. All are being gradually renovated to modern, pastel comfort. As it's tucked away on a small street in the Graça area, you'll probably want to take a cab the first time. After that, it's a short walk to the tram that goes into the heart of town.

5. BUDGET DINING

By far the best areas for scouting out restaurants are the Bairro Alto and the rua das Portas de Santo Antão. Some restaurants offer an *ementa turística,* or tourist menu.

Lisbon's meals are still relatively cheap and built around a number of classic, hearty dishes. One is *caldo verde* (a soup with mashed potatoes, finely shredded kale, and pieces of peppery sausage cooked in a beef broth). Then there's the ubiquitous *bacalhau* (codfish), Portugal's national dish, available in over 200 different styles.

Carne de porco a alentejana is pork stewed with clams in a sauce spiced with herbs. *Barrigas de freira* (literally, "nuns' tummies") is a delightful egg dish. So is *acorda*, made with bread, eggs, parsley, and usually shrimp. *Cozido a portuguesa* is a tasty Portuguese version of the New England boiled dinner. One other very common and savory meal is grilled sardines (large ones, not like the ones you usually find in cans) with a fresh salad. As for wine, you can hardly go wrong ordering the house wine. For dessert, try *pudim Molotov*, a cross between a sponge cake and a pudding served with crème caramel. Any of a dozen types of cheese are also eaten for dessert. One, a creamy, smoked, sheep cheese called *serra da estrêla*, is a delicacy. Breakfast usually consists of coffee and a croissant.

Coffee is a connoisseur's matter in Lisbon. Here is a brief lexicon of its varying forms: *bica* is espresso without milk, *carioca* means light espresso, *garoto* is espresso with milk, and *galão* is a large glass of coffee with milk.

The unfortunate practice of charging a *couvert* (cover) is beginning to spring up around town—a sign of the progressive times.

MEALS FOR LESS THAN 2,200 ESC [$16.05]

NEAR ROSSIO SQUARE

A BRASILEIRA, rua Garrett, 120-122. Tel. 346-95-41.
   Cuisine: SANDWICHES/SNACKS. **Metro:** Rossio.
$ Prices: 600–1,430 Esc ($4.35–$10.45). No credit cards.
   Open: Daily 7:30am–2am.
The city's oldest coffee shop, a block from praça de Camões, it serves a strong, aromatic Brazilian espresso for 55 Esc (40¢) if you're standing and 75 Esc (55¢) if you're sitting. The outside tables (don't miss the sculpture of the permanent patron) are fun for coffee or quick lunches, but at these tables coffee is served in double portions only, for 165 Esc ($1.20). Inside, you'll find the quintessential, fin-de-siècle coffeehouse where conversations swirl and cards and chess are played.

BERNARD', rua Garrett, 104. Tel. 347-31-33.
   Cuisine: SANDWICHES/SNACKS. **Metro:** Rossio.
$ Prices: Continental breakfast 220 Esc ($1.60) at the bar, 440 Esc ($3.20) at a table. AE, DC, EURO, MC, V.
   Open: Mon–Sat 8am–11:30pm.
This charming old café near A Brasileira (see above) is great for a breakfast of coffee and pastries or fresh croissants ranging from 70 Esc (50¢) for a plain one to 375 Esc

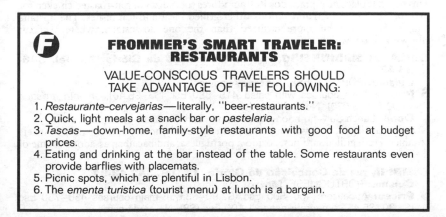

ⓕ FROMMER'S SMART TRAVELER: RESTAURANTS

VALUE-CONSCIOUS TRAVELERS SHOULD
TAKE ADVANTAGE OF THE FOLLOWING:

1. *Restaurante-cervejarias*—literally, "beer-restaurants."
2. Quick, light meals at a snack bar or *pastelaria*.
3. *Tascas*—down-home, family-style restaurants with good food at budget prices.
4. Eating and drinking at the bar instead of the table. Some restaurants even provide barflies with placemats.
5. Picnic spots, which are plentiful in Lisbon.
6. The *ementa turistica* (tourist menu) at lunch is a bargain.

($2.75) for a croissant stuffed with chocolate, cheese, or smoked ham. Also ideal for an afternoon or late-night hot chocolate or snack. Prepayment is required at the bar.

PASTELARIA SUIÇA, praça Dom Pedro IV, 105. Tel. 32-80-92.
  Cuisine: PORTUGUESE. **Metro:** Rossio.
  $ Prices: Main courses 510–1,430 Esc ($3.70–$10.45). No credit cards.
  Open: Daily 7am–9:30pm.

A quintessential café experience in the heart of Rossio Square, this coffee shop serves Brazilian coffee in a glass for 135 Esc ($1), omelets and salads for 275–1,175 Esc ($2–$8.55), and sandwiches for 185–340 Esc ($1.35–$2.50). At lunchtime you may be asked to move inside from the sidewalk tables unless you've ordered a platter.

NEAR AVENIDA DA LIBERDADE

CASA GERALDINOS, rua de Santo António dos Capuchos, 1 and 3. Tel. 53-15-83.
  Cuisine: PORTUGUESE. **Metro:** Avenida or Rotunda.
  $ Prices: Main courses 425–880 Esc ($3.10–$6.40); *ementa turística* 1,050 Esc ($7.65). No credit cards.
  Open: Lunch Mon–Sat noon–3pm; dinner Mon–Sat 7–10pm.

On a steep, sloping street (walk first up rua Telhal), this place, where the name is nowhere in evidence, is always crowded at lunch. Specialties include sopa do carne (beef broth with rice and vegetables), bacalhau, cozido a portuguesa (a potpourri of pork, beef, sausage, cabbage, rice, and carrots—enough for two), and carne de porco portuguesa.

RESTAURANTE BONJARDIM [REI DA BRASA], travessa de Santo Antão, 10. Tel. 342-74-24.
  Cuisine: GRILLED MEATS AND FISH. **Metro:** Restauradores.
  $ Prices: Appetizers 150–400 Esc ($1.10–$2.90); main courses 650–2,000 Esc ($4.75–$14.60); *ementa turística* 1,600 Esc ($11.65). AE, DC, EURO, MC, V.
  Open: Daily noon–11:30pm. **Closed:** May 1.

An ever-so-slight cut above its neighbor "Rei dos Frangos" (see below), the Rei da Brasa specializes in grilled meats and finer fish, with spit-roasted chicken a secondary specialty. Downstairs dining here is preferable to upstairs.

RESTAURANTE BONJARDIM [REI DOS FRANGOS], travessa de Santo Antão, 11. Tel. 342-43-89.
  Cuisine: GRILLED MEATS AND FISH. **Metro:** Restauradores.
  $ Prices: Appetizers 150–350 Esc ($1.10–$2.55); main courses 650–1,650 Esc ($4.75–$12.05); *ementa turística* 1,430 Esc ($10.45). AE, DC, EURO, MC, V.
  Open: Daily noon–11:30pm. **Closed:** May 1.

This no-frills place near praça dos Restauradores specializes in spit-roasted chicken for two for 925 Esc ($6.75) and various other grilled meat and fish dishes. The upstairs dining room is a bit more civilized than the one downstairs, where you eat elbow-to-elbow with strangers.

TASCA DO MARINHEIRO, rua da Conceição da Glória, 38. Tel. 346-94-43.
  Cuisine: PORTUGUESE. **Metro:** Avenida.
  $ Prices: Main courses with salad 415–880 Esc ($3–$6.40); *ementa turística* 1,000 Esc ($7.30). No credit cards.
  Open: Lunch Sun–Fri noon–3pm; dinner Sun–Fri 8pm–midnight.

Near praça Alegria, this working-class tasca is humbly homey and has only four sets of tables. Fresh grilled sardines, cozido a portuguesa, and bacalhau assado are some of the specialties.

ZAMBI II, rua da Conceição da Glória, 14. Tel. 342-43-81.
  Cuisine: PORTUGUESE. **Metro:** Avenida.
  $ Prices: Appetizers 400–500 Esc ($2.90–$3.65); main courses 450–750 Esc ($3.30–$5.45); *ementa turística* 1,100 Esc ($8). No credit cards.

Open: Lunch daily noon–4pm; dinner daily 6–11pm; drinks and nibbles available at the bar daily 10am–2am.

This bright, friendly place just off avenida da Liberdade near the Tasca do Marinheiro consists of a bar and several rows of tables. The house specialties include arroz de mariscos, "fondue bourguignnonn," bacalhau a casa (grilled cod), and bacalhau minhota (fried cod). There are also half a dozen omelet choices.

IN BAIRRO ALTO

RESTAURANTE BARALTO, rua Diário de Noticias, 31. Tel. 342-67-39.
   Cuisine: PORTUGUESE. **Metro:** Rossio. **Tram:** 24.
$ Prices: Main courses 660–1,100 Esc ($4.80–$8); *ementa turística* 1,385 Esc ($10.10). No credit cards.
   Open: Lunch Mon–Fri noon–4pm; dinner daily 6:30pm–midnight.

⭐ This small, down-home restaurant is frequented at lunch by many professionals working in the area. Avelino Pereira is both owner and waiter, and his wife, Rosa, is the cook, whose rendition of the corvina fish, rojoes (lean, marinated pork), and orange cake are highly recommended.

RESTAURANTE "O SOL," calçada do Duque, 21-25. Tel. 347-35-44.
   Cuisine: VEGETARIAN/MACROBIOTIC. **Metro:** Rossio.
$ Prices: Appetizers 65–125 Esc (45¢–90¢); main courses to 425 Esc ($3.10); fixed-price meal 700 Esc ($5.10). No credit cards.
   Open: Mon–Fri 9am–9pm, Sat 9am–2:30pm.

A healthful, hole-in-the-wall eatery where the kitchen is in full view and the offering includes all kinds of organic goods and good-for-you juices.

TASCA DO MANEL, rua da Barroca, 24. Tel. 346-38-13.
   Cuisine: PORTUGUESE. **Metro:** Rossio. **Tram:** 24.
$ Prices: Appetizers 100–1,300 Esc (70¢–$9.50); main courses 880–2,200 Esc ($6.40–$16.05); *ementa turística* 1,430 Esc ($10.45). EURO, MC, V.
   Open: Lunch daily noon–4pm; dinner daily 7pm–midnight.

⭐ Everything is good at this very pleasant place frequented by journalists and assorted other Bairro Alto professionals. The fish is fresh and the grilled pork, veal, and beef are prime choices. The arroz de mariscos is a house specialty. In fall and winter look for game, especially partridge and hare.

NEAR PRAÇA DO COMÉRCIO

ATINEL BAR, off praça do Comércio. Tel. 87-74-19.
   Cuisine: PORTUGUESE/SNACKS. **Tram:** 24.
$ Prices: Appetizers: 150–300 Esc ($1.10–$2.20); main courses 500–2,000 Esc ($3.65–$14.60); *ementa turística* 1,575 Esc ($11.50). No credit cards.
   Open: Daily 6am–9:30pm (lunch noon–3:30pm; snacks, sweets, hamburgers, etc., at other hours).

Though on the river, the Atinel is in no way romantic as it's right by the ferryboat dock. If you can't eat outdoors, try for a table by the picture windows. The diverse menu is in diverse languages. The grilled squid is great.

CUBATA, rua dos Bacalhoeiros, 133. Tel. 87-08-77.
   Cuisine: PORTUGUESE. **Tram:** 24.
$ Prices: Appetizers and salads 170–800 Esc ($1.25–$5.85); main courses 500–2,000 Esc ($3.65–$14.60); *ementa turística* 1,200 Esc ($8.75). No credit cards.
   Open: Sun–Fri 8am–midnight (food served from noon on).

⭐ Though unpretentious in appearance both inside and out, the Cubata serves delicious, economical fare. In addition to the standard repertoire of specialties (including caldo verde, haddock filet with steamed tomatoes, and grilled shrimp), there are about 10 daily specials.

MEALS FOR LESS THAN 3,300 ESC
[$24.05]

NEAR ROSSIO SQUARE

CAFE NICOLA, praça Dom Pedro IV, 24 and 25, in Rossio Sq. Tel. 346-05-79.
Cuisine: PORTUGUESE. **Metro:** Rossio.
$ Prices: Appetizers 130–1,000 Esc (95¢–$7.30); main courses 800–1,800 Esc ($5.85–$13.15); *ementa turística* 1,925 Esc ($14.05). AE, DC, MC, V.
Open: Mon–Fri 7am–8pm, Sat 7am–3pm.
Dating from 1777, this is Lisbon's most popular café and all-purpose eatery, even though it lacks the charm of some others. Coffee, pastries, and meals are served indoors and out; items consumed at the bar must be prepaid at the cashier.

IN BAIRRO ALTO

CANTO DO CAMÕES, travessa da Espera, 38. Tel. 346-54-64.
Cuisine: PORTUGUESE/INTERNATIONAL. **Metro:** Rossio. **Tram:** 24.
$ Prices: Appetizers 200–1,320 Esc ($1.45–$9.65); main courses 1,150–2,200 Esc ($8.40–$16.05); *ementa turística* 2,750 Esc ($20.10). AE, DC, EURO, MC, V.
Open: Lunch Tues–Fri noon–3pm; dinner Tues–Sun 7pm–2am.
This sedate, stylish, air-conditioned restaurant features Swiss specialties (including fondue), and now offers piano and *fado* entertainment at night.

CASANOSTRA, travessa Poço da Cidade, 60 (at the corner of rua da Rosa). Tel. 342-59-31.
Cuisine: ITALIAN. **Reservations:** Recommended. **Metro:** Rossio.
$ Prices: Appetizers 400–1,650 Esc ($2.90–$12.05); main courses 1,300–2,860 Esc ($9.50–$20.85); pastas 750–1,210 Esc ($5.45–$8.85); *ementa turística* 3,630 Esc ($26.50). EURO, MC, V.
Open: Lunch Tues–Fri noon–3pm, Sun 1–2:30pm; dinner Tues–Sun 8–11pm.
★ Casanostra is the province of Maria Paola, a Lisbon resident of 20 years, who imports many of her ingredients from Italy and London to produce authentic Italian cuisine like mama used to make (only better). The pastas, sorbets, and ice creams are homemade. The modern decor is the work of a prominent Portuguese architect. The place seats only 30, so reserve or go early.

CERVEJARIA TRINDADE, rua Nova da Trindade, 20C. Tel. 342-35-06.
Cuisine: PORTUGUESE. **Metro:** Rossio. **Tram:** 24.
$ Prices: Appetizers 75–1,375 Esc (55¢–$10.05); main courses 275–2,200 Esc ($2–$16.05); *ementa turística* 3,000 Esc ($21.90).
Open: Daily noon–2am.
★ In business since 1836, this large, lively, cavernous cervejaria occupies the site of the former 13th-century Convento dos Frades Tinos leveled by the 1755 earthquake. The beautiful tilework within is, in part, from the convent. The patrons of this Lisbon institution include writers, journalists, actors, and a few seafaring types. The offerings include appetizer-size portions of ham, cheese, and assorted cold cuts; sandwiches and omelets; and full meals served at either the tables or the bar.

MAMMA ROSA PIZZERIA, rua do Grémio Lusitano, 14. Tel. 346-53-50.
Cuisine: PIZZA/ITALIAN. **Metro:** Rossio. **Tram:** 24.
$ Prices: Pizzas from 865 Esc ($6.30); pastas and main courses 1,000–2,200 Esc ($7.30–$16.05); *ementa turística* 1,925 Esc ($14.05).
Open: Lunch Mon–Sat 12:30–3pm; dinner daily 7:30pm–2am. **Closed:** Second and third week of Nov.

A charming, checkered-tablecloth trattoria with some of the best pizza in town. The desserts are yummy, too.

NEAR AVENIDA DA LIBERDADE

RESTAURANTE ANDORRA, rua das Portas de Santo Antão, 82. Tel. 342-60-47.
   Cuisine: PORTUGUESE. **Metro:** Restauradores.
$ **Prices:** Appetizers 180–1,000 Esc ($1.30–$7.30); main courses 980–2,090 Esc ($15.25); *ementa turística* 1,980 Esc ($14.45). EURO, MC, V.
   Open: Lunch Mon–Sat 12:30–3pm; dinner Mon–Sat 6–11pm.
Off praça dos Restauradores behind the Central Post Office, this restaurant is informal downstairs and more formal upstairs. Try the arroz de cherne (rice with mixed fish) or açorda de mariscos.

THE CHAINS

ABRACADABRA, Centro Comerical Imaviz, next to the Sheraton Hotel. Tel. 352-04-50.
   Cuisine: FAST FOOD. **Metro:** Rotunda.
$ **Prices:** 190–1,375 Esc ($1.40–$10). No credit cards.
   Open: Daily 9am–2am. **Closed:** Jan 1, Dec 25.
A fast-food joint, this cafeteria offers hamburgers for 250 Esc ($1.80), pizza for 600–1,375 Esc ($4.35–$10), and hot dogs for 240 Esc ($1.75).
   There's another branch at rua do Ouro, 117-119 (tel. 342-45-75), near Rossio Square. It's open Monday through Friday from 8am to 10pm and on Saturday from 11am to 3pm.

MCDONALD'S, avenida da República, 10-F. Tel. 315-31-40.
   Cuisine: FAST FOOD. **Metro:** Saldanha.
$ **Prices:** Hamburgers 230–430 Esc ($1.65–$3.15). No credit cards.
   Open: Mon–Sat 10am–midnight, Sun 11am–midnight.
Lisbon's first McDonald's has supplanted the old, elegant Colombo teahouse, which opened in the late 1930s. No vestige of its former grace remains to mitigate the homogeneous, modern-day, fast-food, McDonald's experience.

PIZZA HUT, avenida Fontes Pereira de Melo, 31. Tel. 57-54-56.
   Cuisine: PIZZA/FAST FOOD. **Metro:** Rotunda.
$ **Prices:** Appetizers 190–550 Esc ($1.40–$4); individual pizzas 553–1,335 Esc ($4.05–$9.75); pastas 860–1,100 Esc ($16.25–$8). No credit cards.
   Open: Daily 11:30am–11:30pm.
The first of the familiar American chains to establish itself in Lisbon, it also offers a salad bar for about 475 Esc ($3.45).

PICNIC SUPPLIES & WHERE TO EAT THEM

Celeiro, rua 1 de Dezembro, 81 (tel. 342-74-95), is a fine soup-to-nuts supermarket near Rossio Square that also offers such ready-cooked fare as roast chicken at 900 Esc ($6.55) per kilo. Open Monday through Friday from 8:30am to 7pm and on Saturday from 8:30am to 1pm. MC, V. Metro: Rossio.
   You can enjoy a picnic in many of the city's numerous parks. My favorites are **San Pedro de Alcantara** and **Parque Eduardo VII,** which has picnic tables.

WORTH THE EXTRA BUCKS

VARANDA RESTAURANT, in the Hotel Eduardo VII, avenida Fontes Pereira de Melo, 5. Tel. 53-01-41.
   Cuisine: PORTUGUESE. **Metro:** Rotunda.

$ Prices: Salads 900–2,530 Esc ($6.55–$18.45); main courses 1,600–2,970 Esc ($11.65–$21.65). AE, DC, V.

Open: Breakfast daily 7–10am; lunch daily 12:30–2:30pm; dinner daily 7:30–9:30pm.

This modern restaurant on the 10th floor of the three-star Hotel Eduardo VII serves up a fine view of Lisbon along with its equally fine fare. Among its charcoal-grilled specialties is a delicious espatada de fruta de mar (shellfish shish kebab). Among the wonderful daily specials is the feijoada, served once or twice a week.

6. ATTRACTIONS

SUGGESTED ITINERARIES

Since the majority of Lisbon's sights are concentrated within the historic heart of the city, those with limited time can still see most of them. Those with more time can indulge in the city's endless reserve of winsome nooks and crannies. If you have only one to five days, the suggested itineraries below will ensure that you see the main attractions.

IF YOU HAVE ONE DAY   After breakfast at Bernard' (see "Budget Dining," above), take your map and head for the maze of spiraling streets that lace the Alfama district. From Rossio Square, head past the shops and boutiques of rua Augusta and turn left onto rua da Conceição. Follow the signs to the Sé (cathedral), a 12th-century structure that has undergone various facelifts. Continue left beyond the Sé and, a bit farther along on your right, stop for the view from the belvedere of Santa Luzia. Follow largo do Contador Mor (directly opposite) to the end and turn left onto chão da Feira to enter the grounds of the Castelo São Jorge (Saint George's Castle). From its ramparts you'll be able to see all of Lisbon.

Wind your way down again to the praça do Comércio and catch a tram or bus (or taxi) to the Belém area to visit the Mosteiro dos Jerónimos (Jerónimos Monastery). Down by the river you'll see the Torre de Belém (Tower of Belém) and the Monument of the Discoveries.

After lunch in a restaurant in the Bairro Alto, head for the Museu da Fundação Calouste Gulbenkian (Gulbenkian Foundation Museum), whose select collection of exquisite art is superbly displayed in a custom-made setting.

IF YOU HAVE TWO DAYS   Spend the morning as outlined above, but have lunch in Belém and then visit the Mosteiro dos Jerónimos, the Museu da Marinha (Marine Museum) at its western end, and the nearby Museu dos Coches (Coach Museum).

On the second day, spend the morning at the Museu da Fundação Calouste Gulbenkian. After lunch in the Bairro Alto, head for the Jardim Botânico and stroll back toward the river along rua Dom Pedro V and rua de São Pedro de Alcantara, where you'll find a small park with a lovely view of downtown Lisbon. Next, visit the 16th-century Igreja de São Roque (San Roque Church), whose most dazzling chapel, dedicated to St. John the Baptist, was constructed in Rome in 1742 of lapis lazuli, alabaster, and amethyst. Continue along rua da Misericórdia to praça de Camões and turn left through largo do Chiado to rua Garrett, where massive reconstruction is under way in the wake of the disastrous fire of August 1988. At the end of rua Garrett, turn left onto rua do Carmo. Both these streets are lined with chic shops and boutiques. At rua de Santa Justa off to the right, you'll see the Elevador de Santa Justa, built by Raul Mesnier de Ponsard, a Portuguese engineer, not by Eiffel as often claimed. Follow rua do Carmo into Rossio Square with its wonderful Moorish train station and stop for a leisurely coffee at one of its cafés.

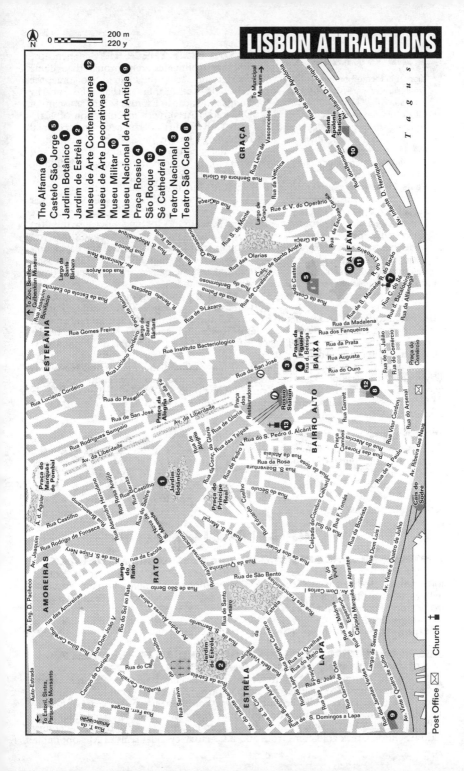

LISBON ATTRACTIONS

The Alfama 6
Castelo São Jorge 5
Jardim Botânico 1
Jardim de Estrêla 2
Museu de Arte Contemporanea 12
Museu de Arte Decorativas 11
Museu Militar 10
Museu Nacional de Arte Antiga 9
Praça Rossio 4
São Roque 13
Sé Cathedral 7
Teatro Nacional 3
Teatro São Carlos 8

0   200 m
     220 y
N

Post Office ⊠   Church ✝

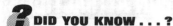

IF YOU HAVE THREE DAYS Spend the first day strolling leisurely through the Alfama district and seeing the Castelo São Jorge; the belvedere of Santa Luzia; the nearby Fundação Ricardo Espirito Santo (Museum of Decorative Arts), with its collection of 17th- and 18th-century Portuguese and colonial furnishings and art objects; the Sé (cathedral) and the nearby Igreja Santo António and Igreja São Vicente, an impressive building whose cloisters feature exquisite 18th-century tiles. At lunchtime you'll likely see many Alfama families grilling sardines on their stoops. In the vicinity of the castle there are several restaurants for lunch. Because this area is so uniquely picturesque, I suggest that you stroll at your leisure for part of the day. Don't worry about getting lost—the Alfama isn't that big and the natives are very helpful (keep your map handy).

Spend the morning of the second day at the Museu da Fundação Calouste Gulbenkian. Head to Belém for lunch and in the afternoon visit the Mosteiro de Jerónimos, the Museu da Marinha, Torre de Belém (Tower of Belém), the Monument of the Discoveries, the Museu dos Coches, and the Museu Nacional de Arte Antiga (National Museum of Ancient Art).

Spend the third morning in the Bairro Alto as outlined above in "If You Have Two Days" and the afternoon exploring the shops of the Baixa area between Rossio Square and praça do Comércio. Catch tram no. 28 (Graça) on rua da Madalena to the Igreja da Graça and have a sunset drink at the bar of the Albergaria da Senhora do Monte, calçada do Monte, 39.

IF YOU HAVE FIVE DAYS Spend three of the days as outlined above, reserving Tuesday or Saturday for a morning visit to the Feira da Ladra flea market. On the afternoon of the fourth day visit the Igreja da Madre de Deus (Church of the Mother of God), beautifully restored inside with tile murals and carved wood, and the nearby Museu do Azulejo (Tile Museum). On the fifth day, go to Sintra, the lush mountain retreat whose fairytale Pena Palace and Paço Real attest to bygone royalty's fondness for this magical place.

TOP ATTRACTIONS

CASTELO SÃO JORGE [Saint George's Castle], Alfama District.

Over 2,000 years ago this strategic hill was the site of important Roman fortifications. Today it is a place for relaxation (not to mention a spectacular view) with gardens, artificial lakes, a playground, peacocks, swans, ducks, geese, and a great many stone benches and tables.

Admission: Free.
Open: Daily 8am–sunset. **Bus:** 37.

MUSEU DA FUNDAÇÃO CALOUSTE GULBENKIAN [Gulbenkian Foundation Museum], avenida de Berna, 45. Tel. 793-51-31.

One of Europe's great art treasures, this museum houses one of the largest privately amassed collections of paintings, furniture, ceramics, sculptures, tapestries, and coins in the world. As you travel through 5,000 years of history in this tailor-made museum, you will pass Egyptian artifacts from the third millennium B.C., 14th-century Chinese porcelain, Japanese prints of the 17th-century Ukio-e School, Greek gold coins from 500 B.C., stone cylinder seals of Mesopotamia

(3000 B.C.), silk carpets from Armenia, and paintings by Rubens, Rembrandt, Gainsborough, Renoir, Turner, Ghirlandaio, and Watteau.
Admission: 225 Esc ($1.65) Tues–Sat, free Sun.
Open: Tues–Sun 10am–5pm. **Closed:** Hols. **Metro:** Palhava. **Bus:** 16, 26, or 30 to praça de Espanha.

MOSTEIRO DOS JERÓNIMOS [Jerónimos Monastery], praça do Império, Belém. Tel. 362-00-34.

⭐ An extravagant expression of thanksgiving for the discoveries of Vasco da Gama (he's buried here) and other Portuguese navigators, the monastery contains the Gothic-Renaissance Church of Santa Maria, famed for the lacy stonework of its two-tiered octagonal cloisters. Formerly situated on the bank of the river (which has since shifted), the church evolved from a chapel built by Prince Henry the Navigator to its current soaring majesty, replete with decorative allusions to the sea and the fruits of the empire it spawned. Besides Vasco da Gama, Luis da Camões (Portugal's "Shakespeare"), and three Portuguese kings (their sarcophagi decorated with elephants) are also buried here.
Admission: June–Sept, 425 Esc ($3.10); Oct–May, 275 Esc ($2).
Open: Tues–Sun 10am–5pm. Guided visits by appointment (tel. 362-00-36).
Closed: Hols. **Tram:** 15, 16, or 17. **Bus:** 12, 27, 28, 29, 43, or 49.

MUSEU DOS COCHES [Coach Museum], praça Afonso de Albuquerque, Belém. Tel. 363-81-64.

Originally a riding school for the royal family, this is now a museum displaying more than 60 royal and aristocratic coaches, the Cadillacs and Rolls-Royces of their day. The oldest dates from 1581; the newest, from 1824, was actually used by Queen Elizabeth II of England during her 1958 state visit to Lisbon.
Admission: June–Sept, 425 Esc ($3.10); Oct–May, 275 Esc ($2); free Sun and mornings of national hols.
Open: Tues–Sun 10am–1pm and 2:30–5:30pm. **Tram:** 15, 16, or 17. **Bus:** 12, 27, 28, 29, 43, or 49.

MORE ATTRACTIONS

SÉ [Cathedral], largo da Sé. Tel. 86-67-52.

Built in the 12th century by Portugal's first king, Afonso Henriques, this is Lisbon's oldest surviving church, its Romanesque facade and towers left undamaged by two violent earthquakes.
Admission: Free.
Open: Daily 9am–noon and 2:30–6pm. **Tram:** 28 (Graça). **Bus:** 37.

FUNDAÇÃO RICARDO ESPIRITO SANTO (Museum of Decorative Arts), largo das Portas do Sol, 2. Tel. 85-21-83.

⭐ Located in a 17th-century palace, this museum displays Portuguese decorative pieces and furniture from the 17th and 18th centuries, most in the Indo-Portuguese style derived from Portugal's Far Eastern colonial experience. On the premises is a school of decorative arts—the work of the foundation includes restoration and reproduction. The artisans here are masters of wood carving, cabinetry, inlay, painting, lacquerwork, and gilding, and they have done restorations for Versailles, Fontainebleau, the Paris Library, and the Rockefellers. They will also make reproductions of almost any piece in the museum, so if you see something you like (and money is no object), you can place your order on the spot. **Note:** As of this writing the museum is closed for restoration. Call before you go.
Admission: 350 Esc ($2.55).
Open: Tues–Sun 10am–1pm and 3–6pm. **Tram:** 28 (Graça). **Bus:** 37.

TORRE DE BELÉM [Tower of Belém], off avenida Brasilia, Belém. Tel. 61-68-92.

Blending elements of the Gothic and Renaissance styles with seafaring motifs and allusions to the fruits of the colonies (Manueline motifs), this 16th-century watchtower was built as protection against pirates. It now contains a small museum of arms and armor. Its upper platform delivers a panoramic view of the Tagus.

Admission: June–Sept, 425 Esc ($3.10); Oct–May, 275 Esc ($2).
Open: Tues–Sun 10am–5pm. **Closed:** Hols. **Tram:** 15 or 16. **Bus:** 29, 43, or 49.

PADRÃO DOS DESCOBRIMENTOS [Monument of the Discoveries], avenida Brasilia, Belém. Tel. 61-62-20.

Several hundred yards from the Torre de Belém, this imposing monument was built in 1960 to commemorate the 500th anniversary of the death of Prince Henry the Navigator, who founded Portugal's first observatory and the Sagres Nautical School. It depicts the prince himself leading a throng of sailors, captains, priests, and poets into the jaws of hard-won imperial glory. In the pavement is a map chronicling Portuguese discoveries from 1427 to 1541.

Admission: Free.
Open: Daily 24 hours. **Tram:** 15 or 16. **Bus:** 29, 43, or 49.

MUSEU DA MARINHA [Naval Museum], praça do Império, Belém. Tel. 362-00-19.

At the western end of the Mosteiro dos Jerónimos, this museum contains a large collection of maps, maritime paraphernalia, and finely detailed models of ships old and new, including Egyptian and Greek warships dating from 3000 B.C. In an annex across the way is an exhibit of life-size royal barges, galleons, and sailing ships.

Admission: 225 Esc ($1.65) adults, 110 Esc (80¢) students 10–18 years, free for children under 10.
Open: Tues–Sun 10am–5pm. **Tram:** 15, 16, or 17. **Bus:** 12, 28, 29, 43, or 49.

MUSEU NACIONAL DE ARTE ANTIGA [National Museum of Ancient Art], rua das Janelas Verdes, Belém. Tel. 67-60-01.

Here you'll find a sampling of eight centuries of art (the 12th through the 19th); one of Europe's great collections of ceramics, silver, and tapestries; the most important national collection of Portuguese paintings; and works by Lucas Cranach, Veláquez, Pieter Brueghel, Hans Holbein, Albrecht Dürer, Murillo, and that "must-see" masterpiece by Hieronymus Bosch, *The Temptations of St. Anthony*. Don't miss the enormous 17th-century silver platter weighing 2,000 pounds!

Admission: 225 Esc ($1.65); free Sun morning.
Open: Tues–Sat 10am–1pm and 2–5pm. **Tram:** Alcantara. **Bus:** 27, 40, 49, or 54.

PARKS & GARDENS

Among Lisbon's numerous gardens, the finest are the **Jardim Botânico (Botanical Garden)** and the **Jardim da Estrêla.** Its largest parks are the **Parque de Monsanto** and the **Parque Eduardo VII.**

The following small parks and terraces offer fine views of the city: ***Cristo Rei,*** across the Tagus, a replica of the statue in Rio de Janeiro; **Alto de Santa Catarina,** rua de Santa Catarina; **Castelo São Jorge; Luneta dos Quarteis, Moinho dos Mochos, Alto da Serafina,** and **Montes Claros** in Parque de Monsanto; **Ponte,** viaduto Duarte Pacheco; belvedere of **Santa Luzia; Senhora do Monte** (great for sunsets); **Zimborio da Basilica da Estrêla,** on largo da Estrêla; and **São Pedro de Alcantara.**

TRAM & WALKING TOURS

A TRAM TOUR

If you take **tram no. 28** along its entire route, you'll pass through Lisbon's most picturesque neighborhoods—the Bairro Alto, Alfama, and Graça.

WALKING TOURS

TOUR 1   Start at Rossio Square in the heart of town. Follow rua do Ouro to praça do Comércio with its statue of King José I. Follow rua da Alfândego de Santarém east out of praça do Comércio and turn left along rua da Madalena to the sign indicating that the Sé (cathedral) is up to your right. On your left you'll come to the Igreja São António and, a little farther up, to the Sé. Follow rua Augusta Rosa (which becomes São Martinho and then rua Limoeiro) to the belvedere of Santa Luzia with a wonderful view of Lisbon and the Tagus.

A little farther up on your left, in largo Portas do Sol, is the Fundação Ricardo Espirito Santo (Museum of Decorative Arts). Returning to the Santa Luzia belvedere and turning right through largo Contador Mor and then going up rua do Funil, you will come upon the Chão da Feira leading up to Castelo São Jorge (Saint George's Castle). Go back along Chão da Feira and follow rua de São Tomé, which becomes calçada da Graça, to the Igreja da Graça by Graça Square. Upon leaving Graça Square, visit the Chapel of Ermida da Senhora do Monte. Turning back a little, go down rua da Voz do Operário until you reach São Vicente Square with the church of the same name. Flanking the church is a wide-open space where the Feira da Ladra is held.

TOUR 2   Start at praça dos Restauradores with its obelisk in memory of national independence won from the Spanish in 1640. Go one block past Rossio Square along rua do Ouro to the Santa Justa Elevator, off to the right. From the top there is a marvelous view of downtown Lisbon, the castle, and the Graça area. The adjacent Convent do Carmo houses the Archeological Museum. From the base of the elevator, follow rua do Carmo to the left and go right on rua Garrett to praça de Luís Camões. Take a right onto rua da Misericórdia, leading off the praça, and you will soon come to the São Roque Church. Next to it is the Museum of Sacred Art. Continue up the street a short distance to the park of São Pedro de Alcantara with its lovely view. Continue in the direction of praça do Príncipe Real along rua Escola Politécnica. On the right is an entrance to the Jardim Botânico.

ORGANIZED BUS TOURS

RN Tours, avenida Fontes Pereira de Melo, 14-12° (tel. 57-75-23), offers various city tours. "Lisboa Turística" is a half-day tour including Rossio, Castelo de São Jorge, Alfama, Praça do Comércio, Torre de Belém, Padrão dos Descobrimentos, Mosteiro dos Jerónimos, and Museu dos Coches. It departs from Parque Eduardo VII daily at 9:30am and 2:30pm. The price is 4,150 Esc ($30.30); children under 4 go free and children 4–10 are charged half price. "Lisboa a Noite e Casino" includes a panoramic view of Lisbon by night, dinner at a restaurant with performances of Portuguese folk dances and fado, and an optional cabaret show at the Casino Estoril (two drinks included; jacket and tie required). This tour departs from Parque Eduardo VII at 8:30pm on Tuesday, Thursday, and Saturday from November to March, and daily from April to October. The tour of only Lisbon costs 8,925 Esc ($65.15); with the casino visit it costs 11,000 Esc ($80.30).

Similar tours are also available through **Portugal Tours,** rua D. Estefania, 124-2° (tel. 352-29-02).

7. SAVVY SHOPPING

The Value-Added Tax (I.V.A. in Portugal) is about 17%. You are entitled to a refund of the tax if your purchases in one store tally at least 10,000 Esc ($73), exclusive of VAT. To obtain the refund, have the shop fill in the front of the Tax-Free Check and you fill in the back. When leaving Portugal, present your purchases (carry them in your hand luggage), Tax-Free Checks, and passport to Customs. Redeem the stamped checks at the Tax Refund counter for cash. You may also send in the checks, which are valid for three months, for a refund by mail. There are Tax Refund counters at the Lisbon airport and the Lisbon harbor. For information, call 418-87-03. Participating stores display the TAX-FREE FOR TOURISTS sign.

Except for several minimalls (such as **Imaviz,** next to the Sheraton Hotel) and one mega-mall (**Amoreiras,** with over 350 shops), small establishments are the norm. The best buys are ceramics, porcelain, pottery, and embroidered and leather goods. The smartest shops are on rua Garrett and the surrounding streets in an area known as the **Chiado,** part of which was razed by the August 1988 blaze; much remains standing though, and reconstruction is well under way.

Rua da Escola Politécnica is the upper end of a long street with five names (rua do Alecrim, rua da Misericórdia, rua de São Pedro de Alcantara, rua Dom Pedro V, and rua da Escola Politécnica). Scattered all along here are antiques shops.

MARKETS   On Tuesday and Saturday the **Feira da Ladra ("Thieves'" or Flea Market)** goes on until 5pm in campo de Santa Clara behind the Igreja São Vicente. Take bus no. 12 from Santa Apolónia Station.

8. EVENING ENTERTAINMENT

Lisbon's nightlife is gaining momentum. For information on performances and productions, contact the tourist office or the **Agência de Bilhetes para Espectáculos Públicos** in praça dos Restauradores, open daily from 9am to 10pm. The latter sells tickets to all cinemas and theaters except the National Theater of São Carlos.

The *Diário de Noticias* also has the latest listings (in Portuguese).

THE PERFORMING ARTS

The season for opera, theater, ballet, and concerts runs from October to May, with additional performances throughout the year. The main venues are the **Nacional D. Maria II Theater,** in Rossio Square (tel. 37-10-78); the **National Theater of São Carlos,** at rua Serpo Pinto, 9 (tel. 36-86-64); the **Gulbenkian Foundation,** avenida de Berna, 45 (tel. 793-51-31); the **São Luís Municipal Theater,** rua António Maria Cardosa (tel. 32-71-72); and the **Trindade Theater** (tel. 32-00-00).

Opera tickets run 500–3,000 Esc ($3.65–$21.90); theater tickets 1,000–2,500 Esc ($7.30–$18.25). Ballet and concert tickets vary greatly depending on the performance.

MUSIC CLUBS

Fado is to Lisbon what jazz is to New Orleans and flamenco is to Seville—a native art that relies on emotion and spontaneity. Don't leave Lisbon without experiencing it. Fado clubs (known as *adegas típicas* or *restaurantes típicos*) serve dinner before and during the entertainment, which usually starts about 10pm. You can also dine elsewhere and arrive around 11pm to enjoy the show for a minimum cover charge, which usually includes one drink.

PARREIRINHA DE ALFAMA, Beco do Espírito Santo, 1. Tel. 86-82-09.

One of the more inexpensive quality fado clubs, this place is cozy, and local patrons often join in the singing. Sets are every 20 minutes from 10pm to 3am.

Prices: Main courses 850–2,450 Esc ($6.20–$17.90). If you go later for drinks, there's a 1,600-Esc ($11.65) minimum from 10:30pm on (includes one drink).

Open: Daily 8pm–3am. **Bus:** 37.

HOT CLUBE DE PORTUGAL, praça da Alegria, 39. Tel. 346-73-69.

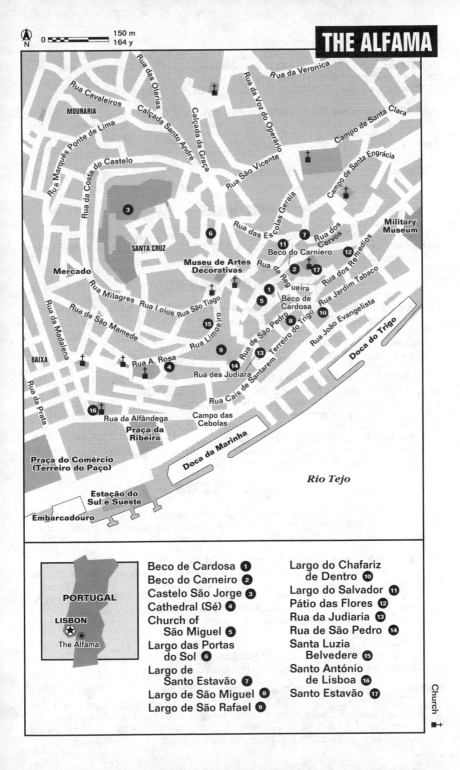

THE ALFAMA

0 — 150 m / 164 y

MOURARIA

Rua Cavaleiros
Rua das Olarias
Calçada Santo André
Calçada da Graça
Rua das Ponte de Lima
Rua Marques Ponte de Lima
Rua da Costa do Castelo

Rua da Voz do Operário
Rua da Veronica
Campo de Santa Clara
Campo de Santa Engrácia

Rua São Vicente

SANTA CRUZ

Rua das Escolas Gerais
Rua dos Corvos
Beco do Carniero
Rua da Regueira
Rua dos Remedios
Rua Jardim Tabaco

Military Museum

Mercado

Museu de Artes Decorativas

Beco de Cardosa
Rua São Tiago
Rua Loios
Rua Milagres
Rua de São Mamede
Rua da Madalena
Rua Limoeiro
Rua de São Pedro
Terreiro do Trigo
Rua João Evangelista

BAIXA

Rua A. Rosa
Rua des Judiara
Rua Cais de Santarem
Rua da Prata
Rua da Alfândega

Doca do Trigo

Campo das Cebolas

Praça da Ribeira

Praça do Comércio (Terreiro do Paço)

Estação do Sul e Sueste

Embarcadouro

Doca da Marinha

Rio Tejo

PORTUGAL

LISBON
The Alfama

Beco de Cardosa ❶
Beco do Carniero ❷
Castelo São Jorge ❸
Cathedral (Sé) ❹
Church of São Miguel ❺
Largo das Portas do Sol ❻
Largo de Santo Estavão ❼
Largo de São Miguel ❽
Largo de São Rafael ❾

Largo do Chafariz de Dentro ❿
Largo do Salvador ⓫
Pátio das Flores ⓬
Rua da Judiaria ⓭
Rua de São Pedro ⓮
Santa Luzia Belvedere ⓯
Santo António de Lisboa ⓰
Santo Estavão ⓱

Church ✝

Come here for the hot sounds of cool jazz in a fitting subterranean atmosphere.
Prices: Beer 225 Esc ($1.65). **Admission:** 500–1,100 Esc ($3.65–$8) when there is live music, which begins about 11:30pm.
Open: Tues–Sat 10pm–2am; live music Thurs–Sat. **Metro:** Avenida.

XAFARIX, avenida Dom Carlos I, 69. Tel. 396-94-87.

One of my favorite Lisbon nightspots, this small, friendly club with nightly live music is owned by Luís Represas, one of Portugal's hot, heartthrob vocalists. The musical idiom varies, but the caliber of the performers is consistently high.
Prices: Beer 475 Esc ($3.45).
Open: Daily 10pm–4am. **Tram:** 15, 16, 17, 18, 29, or 30. **Bus:** 14, 28, 32, 40, 43, or 54.

MOVIES

Foreign films are usually subtitled. Monday matinees are cheapest. First-run theaters include the **Tivoli,** avenida da Liberdade, 188 (tel. 57-05-95), and the **Eden,** praça dos Restauradores, 21 (tel. 32-07-68).

THE BAR SCENE

PAVILHÃO CHINES BAR, rua Dom Pedro V, 89. Tel. 342-47-29.

This unusual bar goes on for several rooms that display owner Luís Pinto Coleho's eclectic collection of toys and vast array of collectibles from the Far East.
Prices: Beer 425 Esc ($3.10).
Open: Mon–Fri 2pm–2am, Sat 6pm–2am, Sun 9pm–2am.

BAIRRO ALTO, travessa dos Inglesinhos, 50. Tel. 342-02-38.

In the vanguard of contemporary design, the Bairro Alto is an outpost in the trendy postmodern mold. Though billed as a "bar/pub," it also has a dance floor and, on the upper level, a billiard table. A mixed crowd converses leisurely at the curvaceous bar.
Prices: 650–1,000 Esc ($4.75–$7.30) minimum.
Open: Daily 8pm–3:30am. **Directions:** This one is tucked away in the labyrinthine upper reaches of the Bairro Alto, so take a cab.

DANCE CLUBS

Lisbon's classier nightspots are permitted to charge an outrageous cover to keep out the riffraff, but well-dressed, respectable-looking types are usually admitted free. A moderate cover may be charged if the place is full, however.

PRIMOROSA, avendia E.U.A., 128-D. Tel. 797-19-13.

One of Lisbon's four enduring discos (Bananas, Ad Lib, and Stones are the others), Primorosa also has a sedate piano bar (quippingly called "Cyrrose," meaning cirrhosis) with live entertainment Monday through Saturday beginning at 11pm. Those who prefer intimacy to the trendy, warehouse expanse of today's discos will appreciate the cozy nooks and crannies of this club's attractive, cavelike decor.
Prices: Beer 1,000 Esc ($7.30); cocktails 1,500 Esc ($10.45); sandwiches and snacks 600–2,200 Esc ($4.35–$16.05). **Admission:** Cover charge varies.
Open: Tues–Sun 11pm–4am. **Metro:** Entrecampos.

KREMLIN, escadinhas da Praia, 5. Tel. 60-87-68.

The last stop on the beautiful people's nocturnal circuit, this most popular of loud, pounding discos doesn't hit full stride until about 4am and holds a party every month or two when it completely changes its interior decor. The crowd is mixed, but those in their 20s and early 30s predominate.

Prices: Drinks from 550 Esc ($4).
Open: Daily midnight–4am, also Sat 6–9:30am also. **Tram:** 15, 16, 17, 18, 29, or 30. **Bus:** 14, 28, 32, 40, or 43.

PLATEAU, escadinhas da Praia, 7. Tel. 396-51-16.
Next door to Kremlin, this is the next-to-last stop on the beautiful people's nocturnal circuit. It is smaller and less distinctive of decor, but the crowd, the mood, and the music are much the same.
Prices: Drinks from 630 Esc ($4.50).
Open: Daily midnight–4:30am. **Tram:** 15, 16, 17, 18, 29, or 30. **Bus:** 14, 28, 32, 40, or 43.

9. EASY EXCURSIONS

THE ESTORIL COAST   This stretch of Atlantic shore was once favored by the native aristocracy and continues to draw some of Europe's more reclusive nobility. Unfortunately, development and pollution have taken their toll. **Estoril** itself is some 15 miles from Lisbon and has a casino with a nightclub (tel. 468-45-21), open daily, except Christmas Eve, from 3pm to 3am. Bring your passport. The cabaret show without dinner costs 3,850–4,500 Esc ($28.10–$32.85), including two drinks.
Cascais, a few miles farther along, has a pretty beach, umbrella-covered sidewalk cafés, souvenir shops, and a lively nightlife that attracts a younger crowd.
For a day in the surf and sun, just hop on the train that leaves every half hour or so from the Cais do Sodré Station and get off at Estoril (a half-hour ride), Cascais (a 40-minute ride), or any other stop along the way that strikes your fancy. Round-trip fare to Cascais is 285 Esc ($2.10).

SINTRA   About 18 miles from Lisbon, this small town (deemed a "glorious Eden" by Byron) of 15,000 swells regularly with daytrippers from the capital. Botanists thrill to some 90 species of unusual plants thriving in the Sintra hills. Romantics revel in Sintra's two marvelous palaces.
The **Paço Real** (tel. 923-41-18), dates back 1,000 years and was the scene of many memorable moments in Portuguese history. What you see today dates mainly from the 14th to the 16th century and is primarily in the baroque style (with Gothic, Manueline, and Islamic flourishes). Impressive are the decorative tilework, gilded ceilings, and the kitchen whose two chimneys are a Sintra landmark. It's open Thursday through Tuesday from 10am to 1pm and 2 to 5pm.
The **Palácio da Pena** (tel. 923-02-27), perched 1,300 feet up on a panoramic mountaintop, is an exemplary piece of Romantic architecture, dating from 1839 when the ruins of a 16th-century monastery began to be adapted for use as a residence. Inspired by the lavish palaces and castles of Bavaria, Pena is a fanciful pastiche of Moorish, Gothic, and Manueline motifs. The Manueline cloister and the chapel remain from the monastery. It's open Tuesday through Sunday from 10am to 1pm and 2 to 5pm.
Admission to both Sintra palaces is 250 Esc ($1.80) October to May, 450 Esc ($3.30) June to September.
Frequent trains run to Sintra from Lisbon's Rossio Station. The trip takes about 45 minutes and costs 285 Esc ($2.10). The local tourist office in praça da República (tel. 923-11-57) is open daily from 9am to 7pm.

QUELUZ   Just nine miles from Lisbon, the pink rococo Queluz Palace (tel. 435-00-39) is Portugal's rendition of Versailles. Built in 1747, it had for 200 years been a hunting lodge before being transformed into a royal residence. Most notable are the Throne Room, Queen's Dressing Room, Don Quixote Chamber, and Music Salon. You'll find Portuguese antiques and tapestries, splendid examples of Arraiolo carpets from the Alentejo region, Italian glassware and marble, Dutch tiles, Austrian porcelain, and Chinese screens throughout the palace. One wing serves as a guesthouse for state visitors (Queen Elizabeth II and former President Reagan are among the ranks). The well-manicured, Versailles-like gardens are a fragrant as well as visual delight. Queluz Palace is open Wednesday through Monday from 10am to 1pm and 2 to 5pm. Admission October through May is 250 Esc ($1.80); June through September, 450 Esc ($3.30).

Unless you have a car, Queluz is best visited as part of an organized tour. Trains do run from Rossio Station to Queluz, but once there you must take a cab.

LONDON

London attracts more American visitors than any other city in Europe, and even the briefest glance at this capital's vast and unique offerings makes it clear why. Tourists are drawn by world-class museums, top shops, unparalleled theater, and a pulsating nightlife. Famous sights, a strong sense of tradition, and the mystique of the monarchy are also compelling attractions. Combine all this with affordable hotels and restaurants, and a public transportation network unrivaled in size, and London's popularity is no mystery. An air of excitement electrifies London—it grips you the moment you arrive. Cars, buses, taxis, and people swirl through the streets with direction and purpose. And yet, even though the city is fast and frenetic, large and lively, it is somehow never impersonal. Pop into any pub and you will discover both warm hospitality and good conversation. In general, English people are slow to break the ice, but once it's broken, they respond with kindness and humor.

Many tourists who visit London hoping to see some history are disappointed when they arrive in this modern city where all too often the only things marking the past are the little blue plaques commemorating former residences. Don't despair: The past is alive and well in London—you just have to know how to look for it. With few notable exceptions, history in the capital is more pronounced *socially* than it is *architecturally*. Indeed, the British class system is the most striking relic of the nation's past, though it's sometimes easy for visitors to miss. The royal family does not exist solely as a tourist attraction; rather, it is at the head of the aristocracy, and it remains a potent symbol of the importance the British still place on breeding. In government, more than three-quarters of the members of the House of Lords are hereditary peers; they inherit their seats as a birthright to this upper house of Parliament. Buckingham Palace and the Houses of Parliament may be less than 150 years old, but along with the Changing of the Guard, the Ceremony of the Keys, the Lord Mayor's Show, and other pageantry parades, these buildings represent something much older.

When you are in London you are in one of the world's most exciting cities. Take advantage of its terrific offerings and unique opportunities. Explore the narrow alleyways of The City, enjoy lunch in a local pub, attend a free concert in a church, and strike up a conversation with the locals. Even though the British Empire is no more, its former capital still flourishes with more than its fair share of cultural activities, entertainment houses, special events, and of course, history. Have fun!

WHAT THINGS COST IN LONDON U.S. $

	U.S. $
Taxi from Victoria Station to a Bayswater hotel	12.30
Underground from Heathrow Airport to central London	5.50
Local telephone call	.20
Double room at the Dorchester Hotel (deluxe)	523.00
Double room at the Strand Palace Hotel (moderate)	190.00
Double room at the Oakley Hotel (budget)	68.40
Lunch for one at the Hard Rock Café (moderate)	14.25
Lunch for one at most pubs (budget)	6.15
Dinner for one, without wine, at Le Gavroche (deluxe)	104.50
Dinner for one, without wine, at Khan's (moderate)	12.40
Dinner for one, without wine, at The Green Café (budget)	5.70
Pint of beer	2.50
Coca-Cola in a restaurant	1.50
Cup of coffee	1.20
Roll of ASA 100 film, 36 exposures	8.00
Admission to the British Museum	Free
Movie ticket	8.55
Cheapest West End theater ticket	11.90

1. FROM A BUDGET TRAVELER'S POINT OF VIEW

LONDON BUDGET BESTS

Not only does London offer many of the world's "bests," but most of these attractions are either free or priced well below comparable sights stateside. Most of London's museums are free, as are the main sections of such major attractions as Westminster Abbey and the Houses of Parliament. The Changing of the Guard at Buckingham Palace is also free, along with the often-acerbic Speaker's Corner every Sunday in Hyde Park (see "Parks and Gardens" in "Attractions," below). Tickets to the London stage are still cheaper than to comparable New York productions, and cheap seats are regularly available to the opera, ballet, and symphony. Whether you're window-shopping in the West End or sightseeing in The City, the following pages will convince you that London is enjoyable on a budget.

SPECIAL DISCOUNT OPPORTUNITIES

FOR STUDENTS Students in England enjoy discounts on travel, theater and museum tickets, and at some nightspots. The **International Student ID Card** is the most readily accepted proof of student status. This card should be purchased before you leave home, but if you've arrived without one and are a good enough talker (or just happen to be carrying a registrar-stamped and -signed copy of your current school transcript), you can obtain one for about £5.50 ($10.45) at S.T.A. Travel, 74 Old Brompton Road, S.W.7 (tel. 071/937-9962), near the South Kensington tube station. The office is open Monday through Friday from 9am to 6pm and on Saturday

✔ WHAT'S SPECIAL ABOUT LONDON

Attractions
- ☐ The Tower of London, combining fascinating history with awesome architecture, colorful pageantry, and good humor.
- ☐ The British Museum, as big as it is famous, and the standard by which other great museums are often judged.
- ☐ Westminster Abbey, where British monarchs have been crowned for 900 years.

Food and Drink
- ☐ Harrods Food Halls, the only food market I know of that doubles as a museum.
- ☐ Pubs—architecturally or culturally, nothing in England is more unique, special, and ubiquitous.

Spectacles
- ☐ Covent Garden, once a marketplace and now an upbeat meeting space in the heart of the West End, which reveals London's lightest side.

- ☐ Speaker's Corner, where comedians, anarchists, religious fanatics, and would-be politicians compete for your ear every Sunday.

Special Events
- ☐ The Chelsea Flower Show, the Notting Hill Carnival, and the Wimbledon Lawn Tennis Championships—so special they're worth planning your trip around.

Flea Markets
- ☐ Particularly Portobello Road and Camden High Street, which seem to go on forever and which offer a full day of fun.

Evening Entertainment
- ☐ Great theater—no other city in the world offers such a wide variety of high-quality productions, and best of all, good government support for many of the repertory theaters makes tickets quite affordable.

from 10am to 4pm. Special student discounts and prices are listed throughout this chapter under their appropriate headings.

FOR SENIORS In Britain, "senior citizen" usually means a woman at least 60 years old and a man at least 65. Seniors often receive the same discounts as students, set forth below under their appropriate headings. Unfortunately for tourists, some discounts are available only to seniors who are also British citizens. More often, however, your passport or other proof of age will also be your passport to cutting costs.

FOR EVERYONE You can start saving money even before you leave home by requesting information from your local British Tourist Authority (BTA). Many of their **tourist publications** that carry a price tag in Britain are distributed free at BTA offices overseas. Ask for a London map as well as a copy of *London Planner*, a monthly events magazine. You can also request any specialized information you might need. BTA's foreign offices are listed in this book's appendix.

If you have forgotten your camera, don't despair: Kodak sponsors a **free camera-loan service** at the British Travel Centre, 12 Regent St., just off Piccadilly Circus. The cameras are good-quality 35mm automatics, and require a credit-card imprint or a refundable £30 ($57) deposit.

If you want to get a **European haircut** for a fraction of the usual cost, visit one of London's hairdressing schools. The **Vidal Sassoon Training School,** 56 Davies Mews, W.1 (tel. 071/629-4635), at the Bond Street tube, charges £8 ($15.20) for a cut and blow-dry. Tints and perms are also available at modest charge. Vidal is open Monday through Friday, and an appointment is required.

2. PRETRIP PREPARATIONS

DOCUMENTS Citizens of the United States, Canada, Australia, and New Zealand need only a valid passport to enter Great Britain. However, Customs officials tend to ask younger travelers and suspicious-looking others to prove that they have enough cash and/or an onward ticket before admitting them into the country. Some street-wise student travelers avoid this hassle at Passport Control by writing the name of an expensive hotel on their landing cards.

WHAT TO PACK Unless you plan to buy an umbrella abroad, or want to use the rain as yet another excuse to duck into a pub, pack this essential item. In addition, few budget hotels provide hairdryers or electrical-current transformers. If you take appliances that need to be plugged in, you'll need an adapter. In Britain, electric appliances run on 240 volts AC and plug into a three-pronged socket different from those used in North America and on the Continent. Virtually everything can be purchased in London, so keep the "lug" out of your luggage by eliminating items that you might need "just in case."

Winter temperatures in London rarely drop below freezing, and in summer, 80°F is considered a heat wave. But because of the unpredictability of island weather, you should be prepared for anything. A warm sweater is essential, no matter what time of year, as well as a jacket or coat (preferably waterproof) appropriate to the season.

Like most cities, London is best explored on foot, and most enjoyable in a comfortable and sturdy pair of shoes.

Finally, Londoners are a rather conservative lot when it comes to dress. Although you will rarely be turned away because of your dress, simple styles and dark colors are best.

WHEN TO GO Seasonal spirit is strong in London. Spring is celebrated with festive fairs and a fresh, friendly attitude as locals shed their coats and restaurateurs return their tables to the sidewalks. Summer means open-air theaters, park picnics, and late-night laughter around bustling Leicester Square. In the autumn, London's trees blaze orange and red, and churches are decorated with flowers and fruits of the harvest. And winter is best for culture. The opera and ballet seasons are in full swing, and theaters, museums, restaurants, and all the major sights are mercifully free of crowds.

London's Average Daytime Temperature & Rainfall

	Jan	Feb	Mar	Apr	May	June	July	Aug	Sept	Oct	Nov	Dec
Temp. (°F)	40	40	44	49	55	61	64	64	59	52	46	42
Rainfall "	2.1	1.6	1.5	1.5	1.8	1.8	2.2	2.3	1.9	2.2	2.5	1.9

SPECIAL EVENTS Specialty and trade shows, including boats, stamps, cars, and comic books, are scheduled throughout the year. The tourist offices can supply you with schedules of current events and exhibitions. Some top annual offerings are listed below.

The **Charles I Commemoration,** on the last Sunday in January, is solemnly marked by hundreds of cavaliers marching through central London in 17th-century dress. Prayers are said at Banqueting House in Whitehall where, on January 30, 1649, King Charles I was executed "in the name of freedom and democracy." Free.

The **Chinese New Year** falls in late January or early February (based on the lunar calendar) and is celebrated on the nearest Sunday. Festive crowds line the decorated streets of Soho to watch the famous Lion Dancers. Free.

The **Easter Parade** is London's largest. Brightly colored floats and marching bands circle Battersea Park, kicking off a full day of activities. Free.

Hotel rooms become scarce during the **Chelsea Flower Show,** held in May every year. This international spectacular features the best of British gardening, with displays of plants and flowers of all seasons. The location, on the breathtakingly beautiful grounds of the Chelsea Royal Hospital, helps make this exposition a world-class affair. For ticket information, see "Parks and Gardens" in "Attractions," below.

Trooping the Colour celebrates the queen's official birthday on a Saturday in early June. Visitors can catch a glimpse of the royal party as it parades down The Mall from Buckingham Palace. Free.

The end of June signals the start of the **Wimbledon Lawn Tennis Championships,** the most prestigious event in tennis. Tickets are usually available at the gate for early rounds of play, but to attend later rounds usually requires planning. For information on booking seats in the center court, see "Sports and Recreation," below.

The **Notting Hill Carnival,** held in late August, is one of the largest annual street festivals in Europe. This African-Caribbean street fair in the community of Notting Hill attracts over half a million people during its 2 days. Live reggae and soul music combine with great Caribbean food to ensure that a great time is had by all. Free.

Visitors have another chance to see the royals during the **State Opening of Parliament** in late October or early November. Although the ceremony itself is not open to the public, crowds pack the parade route to see the procession. Free.

Early November is also the season for **Guy Fawkes Day,** commemorating the anniversary of the "Gunpowder Plot," an attempt to blow up King James I and his parliament. Huge organized bonfires are lit throughout the city and Guy Fawkes, the plot's most famous conspirator, is burned in effigy. Free.

In the middle of November, the **Lord Mayor's Show** takes to the streets with an elaborate parade celebrating the inauguration of the new chief of The City of London. Colorful floats, military bands, and the Lord Mayor's 1756 gold State Coach are all part of this famous event. Free.

BACKGROUND READING   There are too many brilliant British bards to list them all here, but I do feel obliged at least to mention Shakespeare and Dickens. Listed below are some very accessible academic works on British social history. *London Life in the Eighteenth Century* by M. Dorothy George (Academy Chicago Publishers, 1985) is an enlightened and readable study of life in the Georgian period. *The Making of Modern London* by Gavin Weightman and Steve Humphries (Sidgewick and Jackson) is my pick from the mountain of books on the Victorian development of London, and *The Long Weekend* by Robert Graves and Alan Hodge (Norton, 1963) offers a fascinating and straightforward account of Britain between the wars.

3. ORIENTATION & GETTING AROUND

ARRIVING IN LONDON

FROM THE AIRPORT   London is served by three major airports: Heathrow, Gatwick, and Stansted. All have good public transport links to central London.

The cheapest route from **Heathrow Airport** is by Underground railway or subway (often called "the tube"). The 15-mile journey takes approximately 45 minutes and costs £2.90 ($5.50) to any downtown station (see "Getting Around," below, for information on transportation discounts). Service is convenient, as the Underground platforms are directly below the airport terminals. But Heathrow is big, and even those with light luggage are advised to use one of the free baggage carts for the long walk to the train. Trains depart every 4 to 10 minutes from 6am to midnight.

Convenient nonstop trains make the 25-mile trek from **Gatwick Airport** to Victoria Station in about 30 minutes. Unfortunately, it costs a hefty £7 ($13.30) each way. The station is just below the airport, and trains depart every 15 minutes from 6am to 10pm (hourly, on the hour, at other times).

Stansted Airport is 30 miles northeast of London. Bus service to and from Victoria Station is provided by National Express (tel. 071/730-3499) five times a day Monday through Saturday, three times on Sunday. Service is also available to Heathrow and Gatwick. The Stansted Express train (no. 322) makes the 40-minute journey to the airport from Liverpool Street Station for £13.50 ($25.65) in first class, £9 ($17.10) standard class, daily from 5:30am to 11pm.

FROM THE TRAIN STATION   Trains from Paris arrive at Victoria Station, visitors from Amsterdam are deposited at Liverpool Street Station, and arrivals from Edinburgh pull into King's Cross Station. All three are well connected to the city's extensive bus and Underground network. The stations all contain London Transport Information Centres, luggage lockers, telephones, restaurants, and, of course, pubs!

INFORMATION

The **London Tourist Board (LTB)** maintains several Information Centres throughout the capital. They distribute city maps, answer questions, and, in a pinch, can help you find accommodations. When entering England via Heathrow, visit the LTB in the arrivals terminal before making your journey into the city; it's open daily from 9am to 6pm. Those arriving via Gatwick, or by train from Paris, can visit the well-staffed office in Victoria Station's forecourt. The office is open Easter to October, daily from 9am to 8pm; the rest of the year, Monday through Saturday from 9am to 7pm and on Sunday from 9am to 5pm. Other LTB Information Centres are located in Harrods and Selfridges department stores, both open year round during store hours, and at the Tower of London, open Easter to October only, daily from 10am to 6pm. For information by phone, call 071/730-3488 weekdays between 9am and 6pm.

The **British Travel Centre,** 12 Regent St., W.1, just steps from Piccadilly Circus, provides information on all of Britain. It's open from 9am to 6:30pm Monday through Friday, 9am to 5pm on Saturday, and 10am to 4pm on Sunday. Hours are usually slightly reduced in winter.

For information on Scotland, dial 071/930-8661; for Wales, dial 071/407-0969; for Northern Ireland, dial 071/493-0601; for London, call the London Tourist Board (see above).

For information about travel by bus, tube, or British Rail, visit a **London Transport Information Centre** in any of the major train stations, or call the **London Regional Transport Travel Information Service** (tel. 071/222-1234), open 24 hours daily.

NEIGHBORHOODS IN BRIEF

The City   London is often referred to as a "city of villages" that sprang up around the square mile of the original walled Roman city. Most of the walls have long since disappeared, but the political autonomy of The City of London still separates it from the surrounding areas. The City has always been London's financial center, and is crammed with tiny streets and a sense of history befitting its ancient beginnings. The boroughs of Greater London, which flank The City, encompass over 600 square miles, though mercifully, the main tourist attractions are fairly close together.

The West End   West of The City, to Hyde Park, lies the West End. You'll get to know this area well. The Houses of Parliament, Buckingham Palace, and the nation's densest cluster of shops, restaurants, and theaters all make their homes here. Oxford Street, which runs the length of the West End, challenges nearby Covent Garden and Soho for the attentions of shoppers and tourists.

South Kensington and Chelsea Beyond the West End, south of Hyde Park, are the fashionable residential areas of South Kensington and Chelsea. Take a close look at these neighborhoods—you've probably never seen so many beautiful city buildings that you'd like to own.

The East End Hugging The City's eastern side is one of London's poorest areas. Traditionally, the East End was undesirable because both the prevailing winds and the flow of the River Thames move from west to east. In the plague-ridden days before sewers, life on the "wrong" side of The City was dangerous indeed. Today the East End is still home to poorer immigrants as well as the capital's famous Cockneys.

Southwark The borough of Southwark lies across the river from The City, on the south bank of the Thames. Now under heavy reconstruction, Southwark became famous as London's entertainment quarter during Elizabethan times, when theaters and brothels were banned from The City.

GETTING AROUND

BY UNDERGROUND [SUBWAY] AND BUS Commuters constantly complain about it, but to tourists, London's public transportation network is both vast and efficient. Underground stations are abundant, and above ground you can catch one of the famous red double-decker buses. Both the Underground and buses are operated by London Regional Transport (LRT), which maintains fares based on a zone system—you pay for each zone you cross. For most tube trips you will be traveling within the same zone and the fare will be 80p ($1.50). A **1-day Travelcard** is good for unlimited transportation within two zones on the bus and tube after 9:30am Monday through Friday and any time during weekends and public holidays. The card costs £2.30 ($4.35) for adults and £1.10 ($2.10) for children aged 5 to 15. Children 4 and under always ride free. **Weekly Travelcards** valid within the Central London Zone cost £7.80 ($14.80) for adults and £3 ($5.70) for children aged 5 to 15. You will need to present a photo to buy and use the weekly ticket; photo booths are located in tube stations—four passport-size photographs cost £2 ($3.80).

The tube runs every few minutes from about 5:30am to midnight (7:30am to 11pm on Sunday). Tickets can be purchased from the station ticket window or an adjacent coin-operated machine. Hold onto your ticket throughout your ride; you'll need it to exit. Pick up a handy tube map, distributed free at station ticket windows.

It looks as though the red open-back-platform **buses** will one day be a thing of the past, in favor of the more economical driver-only type. But for now, you can still make a flying leap onto the departing vehicle. Take a seat, either upstairs or down, and wait for the conductor to collect your fare. On the newer type of buses, pay the driver as you enter, and exit through the rear doors. The bus fare within the Central London Zone 1 is 80p ($1.50); short hops (two or three stops) cost 60p ($1.15).

Many tourists shy away from riding buses because their routes can be confusing. Get a free bus map from the tourist office, or just ask any conductor about the route, and take advantage of a "top deck" sightseeing adventure. Like the tube, regular bus service also stops after midnight, sometimes making it difficult to get back to your hotel. At night, buses have different routes and different numbers from their daytime counterparts, and service is not as frequent. If you've just missed your night bus, expect a long wait for the next one or hunt down a minicab (see below). The central London night-bus terminus is Trafalgar Square.

BY TAXI For three or four people traveling a short distance, **black cabs** can almost be economically viable. The fare begins at £1 ($1.90), then climbs at a fast clip. There is an additional charge of 20p (40¢) per person, 10p (20¢) per large piece of luggage, and 60p ($1.15) on weekends and after midnight. But the thrill of viewing London's famous monuments from the roomy back seat of a black taxi is almost enough to get your eye off the meter.

Minicabs are meterless cars driven by any entrepreneur with a license. Technical-

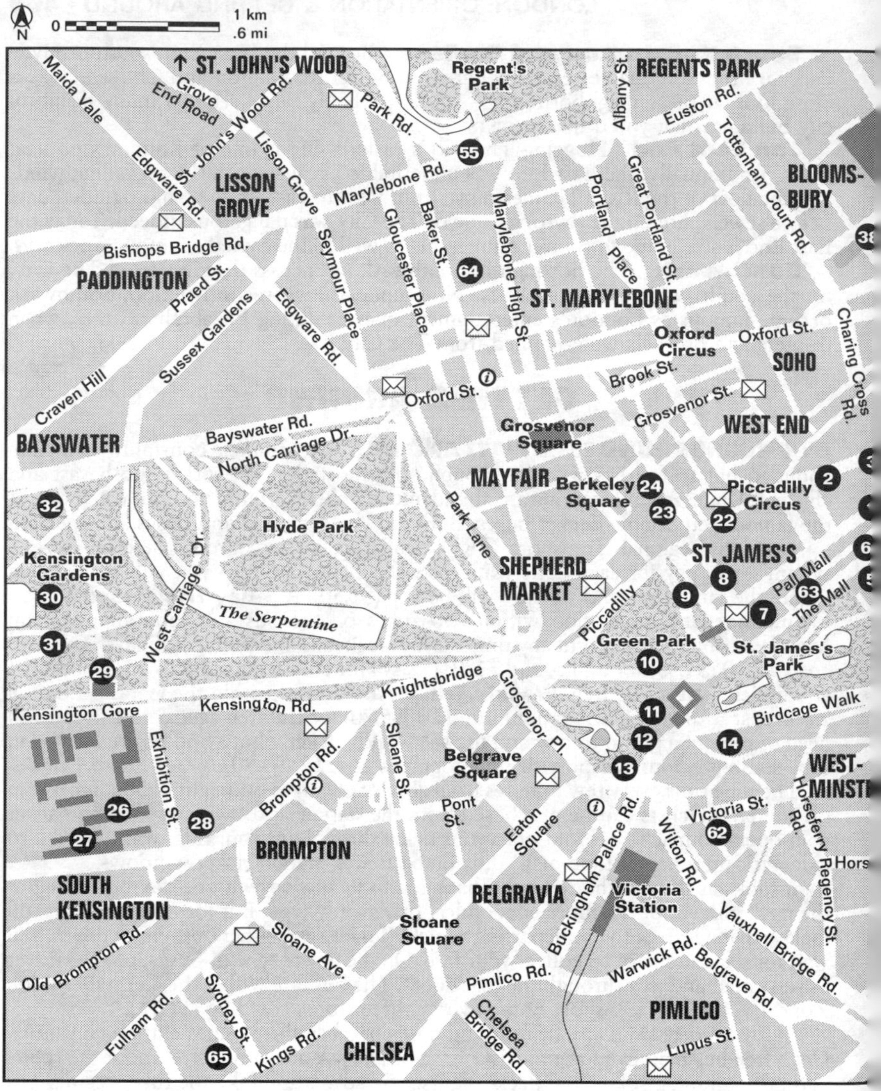

Admiralty Arch ⑤
Albert Memorial ㉙
Apsley House ⑭
Bank of England ㊻
Banqueting House ⑳
Barbican Centre ㊸
Big Ben ⑰
British Museum ㊳
Buckingham Palace ⑪
Cabinet War Rooms ⑮
Carlton House Terrace ⑥
Cenotaph ⑲

Clarence House ⑩
Courtald Institute ㊴
Covent Garden ㉝
10 Downing Street (66)
Dr. Johnson's House (58)
Guildhall ㊹
Horse Guards Building ㉑
Hyde Park Corner ㉕
Imperial War Museum (53)
Institute of Contemporary Arts (ICA) (63)
Kensington Palace ㉛

Lancaster House ⑨
Leadenhall Market ㊾
Lloyd's of London ㊿
London Transport Museum ㉟
Madam Tussaud's (55)
Mansion House ㊽
Museum of the Moving Image (MOMI) (61)
Museum of London ㊶
Museum of Mankind ㉔
National Gallery ②
National Portrait Gallery ③

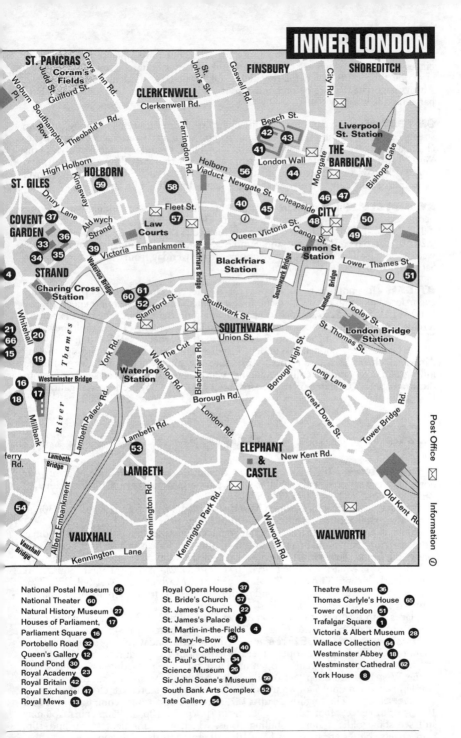

INNER LONDON

ST. PANCRAS
Coram's Fields
CLERKENWELL
Clerkenwell Rd.
FINSBURY
SHOREDITCH
Grays Inn Rd.
Judd St.
Guilford St.
Woburn Pl.
Southampton Row
Theobald's Rd.
High Holborn
HOLBORN
Kingsway
Drury Lane
ST. GILES
Aldwych
Strand
COVENT GARDEN
STRAND
Charing Cross Station
Whitehall
Millbank
River Thames
Westminster Bridge
ferry Rd.
Lambeth Bridge
LAMBETH
VAUXHALL
Vauxhall Bridge
Kennington Lane
Albert Embankment
Lambeth Palace Rd.
Lambeth Rd.
Kennington Rd.
Kennington Park Rd.

St. John's St.
Goswell Rd.
Beech St.
London Wall
Moorgate
City Rd.
Bishops Gate
Liverpool St. Station
THE BARBICAN
CITY
Farringdon Rd.
Holborn Viaduct
Newgate St.
Cheapside
Fleet St.
Law Courts
Queen Victoria St.
Canon St.
Cannon St. Station
Lower Thames St.
Victoria Embankment
Blackfriars Bridge
Blackfriars Station
Southwark Bridge
London Bridge
Stamford St.
Southwark St.
SOUTHWARK
Union St.
Tooley St.
St. Thomas St.
London Bridge Station
Waterloo Station
York Rd.
The Cut
Waterloo Rd.
Blackfriars Rd.
Borough Rd.
London Rd.
Borough High St.
Long Lane
Great Dover St.
ELEPHANT & CASTLE
New Kent Rd.
WALWORTH
Walworth Rd.
Old Kent Rd.
Tower Bridge Rd.

Post Office ⊠   Information ⊙

National Postal Museum 56	Royal Opera House 37	Theatre Museum 36
National Theater 60	St. Bride's Church 57	Thomas Carlyle's House 65
Natural History Museum 27	St. James's Church 22	Tower of London 51
Houses of Parliament, 17	St. James's Palace 7	Trafalgar Square 1
Parliament Square 16	St. Martin-in-the-Fields 4	Victoria & Albert Museum 28
Portobello Road 32	St. Mary-le-Bow 45	Wallace Collection 64
Queen's Gallery 12	St. Paul's Cathedral 40	Westminster Abbey 18
Round Pond 30	St. Paul's Church 34	Westminster Cathedral 62
Royal Academy 23	Science Museum 26	York House 8
Royal Britain 42	Sir John Soane's Museum 59	
Royal Exchange 47	South Bank Arts Complex 52	
Royal Mews 13	Tate Gallery 54	

ly, these taxis are not allowed to cruise for fares, but must operate from sidewalk offices—many of which are centered around Leicester Square. Minicabs are handy after the tube shuts down for the night and black cabs suddenly become scarce. Always negotiate the fare beforehand, and if you're approached by a lone driver, hard bargaining is in order.

ON FOOT London can be a difficult city to negotiate. It seems as though no two streets run parallel, and even locals regularly consult maps. Construction sites further challenge walkers, but in the winding streets of The City and in the tourist area of the West End, there's no better way to go. Don't forget that cars drive on the left, and look both ways before stepping off the curb. Also, cars have the right-of-way over pedestrians; take care even when the light seems to be in your favor.

BY BICYCLE Bike lanes are unheard of and cars are unyielding—still, some people do ride. If you want to rent a bike, try **On Your Bike,** 22 Duke St. Hill, S.E.1 (tel. 071/407-1309). A 10-speed bike rents for £10 ($19) per day during the week, £15 ($28.50) per day on Saturday and Sunday. Substantial discounts are available for weekly rentals. The shop is open Monday through Friday from 9am to 6pm and on Saturday from 9:30am to 5:30pm. MC, V.

BY CAR It's not smart to keep a car in the city, but if you're planning any excursions, a rental is well worth looking into. Rates vary, but expect to pay £100–£125 ($190–$237.50) per week, depending on the season. The least expensive rentals I have found are from **Practical Used Car Rental,** 111 Bartholomew Rd., N.W.5 (tel. 071/284-0199); and **Supercars,** 16 Warner St., E.C.1 (tel. 071/278-6001). Look in the phonebook under "Car Rental" for alternatives and use the big American chains as a last resort. Make sure the rate you pay includes unlimited mileage, all taxes, and the collision-damage waiver, as these extras can send prices into the stratosphere. Gasoline (petrol) costs about £1.75 ($3.35) per Imperial gallon (1.2 U.S. gallons).

 LONDON

Babysitters If your request for a recommendation from a member of your hotel staff is answered with a blank stare, phone **Babysitters Childminders,** 9 Paddington St., W.1. (tel. 071/935-9763).

Banks Most banks are open Monday through Friday from 9:30am to 3:30pm. Some also open Saturday from 9:30am until noon.

Banks generally offer the best exchange rates, but American Express and Thomas Cook are competitive and do not charge a commission for cashing traveler's checks no matter the brand. **American Express** maintains several offices throughout the city, including 6 Haymarket, S.W.1 (tel. 071/930-8422), near Trafalgar Square. A conveniently located **Thomas Cook** office is at 1 Marble Arch, W.1 (tel. 071/723-1668). Both offices are open Monday through Friday from 9am to 5pm and on Saturday from 9am to noon.

Places with the longest hours (sometimes open all night) also offer the worst rates. Beware of Chequepoint and other high-commission bureaux de change.

Business Hours Stores are usually open Monday through Saturday from 10am to 6pm, but most stay open at least 1 extra hour 1 night during the week. Shops in Knightsbridge usually remain open until around 7pm on Wednesday, while stores in the West End are open late on Thursday. Some shops around touristy Convent Garden stay open until 7 or 8pm nightly. By law, most stores are closed Sunday.

Currency The English **pound (£),** a small, thick, round coin, is divided into 100 **pence.** Pence, often called "p," come in 1p, 2p, 5p, 10p, and 50p coins. You may still see some older 1- and 2-shilling coins, which are equivalent to 5p and 10p, respectively. Notes are issued in £5, £10, £20, and £50 denominations.

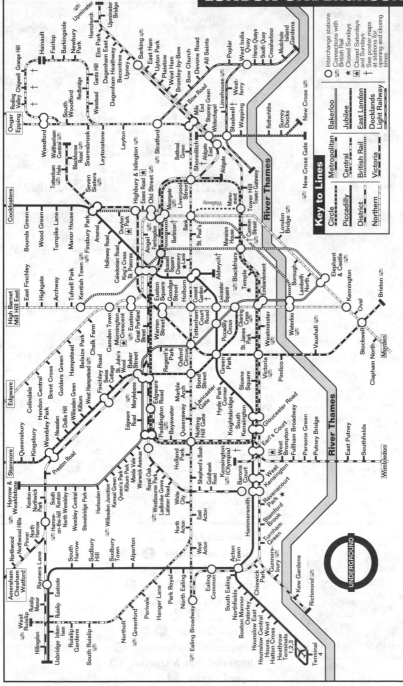

LONDON UNDERGROUND

Key to Lines

Circle	Metropolitan
Piccadilly	Central
District	British Rail
Northern	Victoria
Bakerloo	
Jubilee	
East London	
Docklands Light Railway	

○ Interchange stations

≈ Connections with British Rail

★ Closed Sundays

Ⓧ Closed Saturdays and Sundays

† See poster maps at stations for opening and closing times

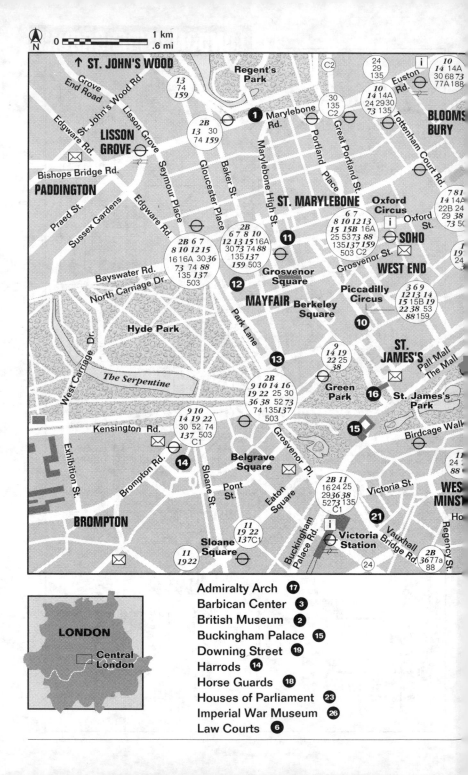

LONDON

Central London

Admiralty Arch **17**
Barbican Center **3**
British Museum **2**
Buckingham Palace **15**
Downing Street **19**
Harrods **14**
Horse Guards **18**
Houses of Parliament **23**
Imperial War Museum **26**
Law Courts **6**

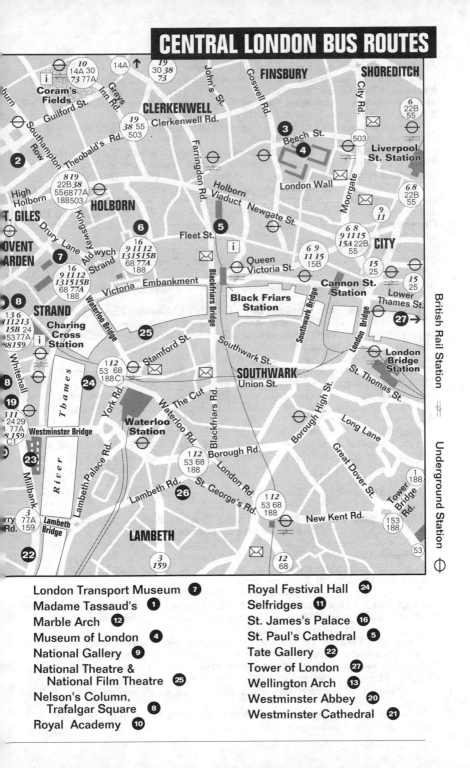

CENTRAL LONDON BUS ROUTES

London Transport Museum ❼
Madame Tassaud's ❶
Marble Arch ⓬
Museum of London ❹
National Gallery ❾
National Theatre &
    National Film Theatre ㉕
Nelson's Column,
    Trafalgar Square ❽
Royal Academy ❿

Royal Festival Hall ㉔
Selfridges ⓫
St. James's Palace ⓰
St. Paul's Cathedral ❺
Tate Gallery ㉒
Tower of London ㉗
Wellington Arch ⓭
Westminster Abbey ⓴
Westminster Cathedral ㉑

British Rail Station

Underground Station ⊖

Doctors and Dentists If you need a physician or dentist and your condition is not life-threatening, call the operator (dial 100) and ask for the local police; they will put you in touch with a specialist. Alternatively, visit **Medical Express,** Chapel Place, W.1 (tel. 071/499-1991). This private walk-in clinic is open Monday through Friday from 9am to 5:30pm and on Saturday from 9:30am to 2:30pm. Consultations begin at £60 ($114).

Citizens of Australia and New Zealand are entitled to free medical treatment and subsidized dental care while in Britain.

Embassies The **U.S. Embassy,** 24 Grosvenor Sq., W.1 (tel. 071/499-9000), is open to walk-in visitors Monday through Friday from 8:30 to 11am. The **Canadian High Commission,** Macdonald House, 1 Grosvenor Sq., W.1 (tel. 071/629-9492), is open Monday through Friday from 9am to 5pm. The **Australian High Commission** is in Australia House on The Strand, W.C.2 (tel. 071/379-4334), and is open Monday through Friday from 9am to 1pm. The **New Zealand High Commission** is in New Zealand House, Haymarket, S.W.1 (tel. 071/930-8422), open Monday through Friday from 9am to 5pm.

Emergencies Police, fire, and ambulance services can be reached by dialing **999** from any phone. No money is required. **Bliss Chemist,** 5 Marble Arch, W.1 (tel. 071/723-6116), is open daily from 9am to midnight. Phone the operator (100) and ask for the police for the opening hours and addresses of other late-opening pharmacies.

Eyeglasses The **Contact Lens Centre,** 32 Camden High St., N.W.1 (tel. 071/383-3838), is one of the cheapest shops for contacts as well as glasses. Even if you forgot to bring your prescription with you, chances are you can be tested and fitted the same day. It's open Monday through Friday from 9am to 7pm, on Saturday from 9am to 5pm, and on Sunday from 10am to 4pm. MC, V.

Holidays Most businesses are closed December 25 and 26, January 1, Good Friday, Easter Monday, and May 1. In addition, many stores close on bank holidays, which are scattered throughout the year. There is no uniform policy for museums, restaurants, and attractions with regard to holidays. To avoid disappointment, always phone before setting out.

Hospitals In an emergency, dial 999 from any phone; no money is needed. **St. Mary's Hospital,** Praed Street, Paddington, W.2. (tel. 071/262-1280), is one of the most centrally located. A dozen other city hospitals also offer 24-hour walk-in emergency care. Dial 100 and ask the operator to connect you with the police; they will tell you which is closest.

Information See "Information" in "Orientation and Getting Around," above.

Laundry/Dry Cleaning Laundries abound and most are open every day. Near Russell Square, try **Red and White Laundries,** 78 Marchmont St., open daily from 8am to 10pm; a wash costs £2 ($3.80) and dryers and soap are 50p (95¢). **Ashbourne Laundry,** 93 Pimlico Rd., is similarly priced and convenient to Victoria Station hotels. **Launderette House,** 18 London St., is open daily from 8am to 8pm and is a good pick in the Bayswater area.

Dry cleaning is very expensive in London. Expect to pay about £2 ($3.80) per shirt, and £4.50 ($8.55) for a pair of pants. With over 40 branches, **Sketchley,** 49 Maddox St., W.1 (tel. 071/629-1292), is one of the city's largest cleaning chains. Check the telephone directory for other locations.

Lost and Found If you lose something **on the bus or tube,** allow 2 days before contacting London Regional Transport, 200 Baker St., N.W.1 (tel. 071/486-2496), open Monday through Friday from 9:30am to 2pm. The **Taxi Lost Property Office,** 15 Penton St., N.1 (tel. 071/833-0996), is open Monday through Friday from 9am to 4pm. Lost property offices are also located in all the major British Rail stations.

If you need **to report a loss or theft,** call the local police by dialing 100 and asking the operator to connect you.

Mail   Post offices are plentiful and are normally open Monday through Friday from 9am to 5pm and on Saturday from 9am to noon. The **Main Post Office,** St. Martin's Place, Trafalgar Square, W.C.2 (tel. 071/930-9580), is open Monday through Saturday from 8am to 8pm. Mail boxes are round and red, and well distributed throughout the city. Airmail letters weighing up to 10 grams cost 39p (75¢) and postcards require a 35p (65¢) stamp to all destinations outside Europe. Budget travelers can get more post for the pound by purchasing aerograms for 34p (65¢) each; the deal is even sweeter at £1.90 ($3.60) per half dozen.

Newspapers/Magazines   There are a lot of local newspapers in London. In general you will find that the tabloids sensationalize news more than the respected, larger-format papers.

The listings magazines *Time Out* and *City Limits* are indispensable for comprehensive information on what's happening in the city. Newsstands are located outside almost every tube station, and an unusually good selection of international newspapers and magazines is available at almost every little tobacco shop and food market.

Photographic Needs   Photo processing in London is more expensive than similar services Stateside. **Dixons,** 88 Oxford St., W.1 (tel. 071/636-8511), with over 80 branches in London, is the best source for most photographic needs. It's open Monday through Friday from 9:30am to 7pm, on Saturday from 9:30am to 6:30pm, and on Sunday from 10am to 4pm.

Police   In an emergency, dial **999** from any phone; no money is needed. At other times, dial the operator (100) and ask to be connected with the police.

Radio/TV   The BBC produces some great television programs, but they're few and far between. Unless your hotel is hooked in to the European Cable Network, you'll have to settle for one of the four local stations.

Radio in London also leaves a lot to be desired. There are only five BBC-run stations, and about half a dozen private broadcasters, including Jazz FM (102.2), easy-listening Melody FM (104.9), and Kiss FM (100.0) which plays dance music all day.

Religious Services   It sometimes seems that the only things in London more ubiquitous than pubs are churches. **Church of England** houses of worship are on almost every street in The City, and you're welcome to attend Sunday services in any one of them. The London Tourist Board can provide you with a complete list. For a special treat, think about spending Sunday morning in St. Paul's Cathedral (tel. 071/248-2705) or Westminster Abbey (tel. 071/222-5152). Services are held at the Abbey at 8am, 10am, 11:15am, 3pm, 5:45pm, and 6:30pm. Times vary at St. Paul's; call for information. **Westminster Cathedral,** Ashley Place, S.W.1 (tel. 071/834-7452), is England's Roman Catholic headquarters, and a spectacular sightseeing destination in its own right (see "Attractions," below). Services are held at 7am, 8am, 9am, 10:30am, noon, 5:30pm, and 7pm. The **Liberal Jewish Synagogue,** 152 Loudoun Rd., N.W.8 (tel. 071/722-8872), holds services on Friday at 8pm and Saturday at 11am. The **Buddhist Society,** 58 Eccleston Sq., S.W.1 (tel. 071/834-5858), holds regular lectures and meditations. Call Monday through Saturday between 2 and 5pm for information.

Shoe Repair   Most of the major tube stations have "heel bars" that can make quick repairs. More extensive work can be performed in any of the major department stores (see "Savvy Shopping," below) or at **Jeeves Snob Shop,** 10 Pont St., S.W.1 (tel. 071/235-1101), open Monday through Friday from 8:30am to 5:30pm and on Saturday from 8:30am to 1pm. AE, MC, V.

Tax   Unlike the United States where tax is tacked on at the register, in England a 17.5% Value-Added Tax (VAT) is already figured into the ticket price of most items. Foreign tourists can reclaim the VAT for major purchases. See "Savvy Shopping," below, for details.

Taxis   London's famous black cabs can be hailed in the street; an illuminated yellow roof light means they're available. If you'll need a taxi from your hotel early in the morning, make a reservation the night before. Try **Computer-cab** (tel.

071/286-0286) or **Radio Taxicabs** (tel. 071/272-0272). For more information on taxis, see "Orientation and Getting Around," above.

Telephone   London now has two **area codes:** 071 (for central London) and 081 (for outer London). You only need to use these codes when phoning from *outside* the calling area. All the telephone numbers in this chapter include area codes for your convenience—use them when applicable.

There are two kinds of **pay phones** in normal use. The first accepts coins, while the other operates exclusively with a Phonecard, available from newsagents in £1, £2, £4, £10, and £20 denominations. The minimum cost of a local call is 10p (19¢) for the first 2 minutes (peak hours). You can deposit up to four coins at a time, but telephones don't make change, so unless you're calling long distance, use 10p coins exclusively. Phonecard telephones automatically deduct the price of your call from the card. Cards are especially handy if you want to call abroad, as you don't have to continuously pop in the pounds. Some large hotels and touristy street corners also have credit-card telephones that accept major credit cards. Lift the handle and follow the instructions on the screen.

To reach the **local operator,** dial 100. The **international operator** is 155. **London phone information** (called "directory inquiries") can be reached by dialing 142, and is free of charge.

Tipping   Most **restaurants** automatically add a discretionary service charge, but not all. The restaurant's policy will be written on the menu. Where a service charge is not included, a 10% to 15% tip is customary. **Taxis** also expect 10% to 15% of the fare. Note that tipping is rare in both pubs and theaters.

4. BUDGET ACCOMMODATIONS

The bed-and-breakfast is one of England's greatest traditions. Morning-meal menus differ, but most hotels serve up a whopper that usually includes cereal, eggs, bacon or sausage, toast, and all the coffee or tea you can drink. It's hearty, and just might last you through the day. The bad news is that, in general, London's budget hotels are not as nice or as cheap as those on the Continent. Rooms are uniformly small and wear is often in evidence. But British hoteliers are famous for their good-humored hospitality, and have an uncanny ability to turn an ordinary stay into a memorable experience. The huge free breakfast helps you stay on budget in London even if you have to pay a little more for a room here than on the Continent.

Summer is a seller's market. Hordes of tourists jousting for coveted hotel rooms keep rates high. But if you sense that rooms are going unoccupied, asking for a reduced rate is definitely in order. In the off-season, prices tumble—sometimes by as much as 30%—and there is often room for further negotiation. Never accept a room until you are sure you've secured the lowest price. Make it clear that you are a budget traveler and be willing to lower your standards. If you're shopping around, make this fact clear. Always ask if they have anything cheaper, and note that many hotels will offer a discount for a stay of a week or more. Everyone, especially single travelers, should ask to see the room before renting it. Most hotels will accommodate a single person in a larger room if it's available, and asking to view it beforehand will encourage this.

Here are a few things to keep in mind when renting a room in London. Although beds are made up daily, sheets are usually not changed during a stay of less than a week. If you need new bedding, request it. Remember that even local telephone calls

THE POUND & THE DOLLAR

At this writing $1 = approximately 53p (or £1 = $1.90), and this was the rate of exchange used to calculate the dollar values given in this chapter (rounded to the nearest nickel). This rate fluctuates from time to time and may not be the same when you travel to the U.K. Therefore the following table should be used only as a guide:

£	U.S.$	£	U.S.$
.01	.02	6	11.40
.05	.10	7	13.30
.10	.19	8	15.20
.25	.48	9	17.10
.50	.95	10	19.00
.75	1.43	15	28.50
1	1.90	20	38.00
2	3.80	25	47.50
3	5.70	30	57.00
4	7.60	40	76.00
5	9.50	50	95.00

made from your room can be deathly expensive—inquire about the rate before dialing. And finally, a personal observation: The guest lounge is the hearth of a hotel—a place where travelers can meet, exchange ideas, and make new friends. Unfortunately, these public areas are quickly fading from budget hotels in favor of an additional money-making bedroom. If you're lucky enough to stay in a hotel with a comfortable lounge area, don't ignore it. Many hotels offer "multishare" accommodations where single visitors share a room with other travelers.

Note: Rates quoted below are accurate for the *summer of 1993.* Expect reductions before and after the season.

Also, if you're phoning an establishment from North America, use the area code given in this section (71 or 81). If you're calling from inside the U.K. but outside the area code, dial 071 or 081.

DOUBLES WITHOUT BATH FOR LESS THAN £37 ($70.30)

BAYSWATER & PADDINGTON

The unofficial district of Bayswater runs along the northern edge of Hyde Park and encompasses Paddington Station, one of the city's major gateways to the north. It is a densely packed residential community, populated by a large number of Indians and Pakistanis. It is also jammed with budget hotels. The area's proximity to the park, good restaurants (especially along Queensway and Westbourne Grove), and transportation links to the West End make Bayswater a desirable place to locate. The Central and District Underground lines run to Bayswater and Paddington Stations, while buses no. 12, 88, and 289 travel the length of Bayswater Road.

DEAN COURT HOTEL, 57 Inverness Terrace, London W.2. Tel. 071/229-2961. 16 rms (25 multishare beds; none with bath) **Tube:** Bayswater.
$ Rates (including continental breakfast): £32 ($60.80) twin; £45 ($85.50) triple; £9.50 ($18.05) per person per night, £62 ($117.80) per week in a multishare. No credit cards.
This hotel overlooks a quiet Bayswater street, just 50 yards from bustling Queensway.

Nicely decorated rooms, a large breakfast, capable management, and an exceptionally kind budget philosophy are all hallmarks of this top budget hotel.

HYDE PARK HOUSE, 48 St. Petersburgh Place, London W.2. Tel. 071/229-1687. 18 rms (none with bath). TV **Tube:** Bayswater.
$ Rates (including continental breakfast): £21 ($39.90) single; £32 ($60.80) twin. No credit cards.

⭐ "Charming" may sound corny, but no other word accurately describes this top pick for good, clean, honest, quiet accommodations. Announced by a small awning in the middle of a block of rowhouses, this family-run B&B puts a quilt on every bed and a refrigerator in every room. Prices include free use of the kitchen, and unlimited attention from the family's friendly small dogs.

From the Bayswater Underground station, turn left onto Moscow Road and left again at the church.

ST. CHARLES HOTEL, 66 Queensborough Terrace, London W.2. Tel. 071/221-0022. 16 rms (all with shower, 4 also with toilet). **Tube:** Queensway.
$ Rates (including English breakfast): £25 ($47.50) single without toilet, £30 ($57) single with toilet; £37 ($70.30) twin without toilet, £40 ($76) twin with toilet. £2 ($3.80) surcharge for 1-night stays. No credit cards.

Mr. and Mrs. Wildrige are this hotel's caring proprietors, and indeed, the interior is beautifully kept. Opulent wood paneling and carefully restored ceilings suggest a high tariff, but a few of the bathless rooms are within our budget.

From the Queensway Underground station, turn left onto Bayswater Road and, after two blocks, take another left onto Queensborough Terrace.

Sussex Gardens

Despite its quiet-sounding name, Sussex Gardens is one of Bayswater's busiest thoroughfares. Beginning as a traffic circle south of Paddington Station, the long street runs straight up to Edgeware Road. Along both sides of Sussex Gardens there's hardly a house that doesn't announce itself as a hotel. Accommodations are uniformly nondescript, but rates are good, and fierce competition in the off-season means that everything's negotiable.

ABC HOTEL, 121 Sussex Gardens, London W.2. Tel. 071/723-3945. 16 rms (none with bath). TV TEL **Tube:** Paddington.
$ Rates (including English breakfast): £26 ($49.40) single; £37 ($70.30) twin. MC, V.

In addition to competent accommodations, tariffs include a good breakfast and free use of the kitchen.

Ⓕ **FROMMER'S SMART TRAVELER: HOTELS**

VALUE-CONSCIOUS TRAVELERS SHOULD TAKE ADVANTAGE OF THE FOLLOWING:

1. Off-season rates. Prices tumble—sometimes by as much as 30%—and often there is room for further negotiation.
2. Long-term stays. Many hotels offer discounts to guests staying a week or more.

QUESTIONS TO ASK IF YOU'RE ON A BUDGET

1. Do you have anything cheaper?
2. Can I see the room first? (Hoteliers are more likely to offer their nicest rooms to travelers who look before they buy.)

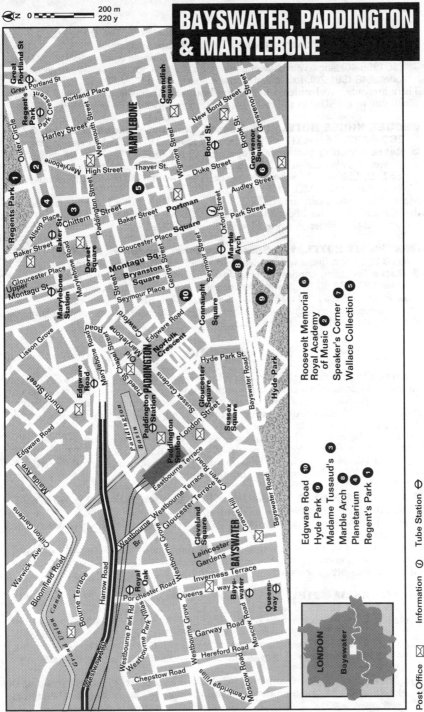

BAYSWATER, PADDINGTON & MARYLEBONE

0 200 m
0 220 y

Edgware Road 🔟
Hyde Park 9️⃣
Madame Tussaud's 3️⃣
Marble Arch 8️⃣
Planetarium 4️⃣
Regent's Park 1️⃣

Roosevelt Memorial 6️⃣
Royal Academy
of Music 2️⃣
Speaker's Corner 7️⃣
Wallace Collection 5️⃣

LONDON
Bayswater

Post Office ⊠   Information ⊙   Tube Station ⊖

GOWER HOTEL, 129 Sussex Gardens, London W.2. Tel. 071/262-2262. 22 rms (20 with shower and toilet). TV TEL **Tube:** Paddington.
$ Rates (including English breakfast): £26 ($49.40) single without shower or toilet, £36 ($68.40) single with shower and toilet; £37 ($70.30) double without shower or toilet, £48 ($91.20) double with shower and toilet. MC, V.
There are only two bathless rooms here, both on the top floor. Although they are small, due to the slant in the roof, good, clean facilities make it worth the climb.

RHODES HOUSE HOTEL, 195 Sussex Gardens, London W.2. Tel. 071/262-0537. 16 rms (12 with shower and toilet). TV TEL **Tube:** Paddington.
$ Rates (including continental breakfast): £20–£25 ($38–$47.50) single without shower or toilet, £30–£35 ($57–$66.50) single with shower and toilet; £30–£35 ($57–$66.50) double without shower or toilet, £40–£47 ($76–$89.30) double with shower and toilet. MC, V.
Most of the rooms here are equipped with private bath, but a few basic singles and doubles are within our budget. If Rhodes House is full, owner Chris Crias will send you around the corner to Argos House, his other hotel.

WESTPOINT HOTEL, 170 Sussex Gardens, London W.2. Tel. 071/402-0281. 66 rms (most with shower and toilet). TV **Tube:** Paddington.
$ Rates (including continental breakfast): £25 ($47.50) single without shower or toilet, £35 ($66.50) single with shower and toilet; £37 ($70.30) twin without shower or toilet, £48 ($91.20) twin with shower and toilet. MC, V.
Farther along the street, this hotel is slightly larger than most. It's somewhat plain, but clean and thoroughly recommendable.

VICTORIA

The rebuilding of Buckingham House into Buckingham Palace in the 1820s helped transform Victoria into a fashionable neighborhood. Bustling Victoria Station bisects the area, separating pricey Belgravia on its northwest from more accessible Pimlico to the southeast. Much of the area was destroyed during World War II when houses took the near misses directed at Victoria Station. Happily, most of the rebuilding has been faithful to the original Greco-Roman style. If you're shopping around, note that although there are hundreds of hotels here, the majority are not up to standard. Victoria is known not for its sights, shopping, or entertainment, but for its proximity to Victoria Station, London's transportation hub.

MELBOURNE HOUSE, 79 Belgrave Rd., London S.W.1. Tel. 071/828-3516. 15 rms (none with bath). **Tube:** Victoria.
$ Rates (including English breakfast): £23 ($43.70) single; £33 ($62.70) double. No credit cards.
Melbourne House is far and away the best B&B on Belgrave Road, and the only one to earn a listing here. The crumbling front belies a clean, though plain, interior. And the airy rooms here are something of a novelty.

MELITA HOUSE HOTEL, 33-35 Charlwood St., London S.W.1. Tel. 071/828-0471. 18 rms (6 with shower and toilet). TV **Tube:** Victoria.
$ Rates (including continental breakfast): £25 ($47.50) single without shower or toilet, £29 ($55.10) single with shower, £33 ($62.70) single with shower and toilet; £37 ($70.30) double without shower or toilet, £42 ($79.80) double with shower, £47 ($89.30) double with shower and toilet. Add 5% when paying by credit card. AE, V.

 In this spotless and charming hotel, located on a quiet side street, breakfast is served in a ground-floor dining room, a refreshing change from the basements of most hotels.
To reach Charlwood Street, turn right off Belgrave Road, south of Warwick Way.

THE OAK HOUSE, 29 Hugh St., London S.W.1. Tel. 071/834-7151. 6 rms (none with bath). **Tube:** Victoria.
$ Rates: £27 ($51.30) twin. No credit cards.

⭐ One of my favorite hotels in this area is also one of the closest to Victoria Station, between Eccleston and Elizabeth Bridges. Like the hotel itself, the sign hanging outside stands out from the other B&Bs on the block. It doesn't take a genius to figure out that resident proprietors Mr. and Mrs. Symington are Scottish. The use of tartan carpeting throughout the hotel is only slightly heavier than the couple's charming accents. There are only six rooms here, all twins, and each is very small. The conscientious owners have fitted all with orthopedic mattresses, hairdryers, electric shaver outlets, tea/coffee-making facilities, a cutting board, knife, and even a bottle opener. No advance reservations are accepted, so when you get to the station just cross your fingers and call.

Warwick Way

Warwick Way is another hotel-lined thoroughfare, for the most part as undesirable as Belgrave Road. Out of dozens, only two hotels are recommendable, and then only when your other options in the area have been exhausted.

ELIZABETH HOUSE, 118 Warwick Way, London S.W.1. Tel. 071/630-0741. 27 rms (9 with shower and toilet). **Tube:** Victoria.
$ Rates (including continental breakfast): £21 ($39.90) single without shower or toilet, £26 ($49.40) single with shower and toilet; £37 ($70.30) twin without shower or toilet, £44 ($83.60) twin with shower and toilet; £15 ($28.50) per person in multishare room. No credit cards.
This is a YWCA guesthouse that accommodates men as well as women. The atmosphere is friendly, the house is clean, and the sparsely furnished rooms will please minimalists. Multishare "dormitory-style" accommodations never group more than four persons per room.

ENRICO HOTEL, 77-79 Warwick Way, London S.W.1. Tel. 071/834-9538. 26 rms (none with bath). **Tube:** Victoria.
$ Rates (including English breakfast): £28 ($53.20) single; £34 ($64.60) double. Prices increase by £2 ($3.80) if you stay only 1 night. MC, V.
Enrico gets marks for its comfortable beds and cheery breakfast room.

NORTHERN BLOOMSBURY

At Bloomsbury's northern edge, opposite King's Cross and St. Pancras Stations, are several hotel-packed streets including Birkenhead, Crestfield, Argyle, and Argyle Square. The area is somewhat shabby and cannot compare with the attractiveness of the more expensive Russell Square area or with the bustle of Bayswater. But the many decrepit, several decent, and even some desirable hotels here are relatively unknown to American tourists, and are very competitively priced (read: cheap).

CENTRAL HOTEL, 16-18 Argyle St., London, W.C.1. Tel. 071/278-8682. 31 rms (none with bath). TV **Tube:** King's Cross.
$ Rates (including English breakfast): £25 ($47.50) single; £31 ($58.90) double; £37 ($70.30) triple. MC, V.
One of the four Caruana brothers, the hotel's proprietors, will happily show you to a simple, reasonably sized room. If the Central is full and you're steered toward their other hotel across the street (the Fairway), be choosy.

ELMWOOD HOTEL, 19 Argyle Sq., London, W.C.1. Tel. 071/837-9361. 11 rms (none with bath). TV **Tube:** King's Cross.
$ Rates (including English breakfast): £21 ($39.90) single; £28 ($53.20) double. No credit cards.

An orange-and-white sign announces this nice B&B, which has been owned by the same resident proprietors for more than 15 years. Enter through the wooden front door into a hotel better than most in the area.

MYRTLE HOTEL, 20 Argyle Sq., London W.C.1. Tel. 071/837-5759. 14 rms (none with bath). TV **Tube:** King's Cross.
$ Rates (including English breakfast): £21 ($39.90) single; £26 ($49.40) double. No credit cards.

This hotel is typical of the area with regard to comfort, services, and price. Like most hotels here, the Myrtle is centrally heated and has a TV, and there's hot and cold running water in the bathless rooms. Accommodations are sparse but clean.

Hunter Street

CAMBRIA HOUSE, 37 Hunter St., London W.C.1. Tel. 071/837-1654. 39 rms (8 with bath). **Tube:** Russell Square.
$ Rates (including English Breakfast): £18 ($34.20) single without shower or toilet; £28 ($53.20) double without shower or toilet, £37 ($70.30) double with shower and toilet. Weekly discounts available. MC, V.

Located at the corner of Tavistock Place, south of Cartwright Gardens, Cambria House is a Salvation Army establishment in a large red-brick building. Simple rooms and fairly strict rules are balanced by low rates. No alcohol is allowed and the house closes at 11pm, but there is a pub around the corner and late-night keys are available for a £2 ($3.80) deposit. As with most religious-run places, the decorator is obviously an ascetic.

CHELSEA & SOUTH KENSINGTON

The expensive residential areas of Chelsea and South Kensington offer little in the way of accommodations for budget travelers. With few notable exceptions, the cost of lodging here reflects location rather than quality. Chelsea gained fame as London's bohemia, a place for writers and artists. Thomas Carlyle, George Eliot, Oscar Wilde, Henry James . . . the list of famous former residents is endless. A room in adjacent South Kensington is only steps away from more than half a dozen top museums and the ritzy boutiques of Knightsbridge. Like Chelsea, it's unlikely that South Kensington will again be home to impoverished artists, as these posh areas are now two of the swankiest neighborhoods in the world.

In addition to the recommendations listed below, a couple more Chelsea and South Kensington hotels appear in the next price category.

MORE HOUSE, 53 Cromwell Rd., London S.W.7. Tel. 071/584-2040. 55 rms (none with bath). **Tube:** Gloucester Road.
$ Rates (including English breakfast): £23 ($43.70) single; £36 ($70.30) twin; £49 ($93.10) triple. 10% discount for stays of 1 week or more. No credit cards. **Open:** June–Sept.

This Catholic-run dormitory with an institutional feel is home to foreign students during the school year, but singles and twins are rented to visitors of all faiths from June to September. The house is well located across from the Science Museum, and extremely functional. There is a refrigerator on every floor, microwave ovens for guests' use, laundry facilities, and a licensed bar.

Turn right from the Gloucester Road Underground and walk five short blocks along Cromwell Road.

OAKLEY HOTEL, 73 Oakley St., London S.W.3. Tel. 071/352-5599. 11 rms (none with bath). **Tube:** Sloane Square.
$ Rates (including English breakfast): £19 ($36.10) single; £36 ($68.40) double; £45 ($85.50) triple; £10 ($19) per person in multishare rooms. No credit cards.

 Well decorated rooms and a fun, friendly atmosphere make this economical hotel a welcome oasis in tab-happy Chelsea. The local council of this chic neighborhood forbids a "hotel" sign, but a knock on the green door will be answered by a friendly Australian. Aside from singles and twins, the hotel has several multishare rooms at great rates. All prices include a large breakfast and free use of the kitchen.

From the Sloane Square Underground, take a long walk, or the no. 11 or 22 bus, down Kings Road to Oakley Street.

EARL'S COURT

Although it is located just west of exclusive Chelsea and Knightsbridge, Earl's Court has been slow to achieve the classy status of its neighbors. There are dozens of hotels here; many are hostel-type multishare accommodations, and quality is often suspect. But the multitude of ultra-budget accommodations means that cheap restaurants, pubs, and services are nearby. The Earl's Court tube station is located in the middle of Earl's Court Road, which, along with Old Brompton Road to the south, is the area's chief shopping strip. Affectionately dubbed "Kangaroo Court," Earl's Court is the unofficial headquarters of England's large, ever-changing Australian community.

AARON HOUSE, 17 Courtfield Gardens, London S.W.5. Tel. 071/370-3991. Fax 071/373-2303. 22 rms (10 with shower and toilet). TV **Tube:** Earl's Court Road.

$ Rates (including continental breakfast): £21 ($39.90) single without shower or toilet, £26 ($49.40) single with shower and toilet; £34 ($64.60) double without shower or toilet, £38 ($72.20) double with shower and toilet; £45 ($85.50) triple without shower or toilet, £50 ($95) triple with shower and toilet. MC, V.

Announced only by a small gold sign to the left of the hotel's front door, Aaron House is perhaps the nicest budget hotel in Earl's Court. Beveled glass, along with beautiful moldings and cornice work are the trademarks of this understated B&B. The front rooms, all with bath, are particularly large, and overlook a peaceful Victorian Square. Every room is fitted with a color television and coffee/tea-making facilities.

The hotel is about three blocks east of the Earl's Court Underground station, on the west side of Courtfield Gardens.

HOTEL BOKA, 33-35 Eardley Crescent, London S.W.5. Tel. 071/370-1388. 52 rms (23 with shower only). **Tube:** Earl's Court Road.

$ Rates (including English breakfast): £25 ($47.50) single without shower, £29 ($55.10) single with shower; £35 ($66.50) double without shower, £38 ($72.20) double with shower; £16 ($30.40) per person in a multibed room. AE, MC, V.

Boka's bright-blue tiled columns stand out in the middle of a pretty Victorian crescent. Inside, expect a friendly staff, unusually high ceilings, and pretty antique bureaus and dressers, some with wood inlay.

From the Earl's Court Underground station, take the Warwick Road exit, cross the street, and turn left onto Eardley Crescent.

THE MANOR HOTEL, 23 Nevern Place, London S.W.5. Tel. 071/370-6018. 27 rms (12 with shower and toilet). **Tube:** Earl's Court Road.

$ Rates (including continental breakfast): £20 ($38) single without shower or toilet, £26 ($49.40) single with shower and toilet; £30 ($57) double without shower or toilet, £37 ($70.30) double with shower and toilet; £40 ($76) triple without shower or toilet, £46 ($87.40) triple with shower and toilet. Discount for stays of 1 week or more. No credit cards.

Despite threadbare carpets and some peeling wallpaper, the Manor is light and airy, and happily devoid of the dark Dickensian feel that plagues most of the area's hotels.

The hotel is located two blocks north of the Underground station at the corner of Templeton Place.

ELSEWHERE AROUND TOWN

ABBEVILLE GUESTHOUSE, 89 Abbeville Rd., London S.W.4. Tel. 071/622-5360. 7 rms (none with bath). TV **Tube:** Clapham Common.

LONDON

Chelsea,
Knightsbridge
& South
Kensington

Albert Memorial ❶
Botanic Gardens ⑪
Brompton Oratory ❽
Chelsea Antiques
Market ⑩
Geological Museum ❺
Harrods ❾
Natural History
Museum ❹
Royal Albert Hall ❷
Royal Geographical
Society ❸
Science Museum ❻
Victoria and Albert
Museum ❼

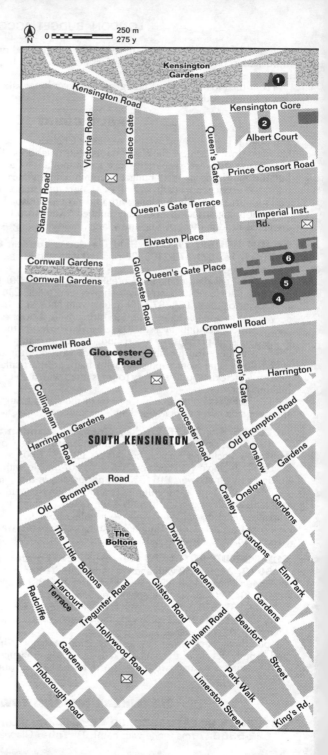

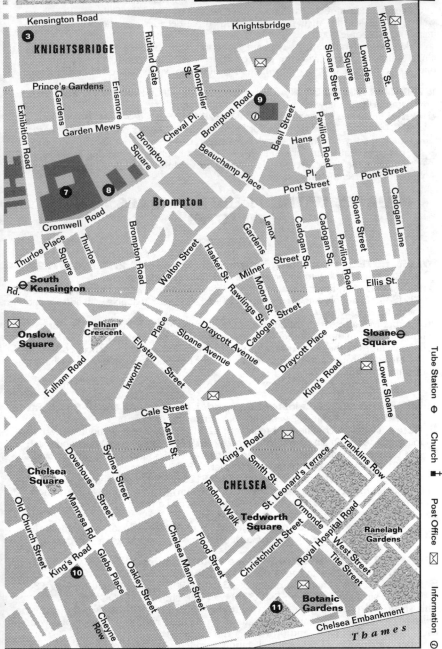

CHELSEA, KNIGHTSBRIDGE & SOUTH KENSINGTON

Kensington Gardens

Kensington Road

Knightsbridge

Kinnerton St.

3

KNIGHTSBRIDGE

Rutland Gate

Montpelier St.

Lowndes Square

Sloane Square

Sloane Street

Prince's Gardens

Enismore Gardens

Garden Mews

Exhibition Road

Brompton Square

Cheval Pl.

Brompton Road

9

Basil Street

Hans

Pavilion Road

Beauchamp Place

Pont Street

Pont Street

Pl.

7 **8**

Brompton

Cromwell Road

Brompton Road

Walton Street

Lenox Gardens

Cadogan Sq.

Sloane Street

Cadogan Lane

Thurloe Place

Thurloe Square

Thurloe

Hasker St.

Milner

Rawlings St.

Moore St.

Cadogan Street

Street

Pavilion Road

Ellis St.

Rd.

South Kensington

Onslow Square

Pelham Crescent

Place

Ixworth

Elystan Street

Draycott Avenue

Sloane Avenue

Cadogan Street

Draycott Place

Draycott Place

King's Road

Lower Sloane

Sloane Square

Fulham Road

Cale Street

Astell St.

Sydney Street

Dovehouse Street

Manresa Rd.

King's Road

Smith St.

St. Leonard's Terrace

Franklins Row

King's Road

Chelsea Square

Old Church Street

King's Road

10

Glebe Place

Oakley Street

Chelsea Manor Street

Flood Street

CHELSEA

Tedworth Square

Radnor Walk

Christchurch Street

Ormonde

Royal Hospital Road

West Street

Tite Street

Ranelagh Gardens

Botanic Gardens

11

Cheyne Row

Chelsea Embankment

Thames

Tube Station ⊖   Church ■✝   Post Office ⊠   Information ⊖

$ Rates (including continental breakfast): £15 ($28.50) single; £25 ($47.50) twin. Discounts offered for stays of 3 nights or more. No credit cards.

In up-and-coming Clapham Common, south of the River Thames, this quiet home offers good accommodations at reasonable rates. Mr. and Mrs. Coleman have been welcoming guests into their home for about three decades and they know how to please picky people.

Take the Underground to Clapham Common, leave at the south exit, and walk along Southside Street (with the park on your right) for about 100 yards. Turn left onto Crescent Lane (not Grove), which after 300 more yards crosses Abbeville Road.

WYNDHAM HOTEL, 30 Wyndham St., London W.1. Tel. 071/723-7204. 11 rms (all with shower). TV **Tube:** Baker Street.

$ Rates (including continental breakfast): £25 ($47.50) single; £34 ($64.60) twin; £40 ($76) triple. These rates are for Frommer guide bearers only. No credit cards.

⭐ Tucked away on a quiet Marylebone street, this hotel stands apart from others both physically and for value. All rooms have coffee/tea-making facilities.

From the Baker Street Underground, cross Marylebone Road and turn right. Wyndham Street is the fifth on your left.

DOUBLES WITHOUT BATH FOR LESS THAN £40 ($76)

BAYSWATER

DYLAN HOTEL, 14 Devonshire Terrace, London W.2. Tel. 071/723-3280. 20 rms (11 with shower and toilet). **Tube:** Paddington.

$ Rates (including English breakfast): £26 ($49.40) single without shower or toilet; £39 ($74.10) double without shower or toilet, £47 ($89.30) double with shower and toilet. AE, DC, MC, V.

Proprietors Mr. and Mrs. Griffiths want travelers to think of this establishment as a "home away from home," and you probably will. Little touches like coffee/tea-making facilities in the bedrooms, cloth tablecloths, and a cup and saucer collection in the breakfast room add to this hotel's charm. Busy designs cover walls, ceilings, floors, and furniture.

From Paddington Station, follow Craven Road six blocks; then turn right.

LORDS HOTEL, 20-22 Leinster Sq., London W.2. Tel. 071/229-8877. Fax 071/229-8377. 42 rms (12 with shower). **Tube:** Bayswater.

$ Rates (including continental breakfast): £25 ($47.50) single without shower or toilet, £31 ($58.90) single with shower, £42 ($79.80) single with shower and toilet; £36 ($68.40) double without shower or toilet, £44 ($83.60) double with shower, £54 ($102.60) double with shower and toilet, £48 ($91.20) triple without shower or toilet, £54 ($102.60) triple with shower, £65 ($123.50) triple with shower and toilet.

This well-run budget establishment offers basic rooms that are both clean and neat. Some rooms are equipped with television and radio, and a few have balconies—all at no extra charge. The hotel caters to people of all ages.

From the Bayswater Underground, turn left onto Moscow Road, then right at the Russian Orthodox church (Ilchester Gardens); Lords is two blocks up on your left.

STRUTTON PARK HOTEL, 45 Palace Court, London W.2. Tel. 071/727-5074. 28 rms (25 with shower). TV TEL **Tube:** Bayswater.

$ Rates (including English breakfast): £31 ($58.90) single without shower, £36 ($68.40) single with shower; £40 ($76) twin with shower. AE, DC, MC, V.

This small and pretty hotel offers twin rooms only, most with shower (no private toilets). There is an elevator to take guests up to their rooms—all equipped with television and telephone—and down to a full breakfast.

From the Bayswater Underground station, turn left onto Moscow Road and walk about six blocks to Palace Court.

Norfolk Square

Norfolk square is a budget-hotel-packed horseshoe around a park just steps south of Paddington Station. There are too many hotels with too few distinguishing marks to mention them all here, but here are two of the best.

DOLPHIN HOTEL, 34 Norfolk Sq., London W.2. Tel. 071/402-4943. 18 rms (7 with shower and toilet). TV **Tube:** Paddington.

$ Rates (including continental breakfast): £24 ($45.60) single without shower or toilet; £34 ($64.60) double without shower or toilet, £42 ($79.80) double with shower and toilet. No credit cards.

In-room refrigerators, coffee makers, and (sometimes) telephones, help this hotel stand out from its neighbors. Otherwise, its recently redecorated rooms are typical of the square and a good bet. There is a £3 ($5.70) supplement for an English breakfast which, like the standard continental, is served in your room.

TUDOR COURT & GALLENCO HOTEL, 10-12 Norfolk Sq., London W.2. Tel. 071/723-6553. Fax 071/723-0727. 35 rms (6 with shower and toilet). TV **Tube:** Paddington.

$ Rates (including English breakfast): £25 ($47.50) single without shower or toilet, £35 ($66.50) single with shower and toilet; £36 ($68.40) double without shower or toilet; £45 ($85.50) double with shower and toilet; £51 ($96.90) triple without shower or toilet, £57 ($108.30) triple with shower and toilet. AE, DC, MC, V.

One of the first hotels you'll encounter is this recommendable B&B, managed by outgoing owner Dave Gupta. Unlike the singles, which tend to be on the small side, doubles here are well proportioned, and all rooms are neat and clean.

VICTORIA

EASTON HOTEL, 36-40 Belgrave Rd., London S.W.1. Tel. 071/834-5938. 55 rms (11 with shower and toilet). **Tube:** Victoria.

$ Rates (including English breakfast): £29 ($55.10) single without shower or toilet, £40 ($76) single with shower and toilet; £40 ($76) double without shower or toilet, £50 ($95) double with shower and toilet; £50 ($95) triple without shower or toilet, £58 ($110.20) triple with shower and toilet. AE, MC, V.

Rooms here are small but adequate, and some on the ground floor let you avoid stairs. An attractive licensed bar almost makes up for the distracting wood paneling on the floor of the breakfast room. The hotel is located on a major thoroughfare just behind Victoria Station.

LUNA HOUSE, 47-49 Belgrave Rd., London S.W.1. Tel. 071/834-5897. 18 rms (10 with shower and toilet). **Tube:** Victoria.

$ Rates (including English breakfast): £21 ($39.90) single without shower or toilet; £31 ($58.90) double without shower or toilet, £40 ($76) double with shower and toilet. No credit cards.

Farther along the street is this friendly, family-run hotel recognizable by the bright-orange lettering on the columns out front. A hearty breakfast is served in twin dining rooms, which are separated into smoking and no-smoking sections. TVs are in most rooms.

OXFORD HOUSE HOTEL, 92-94 Cambridge St., London S.W.1. Tel. 071/834-6467. 17 rms (none with bath). **Tube:** Victoria.

$ Rates (including English breakfast): £28 ($53.20) single; £38 ($72.20) double; £48 ($91.20) triple. Prices increase by £2 ($3.80) if you stay only 1 night. No credit cards.

This hotel is owned by interior designer Yanus Kader and his wife, Terri. Rooms are comfortable and pretty, featuring floral motifs and coordinated curtains. The beautiful dining area with an open kitchen will remind you of home. In the backyard, visit Hannibal, the couple's large and friendly rabbit.

The hotel is south of Belgrave Road near Gloucester Street.

BLOOMSBURY

Bloomsbury's proximity to the West End in general, and to Soho in particular, has long made it a desirable area for tourists. The area gets its energy from its two most important residents: the University of London and the British Museum. Although heavy demand is often reflected in high prices, there are still some good bargains to be found.

Gower Street

Gower Street's budget hotels are some of the city's most popular. Most of the B&Bs that line this street are so similar to one another that only their addresses distinguish them. Stairs are steep, rooms are basic (almost none with bath), and prices are fairly uniform. Special touches and extra-friendly management do set a few apart from the rest. They are ordered here geographically, away from Russell Square. The best way to reach the Gower Street hotels is from the Goodge Street Underground. Cross onto Chenies Street and turn left onto Gower.

ARRAN HOUSE HOTEL, 77 Gower St., London W.C.1. Tel. 071/636-2186. Fax 071/436-5328. 26 rms (4 with shower and toilet). **Tube:** Goodge Street.

$ Rates (including English breakfast): £31 ($58.90) single without shower or toilet; £44 ($83.60) double without shower or toilet, £56 ($106.40) double with shower and toilet. MC, V.

Arran House stands out on the block because of its exceptionally kind resident proprietor, Maj. W. J. Richards. The major has ensured that even guests in the front rooms get a quiet night's sleep by soundproofing all the windows, a modification that I can assure you really works! In addition to laundry and coffee/tea-making facilities, the hotel offers light meals, prepared by the owner's son, a professional caterer.

HOTEL CAVENDISH, 75 Gower St., London W.C.1. Tel. 071/636-9079. 20 rms (none with bath). **Tube:** Goodge Street.

$ Rates (including English breakfast): £28 ($53.20) single; £35–£38 ($66.50–$72.20) twin. No credit cards.

This is a nicely furnished, clean, and cozy home run by Mrs. Phillips. Cheaper twin rooms are slightly smaller than the more expensive ones.

JESMOND HOTEL, 63 Gower St., London W.C.1. Tel. 071/636-3199. 15 rms (none with bath). **Tube:** Goodge Street.

$ Rates (including English breakfast): £26 ($49.40) single; £40 ($76) twin. No credit cards.

The hotel's proprietors, Mr. and Mrs. Beynon, have been to the United States many times and are acutely aware of American habits and desires. All rooms have coffee- and tea-making facilities.

RIDGEMONT PRIVATE HOTEL, 65 Gower St., London W.C.1. Tel. 071/636-1141. 15 rms (none with bath). **Tube:** Goodge Street.

$ Rates (including English breakfast): £26 ($49.40) single; £39 ($74.10) double; £53 ($100.70) triple; £66 ($125.40) quad. No credit cards.

Although it's priced just above our budget, the Ridgemont's friendly atmosphere and warm-hearted Welsh proprietors, Royden and Gwen Rees, make it another good choice along the strip.

Tavistock Place

From the Russell Square Underground, a left turn just before Cartwright Gardens will put you on Tavistock Place.

GOODWOOD HOTEL, 38-40 Tavistock Place, London W.C.1. Tel. 071/837-0855. 18 rms (none with bath). TV **Tube:** Russell Square.

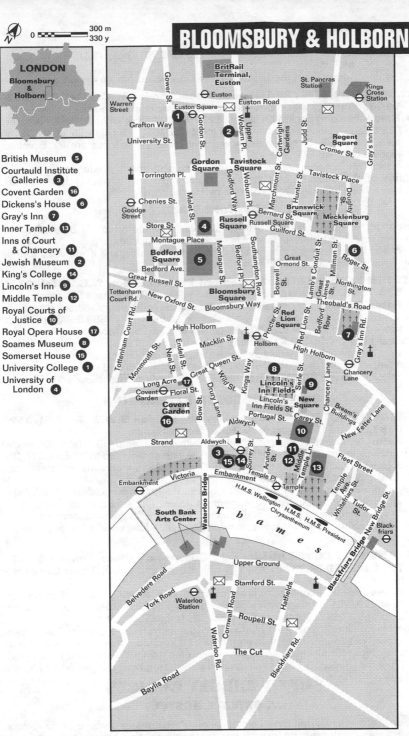

BLOOMSBURY & HOLBORN

0 ━━━━━ 300 m
  ━━━━━ 330 y

LONDON
Bloomsbury
&
Holborn

British Museum ⑤
Courtauld Institute
  Galleries ③
Covent Garden ⑯
Dickens's House ⑥
Gray's Inn ⑦
Inner Temple ⑬
Inns of Court
  & Chancery ⑪
Jewish Museum ②
King's College ⑭
Lincoln's Inn ⑨
Middle Temple ⑫
Royal Courts of
  Justice ⑩
Royal Opera House ⑰
Soames Museum ⑧
Somerset House ⑮
University College ①
University of
  London ④

Church ✠

Post Office ✉

Tube Station ⊖

$ Rates (including continental breakfast): £23 ($43.70) single; £33 ($62.70) double. AE, DC, MC, V.

A few doors down from the St. Athans, the Goodwood has very good rates.

ST. ATHANS HOTEL, 20 Tavistock Place, London W.C.1. Tel. 071/837-9140. 80 rms (3 with shower and toilet). **Tube:** Russell Square.
$ Rates (including English breakfast): £28 ($53.20) single without shower or toilet, £35 ($66.50) single with shower and toilet; £38 ($72.20) twin without shower or toilet, £49 ($93.10) twin with shower and toilet. These rates are for Frommer readers only. AE DC, MC, V.

Owners Hans Geyer guarantees very special rates to guests producing the current edition of this book. Rooms in this well-decorated and terrifically located hotel include a huge breakfast, often cooked by Hans himself.

Bedford Place

Just south of Russell Square, right in the heart of Bloomsbury is Bedford Place, another hotel-lined block that once figured prominently in these pages. Now almost every hotel here charges a around £50 ($97.50) for a double, and if you can afford it, this street is well worth checking out.

REPTON HOUSE HOTEL, 31 Bedford Place, London W.C.2. Tel. 071/636-7045. 38 rms (16 with shower and toilet). **Tube:** Russell Square.
$ Rates (including continental breakfast): £25 ($47.50) single without shower or toilet; £37 ($70.30) double without shower or toilet, £47 ($89.30) double with shower and toilet; £14 ($26.60) per person in a multibed room. MC, V.

The last hotel on the block remaining within our budget is open to tourists during summer months only and definitely worth a stay. The owner stresses cleanliness rather than fanciness, and the sparse but spotless rooms bear this out.

Take the tube to Russell Square, turn left, and walk to the square's south side.

CHELSEA & SOUTH KENSINGTON

MAGNOLIA HOTEL, 104-105 Oakley St., London S.W.3. Tel. 071/352-0187. 21 rms (7 with bath). TV **Tube:** Sloane Square.
$ Rates (including continental breakfast with boiled egg): £29 ($55.10) single without shower or toilet, £35 ($66.50) single with shower and toilet; £39 ($74.10) double without shower or toilet, £44 ($83.60) double with shower and toilet; £50 ($95) triple without shower or toilet. MC, V.

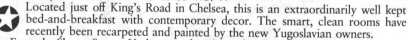

Located just off King's Road in Chelsea, this is an extraordinarily well kept bed-and-breakfast with contemporary decor. The smart, clean rooms have recently been recarpeted and painted by the new Yugoslavian owners.

From the Sloane Square Underground station, take a long walk or bus no. 11 or 22 down Kings Road.

QUEENSBURY COURT HOTEL, 7-11 Queensbury Place, London S.W.7. Tel. 071/589-3693. 35 rms (15 with shower and toilet). **Tube:** Gloucester Road.
$ Rates (including continental breakfast): £26 ($49.40) single without shower or toilet, £29 ($55.10) single with shower and toilet; £34 ($64.60) twin without shower or toilet, £37 ($70.30) twin with shower and toilet. No credit cards.

Home to visiting students from Florida State University, the Queensbury is also open to tourists year round. This small, pretty place offers clean, simple rooms and a great location. Not recommended if you like quiet, as the youngsters are prone to partying.

From the Gloucester Road Underground station, turn right just past More House.

SUPER-BUDGET CHOICES
A PRIVATE HOSTEL

Many hotels offer dormitory accommodations ("multishares") where single visitors share a room with other travelers. If you are traveling with a backpack and arrive at one of London's major railroad stations, you may be handed advertisements for these "unofficial" hostels. These are legitimate, but investigate location before you commit.

NEW KENT HOTEL, 55 Inverness Terrace, London W.2. Tel. 071/229-9982. 16 rms (25 multishare beds; none with bath). **Tube:** Bayswater.
$ Rates (including English breakfast): £32 ($60.80) twin; £45 ($85.50) triple; £9.50 ($18.05) per person per night, £62 ($117.80) per week, in a multishare. No credit cards.

This hotel overlooks a quiet Bayswater street not far from bustling Queensway. It is clean, fun, and friendly. There are rarely, if ever, more than four people sharing a room, but if you require more privacy, ask for one of the well-furnished twins.

From the Bayswater Underground, cross Queensway onto Iverness Place. Inverness Terrace is just one block away.

IYHF HOSTELS

The International Youth Hostel Federation (IYHF) has five establishments in central London, all of which are very crowded during the summer. You have to have a membership card to stay at one of the organization's hostels, available for about £8 ($15.20) at any of the hostels listed below. When staying at a hostel, you can save about £1 ($1.90) per night by supplying your own sheets.

CARTER LANE YOUTH HOSTEL, 36 Carter Lane, London E.C.4. Tel. 071/236-4965. 199 beds. **Tube:** St. Paul's.
$ Rates: £18 ($34.20) per person per night for travelers over 21. MC, V.

After more than 2 years of renovations, the Carter Lane reopened in February 1992 with new walls, beds, and appliances. The hostel boasts a good number of single rooms, and most of the multishare rooms have no more than four beds each. The hostel is situated smack-dab in the heart of The City of London on a small backstreet near St. Paul's Cathedral—a location good for sightseeing, but poor for eats and nightlife, as everything in The City closes when the bankers go home.

From the St. Paul's Underground station, turn right and make your way toward the front steps of the cathedral; follow Dean's Court, a small street, to the corner of Carter Lane.

EARL'S COURT YOUTH HOSTEL, 38 Bolton Gardens, London S.W.5. Tel. 071/373-7083. 100 beds. **Tube:** Earl's Court.
$ Rates: £15 ($28.50) per person per night for travelers over 21. MC, V.

Located near Holland House, in well-positioned, but slightly seedy Earl's Court, it's lively, and stores in the area tend to stay open late.

Exit the Earl's Court Underground and turn right. Bolton Gardens is the fifth street on your left.

HOLLAND HOUSE, Holland Park, London W.8. Tel. 071/937-0748. 190 beds. **Tube:** Holland Park.
$ Rates: £18 ($34.20) per person per night for travelers over 21. MC, V.

This hostel enjoys the most beautiful setting of all London's IYHF hostels. It's located right in the middle of Kensington's green Holland Park.

OXFORD STREET YOUTH HOSTEL, 14-18 Noel St., W.1. Tel. 071/734-1618. 87 beds. **Tube:** Oxford Circus.
$ Rates: £17 ($32.30) per person per night including sheets. MC, V.

London's newest "official" hostel is also the smallest and most centrally located. Not surprisingly, it costs more to locate here, but if you can get a reservation, it's well worth it.

Ys

Several YMCAs and YWCAs offer reliable accommodations at great prices, and most include dinner daily. Some encourage long-term stays with low weekly rates. In a pinch, phone the **National Council of YMCAs** (tel. 081/520-5599) for a list of members with available rooms.

BARBICAN YMCA, 2 Fann St., London E.C.2. Tel. 071/628-0697. 196 rms (none with bath). **Tube:** Barbican.

$ Rates (including English breakfast): £18 ($34.20) per person per day without dinner, £100 ($190) per week including dinner. Reserve at least 2 months ahead. No credit cards.

The good news is that this well-located hotel can accommodate almost 250 people. The bad news is that it often does. Make reservations as early as possible.

INDIAN YMCA, 41 Fitzroy Sq., London W.1. Tel. 071/387-0411. 100 rms (4 with bath). **Tube:** Warren Street.

$ Rates (including English breakfast and dinner): £27 ($51.30) single with or without bath. Discount for stays of 1 week or more. No credit cards.

Although preference is given to Indian citizens and long-term stays, the hotel does maintain a few beds for tourists of other nationalities. Singles only.

LONDON CITY YMCA, 8 Errol St., London E.C.1. Tel. 071/628-8832. 111 rms (none with bath). TV **Tube:** Barbican or Moorgate.

$ Rates (including English breakfast and dinner): £25 ($47.50) per person per night, £117 ($222.30) per week. No credit cards.

Located near the Barbican Y, this hotel offers a similar standard of accommodation, all in single rooms. Although this place is generally filled with students during the school term, you can probably find space here during the summer.

UNIVERSITY ACCOMMODATIONS

From early July to late September (and sometimes during Christmas and Easter), dozens of dormitories open their doors to tourists. Bedrooms are almost all uniformly sparse, and some residence halls offer only singles, but they are relatively inexpensive and centrally located. Try to reserve a space months in advance as the rooms are often packed solid. Even without reservations it can't hurt to call and see if they have a cancellation or a "no-show."

CARR SAUNDERS HALL, 18-24 Fitzroy St., London W.1. Tel. 071/580-6338. 223 rms (3 with bath; 78 self-contained apts.). **Tube:** Warren Street.

$ Rates (including English breakfast): £20 ($38) single with or without bath; £220 ($418) per week apartment for two; £330 ($627) per week apartment for three. No credit cards. **Open:** Early July to late Sept.

The best thing about this hall is its location, near inexpensive restaurants and the West End. There are only single rooms here, and all are small and basic. But there is a communal kitchen and laundry facilities. Couples may be interested in renting one of the hall's apartments with their own private bath and kitchen.

IMPERIAL COLLEGE, 15 Princes Gardens, London S.W.7. Tel. 071/589-5111, ext. 3600. 400 rms (none with bath). **Tube:** South Kensington.

$ Rates: £24 ($45.60) single, including breakfast; £75 ($142.50) per week in shared rooms, without breakfast. No credit cards. **Open:** Early July to late Sept.

This South Kensington dormitory offers luxurious accommodations beside Hyde Park and Royal Albert Hall. The minimum stay in a multishare is 1 week, but if you're going to be in town that long, you won't mind locating here. Singles are more expensive, though still reasonable by London's standards. When phoning, note that the reception is open from 10am to 1pm and again from 2 to 5pm.

PASSFIELD HALL, 1 Endsleigh Place, London W.C.1. Tel. 071/387-3584. 198 beds. **Tube:** Euston Square.

$ Rates (including English breakfast): £20 ($38) single; £40 ($76) double; £47

($89.30) triple. No credit cards. **Open:** Early July to late Sept; Easter and Christmas hols.
This hall is somewhat cheaper and much more basic than nearby John Adams Hall. Facilities are good, however, and include a games room, as well as cooking and laundry facilities.

ROSEBERY HALL, 90 Rosebery Ave., London E.C.1. Tel. 071/278-3251.
170 rms (none with bath). **Tube:** Angel.
$ Rates (including English breakfast): £22 ($41.80) per person, single or twin. No credit cards. **Open:** Early July to late Sept.
This may be the fanciest hotel of the lot, complete with well-furnished modern single rooms, a bar, and a nice breakfast room. Owned by the London School of Economics, the hall is well located near the Camden Passage antiques market.

CAMPING

The Queen's constables are touchy about people sleeping in London's Royal Parks, and for safety's sake, it's probably not a good idea anyway.

ABBEY WOODS CAMPING, Federation Rd., Abbey Wood, London S.E.2. Tel. 081/310-2233. Train: Abbey Wood.
$ Rates: £4.50 ($8.55) per site per night, plus £3 ($5.70) for each adult, £1.75 ($3.35) for youths 5–17. Cars cost £1 ($1.90) additional. MC, V.
Open year round, this large campground can accommodate both tents and RVs. On-site facilities include showers, toilets, a grocery store, laundry room, and children's playground. The grounds are located 7 minutes by foot from Abbey Wood Station. Walk down the hill and turn right to the campground.

LONG-TERM STAYS

When staying for a month or more, it makes financial sense to rent an apartment (a "flat") or a bed-sitting room (a "bed-sit," usually a room in a house, often with cooking facilities). Landlords usually require a security deposit, equal to 1 month's rent, returnable when you vacate the space in good condition. The magazines **Loot,** the **London Weekly Advertiser,** and **Daltons Weekly** are all issued on Thursday and contain good listings. The free, alternative weekly **Capital Gay** also has listings. Every Tuesday at 11am **Capital Radio** distributes a free list of available flat-shares in the lobby of their Euston Tower building at Euston Road, N.W.1 (Tube: Warren Street).

Another good place to look for apartments and flat-shares is on newsstand **bulletin boards** in the area where you're interested in living. The largest and most famous of these is at 214 Earl's Court Rd., next to the Earl's Court Underground station.

Finally, there are a number of accommodation agencies that will do the footwork for you. **Jenny Jones Agency,** 40 S. Molton St., London W.1 (tel. 071/493-4801), specializes in low-cost rentals of 3 months or more, and charges no fees to renters. The office is open Monday through Thursday from 9:30am to 2pm and on Friday from 9:30am to 5:30pm. Contact the London Tourist Board for a list of all of London's rental agencies.

WORTH THE EXTRA BUCKS

Hundreds of hotels fall just slightly beyond our budget, but the following have been selected for their particularly good value.

ASTER HOUSE HOTEL, 3 Sumner Place, London S.W.7. Tel. 071/581-5888. 12 rms (all with bath). TV TEL **Tube:** South Kensington.

$ Rates (including breakfast): £55–£80 ($104.50–$152) single; £67–£87 ($127.30–$165.30) double. AE, MC, V.

Aster House is the most beautiful of a number of small bed-and-breakfasts on this quiet South Kensington street. The pride with which owners Rachel and Peter Carapiet run this hotel is evident the moment you step into the plushly carpeted interior. All rooms have private facilities featuring amenities usually found in more expensive hotels. Take special note of the award-winning garden in the rear. The enormous breakfast buffet includes the usual eggs and sausages, as well as health-oriented fresh fruits, cold meats, cheeses, yogurt, and Muesli. The meal is served in L'Orangerie, the beautiful glass-covered pièce de la résistance of this special hotel.

From the South Kensington Station, walk three blocks down Old Brompton Road to Sumner Place on your left.

CAMELOT HOTEL, 45 Norfolk Sq., London W.2. Tel. 071/262-1980. 44 rms (30 with shower or shower and toilet). TV **Tube:** Paddington.

$ Rates (including English breakfast): £38 ($72.20) single without shower or toilet, £45 ($85.50) single with shower only, £55 ($104.50) single with shower and toilet; £74 ($140.60) double with shower and toilet; £85 ($161.50) triple with shower and toilet. MC, V.

Any way you look at it, this artfully decorated hotel is one of the best-value splurges in London. The ultramodern interior, painted in tasteful pastels, combines the looks and services of a top hotel with the charm and prices of something more modest. All rooms have color TV (with free in-house films), radio, and tea/coffee-making facilities. A cooked breakfast with unlimited helpings is also included. Norfolk Square is in Bayswater, one block south of Paddington Station off London Street.

HARLINGFORD HOTEL, 61-63 Cartwright Gardens, London W.C.1. Tel. 071/387-1551. 44 rms (40 with shower and toilet). TV TEL **Tube:** Russell Square.

$ Rates (including English breakfast): £37 ($70.30) single without shower or toilet, £47 ($89.30) single with shower and toilet; £50 ($95) double without shower and toilet; £61 ($115.90) double with shower or toilet; £71 ($134.90) triple with shower and toilet. MC, V.

The Harlingford is the nicest hotel on Bloomsbury's best-located Georgian crescent. You'll be particularly pleased by the bright ground-floor dining room where a hearty breakfast is served every morning. Rooms are equipped with coffee/tea-making facilities and televisions, but let the well-furnished, cozy communal lounge entice you away from the box. A coffee machine on the landing sits next to a free ice dispenser for chilling your bubbly. Cartwright Gardens is located three blocks north of the Russell Square Underground station.

MERRYFIELD HOUSE, 42 York St., London W.1. Tel. 071/935-8326. 7 rms (all with bath). TV **Tube:** Baker Street.

$ Rates (including English breakfast): £34 ($64.60) single; £46 ($87.40) double; £66 ($125.40) triple. Add £2 ($3.80) per night for stays under 4 nights. No credit cards.

This exceedingly friendly hotel is in the Marylebone section of London, just south of Regent's Park, three blocks from the Baker Street Underground station. Seven compact doubles all have private facilities, a color TV, a hairdryer, and a clock radio. Owner Anthony Tyler-Smith and his cat, Mimi, live on the premises, and if you are lucky enough to get a room in this hotel, you will enjoy their warm hospitality and a full cooked breakfast served each morning in your room.

5. BUDGET DINING

It's not that England lacks a national cuisine; it's just that the national cuisine is lacking! Deep-fried fish and chips is the national dish, and bangers (sausages), fried eggs, and doughy meat pies also enjoy wide popularity. It's all pretty caloric and none too healthy, but it is hearty and filling, and portions are usually large. Meals often begin with an appetizer (called a "starter"), and conclude with coffee and dessert. Vegetables (often just called "veg") are usually served with the main course, and whether they are carrots, peas, or both, they are invariably boiled lifeless.

London's ethnic restaurants are some of the city's best, and several interesting selections are listed below. Indian is probably the most popular foreign food, and it is usually modified to suit the Western palate.

LOCAL BUDGET BESTS

FISH & CHIPS

Fast-food restaurants have taken their toll in London, but "chippies," as the British call them, are still easy to find. Nowadays, fish and chips are usually offered by Middle Eastern places too, but the most authentic joints won't have a kebab in sight. Several kinds of fish are offered, but all taste similar and cod is the cheapest. Sitting down will up the price of the meal considerably, so do as the locals do and get it to "take away"—wrapped in a paper cone, doused with vinegar, and sprinkled with salt. The bill should never top £3 ($5.70).

Two of the most popular chippies include: **Johnnie's Fish Bar,** 494 Kings Rd., S.W.10 (tel. 071/352-3876), just past the World's End Pub in Chelsea, open Monday through Saturday from 11am to 11:30pm; and **North Sea Fish Bar,** 8 Leigh St., W.C.1 (tel. 071/387-5892), just southeast of Cartwright Gardens at Sandwich Street in Bloomsbury, open Monday through Saturday from noon to 2:30pm and again from 5:30 to 11:30pm.

PUB GRUB

Pub food can vary from snacks at the bar to a complete restaurant meal, but it's usually cheap, good, and filling. Most pubs offer food, and there are so many pubs that if you don't like what you see in one, you can move on to the next. Don't be afraid to look at the food before committing—it's usually displayed under glass. When it's not, ask the barkeep for a menu. Popular items include Scotch eggs (a hard-boiled egg surrounded by meat and enclosed in dough), bangers and mash (sausages and mashed potatoes), meat pies (especially during colder months), and ploughman's lunch (bread, cheese, salad, and chutney). Wash it all down with a beer.

The best pubs make their own dishes and keep the food hot on hotplates. Others only offer factory-made pasties (meat-filled pastry) and microwave them on demand. Note that food and drink are ordered separately—they are run as separate enterprises and you must pay for them separately. A good pub lunch will seldom top £4 ($7.60), and careful ordering can cut that amount almost in half.

FROMMER'S SMART TRAVELER: RESTAURANTS

VALUE-CONSCIOUS TRAVELERS SHOULD TAKE ADVANTAGE OF THE FOLLOWING:

1. Budget restaurants on side streets around Covent Garden and Soho—the festive atmosphere of these areas makes finding them fun.
2. Establishments with a number of taxis parked outside—you can be sure the food is good and prices are low.
3. Restaurants that don't have signs welcoming tourists; they usually care about making you a repeat customer.

Many popular pubs are listed in "Evening Entertainment," below. Other pubs known especially for their food include: **Black Friar,** 174 Queen Victoria St., E.C.4 (tel. 071/236-5650), near the Blackfriars Underground station in The City; **De Hems,** 11 Macclesfield St., W.1 (tel. 071/437-2494), in Soho's Chinatown; **The Sun,** 63 Lamb's Conduit St., W.C.1 (tel. 071/405-8278), between the Russell Square and Holborn Underground stations; and the **Lamb and Flag,** 33 Rose St., W.C.2 (tel. 071/497-9504), by Covent Garden Market.

AFTERNOON TEA

As much as the tea itself, it's tradition that makes afternoon tea special. And the pot is usually served with a spread of sandwiches and sweets that more than make a meal. High tea is a pleasant and civilized leisure-class activity. Accordingly, an authentic tea is expensive, and usually served in top hotels, where a jacket and tie is required. A cheap restaurant advertising high tea is just an imitation.

Brown's Hotel, at Albemarle Street and Dover Street, W.1 (tel. 071/493-6020), serves the best fixed-price tea in London. For £12.50 ($23.75), you can sit in one of three wood-paneled, stained-glass lounges and feel like a millionaire. Tailcoated waiters will make sure you don't leave hungry, as they fill your table with tomato, cucumber, and meat sandwiches, as well as scones and pastries. Choose from a variety of teas from East Asia. Served from 3 to 6pm daily. Tube: Green Park. AE, DC, MC, V.

The **Ritz Hotel,** Piccadilly, W.1 (tel. 071/493-8181), is probably the most famous afternoon tea in the world, and even at £14 ($26.60) per person you have to book at least a week in advance. There are two sittings, at 3 and 4:30pm daily. Tube: Green Park. AE, DC, MC, V.

In the rear of the Heal's building, ✪ **Heal's Restaurant,** 196 Tottenham Court Rd., W.1 (tel. 071/636-1666), has a snazzy tea that outshines most hotels both in quality and price. It costs £8 ($15.20) per person, but don't feel like you're settling for less. The green velvet and bentwood furniture is as rich as the smoked-salmon sandwiches and scones with fresh cream. Served Monday through Saturday from 3 to 5:30pm. Tube: Goodge Street. AE, DC, MC, V.

MEALS FOR LESS THAN £5.50 ($10.45)

IN & AROUND SOHO

POLLO, 20 Old Compton St., W.1. Tel. 071/734-5917.
  Cuisine: ITALIAN. **Tube:** Leicester Square.
$ **Prices:** £4.50–£6.50 ($8.55–$12.35). No credit cards.
  Open: Mon–Sat 11:30am–11:30pm.

✪ This is an extremely authentic and popular Italian restaurant, located right in the heart of the hustle. It's packed because the atmosphere is good, the food is great, and the prices are low. There must be 150 menu items, and few top £4.50 ($8.55). Even chicken cacciatore or principessa style (with asparagus) is under £4 ($7.60). And pastas of every shape and size are served with so many different kinds of sauces that even a native Italian couldn't keep up. Carbonara, fiorentina, romana, slavia, Alfredo—you name it, they serve it—and the helpful staff is happy to explain it all in plain English. The list of Italian desserts is impressive too. The restaurant is near Frith Street, a few doors down from the Prince Edward Theater.

THE STAR CAFE, 22b Great Chapel St., W.1. Tel. 071/437-8778.
  Cuisine: ENGLISH. **Tube:** Tottenham Court Road.
$ **Prices:** £3–£5 ($5.70–$9.50). No credit cards.
  Open: Mon–Fri 7am–5pm.

This greasy spoon is on a tiny side street just off Oxford Street near the Tottenham Court Road Underground station. It's a favorite of film-industry types who work in the immediate vicinity. Interesting daily specials such as Irish stew or beef casserole go for about £3.75 ($7.15) and its English stand-bys, such as sausage, beans, and chips, are even cheaper. A mannequin in chef's clothes will greet you at the door, and the tables draped in checkered plastic will tell you that there are no pretensions here.

THE THREE LANTERNS RESTAURANT, 5 Panton St., W.1. Tel. 071/839-5031.

Cuisine: ENGLISH. **Tube:** Piccadilly Circus.
$ Prices: £4–£7 ($7.60–$13.30). No credit cards.
Open: Mon–Sat 11:30am–11pm, Sun 11:30am–8pm.

This restaurant is well priced and well located, between Leicester Square and Piccadilly Circus. Wooden booths in an old-world interior are offset by a modern English menu with a continental influence. Most main courses, such as chicken-mushroom fricassee and moussaka cost just £3.65 ($6.95) each, including vegetables. Soup is £1.10 ($2.10), as are most of the desserts, bringing the grand total of a three-course meal to just £5.85 ($11.10). The owner, Mr. Anastasi, is usually on hand to offer an extra-warm welcome.

WONG KEI, 41-43 Wardour St., W.1. Tel. 071/437-8408.

Cuisine: CHINESE. **Tube:** Leicester Square or Piccadilly Circus.
$ Prices: £4.50–£8 ($8.55–$15.20). No credit cards.
Open: Daily noon–11:30pm.

There are many good and cheap Chinese restaurants in Soho, most serving Cantonese fare. Sitting at the end of Chinatown's Gerrard Street and Lisle Street, Wong Kei is one of the cheapest restaurants in the area, featuring an extensive menu. At least a dozen popular dishes, including chicken with garlic sauce, and beef with vegetables, cost under £4 ($7.60). As is the rule at most Chinese restaurants in London, if you want rice here, you have to order it separately, for 80p ($1.50). Tea is free and hearty eaters can take advantage of a fixed-price meal including three dishes plus rice for only £5 ($9.50) per person (two people minimum).

IN THE CITY

Almost everyone in the square mile of The City of London goes home by 6pm, and restaurant workers are no exception. Below are some good lunch selections.

FERRARI'S, 8 West Smithfield, E.C.1. Tel. 071/236-7545.

Cuisine: ENGLISH. **Tube:** St. Paul's.
$ Prices: £2.50–£4.50 ($4.75–$8.55). No credit cards.
Open: Mon–Fri 5:15am–4pm.

For a little nicer meal in the same area as Piccolo, turn left at the Museum of London and then right onto Little Britain Street until you reach the Smithfield Market, London's wholesale meat center (about six blocks in all, from the St. Paul's Underground station). The restaurant is just across the square. Small and plain, Ferrari's is famous for its very unusual sandwich menu, which includes Norwegian prawn and farmhouse pâté. The shop's cakes are irresistible, too.

MINORIES RESTAURANT, 105a The Minories, E.C.3. Tel. 071/480-6822.

Cuisine: ENGLISH. **Tube:** Tower Hill.
$ Prices: £3.50–£6.50 ($6.65–$12.35). No credit cards.
Open: Mon–Fri 8:30am–3pm.

Just about 150 yards north of the Tower of London, under a railway bridge, this restaurant may have the most unusual location in London—arched ceiling and all. It's also one of the few good-quality budget choices close to one of London's biggest tourist attractions. The small menu features roast beef with chips and peas, spaghetti bolognese, and other home-cooked British standards. The cheerful owner, Mr. Novani, will make you feel at home.

PICCOLO, 7 Gresham St., E.C.2. Tel. 071/606-1492.

Cuisine: ENGLISH. **Tube:** St. Paul's.
$ Prices: £2–£3 ($3.80–$5.70). No credit cards.
Open: Mon–Sat 6am–6pm, Sun 6am–2pm.

This sandwich bar, with fewer than a dozen stools all facing the street, is perfect for a quick bite when visiting St. Paul's Cathedral, and offers quite simply the widest range of sandwiches you're ever likely to come across. Bacon and turkey, roast chicken, and all the standards are priced well below £2.50 ($4.75). The shop is just off Martin's Le Grand Street, between St. Paul's Underground and the Museum of London.

COVENT GARDEN & THE STRAND

FOOD FOR THOUGHT, 31 Neal St., W.C.2. Tel. 071/836-0239.
Cuisine: VEGETARIAN. **Tube:** Covent Garden.
$ **Prices:** £3.50–£5.50 ($6.65–$10.45). No credit cards.
Open: Winter, Mon–Sat noon–8pm. Summer, Mon–Sat 8:30am–8pm.

This most unusual restaurant makes vegetarian food accessible to all palates and pocketbooks. Delicious dishes, such as leek quiche and lasagne, are usually priced around £2.75 ($5.25) and are served downstairs in a small, smoke-free environment. Really tasty soups and salads are also available, as well as a good selection of healthful desserts. Neal Street is across from the Covent Garden Underground station.

TOPPS BAR, 49 Bedford St., W.C.2.
Cuisine: ENGLISH. **Tube:** Covent Garden.
$ **Prices:** £2.50–£4 ($4.75–$7.60). No credit cards.
Open: Mon–Fri 8am–6pm.

Located on the south side of Covent Garden Market, just off The Strand, this is a good place for a cheap lunch in a very touristy area. The restaurant's roast lamb, fish and chips, steak pie with vegetables, and other matter-of-fact English staples won't be easily confused with the Ritz. The food is displayed cafeteria style, and dishes rarely top £3 ($5.70).

PADDINGTON & BAYSWATER

BLUE SKY RESTAURANT, 106 Westbourne Grove, W.2. Tel. 071/229-0777.
Cuisine: ENGLISH. **Tube:** Bayswater.
$ **Prices:** £2.50–£5 ($4.75–$9.50). No credit cards.
Open: Mon–Sat 7am–9:30pm.

The Blue Sky looks like an American diner. Sit at a booth and open the menu to find sandwiches for about £1.25 ($2.40), meat pies for £3.50 ($6.65) and ice cream for 90p ($1.70). The only things missing are the jukebox selectors mounted above each table. The restaurant is close to Chepstow Road.

KHAN'S, 13-15 Westbourne Grove, W.2. Tel. 071/727-5420.
Cuisine: INDIAN. **Tube:** Bayswater.
$ **Prices:** £4–£7 ($7.60–$13.30). AE, DC, MC, V.
Open: Lunch daily noon–3pm; dinner daily 6pm–midnight.

Khan's is famous in these parts for the best Indian food in Bayswater. An airy, cloudlike mural covers the huge walls, as if to create the feeling of a magic-carpet ride. The menu, which includes all the staples, assures that only "halal" meat is used, conforming to the Muslim dietary code. Curry dishes cost about £3 ($5.70), while a whole tandoori chicken, probably enough for two, is under £4.50 ($8.55). Turn left onto Westbourne Grove from Queensway.

SALWA, 4 Crawford Place, W.1. Tel. 071/262-3356.
Cuisine: INDIAN. **Tube:** Edgeware Road.
$ **Prices:** £3.50–£5.50 ($6.65–$10.45). No credit cards.
Open: Daily 11:30am–1am.

Where can you get the most authentic Indian food in London? Competition is tough, but Salwa may take the prize. Don't expect the Taj Mahal—this is a small take-out place that's almost literally a hole-in-the-wall. There are three small tables behind an open kitchen, and although few tourists have been here, the staff is more than happy to serve them. Don't be shy—you can see what's cooking and choose by sight. Try the chicken curry, £3.50 ($6.65), add a plate of pilau rice for £1.30 ($2.45) and a paratha (traditional Indian bread) for 75p ($1.45) and you'll walk out full and smiling.

The restaurant is just east of Edgware Road, about seven blocks north of Oxford Street.

IN BLOOMSBURY

ANWAR'S, 64 Grafton Way, W.1. Tel. 071/387-6664.
   Cuisine: INDIAN. **Tube:** Warren Street.
$ **Prices:** £3–£5 ($5.70–$9.50). No credit cards.
   Open: Daily 10am–10pm.
Anwar's not only maintains a very high standard of quality, but it also is one of the cheapest Indian restaurants in London. Few dishes top £4 ($7.60), and most cost just £3 ($5.70). There is a wide choice of homemade meat and vegetable curries and other Indian specialties, including tandoori chicken for about £3 ($5.70). Anwar's is cafeteria style; help yourself and bring your meal to a basic, Formica-covered table. Despite this "canteen" approach, the food is really top-notch.

AROUND VICTORIA

THE GREEN CAFE, 16 Eccleston St., S.W.1.
   Cuisine: ENGLISH. **Tube:** Victoria.
$ **Prices:** £3–£4 ($5.70–$7.60). No credit cards.
   Open: Mon–Fri 9am–6pm.
This is still one of the best value-for-your-money choices near Victoria Station. Located between Buckingham Palace Road and Ebury Street, this café with only seven tables really is green, both inside and out, and it offers hearty daily specials for about £3 ($5.70). The main course, which might feature roast lamb or steak-and-kidney pie, is usually preceded by soup. A la carte selections are also available, and you won't have to choose carefully to keep the tab under £3.50 ($6.65).

A CHAIN

THE STOCKPOT.
   Cuisine: ENGLISH.
$ **Prices:** £3–£5 ($5.70–$9.50). No credit cards.
   Open: Daily 9am–11pm (sometimes varies by location).

Members of the Stockpot chain are unified by contemporary styling, and a generous, budget-minded philosophy. Menus change daily, and regularly include two homemade soups for 80p ($1.50) each, a dozen main courses like lasagne, roast lamb, and fish and chips for £2–£2.50 ($3.80–$4.75), and an excellent selection of cakes for under £1.50 ($2.85). The food is good and the prices make all the 'Pots popular.

Central London locations include: 273 Kings Rd., S.W.3 (tel. 071/823-3175), in Chelsea, a few blocks past the fire station; 6 Basil St., S.W.3 (tel. 071/589-8627), in ultra-fashionable Knightsbridge between Harrods and Sloane Street; and 40 Panton St., S.W.1 (tel. 071/839-5142), just off Haymarket, one block south of Piccadilly Circus.

MEALS FOR LESS THAN £7 [$13.30]
IN & AROUND SOHO

GABY'S CONTINENTAL BAR, 30 Charing Cross Rd., W.C.2. Tel. 071/836-4233.
   Cuisine: CONTINENTAL. **Tube:** Leicester Square.
$ **Prices:** £3–£6 ($5.70–$11.40). No credit cards.
   Open: Mon–Sat 8am–midnight, Sun noon–10pm.
This restaurant, just off Leicester Square, is one of the best in London for quality and

value. A wonderful assortment of such home-cooked specialties as stuffed eggplant, rolled cabbage, and chicken satay are displayed in the window. Most main courses are less than £4.50 ($8.55), and most are served with salad or rice. Everything is made fresh daily according to the chef's mood and there is always a wide selection of delicious and well-priced meals. The restaurant is also known for its sandwiches, especially salt beef (England's approximation of corned beef), cheapest when you buy it to take out for about £3 ($5.70). Gaby's is fully licensed.

JIMMY'S, 23 Frith St., W.1. Tel. 071/437-9521.

Cuisine: GREEK/CYPRIOT. **Tube:** Leicester Square.
$ Prices: £4.50–£7.50 ($8.55–$14.25). No credit cards.
Open: Lunch Mon–Sat 12:30–3pm; dinner Mon–Sat 5:30–11pm.

Across from Ronnie Scott's jazz club (see "Evening Entertainment," below), Jimmy's is a popular basement bistro with good-quality Greek-Cypriot food for about £5 ($9.50).

NEW PICCADILLY RESTAURANT, 8 Denman St., W.1. Tel. 071/437-8530.

Cuisine: ENGLISH/CONTINENTAL. **Tube:** Piccadilly Circus.
$ Prices: £3.50–£6.50 ($6.65–$12.35). No credit cards.
Open: Daily 11am–9:30pm.

Both the decor and the menu here are straightforward. The long dining room is lined with tables on either side, and diners can choose from a large number of unadventurous but well-prepared English-style specialties like chicken with mushroom sauce, and steak risotto for about £4 ($7.60). For a pound less, try one of their many pizzas, or a pasta dish. Add £1 ($1.90) for soup, plus £1.25 ($2.40) for apple pie or ice cream, and you'll have eaten a satisfying three-course meal for about £6 ($11.40). The restaurant is located just off the bottom of Shaftesbury Avenue, a few feet from Piccadilly Circus, and has no liquor license; patrons are encouraged to bring their own.

IN SOHO'S CHINATOWN

CHUEN CHENG KU, 17 Wardour St., W.1. Tel. 071/437-1398.

Cuisine: CHINESE. **Tube:** Leicester Square.
$ Prices: £4.50–£7.50 ($8.55–$14.25). AE, DC, MC, V.
Open: Daily 11am–11:45pm; dumplings served until 5:45pm.

This huge restaurant serves 21 kinds of steamed, fried, or boiled dumplings, usually around lunchtime. Favorites include steamed-pork buns and shrimp dumplings, each £1.75 ($3.35). It takes a few servings to get a good feed, and a fulfilling experience can be had for about £7 ($13.30).

THE NEW CHAN MAY MAI, 25 Lisle St., W.1. Tel. 071/437-3602.

Cuisine: CHINESE/MALAYSIAN. **Tube:** Leicester Square.
$ Prices: £4–£8.50 ($7.60–$16.15). No credit cards.
Open: Daily noon–midnight.

This is one of the most creative restaurants in Chinatown, dishing out fish with ginger, chicken satay, and other aromatic and flavorful specialties with a Malaysian bite. Begin with their wonderful minced crabmeat-and-sweetcorn soup for about £1.75 ($3.35).

SOUTH KENSINGTON

DAQUISE, 20 Thurloe St., S.W.7. Tel. 071/589-6117.

Cuisine: POLISH. **Tube:** South Kensington.
$ Prices: £5.50–£7.50 ($10.45–$14.25). No credit cards.
Open: Daily 10am–11pm.

Near the major museums and just steps from the South Kensington Underground station, this real find features cabbage in many guises. Stuffed with meat, or served with veal escalope, it costs about £4 ($7.60). Their chlodiak soup (ham stock, beet root, cream, and pickled cucumber) may sound unusual, but it tastes great. A variety of Polish vodkas and beers is also served, and the friendly, if harried, staff encourages diners to nurse their drinks.

THE CHAINS

CRANKS.
Cuisine: VEGETARIAN.
$ Prices: £5.50–£8.50 ($10.45–$16.15). MC, V.
Open: Mon–Sat 10am–10:30pm.

★ When Cranks opened their first health-oriented vegetarian restaurant in the early 1960s, the British public laughed. Today, more than half a dozen eateries continue to "crank out" innovative, high-quality cuisine at prices that have silenced all snickerers. Cheesy lasagne, lentil-and-spinach quiche, satay vegetables, and other tasty dishes are well presented, and served in modern, airy, and somewhat fancy settings. A wide selection of herb teas, at about £1 ($1.90) per pot, is available, as well as a good choice of well-priced and organic wines.

Restaurants include the following downtown locations: Adelaide Street, W.C.2 (tel. 071/379-5919), where The Strand meets Trafalgar Square; The Market, Covent Garden, W.C.2 (tel. 071/379-6508); Tottenham Street, W.1 (tel. 071/631-3912), two blocks from the Goodge Street Underground station off Tottenham Court Road; Barret Street, W.1. (tel. 071/495-1340), across Oxford Street from the Bond Street Underground station; and Marshall Street, W.1 (tel. 071/437-9431), three blocks east of Regent Street in the heart of Soho.

ED'S EASY DINER.
Cuisine: AMERICAN.
$ Prices: £4–£7 ($7.60–$13.30). No credit cards.
Open: Mon–Thurs 11:30am–midnight, Fri–Sat 11:30am–1am, Sun 11:30am–11pm.

Ed's Easys are reconstructions of 1950s-style American diners, complete with bobby-soxed waitresses and jukebox selectors. This place flips one of the most authentic burgers in town, which, along with fries, a cola, or a milkshake, costs about £6.50 ($12.35).

Central London locations include: 12 Moor St., W.1 (tel. 071/439-1955), just off Cambridge Circus; and 362 King's Rd., S.W.3 (tel. 071/352-1956), past the fire station in Chelsea.

RASA SAYANG RESTAURANT.
Cuisine: MALASIAN/SINGAPOREAN.
$ Prices: £5.50–£8.50 ($10.45–$16.15). AE, DC, MC.
Open: Daily noon–10:45pm (varies by location).

These spic-and-span Southeast Asian eateries were some of the first in London. An unusual menu features dozens of meat and vegetarian dishes topped with traditional sauces. Coconut and fruit sauces are common, as are soups and satays. The restaurants are slightly lacking in atmosphere, but are well lit, contemporary in style, and often packed.

Central London locations include: 38 Queensway, W.2 (tel. 071/229-8417), diagonally across from the Bayswater Underground station; 10 Frith St., W.1 (tel. 071/734-8720), in the middle of Soho; and 3 Leicester Place, W.C.2 (tel. 071/427-4556), just southwest of Leicester Square.

PICNIC SUPPLIES

There are plenty of supermarkets around offering the run-of-the-mill staples. Cold-cuts and cheeses from the deli counter are usually cheaper than the prewrapped stuff that hangs in the cooler.

For some unusual picnic goodies, try the big and fascinating **Loon Fung Supermarket** at 42-44 Gerrard St., W.1 (tel. 071/437-7332), right in the heart of Soho's Chinatown. The most adventurous will try the black-jelly fungus or the steamed, congealed chicken's blood. The rest of us will enjoy dried cuttlefish, a traditional snack that goes great with beer. Loon Fung is open daily from 10am to 7pm.

The **Japanese Supermarket** in the Japan Center, 66-68 Brewer St., W.1 (tel. 071/439-8035), off Regent Street near the Piccadilly Circus Underground station, is worth a look for their precooked dishes and unusual Japanese sodas and snacks. It's open Monday through Friday from 10am to 7:30pm, on Saturday from 10am to 6:30pm, and on Sunday from 10am to 6pm.

See "Parks and Gardens," in "Attractions," below, for the top picnic spots.

WORTH THE EXTRA BUCKS

BAHN THAI, 21a Frith St., W.1. Tel. 071/437-8504.
Cuisine: THAI. **Tube:** Tottenham Court Road.
$ **Prices:** £6.50–£16 ($12.35–$30.40). AE, MC, V.
Open: Lunch Mon–Fri noon–2:45pm; dinner Mon–Sat 6–11:15pm, Sun 6:30–10:30pm.

Right in the middle of Soho is one of the best Southeast Asian restaurants in London. Two floors of wooden tables, plants, and decorative wall hangings give this exceptional place a totally authentic feel. But it's the food you've come for, and you won't be disappointed. Excellent, unusual soups, seafood, and rice dishes punctuate a huge and creative menu. Frith Street is near the Tottenham Court Road Underground station, just south of Soho Square.

THE ENGLISH HOUSE, 3 Milner St., S.W.3. Tel. 071/584-3002.
Cuisine: ENGLISH. **Tube:** South Kensington or Sloane Square.
$ **Prices:** £15–£30 ($28.50–$57); fixed-price lunch Mon–Sat £16 ($30.40); fixed-price dinner Sun £21 ($39.90). AE, DC, MC, V.
Open: Lunch daily 12:30–2:30pm; dinner Mon–Sat 7:30–11:30pm, Sun 7:30–10pm.

⭐ Set on a beautiful Chelsea backstreet, the English House looks like the ideal country home. As a fire roars in the cozy dining room, patrons are treated to beautifully prepared traditional English dishes, served by an expertly trained staff. Despite the fact that tables are too close together, dining here is romantic, service is impeccable, and the meal will convince you that English food can be wonderfully good.

PORTERS RESTAURANT, 17 Henrietta St., W.C.2. Tel. 071/836-6466.
Cuisine: ENGLISH. **Tube:** Covent Garden.
$ **Prices:** £8–£11 ($15.20–$20.90). MC, V.
Open: Lunch daily noon–3pm; dinner daily 5:30–11:30pm.

Just one block south of Covent Garden Market, Porters serves traditional English food with a flair. Their large, wood-and-fern restaurant offers over a half dozen meat pies, including steak and mushroom, selling for £8 ($15.20). Weekends are best, when roast beef and Yorkshire pudding with gravy and roast potatoes is £9 ($17.10). Weekends are busy, so expect a wait at the well-stocked bar.

6. ATTRACTIONS

SUGGESTED ITINERARIES

Americans are famous for whizzing around Europe's major sights trying to squeeze in as many of the "hits" as their brief vacations will allow. Europeans (who are both

DID YOU KNOW . . . ?

- London is the most populous city in western Europe.
- In the 1960s London launched two long-lasting fashions: long hair for men and miniskirts for women.
- London's Heathrow airport is the busiest in Europe.
- Harrods is the largest department store in western Europe.

geographically closer to one another and enjoy longer holidays) often poke fun at the hectic pace of the American vacation. But when you've come a long way and have only a few days, moving at a fast clip is in order. If soaking up local culture in a Chelsea café is more your cup of tea, modifications to the itinerary below will have to be made.

IF YOU HAVE ONE DAY Most hotels start serving breakfast at 7:30am. Be there! After breakfast, take the tube to Charing Cross or Embankment (they're within one block of each other) and cross into Trafalgar Square, London's most famous square and the city's unofficial hub. Here the commercial West End meets Whitehall, the main street of government, and The Mall, the regal road that leads to Buckingham Palace. In the center of the square is Nelson's Column. The National Gallery is on the top end of the square, while the northeast side is dominated by the Church of St. Martin-in-the-Fields.

Turn down Whitehall and go inside Banqueting House, in the middle of the block, to view the magnificent ceiling painted by Rubens. Across the street from Banqueting House, visit the home of the Queen's Life Guards, to see the Changing of the Guard Monday through Saturday at 11am and on Sunday at 10am and 4pm (not to be confused with the larger affair at Buckingham Palace). Farther down Whitehall, in the middle of the street, you'll see the Cenotaph, dedicated to the citizens of the U.K. who died during wartime, and just opposite it, behind tall iron gates, is 10 Downing Street, home to the prime minister. At the foot of Whitehall lies Parliament Square, site of Big Ben and the spectacular Houses of Parliament. The famous Westminster Abbey is just across Parliament Square. After a late lunch and a short rest, take the tube into The City and visit St. Paul's Cathedral.

IF YOU HAVE TWO DAYS Follow the itinerary described above, and have time to catch your breath. Take a break from your Whitehall stroll, cross beautiful St. James's Park, and arrive at Buckingham Palace at 11:30am for the Changing of the Guard. Or reverse your Whitehall walk and, starting in Parliament Square, end up at the National Gallery in Trafalgar Square. After visiting the gallery, continue north along Charing Cross Road, turn right on Long Acre, and visit trendy Covent Garden. In the afternoon of your second day, visit one of the museums listed in "Top Attractions," below.

IF YOU HAVE THREE DAYS Spend Days 1 and 2 as described above. On your third day, visit The City of London and its host of interesting financial, legal, religious, and historical sights. Attractions include the Stock Exchange, the Royal Exchange, the Old Bailey, St. Paul's Cathedral, and St. Bride's Church, on Fleet Street. Try to time your sightseeing so that you're at St. Bride's for a free lunchtime recital (on Tuesday, Wednesday, and Friday at 1:15pm, and on Sunday at 11am and 6pm).

In the afternoon of your third day, visit the Museum of the Moving Image on the South Bank, then stroll over to the adjacent South Bank Arts Centre for a late-afternoon drink.

IF YOU HAVE FIVE DAYS Spend Days 1 to 3 as described above. On Days 4 and 5, explore London's historic neighborhoods (most notably Chelsea and South Kensington), or partake in the city's active cultural scene. If you like museums, make a pilgrimage to South Kensington: In addition to the Victoria and Albert Museum, there are no fewer than six other museums in this area, including the Natural History Museum, the Science Museum, the Geological Museum, and the Museum of Instruments. Also worth a stop is Kensington Palace, in Kensington Gardens.

TOP ATTRACTIONS

BRITISH MUSEUM, Great Russell St., W.C.1. Tel. 071/636-1555.

This museum houses an unmatched collection of antiquities—most of which are the spoils of empire. Important finds from Egypt, Greece, Rome, and Cyprus share this warehouse of history with spectacular collections from Asia and the Middle East. The Rosetta Stone, at the entrance to the Egyptian Sculpture Gallery, is interesting as an artifact, and even more fascinating for the way it changed our understanding of hieroglyphics, which were unread for 1,400 years. The sculptures from the Parthenon, known as the Elgin Marbles, are the most famous of the museum's extensive collection of Greek antiquities. Named for Lord Elgin, who took these treasures from Athens, the marbles and other treasures are hotly contested by foreign governments that want their cultural relics back.

To the right of the entrance on the ground floor are the British Library Galleries. Rotating thematic displays come from the library's collection of over eight million books. Included in the permanent exhibit are two copies of the *Magna Carta* (1215), Shakespeare's First Folio (1623), and the Gutenberg Bible (ca. 1453), the first book printed using movable (hence, reusable) type. The adjacent British Library Reading Room was regularly used by Gandhi, Lenin, George Bernard Shaw, and others. Karl Marx wrote *Das Kapital* here. For tourists, admission to the reading room is with a guide only, every hour on the hour from 11am to 4pm.

Admission: Free, £1 ($1.90) donation requested.

Open: Mon–Sat 10am–5pm, Sun 2:30–6pm. **Tube:** Holborn or Russell Square.

BUCKINGHAM PALACE, The Mall.

Buckingham Palace's immense popularity is not due to its great age or its architecture—it is neither old nor spectacular. But as the home to one of the world's last remaining monarchs, the building has strong symbolic interest. It was Queen Victoria who turned the palace into the sovereign's official residence, and it was Victoria who removed the huge Marble Arch from the palace's forecourt and had it deposited in its present location, at the northeast corner of Hyde Park. When the queen is home, the Royal Standard is flown from the flagstaff on the building's roof. Tourists are not allowed inside the palace. The **Changing of the Guard** takes place daily April through August at 11:30am, and on alternate days September through March.

Tube: Victoria, St. James's Park, or Green Park.

HOUSES OF PARLIAMENT. Tel. 071/219-4272 for information.

✪ To most people, the Houses of Parliament, along with their trademark clocktower, are the ultimate symbol of London. Officially known as the Palace of Westminster, the spectacular 19th-century Gothic Revival building contains over 1,000 rooms and 2 miles of corridors. The clocktower at the eastern end houses the world's most famous timepiece. **"Big Ben"** refers not to the clocktower, as many people assume, but to the largest bell in the chime, a 13½-tonner named for the first commissioner of works. Listen to the familiar chime, which has inspired ostentatious doorbells around the world. At night a light shines in the tower whenever Parliament is sitting. Visitors may watch parliamentary debate from the Stranger's Galleries of Parliament's two houses.

Rebuilt in 1950 after a German air-raid attack in 1941, the **House of Commons** remains small. Only 346 of its 650 members can sit at any one time, while the rest crowd around the door and the Speaker's Chair. The ruling party and the opposition sit facing one another, two sword lengths apart.

Debates in the **House of Lords** are not as interesting or lively as those in the more important Commons, but the line to get in is usually shorter, and a visit here will give you an appreciation for the pageantry of Parliament.

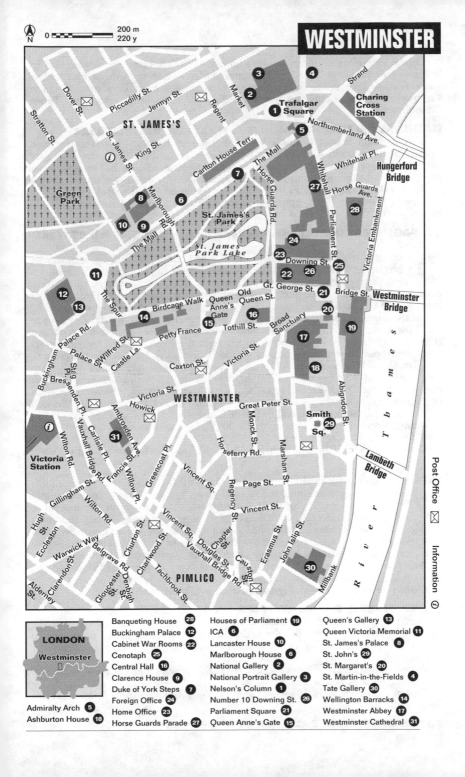

WESTMINSTER

N
0 [scale bar] 200 m
220 y

Trafalgar Square ①

Charing Cross Station

St. James's

Dover St.
Piccadilly St.
Jermyn St.
Regent
Market

Stratton St.
St. James's St.
King St.
Carlton House Terr.
Northumberland Ave.

③
②
④
⑤

Green Park

Marlborough Rd.
The Mall
Horse Guards Rd.

⑧
⑥
⑦

Whitehall Pl.
Hungerford Bridge

The Mall

St. James's Park

⑩
⑨
⑦

Whitehall
Horse Guards Ave.
㉗
㉘

St. James Park Lake

⑪

Parliament St.
Victoria Embankment

㉔
㉓ Downing St.
⑫
⑬

The Spur

Birdcage Walk
Queen Anne's Gate
Old Queen St.
Gt. George St.

㉒
㉖
㉕

Bridge St. **Westminster Bridge**

㉑
㉒

⑭
Petty France
Tothill St.
⑮
⑯
Broad Sanctuary

Caxton St.
Victoria St.
Castle La.
St.Wilfred St.

Palace St.
Buckingham Palace Rd.

⑳
⑰
⑲
⑱

Victoria St.
WESTMINSTER
Great Peter St.

Howick
Ambrosden Ave.
Carlisle Pl.
Francis St.
Willow Pl.
Greencoat Pl.

Monck St.
Marsham St.

Smith Sq. ㉙

Abingdon St.

Lambeth Bridge

Victoria Station
㉛

Wilton Rd.
Vauxhall Bridge Rd.

Horseferry Rd.

Vincent Sq.
Page St.
Regency St.

Gillingham St.
Wilton Rd.
Vincent Sq.
Vincent St.

Eccleston
Hugh St.
Warwick Way
Belgrave Rd.
Churton St.
Charlwood St.
Tachbrook St.
Denbigh St.
Gloucester St.
Chapter St.
Douglas St.
Cau ston
Erasmus St.
John Islip St.

Alderney St.
Clarendon St.
PIMLICO
Vauxhall Bridge Rd.
㉚

Millbank

River Thames

Post Office ✉

Information ⓘ

LONDON
Westminster

Admiralty Arch ⑤
Ashburton House ⑱

Banqueting House ㉘
Buckingham Palace ⑫
Cabinet War Rooms ㉒
Cenotaph ㉕
Central Hall ⑯
Clarence House ⑨
Duke of York Steps ⑦
Foreign Office ㉔
Home Office ㉓
Horse Guards Parade ㉗

Houses of Parliament ⑲
ICA ⑥
Lancaster House ⑩
Marlborough House ⑥
National Gallery ②
National Portrait Gallery ③
Nelson's Column ①
Number 10 Downing St. ㉖
Parliament Square ㉑
Queen Anne's Gate ⑮

Queen's Gallery ⑬
Queen Victoria Memorial ⑪
St. James's Palace ⑧
St. John's ㉙
St. Margaret's ⑳
St. Martin-in-the-Fields ④
Tate Gallery ㉚
Wellington Barracks ⑭
Westminster Abbey ⑰
Westminster Cathedral ㉛

Admission: Free.

Open: House of Commons, public admitted Mon–Thurs starting at 4pm, and Fri 9:30am–3pm; House of Lords, public admitted Mon–Thurs from about 3pm, and on some Fridays. Line up at St. Stephen's Entrance, just past the statue of Oliver Cromwell. Debates usually run into the night, and lines shrink after 6pm. **Tube:** Westminster.

NATIONAL GALLERY, Trafalgar Sq., W.C.2. Tel. 071/839-3321.

This museum houses Britain's best collection of historical paintings by such masters as Rembrandt, Raphael, Botticelli, Goya, and others. The new Sainsbury Wing, which opened in 1991, houses many of the museum's oldest and most precious objects. Special exhibits are also featured here. Phone for details on current shows.

Admission: Main galleries, free; Sainsbury wing, £2–£5 ($3.80–$9.50).

Open: Mon–Sat 10am–6pm, Sun 2–6pm. **Tube:** Charing Cross or Embankment.

ST. PAUL'S CATHEDRAL, St. Paul's Churchyard, E.C.4. Tel. 071/248-2705.

Dedicated to the patron saint of the City of London, St. Paul's is architect Sir Christopher Wren's masterpiece. Wren is buried in the cathedral's crypt, his tomb marked by the Latin inscription "Lector, si monumentum requiris, circumspice" (Reader, if you seek his monument, look around you). Over 515 feet long and 365 feet high (from curb to cross), the great Renaissance edifice is capped by one of the largest domes in Christendom. Hearty travelers can climb the 259 steps to the Whispering Gallery, located just below the dome. Acoustics here are such that even soft sounds can be heard on the other side of the dome, 107 feet away. Another steep climb presents you with a view of London that is unrivaled. Back on the ground, the American Memorial Chapel inside the ambulatory, which was built with contributions from people all over Britain, pays tribute to American soldiers who lost their lives during World War II. The cathedral has been the setting for many important ceremonies, including the funerals of Admiral Lord Nelson (1806) and Sir Winston Churchill (1965), and the wedding of Prince Charles and Lady Diana Spencer (1981).

Admission: Cathedral, free; crypt, £1.30 ($2.45); ambulatories, 70p ($1.35); half price for children under 13.

Open: Mon–Fri 10am–4:15pm, Sat 11am–4:15pm, Sun for services only. **Tube:** St. Paul's.

TATE GALLERY, Millbank, S.W.1. Tel. 071/821-1313.

This is both London's museum of modern art and the primary national gallery for British paintings. Local art connoisseurs complain about the museum's inability to attract major exhibitions, but even if they're not the most prestigious, shows here are usually of high quality. The Tate has an especially good collection of cubist works, as well as a wide selection of other contemporary styles. The Clore Gallery houses an extensive collection of Turner's oils and drawings.

Admission: Permanent collection, free; temporary exhibits, £3 ($5.70) adults, £1.50 ($2.85) students, seniors, and children.

Open: Mon–Sat 10am–5:50pm, Sun 2–5pm. **Tube:** Pimlico.

TOWER BRIDGE, E.1. Tel. 071/403-3761.

Here's a lyrical London landmark you can't miss. You can walk across the footbridges above and examine the hydraulic machinery below, but unless you're particularly fond of heights or Victorian engineering, keep your pounds in your pocket as the best views are from the outside.

Admission: £3 ($5.70) adults, £1.50 ($2.85) seniors and children 5–15 (last tickets sold 45 min. before closing).

Open: Apr–Oct, daily 10am–6:30pm; Nov–Mar, daily 10am–4:45pm. **Tube:** Tower Hill.

TOWER OF LONDON, E.C.3. Tel. 071/709-0765.

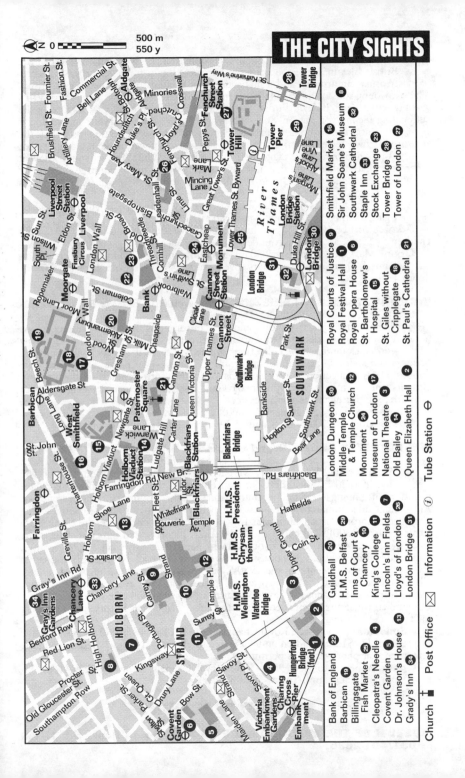

THE CITY SIGHTS

Bank of England	22
Barbican	19
Billingsgate Fish Market	25
Cleopatra's Needle	4
Covent Garden	5
Dr. Johnson's House	13
Grady's Inn	34
Guildhall	20
H.M.S. Belfast	29
Inns of Court & Chancery	10
King's College	11
Lincoln's Inn Fields	7
Lloyd's of London	26
London Bridge	31
London Dungeon	30
Middle Temple & Temple Church	12
Monument	17
Museum of London	3
National Theatre	14
Old Bailey	18
Queen Elizabeth Hall	2
Royal Courts of Justice	9
Royal Festival Hall	1
Royal Opera House	6
St. Bartholomew's Hospital	15
St. Giles without Cripplegate	18
St. Paul's Cathedral	21
Smithfield Market	16
Sir John Soane's Museum	32
Southwark Cathedral	32
Staple Inn	33
Stock Exchange	23
Tower Bridge	28
Tower of London	27

Church ┼   Post Office ⊠   Information ⓘ   Tube Station ⊖

⭐ Begun by William I (The Conqueror) soon after the Norman conquest of the British Isles in 1066, the complex has served as a fortress, a royal palace, a treasury, an armory, and a menagerie, but it is best remembered as a prison. The two young sons of Edward IV were murdered here in 1485, as was Henry VIII's second wife, Anne Boleyn. Today the closest the Tower comes to torture is the suffocating feeling you get on weekends when it seems like everyone in London is here. The Tower is now home to extensive arms and armory collections as well as the treasured Crown Jewels. Even if you're not fascinated by war, make it a point to see Henry VIII's anatomically exaggerated armor in the White Tower (you'll know it when you see it). Below ground, in fortified vaults, jewels like the exquisite Koh-i-noor diamond, which adorns the Queen Mother's Orb and Sceptre, will make your eyes bulge.

A visit to the tower is not cheap, but worth every pound. Upon entering, wait by the first gate for the excellent and free Beefeater-guided tour.

Admission: £6.60 ($12.55) adults, £4.90 ($9.30) students and seniors, £4 ($7.60) children 5–15; free for children under 5.

Open: Mar–Oct, Mon–Sat 9:30am–5:45pm, Sun 2–5:30pm; Nov–Feb, Mon–Sat 9:30am–4:30pm. Beefeater tours given every half hour from 10:45am. **Tube:** Tower Hill.

VICTORIA AND ALBERT MUSEUM, Cromwell Rd., S.W.7. Tel. 071/589-6371.

⭐ Named after Queen Victoria and her consort, this museum is an enormous treasure house devoted to the decorative arts—and is a favorite of many visitors. Comprehensive collections of fine and applied arts cover all countries, periods, and styles. Glass, ceramics, furniture, ivories—you name it, it's here. The famous Dress Collection covers fashions from the 16th century to the present. Upstairs, the Twentieth Century Primary Galleries feature temporary exhibitions of furniture, sculpture, and modern design.

Admission: Free (donation requested).

Open: Mon–Sat 10am–6pm, Sun 2:30–6pm. **Tube:** South Kensington.

WESTMINSTER ABBEY, Broad Sanctuary, S.W.1. Tel. 071/222-5152.

⭐ The Benedictine abbey, which housed a community of monks as early as A.D. 750, was called Westminster (West Monastery) after its location west of The City. In 1050 Edward the Confessor enhanced the site and moved his palace next door, beginning a tradition of church and state that continues to the present day. All of England's monarchs have been crowned in the abbey since William I's (The Conqueror) coronation on Christmas Day in 1066. When not in use, the Coronation Chair (built in 1300) sits behind the High Altar. Incorporated into the chair is the Stone of Scone, which has been associated with Scottish royalty since the 9th century. Captured by Edward I in 1297, the Stone has been stolen back by Scottish nationalists several times (most recently in the 1950s), but always recovered. The abbey's Henry VII Chapel is one of the most beautiful places you may ever see. Its exuberant architectural extravagances and exquisite intricate carvings will take your breath away. Comprehensive "Super Tours" condense the abbey's 900-year history into 1½ hours for £6.50 ($12.35) per person.

Admission: Abbey, free; Royal Chapels, £3 ($5.70) adults, £1.50 ($2.85) students and seniors, £1 ($1.90) children under 15 (free to Henry VII Chapel Wed 6–8pm, the only time that photography is permitted).

Open: Abbey, Mon–Sat 9am–5pm; Royal Chapels, Mon–Fri 9am–4pm, Sat 9am–2pm and 3:45–5pm. **Tube:** Westminster.

MORE ATTRACTIONS

MUSEUM OF THE MOVING IMAGE [MOMI], South Bank, S.E.1. Tel. 081/401-2636.

★ This lively, "hands-on" celebration of film and television is one of the city's newest museums and also one of the best. Chronologically arranged exhibits are staffed by costumed actors who never step out of character. The museum itself is as entertaining as a top movie. Displays strike the perfect balance between technology and the culture it produced. The emphasis here is on things British, but MOMI's extraordinarily popular slant is right out of Hollywood.

Admission: £3 ($5.70) adults, £1.50 ($2.85) students and seniors, £1 ($1.90) children under 15.

Open: Mon–Fri 9am–4pm, Sat 9am–2pm and 3:45–5pm. **Tube:** Waterloo is closer, but the short walk over Hungerford Bridge from the Embankment Underground station is more scenic.

MADAME TUSSAUD'S, Marylebone Rd., N.W.1. Tel. 071/935-6861.

Eerily lifelike figures have made this century-old waxworks world famous. The original moldings of members of the French Court, to whom Madame Tussaud had direct access, are fascinating. But the modern superstars and the Chamber of Horrors, to which this "museum" donates the lion's share of space, is the stuff tourist traps are made of. Madame Tussaud's is expensive, and somewhat overrated. If you have to go, go early to beat the crowds.

Admission: £6.50 ($12.35) adults, £4.50 ($8.55) children 5–15.

Open: Daily 9am–5:50pm. **Tube:** Baker Street.

MUSEUM OF MANKIND, 6 Burlington Gardens, W.1. Tel. 071/437-2224.

Home to the ethnographic department of the British Museum, the Museum of Mankind maintains exhibits relating to a variety of non-Western societies and cultures. One of the world's greatest collections of African art can be found here, while changing exhibitions present themes from Australia, the Pacific Islands, and South America. Don't miss the 9-foot-high Easter Island statue brought back by Captain Cook.

Admission: Free (donation requested).

Open: Mon–Sat 10am–5pm, Sun 2:30–6pm. **Tube:** Piccadilly Circus or Green Park.

SIR JOHN SOANE'S MUSEUM, 13 Lincoln's Inn Fields, W.C.2. Tel. 071/405-2107.

A fantastic array of antiquities, architectural drawings, and works by Hogarth, Turner, and Watteau are housed in the former home of the architect of the first Bank of England. The house is jam-packed with objects, seemingly displayed in a haphazard manner. But enter the small room where Hogarth's *The Rake's Progress* is displayed and ask the guard to show you the room's secret. You'll be convinced that there's a method to the madness.

Admission: Free.

Open: Tues–Sat 10am–5pm. **Tube:** Holborn.

WALLACE COLLECTION, Hartford House, Manchester Sq., W.1. Tel. 071/935-0687.

Also located in a large house, this museum features a fantastic collection of masterpieces by Rembrandt, Rubens, Murillo, and van Dyck. The house also contains a well-preserved selection of 18th-century furniture, ceramics, and armor.

Admission: Free (donation requested).

Open: Mon–Sat 10am–5pm, Sun 2–5pm. **Tube:** Bond Street.

COURTAULD INSTITUTE GALLERIES, Somerset House, The Strand, W.C.2. Tel. 071/873-2526.

Focusing on quality rather than quantity, this small collection of impressionist and post-impressionist paintings is widely considered to be Europe's best. The museum is particularly strong in works by Cézanne.

Admission: £3 ($5.70) adults, £1.50 ($2.85) students, seniors, and children 5–15.

Open: Mon–Sat 10am–6pm, Sun 2–6pm. **Tube:** Temple.

NATIONAL POSTAL MUSEUM, King Edward Building, King Edward St., E.C.1. Tel. 071/239-5420.
This museum has an excellent collection of postage stamps from Britain and the world. Over 150 years of philatelic history is covered, from the "Penny Black" to current issues.
Admission: Free.
Open: Mon–Thurs 9:30am–4:30pm, Fri 9:30am–4pm. **Tube:** St. Paul's.

SAATCHI COLLECTION, 98a Boundary Rd., N.W.8. Tel. 071/624-8299.
In the world of contemporary art, this collection is unrivaled. Charles and Doris Saatchi are Britain's largest private collectors and their personal museum houses rotating displays from their vast holdings. Enter through the unmarked metal gateway of a former paint warehouse.
Admission: Free.
Open: Fri–Sat noon–6pm. **Tube:** St. John's Wood.

INSTITUTE OF CONTEMPORARY ARTS [ICA], The Mall, S.W.1. Tel. 071/930-6393 for recorded information.
A major publicly assisted forum for the expression of artistic ideas, ICA maintains a theater, cinema, café, bar, bookshop, and two galleries for the avant garde. Regular scheduled talks usually relate to current exhibitions.
Admission: Galleries, £1.50 ($2.85).
Open: Daily noon–8pm. **Tube:** Piccadilly Circus or Charing Cross.

COMMERCIAL GALLERIES

Although commercial galleries are primarily interested in sales, works on display can be admired free of charge. The largest cluster of galleries in the West End is on and around **Cork Street,** parallel to Bond Street. You can see an interesting range of contemporary British work as well as established international artists.

PARKS & GARDENS

The English take gardening seriously—planting and pruning are not joking matters. Consequently, London sports a number of well-kept parks and gardens right in the heart of the city.

Hyde Park, the large rectangular expanse that is most often associated with London, is one of the city's most popular greens. As in other Royal Parks, wood and cloth chaise longues are scattered throughout. Fee collectors appear from nowhere extracting 60p ($1.15) from seated tourists, who are usually ignorant of this cost of relaxation. Benches and the grass are free. The park is especially lively on Sunday, when artists hang their wares along the Bayswater Road fence, and the northeast corner, near Marble Arch, becomes "Speaker's Corner," where anyone can stand on a soapbox and pontificate on any subject. Although this tradition is often touted as an example of Britain's tolerance of free speech, few people realize that this ritual began several hundred years ago when condemned prisoners were allowed some final words before they were hanged on Tyburn gallows, which stood on the same spot! Take the tube to Hyde Park Corner.

Lying to London's north is a huge misshapen circle called **Regent's Park.** This is London's playground, famous for its zoo, concerts, and open-air theater in the summer. A band plays free beside the lake twice daily from May through August. Get there by tube to Regent's Park, Baker Street, or Camden Town (to Camden Town for the zoo).

St. James's Park, opposite Buckingham Palace, is perhaps the most beautiful of London's greens. Swans, geese, and other species, including a family of pelicans, make their home here. A central location, a beautiful lake, and plentiful benches make this park perfect for picnicking. Take the tube to St. James's Park.

Adjacent **Green Park** is named for the absence of flowers (except for a short time in spring). But the ample shade from tall trees also makes this park a picnicker's paradise.

Founded in 1673, the **Chelsea Physic Garden,** 66 Royal Hospital Rd., S.W.3 (tel. 071/352-5646), is the oldest botanical garden in Europe. Behind its high walls is a rare collection of exotic plants, shrubs, and trees, many more than 100 years old. Originally founded by the Society of Apothecaries to grow plants for medicinal research, the garden has since expanded to include rare species from the New World. Admission is £2.50 ($4.75) for adults, £1.30 ($2.45) for students and children. Open April through October, on Wednesday and Sunday from 2 to 5pm. The resident English Gardening School holds lectures throughout the summer. Call for details. Take the tube to Sloane Square.

A year-long program of events sponsored by the **Royal Horticultural Society,** Vincent Square, S.W.1 (tel. 071/834-4333), is capped by the spectacular Chelsea Flower Show, held every May on the grounds of the breathtakingly beautiful Chelsea Royal Hospital. Tickets for this rose of garden shows are becoming increasingly hard to obtain, but are available abroad from an overseas booking agent. Check with the British Tourist Authority (see this book's appendix) to find out which agency will be handling ticket sales this year.

The **Royal Botanic Gardens,** better known as ✪ **Kew Gardens** (tel. 081/940-1171), is an important research facility with some of London's most beautiful indoor and outdoor gardens. The architectural splendor of the greenhouses and the 164-foot Chinese-style pagoda combine with chrysanthemums, rhododendrons, peonies, and the like to make a visit to Kew unforgettable. The gardens are open April to mid-September, Monday through Saturday from 9:30am to 6:30pm and on Sunday and holidays from 9:30am to 8pm; mid-September to October, daily from 9:30am to 6pm. Admission is £3 ($5.70) for adults, £1 ($1.90) for students and seniors. Take the tube to Kew Gardens.

KIDS' LONDON

Babies are unwelcome in many restaurants, are not allowed in pubs, and signs barring baby carriages (called "prams") regularly decorate shop windows. But older children are often encouraged with discounts, and activities appealing to youngsters abound. **Kidsline** (tel. 071/222-8070) offers advice on current activities and entertainment for youngsters. The listings magazines *Time Out* and *City Limits* should also be consulted for special events.

LONDON ZOO, in Regent's Park, N.W.1. Tel. 071/722-3333.
The London Zoo rattles and hums with over 7,000 species. This 150-year-old sanctuary features a giant panda and a worldwide reputation for breeding and conservation. The year-round children's zoo is augmented by a summertime "Meet the Animals" program, where camel and pony rides are offered.
Admission: £5.30 ($10.05) adults, £3.30 ($6.25) children aged 5–15.
Open: Apr–Oct, daily 9am–6pm; Nov–Mar, daily 10am–dusk (about 4pm).
Tube: Camden Town.

BRASS RUBBING CENTRE, in St. Martin-in-the-Fields Church, Trafalgar Sq., W.C.2. Tel. 071/437-6023.
Inside one of London's landmark churches, both adults and children can make rubbings of replicas of medieval church brasses. It's interesting, historical, and even artistic.
Admission: Free. Brass rubbings cost 70p ($1.35) and up.
Open: Mon–Sat 10am–6pm, Sun noon–6pm.

SPECIAL-INTEREST SIGHTSEEING
FOR EVERYONE

FREUD MUSEUM, 20 Maresfield Gardens, Hampstead, N.W.3. Tel. 071/435-2002.
This museum is located in the psychoanalyst's former home. Although Freud lived here less than a year, after fleeing from the Nazis in 1938, he was able to re-create his

Viennese consulting room where you can view his famous couch. Other associated memorabilia are also on display.

Admission: £2 ($3.80) adults, £1 ($1.90) students, free for children under 12.
Open: Wed–Sun noon–5pm. **Tube:** Finchley Road.

TWINING'S MUSEUM, 216 The Strand, W.C.2. Tel. 071/353-3511.

It's inside the family's famous tea shop. The world's largest teapot is here, as well as tea bricks once used as currency in China.

Admission: Free (no purchase necessary).
Open: Mon–Fri 9:30am–4:30pm. **Tube:** Aldwych or Temple.

HIGHGATE CEMETERY, Swain's Lane, Hampstead. Tel. 081/340-1834.

Swain's Lane divides London's Highgate Cemetery in two. The old, overgrown "Egyptian" west side filled up years ago and is now accessible only by guided tour. The most famous resident of the east side (where you can roam freely) is Karl Marx, whose grave is topped by a huge bust. The Chinese government helps pay for the upkeep of Marx's grave. Tours are usually scheduled daily, year round. Phone for times and reservations.

Admission: East side, free; west side, £4 ($7.60) donation for tour.
Open: Times vary; call for information. **Tube:** Archway.

FOR THE LITERARY ENTHUSIAST

London boasts an extremely long and rich literary tradition. Geoffrey Chaucer lived above Aldgate, in the easternmost part of The City until 1386, and playwright Joe Orton lived on Noel Road in Islington until his death in 1967. Oscar Wilde, Dylan Thomas, George Orwell, D. H. Lawrence, Shaw, Kipling, Blake—the list of authors who made London their home goes on and on. Unfortunately, a little blue plaque is usually all that's left to mark the past, but there are some exceptions.

DR. JOHNSON'S HOUSE, 17 Gough Sq., Fleet St., E.C.4. Tel. 071/353-3745.

The house where famous lexicographer Samuel Johnson lived and worked, compiling the world's first English dictionary, is now a shrine to him. His original dictionary is on display.

Admission: £2.20 ($4.20) adults, £1.60 ($3.05) students, seniors, and children.
Open: May–Sept, Mon–Sat 11am–5:30pm; Oct–Apr, Mon–Sat 11am–5pm.
Tube: Blackfriars.

KEATS'S HOUSE, Wentworth Place, Keats Grove, N.W.3. Tel. 071/435-2062.

In the home of Romantic poet John Keats, books and memorabilia are on display as well as some of the original furnishings.

Admission: Free.
Open: Apr–Oct, Mon–Fri 1–5pm, Sat 10am–1pm and 2–5pm, Sun 2–5pm; Nov–Mar, Sun–Fri 1–5pm, Sat 10am–1pm and 2–5pm. **Tube:** Hampstead.

THOMAS CARLYLE'S HOUSE, 24 Cheyne Row, S.W.3. Tel. 071/352-7087.

✪ This 18th-century town house is located on a beautiful backstreet in Chelsea. The Scottish writer lived here 47 years, until his death in 1881. His house remains virtually unaltered, to the extent that some of the rooms are without electric light.

Admission: £2.50 ($4.75) adults, £1.25 ($2.40) children under 17.
Open: Apr–Oct, Wed–Sun 11am–5pm. **Closed:** Nov–Mar. **Tube:** Sloane Square.

DICKENS'S HOUSE, Doughty St., W.C.1. Tel. 071/405-2127.

This house was home to one of London's most famous novelists for a short, but prolific, period. It was here that the writer worked on *The Pickwick Papers, Nicholas Nickleby,* and *Oliver Twist.* The author's letters, furniture, and first editions are all on display.

Admission: £2 ($3.80) adults, £1.50 ($2.85) students and seniors, 75p ($1.45) children.

Open: Mon–Sat 10am–5pm. **Tube:** Russell Square.

THE OLD CURIOSITY SHOP, 13-14 Portsmouth St., W.C.2. Tel. 071/405-9891.

⭐ It's debatable whether or not this is the one that Dickens wrote about, but it hardly matters. The amazing Tudor shop dates from 1567, and from the looks of it, you can't dispute its age. Make sure you climb the rickety stairs and see the shop's original fireplace.

Admission: Free (no purchase necessary).

Open: Apr–Oct, Mon–Fri 9am–5:30pm; Nov–Mar, daily 9am–5pm. **Tube:** Holborn.

FOR THE HISTORY BUFF

It's hard to find much "history" on the streets of London because most of the old buildings have either been demolished or stashed away in a museum. But history can be experienced firsthand by observing age-old ceremonies that are carried out as faithfully today as they were hundreds of years ago. In addition to the aforementioned Changing of the Guard, and debates in the Houses of Parliament, plan to attend the **Ceremony of the Keys** at the Tower of London. Every night for the past 700 years the gates of this ancient complex have been ceremoniously locked. You can watch the half-hour-long ritual if you request permission in writing at least 1 month in advance. Tickets are free. Write to the Resident Governor, Constable's Office, HM Tower of London, London EC 3N 4AB. Include an International Reply Coupon.

THE CABINET WAR ROOMS, Clive Steps, King Charles St., S.W.1. Tel. 071/930-6961.

In the British government's World War II underground headquarters, the Cabinet Room, Map Room, Churchill's Emergency Bedroom, and the Telephone Room (where calls to Roosevelt were made) have been restored to their 1940s appearance.

Admission: £3.60 ($6.85) adults, £2.70 ($5.15) students, £1.80 ($3.40) children 5–16.

Open: Daily 10am–6pm (last admission 5:15pm). **Tube:** St. James's Park or Westminster.

FOR THE ARCHITECTURE LOVER

Inigo Jones and Christopher Wren were two of London's most celebrated architects. Both men designed in the English Renaissance style using Italian and French models, themselves inspired by the architecture of classical Greece and Rome. Jones's Banqueting House (see "Suggested Itineraries," above), and St. Paul's Church, overlooking Covent Garden Market, are excellent examples of the era. Wren's most famous work is St. Paul's Cathedral, but his Royal Hospital in Chelsea, and Kensington Palace in Kensington, are equal testaments to his ingenuity.

Whole areas built in the 18th century celebrate the Georgian period's distinct style. Notice the huge windows fronting houses on Cartwright Gardens, Bedford Square, and other squares around Bloomsbury. The Horse Guards buildings on Whitehall date from this period as well.

Although a variety of styles from this era prevent one from making architectural generalizations, London's most striking buildings are pure Victoriana. My favorites are such unabashedly flamboyant ones as St. Pancras Station (tube to Euston), the Houses of Parliament, and the Royal Courts of Justice on The Strand (the last is open Monday through Friday from 10:30am to 4:30pm; take the tube to Aldwych or Temple).

WESTMINSTER CATHEDRAL, Ashley Place, S.W.1. Tel. 071/834-7452.

⭐ Westminster Cathedral, the headquarters of the Catholic church in Britain, was completed in 1903. Just a stone's throw from Victoria Station, this spectacular Byzantine-style building stands in stark contrast to the contemporary office buildings surrounding it. The interior marble columns and detailed mosaics are equally majestic. Take a look at the excellent rendering of the cathedral's interior on the wall just inside the front door. From May to September you can climb to the top of the cathedral's tall tower for an unobstructed view over Victoria and the rest of the city.

Admission: Cathedral, free; tower, £2 ($3.80).

Open: Cathedral, daily 7am–10pm; tower, May–Sept, daily 9am–5pm. **Tube:** Victoria.

THE LLOYDS OF LONDON BUILDING, Lime St., E.C.3. Tel. 071/623-7100.

⭐ There are so many ugly 20th-century buildings in London that Prince Charles is actively fighting against the city's further architectural decline. Located in the center of The City of London, the Lloyds of London building is a stunning exception. Designed by Richard Rogers (co-architect of Paris's Pompidou Center), Lloyds opened in 1986 to much critical attention. All the "guts" of the building (elevators, water pipes, electrical conduits) are on the exterior, and cranes are permanently affixed to the roof, ready to help with further expansion should it become necessary. At night, special lighting lends an extraterrestrial quality to the site. The building is usually not open to the public, but small groups can make reservations to visit the Underwriting Room of this famous insurance market.

Tube: Monument or Bank.

THE ARCHITECTURAL ASSOCIATION, 36 Bedford Sq., W.C.1. Tel. 071/636-0974.

This is London's best architectural college. Its two galleries show major contemporary works.

Admission: Free.

Open: Mon–Fri 10am–6pm, Sat 10am–3pm. **Tube:** Tottenham Court Road.

FOR THE VISITING AMERICAN

Grosvenor Square, W.1, has strong U.S. connections and is known to some as "Little America." John Adams lived on the square when he was the American ambassador to Britain, a statue of Franklin Roosevelt stands in the center of the square, General Eisenhower headquartered here during World War II, and the entire west side is occupied by the U.S. Embassy.

The former **home of Benjamin Franklin,** 36 Craven St., W.C.2 (steps from Trafalgar Square), is just one of many houses formerly occupied by famous Americans. For a complete list, pick up *Americans in London* (paperback; Queen Anne Press, 1988), by Brian Morton, an excellent anecdotal street guide to the London homes and haunts of famous Americans.

ORGANIZED TOURS

WALKING TOURS   London's most interesting streets are best explored on foot, and several high-quality and inexpensive walking-tour companies will help you find your way. The best are offered by ⭐ **Discovery Walks,** 67 Chancery Lane, W.C.2 (tel. 071/256-8973), featuring almost a dozen itineraries led by scholars who are truly interested in their subjects. Brochures listing itineraries can be picked up at London Tourist Board information offices or you can call for daily itineraries. No reservations are necessary—just show up at the appointed time and place. Tours cost £4 ($7.60) for adults, £3.50 ($6.65) for students and seniors, free for children under 14. Several money-saving multiwalk cards are available.

One of London's most popular walks follows the route from Trafalgar Square to Parliament Square, and is presented under "Suggested Itineraries," above.

BUS TOURS   If your time is more limited than your budget, a comprehensive bus tour may be your best bet. These tours guarantee that you will catch all the sights, even though you may not have the foggiest idea of where they are in relation to one another. At £9 ($17.10) per person, the **London Regional Transport** (tel. 071/918-3456) panoramic tours are cheapest. Tours depart frequently from Piccadilly Circus and Victoria Street (Victoria Station). From June 10 to September 22, tours run daily from 9am to as late as 7pm; the rest of the year, daily from 10am to 5pm. Tickets are £1 ($1.90) cheaper when bought in advance at Victoria Station's Travel Information Centre.

Do-it-yourselfers should purchase a **Travelcard** (see "Orientation and Getting Around," above) and climb aboard a famous red double-decker bus. Two of the more scenic bus routes include: no. 11, which passes King's Road, Victoria Station, Westminster Abbey, Whitehall, Horse Guards, Trafalgar Square, the National Gallery, the Strand, Law Courts, Fleet Street, and St. Paul's Cathedral; and no. 53, which passes Regent's Park Zoo, Oxford Circus, Regent Street, Piccadilly Circus, the National Gallery, Trafalgar Square, Horse Guards, Whitehall, and Westminster Square.

SPORTS & RECREATION

Questions pertaining to any London sport, either spectator or participatory, will be answered free of charge by **Sportsline** (tel. 071/222-8000), Monday through Friday from 10am to 6pm.

SOCCER & RUGBY   Soccer (called "football") and rugby seasons run from September to May and attract fiercely loyal crowds. The games are great to watch, but the stands can get rowdy. Think about splurging for seats. Centrally located first-division football clubs include: **Arsenal,** Arsenal Stadium, Avenell Road, N.5 (tel. 071/226-0304), tube to Arsenal; **Tottenham Hotspur,** 748 High Rd., N.17 (tel. 081/801-3323), tube to Seven Sisters; and **Chelsea,** Stamford Bridge, Fulham Road, S.W.6 (tel. 071/381-6221), tube to Fulham Broadway. Tickets cost £7–£17 ($13.30–$32.30), and games are usually played on Saturday.

Twickenham, Whitton Road, T.W.2 (tel. 081/892-8161), is the headquarters of the amateur Rugby Football Union where local and international games are played. Big games are expensive and sell out far in advance, but tickets for smaller matches start at about £6 ($11.40). Take the tube to Richmond, then the Southern Railway.

TENNIS   Center-court seats for the **Wimbledon Championships** are sold by lottery half a year in advance. Unfortunately, there is no system in place allowing foreigners to participate in the draw, but an overseas booking agent usually offers Wimbledon packages. Check with the British Tourist Authority (see this book's appendix) to find out which agency will be handling ticket sales this year. Also, a (very) few center-court seats are sold on the day of the match. To get these seats, camping out in line the night before might be in order; prices range from £16 to £30 ($30.40 to $57). Tickets for the outside courts, where you can see all the stars in earlier rounds of play, are usually available at the gate. Ground entrance for these outside courts costs about £9 ($17.10), £4.50 ($8.55) after 5pm. For further information, call the **All England Lawn Tennis and Croquet Club** (tel. 081/946-2244). To get there, take the tube to Wimbledon.

FITNESS GYMS   The **Chelsea Sports Centre,** Chelsea Manor Street, S.W.3 (tel. 071/352-6985), is the cheapest place to work-out in London, offering a pool and weight room at bargain prices. To use the weights, guests must first take a half-hour "induction," costing £5.50 ($10.45), after which the rate is only £2.20 ($4.20) per session. The pool costs £1.65 ($3.15). Other facilities include a squash court, aerobics classes, a sauna, and a solarium, all at equally low prices. The weight room is open Monday through Saturday from 8am to 10pm and on Sunday from 8am to 6:30pm. The pool is open on Monday, Wednesday, and Thursday from 7:30am to 7pm, on Tuesday from 7:30am to 7pm and 8 to 10pm, on Friday from 7:30am to 10pm, on Saturday from 8am to 10pm, and on Sunday from 8am to 6:30pm.

The gym is a 15-minute walk down King's Road from the Sloane Square tube station.

7. SAVVY SHOPPING

Even the most jaded capitalist may be awed by the sheer quantity of shops in London. The range and variety of goods is so staggering that a quick jump into a store can easily turn into an all-day shopping spree.

The British government encourages tourists to part with their pounds by offering to refund the 17.5% Value-Added Tax (VAT). Not all retailers participate in the refund program, and those that do require a minimum purchase, usually £50 ($95). The reclamation procedure is cumbersome: To reclaim VAT, show the sales clerk your passport and fill out a special form at each shop you visit. Then present the forms and the goods to a Customs officer upon departing Great Britain. After the official validates your VAT forms, mail them back to the stores where you made your purchases. Several months later you will receive your refund—in pounds sterling and minus a small commission charge. You can avoid the bank charges usually encountered when cashing foreign-currency checks by using your credit cards for the purchases and requesting that your VAT refund be credited to your account.

DEPARTMENT STORES

Department stores are the city's most famous shopping institutions, and a handful stand out as top tourist attractions as well.

HARRODS, 87-135 Brompton Rd., S.W.1. Tel. 071/730-1234.

By many estimates, Harrods is the largest department store in the world, selling everything from pins to pianos. The store claims that anything in the world can be bought here, and it may be true. Even if you're not in a shopping mood, the incredible ground-floor food halls are worth a visit. Admire the stained-glass ceiling and the unbelievable fresh-fish fountain in the seafood hall.

Open: Mon–Tues and Thurs–Sat 9am–6pm, Wed 9:30am–7pm. AE, DC, MC, V. **Tube:** Knightsbridge.

SELFRIDGES, 400 Oxford St., W.1. Tel. 071/629-1234.

Selfridges seems almost as big and more crowded than its chief rival, Harrods. Opened in 1909 by Harry Selfridge, a salesman from Chicago, this department store revolutionized retailing with its variety of goods and dynamic displays.

Open: Mon–Wed and Fri–Sat 9:30am–6pm, Thurs 9:30am–8pm. AE, DC, MC, V. **Tube:** Marble Arch or Bond Street.

LIBERTY, 210-220 Regent St., W.1. Tel. 071/734-1234.

Liberty has a worldwide reputation for selling fine textiles in unique surroundings. The pretty, old-world store has an incomparable Asian department.

Open: Mon–Wed and Fri–Sat 9:30am–6pm, Thurs 9:30am–7:30pm. AE, DC, MC, V. **Tube:** Oxford Circus.

LONDON SHOPPING AREAS

The West End This is the heart of London shopping, and mile-long **Oxford Street** is its main artery. Its sidewalks are terminally congested, and with good reason. A solid row of shops stretches as far as the eye can see. So if you only have one day to shop, spend it here. At its mid-section, Oxford Street is bisected by **Regent**

Street, a more elegant thoroughfare, lined with boutiques, fine china shops, and jewelers. At Piccadilly Circus, Regent Street meets **Piccadilly,** which, along with **St. James's Street, Jermyn Street,** and the **Burlington Arcade,** make up one of the swankiest shopping regions in the entire world.

Chelsea   The best shops in Chelsea are located along **King's Road,** a mile-long thoroughfare that straddles the fashion fence between trend and tradition. In the 1970s this was the center of punk fashion. Things have quieted down somewhat since then, but the chain-store boutiques are still mixed with a healthy dose of the avant garde.

Kensington   This is another trendy area for urban designs. The best young fashion flourishes on **Kensington High Street** in general, and in Hyper, Hyper (26-40 Kensington High St.; tel. 071/938-4343), and the Kensington Market (49-53 Kensington High St.; tel. 071/937-1572), in particular.

TRADITIONAL SALES

January sales are as British as Christmas pudding (which is usually reduced by 30% and just as edible the next year as the last). All the big department stores start their annual sales just after Christmas, and the smaller shops usually follow suit. For Londoners, the January sales are a rite, and tourists are no less immune to the fever and passion they induce. Several department stores (chiefly Harrods and Selfridges) compete for all-night lines by offering one or two particularly remarkable specials. Beware: Some goods, shipped in especially for the sales, are not as high quality as those offered the rest of the year.

MARKETS

Outdoor markets are where knowledgeable Londoners and bargain hunters shop for food, clothing, furniture, books, antiques, crafts, and of course, junk. Dozens of markets cater to different communities, and for shopping or just browsing they offer a unique and exciting day out. Few stalls officially open before sunrise. Still, flashlight-wielding professionals appear quite early, snapping up gems before they reach the display table. During wet weather stalls may close early.

PORTOBELLO MARKET, along Portobello Rd., W.11.

Portobello Market is the granddaddy of them all, famous for its overflow of antiques and bric-a-brac along a road that never seems to end. Like all antiques markets, bargaining is in order here. Saturday between 8am and 4pm is best, as the market consists mainly of fruit and vegetable stalls during the week.

Tube: Notting Hill Gate, and ask anyone for directions from there.

CAMDEN PASSAGE MARKET, off Upper St., N.1.

The Market at Camden Passage is smaller than Portobello, and usually cheaper too. Wednesday and Saturday are the best days to pick up bargain jewelry, trinkets, and antiques.

Open: Daily 8:30am–3pm. **Tube:** Angel.

CAMDEN MARKETS, along Camden High St., N.W.1.

Don't confuse Camden Passage (above) with the Camden Markets. This trendy collection of stalls, in parking lots and empty spaces all the way to Chalk Farm Road, specializes in original fashions by young designers, and junk from people of all ages. Cafés and pubs (some offering live music) line the route, making for an enjoyable day out. When you've had enough of shopping here, turn north and walk along the peaceful and pretty Regent's Canal.

Open: Sat–Sun 8am–6pm only. **Tube:** Camden Town.

BRIXTON MARKET, Electric Ave., S.W.9.

Brixton is the heart of African-Caribbean London, and the Brixton Market is its soul. Electric Avenue (immortalized by Jamaican singer Eddie Grant) is lined mostly with exotic fruit and vegetable stalls. But continue to the end and turn right, and you'll see a good selection of the cheapest secondhand clothes in London. Take a detour off the avenue through the enclosed **Granville Arcade** for African fabrics, traditional West African teeth-cleaning sticks, reggae records, and newspapers oriented to the African-British community.

Open: Mon–Tues and Thurs–Sat 8am–5:30pm, Wed 8am–1pm. **Tube:** Brixton.

8. EVENING ENTERTAINMENT

London is a cultural cornucopia. As the sun sets and a hush descends on the rest of the land, the capital's theaters, clubs, screens, and pubs swing into action. **Ticketmaster** (tel. 071/379-0404) makes credit-card bookings for theaters, opera, ballet, and pop music concerts. Their hotline is open 24 hours daily. Ticketmaster locations include the London Tourist Board Information Centre, Victoria Station forecourt (open Monday through Saturday from 9am to 7pm and on Sunday from 9am to 5pm), and Harrods department store, Knightsbridge (open Monday, Tuesday, and Thursday through Saturday from 9am to 6pm and on Wednesday from 9am to 8pm).

Attending a play in London is almost a requirement for any tourist worthy of the name. More theatrical entertainment is offered here than in any other city, at prices far below New York's. Again, the magazines *Time Out* and *City Limits* offer a comprehensive roundup of the week's events.

THE PERFORMING ARTS

THEATER

The term "West End," when applied to theater, refers to commercial theaters around Shaftesbury Avenue and Covent Garden. Currently, there are more than 40 such houses where comedies, musicals, and dramas are regularly staged. Tickets cost £10–£25 ($19–$47.50), and are usually most expensive for musicals as demand for them is highest. But discounts are available. The Society of West End Theatre operates a **discount ticket booth** in Leicester Square, where tickets for many shows are available at half price, plus a £1.25 ($2.40) service charge. Tickets are sold only on the day of performance and there is a limit of four tickets per person. No credit cards are accepted. The booth is open Monday through Saturday from noon on matinee days (which vary with individual theaters), and from 2:30 to 6:30pm for evening performances. All West End theaters are closed Sunday.

Blockbuster shows can be sold out months in advance, but if you just have to see the most popular show, one of the many high-commission **ticket agencies** can help you out. Always check with the box office first for any last-minute returns. Free West End theater guides listing all the current productions are distributed by tourist offices, hotels, and ticket agencies.

If you have an International Student ID Card (ISIC), you can purchase tickets to top shows at drastically reduced prices. Not all theaters participate in this program, so telephone first for availability. Those that do participate offer their student-priced seats on a standby basis half an hour before the performance.

Some of the best theater in London is performed on the "fringe." Dozens of **fringe theaters** devoted to "alternative" plays, revivals, contemporary dramas, and even musicals are often more exciting than established West End productions, and are consistently lower in price. Expect to pay around £4–£7 ($7.60–$13.30). Check one of the listings magazines for show times.

London's best-kept secret? **Cabaret**—usually a combination of song, dance, comedy, and sex. Basically, anything goes, and uniformly low prices make this one of London's best bets. *Note:* Many cabarets are closed during the Edinburgh Festival in August. Look under "Comedy" in the local listings magazines for current offerings.

OPERA & DANCE

Not until the 1946 première of Benjamin Britten's *Peter Grimes* did British opera gain a serious reception. But since then, opera schools have opened, seasons have come into being, and a host of great composers have lifted British opera onto the world stage. The best thing about dance in London (and true to a lesser extent for opera) is that it's really cheap. The major houses all offer inexpensive standby seats sold on the day of performance only, while prices at fringe theaters rarely top £6 ($11.40). Check the listings magazines for major programs and current fringe offerings.

LONDON COLISEUM, St. Martin's Lane, W.C.2. Tel. 071/836-3161 for the box office, 071/836-7666 for recorded information.
The 2,350-seat London Coliseum is home to the English National Opera (ENO), an innovative company that continues to thrill enthusiasts and rock traditionalists. Operas are always sung in English, and many productions have been transported to Germany, France, and the United States. The ENO season lasts from August to May; visiting companies, often dance, perform during the summer months.
  Prices: Tickets, £6.50–£43 ($12.35–$81.70) evenings, £5–£31 ($9.50–$58.90) matinees. AE, DC, MC, V.
  Open: Box office, Mon–Sat 10am–8pm. **Tube:** Leicester Square or Charing Cross.

ROYAL OPERA HOUSE, Bow St., Covent Garden, W.C.2. Tel. 071/240-1066.
Home to both the Royal Opera and the Royal Ballet companies, this posh theater is rich in history, having first hosted an opera in 1817. Cheap seats are usually available on the day of the performance, though they can be pretty far from the stage.
  Prices: Ballet, £13–£54 ($24.70–$102.60); opera, £23–£113 ($43.70–$214.70). AE, DC, MC, V.
  Open: Box office, Mon–Sat 10am–8pm. **Tube:** Covent Garden.

SADLER'S WELLS THEATRE, Rosebery Ave., E.C.1. Tel. 071/278-8916.
  This is one of the busiest stages in London, and also one of the best. Host to visiting opera and dance companies from around the world, the theater offers great sightlines and terrific prices. Seats are available from 10:30am at the advance box office across the road.
  Prices: Tickets, £6–£30 ($11.40–$57). AE, DC, MC, V.
  Open: Box office, Mon–Sat 10:30am–6:30pm (until 7:30pm on performance nights). **Tube:** Angel.

CONTEMPORARY DANCE THEATRE, at The Place, 17 Duke's Rd., W.C.1. Tel. 071/387-0031.
  This showplace usually offers good performances and cheap tickets. The space is small, and, as you can see from the mirrors and barres, is used by a dancing school during the day.
  Prices: Tickets, £8–£11 ($15.20–$20.90). MC, V.
  Open: Box office, Mon–Fri (and Sat performance days) noon–6pm. **Tube:** Euston.

CLASSICAL MUSIC

BRITISH MUSIC INFORMATION CENTRE, 10 Stratford Place, W.1. Tel. 071/499-8567.

Britain's clearinghouse and resource center for "serious" music, the center provides free telephone and walk-in information on current and upcoming events. Free recitals are usually offered weekly, usually on Tuesday and Thursday at 7:30pm; call for exact times.

Admission: Recitals, free.
Tube: Bond Street.

WIGMORE HALL, 36 Wigmore St., W.1. Tel. 071/935-2141.

Perhaps the best auditorium in London for both intimacy and acoustics, Wigmore Hall is scheduled to be reopened in 1992 after a massive refurbishment. Buy the cheapest seats, as it really doesn't matter where you sit.

Prices: Tickets, £4–£16 ($7.60–$30.40). AE, DC, MC, V.
Open: Box office, Mon–Sat 10am–8:30pm. **Tube:** Bond Street or Oxford Circus.

BARBICAN CENTRE, Silk St., E.C.2. Tel. 071/638-8891.

The sprawling, mazelike Barbican Centre has an excellent concert hall that the London Symphony Orchestra calls home. Even if you're not attending a performance, pop down before a show for a free student concert in the foyer.

Prices: Tickets, £8–£25 ($15.20–$47.50). AE, DC, MC, V.
Open: Box office, daily 9am–8pm. **Tube:** Barbican or Moorgate.

SOUTH BANK ARTS CENTRE, South Bank, S.E.1. Tel. 071/928-8800 for the box office, 071/633-0932 for recorded information.

The South Bank Arts Centre contains three well-designed, modern concert halls. Concerts are staged nightly and encompass an eclectic range of styles. The **Royal Festival Hall** is the usual site for major orchestral performances. The smaller **Queen Elizabeth Hall** is known for its chamber-music concerts, and the intimate **Purcell Room** usually hosts advanced students and young performers making their professional debut. In addition, there are free concerts daily in the lobby of the Royal Festival Hall.

Prices: Tickets, £5–£50 ($9.50–$95). AE, DC, MC, V.
Open: Box office, daily 10am–9pm. **Tube:** Waterloo or Embankment.

ROYAL ALBERT HALL, Kensington Gore, S.W.7. Tel. 071/589-3203.

The Royal Albert attracts top symphonies (when there's no rock concert or boxing match), despite its infamous echo.

Prices: Tickets, £7–£45 ($13.30–$85.50). MC, V.
Open: Box office, Daily 9am–9pm. **Tube:** Knightsbridge or Kensington High Street.

Lunchtime Concerts in Churches

In addition to evening performances in the major music halls, lunchtime concerts are regularly scheduled in various churches throughout the city. Church concerts, usually given by young performers, are all free, though it's customary to leave a small donation. A full list of churches offering lunchtime concerts is available from the London Tourist Board.

ST. BRIDE'S CHURCH, Fleet St., E.C.4. Tel. 071/353-1301.

Concerts feature professional musicians or top students on Tuesday and Friday, while Wednesday is devoted to organ recitals. You will want to get there early to explore the ancient crypt of this handsome Wren church.

Admission: Free.
Open: Concerts start at 1:15pm. **Tube:** Blackfriars.

ST. JAMES'S CHURCH, 197 Piccadilly, W.1. Tel. 071/734-4511.

This is one of the few churches outside The City to offer lunchtime recitals. Keep

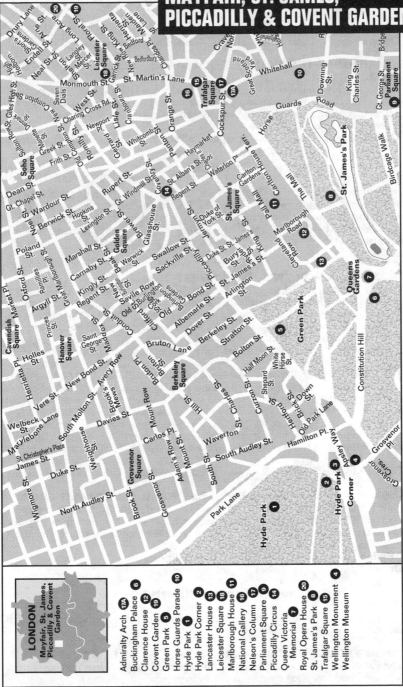

MAYFAIR, ST. JAMES, PICCADILLY & COVENT GARDEN

an eye out for the occasional inexpensive evening concerts here too, usually scheduled during the summer months.

Admission: Free.

Open: Recitals, Thurs–Fri at 1:10pm. **Tube:** Piccadilly Circus.

ST. MARTIN-IN-THE-FIELDS, Trafalgar Sq., W.C.2. Tel. 071/930-1862.

At the weekly chamber-music recitals, works by Debussy and Schubert are favorites. This church is also known for its above-average choir, and a visit to a full choral Sunday service should not be overlooked.

Admission: Free.

Open: Recitals, Mon–Tues at 1:05pm. **Tube:** Embankment or Charing Cross.

ROCK

Since the British rock explosion in the 1960s, London hasn't let up on the number of clubs featuring home-grown talent. The West End in general, and Soho in particular, has a number of intimate places featuring every kind of music known to bandkind. Archaic drinking laws require most late-opening clubs to charge admission, which unfortunately often gets pricey. As usual, check the listings magazines for up-to-the-minute details.

WAG, 35 Wardour St., W.1. Tel. 071/437-5534.

Popular with local rockers, the split-level Wag club is a good local hang-out, despite its attitude-heavy management. The downstairs stage usually attracts newly signed, cutting-edge rock bands, while dance disks spin up top. The door policy can be selective, but if it's your kind of music, you're probably dressed for the part.

Admission: £5–£10 ($9.50–$19). No credit cards.

Open: Mon–Sat 10:30pm–4:30am. **Tube:** Leicester Square or Piccadilly Circus.

ROCK GARDEN, 6-7 Covent Garden Plaza, W.C.2. Tel. 071/240-3961.

Less hip, but with lots of zip, is the fashion-unconscious Rock Garden. Because this small basement club overlooks touristy Covent Garden Market, most of the 250 or so revelers are usually foreigners. The quality of music varies, as the club's policy is to give new talent a stage. But Dire Straits, The Police, and many others played here before fame visited them, and triple and quadruple bills ensure a good variety.

Admission: £4.50–£9 ($8.55–$17.10); you can save £1 ($1.90) by arriving before 11pm on weekends. MC, V.

Open: Mon–Sat 7:30pm–3am, Sun 7:30pm–midnight. **Tube:** Covent Garden.

MARQUEE, 105-107 Charing Cross Rd., W.C.2. Tel. 071/437-6603.

Pink Floyd, David Bowie, Led Zeppelin, The Who, and practically every other rocker you've ever heard of started out playing at Marquee. After more than 30 years, and a change of address, this is still *the* place to hear the bands of the future. Bar prices are refreshingly closer to pub than club.

Admission: £4–£7 ($7.60–$13.30). No credit cards.

Open: Daily 7–11pm. **Tube:** Tottenham Court Road.

In Camden Town & Kentish Town

Many of London's best noise polluters are in Camden Town and adjacent Kentish Town, just east of Regent's Park.

CAMDEN PALACE, 1A Camden Rd., N.W.1. Tel. 071/387-0428.

The Palace features a variety of music from punk to funk. When the bands stop, records spin, and feet keep moving to the beat.

Admission: £5–£10 ($9.50–$19). AE, MC, V.

Open: Mon–Thurs and Sat 9pm–2:30am, Fri 8pm–2:30am. **Tube:** Mornington Crescent or Camden Town.

TOWN & COUNTRY CLUB, 9-17 Highgate Rd., N.W.5. Tel. 071/265-3334.

★ This huge ex-theater with a large dance floor, good seating, and a great, varied line-up of bands is one of London's best clubs. All-day festivals are not unheard-of here, and on weekends after 1am there's free bus service to Trafalgar Square.
Admission: £6–£11 ($11.40–$20.90). AE, DC, MC, V.
Open: Mon–Thurs 7–11:30pm, Fri–Sat 7pm–2am. **Tube:** Kentish Town.

THE BULL & GATE, 389 Kentish Town Rd., N.W.5. Tel. 071/485-5358.
Smaller, cheaper, and often better than its competitors, the Bull & Gate is the unofficial headquarters of London's pub rock scene. Independent and unknown rock bands are often served back-to-back by the half dozen.
Admission: £3–£5 ($5.70–$9.50). No credit cards.
Open: Music, Mon–Sat 8–11pm. **Tube:** Kentish Town.

JAZZ

You can get information on jazz concerts and events from the **Jazz Centre Society** (tel. 071/240-2430) and the listings magazines. Free jazz is offered every Sunday from noon to 2:30pm on Level 5 of the **Barbican Centre,** Silk Street, E.C.2 (tel. 071/638-4141); tube to Barbican or Moorgate.

RONNIE SCOTT'S, 47 Frith St., W.1. Tel. 071/439-0747.
Ronnie Scott's is the capital's best-known jazz room. Top names from around the world regularly grace their Soho stage, but fans be forewarned: This place is pricy. Call for events and show times.
Admission: Usually £10–£15 ($19–$28.50), plus a bar minimum. AE, DC, MC, V.
Open: Mon–Sat 8:30pm–3am, Sun 8–11pm. **Tube:** Leicester Square.

THE 100 CLUB, 100 Oxford St., W.1. Tel. 071/636-0933.
This austere, underground club usually hosts jazz nights on Monday, Wednesday, Friday, and Saturday. The stage is in the center of a smoky basement, looking just the way a jazz club is *supposed* to look.
Admission: £5–£8 ($9.50–$15.20); student discount available. No credit cards.
Open: Mon and Wed 8pm–midnight; Tues, Thurs, and Sun 7:30–11pm; Fri–Sat 8pm–1am. **Tube:** Tottenham Court Road.

BASS CLEF, 35 Coronet St., N.1. Tel. 071/729-2476.

★ Many jazz-loving Londoners swear by this intimate, accessible place. The small club features jazz, Latin, and African music, as well as alternative dance nights.
Admission: Free–£7 ($13.30); usually free Tues. AE, DC, MC, V.
Open: Tues–Sat 8pm–2am, Sun 8pm–midnight. **Tube:** Old Street.

BRAHMS & LISZT, 19 Russell St., W.C.2. Tel. 071/240-3661.
This wine bar presents live jazz nightly in the cellar. Local combos provide a good background to conversation. Bar prices are reasonable for a place within sight of Covent Garden Market.
Admission: Free until 9:30pm, £5 ($13.30) after 9:30pm. No credit cards.
Open: Mon–Sat until 1am, Sun until 10:30pm. **Tube:** Covent Garden.

PIZZA EXPRESS, 10 Dean St., W.1. Tel. 071/437-9595.
One of the city's most popular jazz rooms finds an unlikely location in the

basement of a chain restaurant. The house band shares the stage with visiting musicians. Dinner is compulsory, but inexpensive and tasty.

Admission: £6–£8 ($11.40–$15.20), plus food. AE, DC, MC, V.

Open: Mon–Sat 8:30pm–1am, Sun 8pm–midnight. **Tube:** Tottenham Court Road.

FILMS

FIRST RUN If you want to see a first-run film, go to one of the mega-screens, like the **Odeon** (tel. 071/930-6111) or **Empire** (tel. 071/734-7123), that ring Leicester Square. These grand old theaters show American blockbusters almost exclusively. Avoid the postage-stamp-size screens of the local multiplex. Most Leicester Square cinemas sell reserved seats at prices that range from £5 to £8 ($9.50 to $15.20), depending on the seat's location.

FOREIGN & INDEPENDENT In addition to the Hollywood houses, London is blessed with several top foreign and independent cinemas.

The Premiere, in the Swiss Center, Leicester Square (tel. 071/439-4470), is a comfortable alternative movie house. It's heavy on French films, but movies from other western and eastern European countries are also routinely shown. Tickets are £5.80 ($11). Tube: Leicester Square.

The **Gate Cinema,** at 87 Notting Hill Gate, W.11 (tel. 071/727-4043), alternates between offbeat English- and foreign-language films with double features on Sunday afternoon. Tickets are £5.50 ($10.45), £3.50 ($6.65) for the first performance Monday through Friday and Sunday. Tube: Notting Hill Gate.

REPERTORY CINEMAS Repertory cinemas of note include the **Scala,** 275-277 Pentonville Rd., N.1 (tel. 071/278-0051), tube to King's Cross; and the **Everyman,** Hollybush Vale, N.W.3 (tel. 071/435-1525), tube to Hampstead. Both are known for their triple bills and prices that rarely top £4.50 ($8.55).

PUBS & WINE BARS

PUBS

There's nothing more British than a pub. The public house is exactly that, the British public's place to meet, exchange stories, tell jokes, and drink. Many people have tried to build something that looks like a pub outside Britain, but all fail to capture the unique feel of the real McCoy. Americans tend to think of pubs as evening entertainment, but to the British these institutions are all-day affairs. There's no taboo about spending an afternoon in a pub, and on Sunday afternoon the whole family might go to the pub! (Note, however, that children under 14 are not allowed in pubs at all, and no one under 18 may legally drink alcohol.)

Beer is the main drink sold here; don't even try to order a martini in most places. Sold in Imperial half-pints and pints (20% larger than U.S. measures), the choice is usually between lager and bitter. Expect to pay between £1.20 ($2.30) and £1.75 ($3.35) for a pint. Many pubs serve particularly good "real" ales, distinguishable at the bar by hand-pumps that must be "pulled" by the barkeep. Real ales are natural "live" beers, allowed to ferment in the cask. Unlike lagers, English ales are served at room temperature and may take some getting used to. For an unusual and tasty alternative to barley pop, try cider, a flavorful fermented apple juice that's so good you'll hardly notice the alcohol—until later.

As a rule, there is no table service in pubs, and drinks (and food) are ordered at the bar. Tipping is unusual, and should be reserved for exemplary service.

Most pubs are open Monday through Saturday from 11am to 11pm and on Sunday from noon to 3pm and 7 to 10:30pm. A few close daily between 3 and 7pm.

Carpeted floors, etched glass, and carved-wood bars are the hallmarks of most pubs. But each one looks different, and each has its particular flavor and clientele. Greater London's 5,000-plus pubs ensure that you never have to walk more than a couple of blocks to find one, and part of the enjoyment of "pubbing" is discovering a special one on your own. But a few tried-and-true pubs are listed below to help you on your way.

THE LAMB & FLAG, 33 Rose St., W.C.2. Tel. 071/836-4108.

The Lamb & Flag is an old timber-framed pub in a short cul-de-sac off Garrick Street in Covent Garden. The pub was dubbed the "Bucket of Blood" by the poet Dryden after he was almost beaten to death here (no doubt for being too witty at someone else's expense). The pub can be hard to find, but its great atmosphere and above-average food make the search well worth the effort.

Tube: Leicester Square.

THE SHERLOCK HOLMES, 10 Northumberland St., off Trafalgar Sq., W.C.2. Tel. 071/930-2644.

In the upstairs dining room of this popular pub you'll find a re-creation of Holmes's living room at 221B Baker St., while the head of the hound of the Baskervilles and other relevant "relics" decorate the downstairs bar.

Tube: Charing Cross.

YE OLDE CHESHIRE CHEESE, Wine Office Court, 146 Fleet St., E.C.4. Tel. 071/353-6170.

This 1667 historic wooden pub is where Dr. Johnson took his tipple, and it's an attraction in its own right. Ducking through the low doors will transport you back in time, as the cracked black varnish, wooden benches, and narrow courtyard entrance give it authentic period charm. Meals here are delicious and filling, but expensive.

Tube: St. Paul's.

THE OLD KING LUD, 78 Ludgate Circus, E.C.4. Tel. 071/236-6610.

The "hook" of this pub is its location—built in 1855, on top of the dungeons of the old Fleet Prison. Although it no longer features it, the Old King Lud was the home of the original Welsh rarebit.

Tube: Blackfriars.

MAISON BERLEMONT, 49 Dean St., W.1. Tel. 071/437-2799.

Better known as the French House, this pub is an exceptional reminder of Soho's ethnic past. Still run by a member of the Berlemont family, the pub was the unofficial headquarters of the French Resistance in exile during World War II, and it continues to attract a fiercely loyal French-speaking clientele.

Tube: Tottenham Court Road.

THE SUN, 63 Lamb's Conduit St., W.C.1. Tel. 071/405-8278.

Popular not for its architecture or history, but for its truly remarkable selection of "real" ales and out-of-town brews, the Sun has more than 20 brands on tap, including rotating rare "guest" beers. Landlord Roger Berman will proudly show you his vaulted cellars during slow periods.

Tube: Holborn or Russell Square.

THE FERRET AND FIRKIN, 114 Lots Rd., S.W.10. Tel. 071/352-6645.

The Ferret and Firkin, in Chelsea, offers the best pub night out in London. The beer served here is brewed in the basement and really packs a punch. But the best thing about this pub is the nightly piano player whose amplified instrument turns the place into a raucous sing-along party. You don't have to be under 30 to crowd in here, but only the younger revelers will know all the words. Nine other Firkin pubs are just as fun and flavorful. Unfortunately, most are difficult to reach.

Tube: Sloane Square; then bus no. 11 or 22 down King's Road.

THE FROG & FIRKIN, 41 Tavistock Crescent, W.11. Tel. 071/727-9250.
Just outside Bayswater's northwestern corner, the Frog & Firkin is a carbon copy of the Ferret in Chelsea (see above).
Tube: Westbourne Park.

WINE BARS

Although not as ubiquitous as pubs, wine bars have become fairly common throughout London. Most have a good selection by both the glass and the bottle, and food is almost always served. Menus tend to have a continental flavor, with standards and prices that are higher than most pubs. You don't have to eat, however, and a bottle of the house wine, usually costing £5–£6 ($9.50–$11.40) shared between two or three people may come out cheaper than a visit to a pub. Most wine bars keep pub hours.

THE CORK AND BOTTLE WINE BAR, 44-46 Cranbourne St., W.C.2. Tel. 071/734-7807.
Located between Leicester Square and Charing Cross Road, this basement bar is in the heart of the theater district. The Cork and Bottle is known both for its gourmet food and its extensive wine list.
Tube: Leicester Square.

BRAHMS & LISZT, 19 Russell St., W.C.2. Tel. 071/240-3661.
The name is Cockney rhyming slang for "pissed," which in British English means "drunk." Head downstairs for food, upstairs for rowdier times. The bar features live music nightly (see "Jazz," above, for more information).
Tube: Covent Garden.

THE EBURY WINE BAR, 139 Ebury St., S.W.1. Tel. 071/730-5447.
The Ebury, a stone's throw from Victoria Station, is a typical no-nonsense wine bar. It's popular with younger office workers and executives from the nearby investment bank.
Tube: Victoria or Sloane Square.

DANCE CLUBS

The hippest Londoners go to "One-Nighters," weekly dance events held at established clubs. The very nature of this scene demands frequent fresh faces, outdating recommendations before ink can dry on a page. Weekly listings magazines contain the latest. Discount passes to dance clubs are sometimes available just inside the front door of Tower Records on Piccadilly Circus. Otherwise, expect to part with a mint to get in. Once inside, beware: £4 ($7.60) cocktails are not uncommon.

THE HIPPODROME, Charing Cross Rd., W.C.2. Tel. 071/437-4311.
Located near Leicester Square, the popular Hippodrome is London's big daddy of discos with a great sound system and lights to match. Very touristy, very fun, and packed on weekends.
Admission: £8–£13 ($15.20–$24.70). AE, DC, MC, V.
Open: Mon–Sat 9pm–3:30am. **Tube:** Leicester Square.

LIMELIGHT, 136 Shaftesbury Ave., W.C.2. Tel. 071/434-0572.
This is the London outpost of a small worldwide chain of churches-cum-dance clubs. The cavernous club features several dance floors, and attracts a good-looking crowd. The music is usually mainstream, but phone for special events before heading out.
Admission: £7–£13 ($13.30–$24.70). AE, DC, MC, V.

Open: Mon–Thurs 10:30pm–3am, Fri–Sat 10:30pm–4:30am, Sun 6pm–midnight.

FOR GAY MEN & LESBIANS

FIRST OUT COFFEE SHOP, 52 St. Giles High St., W.C.2. Tel. 071/240-8042.

Breakfast, lunch, and light snacks all day compliment the café au lait in this good-looking Parisian-style café. Good music, a comfortable atmosphere and a bulletin board advertising local happenings has made First Out a natural meeting house.

Open: Mon–Sat 10am–10pm, Sun 1–8pm. No credit cards. **Tube:** Tottenham Court Road.

BRIEF ENCOUNTER, St. Martin's Lane, W.C.2. Tel. 071/240-2221.

Centrally located around the corner from Covent Garden Market, this extremely popular pub attracts a young, business-oriented crowd and tourists, who regularly drink at the pub's outdoor tables.

Open: Mon–Sat 11am–11pm, Sun noon–3pm and 6–11pm. No credit cards. **Tube:** Leicester Square.

BANG, at Busbys, 157 Charing Cross Rd., W.C.2. Tel. 071/734-6963.

Loud music, a large dance floor, and a trendy, cruisy crowd makes Bang one of the best dance spots in the city. The club is open on Monday and Saturday only.

Admission: £5–£10 ($9.50–$19).
Open: Mon 10pm–3am, Sat 11pm–4am. **Tube:** Tottenham Court Road.

HEAVEN, Villiers St., W.C.2. Tel. 071/839-3852.

Hands down, this is the most famous gay club in the city. A stage, where live bands sometimes perform, overlooks a huge dance floor. The crowd varies, but the sound system is always great. The club entrance is on a small street between the Charing Cross and Embankment Underground stations.

Admission: £5–£10 ($9.50–$19).
Open: Tues–Wed and Fri–Sat 10pm–3am. **Tube:** Embankment or Charing Cross.

9. NETWORKS & RESOURCES

STUDENTS

The **University of London,** just north and east of Bloomsbury's Russell Square, is the largest school in the city. Like many urban schools, this university has a majority of commuter students, and doesn't really have a campus. Bloomsbury unfortunately lacks the verve and bustle of a college community, but the pubs and inexpensive restaurants of the neighborhood serve as frequent student hangouts.

The **University of London Student Union (ULU),** Malet Street, W.C.1 (tel. 071/580-9551), caters to over 55,000 students and may be the largest of its kind in the world. In addition to a gym and fitness center, the Malet Street building houses several shops, two restaurants, a health club, two banks, a ticket-booking agency, and an STA travel office. Concerts and dances are also regularly scheduled here. Stop by or phone for information on university activities. The student union building is open Monday through Saturday from 9:30am to 11pm, and on Sunday from 9:30am to noon and again from 12:30 to 10pm. Take the tube to Goodge Street.

GAY MEN & LESBIANS

Despite abundant anti-gay legislation, homophobic hostility is rare. There is a large gay community in London, supported by a plethora of publications, shops, pubs, nightclubs, cafés, and specialized services. **Capital Gay** is the city's première "alternative" paper. Written by and for both men and women, this free weekly features previews, reviews, news, and events listings for the gay and lesbian community. **The Pink Paper** is nationaly distributed, and is also free. Both publications are available at gay bars, bookstores, and cafés. At least two monthlies are regularly available at newsstands around town. **Gay Times** is oriented toward men and is known for both news and features, **HIM** supplements its high-quality reporting with glossy photos. The city's popular listings magazines *Time Out* and *City Limits* also provide excellent coverage.

Several locally produced guidebooks, written for local and visiting gays and lesbians, are available from several dealers, including the **London Tourist Board Bookshop,** in the Tourist Information Centre, Victoria Station Forecourt, S.W.1 (tel. 071/730-3488), open Easter through October, daily from 9am to 8pm; November to Easter, Monday through Saturday from 9am to 6:30pm and on Sunday from 9am to 5pm.

The **Lesbian and Gay Switchboard** (tel. 071/837-7324) offers information, advice, and counseling, as well as a free accommodations agency. The line is open 24 hours, and always busy. The **Lesbian Line** (tel. 071/251-6911) offers similar services to women only. It's open on Monday from 2 to 10pm and Tuesday through Saturday from 7 to 10pm.

THE LONDON LESBIAN & GAY CENTRE, 67-69 Cowcross St., E.C.1. Tel. 071/608-1471.

London's most popular center for gays and lesbians encompasses five floors, and includes a theater, disco, two bars, a café, a bookshop, and a women-only floor. This is a great place to get information on the local scene.
Admission: 80p ($1.50).
Open: Mon–Thurs noon–11pm, Fri–Sat noon–3am (admission until midnight), Sun noon–midnight. **Tube:** Farringdon.

GAY'S THE WORD BOOKSHOP, 66 Marchmont St., W.C.1. Tel. 071/278-7654.

In addition to the largest selection of gay and lesbian biographies, novels, and "how-to" books around, this store also holds regular readings, and stocks calendars, kitsch clothing, jewelry, and associated paraphernalia.
Open: Mon–Fri 11am–7pm, Sat 10am–6pm, Sun 2–7pm. AE, DC, MC, V. **Tube:** Russell Square.

THE ZIPPER STORE, 283 Camden High St., N.W.1. Tel. 071/267-7665.

Leisure wear, leather wear, and a large assortment of "novelties" can be purchased here, at London's only licensed gay sex store.
Open: Mon–Thurs and Sat 10:30am–6:30pm, Fri 10:30am–7pm. AE, MC, V. **Tube:** Camden Town.

WOMEN

London is safer than many other cities, but women are advised to take special precautions. Avoid walking alone at night, especially on small, deserted streets. Always carry some emergency money, and don't hesitate to spend it on a taxi if you feel uneasy. The **London Rape Crisis Centre** (tel. 071/837-1600) offers immediate help, advice, and counseling to victims.

Spare Rib, a widely distributed monthly magazine, features news and commentary on feminist issues. It is available from larger newsstands around the city. **Silver Moon Women's Bookshop,** 68 Charing Cross Rd., W.C.2 (tel. 071/836-7906), is Soho's only dedicated feminist bookseller. Located in the heart of London's book district, Silver Moon boasts a huge selection of fiction and nonfiction titles by and for women, as well as nonsexist children's books. It's open Monday through Saturday from 10:30am to 6:30pm. AE, DC, MC, V. Tube: Leicester Square.

Women-only dance events occur almost every night in London, at nightspots all around the city. These clubs are designed for both straights and lesbians who are not looking to attract the attentions of men. Call **London Friend** (tel. 071/837-7324) or check the listings magazines for the most up-to-date happenings.

10. EASY EXCURSIONS

Even if you only have a short time in London, try to arrange a trip outside the city. Just a few miles from Trafalgar Square you'll be confronted with an England that's strikingly different from the city. The air is cleaner, the people are friendlier, everything is cheaper, and any of the destinations listed below will make you wish you never had to leave.

The **British Travel Centre,** 12 Lower Regent St., W.1 (tel. 071/730-3488), just south of Piccadilly Circus, is worth a visit before heading out. They offer free leaflets and advice, and can also book trains, buses, and tours for you. For train journeys under 50 miles, the cheapest ticket is a "Cheap Day Return." Try to avoid day trips on Friday, when fares increase to catch the mass exodus of city-dwellers.

HAMPTON COURT PALACE   Hampton Court Palace was built in the 16th century by Cardinal Thomas Wolsey, and reluctantly given to King Henry VIII. Five of the king's six wives lived here, and today this mammoth Tudor structure on 50 landscaped acres offers visitors one of the most satisfying day trips outside London. Entrance to the palace, courtyard, and cloister costs £4.60 ($8.75) for adults, £2.90 ($5.50) for children under 16. An additional token charge allows you to get lost in the famous garden maze. The palace is open Monday through Saturday from 9:30am to 5pm and on Sunday from 2 to 7pm.

Hampton Court is only about 15 miles from central London and can be reached by train in 30 minutes from Waterloo Station.

GREENWICH   Greenwich is only a few miles from Piccadilly Circus, but it feels like it's eons away. This famous Thames-side town is the place where Greenwich mean time is fixed, and you can take a picture of yourself straddling the meridian by the Royal Observatory.

The **Royal Naval College** (tel. 081/858-2154) brilliantly illustrates Sir Christopher Wren's architectural talent. Admission is free, and it's open to the public from 2:30 to 5pm Friday through Wednesday.

The *Cutty Sark* (tel. 081/853-3589), now permanently in dry-dock, is open as a museum. This most famous of clipper ships made regular tea runs to China covering almost 400 miles of ocean per day. It's open April to September, Monday through Saturday from 10am to 6pm and on Sunday from noon to 6pm; October to March, the museum closes 1 hour earlier. Admission is £3 ($5.70) for adults, and £2 ($3.80) for children under 15.

There are two interesting ways to get to Greenwich: either by **Waterbus** (a 45-minute journey) from Westminster Pier; or by **Docklands Light Railway** (a 15-minute journey) from the Tower Hill Underground station. Both services operate every few minutes.

KEW GARDENS   Kew Gardens is the site of the massive **Royal Botanic Gardens** and is easily reached by tube. See "Parks and Gardens" in "Attractions," above, for details.

BATH   An excursion to Bath is one of the most popular day trips from London. Founded by the Romans in A.D. 43, the glorious ancient ruins are still fed by the only hot-water spring in Britain. The surrounding town, built in the 18th century, is also worth a visit. The **Roman Baths,** as well as the **Pump Room and Museum,** are open daily in summer from 9am to 6pm; in winter, the sites close 1 hour earlier (opens at 11am on Sunday).

Bath is about 115 miles from London, reached in 80 minutes by high-speed train from Paddington Station, or in 3 hours by bus from Victoria.

WINDSOR CASTLE   Windsor Castle claims to be the largest inhabited castle in the world, and it's on a site that has been a home to monarchs for more than 900 years. Situated on a bend in the Thames about 20 miles from London, the castle sits on 4,800 acres of lawn, woodlands, and lakes. You may see Prince Charles playing polo here. And when the royal family is away, you can explore the State Apartments with their fabulous antiques and paintings. Admission is £2.90 ($5.50); open Monday through Saturday from 10:30am to 5pm and on Sunday from 1:30 to 5pm (the State Apartments close at 3pm in winter).

The exclusive **Eton College** is across a cast-iron footbridge, and is usually combined with a visit to the palace. The prep school's students are famous for attending classes in high collars and tails.

Trains from Paddington Station make the journey to Windsor in 50 minutes.

MADRID

Geographically, governmentally, and spiritually, Madrid is Spain's center of gravity. With most of its citizens "imported" from other parts of Spain, it is a melting pot of the nation's highly diverse strengths, sensibilities, customs, and cultures.

By all accounts Madrid, not New York, is the "city that never sleeps." Any night of the week you're likely to encounter a traffic jam at 3am. Understandable in a country that has a special term for the hours from midnight to dawn—*madrugada* they call it—and it's the Madrileños' time to howl.

Not that they aren't every bit as vital during daylight hours, however. In the post-Franco era Madrid made a breathless sprint from the doldrums of dictatorship to the dynamic promise of the 21st century. The years of economic isolation and social stagnation all but forgotten, Madrid, Europe's highest capital (in altitude) is now also one of its most progressive. Stretched along the expansive Paseo de la Castellana are the corporate headquarters of the nation's vigorous national and international enterprises. Nowadays when you say *mañana* in the Spanish capital it signals progress, not procrastination.

Many first-time visitors to Madrid are surprised by its energy and sophistication. But the beauty of it is that once you scratch the high-tech surface, the core of tradition runs deep and strong. *Tascas, tapas, zarzuela,* and *churros* continue to be enduring passions among a municipal populace that manages to enjoy the best of both the New and Old Worlds.

1. FROM A BUDGET TRAVELER'S POINT OF VIEW

MADRID BUDGET BESTS

Eating in Madrid need not be expensive. At lunchtime, bars and cafeterias post a changing *menu del día,* which offers a choice of two or three vegetables, a main course, and dessert, plus bread and a glass of wine for between 900 and 2,000 pesetas ($9.35 and $20.85). Make this your main meal and then in the evening embark on an exciting round of *tasca* (bar) hopping to sample the tasty and filling assorted hors d'oeuvres called *tapas.*

WHAT THINGS COST IN MADRID	**U.S. $**
Taxi from the airport to the Hotel Villa Magna	20.05
Public transportation within the city	1.40
Local telephone call	.16
Double room at the Palace Hotel (deluxe)	300.00
Double room at the Hotel Arosa (moderate)	225.00
Double room at the Hostal Riesco (budget)	44.10
Lunch for one, without wine, at D'a Queimada (moderate)	14.45
Lunch for one, without wine, at Mesón Pontejos (budget)	11.10
Dinner for one, without wine, at Jockey (deluxe)	110.00
Dinner for one, without wine, at Bali (moderate)	30.00
Dinner for one, without wine, at Casa Rodríguez (budget)	14.00
Glass of wine (or pint of beer)	1.75
Coca-Cola	2.00
Cup of coffee	1.15–1.45
Roll of ASA 100 color film, 36 exposures	6.00
Admission to the Prado Museum	4.70
Movie ticket	2.85–6.30
Cheapest theater ticket	9.35

For the shopper, the best time to visit Madrid is during the *rebajas,* or sales, which take place in January and February and July; all the stores participate, offering amazing discounts that increase as the month goes on.

SPECIAL DISCOUNT OPPORTUNITIES

FOR STUDENTS Students traveling to Madrid should be sure to have an **International Student Identity Card (ISIC)** with them to benefit from discounts offered on travel, lodging, and admission prices. Students who arrive without an ISIC can obtain one at **TIVE** (student tourist offices), at calle José Ortega y Gasset, 71, 28006 Madrid (tel. 347-77-00), or at Fernando El Católico, 88 (tel. 543-02-08), open Monday through Friday from 9am to 2pm. TIVE also provides information on student discount opportunities.

FOR SENIORS Senior citizens can obtain **half-price tickets** on all train travel from the city.

FOR EVERYONE Watch for theaters offering half-price tickets on certain days, as well as some museums that are free one day a week. If you plan to do a lot of traveling on Madrid's public transit system, purchase a *bono* for bus or metro. (See "Getting Around," in "Orientation and Getting Around," below, for details.)
As TAP Air Portugal (tel. toll free 800/221-7370) has increased service to Spain, look for special promotional fares to Madrid via Lisbon. Also ask about Iberia's (tel. toll free 800/772-4642) "Madrid Amigo" offer.

FOR EC CITIZENS Some private museums offer discounted admission charges to EC citizens.

WHAT'S SPECIAL ABOUT MADRID

Attractions
- [ ] The Prado, one of the world's greatest art collections.
- [ ] Royal Palace, exemplifying the grandeur of 18th-century Madrid.
- [ ] The Teleférico, affording a panoramic view of the city in one direction, the Guadarrama Mountains in the other.
- [ ] A bus ride up Paseo de la Castellana to see the contrast of old palaces and 20th-century architecture, and to admire the numerous fountains.
- [ ] Plaza Mayor, where you can soak in the history of Madrid just by sitting and watching.
- [ ] The lobby lounge of the Palace Hotel with its magnificent stained-glass skylight.

Parks
- [ ] Retiro Park on Sunday at noon to join Madrileños in the "paseo."

Restaurants
- [ ] Tapas bars—try Bocaito for the best in town, with the friendliest waiters.

Shopping
- [ ] The Rastro Flea market on Sunday to jostle with the crowds in search of that amazing bargain.

Nightlife
- [ ] La Zarzuela, which is a uniquely Spanish combination of music, dance, and opera.
- [ ] One of the many terrazas on Paseo de la Castellana during a summer evening.

Excursions
- [ ] Toledo, encompassing all of Spanish history, encircled by the River Tagus, and with a magnificent Gothic cathedral.

WORTH THE EXTRA BUCKS

To really get a feel for the spirit of Spain, spend the money you have saved from a diet of tapas on a flamenco show or zarzuela. Alternatively, splurge on dinner at Botín's in its traditional Madrid setting.

---

2. PRETRIP PREPARATIONS

DOCUMENTS   American, British, Canadian, Australian and New Zealand citizens require only a valid passport for stays up to three months.

WHAT TO PACK   From mid-June to mid-September you'll need light cotton clothing, and rarely rain gear or a sweater for the evening. In the spring and fall layers are the answer, for it can become very warm in the sun but cool in the evening. During the winter months warm clothes and a raincoat are necessary, and if you venture north 25 miles to the mountains you'll need a jacket, gloves, and a scarf.

The Spanish, particularly in Madrid, are very clothes conscious, so bring one smart outfit for the theater or that special "splurge" dinner.

For sightseeing, bring shoes that are comfortable on cobblestones.

WHEN TO GO   The saying goes that Madrileños suffer nine months of winter and three months of hell, but it's never humid. If you like it hot, July and August will suit you best, but for more agreeable temperatures, visit during May and June or September and October. From November to April the weather is changeable, but it can be quite glorious with bright blue sky and warm sun. Snow and frost are rare in the city.

Madrid's Average Temperature & Rainfall

	Jan	Feb	Mar	Apr	May	June	July	Aug	Sept	Oct	Nov	Dec
Temp. (°F)	43	45	49	54	61	68	75	74	68	58	48	43
Rainfall "	2	2	1.6	2	1.5	1.2	0.4	0.3	1.3	2	2.4	2

Special Events   Madrid's own **Festival of San Isidro** is celebrated during the middle week of May with special concerts, neighborhood fairs, craft shows, and the most important bullfights of the year.

Both the summer and fall have their seasonal city festivals, **Los Veranos de la Villa** and **Festival de Otoño,** with a myriad of concerts and shows to suit all tastes. For jazz lovers the **International Jazz Festival** in November attracts some of the world's best players.

Religious festivals are celebrated with parades and pageantry, particularly the Procession of the Three Kings on January 5, Carnaval before Lent, and the solemn procession of the penitents during Holy Week.

BACKGROUND READING   The tourist office (address below) publishes many brochures and leaflets in English on Madrid and environs. For an excellent overview of Spain today, read John Hooper's *The Spaniards* (Penguin). Jan Morris's *Spain* (Prentice Hall) and James A. Michener's *Iberia* (Fawcett) are both well worth reading for general background on Spain.

3. ORIENTATION & GETTING AROUND

ARRIVING IN MADRID

FROM THE AIRPORT   Madrid's airport at **Barajas** (tel. 408-52-00 for information) is about nine miles east of the city center. The airport bus runs from 4:45am to 1:50am (with departures every 15 minutes beginning at 6am) between the airport and Plaza de Colón in the center of the city. The fare is 275 ptas. ($2.85). A taxi costs about 1,925 ptas. ($20.05), depending on the traffic, and the journey takes roughly 30 minutes, although it could take up to an hour during rush hour.

FROM THE TRAIN STATION   If you have come down from France and points northeast you will arrive at **Chamartín** station. The south of Spain is served by Charmartín and **Atocha-RENFE** stations and the west by **Príncipe Pío** (also called Norte) Station. All these stations are on the metro (see below) for easy access to anywhere in the city. For information from RENFE (Spanish Railways), call 530-02-02 daily from 7am to 11pm; for reservations, call 527-33-33.

INFORMATION

On arrival, go to the **Tourist Information Center** at either Barajas Airport (tel. 305-86-56) or Chamartín Station (tel. 315-99-76). Both are open Monday through Friday from 8am to 8pm and on Saturday from 8am to 1pm. Two further offices are located in the city at Duque de Medinaceli, 2 (tel. 429-49-51), and in the Torre de Madrid, Princesa, 1, Plaza de España (tel. 541-23-25), open Monday through Friday from 9am to 7pm and on Saturday from 9am to 1pm.

The **Municipal Information Bureau** is located at Plaza Mayor, 3 (tel. 266-54-77). Open Monday through Friday from 10am to 8pm and on Saturday from 10am to 2pm, the bureau provides information, brochures, and maps in English.

In the vicinity of the Plaza de España, Puerta del Sol, Plaza Mayor, and the Prado Museum from July to September, you will encounter friendly young people dressed in a distinctive blue-and-yellow uniform whose express purpose is to help you. They each speak at least two other languages and can offer advice on museums, hotels, restaurants, and special interests.

Even without much Spanish you should be able to find your way around the weekly *Guía del Ocio,* available at newsstands for 100 ptas. ($1.05). It includes information on entertainment, concerts, art exhibitions, sporting events, fairs, processions, and so on. Nondubbed movies are designated "V.O." Thursday's edition of the daily newspaper *El País* has a "Guía" to the week's events, as does Friday's edition of the daily *Diario 16.*

CITY LAYOUT

Madrid is divided into two distinct parts, old and new. In the old part of the city, whose center, historically and geographically, is the **Puerta del Sol,** the streets curve and twist; in the newer area to the north and east, the streets are laid out on a grid system.

You'll find most of my accommodation options around the Puerta del Sol. The streets that will quickly become familiar are: to the north, calle de Alcalá, Gran Vía (with many theaters, cinemas, and stores), and Plaza de España; to the south, calle Mayor (off which is Plaza Mayor), calle de Atocha, and calle de Toledo.

Paseo de la Castellana is the main thoroughfare bisecting the city. South of Plaza de Colón it turns into Paseo de Recoletos, and after crossing Alcalá it becomes Paseo del Prado, where you will find the Prado Museum and, a few blocks farther east, El Retiro Park.

Moncloa, the university area, lies northwest of the city, and **Salamanca,** with its smart shops, is east of Castellana between calle de Goya and calle de Maria de Molina (the airport road).

GETTING AROUND

The tourist office provides a map of Madrid that includes a map of the public transit system. Bus and subway networks are efficient and extensive. Buses travel in their own lanes on often-congested streets. For general information on public transport, call the Consorcio de Transportes (tel. 580-19-80). Taxis are plentiful and inexpensive compared to other capital cities.

BY SUBWAY By consulting a map of the system, you can easily identify the number of the line on which you wish to travel and the name of the station at the end of the line. All the metro stations have a large map at the entrance. A single ticket costs 135 ptas. ($1.40), and a *bono* of 10 tickets is a more economical 530 ptas. ($5.50). The subway runs from 6am to 1:30am.

BY BUS Buses often are more direct than the subway. You'll see both red and yellow buses, the former more numerous, and the latter, called the microbus, more comfortable. Route information is available from the E.M.T. kiosks in Plaza de Callao, Puerta del Sol, Plaza de Cibeles, and Atocha. Here you can buy a *bonobus* of 10 tickets for 530 ptas. ($5.50). A single ticket is 135 ptas. ($1.40). Buses run from 6am to midnight.

ON FOOT Traffic being as bad as it is in Madrid, it's often faster to walk.

BY TAXI Taxis in Madrid abound. If they are available, they display a green light on the roof and/or a green sign on the windshield saying LIBRE. The meter starts at 155 ptas. ($1.60) and increases 70 ptas. (75¢) per kilometer. There is an airport supplement of 325 ptas. ($3.40); from the railway stations and 165 ptas. ($1.70), and after 11pm, and all day Sunday and holidays, taxis charge 165 ptas. ($1.70) extra.

BY CAR Renting a car in Spain is expensive. It's far cheaper to book a fly/drive package before you go. The cheapest options at this writing are **Budget,** Gran Vía, 49, first floor (tel. 247-20-48), open Monday through Friday from 9:30am to 1:30pm and 4 to 7:30pm, and on Sunday from 10am to 1pm, where the basic daily rate starts at 5,700 ptas. ($59.40); and **Rent Me,** Plaza de Herradores, 6 (tel. 559-08-22), open

Monday through Saturday from 9am to 2pm and 4 to 8pm, and on Sunday from 9am to 2pm. But offerings change, so shop around for the best deal.

 MADRID

Babysitters   Babysitters are known as *canguros* in Spanish. As many hostals are family-run, the daughter or son of the house may oblige. Failing that, check under "Servicio Doméstico" in the telephone directory for agencies that offer babysitting services. Always ask for references.

Banks   Money can be changed at any bank advertising CAMBIO; a commission is always charged, which makes cashing small amounts of traveler's checks expensive. A number of U.S. banks have representation in Madrid, the largest of which is Citibank España, Plaza de la Independencia, 6 (tel. 431-50-50), which offers complete domestic retail banking with many branches in the city.

Some Puerta del Sol bank offices are open in the afternoon and on weekends in summer. If you're really in a bind, Chequepoint in Plaza Callao is open off-hours and weekends, but charges a hefty commission.

The airport branch of Banco Exterior de España is also open 24 hours. The American Express office, at Plaza de las Cortes, 2 (tel. 429-57-75), is open Monday through Friday from 9am to 5:30pm and on Saturday from 9am to noon.

Business Hours   The Spanish siesta survives despite influence from across the Atlantic and northern Europe. Most **businesses** operate Monday through Friday from 9am to 6pm, taking a long lunch hour between 2 and 4pm. **Banks and government offices** are open Monday through Friday from 9am to 2pm and on Saturday from 9am to 1pm. **Shops** and many attractions open at 10am, close for lunch from 1:30 to 5pm, and then remain open until 8pm. One consequence of these working hours is four rush hours a day instead of the usual two.

Consulates   The **U.S. Consulate** is located in the embassy at calle Serrano, 75 (tel. 577-40-00), open Monday through Friday from 9am to noon and 3 to 5pm. You'll find the **British Consulate** is at Centro Colón, Marqués de la Ensenada, 16, 2nd floor (tel. 308-52-01), open Monday through Friday from 8am to 2:30pm; the **Canadian Consulate** is in the embassy at Núñez de Balboa, 35 (tel. 431-43-00), open Monday through Friday from 8:30am to 1pm and 2 to 5pm; and the **Australian Consulate** is at Paseo de la Castellana, 143 (tel. 279-85-04), open Monday through Thursday from 8:30am to 1pm and 1:30 to 4:45pm and on Friday from 8:30am to 2:15pm only.

Currency   The unit of currency is the Spanish **peseta (pta.)** with coins of 1, 5, 25, 50, 100, 200, and 500 pesetas. Be aware that the 500-peseta coin is only marginally larger than the 100-peseta coin. Notes are issued in 500- (only a few left in circulation), 1,000-, 2,000-, 5,000-, and 10,000-peseta denominations.

Watch out for the new 1- and 5-peseta coins. The former is tin-colored and tiny, the latter pale bronze and much smaller than the familiar 5 pesetas.

Dentists and Doctors   For bilingual dental and medical attention, the **Unidad Medica** provides a 24-hour service throughout the year. Outside office hours, the telephone-answering service will put you in touch with the duty doctor. The consulting offices, located just behind Plaza de Colón at Conde Aranda, 1 (tel. 435-18-23), are open Monday through Friday from 9am to 8pm and on Saturday from 10am to 2pm. You could also check with your consulate for their list of approved dentists and doctors.

Emergencies   For the police, dial 091; the fire brigade, 080; Red Cross ambulance, 734-47-94; the municipal ambulance, 230-71-44. For a 24-hour pharmacy, phone 098, or go to any pharmacy; if it is closed, it will post a notice advising you where to find the closest open one.

Eyeglasses   General Optica is one of the larger chains in the country. Most eyeglasses can be made within one hour. Their central location is at Preciados, 22, and Carmen, 23 (tel. 522-21-21).

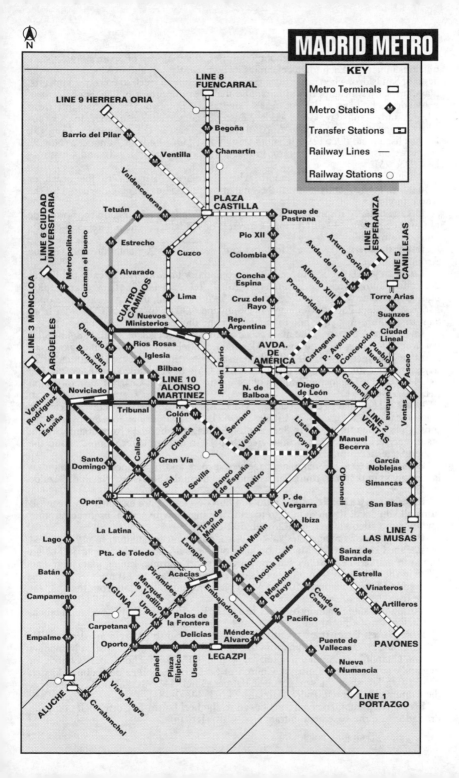

Holidays Like many Catholic countries, the majority of Spain's holidays are religious in nature. Each town celebrates its own saint's day, and in Madrid this is the fiesta of San Isidro, when many businesses close at 2pm all week to enjoy the concerts, plays, art shows, neighborhood fairs, and the most important bullfights of the year.

Madrid's holidays are: New Year's Day (Jan 1), Epiphany (Jan 6), San José (Mar 19), Maundy Thursday, Good Friday, Easter Sunday, San Isidro (May 15), Corpus Christi (May or June), Santiago Apóstol (July 25), Feast of the Assumption (Aug 15), Fiesta Hispanidad (Oct 12), All Saints Day (Nov 1), Our Lady of Almudena (Nov 9), Spanish Constitution Day (Dec 6), Immaculate Conception (Dec 8), and Christmas Day (Dec 25).

August is the traditional month when Spaniards disappear to the beach or mountains; consequently many of the smaller shops and businesses close down for the whole month.

Hospitals Hospital La Paz, Castellana, 261 (tel. 734-26-00), on the north side of town, or Hospital 12 de Octubre, Carretera de Andalucia, Km. 5.4 (tel. 390-80-00), on the south side.

Information See the "Information" section of "Orientation and Getting Around," above.

Laundry There is a centrally located laundry (*lavanderia*) at calle del Barco, 26, called Autoservicio de Lavandería "Alba" (tel. 522-44-63). They charge 1,000 ptas. ($10.40) for washing and drying up to 5 kilos (11 lb.); ironing is extra. It's open Monday through Friday from 9am to 1:30pm and 4:30 to 8pm, and on Saturday from 9am to 1:30pm. Ask your hotel manager for the one nearest to you.

Lost and Found The main office is at Plaza de Legazpi, 7 (tel. 588-43-46). If you lose something on a bus, go to Alcántara, 26 (tel. 401-31-00); if in a taxi, go to Plaza de Chamberi, 4 (tel. 448-79-26). Items will be held at these two locations for 20 days; after that you must go to the Almacén de Objetos Perdidos, Santa Engracia, 120 (tel. 441-02-11). The lost-and-found office for the metro is at Cuatro Caminos station (tel. 233-20-00).

Mail The main post office, "Correos," is the very grand Palacio de Comunicaciones at Plaza de las Cibeles (tel. 521-40-04). It is open for stamps Monday through Saturday from 9am to 8pm and on Sunday and holidays from 10am to 1pm. Stamps are also sold at tobacconists (*estancos*). An airmail letter or postcard to the United States is 95 ptas. ($1).

Newspapers Foreign-language newspapers and magazines can be found at larger kiosks in the main tourist areas, such as Puerta del Sol, Gran Vía, and Plaza de las Cibeles.

Photographic Needs Film and film developing are expensive in Spain, so bring all you need. If you didn't, go to El Corte Inglés, with several branches around town, or to Galeote, Gran Vía, 26 (tel. 532-24-59).

Police See "Emergencies" above. Also, during recent summer months, parked outside the Comunidad de Madrid building on the south side of the Puerta del Sol is a large van marked DENUNCIAS, where you can report a crime. Failing that, there's an office in the Sol Metro station (south side) open from 8am to 11pm.

Radio/TV Tune in to 100.2 FM to pick up Radio Torrejon from the U.S. Air Force base.

During the summer months news broadcasts in English (from London), French, and Italian can be heard on TVE Channel 1 around lunchtime.

Religious Services Catholic services in English are held at Alfonso XIII (tel. 233-30-32). Other denominations to be found in Madrid are Baptist, at Immanuel Baptist Church, Hernández de Tejada, 4 (tel. 407-43-47); Episcopal (Church of England), at the British Embassy Church of St. George, Núñez de Balboa, 43 (tel. 576-51-09); Jewish at the synagogue at Balmes, 3 (tel. 445-98-35); and Protestant, at the Community Church, Padre Damián, 23 (tel. 446-26-81).

Shoe Repair For convenience, go to the heel bar in El Corte Inglés on calle Preciados (use the basement entrance off Calle Tetuan).

THE PESETA & THE DOLLAR

At this writing $1 = approximately 96 ptas. (or 1 pta. = 1¢), and this was the rate of exchange used to calculate the dollar values given in this chapter (rounded to the nearest nickel). This rate fluctuates from time to time and may not be the same when you travel to Spain. Therefore the following table should be used only as a guide:

Ptas.	U.S.$	Ptas.	U.S.$
5	.05	1,000	10.42
10	.10	1,500	15.63
15	.16	2,000	20.83
20	.21	2,500	26.04
25	.26	3,000	31.25
30	.31	3,500	36.46
40	.42	4,000	41.67
50	.52	4,500	46.88
75	.78	5,000	52.08
100	1.04	5,500	57.29
150	1.56	6,000	62.50
200	2.08	6,500	67.71
250	2.60	7,000	72.92
500	5.21	7,500	78.13

Tax   The government sales tax, known as IVA (value-added tax), is currently 6% on most items and 12%–33% on luxury goods. IVA is generally included in the price and can be recovered on goods taken out of the country (see "Savvy Shopping," below, for more details).

Taxis   To call a taxi by telephone, try Radiotaxi (tel. 405-13-13), Radioteléfono taxi (tel. 247-82-00), or Teletaxi (tel. 445-90-08). See "Orientation and Getting Around," above, for further details.

Telephone   The minimum charge for local telephone calls is 15 ptas. (16¢). If you call from your hotel or hostal, expect a hefty surcharge.

Most public phones have clear instructions in English. Simply place at least 15 pesetas' worth of coins in the rack at the top and let them roll in as required. Some new, high-tech public phones provide on-screen instructions in four languages and qaccept the Tarjeta Telefónica, available in 1,000-pta. ($10.40) and 2,000-pta. ($20.85) denominations at *estancos* (tobacconists), post offices, and the *locutorios telefónicas* (central telephone offices) in Plaza Colón and at Gran Vía, 30 (both of which have one Direct USA phone); the *locutorios* are open Monday through Friday from 9am to midnight and on Saturday, Sunday, and holidays from noon to midnight. Other central telephone offices where you can call first and pay afterward are found in the metro station at Sol, in branches of the El Corte Inglés department store, and at the main post office, Puerta H, in Plaza Cibeles, open Monday through Friday from 8am to midnight and on Saturday, Sunday, and holidays 8am to 10pm.

To call collect or at more economical calling-card rates, dial 900-99-00-11 to access AT&T's USA Direct (to do so from a public phone might require coins or a phone card) or 900-99-00-14 to access MCI's Call USA. When calling from a hotel, check first to make sure there is no service charge or surcharge.

To call long distance to the United States and Canada, dial 07, wait for another tone, then dial 1, followed by the area code and number. The average cost of a three-minute call to the United States is approximately 1,700 ptas. ($17.70). Telegram and Telex facilities are available at the main post office (tel. 522-20-00).

The **telephone area code** for Madrid is 1.

Tipping   The custom is widespread, although you are not expected to tip as much as in other countries. The following is a rough guide: In bars, round up the change and always leave at least 10 ptas. (10¢), even after a cup of coffee. In hotels, a service charge is included in the bill, but give the porter 75 ptas. (80¢) per bag; the maid, 300 ptas. ($3.10) per week; the doorman, 50 ptas. (50¢). In restaurants, if the service charge is not included, leave a 10% tip. Give taxi drivers between 5% and 10%, tour guides 10%, and ushers (theater or bullfight) 25 ptas. (25¢).

4. BUDGET ACCOMMODATIONS

There are literally hundreds of *hostals* in Madrid, all strictly graded and controlled by the tourist office. While they may not have some of the conveniences of a hotel, they are usually family-run and therefore more personal.

All the places listed below are in the old part of the city around the Puerta del Sol and Gran Vía. For some of the listings there are several other hostals in the same building; look at the signs at the entrance to the building. If one is all booked up, it's easy to check out its neighbor on another floor. Ask to see the room and bathroom before you commit yourself. Most of the hostals are in interesting old houses that date from the 18th and 19th centuries, with high ceilings, wonderful moldings, and some ornate furnishings to match. Don't be put off by the entrances, which can be quite scruffy-looking—they're in sharp contrast to the well-run and squeaky-clean rooms above.

Note: Rooms that advertise "shower only" usually have a small half-bath with shower and washbasin, sometimes only curtained off from the rest of the room. Rates given below do *not* include VAT unless so indicated.

DOUBLES FOR LESS THAN 4,500 PTAS. [$46.85]

HOSTAL CORUÑA, Paseo del Prado, 12 (3rd Floor), 28014 Madrid. Tel. 1/429-25-43. 8 rms (all with basin only). **Metro:** Antón Martín or Atocha.

$ Rates: 1,980 ptas. ($20.60) single; 3,520 ptas. ($36.65) double; 4,620 ptas. ($48.10) triple. No credit cards.

Hostal Coruña is friendly and is sparkling clean. Ask for a room at the front to enjoy the view and brightness.

HOSTAL DON JUAN, Plaza Vázquez de Mella, 1 (3rd Floor), 28004 Madrid. Tel. 1/522-31-01. 28 rms (27 with complete bath with abbreviated tubs). **Metro:** Gran Vía.

$ Rates: 2,970 ptas. ($30.95) single; 4,290 ptas. ($44.65) double; 6,270 ptas. ($65.30) triple. No credit cards.

⭐ Though this area can be seedy at night—drugs and prostitution abound in the surrounding streets—the prices for the perfectly comfortable accommodations here are right. The Don Juan is completely Spanish in character and decor, and the people who run it and work here are helpful and friendly. The 16 exterior rooms are bright and have little balconies. Most rooms have desks of some kind. Everywhere all is spotless.

HOSTAL LA BARRERA, Atocha, 96 (2nd Floor), 28012 Madrid. Tel. 1/527-53-81. 15 rms (3 with complete bath, 6 with bath but no toilet, 6 with basin only). **Metro:** Atocha.

$ Rates: 1,540 ptas. ($16.05) single with basin; 3,190 ptas. ($33.20) double with shower, 3,190 ptas. ($33.20) double with basin or tub, 3,630 ptas. ($37.80) double with complete bath. No credit cards.

If you are arriving by train at Atocha Station and want to stay nearby, Sr. Mollo at the Hostal La Barrera offers small but spotlessly clean rooms. He warns, however, that if you ask for directions to his hostal at the train station information office, they might try to steer you elsewhere (to an establishment where they get a cut).

HOSTAL RIESCO, Correo, 2 (3rd Floor), 28012 Madrid. Tel. 1/522-26-92 or 532-90-88. 25 rms (13 with bath, 12 with shower only). **Metro:** Sol.

$ Rates (including VAT): 2,200 ptas. ($22.90) single with shower only, 3,080 ptas. ($32.10) single with bath; 3,850 ptas. ($40.10) double with shower only, 4,400 ptas. ($45.85) double with bath. No credit cards.

Right across from the Communidad de Madrid building is the Riesco. Pass through the marble lobby up to the third floor and you'll encounter a hostal featuring a very relaxing sitting room with deep leather sofas around an inviting fireplace. Wood-paneled walls and an Oriental rug complete the picture. There is a TV lounge, and a pay phone. The rooms are well appointed, some with a terrific view of the Puerta del Sol.

HOSTAL SUD AMERICANA, Paseo del Prado, 12 (6th Floor), 28014 Madrid. Tel. 1/429-25-64. 8 rms (all with basin only). **Metro:** Antón Martín or Atocha.

$ Rates: 1,980 ptas. ($20.60) single; 3,520 ptas. ($36.65) double. Showers 375 ptas. ($3.80) extra. No credit cards.

⭐ From the front rooms of this hostal you can't beat the view of the Prado, so ask for one of the larger front rooms. Sr. Pedro Alonso Garrida has been welcoming Frommer readers for more than 30 years to his well-run, nicely decorated hostal.

DOUBLES FOR LESS THAN 5,200 PTAS. ($54.15)

HOSTAL CONTINENTAL, Gran Vía, 44 (3rd Floor), 28013 Madrid. Tel. 1/521-46-40. 29 rooms (all with bath). TEL **Metro:** Callao.

$ Rates: 3,850 ptas. ($40.10) single; 4,840 ptas. ($50.40) double; 6,225 ptas. ($64.85) triple. Continental breakfast 325 ptas. ($3.40) extra. AE, MC, V.

Along with the slightly more expensive Valencia below, the Continental is one of several hostals in a centrally located building. It stands out, though, because the management continues to make improvements. There is a small TV lounge with red leather chairs adjoining the breakfast room. Light refreshments are available in the lounge or in the cheerful-looking bedrooms.

HOSTAL LA MACARENA, Cava de San Miguel, 8, 28005 Madrid. Tel. 1/265-92-21. 23 rms (all with bath). TEL **Metro:** Sol.

$ Rates (including VAT): 3,300 ptas. ($34.35) single; 4,950 ptas. ($51.55) double. AE, MC, V.

A warm welcome awaits you from manager Ricardo González at this hostal behind Plaza Mayor in the street with all the *mesones*. Although the rooms are small, they are attractive, and there are five newer ones upstairs. The TV lounge and breakfast area are especially cozy.

HOSTAL MARÍA CRISTINA, Fuencarral, 20 (2nd Floor), 28004 Madrid. Tel. 1/531-63-00 or 531-63-09. 20 rms (18 with bath, 2 with shower). TEL **Metro:** Gran Vía.

$ Rates: 3,025 ptas. ($31.50) single with shower, 3,630 ptas. ($37.80) single with bath; 4,840 ptas. ($50.40) double with bath; 7,200 ptas. ($75) triple with bath. No credit cards.

This hostal is immaculate, from the TV lounge and cozy sitting room with its

---

FROMMER'S SMART TRAVELER: HOTELS

VALUE-CONSCIOUS TRAVELERS SHOULD
TAKE ADVANTAGE OF THE FOLLOWING:

1. Accommodations without TV lounges, bars, and private bathrooms—amenities cost money. Almost without exception there will be a basin in the room.
2. Areas away from Puerta del Sol and Gran Vía, the tourist meccas. The farther away you get, the cheaper the room.
3. The Centro de Información Juvenil in the Sol Metro station, if you're carrying an international student ID card. This office will give you information on which hostals offer a discount.

QUESTIONS TO ASK IF YOU'RE ON A BUDGET

1. Are hot water and a shower included in the price of the room.
2. Ask for a discount—you're likely to get it especially off-season or for longer stays.

---

wood-paneled walls and Oriental rug to the attractive rooms upstairs (no elevator) furnished with Scandinavian-style pine beds and tables. The bathrooms are small but well appointed. Light refreshments available.

HOSTAL NUESTRA SEÑORA DE SONSOLES, Fuencarral, 18 (2nd Floor), 28004 Madrid. Tel. 1/532-75-23 or 532-75-22. 27 rooms (all with bath). TEL **Metro:** Gran Vía.

$ Rates: 3,300 ptas. ($34.35) single; 4,950 ptas. ($51.55) double; 6,700 ptas. ($69.80) triple. AE, DC, MC, V.

This has to be one of the best-value and best-run hostals in Madrid, and with the special discount for Frommer readers (who consistently rave about the place), falls into our budget bracket. A dim entrance gives way to sparkling marble floors and an attractively furnished lobby and TV lounge with stairs leading to the second floor. A third sitting room has been created, featuring a stunning fishtank. Señora Veronica offers bearers of a copy of this book a 15%–20% discount. Double-glazing in the rooms facing Fuencarral ensures a tranquil stay in this family-run and very secure hotel. Señora Veronica's husband and children speak some English.

HOSTAL RESIDENCIA LA PERLA ASTURIANA, Plaza de Santa Cruz, 3, 28012 Madrid. Tel. 1/266-46-00. Fax 1/266-46-08. 30 rms (20 with bath). TEL **Metro:** Sol.

$ Rates (including VAT): 2,915 ptas. ($30.35) single without bath, 3,845 ptas. ($40.05) single with bath; 5,130 ptas. ($53.45) double with bath; 7,230 ptas. ($75.30) triple with bath. Continental breakfast 325 ptas ($3.40) extra. MC, V.

This hostal couldn't be closer to Plaza Mayor, and it affords great views of the attractive Plaza Santa Cruz. Ask for a room on the south side, since buses stop just outside the east side. The hostal includes a comfortable TV lounge with a small dining room for breakfast and refreshments.

HOSTAL RIFER, calle Mayor, 5 (4th Floor), 28013 Madrid. Tel. 1/532-31-97. 12 rms (4 with bath, 8 with shower only). **Metro:** Sol.

$ Rates (including VAT): 3,300 ptas. ($34.35) single with shower only; 4,015 ptas. ($41.80) double with shower only, 4,730 ptas. ($49.25) double with bath. No credit cards.

Only a stone's throw from the Puerta del Sol and Plaza Mayor is the handsome entrance to this small hostal, where you will be warmly greeted by Señora Julia, who speaks English. The rooms are simply furnished, but sparkling clean, and very light and airy. Those rooms with shower and basin have them enclosed by a curtain. There is a lounge as well.

HOSTAL RIOSOL, calle Mayor, 5 (2nd Floor), 28013 Madrid. Tel. 1/532-31-42. 12 rms (6 with bath, 6 with shower only). **Metro:** Sol.
$ Rates (including VAT): 2,530 ptas. ($26.35) single with shower only, 2,750 ptas. ($28.65) single with bath; 4,070 ptas. ($42.40) double with shower only, 4,510 ptas. ($46.95) double with bath. No credit cards.

Two floors down from the Rifer (see above) is this small hostal. Although it's not quite so attractively presented, it nevertheless has 12 rooms that are all clean and tidy.

HOSTAL TRIANA, Salud, 13, 28013 Madrid. Tel. 1/532-68-12. 29 rms (2 with shower only, 27 with bath). TEL **Metro:** Gran Vía, Callao, or Sol.
$ Rates (including VAT): 2,530 ptas. ($26.35) single with shower only, 2,725 ptas. ($28.40) single with bath; 4,755–5,140 ptas. ($49.55–$53.55) double with bath. No credit cards.

Just down from the Gran Vía, overlooking the attractive and quiet Plaza del Carmen, is this very welcoming hostal. The family of Laya Gómez ensures your comfort. Double glass doors open onto a bright lobby with comfortable-looking chairs, and there is a TV lounge. Some of the decoration—pretty floral fabrics, lots of white paint and wood—is unusual for Madrid. Each room has a small fan, and those overlooking the plaza have a small balcony.

HOSTAL VICTORIA, calle Carretas, 7 (2nd Floor), 28013 Madrid. Tel. 1/522-99-82. 18 rms (15 with bath). A/C TV TEL **Metro:** Sol.
$ Rates (including VAT): 2,770 ptas. ($28.85) single without bath, 3,300–3,850 ptas. ($34.35–$40.10) single with bath; 4,950–5,390 ptas. ($51.55–$56.15) double with bath; 7,150 ptas. ($74.45) triple with bath. AE, MC, V.

This small and conveniently located hostal just off the Puerta del Sol has recently been renovated, right down to the attractive matching curtains and bed linen. Señora María Teresa is attentive and justifiably proud of her hostal. It's popular year round, so book ahead.

DOUBLES FOR LESS THAN 7,200 PTAS. ($75)

HOSTAL EDREIRA, Atocha, 75 (2nd Floor), 28012 Madrid. Tel. 1/429-01-84. 16 rms (8 with bath). **Metro:** Atocha.
$ Rates: 2,970 ptas. ($30.95) single without bath; 4,400 ptas. ($45.85) double without bath, 5,280 ptas. ($55) double with bath; 2,530 ptas. ($26.35) per person triple with bath. No credit cards.

Another well-run hostal is the Edreira, where all the rooms have a cupboard and basin, and pretty floral bedcovers. The hostal feels light and bright, especially with the new parquet flooring. There is a TV lounge. The daughter of the house speaks good English.

HOSTAL LISBOA, Ventura de la Vega, 17, 28014 Madrid. Tel. 1/429-98-94. 23 rms (all with bath). TEL **Metro:** Antón Martín or Sol.
$ Rates (including VAT): 3,850 ptas. ($40.10) single; 5,060–5,500 ptas. ($52.10–$57.30) double; 6,050 ptas. ($63) triple. AE, DC, MC, V.

Set right in the midst of Madrid's restaurants and bars, the Lisboa's attractive facade is most inviting. Its rooms are spread over four floors (with elevator access), and some have double beds made of bronze. There is a small lounge with a TV and VCR. There is no restaurant or bar on the premises, but you won't have to go far to find whatever you want at any time of the day or night.

HOSTAL MATUTE, Plaza de Matute, 11, 28012 Madrid. Tel. 1/429-55-85. 25 rms (most with shower or full bath). TEL **Metro:** Antón Martín.

$ Rates (including VAT): 3,080 ptas. ($32.10) single with shower, 3,850 ptas. ($40.10) single with bath; 4,620 ptas. ($48.10) double with shower, 5,720 ptas. ($59.60) double with bath. Continental breakfast 225 ptas. ($2.35) extra. No credit cards.

⭐ Despite the fact that Plaza de Matute is located right in the middle of calle de las Huertas, one of the prime bar-hopping streets, it's surprisingly quiet. A fascinating staircase decorated with inlaid marble winds up to the hostal, where you will be greeted by Alberto, who speaks good English and is obsessed with proper lighting. This hostal is well appointed; most rooms have just been redecorated and—unusual—there are shelves and storage. You'll sleep on box springs—no sagging beds. There is also a TV lounge.

HOSTAL VALENCIA, Gran Vía, 44 (5th Floor), 28013 Madrid. Tel. 1/522-11-15. 29 rms (10 with bath, 17 with shower and toilet). TEL **Metro:** Callao.

$ Rates: 3,300 ptas. ($34.35) single; 4,950 ptas. ($51.55) double with shower, 5,280 ptas. ($55) double with bath; 7,920 ptas. ($82.50) triple with bath. Continental breakfast 275 ptas. ($2.85) extra. MC, V.

As you walk through the front door you will immediately be made to feel at home by the warmth and coziness emanating from the TV lounge. A continuing favorite, this comfortable hostal is run by Antonio Ramírez and his American wife, Laurie, with an exceptional degree of friendliness.

HOSTAL PER-SAL, Plaza del Angel, 12, 28012 Madrid. Tel. 1/369-46-43. Fax 1/369-19-52. 100 rms (all with bath). TEL **Metro:** Antón Martín or Sol.

$ Rates (including VAT): 4,730 ptas. ($49.25) single; 7,150 ptas. ($74.45) double; 10,230 ptas. ($106.55) triple; 14,080 ptas. ($146.65) quad. Continental breakfast 525 ptas. ($5.45) extra. AE, MC, V.

Spread over four floors, with its own private elevator, this is one of Madrid's larger hostals. It has a good-sized bar and lounge, somewhat plainly decorated with Formica-topped tables, leather chairs, and a marble-chip floor. The bedrooms offer the essentials in terms of furnishings; some have air conditioning. If there are four of you traveling together, ask for one of their quads, which has a wall dividing the room nearly in two.

SUPER-BUDGET CHOICES

HOSTAL BENAMAR, San Mateo, 20 (2nd Floor), 28004 Madrid. Tel. 1/308-00-92. 22 rms (none with bath). **Metro:** Tribunal or Alonso Martínez.

$ Rates (including VAT): 1,760 ptas. ($18.35) single; 3,080 ptas. ($32.10) double; 5,060 ptas. ($52.70) triple. No credit cards.

Señor Benjamin Viñuela's hostal is terrific value for the money. While the rooms do not have a bath, each has a basin and all are very clean and bright and nicely furnished—certainly as comfortable as some of the more expensive hostals. Señor Vinuela speaks four languages, including English. There is no elevator.

HOSTAL VICTORIA II, calle Carretas, 3 (2nd Floor), 28013 Madrid. Tel. 1/522-15-49. 21 rms (none with bath). **Metro:** Sol.

$ Rates (including VAT): 1,650 ptas. ($17.20) single; 2,750 ptas. ($28.65) double; 3,850 ptas. ($40.10) triple.

Under the same management as the nearby (and more expensive) Hostal Victoria (above), this hostal provides basic accommodation on two floors. Despite the scruffy entrance from the street, the rooms are clean and neat, all with basins, and the management is very helpful. It is popular with students who like the central location at Puerta del Sol.

YOUTH HOSTELS

For information about reservations at Madrid's youth hostels, call the **International Youth Hostel Federation** (tel. 521-44-27).

INTERNATIONAL YOUTH HOSTAL, calle de Santa Cruz de Marcenado, 28, 28015 Madrid. Tel. 1/247-45-32. 72 beds. **Metro:** Argüelles.

$ Rates (including breakfast): 600 ptas. ($6.25) per person per night for members under 26 years, 715 ptas. ($7.45) for members over 26. No credit cards.

This youth hostel is heavily used by groups, so always phone first.

RICHARD SCHIRRMANN YOUTH HOSTEL, Recinto de la Casa de Campo, 28011 Madrid. Tel. 1/463-56-99. 134 beds. **Metro:** Lago.

$ Rates (including breakfast): 600 ptas. ($6.25) per person per night for members under 26, 715 ptas. ($7.45) for members over 26. No credit cards.

Same as above.

CAMPING

CAMPING MADRID, Carretera Nacional-I, Madrid-Burgos, Km. 11. Tel. 1/202-28-35. 764-tent capacity.

$ Rates: 385 ptas. ($4) per night per adult, 300 ptas. ($3.10) per child; 385 ptas. ($4) per individual tent, 440 ptas. ($4.60) per family tent; 385 ptas. ($4) per car or caravan (RV). No credit cards.

You'll find the following modern facilities here: phone, post box, money exchange, supermarket, restaurant, cafeteria and bar, hot water, swimming pool, and playground. It's all set in an open and attractive countryside, with lots of pines, acacias, and poplars.

WORTH THE EXTRA BUCKS

HOTEL FRANCISCO I, Arenal, 15, 28013 Madrid. Tel. 1/248-02-04. Fax 1/531-01-88. 58 rms (all with bath). TEL **Metro:** Opera.

$ Rates (including continental breakfast and VAT): 6,135 ptas. ($63.90) single (one person in a double room); 8,500 ptas. ($88.55) double; 10,000 ptas. ($104.15) triple. Half- and full-board rates available. AE, MC, V.

Under the same ownership as the París, below, this hotel is only seconds from the Puerta del Sol and run by the very amicable Francisco Martín. The wood-paneled and marble lobby sets the tone for the rest of the hotel. Near the deep leather chairs of the TV lounge is a well-stocked bar. The restaurant in the hotel is as good as you'll find in its price range. The bedrooms (12 of them air-conditioned) are a sensible size and well appointed.

HOTEL INGLÉS, Echegaray, 8, 28014 Madrid. Tel. 1/429-65-51. Fax 1/420-24-23. 58 rms (all with bath). TV TEL **Metro:** Sol.

$ Rates: 5,610–8,470 ptas. ($58.45–$88.20) single; 8,470–11,000 ptas. ($88.20–$114.60) double, 11,100 ptas ($115.60) double with sitting room. Continental breakfast 550 ptas. ($5.70) extra. AE, DC, MC, V. **Parking:** Available.

The Hotel Inglés welcomes you into its brightly lit lobby and comfortable TV lounge, with its deep sofas and armchairs. Just beyond is the bar/cafeteria, where you can have a drink and take breakfast in the morning. The rooms are well appointed with good cupboards and dresser drawers. All rooms have a radio, and many have a large sitting area. Safe-deposit boxes are available.

HOTEL PARÍS, Alcalá, 2, 28014 Madrid. Tel. 1/521-64-96. Fax 1/531-01-88. 22 rms (all with bath). TEL **Metro:** Sol.

$ Rates (including continental breakfast and VAT): 7,095 ptas. ($73.90) single; 9,790 ptas. ($101.95) double. MC, V.

At the París, conveniently located on the Puerta del Sol, the ambience is traditionally Spanish, with lots of marble, glass, brass, and red plush covering the walls in the entrance. The bedrooms are well appointed, with marble-and-tile bathrooms, some with air conditioning; for a great view, ask for the room overlooking Sol. In addition to a bar, restaurant, and TV lounge, there is a pretty patio terrace in the interior of the building, a great place to sit in warm weather.

HOTEL RESIDENCIA SANTANDER, Echegaray, 1, 28014 Madrid. Tel. 1/429-95-51 or 429-66-44. 40 rms (all with bath). TEL **Metro:** Sol.

$ Rates (including VAT): 5,100 ptas. ($53.10) single (one person in a double room); 7,040 ptas. ($73.35) double, 7,975 ptas. ($83.05) double with a comfortably large sitting area. Continental breakfast 375 ptas. ($3.90) extra. No credit cards.

⭐ The shiny glass-and-brass doorway on Echegaray at the corner of Carrera de San Jerónimo leads into a pleasing foyer with marble walls and a carved-wood reception desk. The rooms are a good size, with parquet floors, dressing table, and wardrobe. Some rooms have giant tubs. There is a TV lounge, a cafeteria, and a bar.

5. BUDGET DINING

There is no shortage of restaurants in Madrid, and for relatively little expense you can eat well. In the old part of the city around the Puerta del Sol, the selection of cafeterias offering good, wholesome Spanish cooking is enormous, especially around Plaza Mayor and Puerta del Sol. A little to the east in the area bounded by calle de las Huertas, carrera de San Jerónimo, along calle de León, calle de Echegaray, and Ventura de la Vega you will find lively bars and cafeterias. Head north to calles de Hartzenbusch and Cardenal Cisneros and the surrounding few blocks for scads of inexpensive restaurants and bars serving everything from tortillas and tapas to Italian and German cuisine.

FAVORITE MEALS A Spanish-style *tortilla* is an omelet made with potato, onion, and garlic, generally served cold when eaten as a tapa (see below). *Gazpacho*, imported from Andalusía and available during the summer only, is a cold vinegar-based soup made with garlic, tomato, various vegetables, bread, and olive oil, served with helpings of onions, green pepper, or chopped egg, to name but a few. *Paella*, another import to Madrid, is rice cooked in saffron with bits of chicken and seafood. *Cocido madrileño* is a three-course meal: first a soup, then a vegetable dish, followed by a stew of beans, sausage, and meat. A popular first course is *judias* (beans), made into a tasty stew. *Perdíz* (partridge) and *codorniz* (quail) appear regularly in Spanish restaurants along with *cochinillo* (suckling pig) and *cordero asado* (roast leg of baby lamb).

And then there are *tapas,* small portions of food that are served in every bar. They vary in size, quality, and diversity, and you can certainly have a complete and interesting meal of tapas alone. Popular tapas include *boquerones* (deep-fried fish), *croquetas* (also deep-fried and filled with béchamel sauce), *empanadillas* (tuna and tomato, deep-fried), *setas* (enormous mushrooms dripping in garlic), *morcilla* (black pudding, rice or onion based), *pimientos fritos* (fried peppers), *pimientos del padrón* (the saying goes "*unos pican, otros no,*" "some are hot, others not"—tiny, fiery-hot peppers mixed in with ordinary ones), *patatas bravas* (potatoes with a piquant sauce), *mejillones* (clams), *chipirones* (baby squid in their ink), *calamares* (squid), *chorizo* and *salchichón* (Spanish sausage), and *queso manchego* (cheese from La Mancha). One word of warning: Don't be pressed into selecting *jamón* (ham) *de Serrano*—it's very tasty, but very expensive too.

MEALS FOR LESS THAN 1,000 PTAS. ($10.40)

CASA MINGO, Paseo de la Florida, 2. Tel. 247-50-31.
Cuisine: SPANISH. **Metro:** Norte. **Bus:** 46.
$ Prices: Main courses 400–1,000 ptas. ($4.15–$10.40). No credit cards.

Open: Daily 10am–1:30am.
Come to this vast high-ceilinged place for some of the best-tasting chicken around. No frills, but cheap and cheerful, and popular with students and young families. As there is no system for lining up, look for a table that's about to be vacated and ask the occupants if it's spoken for—if it's not, claim it. Although chicken accompanied by cider, a salad, and a teriffic tarta de Santiago (almond cake) costs about 1,300 ptas. ($13.55), the chicken is a whole one and easily feeds two.

LA BIOTIKA VEGETARIAN RESTAURANT, Amor de Dios, 3. Tel. 429-07-80.
 Cuisine: VEGETARIAN/MACROBIOTIC. **Metro:** Antón Martín.
 $ Prices: Appetizers 250–775 ptas. ($2.60–$8.05); main courses 600–825 ptas. ($6.25–$8.60); menu del día 875 ptas. ($9.10). No credit cards.
 Open: Lunch daily 1:30–4:30pm; dinner daily 8:30–11:30pm.
Walk through the health-food shop to this small, plain restaurant for delicious macrobiotic and vegetarian cuisine at a very reasonable price.

RESTAURANTE PAULINO, Alonso Cano, 34. Tel. 441-87-37.
 Cuisine: SPANISH. **Reservations:** Essential. **Metro:** Iglesia.
 $ Prices: Menu del día 950 ptas. ($9.90). V.
 Open: Lunch Mon–Sat 1:30–4pm; dinner Mon–Sat 9–11pm. **Closed:** Aug.
You'll find this small, excellent restaurant off the tourist track, but not far from the Sorolla Museum. Lunchtime is the best time to come because in the evening the à la carte menu is more expensive.

RESTAURANTE RAPIDO, Puerta del Sol, 14. Tel. 521-66-16.
 Cuisine: SPANISH. **Metro:** Sol.
 $ Prices: Appetizers 225–650 ptas. ($2.35–$6.75); main courses 550–1,650 ptas. ($5.70–$17.20). No credit cards.
 Open: Mon–Fri 9am–11:30pm, Sat 12:30–11:30pm, Sun and hols 1–11:30pm.
This pleasant self-service restaurant is a good value for your money at breakfast, lunch, and dinner. No frills, just solid fare, including sandwiches and hamburgers.

RESTAURANTE RODRÍGUEZ, San Cristóbal, 15. Tel. 531-11-36.
 Cuisine: SPANISH. **Metro:** Sol.
 $ Prices: Appetizers 190–950 ptas. ($1.95–$9.90); main courses 385–1,650 ptas. ($4–$17.20); menu del día 935 ptas. ($9.75). No credit cards.
 Open: Lunch Fri–Wed 1–4pm; dinner Fri–Wed 8–11:30pm.
This highly popular and friendly restaurant is family run and is known for its hearty stews and cocidos. A star value for your money.

RESTAURANTE ZARA, Infantas, 5. Tel. 532-20-74.

ⓕ FROMMER'S SMART TRAVELER: RESTAURANTS

VALUE-CONSCIOUS TRAVELERS SHOULD TAKE ADVANTAGE OF THE FOLLOWING:

1. The menu del día at lunch, which usually comprises a first course of vegetables or salad, a main course of meat or fish, sometimes dessert and coffee, and always bread and wine.
2. Restaurants filled with Spaniards—the Madrileño is very discerning.
3. Tapas bars in the evening.
4. Standing up to eat or drink. Many establishments have two prices: mesa (table) and barra (bar).

Cuisine: SPANISH/CUBAN. **Metro:** Gran Vía.
$ **Prices:** Appetizers 190–650 ptas. ($1.95–$6.75); main courses 250–1,760 ptas. ($2.60–$18.35); *menu del día* 1,650 ptas. ($17.20). AE, DC, MC, V.
Open: Lunch Mon–Fri 1–5pm; dinner Mon–Fri 8–11:30pm. **Closed:** Hols. and Aug.

Rough white walls and green checkered tablecloths mark this simple, small restaurant. The señora hails from Cuba and has brought her national cuisine to Madrid, combining it with typical Spanish fare. The specialties change daily, so you may find a roast one day, meatballs and fried eggs another, all served with rice.

MEALS FOR LESS THAN 1,500 PTAS. ($15.60)

A HUEVO, Jacometrezo, 6. Tel. 248-51-02.
Cuisine: SPANISH FAST FOOD. **Metro:** Sto. Domingo.
$ **Prices:** Breakfast 225 ptas. ($2.35); combination plates 250–1,870 ptas. ($2.60–$19.45); *menu del día* 950 ptas. ($9.90). MC, V.
Open: Sun–Thurs 8am–1:30am, Fri–Sat 8am–3:30am.

This is a very plain but popular self-service cafeteria just off the Gran Vía, and useful because it's open from 8am. The menu is of the basic steak- or chicken-and-fries variety.

D'A QUEIMADA, Echegaray, 17. Tel. 429-32-63.
Cuisine: SPANISH/GALLEGAN. **Metro:** Sol.
$ **Prices:** Appetizers 475–1,650 ptas. ($4.95–$17.20); main courses 975–2,500 ptas. ($8.05–$26.05); *menu del día* 1,650 ptas. ($17.20); paella 1,075 ptas. ($11.20). MC, V.
Open: Lunch daily 11:30am–5pm; dinner daily 8pm–midnight.

For good and inexpensive paella this should be your first choice, and you won't have to wait hours for its preparation—the demand is such that they always have some ready. It's a fun and friendly restaurant and also features Gallegan cooking.

EL PALETO, Cardenal Cisneros, 38. Tel. 445-40-27.
Cuisine: SPANISH. **Metro:** Bilbao.
$ **Prices:** From 350 ptas. ($3.65). V.
Open: Lunch daily 10am–4:30pm; dinner daily 7pm–1am.

At this narrow bar, ask for a paleto, a slice of spicy veal served between two pieces of French bread, lightly grilled, or a paleto with tomato and pepper. There is a restaurant here also, but it's more fun to sit at the bar with its dusty pink tiles and bullfighter posters.

EL RESTAURANTE VEGETARIANO, Marqués de Santa Ana, 34. Tel. 532-09-27.
Cuisine: VEGETARIAN. **Metro:** Tribunal.
$ **Prices:** Appetizers 395–560 ptas. ($4.10–$5.85); salad bar 545–785 ptas. ($5.65–$8.20); main courses 715–895 ptas. ($7.45–$9.30). V.
Open: Lunch Tues–Sun 1:30–4pm; dinner Tues–Sat 9–11pm.

In a quiet neighborhood north of the Gran Vía, this excellent vegetarian restaurant is simply furnished with pine tables and lots of plants. On the concise menu you'll find such things as cream of leek or avocado soup and broccoli mousse or couscous with vegetables. Wash it all down with alcohol-free beer, *vino ecológico*, or fresh fruit juice.

HUE-PIN, Villalar, 8 (1st Floor). Tel. 431-11-31.
Cuisine: CHINESE. **Metro:** Retiro 1.
$ **Prices:** Appetizers 140–675 ptas. ($1.45–$7.05); main courses 590–1,175 ptas. ($6.15–$12.25). No credit cards.
Open: Lunch daily noon–4pm; dinner daily 8pm–midnight.

Just by Plaza de la Independencia, this small but well-established family-run Chinese restaurant offers traditional fare in an Asian-style setting with lots of lanterns and mirrors. Consider a take-out to carry off to nearby Retiro Park.

LA TARTERIE, Cardenal Cisneros, 24. Tel. 447-05-34.

Cuisine: PIZZA/SNACKS. **Metro:** Bilbao.

$ Prices: Salads 525–715 ptas. ($5.45–$7.45); pizzas 650–1,120 ptas. ($6.75–$11.65); *menu del día* 785 ptas. ($8.15). AE, DC, V.

Open: Daily 9am–3am.

Just one of many restaurants in the area, La Tarterie serves a good selection of quiches and salads, but is best known for its desserts. You can enjoy restaurant or cafeteria-style eating in a contemporary setting with marble-top tables and changing art exhibitions on the walls.

MESÓN RESTAURANTE PONTEJOS, San Cristóbal, 11. Tel. 531-01-54.

Cuisine: SPANISH. **Metro:** Sol.

$ Prices: Appetizers 450–1,760 ptas. ($4.70–$18.35); main courses 600–1,980 ptas. ($6.25–$20.60). MC, V.

Open: Thurs–Tues 9am–midnight.

One of the many restaurants by Plaza Mayor, this small, unpretentious establishment with its tiled bar and blue-and-white-checkered tablecloths has an excellent *menu del día* for 1,045 ptas. ($10.90). On certain days you can get a hefty helping of paella along with crusty homemade bread for 650 ptas. ($6.75).

RESTAURANT BALLESTEROS, Ventura da la Vega, 6. Tel. 429-67-64.

Cuisine: SPANISH. **Metro:** Sol.

$ Prices: Appetizers 300–900 ptas. ($3.10–$9.35); main courses 450–1,800 ptas. ($4.70–$18.75); *menu del día* 1,100 ptas. ($11.45). No credit cards.

Open: Lunch Mon–Sat 1–4pm; dinner Mon–Sat 9pm–midnight. **Closed:** Aug.

In a long, narrow room with tables on either side, owner Manolo Ballesteros offers a simple but clean restaurant featuring typical Spanish dishes such as stuffed eggplant, veal chops, and steak with a house sauce. His paintings decorate the walls.

CAFES

CAFE GIJÓN, Paseo de Recoletos, 21. Tel. 521-54-25.

Cuisine: SPANISH. **Metro:** Banco de España.

$ Prices: Appetizers 300–1,000 ptas. ($3.10–$10.40); main courses 750–4,180 ptas. ($7.80–$43.55); *menu del día* 1,485 ptas. ($15.45). No credit cards.

Open: Lunch Mon–Sat 1–4pm; dinner Mon–Sat 9pm–midnight.

Hemingway made Cafe Gijón famous among Americans, and it is still home to the Spanish tradition of the *tertulia* (when like-minded friends get together for amicable discussion). Outside in the summer or inside in cooler weather, this is a relaxing place to come and sip a coffee or beer, read a newspaper, and watch the other folks.

CIRCULO DE BELLAS ARTES, Alcalá, 42. Tel. 531-77-00 or 531-77-06.

Cuisine: SPANISH. **Metro:** Banco de España.

$ Prices: From 290 ptas. ($3). No credit cards.

Open: Daily 9am–midnight.

Not just a café, but also a cultural center with changing exhibitions upstairs, this place is usually packed. Winter or summer, it's a great place to come and relax. Inside there are lots of deep, comfy chairs from which to admire the painted ceiling and wooden floors; outside you can enjoy the sun. There is a 135-pta. ($1.40) entrance charge to the center. Coffee and a croissant will set you back about 350 ptas. ($3.65).

THE CHAINS

If you're feeling homesick, you may be glad to know that you're never far from **McDonald's, Burger King, Wendy's, Kentucky Fried Chicken,** and **Pizza Hut,** all of which have several locations throughout the busiest parts of the city, especially in Gran Vía, Puerta del Sol, and Orense to the north. Depending on the trimmings, burgers cost 175–395 ptas. ($1.80–$4.10). Local chains include the following:

BOB'S.
Cuisine: FAST FOOD.
$ Prices: 200–1,120 ptas. ($2.10–$11.65). No credit cards.
Open: Daily 9am–3am.
Bob's is an establishment similar to Vip's, below, in every way. Locations include Glorieta de Quevedo, 9; Padro Damián, 38; Miguel Angel, 11; Zurbano, 26; and Serrano, 41.

FOSTER'S HOLLYWOOD.
Cuisine: FAST FOOD.
$ Prices: Hamburgers and fries 675 ptas. ($7.05); *menu del día* 1,455 ptas. ($15.15). No credit cards.
Open: Sun–Thurs 1pm–1:30am, Fri–Sat 1pm–2:30am.
At this popular hamburger joint you can also get a delicious grilled sandwich with spareribs and barbecue sauce. Beer to wash it down costs 225 ptas. ($2.35).
Locations in and around Madrid include Tamayo y Baus, 1; Velázquez, 80; Guzmán el Bueno, 100; Magallanes, 1; Antonio Morales, 3; and Avenida de Brasil, 14–16.

NEBRASKA.
Cuisine: FAST FOOD.
$ Prices: 215–1,120 ptas. ($2.25–$11.65). No credit cards.
Open: Daily 9am–midnight.
This home-grown cafeteria chain offers a *menu del día* for 1,120 ptas. ($11.65) in the bar area, and coffee and pastry for 225 ptas. ($2.35). For the unadventurous, menus are in English.
Locations in Madrid include Alcalá, 18; Gran Vía, 32 and 55; Calle Mayor, 1; Goya, 39; and Bravo Murillo, 109 and 291.

VIP'S.
Cuisine: FAST FOOD.
$ Prices: 200–1,120 ptas. ($2.10–$11.65). No credit cards.
Open: Daily 9am–3am.
Vip's offers cafeteria-style eating along with the sale of books, magazines, records, tapes, videos, beer, wine, cookies, and meats. It's a very popular place for late-night munchies. Breakfast, consisting of toast and marmalade with coffee or tea, is 225 ptas. ($2.35).
Locations in Madrid include Gran Vía, 43; Princesa, 5; Velázquez, 84 and 136; O'Donnell, 17; Paseo de la Castellana, 85; Orense, 16 and 79; Paseo de la Habana, 17; Julian Romea, 4; and Alberto Aguitera, 56.

MEALS FOR LESS THAN 2,000 PTAS.
($20.85)

A TODO MÉXICO, San Bernardino, 4. Tel. 241-93-59.
Cuisine: MEXICAN. **Metro:** Plaza de España.
$ Prices: Appetizers 275–1,120 ptas. ($2.85–$11.65); combination platters 1,225–1,675 ptas. ($12.75–$17.45); *menu del día* 1,795 ptas. ($18.70). No credit cards.
Open: Lunch daily 1–4pm; dinner daily 8:30pm–midnight.
Almost next door to the Bali Indonesian Restaurant (below) you'll find this Mexican restaurant with ceramic-tiled walls and checked tablecloths. A margarita is 500 ptas. ($5.20).

BALI INDONESIAN RESTAURANT, San Bernardino, 5. Tel. 541-91-22.
Cuisine: INDONESIAN. **Metro:** Plaza de España.

$ Prices: Appetizers 280–800 ptas. ($2.90–$8.35); main courses 1,120–1,680 ptas. ($11.65–$17.50). AE, V.
Open: Lunch Tues–Sun 12:30–3:30pm; dinner Tues–Sat 8–11:30pm.

⭐ Just north of Plaza de España, in an area known for its cheap restaurants, is the slightly more expensive Bali Indonesian Restaurant. The decor is tasteful and contemporary, with lots of plants. Try rijstaffel Bali—12 small portions of veal, chicken, pork, and vegetables in different sauces of coconut, peanut, curry, and pepper. With rice this is quite enough for two people and will set you back a total of 4,200 ptas. ($43.75).

CARMENCITA, Libertad, 16. Tel. 531-66-12.
Cuisine: SPANISH. **Metro:** Chueca.
$ Prices: Appetizers 550–1,120 ptas. ($5.70–$11.65); main courses 800–2,250 ptas. ($8.35–$23.45); *menu del día* 1,680 ptas. ($17.50). AE, DC, V.
Open: Lunch Mon–Fri 1–4pm; dinner Mon–Fri 9pm–midnight.

⭐ North of Gran Vía, this charming restaurant decorated with Spanish tiles has long been popular. Favorite dishes include croquettes, meatballs, and tripe. A typical *menu del día* (served at lunch only) will consist of lentils followed by deep-fried fish, a digestif, and wine.

CASA GADES, Conde de Xiquena, 4. Tel. 522-75-10.
Cuisine: ITALIAN. **Metro:** Chueca.
$ Prices: Appetizers 450–950 ptas. ($4.70–$9.90); pastas 600–800 ptas. ($6.25–$8.35); pizza 625–800 ptas. ($6.50–$8.35); main courses 850–2,350 ptas. ($8.85–$24.45); *menu del día* 1,500 ptas. ($15.60). No credit cards.
Open: Lunch daily 1:30–4pm; dinner daily 9pm–12:15am.
Red-and-white checked tablecloths, old photos on the walls, and two galleried seating areas attract a mixed crowd of yuppies and office workers to sample the pizza and pasta. The *menu del día* consists of soup or salad, pasta or fish, dessert, beer or wine, and bread.

EL CUCHI, Cuchilleros, 3. Tel. 266-31-08.
Cuisine: INTERNATIONAL. **Metro:** Sol.
$ Prices: Appetizers 225–1,475 ptas. ($2.35–$15.35); main courses 900–2,970 ptas. ($9.35–$30.95); *menu del día* 1,045 ptas. ($10.90). AE, DC, MC, V.
Open: Lunch daily 1–4pm; dinner daily 8pm–midnight.
The greeting above the door of this restaurant located right behind Plaza Mayor says: "We don't speak English, but we won't laugh at your Spanish"—and the staff couldn't be more fun or helpful (menus are in fact in English). The place is simply crammed with stuff—pictures, tiles, matchbox collections, hat collections (above the bar), and all kinds of dried foods hanging on the walls. The menu is a bit expensive, but if you choose carefully—barbecued chicken and a salad, for example—you can get away with less than 1,875 ptas. ($19.55).

EL LUARQUÉS, Ventura de la Vega, 16. Tel. 429-61-74.
Cuisine: ASTURIAN. **Reservations:** Recommended. **Metro:** Sol.
$ Prices: Appetizers 150–650 ptas. ($1.55–$6.75); main courses 500–1,550 ptas. ($5.20–$16.15); *menu del día* 1,600 ptas. ($16.65). No credit cards.
Open: Lunch Tues–Sun 1–4:30pm; dinner Tues–Sat 9–11:30pm. **Closed:** Aug.
This plain-looking restaurant is always full of knowing locals who come for the excellent home-cooked Asturian cuisine, including such fine bean dishes as garbanzos, fritos, judias, pintas, and fabada. It's best to reserve ahead.

LA TRUCHA, Núñez de Arce, 6. Tel. 532-08-82.
Cuisine: SPANISH/SEAFOOD. **Metro:** Sol.
$ Prices: Appetizers 160–2,475 ptas. ($1.65–$25.80); main courses 500–2,750 ptas. ($5.20–$28.65); *menu de la casa* 2,750 ptas. ($28.65). No credit cards.
Open: Lunch Mon–Sat 12:30–4pm; dinner Mon–Sat 7:30pm–midnight.
Closed: July.
As the name implies, the reason people come here is the trout. Trucha a la Trucha is a

deep-fried trout, split open and filled with chopped ham and garlic. Also popular for tapas.

MI PUEBLO, Costanilla de Santiago, 2. Tel. 248-20-73.
   Cuisine: SPANISH. **Metro:** Sol.
$ Prices: Appetizers 135–625 ptas. ($1.40–$6.50); main courses 825–1,570 ptas. ($8.60–$16.35); *menu del día* 1,500–1,775 ptas. ($15.60–$18.50). MC, V.
   Open: Lunch Tues–Sun 1:30–4:30pm; dinner Tues–Sat 8:30–11:30pm.
   Closed: First three weeks of Aug.
This country-style restaurant with an attractive red-tile floor and lots of local crafts decorating the walls offers Spanish *casera* (home-style) cuisine. Typical dishes include pollo provincial (chicken in tarragon sauce with rice), brocheta catalona (shish kebab with tender steak and vegetables), and rellenos madrileños (five vegetables stuffed with meat).

PICNIC SUPPLIES & WHERE TO EAT THEM

For one-stop shopping, go to the **supermarket** at El Corte Inglés (see "Savvy Shopping," below), visit **Casa Mingo** (see above) for their take-out chicken, cider, and salad (take-out service closed Sunday and holidays). Now go to El Retiro, Parque del Oeste, or the Casa de Campo.

WORTH THE EXTRA BUCKS

CASA BOTÍN, Cuchilleros, 17. Tel. 266-42-17.
   Cuisine: SPANISH. **Reservations:** Recommended. **Metro:** Sol.
$ Prices: Appetizers 380–2,325 ptas. ($3.95–$24.20); main courses 600–3,960 ptas. ($6.25–$41.25); *menu de la casa* 3,400 ptas. ($35.40). No credit cards.
   Open: Lunch daily 1–4pm; dinner daily 8pm–midnight.
A Madrid institution favored by locals and visitors alike, Casa Botín has been in business since the 16th century, and the oven that they use was built just a few hundred years later. Countless different rooms make up the restaurant, from the vaulted cellars to the rooms up the winding staircase. The decoration is very Spanish with lots of tiles, wood beams, and whitewashed walls. Each evening a *tuna* (a group of minstrels dressed in 16th-century costume) entertains—another ingredient that makes this a very special place.

6. ATTRACTIONS

SUGGESTED ITINERARIES

The magic of Madrid, capital of Spain for more than four centuries, will make itself felt as you absorb its history and culture. The variety of museums, the parks and gardens, and the glimpses into the golden age of Spain will intrigue and delight. The more time you have, the more you will enjoy it, but if your trip is limited, the following suggestions will help you spend your time wisely.

Always check hours of the museums before setting out, particularly at the smaller ones.

IF YOU HAVE ONE DAY Your first stop must be the Prado. World-famous and justifiably so, this 18th-century neoclassical building houses a notable collection of old masters, especially Spanish painting.

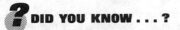

From the Prado, walk or take a bus up to Plaza de las Cibeles and then along Alcalá to the Puerta del Sol. Along the way you'll pass the Fountain of Cibeles, the Goddess of Fertility, and the magnificent Communications Palace (post office to you and me) opened in 1918.

In the Puerta del Sol, the heart of Madrid, Kilometer 0 marks all national roads radiating from Madrid. Calle de Preciados, a pedestrian shopping area, leads off to the north. You will notice a statue of a bear leaning against a tree, which is the emblem of Madrid. Opposite, the Comunidad de Madrid building is topped by a great clock, around which the New Year's crowds gather and try to swallow 12 grapes while the old year is rung out.

Continue west down calle Mayor a few blocks and you'll see a ramp leading up off the street through an archway into Plaza Mayor, where you can sit back, relax with a well-earned drink, and soak in the spirit of Madrid. (Unfortunately, even the cost of a few tapas is exorbitantly high in the plaza, so I don't recommend that you eat lunch here.) Philip III, who sits astride his horse in the center of the plaza, was responsible for the construction of this municipal focal point. Since the 17th century it has been the site of various dramas, from executions during the Spanish Inquisition to fiestas and bullfights. If you are a stamp or coin collector, come on Sunday morning when the surrounding arcades buzz with dealers.

Next on the list of "must-sees" is the Palacio Real (Royal Palace). Walk west on calle del Arenal from Puerta del Sol past the back of the Teatro Real to Plaza de Oriente and the palace directly in front of it. Go through the gate on the left and cross the courtyard to the far side for a stunning view of the Guadarrama Mountains. The palace has over 2,000 rooms but only about 60 are open to the public. The tour includes the State Apartments, the Library, Royal Pharmacy, Armory, and Carriage Museum.

IF YOU HAVE TWO DAYS   Spend your first day as above, but on the second day, leave Madrid for a visit to Toledo. See "Easy Excursions" for details of the sights there.

IF YOU HAVE THREE DAYS   Three days in Madrid will allow you to spend more time at the Prado and follow up your visit there by going to the Casón del Buen Retiro (included in your Prado ticket). There you can see Picasso's *Guernica*, along with his preliminary sketches for it, which shed a fascinating light on the development of this allegorical condemnation of war. Step across calle de Alfonso XII and into the Parque del Retiro, which is delightful at any time but particularly from midday on Sunday when Madrileños, dressed in their best, are outside for the *paseo*, and the main thoroughfares are crowded with mimes, musicians, and acrobats. There is something for everyone here in the park, with formal landscaped gardens and densely wooded areas, boating on the lake, and outdoor bars for people-watching.

On Day 2 visit Toledo as above and on Day 3 go to the Royal Palace in the morning as described above, spend more time exploring the vicinity of Plaza Mayor, visit the nearby covered market of San Miguel (closes at 2pm), and then wander down calle Mayor to see Plaza de la Villa, Madrid's City Hall. The Convento de las Descalzas Reales, founded by Juana de Austria, is quite sumptuous and deserves a visit. The wealth of art at this still-functioning convent is the bequest of its aristocratic residents.

IF YOU HAVE FIVE DAYS   Spend your first three days as described above. On Day 4 choose between a number of fascinating museums, depending on your interest. If you enjoy tapestries, visit the Real Fábrica de Tapices (Royal Tapestry Factory), where tapestries and rugs have been made the same way since the 15th century. The Museo de Artes Decorativas highlights Spanish trends in the decorative arts through the centuries with an emphasis on ceramics. At the Museo Lázaro Galdiano you'll see one man's collection of art including paintings, sculpture, silverware, and marvelous enamels and ivories, all of which he left to the state with his palace. The Museo Sorolla, which is in the artist's house, displays numerous examples of this Valencian impressionist's work from the turn of the century. Finally, for archeology enthusiasts, the Museo Arqueológico Nacional is excellent, especially the Iberian and classical antiquities.

On your final day, take another trip out of Madrid to Philip II's Monasterio de San Lorenzo del Escorial (see "Easy Excursions," below, for travel details). In the foothills of the Guadarrama Mountains, this somber granite testament to Philip and pantheon for Spanish kings dominates the plains below. Along with Philip's austere apartments, the basilica, and museum, you can visit the great library with its beautifully illuminated manuscripts.

TOP ATTRACTIONS

EL PRADO, Paseo del Prado. Tel. 420-28-36.

⭐ Spanish painting from the 12th to the 18th centuries as well as Italian masters and painters from the Venetian and Flemish schools. Only a small portion of the holdings are on display at any given time.

If you have a limited amount of time to enjoy this awe-inspiring museum, don't miss the works of Goya, Velázquez, and El Greco, whose *Adoration of the Shepherds* enthralls with its detail and emotion. In the Velázquez rooms, see his portrait of *Don Baltasar Carlos*, the expressions on the faces of *Los Borrachos* (The Drunkards), and from the last years of his life, *Las Meninas*. Both Velázquez and Goya were court painters, hence the multitude of their paintings here. Goya's cartoons are especially popular, though his portraits and his series of "Black Paintings" also have their admirers. Notice the effect he creates when painting lace—it almost looks translucent. Other famous works to look for are those of the Spanish painters Ribera, Zurbarán, and Murillo, as well as masterpieces by Hieronymus Bosch (*The Garden of Earthly Delights*), Dürer, Titian, Tintoretto, Rubens, and van Dyck.

When you have exhausted the Prado, walk up the hill to the Casón del Buen Retiro (included on your ticket) to see Picasso's *Guernica*.

Admission: 450 ptas. ($4.70).

Open: Tues–Sat 9am–7pm, Sun 9am–2pm. **Closed:** Jan 1, Good Friday, May 1, Dec 25. **Metro:** Atocha or Banco de España. **Bus:** 10, 14, 27, 34, 37, 45, or M6.

PALACIO REAL (Royal Palace), calle de Bailen. Tel. 248-74-04.

⭐ Built by Philip V on the site of the medieval Alcázar, which burned down in the mid-18th century, the opulent Royal Palace, or Palacio de Oriente, was designed by Giovan Battista Sacchetti in the baroque and neoclassical style. Of particular note are Italian architect Sabatini's majestic staircase, the many wonderful chandeliers, some of which were made locally at La Granja, Gasparini's flamboyant rococo drawing room, the Throne Room with its ceiling by Tiepolo, and the great collection of tapestries.

Although King Juan Carlos declined to live here, the palace is still used for state functions, and if you're lucky you may see the State Dining Room laid for a banquet; the table, which can seat over 100 guests, stretches off into the distance, gleaming with silver, gold, and cut glass. Next door is the Clock Room, where over 60 clocks, mostly French, all strike the hour together.

As well as the palace apartments, you can also see the library, coin and music museums, the Royal Pharmacy, the Armory, and the Carriage Museum.

You must take a guided tour, and if there are enough English speakers they will use a bilingual guide.

Admission: Palace, 550 ptas. ($5.70), including the State Apartments, Library, and Armory; Carriage Museum, 200 ptas. ($2.10); Royal Pharmacy, free.

Open: Mon–Sat 9:30am–5:15pm, Sun 9am–3pm. **Closed:** Jan 1, Jan 6, Good Friday, May 1, Dec 25, and for State Receptions. **Metro:** Opera or Plaza de España. **Bus:** 3, 25, 33, 39, or M4.

CONVENTO DE LAS DESCALZAS REALES, Plaza de las Descalzas, 3. Tel. 248-74-04.

Located in the heart of Old Madrid, this richly decorated royal convent was founded in the mid-16th century in the palace where Juana of Austria, Philip II's sister, was born. She used it as a retreat and brought the Poor Clare nuns here. For many years the convent sheltered only royal women and thus it acquired an immense wealth of religious artwork, including tapestries, sculpture, and paintings by Rubens, Brueghel the elder, Gerard David, and Titian. The main staircase features trompe l'oeil wall paintings and frescoes.

Admission: 375 ptas. ($3.90).

Open: Tues–Thurs 10:30am–12:30pm and 4–5:30pm, Fri–Sat 10:30am–12:30pm, Sun 11am–1:30pm. **Closed:** Jan 1, Holy Week, May 1, Dec 24–25. **Metro:** Sol, Callao, or Opera. **Bus:** 1, 2, 5, 20, 46, 52, 53, 74, M1, M2, M3, M5, or M10.

REAL FÁBRICA DE TAPICES (Royal Tapestry Factory), Fuenterrabia, 2. Tel. 551-34-00.

★ Step back in time to see tapestries being made as they were when the factory opened in the 18th century. Many of the tapestries in the Palacio Real or at El Escorial were made here. The tour takes you first through a room where custom-made carpets of incredible dimensions are created, then to the room where ancient tapestries are painstakingly mended. The final stop is the room where new tapestries are made on vast antique wooden looms. The tour is in Spanish, but just to observe is illuminating and fascinating.

Admission: 75 ptas. (80¢).

Open: Mon–Fri 9am–12:30pm. **Closed:** Aug. **Metro:** Menéndez Pelayo. **Bus:** 10, 14, 26, 32, 37, C, or M9.

MUSEO DE ARTES DECORATIVAS (National Museum of Decorative Arts), Montalban, 12. Tel. 521-34-40.

Located just off Plaza de las Cibeles, this museum is stuffed with furniture, leatherwork, wall hangings, ceramics, porcelain, glass, jewelry, toys, dollhouses, clothes, and lace. After the first floor the museum progresses in chronological order, tracing the development of Spanish decoration from the 16th to the 19th century. By the time you reach the fifth floor, you may be exhausted both physically and mentally, but the variety of objects will continue to intrigue and delight.

Admission: 225 ptas. ($2.35).

Open: Tues–Fri 9am–3pm, Sat–Sun 10am–2pm. **Closed:** Weekday hols. **Metro:** Banco de España. **Bus:** 14, 27, 34, 37, 45, or M6.

MUSEO LÁZARO GALDIANO, Serrano, 122. Tel. 561-60-84.

Madrid was indeed fortunate to be the beneficiary of patron of the arts José Lázaro Galdiano. When he died, he left the city his turn-of-the-century house, complete with his vast private collection. Every floor attests to his devotion to art: there are paintings from Spain's golden period including works by El Greco, Ribera, Zurbarán, Murillo, and Goya; the Italians are represented by Guardi, Tiepolo, and Leonardo da Vinci; and there are the English painters too, including Gainsborough and Constable. There are also tapestries, embroideries, gold- and silverwork, fans, jewelry, and a fascinating collection of enamels and ivories.

Admission: 325 ptas. ($3.40).

Open: Tues–Sun 10am–2pm. **Closed:** Hols and Aug. **Metro:** Avenida America. **Bus:** 9, 16, 19, 51, or 89.

SPAIN

Madrid

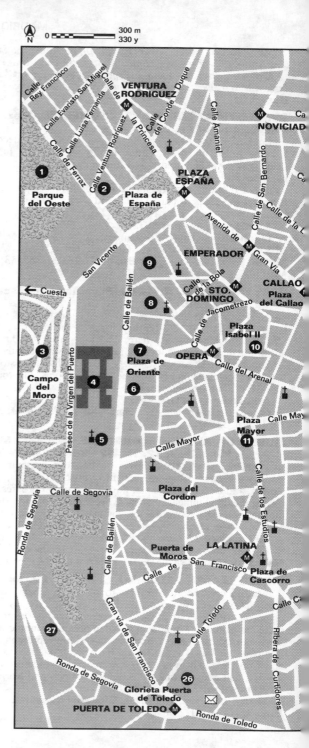

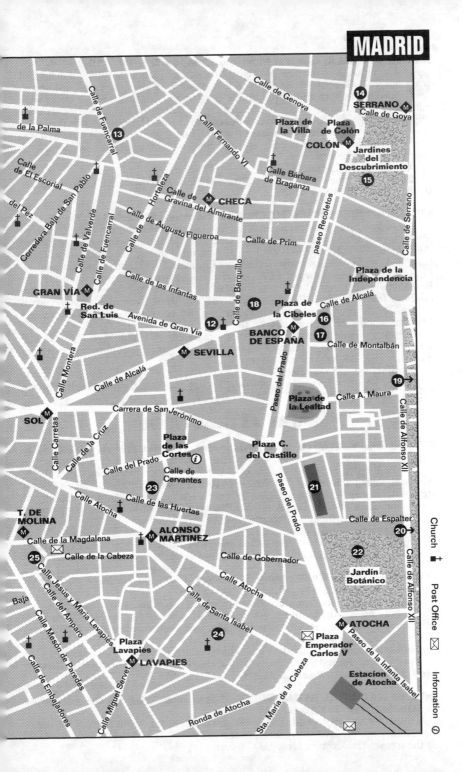

MUSEO SOROLLA, General Martínez Campos, 37. Tel. 410-15-84.

⭐ The museum of the turn-of-the-century painter Joaquín Sorolla is a delightful surprise, especially after the grandeur of some of the museums listed above. Sorolla was born and reared on the coast at Valencia and his later works were influenced by the French impressionists. Many are seascapes, and he had a particular way of painting water so that it appears wet on the canvas. The museum is in the house where he lived and painted, and it has been kept, on the ground floor at least, as it was when he died. He was an avid collector, and along with his paintings you'll see a large quantity of Spanish ceramics.

Admission: 225 ptas. ($2.35).

Open: Tues–Sun 10am–2:30pm. **Closed:** Hols. **Metro:** Rubén Dario or Iglesia. **Bus:** 5, 7, 16, 61, 40, or M3.

MUSEO ARQUEOLÓGICO NACIONAL, Serrano, 13. Tel. 577-79-12.

Located in the same vast building as the National Library, the National Archeological Museum houses an impressive array of antiquities from prehistory to the Middle Ages. Arranged chronologically on three floors, the displays are clearly labeled. As well as Iberian artifacts, there are Egyptian, Greek, and Roman antiquities. Look for the famous *Lady of Elche,* a delightful example of Iberian sculpture; the Roman mosaic depicting the months and seasons; the Visigothic bronzes and funerary offerings from Mérida (a Roman stronghold), and some fascinating votive crowns. Etruscan pottery and Greek vases; ivory, bronze and iron ware; Gothic sculpture; and Mudéjar woodwork further enhance the collection.

Outside the entrance, the Caves of Altamira have been faithfully reproduced, and since tourists are no longer allowed into the real thing, this is your chance to marvel at these simulated 15,000-year-old paintings.

Admission: 225 ptas. ($2.35).

Open: Tues–Sat 9:30am–8:30pm, Sun 9:30am–2:30pm. **Closed:** Hols. **Metro:** Serrano or Retiro. **Bus:** 1, 9, 19, 51, 74, or M2.

MORE ATTRACTIONS

MUSEO DEL EJÉRCITO (Army Museum), Méndez Núñez, 1. Tel. 522-89-77.

One of the two remaining buildings of the Buen Retiro Palace houses the Army Museum, which was founded by Manuel Godoy, who made his spectacular climb from obscurity into the arms of Carlos IV's wife, Maria Luisa of Parma. Weaponry of every kind, from El Cid's sword to Civil War firearms, is displayed alongside armor, uniforms, flags, and thousands of other bits of memorabilia.

Admission: 75 ptas. (80¢).

Open: Tues–Sun 10am–2pm. **Closed:** Holy Week, May 1, Dec 25. **Metro:** Banco de España. **Bus:** 15, 19, 27, 34, 37, or 45.

MUSEO TAURINO (Bullfighting Museum), Plaza de las Ventas, Alcalá, 237. Tel. 255-18-57.

A must-see for the aficionado, the Bullfighting Museum is located behind Las Ventas bullring. Anything and everything to do with bullfighting is here—from busts of famous fighters to heads of famous bulls, from swords and capes to sketches, paintings, and scale models.

Admission: Free (though that may change when remodeling is complete).

Open: Tues–Fri and Sun 9am–2pm (this, too, may change, so call first). **Closed:** Hols. **Metro:** Ventas. **Bus:** 12, 21, 38, 53, M1, or M8.

MUSEO NACIONAL REINA SOFIA, Santa Isabel, 52 (at the corner of Atocha). Tel. 467-50-62.

Called the "MOMA of Madrid," this newly opened museum displays the art of our century (mostly Spanish, by such masters as Picasso, Dalí, Miró, Gris, and Solana) in the former 18th-century Hospital General.

Admission: 450 ptas. ($4.70).
Open: Wed–Mon 10am–9pm. **Metro:** Atocha. **Bus:** 6, 14, 26, 27, 32, 45, 57, or C.

CASA DE LOPE DE VEGA (Lope de Vega's House), Cervantes, 11. Tel. 429-92-16.

Playwright extraordinaire of the 17th century, Lope de Vega lived in this house on, funnily enough, calle Cervantes. The house has been carefully reconstructed and is now a national monument. Inside you can see his study, bedroom, and kitchen, and outside, his garden.

Note: Currently being completely renovated, this museum may still be closed when you arrive.

Admission: 75 ptas. (80¢).
Open: Tues and Thurs 10am–2pm. **Closed:** July 15–Sept 15. **Metro:** Antón Martín. **Bus:** 6, 26, 32, 57, or M9.

MUSEO MUNICIPAL, Fuencarral, 78. Tel. 522-57-32.

Here the history of Madrid is explained through paintings and prints, documents, scale models, carriages, and costumes. Just as interesting is the amazing rococo doorway, designed by Pedro de Ribera to grace what was formerly a hospice for the city's poor.

Admission: Free.
Open: Tues–Sun 10am–2pm. **Closed:** Hols. **Metro:** Tribunal. **Bus:** 3, 7, 40, or M10.

MUSEO NAVAL, Paseo del Prado, 5. Tel. 521-04-19.

For most Americans the highlight of this museum is Juan de la Cosa's map, drawn in 1500, on which America appears for the first time. There are also some wonderful models of ships, huge paintings of sea battles, and lots of nautical instruments. A real treasure trove for the naval buff.

Admission: Free.
Open: Tues–Sun 10:30am–1:30pm. **Closed:** Jan 1 and Dec 25. **Metro:** Banco de España. **Bus:** 10, 14, 27, 34, 37, 45, or M6.

PANTEÓN DE GOYA, Glorieta de San Antonio de la Florida. Tel. 542-07-22.

Charles IV commissioned Goya to decorate the ceiling in the chapel on the right. The frescoes depict the story of St. Anthony of Padua, with cheeky-looking cherubs and blowzy women who were modeled after society people of the day. Goya is buried here, but somehow his head got lost in transit from Bordeaux where he was first interred.

Note: The Pantheon is currently undergoing restoration, so check with the tourist office before you go.

Admission: 100 ptas. ($1.05).
Open: Summer, Thurs–Tues 10am–1pm and 4–7pm; winter, Thurs–Tues 10am–2pm and 4–8pm. **Closed:** Hols. **Metro:** Norte. **Bus:** 41, 46, 75, or C.

PARQUE DE ATRACCIONES, Casa de Campo. Tel. 463-29-00.

Not merely a marvelous funfair for all ages, the Parque de Atracciones, set in the spacious Casa de Campo, also has an auditorium that stages spectacular shows in the summer (free with admission). Restaurants, electronic games, and a cinema round out the entertainment.

Admission: 200 ptas. ($2.10) adults, 50 ptas. (50¢) children; including three attractions, 650 ptas. ($6.75) adults, 350 ptas. ($3.65) children; global admission including all attractions, 1,325 ptas. ($13.80).

Open: Apr–June, Tues–Fri 3–9 or 11pm, Sat noon–9pm or midnight, Sun 11am–10 or 11pm; July–Aug, Tues–Fri 6pm–1am, Sat 6pm–2am, Sun noon–1am; Sept, Tues–Sun hours vary greatly; Oct–Mar, Sat–Sun noon–8pm. Call first to verify times. **Closed:** Public hols. **Metro:** Batán. **Bus:** 33 (from Plaza de Isabel II) or 65, and on Sun also from Ventas, Puente de Vallecas, and Estrecho.

MUSEO ROMÁNTICO (Romantic Museum), San Mateo, 13. Tel. 448-10-45.

This museum houses a charming collection of furniture, paintings, and objets d'art from the 19th century. It was established during the 1920s by the Marquis of La Vega Inclán in a baroque house of the 18th century.

Admission: 225 ptas. ($2.35); free for students and residents of EC countries.

Open: Tues–Sat and every other Sun 9am–2:30pm. **Closed:** Hols and Aug. **Metro:** Alonso Martínez. **Bus:** 37, 40, or M10.

REAL ACADEMIA DE BELLAS ARTES DE SAN FERNANDO (Royal Academy of Fine Arts of San Fernando), Alcalá, 13. Tel. 532-15-46.

Located just east of the Puerto del Sol, this center offers a wide variety of works by such artists as El Greco, Sorolla, Rubens, and Fragonard, plus one room filled with Goyas. An unusual and inexpensive souvenir is a Goya print made from the original plate.

Admission: 225 ptas. ($2.35).

Open: Tues–Fri 9am–7pm, Sat–Mon 9am–3pm. **Metro:** Sol or Sevilla. **Bus:** 3, 5, 15, 20, 51, 52, or M12.

MUSEO DE LAS FIGURAS DE CERA (Wax Museum), Paseo de Recoletos, 41. Tel. 308-08-25.

More than 400 wax figures will thrill and amuse you in this museum under Centro Colón. Prominently featured are scenes from *Don Quixote,* famous bullfighters, and a host of famous and not-so-famous historical and contemporary personages.

Admission: 650 ptas. ($6.75) adults; 450 ptas. ($4.70) children 4–12.

Open: Daily 10:30am–2pm and 4–8:30pm (ticket window closes at 1:30pm and 8pm). **Metro:** Colón. **Bus:** 5, 14, 27, 45, 53, M6, or M7.

ZOO, Casa de Campo. Tel. 711-99-50 or 711-54-16.

Madrid's zoo is one of Europe's best. Most of the animals are housed in attractive, well-kept open pens, separated from the public by ditches. Over 2,000 mammals, birds, and reptiles are grouped according to their continent of origin. A highlight is the two pandas, Chang-Chang and his offspring, Chu-Lin, who was the first panda to be born in captivity in Europe; sadly, his mother died. The Dolphin Show (at 1 and 5pm) is also worth your attention.

Admission: 800 ptas. ($8.35) adults, 540 ptas. ($5.60) children 3–8 and seniors over 65.

Open: Nov–Feb, daily 10:30am–6:30pm; Mar–Oct, daily 10:30–7pm (ticket office closes half an hour earlier). **Metro:** Batán. **Bus:** 33 from Plaza de Isabel II, and on Sun and hols also from Ventas, Puente de Vallecas, and Estrecho.

PARKS & GARDENS

Parque del Retiro means a park to retire in, and this 321-acre oasis is just that. Along with the Casón del Buen Retiro and the building housing the Army Museum, this is all that is left of a 17th-century palace built by Philip IV. Now the tree-lined avenues, formal rose garden, Crystal Palace, boating lake, monuments, and grottoes offer a tranquil retreat from the hubbub of the city. Madrileños like to see and be seen, and on the weekend the whole family dresses up for the *paseo* through this park.

To the south of the Prado is the **Jardín Botánico**, in its current location since the 18th century, where visitors can enjoy a wide range of exotic flora. North and west of the Royal Palace, respectively, you'll find the **Jardines de Sabatini** and the **Campo del Moro.** Just to the north of these are **Parque del Oeste (West Park)** and **La Rosaleda (Rose Garden)** and just north of them on Paseo Pintor Rosales, several open-air bars.

The **Casa de Campo,** west of the city, is an enormous playground for all Madrileños. Here you will find the zoo, the Parque de Atracciones, IFEMA (an exhibition center), a boating lake, sports center, restaurants, and plenty of space to get away from it all.

SPECIAL-INTEREST SIGHTSEEING

If you have a special interest, in history or architecture for example, visit the **Patronato Municipal de Turismo** (Municipal Tourist Board) at calle Mayor, 69 (tel. 580-00-00). They will provide information and help on more than 40 special-interest routes to follow.

A STROLL THROUGH MADRID

Arm yourself with a good map from the tourist office, allow yourself at least an hour (more to meander), and take yourself off to the Retiro Park to the Puerta de Felipe IV, halfway down on calle Alfonso XII.

With your back to the park, you are facing the **Casón del Buen Retiro,** once part of the huge Palace of the Buen Retiro built in 1631, most of which was destroyed by the French during the War of Independence (1808–14). The Casón, part of the Prado, now houses a small collection of 19th-century Spanish painting, as well as Picasso's *Guernica*. With the Casón on your left, walk west down calle de Felipe IV past the neo classical **Army Museum,** (see "More Attractions," above) on your right. On your left is the **Royal Spanish Academy,** built later, but in the same style as the Casón. (The first woman member was elected as recently as 1979.) Next on your left is the **Church of San Jerónimo El Real.** This church has always had strong royal connections and was moved from its original site near the river to the more healthy heights of the Prado by Isabel and Ferdinand. Built in 1505 in the Gothic style, it had a room known as *cuarto viejo,* where Spanish monarchs could retire in times of mourning and at Lent. Here princes of Asturias were sworn in, Alfonso XIII was married, and his grandson, the current King Juan Carlos, celebrated his accession to the throne in 1975.

You will recognize the **Prado Museum** (see "Top Attractions," above), down the hill to your left, also built in the neoclassical style. It consists of three elements—the rotunda on the north side, the temple in the middle, and the palace overlooking the Botanical Gardens. Construction was begun in 1796, but it, too, suffered during the War of Independence, and it was not finished until María Isabel de Braganza, wife of Ferdinand VII, got busy in 1814. In 1819 it opened as an art gallery with 311 pictures. Continuing west, cross over Paseo del Prado at Plaza Cánovas del Castillo. On your right is the **Palace of Villahermosa,** now housing numerous paintings from Baron Heinrich von Thyssen's collection.

On your left is the refurbished **Palace Hotel,** on the site of the former Lerma Palace. Just past the Palacio Villahermosa on the right is the **Palacio del Congresso de Diputados** overlooking **Plaza de las Cortes.** The neoclassical Spanish parliament building was constructed between 1843 and 1850. The two rather fierce-looking lions guarding the entrance were made from bronze cannons taken from the Moors during the African wars.

Fork left on calle del Prado (if you want to pop into a tourist office, there's one on the corner of Duque Medinaceli). Take the next left onto calle de San Agustin, then the first right onto calle de Cervantes, which takes you past **Lope de Vega's House** at no. 11 (see "More Attractions," above). A right turn at the end onto calle del León brings you back to calle del Prado. Just across the street is the **Ateneo,** marked by two lanterns, a gathering place for writers since 1835. Continue west along calle del Prado to **Plaza Santa Ana,** famous for its cafés. On your right as you enter the square is the **Teatro Español,** where plays have been performed since 1582; the current emphasis is on classic Spanish works. Walk west along the left side of the plaza through Plaza del Angel, along the end of calle de las Huertas, turn left, and then right onto calle de Atocha, traversing Plaza Jacinto Benavente as you go.

At Plaza de Provincia, walk past the **Church of Santa Cruz,** on your left, to the **Ministry of Foreign Affairs,** also on your left. This building is strictly neoclassical in style, but with an Italian portal, and once a place to be feared as the court prison.

Continue west along calle de Atocha into **Plaza Mayor,** where you deserve to rest your feet in preparation for the next leg.

Take the right-hand exit on the north side and cross calle Mayor onto calle Bordadores. Walk north on Bordadores, cross calle del Arenal, and with the **Church of San Ginés** on your right, go north on calle San Martín to Plaza San Martín on your left and Plaza de las Descalzas on your right. Straight ahead is the **Monastery of Descalzas Reales** (see "Top Attractions," above). On the west side of Plaza San Martín, pick up calle de la Flora and walk west; it then becomes calle de la Priora. On your left as you pass calle Donados is the little chapel of **El Niño de Remedio,** its walls lined with votive offerings from those on whom miracles were bestowed after praying to the image of the Child Jesus. Continue west along calle de la Priora to **Plaza de Isabel II,** where her statue stands in the middle. On the far side of the plaza is the back entrance of the Teatro Real. Walk up calle de Arrieta to **Plaza de la Encarnación** and the **Monastery** (see above). From the plaza turn left (south) onto calle de la Pavia and come out into Plaza de Oriente. The front entrance of the **Teatro Real** is on your left. Built in the mid-19th century on a site that was once outside the city walls and the location of the local washhouse, this was until recently the home of the National Orchestra of Spain; it is undergoing renovation and will open as the new home of Madrid's opera.

Plaza de Oriente seems rather a misnomer, being on the west (not east) side of the city (from the Royal Palace's point of view it is, of course, on the east side). In the middle of the plaza sits Philip IV on his rearing horse. This position proved technically difficult for sculptor Pedro Tacco, so on the recommendation of his friend Galileo, he made the rear legs solid metal and left the front ones hollow. The **Royal Palace** sits magnificently on the far side of the plaza. On the plaza's south side is the unfinished cathedral of Madrid called **Nuestra Señora de la Almudena,** begun in 1881, but interrupted in 1931. Only since 1985 were enough funds amassed to begin building again.

Now you can take a seat and survey the whole scene from the outdoor Café de Oriente, which is to the right of the Teatro Real.

ORGANIZED TOURS

Three bus companies offer a variety of tours, ranging from a half-day panoramic tour of Madrid to day-long excursions to such places as Toledo, El Escorial, and Segovia. A morning tour of Madrid costs 4,250 ptas. ($44.25) and a full-day tour to Toledo is 7,000 ptas. ($72.90). For further information, consult one of these three centrally located offices: **Juliá Tours,** Gran Vía, 68 (tel. 248-96-05); **Pullmantur,** Plaza de Oriente, 8 (tel. 241-18-01); and **Trapsatur,** San Bernardo, 23 (tel. 542-66-66).

SPECIAL & FREE EVENTS

Every year Madrid launches itself into fiesta after fiesta, at which time the citizens enjoy parades, dancing in the streets, craft fairs, and concerts. You should check the *Guía del Ocio* for full details, but the following are the highlights:

Around Christmas and New Year's the city is alive with excitement which culminates in a great gathering around the big clock in the Puerta del Sol on **New Year's Eve.** Arm yourself with 12 grapes and join in the effort to eat them before the clock stops striking midnight. If you succeed, it is said that you'll have good luck all year (the secret is to take the pits out first). On January 5 the **Three Kings (Los Reyes)** arrive (by helicopter nowadays) for a marvelous parade on horseback through the streets of Madrid, during which the children are showered with candy.

In March, the **Madrid Theater Festival** attracts a galaxy of international companies. On the Saturday before Lent begins, hundreds of gaily decorated floats parade down Paseo de la Castellana in a **Carnaval** procession. **Holy Week (Semana Santa)** is celebrated with due solemnity, and processions of the penitents take place all over Madrid, including around the Puerta del Sol. Around **Easter** there is a great gathering of horses and their riders from Seville, who step through the streets attired in colorful traditional style, beginning and ending in the Retiro Park.

The most important festival celebrates the patron saint of Madrid, **San Isidro,** in the middle of May, with a protracted program of activities and the best bullfights of the year. **"Veranos de la Villa"** provides summer entertainment for the long, warm evenings, including open-air movies at the Cine del Retiro and flamenco shows in another corner of the park. Fall brings Madrid's acclaimed **jazz festival** and the **Feriarte,** Spain's major antiques fair.

The **Fundación Juan March,** Castelló, 77 (tel. 435-42-40), offers free concerts from fall to spring, on Monday and Saturday at noon and on Wednesday at 7:30pm, changing the theme monthly.

7. SAVVY SHOPPING

Madrid's shopping selection is enormous and the service, particularly in the smaller stores, is friendly. You will find everything from modish clothes boutiques to pipe shops between Gran Vía and the Puerta del Sol along the two pedestrian walkways— **calle Preciados** and **calle Carmen.** If you feel like a splurge or just a bit of upscale window-shopping, head for the **Salamanca district,** between Serrano and Velázquez, Goya and Juan Bravo, where all the ritzy designer stores compete for attention. The developing **AZCA area,** between Paseo de la Castellana and Orense, Raimundo Fernández Villaverde and avenida General Perón, is also worth a visit (Metro: Nuevos Ministerios) for its range of stores, El Corte Inglés department store, and the new high-fashion mall, La Moda. A North American–style mall is to be found at La Vaguada. Known as **Madrid-2** (Metro: Barrio del Pilar), you will find over 350 stores offering just about everything you could want, including an excellent market.

Right across from the Prado in the lower reaches of the Palace Hotel is **La Galeria del Prado,** where gleaming marble, brass, glass, and plants set the stage for Madrid's most elegant stores. The mercado **Puerta de Toledo,** on the site of the old Fish Market, purveys all the latest trends in fashion and design, the best of Spanish crafts and contemporary jewelry, and quantities of antiques in over 150 expensive shops. Open Tuesday through Saturday from 11:30am to 9pm and on Sunday and holidays from 11:30am to 3pm.

The major department stores are **El Corte Inglés** and **Galerias Preciados,** both of which have bargain basements (Oportunidades) in some of their stores. Branches of El Corte Inglés include Preciados, 3; Goya, 76; Princesa, 40; and Raimundo Fernández Villaverde, 79 (at the corner of Paseo de la Castellana). Galerias Preciados is at Plaza del Callao, 2; Goya, 85; Arapiles, 10; Ortega y Gasset, 2 (at the corner of Serrano); and Madrid-2/La Vaguada. Both these stores have some English-speaking salespeople and offer information on VAT refunds, obtainable only on single purchases of more than 78,800 ptas. ($820.85). If you're leaving the country from Madrid airport, you can obtain a refund from the Banco Exterior de España (located through Passport Control) upon presentation of the store's signed form subsequently stamped by Spanish Customs.

El Corte Inglés, Galerias Preciados, and the larger shopping centers are open from 10am to 9pm; however, almost everything else closes for lunch at 1:30 or 2pm and doesn't reopen until 5pm. In July and August many stores close on Saturday afternoon, and smaller ones may even close down completely for their month's vacation.

January to February and July are the times for the big sales (*rebajas*), when every store in Madrid offers tremendous discounts that increase as the month proceeds.

If it's a bargain you're after, head for Madrid's flea market, **✪ El Rastro,** in the triangle between San Isidro Cathedral, Puerta de Toledo, and Glorieta de Embajadores. Ribera de Curtidores is its main street. On Sunday mornings thousands of Madrileños throng these streets to purchase everything from a songbird to an old masterpiece. Saturday morning is quieter and a better time for browsing through the antiques shops and secondhand stalls. You are expected to bargain. Watch your purse or wallet.

---

8. EVENING ENTERTAINMENT

THE PERFORMING ARTS

Madrid's performing arts are undergoing a renaissance. At any one time you can enjoy a diverse selection ranging from traditional Hispanic theater to grand opera to contemporary dance. And, of course, there is the ever-popular zarzuela, a uniquely Spanish operetta. Theater tickets range from 900 to 2,500 ptas. ($9.35 to $26.05), and on certain days of the week (usually Wednesday, or Sunday's first performance) you can get up to a 50% discount—check in the **Guía del Ocio.** The first performance is around 7:30pm, the second at 10:30pm.

It's best to go to the theater to buy tickets, since agencies charge a considerable markup. If the theater of your choice is sold out, you may be able to get tickets at the **Localidades Galicia,** at Plaza del Carmen, 1 (tel. 531-27-32), to the left of the Madrid Multicine. It's open Tuesday through Sunday from 10am to 1pm and 4:30 to 7:30pm (closed Monday and holidays). It also sells bullfight and soccer tickets.

THEATER, OPERA & ZARZUELA

TEATRO CALDERON, Atocha, 18. Tel. 369-14-34.
This popular spot produces good revues, plus flamenco, folkloric, and singing festivals.
Metro: Tirso de Molina.

TEATRO DE LA COMEDIA, Príncipe, 14. Tel. 521-49-31.
This theater shows classic Spanish plays by such authors as García Lorca and Valle Inclán.
Metro: Sevilla.

TEATRO ESPAÑOL, Príncipe, 25. Tel. 429-62-97.
Along with the Teatro María Guerrero, this is the official state theater, and is subsidized as such. Classic plays and visiting theater companies are featured as well as the winning play of the important annual Lope de Vega prize.
Metro: Sevilla.

TEATRO MARÍA GUERRERO, Tamayo y Baus, 4. Tel. 319-47-69.
Named after the actress, this state-sponsored theater is also home to the classics.
Metro: Banco de España.

TEATRO LIRICO NACIONAL LA ZARZUELA, Jovellanos, 4. Tel. 429-82-25.
The opera is currently located here until its new home at the Teatro Real is finished in 1992. As its name implies, this is where you come for the zarzuela, and ballet, too.
Metro: Banco de España or Sevilla.

TEATRO DE LA VILLA DE MADRID, Plaza de Colón, Jardines del Descubrimiento. Tel. 575-60-80.
Run by City Hall, this smallish theater underneath the plaza puts on plays and concerts of all kinds, and is the scene of much activity during the Fall Festival (Festival del Otoño).
Metro: Colón.

NUEVO APOLO, Plaza de Tirso de Molina, 1. Tel. 369-14-67.
This privately run theater shows mainly musicals and ballet, plus some zarzuela.
Metro: Tirso de Molina.

LA LATINA, Plaza de la Cebada, 2. Tel. 265-28-35.

This showplace presents popular revues and musicals.
Metro: Latina.

LA CORRALA, Sombrerete at the corner of Mesón de Paredes.
In the summer months, enjoy your zarzuela outside while munching your dinner.
Check with the tourist office for what's on when. The show usually starts at 10:30pm.
Prices: 2,100 ptas. ($21.85) including dinner, 1,625 ptas. ($16.90) including one
drink; half price for seniors and children.
Metro: Lavapies.

CLASSICAL MUSIC

Auditorio Nacional de Música (National Auditorium of Music), Príncipe de
Vergara, 146 (tel. 337-01-00). Three years ago the National Orchestra of Spain moved
into these new quarters, where 2,000 music lovers can enjoy the best of Spanish and
international classical music in a modern and functional setting of wood and marble
with fantastic acoustics. There is also a smaller concert hall, seating 600. Take the
metro to Cruz del Rayo.

FLAMENCO SHOWS

Although not the home of flamenco, Madrid's *tablaos* are enormous fun, but
expensive. For the best value, try the **Torres Bermejas,** Mesonero Romanos, 11
(tel. 532-33-22); **Corral de la Morería,** Morería, 17 (tel. 265-84-46); or the **Café
de Chinitas,** Torija, 7 (tel. 248-51-35). Doors usually open at 9 or 9:30pm and the
show starts at about 10:45pm and ends at 12:30am or even later. The cheapest dinner
at Torres Bermejas is 9,365 ptas. ($97.40), at the Corral the minimum charge is 3,190
ptas. ($33.20), and at the Café de Chinitas, 3,935 ptas. ($41), including one drink.

MOVIES

Recently released movies come to Madrid swiftly. Check in the *Guía del Ocio* or
Friday's *Guía de Diário 16* for what's on.
Undubbed movies (labeled "V.O." in the listings) can be found at: **Alexandra,**
San Bernardo, 29 (tel. 542-29-12); **Alphaville** (four cinemas), Martín de los Héroes,
14 (tel. 248-72-33); **Bellas Artes,** Marqués de Casa Ríera, 2 (tel. 522-50-92);
Bogart, Cedaceros, 7 (tel. 429-80-42); **California,** Andrés Mellado, 47 (tel.
244-00-58); **Infantas,** Infantas, 21 (tel. 522-56-78); and **Renoir** (five cinemas),
Martín de los Héroes, 12 (tel. 248-57-60).
For classic movies, film commentaries, and foreign films, **Filmoteca,** in the Cine
Doré, Santa Isabel, 3 (tel. 227-38-66), is the place to go. Movies are generally shown in
their original language. Tickets cost 170 ptas. ($1.75); a *bono* for 10 sessions is 1,455
ptas. ($15.20). There's a bar, restaurant, and library here, too.

BARS

PLAZA SANTA ANA

CERVECERÍA ALEMANA, Plaza de Santa Ana, 6. Tel. 429-70-33.
As its name suggests, this was a popular haunt of local Germans (it has been in
business since 1904), but it's now packed with one and all at any time. Its bullfighting
prints on wood-paneled walls, marble-top tables, and beamed ceiling conjure a
vintage atmosphere.
Open: Sun–Mon and Wed–Thurs 9am–12:30am, Fri–Sat 9am–1:30am.

CERVECERÍA SANTA ANA, Plaza de Santa Ana, 10. Tel. 429-43-56.

Two doors up from the Alemana, a congenial crowd hangs out in this no-seat bar, which also serves good tapas. It's very popular with students, maybe because the beer is some of the cheapest.

Prices: Beer about 100 ptas. ($1.05).

Open: Thurs–Tues 10am–1am.

LOS GABRIELES, Echegaray, 17. Tel. 429-62-61.

Pop in here for a quick drink just to admire the extraordinary variety of clashing tiles covering the walls.

Open: Daily noon–2am.

VIVA MADRID, Manuel Fernández González, 7. Tel. 410-55-35.

Another student hangout, with a wonderful facade of Spanish tiles, Viva Madrid serves good sandwiches, burgers, etc.

Open: Sun–Fri noon–1am, Sat noon–2am.

HUERTAS

For bar-hopping, you can't do better than the calle de las Huertas area. Some favorites are:

CASA ALBERTO, calle de las Huertas, 18. Tel. 429-93-56.

This narrow bar with cream-colored walls and elaborate carved-wood cornices is popular with an older crowd.

Prices: Glass of wine 190 ptas. ($1.95); hefty portion (*ración*) of sliced pork on pieces of bread 465 ptas. ($4.85).

Open: Daily 10:30am–2am.

EL HECHO BAR, calle de las Huertas, 56. Tel. 429-95-90.

Here you'll find a young, trendy crowd drinking daiquiris at the bar. It's not exactly a budget place, so stick to beer or wine.

Prices: Daiquiris 435 ptas. ($4.55).

Open: Mon 6pm–3am, Tues–Sun noon–2 or 3am.

TABERNA DE DOLORES, Plaza de Jesús, 4. Tel. 468-59-30.

This popular tapas bar near the Palace Hotel and the Prado is famed not only for its vintage atmosphere but for the quality of its fare. The potato chips are some of the best in the city, and the canapés make a savory snack or a satisfying lunch or tapas dinner.

Prices: Canapés or raciones of cheese, salmon, and assorted seafood 195–2,750 ptas. ($2.05–$28.65).

Open: Sun–Thurs 11am–1am, Fri–Sat 11am–2am.

GRAN VÍA

MUSEO CHICOTE, Gran Vía, 12.

This popular watering hole draws a middle-aged clientele and their kids. You can also get sandwiches and tapas.

Open: Daily 1pm–2am.

PLAZA DE SANTA BARBARA & SOUTH

BOCAITO, Libertad, 6. Tel. 532-12-19.

For the best tapas around, head for Bocaito. There are no seats in the bar area, but you can have your dinner of tortillas, croquetas, and mejillones (mussels stuffed and deep-fried) standing up.

Prices: 200–1,155 ptas. ($2.10–$12.05); glass of beer or wine 150 ptas. ($1.55).

Open: Lunch Mon–Sat 1:30–5pm; dinner Mon–Sat 8:30pm–midnight.

CERVECERÍA SANTA BÁRBARA, Plaza de Santa Bárbara, 8. Tel. 319-04-49.

An enormously long bar is host to a wide variety of Madrileños, and this is where you should be, too. A marble floor, red-painted walls with wrought-iron screens, and friendly waiters add to the pleasantness. It is also known for its seafood (expensive)—stick to the beer.

Open: Daily 11am–11pm.

LA CERVECERÍA INTERNACIONAL, Regueros, 8. Tel. 419-48-68.

The strongest beer in the world is served here, they say, and there is certainly a selection from all over the world. There's a beer shop too, and a restaurant.

Open: Daily noon–12:30am.

SANTA BÁRBARA PUB, Fernando VI, 3. Tel. 319-08-44.

Right around the corner from its cousin the Cervecería Santa Bárbara and across from the art nouveau headquarters of the Spanish Society of Authors is what is billed as the first English pub in Madrid. Although you won't find warm beer, you will find a congenial ambience in an authentic setting, right down to the central bar and low, round tables.

Open: Sun–Thurs noon–2am, Fri–Sat noon–3am.

JAZZ BARS

CAFE CENTRAL, Plaza del Angel, 10. Tel. 468-08-44.

This is *the* place for live jazz in Madrid, and as a result is usually packed. Black bench seating, marble-top tables, and glistening brass set the scene. Performances are from 11pm to 12:30am, but it's a good place to come at other times as well, when you'll meet students, tourists, and Madrid's "beautiful people."

Admission: Depends on who's playing, but is usually about 450–950 ptas. ($4.70–$9.90) Mon–Thurs, 550–1,100 ptas. ($5.70–$11.45) Fri–Sun.

Open: Daily 1pm–2 or 3am.

CLAMORES, Albuquerque, 14. Tel. 445-79-38.

This is one of the more popular jazz spots, particularly on Monday when there is dancing, too. It is also a *champañería*, with a great variety of champagnes and Spanish *cavas* (Spanish champagne).

Prices: 450 ptas. ($4.70) cover charge during performances.

Open: Daily 3pm–3am; live jazz nightly at 11:30pm and 1:30am.

MESONES

On Cava de San Miguel, just west of Plaza Mayor, you'll find several little bars known as *mesones,* each specializing in something different. **La Guitarra** features guitar playing, and its ceiling is covered with sangría jugs, which you can buy. **La Tortilla** has tortilla and beer for two for about 855 ptas. ($8.90). The accordionist here will ask you where you are from and play a song to suit. There is the **Queso Mesón** for cheese and the **Mesón de Champiñón,** where a plate of about eight wonderful mushrooms costs 525 ptas. ($5.45). The best time to go is Thursday through Saturday between 10pm and 1am.

SUMMER TERRAZAS

As the nights become warm in Madrid, outdoor bars spring up. The most popular are those along **Paseo de la Castellana** between Cibeles and Emilio Castelar, but they are also expensive. The busiest time is late at night, and on Friday and Saturday you can hardly move down the sidewalk at 2 in the morning. For quieter bars frequented by those over 25, head to **Paseo Pintor Rosales** overlooking the Parque del Oeste.

DISCOS

Madrid's most popular discos tend to operate a selective entrance policy, so dress up and don't wear sneakers if you want to get in. Cover charges, including one drink, run up to 1,900 ptas. ($19.80); a soda inside can cost over 1,000 ptas. ($10.40). They are usually open daily until 4 or 5 in the morning, and you won't see much action before 1am.

ARCHY, Marqués del Riscal, 11. Tel. 308-31-62.
Currently the No. 1 place to go, located in the basement of an old apartment building and decorated in an art deco style, with a restaurant and pub too.
Open: Daily midnight–4am.

JOY ESLAVA, Arenal, 11. Tel. 266-37-33.
An old theater is the home' for this popular venue with great laser shows and interesting people. The best nights are Friday and Saturday.
Open: Main session daily 11:30pm–4am, Fri–Sun early session 7–10:15pm as well (mainly frequented by teenagers).

KEEPER, Juan Bravo, 31. Tel. 262-23-79.
This enormous disco is spread over three floors, with a pub and a spot to retreat from the music.
Open: Sun–Fri 9pm–3am, Sat 9pm–4am.

OBA-OBA, Jacometrezo, 4. Tel. 531-06-40.
Not at all upscale or selective, just great Brazilian music and sambas.
Open: Daily 7pm–5am.

PACHA, Barceló, 11. Tel. 446-01-37.
Once the most popular disco in Madrid, Pacha has its faithful who still frequent this reformed theater of the '30s.
Open: Daily midnight–5am.

9. NETWORKS & RESOURCES

STUDENTS

THE UNIVERSITIES

There are three universities in and around Madrid—Complutense, Autonoma, and one of the oldest universities in the country, Alcalá de Henares, located 12 miles east of the city.

Complutense, the largest, is in the northwest corner of Madrid, its many faculties sprawled over several miles of University City. Head for the Faculty of Philology (Facultad de Filología) in Building A of the Faculty of Philosophy and Letters, where courses for foreigners are held year round. The bar in the basement is a great meeting place and one of the most popular bars on campus. You can get a cheap breakfast here, and the *menu del día* is 600 ptas. ($6.25). Check the notice board for offers of accommodation. During May and June the *Colegios Mayores* (dorms) sometimes have information concerning vacancies in the *Cursos para Extranjeros* (Courses for Foreign Students).

For general information, go to the **Centro de Información Juvenil de la Comunidad de Madrid,** at Caballero de Grácia, 32 (tel. 521-39-60), open Monday through Friday from 9am to 3pm; or in the Sol metro station (tel. 521-95-11), open Monday through Friday from 9am to 3pm. Although the center is directed to the youth of Madrid and their English is limited, the personnel are extremely helpful and will provide computer printouts on just about any topic, from the cheapest hotels and restaurants to friendly bars and discos.

STUDENT HANGOUTS

Hollywoods is the place for hamburgers and spareribs with a U.S. ambience. And **Bob's** and **Vip's** are both extremely popular with students (see "Budget Dining," above, for locations and details). Also very popular with students are:

CAFE DE RUIZ, Ruiz, 11.
For chocolate lovers, tea connoisseurs, or pastry freaks, this is a great place to meet people or catch up on the international press.
Open: Daily 3pm–3am.

CHOCOLATERÍA SAN GINÉS, Pasadizo de San Ginés, 5.
Another venue for the chocoholic, which has been in business since 1894. Drop in for hot chocolate and churros after disco-hopping (it's right behind Joy Eslava).
Open: Wed and Fri–Sun 7–10pm, and 1–8am, Tues and Thurs 1–8am.

FASS, Cardenal Cisneros, 21.
German beer and food specialties, plus other imported beers.
Open: Lunch Tues–Sat 1–4pm; dinner Tues–Sun 7pm–1am.

GAY MEN & LESBIANS

In the area known as Chueca (between calle Hortaleza and calle Barquillo), several establishments have sprung up in recent years. Most popular at the moment is **Cafe Figueroa,** Augusto Figueroa, 17 (tel. 521-16-73). A couple of blocks away at Libertad, 34, is **Blanco y Negro** (tel. 231-11-41). Also look on calle Pelayo and calle Hortaleza for one to suit you.

WOMEN

If women travelers have a problem or need information, try at the **Instituto de la Mujer** and **Asociación de Mujeres Jóvenes,** both located at Almagro, 36 (tel. 419-68-46).

10. EASY EXCURSIONS

SEGOVIA   A trip to Segovia will take you through beautiful countryside at any time of the year, as pine-covered hills give way to a dusty plain covered with vines and olive trees.

The town sits perched on a rocky outcrop, its mellow golden buildings glowing gently. Its fine Gothic **cathedral** and 11th-century **fortress** lie 54 miles north of Madrid and can be reached by train from the Atocha, Chamartín, Recoletos, and

Nuevos Ministerios stations. Trains depart every 2 hours and the 2-hour trip costs 1,050 ptas. ($10.95) round-trip. Buses (tel. 247-52-61 for information) go from Empresa La Sepulvedana, Paseo de la Florida, 11, daily, take 1½ hours, and cost 1,100 ptas. ($11.45).

Segovia is an old Roman city, and its 10-mile-long **aqueduct,** built by Augustus, is still intact and operational. There are a number of important Romanesque churches set among the winding streets, and charming houses with Mudéjar and hexagonal designs.

ARANJUEZ ✪ On the banks of the River Tagus, Aranjuez is a little closer to Madrid, only 29 miles south. The baroque **Royal Palace** was a summer residence in the late 18th century, and the leisurely lifestyle shows through in the parks and gardens, in the "Laborer's House" and in the palace itself. Of special note in the palace is the Porcelain Room, its walls and ceilings covered in beautifully painted porcelain made in the factory of Buen Retiro.

There are trains about every 45 minutes from Atocha Station that take 45 minutes and cost 550 ptas. ($5.70) round-trip, as well as buses from the Sur Bus Station, Canarias, 17 (tel. 468-42-00), that cost 650 ptas. ($6.75).

Something different is the "strawberry train" to Aranjuez that leaves Atocha Station every Saturday and Sunday morning in the summer and returns in the evening. Tickets cost 1,825 ptas. ($19) for adults, 1,525 ptas. ($15.90) for those under 12, and include a visit to the Prince's House, strawberries, and a drink. Call 530-02-02 daily from 7am to 11:30pm for full details.

TOLEDO Toledo is an easy day trip from Madrid. Leave early and wear comfortable shoes to tackle the cobbled hills of El Greco's city. Once there, head for the **cathedral.** One of the most glorious examples of Spanish Gothic architecture, it was built between the 13th and the 16th centuries. Like many Spanish cathedrals, it is nearly enclosed by the town. The cathedral is open Monday through Saturday from 10:30am to 1pm and from 3:30 to 6pm; on Sunday from 10:30am to 1:30pm and from 4 to 6pm (in summer until 7pm); the last tour is at 12:30pm. Tickets for the cathedral treasury cost 385 ptas. ($4). Next stop at the **Church of St. Thomas (Santo Tomé)** to see El Greco's famous painting *The Burial of the Count Orgaz;* tickets cost 115 ptas. ($1.20).

Go on to **El Greco's House and Museum,** interesting as a charming example of a 16th-century Toledan house as well as for his paintings (the house, in fact, wasn't actually El Greco's); then visit the **Santa Cruz Museum.** Both these museums are open from 10am to 2pm and 3:30 or 4 to 6pm (closed Sunday afternoon and Monday); tickets cost 225 ptas. ($2.35). Also try to see the **Alcázar** (same hours as above) and the **Synagoga del Trásito.** Tickets for the Alcázar cost 135 ptas. ($1.40). If you have time (and transportation) you may wish to venture across the River Tagus to the **parador** (signposted). From its terrace you have a wonderful view of Toledo spread before you.

Toledo can be reached by taking the train from Atocha Station, or by bus from calle Canarias Sur bus station. For further information, call the **Toledo Tourist Office** (tel. 0925/22-08-43), which is open Monday through Friday from 9am to 2pm and from 4 to 6pm, on Saturday from 9am to 7pm, and Sunday from 9am to 3pm. Round trip train fare is 825 ptas. ($8.60).

EL ESCORIAL Trains for El Escorial leave frequently from Atocha, Chamartín, Recoletos, and Nuevos Ministerios station; take one hour; and cost 420 ptas. ($4.35) round-trip. Buses leave from Empresa Herranz, Isaac Peral, 10, Moncloa (tel. 243-36-45) and cost 650 ptas. ($6.75) round-trip.

The sight to see here is the **Monasterio de San Lorenzo del Escorial,** built as Philip II's retreat. An all-inclusive ticket for the monastery and the Prince's House is 575 ptas. ($6). The monastery is open Tuesday through Sunday from 10am to 1:30pm and 3:15 to 6pm (ticket office closes at 5:30pm). The **tourist office** at El Escorial can be reached at 890-15-54.

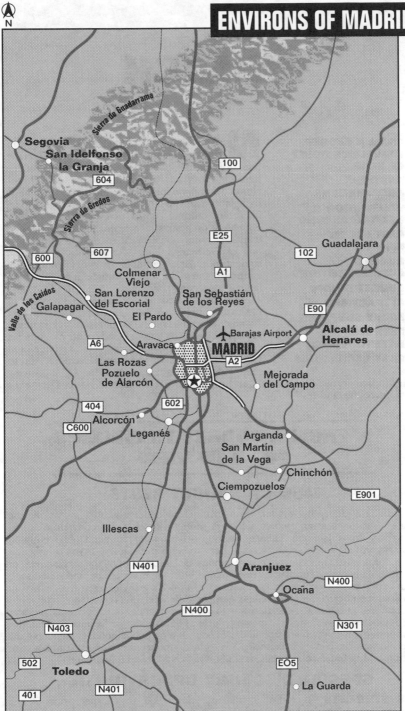

ENVIRONS OF MADRID

N

Segovia

San Idelfonso la Granja
604

Sierra de Guadarrama

Sierra de Gredos

100

E25

600

607

Guadalajara
102

Valle de los Caídos

Colmenar Viejo

San Lorenzo del Escorial

A1

San Sebastián de los Reyes

E90

Galapagar

El Pardo

Alcalá de Henares

A6

Aravaca

Barajas Airport

MADRID

A2

Las Rozas
Pozuelo de Alarcón

Mejorada del Campo

404

602

Alcorcón

Leganés

Arganda

C600

San Martín de la Vega

Chinchón

Ciempozuelos

E901

Illescas

N401

Aranjuez

N400

N400

Ocaña

N403

N301

502

EO5

Toledo

N401

La Guarda

401

MUNICH

Named after the "Munichen," monks who settled here more than 1,200 years ago on the banks of the Isar River, Munich is the capital of the state (or *Land*) of Bavaria and a sprawling city of almost 1.3 million inhabitants. Home of such industrial giants as BMW and Siemens, Munich is also an important cultural capital of Germany, with four symphony orchestras, two opera houses, dozens of world-class museums, more than 20 theaters, and one of Germany's largest universities. Its diverse student population ensures an active avant-garde cultural scene and a liberal attitude in an otherwise largely conservative region.

Munich is a striking city, largely the product of the exuberant imagination and aspirations of past Bavarian kings and rulers. Royal residences, majestic museums, steepled churches, and ornate monuments celebrate architectural styles from baroque and Gothic to neoclassical and postmodernistic. Add to that wide boulevards, spacious parks, a thriving nightlife, and at least six breweries, and you have what amounts to one of Germany's most interesting and festive cities.

---

1. FROM A BUDGET TRAVELER'S POINT OF VIEW

MUNICH BUDGET BESTS

You can save money by standing up in Munich, whether it's eating or visiting the theater. Eat lunch at an *Imbiss*, which is simply a food stall or tiny store selling everything from German sausages and grilled chicken to pizza. Concentrated primarily in Old Town, some even sell beer to wash it all down. If you'd rather sit down for a meal, you can often save money by ordering from the *Tageskarte,* or changing daily menu, for platters that include both the main course and side dishes. Even better, pack a meal and take it to one of Munich's many beer gardens, where all you'll have to buy is beer. Some beer gardens even offer free concerts.

Standing up is also the cheapest way to see performances of the National Theater and Staatstheater, with tickets costing as little as $5. And as for Munich's wonderful museums, many of them are free all day Sunday and on public holidays, including the Alte Pinakothek, Neue Pinakothek, Glyptothek, Antikensammlungen, the Bavarian National Museum, Lenbachhaus, and the Munich Municipal Museum.

SPECIAL DISCOUNT OPPORTUNITIES

FOR STUDENTS If you're a student, your ticket to cheaper prices is the **International Student ID Card.** With it you can realize substantial savings on museum admission fees, with a deduction of 50% or more off the regular price. In addition, both the opera and theater offer student discounts for unsold seats on the night of performance—show up about an hour before the performance to see what's available. Make sure to bring your card with you—you cannot secure one in Germany.

WHAT THINGS COST IN MUNICH	U.S. $
Taxi from the airport to Munich's main train station	50.00
Underground from main train station to Schwabing	1.55
Local telephone call	.20
Double room at the Continental Grand Hotel (deluxe)	233.00
Double room at the Hotel Uhland (moderate)	87.50
Double room at the Pension am Kaiserplatz (budget)	41.85
Lunch for one at Donisl (moderate)	8.00
Lunch for one at Bratwurst Herzl (budget)	6.00
Dinner for one, without wine, at Aubergine (deluxe)	75.00
Dinner for one, without wine, at Hundskugel (moderate)	25.00
Dinner for one, without wine, at Weinbauer (budget)	6.00
Liter of beer	5.00
Glass of wine	2.20
Coca-Cola in a restaurant	1.65
Cup of coffee	1.40
Roll of 200 ASA color film, 36 exposures	5.50
Admission to Museum Alte Pinakothek	2.50
Movie ticket	5.60
Nationaltheater ticket (standing room)	5.00

If you need assistance with travel plans, a travel agency that deals with student and youth travel is **ASTA Reisen,** Amalienstrasse 73 (tel. 089/28 07 68). Open Monday through Friday from 9:30am to 12:30pm and located in the university district called Schwabing, this travel agency also offers concert and theater tickets, youth-hostel cards, and train and plane tickets.

FOR SENIORS Students aren't the only ones who get a break. If you're a senior citizen (at least 65 years old), you're entitled to a 50% discount at most museums in Munich.

FOR EVERYONE If you're an avid museum fan, consider purchasing a **museum pass** for 20 DM ($12.50), which is good for all 23 state-owned museums and is valid for eight days. And if you plan on doing a lot of traveling back and forth on Munich's excellent subways, buses, and trams, you can save money by purchasing a **one-day transportation pass** for 8 DM ($5), outlined in more detail below.

2. PRETRIP PREPARATIONS

DOCUMENTS The only document needed for citizens of the United States, Canada, Australia, and New Zealand is a valid passport, which allows stays up to three months. Visitors from the United Kingdom need only an identity card.

WHAT'S SPECIAL ABOUT MUNICH

The Beer Capital of the World
- ☐ Six major breweries, in a town of only 1.3 million people.
- ☐ Oktoberfest, the largest beer festival in the world.
- ☐ Beer halls, including the 400-year-old Hofbräuhaus, for a brew and hearty Bavarian meals.
- ☐ Beer gardens, more than 35.

Museums
- ☐ 49 museums, galleries, and collections, making Munich one of Germany's most important cultural centers.
- ☐ The Alte Pinakothek, one of Europe's most important collections of the old masters.

- ☐ The Deutsches Museum, the largest technological museum in the world, where visitors could spend a lifetime.

Architectural Highlights
- ☐ Nymphenburg Palace, Germany's largest baroque palace.
- ☐ The Cuvilliés Theater, the finest rococo tier-boxed theater in Germany.
- ☐ The Alte Pinakothek and the Glyptothek, both built in the 19th century by Leo von Klenze, one of Munich's most important architects.
- ☐ The Residenz, the royal residence of the Wittelsbach family.

Students should be sure to bring an International Student ID Card as well.

WHAT TO PACK   You should be prepared for anything, including unexpected cool days in the summer or sudden warm days in the winter. If it's autumn or spring, be sure to bring a warm jacket—the temperature can dip sharply at night. Even in the summer you may need a light jacket or sweater. In winter you'll need a winter coat. Otherwise, dress is fairly casual. Bring one dressy outfit if you plan on going to the opera. But most important of all, bring rain gear. An umbrella is an absolute necessity.

WHEN TO GO   Anytime! Summers can be glorious in Bavaria, and the main tourist season stretches from about April to mid-October. Winters tend to be mild, though snow can fall on the stalls of Munich's outdoor Christmas market.

Munich's Average Daytime Temperature & Rainfall

	Jan	Feb	Mar	Apr	May	June	July	Aug	Sept	Oct	Nov	Dec
Temp. (°F)	33	35	40	50	60	65	70	73	65	50	39	33
Days of Rain	19	16	19	19	21	24	18	17	18	15	17	18

Special Events   Munich's most famous festival is of course its **Oktoberfest**—which is actually held in September, from the middle of the month to the first Sunday in October. Although it's certainly worth experiencing at least once, it's also the busiest time of the year for Munich. Hotels are full, with rooms often going for about 10%–20% more than the usual rate, so be sure to reserve far in advance.

Other annual events in Munich include its **Christkindlmarkt,** an outdoor Christmas market held on Marienplatz from the end of November to Christmas Eve; and **Fasching,** Germany's version of carnival, with elaborate costume balls. Celebrated from January 7 to Shrove Tuesday, Fasching reaches its frenzied peak on

Fasching Sunday and Shrove Tuesday, with special events staged at the Viktualienmarkt and Munich's pedestrian-zoned inner city. These two winter events do not draw nearly the crowds that the Oktoberfest does, which means you should have no trouble finding a hotel room.

BACKGROUND READING For a pictorial essay on Munich and general background information, pick up a copy of *Munich,* of "The Great Cities" series by George Bailey (Time-Life, 1980). If you're interested in learning more about Bavaria's most famous king, read Wilfrid Blunt's *The Dream King: Ludwig II of Bavaria* (Penguin, 1978).

3. ORIENTATION & GETTING AROUND

ARRIVING IN MUNICH

FROM THE AIRPORT Unsurprisingly, Germany's own Lufthansa provides the most flights to Munich's newly opened airport in Erding, located about 17 miles northeast of Munich. After stopping by the tourist information counter to pick up a map and brochures, proceed to the S-Bahn station, where you can board the S-8, bound for Marienplatz (the center of the city), or the Hauptbahnhof (main train station). Cost of the ticket is 10 DM ($6.25), though if you have a Eurailpass you use the S-Bahn for free. The trip to the Hauptbahnhof takes about 40 minutes. A taxi, on the other hand, is prohibitive, costing as much as $50 one way.

FROM THE TRAIN STATION If you come by train, you'll arrive at the **Hauptbahnhof,** Munich's main train station. It's located near the center of town and serves as a nucleus for the city's many tram, U-Bahn (underground subway), and S-Bahn (metropolitan railway) lines. In the train station itself you'll find a tourist information office, a post office, and an information office for obtaining train schedules and making train reservations for travel onward in the rest of Europe.

INFORMATION

Munich's main **city tourist office (Fremdenverkehrsamt)** is located in the Hauptbahnhof at its south exit onto Bayerstrasse. Open Monday through Saturday from 8am to 10pm and on Sunday from 11am to 7pm, it distributes free maps of the city. For a fee of 5 DM ($3.10) the tourist office here and at the airport will also find a hotel room for you, a valuable service if the accommodations listed in this book happen to be full. Other tourist offices are located at Munich's airport, open Monday through Saturday from 8:30am to 10pm and on Sunday from 1 to 9pm, and in the center of the city just off Marienplatz at Rindermarkt and Pettenbeckstrasse (tel. 239 12 72). To reach the latter tourist office, walk south on Rosenstrasse from Marienplatz and take the first left onto Rindermarkt. This office is open Monday through Friday from 9:30am to 6pm. For more information, call the Fremdenverkehrsamt at 089/23911. For **recorded information in English,** call 23 91 62 for open hours of museums and 23 91 72 for information on castles and other attractions.

If you want to know what's going on in Munich, pick up a copy of the **Monatsprogramm,** available at the tourist office. Costing 2 DM ($1.25) it tells you what's being performed when in Munich's theaters and opera houses and how to obtain tickets. In addition, it also lists concerts, both modern and classical, museum hours, and special exhibitions. Although much of the information contained in this pocket-size booklet is in German only, non-German-speakers will also find it useful.

CITY LAYOUT

The heart of Old Munich lies directly east of the Hauptbahnhof. Its very center is **Marienplatz,** a cobblestone plaza only a 15-minute walk from the train station and connected to the rest of the city by an extensive subway network. Throughout the centuries it served as a market square, as a stage for knightly tournaments, and as the site of public executions. Today it is no less important, bordered on one side by the impressive New Town Hall.

Much of the Old Town is a **pedestrian zone,** and it's here that you'll find Munich's smartest boutiques, its most traditional restaurants, its oldest churches, and its outdoor market, the Viktualienmarkt. Most of Munich's museums are located within an easy walk or short subway ride from the city center.

Schwabing, located north of the city center and easily reached by U-Bahn, is home to both Munich's university and its nightlife. Its bohemian heyday was back at the turn of the century, when it served as a mecca for Germany's most talented young artists and writers, including Wassily Kandinsky, Paul Klee, Thomas Mann, and Rainer Maria Rilke. Today Schwabing is known for its sidewalk cafés, fashionable bars, and discos, most of which are found on Leopoldstrasse and Occamstrasse. Although tourist brochures like to call Schwabing "the Greenwich Village of Munich," most of the people milling about here are visitors and tourists, including lots of young people from outlying villages in for a night on the town.

As for other areas worth exploring, the **Englischer Garten** with its wide green expanses and beer gardens stretches northeast from the city center. Munich's Oktoberfest is held at **Theresienwiese** just south of the Hauptbahnhof, while the **Olympiapark,** home of the 1972 Olympics, is on the northern edge of town. **Schloss Nymphenburg,** the royal family's summer residence, lies to the northwest of town, accessible by subway and then streetcar.

GETTING AROUND

Munich's public transportation system is efficient and convenient, one of the best in the world. But even though it's a large city, many of its major attractions are located within walking distance of Marienplatz.

BY SUBWAY Munich's wonderful underground network, which was created in conjunction with the 1972 Olympics, is the ultimate in German efficiency. I have seldom waited more than a few minutes for a train. What's more, Munich's subway stations have something I wish every city in the world would adopt—maps of the surrounding streets. That means you never have to emerge from a subway station wondering where you are.

Munich's subway system is divided into the **U-Bahn** (underground subway) and **S-Bahn** (metropolitan railway). Because the S-Bahn is part of the German Federal Railroad, you can use your Eurailpass on these lines. Otherwise purchase a ticket and validate it yourself by inserting it into one of the little machines at the entrance to the track. It's all on the honor system—that is, there's no ticket collector to make sure you have a ticket. However, there are frequent spot checks by undercover controllers—if you're caught without a ticket you'll pay a stiff fine. Munich's public transportation system operates from about 5am to 1am.

One of the best things about Munich's system is that you can make as many free transfers between subways, buses, and streetcars (trams) as you need to reach your destination. A single journey to most destinations in Munich costs 2.50 DM ($1.55). Shorter journeys—trips of at most only two stops on the subways or four stops on the streetcar or bus—cost only 1.30 DM (80¢). A short journey, for example, is the stretch from the Hauptbahnhof to Marienplatz; a regular journey requiring the 2.50 DM ticket would be from the Hauptbahnhof to Universität.

Much more economical than the single-journey tickets is the **Streifenkarte,** a strip-ticket that allows for multiple journeys. These are available for 10 DM ($6.25) and consist of strips worth 1 DM (60¢) each. For short journeys you use only one strip. Most trips in the city, however, require two strips (a total of 2 DM for the ride, which is considerably less than the 2.50 DM for the single ticket described above). Simply fold up two segments of the Streifenkarte and insert them into the validating machine.

A simpler solution is to purchase a **Tageskarte,** or day ticket, which allows unlimited travel on all modes of transportation for one calendar day. An 8-DM ($5) Tageskarte is valid for most of Munich proper; if you want to travel to the far outskirts, purchase the 16 DM ($10) card for the entire metropolitan area (about a 50-mile radius).

You can purchase Streifenkarte, Tageskarte, and single tickets at the blue vending machines located at U- and S-Bahn stations, as well as from vending machines located at some tram stops and in the second wagon of streetcars that bear a white-and-green K sign. In addition, bus drivers sell single tickets and the Streifenkarte, while tram drivers sell only single tickets. Strip tickets and day tickets are also sold at tobacco and magazine kiosks that display the green-and-white K in their window. In addition, day tickets are sold at Munich's tourist offices.

For more information on the various tickets, how to use them, and where to buy them, pick up a free copy of "Rendezvous with Munich" at the city tourist office at the Hauptbahnhof. **Information about Munich's public transportation system** is also available by calling 23 80 30.

BY BUS & TRAMS   Buses and trams go everywhere the subway doesn't. As mentioned above, one ticket allows for as many transfers as necessary to reach your destination. The free map provided by the tourist office indicates bus and tram routes for the inner city.

BY TAXI   Munich's public transportation system is so efficient that you should never have to fork over money for a taxi. If you do take a taxi, you'll pay 3.60 DM ($2.25) as soon as you step inside. If you need to call a taxi, phone 21610, or 19410. Taxis ordered by phone bring a 1-DM (60¢) surcharge to the bill.

ON FOOT   Another by-product of the 1972 Olympics is Munich's extensive **pedestrian zone,** making it a perfect city to explore on foot. In fact, many of its museums can be reached on foot from the city center. All you need is the map issued by the tourist office to set you off in the right direction.

BY BICYCLE   If you're serious about cycling your way through Munich, be sure to purchase a brochure called "Radl-Touren für unsere Gäste" for 50 Pfennig (30¢) at the tourist office. Although in Germany, it comes complete with suggested routes and maps for touring Munich by bike.

One of the most convenient places to rent bicycles is at **Radius Touristik,** located right inside the Hauptbahnhof near Track 33 (tel. 59 61 13). Open May to October, daily from 8:30am to 6:30pm, this company charges 16 DM ($10) for one day's rental of a single-gear bike. More elaborate bikes are available too, as well as guided bicycle tours.

Another well-known shop renting bicycles is **Lothar Borucki,** Hans-Sachs-Strasse 7 (tel. 26 65 06), located near the Frauenhoferstrasse U-Bahn station. Open Monday through Friday from 9am to 1pm and 3 to 6pm, and on Saturday from 9am to noon, it charges 18 DM ($11.25) for the whole day and 90 DM ($56.25) for a week. **Park & Bike,** Zweibrückenstrasse 8, near Isartorplatz (tel. 22 32 72), is open Monday through Friday from 8am to 5pm. Its rates begin at 15 DM ($9.35) for the day and 70 DM ($43.75) for a week.

In addition, bicycles are for rent at several train and S-Bahn stations in outlying villages of Bavaria, including Freising, Holzkirchen, Ismaning, and Starnberg. These bicycles rent for only 6 DM ($3.75) a day if you arrive by S-Bahn or train (hang on to your ticket for proof) or have a Eurailpass; otherwise you'll pay 10 DM ($6.25) for the day.

CAR RENTAL   It pays to shop around, since car-rental prices can vary widely depending on the time of the year, the day of the week, and the type of car.

Autohansa, one of the bigger firms, has offices both at the airport in Erding and at Schiesstättstrasse 10-12, near the train station (tel. 50 40 64). Or call **Avis** (tel. 12 60 00-20) or **Hertz** (tel. 129 50 01). Other car-rental agencies can be found in the telephone book under the heading "Autovermietung."

Prices vary, but expect to pay about 145–165 DM ($90.60–$103.10) for a one-day rental of a Ford Fiesta or Opel Corsa with unlimited mileage and including tax.

FAST FACTS MUNICH

Babysitters Call 22 92 91 for babysitting service in Munich.

Banks Banks are open Monday through Friday from 8:30am to 12:30pm and 1:30 to 3:30pm (until 5:30pm on Thursday). If you need to exchange money outside bank hours, your best bet is the exchange office at the Hauptbahnhof, open every day from 6am to 11:30pm. In addition, the main post office, described below under "Mail," is open for money exchange 24 hours. **American Express,** Promenadeplatz 6 (tel. 21 990), is open Monday through Friday from 9am to 5:30pm and on Saturday from 9am to noon. No fee is charged to cash American Express traveler's checks here—as the clerk acknowledged, the current exchange rate is bad enough.

Business Hours Downtown businesses and shops are open from 9am to 6pm Monday through Friday and from 9am to 2pm on Saturday. On the first Saturday of the month (called *langer Samstag*), shops remain open until 6pm. Most shops, particularly those in the city center, also stay open until 8 or 9pm on Thursday evening. Note, however, that smaller neighborhood shops may not open for langer Samstag and will generally close from about 12:30 to 2 or 3pm for lunch.

Consulates The **U.S. Consulate** is at Königinstrasse 5 (tel. 28 881) and is open Monday through Friday from 8am to 11:30am. The **Consulate of Great Britain,** at Amalienstrasse 62 (tel. 381 62 80) is open Monday through Friday from 8:45 to 11:30am and 1 to 3:15pm. The **Canadian Consulate,** Tal Strasse 29 (tel. 22 26 61), is open Monday through Thursday from 9am to noon and 2 to 5pm, and on Friday from 9am to noon.

Currency The German **Deutsche mark (DM)** is divided into 100 **Pfennig.** Coins come in 1, 2, 5, 10, and 50 Pfennig and 1, 2, and 5 DM. Notes are issued in denominations of 5, 10, 20, 50, 100, 200, 500, and (though most of us never see it) 1,000 DM. Note that in 1991 new notes were introduced that are valid along with the older notes.

Dentists If you need a dentist in Munich, your best bet is the Universitäts-Zahnarzt Klinik, Goethestrasse 70 (tel. 51 601), the university's dental clinic. It's open day and night and handles emergency dental problems.

Doctors If you need an English-speaking doctor, ask the American and British consulates for their list of English-speaking doctors in Munich, or contact an international *Apotheke* (pharmacy).

Emergencies Important numbers include 110 for the police, 112 for the fire department, and 19 222 for an ambulance. The number for medical emergency service is 55 86 61.

If you're looking for a conveniently located pharmacy, the Internationale Ludwigs-Apotheke, Neuhauser Strasse 8 (tel. 260 30 21 or 260 80 12), is on Munich's famous pedestrian lane. It's open Monday through Wednesday and Friday from 9am to 6:30pm, on Thursday from 9am to 8:30pm, and on Saturday from 9am to 2pm (to 6pm the first Saturday of the month). It's one of the best places to fill international prescriptions; it will also recommend English-speaking doctors. For information regarding the nearest open pharmacy, call 59 44 75.

Eyeglasses If you need new eyeglasses or repairs to your old ones, Söhnges Optik, Kaufingerstrasse 34 (tel. 27 29020), can provide service within a few hours.

THE MARK & THE DOLLAR

At this writing $1 = approximately 1.60 DM (or 1 DM = 62¢), and this was the rate of exchange used to calculate the dollar values given in this chapter (rounded to the nearest nickel). This rate fluctuates from time to time and may not be the same when you travel to Germany. Therefore the following table should be used only as a guide:

DM	U.S.$	DM	U.S.$
.25	.16	15	9.35
.50	.31	20	12.50
.75	.47	25	15.60
1	.62	30	18.75
2	1.25	35	21.85
3	1.85	40	25.00
4	2.50	45	28.10
5	3.10	50	31.25
6	3.75	60	37.50
7	4.35	70	43.75
8	5.00	80	50.00
9	5.60	90	56.25
10	6.25	100	62.50

Open Monday through Friday from 9:15am to 6pm and on Saturday from 9:15am to 1pm, it's conveniently located near Marienplatz in the center of the city.

Holidays Because of its large Catholic population, Munich has more holidays than much of the rest of the country. While many museums and restaurants remain open, shops and businesses close. Holidays in Bavaria are: New Year's (Jan 1), Epiphany (Jan 6), Good Friday, Easter Sunday and Monday, Labor Day (May 1), Ascension Day, Whit Sunday and Monday, Corpus Christi, Assumption Day (Aug 15), German Reunification Day (Oct 3), All Saints Day (Nov 1), Day of Prayer and Repentance (third Wednesday in Nov), and Christmas (Dec 25–26).

Although it's not an official holiday, note that many museums and shops are also closed for the parade on Faschings Dienstag, the Tuesday before Ash Wednesday.

Hospital If you need to go to a hospital, contact your consulate for advice on which one is best for your ailment. Otherwise, call for an ambulance or the medical emergency service, described above under "Emergencies."

Information The main tourist office (Fremdenverkehrsamt) is located in the main train station (Hauptbahnhof). See the "Information" section of "Orientation and Getting Around," above, for information regarding Munich's tourist offices and useful publications on events in Munich.

Laundry/Dry Cleaning A *Reinigung* is a dry cleaner; a *Wäscherei* or *Waschsalon* is for washing clothes. Coin-operated laundries are found at: Pestalozzistrasse 16 (near Sendlinger-Tor-Platz), Baaderstrasse 19 (near Isartorplatz), Amalienstrasse 61 (near the university), and Kurfürstenstrasse 10 and 14 (in Schwabing). Most laundries close at 6pm. A 24-hour laundry is at Landshuter Allee 77 (near Rotkreuzplatz). Ask the staff at your hotel or pension for the location of the closest Waschsalon. A wash load costs 5.50 DM ($3.45) while a dryer costs 1 DM (60¢). Detergent is 1 DM (60¢).

Lost and Found If you lose something on the street or on public transportation, contact the city **lost-and-found office** (Fundburo) at Rupperstrasse 19 (tel. 233-1), open Monday through Friday from 8am to noon and on Tuesday from 2 to 5:30pm as well. Items lost on the S-Bahn or on German trains are turned in to the

Hauptbahnhof lost-and-found office across from Track 26 (tel. 128 66 64). It's open daily from 6:30am to 11:30pm.

Mail Munich's main post office, Postamt 32, is located across the street from the Hauptbahnhof at Bahnhofplatz 1, 8 Munich 2 (tel. 5388-2732). Open 24 hours a day for long-distance telephone and telegram service, it's also the place where you can have your mail sent "Poste Restante." Other post offices are located in the Hauptbahnhof and at Residenzstrasse 2 near Marienplatz. Mailboxes in Germany are yellow.

Airmail letters to North America cost 1.65 DM ($1.05) for the first five grams, while postcards cost 1.05 DM (65¢). If you want to mail a package back home, you can buy a box that comes with tape and string at the post office. Boxes come in five sizes and range in price from 1.10 DM to 3.60 DM (70¢ to $2.25).

Newspapers Looking for the news in English? Check the Internationale Presse newsstand in the Hauptbahnhof (tel. 55 11 717), where you can pick up *USA Today*, the *International Herald Tribune*, and the *Wall Street Journal*. It's open daily from 7am to 10:45pm.

Photographic Needs There are photography shops throughout the center of Munich, but for film try one of the department stores, where prices are likely to be lower. Kaufhof has two convenient locations, on Marienplatz and Karlsplatz, while Hertie is right across from the train station at Bahnhofplatz 7.

Police The emergency telephone number for the police is 110.

Radio You can listen to the American Forces Network (AFN) by tuning in to 1107 AM. The Voice of America can be heard on 1197 AM.

Religious Services The *Monatsprogramm*, available from the Munich tourist office for 2 DM ($1.25), lists churches in various denominations throughout Munich and hours of weekly services.

Shoe Repair If you've worn your shoes out with walking, give them a tuneup at Mister Minit, a chain of shoe-repair shops. They can be found in most department stores, including Hertie located across from the train station and the Kaufhof on Marienplatz. There's also a Schuh Reperatur shop in the Hauptbahnhof.

Tax Germany's 14% federal tax is already included in most hotel and restaurant bills, including all the locales listed in this book. Tax is likewise included in the price of goods, which you can partially recover on items taken out of the country. For information on how you can recover the Value-Added Tax (VAT), refer to this chapter's "Savvy Shopping" section, below.

Taxis Refer to "Orientation and Getting Around," above, for information regarding taxis, including telephone numbers in case you need to call a taxi.

Telephone A local telephone call costs 30 Pfennig (20¢) for the first three minutes, so put more coins in to be sure you're not cut off (unused coins will be returned). Otherwise, you might wish to purchase a telephone card, available in values of 12 DM ($7.50) and 50 DM ($31.25). The 12-DM card gives you approximately 40 minutes of local telephone calls; the 50-DM card is useful for long-distance calls. Telephone cards are becoming so popular in Germany that many public telephones accept only cards. You can purchase them at any post office.

Incidentally, if you come across a number with a dash, the numbers after the dash are the extension number. Simply dial the entire number as you would any telephone number.

If you're calling Munich from outside the city, use the **area code** 089.

For long-distance calls, go to the post office instead of calling from your hotel, since hotels usually add a stiff surcharge—even a local call made from your hotel room is likely to cost upward of 50 Pfennig (30¢). The main post office, located across from the Hauptbahnhof, is open 24 hours. It costs 14.40 DM ($9) to make a three-minute long-distance phone call to the United States.

Tipping Tipping is already included in hotel and restaurant bills. However, it's customary to round restaurant bills up to the nearest mark; if a meal costs more than 20 DM, most Germans will give a 10% tip. Don't leave a tip on the table—rather, include it in the amount you give your waiter. For taxi drivers, it's sufficient to round up to the nearest mark. Porters should receive 2 DM ($1.35) per bag.

4. BUDGET ACCOMMODATIONS

Most of Munich's accommodations are clustered around the main train station, the Hauptbahnhof, particularly along Schillerstrasse. While this area may not be Munich's most charming, what it lacks in atmosphere it certainly makes up for in convenience. The farther you walk from the station, the more quaint and quiet the neighborhoods become.

Although a *pension,* the German equivalent of a bed-and-breakfast, is generally less expensive than a hotel, there is often only a fine line between the two. In any case, the cheaper the room, the greater the likelihood that you'll be sharing a bath down at the end of the hall. Pensions in Munich often charge a small fee for use of the shower, unless, of course, you have a shower in your room. All rooms in pensions and hotels, however, have their own sink. Single rooms, unfortunately, are expensive in Munich; you can save a lot of money by sharing a room.

Private rooms—those rented out in a private home to tourists—offer some of the cheapest accommodations in the city. They also offer a personal touch to your stay, since you're living right in someone's home.

Note that floors begin with "ground floor" (the same as the American first floor) and go up to the first floor (American second), and so on. And remember, if the accommodations below are full, try the tourist office, which will find a room for you for a 5-DM ($3.10) fee. All prices here include tax and service charge. The higher prices are those charged in the summer and during Oktoberfest.

ROOMS IN PRIVATE HOMES FOR LESS THAN 40 DM ($25) PER PERSON

Private homes offering rooms are spread throughout the city and are listed here in alphabetical order. With the exception of the first one, no rooms have a private bathroom and breakfast is not offered. Also except for the first one, these homeowners all prefer guests who stay at least three nights.

Ⓕ FROMMER'S SMART TRAVELER: HOTELS

VALUE-CONSCIOUS TRAVELERS SHOULD TAKE ADVANTAGE OF THE FOLLOWING:

1. Rooms without private shower, which are usually cheaper than rooms with private shower—but you may be charged extra for each shower you take down the hall.
2. Accommodations that offer cooking facilities, which helps save on dining bills.

QUESTIONS TO ASK IF YOU'RE ON A BUDGET

1. Is breakfast included in the price? Is it buffet style, allowing you to eat as much as you wish?
2. How much is the surcharge on local and long-distance telephone calls?
3. Are showers free? If the charge for a shower is high and there are more than two of you, you might save by taking a room with private shower.
4. How far is the accommodation from the center of town? Will you end up spending as much on transportation as the cost of a room in the center of town?

FRAU AUDREY BAUCHINGER, Zeppelinstrasse 37, 8 Munich 80. Tel.
089/48 84 44. 6 rms (2 with tub/shower and toilet, 3 with shower only). **Bus:** 52 from Marienplatz to Schweigerstrasse (the first stop after the river).

$ Rates (including showers): 40 DM ($25) single with shower only; 70 DM ($43.75) double without shower or toilet, 80–90 DM ($50–$56.25) double with shower, 105 DM ($65.60) double with tub/shower and toilet; 35 DM ($21.85) per person triple without shower or toilet. Breakfast (continental or American with coffee refills) 10 DM ($6.25) extra. AE, DC, MC, V.

⭐ The most expensive of the private homes, it's also the most modern and best equipped. Run by a former teacher from Virginia who married a local antiques dealer, its rooms are clean and pleasant and are provided with towels, soap, tissues, fresh flowers, and even a nightly chocolate on your pillow. Each room is different: There is only one single, which has a shower; others are doubles, some without private bathroom, others with shower only or with private bathroom across the hall. There's also a simple triple room ideal for students. Bicycles are for rent. Frau Bauchinger gives new arrivals a 20-minute introduction to what to see in Munich. If you notify her in advance, someone will pick you up at the train station. Frau Bauchinger's establishment is located across the Isar River from the Deutsches Museum. Note that if you pay by credit card, a 5% surcharge will be added to your bill.

FRAU ROSWITHA WOLFER, Blutenburgstrasse 42, 8 Munich 19. Tel.
089/18 46 18. 3 rms (none with bath). **U-Bahn:** U-1 from the Hauptbahnhof to Maillingerstrasse; take the Maillingerstrasse exit and then walk down Maillingerstrasse.

$ Rates (including showers): 35 DM ($21.85) per person. No credit cards.

A very friendly woman, Frau Wolfer speaks excellent English. She rents one tiny single room, as well as two doubles equipped with sink with hot and cold water. The disadvantage of the doubles, however, is that you have to walk through one to get to the other. But Frau Wolfer says young people traveling together don't mind, and it's also good for families (strangers are never put in the connecting room). There is a radio in each room, and a long balcony outside planted with flowers, where it's very pleasant to sit.

FRAU THERESA BOIGER, Hans-Sachs-Strasse 9, 8 Munich 5. Tel. 089/
260 38 35. 3 rms (none with bath). **Tram:** 20, 25, or 27 from the Hauptbahnhof to Fraunhofer-Müllerstrasse (three stops); then a three-minute walk.

$ Rates (including shower): 40 DM ($25) per person. Heating in winter 3 DM ($1.85) extra. No credit cards.

Frau Boiger's apartment is cluttered with mementos of a lifetime spent in a house more than 100 years old. Frau Boiger, who is nearing 80, is a bit of a character. With her smattering of English, she tells guests to ring the doorbell at the front door and then wait for the "modern door-opener"—a key thrown from her upstairs apartment to the street below. (This building predates automatic door buzzers.) Once upstairs, you'll be greeted by her friendly poodle, Bobby. She maintains a refrigerator for guests, who can even cook their own meals if they want to, and everyone is welcome to join her in an evening in front of the television. Two of her rooms are singles or doubles; the third can accommodate two to four people. This area is an interesting part of town, a mixture of antiques shops and gay bars.

FREMDENHEIM WEIGL, Pettenkoferstrasse 32, 8 Munich 2. Tel. 089/
53 24 53. 3 rms (none with bath). **Bus:** 58 to Georg-Hirth-Platz. **Directions:** From the Hauptbahnhof's south exit, walk down Goethestrasse to Pettenkoferstrasse, then turn right (a 15-minute walk).

$ Rates: 35 DM ($21.85) single, 60 DM ($37.50) double. Showers 2.50 DM ($1.55) extra. No credit cards.

These simple rooms are about a 15-minute walk from the train station. Herr Heinrich Dorsch, now in his 80s, has been renting rooms since 1953. He's kind and friendly and extremely proud of his home. Located on the second floor, the Weigl has one single room without a sink and two doubles with washbasins. Herr Dorsch speaks no English, but his granddaughter, who lives upstairs, does.

DOUBLES FOR LESS THAN 90 DM [$56.25]
SOUTH OF THE HAUPTBAHNHOF

HOTEL-PENSION ERIKA, Landwehrstrasse 8, 8 Munich 2. Tel. 089/55 43 27. 30 rms (6 with shower and toilet, 10 with shower only).
$ Rates (including continental breakfast and showers): 55 DM ($34.35) single without shower, 65 DM ($40.60) single with shower only; 90 DM ($56.25) double without shower, 100 DM ($62.50) double with shower, 120 DM ($75) double with shower and toilet. AE, DC, MC, V.
This small, personable hotel is owned by Frau Heu. The only building left standing on the street by the end of World War II, it has large rooms with high ceilings, and even a very tiny elevator. In summer breakfast is served on an outdoor patio. Rooms are pleasant and clean, and some have a telephone and TV; those facing the back of the building are virtually free of traffic noise. It's just a five-minue walk from the train station.

PENSION AUGSBURG, Schillerstrasse 18, 8 Munich 2. Tel. 089/59 76 73. Fax 089/523 16 23. 26 rms (9 with shower only).
$ Rates: 45 DM ($28.10) single without shower, 50 DM ($31.25) single with shower; 65 DM ($40.60) double without shower, 75 DM ($46.85) double with shower; 93 DM ($58.10) triple without shower, 108 DM ($67.50) triple with shower. Breakfast 6 DM ($3.75) extra; showers, 3.50 DM ($2.20). No credit cards.
One of many hotels and pensions on Schillerstrasse, Pension Augsburg is probably the most economical and the best for its price. Its reception is on the third floor—there is no elevator—and though rooms are rather bare, no one is complaining at these prices. Rooms are carpeted and clean, and there's hot water all the time. It's owned and managed by Anna and Heinz Paintner. This pension is a two-minute walk from the south side of the train station.

PENSION HERZOG HEINRICH, Herzog-Heinrich-Strasse 3, 8 Munich 2. Tel. 089/538 25 75 or 538 07 50. 8 rms (none with bath). **Bus:** 58 from the Hauptbahnhof to the Georg-Hirth-Platz stop; or a 15-minute walk.
$ Rates (including breakfast and showers): 60 DM ($37.50) single; 80 DM ($50) double; 110 DM ($68.75) triple. No credit cards.
This clean and pleasant pension is owned by a Turkish family, the Ergüls, and offers simple but spotless rooms decorated with wood furniture—a couple of the largest rooms for three or more people even have balconies. It's located on the second floor (there's no elevator).

PENSION SÜZER, Mitterstrasse 1, 8 Munich 2. Tel. 089/53 35 21. Fax 089/53 60 80. 11 rms (4 with shower and toilet).
$ Rates (including continental breakfast and showers): 80 DM ($50) double without shower or toilet, 100 DM ($62.50) double with shower and toilet; 110 DM ($68.75) triple without shower or toilet; 140 DM ($87.50) quad without shower or toilet. AE, DC.
⭐ Located just 150 yards from the train station (take a right from the station at the tourist office) near Bayerstrasse, this tiny pension is up on the third floor. (Take the elevator to the left or you'll end up at a doctor's office.) It's owned by Herr Süzer, an outgoing and friendly Turk who speaks excellent English and who is eager to answer questions about Munich. You can even sign up here for tours of the city. There are no single rooms. Four rooms have their own refrigerator (with ice cubes!), television, and radio alarm clock. There's also a TV in the tiny dining/reception area, where you can buy a beer or coffee for 2 DM ($1.25). A public phone is available. One load of laundry washed and dried costs 10 DM ($6.25). The rates quoted above are special for bearers of this book (not photocopies), which you should show upon arrival.

NEAR THERESIENWIESE

These two pensions with the same rates year round are located on the edge of Theresienwiese, site of Oktoberfest, about a 15-minute walk from the Hauptbahnhof.

PENSION SCHUBERT, Schubertstrasse 1, 8 Munich 2. Tel. 089/53 50 87. 7 rms (2 with shower). **U-Bahn:** U-3 or U-6 from Sendlinger Tor to Goetheplatz (one stop).

$ Rates (including continental breakfast): 45 DM ($28.10) single without shower; 85 DM ($53.10) double without shower, 95 DM ($59.35) double with shower. Showers 3 DM ($1.85) extra. No credit cards.

★ Located in an older, unadorned building on a tree-lined street, this small pension is a true find. Owned by outgoing Frau Käthe Fürholzer, who speaks some English, its walls are decorated with Bavarian mementos and pictures, including a collection of beer-stein tin tops (designed to keep the flies out and the beer fresh in former days). Rooms are clean and orderly in good German fashion.

PENSION WESTFALIA, Mozartstrasse 23, 8 Munich 2. Tel. 089/53 03 77 or 53 03 78. 19 rms (11 with tub or shower and toilet). TEL **U-Bahn:** U-3 or U-6 from Sendlinger Tor to Goetheplatz.

$ Rates (including buffet breakfast): 60 DM ($37.50) single without shower or toilet, 80 DM ($50) single with tub or shower and toilet; 85 DM ($53.10) double without shower or toilet, 95–110 DM ($59.35–$68.75) double with tub or shower and toilet; 105 DM ($65.60) triple without shower or toilet, 130 DM ($81.25) triple with tub or shower and toilet. Showers 3 DM ($1.80) extra. No credit cards.

★ A century old, this imposing and elaborate building is located on the corner of Mozartstrasse and Kobellstrasse just across from the Oktoberfest meadow. The lobby is on the top floor, reached by elevator, where you'll be met by owner Peter Deiritz and his family. After acquiring the pension in 1990, the Deiritzes totally renovated it, making it brighter and more cheerful. The pension itself is cozy, clean, and comfortable, and the breakfast room features 19th-century paintings, all by Munich artists. In short, this is just the kind of place many visitors to Bavaria are looking for.

NORTH OF THE HAUPTBAHNHOF

The accommodations here are all within walking distance of both the train station and Munich's main cluster of museums, including the Alte and Neue Pinakothek and the Glyptothek.

PENSION ARMIN, Augustenstrasse 5, 8 Munich 2. Tel. 089/59 31 97. Fax 089/59 52 52. 20 rms (none with shower or toilet). **Directions:** Walk one block north from the Hauptbahnhof on Dachauerstrasse and turn right onto Augustenstrasse.

$ Rates (including continental breakfast): 55–65 DM ($34.35–$40.60) single; 85–95 DM ($53.10–$59.35) double; 115–120 DM ($71.85–$75) triple. Showers 2.50 DM ($1.55) extra. No credit cards. **Parking:** 10 DM ($6.25). **Closed:** From Fri before Christmas to Jan 7.

Popular with student groups, backpackers, and families, this reasonably priced pension offers plain, uncluttered rooms decorated with dark, wooden furniture. Iranian-born owner Armin Georgi speaks English and is happy to dispense information on his adopted hometown. A washer and dryer are available to guests for 11 DM ($6.85) per load.

PENSION FLORA, Karlstrasse 49, 8 Munich 2. Tel. 089/59 70 67 or 59 41 35. Fax 089/59 41 35. 45 rms (11 with shower and toilet, 5 with shower only). **Directions:** Walk six minutes from the north exit of the Hauptbahnhof, near the corner of Dachauerstrasse and Karlstrasse.

$ Rates (including continental breakfast): 65 DM ($40.60) single without shower or toilet, 75 DM ($46.85) single with shower and toilet; 90 DM ($56.25) double without shower or toilet, 130 DM ($81.25) double with shower and toilet; 120 DM

($75) triple without shower or toilet, 145 DM ($90.60) triple with shower and toilet; 145 DM ($90.60) quad without shower or toilet, 170 DM ($106.25) quad with shower and toilet. Showers 2 DM ($1.25) extra. No credit cards.

A family-owned operation since 1956, the first-floor Pension Flora is now run by the original owner's son, Adolf, and granddaughter, Judith. Great for the price, it features small but clean rooms with wall-to-wall carpeting. A couple of rooms that face away from the street have small balconies. Breakfast is served in a cheerful dining room with a stucco ceiling.

PENSION GEIGER, Steinheilstrasse 1, 8 Munich 2. Tel. 089/52 15 56. 17 rms (10 with shower). **U-Bahn:** U-2 to Theresienstrasse (or less than a 10-minute walk from the train station).

$ Rates (including continental breakfast): 38–50 DM ($23.75–$31.25) single without shower, 57 DM ($35.60) single with shower; 78 DM ($48.75) double without shower, 89 DM ($55.60) double with shower; 120 DM ($75) triple with shower. Showers 2 DM ($1.25) extra. No credit cards. **Parking:** 2 DM ($1.25).

Owned and managed by the personable Frau Huber for more than 20 years, this clean and well-run pension is located near the Technical University. It's up on the second floor; there's no elevator.

PENSION HUNGARIA, Briennerstrasse 42, 8 Munich 2. Tel. 089/52 15 58. 12 rms (none with bath). **U-Bahn:** U-2 to Königsplatz (one stop, or less than a 10-minute walk from the Hauptbahnhof).

$ Rates (including continental breakfast): 50 DM ($31.25) single; 75–80 DM ($46.85–$50) double; 96 DM ($60) triple; 114 DM ($71.25) quad. Showers 3 DM ($1.85) extra. No credit cards.

⭐ Charming English-speaking Dr. Erika Wolff has owned and managed this delightful small pension since 1957. The reception area, decorated with shadow puppets from Java, is up on the second floor, to which there's unfortunately no elevator. Rooms are bright and cheerful. Highly recommended.

IN SCHWABING

If you want to be close to the nightlife in Schwabing, yet stay in a quiet neighborhood, these two establishments are your best bet.

HAUS INTERNATIONAL, Elisabethstrasse 87, 8 Munich 40. Tel. 089/12 00 60. Fax 089/1200-6251. 168 rms (133 with shower and toilet). **U-Bahn:** U-2 from the Hauptbahnhof to Hohenzollernplatz; then bus no. 33 to Barbarastrasse.

$ Rates (including continental breakfast and showers): 50 DM ($31.25) single without shower or toilet, 75 DM ($41.85) single with shower and toilet; 90 DM ($56.25) double without shower or toilet, 130 DM ($81.25) double with shower and toilet; 130 DM ($81.25) triple with shower and toilet; 165 DM ($103.10) quad with shower and toilet. No credit cards.

Built for the Olympic Games in 1972, this tall, modern youth hotel is popular with international school and youth groups, but there's no age limit. Rooms are very basic but the facilities—restaurant, bar, disco, and swimming pool—are very good. Reserve in advance in writing if you want to stay here, and then call a few days before arrival.

PENSION AM KAISERPLATZ, Kaiserplatz 12, 8 Munich 40. Tel. 089/34 91 90 or 39 52 31. 10 rms (6 with shower). **Directions:** Any S-Bahn in the direction of Marienplatz, changing there to U-Bahn U-3 or U-6 for Münchner Freiheit.

$ Rates (including continental breakfast and showers): 37–45 DM ($23.10–$28.10) single without shower; 67–75 DM ($41.85–$46.85) double without shower, 75 DM ($46.85) double with shower; 89–95 DM ($55.60–$59.35) triple without or with shower; 120 DM ($75) quad without or with shower; 140 DM ($87.50) five-bed room without or with shower; 155–160 DM ($96.85–$100) six-bed room without or with shower. No credit cards.

⭐ If you like touches of the Old World, you can't do better than this place for its price category. Located on the ground floor of a Jugendstil building almost a century old (several architects have offices here—always a good sign), this pension features many rooms decorated with antiques, each in a different style. There is, for example, the English Room, the Farmer's Room, and the Baroque Room, all of which have high ceilings and a feeling of spaciousness. Extravagantly furnished with chandeliers, sitting areas, lace curtains, or washbasins shaped like seashells, the rooms here are highly recommended. Frau Jacobi, who has run the place for more than 16 years, is very friendly, and what's more, she's a native of Munich.

IN THE CITY CENTER

HOTEL ERBPRINZ, Sonnenstrasse 2, 8 Munich 2. Tel. 089/59 45 21. 24 rms (12 with tub or shower and toilet). TEL **Directions:** Walk five minutes east of the Hauptbahnhof on Schützenstrasse or Bayerstrasse, and take a right on Sonnenstrasse.

$ **Rates** (including continental breakfast): 62 DM ($38.75) single without tub/shower or toilet, 85 DM ($53.10) single with tub or shower and toilet; 82–89 DM ($51.25–$55.60) double without tub/shower or toilet, 99–122 DM ($61.85–$76.25) double with tub or shower and toilet; 117 DM ($73.10) triple without tub/shower or toilet, 153 DM ($95.60) triple with tub or shower and toilet. Showers 3 DM ($1.85) extra. AE, MC, V.

This older, second-floor pension has a good location just off Karlsplatz. Its rooms are simple but adequate, and its breakfast room provides a sunny outlook over the action of Karlsplatz. Most of its rooms, however, face toward the back where it's much quieter. Note that its cheapest doubles are actually single rooms with a bed only 4½ feet wide—unless you're more interested in price over comfort, you'll probably want to book the normal, higher-priced double.

PENSION DIANA, Altheimer Eck 15, 8 Munich 2. Tel. 089/260 31 07. 17 rms (none with bath). **S-Bahn and U-Bahn:** Karlsplatz; then a three-minute walk.

$ **Rates** (including breakfast and showers): 55–75 DM ($34.35–$46.85) single; 75–90 DM ($46.85–$56.25) double. Extra person 40 DM ($25). AE, MC, V.

This simple pension has a great location, between Karlsplatz and Marienplatz in the city center. Located on the third floor (there is no elevator), it offers small but perfectly adequate rooms; those toward the back are quieter. Corridors, however, are also rather narrow—not for the claustrophobic.

BETWEEN THE CITY CENTER & THE ISAR RIVER

HOTEL-PENSION BECK, Thierschstrasse 36, Munich 22. Tel. 089/22 07 08 or 22 57 68. Fax 089/22 09 25. 44 rms (8 with shower and toilet). TEL **Tram:** 19 from the Hauptbahnhof to Maxmonument or 20 from the Hauptbahnhof to Marienplatz. **S-Bahn:** Isartor (then a five-minute walk). **U-Bahn:** U-4 or U-5 from the Hauptbahnhof to Lehel.

$ **Rates** (including continental breakfast and showers): 40–48 DM ($25–$30) single without shower or toilet, 68 DM ($42.50) single with shower and toilet; 72–82 DM ($45–$51.25) double without shower or toilet, 88–108 DM ($55–$107.50) double with shower and toilet; 38 DM ($23.75) per person in a three- to five-bed room without shower or toilet, 45–50 DM ($28.10–$31.25) per person in a three- to five-bed room with shower and toilet. Crib available. No credit cards. **Parking:** 5 DM ($3.10).

It's hard to believe that Frau Beck is nearing 70, so energetically does she run this astonishingly cheap pension. Owner since 1950, she speaks very good English, is talkative, and makes sure guests know what to see in her beloved Munich. The building itself is more than 100 years old, with rooms spread over four floors. There is no elevator, and the cheaper rooms are on the upper floors. One of the best things about this old apartment building is that there are small kitchens and refrigerators on each floor that you can use for free, saving money on meals (ask the reception for pots and pans and utensils). Frau Beck welcomes families, with one room large enough for a family of five. The rooms, though old, are large and perfectly adequate, with modern wooden furniture and carpeting, most with TVs. This pension is within a 10-minute walk of both the city center and the Deutsches Museum.

DOUBLES FOR LESS THAN 110 DM
($68.75)
SOUTH OF THE HAUPTBAHNHOF

HOTEL BAYERNLAND, Bayerstrasse 73, 8 Munich 2. Tel. 089/53 31 53.
Fax 089/532 85 32. Telex 5218184. 42 rms (17 with shower and toilet, 25 with shower only). TEL **Directions:** From the south exit of the train station, turn right onto Bayerstrasse.
$ Rates (including breakfast): 69 DM ($43.10) single with shower only, 79 DM ($49.35) single with shower and toilet; 102 DM ($63.75) double with shower only, 128 DM ($80) double with shower and toilet; 140 DM ($87.50) triple with shower only, 160 DM ($100) triple with shower and toilet; 178 DM ($111.25) quad with shower only, 195 DM ($121.85) quad with shower and toilet; 215–250 DM ($134.35–$156.25) for an apartment. Rates are 10–25 DM ($6.25–$15.60) higher during Oktoberfest and major conventions. MC, V. **Parking:** 7 DM ($4.35).

This postwar hotel offers simple, clean rooms, most of which face quiet side streets. Efficiently equipped with an elevator and a small bar, it caters to people mostly in their 20s–40s who are interested in a no-nonsense place to sleep. There are many four- and five-bed rooms here, as well as several two-room apartments (without cooking facilities, alas), making it a good choice for families.

HOTEL DAHEIM, Schillerstrasse 20, 8 Munich 2. Tel. 089/59 42 49. 26 rms (2 with tub/shower and toilet, 2 with shower only). TEL
$ Rates (including continental breakfast and showers): 85 DM ($53.10) single without shower or toilet, 105 DM ($65.60) single with shower only; 105 DM ($65.60) double without shower or toilet, 125 DM ($78.10) double with shower only, 130–150 DM ($81.25–$93.75) double with shower or bath and toilet; 150 DM ($93.75) triple without shower or toilet, 175 DM ($109.35) triple with shower only, 160–170 DM ($100–$106.25) triple with shower and toilet. Rates are 30% higher during Oktoberfest. AE, MC, V.

On busy Schillerstrasse with its many hotels and pensions, the Hotel Daheim is a family-run establishment. The building is a bit old, but the pension itself is perfectly acceptable for the price. Breakfast is served in a lace-curtained room with a good view of Schillerstrasse. Single travelers should note that there are only three single rooms here—the rest are doubles, many of which can be converted into triples. About half the rooms have TVs. Hotel Daheim is a three-minute walk from the south exit of the Hauptbahnhof.

HOTEL HABERSTOCK, Schillerstrasse 4, 8 Munich 2. Tel. 089/55 78 55 or 55 78 56. Fax 089/523 47 34. 67 rms (15 with tub/shower and toilet, 24 with shower only). TEL
$ Rates (including breakfast and one shower daily): 60–70 DM ($37.50–$43.75) single without shower or toilet, 80 DM ($50) single with shower only, 100 DM ($62.50) single with shower and toilet; 106 DM ($66.25) double without shower or toilet, 125 DM ($78.10) double with shower only, 170 DM ($106.25) double with shower and toilet. AE, DC, MC, V.

Also located on Schillerstrasse, the Hotel Haberstock welcomes guests of all ages, businesspeople and tourists alike. Outfitted in the old-fashioned way with two separate doors to eliminate all corridor noise, rooms are simple but tastefully decorated. The hotel itself, typically Bavarian, has nice touches throughout, including ornate gilded mirrors in the lobby, and chandeliers. It's less than a two-minute walk from the Hauptbahnhof.

HOTEL HELVETIA, Schillerstrasse 6, 8 Munich 2. Tel. 089/55 47 45. 46 rms (none with bath). TEL

$ **Rates** (including continental breakfast and showers): 60 DM ($37.50) single; 90 DM ($56.25) double; 40 DM ($25) per person in triple, quad, and five-bed rooms. No credit cards.

Another good choice on Schillerstrasse is the Hotel Helvetia, which is also pleasantly decorated in old-fashioned Bavarian style. The breakfast room has fresh flowers on every table and a TV. Rooms are fairly large with pine furniture, and many double rooms even have two sinks. Most of its rooms face away from the street, assuring a quiet night's rest. Just a few minutes' walk from the Hauptbahnhof's south exit.

HOTEL JEDERMANN, Bayerstrasse 95, 8 Munich 2. Tel. 089/53 32 67. Fax 089/53 65 06. 55 rms (34 with shower and toilet). **Directions:** From the south exit of the train station (near the tourist office), turn right onto Bayerstrasse.

$ **Rates** (including buffet breakfast): 65 DM ($40.60) single without shower or toilet, 90–110 DM ($56.25–$68.75) single with shower and toilet; 95–110 DM ($59.35–$68.75) double without shower or toilet, 130–160 DM ($81.25–$100) double with shower and toilet; 110–130 DM ($68.75–$81.25) triple without shower or toilet. 165–200 DM ($103.10–$125) triple with shower and toilet. Crib available. Showers 3 DM ($1.85) extra. No credit cards. **Parking:** 8 DM ($5).

Less than a 10-minute walk from the train station, this delightful and comfortable establishment has been owned by English-speaking Werner Jenke and his family since 1962. Its lobby was recently renovated, and the breakfast room is a cheerful way to start the day—with an all-you-can-eat breakfast buffet. There are nice touches of antiques and traditional Bavarian furniture throughout, and rooms with bathrooms have the extras of radio, alarm clock, TV, and hairdryer. There are safes in most of the rooms.

IN SCHWABING

HOTEL-PENSION SCHWABINUS, Georgenstrasse 2, 8 Munich 40. Tel. 089/39 59 28 or 39 54 18. Fax 089/34 29 47. 22 rms (7 with shower and toilet, 6 with shower only). TEL **Directions:** S-Bahn to Marienplatz, then U-Bahn U-3 or U-6 to Giselastrasse.

$ **Rates** (including buffet breakfast and showers): 75 DM ($46.85) single without shower or toilet, 85 DM ($53.10) single with shower only, 99 DM ($61.85) single with shower and toilet; 95 DM ($59.35) double without shower or toilet, 125 DM ($78.10) double with shower only, 149 DM ($93.10) double with shower and toilet. Crib available. DC, MC, V. **Parking:** 9 DM ($5.60).

This modern establishment on the ground floor of an apartment house is decorated with cheerful posters and prints, including rows of Hundertwasser prints adorning its corridor. Rooms are large and pleasant (TVs are available), and most face onto a quiet backyard. A calm oasis near Munich's lively nightlife district, it's a good choice despite its high prices.

IN THE CITY CENTER

Located just a few minutes' walk from Marienplatz, these two older hotels are good if you want to be in the middle of the action.

HOTEL AM KARLSTOR, Neuhauser Strasse 34, 8 Munich 2. Tel. 089/59 35 96 or 59 66 21. Fax 089/523 46 81. 28 rms (3 with shower only). TEL **S-Bahn:** Karlsplatz (one stop, or a five-minute walk east from the Hauptbahnhof on the other side of Karlsplatz).

$ **Rates** (including continental breakfast): 68–75 DM ($42.50–$46.85) single without shower, 85–90 DM ($53.10–$56.25) single with shower; 100 DM ($62.50) double without shower, 120–125 DM ($75–$78.10) double with shower; 130–135 DM ($81.25–$84.35) triple without shower, 150 DM ($93.75) triple with shower; 150–155 DM ($93.75–$96.85) quad without shower. Showers 5 DM ($3.10) extra. MC, V.

⭐ More than 30 years old, this homey hotel is located just off Karlsplatz (popularly known as Stachus) on the main pedestrian street leading from the train station to Marienplatz. The elevator, situated next to a movie theater, takes you up to the reception area on the fourth floor, which is surprisingly quiet and peaceful considering the traffic outside. Rooms have modern wooden furniture, and there are a lot of repeat guests. With 16 single rooms, it's a good bet for those traveling alone. Owner Herr Rosenfeld speaks good English.

HOTEL AM MARKT, Heiliggeistrasse 6, 8 Munich 2. Tel. 089/22 50 14. 31 rms (12 with shower and toilet). TEL **S-Bahn:** From the Hauptbahnhof, any S-Bahn in the direction of Marienplatz (two stops).

$ Rates (including continental breakfast and showers): 60–65 DM ($37.50–$40.60) single without shower or toilet; 100–110 DM ($62.50–$68.75) double without shower or toilet, 120–140 DM ($75–$87.50) double with shower and toilet; 148 DM ($92.50) triple without shower or toilet, 180 DM ($112.50) triple with shower and toilet. No credit cards. **Parking:** 8 DM ($5).

⭐ Located next to Munich's colorful outdoor market, the Viktualienmarkt, this hotel, which was renovated in 1988, has flair. The rooms are a bit small, but the breakfast room and entryway are very pleasant, tastefully decorated and displaying photographs of some celebrities who have stayed here—and some who haven't. At any rate, the hotel looks more expensive than it is, and you can't beat its location near Marienplatz.

SUPER-BUDGET CHOICES
YOUTH HOSTELS

To sleep in a youth hostel (*Jugendherberge*) in Bavaria, you cannot be older than 26 and must have a youth-hostel card. If you don't have a youth-hostel card, you can purchase one at the youth hostel itself for 30 DM ($18.75) which is good for one year around the world.

DJH JUGENDHERBERGE MÜNCHEN, Wendl-Dietrichstrasse 20, 8 Munich 19. Tel. 089/13 11 56. 535 beds. **U-Bahn:** U-1 from the Hauptbahnhof to Rotkreuzplatz; then follow the triangular DJH signs.

$ Rates (including breakfast, sheets, and shower): 19 DM ($11.85) per person per night. No credit cards.

Munich's largest and oldest youth hostel opens for check-in at 10am and closes its doors at 1am. Like most youth hostels, it offers multiple bunk beds per room. Note that the entrance to the youth hostel is not on Wendl-Dietrichstrasse, but around the corner on Renatastrasse.

DJH JUGENDGÄSTEHAUS MÜNCHEN, Miesingstrasse 4, 8 Munich 70. Tel. 089/723 65 50. 344 beds (no rms with bath). **Directions:** S-Bahn from the Hauptbahnhof to Marienplatz and then U-Bahn U-3 from Marienplatz to Thalkirchen, from which it's a three-minute walk.

$ Rates (including breakfast, sheets, and showers): 30 DM ($18.75) single; 26 DM ($16.25) per person double; 24 DM ($15) per person triple or quad; 22 DM ($13.75) per person in a dormitory room. No credit cards.

Newer, nicer, and classier than the Jugendherberge above, this youth hostel is also a bit farther from the center. Curfew here is also 1am, but this youth hostel has the choice of singles, doubles, triples, and quads in addition to its dormitories.

A YOUTH HOTEL

CHRISTLICHER VEREIN JUNGER MÄNNER (CVJM), Landwehrstrasse 13, 8 Munich 2. Tel. 089/552 14 10. 34 rms (none with bath).

$ Rates (including breakfast and showers): 45–49 DM ($28.10–$30.60) single; 39 DM ($24.35) per person double; 36 DM ($22.50) per person triple. No credit cards.

Accommodating both males and females, this YMCA is popular with groups, particularly from May through October, so be sure to reserve early. Visitors older than 27 years of age must pay a 14% supplement to the rates above, and note that unmarried couples must sleep in separate rooms. Rooms, mostly twins, are spartan but adequate, and come with sinks. Curfew is at 12:30am, and there's an adjoining restaurant (open evenings only) serving good meals at reasonable prices. The Y is less than a five-minute walk from the Hauptbahnhof's south exit.

CAMPING

CAMPINGPLATZ THALKIRCHEN, Zentralländstrasse 49, 8 Munich 70. Tel. 089/723 17 07. Approximately 2,000 people can be accommodated. **U-Bahn:** U-3 to Thalkirchen; then a 10-minute walk.

$ Rates: 5.50 DM ($3.45) per person; 4–5.50 DM ($2.50–$3.45) per tent, depending on size; 7 DM ($4.35) per auto; 7.50–14.50 DM ($4.70–$9.05) per camping trailer or RV, depending on size. Showers 1 DM (60¢). No credit cards. **Open:** Mid-Mar to Oct.

Open from mid-March to the end of October, this municipal campground is Munich's largest. It's located only 2½ miles from the city center in a parklike setting along the Isar River, with facilities that include washrooms and showers, a bank for money exchange, a snack bar, a supermarket, and even small kitchens. Nearby are the Hellabrunn Zoo and an outdoor heated pool.

YOUTH CAMP AM KAPUZINERHÖLZL, Franz-Schrank-Strasse, 8 Munich 19. Tel. 089/141 43 00. 400 sleeping spaces. **Directions:** U-Bahn U-1 from the Hauptbahnhof to Rotkreuzplatz, then tram no. 12 (marked AMALIENBURGSTRASSE) from Rotkreuzplatz to Botanischer Garten.

$ Rates: 6 DM ($3.75) per person. No credit cards. **Open:** End of June to Aug.

Run by the city of Munich from the end of June through August only, this huge circuslike tent accommodates young people from around the world who want nothing more than a place to sleep. Located in the Nymphenburg–Botanical Garden area, it's stocked with mattresses and blankets, and tea is served free in the morning. There's also a canteen, showers, and an information bureau. There's no curfew, and the maximum stay is three nights. It's wise to call beforehand—to see whether there's space, and also to make sure that the city is still operating it. Every year they talk about doing away with the tent, but the demand is definitely there.

LONG-TERM STAYS

In addition to the two recommendations here, Hotel-Pension Beck (listed under "Doubles for Less Than 90 DM," above) has cooking facilities on each floor.

JOST HÜBNER, Bethmannstrasse 15, Munich-Ismaning. Tel. 089/96 88 37. 2 apts (both with shower and toilet). **S-Bahn:** S-3 from the Hauptbahnhof to Ismaning (a 30-minute trip); then a seven-minute walk.

$ Rates: 320 DM ($200) per week for two people. No credit cards.

English-speaking Herr Hübner rents two apartments, each with private bathroom and kitchenette equipped with electric stove, refrigerator, toaster, pots and pans, and utensils. He also has bicycles for his guests to use, and the castle Schleissheim and a lake are nearby. Ismaning, by the way, is older than Munich and is near the airport, only 7½ miles from the city center. An architect by trade and an enthusiast of old buildings, Herr Hübner has many books on old churches, castles, and buildings in Munich.

PENSION WELTI, 45 Uhdestrasse, 8 Munich 71. Tel. 089/791 15 42. 16 apts (all with tub/shower and toilet). TV TEL **U-Bahn:** U-2 to Aidenbachstrasse; then bus no. 64 from Aidenbachstrasse to Plattlinger Strasse.

$ Rates: 65 DM ($40.60) single; 85 DM ($53.10) double. No credit cards. **Parking:** 3 DM ($1.85).

Each of the apartments in this pension located in the quiet residential neighborhood of Solln has a bathroom and a fully equipped kitchen. There's even daily maid service and a shopping center nearby where you can buy all your provisions. Although rooms are rented on a daily basis, it's great for longer stays. The owner, Rudolph Keis, was born in Germany but lived in the United States for 12 years.

WORTH THE EXTRA BUCKS

Although slightly beyond our usual budget, these hotels are worth the extra money if it's time for a splurge and you want some extra pampering. All are located south of the train station within walking distance.

EUROPÄISCHER HOF, Bayerstrasse 31, 8 Munich 2. Tel. 089/55 15 10. Fax 089/55151-222. Telex 522642. 155 rms (130 with tub or shower and toilet). TEL **Directions:** Walk one minute south from the Hauptbahnhof.

$ **Rates** (including buffet breakfast and showers): 75–95 DM ($46.85–$59.35) single without shower or toilet, 112–170 DM ($70–$106.25) single with shower and toilet; 110–150 DM ($68.75–$93.75) double without shower or toilet, 140–230 DM ($87.50–$143.75) double with shower and toilet; 190–280 DM ($118.75–$175) triple with shower and toilet. The higher prices are for the main tourist season (Sept–Oct), including Oktoberfest. AE, DC, MC, V. **Parking:** 12 DM ($7.50).

You can't get any closer to the train station than this. Located just across the street from the Hauptbahnhof's south side, this modern hotel has a sleek marbled lobby with a courteous staff. Most rooms have been recently renovated with new wallpaper, and TVs are available on request. There's a restaurant, and in its elegant breakfast room you can eat as much as you want. All in all, from its appearance you'd expect it to be more expensive than it is.

HOTEL METROPOLE, Bayerstrasse 43, 8 Munich 2. Tel. 089/53 07 64. Fax 089/532 81 34. 260 rms (230 with tub or shower and toilet, 10 with shower only). TV TEL

$ **Rates** (including breakfast and shower): 75–85 DM ($46.85–$53.10) single without tub/shower or toilet, 125–150 DM ($78.10–$93.75) single with tub or shower and toilet; 110–130 DM ($68.75–$81.25) double without tub/shower or toilet, 170–230 DM ($106.25–$143.75) double with tub or shower and toilet. Extra bed 45 DM ($28.10). AE, DC, MC, V. **Parking:** 15 DM ($9.35).

Conveniently located across the street from the main train station (take the south exit; the hotel entrance is on Goethestrasse), this modern hotel has a light and airy lobby with a two-story atrium topped with a skylight, a friendly staff, and clean, comfortable rooms featuring soundproof windows and TV with remote control. Rooms with showers instead of tubs are cheaper. The higher prices in each category above reflect rates during peak season. Since there are only a few rooms without bathrooms, be sure to reserve in advance if that's important to you. The hotel restaurant serves international food.

HOTEL MONACHIA, Senefelderstrasse 3, 8 Munich 2. Tel. 089/55 52 81. Fax 089/59 25 98. 30 rms (7 with shower and toilet, 14 with shower only). TEL **Directions:** Walk three minutes south from the train station.

$ **Rates** (including breakfast and shower): 75 DM ($46.85) single without shower or toilet, 85 DM ($53.10) single with shower only; 145 DM ($90.60) double without shower or toilet, 165 DM ($103.10) double with shower only, 185 DM ($115.60) double with shower and toilet; 165 DM ($103.10) triple without shower or toilet, 185 DM ($115.60) triple with shower only, 220 DM ($137.50) triple with shower and toilet. AE, CB, DC, MC, V. **Parking:** 15 DM ($9.35).

More economical is this older hotel, owned by Herr Schieferle, who is fluent in English and Spanish. Rooms are spacious and there's an elevator. Breakfasts are substantial.

HOTEL UHLAND, Uhlandstrasse 1, 8 Munich 2. Tel. 089/53 92 77. Fax 089/63 11 14. Telex 528368. 30 rms (all with tub or shower and toilet). MINIBAR TV TEL **Bus:** 58 from the Hauptbahnhof to Georg-Hirth-Platz (third stop).

$ **Rates** (including buffet breakfast): 100–160 DM ($62.50–$100) single; 140–230 DM ($87.50–$143.75) double; 170–260 DM ($106.25–$162.50) triple; 190–300 DM ($118.75–$187.50) quad. Crib available. No credit cards. **Parking:** Free.

⭐ The facade of this 100-year-old building is striking—ornate baroque with flower boxes of geraniums (evergreens in winter) at all the windows. In former days each floor of the building was its own grand apartment. It was converted into a hotel about 40 years ago, and each room is different. Some have been renovated, and a few rooms even have balcony. Parents take note—there's even a "children's room," complete with bunk beds and a stereo. Note that the higher prices in each category are those charged during Oktoberfest and major conventions. Highly recommended, this hotel is located near the Oktoberfest meadow.

5. BUDGET DINING

It's worth coming to Munich solely for its restaurants. Not, perhaps, just for the cuisine—unless, of course, you love pork or calf and crave huge portions of it—but also for the atmosphere. Bavarian restaurants are boisterous affairs, typically with wooden tables and chairs, beamed ceilings, and half-paneled walls studded with simple hooks where you can hang your hat. You sit wherever there's an empty chair (no one will seat you), making it easy to strike up conversation with others at your table, especially after a few rounds of beer. In fact, I suspect that restaurants in Munich evolved solely so that its citizenry could eat something as they imbibed their favorite brew. And this being Bavaria with its tendency toward excess, the meals are hearty and huge. You don't have to spend a fortune here for atmosphere or the food.

Most of Munich's restaurants are in the city center, clustered around the train station and in nightlife districts like Schwabing. Since menus are almost always posted outside the front door, you're never left in the dark about prices. Many restaurants offer a *Tageskarte,* or daily menu, with special complete meals of the day. In fact, most of the entrées in Munich's restaurants are complete meals, including a main course and a couple of side dishes (often potatoes and sauerkraut). Prices listed below are for complete meals.

If you want to save money, eat at an *Imbiss,* a stall or tiny hole-in-the-wall where food is served over the counter and you eat standing up. And for your breakfast coffee, go to Tcshibo or Eduscho, two chain coffee stores that sell both the beans and brew. You can bring your own pastry and drink a cup of coffee standing up for 1.95 DM ($1.20).

In addition to the restaurants listed below, the beer halls in the "Evening Entertainment" section later in this chapter also serve food.

FAVORITE MEALS

With its six breweries and the largest beer festival in the world, Munich is probably best known for beer, which is almost a complete meal in itself. Bavarians even drink it for breakfast. The freshest beer is draft beer, called *vom Fass. Weissbier* is made from wheat instead of barley and is full of nutritious (that's one way to look at it) sediment. In summer, a refreshing drink is a *Radler,* half beer and half lemon soda.

To accompany your beer you might want to order food. For breakfast try *Weisswurst,* literally white sausage, a delicate blend of veal, salt, pepper, lemon, and parsley. Don't eat the skin unless you want to astound those around you—it would be like eating the plastic wrapper around a hamburger. Another popular dish is *Leberkäs,* which translates as liver-cheese but is actually neither one. It's a kind of German meatloaf that looks like a thick slab of bologna, and it's great with a roll, some mustard, and sauerkraut.

Other Bavarian specialties include *Leberknödl* (liver dumplings, often served in a soup or with sauerkraut), *Kalbshaxe* (grilled knuckle of veal), *Schweinshaxe* (grilled knuckle of pork), *Schweinsbraten* (pot-roasted pork), *Sauerbraten* (marinated beef in a thick sauce), and *Spanferkel* (suckling pig).

MEALS FOR LESS THAN 10 DM [$6.20]

IN THE CITY CENTER

BELLA ITALIA, Sendlingerstrasse 66. Tel. 260 93 77.
   Cuisine: ITALIAN. **U-Bahn:** Marienplatz or Sendlinger-Tor.
$ Prices: 6–17 DM ($3.75–$10.60). No credit cards.
   Open: Daily 11:30am–midnight.
This popular chain of Italian-staffed restaurants is the best place in town for inexpensive pizza or pasta, including lasagne, tortellini, cannelloni, and spaghetti, all priced between 6 DM and 15 DM ($3.75 and $9.35). This restaurant, conveniently located between Marienplatz and Sendlinger-Tor-Platz, offers indoor seating as well as outdoor tables in a fashionable courtyard called Asam-Hof. The pizza Bella Italia, topped with ham, mushrooms, olives, peppers, artichoke, and salami, is especially good.

    Other Bella Italias, with the same menu and hours, are located at Rosenheimer Platz in Haidhausen (tel. 48 61 79), Leopoldstrasse 44 in Schwabing (tel. 33 89 50), Türkenstrasse 50 in south Schwabing (tel. 28 07 39), and Hohenzollernplatz 8 (tel. 300-63318).

BEL TERRINE, 6th floor of the Kaufhof Department Store, Karlsplatz. Tel. 51 251.
   Cuisine: GERMAN/VARIED. **S-Bahn:** Karlsplatz/Stachus.
$ Prices: 7–13 DM ($4.35–$8.10). No credit cards.
   Open: Mon–Wed and Fri 9am–6pm, Thurs 9am–8pm, Sat 8:30am–1:30pm (8:30am–5:30pm on langer Samstag).
This self-service cafeteria on the top floor of the Kaufhof Department Store is your best bet for a meal with a panoramic view of the city. Every day there's a changing menu for 13 DM ($8.10); the soups and salad bar are cheaper. If you want to splurge, try one of their delicious desserts.

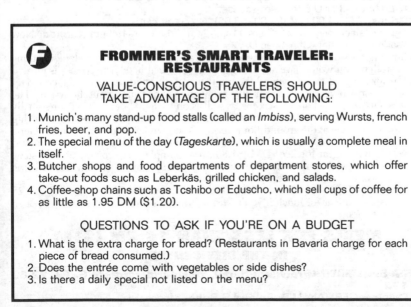

(F) FROMMER'S SMART TRAVELER: RESTAURANTS

VALUE-CONSCIOUS TRAVELERS SHOULD
TAKE ADVANTAGE OF THE FOLLOWING:

1. Munich's many stand-up food stalls (called an *Imbiss*), serving Wursts, french fries, beer, and pop.
2. The special menu of the day (*Tageskarte*), which is usually a complete meal in itself.
3. Butcher shops and food departments of department stores, which offer take-out foods such as Leberkäs, grilled chicken, and salads.
4. Coffee-shop chains such as Tschibo or Eduscho, which sell cups of coffee for as little as 1.95 DM ($1.20).

QUESTIONS TO ASK IF YOU'RE ON A BUDGET

1. What is the extra charge for bread? (Restaurants in Bavaria charge for each piece of bread consumed.)
2. Does the entrée come with vegetables or side dishes?
3. Is there a daily special not listed on the menu?

NEAR THE HAUPTBAHNHOF

NORDSEE, Schützenstrasse 10. Tel. 59 80 52.
   Cuisine: SEAFOOD. **Directions:** Walk a few minutes east of the Hauptbahnhof.
$ **Prices:** 6.50–10 DM ($4.05–$6.25). No credit cards.
   Open: Mon–Wed and Fri 9am–7pm, Thurs 9am–8pm, Sat 9am–3pm (to 6:30pm
   on langer Samstag), Sun 11am–6pm.
A chain of fast-food fish restaurants originating on Germany's northern coast,
Nordsee makes ordering easy by putting the entire menu (about a dozen choices) on a
lighted board with photographs. Simply go through the cafeteria line and choose from
the selections of fish sticks, fish sandwiches, fish paella, herring, fish soup, and sole.
There's also take-out service.
   There's another branch at the Viktualienmarkt (Munich's open-air market) near
Marienplatz, and at Leopoldstrasse 68 in Schwabing.

WIENERWALD, Arnulfstrasse 12. Tel. 59 70 69.
   Cuisine: GERMAN.
$ **Prices:** 6–17 DM ($3.75–$10.60). No credit cards.
   Open: Daily 9am–midnight.
The Wienerwald chain is one of the great success stories of postwar Germany, with
more than 20 locations in Munich and hundreds throughout Germany and Austria.
Legend has it that the founder came to Oktoberfest, saw the mass consumption of
grilled chicken, and decided to open his own restaurant serving only one item—roast
chicken—at a price people could afford. Other items on the menu now include
Schnitzel, Gulasch, and fish; there's also a salad bar.
   This Wienerwald is a minute's walk north of the Hauptbahnhof. Other convenient
branches are at Odeonsplatz 6-7 (tel. 22 58 30), Amalienstrasse 23 (tel. 28 23 92), and
Wendl-Dietrich-Strasse 5 (tel. 16 04 43).

IN SCHWABING

In addition to the restaurant listed here, chain restaurants described above with
locations in Schwabing include Nordsee, Wienerwald, and Bella Italia.

MENSA UNIVERSITÄT, Leopoldstrasse 13. Tel. 38 19 60.
   U-Bahn: U-3 or U-6 to Giselastrasse.
$ **Prices:** 2.90–4.90 DM ($1.80–$3.05). No credit cards.
   Open: Lunch only, Mon–Thurs 11am–2pm, Fri 11am–1:45pm. **Closed:** New
Year's Day, Easter, Christmas Day.
Technically for students, this cafeteria is so big and so busy that if you look anything
like a student you won't have any trouble getting a meal here. The Mensa is located
back from Leopoldstrasse, behind the multistory pink building, in a plain, concrete-
and-glass two-story structure. Your only problem may be figuring out the system. The
daily menus are posted on TV screens, as well as on bulletin boards. There are usually
four different meals available at four different prices—each with its own colored chip
that you buy at one of the ground-floor booths. You then head upstairs to the cafeteria
that is dishing out the meal you've selected and hand in the chip when you've picked
up your tray. A meal for 2.90 DM ($1.80), for example, may consist of beef stew,
potatoes, salad, and a roll. If in doubt about what's being offered and which cafeteria
to go to, ask one of the students.
   A second Mensa, the **Mensa Technische Universität,** Arcisstrasse 17 (tel. 28
14 57), is convenient for lunch if you're visiting the Alte and Neue Pinakothek, open
the same hours.

MEALS FOR LESS THAN 16 DM [$10]
IN THE CITY CENTER

**BEIM SEDLMAYR (Bratwurst-Herzl), Westenriderstrasse 6. Tel. 22 62
19.**
   Cuisine: GERMAN. **U-Bahn and S-Bahn:** Marienplatz.

$ Prices: 6.50–17 DM ($4.05–$10.60). No credit cards.
Open: Mon–Sat 7:45am–3pm. **Closed:** Hols.
This unpretentious restaurant reputedly serves the best Weisswurst in all of Munich, made fresh on the premises each day. Most customers are regulars, locals who stop in before going to work or a day of shopping. It's lcoated near the Viktualienmarkt, Munich's large open-air market. The menu is simple and the prices reasonable. Other good choices in addition to the Weisswurst include Leberkäs, one-pot stews, Spanferkel, Schnitzel, or the Schweinsbraten.

Note: The restaurant's permanent address (Heiliggeiststrasse 3) is undergoing renovation; the restaurant has therefore moved temporarily to Westenriederstrasse around the corner and is called Beim Sedlmayr. Renovations are expected to be completed by the end of 1993, after which it will resume its old name, Bratwurst-Herzl.

DONISL, Weinstrasse 1. Tel. 22 01 84.
 Cuisine: GERMAN. **U-Bahn and S-Bahn:** Marienplatz.
$ Prices: 6.80–35 DM ($4.25–$21.85). AE, DC, MC, V.
 Open: Daily 8am–11:30pm.
Whereas the Bratwurst-Herzl is filled with natives, the Donisl is popular with tourists in part because of its convenient location right off Marienplatz. Its cheapest dish is its Weisswurst for 6.80 DM ($4.25), so if you're on a budget come here for breakfast or lunch. It has a bright interior, with an inner atrium complete with skylight, and on its walls are portraits of famous actors. At the front of the restaurant is a small *Imbiss* with even cheaper dishes. Otherwise, if you feel like splurging, I recommend the pepper steak, Leberkäs, Spanferkel, Schweinsbraten, or the Wurst salad with onions.

MANGO, Rosental 3-4. Tel. 260 89 07.
 Cuisine: VEGETARIAN. **U-Bahn and S-Bahn:** Marienplatz.
$ Prices: 9–16 DM ($5.60–$10). No credit cards.
 Open: Mon–Wed and Fri 11am–7pm, Thurs 11am–9pm, Sat 11am–4pm, Sun 11am–6pm.

★ This simple and pleasant restaurant, decorated with plants and soothing, natural woods, offers a great alternative to the typical pork dishes of German restaurants. Its self-service counter offers approximately 20 selections of vegetarian dishes and salads, from quiches and soups to pasta, stews, and tofu dishes. (How about a tofu Schnitzel?) There's a salad bar where you can help yourself. Note that in the evenings the only entryway is around the corner on Rindermarkt. It's a three-minute walk south of Marienplatz, across from the tourist office.

NÜRNBERGER BRATWURST GLÖCKL AM DOM, Frauenplatz 9. Tel. 22 03 85 or 29 52 64.
 Cuisine: GERMAN. **U-Bahn and S-Bahn:** Marienplatz.
$ Prices: 7.50–24 DM ($4.70–$15). No credit cards.
 Open: Mon–Sat 9:30am–midnight.

★ Although you could easily spend 30 DM ($18.75) here eating such Bavarian specialties as pork filet or Schweinshaxe, all you have to order for the privilege of experiencing a great establishment is the Schweinswurst (four small sausages with Sauerkraut) for a meal costing less than 8 DM ($5). A half liter of beer will cost 4.50 DM ($2.80). Located in the shadows of the Frauenkirche (Church of Our Lady), this is Bavaria at its finest: a rough wooden floor, wooden tables, hooks for clothing, and beer steins and tin plates lining a shelf on the wall. The restaurant was founded in 1893, totally destroyed in 1945, and rebuilt exactly as it was. Upstairs is the Albrecht Dürer Room, quieter and more intimate, but I prefer the liveliness of the ground floor. An evening here could possibly be your most memorable in Munich.

RATSKELLER (under the Town Hall), Marienplatz. Tel. 22 03 13.
 Cuisine: GERMAN. **U-Bahn and S-Bahn:** Marienplatz.
$ Prices: 11–26 DM ($6.85–$16.25). AE, DC, MC, V.
 Open: Daily 10am–midnight.

Many town halls have a restaurant in their cellar, and Munich's is no exception. This one is cavernous, with low, vaulted ceilings, archways, white tablecloths, and flowers on every table. Popular with businesspeople and middle-aged shoppers, this dignified restaurant has an English menu. There's no dress code, but shorts would not be appropriate. In addition to its Bavarian specialties of Spanferkel or suckling pig, it also has a salad bar and vegetarian dishes for those who are tired of pork, as well as Wurst, spaghetti, and Leberkäs. This is a good choice for Weisswurst in the morning, or you might want to come for an afternoon coffee and dessert. Beer and wines available.

WEISSES BRÄUHAUS, Im Tal 10. Tel. 29 98 75.
   Cuisine: GERMAN. **U-Bahn and S-Bahn:** Marienplatz.
$ Prices: 8–23 DM ($5–$14.35). No credit cards.
   Open: Daily 9am–11pm.
This boisterous place is famous for its beer—*Bräuhaus* means brewery—and the beer to order is its wheat beer, either the Weizenbier or Weissbier. A simple, white interior with a wooden floor and long wooden tables, this typical Bavarian restaurant has an English menu, whose cheapest meal is its Weisswurst (available only until noon). If you're hungry, order the Bavarian Farmer's Feast, which comes with roast and smoked pork, pork sausage, liver dumpling, mashed potatoes and Sauerkraut. Other choices include Leberkäs, suckling pig, and breaded calf's head. Or if you want, just order a beer; a half liter costs 4.90 DM ($3.05).

WEINSTADL, Burgstrasse 5. Tel. 523 27 01.
   Cuisine: GERMAN. **U-Bahn and S-Bahn:** Marienplatz.
$ Prices: 10–30 DM ($6.25–$18.75). AE, DC, MC, V.
   Open: Mon–Sat 11am–11:15pm, Sun and hols 5–11:15pm.
In contrast to the other restaurants in this section, this one specializes in German wines instead of beer (Munich was, apparently, a wine town long before beer took over). First built in 1551, and later serving as a Customs house for wines brought in from Austria, Italy, Hungary, and France to be traded for those of Germany, this is a restaurant full of architectural character—a narrow spiral staircase, windows with bull's-eye glass, an arbored courtyard, and a cellar with vaulted ceilings. One of Munich's oldest buildings, it has three floors of dining and there's an English menu listing such specialties as roast pork with potato dumplings and salad, grilled sausage, and Schnitzel, as well as changing daily specials.

ZUM FRANZISKANER, Perusastrasse 5 (with another entrance around the corner at Residenzstrasse 9). Tel. 231 81 20.
   Cuisine: GERMAN. **U-Bahn and S-Bahn:** Marienplatz.
$ Prices: 10–30 DM ($6.25–$18.75). AE, DC, MC.
   Open: Daily 8am–midnight.
A lively Bavarian favorite, this restaurant gets so crowded you may find it difficult to find a seat at prime lunch or dinner times. There are several separate dining rooms, so simply wander through until you find a seat. If you're starving try the Wurst platter, which comes with various kinds of Wurst (smoked, blood, liver, onion, and more), as well as radish and bread. Other sections on the English menu include fresh trout, Leberkäs served with a fried egg and potato salad, knuckle of pork with potato dumpling and cabbage salad, Sauerbraten with dumpling, and Wiener Schnitzel. There are also many changing daily specials which, unfortunately, aren't listed on the English menu. If you're on a budget, you can dine for less than 10 DM ($6.25) if you order the Weisswurst, served here until 9pm. It's three minutes north of Marienplatz.

SOUTH OF THE HAUPTBAHNHOFF

GASTSTÄTTE GRÜNER HOF, 35 Bayerstrasse. Tel. 59 55 71.
   Cuisine: GERMAN.
$ Prices: 9–30 DM ($5.60–$18.75). No credit cards.
   Open: Daily 7:30am–midnight.
Located just across from the train station's south side (where the tourist office is), the Grüner Hof is known for its large, hearty portions. Specialties on the English menu

include pork steak with noodles and vegetables, Bavarian Wurst platter, and the chicken platter (a quarter of a chicken) with side dishes—a great meal for less than 10 DM ($6.25). Weisswurst here is 5.60 DM ($3.50). The Grüner Hof is popular with the locals for its good, German-style home-cooking, as well as for the fact that it has its own butcher shop. A simple dining area with plain wooden tables, red-checkered tablecloths, and wooden floors, this unpretentious Bavarian locale has been dishing out inexpensive meals for more than 30 years.

MARIANDL RESTAURANT, Goethestrasse 51. Tel. 53 51 58.
   Cuisine: GERMAN/VARIED.
$ **Prices:** 8–30 DM ($5–$18.75). No credit cards.
   Open: Lunch Mon–Fri 11:30am–2:30pm; dinner Mon–Fri 6–10:30pm. **Closed:** Hols.

This rather elegant and refined restaurant with a parlorlike atmosphere offers free entertainment as well as dining. From 8pm Monday through Friday musicians play classical music; on Monday it's open mike. Portraits of famous classical composers line the walls, and there are fresh flowers on each table. A changing menu offers a few select complete meals such as Schnitzel or Sauerbraten, but lighter meals such as spaghetti are always available, as well as beer, wine, and champagne. It's located less than a 10-minute walk from the Hauptbahnhof, near Beethovenplatz.

IN SCHWABING

GASTSTÄTTE ATZINGER, Schellingstrasse 9. Tel. 28 28 80.
   Cuisine: GERMAN. **U-Bahn:** U-3 or U-6 to Universität.
$ **Prices:** 8–20 DM ($5–$12.50). No credit cards.
   Open: Daily 11:30am–midnight.

Very popular with students who come here to eat, drink, smoke, and talk, this pub/restaurant has terrific prices and atmosphere. Specialties include Schweinsbraten, Schweinshaxe, Schnitzel, fish, spaghetti, Wurst, and Leberkäs. It's located in the southern part of Schwabing on the corner of Schellingstrasse and Amalienstrasse in an area of bookshops, cheap restaurants, and bars. Its daily specials—giant single-platter meals with a main dish and side dishes—are often big enough to feed two people. A quarter liter of beer is 2 DM ($1.25).

GASTSTÄTTE LEOPOLD, Leopoldstrasse 50. Tel. 39 94 33.
   Cuisine: GERMAN. **U-Bahn:** U-3 or U-6 to Giselastrasse.
$ **Prices:** 10–25 DM ($6.25–$15.60). No credit cards.
   Open: Daily 11:30am–11pm.

Popular with the middle-aged, this Bavarian restaurant can be a haven away from the throngs of Schwabing, though later at night it can get quite crowded. In the summer there are tables and chairs outside where you can watch the passing parade of humanity on busy Leopoldstrasse, the center stage of nightlife in Schwabing. A large, open dining area with a beer-hall atmosphere, it serves a half liter of beer for 4.50 DM ($2.80). Watch for the changing daily menu or order from the menu listing such specialties as Schnitzel, Wurst (including Weisswurst), and Bauernschmaus (Schweinsbraten, smoked pork, sausage, sauerkraut, and dumplings).

GASTSTÄTTE WEINBAUER, Fendstrasse 5. Tel. 39 81 55.
   Cuisine: GERMAN. **U-Bahn:** U-3 or U-6 to Münchener Freiheit.
$ **Prices:** 7–17 DM ($4.35–$10.60). No credit cards.
   Open: Thurs–Tues 11:30am–11:30pm.

This is a good, plain eating establishment typical of neighborhood restaurants everywhere. Tablecloths, flowers, and a few pictures on the walls are the only attempts at decoration; it's the food everyone comes for. Again, portions are huge, and the daily changing menus are a particularly good value. Ask the waiter to translate. Otherwise, items always on the menu include Sauerbraten, Schweinsbraten, Weisswurst, Leberkäs, pepper steak, and Wiener Schnitzel. A half liter of beer is 3.40 DM ($2.10). This is a great place to start an evening in Schwabing, just off Leopoldstrasse near Münchener Freiheit.

STREET FOOD

In addition to the locales mentioned here, both the Viktualienmarkt and the Schmankerlgasse, described in the picnic section below, offer unlimited choices in fast food and stand-up food stalls. Restaurants listed above with an adjoining *Imbiss* or take-out service include Wienerwald, Nordsee, and Donisl.

NEAR THE HAUPTBAHNHOF

MATHÄSER BIERSTADT, Bayerstrasse 5. Tel. 59 28 96.
  Cuisine: GERMAN.
$ Prices: 4–8 DM ($2.50–$5). No credit cards.
  Open: Daily 10am–10pm.
This beer hall a short walk from the main train station has an outdoor *Imbiss* at its main entryway, where it sells Wiener (hot dog), Eintopf mit Rindfleisch (a beef stew), Brathuhn (grilled chicken), Weisswurst, and Leberkäs. You can take your order inside and eat it at one of the stand-up tables just inside the door, where you can also order a beer. This is, after all, a beer hall.

IN THE CITY CENTER

DANMARK, underground passage at Stachus (Karlsplatz).
  Cuisine: INTERNATIONAL. **S-Bahn and U-Bahn:** Karlsplatz/Stachus.
$ Prices: 3–7 DM ($1.85–$4.35). No credit cards.
  Open: Mon–Wed and Fri 9am–7pm, Thurs 9am–9pm, Sat 9am–3pm (to 7pm on langer Samstag).
It's hard to miss this busy *Imbiss,* located in the middle of the passageway underneath the Stachus at Karlsplatz. Different counters offer different things, ranging from Wurst and hot dogs to pizza, hamburgers, sandwiches, gyros, Chinese dishes, and beer. There are stand-up counters where you can eat.

RÄUCHERONKEL, Orlandostrasse 3. Tel. 22 45 09.
  Cuisine: GERMAN.
$ Prices: 4.50–11 DM ($2.80–$6.85). No credit cards.
  Open: Mon–Fri 7am–6pm, Sat 7am–1pm.
Located near the Hofbräuhaus, and just a seven-minute walk from Marienplatz, this cafeteria-style *Imbiss* is connected to its own butcher shop and has chest-high tables where you can stand and eat your food. It's popular with the working class, so no one here speaks English—you'll just have to point. Choices usually include Weisswurst, Leberknödel soup, Schweinsbraten, dumplings, Gulasch, Kalbsbraten, Leberkäs, grilled chicken, and sausages. This is also a good place to buy picnic ingredients.

VINZENZ MURR, Rosenstrasse 7. Tel. 260 47 65.
  Cuisine: GERMAN.
$ Prices: 3–13 DM ($1.85–$8.10). No credit cards.
  Open: Mon–Wed 8am–6:30pm, Thurs 8am–8:30pm, Fri 7:45am–6:30pm, Sat 8am–2pm (to 6pm on langer Samstag).
This is the most convenient location (a minute from Marienplatz) of a chain of butcher shops in Munich, which has a stand-up *Imbiss* in addition to its meats and take-out service. Sandwiches, Schweineschnitzel, salads, cheeses, breads, and Leberkäs are just some of the many selections.

IN SCHWABING

HUT'S PIZZA STATION, Feilitzschstrasse 11. Tel. 34 24 97.
  Cuisine: PIZZA. **U-Bahn:** U-3 or U-6 to Münchener Freiheit.
$ Prices: 3–5.50 DM ($1.85–$3.45). No credit cards.
  Open: Daily noon–1am.
This is one of several take-out establishments in Schwabing, catering primarily to the hordes of young people who come here for a night on the town. Although its main

seller is pizza by the slice for 3.50 DM ($2.20), it also sells curry Wurst and gyros with tzaziki.

PICNIC SUPPLIES & WHERE TO EAT THEM

Read over the selections presented above under "Street Food and the Stand-Up *Imbiss*," since the localities there all offer take-out food.

Department stores (such as Hertie across from the train station or Kaufhof Marienplatz) have food departments in their basements. These sell fruits and vegetables, cheese, sausages, breads, and cakes, as well as ready-made salads, Leberkäs, grilled chicken, and more.

If you want more traditional surroundings, the **Viktualienmarkt** can't be beat. Munich's most famous outdoor market, dating from the early 1800s, it's a colorful affair with permanent little shops and booths and stalls set up under umbrellas. Wurst, bread, cakes, honey, cheese, wine, fruits, vegetables, flowers, and meats are sold here, and in the middle of the market there's even a beer garden, where you're welcome to sit at one of the outer tables (only those without a tablecloth) and eat your purchase. There are also a lot of stand-up fast-food counters. The market is open Monday through Friday from 8am to 6pm and on Saturday from 8am to 2pm.

Another good place to search for picnic ingredients is **Schmankerlgasse,** an underground passage leading from the Hertie department store to Karlsplatz. Schmankerlgasse is lined with booth after booth of food stalls, each specializing in something different, including pita-bread sandwiches, Chinese food, sausages, desserts, croissants, fresh fruit juices, salads, cheeses, and vegetables. You can either stand and eat it here or take it with you. Schmankerlgasse is open Monday through Wednesday and Friday from 9am to 6:30pm, on Thursday from 9am to 8:30pm, and on Saturday from 8:30am to 2pm (first Saturday of the month, 8:30am to 6pm). It's closed on Sunday.

If you want to picnic in style, head for the finest delicatessen in town, **Alois Dallmayr,** at Dienerstrasse 14 (tel. 21350). Its meats, cheeses, wines, grilled chicken, breads, fruits, vegetables, caviar, chocolates, teas, coffees, and cakes are expensive— you can even have things gift-wrapped here. It's open Monday through Wednesday and on Friday from 9am to 6:30pm, on Thursday from 9am to 8:30pm, and on Saturday from 9am to 2pm.

And where can you go to eat your goodies? Try along the **Isar River** or somewhere in the huge expanse of the **Englischer Garten.** Better yet, take your food to one of the **beer gardens** in the section below, where all you have to buy is one of those famous mugs of foaming beer.

BEER GARDENS

Munich's beer gardens are as fickle as the weather—that is, if the weather's bad, the beer gardens don't open. By the same token, if suddenly in the middle of February the weather turns gloriously warm, the beer gardens start turning on the tap.

Generally speaking, however, beer gardens are open on sunny days from May to September or October, usually from 10 or 11am to midnight. Ranging in size from tiny, neighborhood gardens that accommodate a few hundred people to those that seat several thousand, beer gardens number about 35 in and around Munich, making it the beer-garden capital of the world. Many of the larger ones boast traditional Bavarian bands on weekends. The smallest beer available is a liter—after all, you're here to drink beer—which costs about 8 DM ($5). *A Word of Caution:* Many of the beer gardens are located in the middle of huge parks, making them a bit difficult to find. Take note of how you got there; it's even harder to find your way out of the park after you've had a few liters of beer.

The four beer gardens listed here allow you to bring your own food: **Augustiner Keller,** Arnulfstrasse 52 (tel. 59 43 93), located about a 10-minute walk northwest of the Hauptbahnhof; **Viktualienmarkt,** located in the city center near Marienplatz (tel. 29 75 45), closed Sunday and holidays (described in the picnic section, above); **Chinesischer Turm,** in the Englischer Garten (tel. 39 50 28), reached by taking the

U-Bahn (U-3 or U-6) to Giselastrasse; and **Hirschgarten,** Hirschgartenstrasse 1 (tel. 17 25 91), near Nymphenburg Palace (take the S-Bahn to Laim).

WORTH THE EXTRA BUCKS

HAXNBAUER, Münzstrasse 8. Tel. 22 19 22.
   Cuisine: GERMAN. **U-Bahn and S-Bahn:** Marienplatz.
$ Prices: 15–25 DM ($9.35–$15.60). AE, DC, MC, V.
   Open: Dinner only, Mon–Sat 5pm–midnight. **Closed:** Christmas to mid-Jan.

This restaurant claims to sell more pork and veal Haxn than any other place in the world. You can see meats roasting in the front window. Inside, the atmosphere is subdued and dignified, a good place to come for a quiet evening. Note the old copper bar (it's polished every day) and the collection of old firemen's helmets, some 100 years old. Located near the Hofbräuhaus, Haxnbauer has an English menu.

There's another Haxnbauer around the corner at Sparkassenstrasse 2 (tel. 22 19 22) with the same English menu, open daily from 11am to midnight year round. However, it's modern and does not have the same old-world atmosphere as the one above. If you're making reservations by phone, make sure to ask for a table at the Münzstrasse location, since the telephone number is the same for both. A five-minute walk from Marienplatz.

HUNDSKUGEL, Hotterstrasse 18. Tel. 26 42 72.
   Cuisine: GERMAN. **U-Bahn and S-Bahn:** Marienplatz.
$ Prices: 15–45 DM ($9.35–$28.10). No credit cards.
   Open: Daily 11am–11pm.

In operation since 1440, this may well be Munich's oldest restaurant. Its facade, brightly lit and decorated with flower boxes, hints at what's waiting inside — tiny, intimate rooms with low-beamed ceilings, little changed over the centuries. It serves Bavarian and German traditional food, including such specialties as Spanferkel with dumplings and Kraut salad, Tellerfleisch (beef cooked in meat stock and cut into slices), and the Hundskugel Spezial (broiled pork tenderloin with potatoes, mushrooms, and vegetables, baked with cheese), an experience you won't forget. It's just a five-minute walk from Marienplatz.

PRINZ MYSHKIN, Hackeanstrasse 2. Tel. 26 55 90.
   Cuisine: VEGETARIAN. **U-Bahn and S-Bahn:** Marienplatz.
$ Prices: Appetizers and soups 7–11 DM ($4.35–$6.85); pizza 13–18 DM ($8.10–$11.25); main courses 17–27 DM ($10.60–$16.85). AE, MC, V.
   Open: Mon–Thurs 11am–midnight, Fri–Sat 11am–1am.

If you want to splurge on something other than German cuisine, this trendy restaurant serves vegetarian dishes in a refined, relaxed setting. Boasting a high vaulted ceiling, artwork, candles on every table, and background music that's likely to be soft jazz, it serves a variety of changing salads, soups, and appetizers, which may include such choices as vegetarian quiche, Japanese miso soup, or a wild rice salad. In addition to pizza, it also offers innovative main dishes that may range from various ravioli to a Thai-inspired dish of paprika, mushrooms, onions, pineapple, and bananas in a coconut-curry sauce. During lunchtime it offers a fixed-price business lunch for less than 15 DM ($9.35). It's located just a few minutes' walk from Marienplatz, off Sendlinger Strasse.

6. ATTRACTIONS

SUGGESTED ITINERARIES

To see the best of what Munich has to offer, you could easily spend a week in the city. After all, with the possible exception of Berlin, Munich has more first-class museums

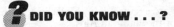
DID YOU KNOW . . . ?

- Munich means "home of the monks."
- In 1919, workers and soldiers in Munich proclaimed a Communist republic—it was short-lived.
- The Nazi party was founded in Munich.
- Nearly 40% of Munich was destroyed during World War II.
- Several of Wagner's operas were first performed in the city.
- During Oktoberfest, 72 oxen broiled whole on the spit, 30,000 grilled fish, 400,000 pairs of pork sausage, and 700,000 chickens are devoured—and over a million gallons of beer is consumed.

than any other city in Germany and is the cultural capital of the nation. If, however, you have less than a week to devote to Munich, the suggested itineraries below will guide you to the most important attractions.

IF YOU HAVE ONE DAY Begin with a breakfast of Munich's famous Weisswurst sausages at a traditional Bavarian restaurant. Then, to get a feel for the atmosphere of this Bavarian capital, stroll through Old Town. Start at Stachus (Karlsplatz) and walk down the pedestrian lane of Neuhauser Strasse with its many shops and boutiques, stopping at the venerable Frauenkirche, Munich's largest church and most celebrated landmark. Continue to Marienplatz, heart of the city, where you'll find the Neues Rathaus (New Town Hall). If you want, take an elevator up to the Rathaus tower for a view over the city.

From Marienplatz head for St. Peter's Church, affectionately called Alte Peter (Old Peter) by the townspeople. From Alte Peter visit the Viktualienmarkt, Munich's colorful open-air market, where you might want to eat lunch at one of its many stand-up food stalls or at the beer garden located in its center.

In the afternoon, head toward the Deutsches Museum, the world's largest technological museum. If you still have the energy, the time, and the inclination, rush to the Alte Pinakothek with its collection of famous masterpieces. Spend the evening at one of Munich's famous beer halls.

IF YOU HAVE TWO DAYS Spend the morning in Old Town as outlined above, but in the afternoon devote yourself to the Alte Pinakothek and its modern counterpart across the street, the Neue Pinakothek, with its collection of late 18th- and 19th-century works.

On Day 2, spend your morning at the Deutsches Museum. In the early afternoon visit Nymphenburg Palace, summer residence of the Wittelsbach Electors of Bavaria and Germany's largest baroque palace.

IF YOU HAVE THREE DAYS Spend your first day in Old Town as outlined above, but include in your walk visits to the Residenz, the official residence of the Wittelsbach family, and its Treasure House. Nearby is the de Cuvilliés Theater, one of the most beautiful rococo theaters in Germany. You should also pay a visit to the Stadtmuseum, the Municipal Museum, with displays relating to the history and development of Munich. End the day with a stroll through the Englischer Garten, stopping off for a liter at its Chinesischer Turm beer garden.

Spend Day 2 as outlined above. On Day 3 visit both the Alte and Neue Pinakothek; the Antikensammlungen, with its collection of antiquities; the Glyptothek, with one of the finest collections of Greek and Roman sculpture in Europe; and the Lenbachhaus, devoted to Munich's artists.

IF YOU HAVE FIVE DAYS Spend the first three days as outlined above. On Day 4, head for the Haus der Kunst, repository for art since the beginning of the 20th century. Nearby is the Bavarian Museum, a great museum relating to the history of than any other city in Germany and is the cultural capital of the nation. If, however, Bavaria with an outstanding collection of nativity scenes. Spend the afternoon shopping or visiting the BMW museum and the Olympic Village. Or go to Dachau, a former concentration camp that has been set up as a memorial to those who died under Hitler's regime. On the fifth day, take an excursion to Neuschwanstein, Germany's most famous castle, in the foothills of the Bavarian Alps.

TOP ATTRACTIONS

If museums are high on your list, you can save money by purchasing a ticket for 20 DM ($12.50) that will allow entrance into all 23 state museums, including the Alte and Neue Pinakothek, Bavarian National Museum, Glyptothek, Antikensammlungen, and the Haus der Kunst. Valid for eight days, it can be purchased at any of the state museums. Remember, too, that many museums (with the exception of the Deutsches Museum and Nymphenburg) are free on Sunday and holidays.

ALTE PINAKOTHEK, Barer Strasse 27. Tel. 238 05215.

✪ If you visit only one museum in Munich, this should be the one. Begun as the private collection of the Wittelsbach family in the early 1500s, it contains virtually all European schools of painting from the Middle Ages to the beginning of the 19th century. It has the largest collection of Rubens in the world, not to mention galleries filled with German, Dutch, Flemish, Italian, Spanish, and French masterpieces. Represented are Dürer, Cranach, Altdorfer, Brueghel, Rembrandt, Raphael, da Vinci, Titian, Tiepolo, El Greco, Velázquez, Murillo, Poussin, and Lorrain. The museum contains galleries of religious allegorical paintings, portraits of peasants and patricians, Romantic landscapes, still-lifes, and scenes of war and hunting. They are housed in an imposing structure built by Leo von Klenze between 1826 and 1836 and modeled on Renaissance palaces of Venice.

Although it's difficult to pick out the stars in the collection, Dürer is well represented with his *The Four Apostles, The Baumgartner Altar, Lamentation for the Dead Christ,* and, my favorite, his famous *Self-Portrait.* Watch for Titian's *Crowning with Thorns,* Rembrandt's *Birth of Christ* with his remarkable use of light and shadows, Rubens's *Self-Portrait with His Wife in the Arbon* and *Last Judgment,* and Brueghel's *Land of Cockaigne.*

In Albrecht Altdorfer's *Battle of Alexander,* which took him 12 years to complete, notice the painstaking detail of the thousands of lances and all the men on horseback. Yet Alexander the Great on his horse is easy to spot amid the chaos, as he pursues Darius fleeing in his chariot. Another favorite of mine is Adriaen Brouwer of the Netherlands, one of the best painters of the peasant genre. The Alte Pinakothek has 17 of his paintings, the largest collection in the world. Cabinet 10, where Brouwer has captured the life of his subjects as they drink at an inn, play cards, or engage in a brawl is delightful.

Admission: 4 DM ($2.50) adults, 2 DM ($1.85) senior citizens, 1 DM (60¢) students and children; combination ticket for both Alte and Neue Pinakothek, 7 DM ($4.35) adults, 3.50 DM ($2.20) senior citizens; free for everyone Sun and hols.

Open: Tues and Thurs 9am–4:30pm and 7–9pm, Wed and Fri–Sun 9am–4:30pm. **U-Bahn:** U-2 to Königsplatz. **Tram:** 18 to Pinakothek. **Bus:** 53 to Schellingstrasse.

NEUE PINAKOTHEK, Barer Strasse 29. Tel. 238 05195.

Across the street from the Alte Pinakothek is the Neue Pinakothek, with its comprehensive view of European painting in the 19th century. Included in the collection are examples of international art from around 1800 (David, Goya, Gainsborough, Turner), as well as German and French impressionism, symbolism, and art nouveau. Corinth, Slevogt, Liebermann, Cézanne, Gauguin, Rodin, van Gogh, Degas, Manet, Monet, and Renoir all have canvases here.

The building itself is a delight, designed by Alexander von Branca and opened in 1981 to replace the old museum destroyed in World War II. Using the natural lighting of skylights and windows, it's the perfect setting for the paintings it displays. Follow the rooms chronologically starting with Room 1.

Admission: 4 DM ($2.50) adults, 2 DM ($1.85) senior citizens, 1 DM (60¢) students and children; combination ticket for both Alte and Neue Pinakothek, 7 DM ($4.35) adults, 3.50 DM ($2.20) senior citizens; free for everyone Sun and hols.

Open: Tues 9am–4:30pm and 7–9pm, Wed–Sun 9am–4:30pm. **U-Bahn:** U-2 to Königsplatz; then a 15-minute walk. **Tram:** 18 to Pinakothek. **Bus:** 53 to Schellingstrasse.

DEUTSCHES MUSEUM, Museuminsel 1 (Ludwigsbrücke). Tel. 21791.

✪ I've been to the Deutsches Museum more than any other museum in Munich—and I still haven't seen it all. The largest technological museum of its kind in the world, the Deutsches Museum is divided into 30 different departments, including those relating to physics, shipping, rocks and minerals, vehicles, musical instruments, aviation, glass technology, writing and printing, photography, textiles, and weights and measures. There's also a planetarium.

You can see the first German submarine, 50 historic automobiles (including the first Benz of 1886), and the original airplanes of the Wright brothers. You can descend into the bowels of a salt mine or test your memory. Would you like to watch the development of a black-and-white print? What was Columbus's route to the New World? What does the nervous system of a turtle look like? What makes the museum fascinating for adults and children alike is that there are buttons to push, gears to crank, and levers to pull.

Admission: 8 DM ($5) adults, 4 DM ($2.50) senior citizens, 2.50 DM ($1.55) students and children.

Open: Daily 9am–5pm. **Tram:** 18 to Deutsches Museum. **S-Bahn:** Isartor.

NYMPHENBURG PALACE AND MARSTALLMUSEUM, AMALIENBURG, AND ROYAL PAVILIONS, Schloss Nymphenburg 1. Tel. 17 90 81.

The former summer residence of the Wittelsbach family who ruled over Bavaria, **Nymphenburg Palace** is Germany's largest baroque palace. Construction began in 1664 but took more than a century to complete; then the palace stretched 625 yards long and looked out over a park of some 500 acres. You could spend a whole day just in the sculptured garden with its statues, lakes, and waterfalls, and in its park pavilions (each a miniature palace in itself). But first visit the main palace and the nearby Marstallmuseum with its outstanding collection of carriages.

There are no tours of the palace—you simply wander around on your own in the two wings that are open to the public. The main attractions of the palace include the glorious Grand Marble Hall richly decorated with stucco work and frescoes, the Brussels tapestries, and the Chinese lacquer cabinet, but the most interesting in gossip circles is King Ludwig I's Gallery of Beauties. The 36 portraits here, commissioned by Ludwig, represent the most beautiful women in Munich in his time. Among them are Marie, Queen of Bavaria (and mother of Ludwig II), and Lola Montez, a dancer whose scandalous relations with Ludwig I prompted an 1848 revolt by a disgruntled people who forced Ludwig's abdication. (Lola Montez, by the way, was banished from the country and moved far away to California, where she made a name for herself during the Gold Rush days.)

Just outside the main palace (to the left as you face the ticket booth) is the **Marstallmuseum,** with its splendid collection of state coaches, carriages, and sleds used for weddings, coronations, and special events. Housed in what used to be the royal stables, the museum culminates in the fantastic fairytale like carriages of Ludwig II, which are no less extravagant than his castles. Up on the first floor above the Marstallmuseum is a collection of Nymphenburger porcelain, with its beautiful and delicate figurines, tea services, plates, and bowls.

Now head for the park. To your left is the **Amalienburg,** a small and delightful pink hunting lodge unlike anything you've ever seen. Considered one of the world's great masterpieces of rococo art, this lodge was built by architect de Cuvilliés for Maria Amalia, Charles Albert's wife. She used to station herself on a platform on the roof to shoot game that were driven past her. The first couple of rooms in this tiny

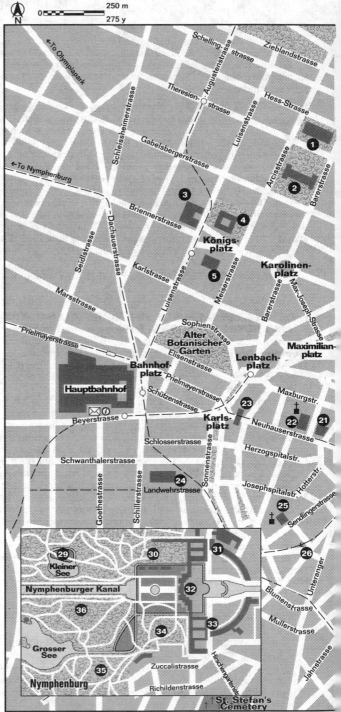

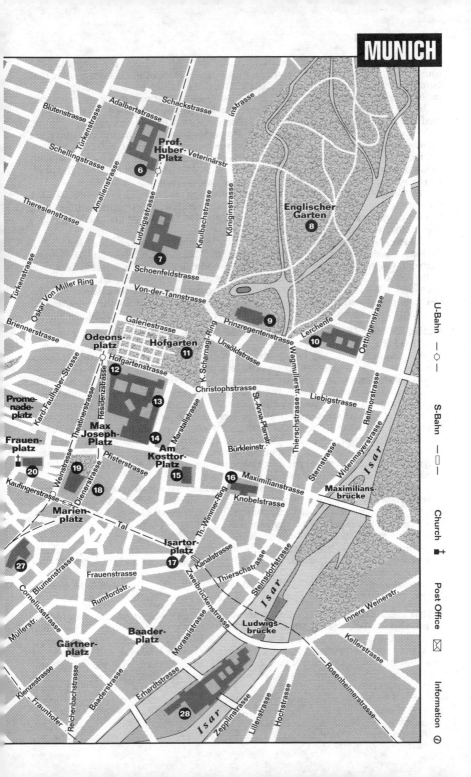

MUNICH

Blütenstrasse
Adalbertstrasse
Schackstrasse
Instrasse
Türkenstrasse
Schellingstrasse
Amalienstrasse
Prof. Huber-Platz
Veterinärstr
⑥
Theresienstrasse
Ludwigstrasse
Kaulbachstrasse
Königinstrasse
⑦
Englischer Garten
⑧
Schoenfeldstrasse
Türkenstrasse
Oskar Von Miller Ring
Von-der-Tannstrasse
Briennerstrasse
Galeriestrasse
Prinzregentenstrasse
⑨
Lerchenfe
Odeons-platz
Hofgarten
Wagmullerstr
⑩
Oettingenstrasse
Hofgartenstrasse
⑪
Unsöldstrasse
Karl-Faulhaber-Strasse
Residenzstrasse
⑫
K. Scharnagl-Ring
Christophstrasse
Liebigstrasse
Theatinerstrasse
⑬
Marstallstrasse
St.-Anna-Pl.
St.-Anna-Strasse
Thierschstrasse
Reitmorstrasse
Promenade-platz
Max Joseph-Platz
⑭
Bürkleinstr.
Sternstrasse
Widenmayerstrasse
Isar
Frauen-platz
Am Kosttor-Platz
⑳
⑲
⑮
⑯
Maximilianstrasse
Maximilians-brücke
Weinstrasse
Pfisterstrasse
Knobelstrasse
Kaufingerstrasse
⑱
Th.-Wimmer-Ring
Dienerstrasse
Marien-platz
Tal
⑰
Isartor-platz
⑳⑦
Blumenstrasse
Frauenstrasse
Kanalstrasse
Thierschstrasse
Steinsdorfstrasse
Isar
Corneliusstrasse
Rumfordstr.
Zweibrückenstrasse
Innere Weinerstr.
Müllerstr.
Baader-platz
Morassistrasse
Ludwigs-brücke
Kellerstrasse
Gärtner-platz
Baaderstrasse
Rosenheimerstrasse
Klenzestrasse
Reichenbachstrasse
Erhardtstrasse
Lilienstrasse
Hochstrasse
Fraunhofer-
⑳⑧
Zepplinstrasse
Isar

U-Bahn —◇—

S-Bahn —□—

Church ■✝

Post Office ⊠

Information ⊖

lodge are simple enough with drawings in the spirit of the hunt, but after that, the rooms take off in a flight of fantasy, with an amazing amount of decorative silver that covers the walls with vines, grapes, and cherubs. Its Hall of Mirrors is as splendid a room as you're likely to find anywhere, far surpassing anything in the main palace.

In the park are also three pavilions: the **Magdalenenklause,** designed as a meditation retreat for Max Emanuel, complete with artificially made cracks in the walls to make it look like a ruin; the **Pagodenburg,** an elegant two-story tea pavilion, with an interior of Dutch tiles on the ground floor and Chinese black-and-red lacquered chambers upstairs; and **Badenburg,** Max Emanuel's bathhouse with its Chinese wallpaper and two-story swimming pool faced with Dutch tiles. The pool, by the way, qualifies as Europe's first indoor swimming pool.

Admission: Combination ticket to everything, 6 DM ($3.75) adults, 4 DM ($2.50) senior citizens, students, and children; for Nymphenburg Palace, Amalienburg, and Marstallmuseum only, 4.50 DM ($2.80) adults, 3 DM ($1.85) senior citizens, students, and children.

Open: Nymphenburg Palace and Amalienburg, summer, Tues–Sun 9am–12:30pm and 1:30–5pm; winter, Tues–Sun 10am–12:30pm and 1:30–4pm. Marstallmuseum, summer, Tues–Sun 9am–noon and 1–5pm; winter, Tues–Sun 10am–noon and 1–4pm. Badenburg, Pagodenburg, and Magdalenenklause, summer, Tues–Sun 10am–12:30pm and 1:30–5pm; closed Oct–Mar. **Directions:** U-Bahn U-1 to Rotkreuzplatz; then tram no. 12 (going in the direction of Amalienburg Strasse) to Schloss Nymphenburg.

RESIDENZMUSEUM AND SCHATZKAMMER, Max-Joseph-Platz 3. Tel. 29 06 71.

Whereas Nymphenburg Palace was the Wittelsbach summer home, the Residenz was the family's official in-town residence for four centuries up until 1918. The **Residenzmuseum,** only a small part of the total residence, is open to the public and here you can wander at will. Even though it's a mere fraction of the total palace, it's so large that I wonder how its inhabitants ever managed to find their way around. There are court rooms, apartments, bedrooms, and arcades in everything from Renaissance and baroque to rococo and neoclassical. The Antiquarium is the largest Renaissance room north of the Alps; in the Silver Chamber is the complete table silver of the House of Wittelsbach—some 3,500 pieces. The Ancestors Hall contains the portraits of 121 members of the Wittelsbach family—eerie because of the way their eyes seem to follow you as you walk down the hall.

In the Residenz is the **Schatzkammer (Treasure House),** housing an amazing collection of jewelry, gold, silver, and religious items belonging to the Bavarian royalty, including swords, scepters, goblets, bowls, toiletry objects, serving platters, and more, each more fantastic than the last. Nothing is plain and simple—indeed, most items are studded with bulging diamonds, rubies, and emeralds.

Admission: Residenzmuseum and Schatzkammer each charges a separate admission of 3.50 DM ($2.20) adults, 2 DM ($1.25) senior citizens and students, free for children up to age 15.

Open: Tues–Sun 10am–4:30pm. **U-Bahn:** U-3, U-4, U-5, or U-6 to Odeonsplatz. **Tram:** 19 to Nationaltheater (or easy walking distance from Marienplatz).

CUVILLIES THEATER, Residenzstrasse 1 (just north of the Residenzmuseum). Tel. 29 68 36 or 29 06 71.

Also known as the Altes Residenztheater, this small but sumptuous work of art is considered the finest rococo tier-boxed theater in Germany. Seating 500 spectators, it was built by François de Cuvilliés in the mid-1700s, destroyed in World War II, and painstakingly rebuilt with some original materials—the magnificently carved and gilded woodwork had been stored in safety during the war. De Cuvilliés, by the way, was considered the best architect and interior decorator of the South German rococo style. A dwarf, he began his career as a court jester. Another of his masterpieces is Amalienburg at Nymphenburg Palace.

Admission: 2 DM ($1.25) adults, 1.50 DM (95¢) senior citizens and students, free for children up to age 15.

Open: Mon–Sat 2–5pm, Sun and hols 10am–5pm. **U-Bahn:** U-3, U-4, U-5, or U-6 to Odeonsplatz.

GLYPTOTHEK, Königsplatz 3. Tel. 28 61 00.

Together with the Antikensammlungen across the square, the Glyptothek forms the largest collection of classical art in what was West Germany. The Glyptothek houses Greek and Roman statues, busts, and grave steles in a beautiful setting of plain white brick and domed ceilings, reminiscent of a Roman bath, and one of the best examples of neoclassicism in Germany. Built by architect Leo von Klenze, the building was commissioned by King Ludwig I, whose dream was to transform Munich into another Athens. Indeed, the Glyptothek does resemble a Greek temple.

In Room II (located to your left as you enter the museum) is the famous *Barberini Faun*, a large sleeping satyr dating from about 220 B.C. In Room IV is the grave stele of Mnesarete, which depicts a dead mother seated in front of her daughter. Also in the museum are sculptures from the pediments of the Aphaia Temple in Aegina, with scenes of the Trojan War, as well as a room filled with Roman busts.

Admission: 3.50 DM ($2.20) adults, 1.80 DM ($1.10) senior citizens, 1 DM (60¢) students; combination ticket for both Glyptothek and Antikensammlungen, 6 DM ($3.75) adults, 3 DM ($1.85) senior citizens and students; free for everyone Sun.

Open: Tues–Wed and Fri–Sun 10am–4:30pm, Thurs noon–8:30pm. **U-Bahn:** U-2 to Königsplatz.

ANTIKENSAMMLUNGEN, Königsplatz 1. Tel. 59 83 59.

The architectural counterpart of the Glyptothek across the square, the Antikensammlungen houses the state's collection of Greek, Roman, and Etruscan art. The focus is on Greek vases (primarily Attic from the 6th and 5th centuries B.C.). Small statues, terra-cotta and bronze objects, round out the collection. Particularly striking is the collection of Greek and Etruscan gold jewelry, including necklaces, bracelets, and earrings.

Admission: 3.50 DM ($2.20) adults, 1.80 DM ($1.10) senior citizens, 1 DM (60¢) students; combination ticket for both Glyptothek and Antikensammlungen, 6 DM ($3.75) adults, 3 DM ($1.85) senior citizens and students; free for everyone Sun.

Open: Tues and Thurs–Sun 10am–4:30pm, Wed noon–8:30pm. **U-Bahn:** U-2 to Königsplatz.

MORE ATTRACTIONS

STÄDTISCHE GALERIE IM LENBACHHAUS, 33 Luisenstrasse. Tel. 52 10 41.

Located off Königsplatz not far from the Glyptothek, the City Gallery in the Lenbach House is the showcase for Munich's artists, in a setting that couldn't be more perfect. The museum is the former Italianate villa of artist Franz von Lenbach, built at the end of the last century. Some of the rooms have been kept as they were then.

Although landscape paintings from the 15th to the 19th century as well as examples of German Jugendstil are part of the collection, the great treasure of the gallery is the collection of the *Blaue Reiter* (Blue Rider) group of artists. Wassily Kandinsky, one of the great innovators of abstract art, was a key member of this Munich-based group, and the Lenbach House has an outstanding collection of Kandinsky's work from his early period shortly after the turn of the century to the outbreak of World War I. Other Blue Rider artists represented include Paul Klee, Franz Marc, August Macke, and Gabriele Münter.

Admission: 6 DM ($3.75) adults, 3 DM ($1.85) senior citizens and students; free for everyone Sun and hols.

Open: Tues–Sun 10am–6pm. **U-Bahn:** U-2 to Königsplatz.

STAATSGALERIE MODERNER KUNST (State Gallery of Modern Art), in the Haus der Kunst, Prinzregentenstrasse 1. Tel. 29 27 10.

The State Gallery of Modern Art is housed in the west end of a massive, columned building called the Haus der Kunst. The building is a product of Hitler's regime, built in 1937, and it now displays much of the modern art Hitler tried to suppress. Devoted to art of the 20th century, it has a large collection of German art, particularly Klee, Marc, Kirchner, and Beckmann. Other highlights are cubism, American abstract expressionism, surrealism, and art of the 1920s and 1930s. On display are works by Braque, Corinth, Salvador Dalí, Kandinsky, Kokoschka, Matisse, Mondrian, Moore, Picasso (14 of his works), and Warhol. The east wing of the Haus der Kunst features changing exhibitions, for which there's a separate entrance fee.

Admission: 3.50 DM ($2.20) adults, 1.80 DM ($1.10) senior citizens, 1 DM (60¢) students, 50 Pfennig (30¢) children; free for everyone Sun and hols.

Open: Tues–Wed and Fri–Sun 9:15am–4:30pm, Thurs 9:15am–4:30pm and 7–9pm. **U-Bahn:** U-3, U-4, U-5, or U-6 to Odeonsplatz; then a 10-minute walk. **Tram:** 20. **Bus:** 53.

BAYERISCHES NATIONALMUSEUM, Prinzregentenstrasse 3. Tel. 21681.

Down the street from the Haus der Kunst, the Bavarian National Museum emphasizes the historical and cultural development of Bavaria, as well as the rest of Europe, from the Middle Ages through the 19th century. The museum complements the Alte Pinakothek, showing what was happening in other genres of art and crafts at the same time painters were producing their masterpieces.

Glass, miniatures, ivory carvings, watches, jewelry, clothing, textiles and tapestries, toys, porcelain (particularly Nymphenburger and Meissner), medieval armor, and religious artifacts and altars are just some of the 20,000 items on display. Outstanding are the wood carvings of Tilman Riemenschneider (notice the facial expressions of the 12 apostles in Room 12), as well as works by Erasmus Grasser, Michael Pacher, Johann Baptist Staub, and Ignaz Günther, to name only a few.

One delightful thing about this museum is that the architecture complements the objects on display. The Late Gothic Church Art Room, for example (Room 15), is modeled after a church in Augsburg, providing a perfect background for the religious art it displays. Similarly, Room 9 is the Augsburg Weavers Room, while Room 10 is the interior of a cozy inn from Gothic times in Passau.

My favorite floor of the museum is the basement. Part of it is devoted to folk art, including furniture and complete rooms showing how people lived long ago. Notice the wooden floors and the low ceiling (to save heat). The other half of the museum houses an incredible collection of nativity scenes (*Krippe*) from around Europe. Some of the displays are made of paper, while others are amazingly lifelike. Both the vastness and the quality of this collection are impressive. Don't miss it.

Admission: 3 DM ($1.85) adults, 1.50 DM (95¢) senior citizens, 1 DM (60¢) students, 50 Pfennig (30¢) children; free for everyone Sun and hols.

Open: Tues–Sun 9:30am–5pm. **U-Bahn:** U-4 or U-5 to Lehel. **Tram:** 20.

MÜNCHNER STADTMUSEUM, Jakobsplatz 1. Tel. 233 223 70.

Whereas the Bavarian National Museum traces the history of the state, the Munich City Museum relates the history of the city—but that's not all. The Puppet-Theater Collection is outstanding, with puppets and theater stages from around the world, while the musical-instrument collection on the fourth floor displays instruments of Europe from the 16th to the 20th century and primitive instruments from around the world.

There are sections devoted to beer brewing (unfortunately with explanations in German only), medieval weaponry, and the history of photography. The museum's most valuable pieces are the 10 *Morris Dancers* carved by Erasmus Grasser, completed in 1480 for display in Munich's old town hall. The morris (or morrice) dance, popular in the 15th century, was a rustic ambulatory dance performed by companies of actors at festivals. The museum also features rooms illustrating life in Munich in the 17th, 18th, and 19th centuries, including parlors, dining rooms, kitchens, and bedrooms.

Admission: 5 DM ($3.10) adults, 2.50 DM ($1.55) senior citizens and students, free for children under 6; free for everyone Sun and hols.

Open: Tues and Thurs–Sun 10am–5pm, Wed 10am–8:30pm. **Directions:** It's an easy walk from Marienplatz, in the direction of Sendlinger-Tor-Platz.

BMW MUSEUM, Petueilring 130. Tel. 389 53307.

Anyone interested in cars, motorcycles, and the history of the automobile should see this museum. Housed in a super-modern building, it features video films (including one describing how the future was imagined by people in the past— essentially, technology as threat), slide shows, and actual displays of motors and cars from the days of the "oldies" to the age of the robot. What's more, the museum relates it all to what was taking place in the world at the time, putting it in historical perspective.

Admission: 4.50 DM ($2.80) adults, 3 DM ($1.85) students and senior citizens, 2 DM ($1.25) children.

Open: Daily 9am–5pm (you must enter by 4pm). **U-Bahn:** U-2 or U-3 to Olympiazentrum; then a five-minute walk.

ZAM—ZENTRUM FÜR AUSSERGEWÖHNLICHE MUSEEN (Center for Out-of-the-Ordinary Museums), Westenriederstrasse 26. Tel. 290 41 21.

Munich's newest museum complex is actually seven museums in one, each one unique. Where else, for example, can you find a museum devoted to the chamber pot? Other collections are devoted to pedal cars (the largest collection in the world, according to the *Guinness Book of World Records*), the life of Kaiserin Elisabeth of Austria, cork screws, keys, and the Easter rabbit! Each collection has its own room, and the entire complex can be viewed in about an hour. Explanations are only in German but there's an English pamphlet.

Admission: 8 DM ($5) adults, 5 DM ($3.10) students, senior citizens, and children.

Open: Daily 10am–6pm. **Directions:** Walk five minutes from Marienplatz or a couple of minutes from Isartorplatz.

BAVARIA FILM TOUR, Bavariafilmplatz 7, Geiselgasteig. Tel. 64 90 67.

Although tours of Germany's largest film studio are only in German, you may wish to join the 1½-hour tour if you're a film buff or speak German. Among the internationally known films produced by Bavaria Film are *Cabaret, Das Boot,* and *The Never-Ending Story.*

Admission: 11 DM ($6.85) adults, 9.50 DM ($5.95) students and senior citizens, 7 DM ($4.35) children.

Open: Mar–Oct, daily 9am–4pm. **Closed:** Nov–Feb. **Tram:** 25 to Bavariafilmplatz.

PARKS & GARDENS

The **Englischer Garten** is one of the largest city parks in Europe. Despite its name it owes its existence to an American rather than an Englishman. Benjamin Thompson, who fled America during the Revolution because of his British sympathies, was instrumental in the park's creation and landscaping. Stretching three miles along the Isar River right in the heart of the city, today it offers beer gardens, sunbathing (including nude, a surprise to quite a few unsuspecting tourists), and recreation.

Much more formal are the 500 acres of **Nymphenburg Park,** already described in "Top Attractions," above. On the north end of Nymphenburg Park is the **New Botanical Garden,** but the most conveniently located garden is the **Hofgarten,** located right off Odeonsplatz and laid out in Italian Renaissance style of the 17th century.

ORGANIZED TOURS

With this guidebook and a good map, and with the help of Munich's great transportation system, you shouldn't need to spend money on an organized tour. For those who prefer to be guided, **Panorama Tours** of the Gray Line offers sightseeing trips of Munich lasting from 1 to 2½ hours. The 1-hour trip is adequate, with buses departing from the front of Hertie Department Store, across from the Hauptbahnhof every day at 10am and 2:30pm (also at 11:30am May through October). The fare is 15 DM ($9.35). Day-long excursions are also offered, including those to castles (Neuschwanstein among them), and to Rothenburg, Herrenchiemsee, Berchtesgaden, and Dachau.

For more information, drop by the Panorama Tours office at Arnulfstrasse 8 (tel. 120 42 48 or 59 15 04), located just to the north of the Hauptbahnhof. The office is open Monday through Friday from 9am to 6pm, on Saturday from 7:30am to noon, and on Sunday from 7:30 to 9am.

SPECIAL & FREE EVENTS

Munich's most famous event of the year is the **Oktoberfest,** which is held from the middle of September to the first Sunday in October. The celebration began in 1810 to honor King Ludwig I's marriage, when the main event consisted of a horse race in a field called Theresienwiese. Everyone had so much fun that the celebration was held again the following year, and then again and again. Today the Oktoberfest is among the largest fairs in the world.

Every year the festivities get under way with a parade on the first Oktoberfest Sunday, with almost 7,000 participants marching through the city streets in folk costumes. Most activities, however, are at the Theresienwiese, where huge beer tents sponsored by local Munich breweries dispense both beer and merriment, complete with Bavarian bands and singing. Each tent holds up to 6,000 people, which gives you at least some idea how rowdy things can get. During the 16-day period of the Oktoberfest, an estimated six million visitors guzzle over a million gallons of beer and eat 700,000 broiled chickens. Pure gluttony, and a lot of fun. In addition to the beer tents, there are also carnival attractions and amusement rides. Entry to the fairgrounds is free, though rides—and of course, beer—cost extra.

Munich's other major event is **Fasching,** which culminates in a parade through town on Ash Tuesday.

7. SAVVY SHOPPING

As Germany's fashion center, Munich has upscale boutiques, department stores, and designer names, all located primarily in the pedestrian-zoned Old Town. If you're interested in souvenirs—beer mugs, the blue-and-white simple pottery of Bavaria, porcelain—your best bet in terms of price is the department stores, including **Hertie** (located across from the Hauptbahnhof), **Karstadt** (on Karlstor right off Stachus and at Neuhauser Strasse 44), and **Kaufhof** (Karlsplatz 21-24 and on Marienplatz).

Another good place to hunt for Bavarian and German souvenirs and gifts is along **Orlandostrasse,** located about a five-minute walk from Marienplatz near the Hofbräuhaus. This small pedestrian lane has several souvenir shops selling T-shirts, beer steins, dolls in Bavarian costume, pipes, postcards, Christmas-tree ornaments, and nutcrackers.

If you have lots of money and want to purchase a Bavarian dirndl, check out **Wallach,** Residenzstrasse 3, which has been selling traditional clothing since 1900. This shop also sells ceramics, some toys and gift items, shawls, bed sheets, beer steins, and pewter.

Most shops are open Monday through Friday from 9am or 9:30am to 6pm and on Saturday from 9am to 2pm. In addition, most shops are also open Thursday evening until 8:30pm and on the first Saturday of the month (*langer Samstag*) until 6pm.

If you're taking your purchases out of the country, you can recover part of the Value-Added Tax (VAT), 14% in Germany. Many shops, including those listed above, will issue a Tax Cheque at the time of purchase. Fill in the reverse side, and upon leaving Germany present the articles to Customs. Airports in Berlin, Frankfurt,

Munich, and other large cities have offices that will refund your money immediately. At other points of departure it's a bit more complicated; if you leave the country by train, ask the Customs official to stamp your check. For more information on recovering VAT, purchase a copy of *International Shopping Guide München* for 2 DM ($1.25). It also lists more than 100 shops in Munich.

MARKETS   Munich's most famous market is the **Viktualienmarkt,** dating from the early 1800s. Here you can buy bread, cheese, honey, cakes, fruit, wine, vegetables, and much, much more. It's a wonderful place to obtain picnic supplies. The market is open year round, Monday through Friday from 8am to 6pm and on Saturday from 8am to 2pm.

If you're here in December, enjoy the **Christkindlmarkt** on Marienplatz, a colorful hodgepodge of stalls offering everything from Bavarian foods to Christmas decorations. It's held from the beginning of December to Christmas Eve.

Even better is the **Auer Dult,** a flea market lasting eight days and held three times a year, in April, July, and October. It has been a Munich tradition for more than 600 years, currently held on Mariahilfplatz (take bus no. 52 from Marienplatz). Everything from spices, leather goods, jewelry, and sweaters to antiques, kitchen gadgets, and ceramics is sold, and there are also rides and amusements for children. For more information, contact the tourist office.

8. EVENING ENTERTAINMENT

Since commercial ticket agencies sell opera and theater tickets at a higher price to make a profit, it makes sense to buy your tickets directly from the theater or opera. To find out where to purchase tickets in advance, buy a copy of the *Monatsprogramm,* issued monthly for 2 DM ($1.25). It lists all the major theaters and what's being played when. Another publication listing operas, plays, classical concerts, rock and jazz concerts, movies, and more is *Munich Found.*

Both the Nationaltheater (the Bavarian State Opera House) and the Staatstheater am Gärtnerplatz (opera, operettas, ballet, and musicals) offer **standing-room tickets** for 8–18 DM ($5–$11.25). You can purchase these tickets in advance, and they may be your best bet to see popular performances. For performances that are not sold out students can get a **discount** at the Nationaltheater by standing in line about an hour before the show and presenting their International Student ID Card. These are discount tickets for seats, starting at about 6 DM ($3.75). Otherwise the normal price of a seat runs about 15–65 DM ($9.35–$40.60).

THE PERFORMING ARTS
THEATER & OPERA

NATIONALTHEATER (Bayerische Staatsoper), Max-Joseph-Platz (box office at Maximilianstrasse 11). Tel. 22 13 16.
With opera performed in its original language, the Nationaltheater's Bavarian State Opera House is famous for its progressive versions of the familiar classics. It also stages ballet. It's just a three-minute walk from Marienplatz.
Prices: Opera tickets, 11–252 DM ($6.85–$157); ballet tickets, 9–100 DM ($5.60–$62.50).
U-Bahn and S-Bahn: Marienplatz.

STAATSTHEATER AM GÄRTNERPLATZ, Gärtnerplatz 3. Tel. 201 67 67.
Light opera, operetta, ballet, and musicals are beautifully performed here, usually in German.
Prices: Tickets, 16–67 DM ($10–$41.85).
Bus: 52 or 56 to Gärtnerplatz.

CUVILLIÈS THEATER, Residenzstrasse 1. Tel. 22 13 16.

Also known as the Altes Residenztheater, this tiny theater (seating 500) is considered the finest rococo tier-boxed theater in Germany. It features opera and classical plays.

Prices: Opera tickets, 9–173 DM ($5.60–$108.10); play tickets, 6–46 DM ($3.75–$28.75).
U-Bahn: U-1 or U-2 to Fraunhoferstrasse.

RESIDENZTHEATER, Max-Joseph-Platz 1. Tel. 22 57 54.

The Bayerisches Staatsschauspiel performs classics in German, including Schiller, Goethe, Shakespeare, and Pirandello.
Prices: Tickets, 16–50 DM ($10–$31.25).
S-Bahn: Marienplatz.

MÜNCHNER KAMMERSPIELE, Maximilianstrasse 26. Tel. 237 213 28.

Contemporary plays from German playwrights, including Böll, Goethe, and Brecht.
Prices: Tickets, 6–40 DM ($3.75–$25).
Tram: 19 to Maximilianstrasse.

GASTEIG, Rosenheimer Strasse 5. Tel. 48 09 80.

Completed in 1985, the Gasteig serves as the stage for Munich's major concerts. Its largest concert hall, the Philharmonie, seats 2,400 and features performances of the Munich Philharmonic Orchestra, the Munich Bach Orchestra and Chorale, the Bavarian Radio Symphony Orchestra, and guest orchestras and ensembles. The Kleiner Konzertsaal (Small Concert Hall) features a wide range of musical talent, from flamenco guitar to concerts of Renaissance and baroque music. The Gasteig also contains several smaller concert halls, as well as the Munich City Library and the Richard Strauss Conservatory.
Prices: Tickets, Munich Philharmonic Orchestra 15–66 DM ($9.35–$41.25).
Tram: 18 to Gasteig. **S-Bahn:** Rosenheimer Platz.

LIVE-MUSIC HOUSES

WIRTSHAUS IM SCHLACHTHOF, Zenettistrasse 9. Tel. 76 54 48.

Schlachthof means slaughterhouse, and there are several nearby, but that doesn't prevent this Wirtshaus from being Munich's most popular nightspot for live music. The building itself is 120 years old, a square brick structure with character, containing a pub, a restaurant, and a large, open room where there are performances of jazz, punk, rock, blues, and even classical music. On Sunday in winter, admission includes a breakfast buffet and live jazz.
Admission: 10–20 DM ($6.25–$12.50) Mon–Sat, depending on the show; 27 DM ($16.85) Sun.
Open: Mon–Sat 8pm–1am, Sun 10:30am–1am. **U-Bahn:** U-3 or U-6 to Poccistrasse or Goetheplatz.

ALLOTRIA, Oskar-von-Miller-Ring 3, Schwabing. Tel. 28 58 58.

An intimate, cozy place with candles on all the tables, Allotria features both American and German jazz musicians. On Monday it's rock 'n' roll. Beer, Coke, wine, and cocktails available.
Admission: 8–30 DM ($5–$18.75).
Open: Mon–Sat 8pm–1am (music begins at 9:30pm), Sun performances 2–7pm.
U-Bahn: U-3 or U-6 to Odeonsplatz.

SCHWABINGER BRETTL, 11 Occamstrasse, Schwabing. Tel. 34 72 89.

My favorite nightspot in Schwabing, the 25-year-old Schwabinger Brettl is the only establishment that carries on the bohemian spirit of old Schwabing, where musicians from around the world can perform to an appreciative audience. Not just anyone can get up and play. Musicians audition beforehand, so you can be assured they're good. This place is tiny, so come early for a seat.
Admission: Free Sun–Tues, Wed–Sat 5 DM ($3.10).
Open: Daily 8pm–1am. **U-Bahn:** U-3 or U-6 to Münchener Freiheit.

UNTERFAHRT, Kirchenstrasse 96, Haidhausen. Tel. 448 27 94.
This jazz locale is more proof that Munich is fast becoming one of Europe's prime spots for jazz. It features modern jazz, "from old-time to no time." On Sunday from October to April there's free jazz in the morning from 10am. On Sunday from 9pm there's a jam session.
   Admission: 13–18 DM ($8.10–$11.25); Sun jam session 5 DM ($3.10).
   Open: Tues–Sun 8pm–1am. **S-Bahn and U-Bahn:** Ostbahnhof; then a five-minute walk.

BEER HALLS

HOFBRÄUHAUS, Platzl 9. Tel. 22 16 76.
Without a doubt, the Hofbräuhaus is the most famous beer hall in the world. In 1989 it celebrated its 400th birthday. Everyone who has ever been to Munich has probably spent at least one evening here, and you'll probably want to do the same. There are several floors in this huge place, but the main hall is the Schwemme on the ground floor. It features your typical Bavarian brass band, waitresses in dirndls, and tables full of friendly Germans who often break into song and link arms as they sway back and forth. If you've never been to the Oktoberfest, this place will give you an idea what it's like. German food is available (there's also a restaurant up on the first floor), including various sausages, Leberkäs, boiled pork knuckle with Sauerkraut and potatoes, a plate of sliced radish, and roast chicken. The Hofbräuhaus, owned by the State of Bavaria, is located in the center of the city in Old Town.
   Prices: Liter of beer 7.90 DM ($4.95).
   Open: Daily 9am–11:30pm. **U-Bahn and S-Bahn:** Marienplatz.

MATHÄSER BIERSTADT, Bayerstrasse 5. Tel. 59 28 96.
This place is massive with various different rooms, but follow the oompah-pah music up a half flight of stairs to the beer hall. Claiming that it pours more beer than anywhere else (it advertises 5,000 seats), the Bierstadt caters to locals rather than to tourists and is sometimes packed even in the middle of the day. In summer you can sit in an outdoor courtyard, and in the morning you can come here for Weisswurst. The menu lists the usual fare of roasted Schweinshaxe, sausages, suckling pig, Leberkäs, sliced radish, chicken, and more. The beer is Löwenbräu. Mathäser is located between Stachus and the Hauptbahnhof.
   Prices: Liter of beer 8.40 DM ($5.25).
   Open: Daily 10am–midnight. **U-Bahn and S-Bahn:** Stachus.

AUGUSTINER BIERHALLE, Neuhauser Strasse 16. Tel. 260 41 06.
About 10% cheaper than its sister Augustiner Restaurant next door, the Bierhalle is much smaller than the other two establishments listed above, with correspondingly lower prices. It still, however, has typical Bavarian decor, with dark wood-paneled walls, wooden tables, and simple hooks for hats and coats. Specialties here include pancake soup with browned onions, Leberkäs, sliced radish, and a menu that changes daily. It's located right on Munich's main pedestrian lane in Old Town, between Stachus and Marienplatz.
   Prices: Half liter of beer from 4 DM ($2.50).
   Open: Mon–Sat 9am–midnight. **U-Bahn and S-Bahn:** Stachus or Marienplatz.

MOVIES

To find out what's playing, either buy a newspaper or try to get a copy of *Munich Found,* which lists the various cinemas and their schedules. Those that show movies in their original language include:

THE FILMMUSEUM, Jakobsplatz 1. Tel. 233 23 48.
This is part of the Munich City Museum, with film festivals held on different themes (recent festivals have included Charlie Chaplin films, Fritz Lang films, and samurai flicks from Japan).
   Admission: 6 DM ($3.75).

Open: Usually two showings daily. **U-Bahn and S-Bahn:** Marienplatz; then a three-minute walk southeast.

NEUES ARENA, Hans-Sachs-Strasse 7. Tel. 260 32 65.

This cinema shows international cult, avant-garde, science fiction, and old and new classics, often in original language.

Open: Several showings nightly. **Tram:** 20, 25, or 27 from the Hauptbahnhof to Fraunhofer-Müllerstrasse; then a three-minute walk.

CINEMA, Nymphenburger Strasse 31. Tel. 55 52 55.

This cinema specializes in contemporary films in both German and English. This is your best bet for seeing Hollywood's most recent releases.

U-Bahn: U-1 to Stiglmaierplatz.

THE BAR SCENE
IN SCHWABING

Once the center of everything bohemian in Munich, Schwabing today is more likely to be filled with out-of-towners than with natives. Still, it's definitely worth a stroll through Munich's most famous night district, and the crowds are still huge. The busiest streets are the main boulevard of **Leopoldstrasse** and the smaller side streets of **Feilitzschstrasse** and **Occamstrasse** near the Münchener Freiheit subway station. Below are a few recommendations to whet your thirst (and don't forget Schwabinger Brettl and Allotria, listed under "Live-Music Houses," above).

HAUS DER 111 BIERE, Franzstrasse 3. Tel. 33 12 48.

The 111 different kinds of beer from 25 countries around the world are the claim to fame of this establishment. Its two floors are often packed with people from around the world as well, and it's easy to strike up a conversation.

Prices: Bottles and cans of beer around 6–12 DM ($3.75–$7.50).

Open: Mon–Fri 5pm–1am, Sat–Sun and hols 3pm–1am. **U-Bahn:** U-3 or U-6 to Münchener Freiheit.

TURBO, Occamstrasse 5. Tel. 34 99 01.

This tiny place, complete with a disk jockey who plays oldies, really packs them in, and in case you're interested, there seem to be many more men than women. The specialty here is the "ein meter Pils oder Alt," which is a one-meter wooden board with 15 small beers on it.

Prices: Smallest beers 2.80 DM ($1.75); "ein meter Pils or Alt" 39 DM ($24.35).

Open: Daily 7pm–1am. **U-Bahn:** U-3 or U-6 to Münchener Freiheit.

NACHTEULE, Occamstrasse 7. Tel. 39 96 56.

Its name means "night owl," and it claims to be the oldest bar left in Schwabing, established in the dark ages of 1960. A small, simple locale with an even tinier dance floor, Nachteule is a place where anyone can feel at home—and judging from the rather mixed clientele, it's a place where many of them do.

Prices: Half liter of beer 4.40 DM ($2.75).

Open: Tues–Sun 7pm–1am. **U-Bahn:** U-3 or U-6 to Münchener Freiheit.

FLOTTE, Occamstrasse 8. Tel. 39 01 80.

Also on Occamstrasse, this bar has been here for 15 years and features free live music on Sunday, Monday, Wednesday, and Thursday evenings, usually rock 'n' roll or golden oldies of the '50s and '60s. It's simply decorated, with the usual wooden floor, large bar area, and wooden tables.

Prices: Half liter of beer 4.80 DM ($3).

Open: Daily 7pm–1am. **U-Bahn:** U-3 or U-6 to Münchener Freiheit.

IN THE CITY CENTER

IWAN, Josephspitalstrasse 15. Tel. 55 49 33.

This trendy bar decorated in red, black, and gray is a convenient place for a drink, day or night. It's located on the corner of Josephspitalstrasse and Sonnenstrasse, nestled in an inner courtyard. In summer there's outdoor seating, and the liquor menu is extensive.

Prices: Third liter beer from 4.50 DM ($2.80); wine from 3.50 DM ($2.20).
Open: Daily 11am–3am (to 1am in winter). **S-Bahn:** Karlsplatz/Stachus.

DISCOS

Unfortunately, discos in Munich are suffering from a tendency toward elitism. Most have doors with one-way mirrors that can be opened only from the inside—so the bouncer can look over potential customers and decide whether they're of the right material to be let in. Far Out, in the center of Old City, gets so crowded on the weekends that you might not get in.

FAR OUT, Am Kosttor 2. Tel. 22 66 62 or 22 66 61.
People come here primarily to dance, evident from the conspicuous lack of seating. It gets so crowded on weekends that the doorman lets in only regular patrons. Go on a week night, when the admission is also lower. There are more than 70 cocktails on its menu, and sandwiches and ice cream are also available. It's located near the Hofbräuhaus in the city center, a seven-minute walk northeast of Marienplatz.

Prices: Half liter of beer 6.50 DM ($4.05). **Admission:** Free Sun–Wed, 5 DM ($3.10) Thurs, 10 DM ($6.25) Fri–Sat.
Open: Daily 10pm–4am.

SUNSET, Leopoldstrasse 69. Tel. 39 03 03.
This small basement establishment is more democratic than most, allowing as many as will fit through its doors.

Prices: Half liter of beer 5.70 DM ($3.55). **Admission:** Free.
Open: Daily 8pm–4am. **U-Bahn:** U-3 or U-6 to Münchener Freiheit.

9. EASY EXCURSIONS

DACHAU Located about 12 miles from Munich is Dachau, site of Germany's first concentration camp under the Hitler regime and now a memorial to those who died under the Nazis. Some 200,000 prisoners—mainly Jews, Gypsies, and opponents of the regime—passed through Dachau's gates, of whom 32,000 lost their lives.

At the **KZ-Gedenkstätte Dachau** (Concentration Camp Memorial), Robert-Bosch-Strasse (tel. 08131/1741), two of the camp's original 30 barracks have been rebuilt, and also on display is the crematorium. The former workshops and offices have been made into a museum, with photograph after photograph illustrating the horrors of the Holocaust. They show the expressionless faces of children with eyes of the old. There are bodies piled high on top of one another, and there are lines of people quietly waiting to be executed. Documentaries are shown in English at 11:30am and 3:30pm.

Visiting the Dachau concentration camp is not a pleasant experience, but perhaps a necessary one: A plaque near the exit of the museum reminds us that those who forget the past are destined to repeat it. If you need something a bit uplifting after visiting the concentration camp, walk through the older medieval city in the center of Dachau, which has a history stretching back 1,200 years.

Admission to the Dachau memorial is free and it's open Tuesday through Sunday from 9am to 5pm. To get there, take the S-Bahn going toward Petershausen to Dachau (about a 20-minute ride), and then bus no. 722 to Robert-Bosch-Strasse.

NEUSCHWANSTEIN You've probably seen pictures of Neuschwanstein—a fairy-tale castle perched up on a cliff above the town of Hohenschwangau (tel.

08362/81035), created by the extravagant Bavarian King Ludwig II. Even if you've never seen it, you'll probably still recognize it, for this is the castle that served as the model for the castle at Disneyland.

Construction on King Ludwig II's most famous castle began in 1869, but it was still not finished at the time of Ludwig's mysterious death in 1886 (his body, as well as the body of his doctor, was found floating in a lake, but no one has ever proven whether he was murdered or committed suicide). Neuschwanstein, one of several overly ornate castles Ludwig left to the world, is a lesson in extravagance, with almost every inch covered in gilt or stucco.

Admission to the castle is 8 DM ($5) for adults and 5 DM ($3.10) for students and senior citizens. It's open April through September, daily from 8:30am to 5:30pm; October through March, daily from 10am to 4pm. To get here, take the train from Munich's Starnberger Bahnhof (next to the Hauptbahnhof) to Füssen, about a two-hour trip; from Füssen, take a bus to Hohenschwangau.

CHAPTER 20

NAPLES

Visiting Naples is like finding an old, tattered, mildewy copy of your favorite novel in the attic. Once you get beyond its deteriorating cover and begin to lose yourself in the story, you enjoy it tremendously and remember it for some time.

Most Neapolitans live a rough, poor life, and the city as a whole carries a chip on its shoulder when it comes to "the north." Northern Italians will tell you that it's "another country" down here, while southern Italians call northerners condescending. But beyond the city's squat buildings and its grime and poverty, the region surrounding Naples and the islands off its shores contain some of the most stunning scenery and historically significant sites that the country—north or south—has to offer.

Is Naples as dirty and dangerous as it's made out to be? Yes and no. There's no denying that the streets are cluttered with litter or that car and diesel exhaust leaves a thin black film on just about everything or that Naples has more than its fair share of pickpockets and petty hustlers. But despite the reputation that Naples has for being crime-ridden, tourists have little to fear from the presence of the Mafia, known as *La Cosa Nostra*.

A few simple precautions will help make your stay in Naples trouble-free: Wear a moneybelt, store your valuables at your hotel, avoid wearing a purse or knapsack that rests anywhere but in front of you where you can see it and hang onto it, and be especially wary on buses, while walking on crowded streets, and in restaurants.

Finally, the good news: Just about everything is significantly cheaper in this area than in the rest of the country!

1. FROM A BUDGET TRAVELER'S POINT OF VIEW

NAPLES BUDGET BESTS   Compared with the rest of Italy, Naples is a budget best. As you can tell by the price chart and from perusing the listings below, the costs of food, lodging, and even the *coperto* (cover charge) at restaurants are lower here than in Venice, Florence, or Rome.

The real budget bests here are the numerous picturesque villages along the coast between Sorrento and Salerno. Amalfi and Positano, two nearby towns that I'll cover, are quite affordable and offer some of the best territory for sun worshipers between the Riviera and Greece. Less expensive still are the many tiny villages in between.

Within the big city itself, pizza—Naples's hometown specialty—is the budget traveler's staple. You'll be able to sustain yourself easily on an endless and delicious supply of *pizza margherita,* which averages under 5,000 lire ($4.35) for a full-meal pie.

Remember that you can always save money on food and drink by consuming them standing up at one of the city's ubiquitous bars. A 1,700-lira ($1.50) *panino* (sandwich) and a cappuccino at 1,000 lire (85¢) make a quick and satisfying lunch. Prices double if you sit down.

WHAT THINGS COST IN NAPLES	U.S. $
Taxi (from the train station to the port)	11.30
Public bus (from any point within the city to any other point)	.85
Local telephone call	.18
Double room at the Hotel Britannique (deluxe)	191.40
Double room at the Hotel Cavour (moderate)	114.80
Double room at the Albergo Casanova (budget)	36.50
Continental breakfast (cappuccino and croissant)	
(at a café/bar)	1.75
(at most hotels)	7.40
Lunch for one at Trattoria Avellinese (moderate)	9.55
Lunch for one at Pizzeria da Michele (budget)	4.35
Dinner for one, without wine, at Antica Trattoria il Vicoletto (deluxe)	30.45
Dinner for one, without wine, at Trattoria alla Brace (moderate)	13.90
Dinner for one, without wine, at the Mergellina youth hostel (budget)	8.70
Coca-Cola (to take out)	1.30
Cappuccino at a café	.85
Roll of color film, 36 exposures	5.85
Admission to the Museo Nazionale Archeologico	6.95
Movie Ticket	6.10

WORTH THE EXTRA BUCKS   Good lodging is important in Naples itself, even if it means paying more for it. The bad places in this poor and sometimes unsafe city can be really bad. While there may be cheaper places to lay your head than those I've listed, you may find it difficult to get much rest or relaxation there. All my suggestions, in all price categories, are safe and agreeable accommodations.

Is Capri worth the extra bucks? Certainly. While everything, right down to the fresh water that must be piped in from the mainland, costs at least twice as much on this tiny rock as on the mainland, its dazzling cliffs and winding whitewashed alleys live up to the island's legendary reputation.

2. PRETRIP PREPARATIONS

DOCUMENTS & WHAT TO PACK   For suggestions on documents and wardrobe, see the Rome chapter.

WHEN TO GO   Naples's climate is more comfortable than that of its northern

WHAT'S SPECIAL ABOUT NAPLES

Ancient Monuments
- ☐ Pompeii, one of the best-preserved cities of antiquity in the world.
- ☐ Herculaneum, another astonishingly well preserved ancient Roman city with many small houses.

Natural Landmarks
- ☐ Mount Vesuvius, with a great view from its 4,000-foot peak.

Museums
- ☐ Museo Archeologico Nazionale, filled with mosaics and treasures from nearby Pompeii.

Food
- ☐ Pizza—local chefs take pride in preserving their city's culinary invention.

Coastal Towns
- ☐ Amalfi, a quintessentially southern Italian city on the sea with a small central piazza and winding streets.
- ☐ Positano, a charming town spread out on a steep hillside toward the beach.

Islands
- ☐ Capri, a small isle of stark beauty and chic visitors.
- ☐ Ischia, an island favored by Germans and others who enjoy the thermal springs.

neighbors as early as March and as late as November. July and August are sweltering in the city, but the islands and coastal villages are delightful. During those months, of course, they are terrifically crowded. At this time all of Italy and a good portion of the rest of Europe heads for the seashore. Since the area around Naples boasts the best beaches in Italy, budget travelers may be frustrated in looking for a room, especially for stays of less than a few weeks.

Naples's Average Daytime Temperature & Rainfall

	Jan	Feb	Mar	Apr	May	June	July	Aug	Sept	Oct	Nov	Dec
Temp. (°F)	50	54	58	63	70	75	83	79	74	66	60	52
Rainfall "	4.7	4	3	3.8	2.4	.8	.8	2.6	3.5	5.8	5.1	3.7

3. ORIENTATION & GETTING AROUND

ARRIVING IN NAPLES

FROM THE AIRPORT   Bus no. 14 connects tiny **Capodichino Airport** with downtown Naples, just four miles away. Exit the air terminal and look for the bus stop sign to the left side of the platform. When returning from the train station, you'll find the airport bus on the right-hand corner of piazza Garibaldi, just outside the Hotel Cavour. The fare is the same as other city buses—1,000 lire (85¢). Buy your ticket from an agent on the piazza before boarding.

FROM THE TRAIN STATION   Most Naples-bound trains arrive at **Stazione Centrale** (tel. 533-4188). This busy terminal occupies an entire side of bustling piazza Garibaldi, where you can get a bus to the port and other corners of the city.

The **Metropolitana,** to piazza Cavour, Mergellina, and beyond, is located downstairs, as is the **Circumvesuviana** suburban rail line to Sorrento.

The **Ente Provinciale per il Turismo (E.P.T.),** the city's official tourist office for the entire Bay of Naples region, staffs a small office near the station's ticket windows (tel. 26-8779). Open Monday through Saturday from 9am to 8pm and sometimes on Sunday from 9am to 1:30pm, this office offers hotel booking without charge, and will provide you with a free, if sketchy, map of the city, bus and boat schedules, and other information on the region.

Some trains terminate at **Stazione Mergellina,** a few miles west of piazza Garibaldi. This stop is perfect for those staying at the youth hostel close by, but others will want to board the adjacent Metropolitana subway to piazza Garibaldi.

INFORMATION

The city's **main tourist office** is located on piazza Gesu Nuovo, toward the center of the city (tel. 552-3328 or 551-2701). It's open Monday through Saturday from 9am to 2pm and 3-7pm.

Be sure to ask the tourist office for the free and indispensable *Qui Napoli,* a multilingual monthly booklet with all sorts of useful information, including train and boat schedules, as well as listings of concerts and lectures. Also look for *Napoli Top,* a similarly helpful guide to the city.

CITY LAYOUT

The huge **piazza Garibaldi** is the center of town for most tourists, as many of the best budget hotel and restaurant selections are on or very near this square. The broad **corso Umberto I,** by way of piazza Bovio and via Depretis, connects this hub with **piazza Municipio** and the regal **piazza del Plebiscito** nearby. Most ferries and hydrofoils to Capri and Ischia leave from the **Molo Beverello** wharf behind the Castel Nuovo, which looms over piazza Municipio.

Piazza del Plebiscito marks one edge of the bayside **Santa Lucia** area, which becomes the **Mergellina** quarter as it stretches to the west along the water. Via Toledo and subsequently via Roma connect piazza del Plebiscito with piazza Dante and the **university quarter,** passing on the left the narrow streets of **Spacca Napoli,** or Old Naples, sometimes also called the Spanish Quarter. Beyond piazza Dante is **piazza Cavour** and the important Museo Archeologico Nazionale. High above it all is the **Vomero** neighborhood and the **Capodimonte Park** in the hills above.

GETTING AROUND

Unlike Florence or Venice, which are compact and easily navigated on foot, or Rome with its convenient subway system, Naples is a big, sprawling city with only a token underground rail network. The public bus system is plagued with choking traffic, sardine-packed coaches, and occasional pickpockets who take advantage of the crowded conditions.

BY BUS   Orange Neapolitan **ATAN city buses** can take you just about anyplace in the city, but they aren't the most pleasant mode of transportation, to put it mildly. Ovenlike in summer, they're always jammed, and so, a good hunting ground for pickpockets. Be careful when boarding; people have been known to fall off. Tickets, which cost 1,000 lire (85¢) and must be validated in one of the red boxes located at both the front and rear doors, can be purchased at the blue booth just outside the train station or at tobacconists (*tabacchi*) and most newsstands for no additional service fee. Half-day tickets are 1,500 lire ($1.30) and full-day tickets, 2,500 lire ($2.20). Bus nos. 150 and 152 connect piazza Garibaldi with piazza Municipio and the port area, continuing from there to Mergellina, where you'll find the youth hostel.

The **S.I.T.A. Long-distance bus terminal,** at via Pisanelli, 4 (tel. 552-2176), located off the inland side of piazza Municipio, serves Sorrento and points on the Amalfi Coast.

BY SUBWAY Naples's **Metropolitana** subway system consists of just one line with 11 stops, connecting piazza Garibaldi with Pozzuoli, via piazza Cavour, piazza Amedeo, and the Mergellina quarter, among other stations. The fare is 1,000 lire (85¢). Trains run every 10–15 minutes from 6am to about 10pm, with limited service at other times.

BY TRAIN The suburban rail line, **Ferrovia Circumvesuviana,** connects Naples with Herculaneum, Pompeii, and ultimately, Sorrento. The fare is based on distance traveled, with a maximum one-way price, from piazza Garibaldi all the way to Sorrento, of 7,000 lire ($6.05). There are several branches and offshoots of the Circumvesuviana; be sure to get on the right train. Note that Eurailpasses are *not* valid on this privately operated rail line. You'll find the schedule in the free tourist publication *Napoli Top.*

BY TAXI Taxis are quite expensive, beginning at 3,500 lire ($3.05) and rapidly increasing by 100 lire (9¢) for each 118 meters (129 yards). From 10pm to 7am they charge a supplement of 2,200 lire ($1.90) and on Sunday a supplement of 1,000 lire (85¢). Bags cost 400 lire (35¢) apiece.

CAR RENTAL Only the brave rent cars to explore the Naples area. Even more nerve-wracking than reckless drivers are the cliff-hugging roads that snake along much of the coastline. While the roads are in good condition and equipped with steel guard rails, the constant hairpin turns may make for a more stressful than enjoyable ride.

For **Avis,** try the agency in the train station (tel. 28-4041) or at via Partenope, 32 (tel. 40-7333), in the Santa Lucia area. **Hertz** is outside the station at piazza Garibaldi, 69 (tel. 20-6228), and at via Partenope, 29 (tel. 40-0400). **Eurodollar** is nearby at via Partenope, 13 (tel. 764-6364 or 764-5464).

Keep in mind that rates can be considerably less—as much as half the price, or better—if you make a reservation before you leave home at least 48 hours in advance. Plan ahead, or consider phoning a friend or relative back home to have the reservations made for you.

 NAPLES

Banks Banks are open for money exchange Monday through Friday from 8:20am to 1:20pm and 2:45 or 3 to 3:45pm or 4pm; a very few banks are also open on Saturday. The train station has a limited currency-exchange office, open daily. The American Express office, in the offices of Ashiba Travel at piazza Municipio, 1 (tel. 551-5303), does not change money. Trying to buy traveler's checks through this less-than-helpful service office is a costly and positively byzantine experience. It's open Monday through Friday from 9am to 1pm and 3:30 to 7:30pm, and on Saturday from 9am to 1pm.

Business Hours In summer, most **businesses and shops** are open Monday through Friday from 9 or 9:30am to 1:30pm and 4 to 7:30 or 8pm. On Saturday, shops are open in the morning only. From mid-September through mid-June, most shops are open Tuesday through Saturday from 9 or 9:30am to 1 or 1:30pm and 3:30 to 8pm, and in the winter, shops don't open on Monday until the afternoon. Just about everything is closed on Sunday. Standard **bank hours** are Monday through Friday from 8:20am to 1:20pm and 2:45 or 3 to 3:45 or 4pm. **Restaurants** are required to close at least one day per week, though the particular day varies from one *trattoria* to another. Serving hours are usually about noon to 2:30 or 3pm and 7 to 10 or 11pm.

Consulates   The **U.S. Consulate** is located on piazza della Repubblica (tel. 761-4303). It's open Monday through Friday from 8am to noon and 2 to 4:30pm. The **British Consulate,** located at via Crispi, 122 (tel. 66-3511), is open in summer from 9am to 12:30pm and 3 to 5:30pm.

Citizens of **Australia, Canada,** and **New Zealand** should consult their missions in Rome.

Currency   The Italian unit of currency is the **lira,** almost always used in the plural form, **lire.** The lowest unit of currency these days is the silver 50-lira coin. There is also a silver 100-lira piece, a gold 200-lira coin, and a combined silver-and-gold 500-lira coin. Notes come in the following denominations: 1,000, 2,000, 5,000, 10,000, 50,000, and 100,000 lire.

Emergencies   As elsewhere in Italy, dial 113 to reach the police. Some Italians recommend the *Carabinieri* (tel. 112) instead, which many consider to be a better-trained police force. For an ambulance, dial 752-0696, or, during the day only, 752-0850. For a list of English-speaking doctors or dentists, consult the American or British consulate.

Holidays   See the Rome chapter for details.

Information   For the location of tourist information offices, see the "Information" section of "Orientation and Getting Around," above.

Lost and Found   If you've lost something in the train station, ask for the Ufficio Oggetti Smarriti. Elsewhere, go to via G. B. Marino (tel. 61-1722). If you left something on public transportation, go to via Laopadi, 120 (tel. 61-5722).

Mail   Naples's massive central post office is on piazza Matteotti (tel. 551-1456), a short walk up via San Felice/via Diaz from piazza Bovio. They're open for stamps and *Fermo Posta* (Poste Restante) Monday through Saturday from 8am to 7:40pm and on Sunday from 8 to 11:50am.

Remember that you can buy stamps (*francobolli*) at any *tabacchi;* ask at your hotel about current postal rates.

Tax and Tipping   See the Rome chapter for information.

Telephone   To make an international phone call, there are two convenient, 24-hour **ASST offices** to serve you: inside the train station, and at via Depretis, 40, between piazza Bovio and piazza Municipio. For other tips on international calls, see the Rome chapter. The **telephone area code** for Naples is 081.

4. BUDGET ACCOMMODATIONS

Staying in an establishment where you trust and feel comfortable with both the management and the other guests is important in Naples. All the places below are run by honest managers who exercise some discretion regarding clientele.

If you can't get a place in one of the hotels recommended below, I would strongly suggest that you base yourself in some other city, such as Sorrento. If you're feeling jittery about the tales of pickpockets and petty thievery on the streets or in your room, don't hesitate to leave your valuables with the front desk.

Italian hoteliers are continually raising their prices; those you encounter may be a

THE LIRA & THE DOLLAR

At this writing $1 = approximately 1,150 lire (or 100 lire = 0.9¢), and this was the rate of exchange used to calculate the dollar values given in this chapter (rounded to the nearest nickel). This rate fluctuates from time to time and may not be the same when you travel to Italy. Therefore the following table should be used only as a guide:

Lire	U.S.$	Lire	U.S.$
50	.04	10,000	8.70
100	.09	15,000	13.04
200	.17	20,000	17.39
300	.26	25,000	21.74
400	.35	30,000	26.09
500	.43	35,000	30.43
750	.65	40,000	34.78
1,000	.87	45,000	39.13
1,500	1.30	50,000	43.48
2,000	1.74	55,000	47.82
2,500	2.17	60,000	52.17
3,000	2.61	65,000	56.52
4,000	3.48	70,000	60.87
5,000	4.35	75,000	65.21

bit more. By Italian law, the maximum price for the room and any additional services (like breakfast or a shower) must be posted in the room.

DOUBLES FOR LESS THAN 43,000 LIRE [$37.40]

ALBERGO CASANOVA, corso Garibaldi, 333, or via Venezia, 2, 80142 Napoli. Tel. 081/26-8287. Fax 081/554-3768. 18 rms (9 with shower and toilet). TEL **Directions:** See below.

$ Rates: 21,000 lire ($18.25) single without shower or toilet, 24,200 lire ($21.05) single with shower and toilet; 42,000 lire ($36.50) double without shower or toilet, 50,400 lire ($43.80) double with shower and toilet; 63,000 lire ($54.80) triple without shower or toilet, 68,300 lire ($59.40) triple with shower and toilet; 73,500 lire ($63.90) quad without shower or toilet, 86,100 lire ($74.85) quad with shower and toilet. Breakfast 5,000 lire ($4.35) extra. 10% discount for bearers of this book. AE, DC, MC, V.

The helpful, English-speaking Arzillo family offers 18 clean, simply furnished rooms, always watched over carefully by one of the family and their aging German shepherd. The roof garden is a remarkable touch for such an inexpensive place. Off-season especially, there's no reason not to stay here, as this is virtually the only budget establishment that is selective about its guests during that time. Since it's located at the end of two dead-end streets, its quarters are exceptionally quiet. They also have a handy luggage-storage room, and will graciously allow guests to call collect from the hotel, without charge.

To reach the Casanova during the day, walk up via Milano from piazza Garibaldi, and turn left when the street ends after three blocks. After dark it's safer to walk up corso Garibaldi.

ALBERGO FIORE, via Milano, 109 (4th Floor), 80142 Napoli. Tel. 081/553-8798. 10 rms (1 with bath).

$ Rates: 17,500 lire ($15.30) single without bath; 32,500 lire ($28.26) double without bath, 39,500 lire ($34.35) double with bath. You'll need 50 lire (5¢) for the elevator. No credit cards.

Albergo Fiore is a favorite of Polish visitors to Naples, and indeed, when I last visited, the place was full of Poles wrapping packages to bring back home. Why so many Polish travelers here? The previous owner was a Pole who moved to Italy, and the contacts he set up with his homeland continue to this day. Although the Fiore is just two doors up via Milano from the central, raucous piazza Garibaldi, it's exceptionally quiet. The management doesn't speak much English.

ALBERGO ZARA, via Firenze, 81 (2nd Floor), 80142 Napoli. Tel. 081/28-7125. 10 rms (3 with shower and toilet, 1 with shower only). **Directions:** See below.

$ Rates: 42,000 lire ($36.50) double without shower, 47,300 lire ($41.15) double with shower; 60,500 lire ($52.60) triple without shower, 63,000 lire ($54.80) triple with shower. No credit cards.

Owned by an uncle of the family that runs the Albergo Casanova (see above), this 10-room hotel features large, clean rooms with colorful stone floors, and even three rooms with frescoed ceilings (though admittedly the frescoes are rather amateurishly executed). Alda and Rafaella Amendola don't speak English, but their daughter, Maria Vittoria, is sometimes around to help translate.

To find the albergo, walk up corso Novara from the station and take the first left onto via Firenze; the Zara will be on the left, on the third block. Corso Novara is the street leading away from the station immediately to your right as you exit (look for the half-built expressway ramp).

TERESITA HOTEL, via Santa Lucia, 90 (2nd Floor), 80142 Napoli. Tel. 081/41-2105. 12 rms (none with bath). **Directions:** See below.

$ Rates: 26,000 lire ($22.60) single; 37,000 lire ($32.20) double; 47,000 lire ($40.85) triple. Showers 2,000 lire ($1.75) extra. No credit cards.

Can fake plants, dubious bathrooms, and a contentious management still garner a recommendation in this guidebook? Usually not, but Naples is not your usual town, and this hotel is one of the cheapest around, located in a good neighborhood in the high-rent part of town. Did I mention that the large rooms are a bit noisy, and they charge a fee each time you shower? Enter the hotel through the faux etched-glass doors.

To reach Teresita, take bus no. 106, 150, or "FT" from the train station, and tell the driver where you're going. The stop will be on via Santa Lucia, about two blocks from the hotel.

DOUBLES FOR LESS THAN 73,000 LIRE ($63.50)

HOTEL CASA BETANIA, via Settembrini, 42, 80139 Napoli. Tel. 081/44-4833. Fax 081/44-4646. 55 rms (25 with shower). TEL **Metropolitana:** Piazza Cavour.

$ Rates: 44,000 lire ($38.25) single without shower, 52,500 lire ($45.65) single with shower; 67,200 lire ($58.45) double without shower, 80,900 lire ($70.35) double with shower. No credit cards.

The Casa Betania is an exceptional value, with tastefully furnished interiors, telephones, and terrazzo floors in every room, and even a restaurant on the second floor. They keep the front door locked at all times and asked to see my passport before opening up when I last arrived.

HOTEL EDEN, corso Novara, 9, 80142 Napoli. Tel. 081/28-5344 or 28-5690. Fax 081/20-2070. 45 rms (all with bath). TEL

$ Rates: 42,000 lire ($36.50) single; 72,600 lire ($63.15) double; 96,800 lire ($84.20) triple; 114,400 lire ($99.50) quad. Breakfast 5,000 lire ($4.35) extra. AE, CB, DC, MC, V.

If you can't afford the three-star Hotel Cavour listed in "Worth the Extra Bucks," below, but want well-run accommodations at a significant discount, try this place. The rates listed above, available only to bearers of this book, are a discount of more than 15% off their everyday rates. Rooms are large, well furnished (although with aging wallpaper), and bright, and all come with private bath. The Hotel Eden is an excellent choice for older readers on a budget. If for any reason the special Frommer discount is not known to the desk clerk, ask to speak to the English-speaking owner, Nicola Lopomo. Corso Novara is the street leading away from the station, immediately to your right as you exit (look for the half-built expressway ramp).

A SUPER-BUDGET CHOICE

OSTELLO MERGELLINA, salita della Grotta a Piedigrotta, 23, 80122 Napoli. Tel. 081/761-2346. 250 beds. Directions: See below.

$ Rates (including continental breakfast and sheets): 17,500 lire ($15.20) per person. No credit cards.

Naples has an outstanding youth hostel, with almost all double rooms and no more than six bunks per room, showers in almost every room, a spacious lobby, free parking out front, and meals at bargain prices. Married couples can almost always count on getting a double room here. The only drawback to the fine double rooms that make up most of the hostel are private bathrooms with toilets missing seat covers.

Membership in the International Youth Hostel Federation is a requirement, but you can buy a youth hostel card at the desk here for 30,000 lire ($26.10), or simply pay a 5,000-lire ($4.35) supplement per night. Dinner, served nightly from 6 to 10pm, is a rock-bottom 9,000 lire ($7.85). Remember that despite the federation's name, there are no age restrictions in Italian youth hostels. The reception desk is open from 7 to 9am and 4:30pm until the 11:30pm curfew, though the rooms are locked up from 9am to 4:30pm.

To get there, take the Metropolitana to the Mergellina. Go right as you exit the station, then right again on via Piedigrotta toward the tunnel. Just after you go under a bridge, turn right and walk uphill to the hostel. The street leading up to the hostel looks like it's still suffering the effects of Mount Vesuvius's last blast, but the hostel itself is a very pleasant surprise.

WORTH THE EXTRA BUCKS

The two hotels listed below are both exceptional choices, highly recommended for travelers of all ages who yearn to be a bit removed from the ordinary chaos of Naples.

HOTEL CAVOUR, piazza Garibaldi, 32, Napoli. Tel. 081/28-3122. 98 rms (9 with bath). TEL

$ Rates: 82,500 lire ($71.75) single without bath, 102,900 lire ($89.50) single with bath; 132,000 lire ($114.80) double without bath, 165,000 lire ($143.50) double with bath. 18% discount for bearers of this book. Breakfast 8,500 lire ($7.40) extra. AE, DC, MC, V.

Once you enter the spacious, luxurious lobby of this three-star hotel you'll feel removed from the clamor of the piazza outside. If you believe all the horror stories you've heard about Naples and are willing to pay more to feel safe, splurge here. Carpeted corridors lead to perfectly adequate rooms that recall the 1950s, all literally within sight of the front door of the train station; it's at the far right corner of the square, on the block following via Milano. A popular place among our readers.

HOTEL LE FONTANE AL MARE, via Niccolo Tommaseo, 14, Napoli. Tel.

081/764-3470 or 764-3811. 25 rms (6 with bath). TEL **Directions:** See below.

$ Rates: 63,000 lire ($54.80) single without bath, 78,800 lire ($68.50) single with bath; 78,800 lire ($68.50) double without bath, 110,300 lire ($95.90) double with bath. Breakfast 12,000 lire ($10.45) extra. AE, DC.

This is my top splurge recommendation in Naples, with enormous, high-ceilinged rooms, most of which include a large sofa and marble coffee table, not to mention a stunning floor-to-ceiling view of the Bay of Naples from 18 of the 25 rooms. The owners literally roll out the red carpet here, and even have a uniformed doorman. Breakfast on the roof garden overlooking the bay is a wonderful way to start the day. Its location and view make Le Fontane al Mare especially popular in summer, so make a reservation. An excellent selection for families.

Take bus no. 106, 150, or 152 to piazza Vittoria from the station; via Niccolo Tommaseo will be the first left as you walk back along the water toward the Castel dell'Ovo. Alternatively take tram no. 1 to piazza Vittoria.

---

5. BUDGET DINING

For important information on dining in Italy, see the introduction to "Budget Dining" in the Rome chapter.

I could go on and on about the special dishes of Naples, and how spaghetti *alle vongole* (in a clam sauce) is as ubiquitous and sought after by Neapolitans as spaghetti *alla bolognese* is to the denizens of Bologna. Or how "fresh" fish here means netted that afternoon. But I'll drop those formalities, because the only culinary specialty that really matters in Naples is pizza, for this is the place where that staple of North American life was born. And while you may hear tourists say that Italian pizza can be a disappointment, you'll hear that only from those who've never been to Naples. The ingredients here are better, and the chefs know what they're doing—pizza making is a prideful profession in Naples, the traditions of which are passed on like heirlooms from one generation to the next. As elsewhere in Italy, Neapolitan pizza is almost always cooked *al forno*—in a dome-shaped, open-mouthed, wood-burning oven.

Keep in mind that in the listings below, prices are given for pasta and meat courses only. Don't forget to add in charges for bread and cover, service, and vegetable side dishes when calculating what you should expect to pay.

MEALS FOR LESS THAN 6,000 LIRE ($5.20)

ANTICA PIZZERIA DA MICHELE, via Cesare Sersale, 1-3. Tel. 553-9204.

Cuisine: PIZZA. **Directions:** See below.

$ Prices: Regular-size pizza 4,000 lire ($3.50). No credit cards.

Open: Mon–Sat 8am–11pm. **Closed:** 15 days in Aug.

★ Eating pizza at da Michele isn't just dinner—it's a rite of passage. This is the oldest and arguably the best pizzeria in Naples, the birthplace of pizza. There are just two items on the menu: pizza marinara (with tomato sauce, garlic, oregano, and oil, but with no cheese) and pizza margherita (with tomato sauce and mozzarella cheese). The decor is similarly simple, almost like a cafeteria: Fluorescent lights hang from the 25-foot-high ceilings, over marble-top tables in two rooms, separated by the pizza ovens. The place is always jammed with locals and pilgrims, and they don't take reservations.

Da Michele is on the left side of the street one short block from corso Umberto I; turn right onto via Pietro Colletta, the eighth street as you walk along corso Umberto

I from piazza Garibaldi. (Count the blocks and look for the Pop 84 shop at the corner—the street itself is poorly marked.)

PIZZERIA TRIANON, via Pietro Colletta, 42.
Cuisine: PIZZA.
$ Prices: 5,300–9,500 lire ($4.60–$8.25). No credit cards.
Open: Lunch Mon–Sat 10am–3:30pm; dinner Mon–Fri 6:30–11pm, Sat–Sun 6:30pm–midnight.

⭐ Mention da Michele to some Neapolitans and a knowing grin will cross their face as they offer this gentle advice: "You're a nice guy, but you don't *really* know the best pizza in Naples." Like da Michele, Trianon has been in business for many years, and like its rival, many local locals will declare it the best pizzeria in the city. But unlike their competitor, Trianon serves a full range of pies—though you'll see most Italians sticking to the traditional margherita. And the atmosphere is more subdued and romantic, with carved ceilings and marble tables, floors, and walls. Which is better? You'll have the gastronomic time of your life judging for yourself! Trianon's pizza comes in two sizes. Their standard pie (*normale*) is more than 12 inches across, considerably bigger than any other pizza in the country; their house specialty is *max*, a monstrous 24-inch pie big enough to feed a family of four, at about twice the price of the *normale*. Trianon is on the right side of the road, half a block beyond da Michele.

MEALS FOR LESS THAN 16,000 LIRE [$13.90]

FRATELLI AIELLO RISTORANTE E PIZZERIA, via Costantinopoli, 2. Tel. 34-1263.
Cuisine: ITALIAN.
$ Prices: Pizza and pasta courses 5,000–8,000 lire ($4.35–$6.95); meat and fish courses 7,500–10,000 lire ($6.50–$8.70). No credit cards.
Open: Lunch Mon–Sat 11am–3pm; dinner daily 6–11pm.
Cloth-topped tables fill two small, understated, and pretty rooms in the geographical center of the city. The traditional Italian menu is huge, and the food here is good. Look for pasta with various shellfish toppings, steak, veal, and various fresh fish sold by weight. The antipasti table is impressive; help yourself, and they'll charge by the plate.

The restaurant is located steps from the Museo Archeologico Nazionale. With your back to the museum, turn left and walk through the piazza Museo, then turn right onto via Costantinopoli and the restaurant will be immediately on your left.

TRATTORIA ALLA BRACE, via Silvio Spaventa, 14. Tel. 26-1260.
Cuisine: ITALIAN.
$ Prices: *Menu turistico* 16,000 lire ($13.90); pizza 3,500–8,000 lire ($3.05–[$6.95); pasta courses 3,500–8,500 lire ($3.05–$7.40); meat courses 6,500–10,000 lire ($5.65–$8.70). DC, MC, V.
Open: Mon–Sat noon–midnight.
Located just one block south of piazza Garibaldi, this is one of the most popular trattorias in Naples, crowded with Italians enjoying its good food and unusually attentive service. Fluorescent lights hang from the ceiling, a bothersome TV beams the latest football match or television drama, and animated conversation fills the air. While owner Carmine Zambello can't boast that pizza was born here, it is very cheap and exceptionally popular, especially considering that all the rest of the food is so good. Most of the time, at least half the clientele is feasting on a pie fresh from the wood-burning oven immediately to the left as you enter. The *menu turistico* includes wine, and a very wide selection of pasta and fish courses.

TRATTORIA AVELLINESE, via Silvio Spaventa, 31-35. Tel. 28-3897.

Cuisine: ITALIAN.

$ Prices: *Menu turistico* 16,000 lire ($13.90); pasta courses 4,500–6,500 lire ($3.90–$5.65); meat courses 6,500–10,000 lire ($5.65–$8.70). DC, MC, V.

Open: Sun–Fri 9am–12:30am.

It's hard to choose between this place and its rival across the street, the alla Brace (see above). Its clientele is just as faithful. Why not try both, and decide for yourself on the third night? Owner Giuseppe Illiano often stands watch in the dining room, and will proudly tell you that he treats Italians and tourists alike. The very reasonably priced tourist menu includes spaghetti alle vongole (with clams) and fresh seafood, and servings are unusually generous.

6. ATTRACTIONS

SUGGESTED ITINERARIES

IF YOU HAVE ONE DAY   It's a shame to have just one day in Naples, since the most important attractions are outside the city in the surrounding region, making it difficult to see much in a whirlwind one-day tour. Nonetheless, make your one day in Naples a Pompeii day. Start at Naples's Museo Archeologico Nazionale, home to nearly all of the treasures unearthed at Pompeii, the ancient city outside Naples that was frozen in time by Mount Vesuvius's terrific eruption nearly 2,000 years ago. After the museum, hop on the Circumvesuviana train for the journey to the ghostly place where the museum's mosaics and sculptures were discovered. If you have the time and energy, make a quick stop at Herculaneum, the less stunning but equally interesting city buried along with Pompeii on August 24, A.D. 79.

IF YOU HAVE TWO DAYS   If you've made it this far south in Italy, you may have had enough of ancient stone architecture and city parks for the time being. You're in luck, then, because beyond the Museo Nazionale there's not that much within the city limits that demands attention. So get away from it all to one of the resort areas in the region. The first stop on any sun lover's itinerary is Capri, Italy's most famous and most popular sunshine destination.

IF YOU HAVE THREE DAYS   On your third day, sample one of the region's coastal villages. Choose for yourself from among the three Amalfi Coast towns covered below: Sorrento, Amalfi, and Positano. Or strike out on your own and find a secluded beach in one of the tiny towns in between these three main resorts.

IF YOU HAVE FIVE DAYS   An all-out tour of the Naples area is likely to be more exhausting than exhaustive. Rather than setting out to touch every base, why not plan to spend three or more days on your favorite island or at the coastal village that suits you best.

TOP ATTRACTIONS

MUSEO ARCHEOLOGICO NAZIONALE, piazza Museo, 35. Tel. 44-0166.

⭐ This is the one "must-see" attraction for visitors to Naples. One of the most important archeological museums in Europe, its collection includes astonishingly well preserved mosaics and art treasures from the excavations of Pompeii and Herculaneum, as well as the bronze *Hermes at Rest,* and the stunning *Farnese Bull,* modeled from a single block of marble. Other notable works here include a larger-than-life *Hercules,* a mosaic uncovered at Pompeii of *Alexander's Battle of Issos* from the 4th century B.C., and a captivating *Aphrodite.* The museum is located on piazza Museo, adjacent to piazza Cavour, which is on the Metropolitana line.

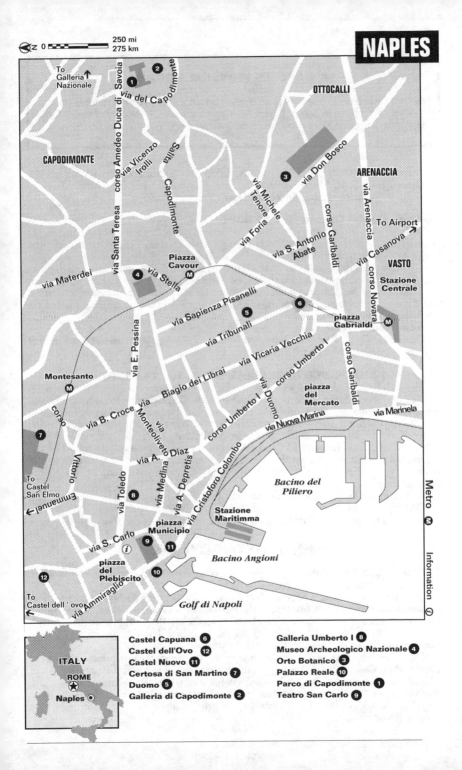

NAPLES

250 mi
0
275 km

OTTOCALLI

CAPODIMONTE

To Galleria Nazionale

via del Capodimonte

corso Amedeo Duca di Savoia

via Vicenzo Irolli

Salita Capodimonte

via Santa Teresa

via Materdei

ARENACCIA

via Don Bosco

via Michele Tenore

via Foria

corso Garibaldi

via Arenaccia

To Airport

via Casanova

corso Novara

VASTO

Stazione Centrale

via S. Antonio Abate

Piazza Cavour

via Stella

via Sapienza Pisanelli

via E. Pessina

via Tribunali

piazza Gabrialdi

Montesanto

via B. Croce Via

Biagio dei Librai

via Vicaria Vecchia

corso Umberto I

corso Garibaldi

piazza del Mercato

via Monteoliveto

via A. Depretis

corso Umberto I

via Duomo

via Nuova Marina

via Marinela

corso Vittorio Emmanuel

To Castel San Elmo

via Toledo

via A. Diaz

via Medina

via Cristoforo Colombo

Bacino del Piliero

Stazione Maritimma

via S. Carlo

piazza Municipio

Bacino Angioni

piazza del Plebiscito

via Ammiraglio

Golf di Napoli

Metro **ⓜ**

Information **ⓘ**

ITALY

ROME

Naples

Castel Capuana **❻**
Castel dell'Ovo **⓬**
Castel Nuovo **⓫**
Certosa di San Martino **❼**
Duomo **❺**
Galleria di Capodimonte **❷**

Galleria Umberto I **❽**
Museo Archeologico Nazionale **❹**
Orto Botanico **❸**
Palazzo Reale **❿**
Parco di Capodimonte **❶**
Teatro San Carlo **❾**

A NOTE ON MUSEUM HOURS

Before setting off to one of Naples's museums, it's always best to double-check the hours it's open in one of the tourist publications, *Qui Napoli* or *Napoli Top*. Hours can change from month to month depending on municipal finances.

Admission: 8,000 lire ($6.95) adults, 4,000 lire ($3.50) children 17 and under. **Open:** July–Sept, Mon–Sat 9am–7:30pm, Sun 9am–1pm; Oct–June, Mon–Sat 9am–2pm, Sun 9am–1pm. **Metropolitana:** Piazza Cavour.

DUOMO, via del Duomo. Tel. 44-9097.

Built in the 13th century on the foundations of a Roman temple, and richly fashioned in Gothic and subsequently baroque style, Naples's cathedral is dedicated to the city's patron saint, San Gennaro. His skull and two golden flasks containing his blood are kept in the Cappella di San Gennaro, the third side chapel to your right as you enter. According to legend, the blood liquefies three times a year: on the first Saturday in May, September 19, and December 16. It's considered a bad omen for the city if it doesn't happen. The Duomo is located on via del Duomo, at the corner of via dei Tribunali, near piazza de Nicola.

Admission: Free.
Open: Daily 7:30am–12:30pm and 4:30–7:30pm. **Metropolitana:** Piazza Cavour.

GALLERIA AND PARCO DI CAPODIMONTE. Tel. 744-1307.

The lush Capodimonte Park crowns the hill a mile north of the Museo Nazionale. The centerpiece of the park is the **Galleria di Capodimonte,** a portrait and porcelain museum housed in an 18th-century royal palace. Though largely unknown, the museum is home to an excellent collection of paintings and drawings by a fine roster of artists, including Botticelli, Masaccio, Bellini, Titian, Michelangelo, Tintoretto, Rubens, Breughel, and El Greco. Most of these masterpieces are found on the second floor, while downstairs are displays of china, majolica, faïence, glassware, and enamels from the porcelain factory on this site which, 200 years ago, was one of the most famous in Europe.

Admission: Galleria, 8,000 lire ($6.95); park free.
Open: Galleria, summer, Tues–Sat 9am–7:30 or 8pm, Sun 9am–1pm; winter, Tues–Sat 9am–2pm, Sun 9am–1pm. **Bus:** 110 or 127 from the train station.

MORE ATTRACTIONS

THE CASTLES OF NAPLES Naples boasts an impressive array of castles from its days as a formidable naval power.

Located between piazza Municipio and piazza del Plebiscito, near the docks where the ferries for Capri and Ischia depart, the massive 13th-century fortress known as the **Castel Nuovo** was used as a royal residence from the 15th through the 18th century. Unfortunately, the interior of the castle, which has five turrets and a deep surrounding moat, is closed to the public.

The Castel Nuovo was considered a more secure defensive position than the **Castel dell'Ovo,** which stands in the harbor off the Santa Lucia district near piazza Municipio, and marks the city's seascape for many travelers. Begun in the 12th century on the former site of hedonist Lucullus's summer villa, the castle is now open only for special exhibits, but it may be open for visitors in 1993, after a massive interior restoration.

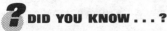

DID YOU KNOW . . . ?

- Naples is the third-largest city in Italy, after Rome and Milan.
- Mt. Vesuvius, southeast of the city, is the only active volcano on the European mainland.
- The Villa of the Papyri, near Herculaneum, inspired California's Getty Museum.
- Naples was a Spanish possession from 1503 to 1707.
- The first steamboat on the Mediterranean was launched from shipyards at Naples in 1818.
- Italy's first railway was inaugurated between Naples and Portici, five miles away, in 1826.
- Enrico Caruso was born and died in Naples.

Situated securely atop the Vomero Hill, the **Castel Sant'Elmo** (tel. 578-4030) is the largest of Naples's several castles. The view from the grounds of the castle is outstanding, and visitors are permitted inside for 1,000 lire (85¢)—though don't expect much. The castle is open year round, Tuesday through Sunday from 9am until 1pm. To reach Sant'Elmo, take the 1,000 lire (85¢) funicular from via Toledo.

Behind Saint Elmo's Castle is the ✪ **Certosa di San Martino** (tel. 578-1769), a 17th-century monastery that today is a museum with assorted displays on naval history, Neapolitan folklore, local costumes, and nativity scenes. Constructed after the World War II bombings, this is one of the city's most important galleries for art treasures and historical references. Its halls are open October through July, Tuesday through Saturday from 9am to 2pm and on Sunday and holidays from 9am to 1pm; August through September, on Tuesday, Thursday, and Saturday from 9am to 8pm, on Wednesday and Friday from 9am to 2pm, and on Sunday and holidays from 9am to 1pm. Admission is 6,000 lire ($5.20).

7. EASY EXCURSIONS

Whatever you do, make an excursion out of Naples. Outside this hot, gritty, workaday city is a wonderland of beauty and history.

POMPEII & HERCULANEUM

Quite simply, these are among the best-preserved 2,000-year-old ruins on the continent. Both Pompeii and Herculaneum can easily be visited in a single-day trip from Naples. Allow about two hours at Herculaneum and four or more at Pompeii.

POMPEII (POMPEI)

✪ Pompeii, once a flourishing city of 25,000 was destroyed suddenly on August 24, A.D. 79, by Mount Vesuvius's most notorious eruption. A layer of lava and cinders 10–20 feet deep covered the entire area, preserving for nearly two millennia these once-prosperous cities. Seventeen centuries later, local residents and archeologists discovered the lost cities, which have been nearly completely excavated. The roofless homes, the partially destroyed city walls, the lonely columns that once supported temples, the 12,000-seat amphitheater, and colorful frescoes offer a moving and fascinating glimpse into life during the 1st century A.D.

While many of the best artifacts and sculptures have been moved to the Museo Nazionale in Naples, to see them in their original context is simply breathtaking. And to see just how sudden Vesuvius's blast was, find the grisly castings of several residents, frozen forever in the throes of death by the powerful eruption. There are about half a dozen such corpses stored in the Horrea (Granari del Foro) at the northwest side of the Forum, just inside the Villa dei Misteri entrance; and in a room just to the right as you enter the Stabian Baths (Terme Stabiane).

There are two ways to get to Pompeii by rail. The first, and most convenient, is via the Circumvesuviana, a privately owned railway that travels around the Bay of Naples. Take the Sorrento line, and get off at "Pompei Scavi–Villa dei Misteri," the first stop after Torre Annunziata. Turn right as you exit and the main entrance to the ruins will be about 100 yards ahead on your left. Circumvesuviana trains depart from Naples's main railway station every few minutes, make the journey in about 20 minutes, and cost 5,000 lire ($4.35) round-trip.

The second train route to Pompeii is via state railway, aboard any local train destined for Salerno or Battipaglia (check the electronic board in the station, or ask at the information window). Get off at the "Pompei" stop, walk straight ahead for two blocks, turn right and head across the pedestrian piazza Bartolo Longo in front of the cathedral, and continue straight ahead on via Roma (a 10-minute walk in all). Trains leave Naples station every 20–40 minutes, make the journey in about 25 minutes, and cost 5,000 lire ($4.35) round-trip. Unlike the Circumvesuviana, the state railway is free to Eurailpass holders.

The ruins at Pompeii are open daily, from 9am until roughly an hour before sunset; in this part of the world, "an hour before sunset" means 8pm June through mid-August and 3:45pm in December, with the closing hour moving forward or backward 15–20 minutes every 15 days. Unfortunately, many of the houses at Pompeii are closed in winter. Admission is 10,000 lire ($8.70) no matter what the sun does. For further information, call 861-0744.

At Pompeii, maps of the site for 3,000 lire ($2.60) are only sometimes available, so you'd do well to also pick up the tourist pamphlet on Pompeii available for free from the tourist office in the Naples train station; this publication has a decent map inside. And try to wear flexible-soled shoes. The ancient streets and alleys of the city were paved with enormous stones that have been known to twist modern ankles and can be hard on your feet.

HERCULANEUM (ERCOLANO)

Herculaneum, also destroyed in the A.D. 79 eruption of Vesuvius, is smaller and less stunning, but much less crowded, than Pompeii. There are no towering columns or majestic amphitheaters at Herculaneum, but the common dwellings of the city's 1st-century inhabitants are in a remarkable state of preservation. Indeed, many of the structures are still covered by the same roofs and held together by the original wooden beams. The mosaic floors and ceilings of the Terme Maschili (Men's Baths) are particularly interesting, as is the colorful and entirely intact mosaic of a couple preparing to bathe in the home at no. 7 Insula V.

Compared to Pompeii, Herculaneum is quite tranquil. Far fewer tourists visit here, and bus tours rarely include this stop on their itineraries. Independent tourists are free to explore the ruins in relative solitude.

To get to the ruins at Herculaneum, take the Circumvesuviana to the "Ercolano" stop. Turn right as you exit the train station, look for the yellow SCAVI DI ERCOLANO sign, and walk straight ahead along via Vittorio Veneto and then along via 4 Novembre to the site entrance at the base of the street. Trains leave piazza Garibaldi in Naples every 20–40 minutes, arriving at Ercolano after 10 stops and 20 minutes. Round-trip fare to Herculaneum is 3,000 lire ($2.60).

The ruins at Herculaneum are open seven days a week, from 9am until roughly one hour before sunset, with the last visitors admitted one hour before closing. Admission is 8,000 lire ($6.95).

If you're having trouble verifying transportation and site hours for Herculaneum and/or Mount Vesuvius, contact the **Herculaneum tourist office** located at via 4 Novembre, 84 (tel. 788-1243 or 777-4221), on the way to the ruins at Herculaneum from the train station. They can also give you a map of the ruins in Herculaneum. They're open Monday through Saturday from 8:30am to 1:30pm.

MOUNT VESUVIUS

✪ Though the postcards show ash billowing from the summit of Naples's hometown volcano, Mount Vesuvius (Monte Vesuvio) has been silent since 1944. Local seismologists watch it carefully for signs of activity. As long as it remains quiet, tourists are welcome to visit the mountain, walk along the volcano's crater, and enjoy the spectacular view from the 4,000-foot-high peak. Go on a clear day.

To reach Vesuvius, take the Circumvesuviana to Ercolano, the 10th stop. Trains leave Naples's piazza Garibaldi every 20–40 minutes, and arrive in Ercolano after 20 minutes; round-trip fare is 3,000 lire ($2.60). A blue or red bus, usually marked VESUVIO, costs 4,000 lire ($3.50) and travels from the piazza directly outside the Ercolano train station to a point a 20-minute hike across a barren moonscape from the summit. (You could walk from the train station, but it would take over an hour.) The obligatory English-speaking guide service at the peak costs 5,000 lire ($4.35); for the same money, the guides will usually stay their distance, if you prefer to explore a bit on your own.

The bus makes the 40-minute trip from Ercolano to Vesuvius roughly every two hours from May through September; departures are at 7:30, 9:25, and 11:20am, and 12:35, 2:50, and 4:50pm. Buses return from the mountain at 8:30 and 10:30am, and 12:30, 2, 4, and 5:50pm. During the off-season there are just three departures, at 8:10am, 10:40am, and 2:30pm, with returns from the summit at 9:30am, 1:30pm, and 4:30pm. In winter the timing is such that it's very difficult to make the complete trip in less than six or seven hours. If you take the 8:10am bus to the peak, you'll have to wait for the 1:30pm bus back to Ercolano. Similarly, trekkers on the 10:40am bus will have to wait for the last bus back down, at 4:30pm.

CAPRI

The beauty of the island of Capri (pronounced *Cap*-ri) is legendary. It's a tiny island—just some four square miles—but it's a lovely one. Don't make the trip in search of long, sandy beaches here, though; what you'll find instead is the occasional pebble cove.

Equally as stunning as Capri's beauty is its extraordinary popularity. Just as the main town of Capri is squeezed between the twin summits of Monte Tiberio and Monte Solaro, travelers are packed into every space big enough for a bed in summer. That also means that everything is at least twice as expensive here as elsewhere in Italy: a 1,500-lire ($1.30) Roman cappuccino is a whopping 3,000 lire ($2.60) at the Gran Caffé on piazza Umberto I, for instance.

In winter, it seems as though the majority of the island's hotels, restaurants, and shops are closed, but this is no reason to avoid Capri. The off-season skies are traditionally sunny, crowds are lighter, everything's cheaper, and you can have much of the island to yourself.

There are four main settlements on Capri: **Marina Grande,** the unremarkable port area where the boats from Naples, Sorrento, and Amalfi dock; **Capri** town, the main city on the island and home to all the trendy shops, expensive cafés, and wealthy tourists, on the hill above the port; the more sedate, traditional **Anacapri,** a short bus ride from Capri town, at the top of the island near Monte Solaro; and **Marina Piccola,** on the south side of the island. The main beaches are at Marina Piccola, Punta Carena, and Bagni di Tiberio, and adjacent to the Marina Grande.

In addition to bathing and sunning here, you'll enjoy exploring some of the island's rugged beauty. For 6,000 lire ($5.20) round-trip you can take a chair lift up **Mount Solaro,** Capri's highest vantage point, for a stunning view in all directions (the chair lift usually runs from 9am to one hour before sunset, depending on the weather, from the main square in Anacapri; tel. 837-1428). You may also want to walk up to **Villa Jovis,** a 40- to 60-minute hike from Capri town to another memorable hilltop where Roman Emperor Tiberius constructed a villa in the 1st century A.D.

ORIENTATION

Most boats will deposit you at Marina Grande, a quick but expensive 2,000-lira ($1.75) **funicular ride** from the town of Capri. The funicular runs every 15 minutes between 6:30am and 8:40pm, May through October only; orange minibuses connect Capri with Anacapri and the two marinas every 15 minutes between 6:30am and 9pm, then every 30 minutes until midnight. Bus fare is 1,500 lire ($1.30). You'll find the **bus depot** in Capri opposite via Roma, 27, next to the Ristorante Campanile.

There are three offices of the **Azienda Autonoma di Cura, Soggiorno, e Turismo** on Capri: on the docks at Marina Grande (tel. 837-0634); on piazza Umberto I (tel. 837-0686), the main square in Capri town; and at via Orlandi, 19a (tel. 837-1524) in Anacapri. Most are open daily from 8am to 8pm June through October, and Monday through Saturday from 8:30am to 2:30pm in the off-season. All three will try to help those who arrive on the island without hotel reservations.

Boat tours to Capri's famous **Grotta Azzurra (Blue Grotto)** are expensive tourist traps; most Caprese will tell you "it's the last thing to see on your tour of the island." Tours can cost as much as 18,000 lire ($15.65) for a 15-minute look at a mildly remarkable sea cave. Still, it might be hard to admit to your friends back home that you visited Capri without viewing the grotto. Go if you must.

The **telephone area code** for Capri is the same as Naples's, 081, but calls to Naples are billed as long distance.

GETTING THERE

FROM NAPLES Boat fares from Naples to Capri differ by only a few hundred lire from one company to the next. Of the countless ship lines that ply the waters of the Bay of Naples, Caremar is the largest. Ferries (*traghetto*) and hydrofoils (*aliscafo*) leave from the docks at Naples's Molo Beverello. To reach the docks, take bus no. 150 from the train station to piazza Municipio; from the piazza, walk toward the water, turn right, and continue along the seawall for a few hundred yards.

The different ferry companies run fairly frequently every day, with the number of departures increasing in summer. Fare is about 9,000 lire ($7.85) for the 70-minute ferry trip and about 13,000 lire ($11.30) for the hydrofoil, which makes the crossing in 40 minutes.

FROM SORRENTO Capri is also connected with Sorrento's Marina Piccola by regular ferries in summer, which make the crossing in 45 minutes. One-way fare is 6,000–7,000 lire ($5.20–$6.10), depending on the company you choose. Compare prices and departure times at the dock.

BUDGET ACCOMMODATIONS

In Capri Town

ALBERGO AÏDA, via Birago, 18, 80073 Capri. Tel. 081/837-0366. 14 rms (all with bath). **Directions:** See below.

$ **Rates** (including breakfast): 95,000 lira ($82.60) double. No credit cards. **Closed:** Oct–Mar.

Just down the street from the Albergo La Tosca (below) is Aïda, with more comfortable, if more expensive, rooms. Both big and bright, this cheery *albergo* features a large outdoor, vine-covered dining and relaxing patio surrounded by palm and fruit trees. This is how you imagined Capri is *supposed* to be. The Aïda is located just before the Margherita on the left (see directions to the Tosca, below).

ALBERGO LA TOSCA, via Birago, 5, 80073 Capri. Tel. 081/837-0989. 12 rms (6 with bath). **Directions:** See below.

$ **Rates:** 31,500 lire ($27.40) single without bath; 57,800 lire ($50.25) double without bath, 73,500 lire ($63.90) double with bath. Prices fall about 10% in low season. No credit cards.

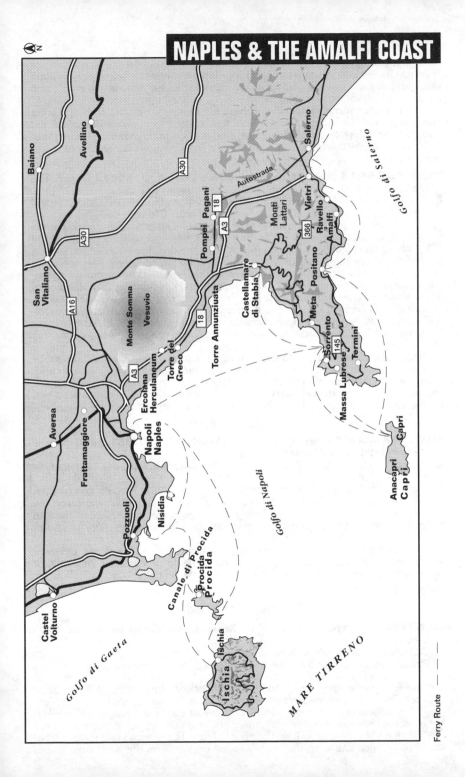

NAPLES & THE AMALFI COAST

Baiano

Avellino

San Vitaliano

A30

A30

A16

Autostrada

Salerno

Golfo di Salerno

Pagani

Pompei

18

A3

Vietri

Monti Lattari

Ravello

366

Amalfi

Monte Somma

Vesuvio

Castellamare di Stabia

Positano

Meta

Aversa

Frattamaggiore

18

Torre Annunziata

Sorrento

145

Termini

A3

Ercolano Herculaneum

Torre del Greco

Massa Lubrense

Napoli Naples

Pozzuoli

Nisidia

Golfo di Napoli

Capri Capri

Anacápri Capri

Castel Volturno

Canale di Procida

Procida Procida

Golfo di Gaeta

Ischia Ischia

MARE TIRRENO

Ferry Route — — —

Some of the cheapest accommodations on the island are the clean and pleasant rooms of Franco de Stefano's Albergo La Tosca. Six rooms enjoy private balconies with water views, and all guests are welcome to use the piano in the entryway, as well as the patio out front which sports a stunning view.

Tosca is open year round, and is a short five-minute walk from the Capri town funicular station. To find the albergo, head up the stairs from piazza Umberto I and walk past the church to the administrative headquarters of the Azienda Autonoma di Turismo. Turn left and follow the signs for the Villa Margherita. The Tosca is just beyond it on the right.

PENSIONE VILLA BIANCA, via Belvedere Cesina, 9, 80073 Capri. Tel. 081/837-8016. 8 rms (all with bath). **Directions:** See below.

$ Rates (including breakfast): 95,500 lire ($80.04) double; 123,000 lire ($106.95) triple; 141,000 lire ($122.60) quad. No credit cards. **Closed:** Dec–Feb.

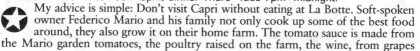 Chances are, you won't want to leave Pensione Villa Bianca. A stunning violet bougainvillea vine twists up the four stories, nearly enveloping this delightful place, and adding a wonderful fragrance to the already-enchanted air. Four of the eight spacious rooms (all of which have colorfully tiled floors) have enormous terraces with a spectacular view of the ocean to the south. Those without a terrace enjoy access to the flower-covered roof, which does double duty as a breakfast area. There is also a kitchen for guests' use (at a nominal fee for cooking). Owner Augusto Ferraro and his German wife, Helga, both speak excellent English. If possible, book well ahead—the best rooms are booked almost a year in advance. Here, as at most hotels on the island, it's difficult to get a room for less than a week or two during July and August.

To find the Villa Bianca from Capri town's piazza Umberto I, walk through the arch on the ocean side of the piazza (opposite the staircase), onto via Longano. Continue straight ahead until this narrow street curves to the right, climbs six stairs, and becomes via Sopramonte. Walk straight for about 200 yards until you see a sign for the hotel on the left. Walk up the stairs, and keep right to reach the villa.

Near Anacapri

VILLA EVA, via la Fabbrica, 8, 80071 Capri. Tel. 081/837-2040. 15 rms (11 with bath). **Directions:** See below.

$ Rates: 55,000 lire ($47.80) double with bath. Breakfast 7,000 lire ($6.10) extra. No credit cards.

Staying outside Anacapri at the remote but spectacular Villa Eva is a rare treat. A mini stone castle with Gothic and romanesque arches, many little staircases and outside entrances to the rooms, and lush gardens about, this is the place to come to really get away from it all—and here you can enjoy secluded splendor at budget prices.

To reach Villa Eva, take an orange shuttle bus from Marina Grande or Capri town to Anacapri's main piazza Vittoria. From there, call Eva or Vincenzo for a ride, or continue on the Anacapri bus to the third stop past the center of town, and follow the signs.

BUDGET DINING

LA BOTTE, via Provinciale Marina Grande, 34, Capri town. Tel. 837-6967.

Cuisine: ITALIAN. **Directions:** See below.

$ Prices: Pasta courses 5,500–9,000 lire ($4.80–$7.80); poultry courses 9,000–11,000 lire ($7.80–$9.55). No credit cards.

Open: July–Aug, lunch daily noon–3pm; dinner daily 7pm–midnight. Sept–June, lunch Thurs–Tues noon–3pm; dinner Thurs–Tues 7pm–midnight.

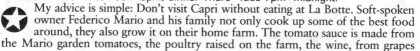 My advice is simple: Don't visit Capri without eating at La Botte. Soft-spoken owner Federico Mario and his family not only cook up some of the best food around, they also grow it on their home farm. The tomato sauce is made from the Mario garden tomatoes, the poultry raised on the farm, the wine, from grapes

harvested by Mr. Mario's father, and the fish personally caught by his brother! I enjoyed the exceptionally fresh ravioli his mother made. You dine either indoors among stucco walls covered by rustic objects or outdoors on a lovely terrace overlooking the sea and Mount Vesuvius in the distance.

To get here, exit Capri town's main square past the bus station and continue straight ahead; when you reach the intersection at the Agip gas station, turn right. The restaurant is shortly after, on the right just before the Carabinieri station.

LA CANTINA DEL MARCHESE, via Tiberio, Capri town. Tel. 837-0857.
   Cuisine: ITALIAN. **Directions:** See below.
$ Prices: Pizza 6,500–10,500 lire ($5.65–$9.15); pasta courses 6,500–10,500 lire ($5.65–$9.15); meat courses 9,500–15,000 lire ($8.25–$13.05). AE, MC, V.
   Open: Apr–Oct, Fri–Wed 11:45am–midnight (with a break in the middle of the afternoon in Aug). Nov–Mar, lunch Fri–Wed 11:45am–2 or 3pm; dinner Fri–Wed 5:30pm–midnight.

With about 12 tables, an open kitchen, and a good compact disc collection, this attractive restaurant is a charming all-around winner. The menu features Caprese specialties, with an particular emphasis on pasta. Garlic and herbs hang from a blond-wood ceiling, putting an Italian slant on an otherwise tropical ambience.

The cantina is about a 15-minute walk from piazza Umberto I. To get here, walk uphill, past the sign pointing to the Pensione Villa Bianca (see above for directions) and turn left just before a tiny piazza with a bar to one side. Follow the signs for the Villa Jovis, and you will pass the restaurant, located across from the elementary school.

ROSTICCERIA SCIALAPOPOLO, via Le Botteghe, 31, Capri town. Tel. 837-0246.
   Cuisine: ITALIAN. **Directions:** See below.
$ Prices: Pasta courses 7,500–10,500 lire ($6.50–$9.15); meat and fish courses 7,500–14,000 lire ($6.50–$12.20). No credit cards.
   Open: Summer, Tues–Sun 8am–11pm. Rest of the year, 8am–8pm.
There's not much to the decor, which includes about 50 bare tables surrounded by plain blond-wood walls. But this self-service cafeteria, without cover or service charges, offers some of the lowest-priced meals in town. A full menu of pasta and meat selections is available from April to December, displayed under glass so you can see before selecting. During the off-season, the *rosticceria* is limited to little pizzas, calzone, desserts, and coffee.

To get here, take the lane just to the left of the Gran Café in Capri town's central square.

ROSTICCERIA SCIUÈ SCIUÈ DI RAFFAELE BUONOCORE, via Vittorio Emanuele, 35, Capri town. Tel. 837-7826.
   Cuisine: ITALIAN. **Directions:** See below.
$ Prices: Pasta courses 7,000 lire ($6.10); meat courses 7,500–10,500 lire ($6.50–$9.15). No credit cards.
   Open: July–Sept, daily 7:30am–1am. Oct–June, Wed–Mon 7:30am–9pm.
A smaller *rosticceria* with only a few counter seats, this place makes good home cuisine for moderate prices. To get there, exit the main square of Capri town just to the right of the Gran Café and follow the curve of the street; you'll soon see the *rosticceria* on the left.

ISCHIA

Ischia suffers in all comparisons to Capri save one: economy. There are no towering white cliffs or narrow alleyways, but everything here is considerably less expensive.

Travelers have long flocked to this island for the innumerable thermal springs. Curiously enough, more than two-thirds of modern tourists are German; indeed, most hoteliers and waiters speak German, and German culinary specialties are available at most restaurants.

Most boats land at **Ischia Porto,** the main town on the island. A few ferries check in at the smaller and more peaceful town of **Casamicciola,** about 2½ miles farther along. Compact **Lacco Ameno** is just half a mile past Casamicciola, and **Forio** is another mile farther along the main road.

You can't miss the island's **tourist office** (tel. 081/99-1146) right on the docks at Ischia Porto, open Monday through Saturday from 9am to 8pm.

Orange **S.E.P.S.A. buses** connect the island's six main towns; fare is 1,200– 1,500 lire ($1.05–$1.30), depending on how far you go. Purchase tickets at the blue *biglietteria* opposite the main bus lot in Ischia Porto (to the right as you come off the wharf), or at the Café Calise on piazza Marina in Casamicciola.

Caremar has seven ferries (*traghetto*) and six hydrofoils (*aliscafo*) running daily from Naples to Ischia and back again. Fare is 7,000 lire ($6.10) each way for the 70-minute ferry trip and 13,000 lire ($11.30) for the hydrofoil, which makes the crossing in half the time. Fares drop slightly in the off-season.

The **telephone area code** here is 081.

BUDGET ACCOMMODATIONS

PENSIONE LA PERGOLA, via Casa Mennella, 1, 80077 Ischia. Tel. 081/99-4902. 20 rms (all with bath). **Bus:** 3 from Ischia Porto, or 3-bis from piazza Marina, the main square in Casamicciola.

$ Rates (including continental breakfast): Apr–Sep, 49,500–60,500 lire ($43.05– $52.60) per person double. Oct and Mar, 41,800–49,500 lire ($36.35–$43.05) per person double. No credit cards. **Closed:** Nov–Feb.

Have you ever wondered what a good old-fashioned European spa would be like? Try the Pensione La Pergola, perched high above Casamicciola in the tiny hamlet of Larita. Both of its pools, on a panoramic terrace overlooking the sea, are filled with naturally heated thermal spring water, which comes out of the hillside at a piping 136°F (it cools down to 98.6°F by the time the pool's full). They also do massages, mudpacks, facials, and steam-inhalation treatment, and at modest rates. Most of the 20 rooms have balconies that overlook the sea and the grape arbors that cling to the nearby hillside. Should you ever want to leave the thermal pools, the Catagna family will point you down the hill to the beach at Lacco Ameno, a 10-minute hike away.

PENSIONE ATLANTIC, via Leonardo Mazzella, 28, 80077 Ischia. Tel. 081/99-1093. 25 rms (all with bath).

$ Rates (including breakfast): 82,500 lire ($71.75) double. No credit cards.

Near Ischia Porto (about 20 minutes on foot) is this establishment run by the ever-gracious Balestrieri family, located in a peaceful residential quarter just a five-minute walk from the beach. Each room has colorful floor tiling and a private bath. Signor Balestrieri will meet you at the bottom of the boat ramp if you call before leaving Naples. Alternatively, call when you land and he'll come fetch you.

BUDGET DINING

TAVERNA JANTO, via Larita, 3.
  Cuisine: ITALIAN.
$ Prices: Pizza 4,500–7,000 lire ($3.90–$6.10); complete meals 14,500–24,000 lire ($12.60–$20.85). No credit cards.
  Open: Lunch daily 12:30–3pm; dinner daily 7:30pm–midnight. **Closed:** Nov– Mar.

Pensione La Pergola's Castagna family also runs this establishment about 100 yards past their place on via Larita (see above for directions).

RISTORANTE MONFALCONE, corso Luigi Manzi, 12. Tel. 99-4401.
  Cuisine: ITALIAN.
$ Prices (most including salad): Pasta courses 5,000–11,000 lire ($4.35–$9.55); meat and fish courses 7,000–17,000 lire ($6.10–$14.80). No credit cards.
  Open: Daily noon–8pm.

For eating down in Casamicciola, try the 75-year-old Ristorante Monfalcone, which claims to be the island's original eatery. The menu is limited, but there's no cover or service charge, and no pressure to eat a full meal.

SORRENTO

According to an early Greek tradition, it was at Sorrento that Odysseus heard the tempting song of the Sirens, those nymphs who labored long hours at seducing and shipwrecking passing sailors. The emperor Augustus apparently heard their voices as well, for this lovely resort community has been a popular vacation spot ever since.

The Sirens apparently are silent today, but something still lures the countless Italians and Europeans who come to enjoy Sorrento's romantic tree-lined streets and to take advantage of its central location in the midst of Italy's most beautiful region. Chock full of reasonably priced hotels and restaurants, it certainly makes the best base from which to explore the Amalfi Coast and the islands, and in fact you might want to forgo spending the night in Naples and simply come directly here.

To find the tourist office, **Azienda Autonoma di Turismo,** via Luigi de Maio, 35 (tel. 081/878-1115, 878-2229, or 878-2104), from the Circumvesuviana train station, walk straight ahead as you exit and take the first left onto corso Italia until you reach piazza Tasso. Exit this piazza at the far right corner, by Rosy's Souvenir Shop, onto via Luigi de Maio. The tourist office will be on the first right past piazza San Antonino beyond a driveway with a sign ARCOLO DEI FORESTIERI in cursive script above. The office is open Monday through Saturday from 8:30am to 2:30pm and 4 to 7pm (5 to 8pm from July through the first half of September). *Note:* The agencies in piazza San Antonino advertising "tourist information" are not the official tourist office.

Sorrento is the final stop on the Circumvesuviana rail line. The last train back to Naples from Sorrento leaves at about 10:40pm. Fare each way for the 65-minute trip is 2,600 lire ($2.25). You can also approach the town from Capri. There are numerous ferries daily in summer, fewer during the off-season. One-way fare for the 45-minute trip is about 4,500 lire ($3.90), depending on the ferry company. See the Capri section for more details.

The most exciting way around the coast is by moped; adventurers would do well to drop their heavy bags in Sorrento and rent an Italian Vespa. There are plenty of rental outlets here, including **Sorrento Rent-a-Car,** corso Italia, 210a (tel. 878-1386). Expect to pay about 28,000 lire ($24.35) per day.

BUDGET ACCOMMODATIONS

HOTEL CITY, corso Italia, 221, 80067 Sorrento. Tel. 081/877-2210. 13 rms (all with bath). **Directions:** See below.
$ Rates: 36,800 lire ($32.00) single; 57,800 lire ($50.25) double; 73,500 lire ($63.90) triple; 89,300 lire ($77.65) quad. V.
This simple little place is the best budget choice in Sorrento. All the rooms are small, cozy, clean, and downright cheap. Owner Gianni Magliulo has decorated the whitewashed halls with paintings by young local artists. The hotel is halfway between the train station and piazza Tasso, on the main road running between the two. Ask for a room away from the noisy street.

HOTEL IL FARO, Marina Piccola, 80067 Sorrento. Tel. 081/878-1390. 30 rms (all with bath). **Directions:** See below.
$ Rates: 66,000 lire ($57.40) single; 120,000 lire ($104.35) double. No credit cards.
★ Located at dockside below the main part of town is the most convenient lodging for those using Sorrento as a base from which to explore the Bay of Naples's twin jewels, Capri and Ischia. More than half the rooms in this recently renovated seaside *albergo* feature ocean views, as does the terrace of the romantic restaurant in front.

To reach the il Faro from the train station, take the orange bus marked MARINA PICCOLA. If you prefer to take the 15-minute walk, exit the station, walk downhill, and turn left on corso Italia. Continue on until you reach piazza Tasso, and walk down the stairs to the right, just past the Hotel Apollo and just before the Bar Vittoria. At the bottom of these stairs, walk a few yards uphill to a second, and final, stairway down to the port.

HOTEL SAVOIA, via Fuorimura, 50, 80067 Sorrento. Tel. 081/878-2511. 25 rms (all with bath). **Directions:** See below.
$ Rates: 42,700 lire ($37.15) single; 62,900 lire ($54.70) double; 78,700 lire ($68.45) triple; 96,800 lire ($84.20) quad. AE, DC, MC.
Farther inland you'll find the Hotel Savoia, owned and operated by the efficient Rosamaria Gargiulo. Rooms are plain, but with 25 rooms (all at budget rates), there is almost always space, often even in the busiest season or late at night. Via Fuorimura begins to the left of piazza Tasso; the hotel is five minutes down the road.

IYHF YOUTH HOSTEL, via Capasso, 5, 80067 Sorrento. Tel. 081/878-1783. 120 beds. **Directions:** See below.
$ Rates: 10,500 lire ($9.15) per person. Breakfast 4,000 lire ($3.50) extra; lunch or dinner, 10,000 lire ($8.70). No credit cards. **Closed:** Nov–Feb.
Sorrento's youth hostel is open from March through October only. There is a midnight curfew, and the hostel closes from 10am to 5pm daily. Rooms contain 6–22 beds each.

To find the hostel, turn right onto corso Italia as you leave the train station; via Capasso is the first major left off this street.

BUDGET DINING

LA FENICE, via degli Aranci, 11. Tel. 878-1652.
Cuisine: ITALIAN. **Directions:** See Below.
$ Prices: Pasta 5,000–8,000 lire ($4.35–$6.95); meat and fish courses 7,500–10,000 lire ($6.50–$8.70). No credit cards.
Open: Lunch Tues–Sun noon–3pm; dinner Tues–Sun 7pm–1am.
Lattice dividers, potted greenery, and colorful walls make La Fenice look more like a trellised garden than the Venetian opera house it was named for. Both bright and comfortable, the restaurant's 25 tables are often filled with knowledgeable diners who come for excellent antipasti, fresh fish, and a good selection of wines. Like the house wine, which costs only 5,000 lire ($4.35) per bottle, this restaurant feels much more expensive than it is. Indeed, La Fenice is one of the great finds of Sorrento.

To reach the restaurant from piazza Tasso, walk down corso Italia about five blocks with the water on your right. Turn left at via degli Aranci, and you'll see the restaurant immediately on your right.

AMALFI

At Amalfi, the largest of the many resort towns on the coast between Sorrento and Salerno, you'll expect the majestic white cliffs, which seem to lean seaward, to topple over on you at any moment. With whitewashed alleys and a cozy main piazza dominated by a cathedral facade reminiscent of Florence's famous Duomo, this coastal village has become the most popular destination in the Naples region after Capri.

During the 10th and 11th centuries Amalfi was one of the four great maritime powers of Italy (along with Pisa, Genoa, and Venice), supporting a population of more than 100,000. But instead of spices, coffee, and silk from the East, today Amalfi's 10,000 residents import sun-worshiping tourists from the West.

While literally every travel agency in Amalfi bills itself as a "tourist information office," the official, genuine **Azienda Autonoma di Turismo tourist office** is inside the courtyard at via Roma, 21 (tel. 089/87-1107 or 87-2619), on the road toward Salerno from the bus station. June through September, it's open Monday through Friday from 8am to 2pm and 4:30 to 7pm, and on Saturday from 8am to 1pm; in winter they're open during the morning only.

The **telephone area code** for Amalfi is 089.

GETTING THERE

To reach Amalfi, take the Circumvesuviana from Naples all the way to Sorrento at the end of the line. From right out in front of the station there, blue **S.I.T.A. buses** wind their tortuous way along the breathtaking Amalfi coast, by way of Positano, with departures roughly every two hours between 6:30am and 8:10pm. For up-to-date schedules, check at the S.I.T.A. terminal in Naples or phone the tourist office in Sorrento. The schedule is posted on a bulletin board outside the Sorrento train station.

The fare for the 80-minute Sorrento–Amalfi trip is about 3,000 lire ($2.60) each way, with the last bus back to Sorrento leaving Amalfi at 8:20pm; tickets are sold on the bus. The trip is an experience in and of itself, as the drivers fearlessly wheel their coaches around countless hairpin turns, with the stark-white coastal cliffs towering hundreds of yards above the road and tumbling several hundred more to the turquoise sea below.

EurailPass travelers can save some money by taking the state railway from Naples down to Salerno, the best link to the Amalfi Coast. Buses marked AMALFI leave Salerno's piazza Concordia on a regular basis; ask at the tourist office for specific times.

You can also travel direct to Amalfi from downtown Naples, with buses departing from the S.I.T.A. terminal at via Giuseppe Pisanelli, 4 (tel. 552-2176), located off the inland side of piazza Municipio. Fare for the two-hour journey, via Salerno, is 5,000 lire ($4.35) each way.

From May through September only, **ferry service** connects Amalfi and Positano with Capri.

BUDGET ACCOMMODATIONS

HOTEL AMALFI, Salita San Giacomo, 84011 Amalfi. Tel. 089/87-2440.
   40 rms (all with bath). TEL **Directions:** See below.
$ Rates: July–Aug, 48,500 lire ($42.20) single; 60,500 lire ($52.60) double; 85,000 lire ($73.90) triple. Sept–June, about 25% less. Breakfast 9,000 lire ($7.80) extra. No credit cards.
Although it lacks the charms of the Lidomare, the Amalfi has been nicely remodeled recently and now boasts sparkling-clean private bathrooms. Unfortunately, the rooms' tiny round windows don't let in much light, making it hard to see the ocean or the small courtyard filled with orange trees.

To find the Hotel Amalfi, walk up via Genova, the main boulevard running through town, and look for signs on the left.

HOTEL LIDOMARE, via Piccolomini, 9, 84011 Amalfi. Tel. 089/87-1332.
   Fax 089/85-7972. 13 rms (all with bath). TEL **Directions:** See below.
$ Rates (including breakfast): 57,000 lire ($49.55) single; 83,500 lire ($72.60) double. AE, DC, MC, V.

The best budget lodging choice in town, if not the entire coastal area, is the Hotel Lidomare. The huge rooms are kept immaculately clean, and each has its own special feature: a piece of priceless antique furniture, a large terrace, air conditioning (in seven rooms), or a terrific view of the ocean, to name just a few. Antiques, sculpture, and the books that owners Nicolò and Evalina Camera have fill the whitewashed halls, and there is a grand piano and TV in the guests' common room. All this is available at prices only a bit higher than at other pensiones listed here.

To find the Hotel Lidomare, take the only street running left off piazza del Duomo as you walk up from the water, and take an immediate left up the stairs. Reservations are strongly recommended.

SPLURGING IN A VILLA

VILLA GRAF FIORENTINO DISTEFANO, via Fontanelle, in Valle dei Mulini, 84011 Amalfi. Tel. 089/87-2390 at the villa or 089/87-1353 at the

owner's office. 3 rms (1 with bath; the other 2 share a bath across the hall). TEL
Directions: See below.

$ **Rates** (special for bearers of this book): $83 double; $105 triple. Breakfast
(available when the owner is around), with champagne and fresh orange juice, $5
extra. No credit cards.

⭐ Although this place is a splurge, it's one of my best finds: a restored
13th-century villa on a large lemon and orange farm at the foot of stunning
mountains. Just three rooms with full comforts can be rented (two rooms have
TVs). Everything inside is spic-and-span clean, and so up-to-date that you'd never
guess that the villa is 700 years old! Modern comforts include a 35-foot swimming
pool filled with river water, a kitchen for guests, and a roof deck for sunning and
relaxing. The area, away from the central part of Amalfi overlooking the mountains, is
blissfully silent.

The entire villa is rented out in August and part of July, but during the rest of the
year Michele Fiorentino, the English-speaking owner, is anxious to attract clients and
has offered an exceptional price for the individual rooms. If you want to reserve for a
longer stay, write to Michele Fiorentino, Medico Chirurgo, via Corte del Bayulo,
84011 Amalfi. In any case, call before coming and he'll pick you up in town (the villa is
difficult to find on your own—it's 15–20 minutes away from the center of town up a
tiring path that includes many stairs, 200 yards beyond Pizzeria il Mulino—and
there's no reception at the villa anyway).

BUDGET DINING

RISTORANTE-PIZZERIA IL MULINO, via Martiri d'Ungheria, 34. Tel. 87-2223.

Cuisine: ITALIAN.

$ **Prices:** *Menu turistico* 18,700 lire ($16.25); pizza 4,500–8,000 lire ($3.90–
$6.95); pasta courses 5,000–8,500 lire ($4.35–$7.40); meat courses 7,000–
8,500 lire ($6.10–$7.40). No credit cards.

Open: May–Sept, lunch daily noon–3pm; dinner daily 7pm–midnight. Oct–Apr,
lunch Tues–Sun noon–3pm; dinner Tues–Sun 7pm–midnight.

Giuseppina Orlando's charming *trattoria* appears in a number of guidebooks and,
with good reason, it has become a favorite of many tourists. Amalfi residents, of
course, have known about this place for years. Dine outside on the veranda or inside in
the open kitchen. There are 18 varieties of pizza, all reasonably priced. Prices for fresh
fish vary with the season; in general, you can plan on spending about 36,000 lire
($31.30) for a full meal of pasta, seafood, and wine for two. Via Martiri d'Ungheria is
the continuation of the main road (via Genova) through town.

TRATTORIA LA BARACCA, piazza dei Dogi (off piazza del Duomo). Tel. 87-1285.

Cuisine: ITALIAN.

$ **Prices:** *Menu turistico* 19,500 lire ($16.95); pasta courses 5,000–10,500 lire
($4.35–$9.15); meat courses 8,500–9,500 lire ($7.40–$8.25); fish courses
10,000–22,000 lire ($8.70–$19.15). No credit cards.

Open: June–Sept, lunch daily noon–3pm; dinner daily 7–11pm. Oct–May, lunch
Thurs–Tues noon–3pm; dinner Thurs–Tues 7–11pm.

In addition to the two very popular house specialties here—zuppa di pesce (fish stew)
and spaghetti alla Baracca (with garlic, anchovies, capers, and olives)—there is a *menu
turistico* for 19,500 lire ($16.95). A bottle of the house wine costs 5,000 lire ($4.35).

POSITANO

⭐ An avalanche of whitewashed houses spills down the hillside between the
coastal highway above Positano and the turquoise sea below. A seemingly
endless series of staircases wind through the town, ending at the compact
cathedral square and the tiny harbor nearby where colorful fishing boats rock gently
back and forth.

Positano is small and beautiful enough to delight, but at the same time is so steep and—relatively—difficult to get around that it has not yet been overrun like some of its neighbors on the coast. While many Italians converge on the largest and best-known resorts—Capri, Sorrento, Amalfi—Positano remains a favorite spot of Neapolitans and others who really *know* the area.

The **Spiaggia Fornillo,** in front of the Hotel Pupetto, and the **Spiaggia Grande,** near the town square, are the largest and most popular of Positano's beaches. An umbrella and seat for the day costs 8,000 lire ($6.95) per person. For the smaller, more tranquil **Spiaggia delle Inglese** to the east, and even cozier beaches to the west, you'll need a car or boat.

Ask at the **tourist office,** via del Saracino, 4 (tel. 089/87-5067), located in the red building opposite the town cathedral and just below the main square, for directions to the beaches and other travel inquiries. Here you can also get advice on mountain hikes nearby. If you are particularly adventurous, you might set your sights on **Nocelle,** a small mountain hamlet above Positano where there are still no roads connecting it to the outside world (only mules make the journey)!

Positano is on the Sorrento–Amalfi **S.I.T.A. bus** line. The 40-minute trip from Sorrento to Positano costs about 1,500 lire ($1.30) each way; last departure from Positano back to Sorrento is at 9:10pm. **Ferries and hydrofoils** also connect with Capri, Naples, and Salerno from May to October.

The **telephone area code** for Positano is 089.

BUDGET ACCOMMODATIONS & DINING

CASA CELESTE, via Fornillo, 10, 84017 Positano. Tel. 089/87-5363. 6 rms (3 with shower). **Directions:** See below.

$ Rates: 71,500 lire ($62.20) double without or with shower, 82,500 lire ($71.75) double with breakfast. Slight discount off-season (but no heating). No credit cards.

All the rooms in Celeste Desiderio's lovely Casa Celeste have terrific views of the town spread over the hill running down to the sea. If you're tired of staying in resort hotels with look-alike rooms, this is the place for you. You'll feel like you're staying in an Italian grandmother's memory-filled 18th-century *casa* because, quite simply, that's what this place is. The halls and rooms are wall-to-wall with paintings and art objects, many of them crafted by students at a now-defunct American-run art workshop in town. Most of the time, Mama Celeste's son, Marco, is around to translate. Breakfast includes homemade jam and is served on a terrace overlooking the sea.

Mama Celeste will cook dinner for you for about 16,000 lire ($13.90), or you could also drop by the nearby Trattoria da Vincenza, viale Pasitea (tel. 87-5128), which is run by her daughter and open from Easter through November; a full meal there should set you back about 18,000 lire ($15.65).

If, like most visitors, you are traveling by bus, ask to be let off at "la Chiesa Nuova" stop; you'll recognize the stop by the Starcross Boutique located on the corner. To get to Casa Celeste from there, walk for about 15 minutes along the main road leading from the coastal highway down into town, and take the first stairway on your right at the hotel signs. The hotel is on your right shortly before you come to the Hotel Vittoria. Alternatively, take the twice-hourly orange "piccolo bus" from the main highway and ask to be left off at via Fornillo; the fare is 800 lire (70¢).

HOTEL VITTORIA, via Fornillo, and HOTEL PUPETTO, on the beach, 84017 Positano. Tel. 089/87-5049. 24 and 30 rms respectively (all with bath). TEL **Directions:** See below.

$ Rates: 47,500 lire ($41.30) single; 80,500 lire ($70) double. 10% discount in low season. MC, V.

Closed: Nov 4–Apr 1.

Every room in the Celentano family's Hotel Vittoria and its twin on the beach, the Hotel Pupetto, has a private bath and a telephone, and nearly all have balconies overlooking the sea. The rooms are exceptionally clean, with whitewashed walls and richly stained shutters and trim. If you arrive in Positano by boat, the Vittoria/Pupetto management will pick you up at the docks. If, like most visitors, you are traveling by bus, ask to be left off at "la Chiesa Nuova" stop; you'll recognize the stop by the Starcross Boutique located on the corner.

To get to the Hotel Vittoria, follow the directions for the Casa Celeste, above. The Vittoria is just beyond the Casa Celeste. To reach the Pupetto, take the "piccolo bus" all the way to the port. Alternatively, stop by the Vittoria, where they will send you down about six stories by elevator to the stairs leading down to the beach.

NICE

"I kissed her and she kissed me and we sat in the car and I felt very strange and then we drove into Nice," wrote Hemingway in his posthumous novel *The Garden of Eden*. It's easy to understand passion as one approaches Nice, for the Côte d'Azur—the French Riviera—must be one of the most sensual regions on earth. Poet Sylvia Plath wrote in her *Letters Home:* "How can I describe the beauty of the country? Everything is so small, close, exquisite, and fertile. Terraced gardens on steep slopes of rich, red earth, orange and lemon trees, olive orchards, tiny pink and peach houses." And then there are the cypress trees and mimosa, the roses and jasmine, the deep blue sea.

At the very center of the Côte d'Azur lies Nice, the largest town in this most famous resort area. It is an attractive city of tidy 19th- and 20th-century buildings, some with domes and ornate decorations, others quite simple and unassuming, many painted Mediterranean white and pink. In Vieux Nice, the medieval part of the city, streets barely wide enough for a small car meander between dark, towering palaces, and bistros ring with the laughter of customers. Not far away, the promenade des Anglais glimmers in the sun and stretches for miles around the curve of the beautiful bay; some people jog and a silver-haired dowager proudly walks her poodle.

Many artists—Picasso, Matisse, Chagall—chose to live on the Côte d'Azur. When you arrive in Nice, you'll understand why.

1. FROM A BUDGET TRAVELER'S POINT OF VIEW

BUDGET BESTS

Most of the **beach** is free in Nice, though it's a beach of pebbles and stones rather than one of comfy sand. The beach gives Nice's **museums** fierce competition of course, but many museums fight back by offering free admission as well.

When it comes to food, the local budget best is the *pan bagnat,* a small round loaf of bread stuffed with salade niçoise–type goodies and selling for 18–24F ($3.35–$4.45). The pan bagnat easily satisfies even the most ravenous appetites (or two less-than-ravenous ones), and is delicious to boot. Look for pan bagnat in streetside kiosks, in bakeries, and in *charcuteries* (France's delicatessens).

WHAT THINGS COST IN NICE	U.S. $
Taxi from the airport to the city center	33.35
Public transportation for an average trip within the city limits	1.50
Local telephone call	.20
Double room at the Hôtel Negresco (deluxe)	350.00
Double room at the Hôtel Solara (moderate)	70.35
Double room at the Hôtel Darcy (budget)	37.05
Lunch for one, without wine, at La Petite Biche (moderate)	14.90
Lunch for one, without wine, at Flunch (budget)	11.10
Dinner for one, without wine, at Chantecler (deluxe)	75.00
Dinner for one, without wine, at La Taverne de l'Opéra (moderate)	18.50
Dinner for one, without wine, at Au Soleil (budget)	10.20
Glass of wine	2.50
Coca-Cola	3.00
Cup of coffee	2.40
Roll of ASA 100 color film, 36 exposures	6.50
Admission to Musée Masséna	free
Movie ticket	7.40
Train ticket (one way) to Monte Carlo	2.60

SPECIAL DISCOUNT OPPORTUNITIES

FOR STUDENTS Students can save some money at some museums by showing the International Student Identity Card (ISIC). As for the buses, students are entitled to discount tickets (bought in books of 10), but first you must apply for a special student identity card, which costs 45F ($8.35), at the ticket kiosk in the Station Central bus station, 10, avenue Félix-Faure, or at Bus Masséna, Galerie Marchande du Parc Autos, place Masséna.

Nice has a major university and a rather large student population. For all sorts of information on inexpensive youth and student fares, tours, charter flights, and other special deals, head for **Usit Voyages,** rue Paganini at rue Belgique (tel. 93-87-34-96)—they are the Council Travel representatives in Nice—or the **Office du Tourisme Universitaire,** 18, avenue des Fleurs (tel. 93-96-85-43).

FOR EVERYONE Nice cannot boast of many special discount opportunities. However, you should know that buying tickets right on a city bus costs far more than buying them beforehand at a kiosk, newsstand, bookstore, or shop. One ticket on the bus costs 8F ($1.50), but if you buy a *carnet* (book) of five tickets at an authorized sales agent before boarding the bus, the price drops to 5.48F ($1). Another way to save money on transportation is to buy a *billet touristique,* or tourist ticket, which allows you to board any bus and travel as much as you like during one full day for 20F ($3.70). The *cartes touristiques* are bus passes good for several days of unlimited travel on the TN (Transports Urbains de Nice) network; the five-day pass costs 77F ($14.25) and the seven-day pass costs 107F ($19.80). For information on these cost-cutting deals, ask at the tourist office or any shop or newsstand that sells bus tickets; or drop in at the Centre d'Information TN, 10, avenue Félix-Faure (tel. 93-62-08-08), open Monday through Friday from 7:15am to 7pm and on Saturday from 8am to 6pm.

Another point for discount hunters to note is that some Côte d'Azur **museums** offer discounted (even half-price) tickets on Sunday.

✓

WHAT'S SPECIAL ABOUT NICE

Attractions
☐ Beaches along the promenade des Anglais and the quai des Etats-Unis, half of them public.
☐ Museums devoted to modern artists—Chagall, Matisse, Picasso—both in Nice and elsewhere along the Riviera.
☐ Le Château, a hill affording great vistas of the city and the coast.

Excursions
☐ Along the Côte d'Azur: Monaco, Antibes, Cannes, Beaulieu-sur-Mer.

Exploring
☐ Vieux Nice, with its narrow streets, colorful markets, and great bistros and restaurants.
☐ Cimiez, with its beautiful villas and Mediterranean vegetation.

WORTH THE EXTRA BUCKS

You should spend any slack in your budget on meals. For the price, you'll find no tastier food, more carefully prepared and professionally served, in France. And Nice, being cheaper than Paris, means that you'll be getting extra value for your money.

2. PRETRIP PREPARATIONS

DOCUMENTS   For tourism or business visits of less than three months, all you need is a valid passport.

WHAT TO PACK   Besides your bathing suit, you may want to have one semi-dressy, conservative outfit for an evening in snazzy Monte Carlo. This may mean yachting whites in summer, muted colors in winter.

Nice has a Mediterranean climate, which means it's cool in winter, hot in summer. Light cotton clothing is essential in the summer, with a light sweater or jacket for cool evening breezes. Hat, sunglasses, and sun screen are advised. In spring and fall, add another layer, plus a light raincoat. Rain is heaviest (and quite heavy at that) in October and November. In the winter you must be prepared for rain and for cool temperatures—it can get downright cold in Nice when the *mistral* (north wind) blows. Bring a warm jacket or sweater as well as a raincoat.

WHEN TO GO   The French Riviera built its fame on entertaining the wealthy and powerful who came from chilly climates during the winter. But today Nice is busy with visitors, both rich and not so rich, all year long.

In the summer Nice is crowded and hotel space can be very difficult to find. During July and August, when the French take their annual vacations, space is especially tight. The weather is hot and dry, the water warm and inviting.

Spring and fall are perhaps the best times to visit the Riviera. The air and water temperatures are perfect, hotels and restaurants are not booked solid, and everyone is more relaxed. But note that November is not recommended: It's the rainiest month, and many of the best art museums and other attractions are closed (some remain closed until mid-December, when the winter tourist season begins to pick up).

Winter is the surprise season here. In December, January, and February some restaurateurs take their *fermeture annuelle* (annual closing for a month's vacation), and some hotels do painting and fix-up work; but in general everything is open for business, cheaper than usual, uncrowded, and delightful. The weather may or may not cooperate—you may have rain and cool weather, or bright sun and warm air.

Nice's Average Daytime Temperature & Rainfall

	Jan	Feb	Mar	Apr	May	June	July	Aug	Sept	Oct	Nov	Dec
Temp. (°F)	46	47	51	56	62	68	73	73	69	61	53	47
Rainfall "	4.1	5.1	4.3	4.3	2.4	2.3	1.3	2.3	5.1	6.7	9.6	5.6

Special Events   Carnival is Nice's big event, beginning two or three weeks before Mardi Gras (Fat Tuesday), just before Ash Wednesday, the beginning of Lent.

Depending on the religious calendar, Nice's Carnival season can begin in January or in February; most of the action takes place during the weekends. Festive decorations fill the city: by day, parades—the *corsi* and the *batailles de fleurs* ("flower battles")—with marchers and floats passing by reviewing stands in place Masséna; by night, parties and masked balls continue till all hours. On Mardi Gras, the last day of Carnival, the city puts on a grand fireworks show over the Mediterranean.

BACKGROUND READING   The south of France has inspired writers from many countries. Fitzgerald's *Tender Is the Night* (Scribner's, 1934) and Hemingway's posthumous *The Garden of Eden* (Macmillan, 1987) are both partially set on the Riviera. Those who read French may enjoy Jules Romains's *La douceur de la vie*, a novel set in Nice in the 1920s.

3. ORIENTATION & GETTING AROUND

Downtown Nice is a fairly compact area. You should find almost everything there—hotels, restaurants, the train and bus stations, the beach—easy to reach on foot. City buses are useful for going to some outlying museums. Many of the most interesting sights are outside Nice, but they can easily be reached by train or bus.

ARRIVING IN NICE

FROM THE AIRPORT   Nice's airport, the **Aéroport Nice–Côte d'Azur,** ranks just after the airports of Paris in terms of activity. It is located at the western edge of town right on the coast only five miles from downtown. Public **bus no. 23** runs the route between the airport and the central train station. The bus will trundle you into the center on weekdays about every 20 minutes, on weekends about every 30 minutes, throughout the day from 6am to 10:30pm, charging 8F ($1.50) for the 30-minute trip.

There's also the **Nice Airport Shuttle** (*navette*), which runs between the central train station and the airport nine times a day. The 20-minute trip costs 25F ($4.60) and makes 20 stops on the way. There's a shuttle booth at the airport, and another in the train station's main hall; the shuttle office is at 35, corniche Fleurie (tel. 93-88-48-43).

A **taxi,** by contrast, will cost about 180F ($33.35) for the trip from the airport into town, depending on your final destination.

FROM THE TRAIN STATION   If you are traveling to Nice from Paris, you can save on accommodations by taking the overnight train. But you may prefer to experience France's state-of-the-art TGV, which will get you to Nice in just seven hours. There are three daily Paris–Nice TGVs from June through September, two from October through May; seat reservations are required and can be made at any travel agency in Paris or directly at a train station.

Nice has two train stations, of which the largest and most convenient is the **Gare Nice-Ville** or central train station (tel. 93-87-50-50), normally called the Gare SNCF (the Société Nationale des Chemins de Fer is France's national railway company). Nice's station has luggage lockers as well as showers, sinks, and toilets kept extremely clean by paid attendants. The city's helpful tourist office is right next to the station—out the doors and to the left—and there are numerous good hotels and restaurants nearby. There are several *bureaux de change* outside the station as well, where you can change money.

To go straight to the waterfront, take bus no. 12 from the west end of the station (out the doors and to the right), or bus no. 5 or 17 from in front of the station.

FROM THE BUS STATION If you arrive by bus, you'll pull into Nice's **Gare Routière** (tel. 93-80-08-70), between Vieux Nice and place Masséna.

ARRIVAL BY CAR Coming by car, you'll approach the city on Autoroute A8, "La Provençale," which skirts the city on its northern boundary. Follow signs for "Centre-ville" (downtown) and "place Masséna" to get downtown.

INFORMATION

The **Office de Tourisme** in Nice is located right outside the train station (tel. 93-87-07-07). It's open July to September, daily from 8:45am to 7pm; and October to June, Monday through Saturday from 8:45am to 12:30pm and 2 to 6pm.

CITY LAYOUT

Imagine downtown Nice as a triangle pointed north. At its apex, the northern point, is the **central train station.** Near the train station there are numerous hotels and restaurants as well as the tourist office. The base of the triangle lies along the waterfront. The eastern point is **Vieux Nice,** the old city, and **Le Château,** a hill on which a castle once stood; the western point is at **Pont Magnan** to the west of the deluxe Hôtel Negresco and the Musée Masséna.

Near the center of the triangle's base, closer to Vieux Nice than to Pont Magnan, is **place Masséna,** the city's main square, where you'll find several luxury hotels. Near place Masséna is a pedestrian zone that covers several blocks of rue Masséna, rue de France, rue Halévy, and rue Paradis; people come here to stroll, window-shop, and eat at the numerous restaurants.

Avenue Jean-Médecin is the main north-south street, beginning at place Masséna and heading north through the heart of the shopping district, then passing just to the east of the train station. Along the waterfront, the wide **promenade des Anglais** is the name of the shore road from the center of town westward; the **quai des Etats-Unis** is its name eastward through Vieux Nice to Le Château.

GETTING AROUND

As you've already read, Nice is a good town for walking, with the occasional bus ride thrown in. (For information on bus tickets, see "Special Discount Opportunities," above.) There is a route map posted at each major bus stop, and also a sign indicating the *point de vente le plus proche,* the nearest place where booklets of bus tickets are sold. Free maps of the bus network are handed out at the tourist offices, in hotels, and at the TN bus information office at 10, avenue Félix-Faure.

For your first sightseeing excursion in Nice, consider the **Trains Touristiques de Nice,** rubber-tired tourist "trolleys" that travel a ring route passing Nice's downtown attractions. See "Attractions," below.

BY TAXI Taxis are rather expensive; the average fare within the city limits is 80F ($14.80). If you're traveling in a group of three people, the price per person isn't so bad.

BY TRAIN Perhaps the best way to move along the Côte d'Azur is by train. Trains run about every hour or two, sometimes much more frequently, depending on the destination. Some of the stations connected by the rail line are (from west to east): St-Raphaël Valescure, Cannes, Juan-les-Pins, Antibes, Biot, Cagnes-sur-Mer, Nice-Ville, Beaulieu-sur-Mer, Eze-sur-Mer, Monaco–Monte Carlo, Menton, and Vintimille (Ventimiglia) on the Italian border.

You can buy tickets for these destinations from one of the machines in the station's main hall. Push the proper buttons to make the following choices: destination, first or second class, adult or child, one way (*aller simple*) or round-trip (*aller-retour*). The machine will display the fare—just insert the proper amount in coins and the ticket will be issued. Before going to your platform (*quai*), punch (*compostez*) your ticket in one of the orange pillarlike punchers—you'll see other people doing it.

BY CAR   Car rentals are quite expensive, and are accelerated by a 28% Value-Added Tax. Renting a small car for a day can easily top $65–$80 once the costs of mileage and fuel are included. Total cost for a week might be $500–$550. It's usually better to make arrangements and pay a deposit before leaving home. Be sure to ask about all the applicable charges, including the basic daily or weekly rental, charge per kilometer, collision-damage-waiver fee, refueling costs, and taxes. Then make a realistic estimate of the number of kilometers you will drive and the amount of fuel you will have to buy. Auto fuel costs $4 per American gallon in France.

In Nice, call **Hertz** toll free at 19/05-30-53-05. **Avis** has three offices: at the train station (tel. 93-87-90-11), at the airport (tel. 93-21-36-33), and downtown off place Masséna at 2, avenue Phocéens (tel. 93-80-63-52). **Europcar** (National, Tilden) has an office in each of the two terminals at the airport, in Aérogare 1 (tel. 93-21-36-44) and in Aérogare 2 (tel. 93-21-42-53); the downtown office is at 6, avenue de Suède (tel. 93-88-64-04), two short blocks west of place Masséna.

A Note on Parking   If you find a place to park in Nice, you will probably have to pay for the privilege. Along the promenade des Anglais there are American-style parking meters that take 1F (18¢) for every 15 minutes. In other parts of town, you may have to pay even though you see no parking meter. Is there a sign nearby with the word TICKETS and an arrow? Are there white lines on the road surface marked PAYANT? If the answer is yes, then you must pay. Find the nearby parking-ticket machine, insert 2F (35¢) for each 20 minutes' time you want, push the button to get your ticket, and then place the ticket on your dashboard where it will be visible from outside the car. When your time is up, either move the car or buy another ticket. By the way, fines for parking illegally are breathtakingly high in France.

Even parked legally, you may return to find your car trapped by the cars behind and ahead, which have been parked bumper-to-bumper with yours.

BY MOPED & BICYCLE   There's an alternative to the expensive rental car if you've got a good sense of balance and are a careful driver. You can rent a moped (motorbike) from the **Arnaud** agency, 4, place Grimaldi (tel. 93-87-88-55), at the corner of rue de la Liberté and rue Grimaldi, only 250 yards northwest of place Masséna. Rental rates are 150F ($27.75) per day for a moped, 90F ($16.65) per day for a regular bicycle. Unless you charge your rental to a credit card, you'll have to put down a hefty (but refundable) deposit of $200 per bike, $650 per moped. Arnaud is open Monday through Saturday from 9am to noon and 2 to 7pm. Unless you already have extensive motorbike- or motorcycle-riding experience, you should drive very carefully on a moped. It's much easier to have a serious accident on a moped than in a car.

 NICE

Babysitters   Call Allo Nursing Service (tel. 93-98-60-98) or the Association Niçoise de Services (tel. 93-98-60-98).

Banks   Banks are normally open Monday through Friday from 9am to noon and 1 or 1:30 to 4:30pm. Some banks are open on Saturday morning, and some currency-exchange booths have very long hours (see "Currency Exchange," below).

Business Hours   Most **museums, shops, and offices** open around 9am, close for lunch at noon, and reopen about 2pm, staying open until 7pm in summer, 5 or 6pm in winter. Most shops are open on Saturday, but closed Sunday and sometimes Monday as well. **Post offices** are normally open from 8am to 7pm Monday through Friday, and on Saturday from 8am to noon.

Currency   The French **franc (F)** is divided into 100 **centimes.** You will find coins of 5, 10, and 20 centimes, and ½, 1, 2, 5, and 10 francs. In a few cases there are two types of coins for one denomination and confusion can result. Look coins over carefully until you're used to them. Bills come in denominations of 20, 50, 100, 500, and 1,000 francs.

Currency Exchange   When changing money, ask if there is a fee or commission charged—a large one can wipe out the advantage of a good exchange rate. Banks and *bureaux de change* (exchange offices) usually offer better exchange rates than hotels, restaurants, and shops. At the intersection of rue de France and rue Halévy, in the center of town near the waterfront next to a pharmacy, is the **Change Bureau,** 2, rue de France, marked by a gigantic $100 bill over the door. It's open daily from 9am to 6 or 7pm. A block to the west on rue de France at rue Massenet is another exchange office. Check to see which offers you more francs for your dollar. As of this writing, neither one exacts a commission or fee for the transaction.

The office of **American Express** is located at 11, promenade des Anglais (tel. 93-87-29-82 for exchange, 93-87-67-99 for tours), at the corner of rue du Congrès and next to a building called the Palais de la Méditerranée. They are open May through September, Monday through Friday from 9am to 6pm and on Saturday from 9am to noon; October through April, Monday through Friday from 9am to noon and 2 to 6pm, and on Saturday from 9am to noon. American Express card holders can use the Express Cash machine on the rue du Congrès side of the building. For 24-hour traveler's check refunds, call toll free 19/05-90-86-00.

Doctors   Call S.O.S. Médecins (tel. 93-85-01-01), open 24 hours.

Emergencies   The emergency number for the police is 17; in other cases, call 93-13-20-00. To report a fire, dial 18. For medical emergencies, call 93-92-55-55. For a doctor, call S.O.S. Médecins (tel. 93-85-01-01), open 24 hours. Hôpital St-Roch, 5, rue Pierre-Dévoluy (tel. 93-13-33-00), has an emergency room open 24 hours. The pharmacy at 7, rue Masséna (tel. 93-87-78-94), is open daily from 7:30pm to 8:30am.

Holidays   France has lots of national holidays, most of them tied to the church calendar. On these days, shops, businesses, government offices, and most restaurants will be closed. They include New Year's Day (Jan 1), Easter Monday (late Mar or Apr); Labor Day (May 1); Ascension Thursday (in May or June, 40 days after Easter); Whit Monday, also called Pentecost Monday (51st day after Easter, in June or July); Bastille Day (July 14); Assumption Day (Aug 15); All Saints Day (Nov 1); Armistice Day (Nov 11); and Christmas Day (Dec 25).

In addition, schedules may be disrupted on Shrove Tuesday (the Tuesday before Ash Wednesday) and Good Friday. For information on Nice's big annual celebration of carnival, see "Special Events" in "Pretrip Preparations," above.

Information   See "Information" in "Orientation and Getting Around," above.

Laundry   Nice has many convenient laundries. Most are open seven days a week from 7am to 9pm. They charge around 17F ($3.15) to wash 5 kilos (11 lb.) of clothing, and 2F (35¢) for five minutes of drying for 15 kilos (15½ lb.) of wet clothes.

There's a laundry in the east wing of the Central Bus Station. Near the train station, look for the Lavishore, 8, rue Belgique, between rue Paganini and rue d'Angleterre. East of the train station, near the Hôtel Sybill's and Hôtel Pastoral, try Taxi-Lav, at the corner of rue Pertinax and rue Lamartine. In the center of the triangular downtown area there's the Laverie Automatique Mourton, 3, rue de Russie, between rue Offenbach and rue Déroulède. Behind Notre-Dame church at 16, rue d'Angleterre, at rue de Suisse, is Le Salon Lavoir. Another one in this area is the Laverie Automatique Swiss Launderette, 12, rue de Suisse, between rue d'Angleterre and rue Paganini. Opposite the Palais Lascaris in Vieux Nice is the Point Laverie, 14, rue Droite. Finally, there's Le Salon Lavoir, 14, avenue Borriglione, at rue Michel-Ange, north of the train station near the Hôtel Riviera and Hôtel Alp Azur.

Lost and Found   If you lose something, contact Objets Trouvés, 27, rue de Châteauneuf (tel. 93-96-60-59). For things left on buses, contact the Société des Transports Urbains de Nice, 24, rue de l'Hôtel des Postes (tel. 93-62-08-08).

Mail   Post offices are open Monday through Friday from 8am to 7pm and on

THE FRANC & THE DOLLAR

At this writing $1 = approximately 5.40F (or 1F = 18½¢), and this was the rate of exchange used to calculate the dollar values given in this chapter (rounded to the nearest nickel). This rate fluctuates from time to time and may not be the same when you travel to France. Therefore the following table should be used only as a guide:

F	U.S.$	F	U.S.$
1	.18	100	18.52
2	.37	125	23.15
3	.56	150	27.78
4	.74	175	32.41
5	.93	200	37.04
6	1.11	225	41.67
7	1.30	250	46.30
8	1.48	275	50.93
9	1.67	300	55.55
10	1.85	325	60.19
15	2.78	350	64.81
20	3.70	375	69.44
25	4.63	400	74.07
50	9.26	500	92.59

Saturday from 8am to noon. The city's main post office is at 23, avenue Thiers (tel. 93-88-55-41), across the street from the train station. Poste Restante is held at the post office on place Wilson (tel. 93-85-94-20), four blocks east of avenue Jean-Médecin along rue de l'Hôtel des Postes.

Newspapers *Nice-Matin* is the city's daily newspaper. *La Semaine des Spectacles* is a weekly paper with entertainment listings. English-language newspapers are available at many locations in Nice.

Tax France's **TVA** (Value-Added Tax) should already be included in the cost of items you buy, and prices quoted to you should be TTC (*Toutes Taxes Compris,* all taxes included). The rate of tax varies depending on the item or service being purchased.

For information on how to get a tax refund on large purchases, see the Paris chapter.

Taxis See "Getting Around" in "Orientation and Getting Around," above.

Telephone Avoid making phone calls from your hotel; many hotels charge at least 2F (35¢) for a local call. Refer to the Paris chapter for more detailed information.

Tipping Service is included at your hotel, but it is still customary to tip the bellhop about 6F ($1.10) per bag, more in expensive splurge hotels. You might use 5% of the daily room rate as a guideline. If you have lots of luggage, tip a bit more. In restaurants, though your *addition* (restaurant bill) or *fiche* (café check) will bear the words *"service compris"* (service charge included), it's customary to leave a tip. In a fancy restaurant, 10%–12% will do; in a cheap place, 8%–10% is fine; in a café, a few perhaps totaling mout less than 10%, is good. Remember, service has supposedly already been paid for. Taxis expect 10% of the fare as a tip. At the theater and cinema, tip 2F (35¢) to the usher who shows you to your seat. In public toilets, there is often a posted fee for using the facilities. If not, the maintenance person will expect a tip of about 2F (35¢). Put it in the basket or on the plate at the entrance. Porters and cloakroom attendants are usually governed b set prices, which are displayed. If not, give a porter 6–8F ($1.10–$1.50) per suitcase, and a cloakroom attendant 2–4F (35¢–75¢) per coat.

4. BUDGET ACCOMMODATIONS

Hotels in Nice are scattered throughout town. Distance from the waterfront lowers the price somewhat. Like elsewhere in Europe, each hotel room is different. In the same little hotel you might find rooms that you think are wonderful and rooms that you can't bear to stay in. Ask to see the room before checking in, and if you don't like it, ask to see another.

In the 19th century Nice developed as a fashionable winter resort, but since the end of the war most of its visitors have come in the summer months. Prices given here are for the high summer season; in those months you may also be required to eat breakfast at your hotel. Outside the high season, many hotels sometimes lower their prices, so always inquire about possible discounts.

In June, July, August, and early September, your problem might be finding a room at all. Many of the city's cheaper rooms are booked up by French vacationers. If you have not reserved a room, plan to arrive early in the day to look for one. If you can't find exactly the one you want, take a room that will do for one night, and then spend a little time reserving another for the rest of your stay.

The city tourist office at the train station will help you find a room for a fee. In summer, this service is likely to be in demand, and there may be quite a line of people waiting, so get in line early. The tourism agents won't start calling until 10am, because that's when most hotels know whether or not they'll have vacant rooms. When they find you a room, you'll pay a fee at the tourism office of 10F ($1.85) for a room in a one-star hotel, 20F ($3.70) for a two-star, 35F ($6.50) for a three-star, and 40F ($7.40) for a four-star. However, when you check in at the hotel, you'll be entitled to a discount on your first night's stay: one star, no discount; two star, 10F ($1.85) discount; three star, 15F ($2.75) discount; four star, 20F ($3.70) discount. Thus the actual fee you pay for the room-finding service is only 10F ($1.85) for one- and two-star hotels, or 20F ($3.70) for three- and four-star ones. In the summer, you'll probably need this service.

DOUBLES FOR LESS THAN 240F ($44.45)

Hotels offering double rooms for less than 240F ($44.45) tend to rate one star in the official ranking. You will find a wide range of rooms in this category, from those with *eau courante* (running water, meaning a sink) to those with a private shower or bath, TV, maybe even a kitchenette. A room with shower or bath does not necessarily have a toilet as well. There are rooms with toilet and shower, rooms with toilet only, and rooms with shower only. Make sure that you know exactly what you want and need—prices often vary greatly according to how much plumbing the room contains.

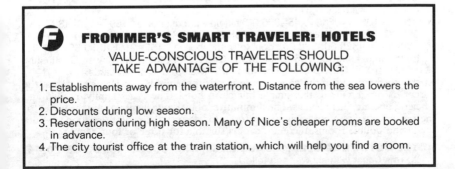

Ⓕ FROMMER'S SMART TRAVELER: HOTELS

VALUE-CONSCIOUS TRAVELERS SHOULD
TAKE ADVANTAGE OF THE FOLLOWING:

1. Establishments away from the waterfront. Distance from the sea lowers the price.
2. Discounts during low season.
3. Reservations during high season. Many of Nice's cheaper rooms are booked in advance.
4. The city tourist office at the train station, which will help you find a room.

SOUTH OF THE TRAIN STATION

The district south of the train station and avenue Thiers is fairly quiet. Hotels cluster on nearly every street and the sea is only a 15-minute walk away. To get here, simply walk out the station door, turn left, and take the *passage souterrain* (underground walkway); you will emerge at avenue Durante and rue de Belgique.

HOTEL CLAIR MEUBLE, 6, rue d'Italie, Nice 06000. Tel. 93-87-87-61. 15 rms.

$ **Rates:** 120F ($22.20) single; 180F ($33.35) double; 240F ($44.45) triple; 300F ($55.55) quad. No credit cards.

On two floors in a modern apartment building, equipped with a shower and kitchenette, the hotel is centrally located, three blocks from the train station, 100 yards off avenue Jean-Médecin. The reception is one floor up, and the owners are very helpful.

HOTEL DARCY, 28, rue d'Angleterre, 06000 Nice. Tel. 93-88-67-06. 28 rms (some with shower).

$ **Rates** (including continental breakfast): 140F ($25.90) single without shower, 200F ($37.05) single with shower; 200F ($37.05) double without shower, 270F ($50) double with shower; 290F ($53.70) triple without shower. 340F ($62.95) triple with shower. Showers 10F ($1.85) extra.

The Darcy is a favorite of low-budget travelers carrying this book. It's close to the train station, on a fairly quiet street, and though a number may be missing here and there from a room door, the hotel is very clean and its owners, M. Alain and Mme Marie Hassoun, have welcomed many readers of this book over the years. Every morning at 8 you can watch an English-language news broadcast in the TV lounge. Lower rates might be offered in the low season.

HOTEL LES ORANGERS, 10 bis, av. Durante, 06000 Nice. Tel. 93-87-51-41. 12 rms (some with shower). TEL

$ **Rates:** 80–130F ($14.80–$24.05) single without shower; 160F ($29.60) double without shower, 200F ($37.05) double with shower; 300F ($55.55) triple with shower; 350F ($64.80) quad with shower; 80F ($14.80) per person in dormitory rooms. Continental breakfast 15F ($2.75) extra; showers, 10F ($1.85). V.

Over the years, Jocelyne and Marc Servole, the charming English-speaking couple who own and operate the Hôtel Les Orangers, have played host to scores of readers. Their little hotel is in an old town house just half a block south of avenue Thiers. Each of the dozen rooms here is equipped with a hotplate, pots, pans, and cutlery, and there's a grocery store 1½ blocks away on rue d'Italie so you can make your own breakfasts, snacks, and light suppers to save money. Their prices are unbeatable. The Orangers is small and in demand—reserve ahead if you can.

HOTEL LYONNAIS, 20, rue de Russie, 06000 Nice. Tel. 93-88-70-74. 31 rms (some with shower). TEL

$ **Rates:** 105–140F ($19.45–$25.90) single without shower, 150F–190F ($27.75–$35.20) single with shower; 120–160F ($22.20–$29.60) double without shower, 160–210F ($29.60–$38.90) double with shower; 165–210F ($30.55–$38.90) triple without shower, 195–260F ($36.10–$48.15) triple with shower. Continental breakfast 20F ($3.70) extra; showers, 16F ($2.95). No credit cards.

At the northern end of the quiet rue de Russie, near the Notre-Dame church at the corner of rue d'Italie, is this simple but clean hotel. The Pages family, cordial and efficient, operate the Lyonnais. The diminutive lobby is one flight up, and the prices for the tidy rooms are gratifyingly down to earth, despite the central location. Besides single and double rooms, there are rooms suitable for three or four people.

HOTEL NOTRE DAME, 22, rue de Russie, Nice 06000. Tel. 93-88-70-44. 20 rms (most with shower and toilet).

$ Rates: 140F ($25.90) single; 160F ($29.60) double; 250F ($46.30) triple; 300F ($55.55) quad. Continental breakfast 20F ($3.70) extra. No credit cards.
If your group has four people, try to book Room 3, which has doubledeckers. The hotel is on four floors and has an elevator. It's three blocks from the train station, near avenue Jean-Médecin.

HOTEL NOVELTY, 26, rue d'Angleterre, 06000 Nice. Tel. 93-87-51-73.
35 rms (some with shower).
$ Rates: 120F ($22.20) single without shower, 200F ($37.05) single with shower; 150F ($27.75) double without shower, 250F ($46.30) double with shower; 80F ($14.80) per person in a five- to eight-bed dorm. Breakfast 30F ($5.55) extra; showers, 110F ($1.85), free in dorm room. AE, MC, V.

★ The Novelty promises to become one of Nice's best budget hotels. Owner M. Richter, who speaks French, German, and English, is presently renovating and expanding it. Rooms will have all kinds of creature comforts—TV, radio, telephone—and will be rented at very reasonable prices. The building doesn't have an elevator yet, but M. Richter has fashioned other outstanding hotels in Nice, and his vision and commitment to budget travel will no doubt turn the Novelty into a top-notch establishment. And to make it even better, after high season he is willing to offer lower rates.

NORTH OF THE TRAIN STATION

The area north of the train station is somewhat farther from the sea and the center of town, and you'll find yourself taking short bus rides or walking to your hotel. The advantages here are quiet streets and, on Saturday morning, an open-air market along avenue Malausséna and avenue Borriglione, the northern continuation of avenue Jean-Médecin just a block north of avenue Thiers.

HOTEL ALP'AZUR, 15, rue Michel-Ange, 06100 Nice. Tel. 93-84-57-61.
16 rms (some with shower). TEL **Bus:** 24 from the south side of avenue Thiers, across the street from the train station, to rue Michel-Ange.
$ Rates: 150F ($27.75) single or double without shower, 180–240F ($33.35–$44.45) single or double with shower. Continental breakfast 20F ($3.70) extra; use of the kitchenettes, 25F ($4.60). No credit cards.
This little five-story hotel is half a block east of avenue Borriglione on the right-hand side of rue Michel-Ange, and it's a quiet, tidy, and pleasant spot. The hotel has a sunny lounge and breakfast room with southern exposure, and a helpful, English-speaking proprietor, M. Zerbib. A small library with books in several languages is at your disposal. All rooms have direct-dial telephones, and some have TV sets. Prices are surprisingly good, and the rooms here, particularly those with kitchenettes, are in high demand. Reserve in advance.

HOTEL ANN MARGARET, 1, av. St-Joseph, 06100 Nice. Tel. 93-96-15-70. 42 rms (some with shower). TEL **Bus:** 5 from the front of the train station to Vernier.
$ Rates: 100F ($18.50) single without shower; 160F ($29.60) double without shower, 260F ($48.15) double with shower; 330F ($61.10) triple with shower. Continental breakfast 30F ($5.55) extra; showers, 15F ($2.75). AE, DC, EURO, MC, V.
Besides its quiet location, good prices, and friendly English-speaking management, the Ann Margaret has a small swimming pool in the garden. It is advertised on the hotel map in Nice's train station with a note saying: "Call us and we'll come pick you up!" Even though the hotel is not far from the station, you must take a roundabout route because of the pattern of roads and rail. For the record, here are walking directions: Leave the station, turn right, walk to boulevard Gambetta, and turn right again; take the sixth little street on the left, which is avenue St-Joseph.

EAST OF AVENUE JEAN-MEDECIN

Directly across avenue Jean-Médecin from Notre-Dame church is a quiet residential area with several excellent budget hotels. The area is a short walk from the train station, and buses along avenue Jean-Médecin make access to the waterfront easy.

HOTEL DU PETIT LOUVRE, 10, rue Emma-Tiranty, 06000 Nice. Tel. 93-80-15-54. 34 rms (all with shower). TEL **Directions:** See below.

$ Rates: 160F ($29.60) single; 200F ($37.05) double. Continental breakfast 24F ($4.45) extra. No credit cards. **Closed:** Nov–Jan.

M. and Mme Vila (she speaks English) run this neat and attractive place, and will welcome you enthusiastically. Though the location is superb and the facilities are a cut above the budget range, the prices are delightfully reasonable.

To find the hotel, go to Notre-Dame church on avenue Jean-Médecin and look for rue Tiranty on the east side of the street just a bit to the south. The hotel is a block along rue Tiranty, near the corner of rue Lamartine.

HOTEL PASTORAL, 27, rue Assalit, 06000 Nice. Tel. 93-85-17-22. 10 rms (some with shower). TEL

$ Rates: 95F ($17.60) single without shower; 100–110F ($18.50–$20.35) double without shower, 140–160F ($25.90–$29.60) double with shower. Continental breakfast 18F ($3.35) extra; showers, 10F ($1.85). Use of kitchenette 16F ($2.95) per person per day. No credit cards.

The Pastoral isn't exactly in the country, but with a stretch of the imagination you can make this apartment-house ground-floor establishment seem countrified. Some rooms open onto a little walled terrace with a few potted plants, and most rooms are bright and cheery. The Pastoral also offers rooms with equipped kitchenettes. The location is good, on rue Assalit at St-Siagre, just a block east of the intersection of avenue Jean-Médecin and avenue Thiers.

NEAR THE SEA

If you simply *must* be near the Mediterranean, don't despair. Several hotels located mere steps from the water rent attractive rooms at affordable prices. In summer, though, these rooms become even more enticing, so try to reserve early. A good place to look is the pedestrian mall formed by rue de France and rue Masséna between rue du Congrès and avenue Jean-Médecin.

HOTEL MEUBLE CELIMENE, 63, rue de France, 06000 Nice. Tel. 93-88-61-51. 9 studios (all with shower). **Bus:** 12 from the train station to Rivoli.

$ Rates: 190–200F ($35.20–$37.05) single or double studio. Studios for three people are also available. No credit cards.

⭐ Many of Nice's hotels feature kitchenettes in the rooms, making the accommodations what we would call "efficiency apartments"; a *hôtel meublé* is precisely that. The Célimène is a wonderful hôtel meublé, with a quiet location next to the Musée Masséna and with cheery second-floor rooms. Not only is it charming— it's cheap. The Célimène is usually booked up by guests staying a week or longer; indeed, the office is open for only two hours a day, from 10:30am to 12:30pm. If you can plan your stay well in advance, try for a place at the Célimène.

HOTEL REX, 3, rue Masséna, 06000 Nice. Tel. 93-87-87-38. 9 rms (some with shower, some with shower and kitchenette). TEL **Bus:** 5 or 12 from the train station to place Masséna.

$ Rates: 170F ($31.50) single without shower; 230–250F ($42.60–$46.30) single or double with shower; 300–325F ($55.55–$60.20) triple with shower. For stays of one week or more: 215F ($39.80) single with shower, toilet, and kitchenette; 240–280F ($44.45–$51.85) studio for two people, 335–350F ($52–$64.80) studio for three. Continental breakfast 23F ($42.60) extra; showers, 12F ($2.20). No credit cards.

 Located far from the street in an interior courtyard, the one-star Hôtel Rex is marvelously quiet yet convenient to the beach and the nightlife of the waterfront. M. and Mme Lhomer will welcome you in French, English, or Italian, and show you to a clean, comfortable room. If you plan to stay at least a week in Nice, the Lhomers can rent you a room with a kitchenette or a studio, complete with pots and pans and spotless glasses. The Rex is truly an exceptional place.

DOUBLES FOR LESS THAN 370F ($68.50)

If you spend slightly more on your room in Nice, you get a lot of advantages, including more comfort, private facilities, and, in a few cases, near-waterfront locations. Most of these hotels get two stars in the official ratings.

SOUTH OF THE TRAIN STATION

HOTEL DURANTE, 16, av. Durante, 06000 Nice. Tel. 93-88-84-40. 26 rms (all with kitchenette and bath or shower). TV TEL **Directions:** See below.
$ Rates: 330F ($61.10) single or double with shower and kitchenette; 380F ($70.35) single or double with bath and kitchenette. Continental breakfast 40F ($7.40) extra. No credit cards.

 The two-star Hôtel Durante is a beautiful, tastefully decorated place, with a superb location on a quiet little dead-end street. Everything here has a touch of elegance. The cheery rooms have French windows that open onto a verdant courtyard with flowers. They have fully equipped modern kitchenettes complete with refrigerator, two-burner hotplate, dishes, and utensils. Management is cordial and distinguished, and in the fall and winter—except for Christmas and Carnival—will offer a one-night discount to guests staying for a week.

To find the Durante, first find the easily visible Hôtel Excelsior on avenue Durante. Opposite is a dead-end street, with the Hôtel La Résidence at the far end. The Hôtel Durante is to the right of La Résidence.

HOTEL NORMANDIE, 18, rue Paganini, 06000 Nice. Tel. 93-88-48-83. 44 rms (all with shower). TEL
$ Rates: 230F ($42.60) single; 300F ($55.55) double; 350F ($64.80) triple; 400F ($74.05) quad. Breakfast 24F ($4.45) extra. AE, MC, V.

Rooms are extremely comfortable and cheerfully decorated in red, white, and blue, and all contain very modern bathrooms. The cordial young proprietors offer lower rates in the off-season. The Normandie is at the corner of rue d'Alsace-Lorraine, two blocks from the train station and a block east of avenue Durante.

HOTEL PARIS-NICE, 58, rue de France, 06000 Nice. Tel. 93-88-38-61. 28 rms (some with shower and toilet). TEL **Bus:** 12 from the train station to Gambetta-France.
$ Rates: 125F ($23.15) single without shower or toilet, 220F ($40.75) single with shower and toilet; 260F ($48.15) double with shower and toilet; 350F ($64.80) triple with shower and toilet. Continental breakfast (with a fruit juice) 30F ($5.55) extra. AE, MC, V.

The Hôtel Paris-Nice is an outstanding budget establishment. Recently renovated, the hotel features handsome rooms with pleasing colors and modern bathrooms. Twenty rooms have TV sets. Mme Martine Voge, the English-speaking manager, will help you make the most of your visit to Nice. The hotel is wonderfully located, just behind the Hôtel Negresco and a block away from the waterfront.

NORTH OF THE TRAIN STATION

HOTEL RIVIERA, place da la Gare du Sud, 06000 Nice. Tel. 93-84-98-58. 32 rms (all with shower). TEL **Directions:** See below.
$ Rates: 280–320F ($51.85–$59.25) double. Continental breakfast 30F ($5.55) extra. AE, EURO, MC, V.

The two-star Riviera must have been a rather glamorous place when lots of trains still arrived and departed at the neighboring Gare du Sud de Provence. Most of the activity at the station died with the Age of Steam, and along with it probably the Riviera's natural clientele. But the hotel preserves a certain elegance in its creamy marble staircase, potted palms, and mirrors. The guest rooms have been renovated, and the bathrooms are new and very attractive. The Riviera is a good choice in high summer when hotels closer to the waterfront may be booked solid.

To find the hotel, walk three blocks from avenue Thiers along avenue Malausséna (the continuation of avenue Jean-Médecin) to place Charles-de-Gaulle. You'll spot the Gare du Sud on your left, and on its right, a block in, the hotel.

NEAR AVENUE JEAN-MEDECIN

HOTEL ANTARES, 5, av. Thiers, 06000 Nice. Tel. 93-88-22-87. 40 rms (all with shower and toilet). TEL
$ Rates: 200F ($37.05) single; 300F ($55.55) double; 400F ($74.05) triple. Continental breakfast 22F ($4.05) extra. AE, EURO, MC, V.

In a modern building, this hotel is ideally located 50 yards from avenue Jean-Médecin and 100 yards from the central train station.

SIBILL'S HOTEL, 25, rue Assalit, 06000 Nice. Tel. 93-62-03-07. 56 rms (all with bath or shower). TV TEL
$ Rates (including continental breakfast): 300F ($55.55) single; 360F ($66.65) double; 440F ($81.50) triple. EURO, MC, V.

This quiet hotel rises at the corner of Assalit and St-Siagre, just one short block east of avenue Jean-Médecin, a substantial limestone edifice of obvious comfort and style. At Sibill's, which rates two official stars, you stay in accommodations that border on three stars, yet the prices are surprisingly and refreshingly moderate. The train station is a five-minute walk away, as is the busy shopping district on avenue Jean-Médecin.

NEAR THE SEA

HOTEL ALIZE, 65, rue de la Buffa, Nice 06000. Tel. 93-88-99-46. 11 rms (all with shower and toilet). A/C TEL
$ Rates: 150F ($27.75) single; 330F ($61.10) double; 400F ($74.05) triple; 440F ($81.50) quad. Breakfast 30F ($5.55) extra.

This charming little hotel, located 50 yards from the Hôtel Negresco and 100 yards from the beach, is tastefully furnished and has a very friendly owner. Breakfast is served in your room.

HOTEL CANADA, 8, rue Halévy, 06000 Nice. Tel. 93-87-98-94. 18 rms (all with shower and toilet, some also with kitchenette). TV TEL **Bus:** 12 from the train station to Grimaldi.
$ Rates: 220–350F ($40.75–$64.80) single or double without kitchenette, 260–350F ($48.15–$64.80) with kitchenette. Continental breakfast 25F ($4.60) extra. AE, MC, V.

 In the midst of Nice's pedestrian zone is the shiny doorway to the Hôtel Canada, and up a flight of creamy marble stairs between mirrored walls is the bright, modern lobby. The rooms all have tiny tiled bathrooms and TV sets, and each one has its own particular touch: a special piece of artwork here, a brass headboard there. They are very nice, and very much in demand in summer, so reserve ahead. The friendly management has offered a 10% discount to holders of this book.

HOTEL HARVEY, 18, av. de Suède, 06000 Nice. Tel. 93-88-73-73. 64 rms (all with bath). A/C TV TEL **Bus:** 12 from the train station to Jardin Albert 1er.
$ Rates: 263F ($48.70) single; 356F ($65.92) double or twin; 422F ($78.15) triple; 562F ($104.05) quad. Continental breakfast 28F ($5.20) extra.
The Hotel Harvey is centrally located, just off the promenade des Anglais. All rooms in this recently renovated hotel have been modernized with basic conveniences.

HOTEL LE MEURICE, 14, av. de Suède, 06000 Nice. Tel. 93-87-74-93. TV TEL **Bus:** 12 from the train station to Jardin Albert 1er.
$ Rates: 290F ($53.70) single; 350F ($64.80) double; 420F ($77.75) triple. Continental breakfast 30F ($5.55) extra. EURO, MC, V.
As you enter the very fancy lobby of Le Meurice, you will probably be greeted by M. or Mme Leal, the owners. They will happily show you to one of their well-kept guest rooms carved from the grand spaces of this 19th-century building. Bits of cornice along the top of the wall or a huge old wardrobe will bring you a whiff of Nice a century ago. Every room has a modern tiled bath, as well as color TV and direct-dial phone. The promenade des Anglais is only half a block away.

HOTEL SOLARA, 7, rue de France, 06000 Nice. Tel. 93-88-09-96. 14 rms. TV TEL **Bus:** 5 from the train station to place Masséna, or 12 from the train station to Grimaldi.
$ Rates: 250F ($46.30) single with shower; 350F ($64.80) double with shower; 390F ($72.20) triple with shower. Continental breakfast 30F ($5.55) extra. AE, EURO, MC, V.
The Solara is aptly named. This marvelous hotel occupies the top floors of a coolly quiet building—ring the bell and take the elevator up. Rooms are modern and luminous, with beige walls, handsome lamps, TV sets, and minibars. Some rooms have balconies and sunny Mediterranean views, even if you can't actually see the water. Rooms on the fifth floor are the nicest.

PONT MAGNAN

A 20-minute stroll from place Masséna west along the promenade des Anglais brings you to Pont Magnan, an upscale residential district with white and pastel apartment blocks facing the Mediterranean. It's not near the center of town, but bus transportation is fast and frequent. Take bus no. 24 from the train station, bus no. 3, 10, 12, or 22 from downtown, or bus no. 8 or 11 along the promenade des Anglais and get off at Magnan.

HOTEL EDEN, 99 bis, promenade des Anglais, 06200 Nice. Tel. 93-86-53-70. 10 rms (some with shower). TEL **Bus:** 24 from the train station to Magnan.
$ Rates: 170F ($31.50) single without shower, 290F ($53.70) single with shower; 310F ($57.40) double without shower, 330F ($61.10) double with shower. Continental breakfast 25F ($4.60) extra. No credit cards.
Believe it or not, its possible to stay in a beautiful villa on the promenade des Anglais, directly across from the beach, and still be within our budget. M. and Mme Prone, who speak English and Italian as well as French, provide homey quarters in high-ceilinged rooms with some period furnishings, plus a sunny little terrace out front and even, from a few points in the villa, a small slice of Mediterranean view. If you reserve in advance, you might even be able to stay here in the high summer season. The villa is near square Général-Ferrié, about eight streets west of the grand Hôtel Negresco.

HOTEL MAGNAN, square Général-Ferrié, 06200 Nice. Tel. 93-86-76-00.
25 rms (all with shower). TV TEL **Bus:** 24 from the train station to Magnan.
$ Rates: 250–380F ($46.30–$70.35) single or double. Continental breakfast 28F ($5.20) extra. EURO, MC, V.
This large two-star hotel is popular, and it's easy to see why. All rooms have balconies and color TV, and some have a minibar. The rooms facing the square have partial sea views, a rare luxury at these prices. The location is very good, only a few steps away from the waterfront and a short bus ride away from the center of town. The hotel is usually full every day in the high summer season, so be sure to reserve in advance.

SUPER-BUDGET CHOICES

AUBERGE DE JEUNESSE, route Forestière, Mont Boron, 06000 Nice. Tel. 93-89-23-64. 56 beds. **Directions:** See below.
$ Rates: 60F ($11.10) per person for members, 80F ($14.80) for nonmembers. Sheets 16F ($2.95) extra for one to seven nights.
Nice's official youth hostel, where you will need your hostel card, is a few miles east of place Masséna on the wooded slopes of Mont Boron. It's a good idea to phone for information before you head out there. Before 10am and after 5pm you can talk to an actual person; between 10am and 5pm the hostel is closed and you'll get a taped message. There's an 11pm curfew (12:30am in summer). Accommodations are in eight dorm rooms.
To get to the hostel, take bus no. 14 (marked "place du Mont Boron") from the Congrès or Gustave V stop on the promenade des Anglais to the L'Auberge stop. (If by mistake you get the no. 14 marked "Castel," get off at route Forestière and walk the short distance to the hostel.) Note that the bus runs only from about 7am to 7:30pm, about every half hour.

RELAIS INTERNATIONAL DE LA JEUNESSE "CLAIRVALLON," 26, av. Scuderi, Cimiez, 06100 Nice. Tel. 93-81-27-63. 150 beds. **Bus:** 15 or 22 from place Masséna or the train station to Scuderi.
$ Rates: 60F ($11.10) per bed. Half board (demi-pension) 120F ($22.20) extra; full board (pension complète), 150F ($27.75).
This private hostel operated by young people is located in the northern reaches of Cimiez, one of Nice's finest residential districts. Surrounded by aristocratic villas, the hostel, with its swimming pool, tennis courts, and pretty grounds, was itself once a villa. You don't have to have a hostel card, or be a certain age, to stay here. Registration is after 5pm, and curfew is 11:30pm. Accommodation is in four- to eight-bed rooms with free showers.
It's located about three miles north of place Masséna, but the bus runs every 10 minutes on weekdays, every 15 or 20 minutes on weekends. When you get off the bus, turn left onto the winding avenue Scuderi, walk about 500 yards past imposing villas and palm trees, and you'll see the relais on the right, near some big cypress trees.

LONG-TERM STAYS

Many of Nice's hotels offer special rates for stays of a week, a month, even a year. This is particularly true of the hôtels meublés, where you can get a room with a kitchenette. Even if no special rates are officially advertised, they can frequently be negotiated.

WORTH THE EXTRA BUCKS

NOUVEL HOTEL, 19 bis, bd. Victor-Hugo, 06000 Nice. Tel. 93-87-15-00.
60 rms (all with shower). TV TEL
$ Rates (including continental breakfast): 400F ($74.05) single; 550F ($101.85) double; 650F ($120.35) triple. AE, DC, EURO, MC, V.

⭐ The ornate facade of the Nouvel Hôtel stands behind a small garden on leafy boulevard Victor-Hugo, one of the most beautiful in Nice. This is a fine residential and commercial neighborhood about midway from the train station to the sea. The rooms are bright and modern, and many have great views of the neighboring Eglise Réformée, a handsome church. Breakfast is served in a rather elegant dining room. A very professional staff will welcome you here.

5. BUDGET DINING

Authentic French cuisine is cheaper in Nice than in Paris, and good restaurants abound. If you want a break from the restaurant routine, there are several good cafeterias as well as the ever-popular cafés serving light meals. Snack stands on the streets sell crêpes, pizza, and Nice's own hearty pan bagnat.

In high summer, you may be required to eat breakfast at your hotel. If not, the traditional spot for breakfast is a café. Remember, if you sit down and have waiter service for your café au lait and croissants, the price will be about 30% higher than if you stand at the counter.

For lunch or dinner you can have a snack or sandwich, or a full *menu du jour* of three to five courses. Ordering the *menu* (the fixed-price meal) is economical, and often the tastiest choice to make. Compare prices for a *menu du jour* among restaurants, count the number of courses, and look for the words *"vin compris"* or *"vin non compris"* on the menu. Some places include a quarter liter of house wine in the price; others charge extra for it. An alternative to a multicourse meal is a *plat du jour*, a main-course platter garnished with vegetables and little extras that easily constitutes a filling meal. It's usually a good deal cheaper than a full *menu du jour*.

Virtually all restaurants post a menu outside the front door giving prices and dishes in detail. Note these other particularities about Nice restaurants: The *menu du jour* may be served either at lunch or at supper. The standard measure of wine is a quarter-liter (*un quart*) carafe—two good glassfuls—of the house variety. You get your choice, red or white. Service charge and tax are included in prices. Leave a tip according to the "Tipping" guidelines given in "Fast Facts," above.

A particular restaurant may choose any day (or part of a day) to close, so be sure to check the hours of operation before heading out to eat.

LOCAL BUDGET BESTS

Seafood is a specialty in Nice, and you should enjoy *bouillabaisse,* the hearty seafood stew, if you see it. Also recommended is the local *soupe au poisson* (fish soup), a deep-red and savory liquid made from fish, tomatoes, and garlic, and served with cheese, croutons, and aioli (Provençal garlic, mayonnaise).

Have a *salade niçoise* at least once, and you may find yourself addicted to this delicious concoction of lettuce, boiled potatoes, green beans, tomatoes, olives, capers, and anchovies.

For snacks, the famous *pan bagnat* consists of *salade niçoise* in a round loaf of bread, filling and delicious. Because of Nice's closeness to Italy, pizza is also a traditional specialty here.

MEALS FOR LESS THAN 70F [$12.95]

SOUTH OF THE TRAIN STATION

RESTAURANT AU SOLEIL, 7 bis, rue d'Italie. Tel. 93-88-77-74.
   Cuisine: FRENCH.

$ Prices: 50–60F ($9.25–$11.10). No credit cards.
Open: Daily 9am–11pm. **Closed:** Nov–Jan.

⭐ Big display windows let lots of light into this large eatery named after the sun. Owner Roger Germain has been serving readers of this guide for years with obvious pleasure. For a very reasonable price you might have a salade niçoise to start, followed by roast turkey with vegetable and french fries, ending with the day's freshly prepared fruit tart. A filling breakfast is also available for 30F ($5.55). And the location, at the corner with rue d'Italie, almost facing the Notre-Dame church, is very convenient. Show a copy of this book for a discount.

RESTAURANT DAVIA, 11 bis, rue Grimaldi. Tel. 93-87-91-39.
Cuisine: FRENCH/ITALIAN.
$ Prices: 50–70F ($9.25–$12.95). No credit cards.
Open: Lunch Thurs–Tues noon–2:30pm; dinner Thurs–Tues 7–11pm.
Davia, owned and run by an Italian woman who does much of the cooking, is a homey place with an eclectic decoration: prints, candle lamp sconces, a huge old Coldspot refrigerator. A radio is tuned to a local station. Near the kitchen, a table groans beneath the weight of a dozen delicious tarts and other baked delicacies. Their two four-course *menus du jour* may include a good salade niçoise, aioli provençale (fish filet garnished with vegetables, garlic mayonnaise on the side), and a slice of apple tart. The Davia is next to the Hôtel King George south of boulevard Victor-Hugo.

RESTAURANT DE PARIS, 28, rue d'Angleterre. Tel. 93-88-64-29.
Cuisine: FRENCH.
$ Prices: 35–65F ($6.50–$12.05). AE, MC, V.
Open: Lunch Mon–Sat 11:30am–3pm; dinner Mon–Sat 6:30–10:30pm.

⭐ M. Jacques Briey, the owner of the Restaurant de Paris, used to be a butcher, which explains the superior quality of the meat served here. The three *menus du jour* offer lots of choices for each course, and the prices are great—38–60F ($7.05–$11.10). Or else you can order a *plat du jour,* such as beef bourguignon, for only 38F ($7.05). The restaurant itself is charming, with French country decor, checkered tablecloths, and sidewalk tables. Look for the Restaurant de Paris at the northern end of rue d'Angleterre, just south of avenue Thiers, quite near the train station.

RESTAURANT LE SAETONE, 8, rue d'Alsace Lorraine. Tel. 93-87-17-95.
Cuisine: FRENCH.
$ Prices: 60–75F ($11.10–$13.90). AE, MC, V.
Open: Lunch Thurs–Tues 11:45am–2pm; dinner Thurs–Tues 6–10pm.
Le Saetone pleases with its homey decor and good food at unbeatable prices. They offer several three-course *menus du jour* and one four-course *menu,* for the prices indicated above. Its convenient location—only a few minutes' walk from the train station between rue Paganini and rue d'Angleterre—also helps draw the crowds. The tables often fill at mealtimes, so get here early.

ON AVENUE JEAN-MEDECIN

CAFETERIA NICE-ETOILE, 30, av. Jean-Médecin. Tel. 93-80-21-57.
Cuisine: FRENCH.
$ Prices: 25–65F ($4.65–$12.05). No credit cards.
Open: Lunch Mon–Sat 11:30am–2:30pm; "tea" Mon–Sat 2:30–6:30pm; dinner Mon–Sat 6:30–8:30pm.

⭐ Cafeterias in Nice are often lavish affairs with many French delicacies offered along with standard fare. Among the best is this pleasant cafeteria located on the third floor of the modern Nice-Etoile shopping complex near the carousel, on avenue Jean-Médecin. Displays are attractive, as are the surroundings. Besides such

FROMMER'S SMART TRAVELER: RESTAURANTS

VALUE-CONSCIOUS TRAVELERS SHOULD
TAKE ADVANTAGE OF THE FOLLOWING:

1. Cafeterias, cafés, and snack stands on the street.
2. Standing up at the counter rather than sitting at a table.
3. The *menu du jour* (the fixed-price meal), the most economical and tastiest choice.
4. The *plat du jour*, cheaper and less filling than the *menu*.

staples as steak haché (chopped sirloin), you'll find smoked salmon for 38F ($7.05) and lobster for 55F ($10.20).

McDONALD'S, 20, av. Jean-Médecin. Tel. 93-62-09-04.
Cuisine: AMERICAN/FRENCH.
$ Prices: 26–42F ($4.80–$7.75); Big Mac 18.50F ($3.40); large french fries 7F ($1.30); beer 10F ($1.85); large soft drink 11F ($2). No credit cards.
Open: Mon–Sat 10am–midnight, Sun 11am–midnight.

The scene is familiar and yet there are some unusual twists: colorful dining areas, the inevitable fast-food lines, customers weighing the choices for hours, elderly dowagers chatting for hours over a cup of tea, kids happily munching, young people enjoying a Big Mac *and a cold beer* (this is France, after all!). Everything is slightly less *à emporter* (to take out).

There's a second McDonald's at 1, promenade des Anglais (tel. 93-87-24-40).

NORTH OF AVENUE JEAN-MEDECIN

COQUILLAGES ANDRE, 6 bis, av. Borriglione. Tel. 93-51-99-99.
Cuisine: FRENCH/SEAFOOD. **Directions:** See below.
$ Prices: 40–75F ($7.40–$13.90); *menu de mer* 70F ($12.95). No credit cards.
Open: Lunch Tues–Sun 11am–3pm; dinner Tues–Sun 6:30–10:30pm.

This very popular eatery is five blocks north of the upper end of avenue Jean-Médecin. The dining room, decorated with fishing nets and a stuffed moonfish and containing only 15 small tables, offers mussels, oysters, sea urchins, coquilles St-Jacques, shrimp, and other fruits de mer—all local catch. The best-selling item here is the *menu de mer*. You'll find no tourists at this highly recommended place, only Niçois.

The best way to reach Coquillages André is to cross under the railway bridge near the train station and walk four blocks up. The restaurant is on the right-hand side, after the Gare du Sud.

NEAR THE SEA

FLUNCH, 7, rue Halévy. Tel. 93-82-17-73.
Cuisine: FRENCH.
$ Prices: 40–60F ($7.40–$11.10). MC, V.
Open: Lunch daily 11am–2:30pm; "tea" daily 2:30–5:30pm; dinner daily 5:30–9:30pm.

The offerings at the Flunch on rue Halévy are truly bewildering in their variety. You will see half a dozen types of bread; cold salads of shrimp, crab, egg, and mayonnaise; cold ham, rare roast beef, smoked salmon; coq au vin, steak haché (chopped sirloin), entrecôte (steak), couscous; desserts, including blueberry pie, chocolate mousse, and little glass jars of freshly made yogurt. The drinks are surprisingly expensive, but you'll find everything else to be quite tasty and reasonably priced.

Another branch is next to the central train station.

LA PIZZA, 34, rue Masséna. Tel. 93-87-70-29.
   Cuisine: ITALIAN.
$ Prices: 18–50F ($3.35–$9.25); pizza 34–50F ($6.30–$9.25); salad 19–45F ($3.50–$8.35); omelets 25–35F ($4.65–$6.50); *plat du jour* 48F ($8.90). No credit cards.
   Open: Lunch daily 11:30am–3pm; dinner daily 6–11:30pm.

⭐ Crowded every afternoon and evening, both winter and summer, La Pizza has found the formula: fresh, delicious pizzas and fast service at good prices. Salads, omelets, and a *plat du jour*, plus wine and beer, are served as well. You might have a short wait for a table, as crowds of young and old press into this place.

MEALS FOR LESS THAN 80F [$14.80]
SOUTH OF THE TRAIN STATION

PALAIS DE CHINE, 41, rue d'Angleterre. Tel. 93-82-22-98.
   Cuisine: CHINESE/THAI.
$ Prices: 55–100F ($10.20–$18.50). MC, V.
   Open: Lunch Fri–Wed noon–2:30pm; dinner Fri–Wed 7–11pm.
Chinese restaurants are not as widespread in France as they are in North America, so this fine restaurant is a welcome surprise. The cordial proprietors offer two four-course *menus du jour*, for 55F and 75F ($10.20 and $13.90), as well as a more elaborate menu for 100F ($18.50), which includes wine. Soups cost 25–38F ($4.60–$7.05). They also prepare delicious Thai dishes for 32–75F ($5.90–$13.90). The Palais de Chine is near the train station, on rue d'Angleterre almost at the corner of avenue Thiers.

RESTAURANT LA PETITE BICHE, 9, rue d'Alsace-Lorraine. Tel. 93-87-30-70.
   Cuisine: FRENCH/NIÇOISE.
$ Prices: 65–100F ($12.05–$18.50). No credit cards.
   Open: Lunch Sat–Thurs 11:30am–2:30pm; dinner Sat–Thurs 6:30–10:30pm.

⭐ The "Little Doe," as its name translates, is a charming and very French place with a country ambience: rough chandeliers, stone pillars, burnished copper vessels, big oil paintings, and mirrors. Though they specialize in seafood, a full range of dishes is offered. The fixed-price dinner allows you to choose from among 21 appetizers, 10 main courses with vegetables, and seven desserts. You can have soupe du pêcheur (fisherman's soup), a dark-red soup made with fish, tomatoes, and garlic, garnished with croutons, grated cheese, and aioli; then a tender, four-egg omelet with potato puffs, and a separate, gigantic plate of french fries; and for dessert, a slice of apricot tart. The restaurant is near the station on Alsace-Lorraine between rue Paganini and rue d'Angleterre, right next door to the Hôtel Normandie.

EAST OF AVENUE JEAN-MEDECIN

RESTAURANT LE COQUET, 18, rue Pertinax. Tel. 93-56-12-71.
   Cuisine: FRENCH/NIÇOISE.
$ Prices: 36–85F ($6.65–$15.75). No credit cards.
   Open: Lunch Mon–Fri 11:30am–3pm; dinner Mon–Fri 6:30–11pm.
Le Coquet is a simple place frequented mainly by local folk—shopkeepers and store clerks—and the occasional tourist. There's not much in the way of decor here, but the food is very tasty. This is a good place to try local specialties such as tripes niçois.

IN VIEUX NICE

RESTAURANT ACCHIARDO, 38, rue Droite.

Cuisine: FRENCH. **Directions:** See below.
$ Prices: 40–75F ($7.40–$13.90). No credit cards.
Open: Lunch Mon–Sat noon–3pm; dinner Mon–Fri 7–10:30pm.

Corn cobs and other farm souvenirs decorate the ceiling beams and walls of this tiny place near the St-Jacob church, presaging good eating. The feeling here is certainly French provincial, though the smiling staff can get by in English. Seafood, as usual, is particularly good, including loup de mer (steamed whitefish in a garlick sauce); with potatoes, carrots, and celery, this would make a typical big *plat du jour*.

Follow signs to the Palais Lascaris, which is on rue Droite, and walk past the palace and the church to the Acchiardo, near the corner with rue du Château.

RESTAURANT CHEZ PALMYRE, 5, rue Droite. Tel. 93-85-72-32.
Cuisine: FRENCH. **Directions:** See below.
$ Prices: 55–70F ($10.20–$12.95). No credit cards.
Open: Lunch Mon–Sat noon–3pm; dinner Mon–Sat 7–11pm.

Whether it's the popularity of the food or the small size of the restaurant (only eight tables), Chez Palmyre always seems busy at mealtime—you may have to wait in line unless you arrive as it opens. A typical *menu du jour* includes appetizer and main course (you get five or six choices of each), plus fruit, cheese, or yogurt.

To find this tiny place in Vieux Nice's bewildering maze of narrow streets, follow signs to the Palais Lascaris, midway along rue Droite. Chez Palmyre is near the corner with rue St-François; street numbers are virtually nonexistent in these parts.

STUDENT EATERIES

For names and addresses of many student eateries, contact **C.R.O.U.S.**, 18, avenue des Fleurs (tel. 93-96-73-73); avenue des Fleurs is the westward continuation of boulevard Victor-Hugo, on the western side of boulevard Gambetta.

RESTAURANT UNIVERSITAIRE, 3, av. Robert-Schumann. Tel. 93-97-10-20.
Cuisine: FRENCH. **Directions:** See below.
$ Prices: 30–40F ($5.55–$7.40). No credit cards.
Open: Sept–June, lunch Mon–Sat 11:30am–1:30pm; dinner Mon–Sat 6:30–8:30pm. **Closed:** July–Aug.

A student ID is not necessary to eat in this 600-seat cafeteria, somewhat out of the way, but certainly cheap and filling. Just ask for a *tarif passager*. Watch the hours—they're short.

To find it, walk west along avenue Thiers, cross boulevard Gambetta, and continue along rue de Châteauneuf to place St-Philippe. Pass under the highway (*autoroute*) and turn left onto the winding road, avenue Robert-Schumann. You'll pass some palm trees, a small restaurant, and then, on your left, you'll see the establishment.

STREET FOOD

You can pick up a pan bagnat or other sandwiches at many streetside kiosks. These sandwiches cost only 10–20F ($1.85–$3.70), and are quite filling; the baguettes they're made with are always delicious.

PICNIC SUPPLIES & WHERE TO EAT THEM

To make your own meals, head first for the **Prisunic** department store, on avenue Jean-Médecin between rue Biscarra and avenue Maréchal-Foch. Most department stores in France have large grocery departments, as this one does. Enter at the corner of rue Biscarra and avenue Jean-Médecin, turn right, and go to the back of the store past the café. You'll find huge chunks of cheese for 7.50F ($1.40), liters of milk for 6F ($1.10), lunch meat to make three large sandwiches for 23F ($4.25), and various salads and side dishes at only a few francs for a 200-gram portion. A bottle of mineral water sells for a mere 5F (90¢); a liter bottle of Coca-Cola is yours for 8F ($1.50). When you're done in the grocery section, head for the doors at the corner of Jean-Médecin and avenue Maréchal-Foch, where the store's bakery is located. Choose from among a dozen different types of bread, all unforgettably delicious and satisfyingly low in price. There are tarts and other baked dessert treats as well. You can even get a "mini pan bagnat" for 15F ($2.75). The store is open Monday through Saturday from 8:30am to 7:15pm (on Friday till 8pm).

Another convenient supermarket is the **Timy Supermarché,** 15, rue d'Italie, at rue Paganini, just a few blocks south of the train station. Wander along this section of rue d'Italie and you'll pass other fish markets, grocery shops, and bakeries (*boulangerie*). **Cave Paganini,** 13, rue Paganini, between rue d'Italie and Clemenceau, is an authentic old-fashioned wine shop where you can buy your vintage in bottles, or bring your own bottle and have it tapped right from the barrel (*vin à la tireuse*) for only about 7.50–10F ($1.40–$1.85) per liter. They also stock beer, mineral water, and fruit juices. Open Monday through Saturday until well into the evening.

Other places to search for picnic supplies are at Nice's **open-air markets.** France is famous for its weekly markets, and no matter how many grocery shops or supermarkets exist in town, there will always be at least one weekly market, and perhaps several. Vendors bring their trucks laden with fresh fruits, vegetables, meats, seafood, chickens, guinea hens, flowers, spices, even clothes and housewares, and lay out their goods on rough tables beneath awnings and umbrellas. Early in the morning the market appears as if by magic and is completely swept away by lunchtime, with only a few tomato crates and banana peels to testify to its earlier existence.

There are many terrific places where you can consume your picnic: on the beach; on a bench along the promenade des Anglais or the quai des Etats-Unis; on place Masséna and the bosky Jardin Albert 1er at the end of avenue Jean-Médecin; or in the park on top of Le Château beside Nice's port, where stands the city's ruined castle.

WORTH THE EXTRA BUCKS

CHANTECLER, in the Hôtel Negresco, 37, promenade des Anglais. Tel. 93-88-39-51.
  Cuisine: FRENCH. **Reservations:** Essential.
$ Prices: 200–500F ($37.05–$92.60). AE, DC, EURO, MC, V.
  Open: Lunch daily noon–2:30pm; dinner daily 7–10:30pm.

★ This is the best restaurant on the Côte d'Azur, and among the best in France—even in the world. The dining rooms glint with the shine of crystal from the chandeliers and the stemware. Service is impeccable, the cuisine distinguished, delicate, and unforgettable. For a budget traveler, the price is unforgettable as well. Is the memory worth it? Make reservations.

LA TAVERNE DE L'OPERA, 8, rue St-François-de-Paule. Tel. 93-85-72-68.
  Cuisine: FRENCH/NIÇOISE.
$ Prices: 70–120F ($12.95–$22.20).
  Open: Lunch Mon–Sat noon–2:30pm; dinner Mon–Sat 7–10:30pm. **Closed:** Dec.

★ Down by the waterfront in Vieux Nice, only a carnation's throw from the flower market and even closer to the opera house, is this grand old tavern heavy with charm and atmosphere. La Taverne de l'Opéra is a great place to try some of the specialties of Nice's cuisine; the seafood is simply splendid. Seating is either outdoors or in.

6. ATTRACTIONS

What you do in Nice will probably depend on the season. In summer, of course, the beaches will entice you. All year long, though, there's a lot to see. Nice has beautiful

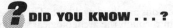

DID YOU KNOW . . . ?

- From 1814 to 1860, Nice belonged to the Kingdom of Sardinia.
- Arabic is widely spoken in some districts of Nice.
- Nice's large English colony built a path bordering the coast in 1822—it eventually became the glitzy promenade des Anglais.
- Monaco, nine miles east of Nice, is the second-smallest country in the world (after Vatican City).
- Rain falls only 60 days of the year on the Riviera.

neighborhoods to stroll around and several fine museums to visit. It's also an excellent base from which to explore all the other towns and villages of the French Riviera (see "Easy Excursions," below).

SUGGESTED ITINERARIES

The beaches are open every day of course, but the museums aren't. Some museums are closed on Monday, others on Tuesday, and many for a month every year, often in rainy November. Check the hours to be sure before heading out. For a complete list of museums and hours, get the free brochure "Les Musées de Nice" at the tourist office.

IF YOU HAVE ONE DAY　With only one day, you can divide your time between the beach, the Musée Matisse or the Musée Chagall in the beautiful Cimiez district, or around Vieux Nice, the labyrinthine old part of town.

IF YOU HAVE TWO DAYS　With two days you can see the chief sights of Nice and make an excursion to at least two other places along the Riviera. Consider Monaco and the Fondation Maeght in St-Paul-de-Vence, for instance. With the fast and frequent train service, you can easily travel both east and west of Nice on the same day.

IF YOU HAVE THREE DAYS　With three days at your disposal, you can spend the first one in Nice, the second one east of Nice (in Monaco and visiting the beautiful Villa Kérylos in Beaulieu-sur-Mer), the third one to the west (in St-Paul-de-Vence and at the Matisse Chapel in Vence).

IF YOU HAVE FIVE DAYS　Five days are plenty for a good first-time exploration of the Côte d'Azur, though you could obviously spend months here and still keep yourself amused. Add the Musée Picasso at the Château Grimaldi in Antibes, and spend a few hours in Cannes as well.

TOP ATTRACTIONS

MUSEE MATISSE, 164, av. des Arènes de Cimiez. Tel. 93-53-17-70.

The works of Henri Matisse (1869–1954) are on display in the 17th-century Villa des Arènes. It's fascinating to view the artist's works—paintings, drawings, sculptures, and studies for the chapel at Vence—right in the place, among the trees, the vistas, even the furniture.

The Musée Matisse is located in the district of Cimiez, an important Roman town north of the center of Nice. Outdoors, all around the Villa des Arènes, are the ruins of Roman Cemenelum, including baths and a theater still used for performances. In the 19th century Queen Victoria and her court made Cimiez their winter vacation home. Even without the museums, Cimiez merits a visit.

Admission: Free.

Open: Tues–Sun 10am–noon and 2–5pm. **Bus:** 15, 17, 20, or 22 from place Masséna to Arènes or Monastère.

MUSEE D'ARCHEOLOGIE, 160, av. des Arènes de Cimiez. Tel. 93-81-59-57.

Nice's new archeological museum was opened in 1989. Roman Cemenelum was the capital of the province of the Maritime Alps, an important passageway to Gallia and Hispania. Many artifacts found at local excavations are displayed here. There are also Greek and Etruscan pieces. Enter the museum through the archeological site on avenue Montecroce.

Admission: Free.

Open: May–Sept, Tues–Sat 10am–noon and 2–6pm, Sun 2–6pm; Oct–Apr, Tues–Sat 10am–noon and 2–5pm, Sun 2–5pm. **Closed:** Nov. **Bus:** 15, 17, 20, or 22 from place Masséna to Arènes or Monastère.

MUSEE NATIONAL MESSAGE BIBLIQUE MARC CHAGALL, av. du Docteur-Ménard at bd. de Cimiez. Tel. 93-81-75-75.

The Chagall family donated 450 of the painter's finer works on biblical subjects to France, his adopted homeland, and they have been put on permanent exhibition in this squat, modern building of white stone built at French government expense and set in its own park. It's pleasantly light and airy inside, which is just the right mood for Chagall's lyrical works: three large stained-glass windows in the concert hall, a room of stunning paintings illustrating *The Song of Songs,* and several rooms hung with grand-scale canvases portraying *Moses and the Burning Bush, The Sacrifice of Isaac,* and similar themes.

Admission: 20F ($3.70) adults, 10F ($1.85) ages 18–24 years and over 60 years, free for children 17 and under; higher prices during special exhibitions.

Open: July–Sept, Wed–Mon 10am–7pm; Oct–June, 10am–12:30pm and 2–5:30pm. **Bus:** 15 or 15A from place Masséna to Musée Chagall.

MUSEE DES BEAUX-ARTS, 33, av. des Baumettes. Tel. 93-44-50-72.

Nice's municipal fine-arts museum is housed in a mansion built for the Ukrainian Princess Kotschoubey in the 1870s. Here you can see paintings from the 17th and 18th centuries as well as works by Degas, Monet, Sisley, and Bonnard. There is a particularly good collection of works by Raoul Dufy, a painter of bright colors and Mediterranean themes, and of the works of Jules Chéret, who painted around the same time and in the same manner as Toulouse-Lautrec.

Admission: Free.

Open: May–Sept, Tues–Sun 10am–noon and 3–6pm; Oct–Apr, Tues–Sun 10am–noon and 2–5pm. **Bus:** 38 to Chéret, or 3, 7, 12, 18, or 22 to Grosso.

LE CHATEAU, above Vieux Nice.

✪ This hill at the eastern end of the quai des Etats-Unis is named after the fortress that once stood here. There are beautiful groves of evergreens and plantings of cacti, with a path to take you around the hilltop. Several viewpoints afford breathtaking vistas of the town and the sea. An elevator at the end of the quai des Etats-Unis will whisk you to the top for 4F (75¢); you can come down the same way or on foot. Also here is the **Tour Bellanda,** an old tower where Berlioz lived for some time and that now houses a small naval museum.

MORE ATTRACTIONS

EGLISE ET MONASTERE DE CIMIEZ (Church and Monastery of Cimiez), place du Monastère. Tel. 93-81-00-04.

Not far from the Musée Matisse is this medieval monastery, which now houses a museum dedicated to the art and history of the Franciscan order. The church contains a few very fine paintings by the Niçois primitives and a school that flourished here in the 15th and 16th centuries. Writer Roger Martin du Gard and artist Raoul Dufy are buried in the cemetery, and so is Matisse, near an olive grove.

Admission: Free.

Open: Mon–Sat 10am–noon and 3–6pm. **Bus:** 15, 15A, or 17 from place Masséna to Monastère.

MUSEE MASSENA, 35, promenade des Anglais, next to the Hôtel

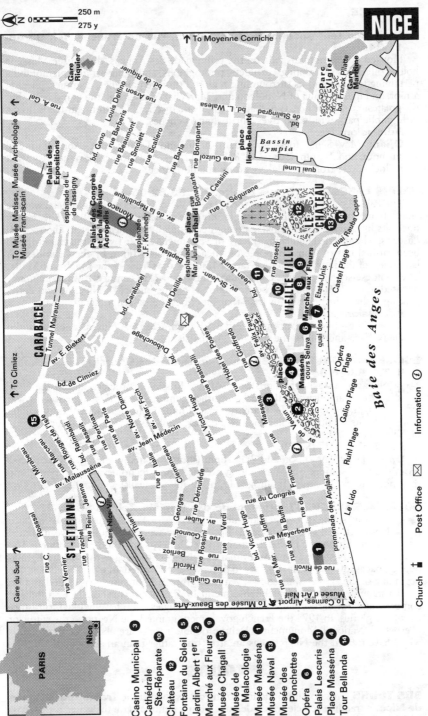

NICE

Z 0 ══════ 250 m
　　　　　 275 y

To Moyenne Corniche →

Baie des Anges

Church ✝　　Post Office ⊠　　Information ⓘ

Casino Municipal ③	Musée de Malacologie ⑧
Cathédrale Ste-Réparate ⑩	Musée Masséna ①
Château ⑫	Musée Naval ⑬
Fontaine du Soleil ⑤	Musée des Ponchettes ⑦
Jardin Albert 1er ②	Opéra ⑥
Marché aux Fleurs ⑨	Palais Lescaris ⑪
Musée Chagall ⑮	Place Masséna ④
	Tour Bellanda ⑭

PARIS
Nice ●

Negresco (entrance in the back at 65, rue de France). Tel. 93-88-11-34.

Housed in a sumptuous villa on the promenade des Anglais, the Musée Masséna holds collections of paintings, artifacts, photographs, and other art and memorabilia pertaining to Nice and its surrounding region. Primitive paintings, ceramics, jewelry, armor, and memorabilia of Napoleon and Maréchal Masséna fill the grand halls, but the greatest attraction here is perhaps the halls themselves. The front garden is now a little public park with palm trees, shrubs, and benches.

Admission: Free.

Open: May–Sept, Tues–Sun 10am–noon and 3–6pm; Oct–Apr, Tues–Sun 10am–noon and 2–5pm. **Bus:** 3, 7, 8, 9, 10, 12, 14, or 22 to Rivoli; or an easy walk four blocks west from rue Halévy along rue de France.

PALAIS LASCARIS, 15, rue Droite. Tel. 93-62-05-54.

The Palais Lascaris, deep within the maze of Vieux Nice's winding streets, was the grand home of a prominent Niçois family, the Lascaris-Ventimiglias. The family traces its lineage back to Eudoxia, a daughter of the Byzantine emperor Theodore II Lascaris, who married Guillaume-Pierre of Ventimiglia in 1261 when the emperor had been pushed out of Constantinople to Nicaea, in Asia Minor, by the Crusaders. A later scion of the family was 55th Grand Master of the Order of the Knights of Malta. The Genoese-style palace was constructed in the mid-17th century. It was completely restored in the 1960s and now houses exhibits on the history of Nice. As you enter, pick up a sheet (in English, for free) that describes the palace in detail.

Admission: Free.

Open: Tues–Sun 9:30am–noon and 2:30–6pm. **Closed:** Nov. **Directions:** Go to Vieux Nice and follow the signs for the palais.

EGLISE ORTHODOXE RUSSE (Russian Orthodox Church), av. Nicholas II. Tel. 93-96-88-02.

Nice was always a fashionable resort for Russian aristocrats, and in the early 1900s Tsar Nicholas II and his mother commissioned this cathedral. It was inaugurated in 1912. Its richly decorated interior includes several outstanding icons. With its six onion domes and vivid colors, the Russian church has become one of Nice's landmarks.

Admission: 12F ($2.20).

Open: Daily 9am–noon and 2:30–6pm (shorter hours in winter). **Directions:** From the train station, walk west along avenue Thiers to boulevard Gambetta, and then north to av. Nicholas II (altogether, a five-minute walk).

HOTEL NEGRESCO, 37, promenade des Anglais. Tel. 93-88-35-68.

On the splendid promenade des Anglais, the Hôtel Negresco is a Nice landmark and one of the great hotels of the world. Its guests have included Queen Elizabeth, Harry Truman, Walt Disney, and Elton John. Opened in 1913 by Henri Negresco, a native Romanian, the sumptuous guest rooms and grand public spaces of this Belle Epoque palace were converted into a hospital at the beginning of the "Great War," only a year later. By 1918 Negresco was ruined and his hotel a shambles. The hotel's rebirth came in 1957, when it was bought by a Belgian company and put in the charge of M. and Mme Augier, who have worked to restore its former glories. In 1974 the French government granted the Negresco the status of "Perpetual National Monument." Deluxe double rooms are about $350, which is why I have treated the Negresco as an attraction rather than an accommodation.

TOURS

BUS TOURS A good introduction to the city is aboard the **Trains Touristiques de Nice,** a trainlike vehicle which departs from a signboard on the waterfront across from the Jardin Albert 1er every 20 minutes from 10am to 7pm during the summer season. The "trains" make a 40-minute tour of the city's high points, including Le Château. The purchase of one ticket at 25F ($4.60) allows you to reboard anywhere along the route throughout the day. For information and reservations, call 93-71-44-77.

For guided bus tours of Nice and the Riviera, contact **Santa Azur,** 11, avenue Jean-Médecin (tel. 93-85-46-81). The tours offered cover many of the towns and sights of both the French and Italian Rivieras. An afternoon tour of Nice, at 75F ($13.90), includes a walk through Vieux Nice, then a bus tour along the promenade des Anglais, Cimiez, the Franciscan monastery, the Roman amphitheaters, plus a trip to the top of Mont Boron for the view and a visit to a candy factory.

WALKING TOURS Walking tours of Vieux Nice, called *visites commentées,* are sponsored by **CAIDEM,** 4, rue Blacas (tel. 93-62-18-12), and begin from the Palais Lascaris at 3pm on Tuesday and Sunday throughout the year. They're in French, with a few words of explanation in English. The cost is 25F ($4.60) per person.

SPECIAL & FREE EVENTS

There are 30 **beaches** in Nice, and 15 of them are public. Many of the events surrounding the **Carnival** are also free (see "Special Events" in "Pretrip Preparations," above).

Other yearly celebrations include the **Festin des Cougourdons** in March, held at the Jardins des Arènes in Cimiez. This is a popular feast with songs and dances, and you can buy the *cougourdons,* which are all kinds of arts and crafts. Also at the Jardin des Arènes, every Sunday in May, is the **Fête des Mais,** which celebrates the return of spring with folkloric shows and picnics.

Other special events along the Riviera include, of course, the **Festival International du Film** held every May in Cannes. In Nice itself, there is a **Festival de Musique Contemporaine** in January, a **Festival de Musique Sacrée** in June, and both a **Grande Parade de Jazz** and a **Festival du Folklore International** in July.

7. SAVVY SHOPPING

If you go to Nice from Paris, you'll probably find shopping in Nice less enthralling. Still, there are some interesting stores along avenue Jean-Médecin, in the pedestrian zone of rue Masséna and rue de France, and in and around posh place Masséna.

More interesting than the boutiques are the different markets. The **Marché aux Fleurs** (Flower Market) is held Tuesday through Sunday from 6am to 5:30pm (except Sunday afternoon) in Vieux Nice at the Cours Saleya, east of the Opera House and just inland from the quai des Etats-Unis.

One block away is a tiny store, **Aux Parfums de Grasse,** selling 80 different scents in flasks and bottles costing from 13F ($2.40) for a lipstick-sized container to 105F ($19.45) for one liter; it's open Monday through Friday, from 9:30am to noon and 2:30 to 7:30pm, and on Saturday from 9:30am to noon. The owner will help you combine various brands to create your personal fragrance.

Also in the general vicinity of Vieux Nice, at rue Antoine-Gauthier, rue Catherine-Ségurane, and rue Emmanuel-Philibert, behind Le Château, is the **Marché d'Art des Antiquaires,** featuring antiques Monday through Saturday from 10am to noon and 3 to 6:30pm. These markets are interesting to visit even if you're not planning to take any pictures.

Forgot your beach novel? Need a *Newsweek*? Nice has several bookstores that carry books in English. Head for one of these: **Nice English Books—Home de la**

Presse, 29, avenue Jean-Médecin (tel. 93-88-84-16); **Riviera Bookshop,** 10, rue Chauvain (tel. 93-85-84-61); or **The Cat's Whiskers,** 26, rue Lamartine (tel. 93-80-02-66), located a block east of Notre-Dame church, just off avenue Jean-Médecin, which is owned and run by an English woman.

8. EVENING ENTERTAINMENT

Nice has an active nightlife, from jazz to opera, from movies to café life. Cultural offerings are outlined in *L'Info,* a quarterly booklet distributed for free at the tourist office and at hotels, and in *La Semaine des Spectacles,* which catalogs the week's entertainment possibilities for all the towns of the Côte d'Azur.

THE PERFORMING ARTS

OPERA, SYMPHONY & BALLET

L'Opéra de Nice, 4, rue St-François-de-Paule (tel. 93-85-67-31), has an active winter season. Performances can include anything from the classics done by European masters to Duke Ellington's *Sophisticated Ladies* presented by New York's Opera Ensemble. The concerts and recitals performed at the Opéra are equally varied. Ballets here are often new works or modern interpretations of classical pieces. The box office is open Tuesday through Saturday from 11am to 7pm. Ticket prices range from 50F to 240F ($9.25 to $44.45).

The City of Nice also sponsors a series of concerts in local churches every Sunday at 3pm. For details, contact **Orchestre d'Harmonie de la Ville de Nice,** 34, boulevard Jean-Jaurès (tel. 93-80-08-50).

THEATER

The city's theatrical venues include the **Théâtre Municipal du Vieux Nice,** rue St-Joseph (tel. 93-62-00-03), and the **Nouveau Théâtre de Nice,** esplanade des Victoires (tel. 93-56-86-86). The plays are in French, of course.

JAZZ & ROCK

One of Nice's prime locations for officially sponsored jazz is **CEDAC de Cimiez,** 49, avenue de la Marne (tel. 93-81-09-09). Contact them for current programs.

During July, the **Grande Parade de Jazz** brings famous musicians to the Parc et Arènes de Cimiez (tel. 93-21-22-01) for outdoor concerts that last long into the night.

MOVIES

As well as several downtown commercial cinemas, there is the **Cinémathèque de Nice,** Acropolis, 3, esplanade Kennedy (tel. 93-92-81-81). Their afternoon and evening screenings might include anything from French movie classics to former Hollywood hits. Tickets cost 40F ($7.40).

THE BAR SCENE

Most of Nice's nighttime activity is in the sidewalk café-bars along the promenade des Anglais, on rue Halévy or avenue Gustave-V, or near place Masséna. The thing to do is stroll along the promenade or circulate in place Masséna, looking for a spot with interesting sounds and the right clientele.

9. EASY EXCURSIONS

The French Riviera is one of the continent's most beautiful regions. You'll soon find that sights in Nice are only half the story—many great attractions are found within an hour's train or bus ride from the city.

Trains to points east and west of Nice are cheap and fast. The train to Monaco, for example, runs at least every hour, takes 22 minutes, and costs only 14F ($2.60). To help you plan your day trips, get the train schedule (*fiche horaire*) for St-Raphaël–Vintimille at the station; it lists the hours for trains along the coast from St-Raphaël to the Italian border, via Cannes, Antibes, Nice, and Monaco.

Buses will be particularly useful for trips to Vence and St-Paul-de-Vence, sites of the splendid Matisse Chapel and the Fondation Maeght. Buses to both destinations depart from Nice's Gare Routière, the central bus station.

EAST OF NICE

BEAULIEU-SUR-MER

The name of this town means "beautiful place by the sea," and it's a fitting name for the site of one of the most beautiful villas on the Riviera.

The ✪ **Villa Kérylos,** Beaulieu-sur-Mer (tel. 93-01-01-44), is an architectural masterpiece. Archeologist Théodore Reinach, fascinated with ancient Greece, had this amazing classical villa built on a rocky peninsula. His design is purely Hellenic down to its furniture and mosaics, with minimal concessions to the 20th century. But where does neoclassicism end and art deco start? The courtyard, the library, the gardens, even the bathrooms—everything is lovingly created.

Admission is 15F ($2.75), with a guided tour included. It is open September, October, and December through June, Tuesday through Sunday from 2 to 6pm; in July and August, Tuesday through Sunday from 2:30 to 6:30pm; closed November. Take the train to Beaulieu-sur-Mer.

ST-JEAN-CAP-FERRAT

Facing Beaulieu-sur-Mer and Villa Kérylos across the water is another idyllic spot, with another exceptional villa.

The Mediterranean-style **Foundation Ephrussi de Rothschild,** St-Jean-Cap-Ferrat (tel. 93-01-33-09), set in lovely gardens, was once the home of the Baroness Ephrussi de Rothschild, who gave it to the Institut de France in the 1930s. Presently the Musée Ile-de-France, the sumptuous house is filled with her collected treasures: Renaissance tapestries, furniture (including pieces that belonged to Marie Antoinette), porcelain and art objects from Asia, and masterpieces by European painters.

Admission to the villa and garden is 35F ($6.50) for adults, 20F ($3.70) for ages 18–24 and over 60 years, with a guided tour included. The villa is open July and August, Tuesday through Sunday from 3 to 7pm; and September to June, Tuesday through Sunday from 2 to 6pm. The gardens are open Tuesday through Sunday from 9am to noon. Both are closed in November. To get there, take the train to Beaulieu-sur-Mer and then the bus toward St-Jean-Cap-Ferrat; or take the bus from Nice's Gare Routière to St-Jean-Cap-Ferrat. One-way bus fare is 10F ($1.85).

EZE

The Azure Coast is sprinkled with picturesque Mediterranean mountain villages built high on the craggy rocks, well defended by battlements and the occasional tumbledown fort. Pirate raids made these inaccessible spots popular places to live in the Middle Ages. Today they are popular again because of their antique charm and sweeping panoramas. The village of Eze, on the Moyenne Corniche (middle coast road) is perhaps the most charming of these. Hop a bus from Nice's Gare Routière, and get off at Eze to climb up its narrow, mazelike streets. The farther up you go, the farther back in time. Bus fare to Eze is 12.50F ($2.30).

You might continue along the Haute Corniche (upper coast road) to **La Turbie,** passing **La Trofée des Alpes** (the Trophy of the Alps), built in 6 B.C. at the order of Augustus, Emperor of Rome, to celebrate the defeat of the Alpine peoples by the Roman legionnaires. The **Musée de la Trofée des Alpes** is open daily from 10am to noon and 2 to 5:30pm.

MONACO

We expect the Principality of Monaco to be a fairytale land, and in many ways it is. Monaco is tiny (only Vatican City is a smaller country), it is beautiful (a lofty promontory over the bluest of seas), and it has its princes and its princesses, looming large (and beautiful) over our collective New World imagination. When you arrive here, though, you might be surprised to find such prosaic things as a train station and a post office. But, then, the principality needs its millions of yearly visitors, and it likes the revenues from its not-so-tiny but oh-so-beautiful stamps.

You don't need your passport when you travel from Nice to Monaco. For all intents and purposes, Monaco is part of France. The principality does issue its own stamps and red-and-white license plates, but most other matters—electricity and water, education, even finance and foreign affairs—are handled by France.

Monaco can be reached by train or bus from Nice. Train fare one way is 14F ($2.60); bus fare is 17F ($3.15).

In its tiny territory, Monaco squeezes several different districts. There's the **Rocher de Monaco,** the oldest part of town on a rocky hillside graced by the princely palace, the Oceanographic Museum, lush gardens, and narrow streets; **La Condamine,** the harbor district at the foot of the Rocher, where most of the Monegasque people live; and of course, **Monte Carlo,** famous and infamous, just uphill from La Condamine.

You can walk around virtually all of Monaco in a few hours. On your way, drop in at the famous **Casino,** in Monte Carlo. Designed by Charles Garnier, the architect of the Paris Opéra, it provided government income for the once-struggling principality. Wander into its posh turn-of-the-century gaming rooms, but don't expect anything as exciting as Mata Hari shooting a Russian spy, which happened here once upon a time. The Casino opens at 10am and remains receptive, as it were, late into the night. Also in Monte Carlo, a villa designed by the same Garnier houses the **Musée de Poupées et Automates (Doll and Automata Museum),** which, interestingly enough, is also known as the Musée National.

If you get to the old city of Monaco in the morning, and if the prince and his family are not in residence, you can tour some apartments of the **Palais du Prince,** with its paintings and tapestries, and then issue forth to witness the changing of the guard just before noon. A wing of the palace is occupied by the **Musée Napoléonien et des Archives du Palais,** an outstanding collection of objects linked to Bonaparte, whose family, incidentally, was related to the princely Grimaldis. Also in the Rocher is the **Musée de l'Océanographie,** founded by Prince Albert I in 1910 and directed by Jacques Cousteau. The nearby **Jardins St-Martin** is a lush collection of cacti and tropical plants not native to this region; they were also created by Prince Albert, whose statue you can see here gazing at the sea. Also in this area is the white, patrician **cathédrale,** which contains some beautiful paintings by the Niçois natives, including a masterful retable by Louis Bréa, "the Provençal Fra Angelico." Princess Grace—Philadelphian Grace Kelly of Hitchcock's *Rear Window* and *To Catch a Thief*—is entombed in the cathedral, under a marble slab reading "Gratia."

ROQUEBRUNE

Roquebrune, like Eze, is one of those picturesque fortified villages, but this one has a fairytale castle, the **Château de Roquebrune,** dating from the 10th century but

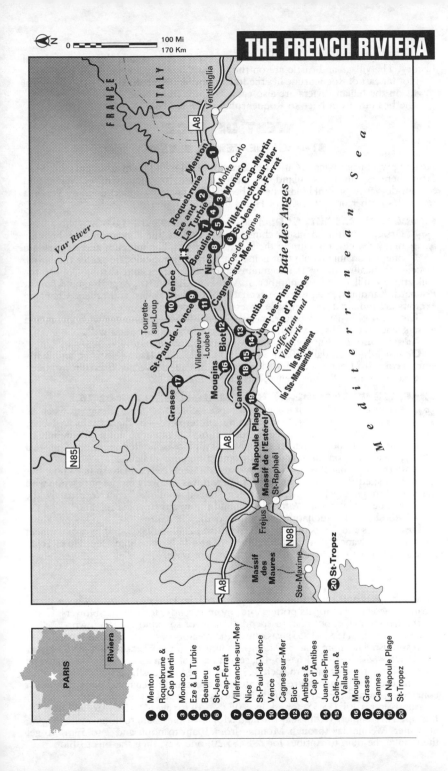

THE FRENCH RIVIERA

0 ____ 100 Mi
____ 170 Km

Var River

FRANCE

ITALY

Ventimiglia

Menton ❶

Roquebrune

Eze and
La Turbie ❷

Monte Carlo

Monaco ❸

Cap-Martin

Villefranche-sur-Mer ❹

St-Jean-Cap-Ferrat ❺

Cros-de-Cagnes

Cagnes-sur-Mer

Beaulieu ❼

Nice ❽

Baie des Anges

Tourette-sur-Loup

Vence ❾

St-Paul-de-Vence ❿

Villeneuve-Loubet

Biot ⓬

Antibes ⓭

Juan-les-Pins

Cap d'Antibes ⓮

Golfe-Juan and Vallauris

Île St-Honorat

Île Ste-Marguerite

Mougins ⓰

Grasse ⓱

Cannes

⓲ ⓳

La Napoule Plage

Massif de l'Estérel

St-Raphaël

Fréjus

Massif des Maures

Ste-Maxime

St-Tropez ⓴

Mediterranean Sea

N85

N98

A8

PARIS

Riviera

❶ Menton
❷ Roquebrune &
Cap Martin
❸ Monaco
❹ Eze & La Turbie
❺ Beaulieu
❻ St-Jean &
Cap-Ferrat
❼ Villefranche-sur-Mer
❽ Nice
❾ St-Paul-de-Vence
❿ Vence
⓫ Cagnes-sur-Mer
⓬ Biot
⓭ Antibes &
Cap d'Antibes
⓮ Juan-les-Pins
⓯ Golfe-Juan &
Vallauris
⓰ Mougins
⓱ Grasse
⓲ Cannes
⓳ La Napoule Plage
⓴ St-Tropez

extensively rebuilt in the 13th. A museum in the castle details the area's colorful history. The village and castle are on the Grand Corniche, accessible by bus.

Not far east of Roquebrune lies the Italian border: **Portofino** and other beautiful towns on the Italian Riviera are also easy day trips from Nice.

The bus fare from Nice to Roquebrune is 22F ($4.05).

WEST OF NICE
ST-PAUL-DE-VENCE & VENCE

Heading west from Nice, 14 minutes away by train is the town of Cagnes-sur-Mer. From here, a bus leads inland, up into the hills, to the towns of Vence and St-Paul-de-Vence. St-Paul holds one of the Riviera's finest art collections, and Vence, a few miles farther on, is the site of Henri Matisse's masterful chapel.

FONDATION MAEGHT, St-Paul-de-Vence. Tel. 93-32-81-63.

⭐ Designed by the Spanish architect José Luís Sert, the Fondation Maeght is for many the best museum in the south of France. The museum and its park are one, an organic whole that is itself a work of art. Sculpture graces the lawns, placed artistically among the fountains and pools, trees and shrubs. As for the collection, you'll see a large number of works by Giacometti, Arp, Braque, Chagall, Bonnard, Kandinsky, Hepworth, Léger, Miró, Calder, Tàpies, and others. Changing exhibits are mounted frequently. A cafeteria provides sustenance.

The town of St-Paul, a picture-perfect medieval village popular with artists and writers since the 1920s, is worth spending some time exploring as well.

Admission: 24–30F ($4.45–$5.55), depending on exhibits.

Open: July–Sept, daily 10am–7pm; Oct–June, daily 10am–12:30pm and 2:30–6pm. **Train:** To Cagnes-sur-Mer, then bus to St-Paul-de-Vence. **Bus:** From Nice's Gare Routière to St-Paul-de-Vence; bus fare is 17F ($3.15).

CHAPELLE DU ROSAIRE, av. Henri Matisse. Tel. 93-58-03-26.

⭐ Art lovers may be familiar with Matisse's chapel at Vence, designed when he was 77 years old and celebrated as his masterpiece—by the artist as well as by his admirers. The chapel is that of the local Dominican nuns. Its interior, by plan, is quite small but brilliantly conceived as a place of limited space but "spiritual infinity," with the conventions met by inspired minimal designs.

Note that the chapel is open only two days a week. Sylvia Plath didn't know this when she visited and she began to cry: "I knew it was so lovely inside, pure white with the sun through blue, yellow, and green stained windows." But fortunately the Mother Superior let her in, "after denying all the wealthy people in cars."

Admission: Free (donations recommended).

Open: Tues and Thurs only, 10–11:30am and 2:30–5:30pm, and by appointment 48 hours in advance; call for particulars. **Closed:** Nov to mid-Dec. **Bus:** From Nice's Gare Routière to Vence, then a 30-minute walk.

BIOT

Although roses and carnations are grown here, the village of Biot has been noted through the centuries for its potters and, more recently, for its glass-blowers. Come for the Musée Léger, but plan to spend an hour or so exploring the town.

Fernand Léger (1881–1955) was one of the creators of cubism, but he started as an impressionist. The more than 340 paintings housed in the **Musée Fernand-Léger,** Biot (tel. 93-65-63-61 or 93-65-63-49), reflect his evolution as a painter. Fascinated by the transformations of modern society, he developed an "aesthetics of the machine," painting even the human figure as a system of tubes and mechanical parts. His brash conception earned critical brickbats, but his work speaks for itself.

Admission is 30F ($5.55) for adults, 20F ($3.70) for ages 18–24 years and over 60. It is open in summer, Wednesday through Monday from 10am to noon and 2 to 6pm; in winter, Wednesday through Monday from 10am to noon and 2 to 5pm. To get there, take the train to Antibes for 28F ($5.20) one way, then the bus to Biot.

ANTIBES

Greek settlers from Marseille founded Antibes in the 4th century B.C. and called it Antipolis ("the opposite city"), a reference to its location across the baie des Anges from Nice.

MUSEE PICASSO AND CHATEAU GRIMALDI, place Marie-Jol. Tel. 93-34-91-91.

⭐ The 12th-century granite Château Grimaldi was built on the ruins of a Roman camp. Picasso came here in 1946 and spent the fall painting and potting. Many of the works you'll see here were created in that one season. Picasso's works are displayed along with those of several contemporaries.

Admission: 22F ($4.05) adults, 12F ($2.20) ages 17–24 and over 60 years.

Open: Summer, Wed–Mon 10am–noon and 3–7pm; winter, Wed–Mon 10am–noon and 2–6pm. **Closed:** Nov to mid-Dec. **Train:** To Antibes.

MUSEE ARCHEOLOGIQUE, on the bastion St-André. Tel. 93-34-48-01.

This museum on the ramparts depicts the town's Greek and Roman history through artifacts—there are some very beautiful amphoras—found in the excavations and coastal waters.

Admission: 10F ($1.85) adults, 5F (90¢) ages 18–24 and over 60 years.

Open: July–Aug, daily 9am–noon and 2–7pm; Sept–June, Wed–Mon 9am–noon and 2–6pm. **Closed:** Nov. **Train:** To Antibes.

CANNES

⭐ Famed for its celebrities and its film festival (in May), Cannes is a much more glamorous resort town than Nice—and prices reflect that difference. For 25F ($4.60) you can take the train from Nice and wander along the boulevard de la Croisette, the elegant waterfront promenade, head down to the beach, gawk at the **Palais des Festivals et des Congrès,** have a snack, and be back at your comfortable, inexpensive Nice headquarters in only a few hours.

OSLO

When you first emerge from Oslo's modern Central Station the city appears as bustling as any. Buses and trams maneuver through people-packed streets. The revolving doors of the adjacent Oslo City shopping complex never cease spinning.

It's ironic that this capital's first impression should be so bold because up until a few years ago this city of almost half a million seemed like a sleepy hamlet. In many ways it still is, and, first impressions notwithstanding, the city's small size has everything to do with its charm. You can easily explore the compact town center on foot, and at no point are the pretty port and the tree-covered mountains more than a stroll or short ride away.

Most locals would say that their favorite aspect of Oslo is its natural setting, surrounded by forest and fronting the vast Oslo Fjord. Indeed, the city's beggarless streets and clean air look very much like the invention of an optimistic imagination. Oslo's perfect combination of cosmopolitan city and spacious country is its greatest asset, and its encircling ring of forest, delightful cafés, and larger-than-life Vigeland Sculpture Garden are incomparable.

The city of 454,000 is forward thinking, and a major concern has been the reduction of pollution, which by most standards is negligible (much through traffic has been rerouted under the city).

You have no doubt heard that Oslo's special beauty has its price. Before you decide that a visit here will take too much weight out of your wallet, read on. By choosing carefully, you can maintain your budget and experience the new Oslo. No longer a modest little town, it has blossomed dramatically to become a city in vibrant full bloom. Don't miss it.

1. FROM A BUDGET TRAVELER'S POINT OF VIEW

OSLO BUDGET BESTS

Bicycling around Oslo's northern hills is not only inexpensive, it is, hands down, one of the city's best experiences. Even if you're not feeling particularly strong, you can take your bike up by train and coast the whole way back into the city! Don't miss this unique opportunity.

Because tickets to the National Theater are substantially subsidized, a great night out will only cost 105–155 Kr ($16.15–$23.85), and is discounted an additional 20% with the Oslo Card (see "Special Discount Opportunities," below).

Opera and ballet tickets for all seats at the Norske Opera, the city's main stage, fall to half price two hours before the performance.

WHAT THINGS COST IN OSLO	U.S. $
Taxi within the town center	10.65
Underground from the train station to an outlying neighborhood	2.30
Local telephone call	.30
Double room at the Grand Hotel (deluxe)	314.00
Double room at Cochs Pensjonat (moderate)	75.40
Double room at Oslo Sjømannshjem (budget)	43.10
Lunch for one, without wine, at Cafe Norrøna (moderate)	9.00
Lunch for one, without wine, at Aulakielleren (budget)	6.50
Dinner for one, without wine, at the Theatercaféen (deluxe)	25.50
Dinner for one, without wine, at Onkel Oswald (moderate)	15.50
Dinner for one, without wine, at Cafe Norrøna (budget)	9.40
Pint of beer or glass of wine	5.55
Coca-Cola at a café	3.10
Cup of coffee at a café	2.20
Roll of ASA 100 color film, 36 exposures	10.45
Admission to Viking Ships Museum	2.30
Movie ticket	6.90
Theater ticket (National Theater)	16.15

SPECIAL DISCOUNT OPPORTUNITIES

FOR STUDENTS Students with an ID to prove their status get discounted admission to most of the city's museums and half-price tickets to the National Theater and the Oslo Concert Hall. **Univers Reiser,** Universitetssentret (Postboks 54/55), Blindern 0313 Oslo 3 (tel. 02/85-32-00), sells discount train and plane tickets to students and young people under 26. It's open Monday through Friday from 8:15am to 3:45pm.

FOR SENIORS Those 65 years old and over are entitled to deep discounts at the Oslo Concert Hall, the Norske Opera, and the National Theater. See individual listings below for details.

Lower entrance fees at museums and other attractions are available only to Scandinavians who are older than 65. However, those from elsewhere who are older than 60 with an ID to prove it may buy the economical Oslo Card for half price; this card allows them free admittance to museums and other attractions.

FOR EVERYONE The **Oslo Card** entitles tourists to free museum entry, free public transportation, and good discounts on a variety of activities throughout the capital, including half price on sightseeing tours by bus or boat. The card is for one, two, or three days, and costs 95, 135, and 165 Kr ($14.60, $20.75, and $25.40), respectively. Even if this sounds expensive, you will find that on heavy sightseeing days it will save you money. Cards can be bought at the tourist information centers (listed below in "Information" in "Orientation and Getting Around"), in Oslo City and Aker Brygge shopping complexes, and at post offices throughout Norway.

WHAT'S SPECIAL ABOUT OSLO

The "Marka"
☐ Dense forest surrounding the city, perfect for biking, hiking, and skiing.

Food
☐ Fresh, sweet shrimp arriving daily and sold right off the boats in the morning.
☐ Smorrbrod, a type of open-face sandwich served with delectable toppings.
☐ Norwegian salmon.

Cafés
☐ Theatercaféen, one of the world's last "grand cafés."
☐ The cafés along Karl Johans Gate and Bogstadveien—so comfortable you can easily spend an afternoon relaxing in them.

Aker Brygge
☐ Former shipyard turned waterfront shopping, dining, entertainment complex.

The Museums of Bygdøy
☐ Mostly nautical in theme.
☐ One of the biggest thrills is getting there by ferry.

Sculpture
☐ The Vigeland Sculpture Garden in Frogner Park, powerful and provocative.

Picnicking
☐ Munching in Frogner Park, the Norwegian Folk Museum, or on the cliffs of Akershus Fortress.

WORTH THE EXTRA BUCKS

Enjoying Oslo doesn't mean unloading a bundle of money on a single extravagance. Sure, you can go dog sledding, or take a Land Rover "safari" through the woods (contact the tourist board for more information), but that's not what Oslo is really about. Spend your money relaxing in a special café (Theatercaféen, perhaps?) or biking around the city. Enjoy the seafood. Experience the city's pulsating nightlife. These activities are truly worth the money.

2. PRETRIP PREPARATIONS

DOCUMENTS Citizens of the United States, Great Britain, Canada, Australia, and New Zealand need no special documents other than a passport to visit Norway.

WHAT TO PACK As always, good walking shoes are a must. Not only will you be strolling downtown, on the docks, and through the malls, but sturdy shoes are needed for bicycling and exploring the beautiful countryside. Summers are usually cooler here than on the Continent, so a sweater or medium-weight jacket can come in handy. For a winter visit, pack warm undergarments (don't laugh at long-johns), and a heavy coat.

Norway's enormously high taxes on alcohol are quite sobering, so if you want to drink without taking out a mortgage, buy a bottle duty-free before entering the country. Ditto for tobacco. Overseas visitors may import up to one liter of alcohol and 200 cigarettes.

WHEN TO GO Oslo greets visitors most hospitably in the summer, when the sun hangs long in the sky (more than 18 hours a day in June and July) and the air is warm. Although the Gulf Stream protects the city from extreme winter temperatures, the sun only shines for a few hours a day. Locals recommend a visit in the month of May, when the fruit trees are flowering and the city takes on added festivity for its National Day, May 17. (In western Norway in May you'll find a striking panorama of flowers, green valleys, and snow still on the mountains.)

Oslo's Average Daytime Temperature & Rainfall

	Jan	Feb	Mar	Apr	May	June	July	Aug	Sept	Oct	Nov	Dec
Temp. (°F)	23	24	31	41	51	59	64	61	53	43	34	28
Rainfall "	1.9	1.4	1	1.7	1.7	2.8	3.2	3.7	3.2	2.9	2.5	2.5

Special Events   During the summer, hardly a week passes without a special event worthy of a visit. Whether it's the **Opera Festival** in July, the **Jazz Festival** and **Chamber Music Festival** in August, the **Ibsen Festival** from late August to mid-September, or the **marathon** in September, something's always bubbling.

In winter, there's the **Oslo Snow Festival** in February and March. In 1993 the city will host the **World Cycling Championship.**

The 10-day **Holmenkollen Ski Festival** in March is one of the year's most popular events. More than 60,000 spectators jostle for space on the last day to witness the thrilling ski-jumping competition.

May 17 is **Constitution Day,** Norway's celebration of itself. A colorful children's parade is one of the day's highlights, when costume-clad kids wind their way through the streets of Oslo.

On **December 10,** when the Nobel Peace Prize is awarded, the city shines under the spotlight of international attention.

3. ORIENTATION & GETTING AROUND

ARRIVING IN OSLO

FROM THE AIRPORT   **Fornebu Airport** (tel. 59-36-13), located 5½ miles from the city center, is modern, welcoming, and the country's most important airport for domestic and international flights, and entry into it affords a picturesque view of Oslo and the Oslo Fjord. Airport services include a baggage-check office (tel. 59-31-44) and a bank, both of which are open long hours. It costs 20 Kr ($3.10) to check a bag for 24 hours and at least that much to change money.

Airport buses (*flybussen*) shuttle between the main terminal and Oslo's Airport Bus Terminal behind Central Station—a 20- to 25-minute ride—and cost 35 Kr ($5.40) (free for children under 16). The bus generally departs every 15 minutes from 6:30am to 10:30pm; there is also an 11:10pm bus.

Less-frequent, slower **city buses** make the same trip and only charge about 17 Kr ($2.60). Bus no. 31 leaves from just outside the terminal and is free with an Oslo Card (see "Special Discount Opportunities" in "From a Budget Traveler's Point of View," above).

A **taxi** to central Oslo will cost about 90 Kr ($13.85), a good option if you are traveling in a group of three or four.

If you've flown in on a charter, you may arrive at **Gardermoen Airport,** 31 miles (50 minutes) from the city center. Airport buses meet these flights and cost 60 Kr ($9.25). Buses to Gardermoen depart from the Airport Bus Terminal two hours before each charter flight.

The SAS telephone number is 06/17-00-20.

FROM THE TRAIN STATION   Oslo's new **Central Station** is reminiscent of an airport—moving walkways and all. Located downtown, the station is an important hub housing several useful services.

The **Oslo Tourist Board** staffs a window (tel. 17-11-24) that's very useful for general information and hotel accommodations (see "Budget Accommodations," below). It's located on the right-hand side, just before the main exit, and is open daily from 8am to 11pm (hours are more restricted in winter).

A **post office and a bank** flank the tourist board's window. The bank offers good rates and is open Monday through Friday from 8am to 7:30pm, on Saturday from 10am to 5pm, and on Sunday from noon to 6pm. The post office (tel. 40-73-99) is open Monday through Friday from 7am to 6pm and on Saturday from 9am to 2pm.

Baggage lockers are located on the promenade above the main hall and cost 20 or 30 Kr ($3.10 or $4.60) per day, depending on size. The area is open from 7am to 11pm, and locked at night. A **checked-baggage area,** open long hours, is in the main hall; bags may be left for 10 Kr ($1.55) per piece for two days.

The new **Interrail Center** at Central Station has showers available from mid-June through September; towels may be rented. Pay toilets in the station cost 5 Kr (75¢); no free ones are available here or in Oslo City mall, next door.

Train tickets are sold from 6:30am to 11pm (until 11:30pm on Sunday) in the central hall. The **Railway Information Office** (tel. 17-14-00) has schedules.

To reach the metro (T-Bane), exit from the station and follow the "T" signs. For trams heading west, exit and walk to the stop on the right-hand side in front of the Oslo City mall.

INFORMATION

To ask questions, browse through brochures, book a tour, buy the Oslo Card or a specialized guidebook, or pick up the free publications *What's On in Oslo* and *Oslo Guide '93,* visit the **Norway Information Center,** across the street from City Hall (tel. 02/33-43-86). It's open Monday through Friday from 9am to 6pm and on Saturday and Sunday from 9am to 4pm; closed major holidays. The Norway Information Center provides more than information; you can book hotel accommodations and buy postcards, T-shirts (some with '93 Winter Olympics logos), Oslo bags, and even lunch or early supper in the café on the premises. There are also exhibitions, telephones, restrooms, and a continuously shown film about Norway.

You can also get help from the **Tourist Information Window** (tel. 17-11-24) in Central Station, open conveniently longer hours, daily from 8am to 11pm, except holidays. This window also has an excellent accommodations-booking service (see "Budget Accommodations," below).

Trafikanten, under the modern neon clock tower in front of Central Station (tel. 17-70-30), answers questions about public transportation and distributes a free transport map. Even if you don't plan to make extensive use of the buses and subways, pick up the map; it's far superior to the tourist board's freebie. Open Monday through Friday from 7am to 8pm and on Saturday, Sunday, and holidays from 8am to 6pm; or you can call 17-70-30 until 11pm.

For **intercity rail information** by phone, dial 02/17-14-00.

For **SAS reservations,** call 17-00-20, 24 hours a day; the office is at Ruseløkkveien 6.

CITY LAYOUT

Oslo occupies a magnificent site, surrounded by high hills on three sides and a fabulous fjord on the fourth. In general, the city's compact and straightforward design makes getting around on foot easy. Jaywalking appears to be a national pastime.

Karl Johans Gate is Oslo's principal mile, running the length of the city's downtown, from Central Station to the Royal Palace. Much of this street is a car-free pedestrian thoroughfare, and many of the city's most important buildings, stores, and hotels (including Parliament and the National Theater) make Karl Johans Gate their address. A pedestrian park is created between Karl Johans Gate and **Stortingsgata,** an important parallel street running from Parliament to the Royal Palace.

Several blocks south, **City Hall** fronts Oslo's active port, creating a triangle with Central Station and the Royal Palace. City Hall is across the street from the main Norway Information Center and its steps are the departure point for guided city bus tours. Across the park from City Hall, ferries make regular runs to the **Bygdøy Peninsula,** site of several top museums. Step lively along the pier, however, as the city's famous shrimp fishermen unload their catch here as well!

Frogner Park, with its famous Vigeland Sculpture Garden, lies about a mile northwest of the **Royal Palace.** The park and the palace sandwich an exclusive neighborhood of tree-lined streets and turn-of-the-century homes, and should definitely be explored.

The **Aker River** divides the city into east and west; in general, prices in shops and restaurants are lower on the east side, but you'll most often find yourself on the west side.

GETTING AROUND OSLO

Because this is such a small city, you will rarely have to rely on public transportation. But when you do, tram, bus, subway, and ferry service is frequent and convenient. All four modes of public transportation share the same fare system. A one-way ride to any point in the city costs 15 Kr ($2.30). In addition to the **Oslo Card** (described above), a number of transportation discounts are available.

A **Tourist Ticket,** costing 40 Kr ($6.15), half price for children, is valid for unlimited rides within a 24-hour period, and can be purchased from either of the tourist information offices (see "Information," above).

A **"Maxi" card,** available from Trafikanten, the local transportation information center in front of Central Station, is good for seven days and sells for 140 Kr ($21.55), half price for children.

BY TRAM The capital's five tram lines, powered by overhead electrical cables, are one of Oslo's most charming features. The trolleys run roughly east-west, on either side of Karl Johans Gate. When waiting at smaller stops, signal the driver to stop. When you get on, either pay the driver, stamp your ticket in the machine, or, if you have an Oslo Card or day pass, just sit down.

BY BUS Buses are marked with two-digit numbers, and all routes converge at **Jernbanetorget,** the square in front of Central Station. Another major bus terminus is at Majorstuen. Upon entering a bus, pay the driver or let him stamp your strip ticket. On reticulated (double-length) buses, stamp your ticket in the machine.

BY SUBWAY (CALLED TUNNELBANE OR T-BANE) The eight T-Bane lines all converge at the **Stortinget** station, behind the National Theater. Either pay the person at the ticket window, stamp your card, or, if you have a pass, just walk through. The Central Station stop is called Jernbanetorget. The subway runs on a schedule you could set your watch by. One ride, within one hour, with a free transfer is 14 Kr ($2.15), half price for children. To spot a station, look for the easily recognizable blue T in a circle.

BY FERRY Ferries connect mainland Oslo with neighboring islands and the Bygdøy Peninsula. **Peninsula ferries** depart from Pier 3, in front of City Hall, and operate daily from April to the end of September and on weekends the first half of October. **Island service** runs all year, and boats depart from the point just below the castle. Ferry fares are the same as other forms of public transportation.

BY TAXI Oslo's taxis run an expensive meter. Even short rides will set you back about 50 Kr ($7.70); the flag drops at 21.30 Kr ($3.30). Prices rise 15% after 7pm. Taxis can be hailed in the street. An illuminated sign on the car's roof indicates that the cab is free for hire. To make an advance booking, call 38-80-90, but be forewarned that you'll be charged from the time the taxi leaves the stand.

BY BICYCLE Bicycling through the "Marka," the forest that surrounds the city, is the quintessential Oslo experience. Locals love the natural beauty that is literally on their doorsteps, and cycling around the city is very popular. There's no better way to spend a day in Oslo.

BY CAR If you decide to travel beyond Oslo, you might consider renting a car. Most major rental firms are represented here, including **Avis,** Munkedamsveien 27 (tel. 83-58-00); **Europcar,** Fornebu Airport (tel. 53-09-39); and **Hertz,** Fornebu Airport (tel. 53-36-47). Compare prices with a local firm, **Bislet Car Rental,** Pilestredet 70 (tel. 60-00-00).

 OSLO

American Express The Oslo agent, Winge, Karl Johans Gate 33 (tel. 42-76-50), does not cash traveler's checks of any kind; it does, however, have a machine out front that dispenses cash or traveler's checks, which can save you from having to wait in line (it's the only such machine you'll find in Norway, though American Express offices are located throughout the country). It's open Monday through Friday from 9am to 5pm (on Thursday to 6pm) and on Saturday from 10am to 2pm. Also, see "Mail," below.

Babysitters There is no central babysitting service in the city, but most hotels can make arrangements for your child.

Banks Banks are open Monday through Friday from 8:15am to 3:30pm (on Thursday until 5pm). From June through the end of August, banks close at 3pm (at 5pm on Thursday). Norwegian banks charge an unusually large commission to change money. Rates are per traveler's check, so it's best to have large denominations. Several post offices, including the Oslo Central Post Office (see "Mail," below), provide a **currency-exchange service,** Monday through Friday from 8am to 8pm and on Saturday from 9am to 3pm. At the Central Post Office, go to Windows 26–29. The rate beats the bank rate. You may find it cheaper to pay by check at stores and restaurants that accept them; the exchange rate may be lower, but you usually avoid a service fee.

Bookstores For a good selection of guidebooks and paperback fiction and nonfiction in English, go to Tanum Libris, Karl Johans Gate 41 (tel. 42-93-10), which is open Monday through Friday from 10am to 8pm and on Saturday from 10am to 5pm; or Norli, Universitets Gate 20-24 (tel. 42-91-35), open Monday through Wednesday and Friday from 9am to 5pm, on Thursday from 9am to 6pm, and on Saturday from 10am to 3pm.

Business Hours **Government offices** are open Monday through Friday from 9am to 4pm (closed weekends); some offices close in summer at 3pm. **Shops** are generally open Monday through Friday from 9am to 6pm (on Thursday to 7pm) and on Saturday from 9am to 3pm. Stores tend to stay open longer in summer, and larger stores may maintain longer hours.

Currency The Norwegian currency is the **krone** (crown), or **kroner (Kr)** in its plural form, made up of 100 **öre.** Banknotes are issued in 10, 50, 100, 500, and 1,000 kroner, and there are coins of 10 and 50 öre and 1 krone, 5 kroner, and 10 kroner.

Dentists Dentists are listed in the phone book (Vol. 1B) under "Tannlege" (tooth doctor). Emergency dental care is provided by Oslo Kommunale Tannlegevakt, Toyen Senter, Kolstadgata 18 (tel. 67-48-46), Monday through Friday from 8 to 11pm and on weekends and holidays from 11am to 2pm.

Doctors For emergency medical care, visit Oslo Kommunale Legevakt, Storgaten 40 (tel. 20-10-90), open 24 hours daily.

Drugstore **Jernbanetorgets Apotek,** Jernbanetorget 4B (tel. 41-24-82), is open 24 hours a day. For those essential supplies you forgot or have run out of, such as toiletries or a washcloth, head for Drogeri Vita, Nedre Slotts Gate 13 (tel. 42-34-21), just off Karl Johans Gate opposite Steen & Strøm department store.

Electricity Electrical appliances run on 220 volts, 50–60 cycles, in Norway. Plugs have two round pins, so you'll probably need an adapter and a transformer.

Embassies The **U.S. Embassy** is at Drammensveien 18 (tel. 44-85-50); the **Canadian Embassy** is at Oscars Gate 20 (tel. 46-69-55); and the **British Embassy**

is at Thomas Heftyesgate 8 (tel. 55-24-00). Since the nearest Australian Embassy is in Stockholm, Sweden, and the nearest New Zealand Embassy is in The Hague, Netherlands, visitors from these countries should refer themselves to the British Embassy. Addresses for other embassies can be found in *Oslo Guide '93* or the telephone book (Vol. 1B) under "Ambasador og Legasjoner."

Emergencies   For police, dial 002 or 66-90-50; to report a fire, dial 001 or 11-44-55; to request an ambulance, call 003 or 20-10-90. Jernbanetorgets Apotek, Jernbanetorget 4B (tel. 41-24-82), is a 24-hour pharmacy, located directly opposite the Central Station.

Eyeglasses   Ulf Jacobsen Optiker, Karl Johans Gate 20 (tel. 42-85-14), is located in the middle of the major shopping street. There's a good selection of frames, and an optometrist on duty. It's open Monday and Wednesday through Friday from 9am to 5pm, on Tuesday from 9am to 6pm, and on Saturday from 10am to 2pm. Krogh Optikk, opposite Ulf Fakobsen, Karl Johans Gate 19 (tel. 42-70-32), has a large selection of frames, and is open Monday through Friday from 9am to 6pm and on Saturday from 9am to 3pm; there's another location in Oslo City.

Holidays   January 1 (New Year's Day), Holy Thursday and Good Friday, Easter Monday, Ascension Day, Whit Monday, May 1 (Labor Day), May 17 (National Day), and December 25 and 26 (Christmas).

Hospitals   The Oslo Kommunale Legevakt, Storgaten 40 (tel. 20-10-90 or 11-70-80), provides 24-hour service for accidents, ambulance, and hospital admissions. The Oslo Red Cross, Frederik Stangs Gate 11-13 (tel. 44-39-80), is open Monday through Friday from 8am to 3pm and on Saturday from 7:30am to 1pm.

Information   Oslo boasts the excellent Norway Information Center, across the street from the City Hall (tel. 33-43-86), and a smaller office in Central Station (tel. 83-00-50), which keeps longer hours. See "Orientation and Getting Around," above, for more information.

Laundry   Expect to pay about 50 Kr ($7.70) for soap, washing, and drying, more if an attendant loads for you, so ask in advance. It's a good idea to call and check hours (the Tourist Information Office keeps an up-to-date listing of laundries and their

THE KRONE & THE DOLLAR

At this writing $1 = approximately 6.5 Kr (or 1 krone = 15¢) and this was the rate of exchange used to calculate the dollar values given in this chapter (rounded to the nearest nickel). This rate fluctuates from time to time and may not be the same when you travel to Norway. Therefore the following table should be used only as a guide:

Kr	U.S.$	Kr	U.S.$
1	.15	50	7.69
2	.31	75	11.54
3	.46	100	15.38
4	.62	150	23.08
5	.77	200	30.77
6	.92	250	38.46
7	1.08	300	46.15
8	1.23	350	53.85
9	1.38	400	61.54
10	1.54	450	69.23
15	2.31	500	76.92
20	3.08	550	84.62
25	3.85	600	92.31

locations); figure on spending a couple of hours when you go. Bislett Bask og Rens, Theresesgate 25 (tel. 46-21-79), is open Monday through Friday from 9am to 7pm and on Saturday from 9am to 3pm. Majorstua Myntvaskeri, Vibes Gate 15 (tel. 69-43-17), is open Monday through Friday from 8am to 8pm, on Saturday from 8am to 5pm, and on Sunday from noon to 5pm. AS Myntvask, 15 Ullevålsveien (tel. 14-00-08), maintains the longest hours, daily from 7am to 9pm; it's about eight blocks north of Stortinget. It has an extra-large machine for sleeping bags.

Lost and Found   The Hittegodskontoret (Lost Property Office), Gronlandsleiret 44 (tel. 66-98-65), is open Monday through Friday from 8:15am to 3pm (from May 15 to September 14, until 2:15pm). If you lost something on a train, try Central Station's Lost Property Office (tel. 36-80-47), open Monday through Saturday from 9am to 4pm.

Mail   The Oslo Central Post Office, Dronningensgate 15, Oslo 1 (tel. 40-90-50), has its entrance on the corner of Prinsensgate. Aside from the usual services, this office has a currency-exchange desk (see "Banks," above), and can hold mail addressed to you and marked "Poste Restante." It's open Monday through Friday from 8am to 8pm and on Saturday from 9am to 3pm. It usually takes about a week for a letter from abroad to arrive in Oslo, and vice versa. Mail between the Scandinavian countries takes two to three days. If you're particularly frugal, you may want to bring postcards from home; otherwise, you'll often pay about $1 per card. Postage is an additional 5.20 Kr (80¢) in postage, for cards or letters. Buy stamps from windows marked FRIMERKER, usually nos. 14 and 15. Poste Restante pickup is at Windows 20 and 21.

American Express card and traveler's check holders can collect their mail from **American Express,** c/o Winge, Postboks 1705, Vika, 0121 Oslo 1. The Winge office, at Karl Johans Gate 33 (tel. 42-76-50), is open Monday through Friday from 9am to 5pm (on Thursday to 6pm) and on Saturday from 10am to 2pm.

Newspapers   The newsstand at the National Theater end of Karl Johans Gate, beside the subway entrance, has the best selection of international publications and keeps long hours: Monday through Friday from 7am to 11pm, on Saturday from 9am to 11pm, and on Sunday from 10am to 11pm. A kiosk selling newspapers at the other end of Karl Johans Gate, at the Domed Church, is open 24 hours a day.

In the second-floor reading room of the Deichman Library, Henrik Ibsens Gate 1 (tel. 20-43-35), you can read English-language newspapers and magazines. It's open Monday through Friday from 10am to 8pm and on Saturday from 9am to 3pm (in summer, Monday through Friday to 6pm).

Photographic Needs   Film and processing can be bought all over town, especially along Karl Johans Gate. Moto Foto, Stranden 3, Aker Brygge (tel. 83-06-24), does one-hour photo finishing, but it doesn't come cheaply: 195 Kr ($30) for 36 prints. It's open Monday through Friday from 10am to 8pm and on Saturday from 10am to 6pm.

Police   For emergencies dial 002 or 66-90-50. Police Headquarters is at Grønlandsleiret 44 (tel. 66-90-50).

Radio/TV   There are two state-owned radio stations and a lot of private ones. During summer, Oslo tourist information is broadcast on 109.2 FM during the first five minutes of every hour.

Television sets in Oslo can receive two Swedish stations and the single Norwegian signal. A second Norwegian station, TV2 from Bergen, is in the works. Happily, many hotels are wired for cable. American and English programs are popular, and are all broadcast in their original language.

Religious Services   Norway is officially Lutheran. The American Lutheran Church, Fritnersgate 15 (tel. 44-35-84), holds Sunday services at 11am from September to May, and at 10am during the summer. St. Olav's Church, Akersveien 1 (tel. 36-23-60), is a well-located Catholic church; the Quaker congregation, Vennenes Samfunn Kvekerne, Meltzers Gate 1 (tel. 44-01-87), holds Quaker meetings; Det Mosaiske Trossamfund Synagogue, Bergstien 13 (tel. 69-29-66), holds Jewish services; and the Islamic Cultural Center, Youngsgate 7 (tel. 20-87-51), can refer Muslims to the appropriate mosque.

Shoe Repair   In the department store Steen and Strøm, Kongensgate 23 (tel. 41-68-00), Mister Minit maintains a shoe-repair booth on the ground floor, which closes one hour before the store does. There's also a Mister Minit in the Oslo City shopping complex near the train station (tel. 17-09-38).

Student Resources   Oslo University is divided into two campuses: one on Karl Johans Gate and the other (newer) to the north. Stick to the city, as the brick-and-concrete suburban campus is hardly worth the trek. Downtown, most students hang out in the square in front of the National Theater, on the steps in front of the university building on Karl Johans Gate, and in Aulakielleren, a university cafeteria listed below under "Budget Dining."

Tax   The Value-Added Tax (VAT), 18% in Norway, is already figured in all hotel, restaurant, and store price tages. See "Savvy Shopping," below, to learn how you can recover VAT for purchases over 300 Kr ($50.40).

Taxis   As mentioned above under "Orientation and Getting Around," taxis in Oslo can be very expensive. Even a group of four rarely justifies a cab's prices. Taxis can be hailed on the street, at Central Station, and at major hotels. Make advance reservations one hour ahead by dialing 33-80-90.

Telephone   The area code for Oslo is 02, and all telephone numbers in this chapter assume this prefix, unless otherwise noted. Directory Inquiries (information) for numbers throughout Scandinavia can be reached free by dialing 0180; for numbers outside Scandinavia, call the international operator at 0115.

Some pay phones work like the ones you're used to. In others, you must put two 1-krone coins on the ramp on top of the phone, then dial the number. When the call is answered, the coins should drop; if they don't, the phone is broken and the call cannot be completed. Local calls start at 2 Kr (30¢); a tone will sound after a few minutes if you have to insert more coins. After 5pm, 2 Kr buys nine minutes of talk time.

To call the United States collect or with your AT&T Calling Card, dial USA Direct (tel. 050-12-011). This local phone number will put you in touch with an American operator. Alternatively, you can make long-distance calls from the pleasant Telecommunications Office, Kongensgate 21 (tel. 40-55-09), with an entrance on Prinsensgate. It's open Monday through Friday from 8am to 9pm and on Saturday and Sunday from 10am to 5pm. Calls to the United States cost about 12 Kr ($1.85) per minute Monday through Friday from 10am to 10pm, 10 Kr ($1.55) after 10pm and all day Sunday. It's cheaper, however, if you call collect or use a calling card. The office has phone books for Sweden, Denmark, and Finland.

Tipping   Restaurants and hotels usually include a 10% service charge in the menu price, so it's rarely necessary to tip. If you've particularly enjoyed the service, round up the bill to the nearest 5% or 10%; this is true for taxis, too. For example, if the taxi fare is 84 Kr, give the driver 90 Kr.

4. BUDGET ACCOMMODATIONS

Budget accommodations exist in Oslo—it just takes a little effort to unearth them. Price-wise, your best bet is a private room. Then try some of the smaller hotels and pensions. Keep in mind that most hotels that are usually above this book's budget offer phenomenal summer and/or weekend bargains—one third to one quarter the regular rates. The list below is by no means exhaustive.

If you prefer to reserve a hotel room before you arrive, write at least three weeks in advance to **Oslo Promotion,** Tourist Information, Vestbarneplassen 1, 0205 Oslo 2. Send your name and address, the dates of your stay, your price category and comfort standards, and a 100-Kr ($15.35) deposit, including a 30-Kr ($4.60) service charge.

You will receive a written confirmation. Note that they will not reserve private rooms ahead of time, nor do they work with all the hotels listed below.

Oslo's best bargain bed cannot be reserved in advance, so cross your fingers (unlike Stockholm and Copenhagen, Oslo does not have many private homes that offer rooms to travelers) and belly up to the **Oslo Information** window in Central Station (tel. 17-11-24), located on your right side before the main exit. This office places tourists in private homes and charges 150 Kr ($23.10) single, 250 Kr ($38.45) double. There is an additional 35 Kr ($5.40) charge if you plan to stay only one night. Most rooms are a 15- to 20-minute public transport ride. There is a 17-Kr ($2.60) per-person booking fee. Additionally, this handy office sells unused hotel rooms on the day of arrival for up to 50%–75% off. Hotels offer such large discounts because business travel drops sharply in summer. This competition makes some of the small hotels and pensions more willing to negotiate their own room rates. The window at the train station is open daily from 8am to 11pm in summer; hours are more restricted off-season.

DOUBLES FOR LESS THAN 265 KR [$40.75]

NEAR CENTRAL STATION

OSLO SJØMANNSHJEM, Tollbugata 4, 0154 Oslo. Tel. 02/41-20-05. 48 rms (none with toilet; 8 with shower). **Directions:** Enter the hotel from Frederik Olsensgate, on a quiet street just a two-block walk from Central Station; look for the sign SJØMANNSHJEMMET.

$ Rates: On the women-only and coed floors, 210 Kr ($32.30) single; 280 Kr ($43.10) double. On the men-only floor, 240 Kr ($36.90) double (no singles). Breakfast, available only in summer, about 35 Kr ($5.40). No credit cards.

 Originally an international seamen's home, today the Sjømannshjem accepts more tourists than sailors. The rooms (20 singles, 28 doubles) are spare but clean, with some furniture dating from the 1950s. Some rooms include a shower stall, but all share public toilets. Rooms are on the sixth and seventh floors, an elevator ride away from the ground-floor reception. There is a TV lounge on each floor (the sixth-floor lounge is nicer), and the staff is nice and helpful. Fancy? No, but this establishment is firmly anchored against the tide of high hotel costs.

BETWEEN THE ROYAL PALACE & FROGNER PARK

ELLINGSEN'S PENSJONAT, Holtegata 25, 0355 Oslo 3. Tel. 02/60-03-59. 20 rms (none with bath). **Tram:** 1 from Central Station to Uranienborgveien and the Uranienborg Church, four blocks past the Royal Palace; then a two-minute walk.

F   FROMMER'S SMART TRAVELER: HOTELS

VALUE-CONSCIOUS TRAVELERS SHOULD
TAKE ADVANTAGE OF THE FOLLOWING:

1. Private homes, the cheapest type of accommodation.
2. Pensions, called *pensonjats*, which provide basic but clean, comfortable, well-situated accommodations.
3. Summer and weekend bargains at many hotels.
4. The Oslo Information window in Central Station, which will place you in a private home or help you find a hotel room.

$ Rates: 160 Kr ($24.60) single; 260 Kr ($40) double. No credit cards.
The Ellingsen's friendly English-speaking owner, Ms. Malfrid Wecking, has been offering incredible value in this stately residential area since 1966. The rooms (17 singles and 3 doubles, none with bath) are sparsely furnished, but very clean, and the bathrooms are sparkling. No breakfast is served here, but cafés are nearby, as is a laundromat. The house, which has no identifying sign out front, is a pretty building with a wrought-iron fence out front; buzz no. 1 when you arrive.

FARTHER OUT

CARL AND SYNNØVE CASPARI, Heggeliveien 55, 0375 Oslo. Tel. 02/14-57-70. 3 rms (sometimes 4). **T-Bane:** 14 or 16 to Heggeli (from Central Station, change to the 14 or 16 at Stortinget); they're across the street, the first house on the right.
$ Rates: 250 Kr ($38.45) double. Breakfast, served in your room, 45 Kr ($6.90) extra. No credit cards.
Mr. Caspari and his wife, born of American parents, are both teachers, and they rent attractive rooms in their two-story white home in a pleasant neighborhood just northwest of Frogner Park. It's a 10-minute ride from the city center, and the good public transportation links and great value earn it special recognition. Add to that a garden filled with fruit trees in which to relax, a grocery store next door, and the Vigeland Sculpture Park a five-minute walk away. A white house peeking over a brown fence, it's easy to spot from the train platform. The Casparis prefer that you do not write ahead, but call just before or upon arrival.

DOUBLES FOR LESS THAN 500 KR [$76.90]

BETWEEN THE ROYAL PALACE & FROGNER PARK

COCHS PENSJONAT, Parkveien 25, 0350 Oslo 3. Tel. 02/60-48-36. Fax 02/46-54-02. 64 rms (most with shower). **Tram:** 1, 2, or 11 from Central Station to Parkveien.
$ Rates: 290 Kr ($44.60) single without shower, 370 Kr ($56.90) single with shower; 370 Kr ($56.90) double without shower, 490 Kr ($75.40) double with shower; 450 Kr ($69.25) triple without shower, 570 Kr ($87.70) triple with shower; 520 Kr ($80) quad without shower, 640 Kr ($98.45) quad with shower. V.
Cochs offers an excellent value in a prime location—half a block from the Royal Palace grounds, behind the palace at the beginning of Hegdehaugsveien. The recently renovated rooms (10 singles, 29 doubles, 13 triples, 12 quads) include new baths, furniture, and contemporary decor. Most rooms are equipped with a small kitchen (utensils must be borrowed from reception), and all are well lit and kept very clean. Travelers have found lodging here since 1905. There's a handy market a block away, plus guests receive a 20% discount at a popular restaurant up the street. You can walk to almost all of Oslo's attractions from Cochs; if you will be arriving via airport bus, get off at the last stop. The pension is a particular bargain for three or four people traveling together.

PENSION HALL HOTEL, Fritnersgate 21 (off Bygdøy Allé), 0264 Oslo 2. Tel. 02/44-32-33 or 55-77-26. 34 rms (2 with shower). TV TEL **Bus:** 30, 31, 41, 72, or 73 from Central Station; ask the driver to let you off at Frogner Church, a two-minute walk from the hotel.
$ Rates: 405 Kr ($62.30) single without shower; 540 Kr ($83.10) double without shower, 660 Kr ($101.55) double with shower. Laundry free to 30 Kr ($4.60) for a wash and dry. AE, DC, EURO, MC, V.
Although this hotel is home mostly to permanent residents, you can usually find a room here (16 singles, 13 twins, 5 family rooms). Attributes include unusually large

rooms, very clean, tiled public bathrooms, large tiled showers, 24-hour reception, and an easy-going ambience. Call a couple of days ahead.

NEAR CENTRAL STATION

CITY HOTEL, Skippergate 19 (Postboks 763), Sentrum, 0106 Oslo 1. Tel. 02/41-36-10. Fax 02/42-24-29. 56 rms (23 with shower).
$ Rates (including breakfast): 375 Kr ($57.70) single without shower, 480 Kr ($73.85) single with shower; 550 Kr ($84.60) double without shower, 650 Kr ($100) double with shower. AE, DC, EURO, MC, V.

Since warm and welcoming Aud Eggum took over as owner/manager in 1991, the City Hotel has undergone a metamorphosis of redecorating and general sprucing up. Soft colors and pleasant furnishings have replaced the haphazard decor of years past, and each room has a sink and a desk; happily, the prices remain reasonable, albeit slightly higher than the other listings in this category. The hotel is cozy (you're free to use the piano in the lounge upstairs) and well located—two blocks from the train station and one block from Karl Johans Gate and from the post office. Rooms on the fifth floor are the nicest. Complimentary coffee and snacks are served at 5pm daily, and guests may buy snacks from reception at other times.

HOTEL FØNIX, Dronningens Gate 19, N-0154 Oslo 1. Tel. 02/42-59-57. Fax 02/33-12-10. 56 rms (16 with shower and toilet, 4 with toilet only). TEL
$ Rates (including breakfast): 300–370 Kr ($46.15–$56.90) single without shower, 400–460 Kr ($61.55–$70.75) single with shower; 450–550 Kr ($69.25–$84.60) double without shower, 500–650 Kr ($76.90–$100) double with shower. Extra bed 200 Kr ($30.75). Prices drop 100 Kr ($17.25) on weekends if rooms are available. AE, DC, EURO, MC, V.

Located just south of Karl Johans Gate, three blocks from the train station, the Fønix is well situated and physically appealing, but it's a better bet for those who choose a room with a private bath than without. Otherwise, you may have to go to a different floor, at the end of a long hallway, to get to a toilet or shower. All the rooms, however, have sinks and modern Scandinavian furnishings. Choose one in the back, away from the city noise. The hotel has a restaurant and pub, and homemade apple-jack is served at breakfast.

WEEKEND & SUMMER SPECIALS

Many hotels catering to businesspeople lower their rates on weekends and from June to the end of August. Normally these well-appointed hotel rooms far exceed our budget, making the special rates listed below really special.

AMI HOTELL, Norhadl Bruns Gate 9, 0165 Oslo. Tel. 02/36-18-01. Fax 02/11-61-10. 38 rms (most with shower). TV TEL **Bus:** 37 from Central Station.
$ Rates (including breakfast): Weekends 340 Kr ($52.30) single without shower, 440–540 Kr ($67.70–$83.10) single with shower; 590 or 640 Kr ($90.10 or $98.45); Extra person 140 Kr ($21.55). DC, EURO, MC, V.

Opened in June 1991, near the National Gallery, the Ami is modern, quiet, and pleasantly decorated with dark wood, soft colors, and art prints, and it's one of Oslo's best weekend bargains. The staff will even order in pizza for you, and on a warm day you can eat it outside in a small courtyard. Most rooms, except for some singles, have private bath, telephone, and cable TV. Rooms are in two buildings, one with an elevator; some can accommodate three to four people; and some no-smoking rooms are available. The hotel is a five-minute walk from Karl Johans Gate.

CECIL HOTEL, Stortings Gate 8, 0161 Oslo 1. Tel. 02/42-70-00. Fax 02/42-26-70. 112 rms (all with toilet and shower). TV TEL MINIBAR **Tram:** Stortinget or Nationaltheatret.
$ Rates (including breakfast): Weekends, 400 Kr ($61.55) single; 500 Kr ($76.90) single bed and sofa bed; 600 Kr ($92.30) double. Weekday rates about 50% higher. Children under 12 stay free in parents' room. AE, DC, EURO, MC, V.

Opened in late 1989, this hotel with its sophisticated lobby and nine-story atrium looks pricier than it is. Ideally located in the heart of town, it features 100 single and combination rooms with a single bed and sofa bed, 10 double rooms, and two suites, all with cheerful decor. Breakfast is served until 11am on Saturday and 12:30pm on Sunday for slugabeds, and complimentary coffee and tea are available from 7am to 11pm. Note to the claustrophobic: Most rooms are climate-controlled and most windows cannot be opened.

GYLDENLØVE HOTEL, Bogstadveien 20, 0355 Oslo 3. Tel. 02/60-10-90.
Fax 02/60-33-90. 159 rms (100 with shower). TV TEL **Tram:** 1 or 11 from Central Station to Bogstadveien.

$ **Rates** (including breakfast): In summer and on weekends year round, 290 Kr ($44.60) single without shower, 320–420 Kr ($49.25–$64.60) single with shower; 400 Kr ($61.55) double without shower, 450–600 Kr ($69.25–$92.30) double with shower. Weekdays the rest of the year, prices jump 30%–40%. AE, DC, EURO, MC, V.

This hotel gets mention for its good location (between the Royal Palace and the Vigeland Sculpture Park), its large, well-decorated rooms, its two no-smoking floors, its smart marble lobby, and its good rates. Almost all the rooms are spacious and quiet, and the shared baths are well tended and modern. A couple of the rooms with private bath have a tub, for those who prefer one, and all rooms have a sink. Some of the private baths are tiny with no shower curtain, so check it out before checking in. Coffee is provided for guests 24 hours a day. Reserve ahead in summer.

NORRØNA HOTELL, Grensen 19, 0159 Oslo 1. Tel. 02/42-64-00. Fax 02/33-25-65. 49 rms (46 with shower, 2 with bath). TV TEL **T-Bane:** Stortinget.

$ **Rates** (including breakfast): Weekends year round, 395 Kr ($60.75) single; 550 Kr ($84.60) double. Weekdays June–Sept, 550 Kr ($84.60) single; 650 Kr ($100) double; extra bed 120 Kr ($18.45). Weekdays the rest of the year, prices shoot up 30%–50%. AE, DC, EURO, MC, V.

Centrally located near the major shopping streets, the Norrøna boasts a restaurant and modern conveniences like hairdryers, cable TV, and radios in the rooms. This is a quiet, comfortable hotel with a TV lounge, and soda, milk, and open-face sandwiches available for guests. No-smoking rooms are available, as well as comfortable family rooms for three to five people. All rooms have twin beds; 10 have balconies. Its popular cafeteria features reasonably priced meals and filling Norwegian home-cooking. The hotel and cafeteria are owned by the Norwegian Lutheran Mission and no alcohol is served.

NORUM HOTEL, Bygdøy Allé 53, 0265 Oslo 2. Tel. 02/44-79-90. Fax 02/44-92-39. 59 rms (all with bath). MINIBAR TV TEL **Bus:** 30, 31, 40, or 41.

$ **Rates** (including breakfast): Fri–Sun, 500 Kr ($76.90) single; 600 Kr ($92.30) double. Mon–Thurs, rates rise about 100 Kr ($15.40). ACCESS, AE, DC, EURO, MC, V.

Only a five-minute walk from the Vigeland Sculpture Park, this old-fashioned hotel, with rooms wallpapered with delicate patterns, high ceilings, tall windows, and a spiral stair, has been in the Mathison family for three generations. Personal touches are everywhere—from the homey atmosphere to the helpful staff to the grandfather clocks scattered throughout the hallways. There is a bright, country-style breakfast room and also a restaurant and bar on the premises. The building itself is striking: ivy-covered and somewhat castlelike. The downside is that the baths are quite small and there is not enough closet space for two people. Ask for a room facing a side street and you can peek across into the windows of a genteel European apartment building. Downtown Oslo is a quick bus ride away.

SUPER-BUDGET CHOICES

A HOSTEL

HARALDSHEIM VANDRERHJEM, Haraldsheimvn. 4 (Postboks 41),

Grefsen, 0409 Oslo 4. Tel. 02/15-50-43 or 22-29-65. Fax 02/71-34-97. 270 beds. **Tram:** 1 or 7 to Sinsen, the last stop; then a five-minute walk up the hill. **Train:** EurailPass holders can commute free by local train (25 daily departures from Central Station).

$ Rates (including breakfast): IYHF members, 140 Kr ($21.55) per person in a shared room without shower or toilet, 160 Kr ($24.60) per person in a shared room with shower and toilet; 225 Kr ($34.60) single without shower or toilet, 315 Kr ($48.45) single with shower and toilet; 385 Kr ($59.25) double without shower or toilet, 455 Kr ($70) double with shower and toilet. Nonmembers pay 25 Kr ($3.85) additional. Sheets 35 Kr ($5.40) extra; towels, 7 Kr ($1.10). No credit cards. **Closed:** Dec 23–Jan 3.

The hostel is 20 minutes from downtown Oslo, but its low prices and great facilities make up for the slight inconvenience. Most rooms have four beds, and some rooms in the newer section have a shower and toilet. In addition to its cafeteria, and cooking and laundry facilities, the hostel offers what may be the best breakfast in Oslo—an all-you-can-eat buffet. Lunch and dinner are available for 55 Kr and 70 Kr ($8.45 and $10.75), respectively, and a picnic lunch goes for 30 Kr ($4.60). The hostel imposes no curfew; there's a three-day maximum stay in summer.

OSLO'S YMCA

INTERRAIL POINT, KFUM, Møllergata 1, 0179 Oslo 1. Tel. 02/42-10-66. 60 beds. **Directions:** Walk from Central Station.

$ Rates: About 90 Kr ($13.85) per person per night. No credit cards. **Open:** Early July to mid-Aug.

For most of July and half of August only, the local YMCA spreads mattresses across its cellar in two rooms—one for men, the other for women. Although it's not as comfortable as the hostel, the rates and location are better. You must have a sleeping bag, and there is a three-night maximum stay. It's open from 8 to 11am and 5pm to midnight, when the doors are locked and a curfew is imposed. Enter from Grubbegata under the KFUM sign.

CAMPING

If you have a tent, you can camp free on the island of Langøyene, just a 10-minute ferry ride from the Aker Brygge dock June through August. There is also a nude beach on this pretty island. The only drawback is that the last ferry departs at 7:30pm.

BOGSTAD CAMPING AND TURISTSENTER, Akersveien 117, 0757 Oslo 7. Tel. 02/50-76-80. 40 cabins. **Bus:** 41 to Bogstad.

$ Rates: 410 Kr ($63.10) small cabins without bath for up to four campers; 670 Kr ($103.10) large cabins with bath for up to six campers. Sheets 50 Kr ($7.70) extra. Tent sites 100 Kr ($15.40) for one or two people. AE, EURO, MC, V.

Located in the Holmenkollen Ski Jump area, Bogstad boasts the largest campground in northern Europe. This is no ordinary campground either. The heavily wooded complex is surrounded by shops, a restaurant, a laundry, and a post office, and is so pretty that it could have served as the set for *Song of Norway*. Large and small cabins, accommodating up to six and four people respectively, are so well equipped it's hardly camping. Each has beds, a stove, a refrigerator, and utensils; in addition, the large cabins have TVs. Write in advance to reserve cabin space as demand is heavy. Of course, there is a large area for tents, too.

WORTH THE EXTRA BUCKS

HOTELL BONDEHEIMEN, Rosenkrantz Gate 8, 0159 Oslo 1. Tel. 02/42-95-30. Fax 02/41-94-37. 76 rms (all with bath). MINIBAR TV TEL **Tram:** Stortinget or Nationaltheatret.

$ Rates (including breakfast, service charge, and tax): May 15–Sept 15 with Best Western Hotel Cheques, 450 Kr ($75.65) single; 280 Kr ($47.05) per person double. July and weekends year round, 530 Kr ($81.55) single; 630–680 Kr double. Weekdays the rest of the year, from 780 Kr ($120) single; 1,040–1,090 Kr ($160–$167.70) double. Two children up to age 15 stay free in parents' room. AE, DC, EURO, MC, V.

Built in 1913 as a refuge for Norwegian farmers on business in the big city, the Hotell Bondeheimen still attracts primarily Norwegians but is ideal for anyone with a hankering for Norwegian design, food, and hospitality. The rooms (26 singles, 44 doubles, 6 family rooms), tastefully furnished in Norwegian pine and dusty-blue decor, feature hairdryers and a trouser press; no-smoking rooms are available. Guests may enjoy the sauna for free, and they receive a 10% discount in the hotel's outstanding cafeteria and gift shop; breakfast, included in the room price, is the heartiest in Oslo. The hotel's shop has outstanding Norwegian crafts and costumes, and the hotel staff is so helpful they even keep extra umbrellas at the desk for guests. If tram noise bothers you, ask for a room in back. Expansion plans are in the works.

5. BUDGET DINING

Nowhere is Oslo's metamorphosis into a cosmopolitan European city more apparent than on the restaurant front. There has been an explosion of upscale international eateries, most of them out of the budget-traveler range. The most economical meal of the day is lunch, when restaurants offer specials. In Norway, people eat four times a day: a hearty breakfast; a light lunch (a cold one, even in winter; workers usually bring their lunch rather than eat out since their midday break is brief and often unpaid); a heartier dinner, called *middag*, at 5pm; and tea and a snack around 8pm.

As in other Scandinavian countries, the government levies heavy taxes on alcohol, making its consumption extremely expensive. You should also know that Norway is one of the few countries defying an international ban on whaling. If you care about this endangered species, do not order whale in restaurants.

In general, Oslo's restaurants are expensive. But don't worry—you won't starve. You will, however, have to rely on supermarkets, fast-food chains, and self-service cafeterias. These eateries, and a few exceptional restaurants, are listed below.

MEALS FOR LESS THAN 45 KR ($6.90)

ARARAT, Storgata 39.
Cuisine: TURKISH. **Bus:** 2, 7, or 11.
$ Prices: Kebabs in pita bread 35–45 Kr ($5.40–$6.90); other items 20–70 Kr ($3.10–$10.75).
Open: Mon–Sat 11am–9pm.

You're guaranteed to eat well and fillingly here, yet still stick to your budget. They don't speak English, but everything—food and prices—is displayed so that you can point and order. It does help to know that *varme retter* means "warm dishes" and *sterk* (pronounced "stark") means "hot," as in spicy. Selections include yogurt and lentil soup, miniature pizzas, kebabs in pita bread, meat dishes served with a hefty salad, and baklava. With a main dish, you get all the bread you can eat. The entrance to this bright, clean eatery is on Ebbels Gate.

AULAKIELLEREN, Karl Johans Gate 47.
Cuisine: NORWEGIAN.
$ Prices: Sandwiches and pastries 10–28 Kr ($1.55–$4.30); hot meals 35–45 Kr ($5.40–$6.90). No credit cards.
Open: Mon–Fri 8am–6pm.

Although it's officially for the law students of Oslo University, no one cares who is taking advantage of one of the cheapest meals in town. Heaping portions and low prices are the norm; coffee is 5 Kr (75¢), or 1.50 Kr (15¢) for hot water if you've brought your own instant brew or tea bag, as the students do. If you want to heat up your food, use the microwave beside the soft-drink cabinet. And clean your table when you've finished. The cafeteria's location can't be beat—just across from the National Theater. Enter at the left side of the main building where the bikes are parked and follow the noise.

HOTDOG STAND, Karl Johans Gate 17, near Kongens Gate.
  Cuisine: FAST FOOD.
$ Prices: 12–20 Kr ($1.85–$3.10).
Grabbing a hot dog at the tiny kiosk on Karl Johans Gate is a long-standing Oslo tradition. Grill med brod, a little smaller than the American version, is a good choice. The kiosk is in the same buildiing as the Scotsman pub, and there's a bench nearby for munching.

KARL P. NORDBY, Dronningens Gate 25. Tel. 41-17-65.
  Cuisine: NORWEGIAN.
$ Prices: 24–40 Kr ($3.70–$6.15). No credit cards.
  Open: Mon–Fri 7:30am–5pm, Sat 9am–2:30pm.
This unassuming spot, where you're likely to be the only out-of-towner, is only half a block from Karl Johans Gate and offers sandwiches, desserts, and coffee.

MEALS FOR LESS THAN 70 KR [$10.75]

CAFE NORRØNA, in the Hotel Norrøna, Grensen 19. Tel. 42-64-00.
  Cuisine: NORWEGIAN. **T-Bane:** Stortinget.
$ Prices: Sandwiches 20–40 Kr ($3.10–$6.15); salad 18 Kr ($2.75); daily special, including coffee, 51 Kr ($7.85) noon–2pm, 61 Kr ($9.40) other hours, 85 Kr ($13.10) Sat (including dessert). No credit cards.
  Open: July–Aug 15, daily noon–5pm; Aug 16–June, Mon 10:30am–6pm, Tues–Fri 8am–6:30pm, Sat 9am–4pm. Sun noon–5pm.
Attractive butcher-block tables and plants add to the appeal of this pretty, spacious self-service cafeteria. The menu is on the counter (English translation on the back). The daily special is a hot, filling meal, served all day but at a reduced price from noon to 2pm. You might want to sample the hot sour-cream porridge, served with juice, a local favorite. The cafeteria is on the second floor of the Hotel Norrøna.

CAFE SJAKK MATT, Haakon VII Gate 5. Tel. 83-41-56.
  Cuisine: LIGHT FARE.

 **FROMMER'S SMART TRAVELER:
RESTAURANTS**

VALUE-CONSCIOUS TRAVELERS SHOULD
TAKE ADVANTAGE OF THE FOLLOWING:

1. Self-service cafeterias, where two people can order one large dish and share it.
2. Supermarkets and smaller markets, for essential picnic ingredients and ready-made sandwiches.
3. Short-order places in Aker Brygge, Paleet, and Oslo City shopping complexes.
4. Lunch and *middag* (early supper) specials at restaurants; look for the sandwich board out front displaying the price.
5. Pasta dishes, invariably the least expensive on any menu; meat and fish dishes are pricier.

$ Prices: 30–62 Kr ($4.60–$9.55). DC, V.
Open: Mon–Thurs 10am–2am, Fri 10am–3:30am, Sat noon–3:30am, Sun noon–2am.

 The prices are good, the crowd's young, and it's too old to be trendy (dating from 1983, it claims to be Oslo's first café). The name means "checkmate," and you'll find sandwiches, pasta, salad, and vegetarian dishes; breakfast is served until noon. It's a block from the Konsert Hus, tucked off Munkedamsveien.

PASTA PRONTO, Pilestredet 63A. Tel. 60-73-11.
Cuisine: ITALIAN. **Tram:** 7 from Central Station.
$ Prices: 40–60 Kr ($6.15–$9.25). No credit cards.
Open: Mon–Fri 11am–7pm, Sat 10am–3pm.

This pint-size noodle factory has a short menu and only four stools. But each of the five pasta dishes, including lasagne and tortellini, is delicious and made fresh daily. It's strictly pasta here—no salads, no side dishes. To-go orders make up the bulk of their business. The restaurant is a 10-minute walk from the Royal Palace, north of Parkveien.

STEEN & STRØM CAFETERIA, in the Steen & Strøm department store, Kongens Gate 23 (6th floor). Tel. 41-68-00.
Cuisine: NORWEGIAN.
$ Prices: Salads 39 Kr ($6) small, 58 Kr ($8.90) large; other items 25–58 Kr ($3.85–$8.90).
Open: Mon 10am–6pm, Tues–Fri 9am–6pm, Sat 9am–4pm.

You'll see people of all ages and occupations here—but few, if any, tourists. The big draw is the lunchtime salad bar, where you can choose from tuna, mussels, or shrimp mixed with corn, tomatoes, sprouts, lettuce, cottage cheese, peppers, or celery—you name it (or point to it). Vegetarian salads cost less; 25 Kr ($3.85) small or 40 Kr ($6.15) large. Sandwiches and desserts are also available, and the cafeteria has a no-smoking area.

For heartier fare and greater variety at somewhat higher prices, consider the adjacent full-service restaurant, Gamle Stua, with its Norwegian country-inn decor and ambience; the fare here includes daily specials, Norwegian porridge, sandwiches, omelets, and meat and fish dishes. Steen & Strøm is just off Karl Johans Gate.

LORRY, Parkveien 12, at Hegdehaugsveien. Tel. 69-69-04.
Cuisine: NORWEGIAN/LIGHT FARE. **Tram:** 1, 2, or 11 from Central Station to Parkveien.
$ Prices: Breakfast 33–53 Kr ($5.10–$8.15); hamburger with fries, 59 Kr ($9.10); daily specials 59–78 Kr ($9.10–$12); fish dishes 69–95 Kr ($10.60–$14.60). AE, DC, EURO, MC.
Open: Mon–Fri 8am–3am, Sat 9am–3am, Sun 11am–3am.

Popular in summer for its congenial outdoor seating and in winter for its cozy pub atmosphere, this place has something for everyone: breakfast, open-face sandwiches, burgers, daily specials, and 81 kinds of beer. If you order a brew before 5pm, it'll cost 29 Kr ($4.45); afterward, 36 Kr ($5.55). Locals congregate here morning, noon, and night, but especially at night, as they have since it opened in 1887. Lorry's is a block from the Royal Palace grounds.

NYE KAFFISTOVA, in the Hotell Bondeheimen, Rosenkrantz Gate 8. Tel. 42-95-30.
Cuisine: NORWEGIAN.
$ Prices: Hot platters 65–95 Kr ($10–$14.60); sandwiches 39–45 Kr ($6–$6.90); salads 20–31 Kr ($3.10–$4.90); homemade soup and bread 20 Kr ($3.10).
Open: Mon–Fri 10:30am–8pm, Sat 11am–5pm, Sun noon–6pm (specials served Mon–Fri 2–8pm, Sat 11am–5pm, Sun noon–6pm).

This main branch of the Kaffistova ("coffee living room") chain offers large, well-prepared Norwegian fare, with all the salad, potatoes, sauerkraut, rice, and vegetables you can eat. Main courses are served cafeteria style. Often, fruit is offered at the self-service salad bar, making a fine dessert. Lunch is served until 2pm. Rosenkrantz Gate bisects Karl Johans Gate. The entrance to the cafeteria, which is in the Hotell Bondeheimen, is just around the corner on Kristian IV Gate.

ONKEL OSWALD, Hegdehaugsveien 34. Tel. 69-05-35.
Cuisine: CONTINENTAL. **Tram:** 11.

$ **Prices:** Specials 35–79 Kr ($5.40–$12.15); main dishes 65–115 Kr ($10–$17.70). ACCESS, AE, DC, EURO, MC, V.

Open: Mon–Fri 9am–2am, Sat 10am–2am, Sun noon–2am.

Popular and lively, and named after the book by Roald Dahl, this is one of the few restaurants in Oslo that serves breakfast all day. The menu features excellent pasta dishes, along with salads and such heavier fare as lamb with garlic and creamed potatoes. You'll also find 49 kinds of beer, coffee with unlimited refills, a relaxing lounge, and outdoor dining in summer.

IN THE SHOPPING MALLS

BEACH CLUB, in Aker Brygge, Bryggetorget 14. Tel. 83-83-82.
Cuisine: AMERICAN.

$ **Prices:** Sandwiches and burgers 39–79 Kr ($6–$12.15). AE, DC, EURO, MC, V.

Open: Mon–Sat 11am–1am, Sun 1pm–1am.

The location is superb, right by the water, and in summer you can munch your tuna melt, grilled cheese sandwich, or beach burger and sip your shake at tables outside. Inside, there's a soda fountain, booths, a pool table, and various touches from Miami and L.A.; there's a DJ (the owner) on weekends from 9pm. You can get main courses here, but they'll run you $20 or so.

CHOP STICKS, in the basement of Oslo City. Tel. 17-06-05.
Cuisine: CHINESE.

$ **Prices:** 25–59 Kr ($3.85–$9.10). No credit cards.

Open: Mon–Sat 11am–9pm, Sun noon–6pm.

The Hong Kong chefs specialize in Cantonese-style food, and for a shopping mall it's pretty good. The daily special might include sweet-and-sour pork, beef chop suey, or chicken curry with rice. There is a second branch in Aker Brygge in the Hallene building.

DENIZ KEBAP, in Aker Brygge, in the Hallene building. Tel. 83-23-61.
Cuisine: TURKISH.

$ **Prices:** 20–60 Kr ($3.10–$9.25). No credit cards.

Open: Daily 10am–8pm.

Pleasant and tucked in a corner, this fast-food grill with perky blue and white tiles serves inexpensive food prepared by the Turkish owner-chef. The barekas (meat-filled filo dough pies) come in chicken or beef, and are quite tasty.

EDDI'S LILLE BAKERITEATER, in Aker Brygge, in the Hallene building. Tel. 83-06-20.
Cuisine: LIGHT FARE.

$ **Prices:** 30–40 Kr ($4.75–$6.30). No credit cards.

Open: Mon–Fri 9am–8pm, Sat 10am–6pm, Sun noon–6pm.

It's a bakery but you can also get sandwiches, rolls, and loaves of fresh-baked bread, and sit down in a relaxed setting. This little place is particularly popular with families. There's occasional free entertainment in the afternoon.

SMØR PETERSEN, in Aker Brygge. Tel. 83-83-70.
Cuisine: NORWEGIAN.

$ **Prices:** 25–80 Kr ($3.85–$12.30). No credit cards.

Open: Mon–Fri 8am–8pm, Sat 10am–6pm.

⭐ This gourmet food store sells a host of hot dishes, including grilled chicken, quiche, and lasagne. Café and bar tables sit just inside the front door. Or you can order your meal to go. A small sandwich and a cup of coffee will run about 25 Kr ($3.85) at Smør Petersen; it's located in the modern building housing the theater in the Aker Brygge complex, on Holmens Gate at Bryggetorget.

TYSK CITY GRILL, in the basement of Oslo City. Tel. 17-05-12.

Cuisine: GERMAN.

$ **Prices:** Fast food 13–49 Kr ($2.25–$8.45); dinners and beef dishes 69–108 Kr ($10.60–$16.60). No credit cards.

Open: Mon–Fri 9am–9:30pm, Sat 9am–6pm.

Come here for bratwurst and wienerschnitzel served with homemade potato salad or pea soup. Much of the fast food is served in pita bread; dinners and beef dishes exceed our budget category. Schnapps and Beck's beer are sold.

MEALS FOR LESS THAN 95 KR ($14.25)

FROGNERSTEREN, Holmenkollveien 200. Tel. 14-37-36.

Cuisine: NORWEGIAN. **T-Bane:** Holmenkollen.

$ **Prices:** Café, 65–155 Kr ($10–$23.85); sandwiches 30–80 Kr ($4.60–$12.30). Restaurant, prices double. AE, DC, EURO, MC, V.

Open: Café, daily 11am–11pm; restaurant, daily noon–11:30pm. **Closed:** Dec 24.

This mountain lodge, with a large fireplace, antler chandeliers, and a roof topped with carved dragon heads, was built in 1896. It is less famous and less touristic than the nearby Holmenkollen restaurant, and better known locally for its view than for its cuisine. The lodge's restaurant, to the left as you enter, is expensive, but the café, with several rustic rooms including a cozy nook at the top of the stairs, is reasonably priced. Both feature fish and meat dishes, including reindeer.

MAMMA ROSA, Øvre Slottsgate 12. Tel. 42-01-30.

Cuisine: ITALIAN.

$ **Prices:** Pizzas and pasta courses 65–80 Kr ($9.25–$12.30); fish and meat courses 85–160 Kr ($13.10–$24.60). AE, DC, EURO, MC, V.

Open: Mon–Sat noon–11:30pm, Sun 1–10:30pm.

This large trattoria is especially favored by tourists looking for a taste of something familiar. And that they get! Tasty, good-sized portions are served in classic Italian-American restaurant surroundings: mirrored walls, faux columns, gold-leafed lamps, and marblelike tables. Mamma Rosa overlooks Karl Johans Gate.

SAMSON, Øvre Slottsgate 21. Tel. 42-55-62.

Cuisine: NORWEGIAN.

$ **Prices:** Smorrbrod 18–48 Kr ($2.75–$7.40); main dishes 58–120 Kr ($8.90–$18.45). No credit cards.

Open: Mon–Fri 9am–7:30pm, Sat 9am–5pm.

Order at the counter and a waiter will deliver your meal to your table (table service after 3pm). The food is good and can be eaten by one of the large front windows overlooking the busy shopping streets. The interior is attractive, with its ornamental wrought iron dividing the seating areas. The restaurant is on the second floor opposite Mama Rosa's just off Karl Johans Gate.

TAJ MAHAL, Olavs Gate 10. Tel. 36-21-15.

Cuisine: INDIAN.

$ **Prices:** Daily special, 59 Kr ($9.10); main dishes 69–149 Kr ($10.60–$22.90). No credit cards.

Open: Daily 3–11pm.

This small restaurant has soft lighting, near-elegant decor, sitar background music, and well-prepared and -presented food, including a number of vegetarian dishes. The daily special is served until 6pm. Enter around the corner on Peder Claussons Gate.

VEGETA VERTSHUS, Munkedamsveien 3B. Tel. 42-85-57.
   Cuisine: VEGETARIAN.
$ **Prices:** Buffet meal, 60 Kr ($9.25) for a small plate, 65 Kr ($10) for a large plate, 98 Kr ($15.10) for all you can eat (including tea or coffee), for soup, bread, and cheese. AE, DC, EURO, MC, V.
   Open: Daily 10am–11pm (last serving 10pm).

⭐ Quantity and variety are the specialties of the house, and they're palatable enough for the most stubborn carnivore. This super-fresh vegetarian smørgåsbord includes a full salad bar, hearty homemade bread and a tempting hot buffet of soups and unusual, healthful specialties. Don't be shy about loading up your plate—nobody else is. Nonalcoholic beer is available. Reasonable prices and a laid-back atmosphere have been the hallmark here since 1938, and owner Ernst Røgler is keen on keeping it that way. Vegeta Vertshus is two blocks from the National Theater. Go downstairs after entering. No smoking.

CAFES

Some are grand, some sophisticated, some bohemian, but most of the city's cafés serve tasty lunches and dinners. Of course you can just linger over coffee, beer, or wine, but don't overlook eating in this relaxed atmosphere.

CAFE BACCHUS, Dronningens Gate 27. Tel. 42-45-49.
   Cuisine: LIGHT FARE.
$ **Prices:** 35–60 Kr ($5.40–$9.25). V.
   Open: Mon–Thurs 11am–1am, Fri–Sat 11am–2am, Sun 1pm–midnight.
If it's been too long since you've had decaffeinated coffee, a BLT, tuna fish, or an egg-salad sandwich (served on walnut bread), this place will come as a godsend. The food is fresh, filling, and delicious. The unique decor features oak paneling from France, a railing (over the bar) from a German church, a spiral staircase from England, and two hanging lamps from a Dutch railway station. The building, behind the domed church and just off Karl Johans Gate, dates from 1848, the café from 1990. Owners Bob De Young, originally from New Jersey (but you'd never know it from his Norwegian accent), and his wife, Marte Kristiansen, make this a most welcoming place, one that's particularly popular with students.

CAFE BROKER, Bogstadveien 27. Tel. 69-36-47.
   Cuisine: NORWEGIAN/CONTINENTAL. **Tram:** 1 or 11 to Bogstadveien.
$ **Prices:** Daily specials 53–71 Kr ($8.15–$10.90); salads 58–68 Kr ($8.90–$10.45). AE, DC, EURO, MC, V.
   Open: Mon–Thurs 11am–1:30am, Fri–Sat 11am–2:30am, Sun noon–1:30am.
A popular meeting and newspaper-perusing place between the Royal Palace and Frogner Park, Café Broker is strikingly decorated with a wood-and-glass exterior and a beautiful hand-painted ceiling. The bar in back is more modern and features a changing exhibition of local artworks. The espresso at 14 Kr ($2.35) is *fabulissimo!*

CAFE CAPUCCHINO, in the courtyard of the Domed Church. Tel. 33-34-30.
   Cuisine: LIGHT FARE.
$ **Prices:** Daily special 65 Kr ($10); sandwiches 35–45 Kr ($5.40–$6.90); salads and tacos 60 Kr ($9.25). V.
   Open: Mon–Sat 11am–6 or 7pm. **Closed:** Whenever it rains—this is strictly an outdoor café.
Owned and managed by the folks at Café Bacchus (see above), it is *barnevennelig*, or "children friendly." Kids can play on the grass and around the fountain, and service is

fast. No alcohol is served here, just hefty salads, tacos, and sandwiches featuring chicken, beef, avocado, shrimp, and salmon. The bread and cakes are homemade. The daily special includes bread and a salad. Check off what you want on the multi-language menu.

CLODION ART CAFE, Bygdøy Allé 63, at Thomas Heftyes Gate. Tel. 44-97-26.

Cuisine: LIGHT FARE.
$ Prices: Brunch 29–53 Kr ($4.45–$8.15); individual dishes 41–136 Kr ($4.15–$20.90). V.
Open: Daily 10am–1am.

Opened in 1989 and a mixture of art deco, modern, and bohemian, it draws a neighborhood crowd and even has a special play nook for toddlers downstairs. Brunch, mainly egg dishes, is served daily from 10am to 3pm, and there are daily specials as well. Music, which is live in winter, may include violin, piano, or harp. Don't miss the arty bathrooms and bar downstairs. The café is a short walk from Frogner Park.

COCO, Ovre Slottsgate 8. Tel. 33-32-66.

Cuisine: LIGHT FARE/DESSERTS.
$ Prices: 20–75 Kr ($3.10–$11.55). AE, V.
Open: Mon–Thurs 11am–2am, Fri–Sat 11am–3am, Sun 3pm–1am.

You have to go out of your way to find this place, but it's worth it for the old-world charm and the desserts. You can also get meals here. The crowd is arty, and there's occasional live music in off-season months. The same owners also have the stylish Recepten Bar, across the street on Prinsens Gate; it serves vegetarian food during the day.

FRU BLOM WINE BAR, Karl Johans Gate 41B. Tel. 42-73-00.

Cuisine: LIGHT FARE.
$ Prices: 31–75 Kr ($4.75–$11.55); glass of wine 29–72 Kr ($4.45–$11.10). AE, DC, EURO, MC, V.
Open: Mon–Thurs 11am–12:30am, Fri–Sat 11am–1:30am.

In the Paleet shopping center, this wine bar is popular for its location and for serving wines by the glass. Daily specials—wines and food—are posted on the blackboard. If you're hungry, they've got lasagne, croque monsieurs, salad, soup, and chili con carne, plus sweets. Beer is available, too. This place sprouted in 1984 from the adjacent Blom restaurant, founded as a tavern by wine merchant C. P. Blom in 1886, and is, in its own way, as much an Oslo landmark as Theatercaféen. The modern Paleet complex grew up around it, but this old survivor held its ground. If you find yourself in the wine bar in the afternoon when the restaurant is not likely to be busy, pop in and ask if you can look around; you might just get an informal tour and learn about the Purple Nose Order and the whimsical paintings and shields on the walls.

OLSEN'S CAFE, Bogstadveien 8. Tel. 46-39-65.

Cuisine: LIGHT FARE.
$ Prices: 24–68 Kr ($3.70–$10.45). AE, V.
Open: Mon–Thurs 11am–12:30am, Fri–Sat 11am–2:30am, Sun 1pm–12:30am.

Small and crowded, Olsen's bubbles each evening with cognoscenti clutching their cappuccinos. Food from the tiny blackboard menu barely fits onto even tinier tables. And although it may not be as "in" as some others, this candlelit café with large windows, bright-yellow walls, and a profusion of plants is still warm and inviting.

THE CHAINS

There are half a dozen **Malik's Bistros** around town, serving hearty meals at low prices. Although they're owned and operated by Pakistani immigrants, Malik's menu is not as foreign as the name suggests. In fact, it is heavy on hamburgers, fish and chips, steaks, chicken, and huge salads; check out selections nos. 5 and 22, two popular meat items. Meals costing 30–90 Kr ($4.60–$13.85) make Malik's Oslo's best budget chain. The two most convenient branches are at Skippergata 27 (tel. 42-25-87), at Karl Johans Gate, where you'll find owner Ayub Malik behind the counter; and at Niels Juels Gate 38 (tel. 44-11-55), west of the Royal Palace. The former is open Monday through Thursday from 10am to 1am, on Friday and Saturday from 10am to 4am, and on Sunday from noon to 1am; the latter, daily from 1pm to midnight. The prettiest location is north of the Royal Palace; devoid of the usual fast-food ambience, Malik's Corner Bistro is slightly less central, at Hegdehaugsveien 32 (tel. 46-86-91); call for hours.

Most locals claim that **Peppe's Pizza** is the best pizza place around. No one can argue with their 11am to 2:30pm lunchtime all-you-can-eat pizza-and-salad special for 65 Kr ($10). At other times a pie for two will set you back 99–139 Kr ($15.25–$21.40). The Stortingsgata 4 (tel. 41-22-51) branch, opposite the Parliament, is the most conveniently located. Other branches are located at Frognerveien 54 (tel. 44-51-05), between the Royal Palace and Frogner Park; and at Drammensveien 40 (tel. 44-77-38), two blocks south of the Royal Palace grounds and the most fun with nice bowling lanes downstairs. All are open Monday through Saturday from 11am to 12:30am and on Sunday from noon to 11:30pm. AE, DC, EURO, MC, and V accepted.

McDonald's has proliferated like weeds in Oslo, and both **Burger King** and McDonald's have places on Karl Johans Gate. But beware: A large burger, fries, and a soda will cost more than $10!

PICNIC SUPPLIES

Shrimp boats pull into the harbor by 8am and unload their catch in front of City Hall, where 30- and 50-krone-size bags (about $5 and $8) of cooked (but unpeeled) shrimp are sold to passersby all day. Add a jar of cocktail sauce from a local market, and bring your gourmet feast to a local park or to the edge of the dock—where seagulls will become your fast friends.

Smør-Petersen, in Aker Brygge mall, on Holmens Gate at Bryggetorget (tel. 83-83-70), is the city's best gourmet delicatessen with more than 100 prepared dishes to go, as well as the usual meats, cheeses, smoked fish, pâtés, and more. It's open Monday through Friday from 8am to 8pm and on Saturday from 10am to 6pm.

There is an **open-air produce market** in front of Central Station, and two inside it. You'll find **7-Eleven** markets throughout the city. The one at Hegdehaugsveien 28 (tel. 60-60-56), north of the palace grounds, is well stocked; another, at Industrigate 41 (tel. 60-85-18), is open 24 hours.

Take your picnic to one of Oslo's nearby islands, or to one of the city's parks, listed under "Attractions," below.

WORTH THE EXTRA BUCKS

ENGEBRET CAFÉ, Bankplassen 1. Tel. 33-66-94.
    Cuisine: NORWEGIAN/FRENCH. **Tram:** 1, 2, or 9. **Bus:** 29.
$ **Prices:** Appetizers 58-76 Kr ($8.90–$11.70); main courses 109–196 Kr ($16.75–$30.15). AE, DC, EURO, MC, V.
    Open: Mon–Fri 11am–11pm, Sat noon–11pm (dinner served anytime after 2pm).
Engebret Christoffersen established this little café in 1857, and actors from the Christiania Theater, forerunner to the National Theater, which used to stand across the street, were its habituées. Now the city's movers and shakers are, and probably some well-heeled actors, too. For a splurge, Theatercaféen is the sentimental choice,

while Engebret is the culinary one. Start with fish soup, mussels in white wine with vegetables and cream, or marinated salmon with tarragon-and-mustard sauce, and for a main course, consider poached leg of lamb, reindeer filets, or Engebret's fish and shellfish pot. The small room to the right of the entrance has photographs of Engebret and some of his famous diners.

THEATERCAFÉEN, in the Hotel Continental, Stortingsgata 24. Tel. 41-90-60.

Cuisine: NORWEGIAN. **Reservations:** Recommended.

$ Prices: 80–250 Kr ($12.30–$38.45); weekday meal specials 80–100 Kr ($12.30–$15.40) for main dish; Norwegian Sunday supper about 100 Kr ($15.40). AE, DC, EURO, MC, V.

Open: Daily 11am–12:30am (last orders at 11pm).

✪ Fairy tales tell you that this is how kings and queens used to dine—in cavernous columned rooms with vaulted ceilings and a waltz band on the balcony. As you can also imagine, prices can be high, but for reindeer with red whortleberries and other old-fashioned Norwegian dishes you don't have to prove your pedigree or empty your wallet. You may even opt for just coffee and dessert, which management doesn't frown upon if you come in before 3pm. But by no means miss this elegant hangout—Ibsen's favorite—for artists, office workers, heads of corporations, and actors alike. Music Tuesday through Sunday, usually from 8pm. Jacket and tie are optional for men.

---

6. ATTRACTIONS

SUGGESTED ITINERARIES

IF YOU HAVE ONE DAY Tackle a couple of the nautical museums on the Bygdøy Peninsula, then visit the Vigeland Sculpture Garden in Frogner Park. Spend the late afternoon and evening exploring the center of Oslo around Karl Johans Gate.

IF YOU HAVE TWO DAYS Take the time to explore the Norwegian Folk Museum on the Bygdøy Peninsula and get to know the city center. On Day 2, visit Tryvann Hill for a thrilling panorama of the Oslo area and a closeup look at the famous Holmenkollen ski jump. In the afternoon, visit the Munch Museum or the National Gallery, which displays the works of Norway's most famous artists. At night, see a play, a ballet, or hear some music.

IF YOU HAVE THREE DAYS On the third day, tour Akershus Castle in the morning, then rent a bicycle and ride around Oslo's beautiful countryside all afternoon. Pack a lunch. You will need a rest before going out to one of the city's many dance clubs.

IF YOU HAVE FIVE DAYS On these extra days, add the Museum of Applied Art, City Hall, the Historical Museum, the Henie-Onstad Art Center, and refer to the *Oslo Guide '93* for other events and museums of particular interest to you. Have fun!

TOP ATTRACTIONS

ON THE BYGDØY PENINSULA

Happily, someone had the good sense to cluster some of Oslo's best museums along the city's scenic Bygdøy (rhymes with "big boy") Peninsula. Most of the collections

DID YOU KNOW . . . ?

- Oslo is the oldest capital in Europe, settled in 1050.
- Norway has been an independent nation only since 1905.
- Oslo was called Cristiania (after a conquering Swedish king) from 1629 to 1925, when it reclaimed its original name.
- Norwegian artist Edvard Munch (1863–1944) bequeathed all his works of art to the city of Oslo in 1940.
- The Nobel Peace Prize is awarded annually in Oslo by a five-person committee elected by the Norwegian Parliament and presented on December 10.
- There are more ski resorts in the Oslo metropolitan area than in any other European capital.
- Oslo hosted the Winter Olympics in 1952. Nearby Lillehammer will host them in 1994.
- Over the years, close to a million Norwegians immigrated to the United States; nearly one in every four eventually returned.
- Oslo has more public sculpture than any other Scandinavian city.

here celebrate Norway's seafaring tradition—a powerful cultural influence that still exists today. No wonder the museums' seaside site is most conveniently reached by ferry; to miss a boat ride in Oslo is to miss an important part of Nordic life.

From Easter through September only, ferries shuttle between Pier 3 (in front of City Hall) and Bygdøy's *Fram* Ship/*Kon-Tiki* Museum complex. The ride takes about 10 minutes and departs every 15 minutes from 8am in summer, every half hour in other months. The last boat back to Oslo proper leaves at 6 or 8pm, depending on the month.

At other times of the year, take bus no. 30 from Central Station or the National Theater directly to the Viking Ships, or to a stop within 10 minutes of the *Fram* Ship/*Kon-Tiki* Museum complex. You might want to ask the Tourist Information Office for a bus schedule, as it only departs two to four times an hour.

Note that it's a half-hour walk from the Viking Ship Museum to the *Kon-Tiki, Fram,* and Norwegian Maritime Museums, clustered together at the tip of the peninsula by the ferry landing. All the attractions on the Bygdøy Peninsula accept the Copenhagen Card, which comes in particularly handy here (see Section 1, "Special Discount Opportunities," in Chapter 10).

VIKINGSKIPSHUSET (Viking Ships Museum), Huk Aveny 35. Tel. 43-83-79.

Three thrilling 9th-century Viking ships have found their final resting place in this specially built museum with vaulted ceilings. These primitive yet awesome ships speak eloquently about a Scandinavian culture that flourished between A.D. 800 and 1050. It is mind-boggling even to imagine that one of these long, low boats, built for long-distance travel, may have visited North America. And now here they are, 10 centuries later, intact to tell their tale.

According to Viking tradition, treasure-laden ships were routinely buried with the wealthy. The ships displayed here were recovered between 1867 and 1904 from burial mounds in the Oslo Fjord area, and two of them are remarkably complete, displayed alongside a variety of tools, provisions, and artifacts that were included in the burials. The 70-foot-long Oseburg ship, exhibited with its wagon and sleighs, is nothing short of magnificent. In 1893 an exact replica of one of the ships was sailed from Norway to the Chicago World's Fair. All three ships are excellently presented, surrounded by elevated viewing platforms. The museum has a gift shop and bookstore.

Admission: 15 Kr ($2.30) adults, 7 Kr ($1.10) students and children 7–16.

Open: May–Aug, daily 10am–6pm; Sept, daily 11am–5pm; Oct and Apr, daily 11am–4pm; Nov–Mar, daily 11am–3pm. **Closed:** May 1, May 17, major hols.

NORSK FOLKEMUSEUM (Norwegian Folk Museum), Museumsveien 10. Tel. 43-70-20.

It's hard to believe that you're in a city, or even a museum, when visiting this outdoor pine-forest town, a five-minute walk from the Viking Ships Museum. Oslo's folk museum consists of 170 historic Norwegian homes displayed in a natural setting on 3,500 acres. Open your eyes and imagine yourself in an 18th-century Norwegian hamlet, or attend a summer Sunday service in the still-functioning 12th-century Gol Stav Church. At the entrance to the grounds lie several traditional museum buildings with collections of old dolls, toys, furniture, flatware, and other home furnishings. Don't miss the Old Parliament Hall, in use from 1814 to 1854, or the re-creation of Henrik Ibsen's 1895 study—both in the building to your right after you enter. A large museum shop (in the building to your left, near the entrance) is filled with crafts, books, dolls, jewelry, and other gift items.

Admission: Summer, 35 Kr ($5.40) adults, 20 Kr ($3.10) students, 15 Kr ($2.30) children; winter, half price.

Open: May 15–Sept 14, Mon–Sat 10am–6pm, Sun 11am–3pm; Sept 15–May 14, Mon–Sat 11am–4pm, Sun noon–4:30pm. **Closed:** Jan 1.

KON-TIKI MUSEUM, Bygdøynesveien 36, at the tip of the peninsula. Tel. 43-80-50.

In 1947 Norwegian explorer Thor Heyerdahl, with a five-person crew and a parrot, crossed the Pacific Ocean on his home-built raft, the *Kon-Tiki*. The journey from Peru to Polynesia covered 4,300 miles, took 101 days, and proved that even in antiquity South American boats could have traveled to the Pacific islands. Did the Incan culture spread throughout the South Pacific? Maybe so, and this raft—composed of a straw hut atop balsa-wood logs and propelled by a simple sail—makes a strong case.

Adjacent to the *Kon-Tiki* is another Heyerdahl vessel, the 15-ton *RA II*, built of papyrus in 1970 to prove that ancient Egyptians could have crossed the Atlantic. The raft's traditional design and proven seaworthiness help explain long-distance cultural similarities.

Admission: 15 Kr ($2.30) adults, 8 Kr ($1.25) students, 6 Kr (90¢) children; 30 Kr ($5.20) for families.

Open: May 18–Aug, daily 10am–6pm; Sept–Oct and Apr–May 16, daily 10:30am–5pm; Nov–Mar, daily 10:30am–4pm. **Closed:** May 17.

FRAM MUSEUM, Bygdøynes, at the tip of the peninsula. Tel. 43-83-70.

The massive Norwegian-built polar vessel *Fram* reached the Arctic in 1893 and Antarctica in 1910, and is now permanently housed in a museum shaped like an oversize A-frame. The most innovative aspect of this ship is the rounded hull that enabled it to ride over ice, rather than into it. On board, you can pretend to be Roald Amundsen or Fridtjof Nansen at the ship's helm and investigate the authentic cabins and rooms inside. There are several viewing levels from which to marvel at this brute of a ship, with relevant exhibits on each.

Admission: 15 Kr ($2.30) adults, 8 Kr ($1.25) students, children, and seniors; 30 Kr ($4.60) families.

Open: May 16–Aug, daily 10am–5:45pm; Sept and the first half of May, daily 11am–4:45pm; Apr and Oct, daily 11am–2:45pm; Nov, Sat–Sun 11am–2:45pm. **Closed:** Dec–Mar.

NORSK SJØFARTSMUSEUM (Norwegian Maritime Museum), Bygdøynesveien 37, at the tip of the peninsula. Tel. 43-82-40.

This is the granddaddy of Oslo's boat museums, with encyclopedic displays of everything from rowboat to cruise ship. Full-size reproductions of ship interiors are next to rooms packed with all sorts of "exhibita nautica." Portholes overlooking the water make the museum's galleries feel like ships' galleys. If you are prone to seasickness, don't attempt to cover every inch of this vast nautical warehouse. There actually are two buildings to explore, one opposite the other. The second building, called the Boat Hall, is filled with wooden boats and details the culture of the coast, including the cod-fishing industry.

Admission: 15 Kr ($2.30) adults, 10 Kr ($1.55) students and children; 35 Kr ($5.80) for families.

Open: May–Sept, daily 10am–7pm; Oct–Apr, Mon, Wed, and Fri–Sat 10:30am–5pm, Tues and Thurs 10:30am–7pm, Sun 10:30am–4pm.

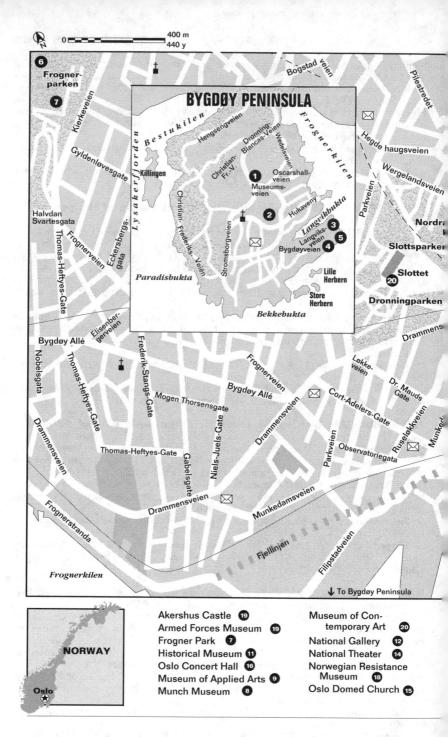

BYGDØY PENINSULA

Akershus Castle ⑲
Armed Forces Museum ⑲
Frogner Park ⑦
Historical Museum ⑪
Oslo Concert Hall ⑯
Museum of Applied Arts ⑨
Munch Museum ⑧

Museum of Con-
    temporary Art ⑳
National Gallery ⑫
National Theater ⑭
Norwegian Resistance
    Museum ⑱
Oslo Domed Church ⑮

NORWAY

Oslo ★

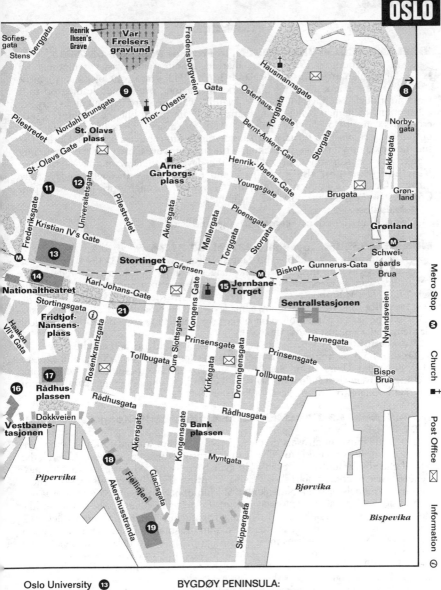

OSLO

Metro Stop   **M**

Church   ■╪

Post Office   ☒

Information   ⓘ

Oslo University ⑬
Town Hall ⑰
Royal Palace ⑳
Parliament ㉑
Vigeland Sculpture
   Park ⑥

BYGDØY PENINSULA:
Museum ⑤
Fram Kon-Tiki Museum ③
Norwegian Folk Museum ②
Norwegian Maritime Museum ④
Viking Ships Museum ①

ELSEWHERE

VIGELAND SCULPTURE GARDEN, in Frogner Park. Tel. 55-28-84.

⭐ A collection of 192 bronze, marble, granite, and plaster sculptures by Norwegian artist Gustav Vigeland (1869–1943) graces one of the city's most beautiful parks. Most of the works line a long promenade leading up to a mammoth obelisk-topped fountain. Vigeland's sculptures are fanciful and energetic celebrations of human beings being human. All are nude, but the sculpture is not erotic. As you get closer to the obelisk, carved from a single piece of granite, an orgy of humanity comes into focus, a startling testament to the artist's genius. During the summer, plan on visiting in the evening—the museums are closed but the restaurants aren't, and the sun still shines. (During the day, you may want to visit the free **Vigeland Museum,** also in the park and open Tuesday through Sunday: May through October from noon to 7pm, and November through April from 1 to 7pm. Concerts are held in the courtyard in summer.)

Admission: Free.

Open: Daily 24 hours. **Tram:** 2 to Vigeland Park.

MUNCH MUSEUM, Toyengate 53. Tel. 67-37-74.

⭐ The tormented world of expressionist Edvard Munch (1863–1944) doesn't get more vivid than this. Stark, silent images of shock and horror are reflected in the expressionless stares on the faces of paintings and visitors alike. *The Scream, The Madonna, The Murderer/The Murderess, Weeping Girl, The Drowned Boy,* and other well-known images are all here. Saddest of all are the artist's many self-portraits. (After your visit here, take some time to explore the Botanical Gardens and Zoo, just across the road.)

Admission: 40 Kr ($6.15) adults, 15 Kr ($2.30) students and children.

Open: June to mid-Sept, Mon–Sat 10am–8pm, Sun noon–8pm; mid-Sept to May, Tues and Thurs 10am–8pm, Wed and Fri–Sat 10am–4pm, Sun noon–8pm. **T-Bane:** Tøyen; then follow the signs to the modern white building. **Bus:** 29 from City Hall Square to Tøyen Skole.

SKI MUSEUM AND HOLMENKOLLEN SKI JUMP, Kongeveien 5. Tel. 92-32-00.

This little museum answers everything you've always wanted to know about the history and utility of the ski. You'll view the Norway's longest ski (3.74m/12½ ft.), the skis of the royal family, and even a 30-inch barrel-stave ski with leather bindings. Generous use of photographs shows civilians, royals, and professionals on skis. There are various models of the Holmenkollen Ski Jump, beginning in 1892 when it was a natural slope. You also get a closeup view of the present ski jump, one of the world's most famous, and certainly one of the most frightening. The record jumper flew 362 feet, more than the length of a football field, into the small bowl below. You can go to the top of the ski jump (tokens for it are sold at the museum ticket window), but be forewarned that the lift takes you only partway, and you have to maneuver the remaining 100 steep steps on your own. At the top, the viewing area is crowded and not good for photographs, plus there is no explanation of what you're looking out at. Still, it does provide a sweeping view of Oslo and the mighty fjords beyond.

Admission: Museum, 25 Kr ($3.85) adults, 15 Kr ($2.30) students and seniors, 20 Kr ($3.10) children; museum and ski jump, about 15 Kr ($2.30) extra.

Open: June, daily 10am–7pm; July, daily 9am–10pm; Aug, daily 9am–9pm; Sept and May, daily 10am–5pm; Oct–Apr, Mon–Fri 10am–3pm, Sat–Sun 11am–4pm. **T-Bane:** Holmenkollen. **Tram:** 15 from Central Station to the Holmenkollen stop (sit on left-hand side for best views of the fjord); then cross the highway and follow the road past Holmenhollen Restaurant up the hill.

TRYVANNSTÅRNET (Tryvann Observation Tower), Voksenkollen. Tel. 14-67-11.

This 1,928-foot tower on Tryvann Hill offers the highest perspective in Oslo and overlooks the vast Oslo Fjord and the Swedish border.

Admission: 20 Kr ($3.10) adults, 15 Kr ($2.30) students, 10 Kr ($1.55) children.

Open: May and Sept, daily 10am–5pm; June and Aug 20–31, daily 10am–7pm; July, daily 9am–10pm; Aug 1–19, daily 9am–8pm; Oct–Apr, Mon–Fri 10am–3pm, Sat–Sun 11am–4pm. **Tram:** 15 to Voksenkollen; then a 20-min. walk up the hill.

MORE ATTRACTIONS

IN THE AKERSHUS FORTRESS

Just three blocks south of bustling, modern Karl Johans Gate are the stone walls and relative silence of Oslo's old Akershus Fortress. Within the compound are several centuries-old government buildings and a couple of museums with military themes. The fortress grounds overlook the city's harbor and are open from 6am to 9pm (until 7pm from September to April). This is a great area for a stroll and picnicking. The statue of F.D.R. was donated by the Norwegian people in 1950 in memory and gratitude.

AKERSHUS CASTLE AND FORTRESS. Tel. 41-25-21.

This stone-and-brick castle dates from the 14th century when it served as the royal residence and impregnable fortress. In the 17th century most of the rooms were extensively renovated; today several of them are open to the public. In addition to visiting the old State Apartments, tourists can explore the ancient crypt below the castle's church. During the summer, guided tours are offered Monday through Saturday at 11am, 1pm, and 3pm; on Sunday at 1 and 3pm. The ramparts are open year round from 6am to 10pm, and concerts are given in the chapel on Sunday at 2pm, summer only.

Admission: 10 Kr ($1.55) adults, 5 Kr (75¢) seniors, students, and children.

Open: May 2–Sept 15, Mon–Sat 10am–4pm, Sun 12:30–4pm; Sept 16–Oct 30 and Apr 15–May 1, Sun only 12:30–4pm. **Closed:** Oct 31–Apr 14.

NORGES HJEMMEFRONTMUSEUM (Norway Resistance Museum). Tel. 40-31-38.

Learn about life under Nazi occupation from 1940 to 1945. Maps detail the German invasion of Norway in April 1940, while models depict prison camps and cells. See models of sabotage actions, as well as tools of the underground resistance, such as radios and newspapers.

Admission: 15 Kr ($2.30) adults, 5 Kr (75¢) students and children; 30 Kr ($4.60) for families.

Open: Apr 15–Sept, Mon–Sat 10am–4pm, Sun 11am–4pm; Oct–Apr 14, Mon–Sat 10am–3pm, Sun 11am–4pm.

ELSEWHERE

MUSEET FOR SAMTIDSKUNST (Museum of Contemporary Art), Bankplassen 4, at Kongens Gate. Tel. 33-58-20.

Norway's newest national museum opened in January 1990 in the former headquarters of Norges Bank's impressive century-old building. It displays Norwegian and international contemporary art, including some photography. Exhibits change three times a year. The museum also has a bookshop and a stylish café.

Admission: Free.

Open: Tues–Fri 11am–7pm, Sat–Sun 11am–4pm. **Tram:** 1, 2, or 9. **Bus:** 29.

NATIONAL GALLERY, Universitetsgate 13. Tel. 20-04-04.

Norway's largest fine-art museum boasts its share of masters: Renoir, Monet, Manet, Cezanne, Rodin, Rembrandt, Rubens, and El Greco, but the best collection here is of 19th-century Norwegian landscapes, hanging on the second floor. It's fascinating to compare and contrast the icy-hard visions of northern artists to the more subdued scenes and techniques of those who lived in the less-brutal south. The museum's large, labyrinthine Munch collection includes his masterpiece *Shrik* ("The Shriek," 1893). Don't miss the works of Christian Krogh (1852–1925).

Admission: Free.

Open: Mon, Wed, and Fri–Sat 10am–4pm; Thurs 10am–8pm; Sun 11am–3pm.

Directions: Walk two blocks north of Karl Johans Gate.

KUNSTINDUSTRIMUSEET (Museum of Applied Art), St. Olavs Gate 1. Tel. 20-35-78.

If it's pretty and usable, it's here. Old and new furniture, arts and crafts, tapestries, clothing, porcelain, and more are displayed chronologically from the Middle Ages. On the fourth floor you can relax on the Scandinavian-design chairs. A recent addition to the museum's collection is Queen Maud's wardrobe from 1920 to 1934. The museum is near St. Olav's Church, at the corner of Ullevålsveien.

Admission: 15 Kr ($2.30) adults, 10 Kr ($1.55) students and children; there's an additional charge for special exhibits.

Open: Tues–Fri 11am–3pm, Sat–Sun noon–4pm.

TEATERMUSEET (Oslo Theater Museum), Nedre Slottsgate 1, 2nd Floor. Tel. 41-81-47.

If you love the theater, you'll adore this museum—from the old costumes and photographs (including one of Mae West, who performed in Oslo in 1937) to the re-created dressing rooms of two competitive Norwegian divas, one who was still performing at age 90. Special exhibits on Ibsen are mounted every summer, and any permanent exhibits that relate to the famous playwright are tagged with a red dot. The museum is only open two days a week for a few hours at a time, so arrange your schedule accordingly. A historic Oslo restaurant, Gamle Raadhus, is on the ground floor of the same building, which dates from 1641 and was Oslo's first town hall as well as the site of its first theatrical performance, in 1667.

Admission: 10 Kr ($1.55) adults, 5 Kr (75¢) students, seniors, and children 7–16.

Open: Wed 11am–3pm, Sun noon–4pm. **Tram:** 1, 2, or 9. **Bus:** 27 or 29.

HENIE-ONSTAD ART CENTER, Sonja Heniesveien 31, Høvikodden. Tel. 54-30-50.

The best private art collection in Norway is 7½ miles from Oslo and, despite the short trip and the relatively high admission fee, is well worth visiting. The emphasis is on 20th-century works, and includes paintings by Matisse, Picasso, Léger, and Miró. Owned by Norwegian shipping tycoon Niels Onstad and his figure-skating-champion wife, Sonja Henie, the museum houses more than 1,800 works of art, not including Sonja's 600 or so medals and trophies. There is also a sculpture garden, shop, and café facing a fjord. Guided tours are available by appointment.

Admission: 20 Kr ($3.10) adults, 10 Kr ($1.55) seniors, students, and children.

Open: Mon 11am–5pm, Tues–Fri 9am–9pm, Sat–Sun 11am–5pm (until 7pm Sat–Sun June–Aug). **Bus:** 151, 153, 161, 162, 251, or 261 to Høvikodden.

PARKS & GARDENS

Oslo is more town than city, and it has ample parks and countryside to prove it. Aside from **Frogner Park,** mentioned above, try picnicking or strolling through the smaller green around **Akershus Fortress.** The woods in and around the Norwegian **Folk Museum** are really far removed from the hustle, and nothing can beat the thick forests, called the **"Marka,"** that completely encircle the city. Sunday is the traditional day for families to visit the Marka, with kids, dogs, bikes, and baby carriages in tow.

If you love to explore old cemeteries, the parklike **Vår Frelsers Gravlund,** the final resting place of Henrik Ibsen, is a must. Filled with tranquil lanes, roses, geraniums, hedges, ferns, and towering trees, it is a spot where tranquility reigns. Ibsen's grave is marked with a black obelisk. Across the street from the cemetery is lovely Gamle Aker Church (1100), Oslo's oldest. If you're energetic, wander along short Telthusbakken street (pick it up at the church) and admire the tiny houses with lace curtains at the windows, red-tile roofs, and white picket fences and roses in front (retrace your steps to go back to the center of town, or you'll end up taking the long way home).

COOL FOR KIDS

Like adults, kids can get caught up in the Norwegian spirit of adventure that is the theme of most of the city's museums. The ferry ride out to the Bygdøy Peninsula and its treasures will certainly grab your child's attention. Is there a kid who could resist playing hide-and-seek in and around the polar exploration vessel *Fram* or taking a fantasy trip on a *real* Viking ship? For more adventures, take the tykes to:

DET INTERNASJONALE BARNEKUNSTMUSEET (International Museum of Children's Art), Lille Frøensveien 4. Tel. 46-85-73.

The exhibits feature the artwork of children from more than 150 countries, depicting what is closest to their hearts and experience. Works focus on animals, plants, village life, people, nature, and relationships. Hours are limited.

Admission: 25 Kr ($3.85) adults, 15 Kr ($2.30) students, seniors, and children.

Open: June 25–Aug 15, Tues–Thurs and Sun 11am–4pm; Sept 10–June 24, Tues–Thurs 9:30am–2pm, Sun 11am–4pm. **Closed:** Aug 16–Sept 9. **T-Bane:** Frøen.

NORSK TEKNISK MUSEUM (Nordic Technical Museum), Kjelsåsveien 143. Tel. 22-25-50.

Children gravitate to the hands-on exhibits that demonstrate technical and scientific concepts. There's a cafeteria and picnic area.

Admission: 20 Kr ($3.10) adults, 10 Kr ($1.55) students and children 7–17; 40 Kr ($6.15) for families.

Open: Mid-June to Aug, Tues–Sun 10am–7pm; Sept to mid-June, Tues 10am–9pm, Wed–Sat 10am–4pm, Sun 10am–5pm. **T-Bane:** Kjelsås.

TUSENFRYD, Vinterbro, Ås. Tel. 09/94-63-63.

One of Oslo's top 10 attractions, this fun-filled amusement park lures kids of all ages and is only 20 minutes from Central Station. Besides rides—everything from a fearsome roller coaster to bumper cars to a merry-go-round—there is plenty of entertainment and food.

Admission: 120 Kr ($18.45) adults, 90 Kr ($13.85) children; 60 Kr ($9.90) for everyone after 5:30pm.

Open: Mid-May to mid-Sept, daily 11am–8:30pm. **Closed:** Mid-Sept to mid-May. **Bus:** 541 from Central Station.

SPECIAL-INTEREST SIGHTSEEING

FOR THE HISTORY BUFF The **Historical Museum,** Frederiksgate 2 (tel. 41-63-00, ext. 956), features a mixed bag of artifacts, including archeological exhibits, religious icons from the Middle Ages, international ethnographic displays, and an excellent numismatic collection. It's located behind the National Gallery, four blocks north of Karl Johans Gate, and admission is free. It's open May 15 to September 14, Tuesday through Sunday from 11am to 3pm; the rest of the year, Tuesday through Sunday from noon to 3pm (closed major holidays).

FOR THE ARCHITECTURE LOVER Whether you're interested in pretty buildings for professional or personal reasons, no one should miss a walk through **Homans byen,** the city's 100-year-old residential and embassy district between the Royal Palace and Frogner Park and Bygdøy Allé and Hegdehaugsveien/Bogstadveien. The

Norwegian Architecture Museum, Josefines Gate 32-34 (tel. 60-22-90), is in this historic neighborhood. Founded in 1975, the museum has changing displays primarily concerned with national architecture since the turn of the century. It's open Monday through Friday from 9am to 3pm (until 8pm on Thursday from September to May 15). Admission is free. Take tram no. 1 to Hegdehaugen Skole. The museum may be moving, so call before heading out.

ORGANIZED TOURS

Oslo's relatively small size and easy-to-get-to sights mean that if you have a couple of days, you'll pretty much see everything by walking around on your own. If you're really pressed for time, **H. M. Kristiansen** (tel. 20-82-06) and **Båtservice** (tel. 20-07-15) offer a comprehensive bus tour that whizzes you past some of the city's highlights in three hours. Adults are charged 150 Kr ($23.10), while students and children pay half price. Most bus and boat tours are half price with the Oslo Card, making them much more affordable.

During the summer several companies offer combination bus and boat tours that depart from Pier 3, in front of City Hall. Contact the city tourist board (see "Information" in "Orientation and Getting Around," above) for itineraries, times, and tickets.

You may also tour Oslo and environs by bicycle—on your own with a rented bike, or as a participant in a guided tour—but it's expensive. **Den Rustne Eike** (The Rusty Hub), Enga 2 (tel. 83-72-31), next door to the Norway Information Center, offers six-hour rides in the peaceful Marka (forest) surrounding Oslo; the tour includes food but costs a hefty 450 Kr ($69.25). Seven- and 10-day tours in the mountain and fjord regions of Norway are also offered. The tours are often led by owner Lars Hotvedt. Bicycle rentals cost about 110 Kr ($16.90) for 6 hours, 170 Kr ($26.15) for 24 hours, with an unusually high 1,500 Kr ($230.75). The bike shop is open daily from 10am to 3:30pm.

SPECIAL & FREE EVENTS

Summer offers a cavalcade of free events, including Saturday jazz concerts in front of the National Theater, and street performances by jugglers, clowns, and musicians along Karl Johans Gate.

Throughout the year, check with the tourist office, and pick up their guide *What's On in Oslo* for the most up-to-date information.

7. SAVVY SHOPPING

Norway is known the world over for its sweaters with their distinctive patterns (a new one has been designed for the Norwegian ski team every year since 1952). Sweaters are sold everywhere, but the most appealing place to buy is at Carl and Reidun Olsen's small, well-stocked shop, **Maurtua,** near City Hall at Fridtjof Nansens Plass 9 (tel. 41-31-64). **William Schmidt & Co.,** in Paleet, Karl Johans Gate 41 (tel. 42-02-88), has a huge selection. Expect to pay at least $100 for a sweater, unless you go to a secondhand clothing store, such as the large **Salvation Army shop,** St. Olav's Plass 3 (tel. 20-48-66), or **UFF,** at Bernt Ankers Gate and Calmeyers Gate. Norwegian knit coats are equally distinctive, and you can readily find caps and mittens (none inexpensive).

Other traditional items are porcelain, glassware, and wood crafts. **Hadeland Glassverk,** in Jevnaker, 44 miles north of Oslo (tel. 063/11-000), sells crystal "seconds" at good value; its museum/gallery, open daily, features glass-blowing exhibitions. The trip, by car or bus, is scenic, and the glassworks, founded in 1762, is one of Scandinavia's largest.

Modern Norwegian silver jewelry influenced by ancient Viking designs may be purchased at **David Andersen,** Karl Johans Gate 20 (tel. 41-69-55), founded in 1876 and supposedly Scandinavia's largest jewelry store; ask to see the Saga line. Even-more-modern designs—in jewelry, clothing, and household items—are displayed at **Norway Designs,** on Roald Amundsens Gate near the Saga cinema (tel. 83-11-00). The stock is unusual, and expensive, but it's fun to browse.

In general, stores are clustered into two manageable shopping areas: **Karl Johans Gate** and the surrounding side streets for major stores, and for smaller shops, **Hegdehaugsveien** and **Bogstadveien,** a single street shooting out northwest from the Royal Palace. Other plunderable shopping streets include **Grensen, Storgata, Stortingsgata,** and **Torggata,** and don't overlook **Oslo City, Aker Brygge** (a former shipyard and an attraction in itself), and the elegant **Paleet** shopping centers. For a variety of crafts, visit **Husfliden,** Møllergata 4 (tel. 42-10-75), and **Heimen Husflid,** Rosenkrantz Gate 8 (tel. 11-11-25).

Typical Norwegian furniture is at **Aarstrand,** Torggata 22 (tel. 20-14-15), where the stools and wine holders can be transported home fairly easily, and **Tannum Mobler,** Stortingsgata 28 at Munkedamsveien (tel. 83-49-25). Camping and outdoor supplies are available at **Schou,** Prinsens Gate 6 at Dronningens Gate (tel. 42-29-19), half a block from the post office.

Always be on the lookout for the word *salg,* which means "sale." Stores have major ones in January and February and in July and August, with reductions up to 50%. Baskets and travel bags are always reasonably priced.

Many stores offer non-Scandinavian tourists the opportunity to recover the VAT on purchases over 300 Kr ($46.15). Here's how to get the refund: When you make your purchase, ask the retailer for a Tax Free Check, and leave your purchase sealed until you exit the country. When you leave Norway (by plane, train, or ferry), show both the check and the purchase to an official at the tax-free office. You will get a cash refund (minus a small commission charge). The highest refundable amount at Oslo Central Station is 400 Kr ($61.55); the rest must be collected outside Norway. Remember not to check luggage containing a purchase until you have received your refund! Questions about tax refunds can be answered by Norway Tax-Free Shopping Postboks 48, Østerdalen 27, 1345 Østerås (tel. 24-99-01).

8. EVENING ENTERTAINMENT

Oslo has probably changed more in the last decade than any other European capital, and nowhere is this more apparent than in the recent explosion of bars, clubs, and nightspots. Some would argue that Oslo offers better nightlife than London, and in many respects it's true. The city has some great bars, dance clubs, a thriving late-night café culture, and a growing gay scene.

Because of Oslo's small size, "serious" cultural events such as opera and theater are few but of high quality, and last-minute seats are often available. Keep an eye out for special events, and refer to the free tourist board publication *What's On in Oslo* for a good, but not exhaustive, list of current events.

THE PERFORMING ARTS

THEATER

There are over a dozen legitimate theaters in the city, with about half these stages usually dedicated to American or British productions translated into Norwegian.

Most of the other theaters feature plays authored by locals. Most are new plays, but revivals and classics, by Ibsen and others, are still performed.

THE NATIONAL THEATER, Stortingsgata 15. Tel. 41-27-10.
This is the city's largest and most prestigious stage. In a monumental building right on Karl Johans Gate, this playhouse specializes in traditional interpretations of modern and classic dramas, and presents many productions of Ibsen's plays. Guest companies occasionally perform in English. Don't hesitate to sit in the rear—all the seats in the theater, built in 1899, are good. Tours of the theater are given on Friday at 3pm for 30 Kr ($4.60).
Prices: Tickets, 105–155 Kr ($16.15–$23.65), half price for students and seniors.
Open: Box office, Mon–Fri 8:30am–6:30pm, Sat 11am–5pm.

MUSIC & DANCE

KONSERT HUS (Oslo Concert Hall), Munkedamsveien 15. Tel. 83-45-10.
This hall just two blocks from the National Theater is home to the Oslo Philharmonic, which performs here on Thursday and Friday evenings from mid-August to mid-June. Guest performers usually take to the stage on off-nights, and in July and August traditional folk concerts and dances are held here on Monday and Thursday at 9pm, and you can talk with the performers afterward. The two pieces of sculpture in front of the Konsert Hus are *Heptakord* by Turid Eng and the soaring *Jord Musikk* by Harald Orebam.
Prices: Tickets, 115–150 Kr ($17.70–$23.10), half price for students on the day of the concert and retirees at all times.
Open: Box office, Mon–Fri noon–8pm, Sat 10am–1pm.

DEN NORSKE OPERA (The Norwegian Opera), Storgata 21. Tel. 42-94-75.
The company is close to 100 years old, but the theater, inside a modern shopping arcade (enter at Storgata 23C), is much newer. Programs vary widely, from traditional opera to highly experimental postmodern dance pieces.
Prices: Tickets, 60–260 Kr ($9.25–$40); seats drop to half price two hours before show time.
Open: Box office, Mon–Fri 10am–6pm (until 7:30pm on performance nights), Sat 11am–4pm. **Closed:** Late June to Aug.

OSLO SPEKTRUM, Holtegate 29. Tel. 17-80-50.
Oslo's new multipurpose hall, opened in spring 1991, holds 9,500 spectators for concerts, sports events, and other mass gatherings. Performers who have graced the stage here have been as divergent as Frank Sinatra and New Kids on the Block.

FILMS

First-run American blockbusters come here two to six months late, but all foreign films are shown in their original language with Norwegian subtitles. Cinema tickets usually cost 45 Kr ($6.90), but special showings may be more. Many theaters offer matinee shows for 35 Kr ($5.40). Check the local newspapers, or ask at the tourist board, for listings.
Filmteatret, Stortingsgata 16 (tel. 41-83-90), is a beautiful old theater with evening showings only.

THE BAR SCENE

If your interest in bars leans mainly toward meeting people, **Studenten** (see below) and **Costa,** Klingenberggata 4 (tel. 42-41-30), are particularly popular, lively, and congenially crowded. For a quieter setting, try **Tut-Ankh-Amon,** Rosengrantz Gate 16 (tel. 42-50-49). Both are near Karl Johans Gate. If you prefer places with live music, Oslo also won't disappoint.

ROCK, BLUES & JAZZ BARS

SMUGET, Kirkegata 34. Tel. 42-52-02.

In Oslo's great nightlife scene, Smuget is the Jack-of-all-trades. It has everything—a café, an intimate stage for live jazz, blues, and rock, and a good dance floor—and executes all of it well. Expect long lines on weekends. Everyone from Harry Belafonte to heavy metaler Yngwie Malmstein has hit some high notes here (usually unannounced), and their good booking policy means top home-grown acts, too. Enter through an alley, where a sign reads FROLICHGARDEN.

Admission: 40 Kr ($6.15) Sun–Thurs, 60 Kr ($9.25) Fri–Sat.

Open: Daily 8pm–4am; bands start about 11pm.

CRUISE CAFE, in Aker Brygge, in the Hallandene building. Tel. 83-64-30.

Cruise Café does a good impression of a great American bar. There's some live rock but mostly blues (a little country and western) almost every other night, featuring American bands, and even when the stage is dark, records spin, attracting a fun crowd. Bands here are meant to be listened to, so the quality is usually pretty good. The grill is hot until 10:30pm, and specializes in burgers, for 70 Kr ($10.75).

Admission: Free–200 Kr ($30.75), depending on the entertainment; music starts at 11pm.

Open: Mon–Tues noon–1am, Wed–Thurs noon–1:30am, Fri–Sat noon–2am, Sun 1pm–1am.

STUDENTEN—JOH. ALBRECHT, Karl Johans Gate 45. Tel. 42-56-80.

Live jazz is featured in this sophisticated, friendly, centrally located bar on Saturday and Monday nights on the ground floor; there's a piano bar downstairs where the music starts nightly at 8pm. It's a blessed relief to find a place like this one, that's spacious, with half a dozen seating areas that include both bar stools and tables. You can get a glass of white wine here for 35 Kr ($5.40) and a glass of red for 42 Kr ($6.45); beer—they make their own—will cost you either 18 Kr or 36 Kr ($2.75 or $5.55) for 2% or 4% alcohol content, respectively. Minimum age is 20 on weekdays, 22 on weekends. The entrance is on the corner of Universitetsgate.

Admission: Free.

Open: Daily 10am–4am.

STORTORVETS GJÆSTGIVERIET, Grensen 1. Tel. 42-88-63.

A Saturday-afternoon tradition in Oslo: in the midst of running weekend errands or a treat after brunch, stopping by this jazz club to hear free music. There's live music Friday night too, but Saturday afternoon is when the place is at its best—and during the Oslo Jazz Festival.

Admission: Free.

Open: Sat 1–5pm.

ROCKEFELLER, Torggata 16. Tel. 20-32-32.

This place, which manages to be large and intimate at the same time, is known for top international acts and some of the longest hair in town. In addition to its penchant for pop, Rocky's dance floor offers an unpretentious good time even when no band is scheduled. It also shows movies like *The Deer Hunter* and *sex, lies, and videotape.* Call the club for schedules and prices.

Admission: Usually 50 Kr ($7.70), but more for big acts; double-feature movies, 70 Kr ($10.75).

Open: Daily 8pm–4am (occasionally it's closed, so call ahead).

DISCOS & CLUBS

The following dance floors don't heat up until about 11pm (midnight on Friday and Saturday), but most people arrive about an hour before to socialize.

BAROCK, Universitetsgate 26. Tel. 42-44-20.
Even though Barock (it's pronounced almost like "baroque") has been around since 1986, it has somehow been able to maintain its air of exclusivity. Some people eat dinner at the expensive restaurant here, but most show up when the music starts. Though there's no fee to enter, you must first pass the bouncer's discriminating eye. Besides the dance floor, there's a pub downstairs; a second disco, called Exit, is upstairs. The minimum age is 24.
Admission: Free.
Open: Sun–Mon 8pm–2:30am, Tues–Sat 6pm–2:30am.

COME BACK, Rosenkrantz Gate 11. Tel. 33-46-40.
Popular with students, this labyrinthine place has two dance floors and a line that stretches down the block on weekends. One dance floor features the latest music; the other, hits from the late '70s and early '80s.
Admission: 50 Kr ($7.70).
Open: Thurs–Fri 9pm–4am, Sat 6pm–4am.

THE GAY SCENE

Oslo is an open city and the gay and straight communities are not so separate as they are in other cities. The gay scene has grown here in the past few years, and new clubs spring up, then fade away. An old standby, Den Sorte Enke, is listed below, and it's a good place to get information about the latest gay hot spots for men and women.

DEN SORTE ENKE, Møllergaten 23. Tel. 11-05-60.
This casual club attracts men of all ages, as well as women. There are three bars downstairs, including a leather bar open on Friday and Saturday only, a mirror-lined disco, which starts at 11pm (no dancing Monday or Thursday), and a roulette wheel. Upstairs, they spin discs described as "Sixties eclectic." Call about upcoming special events.
Admission: Free Sun–Thurs, 45 Kr ($6.90) Fri–Sat.
Open: Daily 6pm–4am.

9. EASY EXCURSIONS

OSLO'S ISLANDS You don't need a lot of time or money to take a short trip out of the city. In fact, all you need is a few hours and 15 Kr ($2.30) for a ferry ticket to one of the port islands. **Hovedøya,** known for its centuries-old cloister, is popular for swimming and exploring. And **Langøyene** is famous for its nude beaches and warm-weather walking. Ferries leave from early morning to 7:30pm from Vippetangen pier, south of Akershus. Although there are island cafés, it's probably best to pack a lunch. Check with the tourist board for current ferry times and further information.

LILLEHAMMER Site of the 1994 winter Olympic games (February 12–27), little Lillehammer is home to 22,000 people and an incredibly beautiful open-air museum called **Maihaugen.** With more than 130 preserved buildings, many with sod roofs, it is also the largest such site in northern Europe. Admission to the park and buildings is 40 Kr ($6.15) for adults, 15 Kr ($2.30) for children. The **Tourist Information Center** is conveniently located beside the train station. The **Olympics Information Center,** just off Storgata, the pedestrian walking street, has an exhibition hall and an excellent slide show about the area in English.

Lillehammer is due north of Oslo and a 2¾-hour train ride away; sit on the left side of the train for scenic views of **Lake Mjosa,** the largest in Norway. The round-trip will cost about $60 unless you have a Eurail or ScanRail pass.

"NORWAY IN A NUTSHELL" & BERGEN In just a couple of days it's possible to experience the breathtaking beauty that makes Norway the most spectacular of all the Scandinavian countries. From Oslo, you can travel to Bergen by train along one of the prettiest routes in Europe—a 291-mile (470km), 6½-hour odyssey that winds through towns, forests, farmland, mountains, lakes, waterfalls, glaciers, and fjords. If you're really strapped for time and don't have even two days to invest, you can see an amazing variety of scenery on an unguided excursion called **"Norway in a Nutshell"** (no guide necessary; the brochures and maps explain everything in vivid detail).

It's an action- and image-packed 12 hours, and with a Eurail, Scanrail, or Nordtourist pass, not expensive at all. All you'll pay extra is boat and bus fare, about 40 Kr ($6.15) and 55 Kr ($8.45). Without the train pass, you're looking at a total tour price of about 400 Kr ($61.55), half price for children. You can do the trip from either Oslo or Bergen as a round-trip, or leave one city and arrive in the other at the end of the day.

Starting out in Oslo, you'll depart by train at 7:30am (same time from Bergen; both trains meet up in Myrdal five hours later). Either side of the train affords gorgeous vistas, perhaps slightly more so on the right side. As it travels west, the train climbs past the popular ski area of **Geilo** (pronounced y-*Eye*-lo) to a stark 62-mile-long (100km) mountain plateau that separates eastern Norway from the western fjords. Four hours into the trip, you'll come to the highest point on the Bergen Line, at 4,267 feet (108m), just before Finse, and then a rapid succession of snow tunnels that blot out the panorama outside. (Bikers might like to know that at Finse there is a mountain-bike trail that goes all the way to Flåm.) At Myrdal, you'll change trains to begin a breathtaking, 50-minute train ride to **Flåm.** The small train dips 2,841 feet while whisking you past snow-capped peaks and cascading waterfalls. There are a couple of stops along the way where you can snap photos and luxuriate in the views; otherwise, it's difficult to maneuver a camera, so put it down, sit back, and enjoy the ride.

In Flåm, you'll have an hour to catch your breath before the next leg of the journey, a boat trip; or you can overnight in this peaceful hamlet quite inexpensively in basic cabins for about 75 Kr ($11.55) per night (a four-minute hot shower will cost another 75¢), or at the pretty Fretheim Hotel (tel. 056/32-200; fax 056/32-303), where a double room with bath and breakfast starts at about 400 Kr ($61.55); the hotel has a heated pool and complimentary rowboats. Walk up the road behind the railroad station for a sweeping view of the Aurland Fjord; it'll take only five minutes.

From Flåm, a river steamer will take you down the **Aurland and Nerøy Fjords,** including one of the narrowest in Norway, to Gudvangen (choose the slower boat over the newer, faster, and bumpier ferry); the trip takes a couple of hours, and refreshments are available on board. From Gudvangen, a bus transports you through a scenic valley and on to a summit providing yet another spectacular view before linking you up in Voss with the train to Bergen (or back to Oslo). The "Norway in a Nutshell" tour, available year round (daily May through October, weekdays only off-season), may be booked through a travel agent in Oslo or through the tourist information office in Bergen.

Bergen Norway's second-largest city, with a population of 214,000, Bergen was founded in 1070 and was the home of composer Edvard Grieg. Besides being the gateway to some of the country's most stunning fjords, "the city of the seven hills" is filled with old-world charm and definitely deserves exploration on its own merits. The **Tourist Information Center,** Torgalmenning (tel. 05/32-14-80), can provide information on "Norway in a Nutshell," answer questions, and provide maps, brochures, and a copy of the *Bergen Guide 1993;* ask about the **Norway Fjord Pass** and the savings on bed-and-breakfast accommodation it represents.

While in Bergen, be sure to see **Bryggen,** the city's row of medieval buildings.

Bryggen is on UNESCO's World Heritage List and today is filled with shops, clubs, restaurants, and a handy fruit market; if the buildings look vaguely familiar, you may have seen replicas of them at Walt Disney's Epcot Center in Florida. Near Bryggen is the lively **fish market,** held Monday through Friday from 8am to 3pm. Flowers, produce, and souvenirs are also sold here. Go early.

For fun and a thrilling view, take the **funicular,** opposite the fish market, to the top of 1,050-foot-high (320m) Mount Fløien. It runs every half hour from early morning until 11pm and is as practical as it is touristic, serving as a vertical subway for residents who live on the steep slope. The price of the trip is 13 Kr ($2) each way, 6 Kr (90¢) for children. You can hike in the woods on marked trails .8 to 3.3 miles long before the return trip down, or walk all the way back (allow about an hour), getting some good exercise and saving on the return fare (ask at tourist information for a map of trails).

If you are interested in Norwegian painting, be sure to see the **Rasmus Meyers Collection,** Rasmus Meyers Allé 7 (tel. 97-80-00), which contains many works of Edvard Munch. It's open mid-May to mid-September, Monday through Saturday from 11am to 4pm and on Sunday from noon to 3pm; off-season, daily except Tuesday from noon to 3pm. Admission is 10 Kr ($1.55), free off-season.

If you have time, **Troldhaugen,** the home and final resting place of Edvard Grieg, where there is a museum, garden, and chamber music hall (you might visit on a day when a concert is scheduled), or **Fantoft Stavkirke,** an early 12th-century stave church, or take one of the numerous sightseeing tours or fjord excursions that are available. Both Troldhaugen and the church take about half an hour to reach by bus and then walking a short distance; both charge a small admission fee, and are open May through September (check exact dates and times).

The annual **Bergen International Festival** is celebrated with music and other activities from mid-June to mid-August. In 1993 the 150th anniversary of the birth of Edvard Grieg will attract additional attention to this exuberant city.

In Bergen, you can get reasonably priced pizza and pasta at **Jeppe's Kro & Pizzeria,** Vågsalmenning 6, open daily for lunch and dinner. For Norwegian food (at higher prices), sample the fare at the **Tracteursted,** a historic tavern in Bryggen (tel. 31-40-46), open for meals May through August only; if you bring your own fish, they'll cook it for you. They serve libations year round, and sometimes there's live music. **Baker Brun,** in the Havtrygd building at the fish market, is a good choice for coffee and sweets.

For an inexpensive overnight, book one of the 11 modest rooms, two with private bath, at the quiet home of **Svien Ølfarnes,** Skivebakken 24, 5018 Bergen (tel. 05/312-044 or 05/317-278). It's a five-minute walk from the train station, and you get kitchen privileges. If you prefer a hotel room, the family-run **Romantik Hotel Park,** near the university at Harald Hårfagres Gate 35, N-5007 Bergen (tel. 05/32-09-60; fax 05/31-03-34), has 20 rooms with private bath (with shower) and TV; the special summer double rate is 310 Kr ($47.70). For about $10 more, you can stay in Best Western's lovely, centrally located 43-room **Victoria Hotel,** where a double room runs 360 Kr ($55.40) a night in summer.

THE SEACOAST Norway's beaches are actually closer to Oslo than its fjords. To experience a few of them firsthand, head due south by train to Tonsberg, a seafaring town that predates the Vikings (A.D. 871). There's swimming and sunning on Notteroy and Tjome islands and plenty of sightseeing in the town itself, including Sem Church, built in 1100. To explore the coast further, take a connecting bus or local train south to the villages of Kragerø and Risør, and visit the archipelago along the coast. This excursion could easily mark the beginning of a trip to Telemark (see below).

TELEMARK Southwest of Oslo, this idyllic region stretches from the Skagerrak coast to the high mountain moors of Hardanger. Telemark is filled with seaswept rocky shores, forests, mountains, moors, valleys, rivers, lakes, canals, open farmland, and picturesque Nordic villages. A highlight of a visit here in summer is a 10-hour boat trip along the Telemark Canal from Skien to Dalen. The area offers ample opportunities for hiking, fishing, sailing, windsurfing, horseback riding, and canoeing. Equally popular in winter, it is a magnet for skiers. The term "Telemark skiing" takes its name from the region, which is also the natural haunt of trolls. These wily creatures have eight fingers and eight toes, carry their heads under their arms, live in the dark, and turn to stone in the sun. Norway's foremost painter of trolls and elves, Theodor Kittelsen, was born in 1857 in Telemark, in Kragerø.

PARIS

What do Chopin, Oscar Wilde, Isadora Duncan, and Jim Morrison have in common? Two things: None of them was a native Parisian, yet all of them died in the French capital and are buried in the city's grand and melancholy Père-Lachaise Cemetery. Of all cities, Paris has lived deepest in the imagination of the world, as much a legend or an archetype, a dream or a myth, as a real city. People have come here from every continent, and when you see the graves of so many legendary foreigners at Père-Lachaise, next to Molière, Proust, Edith Piaf, and other French greats, you understand that Paris is not only the capital of France but also, to a large extent, the capital of the world.

What is no legend is the urban splendor of Paris. Each of the city's famous landmarks is like a vision: the Seine and Notre-Dame, the Arc de Triomphe, the lacelike Eiffel Tower. You'll wander through streets, parks, and entire neighborhoods that are astoundingly beautiful: the Latin Quarter and its labyrinthine side streets, the 17th-century mansions in the Marais, the grand avenue Foch and the diminutive place de Furstemberg. Even the art nouveau gateways to the Métro are endearing.

Yet millennia-old Paris is no dusty museum. It is more modern in many ways than most North American cities. Sleek designs brighten the solid gray facades, computers called *minitel* have replaced phone books, and the swift RER trains, part of the Métro, traverse the city in minutes. And then there are the futuristic, controversial public works of the last two decades: the Centre Pompidou, the Louvre pyramids, and the new Opéra on place de la Bastille. Despite its many illustrious dead, Paris is very much alive and vibrant.

1. FROM A BUDGET TRAVELER'S POINT OF VIEW

Many people imagine that Paris is breathtakingly expensive. That's not true. Some things in Paris are expensive, some are moderate in price, and others are positively dirt cheap. And then there's the question of value for money. An excellent 80F ($14.80) lunch is a bargain; a terrible 45F ($8.35) lunch is a ripoff. Dollar for dollar and franc for franc, Paris offers excellent value for money.

Food costs more in Paris than in some other European cities, but it is generally excellent, as is the service in restaurants. Hotels are moderately priced, and if you plan ahead you will find a small, clean, friendly hotel well within your budget. Transportation on the fast, relatively safe Métro is an indisputable bargain. Paris's beautiful churches and parks are all free, and so are many of its renowned museums one day a week, and if not they may have reduced rates. Refreshments in a café may seem expensive until you realize you are not just paying for a cup of coffee or a glass of wine but for *ambience.*

WHAT THINGS COST IN PARIS	U.S. $
Taxi from Charles de Gaulle Airport to the city center	46.00
Taxi from Orly Airport to the city center	37.00
Public transportation for an average trip within the city (from a Métro *carnet* of 10)	.65
Local telephone call	.20
Double room at the Ritz (deluxe)	470.00
Double room at the Hôtel Jardin des Plantes (moderate)	96.30
Double room at the Hôtel Marignan (budget)	45.00
Lunch for one, without wine, at Au Vieux Casque (moderate)	17.00
Lunch for one, without wine, at Ma Normandie (budget)	10.00
Dinner for one, without wine, at Maxim's (deluxe)	125.00
Dinner for one, without wine, at Bofinger (moderate)	33.00
Dinner for one, without wine, at La Petite Hostellerie (budget)	11.00
Glass of wine	3.70
Coca-Cola	3.70
Cup of coffee	3.50
Roll of ASA 100 color film, 36 exposures	6.50
Admission to the Louvre	6.00
Movie ticket	7.50
Theater ticket (at the Comédie Française)	23.00

PARIS BUDGET BESTS

Choose a hotel room with only as much plumbing as you want. Every room has a private sink with hot and cold water, others also have a shower, still others a bathroom complete with bathtub. Walking a few steps down the hall to the bath or shower will save you quite a lot of money. The price of a single room with full private bath at the Hôtel St. Jacques is 275F ($50.90); for a single room without a private bath it's as low as 146F ($27.05), a saving of nearly 50%.

For lunch and dinner, order the *menu du jour,* the daily fixed-price meal of three or four courses, or just have the *plat du jour* (daily special plate). These offerings are invariably fresh and delicious, and come to you at the best possible price, much cheaper than if you ordered them à la carte. Also, avoid ordering special wines, which can be quite expensive. Order *vin ordinaire* (table wine in a carafe); in fact, if you ask simply for *vin,* that's what the waiter will bring.

In a café, if it's not the ambience but only the drink that you want—a quick cup of coffee or tea, a cooling soft drink, a warming glass of wine or beer—have it while standing at the counter. It costs 40% more to sit down.

To get around town, avoid taxicabs and take the Métro, or just walk. To save on the Métro, buy tickets 10 at a time as a *carnet* (booklet), or get one of the special discount deals listed below.

SPECIAL DISCOUNT OPPORTUNITIES

FOR EVERYONE The best discount opportunities are provided by the RATP (public transportation) cards and the Carte Intermusées.

WHAT'S SPECIAL ABOUT PARIS

Attractions

☐ The smaller museums, such as the Musée de l'Orangerie and the Musée Nissim de Camondo.

☐ Viewing the city from the top of the Eiffel Tower or the Arc de Triomphe.

☐ Exploring historical neighborhoods such as the Latin Quarter and the Marais.

☐ Walking along the Seine, Paris's moody river.

☐ Biking around the vast Bois de Boulogne and relaxing in the intimate place des Vosges, two of Paris's many beautiful parks and squares.

☐ The spectacular Euro Disney Resort, 20 miles outside the city.

Architecture

☐ New, ultramodern structures: the Centre Pompidou, the Louvre pyramids, the Grande Arche de la Défense.

Performing Arts

☐ Performances at Paris's world-renowned stages: the Comédie Française, the Opéra-Garnier, the Opéra-Bastille.

Restaurants

☐ Paris's great restaurants, among the best in the world, definitely worth the splurge.

☐ Sidewalk cafés, where you can watch the world go by.

If you plan to use public transportation frequently, you should consider the **Carte Orange,** a weekly or monthly pass that is quite economical—54F ($10) for a week's unlimited travel (*coupon hebdomadaire*), or 190F ($35.20) for a month's pass (*coupon mensuel*). The only catch is that you must provide a little photo of yourself, and this will increase the price a bit. The weekly Carte Orange must be bought any time from Monday through Wednesday morning, and it is valid through Sunday; get the monthly card on the first or second day of each month.

Otherwise, buying a *carnet* for 34.50F ($6.40) is also a good deal; a single ticket is 5.50F ($1).

The **Carte Intermusées,** good for entry into 62 museums and monuments in Paris and the Ile-de-France region, is on sale at the museums and at major Métro stations. It comes in three varieties: 55F ($10.20) for one day, 110F ($20.35) for three days, and 160F ($29.60) for five days. For the price of the card, you can avoid the ticket lines and walk right into the Louvre, the Musée d'Orsay, the Orangerie, the Picasso Museum, the Panthéon, and the châteaux de Versailles, Malmaison, and Fontainebleau, to mention only a few. But even if you don't buy this card, you can save money by visiting the museums on the day when they have free or reduced admissions. The Louvre, for instance, has reduced admission on certain days of the week.

Another money-saver is the **VAT refund.** As in other countries of the European Community, you can often get a refund on the hefty Value-Added Tax ("TVA" in French) levied on retail purchases. If you purchase more than 2,000F ($370) worth of goods in a single shop, you should request the shopkeeper to make out an export sales invoice (*bordereau*), which you will show to the French Customs officer when you leave the country (at the airport, on the train, at the highway border post—remember to show it!). In a number of weeks the shop will send you a check for the amount of the refund. Not all shops participate in the program, so ask before you buy.

FOR CHILDREN & YOUTHS Anyone under age 18 is admitted free to France's national museums.

If you have a child under age 16 and you plan to travel in France by train, you should explore the possibility of buying a **Carte KIWI** for the child. At 395F ($73.15) it's not cheap, but it may be a good deal in the long run. With this card, the child gets a 50% discount on trips that start in the *période blanche* or *période bleue* (white or blue periods) of the train riders' calendar, some 300 days a year, and everybody accompanying the child (up to four people who do not need to be relatives) also benefits from a 50% discount. For more information, get the brochure "Votre enfant voyage en train," with an English section, from any train station.

FOR STUDENTS & PEOPLE UNDER AGE 25   Students are privileged people in France. All sorts of reductions are offered to holders of a valid **ISIC (International-al Student Identity Card)**. ISIC cards are sold at the **AJF,** 119, rue St-Martin (see "Information" in "Orientation and Getting Around," below), for 45F ($8.35), provided you show proof of your student registration and bring a photograph. You can gain admission to national museums at half price and reductions on train, bus, plane, and even movie and theater tickets. Flash your ISIC whenever you take out your wallet to pay for something—even if no reduction is advertised. You'll be astounded at the number of discounts granted. For more on student savings, see "Information" in "Orientation and Getting Around," below.

Even if you are not a student, but are between ages 18 and 24, you may be entitled to many of the same reductions on all sorts of sights and transportation tickets that students are. Ask whenever you are going to pay for something—your passport should serve as proof of your age.

FOR SENIORS   Drop in at one of Paris's railroad stations and buy a **Carte Vermeil** for 165F ($30.55), valid for one year. With the card, travelers over age 60 will get reductions of up to 50% on certain train trips (starting in the *période bleue*), plane and bus fares, theater tickets, and national museum admissions.

Even without the Carte Vermeil you may be entitled to some discounts, especially on museums and sights. Always ask before paying.

WORTH THE EXTRA BUCKS

The restaurants of Paris are well worth a splurge. Food may seem expensive here, so look on it as the French do: one of life's greatest pleasures. Dining in Paris, albeit expensive, can be a truly memorable experience.

2. PRETRIP PREPARATIONS

DOCUMENTS   For visits of less than three months, all that American and Canadian travelers need is a valid passport.

WHAT TO PACK   Parisians dress well. You can wear whatever you want, but you'll feel much more at home if you dress carefully, whatever the style. Have at least one dressy outfit for the theater and for that splurge in a more expensive restaurant. How much do people dress up in Paris? On Friday, diners at Maxim's come in gowns and tuxedos.

Most of the time, though, tidy, casual clothing is what's wanted. That's what most Parisians at leisure will be wearing.

In summer the city can be hot and humid; in winter, quite cold and chilly, without much sunshine. Take light cottons for summer days, but a sweater or jacket at night; a sweater or jacket or topcoat for spring and autumn; woolens for winter. Take rain gear also. As you can see from the chart below, Paris can be a rainy place at any time of year.

WHEN TO GO Although April in Paris may sometimes be too cold for some travelers, spring and fall are normally the best times to be in the city. Temperatures are usually mild, and the performing arts and other cultural activities are in full bloom. In winter, the lack of sunshine and the occasional bitter-cold wind can be disappointing, but then again, there is so much to see and do inside the buildings of Paris that you won't miss the picnics in the parks.

Like winter, summer can be mild or extreme, depending on the year and your luck. The number of foreign tourists increases, and many Parisians, especially in August, head for the coast or the mountains. The city is transformed, and the banks of the Seine become a make-shift beach: Paris-Plage. Cultural life dwindles and many restaurants, cafés, and shops close for up to a month, what the French call the *fermeture annuelle* (annual closing). The long hours of daylight, though, will give you more time to explore the city and its street life.

Paris's Average Daytime Temperature & Rainfall

	Jan	Feb	Mar	Apr	May	June	July	Aug	Sept	Oct	Nov	Dec
Temp. (°F)	38	39	46	51	58	64	66	66	61	53	45	40
Rainfall "	3.22	2.9	2.4	2.7	3.2	3.5	3.3	3.7	3.3	3.0	3.5	3.1

Special events In the first weeks of January, the big Parisian stores have their annual sales, and there are bargains galore. This is also the month when Paris's boat show is held at La Défense: the **Salon International de la Navigation de Plaisance.**

July 14 is **Bastille Day** and there are enormous celebrations throughout the city, ending with fireworks near the Eiffel Tower. Also in July is the end of the **Tour de France,** and thousands of spectators crowd the Champs-Elysées to witness the finish of this passion-inspiring, month-long bicycle race.

New Year's Eve is called the **Fête de St-Sylvestre,** and it's a night when people go out for enormous multicourse table d'hôte meals in their favorite restaurants. Places at the banquet table are reserved in advance, and can cost as much as $185 per person—but what a feast! It can be difficult to find a simple, normal meal on New Year's Eve.

At virtually any time of the year, there seems to be some sort of music, dance, or drama festival taking place in Paris. Contact the French National Tourist Board in the United States for a complete list (see the Appendix for a complete mailing address and phone number).

BACKGROUND READING Probably more books have been written about Paris than about any other European capital. Here are some personal favorites. Janet Flanner's *Paris Was Yesterday* (Harcourt Brace Jovanovich) is a collection of articles written for *The New Yorker* on diverse aspects of the city's life in the 1920s and '30s; many of the themes portrayed can still be observed today. Dealing with the same period—and America's Lost Generation—is Hemingway's *A Moveable Feast* (Scribner's). Some classic novels include Dickens's *A Tale of Two Cities* (Putnam), set during the French Revolution, and Henry James's *The American* (Norton) and *The Ambassadors* (Penguin), tales that contrast France and America. French writers, of course, have also masterfully captured Paris in literature: Proust's long, rich *Remembrance of Things Past* (Random House); Colette's romantic novels like *Chéri* (Ballantine) and *Gigi* (Farrar, Straus & Giroux); and Simone de Beauvoir's *Memoirs of a Dutiful Daughter* (Schoenhof), a critical account of the author's bourgeois upbringing. Finally, Julio Cortázar, an Argentinean, wrote *Hopscotch* (Pantheon), an experimental novel on literature and bohemia set in the city's streets, bridges, and garrets.

3. ORIENTATION & GETTING AROUND

ARRIVING IN PARIS

FROM THE AIRPORTS   Paris has two airports handling international traffic: Charles de Gaulle and Orly.

Largest, busiest, and most modern is **Aéroport Charles-de-Gaulle** (CDG, sometimes called Roissy–Charles-de-Gaulle), 14½ miles northeast of downtown. Terminal 1 (*Aérogare 1*) is devoted to foreign airlines; Terminal 2 (*Aérogare 2*) is reserved for Air France and a few of its affiliates. A shuttle bus (*navette*) connects the two giant terminals with one another and with the Roissy–Charles-de-Gaulle station of the RER suburban train line. From the station, RER Line B3 trains depart about every 15 minutes on the half-hour trip into town, stopping at Gare du Nord, the mammoth Châtelet–Les Halles Métro interchange, and the RER stations of St-Michel, Luxembourg, Port-Royal, and Denfert-Rochereau, before heading southward out of the city again. A ticket into town on the RER costs 31F ($5.75), or 47F ($8.70) if you want to go first class (not worth it).

Besides the RER, Air France runs shuttle buses from both terminals to the Porte-Maillot Métro station, next to Paris's huge convention center on the western end of the city, and to place Charles-de-Gaulle and the Arc de Triomphe, near some of the budget hotels listed below. There are several buses per hour and they charge 39F ($7.20) for the 40-minute trip.

A taxi into town from Charles-de-Gaulle takes between 40 and 50 minutes and costs about 200F ($37.05) from 7am to 8pm, about 35% more at other times.

Aéroport d'Orly (ORY), 8½ miles south of the city center, receives mostly charter and tour flights at its two terminals, Orly-Ouest for French domestic flights and Orly-Sud for inter-European and intercontinental flights. Shuttle buses connect the two terminals, and other shuttles run between Orly and Charles-de-Gaulle airports every half hour or so.

To get downtown from Orly, take the shuttle bus (every 15 minutes) to the RER station named Pont-de-Rungis–Aéroport d'Orly, and catch a Line C2 train for 25F ($4.60) for the 25-minute trip into town. The train has several downtown stops; at Gare d'Austerlitz, St-Michel, and Invalides you can change to the Métro to reach your final destination.

There's also an Air France shuttle bus for 33F ($6.10) from Orly to the Air France bus terminal, the Aérogare des Invalides, right at the Invalides Métro station just across the Seine from place de la Concorde. The bus runs about five times per hour, and takes a half hour to reach the center. On the way, it makes a stop at Gare de Montparnasse just south of downtown.

A taxi from Orly into the city costs about 160F ($29.60) and takes 40–50 minutes.

FROM THE TRAIN STATIONS   Paris has six major train stations. For information, call the SNCF (Société Nationale des Chemins de Fer) at 45-82-50-50, and ask for someone who speaks English, or go to a travel agent or the information booths at the stations.

Coming from northern Germany and Belgium, you'll probably arrive at **Gare du Nord** (some trains from London arrive here as well). Other trains from London and Normandy come into **Gare St-Lazare,** in northwest Paris. Trains from the west (Brittany, Chartres, Versailles) head to **Gare de Montparnasse;** those from the southwest (the Loire Valley, Bordeaux, the Pyrenees, Spain) to **Gare d'Austerlitz;** those from the south and southeast (the Riviera, Lyon, Italy, Geneva) to **Gare de Lyon.** From Alsace and eastern France, Luxembourg, southern Germany, and Zurich, the arrival station is **Gare de l'Est.** All train stations are next to a Métro station bearing the same name.

FROM THE BUS STATION   International buses pull into Paris's **Gare Routière**

Internationale (International Bus Terminal) at 35, avenue Porte-de-la-Villette, in the 19th arrondissement, the northeastern part of the city. This is not a wonderful part of town, and there are crime problems. The Métro station here is Porte-de-la-Villette; to go downtown, take Line 7 in the direction of either Mairie d'Ivry or Villejuif–Louis-Aragon. For information on bus schedules and fares, call 40-38-93-93.

INFORMATION

FOR EVERYONE   There are small information offices at the airports, and for a fee they will help you to make a hotel reservation. But the prime source of information is the **Office de Tourisme de Paris,** 127, Champs-Elysées, 8e (tel. 46-23-61-72; Métro: Charles-de-Gaulle–Etoile or George-V), open daily from 9am to 8pm. For a fee, they will make a hotel reservation for you on the same day that you want a room: 7F ($1.30) for hostels and *foyers,* 18F ($3.35) for one-star hotels, 25F ($4.60) for two-star hotels, 40F ($7.40) for three-star hotels. The office and its reservation service are often very busy in the summer season—you will probably have to wait in line.

The Office de Tourisme has five auxiliary offices: at Gare du Nord (open May through October, Monday through Saturday from 8am to 9pm and on Sunday from 1 to 8pm; November through April, Monday through Saturday from 8am to 8pm); at Gare de l'Est and Gare de Lyon (open May through October, Monday through Saturday from 8am to 10pm; November through April, until 8pm); at Gare d'Austerlitz (open May through October, Monday through Saturday from 8am to 10pm; November through April, until 3pm); and at the Eiffel Tower (open May through September, daily from 11am to 6pm).

FOR STUDENTS   Paris, with its huge student population both native and foreign, has all sorts of organizations providing information on student-travel discounts:

AJF (Accueil des Jeunes en France), 119, rue St-Martin, 4e (tel. 42-77-87-80; Métro: Rambuteau; RER: Châtelet–Les-Halles), across place Pompidou from the entrance to the Centre Pompidou. AJF helps students and people up to age 35 find student restaurants and obtain inexpensive lodgings, meal vouchers, student cards, and discount train, bus, and plane tickets. This central booking office is open all year, Monday through Saturday from 9am to 5:30pm. They also have a smaller, usually less busy office in the Marais at 16, rue du Pont-Louis-Philippe, 4e (tel. 42-78-04-82; Métro: Pont-Marie, Hôtel-de-Ville, or St-Paul), as well as an office in the Latin Quarter, at 139, boulevard St-Michel, 5e (tel. 43-54-95-86), usually open March to October, Monday through Friday from 10am to 6:30pm, and an office at the Gare du Nord (tel. 42-85-86-19; Métro: Gare du Nord), normally open March to October, Monday through Friday from 9:30am to 6:30pm (in June, July, and August, daily from 8am to 10pm).

OTU (Office pour le Tourisme Universitaire), 137, boulevard St-Michel, 5e (tel. 43-29-12-88; Métro: Port-Royal), open in summer only, can help you find a bed in a hostel or *foyer,* and provide information on student travel both in France and abroad.

UCRIF (Union des Centres de Rencontres Internationales de France), 4, rue Jean-Jacques-Rousseau, 1er (tel. 42-60-42-40; Métro: Louvre-Rivoli), operates more than 60 hostels throughout France, and though they cater to groups, they have an information and reservation service for individuals.

CITY LAYOUT

Medieval Paris was at the heart of the modern city, but since medieval times Paris has grown and absorbed many surrounding communities. Some of these former villages live on as the *arrondissements,* or "municipal boroughs," each with its own local government. The arrondissements are numbered from 1 to 20, starting at the old center of town, around the Louvre, and progressing in a clockwise spiral. Most Parisian addresses will bear the number of the arrondissement: for example, 1er is for the first (*premier*), 2e for the second (*deuxième*), and so on. The arrondissement number is usually (but not always) the last three digits in the postal code. Thus the tourist office is in postal zone 75008—"75" for Paris and "008" for the 8e arrondissement.

Each arrondissement has a character and a meaning for Parisians. The 1er is the Louvre, the Comédie Française, the Banque de France—museums, theater, commerce. Most of the 3e and the 4e is the Marais, the ancient Jewish quarter and home of the aristocracy in the 17th century, now a trendy area of boutiques and restored mansions. The 5e is the Sorbonne, the university, students, bookstores, and cafés. Parts of the 7e, the 8e, and the 16e are well-heeled residential districts. The 18e and the 19e include some of Paris's poorer neighborhoods.

The Seine divides Paris into a **Right Bank** (*rive droite*) and a **Left Bank** (*rive gauche*). The right (north) bank of the river is where you'll find the Louvre, the Opéra, the posh boutiques along rue du Faubourg-St-Honoré, and, *very generally speaking,* the higher-priced part of town. On the left (south) bank are the boulevards St-Michel and St-Germain-des-Prés, the Sorbonne and the Latin Quarter, and, again, generally speaking, much of the city's lower-priced lifestyle. These distinctions are more traditional than hard and fast.

Paris streets change names as they make their way through the city. If you come to a corner and don't see the street name you expect, look on the opposite corner.

The 20 arrondissements are surrounded by Paris's vast *banlieue,* the suburbs. People often speak of *la région parisienne* (the Parisian region) to refer to the Greater Paris area.

GETTING AROUND

The best way to get around Paris is to walk, and entire neighborhoods such as the Latin Quarter and the Marais can be easily negotiated that way. For longer distances, the Métro is best.

BY SUBWAY [METRO] Fast, clean, quite safe, and easy to navigate, the Métro opened its first line in 1900. It is operated by the RATP (Régie Autonome des Transports Parisiens), just like city buses. The Métro has 13 lines and more than 360 stations (there is bound to be one near your destination), and it is connected to the RER (Réseau Express Régional), with four lines that stop only at a few stations, crisscrossing the city in minutes and connecting downtown Paris with its airports. The trains run from 5:30am to past midnight, finishing up their final runs before 1am. The Métro and the RER operate on a zone system, at a different fare per zone, but it is unlikely that you will be traveling any farther than the first zone.

A single ticket (*un billet*) costs 5.50F ($1) but if you ask for *un carnet* (a booklet) you will get 10 (loose) tickets for 34.50F ($6.40) dropping the price per ticket to only 64¢. If you are going to be in Paris for a few days, it may be a better idea to get a weekly or monthly unlimited-ride Carte Orange; see "Special Discount Opportunities" in "From the Budget Traveler's Point of View," above.

Make sure to keep your ticket until you exit the train platform and pass the *limite de validité des billets.* An inspector may ask to see it at any time before that.

The older Métro stations are marked by playful art nouveau gateways reading "Métropolitain"; others are marked by M signs. Every Métro stop has maps of the system, and these are also available at ticket booths. Once you decide which Métro line you need, make sure you are going in the right *direction:* On Métro Line 1, "Direction: Pont de Neuilly" indicates a westbound train, while "Direction: Château de Vincennes" is just the opposite. To change train lines, look for the orange *correspondance* signs; blue signs reading *sortie* mark the exits.

Near the exits there is always a *plan du quartier,* a pictorial and very detailed map of the streets and buildings surrounding each Métro station, with all exits marked. It's often a good idea to consult the *plan du quartier* before you climb the stairs, especially at very large stations; you may want to use a different exit stairway so as to be on the other side of a busy street, or closer to where you are going.

For more information on the city's public transportation, stop in at any of the two offices of the Services Touristiques de la RATP, at 53 bis, quai des Grands-Augustins, 6e (Métro: St-Michel), or at place de la Madeleine, 8e (Métro: Madeleine), or call 43-46-14-14.

Picketpocket Warning   Most of the time the Métro is quite safe. Precautions are in order in the northern parts of the city, in deserted stations late at night, and in those long corridors between stations late at night. As a tourist, you are a special mark. You may feel safer riding in the first train car, where the engineer is. A special warning is in order against pickpockets, who operate in every subway system in the world. In Paris, these include bands of ragamuffins who will quickly surround you, distract you by waving something in your face, pick your pockets clean, and disappear, all within seconds. *Don't let them near you.* Be rude if you have to, but keep them at bay if you value your valuables. Similar situations may occur near tourist attractions.

BY BUS   Although generally slower than the Métro, buses allow you to see the sights as you ride. They take the same tickets as the Métro and also operate on a zone system, shown on charts in each bus.

BY TAXI   Parisian taxis are fairly expensive, but you should know a few things just in case you need one. For one to three people, the drop rate in Paris proper is 10F ($1.85) plus 2.62F (48¢) for every kilometer—or 4.32F (80¢) per mile—from 7am to 8pm, after which rates rise to 4.08F (75¢) for every kilometer. You will pay supplements from taxi ranks at train stations and at the Air France shuttle-bus terminals of 4.50F (85¢), for luggage of 4F (75¢) and, if the driver agrees to do so, 6F ($1.10) for transporting a fourth person or 4F (75¢) for a pet.

Taxi drivers are required by law to transport disabled customers and to help them with wheelchairs, etc.

BY CAR   With its narrow streets and difficult parking, it would be crazy to drive from place to place in Paris. Even for excursions, the best way to go is on the extensive train and bus network. Rental cars are very expensive, fuel is expensive, and traffic fines are positively breathtaking. Renting a car can easily cost around 3,000F ($555) per week for the very cheapest one offered, even at special weekly rates with unlimited mileage, when all charges (including Collision Damage Waiver and fuel) are included. If you must, call **Hertz** in Paris (tel. 1/47-88-51-51); **Avis** (tel. 1/45-50-32-31); **Europcar** (National, Tilden) (tel. 1/30-43-82-82). All these companies and others have car-rental desks at the airports, train stations, and at Air France's Aérogare des Invalides (Métro: Invalides).

FAST
PARIS

Babysitters   There are several agencies in Paris offering babysitting services. Call one of these: Allo Maman Poule (tel. 47-47-78-78); Baby-Sitting Service, 18, rue Tronchet, 8e (tel. 46-37-51-24; Métro: Madeleine); and Kid Service, 159, rue de Rome, 17e (tel. 47-66-00-52; Métro: Gare-St-Lazare).

Banks   Banks are normally open Monday through Friday from 9am to noon and 1 or 1:30 to 4:30pm. Some banks have hours on Saturday morning. Some currency-exchange booths are open very long hours; see "Currency Exchange," below.

Business Hours   The *grands magasins* (department stores) are generally open Monday through Saturday from 9:30am to 6:30pm; smaller shops close for lunch and reopen around 2pm, but this has become rarer than it used to be. Many stores stay open until 7pm in summer; others are closed on Monday, especially in the morning. Large offices remain open all day, but some also close for lunch.

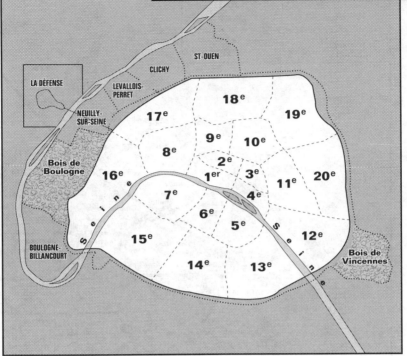

For banking hours, see "Banks," above.
For museum hours, see "Attractions," below.
For post office hours, see "Mail," below.
For restaurant hours, see "Budget Dining," below.

Consulates   If you have a passport, immigration, legal, or other problem, contact your consulate. Call before you go there, as they often keep strange hours and observe both French and home-country holidays. Here are the specifics: **Australia**—4, rue Jean-Rey, 15e (tel. 40-59-33-00); Métro: Bir-Hakeim. **Canada**—35, avenue Montaigne, 8e (tel. 47-23-01-01); Métro: Franklin-D.-Roosevelt or Alma-Marceau. **New Zealand**—7 ter, rue Léonard-de-Vinci, 16e (tel. 45-00-24-11); Métro: Victor-Hugo. **United Kingdom**—16, rue d'Anjou, 8e (tel. 42-66-91-42); Métro: Madeleine. **United States**—2, rue St-Florentin, 8e, just off the northeastern corner of place de la Concorde (tel. 42-96-12-02); Métro: Concorde.

Currency   The French franc (F) is divided into 100 centimes. There are coins of 5, 10, and 20 centimes, and ½, 1, 2, 5, and 10 francs. Sometimes there are two types of coins for one denomination, especially after the bicentennial of the French Revolution, when new commemorative coins were minted; many machines do not take the new 10F coins. Bills come in denominations of 20, 50, 100, 500, and 1,000 francs.

Currency Exchange   Call a commercial bank or look in the financial pages of your newspaper to find the current rate of exchange. You will get slightly less than this rate when you exchange money. Always ask if there is a fee or commission

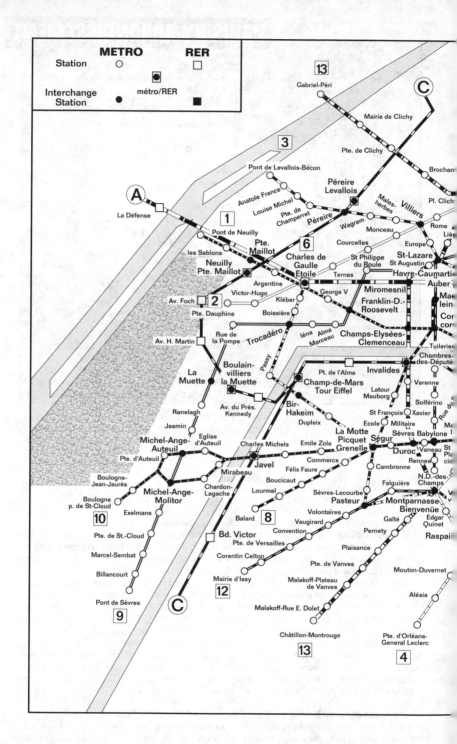

PARIS METRO AND RER

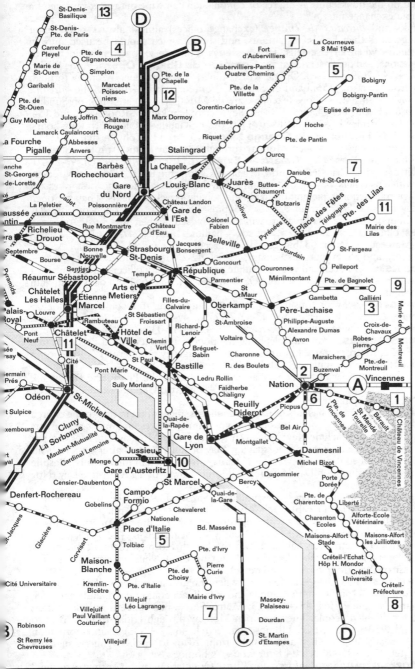

charged on the transaction. A big fee or commission can wipe out the advantage of a favorable exchange rate.

Banks and *bureaux de change* (exchange offices) almost always offer better exchange rates than hotels, restaurants, and shops, which should be used only in emergencies when all else fails. I have always found very good rates, no fees or commissions, and quick service at the **Comptoir de Change Opéra,** 9, rue Scribe, 9e (tel. 47-42-20-96; Métro: Opéra; RER: Auber). They are open Monday through Friday from 9am to 5:15pm and on Saturday from 9:30am to 4:15pm. The *bureaux de change* at all train stations (except Gare de Montparnasse) are open on Sunday; those at 66, avenue des Champs-Elysées, 8e (Métro: Franklin-D.-Roosevelt), and 154, avenue des Champs-Elysées, 8e (Métro: Charles-de-Gaulle–Etoile), keep long hours. The **Société Financière de Change Lincoln,** 11, rue Lincoln, 8e (tel. 42-25-22-57; Métro: George-V), is open Monday through Saturday from 10am to 7:30pm.

With a grand Paris office, **American Express,** 11, rue Scribe, 9e (tel. 47-77-70-00; Métro: Opéra, Chaussée-d'Antin, or Havre-Caumartin; RER: Auber), is extremely busy with customers buying and cashing traveler's checks (not the best rates for exchange transactions), picking up mail, and solving travel problems. They are open Monday through Friday from 9am to 5:30pm; the bank is also open on Saturday (same hours), but the mail-pickup window is closed. Other, less busy American Express offices are located at 5, rue de Chaillot, 16e (tel. 47-23-61-20; Métro: Alma-Marceau or Iéna); 83 bis, rue de Courcelles, 17e (tel. 47-66-03-00; Métro: Courcelles); and 38, avenue de Wagram, 8e (tel. 42-27-58-80; Métro: Ternes).

Dentists You can call your consulate and ask the duty officer to recommend a dentist. For dental emergencies, call SOS Dentaire (tel. 43-37-51-00) daily from 9am to midnight.

Doctors Call your consulate and ask the duty officer to recommend a doctor. Otherwise, call SOS Médecins (tel. 43-37-77-77 or 47-07-77-77), a 24-hour service. Doctors making house calls can be reached at 45-45-31-03.

Emergencies You can telephone the police, 9, boulevard du Palais, 4e (tel. 42-60-33-22; Métro: Cité), 24 hours a day; the emergency number is 17. To report a fire, dial 18. For an ambulance, call SAMU (tel. 45-67-50-50).

Paris has a number of all-night pharmacies, including the Pharmacie Dhéry, 84, avenue des Champs-Elysées, 8e (tel. 45-62-02-41; Métro: George-V), in the Galerie des Champs shopping center.

Holidays France has lots of national holidays, most of them tied to the church calendar. On these days, shops, businesses, government offices, and most restaurants will be closed. They include New Year's Day (Jan 1), Easter Monday (late Mar or Apr); Labor Day (May 1); Ascension Thursday (in May or June, 40 days after Easter); Whit Monday, also called Pentecost Monday (51st day after Easter, in June or July); Bastille Day (July 14); Assumption Day (Aug 15); All Saints Day (Nov 1); Armistice Day (Nov 11); and Christmas Day (Dec 25).

In addition, schedules may be disrupted on Shrove Tuesday (the Tuesday before Ash Wednesday, in Jan or Feb), and Good Friday (late Mar or Apr).

Hospitals Two hospitals with English-speaking staff are the American Hospital of Paris, 63, boulevard Victor-Hugo, Neuilly-sur-Seine (tel. 47-47-53-00), just west of Paris proper (Métro: Les Sablons); and the British Hospital of Paris, 48, rue de Villiers, Levallois-Perret (tel. 47-58-13-12), just north of Neuilly, over the city line northwest of Paris (Métro: Anatole-France).

Hotlines SOS Help is a crisis line where English is spoken; call 47-23-80-80 daily from 3 to 11pm. Comité National pour la Réadaptation des Handicapés, 38, boulevard Raspail, 7e (tel. 45-48-90-13; Métro: Sèvres-Babylone), is an information service for disabled people. They are open Monday through Friday from 9:30am to noon and 2:30 to 8pm. SOS Homosexualité (tel. 46-27-49-36) is an information service for gay people. They answer calls from 10am to 1am. Organisation Flora Tristan (tel. 47-36-96-48) is a 24-hour women's hotline.

Information See "Information" in "Orientation and Getting Around," above.

Laundry/Dry Cleaning To find a laundry near you, ask at your hotel or consult the *Yellow Pages* under "Laveries Automatiques." Take as many 10F, 2F, and 1F pieces as you can. Dry cleaning is "nettoyage à sec"; look for shop signs with the word PRESSING. Washing and drying 6 kilos (13¼ lb.) of stuff usually costs about 30F ($5.55).

Lost and Found The central office is Objets Perdus, 36, rue des Morillons, 15e (tel. 45-31-14-80; Métro: Convention), at the corner of rue de Dantzig; for objects left in a taxi, ask for extension 4208. They are open daily from 8am to 6pm, with longer hours on Tuesday and Thursday in the summer.

If you lose your VISA or MasterCard (both come under the name Carte Bleue in France), call 42-77-11-90, 24 hours a day. For lost American Express traveler's checks, call toll free 19/05-90-86-00.

Mail Large post offices (PTT) are normally open Monday through Friday from 8am to 7pm and on Saturday from 8am to noon; small post offices may have shorter hours. There are many post offices scattered around the city; ask anybody for the nearest one.

The city's main post office is at 52, rue du Louvre, 75001 Paris (tel. 40-28-20-00). It is open 24 hours a day for urgent mailings, telegrams, and telephone calls. This is where you should go to pick up Poste Restante (general delivery) mail; be prepared to show your passport and pay a small fee for each letter you receive.

Police Dial 17 in emergencies; otherwise 42-60-33-22.

Radio/TV The English-language *Paris Passion* magazine has an excellent "TV & Radio" section that highlights the more interesting programs currently on the air.

Religious Services All major religions are represented in Paris. Here are some specifics: St. Joseph's Roman Catholic Church, 50, avenue Hoche, 8e (tel. 42-27-28-56; Métro: Charles-de-Gaulle–Etoile); American Church (Episcopal), 65, quai d'Orsay, 7e (tel. 47-05-07-99; Métro: Invalides); International Baptist Fellowship, 123, avenue du Maine, 14e (tel. 47-49-15-29; Métro: Mouton-Duvernet); Lutheran Church, 16, rue Chauchat, 9e (tel. 47-70-80-30; Métro: Richelieu-Drouot); Eglise Grecque Orthodoxe (Greek Orthodox), 7, rue Georges-Bizet, 16e (tel. 47-20-82-35; Métro: Alma-Marceau); Cathédrale Orthodoxe Alexandre-Nevsky (Russian Orthodox), 12, rue Daru, 8e (tel. 42-27-37-34; Métro: Courcelles); Association Israélite de Paris (Jewish), 17, rue St-Georges, 9e (tel. 42-85-71-09; Métro: Le Peletier); Mosquée de Paris (Muslim), place du Puits-de-l'Ermite, 5e (tel. 45-35-97-33; Métro: Monge).

Tax For information on France's TVA (Value-Added Tax), see "Special Discount Opportunities" in "From a Budget Traveler's Point of View," above.

Taxis See "Orientation and Getting Around," above.

Telephone Pay telephones take coins of ½, 1, 2, and 5F; the minimum charge is 1F (18¢). Most pay phones, though, take only telephone debit cards called *télécartes* that can be bought at post offices and at *tabacs* (cafés and kiosks that sell tobacco products). The minimum charge using a *télécarte* is 80 centimes (15¢), so you save some money by using a card. All you do is insert the card into the phone and make your call; the cost of the call is automatically deducted from the "value" of the card as recorded on its magnetized strip. The *télécarte* comes in 50- and 120-unit values, costing 40F ($7.40) and 96F ($17.75) respectively. If you do not plan to make many phone calls, a *télécarte* may not be a very good idea, since you may end up not using its entire value. They come in very handy, though, for making long-distance calls.

For placing **international calls** to other countries, dial 19, then the country code (for the U.S. and Canada it's "1"), then the area or city code, then the local number. To place a collect call to North America, dial 19/33-11 and an English-speaking operator will assist you. Dial 19/00-11 for an American AT&T operator.

For calling France outside Paris (*province*), dial 16, then the local number.

Avoid making any phone calls from your hotel room; many hotels charge at least 2F (37¢) for local calls.

Tipping Service is supposedly included at your hotel, but it is still customary to tip the bellhop about 6F ($1.10) per bag, more in expensive splurge hotels. You might use 5% of the daily room rate as a guideline. If you have lots of luggage, tip a bit more. Though your *addition* (restaurant bill) or *fiche* (café check) will bear the words

THE FRANC & THE DOLLAR

At this writing $1 = approximately 5.40F (or 1F = 18½¢), and this was the rate of exchange used to calculate the dollar values given in this chapter (rounded to the nearest nickel). This rate fluctuates from time to time and may not be the same when you travel to France. Therefore the following table should be used only as a guide:

F	$U.S.	F	$U.S.
1	.18	100	18.52
2	.37	125	23.15
3	.56	150	27.78
4	.74	175	32.41
5	.93	200	37.04
6	1.11	225	41.67
7	1.30	250	46.30
8	1.48	275	50.93
9	1.67	300	55.56
10	1.85	325	60.19
15	2.78	350	64.81
20	3.70	375	69.44
25	4.63	400	74.07
50	9.26	500	92.59

"*service compris*" (service charge included), it's customary to leave a tip. In a fancy restaurant, 10%–12% will do; in a cheap place, 8%–10% is fine; in a café, a few coins, perhaps totaling more than 5% but less than 10%, is good. Remember, service has supposedly already been paid for. Taxis expect 10% of the fare as a tip. At the theater and cinema, tip the usher who shows you to your seat 2F (35¢). In public toilets, there is often a posted fee for using the facilities. If not, the maintenance person will expect a tip of about 2F (35¢). Put it in the basket or on the plate at the entrance. Porters and cloakroom attendants are usually governed by set prices that are displayed. If not, give a porter 5–8F (90¢–$1.50) per suitcase, and a cloakroom attendant 2–4F (35¢–75¢) per coat.

Useful Telephone Numbers   For weather information, call 36-69-00-00.

4. BUDGET ACCOMMODATIONS

Anyone who has ever seen *An American in Paris* and planned a trip to the capital of France has probably dreamed of staying in some quaint, cozy little hotel on a pretty square or a narrow side street, right in the midst of a neighborhood bursting with charm. Well, there aren't many such hotels left in the 1990s, but with careful planning you can stay in one, and on a budget, too.

Keep in mind that each room in one of these little hotels is different and unique. In the same place you might find charming, airy rooms and rooms that you can't bear to stay in. You will often find a variety of plumbing arrangements as well, from rooms with "EC" (*eau courante,* or running water, meaning a sink) to those with private shower or bath.

Also, if you're looking for a double room, note that in France you usually pay more for a room with two twin beds than for a room with one double bed. When you make a reservation, ask about the beds, so that you know exactly what you're getting and what you're paying for.

Note that a room with shower or bath does not necessarily mean that the room has a toilet as well. There are rooms with toilet and shower, rooms with toilet only, and rooms with shower only. The trend these days is to renovate small hotels and put a shower, toilet, bidet, and sink in each room, so those marvelously cheap bathless rooms are dwindling in number, but there's a long time to go before they all disappear.

Ask to see a room before checking in, and if you don't like it, ask to see another. As for price, the rates given below are for the high summer season, and are correct as this book goes to press. No one has promised to maintain the rates quoted here, so the rate you pay may be a bit higher or lower than that quoted. Also, in high season you may be required to take breakfast with your room.

In summer, many of Paris's budget hotel rooms may be occupied. If you don't have a room reserved, plan to arrive early in the day to look for one. If you can't find the exact room that you want, take a room that will do for one night, and then spend a little time reserving the one you want for the following day.

The **Office de Tourisme de Paris,** on the Champs-Elysées, will help you find a room for a fee (see "Information" in "Orientation and Getting Around," above). In summer, this service is likely to be in demand, and there may be quite a line of people waiting, so get there early. The French government rates each hotel from one to four stars—one star denotes a simple, basic hotel; four stars signify a high-class one. In many of the following descriptions I have noted this rating.

DOUBLES FOR LESS THAN 500F [$92.60]
NEAR THE SORBONNE

The area of the Sorbonne, with its bookstores, café life, and famous boulevards, lives deep in the imagination of many visitors to Paris. Besides the university and the busy intersections of boulevards St-Michel and St-Germain, you'll find several other Parisian icons: the green Jardin du Luxembourg, the dome of the Panthéon, and, only 15 minutes away on foot, the towers of Notre-Dame.

Hotels in this area cater to the student, both French and foreign, and to budget travelers. You can find rock-bottom digs or very comfortable lodgings, as you wish.

GRAND HOTEL ST-MICHEL, 19, rue Cujas, 75005 Paris. Tel. 1/46-33-33-02 or 46-33-65-03. 67 rms (all with shower). TEL **Métro:** Cluny–La Sorbonne. **RER:** Luxembourg.
$ Rates: 220–240F ($40.75–$44.45) single; 280–320F ($51.85–$59.25) double; 400–460F ($74.05–$85.20) triple; 500–550F ($92.25–$101.85) quad. MC, V.

ⓕ FROMMER'S SMART TRAVELER: HOTELS

VALUE-CONSCIOUS TRAVELERS SHOULD
TAKE ADVANTAGE OF THE FOLLOWING:

1. Rooms with one double bed instead of two twin beds.
2. Reservations, especially in summer, when budget rooms may be occupied.
3. Rooms without bath—marvelously cheap.

The Grand Hôtel St-Michel has been owned by the same family since 1896 and managed by Mme Salvage, the original owner's daughter, since after the war. She is now 87 years old and still very much in charge. Her hotel has six floors of basic rooms, most with little balconies, and some (especially nos. 64 and 67) with fine views *sur les toits de Paris*. Breakfast is not served, but nearby cafés can provide it easily and cheaply, and there's also a vending machine for hot beverages.

HOTEL DE LA FACULTE, 1, rue Racine, 75006 Paris. Tel. 1/43-26-87-13. 19 rms (all with shower). TEL **Métro:** Cluny–La Sorbonne.

$ Rates: 290F ($53.70) single or double; 370F ($68.50) triple. Continental breakfast 20F ($3.70) extra. MC, V.

In a prime Latin Quarter location just steps off the busy boulevard St-Michel, this modest hotel holds some surprises. The tiny lobby leads to a minuscule elevator and to a winding staircase. Down the narrow hallways are rooms with older furnishings still in serviceable shape. Everything may seem a bit squeezed in here, but the prices sure won't squeeze your budget.

HOTEL GERSON, 14, rue de la Sorbonne, 75005 Paris. Tel. 1/43-54-28-40. 29 rms. **Métro:** Cluny–La Sorbonne. **RER:** Luxembourg.

$ Rates: 170F ($31.50) single without shower, 270F ($50) single with shower; 230F ($42.60) double without shower, 340F ($62.95) double with shower; 400F ($74.05) triple without shower. Continental breakfast 30F ($5.55) extra; showers 25F ($4.65). MC, V.

The one-star Gerson is in the very heart of the Latin Quarter, just a few steps down the hill from place de la Sorbonne. It is the quintessential low-budget hotel, with soft beds and many nicks in the woodwork, but it has clean rooms, some with private baths that are newish and quite presentable.

HOTEL MARIGNAN, 13, rue du Sommerard, 75005 Paris. Tel. 1/43-54-63-81 or 43-25-31-03. 30 rms (all with sink only). TEL **Métro:** Maubert-Mutualité.

$ Rates (including buffet-style continental breakfast and showers): 160F ($29.60) single; 245F ($45.35) double; 260–280F ($48.15–$51.85) twin; 320–370F ($59.25–$68.50) triple; 410–440F ($75.90–$81.50) quad. Minimum stay 3 nights. No credit cards.

⭐ The Marignan is a friendly place owned since 1956 by an English-speaking couple—he's French and she's from California. Guests appreciate the great hospitality. For instance, they'll supply hot water in the evening if you provide your own cup and coffee or tea, set you up with a babysitter, provide washing and ironing facilities, and let you use their excellent collections of specialized guidebooks. And the prices at the well-located, one-star Marignan are unbeatable.

NEAR ST-MICHEL & NOTRE-DAME

Even closer to the Seine, still in the midst of the vibrant street life of the Latin Quarter, are several other good lodging choices.

HOTEL ESMERALDA, 4 rue Saint-Julien-le-Pauvre, 75005 Paris. Tel. 1/43-54-19-20. 19 rms (most with bath). TEL **Métro:** St-Michel.

$ Rates: 135F ($25) single without shower; 320F ($59.25) single or double with shower; 410–460F ($75.90–$85.20) double with bath and view of Notre-Dame. Breakfast 40F ($7.40) extra; showers, 20F ($3.05). No credit cards.

⭐ The Hôtel Esmeralda, with its beamed ceilings and stone walls, has considerable charm and an excellent location. But what attracts travelers from all over the world are the views of Notre-Dame, obliquely across the little Square René-Viviani. The front rooms, which are larger and nicer and have the views of Notre-Dame, are in high demand at all times, and you must reserve ahead to get one.

Leave the St-Michel Métro station through the exit that emerges at the corner of quai de Montebello and rue St-Jacques; walk east along the river from rue St-Jacques, and turn right just past Shakespeare and Company, before the park.

HOTEL SAINT-ANDRE-DES-ARTS, 66, rue Saint-André-des-Arts, **75006 Paris. Tel. 1/43-26-96-16.** 34 rms (most with shower or bath). TEL **Métro:** Odéon.

$ Rates (including continental breakfast): 200F ($37.05) single without shower or bath, 250–290F ($46.30–$53.70) single with shower; 350–400F ($64.80–$74.05) double with shower or bath; 450F ($83.35) triple with shower or bath; 480F ($88.90) quad with shower or bath. No credit cards.

The Saint-André is the stereotype of the romantic Latin Quarter hotel: a crooked street, art galleries and cafés, a half-timbered building, rough stone. Housed in a 17th-century building, the hotel has tiny rooms, high ceilings, and very good prices. The front-desk clerk speaks English.

When you exit the Odéon Métro station, cross boulevard St-Germain and walk down rue de l'Ancien-Comédie to rue Saint-André-des-Arts, on the right.

SOUTH OF THE JARDIN DU LUXEMBOURG

There is an exceptional hotel several blocks from the southwest corner of the Jardin du Luxembourg. The neighborhood is quite nice, and the Métro will whisk you over to Odéon or St-Michel in a matter of minutes.

HOTEL DES ACADEMIES, 15, rue de la Grande-Chaumière, 75006 Paris. Tel. 1/43-26-66-44. 21 rms. TEL **Métro:** Vavin.

$ Rates (including showers): 140F ($25.90) single with sink and toilet only, 200F ($37.05) single with shower only; 230–260F ($42.60–$48.15) double with shower and toilet. Continental breakfast 25F ($4.60) extra. No credit cards.

On a quiet side street southwest of the Jardin du Luxembourg, the Hôtel des Académies is proper and comfortable, with hearteningly low prices. Chez Wadja, a great low-budget eatery, is virtually across the street. Decor in the lobby and guest rooms is eclectic at worst, kitschy at best. There's no elevator, but rooms on the fourth and fifth floors are cheaper, so the climb pays for itself.

NEAR THE EIFFEL TOWER

The neighborhood around the Eiffel Tower belongs to the seventh arrondissement, and here you'll find a very proper district of leafy streets and fine residential buildings, including the art nouveau creations of architect Jules Lavirotte on avenue Rapp (no. 29 is his masterpiece), and, yes, sudden visions of the Eiffel Tower. There are many restaurants and food shops on avenue Bosquet, rue de Grenelle, and rue St-Dominique, but this is an eminently tranquil area, and you'll soon feel like an old-time resident.

GRAND HOTEL LEVEQUE, 29, rue Cler, 75007 Paris. Tel. 1/47-05-49-15. 50 rms (25 with shower and toilet, 6 with shower only). **Métro:** Ecole-Militaire or Latour-Maubourg.

$ Rates: 200F ($37.05) single or double without shower or toilet, 280F ($51.85) single or double with shower only, 300–330F ($55.55–$61.10) single or double with shower and toilet; 300F ($55.55) triple without shower or toilet, 380F ($70.35) triple with shower and toilet. Continental breakfast 25F ($4.60) extra. EURO, MC, V.

The Grand Hôtel Léveque is a large establishment on a colorful pedestrian street with a busy marketplace during the day and the sound of silence at night. New carpets have recently been placed in many of the rooms. The staff is very friendly and helpful and, if you ask, they may be able to give you one of the rooms on the fifth floor with partial but wonderful views of the Eiffel Tower.

HOTEL DE LA PAIX, 19, rue du Gros-Caillou, 75007 Paris. Tel. 1/45-51-86-17. 23 rms (most with shower). **Métro:** Ecole-Militaire.

$ Rates: 135F ($25) single without shower, 195F ($36.10) single with shower; 280F ($51.85) double with shower; 400F ($74.05) triple with shower. Continental breakfast 30F ($5.55) extra; showers, 16F ($2.95). No credit cards.

On a very quiet side street, the Hôtel de la Paix is simple and pleasant, with its old-fashioned wallpaper and spiral staircase. The furniture in the rooms is modest, but the long French windows with flowers liven things up. Many families stay here, and it's also popular among Japanese tourists, who appreciate the linguistic skills of the multilingual Sri Lankan manager. He has promised a 3% discount for Frommer's readers, and, maybe, 5% discounts for those who travel in the low season or who stay for more than seven nights.

NEW HOTEL, 40 rue St-Quentin, 75010 Paris. Tel. 1/48-78-04-83. 40 rms (all with shower and toilet, or bath). TV **Métro:** Gare du Nord.

$ Rates (including continental breakfast): 310F ($57.40) single with shower and toilet, 340F ($62.95) single with bath; 340F ($62.95) double with shower and toilet, 370F ($68.50) double with bath; 500F ($92.60) triple with shower and toilet, 530F ($98.15) triple with bath; 520F ($96.30) quad with shower and toilet, 550F ($101.85) quad with bath.

This hotel, spread out over six floors, is one of the best deals in town. The building, with an elevator, is located 50 yards off Gare du Nord, to your left as you leave the station.

NORTH OF THE ARC DE TRIOMPHE

Place de l'Etoile, renamed place Charles-de-Gaulle, holds the tremendous Arc de Triomphe. Twelve grand avenues, including the Champs-Elysées, radiate from the vast square. The neighborhoods north of here hold offices, showrooms, restaurants, and hotels. It may lack the immediate charm of the Latin Quarter, but it's quite proper and respectable.

When you arrive at the enormous Charles-de-Gaulle Métro station, consult the address of your hotel, look at the *plan du quartier,* and choose the Métro exit nearest to the street you're going to. This will save you a good 15 minutes of circling the vast square above ground, waiting at corners, and crossing heavily trafficked streets.

HOTEL NIEL, 11, rue Saussier-Leroy, 75017 Paris. Tel. 1/42-27-99-29. 36 rms (some with shower or bath). TEL **Métro:** Ternes.

$ Rates (including continental breakfast): 220F ($40.75) single without shower or bath; 305F ($56.50) double without shower or bath, 350F ($64.80) double with shower or bath; 320F ($59.25) triple without shower or bath, 390F ($72.20) triple with shower or bath. Showers 25F ($4.65) extra. MC, V.

This large hotel has a feeling of simplicity, propriety, and tidiness. The helpful receptionist will tell you that each room is different, but you will see that all are good and clean, and have reading lamps over the beds—rare in Paris. The hotel is located on a quiet street half a block from a colorful street market (see the Hôtel Wagram, below).

HOTEL WAGRAM, 5, rue Poncelet, 75017 Paris. Tel. 1/47-64-13-17. 24 rms (all with shower or bath). TEL **Métro:** Ternes or Charles-de-Gaulle–Etoile.

$ Rates: 210F ($38.90) single with shower; 235–265F ($43.50–$49.05) double with shower or bath. Continental breakfast 22F ($4.05) extra. No credit cards.

This could be the setting for a movie: the young, adventurous couple wandering through a colorful street market, disappearing between the vegetable and fruit stands to enter an unpretentious hotel door. They are greeted by the Padellis, a smiling French-Spanish couple, and handed the key to their room. Up the stairs (there's no elevator, and some rooms are six flights up), their room is simple and neat, with well-used furniture, drapes, and spreads, but clean baths (many newly tiled, some with minitubs). This is the one-star Hôtel Wagram.

IN THE MARAIS

Comprising most of the third and fourth arrondissements in the Right Bank, the Marais district was the seat of Parisian noble life in the 17th century, before the Faubourg St-Germain became fashionable. The splendid *hôtels particuliers* (private mansions) fell into disrepair until the 1960s, when Minister of Culture André Malraux took a personal interest in the area's survival. Despite gentrification and trendiness, the Marais is still home to various ethnic communities—Jewish, Asian, Yugoslav—and artisan groups, and you'll see magnificent architecture and fashionable boutiques standing next to modest workshops and homey *pâtisseries*.

GRAND HOTEL MALHER, 5, rue Malher, 75004 Paris. Tel. 1/42-72-60-92. 36 rms (all with shower and toilet). **Métro:** St-Paul.
$ Rates (including buffet breakfast): 325F ($60.20) single; 490F ($90.75) double; 600F ($111.10) triple.
The rooms at the Grand Hôtel Malher were completely modernized in 1992. The management is cordial and polite. What makes the Malher a special place is its location in the Marais, on a street just off rue St-Antoine, one of the area's major throughfares, and a few minutes' walk from place des Vosges, Paris's most beautiful square. This is a great place from which to explore the area.

DOUBLES FOR LESS THAN 600F ($111.10)

NEAR THE SORBONNE

HOTEL CLAUDE-BERNARD, 43, rue des Ecoles, 75005 Paris. Tel. 1/43-26-32-52. 34 rms. TV TEL **Métro:** Maubert-Mutualité.
$ Rates: 380–600F ($70.35–$111.10) single or double with bath. Triples and quads are also available (call for rates). Continental breakfast 35F ($6.50) extra. AE, DC, MC, V.
It's evident from the moment you enter its lobby that the three-star Hôtel Claude-Bernard keeps very high standards. The congenial rooms have a tasteful crimson wallpaper, sleek bathrooms, and perhaps a semi-antique piece like a writing desk. There are also some suites, and these are particularly attractive, with great couches and seats.

NEAR ST-MICHEL & NOTRE-DAME

GRAND HOTEL DE LIMA, 46, bd. St-Germain, 75005 Paris. Tel. 1/46-34-02-12. 40 rms (all with bath or shower). TEL **Métro:** Maubert-Mutualité.
$ Rates: 350–450F ($64.80–$83.35) single with shower or bath; 420F ($77.75) double with shower only, 480F ($88.90) double with bath and TV. Continental breakfast 34F ($6.30).
⭐ The higher you climb in the Grand Hôtel de Lima, the better it gets. You enter through a little hallway of mirrors and faux marbre, and climb a flight of stairs to the pleasant reception area. From there, an elevator will take you to cheerful, airy rooms, some of which have French windows with views of Notre-Dame or the Panthéon. All this plus cordial proprietors and a superb location.

HOTEL ST-JACQUES, 35, rue des Ecoles, 75005 Paris. Tel. 1/43-26-82-53. 40 rms. **Métro:** Maubert-Mutualité.
$ Rates: 102–146F ($18.90–$27.05) single without shower, 275F ($50.90) single with shower only; 370–415F ($68.50–$76.85) double with bath; 480F ($88.90) triple with bath. Continental breakfast 25F ($4.65) extra; showers, 20F ($3.70). AE, MC, V.
On busy rue des Ecoles, at the corner of rue Valette, the two-star Hôtel St-Jacques has attractive prices and rooms that for the most part are large. The furniture is rather basic, but there are some fine architectural details. When you choose a room, keep in mind the traffic on the main street.

IN THE FAUBOURG ST-GERMAIN

In the 18th century, Parisian aristocrats built elegant *hôtels particuliers* west of boulevard St-Germain in what soon became the *quartier chic* par excellence. Those mansions still stand, occupied for the most part by embassies and ministries. But rather than being a frozen museum, the Faubourg St-Germain is one of the most active areas of Paris, with countless boutiques and antique shops as well as *épiceries* (food shops), *pâtisseries* (pastry shops), and *boulangeries* (bakeries). And there are hotels as well, like the outstanding Hôtel de Nevers. You're a few blocks away from the tourist maelstrom, and this relative calm will allow you to get better acquainted with the subtle moods of the city.

HOTEL DE NEVERS, 83, rue du Bac, 75007 Paris. Tel. 1/45-44-61-30. 11 rms (all with shower or bath). MINIBAR **Métro:** Rue du Bac.

$ Rates: 320F ($59.25) single with shower; 380F ($70.35) double with shower or bath; 450F ($83.35) triple with shower or bath. Continental breakfast 27F ($5) extra. No credit cards.

The building that houses the Hôtel de Nevers used to be a convent, and it's presently *classé*, which means that any restorations must respect the original architecture, which means that there's no elevator, which means that you'll have to climb the beautiful, white, never-ending staircase. Rooms, in their antique primness, are cozy and pleasant, and two of them (nos. 10 and 11) have large terraces; all have well-assorted minibars. And there's a sauve black poodle in the lobby to complete the feeling of hominess.

NEAR THE EIFFEL TOWER

HOTEL DE LA TOUR EIFFEL, 17, rue de l'Exposition, 75007 Paris. Tel. 1/47-05-14-75. 23 rms (all with shower). TV TEL **Métro:** Ecole-Militaire.

$ Rates: 330F ($61.10) single; 380F ($70.35) double. Continental breakfast 25F ($4.65) extra. MC, V.

Next to the Romanian embassy, and with a view of the statues in its garden, the Hôtel de la Tour Eiffel is neither quaint nor romantic, but rather modern and very comfortable. The well-appointed rooms have pleasant furnishings and color TVs, and the bathrooms are very up-to-date. The management is efficient and cordial and, if you wish, they'll serve you a fine breakfast in your room—the *oeufs au plat* are more delicious than any fried eggs you may have eaten back home.

HOTEL RAPP, 8, av. Rapp, 75007 Paris. Tel. 1/45-51-42-28. 16 rms (all with shower or tub). TEL **Métro:** Alma-Marceau. **RER:** Pont de l'Alma.

$ Rates: 290F ($53.70) single; 370–410F ($68.50–$75.90) double. Continental breakfast 28F ($5.20) extra. No credit cards.

Virtually in the shadow of the Eiffel Tower and very close to the Seine (in fact, the nearest Métro is across the river in the Right Bank), the Hôtel Rapp is small, quiet, and rather modern. The manager, who speaks English, extols the convenience and security of being located near several embassies. The rooms are well appointed, with fine dark furniture and yellow drapes, and everything is very clean. Parking is easy on this street, and you pay 15F ($2.75) with a hotel card.

NORTH OF THE ARC DE TRIOMPHE

HOTEL DES DEUX ACACIAS, 28, rue de l'Arc de Triomphe, 75017 Paris. Tel. 1/43-80-01-85. Fax 1/40-53-94-72. 31 rms (all with shower or bath). TV TEL **Métro:** Charles-de-Gaulle–Etoile.

$ Rates (including continental breakfast): 320–380F ($59.25–$70.35) single; 380–420F ($70.35–$77.75) double. No credit cards.

This quiet street just two blocks north of the Arc de Triomphe holds an excellent budget hotel. The rooms are plain, but neat and not faded, and have private showers or baths and color TVs. The woman at the front desk is efficient and amiable. Take the avenue Carnot exit from the Métro.

NEAR PORTE MAILLOT

Porte Maillot is the site of the Palais des Congrès, Paris's convention center, and is several blocks west of the Arc de Triomphe along avenue de la Grande-Armée. This is where the Air France bus from Charles-de-Gaulle Airport drops you, and you can connect with the Métro ("Porte Maillot") or the RER ("Neuilly–Porte-Maillot). The area has many hotels, some of which afford good bargains. Though you're out at the edge of the city, the Métro whisks you to the center easily and cheaply.

HOTEL DE PALMA, 46, rue Brunel, 75017 Paris. Tel. 1/45-74-74-51. 37 rms (all with shower or bath). TV TEL **Métro:** Argentine. **RER:** Neuilly–Porte-Maillot.

$ Rates (including continental breakfast): 385F ($71.30) single with shower or bath; 420F ($77.75) double with shower or bath; 540F ($100) triple with bath.

If you like comfort but don't want to pay top franc for it, head for the Hôtel de Palma. It may be a bit far from the center of things, but the Château-de-Vincennes Métro line will take you rapidly and directly to the Champs-Elysées, place de la Concorde, the Louvre, and the Bastille—with easy connections to the Latin Quarter. The Palma has a large, pleasant lobby and well-kept rooms with modern tiled bathrooms and color TV. The management is very professional.

SUPER-BUDGET CHOICES
YOUTH HOSTELS

Paris has plenty of youth hostels (*auberges de jeunesse*) and *foyers* (literally "homes") to accommodate the hordes of young travelers who descend on the city every summer. Quality differs greatly from place to place, but the superior hostels offer excellent value for your money. While some are huge and impersonal and occupy similarly huge and impersonal buildings, other hostels are friendly, warm places where you can meet people from all over the world. Some of these places, as you'll see from my listings, are housed in historical buildings that are both comfortable and handsome. Many of these hostels welcome travelers regardless of their age.

Hostels in Paris are an especially good deal for solo travelers. As single rooms in hotels become scarce in summer and other periods, you may have to choose between paying for a double room or paying for a bed at a hostel. The latter option can be especially attractive, and not only from a financial point of view. As I said, hostels are a great place to hook up with other travelers, exchange stories, and simply have pleasant company. The major drawback for some people—whether traveling alone or not—is the day lock-out and the night curfew. If having a place to take an afternoon nap is essential to you, or late nightlife is what you came to Paris for, then perhaps staying at a hostel, with all the savings this implies, is not the best choice.

Many hostels do not accept reservations from individual travelers (they do so only for school and other large groups). In those cases, the best strategy is to show up at the hostel where you want to stay as early as possible in the morning—8 o'clock or earlier. You can also call ahead to find out what your chances are for getting a bed. Believe me, for some hostels, like those run by the Accueil des Jeunes en France (see below), all this trouble is really worth it. Once you're "accepted," make sure you tell your host how many nights you plan to stay (five is the maximum at some places).

If you arrive late in the day and don't want to start calling up or going to hostels that may already be full, it's a good idea simply to head for one of the offices of the **Accueil des Jeunes en France (AJF).** This organization exists to find inexpensive beds for young people, and they will book you a bed for that night. If you want to stay at one of their own hostels (they're all great), tell them so. Their main office is at 119, rue St-Martin, 4e (tel. 42-77-87-80; Métro: Rambuteau; RER: Châtelet–Les-Halles), and it's located across from the entrance to the Pompidou Center. See "Information" in "Orientation and Getting Around," above, for the location of their other offices.

The **Office de Tourisme de Paris** will also book you a bed in a hostel for a 7F ($1.30) fee. See "Information" in "Orientation and Getting Around," above, for other organizations that specialize in providing information on budget accommodations.

CENTRE INTERNATIONAL DE PARIS/OPERA, 11, rue Thérèse, 75001 Paris. Tel. 1/42-60-77-23. 68 beds. **Métro:** Pyramides or Palais-Royal–Musée-du-Louvre.

$ Rates (including continental breakfast): 110F ($20.35) per person per night. Lunch or dinner 65F ($12.05) extra. No credit cards. **Open:** July 1–Oct 15.

Run by the UCRIF (Union des Centres de Rencontres Internationales de France), this small hostel is clean and friendly, and at times it feels even cozy. Its location is excellent: off avenue de l'Opéra, not far from the Louvre and the Palais-Royal.

The same people run several other hostels in Paris, including those at 20, rue Jean-Jacques-Rousseau (tel. 1/42-36-88-18; Métro: Louvre-Rivoli, Palais-Royal–Musée-du-Louvre, or Châtelet–Les-Halles); and 44, rue des Bernardins (tel. 1/43-29-34-80; Métro: Maubert-Mutualité), in the Latin Quarter.

YOUTH HOSTEL LE FAUCONNIER, 11, rue du Fauconnier, 75004 Paris. Tel. 1/42-74-23-45. 100 beds. **Métro:** St-Paul or Pont-Marie.

$ Rates (including continental breakfast): 105F ($19.45) per person per night. No credit cards.

⭐ Of all Parisian youth hostels, Le Fauconnier is my favorite. Run by Les Maisons Internationales de la Jeunesse et des Etudiants, it is located in a historic *hôtel particulier* on a quiet street in the Marais, not far from the Seine. Despite the groups that sometimes overrun it, Le Fauconnier has a touch of elegance, with a pleasant courtyard and a beautiful staircase. Some rooms have private showers and no more than two beds, thus affording more privacy than is customary at youth hostels.

Other hostels are located nearby at 12, rue des Barres (tel. 1/42-72-72-09); and 6, rue de Fourcy (tel. 1/42-74-23-45).

UNIVERSITY ACCOMMODATION

FOYER INTERNATIONAL DES ETUDIANTS, 93, bd. St-Michel, 75006 Paris. Tel. 1/43-54-49-63. 160 beds. **Métro:** Luxembourg.

$ Rates (including continental breakfast and showers): 145F ($26.85) single; 200F ($37.05) double. No credit cards. **Open:** July–Sept.

Open to traveling students from July through September, this university residence has an excellent location and is quite comfortable.

WORTH THE EXTRA BUCKS

HOTEL JARDIN DES PLANTES, 5, rue Linné, 75005 Paris. Tel. 1/47-07-06-20. 33 rms (all with shower or bath). MINIBAR TV TEL **Métro:** Jussieu.

$ Rates: 390F ($72.20) single with shower, 450–510F ($83.35–$94.45) single with bath; 510F ($94.45) double with shower, 520–560F ($96.30–$103.70) double with bath; 590–640F ($109.25–$118.50) terrace rooms. Continental breakfast 40F ($7.40) extra; extra bed, 100F ($18.50). AE, DC, MC, V.

⭐ This great two-star hotel owes its name to its location across from the vast Jardin des Plantes, the botanical gardens created on the order of Louis XIII's doctors in 1626 and called, at the time, the Jardin Royal des Plantes Médicinales. There are still some 15,000 medicinal herbs at the gardens, and some regal comforts at the nearby hotel: a roof terrace, a sauna, a vaulted cellar with a fireplace, a glass-fronted sidewalk café adjoining the lobby. All rooms have minibars, and baths have hairdryers. The more expensive rooms open onto the sunny terrace.

5. BUDGET DINING

Brillat-Savarin, author of the 1825 gastronomic classic *Physiology of Taste,* wrote: "To eat is a necessity; to eat well is an art." This dictum still defines the attitude of many a Parisian toward food. Eating is such a passion here that it even shapes the cityscape. Almost every street corner has a bistro or a café, and these, not banks or department stores, dominate the major intersections. It's not unusual to find entire streets lined with small restaurants.

In France, a meal is often a ceremony. A maître d' will usually welcome you and find you a suitable table. Your waiter will be polite and efficient. The chef will be careful in his or her work. The part that you play in this ceremony is crucial. Never underestimate the importance of phrases such as "Bonjour, monsieur" and "Merci, madame," and be aware of the traditional order of things: cocktails precede the meal, and coffee follows dessert.

Despite what you may have learned in high-school French, never say "Garçon!" to call a waiter. Use "Monsieur, s'il vous plaît!" or "Madame, s'il vous plaît!"

Most restaurants in Paris have regular mealtimes: usually noon to 2:30pm for lunch and 7 to 10pm for dinner. For a quick meal outside these times, go to a café: Most serve light one-course meals. But choose your café carefully: A prime location often entails a higher-than-usual price. Buying a sandwich or a crêpe from a sidewalk booth is the cheapest alternative (see "Street Food," below).

Food can be expensive in France. The reason is, to a certain extent, social. The French demand a standard of food quality, preparation, and service higher than the norm in other countries, and they're willing to pay for it. A meal can easily become a memorable experience. Learning a few tips will help you get the best out of eating in Paris, while at the same time minimizing the cost.

Unless breakfast is included in the price of your hotel room, go to a sidewalk café for your morning café au lait and croissant. If you stand at the counter, munch, and sip, the price will be about 40% lower than if you sit down and have a waiter serve you.

For lunch or dinner, the best deal is usually a *menu du jour,* a fixed-price meal of three to five courses, usually with some choice offered for the various courses. House wine, either red or white, is often included, the standard measure being a quarter-liter carafe (*un quart*).

An alternative to a multicourse meal is the *plat du jour* or *plat garni*, a main-course platter garnished with vegetables and little extras that easily constitute a filling meal. It's usually quite a bit cheaper than a full-course *menu du jour.*

For a simple meal, head for a café and order an omelet, sandwich, soup, or salad. French sandwiches, made on a crusty fresh baguette, are disappointing at first glance, with somewhat meager stuffing, but they taste wonderful. Omelets come plain with just a sprinkling of herbs, or filled with cheese, ham, or other hearty additions. Or try a *salade niçoise*, a huge bowl filled with lettuce, boiled potato, hard-boiled egg, capers, tomatoes, olives, and anchovies. These dishes make a filling, pleasant meal for 40–60F ($7.40–$11.10).

If you want a free glass of water (as opposed to its bottled counterpart), ask for *une carafe d'eau* ("ewn kah-rahf *doh*"). **Café** means an espresso.

By the way, Paris has a full complement of American-style fast-food eateries such as McDonald's and Pizza Hut. Parisians, too, respond to the appeal of uniform quality and (relatively) quick service, but you'll discover that fast-food prices are higher here than in the United States.

MEALS FOR LESS THAN 70F ($12.95)

IN THE LATIN QUARTER

A LA BONNE CREPE, 11, rue Grégoire-de-Tours, 63. Tel. 43-54-60-74.
Cuisine: FRENCH/BRETON. **Métro:** Odéon.
$ Prices: Three-course lunch with crêpe for the main course 47F ($8.70); crêpes à la carte 40–65F ($7.40–$12.05); .7-liter pitcher of cider 11F ($2.05). No credit cards.
Open: Lunch Mon–Sat noon–2pm; dinner Mon–Sat 7–11pm.

Brittany is known for its crêpes (French pancakes) and its ciders, and here you can combine these goodies into lunch or dinner. Savory crêpes filled with cheese, meat, seafood, or other hearty ingredients make the main course, and sweet crêpes filled with jam or chocolate are a wonderful dessert. The cider is the alcoholic kind, Brittany's answer to beer. The restaurant seats 30.

Rue Grégoire-de-Tours is a tiny street that begins between nos. 140 and 142 boulevard St-Germain and runs north toward the Seine.

LA DINETTE, 59, rue Dauphine, 6e. Tel. 43-54-35-15.
   Cuisine: CHINESE. **Métro:** Odéon.
$ **Prices:** Three-course meal 40F ($7.40); drinks 12–16F ($2.20–$2.95). No credit cards.
   Open: Daily 11am–11pm.
This very attractive Chinese take-out place also has dining tables. The food, on display in steam tables by the door, is a blend of Asian and French tastiness and beauty. The *menu du jour* offers soup, pâté, or salad, then shrimp dumplings or a main dish made with beef, pork, or chicken, plus Cantonese rice, all for one low price.

WEST & SOUTH OF THE JARDIN DU LUXEMBOURG

ALLIANCE FRANÇAISE, 101, bd. Raspail, 6e. Tel. 45-44-38-28, ext. 254.
   Cuisine: FRENCH. **Métro:** St-Placide.
$ **Prices:** Three-course meal 38F ($7.05); main courses 24F ($4.45). No credit cards.
   Open: Lunch only, Mon–Fri 11:45am–2:30pm.
France's linguistic and cultural institute has a large, simple dining room in its classroom building, and on weekdays you can go to the door, buy a ticket, and get a good, filling meal at a great price. The dining room is intended for those studying French, but no one seems to mind who eats here as long as they pay. Enter the Alliance Française compound and walk straight back to the door in the left corner; go through the door, turn left, and head up the stairs to the dining room, on the left.

CHEZ WADJA, 10, rue da la Grande-Chaumière, 6e. Tel. 43-25-66-90.
   Cuisine: FRENCH/POLISH. **Métro:** Vavin.
$ **Prices:** Three-course *menu du jour* 50F ($9.25); main courses 38F ($7.05). No credit cards.
   Open: Lunch Mon–Sat noon–2:30pm; dinner Mon–Sat 7–9:30pm.
In Paris's large Polish community, Chez Wadja is well known for its remarkably low prices. A bit off the beaten track, off place Picasso, this is a small, one-room family-style eatery. Hungry hordes of thrifty travelers have descended on it since the end of World War II. Atmosphere is minimal, but the value can't be beat. Get here early for a seat.

NEAR THE CHAMPS-ELYSEES

FERI'S RESTAURANT A EMPORTER, 8, rue de Ponthieu, 8e. Tel. 42-56-10-56.
   Cuisine: FRENCH/DELI. **Métro:** Franklin-D.-Roosevelt.

FROMMER'S SMART TRAVELER: RESTAURANTS

VALUE-CONSCIOUS TRAVELERS SHOULD TAKE ADVANTAGE OF THE FOLLOWING:

1. Sandwiches and crêpes from sidewalk booths.
2. Sidewalk cafés for breakfast, unless the meal is included in the price of your hotel room.
3. The *menu du jour* for lunch or dinner.
4. The *plat du jour* or *plat garni*—usually cheaper than the full-course menu.
5. Standing at the counter rather than being served at a table.
6. Restaurants along rue de la Huchette and rue Xavier-Privas.

$ Prices: Main courses 28–40F ($5.20–$7.40); less for salads and sandwiches. No credit cards.
Open: Daily 8am–6am.
Feri's is a little storefront deli and take-out with excellent food at good prices. After 11am a line begins to form for lunch pickup, and it stays busy until after supper. Main courses might be roast chicken, pot au feu (a hearty stew), or spaghetti. You can drop in anytime for croissants, pain au chocolat, and other snacks, and from dinnertime right through until 6am they serve fresh pizzas.

LES MUSES, 45, rue de Berri, 8e. Tel. 45-62-43-64.
   Cuisine: FRENCH/BRETON. **Métro:** St.-Philippe-du-Roule or George-V.
$ Prices: Two-course crêpe meal, cider included, 48F ($8.90). EURO, MC, V.
   Open: Lunch Mon–Sat 11:30am–3pm; dinner Mon–Sat 6:30–10pm.
Les Muses is an attractive little place with mesh curtains, lots of wood, and paintings on the wall. Like A la Bonne Crêpe on the Left Bank, this is a Brittany crêpe shop. The main course is usually a crêpe with meat, seafood, or vegetable filling, garnished with salad or crudités (sliced or grated raw vegetables), followed by a sweet dessert crêpe, all washed down with a bowl of cider. By the way, *crêpes de froment* means wheat-flour crêpes; *galettes de sarrasin* means buckwheat griddlecakes.

NORTH OF THE LOUVRE

MA NORMANDIE, 11, rue Rameau, 2e. Tel. 42-96-87-17.
   Cuisine: FRENCH. **Métro:** Pyramides, 4 Septembre, or Bourse.
$ Prices: *Menus du jour* 55F ($10.20) or 110F ($20.35). AE, EURO, MC, V.
   Open: Lunch Mon–Fri 11:30am–2:30pm; dinner Mon–Fri 7–10pm.
Near the small square in front of the Bibliothéque Nationale, Ma Normandie serves well-prepared food in homey surroundings. Cheerful waiters will greet you when you come in and show you to a table in the ground-floor dining room or upstairs. This is a good place to order such French staples as oeufs mayonnaise (hard-boiled eggs served with mayonnaise) and steak haché (chopped sirloin) as well as more elaborate dishes, and there's lots of delicious bread and great wine.

RESTAURANT L'INCROYABLE, 26, rue de Richelieu, or 23, rue Montpensier, 1er. Tel. 42-96-24-64.
   Cuisine: FRENCH. **Métro:** Palais-Royal–Musée-du-Louvre.
$ Prices: Five-course *menu du jour*, wine included. 60F ($11.10) at lunch, 69F ($12.75) at dinner. No credit cards.
   Open: Lunch Mon–Sat 11:45am–2:15pm; dinner Tues–Fri 6:30–9pm. **Closed:** Jan 1–15.
This little place, in business for 50 years, is justly named "the Incredible," for where else could you have a five-course lunch in appealing old-fashioned surroundings for such a low price? Dark bentwood furniture, old plaques and pictures on the walls, and, in good weather, a few little tables out in the passageway make this restaurant very French. The food is simple but good, with many choices on the *menu du jour*.
   To find L'Incroyable, walk up either rue de Richelieu or rue de Montpensier behind the Comédie-Française.

MEALS FOR LESS THAN 90F ($16.65)

IN THE LATIN QUARTER & ST-GERMAIN-DES-PRES

AU VIEUX CASQUE, 19, rue Bonaparte, 6e. Tel. 35-49-99-46.
   Cuisine: FRENCH. **Métro:** St-Germain-des-Prés or Pont-Neuf.
$ Prices: *Menu du jour*, wine included, 89F ($16.50). No credit cards.
   Open: Dinner only, Mon–Sat 7–11:15pm.
Open for dinner only, Au Vieux Casque has lots of atmosphere, with a wood-and-stucco ground-floor dining room, a stone-vaulted cellar, and an upstairs room with

rough-hewn beams. You can see the chef at work on the ground floor, preparing meals that are a cut above the rest, such as a delicate tomato salad to start, then a turkey cutlet in a cream sauce with rice, followed by camembert or fruit. With its updated classic French dishes and great atmosphere, this is definitely a superior establishment.

AUX CHARPENTIERS, 10, rue Mabillon, 6e. Tel. 43-26-30-05.
   Cuisine: FRENCH. **Métro:** Mabillon.
   $ Prices: *Plats du jour* 70–80F ($12.95–$14.80). AE, DC, MC, V.
   Open: Lunch Mon–Sat noon–3pm; dinner Mon–Sat 7–11:30pm.

During the Middle Ages and Renaissance, the carpenters' guildhall was next door to this restaurant, and it is from this that Aux Charpentiers takes its name. The walls are decorated with photographs and plans of carpentry, including models of wooden vaults and roof structures. The restaurant seats 170 on two levels. The clientele is mostly local, and the choices are very reasonable for traditional and hearty dishes.

LA PETITE HOSTELLERIE, 35, rue da la Harpe, 5e. Tel. 43-54-47-12.
   Cuisine: FRENCH. **Métro:** St-Michel or Cluny–La Sorbonne.
   $ Prices: *Menu du jour* 60F ($11.10) for three courses, 80F ($14.80) for four courses; wine 10F ($1.85). MC, V.
   Open: Lunch Tues–Sat noon–2pm; dinner Mon–Sat 6:30–10pm.
This little place, with its tables and chairs pretty tightly packed in the single dining room, is a typical Latin Quarter bistro. People come here for its small-restaurant ambience and decor, decent French country cooking, polite service, and excellent prices. And the location is great. Rue de la Harpe is a side street running north off boulevard St-Germain just east of boulevard St-Michel.

LE GRENIER DE NOTRE-DAME, 18, rue de la Bûcherie, 5e. Tel. 43-29-98-29.
   Cuisine: FRENCH/VEGETARIAN. **Métro:** Maubert-Mutualité.
   $ Prices: *Menu du jour* 78F ($14.45) for three courses. AE, DC, MC, V.
   Open: Lunch Wed–Mon noon–2:30pm; dinner Wed–Mon 7:15–10:45pm.
Located near Notre-Dame and boulevard St-Michel, Le Grenier is a well-established vegetarian restaurant. There are green tablecloths, fresh flowers, and small lamps on every table, and the food on the plates is outstanding. I especially recommend the cassoulet végétarien, with white beans, onions, tomato, and soy sausage; the lentilles maraîchères, with lentils, carrots, and onions is also delicious. And don't forget the desserts, such as tarte de tofu, for which Le Grenier has a well-deserved reputation.

RESTAURANT DES BEAUX ARTS, 11, rue Bonaparte, 6e. Tel. 43-26-92-64.
   Cuisine: FRENCH. **Métro:** St-Germain-des-Prés.
   $ Prices: Three-course *menu du jour*, wine included, 65F ($12.05). No credit cards.
   Open: Lunch daily noon–2:30pm; dinner daily 7–10:45pm.

Located across the street from Paris's famous Ecole Nationale Supérieure des Beaux Arts (School of Fine Arts) is what many picture as a typical Parisian artists' eatery, with its bentwood furniture, long tables covered in white paper, and wood-paneled walls. The *menu du jour* has numerous offerings of traditional dishes, and the portions are large. If the downstairs dining room is full, try upstairs.

IN THE 15TH ARRONDISSEMENT

LE CAFÉ DU COMMERCE, 51, rue du Commerce, 15e. Tel. 45-75-03-27.
   Cuisine: FRENCH. **Métro:** Emile-Zola, Commerce, or La Motte–Picquet.
   $ Prices: Three-course meal, wine included, 60–100F ($11.10–$18.50).
   Open: Daily noon–midnight.
Located not very far from the Eiffel Tower, Le Café du Commerce is one of the best dining bargains in this general area of unpretentious stores and busy commercial streets. The list of dishes is astounding: about 20 appetizers, seven fish dishes, 16 main courses, seven vegetable side dishes, seven cheeses, and over a dozen desserts.

NEAR THE CHAMPS-ELYSEES

CAFE BAR BRASSERIE LE ROND POINT, 5 rue de Ponthieu, 8e. Tel. 43-59-34-02.
   Cuisine: FRENCH. **Métro:** Franklin-D.-Roosevelt.
   $ Prices: Three-course *menu du jour,* wine included, 85F ($15.75); à la carte dishes 55–70F ($10.20–$12.95); sandwiches 15–26F ($2.75–$4.80).
This restaurant is heavily frequented by locals working in the Champs-Elysées. If you're looking for a typical French atmosphere, you'll find it here. Main courses might be choucroute and spaghetti bolognese; there's a large choice of sandwiches.

CHEZ GERMAIN, 19 rue Jean-Mermoz, 8e. Tel. 43-59-29-24.
   Cuisine: FRENCH/PERIGORDINE. **Métro:** Franklin-D.-Roosevelt.
   $ Prices: *Menus du jour* 85F ($15.75) or 130F ($24.05); main courses 60–95F ($11.10–$17.60). No credit cards.
   Open: Lunch Mon–Sat noon–2:30pm; dinner Mon–Sat 8–9:30pm.
The cuisine of the Périgord revels in foie gras, the delicious liver of the force-fed goose, and in every other sort of thing that can be made from goose meat or with goose fat. The cooking is hearty and absolutely delicious, and you can get an inkling of it at Chez Germain.

EAST OF THE OPERA

CHARTIER, 7, rue du Faubourg-Montmartre, 1er. Tel. 47-70-86-29.
   Cuisine: FRENCH. **Métro:** Richelieu-Drouot.
   $ Prices: Three-course *menu suggestion,* wine included, 70F ($12.95). No credit cards.
   Open: Lunch daily 11am–3pm; dinner daily 6–9:30pm.
Not far from Montmartre in a former library building, Chartier is a long-standing budget restaurant offering very good value in authentic French surroundings. There are about 100 items on the menu. Prices are low enough that a three-course repast is easy on the budget, even if you don't choose the fixed-price meal.

LE DROUOT, 103, rue de Richelieu, 2e, Tel. 42-96-68-23.
   Cuisine: FRENCH. **Métro:** Richelieu-Drouot.
   $ Prices: Three-course *menu du jour,* wine included, 75–80F ($13.90–$14.80). No credit cards.
   Open: Lunch daily 11:45am–3pm; dinner daily 6:30–10pm.
Le Drouot is another of Paris's old faithful budget eateries, with an upstairs working-class dining room straight out of the World War II era. The food is delicious, the waiters efficient, and the clientele loyal.

IN LE MARAIS

MARAIS PLUS, 20, rue des Francs-Bourgeois, 3e. Tel. 48-87-01-40.
   Cuisine: FRENCH. **Métro:** St-Paul.
   $ Prices: Breakfast, brunch, light lunch, or dinner 40–75F ($7.40–$13.90). AE, MC, V.
   Open: Daily 10am–7:30pm.

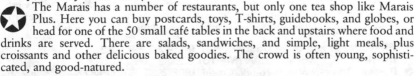

The Marais has a number of restaurants, but only one tea shop like Marais Plus. Here you can buy postcards, toys, T-shirts, guidebooks, and globes, or head for one of the 50 small café tables in the back and upstairs where food and drinks are served. There are salads, sandwiches, and simple, light meals, plus croissants and other delicious baked goodies. The crowd is often young, sophisticated, and good-natured.

STREET FOOD

Paris has a large variety of very affordable street food. Sidewalk booths in many parts of the city—like the Latin Quarter and near the *grands magasins* in the Right Bank—sell tasty sandwiches and crêpes, and, in cold weather, delicious roast chestnuts. I find the crêpes especially good. You can buy them freshly made and stuffed with your choice of ingredients: cheese, ham, egg (or a combination of these); chocolate and nuts; apricot jam; or some other treat. Prices run 10–25F ($1.85–$4.65), depending on stuffing.

LATE-NIGHT/24-HOUR RESTAURANTS

GRAN CAFE DES CAPUCINES, 4, bd. des Capucines, 9e. Tel. 47-42-19-00.
 Cuisine: INTERNATIONAL. **Métro:** Opéra.
 $ Prices: Meals 65–165F ($12.05–$30.55); full breakfast 70F ($12.95); dry martini 48F ($8.90).
 Open: Daily 24 hours.
This place lives up to the traveler's expectations of what an elegant café-restaurant 50 yards off place de l'Opéra should be like—waiters in black and white, a tuxedo-clad maître d', comfortable seats inside and outside, a Belle Epoque decor. If you choose carefully, and remember that you're buying ambience as well as sustenance, the restaurant is a good deal. The food is excellent, the view and the people-watching superb. Note: On the menu, next to the franc prices you'll find the equivalent in ECU, the proposed European currency (example: 12 escargots: 93F or 13.30 ECU)

PICNIC SUPPLIES & WHERE TO EAT THEM

For a very French picnic, the magic words are *charcuterie, épicerie, boulangerie, pâtisserie* (butcher shop, grocery, bakery, pastry shop). A charcuterie used to be just a pig butcher's, but it now designates what might be called a gourmet food shop, with cold meats, pâtés, salads, breads, rolls, cakes, and pastries all on delectable display at the best stores. Prices are not low, but, then, the food is outstanding.
 The best place to eat your picnic lunch is in the nearest park. My favorites are the serene Jardin des Tuileries and the well-bred Parc Monceau, both in the Right Bank, but there is also the place des Vosges in the Marais, with intimate benches, the vast Jardin du Luxembourg in the Left Bank, and the Parc du Champ-du-Mars by the Eiffel Tower. And then there are the benches overlooking the Seine.

WORTH THE EXTRA BUCKS

A PRIORI THE, 35-37, Galerie Vivienne (entrances at 6, rue Vivienne, and 4, rue des Petits-Champs), 2e. Tel. 42-97-48-75.
 Cuisine: FRENCH/TEA ROOM. **Métro:** Bourse, Palais-Royale–Musée-du-Louvre, or Pyramides.
 $ Prices: Light lunch or supper 85–130F ($15.75–$24.05); Sunday brunch 165F ($30.65). MC, V.
 Open: Mon–Sat noon–6:30pm, Sun 1–6:30pm.
 Among the most beautiful of Paris's 19th-century shopping arcades is the Galerie Vivienne, with its high ceilings and elegant stores. You can enjoy both the gallery and a good repast at A Priori Thé, a cleverly named tea room that serves coffee, a large assortment of teas, light meals, sandwiches, salads, and desserts. Management is American, and has created a harmonious and appealing blend of Parisian and New World styles. You can have a brownie for 33F ($6.10).

BOFINGER, 5, rue de la Bastille, 4e. Tel. 42-72-87-82.
 Cuisine: FRENCH/ALSATIAN. **Métro:** Bastille.
 $ Prices: Three-course fixed-price meal 180F ($33.35); three-course à la carte meal, wine included, 260F ($48.15). AE, MC, V.
 Open: Lunch daily noon–3pm; dinner daily 7:30pm–1am.
Bofinger began in the 1860s as a brasserie with the flavor of France's German-influenced Alsace region, and it is now one of the best-loved French restaurants in the city. Its Belle Epoque decor—dark wood, gleaming brass, bright lights, waiters with

long white aprons—will transport you back to the 19th century. The menu features many Alsatian specialties, and there are excellent French classics, including seafood, as well. And the prices are actually quite moderate for Paris. There are 200 seats on two levels.

FAUCHON, 26, place de la Madeleine, 8e. Tel. 47-42-60-11.
   Cuisine: FRENCH. **Métro:** Madeleine.
 $ Prices: *Plats du jour* 15–90F ($9.25–$16.65). AE, EURO, MC, V.
   Open: Mon–Sat 9:40am–7pm.

Founded in 1886, Fauchon is one of the world's great food stores. During lunchtime, long lines of Parisians wait patiently to partake of a delicious hot meal at a crowded stand-up counter while others go to the new cafeteria downstairs. But this is only one aspect of Fauchon. Two buildings and several impeccable rooms feature delicacies from every corner of France and the globe: intricate pastries, fresh meats, perfect fruits from far-away places, and much more. Prices are not low, but then the quality and the presentation are truly outstanding. Even if you don't buy anything, a visit is well worth it: Fauchon has all the richness of a great museum.

PROCOPE, 13, rue de l'Ancienne Comédie, 6e. Tel. 43-26-99-20.
   Cuisine: FRENCH. **Métro:** Odéon.
 $ Prices: Main course plus appetizer or dessert at lunch 75F ($13.90); *menu complet* at lunch 110F ($20.35); oysters around 130F ($24.05); full lunch or dinner 300F ($55.55). AE, MC, V.
   Open: Daily 8am–2pm.

In operation since 1686, Procope bills itself as the oldest restaurant in the world and has entertained guests such as Voltaire, Benjamin Franklin, Marat, and Verlaine. It is a great place for a memorable Parisian meal, with its little crystal chandeliers, mirrors, dark oil paintings, and snowy linens. Many French classics are represented on the long menu, so you can choose from history's best. To save, order the two-course fixed-price lunch, or just drop in for coffee and pastry.

6. ATTRACTIONS

SUGGESTED ITINERARIES

On a first, second, even third visit to Paris, you will get the merest taste of everything that you could want to see in this astoundingly rich city. Don't try to see it "all." Remember, it's better to see just a few things well than to run from museum to monument to park without stopping to reflect.

As you plan your touring, keep in mind that most museums close on either Monday or Tuesday, and that at many of them there is one day each week where admission is free or reduced. Check my listings below for details.

IF YOU HAVE ONE DAY   To start seeing Paris as early as possible, try to have breakfast in a sidewalk café rather than in your hotel, and then begin at Kilometer 0: All distances in France are measured from Notre-Dame, on the Ile de la Cité. From here, cross the River Seine to the Louvre. Pick a section, then a few rooms, for your first visit, for it takes months to see it in its entirety.

From the museum, stroll through the beautiful Jardin des Tuileries to place de la Concorde. Walk down the renowned Champs-Elysées to the Arc de Triomphe; there are several budget restaurants near the Champs-Elysées where you can have lunch. Note that Métro Line 1 runs in a straight line from the Louvre to the Arc de Triomphe (Métro: Charles-de-Gaulle–Etoile), with several stops along the way, an alternative to walking that will also save you some time.

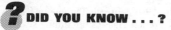

From the Arc de Triomphe, walk down avenue Kléber to place du Trocadéro (or take the Métro to Trocadéro) for some splendid views of the Eiffel Tower. From the top, you will be able to retrace your steps and see some attractions that you did not have time to visit, like the multicolored Centre Pompidou or the white-domed Sacré-Coeur in Montmartre.

Finally, head for the Latin Quarter (catch the RER at Champ-de-Mars, southwest of the Eiffel Tower on the Seine, to St-Michel) and get lost in its little mazelike streets between the river and boulevard St-Germain-des-Prés. This is an excellent area for dinner.

IF YOU HAVE TWO DAYS On the first day, follow the above itinerary from Notre-Dame to the Arc de Triomphe, but see the Louvre in a more relaxed fashion, and take a different route from place de la Concorde to the Champs-Elysées: Walk up rue Royale (with a view of the Eglise de la Madeleine, the church with the Greek columns, at the end) and turn left on rue du Faubourg-St-Honoré to stroll past the Palais de l'Elysée and the poshest shops in Paris. To head back to the Champs-Elysées, turn left on avenue Marigny at place Beauveau. After visiting the Arc de Triomphe, take Métro Line 1 to St-Paul, in the heart of the Marais; walk east on rue St-Antoine and turn left on rue de Brague to see place des Vosges. The Musée Picasso and place de la Bastille are both near here.

Explore the Left Bank on your second day. Start at the Eiffel Tower and stroll past the Invalides, with the Tomb of Napoleon, through the Faubourg St-Germain, a district of elegant 18th-century mansions (both the Musée Rodin and the Musée d'Orsay are here). Head back to the Latin Quarter.

IF YOU HAVE THREE DAYS Combine the above itineraries with visits to the Centre Pompidou and to Montmartre and the Sacré-Coeur. You will also have time to explore the parks: the Jardin du Luxembourg in the Left Bank or Parc Monceau in the Right Bank.

IF YOU HAVE FIVE DAYS Five days is a sensible time to stay in Paris, and if you have a week or 10 days, so much the better. You will probably have time to see the Sainte Chapelle and the Conciergerie on the Ile de la Cité, explore more museums, and visit Versailles, Chartres, or the Euro Disney Resort outside the city.

TOP ATTRACTIONS

CATHEDRALE DE NOTRE-DAME, Ile de la Cité, 4e. Tel. 43-26-07-39.

The Gothic loftiness of Notre-Dame dominates both the Seine and the history of Paris. It was begun in 1163, completed in the 14th century, pillaged during the French Revolution, and restored by Viollet-le-Duc in the 19th century. Polyphonic music developed here and Napoleon crowned himself in this sanctuary. But for all its history, it is the art of Notre-Dame that still awes. Built in an age of illiteracy, the cathedral retells the stories of the Bible in its portals, paintings, and stained glass; its three rose windows are masterful.

For a look at the upper parts of the church, the river, and much of Paris, climb the 387 steps up to the top of one of the towers. The south tower (the one on the right as you face the cathedral) holds Notre-Dame's 16-ton bell, rung on special occasions. The cathedral's museum features exhibits dealing with the history of Notre-Dame.

Admission: Cathedral, free; towers, 30F ($5.55) adults, 16F ($2.95) ages 18–24 and over 60, 5F (90¢) children 7–17, free for children under 7.

Open: Cathedral, daily 8am–7pm; towers and crypt, daily 9:30am–7:30pm (5pm Oct–Mar); museum, Wed and Sat–Sun 2:30–6pm. Free organ concerts at 5:45pm. **Métro:** Cité or St-Michel. **RER:** St-Michel.

SAINTE CHAPELLE, Palais de Justice, lle de la Cité, 4e. Tel. 43-54-30-09.

More valued in medieval times than any martyr's skull, the Crown of Thorns, said to have been gathered at Christ's Crucifixion, was bought by the Crusaders in Constantinople and sent to Paris for safekeeping. Saint Louis, King of France, ordered the "Holy Chapel" to be built as a fitting repository for the precious relic.

In the *chapelle haute* (upper chapel), Old and New Testament scenes are emblazoned in 15 perfect stained-glass windows that are among the highest achievements of 13th-century art. The Sainte Chapelle survived a fire in the 17th century as well as plans for its destruction during the French Revolution, and the beauty created by its master artisans lives on today as strong as ever.

Admission: 24F ($4.45) adults, 13F ($2.40) for ages 18–24 and over 60, 5F (90¢) children 7–17, free for children under 7.

Open: Apr–Sept, daily 9:30am–6:30pm; Oct–Mar, daily 10am–4:20pm. **Métro:** Cité or St-Michel. **RER:** St-Michel.

MUSEE DU LOUVRE, rue de Rivoli, 1er. Tel. 40-20-53-17.

✪ Formerly a royal palace, the Louvre is perhaps the greatest museum in the world. It is certainly one of the largest: If you were to spend five minutes looking at each object in its collection from opening to closing time, it would take you almost a decade to see it all. The *Venus de Milo,* the *Winged Victory,* and the *Mona Lisa* are only three of the masterpieces housed in its collections, which are divided into six departments: Asian antiquities; Egyptian antiquities; Greek, Roman, and Etruscan antiquities; sculpture; paintings; and objets d'art. A very good way to begin exploring this wealth of art is to take the 75-minute guided tour.

The enormous glass pyramid designed by I. M. Pei is the museum's exciting entrance. Of all the *grands projets* supported by President Mitterrand during the last decade, this was probably the most controversial: While many admired the audacious design, others feared that its modernism would clash with the Louvre's classical lines. Oblivious to it all, the photogenic pyramid is well on its way to becoming one of Paris's landmarks. The renovations have also greatly expanded exhibition space and turned the Louvre into a most comfortable museum, with good cafeterias and excellent book and gift shops.

Admission: 33F ($6.10) adults (16F/$2.95 Thurs–Fri, Sat after 5pm, and Sun), 15F ($2.75) ages 18–25 and over 60, free for children under 18.

Open: Mon and Wed 9am–9:45pm, Thurs–Sun 9am–6pm. Call for hours of tours in English. **Métro:** Palais-Royal–Musée-du-Louvre.

ARC DE TRIOMPHE, place Charles-de-Gaulle, 8e. Tel. 43-80-31-31.

The largest triumphal arch in the world was commissioned by Napoleon in honor of his Grande Armée and its 128 victorious battles. The arch was far from complete by the time France's imperial army had been swept from the field at the Battle of Waterloo, and, in fact, some French defeats have been signalized here, as when German armies marched through the arch and down the Champs-Elysées in 1871 and again in 1940. But it has come to symbolize France and to embody some of the greatness of the French spirit: Victor Hugo's death in 1885 was commemorated under the arch and General de Gaulle came here after the liberation of Paris in 1944.

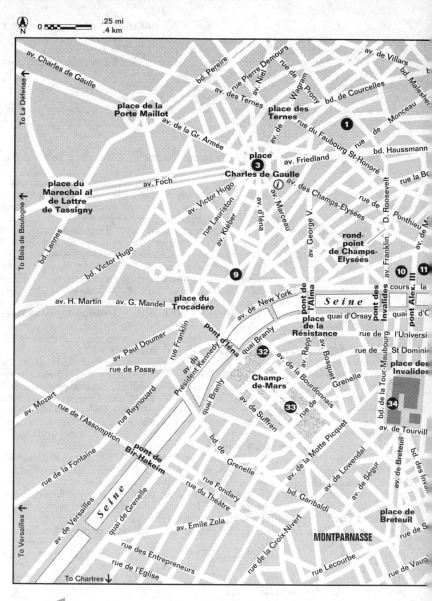

N 0 ⚑⚑⚑⚑⚑   .25 mi
              .4 km

To La Défense ←
av. Charles de Gaulle

bd. Pereire

av. rue Pierre Demours
rue de

av. Niel
av. Wagram Prony

bd. de Courcelles

av. de Villars
bd. Maleshe

de Monceau

place de la
Porte Maillot

av. de la Gr. Armée

place des
Ternes

av. des Ternes

rue du Faubourg St-Honoré

bd. Haussmann

❶

rue de Monceau

place
Charles de Gaulle ❸

av. Friedland

av. de la Bœ

rue de la

av. Foch

av. des Champs-Elysées

rue de

D. Roosevelt

Ponthieu

place du
Marechal al
de Lattre
de Tassigny

av. Victor Hugo

rue Lauriston

av. Kleber

av. d'Iéna

av. Marceau

av. George V.

av. Franklin

rond-
point
de Champs-
Elysées

av. de Ma

bd. Lannes

To Bois de Boulogne ←

bd. Victor Hugo

❾

❿ ⓫

pont Alex. III

Seine

av. H. Martin   av. G. Mandel

place du
Trocadéro

av. de New York

pont de
l'Alma

quai d'Orsay

cours la

quai d'O

la

pont des Invalides

av. Paul Doumer

rue Franklin

pont d'Iéna

quai Branly

place
de la
Résistance

av. Rapp

av. Bosquet

rue de l'Universi

rue de St Domini

bd. de la Tour-Maubourg

place des
Invalides

rue de Passy

av. du Président Kennedy

quai Branly

❸❷

av. de la Bourdonnais

rue de Grenelle

❸❹

av. Mozart

rue de l'Assomption

rue Raynouard

Champ-
de-Mars

av. de Suffren

❸❸

rue de

av. de Tourvill

av. de Breteuil

bd. des Inval

rue de la Fontaine

pont de
Bir-Hakeim

Seine

quai de Grenelle

bd. de Grenelle

rue Fondary

av. de la Motte Picquet

av. de Lowendal

av. de Ségur

place de
Breteuil

rue de S

rue du Théâtre

bd. Garibaldi

To Versailles ←

av. de Versailles

av. Emile Zola

rue de la Croix-Nivert

MONTPARNASSE

rue de S

rue des Entrepreneurs

rue de l'Eglise

rue Lecourbe

rue de Vaug

To Chartres ↓

★ Paris

FRANCE

Arc de Triomphe ❸	Ecole Nationale des Beaux-Arts ㉚	Hôtel et Musée de Cluny
Archives Nationales ㉒	Eglise de la Madeleine ❺	Hôtel de Sens ㉕
Beaubourg ㉑	Folies Bergère ❷	Hôtel de Ville ㉘
Bibliothèque Nationale ❽	Forum des Halles ⑳	Jardin des Plantes
Bourse du Commerce ⑱	Grand Palais ❿	Jardin des Tuileries
Centre Pompidou ㉑	Hôtel Carnavalet ㉔	Jardin du Luxembou
Comédie-Française ⑯	Hôtel des Invalides ㉞	Louvre ⑲
Conciergerie ㉗		

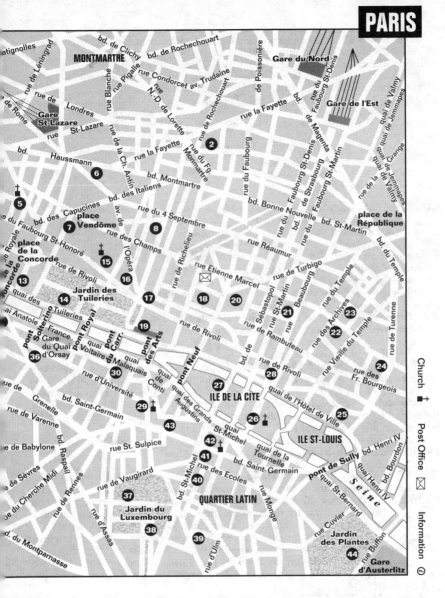

PARIS

MONTMARTRE

bd. de Clichy bd. de Rochechouart

Gare du Nord

Gare de l'Est

Gare St-Lazare

bd. Haussmann

place Vendôme

place de la Concorde

place de la République

Jardin des Tuileries

ILE DE LA CITE

ILE ST-LOUIS

QUARTIER LATIN

Jardin du Luxembourg

Jardin des Plantes

Gare d'Austerlitz

Seine

Church ✠
Post Office ⊠
Information ☉

Beneath the arch, under a gigantic tricolor flag, burns an eternal flame for France's Unknown Soldier. Several outstanding 19th-century sculptures cover the arch, including Rude's *La Marseillaise,* seen on the Champs-Elysées side.

To reach the stairs and elevators that climb the arch, take the underpass (via the Métro entrances). From the top, 162 feet high, you can see in a straight line the Champs-Elysées, the obelisk in place de la Concorde, and the Louvre. On the other side is the Grande Arche de la Défense, a multipurpose structure shaped like an open cube so large that Notre-Dame could fit beneath it. Also from the top you can see the elegant parklike avenue Foch, leading to the vast Bois de Boulogne.

Admission: 30F ($5.55) adults, 16F ($2.95) ages 18–24 and over 60, 5F (90¢) children 7–17, free for children under 7.

Open: Apr–Sept, daily 10am–6pm; Oct–Mar, daily 10am–5pm. **Métro:** Charles-de-Gaulle–Etoile.

TOUR EIFFEL, Parc du Champs-de-Mars, 7e. Tel. 45-50-34-56.

Built as a temporary structure to add flair to the World's Fair of 1889, the Eiffel Tower managed to remain standing and become the soaring symbol of Paris. Praised by some and damned by the likes of Maupassant and the writer Huysmans (who called it "a hollow candlestick"), the tower created as much controversy in its time as Pei's Louvre pyramids did in the 1980s.

Take the Métro to Trocadéro and walk from the Palais de Chaillot to the Seine in order to get the full effect of the tower and its surroundings. Besides fabulous views (especially when the Trocadéro fountains are in full force), you get a free show from the dancers and acrobats in front of the Palais de Chaillot.

The tower has elevators in two of its pillars, and frequently you have a long wait to get one of them. The best view is from the top level, where historians have re-created the office of engineer Gustave Eiffel. The tower has several restaurants and bars.

The vast green esplanade beneath the Eiffel Tower is the Parc du Champs-de-Mars, which extends all the way to the 18th-century Ecole Militaire (Military Academy) at its southeast end. This is a formal lawn, once a parade ground for French troops.

Admission: 18F ($3.35) for the elevator to the first level (188 ft.), 36F ($6.65) to the second level (380 ft.), 53F ($9.80) to the highest level (1,060 ft.). Walking up the stairs to the first and second levels costs 10F ($1.85).

Open: Sun–Thurs 10am–11pm, Fri–Sat 10am–midnight. **Métro:** Trocadéro, Bir-Hakeim, or Ecole-Militaire. **RER:** Champs-de-Mars.

MUSEE D'ORSAY, 1, rue de Bellechasse, 7e. Tel. 40-49-48-14.

Once a railroad station, this turn-of-the-century building (featured in Orson Welles's *The Trial*) houses an astounding collection of art from the second half of the 19th century. Works from the Louvre and the old Musée du Jeu de Paume—repository of an unsurpassed collection of impressionist masterpieces—were transferred here in the mid-1980s, and the Musée d'Orsay is now one of the world's great art museums. Thousands of paintings, sculptures, objets d'art, items of furniture, architectural displays, and even photographs and movies illustrate the diversity and richness of 19th-century art, including realism, impressionism, post-impressionism, and art nouveau.

Admission: 31F ($5.75) adults, 16F ($2.95) ages 18–24 and over 60 and for adults on Sun, free for children under 18.

Open: Tues–Wed and Fri–Sun 10am–6pm, Thurs 10am–9:15pm. **Métro:** Solférino. **RER:** Musée-d'Orsay.

MORE ATTRACTIONS

CONCIERGERIE, Palais de Justice, Ile de la Cité, 1er. Tel. 43-54-30-06.

Every French schoolchild must shudder on passing the Conciergerie. This building dates from the Middle Ages, when it was an administrative office of the Crown, but it is most famous for its days as a prison during the French Revolution. Those destined for beheading at the guillotine under the Reign of Terror were imprisoned here, including Marie Antoinette and other members of the royal family and the nobility. You can visit the dank cells where these unfortunates spent their last days and hours, and marvel at the vagaries of fate.

Admission: 31F ($5.75) adults, 16F ($2.95) ages 18–24 and over 60, free for children under 18.

Open: June–Aug, daily 9:30am–6:30pm; Sept and Apr–May, daily 9:30am–6:30pm; Oct–Mar, daily 10am–5pm. **Métro:** Cité, Châtelet, or St-Michel. **RER:** St-Michel.

BASILIQUE DU SACRE-COEUR, place St-Pierre, 18e. Tel. 42-51-17-02.

Made famous by Utrillo and a hundred lesser artists who lived in Montmartre, the Sacré-Coeur is a vaguely Byzantine-Romanesque church built from 1876 to 1919. It is not as familiar as the Eiffel Tower or the Arc de Triomphe, but it, too, is a romantic symbol of Paris. Be sure to visit the dome. You must climb lots of stairs (that's why it's a good idea to take the elevator up from the Métro and the *funiculaire*), but the view is fabulous: 30 miles across the rooftops of Paris, on a clear day.

Some squares in Montmartre, like place du Tertre, cater to tourists in search of a stereotypical Paris; the artists madly painting away are often better salespeople than anything else. The side streets are worth exploring, and so is the cemetery, which holds the remains of several illustrious writers and musicians.

Admission: Basilica, free; to climb to the dome and visit the crypt, 16F ($2.95).

Open: Basilica, daily 6:30am–11pm. Dome and crypt, Apr–Sept, daily 9am–7pm; Oct–Mar, daily 9am–6pm. **Métro:** Abbesses; take the elevator to the surface and follow the signs to the *funiculaire,* which takes you up to the church for one Métro ticket.

PANTHEON, place du Panthéon, 5e. Tel. 43-54-34-51.

This neoclassical building with a huge dome was originally a church: It was ordered by Louis XV in thanksgiving for his having recovered from a serious illness and it was called the Eglise Ste-Geneviève. After the Revolution it was renamed the Panthéon and was rededicated as a necropolis for France's secular heroes. In the crypt beneath the dome are the tombs of Voltaire, Jean-Jacques Rousseau, Victor Hugo, Louis Braille (inventor of the reading system for the blind), Emile Zola, and other outstanding figures.

Admission: 24F ($4.45) adults, 13F ($2.40) ages 18–24 and over 60, 5F (90¢) children 7–17, free for children under 7.

Open: Apr–Sept, daily 10am–4:45pm; Oct–Mar, daily 10am–12:30pm and 2–5:30pm. **Métro:** Cardinal-Lemoine or Maubert-Mutualité.

LES EGOUTS DE PARIS (Paris Sewers), pont de l'Alma, 7e. Tel. 47-05-10-29.

Those who have read Victor Hugo's *Les Misérables* or seen old movies of World War II resistance fighters will want to visit the sewers of Paris—not as beautiful as the city above the ground, but enormously interesting. Paris's sewer system is actually an engineering marvel, laid out under Napoléon III by Belgrand, at the same time when the *grands boulevards* were being laid. If the mechanical guts of a great city interest you, get in line for a visit on one of the few afternoons when a glimpse is offered.

Admission: 22F ($4.05) adults, 17F ($3.15) ages 18–24 and over 60.

Open: Sat–Wed 11am–5pm. **Closed:** During bad weather. **Métro:** Alma-Marceau. **RER:** Pont de l'Alma.

HOTEL DES INVALIDES, place des Invalides, 7e. Tel. 45-55-37-70.

Louis XIV built this majestic building as a hospital and home for wounded war veterans. These functions are still performed here, and there's office space for numerous departments of the French armed forces. But most visitors come to see the **Tomb of Napoleon,** a great porphyry sarcophagus lying beneath the golden dome of the Invalides. The emperor's body was transferred to this monumental resting place in 1840, almost two decades after his death on the remote South Atlantic island of St. Helena, where he was in exile.

If you like military lore, you must see the **Musée de l'Armée** here, perhaps the greatest in the world. It features thousands of weapons, spear- and arrowheads, suits of armor, cannons, battle flags, booty, and every other sort of military paraphernalia.

Admission: 30F ($5.55) adults, 20F ($3.70) children 7–18 and seniors over 60, free for children under 7.

Open: Apr–Sept, daily 10am–6pm; Oct–Mar, daily 10am–5pm. **Métro:** Latour-Maubourg or Varenne.

MUSEE DE L'ORANGERIE, place de la Concorde, 1er. Tel. 42-97-48-16.

⭐ Since 1984 the Orangerie has housed the renowned Jean Walter and Paul Guillaume art collection. It was donated to the Louvre by Domenica Walter, who was married to both men (not at the same time, of course). The collection, though small (it comprises fewer than 150 paintings, all from the periods of impressionism to the 1930s), is truly remarkable. Among the painters represented here are Cézanne, Renoir, Rousseau, Matisse, Derain, Picasso, Laurencin, and Soutine. The lower floor contains Monet's aqueous *Nymphéas*. The Orangerie's intimate rooms are refreshing after the vastness of the Louvre.

Admission: 26F ($4.80) adults (14F/$2.60 Sun), 14F ($2.60) ages 18–24 and over 60, free for children under 18.

Open: Wed–Mon 9:45am–5:15pm. **Métro:** Concorde.

CENTRE POMPIDOU, place Georges-Pompidou, 3e. Tel. 42-77-12-33.

The full name of this gigantic, futuristic arts center is Centre National d'Art et de Culture Georges Pompidou, and it was despised by many when it was built. Its bold "exoskeletal" architecture and bright colors were seen as out of place in the traditional old Beaubourg neighborhood. Since then, many detractors have become grudging admirers. You'll recognize the center when you see it. Enormous colorful pipes run in mazes to bind its exterior, and translucent escalators of incredible length run along the outer walls, trundling visitors among the various levels.

Besides being a venue for changing exhibits, the center houses the **Musée d'Art Moderne**—with art from the turn of the century to the present—and the **Bibliothèque Publique d'Information,** a public library. The vast square in front of the center features acrobats and other street performers at all times.

Admission: Musée d'Art Moderne, 27F ($5) adults, 18F ($3.35) ages 18–24 and over 60; one-day pass to all exhibits, 55F ($10.20) adults, 50F ($9.25) ages 18–24 and over 60, free for everyone Sun 10am–2pm; free at all times for children under 18.

Open: Mon and Wed–Fri noon–10pm, Sat–Sun 10am–10pm. **Métro:** Rambuteau, Hôtel-de-Ville, or Châtelet-Les-Halles.

PLACE DES VOSGES, in the Marais, 4e.

⭐ Serene and rational yet intimate and endearing, the place des Vosges is Paris's oldest and perhaps most beautiful square. Henri IV planned it in the early 17th century on the spot where Henri II had been killed in a tournament. Originally known as place Royale, it retains its monarchal bonds in the white fleurs-de-lys crowning each row of pink-brick houses. After the Revolution, it became place de l'Indivisibilité and later place des Vosges, in honor of the first départment that completely paid its taxes. Among the famous figures connected with the square are Madame de Sévigné, who was born at no. 1 bis, and Victor Hugo, who lived at no. 6 for 16 years, and whose house presently contains the Musée Victor-Hugo.

The fashionable promenades and romantic duels of the 17th century are long gone, and antiques dealers, booksellers, and cafés compete today for your attention. Children play and older residents chat—all in all, an affable slice of Parisian life.

Admission: Free.

Open: Daily, 24 hours. **Métro:** St-Paul; then walk east on rue St-Antoine and turn left on rue de Brague.

MUSEE PICASSO, in the Hôtel Salé, 5, rue de Thorigny, 3e. Tel. 42-71-25-21.

The Hôtel Salé, a renovated mansion in the Marais, houses the greatest collection of Pablo Picasso's works in the world. After his death in 1973, the artist's estate arranged to donate this enormous collection in lieu of French inheritance taxes, which were also enormous. Besides Picasso's own paintings, sculptures, ceramics, engravings, and sketches, which number in the thousands, the museum displays works by the artist's favorite painters, including Corot, Cézanne, and Matisse.

Admission: 28F ($5.20) adults (16F/$2.95 Sun), 16F ($2.95) ages 18–24 and over 60, free for children under 18.

Open: Wed 9:15am–10pm, Thurs–Mon 9:15am–5:15pm. **Métro:** Chemin-Vert or St-Paul.

MUSEE CARNAVALET, 23, rue de Sévigné, 3e. Tel. 42-72-21-13.

Located in the Marais, the Musée Carnavalet is also known as the Musée de l'Histoire de Paris, and it details the city's history from prehistoric times to the present. Paintings, signs, items of furniture, models of the Bastille, and Marie Antoinette's personal items are all on display. The museum is housed in two splendid mansions, the Hôtel Le Peletier de St-Fargeau and the Hôtel Carnavalet, which was once the home of Madame de Sévigné, the 17th-century writer of masterful letters.

Admission: 30F ($5.55) adults, 20F ($3.70) ages 18–24 and over 60, free for children under 18.

Open: Tues–Sun 10am–5:40pm. **Métro:** St-Paul; then walk east on rue St-Antoine and turn left on rue de Sévigné.

MUSEE DE CLUNY, 6 place Paul-Painlevé, 5e. Tel. 43-25-62-00.

The Cluny is Paris's museum of medieval art. The exhibits here contain wood and stone sculptures, brilliant stained glass and metalwork, and rich tapestries, including the famous 15th-century *The Lady and the Unicorn,* with its representation of the five senses. The Hôtel de Cluny, where the museum is housed, is one of the city's foremost examples of medieval architecture. Some parts date back to Roman times, and you can see the ruins of thermal baths.

Admission: 16F ($2.95) adults, 8F ($1.50) ages 18–24 and over 60, free for children under 18.

Open: Wed–Mon 9:45am–12:30pm and 2–5:15pm. **Métro:** Cluny-Sorbonne.

MUSEE RODIN, in the Hôtel Biron, 77, rue de Varenne, 7e. Tel. 47-05-01-34.

Sixteen rooms in the 18th-century Hôtel Biron contain many of Auguste Rodin's masterpieces. *The Thinker* is here, in several incarnations, and so are *The Age of Iron, The Bourghers of Calais,* and *The Gates of Hell.* The sculpture garden is delightful.

Admission: 22F ($4.05) adults (11F/$2.05 Sun), 11F ($2.05) ages 18–24 and over 60, free for children under 18.

Open: Apr–Sept, Tues–Sun 10am–6pm; Oct–Mar, Tues–Sun 10am–5pm. **Métro:** Varenne.

PLACE VENDOME, 1er.

Place Vendôme features some of the poshest addresses in all of Paris. Here you will find the Hôtel Ritz and such luxurious stores as Van Cleef et Arpels. The column in the center was commissioned by Napoleon to honor those who fought and won the Battle of Austerlitz, and Austrian cannons were used in its construction. Among its famous residents was Chopin, who died at no. 12 in 1849.

Métro: Tuileries, Concorde, or Madeleine.

CIMETIERE DU PERE-LACHAISE, 20e.

Located in eastern Paris, in the 20th arrondissement, Père-Lachaise is the most famous cemetery in the city and one of the most beautiful in the world. The illustrious men and women buried here include greats from the worlds of art, letters, music, and the stage: Molière, Ingres, Balzac, Chopin, Bizet, Oscar Wilde, Sarah Bernhardt, Proust, Modigliani, Apollinaire, Isadora Duncan, Colette, Gertrude Stein, Edith Piaf, Jim Morrison, and Simone Signoret. A map of the cemetery costs 10F ($1.85) and has many of the famous gravesites marked on it.

Open: Mar 15–Nov 5, Mon–Fri 7:30am–6pm, Sat 8:30am–6pm, Sun 9am–6pm; Nov 6–Mar 14, Mon–Fri 8am–5:30pm, Sat 8:30am–5:30pm, Sun 9am–5:30pm. **Métro:** Père-Lachaise.

PARKS & GARDENS

JARDIN DES TUILERIES, between the Louvre and place de la Concorde, 1er. Tel. 42-60-38-01.

This serene garden of forking paths was laid out in the 1560s by Catherine de' Medici, the Queen Mother. A century later, Le Nôtre, creator of French landscaping, redesigned it in the classical style. Today it's a restful green space adorned with white statues in the midst of Paris. Its odd name comes from the clay earth of the land here, once used to make roof tiles called *tuiles*.

Métro: Tuileries or Concorde.

JARDIN DU LUXEMBOURG, 6e. Tel. 43-29-12-78.

Commissioned by King Henry IV's Queen Marie de' Medici, the Jardin du Luxembourg is one of Paris's best-loved parks. It's located south of the Latin Quarter, and is quite popular with students and a favorite with children, who love the *parc à jeux* (playground) and the *théâtre des marionettes* (puppet theater). Besides pools and fountains and statues of queens and poets—including those of Hérédia, Baudelaire, and Verlaine—there are tennis courts and spaces for playing *boules*.

Métro: Odéon. **RER:** Luxembourg.

BOIS DE BOULOGNE, in western Paris, 16e. Tel. 40-67-97-02.

Formerly a forest and a royal hunting preserve, the Bois de Boulogne is the largest park in Paris. Napoléon III donated the bois to the city of Paris, and Baron Haussmann, his town planner, created the Service Municipal des Parcs et Plantations to help transform it into a park. Today it's a vast reserve of more than 2,200 acres with jogging, horseback riding, bicycle trails (you can rent a bike at the bois), two lakes for boating, the famous Longchamp and Auteuil racecourses, the beautiful Jardin Shakespeare in the Pré Catelan, and the Jardin d'Acclimatation, Paris's children's amusement park.

Métro: Les-Sablons, Porte-Maillot, or Porte-Dauphine.

PARC MONCEAU, 8e. Tel. 42-27-39-56.

Of Paris's parks and squares, the English-style Parc Monceau is probably the most romantic. A favorite of Marcel Proust, it contains a number of odd features, including a pyramid, ancient columns, and several tombs of an unknown origin. The park is located in the heart of a well-heeled residential district, and some nearby streets like rue Rembrandt and avenue Vélasquez feature handsome architecture. Two excellent small museums are also in this area: the **Musée Nissim-de-Camondo,** 63, rue de Monceau, 8e (tel. 45-63-26-32), with an extraordinary collection of 18th-century furniture and decorative arts; and the **Musée Cernuschi,** 7, avenue Vélasquez, 8e (tel. 45-63-50-75), specializing in Chinese art.

Métro: Monceau or Villiers. **Bus:** 30 or 94.

SPECIAL-INTEREST SIGHTSEEING

No matter what special interest you may have, there's probably something in Paris just for you. Start with the museums. There are more than 100 of them, and they specialize in all sorts of subjects, arcane and otherwise. The following list barely starts to scratch the surface: **Fondation Le Corbusier** (20th-century architecture), 8–10, square du Docteur-Blanche, 16e (tel. 42-88-41-53; Métro: Jasmin); **Musée d'Art Juif** (Jewish art), 42, rue des Saules, 18e (tel. 42-57-84-15; Métro: Lamarck-Caulaincourt); **Musée de l'Homme** (anthropology and ethnography), in the Palais de Chaillot, 17, place du Trocadéro, 16e (tel. 45-53-70-60; Métro: Trocadéro); **Musée des Arts de la Mode** (fashion), 109, rue de Rivoli, 1er (tel. 42-60-32-14; Métro: Tuileries or Palais-Royal–Musée-du-Louvre); **Musée du Cinéma,** in the Palais de Chaillot, 17, place du Trocadéro, 16e (tel. 45-53-74-39; Métro: Trocadéro); and the **Musée National des Arts Africains et Océaniens** (African and Pacific art), 293, avenue Daumesnil, 12e (tel. 43-43-14-54; Métro: Porte-Dorée).

ORGANIZED TOURS

BUS TOURS   Paris is the perfect city to explore on your own, but if time or leg muscles do not permit, consider taking an introductory tour. The most prominent company is **Cityrama,** 4, place des Pyramides, 1er (tel. 42-60-30-14; Métro: Palais-Royal–Musée-du-Louvre). Their two-hour "orientation tour" of Paris costs 150F ($27.75) and they also feature half- and full-day tours for 240F ($44.45) and 420F ($77.75) respectively. Tours to Versailles and Chartres are a better bargain, but the popular nighttime tours of Paris are expensive.

BOAT TOURS   Among the most favored ways to see Paris is by the **bateaux-mouches,** sightseeing boats that cruise up and down the Seine. They sail from the pont de l'Alma in the Right Bank (tel. 48-59-30-30 for reservations, 42-25-96-10 for schedules; Métro: Alma-Marceau). From March through mid-November departures are usually on the hour and the half hour, while in winter there are 4–16 cruises per day, depending on demand. The voyage lasts 1¼ hours and costs 33F ($6.10). Special reserved-seats tours including meals are run at lunchtime for 300F ($55.55), at tea-time on weekends for 80F ($14.80), and at dinner for 500F ($92.60).

Cheaper than the bateaux-mouches are the **bateaux-bus,** a relatively new ferry service that cruises for several miles through the heart of Paris. There are stops at La Bourdonnais–Tour Eiffel, near the Eiffel Tower (Métro: Trocadéro or Bir-Hakeim; RER: Champs-de-Mars); Solférino–Musée-d'Orsay; quai Malaquais, opposite the Louvre; quai Montebello–Notre Dame; and Hôtel de Ville (Métro: Hôtel-de-Ville). Hop on or off the boat at any stop. Fare is 38F ($7.05) and there are one-, three-, and seven-day passes as well.

SPECIAL & FREE EVENTS

The Office de Tourisme de Paris publishes a monthly list of special events currently taking place, including music festivals, concerts, opera performances, exhibits, plays, and sports events. Ask for the *Manifestations du mois.*

Also see "When to Go" in "Pretrip Preparations," above, for a list of annual special events.

7. SAVVY SHOPPING

Paris is at the forefront of the world of fashion and design. These are some of the world-renowned boutiques: **Chanel,** 31, rue Cambon, 1er (tel. 42-86-28-00; Métro: Concorde or Madeleine); **Lanvin,** 22, rue du Faubourg-St-Honoré, 8e (tel. 42-65-14-40; Métro: Concorde); **Hermès,** 24, rue du Faubourg-St-Honoré, 8e (tel. 40-17-47-17; Métro: Concorde); and **Dior,** 30, avenue Montaigne, 8e (tel. 40-73-54-44; Métro: Franklin-D.-Roosevelt).

More to the point for our budget are the *grands magasins*, Paris's great **department stores.** They sell all sorts of French goods, often at very good prices, and are very experienced at helping you with VAT refunds (see "Special Discount Opportunities" in "From the Budget Traveler's Point of View," above). Try **Galeries Lafayette,** 40, boulevard Haussmann, 9e (tel. 42-82-34-56; Métro: Chaussée-d'Antin), and **Printemps,** 64, boulevard Haussmann, 9e (tel. 42-82-50-00; Métro: Chaussée-d'Antin). These most attractive stores stand directly behind the Opéra and are open Monday through Saturday from 9:30am to 6:30pm.

Largest of all department stores is **La Samaritaine,** 19, rue de la Monnaie, 1er (tel. 44-50-11-20; Métro: Pont-Neuf or Châtelet–Les Halles), between the Louvre and pont Neuf. It's housed in several buildings with art nouveau touches and has an art deco facade on quai du Louvre. The ninth floor of store no. 2 has a fine restaurant that's not expensive; look for signs to the *panorama,* a free observation point with a wonderful view of Paris. La Samaritaine is open on Monday, Wednesday, Thursday, and Saturday from 9:30am to 7pm, and on Tuesday and Friday from 9:30am to 8:30pm.

Many of the city's museums have great **museum shops** that sell arts, crafts, books, and high-quality souvenirs at reasonable prices.

Paris has several English-language **bookstores** carrying American and English books and maps and guides to the city and other destinations. Try **Brentano's,** 37, avenue de l'Opéra, 2e (tel. 42-61-52-50; Métro: Opéra), open Monday through Saturday from 10am to 7pm; or **Galignani,** 224, rue de Rivoli, 1er (tel. 42-60-76-07; Métro: Tuileries), open Monday through Friday from 9:30am to 7pm.

Most famous of all is ✪ **Shakespeare and Company,** 37, rue de la Bûcherie, 5e (no phone; Métro or RER: St-Michel), Sylvia Beach's congenial literary watering hole frequented by Hemingway, Fitzgerald, Gertrude Stein, and other luminaries in the 1920s, when she published the first complete version of Joyce's *Ulysses.* The shop was located then on rue de l'Odéon; its successor is just off place St-Michel.

MARKETS   For a real shopping adventure, come to the vast **Marché aux Puces de la Porte de St-Ouen,** 18e (Métro: Porte-de-Clignancourt). The Clignancourt flea market, as it is commonly known, features several thousand stalls, carts, shops, and vendors selling everything from used blue jeans to antique paintings and furniture. Watch out for pickpockets. It's open on Saturday, Sunday, and Monday from 9am to 8pm.

More comprehensible, and certainly prettier, is the **Marché aux Fleurs** (Métro: Cité), the flower market in place Louis-Lépine on the Ile de la Cité. Come Monday through Saturday to enjoy the flowers, whether you buy anything or not; on Sunday it becomes the **Marché aux Oiseaux,** an equally colorful bird market.

8. EVENING ENTERTAINMENT

Nightlife in Paris is bewilderingly diverse. Whatever you want to see or do is here. Theater is wonderful. Opera, ballet, and classical music performances are world-class. Movie listings are incredibly varied, and there are numerous bars and dance clubs.

Several local publications provide up-to-the-minute listings of performances and other evening entertainment. Foremost among these is *Pariscope: Une Semaine de Paris,* a weekly guide with thorough listings of movies, plays, ballet, art exhibits, clubs, etc. You can buy it at any newstand for 3F (55¢).

For **half-price theater tickets,** go to the Kiosque-Théâtre at the northwest corner of the Madeleine church (Métro: Madeleine). You can buy tickets only for that same day's performance. The little panels all around the kiosk indicate whether the performance is sold out (little red man) or whether they still have tickets (little green man). The Kiosque-Théâtre is open Tuesday through Friday from 12:30 to 8pm, on

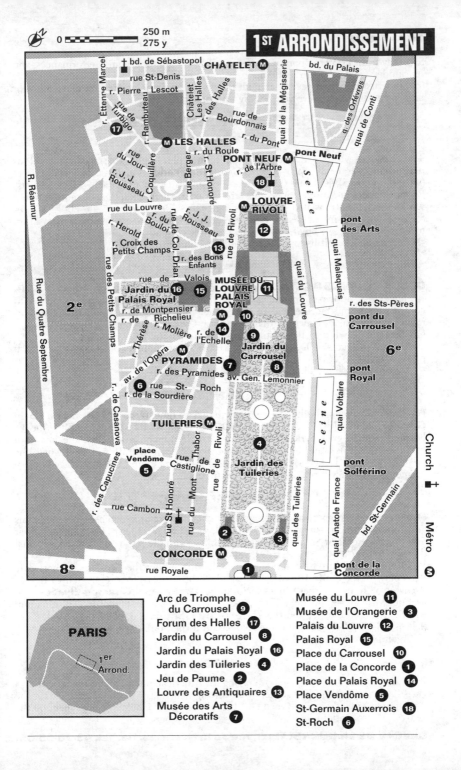

1ST ARRONDISSEMENT

PARIS

1ᵉʳ Arrond.

Arc de Triomphe
  du Carrousel ⑨
Forum des Halles ⑰
Jardin du Carrousel ⑧
Jardin du Palais Royal ⑯
Jardin des Tuileries ④
Jeu de Paume ②
Louvre des Antiquaires ⑬
Musée des Arts
  Décoratifs ⑦

Musée du Louvre ⑪
Musée de l'Orangerie ③
Palais du Louvre ⑫
Palais Royal ⑮
Place du Carrousel ⑩
Place de la Concorde ①
Place du Palais Royal ⑭
Place Vendôme ⑤
St-Germain Auxerrois ⑱
St-Roch ⑥

Church ✝

Métro Ⓜ

Saturday from 12:30 to 2pm for matinees and 2 to 8pm for evening performances, and on Sunday from 12:30 to 4:30pm.

Students can often get last-minute tickets by applying at the box office an hour before curtain time. Have your ISIC with you.

THE PERFORMING ARTS

THEATER

The classics of Molière, Racine, and other French playwrights are staged in marvelous performances at the 300-year-old ✪ **Comédie Française,** 2, rue de Richelieu, 1er (tel. 40-15-00-15, 40-15-00-00 for recorded information in French; Métro: Palais-Royal–Musée-du-Louvre). Schedules are varied with the addition of more modern works and plays translated from other languages. Prices average 45–200F ($8.35–$37.05), with last-minute seats even cheaper. The box office is open daily from 11am to 6pm, and you can buy tickets up to two weeks in advance.

Pariscope has full listings of the other theaters in the city.

OPERA

OPERA DE PARIS BASTILLE, place de la Bastille, 12e. Tel. 40-01-17-89.

The city's principal operatic stage is the Opéra de Paris Bastille. Opened to commemorate the bicentennial of the French Revolution, this modernistic performance center was designed by the Uruguayan-Canadian architect Carlos Ott, and it has brought new life to the Bastille neighborhood.

Prices: Tickets, 50–560F ($9.25–$103.70) available two weeks before each performance.

Open: Box office, 11am–6:30pm. **Métro:** Bastille.

DANCE

For classical ballet and other dance performances, come to the ✪ **Opéra de Paris Garnier,** place de l'Opéra, 9e (tel. 40-17-35-35; Métro: Opéra; RER: Auber). Formerly Paris's great lyrical stage—and also the Opera House that the Phantom called home—this grand building from the age of Napoléon III is in itself worth the price of a ticket. Tickets cost 30–560F ($5.55–$103.70) and the box office is open Monday through Saturday from 11am to 6:30pm.

CLASSICAL MUSIC

Over a dozen Parisian **churches** regularly schedule free or inexpensive organ recitals and concerts, among them Notre-Dame (tel. 43-29-50-40; Métro: Cité), on Sunday at 5:45pm; the Eglise St-Sulpice (Métro: St-Sulpice); and the American Church, 65, quai d'Orsay (tel. 47-05-07-99; Métro: Invalides).

Other concerts are held in numerous halls throughout the city. The Orchestre de Paris plays in the **Salle Pleyel,** 252, rue du Faubourg-St-Honoré, 8e (tel. 45-61-16-99; Métro: Ternes). Other venues include the **Théâre des Champs-Elysées,** 15, avenue Montaigne, 8e (tel. 47-20-36-37, 47-23-47-77 for recorded information; Métro: Alma-Marceau); and the **Théâtre du Châtelet,** 2, place du Châtelet, 1er (tel. 40-28-28-40, 42-33-00-00 for recorded information).

Again, *Pariscope* carries full listings.

JAZZ

Parisians seem to have an insatiable craving for American music, especially jazz, and so Paris has a very vibrant jazz scene. Look through current listings in *Pariscope* for the jazz masters you admire, and then take the Métro to the club (all listings mention the nearest Métro station).

CAVEAU DE LA HUCHETTE, 5, rue de la Huchette, 5e. Tel. 43-26-65-05.

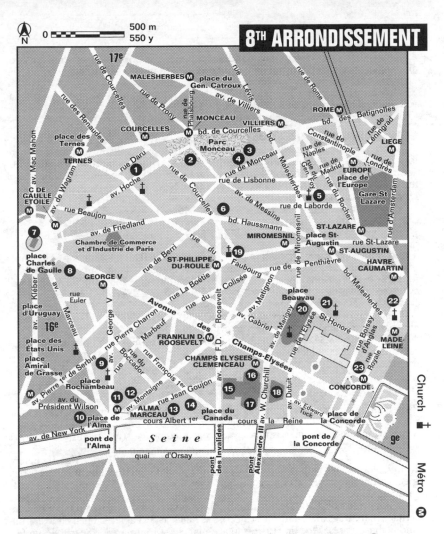

8TH ARRONDISSEMENT

0 | 500 m
0 | 550 y

N

Church ✝

Métro Ⓜ

8e Arrondissement

PARIS

American Cathedral in Paris ❾
Arc de Triomphe ❼
Crazy Horse Saloon ⓫

Eglise de la Madeleine ㉒
Grand Palais ⑯
Hôtel Crillon ㉓
Musée Cernuschi ❸
Musée d'Art Moderne ❿
Musée Jacquemart André ❻
Musée Nissim de Camondo ❹
Notre Dame de la Consolation ⑬
Office du Tourisme ❽
Palais de la Découverte ⑮

Palais de l'Elysée ⑳
Parc Monceau ❷
Petit Palais ⑱
St-Alexandre-Nevsky ❶
St-Augustin ❺
St-Jean-Baptiste ⑭
St. Michael's English Church ㉑
St-Philippe-du-Roule ⑲
Théâtres des Champs Elysées ⑫
Université Paris IV ⑰

This is Paris's jazz club of long standing, popular with both foreigners and locals of all ages who want to listen and dance to good jazz. With a capacity of 400 guests, the club has four rooms and two levels.

Prices: Drinks from 18F ($3.35), but there's no minimum so you buy only what you want. **Admission:** 55F ($10.20) Sun–Thurs, 60F ($11.10) Fri–Sat.
Open: Daily 9:30pm–4am. **Métro:** St-Michel. **RER:** St-Michel.

NEW MORNING, 7-9, rue des Petites-Ecuries, 10e. Tel. 45-23-51-41.

When the Lounge Lizards played here, the audience was skeptical until they were totally seduced by the music, but once they were convinced, the concert lasted until 4am. New Morning is probably Paris's best jazz club, and the audience must be one of the toughest to win over in the world. The best New York groups perform here.

Admission: 110F ($20.35).
Open: Concerts usually start at 9:30pm. **Métro:** Château-d'Eau.

FILMS

The diversity of movies being shown at any time in Paris is bewildering. The glitzy theaters along the Champs-Elysées show new big-name films, both French and foreign. Smaller cinemas located on both banks of the Seine show the classics, as well as lesser-known titles from all over the world. Look in *Pariscope* for what's on.

"V.O." next to a listing stands for *version originale*, which means the soundtrack will be in the original language of the film; "V.F." (*version française*) means that the film has been dubbed in French; *sous-titres* are subtitles. Movie tickets cost about 40–45F ($7.40–$8.35) depending on the cinema and the film that's playing. Students can sometimes get reductions on ticket prices; other discounts are offered during the daytime, and on Monday.

NIGHTCLUBS

Paris nightclubs are world famous. The names Lido, Folies Bergère, Crazy Horse Saloon, and Moulin Rouge are mimicked in dozens of other big cities, and grand revues with music, colorful costumes, variety acts, comedians, and plentiful nudity are a Paris specialty.

The heyday of the great supper-club revues was before World War II, before Technicolor movies with stereo sound, and certainly before the advent of television. Spectacular shows are still staged, but they are expensive and somewhat self-conscious.

If you must see a Paris spectacular, be prepared to spend at least $100 per person, perhaps as much as $200—drinks can cost as much as $35 apiece. Then choose from among these places: **Moulin Rouge,** place Blanche, Montmartre, 18e (tel. 46-06-00-19; Métro: Place-Blanche); **Folies Bergère,** 32, rue Richer, 9e (tel. 42-46-77-11; Métro: Rue-Montmartre or Cadet); **Lido Cabaret Normandie,** 116 bis, avenue des Champs-Elysées, 8e (tel. 40-76-56-10; Métro: George-V); and the **Crazy Horse Saloon,** 12, avenue George-V, 8e (tel. 47-23-32-32; Métro: George-V).

DANCE CLUBS

The clubs of Paris must be among the hippest/chicest in the world. At present, many Parisian circles seem to favor salsa, rap, reggae, and Eurotechdisco, and they fastidiously extol the virtues of going out on weeknights, to avoid the suburban crowds who come into the city on Friday and Saturday nights. The later you go, the better. But everything can change, well, overnight.

REX CLUB, 5, bd. Poissonière, 2e. Tel. 42-36-83-98.

Go down about a thousand steps. Everything is gray and high-tech. It's big. There are mirrors. There is smoke that smells like strawberry. Are things made of rubber? One is young. One wears clothes like silver. One dances by oneself. Tuesday is a big rap party; Wednesday is for bands; Friday is Eurodisco.

Prices: Drinks 50 F ($9.25); beer 30F ($5.55). **Admission:** 70F ($12.95), including one drink.

Open: Daily 11:30pm–dawn. **Métro:** Bonne-Nouvelle.

PIGALLS, 77, rue Pigalle, 9e. Tel. 45-26-04-43.

A somewhat decadent feeling pervades this place, perhaps because of the neighborhood in which it's located. The music is disco and new wave. There are sculptures on the walls. The crowd is less than wild, but fashion-conscious nevertheless. If you come around 2am, you may have to wait around half an hour to get in, but at 4am you'll be admitted right away.

Prices: Drinks 60F ($11.10). **Admission:** 100F ($18.50).

Open: Daily, midnight–?. **Métro:** Pigalle.

AFTER HOURS

Where do you go after it's all over? In the old days, late-night revelers would make their unsteady way to Les Halles to watch the market open and have one last wake-up drink. Les Halles is gone, but not completely.

Le Cochon à l'Oreille, 15, rue Montmartre, 1er (tel. 42-36-07-56). Perhaps the last vestige of Les Halles is the fishmongers' stands set up along rue Montmartre in the early morning. If a fishmonger is going to get up at 2:30 or 3am to set up shop, he or she is going to need something bracing to open the eyes and fight off the chill. This is where they come to get it, among tiled murals of the old produce markets. Always noisy and reassuring, Le Cochon à l'Oreille ("A Pig in Your Ear") will revive and delight you if anything can. It's open Monday through Saturday from 4am to 4pm. Take the Métro to Les Halles.

9. EASY EXCURSIONS

VERSAILLES Louis XIV, who reigned from 1643 to 1715, commissioned the **Château de Versailles** (tel. 30-84-74-00) and its vast grounds and gardens. Construction was under way for 50 years, and the result is simply astounding. Fourteen miles southwest of Paris, Versailles is justifiably one of France's great tourist attractions.

Guided tours take you through parts of the château. Highlights include the royal apartments and the famous **Hall of Mirrors,** where the armistice ending World War I was signed. Save time for the **Grand Trianon,** which functioned as the royal guesthouse, and the **Petit Trianon,** loved by Marie Antoinette. The **gardens** at Versailles, with its fabulous system of waterworks, are also worth special consideration. Water shows called the "grandes eaux" are played May through September on Sunday afternoon, and there is also one night show per month, with the fountains marvelously illuminated. For schedules, ask at the tourist office in Paris, or at the tourist office in the town of Versailles, 7, rue des Réservoirs (tel. 39-50-36-22), only a short walk from the palace.

The palace is open Tuesday through Sunday from 9:45am to 5pm; the grounds are open daily from dawn to dusk. Admission to the palace is 30F ($5.55) for adults, for ages 18–24 and over 60, and for everyone on Sunday. Admission to the Grand Trianon is 16F ($2.95), and 11F ($2.05) for the Petit Trianon or 20F ($3.70) for both the Grand and Petit Trianons.

To get to the palace at Versailles, catch RER Line C5 at the Gare d'Austerlitz, St-Michel, Musée d'Orsay, Invalides, Pont de l'Alma, Champs-de-Mars, or Javel station, and take it to the Versailles Rive Gauche station, from which there's a shuttle bus to the château. The 22.60F ($4.20) trip takes about half an hour. A regular train also leaves from the Gare St-Lazare to the Versailles Rive Gauche RER station.

CHARTRES "For a first visit to Chartres, choose some pleasant morning when the lights are soft, for one wants to be welcome, and the Cathedral has moods, at times severe." Thus wrote Henry Adams in *Mont Saint Michel and Chartres,* and, yes, the cathedral may at times have severe moods—gray and cold like winter weather in the Ile de France region—but it is always astoundingly beautiful, with its harmonious architecture and lofty stained-glass windows.

The ✪ **Cathedral of Chartres** is one of the greatest creations of the Middle Ages. It survived both the French Revolution, when it was scheduled for demolition, and the two world wars. Take one of the excellent guided tours of the cathedral (try to catch one by Malcolm Miller), and save some time to stroll through the graceful, tranquil town of Chartres.

Admission to the cathedral is free. It is open daily: April through September, from 7:30am to 7:30pm; October through March, from 7:30am to 7pm. French-language tours of the cathedral are given in summer Tuesday through Saturday at 10:30am and daily at 3pm; in winter, they are given daily at 2:30pm. Ask at the Chartres tourist office outside the cathedral about tours in English.

Tours of the crypt are given at 11am and 2:15, 3:30, and 4:30pm (in summer, also at 5:15pm). The crypt tour costs 10F ($1.85) for adults, 7F ($1.30) for ages 18–24 and over 60, free for children under 18.

The tower is open April through September, Monday through Saturday from 9:30 to 11:30am and daily from 2 to 5:30pm; October through March, Monday through Saturday from 10 to 11:30am and daily from 2 to 4pm. Admission to the tower is 15F ($2.75) for adults, 9F ($1.65) for young people and seniors.

Trains run frequently from Paris's Gare Montparnasse to Chartres. A round-trip ticket costs 116F ($21.50) and the trip takes about an hour each way.

EURO DISNEY RESORT. Tel. 49-41-49-10.

This spectacular entertainment park, 20 miles east of Paris, about halfway between Charles de Gaulle and Orly airports, opened in April 1992 and immediately became a top sightseeing attraction. It's one-fifth the size of Paris itself, and features Main Street U.S.A., Frontierland, Adventureland, Fantasyland, and Discoveryland. There are six hotels with 5,200 rooms, a golf course of 18 holes (to be enlarged to 27), swimming pools, tennis courts, restaurants, and a Congress Center, Le New York Coliseum, complete with a grand ballroom and a Radio City Music Hall.

Admission: 225F ($41.66) adults, 150F ($27.75) children, free for children under 3; 440F ($81.50) for a three-day ticket.

Open: Mon–Fri 9am–6pm, Sat–Sun 10am–7pm. **RER:** Line A to Chessy, a 40-minute trip; 34F ($6.30) for a second-class ticket. Frequent trains shuttle to and from Chessy and the resort (dial 43-46-14-14 for information). **Directions:** Take Hwy. A-4; ample parking space available.

ROME

Rome is many things to many people. It's the Forum and the Palatine Hill, where the intrigue of the empire played itself out each day, and whence the emperors dispatched armies to conquer most of Europe and the Middle East. It's the pope and the Vatican, the headquarters of Catholicism and a pilgrimage destination for millions of the faithful from throughout the world. It's the Colosseum and the Circus Maximus, where slaughter and sport were one and the same. It's the Sistine Chapel, an artistic achievement that seems to dwarf all other artistic achievements put together. It's the Pantheon, the best-preserved piece of the Eternal City.

It's the chaos of a place that was settled 2½ millennia before the advent of the automobile. It's the city bursting at the seams with the economic refugees of the impoverished provinces of the south. It's a contemporary city packed with high-fashion shops, and fantastic restaurants. And it's the capital of a nation and the cultural, financial, and intellectual center of a major modern power.

Rome is all of these things, but most of all, it's the center of what was for many centuries the dominant civilization in the West. Beyond the crowds and the noise and the heat, it's a living history book, home to ruins and relics that no other city in Europe can match.

1. FROM A BUDGET TRAVELER'S POINT OF VIEW

ROME BUDGET BESTS In general, Rome is a very expensive city, with almost nothing that can be called a genuine bargain. A number of key sights are free though, including all the churches listed in "More Attractions," below, the Pantheon, and one of the great joys of Italian life—the evening *passeggiata* (stroll) on via del Corso and around piazza di Spagna.

WORTH THE EXTRA BUCKS Don't be discouraged by the 10,000-lira ($8.70) admission to the Vatican Museums and the Sistine Chapel. While this is one of the most expensive attractions in Italy, it's also the most stunning and, most important, worth every lira.

Spending a little extra on accommodations is also worth the money. Even a top budget hotel is far from spectacular, but it will get you a room away from the unappealing area around the Stazione Termini, where most cheap rooms are located. It's a shame to come all the way to a city so rich in history and stay in a modern, seedy location.

WHAT THINGS COST IN ROME

	U.S. $
Taxi (from the train station to piazza di Spagna)	8.70
Public bus (from any point within the city to any other point)	.70
Local telephone call	.18
Double room at the Excelsior (deluxe)	426.10
Double room at the Hotel Venezia (moderate)	167.85
Double room at Pensione Papa Germano (budget)	43.05
Continental breakfast (cappuccino and croissant)	
(at any café/bar)	2.60
(at most hotels)	6.70
Lunch for one at Fiaschetteria Beltramme (moderate)	20.90
Lunch for one at Volpetti (budget)	8.70
Dinner for one, without wine, at Patricia e Roberto (deluxe)	113.05
Dinner for one, without wine, at Taverna Fieramosca (moderate)	21.75
Dinner for one, without wine, at the Marco Polo Bar (budget)	9.60
Pint of beer (at the Fiddler's Elbow)	3.50
Glass of wine (at the Druid's Den)	2.60
Coca-Cola to take out	1.75
Cup of coffee (cappuccino) (at any café in town)	1.30
Roll of color film, 36 exposures	5.85
Admission to the Vatican Museums and the Sistine Chapel	8.70
Movie ticket	7.85
Theater ticket (at the Terme di Caracalla)	21.75

For discounted plane, train bus, and boat journeys, students should try the **Centro Turistico Studentesco (CTS),** via Genova, 16 (tel. 4-6791), off via Nazionale. Their discounts are detailed in a publication "Partire Senza Frontiere." Open Monday through Friday from 9am to 1pm and 3 to 7pm, and on Saturday from 9am to 1pm.

2. PRETRIP PREPARATIONS

DOCUMENTS   Italy requires all non-E.C. visitors to carry a passport, but it does not require visas from American, Canadian, British, Australian, or New Zealand travelers.

WHAT TO PACK   Italy enjoys a cool climate in the fall and winter. May through October are generally quite warm, and July and August can be scorching, with temperatures well into the 80s and 90s Fahrenheit. If you're traveling during any season other than summer, you'll get a bit more rain than you're accustomed to in North America or Oceania; waterproof shoes and rain ponchos will come in very handy.

Many of the most important sights in this very traditional country are churches or

WHAT'S SPECIAL ABOUT ROME

Ace Attractions
- Piazza Navona, filled with cafés, artists, and tourists.
- The Spanish Steps, a favorite gathering point of locals and tourists alike during the early evening *passeggiata* (walk).
- The Fountain of Trevi, where tossing a coin over your shoulder into the fountain assures a return visit to the Eternal City.

Ancient Monuments
- The Colosseum, the 50,000-seat stadium of the Roman Empire.
- The Roman Forum, the political and economic center of the vast empire.
- The Pantheon, one of the ancient city's best-preserved structures—an inspiration for all of Western architecture.
- Ostia Antica, a vast, well-preserved Roman city from the 2nd century A.D.

Food
- So many excellent restaurants—it's hard to get a bad meal.

Museums
- The Vatican Museums, home to the Sistine Chapel and 4½ miles of art.
- Capitoline Hill, one of the world's finest sculpture museums.

Parks
- Villa Borghese, a large park of rolling hills near the town center.

Spectacles
- Wednesday audiences with the pope and Sunday blessing.
- Opera at the Terme di Caracalla; summertime opera performances inside ancient Roman baths.

Shopping
- Some of Europe's trendiest stores near piazza di Spagna.
- Porta Portese, a vast Sunday flea market.

Religious Shrines
- St. Peter's, the spiritual center for the world's Catholics.
- Six other Catholic pilgrimage churches, and many lesser churches filled with rich artwork.

---

are located inside churches, which sometimes enforce dress codes. This means, basically, no shorts, no skirts above the knee, and no bare shoulders. Finally, a pair of good walking shoes will help you overcome Rome's many cobblestone streets, not to mention ruins and other pedestrian trials.

WHEN TO GO The main tourist season is April through October, when temperatures are—with the exception of the height of summer—most comfortable.

August is not the best time to visit. The heat is oppressive and the city is just about deserted, since thousands of Romans take this time to vacation. Many shops close down for the entire month. Indeed, there's a saying that "Only the dogs remain in Rome during *Ferragosto*," and that's not far from the truth. All hotels and sights, as well as most restaurants, remain open, but there are few Romans around, and most small businesses, such as laundries and small grocers, are closed.

Rome's Average Daytime Temperature & Rainfall

	Jan	Feb	Mar	Apr	May	June	July	Aug	Sept	Oct	Nov	Dec
Temp. (°F)	49	52	57	62	70	77	82	78	73	65	56	47
Rainfall "	3.6	3.2	2.9	2.2	1.4	0.7	0.2	0.7	3.0	4.0	3.9	2.8

Special Events There are two very special times to be in Rome: Easter and

Christmas. If you plan to visit Rome at these holiest of times, especially during Easter, make reservations *long* in advance. Rome honors its patron saints, Peter and Paul, on June 29.

BACKGROUND READING   History, history, history. Rome's ruins are all the more fascinating if you know something about the context in which they were built and used.

Edward Gibbon's *History of the Decline and Fall of the Roman Empire* (Fawcett, 1987) has been a landmark scholarly work ever since it was written in the 18th century. Robert Graves's *I, Claudius* and *Claudius the God* (Random House, 1977) and H. V. Morton's *A Traveller in Southern Italy* (Dodd, 1987) are lighter reading, but still succeed in taking the reader back into the age of the emperors.

While it may at times be a bit dense for the average train ride, there is nothing quite like Latin literature for setting the scene of ancient Rome. Key works include Virgil's *Aeneid,* an epic poem about the founding of Rome; Plutarch's *Lives* (Modern Library, 1967), which contrasts the Roman and Greek civilizations by comparing individual Greeks and Romans; Petronius's *Satyricon* (Harvard University Press), one of the few surviving examples of an ancient novel and the best portrait of decadent Rome; and the moving and powerful orations of Cicero (Penguin), which offer an interesting window into politics and society of ancient Rome.

Worth reading is a travel guidebook, *Frommer's Rome '93–'94* (Prentice Hall). Finally, Luigi Barzini's classic *The Italians* (Macmillan, 1977) offers a frank, refreshing, and opinionated discussion of the history and culture of his homeland, past and present.

3. ORIENTATION & GETTING AROUND

ARRIVING IN ROME

FROM THE AIRPORT   Most international flights land at **Leonardo da Vinci Airport,** also known as **Fiumicino** (tel. 6-5951), 18 miles from downtown Rome. Immediately after Passport Control (still before Customs) you'll see two tourist information desks to your left, one for Rome and the other for the rest of Italy. The Rome desk has a good map and some useful brochures; it's open daily from 8:30am to 7pm. When it's closed, maps are available from nearby racks. An adjacent bank changes money at reasonable rates; it's open daily from 7:30am to 11pm. After you pass Customs, ignore the rip-off artists at the air terminal who claim to dispense tourist information and hotel reservations. They work for privately run travel agencies with no ties to the official Ente Provinciale per il Turismo.

In the main arrivals hallway you'll find a luggage-storage office, open 24 hours daily, which charges 3,900 lire ($3.40) per bag per day.

There is rail service from the airport to downtown Rome. It's a little inconvenient, because you have to change trains mid-trip, but it's cheap and easily accessible. The airport's train station is connected by walkway to the second floor of the main terminal. The 5,000-lira ($4.35) ticket will take you as far as the suburban rail line's Pyramide station. From there, change to the Metropolitana (subway), which costs 700 lire (60¢), and continue your journey to Rome's main train station, or beyond. Trains leave every 20 minutes or so, from about 6am to 11pm. The complete journey takes about 25 minutes.

Charter flights sometimes land at the city's smaller **Ciampino Airport** (tel. 7934-0297). Yellow ACOTRAL buses leave this airport every half hour or so, and deposit passengers at Cinecittà station, the last stop on Line A of the Metropolitana. From there, take the subway to Rome's central rail station, or beyond. The complete journey takes about 45 minutes, and costs 1,400 lire ($1.20).

Taxis to and from the airports are prohibitively expensive, running about 60,000 lire ($52.20) one way, including surcharges.

FROM THE TRAIN STATION Most Rome-bound trains arrive at the sprawling silver **Stazione Termini.** You'll almost certainly be accosted by hotel hawkers and official-looking touts as soon as you set foot into the station. It's best to avoid these people and head straight toward your preselected hotel, or the official tourist board window at the head of Track 4.

There are exits to either side of the main part of the station. Head toward Track 22 for hotels to the left of the station. Turn right toward Track 1 for the right-side lodgings.

The entrance to the Metropolitana, Rome's two-line subway system, is straight ahead and downstairs (you'll see an illuminated M surrounded by a red circle pointing the way). For buses, continue straight through the outer hall of the train station and walk out the front door to the gigantic bus lot on piazza dei Cinquecento. The bus ticket and information booths are at the near left corner of the lot.

There's a branch of the Banca Nazionale delle Communicazioni between the entrance to Tracks 8–11 and 12–15. You can exchange currency here Monday through Saturday from 8:30am to 7:30pm and on Sunday from 8am to 2:15pm.

In the massive outer hallway you'll find the Informazioni Ferroviarie, which answers questions about train times to other destinations, and nearby, a long, almost-always-crowded bank of ticket windows.

INFORMATION

The most convenient **tourist office** for those arriving by train is *inside* the track area, at the head of Track 4 (tel. 482-4078); visit it before you venture out into the main part of the station. This office is usually open daily from 8:15am to 7:15pm. Pick up an excellent free map here, as well as a list of hotels, a brochure on museums, and other information. This office also makes hotel reservations: Either tell them a price range or a specific name from this book. However, lines can be long at this small window.

Rome's main tourist office, **Ente Provinciale per il Turismo (EPT),** is at via Parigi, 5 (tel. 488-3748), behind the Grand Hotel. They make same-day hotel reservations as well, which are easiest during the morning. This office is open Monday through Saturday from 8:15am to 7:15pm. To get here from the train station, walk around the left side of the Museo Nazionale Romano up to piazza della Repubblica. Take a right behind the museum, walk a few yards, turn left and then right for via Parigi.

CITY LAYOUT

Stazione Termini, the main railroad station, located on piazza dei Cinquecento, marks the eastern edge of the tourist's city. The broad, busy **via Nazionale** begins at **piazza della Repubblica,** just a short walk away, and stretches down to **piazza Venezia,** at the eastern edge of Old Rome. Southeast of piazza Venezia are the **Roman Forum and the Palatine Hill** (the centermost of the seven hills upon which the city was founded), stretching along the ostentatious **via dei Fori Imperiali,** which connects piazza Venezia with the Colosseum.

Via del Corso stretches north from piazza Venezia to **piazza del Popolo,** which marks the northern edge of tourist Rome. About two-thirds of the way to piazza del Popolo, via Condotti runs east to **piazza di Spagna** and the **Spanish Steps,** the city's chic shopping area. East of piazza del Popolo (and north of piazza di Spagna) is **Villa Borghese,** the city's principal park.

To the west of piazza Venezia and stretching toward the river lies **Old Rome,** an area of narrow winding streets, aging buildings, and, generally, excellent restaurants and charming cafés. **Corso Vittorio Emanuele** is the main boulevard traversing this neighborhood. Across the **Tiber (Tevere) River** is **Vatican City** and south of the Holy See is **Trastevere,** for many people the most interesting and colorful corner of the city.

GETTING AROUND

The free **map of Rome** distributed by the tourist office is remarkably comprehensive for a city this size, though its lack of an index makes street-finding tough. The best map of Rome, listing every *vicolo* and *largo,* is the yellow city plan produced by the Istituto Geografico de Agostini, available at bookstores for a whopping 10,000 lire ($8.70). If you plan to dart around the city by bus, pick up the *Roma in Metro-Bus* map by Editrice Lozzi, sold for 6,000 lire ($5.20).

BY SUBWAY   Rome's **Metropolitana** subway system does a good job of connecting you with many major points in the city, but unfortunately it doesn't go anywhere near the Old City or Trastevere. Conveniently enough, the system's two lines intersect at Stazione Termini.

Line A is likely to be most useful to the average tourist, with stops at piazza della Repubblica, piazza Barberini, piazza di Spagna, piazza del Popolo (Flaminio), and the Vatican (Ottaviano). In the opposite direction from Termini, Line A travels southeast past piazza San Giovanni to the Catacombs and other outlying sights. Line B, meanwhile, begins at Termini and heads southwest by way of via Cavour and the Colosseum to the EUR area. The fare is 700 lire (60¢); tickets can be purchased at tobacco shops (*tabacchi*), most newsstands, and from machines in the stations, but *not* from the station personnel. The Metropolitana operates daily from 5:30am to midnight.

BY BUS   There are three major drawbacks to Rome's **A.T.A.C. public bus system**—traffic, crowds, and most of all, pickpockets. Downtown congestion can be so bad that you're better off on foot, especially during the workday, and the overcrowding makes buses prime hunting grounds for the city's petty thieves. Be careful, and take the obvious precautions: secure any valuables in a moneybelt, and keep in front of you any bags you might have.

When navigating this sprawling city by bus, remember one number: **Bus no. 64.** This indispensable line begins right behind the ticket booth at the train station, travels along via Nazionale, passes through piazza Venezia, and continues through the heart of the Old City along via Vittorio Emanuele, ending its journey just off St. Peter's Square. Use caution: The many tourists on this line attract many pickpockets.

Bus no. 492 also makes the Termini–Vatican trip, on a longer route traveling by way of piazza Barberini, piazza Colonna, piazza Venezia, largo di Torre Argentina, and piazza Navona. bus no. 492's western terminus is piazza Risorgimento, up via della Porta Angelica from the entrance to St. Peter's Square, and convenient to the entrance to the Vatican Museums. Other key lines from the station include no. 27, which travels to the Colosseum, and no. 75 and no. 170, which cross the river into Trastevere.

At Stazione Termini, buy bus tickets and inquire about routes at the gray-metal office at the near left corner of the enormous bus lot as you step out of the station. The ticket booth is open daily from 6am to 11:30pm, while the information desk, at the next window over, dispenses advice daily from 7:30am to 7:30pm.

Bus fare is 800 lire (70¢); tickets must be stamped in the red boxes at either end of the bus. You can also buy a **one-day pass,** good on all buses and the Metropolitana, for 2,800 lire ($2.45); a **one-week pass** costs 10,000 lire ($8.70).

ON FOOT   Good luck. Unlike the other major Italian cities, Rome is not a pedestrian's paradise. It seems to spread endlessly, and most maps make things appear closer together than they actually are. Streets originally built for pedestrians are now crowded with cars, and sidewalks are extremely narrow, if they exist at all. Old Rome is about the only area that is actually pleasant to wander. Undoubtedly, you'll need to use the subway and buses to get around at some point. On the other hand, surface transport in the center is often so slow that it makes walking a moderate distance a good idea.

BY TAXI   Taxi fares begin at 6,400 lire ($5.55), and click upward by 300 lire (25¢) every 250 meters (roughly 800 feet). There's a 3,000-lira ($2.60) supplement for all rides between 10pm and 7am, a 1,000-lira (85¢) add-on for travel on Sunday and holidays, and 500 lire (45¢) per bag. If you order a taxi by telephone, the meter goes on when they receive the call, not when you begin riding. Finally, there's a whopping 14,000-lira ($12.15) surcharge for rides to the airport, though curiously they tack on just 10,000 lire ($8.70) for travel from the airport downtown.

Beware of drivers of unmetered cabs at the train station or at the airport who offer you taxi rides (instead, go to the official taxi line at these locations). These offers are from illegal gypsy cabs, which charge exorbitant, uncontrolled rates. To call a taxi, dial 3570, 3875, or 4994.

CAR & SCOOTER RENTAL   Renting a car to get around Rome is pointless, since parking spots are very scarce in this high-rent city and many sights are out of reach of a car. For excursions out of the city, try **Hertz,** via Veneto, 156 (tel. 54-7991); **Avis,** at piazza Esquilino, 1c (tel. 470-1216); or **Budget,** via Boncompagni, 14c (tel. 48-4810).

Keep in mind that rates can be considerably less—as much as half the price, or better—if you make reservations from your home country at least 48 hours in advance. Plan ahead, or consider phoning a friend or relative back home to have reservations made for you.

For scooters and motorcycles, visit the **Scoot-A-Long** agency at via Cavour, 302 (tel. 678-0206), near largo Ricci, two long blocks from the Cavour Metropolitana stop. Mopeds, with a top speed of 30 m.p.h., cost 35,000 lire ($30.45) per day, including insurance and unlimited mileage; there is a 200,000-lira ($173.90) refundable deposit, which you can pay with a credit card; the actual rental fee must be paid in cash. Vespas that reach 60 m.p.h. at full throttle are 40,000 lire ($39.15) a day, with a 300,000-lira ($260.85) deposit. For weekly rates, multiply the daily rate by six. They're open daily from 9am to 7pm. You can take their bikes out of the country, but not on the autostrada. They hope to soon rent bicycles as well.

BY BICYCLE   Navigating Rome by bicycle can be somewhat unnerving because of the heavy traffic, but it gives you unexcelled mobility in the center of town. **Danilo Collalti,** at via del Pellegrino, 80–82 (tel. 654-1084), near campo de' Fiori, rents bikes for 10,000 lire ($8.70) a day, 60,000 lire ($52.15) a week. They're open Tuesday through Sunday from 8:30am to 8pm in summer, 8:30am to 1pm and 3 to 8pm in winter. You can also rent bikes immediately to your right as you exit the piazza di Spagna Metropolitana stop. Prices are 3,200 lire ($2.80) an hour, or 12,000 lire ($10.45) a day. They're open from 9am to midnight March to October, from 9am to 8pm the rest of the year. Both places require a document as deposit.

 ROME

First, a warning: Watch out for **pickpockets** and **Gypsy children.** The former are quite clever, preying on unwary travelers, especially on buses and the Metropolitana. If you take the obvious precautions, however, you shouldn't have much trouble. The ubiquitous Gypsy children, on the other hand, are brash, bothersome, and represent a real social problem. Routinely, a band of six or more unaccompanied children rove major tourist areas, wielding pieces of cardboard or a newspaper. They'll approach their target and begin babbling plaintively, waving or shoving the cardboard or newspaper into your face. Meanwhile, their free hand is rummaging through your pockets or purse. I've found that a modest challenge, rather than retreat, is the most

ITALY

ROME ★

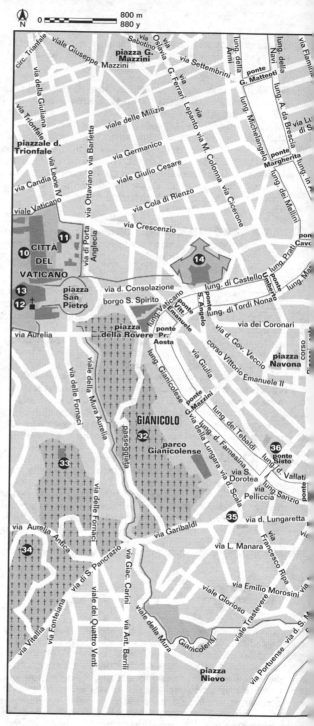

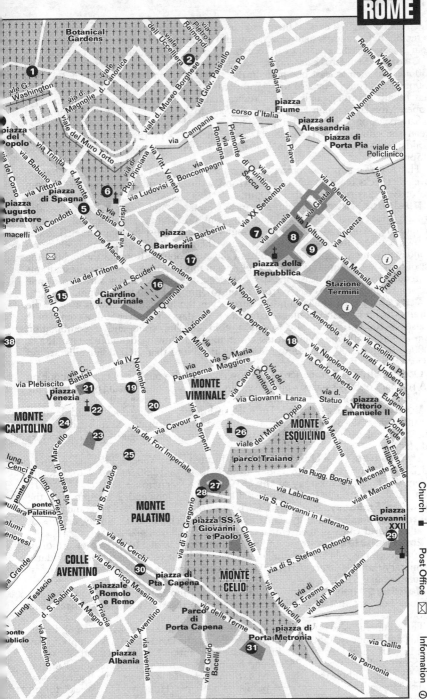

ROME

Botanical Gardens

piazza del Popolo

piazza Augusto Imperatore

macelli

piazza di Spagna

piazza Barberini

piazza della Repubblica

Stazione Termini

piazza Fiume

corso d'Italia

piazza di Alessandria

piazza di Porta Pia

viale d. Policlinico

Giardino d. Quirinale

piazza Venezia

MONTE CAPITOLINO

MONTE VIMINALE

MONTE ESQUILINO

parco Traiano

piazza Vittorio Emanuele II

piazza Giovanni XXII

MONTE PALATINO

piazza SS. Giovanni e Paolo

piazza di Pta. Capena

MONTE CELIO

COLLE AVENTINO

piazzale Romolo e Remo

Parco di Porta Capena

piazza Albania

piazza di Porta Metronia

via G. Washington
via d. Magnolie
viale di Canonica
viale d. Museo Borghese
via Giov. Paisiello
via Po
via Raimondi
viale dell'Uccelliera
via Pierluigi da Palestrina
via Salaria
via Piave
via Nomentana
viale Regina Margherita
via Castro Pretorio
via del Muro Torto
via di Porta Pinciana
via Campania
via Romagna
via Piemonte
via Vitt. Veneto
via Boncompagni
via di Quintino Sella
via XX Settembre
via Gaeta
via Palestro
via Cernaia
via Volturno
via Vicenza
via Marsala
via Castro Pretorio
via del Corso
via Babuino
via Vittoria
via Condotti
via d. Due Macelli
via Sistina
via F. Crispi
via d. Quattro Fontane
via del Tritone
via d. Scuderi
via d. Quirinale
via Nazionale
via Milano
via Panisperna
via S. Maria Maggiore
via Napoli
via Torino
via A. Depretis
via G. Amendola
via Giolitti
via F. Turati
via Pr. Umberto
via Cavour
via del Quattro Cantoni
via Giovanni Lanza
via d. Statuo
via Napoleone III
via Carlo Alberto
via Eugenio
via Conte Verde
via Emanuele Filiberto
via Merulana
via Mecenate
viale Manzoni
via Rugg. Bonghi
via Labicana
via S. Giovanni in Laterano
via di S. Stefano Rotondo
via Claudia
via di S. Erasmo
via dell' Amba Aradam
via di Navicella
via Gallia
via Pannonia
via IV Novembre
via C. Battisti
via Plebiscito
via del Teatro di Marcello
via dei Fori Imperiali
via di S. Teodoro
via di Pierleoni
via dei Cerchi
via del Circo Massimo
via di S. Gregorio
via delle Terme
viale Guido Bacelli
via Guido Bacelli
viale Aventino
via Aventina
via A. Magno
via S. Priscia
via S. Sabina
via Anselmo
lung. Testaccio
ponte Sublicio
ponte Palatino
ponte Cestio
lung. Cenci
lung. d. Aguillara

Church ✝
Post Office ⊠
Information ⓘ

effective defense. Yell back at them, stamp your foot, invoke the name of the *polizia*, preferably before they actually reach you and begin their ploy. Of course, if you spot them ahead, do whatever you can to avoid these fearless, obnoxious criminals.

Banks Standard bank hours are Monday through Friday from 8:30am to 1:30pm, and then at least one hour in the afternoon, somewhere between 2:45 and 4:30pm, most commonly 2:45 to 3:45pm; only a few banks are open on Saturday, and then usually mornings only. The Credito Italiano bank, at piazza di Spagna, 19, is open Monday through Friday from 8:35am to 1:35pm and 2:45 to 4:15pm, and on Saturday from 8:35am to 1:35pm. There's a bank in the train station, situated between the entrance to Tracks 8–11 and Tracks 12–15 that exchanges currency Monday through Saturday from 8:30am to 7:30pm and on Sunday from 8am to 2:15pm.

The American Express office, at piazza di Spagna, 38 (tel. 6-7641), exchanges traveler's checks fee free, and is open Monday through Friday from 9am to 5:30pm and on Saturday from 9am to 12:30pm.

Business Hours In summer, most businesses and shops are open Monday through Friday from 9am to 1pm and 4 to 8pm; on Saturday shops are only open in the morning. From mid-September through mid-June, most shops are open Tuesday through Saturday from 9am to 1pm and anywhere from 3:30 or 4:30 to 7:30pm; on Monday in winter, shops don't open until the afternoon. In Rome as throughout the rest of Italy, just about everything except restaurants is closed on Sunday. Restaurants are required to close at least one day per week; the particular day varies from one trattoria to another. Most serve from noon to 3pm and 7:30 to 10:30pm.

Currency The Italian unit of currency is the lira, almost always used in the plural form, lire. The lowest unit of currency these days is the silver 50-lira coin. There is also a 100-lira piece, also silver; a gold 200-lira coin; and a combination silver-and-gold 500-lira coin. Notes come in the following denominations: 1,000, 2,000, 5,000, 10,000, 50,000 and 100,000 lire. Note that 20,000-lira bills are no longer valid.

Occasionally you'll come across a grooved coin with a pictogram of a telephone on it. A remnant of Italy's old pay-phone system, which is gradually being phased out, the telephone *gettone* is worth 200 lire (18¢), the price of a phone call.

Doctors and Dentists For a list of English-speaking doctors and dentists, consult your embassy. At the private (and expensive) Salvator Mundi clinic, viale Mura Gianicolensi, 67 (tel. 58-6041), you're certain to find English-speaking doctors and staff.

Embassies The **U.S. Embassy** is located at via Veneto, 119a (tel. 4-6741), and is open Monday through Friday from 8:30am to 12:30pm and 2 to 5:30pm. Britons will find the **Embassy of the U.K.** at via XX Settembre, 80a (tel. 475-5441), open Monday through Friday from 9:30am to 12:30pm and 2 to 4pm. For the **Canadian Embassy,** head to via G. B. de Rossi, 27 (tel. 841-5341), and for the **Australian Mission,** stop by via Alessandria, 215 (tel. 83-2721). Finally, citizens of **New Zealand** can visit their embassy at via Zara, 28 (tel. 440-2928).

Emergencies In Rome and throughout Italy, dial 113 in case of fire or in order to reach the police. Some Italians recommend that you forgo the police and use the military-trained *Carabinieri* (tel. 112), in their opinion a better police force. For an ambulance, dial 5100.

Holidays Italy is a very Catholic country, and it celebrates a few national religious holidays that may be unfamiliar to North Americans, Australians, and Britons.

The comprehensive list includes New Year's Day (Jan 1), Epiphany (Jan 6), Easter Sunday and Monday, Liberation Day (Apr 25), Labor Day (May 1), Assumption Day (Aug 15), All Saints Day (Nov 1), Immaculate Conception Day (Dec 8), and Christmas and Santo Stefano (Dec 25–26). Rome honors its patron saints, Peter and Paul, on June 29. Remember that the *International Herald Tribune*, the international English-language daily newspaper, publishes a list of "Holidays This Week" for all countries.

Information   For the location of tourist information offices, see "Information" in "Orientation and Getting Around," above. You should also write the Italian Government Tourist Office in your homeland for a free copy of *General Information for Travelers to Italy*. See the Appendix for a list of tourist offices in the U.S.

Laundry   In Rome and other Italian cities, there are almost no self-service coin-operated laundries. Instead, the laundry staff washes your clothes for you, usually that same day, and charges a set price per load, up to a maximum of 8 or 10 pounds per load. Remember that if you separate your wash into whites and colors, that's considered two loads and is priced accordingly.

There's a *lavanderia* near the train station at via Montebello, 11 (tel. 474-5503), where washing and drying of 3 kilos (6½ lb.) costs 15,000 lire ($13.05) and up to 5 kilos (11 lb.) costs 22,000 lire ($19.15). They're open Monday through Friday from 9am to 7pm and on Saturday from 9am to 1pm. There are many others around town as well.

Lost and Found   Oggetti Rinvenuti is located at via Nicolò Bettoni, 1 (tel. 581-6040), open Monday through Saturday from 9am to noon.

Mail   Rome's main post office is at piazza San Silvestro, 19, near piazza di Spagna. For stamps, visit Windows 22–24, on the right side as you enter. For "Fermo Posta" (Poste Restante), go to Windows 58–60, on the left side (have friends write to you "c/o Fermo Posta, S. Silvestro, 00187 Roma"). They'll hold letters up to a month, and charge you 500 lire (45¢) for the service. This office is open Monday through Friday from 8:25am to 7:40pm and on Saturday from 8:25am to 12:50pm. Most other post offices close at 1:50pm Monday through Friday and are not open on Saturday.

In addition to post offices, you can buy stamps (*francobolli*) at *tabacchi* (tobacconists) with no additional service charges; ask at your hotel about the current postal rates.

Romans prefer to use the more efficient postal service at the Vatican, and I recommend those passing by the Vatican to avail themselves of this option as well. Postage costs the same as in the Italian mail, but delivery is quicker (packages weighing more than 1 kilo/2.2 lb. are not accepted). The main Vatican post office is adjacent to the information office in St. Peter's Square in the left wing, open Monday through Friday from 8:30am to 7pm and on Saturday from 8:30am to 6pm. There is also a mobile postal stand on the right side of the square.

Police   Dial 113 to reach the police. Some Italians recommend that you forgo the police and use the *Carabinieri* (tel. 112), in their opinion a better-trained police force.

Tax   There is a Value-Added Tax (called I.V.A.) in Italy on all consumer products and most services. This tax is refundable if you spend more than 525,000 lire ($456.50) on an item. See "Savvy Shopping," below, for details.

Telephone   To make an international phone call, visit the ASST office located next to the main post office at piazza San Silvestro, 20 (to the right if you're facing the post office). This office is open Monday through Saturday from 8am to 11:30pm and on Sunday from 9am to 8:30pm. A second ASST office, on the lower level of Stazione Termini remains open—and mobbed—24 hours a day. Calls average 5,000 lire ($4.35) a minute to the United States, with rates falling to 4,000 lire ($3.50) a minute from 11pm to 8am and on Sunday.

A less expensive way to call America is through AT&T's USA Direct (tel. 172-1011) or MCI's Call USA (tel. 172-1022). By dialing these local toll-free numbers in Rome you'll reach an American operator who will allow collect calls or calls charged to your AT&T or MCI telephone card. You can also call 172-1001 for Canada Direct and 172-1061 for Australia Direct.

For local calls, there are two types of public pay phones in regular service. The first accepts coins or special slugs, called *gettone*, which you will sometimes receive in change. The second operates with a phonecard, available at *tabacchi* and bars in 5,000-lira ($4.35) and 10,000-lira ($8.70) denominations; break off the perforated corner of the card before using it. Local phone calls cost 200 lire (18¢). To make a call, lift the receiver, insert a coin or card, and dial.

THE LIRA & THE DOLLAR

At this writing $1 = approximately 1,150 lire (or 100 lire = 9¢), and this was the rate of exchange used to calculate the dollar values given in this chapter (rounded to the nearest nickel). This rate fluctuates from time to time and may not be the same when you travel to Italy. Therefore the following table should be used only as a guide:

Lire	U.S.$	Lire	U.S.$
50	.04	10,000	8.70
100	.09	15,000	13.04
200	.17	20,000	17.39
300	.26	25,000	21.74
400	.35	30,000	26.09
500	.43	35,000	30.43
750	.65	40,000	34.78
1,000	.87	45,000	39.13
1,500	1.30	50,000	43.48
2,000	1.74	55,000	47.82
2,500	2.17	60,000	52.17
3,000	2.61	65,000	56.52
4,000	3.48	70,000	60.87
5,000	4.35	75,000	65.21

The **area code** for Rome is 06.

Keep in mind that telephone numbers change frequently in Italy, and a recording announcing the change lasts only a few weeks before the number is reassigned. No one is immune to these haphazard changes: Once when I visited Rome, the state telephone company had just altered the telephone number of Rome's top address, the Colosseum. If a phone number listed in this chapter has changed, you can request the new number by dialing 12.

Tipping In almost all sectors of the Italian economy, service charges are already built into the prices. If service is exceptional, an additional tip of 5% or more is appropriate, though not expected. In cafés, it's customary to leave a 100-lira (9¢) or 200-lira (17¢) coin on the counter with your empty espresso cup. If you've been sitting down, 200–500 lire (17¢–45¢) is more like it. A tip of 1,000 lire (85¢) per day is acceptable for chamber service. For taxis, tip up to 10%; service is not included in their fares.

4. BUDGET ACCOMMODATIONS

Rome's golden age of budget travel is quickly drawing to a close. In previous years, the Italian capital boasted clusters of inexpensive pensiones—small family hotels often run by kindly types more interested in helping travelers than in helping themselves by piling up profits. Today, unfortunately, the old-style pensiones, which usually offer only basic comforts, are dying out, and accommodation prices are skyrocketing as facilities grow more modern (with, for example, private bathrooms in more and more small hotels).

The largest remaining group of budget hotels is near the Stazione Termini, a run-down neighborhood where every language from Arabic to Yoruba seems just as common as Italian. Some budget travelers will likely feel uncomfortable in many of the hotels in that area as they cater to recent immigrants and laborers from the provinces.

In the section that follows I've listed the rare remaining budget pensiones and hotels in central Rome as my first picks. If these choices in the center are full, I've also listed a select number of hotels near the train station—all places that cater to budget travelers from Europe, North America, and Oceania and are discriminating about their clientele.

As in any major tourist destination, reservations are strongly recommended during the summer. Nearly every place listed, except for a few of the smallest ones, accept reservations if you include one night's deposit. Increasingly, however, they won't honor phone reservations made from elsewhere in Italy or Europe unless you follow it up with a deposit that arrives before you do. If you must arrive without a reservation, try to arrive early; the best places fill up by around midday. The tourist office in the train station or at the main office will help you find a room, but their lines can stretch on forever.

The prices listed in this edition are those expected by hotel proprietors for the summer of 1993. In very few cases would hotel owners unequivocally commit to those prices; those you encounter may be a bit more or less; use this book as a guide. By Italian law, the maximum price for the room and any additional services (like breakfast or a shower) must be posted in the room. If you feel that you have been overcharged, contact the local tourist office.

If you arrive in the off-season you'll probably find it substantially easier to locate an available room. You should also receive rates lower than those listed here, especially if you bargain with the owners and remind them that their empty rooms may go unsold if they don't lower their prices.

Another note: Many hotels listed below offer triple rooms, which by Italian law cost 35% more than double rooms.

A continental breakfast in an Italian hotel is one of the great budget-travel disappointments. The usual charge for a roll, butter, jam, and coffee is about 8,000 lire ($6.95). You can get the same breakfast for about half that price at any café in Rome. Unfortunately, many hotels, especially in the medium- and high-priced categories, require their guests to take breakfast. In the descriptions below, if prices are listed "including continental breakfast," then you can assume that breakfast is more or less obligatory; otherwise it's optional, and almost without exception, not worth the price.

DOUBLES FOR LESS THAN 53,000 LIRE [$46.10]

Those seeking to spend the minimum amount of money in Rome won't find many comforts. But if funds are tight, the following provide Rome's rock-bottom rates, usually with few frills.

NEAR THE ROMAN FORUM

PENSIONE BEATRICE, via dei Serpenti, 137, 00184 Roma. Tel. 06/482-4007 or 481-2525. 14 rms (none with bath). **Metropolitana:** Cavour.

$ Rates: 30,800 lire ($26.80) single; 49,500 lire ($43.05) double; 63,800 lire ($55.50) triple. Breakfast 8,000 lire ($6.95) extra. No credit cards.

The Beatrice offers very simple, somewhat run-down rooms, but in an attractive Roman neighborhood at prices that reflect an earlier era in Roman pensiones. It's located halfway between the Colosseum and the Quirinale, just a short walk from the Roman Forum. From the Cavour Metropolitana stop, walk downhill on via Cavour;

take the first right onto via Serpenti and continue right for two blocks. The owners speak no English.

TO THE RIGHT OF THE TRAIN STATION

The neighborhood on either side of the Stazione Termini is rather unappealing, but there are scads of budget accommodations in this area. The area to the right of the station (exit by Track 1) is marginally more attractive and peaceful than the area to the left, a fact vehemently disputed, naturally, by all those in the hotel business on the opposite side of the station.

HOTEL BOLOGNESE, via Palestro, 15 (1st, 2nd, and 3rd Floors), 00185 Roma. Tel. 06/49-0045. 21 rms (2 with bath, 7 with shower only). **Directions:** See below.

$ Rates: 31,500–36,800 lire ($27.40–$32) single without bath, 47,300 lire ($41.15) single with shower only; 52,500 lire ($45.65) double without bath, 63,000 lire ($54.80) double with shower only, 68,300 lire ($59.40) double with bath; 73,500 lire ($63.90) triple without bath, 94,500 lire ($82.20) triple with bath. No credit cards.

When owner Giorgio Calderara isn't carefully watching over his hotel and ensuring the happiness of his guests, you'll find him in a closet-sized studio painting—in fact, all the canvases you see in the halls and rooms are his. The five newly renovated rooms on the first floor, three of which have balconies, are a remarkable bargain, but that's not to take anything away from the well-kept rooms on the two upper floors. Breakfast is not available.

As you exit Stazione Termini by Track 1, turn left and walk along via Marsala, which becomes via Volturno. After three blocks, turn right on via Montebello. The hotel is four blocks ahead past the corner of via Palestro.

HOTEL GALLI, via Milazzo, 20 (2nd Floor), 00185 Roma. Tel. 06/445-6859. 13 rms (1 with bath). **Directions:** See below.

$ Rates: 33,000 lire ($28.70) single without bath; 49,500 lire ($43.05) double without bath, 55,000 lire ($47.80) double with bath; 71,500 lire ($62.20) triple without bath, 88,000 lire ($76.50) triple with bath. Breakfast 8,000 lire ($6.95) extra. No credit cards.

They speak only enough English here to check you in, but the Galli is inexpensive in any language. Rooms are ample, but basic and rather nondescript. Don't worry—the musty odors dissappear quickly once a window is opened.

The hotel is located just 100 yards from the station. Exit by Platform 1, turn right, and take the first left onto via Milazzo.

LOCANDA MARINI, via Palestro, 35 (3rd Floor), 00185 Roma. Tel. 06/44-0058. 10 rms (none with bath). **Directions:** See Pensione Katty, below.

$ Rates: 40,700 lire ($35.40) double; 69,000 ($60) double or triple; 18,200 ($15.80) per person in shared rooms. No credit cards.

The rooms at the Marini are just as spartan as those at the Katty across the hall, but

 FROMMER'S SMART TRAVELER: HOTELS

VALUE-CONSCIOUS TRAVELERS SHOULD
TAKE ADVANTAGE OF THE FOLLOWING:

1. Reservations, which usually require one night's deposit. During the summer, these are a necessity.
2. The tourist office in the train station or at the main office, which will help you reserve a room.

they are a little brighter—meaning that the place feels less like a dormitory—and owner Antonia Marini is just as gracious and friendly. Likewise, prices here are nearly identical to the Katty's, and Antonia never puts more than three guests in a room together. There's no elevator.

LOCANDA OTELLO, via Marghera, 13 (4th Floor), 00185 Roma. Tel. 06/49-0383. 6 rms (none with bath). **Directions:** Walk only a few steps from the side exit of Stazione Termini by Track 1.

$ Rates: 26,700 lire ($23.20) single; 49,500 lire ($43.05) double. No credit cards. The Locanda Otello has exceptionally big, bright rooms for a location so close to the station. Its friendly proprietors only understand a bit of English, and likewise ask only a bit of money from their guests.

PENSIONE KATTY, via Palestro, 35 (3rd Floor), 00185 Roma. Tel. 06/444-1216. 10 rms (2 with bath). **Directions:** See below.

$ Rates: 40,700 lire ($35.40) double without bath; 69,000 lire ($60) double or triple with bath; 18,200 lire ($15.80) per person in shared rooms. Refundable 2,000-lira ($1.75) key deposit required. No credit cards.

Luigi and Maria Idda offer accommodations at bargain-basement rates—indeed, some of the lowest in Rome. This is a one-of-a-kind place, the last of a dying breed of pensione that rents by the bed rather than by the room. There are never more than three beds per room, and there's no elevator. Four blocks from the station, this hotel is just far enough away to be out of earshot and sight of the cacophony and seediness that blights the area near the station.

To get there, head up via Marghera, which begins directly opposite the train station exit by Track 1. Walk up four blocks to via Palestro and turn left; the hotel is on the left side of the street between via San Martino della Battaglia and via Gaeta.

If the Katty is full, they'll send you to the nearby Pensione Lucy, via Magenta, 13 (tel. 495-1740), with similar prices.

PENSIONE PAPÀ GERMANO, via Calatafimi, 14a, 00185 Roma. Tel. 06/48-6919. 13 rms (2 with bath). **Directions:** See below.

$ Rates: 31,500 lire ($27.40) single without bath; 49,500 lire ($43.05) double without bath; 60,000 lire ($52.20) double with bath; 68,300 lire ($59.40) triple without bath; 78,800 lire ($68.50) triple with bath; 22,000 lire ($19.15) per person in a shared room. No credit cards.

While he's at the top of the list in just about every budget guidebook under the sun, owner Gino insists that word of mouth is his best advertising, and that's what keeps his pensione filled 365 days a year. In any case, this place really is a budget standout, mostly because of Gino himself. Terminally happy, he loves his job, tirelessly offering help, advice, books, maps, everything but his own kitchen sink, to even the one-day visitor. He keeps his 13 modern rooms spotless, despite the heavy traffic, and he's also one of the very few hoteliers left in Rome who rent by the bed, an important factor for solo travelers. Perhaps the one drawback is that because the place is so small, noise carries far—don't expect to sleep late. In the end, though, the Pensione Papà Germano is worthy of all the accolades it gets. (In case you're wondering, the place is named for Gino's father.)

The hotel is located about eight blocks from the central train station. Exit by Track 1, turn left, and walk along via Marsala, which becomes via Volturno. Turn right onto via Calatafimi and the hotel is just half a block ahead on your left.

TO THE LEFT OF THE TRAIN STATION

In the area to the left of the station, the streets are wider, the traffic heavier, and the noise level is higher than the area to the right of the station. There are scores of hotels here, and a few are even good choices for budget-minded, safety-conscious travelers.

SOGGIORNO PEZZOTTI, via Principe Amedeo, 79a (2nd Floor), 00185 Roma. Tel. 06/731-1561, 731-4633, or 731-1513. 14 rms (4 with shower only). **Directions:** See below.

$ Rates: 27,500 lire ($23.90) single without shower, 33,000 lire ($28.70) single with shower only; 49,500 lire ($43.05) double without shower, 60,500–82,500 lire ($52.60–$71.75) double with shower only; 66,000–72,600 lire ($57.40–$63.15) triple without shower, 99,000–105,500 lire ($86.10–$91.75) triple with shower only. No credit cards.

This is a clean and attractive place at rock-bottom prices, with balconies in half the spacious rooms, which is quite unusual at these rates. If this hotel is full, the owners will send you to the equally nice Albergo Stella on the next floor up (same telephone number).

To reach the hotel, exit the train station by Track 22, turn left, walk half a block, and turn right onto via Gioberti (Bar Tavola Calda Etna is on the corner). After two blocks, turn left onto via Principe Amedeo. When you reach no. 79a, take the stairs on the left side of the courtyard.

NEAR THE ROMAN FORUM

ALBERGO PERUGIA, via del Colosseo, 7, 00184 Roma. Tel. 06/679-7200. 11 rms (2 with bath, 4 with shower only). TEL **Metropolitana:** Colosseo.
$ Rates: 34,000 lire ($29.55) single without bath; 49,500 lire ($43.05) double without bath, 61,500 lire ($53.50) double with shower only or full bath; 71,500 lire ($62.20) triple without bath, 83,500 lire ($72.60) triple with shower only or full bath. No credit cards.

Location is everything for the Albergo Perugia. Just a short walk from the Colosseum in a very quiet neighborhood, this budget-priced place has unfortunately ignored the basics: The floors and curtains could use a wash, the walls could use some decoration, and everything could use a fresh coat of paint. But the owners are nice, and their prices are relatively low. Note that there are four floors here and no elevator. Breakfast is not available.

From the Colosseo stop on the Metropolitana, turn right down the massive via dei Fori Imperiali, and then right again onto the first small street, called via del Tempio della Pace. A third right turn, at the intersection with via del Colosseo, and the hotel is just ahead on your left.

DOUBLES FOR LESS THAN 75,000 LIRE [$65.20]

NEAR CAMPO DE' FIORI

The area surrounding Campo de' Fiori, Rome's best open-air flower market, is beautiful, historic, and well located. From here you can walk to the Pantheon, the Trevi Fountain, and even the Spanish Steps. When you're tired of walking, it's nice to know that hotels near this campo are also close to the no. 64 bus route.

ALBERGO DELLA LUNETTA, piazza del Paradiso, 68, 00186 Roma. Tel. 06/686-1080. Fax 06/689-2028. 37 rms (15 with bath). **Bus:** 26 from the train station to largo di Torre Argentina.
$ Rates: 33,000 lire ($28.70) single without bath, 57,800 lire ($50.25) single with bath; 63,000 lire ($54.80) double without bath, 93,500 lire ($81.30) double with bath. No credit cards.

A favorite of American students studying in Rome, the labyrinthine Lunetta is simply decorated with fading floral wallpaper and has small bathrooms. Its best virtue is its fine location, near the large corso Vittorio Emanuele toward campo de' Fiori.

From largo Argentina, continue west (in the direction of the bus) along corso Vittorio Emanuele. After three blocks, turn left on via Paradiso. The hotel is half a block ahead.

ALBERGO SOLE, via del Biscione, 76, 00186 Roma. Tel. 06/654-0873 or 687-9446. 60 rms (25 with bath, 4 with shower only). **Bus:** 26 from the train station to largo di Torre Argentina.
$ Rates: 55,700 lire ($48.75) single without bath, 63,000 lire ($54.80) single with

shower only, 71,400 lire ($62.10) single with bath; 73,500 lire ($63.90) double without bath, 78,800 lire ($68.50) double with shower only, 84,000–100,800 lire ($73.05–$87.68) double with bath. No credit cards.

A longtime favorite of Rome *cognoscenti*, the Albergo Sole offers simple aging rooms in what the owner says is the oldest hotel in Rome, dating from 1462! Of course, the area is even more ancient; the hotel is built above the remains of a Roman theater from 55 B.C. The attractive courtyard garden in back is the highlight of the hotel.

Follow directions for the Lunetta, above. Continue across piazza Paradiso onto via Biscione.

HOTEL PICCOLO, via dei Chiavari, 32, 00186 Roma. Tel. 06/654-2560 or 689-2330. 16 rms (3 with bath, 6 with shower only). **Bus:** 64 to largo di Torre Argentina.

$ Rates: 50,400 lire ($43.80) single without bath, 63,000 lire ($54.80) single with shower only; 73,500 lire ($63.90) double without bath, 84,000 lire ($73.05) double with shower only, 99,800 lire ($86.80) double with bath. No credit cards.

Enter this smartly modern hotel through a contemporary cast-iron gate that contrasts well with the small, old-fashioned stone street in front. A modern marble-lined entrance leads up to the first-floor reception and rooms that will not disappoint. Recently redecorated guest quarters are spacious, with spotless bathrooms. The Piccolo is a shining star in one of Rome's top locations.

From largo di Torre Argentina, continue west (in the direction of the bus) two blocks and turn left onto via dei Chiavari. The hotel is three blocks ahead on your right.

BETWEEN PIAZZA DI SPAGNA & PIAZZA DEL POPOLO

The ritzy area around the Spanish Steps is a favorite of visitors to Rome, and perhaps the most expensive in everything from stores to hotels. The following listing, therefore, offers unusually good values.

PENSIONE FIORELLA, via Babuino, 196, 00187 Roma. Tel. 06/361-0597. 8 rms (none with bath). **Metropolitana:** Flaminio.

$ Rates (including continental breakfast): 42,000 lire ($36.50) single; 73,500 lire ($63.90) double. No credit cards.

The orange-and-green tile floors of this simple, delightful little pensione are kept spotless and sparkling by Antonio and Caterina Albano. This is the sort of place that will make you want to extend your stay in Rome just so you can be here. It's one of the nicest places in this price range, in any part of town. Note that reservations are accepted only a day before checking in, and the doors are locked shut nightly at 1am.

Take Line A of the Metropolitana to Flaminio and walk through the arch to piazza del Popolo; via Babuino is the leftmost of the three streets that fan out from the piazza.

TO THE RIGHT OF THE TRAIN STATION

PENSIONE CORALLO, via Palestro, 44 (6th Floor), 00185 Roma. Tel. 06/445-6340. 11 rms (5 with bath). **Directions:** See below.

$ Rates: 41,000 lire ($35.65) single without bath, 49,500 lire ($43.05) single with bath; 59,500 lire ($51.75) double without bath, 71,500 ($62.20) double with bath; 82,500 lire ($71.75) triple without bath, 93,500 lire ($81.30) triple with bath. No credit cards.

This is a classic family-run place, where the ever-professional and courteous Toni Cellestino or his wife is always on hand to make sure their guests are properly cared for. The couple doesn't speak much English, but a bargain is a bargain in any tongue. While the slightly musty rooms can best be described as "unremarkable," eight come complete with a modest, flower-decked balcony, most overlooking a quiet courtyard.

To reach the hotel, exit the train station by Track 1, walk straight for four blocks along via Marghera, and turn left onto via Palestro. The hotel is three blocks ahead. Take the back elevator up to the fire-engine-red reception desk.

TO THE LEFT OF THE TRAIN STATION

HOTEL GIUGIU, via dei Viminale, 8 (2nd Floor), 00184 Roma. Tel. 06/482-7734. 12 rms (4 with bath, 2 with shower only). **Directions:** See below.

$ **Rates** (including continental breakfast): 49,500 lire ($43.05) single without bath; 66,500 lire ($57.85) double without bath, 77,000 lire ($66.95) double with shower only, 94,500 lire ($82.20) double with bath. No credit cards.

A neon sign sticks out over a slightly forbidding entrance, but once inside, the friendly owner, Mr. Chindamo, will make you feel at home. This small pensione boasts 14-foot ceilings and medium-sized rooms that show some wear. Still, the location is good, in a safe neighborhood a block from the Teatro dell'Opera.

To reach the hotel, exit the train station by Track 22, turn right, and walk about four blocks, with the bus lot on your right. Turn left onto largo di Villa Peretti and the hotel will be two blocks ahead on your left, across from the Hotel Columbia, at the head of via dei Viminale.

PENSIONE CORTORILLO, via Principe Amedeo, 79a (5th Floor), 00185 Roma. Tel. 06/446-6934. 7 rms (none with bath). **Directions:** See above.

$ **Rates:** 55,000 lire ($47.80) single; 66,000 lire ($57.40) double; 82,500 lire ($71.75) triple. Prices discounted up to 30% during slow periods. Breakfast 8,000 lire ($6.95) extra. No credit cards.

Signora Iolanda Cortorillo is happy to have celebrated her silver anniversary in this book, and she's still as warm and gracious as she was more than 25 years ago, and she still runs one of the less expensive listings in this chapter. The rooms are quite spacious and clean, especially considering the price. All overlook the interior courtyard, which makes them feel peaceful despite the noisy neighborhood. All in all, this is an exceptional value. Another thing that hasn't changed in all these years: Signora Cortorillo still speaks hardly a word of English, though her daughter is almost always there to help. Also note that they prefer not to take reservations in summer.

PENSIONE DI RIENZO, via Principe Amedeo, 79a (2nd Floor), 00185 Roma. Tel. 06/446-7131. 20 rms (6 with shower). **Directions:** See below.

$ **Rates:** 55,000 lire ($47.80) single without shower, 66,000 lire ($57.40) single with shower only; 71,500 lire ($62.20) double without shower, 82,500 lire ($71.75) double with shower only. Prices discounted up to 30% during slow periods. Breakfast 8,000 lire ($6.95) extra. No credit cards.

Owner Balduino di Rienzo hosts budget travelers in what is certainly one of the best rock-bottom-priced hotels in Rome. Indeed, when you inquire about his prices, he's *proud* to say, "Little, very little." A shy, pleasant man, he speaks enough English to check you in and out, with his daughter often at hand for the big questions. His rooms are generally spacious and quite clean, and the bathroom facilities are modern.

To reach the hotel, exit the train station by Track 22, turn left, walk half a block, and turn right onto via Gioberti (Bar Tavola Calda Etna is on the corner). After two blocks, turn left onto via Principe Amedeo. When you reach no. 79a, take the stairs on the right side of the courtyard.

NEAR PIAZZA NAVONA

ALBERGO ABRUZZI, piazza della Rotonda, 69, 00186 Roma. Tel. 06/679-2021. 25 rms (none with bath). **Bus:** 64 to largo di Torre Argentina.

$ **Rates:** 47,300–57,800 lire ($41.15–$50.25) single; 73,500–82,000 lire ($63.90–$71.30) double. No credit cards.

Unbelievably, this basic budget hotel directly overlooks the Pantheon and the adjacent piazza. It's somewhat noisy, but you can't get more central than this. The hotel's four floors are filled with medium-sized rooms, most with queen-size beds. The more expensive rooms have the piazza view, while the cheaper (and quieter) ones are in the rear.

From largo di Torre Argentina, walk four blocks north along Minerva or via Argentina. The hotel is directly ahead, in front of the Pantheon.

NEAR CASTEL SANT' ANGELO

Located near the Vatican, just across the river from the city's historic center, hotels in this region are a good bet for quiet and a local charm that is often missing from lodgings in more bustling tourist areas.

PENSIONE MARVI, via Pietro della Valle, 13, 00193 Roma. Tel. 06/686-5652 or 654-2621. 7 rms (all with bath). **Bus:** 492 or 910 from the train station to the first stop across the river.
$ Rates (including continental breakfast): 34,500 lire ($30) single; 69,000 lire ($60) double; 138,000 lire ($120) triple. No credit cards.

⭐ Adventurers looking for a wonderfully authentic Roman homestay would do well to look no further than this homey pensione on a quiet residential street.
No English is spoken here, but guests are welcomed by a warm smile and simple yet comfortable surroundings. Breakfast is included, and served in a pretty dining room.

To find one of Rome's best values, walk from the bus stop to the "far" side of Castel Sant' Angelo. Via Pietro della Valle is between the castle and via Crescenzio. There is no sign, just a gold doorbell high up to the left of the building's big green door.

AT PIAZZA DELLA REPUBBLICA, 47

Piazza della Repubblica is like a faded movie star: You recognize the face, and can tell that that person must have been someone special "in their day." This circular piazza, dominated by the Esedra Fountain at its center, has become a squalid, run-down gallery of cheap bars and street vendors, with only a hint of the square's former charm. As our two choices are sandwiched between two adult-film theaters, women traveling alone may want to find other lodgings. Yet, inside, these are all decent choices, even with some elegant flair from an earlier era, at relatively moderate prices.

How to get there? As you exit the train station, head diagonally left across piazza dei Cinquecento to the block-long via Einaudi. As you come upon piazza della Repubblica, walk clockwise (left) under the arcade to reach these hotels.

PENSIONE ESEDRA, piazza della Repubblica, 47 (3rd Floor), 00185 Roma. Tel. 06/488-3912. 8 rms (none with bath). **Directions:** See above.
$ Rates (including continental breakfast): 38,900 lire ($33.80) single; 71,400 lire ($62.10) double; 94,500 lire ($82.20) triple; 126,000 lire ($109.55) quad. 10% discount Nov–Feb. No credit cards.
The 70-year-old Esedra is as faded as the piazza it overlooks. The rooms are enormous and grand, with 20-foot-high ceilings and yards and yards of floor space, but with worn furniture and fixtures that bespeak better times. Nonetheless, Signora Alvieri's once-stately place is the least expensive in the building, and in the end, a bargain.

PENSIONE EUREKA, piazza della Repubblica, 47 (3rd Floor), 00185 Roma. Tel. 06/482-5806 or 488-0334. 33 rms (15 with shower). TEL **Directions:** See above.
$ Rates (including continental breakfast): 34,700 lire ($30.20) single without shower, 37,800 lire ($32.85) single with shower only; 58,800 lire ($51.15) double without shower, 67,200 lire ($58.45) double with shower only; 80,900 lire ($70.35) triple without shower, 93,500 lire ($81.30) triple with shower only. 10% discount offered to bearers of this book. No credit cards.
Like this book, the Eureka has been in business since the late 1950s—indeed, it was

listed in the inaugural edition, and later mentioned in a 1963 story in *Time* magazine, which you'll find proudly displayed just inside the door. Owner Luigi Imperoli, the brother of the woman who owns the Esedra next door, is an amateur archeologist, and he has filled his reception area with his finds. Breakfast is served in an elegant dining room, with old-fashioned tile floors, antique chairs, candelabras on the walls, and a floor-to-ceiling reproduction of a scene from the Sistine Chapel along one wall. Despite the attractive dining room, many of the rooms are run-down and musty, making them less attractive—and less expensive—than other hotels in the building. Yet it does have one special bonus: Luigi says that Frommer's readers staying here can use the gym he owns nearby (called the American Sport Connection) for free, a potential value of 10,000 lire ($8.70) a day.

NEAR THE ROMAN FORUM

ALBERGO APOLLO, via dei Serpenti, 109, 00184 Roma. Tel. 06/488-5889. 11 rms (none with bath). **Bus:** 64 from the train station to the Palazzo delle Esposizioni on via Nazionale (about five stops).
$ Rates: 59,900 lire ($52.10) double. No credit cards.

Rooms are bare and run-down here with some antique closets and desks, but the area is very respectable, across from the Bank of Italy in a characteristic Roman neighborhood. You'll especially enjoy leaving your hotel and seeing the Colosseum in the distance down the street. No room has private plumbing; rather, four rooms on each floor share two bathrooms.

From the bus stop in front of Palazzo delle Esposizioni, walk two blocks west and turn left onto via dei Serpenti. The hotel is two blocks down on your left.

DOUBLES FOR LESS THAN 100,000 LIRE [$86.95]

NEAR THE PANTHEON

PENSIONE MIMOSA, via S. Chiara, 61 (2nd Floor), 00186 Roma. Tel. 06/654-1753. 12 rms (3 with bath). **Bus:** 54 from the train station to largo di Torre Argentina.
$ Rates (including continental breakfast): 50,400 lire ($43.80) single without bath; 79,800 lire ($69.40) double without bath, 90,300 lire ($78.50) double with bath. No credit cards.

An aging place (the building is from the 1500s) with few frills, the Mimosa features an excellent location a block and a half from the Pantheon in the very heart of Rome. The low rates and location make the place a favorite of American students spending a semester in Rome. Guests get copies of the front-door key so they can return at any hour. The owner's two sons speak English.

From largo di Torre Argentina, walk two blocks north on via de Torre Argentina. Turn left on via S. Chiara; the hotel is a half block up on the left.

NEAR CAMPO DE' FIORI

HOTEL CAMPO DE' FIORI, via del Biscione, 6, 00186 Roma. Tel. 06/654-0865 or 687-4886. 27 rms (9 with bath, 4 with shower only). TEL **Bus:** 64 from the train station to largo di Torre Argentina.
$ Rates (including continental breakfast): 99,500 lire ($86.50) double without bath, 105,000 lire ($91.30) double with shower only, 147,000 lire ($127.80) double with bath. MC, V.

They've mastered the art of the unique at this hotel in the heart of the historic district. Each of the nine small rooms with private bath is decorated in a different regional style, carried out in meticulous detail with generous use of mirrors and occasionally gaudy details. The "rustic" room, for instance, feels uncannily like a Tuscan farmhouse. The rooms without private facilities have average furnishings, mini-chandeliers hanging over the beds, and floral wallpaper. Half a dozen rooms enjoy a view of the vibrant campo de' Fiori, Rome's open-air flower market, and all guests have access to the pocket-size roof garden, with its view of St. Peter's. There's no elevator connecting the hotel's six stories, but the management here has made up for it by providing the most elegant four-story climb in Rome: There are few windows on the way up the marble stairs, but they've painted colorful floral scenes to brighten the ascent. The management is gradually adding a private bath—and an individual style—to each room.

From largo di Torre Argentina, continue west (in the direction of the bus) along corso Vittorio Emanuele. After three blocks, turn left onto via Paradiso, a small street that spills into piazza del Paradiso, and continues as via del Biscione to the hotel. It's a seven-block walk in all.

HOTEL SMERALDO, vicolo dei Chiodaroli, 9, 00186 Roma. Tel. 06/687-5929. Fax 06/654-5495. 35 rms (4 with bath, 14 with shower only). TEL **Bus:** 26 from the train station to largo di Torre Argentina.

$ Rates: 57,800 lire ($50.25) single without bath, 78,800 lire ($68.50) single with bath; 78,800 lire ($68.50) double without bath, 99,800 lire ($86.80) double with bath; 104,800 lire ($91.15) triple without bath, 132,700 lire ($115.40) triple with bath. Breakfast 5,000 lire ($4.35) extra. AE, MC, V.

✪ An incredible value in a charming area of the *centro storico* (historic center), this highly recommended choice features a modern reception behind granite floors. An elevator takes you to all four floors, where rooms are simple but clean. Rooms with bathrooms are some of the shiniest I've seen in accommodations of this category. The place is often full, so it's a good idea to reserve ahead of time.

Tiny vicolo dei Chiodaroli is not printed on most maps, but it's not hard to find. From largo di Torre Argentina, turn south (left) onto via de Torre Argentina. Take the second right, via di S. Anna, and Chiodaroli is just ahead on your left.

BETWEEN PIAZZA DI SPAGNA & PIAZZA DEL POPOLO

RESIDENZA BROTZKY, via del Corso, 509 (3rd Floor), 00186 Roma. Tel. 06/361-2339. 13 rms (all with bath or shower). **Metropolitana:** Flaminio.

$ Rates: 63,000 lire ($54.80) single; 89,300 lire ($77.65) double; 120,800 lire ($105.05) triple. No credit cards.

✪ Located on via del Corso, one of Rome's main shopping streets, where the ancient Romans once held chariot races, the Brotzky is very quiet, as many rooms overlook an inner courtyard. Although rooms are simple, with aging plumbing, the Brotzky features a panoramic terrace upstairs affording some of the best views of town. Although they don't serve breakfast, there are tables here for a picnic or relaxation. The *residenza* is often full, so try to reserve ahead of time.

Take the Metropolitana from the train station to Flaminio; from there, walk through the large Roman arch (Porta del Popolo) to piazza del Popolo and then continue straight across the square and two blocks down via del Corso.

IN THE VIA NAZIONALE AREA

Via Nazionale is the wide boulevard running between piazza della Repubblica and piazza Venezia. From the front door of Stazione Termini, walk up to piazza della Repubblica (diagonally to the left across piazza del Cinquecento), walk to the left around this circular piazza, and turn left onto via Nazionale.

PENSIONE ELIDE, via Firenze, 50 (1st Floor), 00184 Roma. Tel. 06/488-3977 or 474-1367. 14 rms (5 with bath, 4 with shower only). TEL **Directions:** See below.

$ Rates: 63,000 lire ($54.80) single without bath, 73,500 lire ($63.90) single with shower only; 84,000 lire ($73.05) double with shower only, 94,500 lire ($82.20) double with bath. Breakfast 7,000 lire ($6.10) extra. V.

✪ This remarkable little place is operated by one of the friendliest families in Rome—appropriately named the Roma family. The floors and the new modern bathrooms always sparkle, and the prices are surprisingly low. They even change the wallpaper and paint the ceilings every year, which is quite an undertaking for such a small and inexpensive place. Ask for Room 16 or 18, both of which have unique carved and painted wooden ceilings. Everyone gets to enjoy the similarly decorated breakfast room. There's a 1:30am curfew.

From the train station, walk clockwise around piazza della Reppublica to via Nazionale. Via Firenza is the second street on the right. Look for the RECOMMENDED BY FROMMER'S GUIDE sign displayed proudly out front.

ACROSS THE RIVER

This one place is not convenient to much of anything, but it's cozy, comfortable, and very modestly priced.

FORTI'S HOTEL, via Fornovo, 7, 00192 Roma. Tel. 06/320-0738 or 321-2256. Fax 06/321-2222. 22 rms (10 with bath, 2 with shower only). TEL **Metropolitana:** Lepanto.

$ Rates (including full breakfast): 55,000 lire ($47.80) single without bath, 66,000 lire ($57.40) single with shower only or bath; 82,500 lire ($71.75) double without bath, 99,000 lire ($86.10) double with shower only or bath; 126,500 lire ($110.00) triple with shower only or bath.

When I last visited, there was a lovely bouquet of flowers brightening the reception area and another in the dining room of this charming hotel run by American expatriate Charles Cabell and his Italian wife. In fact, this place has such a homey feel that a number of embassies in Rome billet their new arrivals here while they look for more permanent housing. Forti's has been in business since 1959, and in this book since 1967, with many happy returns. It's not surprising that you get a full American-style breakfast buffet here, including yogurt, eggs, meat, juice, and other goodies.

To find this home-away-from-home, take Line A of the Metropolitana to Lepanto, the first stop across the river. Walk back toward the river on via Giulio Cesare, and via Fornovo is the second street on your left.

NEAR PIAZZA DI SPAGNA

This handful of hotels is in one of the ritziest neighborhoods in town—and the prices certainly reflect that fact.

HOTEL MARCUS, via del Clementino, 94, 00186 Roma. Tel. 06/687-3679 or 683-2567. 15 rms (all with bath). TEL TV **Metropolitana:** Spagna.

$ Rates: 79,000 lire ($68.70) single; 99,500 lire ($86.50) double; 126,000 lire ($109.55) triple. Breakfast 10,000 lire ($8.70) extra. AE, V.

Located on a large street just a few blocks from the Spanish Steps, the Hotel Marcus offers large, serviceable rooms right in the middle of the city. Salvatore, the owner, has managed this pleasant-enough pensione for over 25 years. And even though it's in the center of the hustle and bustle, the double windows he installed in all the guest rooms help cut out the noise.

To reach the hotel from the Spagna Metropolitana station, exit into piazza di Spagna, turn left, and then turn right onto via Condotti, the street that runs right into the Spanish Steps. Follow this street for seven blocks; its name changes to become via Fontanella Borghese, then via del Clementino.

PENSIONE LIDIA VENIER, via Sistina, 42, 00187 Roma. Tel. 06/679-3815. Fax 06/884-1480, Attn: Lidia Venier. 30 rms (10 with bath, 10 with shower only). **Metropolitana:** Piazza Barberini.

$ Rates (including continental breakfast): 71,500 lire ($62.20) single without bath, 82,500 lire ($71.75) single with shower only, 88,000 lire ($76.50) single with bath; 99,000 double without bath, 115,500 lire ($100.45) double with shower only, 212,000 lire ($105.20) double with bath. AE, DC, V.

Guests ascend an elegant winding marble staircase to the reception area, and from here they are dispatched to their clean, modern rooms, some even complete with frescoed ceilings. Guests take breakfast in a room with painted ceilings and picnic tables and hard wooden benches. Despite these fine touches, prices remain moderate. There is a 2am curfew.

Walk up via Sistina from the piazza Barberini Metropolitana station and you'll come upon the pensione on the left just after the intersection with via Crispi.

NEAR PIAZZA NAVONA

PENSIONE NAVONA, via dei Sediari, 8, 00186 Roma. Tel. 06/686-4203 or 654-3802. 22 rms (10 with bath). **Bus:** 64 to largo di Torre Argentina.

$ Rates (including continental breakfast; with or without bath): 63,000 lire ($54.80) single; 94,500 lire ($82.20) double. No credit cards.

Wrapped around an open courtyard, this pretty first-floor pensione is full of character. Recent renovations have made rooms comfortable if not stylish. The hotel occupies a grand palace built in 1360, and holds architectural surprises at every turn. Bathrooms are fully tiled, and high ceilings lend an open, airy feel. The owners, the Australian-born Natale family, speak fluent English.

Via dei Sediari is a small street between piazza Navona and the Pantheon. It is best reached from piazza S. Andrea d. Valle. Walk a long block north on Rinascimento and turn right on via dei Sediari. The hotel is just ahead on your right.

NEAR THE VATICAN

Neither of the two hotels listed in this section is anything to write home about, but they do give you the opportunity to stay just moments from the Vatican.

HOTEL ADRIATIC, via Vitelleschi, 25, 00193 Roma. Tel. 06/686-9668 or 654-0386. 27 rms (22 with shower only). TEL **Bus:** 64 from the train station to borgo Sant' Angelo.

$ Rates: 53,200 lire ($42.10) single without shower, 70,500 lire ($61.30) single with shower only; 86,500 lire ($75.20) double without shower, 118,500 lire ($103.05) double with shower only; 119,800 lire ($104.20) triple without shower, 159,700 lire ($138.90) triple with shower only. No credit cards.

Lanfranco Mencucci, his wife, and his son, Marino, take great pride in their hotel, and see to it that their modern rooms and bathrooms are kept very clean and attractive. They also have a small terrace with fruit trees and a rose trellis.

To get there, take bus no. 64 to borgo Sant' Angelo near St. Peter's, pass under the nearby portal, and continue along via Porta Castello until you reach via Vitelleschi, where you turn left.

HOTEL BRAMANTE, vicolo delle Palline, 25, 00193 Roma. Tel. 06/654-0426 or 687-9881. 20 rms (10 with shower). **Bus:** 64 from the train station to the last stop.

$ Rates: 55,000 lire ($47.80) single without shower, 68,200 lire ($59.30) single with shower only; 80,300 lire ($69.80) double without shower, 104,500 lire ($90.85) double with shower only. Breakfast 10,000 lire ($8.70) extra. AE, DC, MC, V.

Situated in a charming old building begun in the 14th century, this place is clean, comfortable, and about as close to the Vatican as you can get, even if the linoleum floors and tan wallpaper don't really match the old-Roman flavor of the neighborhood. The ivy-covered breakfast terrace has a view of the Colonnato del Vaticano, the special escape wall that connects the Vatican with the Castel Sant' Angelo. Owner Giuliana Belli was actually born in this building.

To find the Bramante, take bus no. 64 to the last stop, walk through the nearby portal, and continue along largo del Colonnato for three portals; at the third, go left and the hotel will be right there on your right.

TO THE RIGHT OF THE TRAIN STATION

HOTEL PENSIONE ASTORIA GARDEN AND MONTAGNA, via Vittorio Bachelet, 8, 00185 Roma. Tel. 06/446-9908. 32 rms (20 with bath). TEL **Directions:** See below.

$ Rates (including continental breakfast): 56,700 lire ($49.30) single without bath, 67,200 lire ($58.45) single with bath; 97,700 lire ($84.95) double without bath, 121,200 lire ($105.90) double with bath; 135,500 lire ($117.80) triple without bath, 175,500 lire ($152.60) triple with bath. 10% discount offered to bearers of this book. AE, CB, DC, MC, V.

Manager Signor Vannutelli runs this hotel for the Montagna family in good old-fashioned Roman style, with a spacious lobby, lots of old wood, and colorful floral bedspreads that add an air of distinction to the place. Breakfast is served on the glass-enclosed veranda in the lovely back garden/courtyard during the warmer months.

Via Vittorio Bachelet is not listed on most maps, and is in fact the continuation of via Varese between via Vicenza and piazza dell'Independenza. From the train station, walk up via Marghera and go left on via Varese for three blocks.

TO THE LEFT OF THE TRAIN STATION

HOTEL MORGANA, via Turati, 37, 00185 Roma. Tel. 06/446-7338 or 446-7339. Fax 06/446-7230. 58 rms (56 with bath). TV TEL **Directions:** See below.

$ Rates (including continental breakfast): 88,000 lire ($76.50) single with bath; 77,000 lire ($66.95) double without bath, 143,000 lire ($124.35) double with bath; 176,000 lire ($153.05) triple with bath; 220,000 lire ($191.30) quad with bath. AE, DC, MC, V.

★ It's hard to say enough good things about brothers Mauro, Nicolà, and Roberto di Rienzo and their big, comfortable, budget-priced hotel, where they offer exceptionally discounted rates to bearers of this book. With spotless white walls, recessed lighting, and some of the brightest, cleanest, most modern bathrooms in Rome, their ultramodern hotel is one of the best values in the city. The breakfast room, where the all-you-can-eat breakfast is served, is spacious and bright, and some rooms even have brass beds. They boast that they "won't rent a room that they wouldn't sleep in themselves." Always extraordinarily professional, all speak excellent English, and one of them is always around to dispense information about the city. By the way, one reason that they're all so fluent in English is that the two older brothers are married to American women.

To find this excellent albergo, exit the train station by Track 22, go left half a block, and turn right up via Gioberti. Via Turati is the first left off via Gioberti, and the Morgana is on the left on the first block. Keep in mind that via Turati is a continuation of via Amendola. You'll find the hotel just a block after the name change.

ON PIAZZA DELLA REPUBBLICA

HOTEL PENSIONE TERMINUS, piazza della Repubblica, 47 (2nd Floor), 00185 Roma. Tel. 06/488-1505. 18 rms (14 with bath). TEL **Directions:** See above.

$ Rates (including continental breakfast): 73,500 lire ($63.90) single without bath, 89,300 lire ($77.65) single with bath; 99,800 lire ($86.80) double without bath, 126,000 lire ($109.55) double with bath. 10% discount offered to bearers of this book. AE, CB, DC, MC, V.

In addition to high ceilings and antique furniture in some of the rooms, the Terminus offers an airy art deco breakfast room with antique mirrors and cabinets recalling the 1920s. There's also a piano nearby. Some rooms are run-down, with aging wallpaper;

try to get Room 32 or 38, the biggest in the house. Owner Terrinoni Pietro has promised a 10% discount to readers bearing this book.

SUPER-BUDGET CHOICES

Each summer a handful of Roman university dormitories are turned into **unofficial youth hostels,** charging ultra-low rates usually similar or identical to those at the Ostello Foro Italico. Their locations change just about every year, so you'll need to check with the tourist office in Rome when you arrive. Consider, however, that these locations, like the official IYHF hostel, are often quite distant from the central part of the city.

CENTRO UNIVERSITARIO MARIANUM, via Matteo Boiardo, 30, 00185 Roma. Tel. 06/700-5453. 90 rms (none with bath). TEL **Metropolitana:** Manzoni.

$ Rates (including three meals daily): 55,000 lire ($43.50) per person per night, in singles and doubles. No credit cards. **Open:** June 15–July 31 and Aug 21–Oct 30.
A dormitory for local students much of the year, this place has that unmistakable institutional air, but it's good for those who want to pay one modest price for a bed and three square meals (served at 8am, 1pm, and 8pm). The Centro caters primarily to groups, but individual travelers are welcome if there is a vacancy. Note that there is a midnight curfew.

The dorm is just two blocks from piazza San Giovanni in Laterano, and is best approached by Metropolitana to Manzoni. Walk two blocks toward the Colosseum on viale Manzoni, and turn left onto via Matteo Boiardo.

OSTELLO FORO ITALICO, viale Olimpiadi, 61, 00194 Roma. Tel. 06/396-4709. 350 beds. **Metropolitana:** Ottaviano; then bus no. 32.

$ Rates (including continental breakfast and sheets): 19,800 lire ($17.20) per bed per night. Dinner 11,000 lire ($9.55) extra. No credit cards.
With few windows and no neighborhood charm, this rates as one of the less appealing youth hostels in Italy. Rooms contain 6, 7, 12, or 20 beds. An International Youth Hostel Federation membership card is required, but it can be purchased on the spot for 35,000 lire ($30.45). Despite its name, the youth hostel accepts travelers of any age. It's open from 7 to 9am and from 2pm until the 11pm curfew. Entrance is in the rear.

Unfortunately, the hostel is quite distant from anything else in Rome, located out by the Olympic Stadium, about an hour's commute from the train station and the rest of the city center. To get there, take Line A of the Metropolitana to Ottaviano, the end of the line, and then bus no. 32 to the sixth stop.

WORTH THE EXTRA BUCKS

HOTEL VENEZIA, via Varese, 18, 00185 Roma. Tel. 06/445-7101 or 446-3687. Fax 06/495-7687. 59 rms (all with bath). TV TEL **Directions:** See below.

$ Rates (including full breakfast): 126,000 lire ($109.55) single; 178,500 lire ($155.20) double; 252,000 lire ($219.15) triple. AE, CB, DC, MC, V.

For decades, Swiss expatriate Rosemarie Diletti and her daughter, Patrizia, have been beautifying this unique 18th-century building with an extremely personal touch. Antiques, rugs, and various historical pieces fill ample-sized rooms. Several top-floor accommodations have sunny balconies, and all rooms have traditional Murano-glass chandeliers and hairdryers. The staff is both fluent in English and exceedingly helpful around the clock. And when the clock strikes breakfast, look forward to a huge buffet, which usually includes fruit from the owner's garden.

The Hotel Venezia is close enough to the train station to be convenient and easily reached, but in a quiet neighborhood nonetheless. Walk three blocks up via Marghera (which begins opposite the exit by Track 1) to its intersection with via Varese; the hotel is right there on the left.

PENSIONE FABRELLO-WHITE, via Vittoria Colonna, 11 (3rd Floor),

00193 Roma. Tel. 06/320-4446 or 320-4447. Fax 06/562-1617. 36 rms (33 with bath). TEL **Bus:** 492 or 910 from the train station to the first stop across the river.

$ Rates (including continental breakfast; with or without bath): 60,500 lire ($52.60) single; 106,500 lire ($92.60) double; 148,000 lire ($129.15) triple; 174,200 lire ($151.50) quad. DC, MC, V.

✪ Think wood—rich, dark, stained wood. The doors, the shutters, and the antique furniture that fills the rooms and halls. And the inlaid wooden ceilings, which you'll find in almost all the enormous rooms. They've been in business here since the turn of the century, and they've clearly worked hard to preserve the character it must have had back then. Even the entranceway is impressive, and will make the weariest budget traveler feel like a returning emperor. Yet modern convenience is not lacking. Modern bathrooms resembling ship-cabin facilities were recently installed in almost all rooms. Ask for one of the seven rooms that have their own terrace. A delightfully European, Roman kind of place—highly recommended.

The hotel is on the Vatican side of the Tiber, halfway between the ponte Cavour and piazza Cavour. Take bus no. 492 or 910 from the train station and get off at the first stop after you cross the river. Look for the large bust of Minerva on the wall to the right as you step off the elevator.

---

5. BUDGET DINING

"*Pane e coperto*," or "bread and cover charge," is an inexpensive, but unavoidable, menu item that will be new to most travelers. For better or for worse, it's a charge you'll have to pay at restaurants simply for the privilege of eating there. Cover is usually about 1,000 lire (85¢) per person in the least expensive restaurants I've listed and 2,000–2,500 lire ($1.75–$2.20) in the more moderately priced and "Worth the Extra Bucks" section. Also note that a tip (*servizio*) of 10%–15% will automatically be added to your bill.

A traditional Italian meal consists of a first course (*primo piatto*), usually a pasta dish; a second course (*secondo piatto*), meat, fish, or chicken; a vegetable side dish to accompany the main course (*contorno*); and dessert (*dolce*). Most places expect their diners to take at least two courses, and will invariably "remind" you of this lest you "forget."

The ubiquitous tourist menu (*menu turistico* or *menu del giorno*) is an all-inclusive, fixed-price meal that usually ranges from 12,000 to 20,000 lire ($10.45 to $17.40), and which consists of a pasta course, a main course, a vegetable side dish, bread, cover and service charges, and often wine and dessert or fruit. The one disadvantage to this budget option is that you'll usually be offered only a very limited selection of ordinary, uninteresting dishes from which to choose (for this reason, Italians usually avoid the *menu turistico*).

Keep in mind that in the listings below, prices are given for pasta and main courses only. Don't forget to add in charges for bread and cover, service, and vegetable side dishes when calculating what you can actually expect to pay.

To follow a $45-a-day budget best, you should dine at regular restaurants only once a day and rely on one of a few options for your second meal. The most satisfying alternative to a real restaurant is a *rosticceria* (sometimes called a *tavola calda* or *bar/tavola calda*), a sort of Italian cafeteria where glass cases display long trays of usually delicious pastas and meats. You order from the counter, and then eat either at tables or at stand-up counters. Although prices may not be considerably lower than in restaurants, you don't pay service or cover charge, and you can order only one item if you choose (no one will "remind" you to order a second course if you get just a plate of pasta!). I've listed several rosticcerias below, but there are also others in town you may come across.

Another good budget option for lighter meals are self-service pizzerias, which proclaim themselves with signs reading PIZZA RUSTICA or just PIZZA. Here you see large trays of square pizza and usually an area of counters and stools. Based on how hungry you are, tell the server what size piece you want. You'll find many of these places across the center of Rome.

Italian café-bars can also provide budget refuge for lunch. Many bars serve a variety of sandwiches (called *panini* for Italian rolls or *tramezzini* for white-bread sandwiches with the crust cut off), which can save you money and time. Many *alimentari* (general food stores) can also prepare you a sandwich on the spot.

A Note on Breakfast As mentioned in the introduction to "Budget Accommodations," avoid hotel breakfasts if at all possible. Always expensive and often unsatisfying, they cannot compare with a visit to an Italian café-bar where you stand at the counter for a delicious cappuccino and a pastry or two for 3,000–4,000 lire ($2.60–$3.50).

Stand Up Another uniquely Italian custom to watch out for in Italian bars and cafés is the difference between prices *alla banca* (at the bar), and those *alla tavola* (at a table). You'll rarely see Italians sitting down to savor their cappuccino because sit-down prices on *all* items are at least twice those if you stand at the bar, three times as much in the most touristed places.

Favorite Roman Dishes In New York, London, and other world capitals, it's often not the native dishes that are so special, but rather those that the countless immigrants who settle and open restaurants import from home. The same can be said of Rome. Here you can sample foods from the farthest provincial reaches of the Republic without ever stepping out of range of the Metropolitana. Most restaurants in Rome proudly announce somewhere on their menu or business card (*bigliettino*) the region where their specialties originated, and often go further to identify one or two particular house specialties. Spaghetti *alla carbonara* (with a sauce of bacon and eggs) and *saltimbocca alla romana* (veal wrapped or covered in ham slices) top the list of homespun Roman specialties, but don't be afraid to go beyond these staples. Ask the host for recommendations of the region—*carbonara* may not be the wisest selection at an Abruzzese trattoria.

Because Rome is such a cosmopolitan city, many of the trattorias in the city have multilingual menus.

MEALS FOR LESS THAN 10,500 LIRE ($9.15)

NEAR THE MAIN TOURIST OFFICE

MARCO POLO BAR, largo S. Susanna, 108. Tel. 482-4869.
   Cuisine: ITALIAN. **Directions:** See below.
$ **Prices:** Complete meal 11,000 lire ($9.60). No credit cards.
   Open: Lunch Mon–Sat noon–3pm; dinner Mon–Sat 6:30–10pm.

FROMMER'S SMART TRAVELER: RESTAURANTS

VALUE-CONSCIOUS TRAVELERS SHOULD
TAKE ADVANTAGE OF THE FOLLOWING:

1. The *menu turistico* and *menu del giorno*, which are all-inclusive, fixed-price meals.
2. *Rosticcerias*, which are "Italian cafeterias."
3. Self-service pizzerias.
4. Café-bars—budget refuges for lunch.

★ A popular café-bar, Marco Polo offers the lowest full-meal price around in a small self-service area beyond the cappuccino makers and the pastry counters. The dining area is attractive for self-service, with dark-wood walls and private tables after you collect your food. Since you fetch the food yourself, you don't pay a service or cover charge.

You'll find this bargain just off largo S. Susanna toward via Veneto, a five-minute walk from the Repubblica Metropolitana stop.

OFF VIA NAZIONALE

PIZZERIA EST! EST! EST!, via Genova, 32. Tel. 488-1107.
Cuisine: ITALIAN. **Directions:** See below.
$ **Prices:** 8,400–10,500 lire ($7.30–$9.15), cover and service included. No credit cards.
Open: Dinner only, Tues–Sun 6–11:30pm. **Closed:** Three weeks in Aug.

★ In business since the turn of the century, this is the oldest pizzeria in Rome. Is it the best? Only you can judge that. The decor of the place hasn't changed much in more than 90 years—diners still eat at wooden tables astride antique woodwork. And while it's not the cheapest pizzeria in Rome, it's certainly the most storied and just maybe the best.

Take a left off via Nazionale onto via Genova if you're coming from piazza della Repubblica.

NEAR PIAZZA NAVONA

PIZZERIA BAFFETTO, via del Governo Vecchio, 114. Tel. 686-1617.
Cuisine: ITALIAN. **Directions:** See below.
$ **Prices:** 7,000–10,000 lire ($6.10–$8.70). No credit cards.
Open: Mon–Sat 6:30pm–1am. **Closed:** 15 days in Aug.
Ask any Roman where to go for pizza and invariably this place will be mentioned first. Of the three pizzerias that I list in Rome, this is the cheapest, smallest, and most crowded, its two bright rooms always packed with young Romans, no matter what the time or the weather (and spilling out to a few streetside tables in summer). If you're in a hurry or especially hungry, arrive to grab a table as soon as they open.

You'll find Baffetto near piazza Navona on via del Governo Vecchio, at its corner with via Sora, in the area behind the Chiesa Nuova.

VOLPETTI, via della Scrofa, 31-32. Tel. 686-1940.
Cuisine: ITALIAN. **Directions:** See below.
$ **Prices:** Pasta courses 5,000–5,500 lire ($4.35–$4.80); meat courses 5,500–10,000 lire ($4.80–$8.70). No credit cards.
Open: Mon–Sat 7am–8:30pm.
An upscale food store and *rosticceria*, Volpetti is best suited for a quick meal as they offer only stand-up dining at metal counters. Despite this inconvenience, the place is quite attractive and the food excellent. It's located near the intersection of via dei Portoghese and via della Scrofa (a street that runs roughly parallel to the Tiber River), just a few minutes from the north end of piazza Navona.

NEAR THE COLOSSEUM

ASSO BAR, via Cavour, 253.
Cuisine: ITALIAN. **Metropolitana:** Cavour.
$ **Prices:** Pasta courses 5,500 lire ($4.80); meat courses 8,000 lire ($6.95). No credit cards.
Open: Mon–Sat 11:30am–11:30pm (until 1 or 2am in summer).
A sizable place that looks more like an American cafeteria than most Italian *rosticcerie,* Asso Bar offers a wide selection of foods as well as an ample number of

tables. It's located at the intersection of via dei Serpenti and via Cavour, a few blocks north of the Colosseum.

SNACK BAR VENEZIA, via Cavour, 207. Tel. 48-4540.
Cuisine: ITALIAN. **Metropolitana:** Cavour.
$ Prices: Pasta courses 5,500–7,000 lire ($4.80–$6.95); meat courses 6,000–10,000 lire ($5.20–$9.15). No credit cards.
Open: Lunch only, Mon–Sat noon–2:30pm.

A clean, modern café-bar, the Venezia serves up some tasty pasta for lunch only from the back of the bar. You can eat at a counter or at one of the few tables here. It's near the Cavour Metropolitana stop, toward the Colosseum.

MEALS FOR LESS THAN 16,000 LIRE ($13.90)

NEAR PIAZZA NAVONA & LARGO DI TORRE ARGENTINA

L'INSALATA RICCA, largo dei Chiavari, 85. Tel. 654-3656.
Cuisine: ITALIAN. **Directions:** See below.
$ Prices: Pasta courses 5,500–8,000 lire ($4.80–$6.95); meat courses 7,700–11,000 lire ($6.70–$9.60); salads 4,000–7,000 lire ($3.50–$6.10). No credit cards.
Open: Lunch Thurs–Tues 12:30–3pm; dinner Thurs–Tues 6:45–11pm.

⭐ Translated literally, this excellent budget-priced trattoria's name means "the rich salad." Guess what their specialty is. . . . Their selection of second courses is relatively limited, but they always have at least 10 different salads, eight delicious and unique first courses, and a handful of daily specials. You'll find it easy to save money here by ordering just a pasta dish and a salad, which will satisfy the heartiest appetite for little more than 15,000 lire ($13.05). Indeed, unlike many places where they insist that you take a full meal, here the management boasts that their trattoria was created to provide a place where diners could take just one course or a salad. Their menu is multilingual, and there's always a line for the excellent and inexpensive food served at this tiny one-room restaurant. No smoking allowed.

L'Insalata Ricca is situated just a few steps from corso Vittorio Emanuele, on the left just past largo di Torre Argentina (from the station), and like its cousin listed below, is not far from piazza Navona.

PIZZERIA LE MASCHERE, via dei Monte della Farina, 29.
Cuisine: ITALIAN. **Bus:** 64 from the train station to largo di Torre Argentina.
$ Prices: Pizza 8,000–11,000 lire ($6.95–$9.60), plus a steep 2,000-lira ($1.75) *coperto* per person and 15% service. AE, DC, MC, V.
Open: Dinner only, Tues–Sun 7pm–midnight.

Stick to the thin-crust pizza here or you'll end up spending 21,000 lire ($18.25) or more on a full meal of specialties from Calabria, the owner's home province. As pizza goes, the pies are quite expensive, but the setting is enchanting. *Maschere* means "masks," and the walls of the often-crowded large dining area inside are covered with them. They have outdoor tables on a quiet piazza in summer.

The pizzeria is one short block in from via Arenula, the main boulevard running between largo di Torre Argentina and ponte Garibaldi.

RISTORANTE IL DELFINO, corso Vittorio Emanuele, 67. Tel. 686-4053.
Cuisine: ITALIAN. **Bus:** 64 from the train station or piazza Venezia to largo di Torre Argentina.
$ Prices: *Menu turistico* 16,500 lire ($14.35); pizza 7,000–8,000 lire ($6.10–$6.95); pasta courses 5,500–7,000 lire ($4.80–$6.10); meat courses 8,000–10,000 lire ($6.95–$8.70). AE, DC, MC, V.
Open: Tues–Sun 8am–9pm.

⭐ This is Rome's biggest self-service restaurant, with an exceptionally wide selection of dishes, including pizza that's available continuously (unlike most pizzerias, where the ovens are fired up only for the dinner hour). It's a bright, cheery place, with polished green stone floors and piped-in pop music, and less of a fast-food atmosphere than many of the newer self-services in town. They even offer an English/American-style breakfast of two eggs, bacon, toast, juice, and coffee for about 9,000 lire ($7.80). The restaurant is just past largo di Torre Argentina, on the no. 64 bus line.

TRATTORIA DA SERGIO, vicolo delle Grotte, 27. Tel. 686-4293.

Cuisine: ITALIAN. **Bus:** 64 from the train station to largo di Torre Argentina.
$ Prices: Pizza 5,000–8,000 lire ($4.35–$6.95); pasta courses 4,000–7,000 lire ($3.50–$6.10); meat courses 8,000–12,000 lire ($6.95–$10.50). No credit cards.
Open: Lunch Mon–Sat 12:30–3:30pm; dinner Mon–Sat 7:30pm–midnight.

For good home-cooking at moderate prices you'll enjoy Da Sergio, where every day a new pasta specialty emerges. When I visited, I enjoyed gnocchi, which the owner had made earlier in the day. The simple interior includes hams hanging from the ceiling as well as a crowd of loyal locals.

From largo di Torre Argentina, go down via Arenula toward the river and continue until piazza Cairoli; then turn right onto via dei Giubbonari and take the fifth left.

TRATTORIA L'INSALATA RICCA 2, piazza Pasquino, 72. Tel. 654-7881.

Cuisine: ITALIAN. **Directions:** See below.
$ Prices: Pasta courses 5,500–8,000 lire ($4.80–$6.95); meat courses 7,700–11,000 lire ($6.70–$9.60); salads 4,000–7,000 lire ($3.50–$6.10). No credit cards.
Open: Lunch Tues–Sun 12:30–3pm; dinner Tues–Sun 7:15–11:30pm.

Eat here and you'll discover why the owners decided to open a second place under the same name. The atmosphere is rustic—rare in Rome—with wood-beamed ceilings, copper pots and wine jugs dangling from the roof, and a hand-painted sign out front. This refreshing find is situated near piazza Navona, at one end of via Santa Maria dell'Anima.

NEAR THE COLOSSEUM

DA SABATINO, via del Boschetto, 28.

Cuisine: ITALIAN. **Metropolitana:** Cavour.
$ Prices: Pasta courses 4,000–5,500 lire ($3.50–$4.80); meat and poultry courses 5,500–9,000 lire ($4.80–$7.80). No credit cards.
Open: Lunch Mon–Sat noon–4pm; dinner Mon–Sat 7pm–midnight.

⭐ A simple, very Roman restaurant with imitation woodwork and a mix of prints and paintings on the wall, Da Sabatino offers some of the lowest à la carte food prices in town. Only two people work here: Sabatino, who serves the tables and chats with the loyal Roman clientele, and his wife, who tends to all the cooking. Both have honed their skills—Sabatino entering his 45th year at the place.

Via del Boschetto runs between via Nazionale and the Colosseum, about five minutes from the Cavour Metropolitana stop. Outside you'll see only a sign reading FRASCATI above the small plain door.

TRATTORIA DA PASQUALINO, via dei Santi Quattro, 66. Tel. 700-4576.

Cuisine: ITALIAN. **Directions:** See below.
$ Prices: Pasta courses 6,000–9,000 lire ($5.20–$7.80); meat and fish courses 7,000–14,500 lire ($6.10–$12.60). AE, V.
Open: Lunch Tues–Sun noon–3pm; dinner Tues–Sun 8pm–midnight.

The 100-year-old Da Pasqualino boasts a remarkable location just a block from the Colosseum. Yet despite its proximity to Rome's foremost sight, prices are remarkably reasonable and the ambience very typical with mostly Italians dining. The street is toward San Giovanni in Laterano from the Colosseum. Follow via dei Fori Imperiali past the Colosseum and just before it turns into via Labicana, turn right; then take the second left.

NEAR THE TREVI FOUNTAIN

Tourists flock by the busload to throw their loose lire into the gaudy, baroque Trevi Fountain; legend has it that those who do so will be sure to return to Rome. Tourists also come for the neighborhood's several moderately priced trattorias.

Here are several good picks, but you might shop around in this compact area, since others offer competitive prices.

ROSTICCERIA/TAVOLA CALDA AL PICCHIO, via del Lavatore, 39-40. Tel. 678-9926 or 678-1602.

Cuisine: ITALIAN.

$ Prices: *Menu turistico* (with six different options, all including wine) 16,500–22,000 lire ($14.35–$19.15); pasta courses 4,000–7,000 lire ($3.50–$6.10); meat courses 6,000–12,000 lire ($5.20–$10.45). No credit cards.

Open: Lunch Tues–Sun noon–3:30pm; dinner Tues–Sun 6–10:30pm. **Closed:** Two weeks in Feb.

This restaurant is a bit more pleasant than its neighbors, and can cater to your every whim, with six different *menu turistico* options. Its choices are advertised in six languages. The ambience is a bit unusual for Rome: tables under a long barrel vault more reminiscent of a Czechoslovakian beer hall than an Italian eatery. If you prefer, they also offer a self-service *rosticceria* with counter seating to the front of the restaurant.

TRATTORIA DELLA STAMPA, via dei Maroniti, 32. Tel. 678-9919.

Cuisine: ITALIAN. **Metropolitana:** Barberini.

$ Prices: Pasta courses 5,500–7,000 lire ($4.80–$6.10); meat courses 8,000–11,000 lire ($6.95–$9.60). No credit cards.

Open: Lunch Mon–Sat 12:30–3pm; dinner Mon–Sat 6:30 or 7–10 or 10:30pm.

A very typical place in the heart of Rome and a favorite of journalists (the name means "trattoria of the press"). The plain woodwork is decorated with onions, red peppers, and wine, all ingredients favored by owner Antonio Bucci, who presides over the kitchen.

The restaurant is on a small street that begins at largo del Tritone off via del Tritone, not far from the Barberini Metropolitana stop.

TRASTEVERE

"Everyone has his own favorite trattoria in Trastevere," so the Romans tell you. My favorite budget value is this one, but there are many others in this area just waiting to be discovered.

TRATTORIA MARIO'S, via del Moro, 53. Tel. 580-3809.

Cuisine: ITALIAN. **Bus:** 170 from the train station or piazza Venezia.

$ Prices: *Menu turistico* 15,000 lire ($13.05); pasta courses 4,000–5,500 lire ($3.50–$4.80); meat courses 7,000–9,000 lire ($6.10–$7.80). No credit cards.

Open: Lunch Mon–Sat noon–4pm; dinner Mon–Sat 7pm–midnight. **Closed:** Second half of Aug.

This charming place, decorated with the work of neighborhood artists, and operated by three generations of Mario's family, offers one of the better food values in Rome. The 15,000-lira ($13.05) *menu turistico* is the cheapest outside the immediate vicinity of the train station and full of variety, making it a big favorite of foreigners in Rome.

Mario's is situated in Trastevere, the artists' and writers' quarter of Rome. Get off bus no. 170 at the first stop after ponte Garibaldi, turn right onto via del Moro and walk toward ponte Sisto, and look for the trattoria halfway down on the left.

NEAR STAZIONE TERMINI

This is certainly the best Roman neighborhood for budget dining, though neither the surroundings nor the food is particularly pleasant in this area. Here are a few exceptions to the rule:

HOSTARIA-PIZZERIA LA REATINA, via San Martino della Battaglia, 17. Tel. 49-0314.

Cuisine: ITALIAN. **Directions:** See below.

$ Prices: Pizza 5,000–8,500 lire ($4.35–$7.40); pasta courses 4,000–6,000 lire ($3.50–$5.20); meat courses 6,000–11,000 lire ($5.20–$9.60). *Coperto* and service 2,000 lire ($1.75) extra. No credit cards.

Open: Lunch Sun–Fri noon–3pm; dinner Sun–Fri 6:30–11:30pm. **Closed:** 15 days in Aug.

There's no *menu turistico* here, but with moderate à la carte prices you'll have no trouble filling up for *less* than you'd pay for a fixed-price dinner someplace else. A three-course meal here (without wine) shouldn't be more than 16,000 lire ($13.90). Don't expect much in the way of atmosphere—just hearty, inexpensive food and a loyal, satisfied local clientele. Pizza is served, but only in the evening. The service is not always the most attentive.

Via San Martino della Battaglia runs between piazza Indipendenza and viale Castro Pretorio. The restaurant is on the right just past the intersection with via Villafranca.

TRATTORIA DA BENEDETTO, via Vicenza, 44.

Cuisine: ITALIAN. **Directions:** See below.

$ Prices: Pasta courses 7,000 lire ($6.10); meat courses 8,000–15,500 lire ($6.95–$13.50). No credit cards.

Open: Lunch Mon–Sat noon–3:15pm; dinner Mon–Sat 6:30–11pm. **Closed:** 10 days in Aug.

This is yet another of the recommendable and inexpensive trattorias in this area. You'll find it at the corner of via Vicenza and via Palestro.

TRATTORIA L'ARCHETTO, via Turati, 104-106. Tel. 446-0318.

Cuisine: ITALIAN. **Directions:** See below.

$ Prices: *Menu turistico* 15,400 lire ($13.40); pasta courses 5,500–7,000 lire ($4.80–$6.10); meat courses 8,000–14,500 lire ($6.95–$12.60). AE.

Open: Lunch Mon–Sat noon–3pm; dinner Mon–Sat 6:30–11pm.

This is a simple but friendly family-style place, with plain pine walls, curtains, and outdoor tables in summer. It's situated off the beaten track, but it's worth the walk for the food, particularly the pasta dishes, and the prices are among the most reasonable around. This is one of the few places I found with veal as a selection on the *menu turistico;* pizza is available in the evening only. Gino and his friend and partner, Angelo, don't speak much English, but they do have an English menu.

The restaurant is located on the left side of the station, on via Turati between via Rattazza and via Capellini, on the block past piazza Manfredo Fanti.

MEALS FOR LESS THAN 23,000 LIRE [$20]

NEAR PIAZZA NAVONA

Again, this is a top-notch neighborhood for finding good food at reasonable prices.

ANTICA TRATTORIA PIZZERIA POLESE, piazza Sforza Cesarini, 40. Tel. 686-1709.

Cuisine: ITALIAN. **Directions:** See below.

$ Prices: Pasta courses 7,000–10,000 lire ($6.10–$8.70); meat courses 8,500–18,000 lire ($7.40–$15.65). MC, V.

Open: Lunch Wed–Mon 12:15–3pm; dinner Wed–Mon 7–11pm.

The menu here, which changes regularly, is large—the last time I visited they were featuring no fewer than 17 second-course selections. The menu is not translated, but most of the waiters speak English. You can order such specialties as fettuccine alla Sforza (with a sauce of cream and mushrooms), fracostine di vitello alla fornata (veal in a white-wine sauce), or abbacchio al forno (roast lamb). The Polese remains busy year round, with tables outside on the piazza in summer and rustic old chandeliers over the tables inside. All in all, this is an excellent selection for the medium-priced category, where you can expect to spend 20,000–30,000 lire ($17.40–$26.10) for a plentiful, hearty, and delicious meal, including wine.

Piazza Sforza Cesarini is just off corso Vittorio Emanuele, the main boulevard running through Old Rome, between piazza di Chiesa Nuova and the Tiber.

TRATTORIA DA LUIGI, piazza Sforza Cesarini, 24. Tel. 686-5946 or 654-5463.
   Cuisine: ITALIAN. **Directions:** See Antica Trattoria Pizzeria Polese, above.
$ Prices: Pasta courses 7,500–8,500 lire ($6.50–$7.40); meat courses 10,000–14,500 lire ($8.70–$12.60). AE, DC, V.
   Open: Lunch Tues–Sun noon–3pm; dinner Tues–Sun 7pm–midnight.
Located on the same square as the Polese, listed above, this place is similarly priced, and just about as popular and well established. Also like its nearby competitor, it has outdoor tables in summer and red lampshades over the tables. It's kept darker and more romantic, though, and is tastefully decorated with old theater posters and mirrors advertising various English liquors. Perhaps it's the latter that makes tourists and expatriates prefer this place, while more Italians can be found at the Polese. They don't seem to mind if you order only a pasta dish here; I especially recommend the penne alla vodka in a rich tomato cream sauce.

NEAR THE VATICAN

TAVERNA-RISTORANTE TRE PUPAZZI, borgo Pio, 183. Tel. 686-8371.
   Cuisine: ITALIAN. **Directions:** See below.
$ Prices: *Menu turistico* (including dessert) 22,000 lire ($19.15); pizza 7,500–9,000 lire ($6.50–$7.80); pasta courses 7,500–10,000 lire ($6.50–$8.70); meat courses 10,000–19,000 lire ($8.70–$16.50). AE, MC, V.
   Open: Lunch Mon–Sat noon–3pm; dinner Mon–Sat 7–11:30pm.
This cozy and charming 17th-century-style taverna comes highly recommended from nearby hoteliers and many other Romans as well. Its 22,000-lira ($19.15) *menu turistico* is acceptable considering the restaurant's delightful atmosphere and proximity to St. Peter's. Service can be slow, however.

The restaurant is situated on borgo Pio at its intersection with via dei Tre Pupazzi. Borgo Pio is two short blocks from, and parallel to, via della Conciliazione.

NEAR STAZIONE TERMINI

If you must eat in this neighborhood and can afford this price range, you'll find either of these places acceptable:

HOSTARIA ANGELO, via Principe Amedeo, 104. Tel. 731-2263.
   Cuisine: ITALIAN. **Directions:** See below.
$ Prices: *Menu turistico* 21,000 lire ($18.25); pasta courses 4,500–7,000 lire ($3.90–$6.10); meat courses 7,500–11,000 lire ($6.50–$9.60). AE, DC, MC, V.
   Open: Lunch Thurs–Tues 11am–3pm; dinner Thurs–Tues 6–11pm.
Angelo's atmosphere is pleasant enough, featuring checkered floors and wood paneling. Its clientele includes a good mix of Italians and tourists. Stick to the ample *menu turistico*, which includes a choice from among 10 second courses—otherwise you're likely to spend 22,000 lire ($19.15) or more.

The restaurant is located between via Gioberti and via Cattaneo.

TRATTORIA DA ALFREDO, via Principe Amedeo, 126a. Tel. 446-4298.
   Cuisine: ITALIAN. **Directions:** See below.

$ Prices: *Menu turistico* 19,500 lire ($16.95) without wine, 22,000 lire ($19.15) with wine; pasta courses 4,500–6,000 lire ($3.90–$5.20); meat courses 8,500–11,000 lire ($7.40–$9.60). AE, MC, V.

Open: Lunch Mon–Sat noon–3pm; dinner Mon–Sat 6:30–11pm.

Located a few steps beyond the Trattoria Angelo, with atmosphere and service a few notches below, Alfredo's is nonetheless a good choice. The *menu turistico* includes an unusually wide selection of second courses, including veal, chicken, liver, and fish.

PICNIC SUPPLIES & WHERE TO EAT THEM

Piazza Vittorio Emanuele, near the train station, is Rome's principal open-air daily food market. There's also a modest-sized outdoor covered market (the **Mercato Rionale**) at via Flaminia, 60, near piazza del Popolo, and plenty of little shops in between where you can pick up meat, cheese, and drinks; the market's open Monday through Saturday from 7am to 2pm. The market in **campo de' Fiori** is especially characteristic and photogenic. There's an open-air food market near the train station year round, Monday through Saturday from 6am to about 2pm, on **via Montebello,** on the two blocks between via Volturno and via Goito. There are numerous *panetterie, pasticcerie,* and *salumerie* in the storefronts behind the street vendors.

Doing your own shopping for food in Italy can be an interesting cultural experience in and of itself, since supermarkets are very rare. Cold cuts are sold at a *salumeria*. To pick up cheese or yogurt, you'll have to find a *latteria*. Vegetables can usually be found at an *alimentari*, the closest thing Italy has to a grocery store. For bread to put all that between, visit a *panetteria*. Wander into a *pasticceria* to find dessert. And for a bottle of wine to wash it down, search out a *vinatteria*.

The **Villa Borghese,** Rome's only downtown park, is the place to take your fixings for an imperial picnic.

WORTH THE EXTRA BUCKS

NEAR THE FORUM & THE COLOSSEUM

RISTORANTE-PIZZERIA SU RECREU, via del Buon Consiglio, 17. Tel. 679-4918.

Cuisine: ITALIAN. **Metropolitana:** Cavour.

$ Prices: Pizza 10,000–12,000 lire ($8.70–$10.45); pasta courses 9,000–12,000 lire ($7.80–$10.45); meat courses 15,500–18,000 lire ($13.50–$15.65); fresh fish 10,000–19,000 lire ($8.70–$16.50) per 100 grams (roughly a quarter pound). AE, DC, MC, V.

Open: Lunch Sun–Tues noon–3pm; dinner Sun–Tues 7:30pm–1:30am.

The sign over the door—LOCALE TIPICO SARDO—means "typical Sardinian restaurant." That tells it all about this popular restaurant with white stucco walls, closely packed tables, and Sardinian artifacts hanging from walls and ceiling. The food is outstanding, and the atmosphere lively. Popular dishes include risotto alla pescatore (a rice-and-seafood combination), pane frattau (very thin bread stuffed with tomato, cheese, and egg), linguine con bottarga (with fish roe), homemade ravioli stuffed with spinach and ricotta cheese, and fresh fish.

From the Cavour Metropolitana stop, walk along via Cavour away from the train station and take the third left onto via del Cardello, one block past via degli Annibaldi. The pocket-sized via del Buon Consiglio is immediately on your right.

IN TRASTEVERE

TAVERNA FIERAMOSCA, piazza de' Mercanti. Tel. 589-0289.

Cuisine: ITALIAN. **Bus:** 170 from the train station or piazza Venezia to viale Trastevere.

$ Prices: Pizza 6,500–15,500 lire ($5.65–$13.50); meat courses 8,000–22,000 lire ($6.95–$19.15); vegetables 5,500–7,000 lire ($4.80–$6.10). No credit cards.

Open: Dinner only, Mon–Sat 7pm–midnight. **Closed:** One week in Aug.

This delightful place bills itself as an authentic medieval taverna, and that's exactly what it is. Cannons hang from the ceiling, suits of armor stand at attention in the corner, and all eating is done at long wooden tables. They carry the theme to the extreme, and don't serve any pasta, which came to Italy with Marco Polo toward the end of the Middle Ages. Indeed, the only modern intrusion is the eating utensils. This Middle Ages mess hall enjoys a devout following of Romans and tourists alike. The menu here is a 24- by 36-inch souvenir poster, and during the evening, guitar and accordion players add to the revelry. In summer there are 200 seats on the piazza outside.

You can get here aboard bus no. 170 (from the Termini and piazza Venezia areas); get off at the first stop across the river on viale Trastevere, walk along via dei Genovesi for five short blocks, and turn right onto via Santa Cecilia to piazza de' Mercanti.

NEAR THE HISTORIC CENTER

FIASCHETTERIA BELTRAMME, via della Croce, 39.
   Cuisine: ITALIAN. **Metropolitana:** Piazza di Spagna.
 $ Prices: Pasta courses 8,500–12,000 lire ($7.40–$10.45); meat courses 12,000–22,000 lire ($10.45–$19.15). No credit cards.
   Open: Lunch Mon–Sat noon–3pm; dinner Mon–Sat 7:45–10:30pm. **Closed:** Aug.

The sketches on the wall were done by artists who frequent this tiny one-room institution that has been serving Roman specialties here for more than a century. In fact, it's so well known among the city's artists and intellectuals that there's neither a menu nor a sign (other than FIASCHETTERIA) out front identifying it as a place to eat. Owner Luciano Guerra points out that this is a "*locale*" known to the national art authorities," though he doesn't say whether it's the food or the milieu—or the combination of the two—that attracts them.

Via della Croce begins at piazza di Spagna, at the corner where the Mondi shop is situated.

RISTORANTE VALLE "LA BIBLIOTECA," largo Teatro Valle, 9. Tel. 654-1357 or 654-1292.
   Cuisine: ITALIAN. **Reservations:** Recommended, especially on Sat. **Bus:** 64 or 170 from the train station to largo di Torre Argentina.
 $ Prices: Pasta courses 10,000–11,000 lire ($8.70–$9.55); meat courses 15,500–24,000 lire ($13.50–$20.85). AE, DC, MC, V.
   Open: Dinner only, Mon–Sat 8pm–1 or 2am.

This is one of Rome's older restaurants, known to everyone simply as "La Biblioteca" (The Library), for its exceptionally exhaustive wine collection that lines almost every inch of its walls. Some might call the place gaudy or even tacky, but it does have a certain charm, and the food is excellent. You don't get to be this old without it. They also feature live music and dancing every night. Expect to spend at least 35,000 lire ($30.45) per person without wine.

To get here, take bus no. 64 or 170 to largo di Torre Argentina; continue on foot in the same direction the bus was traveling, and turn right at piazza di Sant' Andrea della Valle.

---

6. ATTRACTIONS

SUGGESTED ITINERARIES

A word to the wise about sightseeing in Rome, especially if you're considering a brief visit: Time your visit in general, and your individual days in particular, to make sure

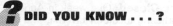

DID YOU KNOW . . . ?

- Rome's population at the end of the 1st century was one million people; by the 6th century it was less than 50,000.
- Construction of Rome's subway had to be stopped frequently so that archeologists could examine newly found vestiges of the city's past.
- There are more than 300 monumental fountains in Rome.
- According to author John Gunther, by the mid-1960s there had been no fewer than 230,000 books written about Rome.
- The 1985 treaty between Italy and the Vatican ended Rome's title of "sacred city."
- The Vatican may be the smallest country in the world, but it contains the largest residence—the Vatican Palace.
- The Spanish Steps were actually designed by the French, but received their name from the nearby Spanish Embassy.

you don't come all this way only to find everything locked up. Just about all the sights of significance, except the Vatican and other churches, are closed on Monday. During the rest of the week many places close by 2pm, and stop admitting visitors 30–60 minutes before that.

IF YOU HAVE ONE DAY   Rome was not built in a day, and don't expect even to scratch its surface in just one day of touring. Frankly, what you see in one day depends on your own interests. The Colosseum and Forum will delight history buffs, while those with a more spiritual interest in the Eternal City will want to focus on St. Peter's and the Vatican area. Either could easily consume not just one but several days, so get an early start.

IF YOU HAVE TWO DAYS   Spend your second day at whichever place—the Forum/Colosseum or St. Peter's/Vatican area—you weren't able to get to on your first day.

IF YOU HAVE THREE DAYS   What should you not miss once you've covered the most significant historic and religious areas? The Pantheon is something of a must-see, as are the twin museums on Capitoline Hill, followed by the Etruscan Museum and the Galleria Borghese in the Villa Borghese.

IF YOU HAVE FIVE DAYS   If you have managed to see everything that I suggested above—an especially difficult task considering the capricious opening days and hours of most sights—move on to Tivoli, Ostia Antica, or the various pilgrimage churches listed below.

TOP ATTRACTIONS

With the exception of churches, all the sights listed below stop admitting visitors at least 30, and in some cases as much as 60, minutes before the listed closing time. Tourists can remain inside until the posted closing time, but entrance is forbidden in the last half hour or more.

THE COLOSSEUM AND THE ARCH OF CONSTANTINE, via dei Fori Imperiali. Tel. 700-4261.

Every city has one icon that symbolizes the city. In Paris it's the Eiffel Tower, in Venice the gondola, and in Rome the Colosseum (Colosseo). It's most impressive from the outside, a mammoth remnant of the golden age of the Roman Empire. Completed in the 1st century A.D., it was in this 50,000-seat stadium that Christians were thrown to the lions and other public events took place. Its legendary crumbled look is due mostly to the fact that it was used for centuries as a quarry for other Roman construction projects. The original "floor" of the structure is also gone, revealing the labyrinthine underground network where prisoners, lions, and general provisions were kept.

To clamber up to the higher levels, go to the stairway just to the left as you face the main entrance. Note that in recent years, various of the three upper levels have been closed for reconstruction and reinforcement.

As you step out of the Colosseum, you'll see the grandest triumphal arch of them all, the Arch of Constantine, to the left.

Admission: Colosseum, free to street level of interior, 6,000 lire ($5.20) to the upper levels.

Open: Wed and hols, year round 9am–2pm; Mon–Tues and Thurs–Sat, June 1–July 15 9am–7pm, May and July 16–Aug 15 9am–6:30pm, Apr 16–30 and Aug 16–31 9am–6pm, Mar 16–Apr 15 and Sept 9am–5:30pm, Feb 16–Mar 15 and Oct 9am–5pm, Nov–Jan 15 9am–4:30pm. Last admission to the upper levels is one hour before closing. **Closed:** Jan 16–Feb 15. **Metropolitana:** Colosseo.

THE FORUM, PALATINE HILL, AND CIRCUS MAXIMUS, via dei Fori Imperiali.

⭐ The **Roman Forum (Foro Romano)** (tel. 678-0782) is a wonderful, intact slice of ancient Rome, where, with a little imagination, you can envision the life and vibrancy of the city as it was 2,000 years ago. This area was for a long time the seat of commerce and government, where Romans came to conduct all business, imperial and mercantile.

Archeologists began uncovering the site early in the last century, and are still digging here today. As you descend into the main part, the life of the Eternal City flowers before you—the triumphal arches at either end, the remains of several imperial temples, the odd, lonely marble column sprouting up from the earth, or the slice of marble edifice lying on the ground carved with a few letters or words of an inscription.

The Arch of Titus marks the east end of the Forum, nearest the Colosseum, while the bigger and more impressive Arch of Tiberius stands at the west end. Rising above the Forum, and accessible from stairs near the Arch of Titus, is the **Palatine Hill.** Rome was built on seven hills, beginning with this one. The palace ruins and the remains of the other buildings and gardens here are less impressive than those of the Forum below, but significant nonetheless.

Only the outline of the narrow oval known as the **Circo Massimo (Circus Maximus),** where Roman chariot races took place, remains. To view the Circus, now an open expanse of grass, go to the southern side (far left edge, as you enter) of the Palatine Hill. You can also jog there today.

The main entrance to the Forum is on via dei Fori Imperiali, a huge boulevard created by World War II dictator Benito Mussolini as a place to hold military parades. Another entrance to the Palatine Hill and Forum is down via di San Gregorio from the Colosseum, to the left as you exit. If you're in a hurry and would prefer to see only the Forum, you can make a quick getaway (and it's only an exit, not an entrance) behind the Arch of Titus, the closest exit to the Colosseum.

Admission: Forum and Palatine Hill, 10,000 lire ($8.70); Circus Maximus, free.

Open: Sun, Tues, and hols, year round 9am–2pm; Mon and Wed–Sat, June 1–July 15 9am–7pm, May and July 16–Aug 15 9am–6:30pm, Apr 16–30 and Aug 16–31 9am–6pm, Mar 16–Apr 15 and Sept 9am–5:30pm, Feb 16–Mar 15 and Oct 9am–5pm, Nov–Jan 15 9am–4:30pm. Last admission is one hour before closing. **Closed:** Jan 1 and May 1.

AUGUSTUS'S AND TRAJAN'S FORUMS, via dei Fori Imperiali.

If you walk away from the Colosseum on via Alessandrina, you'll see Augustus's Forum on the right side, and Trajan's Forum on the left. Neither of these is open to the public, but you can see everything you need to from the sidewalk above.

Trajan's Forum is certainly the highlight of this imperial walk, with its 25 standing columns, including the intricately carved Trajan's Column (Colonna Traiano), a stunning series of bas-reliefs winding up a monumental pillar.

Via dei Fori Imperiali ends at piazza Venezia, which is dominated by the stark-white winged chariots of the ostentatious 19th-century Vittorio Emanuele Monument.

THE PANTHEON, piazza della Rotonda. Tel. 36-9831.

⭐ The Pantheon was not the first building in Rome, but it's certainly the oldest structure in the city still entirely intact. The original building, built by Marcus Agrippa in the reign of Augustus Caesar (around 27 B.C.) as a temple to all the gods, was a rectangular structure. All but the front columns and portico were later destroyed by fire, and when it was rebuilt by the Emperor Hadrian (A.D. 130), it took on its present round form. It served later for a time as a church and even for a while as a fish market, and today it is the best-preserved monument to the industry of classical Roman civilization. Note that all light for this marvelous structure comes from the hole in the center of the ceiling.

To the layperson, this dome is much more impressive than the Duomo in Florence, since the dome here is so immediate, beginning just about 50 feet above the patterned marble floors. The great artist Raphael is buried here, in the illuminated tomb to the left as you enter.

Admission: Free.

Open: July–Sept, daily 9am–6pm (light permitting); Oct–June, Mon–Sat 9am–4pm, Sun 9am–1pm. **Bus:** 64, 170, or 175 to largo di Torre Argentina; then walk up via de' Cestari for three blocks to piazza della Rotonda.

CAPITOLINE HILL, piazza del Campidoglio.

⭐ This smallest of Rome's seven hills was the political and religious center of the imperial city, and for many centuries since it has been home to Rome's **Palazzo Senatorio** (city hall). The hill's sweeping front steps, designed by Michelangelo, lead from piazza Venezia up to this majestic plateau, while the back side of the summit enjoys a terrific view of the Forum below.

Two museums share this tiny square. The **Museo dei Conservatori,** on the right side as you reach the top, and the **Museo Capitoline** opposite (tel. 678-2862 for both), together make up the oldest and perhaps the finest sculpture museum in the world. Don't miss the mosaics from Hadrian's villa, or the collection's most famous works, including *The Dying Gaul, Boy Extracting a Thorn from His Foot, Old and Young Centaurs,* and the *Capitoline Wolf.*

Admission: Piazza, free; museums, 6,000 lire ($5.20) for both, free the last Sun in each month.

Open: Piazza, daily 24 hours. Both museums, Apr–Sept, Tues 9am–1:30pm and 5–8pm, Wed–Fri 9am–1:30pm, Sat 9am–1:30pm and 8–11pm, Sun 9am–1pm; Oct–Mar, Tues 9am–1:30pm and 5–8pm, Wed–Fri 9am–1:30pm, Sat 9am–1:30pm and 5–8pm, Sun 9am–1pm; last entrance is 30 minutes before closing.

SAINT PETER'S SQUARE AND BASILICA.

⭐ Saint Peter's Square is in fact not a square at all, but a beautiful oval piazza ringed by a majestic colonnade and dominated by two stately fountains at the center.

The absolutely enormous Saint Peter's Basilica is the second-largest church in the world (a pale imitation in the Ivory Coast recently became the largest), and of course the spiritual center for millions of Catholics. Throughout the center aisle of the church are markers indicating the size of other major cathedrals in the world—dwarfs by comparison.

Although there has been a church on this site since the 4th century—as long as Christianity has been the official Roman religion—the present structure was not begun until the early 16th century, and completed more than 100 years later. Immediately to the right as you enter is Michelangelo's best and most moving *Pietà*—he did four of these statues, this one when he was 25 years old. The sculpture is now protected by bulletproof glass after a 1978 terrorist attack on the artwork.

Saint Peter's tomb is said to be beneath Bernini's captivating canopied altar. Downstairs you'll find the tombs of a number of popes and other saints.

Visitors can climb the cupola for a terrific view of the Vatican complex and the rest

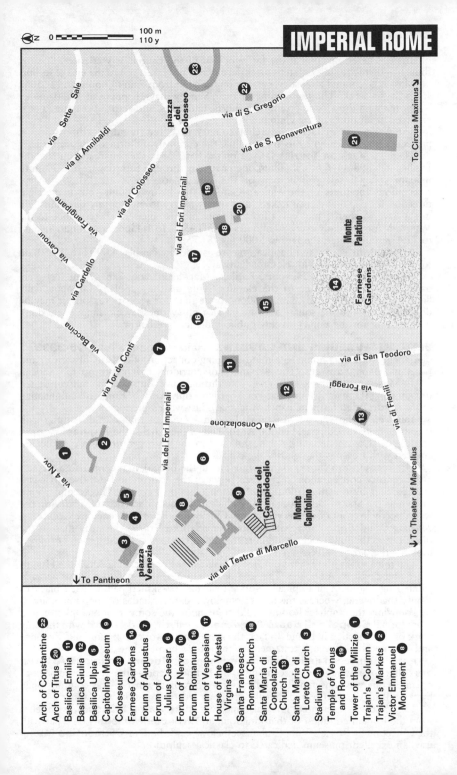

IMPERIAL ROME

of Rome. The entrance is at the far right end of the church as you enter. Beware, though—there are still 330 steps *after* the elevator has taken you to the end of its line.

Mass is celebrated almost every hour on the hour from 7am to noon, and at 5pm, seven days a week. The *pontificale,* or main Sunday mass, happens at 10:30am.

Note that a dress code prohibiting shorts, tank tops, and skirts above the knee is enforced at all times in the church.

The Vatican is in fact a sovereign country of a few hundred citizens and is protected (theoretically) by its own militia, the curiously uniformed Swiss guards.

There's a **Vatican Tourist Office** on the left side of the square as you face the basilica (tel. 698-4466 or 698-4866) open Monday through Saturday from 8:30am to 6:30pm. They'll sell you a map of the Vatican for 1,500 lire ($1.30), accept reservations for tours of the Vatican Gardens (see below), point you in the right direction for papal-audience tickets, and otherwise try to answer any questions you might have. A shuttle bus leaves from in front of this office for the entrance to the Vatican Museums daily every 30 minutes from 8:45am to 1:45pm in summer, 8:45am to 12:45pm in winter; the fare is 2,000 lire ($1.75).

Admission: Piazza and basilica, free; to ascend the cupola, 4,000 lire ($3.50) on foot, 5,000 lire ($4.35) with elevator halfway.

Open: Piazza, daily 24 hours. Basilica, Mar–Sept, daily 7am–7pm; Oct–Feb, daily 7am–6pm. Entrance to the elevator/stairs up the cupola, Mar–Sept, daily 8am–6pm; Oct–Feb, daily 8am–4:30pm. Note that, for security reasons, it may be difficult to get into the square and the basilica on Wednesday morning if you don't have a ticket for the pope's weekly public audience (see below).

VATICAN MUSEUMS AND GARDENS, viale Vaticano. Tel. 698-3333.

The Vatican is home to a mind-boggling collection of artistic, historical, and monetary treasures. The 4½ miles of corridors that make up the Vatican Museums complex will take you through five outstanding museums, the breathtaking Raphael Rooms, and Fra Angelico's only work in Rome, all culminating in the unparalleled Sistine Chapel. And that's just what's indoors.

You'll enter the Vatican Museums through a series of long corridors hung with tapestries from the Raphael School. At the end of these halls, the **Raphael Rooms** commence. Commissioned by Pope Julius II in the 16th century, these salons are covered with frescoes that glorify the papacy.

The intense, grim *Incendio di Borgo* (Fire in the Borgo), in the first room, depicts a 9th-century conflagration in the area between the Vatican and the river that was extinguished by the miraculous intervention of Pope Leo IV. The second room, known as the Stanza della Segnatura, includes Raphael's depiction of *Truth* (on the wall directly in front of you as you enter). Clockwise, the other scenes are *Goodness, Theology,* and *Beauty.* Raphael painted himself into *Truth*—he's the man in the black cap in the lower right-hand corner. And in the lower left corner of *Theology,* look for the old Saint Peter's Basilica.

The third room, the Stanza di Eliodoro, shows the pope asking Attila the Hun to cease and desist in A.D. 410. The Sala di Costantino, the final room, was actually painted by a student of Raphael. Notice that this less-skilled painter used black to signify shadowing, whereas the master employed darker shades of the same color.

Following the Raphael Rooms you'll come upon the somber, contemplative, and more formal **Cappella di Beato Angelico,** a small chapel decorated with the only work of Fra Angelico in Rome. In fact, the scenes in his work look more like Florence and Tuscany than Rome, a testament to the artist's homesickness.

If you're interested in the Vatican's **Museum of Modern Religious Art,** visit this collection now, before descending to the Sistine Chapel—the Vatican traffic cops operate a one-way museum. This collection—55 rooms' worth—was commissioned by Pope Paul VI, who feared that the religious artistic tradition was fading.

The Vatican Museum complex also includes an **Egyptian Museum,** with relics from the Roman conquest of that kingdom; an **Etruscan Museum,** on a par with the collection at Rome's Villa Giulia (see below); and the **Pio-Clementine Museum,** an excellent museum dedicated to classical sculpture.

The Vatican has graciously put together a brochure outlining four suggested itineraries of its enormous complex, ranging in length from 90 minutes to five hours, which you can pick up at the entrance.

From the corridors of tapestries you'll doubtless see the lush **Vatican Gardens.** Guided tours of the Vatican City grounds are the only sort available—public access is otherwise not allowed. From March through October, tours leave Monday, Tuesday, and Thursday through Saturday at 10 or 11am from the tourist information office on St. Peter's Square; November to February, tours run only on Tuesday, Thursday, and Saturday. The tour costs 15,000 lire ($13.05). Reservations for garden tours are required year round; in summer, it's recommended that you reserve several days in advance. Reservations can be made in person only (with a passport or ID in hand), and payment is required when you make the reservation.

Admission: Gardens, see text above; museums, 10,000 lire ($8.70), free to all the last Sun of the month. Cassette guide to the Sistine Chapel costs 4,000 lire ($3.50); to the Chapel and the Raphael Rooms, 6,000 lire ($5.20).

Open: Gardens, see text above. Museums, July–Sept and the two weeks before and after Easter, Mon–Sat and last Sun of the month 8:45am–5pm; Oct–June, Mon–Sat and last Sun of the month 9am–1:45pm. Last visitors are admitted one hour before closing. **Directions:** The entrance to the Vatican Museums is on viale del Vaticano, a fair hike from St. Peter's Square, on the north side of Vatican City. If you're not up to a 10- to 15-minute trek, take the shuttle bus from the Vatican City Tourist Office on St. Peter's Square (see the text above). **Metropolitana:** Ottaviano; then about a six-block walk to the entrance. **Bus:** 492 from the train station and old city area.

CAPELLA SISTINA [Sistine Chapel], Vatican Museums, viale Vaticano.

✪ In Italy, all roads lead to Rome. In Rome, all roads lead to the Vatican. And in the Vatican, all roads lead to the Sistine Chapel. Thousands of slightly distracted tourists wander anxiously through the Raphael Rooms and other parts of the Vatican Museums, through which all visitors must pass to get to the chapel, with that inquiring "Are we there yet?" look on their face.

What they're all waiting for is, of course, the enormous, stunning ceiling painted by Michelangelo between 1508 and 1512. Everything about the Sistine Chapel is simply awe-inspiring. Besides the absolute splendor of Michelangelo's work, and the fact that he worked on such a huge horizontal surface, consider that he did it in 30-minute bursts of effort, since frescoes are painted on wet plaster. Also consider, as your neck gets sore bending backward to gaze at the work, what it must have been like to stand like that continually and still produce one of the greatest works of art ever.

What's more, anxious to return to his native Florence, he got the job done quite quickly. The same cannot be said for the cleaning and restoration, which are expected to take decades.

The Sistine Chapel was in fact not built as a chapel at all, but rather was meant to be a vault—note its rectangular shape. Its homeliness as a place of worship was not lost on Pope Sixtus IV, and he commissioned the frescoes that adorn its walls; the left wall shows the story of Moses, while the right side details the life of Jesus. Sixtus IV's successor and nephew, Pope Julius II, still wasn't pleased with the look of the place, so he asked Michelangelo to connect the two walls. Michelangelo, a sculptor by trade, had no interest in doing the ceiling, but the pope forced him to do it. (Indeed, if you study his figures, you'll see that they appear more like sculptures than paintings.)

Each of the scenes on the ceiling displays a different day in the Creation, as told in the book of Genesis. The crowning glory of the room is the tremendously powerful *Last Judgment,* commissioned years later by Pope Paul III, who insisted that it be painted over the altar (until that time, depictions of the Last Judgment had always been displayed at the church exit). Look for both the face of Michelangelo and St. Bartholomew, who's holding his own skin.

Debate has raged for years now over the ground-breaking cleansing of the ceiling, which took place during much of the 1980s. Only two individuals—the best art conservators in the world—were allowed to touch the priceless plaster. Some in the art world insist that Michelangelo's work has been forever altered, while others, myself included, are awe-struck by the stunning palate—and the creative use of shadow—that the restoration has uncovered. Compare the restored ceiling with the *Last Judgment* and decide for yourself. Indeed, there's a saying that older Romans keep themselves going by waiting for the day when the cleaners complete work on the *Last Judgment*. They're soon scheduled to begin the process.

There is no flash photography allowed, no guided-tour operating (briefings are conducted in the halls and museum rooms preceding the chapel), and—ostensibly—no talking allowed inside the Sistine Chapel.

Admission: Included in the 10,000-lira ($8.70) admission to the Vatican Museums.

Open: The Sistine Chapel is part of the Vatican Museums complex, and so follows the same hours (see above).

PAPAL AUDIENCES, piazza San Pietro.

Each Wednesday that the pope is in Rome, he speaks with the general public. The regular time for the pope's weekly public session is 11am—usually 10am during the summer. However, this can change from one week to the next, so be sure to check when you arrive in Rome.

Audiences take place outside in St. Peter's Square during the warmer months, and in various interior rooms when it's cold or wet; again, check when you pick up your tickets.

There are several ways to get tickets to see the pope, which, of course, are free. Tickets are rarely "sold out," but you must request them at least the day before.

The most convenient way to reserve tickets is to call the American Paulist fathers at the **Church of Santa Susanna,** via XX Settembre, 14 (tel. 482-7510), to reserve tickets, which must be picked up on Tuesday afternoon between 4 and 6pm. Via XX Settembre runs parallel to via Nazionale, one block farther away from the train station. Santa Susanna is on the block between via Orlando, which radiates from piazza della Repubblica, and via Torino.

Alternatively, you can contact the very helpful **Foyer Unitas,** via S. Maria dell'Anima, 30 (tel. 686-5951), to reserve tickets a few days before the event. (See "Organized Tours," below, for more information on this group.)

You can also reserve tickets at the **Prefettura,** up the stairs under the colonnade on the right side of St. Peter's Square as you face the basilica (where the ellipse meets the rectangular area directly in front of the church). The Prefettura is open Monday through Saturday from 9am to 1pm. Their address for written inquiries is: Prefettura della Casa Pontificia, Città del Vaticano 00120.

Finally, you can also work through the **Bishop's Office for United States Visitors to the Vatican,** via dell'Umiltà, 30, 00187 Roma (tel. 06/678-9184; fax 06/686-7561), but only by writing before you arrive in Rome or calling at least a week beforehand. In any case, it's best to have a letter of introduction from your local pastor.

If you can't make a Wednesday audience, you can catch up with the pope on Sunday promptly at noon, when he appears at his library window on St. Peter's Square to recite the Angelus, a traditional prayer, and issue his blessing to the world for that week.

CASTEL SANT' ANGELO, lungotevere Castello. Tel. 687-5036.

On the banks of the Tiber, and connected to the Vatican by a wall that includes a secret escape tunnel, is the imposing Castel Sant' Angelo. Built by the Emperor Hadrian in A.D. 139 as his mausoleum, it has subsequently served many purposes, at various times having been used as a fort, a prison (Cellini slept here, as did the notorious Cenci family), and most notably, a papal refuge. Highlights of the fortress include the weapons and uniform exhibits, Pauline Hall, the Perseus Room, and the Library.

Admission: 5,000 lire ($4.35).

Open: Mon 2–5:30pm, Tues–Sat 9am–1pm, Sun 9am–noon.

MUSEO DI VILLA GIULIA [Etruscan Museum], piazza Villa Giulia, 9. Tel. 320-1951 or 320-1993.

This fine museum happens to be situated in a lovely villa at one end of the Villa Borghese, Rome's main urban park. As archeological museums go, this one is rather impressive, home to the world's finest collection of Etruscan relics. No one is quite sure where the Etruscans came from or when or where they landed, but they apparently settled in southern Tuscany, where the artifacts that fill this museum were discovered. Scholars agree that they brought with them a highly developed culture, as evidenced by their exceptionally advanced art and sculpture. They are believed to have ruled Rome for a century or more beginning in the 7th century B.C.

The museum, packed with archeological treasures, offers a stunning window into their civilization, mostly in the form of pottery (downstairs), though there is also a fine collection of bronze implements (upstairs), and several outstanding larger sculpted pieces as well. The highlights of the first floor include the two figures of *Apollo* in Room 7, and the *Sarcofago degli Sposi* in Room 9, a remarkably well-preserved sarcophagus with a half-reclining married couple on top. Among the most impressive pieces upstairs is a two-foot-tall bronze figure in Room 15, *Veiovis di Monterazzano* from the 1st century A.D., found near Viterbo in October 1955, and an Etruscan chariot in Room 18.

Admission: 5,000 lire ($4.35).

Open: Tues–Sat 9am–7:30pm, Sun 9am–1pm. **Metropolitana:** Flaminio; then a good 30-minute walk or take bus no. 48. **Bus:** 910 from the train station, or 48 from the Flaminio Metropolitana stop.

GALLERIA BORGHESE, piazzale del Museo Borghese. Tel. 85-8577.

At the opposite end of the Villa Borghese park from the Etruscan Museum is the Galleria Borghese, with an excellent collection of both paintings and sculpture. Indeed, it's about the only good old-fashioned art museum in Rome. The first floor is home to Bernini's moving *Rape of Persephone*, as well as his *Apollo and Daphne*, and Canova's erotic sculpture of the housemaster herself, Pauline Bonaparte (Napoleon Bonaparte's sister). Upstairs you'll come upon Raphael's *Descent from the Cross;* paintings by Titian, Botticelli, and Rubens; and a wide collection of grim portraits by Caravaggio. Unfortunately, the building has been undergoing major renovation; parts of the museum may be closed this year.

Admission: Free.

Open: Tues–Sat 9am–2pm, Sun 9am–1pm. Last admission is 30 minutes before closing. **Bus:** 910 from the train station, or 56 from piazza Barberini or piazza Venezia, will take you to the park entrance closest to the museum. **Directions:** To get here from the Villa Giulia, walk around behind the museum along viale delle Belle Arti, past the Modern Art Museum on your left, and straight into the heart of the park on viale di Villa Giulia. When you get to the top of the hill, you'll see a path branching off to the left and a sign directing you to the Galleria Borghese. This very pleasant 20-minute amble looks longer on a map than it actually is.

BASILICA DI SAN GIOVANNI IN LATERANO [Saint John in Lateran], piazza San Giovanni in Laterano, 4. Tel. 698-6433.

The oldest church in Rome, San Giovanni in Laterano is the city's hometown cathedral, where the pope comes to celebrate mass on certain holidays. Indeed, the crimson building to the right as you face the church was the papal residence from the 4th through the 14th century.

Statues of the 12 Apostles line the main hall of the church. Those on the left (as you enter) are by Bernini, and those on the right by Borromini, the principal architect for most of the structure you see today.

Admission: Free.

Open: Daily 7am–6pm. **Metropolitana:** San Giovanni; then walk through the portal at the walls of Rome and the church will come into sight.

CHIESA DI SANTA MARIA DEGLI ANGELI [Saint Mary of the Angels], piazza della Repubblica. Tel. 488-0812.

Michelangelo converted part of the Baths of Diocletian into this church just around the corner from the Museo Nazionale Romano delle Terme. Its airy interior and beautiful marble floors are surrounded by huge paintings that would be the pride of any less-ornamented city.

Admission: Free.

Open: Daily 7:30am–noon and 4–6:30pm.

MORE ATTRACTIONS

CHIESA DI SAN PIETRO IN VINCOLI [Saint Peter in Chains], piazza di San Pietro in Vincoli, 4a. Tel. 488-2865.

The chains that held St. Peter, the patron saint of Rome, can be seen under the high altar of this church. The chief attraction is not the chains, however, but rather Michelangelo's fabulous, if unfinished, *Moses,* complete with a marvelously carved waist-length beard, and sitting on top of the tomb of Pope Julius II, to the right as you face the altar.

Among the treasures of the church are a piece of the table from the Last Supper (facing the apse door), the heads of Saints Paul and Peter (in the tabernacle), and a great bronze door from the Senate of the Roman Forum (now in the middle part of the main entrance).

Admission: Free.

Open: Daily 7am–12:30pm and 3:30–6pm. **Metropolitana:** Piazza Cavour; then walk left across via Giovanni Lanza to via di Monte. Polacco, trudge up the three endless flights of stairs that are this street, and turn right at the top (after a few hundred yards you'll come upon a piazza, and the church to the left). **Directions:** From the Colosseum, walk up largo Polveriera and go left on via Eudossiana to the church.

SANTUARIO SCALA SANTA, piazza San Giovanni in Laterano. Tel. 759-4619.

The building off to the left and across the street as you exit the Basilica of San Giovanni in Laterano houses the Holy Stairs (Scala Santa), the original 28 marble steps from Pontius Pilate's villa—now covered with wood for preservation—that Christ is said to have climbed on the day that he was condemned to death. According to a medieval tradition they were brought from Jerusalem to Rome by Constantine's mother, Helen, in 326, and the stairs have been in their present location since 1589. Today pilgrims from all over the world come here to climb the steps on their knees. This is one of the holiest sites in Christendom; please show respect for those worshipping here and refrain from talking or taking pictures.

Admission: Free.

Open: Daily 6:15am–12:30pm and 3–7pm. **Metropolitana:** San Giovanni; then walk through the portal at the walls of Rome and the church will come into sight.

BASILICA DI SAN CLEMENTE, piazza di San Clemente, via San Giovanni in Laterano. Tel. 731-5723.

While so much of Rome is glorious and monumental, a visit to the several layers of San Clemente will give you a feel of what it was like to have been an early Christian in Rome. Beneath this plain 12th-century structure are the remains of two earlier structures, dating from the 4th and 1st centuries A.D., respectively.

The medieval *Triumph of the Cross* mosaic in the apse of the church is particularly noteworthy, as are the two intact and well-preserved 11th-century frescoes: one, scenes from the legend of St. Alexis, and the other, St. Clement celebrating mass.

Admission: Main church, free; excavations, 2,000 lire ($1.75).

Open: Mon–Sat 9am–noon and 3:30–6pm, Sun 10am–noon and 3:30–6pm. **Directions:** San Clemente is located one long block from the Colosseum, and a 10-minute walk from the Chiesa di San Giovanni in Laterano.

BASILICA DI SANTA MARIA MAGGIORE [Saint Mary Major], piazza Santa Maria Maggiore. Tel. 48-3195.

One of the seven pilgrimage churches in Rome, this basilica houses relics of the Holy Crib below the altar and a 5th-century triumphal arch above the altar. Its other features include two richly decorated chapels, the right one in the Renaissance style, the left one baroque, and a stunning 13th-century mosaic in the apse. The ceiling is decorated with gold brought back from America by Columbus.

Admission: Free.

Open: Summer, daily 7am–8pm; winter, daily 7am–7pm. **Directions:** You can enter the church, which is situated a short walk from the train station, at either end, from piazza Santa Maria Maggiore in the front or via Cavour in the back.

CIMITERO MONUMENTALE DEI PADRI CAPPUCINI, via Veneto, 27.

This is perhaps the most unusual and unique sight in the country: Every inch of its walls and ceilings are adorned with the skeletal remains of 4,000 Capuchin friars who died between 1528 and 1870. It's of no special religious significance; their sign of explanation reads simply that these bones "speak eloquently to the visitors about the drama of a life which is passing" and urges prayer and meditation. This is a grisly, haunting, and curiously popular place.

Admission: 1,000 lire (90¢).

Open: Summer, daily 9am–noon and 3–6:30pm; winter, daily 9am–noon and 3–6pm. **Metropolitana:** Barberini; then walk up the right side of via Veneto and take the stairs on the right side of the Chiesa Immacolata Concezione at via Veneto, 27.

PARKS & GARDENS

Rome is a city of stone, not of green. Nonetheless, those who need a fix of fresh air should venture into the ✪ **Villa Borghese,** Rome's urban park, located on the north side of the Old City. You'll find some of the best views over Rome from the edge of the park here, as well as countless hills and trees and a duck pond inside the massive area. The park is best approached from the Spagna or Flaminio Metropolitana stations, on the south and west sides of the park, or by taking bus no. 910 from the station, or bus no. 56 from piazza Barberini or piazza Venezia, to the east side of the greenlands.

For other natural edification, turn to the **Vatican Gardens** (see "Top Attractions," above) or **Tivoli** (see "Easy Excursions," below).

ORGANIZED TOURS

INTENSIVE TOURS Rome's best tours—and, indeed, perhaps Europe's most remarkable guided visits—are free, and operated by Josefa Koet and Leideke Galema, two Dutch nuns who run the **Foyer Unitas Ecumenical Centre,** an ecumenical study center on the fourth floor of the Palazzo Pamphilj at via Santa Maria dell'Anima, 30 (tel. 686-5951), just off piazza Navona. Their tours and evening slide presentations were prompted by the fact that while there were countless Catholic groups in the city offering guidance and tours for Catholic visitors, there were few organizations catering to non-Catholic visitors. Their tours were designed with non-Catholics in mind, but travelers of any faith are welcome to join.

What's the catch? Well, these are not ordinary tours. They are for the budget traveler who has a serious and intense interest in the history and culture of this spectacular city—and in examining particular sights in great depth. They may spend an entire morning, for example, showing a group a single building, or one particular area of the Forum. They may spend hours discoursing on the history of one of the city's catacombs, or conducting a group through a few of the Vatican Museums. They don't rush from place to place, but rather relate to you everything they know about a particular place.

Sign up for these unique excursions only if you are ready and willing to give the kind of serious attention that these women deserve. If you are, you'll come away with a terrific educational experience, for an entirely voluntary contribution. The slate of topics for their slide presentations and walking tours (which usually go hand-in-hand) varies from one month to the next.

The Palazzo Pamphilj is one short block up via di Sant' Agnese in Agone from piazza Navona. If you're coming from corso Vittorio Emanuele, you'll find via Sant' Agnese on the left just past the fountain at the center of piazza Navona. They're open Monday through Friday from 9am to noon and then again from 4:30 until 6:30pm, and on Saturday from 9am to noon only. If you come at another time, you can take a program from the elevator door and call in a reservation later during office hours. You can simply show up at the date, time, and meeting point listed, but they recommend that you call to confirm, in case one of them is not feeling well, or museum hours have changed. Note that they do not operate their tours during July and August.

BUS TOURS   For the standard bus tour, my recommendation is **Carrani Tours,** via Vittorio Emanuele Orlando, 95 (tel. 488-0510 or 474-2501). They've been in the bus-tour business since 1927—about as long as buses have roamed the Roman roads. Their claim to fame today is that they offer a 20% discount to bearers of this book. Most of their 20 tours range in price from 32,000 to 38,000 lire ($27.85 to $33.05). You can pick up their brochure in just about every hotel and pensione in Rome, or at their headquarters a block up from piazza della Repubblica. Note that they'll usually come and pick you up at your hotel.

WALKING TOURS   Finally, the local **Ente Proviciale per il Turismo** has put together six half-day walking tours through various quarters of the city in the back pages of "Here Rome."

---

7. SAVVY SHOPPING

There's a value-added tax (called I.V.A.) in Italy on all consumer goods and most services. The average tax is 19%, but it goes as high as 35% on some luxury items. You are entitled to a refund of the tax paid if you spend more than 525,000 lire ($456.50) on one item. Remember to get a receipt from the shopkeeper. Show the invoice to the Customs official at the border (who can ask to see the goods) and he or she will stamp it and return it to you. Take the receipt home and mail it to the merchant within 90 days. Your refund will be mailed to you.

BEST BUYS   **Piazza di Spagna** is the most exclusive address in fashion in Rome. Along the streets to the west of the square, particularly **via Condotti,** you'll find all the best Italian and international names in clothing and footwear. Needless to say, prices in this high-rent neighborhood are as high as the fashion.

Rome's most popular—and most popularly priced—shopping area is **via Cola di Rienzo** near the Vatican, running from piazza del Risorgimento to the ponte Margherita. Walking along this mile-long strip, you'll pass scads of clothing, shoe, and souvenir shops, as well as pharmacies, supermarkets, and small department stores, all with prices considerably more moderate than those across the river. This is where the average middle-income Roman comes to shop. To get there, take the Metropolitana to Lepanto or Ottaviano.

Via Nazionale and **via del Corso** are also fine areas for window-shoppers (and those with fewer lire to spend, too). Here you'll find many of Rome's department stores.

Finally, **Old Rome,** particularly north of piazza Venezia and between piazza Navona and the Trevi Fountain, is the place to wander for handcrafts and one-of-a-kind shops and boutiques.

MARKETS   You can find everything from 17th-century candelabra and antique doorknockers to 5,000-lira ($4.35) cassette tapes and 20,000-lira ($17.40) shoes at Rome's seemingly endless flea market at ✪ **Porta Portese** in Trastevere. Count-

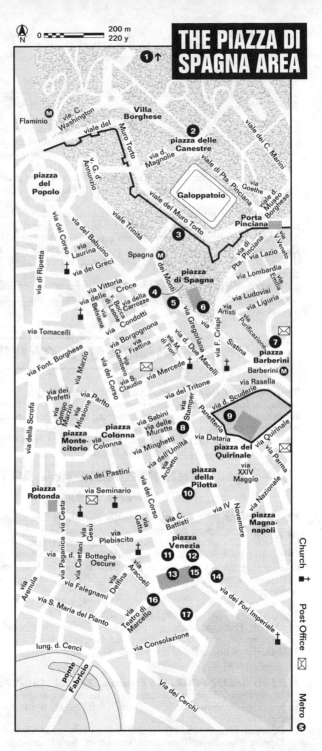

THE PIAZZA DI SPAGNA AREA

0 — 200 m
0 — 220 y

ROME
Piazza di Spagna

Campidoglio **16**
Fontana di Trevi **8**
Foro di Augusto **14**
Foro di Cesare **17**
Foro Traiano **12**
Galleria Borghese **1**
Monumento Vittorio Emanuele **13**
Palazzo Barberini **7**
Piazza di Spagna **4**
Piazza Venezia **11**
Quirinale **9**
Santa Maria Aracoeli **15**
Santa Trinità dei Monti **6**
Santi Apostoli **10**
Scalinata **5**
Villa Borghese **2**
Villa Medici **3**

Church ✝
Post Office ✉
Metro Ⓜ

less vendors and just plain folks set up shop here every Sunday from roughly 7 or 8am to about 1 or 2pm. Most of the wares (mostly clothes) on sale here are pretty chintzy and of little interest to the tourist, but the market is a sight in and of itself. Unlike the open-air market in Florence, you'll see precious few tourists and thousands of Romans. Still, watch out for pickpockets.

Bus no. 27 will take you here from the train station and downtown; get off at the second stop after the river, on via Ettore Rolli, just past the corner of via Panfilo Castaldi; the market, whose size varies with the meteorological and economic climate, stretches at least to via Pietro Ripari and piazza Ippolito Nievo, which is on the no. 170 bus line.

One of many markets specializing in flowers and produce is on **✪ piazza Campo de' Fiori.** Most vendors are here Monday through Saturday from 7 or 8am until 1:30pm.

A handful of pushcarts offering used books, etchings, lithographs, art reproductions, antique jewelry, and other old odds and ends and one-of-a-kind items sets up Monday through Saturday from 9am until about 6pm (4:30pm in winter) at **piazza Borghese,** near the ponte Cavour. To find them, walk out via Condotti from piazza di Spagna and continue for 2½ blocks past via del Corso on via della Fontanella Borghese.

Piazza Vittorio Emanuele, south of Stazione Termini, is the site of Rome's biggest daily open-air food market, open Monday through Saturday roughly from 8am to 2pm.

8. EVENING ENTERTAINMENT

This Week in Rome, a free magazine available from the concierge desks of top hotels, is full of current information on what's happening around town. *Trova Roma,* a weekly listings magazine inserted in the Thursday edition of *La Repubblica* newspaper, is indispensable for its coverage of movies, music, art, opera, dance, and the like. Most newsstands stock extra, free copies of *Trova Roma* in case you weren't able to pick it up on Thursday. Ask for it.

THE PERFORMING ARTS
OPERA & BALLET

TERME DI CARACALLA, via delle Terme di Caracalla.

✪ Open-air opera and ballet at the Terme di Caracalla are one of the great summer events of Europe. The stage is set amid the ruins of this one-time Roman bathhouse, which indeed often becomes part of the production. Usually they put on two operas and a ballet here each summer, with shows three or four times a week in July and August. Their production of *Aïda* is particularly memorable.

Prices: Tickets, 25,000–65,000 lire ($21.75–$56.50) for the opera, 20,000–50,000 lire ($17.40–$43.50) for the ballet.

Open: The main opera house ticket office on via Firenze, on the block between via Nazionale and via del Viminale (tel. 488-3641 for information), Tues–Sun 9:30am–6pm; box office at the Terme, 8–9:30pm on performance days. **Bus:** 93 from the train station to the Terme.

TEATRO DELL'OPERA, via Firenze, 72. Tel. 488-1755.

If there are no performances at the Terme di Caracalla when you visit, you can attend a performance at the Teatro dell'Opera, a plain, white building almost remarkable for its ugly facade.

Prices: Tickets, 15,000–100,000 lire ($13.05–$86.95).

Open: Box office, Tues–Sat 10am–4pm, Sun 10am–1pm.

JAZZ

Rome also sports a fair variety of small jazz clubs with frequent performances of local musicians (you'll find most of them listed in the entertainment sections of Italian newspapers).

One favorite is the **Saint Louis Music City,** via del Cardello, 13A (tel. 474-5076). A long cavernous club with a jazz stage to one end, this place also has a restaurant area and a pool table off to the side. Entrance is free, but you must become a club member first, a formality which will set you back 10,000 lire ($8.70). Happily, club owner Mario Ciampa has traditionally offered a 50% discount on memberships to bearers of this book. It's still not cheap, however. If you sit at one of the tables near the stage, expect to pay 5,000–10,000 lire ($4.35–$8.70) per drink. There's live music almost every night from 10:30pm or so. Via del Cardello is halfway between the Colosseum and via Cavour.

MOVIES

English-language movies in Italy are almost always dubbed. The one exception in Rome is at the ✪ **Pasquino,** in Trastevere at vicolo del Piede, 19A (tel. 580-3622), which maintains a cult following among American expatriates in Rome. Prices here are lower than at most other theaters, only 6,000 lire ($5.20) as opposed to 9,000 lire ($7.85) elsewhere in town. Films at the Pasquino change every day or two; check the local newspapers for listings.

CAFES & GELATERIAS

When in Rome, do as the Romans do. Enjoy a leisurely dinner at some hidden-away trattoria's outdoor tables, or while away the night at a café in a peaceful neighborhood.

The outdoor cafés on the pedestrians-only **piazza della Rotonda,** in the shadow of the Pantheon, are perhaps the best places to be on warm summer nights. Cappuccino prices are a steep 4,000 lire ($3.50). The long, oval **piazza Navona,** with the overly baroque fountain in the center, is also popular at night.

The **Spanish Steps** on piazza di Spagna are almost a sight in and of themselves. There are no cafés actually on the staircase, but on warm summer nights the place is abuzz with the sounds of (mostly) young people from all over the world just sitting around, hanging out, and generally having a good time.

And from piazza di Spagna it's always pleasant to stroll over to the **Fontana di Trevi** by night.

GELATERIA TRE SCALINI, piazza Navona, 28.

✪ The famous Gelateria Tre Scalini is the headline hangout on this square. Its most noteworthy dessert is *tartufo,* the ice-cream confection by which all other ice-cream confections in this gelato-rich country are judged. This homemade delicacy is the richest mound of chocolate you can imagine, packed with bittersweet chocolate chips and a cherry buried somewhere inside—or as some would say, a mound of bittersweet chocolate chips held together by a smidgen of chocolate ice cream all crowned with whipped cream.

Prices: Tartufo, 5,000 lire ($4.35) inside at the bar, 9,000 lire ($7.85) at an outdoor table.

Open: Summer, Thurs–Tues 8am–1:30am; winter, Thurs–Tues 8am–1am.

GIOLITTI, via Uffici del Vicario, 40. Tel. 679-4206.

✪ Some locals prefer the ice cream at Giolitti, a fancy café with a turn-of-the-century look with marble floors and hanging chandeliers, but no outdoor tables. It's on a small street between piazza Navona and piazza Colonna.

Prices: Cones (to go) 2,000–3,000 lire ($1.75–$2.60); sundaes (at a table) 6,000–10,000 lire ($5.20–$8.70).

Open: Tues–Sun 7am–2am.

CAFE GRECO, near the Spanish Steps.

Of the cafés near the Spanish Steps, the Café Greco is the standout, being the oldest in Rome.

Open: Mon–Sat 8am–8:40pm.

CAFE GELATERIA FONTANA DI TREVI, piazza Fontana di Trevi, 90.

This is the most popular of the several *gelaterie* (ice-cream shops) ringing the piazza. Try their *cornetto,* a chocolate-covered croissant stuffed with whipped cream, chocolate cream, or custard. Small pizzas and sandwiches are also sold here.

Open: Summer, daily 7am–2am; winter, Thurs–Tues 7am–midnight.

BARS

For a budget drink, you can't do better than the **Vineria Reggio,** on campo de' Fiori, 15 (tel. 654-3268). A quintessentially Roman place, this is both a wine store and a bar, specializing in small glasses of *prosecco* (sparkling wine) for only 1,500–2,000 lire ($1.30–$1.75). You can either drink standing along the long bar or seated at the wooden benches. Open Monday through Saturday from 9:30am to 2:30pm and 5pm to 1am.

Several other local favorites for nighttime drinks are along **via del Governo Vecchio,** a narrow back street near piazza Navona and the Chiesa Nuova. Among the cozy, little romantic cafés here are the **Enoteca il Piccolo** at no. 74–76, the **Creperie Mizzi** at no. 112, and **Il Merlo Maschio** at no. 12. This is one of the few areas in Rome—or in Italy, for that matter—where you can find a subdued, comfortable place to sit and leisurely enjoy a few drinks. Small snacks are also available. Most bars along this street are open every night until 2am.

TWO IRISH PUBS

It may seem absurd to recommend an Irish bar in an Italian city, but the fact is that Romans have few bars where they sit for hours over a few drinks. Rather, they'll pop in for 10 minutes on their way home, remain standing, and toss back a small glass of wine or an apéritif, often alone. And most bars close by about 9pm. Only at "foreign-style" pubs such as the two listed below can you find the atmosphere and conviviality—and even the tables—for the kind of lounging that North American, English, and Australian natives are accustomed to.

THE FIDDLER'S ELBOW, via della Olmata, 43.

This is just about a one-of-a-kind place in Rome, and as such is extremely popular. When I last visited, on a Thursday in midwinter, there was not a seat free. They also happen to be the biggest seller of Guinness in Italy. Via della Olmata begins at piazza Santa Maria Maggiore, on the side of the square farthest from the train station.

Prices: Half pint of beer 4,000 lire ($3.50); pint of beer 6,000 lire ($5.20).

Open: Tues–Sun 4:30pm–12:15am.

THE DRUID'S DEN, via San Martino ai Monti, 28.

Taped Irish music and lively conversation fill the air, Harp, Guinness, and Twyford fill the glasses, and young Romans fill the tables at this cozy hideaway near the train station where the walls are covered with Irish-pub icons. As you walk along via Merulana from piazza Santa Maria Maggiore, via San Martino ai Monti will be the second right; look for the green-lit arch on the right.

Prices: Half pint of beer 4,000 lire ($3.50); pint of beer 6,000 lire ($5.20); glass of wine 3,000 lire ($2.60).

Open: Daily 6pm–midnight.

DISCOS

One thing Romans who aren't millionaires don't do is dance much, since it can be prohibitively expensive: expect to spend 40,000–50,000 lire ($34.80–$43.50) just for entrance and a few drinks.

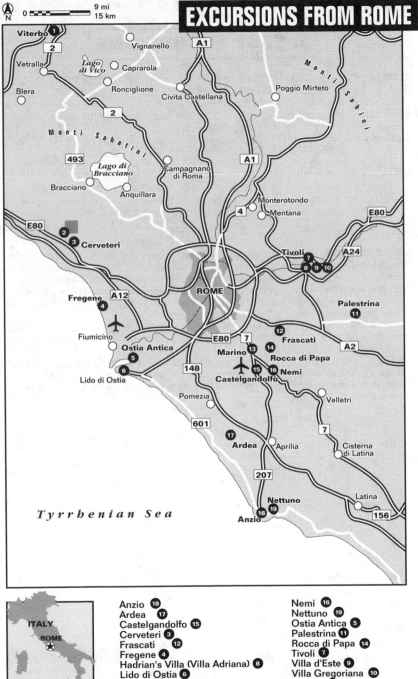

EXCURSIONS FROM ROME

0   9 mi
    15 km

Viterbo ①
Vignanello
② Vetralla
Lago di Vico
Caprarola
Blera
Ronciglione
Civita Castellana
Poggio Mirteto

Monti Sabatini

2

493
Lago di Bracciano
Campagnano di Roma
Bracciano
Anquillara
A1

Monterotondo
4   Mentana
E80

E80
② ③ Cerveteri

Tivoli ⑦
⑧ ⑨ ⑩
A24

Fregene
A12
④

Palestrina
⑪

Fiumicino
Ostia Antica
⑤

E80 7

⑫ Frascati
A2

Marino ⑬ ⑭
⑮ Rocca di Papa

Lido di Ostia
⑥
148
Castelgandolfo
⑯ Nemi

Pomezia

Velletri

601
⑰
Ardea
Aprilia

7
Cisterna di Latina

207

Latina

Nettuno
⑱ ⑲
Anzio
156

Tyrrhenian Sea

ITALY
ROME

Anzio ⑱		Nemi ⑯	
Ardea ⑰		Nettuno ⑲	
Castelgandolfo ⑮		Ostia Antica ⑤	
Cerveteri ③		Palestrina ⑪	
Frascati ⑫		Rocca di Papa ⑭	
Fregene ④		Tivoli ⑦	
Hadrian's Villa (Villa Adriana) ⑧		Villa d'Este ⑨	
Lido di Ostia ⑥		Villa Gregoriana ⑩	
Marino ⑬		Viterbo ①	
Necropolis of Cerveteri ②			

9. EASY EXCURSIONS

TIVOLI ✪ Tivoli is lov-e-ly, even if it is a bit worn out from all the tourists who flock here each day. The **Villa d'Este** (tel. 0774/2-2070), a delightful tiered water park built by Cardinal d'Este in the 16th century, is the more interesting of the two villas here. Amazingly enough, the villa's 500 fountains, conduits, and waterfalls operate entirely by gravity—quite an engineering feat. Nearby is the much older **Villa Adriana** (tel. 0774/53-0203), a motley collection of replicas of all the beautiful places that the Emperor Hadrian had seen in the world.

Both are open daily from 9am until an hour before sunset. Entrance is 5,000 lire ($4.35) for the Villa d'Este, 4,000 lire ($3.50) for the Adriana.

Tivoli is located some 45 minutes outside Rome, accessible by a bus marked "Autobus per Tivoli," which leaves every 15–20 minutes from via Gaeta just west of via Volturno, near Stazione Termini; fare is 2,500 lire ($2.20) each way. It's easiest to take the bus to the Villa d'Este, then take bus no. 2 or 4 from there to the Villa Adriana.

OSTIA ANTICA ✪ A vast, astonishingly well preserved ancient Roman city in a pastoral setting without any nearby sign of modernity, Ostia Antica captures the essence of Imperial Rome in the middle of the 2nd century A.D. It's especially worth visiting if you won't have a chance to go to Pompeii, for here you will see such dazzling details of Roman architecture as mosaic floors, marble walls, a few wall paintings—details and large missing from the Roman Forum.

Ostia Antica is open daily from 9am to 7pm March through September, and daily from 9am to 5pm the rest of the year. Last entrance is one hour before closing. Admission is 6,000 lire ($5.20).

To get to Ostia Antica, take the Metropolitana Line B to the Pyramide station and transfer there to a suburban train which connects with Ostia Antica in half an hour. When you arrive, walk onto a bridge over a highway and continue straight in that direction for 5–10 minutes.

SALZBURG

Salzburg is famous for its magnificent Alpine scenery, its perfectly preserved baroque inner city, and its music festivals, as well as for being Mozart's birthplace. Although it has only 150,000 inhabitants, it is one of the world's leading cultural centers, especially for classical music. A short journey by train or car from Munich, it's a convenient stopover for anyone traveling from Germany to Vienna or Italy. Like most European cities, it is divided by a river, the Salzach, into left and right banks, connected by 10 bridges. The names of both the town and the river derive from the salt mines in the region, which brought Salzburg fame and fortune.

Mozart's Birthplace on Getreidegasse is a magnet, attracting more than a million visitors each year. Every year in January, July, August, and on Easter, Wolfgang Amadeus's genius is celebrated in world-renowned music festivals, with such conductors in the past as Leonard Bernstein, James Levine, and Herbert von Karajan, and such singers as Fischer-Dieskau, Pavarotti, and Baltsa. Salzburg's perfectly preserved center on the left bank, with its baroque structures, its brooding fortress above the old city, its 17th-century streets, gaily flowered horsecarts, and strolling shoppers, many dressed in colorful dirndls, creates an enthralling setting and mood, made even more magical by the Alpine scenery on every side. The city, filled with architectural wonders, is known as the Austrian Rome. Little wonder that many travelers count Salzburg as one of Europe's most beautiful and charming towns.

---

1. FROM A BUDGET TRAVELER'S POINT OF VIEW

SALZBURG BUDGET BESTS In Salzburg, you'll find **open-air food and drink stalls**—called *Imbiss,* Quick Snack, Fast Food, or Würstelbude—at every second street corner. They sell wieners, hamburgers, sandwiches, Leberkäse, soft drinks, and beer (in cans) for much less than a restaurant would charge: a Coke is 15 S ($1.35); a hot dog, 25 S ($2.25); a beer, 24 S ($2.20). On a rainy or cold day, the **self-service counters** in department stores, butcher shops, or youth hostels can be considerable moneysavers. One of the most central and easiest to find is **Bosna,** Getreidegasse 40, a block from Mozart's Birthplace.

Finally, it can be very relaxing and enjoyable indeed to sit in the small open-air café at **Mirabellgarten,** Salzburg's most scenic and popular public park and garden, sipping a small beer and munching a buttered roll—total cost is 40 S ($3.65)—while admiring the surrounding baroque buildings, the Hohensalzburg silhouette, and the Alpine skyline (and the pigeons hunting for your breadcrumbs).

WHAT THINGS COST IN SALZBURG	U.S. $
Taxi from the airport to the train station or hotel	10.90
Public transportation (bus or trolleybus)	1.65
Local telephone call	.09
Double room, with continental breakfast, at the Hotel Zum Hirschen (deluxe)	142.00
Double room, with continental breakfast, at the Goldene Krone (moderate)	77.25
Double room, with continental breakfast, at Pension Bergland (budget)	42.70
Lunch for one, without wine, at Sternbräu (moderate)	9.00
Lunch for one, without wine, at Mensa im Mozarteum (budget)	4.55
Dinner for one, without wine, at K & K (deluxe)	22.00
Dinner for one, without wine, at Wienerwald (moderate)	10.00
Dinner for one, without wine, at Wilder Mann (budget)	7.00
Half liter of beer	1.90
Glass of wine (one-eighth liter)	2.00
Coca-Cola (in a restaurant)	1.70
Cup of coffee with milk (in a restaurant)	2.40
Roll of ASA 100 color film, 36 exposures	6.25
Admission to Mozart's Birthplace	4.55
Movie ticket	5.90–7.70
Concert ticket (to Festspielhaus)	19.10

Make sure to visit the City Tourist Office, Mozartplatz 5 (tel. 0662/847568), for up-to-date information on **free events** such as concerts or folklore evenings that may take place during your stay. During the summer months, for example, there are free brass-band concerts in the Mirabellgarten on Wednesday evening at 8:30pm and on Sunday at 10:30am. There are also free concerts given throughout the school year by students at the music school Mozarteum.

SPECIAL DISCOUNT OPPORTUNITIES   There are **discounts** on admission fees to museums and reduced cable-car fares granted to students and children under 15, provided you can show proof of age (passport) or an International Student ID Card. These reductions vary from 20% to 50%.

Anyone under 26 can purchase heavily reduced rail and flight tickets by contacting **Ökista,** Wolf-Dietrich-Strasse 31 (tel. 0662/883252), open Monday through Friday from 9:30am to 5:30pm.

WORTH THE EXTRA BUCKS   Salzburg is famous throughout the world for its music, presented throughout the year in a number of **festivals and concerts.** Tickets to these concerts are not always inexpensive and are not even always available unless you order them months in advance. But it's worth the effort and the money to take advantage of being in one of the music capitals of the world. See "Special and Free Events" in "Attractions" and "Evening Entertainment," below, for more information.

WHAT'S SPECIAL ABOUT SALZBURG

Music

☐ The Salzburg Festival in August, one of the world's best for classical music and opera.

☐ Concerts almost daily in Mirabell Palace, the Residenz, or the Fortress.

☐ Other festival extravaganzas throughout the year.

Film Locations

☐ *The Sound of Music*, filmed at Schloss Leopoldskron (closed to the public), the Nonnberg Abbey, Festspielhaus, and Mirabell Garden.

Romantic Walk

☐ Along the Salzach River at night, with a view of floodlit Hohensalzburg Fortress.

Architectural Highlights

☐ Hohensalzburg Fortress, a medieval landmark above the city.

☐ The Residenz, residence of the archbishop of Salzburg, rebuilt in the baroque style.

☐ The Dom (cathedral), the finest example of an early baroque building north of the Alps.

☐ Hellbrunn Palace, a summer residence for the archbishops and famous for its trick fountains.

☐ Churches in Salzburg by famed architect Fischer von Erlach, including the Collegiate Church, Holy Trinity Church, and St. John's Hospital Church.

2. PRETRIP PREPARATIONS

DOCUMENTS   All Canadian and U.S. citizens need for entry into Austria for stays up to 90 days is a valid passport.

WHAT TO PACK   For your ideal wardrobe, see the Vienna chapter.

WHEN TO GO   Salzburg's season is all year around. In fact, winter is one of the most beautiful times of year, when a fresh blanket of snow covers the hills surrounding the city. Summers are pleasant and are rarely so hot that they're uncomfortable. The main tourist season is during the months of July, August, and September, when many hotels in the medium and upper range raise their rates.

Salzburg's Average Daily Temperature & Rainfall

	Jan	Feb	Mar	Apr	May	June	July	Aug	Sept	Oct	Nov	Dec
Temp. (°F)	28	35	37	45	55	64	68	67	60	50	39	33
Rainfall ″	2.5	2.6	2.8	3.5	5.3	6.8	7.5	6.4	3.6	2.9	2.7	2.7

Special Events   There are annual music festivals in Salzburg throughout the year. The year kicks off with **Mozart Week,** held at the end of January, followed by the **Salzburg Easter Festival.** Most famous is the **Salzburg Festival,** which is held throughout August and has a history stretching back 70 years. It features opera, plays, concerts, chamber music, and a number of other events. Autumn brings the **Salzburg Cultural Days,** a two-week musical event held in October with more opera, ballet, and concerts. Since these festivals are very popular, you should make hotel reservations at least a month in advance if you wish to visit Salzburg during these times, especially in August.

3. ORIENTATION & GETTING AROUND

ARRIVING IN SALZBURG

FROM THE AIRPORT **Flughafen Airport,** Innsbrucker Bundesstrasse 95 (tel. 8055-0), a mile southwest of the city, is larger than Innsbruck's and much smaller than Munich's. Daily flights are operated to and from Frankfurt, London (Heathrow), Amsterdam, Paris, Zurich, and Vienna. Bus no. 77 takes you to Salzburg's main train station for 18 S ($1.65); taxis charge 120 S ($10.90) for the same trip.

FROM THE TRAIN STATION Salzburg is about 2½ hours from Munich by train, and about 3 hours from Vienna. All trains arrive at the **Hauptbahnhof** (main train station) on the right bank of the city center at Südtiroler Platz (tel. 1717). Buses depart from Südtiroler Platz to various parts of the city, including the Old City (*Altstadt*) across the river. It's about a 20-minute walk from the Hauptbahnhof to the heart of Alstadt.

BY CAR If you come by car, ask the hotel proprietor where the nearest garage is located. Street parking for cars is practically impossible, especially on the left bank with its narrow streets and pedestrians-only zones.

INFORMATION

There's a small **tourist information kiosk** on Platform 10 of the Hauptbahnhof, Südtiroler Platz (tel. 0662/87 17 12 or 87 36 38), where you can pick up a free map or obtain hotel reservations by paying a 50-S ($4.55) deposit per person that goes toward your hotel payment. In addition, there's also a 25-S ($2.25) fee for the service. This office is open during the winter, daily from 8:45am to 7:30pm; in the summer, daily from 8:30am to 8:30pm (to 9:30pm in July and August). Be sure to pick up a free map of the city.

The main **City Tourist Office (Stadtverkehrsbüro)** is located in the heart of the Old City at Mozartplatz 5 (tel. 0662/84 75 68, 88987-330 or 88987-331). Open in the summer daily from 8am to 8pm, and in the winter daily from 9am to 6pm, it also books hotel rooms, hands out free city maps and brochures, and sells sightseeing, concert, and theater tickets. Be sure to pick up a free copy of *Wochenspiegel*, which lists what's going on in Salzburg's many music halls. There's also a brochure printed monthly that lists the various concerts.

In the same office is also a counter for Salzburger Land, the province of Salzburg. Stop here for information on the region outside the city, including Untersberg and Hallein.

CITY LAYOUT

Most attractions are located on the left bank of the Salzach River, in the **Old City (Altstadt).** Much of the Alstadt is now a pedestrian zone, including Getreidegasse with its many shops, Domplatz, and Mozartplatz. The Altstadt is where you'll find such attractions as Mozarts Geburtshaus (Mozart's Birthplace), the Festival House complex, the cathedral, the Catacombs of St. Peter, the Haus der Natur (Museum of Natural History), and Salzburg's landmark, the Hohensalzburg Fortress. In fact, it's the **Hohensalzburg,** towering above the Altstadt on a sheer cliff, that makes Salzburg such a beautiful city, even from afar. It's lit up at night, making a walk along the **Salzach River** one of the most romantic in Austria.

The **Hauptbahnhof** is located on the opposite (right) side of the Salzach River, about a 20-minute walk from the Altstadt. This part of the city is newer and also contains the Mirabellgarten and a number of hotels and shops.

GETTING AROUND

BY PUBLIC TRANSPORTATION   A quick, comfortable public transportation system is provided by 14 bus lines, charging 18 S ($1.65) per ticket or 60 S ($5.45) for a set of five, which reduces the single-trip price to $1.10. Tickets are good for a single journey, including transfers to reach your final destination. If you think you'll be traveling a lot by bus, you might also wish to purchase a 24-hour ticket for 48 S ($4.35) or a three-day pass for 96 S ($8.70), which allows you to use all of Salzburg's buses, ride the funicular up to the fortress, take the Mönchsberg lift and the tramway (Salzburg-Bergheim). Note that children the age of 6 can travel for free on Salzburg's buses and that children 6–15 years of age can travel for half the prices quoted above.

You can purchase only single tickets from bus drivers. Sets of five reduced-fare tickets and the one- and three-day passes can be purchased from more than 120 tobacco shops throughout the city, marked with a sign that says TABAK TRAFIK. For more information about Salzburg's public transportation system, call 20551.

BY TAXI   Average taxi fare from the train station to a hotel or private home within the city limits is 80 S ($7.25), and 120 S ($10.90) to the airport or into the outskirts. Fares start at 30 S ($2.70) as soon as you climb into a taxi; luggage is an extra 5 S (45¢) each. To telephone for a taxi, call 8111 or 76111.

ON FOOT   Walking around Salzburg, especially in the Old City on the left bank, with its many pedestrian zones, is a pleasure. In fact, because Salzburg is rather small and compact, you can walk to most of its major attractions. One of the best walks in the city is along the top of Mönchsberg from Café Winkler to the fortress, about a 30-minute walk.

BY BICYCLE   Cycling is becoming more and more popular in Salzburg, evident from the ever-increasing bike paths through the city. If you feel like a long ride, try the bike path beside the Salzach River that goes all the way to Hallein, nine miles away.

You can rent bicycles year round at the Hauptbahnhof (train station) at Counter 3 (tel. 8887-5427). About 30 standard bikes are available (no racing bikes or mountain bikes) for 90 S ($8.20) a day. If you have a Eurailpass or a ticket valid for that day, the cost is only 45 S ($4.10).

BY CAR   It's much less expensive if you arrange for car rental before coming to Europe. If you need a car in Salzburg, go to **Hertz,** Ferdinand-Porsche-Strasse 7 (tel. 87 66 74), across the street from the train station near the Hotel Europa, or to their airport office (tel. 85 20 86). Both offices are open Monday through Friday from 8am to 6pm and on Saturday from 8am to 1pm (the airport branch is open on Sunday too, from 9am to noon and 3 to 9pm). Daily rental of a Fiat Panda is 350 S ($31.80), plus 20% tax and 3.50 S (30¢) per kilometer.

Nearby is **Avis,** Ferdinand-Porsche-Strasse 7 (tel. 87 72 78). It's open Monday through Friday from 7:30am to 6pm and on Saturday and Sunday from 9am to noon, and charges 846 S ($76.90) for a one-day rental of an Opel Corsa, including unlimited mileage and 20% tax. However, because there are often special weekend prices and other promotions, it pays to shop around.

FAST FACTS: SALZBURG

Babysitters   Students at Salzburg's university earn extra money by babysitting. Call 8044-6002, Monday through Thursday from 9am to noon and 1:30 to 3:30pm, and on Friday from 9am to noon.

Banks   Banks are open Monday through Friday from 8am to noon and 2 to 4:30pm. If you need to **exchange money** outside these hours, try the Wechselstube (Exchange Office; tel. 804 85 50) at the Hauptbahnhof, open daily from 7am to 10pm in summer and from 7:30am to 9pm in winter. You can also exchange money at the post office in the train station, open 24 hours, as well as at the main post office, Residenzplatz 9 (tel. 844127), Monday through Friday from 7am to 7pm and on Saturday from 8 to 10am. The **American Express** office is at Mozartplatz 5-7 (tel. 84 25 01), right next to the tourist office. It's open Monday through Friday from 9am to 5:30pm and on Saturday from 9am to noon.

Business Hours   Shops are usually open Monday through Friday from 9am to 6pm (some close for an hour or two at noon) and on Saturday from 9am to noon. On the first Saturday of the month (called *langer Samstag*), many shops remain open until 5pm.

Consulates   The **U.S. Consulate General** is at Gisela Kai 51 (tel. 28601), open Monday through Friday from 9 to 11am and 2 to 4pm. The **Consulate of the United Kingdom** is at Alter Markt 4 (tel. 84 81 33), open Monday through Friday from 9am to noon.

Currency   The Austrian currency is the **Schilling,** written ASch, ÖS, or simply **S** (as I have). A Schilling is made up of 100 **Groschen** (which are seldom used). Coins are minted as 2, 5, 10, and 50 Groschen, and 1, 5, 10, and 20 Schilling. Banknotes appear as 20, 50, 100, 500, 1,000, and 5,000 Schilling.

Dentists and Doctors   If you need a doctor or dentist, your best bet is to head to one of Salzburg's hospitals; the largest is the St. John's Hospital, Müllner Hauptstrasse 48 (tel. 4482-0). Or ask your hotel concierge for the address of the hospital closest you, or inquire at your consulate. If you need an English-speaking doctor during the weekend, call 141.

Emergencies   For the police, phone 133; to report a fire, 120. For urgent medical assistance on the weekend, or an English-speaking doctor, call 141; for an ambulance, 144.

Two pharmacies useful to travelers are the 400-year-old Alte Hofapotheke, Alter Markt 6 (tel. 843623), a wonderful old-world drugstore a few blocks from the Mozart house; and Salvator Apotheke, Mirabellplatz 5 (tel. 87 14 11). Both are open Monday through Friday from 8am to 12:30pm and 2:30 to 6pm, and on Saturday from 8am to noon. The names and addresses of pharmacies that are open on Saturday afternoon, Sunday, and holidays are posted in every pharmacy window (they take turns staying open weekends).

Holidays   Holidays celebrated in Salzburg are New Year's Day (Jan 1), Epiphany (Jan 6), Easter Monday, Labor Day (May 1), Ascension Day, Whit Monday, Corpus Christi, Assumption Day (Aug 15), Austria Day (Oct 26), All Saints' Day (Nov 1), Immaculate Conception (Dec 8), and Christmas (Dec 25–26).

Hospitals   Hospitals in Salzburg include St. John's Hospital, Müllner Hauptstrasse 48 (tel. 4482-0); Accident Hospital, Dr.-Franz-Rehrl-Platz 5 (tel. 6580-0); Hospital of the Barmherzigen Brüder, Kajetanerplatz 1 (tel. 84 45 31-0); and Diakonissen Hospital, Imbergstrasse 31 (tel. 87 75 81-0).

Information   The main tourist office is located at Mozartplatz 5 (tel. 84 75 86). For more information, refer to "Orientation and Getting Around," above.

Laundry   There's a self-service laundry located on Südtirolerplatz in front of the train station: Constructa, Kaiserschützenstrasse 10 (tel. 87 62 53), open Monday through Friday from 6:30am to 7pm and on Saturday from 6:30am to 1pm. It charges 102 S ($9.25) for 6 kilos (13¼ lb.) washed and dried.

Lost and Found   All lost-and-found objects are registered with the Polizei (police) at Alpen Strasse 90. The Fundbüro (tel. 29511-2330 or 29511-2331) is the lost-and-found office, open Monday through Friday from 7:30am to 12:30pm. Phone information is given Monday through Friday from 7:30am to 3:30pm.

Mail   The main post office (Hauptpostamt) is located in the center of the Old City at Residenz Platz 9 (tel. 844 12 10). It's open Monday through Friday from 7am to 7pm and on Saturday from 8 to 10am. Have your mail sent here for Poste Restante. There's a branch post office beside the train station at Südtiroler Platz (tel. 70 55 10), open 24 hours daily. Postcards to North America cost 8.50 S (75¢), while airmail letters cost 10 S (90¢), plus 1.50 S (14¢) for each gram.

Photographic Needs   For film or quick development of prints, there's a Herlango photo shop at Schwarzstrasse 10 (tel. 87 36 41), located on the right bank of the Salzach River between Staatsbrücke and Makartsteg bridges. It's open Monday through Friday from 8:30am to 6pm and on Saturday from 8:30am to noon (to 5pm on the first Saturday of the month).

Police   The emergency number for the police is 133.

Shoe Repair   There's a Mister Minit, which provides quick service for shoe repairs, in a shopping mall called Kiesel-Passage at the corner of Rainer and Elisabethstrasse, about a two-minute walk from the Hauptbahnhof. It's open Monday through Friday from 9am to 6:30pm and on Saturday from 9am to 1pm.

Tax   Government tax and service charge are already included in restaurant and hotel bills. If you have purchased goods for more than 1,000 S ($90.90), you're entitled to a refund of part of the Value-Added Tax; see "Savvy Shopping," below.

Taxis   See "Orientation and Getting Around," above.

Telephone   Telephone booths are painted silver with a yellow top and are found on major roads and squares. For **local calls,** use a 1-S (9¢) coin for each minute—insert more coins to avoid being cut off (unused coins will be returned).

Note that telephone numbers are gradually being changed in Salzburg. If you have problems making a connection or need a number, dial 08 for information. And if you come across a number with a dash, as in 6580-0, the number after the dash is the extension number. Simply dial the entire number.

Because hotels add a surcharge to telephone calls made from guest rooms, make your **international calls** from a post office. The cost of a three-minute call to the United States is 54 S ($4.90). If you're going to make a lot of local calls or wish to make

THE SCHILLING & THE DOLLAR

At this writing $1 = approximately 11 S (or 1 S = 9¢), and this was the rate of exchange used to calculate the dollar values given in this chapter (rounded to the nearest nickel). This rate fluctuates from time to time and may not be the same when you travel to Austria. Therefore the following table should be used only as a guide:

S	U.S.$	S	U.S.$
1	.09	100	9.09
2	.18	150	13.63
3	.27	200	18.18
4	.36	250	22.72
5	.45	300	27.27
6	.54	350	31.82
7	.64	400	36.36
8	.73	450	40.90
9	.82	500	45.45
10	.91	600	54.54
15	1.36	700	63.63
20	1.81	800	72.72
25	2.27	900	81.81
50	4.54	1,000	90.90

international calls from a pay phone, purchase a **telephone card** from any post office, available in values of 50 S ($4.55) or 100 S ($9.10); then just insert the card into slots of special telephones found virtually everywhere.

Salzburg's **city telephone code** is 0662 within Austria, 662 if you're calling Salzburg from another country.

Tipping   A service charge is included in hotel and restaurant bills, and taxi fares. Still, it's customary to round up to the nearest 10 S (95¢) for both restaurant bills and taxi fares. If you feel a tip is necessary, add only 10% to any bill.

4. BUDGET ACCOMMODATIONS

Most of Salzburg's budget accommodations are located on the outskirts of town and in neighboring villages, easily reached in less than 30 minutes by bus. The cheapest rooms are those rented out in private homes, with a shared bathroom down the hall. However, they are usually equipped with a sink and are clean.

A bit higher priced are bathless doubles in smaller pensions (often called a *Gasthof* or *Gästehaus*). Not surprisingly, prices are usually higher for establishments more centrally located. In addition, many of the higher-priced accommodations charge even more during peak season, from July through September. In January, when tourism is at its lowest, some hotels close down completely.

If the recommendations below are full, the **Salzburg City Tourist Office** at the train station and on Mozartplatz will book a room for you for a fee and deposit.

Remember that telephone numbers are being changed in Salzburg. If you can't reach any of the accommodations below, dial 08 for information.

DOUBLES (IN PRIVATE HOMES) FOR LESS THAN 445 S ($40.45)

These accommodations are in private homes, which sometimes offer less privacy but are good opportunities for getting to know the Austrians better. Note, however, that they all prefer guests to stay longer than one night.

IN THE CITY

FRAU BRIGITTE LENGLACHNER, Scheibenweg 8, 5020 Salzburg. Tel. 0662/43 80 44 or 38044. 6 rms (2 with shower and toilet).

$ Rates (including continental breakfast and showers): 270 S ($24.55) single without shower or toilet; 440 S ($40) double without shower or toilet, 500 S ($45.45) double with shower and toilet; 650 S ($59.10) triple without shower or toilet. No credit cards.

This small two-story cottage is owned by a traditionalist who wears dirndl costumes and speaks English. Look at her guestbook—it's full of praise. Rooms, all with sinks, are pleasant and spotlessly clean, and have the look of traditional Austria. In addition to the rooms listed above there's also a double room equipped with a bunk bed for 400 S ($36.35). This place is very popular, so try to reserve in advance. It's a 10-minute walk from the Hauptbahnhof, across the Salzach River via Pioniersteg bridge.

FRAU HILDE RADISCH, Scheibenweg 5, 5020 Salzburg. Tel. 0662/32 99 32. 3 rms (none with bath).

F **FROMMER'S SMART TRAVELER: HOTELS**
VALUE-CONSCIOUS TRAVELERS SHOULD
TAKE ADVANTAGE OF THE FOLLOWING:

1. Winter discounts offered by medium- and upper-range hotels.
2. Lower prices charged for accommodations in surrounding villages.
3. Accommodations offering cooking facilities, which help save on dining bills.

QUESTIONS TO ASK IF YOU'RE ON A BUDGET

1. Is there an extra charge for taking a shower?
2. Is breakfast included in the price?
3. How much is the surcharge on local and long-distance calls?

$ Rates (including continental breakfast and showers): 260 S ($23.65) single; 420 S ($38.20) double. No credit cards.
Located a 10-minute walk from the Hauptbahnhof right down the street from Frau Lenglachner, listed above, this is another good choice in private accommodations. Frau Radisch, a talkative septuagenarian, has an ivy-covered two-story house with a garden. She has one single room (without a sink) and two double rooms with a sink and adorned with such antiques as a coffee grinder and kitchen scales.

FRAU TRUDE POPPENBERGER, Wachtelgasse 9, 5020 Salzburg. Tel. 0662/43 00 94. 2 rms (neither with bath).
$ Rates (including continental breakfast): 250 S ($22.70) single; 400 S ($36.35) double. Showers 20 S ($1.80) extra. No credit cards.
Frau Poppenberger offers two rooms with balcony in her private home. She will pick you up at the train station, and her husband speaks fluent English. It's a 20-minute walk from the Hauptbahnhof, across the Salzach River.

RUDY AND FRIEDL SIMMERLE, Wachtelgasse 13, 5020 Salzburg. Tel. 0662/35 67 95. 2 rms (1 with toilet).
$ Rates (including continental breakfast): 400 S ($36.35) double. Showers 20 S ($1.80) extra. No credit cards.
The Simmerles are a retired couple who speak fluent English. Their two rooms—one with its own toilet and the other with a sink—are large and well furnished. Living here is like being their guest, and if you phone one or two days in advance and let them know when you're arriving, they'll come pick you up after receiving a second phone call confirming that you've arrived. This home is in the northwestern part of the city, a 20-minute walk from the Hauptbahnhof, across the Salzach River.

IN THE OUTSKIRTS

EVELYN TRUHLAR, Lettensteig 11, 5082 Fürstenbrunn. Tel. 06246/ 3377 or 73377. 1 rm (with shower and toilet). **Bus:** 1 from the Hauptbahnhof to Hanuschplatz, then 60 from Hanuschplatz to the last stop in Fürstenbrunn.
$ Rates (including continental breakfast): 400 S ($36.35) double; 760 S ($69.10) quad. No credit cards.
Last but certainly not least in this list of inexpensive accommodations is Evelyn's spacious room with its very modern bathroom and a huge terrace with a panoramic view. The owner, who has managed Bob's Bavarian Tours for more than 15 years,

speaks excellent English and knows Salzburg in and out; she'll even pick you up at the station. This is one of the best bargains around, and the tiny village of Fürstenbrunn should appeal to those who enjoy the countryside and walks through the woods.

FRAU ELFRIEDE KERNSTOCK, Karolingerstrasse 29, 5020 Salzburg. Tel. 0662/82 74 69. 6 rms (4 with shower and toilet). **Bus:** 77 from the Hauptbahnhof to Karolingerstrasse.

$ Rates (including continental breakfast and showers): 440 S ($40) double without shower or toilet, 500 S ($45.45) double with shower and toilet; 750 S ($68.20) triple with shower and toilet; 1,000 S ($90.90) quad with shower and toilet. No credit cards.

Located on the western edge of town, this beautiful private bungalow has handpainted furniture, spacious rooms and closets, and very clean toilets. One of the rooms with private bathroom has a small kitchen; another has a balcony. If she's not busy with guests, English-speaking Frau Kernstock will pick you up at the bus stop if you call from the station. While you are having breakfast, you'll hear the soundtrack from *The Sound of Music*.

FRAU MATHILDE LINDNER, Kasern am Berg 64, 5020 Salzburg. Tel. 0662/45 66 81 or 45 67 73. 8 rms (none with bath). **Bus:** 1, 2, 5, or 6 from the Hauptbahnhof to Mirabellplatz, then 15 from Mirabellplatz to Kasern (15 minutes); then a 10-minute walk uphill.

$ Rates (including continental breakfast and showers): 350 S ($31.80) double; 600 S ($54.55) quad. No credit cards.

This nice Alpine cottage is on top of a high hill northeast of Salzburg with a great view of the mountains. Four of the rooms have access to a balcony, and there's a garden for sunbathing. The rooms are furnished with beds made of wood, wardrobes, chairs, tables, and sinks. Frau Lindner will pick you up from the station; if you're arriving by car, take the Autobahn Nord exit. If you have a Eurailpass, you can ride for free on a local train from the Salzburg train station to Kasern, a four-minute ride. Families are welcome.

FRAU MOSER, Kasern am Berg 59, 5020 Salzburg. Tel. 0662/45 66 76. 4 rms (none with bath). **Bus:** 1, 2, 5, or 6 from the Hauptbahnhof to Mirabellplatz, then 15 from Mirabellplatz to Kasern (15 minutes); then a 10-minute walk uphill.

$ Rates (including continental breakfast and showers): 160 S ($14.55) single; 330–350 S ($30–$31.80) double. No credit cards.

Frau Moser's husband is a hunter, evident from the more than 100 antlers that decorate the walls of this private home. Not far from Frau Lindner's, above, it also offers a great view of Salzburg, and its upper-priced doubles have their own balcony. The breakfast room has a panoramic view of the Alpine scenery as well, and there is a terrace and garden. If you telephone, she'll pick you up from the station.

FRAU ROSEMARIE STEINER, Moosstrasse 156c, 5020 Salzburg. Tel. 0662/83 00 31. 6 rms (3 with shower and toilet). **Bus:** 1 from the Hauptbahnhof to Hanuschplatz, then 60 from Hanuschplatz to Kaserer (about 20 minutes); then a couple of minutes' walk.

$ Rates (including continental breakfast and showers): 210 S ($19.10) single without shower or toilet; 360 S ($32.70) double without shower or toilet, 400 S ($36.35) double with shower and toilet. No credit cards.

This modern three-story house south of town offers adequately furnished and clean rooms, three of which have balconies. There's also a TV lounge, and the owner, who speaks English, is happy to give sightseeing advice.

GÄSTEHAUS GASSNER, Moosstrasse 126b, 5020 Salzburg. Tel. 0662/ 82 49 90. 9 rms (7 with shower and toilet). **Bus:** 1 from the Hauptbahnhof to Hanuschplatz, then 60 from Hanuschplatz to Felleitner (10 minutes).

$ Rates (including continental breakfast): 400 S ($36.35) double without shower or toilet, 440–500 S ($40–$45.45) double with shower and toilet. No credit cards.

This modern home is south of the city, with well-furnished, clean, spacious rooms, some with TV and telephone. The breakfast room faces a field, and there's an outdoor terrace where guests can eat breakfast in the summer. Except in the morning, someone will pick you up at the station.

DOUBLES (IN PRIVATE HOMES) FOR LESS THAN 510 S ($46.35)

IN THE CITY

FRAU MARIA RADERBAUER, Schiesstattstrasse 65, 5020 Salzburg. Tel. 0662/43 93 63. 5 rms (3 with shower and toilet).
$ Rates (including continental breakfast and showers): 270 S ($24.55) single without shower or toilet; 500 S ($45.45) double without or with shower and toilet; 750 S ($68.20) triple with private shower and toilet across the hall. No credit cards.
This two-story private house in a quiet neighborhood is surrounded by rose bushes and has sparkling-clean rooms. The triple room has a balcony, as well as its own bathroom across the hall. Frau Raderbauer will pick up guests at the station. The house is a 20-minute walk from the Hauptbahnhof, across the Salzach River via Pioniersteg Bridge and across the park.

IN THE OUTSKIRTS

BLOBERGERHOF, Hammerauerstrasse 4, 5020 Salzburg. Tel. 0662/83 02 27. 6 rms (all with shower and toilet). **Bus:** 1 from the Hauptbahnhof to Hanuschplatz, then 60 from Hanuschplatz to Kaserer (about 20 minutes); then a couple of minutes' walk.
$ Rates (including continental breakfast): 350 S ($31.80) single; 500 S ($45.45) double. No credit cards.
This Salzburg-style farmhouse is managed by a mother-and-daughter team who receive repeated kudos from readers. Its rooms are spacious and it's neat as a pin. They raise chickens, so you can always be assured of fresh eggs. They will pick you up at the station.

FRAU MARIANNE SCHOIBL, Saalachstrasse 6, 5020 Salzburg. Tel. 0662/42 21 59. 3 rms (all with shower). **Bus:** 1 from the Hauptbahnhof to Leiner/Stadium, then 29 to Saalachstrasse.
$ Rates (including continental breakfast): 480 S ($43.65) double. No credit cards.
The ideal place for a long stay, this small and cozy bungalow-type private home is located in a very quiet area northwest of town. The host is very helpful. The rate includes use of a kitchenette with a refrigerator and other equipment.

DOUBLES FOR LESS THAN 550 S ($55)

IN THE CITY

GASTHOF JAHN, Elisabethstrasse 31, 5020 Salzburg. Tel. 0662/87 14 05. 26 rms (15 with shower and toilet).
$ Rates (including continental breakfast and showers): 310–320 S ($28.20–$29.10) single without shower or toilet; 520–530 S ($47.25–$48.20) double without shower or toilet, 640–670 S ($58.20–$60.90) double with shower and toilet. No credit cards.
This Gasthof offers adequately furnished and clean rooms, on the third floor above its popular restaurant serving Austrian food (there's no elevator). In summer there's outdoor dining. The higher rates in each category above are those charged during peak season in July, August, and September. It's just a five-minute walk from the Hauptbahnhof.

GASTHOF RÖMERWIRT, Nonntaler Hauptstrasse 47, 5020 Salzburg. Tel. 0662/84 33 91. 35 rms (15 with shower and toilet). **Bus:** 5 from the Hauptbahnhof to Nonntal (10 minutes).
$ Rates (including continental breakfast and showers): 325 S ($29.55) single without shower or toilet, 550 S ($50) single with shower and toilet; 550 S ($50) double without shower or toilet, 650 S ($59.10) double with shower and toilet; 800 S ($72.70) triple without shower or toilet, 950 S ($86.35) triple with shower and toilet. No credit cards. **Parking:** Free. **Closed:** Nov–Feb.

In a quiet area behind Mönchsberg on the left side of the river is this modern three-story pension with spacious but spartanly simple rooms (in fact, it reminds me of a dormitory). Proprietor Herr Wallner is helpful about what to do in Salzburg and speaks English. There is ample free parking.

PENSION BERGLAND, Rupertgasse 15, 5020 Salzburg. Tel. 0662/87 23 18. Fax 0662/872 31 88. 17 rms (12 with shower and toilet). TEL
$ Rates (including continental breakfast and showers): 360 S ($32.70) single with shower only, 430 S ($39.10) single with shower and toilet; 470 S ($42.70) double without shower or toilet, 640–700 S ($58.20–$63.65) double with shower and toilet; 810 S ($73.65) triple with shower and toilet. No credit cards. **Closed:** Mid-Nov to mid-Dec.

This pension is on three floors of a modern building on a residential street, about a 15-minute walk across the river from the Old City. It has a lounge equipped with a piano and a small English library. Rooms are spotlessly clean and cheerfully decorated with Scandinavian furniture and original artwork by the owner, Peter Kuhn. Some rooms have radios; others have TVs. There are bicycles for rent, and the owner speaks English. It's located about a 15-minute walk south of the Hauptbahnhof.

IN THE OUTSKIRTS

GASTHOF FÜRSTENBRUNN, Fürstenbrunnerstrasse 50, 5082 Fürstenbrunn. Tel. 06246/3342. 11 rms (all with shower and toilet). **Bus:** 1 from the Hauptbahnhof to Hanuschplatz, then 60 from Hanuschplatz to Fürstenbrunn (about 20 minutes).
$ Rates (including continental breakfast): 520 S ($47.25) double; 750 S ($68.20) triple; 880 S ($88) quad. No credit cards.

✪ A very quiet location five miles south of Salzburg at the foot of Untersberg mountain, this is a very cheerful guesthouse, with plants in the hallway, large and spotlessly clean rooms, and wooden furniture gaily painted in Austrian style (*Bauernmöbel*). Owners Manfred and Heidelinde Schnöll speak some English and will pick up guests at the train station. The guesthouse's restaurant serves lunch and dinner. It's a great place to stay if you enjoy the wooded countryside.

PENSION HELMHOF, Kirchengasse 29, 5020 Salzburg. Tel. 0662/43 30 79. Fax 0662/43 30 79. TEL 16 rms (12 with tub/shower and toilet). **Bus:** 2 from the Hauptbahnhof to Rudolf-Biebl-Strasse, then 29 to Schmiedingerstrasse.
$ Rates (including continental breakfast and showers): 300 S ($27.25) single without tub/shower or toilet, 360 S ($32.70) single with tub/shower and toilet; 460 S ($41.80) double without tub/shower or toilet, 600 S ($54.55) double with tub/shower and toilet; 600 S ($54.55) triple without tub/shower or toilet, 800 S ($72.70) triple with tub/shower and toilet. No credit cards.

Located in Liefering on the northeastern edge of town, this pension may still have rooms when other pensions in the center of town are booked up. This attractive country house has a red roof, green shutters, balconies off most rooms, and flowers on the windowsills. The owner speaks English, and there's a tiny outdoor swimming pool.

PENSION SCHIESSLING, Anif 17, 5081 Salzburg. Tel. 06246/2485. 12

rms (2 with shower and toilet). **Bus:** 55 from the Hauptbahnhof to Anif Hotel Friesacher (20 minutes).

$ Rates (including continental breakfast and showers): 320 S ($29.10) double without shower or toilet, 400 S ($36.35) double with shower and toilet. 10% surcharge for stays of only one night. No credit cards.

This pension is located in a village called Anif, south of Salzburg. There's a farmhouse and a dairy, with 30 cows and a bull in the barn. Most of the rooms are located in a more modern structure across the street. Breakfast is served in a pleasant room with a terrace. Anif is known for its *Heurige* (wine taverns), so there's more to do here in the evening than in most small villages. This pension is one of the best budget accommodations near Salzburg.

DOUBLES FOR LESS THAN 690 S ($62.70)

IN THE CITY

GASTHOF AUERHAHN, Bahnhofstrasse 15, 5020 Saizburg. Tel. 0662/ 51052. 16 rms (all with shower and toilet).

$ Rates (including continental breakfast): 500 S ($45.45) single, 680 S ($61.80) double; 800 S ($72.70) triple. AE, DC, MC, V. **Closed:** Nov.

This small and well-furnished hotel, a 10-minute walk north of the Hauptbahnhof, is across the streeet from a secondary railroad track (used once or twice a day, causing little noise). It's family owned, with a very pleasant restaurant serving typical Austrian food, popular with people from the neighborhood. The rooms are upstairs, along corridors that have a hunting-lodge feel to them with heavy beams, painted *Bauernmöbel*, and gaily painted doors. Half of the rooms have telephones, and TVs are available on request. The only disadvantage to staying here is that it's a bit far from the Old City.

HOTEL AMADEUS, Linzer Gasse 43-45, 5020 Salzburg. Tel. 0662/87 14 01 or 876163. Fax 0662/876 16 37. Telex 632883. 27 rms (20 with tub/shower and toilet). TEL **Bus:** 1, 2, 5, or 6 from the Hauptbahnhof to Makartplatz.

$ Rates (including continental breakfast and showers): 400–420 S ($36.35–$38.20) single without tub/shower or toilet, 520–680 S ($47.25–$61.80) single with tub/shower and toilet; 600–680 S ($54.55–$60.80) double without tub/ shower or toilet, 860–1,160 S ($78.20–$105.45) double with tub/shower and toilet; 1,150–1,400 S ($104.55–$127.25) triple with tub/shower and toilet. AE, DC.

This small, family-owned hotel has a great location in the center of the city, within walking distance of almost everything. Guests have their choice of rooms facing either the street or a beautiful and peaceful cemetery (where Mozart's wife is buried). Rooms with tub/shower and toilet also have TVs with cable programs in English. The lowest prices in each category are for the off-season, while the higher prices are for the summer months.

PENSION GANSLHOF, Vogelweiderstrasse 6, 5020 Salzburg. Tel. 0662/87 38 53. 15 rms (all with shower and toilet). TEL **Bus:** 1 from the Hauptbahnhof to Mirabellplatz, then 29 from Mirabellplatz to Vogelweiderstrasse.

$ Rates (including continental breakfast): 420–480 S ($38.20–$43.65) single; 680–780 S ($61.80–$70.90) double; 870–990 S ($79.10–$99) triple. No credit cards.

This pension is a 15-minute walk southeast of the train station. Rates cited are for winter and summer respectively, and rooms are clean and simple. It was completely modernized in 1988, and the owner speaks English.

IN THE OUTSKIRTS

PARKPENSION KASERN, Kasern 20, 5020 Salzburg. Tel. 0662/

50062. Fax 0662/51188. Telex 632624. 14 rms (all with tub/shower and toilet).
Bus: 1, 2, 5, or 6 from the Hauptbahnhof to Mirabellplatz, then 15 from Mirabellplatz to Kasern.
$ Rates (including continental breakfast): 400–550 S ($36.35–$55) single; 650–950 S ($59.10–$86.35) double. Extra person 200 S ($18.20). No credit cards.

⭐ This is a lovely country house set in a park in the northern outskirts of town. Built in 1870 as a private mansion, it is now in its fourth generation of owners and features exquisite artistry throughout. Most rooms are large, with tall ceilings and antique furniture; a recent addition includes six modern rooms as well. There's a fine garden where guests can sit outside in the summer. Proprietor Felicitas Eichhausen and her husband speak excellent English. This pension is located 15 minutes by bus from the city center.

SUPER-BUDGET CHOICES

INTERNATIONAL YOUTH HOTEL, Paracelsusstrasse 9, 5020 Salzburg.
Tel. 0662/87 96 49. 150 beds. **Directions:** Walk 10 minutes south of the train station.
$ Rates: 140 S ($12.60) per person double; 120 S ($10.90) per person quad; 110 S ($10) per person in a dorm room. Showers 10 S (90¢) extra. No credit cards.
This is the best budget choice in town. It's centrally located (a 15-minute walk to the Old City), and there's no curfew or age limit. There are three double rooms; the rest are quads and dormitory-style rooms with six to eight beds per room. All rooms have sinks; lockers are available, and there's a coin-operated laundry. A bar is open until midnight, and breakfast and dinner are available. *The Sound of Music* is shown daily at 2:30pm free of charge. The only drawback is that you can reserve a bed only one day in advance of your arrival, so call early in the morning. The young staff all speak English.

JUGENDGÄSTEHAUS SALZBURG, Josef-Preis-Allee 18, 5020 Salzburg. Tel. 0662/842 67 00. Fax 0662/89 14 87. Telex 613622284. 390 beds.
Bus: 5 from the Hauptbahnhof to Justizgebäude; then a five-minute walk.
$ Rates (including continental breakfast and showers): 215 S ($19.55) per person in a double with shower and toilet; 170 S ($15.45) per person in a quad with shower only; 125 S ($11.35) per person in a dorm room. Box lunch or dinner 60 S ($5.45) extra. No credit cards.
This is an official youth hostel that is open all year. If you're not a card-carrying member, you can still stay here for 30 S ($2.70) extra per night. Amenities include a TV room, steel lockers, a coin-operated laundry, a self-service restaurant, rental bike for 55 S ($5) a day, and a games room for table tennis. There is a midnight curfew.

JUGENDHERBERGE AIGNER STRASSE, Aigner Strasse 34, 5026 Salzburg. Tel. 0662/23248. 105 beds. **Bus:** 6 from the Hauptbahnhof to Volksgartenbad, then 49 from Volksgartenbad to the Finanzamt stop.
$ Rates (including continental breakfast, sheets, and showers): 125 S ($11.35) per person. No credit cards.
This is another official youth hostel, open all year and offering rooms that sleep two to eight people. There's no age limit, but if you're not a youth-hostel member you must pay 30 S ($2.70) extra per night. Facilities include a TV room and table tennis. It's located in the southern part of Salzburg, about a 25-minute walk from the Altstadt and the Hauptbahnhof.

CAMPING

CAMPING ASK SALZBURG WEST, Karolingerstrasse 4, 5020 Salzburg.
Tel. 0662/84 56 02. Bus: 77 from the Hauptbahnhof to Karolingerstrasse.
$ Rates: 42 S ($3.80) per adult, 21 S ($1.90) per child; 30 S ($2.70) per tent; 35 S

($3.20) per car; 40–65 S ($3.65–$5.90) per RV. Showers 10 S (90¢) extra. No credit cards. **Closed:** Mid-Sept to mid-May.
This camping ground is located on the western edge of the city. It's open from mid-May to mid-September.

CAMPING OST-GNIGL, Parscherstrasse 4, 5023 Salzburg. Tel. 0662/ 64 41 43 or 64 41 44. **Bus:** 1, 2, 5, or 6 from the Hauptbahnhof to Mirabellplatz, then 29 from Mirabellplatz to Minnesheimstrasse.
$ Rates (including showers): 30 S ($2.70) per adult, 18 S ($1.65) per child; 22 S ($2) per tent; 28 S ($2.55) per car; 25–35 S ($2.25–$3.20) per RV. No credit cards. **Closed:** Oct to mid-May.
This campground has a good location on the eastern edge of town with easy access to the city center by bus. It's open from mid-May through September.

WORTH THE EXTRA BUCKS

GOLDENE KRONE, Linzer Gasse 48, 5020 Salzburg. Tel. 0662/87 23 00 or 87 83 52. 25 rms (all with bath). TEL **Bus:** 1, 2, 5, or 6 from the Hauptbahnhof to Makartplatz.
$ Rates (including continental breakfast): 480–500 S ($43.65–$45.45) single; 850–900 S ($77.25–$81.80) double; 1,000–1,200 S ($90.90–$109.10) triple. No credit cards.
This is a centrally located accommodation on the right bank, just across the Salzach River from the Old City. The building, renovated and clean, dates from the 17th century. The highest prices in each category above are for the peak season in July and August.

HOTEL-PENSION TRUMER STUBE, Bergstrasse 6, 5020 Salzburg. Tel. 0662/87 43 26. Fax 0662/87 43 26. 22 rms (all with shower and toilet). TEL **Bus:** 1, 2, 5, or 6 from the Hauptbahnhof to Mirabellplatz.
$ Rates (including continental breakfast): 480–680 S ($43.65–$61.80) single; 780–1,250 S ($70.90–$113.65) double; 1,100–1,600 S ($100–$145.45) triple; 1,300–1,800 S ($118.20–$163.65) quad. AE.
 This is a great place for a splurge, centrally located just across the river from the Old City, a five-minute walk from Mozart's Birthplace. Ideal for both couples and families, it's owned by a charming young couple, the Hirschbichlers, both of whom speak English and are eager to give tips on sightseeing. The pension was recently renovated, there's an elevator, and rooms are spotlessly clean. Those facing the back are quiet. The above rates reflect both the low- and high-season rates for each category.

HOTEL ZUM HIRSCHEN, St.-Julien-Strasse 21, 5020 Salzburg. Tel. 0662/87 31 41. Fax 0662/731 41 58. Telex 632691. 72 rms (all with tub/shower and toilet). MINIBAR TV TEL
$ Rates (including buffet breakfast): 570–900 S ($51.80–$81.80) single; 950– 1,800 S ($86.35–$163.65) double. AE, DC, MC, V. **Parking:** Free.
This 100-year-old structure was completely renovated in 1989 and now looks like a modern hotel. There's a sauna, which costs 110 S ($10) extra, and a solarium. It's just a five-minute walk from the Hauptbahnhof.

PENSION WOLF, Kaigasse 7, 5020 Salzburg. Tel. 0662/842 42 30 or 843 45 30. Fax 0662/842 42 34. 12 rms (all with tub/shower and toilet). TV TEL **Bus:** 5, 6, 51, or 55 from the Hauptbahnhof to Mozartsteg; then a two-minute walk.
$ Rates (including continental breakfast): 520–720 S ($47.25–$65.45) single; 930–1,290 S ($84.55–$117.25) double. AE.
This small pension has one of the best locations in the city, in a quiet pedestrian zone at the foot of the Hohensalzburg in the Old City. The structure itself dates from the 14th century and is a national monument, but inside it's super-modern

with all the conveniences, including an elevator. Try to book Room 15, 17, or 18—each has antique furniture. Every room in the hotel is different. The owner wears dirndl costumes and speaks excellent English. The highest prices are for August.

5. BUDGET DINING

Salzburg's inexpensive restaurants are evenly distributed on both banks of the Salzach River, many of them conveniently clustered in and around the Old City. Most local restaurants feature specialties typical of Austria and southern Germany, such as *Leberknödelsuppe* (soup with liver dumplings), *Knoblauchsuppe* (garlic soup), *Bauernschmaus* (a combination dish of pork, ham, sausage, dumpling, and sauerkraut), *Tafelspitz* (boiled beef with vegetables), *Gulasch* (Hungarian stew), *Leberkäs* (a German meatloaf), *Wiener Schnitzel* (breaded veal cutlet), or sausage with kraut or knödel. The only real Salzburg dish is *Salzburger Nockerl*, a dessert made of eggs, flour, butter, and sugar, and sometimes called a "pregnant omelet." When served at your table it looks round and fluffy like a blimp, but when you start eating it the air escapes and the Nockerl looks like a plain omelet. It tastes good; try it at least once while in Salzburg.

MEALS FOR LESS THAN 50 S [$4.55]

BOSNA, Getreidegasse 40. Tel. 84 31 94.
   Cuisine: FAST FOOD.
   $ Prices: 25–35 S ($2.25–$3.20). No credit cards.
   Open: Daily 10am–7pm.
Located on the same street as Mozart's Birthplace in the heart of the Old City, this small hole-in-the-wall is a typical *Steh-Imbiss*, which means that customers eat standing up at the small counter or else order their food take-out. An alternative to the McDonald's down the street (yes, there's a McDonald's not far from Mozart's Birthplace, with one of the most discreet golden arches you've ever seen), it sells Grillwurst, hamburgers, french fries, beer, and soda.

MENSA IM MOZARTEUM, Mirabellplatz 1. Tel. 87 35 06.
   Cuisine: AUSTRIAN. **Bus:** 1, 2, 5, or 6 from the Hauptbahnhof to Mirabellplatz.
   $ Prices (for nonstudents): Fixed-price meals 35–50 S ($3.20–$4.55). No credit cards.
   Open: Lunch only, Mon–Fri 11:30am–2pm. **Closed:** July 7–15, Sept 1–16, Dec 22–Jan 6.
This student mensa, located in the Mozarteum music school, serves fixed-price meals to both students and nonstudents, though nonstudents pay about 10 S (90¢) more. The menu changes daily, usually with three or four choices available. It's conveniently located on the right side of the Salzach, between the train station and the Old City, about a 10-minute walk from each. The only problem is that the mensa, buried in a basement, is a bit difficult to find. Ask a student for directions.

MENSA AND BUFFET, Hellbrunnerstrasse 32a. Tel. 24139.
   Cuisine: AUSTRIAN. **Bus:** 5 to Justizbebäude.
   $ Prices (for nonstudents): Fixed-price meals 35–50 S ($3.20–$4.55). No credit cards.
   Open: Lunch only, Sept–June, Mon–Fri 11:30am–2pm. **Closed:** July–Aug, Dec 22–Jan 6.
This student mensa is located about a five-minute walk southeast of the Old City, near

FROMMER'S SMART TRAVELER: RESTAURANTS

VALUE-CONSCIOUS TRAVELERS SHOULD
TAKE ADVANTAGE OF THE FOLLOWING:

1. The daily specials (*Tagesgericht*), which change daily and are usually complete meals at discount prices.
2. Butcher shops and food departments of department stores, which usually offer take-out food such as Leberkäs or grilled chicken.
3. The *Imbiss*, or food stall, selling Wurst, snacks, and beer.

QUESTIONS TO ASK IF YOU'RE ON A BUDGET

1. Is there an extra charge for each piece of bread consumed?
2. Does the main course come with vegetables or side dishes?

the Jugendgästehaus (youth hostel). It serves fixed-price meals to nonstudents for slightly higher prices than students pay, with about four choices available.

MEALS FOR LESS THAN 88 S [$8]

IN THE OLD CITY

AUGUSTINERBRÄU, Linderhofstrasse or Augustinergasse 4. Tel. 43 12 46.

Cuisine: AUSTRIAN. **Bus:** 1, 2, 5, or 6 from the Hauptbahnhof to Mirabellplatz, then 27 from Mirabellplatz to Augustinergasse; or 1 from the Hauptbahnhof to Hanuschplatz, then 27 from Hanuschplatz to Augustinergasse.

$ Prices: 20–60 S ($1.80–$5.45). No credit cards.

Open: Mon–Fri 3–11pm, Sat–Sun and hols 2:30–11pm.

This is a great place for a meal, either in its beer garden or in one of the huge beer halls upstairs. Known among locals as Müllnerbräu (because of the area it's in, Müllner), this is a brewery, where the star of the show is the brew, costing 21 S ($1.90) for a half liter or 42 S ($3.80) for a liter. You can bring your own food if you wish, but there are also various counters selling sausages and cold cuts, cheese, pretzels, bread, hamburgers, grilled chicken, Gulaschsuppe, boiled pork with horseradish, beef with creamed spinach and potatoes, and more. Pick and choose and create your own dinner. This is a crowded and noisy place, just as a brewery should be. It's located north of Mönchsberg.

NORDSEE, Getreidegasse 27. Tel. 842320.

Cuisine: SEAFOOD. **Bus:** 1 from the Hauptbahnhof to Hanuschplatz.

$ Prices: 50–100 S ($4.55–$9.10). MC, V.

Open: Mon–Sat 9am–11pm, Sun and hols 11am–11pm (to 7pm in winter).

Nordsee is a chain of fast-food fish restaurants that originated in northern Germany. This self-service restaurant is conveniently located on the same street as Mozart's Birthplace, offering fishburgers, fish sandwiches, cod filet with potato salad, pickled herring in white-mustard sauce, and more. Take-out service is also available.

PIZZALAND, Getreidegasse 14. Tel. 84 14 00.

Cuisine: PIZZA. **Bus:** 1 from the Hauptbahnhof to Hanuschplatz.

$ Prices: 55–95 S ($5–$8.65). MC, V.

Open: Sun–Wed 10:30am–11:30pm, Thurs–Sat 10:30am–12:30am.

Also near Mozart's Birthplace, this is a chain of pizza parlors that offer pasta and selections such as Weiner Schnitzel and hot chili as well. It also has a do-it-yourself salad bar, with a small plate costing 36 S ($3.25); a large plate, 59 S ($5.35).

SCHWAIGHOFER, Kranzlmarkt 3. Tel. 84 27 09.
    Cuisine: AUSTRIAN. **Bus:** 1 from the Hauptbahnhof to Hanuschplatz.
$ Prices: 55–110 S ($5–$10). No credit cards.
    Open: Mon–Fri 9am–6pm, Sat 8am–12:30pm (to 2pm the first Sat of the month).
This is a tiny Austrian-style deli offering more than 20 different kinds of salads, which range from 20 S to 40 S ($1.80 to $3.65), and such main courses as Gulasch, Schweinebraten with salad, liver with rice, and other Austrian specialties. It's a tiny place, with just a few seats in the back where you can eat your meal. Take-out service is also available.

NEAR THE HAUPTBAHNHOF

FORUM SELF-SERVICE RESTAURANT, Südtirolerplatz 11. Tel. 50536.
    Cuisine: AUSTRIAN.
$ Prices: 40–100 S ($3.65–$9.10). No credit cards.
    Open: Mon–Fri 9am–5:30pm, Sat 9am–noon (to 4pm the first Sat of the month).
This restaurant is up on the first floor of Salzburg's largest department store, which faces the train station. It serves two excellent daily *Tagesgerichte* for 55 S and 70 S ($5 and $6.35) with soup, a main dish, and salad. There are many à la carte choices, and with drinks and dessert, you can eat like royalty for less than $10. There is a no-smoking section.

KIESELPASSAGE, Rainerstrasse 19-23. Tel. 88 26 91.
    Cuisine: AUSTRIAN.
$ Prices: 20–75 S ($1.80–$6.80). No credit cards.
    Open: Mon–Sat 9am–6pm, Sat 9am–noon (to 4:30pm the first Sat of the month).
The Kieselpassage is a small, indoor shopping mall about a three-minute walk from the Hauptbahnhof, on the corner of Elisabethstrasse and Rainerstrasse. In its basement is a food court, with counters selling breads, pastries, salads, and such dishes as grilled chicken, Gulaschsuppe, Wiener Schnitzel, and daily specials. The only disadvantage is that there aren't many places to sit down—you may end up eating at one of the several stand-up counters. Also in the basement is a store selling fruit, vegetables, and food.

MEALS FOR LESS THAN 140 S ($12.70)

IN THE OLD CITY

DON CAMILLO & PEPPONE, Gstättengasse 15. Tel. 84 32 84.
    Cuisine: ITALIAN. **Bus:** 1 from the Hauptbahnhof to Hanuschplatz.
$ Prices: Pizza and pasta 65–120 S ($5.90–$10.90); meat dishes 130–225 S ($11.80–$20.45). DC, MC, V.
    Open: Lunch daily 11:30am–1:30pm; dinner daily 5:30–11:30pm.
You can choose from dozens of pizzas and pasta dishes in this 130-seat restaurant located near the lift to Café Winkler. Specialties include its many pizzas, spaghetti pomodoro, picatta milanese (Italian version of Wiener Schnitzel) with fries, and frittura mista (fried mixed fish).

GASTHAUS WILDER MANN, Getreidegasse 20 or Griesgasse 17. Tel. 43 88 44 or 84 17 87.
    Cuisine: AUSTRIAN. **Bus:** 1 from the Hauptbahnhof to Hanuschplatz.
$ Prices: 45–130 S ($4.10–$11.80). No credit cards.
    Open: Daily 11am–9pm (last order).

★ This simple and popular restaurant has wooden tables, a wood-plank floor, and antlers on the wall. This is where the locals come to drink, eat, and gossip, and you may well be the only non-Salzburger around. The menu lists Bauernschmaus, Gulasch, Bratwurst, Schnitzel with ham and cheese baked over it, turkey with mushroom sauce, and Leberkäs. Watch, too, for the reasonable daily specials. Wilder Mann translates as "Wild Man," an appropriate name. It's located in a narrow passageway between Getreidegasse and Griesgasse.

STERNBRÄU, Getreidegasse 34-36 or Griessgasse 23. Tel. 84 21 40.
    Cuisine: AUSTRIAN. **Bus:** 1 from the Hauptbahnhof to Hanuschplatz.
$ Prices: Main courses 80–185 S ($7.25–$16.80). No credit cards.
    Open: Daily 9am–midnight.
This is considered one of Salzburg's best moderately priced restaurants, a huge place with seating both inside and outside in a courtyard garden (a great place for a beer). The menu is extensive, listing such Austrian favorites as Bauernschmaus, Wiener Schnitzel with fries and salad, rumpsteak with herb butter and salad, pork cutlet, and grilled steak.

STIEGLKELLER, Festungsgasse 10. Tel. 84 26 81.
    Cuisine: AUSTRIAN. **Bus:** 5, 6, 51, or 55 from the Hauptbahnhof to Mozartsteg.
$ Prices: 75–125 S ($6.80–$11.35). No credit cards.
    Open: May–Sept, daily 11am–midnight. **Closed:** Oct–Apr.
Carved out of the rock of a mountain, the Festungsberg, a few hundred yards off Residenz Platz, is a typical Austrian beer-cellar restaurant. It has outdoor beer gardens as well as indoor seating. Try the Leberknödelsuppe, roast chicken, or the Salzburger Nockerl.

WIENERWALD RESTAURANT, Griesgasse 31. Tel. 843 47 07.
    Cuisine: AUSTRIAN. **Bus:** 1 from the Hauptbahnhof to Hanuschplatz.
$ Prices: 65–130 S ($5.90–$11.80). AE, DC, MC, V.
    Open: Daily 9am–1am.
This restaurant on Griesgasse has rooms decorated like a Swiss chalet, with comfortable seats. There are more than 300 restaurants of this chain in Austria, Germany, and Switzerland, where the specialty is spit-roasted chicken. Other items on the menu include Schnitzel, turkey, fish, Gulasch, and chicken Cordon Bleu. It's popular with families.

YUEN CHINA RESTAURANT, Getreidegasse 24. Tel. 84 37 70.
    Cuisine: CHINESE. **Bus:** 1 from the Hauptbahnhof to Hanuschplatz.
$ Prices: 85–180 S ($7.70–$16.35). AE, DC, MC, V.
    Open: Daily 11:30am–11:30pm.
This restaurant, entered via a courtyard and up a flight of stairs, looks quite authentic with its dragon motif on the ceiling, hanging Chinese lanterns, and a tank of exotic goldfish. In addition to the usual beef, chicken, pork, and vegetable dishes, it also offers daily specials.

NEAR THE HAUPTBAHNHOF

GASTHOF JAHN, Elisabethstrasse 31. Tel. 87 14 05.
    Cuisine: AUSTRIAN.
$ Prices: 80–190 S ($7.25–$17.25). No credit cards.
    Open: Lunch daily 11am–2pm; dinner daily 6–10:30pm.
This typical, neighborhood restaurant has an English menu, offering Schnitzel, pepper steak, omelets, fish, Bauernschmaus, Leberkäs, and snacks. In the summer you can sit outside under a chestnut tree. It's a good place to eat if you're waiting for a train, as it's only a five-minute walk from the Hauptbahnhof.

ROSENKAVALIER, in the Hauptbahnhof. Tel. 87 23 77-15.
    Cuisine: AUSTRIAN.
$ Prices: Salads 55–80 S ($5–$7.25); main courses 70–125 S ($6.35–$11.35). AE, DC, MC, V.

Open: Daily 10am–10pm.

Normally I avoid restaurants in train stations, but this one is clearly an exception. It's a very civilized establishment, with tall ceilings and a turn-of-the-century atmosphere embellished with white tablecloths and classical or piano music playing softly in the background. Its menu is fairly standard, including salads, soups, and such Austrian specialties as Kavalierspitz (boiled rump of beef), Schnitzel, Gulasch, Hirtenspiess (mixed skewered meats), and Cordon Bleu, as well as lasagne and spaghetti. As is usual in Austria, main dishes come with such side dishes as salad or potatoes, making them complete meals. A good place for a meal while waiting for a train connection.

CAFES & KONDITOREI

Salzburg is famous for its coffeehouses and pastry shops, where you can linger over pastry and coffee or a glass of wine, read the newspapers available (including the *International Herald Tribune*) and watch the passersby. In summer, many cafés have outdoor seating. Inside you will be tempted by the many varieties of delectable confections, heavily garnished with whipped cream. If you prefer, you can also take some pastries away for consumption on a park bench or in your hotel.

As well as the establishments listed below, other recommended coffeehouses are **Café Glockenspiel,** Mozartplatz 2 (tel. 841403), and **Hagenauerstuben,** on Getreidegasse near Mozart's Birthplace.

CAFE BAZAR, Schwarzstrasse 3. Tel. 84 37 46.
   Cuisine: COFFEEHOUSE/SNACKS.
$ Prices: *Melange* 30 S ($2.70); desserts 20–50 S ($1.80–$4.55).
   Open: Mon 10am–6pm, Tues–Sat 7:30am–11pm.
This fancy coffeehouse, located on the right side of the Salzach River near the Staatsbrücke, features chandeliers and large windows with views of the river. It's popular with students from the nearby Mozarteum as well as older people perusing the daily newspaper. In addition to coffee and desserts, it serves snacks and daily specials.

CAFE MOZART, Getreidegasse 22. Tel. 43746.
   Cuisine: COFFEEHOUSE.
$ Prices: *Mocca* 22 S ($2); desserts from 25 S ($2.25).
   Open: Mon–Sat 9am–10pm, Sun 11am–8pm.
This upstairs coffeehouse is appropriately named, as it's located on the same street as Mozart's Birthplace. Although the house itself is 700 years old, the coffee shop dates back only 150 years. Refined and quieter than the coffeehouses above, this is where the locals tend to go for their meditative cups of coffee (try the *mocca,* a strong Viennese coffee), along with their torte and strudel, of course. The specialty of the house is its rich chocolate cake.

CAFE TOMASELLI, Alter Markt 9. Tel. 84 44 88.
   Cuisine: COFFEEHOUSE.
$ Prices: *Melange* (large coffee with milk) 30 S ($2.70); desserts average 25–60 S ($2.25–$5.45).
   Open: Mon–Sat 7am–9pm, Sun 8am–9pm.
Established in 1705, Café Tomaselli is still going strong. In fact, it's so popular that you may have to wait to get a seat. In the summer, extra chairs are placed outside on the cobblestone square. Have a *Melange* (large cup of coffee with milk) and dessert, or choose from the pastry tray that is carried through the coffee shop or go to the display case. There's also wine, beer, soft drinks, and snacks, and in summer, ice cream.

KONDITOREI FÜRST, Brodgasse 13. Tel. 84 37 59.
   Cuisine: COFFEEHOUSE.
$ Prices: *Melange* 28 S ($2.55); desserts from 30 S ($2.70).
   Open: Mon–Sat 8am–8pm, Sun and hols 9am–8pm.
Across the square from Tomaselli is this younger upstart, founded in 1884. There are

50 varieties of cakes, pastries, and confection here, most heavily garnished with whipped cream. Try the Mohrenkopf, Mozartkugel, or Linzertorte—sinful!

PICNIC SUPPLIES & WHERE TO EAT THEM

Kaufhaus Forum, located across from the Hauptbahnhof at Südtirolerplatz 11 (tel. 50536), has a food department in the basement. Come here for the basics of cheese, sausage, bread, and fruit, as well as prepared foods like Leberkäs. It's open Monday through Friday from 9am to 5:30pm and on Saturday from 9am to noon (to 4:30pm on the first Saturday of the month).

In the Old City, a wonderful place for inexpensive food is **Schwaighofer,** Kranzlmarkt 3 (tel. 84 27 09), located near the Staatsbrücke. This tiny hole-in-the-wall specializes in deli meats and sausages, cheeses, 20 different kinds of salads, and such dishes as Gulaschsuppe, Tafelspitz, and stuffed green pepper. There are even a few tables where you can sit down to eat your goodies. It's open Monday through Friday from 9am to 6pm and on Saturday from 8am to 12:30pm (to 2pm on the first Saturday of the month).

If it's a nice day, you may want to join the other sun worshipers on the benches in the **Mirabellgarten** or along the Salzach River. Another good place to eat your purchases is at the **Augustinerbräu,** a brewery described in "Meals for Less Than 88 S ($8)," above.

WORTH THE EXTRA BUCKS

K & K, Waagplatz 2. Tel. 84 21 56.
   Cuisine: AUSTRIAN.
$ Prices: Appetizers and soups 45–105 S ($4.10–$9.55); main courses 120–230 S ($10.90–$20.90); fixed-price meals 200 S ($18.20) at lunch, 405 S ($36.80) at dinner; table charge 20 S ($1.80) per person. AE, DC, MC, V.
   Open: Lunch daily 11:30am–2pm; dinner daily 6–10pm. **Closed:** Sun in winter.

Located in the Old City, near the tourist office and American Express, this cozy and civilized restaurant features fresh flowers, heavy wooden tables, and classical music playing softly in the background. Note the stone fish tank upstairs—filled with today's fresh trout. The menu is interesting and changes daily, listing typical Austrian cuisine as well as Austrian dishes with a twist. Thus, in addition to the usual Tafelspitz, grilled chicken breast, and trout, there may also be cauliflower and broccoli layered with ham or perhaps a very delicious spinach ravioli with parmesan.

STIFTSKELLER ST. PETER, St. Peter-Bezirk 1. Tel. 841 26 80.
   Cuisine: AUSTRIAN.
$ Prices: 90–200 S ($8.20–$18.20). No credit cards.
   Open: Easter–Nov, daily 9:30am–11pm; Nov–Easter, Tues–Sun 9:30am–11pm.

Located near St. Peter's Monastery at the foot of the Mönchsberg, this is probably the most popular first-class restaurant in Salzburg. It serves international food as well as local specialties, including fresh trout, Wiener Schnitzel, homemade Bratwurst, roast duck, and numerous daily specials. There are various dining rooms, each different but all with a medieval ambience. In short, this place is a delight. It's under the management of St. Peter's Monastery, which dates from 803.

---

6. ATTRACTIONS

SUGGESTED ITINERARIES

IF YOU HAVE ONE DAY   Start the morning with a tour of the Hohensalzburg Fortress and its museums. You might want to take the funicular up the hill, and then

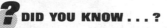

walk back down into the city (about a 20-minute walk). Spend the afternoon in the Old City, strolling through its pedestrian lanes. Be sure to see Mozart's Birthplace on Getreidegasse, which is Salzburg's most famous and picturesque street. Notice the many wrought-iron shop signs; in the days when many people were illiterate, they served a useful purpose. Other places to visit include the Dom (cathedral) and the cemetery at St. Peter's, one of the most beautiful cemeteries I've seen. Top the day off with a beer at Augustinerbräu. In the evening, take a stroll along the Salzach River, where you'll have a view of the fortress all lit up.

IF YOU HAVE TWO DAYS   To the attractions above, add the Hellbrunn Palace, three miles south of the city (open only from April through October). Its park with the trick fountains is unique. Try, also, to include a visit to the Haus der Natur (Museum of Natural History), one of the best of its kind in the world; the Residenz State Rooms; and the National Costume Museum, all in the Old City. In late afternoon, take the lift to Café Winkler, a casino and café. It's worth the trip to the top just for the view, the best in all of Salzburg. If you feel like a hike, you can walk from Café Winkler along the ridge to the fortress in about a half hour, with great photo opportunities along the way. In the evening, get dressed up and go to one of Salzburg's many musical events, such as a concert in the fortress, its Festival Houses, the Mozarteum, or the Residenz.

IF YOU HAVE THREE DAYS   Spend the first two days as outlined above. On the third day, head for Untersberg, a mountain seven miles south of Salzburg where you have a lovely view of the city and the Alps. In the afternoon, take a stroll through the Mirabellgarten, topping it off with a sauna or swim at the adjoining Kurhaus.

IF YOU HAVE FIVE DAYS   Consider taking Bob's Bavarian Mountain Tour, a four-hour guided (in English) excursion covering the major *Sound of Music* film locations and a visit to Berchtesgaden. Another interesting option is to take a do-it-yourself excursion to Hallein's salt mines (open from April through October).

TOP ATTRACTIONS

MOZARTS GEBURTSHAUS (Mozart's Birthplace), Getreidegasse 9. Tel. 84 43 13.

This is, without doubt, the most heavily visited attraction in Salzburg. Wolfgang Amadeus Mozart was born in this third-floor apartment in 1756. The museum exhibits his piano (he started composing when he was 4 years old) and the violin he played as a small boy. A plaque marks the spot where his cradle stood. Of the several paintings of Amadeus and his family, only one is thought to be a true likeness of the musical genius—the unfinished one by the piano, by Mozart's brother-in-law.

In addition to the rooms where the family lived, there are also a few adjoining rooms decorated as a typical burgher's house during Mozart's time. But most fascinating are the models of various stage settings for Mozart's operas, showing the different interpretations through the ages. The dozens of models, all originals, range

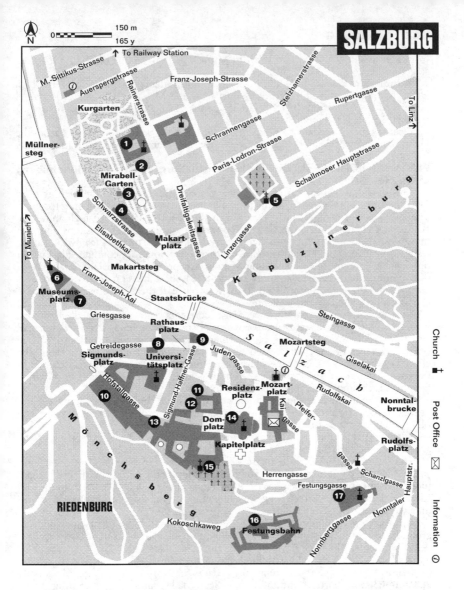

SALZBURG

0 ——————— 150 m
0 ——————— 165 y

↑ To Railway Station

To Linz →

To Munich ↗

Church ■✝

Post Office ☒

Information ⓘ

Street and place labels (on map):

M.-Sittikus-Strasse · Auerspergstrasse · Franz-Joseph-Strasse · Rupertgasse · Stelzhamerstrasse · Schrannengasse · Paris-Lodron-Strasse · Schallmoser Hauptstrasse · Kurgarten · Rainerstrasse · Dreifaltigkeitsgasse · Linzergasse · Schwarzstrasse · Mirabell-Garten · Makart-platz · Makartgasse · Elisabethkai · Müllner-steg · Makartsteg · Franz-Joseph-Kai · Museums-platz · Staatsbrücke · Griesgasse · Rathaus-platz · Getreidegasse · Sigmunds-platz · Universi-tätsplatz · Sigmund-Haffner-Gasse · Juden-gasse · Mozartsteg · Giselakai · Steingasse · Kapuzinerberg · Salzach · Hofstallgasse · Mönchsberg · RIEDENBURG · Residenz-platz · Mozart-platz · Kai-gasse · Rudolfskai · Pfeifer-gasse · Dom-platz · Kapitelplatz · Nonntal-brucke · Rudolfs-platz · Herrengasse · Festungsgasse · Schanzlgasse · Nonntaler Haupstr. · Kokoschkaweg · Festungsbahn · Nonnberggasse

Vienna ★
● Salzburg
AUSTRIA

from a production of *Don Giovanni* in Munich in 1810 to one of *Die Zauberflöte* staged in Berlin in 1930. A must-see.

Admission: 50 S ($4.55) adults, 35 S ($3.20) students and senior citizens, 10 S (90¢) children; combined ticket for Geburtshaus and Mozarts Wohnhaus (described under "More Attractions"); 70 S ($6.35) adults, 45 S ($4.10) students and senior citizens, 15 S ($1.35) children.

Open: June–Aug, daily 9am–7pm; Sept–May, daily 9am–6pm. **Bus:** 1 from the Hauptbahnhof to Hanuschplatz, or 5 or 6 from the Hauptbahnhof to Rathausplatz.

FESTUNG HOHENSALZBURG (Hohensalzburg Fortress), Mönchsberg 34. Tel. 8042-2123.

This medieval fortress-castle dominates the city. Built between the 11th and the 17th centuries as a residence for the prince-archbishops who ruled Salzburg for more than 500 years, it is a perfectly preserved medieval fortress. Perched high above the city on a cliff, it contains the **State Rooms** of the former archbishops and two museums. The State Rooms, with their coffered ceilings and intricate ironwork, can be visited only if you join one of the tours. Unfortunately, tours are conducted in English only when enough English-speaking visitors are present to warrant it. To avoid disappointment, therefore, pay only the 20-S ($1.80) admission fee to the fortress grounds and then head immediately to the tour office. If there's a tour in English, you can always pay the difference there.

The tour takes visitors through dark corridors and unfurnished chambers, including a dismal **torture chamber** where prisoners were hung, stretched, burned, and tortured beyond the limits of the imagination. In the fortress is also a huge open-air **barrel organ**, which used to ring out at the end of the day to signal the closing of the city gates. Now it is played three times a day from Easter to October. In the living quarters of the former archbishops is a late Gothic porcelain stove dating from 1501, the most valuable item in the fortress.

The tour concludes at the **Burg Museum,** with its displays of weapons used in peasant revolts, furniture, and a macabre collection of medieval torture devices. The other museum, the **Rainermuseum,** displays more weapons.

If you don't take the tour, the base admission fee allows you to wander through the grounds of the fortress, its courtyards, and its viewing platforms.

The easiest way to reach the fortress is by funicular. However, it's not cheap, and you still have to pay admission once you reach the top of the hill. If you're on a budget, therefore, you might wish to approach the fortress on foot. A path leads from the Old City and winds up the hill, offering changing vistas on the way. As an alternative, you may wish to go up by funicular and come down on foot.

Admission: Grounds only, 20 S ($1.80) adults, 10 S (90¢) students and children; grounds, tour, and museums, 45 S ($4.10) adults, 40 S ($3.65) senior citizens, 25 S ($2.25) students, 20 S ($1.80) children. The funicular costs 17 S ($1.55) one way or 27 S ($2.45) round-trip for adults; children pay half price.

Open: Conducted tours, June–Sept, daily 9:30am–6:30pm; Oct–May, daily 9:30am–4:30pm. Fortress grounds, Apr–Sept, daily 8am–7pm; Oct–Mar, daily 8am–6pm. **Closed:** Rainer Museum, Oct–Apr. **Directions:** Funicular or 30-minute walk from the Old City.

RESIDENZ, Residenzplatz 1. Tel. 8042-2690.

The Residenz, in the heart of the Old City, dates from the mid-12th century but was rebuilt extensively during the 16th, 17th, and 18th centuries. It served as the official residence of the archbishops when it was deemed safe for them to move down from the fortress into the city (after you've toured both the fortress and the Residenz, you won't blame them for preferring the much more elegant Residenz). Conducted 40-minute tours of the **Residenz Prunkräume (State Rooms)** take visitors through the throne room (considered the most beautiful room of the Residenz), the bedroom of the archbishop, the library, and other chambers. Be sure to visit the **Residenzgalerie,** too. A gallery of European art from the 16th to the 19th century, it includes works by Dutch, French, Italian, and Austrian baroque artists. Of special interest are paintings that depict Salzburg through the centuries.

Admission: Tours of the State Rooms, 40 S ($3.65) adults, 30 S ($2.70) senior citizens and students, free for children to age 15; Residenzgalerie, 40 S ($3.65) adults, 30 S ($2.70) senior citizens and students, free for children. A combined ticket for the State Rooms and the Residenzgalerie costs 60 S ($5.45) for adults.

Open: State Rooms tours, July–Aug, daily 10am–4:40pm (last tour); Sept–June, Mon–Fri at 10am, 11am, noon, 2pm, and 3pm. Residenzgalerie, daily 10am–5pm (closed Wed in winter).

HAUS DER NATUR (Museum of Natural History), Museumplatz 5. Tel. 84 26 53.

On five floors in 80 exhibition rooms, practically everything that lives or grows on our planet is brilliantly displayed. Exhibits include: stuffed prehistoric animals; the twin roots of a fir tree hundreds of years old; live tarantulas; a rock crystal weighing 1,360 pounds; such abnormalities as a calf with two heads, a chicken with four legs, and a deer with three; a giant model of a DNA molecule; models of the *Saturn* V rocket; and pieces of moon rock donated by President Nixon in 1973. There's also an aquarium with fresh- and seawater animals, as well as the Reptile Zoo with 200 scaly creatures, including a collection of poisonous snakes and alligators. Without a doubt, this is one of the best natural-history museums in Europe. Unfortunately, descriptions are only in German.

Admission: 35 S ($3.20) adults, 20 S ($1.80) students and children.

Open: Daily 9am–5pm. **Bus:** 1 from the Hauptbahnhof to Hanuschplatz; then turn right onto Griesgasse and at the end of it is Museumplatz.

HELLBRUNN PALACE, 3 miles south of the city. Tel. 82 03 73.

Built as a hunting lodge and summer residence for Salzburg's prince-archbishops, the palace is an impressive example of the wealth and comfort controlled by absolute rulers at that time. It features, like the palace of the tsars in Leningrad, dozens of hidden trick fountains and water sprays in its large baroque gardens. This is probably the only conducted tour in Europe in which laughing, running, and hiding is expected of the tourist. Tours through the palace last approximately 45 minutes.

Be sure, too, to visit the **Volkskundemuseum (Folklore Museum),** located in the Monatsschlösschen on the palace grounds. (By the way, not far away is the **Hellbrun Zoo,** worth a visit if you have kids.)

Admission: 48 S ($4.35) adults, 24 S ($2.80) students and children.

Open: Apr and Oct, daily 9am–4:30pm; May–Sept, daily 9am–5pm; July–Aug, evening tours 6–10pm. **Closed:** Nov–Mar. **Bus:** 55 from the Hauptbahnhof to Hellbrun (a 20-minute ride).

MORE ATTRACTIONS

If you plan to visit the Museum Carolino Augusteum, the Bürgerspital Museum (Toy Museum), the cathedral excavations, and the Folklore Museum, you can save money by buying a combination ticket to all four for 40 S ($3.65) for adults, and 15 S ($1.35) for students and children.

MOZARTS WOHNHAUS (Mozart's Residence), Makartplatz 8. Tel. 84 43 13.

This house, where Mozart lived as an adult, should not be confused with his birthplace at Getreidegasse 9. Here Mozart lived with his family from 1773 to 1787. The apartment was reconstructed after being bombed in World War II. Today you can see the kitchen and the room where he composed, and a collection of musical instruments; slide shows of Mozart's life are shown four times a day.

Admission: 35 S ($3.20) adults, 25 S ($2.25) senior citizens and students, 5 S (45¢) children; combination ticket to both Mozart's Birthplace and Residence, 70 S ($6.35) adults, 45 S ($4.10) senior citizens and students, 15 S ($1.35) children.

Open: June–Aug, daily 10am–6pm; Sept–May, daily 10am–5pm. **Bus:** 1 or 5 from the Hauptbahnhof to Makartplatz.

ST. SEBASTIAN FRIEDHOF (Cemetery), Linzer Gasse 41.

And now for some ancient gossip! Three of Salzburg's most famous people are buried here. Best known, perhaps, are two members of Wolfgang Amadeus Mozart's family—his father, Leopold, and his wife, Constantia. The talk around Salzburg is that Amadeus was actually in love with Constantia's sister, but when the sister refused him he settled for Constantia, who reputedly resembled her sister. After Amadeus's death, Constantia remarried Georg Nikolaus Nissen, who ended up writing Mozart's first biography.

Another famous person buried here is Archbishop Wolf-Dietrich von Raitenau, who more than anyone else was responsible for the Salzburg of today, turning it from a medieval town into a Renaissance and baroque city. Educated in Rome and related to the Medicis, Wolf-Dietrich wished to transform Salzburg into a dazzling city that would rival the great cities of Italy. He set about rebuilding the Dom (cathedral), started construction on the Residenz, and built a palace (Mirabell Palace) for himself and his mistress, who bore him 12 children. A bit too flamboyant for an archbishop, Wolf-Dietrich was eventually imprisoned.

Finally, Doctor Paracelsus, an alchemist who worked tirelessly to find cures for leprosy and dropsy, is buried here as well.

Admission: Free.

Open: Daily 7am–7pm. **Bus:** 1 or 5 from the Hauptbahnhof to Mirabellplatz or Makartplatz.

MUSEUM CAROLINO AUGUSTEUM, Museumplatz 1. Tel. 84 31 45.

This is a collection of Salzburg art—paintings, sculptures, religious art, ceramics, musical instruments, and glassware from Roman times to the present—giving a vivid presentation of Salzburg's cultural history through the ages.

Admission: 30 S ($2.70) adults, 10 S (90¢) students and children.

Open: Tues 9am–8pm, Wed–Sun 9am–5pm. **Bus:** 1 from the Hauptbahnhof to Hanuschplatz; then turn right onto Griesgasse and at the end of it is Museumplatz.

DOM (Cathedral), Domplatz. Tel. 84 41 89.

Salzburg's Dom was originally built back in the 8th century but was destroyed by a fire in the 16th century. The present Dom, commissioned by Archbishop Wolf-Dietrich and designed by an Italian architect, is considered the finest example of an early baroque building north of the Alps. This is where Mozart was baptized, and it's famed for its three bronze doors and its 4,000-pipe organ. Treasures of the Dom are on display in the museum, to the right of the front door.

Admission: Dom, free (but donations appreciated); Dom museum, 25 S ($2.25) adults, 15 S ($1.35) senior citizens, 10 S (90¢) students, 5 S (45¢) children.

Open: Dom, daily 6am–8pm (6pm in winter); Dom museum, mid-May to mid-Oct, daily 10am–5pm (closed mid-Oct to mid-May). **Bus:** 1 from the Hauptbahnhof to Hanuschplatz; then walk to the end of Sigmund Hafnergasse, turn left, and you've reached Domplatz.

DOMGRABUNGSMUSEUM (Cathedral Excavations), Residenzplatz. Tel. 84 52 95.

Around the corner from the Dom entrance (to the left if you're facing the Dom's massive doors) is a museum showing the history of the Dom since the 8th century, with excavation work showing ruins of the foundation.

Admission: 15 S ($1.35) adults, 10 S (90¢) students and children.

Open: Easter–Oct, daily 9am–5pm. **Closed:** Nov–Easter. **Bus:** 1 from the Hauptbahnhof to Hanuschplatz.

TRACHTENMUSEUM (National Costume Museum), Griesgasse 23. Tel. 84 31 19.

Those who plan to buy dirndls should go here first: Traditional Salzburg dress, past and present (and a few lederhosen, sweaters, hats, and jackets), from the 18th to the 20th century, is on exhibit.

Admission: 30 S ($2.70) adults, 20 S ($1.80) students and children.

Open: Mon–Fri 10am–noon and 2–5pm, Sat 10am–noon. **Bus:** 1 from the Hauptbahnhof to Hanuschplatz; then turn right onto Griesgasse and the museum will be on your left.

CATACOMBS OF ST. PETER'S CHURCH, St. Peter-Bezirk 1. Tel. 844 57 80.

This church in the Old City has a lovely rococo interior. Relatives of Mozart (his sister, Nannerl) and Haydn, among others, are buried here in a cemetery—very beautifully arranged and worth a walk through. There are guided tours of the catacombs for a minimum of five people.

Admission: Church and cemetery, free; catacombs tour, 10 S (90¢) adults, 7 S (65¢) senior citizens, students, and children.

Open: Church, daily 9am–5pm. Catacombs tour, May–Sept, daily 10am–5pm on the hour; Oct–Apr, daily at 11am, noon, and 1:30, 2:30, and 3:30pm. **Bus:** 1 from the Hauptbahnhof to Hanuschplatz; then walk to the end of Sigmund Hafnergasse, turn left to Domplatz, and the church is next to the Dom.

BÜRGERSPITAL MUSEUM (Toy Museum), Bürgerspitalgasse 2. Tel. 84 75 60.

Housed in the former Salzburg Municipal Hospital, this delightful museum displays every conceivable sort of toy, from a hand-carved Noah's Ark to a merry-go-round, from model trains to tin soldiers—all dating from the 16th century to the present. There's also folk art and musical instruments. You'll see more adults than children as visitors here.

Admission (including the Punch-and-Judy show Wed and Fri at 3pm): 25 S ($2.25) adults, 10 S (90¢) students and children.

Open: Tues–Sun 9am–5pm. **Bus:** 1 from the Hauptbahnhof to Hanuschplatz.

THE CARILLON, Mozartplatz 1. Tel. 8042-2276.

Tunes are played on a 35-bell chime cast in Antwerp in the 18th century. The carillon is located in the heart of the Old City across from the tourist office, and a good place to listen to the music is at one of the outdoor tables of the Café Glockenspiel in the same square. If you want to learn more about the carillon, you can join a tour (in good weather) and go up the tower, where the view is great.

Admission: Listening to the chimes, free; tour, 20 S ($1.80) adults, 10 S (90¢) children.

Open: Carillon, played daily at 7am, 11am, and 6pm. Tours, Mar 16–Nov 1, daily at 10:45am and 5:45pm; Nov 2–Mar 14, Mon–Sat at 10:45am and 5:45pm. **Bus:** 5 or 6 from the Hauptbahnhof to the Rathaus.

MÖNCHSBERG AND CAFE WINKLER, Mönchsberg. Tel. 20551.

Salzburg's other conspicuous hilltop building is Café Winkler, which contains a café and a casino (see "Evening Entertainment," below, for more information on the casino) and sits high above the city. The best reason for coming here, however, is for the view, considered the best in the city. After all, in front of you are all the churches, a stretch of the Salzach River, and the Hohensalzburg Fortress (which you don't have, obviously, from the fortress itself). Also of interest is the *Sattler Panorama*, a huge 360° mural of Salzburg painted in 1825. After it was painted, it was taken throughout Europe as proof that Salzburg was a beautiful city worthy of a visit.

If you feel like a hike, take the path that skirts the top of the ridge to the fortress, about a 30-minute walk. Otherwise, the best way to reach Café Winkler is via the Mönchsberg Lift, an elevator that whisks visitors to the top. The elevator is at Gstättengasse 13, departing at least every 15 minutes.

Admission: Mönchsberg Lift, 13 S ($1.20) one way and 21 S ($1.90) round-trip adults, half price for children; *Sattler Panorama* and the view, free.

Open: Elevator, daily 7am–3am. Café summer, daily 11am–3am; winter, Tues 2pm–midnight; Wed–Sat 11am–midnight. **Bus:** 1 from the Hauptbahnhof to Hanuschplatz.

PARKS & GARDENS

The most famous garden in town, now a public park, is the **Mirabell Garden (Mirabellgarten)** on the right bank of the river. The garden was designed in the 17th century in baroque style and decorated with statues, marble putti, fountains, and ponds. It offers a good view of the Hohensalzburg Fortress.

Mirabell is the Italian word for "beautiful view." Both the garden and palace (used for concerts and administrative offices) were built by Archbishop Wolf-Dietrich for his mistress. Today the area is a popular place for a stroll, and its park benches are always full with Salzburg's office workers and older people catching a few rays. The Orangerie is free, and in the spring the garden comes alive with 17,000 tulips. A small open-air cafeteria sells beverages and snacks.

Adjoining the garden is the **Kurpark,** a tree-lined area with a small hill called Rosen-hügel, a good spot for taking snapshots.

Smaller parks are found at the foot of Kapuzinerberg and Mönchsberg, all with benches that invite picnicking.

ORGANIZED TOURS

In a city as small as Salzburg that can be so pleasurably covered on foot, it really isn't necessary to book a bus tour unless you desire (and have the time) to visit out-of-town sights. For readers planning more than a two-day stay, here's a list of the excursions to consider.

Bob's Special Tours (tel. 87 24 84 or 06246/73377) offers two four-hour tours, each of which costs 280 S ($25.45). The "Sound of Music Tour" includes a short city tour and takes in most of the major filming locations of the movie, including Leopoldskron Palace, the lake district, and the church where the wedding took place. The second tour, the "Bavarian Mountain Tour," includes some *Sound of Music* sights, as well as the gardens of Hellbrunn and Berchtesgaden in Germany (passport required). Both tours depart at 9am and 2pm in summer, 9am in winter, with pickup at any guesthouse or hotel in Salzburg. Tours are small and personable, in buses that seat 8–20 people. "Bob," by the way, is a woman named Eveline Truhlar.

Another tour company is **Salzburg Panorama Tours** (tel. 88 32 11-0 or 87 40 29). In addition to its "City Tour," "Sound of Music Tour," and "Bavarian Mountain and Saltmines Tour," it also offers two tours of the surrounding countryside: "Lakes and Mountains" is a 4½-hour circular tour through Salzburg's lake district—Fuschl See, Mondsee, and Wolfgang See, stopping at the famous Weisses Rössl Hotel. This tour operates at 2pm daily, for 280 S ($25.45) per person. The "Bavarian Mountain Tour" is a 4½-hour tour that crosses the German border twice (bring your passport). The tour proceeds via Hellbrunn and Anif to Berchtesgaden and Königssee. You'll see Hitler's former residence (what's left of it, anyway) from your bus window. The tour leaves daily at 2pm, at a cost of 280 S ($25.45) per person.

And finally, one more tour company is **Salzburg Sightseeing Tours,** Am Mirabellplatz 2 (tel. 88 16 15 or 88 16 16), offering similar tours with similar prices, including a "City Tour," a "Sound of Music Tour," and trips to the surrounding countryside. Its four-hour tour of the Berchtesgaden saltmines, for example, departs daily at 9am and 2pm in summer and 2pm in winter and costs 280 S ($25.45), excluding entrance fee to the mines.

SPECIAL & FREE EVENTS

Salzburg's most famous annual event is the **Salzburg Festival,** which attracts music lovers from all over the world. It's therefore understandable that tickets are hard to come by and impossible to get once the festival is under way—from the end of July to the end of August. To find out what's being performed, contact the Salzburg Festival, Postfach 140, 5020 Salzburg (tel. 0662/8045). Among the highlights are Mozart's operas, Hugo von Hofmannsthal's *Everyman,* performances of the Salzburg Marionette Theater, and guest philharmonic orchestras.

For free concerts, your best bet is the **Mozarteum,** where concerts are given regularly by students. In the summer, free brass-band concerts are held in **Mirabell Garden** on Wednesday at 8:30pm and on Sunday at 10:30am.

7. SAVVY SHOPPING

Austrian artisanry is of high quality, with correspondingly high prices for sweaters, dirndls, leather goods, jewelry, and other local goods. Most shops are concentrated in the Old City along Getreidegasse and Alter Markt, as well as across the river along Linzer Gasse.

If you make purchases in any one store that total more than 1,000 S ($90.90), you're entitled to a refund of the Value-Added Tax (which amounts to 10%–32%, depending on the item). Ask the store clerk for a U-34 form, which you present to Austrian Customs upon leaving the country (if you're leaving by train, you can go through Customs at the Salzburg train station).

MARKETS Salzburg has two well-known markets. **Grüner Markt (Green Market)** is held in the Old City, in front of the Universitäts church on Universitätsplatz (behind Mozart's Birthplace). It features stalls selling vegetables, fruit, flowers, and a few souvenirs, as well as a stand-up food stall selling sausages. It takes place Monday through Friday from 6am to 6pm and on Saturday from 6am to 1pm.

On the other side of the river, in front of St. Andrews Church near Mirabellplatz, is the **Schrannenmarkt.** This is where Salzburg's housewives go to shop and socialize, purchasing vegetables and locally grown products. It's held every Thursday (on Wednesday if Thursday is a public holiday) from 6am to 1pm.

8. EVENING ENTERTAINMENT

Salzburg was known throughout the world as a city of music long before Julie Andrews sang that its hills were alive with the sound of music. As the birthplace of Mozart and site of the Salzburg Festival, the city boasts a musical event almost every night of the year.

To find out what's going on where, stop by the City Tourist Office, Mozartplatz 5 (tel. 84 75 68), to pick up a free copy of *Wochenspiegel* as well as a monthly brochure.

The cheapest way to buy theater tickets is by going directly to the theater box office. A ticket agency, such as **Polzer,** Residenzplatz 4 (tel. 846500), will charge a stiff 20% commission. The **Salzburg Ticket Service,** which also charges a 20% commission, is conveniently located at the City Tourist Office on Mozartplatz (tel. 84 22 96 or 84 03 10). Selling tickets for all concerts, it's open Monday through Friday from 9am to 6pm and on Saturday from 9am to noon. In July and August it's open daily from 9am to 7pm.

THE PERFORMING ARTS
OPERA, DANCE & MUSIC

FESTSPIELHAUS, Hofstallgasse 1. Tel. 8045.

This is where opera, ballet, and concerts are performed, and most of the Salzburg Festival takes place here. Performances are usually held in the 1,324-seat Kleines Haus (Small House) or the 2,170-seat Grosses Haus (Large House), and it's best to buy your tickets in advance; the box office is at Waagplatz la, near the City Tourist Office (tel. 84 53 46).

Prices: Tickets, 210–490 S ($19.10–$44.55); during the Salzburg Festival, 500–3,700 S ($45.45–$336.35).

Open: Box office, Mon–Fri 8am–6pm; performances usually at 7:30pm. **Bus:** 1 from the Hauptbahnhof to Hanuschplatz, or 5 or 6 from the Hauptbahnhof to Rathausplatz.

MOZARTEUM, Schwarzstrasse 26. Tel. 87 31 54.

This concert and music hall is where orchestra concerts, chamber music, and organ recitals are presented. As part of a music school, it occasionally features free concerts by students. The Mozarteum is located on the right bank of the river, near Mirabell Garden.

Prices: 180–600 S ($16.35–$54.55) for most tickets.

Open: Box office, Mon–Fri 9am–noon and 2–5pm; performances at 11am and/or 7:30pm. **Bus:** 1, 5, or 6 from the Hauptbahnhof to Mirabellplatz.

MIRABELL PALACE, Mirabellplatz, and the RESIDENZ, Residenzplatz 1.

The Salzburger Schlosskonzerte (Salzburg Palace Concerts; tel. 87 27 88) take place throughout the year in the Mirabell Palace and the Residenz. The chamber-music series presents much of Mozart's music, as well as music from the Viennese classical period, early music, music of the New Vienna School, and contemporary composers. The instrumentation ranges from solo piano to quartets, and everyone from Dvořák and Beethoven to Schubert, Bach, Brahms, ad infinitum, is played. Concerts are held in small ornately baroque rooms, much as they were during Mozart's time.

Prices: Tickets, 270 S ($24.55).

Open: Box office (Makartplatz 9), Mon–Fri 9am–noon and 2–5pm; performances almost daily at 8 or 8:30pm. **Bus:** 1, 5, or 6 from the Hauptbahnhof to Mirabellplatz (Mirabell Palace) or Rathausplatz (Residenz).

FESTUNG HOHENSALZBURG (Fortress), Mönchsberg 34. Tel. 84 88 22 or 82 58 58.

Salzburg's landmark, the Hohensalzburg Fortress, features concerts in the medieval Prince's Chamber from mid-May to mid-October and during Easter and Christmas. The music of Haydn, Mozart, Beethoven, Bach, Schubert, Chopin, and other composers is presented by such local musicians as the Salzburger Mozart-Ensemble as well as guest musicians.

Prices: Tickets, 270 S ($24.55).

Open: Box office (A.-Adlgasser-Weg 22), daily 9am–9pm; performances, mid-May to mid-October, daily at 8 or 8:30pm. **Directions:** Funicular from Festungsgasse.

THEATER

SALZBURGER LANDESTHEATER, Schwarzstrasse 22. Tel. 87 15 12.

Comedies, dramas, and musicals are performed, as well as operas and operettas.

During August the theater takes part in the Salzburg Festival. The Landestheater is located on the right bank of the Salzach, just south of Mirabell Garden.

Prices: Tickets, 180–620 S ($16.35–$56.35).

Open: Box office, Tues–Sat 10am–1pm and 5:30–7pm; performances, usually Tues–Sun at 7 or 7:30pm. **Bus:** 1, 5, or 6 from the Hauptbahnhof to Makartplatz.

SALZBURGER MARIONETTENTHEATER, Schwarzstrasse 24. Tel. 87 24 06.

Located next to the Landestheater, the Salzburger Marionettentheater was founded in 1913 and is one of the largest and most famous marionette theaters in Europe. It has toured throughout the world, including Argentina, Australia, Japan, and the United States, not to mention almost every country in Europe. It presents operas and operettas from Easter through September, including *The Magic Flute, Die Fledermaus, The Barber of Seville, The Marriage of Figaro,* and *Don Giovanni.*

Prices: Tickets, 230–400 S ($20.90–$36.35).

Open: Box office, Mon–Fri 10am–noon and 3–6pm, Sat 10am–noon; performances, usually Mon–Sat at 7:30 or 8pm, matinees occasionally at 4pm July–Aug. **Bus:** 1, 5, or 6 from the Hauptbahnhof to Makartplatz.

MOVIES

The easiest to find are the **Central Lichtspiele,** Linzer Gasse 17 (tel. 872282); **Elmo Kino,** St.-Julien-Strasse 5 (tel. 87 23 73), on the right bank; and **Mozartkino,** Kaigasse 33 (tel. 84 22 22).

The first performance usually starts at 2:30pm, the last at 10pm. Average ticket price is 65–85 S ($5.90–$7.70) for evening shows, 50 S ($4.55) for matinees.

GAMBLING

If you like to gamble, head for the **Casino at Café Winkler,** which sits atop Mönchsberg (tel. 84 56 56) and is best reached by elevator from Gstättengasse 13 (the lift ticket is free if you're going to the casino). Open daily from 3pm to 3am, it features roulette, baccarat, blackjack, poker, and slot machines. You must bring your passport or you won't be allowed in. The entry fee is 210 S ($19.10) but for that you get 250 S ($22.70) in chips. The minimum bet is 20 S ($1.80).

THE BAR SCENE

Salzburg's nightlife tends toward the refined and the classical, but there is a street on the right bank that shows promising signs of developing into an alternative night scene. Called **Steingasse,** it's a narrow, ancient, cobbled street that leads uphill from the Staatsbrücke, hugging the side of the Kapuzinerberg hill. There are some trendy shops here, as well as some rather exclusive nightclubs (with one-way mirrors and no windows). And yes, that tiny house at Steingasse 24 with the red light beckoning brightly is what you think it is.

In addition to a stroll on Steingasse, there are also a couple of breweries in Salzburg that are congenial for an evening out.

FRIDRICH, Steingasse 15. Tel. 87 62 18.

For a drink along Steingasse on the right bank of the river, try this tiny, modern bar. It's housed snugly in what used to be a blacksmith's shop, in a building dating from the 14th century and boasting its original arched ceiling. There's a sign on the door that says this place is for members only, but that's enforced only if the place gets too full.

Prices: A tiny glass of wine from 26 S ($2.35).

Open: Daily 5pm–1am. **Bus:** 1, 2, 5, or 6 to Mirabellplatz.

AUGUSTINERBRÄU, Augustinergasse 4. Tel. 43 12 46.

This brewery is one of the cheapest places in town for a brew, with seating either outdoors in its beer garden or in one of its massive dining halls. There are also counters selling sausages, pretzels, and other foods that go well with beer.

Prices: A half liter of beer 21 S ($1.90).
Open: Mon–Fri 3–11pm, Sat–Sun and hols 2:30–11pm. **Bus:** 27 from Mirabellplatz or Hanuschplatz to Augustinergasse.

DIE WEISSE BRÄUSTÜBERL AND BRAUGASTHOF, Rupertgasse 10 and Virgilgasse 9. Tel. 87 22 46 or 87 64 81.

This brewery, which specializes in wheat beer, serves its beer in two establishments located next to each other. The Braugasthof, on Rupertgasse 10, is a large restaurant with waiter service and changing menus offering such dishes as pepper steak and Gulasch. The Bräustüberl, located behind the Braugasthof, is smaller and less formal—you fetch your own beer and can dine on various sausages and pretzels. In fine weather, you'll probably want to sit outside in the beer garden. It's located on the right bank of the Salzach, about a 15-minute walk from the Old City or the Hauptbahnhof.

Prices: A half liter beer 30 S ($2.70).
Open: Bräustüberl, daily 11am–11pm; Braugasthof, Mon–Fri 5pm–midnight, Sat 10am–2pm. **Bus:** 29.

URBANKELLER, Schallmooser Hauptstrasse 50. Tel. 87 08 94.

This cellarlike establishment with a vaulted ceiling served as a wine cellar and ice-storage room back in 1636. Today it's a *Heuriger* (wine tavern) and it features jazz music every Friday evening except on holidays and during the months of July and August. It offers a self-service counter of salads, cheeses, and sausages, and a glass of wine is 32 S ($2.90). There's also a restaurant with waitress service. The music includes local groups such as the Salzach River Stompers, as well as jam sessions and guest bands. It's located on the right bank of the Salzach, about a 30-minute walk from the Old City or the Hauptbahnhof, or a short bus ride.

Prices: Wine from 32 S ($2.90). **Admission:** Free Mon–Thurs and Sat, 100 S ($9.10) Fri.
Open: Mon–Sat 5pm–midnight. **Bus:** 29 to Canavalstrasse.

---

9. EASY EXCURSIONS

UNTERSBERG Untersberg, the mountain dominating Salzburg, is 6,115 feet above sea level, seven miles south of the city in St. Leonhard. Visiting Untersberg is certainly worth the extra bucks, and probably will be one of the highlights of your stay in Salzburg. To get there, take public bus no. 55 from the train station to St. Leonhard, the last stop, and change to the cable car to ride to the top of the mountain. You'll have a glorious view of Salzburg and the Alps. A marked path leads to the peak in about 20 minutes (bring good walking shoes if you plan to hike); if you prefer, you can sit in the restaurant there and enjoy the view.

The round-trip fare for the cable car (tel. 87 12 17 or 06246/2477) is 160 S ($14.55) for adults, 90 S ($8.20) for children. The cable car operates daily: July to September 15, from 8:30am to 5:30pm; March through June and September 16 through October, from 9:15am to 4:45pm; and December 25 to February 28, from 10am to 4pm. It's closed for maintenance for two weeks in April, November, and the first three weeks in December.

HALLEIN Hallein, 10 miles south of Salzburg, is famous for its **salt mines,** near a mountain, the Dürrnberg. The mines (tel. 06245/52 85 15) have been operated since Roman times. Take an early train from Salzburg station to Hallein. In Hallein, follow the signs to the ground station of the funicular on Dürrnberg. At the top of the mountain, take the footpath (a five-minute walk) to the Dürrnberg salt-mine entrance. A one-hour salt-mine tour (in German only) is conducted by a uniformed miner. He'll give you a coverall to protect you from cold, humidity, and dirt, and then seat you on the bench of a small electric car. You'll see a huge saltwater lake, slide down twice on wooden rails, and listen to lectures on salt production. This excursion will take half a day, and is highly recommended if you travel with kids, even though the tour is in German (if you're lucky, your tour guide may speak some English and make a few translations for your sake).

The salt mines are open May to October from 9am to 5pm. They're closed during the winter months from November to April. Cost of the tour is 105 S ($9.55) for adults and 55 S ($5) for children. Note that children must be at least 4 years old to go on the tour.

STOCKHOLM

On a map, Stockholm appears cold and remote, a city disjointedly dotted across numerous islands, sliced into pieces by frigid arctic waters, and positioned as far north as Siberia. Yet to enter this breathtaking cosmopolitan city is to enter a romantic dream of old-world Europe. With remarkable grace, the Swedes have tamed their environment.

Up close, Stockholm is the most beautiful capital in Scandinavia—indeed, it is one of the most beautiful cities in the world. By day, the cramped, winding streets of Gamla Stan (Old Town) gracefully give way to the vast openness of Skansen. At night, world-class restaurants and glamorous clubs speak eloquently of Stockholm's sophistication, and lights from some of Europe's grandest buildings wink at passersby across well-kept ocean inlets.

Not surprisingly, the Swedish people mimic their environment. From afar, locals may appear distant and cool. Strangers will rarely meet your eye, and everything seems so ordered and quiet. However, when you delve into the Swedish culture and begin to meet individuals, their openness and warmth are endless.

1. FROM A BUDGET TRAVELER'S POINT OF VIEW

STOCKHOLM BUDGET BESTS

Opera and philharmonic tickets can be had practically for a song, and the city's many playhouses are also reasonably priced. Outdoor summer concerts and other warm-weather events are usually free, as are a host of year-round special events and activities (see the appropriate headings below for details).

During winter, open-air ice skating in the heart of the city is both exhilarating and cheap. So is a stroll along the waterfront, or a walk through Old Town.

Try starting your day with an aerobics class. It's very popular with the locals, costs just $5, and is easy to arrange.

SPECIAL DISCOUNT OPPORTUNITIES

FOR STUDENTS   A valid student ID will get you discounts at some museums and at cultural events such as the opera and ballet. See below for details.

FOR SENIORS   Travelers 65 years old and over receive most of the same discounts as students, and more. Take advantage of the 50% reduction on subways and buses. The listings below have even more heartening discount news.

WHAT THINGS COST IN STOCKHOLM	U.S. $
Taxi from Central Station to the National Museum	9.80
T-Bana from train station to an outlying neighborhood	2.00
Local telephone call	.33
Double room at the Grand Hotel (deluxe)	361.40
Double without bath at the Queen's Hotel (moderate)	96.55
Double room at the Wasa Park Hotell (budget)	85.50
Lunch for one, without wine, at Birgir Jarl (moderate)	9.25
Lunch for one, without wine, at Taco Bar (budget)	6.10
Dinner for one, with wines, at Stadhuskällaren (deluxe)	123.75
Dinner for one, without wine, at Slingerbulten (moderate)	18.50
Dinner for one, without wine, at Mamma Rosa (budget)	10.25
Pint of beer in a bar	6.20
Coca-Cola in a café	2.75
Cup of coffee in a café	2.50
Roll of ASA 100 color film, 36 exposures	9.80
Admission to the *Vasa* Museum	4.95
Movie ticket	9.90
Budget theater ticket	11.55

FOR EVERYONE On heavy sightseeing days, the **Stockholm Card** will prove itself one of the city's most outstanding values. Just 135 Kr ($22.30) per day or 285 Kr ($47) for three days buys you unlimited rides on the public transportation network, admission to most of the city's museums, free guided city sightseeing tours, and a guidebook to Stockholm. It also provides boat sightseeing at half price, as well as a one-way ticket to Drottningholm Palace. The card may be purchased at the tourist information counter at Sweden House and at Hotellcentralen at Central Station, and is valid for one adult and two children under the age of 18.

If you visit between October and April, you can take advantage of the special activities and discounts offered through the **Stimulating Stockholm** program. Some of the best deals focus on exercise: ice skating, fitness and Tai Chi classes, cross-country skiing, horseback riding. Ask for the brochure, and more details, at the information counter in Sweden House.

You'll find a reliable **free map** at the back of the free tourist board publication *Stockholm This Week*.

Sweden's enormously high taxes on alcohol are quite sobering. If you want to tipple without taking out a mortgage, buy **duty-free alcohol** before entering the country. Ditto for tobacco. Overseas visitors may import up to one quart of alcohol and 200 cigarettes.

WORTH THE EXTRA BUCKS

Stockholm County encompasses about 24,000 small islands, and each one will make you believe that you're a million miles from anywhere. Most are uninhabited, a few *were* inhabited hundreds of years ago (and contain interesting ruins), and others are jammed every summer with vacationing city-dwellers. The Stockholm Information

Service (see "Information" in "Orientation and Getting Around," below) will be happy to help you plan an excursion, as either a day trip or an overnight stay. Ferries are usually frequent and cheap, hotels are more charming and less expensive than in the city, and camping is always free. It is really unusual to have such a pristine expanse adjacent to a major city. Take advantage of this incomparable opportunity to take to the islands and seas at a relatively low cost. See "Easy Excursions," below, for further details.

2. PRETRIP PREPARATIONS

DOCUMENTS Citizens of the United States, Canada, Great Britain, Australia, and New Zealand need only a passport to visit Sweden.

WHAT TO PACK Even in summer it's a good idea to have a light coat, as temperatures often drop at night (and sometimes during the day as well). Cold weather begins by October and locals usually stay bundled up until April. January and February are coldest. Stockholm's streets are ideal for walking, but those of Gamla Stan (Old Town) are made of cobblestone, so be sure to bring good walking shoes and leave your heels at home. People of all ages in Stockholm wear jeans.

WHEN TO GO Without question, most of Stockholm's special events and free outdoor concerts happen during summer. But spring and autumn are probably the prettiest times of year, and while citizens of many other countries think of winter as something to wait out, Swedes revel in this season.

Stockholm's Average Daytime Temperature & Rainfall

	Jan	Feb	Mar	Apr	May	June	July	Aug	Sept	Oct	Nov	Dec
Temp. (°F)	27	26	31	40	50	59	64	62	54	45	37	32
Rainfall "	1.7	1.1	1	1.2	1.3	1.7	2.4	3	2.4	1.9	2	1.9

Special Events The **Stockholm Marathon** is usually run in early June, attracting thousands of local and world-class runners.

The June **Midsummer Celebration** falls on the Friday nearest to the longest day of the year. Special events, most free, fill parks and other outdoor spaces.

The **Stockholm Jazz and Blues Festival** is held for 10 days from the last weekend of June through the first weekend of July. Programs for this annual event will be available through the Stockholm Information Office.

Bellman Week, in the middle of July, honors the 18th-century court poet Carl Michael Bellman. Revelers, many in period costume, celebrate with poetry and music at Gröna Lund and various other city parks.

The annual 10-day **Stockholm Water Festival** in early August, established in 1991, celebrates the element that makes Stockholm such a unique and lovely city, as well as one in which swimming and fishing in the center of town are long-standing traditions. Festivities include live entertainment, music, dancing, sporting events, fireworks, and the awarding of the Stockholm Water Prize, a cash prize of $150,000 that goes to an individual or organization that has made an outstanding contribution to water conservation.

The **Women's 10K Run,** scheduled each August, has traditionally attracted more than 25,000 entrants.

WHAT'S SPECIAL ABOUT STOCKHOLM

Gamla Stan [Old Town]
☐ Narrow streets and alleyways that make you get lost—in direction and time.
☐ The city's densest cluster of shops, restaurants, and nightspots.

Special Parks
☐ Skansen, a memorable open-air museum and picnic spot.
☐ Djurgården, a forested island in the heart of the city perfect for jogging and strolling.
☐ Kungsträdgården, the city's main park for ice skating, concerts, and people-watching.

Waterfront
☐ Boasting some of Europe's most glorious and grand buildings and views (don't forget your camera when you cross the bridge to Djurgården).

Festivals and Events
☐ Especially during summer, festivals and events include the Jazz and Blues Festival, the Water Festival, Sailboat Day, and the Stockholm Marathon.
☐ The Nobel Prize ceremonies in December, one of the world's biggest annual events.

Sailboat Day, during the first weekend in September, is an excuse for the city's aquatic pleasurecraft to show off. From Sunfish to schooner, the harbor becomes a showcase for boats of all sizes.

The exciting week-long **Stockholm Open** tennis championships are held the last week of October or the first week of November in the Globe Arena.

The **Nobel Prizes,** named after the Swedish inventor of dynamite, Alfred Nobel, are awarded on December 10 for excellence in physics, chemistry, medicine, literature, and economics. The prizes have been awarded since 1901.

Lucia, the festival of lights, is celebrated on December 13, the shortest day (and longest night) of the year. This is one of the most popular and colorful of all Swedish festivals, designed to "brighten up" an otherwise dark period. The festivities continue on the nearest Sunday, when a Lucia Queen is crowned with candles during a ceremony in Skansen. Concerts are held throughout the city from morning till night.

Finally, few locals miss the **Christmas Markets** held every Sunday, beginning four weeks before the holiday. Stalls fill squares in Gamla Stan and Skansen selling traditional foods, handcrafts, gifts, and other seasonal items.

BACKGROUND READING   Noted Swedish authors include: Vilhelm Moberg, most famous for his works on the Swedish-American experience, especially *The Emigrants* (Warner Books); Per-Anders Fogelstrom, whose novels are set in Stockholm; dramatist August Strindberg, famous for the realism of his plays; Selma Lagerlöf, who penned works such as *The Wonderful Adventures of Nils;* and Astrid Lindgren, author of dozens of children's books.

Those interested in the Vikings can try Johannes Brondsted's *The Vikings* (Penguin Books) or Frans Bengtsson's *The Long Ships* (William Collins Sons and Co.).

If you want to read about the politics, economics, and culture of Sweden, you can order free fact sheets from the **Swedish Information Service,** which has offices in the U.S. at 1 Dag Hammarskjöld Plaza, 45th Floor, New York, NY 10017-2201 (tel. 212/751-5900; fax 212/752-4789), and at 10880 Wilshire Blvd., Suite 505, Los Angeles, CA 90024-4314 (tel. 213/470-2154; fax 213/475-4683). In Stockholm, the **Swedish Institute,** with more of the same enlightening pamphlets, is conveniently located on the second floor of Sweden House, at Kungsträdgården (tel. 789-20-00). Dozens of well-written and well-researched publications seem to leave no stone unturned. The institute also sells a wide variety of English-language books about Sweden and by famous Swedish authors. It's open Monday through Friday from 9am to 6pm during summer, and until 5pm in winter.

3. ORIENTATION & GETTING AROUND

ARRIVING IN STOCKHOLM

FROM THE AIRPORT   Stockholm's **Arlanda Airport** is 28 miles north of town. Four rainbow-striped buses (tel. 23-60-00) leave the airport, and you want the one to "Stockholm City." Take it to City Terminal. It costs 50 Kr ($8.25) for everyone, except kids under 16 who ride free with a parent. The journey takes 40 minutes, and buses run about every 10 minutes from 5:45am to 10:05pm. Taxis are available at the airport, but the ride into town will run you about 500 Kr ($82.50).

You can change money in the baggage-claim area, before you reach Customs, at a bank offering reasonable rates. Adjacent red telephones offer local calls for up to three minutes for 2 Kr (35¢). Beyond Customs, you'll find representatives from most of the major car-rental companies. Downstairs is the Left-Luggage Office (tel. 797-60-80); charges are 25 Kr ($4.10) per bag per day, and the office never closes. Lockers cost 20–25 Kr ($3.30–$4.10).

Pick up a city map from the information office at the airport, which is open 24 hours, and you'll soon be making your way easily around the city. There are six day rooms available at the airport if you choose to rest.

FROM THE TRAIN/BUS STATION   Stockholm's train station, **Central Station,** Vasagatan 14, and bus station, **City Terminal (Cityterminalen),** Klarabergsviadukten 72, are across the street from one another and connected underground by escalators. Central Station has three levels and can be confusing in its enormity; the more modern, two-level City Terminal, on the other hand, is easy to maneuver in and seems more like an international airport than a bus station. It has an information desk inside to the left of entrance, a money-exchange window (look for the yellow-and-black sign), a kiosk selling international newspapers, and an SAS office.

Since neither the bus nor the train station is within walking distance of hostels or most budget hotels, you'll probably have to take the subway to your lodging. But that's easy enough: From the lower level of Central Station you can connect directly to the subway system. Just follow the signs that say TUNNELBANA or T-BANA.

The lower level of the train station is also home to the tourist office and the very helpful Hotellcentralen, where you can book hotel rooms (see "Budget Accommodations," below, for further details). Look for an illuminated white "i" on a green background pointing the way.

Baggage carts and photo machines are across the corridor from Hotellcentralen.

Lockers are available for 15, 20, or 25 Kr ($2.50, $3.30, or $4.10), depending on size, per 24 hours, on the same level, but it is much safer to make use of the Left-Luggage Office (Resgods) (tel. 762-25-49) on the ground level (upstairs, near the escalator to the bus station), which charges 40 Kr ($6.60) per bag per day. It's open daily from 6am to 10pm.

Train tickets are sold on the ground floor. Windows 1–10 are for foreign travel; Windows 11–26, for domestic.

The ground floor is also home to telephones, train information (SJ Information), and currency-exchange offices. The currency-exchange office is open daily from 8am to 9pm; look for the big yellow-and-black sign.

There is a large market on the lowest level, along with clean bathrooms—there's a 5-Kr (80¢) charge to use them—and large showers, which cost 20 Kr ($3.30). An attendant is on duty.

For information about rail service within Sweden, call 020/75-75-75; for international rail service, 22-79-40. For bus information, call 700-51-47 between 6am and 10:30pm; for airport bus departures, call 600-10-00.

INFORMATION

After getting settled in your hotel room, your first stop in Stockholm should be Sweden House (Sverige Huset), Hamngatan 27, off Kungsträdgården.

On the ground floor you'll find the **Stockholm Information Service** (tel. 789-20-00), the country's main tourist office. Even if you desire no other information, make sure you get your free copy of *Stockholm This Week* for its lists of special and free events and good map. The Stockholm Card (described above under "Budget Bests" in "From a Budget Traveler's Point of View") can be purchased here, as can city tour and archipelago excursion tickets. Ask for the brochure "Stimulating Stockholm," which lists more than a dozen inexpensive ways to enjoy Stockholm and environs from October through April. This office sells stamps and will reserve a hotel room for you for a service charge of 24 Kr ($3.95), plus a 9% deposit on the room. You can also buy posters, cards, and gift items here. Their 202-page *Discover Stockholm* book for 35 Kr ($5.80) is a good investment and souvenir of your trip; a map of Stockholm and surrounding areas cost 10 Kr ($1.65). There is a convenient, but locked, bathroom on the premises—you have to ask someone to buzz you into it. The Stockholm Information Service is open mid-June to August 31, Monday through Friday from 9am to 6pm and on Saturday and Sunday from 9am to 5pm; the rest of the year, Monday through Friday from 9am to 5pm and on Saturday and Sunday from 9am to 2pm.

The **Swedish Institute Bookshop,** located on the second floor of Sweden House (tel. 789-20-00 from 9:30am to 12:30pm; fax 20-72-48), features an extensive collection of English-language books, coffee-table tomes, records, cassettes, CDs, children's books, art books, and free fact sheets on Sweden's social, political, and economic issues. It's open Monday through Friday from 9am to 6pm June through August, and 9am to 5pm September to May.

Hotellcentralen, on the lower level of Central Station (tel. 24-08-80), makes hotel reservations (see "Budget Accommodations," below), answers general questions, and distributes free maps. It's open May through September, daily from 8am to 9pm; the rest of the year, Monday through Friday from 8am to 5pm, on Saturday and Sunday from 8am to 1pm.

SL Center, on the lower level of Sergels Torg (tel. 786-10-00 daily from 7am to 9pm), offers information about local subway and bus transportation and sells a good transport map as well as tickets for the system. It's open Monday through Thursday from 8:30am to 6:30pm, on Friday from 8:30am to 5:30pm, and on Saturday from 10am to 3pm.

CITY LAYOUT

It helps to picture the city as the group of islands it really is, even though, for all intents and purposes, bridges and tunnels connect them as one. Fortunately for visitors, only a handful of the thousands of islands in the Stockholm archipelago are important tourist destinations.

Norrmalm The heart of modern Stockholm, Norrmalm, is actually on the mainland, in the northernmost part of the city center. It is where you will arrive at the train station, shop in the major stores, and probably find a hotel. **Drottninggatan,** the major pedestrian shopping street, runs approximately north-south, and bisects Norrmalm. Along this thoroughfare are the important squares of **Sergels Torg** (the active center of Norrmalm) and **Hötorget,** home to Åhléns and PUB department stores, respectively. Branching east from Sergels Torg is **Hamngatan,** a short street lined with chain store outlets, the NK department store (Sweden's largest), Sweden House (home of the Stockholm Information Service), and **Kungsträdgården** (half park, half street, and host to many free outdoor events). **Birgir Jarlsgatan,** a few blocks east of Kungsträdgården, is the address of the Royal Dramatic Theater and the American Express office and is filled with interesting shops and cafés as far as **Sturegallerian,** the trendy new shopping gallery at Stureplan.

Kungsholmen   Due west of Norrmalm, Kungsholmen is home to Stockholm's striking City Hall, where the Nobel Prize banquet is held annually.

Gamla Stan   In Swedish, Gamla Stan means **Old Town,** and on the city's tourist maps, this district's small island is always in the center. Rightly so. Pretty buildings, cobblestone streets, narrow alleyways, and interesting shops provide a welcome counterpoint to Norrmalm's big-city landscape. In olden days, fast currents on either side of the island forced sea merchants to portage their goods to vessels waiting on the other side. The paths these porters pounded are now the oldest extant streets in Stockholm and are well worth exploring.

Södermalm   South of Gamla Stan is Södermalm, an area that, up until about 10 years ago, was considered the "bad" side of town. Today, as the city gentrifies, Södermalm's rents have rocketed and chic restaurants, bars, and clubs have moved in. You might stay in one of Södermalm's budget hotels or private rooms, and you're well advised to visit the cliffs overlooking Stockholm Harbor.

Skeppsholmen   East of Gamla Stan, across a narrow channel, lies tiny, pretty Skeppsholmen, containing the Museum of Modern Art and two youth hostels. The quiet streets around the island's perimeter are perfect for strolling.

Djurgården   Farther east still is Stockholm's tour de force, the magnificent Djurgården (Deer Park), which encompasses many of the city's top sights. This shady neck of land with lush oak groves would be any lumberjack's delight but, thankfully, has been protected for centuries by the government, which has historically maintained the area as a grazing ground for the king's deer. The *Vasa* Ship Museum and the massive outdoor Skansen Folk Museum are the area's top draws, though several other good museums are located here, too.

GETTING AROUND

Subways (called Tunnelbana) and buses are operated by SL, the city transportation network, and charge according to a zone system—the price increases the farther you go. Most places you'll visit in central Stockholm will cost 12 Kr ($2.20), payable at the Tunnelbana and bus entrance.

In addition to the **Stockholm Card,** described above under "Special Discount Opportunities" in "From the Budget Traveler's Point of View," several other discounts are available. SL sells **day passes.** A one-day unlimited-use pass for central Stockholm and the Djurgården ferries costs 30 Kr ($4.95); a three-day pass is 105 Kr ($17.30). A pass that encompasses all of greater Stockholm is also available for 55 Kr ($9.10) for one day. All are half price for people under 18 and over 65.

People under 18 and senior citizens can buy half-price tickets for all forms of public transportation. For more information about routes, times, and prices, call 786-10-00.

BY SUBWAY [TUNNELBANA OR T-BANA]   Stockholm is blessed with a fast and far-reaching subway system called the T-Bana. It's easy to use and you'll probably never go more than a few stops or wait more than five minutes for a train. Color-coded maps are on station walls and printed in most tourist publications. Timetables for each train are also posted. Escalators in some subway stations are steep enough to rival London's. More than half the city's 99 subway stations are distinctive for the permanent artwork and other decoration they display. Especially eye-catching are Kungsträdgården, T-Centralen, and Slussen.

One ticket costs 12 Kr ($2) and is good for one hour (use it as often as you want), or you can get a strip of 15 coupons for 55 Kr ($9.10). A 24-hour card for unlimited use in central Stockholm costs 30 Kr ($4.95) for adults, 15 Kr ($2.50) for children; the same pass for use in Greater Stockholm costs 55 Kr ($9.10) for adults, 28 Kr ($4.60) for children. A 72-hour pass is 105 Kr ($17.30) for adults, 53 Kr ($8.75) for children. Unlimited transportation is included in the cost of the Stockholm Card.

If you are paying with cash or using a strip ticket, pass through the gate and tell the person in the ticket booth where you are going. He or she will either ask for your fare or stamp your ticket. If you have a Stockholm Card, just flash it. Sometimes the ticket collector is absent; in these instances, few commuters wait for the collector to return—they just walk through.

Note: Most subway stops have several well-marked exits; save yourself time (and avoid walking several blocks out of your way) by checking your map and choosing the exit closest to your destination. Trains are shorter during less heavily trafficked periods, such as evenings, so stand toward the center of the platform for boarding.

BY BUS   Buses run where subways don't, comprehensively covering the city. Enter through the front door and pay the driver, show your Stockholm Card, or have your strip ticket stamped. If you plan on making extensive use of buses, buy a transport map from the Stockholm Information Office or the SL Center (addresses listed under "Information," above). Many buses depart from Normalmstorg, which is catercorner to Kungsträdgården and two blocks from Sweden House.

BY FERRY   From May to September, ferries ply the waters between Gamla Stan and Djurgården, providing the best link between these two highly touristed areas. In summer, boats depart every 20 minutes from 9am to 1am; in winter, Monday through Friday from 9am to 5pm and on Saturday and Sunday from 9am to 6pm. The ride costs 15 Kr ($2.50) for adults, half price for seniors and those 7–18 years old. Check with the Stockholm Information Service for more information.

BY TAXI   Beware! The meter starts at 24 Kr ($3.95), and a short ride can easily come to 60 Kr ($9.90), but the tip is included in the price. You can order a cab by phone (tel. 15-00-00), but there is an additional charge. Avoid gypsy cabs; always take one with a yellow license plate with a T at the end of the number.

ON FOOT   Walking is the most delightful way to get to know the city. You'll have to explore Gamla Stan on foot as cars are banned from most of the streets. Djurgården and Skeppsholmen are popular haunts for strolling.

BY BICYCLE   Bicycling is particularly recommended for exploring Djurgården and bikes are available for rent just to your right after you cross the bridge onto the island from **Skepp o Höj** (tel. 660-57-57) from April through September.

CAR RENTAL   Unless you are planning an extended trip outside Stockholm, you will find that keeping a car in the city is more trouble than it's worth. Most major American car-rental firms, including Hertz and Avis, have counters at the airport and offices in Stockholm. Local companies are usually cheaper and are listed under "Biluthyrning" in the phone book and in the "Shopping" section of *Stockholm This Week.* Swedish law requires that motorists drive with their lights on day and night.

FAST   STOCKHOLM

American Express   The Stockholm office gets a gold star from travelers for friendliness and helpfulness. Located catercorner from the Royal Dramatic Theater at Birgir Jarlsgatan 1 (tel. 679-78-80), it can exchange money and hold or forward mail (see "Mail," below). There is a cash machine on the premises. The office is open Monday through Friday from 9am to 5pm and on Saturday from 10am to 1pm. For 24-hour refund assistance, call 020-795-155.

Babysitters   To find a babysitter, ask the proprietor of your hotel or guesthouse for a recommendation. Deluxe hotels also usually keep a list of babysitters and might be of assistance.

Banks Most banks are open Monday through Friday from 9:30am to 3pm. Some in central Stockholm keep later hours on Thursday, and conveniently located Nordbanken, across the street from Sweden House, is open until 5pm Monday through Friday.

Exchange rates rarely vary from bank to bank, but commissions do. These fees can be very high, around 30 Kr ($4.95) for a traveler's-check transaction; however, you may often exchange up to six checks per transaction, so it's a good idea to change as much money as you think you will need at one time. There may be no fee to change cash, but the rate is lower. Competitive rates are also offered by many post offices, including the main branch, which keeps long hours (see "Mail," below, for details). The exchange window at the train station keeps long hours, from 8am to 9pm daily. Cash American Express traveler's checks at the American Express office at no extra charge.

Bookstores The best prices, along with a large selection of books, are found at Akademi Bokhandeln, at Regeringsgatan and Master Samuelsgatan (tel. 21-15-90), open Monday through Friday from 9:30am to 6pm and on Saturday from 10am to 2pm (to 3pm in winter); check out the bargain bin. Fiction is upstairs, in the back on the left. Large and impressive, Hedengrens Bokhondel, at Stureplan 4 in Sturegallerian (tel. 611-51-28), has big travel and fiction sections downstairs; you'll also find a nice architecture section. They have a smaller shop a block away, at Kungsgatan 4 (tel. 723-15-81) that sells discounted books in English. A novel by Graham Greene or Marguerite Duras will probably run you 65–85 Kr ($10.70–$14) wherever you buy it.

Business Hours **Shops** are usually open Monday through Friday from 9:30am to 6pm and on Saturday from 9:30am to 2pm. Larger stores may maintain longer hours Monday through Saturday, and may open on Sunday as well. Most offices are open Monday through Friday only, from 9am to 5pm.

Currency You'll pay your way in Stockholm in Swedish kronor (Kr) or crowns (singular, krona), sometimes abbreviated SEK, which are divided into 100 öre. Bills come in denominations of 5, 10, 50, 100, 1,000, and 10,000 kronor. Coins are issued in 5, 10, and 50 öre, as well as 1, 2, and 5 kronor. For money exchange, see "Banks," above, and "Mail," below.

Dentists Emergency dental care is available at St. Eriks Hospital, Fleminggatan 22 (tel. 654-11-17, or 644-92-00 after 9pm). Regular hospital hours for walk-ins are 8am to 7pm. At other times, phone first.

Doctors Normally, emergency medical care is provided by the hospital closest to the area in which you are staying. Medical Care Information (tel. 644-92-00) can provide you with this information as well as advice regarding injuries. City Akuten, a privately run infirmary at Holländargatan 3 (tel. 11-71-02), can also provide help, but at a cost of 300–500 Kr ($49.50–$82.50) a visit. Also check the telephone directory under "vardcentraler" in the blue pages at the beginning of the *Företag* phone book for clinics listed by neighborhood, and you may be able to see a local doctor for less money than the amount noted above.

Embassies The **U.S. Embassy** is at Strandvägen 101 (tel. 783-53-00); the **Canadian Embassy,** Tegelbacken 4 (tel. 23-79-20); the **Irish Embassy,** Ostermalmsgatan 97 (tel. 661-74-09); the **Embassy of the U.K.,** Skarpögatan 6-8 (tel. 667-01-40); the **Australian Embassy,** Sergels Torg 12 (tel. 613-29-00). **New Zealand** does not maintain an embassy in Stockholm; inquiries should be made through the Australian Embassy.

Emergencies For police, fire department, or ambulance service, call 90-000.

Eyeglasses Almost every street has an "Optiker" that can repair or replace broken glasses. **Tollare,** Hamngatan 37, in the center of Gallerian shopping mall (tel. 20-13-33), has friendly service and a good selection of frames in contemporary styles. It's open Monday through Friday from 9:30am to 6:30pm, on Saturday from 9:30am to 4pm, and on Sunday from noon to 4pm. Or try **NK Optik,** in NK department store at Hamngatan 18-20 (tel. 762-87-78), open Monday through Friday from 10am to 7pm, on Saturday from 10am to 5pm, and on Sunday from 11am to 5pm (possibly shorter hours in summer).

Holidays   Sweden celebrates New Year's Day, Epiphany, Good Friday, Easter and Easter Monday, May Day, Ascension Day (Thursday of the sixth week after Easter), Whit Sunday and Monday (also called Pentecost), Midsummer Day (Saturday closest to June 24), All Saints' Day (the Saturday following Oct 30), and Christmas (Dec 24–26).

Hospitals   For the hospital closest to you, phone Medical Care Information (tel. 44-92-00), or visit City Akuten, Holländargatan 3 (tel. 11-71-02), a privately run infirmary.

Information   The Stockholm Information Service is located in Sweden House, Hamngatan 27 (tel. 789-20-00). Other tourist offices and sources of information are mentioned above in "Orientation and Getting Around."

Laundry/Dry Cleaning   Many of the hotels listed below in "Budget Accommodations" offer laundry facilities. There is a self-service laundry, Tvättomatten, at Västmannagatan 61 opposite Gustav Vasa Church (tel. 34-64-80), where for 50 Kr ($9.10) you can wash and dry 5 kilos (11 lb.) of dirty clothes. The cost includes washing powder, and you should plan to arrive at least two hours before closing; it's open Monday through Friday from 9am to 1pm and 2 to 6pm, and on Saturday from 10am to 2pm. Tvättomatten will also wash or dry clean your clothes for you—at a higher price, of course.

Lost and Found   If you lost it on a bus or the T-Bana, check at the SL office at the Rådmansgatan stop (tel. 736-07-80). If you lost it on a train, check the lost-and-found office on the lower concourse of Central Station (tel. 762-20-00). If you lost it somewhere else, check with the Police Lost and Found Office, Tjärhovsgatan 21 (tel. 769-30-75).

Mail   The main Stockholm Post Office, Vasagatan 28-34 (tel. 781-20-00), is

THE KRONA & THE DOLLAR

At this writing $1 = approximately 6.06 kronor (or 1 krona = 16½¢), and this was the rate of exchange used to calculate the dollar values given in this chapter (rounded to the nearest nickel). This rate fluctuates from time to time and may not be the same when you travel to Sweden. Therefore the following table should be used only as a guide:

Kr	U.S.$	Kr	U.S.$
1	.17	100	16.50
2	.33	125	20.63
3	.50	150	24.75
4	.66	175	28.88
5	.80	200	33.00
6	.99	225	37.13
7	1.16	250	41.25
8	1.32	275	45.38
9	1.49	300	49.50
10	1.65	325	53.63
15	2.50	350	57.76
20	3.30	375	61.88
25	4.10	400	66.01
50	8.25	500	82.51

diagonally across from Central Station. It is open Monday through Friday from 8am to 6:30pm; the one in Central Station is open later. Most local post offices are open from 9am to 6pm Monday through Friday and 9am to 1pm on Saturday. A centrally located post office only a couple of blocks from Sweden House and NK department store, at Regeringsgatan 65 (tel. 781-21-38), is open Monday through Friday from 8:30am to 6:30pm and on Saturday from 10am to 1pm.

You can receive mail either at the main post office (marked "Poste Restante" with a "hold until" date) or at American Express. The mail service at American Express, Birger Jarlsgatan 1 (tel. 679-78-80), is free; the mail is delivered here daily about 10am. The charge to forward mail is 20 Kr ($3.30). Open Monday through Friday from 9am to 5pm and on Saturday from 10am to 1pm.

Newspapers Unfortunately, there are no English-language newspapers or magazines printed in Sweden. The *International Herald Tribune* and *USA Today* are available at newsstands all around town and in most hotel news shops. The latest American and British magazines are also readily available. A broad selection of periodicals is available at the service center level of NK department store and at the International Press Center, Regeringsgatan 12 (tel. 21-22-64), open Monday through Friday from 10am to 6:30pm and on Saturday from 10am to 4pm.

Expressen, a liberal tabloid, and *Dagens Nyheter,* an independent newspaper, are Stockholm's largest-selling dailies. Even if you can't read Swedish, you might be interested in scanning their advertising and nightlife pages.

Finally, foreign periodicals can be read free at Culture House (Kulturhuset), Sergels Torg, third floor (see "Information," above), and at the Municipal Library (Stadsbiblioteket), Sveavägen 73 (tel. 23-66-00), open Monday through Thursday from 10am to 8:30pm, on Friday from 10am to 6pm, and on Saturday and Sunday from noon to 4pm.

Pharmacy For 24-hour service, go to C. W. Scheele, Klarabergsgatan 64 (tel. 24-82-80).

Photographic Needs Film can be purchased and processed on almost every street in the city center, especially in the major tourist areas. One-hour film processing is available at Central Station. For camera supplies and one-hour processing, try Hasselblads Foto, Hamngatan 16 (tel. 21-40-42), open Monday through Friday from 9:30am to 6pm and on Saturday from 10am to 2pm.

Department stores often have two-for-the-price-of-one sales on film in the summer.

Police For emergencies, dial 90-000. For other matters, contact Police Headquarters (Polishuset) at Agnegatan 33-37 (tel. 769-30-00). One conveniently located precinct office is inside Central Station.

Radio/TV There are only three FM radio stations in the Stockholm area, all state-run. Radio Stockholm relays the BBC World Service news at 7pm Monday through Friday on 103.3 FM. Radio Sweden, at 89.6 FM, broadcasts programs in English; call 784-74-00 for times. If you have an AM receiver, you may hear broadcasts all the way from Moscow—and beyond.

Television is also a government affair. There are only two national channels, and programming seems to favor nature and news shows. When foreign movies are shown (usually at night), they are subtitled. Good news: no commercials. Stations sign off around 11:30pm.

Religious Services Some 92% of Swedes belong to the Church of Sweden, a Lutheran church. The Stockholm Cathedral (Storkyrkan), Old Town (tel. 723-30-00), consecrated in 1279, holds regular services, and is open to the public. Two Protestant Sunday services in English are held at 9am at Santa Clara Church, Clara Östra Kyrkogatan 8, near Central Station (tel. 723-30-29), and at Immanuel Church, an interdenominational fellowship, at Kungstensgatan 17 (tel. 15-12-25). Other houses of worship include: Stockholm Cathedral (Roman Catholic), Folkungagatan 46 (tel. 40-00-81), and the modern, centrally located Santa Eugenia Catholic Church, Kungsträdgårdsgatan 12 (tel. 679-57-70); the Islamic Congregation, Torsgatan 48A, ground floor (tel. 31-61-75); and the Great Synagogue (Jewish-Conservative), Wahrendorffsgatan 3A (tel. 679-51-60).

Shoe Repair   There is while-you-wait shoe-repair at Mister Minit, in NK department store at Hamngatan 18-20 (tel. 762-85-83); it's open Monday through Friday from 10am to 6pm and on Saturday from 10am to 3pm.

Tax   Sweden is legendary for its painfully high income taxes—as much as 72% in the top bracket. Fortunately, visitors to Stockholm need only concern themselves with the 24.6% VAT (Value-Added Tax) applied to most goods and services. In actuality, you won't really have to worry about this either, as the VAT is already added into the tag price of most store items, restaurant menus, and hotel tariffs.

Many stores offer non-Scandinavian tourists the opportunity to recover the VAT on purchases over 100 Kr ($18.20). See "Savvy Shopping," below, for details.

Taxis   Taxis in Stockholm are expensive. Even a group of four rarely justifies a cab's prices. The meter drops at 24 Kr ($3.95), including tip, and rises rapidly. Advance reservations can be made by dialing 15-00-00, for which there should be no extra charge.

Telephone, Telex, and Fax   The area code for Stockholm is 08, and all numbers listed in this chapter assume that prefix, unless otherwise noted.

Public phones are fairly straightforward. **Local calls** cost 2 Kr (33¢) for the first few minutes, and one more krona for every couple of minutes after that (depending on distance). Phones accept 50-öre, 1-Kr, and 5-Kr coins.

The easiest way to make **international calls** to America is via AT&T's USA Direct service. If you have an AT&T Calling Card, or call collect, you can reach an American operator from any phone by calling 020-795-611. Deposit 2 Kr before dialing.

Alternatively, international calls can be made from the Telecenter Office in Central Station (tel. 780-81-21), open Monday through Friday from 8am to 9pm. A call to the United States or Canada from here costs 14.40 Kr ($2.40) per minute daily from 10pm to 10am; from 10am to 10pm rates rise to 18.75 Kr ($3.10) per minute. If you need to speak with an international operator, dial 0019.

For directory listings or other information for Stockholm or other parts of Sweden only, dial 07975.

The Stockholm telephone directory consists of three different books: the one designated *Företag* is for companies and organizations; *Huskåll*, for individuals; and *Gula Sidorna* is the yellow pages. At this writing, many local numbers are being changed, often simply adding a 6 at the beginning of the number.

The Telecenter will also hold **Telexes** for you sent via no. 17019, as well as **faxes.** Ask the sender to specify "hold for [your name]" on the Telex or fax, or if they include your local telephone number, the office will contact you when it arrives. Receiving a fax costs about 25 Kr ($4.10) per page, with an additional 10-Kr ($1.65) charge if they call to notify you of its arrival. The Telecenter is open in summer, daily from 8am to 9pm. Credit cards are accepted (AE, DC, EURO, MC, V).

Tipping   A 10%–15% service charge is routinely included in hotel, restaurant, and other charges. Further tipping is unnecessary unless service is extraordinary.

4. BUDGET ACCOMMODATIONS

Sure, you've heard about Stockholm's sky-high hotel prices. But less expensive options exist, so armed with this guide, you're sure to find an affordable bed.

There is no budget-hotel-packed street in the city. Budget hotels are few and far between and are listed below along with some accommodation alternatives.

It is surprisingly common for Stockholm's city-dwellers to supplement their incomes by sharing their homes with tourists. Most of the people who open their homes to foreigners are exceedingly friendly, well traveled, and interested in meeting new people, and give a lot of themselves to ensure that their guests are comfortable. There seems to be an unofficial network of private-room renters, so even if the home you phone is full, chances are pretty good that the owners will refer you to a friend who has room.

Here are a few alternatives to emptying your wallet for a room:

A ROOM IN A PRIVATE HOME Some locals have been renting spare rooms to tourists for years, and their rates and locations prove them to be excellent values. Some sure-to-please choices are listed below.

A DISCOUNTING SERVICE On the lower level of Central Station, **Hotellcentralen** (tel. 24-08-80) can sometimes offer cut-price rooms for same-day occupancy during slow periods. Of course, not all hotels discount rooms, but those that do usually lower their rates as the day wears on. There is a 24-Kr ($3.95) booking fee (it's waived if you call from abroad). The office is open May through September, daily from 8am to 9pm; April and October, daily from 8am to 5pm; and November through March, Monday through Friday from 8:30am to 5pm. Credit cards are accepted (AE, EURO, MC, and V). **Hotelltjänst** (see "Room-Finding Services," below) offers a similar service.

HOSTELS Don't shy away from hostels, especially if you're traveling alone. Most of the city's hostels have four-bed rooms with extremely reasonable prices. All have exceptionally high standards and are clean, and two occupy the city's best location. See "Super-Budget Choices," below, for details.

ROOM-FINDING SERVICES

The following companies work with private citizens all around Stockholm, and can offer very good accommodations at great prices. Ask for a place near a subway or bus stop.

ALL-RUM, Wallingatan 34, S-11124 Stockholm. Tel. 08/21-37-89 or 21-37-90.

All-Rum acts as an agent for half a dozen small furnished apartments that can accommodate one to four people. Rates are usually 250 Kr ($41.25) single and 500 Kr ($82.50) double. Weekly rates for apartments with TVs and bathrooms are 2,500 Kr ($412.55) single and 3,500 Kr ($577.55) double. All-Rum is located right in the bend of Wallingatan at the corner of Västmannagatan, about seven blocks north of Central Station.

Open: Mon–Wed 10am–5pm, Thurs 10am–6pm, Fri 10am–3pm. **Closed:** One to two weeks in July.

HOTELLTJÄNST, Vasagatan 15-17 (4th Floor), S-11120 Stockholm. Tel. 08/10-44-37, 10-44-57, or 10-44-67. Fax 08/21-37-16.

Hotelltjänst regularly rents more than 50 private rooms across Stockholm at excellent, set rates. In fact, it's hard to beat their charge of 220 Kr ($36.30) single, 330 Kr ($54.45) double. There are no service fees, but a minimum two-night stay is required.

In addition, this office sometimes offers select hotel rooms at a deep discount, often as much as 50% in summer. This can mean high-quality singles for about 500 Kr ($82.50) and doubles for 700 Kr ($115.50). You can reserve hotel rooms anytime in advance; private rooms, 10 days ahead. The office, which has a 24-hour answering machine, is located two long blocks from Central Station; turn right when you get off the elevator.

Open: Mon–Fri 9am–noon and 1–5pm.

FROMMER'S SMART TRAVELER: HOTELS

VALUE-CONSCIOUS TRAVELERS SHOULD
TAKE ADVANTAGE OF THE FOLLOWING:

1. Rooms in private homes.
2. Room-finding services, which often offer cut-price rooms.
3. Hostels—excellently priced, well-maintained, clean lodgings for people of all ages.

DOUBLES FOR LESS THAN 410 KR ($67.65)

PRIVATE HOMES

Staying in a private home costs less than in a hotel, and it affords the opportunity to get to know Swedish people in their own environment. Call ahead to book a room, and let the hosts know your arrival time so they don't spend hours waiting for you.

MS. ELIZABET VIKLUND, Roslagsgatan 15, S-11355 Stockholm. Tel. 08/15-40-51. 2 rms. **T-Bana:** Odenplan. **Bus:** 53 from Central Station (it stops across the street from her building).
$ Rates: 225 Kr ($37.15) single; 400 Kr ($66) double. Breakfast 25 Kr ($4.15) extra. No credit cards.
A cordial and informative host who prefers that you write ahead, Ms. Viklund will point out the best budget cafés and shops in her neighborhood, a short bus/subway ride from the city center. Her home has the feel of a country house, with large windows, lots of wood furniture, touches of lace, a bottle collection, and dried and fresh flowers everywhere. The White Room is reserved for singles; the large double room has an adjacent bath with tub. Ms. Viklund is flexible and can add a bed or two to accommodate families or small groups traveling together. A fine cook whose guests clamor for her recipes, she lived and studied in New York in the 1960s. A dozen buses one block from her house connect with the Odenplan subway stop.

MS. EIVON LICHTSHINER, Bergsgatan 45, Stockholm. Tel. 08/746-91-66. 3 rms (all with shower and toilet). **T-Bana:** Rådhuset, one stop from Central Station; then walk less than two blocks.
$ Rates: 300 Kr ($49.50) single; 400 Kr ($66) double, 400–500 Kr ($66–$82.50) double with kitchenette, depending on the number of guests. No credit cards.
The friendly Ms. Lichtshiner is conversant in English, German, French, and Russian. Each of her comfortable rooms has a toilet, sink, and shower; one has a loft bed. Guests have use of the kitchen. Additionally, she rents a little "paradise house" in the country, 15 miles outside Stockholm. The city home is on a residential street on the island of Kungsholmen.

MS. ERJA-RIITTA SALONEN, Bastugatan 31 (3rd Floor), S-11725 Stockholm. Tel. 08/658-55-89. 2 rms. TV **T-Bana:** Line 14 from Central Station to Mariatorget, the third stop; then walk five blocks up a steep hill.
$ Rates: 250 Kr ($41.25) single; 400 Kr ($66) double. No credit cards.
If you're interested in communal living, a stay here, on the island of Sodermalm, will be educational as well as pleasant. Eighteen families built, live, and share meals in this modern structure with an oval glass entry. It has a sauna, communal kitchen and dining area, and round tower with a panoramic view of the city. Of the two rooms

that Ms. Salonen rents out, the double is somewhat cramped with a king-size bed and desk; the single has a balcony that overlooks courtyards below. Both rooms have a TV, and they share a large bath with a shower. Guests may use the washing machine and sauna. Ms. Salonen, who is originally from Finland, prefers that you write ahead. An apartment is available for those who plan to stay a week.

MS. EVA ABELIN, Skeppargatan 49B, S-11458 Stockholm. Tel. 08/ 663-49-57. 2 rms. **T-Bana:** Ostermalmstorg; take the Ostermalm exit and then walk three blocks (about five minutes) east to the apartment, which is next to a flag shop.

$ Rates: 275 Kr ($45.40) single; 400 Kr ($66) double. Breakfast 35 Kr ($5.80) extra. No credit cards.

This place has it all: a central location, elegant facilities, and an engaging, gracious host. A lawyer by training, Ms. Gisslar is a consultant to a committee dedicated to human-rights causes that hands out an alternative Nobel Peace Prize. She also has a passion for art and is an avid collector. The single room she rents out is comfortable and the double features a large wooden writing table and a pretty queen-size bed. Guests have use of the kitchen.

MS. INGRID OLLEN, Störtloppsvägen 34, S-12661 Stockholm. Tel. 08/646-68-68. 2 rms. **T-Bana:** Västertorp.

$ Rates: 175 Kr ($28.90) single; 250 Kr ($41.25) double; 300 Kr ($49.50) triple. Discounts available for stays longer than a week. Breakfast 30 Kr ($5.45) extra. No credit cards.

Located a 15-minute ride from the center in a pleasant neighborhood that includes a bank, post office, and several stores and cafés, the two double rooms here come with cooking privileges. Ms. Ollen is a retired nurse, not to mention a world traveler and avid swimmer, who has welcomed people from 30 countries to her home. Guests can use the laundry for 25 Kr ($4.10), and there is an open-air pool nearby.

At the Västertorp T-Bana stop, exit the station following the arrow toward Störtloppsvägen. Turn left on that street and walk two blocks; when you reach the *apotek* (pharmacy), walk behind that building to find the entrance.

MS. PERNILLA WILTON, Bastugatan 48A, S-11825 Stockholm. Tel. 08/84-14-79. 1 rm. TV **T-Bana:** Mariatorget; then walk five blocks north (uphill) to Bastugatan.

$ Rates: 250 Kr ($41.25) single; 390 Kr ($64.35) double. No credit cards.

On the same quiet Sodermalm street as Ms. Salonen, Pernilla Wilton offers a spacious room with a full-size bed, TV, and plenty of books and tourist materials to read. Better still, it's in a 19th-century house with a cozy Swedish ambience and a view of Lake Malaren and the city, most notably the striking City Hall. English and German are spoken. Call ahead to be sure the room is available.

HOTELS

HOTELL GUSTAV VASA, Västmannagatan 61, S-11325 Stockholm. Tel. 08/34-38-01 or 34-13-20. 33 rms (11 with bath). TEL **T-Bana:** Odenplan.

$ Rates (including continental breakfast): 330 Kr ($54) single without bath, 410 Kr ($67.65) single with bath; 430 Kr ($70.95) double without bath, 510 Kr ($84.15) double with bath; 200 Kr ($33) per person in family rooms for three or four people. AE, DC, EURO, MC, V.

The Gustav Vasa's friendly family atmosphere has everything to do with Polish manager Krystyna Öhrling and her Swedish husband, Aarne. Some rooms have attractive personal touches, such as an antique radio or a classic, free-standing wardrobe. Room 1 is a particularly nice double with bath; no. 3, a comfortable single with the bath across the hall. Rooms with bath have shower, no tub. Most rooms have a safe. At night there is usually a video movie in the living room.

The hotel, half a block from the T-Bana station (Västmannagatan exit), is wedged between Odengatan and Karlbergsvägen, across from the monumental domed Gustav

Vasa Church. The reception is on the second floor, and a self-service laundry is in the same building.

For Single Rooms

HOTELL ÖRN SKÖLD, Nybrogatan 6, S-11434 Stockholm. Tel. 08/667-02-85. Fax 667-69-91. 3 rms (1 with bath, 1 with toilet only). **T-Bana:** Line 13, 14, or 15 to Östermalmstorg (Östermalm exit), just one stop from Central Station.
$ Rates: 195 Kr ($32.20) single without bath, 250 Kr ($41.25) single with toilet only, or 450 Kr ($74.25) single with bath.

These small, basic singles rent on a first-come, first-served basis, for the lowest rates in town. There's barely room for you and your bag, and the toilet and shower are a walk away from the room that has neither (it does have a telephone). The room with full bath (with shower) also has a telephone and television; the room with toilet only has neither telephone nor television. Still, the location is central, a block from the American Express office. Other rooms in this upscale hotel are beyond this book's budget.

DOUBLES FOR LESS THAN 550 KR [$90.75]

HOTELL DANIELSON, Wallingatan 31, S-11124 Stockholm. Tel. 08/11-10-76 or 11-10-65. 14 rms (some with shower and/or toilet). **Bus:** 47 or 53 from Central Station to the third stop.
$ Rates: 400 Kr ($66) single without shower or toilet, 500 Kr ($82.50) single with toilet only, 550 Kr ($90.75) single with shower and toilet; 550 Kr ($90.75) double without shower or toilet, 600 Kr ($99) double with toilet only, 650 Kr ($107.25) double with shower and toilet; 750 Kr ($123.75) triple without shower or toilet, 825 Kr ($136.15) triple with shower and toilet. Breakfast 30 Kr ($5.45) extra. No credit cards.

The Danielson is not in top form: The toilets are small and aging, and the room lighting is dim. The location, however, is just great—at the corner of Västmannagatan, a few blocks from some of Norrmalm's main shopping streets and eight blocks (a 10-minute walk) north of Central Station.

PENSIONAT ODEN, Odengatan 38, S-11351 Stockholm. Tel. 08/61-24-349. 9 rms (none with bath). **T-Bana:** Odenplan; then walk four blocks away from the church along Odengatan.
$ Rates (including breakfast): 95–450 Kr ($65.20–$74.25) single; 495–595 Kr ($81.70–$98.20) double. No credit cards.

One of Stockholm's better values, the Oden features large rooms with white wood furniture in bright, cheery surroundings. The rooms facing the street are both nicer and noisier than the ones in the rear. You're likely to feel at home in either. One of the doubles has a refrigerator, and several rooms come with clock radios; no. 7 is an especially comfortable twin. This hotel is on the other end of Odengatan from Vasa Park.

WASA PARK HOTELL, St. Eriksplan 1, S-11320 Stockholm. Tel. 08/34-02-85. Fax 08/30-94-22. 14 rms (none with bath). TV TEL **T-Bana:** St. Eriksplan, four stops from Central Station.
$ Rates: 395 Kr ($65.20) single; 520 Kr ($85.50) double. Extra person 150 Kr ($24.75). Breakfast 35 Kr ($5.80) extra, although in summer it's sometimes included in the room price. EURO, MC, V.

The new double rooms here resemble those you might find in a first-class hotel, with sharp gray carpets, dark-wood furniture, and TVs. A few older rooms are more old-fashioned. Still, rooms vary in quality; no. 16 is a pleasant twin. The public bathrooms, one with a tub, are quite clean. The carefree manner in which the entire hotel is run is slightly disconcerting, but service is good enough, and when business is slow the management is open to price negotiation. The location is great, in Norrmalm's arty quarter. The entrance to the hotel is through the arch to the right of the Thai restaurant on Sankt Eriksplan. The airport bus stops outside, and the T-Bana station is one block away.

WEEKEND & SUMMER DISCOUNTS

The following hotels are good value every day during the summer and on Saturday and Sunday year round, when rates are noticeably reduced.

HOTELL ANNO 1647, Mariagränd 3, S-11646 Stockholm. Tel. 08/44-04-80. Fax 08/43-37-00. 43 rms (21 with bath). TV TEL **T-Bana:** Slussen.
$ Rates (including breakfast): Most days in summer and Fri–Sat year round. 450 Kr ($74.25) single with sink only, 550 Kr ($90.75) single with bath; 650 Kr ($107.25) double with sink only, 740 Kr ($122.10) double with bath. Mini-suites and suites available at reduced rates. Sun–Thurs the rest of the year, prices almost double. AE, DC, EURO, MC, V.

This gorgeous hotel has undergone many renovations since its erection in 1647. And while updating has made it more modern (and expensive), the Anno 1647 still jealously guards its "country inn" roots. The rooms with private bath (with shower) are substantially nicer than those without, but pretty hardwood floors and tasteful furnishings in mauve and green or gray, TVs, telephones, and radios make all more than adequate. All rooms have a desk and good reading light. There's a café that serves lunch and snacks and a no-smoking floor, but no elevator, so if you dislike stairs, ask for a double room on the ground floor. The hotel provides some excellent views of the harbor and Old Town. The entrance is on narrow Mariagränd, off Gotgatan.

QUEEN'S HOTEL, Drottninggatan 71A, S-11136 Stockholm. Tel. 08/24-94-60. Fax 08/21-76-20. 30 rms (7 with shower and toilet, 11 with shower only). TV TEL **Directions:** From Central Station, turn left on Vasagatan, right on Olof Palmes Gata, and left again on Drottningatan—a 10-minute walk in all.
$ Rates (including breakfast): Daily in summer and Sat–Sun year round, 335 Kr ($55.30) single without shower or toilet, 415 Kr ($68.50) single with shower only, 485 Kr ($80.05) single with shower and toilet; 435 Kr ($71.80) double without shower or toilet, 495 Kr ($81.70) double with shower only, 585 Kr ($96.55) double with shower and toilet. Mon–Fri the rest of the year prices rise about 30%. ACCESS AE, DC, EURO, MC, V.

On Stockholm's busiest shopping street, near the intersection of Olof Palmes Gata, this pleasant hotel has 10 new rooms that have full bath (with shower) and in-room iron, plus 20 older rooms (16 doubles and 4 small singles) a TV lounge, and an old-fashioned elevator. The well-furnished rooms have clock radios. Breakfast is served in a cheerful country-style dining room. The staff is friendly and helpful, so much so that if you have an early flight or train, they prepare an early breakfast for you.

SUPER-BUDGET CHOICES

BRYGGHUSET, Norrtullsgatan 12N, Stockholm. Tel. 08/31-24-24. Fax 08/33-29-74. 57 beds. **T-Bana:** Odenplan; take the Odenplan exit and walk three blocks up Norrtullsgatan.
$ Rates: 110 Kr ($18.15) per adult, 93 Kr ($15.70) per child. Sheets 25 Kr ($4.10) extra. No credit cards. **Open:** Early June to Aug.

Most of the year the building serves as a community center, where locals gather for various events. During the summer the "community" is expanded to include world travelers who are accommodated in two-, three-, four-, and six-bed rooms. It's good for families, who can wash clothes here; the atmosphere and prices are inviting; and breakfast is available next door for 35 Kr ($5.80). A 2am curfew is enforced. It's open from early June to the end of August (call for exact dates); no sleeping bags allowed. The entrance is right on the main street, near the corner of Frejgatan.

COLUMBUS HOTELL & VANDRARHEM, Tjärhovsgatan 11, S-11621 Stockholm. Tel. 08/644-17-17. Fax 08/702-07-64. 44 rms (none with bath). **T-Bana:** Medborgarplatsen; Tjärhovsgatan is five blocks east.
$ Rates: Hotel, 390 Kr ($64.35) single; 490 Kr ($80.85) double. Hostel, 250 Kr ($41.25) single or double; 105 Kr ($17.30) per person in family or dorm rooms. Paper sheets 25 Kr ($4.10) extra; cotton sheets, 40 Kr ($6.60) towels, 10 Kr ($1.65). Breakfast 35 Kr ($5.80) extra. No credit cards. **Closed:** Dec 23–Jan 2.

⭐ Another hotel and hostel on the island of Södermalm, the Columbus is capably and cordially run by brothers Dan and Bjorn Collin. The hotel section, separate from the hostel, consists of only eight rooms (seven doubles and one single) that share a shower and toilet; each has a TV but no phone. The hostel has rooms with two to eight beds, lockers, and three showers for men and women on each of the three floors; the public bathrooms are passable but not sparkling. The pleasant and quiet Columbus also has a secure baggage room, a small kitchen for guests open 24 hours, a room with a sun bed for those who want an artificial Nordic tan, a pleasant café for meals or snacks, and an outdoor café in summer. A children's playground, a park, and an indoor pool are nearby. There is no curfew, but the Columbus, in a building dating from 1780, closes from December 23 to January 2. The maximum hostel stay is five nights.

HOTEL/HOSTEL *GUSTAF AF KLINT*, Stadsgårdskajen 153, S-11645 Stockholm. Tel. 08/640-40-77 or 640-40-78. Fax 08/640-64-16. 32 cabins (none with bath). **T-Bana:** Slussen (Södermalmstorg exit); then walk down to the riverbank—the ship is about 200 yards to the right.
$ Rates: In the hostel part, 120 Kr ($19.80) per person. Breakfast 40 Kr ($6.60) extra; paper sheets, 35 Kr ($5.80) cotton sheets, 55 Kr ($9.10) towels, 10 Kr ($1.65). In the hotel part, 380 Kr ($62.70) single; 480 Kr ($79.20) double. AE, DC, EURO, MC, V.
This floating hotel and youth hostel rigged with lights is on the riverbank just across from Old Town. When the *Klint* served as a radar sounder mapping out the ocean floor, the officers lived in what is now the hotel part of the ship (five singles and nine doubles), while the deckhands occupied what is now the hostel part (two doubles, a triple, and 15 quads). The hotel section is slightly more spacious than the hostel's cramped quarters, but all cabins are equipped with bunk beds. During the summer the ship's deck-top bar and café are open, with a lovely view of Stockholm's harbor. Year round, below deck, cheap dinners are served in a small, sometimes smoky, licensed restaurant. The location is convenient, there's an on-board sauna, and general manager Karl-Olof Olofsson is congenial and helpful.

SLEEP INN YOUTH HOSTEL, Döbelnsgatan 56, S-11352 Stockholm. Tel. 08/31-31-18 or 08/32-37-31. 3 dorm rms. **T-Bana:** Rådmansgatan (exit onto Handelshögskolan). **Bus:** 52; get off at the stop opposite the Hard Rock Café.
$ Rates: 95 Kr ($15.70) per person. Sheets 20 Kr ($3.30) extra. **Open:** July 1–Aug 18.
Centrally located, this "unofficial" youth hostel offers basic accommodation: a bed in one of three dormitories, one for women and two mixed. There are separate showers and toilets for women and men, as well as a large sitting/breakfast room that has a TV. The hostel is air-conditioned and has a self-service laundry and refrigerator for guests' use. It closes daily between noon and 4pm. If you're not too loaded down, you can walk here from Central Station in about 20 minutes; otherwise, the subway or bus will get you quite close.

IYHF HOTELS

There are four "official" International Youth Hostel Federation (IYHF) hostels in Stockholm, offering excellently priced, well-maintained clean lodgings. Two, on

Skeppsholmen, probably offer the best-located lodgings in the city (and they fill up by 8am in summer). All are similarly priced, and offer lower rates to IYHF card-carriers. If you are not a member, you have to get a Welcome Card and pay an extra 36 Kr ($5.95) per night for up to six nights, after which you gain member status.

Finally, the Swedish Hostel Federation emphasizes that its hostels are not just for young people. If hosteling suits your style, age is unimportant.

AF *CHAPMAN*, Västra Brobänken, Skeppsholmen, S-11149 Stockholm. Tel. 08/679-50-15. Fax 611-71-55. 136 beds (no rms with bath). **T-Bana:** Kungsträdgården. **Bus:** 65.

$ Rates: 95 Kr ($15.70) per person with the IYHF card, 130 Kr ($21.45) without. Paper sheets 25 Kr ($4.10) towels, 10 Kr ($1.65). Breakfast 40 Kr ($6.60) extra. EURO, MC, V. **Closed:** Mid-Dec to Apr 1.

★ The towering, fully rigged masts of this gallant "Tall Ship" are a Stockholm landmark. The vessel sailed throughout the world under British, Norwegian, and then Swedish flags for about half a century before establishing itself as a hostel in 1949. Today the ship is permanently moored on the island of Skeppsholmen. The hostel is extremely popular, turning away as many as 100 people a day during the summer months. The reception opens at 7am (until noon, then again from 3 to 10pm), and it is suggested that you arrive early to reserve a bed. The hostel imposes a five-night maximum stay, and closes in winter. The ship is also closed daily from 10am to 4pm, and enforces a 2am curfew. Sleeping bags may be used on top of a sheet. You can rent sheets or supply your own. There is no kitchen, laundry, or TV room, but you may wash out small items and watch TV across the street at the STF *Vandrarhem*; there are only two showers for women. Each room has a locker, and the common area (and the café on the deck in summer) is conducive to meeting people; browse through the budget-conscious *Stockholm Guide* compiled by senior deputy warden Catharina Hård af Segerstad.

LÅNGHOLMEN HOSTEL AND HOTEL, Långholmen Island (P.O. Box 9116), S-10272 Stockholm. Tel. 08/668-05-00. Fax 08/84-10-96. 254 beds. TV TEL **T-Bana:** Hornstull; then follow the directions below.

$ Rates: Hostel, 90 Kr ($14.85) per person with the IYHF card, 125 Kr ($20.60) without. Breakfast 50 Kr ($8.25), half price for children under 12; cotton sheets, 35 Kr ($5.80) towels, 10 Kr ($1.65). Hotel (including breakfast), daily in summer and Sat–Sun year round, 430 Kr ($70.95) single cell with shower, 630 Kr ($103.95) double cell with shower; Mon–Fri the rest of the year, 630 Kr ($103.95) single cell with shower, 830 Kr ($136.95) double cell with shower. AE, DC, EURO, MC, V.

For over 2½ centuries Långholmen Prison housed some of the country's worst criminals. Painstaking renovations, true to the integrity of the building, have culminated in one of the fanciest, most unusual hostels in the world. The decor is an enjoyable cross between prison institutional and ultramodern Scandinavian. Most rooms have private baths, radios, videos, TVs, and telephones, and new, high-quality beds that pull down Murphy style from the walls.

A member of the Swedish Hostel Federation, the Långholmen rents similar rooms at both hostel and hotel prices. Sheets and towels are not provided in the hostel half, and you're expected to clean the hostel room when you leave. No curfew is imposed, and guests are permitted to use the kitchen and laundry facilities and borrow an iron or hairdryer. You can even swim in the lake in front of the hotel. On winter weekdays, when the hotel is full, only 26 beds are available at hostel prices.

From the Hornstull T-Bana station, follow Långholmsgatan toward "Väster-broplan." Turn left on Högalidsgatan and cross the first small bridge you come to onto the island, a 10-minute walk in all. It's easier to get here by car, but if you're walking the circuitous route, enter the Långholmen compound where you see the glass walkway. During summer there is boat service from Stadshusbron, near Central Station. Call the reception for departure times.

STF *VANDRARHEM*/HOSTEL SKEPPSHOLMEN, Västra Brobänken, Skeppsholmen, S-11149 Stockholm. Tel. 08/679-50-17. Fax 01/611-

71-55. 152 beds (no rms with bath). **T-Bana:** Kungsträdgården. **Bus:** 65, until 6pm only.

$ Rates: 95 Kr ($15.70) per person with the IYHF card, 130 Kr ($21.45) without; if it's available, a bed in the 15-bed room is a bargain at 60 Kr ($9.90). Paper sheets 25 Kr ($4.10) towels, 10 Kr ($1.65). Breakfast 40 Kr ($6.60) extra. EURO, MC, V.

Closed: Mid-Dec to mid-Jan.

Located just across from the *Af Chapman,* this yellow, three-story hostel often picks up the ship's overflow in its 14 doubles, 14 triples, 14 quads, and one 15-bed room for men and a 6-bed room for women. The doubles, triples, and quads are well sized and have sinks, and some feature magnificent views of Old Town. The reception is open from 7am to noon and again from 3 to 10pm. There are lockers, a small shop for snacks and sundries, museum prints in the rooms and hallways, and several common areas with benches and tables for relaxing or watching TV. The dining room serves terrific porridge (try it the Swedish way, with milk and apple butter). This hostel provides more privacy than the *Chapman.* Curfew is at 2am.

TOURISTGÅRDEN ZINKEN, Zinkens väg 20, S-11741 Stockholm. Tel. 08/668-57-86. 400 beds (no rms with bath). **T-Bana:** Zinkensdamm; then follow the directions below.

$ Rates: 93 Kr ($15.35) per person with the IYHF card, 129 Kr ($21.30) without. Breakfast 40 Kr ($6.60) extra; cotton sheets, 36 Kr ($5.95) towels, 10 Kr ($1.65). No credit cards.

Seven bunk-bedded bungalows make up Touristgården Zinken, the largest hostel in Sweden. Rooms are clean, and a kitchen is available free for guests' use. Several terrific facilities are offered at extra cost, including: a sauna, 20 Kr ($3.30); a large Jacuzzi and solarium, 40 Kr ($6.60); and washing machines and dryers, 30 Kr ($4.65). Reception sells a wide variety of candy and sweets, as well as postcards. The atmosphere is relaxed, like a simple country lodge; the staff is friendly; and the grounds have picnic tables, roses, and trees. The hostel is open 24 hours.

The hostel is a bit of a walk from the Zinkensdamm T-Bana station. Proceed east along Hornsgatan (where there's a good bakery), follow the rock outcropping, turn left down the steps between nos. 103 and 107, and follow the path down the hill. The hostel is the brown building on the left. It's on western Södermalm; as always, call ahead before setting out.

UNIVERSITY ACCOMMODATIONS

HOTELL FRESCATI, Professorsslingan 13, S-10405 Stockholm. Tel. 08/15-94-34; or 08/612-16-05 off-season. 120 rms (all with bath). **T-Bana:** Universitetet; then follow the directions below.

$ Rates: Hostel, 150 Kr ($24.75) per person. Hotel, 275 Kr ($45.40) single; 375 Kr ($61.90) double. Sheets 45 Kr ($7.40) extra; towels, 15 Kr ($2.50). Breakfast 45 Kr ($7.40) extra; dinner, 65 Kr ($10.70). **Open:** June–Aug. No credit cards.

From September through May the Frescati is home to students from several local universities. Come summer, the hotel becomes one of the best deals in town for tourists of all ages. The red-brick complex also houses a restaurant, a supermarket, and various shops, and imposes no curfew.

Although it's far outside the center, to reach the Frescati, take the T-Bana to Universitetet, and then walk for 15–20 minutes or change to bus no. 40 (you can also pick up bus no. 40 from the Odenplan T-Bana stop). There's reasonably priced dining and shopping in the area surrounding the hotel.

WORTH THE EXTRA BUCKS

WELLINGTON HOTEL, Storgatan 6, S-11451 Stockholm. Tel. 08/667-09-10. Fax 08/667-12-54. 51 rooms (all with bath). TV TEL **T-Bana:** Östermalmstorg.

$ Rates (including breakfast): May–Sept, Hotel Cheque $60.45 per person. Daily in summer and Sat–Sun year round, 700 Kr ($115.50) single; 850 Kr ($140.25). Other times almost double the price. AE, EURO, DC, MC, V.

★ Except for the economical Hotel Cheques offered by Best Western and special summer and weekend rates, this prize of a small hotel would far exceed budget status. Its staff is so friendly that guests often linger in the living-room–like lobby chatting with them. From the comfortable rooms, decorated in soft colors and outfitted with a pants press and hairdryer, you can hear the soft sound of church bells on the hour. A sauna, free to guests, is beautifully appointed, with a changing room, terry-cloth robes, soft towels, lotion and shampoo, shower, toilet, and sun bed. Add to that a breakfast room, concierge service, an ironing room, two no-smoking floors, and the most pleasant electronic wake-up call you're likely to get. The top floors afford memorable rooftop views.

5. BUDGET DINING

For tourists on a budget, mealtimes can sometimes seem more like a chore than a delight. Food in Stockholm is priced higher than in most other European cities, but this hardly means you'll starve. In addition to good-value lunch specials (see below) there are a number of great budget eateries.

Although price limitations mean you're unlikely to enjoy a full-fledged Swedish smörgåsbord, you can try other local specialties including herring (*strömming*), pea soup (*ärtsoppa*, usually served on Thursday), eel, Swedish meatballs, dill meat fricassee, and *pytt i panna* (a simple, tasty meat-and-potato hash).

If you're in Stockholm during the Christmas season, when tables are trimmed with traditional colorful holiday cutlery, be sure to sample ginger cookies and *glögg*, a potent traditional drink of fortified hot mulled wine with raisins and almonds.

And don't forget to visit the Swedish pastry shops—some of the best in Europe!

Many restaurants compete for noontime midweek business with fantastic lunch specials. Most only cost 45–60 Kr ($7.40–$9.90), and unless otherwise noted, prices for all lunch specials listed here include a main course, salad, bread, and a nonalcoholic drink. Lunch is usually served from 11am to 2pm (check individual listings). Adjust your eating habits and take advantage of specials that make a large lunch considerably less expensive than dinner. If you don't see a daily special (*dagens rätt*) posted, ask for it.

For dinner, look to pasta and pizza houses or one of a number of vegetarian restaurants (some of Stockholm's prettiest eateries). To save even more money, avoid alcohol; state control keeps prices extremely high.

MEALS FOR LESS THAN 65 KR [$10.70]

BOMBAY KEBAB, Varjedag 11-24. Tel. 658-62-80.
   Cuisine: INDIAN. **T-Bana:** Hornstull.
   $ Prices: 25–65 Kr ($4.10–$10.70). No credit cards.
   Open: Mon–Sat 11am–11pm, Sun 1–11pm.
It can't be beat on several counts: The food's good, plentiful, and includes favorites like shish kebab, beef vindaloo, biriani, samosas, and vegetarian dishes; the price is right; and it's open fairly late.

COFFEE HOUSE, Odengatan 45 (near Dobelnsgatan). Tel. 673-23-43.
   Cuisine: LIGHT FARE.
   $ Prices: 35–55 Kr ($5.80–$9.10); lunch special 45 Kr ($5.80). No credit cards.

Ⓕ **FROMMER'S SMART TRAVELER:**
RESTAURANTS

VALUE-CONSCIOUS TRAVELERS SHOULD
TAKE ADVANTAGE OF THE FOLLOWING:

1. Lunch specials—large lunches are considerably less expensive than dinner.
2. Department-store cafeterias, pasta and pizza houses, and vegetarian restaurants for dinner.

Open: Mon–Fri 7am–5pm, Sat–Sun 9am–5pm.
This friendly place with tiled floor and round tables is filled with local folks and the low hum of conversations. The lunch special, served from 11am to 2pm, includes a sandwich, juice, and coffee. Quiche and large salads are also available, and coffee comes with a free refill (help yourself from the table inside the door). There's a high chair for tots. The Lebanese owners, the three Makdessi-Elias brothers, will make you feel most welcome.

KUNGSTORNET, Kungsgatan 28. Tel. 20-66-43.
Cuisine: LIGHT FARE.
$ Prices: 18–55 Kr ($3–$9.10). No credit cards.
Open: Mon–Thurs 7am–11pm, Fri 7am–midnight, Sat 8am–midnight, Sun 9am–10pm.
What you see is what you get: decor from the 1950s, seating upstairs and down, and a menu heavy on sandwiches. You can also get quiche, stuffed avocados, and salads, and the lunch prices include bread and coffee. It's a block from Sveagatan.

NIKKI'S CAFE, Jungfrugatan 6. Tel. 662-14-74.
Cuisine: LIGHT FARE. **T-Bana:** Östermalmstorg.
$ Prices: Breakfast 14–46 Kr ($2.30–$7.60); sandwiches 15–25 Kr ($2.50–$4.10); hefty salad 45 Kr ($7.40); daily special 50 Kr ($8.25). EURO, V.
Open: Mon–Fri 7:30am–2:30pm. **Closed:** Four weeks in summer, usually July to early Aug.

★ The hours aren't great, but the prices are. This tiny café, tucked just off the main drag less than half a block from Hedvig Eleonara Church, has only nine tables, red-and-white checked tablecloths, and red hanging lamps. Prices are reasonable (for Stockholm), especially if you like breakfast; coffee and tea are 6 Kr ($1) for the first cup and 4 Kr (65¢) for a refill. The special comes with bread, cheese, and coffee. Help yourself to the bread and cheese from the table by the window, as well as to the veggies on your own table. A typical special is a full plate of roast lamb with tasty potatoes au gratin. Make this your big meal of the day.

SILVERHÄSTEN CAFE, Master Samuelsgatan 21. Tel. 20-23-74.
Cuisine: LIGHT FARE. **T-Bana:** T-Centralen.
$ Prices: 39–56 Kr ($6.45–$9.25). EURO, MC.
Open: Mon–Thurs 8am–11pm, Fri–Sat 9am–5am, Sun 11am–11pm.
From outside it appears a small café, but inside it consists of five different eating areas, each of which attracts a different crowd—readers, chatters, diners, a young group, an older group. Fare includes crêpes, croissant sandwiches, lasagne, pasta, stuffed potatoes, large salads, milkshakes, and fresh-squeezed juice. Order at the counter and clear your own table. There's piano music Saturday at lunch.

TACO BAR, Slöjdgatan 2 at Master Samuelsgatan. Tel. 11-16-26.
Cuisine: MEXICAN. **T-Bana:** Hörtorget or T-Centralen.

$ Prices: 26–48 Kr ($4.30–$7.90). No credit cards.
Open: Mon–Fri 11am–7pm, Sat 11am–5pm.
With nachos, enchiladas, tacos, and the like, this is Tex-Mex à la upscale Taco Bell. Order with tongue firmly in cheek—you're a long way from Old Mexico. Slöjdgatan is a small street parallel to Sergelgatan, just one block away. There are smaller versions at Kungsgatan 3 at Birgir Jarlsgatan and at Kungsgatan 44 in Kungshallen.

MEALS FOR LESS THAN 85 KR [$14]

IN GAMLA STAN

LILLA KARACHI, Lilla Nygatan 12. Tel. 20-54-54.
  Cuisine: PAKISTANI. **T-Bana:** Gamla Stan.
$ Prices: 65–110 Kr ($10.70–$18.15). AE, EURO, V.
  Open: Mon–Fri 11am–10pm, Sat–Sun noon–10pm.
This small, well-decorated restaurant with top-notch Swedish-influenced Pakistani cuisine can be considered one of Stockholm's greatest bargains. The aroma alone will start you salivating even before you sit down at one of their cozy, glass-topped tables. Lilla Karachi is especially recommended for its lunch prices and vegetarian meals. The restaurant is near the corner of Tyska Brinken, about two blocks from the Gamla Stan T-Bana.

IN NORRMALM & ÖSTERMALM

ALICE B., Sveavägen 57. Tel. 31-55-33.
  Cuisine: LIGHT FARE. **T-Bana:** Rådmansgatan. **Bus:** 52.
$ Prices: 49–79 Kr ($8.10–$13.05); daily pasta special 59 Kr ($9.75).
  Open: Mon 4pm–1am, Tues–Sun 4pm–3am (food served Mon–Thurs to 11:30pm, Fri–Sat to 12:30am).
This casual restaurant housed in Stockholm's Gay Center serves baguettes, croques monsieurs, big hamburgers, fish 'n' chips, pytt i panna (Swedish stew), and steak, along with a daily pasta special. Besides the food, there are soft lights, soft music, and a pool table. It's half a block from the Rådmansgatan T-Bana station on a pretty tree-lined street. Look for the Gay Center sign that says PRIDE out front.

CAPRI, Nybrogatan 15. Tel. 662-31-32.
  Cuisine: ITALIAN. **T-Bana:** Östermalmstorg.
$ Prices (including bread, salad, and service): Pizza or pasta 65–80 Kr ($10.70–$13.20); other dishes 110–160 Kr ($18.15–$26.40). ACCESS, AE, DC, EURO, MC, V.
  Open: Mon–Fri 4:30pm–midnight, Sat–Sun noon–midnight.
Although this place also serves meat and fish dishes, it's the extensive pasta and pizza menu, not to mention courteous service and well-prepared dishes, that attracts budgeteers. Capri's vaulted ceiling is reminiscent of Italy's Blue Grotto. If you come for dinner, look for the nightly special, which is usually less expensive than the regular menu. The restaurant is located just west of Östermalms food hall, two blocks from the Östermalmstorg T-Bana station.

CITY LEJON, Holländargatan 8. Tel. 20-76-35.
  Cuisine: SWEDISH. **T-Bana:** Hötorget.
$ Prices: 57–98 Kr ($9.40–$16.15); lunch specials from 45 Kr ($7.40). AE, EURO, MC.
  Open: Mon–Thurs 10am–10pm, Fri 10am–11pm, Sat noon–11pm, Sun noon–10pm (lunch special served 10:30am–3pm).
The great draw here is the lunch special, absolutely one of the best values in town. This place bustles, mainly with local office workers, and gets quite busy around noon.

A continuous series of wooden doors covers the restaurant's walls, complemented by wooden tables and low-wattage stained-glass hanging lamps. The food here is good and filling, and the weinerschnitzel and plank steak are particularly popular. The location is great—just off Kungsgatan, 2½ blocks north of Hötorget Square.

GRONA LINJEN, Mäster Samuelsgatan 10. Tel. 611-92-96.
  Cuisine: VEGETARIAN. **T-Bana:** Hötorget.
$ **Prices:** All-you-can-eat meal (including main course, soup, and salad bar) 60 Kr ($9.90) at lunch, 75 Kr ($12.40) at dinner. No credit cards.
  Open: Mon–Fri 10:30am–8pm, Sat 11am–8pm. **Closed:** Hols.

★ This was the house of Sweden's prewar Conservative Party leader, and eating here still feels like dining in a private home. The restaurant, which opened as Sweden's first vegetarian restaurant in 1940, features vintage ceramic fixtures, white furniture, pastel walls, four dining areas including a reading room (don't miss the fireplace in the middle room), and an unlimited supply of a great variety of foods. Enter through a modest doorway, near the corner of Norrlandsgatan. The restaurant is on the third floor, but there's an elevator.

MAMMA ROSA, Sveavägen 55. Tel. 30-40-21.
  Cuisine: ITALIAN. **T-Bana:** Rådmansgatan. **Bus:** 52.
$ **Prices:** Pizza and pasta 53–75 Kr ($8.75–$12.40); fish and meat dishes 110–170 Kr ($18.15–$28.05); lunch special (including bread, salad, espresso, and a small glass of beer, juice, or soda) 49–75 Kr ($8.10–$12.40). AE, DC, EURO, V.
  Open: Mon–Fri 10:30am–midnight, Sat–Sun noon–midnight (lunch special served 10:30am–2:30pm).
A refurbished Stockholm standard, it has gray-and-peach decor, sconces, mirrored walls, and a gleaming cappuccino machine. An authentic staff, a good menu, and great food are the real testaments to this trattoria's success. An attractive special packs them in at lunch, but to stay under budget at dinner, limit yourself to pasta and pizza. The restaurant is half a block from the Rådmansgatan T-Bana station.

ON SÖDERMALM

STRÖMMEN, Södermalms Torg. Tel. 43-44-70.
  Cuisine: SWEDISH. **T-Bana:** Slussen (take the Södermalms Torg exit).
$ **Prices:** 39–60 Kr ($6.45–$9.90); lunch special 45 Kr ($7.40). No credit cards.
  Open: Mon–Fri 7:30am–6:30pm, Sat 7:30am–5pm, Sun 9am–6pm.
It's a coffee shop with a rooftop-restaurant view, and its perch above the harbor, in the free-standing blue building across the square from the Slussen T-Bana station, is one of the best locations in Stockholm! In addition to some of the cheapest dinner dishes in town, Strömmen serves a good breakfast. If you're in the mood for an early-morning walk across Gamla Stan, make this your goal for coffee and a roll. Lunch comes with beer or mineral water, and every seat has a panoramic view.

ON DJURGÅRDEN

CAFE BLÅ PORTEN, Djurgårdsvägen 64. Tel. 662-71-62.
  Cuisine: LIGHT FARE. **Bus:** 44 or 47.
$ **Prices:** 10–70 Kr ($1.65–$11.55). No credit cards.
  Open: Tues–Thurs 11am–9pm, Fri 11am–4:30pm, Sat–Sun 11am–5pm.

★ There are not many restaurants on this museum island, and those that are here cater almost exclusively to hungry, stranded tourists. This bohemian, cafeteria-style café is an exception, catering equally to students and art enthusiasts who visit the adjacent Liljevalch Art Gallery, where exhibits change every 12 weeks. The café has an inviting atmosphere and serves soups, salads, quiche, and cold meals, along with wine and beer. Sandwiches, cookies, and fruit, set out on wooden tables, are also available, and there are no-smoking tables. Café Blå Porten (it means Blue Door, and it has one) is located beside the above-mentioned gallery, and in summer spills out into the art gallery's tree- and plant-filled courtyard.

IN THE DEPARTMENT STORES

Department-store cafés in Stockholm are quiet and well decorated, and some are even moderately priced.

NK CAFETERIA [NK CAFEET], on the 4th floor of the department store, Hamngatan 18-20. Tel. 762-80-00.
Cuisine: LIGHT FARE. **T-Bana:** Kungsträdgården.
$ Prices: Sandwiches 30–60 Kr ($4.95–$9.90); pastries 11–27 Kr ($1.80–$4.45).
Open: Mon–Fri 10am–6:30pm, Sat–Sun 10am–4:30pm.
Cheerful, relaxed, and brightly lit, it's a point-and-pay kind of place, adjacent to a full-service (more expensive) restaurant called Plates. NK also has a small French café on the third floor that opens half an hour later than the cafeteria, and there is a coffee shop in the subbasement that is particularly popular with students.

PUB CAFETERIA, on the fifth floor of PUB department store, Drottninggatan 72-76, Hötorget Sq. Tel. 791-60-00.
Cuisine: LIGHT FARE. **T-Bana:** Hötorget.
$ Prices: Daily special, 60 Kr ($9.90); sandwiches from 20 Kr ($3.30); other dishes, 45–70 Kr ($7.40–$11.55). No credit cards.
Open: Mon–Fri 10am–7pm, Sat 10am–5pm, Sun 10am–4pm.
A pleasant cafeteria, right beside an exhibit on Greta Garbo, the store's most famous salesperson, it has daily lunch specials and coffee refills for 3 Kr (50¢). Hot meals are served from 11am to 3pm. (PUB has two buildings; you want the one called Hötorgshuset.)

FOR THE LUNCH SPECIAL

Stockholm's ubiquitous lunch specials are its saving grace for the budget tourist. Except in the most heavily touristed areas, almost every restaurant in the city offers a good meal at prices that are substantially lower than at dinner. The first two restaurants listed below, like most of the city's best deals, are in the business district of eastern Norrmalm. When striking out on your own, note that a crowded restaurant usually means good food at low prices. The following eateries are above our budget at dinnertime, but offer excellent lunch specials.

BISTRO JARL, Birgir Jarlsgatan 7. Tel. 611-76-30.
Cuisine: SWEDISH/FRENCH.
$ Prices: Lunch specials, 56 Kr ($9.25); tapas, 15 Kr ($2.50) each; appetizers 15–65 Kr ($2.50–$10.70); main courses 72–130 Kr ($11.90–$21.45). ACCESS, AE, DC, EURO, MC, V.
Open: Lunch daily 11am–2:30pm; dinner daily 5pm–midnight.
A most attractive addition to Stockholm's dining scene, the centrally located Bistro Jarl has a lunch special that comes with homemade bread, a salad, and a main dish that's either meat, fish, or vegetarian. And homemade pies are available if you're still hungry at the end of the meal. The elegant and intimate café has lace curtains, high ceilings, and linen tablecloths (but paper napkins), and there are newspapers and backgammon to distract patrons. Check the blackboard menu for the day's offerings.

GETINGBOET, Sveavägen 9-11. Tel. 21-29-35.
Cuisine: SWEDISH.
$ Prices: Lunch specials 46–63 Kr ($7.60–$10.40); appetizers 35–49 Kr ($5.80–$8.10), main courses 64–99 Kr ($10.55–$16.35).
Open: Mon–Fri 11am–11pm, Sat noon–11pm.

A block from the House of Culture, Getingboet ("Wasp's Nest") serves lunch from 11am to 3pm; the lunch (and dinner) menu changes monthly but always includes a pasta and meat or fish dishes. At lunch you can also get an open-face sandwich with bread and salad. The restaurant fills up in the evenings with a lively theater crowd, along with those who simply want to take advantage of the great happy hour served upstairs from 3 or 4pm to 6pm, when free hors d'oeuvres (meatballs, sausages, peanuts, and olives) are served with beer for 28 Kr ($4.60) and with wine for 29 Kr ($4.80). This could be the city's best deal.

RESTAURANG ROSENBRUNN, Brunnsgatan 21. Tel. 11-16-37.

Cuisine: SWEDISH. **T-Bana:** Hötorget.
$ Prices: Lunch special 55 Kr ($9.10). AE, EURO, MC, V.
Open: Lunch Mon–Fri 10:30am–3pm; dinner Mon–Sat 5pm–midnight.

A la carte dishes that cost 75–135 Kr ($12.40–$22.30) are served with bread, salad, and a nonalcoholic drink for a half to a third the price during lunch. Needless to say, this smart serve-yourself place gets crowded. Rosenbrunn is at the corner of Regeringsgatan, four blocks east of Hötorget Square.

TARO, Kammakargatan 11. Tel. 11-05-15.

Cuisine: JAPANESE. **T-Bana:** Rådmansgatan. **Bus:** 52.
$ Prices: Lunch special 52–60 Kr ($8.60–$9.90); fried or grilled dishes 85–150 Kr ($14–$24.75). DC, EURO, MC, V.
Open: Lunch Mon–Fri 11am–1pm; dinner Mon–Sat 5–10am. **Closed:** Fri lunch in winter.

A good lunch spot in the middle of Norrmalm for those with a hankering for Japanese food. A choice of three specials is served in traditional surroundings, and include main course, salad, rice, and green tea, light beer, or tea. The relaxed atmosphere here is atypical of Stockholm's usual midday rush. The restaurant is just off Sveagatan, 2½ blocks from the Rådmansgatan T-Bana station.

MEALS FOR LESS THAN 110 KR [$18.15]

IN GAMLA STAN

MICHELANGELO, Västerlanggatan 62. Tel. 21-50-99.

Cuisine: ITALIAN. **T-Bana:** Gamla Stan.
$ Prices: Pizza and pastas 55–80 Kr ($9.10–$13.20); meat and fish dishes 116–179 Kr ($19.15–$29.55); lunch special 55 Kr ($9.10). AE, DC, EURO, MC, V.
Open: Mon–Fri 11am–midnight, Sat–Sun and hols noon–midnight (lunch special served Mon–Fri 11am–2:30pm).

Stucco walls, pictures of the Sistine Chapel, Italian rock-and-roll, and candlelit tables are the hallmarks of this touristy but good Italian restaurant. Downstairs you can eat in one of several brick cellar rooms with fish tanks and cherub statuettes. The food includes a large assortment of pizza, pasta with smoked salmon and lobster sauce, and steak with cream sauce and onions. The location is great—on the main pedestrian drag, right in the heart of Old Town, a two-minute walk from the Gamla Stan T-Bana station.

SLINGERBULTEN, Stora Nygatan 24. Tel. 10-76-22.

Cuisine: SWEDISH. **Reservations:** Recommended at dinner. **T-Bana:** Gamla Stan.
$ Prices: 69–155 Kr ($11.40–$25.60); lunch special 57 Kr ($9.40). AE, DC, EURO, MC, V.
Open: Daily 11am–11pm (lunch special served 11am–3pm).

Slingerbulten offers excellent food at moderate prices right in the center of Gamla Stan. Two small green rooms decorated with plants, paintings that depict Gamla Stan scenes, and checkered tablecloths give this place a homey,

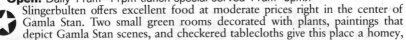

local flavor. Lunch specials change daily, but the emphasis is on seafood, and you always serve yourself at lunch. Dinner is more formal and more expensive, with dishes that include fried herring, Indian-style shrimp with curry and cognac, and trout that's fried and then poached in wine. Stora Nygatan is Gamla Stan's widest street, on the west side of the tiny island. The restaurant (ask them what the name means) is three blocks from the Gamla Stan T-Bana station.

IN NORRMALM & ÖSTERMALM

ARNOLD'S, Birgir Jarlsgatan 20. Tel. 679-71-00.
   Cuisine: CONTINENTAL. **T-Bana:** Östermalmstorg.
   $ Prices: 50–150 Kr ($8.25–$24.75). AE, DC, EURO, MC, V.
   Open: Daily 11am–1am.
An inviting corner restaurant that is especially crowded in the evening, its dining area is surrounded by windows looking out onto lively Stureplan. Childhood memorabilia adorn the walls and ceiling, and there is additional seating in the upstairs balcony. To keep the tab low here, order a stuffed baked potato, barbecued spareribs, or a BLT. The most popular item, however, is the steak-and-salad combo, which costs 97 Kr or 149 Kr ($16 or $24.60), depending on the size of the steak. A large glass of beer here costs 33 Kr ($5.45).

HARD ROCK CAFE, Sveavägen 75. Tel. 16-03-50.
   Cuisine: HAMBURGERS. **T-Bana:** Rådmansgatan.
   $ Prices: 79–129 Kr ($13.05–$21.30). AE, DC, EURO, MC, V.
   Open: Sun–Mon 11am–midnight, Tues–Sat 11am–2am.
Is it a tourist attraction or is it a restaurant? Cynics hate to admit it, but the Hard Rock is perennially packed and, price aside, flips the best burger in town. You can also get a slightly less expensive BLT. The café does have character, with walls exhibiting rock 'n' roll memorabilia, and whether you like it or not, the chain has successfully promoted itself as the unofficial American embassy to the culinary world. It's located at the corner of Odengatan, two blocks north of the Rådmansgatan T-Bana station.

RESTAURANG LE STUDIO DU THEATRE, St. Eriksplan 4. Tel. 33-63-05.
   Cuisine: SWEDISH/FRENCH. **Reservations:** Recommended Sat–Sun. **T-Bana:** St. Eriksplan.
   $ Prices: 60–100 Kr ($9.90–$16.50); daily special 58 Kr ($9.60). AE, DC, EURO, MC, V.
   Open: Mon–Fri 11am–1am, Sat noon–1am, Sun 2pm–1am.
Le Studio is an appealing local place popular with theater-goers (there are numerous stages in the area). Warm and lively, the room seems full even when business is slow—which is rare. The restaurant's intimate size gives it an air of exclusivity, and smart decor complements the good cooking. The wine list is extensive, and at night an American or Irish bartender can mix your favorite. During summer, café tables line the street and the crowd flows out the door. Beware: A cup of tea here will run you 20 Kr ($3.30). The restaurant is a few doors from the St. Eriksplan T-Bana station.

ÖRTAGÅRDEN (Herb Garden), Nybrogatan 31. Tel. 662-17-28.
   Cuisine: VEGETARIAN. **Reservations:** Recommended at night. **T-Bana:** Ostermalmstorg.
   $ Prices: All-you-can-eat mini-smörgåsbord, 65 Kr ($10.70) Mon–Fri until 5pm, 85 Kr ($14) Mon–Fri after 5pm and all day Sat–Sun. DC, EURO, MC, V.
   Open: Mon–Fri 10:30am–9:30pm, Sat 11am–8:30pm, Sun noon–8:30pm.
Floral furniture, pastel-green woodwork, and a ceiling hung with glass chandeliers will have budgeteers convinced that they're in the wrong place. Sit down! Örtagården offers one of the best deals in town with its huge smörgåsbord and comfortable surroundings. Help yourself to the hot and cold dishes and take a seat in the elegant dining room. At night, a classical pianist performs and

reservations are suggested. Örtagården is on the second floor, in the same building as Östermalms food hall (separate entrance).

FAST FOOD & PICNIC SUPPLIES

The high-quality fast-food eateries and fresh food markets around Hötorget Square are essential knowledge for budget travelers.

On the south side of the square, enter through the glass doors of **Hötorgshallen,** and take the escalator down to this great gourmet market. Almost magically, you seem to descend onto a veritable cornucopia of high-quality picnic supplies and prepared foreign foods. Head for the coffee bar, or sample a kebab in pita or a falafel for about 35 Kr ($5.80). Hörtorgshallen has been around since 1880, but was rebuilt in 1958; it houses 50 stands selling fresh breads, meats, fish, and cheeses, with the eating stalls situated along the sides. You can get fresh fish lunches and dinners—and sit down—at a popular spot called **Kajsas Fisk.** Opposite it, by the escalator, Piccolino Café sells sandwiches and a daily hot meal for 50 Kr ($8.25). Hörtorgshallen is open Monday through Friday from 9:30am to 6pm and on Saturday from 9am to 3pm (in summer, on Saturday to 2pm).

Across Hötorget Square is **Kungshallen,** a two-story indoor mall packed with low-cost fast-food stands. It seems as though most of the world's cuisines are represented here, and it's easy to fill up for under 50 Kr ($8.25). Chicken salad, stuffed potatoes, pizzas, pastas, tacos, and more sell for under $8. Hours of individual establishments vary, but the complex is usually open Monday through Friday from 10:30am to 7pm, and on Saturday and Sunday from 11am to 7pm (a couple of stalls stay open until 1am nightly).

Fruits, vegetables, and a variety of other picnic supplies are also available at the **outdoor market** on Hötorget Square itself. It's open year round from 9am to 6pm Monday through Friday and until 4pm on Saturday.

The **Saluhall,** on Östermalmstorg at the corner of Nybrogatan and Humlegårdsgatan, is the fanciest food market of the lot—and Sweden's oldest. Inside the striking brick building, nearly two dozen stalls, a few doubling as restaurants, offer high-quality fish, meats, cheeses, fresh produce, and Swedish specialties. Sample flaskpannkaka (oven pancake with ham), frestelse (baked anchovies and potatoes in cream), or biff Lindstrom (beef patties with capers and beets). Figure on spending 70–120 Kr ($11.55–$19.80). It's open on Monday from 10am to 6pm, Tuesday through Friday from 9am to 6pm, and on Saturday from 9am to 3pm.

For picnic staples and general foods, try the **supermarket** in the basement of Åhléns department store (tel. 24-60-00) on Drottninggatan. alternatively, **ICA** and **Konsum** are two of the largest supermarket chains around.

WORTH THE EXTRA BUCKS

LE BISTROT DE WASAHOF, Dalagatan 46. Tel. 32-34-40.
   Cuisine: SWEDISH. **Reservations:** Suggested. **T-Bana:** Odenplan.
$ **Prices:** 70–165 Kr ($12.70–$30). AE, DC, EURO, MC, V.
   Open: Daily 5pm–1am.
This bubbling bistro is not tremendously above our budget and is recommended for a special night out. Just south of Odengatan, the restaurant is in a theater-infested area known as Stockholm's "off Broadway." The crowd is arty, the food excellent, and the atmosphere convivial. The paintings, which date from 1943, depict the life of 18th-century Swedish musician Carl Michael Bellman. The menu changes monthly. The restaurant is two blocks from the T-Bana stop.

A SUPER-SPLURGE

STADSHUSKÄLLAREN (City Hall Cellar), Stadshuset, Kungholmen. Tel. 650-54-54.

Cuisine: SWEDISH. **Reservations:** Required at least two days in advance. **T-Bana:** T-Centralen.

$ Prices: Nobel dinner, 750 Kr ($123.75) per person; two-course lunch 175 Kr ($28.90). AE, DC, EURO, MC, V.

Open: Mon–Fri 11:30am–11:30pm, Sat 2–11:30pm. **T-Bana:** Rådhuset. **Bus:** 62.

You don't have to be a Nobel Prize winner, or even the significant other of one, to sit down to an authentic Nobel dinner. The restaurant that orchestrates the prestigious banquet each year can also arrange Nobel dinners for individuals—your choice of any Nobel menu since the first, in 1905. Imagine dining (as laureates actually did in 1989) on appetizers of quail eggs and smoked-eel and sole pâté, followed by a main course of tender moose in a berry sauce (game is almost always on the menu), and the perennial Nobel dessert, ice cream enveloped in spun sugar, and petit-fours. Fine champagne, wine, and after-dinner drinks accompany the meal. Granted, you pay mightily for the experience, but it's unforgettable, foodwise and otherwise. The cellar restaurant in City Hall looks much as it did when it opened in 1922, and the service and food were never better.

6. ATTRACTIONS

SUGGESTED ITINERARIES

IF YOU HAVE ONE DAY   Start your day in Djurgården with a visit to the *Vasa* Ship Museum and the vast outdoor Skansen folk museum. After a picnic lunch or a bite to eat in Café Blå Porten, in Djurgården, set your sights on Gamla Stan (Old Town) for an afternoon stroll. Take your time wandering around Stockholm's oldest streets and admiring the city's pretty port views. With few exceptions, Stockholm's best sights are outside.

IF YOU HAVE TWO DAYS   Spend the first day as described above. On the second day, explore the streets of modern Stockholm's Norrmalm district. A visit to Kungsträdgården park is a must and, in winter, might include an ice-skating session. During summer, keep an eye out for the regularly scheduled special events here. It's also easy to go from here to Kungsholmen and tour Stockholm's renowned City Hall.

IF YOU HAVE THREE DAYS   On the third day, make the short trip to Drottningholm Palace to see the Swedish royal couple's house and gardens. Later, back in Stockholm's Old Town, compare it with the older Royal Palace, and visit Storkyrkan, Stockholm's cathedral and the oldest building in town.

IF YOU HAVE FIVE DAYS   Continue your museum-hopping at the Millesgården, the Museum of National Antiquities, the National Art Museum, and any other that might interest you. Take an archipelago cruise or a trip to one of the many islands around the city.

TOP ATTRACTIONS

IN DJURGÅRDEN

Many of Stockholm's best sights are clustered in the Djurgården area, east of Gamla Stan (Old Town). Beautiful, thick forests and sweeping harbor vistas gracefully combine with several well-designed sightseeing attractions.

The most enjoyable way to get here in warm weather is by ferry from Gamla Stan. Buses and a trolley will also get you here; bus nos. 44 and 47 stop at the two top attractions, described below, and bus no. 69 will take you to the tip of the island and other attractions. It's also fun to take just for the inexpensive, pseudo-tour it provides.

VASAMUSÉET (Vasa Museum). Tel. 666-48-00.

⭐ When the warship *Vasa* set sail on its maiden voyage in August of 1628, it was destined to become the pride of the Swedish fleet. But even before it reached the mouth of Stockholm harbor, the 64-cannon man-o'-war caught a sudden gust of wind, fell on its side, and sank to the bottom of the sea. Forgotten for centuries, the boat was discovered in 1956 by marine archeologist Anders Franzén. Today, this highly ornamented, well-preserved wooden vessel is the most frequently visited attraction in Stockholm.

It took five years and advanced technology to raise the fragile ship intact, but in 1961 the *Vasa* was successfully reclaimed and placed in a climatically controlled museum. In the summer of 1990 the *Vasa* moved into a stunning new $27-million building, marking the latest chapter in this ship's long history. Be sure to see the carvings on the bow and stern and the life-size replica of the ship's interior. Children love the computer area, where they can try their hand at raising the *Vasa* from the ocean floor. Two of the original masts and copies of two that did not survive will be added by 1995.

Admission: 30 Kr ($4.95) adults, 10 Kr ($1.65) children 7–15.

Open: June–Aug, daily 9:30am–7pm; Sept–May, daily 10am–5pm (to 8pm Wed). **Closed:** Jan 1, May 1, Dec 24–26, Dec 31. **Ferry:** May–Sept, from Slussen (on Södermalm). **Trolley:** 7, departing in summer and on weekends year round from across the street from the Royal Dramatic Theater. **Bus:** 44 or 47.

SKANSEN. Tel. 663-05-00.

⭐ The year 1991 marked the 100th anniversary of this wonderful 75-acre outdoor museum. Home to over 150 buildings from the 16th to the early 20th century, Skansen is a "Swedish Williamsburg," displaying traditional Nordic log cabins and native stone houses in their original settings. Weather-beaten and imperfect, yet thoroughly charming, many of the buildings here were transported from locations all across Sweden. Some of the cottages (rural dwellings and 18th-century town houses) maintain their original interiors, including painted wooden walls, fireplaces, spinning wheels, old plates, and assorted folk decor. Throughout the museum, craftspeople, using traditional tools and methods, demonstrate the former ways of farming, metalworking, typography, bookbinding, and 15 other trades.

The museum's buildings are interesting in and of themselves, but Skansen's real success is due to its exceptionally peaceful surroundings on a naturally wooded peninsula. In addition, there is a particularly endearing zoo. There may not be many animals here that you haven't seen before, but the open design makes it feel more like a farm than a zoo.

Restaurants and food stands are scattered throughout the area, but, if the weather is nice, it's fun to pack your own lunch and find a welcoming spot for a picnic.

During the summer, try your foot at folk dancing with the locals. Dances are scheduled every evening at 7pm.

A map of Skansen, sold at the museum's entrance, will definitely come in handy. There is also a gift shop.

Admission: May–Aug 28 Kr ($4.60) adults, 13 Kr ($2.15) children; Sept–Apr, 20 Kr ($3.30) adults, 5 Kr (80¢).

Open: Museum grounds, May–Aug, daily 9am–10pm; Sept–Apr, daily 9am–5pm. Historic houses, May–Aug, daily 11am–5pm; Sept–Apr, daily 11am–3pm. **Ferry:** May–Sept, from Slussen (on Söder malm). **Trolley:** 7, departing in summer and on weekends year round from across the street from the Royal Dramatic Theater. **Bus:** 44 or 47.

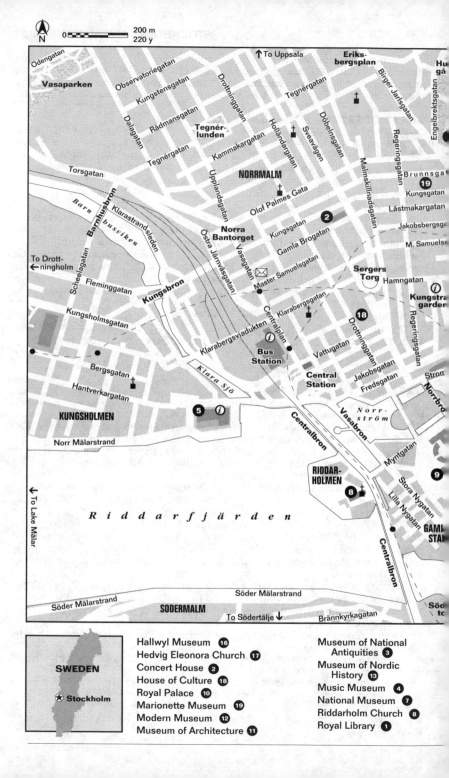

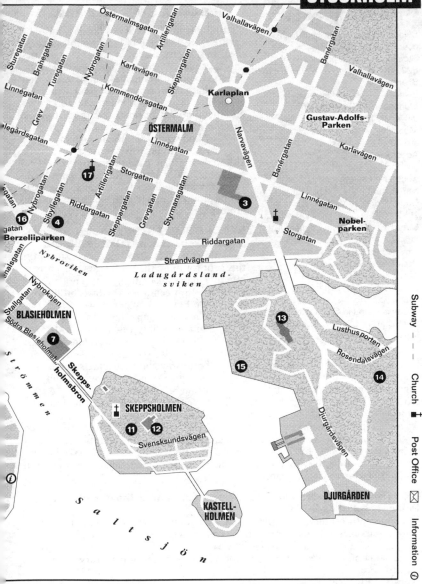

STOCKHOLM

Östermalmsgatan
Valhallavägen
Sturegatan
Brahegatan
Turegatan
Nybrogatan
Artillerigatan
Skeppargatan
Banérgatan
Valhallavägen
Karlavägen
Kommendörsgatan
Linnégatan
Karlaplan
Grev
Gustav-Adolfs-Parken
legårdsgatan
ÖSTERMALM
Linnégatan
Narvavägen
Karlavägen
Banérgatan
gatan
Nybrogatan
Sibyllegatan
Artillerigatan
Storgatan
17
Riddargatan
Skeppargatan
Grevgatan
Styrmansgatan
3
Linnégatan
16
4
gatan
Berzeliiparken
Riddargatan
Storgatan
Nobel-parken
nalsgatan
Nybroviken
Strandvägen
Nybrokajen
Ladugårdslands-sviken
Stallgatan
BLASIEHOLMEN
13
Lusthusporten
Södra Blasieholmsh
7
Skepps-holmsbron
15
Rosendalsvägen
S t r ö m m e n
14
SKEPPSHOLMEN
11
12
Svensksundsvägen
Djurgårdsvägen
(i)
DJURGÅRDEN
KASTELL-HOLMEN
S a l t s j ö n

Subway – – –

Church ■✝

Post Office ⊠

Information ⓘ

oyal Opera House **6**
kansen **14**
wn Hall **5**
athedral **9**
asa Museum **15**

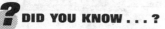

IN GAMLA STAN [OLD TOWN]

Getting lost in Gamla Stan's timeless maze of car-free streets is one of Stockholm's greatest pleasures. Pretty shades of pastel separate the short, squat buildings along cobblestone streets. Exposed drainpipes run past wooden storm shutters protecting first-floor windows. Black metal streetlamps illuminate storefronts and metal hooks for hoisting cargo hang over garret windows.

Also known as Old Town, Gamla Stan is the city's most heavily touristed area and, although you may catch a glimpse of a contemporary office interior or pass some high-fashion window displays, its quiet, historical charm stoically maintains an authentic ancient atmosphere.

STOCKHOLMS SLOTT (Royal Palace), off Skeppsbron. Tel. 789-85-00.

Although a royal residence has stood on this spot for more than 700 years, the current building dates from the 17th century. The 17th and 18th centuries saw Sweden flourish as one of Europe's major powers, and this grand palace, encompassing over 600 rooms, was rebuilt to reflect this status. Today the Swedish king only performs ceremonial tasks, and the palace is used for official state functions. The complex is huge and, although you'll probably find its massive stone facade somewhat uninspired, the 18th-century Royal Apartment interiors are as grand and distinguished as any. Flamboyantly painted ceilings, opulent chandeliers, ornate tapestries, and other royal riches are all on permanent display. Note that the apartments can close without notice for special occasions.

At noon (1pm on Sunday) you can see the Changing of the Guard in the palace courtyard. In summer, the spectacle includes the guards' parade and music.

Admission: 30 Kr ($4.95), adults, 15 Kr ($2.50) students, 10 Kr ($1.65) children.

Open: May–Aug, Tues–Sat 10am–3pm, Sun noon–3pm; Sept–Apr, Tues–Sun noon–3pm. **T-Bana:** Gamla Stan.

STORKYRKAN (Stockholm Cathedral), Trångsund (next to the Royal Palace). Tel. 723-30-00.

Since the 13th century, this church has seen some of Sweden's most important religious ceremonies, including coronations and royal marriages. Many people believe this to be the oldest building in the city. Every Saturday at 1pm, and on Sunday once or twice a month, concerts featuring the church's huge 18th-century organ are performed here.

Admission: Free.

Open: Daily 9am–5pm (until 4pm in winter). **T-Bana:** Gamla Stan.

ON KUNGSHOLMEN

STADHUSET (City Hall), Hantverkargatan 1. Tel. 785-90-00.

Stockholm's lavish, landmark City Hall is home to the annual Nobel Prize banquet and may be visited only by guided tour. The tour's highlight is undoubtedly the Golden Hall, lavishly decorated with over 19 million

23-karat-gold tiles and one of the world's most beautiful rooms. Dinners honoring Nobel Prize winners were originally held in this room, but swelling guest lists have forced the party to relocate to the even-larger Blue Hall (which isn't blue). Marble floors, stone columns, and Gothic motifs throughout make City Hall look and feel much older than its 70 years. You may climb to the top of the distinctive tower, topped by three gleaming crowns, in summer only.

Admission: 20 Kr ($3.30) adults, free for children under 12.

Open: Tours, summer, daily at 10am, 11am, noon, and 2pm; the rest of the year, daily at 10am and noon. Tower visits, May–Sept, daily 10am–3pm. **T-Bana:** Rådhuset.

IN NORRMALM & ON SKEPPSHOLMEN

NATIONAL MUSEUM, Blasieholmen. Tel. 666-42-50.

Although it stocks masterpieces by stars like Rembrandt, Rubens, El Greco, and Renoir, this pleasant and manageable museum, which turned 200 in 1992, is not labyrinthine like the Louvre. There are English-language tours in summer, and the collection is well marked (in Swedish) and nicely displayed. Be sure to visit the third-floor gallery with mid-19th- to mid-20th-century Swedish painters, including Anders Zorn, Carl Larsson, and Ernst Josephson. The second-floor Department of Applied Arts features over 28,000 pieces of porcelain, glassware, silverwork, and jewelry, including a contemporary Swedish design gallery. The third floor also houses works by Renoir, Degas, Rodin, and Corot, along with 16th- and 17th-century French, Italian, Flemish, and Dutch painters. The museum is at the foot of the bridge to Skeppsholmen.

Admission: 40 Kr ($6.60) adults, 20 Kr ($3.30) students and seniors, free for children under 16; free for everyone on Fri.

Open: July–Aug, Tues–Wed and Fri–Sun 11am–5pm, Thurs 11am–9pm; Sept–June, Tues and Thurs 11am–9pm, Wed and Fri–Sun 11am–5pm.

MODERNA MUSÉET (Modern Art Museum), Skeppsholmen. Tel. 666-42-50.

⭐ Open late three times a week, the Modern Art Museum is an excellent choice for evening sightseeing, especially on Thursday, when it's free. The museum features examples from the most popular artists including Picasso, Matisse, Dalí, Warhol, Ernst, Kandinsky, Braque, Miró, and Pollock, as well as some Swedish contemporaries. Although temporary exhibitions often lack star power, they are usually adventurous and tackle unusual themes. The pleasant museum café offers a variety of dishes, and there is a museum shop. Housed in the same building, the small **Museum of Photography** mounts outstanding special exhibits.

Admission: 40 Kr ($6.60) adults, 20 Kr ($3.30) students and seniors, free for children under 16; free to all on Thurs.

Open: Tues–Thurs 11am–9pm, Fri–Sun 11am–6pm. **T-Bana:** Kungsträdgården; then a 10-minute walk. **Bus:** 65 to Skeppsholmen.

MORE ATTRACTIONS

ON DJURGÅRDEN

WALDEMARSUDDE, Prins Eugens väg 6. Tel. 662-18-33.

This former palace of Prince Eugen (1865–1947) is not only known for its glorious architecture and truly palatial view, but has been made famous by the artworks of Prince Eugen himself. The "artist prince," as Eugen is now known, was a prolific painter, and some believe that he was pretty good, too. Although the palace's collection also includes paintings by modern Nordic masters, this art is outnumbered by a ton of works by the prince. The gallery of Swedish art is to the left of the main entrance, and there are also provocative special exhibits. A small café on the premises offers a coffee refill for free. Some sculpture by Carl Milles is in the rose garden, and the small house adjacent to the palace has exhibits on the life of Prince Eugen. The palace is dramatically situated, nestled among thick forest overlooking the port and Södermalm.

Admission: 30 Kr ($4.95) adults, 15 Kr ($2.50) students and seniors, free for children under 16.

Open: June–Aug, Tues and Thurs 11am–5pm and 7–9pm, Wed and Fri–Sun 11am–5pm; Sept–Nov 26 and Dec 26–May, Tues–Sun 11am–4pm (the grounds stay open until 7pm). **Closed:** Nov 25–Dec 25. **Bus:** 47.

THIELSKA GALLERIET (Thiel Gallery), Sjotullsbacken 6-8. Tel. 662-58-84.

⭐ Built as a gallery to house the burgeoning collection of banker and art patron Ernst Thiel, it was bought by Sweden and opened to the public in 1924, when Thiel went bust. One room is devoted to Carl Larsson, and there are works by Gauguin, Vuillard, Anders Zorn, Carl Wilhelmson, and Ernst Josephson. Climb to the tower room to see the two dozen Munchs and a fine view of the archipelago. On the grounds are works by Rodin and Norwegian sculptor Gustav Vigeland.

Admission: 20 Kr ($3.30) adults, 10 Kr ($1.65) students and seniors.

Open: Mon–Sat noon–4pm, Sun 1–4pm. **Bus:** 69.

NORDISKA MUSÉET (Museum of Nordic History), Djurgården. Tel. 666-46-00.

Located in an impressive stone building, this ethnographic museum documents changes in Nordic life over the past 500 years. You'll learn how Swedes lived, dressed, hunted, and fished, and track the culture's evolution to the current day. Don't miss the grandfather clock collection. The museum's café offers a daily lunch special.

Admission: 30 Kr ($4.95) adults, 20 Kr ($3.30) students, 10 Kr ($1.65) children 7–16.

Open: June–Aug, Mon–Wed and Fri 10am–4pm, Thurs 10am–8pm, Sat–Sun noon–5pm; Sept–May, Tues–Wed and Fri 10am–4pm, Thurs 10am–8pm, Sat–Sun 11am–4pm. **Bus:** 47 or 69. **Ferry:** From Gamla Stan to Djurgården. **Trolley:** 7, departing in summer and on weekends year round from across the street from the Royal Dramatic Theater.

IN NORRMALM

HALLWYLSKA MUSÉET (Hallwyl Museum), Hamngatan 4. Tel. 666-44-75.

⭐ Stockholm's most unusual (perhaps eccentric) museum is a magnificent turn-of-the-century private residence filled with 70 years' worth of passionate collecting by Countess Wilhelmina von Hallwyl. On display is everything from buttons to Dutch and Swedish paintings, European china and Chinese silver, umbrellas, and weapons. The Hallwyls, who lived here from 1898 to 1930, had four daughters, one of whom, Ellen, became a sculptor and studied with Carl Milles; and they had a modern bathroom before the king did! Admission to the house is by one-hour guided tour only. Arrive early; they book up quickly. You'll wish you could stay longer.

Admission: 30 Kr ($4.95).

Open: Daily noon–3pm. The English-language tour is at 1pm; off-season, the English-language tour is on Sun only. **T-Bana:** Kungsträdgården.

KULTURHUSET (House of Culture), Sergels Torg 3. Tel. 700-01-62 or 700-01-10.

The Kulturhuset, housed in a 1960s building, is designed to expose Swedes to other cultures, but it is equally effective at exposing other cultures to each other. On its multiple floors are numerous galleries, stages, cafés, a large library, thousands of records (which you may listen to with headsets), 200 newspapers, 500 magazines, a bookshop, and chessboards. People from all over the world come here to catch up on "local" news. The glass sculpture outside the building, *Vertical Accent,* by Edvin Ohrstrom, is particularly striking at night, when it's lit.

Admission: Free, except for theater productions and concerts.
Open: Information, Mon–Thurs 8am–8pm, Fri 8am–6pm, Sat–Sun 11am–5pm.
T-Bana: T-Centralen.

ON SÖDERMALM

KATARINA ELEVATOR, Södermalms Torg, Slussen.

The Katarina Elevator itself is not the attraction—the seven-story view it provides is! Located just over the bridge from Gamla Stan, the elevator lifts visitors to a perch high above the port. If you're feeling strong, make the climb yourself up the cliff behind the elevator, but don't miss this spectacular view of Stockholm.

Admission: 3 Kr (50¢), free for children under 7.
Open: Mon–Sat 7:30am–10pm, Sun and hols 10am–10pm. **T-Bana:** Slussen.

ON LIDINGÖ

MILLESGÅRDEN, Carl Milles väg 2. Tel. 731-50-60.

One of the greatest Swedish artists, sculptor Carl Milles (1875–1955) returned to Stockholm late in life to design and build a garden on a hill on the island of Lidingö. Unfortunately the Milles Garden is a little time-consuming to get to, but those who are eager enough will be rewarded with views of magnificent fountains and sculptures, including the memorable *Hand of God,* overlooking all of Stockholm. Picnickers will agree that this breathtaking site beautifully augments the artist's own works.

Admission: 30 Kr ($4.95) adults, 25 Kr ($4.10) students and seniors, free for children under 12.
Open: May–Sept, daily 10am–5pm; Oct–Apr, Tues–Sun 11am–4pm. **T-Bana:** Ropsten; then bus to Torsvik (the first stop; pedestrians cannot cross the bridge on foot). From here, walk about 8 minutes, following the signs to the Milles Garden. The entire trip will take about 40 minutes.

PARKS & GARDENS

Parks are one of Stockholm's loveliest assets, and many have already been mentioned above. Bring a picnic to **Skansen,** or to anywhere on the wooded peninsula of **Djurgården.** Waldemarsudde and Millesgården are also excellent strolling grounds, as is the entire island of Skeppsholmen. In Norrmalm, take your lunch to **Kungsträdgården,** a bustling urban park and the city's summer meeting place.

Tanto Lunden, with tiny cottages and carefully tended gardens near the city center, is a Stockholm phenomenon, created in 1919 so that city workers who couldn't afford a country home could benefit from country living. The cottages, one room each, look more like dollhouses, with equally tiny yards filled with birdhouses and compost heaps. To get here, take bus no. 43 or the T-Bana to Zinkensdamm. Zinkens väg, where you'll find the Touristgården Zinken youth hostel, dead-ends into Tanto Lunden; climb the wooden steps and enter a world in miniature. Don't overlook delightful house no. 69.

KIDS' STOCKHOLM

The award-winning **Marionett Muséet (Marionette Museum)**, Brunnsgatan 6 (tel. 10-30-61), is an enchanting place, with displays of 1,000 puppets—string puppets, shadow puppets, glove puppets, even battery-driven puppets—from around the world, particularly Sweden and Asia. Children may play with some of them. Ask at the desk for exhibit descriptions in English. There is free coffee for visitors, and you may even sit and have tea in the Japanese room. Admission is 20 Kr ($3.30) for adults and 10 Kr ($1.65) for children. On weekends, admission to the museum and a performance at the adjacent Puppet Theater is 10 Kr ($1.65). The museum is open from January to June and August to September, daily from 1 to 4pm; closed the month of July.

"Please touch" is the modus operandi at the **Musikmuséet (Music Museum)**, Sibyllegatan 2 (tel. 666-42-50). Kids get to play many of the instruments displayed here, among them conga drums, xylophone, harp, accordion, stringed instruments, and synthesizer. Adults can enjoy the texts in English. Downstairs, instruments from the 16th to the 20th century, including a clavichord, lute, and harpsichord, are displayed. There's also an informative exhibit on jazz in Sweden. The museum shop sells cassettes, CDs, records, books (mostly in Swedish), and posters. It's open Tuesday through Sunday from 11am to 4pm; the admission is 20 Kr ($3.30) for adults, 10 Kr ($1.65) for children.

Another favorite with kids is the **Tekniska Muséet (National Museum of Science and Technology)**, Museivagen 7, Djurgården (tel. 663-10-85), where they get to experiment to their hearts' content, as well as view steam engines, aircraft, vintage cars, and more. It's open Monday through Friday from 10am to 4pm and on Saturday and Sunday from noon to 4pm; admission is 25 Kr ($4.10) for adults, 10 Kr ($1.65) for children. Within walking distance is the 155-meter (507-ft.) **Kaknas TV Tower** (tel. 667-80-30), which provides a panoramic view of Stockholm and the archipelago. Inside is a souvenir shop and a tourist information office. The tower is open April 15 through September 15, daily from 9am to 10:30pm; the rest of the year, daily from 9am to 6pm. Admission is 15 Kr ($2.30) for adults and 8 Kr ($1.30) for children, (under 7 free). To get here or to the National Museum of Science and Technology, take bus no. 69.

SPECIAL-INTEREST SIGHTSEEING

FOR THE LITERARY ENTHUSIAST   Admirers of Swedish dramatist August Strindberg (1849–1912) can visit the **Strindberg Museum**, Drottninggatan 85 (tel. 11-37-89), a reconstruction of his last home, built on its original site. The house is filled with authentic furniture and details and includes a reconstruction of the author's library. It's open Tuesday through Friday from 10am to 4pm (on Tuesday also from 6 to 8pm) and on Saturday and Sunday from noon to 4pm. Admission is 15 Kr ($2.50) for adults, free for children under 16; free for everyone on Tuesday evening. Take the T-Bana to Rådmansgatan.

FOR THE HISTORY BUFF   Stockholm was founded in the 13th century and, despite the fancy boutiques that now line the streets of Gamla Stan, you can still get a feeling for what it must have been like here hundreds of years ago. Cars are banned from most streets, and the area's narrow alleyways still claim ancient charm. Wander along Österlånggatan and Västerlånggatan, following the path where the ancient city walls once stood.

Those interested in the Vikings and early Swedish history will enjoy a visit to the **Historiska Muséet (Museum of National Antiquities)**, Narvavägen 13-17 (tel. 783-94-00). Viking stone inscriptions, 10th-century coins, and ancient armor are displayed here. The collection, which complements that of the Nordic museum, shows daily life from the dawn of time to the Middle Ages. The museum shop is worth a visit for its fine collection of English-language history books and copies of Viking jewelry in gold and silver. The museum shop is open Tuesday through Sunday from noon to 5pm (in winter, also on Thursday until 8pm). Admission is 30 Kr ($4.95) for adults, 10 Kr ($1.65) for students, seniors, and children under 16. To get there, take the T-Bana to Karlaplan or bus no. 44, 47, or 69.

Next in the historical chain of progression is **Skansen,** which shows how Swedes have lived (and in what kinds of structures) over the past 400 years, and the **Museum of Nordic History,** which details how Sweden became a modern society (see "Top Attractions" and "More Attractions," above, respectively).

FOR THE ARCHITECTURE LOVER   Stockholm's most stunning edifices line the water, and continue for the length of the city. Most of these gorgeous buildings were erected around the turn of the century and are maintained in excellent condition. The city's picture-postcard beauty can be summed up in one spot: on the bridge Djurgårdsbron, which connects Djurgården (where Skansen is located) to the rest of the city.

The **Museum of Architecture,** Skeppsholmen (tel. 697-75-10), has models, maps, and architectural plans of Stockholm. It's open from 11am to 9pm on Tuesday and 11am to 5pm Wednesday through Sunday. Admission is 20 Kr ($3.30) for adults, 10 Kr ($1.65) for students and seniors, free for children under 15. Take bus no. 65 or the T-Bana to Kungsträdgården.

The **Stockholm Stadsmuséet (Stockholm City Museum),** in Slussen near the subway exit (tel. 700-05-00), depicts Stockholm in centuries past in drawings and models. Texts are in Swedish only, but visitors should still find the first and second floors well done and interesting. The museum, which has a good café, is open Tuesday through Thursday from 11am to 7pm (to 9pm January to mid-May) and Friday through Monday from 11am to 5pm; admission is 15 Kr ($2.50) for adults, free for children under 18.

ORGANIZED TOURS

Some visitors find Stockholm a difficult city to negotiate, because of its island layout and spread-out sights. A tour can save you a lot of time and be quite informative as well. **Stockholm Sightseeing** (tel. 24-04-70) offers the least expensive panoramic tour of the city. Buses leave from in front of Sweden House, and tours take 2½ hours and cost 200 Kr ($33) half price for children, from mid-May through September. From October through mid-May tours are scaled back to 1½ hours and cost 135 Kr ($22.30) for adults, half price for children.

Their **Under the Bridges of Stockholm** tour takes 1½ hours and costs 90 Kr ($14.85) for adults, half price for children. The boat leaves from in front of the ticket booth in front of the Grand Hotel. A similar but shorter (one-hour) water tour, **Cityringen,** is offered by **Stromma's Sightseeing** (tel. 23-33-75) and costs 65 Kr ($10.70) for adults, half price for children 6–11. The sleek, glass-enclosed boat leaves from City Hall and Nybroviken, which is opposite the Royal Dramatic Theater. Visit the Stockholm Information Service (see "Information" in "Orientation and Getting Around," above) for tour times and reservations, and refer to the "Sightseeing" section of *Stockholm This Week* for a full list of tour operators.

SPECIAL & FREE EVENTS

In addition to the special events outlined under "When to Go," in "Pretrip Preparations," above, a full schedule of special and free happenings will keep you busy. Always check with the tourist office and their publication *Stockholm This Week* for the most up-to-date information.

During the summer, Norrmalm's park, Kungsträdgården, adjacent to Sweden House, comes alive almost daily with classical-music concerts, rock bands, theater performances, and various other attractions. During the winter, an outdoor ice rink opens its gates here, providing some of the best inner-city skating anywhere.

Summertime also means frequent, free and almost-free concerts in other parts of Stockholm. **Sommarnättskonserterna (Summer Night Concerts)** are held on the stairs of the National Museum of Fine Art during July and August, and **folk dancing** is performed every afternoon at the Skansen outdoor museum.

7. SAVVY SHOPPING

A whopping 25% goods tax makes shopping in Sweden expensive, and you can get most items at home for less money. On the positive side, Swedish stores usually stock items of the highest quality. Favorite buys include crystal, clothing, and Scandinavian-design furniture. Take a good look at some of the high-tech designs that have made Scandinavia famous. You might decide to take home a souvenir that will bring you joy for years to come.

Many stores offer tax rebates to tourists spending over 101 Kr ($16.65). Here's how to get your refund: When you make your purchase, ask the retailer for a Tax Free Check (valid for one month), and leave your purchase sealed until you leave the country. At any border crossing on your way out of Sweden (or at repayment centers in Denmark, Finland, or Norway), show both the check (to which you have added your name, address, and passport number), and the purchase to an official at the tax-free office. You will get a cash refund of 16%–18% in U.S. dollars (or seven other currencies) after the service charge has been taken out (remember not to check the purchase in your luggage until after you receive the refund). At Arlanda Airport there are separate booths for VAT purchases that are to be checked as baggage and those that are to be carried on the plane, so be sure to get in the right line for your refund.

BEST BUYS & WHERE TO FIND THEM

For the best shopping and window-shopping in Stockholm, stroll along the quiet streets of **Gamla Stan** (particularly Västerlånggatan), filled with boutiques, art galleries, and jewelry stores. Similarly winsome shops may be found along **the Hornsgats-Puckeln** (the Hornsgatan-Hunchback, as its known locally) on Södermalm. Other streets that tempt browsing include **Hamngatan, Birger Jarlsgatan, Biblioteksgatan,** and **Kungsgaton,** all in Normalm.

NK (it stands for Nordiska Kompaniet), Hamngatan 18-20 (tel. 762-80-00), across from Sweden House, is the Harrods of Stockholm. The stunning department store sells quality merchandise beautifully displayed, often at high prices. It's open Monday through Friday from 10am to 7pm, on Saturday from 10am to 5pm, and on Sunday from 11am to 5pm.

PUB, another popular department store, at Hötorget Square (tel. 791-60-00), claims Greta Garbo as its most famous employee. Visit the fifth floor of its Hötorgshuset building to see a small exhibit (conveniently located next to the coffee shop) about the then-unglamorous Greta. The store is open Monday through Friday from 10am to 7pm, on Saturday from 10am to 5pm, and on Sunday from noon to 4pm.

Gallerian, Hamngatan 37, is a centrally located mall, where you can buy toys, cheap postcards, and other items; its upscale cousin, **Sturegallerian,** is at Stureplan 4.

Drottninggatan is a pedestrian street leading from Hörtoget Square past the Kulturhuset into Gamla Stan, but most of the stores along it are less appealing than those you'll find elsewhere.

The **Swedish Institute Bookshop,** on the second floor of Sweden House, Hamngatan 27 (tel. 789-20-00), has a wealth of books about the art and culture of Sweden, CDs, cassettes, records, and children's books, including many by Astrid

Lindgren. For toys, shop at **Stor & Liten,** in the Gallerian shopping center, Hanmgatan 37 (tel. 23-13-90), and **Leka Samman,** in Södermalm, at Hornsgatan 50A (tel. 714-96-00).

For famous Swedish crystal, compare prices at the **Crystal Showroom,** near Sweden House, at Hamngatan 11 (tel. 21-70-34), or **Duka,** at the Consert House, Kungsgatan 41 at Sveavägen (tel. 20-60-41).

For handcrafts, including textiles, yarns, baskets, rugs, pottery, and items in wood and metal, browse through the large **Svensk Hemslöjd,** Sveavägen 44 (tel. 23-21-15), operated by the Swedish Handicraft Society.

For camping or outdoor gear, **Frilufts Magasinet,** with two locations, at Sveavägen 73 at Odengatan (tel. 34-20-00), and Hantverkargatan 38-40 (tel. 652-50-92), has a wide assortment.

Most shops are open Monday through Friday from 9:30am to 6pm and on Saturday from 10am to 2pm. Department stores stay open later (see above).

If Scandinavian-design furniture, lamps, glass, ceramics, and other household objects intrigue you, don't miss **IKEA,** Kungens Kurva (tel. 740-80-00), which claims to be the largest home-furnishings store in the world. The store is 25 minutes from the city center, and is serviced by a special free bus, which leaves from the front of Sweden House hourly, Monday through Friday only, from 11am to 5pm (returning hourly on the half hour). Otherwise, take the T-Bana to Skärholmen. The store does not accept credit cards. IKEA is open Monday through Friday from 11am to 8pm, on Saturday from 10am to 5pm, and on Sunday from 11am to 5pm.

MARKETS & AUCTIONS

THE FLEA MARKET Bargain hunters won't want to miss northern Europe's largest flea market, in the **Skärholmen shopping center** (tel. 710-00-60). Amid plenty of junk are some real finds. The offerings are too numerous to mention. Take T-Bana Line 13 to Skärholmen, a 20-minute ride from the Central Station. From the T-Bana stop, walk ahead and turn left on the square into the shopping mall; look for a yellow sign LOPPMARKNADEN pointing down an escalator to the indoor intersection of Storholmsgatan and Lillhomsgången. Although the market bustles all week long, weekends are liveliest. The market is open Monday through Friday from 11am to 6pm, on Saturday from 9am to 3pm, and on Sunday from 10am to 3pm. Admission is 8 Kr ($1.30) for adults, free for children on weekends and free for all on weekdays.

AN AUCTION Gavels have been finalizing public auctions in Stockholm since 1674, and that tradition continues today at **Auktionsverket (Auction Chambers),** Jakobsgatan 10, in the Gallerian mall (tel. 14-24-40). Visitors are welcome to bid or watch. Viewings are usually held on Friday and Saturday, but call for viewing and auction times, and ask what's up for bids on the day you want to visit.

8. EVENING ENTERTAINMENT

Stockholm's "living arts" are well supported with state funds. As a result, the price of high-quality "serious" entertainment is extremely reasonable. Moreover, good public funding means that performing arts houses don't have to rely on a conservative public—they can experiment with new and interesting ideas.

Stockholm's concert hall, opera house, and theaters are closed in the summer, but, luckily three deals are offered in their place. **Free open-air park performances by Parkteatern** (the Parks Theater) begin every June and continue throughout the summer; **Sommarnättskonserterna (Summer Night Concerts),** on the main staircase of the National Museum, start in July and run through the end of August; and folk-dancing at **Skansen** is nightly at 7pm.

Also in the summer, **jazz cruises** provide an exhilarating way to experience

Stockholm from the water while enjoying upbeat entertainment under the stars. This is a good way to meet Swedish people, and the boats usually stop at a friendly island so revelers can dance on shore.

Churches—the cathedral, on Gamla Stan; Jacob's Church, near the Opera House; and Hedvig Eleonora, in Östermalm, for instance—often host free evening (and afternoon) concerts. Check listings under "Music" in *Stockholm This Week* or look for announcements posted in front of individual churches.

On the late-night front, all is also well. The nightlife in what once was a fairly staid capital has undergone a major change over the last decade or so. Today, late-nighters can engage in the city's thriving café culture, listen to live rock and jazz, and dance into the wee hours—usually at Kungsträdgården or on Gamla Stan or Södermalm.

Always check the tourist office, *Stockholm This Week,* and local newspapers (especially *Dagens Nyheter* from Thursday through Sunday) for details on upcoming events.

THE PERFORMING ARTS

Almost every capital has its "National Houses," where the biggest-budgeted performances are staged. But it is the proliferation of "alternative" theater and music that divides cities with great culture from all the rest. Stockholm is one of those great cities, and an opportunity to visit one of its smaller playhouses should not be passed up. Check *Stockholm This Week* for a full list of current performances. This is a great opportunity to experience some high-quality, inexpensive, cutting-edge entertainment. (Not many theaters are open in summer, but you'll find plenty of concerts.)

CLASSICAL CONCERTS, OPERA, THEATER & BALLET

FILHARMONIKERNA I KONSERTHUSET (Stockholm Concert Hall), Hötorget 8. Tel. 22-18-00 for information, 10-21-10 or 24-41-30 for the box office.

This hall is home to the **Stockholm Philharmonic Orchestra,** and performances are usually on Wednesday, Thursday, and Saturday throughout the season (August through May), while touring companies sometimes light up the stage on other days throughout the year. Carl Milles's sculpture *Orpheus* is outside the building.

Prices: Tickets, 53–165 Kr ($8.75–$27.20); students and seniors get a 20% discount.

Open: Box office, Mon–Fri 11am–6pm, Sat 11am–3pm.

BERWALDHALLEN (Berwald Concert Hall), Strandvägen 69. Tel. 784-18-00.

This award-winning hexagonal structure built into a granite hillside is home to **Stockholm's Radio Symphony Orchestra.** Call or check the entertainment section of local papers for a schedule and times for upcoming concerts.

Prices: Tickets 65–130 Kr ($11–$21.45).

Open: Box office, Mon–Fri 9–11am and 12:30–2:30pm. Performances start at 7:30 or 8pm.

OPERAN (Opera House), Gustav Adolfs Torg. Tel. 24-82-40.

The Operan houses the **Swedish Royal Opera.** Most of the operas performed in this beautifully restored house are translated into Swedish, with an emphasis on popular works (for example, *Don Giovanni, Madame Butterfly,* and *Carmen*). The season runs from the end of August to the beginning of June. Call or visit the box office for a current schedule.

Prices: Tickets, 90–230 Kr ($14.85–$37.95); students can buy most tickets at a discount of almost 50%. There are some side seats (with an obstructed view) for 50 Kr ($8.25) and "listening seats" (no view, but not standing room) for only 20 Kr ($3.30). Children younger than 16 get discounts for certain performances.

Open: Box office, Mon–Fri 11am–7:30pm (to 6pm when no performance is scheduled), Sat 11am–3pm (later on performance days). **Closed:** June–Aug.

KUNGLIGA DRAMATISKA THEATERN (Royal Dramatic Theater), on Nybroplan. Tel. 667-06-80.

This is one of the great playhouses of Europe. The plays performed here are almost exclusively in Swedish, but that shouldn't deter you. Occasionally ballets light up the stage. During the summer the theater offers a daily guided tour for 15 Kr ($2.50) at 3pm; the rest of the year, at 6:30pm on Saturday only. It's closed for two weeks in summer.

Prices: Theater tickets, 70–140 Kr ($11.55–$23.10) for the large stage, 140 Kr ($23.10) for the small stage. Those under 20 pay half price; ages 20–26 get a 10% discount, as do seniors, but only on Sunday.

Open: Box office, Mon 10am–6pm, Tues–Sat 10am–7pm, Sun noon–4pm.

REGINA THEATRE, Drottninggatan 71A. Tel. 20-70-00.

In operation since 1981, the Regina is the largest English-language theater outside England, and Europe's only Equity theater besides Vienna's English Theater. It is Sweden's only English-language theater, though performances may vary in quality. Seating for 300 people is open and all seats are good. Half a dozen or more productions are mounted a year. The theater has its own pub, a congenial place to meet before the 7:30pm curtain.

Prices: Tickets, 150 Kr ($24.75); students get a 20% discount on tickets bought on the performance night.

Open: Box office, Mon noon–6pm, Tues–Sat noon–7pm. **Closed:** June–Aug.

JAZZ, ROCK & BLUES

GLOBEN (Globe Arena), Johanneshov. Tel. 725-10-00 for information, 600-34-00 for the box office.

Stockholm's futuristic Globe Arena measures 85m (279 ft.) high by 110m (361 ft.) wide, and seats 16,000 people. It has hosted such stars as Roxette, Sting, Diana Ross, Liza Minelli, and Ray Charles. If you're not a mega-concert fan, you might enjoy taking in an ice hockey game here. Tours are given daily in summer from 10am to 4pm.

Admission: About 230 Kr ($37.95) for concerts, about 100 Kr ($16.50) for ice hockey.

Open: Box office, Mon–Fri 11am–6pm, Sat 11am–4pm. **T-Bana:** Globen.

STAMPEN, Stora Nygatan 5, in Gamla Stan. Tel. 20-57-93.

Stampen, a Stockholm tradition since 1967, is the city's lively center for jazz, with two bands performing nightly. The upstairs stage is beneath a ceiling sporting a contra bass, a Confederate flag, a wooden sleigh, and other whimsical decor. The second stage is in the more subdued downstairs room. Minimum age is 23. Like many of the city's other live-music clubs, Stampen is located in Gamla Stan. Bengt, the person who's likely to greet you at the door, has worked here since 1969.

Admission: 50–100 Kr ($8.25–$16.50), depending on the band; free music Thurs and Sat afternoon.

Open: Tues–Sat 8am–1am. **T-Bana:** Gamla Stan.

ENGELEN, Kornhamnstorg 59B, in Gamla Stan. Tel. 20-10-92.

Engelen (the name means "Angel") provides a stage for local bands nightly. The live music is upstairs from 8:30pm until midnight, while dance discs spin below until 3am in Kolingen. The early- to mid-20s crowd arrives early (before 10pm), especially on weekends when it's packed. Patrons are welcome to join in an open jam on Sunday from 5:30 to 8:30pm.

Prices: Wine 35 Kr ($5.75); beer 44 Kr ($7.25). **Admission:** 40–50 Kr ($6.60–$8.25) Sun–Thurs, 60–70 Kr ($9.90–$11.55) Fri–Sat.
Open: Daily 5pm–3am. **T-Bana:** Gamla Stan.

KAOS, Stora Nygatan 21, in Gamla Stan. Tel. 20-58-86.

This is an informal, bilevel café and club with live music nightly. Several nights a week, especially on weekends, an additional stage is opened downstairs in the vaulted cellar, where a second band plays. Sunday night from 9pm on is dedicated to the blues, Wednesday is for boogie-woogie, and there's a free jam session at 2pm on Saturday. In a house dating from 1760, Kaos has been around for about 30 years and claims to be the oldest music club in Sweden. There is a sense of walking into the '60s when you enter.

Prices: Wine or beer 30–42 Kr ($4.95–$6.95). **Admission:** Free before 7:30pm; afterward, 20–40 Kr ($3.30–$6.60) Sun–Thurs, 50 Kr ($8.25) Fri–Sat; free jam session at 2pm Sun.
Open: Mon–Fri 5pm–1am, Sat–Sun 2pm–1am. **T-Bana:** Gamla Stan.

FASCHING, Kungsgatan 63. Tel. 21-62-67.

This club is open every day, serving up plenty of contemporary jazz and some blues.

Admission: From 70 Kr ($11.55), depending on the entertainment; occasionally free.
Open: Mon–Thurs 7pm–midnight, Fri–Sat from 8pm; music starts between 8 and 9pm; call to check days and times. **T-Bana:** Hötorget.

TRE BACKAR, Tegnergatan 12-14. Tel. 673-44-00.

The mixture of music in this popular and versatile place is rock, blues, and folk.
Admission: 40–50 Kr ($6.60–$8.25), depending on the entertainment.
Open: Mon–Thurs 10:30am–midnight, Fri–Sun 6pm–1am. **T-Bana:** Rådmansgatan.

MOSEBACKE ESTABLISSEMENT, Mosebacke Torg 1-3. Tel. 641-90-20.

Mosebacke attracts an older crowd with its cabarets, and packs in people of all ages who come to listen to local rock, blues, and jazz bands. The big plus for budgeteers is the free outdoor entertainment in summer from 7 to 11pm nightly. Call for the schedule.

Admission: 40–140 Kr ($6.60–$23.10), depending on the band; free outdoors in mid-Aug.
Open: Daily 5pm–midnight. **T-Bana:** Slussen.

MOVIES

Tickets for most films, including American blockbusters and other international hits, are usually 60 Kr ($9.90). Most foreign films are screened in their original language with Swedish subtitles. **Röda Kvarn,** Biblioteksgatan 5 (tel. 84-05-00 from 12:30 to 9pm), is a centrally located cinema that usually offers one midafternoon and two evening shows; you can reserve your seat in advance.

THE BAR SCENE

Because of the astronomical price of alcohol, most customers nurse their drinks for a long time and understanding waiters don't hurry you. For budget tourists, even a short hop to the local watering hole must be considered a splurge, and with that in mind, here are some favorites.

DIRTY DICK'S BAR, Tyska Brinken 30, in Gamla Stan. Tel. 20-80-22.

Pass the restaurant on the ground level and head upstairs to this honky-tonk that boasts the best-preserved wooden ceiling in Stockholm, dating from 1648. The entrance is on Stora Nygatan.

Prices: Beer 35 Kr ($5.80), 28 Kr ($4.60) 5–9pm; glass of wine 45 Kr ($7.40).
Open: Daily 5:30pm–midnight.

BAKFICKAN (Back Pocket Bar), Operahuset, Kungsträdgården. Tel. 20-77-45.

This well-kept secret—from visitors anyway—is as tiny as its name implies. Patrons sit around the bar (where service is quickest) or at bar stools along the tiled walls. The quietest time is 2–5pm. Good food is available all day and includes dishes such as salmon or venison served with vegetables and bread.

Prices: Glass of wine 37 Kr ($6.10); beer 41 Kr ($6.75); daily food specials 55–105 Kr ($9.10–$17.30).
Open: Mon–Sat 11:30am–11:30pm.

TENNSTOPET, Dalagatan 50, at Odenplan. Tel. 32-25-18.

You'll have to fight local artists and journalists for a seat at the bar of Stockholm's oldest pub, with a bright-red awning outside and equally red decor inside. There's a dart room in back and a couple of cozy tables in between it and the crowded bar area. A restaurant on the premises serves traditional Swedish fare in a pretty setting, but the prices exceed our book's budget.

Prices: Bass Pale Ale, McEwan's Export, Guinness Stout, and other imports, 39 Kr ($6.45).
Open: Mon–Thurs 11:30am–12:30am, Fri 11:30am–1am, Sat 2pm–1am, Sun 4pm–12:30am.

BLACK & BROWN INN, Hornsgatan 50B, in Södermalm. Tel. 644-82-80.

The bartenders wear kilts in this landmark tavern with booths, windowseats, and plaid wallpaper. Scottish and Irish music plays constantly, and fish 'n' chips, Swedish hash, and burgers compliment the beers.

Prices: Bottle of beer 37 Kr ($6.10).
Open: Sun–Thurs 4pm–midnight, Fri–Sat 1pm–midnight.

DANCE CLUBS

If starting late means it's good, then Stockholm's dance clubs are very good. Most are open for dinner, then there's a lull for a few hours before the die-hards arrive around midnight. The very nature of this scene requires constant new places, so ask around, and check the listings in newspapers and magazines for the latest.

CAFE OPERA, on Kungsträdgården, behind the Opera House. Tel. 11-00-26.

Café Opera is one of the most exclusive places in town, one of those upscale spots you read about in the society pages. Although the line to get in can be long, the door policy is not as brutally selective as similar clubs in other cities. Some people eat expensive dinners here, but the real socializing only starts, with the dancing, after midnight. Drinks are appropriately expensive. To escape the frenzy here, turn right when you enter instead of left, pass through the Opera Bar, where artists and journalists strike poses, and make your way to the congenial Bacfickan, or Back Pocket Bar (see separate entry, above).

Prices: Beer 43 Kr ($7.10); glass of wine 53 Kr ($8.75). **Admission:** Free before 11pm, 60 Kr ($9.90) 11pm–2am.
Open: Mon–Sat 11:30am–3am, Sun 1pm–3am. Music starts at 11pm.

THE DAILY NEWS CAFE, Kungsträdgården. Tel. 21-56-55.

Another "in" spot with an exclusive door policy, the Daily News Café is just doors away from Café Opera. With an elaborate light show and good sound, it's more dance oriented than the nearby Opera. The crowd doesn't come until late, and when they do, the scene is pure New York. Drinks are ridiculously priced. The dance floor is small, as is the Backstage bar downstairs. There's live music upstairs, a disco downstairs; both get going around 10pm. Melody, next door and under the same ownership, has a stage, a dance floor with a balcony overlooking it, and a bar; it's only used when big groups are booked and they expect a crowd.

Prices: Beer 42 Kr ($6.95); wine 38 Kr ($5.30). **Admission:** Free Wed–Thurs and Sun, 60 Kr ($9.90) Fri–Sat after 10pm.

Open: Wed–Thurs 8pm–3am, Fri–Sat 8pm–3am, Sun 9pm–3am.

GÖTA KÄLLARE, in the Medborgarplatsen subway stop, in Södermalm. Tel. 42-08-28.

Well-dressed couples, most aged 30–60, who like to dance cheek-to-cheek congregate here to enjoy the live bands, large dance floors, Platters-style music, and each other. Live music for 45 minutes alternates with disco for 15 minutes, and food is served. On Sunday there's a tea dance. You've got to be at least 25 to get into this fun place. Turn right as you come up the stairs from the subway if you're coming from the direction of Norrmalm.

Admission: 85 Kr ($14).

Open: Mon–Sat 8pm–2:30am, Sun tea dance 4–10pm.

9. NETWORKS & RESOURCES

STUDENTS Students who plan to study in Stockholm or elsewhere in Sweden may get a handbook of information about housing, health services, work permits, Swedish-language courses, sports and social activities, and other matters by contacting the **Federation of Student Unions,** Körsbärsvägen 2 (Box 5652), S-11489 Stockholm (tel. 08/15-03-40). To visit them in person, take the T-Bana to Tekniska Högskolan; call ahead for hours.

SFS Resebyrå, Kungsgatan 4 (tel. 23-45-15), is the place for low-cost student and youth rail and air tickets; the maximum age for the latter is 30–35. It's open Monday through Friday from 9:30am to 5pm. The office is one block from Birgir Jarlsgatan at Stureplan.

Transalpino, Birger Jarlsgatan 13 (tel. 679-98-70), offers discount plane tickets for students to age 35 with valid ID. Open Monday through Friday from 10am to 5pm.

GAY MEN & LESBIANS Many local gays gather at **RFSL-Huset,** Sveavägen 57 (tel. 736-02-12 for information, or 24-74-65 for the switchboard 8–11pm; or 736-02-10 for the help line). This large building is headquarters to most of Stockholm's gay organizations, and also houses a restaurant, disco, and bookstore.

Alice B. (tel. 31-55-33) is a casual eatery serving light fare including burgers, pasta, and fish 'n' chips. And if you're in the mood for a beer and a game of pool, that's possible, too (for details, see "Budget Dining," above).

Pride (tel. 31-55-33), a small disco in the back of the building, is open Tuesday through Sunday from 9pm to 3am. The first Friday of the month is lesbian night, but men are still welcome at the bar. Admission of 70 Kr ($11.55) is charged only on Friday and Saturday.

Bokhandeln Rosa Rummet (The Pink Room Bookstore) (tel. 736-02-15) has postcards and a good selection of Swedish- and English-language books on current gay issues. It's open Monday through Thursday from 3 to 9pm and Friday through Sunday from 3 to 6pm.

Get to the RFSL-Huset complex via the T-Bana to Rådmanhuset or bus no. 52, which stops on Sveavägen. Look for the green-and-pink neon sign that says PRIDE out front.

10. EASY EXCURSIONS

DROTTNINGHOLM

The palace of the present-day Swedish King Carl XVI Gustaf and Queen Silvia is open to visitors year round. The 17th-century rococo structure is just seven miles from the city center. In addition to the State Apartments, the palace grounds encompass a theater dating from 1766, and a beautiful Chinese Pavilion.

There are three ways of reaching Drottningholm. The first, and most exciting, is by steamboat, which takes 50 minutes and costs 50 Kr ($9.10) one way, 70 Kr ($12.70) round-trip (half price for children). Boats leave from Stadshusbron, beside Stockholm's City Hall, daily: on the hour from 10am to 4pm plus at 6pm from early June to mid-August, and 10am to 2pm (to 4pm on weekends) from late April to early June. Call Strömma Kanalbolaget (tel. 23-33-75) for more information, including autumn sailings.

Stockholm Sightseeing (tel. 24-04-70) offers trips to Drottningholm in turn-of-the-century boats for 35 Kr ($5.80) one way, 70 Kr ($11.55) round-trip. Boats depart hourly from 9:30am to 4:30pm from late April to early June and from 9:30am to 6:30pm from early June to mid-August. Trips are offered until October.

You can also take the T-Bana to Brommaplan and then connect to any Mälarö bus for Drottningholm.

DROTTNINGHOLM SLOTT (Drottningholm Palace). Tel. 759-03-10.

Built for Sweden's Queen Eleonora in 1662, this four-story palace with two-story wings has often been referred to as a "little Versailles." The interior dazzles with opulent furniture and art from the 17th through the 19th century, including painted ceilings framed by gold, ornate chandeliers, Chinese vases, and other showy details. Ample sculptured gardens surround the palace, and from time to time visitors may even spot the down-to-earth royal couple taking a stroll.

Admission: 25 Kr ($4.10) adults, 10 Kr ($1.65) students.
Open: May–Aug, daily 11am–4:30pm; Sept, Mon–Fri 1–3:30pm, Sat–Sun noon–3:30pm. **Closed:** Oct–Apr.

DROTTNINGHOLM COURT THEATER. Tel. 759-04-06.

The palace theater, one of the oldest extant stages in the world still using original backdrops and props, stands today exactly as it was on opening night in 1766. Here, 18th-century ballets and operas are still performed, authentic down to original costumes. Inquire at the Stockholm Information Service for a schedule of the period operas and ballets held from May to September. Even if no show is scheduled, visit the museum next door; it's definitely worth a visit.

Admission: 25 Kr ($4.10) adults, 15 Kr ($2.50) children.
Open: May–Aug, Mon–Sat 11:30am–4:30pm, Sun 12:30–4:30pm; Sept, daily 12:30–3pm. **Closed:** Oct–Apr.

KINA SLOTT (Chinese Pavilion), near the end of the palace park.

Many of Europe's grand old palaces were inspired by the exotic architecture of Asia. This pavilion was constructed in Stockholm in 1753 as a royal birthday gift and quietly floated downriver so that it would surprise the queen when it arrived. The pavilion was a particular favorite of King Gustavus III, who loved to pass summer days here with his court.

Admission: 25 Kr ($4.10).
Open: Apr, daily 1–3:30pm; May–Aug, daily 11am–4:30pm; Sept, Mon–Fri 1–3:30pm, Sat–Sun noon–3:30pm. **Closed:** Oct–Mar.

MARIEFRED

The perfect day trip, a visit to Mariefred on Lake Mälaren includes a boat ride, a pretty little town that's easy to explore on foot, an "old-time" train station and steam railway, a bookshop that has been around since 1897, and a castle with compelling nooks and crannies and a portrait collection from the 16th century to modern times.

Gripsholm Castle, on a spit of land south of the town, is home to the **National Portrait Gallery,** with 1,200 of its 4,000 portraits on display. There is a multitude of rooms and portraits to see, outstanding among them the ceiling and paneling in Duke Karl's Chamber, the tiled fireplace in Princess Sofia Albertina's Study, the King's Bedchamber with a 17th-century ivory clock, the paneling and wall hangings in the Council Chamber, the White Drawing Room, the domed ceiling of Gustav III's Theater, the Sentry Corridor (Jenny Lind hangs here), the Large Gallery (King Carl XVI Gustaf and his family are here, along with Louisa Ulrika, whose attendants are depicted as hens), and the Tower Room, where you'll find modern portraits, including Dag Hammarskjöld, Greta Garbo, and Ingmar Bergman. Room 52 houses some compelling self-portraits.

A guidebook in English is helpful but pricey, at about $5. Admission is 25 Kr ($4.10) for adults, 10 Kr ($1.65) for children under 16.

There are shops, an inviting café, **Konditori Fredman,** and the **town hall** around the main square, and some charming streets to explore behind it. The **Strand Restaurant,** in the yellow house by the water, serves more substantial meals.

Many visitors never realize there's a **boardwalk** just beyond the restaurant (walk in the opposite direction of the church and the pier) that leads past moored boats and houses with red-tile roofs peaking out to sea. There are benches where you can sit and gaze at the bullrushes, and beyond them, the church steeple and castle domes.

In summer, a coal-fired steamboat called the **S/S Mariefred** makes the trip to Mariefred from Stockholm; off-season it's the sleek tour boat **M/S Kungsholm,** with two enclosed seating levels and a small open deck. (Sit on the right-hand side for the best views and photo opportunities.)

The pretty trip, which offers splendid views of City Hall as the boat leaves Stockholm, takes a little more than an hour and costs 80 Kr ($13.20), half price for children under 12. Snacks and drinks are served on board. (You may reboard the boat 10 minutes before departure time.) In the summer, you may also travel to Mariefred by train—the last leg of the journey, from Laggesta to Mariefred (change trains at the small terminal called Laggesta Södra), in a turn-of-the-century steam-powered train.

VAXHOLM

Local ferries and tour boats make the pleasant trip to Vaxholm, a popular island destination in the archipelago, many times a day. This is a small place and you'll feel at home and be able to get your bearings as soon as you arrive.

To familiarize yourself with Vaxholm once you've disembarked, follow the path along the water, passing the **information office** (tel. 0764/314-80) (ask for a map if it's open) and the sign for the fortress museum (see below), to the **lookout** at the old Portuguese battery. From this serene spot, you may stroll down the hill and sit on the rocks by the water.

From here, make your way to the **main square** of the town; follow Vallgatan, crossing Fiskaregatan and Kilgatan. Turn right on Lotsgatan, which leads to the main square and the **town hall,** built in 1885 and rebuilt in 1925. You'll also find some shops on the square. From here, follow Rådhusgatan back to the waterfront and the information office.

If you want to treat yourself to a good (but not inexpensive), elegantly served meal with a view of the harbor and boats scudding to and fro, visit the restaurant in the **Vaxholm Hotel.**

The **Vaxholm Fortress,** constructed between 1548 and 1863 to protect the inlet to Stockholm, is open from mid-May through August; admission is 10 Kr ($1.65) for adults, 5 Kr (80¢) for seniors and kids 7–12. You can get there in five minutes by boat or in 35 *seconds* by transverse "elevator," or "bridge shuttle," the first of its kind in Sweden.

The ferry to Vaxholm takes about an hour, calling at several islands along the way, and costs 40 Kr ($6.60) one way, 80 Kr ($13.20) round-trip. It departs from in front of the Grand Hotel; call Waxholmsbolaget (tel. 679-58-30) for more information. Bus no. 670 will get you back to Stockholm if you don't want to wait for the return boat.

ARCHIPELAGO EXPLORATION

Vaxholm is only one of Greater Stockholm's 24,000 or so nearby islands. If you want to explore the archipelago in depth, buy the 16-day ferry pass, called a **Bátluffarkortet,** for only 200 Kr ($36.40). Also drop by **Strömma Kanalbolaget,** at Skeppsbron 30 (tel. 23-33-75), for a list of ferryboat cruises and timetables.

CHAPTER 27

VENICE

Sure, the tourists, most of them blindly following some pastel umbrella, are inescapable. Sure, prices can be double what they are anywhere else in Italy. And, yes, it's not the cleanest city in Europe.

But this, after all, is Venice. The tourists come for a very good reason: Venice is beautiful. It's the rio Frescada canal flowing slowly past the houses, in subdued shades of red, green, and violet, that line its waters. It's the truly grand Canale Grande winding its way past stately Renaissance *palazzi*. It's the unparalleled tranquility of campo Santa Margherita, where only the sound of the fish hawker or children playing football pierces the stillness. And it's the gondolas and *motoscafi* that slowly and skillfully ply the waters of the city. Underneath it all, this *is* for real—Venice is a living, breathing city, not just a show for the tourists.

Venice was at the crossroads of Byzantine and Roman worlds for centuries, a fact that lends to its unique heritage of art and architecture. Traders and thinkers no longer pass through "La Serenissima" as they once did, but Venice is nonetheless at a crossroads: an intersection in time between the world of the Renaissance and the modern world, which includes the budget traveler—and that means you!

1. FROM A BUDGET TRAVELER'S POINT OF VIEW

VENICE BUDGET BESTS You've probably heard it said a hundred times, but the best free sight in Venice is the city itself. And there's something else you can't buy anywhere—the quiet. You'll hear conversations going on in dozens of languages, but never an automobile horn, a failing muffler, or a screaming police siren. Just the occasional murmur of a *motoscafo* making its way through the narrow side canals of the city.

Venice's many festivals and special events (see "Special Events" in "Pretrip Preparations," below) are also a budget best. Most of the revelry is free, and even at the Film Festival and the Biennale there are a number of free and inexpensive screenings and exhibits.

You can always save money on food and drink by consuming them standing up at one of the city's ubiquitous bars. A 3,000-lira ($2.60) *panino* (sandwich) and a cappuccino at 1,500 lire ($1.30) make a quick and satisfying lunch. Prices double—at least—if you sit down.

SPECIAL DISCOUNT OPPORTUNITIES Anyone between ages 16 and 26 with a pocket-sized photo can pick up a free **"Venice for the Young" pass** at the tourist office, entitling the holder to various discounts across the city.

WHAT THINGS COST IN VENICE	U.S. $
Water taxi (for any journey up to 7 minutes)	20.85
Public boat (from any point within the city to any other point)	1.90
Local telephone call	.18
Double room at the Gritti Palace (deluxe)	456.50
Double room at the Pensione Seguso (moderate)	90.85
Double room at Albergo Adua (budget)	41.15
Continental breakfast (cappuccino and croissant) (at a café/bar)	3.05
(at most hotels)	6.95
Lunch for one at Trattoria alla Madonna (moderate)	21.75
Lunch for one at any café in town (budget)	6.10
Dinner for one, without wine, at Harry's Bar (deluxe)	104.35
Dinner for one, without wine, at Antica Locanda Montin (moderate)	34.80
Dinner for one, without wine, at Beau Brummel (budget)	6.50
Pint (*grande*) of beer at any café in town	3.50
Glass (*bicchiere*) of wine at any café in town	.85
Coca-Cola (to take out)	2.20
Cup of coffee (cappuccino) at any café in town	1.30
Roll of color film, 36 exposures	9.55
Admission to the Palazzo Ducale	6.95
Movie ticket	6.95
Theater ticket (at Teatro La Fenice)	17.40

WORTH THE EXTRA BUCKS   Just about everything in Venice, from accommodations to public transportation to dry cleaning, costs significantly more than in any other Italian city. But in my opinion, this one-of-a-kind city is worth every lira.

2. PRETRIP PREPARATIONS

DOCUMENTS & WHAT TO PACK   For general suggestions on documents and wardrobe, see the Rome chapter. There is one wardrobe tip unique to Venice though: Beware the *acqua alta* (flooding), and bring waterproof shoes if you visit between November and March. (Is Venice sinking? Take a look at any building, or room for that matter, and notice how everything is askew. But the entire country is committed to keeping the city afloat for many, many years to come.)

WHEN TO GO   May and September are perhaps the best months to visit Venice, for two reasons. The weather is quite seasonable at these times, but, more significantly, the crowds are thinner during these months. June and especially July and August are a perpetual mob scene, though temperatures are a bit cooler than in other Italian cities.

Visiting Venice in April or October is hit or miss; it can still be quite cool and damp here, but delightfully uncrowded.

Venice can be considerably cheaper from the first of November through the middle of March, when many of the hotels in the city observe low-season (*bassa stagione*) prices that are about 25%–40% lower than the regular rates. Of course this is a double-edged sword. If *your* hotel was in a cold, wet, flooded city, you'd discount the room rates, too.

Venice's Average Temperature & Rainfall

	Jan	Feb	Mar	Apr	May	June	July	Aug	Sept	Oct	Nov	Dec
Temp. (°F)	43	48	53	60	67	72	77	74	68	60	54	44
Rainfall "	2.3	1.5	2.9	3.0	2.8	2.9	1.5	1.9	2.8	2.6	3.0	2.1

Special Events   During the week and a half before Ash Wednesday, Venetians take to the streets for **Carnevale.** Revelers dance in the streets dressed in centuries-old costumes and hide behind the colorful porcelain masks that you see in gift shops all over town. Countless other events fill the calendar for the entire month leading up to Ash Wednesday. Contact the tourist office for full details on the 1993 festivities.

The **Voga Longa** (literally the "long row"), a 30km (18-mile) rowing "race" from San Marco to the Lido and back, has been revived recently after centuries of disinterest. It takes place in May; for exact dates for 1993, consult the tourist office. The event itself is colorful, if not much of a race; it's mostly a fine excuse for a party. The 1993 race will be the 19th annual.

Stupendous fireworks fill the night sky and hearty revelry the night air during the **Festa del Redentore,** on the third Saturday night and Sunday in July. The celebration, which marks the lifting—in July of 1578—of a plague that had gripped the city, is centered around the Chiesa del Redentore on the Giudecca. A pair of pontoon bridges link piazza San Marco with the Giudecca for the occasion, and boats full of revelers fill the Giudecca Canal.

The **Venice International Film Festival,** held in late August and early September, is perhaps the finest summer celebration of celluloid in Europe after Cannes. Films from all over the world are shown in various venues across the city, and often outside in the many *campi*. Ticket prices vary, but are usually quite modest; many of the outdoor screenings are free.

Venice hosts the latest in modern painting and sculpture from dozens of countries during the **Biennale,** an international modern-art show that fills the pavilions of the gardens at the east end of Castello throughout the summer of every even-numbered year. Many great modern artists have been "discovered" at this world-famous show. Note that the gardens are marked "Esposizione Internazionale d'Arte Moderna" on most maps; take vaporetto Line 1 or 4 to the Giardini stop.

The **Regatta Storica,** which takes place on the Grand Canal on the first Sunday in September, is a seagoing parade first, an excuse for a party second, and, finally, a genuine regatta. Just about every seaworthy gondola in Venice participates in this maritime cavalcade, richly decorated for the occasion and piloted by *gondolieri* in colorful period costumes.

Finally, the ultimate anomaly. Venice's irrepressible civic boosters have arranged for an annual October **Maratona (Marathon),** starting at Villa Pisani on the mainland and ending up along the Zattere for a finish at the Basilica di Santa Maria della Salute on the tip of Dorsoduro.

Other notable events include the **Festa della Salute,** on November 21, and the **Festa della Sensa,** on the Sunday following Ascension Day.

WHAT'S SPECIAL ABOUT VENICE

The City Itself

☐ The silence—no sirens, no motorcycles, no diesel exhaust, just children playing, dogs barking, fish merchants hawking. . . .

☐ The fact that beneath it all Venice is a living, breathing, proud, even thriving city.

☐ The canals—need I say more?

☐ The subdued, weather-beaten pastel colors of the city's houses, every one of which is somewhat askew.

Events/Festivals

☐ The Carnevale, when Venetians and tourists alike take to the streets in vivid porcelain masks for days of bacchanalian revelry.

☐ The annual Venice International Film Festival, the next best thing to Cannes—including some free screenings.

☐ The Biennale: In Italy's museums, art history is exhibited; at this biennial celebration, art history happens.

Cuisine

☐ Seafood, particularly spaghetti alle vongole.

Sights

☐ The modern art on display at the Peggy Guggenheim Collection, arguably the finest modern art museum in Europe.

☐ The open expanse of piazza San Marco, such a contrast to the rest of this tiny city of narrow, labyrinthine alleys and canals.

☐ Seeing how precious little has changed in Venice since the 15th-century canvases on display at the Accademia.

☐ Watching local artisans make the famous hand-painted porcelain Carnival masks (*maschere*).

The Romance

☐ A moonlight gondola ride—though expensive and exclusively for tourists, it really is wonderfully romantic.

BACKGROUND READING   My favorite is Mary McCarthy's *Venice Observed* (Harcourt Brace Jovanovich). For texts on Renaissance art and architecture, page to the Florence chapter. Luigi Barzini's classic *The Italians* (Macmillan) for a frank, refreshing, and opinionated discussion of the history and culture of Italy, past and present.

3. ORIENTATION & GETTING AROUND

ARRIVING IN VENICE

FROM THE AIRPORT   Flights land at the **Aeroporto Marco Polo,** due north of the city on the mainland (tel. 66-1111 or 66-1262). Of course, the most fashionable and traditional way to arrive in the city is by sea. The **Cooperative San Marco** (tel. 523-5775 or 528-5930) keeps that tradition alive, operating a *motoscafo* (shuttleboat) service between the airport and piazza San Marco for 15,000 lire ($13.05) each way. Call for their daily schedule of 10 or so round-trips, which changes with the season, or drop by their headquarters at San Marco, 978, on calle dei Fabbri. A private **water taxi** into town will cost more than your flight did, about 100,000 lire ($86.95).

The **Azienda Trasporti Veneto Orientale (ATVO) bus** (tel. 520-5530) connects the airport with piazzale Roma. Buses leave roughly every hour, cost 5,000 lire ($4.35), and make the trip in about 30 minutes. Local ACTV bus no. 5 (tel. 78-0111) is cheaper still, at 800 lire (70¢) per person plus 700 lire (60¢) for each large piece of luggage. Buses leave from the airport and piazzale Roma every hour at 40 minutes after the hour.

FROM THE TRAIN STATION   Trains from all over Europe arrive at the **Stazione Venezia—Santa Lucia** (tel. 71-5555). To get there, all trains must pass through a station marked "Venezia—Mestre." Don't be confused: Mestre is a charmless industrial city on the mainland.

At the far right end as you come off the tracks at Santa Lucia is the luggage depot, near the head of Track 8. If you're planning to strike out on your own to look for accommodations, you're very well advised to leave your heavy gear here. They charge 1,500 lire ($1.30) per piece per day, and are open 24 hours daily. There's an Albergo Diurno (day hotel) at the far right side of the station as you face the tracks; it's open daily from 7am to 8pm, and charges 5,000 lire ($4.35) for a shower.

An office for international phone calls is to your right in the main hall as you come off the tracks. See "Fast Facts: Venice" for details.

The official city tourist board, **Azienda Autonoma di Soggiorno e Turismo** (tel. 71-5288) staffs an office located between the station's large front doors. It's open daily from 8am to 8pm.

The **train information** office (tel. 715-5550), marked with a lowercase "i," is located on the left side of the station's main hall. It is staffed daily from 8am to 9pm.

Two banks for **currency exchange** keep long hours (usually until 9pm), and compete with each other for business. Compare rates before exchanging.

Finally, upon exiting the station, you'll find the docks for vaporetto Lines 2 and 5 to your left; Line 1 is to your right.

ARRIVING BY CAR   Traveling by car? Have no fear, as there is parking at **Garage S. Marco,** on piazzale Roma (tel. 523-5101), the one dry point on the Venetian end of the causeway to Mestre and the mainland. Parking in the garage will set you back some 20,000 lire ($17.40) per day, depending on the size of your car.

INFORMATION

In addition to the tourist office located inside the train station (see "Arriving in Venice," above), there's a second **tourist office** at San Marco, 71, just off calle dell' Ascensione (tel. 522-6356), in the far left arcade at the opposite end of piazza San Marco from the basilica. They maintain a remarkably spotty schedule. Their best guess when I last visited was Monday through Saturday from 8:30am to 3:45pm.

CITY LAYOUT

Keep in mind as you wander seemingly hopelessly among the *fondamente* and *calle* of Venice that the city was not built to make sense to those on foot, but rather to those plying its canals. No matter how good your map and your sense of direction, you will repeatedly get wonderfully lost.

Snaking through the city like an inverted S is the **Canale Grande (Grand Canal),** the wide main artery of aquatic Venice. Scores of short and narrow canals cut through the interior of the two halves of the city, flowing gently by the doorsteps of centuries-old *palazzi,* and endlessly frustrating the landlubbing tourists trying to navigate the city on foot.

There are only three bridges (*ponti*) that cross the Grand Canal: the **Ponte Scalzi,** just outside the train station; the elegant, white marble **Ponte Rialto,** which connects the *sestieri* (districts) of San Marco and San Polo at the center of town; and the wooden **Ponte Accademia,** connecting campo Morosini in San Marco with the Accademia museum across the way in Dorsoduro.

The city is divided into six districts, or sestieri. **Cannaregio** stretches from the train station east to the Rialto Bridge. To the east beyond Cannaregio (and skirting piazza San Marco) is the **Castello** quarter. The sestiere of **San Marco** shares this side of the Grand Canal with Castello and Cannaregio, occupying (roughly) the area west of piazza San Marco and the Rialto Bridge. **San Polo** is across the Rialto Bridge, stretching west to just beyond campo dei Frari and campo San Rocco. **Santa Croce** is next, moving north and west, stretching all the way to piazzale Roma. Finally, you'll find **Dorsoduro** on the opposite side of the Accademia Bridge from San Marco. Not confused enough yet? For the record, each sestiere is divided further into an indeterminate number of *parrochie,* or neighborhoods. These indications appear on no maps, and are of little or no use to the navigating tourist.

Within each sestiere, there are no street numbers, but simply one continuous string of 6,000 or so house numbers, which wind their way among the canals and calle in a fashion known to no living person. The format for **addresses** in this chapter is the name of the sestiere, followed by the house number within that district, followed by the name of the street on which you'll find that address: for example, San Marco, 1471, on salizzada San Moisé.

Venice shares its lagoon with several other islands. Opposite piazza San Marco and Dorsoduro is the **Giudecca,** a tranquil, working-class place where you'll find the youth hostel and a handful of hotels, restaurants, and bars. The **Lido di Venezia** is the city's beach; it separates the lagoon from the open sea. **Murano, Burano,** and **Torcello** are popular tourist spots northeast of the city.

Finally, the industrial city of **Mestre,** on the mainland, is the gateway to Venice.

GETTING AROUND

The successful tourist in Venice is like one of those miniature battery-operated toy cars that children play with, which, when driven into a wall or other obstacle, instantly turn and continue on their way. Inevitably, time and again, you'll think you know exactly where you're going, only to wind up at the end of a dead-end street, or at the side of a canal with no bridge to get to the other side. Just remind yourself that the city's physical complexity—that is, getting lost—is an integral part of its charm. But Venice, with its countless stepped footbridges and almost no elevators in any of the buildings, is one of the worst cities in the world for the physically disabled.

The free map offered by the tourist office has good intentions, but it doesn't even show, much less name or index, all the pathways of Venice. For that, pick up the yellow-jacketed map (*pianta di città*) produced by **Studio F.M.B. Bologna,** for 8,000 lire ($6.95) at any newsstand. This map also shows all the vaporetto stops and lines.

BY BOAT The various areas and islands of the city are linked by a comprehensive ***vaporetto*** system of some two dozen lines, operated by the Azienda del Consorzio Trasporti Veneziano (ACTV) (tel. 78-0111 or 528-9820). The tourist office and most ACTV stations, offer a map of the system as well.

Fare on most boats, including Lines 1, 5, and 34 (the most frequently used by the average traveler) is 2,200 lire ($1.90). Express boats, most notably Line 2, and those that cross the lagoon, cost 3,300 lire ($2.85). Most lines run every 10–15 minutes from 7am to midnight, then hourly until morning. Note, however, that not all stations sell tickets after dark; settle up with the conductor on board, or gamble on a 30,000-lira ($26.10) fine.

The 13,000-lira ($11.30) **Biglietto 24 Ore** entitles the bearer to 24 hours of unlimited travel on any ACTV vessel except Lines 2 and 28. The **Biglietto 3 Giorni,** which covers three full days of unlimited travel on all boats but Lines 2 and 28, may seem steep at 22,000 lire ($19.15), but the single-fare trips can add up quite quickly.

Line 1, an *accellerato,* is the most important one for the average tourist, making all stops along the Grand Canal and continuing on to the Lido. **Line 2,** a *diretto,* also travels the Grand Canal, though it stops only at piazzale Roma, the train station, the Rialto Bridge, the Accademia Bridge, and piazza San Marco before heading out to the Lido. **Line 5,** the *circolare,* is another major line, circling the perimeter of the city, and crossing the lagoon to Giudecca and Murano. **Line 12** also crosses the waves to Murano, continuing on to Burano and Torcello.

There are just three bridges spanning the Grand Canal. To fill in the gaps, ***traghetti* gondolas** cross the canal at seven or so intermediate points. You'll find a traghetto station at the end of any street named "calle del Traghetto" on your map (see "Suggested Itineraries" in "Attractions," below). The fare, regulated by the local government, is 500 lire (45¢).

BY WATER TAXI *Taxi acquei* (water taxis) prices are high and not for the average tourist. For journeys up to seven minutes, the rate is 24,000 lire ($20.85); 430 lire (40¢) click off for each additional 15 seconds. There's an 8,000-lira ($6.95) supplement for night service (10pm to 7am), and a 9,000-lira ($7.85) surcharge on Sunday and holidays; note that these two supplements cannot be applied simultaneously. If they have to come get you, tack on another 7,500 lire ($6.50).

There are six **water-taxi stations** serving various key points in the city: the train station (tel. 71-6286), piazzale Roma (tel. 71-6922), the Rialto Bridge (tel. 523-0575), piazza San Marco (tel. 522-9750), the Lido (tel. 526-0059), and Marco Polo Airport (tel. 541-5084). **Radio Taxi** (tel. 523-2326 or 522-2303) will come pick you up any place in the city, for a surcharge of course.

ON FOOT Get a map, but don't get frustrated if it's hard to follow. Look for the ubiquitous yellow signs that direct travelers toward five major landmarks: Ferrovia (the train station), piazzale Roma, the Rialto Bridge, piazza San Marco, and the Accademia Bridge.

FAST FACTS   *VENICE*

Banks Standard bank hours are Monday through Friday from 8:35am to 1:35pm and 2:45 to 3:45pm or 3 to 4pm (usually the latter); only a few banks, and the American Express office (see "Currency Exchange," below), are open on Saturday; those banks that are open on Saturday follow an 8:35 to 11:35am schedule. Both exchange offices at the train station are open seven days a week.

Business Hours Standard hours for **shops** are 9am to 12:30pm and 3 to 7:30pm Monday through Saturday. In winter shops are closed on Monday morning, while in summer it's usually Saturday afternoon that they're closed; most grocers are closed on Wednesday afternoon throughout the year. In Venice and throughout Italy, just about everything is closed on Sunday. **Restaurants** are required to close at least one day per week, though the particular day varies from one trattoria to another.

Consulates The **British Consulate** is at Dorsoduro, 1051 (tel. 522-7207), at the foot of the Accademia bridge. It's open Monday through Friday from 9am to noon and 2 to 4pm.

The **United States, Canada,** and **Australia** have consulates in Milan, about three hours away by train. (The **U.S. Consulate in Milan** is at largo Donegani, 1 [tel. 392/65-2841], open Monday through Friday from 9am to noon and 2 to 4pm.) Along with New Zealand, they all maintain embassies in Rome (see the Rome chapter).

Currency The Italian unit of currency is the **lira,** almost always used in the plural form, **lire.** The lowest unit of currency these days is the silver 50-lira coin. There is also a 100-lira piece, also silver; a gold 200-lira coin; and a combination silver-and-gold 500-lira coin. Notes come in the following denominations: 1,000, 2,000, 5,000, 10,000, 50,000 and 100,000 lire. Note that 20,000-lira bills are no longer valid.

Currency Exchange In addition to the banks mentioned under "From the Train Station" in "Orientation and Getting Around," above, you can change money at the **American Express** office, San Marco, 1471, on salizzada San Moisé (tel. 520-0844). If you're standing in front of San Marco, exit the piazza by way of the arcade at the far left end, and bear slightly to the right; you'll see a mosaic sign in the pavement pointing the way. In summer, they're open for banking Monday through

Friday from 8am to 8pm and on Saturday from 9am to 12:30pm; in winter, it's Monday through Friday from 9am to 5:30pm and on Saturday from 9am to 12:30pm. For all other services, throughout the year their hours are Monday through Friday from 9am to 6pm and on Saturday from 9am to 1pm.

Dentists and Doctors　For a short list, check with the British Consulate or the American Express office.

Emergencies　In Venice and throughout Italy, dial 113 to reach the police. Some Italians will recommend that you forgo the police and try the military-trained *Carabinieri* (tel. 112), in the opinion of some a better police force. For an ambulance, phone 523-0000. To report a fire, dial 522-2222; on the Lido, 526-0222. For a (short) list of English-speaking doctors or dentists, contact the American Express office or the British Consulate.

Holidays　See the Rome chapter for detailed information.

Information　The most convenient and most helpful tourist office is located in the outer hall of the train station. For the location of other tourist information offices, see "Information" in "Orientation and Getting Around," above.

Laundry　The most convenient self-service laundry to the train station is the Lavaget at Cannaregio, 1269, to the left as you cross the Ponte alle Guglie from Lista di Spagna. The Lavanderia a Gettone Gabriella, San Marco, 985, on calle Terrà delle Colonne, is the best place in the piazza San Marco neighborhood. To find it, exit the piazza underneath the clock tower, continue straight along Merceria dell' Orologio, turn left onto Merceria San Zulian, cross a small bridge onto calle Fiubera, then take your first right and then your first left. If you get lost, ask someone to point you toward the Hotel Astoria. Both are open Monday through Friday from 8:30am to 12:30pm and 3 to 7pm; the rate at both locations is about 15,000 lire ($13.05) for up to 4.5 kilos (10 lb.).

At the Lavanderia a Gettone SS. Apostoli, at Cannaregio, 4553a, on salizzada del Pistor, just off campo SS. Apostoli (tel. 522-6650), you pay 10,000 lire ($8.70) for a load of 4.5 kilos (10 lb.) or more or 18,000 lire ($15.65) for 8 kilos (17 lb.)

THE LIRA & THE DOLLAR

At this writing $1 = approximately 1,150 lire (or 100 lire = 9¢), and this was the rate of exchange used to calculate the dollar values given in this chapter (rounded to the nearest nickel). This rate fluctuates from time to time and may not be the same when you travel to Italy. Therefore the following table should be used only as a guide:

Lire	U.S.$	Lire	U.S.$
50	.04	10,000	8.70
100	.09	15,000	13.04
200	.17	20,000	17.39
300	.26	25,000	21.74
400	.35	30,000	26.09
500	.43	35,000	30.43
750	.65	40,000	34.78
1,000	.87	45,000	39.13
1,500	1.30	50,000	43.48
2,000	1.74	55,000	47.82
2,500	2.17	60,000	52.17
3,000	2.61	65,000	56.52
4,000	3.48	70,000	60.87
5,000	4.35	75,000	65.21

or more. This place is open from 8:30am to 12:30pm and 3 to 7pm Monday through Friday. It's (relatively) convenient to the Rialto Bridge area.

Lost and Found   The central Ufficio Oggetti Rinvenuti (tel. 78-8225) is in the *annex* to the City Hall (known as the "Municipio" in Italian), at San Marco, 4134, on calle Piscopia o Loredan, just off riva del Carbon on the Grand Canal, near the Rialto Bridge (on the same side of the canal as the Rialto vaporetto station). Look for *scala* (stairway) C; the lost-and-found office is in the "Economato" section on the "Mezzanino" level, one flight up. The office is ostensibly open only on Monday, Wednesday, and Friday from 9:30am to 12:30pm, but there's usually someone available five days a week, from 9:30am until the building closes at 1:30pm.

There's also an Ufficio Oggetti Smarriti at the airport (tel. 66-1266), and an Ufficio Oggetti Rinvenuti at the train station (tel. 71-6122); it's located right at the head of Track 14, and is open Monday through Friday from 8am to 4pm.

Mail   Venice's Posta Centrale is at San Marco, 5554, on salizzada Fontego dei Tedeschi (tel. 528-62-12), just off campo San Bartolomeo, near the foot of the Rialto Bridge on the San Marco side of the Grand Canal. This office is usually open Monday through Saturday from 8:15am to 7pm. Stamps are sold at Window 12, while *Fermo Posta* mail can be picked up at Window 4.

If you're at piazza San Marco and need postal services, walk through sottoportego San Geminian, the center portal at the opposite end of the piazza from the basilica. This post office is open Monday through Friday from 8:15am to 1:30pm and Saturday from 8:15am to 12:10pm.

Remember that you can buy stamps (*francobolli*) at any *tabacchi* with no additional service charge; ask at your hotel about the current postal rates.

Pharmacies   Venice's many drugstores take turns staying open all night. To find out which one is on call tonight in your area ask at your hotel or dial 523-0573.

Police   In an emergency, dial 112 or 113. For other business, dial 522-2331 or 523-5333.

Shoe Repair   If your hotel manager doesn't know of one closer, try the shoe repair shop at Dorsoduro, 871, on calle Nuova Sant'Agnese, on the main route between the Accademia and the Peggy Guggenheim Collection.

Tax and Tipping   See the Rome chapter for information.

Telephone   To make an international phone call, visit the Azienda Stato Servizi Telefonici (ASST) office in the main (outer) hall of the train station, to the right if the tracks are at your back. This office is normally open Monday through Friday from 8am to 8pm and on Saturday from 8am to 2pm. An ASST office nearby at piazzale Roma is open Monday through Friday from 8am to 9:30pm and on Saturday from 8am to 2pm. Finally, there's an ASST office next door to the main post office, at San Marco, 5550, on salizzada Fontego dei Tedeschi, which is open daily from 8am to 8pm. For further information on long-distance dialing, as well as information on local calls, see the Rome chapter.

The telephone area code for Venice is 041.

4. BUDGET ACCOMMODATIONS

The heading above has to be one of the great oxymorons of European travel. Hotels are more expensive in Venice than in any other city in Italy. Whatever you've been spending in other parts of the country, you can plan on spending about 1½ times that amount here. But it's worth it.

In summer, it can seem that there are no budget lodgings in Venice, especially if you arrive in the city after noon. Arrive as early as you can, for time literally is money.

The tourist office in the train station will book rooms for you, but their lines are long, and, understandably, their patience sometimes thin.

If you're on a tight budget, or can't help but arrive late, consider spending your first night in Padova, a pleasant university city some 30 minutes by train from Venice. Whatever you do, don't be lured to Mestre, a mere 10 minutes across the lagoon from Venice. It's a charmless industrial city that doesn't live up to any of the nice things that you might hear said about it.

Finally, keep in mind that hotels observe a high- and a low-season price schedule. Be sure to ask when you arrive at a hotel whether they in fact have an off-season price. High season in Venice runs from March 16 through October 31; some hotels close altogether after this period, especially in December, January, and February.

A continental breakfast in an Italian hotel is a great disappointment. The usual rate for a roll, butter, jam, and coffee is 6,000–10,000 lire ($5.20–$8.70). You can get the same breakfast for about half that price at any Venetian café. Unfortunately, many of the hotels I've listed, especially in the medium-, and high-priced categories, require their guests to take breakfast. In the descriptions below, if prices are listed "including continental breakfast," then you can assume that breakfast is more or less obligatory; otherwise it's optional, and almost without exception, not worth the price.

DOUBLES FOR LESS THAN 64,000 LIRE [$55.65]

ON OR NEAR LISTA DI SPAGNA

The Lista di Spagna, immediately to the left as you exit the train station, is the best in the city for budget accommodations, if a little charmless.

ALBERGO ADUA, Cannaregio, 233a, on Lista di Spagna, Venezia. Tel. 041/71-6184. 12 rms (4 with bath). **Directions:** See below.

$ Rates: 33,600 lire ($29.20) single without bath, 42,000 lire ($36.50) single with bath; 47,300 lire ($41.15) double without bath, 78,800 lire ($68.50) double with bath; 73,500 lire ($63.90) triple without bath, 94,500 lire ($82.20) triple with bath; 84,000 lire ($73.05) quad without bath, 126,000 lire ($109.60) quad with bath. Breakfast 7,000 lire ($6.10) extra. No credit cards.

This is a delightful family operation, with an unusually elegant entrance, very comfortable rooms, and one of the friendliest families in Venice. Patriarch Stefani's son Luciano and daughter Lucia are bubbly, helpful, and efficient, and speak perfectly adequate English. They've been in business some 31 years—almost all of them in this book—and it hasn't gotten old yet. Breakfast is served in their kitchen, or, if you prefer, in bed.

You'll find their place on the right side of Lista di Spagna, about two blocks from the train station.

ARCHIE'S HOUSE, Cannaregio, 1814, just off rio San Leonardo, 30 Venezia. Tel. 041/72-0884. 7 rms (1 with bath). **Directions:** See below.

$ Rates: 19,800–25,300 lire ($17.20–$22.00) per person in shared rooms. Showers 500 lire (45¢) extra. Call to check their rates in low season (Oct–May), which are usually about 30% off the standard price. Singles not available in summer. No credit cards.

This place is one of those ultra-budget institutions, where Archie Baghin (an English version of Arcadio) and his Taiwanese wife, Chuen-Lih, offer very simple accommodations that are just about the cheapest in Venice. Though he hails from nearby Vicenza, Archie has lived in 12 countries and has picked up a Ph.D., as well as French, German, English, Greek, and Chinese, among other languages, along the way. In 1977 he settled down here and, "for fun," got into the rooming-house business. Archie is full of helpful hints about all the countries he's called home at one time or another, not to mention Venice. No reservations are accepted.

To find his place from the train station, turn left and walk straight along Lista di Spagna, cross the first bridge (Ponte alle Guglie), and continue on rio San Leonardo. You'll find Archie's on your right just past Cannaregio, 1745 (on the right), and the Hotel Leonardo (on the left).

CASA DAVID, Cannaregio, 180 (2nd Floor), a few steps in from Lista di Spagna, Venezia. Tel. 041/71-5446. 4 rms (none with bath). **Directions:** See below.

$ Rates: 29,400 lire ($25.55) single; 50,400 lire ($43.80) double; 69,300 lire ($60.25) triple. No credit cards.

With only four rooms to rent, compact Casa David really feels like the home it is. In addition to great prices, guests are treated to roomy double rooms, and big smiles from the proprietors, who speak very little English. Look for the FROMMER'S sign on the door.

To reach the house from the station, walk about two blocks along Lista di Spagna and turn right down a narrow alley, just past the Hotel Continental at Cannaregio, 170. The *casa* is a few doors ahead on your left.

CASA NIVES OTTOLENGHI, Cannaregio, 180 (3rd Floor), a few steps in from Lista di Spagna, Venezia. Tel. 041/71-5206. 5 rms (none with bath). **Directions:** See below.

$ Rates: 48,500 lire ($42.20) double. No credit cards.

Signora Nives is a fiercely proud woman, and the words "very clean, very clean" roll off her lips as though they were the first words that she ever spoke. This is just a tiny place, with only five rooms, but her prices are just as small. Breakfast is not available.

To find this cozy *casa* from the station, walk about two blocks down Lista di Spagna and turn right down a narrow alley, just past the Hotel Continental at Cannaregio, 170. The *casa* is a few doors ahead on your left.

LOCANDA BERNARDI-SEMENZATO, Cannaregio, 4366, on calle de l'Oca, Venezia. Tel. 041/522-7257 or 522-2424. 18 rms (5 with bath). **Directions:** See below.

$ Rates: 33,600 lire ($29.20) single without bath, 41,300 lire ($35.90) single with bath; 48,400 lire ($42.10) double without bath, 66,000 lire ($57.40) double with bath; 63,800 lire ($55.50) triple without bath, 82,500 lire ($71.75) triple with bath. Breakfast 4,000 lire ($3.50) extra. MC, V. **Closed:** Jan–Feb.

The rooms at this cozy little locanda are plain, with little on the walls, but kept very clean and homey—and remarkably cheap—by the young, English-speaking Pepoli family and their two charming children. Access to the rooftop terrace is included in these ultra-budget rates. A top recommendation.

From the Ca d'Oro vaporetto stop (no. 6), walk straight ahead to the Strada Nova, turn right, and look for the sign on your left above Cannaregio, 4309, just before you reach campo SS. Apostoli. This will be calle Duca; walk up and take the first right onto calle de l'Oca.

NEAR THE TRAIN STATION

LOCANDA STEFANIA, Santa Croce, 181a, on fondamenta Tolentini, Venezia. Tel. 041/520-3757. 17 rms (7 with bath). **Directions:** See below.

$ Rates: 32,500 lire ($28.25) single without bath, 44,000 lire ($38.25) single with bath; 52,800 lire ($45.90) double without bath, 71,500 lire ($62.15) double with bath; 71,500 lire ($62.15) triple without bath, 99,000 lire ($86.10) triple with bath. No credit cards. **Closed:** Nov 15–Mar.

The Stefania has a falling-down look from the outside, but once indoors you'll find a refreshing and excellent budget choice run by the Girardi family. It features plain, exceptionally spacious rooms with large windows, in a relatively quiet neighborhood. Ask for one of the three rooms with frescoed ceilings.

From the train station, cross Ponte Scalzi right out front, turn right, and walk along

FROMMER'S SMART TRAVELER: HOTELS

VALUE-CONSCIOUS TRAVELERS SHOULD
TAKE ADVANTAGE OF THE FOLLOWING:

1. If possible, hotels where breakfast is not obligatory.
2. Arriving in the city before noon, when it's more likely you'll find a budget room.
3. Spending the night in Padova, if you're on an especially tight budget.

---

the Grand Canal until you reach the first canal, rio Tolentini. Here, turn left along fondamenta Tolentini; when this canal makes a sharp right at campazzo dei Tolentini, follow the canal and the locanda will be on your left.

NEAR PIAZZA SAN MARCO

This is the highest-rent neighborhood in this high-rent city, with the exception of the handful of places listed below.

ALLOGGI AI DO MORI, San Marco, 658, on calle Larga San Marco, Venezia. Tel. 041/520-4817. 12 rms (3 with bath). **Directions:** See below.
$ Rates: 42,000 lire ($36.50) single without bath; 60,900 lire ($52.95) double without bath, 81,900 lire ($71.20) double with bath; 85,100 lire ($74.00) triple without bath; 105,000 lire ($91.30) quad without bath. Breakfast 6,000 lire ($5.20) extra. AE. 5% discount on the above rates for bearers of this book.

Tony, the genial, effusive owner of this budget-priced place just steps from piazza San Marco, learned his trade during 25 years in England. Ask for the "painter's room," a pocket-sized room that opens onto a spacious rooftop patio, from which you can almost reach out and touch San Marco. Rooms 8 and 9 are also noteworthy, featuring beamed ceilings and a good view of the basilica; in fact, only Room 7 doesn't have a view. Though exceptionally small, all the rooms in this 17th-century building feel very cozy—probably a consequence of Tony's charm. Tony's place is named for the two Moors who can be seen ringing the bells atop the nearby San Marco clock tower.

To find Do Mori from the San Marco vaporetto stop (no. 15), head to the piazza, where you should exit underneath the clock tower; turn right at the first opportunity and you'll find the hotel on the left, just before Wendy's.

LOCANDA CASA PETRARCA, San Marco, 4386, on calle Schiavone, Venezia. Tel. 041/520-0430. 6 rms (3 with bath). **Directions:** See below.
$ Rates: 34,600 lire ($30.10) single without bath; 63,800 lire ($55.50) double without bath, 86,900 lire ($75.55) double with bath; 91,300 lire ($79.40) triple without bath, 115,500 lire ($100.45) triple with bath. Breakfast 7,000 lire ($6.10) extra. No credit cards.

Nellie must be one of the kindest and most delightful women in Italy. Always smiling and happy, she could bring sunshine to the Bridge of Sighs. She patiently dispenses advice in English more refined than that of most of her guests, and maintains a sunny, spotless place. What's the catch? She has just six rooms, and could never accommodate even a fraction of those who want to be her guests. A real one-of-a-kind place, tucked away at canalside on a dead-end calle, Nellie's nest is hard to find—but patience, like her warmth, is a virtue.

From campo San Luca, near the Rialto Bridge (vaporetto: Rialto), walk away from the Grand Canal on calle dei Fuseri (look for the Tarantola Bookstore on the corner), take the first left onto calle Ungheria, and then go right onto calle Schiavone; no. 4386 is on the left. Be careful at night, as two budget travelers somehow missed her door and walked right into the canal at the end of the calle. Having trouble finding campo

San Luca? As you step off the vaporetto at Rialto, turn right and walk along the Grand Canal, and turn left on calle del Carbon (just after San Marco, 4176), which runs right into campo San Luca.

PENSIONE CASA VERARDO, Castello, 4765, at the foot of Ponte Storto, Venezia. Tel. 041/528-6127. 12 rms (2 with bath, 8 with shower only). **Directions:** See below.

$ **Rates:** 38,900 lire ($33.80) single without bath; 57,800 lire ($50.25) double without bath, 68,300 lire ($59.40) double with shower only, 78,800 lire ($68.50) double with bath; 94,500 lire ($82.20) triple with shower only, 99,800 lire ($86.30) triple with bath; 31,500 lire ($27.40) per person in quads or quints with bath. Breakfast 6,000 lire ($5.20) extra. No credit cards.

⭐ You know you're staying in a friendly family's home the moment you step through the door of this centrally located and exceptionally reasonably priced pensione. Copies of famous Renaissance masterpieces decorate the walls of the oversize rooms, which are charmingly cluttered with huge antiques. Though it's just a short walk from piazza San Marco, the Verardo is located on a quiet canal, and is one of the few places where you can step outside and not see anyone selling anything.

To get there, take the Line 1 or 2 vaporetto to San Zaccaria; walk up calle delle Rasse to campo SS. Filippo e Giacomo; exit the *campo* on calle Rimpeto la Sacristia, which begins at Bar Europa, and the door to the pensione will be right there once you cross Ponte Storto, the first bridge.

IN SAN POLO

LOCANDA CA' FOSCARI, Dorsoduro, 3887, on calle Marconi, at the foot of Crosera, Venezia. Tel. 041/522-5817. 12 rms (1 with bath, 2 with shower only). **Directions:** See below.

$ **Rates** (with or without bath): 36,300 lire ($31.55) single; 57,500 lire ($50.00) double; 80,300 lire ($69.80) triple; 101,200 lire ($88.00) quad. Breakfast 6,000 lire ($5.20) extra. No credit cards. **Closed:** Two months between Nov and Feb.

Though one of the most modestly priced hotels I've listed in Venice, this family-run locanda is remarkably bright and spacious, with big windows in most rooms, soothing pink and lavender ceilings, even textured wallpaper and a roof garden—all the details that really make a difference for the traveler on a shoestring budget. A fine choice, especially for groups of three or four.

To get to the Ca'Foscari from the train station, take vaporetto Line 1 to San Tomà; from the wharf, walk up to calle Campaniel and turn left; once across the first canal, turn immediately right onto fondamenta Frescada, then left onto calle Marconi.

IN THE EASTERN END OF CASTELLO

LOCANDA SANT' ANNA, Castello, 269, on corte dei Bianco, Venezia. Tel. 041/520-4203 or 528-6466. 8 rms (3 with bath, 3 with shower only). **Directions:** See below.

$ **Rates:** 36,800 lire ($32.00) single without bath; 46,200 lire ($40.20) double without bath, 65,100 lire ($56.60) double with shower only, 77,700 lire ($67.55) double with bath; 101,200 lire ($88.00) triple with shower only, 106,700 lire ($92.78) triple with bath. Breakfast 6,000 lire ($5.20) extra. No credit cards. **Closed:** Mid-Jan to mid-Feb.

⭐ Though one of the most remote hotels listed in this chapter, the Sant' Anna is one of my top choices in the city. In a very quiet, peaceful location far from the major tourist traffic, this ultramodern, elegant locanda is an ideal selection for families or any others who want to come home in the evening and simply relax. The locanda has a newer, almost institutional feel, but rooms are good-sized, and many feature large windows overlooking a wide canal. The sitting room, a veritable jungle of plants kept in perfect health by the ever-attentive Vianello family, is especially nice, with Murano chandeliers.

From the Giardini vaporetto stop (no. 18) on Line 1, walk through the park ahead of you and slightly to your left (viale Garibaldi on your map). Turn right when this tree-lined boulevard ends, walk along the right side of rio di Sant' Anna canal, at which point you'll be walking along fondamenta di Sant' Anna. Go left over the second bridge, walk straight ahead, and take the second right onto corte di Bianco.

DOUBLES FOR LESS THAN 95,000 LIRE ($82.60)

ON OR NEAR LISTA DI SPAGNA

Exit the train station and turn left for this wide boulevard, which begins just past Ponte Scalzi.

ALBERGO SANTA LUCIA, Cannaregio, 358, on calle della Misericordia, Venezia. Tel. 041/71-5180. 18 rms (7 with bath). **Directions:** See below.
$ Rates (including continental breakfast): 39,900 lire ($34.70) single without bath; 49,400 lire ($42.95) double without bath, 83,000 lire ($72.20) double with bath; 87,200 lire ($75.80) triple without bath, 129,200 lire ($112.35) triple with bath. MC, V. **Closed:** Two weeks in Jan or Feb.
You'll recognize this place by its flower-decorated stone terrace with sun chairs, a place filled with roses, oleander, ivy, and birds chirping—though the rooms themselves are rather plain. Breakfast is served in an old-fashioned way, with coffee and tea brought in sterling-silver pots. Owner Emilia Gonzato Parcianello doesn't speak English, but her son, Gianangelo, does. The friendly owners close for two weeks at some indeterminate time during the winter.
    Calle della Misericordia is the second left off Lista di Spagna.

HOTEL DOLOMITI, Cannaregio, 73, on calle Priuli, Venezia. Tel. 041/71-5113 or 71-6635. Fax 041/71-6635. 50 rms (20 with bath). TEL **Directions:** See below.
$ Rates: 46,200 lire ($40.20) single without bath, 76,700 lire ($66.70) single with bath; 52,500 lire ($45.65) twin without bath, 86,100 lire ($74.85) twin with bath; 57,800 lire ($50.25) double without bath, 95,600 lire ($83.15) double with bath; 73,500 lire ($63.90) triple without bath, 119,700 lire ($104.10) triple with bath. Breakfast 10,000 lire ($8.70) extra. No credit cards. **Closed:** Nov 15–Feb.
An unremarkable exterior gives way to large, clean, but ordinary rooms at this lodging house just a few steps from the train station. There are four floors, though, unfortunately, no elevator. Sergio, the manager, speaks good English. Calle Priuli is the first left off Lista di Spagna.

HOTEL GUERRINI, Cannaregio, 265, on calle delle Procuratie, Venezia. Tel. 041/71-5114. 32 rms (23 with bath). **Directions:** See below.
$ Rates: 43,100 lire ($37.50) single without bath, 72,500 lire ($63.05) single with bath; 57,800 lire ($50.25) double without bath, 90,300 lire ($78.50) double with bath; 113,400 lire ($98.60) triple with bath; 135,500 lire ($117.80) quad with bath. Breakfast 13,000 lire ($11.30) extra in season, 6,000 lire ($5.20) during winter. No credit cards. **Closed:** Mid-Jan to mid-Mar.
The Guerrini has been in the Mazzo family for half a century, a fact reflected in the efficient professionalism and helpfulness of their English-speaking staff. Their place is clean, if a bit sterile, with uninspiring yellow walls and a few objets d'art thrown in to keep the place interesting. If only they could put as much effort and elegance into their rooms as they have in their marble-tiled, chandelier-bedecked lobby. . . . Ask for one of the new rooms in the main building, as opposed to the more mundane quarters in the annex across the street.
    Calle delle Procuratie is the fourth left off Lista di Spagna.

HOTEL LEONARDO, Cannaregio, 1385, on calle della Masena, Venezia. Tel. 041/71-8666. 16 rms (8 with bath). TEL **Directions:** See below.
$ Rates (including continental breakfast): 49,400 lire ($42.95) single without bath, 68,300 lire ($59.40) single with bath; 76,700 lire ($66.70) double without bath,

110,300 lire ($95.90) double with bath; 110,300 lire ($95.90) triple without bath, 142,800 lire ($124.20) triple with bath. Showers (for those in rooms without plumbing), 3,000 lire ($2.60) extra. MC, V. **Closed:** Jan.

⭐ There's an air of faded elegance (read: time for a renovation) about this homey place, operated by Maria Teresa Gonzato, the sister of the woman who owns the Albergo Santa Lucia, listed above. Nonetheless, the place is clean and tastefully decorated, and all the furniture and headboards are either upholstered or carved.

To find the Leonardo from the train station, walk along Lista di Spagna and cross the first bridge, Ponte alle Guglie; continue straight on rio Terrà San Leonardo and calle della Masena will be the sixth left after the bridge (look for the sign on the left above Cannaregio, 1382, just before campiello Anconetta).

HOTEL ROSSI, Cannaregio, 262, on calle delle Procuratie, Venezia. Tel. 041/71-5164 or 71-7784. 20 rms (8 with bath). TEL **Directions:** See below.
$ Rates (including continental breakfast): 38,000 lire ($33.05) single without bath, 52,800 lire ($45.90) single with bath; 69,300 lire ($60.25) double without bath, 92,400 lire ($80.35) double with bath; 92,400 lire ($80.35) triple without bath, 117,200 lire ($101.90) triple with bath. In low season you may be able to avoid the mandatory breakfast. AE, MC, V. **Closed:** Early Jan to mid-Feb.

This is a pleasant little place, with adequate rooms and a quiet courtyard next door—not my favorite, but an acceptable standby in this convenient neighborhood. They're closed for about six weeks from early January through mid-February. Calle delle Procuratie is the fifth left as you walk along Lista di Spagna from the train station, just before campo San Geremia.

NEAR SAN MARCO

HOTEL ATLANTICO, Castello, 4416, on calle del Rimedio, Venezia. Tel. 041/520-9244. 36 rms (26 with bath). TEL **Directions:** See below.
$ Rates (including continental breakfast): 61,100 lire ($53.15) single without bath, 91,000 lire ($79.15) single with bath; 90,800 lire ($78.95) double without bath, 125,400 lire ($109.05) double with bath; 121,000 lire ($105.20) triple without bath, 164,000 lire ($142.60) triple with bath. 10% discount on rooms with bath for bearers of this book. No credit cards.

Laura Innocenti's spacious rooms are complimented by pretty common areas, modern baths, and old-world charm. Some top-floor accommodations have a view of the nearby Bridge of Sighs.

Though the Atlantico is centrally located about five minutes from piazza San Marco, it's very quiet for the area. From piazza San Marco, head out calle Larga San Marco, which is the first right as you exit the piazza under the clock tower; go left at calle va al Ponte de l'Anzolo (the last calle before calle Larga San Marco goes over a small bridge—you'll find the Ristorante all' Angelo on the corner), and the first right will be ramo dell' Anzolo, which becomes calle del Rimedio once you cross the first bridge.

HOTEL SAN GALLO, San Marco, 1093a (1st Floor), on campo San Gallo, Venezia. Tel. 041/522-7311 or 528-9877. Fax 041/522-5702. 14 rms (9 with bath). TEL **Directions:** See below.
$ Rates (including continental breakfast): 62,500 lire ($54.35) single without bath, 94,500 lire ($82.20) single with bath; 94,500 lire ($82.20) double without bath, 126,000 lire ($109.55) double with bath; 123,000 lire ($106.95) triple without bath, 169,500 lire ($147.40) triple with bath. V.

⭐ The San Gallo only opened in the last few years, but owner Sandro Rossi has put so much effort into selecting period furnishings and room styling—right down to the chandeliers and the fogged windows—that you'll believe you've stepped back in time. From April through October, breakfast is served on a rooftop patio where you can enjoy an excellent view of San Marco.

Take vaporetto Line 1 or 2 to the San Marco–Vallaresso stop (no. 15). Walk straight up calle Vallaresso until it ends. Go left, then immediately right onto Frezzeria, and turn right onto calle Tron (at San Marco, 1133a), which opens onto campo San Gallo. Alternatively, from the Rialto Bridge area, walk straight down calle dei Fabbri and turn right on calle San Gallo into the piazza.

PENSIONE DONI, Castello, 4656, on fondamenta del Vin, Venezia. Tel. 041/522-4267. 13 rms (none with bath). **Directions:** See below.

$ **Rates** (including continental breakfast): 49,500 lire ($43.05) single; 70,900 lire ($61.65) double; 94,600 lire ($82.25) triple; 121,000 lire ($105.20) quad. No credit cards. **Closed:** Dec–Feb.

This quaint little canalside place has adequate rooms with soothing garden and terrific views at remarkably reasonable prices. The rooms, most of which overlook a peaceful interior courtyard, are downright ordinary, but the prices are genuinely extraordinary for the neighborhood. The effusive Annabella Doni is proud of her family-run place, and happier than the average hotelier to see Frommer readers step through the door.

From piazza SS. Filippo e Giacomo, head out on salizzada San Provolo, the street leading away from piazza San Marco; fondamenta del Vin is the first street on your right as soon as you cross Ponte San Provolo. Alternatively, take vaporetto Line 1 or 2 to the San Zaccaria–Danieli stop (no. 16); from the landing, cross the bridge to the right, take the first left onto calle del Vin, and bear left.

LOCANDA SILVA, Castello, 4423, on fondamenta del Rimedio, Venezia. Tel. 041/522-7643. 25 rms (7 with bath). **Directions:** See below.

$ **Rates** (including continental breakfast): 45,000 lire ($39.15) single without bath; 69,300 lire ($60.25) double without bath, 84,200 lire ($73.20) double with bath; 99,000 lire ($86.10) triple without bath, 129,800 lire ($112.90) triple with bath. No credit cards. **Closed:** Dec–Jan.

I've seen better, and then again I've seen worse. This spacious 25-room place, situated on a peaceful canal not far from piazza San Marco, is kept clean and comfortable— and modestly priced—by Signor Ettore and his daughter, Sandra.

To find it, exit piazza San Marco on calle dell' Anzolo, take the second right, and cross the canal (you'll be on calle del Rimedio at this point); turn left onto fondamenta del Rimedio when this street ends.

NEAR THE RIALTO BRIDGE

PENSIONE STURION, San Polo, 679, on calle del Sturion, Venezia. Tel. 041/523-6243. Fax 041/522-6748. 12 rms. A/C TV TEL **Directions:** See below.

$ **Rates** (including continental breakfast): 84,000 lire ($73.05) single with bath; 84,000–89,300 lire ($73.05–$77.65) double without bath, 115,500–120,800 lire ($100.45–$105.05) double with bath; 157,500 lire ($136.95) triple with bath; 199,500 lire ($173.50) quad with bath. No credit cards.

Though there has been a pensione on this site since 1290, a 1992 gutting and rebuilding has rendered the Sturion one of the city's most contemporary moderately priced hotels. Owned and operated by Sandro Rossi and his Scottish wife, Helen, the hotel is perched four flights, and 69 tiring steps, above the Grande Canal—one of the only reasonably priced places in Venice where you can savor a view of the city's bustling central waterway and your morning cappuccino at the same time. Unfortunately, only two rooms offer water views; the rest have a charming lookout over the Rialto rooftops.

From the Rialto vaporetto stop, cross the bridge, turn left at the other side, and walk along the water; calle del Sturion will be the fifth street on the right, just before San Polo, 740.

NEAR THE ACCADEMIA

ANTICA LOCANDA MONTIN, Dorsoduro, 1147, on fondamenta di Borgo, Venezia. Tel. 041/522-7151. Fax 041/522-3307. 7 rms (none with bath). **Directions:** See below.

$ **Rates:** 37,800 lire ($32.85) single; 65,100 lire ($56.60) double; 76,700 lire ($66.70) triple. Breakfast 5,000 lire ($4.35) extra. AE, DC, MC, V. **Closed:** Jan or Feb.

⭐ Part of the Carretin family for over 45 years, Locanda Montin's unique, offbeat interior warrants high marks from a trendy, budget-conscious clientele. Rooms, which enjoy views of a quiet canal or an interior courtyard, are furnished with oversize wooden beds, and a clutter of art. The hotel closes at 1am.

The Montin is about equidistant from the Zattere vaporetto stop (Line 5) on the Giudecca Canal, and the Ca' Rezzonico stop (Lines 1 and 2) on the Grand Canal. From the former, turn left along the Zattere and take the first right onto calle Trevisan, which becomes fondamenta di Borgo after the first bridge. From Ca' Rezzonico, walk straight ahead on calle del Traghetto and take the third left after you pass campo San Barnabà; this is calle delle Turchette, which, after the first bridge, becomes fondamenta di Borgo.

HOTEL GALLERIA, Dorsoduro, 878a, at the foot of the Accademia Bridge, Venezia. Tel. 041/520-4172. 10 rms (6 with bath). **Directions:** See below.

$ **Rates** (including continental breakfast): 52,500 lire ($45.65) single without bath; 74,600 lire ($64.85) double without bath, 107,100 lire ($93.15) double with bath; 134,400 lire ($116.85) triple with bath; 162,800 lire ($141.55) quad with bath. No credit cards.

⭐ Spending the night here is like staying at the Ca' d'Oro. Step through the great green doors, with brass gargoyle doorknobs, and saunter up the marble staircase to the reception area, complete with red velvet wallpaper and designer carpets. From there you'll be led to the modern rooms, where you'll rest under enormous down comforters, beneath what must be the only carved ceilings in a hotel in Italy. Six of the rooms overlook the Grand Canal; this is perhaps the only place remotely in this price range with Grand Canal views.

As you cross the Accademia Bridge from San Marco, or step off the vaporetto (Line 1, 2, or 4) at the Accademia stop, you'll see the Galleria to the left of the museum.

PENSIONE ALLA SALUTE (DA CICI), Dorsoduro, 222, on fondamenta Ca' Balà, Venezia. Tel. 041/523-5404 or 522-2271. 68 rms (30–32 with shower or bath). TEL **Directions:** See below.

$ **Rates** (including continental breakfast): 52,500 lire ($45.65) single without bath, 78,800 lire ($68.50) single with bath; 75,600 lire ($65.75) double without bath, 110,300 lire ($95.90) double with bath; 99,800 lire ($86.30) triple without bath, 141,800 lire ($123.30) triple with bath. No credit cards.

The elegant lobby, lovely terrace garden, and cozy cocktail bar of this exceptionally large hotel give way to 68 excellent rooms, most of which have high ceilings and huge windows. The Salute is situated in a very quiet residential neighborhood, near the Guggenheim Collection, that sees few tourists. Breakfast is served outdoors in summer. This is the medium-priced place to try when you arrive in the late afternoon and every place else is *completo* (full).

To find the Pensione alla Salute, take vaporetto Line 1 to the Santa Maria della Salute stop (no. 14). Walk straight ahead to the first bridge on your right, cross it, and walk as straight ahead as you can to the next canal, where you'll turn left (before crossing the bridge) onto fondamenta Ca' Balà.

IN SAN POLO

HOTEL IRIS, San Polo, 2910a, on calle del Cristo, just off fondamenta della Dona Onesta, Venezia. Tel. 041/522-2882. 30 rms (12 with bath). **Directions:** See below.

$ **Rates** (including continental breakfast): 50,400 lire ($43.80) single without bath,

79,800 lire ($69.40) single with bath; 71,400 lire ($62.10) double without bath, 105,000 lire ($91.30) double with bath. AE, MC, V. **Closed:** Early Jan to early Feb.

⭐ Big, dark rooms and hallways are cluttered with good-quality, original modern art. Everything is kept spotlessly clean and tastefully decorated by owners Livio and Flora Fullin. Ask for one of their five rooms with frescoed ceilings. This is an especially good choice for those who would like to get off the beaten tourist track. Downstairs, they operate a fine restaurant/pizzeria with a *giardinetto* (patio) on the canal (the Ristorante al Giardinetto; see "Budget Dining," below).

To reach their place, take vaporetto Line 1 or 4 to San Tomà, walk straight ahead along calle del Traghetto, turn left at the end of this short calle, and then take the first right (before you go over the bridge) onto fondamenta del Forner, which becomes fondamenta della Dona Onesta.

SUPER-BUDGET CHOICES

FORESTERIA DELLA CHIESA VALDESE, Castello, 5170, at the end of calle Lunga Santa Maria Formosa, Venezia. Tel. 041/528-6797. 43 beds (no rms with bath), 2 apartments. **Directions:** See below.

$ **Rates:** 18,700 lire ($16.25) per person in dormitory rooms, 27,500 lire ($23.90) in a double or triple; 104,000 lire ($90.45) four-bed apartment with bath and kitchen (four- to seven-night minimum). Their 7,000 lire ($6.10) breakfast is often mandatory. No credit cards.

Those lucky enough to find a place at this elegant 16th-century palazzo will find wonderfully charming accommodations at almost impossibly low prices. Each of the rooms of this old-world hideaway opens onto a balcony overlooking a quiet canal. The frescoes that grace the high ceilings in the doubles and two of the dorms are by the same artist who decorated the Correr. The four-room apartments, complete with kitchen facilities, are the best budget choice in town for traveling families. The reception is open from 9am to 1pm and 6 to 8pm only.

You'll find the Valdese by walking to the end of calle Lunga Santa Maria Formosa; the calle begins at the Bar all' Orologio on campo Santa Maria Formosa, which is just about equidistant from piazza San Marco and the Rialto Bridge.

HOSTELS & DORMITORIES

FORESTERIA DOMUS CAVANIS, Dorsoduro, 912a, on rio Antonio Foscarini, Venezia. Tel. 041/528-7374. 90 beds in 45 rms (none with bath). **Directions:** See below.

$ **Rates** (including continental breakfast): 39,000 lire ($33.90) single; 69,500 lire ($60.45) double; 98,000 lire ($85.20) triple; 121,000 lire ($105.20) quad. Full board also available. No credit cards. **Open:** June–Sept only.

While the rooms in this converted dormitory—open to tourists June through September only—are rather plain, the beds are narrow, and the place is popular with groups, Padre Ferdinando Fietta runs a tip-top place and the prices are extraordinary. The institutional-looking building surrounds a concrete playground.

To reach it from the Accademia stop on vaporetto Line 1 or 2, walk to the left around the museum, then walk straight ahead on rio Antonio Foscarini. The Domus Cavanis will be halfway down on your right.

OSTELLO VENEZIA, Giudecca, 86, on fondamenta Zitelle, Venezia. Tel. and Fax 041/523-8211. 300 beds. **Directions:** See below.

$ **Rates** (including continental breakfast, sheets, and showers): 18,000 lire ($15.65) per person. Youth hostel card available on premises for 30,000 lire ($26.10), or you can buy a hostel card on an installment basis for 5,000 lire ($4.35) per night for six nights. No credit cards.

Modern, spotless, and efficiently run by Claudio Camillo, this is one of the finest hostels around. What's more, the view of the tip of Dorsoduro and piazza San Marco off in the distance is positively awesome. There's a three-night maximum stay, which is usually enforced only in summer. Arrive by midafternoon to guarantee yourself a bed in the summer. From July 1 through September 30 registration opens at noon; the remainder of the year the check-in starts at 5pm. The rooms are closed until 5pm all year, and curfew is 11pm. This youth hostel is open to budget travelers of all ages. Remember to add the cost of the vaporetto fare to the net cost of staying at this hostel. The ample dinner, at 12,600 lire ($10.95) for three courses and fruit, is one of the best food values in town. Mealtimes are usually 6 to 9pm.

To get to the youth hostel, take vaporetto Line 5, the "Circolare Destra," from the docks to the right as you exit the train station, or *motoscafo* Line 8, to the Zitelle stop, at the eastern end of the Giudecca, and turn right as you step off the boat.

FOR WOMEN ONLY

CASA DELLE STUDENTE DOMUS CIVICA, San Polo, 3082, at the corner of calle Chiovere and calle Campazzo, Venezia. Tel. 041/72-1103. 95 beds (no rms with bath). **Directions:** See below.
   $ Rates: 27,500 lire ($23.90) single; 44,000 lire ($38.25) double. No credit cards.
   Open: June–July and Sept (*not* Aug).
This is an unremarkable institutional place for women only. They're open just June, July, and September (*not* August); the rest of the year it's a dormitory for students at the local university. Don't plan on any carousing, as they enforce an 11pm curfew. All rooms are singles and doubles, and breakfast is not available.

From the train station, cross Ponte Scalzi right out front, turn right, and walk along the Grand Canal until you reach the first canal, rio Tolentini. Here, turn left along fondamenta Tolentini; when this canal makes a sharp right at campazzo dei Tolentini, turn left onto corte dei Amai, which will lead you right to the corner of calle Chiovere and calle Campazzo, just after you cross the rio delle Meneghette canal.

ISTITUTO SUORE CANOSSIANE, Giudecca, 428, on fondamenta del Ponte Piccolo, Venezia. Tel. 041/522-2157. 35 beds. **Directions:** See below.
   $ Rates: 12,500 lire ($10.85) per person. No credit cards.
This private Catholic kindergarten by day is used as a budget hostel for women at night. But with an 8:30am lockout and an 11pm curfew in summer (10pm in winter), this is for the die-hard budget traveler only. The reception and the rooms are open from 6pm. Breakfast is not available.

The istituto is most conveniently reached from the Sant' Eufemia vaporetto stop on Line 5. Turn left and walk along the water as you get off the boat and you'll find it just beyond the first bridge.

WORTH THE EXTRA BUCKS

Venice will cost you more across the board than you're accustomed to paying elsewhere in Italy. Here are my two splurge recommendations in this city of splurge.

CASA FROLLO, Giudecca, 50, on fondamenta Zitelle, Venezia. Tel. 041/522-2723. 26 rms (14 with bath). TEL **Directions:** See below.
   $ Rates (including continental breakfast): 55,000 lire ($47.80) single without bath, 71,500 lire ($62.20) single with bath; 99,000 lire ($86.10) double without bath, 121,000 lire ($105.20) double with bath; 144,700 lire ($125.80) triple without bath, 165,000 lire ($143.50) triple with bath. No credit cards. **Closed:** Dec–Mar.

If you can't stay in the Ca' Rezzonico, book a room at this gem on the peaceful island of Giudecca. This is the only hotel I've ever known with its own historic-preservation society, and it possesses perhaps the most remarkable antique collection of any hotel in this book. The building itself was constructed at the end of the 16th century, and has been altered little since then. It has been in service as a hotel since 1892; the Flora Soldan family has been in charge for the last 34 years. The view from the breakfast room, which has a whole bank of 12-foot-high windows that look out on the Salute Church at the tip of Dorsoduro, is simply spectacular. Half the rooms also enjoy this same terrific view. If frescoed ceilings are your thing, ask for the bathless double just off the main hall. A very special place.

Take the Line 5 vaporetto or the Line 8 *motoscafo* to the Zitelle stop on the Giudecca, and turn right along fondamenta Zitelle (remember that the vaporetto does not run all night).

PENSIONE SEGUSO, Dorsoduro, 779, on the Zattere, Venezia. Tel. 041/522-2340 or 528-6858. 36 rms (14 with bath). TEL **Directions:** See below.
$ Rates (including continental breakfast): 67,000 lire ($58.25) single without bath, 98,000 lire ($85.20) single with bath; 104,500 lire ($90.85) double without bath, 135,300 lire ($117.65) double with bath. The 13,000-lira ($11.30) breakfast is sometimes mandatory. AE, CB, DC, MC, V. **Closed:** Dec–Feb.

The Seguso boasts just about the most impressive set of antiques anywhere, and certainly the most elegant sitting room in town. Located smack on the Giudecca Canal, it has an uncanny old-world feel—you feel like your three-masted sailing ship should be parked out front.

Those without their own boats can reach the Seguso as follows: Take vaporetto Line 5 or 8 to the Zattere stop, on the Guidecca Canal, and turn right along the water as you step off the boat; you'll find the Seguso behind the Pensione Calcina. Alternatively, take vaporetto Line 1 or 2 to the Accademia stop, walk to the left around the museum, then walk straight ahead on rio Antonio Foscarini to the Zattere, where you'll turn left.

5. BUDGET DINING

Venice does not lack for restaurants. Finding a place that's a cut above the rest, though, is another story altogether. I've listed a dozen or so places below that are either notably inexpensive or good—or both.

Eating cheap in Venice is not easy. Pizza is by no means a local specialty, but it nonetheless represents about the only way to save money. Standing up at a café or *rosticceria* is uniformly less expensive than sitting down, if not very comfortable.

Keep in mind that the listings below show prices for pasta and meat courses only. Don't forget to add in charges for bread and cover, service, and vegetable side dishes when calculating what you can actually expect to pay.

LOCAL BUDGET BESTS

Local cuisine always reflects the surrounding region. Venice is situated literally in the middle of the ocean, so guess what dominates the city's culinary life.

Spaghetti *alle vongole* (in a clam sauce) is a staple. Spaghetti *bigoli in salsa* (with a sauce of anchovies and onions) is harder to find, but equally distinctive. *Seppie nere con polenta* is stewed cuttlefish, a sharp, salty delicacy served in its own black ink over polenta, a thick porridge made from corn flour. *Risotto di seppie nere* means rice with cuttlefish, a creature common to this area but otherwise rare in Italy. (The squeamish should note that cuttlefish exude a black ink that'll color your plate—and your tongue.) Needless to say, fresh grilled fish (*pesce alla griglia*) is always available. Finally, there's the ubiquitous *frittura mista,* a mixture of fried seafood. Other, more earthly dishes include *risi e bisi* (rice with peas), *pasta fagioli* (bean-and-pasta soup), and every youngster's favorite, *fegato alla veneziana,* or liver and onions.

MEALS FOR LESS THAN 13,500 LIRE [$11.75]

ON OR NEAR LISTA DI SPAGNA

This is the most heavily touristed area of town, and you're not likely to get much in the way of authentic Venetian cuisine, but the restaurants along this stretch are cheap and convenient to the many hotels recommended in the neighborhood.

GINO'S, Cannaregio, 158, on Lista di Spagna. Tel. 71-6072.
Cuisine: ITALIAN.
$ Prices: *Menu turistico,* 9,000 lire ($7.80) for pasta and salad, 13,000 lire ($11.30) for a standard meal, 17,500 lire ($15.20) for the deluxe "Venetian" meal; pizza and pasta courses 4,500–10,500 lire ($3.90–$9.15); meat courses 8,000–10,000 lire ($6.95–$8.70); grilled fish 13,000–14,000 lire ($11.30–$12.20). No cover charge. AE, DC, MC, V.
Open: Fri–Wed 9am–midnight.

There's nothing very spectacular or remarkable about this place except for its very modest prices and the fact that there's no *coperto* tacked onto the bill. Curiously, this place is reasonably popular with Italian young people.

TRATTORIA SPACCANAPOLI, Cannaregio, 1518, on rio Terrà San Leonardo. Tel. 71-6170.
Cuisine: ITALIAN. **Directions:** See below.
$ Prices: *Menu turistico* 11,000–28,000 lire ($9.55–$24.35). Minimum 13,000 lire ($11.30) per person. MC, V.
Open: Lunch Wed–Mon noon–2:30pm; dinner Wed–Mon 5–10pm. **Closed:** Jan–Feb.

With outdoor tables and a dark, romantic interior, this place is a cut above some of its tackier, more touristy neighbors along this strip leading from the station. Nonetheless, they cater to every traveler's whim and budget with countless fixed-price meals. Indeed, it's functionally impossible to order à la carte, since every combination you could come up with is covered by one of their all-inclusive specials; they offer a dozen fixed-price options in the 10,000 to 11,000-lira ($8.70 to $9.55) price range alone. Exceptionally pleasant and authentic.

You'll find it on the right side of the road at the far foot of Ponte alle Guglie, the bridge that crosses Canale di Cannaregio at the end of Lista di Spagna.

SNACK-PIZZERIA BEAU BRUMMEL, Cannaregio, 160a, on Lista di Spagna. Tel. 71-5707.
Cuisine: ITALIAN.
$ Prices: Pizza-and-beer or spaghetti-and-wine fixed-price meal 8,000 lire ($6.95); *menu turistico* 14,500 lire ($12.60) or 20,000 lire ($17.40); pizza and pasta courses

---

 FROMMER'S SMART TRAVELER: RESTAURANTS

VALUE-CONSCIOUS TRAVELERS SHOULD TAKE ADVANTAGE OF THE FOLLOWING:

1. Standing up at a café or *rosticceria*—uniformly less expensive than sitting down.
2. Pizza—not a *local* specialty, but a way to save money.

6,300–8,400 lire ($5.50–$7.30); meat courses 10,000–16,000 lire ($8.70–$13.90). No cover charge. AE, DC, MC, V.
Open: Thurs–Tues 9am–10pm.
While throughout most of Venice and Italy you'll be frowned upon and still charged a dollar or more for *coperto* if you order just one course and a drink, at this tacky tourist spot they encourage it. You can choose from pizza and a beer, or spaghetti and a glass of wine, both priced at 8,000 lire ($6.95), with no added charges. Its atmosphere is slightly less tacky and more Italian than its neighbor and competition next door, Gino's.

NEAR PIAZZA SAN MARCO

PIZZERIA AL VECIO CANTON, Castello, 4738a, at the corner of Ruga Giuffa, calle Ruta, and calle della Corona, off campo Santa Maria Formosa. Tel. 528-5176.
  Cuisine: ITALIAN. **Directions:** See below.
$ **Prices:** Pizza 5,300–9,500 lire ($4.60–$8.25); pasta courses 6,300–8,400 lire ($5.50–$7.30); meat courses 9,500–16,000 lire ($8.25–$13.90). AE, CB, DC.
  Open: Lunch Thurs–Mon noon–2:30pm; dinner daily 7–10:30pm.
  Closed: Aug, and for one to two weeks at Christmas.

Good pizza is hard to find in Venice, and I mean that in the literal sense. Really tucked away, on the corner of two tiny streets, this may be one of the best-hidden *pizzerie* in Italy, but its charming atmosphere and tasty fixings are worth the time you'll spend looking for the place. Inside is both intimate and friendly, with just 10 tables surrounded by wooden chairs, and a service staff that speaks decent English.

To get there from campo SS. Filippo e Giacomo, exit on salizzada San Provolo, cross the bridge and take the first left, then go left again over the next bridge onto corte Rotta.

NEAR CAMPO DEI FRARI

RISTORANTE AL GIARDINETTO, San Polo, 2909, on calle del Cristo, just off fondamenta della Dona Onesta. Tel. 522-4100 or 522-2882.
  Cuisine: ITALIAN. **Directions:** See below.
$ **Prices:** *Menu turistico* 19,000 lire ($16.50); pizza and pasta courses 5,300–9,500 lire ($4.60–$8.25); meat courses 9,000–17,000 lire ($7.85–$14.80). AE, MC, V.
  Open: Lunch Tues–Sun noon–2pm; dinner Tues–Sun 7–10pm. **Closed:** Dec 20–Jan 31.

It's hard to resist their budget-priced pizza, served outside under a charming grape arbor and just steps from a quiet canal. But the fish is outstanding as well—owner Livio picks up fresh seafood at the nearby campo della Pescaria each morning. You may never want to leave.

To find it, take vaporetto Line 1 or 4 to San Tomà, walk straight ahead along calle del Traghetto, turn left at the end of this short calle and then take the first right (before you go over the bridge) onto fondamenta del Forner, which becomes fondamenta della Dona Onesta.

NEAR THE RIALTO BRIDGE

ANTICA TRATTORIA DA MARCO, San Polo, 900, on campiello del Sansoni. Tel. 522-6565.
  Cuisine: ITALIAN. **Directions:** See below.
$ **Prices:** Pizza 6,300–10,500 lire ($5.50–$9.15), most priced at 7,400–9,500 lire ($6.45–$8.25). No credit cards.
  Open: Lunch Tues–Sun noon–2:30pm; dinner Tues–Sun 7–10pm.
The old-fashioned feel of this cozy place is complimented by the soothing jazz and rhythm and blues that is played continuously. Their pizza is so good that at the end of their first year in business they dropped everything else from their menu.

From the foot of the Rialto Bridge on the San Polo side of the Grand Canal, turn left and walk along the Grand Canal for five blocks, where you should turn right onto calle del Paradiso and walk ahead for about four blocks to the campiello del Sansone.

PIZZERIA BORA BORA, San Marco, 5252 or 5260, with entrances on calle dei Stagneri and calle Gallazza. Tel. 523-6583.
Cuisine: ITALIAN. **Reservations:** Recommended. **Directions:** See below.
$ **Prices:** Pizza 6,300–8,400 lire ($5.50–$7.30); pasta courses 6,500–9,000 lire ($5.65–$7.80); meat and fish courses 11,000–13,000 lire ($8.70–$11.30); jumbo salad 10,000 lire ($8.70). 10% discount for bearers of this book. No cover charge, but 12% service charge. No credit cards.
Open: Lunch Thurs–Tues noon–3:30pm; dinner Thurs–Tues 7–10:30pm.
Closed: Two weeks in Jan and two weeks in July.

⭐ With no fewer than 40 different kinds of pizza, Bora Bora can satisfy any palate. It's got a nouveau, trendy atmosphere heavy on the tropical/aquatic, right down to the turquoise floor tiling and the Hawaiian shirts sported by the waiters. The place is tiny and extremely popular—one of the only pizzerias in Italy where reservations are recommended. Their prices are discounted a generous 10% for bearers of this book.

You'll find calle dei Stagneri off campo San Bartolomeo, which is at the foot of the Rialto Bridge on the San Marco side of the Grand Canal. Calle dei Stagneri begins at the right end of campo San Bartolomeo if you're coming off the bridge; look for the Banca Commerciale Italiana on the corner.

ROSTICCERIA SAN TEATRO GOLDONI, San Marco, 4747, on calle dei Fabbri. Tel. 522-2446.
Cuisine: ITALIAN.
$ **Prices:** *Menu turistico* 17,500 lire ($15.20); pizza and pasta courses 5,500–8,000 lire ($4.80–$6.95); meat courses 8,000–11,000 lire ($6.95–$8.70). No credit cards.
Open: Lunch Thurs–Tues 10am–2:30pm; dinner Thurs–Tues 5–9pm. **Closed:** One week sometime in Jan or Feb.

As at all *rosticcerie,* you can see exactly what you're getting and don't have to pay any cover charge. Specialties here include pollo alla veneta (Venetian-style chicken) and fegato alla veneziana (liver and onions). It's just off campo San Luca, near the Rialto Bridge.

ROSTICCERIA SAN BARTOLOMEO, San Marco, 5423, on calle della Bissa. Tel. 522-3569.
Cuisine: ITALIAN. **Directions:** See below.
$ **Prices:** *Menu turistico* 9,500 lire ($8.25), 12,600 lire ($10.95), and 16,800 lire ($14.60) in the ground-floor dining room, and 19,000 lire ($16.50) and 27,000 lire ($23.50) upstairs; pasta courses 5,300–6,300 lire ($4.60–$5.50) in the ground-floor dining room, about 20% more upstairs; meat and fish courses 9,500–12,600 lire ($8.25–$10.95) in the ground-floor dining room, about 20% more upstairs. No cover charge downstairs. MC, V.
Open: Summer, lunch Tues–Sun 9am–2:30pm; dinner Tues–Sun 4:30–9:30pm. Winter, lunch Tues–Sun 9am–2:30pm; dinner, Tues–Sun 4:30–8:40pm. **Closed:** Two weeks in Jan.

⭐ With 17 different pasta dishes, 12 meat courses, and about that many seafood dishes, all displayed under the long glass counter, this place can satisfy any combination of culinary desires. What's more, since all the food is displayed under glass counters, you don't have to worry about any mistranslation—you'll know exactly what you're ordering. There's no *coperto* if you take your meal standing up (or sitting on stools) in the aroma-filled ground-floor eating hall, and of course, as in any stand-up place, there's no implicit or explicit requirement that you take more than one course. For those who prefer to linger, head to the dining hall upstairs, though you can do much better than this institutional setting. This appears to be the most popular *rosticceria* in Venice, and for good reason.

From campo San Bartolomeo, at the foot of the Rialto Bridge on the San Marco side of the Grand Canal, take the underpass to your left (if the bridge is at your back) marked SOTTOPORTEGO DELLA BISSA; you'll come across the *rosticceria* at the first corner. Note that while this place still calls itself the "San Bartolomeo" on its menus and business cards, the sign above the entrance reads GISLON.

MEALS FOR LESS THAN 26,500 LIRE [$23.05]

NEAR SAN MARCO

TRATTORIA ALLA RIVETTA, Castello, 4625, on salizzada San Provolo. Tel. 528-7302.
   Cuisine: SEAFOOD. **Directions:** See below.
$ Prices: Pasta courses 5,500–8,000 lire ($4.80–$6.95); fish courses 8,400–13,000 lire ($7.30–$11.30); other second courses 9,000–12,600 lire ($7.80–$10.95). AE, MC, V.
   Open: Lunch Tues–Sun noon–2:30pm; dinner Tues–Sun 7–10pm. **Closed:** Mid-July to mid-Aug.

⭐ There are scores of places in this price range throughout Venice, but alla Rivetta has that extra something that makes all the difference in a meal. A lively, popular, and thoroughly authentic place, this is your best bet for genuine Venetian cuisine and company in the immediate area of San Marco. All sorts of fish—their specialty—decorate the window of this plain, brightly lit place, where you'll be welcomed heartily by the bustling staff. Be sure to try the antipasto di pesce and whatever is penciled in as the daily special. Expect to wait for a table, even in winter. An excellent place to experiment, as they do everything well.

The trattoria is literally tucked away next to a bridge, just off the side of campo SS. Filippo e Giacomo with the FARMACIA sign at the corner. Campo SS. Filippo e Giacomo is just behind Basilica di San Marco.

TRATTORIA BANDIERETTE, San Marco, 813, on calle Fiubera. Tel. 522-0625.
   Cuisine: ITALIAN. **Directions:** See below.
$ Prices: *Menu turistico* 16,500 lire ($14.35); pasta courses 6,000–6,500 lire ($5.20–$5.70); meat courses 11,000–13,000 lire ($8.70–$11.30). No credit cards.
   Open: Lunch Wed–Mon noon–2:30pm; dinner Wed–Mon 7–9:30pm. **Closed:** Jan 15–Mar 15.

This family-run trattoria advertises *cucina casalinga* ("home-cooking") and has exceptionally low prices for a place so very close to piazza San Marco. The staff is very friendly, especially considering the location in the heart of the tourist quarter.

Exit the piazza under the clock tower, which is to the left as you face the church; go left, cross Ponte dei Ferali, and the Bandierette will be on your left.

NEAR THE ACCADEMIA

TAVERNA SAN TROVASO, Dorsoduro, 1016, on fondamenta Priuli. Tel. 520-3703.
   Cuisine: ITALIAN. **Directions:** See below.
$ Prices: *Menu turistico* (including wine and dessert) 18,000 lire ($15.65); pizza and pasta courses 5,300–10,500 lire ($4.60–$9.15); meat courses 8,400–12,600 lire ($7.30–$10.95); fish courses 14,700–21,000 lire ($12.80–$18.25). AE, DC, MC, V.
   Open: Lunch Tues–Sun noon–2:30pm; dinner Tues–Sun 7–9:30pm. **Closed:** A few days around Christmas.

Dining here is like eating in a wine cellar. Bottles line the wood-paneled walls, and the vaulted brown ceilings add an intimate touch. They offer a *menu turistico* that includes wine, dessert, and frittura mista (mixed fried seafood). Both the wine-cellar room downstairs and the more modern air-conditioned quarters upstairs are frequently packed with happy patrons enjoying the excellent food and fine service. Fegato alla veneziana (liver and onions) and grilled fish are the taverna's claim to fame. They also prepare an excellent gnocchi and a competent osso bucco.

You'll find this place not far from the Accademia: Walk to the right around the museum, take an immediate right onto calle Gambara, and turn left when this street ends at a canal. The San Trovaso will be right there on your left.

NEAR CAMPO DEI FRARI

TRATTORIA DELLA DONA ONESTA, Dorsoduro, 3922, on calle della Dona Onesta. Tel. 522-9586.
   Cuisine: ITALIAN. **Directions:** See below.
$ **Prices:** Pasta courses 4,500–8,000 lire ($3.95–$6.95); meat courses 9,000–12,000 lire ($7.80–$10.45); lire ($6.95–$9.55). MC, V.
   Open: Lunch Mon–Sat noon–2:30pm; dinner Mon–Sat 7–10pm. **Closed:** Aug, and around Christmas.

★ This is an unpretentious place that might not catch your eye (even if you could find it) unless you peek through the curtains to see that every one of its 11 tables is full. There aren't even pictures on the wall—all their energy is devoted to the food, which is excellent and quite reasonably priced by Venetian standards. Be sure to try the cioccolatina (chocolate liqueur in frozen cream).

The Dona Onesta is difficult to find, but worth the effort. Turn off Crosera, which runs perpendicular to the Grand Canal between campo San Pantalon and campo dei Frari, at Dorsoduro, 3930, near the Hotel Tivoli. The restaurant is right at rio Frescada canal. Alternatively, take vaporetto Line 1 or 4 to San Tomà, walk straight ahead along calle del Traghetto, turn left at the end of this short calle and then take the first right (before you go over the bridge) onto fondamenta del Forner, which becomes fondamenta della Dona Onesta. Continue on Dona Onesta and turn left across the first bridge.

PICNIC SUPPLIES & WHERE TO EAT THEM

Doing your own shopping for food in Italy can be an interesting experience since there's no such thing as a supermarket. See the Rome chapter for details.

Venice's principal market, commonly referred to as the **Mercato Rialto,** begins on the San Polo side of the Rialto Bridge and continues along the Grand Canal to campo della Pescaria, just about directly across the canal from the Ca'd'Oro vaporetto stop. You'll find the vendors there Monday through Saturday roughly from 7am to 1pm, though the fish merchants usually take Monday off.

Each day, an open-air market specializing in fresh fish and vegetables sets up shop on the spacious **campo Santa Margherita,** open roughly Tuesday through Saturday from 8:30am until 1 or 2pm. A more colorful market, however, is the nearby produce market that operates from the side of **a boat moored just off campo San Barnabà.** This market operates roughly from 8am to 1pm and 3:30 to 7:30pm, daily except Wednesday afternoon and Sunday. You should have no trouble filling out your picnic spread with the fixings available at the various shops that line the sides of the campo, including an exceptional *panetteria* (Rizzo Pane) at no. 2772, a fine *salumeria* at no. 2844, and a good shop for wine, sweets, and other picnic accessories next door.

Other open-air produce markets? Try **via Giuseppe Garibaldi,** in the eastern end of the Castello sestiere, where vendors are in business Monday through Saturday, roughly from 8:30am to 1:30pm. This is the second-largest market in the city after Rialto. (On Saturday, you'll find clothes, kitchen utensils, and other miscellaneous items for sale here as well.) You'll find the market along **rio Terrà San Leonardo,** between Ponte alle Guglie and campiello Anconetta, to be the most convenient to the train station. Finally, you might try **campo Santa Maria Formosa.**

Unfortunately, Venice doesn't have much in the way of green space for a picnic. The park at the eastern end of Castello (see "Parks and Gardens" in "Attractions," below) is hardly worth the trek or the money you'll spend getting there.

WORTH THE EXTRA BUCKS

It's remarkably easy to spend 30,000 lire ($26.10) on dinner anywhere in this city. But these are two very special places where your money will be well spent.

ANTICA LOCANDA MONTIN, Dorsoduro, 1147, on fondamenta di Borgo. Tel. 522-7151.
   Cuisine: SEAFOOD. **Directions:** See below.
$ Prices: Pasta courses 6,000–9,500 lire ($5.20–$8.25); meat courses 11,000–18,000 lire ($9.55–$15.65); fish courses 11,000–26,300 lire ($9.55–$22.85). AE, DC, MC, V.
   Open: Lunch Thurs–Tues 12:30–2:30pm; dinner Thurs–Mon 7:30–10pm.

Signora Carrettin, the iconoclastic owner of the Montin, has put together the best modern-art collection outside the Guggenheim on the walls of this popular, unpretentious restaurant. In fact, hardly an inch of wall shows through the paintings and drawings that are stacked five high. You know a place must be good when it's this crowded, at these prices, in such an out-of-the-way location. There's also a terrific garden out back.

The Montin is about equidistant from the Zattere vaporetto stop (Line 5) on the Giudecca Canal, and the Ca' Rezzonico stop (Lines 1 and 2) on the Grand Canal. From the former, turn left along the Zattere and take the first right onto calle Trevisan, which becomes fondamenta di Borgo after the first bridge. From Ca' Rezzonico, walk straight ahead on calle del Traghetto and take the third left after you pass campo San Barnabà; this is calle delle Turchette, which, after the first bridge, becomes fondamenta di Borgo.

TRATTORIA ALLA MADONNA, San Polo, 594, on calle della Madonna. Tel. 522-3824.
   Cuisine: ITALIAN. **Directions:** See below.
$ Prices: Pasta courses 5,500–6,500 lire ($4.80–$5.65); meat courses 11,000–13,000 lire ($9.60–$11.30); grilled fish 6,500 lire ($5.65) per *etto* (roughly a quarter pound). AE, MC, V.
   Open: Lunch Thurs–Tues noon–3pm; dinner Thurs–Tues 7–10pm. **Closed:** Dec 24–Jan 31.

You'll find art, art, and more art here, always original and usually stacked two or three high on the high walls of this trattoria, one of the city's most famous. The place is enormous—the five dining rooms all have high beamed ceilings—but there's rarely an empty table. The food and service are terrific and much sought after. Specialties include risotto con frutti di mare (rice with seafood) and any fish "alla griglia" (grilled). Expect to spend about 38,500 lire ($33.50) for a full meal including wine.

From the foot of the Rialto Bridge on the San Polo side of the Grand Canal, turn left; calle della Madonna will be the second street on your right (look for the big yellow sign).

6. ATTRACTIONS

SUGGESTED ITINERARIES

IF YOU HAVE ONE DAY   I have a radical suggestion: If you have just one day in Venice, don't bother with any of the sights. Not the Basilica di San Marco, not the

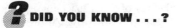

DID YOU KNOW . . . ?

- In the 9th century, the body of St. Mark was supposedly transported from Egypt to Venice.
- Richard Wagner died in 1883 at the Palazzo Loredan-Vendramin-Calergi, overlooking the Grand Canal.
- The Grand Canal is bordered by about 200 palaces.
- UNESCO's worldwide campaign to save Venice was launched in 1966, after terrible floods in November of that year.
- Venice's *vaporetti* were originally fueled by steam, hence their name (''little steamers'').
- In accordance with laws against opulent decoration, gondolas have been painted black since the 16th century.
- The average age of Venetians is the highest in Europe.
- The population of Venice in the 19th century was nearly 200,000; today it's 85,000.
- The population of Venice doubles during Carnival.

Accademia or the Peggy Guggenheim Collection. Instead, just wander aimlessly among the city's labyrinth of streets and passageways, for this city of canals is its own most extraordinary attraction. For its look, way of life, and history, Venice has no match in Europe. Some of the plainer neighborhoods, off the beaten tourist track, include eastern Castello; the Ghetto area (once the Jewish quarter) in northern Cannaregio; and the island of Giudecca.

IF YOU HAVE TWO DAYS Once you've thoroughly taken in the city's best sight—the city itself—move on to the lesser attractions. First among them has to be the Basilica di San Marco and the Palazzo Ducale, both right on piazza San Marco. While you're on the square, you might as well take in the Museo Correr and ride the elevator to the top of Campanile di San Marco for a terrific view of the entire lagoon.

IF YOU HAVE THREE DAYS Turn over your third day in Venice to its art. Visit the Accademia for a look at the city's Renaissance heritage and the nearby Collezione Peggy Guggenheim for one of Europe's best collections of 20th-century artworks. If you have time after this, take in either the Ca' Rezzonico or the Ca' d'Oro for a look at the interior of one of the *palazzi* that line the Grand Canal.

IF YOU HAVE FIVE DAYS The remainder of the city's sights will carry you through a fourth day. For Day 5, I suggest that you explore the rest of the lagoon: Murano, Burano, Torcello, and the Lido.

TOP ATTRACTIONS

BASILICA DI SAN MARCO, San Marco, piazza San Marco. Tel. 522-5697.

⭐ Venice for centuries was Europe's principal gateway to the East, so it's no surprise that the architectural style for the sumptuously Byzantine Basilica di San Marco, complete with several bulbed domes, was borrowed from Constantinople. Legend has it that in 828, four Venetians—a monk, a priest, and two

---

A NOTE ON ADMISSION TIMES

With the exception of churches, all the sights listed below stop admitting visitors at least 30 minutes, and in some cases as much as 60 minutes, before the listed closing time. Tourists can remain inside until the posted closing time, but entrance is forbidden in the last half hour or more.

enterprising merchants—conspired to smuggle the remains of Saint Mark from Alexandria. Thus Saint Mark replaced the Greek St. Theodore as the patron saint of Venice. Through the subsequent centuries, Venetians vied with one another in donating gifts to this church, the saint's final resting place.

And so it is that the interior of San Marco came to be so exquisitely gilded, every inch covered in colorful mosaics added over some seven centuries. For an up-close look at many of the most remarkable of these, pay the admission to go upstairs to the galleries. Also up here is the Loggia dei Cavalli, the patio above the entrance, from which you can enjoy a closer look at the exterior of the church, and you can mingle with copies of the famous four bronze horses brought to Venice from Constantinople in the 13th century (the originals have been moved inside to the otherwise not terribly interesting museum).

The church's greatest treasure is the magnificent jewel-encrusted golden altarpiece known as the Pala d'Oro. Also worth a visit is the Tesoro (Treasury), to the far right as you enter the basilica, with a collection of the Crusaders' plunder from Constantinople and other gold and relics amassed by the church over the years.

Admission: Basilica, free; galleries, museum, and Loggia dei Cavalli, 2,000 lire ($1.75); Tesoro, 2,000 lire ($1.75); Pala d'Oro, 2,000 lire ($1.75).

Open: Summer, Mon–Sat 9:30am–5:30pm, Sun 2–5:30pm; winter, Mon–Sat 9:30am–4:30pm, Sun 1:30–4:30pm. Last entrance 30 minutes before closing time.

PALAZZO DUCALE AND PONTE DEI SOSPIRI (Bridge of Sighs), San Marco, piazza San Marco. Tel. 522-4951.

⭐ The lovely pink Palazzo Ducale, which was the home and government center of the doges (dukes) who ruled Venice for years, stands between the Basilica di San Marco and the water. Its intricately carved columns, famed 15th-century Porta della Carta (the main entrance, where the doges' proclamations were posted), and splendid inner courtyard with a double row of Renaissance arches give way, via the enormous Scala dei Giganti staircase, to the wood-paneled courts and meeting rooms of the interior, richly decorated by the finest Venetian painters, including Veronese, Titian, Carpaccio, and Tintoretto.

The first room you'll come upon is the Sala Quattro Porte, a spacious room with works by Tintoretto. The Sala del Collegio, the next main room, is richly decorated with both Tintorettos and 11 pieces by Veronese. A right turn from this room leads into one of the most impressive of the spectacular interior rooms, the richly adorned Senato (Senate). After passing again through the Sala Quattro Porte, you'll come to the Stanza del Consiglio dei Dieci (Room of the Council of Ten), which is of particular historical interest, as this is the room where justice was dispensed. Just outside the adjacent chamber, the Sala della Bussola, is the last complete Bocca dei Leoni ("lion's mouth"), a slit in the wall into which secret denunciations of alleged enemies of the state were placed for quick action by the much-feared Council of Ten.

The main sight on the next level down—and indeed in the entire palace—is the Sala del Maggior Consiglio (Great Council Hall). This enormous space is made special by Tintoretto's *Paradiso* above the doge's seat, and Veronese's *Il Trionfo di Venezia* (The Glorification of Venice) in the oval on the ceiling. Tintoretto also did the portraits of the doges that encircle the top of this chamber; note that the picture of the Doge Faliero, who was convicted of treason and beheaded in 1355, has been blacked out. Exit the Great Council Hall via the tiny doorway on the opposite side of Tintoretto's *Paradiso* to find the enclosed Ponte dei Sospiri (Bridge of Sighs), which connects the palace with the grim Prigioni (Prisons). The bridge is named for the sighs of Casanova. But contrary to popular myth, it was not despair over a romance that gave it its name, but rather his sadness at being led to the adjacent jail.

Readers who understand Italian may be interested in the Itinerari Segreti del Palazzo Ducale (Secret Itineraries of the Palazzo Ducale)—guided tours of otherwise restricted quarters of this enormous, impressive palace. Make reservations for the

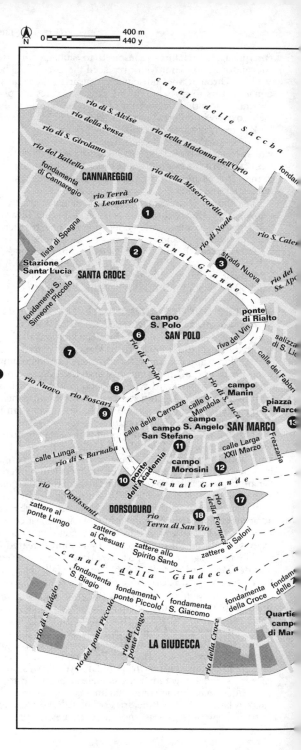

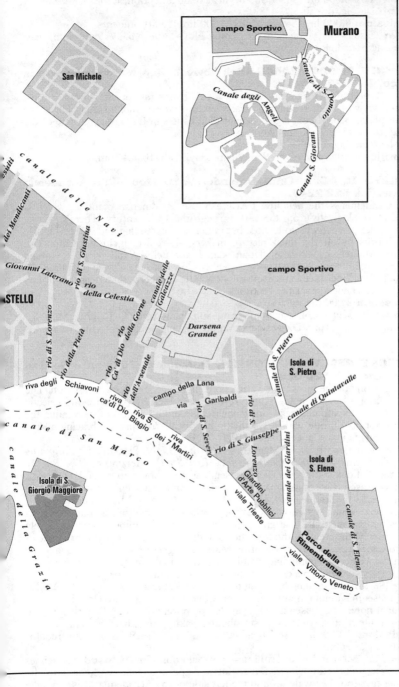

campo Sportivo   **Murano**

Canale di S. Donato

Canale degli Angeli

Canale S. Giovani

Canale S. Giovani

San Michele

esiitti

canale delle Navi

dei Mendicanti

rio di S. Giustina

Giovanni Laterano

rio della Celestia

STELLO

canale delle Galeazze

Darsena Grande

campo Sportivo

rio di S. Lorenzo

rio della Pietà

rio Ca' di Dio della Gorne

rio dell'Arsenale

canale di S. Pietro

Isola di S. Pietro

riva degli Schiavoni

riva ca' di Dio

riva S. Biagio

campo della Lana

via Garibaldi

rio di S. Severo

canale di Quintavalle

canale di San Marco

riva dei 7 Martiri

rio di S. Giuseppe

rio di S. Lorenzo

canale del Giardini

Isola di S. Elena

canale della Grazia

Isola di S. Giorgio Maggiore

Giardini d'Arte Pubblici

viale Trieste

Parco della Rimembranza

canale di S. Elena

viale Vittorio Veneto

tours, which cost 8,000 lire ($6.95) and begin at 10am and noon, at the "Direzione" at the Palazzo Ducale, or call 520-4287.

Admission: 8,000 lire ($6.95) adults, 4,000 lire ($3.50) students.

Open: Easter–Oct, daily 8:30am–7pm; Nov–Easter, daily 9am–4pm. Last entrance one hour before closing.

CAMPANILE DI SAN MARCO (Bell Tower), San Marco, piazza San Marco. Tel. 522-4064.

What's a beautiful Italian city without a bell tower for tourists to climb for a spectacular view of the surrounding area? Well, this *campanile,* located right in the middle of piazza San Marco, is less elegant than others in Italy, but the view of the entire lagoon is really something.

Admission: 3,000 lire ($2.60).

Open: June–Aug, daily 9am–9pm; Sept–May, daily 10am–4pm.

GALLERIA DELL' ACCADEMIA, Dorsoduro, at the foot of the Accademia Bridge. Tel. 522-2247.

The Accademia is the definitive treasure house of Venetian painting, which is exhibited chronologically from the 13th through the 18th century. There's no one hallmark masterpiece in this collection, but rather an outstanding and comprehensive array of works by all the great picture makers of Venice, including Carpaccio, Tintoretto, Mantegna, Veronese, Titian, Canaletto, Bellini, and Tiepolo, among others. Most of all, though, the works open a window onto the Venice of 500 or 600 years ago. Indeed, you'll see in the canvases how little Venice, perhaps least of any city in Europe, has changed over the centuries.

Admission: 8,000 lire ($6.95).

Open: July–Sept, Mon–Sat 9am–7pm, Sun 9am–1pm; Oct–June, Mon–Sat 9am–2pm, Sun 9am–1pm. **Directions:** Vaporetto Line 1, 2, or 4 to the Accademia stop (no. 12).

COLLEZIONE PEGGY GUGGENHEIM, Dorsoduro, 701, on calle San Cristoforo. Tel. 520-6288.

★ This is one of the most visited attractions in Venice, and for good reason. The collection of painting and sculpture was assembled by eccentric and eclectic American expatriate Peggy Guggenheim. She did a fine job of it, creating the only collection in Europe with a systematic historical structure, embracing all the major movements in art since about 1910.

Among the major works are Magritte's *Empire of Light,* Picasso's *La Baignade,* Kandinsky's *Landscape with Church (with Red Spot),* Metzinger's *The Racing Cyclist,* and Pollock's *Alchemy.* The museum is also home to several of Ernst's haunting canvases, Giacometti's unique figures, Brancusi's fluid sculptures, and numerous works by Braque, Dalí, Léger, Mondrian, Chagall, Miró, and others.

The Palazzo Venier dei Leoni, Peggy Guggenheim's home throughout her life in Venice, is a sight in itself. The graves of her canine companions share the lovely interior garden with several of the collection's sculptures, while the patio at the side of the Grand Canal, watched over by Marino Marini's *Angel of the Citadel,* is one of the best spots in Venice to simply linger and watch the canal life.

The posters sold here make excellent inexpensive souvenirs or gifts; posters are 7,000 lire ($6.10), and mailing/carrying tubes are available at 3,000 lire ($2.60). Also note the museum's unique hours—it's open when many others are closed.

One final note: The museum staff is made up entirely of young English-speaking students on internships, so don't be shy about speaking English with them.

Admission: 7,000 lire ($6.10) adults, 4,000 lire ($3.50) students, free for everybody Sat 6–9pm.

Open: Sun–Mon and Wed–Fri 11am–6pm, Sat noon–9pm. **Closed:** Sometimes during a few months in winter. **Directions:** Vaporetto Line 1, 2, or 4 to the Accademia stop (no. 12); walk around the left side of the Accademia Museum, take the first left, and walk straight, following the signs—you'll cross one canal, then walk alongside another, until turning left when necessary.

SCUOLA GRANDE DI SAN ROCCO, San Polo, 3058, on campo San Rocco. Tel. 523-4864.

⭐ This museum adjacent to campo dei Frari and the Frari Church is, simply, a vast monument to the work of Tintoretto—the largest collection anywhere of his work. The collection, the richest of the many schools (*scuole*) that once flourished here, begins upstairs in the Sala dell' Albergo. The most notable of the enormous, powerful canvases is the moving *La Crocifissione* (The Crucifixion). In the center of the gilt ceiling of the Great Hall, also upstairs, is *Il Serpente di Bronzo* (The Bronze Snake). Among the eight huge, sweeping paintings downstairs, each depicting a scene from the New Testament, *La Strage degli Innocenti* (The Slaughter of the Innocents) is the most noteworthy, so full of dramatic urgency and energy that the figures seem almost to tumble out of the frame. As you enter the room, it's on the opposite wall and at the far end of the room.

There's a guide to the paintings inside posted on the wall just *before* the entrance to the museum. There are a few Tiepolos among the paintings, as well as a solitary work by Titian. Note that the works on or near the staircase are not by Tintoretto.

Admission: 6,000 lire ($5.20).

Open: Apr–Oct, daily 9am–1pm and 3:30–6:30pm; Nov–Mar, Mon–Fri 10am–1pm, Sat–Sun 10am–4pm. **Directions:** Vaporetto Line 1 or 4 to the San Tomà stop; from there, walk straight ahead on calle del Traghetto, turn right and then immediately left across campo San Tomà; then walk as straight ahead as you can, on ramo Mandoler, then calle Larga Prima, and finally salizzada San Rocco, which leads into the campo of the same name—look for the crimson sign behind the Frari Church.

MORE ATTRACTIONS

MUSEO CORRER, San Marco, piazza San Marco. Tel. 522-5625 or 520-0552.

This museum, which you enter through an arcade at the opposite end of piazza San Marco from the basilica, is no match for the Accademia, but it does include some interesting scenes of Venetian life among its collection of paintings. And while the Ca' Rezzonico shows what life in a palazzo on the banks of the Grand Canal was like, the fine collection of artifacts on exhibit here gives an interesting feel for the day-to-day aspect of life in this city. There are even a few pieces of armor and old-time weaponry.

Carpaccio's *Le Cortigiane* (The Courtesans), in Room 15 on the upper floor, is the collection's one notable masterpiece. For a lesson in just how little this city has changed in the last several hundred years, head to Room 22 and its anonymous 17th-century bird's-eye view of Venice. Most of the rooms have a sign with a few paragraphs in English explaining the significance of that *sala*'s wares.

Admission: 5,000 lire ($4.35) adults, 2,500 lire ($2.15) students.

Open: Daily 9am–4pm. Last entrance is 30 minutes before closing time; call ahead to check the hours, as they often change as special-event and traveling exhibitions pass through the city.

BASILICA DEI FRARI, San Polo, 3072, on campo dei Frari. Tel. 522-2637.

Just around the corner from the Scuola Grande di San Rocco, this Gothic church houses the melodramatic and grandiose tombs of two famous Venetians, Canova and Titian. It's also home to Titian's *Assumption of the Virgin,* behind the high altar, and his *Virgin of the Pesaro Family* in the left nave. Through a door on the right as you face the altar, in the Sacristy, you'll see Bellini's triptych *Madonna and Child.*

Admission: 1,000 lire (85¢), free on holidays.

Open: Mon–Sat 9am–noon and 2:30–5:30pm, Sun 3–5:30pm; hours can be erratic in winter. **Directions:** Vaporetto Line 1 or 4 to the San Tomà stop; from there, walk straight ahead on calle del Traghetto, turn right and then immediately left across campo San Tomà; then walk as straight ahead as you can, on ramo Mandoler, then calle Larga Prima, and turn right when you reach the beginning of salizzada San Rocco.

CA' REZZONICO (Collezioni del 700 Veneziano), Dorsoduro, on fondamenta Rezzonico. Tel. 522-4543.

This 18th-century canalside palazzo offers an intriguing look into what living in a grand Venetian palazzo was like. Furnished with period paintings, furniture, tapestries, and artifacts, this museum is one of the best windows onto the life of Venice of 200 years ago, as seen through the tastes and fashions of the Rezzonico clan.

Admission: 5,000 lire ($4.35) adults, 2,500 lire ($2.15) students.

Open: Mon–Thurs and Sat 10am–4pm, Sun 9am–12:30pm. **Directions:** Vaporetto Line 1 to Ca' Rezzonico; from the vaporetto dock, walk straight ahead to campo San Barnabà, turn right at the piazza and go over one bridge, then take an immediate right for the museum entrance.

CA' D'ORO (Galleria Giorgio Franchetti), Cannaregio, between 3931 and 3932, on the narrow calle Ca' d'Oro. Tel. 523-8790.

The 15th-century Ca' d'Oro is the best-preserved and most impressive of the patrician *palazzi* that line the Grand Canal. The ornately decorated beamed ceilings provide the setting for sculptures, furniture, tapestries, impressive bronze and iron work from Venetian churches, and an art gallery, whose two most important canvases include Mantegna's gripping, haunting *San Sebastiano* immediately as you enter and Titian's *Venus* on the top floor, as well as lesser paintings by Tintoretto, Carpaccio, van Dyck, Giorgione, and others. For a delightful stop, step out onto the palazzo's balcony, which overlooks the Grand Canal.

Admission: 4,000 lire ($3.50).

Open: Mon–Sat 9am–1:30pm, Sun 9am–1:30pm. **Directions:** Vaporetto to the Ca' d'Oro stop; the entrance is 50 yards away.

PARKS & GARDENS

Alas, there's not much in the way of parks or gardens in this maritime city of stratospheric real-estate values. In fact, the only acceptable set of gardens is at the far eastern end of the Castello sestiere, where the Biennale takes place every two years; look for "Esposizione Internazionale d'Arte Moderna" on your map. Vaporetto Lines 1 and 4 stop at the Giardini station nearby.

SPECIAL-INTEREST SIGHTSEEING

FOR THE BOAT LOVER One of the most interesting sights in Venice is the ✪ **Tramontin Gondola Factory** at Dorsoduro, 1542, on fondamenta Ognissanti. Nearly half the 400 sleek black boats that ply the canals of Venice today have been made by one of the four generations of the Tramontin family who have labored at this craft—and in this location—since 1884.

Though the boats have no modern equipment and are rarely moved at any great speed, putting one together is a fascinatingly exact science. The right side of the gondola is lower, for instance, since the gondolier always stands on the left. If the Tramontini worked continuously, assembling just one of these would take some 40 to 45 working days. As it is, today's father-son team puts just three new boats into service each year, carefully crafting each from the seven types of wood—mahogany, cherry, fir, walnut, oak, elm, and lime—necessary to give the boat its various characteristics. They don't do all the work, but they do put all the pieces together; the painting, the *ferro* (the iron symbol of the city that is affixed to the bow), and the wood carving, for instance, are all farmed out to various local artisans.

To find their place from the Zattere, the seaside boulevard on the Guidecca Canal in Dorsoduro (on vaporetto Line 5), walk up calle Cartelotti (also known as

Corteleto), which begins at no. 1470, and turn left onto fondamenta Ognissanti when this short street ends. (It's near the Ospedale Giustinian, if you're asking directions.) Don't be shy, just walk right in.

They're on the job Monday through Friday from 9am to noon and then from 2 to 6pm; note that they're away on vacation for most of August.

FOR THE ROMANTIC A **gondola ride** is one of the great traditions of Europe, and it really is as romantic as it looks. But only royal Romeos can afford it. The going rate in 1991 was 70,000 lire ($60.85) for up to 50 minutes, for up to five passengers per vessel; there's a 20,000-lira ($17.40) surcharge for travel after dark. And what of the accompanying musicians and serenading *signore* that have made gondoliering so famous? Well, a musical ensemble is so expensive that it must be shared among several boats traveling together. Travel agents are about the only people in town who book musical accompaniment.

There are 12 gondola stations spread throughout Venice, including piazzale Roma (tel. 522-0581), the train station (tel. 71-8543), the Rialto Bridge (tel. 522-4904), and piazza San Marco (tel. 520-0685).

But before your dreams fade away, read on. . . . To tourists, gondolas mean romance, but to Venetians they're a basic form of transportation. There are just three bridges that cross the Grand Canal, and *traghetto* gondolas ferry the general public back and forth at seven other points along the way. You'll find a traghetto gondola station at the end of any street on your map with the name "calle del Traghetto." There's one, for instance, right alongside the San Tomà vaporetto station, and next to Ca' Rezzonico. The ride is short, and you must stand, but it's priced for the local citizenry, not the wealthy tourists. Ask at the tourist office for the going rate (set by the government); when I was last there it was 400 lire (35¢) one way.

7. SAVVY SHOPPING

BEST BUYS & WHERE TO FIND THEM Scores of boutiques fill the narrow pathways between the Rialto Bridge and piazza San Marco. The budget-conscious should know, though, that they'll find better value to the south in Florence and Rome.

Venice is uniquely famous for several local products, including the multicolored, intricately carved **glassware** from the nearby island of Murano and the delicate **lace** of the factories on Burano.

Everywhere—and I mean everywhere—you'll see shops selling hand-painted porcelain **Carnival masks** (*maschere*). These make excellent souvenirs, and since they are priced by size and intricacy of design, they can meet any budget. There's no window-shopping quite like watching the masks being made. There are several ateliers (studio factories) around town where you can watch these artisans in action. My favorite is the **Ca' Macana** at Dorsoduro, 3172, on calle delle Botteghe, around the corner from the Ca' Rezzonico (tel. 520-3229). Other noteworthy studio factories offering these handcrafts and other gifts include **Riflesso di Venezia,** at Dorsoduro, 2856, on calle Lunga San Barnabà; **Metamauco,** at San Marco, 1735, on Frezzeria (tel. 528-5885); and **Cristal Star,** at San Marco, 1017, on calle dei Fabbri (tel. 523-4968).

8. EVENING ENTERTAINMENT

Whether or not you're in Venice during the summer festival season, be sure to visit one of the tourist information centers for current English-language schedules of events. Up-to-date entertainment listings are posted in the offices.

Other sources of information include the music section of the **Venice Depart-**

ment of Culture (tel. 520-9288), for current serious music offerings, and the weekly tourist-oriented magazine *Ospite de Venezia,* available free from most major hotels.

THE PERFORMING ARTS

Several Venetian churches regularly host classical-music concerts by local and international artists. **Chiesa di Vivaldi,** known officially as Chiesa di Santa Maria della Pietà, is a popular venue, as is the Frari Church, and a host of others around the city. Information, schedules, and tickets—which usually average about 15,000 lire ($13.05)—are available from Agenzia Kele & Teo, Ponte dei Baretteri, San Marco (tel. 520-8722), and other ticket agencies around town.

TEATRO LA FENICE, San Marco, 2549, on campo San Fantin. Tel. 521-0161.
   The famous Fenice theater is the city's principal stage for opera, music, theater, and (sometimes) dance. A concert here is not just a show, it's an experience.
   Prices: Tickets, 20,000–80,000 lire ($17.40–$69.55).
   Open: Box office, daily 9:30am–12:30pm and from 30 minutes before curtain time.

TEATRO GOLDONI, San Marco, on calle Goldoni 4650/b, near campo San Luca. Tel. 520-5422.
   Located close to the Rialto Bridge, this theater is known for its winter theater season, which regularly features well-known international productions.
   Prices: Tickets, 15,000–28,000 lire ($13.05–$24.35).
   Open: Box office, Mon–Sat 10am–1pm and 4:30–7pm.

RIDOTTO THEATER, calle Vallaresso, San Marco. Tel. 522-2939.
   Both contemporary and classic plays are staged in Italian at this theater just a stone's throw away from St. Marks Square. Recent productions have included works by Shakespeare, Molière, Alan Ayckbourn, and Neil Simon.
   Prices: Tickets, 14,000–28,000 lire ($12.15–$24.35).
   Open: Box office, Mon–Sat 10:30am–12:30pm and 4:30–6:30pm.

BARS

DEVIL'S FOREST PUB, San Marco, 5185, on calle Stagneri. Tel. 520-0623.
   One of the city's newest watering holes, Devil's Forest is designed to look like a British pub, complete with a carved-wood bar, interior stained glass, and a good selection of draft beers, including Guinness Stout. Dart and backgammon boards are available to patrons, as are simple pasta dishes and sandwiches, which cost 5,000–7,000 lire ($4.35–$6.10).
   Prices: Pint of beer 5,000–6,000 lire ($4.35–$5.20).
   Open: Tues–Fri 8am–midnight, Sat–Sun 8am–1am. **Directions:** You'll find calle Stagneri off campo San Bartolomeo, which is at the foot of the Rialto Bridge on the San Marco side of the Grand Canal. Calle Stagneri begins at the right end of campo San Bartolomeo if you're coming off the bridge; look for the Banca Commerciale Italiana on the corner.

PARADISO PERDUTO, Cannaregio, 2540, on fondamenta della Misericordia. Tel. 72-0581.
   Good food at reasonable prices would be enough to regularly pack this restaurant, but its biggest draw is the live jazz music, performed on a small stage several nights a week. Extremely popular with American and other foreigners living in Venice, this bar

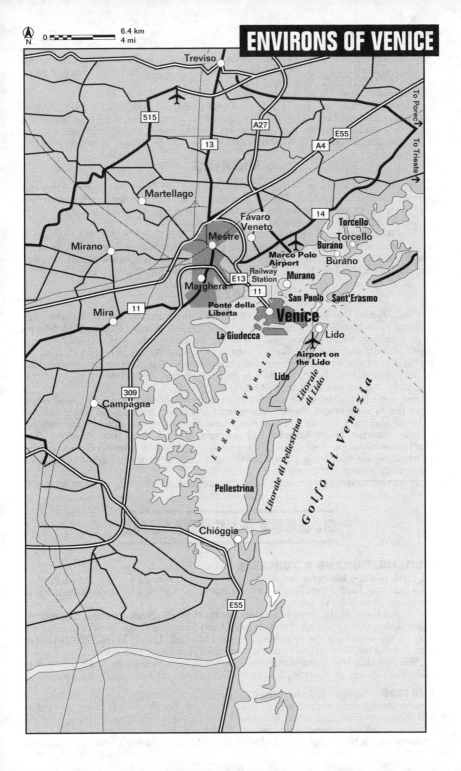

is largely devoid of tourists, primarily because it's hard to find and off the beaten path. If you feel like eating, you'll find a good selection of well-prepared pizzas and pastas for under 9,000 lire ($7.85); arrive early for a table.

Prices: Pint of beer 5,000 lire ($4.35).

Open: Thurs–Tues 7pm–1 or 2am. **Directions:** To find Paradiso from the train station, walk along Lista di Spagna, past campo S. Geremia, and across the first bridge onto rio Terra S. Leonardo. Turn left onto rio Terra Farsetti, cross the bridge, and turn right onto fondamenta della Misericordia. The bar will be straight ahead on your left.

MOVIES

There are five cinemas in Venice and two on the Lido that often screen American, British, and Australian films. Call or check entertainment listings to see whether the movies are *versione originale* (in their original language, with Italian subtitles). On movie posters around town, it is usually abbreviated "v.o."

The **Accademia,** at Dorsoduro, 1019, on calle Corfu (tel. 528-7706), opposite El Souk disco, and the **Olimpia,** campo San Gallo, at San Marco, 1094 (tel. 520-5439), are the two most centrally located theaters, and most likely to show films in English. Tickets cost 8,000 lire ($6.95). The Olimpia is closed Monday.

CAFES

For tourists and locals alike, Venetian nightlife centers around the city's many cafés, themselves tucked away in some of the world's prettiest piazzas. **Piazza San Marco** is far and away the most popular, if also the most expensive and touristed place to linger over cappuccinos. The Caffè Florian, at San Marco, 56a-59a, on the side of the piazza nearest the water, is the most famous (closed Wednesday); on the opposite side of the square at San Marco, 133-134, is the Café Lavena. At both spots, a cappuccino at a table will set you back at least 6,000 lire ($5.20).

For just plain relaxing, at a lower price and level of pretension, I'm fond of the three places on **campo Santa Margherita,** a huge open campo about halfway between the train station and Ca' Rezzonico. Other popular squares for café life include **campo Sant'Angelo** and **campo Santo Stefano. Campo San Bartolomeo,** at the foot of the Rialto Bridge, and nearby **campo San Luca** are the most popular gathering spots in town; you'll see Venetians of all ages milling about engaged in animated conversation.

Note that most cafés are open Monday through Saturday from 8pm to midnight.

9. EASY EXCURSIONS

MURANO, BURANO & TORCELLO Venice shares its lagoon with three other principal islands. **Murano** is famous throughout the world for the products of its glass factories. Lace is the claim to fame of **Burano.** And nearby **Torcello** is home to the oldest church in Venice.

Guided tours of the three islands are operated by the **Serenissima Company;** departures are from a dock between piazza San Marco and the Hotel Danieli, right next to the wharf for the *motonave* to the Lido (tel. 522-8538 or 522-4281). The four-hour, 25,000-lira ($21.75) tours leave daily at 9:30am and 2:30pm.

You can also visit these islands on your own. Vaporetto Lines 5, 12, 13, and 18 make the journey to Murano, and Line 12 continues on to Burano and Torcello.

THE LIDO Venice's Lido **beaches** are more scene than substance. For bathing and sunworshiping, there are much nicer beaches in Italy. But the parade of wealthy Italian and foreign tourists (and a few Venetians) who frequent this *litorale* throughout the summer is an interesting sight indeed. There are two beach areas at the Lido: **Bucintoro,** at the opposite end of viale Santa Maria Elisabetta from the vaporetto station; and **San Niccolò,** a mile away, and reached by bus B. You'll have to pay 10,000 lire ($8.70) per person (standard procedure throughout Italy) unless you patronize the public beach at the end of bus Line B.

Vaporetto Lines 1, 2, and 4 cross the lagoon to the Lido from the San Zaccaria–Danieli stop near San Marco; Lines 6 and 14 also travel to the Lido. From the Lido–Santa Maria Elisabetta vaporetto stop, walk straight ahead along viale Santa Maria Elisabetta to reach the beach (or take bus A). Bus B goes to San Niccolò.

VIENNA

Being in Vienna sometimes makes me wish I had a time machine, not that it would be easy to decide which century to zero in on. Perhaps the last half of the 18th century would be a good choice, when Vienna resounded with the music of Haydn, Mozart, and Beethoven, and Empress Maria Theresa ruled from her glittering Schönbrunn Palace. Or maybe I would choose the first decades of the 20th century, when Sigmund Freud was developing his methods of psychoanalysis, Gustav Klimt was covering canvases with his Jugendstil figures, and Vienna was whirling to the waltzes of Strauss.

But I'll settle gladly for the Vienna of today. Music is still the soul of Vienna, the manifestation of its spirit—from jazz concerts and punk rock to chamber music and opera. The Habsburgs, rulers of Austria for six centuries, left behind a rich architectural legacy of magnificent buildings, from baroque and rococo palaces to Gothic cathedrals and beautifully landscaped gardens.

Vienna, however, is not resting on past laurels. After the Austro-Hungarian Empire was carved up into several countries after the end of World War I, Vienna was a capital without an empire, and when the Iron Curtain fell after World War II, Vienna was suddenly on the edge of western Europe, seemingly far from the other capitals. The recent opening up of eastern Europe, however, has shifted the emphasis farther east, and Vienna is again in the center. A springboard for travel to and from Budapest, Prague, and beyond, Vienna has reblossomed into the international city it once was. Vienna is "in," with chic boutiques, good restaurants, and a burgeoning nightlife.

1. FROM A BUDGET TRAVELER'S POINT OF VIEW

VIENNA BUDGET BESTS

The most wonderful thing you can do for yourself is to go to a performance at the Staatsoper (State Opera). Standing-room tickets start at only $1.35—for which you are treated to extravaganzas held on one of Vienna's most renowned stages. Even sit-down tickets are a bargain, starting at 90 S ($8.20).

WHAT THINGS COST IN VIENNA · U.S. $

	U.S. $
Taxi from the airport to the city center	30.00
U-Bahn from Stephansdom to Schönbrunn	1.80
Local telephone call (1 min.)	.09
Double room at the Hotel Sacher (deluxe)	145.45
Double room at Pension Pertschy (moderate)	85.45
Double room at Pension Wild (budget)	42.70
Lunch for one, without wine, at Gasthaus Witwe Bolte (moderate)	12.00
Lunch for one, without wine, at Naschmarkt (budget)	5.00
Dinner for one, without wine, at Hauswirth (deluxe)	25.00
Dinner for one, without wine, at Crêperie-Brasserie Spittelberg (moderate)	12.00
Dinner for one, without wine, at Schnitzelwirt (budget)	6.00
Half liter of beer	3.25
Glass of wine (one-eighth liter)	2.00
Coca-Cola (in a restaurant)	1.50
Cup of coffee (in a restaurant)	2.00
Roll of ASA 100 color film, 36 exposures	6.25
Admission to Kunsthistorisches Museum	4.10
Movie ticket (depends on where you sit)	6.35–8.20
Theater ticket (standing room at Staatsoper)	1.35

The rest of Vienna is affordable too. Try at least one meal at a *Beisl,* a typical blue-collar pub, where you can get hearty, home-cooked meals for as little as 70 S ($6.35). But don't forget Vienna's wonderful wine cellars, where you can soak in the lively atmosphere for the price of a glass of wine.

And if you want to save money, eat at a *Würstelstand,* a sidewalk food stand selling various kinds of Wurst and a roll for 22–32 S ($2–$2.90). They're located throughout the city and are as much a part of the Viennese scene as the opera house.

SPECIAL DISCOUNT OPPORTUNITIES

FOR STUDENTS If you're a student with bonafide identification, you are entitled to savings of 50% or more off the admission price of museums in Vienna. You can also obtain theater tickets at the Staatsoper, Burgtheater, or Akademietheater for 50 S ($4.55), but only if you can show current student status with a valid university identification card. To be on the safe side, be sure to bring both your university card and an **International Student Identity Card (ISIC).**

If you've arrived in Vienna without an ISIC, you can obtain one at **Ökista,** where you can also purchase cheap airline flights and train tickets (for youths under 26 years). There are three locations: Türkenstrasse 4 (tel. 40 14 80), Karlsgasse 3 (tel. 65 01 28), and Reichsratstrasse 13 (tel. 402 15 61). All three are open Monday through Friday from 9:30am to 5:30pm.

FOR EVERYONE All municipal museums (including the residences of Mozart, Beethoven, Haydn, and Strauss, the Vienna Historical Museum, and the Clock Museum) are free on Friday morning.

☑ WHAT'S SPECIAL ABOUT VIENNA

Music

- ☐ The Staatsoper (State Opera), one of Europe's best—and it offers 500 standing-room tickets starting at only $1.35.
- ☐ Beethoven, Haydn, Mozart, Schubert, and Johann Strauss, whose homes are open to the public.
- ☐ Music festivals galore, including the Operetta Festival, the Haydn Festival, the Schubert Festival, and the Summer of Music.

Museums

- ☐ The Treasury, with its jewels and riches of the Habsburg family.
- ☐ The Museum of Fine Arts, with its paintings by the old masters.
- ☐ Museums of the 19th and 20th centuries, including the gallery at Belvedere and the Museum of Modern Art.
- ☐ Special-interest museums, from the Sigmund Freud Haus to the Clock Museum and the Doll and Toy Museum.

Coffeehouses

- ☐ A wide range of coffeehouses, from the elegant Demel to the egalitarian-minded Café Hawelka.
- ☐ At least 20 different varieties of coffee, from *Mokka* to *Melange*.
- ☐ Tortes, cakes, and desserts!

Architecture

- ☐ Schönbrunn, one of Europe's most impressive baroque palaces.
- ☐ Imposing buildings of the 19th century, including the Museum of Fine Arts and Museum of Natural History, the State Opera House, and the Parliament.
- ☐ Works by innovative architects of the 20th century, including Adolf Loos and Otto Wagner, and, more recently, several whimsical buildings by Hundertwasser.

If you're an avid museum fan, you might want to purchase a **museum pass** good for all municipal and national museums at a price of 150 S ($13.65). It contains 14 coupons worth 15 S ($1.35) each, a savings of 28%. If you're interested in seeing the famous Spanish Riding School, consider going to one of the morning training sessions, when tickets cost 70 S ($6.35). If you're willing to stand, you can see the Vienna Boys' Choir free of charge (they perform at Sunday mass). And if you plan on traveling a lot by public transportation, be sure to buy a "strip ticket," described in more detail below.

2. PRETRIP PREPARATIONS

DOCUMENTS   Citizens of the United States, Great Britain, Canada, Australia, and New Zealand need only a valid passport for stays up to 90 days.

WHAT TO PACK   Warm clothing and shoes or boots with nonskid soles are essential in winter. In spring and fall, be sure to bring a warm sweater and both a raincoat and an umbrella. In summer you'll be comfortable with light cotton clothing, but you'll need a light jacket for cool evenings. Bring at least one dressy outfit—the Viennese dress up for the opera.

WHEN TO GO   Vienna is at the same latitude as Seattle and the northern tip of Maine, and its climate is moderate and generally agreeable. May, June, and September are usually the nicest months; snow can cover the ground from December through February.

Vienna's Average Daytime Temperature & Days of Rain

	Jan	Feb	Mar	Apr	May	June	July	Aug	Sept	Oct	Nov	Dec
Temp. (°F)	30	32	38	50	58	64	68	70	60	50	41	33
Days of Rain	3	3	3	4	5	5	4	5	5	4	4	3

Special Events If your sole reason for coming to Vienna is the theater, avoid July and August like the plague—the Staatsoper, Volksoper, Burgtheater, and Akademietheater are all closed during these months. In addition, in July and August there are no performances of either the Spanish Riding School or the Vienna Boys' Choir. However, there are many musical events that are part of Vienna's Summer of Music festival.

It's not surprising that many of Vienna's festivals and events revolve around music. The **Operetta Festival** in early February stages Volksoper productions. In March there's a **Haydn Festival,** while the **Wiener Festwochen (Vienna Festival)** in May and June features music, theater, dance, and art.

July and August feature Vienna's **Summer of Music** with its many concerts at Schönbrunn Palace, at memorial sites (such as the Haydn House) and at the Rathaus (City Hall). The annual **Schubert Festival** is in November; December is the month of the outdoor **Christmas bazaar,** with stalls selling handcrafted items and decorations in front of the Rathaus, on Spittelberg, and on Freyung.

BACKGROUND READING For a better appreciation of Vienna and its history, read Charles Osborne's *Schubert and His Vienna* (Knopf, 1985) or Hilde Spiel's *Vienna's Golden Autumn, 1866–1938* (Weidenfeld, 1987). A vivid portrayal of Maria Theresa and her times is presented by Edward Crankshaw in *Maria Theresa* (Atheneum, 1969). For a personal account of Vienna's darker pages of history, a gripping story of the fate of a Jewish family is given by George Clare in his *Last Waltz in Vienna: The Rise and Destruction of a Family, 1842–1942* (Holt & Co., 1981).

3. ORIENTATION & GETTING AROUND

ARRIVING IN VIENNA

FROM THE AIRPORT Vienna's airport is called **Schwechat** (tel. 711 10-2231), located about 11 miles southeast of the city center. A shuttle bus departs about every 20 or 30 minutes for the City Air Terminal, located near the center of town next to the Hilton. From the City Air Terminal you can catch the U-Bahn (subway) at the Landstrasse station.

Less frequent are the shuttle buses to the Südbahnhof and Westbahnhof, Vienna's two train stations, with departures every hour. In any case, cost of the shuttle bus to the City Air Terminal or the train stations is 60 S ($5.45) one way. Taxis charge about $30 for the same trip.

FROM THE TRAIN STATION Vienna has two main train stations. If you're arriving from Germany, Switzerland, France, Salzburg, or other points west or north, in most cases you'll arrive at the **Westbahnhof** (West Station). Tram no. 58 travels from the station toward the city center. By the end of 1993 or early 1994, the completion of a new subway line (the U-3), will connect the Westbahnhof with Stephansplatz in the city center.

If you're arriving from the south or east, say, from Italy, Hungary, Yugoslavia, or Greece, you'll most likely arrive at the **Südbahnhof** (South Station). Take Tram D from in front of the station if you're heading for the Ring and the city center. Tram no. 18 travels between the two train stations.

Since the opening of eastern Europe, **Franz-Josefs-Bahnhof** has become important for train travel to and from Prague. Take Tram D for the city Ring and the city center; Tram no. 5 travels to the Westbahnhof. The U-4 Friedensbrücke stop is about a five-minute walk from the station.

For information on train schedules, call 1717.

INFORMATION

For information on Vienna, including the current showings and times for the opera, theater, Spanish Riding School, and the Vienna Boys' Choir, drop by the **Vienna Tourist Board,** Kärntner Strasse 38 (tel. 211 14-0, 513 88 92, or 43 89 89), on the corner of Philharmoniker Strasse and Kärntner Strasse, near the Sacher Hotel. It's open daily from 9am to 7pm. Be sure to pick up a free copy of the **Wien Monatsprogramm,** issued every month and available at the Tourist Board—it tells what's going on in Vienna's concert halls, theaters, and opera houses.

If you're looking for detailed information, be sure to purchase a 30-S ($2.70) English-language booklet called **Vienna from A to Z,** also available at the Tourist Board. Published by the city government, its alphabetical listings are keyed to the unique, numbered plaques you'll find affixed to the front of every building of historical interest in Vienna. You'll spot these plaques everywhere: They are heralded by little red-and-white flags in summer. By referring to the number on the plaque with the corresponding number in *Vienna from A to Z,* you'll have the English translations.

The tourist office will also book hotel rooms for a 35-S ($3.20) fee. Next door to the tourist office is the travel agency **Intropa** (tel. 51514), which sells theater tickets, books sightseeing tours, and exchanges money. In summer it's open daily from 9am to 5:30pm; winter hours are Monday through Friday from 9am to 5:30pm and on Saturday from 9am to noon.

If you're arriving at Vienna International Airport, there's a tourist office in the Arrivals Hall, open daily from 8:30am to 11pm (to 10pm in winter). A tourist office at the Westbahnhof is open daily from 7am to 8:40pm, (to 11pm in summer), while another one at the Südbahnhof is open daily from 6:30am to 10pm (to 9pm in winter). Both will book hotel rooms.

CITY LAYOUT

Vienna's old city center is delightfully compact, filled with tiny cobblestone streets leading to majestic squares. In the center is **Stephansplatz** with Vienna's most familiar landmark, St. Stephen's Cathedral (Stephansdom). From here it's a short walk to the Hofburg (the official residence of the Habsburgs), the Kunsthistorisches Museum (Art History Museum), and the Staatsoper. **Kärntner Strasse,** much of it pedestrian, is Vienna's main shopping street and leads from Stephansplatz past the Staatsoper to **Karlsplatz.**

Circling the Old City (Altstadt) is "the Ring," as Vienna's **Ringstrasse** is commonly called. This impressive boulevard is 2½ miles long and 187 feet wide, built in the mid-1800s along what used to be the city's fortifications (hence its shape as a circle around the Old City). Everything inside the Ring is known as the First *Bezirk* (meaning precinct, denoted by 1010 in addresses). The rest of Vienna is also divided into various precincts.

Trams run along the tree-shaded Ring, which is divided into various sections, known as Opernring (home of the Staatsoper), Kärntner-Ring, Burgring (where you'll find the Hofburg and the Kunsthistorisches Museum), and Schubert Ring. **Schönbrunn,** Vienna's top sight, is located a few miles southwest of the city center, easily reached by U-Bahn from Karlsplatz.

GETTING AROUND

Vienna's transit network consists of five **U-Bahn (subway) lines, trams, buses,** and several **rapid transit** and **commuter trains.** Unfortunately, a good free map depicting tram and bus lines, which are what most tourists need to get around, does not exist. Luckily, most of Vienna's attractions are within walking distance of one another.

If you think you'll be using Vienna's public transportation system extensively, you may wish to purchase a large map with the U-Bahn, bus, and tram lines outlined throughout for 15 S ($1.35) from the **Informationsdienst der Wiener Verkehrs-betriebe,** located in the underground Opernpassage at Karlsplatz and at Stephansplatz. It's open Monday through Friday from 7am to 6pm and on Saturday and Sunday from 8:30am to 4pm. The staff can answer questions, such as which bus to take to reach your destination. You can also call for information by dialing 587 31 86.

Fares   A single ticket (good for the tram, bus, S-Bahn, or the U-Bahn) costs 20 S ($1.80), which permits as many transfers as you need to reach your destination as long as you keep moving in the same direction. It can be purchased from machines found in U-Bahn stations, ticket booths, or from conductors. I suggest, however, that instead of single tickets you purchase the **Vierfahrtenstreifenkarte,** a strip ticket that allows four rides for 60 S ($5.45). These must be purchased in advance, either from ticket booths at the Karlsplatz or Stephansplatz U-Bahn station or from automatic machines at all U-Bahn and train stations (look for the VOR FAHRKARTEN sign). In addition, there's also a **24-hour ticket** available for 45 S ($4.10), a **72-hour ticket** for 115 S ($10.45), or an **eight-day pass** for 235 S ($21.35). You must validate all tickets yourself by inserting them into machines at the entryway of S-Bahn and U-Bahn platforms or on buses and trams. Children up to the age of 6 can travel for free, while those from 7 to 15 travel for half the fare.

BY TAXI   If you find you need a taxi, you can call one (tel. 31300, 1712, 40100, 60160, or 91 011). The base price is 22 S ($2) plus an additional 10 S (90¢) for taxis summoned by phone. Each additional kilometer is 10 S (90¢). Luggage is 10 S (90¢) extra.

BY U-BAHN [SUBWAY]   The most important U-Bahn line for visitors is U-4, which stops at Karlsplatz before continuing to Kettenbrückengasse (site of Vienna's outdoor market and weekend flea market) and Schönbrunn. U-2 travels around part of the Ring, while U-1 has a station at Stephansplatz. U-4, U-2, and U-1 all converge at Karlsplatz. U-3, due to be completed by 1994, will connect the Westbahnhof with Stephansplatz.

BY TRAM   Although the U-Bahn and buses are gradually taking over most of the tram routes, trams are still heavily used for traveling around the Ring (tram nos. 1 and 2) and for transportation between the Südbahnhof and the Ring (tram D) and the Westbahnhof and the Burgring (tram no. 58). Tram no. 18 travels between the Westbahnhof and the Südbahnhof.

BY BUS   Buses crisscross the entire city. Small buses go through the inner city Monday through Saturday and there are eight buses in operation throughout the night from Schwedenplatz to the suburbs (including Grinzing) on weekend nights and nights before public holidays. Information on both buses and trams can be obtained at the **Wiener Verkehrsbetriebe Informationsdienst** (information office of the Vienna transport service), located in the underground passageway linking the Oper and Karlsplatz and at Stephansplatz.

ON FOOT   You can do almost all your sightseeing in Vienna on foot. You can walk from one end of the Old City to the other in about 10 minutes. Even the walk from the Ring to either train station is only a half hour or so.

BY BICYCLE   There are more than 200 miles of marked bike paths in Vienna. During July and August, bikes may be taken along for half fare in specially marked cars of the U-Bahn Monday through Friday from 9am to 3pm and from 6:30pm to the end of the day, and on Saturday and Sunday after 9am.

The most popular places for bike rentals and tours are at the amusement center of Prater and along the banks of the Donaukanal (Danube Canal), with several bike-rental agencies at both these spots. Most centrally located is probably the bike shop **Radverleih Salztorbrücke** at Salztorbrücke, north of Stephansplatz on the Donaukanal (tel. 460 60 72 or 63 82 34). It's open April to mid-October, Monday through Friday from 9am to dusk and on Saturday and Sunday from 9am to 7pm. Other bike shops are located at the Praterstern station and Am Kaisermühlendamm station. Costs are generally 40 S ($3.65) for one hour or 200 S ($18.20) for the whole day.

During the summer, bikes are also available for rent at the Westbahnhof. If you have a Eurailpass or a valid train ticket for that day, cost of a day's rental is 40 S ($3.65). Otherwise, bikes rent for 90 S ($8.20) for one day.

For more information on biking, contact the Vienna Tourist Board, where you can also pick up a pamphlet called "See Vienna by Bike," complete with recommended routes.

CAR RENTAL   Car-rental agencies include **Avis,** Opernring 1 (tel. 587 62 41); **Budget Rent-a-Car,** Hilton Air Terminal (tel. 75 65 65); and **Hertz,** Kärntner Ring 17 (tel. 512 86 77). Prices vary according to day of the week and number of rental days, but expect to pay 792–936 S ($72–$85) a day for an Opel Corsa, including unlimited mileage and a 20% tax.

FAST FACTS   VIENNA

Babysitters   Call the Babysitting Zentrale (tel. 49123) Monday through Friday from 8am to 2pm.

Banks   The main banks of Vienna are open Monday through Friday from 8am to 12:30pm and 1:30 to 3pm (to 5:30pm on Thursday). Note that in Austria, you cannot obtain cash from credit cards. If you need to exchange money outside bank hours, you can do so at Intropa, located beside the Tourist Board office at the corner of Philharmoniker Strasse and Kärntner Strasse, open daily in summer from 9am to 5:30pm and in winter Monday through Friday from 9am to 5:30pm and on Saturday from 9am to noon. In addition, there's an automatic money-exchange machine at the Zentralsparkasse and Kommerzialbank, conveniently located in the heart of the city at Stephansplatz 2 (tel. 512 13 83). Open 24 hours a day, it will change $20 and $50 bills into Austrian currency. Finally, there are also money-exchange counters at the Westbahnhof and Südbahnhof train stations, open daily from 7am to 10pm.

An **American Express** office is located at Kärntner Strasse 21-23 (tel. 51 540), open Monday through Friday from 9am to 5:30pm and on Saturday from 9am to noon.

Business Hours   Shop hours are generally Monday through Friday from 9am to 6pm and on Saturday from 9am to noon or 1pm. Shops outside the city center may close for lunch from noon to 2 or 3pm. On the first Saturday of the month (called *langer Samstag*), shops are open longer, to 5pm.

Consulates   If you have questions or problems regarding American passports or visas, contact the **U.S. Consulate** at Gartenbaupromenade 2 (tel. 31 55 11), in the Marriott Hotel, open Monday through Friday from 8:30am to noon and 1 to 4:30pm. The **Australian Consulate** is at Mattiellistrasse 2-4 (tel. 512 85 80), open Monday through Friday from 9am to 1pm for visa applications and also from 2 to 5pm for other matters such as lost passports. The **Canadian Consulate,** at Dr.-Karl-Lueger-Ring 10 (tel. 533 36 91), is open Monday through Friday 8:30am to 12:30pm and 1:30 to 3:30pm. The **British Consulate,** Jauresgasse 10 (tel. 713 15 75), is open Monday through Friday from 9:15 to noon and (for British passport holders) 2 to 4pm.

Currency   The Austrian currency is the Schilling, written ASch, ÖS, or simply S (as I have done). A Schilling is made up of 100 Groschen (which are seldom used). Coins come in 2, 5, 10, and 50 Groschen, and 1, 5, 10, and 20 Schilling. Banknotes appear as 20, 50, 100, 500, 1,000, and 5,000 Schilling.

Dentists For a list of English-speaking dentists in Vienna, contact one of the consulates above. If you need dental assistance on a weekend or during the night, telephone 512 20 78 for a recorded message of dentists with weekend or night emergency service.

Doctors The consulates above have lists of English-speaking doctors in Vienna, or call the Doctors' Association (tel. 1771) for a referral. If you need an emergency doctor during the night (daily from 7pm to 7am), call 141.

Emergencies Dial 122 for the fire department, 133 for the police, 144 for an ambulance, and 1550 to find out which pharmacy has night hours. Refer above for doctors and dentists.

Eyeglasses For optical needs, a convenient shop in the heart of the city called Trude Kleemann Optik, Kärntner Strasse 37 (tel. 512 84 25), is open Monday through Friday from 9am to 6pm and on Saturday from 9:30am to 12:30pm.

Holidays Vienna celebrates New Year's Day (Jan 1), Epiphany (Jan 6), Easter Monday, Labor Day (May 1), Ascension Day, Whit Monday, Corpus Christi, Assumption (Aug 15), National Holiday (Oct 26), All Saints Day (Nov 1), Feast of the Immaculate Conception (Dec 8), and Christmas (Dec 25–26).

Hospitals There's a general hospital, the Allgemeine Krankenhaus, at the corner of Alser Strasse and Spitalgasse (tel. 48000). Otherwise, free first-aid treatment is available 24 hours a day at the Krankenhaus der Barmherzigen Brüder, Grosse Mohren-Gasse 9 (tel. 21 12 10). A hospital to serve primarily needy people, it also dispenses medications free of charge.

Information See the "Information" section of "Orientation and Getting Around," above, for addresses of the Vienna Tourist Board.

Laundry Ask the proprietor of your hotel for directions to the nearest self-service laundry. Otherwise, a conveniently located coin laundry is the Münzwäscherei Margaretenstrasse, Margaretenstrasse 52 (tel. 587 04 73), open Monday through Friday from 7am to 6pm and on Saturday from 8am to noon. It costs about 85 S ($7.70) to wash 6 kilos (13¼ lb.) of laundry (not including detergent), plus 16 S ($1.45) for drying.

Lost and Found Vienna's main lost-property office is at Wasagasse 22 (tel. 313 44-92 11), open Monday through Friday from 8am to noon. All found items end up here after a few days. First, however, they're turned in to the police. If you know approximately where you lost something, inquire first at the nearest police station.

Mail Most post offices in Vienna are open Monday through Friday from 8am to noon and 2 to 6pm. The main post office (Hauptpostamt), located in the heart of the city inside the Ring at Barbaragasse 2 (tel. 512 78 810), on the corner of Postgasse, is open 24 hours daily for long-distance telephone calls, telegrams, and stamps. You can have your mail sent here Post Restante. Post offices at both the Westbahnhof and the Südbahnhof are also open 24 hours a day. Postcards to North America cost 8.50 S (75¢), while airmail letters cost 10 S (90¢), plus 1.50 S (14¢) for each five grams.

Newspapers *USA Today,* the *Wall Street Journal,* and the *International Herald Tribune* are available at most international kiosk newspaper stands inside the Ring and at the larger hotels.

Photographic Needs Foto Herlango, located in the heart of the Old City just off Stephansplatz at Graben 11 (tel. 512 33 61), is a convenient place for film. More shops are on Kärntner Strasse and throughout the city. Most are open Monday through Friday from 9am to 6pm and on Saturday from 9am to noon (to 5pm the first Saturday of the month).

Police The emergency number for the police is 133.

Radio/TV Tune in to 103.8 FM for "The Blue Danube," a radio program in English about Vienna and things of interest to tourists, including news and music. Likewise, every Saturday at noon on FS1, there's a television program called "Hello Austria" that also covers sightseeing and gives information about Austria.

THE SCHILLING & THE DOLLAR

At this writing $1 = approximately 11 S (or 1 S = 9¢), and this was the rate of exchange used to calculate the dollar values given in this chapter (rounded to the nearest nickel). This rate fluctuates from time to time and may not be the same when you travel to Austria. Therefore the following table should be used only as a guide:

S	U.S.	S	U.S.
1	.09	100	9.09
2	.18	150	13.63
3	.27	200	18.18
4	.36	250	22.72
5	.45	300	27.27
6	.54	350	31.82
7	.64	400	36.36
8	.73	450	40.90
9	.82	500	45.45
10	.91	600	54.54
15	1.36	700	63.63
20	1.81	800	72.72
25	2.27	900	81.81
50	4.54	1,000	90.90

Shoe Repair There are small neighborhood shoe-repair shops everywhere in the city, but one chain to look out for is Mister Minit. You'll find a Mister Minit in department stores, including Gerngross at Mariahilfer Strasse 38-48 (tel. 93 25 25).

Tax Government tax and service charge is already included in restaurant and hotel bills. If you have purchased goods for more than 1,000 S ($90.90), you're entitled to a refund of part of the Value-Added Tax (up to 32%). See "Savvy Shopping," below, for more information.

Taxis See "Orientation and Getting Around," above, for details concerning cost of a taxi and telephone numbers to call one.

Telephone It costs 1 S (9¢) to make a one-minute **local telephone call** (insert several 1-Schilling coins to ensure against being cut off—unused coins will be returned at the end of the call). If you come across a telephone number with a dash at the end (such as 51553-0), it indicates an extension. Treat it as you would any number and simply dial the whole number. Note that all telephone numbers in Vienna are gradually being changed to seven digits (a process that will take years). If you come across a number in this book that has been changed, call information (tel. 1611) to inquire about the new number.

Because hotels add a surcharge on calls made from their rooms, you're best off going to a post office to make **long-distance telephone calls.** It costs 54 S ($4.90) to make a three-minute call to the United States. An alternative is to purchase a **telephone card,** available at any post office in values of 50 S ($4.55) or 100 S ($9.10), which can be used in special telephones found virtually everywhere (in fact, sometimes it's difficult to find a telephone that will accept coins, so popular are telephone cards).

The telephone **area/city code** for Vienna is 01 if you're calling from within Austria; 1 if you're calling from outside Austria.

Tipping A 15% service charge is already included in restaurant bills, but it's customary to round off to the nearest 10 S (90¢) on bills under 100 S ($9.10). For more expensive meals, add 10%. The same rule applies to taxi drivers. Porters receive 10–20 S (90¢–$1.80) per bag.

4. BUDGET ACCOMMODATIONS

The best budget accommodations are in the vicinity of the Westbahnhof train station and near the university along Alser Strasse. If you want to save money, take a room without private bath, but note that some establishments charge extra for showers in communal washrooms. Keep in mind that some rates include breakfast while others do not—a room-only charge may well end up being more expensive than rates that include free showers and breakfast. The most expensive accommodations are those in the old city center.

Recommendations below include rooms in private homes, in pensions (which are usually cheaper than hotels and sometimes cheaper than private homes), and in hotels. I've also listed a few university dormitories that take in tourists and boarders during the summer months. Note that floors are numbered according to the British system, starting with the ground floor and then going up to the first floor (the American second floor).

Incidentally, Vienna's telephone system is being computerized, which means that all households and businesses are gradually receiving new telephone numbers. Although every effort was made to be as up-to-date as possible, some telephone numbers below may no longer be current when you arrive. Call the operator (tel. 1611) if you have any problems. And remember that if the suggested accommodations are full, the **Vienna Tourist Board** will book a room for a fee of 35 S ($3.20), including rooms in private homes.

DOUBLES FOR LESS THAN 570 S [$51.80]
OFF MARIAHILFER STRASSE

HOTEL KUGEL, Siebensterngasse 43/Neubaugasse 46, 1070 Vienna. Tel. 01/93 33 55 or 93 13 30. Fax 01/93 16 78. 38 rms (17 with shower and toilet, 17 with shower only). **Tram:** 49 from the Westbahnhof to Neubaugasse/ Siebensterngasse; or D from Franz-Josefs-Bahnhof to Westbahnstrasse/ Kaiserstrasse. **Bus:** 13A from the Südbahnhof to Kirchengasse.

$ **Rates** (including breakfast and showers): 375 S ($34.10) single without shower or toilet, 430 S ($39.10) single with shower only, 530 S ($48.20) single with shower and toilet; 510 S ($46.35) double without shower or toilet, 680 S ($61.80) double with shower only, 860 S ($78.20) double with shower and toilet. No credit cards.
Located on the corner of Neubaugasse and Siebensterngasse, this century-old hotel has been owned by the same family from the beginning; it's now in its third generation. It shows its age, with small rooms and outdated wallpaper, but it has a good location and is adequate for the price. Showers were added as afterthoughts as free-standing cabinets. Note that street noise tends to be loud.

PENSION LINDENHOF, Lindengasse 4, 1070 Vienna. Tel. 01/93 04 98. 19 rms (10 with shower and toilet). **Tram:** 52 or 58 from the Westbahnhof to Stiftgasse; or tram D from Franz-Josefs-Bahnhof to Burgring, then 52 or 58 to Stiftgasse. **Bus:** 13 A from the Südbahnhof to Kirchengasse.

$ **Rates** (including breakfast): 340 S ($30.90) single without shower or toilet, 440 S

($40) single with shower and toilet; 560 S ($50.90) double without shower or toilet, 780 S ($70.90) double with shower and toilet; 840 S ($76.35) triple without shower or toilet, 1,170 S ($106.35) triple with shower and toilet. Showers 20 S ($1.80) extra. No credit cards.

Located behind the large Herzmansky department store, Pension Lindenhof is owned by George Gebrael, an Armenian with Austrian citizenship who is married to a Bulgarian. Mr. Gebrael in fact speaks seven languages, English among them, and both his daughter and son go to an international school taught in English. The long corridor of the pension is filled with massive plants, and a few of the rooms even have balconies.

NEAR SCHOTTEN RING & THE UNIVERSITY

PENSION FALSTAFF, Müllnergasse 5, 1090 Vienna. Tel. 01/34 91 27 or 34 91 86. Fax 01/349 18 64. 17 rms (2 with shower and toilet, 7 with shower only). TEL **Tram:** D from the Südbahnhof or Franz-Josefs-Bahnhof to Schlichtgasse; or 52 or 58 from the Westbahnhof to Burgring, then D from Burgring to Schlichtgasse.

$ Rates (including continental breakfast): 310 S ($28.20) single without shower or toilet, 440 S ($40) single with shower only; 530 S ($48.20) double without shower or toilet, 650 S ($59.10) double with shower only, 750 S ($68.20) double with shower and toilet. Showers 30 S ($2.70) extra. No credit cards.

This pension is one of the best finds in this price category, with simple but clean rooms—some of them enormous. There's a 50% discount for stays of a month or longer in the winter. It's located on floor "M," the mezzanine floor, and there's an elevator.

PENSION WILD, Lange Gasse 10, 1080 Vienna. Tel. 01/43 51 74. 16 rms (2 with shower and toilet). **U-Bahn:** U-2 to Lerchenfelderstrasse. **Tram:** 52 or 58 from the Westbahnhof to Mariahilfer Strasse, the U-Bahn U-2 from Mariahilfer Strasse to Lerchenfelderstrasse; or D from Franz-Josefs-Bahnhof to Bellaria. **Bus:** 13A from the Südbahnhof to Piaristengasse.

$ Rates (including breakfast and showers): 280–350 S ($25.45–$31.80) single without shower or toilet; 470–520 S ($42.70–$47.25) double without or with shower or toilet. AE, DC, MC, V.

✪ This is the absolute star of the budget pensions. Run by friendly Frau Wild and her English-speaking son, Peter, this place features refrigerators, cooking facilities, pots, pans, and utensils on every floor, making it popular with students and for longer stays (spaghetti, says Frau Wild, is the most frequently cooked dish). The pension started out more than a quarter of a century ago with only one bed, but now covers several floors, accessible by elevator. Rooms are clean, and multibed ones are available. There's even a fitness studio in the basement, with a sauna and steam bath that costs 30 S ($2.70) for guests. It's a true find, so be sure to book ahead.

DOUBLES [IN PRIVATE HOMES] FOR LESS THAN 650 S [$59.10]
NEAR THE WESTBAHNHOF

If you're coming from the Südbahnhof, take tram no. 18 to the Westbahnhof. From Franz-Josefs-Bahnhof, take tram no. 5.

BARBARA KOLLER, Schmalzhofgasse 11, 1060 Vienna. Tel. 01/597 29 35. 5 rms (all with shower and toilet). **Tram:** 52 or 58 to Zieglergasse.

$ Rates (including continental breakfast): 320 S ($29.10) per person. No credit cards.

This cheerful establishment has its own stairway up to the first floor—look for the iron gate. Rooms are large and spotless, with sturdy old-fashioned furniture. This private home wraps itself around an inner courtyard; next door is an Indian restaurant. It's located about a 10-minute walk from the train station, near Mariahilfer

Strasse in the direction of the Ring. Although the rate is a bit higher than the others in this category, keep in mind that all rooms have bathrooms and that breakfast is included.

F. KALED, Lindengasse 42, 1070 Vienna. Tel. 01/93 90 13. 5 rms (2 with shower and toilet). TV **Tram:** 5 to Lindengasse. **Bus:** 13A from the Südbahnhof to Mariahilfer Strasse; or a 10-minute walk from the Westbahnhof.
$ **Rates** (including showers): 350 S ($31.80) single without shower or toilet; 440–500 S ($40–$45.45) double without shower or toilet, 550–600 S ($50–$54.55) double with shower and toilet; 700–750 S ($63.65–$68.20) triple without shower or toilet. Breakfast 50 S ($4.55) extra. No credit cards.
Mr. Kaled, a Tunisian who speaks English, French, and German, offers spacious rooms, each with a radio-cassette player and cable TV with CNN broadcasts. All rooms face a quiet, inner courtyard. Highly recommended by many readers of this book.

FRAU HEDWIG GALLY, Apt. 10, Arnsteingasse 25, 1150 Vienna. Tel. 01/812 90 73 or 830 42 44. 10 rms (3 with shower and toilet, 5 with shower only). **Tram:** 52 or 58 to Kranzgasse.
$ **Rates** (including showers): 250 S ($22.70) single without shower or toilet; 360 S ($32.70) double without shower or toilet, 450 S ($40.90) double with shower only, 550 S ($50) double with shower and toilet; 100 S ($9.10) extra for a triple. Additional cot 50 S ($4.55) extra; breakfast, 45 S ($4.10). No credit cards.
Frau Gally, who speaks good English, has a variety of rooms, including one single, doubles with or without shower, one double with shower and toilet, and even a large apartment with two rooms, appropriate for families with children. Every room is equipped with a hotplate and utensils for cooking, as well as a sink with hot water. Good also for longer stays, it's located about a 10-minute walk southwest of the train station, off Mariahilfer Strasse.

IRMGARD AND SANDY LAURIA, Kaiserstrasse 77, 1070 Vienna. Tel. 01/93 41 52. 5 rms (1 with shower), 1 apt (with shower and toilet). TV **U-Bahn:** U-6 to Stadthalle. **Tram:** 5 from the Westbahnhof or Franz-Josefs-Bahnhof to Burggasse. **Bus:** 13A from the Südbahnhof to Kellermann Gasse, then 48A from Kellerman Gasse to Kaiserstrasse.
$ **Rates** (including showers): 460–500 S ($41.80–$45.45) double without shower, 660 S ($60) double with shower; 660 S ($60) triple without shower, 750 S ($68.20) triple with shower; 800 S ($72.70) quad without shower, 880 S ($80) quad with shower, 660 S ($60) apt for two people, 750 S ($68.20) for three people, 880 S ($80) for four people. No credit cards.

 FROMMER'S SMART TRAVELER: HOTELS

VALUE-CONSCIOUS TRAVELERS SHOULD
TAKE ADVANTAGE OF THE FOLLOWING:

1. Accommodations that offer cooking facilities, which will help you to save money on your dining bills.
2. Winter discounts offered by some hotels and pensions.

QUESTIONS TO ASK IF YOU'RE ON A BUDGET

1. Is there an extra charge for taking a shower?
2. Is breakfast included in the price?
3. How much is the surcharge on local and long-distance calls?

Independent backpackers who don't like the intimate quarters of living in someone's house might prefer staying here, since Frau Lauria lives separately in her own apartment in the same building. The atmosphere is laid back and the rooms are cozy. Although breakfast is not served, rooms have plates and flatware and hot-water kettle; there's a communal fridge. This establishment is located about a 15-minute walk north of the Westbahnhof. Rooms are up on the second floor, Apartment 8.

NEAR THE SÜDBAHNHOF

FRANK HEBERLING, Apt. 31, Siccardsburggasse 42, 1100 Vienna. Tel. 01/625 42 73 or 604 02 29. 6 rms (1 with shower). **Tram:** 18 from the Westbahnhof or D from Franz-Josefs-Bahnhof to the Südbahnhof, then O from the Südbahnhof to Quellenplatz; then a five-minute walk.

$ Rates (including showers): 400 S ($36.35) double; 120 S ($10.90) per person in the dormlike four-bed room. Breakfast 35 S ($3.20) extra. No credit cards.

Be sure to call first, since the Heberlings are an older, retired couple who live in a nearby building (in the summer, however, Frau Heberling usually can be found at Apartment 31). The husband-and-wife team, who prefer guests who stay more than one night, speak very good English and are quite friendly, giving guests a local map with directions on how to reach the city center, where the closest laundry is, etc. The building is 100 years old but is in excellent condition. The rooms are actually small apartments—with a front sitting room in addition to a bedroom—and are comfortable if a bit plain.

NEAR NASCHMARKT & KARLSPLATZ

FRAU HILDE WOLF, Schleifmühlgasse 7, 1040 Vienna. Tel. 01/574 90 94. 4 rms (2 with toilet). **Directions:** Tram no. 6 from the Westbahnhof to Eichenstrasse (four stops), then tram no. 62 from Eichenstrasse to Paulanergasse; or tram D from the Südbahnhof or Franz-Josefs-Bahnhof to Oper, then tram no. 62 or bus no. 65 from Oper to Paulanergasse or bus no. 59A to Schleifmühlgasse.

$ Rates (including continental breakfast): 360 S ($32.70) single; 470 S ($42.70) double; 685 S ($62.25) triple; 800 S ($72.70) quad. Showers 20 S ($1.80) extra. No credit cards.

Both Frau Wolf and her husband, Otto, speak English, and they offer large, high-ceilinged rooms comfortably furnished with fin-de-siècle furniture. Frau Wolf, who loves children and welcomes families, serves a lavish breakfast and says that readers of this book can ask for second helpings of coffee, bread, butter, and marmalade. Her apartment is centrally located, just a few minutes' walk from the Staatsoper and Karlsplatz near the outdoor market.

FRAU RENATE HALPER, Straussengasse 5, 1050 Vienna. Tel. 01/587 12 78. 3 rms and 1 apt (none with bath). **U-Bahn:** U-4 to Pilgramgasse. **Tram:** 52 or 58 from the Westbahnhof to Amerlingstrasse; then 13A (toward the Südbahnhof) to Ziegelofen Gasse. **Bus:** 13A from the Südbahnhof to Ziegelofen Gasse.

$ Rates (including breakfast and showers): 400 S ($36.35) single; 600 S ($54.55) double; 350 S ($31.80) per person in the apt. No credit cards.

Renate Halper is a young, outgoing, friendly woman who speaks English fluently. She has even prepared a small booklet in English for her guests with information regarding restaurants in the vicinity, how to get from her apartment to the various sights, explanations of Vienna's many different kinds of coffee, and more. The four-bed room is outfitted with furniture that used to belong to Renate's grandmother. Another room has a balcony, and the apartment has its own kitchen and TV with cable. She lives less than a 15-minute walk from the city center.

RENATE GAJDOS, Pressgasse 28, 1040 Vienna. Tel. 01/587 74 16. 7 rms (none with bath). **U-Bahn:** U-4 to Kettenbrückengasse.

$ Rates (including breakfast and showers): 350 S ($31.80) single; 500 S ($45.45) double; 700 S ($63.65) triple. No credit cards.

One of the rooms here is a single and two others are joined, appropriate for families. Rooms are large, sunny, and well furnished, and the breakfast room is cheerful with lots of interesting knickknacks on the shelves, giving you something to look at as you eat Frau Gajdos's homemade marmalade along with sausage, bread, and egg. She has been in the business about 30 years. This private home is located near the outdoor market and Karlsplatz.

DOUBLES [IN PRIVATE HOMES] FOR LESS THAN 750 S [$68.20]

INSIDE THE RING

FRAU ADELE GRÜN, Apt. 19, Gonzagagasse 1, 1010 Vienna. Tel. 01/533 25 06. 4 rms (none with bath). **Tram:** D from the Südbahnhof to Oper, then 1 or 2 from Oper to Salztorbrücke; or 52 from the Westbahnhof to Burgring, then 1 or 2 from Burgring to Salztorbrücke; or D from Franz-Josefs-Bahnhof to Börserplatz, then 1 to Salztorbrücke.
$ Rates (including showers): 350–400 S ($31.80–$36.35) single; 750–800 S ($68.20–$72.70) double. No credit cards.
Located in an elegant older building just off Franz Josefs Kai up on the third floor (there's an elevator), the rooms here are pleasant and clean. Frau Grün, in her 70s, speaks English and is friendly. If no one answers the house phone, try her office number (tel. 533 25 06).

FRAU HOFFMANN, Annagasse 3A, 1010 Vienna. Tel. 01/512 49 04. 5 rms (3 with shower). **Tram:** D from the Südbahnhof or Franz-Josefs-Bahnhof to Oper, then a three-minute walk; or 52 from the Westbahnhof to Burgring, then D from Burgring to Oper (one stop), then a three-minute walk.
$ Rates (including continental breakfast and showers): 650 S ($59.10) double without shower, 750 S ($68.20) double with shower. No credit cards.
Once a famous skater, Frau Hoffmann ran her establishment as a pension for 32 years, but in 1988 changed to a private-room status. Rooms are enormous and the location can't be beat (just off Kärntner Strasse). Frau Hoffmann speaks English, serves big breakfasts, and gives advice on what to do in Vienna.

DOUBLES FOR LESS THAN 870 S [$79.10]

NEAR THE WESTBAHNHOF

HOTEL FUCHS, Mariahilfer Strasse 138, 1050 Vienna. Tel. 01/83 12 01. Fax 01/83 12 01. Telex 136413. 86 rms (27 with tub/shower and toilet). TEL **Tram:** 18 from the Südbahnhof or 5 from Franz-Josefs-Bahnhof to the Westbahnhof, then a few minutes' walk.
$ Rates (including breakfast): 350–450 S ($31.80–$40.90) single without tub/shower or toilet, 850 S ($77.25) single with tub/shower and toilet; 750–850 S ($68.20–$77.25) double without tub/shower or toilet, 1,100–1,200 S ($100–$109.10) double with tub/shower and toilet; 1,100 S ($100) triple without tub/shower or toilet, 1,500 S ($136.35) triple with tub/shower and toilet. Discounts of 15%–20% available Nov–Mar. Students with ID receive a 30% discount on rooms without tub/shower or toilet. Showers 45 S ($4.10) extra. AE, DC, MC, V. **Parking:** 70 S ($6.65).
Built in 1880, this old-fashioned hotel has nicely furnished rooms and double-pane windows. There are telephones in all rooms, and TVs in rooms with tub/shower and toilet. It's located just a few minutes' walk from the Westbahnhof (exit where you see the POSTAMT post office sign, and then turn immediately right onto Mariahilfer Strasse). There is a restaurant on the premises, and you can book tickets for the theater, opera, and Spanish Riding School here.

NEAR THE UNIVERSITY

PENSION ADRIA, Wickenburggasse 23, 1080 Vienna. Tel. 01/402 02 38. Fax 01/408 39 06. 14 rms (11 with shower and toilet, 3 with shower only). TEL **Tram:** D from the Südbahnhof to Schottentor, then a 10-minute walk; or 5 from the Westbahnhof or Franz-Josefs-Bahnhof to Alserstrasse.

$ **Rates** (including buffet breakfast and showers): 500 S ($45.45) single with shower only, 550 S ($50) single with shower and toilet; 860 S ($78.20) double with shower and toilet; 1,040 S ($94.55) triple with shower and toilet. AE, MC, V.

This pension is simple and clean, good for people who are looking for a no-nonsense place to sleep. Owned by English-speaking Mr. Hamde, a Jordanian who now has Austrian citizenship, it's located northwest of the Ring, within a 20-minute walk from the old city center. All rooms have radios and some have TVs. The buffet breakfast is all-you-can-eat.

PENSION AMON, Daungasse 1, 1080 Vienna. Tel. 01/42 01 94. 12 rms (all with shower). **Tram:** 5 from the Westbahnhof or Franz-Josefs-Bahnhof to Laudongasse. **Bus:** 13A from the Südbahnhof to Skodagasse (the last stop).

$ **Rates** (including continental breakfast): 450 S ($40.05) single; 650 S ($59.10) double; 850 S ($77.25) triple. AE, DC, MC, V.

English-speaking Herr Amon hunts for a hobby, as is apparent in the rows of antlers lining the corridor of his small pension. His cozy breakfast room, outfitted with a TV, is also decorated in the spirit of the hunt. Rooms are comfortable, if a bit old-fashioned, and Herr Amon will give sightseeing tips.

PENSION ASTRA, Alserstrasse 32, 1090 Vienna. Tel. 01/402 43 54 or 408 22 70. 17 rms (15 with shower and toilet, 2 with shower only). 4 apts. TEL **U-Bahn:** U-6 from the Westbahnhof to Alserstrasse. **Tram:** 5 from Franz-Josefs-Bahnhof to Spittalgasse/Alserstrasse, then a five-minute walk. **Bus:** 13A from the Südbahnhof to Skodagasse (the last stop).

$ **Rates:** 480 S ($43.65) single with shower only, 550 S ($50) single with shower and toilet; 640 S ($58.20) double with shower only, 840–880 S ($76.35–$80) double with shower and toilet; 800 S ($72.70) apt for two people, 1,000 S ($90.90) for three people. Crib available. No credit cards.

Rooms here are quiet and clean (all but one face off the street), managed by friendly, English-speaking Gaby Brekoupil. There is a TV in some rooms, and the apartments come with a small kitchenette and TV, making them especially good for families or for longer stays.

PENSION COLUMBIA, Kochgasse 9, 1080 Vienna. Tel. 01/42 67 57. 8 rms (2 with shower). **Tram:** 5 from the Westbahnhof to Kochgasse, or 5 from Franz-Josefs-Bahnhof to Lederergasse. **Bus:** 13A from the Südbahnhof to Laudongasse.

$ **Rates** (including continental breakfast and showers): 430 S ($39.10) single without shower, 470 S ($42.70) single with shower; 600 S ($54.55) double without shower, 650 S ($59.10) double with shower. Winter discounts of 10 S (90¢) per person are available. No credit cards.

Rooms here are literally large enough to dance in, with high ceilings typical of turn-of-the-century Viennese buildings. Owner Herr Naschenweng has run the pension since 1957 and is used to answering the usual sightseeing questions. The only drawback is that there's no elevator to the pension, located up two flights of stairs.

SUPER-BUDGET CHOICES

YOUTH HOSTELS

BELIEVE-IT-OR-NOT, Apt. 14, Myrthengasse 10, 1070 Vienna. Tel.

01/526 46 58. 9 beds. **U-Bahn:** U-6 from the Westbahnhof to Burggasse-Stadthalle, then tram no. 48A from Burggasse-Stadthalle to Neubaugasse/Myrthengasse. **Bus:** 13A from the Südbahnhof to Kellermanngasse.

$ Rates (including sheets and showers): 110 S ($10) per person per night in winter (except Christmas and Easter), 160 S ($14.55) the rest of the year. No credit cards.

This is a very small establishment, simply one room outfitted with bunk beds, available to both males and females. It's run by a charming young woman who speaks excellent English, and clean sheets are included in the price. No breakfast is served, but guests are welcome to make their own. You'll like this place.

HOSTEL RUTHENSTEINER, Robert-Hamerling-Gasse 24, 1150 Vienna.
Tel. 01/83 46 93 or 830 82 65. 66 beds. **Tram:** 18 from the Südbahnhof or 5 from Franz-Josefs-Bahnhof to the Westbahnhof, then a five-minute walk.

$ Rates (including showers): 199 S ($18.10) single; 199 S ($18.10) per person double; 119–139 S ($10.80–$12.65) per person in multibed rooms. Breakfast 25 S ($2.30) extra. No credit cards.

Although technically a youth hostel, Hostel Ruthensteiner doesn't require a membership card and there's no age limit or curfew. Single, double, and multibed rooms are available, and all rooms have sinks. There's a kitchen where you can cook your own food, and even better is the brick patio where you can eat. Run by Erin and Walter Ruthensteiner (Erin is American), it's near the Westbahnhof.

JUGENDGÄSTEHAUS ZÖHRER, Skodagasse 26, 1080 Vienna. Tel. 01/
43 07 30. 29 beds. **Tram:** 5 from the Westbahnhof to Alserstrasse, or 5 from Franz-Josefs-Bahnhof to Skodagasse. **Bus:** 13A from the Südbahnhof to Skodagasse (the last stop).

$ Rates (including breakfast and showers): 170 S ($15.45) per person per night. No credit cards.

This casual, small establishment offers eight dormitory-style rooms (most with their own shower) with bunk beds, lockers, and a kitchen where you can cook your own meals. The atmosphere is friendly, the rooms are clean, and youth-hostel cards are not required. No age limit, no curfew. It's located northwest of the city center, near the university district.

YOUTH HOSTELS

JUGENDGÄSTEHAUS BRIGITTENAU, Friedrich-Engels-Platz 24, 1200
Vienna. Tel. 01/33 28 294. 282 beds. **U-Bahn:** U-6 from the Westbahnhof to Nussdorfer Strasse, then bus no. 35A from Nussdorfer Strasse to Friedrich-Engels-Platz (the last stop). **Tram:** 31 from Franz-Josefs-Bahnhof to Friedrich-Engels-Platz. **Schnellbahn** (a commuter train): from the Südbahnhof to Traisengasse, then tram N from Traisengasse to Friedrich-Engels-Platz.

$ Rates (including continental breakfast and showers): 150 S ($13.65) per person per night with youth-hostel membership card, 180 S ($16.35) without membership card. Lunch or dinner 60 S ($5.45) extra. No credit cards.

This modern youth hostel requires a membership card, but those who don't have one can stay by paying the 30 S ($2.70) extra per nght. It's located in the northern end of town, near the Danube River.

JUGENDHERBERGE WIEN, Myrthengasse 7 (tel. 01/936 31 60) and
Neustiftgasse 85 (tel. 01/93 74 62), 1070 Vienna. Fax for both 01/52 35 849. 225 beds. **U-Bahn:** U-6 from the Westbahnhof to Burggasse-Stadthalle, then tram no. 48A from Burggasse-Stadthalle to Neuburggasse. **Tram:** D from Franz-Josefs-Bahnhof to Dr.-Karl-Ring, then 48A to Neubaugasse. **Bus:** 13A from the Südbahnhof to Kellermanngasse.

$ Rates (including breakfast and showers): 150 S ($13.65) per person per night. Lunch or dinner 60 S ($5.45) extra. No credit cards.

Although there's no age limit, you must have a youth-hostel card to stay here. The building was built in the Biedermeier style in 1828, but the renovated interior is modern, and a new wing was recently added. Each room has its own shower; those in the new wing also have a toilet. Other facilities include a large dining room, TV room, laundry room, and table tennis and Foosball games. The front doors close at midnight.

SUMMER ONLY ACCOMMODATION

During the summer months, a number of student dormitories rent rooms to travelers.

CITY HOSTEL, Seilerstätte 30, 1010 Vienna. Tel. 01/512 84 63 or 512 79 23. 170 beds. **Tram:** 52 or 58 from the Westbahnhof to Burgring, or D from Franz-Josefs-Bahnhof or the Südbahnhof to Oper.
$ Rates (including continental breakfast and showers): 240 S ($21.80) single; 350 S ($31.80) double. No credit cards. **Open:** July–Sept.
Located right in the city center not far from Kärntner Strasse, this youth hostel is in the International Student House and is in operation from July 1 to September 30. Although technically for youth-hostel members or students with proper identification, anyone can stay here by paying an extra 10%. Rooms are simple, with both singles and doubles available.

TURMHERBERGE DON BOSCO, Lechnerstrasse 12, 1030 Vienna. Tel. 01/713 14 94. 50 beds. **Tram:** 18 from the Westbahnhof or Südbahnhof to Stadionbrücke, then a few minutes' walk.
$ Rates (including showers): 60 S ($5.45) per person per night. No credit cards. **Open:** Mar–Nov.
This youth hostel is open from March to November. Its beds are divided into seven rooms on seven floors of a bell tower. A youth-hostel card is required.

CAMPING

CAMPING RODAUN, An der Au 2, 1238 Wien-Rodaun. Tel. 01/88 41 54.
$ Rates: 60 S ($5.45) per person per night, plus 47 S ($4.25) per night for the campsite. **Open:** Mid-Mar to mid-Nov.
Camping Rodaun is located six miles from the city center (take tram no. 60) and has a swimming pool.

CAMPINGPLATZ SCHLOSS LAXENBURG, Münchendorferstrasse Laxenburg, 2361 Laxenburg. Tel. 02236/71 333.
$ Rates: 52 S ($4.70) per person per night, plus 50 S ($4.55) per night for the campsite. **Open:** End of Mar to the end of Oct.
This campground is in Laxenburg, nine miles from the city center, reachable by bus from the Vienna Centre bus station. Facilities include a restaurant, supermarket, and heated swimming pool with a children's pool.

CAMPINGPLATZ WIEN SUD, Breitenfurterstrasse 269, 1230 Vienna. Tel. 01/86 92 18.
$ Rates: 52 S ($4.70) per person per night, plus 50 S ($4.55) per night for the campsite. **Open:** End of May to mid-Sept.
This campground is located 4.3 miles from the city center (take tram no. 52 or bus no. 62B). Facilities include a recreation room.

CAMPINGPLATZ WIEN WEST I, Hüttelbergstrasse 40, 1140 Vienna. Tel. 01/94 14 49.
$ Rates: 52 S ($4.70) per person per night, plus 50 S ($4.55) per night for the campsite. **Open:** Mid-July to mid-Sept.

It's located four miles from the city center (take tram no. 49 or bus no. 52B). Facilities include a recreation room, laundry room, and supermarket.

CAMPINGPLATZ WIEN WEST II, Hüttelbergstrasse 80, 1140 Vienna. Tel. 01/94 23 14.
$ Rates: 52 S ($4.70) per person per night, plus 50 S ($4.55) per night for the campsite. **Open:** All year.
Located four miles from the city center (via tram no. 49 or bus no. 52B), the campground has a recreation room, laundry room, and store. There are also bungalows renting for 380 S ($34.55), available April to October.

LONG-TERM STAYS

Both Frau Gally and Frau Halper, whose private rooms are listed above, and Pension Astra and Pension Wild, described previously, offer cooking facilities, making them ideal for longer stays. If you plan on staying for a length of time in the winter, Pension Falstaff and Hotel Fuchs, listed above, offer winter discounts. In addition, in the listings below under "Worth the Extra Bucks," Pension Aviano has a couple of rooms with cooking facilities and offers winter discounts. Pension Aviano, Pension Pertschy, and Pension Edelweiss also have lower rates in winter.

WORTH THE EXTRA BUCKS

HOTEL-PENSION ZIPSER, Langegasse 49, 1080 Vienna. Tel. 01/42 02
28. Fax 0222/408 52 66 13. Telex 115544. 50 rms (all with tub/shower and toilet). TV TEL **Tram:** 5 from the Westbahnhof or Franz-Josefs-Bahnhof to Lederergasse. **Bus:** 13A from the Südbahnhof to Theater in der Josefstadt.
$ Rates (including buffet breakfast): 590–615 S ($56.20–$62.70) single; 880–990 S ($80–$90) double without courtyard view. 1,020–1,080 S ($92.70–$98.20) double with courtyard view. Extra person 220 S ($20). AE, DC, MC, V. **Parking:** 120 S ($10.90).
Rooms here are modern and clean, some of which overlook a quiet inner courtyard with trees and have a balcony. All rooms have double doors (to seal out noise) as well as tile bathrooms and radio. The pension is located about a five-minute walk behind the Rathaus.

PENSION AVIANO, Marco-d'Aviano-Gasse 1, 1010 Vienna. Tel. 01/512
83 30. Fax 01/512 81 65-65. Telex 136375. 10 rms (all with shower and toilet). MINIBAR TV TEL **Tram:** 52 or 58 from the Westbahnhof to Burgring, or D from the Südbahnhof or Franz-Josefs-Bahnhof to Oper.
$ Rates (including continental breakfast): Winter, 680 S ($61.80) single; 880–980 S ($80–$89.10) double. Summer, 740 S ($67.25) single; 1,080–1,160 S ($98.20–$105.45) double. MC.
⭐ Centrally located just off Kärntner Strasse, this small and personable pension offers rooms elegantly decorated in Old Vienna Biedermeier style, as well as such modern conveniences as radio, minibar, and a private safe. A couple of rooms are equipped with hotplates, and some rooms also face the famous shopping street, Kärntner Strasse (these have double-pane windows to keep them quiet).

PENSION EDELWEISS, Langegasse 61, 1080 Vienna. Tel. 01/42 23 06.
Fax 01/42 46 31-10. Telex 136375. 20 rms (all with tub/shower and toilet). TV TEL **Tram:** 5 from the Westbahnhof or Franz-Josefs-Bahnhof to Langegasse. **Bus:** 13A from the Südbahnhof to Skodagasse (the last stop).
$ Rates (including continental breakfast): Summer, 620–680 S ($56.35–$61.80) single; 980–1,040 S ($89.10–$94.55) double. Winter, 520–540 S ($47.25–$49.10) single, 760–880 S ($69.10–$80) double. MC.
Owned by the Pertschy family, which also runs the Pension Pertschy (see below), this

pleasant establishment has a friendly, competent, English-speaking staff and newly furnished rooms. The breakfast room is especially cheerful.

PENSION NOSSEK, Graben 17, 1010 Vienna. Tel. 01/533 70 41. Fax 01/535 36 46. 26 rms (22 with tub/shower and toilet, 4 with shower only). TEL **U-Bahn:** U-1 or U-3 to Stephansplatz. **Tram:** D from the Südbahnhof to Oper, then U-Bahn U-1 from the Südbahnhof to Stephansplatz (one stop); or 52 or 58 from the Westbahnhof to Burgring, then bus no. 2A from Burgring to Graben-Petersplatz. **Bus:** 2A from Burgring to Graben-Petersplatz.

$ Rates (including breakfast): 550 S ($50) single with shower only, 700 S ($63.65) single with shower and toilet; 900–950 S ($81.80–$86.35) double with shower and toilet; 1,250–1,500 S ($113.65–$136.35) triple with shower and toilet. No credit cards.

⭐ This pension has a great location, right on Graben Square in the heart of the city. Its owner-manager is Dr. Cremona, who lived in Ohio for 20 years. An interesting feature is that Mozart lived in a third-floor apartment in this building from 1781 to 1782. (Mozart lived in many places in Vienna—moving when he couldn't pay the rent.) Singles have either a shower or shower and toilet; the doubles all have a shower and toilet, and the more expensive doubles face the Graben, a picturesque view. TVs are available on request. The people running this pension care about their guests, and are happy to give advice and suggestions for sightseeing.

PENSION PERTSCHY, Habsburgergasse 5, 1010 Vienna. Tel. 01/534 49. Fax 0222/534 49-49. Telex 136375. 43 rms (all with tub/shower and toilet). MINIBAR TV TEL **Tram:** D from the Südbahnhof to Oper, then bus no. 3A from Oper to Habsburgergasse; or 52 or 58 from the Westbahnhof to Burgring, then bus no. 2A from Burgring to Habsburgergasse.

$ Rates (including buffet breakfast): Winter, 660 S ($60) single; 940 S ($85.45) double. Summer, 680–740 S ($61.80–$67.25) single; 980–1,200 S ($89.10–$109.10) double. MC.

⭐ This is a wonderful place for a splurge. Located just a few steps off the Graben and near Stephansplatz, it occupies the first several floors of an ancient "palais" built in 1725 and now an official historical landmark. The ceilings are high and vaulted, and rooms are outfitted in Biedermeier style, complete with chandeliers and minibars. Three rooms even have tile heaters—one is 200 years old. To get from room to room, you walk along an enclosed catwalk on a balcony that traces around a courtyard. As for the Pertschys, they lived in Canada for 10 years, and the whole family speaks perfect English. Highly recommended.

5. BUDGET DINING

Because many shops and businesses are located inside the Ring and along Mariahilfer Strasse, many of Vienna's best-known eateries are there as well. You don't have to spend a lot of money to eat well in Vienna, and there's enough variety to keep the palate interested.

But first you have to know what you're looking for. A *Billateria* (from the German word *billig*, meaning cheap) is a self-service restaurant where you can create your own multicourse meal at very low prices. Along these same lines, but a bit more upscale, is a chain of cafeterias called the *Naschmarkt*, all with very convenient locations. And finally, a *Beisl* is the Austrian word for pub or tavern, many of which serve hearty and inexpensive meals.

FAVORITE MEALS

Viennese cuisine is the culmination of various ethnic influences, including Bohemian, Hungarian, Croatian, Slovene, German, and Italian. At the top end of the price scale is wild game, followed by various fish, poultry, and beef dishes. Most restaurants serve complete meals—that is, main dish and one or several side dishes. Prices listed for each restaurant below, therefore, are usually for complete meals.

For starters, you might try a **soup,** such as *Griessnockerlsuppe* (clear soup with semolina dumplings), *Leberknödlsuppe* (soup with liver dumplings), *Rindsuppe* (beef broth), or *Gulaschsuppe* (Hungarian goulash).

For **main courses,** popular dishes include *Bauernschmaus* (a combination of many varied sausages and pork items with sauerkraut and dumplings), *Tafelspitz* (boiled beef with vegetables), *Wiener Schnitzel* (breaded veal cutlet), *Schweinebraten* (roast pork), *Spanferkel* (suckling pig), *Backhendl* (fried and breaded chicken), and *Gulasch* (stew). *Nockerl* are little dumplings, usually served with sauce.

And of course, there are **desserts.** Vienna's *Apfelstrudel* (apple strudel) is probably the best in the world. *Palatschinken* are light, sugared pancakes; *Kaiserschmarren* is a diced omelet, served with jam and sprinkled with sugar.

And to top it all off, you'll want **coffee,** of which there are at least 20 different varieties. Introduced 300 years ago by the Turks during their unsuccessful attempt to conquer Vienna, coffee has become an art form, served in veritable institutions known as the Viennese coffeehouses. Among the many different kinds of coffee are the *kleiner Schwarzer,* a small cup without milk; the *kleiner Brauner,* small cup with a little milk; the *Melange,* large cup with milk; *Mokka,* strong black Viennese coffee; *Melange mit Schlag,* same as Mokka but topped with whipped cream; *Einspänner,* glass of coffee with whipped cream; and *Türkischer,* Turkish coffee boiled in a small copper pot and served in tiny cups. Coffee is always served with a glass of water.

LOCAL BUDGET BETS

MENSA, Technische Universität Wien, Turm B, Wiedner Hauptstrasse 8-19.
   Cuisine: AUSTRIAN. **U-Bahn:** U-1, U-2, or U-4 to Karlsplatz.
$ Prices: Fixed-price meals 25–40 S ($2.25–$3.65). No credit cards.
   Open: Lunch only, Mon–Fri 11am–2pm. **Closed:** Christmas–Jan 7, Feb, July–Sept.

Although technically for students, this student cafeteria (Mensa) is so busy that no one would blink twice if you came here for a meal, especially if you're young and look like you know what you're doing. It's located up on the first floor of a modern, light-green

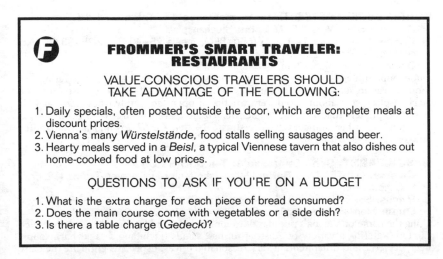

ⓕ FROMMER'S SMART TRAVELER: RESTAURANTS

VALUE-CONSCIOUS TRAVELERS SHOULD TAKE ADVANTAGE OF THE FOLLOWING:

1. Daily specials, often posted outside the door, which are complete meals at discount prices.
2. Vienna's many *Würstelstände,* food stalls selling sausages and beer.
3. Hearty meals served in a *Beisl,* a typical Viennese tavern that also dishes out home-cooked food at low prices.

QUESTIONS TO ASK IF YOU'RE ON A BUDGET

1. What is the extra charge for each piece of bread consumed?
2. Does the main course come with vegetables or a side dish?
3. Is there a table charge (*Gedeck*)?

and glass building not far from Karlsplatz. There are usually four different platters available, from stews to grilled chicken or spaghetti. There are different counters for each, along with additional choices of soups and salad. Pay after choosing your food, and be sure to clear your tray when you're finished. You'll also find an inexpensive snack bar here.

There's another Mensa, this one a student cafeteria of the Universität Wien, at Universitätstrasse 7, near Schottentor. It's open for lunch only, Monday through Friday from 11am to 2pm.

MEALS FOR LESS THAN 80 S ($7.25)

INSIDE THE RING

BIZI, Rotenturmstrasse 4. Tel. 513 37 05.
   Cuisine: ITALIAN. **U-Bahn:** Stephansplatz.
$ Prices: Pizza and pasta 65–80 S ($5.10–$7.25). No credit cards.
   Open: Daily 11am–11:30pm.
Located on the corner of Rotenturmstrasse and Wollzeile just north of Stephansplatz, this enormously popular self-service restaurant serves a variety of pizza and pasta, including ravioli, gnocchi, tagliatelle, tortellini—with a choice in sauces. Pizza by the slice costs 25 S ($2.25), and there's also a salad bar—a large plate costs 50 S ($4.55). The decor is upbeat and pleasant, with modern art on the walls, and there's even a no-smoking section.

BUFFET TRZESNIEWSKI, Dorotheergasse 1. Tel. 512 32 91.
   Cuisine: SANDWICHES. **U-Bahn:** to Stephansplatz.
$ Prices: 7 S (65¢) per sandwich. No credit cards.
   Open: Mon–Fri 9am–7:30pm, Sat 9am–1pm (to 6pm on *langer Samstag*).
⭐ This is one of the most popular cafeterias in all of Vienna, and rightly so. It's a tiny shop centrally located just off Stephansplatz, so small in fact that the mealtime line often snakes through the entire store. It's best, therefore, to come here during off-peak times. Trzesniewski is a buffet of open-face finger sandwiches, each costing only 7 S (65¢) and covered with such spreads as salami, egg salad, herring, tomatoes, or a couple dozen other selections. Four sandwiches are usually enough for me, along with a Pfiff, a very tiny beer (an eighth of a liter) for only 8 S (70¢). Very Viennese in atmosphere, this place is highly recommended.

DURAN SUPERIMBISS, Rotenturmstrasse 11. Tel. 63 71 15.
   Cuisine: SANDWICHES. **U-Bahn:** Stephansplatz.
$ Prices: Sandwiches 7–9.50 S (65¢–85¢); meals 25–40 S ($2.25–$3.65). No credit cards.
   Open: Mon–Fri 9am–7pm, Sat 9am–1pm.
Duran Superimbiss is one of the most popular self-service chains in town, offering fast food to eat in its simple surroundings or to take out. This store, just north of Stephansplatz, sells about two dozen varieties of open-face sandwiches alone, as well as special platters that may include Schweinebraten, grilled sausage, or Schnitzel.

There are other branches at Alserstrasse 14 (tel. 42 67 25) and at Mariahilfer Strasse 91 (tel. 596 23 73).

NASCHMARKT, Schottengasse 1. Tel. 533 51 86.
   Cuisine: AUSTRIAN. **U-Bahn:** U-2 to Schottentor-Universität. **Tram:** 1, 2, or D to Schottentor.
$ Prices: 55–90 S ($5–$8.20). No credit cards.
   Open: Mon–Fri 9am–7:30pm, Sat–Sun and hols 10am–6pm.
Using the name of Vienna's popular outdoor market, the Naschmarkt is a self-service cafeteria offering a variety of Austrian dishes, salads (including a salad bar), soups, beer, desserts, and other items at very reasonable prices. Especially good are the daily

specials, which may include Schnitzel, Schweinebraten, chicken, stews, fish, or spaghetti, along with one or two side dishes. The interior is modern and pleasant. A good old standby.

Other convenient locations are at Schwarzenbergplatz 16 (tel. 505 31 15), open Monday through Friday from 7am to 9pm and on Saturday and Sunday from 9am to 9pm; and at Mariahilfer Strasse 84 (tel. 587 63 06), open daily from 11am to 10pm.

NORDSEE, Kärntner Strasse 25. Tel. 512 73 54.
   Cuisine: FISH. **U-Bahn:** Stephansplatz or Karlsplatz.
   $ Prices: 65–115 S ($5.90–$10.45). No credit cards.
   Open: Daily 9am–10:30pm.

A simple, seafood chain from northern Germany, Nordsee is a cafeteria with pictures on the wall of all the dishes available, making ordering a snap. There are fish sticks, fish soup, fish paella, herring, baked fish, salads, and fish sandwiches, and take-out service is available from its open-fronted streetside display counter. This cafeteria has an envied location right on Kärntner Strasse, between Stephansplatz and the Staatsoper, and there's even outdoor dining.

There's another branch off the Graben in the center of town at Kohlmarkt 6 (tel. 533 59 66), open Monday through Friday from 9am to 7pm and on Saturday and Sunday from 10am to 6pm; and at Mariahilfer Strasse 34 (tel. 93 93 68), open Monday through Friday from 8:30am to 7pm and on Saturday from 8:30am to 2pm.

PIZZA LAND, Petersplatz 2. Tel. 533 70 74.
   Cuisine: PIZZA/PASTA. **U-Bahn:** Stephansplatz.
   $ Prices: 50–90 S ($4.55–$8.20). No credit cards.
   Open: Sun–Wed 10am–midnight, Thurs–Sat 10am–1am.

A chain from England, Pizza Land offers both thin-crust and deep-dish pizza, with about 20 different combinations of toppings. Advertisements claim you'll have your order in 10 minutes; take-out is available. Other items on the menu include spaghetti and lasagne. There's a salad bar.

Other convenient branches are at Krugerstrasse 6 (tel. 512 52 59), inside the Ring, and at Mariahilfer Strasse 112 (tel. 526 49 08), on the way to the Westbahnhof, both open the same hours as above.

WIENERWALD, Annagasse 3. Tel. 512 37 66.
   Cuisine: AUSTRIAN. **U-Bahn:** U-1, U-2, or U-4 to Karlsplatz.
   $ Prices: 70–110 S ($6.35–$10). AE, DC, MC, V.
   Open: Daily 11am–1am.

Wienerwald is a huge and successful chain of grilled-chicken restaurants found throughout Austria and Germany, with almost 20 locations in Vienna alone. The founder of the chain got the idea for his restaurant after visiting Munich's Oktoberfest after World War II and noticing the huge consumption of chicken. Other dishes on the English menu include Wiener Schnitzel, Gulasch, turkey Cordon Bleu, and a mixed grill.

Other branches are at Freyung 6 (tel. 533 14 20), Mariahilfer Strasse 156 (tel. 83 31 65), and Westbahnstrasse 14 (tel. 93 17 43).

OUTSIDE THE RING

NEW AGE, Lichtentalergasse 20. Tel. 310 28 70.
   Cuisine: INTERNATIONAL/VEGETARIAN. **Tram:** D to Althanstrasse.
   $ Prices: 30–70 S ($2.70–$6.35). No credit cards.
   Open: Lunch Mon–Fri 11:30am–2pm; dinner Mon–Fri 7pm–2am. **Closed:** Aug.

Located north of the Ring near the Franz-Josef-Bahnhof, this casual restaurant/bar is a good alternative if you're tired of the usual heavy Austrian cuisine. Its food is lighter, making generous use of vegetables, cheeses, and sauces. Specialties include baked Camembert topped with breadcrumbs, nuts with cranberries, spinach with fried egg and potatoes, green tortelloni in a mushroom-cream sauce, stuffed eggplant, and such soups as garlic or Mexican onion. Popular with young people from Vienna's alternative scene, it's a good place to come even for just a beer.

SCHNITZELWIRT, Neubaugasse 52. Tel. 93 37 71.

Cuisine: AUSTRIAN. **U-Bahn:** U-2 to Volkstheater, then a 10-minute walk. **Tram:** 49 from Dr.-Karl-Renner-Ring to Siebensterngasse. **Bus:** 13A to Siebensterngasse.

$ Prices: 50–80 S ($4.55–$7.25). No credit cards.

Open: Mon–Fri 11am–10pm, Sat 11am–2:30pm and 5–9:50pm. **Closed:** Hols.

Known also as Gaststätte Helene Schmidt, this restaurant, specializing in variations of the Schnitzel, has been one of Vienna's leading budget restaurants for years, heavily patronized by students, shopkeepers, and employees working in the area. Little wonder—the Schnitzel are gigantic, covering the whole plate (if there are two of you, you might consider sharing one). It's located a few blocks north of Vienna's popular shopping street, Mariahilfer Strasse, near the corner of Siebensterngasse. The place is often packed and is highly recommended.

TUNNEL, Florianigasse 39. Tel. 42 34 65.

Cuisine: INTERNATIONAL. **U-Bahn:** U-2 to Rathaus, then a 10-minute walk. **Tram:** 5. **Bus:** 13A.

$ Prices: 40–120 S ($3.65–$10.90). No credit cards.

Open: Daily 9am–2am.

 This informal establishment is actually a combination restaurant and bar, with a live-music house downstairs in the basement. Catering to Vienna's large student population, it starts the day with huge breakfasts (including Arabian breakfast, granola, and omelets) and continues the day with sandwiches, salads, vegetarian dishes, pizza (big enough for two people to share), pasta, and Viennese pancakes. The menu is eclectic, with everything from hummus or gnocchi to moussaka or a dish of Asian vegetables. From 11:30am to 2:30pm there's a daily special for 45 S ($4.10). The bread here is free with your meal. You can stay as long as you wish, and you can come just for a drink. It's located west of the Ring, behind the Rathaus.

MEALS FOR LESS THAN 140 S [$12.70]

INSIDE THE RING

BASTEI BEISL, Stubenbastei 10. Tel. 512 43 19.

Cuisine: AUSTRIAN. **U-Bahn:** Stephansplatz.

$ Prices: 90–200 S ($8.20–$18.20). AE, DC, MC.

Open: Mon–Sat 9am–11:30pm.

This family-style Beisl, located about a five-minute walk east of Stephansplatz, has a homey atmosphere with wooden booths and chairs. It offers a fixed-price lunch menu for 90 S ($8.20) and 110 S ($10), and a changing daily menu. Otherwise, perennial favorites include Wiener Tafelspitz, Beisl Gulasch, Wiener Schnitzel, Cordon Bleu, Zwiebelrostbraten (roast beef with onion), trout, pork medallions, and pepper steak. There's a long wine list in addition to the usual beer.

DOM BEISL, Schulerstrasse 4. Tel. 512 91 81.

Cuisine: AUSTRIAN. **U-Bahn:** U-1 or U-3 to Stephansplatz.

$ Prices: 65–100 S ($5.90–$9.10). No credit cards.

Open: Mon–Fri 7am–5pm.

 A typical neighborhood Beisl, this simple eatery with its wooden floor and plain furniture is conveniently located on the corner of Domgasse directly behind St. Stephen's Cathedral. Maybe that's why it's a favorite eating place of the Fiaker, the famous Viennese horse-carriage drivers stationed around Stephansplatz. A family-run establishment (owner Alfred Massinger is almost always present), it posts its changing daily specials on a blackboard hanging outside the front door. Otherwise, items on the regular menu include Schweinebraten with Knödel (dumplings), Bauernschmaus, Wiener Schnitzel, and Hühnerbrustfilet (chicken breast filet).

FIGLMÜLLER, Wollzeile 5. Tel. 52 61 77.

Cuisine: AUSTRIAN. **U-Bahn:** Stephansplatz.

$ Prices: 80–150 S ($7.25–$13.65). No credit cards.

Open: Mon–Fri 8am–10:45pm, Sat 8am–3pm.

Located on a small alley just off Wollzeile north of Stephansplatz, this cheerful restaurant with waiters in bow ties is famous for its huge Schnitzel and home-style Viennese specialties. The daily changing menu is written on a blackboard (in German only) and may include such specialties as Tafelspitz or chicken breast in addition to its Schnitzel. It has a large selection of wines from its own vineyards.

GÖSSER BIERKLINIK, Steindelgasse 4. Tel. 535 69 82.

Cuisine: AUSTRIAN. **U-Bahn:** U-1 or U-3 to Stephansplatz, then a five-minute walk west.

$ Prices: 85–225 S ($7.70–$20.45). AE, DC, MC, V.

Open: Mon–Sat 9am–midnight. **Closed:** Hols.

First mentioned in documents from 1406, this old building became a restaurant in the 17th century. Since 1924 it has been the property of Gösser Brewery, with dining spread among nine rooms on various floors. One room even displays a Turkish cannonball that hit the place 300 years ago when Vienna lay under siege. Simply and pleasantly decorated, you can either splurge or eat for under $10. Hearty dishes include fresh fish, homemade Gulasch, Bauernschmaus, grilled duck, Wiener Schnitzel, roast beef with onions, steak, and Specklinsen (ham and lentils). Gösser beer starts at 27 S ($2.45) for a *Seidel* (one-third liter). It's located just off the Graben.

MÜLLERBEISL, Seilerstätte 15. Tel. 512 42 65.

Cuisine: AUSTRIAN. **U-Bahn:** U-1, U-2, or U-4 to Karlsplatz.

$ Prices: 95–195 S ($8.65–$17.70). AE, DC, MC.

Open: Lunch daily 11am–2:30pm; dinner daily 5:30–11pm.

This cozy Beisl with its wooden benches and colorful tablecloths has an unmistakably Austrian look. It's located on a street running parallel to Kärntner Strasse, across from the Hochschule für Musik—you may be serenaded by students practicing the piano or violin. There are a few tables outside on the sidewalk where you can sit on nice days. It serves typical Beisl food, including Wiener Schnitzel, liver, Jägerschnitzel (schnitzel with mushrooms in red wine sauce), Gulasch, pepper steak, rumpsteak, and fish.

ORPHEUS, Spiegelgasse 10. Tel. 512 38 53.

Cuisine: GREEK. **U-Bahn:** Stephansplatz or Karlsplatz.

$ Prices: 75–155 S ($6.80–$14.10). No credit cards.

Open: Sun–Wed noon–midnight, Thurs–Sat noon–2am.

A popular Greek eatery on a street paralleling Kärntner Strasse, it's colorfully painted with blue and green walls, accentuated by black furniture. I personally recommend the Orpheus Plate, which comes with samplings of souvlaki, lamb cutlet, pork cutlet, and chicken breast. There's also the usual selection of moussaka, lamb, souvlaki, steaks, and fish selections.

PRONTO, Spiegelgasse 2. Tel. 512 29 58.

Cuisine: ITALIAN. **U-Bahn:** Stephansplatz or Karlsplatz.

$ Prices: 50–80 S ($4.55–$7.25). No credit cards.

Open: Mon–Thurs 11am–midnight, Fri–Sat 11am–2am. **Closed:** Hols.

Pronto is a miniature stand-up eatery with genuine Italian cuisine, offering different dishes every day, from lasagne to minestrone or tortellini. It's extremely popular and packed during lunch and dinner, so try to eat during off-hours.

STADTBEISL, Naglergasse 21. Tel. 533 33 23.
Cuisine: AUSTRIAN. **U-Bahn:** U-1 or U-3 to Stephansplatz, then a five-minute walk west.
$ Prices: 80–180 S ($7.25–$16.35). V.
Open: Daily 11am–11:30pm.

A pleasant locale in the heart of Old Vienna, this Beisl has a history that stretches back to the early 1700s. Once under the ownership of a cloister that offered soup lines to the poor twice a week, the old building has a cellar three stories deep—part of which are old catacombs with underground passageways linked to Stephansdom and other parts of the inner city (you can visit the uppermost cellar with its arched ceilings and brick floor). At any rate, the building has been a restaurant since 1745, with rooms that resemble a hunting lodge. The front room is crowded with antiques, while antlers decorate the back room. Traditional tiled stoves (*Kachelofen*) heat the entire locale. The menu offers such interesting choices as hazelnut steak with curry rice and Hungarian dishes, as well as such standbys as Wiener Schnitzel, fish, and spinach with fried eggs and potatoes.

NEAR MARIAHILFER STRASSE & NASCHMARKT

CREPERIE-BRASSERIE SPITTELBERG, Spittelberggasse 12. Tel. 96 15 70.
Cuisine: FRENCH. **U-Bahn:** U-2 to Volkstheater. **Tram:** 49 from Dr.-Karl-Renner-Ring to Spittelberg.
$ Prices: 90–170 S ($8.20–$15.45). AE, DC, MC, V.
Open: Dinner only, daily 6pm–midnight.

Located in what used to be Vienna's red-light district but has since become a tiny enclave of trendy restaurants, this casual French eatery has salads with a great selection of different dressings, galettes stuffed with such fillings as spinach or turkey, crêpes with sweet fillings, and vegetarian dishes. The restaurant itself is in a modernized old building, with hanging plants and lighting suspended from the super-tall ceiling. There's outdoor seating in the summer. Spittelberggasse is north of Mariahilfer Strasse and west of the Natural History Museum.

GASTHAUS WITWE BOLTE, Gutenberggasse 13. Tel. 93 14 50.
Cuisine: AUSTRIAN. **U-Bahn:** U-2 to Volkstheater. **Tram:** 49 from Dr.-Karl-Renner-Ring to Spittelberg.
$ Prices: 90–180 S ($8.20–$16.35). No credit cards.
Open: Daily 11:30am–1am.

Its facade is fancy baroque, but the interior consists of several small and simple rooms, where the emphasis is on such hearty home-cooked meals as Tafelspitz, Schnitzel, Schweinebraten, and Gulasch. There's also a wonderful outdoor dining area. The restaurant itself is located near the Crêperie-Brasserie Spittelberg (above) on a narrow, lamp-lit cobblestone street that centuries ago used to be the center of Vienna's red-light district. Empress Maria Theresa, a staunch Catholic, tried to curb prostitution but had little success; according to local lore, her son, Joseph II, fled through the door of this very house in 1778 disguised as a regular citizen.

NASCHMARKT BEISL, Linke Wienzeile 14. Tel. 587 53 13.
Cuisine: LEBANESE. **U-Bahn:** U-4 to Kettenbrückengasse, or U-1, U-2, or U-4 to Karlsplatz.
$ Prices: 40–160 S ($3.65–$14.55). No credit cards.
Open: Mon–Sat 8:30am–11pm.

Located right next to Vienna's outdoor market, this place is plain and cheap, good for a sit-down meal after you've strolled through the Naschmarkt. The menu lists tsatsiki, hummus, stuffed pepper, kebabs, pizza with meat and vegetables, a mixed-grill platter, and lamb, as well as Austrian dishes like Wiener Schnitzel and Gulasch. If you're on a budget, order the falafel for 40 S ($3.65).

RESTAURANT DER GRIECHE, Barnabitengasse 5. Tel. 587 74 66.
   Cuisine: GREEK. **Tram:** 52 or 58 to Stiftgasse or Amerlingstrasse.
$ **Prices:** 90–165 S ($8.20–$15). *Gedeck* (table charge), 4 S (40¢) for lunch, 8 S (70¢) for dinner. No credit cards.
   Open: Lunch daily 11:30am–2:30pm; dinner daily 6pm–midnight.
Near Mariahilfer Strasse just half a block from the Gerngross department store, this is a simple restaurant with an outdoor garden for summer dining. Retsina and domestic Greek wines are, of course, available, as well as exochiko (lamb casserole), kleftiko (lamb cooked with cheese and garlic), moussaka, shrimp, fish, souvlaki, lamb chops, and Bauernsalat (Greek salad).

SHALIMAR, Schmalzhofgasse 11. Tel. 56 43 17.
   Cuisine: INDIAN. **Tram:** 52 or 58 to Zieglergasse.
$ **Prices:** 80–190 S ($7.25–$17.25). fixed-price meals 165–210 S ($15–$19.10). *Gedeck,* 16 S ($1.45) per person. AE, DC, MC, V.
   Open: Lunch daily noon–2pm; dinner daily 6–11pm.
Located just south of Mariahilfer Strasse, this brightly decorated Indian restaurant with outdoor seating offers tandoori chicken, curry dishes of chicken, pork, lamb, beef, and fish, and a variety of vegetarian dishes. Indian music plays softly in the background. There's a *Gedeck* (table charge) here, per person, but the food is good enough to warrant coming here.

COFFEEHOUSES INSIDE THE RING

Just as Paris has its sidewalk cafés, Vienna has its coffeehouses, which are institutions in themselves. There are literally dozens of different ways to order coffee (refer to the beginning of the dining section, above). If all you're looking for is a cheap cup of coffee to give you fuel for the day, look for a chain called **Eduscho.** There's one at Graben 12 and another on Kärntner Strasse 12, where a cup of coffee starts at 6 S (55¢). They're open Monday through Friday from 8am to 6pm, and on Saturday from 8am to 12:30pm. There are chest-high tables where you can stand and sip your purchase.

BRÄUNERHOF CAFE, Stallburggasse 2. Tel. 512 38 93.
   Located on a tiny street that connects Dorotheergasse and Bräunergasse, this café falls somewhere between Demel and Hawelka as far as style and decoration go. Rather than the dark-paneled walls of many older coffeehouses, this one has a bright and simple interior with gracefully arching lamps by Hoffmann. There are several expensive antique shops in the immediate area, and on Saturday, Sunday, and holidays from 3 to 6pm a trio entertains customers. A Melange here costs 27 S ($2.45).
   Open: Mon–Sat 7:30am–8:30pm, Sun and hols 10am–8:30pm.

CAFE HAWELKA, Dorotheergasse 6. Tel. 512 82 30.
   Located just off Stephansplatz, Café Hawelka is small and smoky, catering more to commoners than to the high society that frequents Demel. With walls covered with posters and placards, it attracts students, artists, writers, and other bohemian types. It's famous for its Buchtel, a pastry made fresh daily and available only after 10pm. I personally prefer this café to Demel, and its 30 S ($2.70) for a Melange is more acceptable.
   Open: Mon and Wed–Sat 8am–2am, Sun and hols 4pm–2am.

DEMEL, Kohlmarkt 14. Tel. 533 55 16.
   This is the most expensive and most famous coffeehouse in Vienna. Founded in 1785 by a pastry chef who later served as the pastry supplier to the royal family,

Demel's elegant interior looks like the private parlor of a count. A small pot of coffee here costs 45 S ($4.10), worth the cost just for the show of people and waitresses. Tortes and cakes start at 30 S ($2.70). And as though in admission of their high prices, Demel even accepts all major credit cards.

Open: Daily 10am–6pm.

STREET FOOD

The *Würstelstand* (frankfurter stand) is as much a part of the Viennese scene as its coffee shops. Situated throughout the city, they sell Bratwurst, Leberkäs, curry wurst, soft drinks, and beer, with most prices between 22 and 32 S ($2 and $2.90).

Conveniently located stands are those on Seilergasse (just off Stephansplatz), open daily from 7am to 1am; on Kupferschmiedgasse (just off Kärntner Strasse), open Monday through Friday from 9am to 5:30pm; in the Gerngross department store at Mariahilfer Strasse 38-48, open 24 hours a day; and at Schwarzenbergplatz, open 24 hours a day.

Another good place to look for food stalls is at the Naschmarkt, described below under picnic supplies.

PICNIC SUPPLIES & WHERE TO EAT THEM

The best place for picnic supplies—and indeed, one of Vienna's most colorful attractions—is the **Naschmarkt.** It's an open-air market located just a five-minute walk from Karlsplatz, with stalls selling fish, vegetables, fruit, meats, cheeses, Asian foodstuffs, Greek specialties, flowers, and tea. My Viennese friends say that this is the best place to shop because of the freshness of produce and variety of goods, including exotic items. In between the food stalls are a number of stand-up *Imbisse,* fast-food counters where you can buy sausages, sandwiches, beer, grilled chicken, and other ready-made foods. The Naschmarkt is open Monday through Friday from 6am to 6:30pm and on Saturday from 6am to 1pm.

As for picnic settings, Vienna's most accessible parks are its **Stadtpark** and its **Volksgarten,** both located on the Ring. In addition, both Schönbrunn and Belvedere palaces have formal gardens. Keep in mind, however, that the Viennese are a bit stodgy and do not look kindly on people who wander off pathways and sprawl upon the grass. Some of Vienna's younger generation have staged sit-ins in protest of the "Keep Off the Grass" rule, but things change slowly here. In any case, there are always lots of park benches. If you really want to get away from the city, take an excursion to the **Vienna Woods** or the **Danube,** both described in "Easy Excursions," later in this chapter.

WORTH THE EXTRA BUCKS

In addition to the restaurants here, there are a number of wine cellars in the entertainment section that offer meals at prices above our budget. Although you can experience these establishments just for the price of a drink, they are also great for a complete meal, which will cost about $15 and up.

GRIECHENBEISL, Fleischmarkt 11. Tel. 533 19 41 or 533 19 77.
   Cuisine: AUSTRIAN. **U-Bahn:** Stephansplatz or Schwedenplatz.
$ Prices: 150–250 S ($13.65–$22.70). AE, DC, MC, V.
   Open: Daily 11am–1am.
All Viennese know the Griechenbeisl and many of their ancestors have probably dined here, since it dates back to the 15th century. Housed in an ancient-looking, vine-covered building that is divided into several small rooms linked by narrow winding passageways, it offers a typical Viennese menu, including Wiener Schnitzel, Tafelspitz, Bauernschmaus, venison steak, and deer stew. It's a place with a lot of

character, but if the menu is too expensive, you can always come after 11pm just for a drink (see "Evening Entertainment," below, for more information).

HEDRICH, Stubenring 2. Tel. 512 95 88.
Cuisine: AUSTRIAN. **Tram:** 1 or 2 to Dr.-Karl-Lueger-Platz.
$ Prices: Main courses 120–240 S ($10.90–$21.80); fixed-price meal 120 S ($10.90). No credit cards.
Open: Mon–Thurs 11am–9pm.

This small, bistrolike, trendy restaurant is one of several to have opened and blossomed in recent years. It serves traditional Viennese cooking, but in an atmosphere more chic than a Beisl and not as stuffy as a first-class restaurant. Its handwritten menu changes every day, but may include Wiener Schnitzel, lamb, calf's liver, or trout. Main courses come with side dishes, but the best deal is the daily special for 120 S ($10.90), which consists of a soup or appetizer, main dish, and salad. This restaurant is located on the southeast corner of the Ring.

RESTAURANT HAUSWIRTH, Otto Bauergasse 20. Tel. 587 12 61.
Cuisine: AUSTRIAN. **Tram:** 52 or 58 to Zieglergasse or Amerlingstrasse.
$ Prices: Main courses 175–270 S ($15.90–$24.55). AE, DC, MC, V.
Open: Lunch Mon–Fri 11:30am–3pm; dinner Mon–Sat 6:30–11pm. **Closed:** Hols.

★ Come here for an elegant dining experience, complete with chandeliers, fresh flowers, and drawing-room–like dining areas from the turn of the century. In summer there's also outdoor dining that still manages to maintain its high degree of elegance. The menu, featuring light, original cuisine, changes to complement each season, depending on what's available. Thus spring may feature fish; summer, mushrooms and asparagus; and autumn, wild game. There are 11,000 bottles of wine in the restaurant's own cellar, which you can visit upon request.

WIENER RATHAUSKELLER, Rathausplatz. Tel. 421 21 90.
Cuisine: AUSTRIAN. **Reservations:** Recommended Tues–Sat for the fixed-price meal. **U-Bahn:** U-2 to Rathaus. **Tram:** 1, 2, or D to Burgtheater.
$ Prices: Main courses 105–250 S ($9.55–$22.70). AE, DC, MC, V.
Open: Lunch Mon–Sat 11:30am–3pm; dinner Mon–Sat 4–11pm.

A la carte dining is offered in the Rittersaal (Knights' Hall) in the cellar of Vienna's City Hall. It's a beautiful room, with medievallike murals on the vaulted ceilings, pink tablecloths, beautiful lamps, and flowers on every table. In the evenings there's live classical music. Incidentally, farther down the hall is the Grinzinger Keller, where at 8pm Tuesday through Saturday night in the summer a fixed-price meal with traditional Viennese entertainment is offered for a package of 370 S ($33.65) per person. Call for reservations.

6. ATTRACTIONS

SUGGESTED ITINERARIES

The Habsburgs, who ruled over a vast empire for 600 years, left behind a rich collection of art, treasures, buildings, and palaces. These, together with the score of other museums and sights Vienna has to offer, make it necessary to plan your itinerary. Let the suggestions below be your guide.

IF YOU HAVE ONE DAY Start the morning with a tour of Vienna's Old City, beginning at Stephansplatz. Here you'll find the towering St. Stephen's Cathedral,

Vienna ★

AUSTRIA

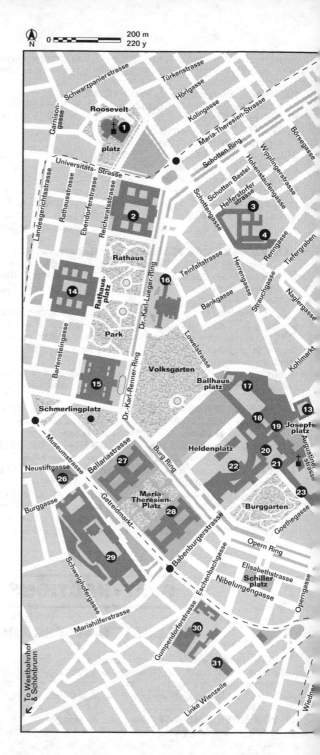

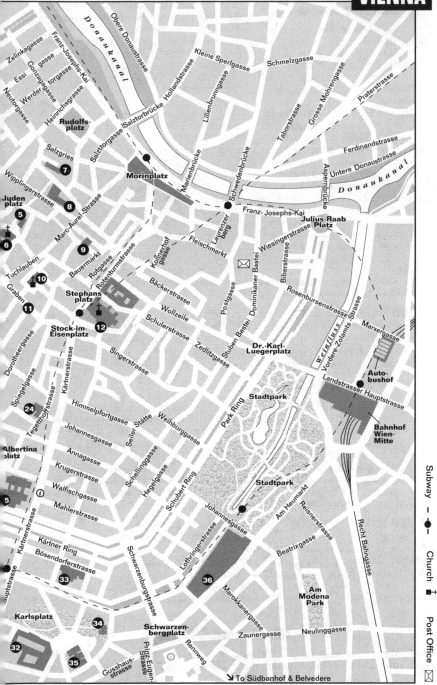

Donau kanal

Obere Donaustrasse

Zelinkagasse

Franz-Josephs-Kai

Essi gasse

Gonzagagasse

Werder torgasse

Neutorgasse

Heinrichsgasse

Rudolfs-platz

Salzgries

Wipplingerstrasse

Salztorgasse

Salztorbrücke

Marc-Aurel Strasse

Juden platz

5

6

Tuchlauben

Bauermarkt

Rotgasse

Rotenturmstrasse

10

Graben

11

Stephans platz

Stock-im-Eisenplatz

12

Dorotheergasse

Singerstrasse

Spiegelgasse

24

Tegetthoffstrasse

Kärntnerstrasse

Himmelpfortgasse

Johannesgasse

Annagasse

Krugerstrasse

Walfischgasse

Mahlerstrasse

Albertina platz

5

Kärntnerstrasse

Kärntner Ring

Bösendorferstrasse

33

Karlsplatz

34

32

35

Gusshaus-strasse

Prinz-Eugen-Strasse

Schwarzen-bergplatz

Schwarzenbergstrasse

Morinplatz

Marienbrücke

Hollandstrasse

Lilienbrunngasse

Kleine Sperlgasse

Schmelzgasse

Grosse Mohrengasse

Praterstrasse

Taborstrasse

Ferdinandstrasse

Untere Donaustrasse

Aspernbrücke

Schwedenbrücke

Franz-Josephs-Kai

Julius-Raab Platz

Lawenzer berg

Fleischmarkt

Wiesingerstrasse

Biberstrasse

Kollnerhof gasse

Bäckerstrasse

Postgasse

Dominikaner Bastei

Rosenbursenstrasse

Marxergasse

Wollzeile

Schulerstrasse

Stuben Bastei

Zedlitzgasse

Dr.-Karl-Luegerplatz

Weihburggasse

Seiler Stätte

Schellinggasse

Hegelgasse

Schubert Ring

Lothringerstrasse

Johannesgasse

Park Ring

Stadtpark

Stadtpark

Am Heumarkt

Reisnerstrasse

Beatrixgasse

Recht Bahngasse

Vordere Zollamts Strasse

Landstrasser Hauptstrasse

Auto-bushof

Bahnhof Wien-Mitte

Marokkanergasse

Am Modena Park

Zaunergasse

Neulinggasse

Rennweg

36

↘ To Südbanhof & Belvedere

Subway —●—

Church ∎ †

Post Office ☒

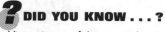

Vienna's most important Gothic building and its best-known landmark. First constructed in the 12th century and then enlarged and reconstructed over the next eight centuries, it has a 450-foot-high south tower with 343 spiral steps—which you can climb round and round and be rewarded with a great view of the city (entrance is outside the church on its south side). If you don't like stairs, you can take an elevator to the top of the never-completed north tower, only about half as high as the south tower.

Radiating from Stephansplatz is the Old City. Of particular beauty are Schön-laterngasse and Annagasse, two lanes reminiscent of what Vienna used to look like, and Am Hof, Vienna's largest square. Have coffee at one of the famous coffeehouses, and then stroll down the Kärntner Strasse pedestrian shopping street for a look at modern Vienna.

After you've seen the inner city, hightail it to Schönbrunn, Vienna's most famous attraction and home of the Habsburg dynasty. Finish the day with a performance at the opera or theater, topped with a drink in one of Vienna's historic wine cellars.

IF YOU HAVE TWO DAYS Spend your first day as outlined above. On the second, head toward the Hofburg, the official residence of the Habsburgs, which now contains a treasury with an astounding collection of riches and the imperial rooms. Nearby is the Kunsthistorisches Museum, a fine-arts museum with its great collection of the old masters. If you have time, walk to the nearby Imperial Crypts, where the Habsburgs have been buried for the last 300 years. Spend the evening in Grinzing or one of Vienna's other wine districts.

IF YOU HAVE THREE DAYS In addition to the sights given above, try to schedule some activities that occur only on certain days of the week. Training sessions of the renowned Spanish Riding School, for example, take place Tuesday through Saturday from 10am to noon (except for the months of July and August), and the Vienna Boys' Choir sings at masses on Sunday.

Other important sights you should include on a three-day stay in Vienna are the open-air market at Naschmarkt (on Saturday there's also a flea market) and Belvedere Palace, where you'll find three art galleries. In the evening go to Prater, Vienna's old-fashioned amusement park.

IF YOU HAVE FIVE DAYS Spend the first three days as outlined above. On the fourth day, explore your own special interests—visiting composers' homes, the Museum of Military History, the Museum of Applied Arts, the Clock Museum, or Vienna's Historical Museum. Architecture buffs should be sure to see the Hundertwasser Haus and KunstHausWien.

On your fifth day, take a trip to Vienna's countryside. Popular destinations include the famous Vienna Woods and the extensive park along the Danube (where you can even go swimming in the summer).

TOP ATTRACTIONS

Remember to purchase a copy of *Vienna from A to Z* for an explanation of the city's many historically important buildings. In addition, the *Wien Monatsprogramm* lists all special exhibitions being held at museums and galleries in Vienna. Both are available at the Vienna Tourist Board.

If you thrive on museums, purchase the **Museum Pass,** good for all municipal and national museums at a price of 150 S ($13.65). It contains 14 coupons worth 15 S ($1.35) each, a savings of 28%. Depending on the museum, one to three coupons may be required for admission. The pass can be used by several people and is transferable.

Note that most museums are closed on January 1, Good Friday, Easter Sunday, May 1, Whitsunday, Corpus Christi, November 1 and 2, December 24 and 25, and for general elections. Exceptions are the Museum of Fine Arts, Schönbrunn Place, the Hofburg, and the Imperial Burial Vault, which remain open on Easter Sunday/Monday and on Whitsunday/Monday.

SCHÖNBRUNN, Schönbrunner Schlosstrasse. Tel. 81113.

★ To visit Vienna without seeing the lovely summer palace of Schönbrunn is like not visiting Vienna at all. A baroque palace with an astounding 1,441 rooms, it was built between 1696 and 1730 in the midst of a glorious garden. Empress Maria Theresa left the greatest imprint on Schönbrunn: In the course of having 16 children (one of whom was Marie Antoinette), running the country, and fighting a war for her right to sit on the Austrian throne, she still found time to decorate and redesign Schönbrunn (1744–49), and it remains virtually as she left it. When the French besieged Vienna in the early 19th century, Napoléon I was so impressed with Schönbrunn that he occupied Maria Theresa's favorite rooms. Emperor Franz Joseph I was born in the palace and lived here with his beautiful wife, Elisabeth. And it was here, too, that Charles I, Austria's last emperor, abdicated and renounced the Imperial Crown.

To see the inside of the predominantly white-and-gilt palace, you must join a 40-minute tour that visits 40 of the palace's many rooms. Immediately upon arrival, check for the next English-language tour. If there's a wait, you can always take a walk through the 500 acres of palace grounds, one of the most important baroque gardens in the French style. At the top of the hill opposite the palace is the Gloriette, a monument to soldiers. There's also the lovely Neptune Fountain, artificial Roman ruins, a zoo, and the Palmenhaus, built in 1883 as the largest glasshouse in Europe. Be sure, too, to visit the Wagenburg, a museum with 36 carriages belonging to the imperial family.

As for the palace tour, among the rooms you'll visit are: the exotic Chinese Rooms; the cheerful breakfast room decorated with appliqué work done by Maria Theresa's daughters; the Hall of Mirrors, where the 6-year-old Mozart played for Maria Theresa; the Napoleon Room, where Napoleon lived and his only legitimate son died; and the Large Gallery, fashioned after a room in Versailles and used for imperial banquets. Most spectacular is perhaps the Millions Room, Maria Theresa's private salon decorated with 260 precious parchment miniatures set under glass in the paneling and brought from Constantinople.

Admission: Schönbrunn tour, 50 S ($4.55) adults, 25 S ($2.25) students with an International Student ID Card (up to age 27), 10 S (90¢) children 6–10; Wagenburg, 30 S ($2.70) adults, 15 S ($1.35) students, free for children to age 10.

Open: Schönbrunn tours, July–Sept, daily 8:30am–5:30pm; Apr–June and Oct, daily 8:30am–5pm; Nov–Mar, daily 9am–4pm (closed Jan 1, Nov 1, Dec 25). Wagenburg, summer, Tues–Sun 10am–5pm; winter, Tues–Sun 10am–4pm. **U-Bahn:** U-4 to Schönbrunn or Hietzing. **Tram:** 58 from anywhere along Mariahilfer Strasse to Schloss Schönbrunn.

HOFBURG (Imperial Palace), Michaeler Platz 1, Burgring. Tel. 587 55 54.

The Hofburg was the Imperial Palace of the Habsburgs for more than six centuries, during which time changes and additions were made in every conceivable architectural style—Gothic, Renaissance, baroque, rococo, classical, and the early

1870s. The entire Hofburg occupies 47 acres, a virtual city within a city, with more than 2,600 rooms. Contained in the vast complex are the Schauräume, the former Imperial Rooms; the Schatzkammer, the Treasury with its magnificent imperial and religious treasures (described below); and the Neue Hofburg, with its collection of medieval armor and weapons and its museum of ancient musical instruments as well as instruments played by Brahms, Haydn, Schumann, and other composers. The Spanish Riding School and the Burgkapelle featuring Sunday masses with the Vienna Boys' Choir are also on the Hofburg grounds (also described below).

The Schauräume will seem a bit plain after the splendor of Schönbrunn, but what I like about it is that you can wander around on your own (guided tours are only in German most of the year). You'll see the apartments of Franz Joseph and his wife, Elisabeth, and of Tsar Alexander I of Russia. There are several portraits of a young Elisabeth, a beautiful woman from the Wittelsbach family of Munich who was married to Franz Joseph in 1854 to further German interests. Known as Sissi, she was a talented, artistic, and vain woman—she would no longer sit for portraits after the age of 30—and in the Hofburg is her own small gymnasium where she kept in shape (much to the disgust of the court, which thought it improper for a lady). Rudolf, the son of Elisabeth and Franz Joseph and the only male heir to the throne, committed suicide in Mayerling. Elisabeth herself was assassinated in 1898 by an anarchist in Geneva.

You'll also see the royal dining room laid out with the imperial place setting—notice how the silverware is laid only on the right side and is turned down, according to Spanish court etiquette, which was the rage of the time. There are five wine glasses for each guest, and the napkins are 3.3 square feet each.

The Hofburg is located inside the Ring, about a seven-minute walk from Stephansplatz.

Admission: Schauräme, 25 S ($2.25) adults, 10 S (90¢) students and children; Weapons Collection or the Collection of Ancient Musical Instruments, 30 S ($2.70) each for adults, 15 S ($1.35) students and children.

Open: Schauräume, Mon–Sat 8:30am–noon and 12:30–4:30pm (last admission at 4pm), Sun and hols 8:30am–12:30pm (closed May 1, Nov 2, Dec 24, Dec 31); Weapons Collection and Collection of Ancient Musical Instruments, Mon, Wed, and Fri 10am–4pm, Sat–Sun 9am–4pm. **U-Bahn:** U-1 or U-3 to Stephansplatz or U-2 to Mariahilfer Strasse. **Tram:** 1, 2, D, or J to Burgring.

SCHATZKAMMER (Treasury), Hofburg, Schweizerhof. Tel. 533 79 31.

The Schatzkammer displays the royal and religious treasures of the Habsburg family, a collection that is nothing short of stunning. Its displays of priceless imperial regalia and relics of the Holy Roman Empire of the German nation include royal crowns inlaid with diamonds, rubies, pearls, sapphires, and other gems, as well as christening robes of the Habsburg family, swords, imperial crosses, altars, and coronation robes. Two prized Habsburg heirlooms are considered to have strange mystical and religious significance—the Agate Bowl, dating from the 4th century, was once thought to be the Holy Grail; and the Ainkhörn, a huge narwhale tusk, was associated with Christ.

Admission: 60 S ($5.45) adults, 30 S ($2.70) senior citizens, students, and children.

Open: Wed–Mon 10am–6pm. **U-Bahn:** U-1 or U-3 to Stephansplatz or U-2 to Mariahilfer Strasse. **Tram:** 1, 2, D, or J to Burgring.

SPANISCHE REITSCHULE (Spanish Riding School), Hofburg, Josefsplatz.

This prestigious school has roots dating back to more than 400 years ago when Spanish horses were brought to Austria for breeding. The famous and graceful Lippizaner horses are a cross of Berber and Arabian stock with Spanish and Italian horses (they are born with dark coats, turning white only between 4 and 10 years of age). Their performances with intricate steps and movements are a sight to be seen, but cheaper and almost as good are the morning training sessions.

In fact, tickets for the regular performances are so hard to come by that your best bet may be for the training sessions. If you're determined to see a performance, write in advance to Spanische Reitschule, Hofburg, 1010 Vienna. Otherwise, there are short 30-minute performances on Saturdays in May and a couple Saturdays in June and September at 9am, tickets for which are sold at theater ticket and travel agencies (including American Express and Intropa, both on Kärntner Strasse). Note, however, that you have to pay the extra 22% commission charged by agencies.

If you decide to go to a training session, get there early and wait in line (Gate 2), since no reservations are accepted for these.

Admission: Regular performances, seats 200–700 S ($18.20–$63.65), standing room 150–160 S ($13.65–$14.55); short performances 165 S ($15), plus 22% commission. Training sessions, 70 S ($6.35) adults, 20 S ($1.80) children.

Open: Regular performances, Mar–June and Sept to mid-Dec, Sun at 10:45am and most Weds at 7pm; short performances, May and Sept, Sat at 9am; training sessions, mid-Feb to June, end of Aug to mid-Oct, and mid-Nov to mid-Dec, Tues–Fri 10am–noon. **U-Bahn:** U-1 or U-3 to Stephansplatz.

WIENER SÄNGERKNABEN (Vienna Boys' Choir), Burgkapelle, Hofburg (entrance on Schweizerhof).

The Vienna Boys' Choir was founded in 1498 to sing at church services for the court. Both Joseph Haydn and Franz Schubert sang in the choir, which now actually consists of several choirs, two of which are usually on world tours. You can hear the Boys' Choir perform every Sunday and religious holiday at 9:15am mass in the Burgkapelle of the Hofburg, from January to the end of June and from mid-September to Christmas. Seats should be ordered at least two months in advance by writing to Hofmusikkapelle, Hofburg, A-1010 Vienna. Do not enclose money or a check, but rather pick up your ticket at the Burgkapelle on the Friday preceding the performance between 11am and noon or on Sunday before 9am. Unsold tickets go on sale also at the Burgkapelle on Friday from 5pm (it's wise to get there by 4:30pm).

Note that standing room for mass is free, but there's room for only 20 people on a first-come, first-served basis, so get there early if you're interested.

Admission: Seats, 50–180 S ($4.55–$16.35); standing room, free.

Open: Mass held Sun and religious hols at 9:15am Jan–June and mid-Sept to Dec. **Closed:** Jan 6, Ascension Day, Dec 8, Dec 26. **U-Bahn:** U-1 or U-3 to Stephansplatz.

KUNSTHISTORISCHES MUSEUM (Museum of Fine Arts), Maria-Theresien-Platz. Tel. 521 77 301.

✪ This great museum owes its existence largely to the Habsburgs, who for centuries were patrons and collectors of art. There are several collections, of which the Egyptian-Oriental Collection and the Picture Gallery are the most outstanding. Other collections include coins and medals and sculpture and applied arts from the medieval, Renaissance, and baroque periods.

The Picture Gallery is up on the first floor, with paintings by Rubens, Rembrandt, Dürer, Memling, Titian, Giorgione, Tintoretto, Caravaggio, and Velázquez. The high point of the entire museum, however, is a room full of Brueghels, including the *Turmbau zu Babel* (Tower of Babel), *Die Jäger im Schnee* (The Hunters in the Snow—you can hardly believe it's not real), the *Kinderspiel* (in which children have taken over an entire town), and *Die Bauernhochzeit* (The Peasant Wedding—notice how the bride is isolated in front of the green cloth, barred by custom from eating or talking).

Admission: 45 S ($4.10) adults, 20 S ($1.80) senior citizens, students, and children to age 10, free for children under age 10.

Open: Tues and Fri 10am–9pm, Wed–Thurs and Sat–Sun and hols 10am–6pm. **U-Bahn:** U-2 to Mariahilfer Strasse. **Tram:** 1, 2, 52, 58, D, or J to Burgring.

BELVEDERE, Prinz-Eugen-Strasse 27 (Oberes Belvedere) and Rennweg 6 (Unteres Belvedere). Tel. 784 15 80.

The Belvedere is a light, airy baroque palace built in the early 1700s as a summer residence for Austria's beloved Prince Eugene (from Savoy), who succeeded in protecting Austria from a couple of Turkish invasions and was rewarded for his service by being made minister of war and later prime minister by Emperor Charles VI. He remained a bachelor his whole life, and when he died his estate fell to his heiress—"frightful Victoria" as the Viennese called her—who promptly sold the palace. The Imperial Court acquired the buildings and gardens in 1752, and it was here that Franz Ferdinand, heir to the throne, lived before taking his fateful trip to Sarajevo in 1914.

Belvedere is actually two palaces, now containing some important galleries. The **Oberes Belvedere** (close to the Südbahnhof) is the more lavish of the two, situated up on a hill with a sweeping view of the city. It's now a gallery for 19th- and 20th-century Austrian art, including Biedermeier paintings by Amerling and Waldmüller. Be sure to go up to the top floor, where you'll find the works of Oskar Kokoschka and Egon Schiele, as well as of Gustav Klimt (1862–1918), considered the foremost representative of Viennese Jugendstil (art nouveau) painting. You'll see his famous *Der Kuss* (The Kiss) and *Judith* (the frame was made by his brother).

A walk through the beautiful landscaped gardens brings you to the **Unteres Belvedere,** now home of the Museum of Austrian Baroque with its works of the 17th and 18th centuries. And finally, in the **Orangerie** is the Museum of Medieval Austrian Art, which includes sculpture and panel paintings from the end of the 12th to the early 16th century.

Admission (including all museums): 60 S ($5.45) adults, 30 S ($2.70) senior citizens, students, and children above age 10, free for children to age 10.

Open: Tues–Sun 10am–5pm. **Tram:** D to Schloss Belvedere (Oberes Belvedere); or 71 to Unteres Belvedere.

MORE ATTRACTIONS

STEPHANSDOM (St. Stephen's Cathedral), Stephansplatz. Tel. 51552 or 51 55 63.

In the heart of the Old City, Stephansdom is Vienna's best-known landmark. First constructed in the 12th century and then enlarged and reconstructed for the next eight centuries, it remains Vienna's most important Gothic structure. Its dimensions are huge—352 feet long with a nave 128 feet high. The highest part is its 450-foot-high south tower, completed in 1433, with 343 spiral steps. The south tower is open to the public (entrance is on the church's south side) and affords one of the best views of the city. If you don't like to climb stairs, you can take an elevator to the top of the north tower, which was never completed and is only about half as high as the south tower. Finally, the Catacombs of the cathedral contain copper urns bearing the intestines of the Habsburg family (their bodies are in the Imperial Burial Vault, described below, while their hearts are in the Augustiner Church).

Admission: Cathedral, free; south tower, 20 S ($1.80) adults, 5 S (45¢) children; north tower, 40 S ($3.65) adults, 15 S ($1.35) children; catacombs, 30 S ($2.70) adults, 20 S ($1.80) students, 10 S (90¢) children.

Open: South tower, summer, daily 9am–5:30pm; winter, daily 9am–4:30pm. North tower, daily 8am–4:45pm. Catacombs, Mon–Sat 10–11:30am and 2–4:30pm, Sun and hols 2–4:30pm. **U-Bahn:** U-1 or U-3 to Stephansplatz.

KAPUZINERKIRCHE, WITH THE KAISERGRUFT (Imperial Burial Vault), Neuer Markt 1. Tel. 512 68 53.

Most visitors to Vienna feel it their duty to make a pilgrimage to the Kapuziner Church (located behind the Opera House on tiny Tegetthoffstrasse), which contains the Imperial Burial Vault and the coffins of 136 Habsburg family members. Some of the coffins are very elaborate; the biggest one belongs to Empress Maria Theresa and her husband. They're surrounded by the coffins of their 16 children, many of whom died in infancy. The only non-Habsburg to be buried here was the governess to Maria Theresa and her children. Each coffin has two keys, which are kept at separate places to prevent foul play. The coffins contain only the embalmed bodies; the intestines are kept in copper urns in the catacombs of Stephansdom, while the hearts are in the Augustiner Church.

Admission: 30 S ($2.70) adults, 20 S ($1.80) senior citizens, students, and children.

Open: Daily 9:30am–4pm. **U-Bahn:** U-1 or U-3 to Stephansplatz.

ALBERTINA GRAPHISCHE SAMMLUNGEN (Albertina Collection of Graphic Art), Augustinerstrasse 1. Tel. 534 83.

Quite simply, this is one of the largest and most important graphic-art collections in the world, with European drawings and prints from the 15th century to the present. However, because these works of art are so sensitive to light and climatic conditions, only a few of them are displayed at any one time. Special exhibitions center on a theme—for example, the works of Albrecht Dürer (the world's largest Dürer collection, including his famous *Hare* and *Praying Hands*). One room has copies of some of the most famous pieces, with works by Dürer, Brueghel, Rembrandt, Rubens, Klimt, and others.

Admission: 45 S ($4.10) adults, 20 S ($1.80) senior citizens, students, and children, free for children up to age 10.

Open: Mon–Tues and Thurs 10am–4pm, Wed 10am–6pm, Fri 10am–2pm, Sat–Sun 10am–1pm. **U-Bahn:** U-1 to Karlsplatz-Oper.

ÖSTERREICHISCHES MUSEUM FÜR ANGEWANDTE KUNST (Museum of Applied Arts), Stubenring 5. Tel. 7 1136 or 2949.

✪ The oldest museum of applied arts on the European continent, this is a fine collection of Austrian ceramics, furniture, silver, and jewelry, housed in a stately 19th-century building constructed in Florentine Renaissance style. It contains a fascinating collection of Viennese chairs from the 1800s, as well as designs of the Wiener Werkstätte, a remarkable workshop founded at the turn of the century by Josef Hoffmann, Kolo Moser, and Fritz Waerndorfer. The museum's Jugendstil and art nouveau collections are particularly outstanding, with works from around Europe. There's also a room devoted to works from Asia, including lacquerware, porcelain, and Buddha statues, while another room shows the similarities between Eastern and Western art. This is a fascinating museum, and what's more, it's never crowded.

Admission: 40 S ($3.65) adults, 20 S ($1.80) students, free for children.

Open: Wed–Mon 11am–6pm (half the museum closed 12:45–1:30pm; the other half closed 1:30–2:15pm). **U-Bahn:** U-4 to Landstrasse Wien Mitte or U-3 to Stubentor. **Tram:** 1 or 2 to Dr.-Karl-Lueger-Platz.

MUSEUM MODERNER KUNST (Museum of Modern Art), Liechtenstein Palace, Fürstengasse 1. Tel. 34 12 59 or 34 63 03.

Housed in a baroque building is the city's Museum of Modern Art, with international works of art from the 20th century. Included in the collection are works by Richard Estes, Malcolm Morley, Andy Warhol, Paul Klee, Wassily Kandinsky, and Austrians Kolo Moser, Max Oppenheimer, Oskar Kokoschka, and Egon Schiele. Emphasis of the museum is on Viennese works since 1900, "classical modern" art from cubism to abstraction, and abstract art since 1950. The permanent exhibitions are on the first and second floors. There are also temporary exhibitions both here and at a second location, Museum des 20. Jahrhunderts, in the Schweizer Garten.

Admission: 30 S ($2.70) adults, 15 S ($1.35) senior citizens and students, free for children.

Open: Wed–Mon 10am–6pm. **Tram:** D to Fürstengasse.

HISTORISCHES MUSEUM DER STADT WIEN (Vienna Historical Museum), Karlsplatz 4. Tel. 505 87 47.

The Vienna Historical Museum is devoted to Vienna's 7,000 years of history, from the Neolithic period and the time of the tribal migrations through the Middle Ages to the blossoming of Biedermeier and Jugendstil. There's armor, booty from the Turkish invasions, models of the city, furniture, glassware, and paintings by Klimt,

Waldmüller, and Schiele among others. One room is the complete interior of poet Franz Grillparzer's apartment; there's also the living room of architect Loos.

Admission: 30 S ($2.70) adults, 15 S ($1.35) senior citizens, 10 S (90¢) students and children.

Open: Tues–Sun 9am–4:30pm. **U-Bahn:** U-1, U-2, or U-4 to Karlsplatz.

SIGMUND FREUD HAUS, Burggasse 19. Tel. 319 15 69.

Sigmund Freud lived and worked here from 1891 to 1938. This small museum documents his life, with photographs of him, his mother, wife, and others who influenced his life. A notebook in English is available that identifies everything in the museum, with translations of passages written by Freud. To enter the house, it's necessary to ring the doorbell and push the door at the same time.

Admission: 45 S ($4.10) adults, 20 S ($1.80) senior citizens, students, and children.

Open: Daily 9am–3pm. **U-Bahn:** U-2 to Schottentor, then a 10-minute walk. **Tram:** D to Schlickgasse.

KUNSTHAUSWIEN, Untere Weissgerberstrasse 13. Tel. 712 04 91.

One of the newest additions to Vienna's art scene, the KunstHausWien is the brain child of Austrian painter and designer Friedensreich Hundertwasser, famous for his whimsical, fantastical, and thought-provoking paintings, prints, and architecture. Created from a former factory building of the Thonet Company (well known for its bentwood furniture), the KunstHausWien is a museum housing approximately 300 works of Hundertwasser, including paintings, prints, tapestries, and architectural models. Typical of Hundertwasser, the building itself is one of the exhibits, a colorful protest against the mundane gray of modern cities.

There's a café that features 100 different Thonet chairs and an uneven, buckled floor, as well as a museum shop. Be sure, too, to see the **Hundertwasser Haus,** a nearby apartment complex Hundertwasser designed on the corner of Kegelgasse and Löwengasse in the mid-1980s (about a four-minute walk from the KunstHausWien). On Kegelgasse is also **Kalke Village,** another Hundertwasser architectural conversion, this time from a former stable and gas station into a small shopping complex housing boutiques and a café.

Admission: 50 S ($4.55) adults, 40 S ($3.65) senior citizens and students, free for children under 12.

Open: KunstHausWien, daily 10am–7pm. Kalke Village, winter, daily 10am–5pm; summer, daily 9am–7pm. **Tram:** N or O to Radetzkyplatz.

UHRENMUSEUM, Schulhof 2. Tel. 533 22 65.

More than 1,000 clocks from all over the world are on display in this delightful museum, including tower clocks (one is from Stephansdom), pocket watches, portable sun clocks, Japanese pillar clocks, and more. The oldest clock dates from the early 15th century (it still works). The museum is located just off the northeast end of Am Hof square.

Admission: 30 S ($2.70) adults, 15 S ($1.35) senior citizens, 10 S (90¢) students and children.

Open: Tues–Sun 9am–4:30pm. **U-Bahn:** U-1 or U-3 to Stephansplatz.

PUPPEN & SPIELZEUG MUSEUM (Doll and Toy Museum), Schulhof 4. Tel. 535 68 60.

Located right beside the Clock Museum is this museum dedicated to dolls and dollhouses. Most of the hundreds of dolls in the collection are German, dating from 1830 to 1930, but also included are dolls from France and other European countries. The displays are excellently laid out, and the museum itself is in a house centuries old. Most of the visitors are adults.

Admission: 60 S ($5.45) adults, 30 S ($2.70) senior citizens, students, and children.

Open: Tues–Sun 10am–6pm. **U-Bahn:** U-1 or U-3 to Stephansplatz.

HEERESGESCHICHTLICHES MUSEUM (Museum of Military History), Arsenal. Tel. 78 23 03.

Housed in a Moorish-Byzantine–style building constructed in the 1850s as part of the Vienna Arsenal, this museum has an admirable collection of weapons, uniforms, and memorabilia from the Thirty Years' War to the present. Included are guns, sabers, planes, tanks, heavy artillery, and model ships. One room commemorates the start of World War I, with displays of the automobile Archduke Franz Ferdinand and his wife were riding in when assassinated in Sarajevo and the uniform the archduke was wearing.

Admission: 30 S ($2.70) adults, 15 S ($1.35) students and children.

Open: Sat–Thurs 10am–4pm. **Directions:** U-1, tram D or 18, or bus no. 13A to the Südbahnhof, then a 10-minute walk, through the Schweizer Garten.

PRATER, Hauptallee. Tel. 512 83 14.

Prater is Vienna's amusement park, first opened to the general public in 1766 on the former grounds of Emperor Maximilian II's game preserve. Most notable is its giant Ferris wheel, built in 1896 (and then rebuilt after its destruction in World War II) and measuring 200 feet in diameter. There are also the usual shooting ranges, amusement rides, game arcades, and beer halls. This is a good place for a stroll on a warm summer's night.

Admission: Free; charges for amusement rides.

Open: Apr–Sept, daily 9am–11pm; Mar and Oct, daily 10am–10pm. **Closed:** Nov–Feb. **Directions:** U-Bahn U-1 or S-Bahn to Praterstern.

PARKS & GARDENS

STADTPARK, Parkring.

The Stadtpark, or City Park, dates from the mid-1800s, covers about 22 acres, and is located in the center of town right on the Ring. At its western edge is the Kursalon, with classical music recitals every evening.

U-Bahn: U-4 to Stadtpark. **Tram:** 1, 2, J, or T.

VOLKSGARTEN, Dr.-Karl-Renner-Ring.

Even older than the Stadtpark is the Volksgarten, which opened in 1820 on the site of fortifications blown up by the French. There's a memorial to Empress Elisabeth here, located just north of the Hofburg on the Ring.

U-Bahn: U-2 or U-3 to Volkstheater. **Tram:** 1, 2, D, or J to Parliament.

BURGGARTEN, Opernring-Burgring.

Slightly smaller and also on the Ring, the Burggarten is just south of the Hofburg. It came into being when Napoleon ordered the bastions of the Burg to be destroyed in 1809. Becoming a public park in 1919, it contains monuments to Mozart and Franz Joseph I.

Tram: 1, 2, 52, 58, D, or J to Burgring.

BOTANISCHER GARTEN, Mechelgasse 3. Tel. 78 71 01.

Located just east of the gardens of Belvedere (see the Belvedere sightseeing entry, above), the Botanical Garden was laid out in 1757 on the order of Empress Maria Theresa as a medicinal garden. Today it's known for its cacti, succulents, and orchids.

Admission: Free.

Tram: 71 to Unteres Belvedere, or D to Schloss Belvedere.

SCHÖNBRUNN PARK, Schönbrunner Schlosstrasse.

The 500 acres of this palace garden are considered one of the most important baroque gardens laid out in the French style. It contains fountains, artificial Roman ruins, a large greenhouse, a butterfly house, a palm house, and a zoo.

U-Bahn: U-4 to Schönbrunn or Hietzing. **Tram:** 58 to Schloss Schönbrunn.

SPECIAL-INTEREST SIGHTSEEING

FOR THE MUSIC LOVER

If you're a fan of Mozart, Schubert, Strauss, Haydn, or Beethoven, you've certainly come to the right city. Here you'll find the houses where they lived, the cemetery where most of them are buried, and statues of these musical giants everywhere (especially in the Stadtpark and the Burggarten).

In addition, you might also like to see the interior of the **Staatsoper,** Opernring 2. (tel. 51444-2955), especially during the months of July and August when there are no performances. Built in 1861–69 and rebuilt after World War II, it is considered one of the world's best opera houses (see "Evening Entertainment," below, for performance information). Tours of the Staatsoper are held throughout the year—check the board outside the entrance for times of the day's tours, usually twice a day in winter and as many as five times a day in summer, in both English and German. Tours cost 40 S ($3.65). The entryway for the tours is on the west side of the building.

You can also visit apartments where the composers lived. Set up as memorial rooms, they are all a bit plain and unadorned, something only devoted music fans might be interested in seeing. All the apartments are open the same hours for the same charge and are free on Friday mornings (except holidays).

BEETHOVEN-GEDENKSTÄTTE, in the Pasqualati House, Mölker Bastei 8. Tel. 637 06 65.

Ludwig van Beethoven (1770–1827) came to Vienna from Germany when he was 22 years old and stayed here until his death. Moody and rebellious, Beethoven had habits so irregular (he sometimes played and composed in the middle of the night) that he was constantly being evicted from apartments all over Vienna. One landlord who loved him, however, was Mr. Pasqualati, who kept Beethoven's apartment free—no one else was allowed to live in it, even when the restless composer was not there. Beethoven lived here on and off from 1804 to 1815 and composed his Fourth, Fifth, and Seventh Symphonies here. Adjoining the Beethoven memorial rooms is the Adalbert Stifter Memorial, with paintings and drawings. (You can also visit other places he lived: at Probusgasse 6 and the Eroica House at Döblinger Hauptstrasse 92.)

Admission: 15 S ($1.35) adults, 5 S (45¢) students and children.
Open: Tues–Sun 9am–12:15pm and 1–4:30pm. **U-Bahn:** U-2 to Schottentor. **Tram:** 1, 2, or D to Schottentor.

HAYDN-WOHNHAUS MIT BRAHMS-GEDENKRAUM, Haydngasse 19. Tel. 596 13 07.

Considered to have invented the symphony, Joseph Haydn (1732–1809) acquired this tiny house in 1793 and lived here until his death. In addition to his letters, manuscripts, and personal mementos are two pianos and his death mask. There's also a memorial room to Brahms.

Admission: 15 S ($1.35) adults, 5 S (45¢) students and children.
Open: Tues–Sun 9am–12:15pm and 1–4:30pm. **Tram:** 52 or 58.

MOZART'S FIGAROHAUS, Domgasse 5. Tel. 513 62 94.

Born in Salzburg and moving to Vienna in 1781, Mozart (1756–91) lived here with his wife and son for three years, from 1784 to 1787. These were his happiest years, and it was here that he wrote *The Marriage of Figaro* and received visits from Haydn and a 16-year-old Beethoven. Located just off Stephansplatz in what used to be a wealthy neighborhood, Figarohaus was already 200 years old when Mozart lived here. His apartment is up on the first floor, which you can reach by walking through a tiny courtyard and then up some dark stairs. Mozart later lived in poverty and died a pauper.

Admission: 15 S ($1.35) adults, 5 S (45¢) students and children.
Open: Tues–Sun 9am–12:15pm and 1–4:30pm. **U-Bahn:** U-1 or U-3 to Stephansplatz.

SCHUBERT'S BIRTHPLACE, Nussdorfer Strasse 54. Tel. 345 99 24.

This is the house where Franz Schubert was born in 1797. A versatile and prolific composer who wrote symphonies, masses, piano pieces, operas, and musical comedies, Schubert died when he was only 31. In addition to his birthplace, you can also visit the place where he died, at Kettenbrückengasse 6.
Admission: 15 S ($1.35) adults, 5 S (45¢) students and children.
Open: Tues–Sun 9am–12:15pm and 1–4:30pm. **S-Bahn:** Nussdorfer Strasse.
Tram: D, 8, or 42.

JOHANN-STRAUSS-WOHNUNG, Praterstrasse 54. Tel. 24 01 21.

This is where Strauss (1825–99) composed his famous *Blue Danube* waltz, which is probably better known than the Austrian national anthem. He lived here from 1863 to 1870.
Admission: 15 S ($1.35) adults, 5 S (45¢) for students and children.
Open: Tues–Sun 9am–12:15pm and 1–4:30pm. **U-Bahn:** U-1 to Nestroyplatz.

ZENTRALFRIEDHOF (Central Cemetery), Simmeringer Hauptstrasse 234. Tel. 76 55 44.

Austria's largest cemetery, it contains the graves of Strauss (both father and son), Brahms, Schubert, Franz von Suppé, and Beethoven, as well as a commemorative grave of Mozart.
Admission: Free.
Open: Summer, daily 7am–7pm; winter, daily 8am–5pm. **Tram:** 71 from Schwarzenbergplatz to the next-to-the-last stop; walk through the main entrance straight ahead to the Graves of Honor, where you'll find all the composers buried within a few feet of each other, near the Dr. Karl Lueger Church.

FOR THE ARCHITECTURE BUFF

Vienna has a wealth of baroque palaces and fine buildings along and outside the Ring, including Schönbrunn, Belvedere, the Hofburg, and the Parliament. Other buildings of special interest to architects include the **Adolf Loos** building at Friedrichstrasse 6, constructed in 1899 and now a coffeehouse called Museum, and the Loos Building on Michaelerplatz, built in 1910 amid controversy because of its strict architectural style, void of any ornamentation. Loos also designed the public toilets on the Graben, which were recently renovated at a tremendous cost to the city—they may well be the most beautiful public toilets in the world. Lovers of art nouveau architecture should also check out the **Otto Wagner** U-Bahn station at Karlsplatz and his Postsparkasse bank at Georg-Coch-Platz 2. Both Loos and Wagner are Vienna's most important architects of the first part of this century.

Of course, the Old City inside the Ring is a treasure trove of architectural styles, particularly patrician houses built in the Middle Ages. **Am Hof, Annagasse, Bäckerstrasse, Fleischmarkt, and Schönlaterngasse** are just some of the streets with famous houses. Information on individual houses, as well as Vienna's most famous buildings, is given in *Vienna from A to Z*, available for 30 S ($2.70) from the Vienna Tourist Board.

In addition to Vienna's baroque palaces and its fine buildings inside the Ring, you might be interested in seeing the **Hundertwasser Haus,** located on the corner of Löwengasse and Kegelgasse. It's an apartment house like none you've ever seen—irregularly shaped, turreted, and almost fluid. You can't visit the apartments inside, but there is a coffee shop up on the first floor. People flock here just to take a photograph of the exterior.

Across the street on Kegelgasse is **Kalke Village,** a shopping complex designed by Hundertwasser, and a four-minute walk away is the **KunstHausWien,** a museum designed by Hundertwasser to house his works (see "More Attractions," above).

ORGANIZED TOURS

WALKING TOURS   There are a number of walking tours conducted in English. **Vienna Tourist Guides,** for example, offers guided walks through medieval Vienna, the old Jewish quarter of Vienna, an art nouveau architectural tour, and other parts of Vienna. Price of a tour is 100 S ($9.10) excluding entrance fees; 50 S ($4.55) for youths, free for children under 15.

Pick up a brochure, "Walks in Vienna," detailing the various tours, times, and departure points from the Vienna Tourist Board, Kärntner Strasse 38. No reservations are necessary for the tours, which last about 1½ hours and are held regardless of the weather.

BUS TOURS   There are a number of tour companies offering general city tours of Vienna and specialized tours, which you can book at travel agencies and at top hotels throughout the city. One tour company is **Cityrama,** Börsegasse 1 (tel. 53 41 30), which offers various tours that include Schönbrunn, the Hofburg, the Spanish Riding School training session, the Vienna Woods, the Mayerling hunting lodge where Crown Prince Rudolph committed suicide, musicians' homes, Grinzing, Prater, Salzburg, and more. A three-hour city tour costs 340 S ($30.90). Departure for tours is at the Kursalon in the Stadtpark.

TRAM TOURS   From May through September, tours of Vienna via a 1929-vintage tram car are conducted on Saturday, Sunday, and holidays. Departure is from Karlplatz; the cost is 150 S ($13.65) for adults and 50 S ($4.55) for children. For more information, contact the Vienna Tourist Board.

BOAT TOURS   Boats cruise the Danube May through September, departing from a pier next to Schwedenbrücke (U-Bahn station is Schwedenplatz, or a five-minute walk from Stephansplatz). Boats depart daily at 10:30am and 1, 2:30, 4:30pm. Tours last three hours and cost 180 S ($16.35), half price for children. For more information, call 21 7500-454.

SPECIAL & FREE EVENTS

For information on Vienna's many musical festivals, refer to "Pretrip Preparations," above. For free entertainment, don't forget that you can hear the famous Vienna Boys' Choir absolutely free during Sunday mass if you're willing to stand and you get there early (see "Top Attractions," above). In addition, there are free organ recitals in St. Stephen's Cathedral from May through October every Wednesday at 7pm.

7. SAVVY SHOPPING

Vienna is known for the excellent quality of its works, which of course do not come cheap. If money is no object, you may want to shop for petit-point items, hand-painted Augarten porcelain, gold jewelry, ceramics, enamel jewelry, and leather goods. Also popular is *Loden,* the boiled and rolled wool fabric fashioned into overcoats, suits, and hats, as well as knitted sweaters. If you're on a budget, Vienna's Saturday flea market is one of Europe's best.

Vienna's most famous shopping streets are in the city center, including the pedestrian Kärntner Strasse, the Graben, Kohlmarkt, and Rotenturmstrasse. Mariahilfer Strasse also has department stores and shops.

If you make a purchase of more than 1,000 S ($90.90) at any store, you are entitled to a refund of part of the Value-Added Tax (VAT), which is 20%–32% on regular items (such as clothing) and 24% on luxury items (such as jewelry). Make sure to ask the store clerk for a U-34 tax-refund form. Visitors leaving Austria by car receive their refund immediately from any Austrian Automobile Club office at the border; airplane passengers can claim their refund from the bank window at the airport (be sure you have your purchase with you and have your receipt stamped by a Customs official). If you're traveling by train, have the Customs officer at the border stamp the tax-refund form, then mail it back to the shop where you made your purchase.

FLEA MARKETS   If you're in Vienna on a Saturday, head straight for the town's best-known flea market, held on **Linke Wienzeile** near the Kettenbrücken U-Bahn station. This is the most colorful place in town to look for curios, antiques, old books, and junk, evident from the hordes of people who descend upon the place. I've bought old coffee grinders here for almost everyone I know (although they aren't quite the bargain they were 15 years ago). Be sure to haggle. It's open on Saturday from about 8am to 6pm.

If you're here only on a weekday, it's still worth a trip to the adjoining **Naschmarkt,** Vienna's outdoor food and produce market (see "Budget Dining," above).

Another market, for arts and crafts and antiques, held only in the summer from May through August, takes place on Saturday from 2 to 6pm and on Sunday from 10am to 6pm along the promenade of the Donaukanal at **Franz-Josephs-Kai** (near the Schwedenplatz U-Bahn station, north of Stephansplatz). It's an art and antiques market, with vendors selling paintings, books, stamps, coins, antique glass, and bric-a-brac, as well as contemporary art and crafts.

SHOPPING FOR THOSE TRAVEL ESSENTIALS   Vienna's main department stores are all conveniently located: **Gerngross,** Mariahilfer Strasse 38-48 (tel. 932 52 50); **Herzmansky,** Mariahilfer Strasse 26-30 (tel. 93 16 36); and **Stafa,** Mariahilfer Strasse 120 (tel. 938 62 10).

8. EVENING ENTERTAINMENT

Everything in Vienna is somewhat theatrical, due perhaps to its majestic baroque backdrop. Small wonder that opera and theater reign supreme here. It would be a shame to come all this way without experiencing something that's very dear to the Viennese heart.

To find out what's being played on Vienna's many stages, pick up a copy of *Wien Monatsprogramm,* available free at the Vienna Tourist Board. In addition to monthly programs, it also lists places where you can purchase tickets in advance, thereby avoiding the 22% surcharge on tickets sold at travel agencies. If you're a student under 27 years old with a valid ID from your college and university, you can purchase tickets for the Staatsoper, the Burgtheater, and Akademietheater for just 50 S ($4.55) on the night of the performance (an International Student Identity Card will not be accepted as proof of student status). Almost all other theaters also offer reduced rates for students, usually about 20% off the usual ticket price. Even if you're not a student, you can see the Burgtheater or Staatsoper (Austrian State Opera) for as little as 15 S ($1.35) for standing-room tickets.

THE PERFORMING ARTS

For advance sales of tickets for the Burgtheater, Akademietheater, Staatsoper, and Volksoper, go to the **Bundestheaterkassen,** Goethegasse 1 (tel. 514 44-2969), located just a minute's walk northwest of the Staatsoper. Tickets go on sale a week before each performance. The Bundestheaterkassen is open Monday through Friday from 8am to 6pm, on Saturday from 9am to 2pm, and on Sunday and holidays from 9am to noon. Tickets for all four stages are also available directly at each box office an hour before the performance, but only for that day's performance. Thus, if you're interested in seeing any production of the Burgtheater, Akademietheater, Staatsoper, or the Volksoper, this should be your first stop upon arrival in Vienna. Otherwise, you can also order tickets for these venues by credit card by calling 01/513 15 13 Monday through Friday from 9am to 5pm, on Saturday from 9am to 2pm, and on Sunday and holidays from 9am to noon. Telephone sales begin six days before the day of performance and can be ordered by holders of American Express, Diners Club, MasterCard, and VISA. Note that standing-room tickets are not sold in advance but only on the night of the performance.

OPERA & BALLET

STAATSOPER, Opernring 2. Tel. 51444-2959 or 51444-2960.

Considered one of the world's leading opera houses, the Staatsoper stages grand productions throughout the year except during July and August. It's tradition to start off each new year with the production of *Die Fledermaus* in January, but the rest of the year features only opera and ballet, accompanied by the Viennese Philharmonic orchestra. The program changes nightly (though there may be repeat performances later in the month), which means that a lot of time and money is spent on preparing and removing the stage sets alone. In fact, the Staatsoper employs 1,200 people, including the stage crew, singers, and production staff. The stage area is 5,300 square feet, one of the largest in Europe and much larger than the spectator floor of the opera house. The theater itself features a red, ivory, and gold interior, is horseshoe-shaped, and its walls are lined with box seats. It holds 2,200 people— 1,700 in seats and 500 in the standing-room sections.

You can spend as much as $136 for a ticket if you want, but the most economical way to see a performance is to purchase one of the 500 standing-room tickets available on the night of the performance. To do so, go to the Staatsoper at least three hours before the performance, stand in line, buy your ticket, and once inside, mark your "seat" by tying a scarf to the rail. You can then leave and come back just before the performance.

Incidentally, even though no operas or ballets are performed in July and August, other events take place, including concerts; check the *Monatsprogramm*.

Tours: Given almost daily throughout the year, two to five times a day (check the board outside the entrance for the times of each day's tours); cost is 40 S ($3.65).

Prices: Seats, 90–1,500 S ($8.20–$136.40) for most productions; standing room, 15 S ($1.35) for the Galerie (upper balcony), 20 S ($1.80) for the slightly better Parterrestehplatz (ground floor). Unsold tickets are available to students with ID for 50 S ($4.55) on the performance night at the box office.

Open: Box office at Bundestheaterkassen, Mon–Fri 8am–6pm, Sat 9am–2pm, Sun and hols 9am–noon; performances nightly Sept–June. **U-Bahn:** U-1, U-2, or U-4 to Karlsplatz-Oper.

VOLKSOPER, Währinger Strasse 78. Tel. 51444-3318.

Spectacular operettas and light operas are featured here, from *Der Zigeunerbaron* by Strauss to *Die Hochzeit des Figaro* by Mozart. Standing-room tickets and discount tickets for students are sold on the night of the performance.

Prices: Seats, 50–600 S ($4.55–$54.55); standing room, 15 S ($1.35) student tickets, 50 S ($4.55).

Open: Box office at Bundestheaterkassen, Mon–Fri 8am–6pm, Sat 9am–2pm, Sun and hols 9am–noon; performances, nightly (closed July–Aug), usually at 7pm, sometimes Sat–Sun matinees. **U-Bahn:** U-6 to Währinger-Strasse–Volksoper. **Tram:** 40, 41, or 42 to Währinger-Strasse–Volksoper.

THEATER

BURGTHEATER, Dr.-Karl-Lueger-Ring 2. Tel. 51444-2959.

Under the direction of Claus Peymann, the Burgtheater stages the great German classics as well as modern plays, from Friedrich Schiller's *Wilhelm Tell* to Georg

Büchner's *Woyzeck*. Actors and actresses consider an engagement here a highlight in their acting careers.

Prices: Seats, 50–450 S ($4.55–$40.90); standing room, 15 S ($1.35); student tickets, 50 S ($4.55).

Open: Box office at Bundestheaterkassen, Mon–Fri 8am–6pm, Sat 9am–2pm, Sun and hols 9am–noon; performances Sept–June, most evenings. **Tram:** 1, 2, or D to Burgtheater.

AKADEMIETHEATER, Lisztstrasse 1. Tel. 51444-2959.

Another important theater, this one features performances of classic and modern playwrights, from Shakespeare to Bertolt Brecht.

Prices: Seats, 50–450 S ($4.55–$40.90); standing room, 15 S ($1.35).

Open: Box office at Bundestheaterkassen, Mon–Fri 8am–6pm, Sat 9am–2pm, Sun and hols 9am–noon; performances Sept–June, most evenings. **U-Bahn:** U-4 to Stadtpark. **Tram:** 1, 2, 71, or D to Schwarzenbergplatz.

THEATER IN DER JOSEFSTADT, Josefstädter Strasse 26. Tel. 402 51 27.

First opened in 1788, this is Vienna's oldest theater in continuous operation. Max Reinhardt (founder of the Salzburg Festival) brought fame here through renovations and major productions in the 1920s. If you understand German, you'll like the intimate coziness of this theater with its performances of light drama and Viennese classics.

Prices: Seats, 50–500 S ($4.55–$45.45).

Open: Performances, most nights at 7:30pm, Sun matinees at 3pm. **U-Bahn:** U-2 to Rathaus. **Tram:** J to Lederergasse. **Bus:** 13A to Theater in der Josefstadt.

THEATER AN DER WIEN, Linke Wienzeile 6. Tel. 588 30-265.

The Theater an der Wien, together with the Raimundtheater, Wallgasse 18–20 (tel. 599 77 27), and Ronacher, Seilerstätte 9 (tel. 513 83 40), stages musicals. All three are part of the Vereinigte Bühnen (United Theaters) under the direction of Peter Weck. Previous productions have included *Les Misérables, Phantom of the Opera, Freudiana* and *Cats.*

Prices: 250–990 S ($22.70–$99).

Open: Box office, daily 10am–1pm and 2–6pm at each theater; performances, throughout the year. **U-Bahn:** U-1, U-2, or U-4 to Karlsplatz-Oper (for Theater an der Wien).

VIENNA'S ENGLISH THEATER, Josefsgasse 12. Tel. 402 12 60.

If you don't speak German, you might prefer a visit to this English-language theater, which presents highly professional productions of both classic and contemporary plays.

Prices and Performances: Contact the English Theater. **U-Bahn:** U-2 to Rathaus.

CLASSICAL MUSIC

Be sure to check the *Wien Monatsprogramm* for a current listing of concerts.

Hübner's Kursalon, Stadtpark, Johannesgasse 33 (tel. 713 21 81). Johann Strauss conducted waltzes here more than 100 years ago, and waltz music is still one of the main attractions of the Kursalon, located in the west end of the Stadtpark. From April to the end of October, concerts are held outside under the stars nightly from 8 to 11pm (indoors in bad weather). There are also afternoon tea-time concerts from 4 to 6pm. Admission is 45 S ($4.10) for the afternoon performance and 120 S ($10.90) for the evening show, which includes one drink. The closest U-Bahn station is Stadtpark, or take tram no. 1 or 2 to Weihburggasse.

LIVE MUSIC

ROCKHAUS, Adalbert-Stifter-Strasse 73. Tel. 33 46 41.

This is one of Vienna's best-known venues for live music, including blues, rock, new wave, and hard rock. International groups provide the main entertainment, while Austrian musicians are usually the warm-up band. Check the daily newspaper for current concerts.

Admission: 100–150 S ($9.10–$13.65) for local bands, 150–200 S ($13.65–$18.20) for international bands.

Open: Tues–Sun; bar opens at 6pm; concerts begin around 8pm. **Tram:** 31, 32, or N. **Bus:** 11A or 35A.

TUNNEL, Florianigasse 39. Tel. 42 34 65.

⭐ Located behind the Rathaus near the university district, this basement establishment features live music nightly, from blues and rock to folk and jazz. Groups are mainly European, including bands from eastern European countries. Monday nights feature jam sessions. If you're hungry, an inexpensive restaurant upstairs on the ground floor serves food until 1am.

Prices: Beer from 26 S ($2.35); long drinks from 36 S ($3.25). **Admission:** 30–90 S ($2.70–$8.20) Tues–Sun; Mon jam sessions free.

Open: Daily 7pm–2am (live music begins around 9pm). **U-Bahn:** U-2 to Rathaus, then a 10-minute walk. **Tram:** 5. **Bus:** 13A.

METROPOL, Hernalser Hauptstrasse 55. Tel. 43 35 43.

The Metropol has served as a mecca of the Viennese youth scene for more than a decade, with productions that range from rock, new wave, jazz, and reggae concerts to cabaret.

Admission: 140–250 S ($12.70–$22.70).

Open: Tues–Sat from 7 or 8pm. **Tram:** 43 from Schottentor.

MOVIES

Stadtkino, Schwarzenbergplatz 7 (tel. 712 62 76 or 72 62 76). A municipally run cinema, the Stadtkino features unconventional films that are seldom shown in commercial theaters, including foreign films from all over the world in their original languages.

Burg Kino, Opernring 19 (tel. 587 84 06). This movie theater shows films in their original languages.

Austrian Film Museum, in the Albertina, Augustinerstrasse 1 (tel. 533 70 54). With a comprehensive archive of rare copies and documents relating to film history, the cinema here shows films in original languages, complete retrospectives, and avant-garde and experimental films. Movies, presented from October to May, often revolve around a special theme. The price here is 45 S ($4.10), plus a 30-S ($2.70) one-day membership.

THE BAR SCENE

HISTORIC WINE CELLARS

Since these wine cellars may be crowded during mealtimes, you might consider coming here for a drink later in the evening—unless, of course, you want to splurge on a meal that will cost $10 or more. They're all inside the Ring.

AUGUSTINER KELLER, Augustinerstrasse 1. Tel. 533 10 26.

With a history stretching back several centuries, the Augustiner Keller does seem rather ancient, with its wooden floors, a vaulted brick ceiling, and long, narrow room. There's traditional *Heurigenmusik* every evening starting at 6:30pm (no cover charge), and the menu here includes grilled chicken, grilled shank of pork, pork cutlet, baked trout, and Apfelstrudel.

Prices: Glass of wine from 27 S ($2.45).

Open: Daily 10am–12:30am. **U-Bahn:** Karlsplatz or Stephansplatz.

MELKERSTIFTSKELLER, Schottengasse 3. Tel. 533 55 30.

This *Heuriger* (Viennese wine tavern) features wine from its own vineyards, served in historic vaulted rooms. Its menu features pork, chicken, veal, Bratwurst with Sauerkraut, and other typical Viennese cuisine.

Prices: Glass of wine from 28 S ($2.55).
Open: Mon–Sat 5pm–midnight. **U-Bahn:** U-2 to Schottentor.

URBANIKELLER, Am Hof 12. Tel. 63 91 02.

Located on one of Vienna's most venerable old squares in the heart of the city, the Urbanikeller gets my vote as the city's most picturesque wine cellar.

Founded in 1906, its dining room looks like the setting of some medieval movie, with its stone walls, arched ceiling, and heavy oak tables. There's live Viennese music from 7pm to midnight, making it a great place to stop off for a late-night drink. Wine is a bit more expensive here, but it's worth it.

Prices: Glass of wine from 38 S ($3.45).
Open: Daily 6pm–1am. **Closed:** Mid-July to mid-Aug. **U-Bahn:** U-1 or U-3 to Stephansplatz.

ZWÖLF APOSTELKELLER, Sonnenfelsgasse 3. Tel. 512 67 77.

This huge wine cellar is two levels deep. The vaulting of the upper cellar is mainly 15th-century Gothic, while the lower cellar is early baroque. Unlike the places above, it's perfectly acceptable to come here anytime just for drinks.

Prices: Glass of wine from 25 S ($2.25).
Open: Daily 4:30pm–midnight. **U-Bahn:** U-1 to Stephansplatz.

DRINKS IN VIENNA'S OLD QUARTER

GRIECHENBEISL, Fleischmarkt 11. Tel. 533 19 41 or 533 19 77.

This historic inn is one of Vienna's most famous locales, dating back to the 15th century. Housed in an ancient-looking, vine-covered building on one of the city's small crooked streets, the Griechenbeisl is fantastically picturesque, with lots of cozy little rooms linked by narrow winding passageways. One of the small rooms has signatures of famous personalities who have been here, including Beethoven, Wagner, Mark Twain, and Count Zeppelin. Since the Griechenbeisl is a restaurant (and too expensive for us), come after 11pm for a drink. Although there's no substantial proof, local legend says that it was in this inn that an anonymous ballad-singer wrote "Lieber Augustin" in 1679 while Vienna suffered from the plague.

Prices: Half liter of beer 40 S ($3.65); quarter liter of wine from 42 S ($3.80).
Open: Daily 11am–1am. **U-Bahn:** U-1 or U-3 to Stephansplatz, or U-1 or U-4 to Schwedenplatz.

KAFFEE ALT WIEN, Bäckerstrasse 9. Tel. 512 52 22.

An old, dimly lit coffeehouse in the heart of old Vienna, this combination café/bar first opened in 1936 and is popular with students, artists, and writers.

Its tired old walls are hidden beneath the barrage of posters announcing concerts and exhibitions. In the afternoon it's a good place to come to read the newspaper, study, write letters, and relax; late at night it can get so crowded that it's hard to get through the front door.

Prices: *Seidel* (one-third liter) of beer from 23 S ($2.10); glass of wine 15 S ($1.35).
Open: Daily 10am–4am. **U-Bahn:** U-1 or U-3 to Stephansplatz.

OSWALD & KALB, Bäckerstrasse 14. Tel. 512 13 71 or 512 69 92.

This restaurant/bar caters to Vienna's young and upwardly mobile, including writers and artists. It's simple, with wooden floors and white tablecloths, and features a handwritten menu that changes daily. Main courses include fish, chicken, and pork dishes, but you may wish to come here just for a drink.

Prices: Main courses 90–140 S ($8.20–$12.70); a *Krügerl* (half liter) of beer 36 S ($3.25).
Open: Daily 6pm–1am. **U-Bahn:** U-1 or U-3 to Stephansplatz.

PANIGL, Schönlaterngasse 11. Tel. 513 17 16.

Another trendy bar in Vienna's old quarter, this one also pulls in artists, journalists, and TV and film personalities. Although it's tiny, people pack in for the Italian antipasti, cheeses, and of course the Italian wines.

Prices: Drinks from about 40 S ($3.65); small glass of wine 22 S ($2).
Open: Mon–Fri 2pm–4am, Sat–Sun and hols 7pm–4am. **U-Bahn:** U-1 or U-3 to Stephansplatz.

SCHWIMMENDE PYRAMIDE, Seilerstätte 3A. Tel. 513 29 70.

This interesting locale with avant-garde artwork on its front door and modern lamps inside offers 70 different kinds of beer. It also has an extensive menu (food is served until 4am), featuring spareribs, fish, spaghetti, chili, Wiener Schnitzel, and Viennese specialties.

Prices: Most main courses under 100 S ($9.10); a *Seidel* (one-third liter) of beer from 20 S ($1.80).
Open: Daily 4pm–4am. **U-Bahn:** U-1 or U-3 to Stephansplatz.

WUNDER BAR, Schönlaterngasse 8. Tel. 512 79 89.

There's no sign outside to identify this place, apparently because everyone knows that it's here. A small locale with a ceiling that could be called a modern interpretation of Gothic, it doesn't get crowded here until after 10pm.

Prices: Glass of wine from 18 S ($1.65); beer from 26 S ($2.35).
Open: Daily 4pm–2am. **U-Bahn:** U-1 or U-3 to Stephansplatz.

DRINKS IN RABENSTEIG

About a 15-minute walk northeast of Stephansplatz brings you to Rabensteig, the old Jewish quarter of Vienna. Today it's one of Vienna's most popular nightspots, with several bars lining Rabensteig, Seitenstettengasse, and other small pedestrians-only streets. These three are my favorites.

CAFE BILLARD ROTER ENGEL, Rabensteig 5. Tel. 535 41 05.

This very popular place has live music in the evenings after 9pm, with everything from jazz to reggae. Upstairs are billiard tables, in case you're itching to shoot some pool.

Prices: *Seidel* (one-third liter) of beer 26 S ($2.35); small glass of wine from 18 S ($1.65). **Admission:** Music charge 40–70 S ($3.65–$6.35).
Open: Sun–Wed 3pm–2am, Thurs–Sat 3pm–4am. Live music from 9pm. **U-Bahn:** U-1 or U-4 to Schwedenplatz.

CASABLANCA, Rabensteig 8. Tel. 533 34 63.

Located directly across the street from Roter Engel, this bar offers the usual wine and beer, along with live music provided by local bands and outdoor seating.

Prices: *Seidel* (one-third liter) of beer 27 S ($2.45). **Admission:** Music charge 15 S ($1.35).
Open: Tues–Sat 6pm–4am, Sun–Mon and hols 6pm–2am (summer, daily from 3pm). Live music from 9pm. **U-Bahn:** U-1 or U-4 to Schwedenplatz.

KRAH KRAH, Rabensteig 8. Tel. 63 81 93.

You can choose from among 40 different kinds of beer. Incidentally, "Krah Krah" is the sound a raven makes, referring to the street Rabensteig, which means Ravens' Path. On Sunday from 11:30am to 2:30pm there's free jazz.

Prices: *Seidel* (one-third liter) of beer from 26 S ($2.35).
Open: Daily 11am–2am. **U-Bahn:** U-1 or U-4 to Schwedenplatz.

DISCOS

ATRIUM, Schwindgasse 1. Tel. 505 35 94.

Conveniently located just off Schwarzenbergplatz, this disco is a cavernous underground club of various rooms. Attracting people in their 20s, it offers beer and wine. On Thursday there's sometimes a rock band.

Prices: Beer or wine from 40 S ($3.65). **Admission:** 30 S ($2.70).

Open: Thurs and Sun 8pm–2am, Fri–Sat 8pm–4am. **Tram:** 1, 2, 71, or D to Schwarzenbergplatz.

MOVE, Daungasse 1. Tel. 43 32 78.

Stars come alive as soon as you descend into this basement establishment, with its black walls and thousands of orange and green neon dots. Holograms line the walls.

Admission: 40 S ($3.65); half the admission goes toward your first drink. Students free Mon and Wed, 20 S ($1.80) other days. Women free Tues and Thurs.

Open: Daily 9pm–4am. **U-Bahn:** U-2 to Rathaus or U-6 to Josefstädter Strasse, then a 10-minute walk. **Tram:** 43 or 44 to Skodagasse, or 5 or 31 to Florianigasse.

P1 DISCOTHEK, Rotgasse 9. Tel. 535 99 95.

This is probably Vienna's hottest disco of the moment, popular with people in their 20s. A former filming studio, it's huge, with a large dance floor and enough room to accommodate 1,500 people throughout. It opened in 1988—and attained instant fame when Tina Turner came here at the start of her European tour. It's conveniently located inside the Ring, not far from Stephansplatz.

Prices: *Seidel* of beer 40 S ($3.65). **Admission:** 50 S ($4.55), which includes one drink; more for an occasional special concert.

Open: Sun–Thurs 9pm–4am, Fri–Sat 9pm–6am. **U-Bahn:** U-1 to Stephansplatz.

THE HEURIGE

Heurige are Viennese wine taverns featuring Viennese wines (called Heurige as well). Today there are about 400 families still cultivating vineyards in Vienna, spread over the wine-growing districts of Grinzing, Nussdorf, Heiligenstadt, Sievering, and Neustift among others.

Of these, **Grinzing** is probably the best known, with about 20 Heurige clustered together. Most of them have wine gardens for summer drinking, but in the winter there's plenty of action indoors. Look for the sprig of pine, usually hung above the entrance, and a small plaque with EIGENBAU written on it, which means that the grower serves his or her own wine. Grinzing is only five miles from the city center, which you can reach by taking tram no. 38 from Schottentor. There's no cover charge; you can buy a quarter-liter mug of wine for 40 S ($3.65) and linger as long as you wish.

9. EASY EXCURSIONS

THE VIENNA WOODS The Vienna Woods surround much of the city, offering mile upon mile of hiking trails, views, and solitude. One of the most popular destinations is **Kahlenberg,** which affords great views over the whole city. To reach Kahlenberg, take tram no. 38 to Grinzing, transferring there to bus no. 38A to Kahlenberg. If you're a hiker, you can also walk to Kahlenberg in about two hours by taking tram D to the last station and then striking out from there.

THE DONAUINSEL How about a swim in the Danube? Actually, it's the Alte Donau (Old Danube), where you'll find beaches, restaurants, paddleboats, rental bikes, and other facilities. The largest and oldest beach is **Gänsehäufel,** a section of which is segregated for nudists. To reach the beach, take U-Bahn U-1 to either the Kaisermühlen or Alte Donau station. Nearby is also the 13-mile-long **Donauinsel,** sandwiched in between the Danube Canal and the New Danube, popular with joggers, cyclists, and strollers. It's the largest recreation area in Vienna's immediate vicinity and also offers bathing opportunities right off its bank. You can reach the Donauinsel by taking U-Bahn U-1 to the Donauinsel station.

BOAT TRIPS ON THE DANUBE   From April to late October there are daily excursion trips from Vienna all the way to Linz, Grein, even Budapest. A popular three-hour trip on the Danube departs daily from Schwedenplatz and costs 180 S ($16.35). For more information, contact the **Danube Steamship Company (DDSG)** (tel. 21 75 00).

ZURICH

Travesties, a play by Tom Stoppard, is set in Zurich, and three of its main characters are Lenin, James Joyce, and Tristan Tzara. During World War I, these revolutionary figures were all living in neutral Zurich. From there, Lenin went on to lead a revolution in Russia, and Joyce did no less for the English novel. And Tzara, the Romanian-born poet, created dadaism—a movement aimed at destroying all semblance of order in literature—in Zurich's very own Cabaret Voltaire. Those were heady times for the largest city in Switzerland.

The bohemian Cabaret Voltaire is now gone, and probably the first thing you'll see in Zurich is Bahnhofstrasse, an urbane boulevard leading from the train station to the Zürichsee, the lake. Here you can get all the finer things in life: a mink coat, a Patek Philippe watch, Havana cigars. You'll see orderly shoppers moving under perfect trees and, in the summer, bright national and cantonal flags. There are no cars, only blue-and-white trams, smoothly gliding by. On clear days nature itself agrees: The Zürichsee turns a deep blue and you can see the snowcapped Alps.

In some ways Zurich seems a perfect city. Visitors are almost always impressed with the atmosphere of honest dealing, cleanliness, and efficiency. The prices may scare you at first, but you'll find that there are no hidden costs, and people are willing to help tourists. Traveling here is so easy that you could almost do it with your eyes closed. Zurich is thus an ideal gateway to Europe.

1. FROM A BUDGET TRAVELER'S POINT OF VIEW

SPECIAL DISCOUNT OPPORTUNITIES

FOR STUDENTS An **International Student Identity Card (ISIC)** will get you considerable reductions on opera and theater tickets, and 10%–50% discounts on the tourist office tours of Zurich and environs. Contact the **Swiss Student Travel Office (SSR),** at Bäckerstrasse 40 (tel. 241-12-08) or Leonhardstrasse 10 (tel. 242-30-00), if you don't have an ISIC—for a SFr 11 ($7.85) fee they'll issue a card if you show them proof of your academic status. The offices are open on Monday from 1 to 8pm and Tuesday through Friday from 10am to 6pm; on Saturday only the Bäckerstrasse 40 office is open, from 10am to noon.

FOR EVERYONE Eating a quick lunch standing up at one of the many **fast-food street stalls**—such as the Gans, at Niederdorfstrasse 8 (near Central), or at a sidewalk counter of one of the great department stores on and near Bahnhofstrasse, or in Shopville, the underground mall between the Hauptbahnhof (central train station) and Bahnhofstrasse—can save you 25% or more of what you'd pay in a restaurant.

Sitting in one of the many sidewalk cafés on Bahnhofstrasse or in the Old City, drinking a coffee or soft drink for SFr 2.80–3.20 ($2–$2.30), watching the crowds walk by and enjoying the atmosphere, is an inexpensive way of relaxing after long walks or sightseeing; in fact, this is static sightseeing at its best.

For SFr 6 ($4.30) you can buy a *Tageskarte,* a ticket valid for 24 hours on all trams and buses inside the city limits (see "Orientation and Getting Around," below).

Admission at several museums and churches is free; visit the Landesmuseum, the Museum Bellerive, the Grossmünster, the Fraumünster, and St. Peterskirche.

Finally, be sure to check with the tourist office (see "Information," in "Orientation and Getting Around," below) about **free folklore evenings** or **open-air concerts.**

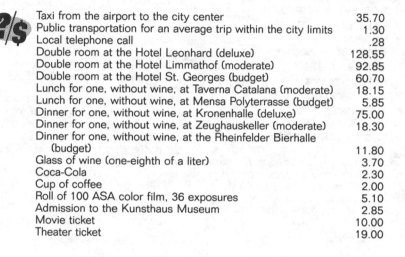

WHAT THINGS COST IN ZURICH	U.S. $
Taxi from the airport to the city center	35.70
Public transportation for an average trip within the city limits	1.30
Local telephone call	.28
Double room at the Hotel Leonhard (deluxe)	128.55
Double room at the Hotel Limmathof (moderate)	92.85
Double room at the Hotel St. Georges (budget)	60.70
Lunch for one, without wine, at Taverna Catalana (moderate)	18.15
Lunch for one, without wine, at Mensa Polyterrasse (budget)	5.85
Dinner for one, without wine, at Kronenhalle (deluxe)	75.00
Dinner for one, without wine, at Zeughauskeller (moderate)	18.30
Dinner for one, without wine, at the Rheinfelder Bierhalle (budget)	11.80
Glass of wine (one-eighth of a liter)	3.70
Coca-Cola	2.30
Cup of coffee	2.00
Roll of 100 ASA color film, 36 exposures	5.10
Admission to the Kunsthaus Museum	2.85
Movie ticket	10.00
Theater ticket	19.00

2. PRETRIP PREPARATIONS

DOCUMENTS Citizens of the United States, Great Britain, Canada, Australia, and New Zealand need only a valid passport for stays up to three months in Switzerland.

WHAT TO PACK The weather in Zurich is similar to that of the northeastern United States, without the extremes. Be prepared for some cool days in summer, some warm days in winter. If you visit in the fall or spring, take a warm jacket. In the summer, pack a sweater; in the winter, carry a coat or parka. And whenever you come, bring an umbrella and rain gear. It doesn't rain for long periods of time, but there are frequent, short thunderstorms.

You may want to keep in mind that people in Zurich are careful dressers, and rather conservative.

WHEN TO GO The main tourist season runs from April to October. If you come between June and early September, make sure to reserve a room in advance. But even

✔ WHAT'S SPECIAL ABOUT ZURICH

Attractions
- ☐ Exploring the Old City, with its churches, fountains, and boutiques.
- ☐ Walking around the Zürichberg, the city's mountain, with great views of the lake and Alps.
- ☐ Visiting the places associated with Zurich's famous former residents: Joyce, Wagner, Einstein.
- ☐ Seeing the Swiss National Museum and historic churches.

Shopping
- ☐ Window-shopping along the Bahnhofstrasse, one of Europe's finest commercial arteries.

Excursions
- ☐ Lucerne, the Jungfraujoch, Titlis, the Black Forest, and other great Alpine destinations.
- ☐ Boating around the Zürichsee, one of Switzerland's most beautiful lakes.

if you visit Zurich during low season, you'll always find lots of activity and a pleasant atmosphere.

Zurich's Average Daytime Temperature & Rainfall

	Jan	Feb	Mar	Apr	May	June	July	Aug	Sept	Oct	Nov	Dec
Temp. (°F)	32	33	39	48	58	65	70	69	63	50	39	33
Rainfall "	2.4	3.5	2.6	3.1	6.1	8.6	6.5	4.9	3.9	1.9	2.5	2.3

BACKGROUND READING George Mikes's *Switzerland for Beginners* (André Deutsch, 1987) is a collection of witty essays on diverse aspects of Swiss life, including banking and the so-called gnomes of Zurich, languages, and feminism. Eugene V. Epstein, an American humorist living in Switzerland, is the author of four collections of "titillating tales of life in Switzerland"; a telling title is *Malice in Wonderland* (Benteli Publishers).

German-language Swiss literature, with the possible exception of Friedrich Dürrenmatt and Max Frisch, is not well known in the United States. H. M. Waidson's *Anthology of Modern Swiss Literature* (Oswald Wolff) gathers English translations of writings by Swiss authors from each of the country's linguistic regions: German, French, Italian, and Romansch. If you read French, try to get a copy of Jean-Pierre Moulin's *Des Villes en Suisse* (Autrement), a collection of penetrating essays on several Swiss cities, including, of course, Zurich.

Finally, for a sharp portrait of Zurich during World War I, read Tom Stoppard's *Travesties* (Grove Press).

3. ORIENTATION & GETTING AROUND

ARRIVING IN ZURICH

FROM THE AIRPORT Zurich's airport, **Kloten,** is located seven miles from the city center. It is one of the 10 busiest airports in Europe, and provides direct connections with 120 cities in 80 countries. Rated best European airline in 1989 by the readers of *Condé Nast Traveler* magazine, Swissair flies to Zurich-Kloten from New York, Boston, Atlanta, Los Angeles, Chicago, Toronto, Montréal, and Anchorage.

The Swiss Federal Railways runs a feeder service to the Hauptbahnhof (Zurich's central train station) every 10–20 minutes (a 10-minute ride) for SFr 5 ($3.55). If you're carrying a lot of bags and are going to a hotel in the 8001 Zurich postal code (most of my hotel listings are here), consider the **Welti-Furrer Limousine Service** (tel. 272-24-44). They leave the airport every 45 minutes and charge SFr 14 ($10) per person. They depart from the arrivals hall in Terminal B; to go from Zurich to Kloten, call ahead for reservations.

There is a **tourist office** at the airport in Terminal B (where transcontinental flights arrive) and is open daily from 10am to 7pm.

FROM THE TRAIN STATION   Built in 1871, Zurich's cavernous **Hauptbahnhof (central train station,** often abbreviated HB) is located in the very heart of the city. Trams, buses, and taxis will transport you from here to anywhere in Zurich.

BY CAR   Check first with your hotel about parking possibilities. Many hotels have parking space for their guests, but some—especially in the old part of town with its narrow streets—may advise you on the nearest garage.

INFORMATION

A very efficient **tourist office** is located in the Hauptbahnhof, Bahnhofplatz 15 (tel. 211-40-00). Look for their signs in English (the German phrase *Verkehrsbüro* is not used here very often). Their multilingual guides hand out maps for SFr 1–3 (70¢–$2.15) and brochures (make sure to buy a copy of the weekly *Zürich News*) costing SFr 1 (70¢); they also sell excursion tickets, and make hotel bookings for a small fee: SFr 5 ($3.55) per room. From March through October, they are open Monday through Friday from 8am to 10pm and on Saturday and Sunday from 8am to 8:30pm. Their hours from November through February are slightly shorter: Monday through Friday from 8am to 8pm and on Saturday and Sunday from 9am to 6pm.

There is another tourist office located at the airport that can help with transportation into the city when you arrive (see "Arriving in Zurich," above).

CITY LAYOUT

Zurich is easy to explore. You'll probably become acquainted first with **Bahnhofstrasse,** the mile-long commercial street that runs north to south from the Hauptbahnhof to the **Zürichsee,** or Zurich Lake. At **Bürkliplatz,** a waterfront square at the end of Bahnhofstrasse, you can view the lake, the surrounding wooded hills, and, weather permitting, at least eight mountain peaks rising as high as 10,000 feet.

The **Altstadt (Old City)** straddles both sides of the Limmat River. On the west bank, it starts at Beatenplatz, near the Hauptbahnhof, and runs west of Bahnhofstrasse all the way to Bürkliplatz. Here you can wander through narrow, hilly streets and pass many historical structures, such as St. Peter's Church and the Fraumünster, with the beautiful Chagall and Giacometti glass. I find this area quieter, and therefore more pleasant to walk around, than its left-bank counterpart.

The old city to the left of the Limmat begins at **Central** and ends at **Bellevueplatz,** two squares bustling with trams and people. Consider walking along the riverside **Limmatquai** or along such streets as Niederdorfstrasse and Münstergasse. If you take the latter walk, you'll tread cobblestone streets, pass houses built from the 15th through the 17th century, guildhalls with carved and stuccoed exteriors, fountains, marble portals, and the twin-towered Grossmünster (cathedral).

Don't overlook the heights of Zurich. A marvelous wooded mountain in the middle of the city, the **Zürichberg** is easily accessible from the Hauptbahnhof by tram no. 6 to Zoo, the last station, or tram no. 10 to Rigiplatz and then the *Seilbahn* (cable car) to the last stop.

GETTING AROUND

BY TRAM & BUS Zurich is easily manageable if you familiarize yourself with the user-friendly tram and bus system, run by the Verkehrsbetriebe der Stadt Zürich (VBZ Züri-Linie, or Zurich Public Transport). All tram and bus stops have names, so you'll know exactly where to get off. Tickets are purchased prior to getting on the tram or bus (same tickets for both) from the blue automatic vending machines with multilingual instructions posted near each stop. Tickets cost SFr 1.80 ($1.30) for short trips and SFr 3 ($2.15) for longer distances. But you'll probably save money by buying a **Tageskarte,** a ticket valid for a full 24 hours; it costs SFr 6 ($4.30). The honor system is observed in Zurich—if you're caught without a ticket you'll be hit with a SFr-50 ($35.70) fine.

If you need more information, go to the tourist office at the Hauptbahnhof, or the Züri-Linie's Abonnementsbüro in Shopville, the underground shopping mall between the Hauptbahnhof and Bahnhofstrasse, the latter open Monday through Friday from 7am to 7pm, on Saturday from 7am to 6pm, and on Sunday from 8am to 7pm.

BY TAXI A taxi ride within the city limits costs about SFr 20 ($14.30); from the airport, about SFr 60 ($42.85).

BY BICYCLE You can rent a bicycle at the Hauptbahnhof for the following daily fees: SFr 16 ($11.40) for an adult bike, SFr 10 ($7.15) for a child's bike, and SFr 26 ($18.55) for mountain bikes. There are special reduced daily rates for families: SFr 40 ($28.55) for two adults' and one child's bikes. Go to the luggage department counter near the Landesmuseum exit of the Hauptbahnhof (tel. 245-34-77). It's open daily from 6am to 9:45pm.

CAR RENTAL For car rental, contact **Hertz,** Lagerstrasse 33, near the Hauptbahnhof (tel. 242-84-84). They charge SFr 180 ($128.55) per day (for a rental of up to three days with unlimited mileage, gas included) for a Fiat Uno, Opel Corsa, or Ford Fiesta, with lower rates for longer rentals and weekends. Hertz is open Monday through Friday from 7am to 7:30pm, on Saturday from 7am to 6pm, and on Sunday from 8am to 6pm. There's another office at the airport (tel. 814-05-11), which is open daily from 6:30am to around 11pm, when the last flights arrive.

 ZURICH

Babysitters To find a babysitter, call Kady (tel. 211-37-86).

Business Hours **Shops** are open Monday through Friday from 8am to 6:30pm and on Saturday from 8am to 4pm. On Thursday, some stores stay open until 9pm, whereas others are closed on Monday morning. **Banks** operate Monday through Wednesday and on Friday from 8:15am to 4:30pm, on Thursday from 8:15am to 6pm. The **money-exchange office** in the Hauptbahnhof and the airport is open daily from 6:30am to 11:30pm. The **American Express** office, at Bahnhofstrasse 20, near Paradeplatz (tel. 211-83-70), is open Monday through Friday from 8:30am to 5:30pm and on Saturday from 8:30am to noon.

Consulates The **Consulate General of the United States** is at Zollikerstrasse 141 (tel. 55-25-66). The **British Consulate** is at Dufourstrasse 156 (tel. 261-15-20). All the embassies are in Berne, Switzerland's capital.

Currency The unit of Swiss currency is the **franc (SFr),** made up of 100 **rappen.** There are bills for 10, 20, 50, 100, 500, and 1,000 francs; and coins for 5, 10, 20, and 50 rappen, and 1, 2, and 5 francs.

Dentist If you have an emergency dental problem, call 255-11-11.

Doctor For an English-speaking doctor, contact the University Hospital (tel. 255-11-11).

Emergencies For the police, call 117; to report a fire, 118; for an ambulance, 361-61-61; for first aid, including dental problems, 255-11-11. For an English-speaking doctor, or if you need a children's doctor, contact the Universitätsspital (University Hospital) (tel. 255-11-11).

The pharmacy (*Apotheke*) at Theaterstrasse 14 (tel. 252-56-00), near Bellevueplatz, between the ABM and EPA department stores, is open daily 24 hours.

Holidays Official holidays in Zurich are New Year's Day (Jan 1), Berchtoldstag (Jan 2), Good Friday, Easter Monday, May Day (May 1), Whit Monday, National Holiday (Aug 1), and Christmas (Dec 25–26).

Hospital The Universitätsspital (University Hospital) is located on Rämistrasse (tel. 255-11-11), near Universitätsstrasse. Take tram no. 6 or 10 from the Hauptbahnhof, or no. 9 from Bellevueplatz, to ETH/Universitätsspital.

Information The Tourist Information Office is located at the Hauptbahnhof. For details, see "Orientation and Getting Around," above.

Laundry Two easy-to-find laundries are Speed Wash, Häringstrasse 14, near Central-Platz (tel. 261-87-40), open Monday through Friday from 8am to 6:30pm; and the Waschanstalt, Mühlegasse 11, just over the Brunbrücke from the Hauptbahnhof (tel. 252-37-95), open Monday through Friday from 7:30am to noon and 1 to 6:30pm. Both charge SFr 17 ($12.15) for 5 kilos (11 lbs.) washed and dried.

Lost and Found For wallets, passports, keys, or umbrellas lost in the city, contact the Fundbüro, Werdmühlstrasse 10, near the Hauptbahnhof (tel. 216-51-11). Its office hours are Monday through Friday from 7:30am to 5:30pm. For items lost on trains, dial 211-88-11.

Mail Zurich has several postal codes, based on the number 8000. The Central Post Office, called Sihl-Post, is located at Kasernenstrasse 95 (tel. 245-41-11), just a few blocks from the Hauptbahnhof. The post office in the Hauptbahnhof (tel. 221-11-81) stays open Monday through Friday from 7:30am to 6:30pm and on Saturday from 7:30 to 11am.

As they do elsewhere, American Express in Zurich, Bahnhofstrasse 20 (tel. 211-83-70), will hold mail for its clients and, for a small fee, for everyone else. It's open Monday through Friday from 8:30am to 5:30pm and on Saturday from 8:30am to noon.

Networks and Resources **Beratungstelle INFRA,** Autonomes Frauenzentrum, Mattengasse 27 (tel. 272-85-03), is an information clearinghouse for women. **Schwules Begegnungszentrum SchwuzZ,** Sihlquai 67 (tel. 271-22-50), is a social center for gay men. **Beratungsstelle Pro Infirmis,** Hohlstrasse 52 (tel. 271-44-11), offers information for disabled people. They are open Monday through Friday from 8am to noon and 1:30 to 5pm.

Newspapers The city's principal newspaper is the *Neue Zürcher Zeitung*. Newspapers in languages other than German, including the *International Herald Tribune,* are readily available in many kiosks around town.

Photographic Needs There are several stores along Bahnhofstrasse that sell film and anything else that you may need for your camera.

Religious Services The International Protestant Church, Schanzengasse 25, has an English service on Sunday at 11:30am; from the Hauptbahnhof, take tram no. 3 to Kunsthaus. There is a Roman Catholic mass in English at St. Anton, Neptunstrasse 60, on Sunday at 11:15am; take tram no. 15 from Central to Englischviertelsstrasse. There are daily services at the orthodox synagogues located at Löwenstrasse 10 (tel. 221-38-92) and Freigutstrasse 37 (tel. 201-49-98); call for details.

Tax Your restaurant and hotel bills in Zurich will include tax. The VAT (Value-Added Tax) of 6.2% levied on items above SFr 500 ($357.15) is refundable; simply ask the store for a VAT form and present it to the Customs official when leaving the country.

Telephone The **International Telephone Office,** inside the Hauptbahnhof, is open Monday through Friday from 7am to 10:30pm and on Saturday and Sunday from 9am to 9pm. For **local telephone calls** from a phone booth, insert two 20-rappen coins. For advice on how to make international calls, dial 221-17-00. Zurich's **area code** is 01.

THE SWISS FRANC & THE DOLLAR

At this writing $1 = approximately 1.40 Swiss francs (or SFr 1 = 71¢), and this was the rate of exchange used to calculate the dollar values given in this chapter (rounded to the nearest nickel). This rate fluctuates from time to time and may not be the same when you travel to Switzerland. Therefore the following table should be used only as a guide:

SFr	U.S.$	SFr	U.S.$
1	.71	35	25.00
2	1.42	40	28.57
3	2.14	45	32.14
4	2.85	50	35.71
5	3.57	55	39.28
6	4.28	60	42.85
7	5.00	65	46.42
8	5.71	70	50.00
9	6.42	75	53.57
10	7.14	80	57.14
15	10.71	85	60.71
20	14.28	90	64.28
25	17.85	95	67.85
30	21.42	100	71.42

Tipping It's not customary to tip in Switzerland, since tips are already included in hotel and restaurant bills and taxi fares. But if someone has been especially helpful, a tip will not be objected to.

4. BUDGET ACCOMMODATIONS

A bad Swiss hotel is not easy to find. Switzerland is the training ground for aspiring hotel managers from every part of the world and the standards at the famous Swiss hotel schools are very high. For instance, aspiring hôteliers are taught which of six glasses to use for serving a bordeaux, and sometimes these amenities trickle down in some form to low-cost establishments. In fact, most budget hotels could not possibly be any cleaner than they are, and the service is usually very polite. Because of that, you should have no qualms about staying at virtually any of the 120 hotels and pensions in the city.

Keep in mind, though, that similarly priced hotels in Zurich may differ greatly in decoration, comfort, and service. A rickety room with unattractive curtains in a hotel with long, dark corridors may cost the same as a sleek, well-lit room in a renovated hotel, and since prices are high in this city, you'll want the very best for your money. It's a good idea to reserve in advance, since Zurich is an important European financial center, often filled with visiting businesspeople who may prefer budget establishments over deluxe palaces. If you arrive in Zurich and have trouble finding a place to stay, keep in mind that the tourist offices at the Hauptbahnhof and the airport will make hotel reservations for a small fee.

Zurich, like the rest of Switzerland, is one European destination where budget travelers may prefer to stay at the youth hostel (Jugendherberge). This is especially true if you're traveling by yourself. Some Swiss hostels, like the ones in Lausanne and Montreux, are excellent values, and may even be worth a detour.

DOUBLES FOR LESS THAN SFR 90 [$64.30]

HOTEL ITALIA, Zeughausstrasse 61, 8004 Zürich. Tel. 01/241-05-55.
36 rms (none with bath). **Tram:** 3 or 14 to Kasernenstrasse.
$ Rates (including continental breakfast and showers): SFr 65 ($46.40) single; SFr 85 ($60.70) double; SFr 120 ($85.70) triple; SFr 140 ($100) quad. No credit cards.
The hotel has been managed by the Papagni family since 1960. It's centrally located, in a quiet area a 3-minute walk from the tram and a 10-minute walk from the city center and train station. Rooms are adequately furnished, clean, and spread over three floors; there is no elevator. Breakfast is served in a street-level restaurant or in the tree-lined garden. The restaurant offers four daily menus ranging from $9 to $14. English is spoken. Parking in the street is possible.

HOTEL LINDE, Universitätstrasse 91, 8033 Zürich. Tel. 01/362-21-09.
10 rms. MINIBAR TV **Tram:** 10 from the Hauptbahnhof to Winkelriedstrasse.
$ Rates (including continental breakfast and showers): SFr 55–70 ($39–$49.70) single; SFr 80–95 ($57.15–$67.85) double; SFr 115–130 ($82.15–$92.85) triple. The higher prices apply in summer.

 This lovely hotel, parts of which date from the 17th century, has a homey atmosphere. It's located in a residential area, and at times it may remind you of a country chalet. Most of the spacious rooms have large windows overlooking private residences and gardens, and all 10 have a color TV and minibar. Breakfast is served in the street-level restaurant.

HOTEL ST. GEORGES, Weberstrasse 11, 8004 Zürich. Tel. 01/241-11-44. 43 rms (none with bath). **Tram:** 3 or 14 to Stauffacher.
$ Rates (including continental breakfast and showers): SFr 60 ($42.85) single; SFr 85 ($60.70) double; SFr 110 ($78.55) triple; SFr 130 ($92.85) quad.
The St. Georges has a very pleasant lobby and clean, comfortable rooms with new furniture. Some rooms have views of a pretty square and a church. The staff is courteous and efficient, and will show you the way to a laundry room where you can use a washer and dryer for a small fee.
Take tram no. 3 or 14 to Stauffacher; from there, take the first street on the left and then the second on the right.

HOTEL SEEFELD, Seehofstrasse 11, 8008 Zürich. Tel. 01/252-25-70. 17 rms. **Tram:** 4 from the Hauptbahnhof to Opernhaus.
$ Rates (including continental breakfast and showers): SFr 55 ($39.30) single

---

Ⓕ FROMMER'S SMART TRAVELER: HOTELS

VALUE-CONSCIOUS TRAVELERS SHOULD
TAKE ADVANTAGE OF THE FOLLOWING:

1. Reserving in advance—many visiting businesspeople prefer budget establishments over deluxe ones.
2. The tourist offices at the Hauptbahnhof and the airport, which will make hotel reservations for a small fee.
3. The youth hostel, a great value.

without bath; SFr 86 ($61.40) double without bath, SFr 110 ($78.55) double with bath; SFr 105 ($75) triple without bath, SFr 145 ($103.55) triple with bath. No credit cards.

Located in a quiet area near the opera house, this hotel has large, well-appointed rooms with high ceilings. The management is friendly, and many Swiss business-people stay here. No elevator.

JUSTINUS HEIM, Freudenbergstrasse 146, 8044 Zürich. Tel. 01/361-38-06. 35–40 beds in summer, about 12 in winter (no rms with bath or shower). **Directions:** See below.

$ Rates (including continental breakfast and showers): SFr 35–50 ($25–$35.70) single; SFr 60–80 ($42.85–$57.15) double; SFr 100–120 ($71.40–$85.70) triple; SFr 120–140 ($85.70–$100) quad. No credit cards.

During the academic year, students from some 42 countries stay here while they attend school in Zurich, giving this modern house a cosmopolitan atmosphere.

Located in a serene residential area near the Zürichberg (a mountain), the Justinus Heim is one of the best deals in town, with perfect rooms and, on clear days, views of the city, the lake, and, yes, the Alps. You can go for long walks in the Zürichbergwald, the forest behind the house, or relax on the terrace in the summer. They also have washers and dryers (SFr 2/$1.45 per load), and a large kitchen you can use for SFr 1 (70¢) per day.

From the Hauptbahnhof, take tram no. 10 to the Rigiblick stop and transfer to the Seilbahn (cable car); get off at Bergstation, the last stop, right across from the Justinus Heim.

MARTAHAUS, Zähringerstrasse 36, 8001 Zürich. Tel. 01/251-45-50. 80 beds (no rms with bath). **Directions:** See below.

$ Rates (including continental breakfast and showers): SFr 60 ($42.85) single; SFr 89 ($63.55) double; SFr 105 ($75) triple; SFr 26 ($18.55) per person in a dorm. No credit cards.

Plain and simple, the friendly Martahaus is an excellent deal, especially for those willing to share a room with five other people of the same sex. Other establishments may have nicer singles, doubles, and triples, but not at these prices, and the two six-bed dorms (with individual lockers and impenetrable-looking red curtains separating the beds) are hard to beat. A red elevator will take you to your room on one of five floors. It's very clean, with a TV room, and is centrally located to boot.

From the Hauptbahnhof, walk to Central (see the directions for the Pension St. Josef, below); Zähringerstrasse starts here.

DOUBLES FOR LESS THAN SFR 120 [$85.70]

HOTEL BRISTOL, Stampfenbachstrasse 34, 8035 Zürich. Tel. 01/261-84-00. 50 rms. TV TEL **Directions:** See below.

$ Rates (including continental breakfast): SFr 80 ($57.15) single without bath, SFr 110 ($78.55) single with bath; SFr 110 ($78.55) double without bath, SFr 160 ($114.30) double with bath.

Recently renovated, the Bristol is one of the most comfortable hotels described in this chapter. Rooms have cozy blankets, lamps for reading and writing, and color TVs with programming (including CNN) in four languages. The staff is efficient and friendly.

To get there from the Hauptbahnhof, walk over the Walchebrücke (the bridge near the Landesmuseum), across Neumühlequai, and up the steps to Stampfenbachstrasse, then turn left; the hotel is 100 yards away.

HOTEL HIRSCHEN, 13 Niederdorfstrasse, 8001 Zürich. Tel. 01/251-42-52. 38 rms. **Tram:** 3 or 14 to Centralplatz.

$ Rates (including continental breakfast): SFr 50 ($35.70) single without shower or toilet, SFr 70 ($50) single with shower only, SFr 80 ($57.15) single with shower and toilet; SFr 80 ($57.15) double without shower or toilet, SFr 100 ($71.40) double with shower only, SFr 120 ($85.70) double with shower and toilet.

Although this hotel has no elevator, creaky stairs, and low ceilings, the rooms are comfortably furnished.

HOTEL LIMMATHOF, Limmatquai 142, 8023 Zürich. Tel. 01/261-42-20. 30 rms (all with bath). **Directions:** See below.

$ Rates (including continental breakfast): SFr 95–110 ($67.85–$78.55) single; SFr 130–160 ($92.85–$114.30) double; SFr 180 ($128.55) triple.

Managed by a father-and-son team, the Nussbaumers, this superior hotel was recently renovated and has comfortable, modern rooms, all with bath, some with traditional furniture and/or color TV. Breakfast, which includes orange juice, is served in a street-level restaurant with Swiss wooden chairs. The service is efficient and pleasant. They take reservations, which should be followed by a deposit.

From the Hauptbahnhof, cross the Bahnhofbrücke to Central; you'll be facing the hotel. (See the directions for the Pension St. Josef, below.)

HOTEL KRONE, Limmatquai 88, 8001 Zürich. Tel. 01/251-42-22. 25 rms. **Tram:** 4 from the Hauptbahnhof to Rudolf Brun-Brücke.

$ Rates (including continental breakfast): SFr 68–78 ($48.55–$55.70) single without bath; SFr 105–115 ($75–$82.15) double without bath, SFr 145 ($103.55) double with bath; SFr 160 ($114.30) triple without bath.

This three-story house facing the Limmat River has plain but clean rooms. The building dates from the 17th century, and the hotel has been in existence for more than 100 years. Their restaurant is open for both lunch and dinner.

HOTEL VILLETTE, Kruggasse 4, 8001 Zürich. Tel. 01/251-23-35. 14 rms (most with bath). TV TEL **Tram:** 11 from the Hauptbahnhof to Bellevueplatz.

$ Rates (including continental breakfast): SFr 80 ($57.15) single with toilet only, SFr 100 ($71.40) single with bath; SFr 110 ($78.55) double with toilet only, SFr 120 ($85.70) double with bath; SFr 145 ($103.55) triple with bath. Reservations by phone accepted when followed by a deposit.

Centrally located in the Old City, this small, superior hotel has rooms with minibars, and all have color TVs as well. The breakfast room and a typical Swiss restaurant are on the first floor, while the reception and the rooms are reached by an elevator.

Kruggasse is a bit hard to find. After exiting the tram at Bellevueplatz, walk along Limmatquai in the direction the tram came; Kruggasse is the second street.

HOTEL ZÜRICHBERG, Orellistrasse 21, 8044 Zürich. Tel. 01/252-38-48. 60 rms (none with bath). **Tram:** 6 from the Hauptbahnhof to Zoo (the last stop).

$ Rates (including buffet breakfast and showers): SFr 65–90 ($46.40–$64.30) single; SFr 115–130 ($82.15–$92.85) double. Rooms with views of the lake are more expensive than those with views of the forest.

The Hotel Zürichberg, rambling and traditional, high above the city, next to a forest and to the cemetery where James Joyce is buried, could be the setting for a detective novel. The rooms are cozy and well appointed, and some have balconies and long windows. The corridors are large and high-ceilinged, and the sitting room, with its view of city, lake, and mountains—or, in winter, maybe just a blanket of snow—has elegant, if faded, furnishings and shelves with German and English books. But the Zürichberg is not bleak. In fact, it's a great hotel for children, with the zoo and a public playground and swimming pool nearby.

PENSION ST. JOSEF, Hirschengraben 64, 8001 Zürich. Tel. 01/251-27-57. 45 rms (none with bath). **Directions:** See below.

$ Rates (including buffet breakfast and showers): SFr 62–65 ($44.30–$46.40) single; SFr 93–100 ($66.40–$71.40) double; SFr 125–135 ($89.30–$96.40) triple; SFr 145–160 ($103.55–$114.30) quad; SFr 180–200 ($125.55–$157.15) five-bed room. Prices vary according to the length of stay (at least three nights preferred) and the season. No credit cards.

★ The three houses that make up the Pension St. Josef are among the nicest places to stay in Zurich. The rooms, which are spotless, have beautiful furniture and feel very cozy, with tasteful paintings and drawings. The atmosphere is very friendly, and you'll feel right at home in the TV room. In order to register you'll have to arrive by 6pm. There is no real curfew, but if you want to come in late you'll have to get a key, for a SFr-10 ($7.15) deposit.

The St. Josef is a 10-minute walk from the Hauptbahnhof across the Bahnhofbrücke (the bridge by the Coop Super-Center) onto Central, a square where many tram lines converge; Hirschengraben is the steep street at very end of the square. (If you have a lot of luggage, you may want to take a cab; you could also take tram no. 3 to Central, but that won't take you uphill.)

SUPER-BUDGET CHOICES

JUGENDHERBERGE, Mutschellenstrasse 114, 8038 Zürich. Tel. 01/ 482-35-44. 375 beds. **Tram:** 7 from the Hauptbahnhof to Morgental.

$ Rates (including continental breakfast): SFr 22 ($15.70) per person for members, SFr 29 ($20.70) per person for nonmembers. A youth-hostel card costs SFr 30 ($21.40) if you buy it here. No credit cards.

Large and modern, Zurich's only official youth hostel has 9 rooms for families, 46 rooms with 6 double-decker beds, and two dorms with 30 double-decker beds in each. For a Swiss hostel it's an impersonal place, but a great value nonetheless, with a self-catering kitchen, a cafeteria, lockers, a TV lounge, games rooms, and laundry facilities.

It's a 15-minute ride on tram no. 7 from the Central Station to Morgental. From there, follow the signs for a 10-minute walk.

FOR WOMEN, FAMILIES & MARRIED COUPLES ONLY

FOYER HOTTINGEN, Hottingerstrasse 31, 8032 Zürich. Tel. 01/261-93-15. 24 rms (none with bath). **Tram:** 3 from the Hauptbahnhof to Hottingerplatz.

$ Rates (including continental breakfast and showers): SFr 42 ($30) single; SFr 70 ($50) double; SFr 76 ($54.30) triple; SFr 84 ($60) quad; SFr 22 ($15.70) per person in a 4-bed dorm, SFr 18 ($12.85) in a 16-bed dorm. No credit cards.

Rooms at the Foyer Hottingen are simple but comfortable and very clean, and there is a small kitchen that you can use. The Catholic staff is warm and efficient, and their rates are among the best in town. They take reservations and will remind you that there is a midnight curfew.

WORTH THE EXTRA BUCKS

HOTEL LEONHARD, Limmatquai 136, 8001 Zürich. Tel. 01/251-30-80. MINIBAR TV **Directions:** See below.

$ Rates (including buffet breakfast): SFr 140 ($100) single with bath; SFr 180 ($128.55) double with bath; SFr 220 ($157.15) triple with bath.

This is a small but very cozy hotel that has been owned by the same family for three generations. The three floors are not served by an elevator, but all rooms in this old house facing the Limmat River have been modernized, and have color TV, hairdryer, and minibar.

From the Hauptbahnhof, cross the bridge to Central (see the directions for the Pension St. Josef, above); the Leonhard is a five-minute walk from here.

RESIDENZ DREI KÖNIGE, Seestrasse 65, Zürich 8002. Tel. 01/281-11-91. 14 rms, 2 suites (all with shower and toilet). TV TEL **Tram:** 7 from the Hauptbahnhof to the Rietberg Museum stop.

$ Rates: SFr 150 ($107.15) single; SFr 175 ($125) double; SFr 280 ($200) suite for two people, 390 ($270.55) suite for three. No credit cards.

This hotel opened in 1991 and is housed in a beautifully modernized art nouveau–style building, directly across the street from the Rietberg Museum. Every room (five singles, nine doubles) has a color TV with CNN, and suites have kitchenettes with microwave ovens. There is an elevator, and a self-service laundry is on each floor. English is spoken. Reserve early—the hotel is often heavily booked.

5. BUDGET DINING

The many restaurants of Zurich cover everything from fast food to gourmet. Although the accent throughout the city may appear to be on international cuisine, I've listed several places where you can taste some of the local specialties. Besides the ever popular *fondue* (melted cheese, into which bread or boiled potatoes are dipped), there are other favorites: *geschnetzeltes* (shredded veal cooked with mushrooms in a cream sauce, and invariably served with grated and fried potatoes), *rösti* (a sort of hash-browned potatoes with onion), *leberspiessli* (calf's liver grilled with bacon and served on a spit), and *Zürcher topf* (baked macaroni, ground meat, and tomato sauce).

Restaurants are concentrated around the Hauptbahnhof, along Bahnhofstrasse, and in the Old City. I've also listed several restaurants located near Helvetiaplatz, a square that's a 10-minute walk from the Hauptbahnhof across the Sihl River. Most restaurants in Zurich tend to be crowded (except on weekends), so come early or late to find a good seat. But don't arrive too late: Restaurants that may be open 18 hours a day stop serving hot meals after normal eating hours. Cheap restaurants in Zurich normally don't accept credit cards (although they often accept traveler's checks), so always inquire before sitting down.

MEALS FOR LESS THAN SFR 10 [$7.15]

CINDY, Central (in same building as the Polybahn cable-car station). Tel. 262-40-79.
   Cuisine: SWISS FAST FOOD.
   $ Prices: Light meals SFr 3–9.90 ($2.15–$7.05). No credit cards.
   Open: Mon–Sat 7am–midnight, Sun 8am–11pm.
This fast-food place offers an unusually large variety of hot and cold dishes and beverages, and is especially popular with students from the nearby universities. Hamburgers, pizzas, roast chicken, fries, wieners, and meatballs are all available.

MENSA POLYTERRASSE, Leonhardstrasse 34. Tel. 251-64-20.
   Cuisine: SWISS. **Tram:** 6 or 10 to ETH/Universitätsspital; or see below.
   $ Prices: SFr 5–8.20 ($3.55–$5.85).
   Open: Mensa, lunch Mon–Fri 11:15am–1:30pm, Sat 11:30am–1pm; dinner Mon–Thurs 5:30–7:30pm, Fri 5:30–7:15pm. Cafeteria, Mon–Fri 6:45am–9pm, Sat 7:30am–1:15pm.
This is the mensa of the ETH Zürich, the prestigious technical university where Albert Einstein once taught. The four daily menus served at this huge restaurant (1,200 total seats) might include hamburger steak with noodles and salad or grilled chicken with french fries and salad. The prices are very good and you may meet some students. Atop the terrace is a cafeteria, operated separately from the mensa.

To reach the mensa, take the tram as noted above, or the Polybahn (cable-car railway) from Central at a cost of SFr .80 (55¢); a Tageskarte is also valid for the Polybahn.

SALVATION ARMY RESTAURANT, Molkenstrasse 6. Tel. 242-90-00.
   Cuisine: SWISS. **Directions:** See below.
   $ Prices: Main courses SFr 3–10 ($2.15–$7.15). No credit cards.
   Open: Restaurant, lunch daily noon–12:45pm; dinner daily 6–6:45pm. Cafeteria, lunch daily 12:30–5pm; dinner daily 7–9:30pm.
The Salvation Army in Zurich provides inexpensive two-course meals to everybody,

---

(F) **FROMMER'S SMART TRAVELER:**
RESTAURANTS

VALUE-CONSCIOUS TRAVELERS SHOULD
TAKE ADVANTAGE OF THE FOLLOWING:

1. Arriving either early or late, to ensure a good seat.
2. Restaurants clustered around the Hauptbahnhof, along Bahnhofstrasse, in the Old City, and near Helvetiaplatz.

---

not only to those in need. Meals include minestrone, spaghetti bolognese, and tea; or rice soup, roast chicken with fries, and tea. The dining room is self-serve and there is also a cafeteria, which serves light meals and snacks (such as tomato soup, cold cuts, coffee, tea, and dessert).

Molkenstrasse is located near Helvetiaplatz, a 10-minute walk across the Sihl River from the station.

SILBERKUGEL, in Shopville, the underground passage leading from the Hauptbahnhof to Bahnhofstrasse. Tel. 221-16-77.
   Cuisine: SWISS FAST FOOD.
$ Prices: Light dishes SFr 3–7 ($2.40–$5.60). No credit cards.
   Open: Mon–Fri 6:15am–10pm, Sat 6:30am–10pm, Sun 9am–7:30pm.
This is one of a chain of popular fast-food eateries serving quick, light meals—there are eight Silberkugels around Zurich. They offer hamburgers in the usual varieties, soups, sandwiches, and salads.

STADTKÜCHE (City Kitchen), Schipfe 16. Tel. 211-21-22.
   Cuisine: SWISS. **Directions:** See below.
$ Prices: Hot lunches SFr 7.50 ($5.35). No credit cards.
   Open: Lunch only, Mon–Fri 11:30am–1pm.
The City Kitchen serves what is probably the cheapest hot lunch in Zurich. Despite the name, it's not a charitable organization, so feel free to eat here. The two-course meal might be spaghetti bolognese, salad, and flan, or some other such dishes. By adding soup, you'll have a three-course meal for half the price it would cost you in any other budget restaurant.

Schipfe is in the Old City, on the same side as Bahnhofstrasse, near the Limmat River between Rudolf Brun-Brücke and Rathausbrücke.

YMCA RESTAURANT, Sihlstrasse 33. Tel. 221-36-73.
   Cuisine: SWISS. **Directions:** See below.
$ Prices: SFr 12–15 ($8.55–$10.70). No credit cards.
   Open: Mon–Fri 8am–7:30pm.
Workers from nearby offices and shops come here for generous portions of good food, served one flight up in this palacelike building. The selection is not extensive, but whatever is on the menu is usually tasty and filling. There are à la carte dishes as well.

Sihlstrasse is off Bahnhofstrasse.

MEALS FOR LESS THAN SFR 15 [$10.70]

BIERHALLE WOLF, Limmatquai 132. Tel. 251-01-30.
   Cuisine: SWISS.
$ Prices: Main courses SFr 7.50–15.50 ($5.35–$11.05). No credit cards.
   Open: Daily noon–1am.
Near Central, this popular eatery is frequented by locals working in this busy part of town. Come early to find a seat. One-plate offerings include Hungarian gulash with

steamed potatoes, spaghetti marinara, and Wiener Schnitzel with noodles and creamy sauce. A music-and-folklore program is performed every afternoon from 4 to 6pm (free) and every evening from 8pm to midnight; Sunday through Thursday there's a SFr-4 ($2.85) supplement, and on Friday and Saturday, a SFr-5 ($3.55) supplement.

RACLETTE STUBE, Zähringerstrasse 16. Tel. 251-41-30.
　Cuisine: SWISS. **Directions:** See below.
$ Prices: Main courses SFr 7.50–37 ($5.35–$26.40).
　Open: Summer, lunch Fri only, noon–2pm; dinner daily 6–11pm; winter, lunch Fri only, noon–2pm, dinner daily 5–11pm.

　　Located in the Old City, this is Zurich's only full-time raclette restaurant. A raclette consists of a platter of melted cheese, accompanied by a boiled potato and pickled baby onions. You season the cheese with salt and pepper, eat it, then request another until you're full. Here you can also have cheese fondue for SFr 18.50 ($13.20) or fondue bourguignonne (meat fondue), for two, for SFr 74 ($52.85). Zähringerstrasse runs almost parallel to Limmatquai, near Central.

RESTAURANT AM HELVETIAPLATZ, Stauffacherstrasse 60. Tel. 242-11-55.
　Cuisine: SWISS. **Directions:** See below.
$ Prices: Main courses SFr 7.50–37 ($5.35–$26.40). No credit cards.
　Open: Mon–Fri 11am–midnight, Sat–Sun noon–midnight.
This highly popular restaurant has a huge 300-seat dining room where you can sample Swiss dishes like rösti for SFr 12 ($8.55) and geschnetzeltes for SFr 24 ($17.15). Other items on the menu include potato soup, sausage grilled with onions and served with roast potatoes, and Italian dishes. The service is very quick.
　Stauffacherstrasse and Helvetiaplatz are a 10-minute walk from the Hauptbahnhof across the Sihl River.

RESTAURANT GESSNERALLEE, Schützengasse 32. Tel. 221-28-33.
　Cuisine: SWISS. **Directions:** See below.
$ Prices: Main courses SFr 12–27 ($8.55–$19.30). No credit cards.
　Open: Mon–Fri 8am–midnight, Sat–Sun 8am–7pm.
This is one of the cheapest eateries near the Hauptbahnhof. Local workers always crowd the dining room, which is decorated with farmer tools and copper pots. There is a large selection of omelets and hearty dishes. In the summer, they also have a pleasant open-air terrace.
　Schützengasse is off Bahnhofstrasse, only one block from the Hauptbahnhof.

RHEINFELDER BIERHAUS, Marktgasse 19. Tel. 251-29-91.
　Cuisine: SWISS. **Directions:** See below.
$ Prices: Main courses SFr 8.50–16.50 ($6.05–$11.80). No credit cards.
　Open: Daily 9am–midnight.
Little English is spoken at this rather basic dining room, with excellent food. Dishes include entrecôte with fries, hamburger, veal cutlet, spaghetti, and roast chicken.
　Near the Rathausbrücke, Marktgasse is the continuation of Niederdorfstrasse.

ZUR KARIN, Limmatquai 86. Tel. 252-11-49.
　Cuisine: INTERNATIONAL.
$ Prices: Main courses SFr 6.50–33 ($4.65–$23.55); fixed-price menus SFr 13.50 ($9.65) and SFr 16 ($11.40). AE, EURO, MC, V.
　Open: Daily 10am–midnight (fixed-price menus Mon–Fri).
Only beef imported from Argentina is served at this popular eatery and steakhouse. Facing the Limmat River, off Centralplatz, it has 120 seats on two levels. Besides the daily menus, à la carte dishes include salads, corn on the cob, and such cuts of beef as rumpsteak, beefsteak, and entrecôte. The atmosphere is lively, and English is spoken. Highly recommended.

MEALS FOR LESS THAN SFR 25 [$17.85]
CAFE RESTAURANT SEIDENHOF, Sihlstrasse 9. Tel. 211-65-44.

Cuisine: SWISS. **Directions:** See below.
$ **Prices:** Main courses SFr 8–21 ($5.70–$15). No credit cards.
Open: Mon–Wed and Fri 6:30am–9pm, Thurs 6:30am–9:30pm, Sat 6:30am–noon.

Businesspeople have lunch at this ultramodern dining room in the Seidenhof Hotel building. Only à la carte dishes are served, such as omelets filled with ham or marmalade, shredded veal with roast potatoes, and filet mignon with salad.

Sihlstrasse is off Bahnhofstrasse.

MÖVENPICK, Bahnhofstrasse 81. Tel. 211-50-34.

Cuisine: SWISS/INTERNATIONAL.
$ **Prices:** Main courses SFr 15.30–29.50 ($10.90–$21.05); salads SFr 7–8.80 ($5–$6.30); soups SFr 5.80–6.80 ($4.15–$4.85).
Open: Daily 11am–11pm.

This pleasant restaurant—one of a chain—is versatile. Choose as much or as little as you wish to eat: a cup of coffee, a pastry, a salad at the salad bar, a sundae, minestrone, Parisian-style onion soup, veal sausage, smoked salmon, ham in a wine sauce with currants and Sauerkraut, or beef with mushrooms in a herb sauce. They have an English-language menu, but it's shorter than the German one, and it doesn't include the *Heute aktuell* (daily specials), which can be quite creative: When I was there, it listed all sorts of lentil dishes.

RESTAURANT DU NORD, Bahnhofplatz 2. Tel. 211-37-90.

Cuisine: INTERNATIONAL.
$ **Prices:** Six two-course menus SFr 13–30 ($9.30–$21.40); main courses SFr 15–20 ($10.70–$14.30); desserts from SFr 6 ($4.30).
Open: Daily 8am–midnight.

The restaurant is in a very central location, across from the main entrance of the Hauptbahnhof (to the left), one flight up. Dishes include a large salad bowl with a boiled egg, sauerkraut with mashed potatoes, stewed rabbit with dumplings, and apple pie with cream. Ask for the English menu.

RESTAURANT HILTL VEGI, Sihlstrasse 28. Tel. 221-38-70 or 221-38-71.

Cuisine: VEGETARIAN. **Directions:** See below.
$ **Prices:** Main courses SFr 7.60–16.90 ($5.40–$12.05). No credit cards.
Open: Mon–Sat 6:30am–9pm, Sun 11am–9pm.

Founded in 1897, Zurich's leading vegetarian restaurant is still managed by the same family. Salads, gnocchi romana, spaghetti with herb sauce, soyburgers, and many types of teas and juices are served in the modern, brightly colored dining rooms. The atmosphere is pleasant and the service is quick. Sihlstrasse is off Bahnhofstrasse.

RESTAURANT WEISSER WIND, Oberdorfstrasse 20. Tel. 251-18-45.

Cuisine: INTERNATIONAL. **Directions:** See below.
$ **Prices:** Two-course meals SFr 16.50–19.80 ($11.80–$14.15). No credit cards.
Open: Mon–Sat 10am–midnight.

This large, somewhat quaint dining room has first-class food and service. Two-course meals are served Monday through Friday during the lunch hour (11:30am to 2pm) and dinner (5:30 to 11pm), and all day on Saturday. A la carte items include pasta, red snapper, nasi goreng, choucroute, and special low-calorie dishes.

Oberdorfstrasse is off Rämistrasse, near Bellevueplatz.

SHANGHAI RESTAURANT, Bäckerstrasse 62. Tel. 242-40-39.

Cuisine: CHINESE/JAPANESE. **Directions:** See below.
$ **Prices:** Soups SFr 8–13 ($5.70–$9.30); main courses SFr 21.50–34.50 ($15.35–$24.65).
Open: Lunch Thurs–Tues 11:45am–2pm; dinner Thurs–Tues 5:45–10pm.

The multilingual menu lists countless Asian dishes, from hot-and-sour soup and spring rolls to spiced boneless duck, and high standards are met throughout. During the week two-course meals are available for lunch. Bäckerstrasse is near Helvetiaplatz, a 10-minute walk from the Hauptbahnhof across the Sihl River.

SPAGHETTI FACTORY, Theaterstrasse 10. Tel. 261-80-70.

Cuisine: ITALIAN/AMERICAN. **Reservations:** Recommended Fri–Sun after 8pm. **Tram:** 2, 4, 5, 9, 11, or 15 to Bellevueplatz.

$ Prices: Main courses SFr 10.50–23.50 ($7.50–$16.80).

Open: Mon–Thurs 8am–2am, Fri–Sat 8am–4am, Sun 11am–2am.

Don't let the names of some of the 20 spaghetti platters in the menu offend you—Al Capone, American Disaster, and Go to Hell, for example. As a former resident of Miami, I was at first insulted by the inclusion of my old hometown as one of those notorious names, but the scrumptious pastas helped me get over it. Pastas are served with various sauces, including smoked-salmon dressing, steak tartare, and curried chicken. Decorated with neon lights and bright colors, the Spaghetti Factory is popular: It's a good idea to make reservations on weekends after 8pm.

TAVERNA CATALANA, Glockengasse 8. Tel. 221-12-62.

Cuisine: SPANISH. **Directions:** See below.

$ Prices: Main courses SFr 10–25 ($7.15–$17.85). No credit cards.

Open: Tues–Sat 11am–11:30pm.

Beef Gulasch, pork chops, veal cutlets, omelets served with peppers, and salads (try their fish salad—it's especially good) are among the most popular dishes here. For less than SFr 25 ($17.85) you can eat well at this taverna where the Spanish waiters speak English. You can also bring food bought elsewhere and rent a knife, fork, and spoon, and eat here for SFr 1.50 ($1.05), a Taverna Catalana tradition. Locals crowd the polished oak tables, and you may not find a seat if you come after noon.

To find it, walk up Augustinerstrasse, off Bahnhofstrasse.

TAVERNA SYRTAKI, Werdstrasse 66. Tel. 242-53-59.

Cuisine: GREEK. **Tram:** 3 or 14 to Stauffacher (the fourth stop).

$ Prices: Main courses SFr 9–36 ($6.40–$25.70). No credit cards.

Open: Lunch Mon–Sat 11:30am–2pm; dinner Mon–Sat 6–10:30pm.

Here you can order dolmata (tomato salad), avgolemono (chicken broth with egg and lemon juice), dolmadakia (stuffed grape leaves), an omelet filled with feta cheese, moussaka, paidakia arnissia (grilled lamb chops with zucchini), baklava (honey cake), and various Greek wines.

ZEUGHAUSKELLER, Bahnhofstrasse 28. Tel. 211-26-90.

Cuisine: SWISS.

$ Prices: Main courses SFr 12–30 ($8.55–$21.40); soups SFr 4.50–7.70 ($3.20–$5.50); salads SFr 4.80–17.70 ($3.40–$12.65); desserts SFr 4.80–7.70 ($3.40–$5.50); beer SFr 2.60–5.80 ($1.85–$4.15).

Open: Daily 11:30am–11pm (last orders at 9:45pm).

Housed in a building that used to be an arsenal and that in 1987 celebrated its fifth centennial, the bustling Zeughauskeller is a great place to taste a variety of Swiss dishes. They don't serve fondue, but you can try a delicious Kalbsgeschnetzeltes nach Zürcher Art (sliced veal and mushrooms in a wine sauce) for SFr 25.60 ($18.30), Zürcher Ratsherrenteller (a mixed grill with rösti) for SFr 30.50 ($21.70), or the hilarious Kanonenputzer, a yard-long sausage from French Switzerland served with potato salad that feeds four people, for SFr 64 ($45.70), also available at half that length and half that price. The main beverage here is beer. Owners Herr Andreae and Herr Hammer head a quick, friendly staff. You can ask for a menu in English.

CAFES

The citizens of Zurich relax at their cafés for hours on end. You can do the same, while having some coffee, tea, ice cream, pastries, or even a light meal: Many cafés actually function as restaurants and have a daily special that often can be an excellent deal.

CAFE LITTERAIRE, Schützenstrasse 19. Tel. 211-16-27.

Cuisine: COFFEEHOUSE/SNACKS.

$ Prices: Cup of coffee SFr 2.80–3.50 ($2–$2.50); lasagne verdi SFr 13.50 ($9.65).

Two blocks south of the Hauptbahnhof and one block west of Bahnhofstrasse, the Café Littéraire boasts no sidewalk tables, but it does have a fine brown and olive-green interior and very good coffee. Yes, people who congregate at this café look literary, though few seem to care about the German-language newspapers available here. Come for the lasagna verde, and bring your own copy of the *International Herald Tribune.* It's crowded during breakfast and lunch, but less so in the evenings.

CAFE ODEON, Limmatquai 2. Tel. 251-16-50.

Cuisine: COFFEEHOUSE/SNACKS.
$ Prices: Cup of coffee or glass of wine SFr 3.20 ($2.30); *Tages Menüs* (daily specials) SFr 11–16 ($7.85–$11.40).
Open: Mon–Thurs 7am–2am, Fri–Sat 7am–4am, Sun 11am–2am.

Near Bellevueplatz, this beautiful café is decorated in art nouveau style.

CAFE SELECT, Limmatquai 16. Tel. 252-43-72.

Cuisine: COFFEEHOUSE/SNACKS.
$ Prices: *Tages Menüs* (daily specials) SFr 9.50–18.50 ($6.80–$13.20).
Open: Mon–Fri 7am–11:30pm, Sat–Sun 7:30am–11:30pm.

Between the Münsterbrücke and the Quaibrücke, the Café Select has about 13 different dishes in its daily specials.

STREET FOOD

Along Zurich's major arteries, such as Bahnhofstrasse and Limmatquai, you'll see fast-food stalls selling all kinds of sausages and sandwiches that will make a decent, cheap, and quick lunch or snack. Try them.

LATE-NIGHT/24-HOUR RESTAURANTS

Many restaurants in Zurich remain open until midnight or later, but often their kitchens close around 10pm or earlier. When all else fails, the Hauptbahnhof will save you. There are six or seven restaurants and cafeterias here, and at least one of them is open at any given time. There is always at least one place to eat here 24 hours a day.

PICNIC SUPPLIES & WHERE TO EAT THEM

Consider having a picnic: Swiss delicatessens carry delicious cold cuts, and buying bread, wine, and chocolate is an inexpensive alternative to restaurant eating. For take-out food such as grilled chicken, herring, potato salad, meatballs, and an enormous variety of cheeses, try the **Coop Super-Center,** on Bahnhofplatz near the Bahnhofbrücke (it has a large sign), or **Bell's,** Bahnhofstrasse 102, one block from the Hauptbahnhof. And there are small shops everywhere offering delicious pastries.

Now that you have your cake, where do you eat it? If you're not too hungry, you'll be able to get to the **lakeshore** at the end of Bahnhofstrasse, or to **Belvoirpark** and **Rieterpark** (see "Parks and Gardens" in "Attractions," below). But my favorite place for a tranquil, solitary picnic is **Zürichberg,** the mountain. To get there, take tram no. 5 or 6 to Zoo, the last stop, or take tram no. 9 or 10 to Seilbahn Rigiblick and then the Seilbahn (cable car) itself to the last stop.

WORTH THE EXTRA BUCKS

KRONENHALLE, Rämistrasse 4. Tel. 252-58-93.

Cuisine: CONTINENTAL. **Reservations:** Strongly recommended. **Tram:** 2, 4, 5, 8, 9, 11, or 15 to Bellevueplatz.
$ Prices: SFr 55–125 ($39.30–$89.30).
Open: Daily noon–midnight.

⭐ This is one of Zurich's first-class restaurants, with a guest list that has included James Joyce, Andy Warhol, Henry Kissinger, and Elizabeth Taylor. Paintings by Picasso, Chagall, Matisse, and Miró decorate the impeccable dining hall and two Giacometti lamps light the cozy bar. Items from the menu include filet of sole with melon dumplings, Norwegian lobster, and rack of lamb provençal. The dessert specialty is chocolate mousse, which was supposedly invented here over 100 years ago. Reservations are strongly recommended.

6. ATTRACTIONS

SUGGESTED ITINERARIES

IF YOU HAVE ONE DAY   If you have only one day to visit Zurich, I recommend the following itinerary. From the Hauptbahnhof, walk along Bahnhofstrasse, the main commercial artery whose banks and expensive stores are emblematic of official Zurich. At the end of Bahnhofstrasse is the Zürichsee, the lake, with wonderful views of the Alps on clear days. Head back and explore the narrow streets of the Old City. This is a great area to have lunch. If you want to visit only one church, make it the Fraumünster. You may still have time to visit a museum: Choose either the Landesmuseum or the Kunsthaus.

IF YOU HAVE TWO DAYS   Spend Day 1 as described above. On Day 2, in the morning you can go to a museum or visit more churches (see the listings below). In the afternoon, try to get away from the city center. Take tram no. 5 or 6 to the last stop and visit the Zoologischer Garten or Fluntern cemetery, or just walk around the wooded Zürichberg. The uphill tram ride is worth it: Along the winding residential streets you'll pass various superb styles of 20th-century architecture. Or leave the city for Uetliberg, a 2,800-foot hill affording great views.

IF YOU HAVE THREE DAYS   Switzerland is a breathtakingly beautiful country, and Zurich is an excellent base for day trips. On Day 3, take a trip to either Lucerne or the Jungfraujoch (see "Easy Excursions," below).

IF YOU HAVE FIVE DAYS   By this time you'll be an old Zurich hand, so I probably don't need to tell you what to do. The city has a number of specialized museums—toys, coffee, decorative arts, and so on—that you may want to visit, and other possible day trips in Switzerland and beyond beckon. Consider Berne, Basel, or the Principality of Liechtenstein.

TOP ATTRACTIONS

SCHWEIZERISCHES LANDESMUSEUM (Swiss National Museum),
Museumstrasse 2. Tel. 218-65-65.

⭐ You'll probably get lost in this many-turreted Victorian building, but so much the better. This is the attic of Switzerland—and of the peoples that preceded the Swiss in this land—and what a wonderful treasure trove it is. You'll see stones, furniture, tools, paintings, weapons, costumes, sleighs, uniforms, toys, clocks, flags, stained glass, textiles, and much more. My favorite exhibits are the 16th-century terrestrial globe in Room 23 and the Celtic gold bracelets in Room 71.

The Landesmuseum is located next to the Hauptbahnhof.
Admission: Free.
Open: Tues–Sun 10am–5pm; guided tours in English given in summer, Thurs at 10:15am.

KUNSTHAUS (Art Gallery), Heimplatz 1. Tel. 251-67-55.

⭐ This world-famous collection is housed in a superbly designed complex with a scenic garden in the center. The permanent collection includes paintings by Breughel the Elder, Memling, Hals, Rembrandt, Rubens, Canaletto, Munch,

Toulouse-Lautrec, Utrillo, Picasso, Chagall, Klee, Kandinsky, Mondrian, and Tanguy. This is a great place to learn about the connections between Zurich and dadaism. There are also changing exhibitions, for which you need a separate ticket.

Admission: SFr 4 ($2.85) adults, SFr 3 ($2.15) students.
Open: Mon 2–5pm, Tues–Thurs 10am–9pm, Fri–Sun 10am–5pm. **Tram:** 3, 5, 8, or 9 to Kunsthaus; or a 15-minute walk from the Hauptbahnhof.

MUSEUM RIETBERG, Gablerstrasse 15. Tel. 202-45-28.

What started as a collection of mostly Asian art, donated to the city by a banker, has grown to encompass many kinds of non-European artistic expressions. There are objects from the Americas, Africa, the Middle East, India, China, and other parts of Asia. Several of the Chinese masterpieces were recovered from East Germany in exchange for some of Lenin's personal effects from his days as a Zurich resident.

Admission: SFr 3 ($2.15).
Open: Tues and Thurs–Sun 10am–5pm, Wed 10am–9pm. **Tram:** 6 or 7 to Museum Rietberg.

GROSSMÜNSTER (Cathedral), Grossmünsterplatz. Tel. 252-59-49.

The two Gothic towers of the Grossmünster are a landmark in Zurich. Construction began around 1100 over the ruins of a former convent, and now the oldest parts of the building are the choir and the very interesting crypt. The Grossmünster has played a major role in the history of the Swiss church; Ulrich Zwingli, the central figure of the Swiss Reformation, preached here from 1519 to 1531, until his execution. The church bears the mark of these troubled times, as it was stripped of all religious ornaments and to this day looks bare and austere.

The Grossmünster is near Münsterbrücke in the Old City across the Limmat River from the Hauptbahnhof.

Admission: Free.
Open: Daily 9am–6pm.

FRAUMÜNSTER, Fraumünsterstrasse. Tel. 202-59-21.

✪ The Fraumünster owes its name to the church's origin in the 9th century as a convent for noble women. Through the centuries the building has undergone many transformations, and little remains of the original architecture. But that's all right: Visitors come here to see something quite different—namely, the luminiscent glasswork by Marc Chagall and Alberto Giacometti in the transept. The Fraumünster is near Poststrasse, just off Bahnhofstrasse.

Admission: Free.
Open: Daily 9am–6pm.

ST. PETERSKIRCHE (St. Peter's Church), St. Peterhofstatt. Tel. 211-25-88.

St. Peter's is Zurich's oldest parish church and has Europe's largest clock on its tower, 28.5 feet wide, with a 12-foot-long minute hand. Until 80 years ago members of Zurich's fire brigade were posted in the four small turreted windows above the clock face, and they'd blow a horn whenever they detected a fire.

St. Peter's is near Augustinergasse, just off Bahnhofstrasse.

Admission: Free.
Open: Daily 8am–6pm.

MORE ATTRACTIONS

ZUNFTHAUS ZUR MEISE, Münsterhof 20. Tel. 221-28-07.

Of the eight guildhalls of Zurich, the Zunfthaus zur Meisen is the only one that hasn't been converted into a public building or a restaurant. Built in 1757 and formerly the wine merchant's guildhouse, it now houses a permanent exhibition of the Landesmuseum's 18th-century porcelain and faïence collection in richly stuccoed showrooms.

Admission: Free.

DID YOU KNOW . . . ?

- Switzerland's borders have remained virtually unchanged since 1815, an anomaly in Europe.
- Swiss watchmakers control nearly half the world market.
- People in Zurich speak a Swiss dialect of German called Schwitzerdeutsch; writing is done in Hochdeutsch, or "proper" German.
- Switzerland was neutral during World War II, but because of its proximity to Germany, some bombs were accidentally dropped on Zurich.
- People in Switzerland travel by train an average of 39 times a year, more than in any other European country.
- Swiss women were only given the right to vote in federal elections as late as 1971.

Open: Tues–Fri and Sun 10am–noon and 2–5pm, Sat 10am–noon and 2–6pm. **Directions:** From Paradeplatz, on Bahnhofstrasse, walk up Waaggasse or Poststrasse to Münsterhof.

MUSEUM BÜHRLE, Zollikerstrasse 172. Tel. 55-00-86.

This private art gallery displays medieval wood sculptures and paintings by such masters as Rembrandt, Tiepolo, and Goya, as well as an extraordinary collection of impressionist paintings, including works by Cézanne, Renoir, Manet, Monet, Gauguin, and van Gogh.

Admission: SFr 6.60F ($4.70) adults, half price for students and children.

Open: Tues and Fri 2–5pm, Wed 5–8pm. **Tram:** 2 (from Paradeplatz or Bellevueplatz) or 4 (from the Hauptbahnhof or Bellevueplatz) to Wildbachstrasse.

MUSEUM BELLERIVE, Höschgasse 3. Tel. 383-43-76.

This small museum of decorative arts features an exquisite collection. The displays include Peruvian and Chinese textiles, Spanish folk art, Tiffany- and Liberty-style objets d'art, antique glassware, marionettes, musical instruments, Japanese basketwork, and English pottery.

Admission: Free.

Open: Tues and Thurs–Sun 10am–5pm, Wed 10am–9pm. **Tram:** 2 (from Paradeplatz or Bellevueplatz) or 4 (from the Hauptbahnhof or Bellevueplatz) to Höschgasse.

ZOOLOGISCHER GARTEN, Zürichbergstrasse 221. Tel. 252-71-00.

Here is one of the best-kept zoos in Europe, two miles east of the Hauptbahnhof on a mountain slope. Animals are kept in natural habitats in a huge park with flower gardens and ponds. Over 2,000 animals of 400 species are kept here, from elephants, rhinos, and tigers to red pandas, turtles, and even giant cockroaches (in a terrarium). There's a large cafeteria and a mini-zoo for children, who will love a visit.

Admission: SFr 10 ($7.15) adults, SFr 6 ($4.30) students, SFr 5 ($3.55) children.

Open: Summer, daily 8am–6pm; winter, daily 8am–5pm. **Tram:** 6 to Zoo (the last stop), then a 250-yard walk.

PARKS & GARDENS

BELVOIRPARK AND RIETERPARK, near Bahnhof Enge.

Belvoirpark, adjoined by Rieterpark, is the largest of Zurich's numerous parks. Both feature terraced flower gardens and shady walks under old trees, and both offer a beautiful view of the city, lake, and mountains. There is an outdoor restaurant amid the trees, but you can sit and eat your picnic on one of the many benches.

Admission: Free.

Open: Daily 24 hours. **Tram:** 6 or 7 to Museum Rietberg.

UETLIBERG, outside the city.

Uetliberg is a very popular parklike area that is actually a 2,800-foot hill. To get here, take the electric orange train at the Central Station. The train stops eight times on the way for a total travel time of 20 minutes. From the final stop, a 10-minute hike will take you to an observation point that offers a grand view over the entire region. Many Zurichers leave the train at one of the first stops and wander

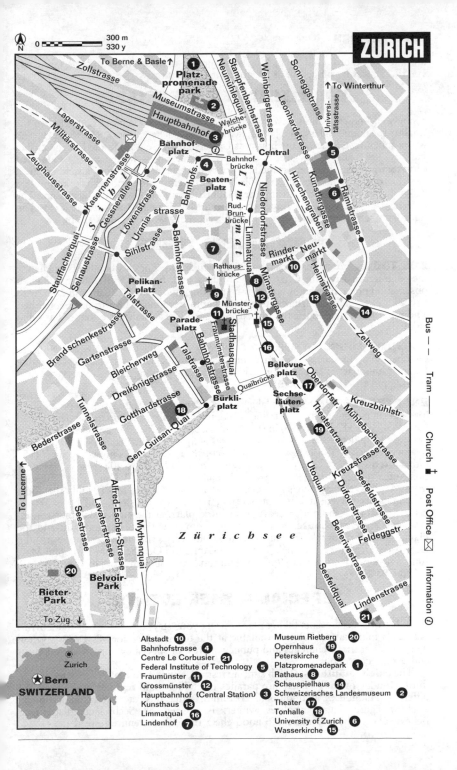

around this beautiful hill, picnicking and enjoying nature. The round-trip fare is SFr 10 ($7.15), less if you get off at the third or fourth stop.

FOR LITERARY ENTHUSIASTS

Many well-known authors have resided in Zurich, but none more significant to the English-speaking reader than James Joyce. He lived here from 1915 to 1919, and wrote much of *Ulysses* at his house at Universitätstrasse 38. He died in the city in January 1941, just a few weeks after his return. He is buried at **✪ Friedhof Fluntern,** a beautifully landscaped cemetery near the woods in the Zürichberg area. A statue of the author holding a book is near the grave. To get here, take tram no. 5 (from Bellevueplatz) or 6 (from the Hauptbahnhof) to Zoo, the last stop. The cemetery is open daily until 7pm, except from May through August when it closes an hour later, and from November 3 through February when it closes at 5pm.

ORGANIZED TOURS

BUS TOURS   A standard city bus tour, which hits Zurich's highlights, including the commercial areas, the Old City, the bridges, and the lake, with a short stop at an observation point, is given by an English-speaking guide daily at 10am and 2pm, with two additional daily departures at noon and 4pm from mid-May through September. The duration is two hours; the price is SFr 24 ($17.15), half price for students and children.

WALKING TOURS   A walking tour through the Old City is operated June to October on Tuesday, Thursday, and Saturday. The tour leaves from the Hauptbahnhof at 9:30am and 3pm with an English-speaking guide. It lasts two hours and the price is SFr 15 ($10.70)

BOAT TOURS   Zurich's great lake, the **✪ Zürichsee,** offers several possibilities for boat tours from April to October. There is a five-hour boat trip to Rapperswil and back that costs SFr 24 ($17.15) in second class, SFr 40 ($28.55) in first class. A shorter afternoon trip departs at 2:40pm and returns at 5pm, costing SFr 15 ($10.70), while a relaxing "lunch trip" leaves at 12:10pm, returns at 1:15, and only costs SFr 7 ($5). Other afternoon trips leave every 30 minutes and cost SFr 9 ($6.40); these are the only boat tours offered in winter, with a single daily departure at 2:30pm. Every Tuesday from May to October, there's a special "Fondue-Schiff" where fondue and other local specialties are served; it leaves at 8:15pm, returns by 10:30pm, and costs SFr 17 ($12.15). All these boat tours leave from Bürkliplatz, at the end of Bahnhofstrasse.

There are **river boats** as well, leaving from near the Landesmuseum and the Hauptbahnhof and taking you past the Old City's beautiful cityscape to the Zürichsee. Departures are every 30 minutes: April and October from 1 to 6pm; May, June, and Sepember from 1 to 9pm; and July and August from 10am to 9pm. The fare is SFr 7.50 ($5.35).

SPECIAL & FREE EVENTS

For a list of special events taking place during your stay, take a look at the *Zürich News,* a bilingual publication available at the tourist office for SFr 1 (70¢). Often there are concerts at churches and public squares, or special exhibitions at museums and private collections.

The **Sechseläuten** is Zurich's spring festival, and it is normally celebrated on the third Monday of April. There are parades of children and representatives from the different guildhouses in traditional costumes. After this, at exactly 6pm, Böögg, a straw figure that symbolizes winter, is burned on Sechseläutenplatz, near Bellevueplatz. There is music and good cheer through the entire festival.

Have you ever considered **candlemaking?** For several days in December, children and grownups congregate at Bürkliplatz for lessons in the fine art of producing your very own candle with bee's wax and a wick. Help is offered in English. Check with the tourist office for details.

7. SAVVY SHOPPING

Zurich is a shopper's paradise, albeit a very expensive one. The exclusive stores along **Bahnhofstrasse** sell dazzling clothes, jewelry, perfumes, leather goods, and watches, but shopping here threatens the very existence of this book: We don't want to become *Europe on $45 an Hour* just yet.

But don't despair: It's still possible to find affordable goods even in Zurich. Bahnhofstrasse itself is flanked by the city's largest department stores, **Globus, Vilan, Jelmoli,** and **St. Annahof,** which often offer merchandise for lower prices than the smaller stores and boutiques. Their food departments—on the ground or lower floors—are great places for buying groceries and picnic supplies.

Most shops, including the department stores, are open Monday through Friday from 9am to 6:30pm and on Saturday to 4pm.

Before buying one of Switzerland's famous watches on Bahnhofstrasse or in a department store, go to **Uhren-Boutique,** Bäckerstrasse 25 (tel. 241-09-22), near Stauffacherplatz. They have a very large selection of watches for lower-than-usual rates. But look closely—with the exchange rate, it might be cheaper to buy a Swiss watch outside Switzerland. The Stauffacherplatz area, incidentally, is better than most for shoppers on a budget.

If you want to buy books in English, drop by **Orell Füssli Buchhandlung,** Pelikanstrasse 10 (tel. 211-27-04), off Bahnhofstrasse, near Augustinergasse. They have an excellent selection of American and English paperbacks, including most of the books on Zurich and Switzerland mentioned in "Background Reading," above. For secondhand paperbacks, try **Buchantiquariat,** Badenerstrasse 41 (tel. 241-81-97), at the corner of Stauffacherstrasse.

8. EVENING ENTERTAINMENT

Zurich is the largest city in Switzerland and as such it has an active, if not wild, night scene. To find out what's going on in town, especially plays and concerts, get a copy of *Zürich News,* a publication available at the tourist office (see "Orientation and Getting Around," above) for SFr 1 (70¢). Also, keep your eyes open for signs posted around public places (such as Shopville) advertising concerts in churches and movies.

THE PERFORMING ARTS

Billettzentrale, also called BIZZ, at Werdmühleplatz (tel. 221-22-83), can help you get tickets to any theater or concert hall in Zurich. It's open Monday through Friday from 10am to 6:30pm and on Saturday from 10am to 2pm.

OPERNHAUS (Opera House), Falkenstrasse 1. Tel. 262-09-09.
Zurich's Opernhaus, near Bellevueplatz, was built in the 1890s. Operas, operettas, ballets, and classical-music concerts are all performed here.

Prices: Tickets, SFr 19–160 ($13.55–$114.30).
Closed: Usually July–Aug.

SCHAUSPIELHAUS ZÜRICH, Rämistrasse 34. Tel. 265-58-58.

The leading theater in the city—and one of the most prestigious in the German-speaking countries—is the Schauspielhaus Zürich, near Bellevueplatz. They publish a monthly schedule of plays—ask for the Schauspielhaus *Monatspielplan* at the tourist office.

Prices: Tickets average SFr 15–64 ($10.70–$45.70), half price for students.

TONHALLE, Claridenstrasse 7. Tel. 201-15-80.

Facing the lake near Bürkliplatz, Tonhalle is Zurich's largest concert hall, with over 1,500 seats. In 1988, in conjunction with the newspaper *Züri Woche*, the Tonhalle began a very popular series of lunch concerts (*Lunchkonzerte*), starting at 12:15pm and lasting for 45 minutes. Reservations are accepted one to two weeks before each concert.

Prices: Tickets, evenings, SFr 5–20 ($3.55–$14.30); lunch concerts, SFr 8 ($5.70).

THEATER AM HECHTPLATZ, Hechtplatz 7. Tel. 252-32-24.

The Theater am Hechtplatz, near Limmatquai, between Rathausbrücke and Münsterbrücke, is small, with only 260 seats, and very popular. Experimental theater and cabaret are performed.

Prices: Tickets, SFr 24 ($17.15) for a good seat.

SWISS FOLKLORE

KANDLI SWISS CHALET, Pfalzgasse 1. Tel. 211-11-82 or 211-53-17.

Kindli Chalet is Zurich's number-one Swiss folklore showplace. Eight musicians—singers, Alp horn players, cowbell players, zither virtuosi, and yodelers—perform traditional Swiss music. Located off Bahnhofstrasse, at the upper end of Rennweg, it seats 120.

Prices: Show supplement SFr 8 ($5.70); first performance combined with obligatory diner costing SFr 80–120 ($57.15–$85.70). After 10pm guests may order à la carte; typical dishes cost SFr 36–43 ($25.70–$30.70). All credit cards. Reservations recommended.

Open: Daily 8:30pm–midnight.

SCHÄFLI RESTAURANT, Badergasse 6. Tel. 251-41-44.

The Schäfli, a few blocks from Centralplatz, offers folklore shows nightly. Five musicians play Swiss, German, and Austrian folk music on accordion, guitar, horn, clarinet, and trumpet. There's no admission charge, but the drink prices include a special music supplement.

Prices (including music supplement): Half liter of beer SFr 8 ($5.70); quarter liter of wine SFr 12 ($8.55). **Admission:** Free.

Open: Daily 8pm–midnight.

BÖRSE RESTAURANT, Bleicherweg 5. Tel. 211-23-33.

Börse Restaurant, near Paradeplatz, features a "Swiss Folklore Music and Dance" show each Thursday at 8pm and American country music (with western food) each Tuesday from 8 to 11pm. This is the most genuine folklore presentation in town—if you happen to be in Zurich on a Tuesday or Thursday, try to go.

Open: Performances Tues and Thurs at 8pm.

MOVIES

Zurich's 30-some cinemas are concentrated near the Hauptbahnhof and Bellevueplatz. The first performances start at 2:15pm, the last at 9:15pm. Films are shown in the original version, with German subtitles; a few are dubbed in German, Italian, or French. Seats normally cost SFr 14 ($10).

DISCOS

MASCOTTE, Theaterstrasse 10. Tel. 252-44-81.

Mascotte, near Bellevueplatz, is one of the leading discos in town. The dance floor is one flight up.

Admission: SFr 15 ($10.70), which includes the first drink.
Open: Daily 9pm–3am.

ROTE FABRIK, Seestrasse 395. Tel. 482-70-84.

This is an avant-garde disco with rock-and-roll bands playing several nights a week (the schedule is published in *Zürich News*). Located in a red-brick building that was once a telephone factory, it holds 1,200 guests. There's an admission charge, and beverages are sold at normal rates.

Admission: SFr 10 ($7.15).
Open: Varies. **Tram:** 2, 5, 8, 9, or 11 to Bürkliplatz (near the lake) and transfer there to bus no. 61 or 65 (Rote Fabrik is the second stop).

ZABI BAR, Leonhardstrasse 19. Tel. 271-22-50.

This weekly meeting bar for Zurich's gay community is near Centralplatz, five walking minutes from the Hauptbahnhof.

Admission: SFr 10 ($7.15).
Prices: Drinks SFr 2–4 ($1.40–$2.85).
Open: Fri only, 10:30pm–3am.

9. EASY EXCURSIONS

Switzerland is a small country with breathtaking scenery and a superb, if expensive, railway system. If you can afford it, try to get out of Zurich at least once. Many interesting cities can be visited as easy day trips from Zurich. There is **Lucerne,** for instance, with its covered bridges and medieval walls and towers. Or **Berne,** the capital of the Swiss Federation, a tranquil city of hilly streets, arcades, and emblematic (you'll see them on flags) as well as real bears (don't worry, they're restricted to the Bärengraben, or Bear Pit). **Basel,** the second-largest city in the country, on the Rhine near the French and German borders, has a vibrant cultural life and a 500-year-old university. Even the **Ticino,** the Italian-speaking canton, is not impossibly far away; with its lively streets and exuberant flora, **Lugano,** the largest town here, represents a lesser-known aspect of Switzerland. And then there's **Liechtenstein,** an Alpine principality near the Austrian border.

But despite the charm of its cities and towns, it is the **Alps** that Switzerland is famous for. In the winter, people come from all over the world to ski at such glittering resorts as **Zermatt, Davos,** and **St. Moritz,** but all year long, if weather conditions are good, you can take a trip that you're bound to remember all your life: an excursion to the Jungfraujoch.

At 11,333 feet, the ✪ **Jungfraujoch** station is the highest on the continent, and this trip to the "top of Europe" affords some of the sublime vistas that so enthralled 19th-century travelers. The journey itself is half the fun. From Zurich you travel first to Interlaken, then to Lauterbrunnen, which is 2,612 feet high, then by rack-railway to Kleine Scheidegg, 6,762 feet high. Here you'll have a view of three famous peaks: Jungfrau, Mönch, and Eiger. And here you also board the Jungfrau-Bahn, another rack-railway, for a one-hour trip to the Jungfraujoch, the last station.

An elevator can take you to the Eispalast (Ice Palace), hewn in a glacier, to stare, speechless, at the beautiful Alps.

The tourist office in Zurich offers a tour to the Jungfraujoch that, for SFr 169 ($120.70) for adults, SFr 152 ($108.55) for students, may actually be cheaper—and certainly easier—than if you do it yourself. The tour operates between May and October on Monday, Tuesday, Thursday, Saturday, and Sunday, leaving the Hauptbahnhof at 8am and returning there by 9pm. The tour returns via Berne to offer a different panorama. Book at least one day in advance with the tourist office, your hotel, or a travel agency, and make sure to wear warm clothing, as it's bitterly cold even in high summer.

A. EUROPEAN TOURIST OFFICES

Austrian National Tourist Office, 500 Fifth Ave., New York, NY 10110 (tel. 212/944-6880); 500 N. Michigan Ave., Chicago, IL 60611 (tel. 312/644-5556); 11601 Wilshire Blvd., Suite 2480, Los Angeles, CA 90025 (tel. 213/477-3332).

Belgian Tourist Office, 745 Fifth Ave., New York, NY 10151 (tel. 212/758-8130).

British Tourist Authority, 40 W. 57th St., New York, NY 10019 (tel. 212/581-4700); 625 N. Michigan Ave., Chicago, IL 60611 (tel. 312/787-0490); 350 S. Figueroa St., Los Angeles, CA 90071 (tel. 213/628-3525); 2580 Cumberland Pkwy., Atlanta, GA 30339 (tel. 404/432-9635).

Danish Tourist Board, 655 Third Ave., New York, NY 10017 (tel. 212/949-2333).

French Government Tourist Office, 610 Fifth Ave., New York, NY 10020 (tel. 212/757-1125); 645 N. Michigan Ave., Chicago, IL 60611 (tel. 312/337-6301); 2305 Cedar Springs Rd., Suite 205, Dallas, TX 75201 (tel. 214/720-4010); 9454 Wilshire Blvd., Beverly Hills, CA 90212 (tel. 213/271-6665). For information and travel brochures, call 900/990-0040 (50¢ per minute).

German National Tourist Office, 122 E. 42nd St. New York, NY 10168-0072 (tel. 212/661-7200); 444 S. Flower St., Los Angeles, CA 90071 (tel. 213/688-7332).

Greek National Tourist Organization, 645 Fifth Ave., 5th Floor, New York, NY 10022 (tel. 212/421-5777); 168 N. Michigan Ave., Chicago, IL 60601 (tel. 312/782-1084); 611 W. 6th St., Suite 2198, Los Angeles, CA 90017 (tel. 213/626-6696).

IBUSZ Hungarian Travel Company, 1 Parker Plaza, Fort Lee, NJ 07024 (tel. 201/592-8585).

Irish Tourist Board, 757 Third Ave., New York, NY 10017 (tel. 212/418-0800).

Italian Government Travel Office, 630 Fifth Ave., New York, NY 10111 (tel. 212/245-4822); 500 N. Michigan Ave., Suite 1046, Chicago, IL 60611 (tel. 312/644-0990); 360 Post St., San Francisco, CA 94108 (tel. 415/392-6206).

Netherlands Board of Tourism, 355 Lexington Ave., New York, NY 10017 (tel. 212/370-7360); 225 N. Michigan Ave., Suite 326, Chicago, IL 60601 (tel. 312/819-0300); 90 New Montgomery St., 3rd Floor, San Francisco, CA 94105 (tel. 415/543-6772).

Norwegian Tourist Board, 655 Third Ave., New York, NY 10017 (tel. 212/949-2333).

Portuguese National Tourist Office, 590 Fifth Ave., New York, NY 10036 (tel. 212/354-4403).

National Tourist Office of Spain, 665 Fifth Ave., New York, NY 10022 (tel. 212/759-8822); 845 N. Michigan Ave., Suite 915E, Chicago, IL 60611 (tel. 312/642-1992); 8383 Wilshire Blvd., Suite 960, Beverly Hills, CA 90211 (tel. 213/658-7188); 1221 Brickell Ave., Suite 1850, Miami, FL 33131 (tel. 305/358-1992).

Swedish Tourist Board, 655 Third Ave., New York, NY 10017 (tel. 212/949-2333).

Swiss National Tourist Office, 608 Fifth Ave., New York, NY 10020 (tel. 212/757-5944); 150 N. Michigan Ave., Suite 2930, Chicago, IL 60601 (tel. 312/630-5840); 260 Stockton St., San Francisco, CA 94108 (tel. 415/362-2260); 222 N. Sepulveda Blvd., Suite 1570, El Segundo, CA 90245 (tel. 213/335-5980).

B. TRAIN FARES & SCHEDULES

FARES

The cost of one-way second-class tickets for trips between the major cities of Europe in early 1993 are shown below.

AMSTERDAM to: Paris, $71; Copenhagen, $141; London, $102; Vienna, $215; Brussels, $33; Frankfurt, $79; Rome, $254; Venice (via Basel), $196

LONDON to: Brussels, $101; Edinburgh, $105; Glasgow, $105; Dublin, $137; Paris, $113; Amsterdam, $102

PARIS to: Brussels, $43; Amsterdam, $71; Madrid, $128; Copenhagen, $208; Frankfurt, $85; Munich, $127; Zurich, $82; Rome, $178; Cannes, $100; Lourdes, $84; Marseille, $85; Nice, $103; Strasbourg, $56

ROME to: Florence, $34; Naples, $19; Genoa, $47; Venice, $51; Milan, $55; Amsterdam, $254; Barcelona, $138; Brussels, $192; Frankfurt, $184; Geneva, $114; London, $291; Madrid, $186; Munich, $100; Nice, $64; Paris, $178; Vienna, $114; Trieste, $63; Zurich, $113

MADRID to: Barcelona, $53; Toledo, $6; Valencia, $35; Lisbon, $49; Paris, $128; Rome, $186; Seville, $42

BARCELONA to: Marseille, $58; Nice, $80; Paris, $106; Rome, $138; Lourdes, $62

FRANKFURT to: Amsterdam, $99; Brussels, $72; Copenhagen, $164; Innsbruck, $102; Milan, $129; Naples, $201; Paris, $85; Rome, $184; Venice, $153; Vienna, $115

MUNICH to: Amsterdam, $150; Brussels, $142; Copenhagen, $204; Innsbruck, $29; Milan, $66; Naples, $119; Paris, $127; Rome, $100; Salzburg, $27; Venice, $73; Vienna, $65; Zurich, $67

SCHEDULES

To plan your European trip, you'll need a timetable of the major European expresses.

The schedules that follow show the trains that depart from major European cities. With very few exceptions, only the major international expresses are listed—the fast, crack trains. But not every international express is here, because many of these famous trains have only first-class accommodations. You can be sure that if a train is mentioned in *Frommer's Europe on $45 a Day,* it has second-class seats or second-class couchettes.

Below we have listed the departure and arrival times of the major international connections, in effect between May 23 and September 25, 1993.

Unless otherwise stated, these trains make their runs every day of the week and in every season. The abbreviation "lv" means "leaves"; the abbreviation "ar" indicates a train's arrival time. Usually, we'll give the train's departure time from all the cities in the country from which it sets out, and provide its arrival time in the various cities of the countries to which it goes. Thus, the schedule of the *Orient Express*—"lv Paris 7:43pm; lv Strasbourg 11:55pm; ar Karlsruhe 1am; ar Munich 4:26am; ar Salzburg 5:53am; ar Vienna 9:25am"—indicates that the *Orient Express* leaves Paris at 7:43pm daily; goes to Strasbourg, from which it then departs at 11:55pm; arrives in Karlsruhe at 1am, in Munich at 4:26am, in Salzburg at 5:53am; and finally pulls into Vienna at 9:25am.

TRAINS LEAVING LONDON

London–Paris   Lv London (Victoria Station) 9:10am; ar Paris 5:21pm; lv London 2:30pm; ar Paris 10:48pm. Both trains go via Dover–Calais.

London–Amsterdam   Lv London (Victoria Station) 11:10am; ar Amsterdam 8:38pm; lv London 9am, ar Amsterdam 8:38pm.

London–Brussels   Lv London (Victoria Station) 9am and 1pm, ar Brussels (Midi Station) 5:43 and 9:43pm.

London–Copenhagen   Lv London (Victoria Station) 9am; ar next day Copenhagen 8:25am. Lv London (Victoria Station) 8:35pm; ar next day Copenhagen 8:20pm. (Both go via Dover–Ostende.)

London–Cologne–Munich   Lv London (Victoria Station) 1pm; ar Cologne 12:49am; ar Munich 7:27am.

London–Edinburgh   Lv London (King's Cross Station) Mon–Sat hourly from 6am to 6pm, Sun hourly from 11am to 6:30pm. Travel time is an average 5 hours.

TRAINS LEAVING PARIS

SIMPLON EXPRESS   Paris–Lausanne–Milan–Venice–Trieste–Belgrade
Lv Paris (Gare de Lyon) 7:32pm; ar Lausanne 12:29pm; ar Milan 4:05am; ar Venice 6:45am; ar Trieste 8:45am; ar Belgrade 8:55pm. Takes passengers only for stations beyond Milan.

ORIENT EXPRESS   Paris–Munich–Vienna
Lv Paris (Gare de l'Est) 7:43pm; lv Strasbourg 11:55pm; ar Karlsruhe 1am; ar Munich 4:26am; ar Salzburg 5:53am; ar Vienna 9:25am.

NAPOLI EXPRESS   Paris–Torino–Genoa–Pisa–Rome–Naples
Lv Paris (Gare de Lyon) 8:56pm; ar Modane 4:12am; ar Torino 6:18am; ar Genoa 8:29am; ar Pisa 10:24am; ar Rome 2:35pm; ar Naples 4:15pm.

THE VIKING EXPRESS   Paris–Hamburg–Copenhagen
Lv Paris (Gare du Nord) 6:40pm; lv Liège 10:15pm; ar Cologne 11:57pm; ar Hamburg 4:15am; ar Puttgarden 6:17am; ar Copenhagen 10:25am.

Paris–Frankfurt   Lv Paris (Gare de l'Est) 6:58am, 9am, 1:03pm, and 5:17pm; ar Frankfurt 1:08pm, 3:08pm, 7:08pm, and 11:08pm.

Paris–Brussels–Amsterdam   Lv Paris (Gare du Nord) 7:47am, 10:20am, 2:46pm, 4:47pm, and 6:36pm; ar Brussels 2:02pm, 4:34pm, 9:06pm, 10:35pm, and 11:59pm; ar Amsterdam 2:02pm, 4:34pm, 9:01pm, 10:32pm, and 11:59pm.

Paris–London   Lv Paris (Gare du Nord) 8:02am, 2:15pm, and 4:22pm; ar London 2:24pm, 8:24pm, and 10:04pm (all via Boulogne and Dover or Folkestone).

Paris–Barcelona   Lv Paris (Gare de Lyon) 11:42am; ar Barcelona 9:18pm. Lv Paris (Gare d'Austerlitz) 9pm; ar Barcelona 8:30am.

Paris–Madrid   Lv Paris (Gare d'Austerlitz) 7:55pm; ar Madrid 8:30am. Lv Paris (Gare d'Austerlitz) 10:30pm; ar Madrid 3:10pm.

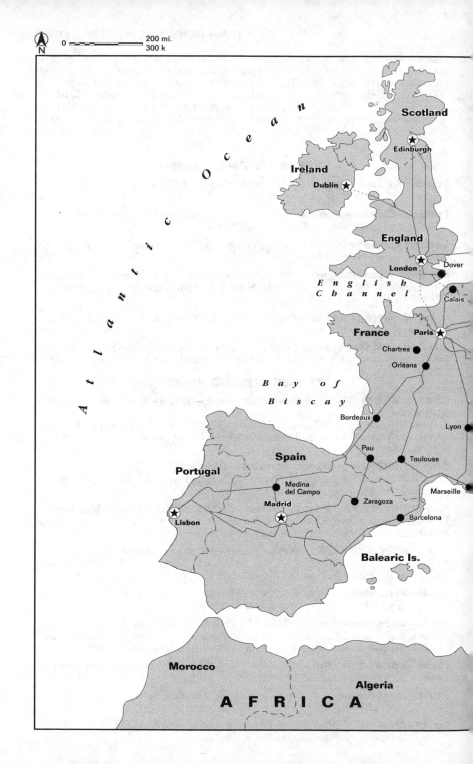

MAJOR EUROPEAN RAIL CONNECTIONS

Paris—Luxembourg   Lv Paris (Gare de l'Est) 6:58am, 10:57am, and 5:16pm; ar Luxembourg 10:35am, 2:36pm, and 8:45pm.

Paris—Rome   Lv Paris (Gare de Lyon) 6:47pm; ar Torino 3:01am; ar Genoa 4:53am; ar Pisa 6:59am; ar Rome 9:35am (Termini).

Paris—Nice   Lv Paris (Gare de Lyon), 9:45pm; ar Nice 7:50am.
  TGV (high-speed) trains from Gare de Lyon. Lv Paris 10:41am, 1:24pm, and 3:05pm; ar Nice 5:38pm, 8:22pm, and 10:02pm.

Paris—Geneva   Lv Paris (Gare de Lyon) 7:35am, 10:36am, 5:40pm, and 7:13pm; ar Geneva 11:08am, 2:05pm, 9:11pm, and 10:45pm. (This is the TGV train.)

Paris—Zurich   Lv Paris (Gare de l'Est) 5:04pm; ar Zurich 10:48pm.
  Lv Paris (Gare de l'Est) 7:30am; ar Basel 12:27am; ar Zurich 1:23pm.

TRAINS LEAVING BRUSSELS

OSTEND—VIENNA EXPRESS Brussels—Cologne—Vienna   Lv Ostend 8:30pm; lv Brussels (Gare du Midi) 9:40pm; lv Liège 10:53pm; lv Aachen 11:36pm; ar Cologne 12:28am; ar Mainz 1:09am; ar Mannheim 3:21am; ar Würzburg 4:08am; ar Passau 7:28am; ar Vienna 10:58am.

Brussels—London   Lv Brussels (Gare du Midi) 6:59am, 9:59am, and 11:45pm; ar London (Victoria Station) 11:06am, 2:06pm, and 3:54pm (all via Ostende–Dover).

Brussels—Rotterdam—Amsterdam   Lv Brussels (Gare du Midi) 11:04am; lv Antwerp 11:47am; ar Rotterdam 12:59pm; ar The Hague 1:18pm; ar Amsterdam 2:02pm.
  Lv Brussels (Gare du Midi) 2:10pm; lv Antwerp 2:49pm; ar Rotterdam 4:02pm; ar The Hague 4:21pm; ar Amsterdam 5:08pm.
  Lv Brussels (Gare du Midi) 5:10pm; lv Antwerp 5:54pm; ar Rotterdam 7:02pm; ar The Hague 7:21pm; ar Amsterdam 8:08pm.

Brussels—Paris   Lv Brussels (Gare du Midi) 8:10am, 10:10am, 2:10pm, and 7:10pm; ar Paris 10:54am, 12:56pm, 5:09pm, and 10:06pm.

Brussels—Luxembourg   Lv Brussels (Gare du Midi) 7:15am, 12:20pm, 2:22pm, 3:22pm, and 6:22pm; ar Luxembourg 9:49am, 2:49pm, 5:11pm, 6:11pm, and 9:11pm.

TRAINS LEAVING AMSTERDAM

HOLLAND—SCANDINAVIA EXPRESS Amsterdam—Copenhagen
Lv Amsterdam 8:02am; ar Hamburg 1:39pm; ar Puttgarden 3:38pm; ar Copenhagen 7:10pm.

NORTH-WEST EXPRESS Amsterdam—Hamburg—Copenhagen—Stockholm   Lv Amsterdam 8:32pm; ar Hamburg 2:15am; ar Puttgarden 4:17am; ar Copenhagen 10am; ar Stockholm 6:59pm.

HOLLAND—VIENNA EXPRESS Amsterdam—Cologne—Frankfurt—Nuremburg—Vienna   Lv Amsterdam 8:56pm; ar Cologne 11:30pm; ar Frankfurt 2am; ar Nuremberg 4:35am; ar Vienna 10:58am.

ERASMUS EXPRESS Amsterdam—Cologne—Munich   Lv Amsterdam 8am; ar Cologne 10:57am; ar Munich 5:12pm.

Amsterdam—London   Lv Amsterdam 9:32am and 7:47pm; ar London (Liverpool Street Station) 8:01pm and 9am (both via Hook of Holland and Harwich).

Amsterdam—Brussels—Paris   Lv Amsterdam 7am; ar Antwerp 9:17am; ar Brussels 9:49am; ar Paris 12:56pm.
  Lv Amsterdam 10:49am; ar Antwerp 1:15pm; ar Brussels 1:46pm; ar Paris 5:09pm.
  Lv Amsterdam 3:53pm; ar Antwerp 6:12pm; ar Brussels 6:43pm; ar Paris 10:06pm.

TRAINS LEAVING COPENHAGEN

THE NORTH EXPRESS Copenhagen—Cologne—Paris Lv Copenhagen 9:05pm; ar Cologne 7:46am; ar Aachen 9:02am; ar Liège 10:14am; ar Paris 1:18pm.

NORTH-WEST EXPRESS Copenhagen—Hamburg—Amsterdam— London Lv Copenhagen 10:05pm; lv Puttgarden 1:56am; ar Hamburg 3:46am; ar Amersfoort 9:04am; ar Rotterdam 10:21am; ar Hook of Holland 10:42am; ar London (Liverpool Street Station) 8pm.

SCANDINAVIA—HOLLAND EXPRESS Copenhagen—Hamburg— Bremen—Amsterdam Lv Copenhagen 10:05pm; lv Puttgarden 1:35pm; ar Hamburg 3:28pm; lv Bremen 4:40pm; ar Amsterdam 9:54pm.

Copenhagen—Stockholm Lv Copenhagen 10:35am and 2:35pm; ar Stockholm 6:59pm and 10:47pm.

Copenhagen—Vienna Lv Copenhagen 3:20pm; ar Hamburg 6:26pm; ar Passau 6:14am; ar Vienna 8:30am.

TRAINS LEAVING STOCKHOLM

Stockholm—Oslo Lv Stockholm 8:42am, 3:30pm, and 11:07pm; ar Oslo 2:42pm, 9:55pm, and 7:55am.

Stockholm—Copenhagen Lv Stockholm 8:06am, 2:06pm, and 10:30pm; ar Copenhagen 4:50pm, 11:09pm, and 6:53am.

TRAINS LEAVING OSLO

Oslo—Copenhagen Lv Oslo 7:30am, 10:00am, and 10:40pm; ar Copenhagen 4:50pm, 8:15pm, and 8:50am.

Oslo—Stockholm Lv Oslo 10:55am, 3:47pm, and 10:50pm; ar Stockholm 5:26pm, 10:25pm, and 6:55am.

TRAINS LEAVING MUNICH

THE GOTTFRIED KELLER EXPRESS Munich—Zurich Lv Munich 11:58am; lv Lindau 2:27pm; ar St. Margarethen 2:52pm; ar Zurich 4:21pm.

THE MICHELANGELO EXPRESS Munich—Florence—Rome Lv Munich 9:30am; lv Innsbruck 11:18am; lv Verona 3:14pm; lv Florence 4:46pm; ar Rome 8:45pm.

SKANDIA EXPRESS Munich—Hamburg—Copenhagen Lv Munich 11:05pm; ar Hamburg 7:49am; ar Copenhagen 1:20pm (sleepers and couchettes only).

THE BAVARIA Munich—Zurich Lv Munich 6:58pm; lv Lindau 8:29pm; ar St. Margarethen 8:54pm; ar Zurich 10:21pm.

Munich—Innsbruck—Verona—Florence—Rome Lv Munich 8:30pm; lv Innsbruck 10:20pm; ar Verona 2:58am; ar Florence 7:30am; ar Rome 8:33am.

Munich—Venice Lv Munich 7:40am and 11:30pm (sleepers only); ar Venice 4:14pm, and 8:45am.

TRAINS LEAVING VIENNA

THE VIENNA—HOLLAND EXPRESS Vienna—Frankfurt—Brussels— London Lv Vienna (Westbahnhof) 7pm; ar Passau 10:04am; ar Frankfurt 1:23am;

ar Cologne 4:50am; ar Aachen 5:48am; ar Liège 6:45am; ar Brussels 7:59am; ar Ostende 9:09am; ar London 2:06pm.

THE ORIENT EXPRESS Vienna–Munich–Paris Lv Vienna (West-bahnhof) 7:40pm; lv Salzburg 11:07pm; ar Munich 12:28am; ar Strasbourg 5am; ar Paris 9:29am.

THE MOZART Vienna–Paris Lv Vienna 9am; ar Paris 10:10pm (via Munich and Strasbourg).

THE ROSENKAVALIER Vienna–Paris Lv Vienna 7:40pm; ar Paris 9:29am (via Munich and Strasbourg).

Vienna–Venice The *Romulus Express* (lv Vienna 7:24am; ar Venice 3:15pm) is your best train for this trip, but there are three other trains that leave Vienna daily for Venice. All depart from the Südbahnhof. For instance, lv Vienna 1:11pm, ar Venice 9:57pm; lv Vienna 7:45pm, ar Venice 3:50am; lv Vienna 10:30pm, ar Venice 8:30am (the last two trains, sleepers only).

Vienna–Belgrade Lv Vienna (Südbahnhof) 8:10pm; ar Zagreb 2:48am; ar Belgrade 8:32am.

TRAINS LEAVING ROME

THE PALATINE EXPRESS Rome–Torino–Paris Lv Rome 4:15pm; lv Pisa 9:51pm; lv Torino 1:53am; ar Paris (Gare de Lyon) 8:52am (sleepers and couchettes only).

THE MICHELANGELO EXPRESS Rome–Florence–Innsbruck–Munich Lv Rome 7:45am; lv Florence 9:59am; lv Bologna 11:00am; lv Verona 1:00pm; ar Innsbruck 4:59am; ar Munich 6:58am.

THE SIMPLON EXPRESS Rome–Florence–Venice–Trieste–Belgrade Lv Rome 11:10pm; ar Florence 2:35am; ar Venice 6:28am; lv Trieste 9:15am; ar Ljubljana 1:15pm; ar Zagreb 3:29pm; ar Belgrade 8:55pm.

Rome–Florence Lv Rome 8:10am, ar Florence 10:10am; lv Rome 9:00am, ar Florence 11:15am; lv Rome 1:10pm, ar Florence 3:10pm; lv Rome 5:00pm, ar Florence 7:08pm; lv Rome 7:45pm; ar Florence 9:24pm. (17 daily departures.)

Rome–Naples Lv Rome 8:35am, ar Naples 10:38am; lv Rome 9:00am, ar Naples 11:04am; lv Rome 4:20pm, ar Naples 7pm; lv Rome 7:20pm, ar Naples 9:50pm. (17 daily departures.)

Rome–Milan Lv Rome 8:10am, ar Milan 1:10pm; lv Rome 1:10pm, ar Milan 6:10pm; lv Rome 4:10pm, ar Milan 9:10pm; lv Rome 11:30pm, ar Milan 8:15am. (15 daily departures.)

Rome–Nice Lv Rome 12:30pm, ar Nice 10:15pm; lv Rome 11:30pm, ar Nice 10:10am.

Rome–Lausanne Lv Rome 6:40am; lv Florence 8:19am; ar Brig 3:50pm; ar Lausanne 5:25pm. (Change trains in Milan.)

Rome–Geneva Lv Rome noon; lv Florence 2:15pm; lv Milan 5:25pm; ar Brig 7:45pm; ar Lausanne 9:11pm; ar Geneva 9:48pm. (Change trains in Milan.)

TRAINS LEAVING NICE

Nice–Rome Lv Nice 8:35am and 8:10pm; ar Rome 6:15pm and 7:00am.

Nice–Zurich Lv Nice 8:20pm; lv Cannes 9:04pm; lv Marseille 11:42pm; lv Avignon 1:31am; ar Geneva 7:43am; ar Lausanne 8:30am; ar Berne 9:42am; ar Zurich 10am.

TRAINS LEAVING ZURICH

ZURICH—HAMBURG   EXPRESS   Zurich—Basel—Hanover—Hamburg Lv Zurich 9:00pm; lv Basel 10:45pm; lv Hanover 5:57am; ar Hamburg 8:01am (sleepers only).

BAVARIA EXPRESS Zurich—Munich Lv Zurich 7:07am; ar St. Margarethen 8:31am; ar Lindau 8:58am; ar Munich 11:24am.

Zurich—Rome Lv Zurich 11:03am; lv Lugano 2:06pm; ar Milan 3:40pm; ar Rome (Termini) 9:00pm.
Lv Zurich 10:10pm; ar Florence 6:26am; ar Rome (Termini) 9:25am.

Zurich—Paris Lv Zurich 7am; ar Basel 8:01am; ar Paris 12:59pm.
Lv Zurich 3:37pm; ar Basel 4:28pm; ar Paris (Gare de L'est) 9:29pm.

Zurich—Nice Lv Zurich 8:03pm; lv Berne 9:18pm; lv Geneva 11:27pm; ar Valence 2:43am; ar Marseille 4:55am; ar Cannes 7:18am; ar Nice 6:57am.

Zurich—Innsbruck—Salzburg—Vienna Lv Zurich 9:33am; ar Innsbruck 11:27am; ar Salzburg 3:36pm; ar Vienna 7pm.
Lv Zurich 1:33pm; ar Innsbruck 5:25pm; ar Salzburg 7:36pm; ar Vienna 11pm.

TRAINS LEAVING MADRID

PUERTA DEL SOL EXPRESS   Madrid—Bordeaux—Paris Lv Madrid (Chamartín) 7:35pm; ar Paris (Gare d'Austerlitz) 8:30am.

LUSITANIA EXPRESS   Madrid—Lisbon Lv Madrid (Atocha) 1:50pm and 11:00pm; ar Lisbon 9:10pm and 8:45am.

TRAINS LEAVING BARCELONA

CATALAN EXPRESS   Barcelona—Geneva Lv Barcelona 9:55am; ar Geneva 7:44pm.

TRAINS LEAVING ATHENS

AKROPOLIS EXPRESS   Athens—Belgrade—Salzburg—Munich Lv Athens 8:30am; lv Thessaloniki 4pm; ar Gevgeli 5:30pm; ar Belgrade 6:28am; lv Zagreb 12:45pm; ar Ljubljana 3:10pm; ar Salzburg 8:25pm; ar Munich 10:42pm (the next day).

VENEZIA EXPRESS   Athens—Belgrade—Trieste—Venice Lv Athens 11pm; lv Thessaloniki 7:00am; ar Belgrade 6:28pm; lv Ljubljana 3:40am; ar Trieste 7:45am; ar Venice 11:38am (arrives 2 days after departure from Athens).

C. WHAT THINGS COST ACROSS EUROPE*

	Amsterdam	Athens	Barcelona	Berlin	Brussels	Budapest	Copenhagen	Dublin	Edinburgh	Florence	Geneva
Local phone call	.15	.40	.20	.20	.35	.25	.09	.36	.20	.18	.28
Dbl. room (deluxe)	294	197	385	312	228	260	340	270	260	390	380
Dbl. room (mod.)	97	91.60	245	87.50	89.50	125	89.50	190	95	97.40	140
Dbl. room (budget)	60	23.15	63	48.85	48.30	25	38.60	52.20	57	40.50	54
Lunch (mod)**	16.50	8.70	14.30	8.50	12.05	10	8.60	14.40	9.50	18.25	12.50
Lunch (budget)**	5.50	5.80	7	4.50	4	2	6.10	7.20	4.75	4.35	7.50
Dinner (deluxe)**	40	20	75	53	105	30	37.55	57.60	78	105	45
Dinner (mod.)**	16	9.45	35.50	17	27.60	14	12.10	21.60	23	25.75	25
Dinner (budget)**	9	6.25	20	5	10.35	3.60	9.25	14.40	9	10.50	14.50
Cup of coffee	1.35	.75	.95	2.05	2.05	.65	2.45	1	1.15	1.30	1.90
Coca-Cola	1.35	.85	1.40	1.70	2.05	.45	2.10	1	1.15	1.75	2.10
Film (36 exp.)	9.10	5.50	5.65	5.60	8.30	5.25	11.05	8.60	7	7.85	5
Movie ticket	7.90	5.25	5	5.60	9	1.50	10.60	7.20	6.25	6.50	10

*Prices are in U.S. dollars.
**Meal prices are for one person, without wine.

Innsbruck	Lisbon	London	Madrid	Munich	Naples	Nice	Oslo	Paris	Rome	Salzburg	Stockholm	Venice	Vienna	Zurich
.09	.08	.20	.16	.20	.18	.20	.30	.20	.18	.09	.33	.18	.09	.28
94.55	320	523	300	233	191	350	314	470	425	142	361	456	145	128
52.70	130	190	225	87.50	115	70	75.40	96	168	77.25	96.55	90.85	85.45	92.83
38.20	30.50	68.40	44.10	41.85	36.50	37	43.10	45	45	42.70	85.50	41.15	42.70	60.70
10	13.25	14.25	14.45	8	9.55	15	9	17	21	9	9.25	21.75	12	18.15
5.90	7.70	6.15	11.10	6	4.35	11.10	6.50	10	9	4.50	6.10	6.10	5	5.85
20	68.25	104	110	75	30.45	75	25.50	125	113	22	124	104	25	75
11.40	22	12.40	30	25	13.90	18.50	15.50	33	22	10	18.50	34.80	12	18.30
8	9.95	5.70	14	6	8.70	10.20	9.40	11	10	7	10.25	6.50	6	11.80
2.25	.65	1.20	1.25	1.40	.85	2.40	2.20	3.50	1.30	2.40	2.50	1.30	2	2
1.80	1	1.50	2	1.65	1.30	3	3.10	3	1.75	1.70	2.75	2.20	1.50	2.30
6.25	5.35	8	6	5.50	5.85	6.50	10.45	7	5.85	6.25	9.80	9.55	8.55	5.10
7	2.50	8.55	3.50	5.60	6.10	7.40	6.90	7.50	7.85	6.50	9.90	6.95	7	10

D. EUROPEAN WEATHER

		Amsterdam	Athens	Barcelona	Berlin	Brussels	Budapest	Copenhagen	Dublin	Edinburgh	Florence	Geneva
JAN	Temp °F	36	52	49	30	35	30	32	45	38	45	34.7
	Rainfall"	2.5	*	*	2.2	2.6	*	1.9	2.7	1.8	3	2.6
FEB	Temp °F	36	54	51	32	38	35	31	45	38	47	28.8
	Rainfall"	1.9	*	*	1.6	2.4	*	1.5	2	1.5	3.3	2.4
MAR	Temp °F	41	58	54	40	43	42	36	49	41	50	40.5
	Rainfall"	1.9	*	*	1.2	2.1	*	1.2	2	1.5	3.7	3.8
APR	Temp °F	46	65	59	48	49	55	44	53	45	60	44.4
	Rainfall"	1.9	*	*	1.6	2.4	*	1.5	1.9	1.5	2.7	2.6
MAY	Temp °F	54	74	64	53	56	64	53	58	50	67	59.7
	Rainfall"	2.4	*	*	2.3	2.2	*	1.7	2.3	1.9	2.2	2.8
JUNE	Temp °F	59	86	72	60	61	68	60	63	56	75	63
	Rainfall"	3.2	*	*	2.9	3	*	1.8	2.1	1.8	1.4	3.3
JULY	Temp °F	62	92	76	64	63	74	64	65	58	77	67.7
	Rainfall"	2.6	*	*	3.2	3.7	*	2.8	2.4	2.7	1.4	3.0
AUG	Temp °F	58	92	76	62	63	71	63	65	58	70	65.1
	Rainfall"	2.6	*	*	2.7	3.1	*	2.6	3	2.9	2.7	3.9
SEPT	Temp °F	51	82	72	56	60	65	57	62	55	64	60
	Rainfall"	2.9	*	*	2.2	2.5	*	2.4	2.9	2.2	3.2	3.8
OCT	Temp °F	44	72	64	49	52	54	49	57	50	63	53.2
	Rainfall"	2.3	*	*	1.6	3.3	*	2.3	2.7	2.2	4.9	3.4
NOV	Temp °F	38	63	57	40	43	46	41	50	42	55	41
	Rainfall"	2.1	*	*	2.4	2.9	*	1.9	2.8	2.3	3.8	3.6
DEC	Temp °F	32	56	51	34	37	35	37	47	40	46	36.1
	Rainfall"	2.6	*	*	1.9	3.5	*	1.9	3.2	2.2	2.9	3.2

Innsbruck	Lisbon	London	Madrid	Munich	Naples	Nice	Oslo	Paris	Rome	Salzburg	Stockholm	Venice	Vienna	Zurich
30 3.4	57 4.3	40 2.1	42.8 2	33 2.1	50 4.7	46 4.1	23 1.9	38 3.2	49 3.6	28 2.5	27 1.7	43 2.3	30 1.5	32 2.4
35 2.5	59 3.0	40 1.6	45.1 2	35 2.2	54 4	47 5.1	24 1.4	39 2.9	52 3.2	35 2.6	26 1.1	48 1.5	32 1.7	33 3.5
42 3.2	63 4.2	44 1.5	49.1 1.6	40 2.1	58 3	51 4.3	31 1	46 2.4	57 2.9	37 2.8	31 1	53 2.9	38 1.7	39 2.6
48 4.1	67 2.1	49 1.5	53.8 2	50 2.9	63 3.8	56 4.3	41 1.7	51 2.7	62 2.2	45 3.5	40 1.2	60 3.0	50 1.8	48 3.1
55 4.5	71 1.7	55 1.8	61 1.5	60 4	70 2.4	62 2.4	51 1.7	58 3.2	70 1.4	55 5.3	50 1.3	67 2.8	58 2.8	58 6.1
65 5.4	77 0.6	61 1.8	68.4 1.2	65 5.4	75 .8	68 2.3	59 2.8	64 3.5	77 0.7	64 6.8	59 1.7	72 2.9	64 2.6	65 8.6
70 5.8	81 0.1	64 2.2	75.2 0.4	70 5.2	83 .8	73 1.3	64 3.2	66 3.3	82 0.2	68 7.5	64 2.4	77 1.5	68 3.3	70 6.5
70 5.3	82 0.2	64 2.3	74.3 0.3	73 4.5	79 2.6	73 2.3	61 3.7	66 3.7	78 0.7	67 6.4	62 3	74 1.9	67 2.8	69 4.9
65 4.2	79 1.3	59 1.9	68 1.3	65 2.9	74 3.5	69 5.1	53 3.2	61 3.3	73 3.0	60 3.6	54 2.4	68 2.8	60 1.7	63 3.9
48 3.5	72 2.4	52 2.2	58 2	50 2.3	66 5.8	61 6.7	43 2.9	53 3.0	65 4.0	50 2.9	45 1.9	60 2.6	50 2.2	50 1.9
38 3.3	63 3.7	46 2.5	48.2 2.4	39 2.3	60 5.1	53 9.6	34 2.5	45 3.5	56 3.9	39 2.7	37 2	54 3.9	41 2.1	39 2.5
32 3.7	58 4.1	42 1.9	43 2	33 2.1	52 3.7	47 5.6	28 2.5	40 3.1	47 2.8	33 2.7	32 1.9	44 2.1	33 1.8	33 2.3

E. CAPSULE VOCABULARIES

DANISH

ENGLISH	DANISH	PRONUNCIATION
Hello	God Dag	go da
How are you?	Hvordan har De det?	vohr-dan hahr dee day?
Very well	Tak, godt	tak gaht
Thank you	Tak	tak
Good-bye	Farvel	fahr-vel
Please	Vaer saa venlig	vayr saw venlee
Yes	Ja	ya
No	Nej	nai
Excuse me	Unkskyld	own-skeel
I don't understand.	Jeg forstaar ikke.	vai fawr-star ik-uh.
Give me . . .	Giv mig . . .	Gee-mai . . .
Where is . . . ?	Hvor er der . . . ?	vohr ayr der . . . ?
the station	jernbanestationen	yayrn-ban-uh-sta-shonun
a hotel	et hotel	it ho-tel
a restaurant	en restaurang	in rest-oh-rahng
the toilet	toalett	twah-let-tud
To the right	Til hojre	till hoi-ruh
To the left	Til venstre	till ven-struh
I would like . . .	Jeg vilde gerne have . . .	yai-vil-luh gayr-nuh-ha . . .
to eat	noget at spise	noh-ud ah spee-suh
a room	et Vaerelse	it vay-rul-suh
How much is it?	Hvor meget?	vohr ma-yud?
When?	Hvornaar?	vohr-nawr?
Yesterday	i Gaar	ee gawr
Today	i Dag	ee da
Tomorrow	i Morgen	ee mawrn
Write it out.	Skriv det.	skreev day.

NUMBERS

1	en (ayn)	12	tolv (tahll)	50	halvtreds (hal-tress)
2	to (toh)	13	tretten (tret-un)	60	tres (tress)
3	tre (tray)	14	fjorten (fyawr-tun)	70	halvfjerds (half-yayrss)
4	fire (fee-rah)	15	femten (fem-tun)	80	firs (feerss)
5	fem (fem)	16	seksten (saiss-tun)	90	halvfems (halfemss)
6	seks (sex)	17	sytten (ser-tun)	100	hundrede (hoon-rud-uh)
7	syv (syee)	18	atten (a-tun)		
8	otte (oh-tuh)	19	nitten (nitun)		
9	ni (nee)	20	tyve (tee-vuh)		
10	ti (tee)	30	tredive (tred-vuh)		
11	elve (el-vuh)	40	fyrre (fer-raw)		

DUTCH

ENGLISH	DUTCH	PRONUNCIATION
Hello	Hallo	ha-loh
How are you?	Hoe gaat het met U?	hoo haht ut met oo?
Very well	Uitstekend	out-stayk-end
Thank you	Dank U	Dahnk ew

ENGLISH	DUTCH	PRONUNCIATION
Good-bye	**Dag**	dahk
Please	**Alstublieft**	ah-stoo-bleeft
Yes	**Ja**	yah
No	**Nee**	nay
Excuse me	**Pardon**	par-dawn
Give me . . .	**Geeft U my . . .**	hayft oo may . . .
Where is . . . ?	**Waar is . . . ?**	vahr iz . . . ?
the station	**het station**	het stah-ssyonh
a hotel	**een hotel**	uhn ho-tel
a restaurant	**een restaurant**	uhn res-to-rahng
the toilet	**het toilet**	het twah-let
To the right	**Rechts**	rekhts
To the left	**Links**	links
Straight ahead	**Rechtdoor**	rekht-dour
I would like . . .	**Ik zou graag . . .**	ik zow hrah . . .
to eat	**eten**	ay-ten
a room	**een kamer**	uhn kah-mer
for one night	**voor een nacht**	voor ayn nakht
How much is it?	**Hoe veel kost het?**	hoo fayl kawst het?
The check	**De rekening**	duh ray-ken-ing
When?	**Wanneer?**	vah-neer
Yesterday	**Gisteren**	his-ter-en
Today	**Vandaag**	van-dahkh
Tomorrow	**Morgen**	mor-hen
Breakfast	**Ontbijt**	ohnt-bayt
Lunch	**Lunch**	lunch
Dinner	**Diner**	dee-nay

NUMBERS

1 **een** (ayn)	12 **twaalf** (tvahlf)	30 **dertig** (dayr-tukh)
2 **twee** (tway)	13 **dertien** (dayr-teen)	40 **veertig** (vayr-tukh)
3 **drie** (dree)	14 **veertien** (vayr-teen)	50 **vijftig** (vahf-tukh)
4 **vier** (veer)	15 **vijftien** (vayf-teen)	60 **zestig** (zes-tukh)
5 **vijf** (vayf)	16 **zestien** (zes-teen)	70 **zeventig**
6 **zes** (zes)	17 **zeventien**	(zay-vun-tukh)
7 **zeven** (zay-vun)	(zay-vun-teen)	80 **tachtig** (takh-tukh)
8 **acht** (akht)	18 **achtien** (akh-teen)	90 **negentig**
9 **negen** (nay-hen)	19 **negentien**	(nay-hen-tukh)
10 **tien** (teen)	(nay-hen-teen)	100 **honderd**
11 **elf** (elf)	20 **twinting** (twin-tukh)	(hon-dayrt)

FRENCH

ENGLISH	FRENCH	PRONUNCIATION
Hello	**Bonjour**	bohn-zhoor
How are you?	**Comment allez-vous?**	koh-mawh tah-lay voo?
Very well	**Très bien**	tray byanh
Thank you	**Merci**	mayr-see
Good-bye	**Au revoir**	aw ruh-vwar
Please	**S'il vous plaît**	sill voo play
Yes	**Oui**	wee
No	**Non**	nawh
Excuse me	**Pardon**	par-dawh
Give me . . .	**Donnez-moi . . .**	duh-nay mwah . . .
Where is . . . ?	**Où est . . . ?**	oo ay . . . ?
the station	**la gare**	lah gar

ENGLISH	FRENCH	PRONUNCIATION
a hotel	un hôtel	uh-no-tel
a restaurant	un restaurant	uh res-tow-rawh
the toilet	le lavabo	luh lah-vah-bo
To the right	A droite	ah drwaht
To the left	A gauche	ah gohsh
Straight ahead	Tout droit	too drwah
I would like . . .	Je voudrais . . .	zhuh voo-dray . . .
to eat	manger	mawh-zhay
a room	une chambre	ewn shawm-bruh
for one night	pour une nuit	poor ewn nwee
How much is it?	Combien ça coûte?	kawm-byanh sah koot?
The check	L'addition	lah-dee-syohnh
When?	Quand?	kawnhn?
Yesterday	Hier	yayr
Today	Aujourd'hui	oh-zhoor-dwee
Tomorrow	Demain	duh-manh
Breakfast	Le petit déjeuner	luh puh-tee day-zhuh-nay
Lunch	Déjeuner	day-zhuh-nay
Dinner	Dîner	dee-nay

NUMBERS

1	**un (uhnh)**	12	**douze (dooze)**	50	**cinquante (san-kawnt)**
2	**deux (duh)**	13	**treize (trezz)**	60	**soixante (swaz-ant)**
3	**trois (trwa)**	14	**quatorze (ka-torze)**	70	**soixante-dix (swaz-ant-deess)**
4	**quatre (kahtr)**	15	**quinze (kanze)**	80	**quatres-vingt (kahtr-vanh)**
5	**cinq (sank)**	16	**seize (sezz)**	90	**quatres-vingt-dix (kahtr-vanh-deess)**
6	**six (seess)**	17	**dix-sept (dee-set)**	100	**cent (sawnh)**
7	**sept (set)**	18	**dix-huit (deez-weet)**		
8	**huit (weet)**	19	**dix-neuf (deez-nuff)**		
9	**neuf (nuff)**	20	**vingt (vahn)**		
10	**dix (deess)**	30	**trente (trawnt)**		
11	**onze (ohnze)**	40	**quarante (ka-rawnt)**		

GERMAN

ENGLISH	GERMAN	PRONUNCIATION
Hello	Guten Tag	goo-ten tahk
How are you?	Wie geht es ihnen?	vee gayt ess ee-nen?
Very well	Sehr gut	zayr goot
Thank you	Danke schön	dahn-keh shern
Good-bye	Auf Wiedersehen	owf vee-dayr-zayn
Please	Bitte	bit-tuh
Yes	Ja	yah
No	Nein	nine
Excuse me	Entschuldigen Sie	en-shool-di-gen zee
Give me . . .	Geben Sie mir . . .	gay-ben zee meer . . .
Where is . . . ?	Wo ist . . . ?	voh eest . . . ?
the station	der Bahnhof	dayr bahn-hohf
a hotel	ein Hotel	ain hotel
a restaurant	ein Restaurant	ain res-tow-rahng
the toilet	die Toilette	dee twah-let-tuh
To the right	Nach rechts	nakh reshts
To the left	Nach links	nakh leenks
Straight ahead	Geradeaus	geh-rah-deh-ous
I would like . . .	Ich möchte . . .	ikh mersh-ta . . .

ENGLISH	GERMAN	PRONUNCIATION
to eat	**essen**	ess-en
a room	**ein Zimmer**	ain tzim-mer
for one night	**für eine Nacht**	feer ai-neh nakht
How much is it?	**Wieviel kostet?**	vee-feel kaw-stet?
The check, please	**Zahlen, bitte**	tzah-len, bit-tuh
When?	**Wann?**	vahn?
Yesterday	**Gestern**	geh-stern
Today	**Heute**	hoy-tuh
Tomorrow	**Morgen**	more-gen
Breakfast	**Frühstück**	free-shtick
Lunch	**Mittagessen**	mi-tahg-gess-en
Dinner	**Abendessen**	ah-bend-ess-en

NUMBERS

1	**eins** (aintz)	13	**dreizehn** (dry-tzayn)	20	**zwanzig** (tzvahn-tzik)
2	**zwei** (tzvai)	14	**vierzehn** (feer-tzayn)	30	**dreissig** (dry-sik)
3	**drei** (dry)	15	**fünfzehn** (fewnf-tzayn)	40	**vierzig** (feer-tzik)
4	**vier** (feer)	16	**sechzehn** (zex-tzayn)	50	**fünfzig** (fewnf-tzik)
5	**funf** (fewnf)	17	**siebzehn** (zeeb-tzayn)	60	**sechzig** (zex-tzik)
6	**sechs** (zex)	18	**achtzehn** (akh-zayn)	70	**siebzig** (zeeb-tzik)
7	**sieben** (zee-ben)	19	**neunzehn** (noyn-tzayn)	80	**achtzig** (akht-tzik)
8	**acht** (ahkht)			90	**neunzig** (noyn-tzik)
9	**neun** (noyn)			100	**hundert** (hoon-dert)
10	**zehn** (tzayn)				
11	**elf** (ellf)				
12	**zwölf** (tzvuhlf)				

GREEK

GREEK ALPHABET

A, α	**álfa**	N, ν	**ní**	
B, β	**víta**	Ξ, ξ	**xí**	
Γ, γ	**gáma**	O, o	**ómikron**	
Δ, δ	**thélta**	Π, π	**pí**	
E, ε	**épsilon**	P, ρ	**ró**	
Z, ζ	**zíta**	Σ, σ	**sígma**	
H, η	**íta**	T, τ	**táf**	
Θ, θ	**thíta**	Υ, υ	**ípsilon**	
I, ι	**yóta**	Φ, φ	**fí**	
K, κ	**kápa**	X, χ	**hí**	
Λ, λ	**lámtha**	Ψ, ψ	**psí**	
M, μ	**mí**	Ω, ω	**oméga**	

ENGLISH	GREEK PRONUNCIATION
Hello or Good-bye (informal)	**Yah-sahs**
Hello or Good-bye (formal)	**Heh-re-te**
Thank you	**Ef-kah-ree-stoh**
You're welcome	**Pah-rah-kah-lo**
Please	**Pah-rah-kah-lo**
Yes	**Neh**
No	**O-hee**
Excuse me	**Sig-no-mee**
I don't understand.	**Then-kah-tah-lah-veh-no.**
Please repeat it.	**Peh-steh-toh pah-lee, pah-rah-kah-lo.**
Where is . . . ?	**Poo-ee-neh . . . ?**

ENGLISH	GREEK PRONUNCIATION
the bus station	stath-mos lee-oh-for-ee-oo
the train station	stath-mos tren-oo
the airport	aero-thro-me-oh
the hotel	kse-noh-tho-hee-oh
Left	A-rees-ter-ah
Right	The-xi-ah
How?	Poss?
How far?	Poh-soh mah-kree-ah?
What?	Tee?
When?	Po-teh?
Today	See-mer-ah
Tomorrow	Ah-vree-oh
Breakfast	Pro-ee-noh
Lunch	Mes-se-meree-a-noh
Dinner	Brah-three-noh

NUMBERS

0	**Mee-den**	20	**Ee-koh-see**	400	**Te-tra-kos-ya**
1	**E-nas**	30	**Tree-an-dah**	500	**Pen-da-ko-sya**
2	**Thee-oh**	40	**Sa-ran-dah**	600	**Ek-sa-kos-ya**
3	**Tree-ah**	50	**Pe-neen-dah**	700	**Ef-ta-kos-ya**
4	**Tes-sera**	60	**Ek-seen-dah**	800	**Oc-ta-kos-ya**
5	**Pend-eh**	70	**Ev-doh-meen-dah**	900	**En-ya-kos-ya**
6	**Ek-see**	80	**Oc-don-dah**	1,000	**Hi-lia**
7	**Ef-tah**	90	**E-ne-neen-dah**	2,000	**Dee-oh**
8	**Oc-to**	100	**E-ka-toh**		**Hi-lia-dess**
9	**E-nay-a**	200	**Dee-ah-kos-ya**	3,000	**Trees**
10	**De-ka**	300	**Tria-ko-sya**		**Hil-lia-dess**

HUNGARIAN

ENGLISH	HUNGARIAN	PRONUNCIATION
Hello	**Jó napot**	yoh naw-poht
How are you?	**Hogy van?**	hoj vawn?
Very well	**Nagyon jól**	naw-jon yohl
Thank you	**Köszönöm**	kur-sur-nurm
You're welcome	**Kérem**	kay-rem
Good-bye	**Viszontlátásra**	vee-sont-lah-tahsh-raw
Please	**Legyen szíves**	leh-jen see-vesh
Yes	**Igen**	ee-gen
No	**Nem**	nem
Excuse me	**Bocsánat**	boh-chah-nawt
Where is the . . . ?	**Hol van . . . ?**	hohl vawn . . . ?
bus station	**az autóbuszállomás**	awz ow-ton-boos-ah-loh-mahsh
train station	**a vasútállomás**	aw vaw-shoot-ah-loh-mahsh
airport	**a repülötér**	aw reh-pee-lur-tayr
baggage check	**a csomag-megörzöo**	aw choh-mawg-meg-ur-zur
check-in counter	**kell bejelent-keznem**	kel beh-jeh-lent-kez-nem
I'm looking for the . . .	**Keresem a . . .**	keh-reh-shem aw . . .
bank	**bankot**	bawn-koht
church	**tamplomot**	tem-ploh-moht
city center	**belvárost**	bel-vah-rosht

ENGLISH	HUNGARIAN	PRONUNCIATION
museum	múzeumot	moo-zeh-oo-moht
pharmacy	patikát	paw-tee-kaht
park	parkot	pawr-koht
theater	színházat	seen-hah-zawt
tourist office	turista	too-reesh-taw
	ügynökséget	eej-nurk-shay-get
embassy	nagykövetséget	nawj-kur-vet-shay-get
How much does it cost?	Mennyibe kerül?	men-yee-beh keh-reel?
Breakfast	Reggeli	reg-geh-lee
Lunch	Ebed	eh-bayd
Dinner	Vacsora	vaw-choh-raw

NUMBERS

1	**egy (ej)**	13	**tizenhárom**	20	**húsz (hoos)**
2	**kettó (ket-tur)**		(teez-en-hah-rohm)	30	**harminc**
3	**három (hah-rohm)**	14	**tizennégy**		(hawr-meents)
4	**négy (nayj)**		(teez-en-nayj)	40	**negyven (nej-ven)**
5	**öt (urt)**	15	**tizenöt (teez-en-urt)**	50	**ötven (urt-ven)**
6	**hat (hawt)**	16	**tizenhat**	60	**hatvan (hawt-vawn)**
7	**hét (hayt)**		(teez-en-hawt)	70	**hetven (het-ven)**
8	**nyolc (nyohlts)**	17	**tizenhét**	80	**nyolcvan**
9	**kilenc (keelents)**		(teez-en-hayt)		(nyohlts-vawn)
10	**tiz (teez)**	18	**tizennyolc**	90	**kilencven**
11	**tizenegy**		(teez-en-nyohlts)		(kee-lents-ven)
	(teez-en-ej)	19	**tizenkilenc**	100	**száz (sahz)**
12	**tizenkettó**		(teez-en-kee-lents)		
	(teez-en-ket-tur)				

ITALIAN

ENGLISH	ITALIAN	PRONUNCIATION
Hello	**Buon giorno**	bwohn djor-noh
How are you?	**Come sta?**	koh-may stah?
Very well	**Molto bene**	mohl-toh bay-nay
Thank you	**Grazie**	grah-tzyeh
Good-bye	**Arrivederci; Ciao**	ah-ree-vay-dehr-chee; chow
Please	**Per piacere**	payr pee-ya-chay-ray
Yes	**Si**	see
No	**No**	noh
Excuse me	**Scusi**	skoo-zee
Give me . . .	**Mi dia**	mee dee-ah
Where is . . . ?	**Dov'è . . . ?**	do-vay . . . ?
the station	**la stazione**	la stah-tzyonay
a hotel	**un albergo**	oon ahl-bayr-goh
a restaurant	**un ristorante**	oon rees-to-rahn-tay
the toilet	**il gabinetto**	eel ga-bee-nay-toh
To the right	**A destra**	ah dess-trah
To the left	**A sinistra**	ah see-nee-strah
Straight ahead	**Avanti**	ah-vahn-tee
I would like . . .	**Vorrei . . .**	vohr-ray . . .
to eat	**mangiare**	mahn-djah-ray
a room	**una camera**	oona kah-may-rah
for one night	**per una notte**	payr oona noh-tay
How much is it?	**Quanto costa?**	kwan-toh kaw-stah?
The check	**Il conto**	eel kohn-toh

ENGLISH	ITALIAN	PRONUNCIATION
When?	**Quando?**	kwahn-doh?
Yesterday	**Ieri**	ee-yay-ree
Today	**Oggi**	aw-djee
Tomorrow	**Domani**	doh-mah-nee
Breakfast	**Colazione**	koh-lah-tzyoh-nay
Lunch	**Pranzo**	prahn-tzoh
Dinner	**Cena**	chay-nah

NUMBERS

1 **uno** (oo-noh)
2 **due** (doo-ay)
3 **tre** (tray)
4 **quattro** (kwah-troh)
5 **cinque** (cheen-kway)
6 **sei** (say)
7 **sette** (set-tay)
8 **otto** (aw-toh)
9 **nove** (noh-vay)
10 **dieci** (dee-ah-chee)
11 **undici** (oon-dee-chee)
12 **dodici** (doh-dee-chee)
13 **tredici** (tray-dee-chee)

14 **quattordici** (kwah-tohr-dee-chee)
15 **quindici** (kween-dee chee)
16 **sedici** (say-dee-chee)
17 **diciasette** (dee-cha-se-tay)
18 **diciotto** (dee-choh-toh)
19 **dicianove** (dee-chay-novay)
20 **venti** (vayn-tee)
30 **trenta** (trayn-tah)

40 **quaranta** (kwah-rahn-tah)
50 **cinquanta** (cheen-kwan-tah)
60 **sessanta** (ses-san-tah)
70 **settanta** (set-tan-tah)
80 **ottanta** (aw-ton-tah)
90 **novanta** (noh-van-tah)
100 **cento** (chayn-toh)

NORWEGIAN

ENGLISH	NORWEGIAN
Good morning	**God morgen**
Good afternoon	**God dag**
Good night	**God natt**
Good-bye	**Adjø**
Thank you	**Takk**
You're welcome	**Vær så god**
Please	**Vær så god**
Yes	**Ja**
No	**Nei**
Excuse me	**Unnskyld**
I don't understand	**Jeg forstår ikke**
Where is . . . ?	**Hvor er . . . ?**
the train station	**Jernbanestasjon**
Right	**Høyre**
Left	**Venstre**
Go straight ahead	**Kjør rett frem**
Can you direct me to . . . ?	**Kan De vise meg veien til . . . ?**
Near	**I nærheten**
Far	**Langt borte**
How much?	**Hvor mye?**
Cheap	**Billig**
Expensive	**Dyrt**
When?	**Når?**
Today	**I dag**
Tomorrow	**I morgen**
What?	**Hva?**
What time is it?	**Hvor mange er klokken?**

NUMBERS

1 **en**	11 **elleve**	20 **tjue**
2 **to**	12 **tolv**	30 **tretti**
3 **tre**	13 **tretten**	40 **førti**
4 **fire**	14 **fjorten**	50 **femti**
5 **fem**	15 **femten**	60 **seksti**
6 **seks**	16 **seksten**	70 **sytti**
7 **sju**	17 **sytten**	80 **åtti**
8 **åtte**	18 **atten**	90 **nitti**
9 **ni**	19 **nitten**	100 **hundre**
10 **ti**		

PORTUGUESE

ENGLISH	PORTUGUESE	PRONUNCIATION
Hello	**Olá**	oh-lah
How are you?	**Como está?**	ko-mo esh-tah?
Very well	**Muito bem**	muy-toh bym
Thank you	**Muito obrigado**	muy-toh ob-ree-gah-doo
Good-bye	**Adeus**	ah-day-ush
Please	**Faça favor**	fas-sah fah-vohr
Yes	**Sim**	sem
No	**Não**	naion
Excuse me	**Desculpe-me**	dash-kul-pah-meh
Give me . . .	**Dê-me . . .**	deh-meh . . .
Where is . . . ?	**Onde fica . . . ?**	on-deh fee-kah . . . ?
the station	**a estação**	o aish-tah-ssaion
a hotel	**um hotel**	oom ho-tel
a restaurant	**um restaurante**	om rash-tah-ran-teh
the toilet	**a casa de banho**	ah kah-zah de bahn-yoo
To the right	**A direita**	aah dee-rai-tah
To the left	**A esquerda**	aah ask-ker-dah
Straight ahead	**Em frente**	ym frain-tah
I would like . . .	**Gostaria de . . .**	goosh-tah-ree-ah de . . .
to eat	**comer**	koh-mehr
a room	**um quarto**	oom kwar-toh
How much is it?	**Quanto custa?**	kwahn-to koosh-tah?
The check, please.	**A conta se faz, favor.**	ah kohn-tah sa fahsh, fah-vohr.
When?	**Quando?**	kwan-doh?
Yesterday	**Ontem**	ohn-tym
Today	**Hoje**	hoyh-je
Tomorrow	**Amanha**	ah-mai-nyayh
Breakfast	**Pequeno almoço**	pai-kai-noh aahl-mohs-soh
Lunch	**Almoço**	aahl-mohs-soh
Dinner	**Jantar**	jain-taah

NUMBERS

1 **um** (oom)	7 **sete** (ssai-teh)	13 **treze** (trai-zeh)
2 **dois** (doysh)	8 **oito** (oy-toh)	14 **catorze** (kah-tohr-zeh)
3 **três** (traish)	9 **nove** (noh-veh)	15 **quinze** (keen-zeh)
4 **quatro** (kwah-troh)	10 **dez** (daish)	16 **dezasseis** (deh-zai-ssaish)
5 **cinco** (sseen-koh)	11 **onze** (on-zeh)	
6 **seis** (ssaish)	12 **doze** (doh-zeh)	

17 **dezassete** (deh-zai-ssai-teh)	30 **trinta** (treehn-tah)	70 **setenta** (ssai-tain-tah)
18 **dezóito** (deh-zoy-toh)	40 **quarenta** (kwah-rain-tah)	80 **oitenta** (oy-tain-tah)
19 **dezanove** (deh-za-noh-veh)	50 **cinquenta** (sseen-kwain-tah)	90 **noventa** (noh-vain-tah)
20 **vinte** (veen-teh)	60 **sessenta** (ssai-ssaihn-tah)	100 **cem** (sym)

SPANISH

ENGLISH	SPANISH	PRONUNCIATION
Hello	**Buenos días**	bway-noss dee-ahss
How are you?	**Como está Usted?**	koh-moh ess-tah oo-steth?
Very well	**Muy bien**	mwee byen
Thank you	**Gracias**	gra-theeahss
Good-bye	**Adiós**	ad-dyohss
Please	**Por favór**	pohr fah-bohr
Yes	**Sí**	see
No	**No**	noh
Excuse me	**Perdóneme**	pehr-doh-neh-may
Give me . . .	**Deme . . .**	day-may . . .
Where is . . . ?	**Donde está . . . ?**	dohn-day ess-tah . . . ?
the station	**la estación**	la ess-tah-thyohn
a hotel	**un hotel**	oon-oh-tel
a restaurant	**un restaurante**	oon res-tow-rahn-tay
the toilet	**el servicio**	el ser-vee-the-o
To the right	**A la derecha**	ah lah day-ray-chuh
To the left	**A la izquierda**	ah lah eeth-kyayr-duh
Straight ahead	**Adelante**	ah-day-lahn-tay
I would like . . .	**Quiero . . .**	kyehr-oh . . .
to eat	**comer**	ko-mayr
a room	**una habitachión**	ooh-nah ah-bee-tah-thyohn
How much is it?	**Cuánto?**	kwahn-toh?
The check	**La cuenta**	la kwen-tah
When?	**Cuándo?**	kwan-doh?
Yesterday	**Ayer**	ah-yayr
Today	**Hoy**	oy
Tomorrow	**Mañana**	mahn-yah-nah
Breakfast	**Desayuno**	deh-sai-yoo-noh
Lunch	**Comida**	co-mee-dah
Dinner	**Cena**	thay-nah

NUMBERS

1 **uno** (oo-noh)	14 **catorce** (kah-tor-thay)	40 **cuarenta** (kwah-ren-tah)
2 **dos** (dos)	15 **quince** (keen-thay)	50 **cincuenta** (theen-kween-tah)
3 **tres** (trayss)	16 **deiciseis** (dyeth-ee-sayss)	60 **sesenta** (say-sen-tah)
4 **cuatro** (kwah-troh)	17 **diecisiete** (dyeth-ee-sye-tay)	70 **setenta** (say-ten-tah)
5 **cinco** (theen-koh)	18 **dieciocho** (dyeth-ee-oh-choh)	80 **ochenta** (oh-chen-tah)
6 **seis** (sayss)	19 **diecinueve** (dyeth-ee-nywaybay)	90 **noventa** (noh-ben-tah)
7 **siete** (syeh-tay)	20 **veinte** (bayn-tay)	100 **cien** (thyen)
8 **ocho** (oh-choh)	30 **treinta** (trayn-tah)	
9 **nueve** (nway-bay)		
10 **diez** (dyeth)		
11 **once** (ohn-thay)		
12 **doce** (doh-thay)		
13 **trece** (tray-thay)		

SWEDISH

ENGLISH	SWEDISH	PRONUNCIATION
Hello	**God dag**	goo dah
How are you?	**Hur står det till**	hoor store det till
Very well	**Tack bra**	tahk brah
Thank you	**Tack**	tahk
Goodbye	**Adjö**	ah-yer
Please	**Var snäll och**	vahr snell oh
Yes	**Ja**	yah
No	**Nej**	nay
Excuse me	**Ursäkta**	oor-sek-tah
I don't understand	**Jag förstår inte**	yah furst-tore in-tuh
Give me	**Ge mig**	yah may
Where is . . . ?	**Var finns det . . . ?**	vahr finss det . . . ?
the station	**stationen**	stah-shoo-nen
a hotel	**ett hotell**	et ho-tel
a restaurant	**en restaurang**	en rest-oh-rahng
a toilet	**toaletten**	twah-let-ten
To the right	**Åt höger**	oht her-ger
To the left	**Åt vänster**	oht yen-ster
Straight ahead	**Rakt fram**	rahkt-frahm
I would like . . .	**Jag vill ha . . .**	ya vill hah . . .
to eat	**mat**	maht
a room	**ett rum**	et ruhm
How much is it?	**Vad kostar det?**	vahd kaw-stahr dayt
That's too expensive	**Det är för mycket**	dayt ayr fer mik-ket
When?	**Nä?**	nayr
Yesterday	**I går**	ee gore
Today	**I dag**	ee dah
Tomorrow	**I morgon**	ee mawr-rawn

NUMBERS

1 **ett** (et)	11 **elva** (el-vah)	20 **tjugo** (chew-goo)
2 **tva** (tvoh)	12 **tolv** (tawlv)	30 **trettio** (tret-tee)
3 **tre** (tray)	13 **tretton** (tret-tawn)	40 **fyrtio** (fur-tee)
4 **fyra** (fee-rah)	14 **fjorton** (fyoor-tawn)	50 **femtio** (fem-tee)
5 **fem** (fem)	15 **femton** (fem-tawn)	60 **sextio** (sex-tee)
6 **sex** (sex)	16 **sexton** (sex-tawn)	70 **sjuttio** (shut-tee)
7 **sju** (shew)	17 **sjutton** (shuht-tawn)	80 **åttio** (awt-tee)
8 **åtta** (awt-tah)		90 **nittio** (neet-tww)
9 **nio** (nee-joh)	18 **aderton** (ahr-tawn)	100 **hundra** (huhn-dran)
10 **tio** (tee-yoo)	19 **nitton** (nit-tawn)	

F. MENU TERMS

DANISH

SOUPS

aspargesuppe asparagus soup **gule ærter** pea soup
blomkaalsuppe cauliflower soup

EGGS

æggekage omelette
blødkogt æg soft-boiled egg
hardkogt æg hard-boiled egg

roræg scrambled eggs
spejlæg fried egg

FISH

al eel
fiske frikadeller fish cakes
helleflynder halibut
hummer lobster
krabber crab
krebs crayfish
laks salmon
makrel mackerel

muslinger mussels
orred trout
pighvar turbot
rejer shrimp
rodspætte plaice
sild herring
torsk cod

MEATS

agerhons partridge
and duck
andesteg roast duck
bof steak
boller meatballs
due pigeon
dyr venison
fasan pheasant
flæskesteg roast pork
gaas goose
hakkebof hamburger
kalkun turkey
kalve veal
kalvesteg roast veal

kylling chicken
lam lamb
lammesteg roast lamb
lever liver
leverpostej liver pâté
okse beef
oksesteg roast beef
polser sausages
skinke ham
spegepolse salami
svin pork
tunge tongue
vildand wild duck

VEGETABLES

ærter peas
agurk cucumber
asparges asparagus
blomkaal cauliflower
bonner string beans
gulerodder carrots
hvidkal cabbage

kartofler potatoes
log onions
ris rice
rodkaal red cabbage
rosenkaal brussels sprouts
tomater tomatoes

FRUITS

æbler apples
ananas pineapple
appelsiner oranges
blommer plums

ferskner peaches
hindbær raspberries
jordbær strawberries
pærer pears

DESSERTS

budding pudding
hindbær med flode raspberries with
  cream

is ice cream
kompot stewed fruit
kager pastry

BEVERAGES

æblemost apple juice
flode cream

kaffe coffee
mælk milk

ol beer
te tea

vand water
vin wine

BASICS

brod bread
ost cheese

salt salt
smor butter

COOKING TERMS

farseret stuffed
grilleret grilled
kogt boiled

ristet fried
stegt roast

DUTCH

SOUPS

aardapplesoep potato soup
bonensoep bean soup
erwtensoep pea soup
groentesoep vegetable soup

kippensoep chicken soup
soep soup
tomatensoep tomato soup
uiensoep onion soup

EGGS

eieren eggs
hardgekookte eieren hard-boiled
  eggs

roereieren scrambled eggs
spiegeleieren fried eggs
zachtgekookte eieren boiled eggs

FISH

forel trout
garnalen shrimp
gerookte zalm smoked salmon
haring herring
kabeljauw haddock
kreeft lobster

makreel mackerel
mosselen mussels
oesters oysters
sardientjes sardines
vis fish
zalm salmon

MEATS

biefstuk steak
chateaubriand filet steak
eend duck
gans goose
gebraden worst fried sausage
kalkoen turkey
kip chicken
konin rabbit

koude schotel cold cuts
lamscotelet lamb chops
lamsvlees lamb
lever liver
niertjes kidneys
ragout beef stew
runder bief beef
spek bacon

VEGETABLES

aardappelen potatoes
asperges asparagus
augurkjes pickles
bonen beans
bieten beets
erwtjes peas
groente vegetables
kool cabbage
patates frites french fried potatoes
prinsesseboontjes green beans

purée mashed potatoes
radijsjes radishes
rapen turnips
rijst rice
sla lettuce
spinazie spinach
tomaten tomatoes
worteltjes carrots
zuurkool sauerkraut

SALADS

sla salad

komkommersla cucumber salad

FRUITS

appelen apples
bananen bananas
citroenen lemons
druiven grapes

fruit fruit
kersen cherries
pruimen plums
sinaasappelen oranges

DESSERTS

ananas pineapple
cake cake
compôte stewed fruits
frambozen raspberries

ijs ice cream
nagerecht dessert
omelette omelette
zwate bessen blackberries

BEVERAGES

bier beer
cognac brandy
koffie coffee
melk milk
rode wijn red wine

thee tea
tomaten sap tomato juice
water water
wijn wine
witte wijn white wine

BASICS

azijn vinegar
boter butter
brood bread
honing honey
jam jam

kaas cheese
mosterd mustard
peper pepper
suiker sugar
zout salt

COOKING TERMS

gebakken fried
gekookt boiled
geroosterd broiled

goed doorgebakken well done
niet doorgebakken rare

FRENCH

SOUPS

bouillabaisse fish soup
consommé clear broth
potage, soupe soup
potage à la reine cream of chicken
 soup
potage au vermicelle noodle soup

potage aux lentilles lentil soup
potage portugais tomato soup
potage Saint-Germain pea soup
potage de volaille chicken broth
soupe à l'oignon onion soup

FISH

aigrefin haddock
anguille eel
brochet pike
crevette shrimp
escargots snails
hareng herring
homard lobster

huîtres oysters
maquereau mackerel
moules mussels
poissons fish
saumon fumé smoked salmon
thon tuna
truite trout

MEATS

agneau lamb
ailes chicken wings
aloyau sirloin
bifteck steak
boeuf beef
canard duck
caneton duckling
cervelles brains
charcuterie cold cuts
chauteaubriand filet steak
chevreuil venison
coq au vin chicken in wine
côtelette d'agneau lamb chop
dindonneau farci stuffed turkey
dinde turkey
foie liver
foie gras goose liver

gigot de mouton leg of mutton
grenouille frog
jambon ham
lapin rabbit
mouton mutton
oie goose
pot au feu beef stew
poulet chicken
poussin squab
ris de veau sweetbreads
rognons kidneys
rôti roast
saucisse grillée fried sausage
tournedos small filet steaks
veau veal
viande en ragoût meat stew
volaille poultry

VEGETABLES

asperge asparagus
aubergine eggplant
choucroute sauerkraut
choux cabbage
cornichon pickle
épinards spinach
haricots verts green beans
légumes vegetables

navets turnips
petits pois green peas
pommes de terres potatoes
pommes frites french fried potatoes
purée de pommes mashed potatoes
radis radish
riz rice

SALADS

crudités vegetable salad
salade de concombres cucumber
  salad

salade de laitue lettuce salad
salade niçoise tuna salad
salade variée mixed salad

FRUITS

ananas pineapple
fraises strawberries
framboises raspberries

oranges oranges
pamplemousse grapefruit
raisins grapes

DESSERTS

compôte de fruits stewed fruit
crème à la vanille vanilla custard
fromage à la crème cream cheese
fruits frais fresh fruit
gâteau cake

glace à la vanille vanilla ice cream
macedoine de fruits fruit salad
petits fours tea cakes
tartes pastries

BEVERAGES

bière beer
café coffee
cognac brandy
crème cream
eau water
jus d'orange orange juice

jus de tomates tomato juice
lait milk
thé tea
vin wine
vin blanc white wine
vin rouge red wine

BASICS

beurre butter
citron lemon
fromage cheese
moutarde mustard
pain bread

poivre pepper
sel salt
sucre sugar
vinaigre vinegar

COOKING TERMS

à point medium
bien cuit well done
farci stuffed
frit fried

meunière, au beurre buttered
rôti roast
saignant rare

GERMAN

SOUPS

Erbsensuppe pea soup
Gemüsesuppe vegetable soup
Hühnerbrühe chicken soup
Kartoffelsuppe potato soup
Königinsuppe cream of chicken soup

Linsensuppe lentil soup
Nudelsuppe noodle soup
Ochsenschwanzsuppe oxtail soup
Schildkrötensuppe turtle soup

EGGS

Eier in Schale boiled eggs
Rühreier scrambled eggs
Spiegeleier fried eggs

mit Speck with bacon
Verlorene Eier poached eggs

FISH

Aal eel
Forelle trout
Hecht pike
Karpfen carp
Krebs crayfish

Lachs salmon
Makrele mackerel
Rheinsalm Rhine salmon
Schellfisch haddock
Seezunge sole

MEATS

Aufschnitt cold cuts
Brathuhn roast chicken
Bratwurst grilled sausage
Deutsches Beefsteak hamburger steak
Eisbein pigs' knuckles
Ente duck
Gans goose
Gefüllte Kalbsbrust stuffed breast of veal
Hammel mutton
Hirn brains
Kalb veal
Kaltes Geflügel cold poultry

Kassler Rippchen pork chops
Lamm lamb
Leber liver
Nieren kidneys
Ragout stew
Rinderbraten roast beef
Rindfleisch beef
Sauerbraten sauerbraten
Schinken ham
Schweinebraten roast pork
Taube pigeon
Truthahn turkey
Wiener Schnitzel veal cutlet
Wurst sausage

VEGETABLES

Artischocken artichokes
Blumenkohl cauliflower
Bohnen beans

Bratkartoffeln fried potatoes
Erbsen peas
Grüne Bohnen string beans

Gurken cucumbers
Karotten carrots
Kartoffelbrei mashed potatoes
Kartoffelsalat potato salad
Knödel dumplings
Kohl cabbage
Reis rice
Rote Rüben beets
Rotkraut red cabbage

Salat lettuce
Salzkartoffeln boiled potatoes
Sauerkraut sauerkraut
Spargel asparagus
Spinat spinach
Steinpilze boletus mushrooms
Tomaten tomatoes
Vorspeisen hors d'oeuvres
Weisse Rüben turnips

SALADS

Gemischter Salat mixed salad
Gurkensalat cucumber salad

Kopfsalat lettuce salad
Rohkostplatte vegetable salad

FRUITS

Ananas pineapples
Apfel apples
Apfelsinen oranges
Bananen bananas
Birnen pears

Kirschen cherries
Pfirsiche peaches
Weintrauben grapes
Zitronen lemons

DESSERTS

Blatterteiggebäck puff pastry
Bratapfel baked apple
Kloss dumpling
Kompott stewed fruit
Obstkuchen fruit tart

Obstsalat fruit salad
Pfannkuchen sugared pancakes
Pflaumenkompott stewed plums
Teegebäck tea cakes
Torten pastries

BEVERAGES

Bier beer
Ein Dunkles a dark beer
Ein Helles a light beer
Eine Tasse Kaffee a cup of coffee
Eine Tasse Tee a cup of tea
Milch milk

Rotwein red wine
Sahne cream
Schokolade chocolate
Tomatensaft tomato juice
Wasser water
Weinbrand brandy

BASICS

Brot bread
Butter butter
Eis ice
Essig vinegar
Käse cheese

Pfeffer pepper
Salz salt
Senf mustard
Zitrone lemon
Zucker sugar

COOKING TERMS

Gebacken baked
Gebraten fried
Gefüllt stuffed
Gekocht boiled

Geröstet broiled
Gut durchgebraten well done
Nicht durchgebraten rare
Paniert breaded

GREEK

FISH

astakos (ladolemono) lobster (with oil and lemon sauce)

bakaliaro (skordalia) cod (with garlic)

barbounia (skaras) red mullet (grilled)
caravides crayfish
garides shrimp
glossa (tiganiti) sole (fried)
kalamarakia (tiganita) squid (fried)
kalamarakia (yemista) squid (stuffed)

oktapodi octopus
soupies yemistes stuffed cuttlefish
taramosalata fish roe with mayonnaise
tsipoura dorado

MEATS

arni avgolemono lamb with lemon sauce
arni souvlas spit-roasted lamb
arni yiouvetsi lamb in tomato sauce
brizola moscharisia beef or veal steak
brizola hirini pork steak or chop
dolmadakia stuffed vine leaves
keftedes fried meatballs
kotopoulo souvlas spit-roasted chicken

kotopoulo yemisto stuffed chicken
loukanika spiced sausages
moussaka meat and eggplant (or potato)
paidakia lamb chops
pilafi, risi rice pilaf
souvlaki lamb (sometimes veal) on the skewer
youvariakia boiled meat balls with rice
yiouvetsi lamb with noodles

SALADS

melitzanosalata eggplant salad
midia fassolia dandelion salad

tzatziki cucumber with yogurt

BEVERAGES

bíra beer
gala milk
kafe(s) coffee
krasí wine

neró water
neró enfialoméno mineral water
tsáï tea

BASICS

aláti salt
avgá eggs
méli honey
psomí bread

soúpa soup
tirí cheese
yiaoúrti yogurt

HUNGARIAN

SOUPS

gulyasleves goulash soup
gombaleves mushroom soup
húsleves bouillon

paradicsomleves tomato soup
zöldborsóleves pea soup
zöldségleves vegetable soup

EGGS

gombás omlett mushroom omelet
kemény tojás hard-boiled eggs
kolbásszal eggs with sausage
lágy tojás soft-boiled eggs
omlett omelet

rántotta scrambled eggs
sonkával eggs with ham
szalonnával eggs with bacon
tükörtojás fried eggs

FISH

csuka pike	**halászlé** fish stew
csuka tejfölben pike with sour cream	**pisztráng** trout
fogas pike-perch	**ponty** carp
	tonhal tuna

MEATS

barany lamb	**malacsült** roast piglet
bécsi szelet wienerschnitzel	**marhahús** beef
borjúhús veal	**nyársonsùlt** shish kebab
csirke chicken	**paprikáscsirke** chicken paprikash
disznóhús pork	**pecsenye** roast
kacsa duck	**pörkölt** goulash
kotlett cutlet	**tokány** ragoût
liba goose	

VEGETABLES

bab beans	**paradicsom** tomato
burgonya potato	**rizs** rice
gomba mushrooms	**spenót** spinach
káposzta cabbage	**zöldbab** green beans
lecsó pickled vegetables	

SALADS

fejes saláta green salad	**uborkasaláta** cucumber salad
paprikasaláta pepper salad	**vegyes saláta** mixed salad

FRUITS

barack apricot	**körte** pears
csereszyne cherries	**narancs** oranges
dinnye melon	**szőlő** grapes

DESSERTS

almás rétes apple strudel	**fagylalt** ice cream
cseresznyes retes cherry strudel	**túrós rétes** cheese strudel
csokoládé torta chocolate cake	

BEVERAGES

barna sör dark beer	**pezsgő** champagne
fehér bor white wine	**sör** beer
kakaó cocoa	**tea** tea
kávé coffee	**tej** milk
koktel cocktail	**viz** water
narancslé orange juice	**vörös bor** red wine
pálinka brandy	

BASICS

bors black pepper	**mustár** mustard
cukor sugar	**olaj** oil
ecet vinegar	**sajt** cheese
kenyér bread	**só** salt
majonéz mayonnaise	**vaj** butter
méz honey	

COOKING TERMS

agyonsütve well done
csipős hot (peppery)
dinsztelve braised
félig nyersen rare
forró hot (in temperature)
főzve boiled
friss fresh
fűszerezve spicy

hideg cold
közepesen kisütve medium
nyers raw
párolva steamed
sós salty
sütve baked
zsírban sütve deep-fried

ITALIAN

SOUPS

brodo consommé
minestra soup
minestrone vegetable soup
pastina in brodo noodle soup

riso in brodo rice soup
zuppa alla pavese egg soup
zuppa di fagioli bean soup
zuppa di pesce fish soup

EGGS

omelette, frittata omelette
omelette alla parmigiana cheese
  omelette
omelette di fegatini omelette with
  chicken livers
omelette di funghi mushroom
  omelette
pan dorato french-fried toast

**strapazzate al
  pomodoro** scrambled with tomato
uova eggs
uova affogate poached eggs
uova a la coque boiled eggs
uova fritte fried eggs
uova strapazzate scrambled eggs

FISH

acciughe anchovies
aragosta lobster
aringhe herring
filetto di sogliola filet of sole
fritto di pesce assorted fried fish
frutta di mare assorted sea food
gamberi shrimp
merluzzo cod

ostriche oysters
pesce fish
sardine sardine
scampi fritti fried shrimp
sgombro mackerel
sogliola sole
tonno tuna fish
trota trout

MEATS

abbachio baby lamb
agnello lamb
anitra duck
bistecca steak
carne meat
carne fredda assortita cold cuts
cervello brains
fegato liver
lepre rabbit
lingua tongue
maiale pork
manzo lesso boiled beef

pancetta bacon
pollo chicken
pollo alla diavolo deviled chicken
cotoletta alla bolognese veal cutlet
  with melted cheese
cotoletta alla milanese breaded
  veal cutlet
fagiano pheasant
fegatini chicken livers
prosciutto ham
reni kidney
rosbif roast beef

VEGETABLES

antipasto hors d'oeuvres
asparagi asparagus
cannelloni pasta with meat filling

carciofi artichokes
carote carrots
cavolfiore cauliflower

cavolo cabbage
cetrioli cucumbers
cipolle onions
fagiolini string beans
fettuccine noodles
funghi mushrooms
insalata mista mixed salad
insalata verde lettuce salad
lattuga lettuce
melanzana eggplant
olive olives
patate potatoes
peperoni green, red, or yellow
 peppers

piselli peas
pizza you know this one
pomodori tomatoes
ravioli alla fiorentina cheese ravioli
ravioli alla vegetariana ravioli with
 tomato sauce
riso rice
risotto rice dish
sedano celery
spinaci spinach
verdura vegetables
zucchini squash

FRUITS

ananasso pineapple
aranci oranges
banane bananas
ciliegie cherries
frutta fruit

frutta cotta stewed fruit
limoni lemons
mele apples
pere pears
uva grape

DESSERTS

budino pudding
cassata ice cream with fruit
dolci dessert
gelato ice cream

macedonia di frutta fruit salad
pasticceria pastry
pesca alla Melba peach Melba
torta cake

BEVERAGES

acqua water
acqua minerale mineral water
aranciata orangeade
bibite beverages
birra beer

caffè coffee
latte milk
limonata lemonade
thè tea
vino wine

BASICS

aceto vinegar
biscotti crackers
burro butter
formaggio cheese
ghiaccio ice
marmellata jam
mostarda mustard

olio oil
pane bread
pepe pepper
sale salt
sott'aceti pickles
zucchero sugar

COOKING TERMS

al sangue rare
arrosto roast

ben cotto well done
lesso, bollito boiled

PORTUGUESE
SOUPS

caldo verde potato and cabbage soup
canja de galinha chicken soup
creme de camarão cream of shrimp
 soup
creme de legumes cream of
 vegetable soup

sopa à Alentejano Alentejo soup
sopa de cebola onion soup
sopa de mariscos shellfish soup
sopa de queijo cheese soup
sopa de tomate tomato soup

EGGS

ovos com presunto ham and eggs
ovos cozidos hard-boiled eggs
ovos escalfados poached eggs
ovos estrelados fried eggs

ovos mexicos scrambled eggs
omeleta omelet
ovos quentes soft-boiled eggs
tortilha Spanish omelet

FISH

ameijoas clams
atum tuna
bacalhau salted codfish
cherne turbot
camarãos shrimp
eiró eel
lagosta lobster
linguado sole
lulas squid

ostras oysters
peixe espada swordfish
percebes barnacles
pescada hake
robalo bass
salmonete red mullet
santola crab
sardinhas sardines

MEATS

bife steak
borracho pigeon
borrego lamb
cabrito kid
carneiro mutton
coelho rabbit
costeletas chops
dobrada tripe
frango chicken
galinha fowl
ganso goose

iscas liver
lingua tongue
pato duck
perdiz partridge
perú duck
porco pork
presunto ham
rim kidney
salchichas sausages
vaca beef
vitela veal

VEGETABLES

aipo celery
alcachôfra artichoke
arroz rice
azeitonas olives
batatas potatoes
berinjela eggplant
beterrabas beets
cebola onion
cenouras carrots
cogumelo mushroom

couve-flor cauliflower
couve cabbage
ervilhas peas
espargos asparagus
espinafres spinach
favas broad beans
feijão bean
nabo turnip
pepino cucumber
tomate tomato

SALADS

agriãos watercress salad
alface lettuce

salada mista mixed salad
salada verde green salad

FRUITS

abacate avocado
alperches apricots
ameixa plum
ananas pineapple
cerajas cherries
figos figs
framboesa raspberry

laranjas oranges
limão lemon
maçãs apples
melancia watermelon
melão melon
morangos strawberries
peras pears

pêssegos peaches
roma pomegranate
tâmara date

toronja grapefruit
uvas grapes

DESSERTS

arroz doce rice pudding
bolo cake
gelados diversos mixed ice creams
maçã assada baked apple
pastelaria pastry
pêssego Melba peach Melba

pudim flan egg custard
pudim de pão bread pudding
salada de frutas fruit salad
sorvetes sherbets
queijo cheese

BEVERAGES

água water
água mineral mineral water
café coffee
chá tea
cerveja beer
com gelo with ice
laranjada orangeade

leite milk
sumo de fruta fruit juice
sumo de laranja orange juice
sumo de tomate tomato juice
vinho branco white wine
vinho tinto red wine

BASICS

açúcar sugar
alho garlic
azeite olive oil
caril curry
compota jam
manteiga butter

mostarda mustard
pão bread
pimenta pepper
queijo cheese
sal salt
vinagre vinegar

COOKING TERMS

assado no forno baked
cozido boiled
estufada braised

frito fried
mal passado rare
bem passado well done

SPANISH

SOUPS

caldo gallego Galician broth
caldo de gallina chicken soup
sopa de ajo garlic soup
sopa de cebolla onion soup
sopa clara consommé
sopa espesa thick soup

sopa de fideos noodle soup
sopa de guisantes pea soup
sopa de lentejas lentil soup
sopa de pescado fish soup
sopa de tomate tomato soup
sopa de verduras vegetable soup

EGGS

huevos escaltados poached eggs
huevos fritos fried eggs
huevos duros hard-boiled eggs

huevos revueltos scrambled eggs
huevos por agua soft-boiled eggs
tortilla omelet

FISH

almejas clams
anchoas anchovies
anguilas eels
arenque herring
atún tuna

bacalao cod
calamares squid
cangrejo crab
caracoles snails
centollo sea urchin

chocos large squid
cigalas small lobsters
gambas shrimp
langosta lobster
langostinos prawns
lenguado sole
mejillones mussels
merluza hake
necoras spider crabs

ostras oysters
pescadilla whiting
pijotas small whiting
pulpo octopus
rodaballo turbot
salmonete mullet
sardinas sardines
trucha trout
vieiras scallops

MEATS

albondigas meatballs
bistec beefsteak
callos tripe
cerdo pork
chuleta cutlet
cocido stew
conejo rabbit
cordero lamb
costillas chops
gallina fowl
ganso goose
higado liver
jamón ham

lengua tongue
paloma pigeon
pato duck
pavo turkey
perdiz partridge
pollo chicken
riñón kidney
rosbif roast beef
solomillo loin
ternera veal
tocino bacon
vaca beef

VEGETABLES

aceitunas olives
alcachofa artichoke
arroz rice
berenjena eggplant
cebolla onion
col cabbage
colifior cauliflower
esparragos asparagus
espinacas spinach
guisantes peas

judías verdes string beans
nabo turnip
patata potato
pepino cucumber
remolachas beets
setas mushrooms
tomate tomato
zanahorias carrots

SALADS

ensalada mixta mixed salad
ensalada de pepinos cucumber
  salad

ensalada verde green salad
lechuga lettuce

FRUITS

albaricoque apricot
aquacate avocado
cerezas cherries
ciruela plum
datil date
frambuesa raspberry
fresa strawberry
granada pomegranate
higo fig

limón lemon
manzana apple
melocoton peach
naranja orange
pera pear
piña pineapple
plátano banana
toronja grapefruit
uvas grapes

DESSERTS

buñuelos fritters
compota stewed fruit

flan caramel custard
fruta fruit

galletas tea cakes
helado ice cream

pasteles pastries
torta cake

BEVERAGES

agua water
agua mineral mineral water
café coffee
cerveza beer
ginebra gin
jerez sherry
jugo de naranjas orange juice
jugo de tomate tomato juice
leche milk

sangría red wine, fruit juice, and soda
sidra cider
sifon soda
té tea
vino blancho white wine
vino tinto red wine

BASICS

aceite oil
ajo garlic
azucar sugar
hielo ice
mantequilla butter
miel honey

mostaza mustard
pan bread
pimienta pepper
queso cheese
sal salt
vinagre vinegar

COOKING TERMS

asado roast
cocido broiled
empanado breaded
frito fried

muy hecho well done
poco hecho rare
tostado toast

SWEDISH

SOUPS

ärtsoppa pea soup
buljong broth

kálsoppa cabbage soup
soppa soup

FISH

anjovis anchovies
fisk fish
hummer lobster
kolja haddock
karp carp
kaviar caviar

makrill mackerel
ostron oyster
sill herring
stör sturgeon
torsk cod

MEATS

anka duck
biffstek steak
fárkött mutton
fläsk pork
gás goose
kalv veal
korv sausage

kyckling chicken
lamm lamb
lever liver
oxe beef
rostbiff roast beef
skinka ham

VEGETABLES

ärta pea
ärwskocka artichoke
blomkál cauliflower

bruna bönor kidney beans
gurka cucumber
kál cabbage

lök onion
makaroner macaroni
morot carrot

potatis potatoes
rödbeta beet
sparris asparagus

FRUITS

apelsiner oranges
avocado avocado
körsbär cherry
päron pear

persika peach
plommon plum
vindruva grape

DESSERTS

kakor pastry
russinkaka plumcake

sockerkaka cake

BEVERAGES

kaffe coffee
karnmjölk buttermilk
mineral vatten mineral water
mjölk milk

öl ale
te tea
vatten water

G. WEIGHTS & MEASURES

LENGTH

1 millimeter (mm)	=	.04 inches (*or* less than $\frac{1}{16}$ in.)
1 centimeter (cm)	=	.39 inches (*or* just under ½ in.)
1 meter (m)	=	39 inches (*or* about 1.1 yards)
1 kilometer (km)	=	.62 miles (*or* about ⅔ of a mile)

To convert kilometers to miles, multiply the number of kilometers by 0.62. Also use to convert speeds from kilometers per hour (kmph) to miles per hour (m.p.h.).
To convert miles to kilometers, multiply the number of miles by 1.61. Also use to convert speeds from m.p.h. to kmph.

CAPACITY

1 liter (l)	=	33.92 ounces	=	2.1 pints	=	1.06 quarts
	=	0.26 U.S. gallons				
1 Imperial gallon	=	1.2 U.S. gallons				

To convert liters to U.S. gallons, multiply the number of liters by 0.26.
To convert U.S. gallons to liters, multiply the number of gallons by 3.79.
To convert Imperial gallons to U.S. gallons, multiply Imperial gallons by 1.2.
To convert U.S. gallons to Imperial gallons, multiply U.S. gallons by 0.83.

WEIGHT

1 gram (g)	=	0.04 ounces (*or* about a paperclip's weight)		
1 kilogram (kg)	=	35.2 ounces		
	=	2.2 pounds		
1 metric ton	=	2,205 pounds	=	1.1 short ton

To convert kilograms to pounds, multiply the number of kilograms by 2.2.
To convert pounds to kilograms, multiply the number of pounds by 0.45.

TEMPERATURE

°C	−18°	−10	0	10	20	30	40
°F	0° 10 20	32 40	50	60	70	80	90 100

To convert degrees Celsius to degrees Fahrenheit, multiply °C by 9, divide by 5, then add 32 (example: 20°C × 9/5 + 32 = 68°F).

To convert degrees Fahrenheit to degrees Celsius, subtract 32 from °F, then multiply by 5, then divide by 9 (example: 85°F − 32 × 5/9 = 29.4°C).

H. SIZE CONVERSIONS

The following charts should help you to choose the correct clothing sizes in Europe. However, sizes can vary, so the best guide is simply to try things on.

WOMEN'S DRESSES, COATS & SKIRTS

American	4	6	8	10	11	12	13	14	15	16	18
Continental	36	38	38	40	40	42	42	44	44	46	48
British	8	10	11	12	13	14	15	16	17	18	20

WOMEN'S BLOUSES & SWEATERS

American	6	8	10	12	14	16
Continental	34	36	38	40	42	44
British	32	34	36	38	40	42

WOMEN'S SHOES

American	5	6	7	8	9	10
Continental	36	37	38	39	40	41
British	3½	4½	5½	6½	7½	8½

MEN'S SUITS

American	34	36	38	40	42	44	46	48
Continental	44	46	48	50	52	54	56	58
British	34	36	38	40	42	44	46	48

MEN'S SHIRTS

American	14½	15	15½	16	16½	17	17½	18
Continental	37	38	39	41	42	43	44	45
British	14½	15	15½	16	16½	17	17½	18

MEN'S SHOES

American	7	8	9	10	11	12	13
Continental	39½	41	42	43	44½	46	47
British	6	7	8	9	10	11	12

CHILDREN'S CLOTHING

American	3	4	5	6	6X
Continental	98	104	110	116	122
British	18	20	22	24	26

CHILDREN'S SHOES

American	8	9	10	11	12	13	1	2	3
Continental	24	25	27	28	29	30	32	33	34
British	7	8	9	10	11	12	13	1	2

INDEX

GENERAL INFORMATION

DESTINATIONS

NOTE: An asterisk (*) indicates that an attraction is an Author's Favorite

1058 · INDEX

1068 · INDEX

Now Save Money On All Your Travels by Joining
FROMMER'S ™ TRAVEL BOOK CLUB
The World's Best Travel Guides at Membership Prices

FROMMER'S TRAVEL BOOK CLUB is your ticket to successful travel! Open up a world of travel information and simplify your travel planning when you join ranks with thousands of value-conscious travelers who are members of the FROMMER'S TRAVEL BOOK CLUB. Join today and you'll be entitled to all the privileges that come from belonging to the club that offers you travel guides for less to more than 100 destinations worldwide. Annual membership is only $25 (U.S.) $35 (Canada and all foreign).

The Advantages of Membership

1. Your choice of three free FROMMER'S TRAVEL GUIDES (you can pick two from our FROMMER'S COUNTRY and REGIONAL GUIDES and one from our FROMMER'S CITY GUIDES).
2. Your own subscription to **TRIPS AND TRAVEL** quarterly newsletter.
3. You're entitled to a **30% discount** on your order of any additional books offered by FROMMER'S TRAVEL BOOK CLUB.
4. You're offered (at a small additional fee) our **Domestic Trip Routing Kits.**

Our quarterly newsletter **TRIPS AND TRAVEL** offers practical information on the best buys in travel, the "hottest" vacation spots, the latest travel trends, world class events and much, much more.

Our **Domestic Trip Routing Kits** are available for any North American destination. We'll send you a detailed map highlighting the best route to take to your destination—you can request direct or scenic routes.

Here's all you have to do to join:
Send in your membership fee of $25 ($35 Canada and foreign) with your name and address on the form below along with your selections as part of your membership package to **FROMMER'S TRAVEL BOOK CLUB, P.O. Box 473, Mt. Morris, IL 61054-0473**. Remember to select 2 FROMMER'S COUNTRY and REGIONAL GUIDES and 1 FROMMER'S CITY GUIDE on the pages following.

If you would like to order additional books, please select the books you would like and send a check for the total amount (please add sales tax in the states noted below), plus $2 per book for shipping and handling ($3 per book for all foreign orders) to:

FROMMER'S TRAVEL BOOK CLUB
P.O. Box 473
Mt. Morris, IL 61054-0473
1-815-734-1104

[ ] **YES**. I want to take advantage of this opportunity to join FROMMER'S TRAVEL BOOK CLUB.

[ ] **My check is enclosed**. Dollar amount enclosed_____*

Name_____

Address_____

City_____ State_____ Zip_____

To ensure that all orders are processed efficiently, please apply sales tax in the following areas: CA, CT, FL, IL, NJ, NY, TN, WA and CAN.

*With membership, shipping and handling will be paid by FROMMER'S TRAVEL BOOK CLUB for the three free books you select as part of your membership. Please add $2 per book for shipping and handling for any additional books purchased ($3 per book for all foreign orders).

Allow 4-6 weeks for delivery. Prices of books, membership fee, and publication dates are subject to change without notice.

FROMMER GUIDES

	Retail Price	Code		Retail Price	Code
Alaska 1990–91	$14.95	C001	Jamaica/Barbados		
Arizona 1993–94	$18.00	C101	1993–94	$15.00	C105
Australia 1992–93	$18.00	C002	Japan 1992–93	$19.00	C020
Austria/Hungary 1991–			Morocco 1992–93	$18.00	C021
92	$14.95	C003	Nepal 1992–93	$18.00	C038
Belgium/Holland/			New England 1992	$17.00	C023
Luxembourg 1993–94	$18.00	C106	New Mexico 1991–92	$13.95	C024
Bermuda/Bahamas			New York State 1992–93	$19.00	C025
1992–93	$17.00	C005	Northwest 1991–92	$16.95	C026
Brazil 1991–92	$14.95	C006	Portugal 1992–93	$16.00	C027
California 1992	$18.00	C007	Puerto Rico 1993–94	$15.00	C103
Canada 1992–93	$18.00	C009	Puerto Vallarta/		
Caribbean 1993	$18.00	C102	Manzanillo/		
The Carolinas/Georgia			Guadalajara 1992–93	$14.00	C028
1992–93	$17.00	C034	Scandinavia 1991–92	$18.95	C029
Colorado 1993–94	$16.00	C100	Scotland 1992–93	$16.00	C040
Cruises 1993–94	$19.00	C107	Skiing Europe 1989–90	$14.95	C030
DE/MD/PA & NJ Shore			South Pacific 1992–93	$20.00	C031
1992–93	$19.00	C012	Switzerland/Liechten-		
Egypt 1990–91	$14.95	C013	stein 1992–93	$19.00	C032
England 1993	$18.00	C109	Thailand 1992–93	$20.00	C033
Florida 1993	$18.00	C104	USA 1991–92	$16.95	C035
France 1992–93	$20.00	C017	Virgin Islands 1992–93	$13.00	C036
Germany 1993	$19.00	C108	Virginia 1992–93	$14.00	C037
Italy 1992	$19.00	C019	Yucatán 1992–93	$18.00	C110

FROMMER $-A-DAY GUIDES

	Retail Price	Code		Retail Price	Code
Australia on $45 a Day			Israel on $45 a Day		
1993–94	$18.00	D102	1993–94	$18.00	D101
Costa Rica/Guatemala/			Mexico on $50 a Day		
Belize on $35 a Day			1993	$19.00	D105
1991–92	$15.95	D004	New York on $70 a Day		
Eastern Europe on $25			1992–93	$16.00	D016
a Day 1991–92	$16.95	D005	New Zealand on $45 a		
England on $60 a Day			Day 1993–94	$18.00	D103
1993	$18.00	D107	Scotland/Wales on $50 a		
Europe on $45 a Day			Day 1992–93	$18.00	D019
1993	$19.00	D106	South America on $40 a		
Greece on $45 a Day			Day 1991–92	$15.95	D020
1993–94	$19.00	D100	Spain on $50 a Day		
Hawaii on $75 a Day			1991–92	$15.95	D021
1993	$19.00	D104	Turkey on $40 a Day		
India on $40 a Day			1992	$22.00	D023
1992–93	$20.00	D010	Washington, D.C. on		
Ireland on $40 a Day			$40 a Day 1992	$17.00	D024
1992–93	$17.00	D011			

FROMMER CITY $-A-DAY GUIDES

	Retail Price	Code		Retail Price	Code
Berlin on $40 a Day 1992–93	$12.00	D002	Madrid on $50 a Day 1992–93	$13.00	D014
Copenhagen on $50 a Day 1992–93	$12.00	D003	Paris on $45 a Day 1992–93	$12.00	D018
London on $45 a Day 1992–93	$12.00	D013	Stockholm on $50 a Day 1992–93	$13.00	D022

FROMMER TOURING GUIDES

Amsterdam	$10.95	T001	New York	$10.95	T008
Australia	$10.95	T002	Paris	$ 8.95	T009
Barcelona	$14.00	T015	Rome	$10.95	T010
Brazil	$10.95	T003	Scotland	$ 9.95	T011
Egypt	$ 8.95	T004	Sicily	$14.95	T017
Florence	$ 8.95	T005	Thailand	$12.95	T012
Hong Kong/Singapore/ Macau	$10.95	T006	Tokyo	$15.00	T016
Kenya	$13.95	T018	Turkey	$10.95	T013
London	$12.95	T007	Venice	$ 8.95	T014

FROMMER'S FAMILY GUIDES

California with Kids	$16.95	F001	San Francisco with Kids	$17.00	F004
Los Angeles with Kids	$17.00	F002	Washington, D.C. with Kids	$17.00	F005
New York City with Kids	$18.00	F003			

FROMMER CITY GUIDES

Amsterdam/Holland 1991–92	$ 8.95	S001	Miami 1991–92	$ 8.95	S021
Athens 1991–92	$ 8.95	S002	Minneapolis/St. Paul 1991–92	$ 8.95	S022
Atlanta 1991–92	$ 8.95	S003	Montréal/Québec City 1991–92	$ 8.95	S023
Atlantic City/Cape May 1991–92	$ 8.95	S004	New Orleans 1993–94	$13.00	S103
Bangkok 1992–93	$13.00	S005	New York 1992	$12.00	S025
Barcelona/Majorca/ Minorca/Ibiza 1992	$12.00	S006	Orlando 1993	$13.00	S101
Belgium 1989–90	$ 5.95	S007	Paris 1993–94	$13.00	S109
Berlin 1991–92	$10.00	S008	Philadelphia 1991–92	$ 8.95	S028
Boston 1991–92	$ 8.95	S009	Rio 1991–92	$ 8.95	S029
Cancún/Cozumel/ Yucatán 1991–92	$ 8.95	S010	Rome 1991–92	$ 8.95	S030
			Salt Lake City 1991–92	$ 8.95	S031
Chicago 1991–92	$ 9.95	S011	San Diego 1993–94	$13.00	S107
Denver/Boulder/ Colorado Springs 1990–91	$ 7.95	S012	San Francisco 1993	$13.00	S104
			Santa Fe/Taos/ Albuquerque 1993–94	$13.00	S108
Dublin/Ireland 1991–92	$ 8.95	S013	Seattle/Portland 1992–93	$12.00	S035
Hawaii 1992	$12.00	S014	St. Louis/Kansas City 1991–92	$ 9.95	S036
Hong Kong 1992–93	$12.00	S015			
Honolulu/Oahu 1993	$13.00	S106	Sydney 1991–92	$ 8.95	S037
Las Vegas 1991–92	$ 8.95	S016	Tampa/St. Petersburg 1993–94	$13.00	S105
Lisbon/Madrid/Costa del Sol 1991–92	$ 8.95	S017	Tokyo 1992–93	$13.00	S039
London 1993	$13.00	S100	Toronto 1991–92	$ 8.95	S040
Los Angeles 1991–92	$ 8.95	S019	Vancouver/Victoria 1990–91	$ 7.95	S041
Mexico City/Acapulco 1991–92	$ 8.95	S020	Washington, D.C. 1993	$13.00	S102

Other Titles Available at Membership Prices—
SPECIAL EDITIONS

	Retail Price	Code		Retail Price	Code
Bed & Breakfast North America	$14.95	P002	Marilyn Wood's Wonderful Weekends (within 250-mile radius of New York City)	$11.95	P017
Caribbean Hideaways	$16.00	P005			
Honeymoon Destinations	$14.95	P006	New World of Travel 1991 by Arthur Frommer	$16.95	P018
			Where to Stay USA	$13.95	P015

GAULT MILLAU'S "BEST OF" GUIDES

Chicago	$15.95	G002	New England	$15.95	G010
Florida	$17.00	G003	New Orleans	$16.95	G011
France	$16.95	G004	New York	$16.95	G012
Germany	$18.00	G018	Paris	$16.95	G013
Hawaii	$16.95	G006	San Francisco	$16.95	G014
Hong Kong	$16.95	G007	Thailand	$17.95	G019
London	$16.95	G009	Toronto	$17.00	G020
Los Angeles	$16.95	G005	Washington, D.C.	$16.95	G017

THE REAL GUIDES

Amsterdam	$13.00	R100	Morocco	$14.00	R111
Barcelona	$13.00	R101	Nepal	$14.00	R018
Berlin	$11.95	R002	New York	$13.00	R019
Brazil	$13.95	R003	Able to Travel (avail April '93)	$20.00	R112
California & the West Coast	$17.00	R102	Paris	$13.00	R020
Canada	$15.00	R103	Peru	$12.95	R021
Czechoslovakia	$14.00	R104	Poland	$13.95	R022
Egypt	$19.00	R105	Portugal	$15.00	R023
Florida	$14.00	R006	Prague	$15.00	R113
France	$18.00	R106	San Francisco & the Bay Area	$11.95	R024
Germany	$18.00	R107	Scandinavia	$14.95	R025
Greece	$18.00	R108	Spain	$16.00	R026
Guatemala/Belize	$14.00	R109	Thailand	$17.00	R114
Holland/Belgium/ Luxembourg	$16.00	R031	Tunisia	$17.00	R115
Hong Kong/Macau	$11.95	R011	Turkey	$13.95	R116
Hungary	$12.95	R012	U.S.A.	$18.00	R117
Ireland	$17.00	R110	Venice	$11.95	R028
Italy	$13.95	R014	Women Travel	$12.95	R029
Kenya	$12.95	R015	Yugoslavia	$12.95	R030
Mexico	$11.95	R016			